T0257411

THE ART OF
COMPUTER PROGRAMMING

DONALD E. KNUTH *Stanford University*

  ADDISON–WESLEY

Volume 4A / **Combinatorial Algorithms, Part 1**

THE ART OF
COMPUTER PROGRAMMING

Boston · Columbus · New York · San Francisco · Amsterdam · Cape Town
Dubai · London · Madrid · Milan · Munich · Paris · Montréal · Toronto · Delhi · Mexico City
São Paulo · Sydney · Hong Kong · Seoul · Singapore · Taipei · Tokyo

The poem on page 437 is quoted from *The Golden Gate* by Vikram Seth (New York: Random House, 1986), copyright © 1986 by Vikram Seth.

For government sales inquiries, please contact governmentsales@pearsoned.com
For questions about sales outside the U.S., please contact intlcs@pearson.com

Visit us on the Web: informit.com/aw

Library of Congress Cataloging-in-Publication Data
```
Knuth, Donald Ervin, 1938-
  The art of computer programming / Donald Ervin Knuth.
  xvi,883 p. 24 cm.
  Includes bibliographical references and index.
  Contents: v. 1. Fundamental algorithms. -- v. 2. Seminumerical
algorithms. -- v. 3. Sorting and searching. -- v. 4a. Combinatorial
algorithms, part 1.
  Contents: v. 4a. Combinatorial algorithms, part 1.
  ISBN 978-0-201-89683-1 (v. 1, 3rd ed.)
  ISBN 978-0-201-89684-8 (v. 2, 3rd ed.)
  ISBN 978-0-201-89685-5 (v. 3, 2nd ed.)
  ISBN 978-0-201-03804-0 (v. 4a)
  1. Electronic digital computers--Programming.  2. Computer
algorithms.   I. Title.
QA76.6.K64   1997
005.1--DC21                                            97-2147
```

Internet page http://www-cs-faculty.stanford.edu/~knuth/taocp.html contains current information about this book and related books.

See also http://www-cs-faculty.stanford.edu/~knuth/sgb.html for information about *The Stanford GraphBase*, including downloadable software for dealing with the graphs used in many of the examples.

And see http://www-cs-faculty.stanford.edu/~knuth/mmix.html for basic information about the MMIX computer.

ISBN-13   978-0-201-03804-0
ISBN-10   0-201-03804-8

Twenty-third printing, October 2023

23 2023

PREFACE

To put all the good stuff into one book is patently impossible,
and attempting even to be reasonably comprehensive
about certain aspects of the subject is likely to lead to runaway growth.
— GERALD B. FOLLAND, "Editor's Corner" (2005)

THE TITLE of Volume 4 is *Combinatorial Algorithms*, and when I proposed it
I was strongly inclined to add a subtitle: *The Kind of Programming I Like Best.*
My editors have decided to tone down such exuberance, but the fact remains
that programs with a combinatorial flavor have always been my favorites.

On the other hand I've often been surprised to find that, in many people's
minds, the word "combinatorial" is linked with computational difficulty. Indeed,
Samuel Johnson, in his famous dictionary of the English language (1755), said
that the corresponding noun "is now generally used in an ill sense." Colleagues
tell me tales of woe, in which they report that "the combinatorics of the situation defeated us." Why is it that, for me, combinatorics arouses feelings of
pure pleasure, yet for many others it evokes pure panic?

It's true that combinatorial problems are often associated with humongously
large numbers. Johnson's dictionary entry also included a quote from Ephraim
Chambers, who had stated that the total number of words of length 24 or less,
in a 24-letter alphabet, is 1,391,724,288,887,252,999,425,128,493,402,200. The
corresponding number when we replace 24 by 10 in Chambers's statement is
11,111,111,110; and it's only 3905 when we reduce the parameter to 5. Thus a
"combinatorial explosion" certainly does occur as the size of the problem grows
from 5 to 10 to 24 and beyond.

Computing machines have become tremendously more powerful throughout
my life. As I write these words, I know that they are being processed by a "lap-
top" whose speed is more than 100,000 times faster than the trusty IBM Type 650
computer to which I've dedicated these books. My current machine's memory
capacity is also more than 100,000 times greater. Tomorrow's computers will be
even faster and more capacious. But these amazing advances have not diminished
people's craving for answers to combinatorial questions; quite the contrary. Our
once-unimaginable ability to compute so rapidly has raised our expectations, and
whetted our appetite for more — because the size of a combinatorial problem can
increase more than 100,000-fold when a parameter n increases by just 1.

Combinatorial algorithms can be defined informally as techniques for the
high-speed manipulation of combinatorial objects such as permutations or graphs.
We typically try to find patterns or arrangements that are the best possible ways
to satisfy certain constraints. The number of such problems is vast, and the art

of writing such programs is especially important and appealing because a single good idea can save years or even centuries of computer time.

Indeed, the fact that good algorithms for combinatorial problems can have a terrific payoff has led to terrific advances in the state of the art. Many problems that once were thought to be intractable can now be polished off with ease, and many algorithms that once were known to be good have now become better. Starting about 1970, computer scientists began to experience a phenomenon that we called "Floyd's Lemma": Problems that seemed to need n^3 operations could actually be solved in $O(n^2)$; problems that seemed to require n^2 could be handled in $O(n \log n)$; and $n \log n$ was often reducible to $O(n)$. More difficult problems saw a reduction in running time from $O(2^n)$ to $O(1.5^n)$ to $O(1.3^n)$, etc. Other problems remained difficult in general, but they were found to have important special cases that are much simpler. Many combinatorial questions that I once thought would never be answered during my lifetime have now been resolved, and those breakthroughs have been due mainly to improvements in algorithms rather than to improvements in processor speeds.

By 1975, such research was advancing so rapidly that a substantial fraction of the papers published in leading journals of computer science were devoted to combinatorial algorithms. And the advances weren't being made only by people in the core of computer science; significant contributions were coming from workers in electrical engineering, artificial intelligence, operations research, mathematics, physics, statistics, and other fields. I was trying to complete Volume 4 of *The Art of Computer Programming*, but instead I felt like I was sitting on the lid of a boiling kettle: I was confronted with a combinatorial explosion of another kind, a prodigious explosion of new ideas!

This series of books was born at the beginning of 1962, when I naïvely wrote out a list of tentative chapter titles for a 12-chapter book. At that time I decided to include a brief chapter about combinatorial algorithms, just for fun. "Hey look, most people use computers to deal with numbers, but we can also write programs that deal with patterns." In those days it was easy to give a fairly complete description of just about every combinatorial algorithm that was known. And even by 1966, when I'd finished a first draft of about 3000 handwritten pages for that already-overgrown book, fewer than 100 of those pages belonged to Chapter 7. I had absolutely no idea that what I'd foreseen as a sort of "salad course" would eventually turn out to be the main dish.

The great combinatorial fermentation of 1975 has continued to churn, as more and more people have begun to participate. New ideas improve upon the older ones, but rarely replace them or make them obsolete. So of course I've had to abandon any hopes that I once had of being able to surround the field, to write a definitive book that sets everything in order and provides one-stop shopping for everyone who has combinatorial problems to solve. The array of applicable techniques has mushroomed to the point where I can almost never discuss a subtopic and say, "Here's the final solution: end of story." Instead, I must restrict myself to explaining the most important principles that seem to underlie all of the efficient combinatorial methods that I've encountered so far.

At present I've accumulated more than twice as much raw material for Volume 4 as for all of Volumes 1–3 combined.

This sheer mass of material implies that the once-planned "Volume 4" must actually become several physical volumes. You are now looking at Volume 4A. Volumes 4B and 4C will exist someday, assuming that I'm able to remain healthy; and (who knows?) there may also be Volumes 4D, 4E, ...; but surely not 4Z.

My plan is to go systematically through the files that I've amassed since 1962 and to tell the stories that I believe are still waiting to be told, to the best of my ability. I can't aspire to completeness, but I do want to give proper credit to all of the pioneers who have been responsible for key ideas; so I won't scrimp on historical details. Furthermore, whenever I learn something that I think is likely to remain important 50 years from now, something that can also be explained elegantly in a paragraph or two, I can't bear to leave it out. Conversely, difficult material that requires a lengthy proof is beyond the scope of these books, unless the subject matter is truly fundamental.

OK, it's clear that the field of Combinatorial Algorithms is vast, and I can't cover it all. What are the most important things that I'm leaving out? My biggest blind spot, I think, is geometry, because I've always been much better at visualizing and manipulating algebraic formulas than objects in space. Therefore I don't attempt to deal in these books with combinatorial problems that are related to computational geometry, such as close packing of spheres, or clustering of data points in n-dimensional Euclidean space, or even the Steiner tree problem in the plane. More significantly, I tend to shy away from polyhedral combinatorics, and from approaches that are based primarily on linear programming, integer programming, or semidefinite programming. Those topics are treated well in many other books on the subject, and they rely on geometrical intuition. Purely combinatorial developments are easier for me to understand.

I also must confess a bias against algorithms that are efficient only in an asymptotic sense, algorithms whose superior performance doesn't begin to "kick in" until the size of the problem exceeds the size of the universe. A great many publications nowadays are devoted to algorithms of that kind. I can understand why the contemplation of ultimate limits has intellectual appeal and carries an academic cachet; but in *The Art of Computer Programming* I tend to give short shrift to any methods that I would never consider using myself in an actual program. (There are, of course, exceptions to this rule, especially with respect to basic concepts in the core of the subject. Some impractical methods are simply too beautiful and/or too insightful to be excluded; others provide instructive examples of what *not* to do.)

Furthermore, as in earlier volumes of this series, I'm intentionally concentrating almost entirely on *sequential* algorithms, even though computers are increasingly able to carry out activities in parallel. I'm unable to judge what ideas about parallelism are likely to be useful five or ten years from now, let alone fifty, so I happily leave such questions to others who are wiser than I. Sequential methods, by themselves, already test the limits of my own ability to discern what the artful programmers of tomorrow will want to know.

The main decision that I needed to make when planning how to present this material was whether to organize it by problems or by techniques. Chapter 5 in Volume 3, for example, was devoted to a single problem, the sorting of data into order; more than two dozen techniques were applied to different aspects of that problem. Combinatorial algorithms, by contrast, involve many different problems, which tend to be attacked with a smaller repertoire of techniques. I finally decided that a mixed strategy would work better than any pure approach. Thus, for example, these books treat the problem of finding shortest paths in Section 7.3, and problems of connectivity in Section 7.4.1.3; but many other sections are devoted to basic techniques, such as the use of Boolean algebra (Section 7.1), backtracking (Section 7.2.2), matroid theory (Section 7.6), or dynamic programming (Section 7.7). The famous Traveling Salesrep Problem, and other classic combinatorial tasks related to coloring and packing, have no sections of their own, but they come up several times in different places as they are treated by different methods.

I've mentioned great progress in the art of combinatorial computing, but I don't mean to imply that all combinatorial problems have actually been tamed. When the running time of a computer program goes ballistic, its programmers shouldn't expect to find a silver bullet for their needs in this book. The methods described here will often work a great deal faster than the first approaches that a programmer tries; but let's face it: Combinatorial problems get huge very quickly. We can even prove rigorously that a certain small, natural problem will *never* have a feasible solution in the real world, although it is solvable in principle (see the theorem of Stockmeyer and Meyer in Section 7.1.2). In other cases we cannot prove as yet that no decent algorithm for a given problem exists, but we know that such methods are unlikely, because any efficient algorithm would yield a good way to solve thousands of other problems that have stumped the world's greatest experts (see the discussion of NP-completeness in Section 7.9).

Experience suggests that new combinatorial algorithms will continue to be invented, for new combinatorial problems and for newly identified variations or special cases of old ones. Experience also suggests that people's appetite for such algorithms will continue to grow. The art of computer programming continually reaches new heights when programmers are faced with challenges such as these. Yet today's methods are also likely to remain relevant.

Most of this book is self-contained, although there are frequent tie-ins with the topics discussed in Volumes 1–3. Low-level details of machine language programming have been covered extensively in those volumes, so the algorithms in the present book are usually specified only at an abstract level, independent of any machine. However, some aspects of combinatorial programming are heavily dependent on low-level details that didn't arise before; in such cases, all examples in this book are based on the MMIX computer, which supersedes the MIX machine that was defined in early editions of Volume 1. Details about MMIX appear in a paperback supplement to that volume called *The Art of Computer Programming*, Volume 1, Fascicle 1, containing Sections 1.3.1′, 1.3.2′, etc.; they're also available on the Internet, together with downloadable assemblers and simulators.

Another downloadable resource, a collection of programs and data called *The Stanford GraphBase*, is cited extensively in the examples of this book. Readers are encouraged to play with it, in order to learn about combinatorial algorithms in what I think will be the most efficient and most enjoyable way.

Many of the computer programs that I wrote while preparing this material are listed on the following webpage:

`http://www-cs-faculty.stanford.edu/~knuth/programs.html`

In particular, you can download BDD14 and BDD15, which are the experimental toolkits that I played with when studying BDDs and ZDDs, respectively, in Section 7.1.4. Another example is a program called SIMPATH, for exercise 7.1.4–225.

Incidentally, while writing the introductory material at the beginning of Chapter 7, I was pleased to note that it was natural to mention some work of my Ph.D. thesis advisor, Marshall Hall, Jr. (1910–1990), as well as some work of *his* thesis advisor, Oystein Ore (1899–1968), as well as some work of *his* thesis advisor, Thoralf Skolem (1887–1963). Skolem's advisor, Axel Thue (1863–1922), was already present in Chapter 6.

I'm immensely grateful to the hundreds of readers who have helped me to ferret out numerous mistakes that I made in the early drafts of this volume, which were originally posted on the Internet and subsequently printed in paperback fascicles. In particular, the extensive comments of Thorsten Dahlheimer, Marc van Leeuwen, and Udo Wermuth have been especially influential. But I fear that other errors still lurk among the details collected here, and I want to correct them as soon as possible. Therefore I will cheerfully award $2.56 to the first finder of each technical, typographical, or historical error. The `taocp` webpage cited on page iv contains a current listing of all corrections that have been reported to me.

Stanford, California   D. E. K.
October 2010

> In my preface to the first edition,
> I begged the reader not to draw attention to errors.
> I now wish I had not done so
> and am grateful to the few readers who ignored my request.
> — STUART SUTHERLAND, *The International Dictionary of Psychology* (1996)

> Naturally, I am responsible for the remaining errors—
> although, in my opinion, my friends could have caught a few more.
> — CHRISTOS H. PAPADIMITRIOU, *Computational Complexity* (1994)

> I like to work in a variety of fields
> in order to spread my mistakes more thinly.
> — VICTOR KLEE (1999)

A note on references. Several oft-cited journals and conference proceedings have special code names, which appear in the Index and Glossary at the close of this book. But the various kinds of *IEEE Transactions* are cited by including a letter code for the type of transactions, in boldface preceding the volume number. For example, '*IEEE Trans.* **C-35**' means the *IEEE Transactions on Computers*, volume 35. The IEEE no longer uses these convenient letter codes, but the codes aren't too hard to decipher: '**EC**' once stood for "Electronic Computers," '**IT**' for "Information Theory," '**SE**' for "Software Engineering," and '**SP**' for "Signal Processing," etc.; '**CAD**' meant "Computer-Aided Design of Integrated Circuits and Systems."

A cross-reference such as 'exercise 7.10–00' points to a future exercise in Section 7.10 whose number is not yet known.

A note on notations. Simple and intuitive conventions for the algebraic representation of mathematical concepts have always been a boon to progress, especially when most of the world's researchers share a common symbolic language. The current state of affairs in combinatorial mathematics is unfortunately a bit of a mess in this regard, because the same symbols are occasionally used with completely different meanings by different groups of people; some specialists who work in comparatively narrow subfields have unintentionally spawned conflicting symbolisms. Computer science — which interacts with large swaths of mathematics — needs to steer clear of this danger by adopting internally consistent notations whenever possible. Therefore I've often had to choose among a number of competing schemes, knowing that it will be impossible to please everyone. I have tried my best to come up with notations that I believe will be best for the future, often after many years of experimentation and discussion with colleagues, often flip-flopping between alternatives until finding something that works well. Usually it has been possible to find convenient conventions that other people have not already coopted in contradictory ways.

Appendix B is a comprehensive index to all of the principal notations that are used in the present book, inevitably including several that are not (yet?) standard. If you run across a formula that looks weird and/or incomprehensible, chances are fairly good that Appendix B will direct you to a page where my intentions are clarified. But I might as well list here a few instances that you might wish to watch for when you read this book for the first time:

- Hexadecimal constants are preceded by a number sign or hash mark. For example, $^\#123$ means $(123)_{16}$.

- The "monus" operation $x \mathbin{\dot-} y$, sometimes called dot-minus or saturating subtraction, yields $\max(0, x - y)$.

- The median of three numbers $\{x, y, z\}$ is denoted by $\langle xyz \rangle$.

- A set such as $\{x\}$, which consists of a single element, is often denoted simply by x in contexts such as $X \cup x$ or $X \setminus x$.

- If n is a nonnegative integer, the number of 1-bits in n's binary representation is νn. Furthermore, if $n > 0$, the leftmost and rightmost 1-bits of n are respectively $2^{\lambda n}$ and $2^{\rho n}$. For example, $\nu 10 = 2$, $\lambda 10 = 3$, $\rho 10 = 1$.

- The Cartesian product of graphs G and H is denoted by $G \square H$. For example, $C_m \square C_n$ denotes an $m \times n$ torus, because C_n denotes a cycle of n vertices.

NOTES ON THE EXERCISES

THE EXERCISES in this set of books have been designed for self-study as well as for classroom study. It is difficult, if not impossible, for anyone to learn a subject purely by reading about it, without applying the information to specific problems and thereby being encouraged to think about what has been read. Furthermore, we all learn best the things that we have discovered for ourselves. Therefore the exercises form a major part of this work; a definite attempt has been made to keep them as informative as possible and to select problems that are enjoyable as well as instructive.

In many books, easy exercises are found mixed randomly among extremely difficult ones. A motley mixture is, however, often unfortunate because readers like to know in advance how long a problem ought to take — otherwise they may just skip over all the problems. A classic example of such a situation is the book *Dynamic Programming* by Richard Bellman; this is an important, pioneering work in which a group of problems is collected together at the end of some chapters under the heading "Exercises and Research Problems," with extremely trivial questions appearing in the midst of deep, unsolved problems. It is rumored that someone once asked Dr. Bellman how to tell the exercises apart from the research problems, and he replied, "If you can solve it, it is an exercise; otherwise it's a research problem."

Good arguments can be made for including both research problems and very easy exercises in a book of this kind; therefore, to save the reader from the possible dilemma of determining which are which, *rating numbers* have been provided to indicate the level of difficulty. These numbers have the following general significance:

Rating   Interpretation

00 An extremely easy exercise that can be answered immediately if the material of the text has been understood; such an exercise can almost always be worked "in your head," unless you're multitasking.

10 A simple problem that makes you think over the material just read, but is by no means difficult. You should be able to do this in one minute at most; pencil and paper may be useful in obtaining the solution.

20 An average problem that tests basic understanding of the text material, but you may need about fifteen or twenty minutes to answer it completely. Maybe even twenty-five.

30 A problem of moderate difficulty and/or complexity; this one may involve more than two hours' work to solve satisfactorily, or even more if the TV is on.

40 Quite a difficult or lengthy problem that would be suitable for a term project in classroom situations. A student should be able to solve the problem in a reasonable amount of time, but the solution is not trivial.

50 A research problem that has not yet been solved satisfactorily, as far as the author knew at the time of writing, although many people have tried. If you have found an answer to such a problem, you ought to write it up for publication; furthermore, the author of this book would appreciate hearing about the solution as soon as possible (provided that it is correct).

By interpolation in this "logarithmic" scale, the significance of other rating numbers becomes clear. For example, a rating of *17* would indicate an exercise that is a bit simpler than average. Problems with a rating of *50* that are subsequently solved by some reader may appear with a *40* rating in later editions of the book, and in the errata posted on the Internet (see page iv).

The remainder of the rating number divided by 5 indicates the amount of detailed work required. Thus, an exercise rated *24* may take longer to solve than an exercise that is rated *25*, but the latter will require more creativity. All exercises with ratings of *46* or more are open problems for future research, rated according to the number of different attacks that they've resisted so far.

The author has tried earnestly to assign accurate rating numbers, but it is difficult for the person who makes up a problem to know just how formidable it will be for someone else to find a solution; and everyone has more aptitude for certain types of problems than for others. It is hoped that the rating numbers represent a good guess at the level of difficulty, but they should be taken as general guidelines, not as absolute indicators.

This book has been written for readers with varying degrees of mathematical training and sophistication; as a result, some of the exercises are intended only for the use of more mathematically inclined readers. The rating is preceded by an *M* if the exercise involves mathematical concepts or motivation to a greater extent than necessary for someone who is primarily interested only in programming the algorithms themselves. An exercise is marked with the letters "*HM*" if its solution necessarily involves a knowledge of calculus or other higher mathematics not developed in this book. An "*HM*" designation does *not* necessarily imply difficulty.

Some exercises are preceded by an arrowhead, "▶"; this designates problems that are especially instructive and especially recommended. Of course, no reader/student is expected to work *all* of the exercises, so those that seem to be the most valuable have been singled out. (This distinction is not meant to detract from the other exercises!) Each reader should at least make an attempt to solve all of the problems whose rating is *10* or less; and the arrows may help to indicate which of the problems with a higher rating should be given priority.

Several sections have more than 100 exercises. How can you find your way among so many? In general the sequence of exercises tends to follow the sequence of ideas in the main text. Adjacent exercises build on each other, as in the pioneering problem books of Pólya and Szegő. The final exercises of a section often involve the section as a whole, or introduce supplementary topics.

Solutions to most of the exercises appear in the answer section. Please use them wisely; do not turn to the answer until you have made a genuine effort to solve the problem by yourself, or unless you absolutely do not have time to work this particular problem. *After* getting your own solution or giving the problem a decent try, you may find the answer instructive and helpful. The solution given will often be quite short, and it will sketch the details under the assumption that you have earnestly tried to solve it by your own means first. Sometimes the solution gives less information than was asked; often it gives more. It is quite possible that you may have a better answer than the one published here, or you may have found an error in the published solution; in such a case, the author will be pleased to know the details. Later printings of this book will give the improved solutions together with the solver's name where appropriate.

When working an exercise you may generally use the answers to previous exercises, unless specifically forbidden from doing so. The rating numbers have been assigned with this in mind; thus it is possible for exercise $n + 1$ to have a lower rating than exercise n, even though it includes the result of exercise n as a special case.

Summary of codes:		*00* Immediate
		10 Simple (one minute)
		20 Medium (quarter hour)
▶	Recommended	*30* Moderately hard
M	Mathematically oriented	*40* Term project
HM	Requiring "higher math"	*50* Research problem

EXERCISES

▶ **1.** [*00*] What does the rating "*M15*" mean?

2. [*10*] Of what value can the exercises in a textbook be to the reader?

3. [*HM45*] Prove that every simply connected, closed 3-dimensional manifold is topologically equivalent to a 3-dimensional sphere.

Art derives a considerable part of its beneficial exercise
from flying in the face of presumptions.
— HENRY JAMES, "The Art of Fiction" (1884)

I am grateful to all my friends,
and record here and now my most especial appreciation
to those friends who, after a decent interval,
stopped asking me, "How's the book coming?"
— PETER J. GOMES, *The Good Book* (1996)

I at last deliver to the world a Work which I have long promised,
and of which, I am afraid, too high expectations have been raised.
The delay of its publication must be imputed, in a considerable degree,
to the extraordinary zeal which has been shown by distinguished persons
in all quarters to supply me with additional information.
— JAMES BOSWELL, *The Life of Samuel Johnson, LL.D.* (1791)

The author is especially grateful to the Addison–Wesley Publishing Company
for its patience in waiting a full decade for this manuscript
from the date the contract was signed.
— FRANK HARARY, *Graph Theory* (1969)

The average boy who abhors square root or algebra
finds delight in working puzzles which involve similar principles,
and may be led into a course of study
which would develop the mathematical and inventive bumps
in a way to astonish the family phrenologist.
— SAM LOYD, *The World of Puzzledom* (1896)

Bitte ein Bit!
— Slogan of Bitburger Brauerei (1951)

CONTENTS

Hommage à Bach.

CHAPTER SEVEN

COMBINATORIAL SEARCHING

> *You shall seeke all day ere you finde them,*
> *& when you have them, they are not worth the search.*
> — BASSANIO, in *The Merchant of Venice* (Act I, Scene 1, Line 117)

> *Amid the action and reaction of so dense a swarm of humanity,*
> *every possible combination of events may be expected to take place,*
> *and many a little problem will be presented which may be striking and bizarre.*
> — SHERLOCK HOLMES, in *The Adventure of the Blue Carbuncle* (1892)

> *The field of combinatorial algorithms is too vast to cover*
> *in a single paper or even in a single book.*
> — ROBERT E. TARJAN (1976)

> *While jostling against all manner of people*
> *it has been impressed upon my mind that the successful ones*
> *are those who have a natural faculty for solving puzzles.*
> *Life is full of puzzles, and we are called upon*
> *to solve such as fate throws our way.*
> — SAM LOYD, JR. (1926)

COMBINATORICS is the study of the ways in which discrete objects can be arranged into various kinds of patterns. For example, the objects might be $2n$ numbers $\{1, 1, 2, 2, \ldots, n, n\}$, and we might want to place them in a row so that exactly k numbers occur between the two appearances of each digit k. When $n = 3$ there is essentially only one way to arrange such "Langford pairs," namely 231213 (and its left-right reversal); similarly, there's also a unique solution when $n = 4$. Many other types of combinatorial patterns are discussed below.

Five basic types of questions typically arise when combinatorial problems are studied, some more difficult than others.

  i) Existence: Are there any arrangements X that conform to the pattern?
 ii) Construction: If so, can such an X be found quickly?
iii) Enumeration: How many different arrangements X exist?
 iv) Generation: Can all arrangements X_1, X_2, ... be visited systematically?
  v) Optimization: What arrangements maximize or minimize $f(X)$, given an objective function f?

Each of these questions turns out to be interesting with respect to Langford pairs.

For example, consider the question of existence. Trial and error quickly reveals that, when $n = 5$, we cannot place $\{1, 1, 2, 2, \ldots, 5, 5\}$ properly into ten positions. The two 1s must both go into even-numbered slots, or both into odd-numbered slots; similarly, the 3s and 5s must choose between two evens or two odds; but the 2s and 4s use one of each. Thus we can't fill exactly five slots of each parity. This reasoning also proves that the problem has no solution when $n = 6$, or in general whenever the number of odd values in $\{1, 2, \ldots, n\}$ is odd.

In other words, Langford pairings can exist only when $n = 4m-1$ or $n = 4m$, for some integer m. Conversely, when n does have this form, Roy O. Davies has found an elegant way to construct a suitable placement (see exercise 1).

How many essentially different pairings, L_n, exist? Lots, when n grows:

$$
\begin{aligned}
L_3 &= 1; & L_4 &= 1; \\
L_7 &= 26; & L_8 &= 150; \\
L_{11} &= 17{,}792; & L_{12} &= 108{,}144; \\
L_{15} &= 39{,}809{,}640; & L_{16} &= 326{,}721{,}800; \\
L_{19} &= 256{,}814{,}891{,}280; & L_{20} &= 2{,}636{,}337{,}861{,}200; \\
L_{23} &= 3{,}799{,}455{,}942{,}515{,}488; & L_{24} &= 46{,}845{,}158{,}056{,}515{,}936.
\end{aligned}
\tag{1}
$$

[The values of L_{23} and L_{24} were determined by M. Krajecki, C. Jaillet, and A. Bui in 2004 and 2005; see *Studia Informatica Universalis* **4** (2005), 151–190.] A seat-of-the-pants calculation suggests that L_n might be roughly of order $(4n/e^3)^{n+1/2}$ when it is nonzero (see exercise 5); and in fact this prediction turns out to be basically correct in all known cases. But no simple formula is apparent.

The problem of Langford arrangements is a simple special case of a general class of combinatorial challenges called *exact cover problems*. In Section 7.2.2.1 we shall study an algorithm called "dancing links," which is a convenient way to generate all solutions to such problems. When $n = 16$, for example, that method needs to perform only about 3500 memory accesses for each Langford pair arrangement that it finds. Thus the value of L_{16} can be computed in a reasonable amount of time by simply generating all of the pairings and counting them.

Notice, however, that L_{24} is a *huge* number — roughly 5×10^{16}, or about 1500 MIP-years. (Recall that a "MIP-year" is the number of instructions executed per year by a machine that carries out a million instructions per second, namely 31,556,952,000,000.) Therefore it's clear that the exact value of L_{24} was determined by some technique that did *not* involve generating all of the arrangements. Indeed, there is a much, much faster way to compute L_n, using polynomial algebra. The instructive method described in exercise 6 needs $O(4^n n)$ operations, which may seem inefficient; but it beats the generate-and-count method by a whopping factor of order $\Theta((n/e^3)^{n-1/2})$, and even when $n = 16$ it runs about 20 times faster. On the other hand, the exact value of L_{100} will probably never be known, even as computers become faster and faster.

We can also consider Langford pairings that are *optimum* in various ways. For example, it's possible to arrange sixteen pairs of weights $\{1, 1, 2, 2, \ldots, 16, 16\}$ that satisfy Langford's condition and have the additional property of being "well-balanced," in the sense that they won't tip a balance beam when they are placed in the appropriate order:

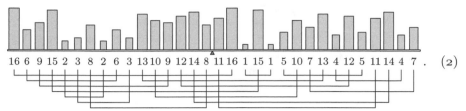

$$16\ 6\ \ 9\ 15\ 2\ \ 3\ \ 8\ \ 2\ \ 6\ \ 3\ 13\ 10\ 9\ \ 12\ 14\ 8\ \ 11\ 16\ 1\ 15\ 1\ \ 5\ 10\ 7\ 13\ 4\ 12\ 5\ 11\ 14\ 4\ \ 7\ . \qquad (2)$$

In other words, $15.5 \cdot 16 + 14.5 \cdot 6 + \cdots + 0.5 \cdot 8 = 0.5 \cdot 11 + \cdots + 14.5 \cdot 4 + 15.5 \cdot 7$; and in this particular example we also have another kind of balance, $16 + 6 + \cdots + 8 = 11 + 16 + \cdots + 7$, hence also $16 \cdot 16 + 15 \cdot 6 + \cdots + 1 \cdot 8 = 1 \cdot 11 + \cdots + 15 \cdot 4 + 16 \cdot 7$.

Moreover, the arrangement in (2) has *minimum width* among all Langford pairings of order 16: The connecting lines at the bottom of the diagram show that no more than seven pairs are incomplete at any point, as we read from left to right; and one can show that a width of six is impossible. (See exercise 7.)

What arrangements $a_1 a_2 \ldots a_{32}$ of $\{1, 1, \ldots, 16, 16\}$ are the *least* balanced, in the sense that $\sum_{k=1}^{32} k a_k$ is maximized? The maximum possible value turns out to be 5268. One such pairing — there are 12,016 of them — is

$$2\ 3\ 4\ 2\ 1\ 3\ 1\ 4\ 16\ 13\ 15\ 5\ 14\ 7\ 9\ 6\ 11\ 5\ 12\ 10\ 8\ 7\ 6\ 13\ 9\ 16\ 15\ 14\ 11\ 8\ 10\ 12. \qquad (3)$$

A more interesting question is to ask for the Langford pairings that are smallest and largest in lexicographic order. The answers for $n = 24$ are

$$\{\texttt{abacbdecfgdoersfpgqtuwxvjklonhmirpsjqkhltiunmwvx,}$$
$$\texttt{xvwsquntkigrdapaodgiknqsvxwutmrpoljecfhbcebmfjlh}\} \qquad (4)$$

if we use the letters a, b, ..., w, x instead of the numbers 1, 2, ..., 23, 24.

We shall discuss many techniques for combinatorial optimization in later sections of this chapter. Our goal, of course, will be to solve such problems without examining more than a tiny portion of the space of all possible arrangements.

Orthogonal latin squares. Let's look back for a moment at the early days of combinatorics. A posthumous edition of Jacques Ozanam's *Recreations mathematiques et physiques* (Paris: 1723) included an amusing puzzle in volume 4, page 434: "Take all the aces, kings, queens, and jacks from an ordinary deck of playing cards and arrange them in a square so that each row and each column contains all four values and all four suits." Can you do it? Ozanam's solution, shown in Fig. 1 on the next page, does even more: It exhibits the full panoply of values and of suits also on both main diagonals. (Please don't turn the page until you've given this problem a try.)

By 1779 a similar puzzle was making the rounds of St. Petersburg, and it came to the attention of the great mathematician Leonhard Euler. "Thirty-six officers of six different ranks, taken from six different regiments, want to march in a 6×6 formation so that each row and each column will contain one officer of each rank and one of each regiment. How can they do it?" Nobody was able to

Fig. 1. Disorder in the court cards:
No agreement in any line of four.
(This configuration is one of many
ways to solve a popular eighteenth-
century problem.)

find a satisfactory marching order. So Euler decided to resolve the riddle — even
though he had become nearly blind in 1771 and was dictating all of his work
to assistants. He wrote a major paper on the subject [eventually published in
*Verhandelingen uitgegeven door het Zeeuwsch Genootschap der Wetenschappen
te Vlissingen* **9** (1782), 85–239], in which he constructed suitable arrangements
for the analogous task with n ranks and n regiments when $n = 1, 3, 4, 5, 7, 8,$
9, 11, 12, 13, 15, 16, ... ; only the cases with $n \bmod 4 = 2$ eluded him.

There's obviously no solution when $n = 2$. But Euler was stumped when $n =$
6, after having examined a "very considerable number" of square arrangements
that didn't work. He showed that any actual solution would lead to many others
that look different, and he couldn't believe that all such solutions had escaped
his attention. Therefore he said, "I do not hesitate to conclude that one cannot
produce a complete square of 36 cells, and that the same impossibility extends
to the cases $n = 10$, $n = 14$ ... in general to all oddly even numbers."

Euler named the 36 officers $a\alpha$, $a\beta$, $a\gamma$, $a\delta$, $a\epsilon$, $a\zeta$, $b\alpha$, $b\beta$, $b\gamma$, $b\delta$, $b\epsilon$, $b\zeta$,
$c\alpha$, $c\beta$, $c\gamma$, $c\delta$, $c\epsilon$, $c\zeta$, $d\alpha$, $d\beta$, $d\gamma$, $d\delta$, $d\epsilon$, $d\zeta$, $e\alpha$, $e\beta$, $e\gamma$, $e\delta$, $e\epsilon$, $e\zeta$, $f\alpha$, $f\beta$, $f\gamma$,
$f\delta$, $f\epsilon$, $f\zeta$, based on their regiments and ranks. He observed that any solution
would amount to having two *separate* squares, one for Latin letters and another
for Greek. Each of those squares is supposed to have distinct entries in rows and
columns; so he began by studying the possible configurations for $\{a, b, c, d, e, f\}$,
which he called *Latin squares*. A Latin square can be paired up with a Greek
square to form a "Græco-Latin square" only if the squares are *orthogonal* to each
other, meaning that no (Latin, Greek) pair of letters can be found together in
more than one place when the squares are superimposed. For example, if we let
$a = \mathtt{A}$, $b = \mathtt{K}$, $c = \mathtt{Q}$, $d = \mathtt{J}$, $\alpha = \clubsuit$, $\beta = \spadesuit$, $\gamma = \diamondsuit$, and $\delta = \heartsuit$, Fig. 1 is equivalent

to the Latin, Greek, and Græco-Latin squares

$$\begin{pmatrix} d & a & b & c \\ c & b & a & d \\ a & d & c & b \\ b & c & d & a \end{pmatrix}, \quad \begin{pmatrix} \gamma & \delta & \beta & \alpha \\ \beta & \alpha & \gamma & \delta \\ \alpha & \beta & \delta & \gamma \\ \delta & \gamma & \alpha & \beta \end{pmatrix}, \quad \text{and} \quad \begin{pmatrix} d\gamma & a\delta & b\beta & c\alpha \\ c\beta & b\alpha & a\gamma & d\delta \\ a\alpha & d\beta & c\delta & b\gamma \\ b\delta & c\gamma & d\alpha & a\beta \end{pmatrix}. \quad (5)$$

Of course we can use *any* n distinct symbols in an $n \times n$ Latin square; all that matters is that no symbol occurs twice in any row or twice in any column. So we might as well use numeric values $\{0, 1, \ldots, n-1\}$ for the entries. Furthermore we'll just refer to "latin squares" (with a lowercase "l"), instead of categorizing a square as either Latin or Greek, because orthogonality is a symmetric relation.

Euler's assertion that two 6×6 latin squares cannot be orthogonal was verified by Thomas Clausen, who reduced the problem to an examination of 17 fundamentally different cases, according to a letter from H. C. Schumacher to C. F. Gauss dated 10 August 1842. But Clausen did not publish his analysis. The first demonstration to appear in print was by G. Tarry [*Comptes rendus, Association française pour l'avancement des sciences* **29**, part 2 (1901), 170–203], who discovered in his own way that 6×6 latin squares can be classified into 17 different families. (In Section 7.2.3 we shall study how to decompose a problem into combinatorially inequivalent classes of arrangements.)

Euler's conjecture about the remaining cases $n = 10$, $n = 14$, ... was "proved" three times, by J. Petersen [*Annuaire des mathématiciens* (Paris: 1902), 413–427], by P. Wernicke [*Jahresbericht der Deutschen Math.-Vereinigung* **19** (1910), 264–267], and by H. F. MacNeish [*Annals of Math.* (2) **23** (1922), 221–227]. Flaws in all three arguments became known, however; and the question was still unsettled when computers became available many years later. One of the very first combinatorial problems to be tackled by machine was therefore the enigma of 10×10 Græco-Latin squares: Do they exist or not?

In 1957, L. J. Paige and C. B. Tompkins programmed the SWAC computer to search for a counterexample to Euler's prediction. They selected one particular 10×10 latin square "almost at random," and their program tried to find another square that would be orthogonal to it. But the results were discouraging, and they decided to shut the machine off after five hours. Already the program had generated enough data for them to predict that at least 4.8×10^{11} hours of computer time would be needed to finish the run!

Shortly afterwards, three mathematicians made a breakthrough that put latin squares onto page one of major world newspapers: R. C. Bose, S. S. Shrikhande, and E. T. Parker found a remarkable series of constructions that yield orthogonal $n \times n$ squares for all $n > 6$ [*Proc. Nat. Acad. Sci.* **45** (1959), 734–737, 859–862; *Canadian J. Math.* **12** (1960), 189–203]. Thus, after resisting attacks for 180 years, Euler's conjecture turned out to be almost entirely wrong.

Their discovery was made without computer help. But Parker worked for UNIVAC, and he soon brought programming skills into the picture by solving the problem of Paige and Tompkins in less than an hour, on a UNIVAC 1206 Military Computer. [See *Proc. Symp. Applied Math.* **10** (1960), 71–83; **15** (1963), 73–81.]

Let's take a closer look at what the earlier programmers did, and how Parker dramatically demolished their approach. Paige and Tompkins began with the following 10×10 square L and its unknown orthogonal mate(s) M:

$$L = \begin{pmatrix} 0 & 1 & 2 & 3 & 4 & 5 & 6 & 7 & 8 & 9 \\ 1 & 8 & 3 & 2 & 5 & 4 & 7 & 6 & 9 & 0 \\ 2 & 9 & 5 & 6 & 3 & 0 & 8 & 4 & 7 & 1 \\ 3 & 7 & 0 & 9 & 8 & 6 & 1 & 5 & 2 & 4 \\ 4 & 6 & 7 & 5 & 2 & 9 & 0 & 8 & 1 & 3 \\ 5 & 0 & 9 & 4 & 7 & 8 & 3 & 1 & 6 & 2 \\ 6 & 5 & 4 & 7 & 1 & 3 & 2 & 9 & 0 & 8 \\ 7 & 4 & 1 & 8 & 0 & 2 & 9 & 3 & 5 & 6 \\ 8 & 3 & 6 & 0 & 9 & 1 & 5 & 2 & 4 & 7 \\ 9 & 2 & 8 & 1 & 6 & 7 & 4 & 0 & 3 & 5 \end{pmatrix} \quad \text{and} \quad M = \begin{pmatrix} 0 & \sqcup & \sqcup & \sqcup & \sqcup & \sqcup & \sqcup & \sqcup & \sqcup & \sqcup \\ 1 & \sqcup & \sqcup & \sqcup & \sqcup & \sqcup & \sqcup & \sqcup & \sqcup & \sqcup \\ 2 & \sqcup & \sqcup & \sqcup & \sqcup & \sqcup & \sqcup & \sqcup & \sqcup & \sqcup \\ 3 & \sqcup & \sqcup & \sqcup & \sqcup & \sqcup & \sqcup & \sqcup & \sqcup & \sqcup \\ 4 & \sqcup & \sqcup & \sqcup & \sqcup & \sqcup & \sqcup & \sqcup & \sqcup & \sqcup \\ 5 & \sqcup & \sqcup & \sqcup & \sqcup & \sqcup & \sqcup & \sqcup & \sqcup & \sqcup \\ 6 & \sqcup & \sqcup & \sqcup & \sqcup & \sqcup & \sqcup & \sqcup & \sqcup & \sqcup \\ 7 & \sqcup & \sqcup & \sqcup & \sqcup & \sqcup & \sqcup & \sqcup & \sqcup & \sqcup \\ 8 & \sqcup & \sqcup & \sqcup & \sqcup & \sqcup & \sqcup & \sqcup & \sqcup & \sqcup \\ 9 & \sqcup & \sqcup & \sqcup & \sqcup & \sqcup & \sqcup & \sqcup & \sqcup & \sqcup \end{pmatrix}. \quad (6)$$

We can assume without loss of generality that the rows of M begin with 0, 1, ..., 9, as shown. The problem is to fill in the remaining 90 blank entries, and the original SWAC program proceeded from top to bottom, left to right. The top left $\sqcup$ can't be filled with 0, since 0 has already occurred in the top row of M. And it can't be 1 either, because the pair $(1, 1)$ already occurs at the left of the next row in (L, M). We can, however, tentatively insert a 2. The digit 1 can be placed next; and pretty soon we find the lexicographically smallest top row that might work for M, namely 0214365897. Similarly, the smallest rows that fit below 0214365897 are 1023456789 and 2108537946; and the smallest legitimate row below them is 3540619278. Now, unfortunately, the going gets tougher: There's no way to complete another row without coming into conflict with a previous choice. So we change 3540619278 to 3540629178 (but that doesn't work either), then to 3540698172, and so on for several more steps, until finally 3546109278 can be followed by 4397028651 before we get stuck again.

In Section 7.2.2 we'll study ways to estimate the behavior of such searches, without actually performing them. Such estimates tell us in this case that the Paige–Tompkins method essentially traverses an implicit search tree that contains about 2.5×10^{18} nodes. Most of those nodes belong to only a few levels of the tree; more than half of them deal with choices on the right half of the sixth row of M, after about 50 of the 90 blanks have been tentatively filled in. A typical node of the search tree probably requires about 75 mems (memory accesses) for processing, to check validity. Therefore the total running time on a modern computer would be roughly the time needed to perform 2×10^{20} mems.

Parker, on the other hand, went back to the method that Euler had originally used to search for orthogonal mates in 1779. First he found all of the so-called *transversals* of L, namely all ways to choose some of its elements so that there's exactly one element in each row, one in each column, and one of each value. For example, one transversal is 0859734216, in Euler's notation, meaning that we choose the 0 in column 0, the 8 in column 1, ..., the 6 in column 9. Each transversal that includes the k in L's leftmost column represents a legitimate way to place the ten k's into square M. The task of finding transversals is, in fact, rather easy, and the given matrix L turns out to have exactly 808 of them; there are respectively $(79, 96, 76, 87, 70, 84, 83, 75, 95, 63)$ transversals for $k = (0, 1, \ldots, 9)$.

Once the transversals are known, we're left with an exact cover problem of 10 stages, which is much simpler than the original 90-stage problem in (6). All we need to do is cover the square with ten transversals that don't intersect — because every such set of ten is equivalent to a latin square M that is orthogonal to L.

The particular square L in (6) has, in fact, exactly one orthogonal mate:

$$
\begin{pmatrix}
0 & 1 & 2 & 3 & 4 & 5 & 6 & 7 & 8 & 9 \\
1 & 8 & 3 & 2 & 5 & 4 & 7 & 6 & 9 & 0 \\
2 & 9 & 5 & 6 & 3 & 0 & 8 & 4 & 7 & 1 \\
3 & 7 & 0 & 9 & 8 & 6 & 1 & 5 & 2 & 4 \\
4 & 6 & 7 & 5 & 2 & 9 & 0 & 8 & 1 & 3 \\
5 & 0 & 9 & 4 & 7 & 8 & 3 & 1 & 6 & 2 \\
6 & 5 & 4 & 7 & 1 & 3 & 2 & 9 & 0 & 8 \\
7 & 4 & 1 & 8 & 0 & 2 & 9 & 3 & 5 & 6 \\
8 & 3 & 6 & 0 & 9 & 1 & 5 & 2 & 4 & 7 \\
9 & 2 & 8 & 1 & 6 & 7 & 4 & 0 & 3 & 5
\end{pmatrix}
\perp
\begin{pmatrix}
0 & 2 & 8 & 5 & 9 & 4 & 7 & 3 & 6 & 1 \\
1 & 7 & 4 & 9 & 3 & 6 & 5 & 0 & 2 & 8 \\
2 & 5 & 6 & 4 & 8 & 7 & 0 & 1 & 9 & 3 \\
3 & 6 & 9 & 0 & 4 & 5 & 8 & 2 & 1 & 7 \\
4 & 8 & 1 & 7 & 5 & 3 & 6 & 9 & 0 & 2 \\
5 & 1 & 7 & 8 & 0 & 2 & 9 & 4 & 3 & 6 \\
6 & 9 & 0 & 2 & 7 & 1 & 3 & 8 & 4 & 5 \\
7 & 3 & 5 & 1 & 2 & 0 & 4 & 6 & 8 & 9 \\
8 & 0 & 2 & 3 & 6 & 9 & 1 & 7 & 5 & 4 \\
9 & 4 & 3 & 6 & 1 & 8 & 2 & 5 & 7 & 0
\end{pmatrix}. \tag{7}
$$

The dancing links algorithm finds it, and proves its uniqueness, after doing only about 1.7×10^8 mems of computation, given the 808 transversals. Furthermore, the cost of the transversal-finding phase, about 5 million mems, is negligible by comparison. Thus the original running time of 2×10^{20} mems — which once was regarded as the inevitable cost of solving a problem for which there are 10^{90} ways to fill in the blanks — has been reduced by a further factor of more than 10^{12}(!).

We will see later that advances have also been made in methods for solving 90-level problems like (6). Indeed, (6) turns out to be representable directly as an exact cover problem (see exercise 17), which the dancing links procedure of Section 7.2.2.1 solves after expending only 1.3×10^{11} mems. Even so, the Euler–Parker approach remains about a thousand times better than the Paige–Tompkins approach. By "factoring" the problem into two separate phases, one for transversal-finding and one for transversal-combining, Euler and Parker essentially reduced the computational cost from a product, $T_1 T_2$, to a sum, $T_1 + T_2$.

The moral of this story is clear: Combinatorial problems might confront us with a huge universe of possibilities, yet we shouldn't give up too easily. A single good idea can reduce the amount of computation by many orders of magnitude.

Puzzles versus the real world. Many of the combinatorial problems we shall study in this chapter, like Langford's problem of pairs or Ozanam's problem of the sixteen honor cards, originated as amusing puzzles or "brain twisters." Some readers might be put off by this emphasis on recreational topics, which they regard as a frivolous waste of time. Shouldn't computers really be doing useful work? And shouldn't textbooks about computers be primarily concerned with significant applications to industry and/or world progress?

Well, the author of the textbook you are reading has absolutely no objections to useful work and human progress. But he believes strongly that a book such as this should stress *methods* of problem solving, together with mathematical ideas and *models* that help to solve many different problems, rather than focusing on the reasons why those methods and models might be useful. We shall learn many beautiful and powerful ways to attack combinatorial problems, and the elegance of those methods will be our main motivation for studying them. Combinatorial challenges pop up everywhere, and new ways to apply the techniques discussed in this chapter arise every day. So let's not limit our horizons by attempting to catalog in advance what the ideas are good for.

For example, it turns out that orthogonal latin squares are enormously useful, particularly in the design of experiments. Already in 1788, François Cretté de Palluel used a 4×4 latin square to study what happens when sixteen sheep — four each from four different breeds — were fed four different diets and harvested at four different times. [*Mémoires d'Agriculture* (Paris: Société Royale d'Agriculture, trimestre d'été, 1788), 17–23.] The latin square allowed him to do this with 16 sheep instead of 64; with a Græco-Latin square he could also have varied another parameter by trying, say, four different quantities of food or four different grazing paradigms.

But if we had focused our discussion on his approach to animal husbandry, we might well have gotten bogged down in details about breeding, about root vegetables versus grains and the costs of growing them, etc. Readers who aren't farmers might therefore have decided to skip the whole topic, even though latin square designs apply to a wide range of studies. (Think about testing five kinds of pills, on patients in five stages of some disease, five age brackets, and five weight groups.) Moreover, a concentration on experimental design could lead readers to miss the fact that latin squares also have important applications to discrete geometry and error-correcting codes (see exercises 18–24).

Even the topic of Langford pairing, which seems at first to be purely recreational, turns out to have practical importance. T. Skolem used Langford sequences to construct Steiner triple systems, which we have applied to database queries in Section 6.5 [see *Math. Scandinavica* **6** (1958), 273–280]; and in the 1960s, E. J. Groth of Motorola Corporation applied Langford pairs to the design of circuits for multiplication. Furthermore, the algorithms that efficiently find Langford pairs and latin square transversals, such as the method of dancing links, apply to exact cover problems in general; and the problem of exact covering has great relevance to crucial problems such as the equitable apportionment of voter precincts to electoral districts, etc.

The applications are not the most important thing, and neither are the puzzles. Our primary goal is rather to get basic concepts into our brains, like the notions of latin squares and exact covering. Such notions give us the building blocks, vocabulary, and insights that *tomorrow's* problems will need.

Still, it's foolish to discuss problem solving without actually solving any problems. We need good problems to stimulate our creative juices, to light up our grey cells in a more-or-less organized fashion, and to make the basic concepts familiar. Mind-bending puzzles are often ideal for this purpose, because they can be presented in a few words, needing no complicated background knowledge.

Václav Havel once remarked that the complexities of life are vast: "There is too much to know... We have to abandon the arrogant belief that the world is merely a puzzle to be solved, a machine with instructions for use waiting to be discovered, a body of information to be fed into a computer." He called for an increased sense of justice and responsibility; for taste, courage, and compassion. His words were filled with great wisdom. Yet thank goodness we do also have puzzles that *can* be solved! Puzzles deserve to be counted among the great pleasures of life, to be enjoyed in moderation like all other treats.

Of course, Langford and Ozanam directed their puzzles to human beings, not to computers. Aren't we missing the point if we merely shuffle such questions off to machines, to be solved by brute force instead of by rational thought? George Brewster, writing to Martin Gardner in 1963, expressed a widely held view as follows: "Feeding a recreational puzzle into a computer is no more than a step above dynamiting a trout stream. Succumbing to instant recreation."

Yes, but that view misses another important point: Simple puzzles often have generalizations that go beyond human ability and arouse our curiosity. The study of those generalizations often suggests instructive methods that apply to numerous other problems and have surprising consequences. Indeed, many of the key techniques that we shall study were born when people were trying to solve various puzzles. While writing this chapter, the author couldn't help relishing the fact that puzzles are now more fun than ever, as computers get faster and faster, because we keep getting more powerful dynamite to play with. [Further comments appear in the author's essay, "Are toy problems useful?", originally written in 1976; see *Selected Papers on Computer Science* (1996), 169–183.]

Puzzles do have the danger that they can be *too* elegant. Good puzzles tend to be mathematically clean and well-structured, but we also need to learn how to deal systematically with the messy, chaotic, organic stuff that surrounds us every day. Indeed, some computational techniques are important chiefly because they provide powerful ways to cope with such complexities. That is why, for example, the arcane rules of library-card alphabetization were presented at the beginning of Chapter 5, and an actual elevator system was discussed at length to illustrate simulation techniques in Section 2.2.5.

A collection of programs and data called the Stanford GraphBase (SGB) has been prepared so that experiments with combinatorial algorithms can readily be performed on a variety of real-world examples. SGB includes, for example, data about American highways, and an input-output model of the U.S. economy; it records the casts of characters in Homer's *Iliad*, Tolstoy's *Anna Karenina*, and several other novels; it encapsulates the structure of Roget's *Thesaurus* of 1879; it documents hundreds of college football scores; it specifies the gray-value pixels of Leonardo da Vinci's *Gioconda* (Mona Lisa). And perhaps most importantly, SGB contains a collection of five-letter words, which we shall discuss next.

The five-letter words of English. Many of the examples in this chapter will be based on the following list of five-letter words:

aargh, abaca, abaci, aback, abaft, abase, abash, ... , zooms, zowie. (8)

(There are 5757 words altogether — too many to display here; but those that are missing can readily be imagined.) It's a personal list, collected by the author between 1972 and 1992, beginning when he realized that such words would make ideal data for testing many kinds of combinatorial algorithms.

The list has intentionally been restricted to words that are **truly** part of the English language, in the sense that the author has encountered them in actual use. Unabridged dictionaries contain thousands of entries that are much more esoteric, like `aalii`, `abamp`, ..., `zymin`, and `zyxst`; words like that are useful primarily to SCRABBLE® players. But unfamiliar words tend to **spoil** the fun for anybody who doesn't know them. Therefore, for twenty years, the author systematically took note of all **words** that seemed **right** for the expository **goals** of *The Art of Computer Programming*.

Finally it was necessary to freeze the collection, in order to have a **fixed point** for reproducible experiments. The English language will always be evolving, but the 5757 SGB words will therefore always stay the same — even though the author has been tempted at times to add a few words that he didn't know in 1992, such as `chads`, `stent`, `blogs`, `ditzy`, `phish`, `bling`, and possibly `tetch`. No; `noway`. The time for any changes to SGB has long since **ended: finis**.

> *The following Glossary is intended to contain all well-known English words*
> *... which may be used in good Society, and which can serve as Links.*
> *... There must be a stent to the admission of spick words.*
> — LEWIS CARROLL, *Doublets: A Word-Puzzle* (1879)

> *If there is such a verb as to tetch, Mr. Lillywaite tetched.*
> — ROBERT BARNARD, *Corpse in a Gilded Cage* (1984)

Proper names like `Knuth` are not considered to be legitimate words. But `gauss` and `hardy` are `valid`, because "gauss" is a unit of magnetic induction and "hardy" is hardy. In fact, SGB words are composed entirely of ordinary lowercase letters; the list contains no hyphenated words, contractions, or terms like `blasé` that require an accent. Thus each word can also be regarded as a vector, which has five components in the range $[0 .. 26)$. In the vector sense, the words `yucca` and `abuzz` are furthest apart: The Euclidean distance between them is

$$\|(24, 20, 2, 2, 0) - (0, 1, 20, 25, 25)\|_2 = \sqrt{24^2 + 19^2 + 18^2 + 23^2 + 25^2} = \sqrt{2415}.$$

The entire Stanford GraphBase, including all of its programs and data sets, is easy to download from the author's website (see page iv). And the list of all SGB words is even easier to obtain, because it is in the file '`sgb-words.txt`' at the same place. That file contains 5757 lines with one word per line, beginning with '`which`' and ending with '`pupal`'. The words appear in a default order, corresponding to frequency of usage; for example, the words of rank 1000, 2000, 3000, 4000, and 5000 are respectively `ditch`, `galls`, `visas`, `faker`, and `pismo`. The notation '`WORDS`(n)' will be used in this chapter to stand for the n most common words, according to this ranking.

Incidentally, five-letter words include many plurals of *four-letter words*, and it should be noted that no Victorian-style censorship was done. Potentially offensive vocabulary has been expurgated from *The Official SCRABBLE® Players Dictionary*, but not from the SGB. One way to ensure that semantically unsuitable

terms will not appear in a professional paper based on the SGB wordlist is to
restrict consideration to WORDS(n) where n is, say, 3000.

Exercises 26–37 below can be used as warmups for initial explorations of the
SGB words, which we'll see in many different combinatorial contexts throughout
this chapter. For example, while covering problems are still on our minds, we
might as well note that the four words 'third flock began jumps' cover 20 of
the first 21 letters of the alphabet. Five words can, however, cover at most 24
different letters, as in {becks, fjord, glitz, nymph, squaw} — unless we resort to
a rare non-SGB word like waqfs (Islamic endowments), which can be combined
with {gyved, bronx, chimp, klutz} to cover 25.

Simple words from WORDS(400) suffice to make a *word square*:

$$
\begin{array}{l}
\texttt{class} \\
\texttt{light} \\
\texttt{agree} \\
\texttt{sheep} \\
\texttt{steps}
\end{array}
\qquad\qquad (9)
$$

We need to go almost to WORDS(3000), however, to obtain a *word cube*,

$$
\begin{array}{lllll}
\texttt{types} & \texttt{yeast} & \texttt{pasta} & \texttt{ester} & \texttt{start} \\
\texttt{yeast} & \texttt{earth} & \texttt{armor} & \texttt{stove} & \texttt{three} \\
\texttt{pasta} & \texttt{armor} & \texttt{smoke} & \texttt{token} & \texttt{arena} \\
\texttt{ester} & \texttt{stove} & \texttt{token} & \texttt{event} & \texttt{rents} \\
\texttt{start} & \texttt{three} & \texttt{arena} & \texttt{rents} & \texttt{tease}
\end{array}
\qquad (10)
$$

in which every 5×5 "slice" is a word square. With a simple extension of the
basic dancing links algorithm (see Section 7.2.2.1), one can show after performing
about 390 billion mems of computation that WORDS(3000) supports only three
symmetric word cubes such as (10); exercise 36 reveals the other two. Surprisingly, 83,576 symmetrical cubes can be made from the full set, WORDS(5757).

Graphs from words. It's interesting and important to arrange objects into
rows, squares, cubes, and other designs; but in practical applications another
kind of combinatorial structure is even *more* interesting and important, namely
a *graph*. Recall from Section 2.3.4.1 that a graph is a set of points called
vertices, together with a set of lines called *edges*, which connect certain pairs
of vertices. Graphs are ubiquitous, and many beautiful graph algorithms have
been discovered, so graphs will naturally be the primary focus of many sections
in this chapter. In fact, the Stanford GraphBase is primarily about graphs, as
its name implies; and the SGB words were collected chiefly because they can be
used to define interesting and instructive graphs.

Lewis Carroll blazed the trail by inventing a game that he called Word-
Links or Doublets, at the end of 1877. [See Martin Gardner, *The Universe in
a Handkerchief* (1996), Chapter 6.] Carroll's idea, which soon became quite
popular, was to transform one word to another by changing a letter at a time:

$$
\texttt{tears} - \texttt{sears} - \texttt{stars} - \texttt{stare} - \texttt{stale} - \texttt{stile} - \texttt{smile}. \qquad (11)
$$

The shortest such transformation is the shortest *path* in a graph, where the vertices of the graph are English words and the edges join pairs of words that have "Hamming distance 1" (meaning that they disagree in just one place).

When restricted to SGB words, Carroll's rule produces a graph of the Stanford GraphBase whose official name is $words(5757, 0, 0, 0)$. Every graph defined by SGB has a unique identifier called its *id*, and the graphs that are derived in Carrollian fashion from SGB words are identified by *id*s of the form $words(n, l, t, s)$. Here n is the number of vertices; l is either 0 or a list of weights, used to emphasize various kinds of vocabulary; t is a threshold so that low-weight words can be disallowed; and s is the seed for any pseudorandom numbers that might be needed to break ties between words of equal weight. The full details needn't concern us, but a few examples will give the general idea:

- $words(n, 0, 0, 0)$ is precisely the graph that arises when Carroll's idea is applied to $\text{WORDS}(n)$, for $1 \le n \le 5757$.
- $words(1000, \{0, 0, 0, 0, 0, 0, 0, 0, 0, 0\}, 0, s)$ contains 1000 randomly chosen SGB words, usually different for different values of s.
- $words(766, \{0, 0, 0, 0, 0, 0, 0, 1, 0\}, 1, 0)$ contains all of the five-letter words that appear in *The TEXbook* and *The METAFONTbook*.

There are only 766 words in the latter graph, so we can't form very many long paths like (11), although

$$\text{basic} — \text{basis} — \text{bases} — \text{based}$$
$$— \text{baked} — \text{naked} — \text{named} — \text{names} — \text{games} \qquad (12)$$

is one noteworthy example.

Of course there are many other ways to define the edges of a graph when the vertices represent five-letter words. We could, for example, require the Euclidean distance to be small, instead of the Hamming distance. Or we could declare two words to be adjacent whenever they share a subword of length four; that strategy would substantially enrich the graph, making it possible for chaos to yield peace, even when confined to the 766 words that are related to TEX:

$$\text{chaos} — \text{chose} — \text{chore} — \text{score} — \text{store}$$
$$— \text{stare} — \text{spare} — \text{space} — \text{peace}. \qquad (13)$$

(In this rule we remove a letter, then insert another, possibly in a different place.) Or we might choose a totally different strategy, like putting an edge between word vectors $a_1a_2a_3a_4a_5$ and $b_1b_2b_3b_4b_5$ if and only if their dot product $a_1b_1 + a_2b_2 + a_3b_3 + a_4b_4 + a_5b_5$ is a multiple of some parameter m. Graph algorithms thrive on different kinds of data.

SGB words lead also to an interesting family of *directed* graphs, if we write $a_1a_2a_3a_4a_5 \to b_1b_2b_3b_4b_5$ when $\{a_2, a_3, a_4, a_5\} \subseteq \{b_1, b_2, b_3, b_4, b_5\}$ as multisets. (Remove the first letter, insert another, and rearrange.) With this rule we can, for example, transform words to graph via a shortest oriented path of length six:

$$\text{words} \to \text{dross} \to \text{soars} \to \text{orcas} \to \text{crash} \to \text{sharp} \to \text{graph}. \qquad (14)$$

Theory is the first term in the Taylor series of practice.
— THOMAS M. COVER (1992)

The number of systems of terminology presently used in graph theory
is equal, to a close approximation, to the number of graph theorists.
— RICHARD P. STANLEY (1986)

Graph theory: The basics. A graph G consists of a set V of vertices together
with a set E of edges, which are pairs of distinct vertices. We will assume that V
and E are *finite* sets unless otherwise specified. We write $u \!-\! v$ if u and v are vertices with $\{u, v\} \in E$, and $u \not\!-\! v$ if u and v are vertices with $\{u, v\} \notin E$. Vertices
with $u \!-\! v$ are called "neighbors," and they're also said to be "adjacent" in G.
One consequence of this definition is that we have $u \!-\! v$ if and only if $v \!-\! u$.
Another consequence is that $v \not\!-\! v$, for all $v \in V$; that is, no vertex is adjacent
to itself. (We shall, however, discuss multigraphs below, in which loops from a
vertex to itself are permitted, and in which repeated edges are allowed too.)

The graph $G' = (V', E')$ is a *subgraph* of $G = (V, E)$ if $V' \subseteq V$ and $E' \subseteq E$.
It's a *spanning* subgraph of G if, in fact, $V' = V$. And it's an *induced* subgraph
of G if E' has as many edges as possible, when V' is a given subset of the
vertices. In other words, when $V' \subseteq V$ the subgraph of $G = (V, E)$ induced by
V' is $G' = (V', E')$, where

$$ E' \;=\; \{\, \{u, v\} \mid u \in V',\, v \in V',\, \text{and } \{u, v\} \in E \,\}. \qquad (15) $$

This subgraph G' is denoted by $G\,|\,V'$, and often called "G restricted to V'." In
the common case where $V' = V \setminus \{v\}$, we write simply $G \setminus v$ ("G minus vertex v")
as an abbreviation for $G \mid (V \setminus \{v\})$. The similar notation $G \setminus e$ is used when
$e \in E$ to denote the subgraph $G' = (V, E \setminus \{e\})$, obtained by removing an edge
instead of a vertex. Notice that all of the SGB graphs known as $words(n, l, t, s)$,
described earlier, are induced subgraphs of the main graph $words(5757, 0, 0, 0)$;
only the vocabulary changes in those graphs, not the rule for adjacency.

A graph with n vertices and e edges is said to have *order* n and *size* e. The
simplest and most important graphs of order n are the *complete graph* K_n, the
path P_n, and the *cycle* C_n. Suppose the vertices are $V = \{1, 2, \ldots, n\}$. Then

- K_n has $\binom{n}{2} = \frac{1}{2}n(n-1)$ edges $u \!-\! v$ for $1 \le u < v \le n$; every n-vertex
  graph is a spanning subgraph of K_n.
- P_n has $n-1$ edges $v \!-\! (v{+}1)$ for $1 \le v < n$, when $n \ge 1$; it is a path
  of length $n{-}1$ from 1 to n.
- C_n has n edges $v \!-\! ((v \bmod n){+}1)$ for $1 \le v \le n$, when $n \ge 1$; it is a graph
  only when $n \ge 3$ (but C_1 and C_2 are multigraphs).

We could actually have defined K_n, P_n, and C_n on the vertices $\{0, 1, \ldots, n{-}1\}$,
or on *any* n-element set V instead of $\{1, 2, \ldots, n\}$, because two graphs that differ
only in the names of their vertices but not in the structure of their edges are
combinatorially equivalent.

Formally, we say that graphs $G = (V, E)$ and $G' = (V', E')$ are *isomorphic*
if there is a one-to-one correspondence φ from V to V' such that $u \!-\! v$ in G if

and only if $\varphi(u) \!-\! \varphi(v)$ in G'. The notation $G \cong G'$ is often used to indicate that G and G' are isomorphic; but we shall often be less precise, by treating isomorphic graphs as if they were equal, and by occasionally writing $G = G'$ even when the vertex sets of G and G' aren't strictly identical.

Small graphs can be defined by simply drawing a diagram, in which the vertices are small circles and the edges are lines between them. Figure 2 illustrates several important examples, whose properties we will be studying later. The Petersen graph in Figure 2(e) is named after Julius Petersen, an early graph theorist who used it to disprove a plausible conjecture [L'*Intermédiaire des Mathématiciens* **5** (1898), 225–227]; it is, in fact, a remarkable configuration that serves as a counterexample to many optimistic predictions about what might be true for graphs in general. The Chvátal graph, Figure 2(f), was introduced by Václav Chvátal in *J. Combinatorial Theory* **9** (1970), 93–94.

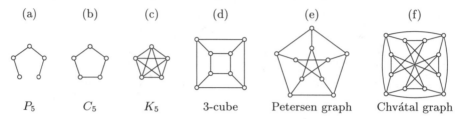

| (a) | (b) | (c) | (d) | (e) | (f) |

P_5 C_5 K_5 3-cube   Petersen graph   Chvátal graph

Fig. 2. Six example graphs, which have respectively $(5, 5, 5, 8, 10, 12)$ vertices and $(4, 5, 10, 12, 15, 24)$ edges.

The lines of a graph diagram are allowed to cross each other at points that aren't vertices. For example, the center point of Fig. 2(f) is *not* a vertex of Chvátal's graph. A graph is called *planar* if there's a way to draw it without any crossings. Clearly P_n and C_n are always planar; Fig. 2(d) shows that the 3-cube is also planar. But K_5 has too many edges to be planar (see exercise 46).

The *degree* of a vertex is the number of neighbors that it has. If all vertices have the same degree, the graph is said to be *regular*. In Fig. 2, for example, P_5 is irregular because it has two vertices of degree 1 and three of degree 2. But the other five graphs are regular, of degrees $(2, 4, 3, 3, 4)$ respectively. A regular graph of degree 3 is often called "cubic" or "trivalent."

There are many ways to draw a given graph, some of which are much more perspicuous than others. For example, each of the six diagrams

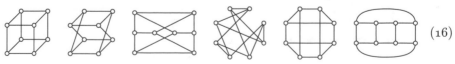

$$(16)$$

is isomorphic to the 3-cube, Fig. 2(d). The layout of Chvátal's graph that appears in Fig. 2(f) was discovered by Adrian Bondy many years after Chvátal's paper was published, thereby revealing unexpected symmetries.

The symmetries of a graph, also known as its *automorphisms*, are the permutations of its vertices that preserve adjacency. In other words, the permutation φ is an automorphism of G if we have $\varphi(u) \!-\! \varphi(v)$ whenever $u \!-\! v$ in G. A well-chosen drawing like Fig. 2(f) can reveal underlying symmetry, but a single diagram isn't always able to display all the symmetries that exist. For example, the 3-cube has 48 automorphisms, and the Petersen graph has 120. We'll study algorithms that deal with isomorphisms and automorphisms in Section 7.2.3. Symmetries can often be exploited to avoid unnecessary computations, making an algorithm almost k times faster when it operates on a graph that has k automorphisms.

Graphs that have evolved in the real world tend to be rather different from the mathematically pristine graphs of Figure 2. For example, here's a familiar graph that has no symmetry whatsoever, although it does have the virtue of being planar:

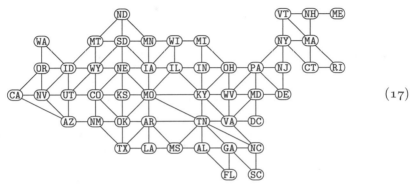

$$(17)$$

It represents the contiguous United States of America, and we'll be using it later in several examples. The 49 vertices of this diagram have been labeled with two-letter postal codes for convenience, instead of being reduced to empty circles.

Paths and cycles. A spanning path P_n of a graph is called a *Hamiltonian path*, and a spanning cycle C_n is called a *Hamiltonian cycle*, because W. R. Hamilton invented a puzzle in 1856 whose goal was to find such paths and cycles on the edges of a dodecahedron. T. P. Kirkman had independently studied the problem for convex polyhedra in general, in *Philosophical Trans.* **146** (1856), 413–418; **148** (1858), 145–161. [See *Graph Theory 1736–1936* by N. L. Biggs, E. K. Lloyd, and R. J. Wilson (1998), Chapter 2.] The task of finding a spanning path or cycle is, however, much older — indeed, we can legitimately consider it to be the oldest problem of graph theory, because paths and tours of a knight on a chessboard have a continuous history going back to ninth-century India (see Section 7.2.2.4). A graph is called *Hamiltonian* if it has a Hamiltonian cycle. (Incidentally, the Petersen graph is the smallest 3-regular graph that is neither planar nor Hamiltonian; see C. de Polignac, *Bull. Soc. Math. de France* **27** (1899), 142–145.)

The *girth* of a graph is the length of its shortest cycle; the girth is infinite if the graph is acyclic (containing no cycles). For example, the six graphs of Fig. 2 have girths $(\infty, 5, 3, 4, 5, 4)$, respectively. It's not difficult to prove that a graph of minimum degree k and girth 5 must have at least $k^2 + 1$ vertices. Further analysis shows in fact that this minimum value is achievable only if $k = 2$ (C_5), $k = 3$ (Petersen), $k = 7$, or perhaps $k = 57$. (See exercises 63 and 65.)

The *distance* $d(u, v)$ between two vertices u and v is the minimum length of a path from u to v in the graph; it is infinite if there's no such path. Clearly $d(v, v) = 0$, and $d(u, v) = d(v, u)$. We also have the triangle inequality

$$d(u, v) + d(v, w) \geq d(u, w). \tag{18}$$

For if $d(u, v) = p$ and $d(v, w) = q$ and $p < \infty$ and $q < \infty$, there are paths

$$u = u_0 \text{---} u_1 \text{---} \cdots \text{---} u_p = v \quad \text{and} \quad v = v_0 \text{---} v_1 \text{---} \cdots \text{---} v_q = w, \tag{19}$$

and we can find the least subscript r such that $u_r = v_s$ for some s. Then

$$u_0 \text{---} u_1 \text{---} \cdots \text{---} u_{r-1} \text{---} v_s \text{---} v_{s+1} \text{---} \cdots \text{---} v_q \tag{20}$$

is a path of length $\leq p + q$ from u to w.

The *diameter* of a graph is the maximum of $d(u, v)$, over all vertices u and v. The graph is *connected* if its diameter is finite. The vertices of a graph can always be partitioned into connected *components*, where two vertices u and v belong to the same component if and only if $d(u, v) < \infty$.

In the graph $words(5757, 0, 0, 0)$, for example, we have $d(\texttt{tears}, \texttt{smile}) = 6$, because (11) is a shortest path from $\texttt{tears}$ to $\texttt{smile}$. Also $d(\texttt{tears}, \texttt{happy}) = 6$, and $d(\texttt{smile}, \texttt{happy}) = 10$, and $d(\texttt{world}, \texttt{court}) = 6$. But $d(\texttt{world}, \texttt{happy}) = \infty$; the graph isn't connected. In fact, it contains 671 words like $\texttt{aloof}$, which have no neighbors and form connected components of order 1 all by themselves. Word pairs such as $\texttt{alpha}$ — $\texttt{aloha}$, $\texttt{droid}$ — $\texttt{druid}$, and $\texttt{opium}$ — $\texttt{odium}$ account for 103 further components of order 2. Some components of order 3, like $\texttt{chain}$ — $\texttt{chair}$ — $\texttt{choir}$, are paths; others, like $\{\texttt{getup}, \texttt{letup}, \texttt{setup}\}$, are cycles. A few more small components are also present, like the curious path

$$\texttt{login} \text{---} \texttt{logic} \text{---} \texttt{yogic} \text{---} \texttt{yogis} \text{---} \texttt{yogas} \text{---} \texttt{togas}, \tag{21}$$

whose words have no other neighbors. But the vast majority of all five-letter words belong to a giant component of order 4493. If you can go two steps away from a given word, changing two different letters, the odds are better than 15 to 1 that your word is connected to everything in the giant component.

Similarly, the graph $words(n, 0, 0, 0)$ has a giant component of order (3825, 2986, 2056, 1186, 224) when $n = (5000, 4000, 3000, 2000, 1000)$, respectively. But if n is small, there aren't enough edges to provide much connectivity. For example, $words(500, 0, 0, 0)$ has 327 different components, none of order 15 or more.

The concept of distance can be generalized to $d(v_1, v_2, \ldots, v_k)$ for any value of k, meaning the minimum number of edges in a connected subgraph that contains the vertices $\{v_1, v_2, \ldots, v_k\}$. For example, $d(\texttt{blood}, \texttt{sweat}, \texttt{tears})$ turns out to be 15, because the subgraph

$$
\begin{array}{l}
\texttt{blood} \text{---} \texttt{brood} \text{---} \texttt{broad} \text{---} \texttt{bread} \text{---} \texttt{tread} \text{---} \texttt{treed} \text{---} \texttt{tweed} \\[4pt]
\texttt{tears} \text{---} \texttt{teams} \text{---} \texttt{trams} \text{---} \texttt{trims} \text{---} \texttt{tries} \text{---} \texttt{trees} \quad \texttt{tweet} \\[4pt]
\hspace{22em} \texttt{sweat} \text{---} \texttt{sweet}
\end{array}
\tag{22}
$$

has 15 edges, and there's no suitable 14-edge subgraph.

We noted in Section 2.3.4.1 that a connected graph with fewest edges is called a *free tree*. A subgraph that corresponds to the generalized distance $d(v_1, \ldots, v_k)$ will always be a free tree. It is misleadingly called a *Steiner tree*, because Jacob Steiner once mentioned the case $k = 3$ for points $\{v_1, v_2, v_3\}$ in the Euclidean plane [*Crelle* **13** (1835), 362–363]. Joseph Gergonne had, however, already posed and solved the problem for *any* k points in the plane [*Annales de mathématiques pures et appliquées* **1** (1811), 292, 375–384 and planche 6].

Coloring. A graph is said to be k-*partite* or k-*colorable* if its vertices can be partitioned into k or fewer parts, with the endpoints of each edge belonging to different parts—or equivalently, if there's a way to paint its vertices with at most k different colors, never assigning the same color to two adjacent vertices. The famous Four Color Theorem, conjectured by F. Guthrie in 1852 and finally proved with massive computer aid by K. Appel, W. Haken, and J. Koch [*Illinois J. Math.* **21** (1977), 429–567], states that *every planar graph is 4-colorable*. No simple proof is known, but special cases like (17) can be colored at sight (see exercise 45); and $O(n^2)$ steps suffice to 4-color a planar graph in general [N. Robertson, D. P. Sanders, P. Seymour, and R. Thomas, *STOC* **28** (1996), 571–575].

The case of 2-colorable graphs is especially important in practice. A 2-partite graph is generally called *bipartite*, or simply a "bigraph"; every edge of such a graph has one endpoint in each part.

Theorem B. *A graph is bipartite if and only if it contains no cycle of odd length.*

Proof. [See D. König, *Math. Annalen* **77** (1916), 453–454.] Every subgraph of a k-partite graph is k-partite. Therefore the cycle C_n can be a subgraph of a bipartite graph only if C_n itself is a bigraph, in which case n must be even.

Conversely, if a graph contains no odd cycles we can color its vertices with the two colors $\{0, 1\}$ by carrying out the following procedure: Begin with all vertices uncolored. If all neighbors of colored vertices are already colored, choose an uncolored vertex w, and color it 0. Otherwise choose a colored vertex u that has an uncolored neighbor v; assign to v the opposite color. Exercise 48 proves that a valid 2-coloring is eventually obtained. ∎

The *complete bipartite graph* $K_{m,n}$ is the largest bipartite graph whose vertices have two parts of sizes m and n. We can define it on the vertex set $\{1, 2, \ldots, m+n\}$ by saying that $u \,$—$\, v$ whenever $1 \le u \le m < v \le m + n$. In other words, $K_{m,n}$ has mn edges, one for each way to choose one vertex in the first part and another in the second part. Similarly, the *complete k-partite graph* $K_{n_1, \ldots, n_k}$ has $N = n_1 + \cdots + n_k$ vertices partitioned into parts of sizes $\{n_1, \ldots, n_k\}$, and it has edges between any two vertices that don't belong to the same part. Here are some examples when $N = 6$:

$$\text{[graph } K_{1,5}\text{]} \quad ; \qquad \text{[graph]} \cong \text{[graph]} \quad ; \qquad \text{[graph]} \cong \text{[graph]} \quad . \qquad (23)$$

$$K_{1,5} \qquad\qquad K_{3,3} \qquad\qquad\qquad K_{2,2,2}$$

Notice that $K_{1,n}$ is a free tree; it is popularly called the *star graph* of order $n+1$.

From now on say "digraph" instead of "directed graph."
It is clear and short and it will catch on.
— GEORGE PÓLYA, letter to Frank Harary (c. 1954)

Directed graphs. In Section 2.3.4.2 we defined *directed graphs* (or *digraphs*), which are very much like graphs except that they have *arcs* instead of edges. An arc $u \longrightarrow v$ runs from one vertex to another, while an edge $u \,—\, v$ joins two vertices without distinguishing between them. Furthermore, digraphs are allowed to have self-loops $v \longrightarrow v$ from a vertex to itself, and more than one arc $u \longrightarrow v$ may be present between the same vertices u and v.

Formally, a digraph $D = (V, A)$ of order n and size m is a set V of n vertices and a multiset A of m ordered pairs (u, v), where $u \in V$ and $v \in V$. The ordered pairs are called arcs, and we write $u \longrightarrow v$ when $(u, v) \in A$. The digraph is called *simple* if A is actually a set instead of a general multiset — namely, if there's at most one arc (u, v) for all u and v. Each arc (u, v) has an initial vertex u and a final vertex v, also called its "tip." Each vertex has an *out-degree* $d^+(v)$, the number of arcs for which v is the initial vertex, and an *in-degree* $d^-(v)$, the number of arcs for which v is the tip. A vertex with in-degree 0 is called a "source"; a vertex with out-degree 0 is called a "sink." Notice that $\sum_{v \in V} d^+(v) = \sum_{v \in V} d^-(v)$, because both sums are equal to m, the total number of arcs.

Most of the notions we've defined for graphs carry over to digraphs in a natural way, if we just insert the word "directed" or "oriented" (or the syllable "di") when it's necessary to distinguish between edges and arcs. For example, digraphs have subdigraphs, which can be spanning or induced or neither. An isomorphism between digraphs $D = (V, A)$ and $D' = (V', A')$ is a one-to-one correspondence φ from V to V' for which the number of arcs $u \longrightarrow v$ in D equals the number of arcs $\varphi(u) \longrightarrow \varphi(v)$ in D', for all $u, v \in V$.

Diagrams for digraphs use arrows between the vertices, instead of unadorned lines. The simplest and most important digraphs of order n are directed variants of the graphs K_n, P_n, and C_n, namely the *transitive tournament* $K_n^{\rightarrow}$, the *oriented path* $P_n^{\rightarrow}$, and the *oriented cycle* $C_n^{\rightarrow}$. They can be schematically indicated by the following diagrams for $n = 5$:

$$K_5^{\rightarrow} \qquad\qquad\qquad P_5^{\rightarrow} \qquad\qquad\qquad C_5^{\rightarrow} \tag{24}$$

There's also the *complete digraph* J_n, which is the largest simple digraph on n vertices; it has n^2 arcs $u \longrightarrow v$, one for each choice of u and v.

Figure 3 shows a more elaborate diagram, for a digraph of order 17 that we might call "expressly oriented": It is the directed graph described by Hercule Poirot in Agatha Christie's novel *Murder on the Orient Express* (1934). Vertices correspond to the berths of the Stamboul–Calais coach in that story, and an arc $u \longrightarrow v$ means that the occupant of berth u has corroborated the alibi of the person in berth v. This example has six connected components, namely $\{0, 1, 3, 6, 8, 12, 13, 14, 15, 16\}$, $\{2\}$, $\{4, 5\}$, $\{7\}$, $\{9\}$, and $\{10, 11\}$, because connectivity in a digraph is determined by treating arcs as edges.

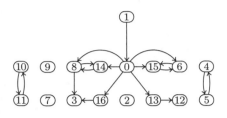

2: Samuel Edward Ratchett, the deceased American
3: Caroline Martha Hubbard, the American matron
4: Edward Henry Masterman, the British valet
5: Antonio Foscarelli, the Italian automobile salesman
6: Hector Willard MacQueen, the American secretary
7: Harvey Harris, the Englishman who didn't show up
8: Hildegarde Schmidt, the German lady's maid
9: (vacancy)
10: Greta Ohlsson, the Swedish nurse
11: Mary Hermione Debenham, the English governess
12: Helena Maria Andrenyi, the beautiful countess
13: Rudolph Andrenyi, the Hungarian count/diplomat
14: Natalia Dragomiroff, the Russian princess dowager
15: Colonel Arbuthnot, the British officer from India
16: Cyrus Bethman Hardman, the American detective

LEGEND
0: Pierre Michel, the French conductor
1: Hercule Poirot, the Belgian detective

Fig. 3. A digraph of order 17 and size 18, devised by Agatha Christie.

Two arcs are *consecutive* if the tip of the first is the initial vertex of the second. A sequence of consecutive arcs $(a_1, a_2, \ldots, a_k)$ is called a *walk* of length k; it can be symbolized by showing the vertices as well as the arcs:

$$v_0 \xrightarrow{a_1} v_1 \xrightarrow{a_2} v_2 \cdots v_{k-1} \xrightarrow{a_k} v_k. \tag{25}$$

In a simple digraph it's sufficient merely to specify the vertices; for example, $1 \longrightarrow 0 \longrightarrow 8 \longrightarrow 14 \longrightarrow 8 \longrightarrow 3$ is a walk in Fig. 3. The walk in (25) is an oriented *path* when the vertices $\{v_0, v_1, \ldots, v_k\}$ are distinct; it's an oriented *cycle* when they are distinct except that $v_k = v_0$.

In a digraph, the directed distance $d(u, v)$ is the number of arcs in the shortest *oriented* path from u to v, which is also the length of the shortest walk from u to v. It may differ from $d(v, u)$; but the triangle inequality (18) remains valid.

Every graph can be regarded as a digraph, because an edge $u \relbar v$ is essentially equivalent to a matched pair of arcs, $u \longrightarrow v$ and $v \longrightarrow u$. The digraph obtained in this way retains all the properties of the original graph; for example, the degree of each vertex in the graph becomes its out-degree in the digraph, and also its in-degree in the digraph. Furthermore, distances remain the same.

A *multigraph* (V, E) is like a graph except that its edges E can be any *multiset* of pairs $\{u, v\}$; edges $v \relbar v$ that loop from a vertex to itself, which correspond to "multipairs" $\{v, v\}$, are also permitted. For example,

$$\text{①—②—③} \tag{26}$$

is a multigraph of order 3 with six edges, $\{1,1\}$, $\{1,2\}$, $\{2,3\}$, $\{2,3\}$, $\{3,3\}$, and $\{3,3\}$. The vertex degrees in this example are $d(1) = d(2) = 3$ and $d(3) = 6$, because each loop contributes 2 to the degree of its vertex. An edge loop $v \relbar v$ becomes *two* arc loops $v \longrightarrow v$ when a multigraph is regarded as a digraph.

Representation of graphs and digraphs. Any digraph, and therefore any graph or multigraph, is completely described by its *adjacency matrix* $A = (a_{uv})$, which has n rows and n columns when there are n vertices. Each entry a_{uv} of this matrix specifies the number of arcs from u to v. For example, the adjacency matrices for $\vec{K_3}$, $\vec{P_3}$, $\vec{C_3}$, J_3, and (26) are respectively

$$\vec{K_3} = \begin{pmatrix} 0 & 1 & 1 \\ 0 & 0 & 1 \\ 0 & 0 & 0 \end{pmatrix}, \quad \vec{P_3} = \begin{pmatrix} 0 & 1 & 0 \\ 0 & 0 & 1 \\ 0 & 0 & 0 \end{pmatrix}, \quad \vec{C_3} = \begin{pmatrix} 0 & 1 & 0 \\ 0 & 0 & 1 \\ 1 & 0 & 0 \end{pmatrix}, \quad J_3 = \begin{pmatrix} 1 & 1 & 1 \\ 1 & 1 & 1 \\ 1 & 1 & 1 \end{pmatrix}, \quad A = \begin{pmatrix} 2 & 1 & 0 \\ 1 & 0 & 2 \\ 0 & 2 & 4 \end{pmatrix}. \tag{27}$$

The powerful mathematical tools of matrix theory make it possible to prove many nontrivial results about graphs by studying their adjacency matrices; exercise 65 provides a particularly striking example of what can be done. One of the main reasons is that matrix multiplication has a simple interpretation in the context of digraphs. Consider the square of A, where the element in row u and column v is

$$(A^2)_{uv} = \sum_{w \in V} a_{uw} a_{wv}, \tag{28}$$

by definition. Since a_{uw} is the number of arcs from u to w, we see that $a_{uw}a_{wv}$ is the number of walks of the form $u \longrightarrow w \longrightarrow v$. Therefore $(A^2)_{uv}$ is the total number of walks of length 2 from u to v. Similarly, the entries of A^k tell us the total number of walks of length k between any ordered pair of vertices, for all $k \geq 0$. For example, the matrix A in (27) satisfies

$$A = \begin{pmatrix} 2 & 1 & 0 \\ 1 & 0 & 2 \\ 0 & 2 & 4 \end{pmatrix}, \qquad A^2 = \begin{pmatrix} 5 & 2 & 2 \\ 2 & 5 & 8 \\ 2 & 8 & 20 \end{pmatrix}, \qquad A^3 = \begin{pmatrix} 12 & 9 & 12 \\ 9 & 18 & 42 \\ 12 & 42 & 96 \end{pmatrix}; \tag{29}$$

there are 12 walks of length 3 from the vertex 1 of the multigraph (26) to vertex 3, and 18 such walks from vertex 2 to itself.

Reordering of the vertices changes an adjacency matrix from A to $P^- AP$, where P is a permutation matrix (a 0–1 matrix with exactly one 1 in each row and column), and $P^- = P^T$ is the matrix for the inverse permutation. Thus

$$\begin{pmatrix} 2 & 1 & 0 \\ 1 & 0 & 2 \\ 0 & 2 & 4 \end{pmatrix}, \quad \begin{pmatrix} 2 & 0 & 1 \\ 0 & 4 & 2 \\ 1 & 2 & 0 \end{pmatrix}, \quad \begin{pmatrix} 0 & 1 & 2 \\ 1 & 2 & 0 \\ 2 & 0 & 4 \end{pmatrix}, \quad \begin{pmatrix} 0 & 2 & 1 \\ 2 & 4 & 0 \\ 1 & 0 & 2 \end{pmatrix}, \quad \begin{pmatrix} 4 & 0 & 2 \\ 0 & 2 & 1 \\ 2 & 1 & 0 \end{pmatrix}, \quad \text{and} \quad \begin{pmatrix} 4 & 2 & 0 \\ 2 & 0 & 1 \\ 0 & 1 & 2 \end{pmatrix} \tag{30}$$

are all adjacency matrices for (26), and there are no others.

There are more than $2^{n(n-1)/2}/n!$ graphs of order n, when $n > 1$, and almost all of them require $\Omega(n^2)$ bits of data in their most economical encoding. Consequently the best way to represent the vast majority of all possible graphs inside a computer, from the standpoint of memory usage, is essentially to work with their adjacency matrices.

But the graphs that actually arise in practical problems have quite different characteristics from graphs that are chosen at random from the set of all possibilities. A real-life graph usually turns out to be "sparse," having say $O(n \log n)$ edges instead of $\Omega(n^2)$, unless n is rather small, because $\Omega(n^2)$ bits of data are difficult to generate. For example, suppose the vertices correspond to people, and the edges correspond to friendships. If we consider 5 billion people, few of them will have more than 10000 friends. But even if everybody had 10000 friends, on average, the graph would still have only 2.5×10^{13} edges, while almost all graphs of order 5 billion have approximately 6.25×10^{18} edges.

Thus the best way to represent a graph inside a machine usually turns out to be rather different than to record n^2 values of elements a_{uv} for an adjacency matrix. Instead, the algorithms of the Stanford GraphBase were developed with a data structure akin to the linked representation of sparse matrices discussed in Section 2.2.6, though somewhat simplified. That approach has proved to be not only versatile and efficient, but also easy to use.

The SGB representation of a digraph is a combination of sequential and linked allocation, using nodes of two basic types. Some nodes represent vertices, other nodes represent arcs. (There's also a third type of node, which represents an entire graph, for algorithms that deal with several graphs at once. But each graph needs only one graph node, so the vertex and arc nodes predominate.)

Here's how it works: Every SGB digraph of order n and size m is built upon a sequential array of n vertex nodes, making it easy to access vertex k for $0 \le k < n$. The m arc nodes, by contrast, are linked together within a general memory pool that is essentially unstructured. Each vertex node typically occupies 32 bytes, and each arc node occupies 20 (and the graph node occupies 220); but the node sizes can be modified without difficulty. A few fields of each node have a fixed, definite meaning in all cases; the remaining fields can be used for different purposes in different algorithms or in different phases of a single algorithm. The fixed-purpose parts of a node are called its "standard fields," and the multipurpose parts are called its "utility fields."

Every vertex node has two standard fields called NAME and ARCS. If v is a variable that points to a vertex node, we'll call it a *vertex variable*. Then NAME(v) points to a string of characters that can be used to identify the corresponding vertex in human-oriented output; for example, the 49 vertices of graph (17) have names like CA, WA, OR, ..., RI. The other standard field, ARCS(v), is far more important in algorithms: It points to an arc node, the first in a singly linked list of length $d^+(v)$, with one node for each arc that emanates from vertex v.

Every arc node has two standard fields called TIP and NEXT; a variable a that points to an arc node is called an *arc variable*. TIP(a) points to the vertex node that represents the tip of arc a; NEXT(a) points to the arc node that represents the next arc whose initial vertex agrees with that of a.

A vertex v with out-degree 0 is represented by letting ARCS$(v) = \Lambda$ (the null pointer). Otherwise if, say, the out-degree is 3, the data structure contains three arc nodes with ARCS$(v) = a_1$, NEXT$(a_1) = a_2$, NEXT$(a_2) = a_3$, and NEXT$(a_3) = \Lambda$; and the three arcs from v lead to TIP(a_1), TIP(a_2), TIP(a_3).

Suppose, for example, that we want to compute the out-degree of vertex v, and store it in a utility field called ODEG. It's easy:

> Set $a \leftarrow$ ARCS(v) and $d \leftarrow 0$.
> While $a \ne \Lambda$, set $d \leftarrow d + 1$ and $a \leftarrow$ NEXT(a).   (31)
> Set ODEG$(v) \leftarrow d$.

When a graph or a multigraph is considered to be a digraph, as mentioned above, its edges $u \,—\, v$ are each equivalent to two arcs, $u \longrightarrow v$ and $v \longrightarrow u$. These arcs are called "mates"; and they occupy two arc nodes, say a and a', where a appears in the list of arcs from u and a' appears in the list of arcs from v. Then TIP$(a) = v$ and TIP$(a') = u$. We'll also write

$$\text{MATE}(a) = a' \qquad \text{and} \qquad \text{MATE}(a') = a, \qquad (32)$$

in algorithms that want to move rapidly from one list to another. However, we usually won't need to store an explicit pointer from an arc to its mate, or to have

a utility field called MATE within each arc node, because the necessary link can
be deduced *implicitly* when the data structure has been constructed cleverly.

The implicit-mate trick works like this: While creating each edge $u — v$
of an undirected graph or multigraph, we introduce *consecutive* arc nodes for
$u \longrightarrow v$ and $v \longrightarrow u$. For example, if there are 20 bytes per arc node, we'll reserve
40 consecutive bytes for each new pair. We can also make sure that the memory
address of the first byte is a multiple of 8. Then if the arc node a is in memory
location α, its mate is in location

$$\left. \begin{cases} \alpha + 20, & \text{if } \alpha \bmod 8 = 0 \\ \alpha - 20, & \text{if } \alpha \bmod 8 = 4 \end{cases} \right\} = \alpha - 20 + \big(40 \mathbin{\&} ((\alpha \mathbin{\&} 4) - 1)\big). \qquad (33)$$

Such tricks are valuable in combinatorial problems, when operations might
be performed a trillion times, because every way to save 3.6 nanoseconds per
operation will make such a computation finish an hour sooner. But (33) isn't
directly "portable" from one implementation to another. If the size of an arc
node were changed from 20 to 24, for example, we would have to change the
numbers 40, 20, 8, and 4 in (33) to 48, 24, 16, and 8.

The algorithms in this book will make no assumptions about node sizes.
Instead, we'll adopt a convention of the C programming language and its descendants, so that if a points to an arc node, '$a + 1$' denotes a pointer to the arc
node that follows it in memory. And in general

$$\texttt{LOC(NODE}(a + k)) \; = \; \texttt{LOC(NODE}(a)) + kc, \qquad (34)$$

when there are c bytes in each arc node. Similarly, if v is a vertex variable, '$v + k$'
will stand for the kth vertex node following node v; the actual memory location
of that node will be v's location plus k times the size of a vertex node.

The standard fields of a graph node g include $\texttt{M}(g)$, the total number of arcs;
$\texttt{N}(g)$, the total number of vertices; $\texttt{VERTICES}(g)$, a pointer to the first vertex
node in the sequential list of all vertex nodes; $\texttt{ID}(g)$, the graph's identification,
which is a string like $\texttt{words(5757,0,0,0)}$; and some other fields needed for the
allocation and recycling of memory when the graph grows or shrinks, or for
exporting a graph to external formats that interface with other users and other
graph-manipulation systems. But we will rarely need to refer to any of these
graph node fields, nor will it be necessary to give a complete description of SGB
format here, since we shall describe almost all of the graph algorithms in this
chapter by sticking to an English-language description at a fairly abstract level
instead of descending to the bit level of machine programs.

A simple graph algorithm. To illustrate a medium-high-level algorithm of
the kind that will appear later, let's convert the proof of Theorem B into a
step-by-step procedure that paints the vertices of a given graph with two colors
whenever that graph is bipartite.

Algorithm B (*Bipartiteness testing*). Given a graph represented in SGB format,
this algorithm either finds a 2-coloring with $\texttt{COLOR}(v) \in \{0, 1\}$ in each vertex v,
or it terminates unsuccessfully when no valid 2-coloring is possible. Here $\texttt{COLOR}$
is a utility field in each vertex node. Another vertex utility field, $\texttt{LINK}(v)$, is a

vertex pointer used to maintain a stack of all colored vertices whose neighbors have not yet been examined. An auxiliary vertex variable s points to the top of this stack. The algorithm also uses variables u, v, w for vertices and a for arcs. The vertex nodes are assumed to be $v_0 + k$ for $0 \leq k < n$.

B1. [Initialize.] Set $\texttt{COLOR}(v_0 + k) \leftarrow -1$ for $0 \leq k < n$. (Now all vertices are uncolored.) Then set $w \leftarrow v_0 + n$.

B2. [Done?] (At this point all vertices $\geq w$ have been colored, and so have the neighbors of all colored vertices.) Terminate the algorithm successfully if $w = v_0$. Otherwise set $w \leftarrow w - 1$, the next lower vertex node.

B3. [Color w if necessary.] If $\texttt{COLOR}(w) \geq 0$, return to B2. Otherwise set $\texttt{COLOR}(w) \leftarrow 0$, $\texttt{LINK}(w) \leftarrow \Lambda$, and $s \leftarrow w$.

B4. [Stack $\Rightarrow u$.] Set $u \leftarrow s$, $s \leftarrow \texttt{LINK}(s)$, $a \leftarrow \texttt{ARCS}(u)$. (We will examine all neighbors of the colored vertex u.)

B5. [Done with u?] If $a = \Lambda$, go to B8. Otherwise set $v \leftarrow \texttt{TIP}(a)$.

B6. [Process v.] If $\texttt{COLOR}(v) < 0$, set $\texttt{COLOR}(v) \leftarrow 1 - \texttt{COLOR}(u)$, $\texttt{LINK}(v) \leftarrow s$, and $s \leftarrow v$. Otherwise if $\texttt{COLOR}(v) = \texttt{COLOR}(u)$, terminate unsuccessfully.

B7. [Loop on a.] Set $a \leftarrow \texttt{NEXT}(a)$ and return to B5.

B8. [Stack nonempty?] If $s \neq \Lambda$, return to B4. Otherwise return to B2. ∎

This algorithm is a variant of a general graph traversal procedure called "depth-first search," which we will study in detail in Section 7.4.1.2. Its running time is $O(m + n)$ when there are m arcs and n vertices (see exercise 70); therefore it is well adapted to the common case of sparse graphs. With small changes we can make it output an odd-length cycle whenever it terminates unsuccessfully, thereby proving the impossibility of a 2-coloring (see exercise 72).

Examples of graphs. The Stanford GraphBase includes a library of more than three dozen generator routines, capable of producing a great variety of graphs and digraphs for use in experiments. We've already discussed *words*; now let's look at a few of the others, in order to get a feeling for some of the possibilities.

• *roget*(1022, 0, 0, 0) is a directed graph with 1022 vertices and 5075 arcs. The vertices represent the categories of words or concepts that P. M. Roget and J. L. Roget included in their famous 19th-century *Thesaurus* (London: Longmans, Green, 1879). The arcs are the cross-references between categories, as found in that book. For example, typical arcs are $\texttt{water} \longrightarrow \texttt{moisture}$, $\texttt{discovery} \longrightarrow \texttt{truth}$, $\texttt{preparation} \longrightarrow \texttt{learning}$, $\texttt{vulgarity} \longrightarrow \texttt{ugliness}$, $\texttt{wit} \longrightarrow \texttt{amusement}$.

• *book*("jean", 80, 0, 1, 356, 0, 0, 0) is a graph with 80 vertices and 254 edges. The vertices represent the characters of Victor Hugo's *Les Misérables*; the edges connect characters who encounter each other in that novel. Typical edges are $\texttt{Fantine} \!-\! \texttt{Javert}$, $\texttt{Cosette} \!-\! \texttt{Thénardier}$.

• *bi_book*("jean", 80, 0, 1, 356, 0, 0, 0) is a bipartite graph with 80+356 vertices and 727 edges. The vertices represent characters or chapters in *Les Misérables*; the edges connect characters with the chapters in which they appear (for instance, $\texttt{Napoleon} \!-\! \texttt{2.1.8}$, $\texttt{Marius} \!-\! \texttt{4.14.4}$).

- *plane_miles*(128, 0, 0, 0, 1, 0, 0) is a planar graph with 129 vertices and 381 edges. The vertices represent 128 cities in the United States or Canada, plus a special vertex INF for a "point at infinity." The edges define the so-called *Delaunay triangulation* of those cities, based on latitude and longitude in a plane; this means that $u - v$ if and only if there's a circle passing through u and v that does not enclose any other vertex. Edges also run between INF and all vertices that lie on the convex hull of all city locations. Typical edges are Seattle, WA — Vancouver, BC — INF; Toronto, ON — Rochester, NY.

- *plane_lisa*(360, 250, 15, 0, 360, 0, 250, 0, 22950000) is a planar graph that has 3027 vertices and 5967 edges. It is obtained by starting with a digitized image of Leonardo da Vinci's *Mona Lisa*, having 360 rows and 250 columns of pixels, then rounding the pixel intensities to 16 levels of gray from 0 (black) to 15 (white). The resulting 3027 rookwise connected regions of constant brightness are then considered to be neighbors when they share a pixel boundary. (See Fig. 4.)

 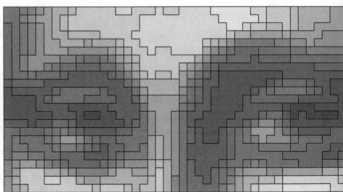

Fig. 4. A digital rendition of *Mona Lisa*, with a closeup detail (best viewed from afar).

- *bi_lisa*(360, 250, 0, 360, 0, 250, 8192, 0) is a bipartite graph with $360 + 250 = 610$ vertices and 40923 edges. It's another takeoff on Leonardo's famous painting, this time linking rows and columns where the brightness level is at least 1/8. For example, the edge r102 — c113 occurs right in the middle of Lisa's "smile."

- *raman*(31, 23, 3, 1) is a graph with quite a different nature from the SGB graphs in previous examples. Instead of being linked to language, literature, or other outgrowths of human culture, it's a so-called "Ramanujan expander graph," based on strict mathematical principles. Each of its $(23^3 - 23)/2 = 6072$ vertices has degree 32; hence it has 97152 edges. The vertices correspond to equivalence classes of 2×2 matrices that are nonsingular modulo 23; a typical edge is (2,7;1,1) — (4,6;1,3). Ramanujan graphs are important chiefly because they have unusually high girth and low diameter for their size and degree. This one has girth 4 and diameter 4.

• *raman*(5, 37, 4, 1), similarly, is a regular graph of degree 6 with 50616 vertices and 151848 edges. It has girth 10, diameter 10, and happens also to be bipartite.

• *random_graph*(1000, 5000, 0, 0, 0, 0, 0, 0, 0, *s*) is a graph with 1000 vertices, 5000 edges, and seed *s*. It "evolved" by starting with no edges, then by repeatedly choosing pseudorandom vertex numbers $0 \leq u, v < 1000$ and adding the edge $u \mathrel{-\!\!-} v$, unless $u = v$ or that edge was already present. When $s = 0$, all vertices belong to a giant component of order 999, except for the isolated vertex 908.

• *random_graph*(1000, 5000, 0, 0, 1, 0, 0, 0, 0, 0) is a digraph with 1000 vertices and 5000 arcs, obtained via a similar sort of evolution. (In fact, each of its arcs happens to be part also of *random_graph*(1000, 5000, 0, 0, 0, 0, 0, 0, 0, 0).)

• *subsets*(5, 1, −10, 0, 0, 0, #1, 0) is a graph with $\binom{11}{5} = 462$ vertices, one for every five-element subset of $\{0, 1, \ldots, 10\}$. Two vertices are adjacent whenever the corresponding subsets are disjoint; thus, the graph is regular of degree 6, and it has 1386 edges. We can consider it to be a generalization of the Petersen graph, which has *subsets*(2, 1, −4, 0, 0, 0, #1, 0) as one of its SGB names.

• *subsets*(5, 1, −10, 0, 0, 0, #1̄0, 0) has the same 462 vertices, but now they are adjacent if the corresponding subsets have four elements in common. This graph is regular of degree 30, and it has 6930 edges.

• *parts*(30, 10, 30, 0) is another SGB graph with a mathematical basis. It has 3590 vertices, one for each partition of 30 into at most 10 parts. Two partitions are adjacent when one is obtained by subdividing a part of the other; this rule defines 31377 edges. The digraph *parts*(30, 10, 30, 1) is similar, but its 31377 arcs point from shorter to longer partitions (for example, 13+7+7+3 ⟶ 7+7+7+6+3).

• *simplex*(10, 10, 10, 10, 10, 0, 0) is a graph with 286 vertices and 1320 edges. Its vertices are the integer solutions to $x_1 + x_2 + x_3 + x_4 = 10$ with $x_i \geq 0$, namely the "compositions of 10 into four nonnegative parts"; they can also be regarded as barycentric coordinates for points inside a tetrahedron. The edges, such as 3.1.4.2 ⎯ 3.0.4.3, connect compositions that are as close together as possible.

• *board*(8, 8, 0, 0, 5, 0, 0) and *board*(8, 8, 0, 0, −2, 0, 0) are graphs on 64 vertices whose 168 or 280 edges correspond to the moves of a knight or bishop in chess.

And zillions of further examples are obtainable by varying the parameters to the SGB graph generators. For example, Fig. 5 shows two simple variants of *board* and *simplex*; the somewhat arcane rules of *board* are explained in exercise 75.

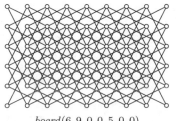
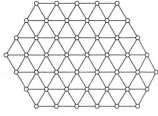

board(6, 9, 0, 0, 5, 0, 0)   *simplex*(10, 8, 7, 6, 0, 0, 0)
(Knight moves on a 6 × 9 chessboard)   (A truncated triangular grid)

Fig. 5. Samples of SGB graphs related to board games.

Graph algebra. We can also obtain new graphs by operating on the graphs that we already have. For example, if $G = (V, E)$ is any graph, its *complement* $\overline{G} = (V, \overline{E})$ is obtained by letting

$$u \!-\! v \text{ in } \overline{G} \quad\Longleftrightarrow\quad u \neq v \text{ and } u \!\not\!-\! v \text{ in } G. \tag{35}$$

Thus, non-edges become edges, and vice versa. Notice that $\overline{\overline{G}} = G$, and that $\overline{K_n}$ has no edges. The corresponding adjacency matrices A and $\overline{A}$ satisfy

$$A + \overline{A} \;=\; J - I; \tag{36}$$

here J is the matrix of all 1s, and I is the identity matrix, so J and $J - I$ are respectively the adjacency matrices of J_n and K_n when G has order n.

Furthermore, every graph $G = (V, E)$ leads to a *line graph* $L(G)$, whose vertices are the edges E; two edges of G are adjacent in $L(G)$ if they have a common vertex. Thus, for example, the line graph $L(K_n)$ has $\binom{n}{2}$ vertices, and it is regular of degree $2n - 4$ when $n \geq 2$ (see exercise 82). A graph is called *k-edge-colorable* when its line graph is k-colorable.

Given two graphs $G = (U, E)$ and $H = (V, F)$, their *union* $G \cup H$ is the graph $(U \cup V, E \cup F)$ obtained by combining the vertices and edges. For example, suppose G and H are the graphs of rook and bishop moves in chess; then $G \cup H$ is the graph of queen moves, and its official SGB name is

$$gunion(board(8, 8, 0, 0, -1, 0, 0), board(8, 8, 0, 0, -2, 0, 0), 0, 0). \tag{37}$$

In the special case where the vertex sets U and V are disjoint, the union $G \cup H$ doesn't require the vertices to be identified in any consistent way for cross-correlation; we get a diagram for $G \cup H$ by simply drawing a diagram of G next to a diagram of H. This special case is called the "juxtaposition" or *direct sum* of G and H, and we shall denote it by $G \oplus H$. For example, it's easy to see that

$$K_m \oplus K_n \;\cong\; \overline{K_{m,n}}, \tag{38}$$

and that every graph is the direct sum of its connected components.

Equation (38) is a special case of the general formula

$$K_{n_1} \oplus K_{n_2} \oplus \cdots \oplus K_{n_k} \;\cong\; \overline{K_{n_1, n_2, \ldots, n_k}}, \tag{39}$$

which holds for complete k-partite graphs whenever $k \geq 2$. But (39) fails when $k = 1$, because of a scandalous fact: The standard graph-theoretic notation for complete graphs is inconsistent! Indeed, $K_{m,n}$ denotes a complete 2-partite graph, but K_n does *not* denote a complete 1-partite graph. Somehow graph theorists have been able to live with this anomaly for decades without going berserk.

Another important way to combine disjoint graphs G and H is to form their *join*, $G \!-\! H$, which consists of $G \oplus H$ together with all edges $u \!-\! v$ for $u \in U$ and $v \in V$. [See A. A. Zykov, *Mat. Sbornik* **24** (1949), 163–188, §I.3.] And if G and H are disjoint *digraphs*, their *directed join* $G \longrightarrow H$ is similar, but it supplements $G \oplus H$ by adding only the one-way arcs $u \longrightarrow v$ from U to V.

The direct sum of two matrices A and B is obtained by placing B diagonally below and to the right of A:

$$A \oplus B = \begin{pmatrix} A & O \\ O & B \end{pmatrix}, \tag{40}$$

where each O in this example is a matrix of all zeros, with the proper number of rows and columns to make everything line up correctly. Our notation $G \oplus H$ for the direct sum of graphs is easy to remember because the adjacency matrix for $G \oplus H$ is precisely the direct sum of the respective adjacency matrices A and B for G and H. Similarly, the adjacency matrices for $G \!-\! H$, $G \rightarrow H$, and $G \leftarrow H$ are

$$A \!-\! B = \begin{pmatrix} A & J \\ J & B \end{pmatrix}, \quad A \rightarrow B = \begin{pmatrix} A & J \\ O & B \end{pmatrix}, \quad A \leftarrow B = \begin{pmatrix} A & O \\ J & B \end{pmatrix}, \tag{41}$$

respectively, where J is an all-1s matrix as in (36). These operations are associative, and related by complementation:

$$A \oplus (B \oplus C) = (A \oplus B) \oplus C, \quad A \!-\! (B \!-\! C) = (A \!-\! B) \!-\! C; \tag{42}$$
$$A \rightarrow (B \rightarrow C) = (A \rightarrow B) \rightarrow C, \quad A \leftarrow (B \leftarrow C) = (A \leftarrow B) \leftarrow C; \tag{43}$$
$$\overline{A \oplus B} = \overline{A} \!-\! \overline{B}, \quad \overline{A \!-\! B} = \overline{A} \oplus \overline{B}; \tag{44}$$
$$\overline{A \rightarrow B} = \overline{A} \leftarrow \overline{B}, \quad \overline{A \leftarrow B} = \overline{A} \rightarrow \overline{B}; \tag{45}$$
$$(A \oplus B) + (A \!-\! B) = (A \rightarrow B) + (A \leftarrow B). \tag{46}$$

Notice that, by combining (39) with (42) and (44), we have

$$K_{n_1, n_2, \ldots, n_k} = \overline{K_{n_1}} \!-\! \overline{K_{n_2}} \!-\! \cdots \!-\! \overline{K_{n_k}} \tag{47}$$

when $k \geq 2$. Also

$$K_n = K_1 \!-\! K_1 \!-\! \cdots \!-\! K_1 \quad \text{and} \quad \vec{K_n} = K_1 \rightarrow K_1 \rightarrow \cdots \rightarrow K_1, \tag{48}$$

with n copies of K_1, showing that $K_n = K_{1,1,\ldots,1}$ is a complete n-partite graph.

Direct sums and joins are analogous to addition, because we have $\overline{K_m} \oplus \overline{K_n} = \overline{K_{m+n}}$ and $K_m \!-\! K_n = K_{m+n}$. We can also combine graphs with algebraic operations that are analogous to multiplication. For example, the *Cartesian product* operation forms a graph $G \square H$ of order mn from a graph $G = (U, E)$ of order m and a graph $H = (V, F)$ of order n. The vertices of $G \square H$ are ordered pairs (u, v), where $u \in U$ and $v \in V$; the edges are $(u, v) \!-\! (u', v)$ when $u \!-\! u'$ in G, together with $(u, v) \!-\! (u, v')$ when $v \!-\! v'$ in H. In other words, $G \square H$ is formed by replacing each vertex of G by a copy of H, and replacing each edge of G by edges between corresponding vertices of the appropriate copies:

$$(49)$$

As usual, the simplest special cases of this general construction turn out to be especially important in practice. When both G and H are paths or cycles, we get "graph-paper graphs," namely the $m \times n$ *grid* $P_m \square P_n$, the $m \times n$ *cylinder* $P_m \square C_n$, and the $m \times n$ *torus* $C_m \square C_n$, illustrated here for $m = 3$ and $n = 4$:

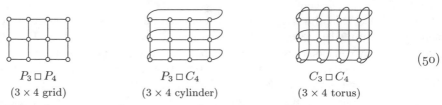

$$\text{(50)}$$

$$P_3 \square P_4 \qquad\qquad P_3 \square C_4 \qquad\qquad C_3 \square C_4$$
$$(3 \times 4 \text{ grid}) \qquad (3 \times 4 \text{ cylinder}) \qquad (3 \times 4 \text{ torus})$$

Four other noteworthy ways to define products of graphs have also proved to be useful. In each case the vertices of the product graph are ordered pairs (u, v).

- The *direct product* $G \otimes H$, also called the "conjunction" of G and H, or their "categorical product," has $(u, v) \,\text{---}\, (u', v')$ when $u \,\text{---}\, u'$ in G and $v \,\text{---}\, v'$ in H.

- The *strong product* $G \boxtimes H$ combines the edges of $G \square H$ with those of $G \otimes H$.

- The *odd product* $G \triangle H$ has $(u, v) \,\text{---}\, (u', v')$ when we have either $u \,\text{---}\, u'$ in G or $v \,\text{---}\, v'$ in H, but not both.

- The *lexicographic product* $G \circ H$, also called the "composition" of G and H, has $(u, v) \,\text{---}\, (u', v')$ when $u \,\text{---}\, u'$ in G, and $(u, v) \,\text{---}\, (u, v')$ when $v \,\text{---}\, v'$ in H.

All five of these operations extend naturally to products of $k \geq 2$ graphs $G_1 = (V_1, E_1), \ldots, G_k = (V_k, E_k)$, whose vertices are the ordered k-tuples $(v_1, \ldots, v_k)$ with $v_j \in V_j$ for $1 \leq j \leq k$. For example, when $k = 3$, the Cartesian products $G_1 \square (G_2 \square G_3)$ and $(G_1 \square G_2) \square G_3$ are isomorphic, if we consider the compound vertices $(v_1, (v_2, v_3))$ and $((v_1, v_2), v_3)$ to be the same as (v_1, v_2, v_3). Therefore we can write this Cartesian product without parentheses, as $G_1 \square G_2 \square G_3$. The most important example of a Cartesian product with k factors is the k-cube,

$$P_2 \square P_2 \square \cdots \square P_2; \tag{51}$$

its 2^k vertices $(v_1, \ldots, v_k)$ are adjacent when their Hamming distance is 1.

In general, suppose $v = (v_1, \ldots, v_k)$ and $v' = (v'_1, \ldots, v'_k)$ are k-tuples of vertices, where we have $v_j \,\text{---}\, v'_j$ in G_j for exactly a of the subscripts j, and $v_j = v'_j$ for exactly b of the subscripts. Then we have:

- $v \,\text{---}\, v'$ in $G_1 \square \cdots \square G_k$ if and only if $a = 1$ and $b = k - 1$;
- $v \,\text{---}\, v'$ in $G_1 \otimes \cdots \otimes G_k$ if and only if $a = k$ and $b = 0$;
- $v \,\text{---}\, v'$ in $G_1 \boxtimes \cdots \boxtimes G_k$ if and only if $a + b = k$ and $a > 0$;
- $v \,\text{---}\, v'$ in $G_1 \triangle \cdots \triangle G_k$ if and only if a is odd.

The lexicographic product is somewhat different, because it isn't commutative; in $G_1 \circ \cdots \circ G_k$ we have $v \,\text{---}\, v'$ for $v \neq v'$ if and only if $v_j \,\text{---}\, v'_j$, where j is the minimum subscript with $v_j \neq v'_j$.

Exercises 91–102 explore some of the basic properties of graph products. See also the book *Product Graphs* by Wilfried Imrich and Sandi Klavžar (2000), which contains a comprehensive introduction to the general theory, including algorithms for factorization of a given graph into "prime" subgraphs.

*Graphical degree sequences. A sequence $d_1 d_2 \ldots d_n$ of nonnegative integers is called *graphical* if there's at least one graph on vertices $\{1, 2, \ldots, n\}$ such that each vertex k has degree d_k. We can assume that $d_1 \geq d_2 \geq \cdots \geq d_n$. Clearly $d_1 < n$ in any such graph; and the sum $m = d_1 + d_2 + \cdots + d_n$ of any graphical sequence is always even, because it is twice the number of edges. Furthermore, it's easy to see that the sequence 3311 is not graphical, because a (simple) graph cannot contain more than one edge between two vertices. Therefore graphical sequences must also satisfy additional conditions. What are they?

A convenient way to decide if a given sequence $d_1 d_2 \ldots d_n$ is graphical, and to construct such a graph if one exists, was discovered by V. Havel [*Časopis pro Pěstování Matematiky* **80** (1955), 477–479]. We begin with an empty tableau, having d_k cells in row k; these cells represent "slots" into which we'll place the neighbors of vertex k in the constructed graph. Let c_j be the number of cells in column j; thus $c_1 \geq c_2 \geq \cdots$, and when $1 \leq k \leq n$ we have $c_j \geq k$ if and only if $d_k \geq j$. For example, suppose $n = 8$ and $d_1 \ldots d_8 = 55544322$; then

$$
\begin{array}{c}
\\
\end{array}
$$

| 1 |
| 2 |
| 3 |
| 4 |
| 5 |
| 6 |
| 7 |
| 8 |

$$(52)$$

is the initial tableau, and we have $c_1 \ldots c_5 = 88653$. Havel's idea is to pair up vertex n with d_n of the highest-degree vertices. In this case, for example, we create the two edges $8 - 3$ and $8 - 2$, and the tableau takes the following form:

$$(53)$$

(We don't want $8 - 1$, because the empty slots should continue to form a tableau shape; the cells of each column must be filled from the bottom up.) Next we set $n \leftarrow 7$ and create two further edges, $7 - 1$ and $7 - 5$. And then come three more, $6 - 4$, $6 - 3$, $6 - 2$, making the tableau almost half full:

$$(54)$$

We've reduced the problem to finding a graph with degree sequence $d_1 \ldots d_5 = 43333$; at this point we also have $c_1 \ldots c_4 = 5551$. The reader is encouraged to fill in the remaining blanks, before looking at the answer in exercise 103.

Algorithm H (*Graph generator for specified degrees*). Given $d_1 \geq \cdots \geq d_n \geq d_{n+1} = 0$, this algorithm creates edges between the vertices $\{1, \ldots, n\}$ in such a way that exactly d_k edges touch vertex k, for $1 \leq k \leq n$, unless the sequence $d_1 \ldots d_n$ isn't graphical. An array $c_1 \ldots c_{d_1}$ is used for auxiliary storage.

H1. [Set the c's.] Start with $k \leftarrow d_1$ and $j \leftarrow 0$. Then while $k > 0$ do the following operations: Set $j \leftarrow j + 1$; while $k > d_{j+1}$, set $c_k \leftarrow j$ and $k \leftarrow k - 1$. Terminate successfully if $j = 0$ (all d's are zero).

H2. [Find n.] Set $n \leftarrow c_1$. Terminate successfully if $n = 0$; terminate unsuccessfully if $d_1 \geq n > 0$.

H3. [Begin loop on j.] Set $i \leftarrow 1$, $t \leftarrow d_1$, $r \leftarrow c_t$, and $j \leftarrow d_n$.

H4. [Generate a new edge.] Set $c_j \leftarrow c_j - 1$ and $m \leftarrow c_t$. Create the edge $n - m$, and set $d_m \leftarrow d_m - 1$, $c_t \leftarrow m - 1$, $j \leftarrow j - 1$. If $j = 0$, return to step H2. Otherwise, if $m = i$, set $i \leftarrow r + 1$, $t \leftarrow d_i$, and $r \leftarrow c_t$ (see exercise 104); repeat step H4. ∎

When Algorithm H succeeds, it certainly has constructed a graph with the desired degrees. But when it fails, how can we be sure that its mission was impossible? The key fact is based on an important concept called "majorization": If $d_1 \ldots d_n$ and $d'_1 \ldots d'_n$ are two partitions of the same integer (that is, if $d_1 \geq \cdots \geq d_n$ and $d'_1 \geq \cdots \geq d'_n$ and $d_1 + \cdots + d_n = d'_1 + \cdots + d'_n$), we say that $d_1 \ldots d_n$ *majorizes* $d'_1 \ldots d'_n$ if $d_1 + \cdots + d_k \geq d'_1 + \cdots + d'_k$ for $1 \leq k \leq n$.

Lemma M. *If $d_1 \ldots d_n$ is graphical and $d_1 \ldots d_n$ majorizes $d'_1 \ldots d'_n$, then $d'_1 \ldots d'_n$ is also graphical.*

Proof. It is sufficient to prove the claim when $d_1 \ldots d_n$ and $d'_1 \ldots d'_n$ differ in only two places,

$$d'_k = d_k - [k = i] + [k = j] \qquad \text{where } i < j, \tag{55}$$

because any sequence majorized by $d_1 \ldots d_n$ can be obtained by repeatedly performing mini-majorizations such as this. (Exercise 7.2.1.4–55 discusses majorization in detail.)

Condition (55) implies that $d_i > d'_i \geq d'_{i+1} \geq d'_j > d_j$. So any graph with degree sequence $d_1 \ldots d_n$ contains a vertex v such that $v - i$ and $v \not\!-j$. Deleting the edge $v - i$ and adding the edge $v - j$ yields a graph with degree sequence $d'_1 \ldots d'_n$, as desired. ∎

Corollary H. *Algorithm H succeeds whenever $d_1 \ldots d_n$ is graphical.*

Proof. We may assume that $n > 1$. Suppose G is any graph on $\{1, \ldots, n\}$ with degree sequence $d_1 \ldots d_n$, and let G' be the subgraph induced by $\{1, \ldots, n-1\}$; in other words, obtain G' by removing vertex n and the d_n edges that it touches. The degree sequence $d'_1 \ldots d'_{n-1}$ of G' is obtained from $d_1 \ldots d_{n-1}$ by reducing some d_n of the entries by 1 and sorting them into nonincreasing order. By definition, $d'_1 \ldots d'_{n-1}$ is graphical. The new degree sequence $d''_1 \ldots d''_{n-1}$ produced by the strategy of steps H3 and H4 is designed to be majorized by every such $d'_1 \ldots d'_{n-1}$, because it reduces the largest possible d_n entries by 1. Thus the new $d''_1 \ldots d''_{n-1}$ is graphical. Algorithm H, which sets $d_1 \ldots d_{n-1} \leftarrow d''_1 \ldots d''_{n-1}$, will therefore succeed by induction on n. ∎

The running time of Algorithm H is roughly proportional to the number of edges generated, which can be of order n^2. Exercise 105 presents a faster method, which decides in $O(n)$ steps whether or not a given sequence $d_1 \ldots d_n$ is graphical (without constructing any graph).

Beyond graphs. When the vertices and/or arcs of a graph or digraph are decorated with additional data, we call it a *network*. For example, every vertex of *words* $(5757, 0, 0, 0)$ has an associated rank, which corresponds to the popularity of the corresponding five-letter word. Every vertex of *plane_lisa* $(360, 250, 15, 0, 360, 0, 250, 0, 22950000)$ has an associated pixel density, between 0 and 15. Every arc of *board* $(8, 8, 0, 0, -2, 0, 0)$ has an associated length, which reflects the distance of a piece's motion on the board: A bishop's move from corner to corner has length 7. The Stanford GraphBase includes several further generators that were not mentioned above, because they are primarily used to generate interesting networks, rather than to generate graphs with interesting structure:

• *miles* $(128, 0, 0, 0, 0, 127, 0)$ is a network with 128 vertices, corresponding to the same North American cities as the graph *plane_miles* described earlier. But *miles*, unlike *plane_miles*, is a complete graph with $\binom{128}{2}$ edges. Every edge has an integer length, which represents the distance that a car or truck would have needed to travel in 1949 when going from one given city to another. For example, 'Vancouver, BC' is 3496 miles from 'West Palm Beach, FL' in the *miles* network.

• *econ* $(81, 0, 0, 0)$ is a network with 81 vertices and 4902 arcs. Its vertices represent sectors of the United States economy, and its arcs represent the flow of money from one sector to another during the year 1985, measured in millions of dollars. For example, the flow value from **Apparel** to **Household furniture** is 44, meaning that the furniture industry paid $44,000,000 to the apparel industry in that year. The sum of flows coming into each vertex is equal to the sum of flows going out. An arc appears only when the flow is nonzero. A special vertex called **Users** receives the flows that represent total demand for a product; a few of these end-user flows are negative, because of the way imported goods are treated by government economists.

• *games* $(120, 0, 0, 0, 0, 0, 128, 0)$ is a network with 120 vertices and 1276 arcs. Its vertices represent football teams at American colleges and universities. Arcs run between teams that played each other during the exciting 1990 season, and they are labeled with the number of points scored. For example, the arc Stanford $\longrightarrow$ California has value 27, and the arc California $\longrightarrow$ Stanford has value 25, because the Stanford Cardinal defeated the U. C. Berkeley Golden Bears by a score of 27–25 on 17 November 1990.

• *risc* (16) is a network of an entirely different kind. It has 3240 vertices and 7878 arcs, which define a *directed acyclic graph* or "dag" — namely, a digraph that contains no oriented cycles. The vertices represent gates that have Boolean values; an arc such as Z45 $\longrightarrow$ R0:7˜ means that the value of gate R0:7˜ is an input to gate Z45. Each gate has a type code (AND, OR, XOR, NOT, latch, or external input); each arc has a length, denoting an amount of delay. The network contains the complete logic for a miniature RISC chip that is able to obey simple commands governing sixteen registers, each 16 bits wide.

Complete details about all the SGB generators can be found in the author's book *The Stanford GraphBase* (New York: ACM Press, 1994), together with dozens of short example programs that explain how to manipulate the graphs and networks that the generators produce. For example, a program called LADDERS shows how to find a shortest path between one five-letter word and another. A program called TAKE_RISC demonstrates how to put a nanocomputer through its paces by simulating the actions of a network built from the gates of $risc(8)$.

Hypergraphs. Graphs and networks can be utterly fascinating, but they aren't the end of the story by any means. Lots of important combinatorial algorithms are designed to work with *hypergraphs*, which are more general than graphs because their edges are allowed to be *arbitrary* subsets of the vertices.

For example, we might have seven vertices, identified by nonzero binary strings $v = a_1a_2a_3$, together with seven edges, identified by bracketed nonzero binary strings $e = [b_1b_2b_3]$, with $v \in e$ if and only if $(a_1b_1 + a_2b_2 + a_3b_3) \bmod 2 = 0$. Each of these edges contains exactly three vertices:

$$[001] = \{010, 100, 110\}; \quad [010] = \{001, 100, 101\}; \quad [011] = \{011, 100, 111\};$$
$$[100] = \{001, 010, 011\}; \quad [101] = \{010, 101, 111\};$$
$$[110] = \{001, 110, 111\}; \quad [111] = \{011, 101, 110\}. \tag{56}$$

And by symmetry, each vertex belongs to exactly three edges. (Edges that contain three or more vertices are sometimes called "hyperedges," to distinguish them from the edges of an ordinary graph. But it's OK to call them just "edges.")

A hypergraph is said to be r-*uniform* if every edge contains exactly r vertices. Thus (56) is a 3-uniform hypergraph, and a 2-uniform hypergraph is an ordinary graph. The complete r-uniform hypergraph $K_n^{(r)}$ has n vertices and $\binom{n}{r}$ edges.

Most of the basic concepts of graph theory can be extended to hypergraphs in a natural way. For example, if $H = (V, E)$ is a hypergraph and if $U \subseteq V$, the subhypergraph $H \mid U$ induced by U has the edges $\{e \mid e \in E \text{ and } e \subseteq U\}$. The complement $\overline{H}$ of an r-uniform hypergraph has the edges of $K_n^{(r)}$ that aren't edges of H. A k-coloring of a hypergraph is an assignment of at most k colors to the vertices so that no edge is monochromatic. And so on.

Hypergraphs go by many other names, because the same properties can be formulated in many different ways. For example, every hypergraph $H = (V, E)$ is essentially a *family of sets*, because each edge is a subset of V. A 3-uniform hypergraph is also called a *triple system*. A hypergraph is also equivalent to a matrix B of 0s and 1s, with one row for each vertex v and one column for each edge e; row v and column e of this matrix contains the value $b_{ve} = [v \in e]$.

Matrix B is called the *incidence matrix* of H, and we say that "v is incident with e" when $v \in e$. Furthermore, a hypergraph is equivalent to a *bipartite graph*, with vertex set $V \cup E$ and with the edge $v - e$ whenever v is incident with e. The hypergraph is said to be *connected* if and only if the corresponding bipartite graph is connected. A *cycle* of length k in a hypergraph is defined to be a cycle of length $2k$ in the corresponding bipartite graph.

For example, the hypergraph (56) can be defined by an equivalent incidence matrix or an equivalent bipartite graph as follows:

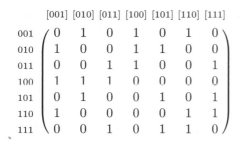 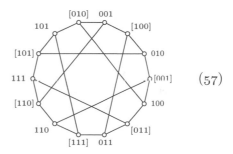

$$(57)$$

It contains 28 cycles of length 3, such as

$$[101] - 101 - [010] - 001 - [100] - 010 - [101]. \tag{58}$$

The *dual* H^T of a hypergraph H is obtained by interchanging the roles of vertices and edges, but retaining the incidence relation. In other words, it corresponds to transposing the incidence matrix. Notice, for example, that the dual of an r-regular graph is an r-uniform hypergraph.

Incidence matrices and bipartite graphs might correspond to hypergraphs in which some edges occur more than once, because distinct columns of the matrix might be equal. When a hypergraph $H = (V, E)$ does not have any repeated edges, it corresponds also to yet another combinatorial object, namely a *Boolean function*. For if, say, the vertex set V is $\{1, 2, \ldots, n\}$, the function

$$h(x_1, x_2, \ldots, x_n) = \big[\{ j \mid x_j = 1 \} \in E \big] \tag{59}$$

characterizes the edges of H. For example, the Boolean formula

$$\begin{aligned} (x_1 \oplus x_2 \oplus x_3) \wedge (x_2 \oplus x_4 \oplus x_6) \wedge (x_3 \oplus x_4 \oplus x_7) \\ \wedge (x_3 \oplus x_5 \oplus x_6) \wedge (\bar{x}_1 \vee \bar{x}_2 \vee \bar{x}_4) \end{aligned} \tag{60}$$

is another way to describe the hypergraph of (56) and (57).

The fact that combinatorial objects can be viewed in so many ways can be mind-boggling. But it's also extremely helpful, because it suggests different ways to solve equivalent problems. When we look at a problem from different perspectives, our brains naturally think of different ways to attack it. Sometimes we get the best insights by thinking about how to manipulate rows and columns in a matrix. Sometimes we make progress by imagining vertices and paths, or by visualizing clusters of points in space. Sometimes Boolean algebra is just the thing. If we're stuck in one domain, another might come to our rescue.

Covering and independence. If $H = (V, E)$ is a graph or hypergraph, a set U of vertices is said to *cover* H if every edge contains at least one member of U. A set W of vertices is said to be *independent* (or "stable") in H if no edge is completely contained in W.

From the standpoint of the incidence matrix, a covering is a set of rows whose sum is nonzero in every column. And in the special case that H is a graph, every column of the matrix contains just two 1s; hence an independent set in a graph corresponds to a set of rows that are mutually orthogonal — that is, a set for which the dot product of any two different rows is zero.

These concepts are opposite sides of the same coin. If U covers H, then $W = V \setminus U$ is independent in H; conversely, if W is independent in H, then $U = V \setminus W$ covers H. Both statements are equivalent to saying that the induced hypergraph $H \mid W$ has no edges.

This dual relationship between covering and independence, which was perhaps first noted by Claude Berge [*Proc. National Acad. Sci.* **43** (1957), 842–844], is somewhat paradoxical. Although it's logically obvious and easy to verify, it's also intuitively surprising. When we look at a graph and try to find a large independent set, we tend to have rather different thoughts from when we look at the same graph and try to find a small vertex cover; yet both goals are the same.

A covering set U is *minimal* if $U \setminus u$ fails to be a cover for all $u \in U$. Similarly, an independent set W is *maximal* if $W \cup w$ fails to be independent for all $w \notin W$. Here, for example, is a minimal cover of the 49-vertex graph of the contiguous United States, (17), and the corresponding maximal independent set:

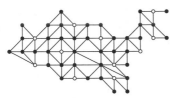 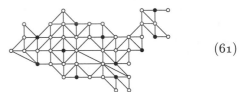 (61)

Minimal vertex cover,   Maximal independent set,
with 38 vertices   with 11 vertices

A covering is called *minimum* if it has the smallest possible size, and an independent set is called *maximum* if it has the largest possible size. For example, with graph (17) we can do much better than (61):

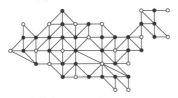 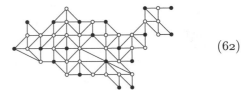 (62)

Minimum vertex cover,   Maximum independent set,
with 30 vertices   with 19 vertices

Notice the subtle distinction between "minimal" and "minimum" here: In general (but in contrast to most dictionaries of English), people who work with combinatorial algorithms use '-al' words like "minimal" or "optimal" to refer to combinatorial configurations that are *locally* best, in the sense that small changes don't improve them. The corresponding '-um' words, "minimum" or "optimum," are reserved for configurations that are *globally* best, when considered over all possibilities. It's easy to find solutions to any optimization problem that are merely optimal, in the weak local sense, by climbing repeatedly until reaching the top of a hill. But it's usually much harder to find solutions that are truly optimum. For example, we'll see in Section 7.9 that the problem of finding a maximum independent set in a given graph belongs to a class of difficult problems that are called *NP-complete*.

Even when a problem is NP-complete, we needn't despair. We'll discuss techniques for finding minimum covers in several parts of this chapter, and those methods work fine on smallish problems; the optimum solution in (62) was found in less than a second, after examining only a tiny fraction of the 2^{49} possibilities. Furthermore, special cases of NP-complete problems often turn out to be simpler than the general case. In Sections 7.5.1 and 7.5.5 we'll see that a minimum vertex cover can be discovered quickly in any bipartite graph, or in any hypergraph that is the dual of a graph; we'll also study efficient ways to discover a maximum *matching*, which is a maximum independent set in the line graph of a given graph.

The problem of maximizing the size of an independent set occurs sufficiently often that it has acquired a special notation: If H is any hypergraph, the number

$$\alpha(H) \ = \ \max\big\{|W| \ \big| \ W \text{ is an independent set of vertices in } H\big\} \qquad (63)$$

is called the *independence number* (or the stability number) of H. Similarly,

$$\chi(H) \ = \ \min\{k \mid H \text{ is } k\text{-colorable}\} \qquad (64)$$

is called the *chromatic number* of H. Notice that $\chi(H)$ is the size of a minimum covering of H by independent sets, because the vertices that receive any particular color must be independent according to our definitions.

These definitions of $\alpha(H)$ and $\chi(H)$ apply in particular to the case when H is an ordinary graph, but of course we usually write $\alpha(G)$ and $\chi(G)$ in such situations. Graphs have another important number called their *clique number*,

$$\omega(G) \ = \ \max\big\{|X| \ \big| \ X \text{ is a clique in } G\big\}, \qquad (65)$$

where a "clique" is a set of mutually adjacent vertices. Clearly

$$\omega(G) \ = \ \alpha(\overline{G}), \qquad (66)$$

because a clique in G is an independent set in the complementary graph. Similarly we can see that $\chi(\overline{G})$ is the minimum size of a "clique cover," which is a set of cliques that exactly covers all of the vertices.

Several instances of "exact cover problems" were mentioned earlier in this section, without an explanation of exactly what such a problem really signifies. Finally we're ready for the definition: Given the incidence matrix of a hypergraph H, an *exact cover* of H is a set of rows whose sum is $(1\,1 \ldots 1)$. In other words, an exact cover is a set of vertices that touches each hyperedge exactly once; an ordinary cover is only required to touch each hyperedge *at least* once.

EXERCISES

1. [*25*] Suppose $n = 4m - 1$. Construct arrangements of Langford pairs for the numbers $\{1, 1, \ldots, n, n\}$, with the property that we also obtain a solution for $n = 4m$ by changing the first '$2m-1$' to '$4m$' and appending '$2m-1\ 4m$' at the right. *Hint:* Put the $m - 1$ even numbers $4m-4$, $4m-6$, $\ldots$, $2m$ at the left.

2. [*20*] For which n can $\{0, 0, 1, 1, \ldots, n-1, n-1\}$ be arranged as Langford pairs?

3. [*22*] Suppose we arrange the numbers $\{0, 0, 1, 1, \ldots, n-1, n-1\}$ in a *circle*, instead of a straight line, with distance k between the two k's. Do we get solutions that are essentially distinct from those of exercise 2?

4. [*M20*] (T. Skolem, 1957.) Show that the Fibonacci string $S_\infty = babbababbabba\ldots$ of exercise 1.2.8–36 leads directly to an infinite sequence $0012132453674\ldots$ of Langford pairs for the set of *all* nonnegative integers, if we simply replace the a's and b's independently by 0, 1, 2, etc., from left to right.

▶ **5.** [*HM22*] If a permutation of $\{1, 1, 2, 2, \ldots, n, n\}$ is chosen at random, what is the probability that exactly k non-k's appear between the two k's, given k? Use this formula to guess the size of the Langford numbers L_n in (1).

▶ **6.** [*M28*] (M. Godfrey, 2002.) Let $f(x_1, \ldots, x_{2n}) = \prod_{k=1}^{n}\left(x_k x_{n+k} \sum_{j=1}^{2n-k-1} x_j x_{j+k+1}\right)$.
   a) Prove that $\sum_{x_1, \ldots, x_{2n} \in \{-1, +1\}} f(x_1, \ldots, x_{2n}) = 2^{2n+1} L_n$.
   b) Explain how to evaluate this sum in $O(4^n n)$ steps. How many bits of precision are needed for the arithmetic?
   c) Gain a factor of eight by exploiting the identities
   $$f(x_1, \ldots, x_{2n}) = f(-x_1, \ldots, -x_{2n}) = f(x_{2n}, \ldots, x_1) = f(x_1, -x_2, \ldots, x_{2n-1}, -x_{2n}).$$

7. [*M22*] Prove that every Langford pairing of $\{1, 1, \ldots, 16, 16\}$ must have seven uncompleted pairs at some point, when read from left to right.

8. [*23*] The simplest Langford sequence is not only well-balanced; it's *planar*, in the sense that its pairs can be connected up without crossing lines as in (2):

$$2\ 3\ 1\ 2\ 1\ 3.$$

Find all of the planar Langford pairings for which $n \leq 8$.

9. [*24*] (*Langford triples.*) In how many ways can $\{1, 1, 1, 2, 2, 2, \ldots, 9, 9, 9\}$ be arranged in a row so that consecutive k's are k apart, for $1 \leq k \leq 9$?

10. [*M20*] Explain how to construct a *magic square* directly from Fig. 1. (Convert each card into a number between 1 and 16, in such a way that the rows, columns, and main diagonals all sum to 34.)

11. [*20*] Extend (5) to a "Hebraic-Græco-Latin" square by appending one of the letters $\{\aleph, \beth, \gimel, \daleth\}$ to the two-letter string in each compartment. No letter pair (Latin, Greek), (Latin, Hebrew), or (Greek, Hebrew) should appear in more than one place.

▶ **12.** [*M21*] (L. Euler.) Let $L_{ij} = (i+j) \bmod n$ for $0 \leq i, j < n$ be the addition table for integers mod n. Prove that a latin square orthogonal to L exists if and only if n is odd.

13. [*M25*] A 10×10 square can be divided into four quarters of size 5×5. A 10×10 latin square formed from the digits $\{0, 1, \ldots, 9\}$ has k "intruders" if its upper left quarter has exactly k elements ≥ 5. (See exercise 14(e) for an example with $k = 3$.) Prove that the square has no orthogonal mate unless there are at least three intruders.

14. [*29*] Find all orthogonal mates of the following latin squares:

(a)	(b)	(c)	(d)	(e)
3145926870	2718459036	0572164938	1680397425	7823456019
2819763504	0287135649	6051298473	8346512097	8234067195
9452307168	7524093168	4867039215	9805761342	2340178956
6208451793	1435962780	1439807652	2754689130	3401289567
8364095217.	6390718425.	8324756091.	0538976214.	4012395678
5981274036'	4069271853'	7203941586'	4963820571'	5678912340
4627530981	3102684597	5610473829	7192034658	6789523401
0576148329	9871546302	9148625307	6219405783	0195634782
1730689452	8956307214	2795380164	3471258906	1956740823
7093812645	5643820971	3986512740	5027143869	9567801234

15. [*50*] Find three 10×10 latin squares that are mutually orthogonal to each other.

16. [*48*] (H. J. Ryser, 1967.) A latin square is said to be of "order n" if it has n rows, n columns, and n symbols. Does every latin square of odd order have a transversal?

17. [*25*] Let L be a latin square with elements L_{ij} for $0 \le i, j < n$. Show that the problems of (a) finding all the transversals of L, and (b) finding all the orthogonal mates of L, are special cases of the general exact cover problem.

18. [*M26*] The string $x_1 x_2 \ldots x_N$ is called "*n*-ary" if each element x_j belongs to the set $\{0, 1, \ldots, n-1\}$ of *n*-ary digits. Two strings $x_1 x_2 \ldots x_N$ and $y_1 y_2 \ldots y_N$ are said to be *orthogonal* if the N pairs (x_j, y_j) are distinct for $1 \le j \le N$. (Consequently, two *n*-ary strings cannot be orthogonal if their length N exceeds n^2.) An *n*-ary matrix with m rows and n^2 columns whose rows are orthogonal to each other is called an *orthogonal array* of order n and depth m.

Find a correspondence between orthogonal arrays of depth m and lists of $m - 2$ mutually orthogonal latin squares. What orthogonal array corresponds to exercise 11?

▶ **19.** [*M25*] Continuing exercise 18, prove that an orthogonal array of order $n > 1$ and depth m is possible only if $m \le n + 1$. Show that this upper limit is achievable when n is a prime number p. Write out an example when $p = 5$.

20. [*HM20*] Show that if each element k in an orthogonal array is replaced by $e^{2\pi k i/n}$, the rows become orthogonal vectors in the usual sense (their dot product is zero).

▶ **21.** [*M21*] A *geometric net* is a system of points and lines that obeys three axioms:
  i) Each line is a set of points.
  ii) Distinct lines have at most one point in common.
  iii) If p is a point and L is a line with $p \notin L$, then there is exactly one line M such that $p \in M$ and $L \cap M = \emptyset$.
If $L \cap M = \emptyset$ we say that L is *parallel* to M, and write $L \parallel M$.
  a) Prove that the lines of a geometric net can be partitioned into equivalence classes, with two lines in the same class if and only if they are equal or parallel.
  b) Show that if there are at least two classes of parallel lines, every line contains the same number of points as the other lines in its class.
  c) Furthermore, if there are at least three classes, there are numbers m and n such that all points belong to exactly m lines and all lines contain exactly n points.

▶ **22.** [*M22*] Show that every orthogonal array can be regarded as a geometric net. Is the converse also true?

23. [*M23*] (*Error-correcting codes.*) The "Hamming distance" $d(x, y)$ between two strings $x = x_1 \ldots x_N$ and $y = y_1 \ldots y_N$ is the number of positions j where $x_j \ne y_j$. A *b-ary code with n information digits and r check digits* is a set $C(b, n, r)$ of b^n strings $x = x_1 \ldots x_{n+r}$, where $0 \le x_j < b$ for $1 \le j \le n+r$. When a codeword x is transmitted and the message y is received, $d(x, y)$ is the number of transmission errors. The code is called *t-error correcting* if we can reconstruct the value of x whenever a message y is received with $d(x, y) \le t$. The *distance* of the code is the minimum value of $d(x, x')$, taken over all pairs of codewords $x \neq x'$.

a) Prove that a code is *t*-error correcting if and only if its distance exceeds $2t$.

b) Prove that a single-error correcting *b*-ary code with 2 information digits and 2 check digits is equivalent to a pair of orthogonal latin squares of order b.

c) Furthermore, a code $C(b, 2, r)$ with distance $r+1$ is equivalent to a set of r mutually orthogonal latin squares of order b.

▶ **24.** [*M30*] A geometric net with N points and R lines leads naturally to the binary code $C(2, N, R)$ with codewords $x_1 \ldots x_N x_{N+1} \ldots x_{N+R}$ defined by the parity bits

$$x_{N+k} = f_k(x_1, \ldots, x_N) = \left(\sum \{x_j \mid \text{point } j \text{ lies on line } k\}\right) \bmod 2.$$

a) If the net has m classes of parallel lines, prove that this code has distance $m + 1$.

b) Find an efficient way to correct up to t errors with this code, assuming that $m = 2t$. Illustrate the decoding process in the case $N = 25$, $R = 30$, $t = 3$.

25. [*27*] Find a latin square whose rows and columns are five-letter words. (For this exercise you'll need to dig out the big dictionaries.)

▶ **26.** [*25*] Compose a meaningful English sentence that contains only five-letter words.

27. [*20*] How many SGB words contain exactly k distinct letters, for $1 \le k \le 5$?

28. [*20*] Are there any pairs of SGB word vectors that differ by ± 1 in each component?

29. [*20*] Find all SGB words that are *palindromes* (equal to their reflection), or mirror pairs (like `regal lager`).

▶ **30.** [*20*] The letters of `first` are in alphabetic order from left to right. What is the lexicographically *first* such five-letter word? What is the last?

31. [*21*] (C. McManus.) Find all sets of three SGB words that are in arithmetic progression but have no common letters in any fixed position. (One such example is {`power`, `slugs`, `visit`}.)

32. [*23*] Does the English language contain any 10-letter words $a_0 a_1 \ldots a_9$ for which both $a_0 a_2 a_4 a_6 a_8$ and $a_1 a_3 a_5 a_7 a_9$ are SGB words?

33. [*20*] (Scot Morris.) Complete the following list of 26 interesting SGB words:

about, bacon, faced, under, chief, ..., pizza.

▶ **34.** [*21*] For each SGB word that doesn't include the letter y, obtain a 5-bit binary number by changing the vowels {a, e, i, o, u} to 1 and the other letters to 0. What are the most common words for each of the 32 binary outcomes?

▶ **35.** [*26*] Sixteen well-chosen elements of WORDS(1000) lead to the branching pattern

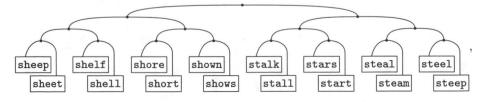

which is a complete binary trie of words that begin with the letter s. But there's no such pattern of words beginning with a, even if we consider the full collection WORDS(5757).

What letters of the alphabet can be used as the starting letter of sixteen words that form a complete binary trie within WORDS(n), given n?

36. [*M17*] Explain the symmetries that appear in the word cube (10). Also show that two more such cubes can be obtained by changing only the two words {stove, event}.

37. [*20*] Which vertices of the graph *words*(5757, 0, 0, 0) have maximum degree?

38. [*22*] Using the digraph rule in (14), change tears to smile in just three steps, *without computer assistance.*

39. [*M00*] Is $G \setminus e$ an induced subgraph of G? Is it a spanning subgraph?

40. [*M15*] How many (a) spanning (b) induced subgraphs does a graph $G = (V, E)$ have, when $|V| = n$ and $|E| = e$?

41. [*M10*] For which integers n do we have (a) $K_n = P_n$? (b) $K_n = C_n$?

42. [*15*] (D. H. Lehmer.) Let G be a graph with 13 vertices, in which every vertex has degree 5. Make a nontrivial statement about G.

43. [*23*] Are any of the following graphs the same as the Petersen graph?

44. [*M23*] How many symmetries does Chvátal's graph have? (See Fig. 2(f).)

45. [*20*] Find an easy way to 4-color the planar graph (17). Would 3 colors suffice?

46. [*M25*] Let G be a graph with $n \geq 3$ vertices, defined by a planar diagram that is "maximal," in the sense that no additional lines can be drawn between nonadjacent vertices without crossing an existing edge.

a) Prove that the diagram partitions the plane into regions that each have exactly three vertices on their boundary. (One of these regions is the set of all points that lie outside the diagram.)

b) Therefore G has exactly $3n - 6$ edges.

47. [*M22*] Prove that the complete bigraph $K_{3,3}$ isn't planar.

48. [*M25*] Complete the proof of Theorem B by showing that the stated procedure never gives the same color to two adjacent vertices.

49. [*18*] Draw diagrams of all the cubic graphs with at most 6 vertices.

50. [*M24*] Find all bipartite graphs that can be 3-colored in exactly 24 ways.

▶ **51.** [*M22*] Given a geometric net as described in exercise 21, construct the bipartite graph whose vertices are the points p and the lines L of the net, with $p \text{ --- } L$ if and only if $p \in L$. What is the *girth* of this graph?

52. [*M16*] Find a simple inequality that relates the diameter of a graph to its girth. (How small can the diameter be, if the girth is large?)

53. [*15*] Which of the words world and happy belongs to the giant component of the graph *words*(5757, 0, 0, 0)?

▶ **54.** [*21*] The 49 postal codes in graph (17) are AL, AR, AZ, CA, CO, CT, DC, DE, FL, GA, IA, ID, IL, IN, KS, KY, LA, MA, MD, ME, MI, MN, MO, MS, MT, NC, ND, NE, NH, NJ, NM, NV, NY, OH, OK, OR, PA, RI, SC, SD, TN, TX, UT, VA, VT, WA, WI, WV, WY, in alphabetical order.

    a) Suppose we consider two states to be adjacent if their postal codes agree in one place (namely AL — AR — OR — OH, etc.). What are the components of this graph?

    b) Now form a directed graph with XY ⟶ YZ (for example, AL ⟶ LA ⟶ AR, etc.). What are the *strongly connected components* of this digraph? (See Section 2.3.4.2.)

    c) The United States has additional postal codes AA, AE, AK, AP, AS, FM, GU, HI, MH, MP, PW, PR, VI, besides those in (17). Reconsider question (b), using all 62 codes.

55. [*M20*] How many edges are in the complete k-partite graph $K_{n_1,\ldots,n_k}$?

▶ **56.** [*M10*] True or false: A multigraph is a graph if and only if the corresponding digraph is simple.

57. [*M10*] True or false: Vertices u and v are in the same connected component of a directed graph if and only if either $d(u,v) < \infty$ or $d(v,u) < \infty$.

58. [*M17*] Describe all (a) graphs (b) multigraphs that are regular of degree 2.

▶ **59.** [*M23*] A *tournament* of order n is a digraph on n vertices that has exactly $\binom{n}{2}$ arcs, either $u \longrightarrow v$ or $v \longrightarrow u$ for every pair of distinct vertices $\{u,v\}$.

    a) Prove that every tournament contains an oriented spanning path $v_1 \longrightarrow \cdots \longrightarrow v_n$.

    b) Consider the tournament on vertices $\{0,1,2,3,4\}$ for which $u \longrightarrow v$ if and only if $(u - v) \bmod 5 \geq 3$. How many oriented spanning paths does it have?

    c) Is $K_n^{\rightarrow}$ the only tournament of order n that has a unique oriented spanning path?

▶ **60.** [*M22*] Let u be a vertex of greatest out-degree in a tournament, and let v be any other vertex. Prove that $d(u,v) \leq 2$.

61. [*M16*] Construct a digraph that has k walks of length k from vertex 1 to vertex 2.

62. [*M21*] A *permutation digraph* is a directed graph in which every vertex has out-degree 1 and in-degree 1; therefore its components are oriented cycles. If it has n vertices and k components, we call it *even* if $n - k$ is even, *odd* if $n - k$ is odd.

    a) Let G be a directed graph with adjacency matrix A. Prove that the number of spanning permutation digraphs of G is per A, the permanent of A.

    b) Interpret the determinant, det A, in terms of spanning permutation digraphs.

63. [*M23*] Let G be a graph of girth g in which every vertex has at least d neighbors. Prove that G has at least N vertices, where

$$N = \begin{cases} 1 + \sum_{0 \leq k < t} d(d-1)^k, & \text{if } g = 2t + 1; \\ 1 + (d-1)^t + \sum_{0 \leq k < t} d(d-1)^k, & \text{if } g = 2t + 2. \end{cases}$$

▶ **64.** [*M21*] Continuing exercise 63, show that there's a *unique* graph of girth 4, minimum degree d, and order $2d$, for each $d \geq 2$.

▶ **65.** [*HM31*] Suppose graph G has girth 5, minimum degree d, and $N = d^2 + 1$ vertices.

    a) Prove that the adjacency matrix A of G satisfies the equation $A^2 + A = (d-1)I + J$.

    b) Since A is a symmetric matrix, it has N orthogonal eigenvectors x_j, with corresponding eigenvalues λ_j, such that $Ax_j = \lambda_j x_j$ for $1 \leq j \leq N$. Prove that each λ_j is either d or $(-1 \pm \sqrt{4d-3})/2$.

    c) Show that if $\sqrt{4d-3}$ is irrational, then $d = 2$. *Hint:* $\lambda_1 + \cdots + \lambda_N = \text{trace}(A) = 0$.

    d) And if $\sqrt{4d-3}$ is rational, $d \in \{3,7,57\}$.

66. [*M30*] Continuing exercise 65, construct such a graph when $d = 7$.

67. [*M48*] Is there a regular graph of degree 57, order 3250, and girth 5?

68. [*M20*] How many different adjacency matrices does a graph G on n vertices have?

▶ **69.** [*20*] Extending (31), explain how to calculate both out-degree ODEG(v) and in-degree IDEG(v) for *all* vertices v in a graph that has been represented in SGB format.

▶ **70.** [*M20*] How often is each step of Algorithm B performed, when that algorithm successfully 2-colors a graph with m arcs and n vertices?

71. [*26*] Implement Algorithm B for the MMIX computer, using the MMIXAL assembly language. Assume that, when your program begins, register v0 points to the first vertex node and register n contains the number of vertices.

▶ **72.** [*M22*] When COLOR(v) is set in step B6, call u the *parent* of v; but when COLOR(w) is set in step B3, say that w has no parent. Define the (inclusive) *ancestors* of vertex v, recursively, to be v together with the ancestors of v's parent (if any).
   a) Prove that if v is below u in the stack during Algorithm B, the parent of v is an ancestor of u.
   b) Furthermore, if COLOR(v) = COLOR(u) in step B6, v is currently in the stack.
   c) Use these facts to extend Algorithm B so that, if the given graph is not bipartite, the names of vertices in a cycle of odd length are output.

73. [*15*] What's another name for *random_graph*(10, 45, 0, 0, 0, 0, 0, 0, 0, 0)?

74. [*21*] What vertex of *roget*(1022, 0, 0, 0) has the largest out-degree?

75. [*22*] The SGB graph generator *board*($n_1, n_2, n_3, n_4, p, w, o$) creates a graph whose vertices are the t-dimensional integer vectors $(x_1, \ldots, x_t)$ for $0 \le x_i < b_i$, determined by the first four parameters (n_1, n_2, n_3, n_4) as follows: Set $n_5 \leftarrow 0$ and let $j \ge 0$ be minimum such that $n_{j+1} \le 0$. If $j = 0$, set $b_1 \leftarrow b_2 \leftarrow 8$ and $t \leftarrow 2$; this is the default 8×8 board. Otherwise if $n_{j+1} = 0$, set $b_i \leftarrow n_i$ for $1 \le i \le j$ and $t \leftarrow j$. Finally, if $n_{j+1} < 0$, set $t \leftarrow |n_{j+1}|$, and set b_i to the ith element of the periodic sequence $(n_1, \ldots, n_j, n_1, \ldots, n_j, n_1, \ldots)$. (For example, the specification $(n_1, n_2, n_3, n_4) = (2, 3, 5, -7)$ is about as tricky as you can get; it produces a 7-dimensional board with $(b_1, \ldots, b_7) = (2, 3, 5, 2, 3, 5, 2)$, hence a graph with $2 \cdot 3 \cdot 5 \cdot 2 \cdot 3 \cdot 5 \cdot 2 = 1800$ vertices.)

The remaining parameters (p, w, o), for "piece, wrap, and orientation," determine the arcs of the graph. Suppose first that $w = o = 0$. If $p > 0$, we have $(x_1, \ldots, x_t) \longrightarrow (y_1, \ldots, y_t)$ if and only if $y_i = x_i + \delta_i$ for $1 \le i \le t$, where $(\delta_1, \ldots, \delta_t)$ is an integer solution to the equation $\delta_1^2 + \cdots + \delta_t^2 = |p|$. And if $p < 0$, we allow also $y_i = x_i + k\delta_i$ for $k \ge 1$, corresponding to k moves in the same direction.

If $w \ne 0$, let $w = (w_t \ldots w_1)_2$ in binary notation. Then we allow "wraparound," $y_i = (x_i + \delta_i) \bmod b_i$ or $y_i = (x_i + k\delta_i) \bmod b_i$, in each coordinate i for which $w_i = 1$.

If $o \ne 0$, the graph is directed; offsets $(\delta_1, \ldots, \delta_t)$ produce arcs only when they are lexicographically greater than $(0, \ldots, 0)$. But if $o = 0$, the graph is undirected.

Find settings of $(n_1, n_2, n_3, n_4, p, w, o)$ for which *board* will produce the following fundamental graphs: (a) the complete graph K_n; (b) the path P_n; (c) the cycle C_n; (d) the transitive tournament $\vec{K_n}$; (e) the oriented path $\vec{P_n}$; (f) the oriented cycle $\vec{C_n}$; (g) the $m \times n$ grid $P_m \square P_n$; (h) the $m \times n$ cylinder $P_m \square C_n$; (i) the $m \times n$ torus $C_m \square C_n$; (j) the $m \times n$ rook graph $K_m \square K_n$; (k) the $m \times n$ directed torus $\vec{C_m} \square \vec{C_n}$; (l) the null graph $\overline{K_n}$; (m) the n-cube $P_2 \square \cdots \square P_2$ with 2^n vertices.

76. [*20*] Can *board*($n_1, n_2, n_3, n_4, p, w, o$) produce loops, or parallel (repeated) edges?

77. [*M20*] If graph G has diameter ≥ 3, prove that $\overline{G}$ has diameter ≤ 3.

78. [*M27*] Let $G = (V, E)$ be a graph with $|V| = n$ and $G \cong \overline{G}$. (In other words, G is *self-complementary*: There's a permutation φ of V such that $u \!-\! v$ if and only if $\varphi(u) \!+\! \varphi(v)$ and $u \neq v$. We can imagine that the edges of K_n have been painted black or white; the white edges define a graph that's isomorphic to the graph of black edges.)
   a) Prove that $n \bmod 4 = 0$ or 1. Draw diagrams for all such graphs with $n < 8$.
   b) Prove that if $n \bmod 4 = 0$, every cycle of the permutation φ has a length that is a multiple of 4.
   c) Conversely, every permutation φ with such cycles arises in some such graph G.
   d) Extend these results to the case $n \bmod 4 = 1$.

▶ **79.** [*M22*] Given $k \geq 0$, construct a graph on the vertices $\{0, 1, \ldots, 4k\}$ that is both regular and self-complementary.

▶ **80.** [*M22*] A self-complementary graph must have diameter 2 or 3, by exercise 77. Given $k \geq 2$, construct self-complementary graphs of both possible diameters, when (a) $V = \{1, 2, \ldots, 4k\}$; (b) $V = \{0, 1, 2, \ldots, 4k\}$.

81. [*20*] The complement of a simple digraph without loops is defined by extending (35) and (36), so that we have $u \to v$ in $\overline{D}$ if and only if $u \neq v$ and $u \nrightarrow v$ in D. What are the self-complementary digraphs of order 3?

82. [*M21*] Are the following statements about line graphs true or false?
   a) If G is contained in G', then $L(G)$ is an induced subgraph of $L(G')$.
   b) If G is a regular graph, so is $L(G)$.
   c) $L(K_{m,n})$ is regular, for all $m, n > 0$.
   d) $L(K_{m,n,r})$ is regular, for all $m, n, r > 0$.
   e) $L(K_{m,n}) \cong K_m \square K_n$.
   f) $L(K_4) \cong K_{2,2,2}$.
   g) $L(P_{n+1}) \cong P_n$.
   h) The graphs G and $L(G)$ both have the same number of components.

83. [*16*] Draw the graph $\overline{L(K_5)}$.

▶ **84.** [*M21*] Is $L(K_{3,3})$ self-complementary?

85. [*M22*] (O. Ore, 1962.) For which graphs G do we have $G \cong L(G)$?

86. [*M20*] (R. J. Wilson.) Find a graph G of order 6 for which $\overline{G} \cong L(G)$.

87. [*20*] Is the Petersen graph (a) 3-colorable? (b) 3-edge-colorable?

88. [*M20*] The graph $W_n = K_1 \!-\! C_n$ is called the *wheel* with n spokes, when $n \geq 3$. How many cycles does it contain as subgraphs?

W_7

89. [*M20*] Prove the associative laws, (42) and (43).

▶ **90.** [*M24*] A graph is called a *cograph* if it can be constructed algebraically from 1-element graphs by means of complementation and/or direct sum operations. For example, there are four nonisomorphic graphs of order 3, and they all are cographs: $\overline{K_3} = K_1 \oplus K_1 \oplus K_1$ and its complement, K_3; $\overline{K_{1,2}} = K_1 \oplus K_2$ and its complement, $K_{1,2}$, where $K_2 = \overline{K_1 \oplus K_1}$.

Exhaustive enumeration shows that there are 11 nonisomorphic graphs of order 4. Give algebraic formulas to prove that 10 of them are cographs. Which one isn't?

▶ **91.** [*20*] Draw diagrams for the 4-vertex graphs (a) $K_2 \square K_2$; (b) $K_2 \otimes K_2$; (c) $K_2 \boxtimes K_2$; (d) $K_2 \triangle K_2$; (e) $K_2 \circ K_2$; (f) $\overline{K_2} \circ K_2$; (g) $K_2 \circ \overline{K_2}$.

92. [*21*] The five types of graph products defined in the text work fine for simple digraphs as well as for ordinary graphs. Draw diagrams for the 4-vertex digraphs (a) $\vec{K_2} \square \vec{K_2}$; (b) $\vec{K_2} \otimes \vec{K_2}$; (c) $\vec{K_2} \boxtimes \vec{K_2}$; (d) $\vec{K_2} \triangle \vec{K_2}$; (e) $\vec{K_2} \circ \vec{K_2}$.

93. [15] Which of the five graph products takes K_m and K_n into K_{mn}?

94. [10] Are the SGB *words* graphs induced subgraphs of $P_{26} \mathbin{\square} P_{26} \mathbin{\square} P_{26} \mathbin{\square} P_{26} \mathbin{\square} P_{26}$?

95. [M20] If vertex u of G has degree d_u and vertex v of H has degree d_v, what is the degree of vertex (u, v) in (a) $G \mathbin{\square} H$? (b) $G \otimes H$? (c) $G \boxtimes H$? (d) $G \bigtriangleup H$? (e) $G \circ H$?

▸ **96.** [M22] Let A be an $m \times m'$ matrix with $a_{uu'}$ in row u and column u'; let B be an $n \times n'$ matrix with $b_{vv'}$ in row v and column v'. The *direct product* $A \otimes B$ is an $mn \times m'n'$ matrix with $a_{uu'}b_{vv'}$ in row (u, v) and column (u', v'). Thus $A \otimes B$ is the adjacency matrix of $G \otimes H$, if A and B are the adjacency matrices of G and H.

Find analogous formulas for the adjacency matrices of (a) $G \mathbin{\square} H$; (b) $G \boxtimes H$; (c) $G \bigtriangleup H$; (d) $G \circ H$.

97. [M25] Find as many interesting algebraic relations between graph sums and products as you can. (For example, the distributive law $(A \oplus B) \otimes C = (A \otimes C) \oplus (B \otimes C)$ for direct sums and products of matrices implies that $(G \oplus G') \otimes H = (G \otimes H) \oplus (G' \otimes H)$. We also have $\overline{K_m} \mathbin{\square} H = H \oplus \cdots \oplus H$, with m copies of H, etc.)

98. [M20] If the graph G has k components and the graph H has l components, how many components are in the graphs $G \mathbin{\square} H$ and $G \boxtimes H$?

99. [M20] Let $d_G(u, u')$ be the distance from vertex u to vertex u' in graph G. Prove that $d_{G \mathbin{\square} H}((u, v), (u', v')) = d_G(u, u') + d_H(v, v')$, and find a similar formula for $d_{G \boxtimes H}((u, v), (u', v'))$.

100. [M21] For which connected graphs is $G \otimes H$ connected?

▸ **101.** [M25] Find all connected graphs G and H such that $G \mathbin{\square} H \cong G \otimes H$.

102. [M20] What's a simple algebraic formula for the graph of *king moves* (which take one step horizontally, vertically, or diagonally) on an $m \times n$ board?

103. [20] Complete tableau (54). Also apply Algorithm H to the sequence 866444444.

104. [18] Explain the manipulation of variables i, t, and r in steps H3 and H4.

105. [M38] Suppose $d_1 \geq \cdots \geq d_n \geq 0$, and let $c_1 \geq \cdots \geq c_{d_1}$ be its conjugate as in Algorithm H. Prove that $d_1 \ldots d_n$ is graphical if and only if $d_1 + \cdots + d_n$ is even and $d_1 + \cdots + d_k \leq c_1 + \cdots + c_k - k$ for $1 \leq k \leq s$, where s is maximal such that $d_s \geq s$.

106. [20] True or false: If $d_1 = \cdots = d_n = d < n$ and nd is even, Algorithm H constructs a *connected* graph.

107. [M21] Prove that the degree sequence $d_1 \ldots d_n$ of a self-complementary graph satisfies $d_j + d_{n+1-j} = n - 1$ and $d_j = d_{j-(-1)^j}$ for $1 \leq j \leq n/2$.

▸ **108.** [M23] Design an algorithm analogous to Algorithm H that constructs a *simple directed graph* on vertices $\{1, \ldots, n\}$, having specified values d_k^- and d_k^+ for the in-degree and out-degree of each vertex k, whenever at least one such graph exists.

109. [M20] Design an algorithm analogous to Algorithm H that constructs a *bipartite graph* on vertices $\{1, \ldots, m + n\}$, having specified degrees d_k for each vertex k when possible; all edges $j \!-\! k$ should have $j \leq m$ and $k > m$.

110. [M22] Without using Algorithm H, show by a direct construction that the sequence $d_1 \ldots d_n$ is graphical when $n > d_1 \geq \cdots \geq d_n \geq d_1 - 1$ and $d_1 + \cdots + d_n$ is even.

▸ **111.** [25] Let G be a graph on vertices $V = \{1, \ldots, n\}$, with d_k the degree of k and $\max(d_1, \ldots, d_n) = d$. Prove that there's an integer N with $n \leq N \leq 2n$ and a graph H on vertices $\{1, \ldots, N\}$, such that H is regular of degree d and $H \,|\, V = G$. Explain how to construct such a regular graph with N as small as possible.

▶ **112.** [*20*] Does the network *miles*(128, 0, 0, 0, 0, 127, 0) have three equidistant cities? If not, what three cities come closest to an equilateral triangle?

113. [*05*] When H is a hypergraph with m edges and n vertices, how many rows and columns does its incidence matrix have?

114. [*M20*] Suppose the multigraph (26) is regarded as a hypergraph. What is the corresponding incidence matrix? What is the corresponding bipartite multigraph?

▶ **115.** [*M20*] When B is the incidence matrix of a graph G, explain the significance of the symmetric matrices $B^T B$ and BB^T.

116. [*M17*] Describe the edges of the complete bipartite r-uniform hypergraph $K_{m,n}^{(r)}$.

117. [*M22*] How many nonisomorphic 1-uniform hypergraphs have m edges and n vertices? (Edges may be repeated.) List them all when $m = 4$ and $n = 3$.

118. [*M20*] A "hyperforest" is a hypergraph that contains no cycles. If a hyperforest has m edges, n vertices, and p components, what's the sum of the degrees of its vertices?

119. [*M18*] What hypergraph corresponds to (60) without the final term $(\bar{x}_1 \vee \bar{x}_2 \vee \bar{x}_4)$?

120. [*M20*] Define *directed hypergraphs*, by generalizing the concept of directed graphs.

121. [*M19*] Given a hypergraph $H = (V, E)$, let $I(H) = (V, F)$, where F is the family of all maximal independent sets of H. Express $\chi(H)$ in terms of $|V|$, $|F|$, and $\alpha(I(H)^T)$.

▶ **122.** [*M24*] Find a maximum independent set and a minimum coloring of the following triple systems: (a) the hypergraph (56); (b) the dual of the Petersen graph.

123. [*17*] Show that the optimum colorings of $K_n \square K_n$ are equivalent to the solutions of a famous combinatorial problem.

124. [*M22*] What is the chromatic number of the Chvátal graph, Fig. 2(f)?

125. [*M48*] For what values of g is there a 4-regular, 4-chromatic graph of girth g?

▶ **126.** [*M22*] Find optimum colorings of the "kingwise torus," $C_m \boxtimes C_n$, when $m, n \geq 3$.

127. [*M22*] Prove that (a) $\chi(G) + \chi(\overline{G}) \leq n + 1$ and (b) $\chi(G)\chi(\overline{G}) \geq n$ when G is a graph of order n, and find graphs for which equality holds.

128. [*M18*] Express $\chi(G \square H)$ in terms of $\chi(G)$ and $\chi(H)$, when G and H are graphs.

129. [*23*] Describe the maximal cliques of the 8×8 queen graph (37).

130. [*M20*] How many maximal cliques are in a complete k-partite graph?

131. [*M30*] Let $N(n)$ be the largest number of maximal cliques that an n-vertex graph can have. Prove that $3^{\lfloor n/3 \rfloor} \leq N(n) \leq 3^{\lceil n/3 \rceil}$.

▶ **132.** [*M20*] We call G *tightly colorable* if $\chi(G) = \omega(G)$. Prove that $\chi(G \boxtimes H) = \chi(G)\chi(H)$ whenever G and H are tightly colorable.

133. [*21*] The "musical graph" illustrated here provides a nice way to review numerous definitions that were given in this section, because its properties are easily analyzed. Determine its (a) order; (b) size; (c) girth; (d) diameter; (e) independence number, $\alpha(G)$; (f) chromatic number, $\chi(G)$; (g) edge-chromatic number, $\chi(L(G))$; (h) clique number, $\omega(G)$; (i) algebraic formula as a product of well-known smaller graphs. What is the size of (j) a minimum vertex cover? (k) a maximum matching? Is G (l) regular? (m) planar? (n) connected? (o) directed? (p) a free tree? (q) Hamiltonian?

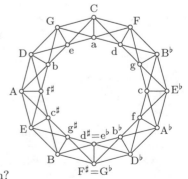

134. [*M22*] How many automorphisms does the musical graph have?

▸ **135.** [*HM26*] Suppose a composer takes a random walk in the musical graph, starting at vertex C and then making five equally likely choices at each step. Show that after an even number of steps, the walk is more likely to end at vertex C than at any other vertex. What is the exact probability of going from C to C in a 12-step walk?

136. [*HM23*] A *Cayley digraph* is a directed graph whose vertices V are the elements of a group and whose arcs are $v \longrightarrow v\alpha_j$ for $1 \le j \le d$ and all vertices v, where $(\alpha_1, \ldots, \alpha_d)$ are fixed elements of the group. A *Cayley graph* is a Cayley digraph that is also a graph. Is the Petersen graph a Cayley graph?

▸ **137.** [*M25*] (*Generalized toruses.*) An $m \times n$ torus can be regarded as a tiling of the plane. For example, we can imagine that infinitely many copies of the 3×4 torus in (50) have been placed together gridwise, as indicated in the left-hand illustration above; from each vertex we can move north, south, east, or west to another vertex of the torus. The vertices have been numbered here so that a northward move from v goes to $(v+4) \bmod 12$, and an eastward move to $(v+3) \bmod 12$, etc. The right-hand illustration shows the same torus, but with a differently shaped tile; *any* way to choose twelve cells numbered $\{0, 1, \ldots, 11\}$ will tile the plane, with exactly the same numbering scheme.

Shifted copies of a single shape will also tile the plane if they form a *generalized torus*, in which cell (x, y) corresponds to the same vertex as cells $(x + a, y + b)$ and $(x + c, y + d)$, where (a, b) and (c, d) are integer vectors and $n = ad - bc > 0$. The generalized torus will then have n points. These vectors (a, b) and (c, d) are $(4, 0)$ and $(0, 3)$ in the 3×4 example above; and when they are respectively $(5, 2)$ and $(1, 3)$ we get

Here $n = 13$, and a northward move from v goes to $(v + 4) \bmod 13$; an eastward move goes to $(v + 1) \bmod 13$.

Prove that if $\gcd(a, b, c, d) = 1$, the vertices of such a generalized torus can always be assigned integer labels $\{0, 1, \ldots, n-1\}$ in such a way that the neighbors of v are $(v \pm p) \bmod n$ and $(v \pm q) \bmod n$, for some integers p and q.

138. [*HM27*] Continuing exercise 137, what is a good way to label k-dimensional vertices $x = (x_1, \ldots, x_k)$, when integer vectors α_j are given such that each vector x is equivalent to $x + \alpha_j$ for $1 \leq j \leq k$? Illustrate your method in the case $k = 3$, $\alpha_1 = (3, 1, 1)$, $\alpha_2 = (1, 3, 1)$, $\alpha_3 = (1, 1, 3)$.

▸ **139.** [*M22*] Let H be a fixed graph of order h, and let $\#(H{:}G)$ be the number of times that H occurs as an induced subgraph of a given graph G. If G is chosen at random from the set of all $2^{n(n-1)/2}$ graphs on the vertices $V = \{1, 2, \ldots, n\}$, what is the average value of $\#(H{:}G)$ when H is (a) K_h; (b) P_h, for $h > 1$; (c) C_h, for $h > 2$; (d) arbitrary?

140. [*M30*] A graph G is called *proportional* if its induced subgraph counts $\#(K_3{:}G)$, $\#(\overline{K_3}{:}G)$, and $\#(P_3{:}G)$ each agree with the expected values derived in exercise 139.

   a) Show that the wheel graph W_7 of exercise 88 is proportional in this sense.

   b) Prove that G is proportional if and only if $\#(K_3{:}G) = \frac{1}{8}\binom{n}{3}$ and the degree sequence $d_1 \ldots d_n$ of its vertices satisfies the identities

$$d_1 + \cdots + d_n = \binom{n}{2}, \qquad d_1^2 + \cdots + d_n^2 = \frac{n}{2}\binom{n}{2}. \qquad (*)$$

141. [*26*] The conditions of exercise 140(b) can hold only if $n \bmod 16 \in \{0, 1, 8\}$. Write a program to find all of the proportional graphs that have $n = 8$ vertices.

142. [*M30*] (S. Janson and J. Kratochvíl, 1991.) Prove that no graph G on 4 or more vertices can be "extraproportional," in the sense that its subgraph counts $\#(H{:}G)$ agree with the expected values in exercise 139 for each of the eleven nonisomorphic graphs H of order 4 that are considered in exercise 90. *Hint:* Observe that $(n-3)\#(K_3{:}G) = 4\#(K_4{:}G) + 2\#(K_{1,1,2}{:}G) + \#(\overline{K_{1,3}}{:}G) + \#(\overline{K_1 \oplus K_{1,2}}{:}G)$.

▸ **143.** [*M25*] Let A be any matrix with $m > 1$ distinct rows, and $n \geq m$ columns. Prove that at least one column of A can be deleted, without making any two rows equal.

▸ **144.** [*21*] Let X be an $m \times n$ matrix whose entries x_{ij} are either 0, 1, or $*$. A "completion" of X is a matrix X^* in which every $*$ has been replaced by either 0 or 1. Show that the problem of finding a completion with fewest distinct rows is equivalent to the problem of finding the chromatic number of a graph.

▸ **145.** [*25*] (R. S. Boyer and J. S. Moore, 1980.) Suppose the array $a_1 \ldots a_n$ contains a *majority element*, namely a value that occurs more than $n/2$ times. Design an algorithm that finds it after making fewer than n comparisons. *Hint:* If $n \geq 3$ and $a_{n-1} \neq a_n$, the majority element of $a_1 \ldots a_n$ is also the majority element of $a_1 \ldots a_{n-2}$.

Yet now and then your men of wit
Will condescend to take a bit.
— JONATHAN SWIFT, *Cadenus and Vanessa* (1713)

If the base 2 is used the resulting units may be called binary digits,
or more briefly bits, *a word suggested by J. W. Tukey.*
— CLAUDE E. SHANNON, in *Bell System Technical Journal* (1948)

bit (bit), n . . . [A] boring tool . . .
— *Random House Dictionary of the English Language* (1987)

7.1. ZEROS AND ONES

COMBINATORIAL ALGORITHMS often require special attention to efficiency, and
the proper representation of data is an important way to gain the necessary
speed. It is therefore wise to beef up our knowledge of elementary representation
techniques before we set out to study combinatorial algorithms in detail.

Most of today's computers are based on the binary number system, instead
of working directly with the decimal numbers that human beings prefer, because
machines are especially good at dealing with the two-state on-off quantities that
we usually denote by the digits 0 and 1. But in Chapters 1 to 6 we haven't made
much use of the fact that binary computers can do several things quickly that
decimal computers cannot. A binary machine can usually perform "logical" or
"bitwise" operations just as easily as it can add or subtract; yet we have seldom
capitalized on that capability. We've seen that binary and decimal computers are
not significantly different, for many purposes, but in a sense we've been asking
a binary computer to operate with one hand tied behind its back.

The amazing ability of 0s and 1s to encode information as well as to encode
the logical relations between items, and even to encode algorithms that describe
the processing of information, makes the study of binary digits especially rich.
Indeed, we not only use bitwise operations to enhance combinatorial algorithms,
we also find that the properties of binary logic lead naturally to new combinatorial problems that are of great interest in their own right.

Computer scientists have gradually become better and better at taming the
wild 0s and 1s of the universe and making them do useful tricks. But as bit
players on the world's stage, we'd better have a thorough understanding of the
low-level properties of binary quantities before we launch into a study of higher-
level concepts and techniques. Therefore we shall start by investigating basic
ways to combine individual bits and sequences of bits.

7.1.1. Boolean Basics

There are 16 possible functions $f(x, y)$ that transform two given bits x and y
into a third bit $z = f(x, y)$, since there are two choices for each of $f(0, 0)$, $f(0, 1)$,
$f(1, 0)$, and $f(1, 1)$. Table 1 indicates the names and notations that have traditionally been associated with these functions in studies of formal logic, assuming
that 1 corresponds to "true" and 0 to "false." The sequence of four values
$f(0, 0)f(0, 1)f(1, 0)f(1, 1)$ is customarily called the *truth table* of the function f.

Let us conceive, then, of an Algebra
in which the symbols x, y, z, *&c. admit indifferently of*
the values 0 *and* 1, *and of these values alone.*
— GEORGE BOOLE, *An Investigation of the Laws of Thought* (1854)

'Contrariwise,' continued Tweedledee, 'if it was so, it might be;
and if it were so, it would be;
but as it isn't, it ain't. That's logic.'
— LEWIS CARROLL, *Through the Looking Glass* (1871)

Such functions are often called "Boolean operations" in honor of George Boole, who first discovered that algebraic operations on 0s and 1s could be used to construct a calculus for logical reasoning [*The Mathematical Analysis of Logic* (Cambridge: 1847); *An Investigation of the Laws of Thought* (London: 1854)]. But Boole never actually dealt with the "logical or" operation $\vee$; he confined himself strictly to ordinary arithmetic operations on 0s and 1s. Thus he would write $x + y$ to stand for disjunction, but he took pains never to use this notation unless x and y were mutually exclusive (not both 1). If necessary, he wrote $x + (1-x)y$ to ensure that the result of a disjunction would never be equal to 2.

When rendering the $+$ operation in English, Boole sometimes called it "and," sometimes "or." This practice may seem strange to modern mathematicians until we realize that his usage was in fact normal English for disjoint sets; we say, for example, that "boys and girls are children," but "children are boys or girls."

Boole's calculus was extended to include the unconventional rule $x + x = x$ by W. Stanley Jevons [*Pure Logic* (London: Edward Stanford, 1864), §69], who pointed out that $(x + y)z$ was equal to $xz + yz$ using his new $+$ operation. But Jevons did not know the other distributive law $xy + z = (x+z)(y+z)$. Presumably he missed this because of the notation he was using, since the second distributive law has no familiar counterpart in arithmetic; the more symmetrical notations $x \wedge y$, $x \vee y$ in Table 1 make it easier for us to remember both distributive laws

$$(x \vee y) \wedge z = (x \wedge z) \vee (y \wedge z); \tag{1}$$

$$(x \wedge y) \vee z = (x \vee z) \wedge (y \vee z). \tag{2}$$

The second law (2) was introduced by C. S. Peirce, who had discovered independently how to extend Boole's calculus [*Proc. Amer. Acad. Arts and Sciences* **7** (1867), 250–261]. Incidentally, when Peirce discussed these early developments several years later [*Amer. J. Math.* **3** (1880), 32], he referred to "the Boolian algebra, with Jevons's addition"; his now-unfamiliar spelling of "Boolean" was in use for many years, appearing in the Funk and Wagnalls unabridged dictionary as late as 1963.

The notion of truth-value combination is actually much older than Boolean algebra. Indeed, propositional logic had been developed by Greek philosophers already in the fourth century B.C. There was considerable debate in those days about how to assign an appropriate true-or-false value to the proposition "if x then y" when x and y are propositions; Philo of Megara, about 300 B.C., defined

Table 1

THE SIXTEEN LOGICAL OPERATIONS ON TWO VARIABLES

Truth table	New and old notation(s)	Operator symbol ∘	Name(s)
0000	0	$\perp$	Contradiction; falsehood; antilogy; constant 0
0001	$xy,\ x \wedge y,\ x \ \& \ y$	$\wedge$	Conjunction; and
0010	$x \wedge \bar{y},\ x \not\supset y,\ [x>y],\ x \mathbin{\dot{-}} y$	$\bar{\supset}$	Nonimplication; difference; and not; but not
0011	x	L	Left projection; first dictator
0100	$\bar{x} \wedge y,\ x \not\subset y,\ [x<y],\ y \mathbin{\dot{-}} x$	$\bar{\mathsf{C}}$	Converse nonimplication; not ... but
0101	y	R	Right projection; second dictator
0110	$x \oplus y,\ x \not\equiv y,\ x\,\hat{}\,y$	$\oplus$	Exclusive disjunction; nonequivalence; "xor"
0111	$x \vee y,\ x \mid y$	$\vee$	(Inclusive) disjunction; or; and/or
1000	$\bar{x} \wedge \bar{y},\ \overline{x \vee y},\ x \bar{\vee} y,\ x \downarrow y$	$\bar{\vee}$	Nondisjunction; joint denial; neither ... nor
1001	$x \equiv y,\ x \leftrightarrow y,\ x \Leftrightarrow y$	$\equiv$	Equivalence; if and only if; "iff"
1010	$\bar{y},\ \neg y,\ !y,\ \sim y$	$\bar{\mathsf{R}}$	Right complementation
1011	$x \vee \bar{y},\ x \subset y,\ x \Leftarrow y,\ [x \geq y],\ x^y$	C	Converse implication; if
1100	$\bar{x},\ \neg x,\ !x,\ \sim x$	$\bar{\mathsf{L}}$	Left complementation
1101	$\bar{x} \vee y,\ x \supset y,\ x \Rightarrow y,\ [x \leq y],\ y^x$	$\supset$	Implication; only if; if ... then
1110	$\bar{x} \vee \bar{y},\ \overline{x \wedge y},\ x \bar{\wedge} y,\ x \mid y$	$\bar{\wedge}$	Nonconjunction; not both ... and; "nand"
1111	1	$\top$	Affirmation; validity; tautology; constant 1

it by the truth table shown in Table 1, which states in particular that the implication is true when both x and y are false. Much of this early work has been lost, but there are passages in the works of Galen (2nd century A.D.) that refer to both inclusive and exclusive disjunction of propositions. [See I. M. Bocheński, *Formale Logik* (1956), English translation by Ivo Thomas (1961), for an excellent survey of the development of logic from ancient times up to the 20th century.]

A function of two variables is often written $x \circ y$ instead of $f(x, y)$, using some appropriate operator symbol $\circ$. Table 1 shows the sixteen operator symbols that we shall adopt for Boolean functions of two variables; for example, $\perp$ symbolizes the function whose truth table is 0000, $\wedge$ is the symbol for 0001, $\bar{\supset}$ is the symbol for 0010, and so on. We have $x \perp y = 0$, $x \wedge y = xy$, $x \bar{\supset} y = x \mathbin{\dot{-}} y$, $x \mathsf{L} y = x$, $\ldots$, $x \bar{\wedge} y = \bar{x} \vee \bar{y}$, $x \top y = 1$.

Of course the operations in Table 1 aren't all of equal importance. For example, the first and last cases are trivial, since they have a constant value independent of x and y. Four of them are functions of x alone or y alone. We write $\bar{x}$ for $1 - x$, the *complement* of x.

The four operations whose truth table contains just a single 1 are easily expressed in terms of the AND operator $\wedge$, namely $x \wedge y$, $x \wedge \bar{y}$, $\bar{x} \wedge y$, $\bar{x} \wedge \bar{y}$. Those with three 1s are easily written in terms of the OR operator $\vee$, namely $x \vee y$, $x \vee \bar{y}$, $\bar{x} \vee y$, $\bar{x} \vee \bar{y}$. The basic functions $x \wedge y$ and $x \vee y$ have proved to be more useful in practice than their complemented or half-complemented cousins, although the NOR and NAND operations $x \bar{\vee} y = \bar{x} \wedge \bar{y}$ and $x \bar{\wedge} y = \bar{x} \vee \bar{y}$ are also of interest because they are easily implemented in transistor circuits.

In 1913, H. M. Sheffer showed that all 16 of the functions can be expressed in terms of just one, starting with either $\bar{\vee}$ or $\bar{\wedge}$ as the given operation (see exercise 4). Actually C. S. Peirce had made the same discovery about 1880, but his work on the subject remained unpublished until after his death [*Collected Papers of Charles Sanders Peirce* **4** (1933), §§12–20, 264]. Table 1 indicates that NAND and NOR have occasionally been written $x \mid y$ and $x \downarrow y$; sometimes they have been called "Sheffer's stroke" and the "Peirce arrow." Nowadays it is best *not* to use Sheffer's vertical line for NAND, because $x \mid y$ denotes bitwise $x \vee y$ in programming languages like C.

So far we have discussed all but two of the functions in Table 1. The remaining two are $x \equiv y$ and $x \oplus y$, "equivalence" and "exclusive-or," which are related by the identities

$$x \equiv y \;=\; \bar{x} \oplus y \;=\; x \oplus \bar{y} \;=\; 1 \oplus x \oplus y; \tag{3}$$

$$x \oplus y \;=\; \bar{x} \equiv y \;=\; x \equiv \bar{y} \;=\; 0 \equiv x \equiv y. \tag{4}$$

Both operations are associative (see exercise 6). In propositional logic, the notion of equivalence is more important than the notion of exclusive-or, which means inequivalence; but when we consider bitwise operations on full computer words, we shall see in Section 7.1.3 that the situation is reversed: Exclusive-or turns out to be more useful than equivalence, in typical programs. The chief reason why $x \oplus y$ has significant applications, even in the one-bit case, is the fact that

$$x \oplus y \;=\; (x + y) \bmod 2. \tag{5}$$

Therefore $x \oplus y$ and $x \wedge y$ denote addition and multiplication in the field of two elements (see Section 4.6), and $x \oplus y$ naturally inherits many "clean" mathematical properties.

Basic identities. Now let's take a look at interactions between the fundamental operators $\wedge$, $\vee$, $\oplus$, and $\bar{}$, since the other operations are easily expressed in terms of these four. Each of $\wedge$, $\vee$, $\oplus$ is associative and commutative. Besides the distributive laws (1) and (2), we also have

$$(x \oplus y) \wedge z \;=\; (x \wedge z) \oplus (y \wedge z), \tag{6}$$

as well as the *absorption laws*

$$(x \wedge y) \vee x \;=\; (x \vee y) \wedge x \;=\; x. \tag{7}$$

One of the simplest, yet most useful, identities is

$$x \oplus x \;=\; 0, \tag{8}$$

since it implies among other things that

$$(x \oplus y) \oplus x \;=\; y, \qquad (x \oplus y) \oplus y \;=\; x, \tag{9}$$

when we use the obvious fact that $x \oplus 0 = x$. In other words, given $x \oplus y$ and either x or y, it is easy to determine the other. And let us not overlook the simple *complementation law*

$$\bar{x} \;=\; x \oplus 1. \tag{10}$$

Another important pair of identities is known as *De Morgan's laws* in honor of Augustus De Morgan, who stated that "The contrary of an aggregate is the compound of the contraries of the aggregants; the contrary of a compound is the aggregate of the contraries of the components. Thus (A, B) and AB have ab and (a, b) for contraries." [*Trans. Cambridge Philos. Soc.* **10** (1858), 208.] In more modern notation, these are the rules we have implicitly derived via truth tables in connection with the operations NAND and NOR in Table 1, namely

$$\overline{x \wedge y} = \bar{x} \vee \bar{y}; \tag{11}$$

$$\overline{x \vee y} = \bar{x} \wedge \bar{y}. \tag{12}$$

Incidentally, W. S. Jevons knew (12) but not (11); he consistently wrote $\bar{A}B + \bar{B}A + \bar{A}\bar{B}$ instead of $\bar{A} + \bar{B}$ for the complement of AB. Yet De Morgan was not the first Englishman who enunciated the laws above. Both (11) and (12) can be found in the early 14th century writings of two scholastic philosophers, William of Ockham [*Summa Logicæ* **2** (1323)] and Walter Burley [*De Puritate Artis Logicæ* (c. 1330)].

De Morgan's laws and a few other identities can be used to express $\wedge$, $\vee$, and $\oplus$ in terms of each other:

$$x \wedge y = \overline{\bar{x} \vee \bar{y}} = x \oplus y \oplus (x \vee y); \tag{13}$$

$$x \vee y = \overline{\bar{x} \wedge \bar{y}} = x \oplus y \oplus (x \wedge y); \tag{14}$$

$$x \oplus y = (x \vee y) \wedge \overline{x \wedge y} = (x \wedge \bar{y}) \vee (\bar{x} \wedge y). \tag{15}$$

According to exercise 7.1.2–77, all computations of $x_1 \oplus x_2 \oplus \cdots \oplus x_n$ that use only the operations $\wedge$, $\vee$, and $^-$ must be at least $4(n-1)$ steps long; thus, the other three operations are not an especially good substitute for $\oplus$.

Functions of n variables. A Boolean function $f(x, y, z)$ of three Boolean variables x, y, z can be defined by its 8-bit truth table $f(0,0,0)f(0,0,1)\ldots f(1,1,1)$; and in general, every n-ary Boolean function $f(x_1, \ldots, x_n)$ corresponds to a 2^n-bit truth table that lists the successive values of $f(0, \ldots, 0, 0)$, $f(0, \ldots, 0, 1)$, $f(0, \ldots, 1, 0)$, $\ldots$, $f(1, \ldots, 1, 1)$.

We needn't devise special names and notations for all these functions, since they can all be expressed in terms of the binary functions that we've already learned. For example, as observed by I. I. Zhegalkin [*Matematicheskiǐ Sbornik* **35** (1928), 311–369], we can always write

$$f(x_1, \ldots, x_n) = g(x_1, \ldots, x_{n-1}) \oplus h(x_1, \ldots, x_{n-1}) \wedge x_n \tag{16}$$

when $n > 0$, for appropriate functions g and h, by letting

$$\begin{aligned} g(x_1, \ldots, x_{n-1}) &= f(x_1, \ldots, x_{n-1}, 0); \\ h(x_1, \ldots, x_{n-1}) &= f(x_1, \ldots, x_{n-1}, 0) \oplus f(x_1, \ldots, x_{n-1}, 1). \end{aligned} \tag{17}$$

(The operation $\wedge$ conventionally takes precedence over $\oplus$, so we need not use parentheses to enclose the subformula '$h(x_1, \ldots, x_{n-1}) \wedge x_n$' on the right-hand side of (16).) Repeating this process recursively on g and h until we're down to 0-ary functions leaves us with an expression that involves only the operators $\oplus$, $\wedge$, and a sequence of 2^n constants, together with the variables $\{x_1, \ldots, x_n\}$. Furthermore, those constants can usually be simplified away, because we have

$$x \wedge 0 = 0 \qquad \text{and} \qquad x \wedge 1 = x \oplus 0 = x. \tag{18}$$

After applying the associative and distributive laws, we end up needing the constant 0 only if $f(x_1, \ldots, x_n)$ is identically zero, and the constant 1 only if $f(0, \ldots, 0) = 1$.

We might have, for instance,

$$\begin{aligned}
f(x, y, z) &= \big((1 \oplus 0 \wedge x) \oplus (0 \oplus 1 \wedge x) \wedge y\big) \oplus \big((0 \oplus 1 \wedge x) \oplus (1 \oplus 1 \wedge x) \wedge y\big) \wedge z \\
&= (1 \oplus x \wedge y) \oplus (x \oplus y \oplus x \wedge y) \wedge z \\
&= 1 \oplus x \wedge y \oplus x \wedge z \oplus y \wedge z \oplus x \wedge y \wedge z.
\end{aligned}$$

And by rule (5), we see that we're simply left with the polynomial

$$f(x, y, z) = (1 + xy + xz + yz + xyz) \bmod 2, \tag{19}$$

because $x \wedge y = xy$. Notice that this polynomial is linear (of degree ≤ 1) in each of its variables. In general, a similar calculation will show that *any* Boolean function $f(x_1, \ldots, x_n)$ has a unique representation such as this, called its *multilinear representation* or *exclusive normal form*, which is a sum (modulo 2) of zero or more of the 2^n possible terms $1, x_1, x_2, x_1 x_2, x_3, x_1 x_3, x_2 x_3, x_1 x_2 x_3, \ldots, x_1 x_2 \ldots x_n$.

George Boole decomposed Boolean functions in a different way, which is often simpler for the kinds of functions that arise in practice. Instead of (16), he essentially wrote

$$f(x_1, \ldots, x_n) = \big(g(x_1, \ldots, x_{n-1}) \wedge \bar{x}_n\big) \vee \big(h(x_1, \ldots, x_{n-1}) \wedge x_n\big) \tag{20}$$

and called it the "law of development," where we now have simply

$$\begin{aligned}
g(x_1, \ldots, x_{n-1}) &= f(x_1, \ldots, x_{n-1}, 0), \\
h(x_1, \ldots, x_{n-1}) &= f(x_1, \ldots, x_{n-1}, 1),
\end{aligned} \tag{21}$$

instead of (17). Repeatedly iterating Boole's procedure, using the distributive law (1), and eliminating constants, leaves us with a formula that is a disjunction of zero or more *minterms*, where each minterm is a conjunction such as $x_1 \wedge \bar{x}_2 \wedge \bar{x}_3 \wedge x_4 \wedge x_5$ in which every variable or its complement is present. Notice that a minterm is a Boolean function that is true at exactly one point.

For example, let's consider the more-or-less random function $f(w, x, y, z)$ whose truth table is

$$1100\ 1001\ 0000\ 1111. \tag{22}$$

When this function is expanded by repeatedly applying Boole's law (20), we get a disjunction of eight minterms, one for each of the 1s in the truth table:

$$\begin{aligned}
f(w, x, y, z) = {}& (\bar{w} \wedge \bar{x} \wedge \bar{y} \wedge \bar{z}) \vee (\bar{w} \wedge \bar{x} \wedge \bar{y} \wedge z) \vee (\bar{w} \wedge x \wedge \bar{y} \wedge \bar{z}) \vee (\bar{w} \wedge x \wedge y \wedge z) \\
& \vee (w \wedge x \wedge \bar{y} \wedge \bar{z}) \vee (w \wedge x \wedge \bar{y} \wedge z) \vee (w \wedge x \wedge y \wedge \bar{z}) \vee (w \wedge x \wedge y \wedge z). \quad \text{(23)}
\end{aligned}$$

In general, a disjunction of minterms is called a *full disjunctive normal form*. Every Boolean function can be expressed in this way, and the result is unique — except, of course, for the order of the minterms. *Nitpick:* A special case arises when $f(x_1, \ldots, x_n)$ is identically zero. We consider '0' to be an empty disjunction, with no terms, and we also consider '1' to be an empty conjunction, for the same reasons as we defined $\sum_{k=1}^{0} a_k = 0$ and $\prod_{k=1}^{0} a_k = 1$ in Section 1.2.3.

C. S. Peirce observed, in *Amer. J. Math.* **3** (1880), 37–39, that every Boolean function also has a *full conjunctive normal form*, which is a conjunction of "min-clauses" like $\bar{x}_1 \vee x_2 \vee \bar{x}_3 \vee \bar{x}_4 \vee x_5$. A minclause is 0 at only one point; so each clause in such a conjunction accounts for a place where the truth table has a 0. For example, the full conjunctive normal form of our function in (22) and (23) is

$$f(w, x, y, z) \; = \; (w \vee x \vee \bar{y} \vee z) \wedge (w \vee x \vee \bar{y} \vee \bar{z}) \wedge (w \vee \bar{x} \vee y \vee \bar{z}) \wedge (w \vee \bar{x} \vee \bar{y} \vee z)$$
$$\wedge \, (\bar{w} \vee x \vee y \vee z) \wedge (\bar{w} \vee x \vee y \vee \bar{z}) \wedge (\bar{w} \vee x \vee \bar{y} \vee z) \wedge (\bar{w} \vee x \vee \bar{y} \vee \bar{z}). \quad (24)$$

Not surprisingly, however, we often want to work with disjunctions and con-junctions that *don't* necessarily involve full minterms or minclauses. Therefore, following nomenclature introduced by Paul Bernays in his *Habilitationsschrift* (1918), we speak in general of a *disjunctive normal form* or "DNF" as *any* disjunction of conjunctions,

$$\bigvee_{j=1}^{m} \bigwedge_{k=1}^{s_j} u_{jk} \; = \; (u_{11} \wedge \cdots \wedge u_{1s_1}) \vee \cdots \vee (u_{m1} \wedge \cdots \wedge u_{ms_m}), \quad (25)$$

where each u_{jk} is a *literal*, namely a variable x_i or its complement. Similarly, any conjunction of disjunctions of literals,

$$\bigwedge_{j=1}^{m} \bigvee_{k=1}^{s_j} u_{jk} \; = \; (u_{11} \vee \cdots \vee u_{1s_1}) \wedge \cdots \wedge (u_{m1} \vee \cdots \vee u_{ms_m}), \quad (26)$$

is called a *conjunctive normal form*, or "CNF" for short.

A great many electrical circuits embedded inside today's computer chips are composed of "programmable logic arrays" (PLAs), which are ORs of ANDs of possibly complemented input signals. In other words, a PLA basically computes one or more disjunctive normal forms. Such building blocks are fast, versatile, and relatively inexpensive; and indeed, DNFs have played a prominent role in electrical engineering ever since the 1950s, when switching circuits were imple-mented with comparatively old-fashioned devices like relays or vacuum tubes. Therefore people have long been interested in finding the simplest DNFs for classes of Boolean functions, and we can expect that an understanding of disjunc-tive normal forms will continue to be important as technology continues to evolve.

The terms of a DNF are often called *implicants*, because the truth of any term in a disjunction implies the truth of the whole formula. In a formula like

$$f(x, y, z) \; = \; (x \wedge \bar{y} \wedge z) \vee (y \wedge z) \vee (\bar{x} \wedge y \wedge \bar{z}),$$

for example, we know that f is true when $x \wedge \bar{y} \wedge z$ is true, namely when $(x, y, z) = (1, 0, 1)$. But notice that in this example the shorter term $x \wedge z$ also turns out to be an implicant of f, even though not written explicitly, because the additional term $y \wedge z$ makes the function true whenever $x = z = 1$, regardless of the value of y. Similarly, $\bar{x} \wedge y$ is an implicant of this particular function. So we might as well work with the simpler formula

$$f(x, y, z) = (x \wedge z) \vee (y \wedge z) \vee (\bar{x} \wedge y). \qquad (27)$$

At this point no more deletions are possible within the implicants, because neither x nor y nor z nor $\bar{x}$ is a strong enough condition to imply the truth of f.

An implicant that can't be factored further by removing any of its literals without making it too weak is called a *prime implicant*, following the terminology of W. V. Quine in *AMM* **59** (1952), 521–531.

These basic concepts can perhaps be understood most easily if we simplify the notation and adopt a more geometric viewpoint. We can write simply '$f(x)$' instead of $f(x_1, \ldots, x_n)$, and regard x as a vector, or as a binary string $x_1 \ldots x_n$ of length n. For example, the strings $wxyz$ where the function of (22) is true are

$$\{0000, 0001, 0100, 0111, 1100, 1101, 1110, 1111\}, \qquad (28)$$

and we can think of them as eight points in the 4-dimensional hypercube $2 \times 2 \times 2 \times 2$. The eight points in (28) correspond to the minterm implicants that are explicitly present in the full disjunctive normal form (23); but none of those implicants is actually prime. For example, the first two points of (28) make the subcube 000∗, and the last four points constitute the subcube 11∗∗, if we use asterisks to denote "wild cards" as we did when discussing database queries in Section 6.5; therefore $\bar{w} \wedge \bar{x} \wedge \bar{y}$ is an implicant of f, and so is $w \wedge x$. Similarly, we can see that the subcube 0∗00 accounts for two of the eight points in (28), making $\bar{w} \wedge \bar{y} \wedge \bar{z}$ an implicant.

In general, each prime implicant corresponds in this way to a *maximal* subcube that stays within the set of points that make f true. (The subcube is maximal in the sense that it isn't contained in any larger subcube with the same property; we can't replace any of its explicit bits by an asterisk. A maximal subcube has a maximal number of asterisks, hence a minimal number of constrained coordinates, hence a minimal number of variables in the corresponding implicant.) The maximal subcubes of the eight points in (28) are

$$000∗, 0∗00, ∗100, ∗111, 11∗∗; \qquad (29)$$

so the prime implicants of the function $f(w, x, y, z)$ in (23) are the terms of

$$(\bar{w} \wedge \bar{x} \wedge \bar{y}) \vee (\bar{w} \wedge \bar{y} \wedge \bar{z}) \vee (x \wedge \bar{y} \wedge \bar{z}) \vee (x \wedge y \wedge z) \vee (w \wedge x). \qquad (30)$$

The *disjunctive prime form* of a Boolean function is the disjunction of all its prime implicants. Exercise 30 contains an algorithm to find all the prime implicants of a given function, based on a list of the points where the function is true.

We can define a *prime clause* in an exactly similar way: It is a disjunctive clause that is implied by f, having no subclause with the same property. And the *conjunctive prime form* of f is the conjunction of all its prime clauses. (An example appears in exercise 19.)

In many simple cases, the disjunctive prime form is the shortest possible disjunctive normal form that a function can have. But we can often do better, because we might be able to cover all the necessary points with only a few of the maximal subcubes. For example, the prime implicant $(y \wedge z)$ is unnecessary in (27). And in expression (30) we don't need both $(\bar{w} \wedge \bar{y} \wedge \bar{z})$ and $(x \wedge \bar{y} \wedge \bar{z})$; either one is sufficient, in the presence of the other terms.

Unfortunately, we will see in Section 7.9 that the task of finding a shortest disjunctive normal form is NP-hard, thus quite difficult in general. But many useful shortcuts have been developed for sufficiently small problems, and they are well explained in the book *Introduction to the Theory of Switching Circuits* by E. J. McCluskey (New York: McGraw–Hill, 1965). For later developments, see Petr Fišer and Jan Hlavička, *Computing and Informatics* **22** (2003), 19–51.

There's an important special case for which the shortest DNF is, however, easily characterized. A Boolean function is said to be *monotone* or *positive* if its value does not change from 1 to 0 when any of its variables changes from 0 to 1. In other words, f is monotone if and only if $f(x) \leq f(y)$ whenever $x \subseteq y$, where the bit string $x = x_1 \ldots x_n$ is regarded as contained in or equal to the bit string $y = y_1 \ldots y_n$ if and only if $x_j \leq y_j$ for all j. An equivalent condition (see exercise 21) is that the function f either is constant or can be expressed entirely in terms of $\wedge$ and $\vee$, without complementation.

Theorem Q. *The shortest disjunctive normal form of a monotone Boolean function is its disjunctive prime form.*

Proof. [W. V. Quine, *Boletín de la Sociedad Matemática Mexicana* **10** (1953), 64–70.] Let $f(x_1, \ldots, x_n)$ be monotone, and let $u_1 \wedge \cdots \wedge u_s$ be one of its prime implicants. We cannot have, say, $u_1 = \bar{x}_i$, because in that case the shorter term $u_2 \wedge \cdots \wedge u_s$ would also be an implicant, by monotonicity. Therefore no prime implicant has a complemented literal.

Now if we set $u_1 \leftarrow \cdots \leftarrow u_s \leftarrow 1$ and all other variables to 0, the value of f will be 1, but all of f's other prime implicants will vanish. Thus $u_1 \wedge \cdots \wedge u_s$ must be in every shortest DNF, because every implicant of a shortest DNF is clearly prime. ∎

Corollary Q. *A disjunctive normal form is the disjunctive prime form of a monotone Boolean function if and only if it has no complemented literals and none of its implicants is contained in another.* ∎

Satisfiability. A Boolean function is said to be *satisfiable* if it is not identically zero — that is, if it has at least one implicant. The most famous unsolved problem in all of computer science is to find an efficient way to decide whether a given Boolean function is satisfiable or unsatisfiable. More precisely, we ask: Is there an algorithm that inputs a Boolean formula of length N and tests it for satisfiability, always giving the correct answer after performing at most $N^{O(1)}$ steps?

When you hear about this problem for the first time, you might be tempted to ask a question of your own in return: "What? Are you serious that computer scientists still haven't figured out how to do such a simple thing?"

Well, if you think satisfiability testing is trivial, please tell us your method. We agree that the problem isn't always difficult; if, for example, the given formula involves only 30 Boolean variables, a brute-force trial of 2^{30} cases — that's about a billion — will indeed settle the matter. But an enormous number of practical problems that still await solution can be formulated as Boolean functions with, say, 100 variables, because mathematical logic is a very powerful way to express concepts. And the solutions to those problems correspond to the vectors $x = x_1 \ldots x_{100}$ for which $f(x) = 1$. So a truly efficient solution to the satisfiability problem would be a wonderful achievement.

There is at least one sense in which satisfiability testing is a no-brainer: If the function $f(x_1, \ldots, x_n)$ has been chosen at random, so that all 2^n-bit truth tables are equally likely, then f is almost surely satisfiable, and we can find an x with $f(x) = 1$ after making fewer than 2 trials (on the average). It's like flipping a coin until it comes up heads; we rarely need to wait long. But the catch, of course, is that practical problems do not have random truth tables.

Okay, let's grant that satisfiability testing does seem to be tough, in general. In fact, satisfiability turns out to be difficult even when we try to simplify it by requiring that the Boolean function be presented as a "formula in 3CNF" — namely as a conjunctive normal form that has only *three* literals in each clause:

$$f(x_1, \ldots, x_n) = (t_1 \lor u_1 \lor v_1) \land (t_2 \lor u_2 \lor v_2) \land \cdots \land (t_m \lor u_m \lor v_m). \qquad (31)$$

Here each t_j, u_j, and v_j is x_k or $\bar{x}_k$ for some k. The problem of deciding satisfiability for formulas in 3CNF is called "3SAT," and exercise 39 explains why it is not really easier than satisfiability in general.

We will be seeing many examples of hard-to-crack 3SAT problems, for instance in Section 7.2.2.2, where satisfiability testing will be discussed in great detail. The situation is a little peculiar, however, because a formula needs to be fairly long before we need to think twice about its satisfiability. For example, the shortest unsatisfiable formula in 3CNF is $(x \lor x \lor x) \land (\bar{x} \lor \bar{x} \lor \bar{x})$; but that one is obviously no challenge to the intellect. We don't get into rough waters unless the three literals t_j, u_j, v_j of a clause correspond to three different variables. And in that case, each clause rules out exactly 1/8 of the possibilities, because seven different settings of (t_j, u_j, v_j) will make it true. Consequently every such 3CNF with at most seven clauses is automatically satisfiable, and a random setting of its variables will succeed with probability $\geq 1 - 7/8 = 1/8$.

The shortest interesting formula in 3CNF therefore has at least eight clauses. And in fact, an interesting 8-clause formula does exist, based on the associative block design by R. L. Rivest that we considered in 6.5–(13):

$$(x_1 \lor x_2 \lor \bar{x}_3) \land (x_2 \lor x_3 \lor \bar{x}_4) \land (x_3 \lor x_4 \lor x_1) \land (x_4 \lor \bar{x}_1 \lor x_2)$$
$$\land (\bar{x}_1 \lor \bar{x}_2 \lor x_3) \land (\bar{x}_2 \lor \bar{x}_3 \lor x_4) \land (\bar{x}_3 \lor \bar{x}_4 \lor \bar{x}_1) \land (\bar{x}_4 \lor x_1 \lor \bar{x}_2). \qquad (32)$$

Any seven of these eight clauses are satisfiable, in exactly two ways, and they force the values of three variables; for example, the last seven imply that we have $x_1 x_2 x_3 = 001$. But the complete set of eight cannot be satisfied simultaneously.

Simple special cases. Two important classes of Boolean formulas have been identified for which the satisfiability problem does turn out to be pretty easy. These special cases arise when the conjunctive normal form being tested consists entirely of "Horn clauses" or entirely of "Krom clauses." A *Horn clause* is an OR of literals in which all or nearly all of the literals are complemented — at most one of its literals is a pure, unbarred variable. A *Krom clause* is an OR of exactly two literals. Thus, for example,

$$\bar{x} \vee \bar{y}, \qquad w \vee \bar{y} \vee \bar{z}, \qquad \bar{u} \vee \bar{v} \vee \bar{w} \vee \bar{x} \vee \bar{y} \vee z, \quad \text{and} \quad x$$

are examples of Horn clauses; and

$$x \vee x, \qquad \bar{x} \vee \bar{x}, \qquad \bar{x} \vee \bar{y}, \qquad x \vee \bar{y}, \qquad \bar{x} \vee y, \quad \text{and} \quad x \vee y$$

are examples of Krom clauses, only the last of which is not also a Horn clause. (The first example qualifies because $x \vee x = x$.) Notice that a Horn clause is allowed to contain any number of literals, but when we restrict ourselves to Krom clauses we are essentially considering the 2SAT problem. In both cases we will see that satisfiability can be decided in linear time — that is, by carrying out only $O(N)$ simple steps, when given a formula of length N.

Let's consider Horn clauses first. Why are they so easy to handle? The main reason is that a clause like $\bar{u} \vee \bar{v} \vee \bar{w} \vee \bar{x} \vee \bar{y} \vee z$ can be recast in the form $\neg(u \wedge v \wedge w \wedge x \wedge y) \vee z$, which is the same as

$$u \wedge v \wedge w \wedge x \wedge y \;\Rightarrow\; z.$$

In other words, if u, v, w, x, and y are all true, then z must also be true. For this reason, parameterized Horn clauses were chosen to be the basic underlying mechanism of the programming language called Prolog. Furthermore there is an easy way to characterize exactly which Boolean functions can be represented entirely with Horn clauses:

Theorem H. *The Boolean function $f(x_1, \ldots, x_n)$ is expressible as a conjunction of Horn clauses if and only if*

$$f(x_1, \ldots, x_n) = f(y_1, \ldots, y_n) = 1 \quad \text{implies} \quad f(x_1 \wedge y_1, \ldots, x_n \wedge y_n) = 1 \quad (33)$$

for all Boolean values x_j and y_j.

Proof. [Alfred Horn, *J. Symbolic Logic* **16** (1951), 14–21, Lemma 7.] If we have $x_0 \vee \bar{x}_1 \vee \cdots \vee \bar{x}_k = 1$ and $y_0 \vee \bar{y}_1 \vee \cdots \vee \bar{y}_k = 1$, then

$$(x_0 \wedge y_0) \vee \overline{x_1 \wedge y_1} \vee \cdots \vee \overline{x_k \wedge y_k}$$
$$= (x_0 \vee \bar{x}_1 \vee \bar{y}_1 \vee \cdots \vee \bar{x}_k \vee \bar{y}_k) \wedge (y_0 \vee \bar{x}_1 \vee \bar{y}_1 \vee \cdots \vee \bar{x}_k \vee \bar{y}_k)$$
$$\geq (x_0 \vee \bar{x}_1 \vee \cdots \vee \bar{x}_k) \wedge (y_0 \vee \bar{y}_1 \vee \cdots \vee \bar{y}_k) \;=\; 1;$$

and a similar (but simpler) calculation applies when the unbarred literals x_0 and y_0 are not present. Therefore every conjunction of Horn clauses satisfies (33).

Conversely, condition (33) implies that every prime clause of f is a Horn clause (see exercise 44). ∎

Let's say that a *Horn function* is a Boolean function that satisfies condition (33), and let's also call it *definite* if it satisfies the further condition $f(1,\ldots,1) = 1$. It's easy to see that a conjunction of Horn clauses is definite if and only if each clause has *exactly* one unbarred literal, because only an entirely negative clause like $\bar{x} \vee \bar{y}$ will fail if all variables are true. Definite Horn functions are slightly simpler to work with than Horn functions in general, because they are obviously always satisfiable. Thus, by Theorem H, they have a unique least vector x such that $f(x) = 1$, namely the bitwise AND of all vectors that satisfy all clauses. The *core* of a definite Horn function is the set of all variables x_j that are true in this minimum vector x. Notice that the variables in the core must be true whenever f is true, so we can essentially factor them out.

Definite Horn functions arise in many ways, for example in the analysis of games (see exercises 51 and 52). Another nice example comes from compiler technology. Consider the following typical (but simplified) grammar for algebraic expressions in a programming language:

$$\begin{aligned}
\langle\,\text{expression}\,\rangle &\to \langle\,\text{term}\,\rangle \mid \langle\,\text{expression}\,\rangle + \langle\,\text{term}\,\rangle \mid \langle\,\text{expression}\,\rangle - \langle\,\text{term}\,\rangle \\
\langle\,\text{term}\,\rangle &\to \langle\,\text{factor}\,\rangle \mid -\langle\,\text{factor}\,\rangle \mid \langle\,\text{term}\,\rangle * \langle\,\text{factor}\,\rangle \mid \langle\,\text{term}\,\rangle / \langle\,\text{factor}\,\rangle \\
\langle\,\text{factor}\,\rangle &\to \langle\,\text{variable}\,\rangle \mid \langle\,\text{constant}\,\rangle \mid (\langle\,\text{expression}\,\rangle) \\
\langle\,\text{variable}\,\rangle &\to \langle\,\text{letter}\,\rangle \mid \langle\,\text{variable}\,\rangle\langle\,\text{letter}\,\rangle \mid \langle\,\text{variable}\,\rangle\langle\,\text{digit}\,\rangle \qquad\qquad (34) \\
\langle\,\text{letter}\,\rangle &\to \text{a} \mid \text{b} \mid \text{c} \\
\langle\,\text{constant}\,\rangle &\to \langle\,\text{digit}\,\rangle \mid \langle\,\text{constant}\,\rangle\langle\,\text{digit}\,\rangle \\
\langle\,\text{digit}\,\rangle &\to \text{0} \mid \text{1}
\end{aligned}$$

For example, the string a/(-b0-10)+cc*cc meets the syntax for $\langle\,\text{expression}\,\rangle$ and uses each of the grammatical rules at least once.

Suppose we want to know what pairs of characters can appear next to each other in such expressions. Definite Horn clauses provide the answer, because we can set the problem up as follows: Let the quantities Xx, xX, and xy denote Boolean "propositions," where X is one of the symbols $\{E, T, F, V, L, C, D\}$ standing respectively for $\langle\,\text{expression}\,\rangle$, $\langle\,\text{term}\,\rangle$, ..., $\langle\,\text{digit}\,\rangle$, and where x and y are symbols in the set $\{+, -, *, /, (,), \text{a}, \text{b}, \text{c}, 0, 1\}$. The proposition Xx means, "X can end with x"; similarly, xX means, "X can start with x"; and xy means, "The character x can be followed immediately by y in an expression." (There are $7 \times 11 + 11 \times 7 + 11 \times 11 = 275$ propositions altogether.) Then we can write

$$\begin{array}{llllll}
\text{xT} \Rightarrow \text{xE} & \Rightarrow -\text{T} & \text{xC} \Rightarrow \text{xF} & \text{Vx} \wedge \text{yL} \Rightarrow \text{xy} & & \Rightarrow \text{Lc} \\
\text{Tx} \Rightarrow \text{Ex} & \text{xF} \Rightarrow -\text{x} & \text{Cx} \Rightarrow \text{Fx} & \text{Vx} \wedge \text{yD} \Rightarrow \text{xy} & \text{xD} \Rightarrow \text{xC} & \\
\text{Ex} \Rightarrow \text{x+} & \text{Tx} \Rightarrow \text{x*} & \Rightarrow (\text{F} & \text{Dx} \Rightarrow \text{Vx} & \text{Dx} \Rightarrow \text{Cx} & \\
\text{xT} \Rightarrow +\text{x} & \text{xF} \Rightarrow *\text{x} & \text{xE} \Rightarrow (\text{x} & \Rightarrow \text{aL} & \text{Cx} \wedge \text{yD} \Rightarrow \text{xy} & \\
\text{Ex} \Rightarrow \text{x-} & \text{Tx} \Rightarrow \text{x/} & \text{Ex} \Rightarrow \text{x)} & \Rightarrow \text{La} & & \Rightarrow \text{OD} \\
\text{xT} \Rightarrow -\text{x} & \text{xF} \Rightarrow /\text{x} & \Rightarrow \text{F)} & \Rightarrow \text{bL} & & \Rightarrow \text{DO} \\
\text{xF} \Rightarrow \text{xT} & \text{xV} \Rightarrow \text{xF} & \text{xL} \Rightarrow \text{xV} & \Rightarrow \text{Lb} & & \Rightarrow \text{1D} \\
\text{Fx} \Rightarrow \text{Tx} & \text{Vx} \Rightarrow \text{Fx} & \text{Lx} \Rightarrow \text{Vx} & \Rightarrow \text{cL} & & \Rightarrow \text{D1}
\end{array} \qquad (35)$$

where x and y run through the eleven terminal symbols $\{+, \ldots, 1\}$. This schematic specification gives us a total of $24 \times 11 + 3 \times 11 \times 11 + 13 \times 1 = 640$ definite

Horn clauses, which we could write out formally as

$$\left(\overline{\texttt{+T}} \lor \texttt{+E}\right) \land \left(\overline{\texttt{-T}} \lor \texttt{-E}\right) \land \cdots \land \left(\overline{\texttt{V+}} \lor \overline{\texttt{OL}} \lor \texttt{+0}\right) \land \cdots \land \left(\texttt{D1}\right)$$

if we prefer the cryptic notation of Boolean algebra to the $\Rightarrow$ convention of (35).

Why did we do this? Because *the core of all these clauses is the set of all propositions that are true in this particular grammar.* For example, one can verify that -E is true, hence the symbols (- can occur next to each other within an expression; but the symbol pairs ++ and *- cannot (see exercise 46).

Furthermore, we can find the core of any given set of definite Horn clauses without great difficulty. We just start out with the propositions that appear alone, on the right-hand side of $\Rightarrow$ when the left-hand side is empty; thirteen clauses of that kind appear in (35). And once we assert the truth of those propositions, we might find one or more clauses whose left-hand sides are now known to be true. Hence their right-hand sides also belong to the core, and we can keep going in the same way. The whole procedure is pretty much like letting water run downhill until it has found its proper level. In fact, when we choose appropriate data structures, this downhill process goes quite fast, requiring only $O(N+n)$ steps, when N denotes the total length of the clauses and n is the number of propositional variables. (We assume here that all clauses have been expanded out, not abbreviated in terms of parameters like x and y above. More sophisticated techniques of theorem proving are available to deal with parameterized clauses, but they are beyond the scope of our present discussion.)

Algorithm C (*Core computation for definite Horn clauses*). Given a set P of propositional variables and a set C of clauses, each having the form

$$u_1 \land \cdots \land u_k \Rightarrow v \qquad \text{where } k \geq 0 \text{ and } \{u_1, \ldots, u_k, v\} \subseteq P, \qquad (36)$$

this algorithm finds the set $Q \subseteq P$ of all propositional variables that are necessarily true whenever all of the clauses are true.

We use the following data structures for clauses c and propositions p:

CONCLUSION(c) is the proposition on the right of clause c;

COUNT(c) is the number of hypotheses of c not yet asserted;

TRUTH(p) is 1 if p is known to be true, otherwise 0;

LAST(p) is the last clause in which p is waiting to be asserted;

PREV(c) is the previous clause that awaits the same hypothesis as c;

START(c) tells where the hypotheses of c appear in MEM.

(A "hypothesis" is the appearance of a proposition on the left-hand side of a clause.) An array called MEM holds all the left-hand sides of the clauses; if START$(c) = l$ and COUNT$(c) = k$, the not-yet-asserted hypotheses of clause c are MEM$[l+1]$, ..., MEM$[l+k]$. We also maintain a stack $S_0, S_1, \ldots, S_{s-1}$ of all propositions that are known to be true but not yet asserted.

C1. [Initialize.] Set LAST$(p) \leftarrow \Lambda$ and TRUTH$(p) \leftarrow 0$ for each proposition p. Also set $l \leftarrow s \leftarrow 0$, so that MEM and the stack are initially empty. Then for each clause c, having the form (36), set CONCLUSION$(c) \leftarrow v$. If $k = 0$ and

$\mathtt{TRUTH}(v) = 0$, simply set $\mathtt{TRUTH}(v) \leftarrow 1$, $S_s \leftarrow v$, and $s \leftarrow s+1$. But if $k > 0$, set $\mathtt{MEM}[l+j] \leftarrow u_j$ for $1 \le j \le k$, $\mathtt{COUNT}(c) \leftarrow k$, $\mathtt{START}(c) \leftarrow l$, $l \leftarrow l+k$, $\mathtt{PREV}(c) \leftarrow \mathtt{LAST}(u_k)$, and $\mathtt{LAST}(u_k) \leftarrow c$.

C2. [Prepare to loop.] Terminate the algorithm if $s = 0$; the desired core now consists of all propositions whose $\mathtt{TRUTH}$ has been set to 1. Otherwise set $s \leftarrow s-1$, $p \leftarrow S_s$, and $c \leftarrow \mathtt{LAST}(p)$. (We'll update the clauses that await p.)

C3. [Done with loop?] If $c = \Lambda$, return to C2. Otherwise set $c' \leftarrow \mathtt{PREV}(c)$, $q \leftarrow \mathtt{CONCLUSION}(c)$, and go to C6 if $\mathtt{TRUTH}(q) = 1$. Otherwise set $l \leftarrow \mathtt{START}(c)$ and $k \leftarrow \mathtt{COUNT}(c) - 1$.

C4. [Done with c?] If $k = 0$, go to C5. Otherwise set $p \leftarrow \mathtt{MEM}[l+k]$. If $\mathtt{TRUTH}(p) = 1$, set $k \leftarrow k - 1$ and repeat this step. Otherwise set $\mathtt{COUNT}(c) \leftarrow k$, $\mathtt{PREV}(c) \leftarrow \mathtt{LAST}(p)$, $\mathtt{LAST}(p) \leftarrow c$, and go to C6.

C5. [Deduce $\mathtt{CONCLUSION}(c)$.] Set $\mathtt{TRUTH}(q) \leftarrow 1$, $S_s \leftarrow q$, $s \leftarrow s+1$.

C6. [Loop on c.] Set $c \leftarrow c'$ and return to C3. ∎

Notice how smoothly the sequential and linked data structures work together, avoiding any need to search for a place to make progress in the calculation. We're doing a bare minimum of work! Algorithm C is similar in many respects to Algorithm 2.2.3T (topological sorting), which was the first example of multilinked data structures that we discussed long ago in Chapter 2; in fact, we can regard Algorithm 2.2.3T as the special case of Algorithm C in which every proposition appears on the right-hand side of exactly one clause. (See exercise 47.)

Exercise 48 shows that a slight modification of Algorithm C solves the satisfiability problem for Horn clauses in general. Further discussion can be found in papers by W. F. Dowling and J. H. Gallier, *J. Logic Programming* **1** (1984), 267–284; M. G. Scutellà, *J. Logic Programming* **8** (1990), 265–273.

We turn now to Krom functions and the 2SAT problem. Again there's a linear-time algorithm; but again, we can probably appreciate it best if we look first at a simplified-but-practical application. Let's suppose that seven comedians have each agreed to do one-night standup gigs at two of five hotels during a three-day festival, but each of them is available for only two of those days because of other commitments:

> Tomlin should do Aladdin and Caesars on days 1 and 2;
> Unwin should do Bellagio and Excalibur on days 1 and 2;
> Vegas should do Desert and Excalibur on days 2 and 3;
> Williams should do Aladdin and Desert on days 1 and 3;   (37)
> Xie should do Caesars and Excalibur on days 1 and 3;
> Yankovic should do Bellagio and Desert on days 2 and 3;
> Zany should do Bellagio and Caesars on days 1 and 2.

Is it possible to schedule them all without conflict?

To solve this problem, we can introduce seven Boolean variables $\{t, u, v, w, x, y, z\}$, where t (for example) means that Tomlin does Aladdin on day 1 and Caesars on day 2 while $\bar{t}$ means that the days booked for those hotels occur in the opposite order. Then we can set up constraints to ensure that no two comedians are booked in the same hotel on the same day:

$$\begin{array}{llll}
\neg(t \wedge w)\ [\text{A1}] & \neg(y \wedge \bar{z})\ [\text{B2}] & \neg(t \wedge z)\ [\text{C2}] & \neg(w \wedge y)\ [\text{D3}] \\
\neg(u \wedge z)\ [\text{B1}] & \neg(\bar{t} \wedge x)\ [\text{C1}] & \neg(v \wedge \bar{y})\ [\text{D2}] & \neg(\bar{u} \wedge \bar{x})\ [\text{E1}] \\
\neg(\bar{u} \wedge y)\ [\text{B2}] & \neg(\bar{t} \wedge \bar{z})\ [\text{C1}] & \neg(\bar{v} \wedge w)\ [\text{D3}] & \neg(u \wedge \bar{v})\ [\text{E2}] \\
\neg(\bar{u} \wedge \bar{z})\ [\text{B2}] & \neg(x \wedge \bar{z})\ [\text{C1}] & \neg(\bar{v} \wedge y)\ [\text{D3}] & \neg(v \wedge x)\ [\text{E3}]
\end{array} \quad (38)$$

Each of these constraints is, of course, a Krom clause; we must satisfy

$$(\bar{t} \vee \bar{w}) \wedge (\bar{u} \vee \bar{z}) \wedge (u \vee \bar{y}) \wedge (u \vee z) \wedge (\bar{y} \vee z) \wedge (t \vee \bar{x}) \wedge (t \vee z) \wedge (\bar{x} \vee z)$$
$$\wedge\ (\bar{t} \vee \bar{z}) \wedge (\bar{v} \vee y) \wedge (v \vee \bar{w}) \wedge (v \vee \bar{y}) \wedge (\bar{w} \vee \bar{y}) \wedge (u \vee x) \wedge (\bar{u} \vee v) \wedge (\bar{v} \vee \bar{x}). \quad (39)$$

Furthermore, Krom clauses (like Horn clauses) can be written as implications:

$$t \Rightarrow \bar{w}, \quad u \Rightarrow \bar{z}, \quad \bar{u} \Rightarrow \bar{y}, \quad \bar{u} \Rightarrow z, \quad y \Rightarrow z, \quad \bar{t} \Rightarrow \bar{x}, \quad \bar{t} \Rightarrow z, \quad x \Rightarrow z,$$
$$t \Rightarrow \bar{z}, \quad v \Rightarrow y, \quad \bar{v} \Rightarrow \bar{w}, \quad \bar{v} \Rightarrow \bar{y}, \quad w \Rightarrow \bar{y}, \quad \bar{u} \Rightarrow x, \quad u \Rightarrow v, \quad v \Rightarrow \bar{x}. \quad (40)$$

And every such implication also has an alternative, "contrapositive" form:

$$w \Rightarrow \bar{t}, \quad z \Rightarrow \bar{u}, \quad y \Rightarrow u, \quad \bar{z} \Rightarrow u, \quad \bar{z} \Rightarrow \bar{y}, \quad x \Rightarrow t, \quad \bar{z} \Rightarrow t, \quad \bar{z} \Rightarrow \bar{x},$$
$$z \Rightarrow \bar{t}, \quad \bar{y} \Rightarrow \bar{v}, \quad w \Rightarrow v, \quad y \Rightarrow v, \quad y \Rightarrow \bar{w}, \quad \bar{x} \Rightarrow u, \quad \bar{v} \Rightarrow \bar{u}, \quad x \Rightarrow \bar{v}. \quad (41)$$

But oops — alas — there is a vicious cycle,

$$u \ \underset{[\text{B1}]}{\Rightarrow}\ \bar{z} \ \underset{[\text{B2}]}{\Rightarrow}\ \bar{y} \ \underset{[\text{D2}]}{\Rightarrow}\ \bar{v} \ \underset{[\text{E2}]}{\Rightarrow}\ \bar{u} \ \underset{[\text{B2}]}{\Rightarrow}\ z \ \underset{[\text{C2}]}{\Rightarrow}\ \bar{t} \ \underset{[\text{C1}]}{\Rightarrow}\ \bar{x} \ \underset{[\text{E1}]}{\Rightarrow}\ u. \quad (42)$$

This cycle tells that u and $\bar{u}$ must both have the same value; so there is no way to accommodate all of the conditions in (37). The festival organizers will have to renegotiate their agreement with at least one of the six comedians $\{t, u, v, x, y, z\}$, if a viable schedule is to be achieved. (See exercise 53.)

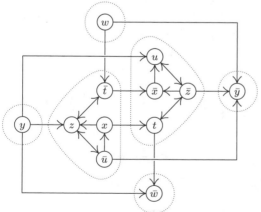

Fig. 6. The digraph corresponding to all implications of (40) and (41) that do not involve either v or $\bar{v}$. Assigning appropriate values to the literals in each strong component will solve a binary scheduling problem that is an instance of 2SAT.

The organizers might, for instance, try to leave v out of the picture temporarily. Then five of the sixteen constraints in (38) would go away and only 22 of the implications from (40) and (41) would remain, leaving the directed graph illustrated in Fig. 6. This digraph does contain cycles, like $z \Rightarrow \bar{u} \Rightarrow x \Rightarrow z$ and $t \Rightarrow \bar{z} \Rightarrow t$; but no cycle contains both a variable and its complement. Indeed, we can see from Fig. 6 that the values $tuwxyz = 110000$ do satisfy every clause of (39) that doesn't involve v or $\bar{v}$. These values give us a schedule that satisfies six of the seven original stipulations in (37), starting with (Tomlin, Unwin, Zany, Williams, Xie) at the (Aladdin, Bellagio, Caesars, Desert, Excalibur) on day 1.

In general, given any 2SAT problem with m Krom clauses that involve n Boolean variables, we can form a directed graph in the same way. There are $2n$ vertices $\{x_1, \bar{x}_1, \ldots, x_n, \bar{x}_n\}$, one for each possible literal; and there are $2m$ arcs of the form $\bar{u} \to v$ and $\bar{v} \to u$, two for each clause $u \lor v$. Two literals u and v belong to the same *strong component* of this digraph if and only if there are oriented paths from u to v and from v to u. For example, the six strong components of the digraph in Fig. 6 are indicated by dotted contours. All literals in a strong component must have the same Boolean value, in any solution to the corresponding 2SAT problem.

Theorem K. *A conjunctive normal form with two literals per clause is satisfiable if and only if no strong component of the associated digraph contains both a variable and its complement.*

Proof. [Melven Krom, *Zeitschrift für mathematische Logik und Grundlagen der Mathematik* **13** (1967), 15–20, Corollary 2.2.] If there are paths from x to $\bar{x}$ and from $\bar{x}$ to x, the formula is certainly unsatisfiable.

Conversely, assume that no such paths exist. Any digraph has at least one strong component S that is a "source," having no incoming arcs from vertices in any other strong component. Moreover, our digraph always has an attractive antisymmetry, illustrated in Fig. 6: We have $u \to v$ if and only if $\bar{v} \to \bar{u}$. Therefore the complements of the literals in S form another strong component $\overline{S} \neq S$ that is a "sink," having no *outgoing* arcs to other strong components. Hence we can assign the value 0 to all literals in S and 1 to all literals in $\overline{S}$, then remove them from the digraph and proceed in the same way until all literals have received a value. The resulting values satisfy $u \leq v$ whenever $u \to v$ in the digraph; hence they satisfy $\bar{u} \lor v$ whenever $\bar{u} \lor v$ is a clause of the formula. ∎

Theorem K leads immediately to an efficient solution of the 2SAT problem, thanks to an algorithm by R. E. Tarjan that finds strong components in linear time. [See *SICOMP* **1** (1972), 146–160; D. E. Knuth, *The Stanford GraphBase* (1994), 512–519.] We shall study Tarjan's algorithm in detail in Section 7.4.1.2. Exercise 54 shows that the condition of Theorem K is readily checked whenever the algorithm detects a new strong component. Furthermore, the algorithm detects "sinks" first; thus, as a simple byproduct of Tarjan's procedure, we can assign values that establish satisfiability by choosing the value 1 for each literal in a strong component that occurs before its complement.

Medians. We've been focusing on Boolean binary operations like $x \lor y$ or $x \oplus y$. But there's also a significant *ternary* operation $\langle xyz \rangle$, called the *median* of x, y, and z:

$$\langle xyz \rangle = (x \land y) \lor (y \land z) \lor (x \land z) = (x \lor y) \land (y \lor z) \land (x \lor z). \tag{43}$$

In fact, $\langle xyz \rangle$ is probably the most important ternary operation in the entire universe, because it has amazing properties that are continually being discovered and rediscovered.

In the first place, we can see easily that this formula for $\langle xyz \rangle$ describes the *majority* value of any three Boolean quantities x, y, and z: $\langle 000 \rangle = \langle 001 \rangle = 0$ and $\langle 011 \rangle = \langle 111 \rangle = 1$. We call $\langle xyz \rangle$ the "median" instead of the "majority" because, if x, y, and z are arbitrary *real* numbers, and if the operations $\wedge$ and $\vee$ denote min and max in (43), then

$$\langle xyz \rangle \;=\; y \qquad \text{when } x \leq y \leq z. \tag{44}$$

Secondly, the basic binary operations $\wedge$ and $\vee$ are special cases of medians:

$$x \wedge y \;=\; \langle x0y \rangle; \qquad\qquad x \vee y \;=\; \langle x1y \rangle. \tag{45}$$

Thus *any* monotone Boolean function can be expressed entirely in terms of the ternary median operator and the constants 0 and 1. In fact, if we lived in a median-only world, we could let $\wedge$ stand for falsehood and $\vee$ for truth; then $x \wedge y = \langle x\wedge y \rangle$ and $x \vee y = \langle x\vee y \rangle$ would be perfectly natural expressions, and we could even use Polish notation like $\langle \wedge xy \rangle$ and $\langle \vee xy \rangle$ if we wanted to! The same idea applies to extended real numbers under the min-max interpretation of $\wedge$ and $\vee$, if we take medians with respect to the constants $\wedge = -\infty$ and $\vee = +\infty$.

A Boolean function $f(x_1, x_2, \ldots, x_n)$ is called *self-dual* when it satisfies

$$\overline{f(x_1, x_2, \ldots, x_n)} \;=\; f(\bar{x}_1, \bar{x}_2, \ldots, \bar{x}_n). \tag{46}$$

We've noted that a Boolean function is monotone if and only if it can be expressed in terms of $\wedge$ and $\vee$; by De Morgan's laws (11) and (12), a monotone formula is self-dual if and only if the symbols $\wedge$ and $\vee$ can be interchanged without changing the formula's value. Thus the median operation defined in (43) is both monotone and self-dual. In fact, it is the simplest nontrivial function of that kind, since none of the binary operations in Table 1 are both monotone and self-dual except the projections L and R.

Furthermore, *any* expression that has been formed entirely with the median operator, without using constants, is both monotone and self-dual. For example, the function $\langle w\langle xyz \rangle \langle w\langle uvw \rangle x \rangle \rangle$ is self-dual because

$$\overline{\langle w\langle xyz \rangle \langle w\langle uvw \rangle x \rangle \rangle} \;=\; \langle \bar{w}\, \overline{\langle xyz \rangle}\, \overline{\langle w\langle uvw \rangle x \rangle} \rangle$$
$$=\; \langle \bar{w}\langle \bar{x}\bar{y}\bar{z} \rangle \langle \bar{w}\, \overline{\langle uvw \rangle}\, \bar{x} \rangle \rangle \;=\; \langle \bar{w}\langle \bar{x}\bar{y}\bar{z} \rangle \langle \bar{w}\langle \bar{u}\bar{v}\bar{w} \rangle \bar{x} \rangle \rangle.$$

Emil Post, while working on his Ph. D. thesis (Columbia University, 1920), proved that the converse statement is also true:

Theorem P. *Every monotone, self-dual Boolean function $f(x_1, \ldots, x_n)$ can be expressed entirely in terms of the median operation $\langle xyz \rangle$.*

Proof. [*Annals of Mathematics Studies* **5** (1941), 74–75.] Observe first that

$$\langle x_1 y \langle x_2 y \ldots y \langle x_{s-1} y x_s \rangle \ldots \rangle \rangle$$
$$= ((x_1 \vee x_2 \vee \cdots \vee x_{s-1} \vee x_s) \wedge y) \vee (x_1 \wedge x_2 \wedge \cdots \wedge x_{s-1} \wedge x_s); \qquad (47)$$

this formula for repeated medianing is easily proved by induction on s.

Now suppose $f(x_1, \ldots, x_n)$ is monotone, self-dual, and has the disjunctive prime form

$$f(x_1, \ldots, x_n) = t_1 \vee \cdots \vee t_m, \qquad t_j = x_{j1} \wedge \cdots \wedge x_{js_j},$$

where no prime implicant t_j is contained in another (Corollary Q). Any two prime implicants must have at least one variable in common. For if we had, say, $t_1 = x \wedge y$ and $t_2 = u \wedge v \wedge w$, the value of f would be 1 when $x = y = 1$ and $u = v = w = 0$, as well as when $x = y = 0$ and $u = v = w = 1$, contradicting self-duality. Therefore if any t_j consists of a single variable x, it must be the only prime implicant — in which case f is the trivial function $f(x_1, \ldots, x_n) = x = \langle xxx \rangle$.

Define the functions $g_0, g_1, \ldots, g_m$ by composing medians as follows:

$$g_0(x_1, \ldots, x_n) = x_1;$$
$$g_j(x_1, \ldots, x_n) = h(x_{j1}, \ldots, x_{js_j}; g_{j-1}(x_1, \ldots, x_n)), \text{ for } 1 \le j \le m; \qquad (48)$$

here $h(x_1, \ldots, x_s; y)$ denotes the function on the top line of (47). By induction on j, we can prove from (47) and (48) that $g_j(x_1, \ldots, x_n) = 1$ whenever we have $t_1 \vee \cdots \vee t_j = 1$, because $(x_{j1} \vee \cdots \vee x_{js_j}) \wedge t_k = t_k$ when $k < j$.

Finally, $f(x_1, \ldots, x_n)$ must equal $g_m(x_1, \ldots, x_n)$, because both functions are monotone and self-dual, and we have shown that $f(x_1, \ldots, x_n) \le g_m(x_1, \ldots, x_n)$ for all combinations of 0s and 1s. This inequality suffices to prove equality, because a self-dual function equals 1 in exactly half of the 2^n possible cases. ∎

One consequence of Theorem P is that we can express the median of five elements via medians of three, because the median of any odd number of Boolean variables is obviously a monotone and self-dual Boolean function. Let's write $\langle x_1 \ldots x_{2k-1} \rangle$ for such a median. Then the disjunctive prime form of $\langle vwxyz \rangle$ is

$$(v \wedge w \wedge x) \vee (v \wedge w \wedge y) \vee (v \wedge w \wedge z) \vee (v \wedge x \wedge y) \vee (v \wedge x \wedge z)$$
$$\vee (v \wedge y \wedge z) \vee (w \wedge x \wedge y) \vee (w \wedge x \wedge z) \vee (w \wedge y \wedge z) \vee (x \wedge y \wedge z);$$

so the construction in the proof of Theorem P expresses $\langle vwxyz \rangle$ as a huge formula $g_{10}(v, w, x, y, z)$ involving 2,046 median-of-3 operations. Of course that expression isn't the shortest possible one; we actually have

$$\langle vwxyz \rangle = \langle v \langle xyz \rangle \langle wx \langle wyz \rangle \rangle \rangle. \qquad (49)$$

[See H. S. Miiller and R. O. Winder, *IRE Transactions* **EC-11** (1962), 89–90.]

*Median algebras and median graphs. We noted earlier that the ternary operation $\langle xyz \rangle$ is useful when x, y, and z belong to any ordered set like the real numbers, when $\wedge$ and $\vee$ are regarded as the operators min and max. In fact, the operation $\langle xyz \rangle$ also plays a useful role in far more general circumstances.

A *median algebra* is any set M on which a ternary operation $\langle xyz \rangle$ is defined that takes elements of M into elements of M and obeys the following three axioms:

$$\langle xxy \rangle = x \quad \text{(majority law)}; \tag{50}$$

$$\langle xyz \rangle = \langle xzy \rangle = \langle yxz \rangle = \langle yzx \rangle = \langle zxy \rangle = \langle zyx \rangle \quad \text{(commutative law)}; \tag{51}$$

$$\langle xw\langle ywz \rangle \rangle = \langle \langle xwy \rangle wz \rangle \quad \text{(associative law)}. \tag{52}$$

In the Boolean case, for example, the associative law (52) holds for $w = 0$ and $w = 1$ because $\wedge$ and $\vee$ are associative. Exercises 75 and 76 prove that these three axioms imply also a *distributive law* for medians, which has both a short form

$$\langle \langle xyz \rangle uv \rangle = \langle x\langle yuv \rangle \langle zuv \rangle \rangle \tag{53}$$

and a more symmetrical long form

$$\langle \langle xyz \rangle uv \rangle = \langle \langle xuv \rangle \langle yuv \rangle \langle zuv \rangle \rangle. \tag{54}$$

No simple proof of this fact is known, but we can at least verify the special case of (53) and (54) when $y = u$ and $z = v$: We have

$$\langle \langle xyz \rangle yz \rangle = \langle xyz \rangle \tag{55}$$

because both sides equal $\langle xy\langle zyz \rangle \rangle$. In fact, the associative law (52) is just the special case $y = u$ of (53). And with (55) and (52) we can also verify the case $x = u$: $\langle \langle uyz \rangle uv \rangle = \langle vu\langle yuz \rangle \rangle = \langle \langle vuy \rangle uz \rangle = \langle \langle yuv \rangle uz \rangle = \langle \langle \langle yuv \rangle uv \rangle uz \rangle = \langle \langle yuv \rangle u\langle vuz \rangle \rangle = \langle u\langle yuv \rangle \langle zuv \rangle \rangle$.

An *ideal* in a median algebra M is a set $C \subseteq M$ for which we have

$$\langle xyz \rangle \in C \quad \text{whenever } x \in C, \, y \in C, \text{ and } z \in M. \tag{56}$$

If u and v are any elements of M, the *interval* $[u \mathbin{..} v]$ is defined as follows:

$$[u \mathbin{..} v] = \{ \langle xuv \rangle \mid x \in M \}. \tag{57}$$

We say that "x is between u and v" if and only if $x \in [u \mathbin{..} v]$. According to these definitions, u and v themselves always belong to the interval $[u \mathbin{..} v]$.

Lemma M. *Every interval $[u \mathbin{..} v]$ is an ideal, and $x \in [u \mathbin{..} v] \iff x = \langle uxv \rangle$.*

Proof. Let $\langle xuv \rangle$ and $\langle yuv \rangle$ be arbitrary elements of $[u \mathbin{..} v]$. Then

$$\langle \langle xuv \rangle \langle yuv \rangle z \rangle = \langle \langle xyz \rangle uv \rangle \in [u \mathbin{..} v]$$

for all $z \in M$, by (51) and (53), so $[u \mathbin{..} v]$ is an ideal. Furthermore every element $\langle xuv \rangle \in [u \mathbin{..} v]$ satisfies $\langle xuv \rangle = \langle u\langle xuv \rangle v \rangle$ by (51) and (55).   ∎

Our intervals $[u \mathbin{..} v]$ have nice properties, because of the median laws:

$$v \in [u \mathbin{..} u] \implies u = v; \tag{58}$$

$$x \in [u \mathbin{..} v] \text{ and } y \in [u \mathbin{..} x] \implies y \in [u \mathbin{..} v]; \tag{59}$$

$$x \in [u \mathbin{..} v] \text{ and } y \in [u \mathbin{..} z] \text{ and } y \in [v \mathbin{..} z] \implies y \in [x \mathbin{..} z]. \tag{60}$$

Equivalently, $[u \mathbin{..} u] = \{u\}$; if $x \in [u \mathbin{..} v]$ then $[u \mathbin{..} x] \subseteq [u \mathbin{..} v]$; and $x \in [u \mathbin{..} v]$ also implies that $[u \mathbin{..} z] \cap [v \mathbin{..} z] \subseteq [x \mathbin{..} z]$ for all z. (See exercise 72.)

Now let's define a graph on the vertex set M, with the following edges:

$$u \relbar v \quad \Longleftrightarrow \quad u \neq v \text{ and } \langle xuv \rangle \in \{u, v\} \text{ for all } x \in M. \qquad (61)$$

In other words, u and v are adjacent if and only if the interval $[u \mathinner{..} v]$ consists of just the two points u and v.

Theorem G. *If M is any finite median algebra, the graph defined by (61) is connected. Moreover, vertex x belongs to the interval $[u \mathinner{..} v]$ if and only if x lies on a shortest path from u to v.*

Proof. If M isn't connected, choose u and v so that there is no path from u to v and the interval $[u \mathinner{..} v]$ has as few elements as possible. Let $x \in [u \mathinner{..} v]$ be distinct from u and v. Then $\langle xuv \rangle = x \neq v$, so $v \notin [u \mathinner{..} x]$; similarly $u \notin [x \mathinner{..} v]$. But $[u \mathinner{..} x]$ and $[x \mathinner{..} v]$ are contained in $[u \mathinner{..} v]$, by (59). So they are smaller intervals, and there must be a path from u to x and from x to v. Contradiction.

The other half of the theorem is proved in exercise 73. ∎

Our definition of intervals implies that $\langle xyz \rangle \in [x \mathinner{..} y] \cap [x \mathinner{..} z] \cap [y \mathinner{..} z]$, because $\langle xyz \rangle = \langle \langle xyz \rangle xy \rangle = \langle \langle xyz \rangle xz \rangle = \langle \langle xyz \rangle yz \rangle$ by (55). Conversely, if $w \in [x \mathinner{..} y] \cap [x \mathinner{..} z] \cap [y \mathinner{..} z]$, exercise 74 proves that $w = \langle xyz \rangle$. In other words, *the intersection $[x \mathinner{..} y] \cap [x \mathinner{..} z] \cap [y \mathinner{..} z]$ always contains exactly one point,* whenever x, y, and z are points of M.

Figure 7 illustrates this principle in a $4 \times 4 \times 4$ cube, where each point x has coordinates (x_1, x_2, x_3) with $0 \leq x_1, x_2, x_3 < 4$. The vertices of this cube form a median algebra because $\langle xyz \rangle = (\langle x_1 y_1 z_1 \rangle, \langle x_2 y_2 z_2 \rangle, \langle x_3 y_3 z_3 \rangle)$; furthermore, the edges of the graph in Fig. 7 are those defined in (61), running between vertices whose coordinates agree except that one coordinate changes by ± 1. Three typical intervals $[x \mathinner{..} y]$, $[x \mathinner{..} z]$, and $[y \mathinner{..} z]$ are shown; the only point common to all three intervals is the vertex $\langle xyz \rangle = (2, 2, 1)$.

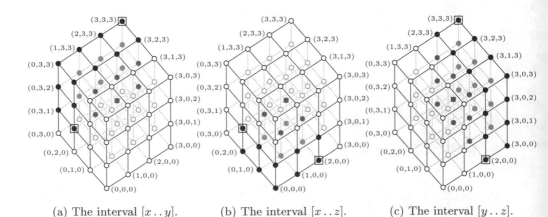

(a) The interval $[x \mathinner{..} y]$.   (b) The interval $[x \mathinner{..} z]$.   (c) The interval $[y \mathinner{..} z]$.

Fig. 7. Intervals between the vertices $x = (0, 2, 1)$,
$y = (3, 3, 3)$, and $z = (2, 0, 0)$ in a $4 \times 4 \times 4$ cube.

So far we've started with a median algebra and used it to define a graph with certain properties. But we can also start with a graph that has those properties and use it to define a median algebra. If u and v are vertices of *any* graph, let us define the interval $[u \mathinner{.\,.} v]$ to be the set of all points on shortest paths between u and v. A finite graph is said to be a *median graph* if exactly one vertex lies in the intersection $[x \mathinner{.\,.} y] \cap [x \mathinner{.\,.} z] \cap [y \mathinner{.\,.} z]$ of the three intervals that tie any three given vertices x, y, and z together; and we denote that vertex by $\langle xyz \rangle$. Exercise 75 proves that the resulting ternary operation satisfies the median axioms.

Many important graphs turn out to be median graphs according to this definition. For example, any free tree is easily seen to be a median graph; and a graph like the $n_1 \times n_2 \times \cdots \times n_m$ hyperrectangle provides another simple example. Cartesian products of arbitrary median graphs also satisfy the required condition.

*Median labels. If u and v are any elements of a median algebra, the mapping $f(x)$ that takes $x \mapsto \langle xuv \rangle$ is a *homomorphism*; that is, it satisfies

$$f(\langle xyz \rangle) \;=\; \langle f(x)f(y)f(z) \rangle, \tag{62}$$

because of the long distributive law (54). This function $\langle xuv \rangle$ "projects" any given point x into the interval $[u \mathinner{.\,.} v]$, by (57). And it is particularly interesting in the case when $u \!-\! v$ is an edge of the corresponding graph, because $f(x)$ is then two-valued, essentially a Boolean mapping.

For example, consider the typical free tree shown below, with eight vertices and seven edges. We can project each vertex x onto each of the edge intervals $[u \mathinner{.\,.} v]$ by deciding whether x is closer to u or to v:

$$
\begin{array}{cccccccccc}
 & ac & bc & cd & de & ef & eg & dh & \\
a \mapsto & a & c & c & d & e & e & d & 0000000 \\
b \mapsto & c & b & c & d & e & e & d & 1100000 \\
c \mapsto & c & c & c & d & e & e & d & 1000000 \\
d \mapsto & c & c & d & d & e & e & d & 1010000 \quad (63)\\
e \mapsto & c & c & d & e & e & e & d & 1011000 \\
f \mapsto & c & c & d & e & f & e & d & 1011100 \\
g \mapsto & c & c & d & e & e & g & d & 1011010 \\
h \mapsto & c & c & d & d & e & e & h & 1010001 \\
\end{array}
$$

On the right we've reduced the projections to 0s and 1s, arbitrarily deciding that $a \mapsto 0000000$. The resulting bit strings are called *labels* of the vertices, and we write, for example, $l(b) = 1100000$. Since each projection is a homomorphism, we can calculate the median of any three points by simply taking Boolean medians in each component of their labels. For example, to compute $\langle bgh \rangle$ we find the bitwise median of $l(b) = 1100000$, $l(g) = 1011010$, and $l(h) = 1010001$, namely $1010000 = l(d)$.

When we project onto all the edges of a median graph, we might find that two columns of the binary labels are identical. This situation cannot occur with a free tree, but let's consider what would happen if the edge $g \!-\! h$ were added to the tree in (63): The resulting graph would still be a median graph, but the columns for eg and dh would become identical (except with $e \leftrightarrow d$ and $g \leftrightarrow h$). Furthermore, the new column for gh would turn out to be equivalent to the column for de. Redundant components should be omitted from the labels in such cases; therefore the vertices of the augmented graph would have six-bit labels, like $l(g) = 101101$ and $l(h) = 101001$, instead of eight-bit labels.

The elements of any median algebra can always be represented by labels in this way. Therefore *any identity that holds in the Boolean case will be true in all median algebras.* This "zero-one principle" makes it possible to test whether any two given expressions built from the ternary operation $\langle xyz \rangle$ can be shown to be equal as a consequence of axioms (50), (51), and (52)—although we do have to check $2^{n-1} - 1$ cases when we test n-variable expressions by this method.

For example, the associative law $\langle xw \langle ywz \rangle \rangle = \langle \langle xwy \rangle wz \rangle$ suggests that there should be a symmetrical interpretation of both sides that does not involve nested brackets. And indeed, there is such a formula:

$$\langle xw \langle ywz \rangle \rangle = \langle \langle xwy \rangle wz \rangle = \langle xwywz \rangle, \tag{64}$$

where $\langle xwywz \rangle$ denotes the median of the five-element multiset $\{x, w, y, w, z\} = \{w, w, x, y, z\}$. We can prove this formula by using the zero-one principle, noting also that median is the same thing as majority in the Boolean case. In a similar way we can prove (49), and we can show that the function used by Post in (47) can be simplified to

$$\langle x_1 y \langle x_2 y \ldots y \langle x_{s-1} y x_s \rangle \ldots \rangle \rangle = \langle x_1 y x_2 y \ldots y x_{s-1} y x_s \rangle; \tag{65}$$

it's a median of $2s - 1$ quantities, where nearly half of them are equal to y.

A set C of vertices in a graph is called *convex* if $[u \mathinner{\ldotp\ldotp} v] \subseteq C$ whenever $u \in C$ and $v \in C$. In other words, whenever the endpoints of a shortest path belong to C, all vertices of that path must also be present in C. (A convex set is therefore identical to what we called an "ideal," a few pages ago; now our language has become geometric instead of algebraic.) The *convex hull* of $\{v_1, \ldots, v_m\}$ is defined to be the smallest convex set that contains each of the vertices $v_1, \ldots, v_m$. Our theoretical results above have shown that every interval $[u \mathinner{\ldotp\ldotp} v]$ is convex; hence $[u \mathinner{\ldotp\ldotp} v]$ is the convex hull of the two-point set $\{u, v\}$. But in fact much more is true:

Theorem C. *The convex hull of* $\{v_1, v_2, \ldots, v_m\}$ *in a median graph is the set of all points*

$$C = \{ \langle v_1 x v_2 x \ldots x v_m \rangle \mid x \in M \}. \tag{66}$$

Furthermore, x is in C if and only if $x = \langle v_1 x v_2 x \ldots x v_m \rangle$.

Proof. Clearly $v_j \in C$ for $1 \leq j \leq m$. Every point of C must belong to the convex hull, because the point $x' = \langle v_2 x \ldots x v_m \rangle$ is in the hull (by induction on m), and because $\langle v_1 x \ldots x v_m \rangle \in [v_1 \mathinner{\ldotp\ldotp} x']$. The zero-one principle proves that

$$\langle x \langle v_1 y v_2 y \ldots y v_m \rangle \langle v_1 z v_2 z \ldots z v_m \rangle \rangle = \langle v_1 \langle xyz \rangle v_2 \langle xyz \rangle \ldots \langle xyz \rangle v_m \rangle; \tag{67}$$

hence C is convex. Setting $y = x$ in this formula proves that $\langle v_1 x v_2 x \ldots x v_m \rangle$ is the closest point of C to x, and that $\langle v_1 x v_2 x \ldots x v_m \rangle \in [x \mathinner{\ldotp\ldotp} z]$ for all $z \in C$. ∎

Corollary C. *Let the label of v_j be $v_{j1} \ldots v_{jt}$ for $1 \leq j \leq m$. Then the convex hull of $\{v_1, \ldots, v_m\}$ is the set of all $x \in M$ whose label $x_1 \ldots x_t$ satisfies $x_j = c_j$ whenever $v_{1j} = v_{2j} = \cdots = v_{mj} = c_j$.* ∎

For example, the convex hull of $\{c, g, h\}$ in (63) consists of all elements whose label matches the pattern $10**0**$, namely $\{c, d, e, g, h\}$.

When a median graph contains a 4-cycle $u \,—\, x \,—\, v \,—\, y \,—\, u$, the edges $u \,—\, x$ and $v \,—\, y$ are equivalent, in the sense that projection onto $[u \mathrel{..} x]$ and projection onto $[v \mathrel{..} y]$ both yield the same label coordinates. The reason is that, for any z with $\langle zux \rangle = u$, we have

$$
\begin{aligned}
y = \langle uvy \rangle &= \langle \langle zux \rangle vy \rangle \\
&= \langle \langle zvy \rangle \langle uvy \rangle \langle xvy \rangle \rangle \\
&= \langle \langle zvy \rangle yv \rangle,
\end{aligned}
$$

hence $\langle zvy \rangle = y$; similarly $\langle zux \rangle = x$ implies $\langle zvy \rangle = v$. The edges $x \,—\, v$ and $y \,—\, u$ are equivalent for the same reasons. Exercise 77 shows, among other things, that two edges yield equivalent projections if and only if they can be proved equivalent by a chain of equivalences obtained from 4-cycles in this way. Therefore the number of bits in each vertex label is the number of equivalence classes of edges induced by the 4-cycles; and it follows that the reduced labels for vertices are uniquely determined, once we specify a vertex whose label is $00 \ldots 0$.

A nice way to find the vertex labels of any median graph was discovered by P. K. Jha and G. Slutzki [*Ars Combin.* **34** (1992), 75–92] and improved by J. Hagauer, W. Imrich, and S. Klavžar [*Theor. Comp. Sci.* **215** (1999), 123–136]:

Algorithm H (*Median labels*). Given a median graph G and a source vertex a, this algorithm determines the equivalence classes defined by the 4-cycles of G, and computes the labels $l(v) = v_1 \ldots v_t$ of each vertex, where t is the number of classes and $l(a) = 0 \ldots 0$.

H1. [Initialize.] Preprocess G by visiting all vertices in order of their distance from a. For each edge $u \,—\, v$, we say that u is an *early neighbor* of v if a is closer to u than to v, otherwise u is a *late neighbor*; in other words, the early neighbors of v will already have been visited when v is encountered, but the late neighbors will still be awaiting their turn. Rearrange all adjacency lists so that early neighbors are listed first. Place each edge initially in its own equivalence class; a "union-find algorithm" like Algorithm 2.3.3E will be used to merge classes when the algorithm learns that they're equivalent.

H2. [Call the subroutine.] Set $j \leftarrow 0$ and invoke Subroutine I with parameter a. (Subroutine I appears below. The global variable j will be used to create a master list of edges $r_j \,—\, s_j$ for $1 \leq j < n$, where n is the total number of vertices; there will be one entry with $s_j = v$, for each vertex $v \neq a$.)

H3. [Assign the labels.] Number the equivalence classes from 1 to t. Then set $l(a)$ to the t-bit string $0 \ldots 0$. For $j = 1, 2, \ldots, n - 1$ (in this order), set $l(s_j)$ to $l(r_j)$ with bit k changed from 0 to 1, where k is the equivalence class of edge $r_j \,—\, s_j$. ∎

Subroutine I (*Process descendants of r*). This recursive subroutine, with parameter r and global variable j, does the main work of Algorithm H on the graph of all vertices currently reachable from vertex r. In the course of processing, all such vertices will be recorded on the master list, except r itself, and all edges between them will be removed from the current graph. Each vertex has four fields called its `LINK`, `MARK`, `RANK`, and `MATE`, initially null.

I1. [Loop over s.] Choose a vertex s with $r - s$. If there is no such vertex, return from the subroutine.

I2. [Record the edge.] Set $j \leftarrow j + 1$, $r_j \leftarrow r$, and $s_j \leftarrow s$.

I3. [Begin breadth-first search.] (Now we want to find and delete all edges of the current graph that are equivalent to $r - s$.) Set `MARK`$(s) \leftarrow s$, `RANK`$(s) \leftarrow 1$, `LINK`$(s) \leftarrow \Lambda$, and $v \leftarrow q \leftarrow s$.

I4. [Find the mate of v.] Find the early neighbor u of v for which `MARK`$(u) \neq s$ or `RANK`$(u) \neq 1$. (There will be exactly one such vertex u. Recall that early neighbors have been placed first, in step H1.) Set `MATE`$(v) \leftarrow u$.

I5. [Delete $u - v$.] Make the edges $u - v$ and $r - s$ equivalent by merging their equivalence classes. Remove u and v from each other's adjacency lists.

I6. [Classify the neighbors of v.] For each early neighbor u of v, do step I7; for each late neighbor u of v, do step I8. Then go to step I9.

I7. [Note a possible equivalence.] If `MARK`$(u) = s$ and `RANK`$(u) = 1$, make the edge $u - v$ equivalent to the edge `MATE`$(u) -$ `MATE`(v). Return to I6.

I8. [Rank u.] If `MARK`$(u) = s$ and `RANK`$(u) = 1$, return to I6. Otherwise set `MARK`$(u) \leftarrow s$ and `RANK`$(u) \leftarrow 2$. Set w to the first neighbor of u (it will be early). If $w = v$, reset w to u's second early neighbor; but return to I6 if u has only one early neighbor. If `MARK`$(w) \neq s$ or `RANK`$(w) \neq 2$, set `RANK`$(u) \leftarrow 1$, `LINK`$(u) \leftarrow \Lambda$, `LINK`$(q) \leftarrow u$, and $q \leftarrow u$. Return to I6.

I9. [Continue breadth-first search.] Set $v \leftarrow$ `LINK`(v). Return to I4 if $v \neq \Lambda$.

I10. [Process subgraph s.] Call Subroutine I recursively with parameter s. Then return to I1. ∎

This algorithm and subroutine have been described in terms of relatively high-level data structures; further details are left to the reader. For example, adjacency lists should be doubly linked, so that edges can readily be deleted in step I5. Any convenient method for merging equivalence classes can be used in that step.

Exercise 77 explains the theory that makes this algorithm work, and exercise 78 proves that each vertex is encountered at most $\lg n$ times in step I4. Furthermore, exercise 79 shows that a median graph has at most $O(n \log n)$ edges. Therefore the total running time of Algorithm H is $O(n(\log n)^2)$, except perhaps for the bit-setting in step H3.

The reader may wish to play through Algorithm H by hand on the median graph in Table 2, whose vertices represent the twelve monotone self-dual Boolean functions of four variables $\{w, x, y, z\}$. All such functions that actually involve all four variables can be expressed as a median of five things, like (64). With

Table 2

LABELS FOR THE FREE MEDIAN ALGEBRA ON FOUR GENERATORS

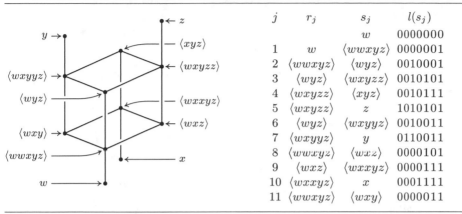

j	r_j	s_j	$l(s_j)$
		w	0000000
1	w	$\langle wwxyz \rangle$	0000001
2	$\langle wwxyz \rangle$	$\langle wyz \rangle$	0010001
3	$\langle wyz \rangle$	$\langle wxyzz \rangle$	0010101
4	$\langle wxyzz \rangle$	$\langle xyz \rangle$	0010111
5	$\langle wxyzz \rangle$	z	1010101
6	$\langle wyz \rangle$	$\langle wxyyz \rangle$	0010011
7	$\langle wxyyz \rangle$	y	0110011
8	$\langle wwxyz \rangle$	$\langle wxz \rangle$	0000101
9	$\langle wxz \rangle$	$\langle wxxyz \rangle$	0000111
10	$\langle wxxyz \rangle$	x	0001111
11	$\langle wwxyz \rangle$	$\langle wxy \rangle$	0000011

starting vertex $a = w$, the algorithm computes the master list of edges $r_j \!-\! s_j$ and the binary labels shown in the table. (The actual order of processing depends on the order in which vertices appear in adjacency lists. But the final labels will be the same under any ordering, except for permutations of the columns.)

Notice that the number of 1-bits in each label $l(v)$ is the distance of v from the starting vertex a. In fact, the uniqueness of labels tells us that *the distance between any two vertices is the number of bit positions in which their labels differ*, because we could have started at any particular vertex.

The special median graph in Table 2 could actually have been handled in a completely different way, without using Algorithm H at all, because the labels in this case are essentially the same as the *truth tables* of the corresponding functions. Here's why: We can say that the simple functions w, x, y, z have the respective truth tables $t(w) = 0000000011111111$, $t(x) = 0000111100001111$, $t(y) = 0011001100110011$, $t(z) = 0101010101010101$. Then the truth table of $\langle wwxyz \rangle$ is the bitwise majority function $\langle t(w)t(w)t(x)t(y)t(z) \rangle$, namely the string 0000000101111111; and a similar computation gives the truth tables of all the other vertices.

The last half of any self-dual function's truth table is the same as the first half, but complemented and reversed, so we can eliminate it. Furthermore the leftmost bit in each of our truth tables is always zero. We are left with the seven-bit labels shown in Table 2; and the uniqueness property guarantees that Algorithm H will produce the same result, except for possible permutation of columns, when it is presented with this particular graph.

This reasoning tells us that the edges of the graph in Table 2 correspond to pairs of functions whose truth tables are almost the same. We move between neighboring vertices by switching only two complementary bits of their truth tables. In fact, the degree of each vertex turns out to be exactly the number of prime implicants in the disjunctive prime form of the monotone self-dual function represented by that vertex (see exercises 70 and 84).

Median sets. A *median set* is a collection X of binary vectors with the property that $\langle xyz \rangle \in X$ whenever $x \in X$, $y \in X$, and $z \in X$, where the medians are computed componentwise as we've done with median labels. Thomas Schaefer noticed in 1978 that median sets provide us with an attractive counterpoint to the characterization of Horn functions in Theorem H:

Theorem S. *The Boolean function $f(x_1, \ldots, x_n)$ is expressible as a conjunction of Krom clauses if and only if*

$$f(x_1, \ldots, x_n) = f(y_1, \ldots, y_n) = f(z_1, \ldots, z_n) = 1$$
$$\text{implies} \quad f(\langle x_1 y_1 z_1 \rangle, \ldots, \langle x_n y_n z_n \rangle) = 1 \qquad (68)$$

for all Boolean values x_j, y_j, and z_j.

Proof. [*STOC* **10** (1978), 216–226, Lemma 3.1B.] If we have $x_1 \vee x_2 = y_1 \vee y_2 = z_1 \vee z_2 = 1$, say, with $x_1 \leq y_1 \leq z_1$, then $\langle x_1 y_1 z_1 \rangle \vee \langle x_2 y_2 z_2 \rangle = y_1 \vee \langle x_2 y_2 z_2 \rangle = 1$, since $y_1 = 0$ implies that $x_2 = y_2 = 1$. Thus (68) is necessary.

Conversely, if (68) holds, let $u_1 \vee \cdots \vee u_k$ be a prime clause of f, where each u_j is a literal. Then, for $1 \leq j \leq k$, the clause $u_1 \vee \cdots \vee u_{j-1} \vee u_{j+1} \vee \cdots \vee u_k$ is not a clause of f; so there's a vector $x^{(j)}$ with $f(x^{(j)}) = 1$ but with $u_i^{(j)} = 0$ for all $i \neq j$. If $k \geq 3$, the median $\langle x^{(1)} x^{(2)} x^{(3)} \rangle$ has $u_i = 0$ for $1 \leq i \leq k$; but that's impossible, because $u_1 \vee \cdots \vee u_k$ was supposedly a clause. Hence $k \leq 2$. ∎

Thus median sets are the same as "2SAT instances," the sets of points that satisfy some formula f in 2CNF.

A median set is said to be *reduced* if its vectors $x = x_1 \ldots x_t$ contain no redundant components. In other words, for each coordinate position k, a reduced median set has at least two vectors $x^{(k)}$ and $y^{(k)}$ with the property that $x_k^{(k)} = 0$ and $y_k^{(k)} = 1$ but $x_i^{(k)} = y_i^{(k)}$ for all $i \neq k$. We've seen that the labels of a median graph satisfy this condition; in fact, if coordinate k corresponds to the edge $u \!-\! v$ in the graph, we can let $x^{(k)}$ and $y^{(k)}$ be the labels of u and v. Conversely, any reduced median set X defines a median graph, with one vertex for each element of X and with adjacency defined by all-but-one equality of coordinates. The median labels of these vertices must be identical to the original vectors in X, because we know that median labels are essentially unique.

Median labels and reduced median sets can also be characterized in yet another instructive way, which harks back to the networks of *comparator modules* that we studied in Section 5.3.4. We noted in that section that such networks are useful for "oblivious sorting" of numbers, and we noted in Theorem 5.3.4Z that a network of comparators will sort all $n!$ possible input permutations if and only if it correctly sorts all 2^n combinations of 0s and 1s. When a comparator module is attached to two horizontal lines, with inputs x and y entering from the left, it outputs the same two values on the right, but with $\min(x, y) = x \wedge y$ on the upper line and $\max(x, y) = x \vee y$ on the lower line. Let's now extend the concept slightly by also allowing *inverter modules*, which change 0 to 1 and vice versa. Here, for example, is a comparator-inverter network (or CI-net, for short), which transforms the binary value 0010 into 0111:

$$(69)$$

(A single dot denotes an inverter.) Indeed, this network transforms

$$
\begin{array}{llll}
0000 \mapsto 0110; & 0100 \mapsto 0111; & 1000 \mapsto 0111; & 1100 \mapsto 0110; \\
0001 \mapsto 0111; & 0101 \mapsto 1111; & 1001 \mapsto 0101; & 1101 \mapsto 0111; \\
0010 \mapsto 0111; & 0110 \mapsto 1111; & 1010 \mapsto 0101; & 1110 \mapsto 0111; \\
0011 \mapsto 0110; & 0111 \mapsto 0111; & 1011 \mapsto 0111; & 1111 \mapsto 0110.
\end{array}
\tag{70}
$$

Suppose a CI-net transforms the bit string $x = x_1 \ldots x_t$ into the bit string $x'_1 \ldots x'_t = f(x)$. This function f, which maps the t-cube into itself, is in fact a *graph homomorphism*. In other words, we have $f(x) \text{---} f(y)$ whenever $x \text{---} y$ in the t-cube: Changing one bit of x always causes exactly one bit of $f(x)$ to change, because every module in the network has this behavior. Moreover, CI-nets have a remarkable connection with median labels:

Theorem F. *Every set X of t-bit median labels can be represented by a comparator-inverter network that computes a Boolean function $f(x)$ with the property that $f(x) \in X$ for all bit vectors $x = x_1 \ldots x_t$, and $f(x) = x$ for all $x \in X$.*

Proof. [Tomás Feder, *Memoirs Amer. Math. Soc.* **555** (1995), 1–223, Lemma 3.37; see also the Ph. D. thesis of D. H. Wiedemann (University of Waterloo, 1986).] Consider columns i and j of the median labels, where $1 \le i < j \le t$. Any such pair of columns contains at least three of the four possibilities $\{00, 01, 10, 11\}$, if we look through the entire set of labels, because median labels have no redundant columns. Let us write $\bar{\jmath} \to i$, $j \to i$, $i \to j$, or $i \to \bar{\jmath}$ if the value 00, 01, 10, or 11 (respectively) is missing from those two columns; we can also note the equivalent relations $\bar{\imath} \to j$, $\bar{\imath} \to \bar{\jmath}$, $\bar{\jmath} \to \bar{\imath}$, or $j \to \bar{\imath}$, respectively, which involve $\bar{\imath}$ instead of i. For example, the labels in Table 2 give us the relations

$$
\begin{array}{ll}
1 \to \bar{2}, 3, \bar{4}, 5, \bar{6}, 7 & 2, \bar{3}, 4, \bar{5}, 6, \bar{7} \to \bar{1}; \\
2 \to 3, \bar{4}, \bar{5}, 6, 7 & \bar{3}, 4, 5, \bar{6}, \bar{7} \to \bar{2}; \\
3 \to \bar{4}, 7 & 4, \bar{7} \to \bar{3}; \\
4 \to 5, 6, 7 & \bar{5}, \bar{6}, \bar{7} \to \bar{4}; \\
5 \to 7 & \bar{7} \to \bar{5}; \\
6 \to 7 & \bar{7} \to \bar{6}.
\end{array}
\tag{71}
$$

(There is no relation between 3 and 5 because all four possibilities occur in those columns. But we have $3 \to \bar{4}$ because 11 doesn't appear in columns 3 and 4. The vertices whose label has a 1 in column 3 are those closer to $\langle wyz \rangle$ than to $\langle wwxyz \rangle$ in Table 2; they form a convex set in which column 4 of the labels is always 0, because they are also closer to $\langle wxxyz \rangle$ than to x.)

These relations between the literals $\{1, \bar{1}, 2, \bar{2}, \ldots, t, \bar{t}\}$ contain no cycles, so they can always be topologically sorted into an anti-symmetrical sequence

$u_1 u_2 \ldots u_{2t}$ in which u_j is the complement of u_{2t+1-j}. For example,

$$1 \; \overline{7} \; 4 \; 2 \; \overline{3} \; \overline{5} \; \overline{6} \; 6 \; 5 \; 3 \; \overline{2} \; \overline{4} \; 7 \; \overline{1} \tag{72}$$

is one such way to sort the relations in (71) topologically.

Now we proceed to construct the network, by starting with t empty lines and successively examining elements u_k and u_{k+d} in the topological sequence, for $d = 2t - 2, 2t - 3, \ldots, 1$ (in this order), and for $k = 1, 2, \ldots, t - \lceil d/2 \rceil$. If $u_k \to u_{k+d}$ is a relation between columns i and j, where $i < j$, we append new modules to lines i and j of the network as follows:

$$\text{If } i \to j \qquad \text{If } i \to \bar{j} \qquad \text{If } \bar{i} \to j \qquad \text{If } \bar{i} \to \bar{j} \tag{73}$$

For example, from (71) and (72) we first enforce $1 \to 7$, then $1 \to \overline{4}$, then $1 \to \overline{2}$, then $\overline{7} \to \overline{4}$ (that is, $4 \to 7$), etc., obtaining the following network:

$$\tag{74}$$

(Go figure. No modules are contributed when, say, u_k is $\overline{7}$ and u_{k+d} is 3, because the relation $\overline{3} \to 7$ does not appear in (71).)

Exercise 89 proves that each new cluster of modules (73) preserves all of the previous relations and enforces a new one. Therefore, if x is any input vector, $f(x)$ satisfies all of the relations; so $f(x) \in X$ by Theorem S. Conversely, if $x \in X$, every cluster of modules in the network leaves x unchanged. ∎

Corollary F. *Suppose the median labels in Theorem F are closed under the operations of bitwise AND and OR, so that $x \,\&\, y \in X$ and $x \mid y \in X$ whenever $x \in X$ and $y \in X$. Then there is a permutation of coordinates under which the labels are representable by a network of comparator modules only.*

Proof. The bitwise AND of all labels is $0 \ldots 0$, and the bitwise OR is $1 \ldots 1$. So the only possible relations between columns are $i \to j$ and $j \to i$. By topologically sorting and renaming the columns, we can ensure that only $i \to j$ occurs when $i < j$; and in this case the construction in the proof never uses an inverter. ∎

In general, if G is any graph, a homomorphism f that maps the vertices of G onto a subset X of those vertices is called a *retraction* if it satisfies $f(x) = x$ for all $x \in X$; and we call X a *retract* of G when such an f exists. The importance of this concept in the theory of graphs was first pointed out by Pavol Hell [see *Lecture Notes in Math.* **406** (1974), 291–301]. One consequence, for example, is that the distance between vertices in X — the number of edges on a shortest path — remains the same even if we restrict consideration to paths that lie entirely in X. (See exercise 93.)

Theorem F demonstrates that every t-dimensional set of median labels is a retract of the t-dimensional hypercube. Conversely, exercise 94 shows that hypercube retracts are always median graphs.

Threshold functions. A particularly appealing and important class of Boolean functions $f(x_1, x_2, \ldots, x_n)$ arises when f can be defined by the formula

$$f(x_1, x_2, \ldots, x_n) = [w_1 x_1 + w_2 x_2 + \cdots + w_n x_n \geq t], \tag{75}$$

where the constants w_1, w_2, $\ldots$, w_n are integer "weights" and t is an integer "threshold" value. For example, threshold functions are important even when all the weights are unity: We have

$$x_1 \wedge x_2 \wedge \cdots \wedge x_n = [x_1 + x_2 + \cdots + x_n \geq n]; \tag{76}$$

$$x_1 \vee x_2 \vee \cdots \vee x_n = [x_1 + x_2 + \cdots + x_n \geq 1]; \tag{77}$$

$$\text{and} \quad \langle x_1 x_2 \ldots x_{2t-1} \rangle = [x_1 + x_2 + \cdots + x_{2t-1} \geq t], \tag{78}$$

where $\langle x_1 x_2 \ldots x_{2t-1} \rangle$ stands for the median (or majority) value of a multiset that consists of any odd number of Boolean values $\{x_1, x_2, \ldots, x_{2t-1}\}$. In particular, the basic mappings $x \wedge y$, $x \vee y$, and $\langle xyz \rangle$ are all threshold functions, and so is

$$\bar{x} = [-x \geq 0]. \tag{79}$$

With more general weights we get many other functions of interest, such as

$$[2^{n-1} x_1 + 2^{n-2} x_2 + \cdots + x_n \geq (t_1 t_2 \ldots t_n)_2], \tag{80}$$

which is true if and only if the binary string $x_1 x_2 \ldots x_n$ is lexicographically greater than or equal to a given binary string $t_1 t_2 \ldots t_n$. Given a set of n objects having sizes w_1, w_2, $\ldots$, w_n, a subset of those objects will fit into a knapsack of size $t - 1$ if and only if $f(x_1, x_2, \ldots, x_n) = 0$, where $x_j = 1$ represents the presence of object j in the subset. Simple models of neurons, originally proposed by W. McCulloch and W. Pitts in *Bull. Math. Biophysics* **5** (1943), 115–133, have led to thousands of research papers about "neural networks" built from threshold functions.

We can get rid of any negative weight w_j by setting $x_j \leftarrow \bar{x}_j$, $w_j \leftarrow -w_j$, and $t \leftarrow t + |w_j|$. Thus a general threshold function can be reduced to a positive threshold function in which all weights are nonnegative. Furthermore, any positive threshold function (75) can be expressed as a special case of the median/majority-of-odd function, because we have

$$\langle 0^a 1^b x_1^{w_1} x_2^{w_2} \ldots x_n^{w_n} \rangle = [b + w_1 x_1 + w_2 x_2 + \cdots + w_n x_n \geq b + t], \tag{81}$$

where x^m stands for m copies of x, and where a and b are defined by the rules

$$a = \max(0, 2t - 1 - w), \quad b = \max(0, w + 1 - 2t), \quad w = w_1 + w_2 + \cdots + w_n. \tag{82}$$

For example, when all weights are 1, we have

$$\langle 0^{n-1} x_1 \ldots x_n \rangle = x_1 \wedge \cdots \wedge x_n \quad \text{and} \quad \langle 1^{n-1} x_1 \ldots x_n \rangle = x_1 \vee \cdots \vee x_n; \tag{83}$$

we've already seen these formulas in (45) when $n = 2$. In general, either a or b is zero, and the left-hand side of (81) specifies a median of $2T - 1$ elements, where

$$T = b + t = \max(t, w_1 + w_2 + \cdots + w_n + 1 - t). \tag{84}$$

There would be no point in letting both a and b be greater than zero, because the majority function clearly satisfies the cancellation law

$$\langle 01x_1x_2\ldots x_{2t-1}\rangle \;=\; \langle x_1x_2\ldots x_{2t-1}\rangle. \tag{85}$$

One important consequence of (81) is that every positive threshold function comes from the pure majority function

$$g(x_0, x_1, x_2, \ldots, x_n) \;=\; \langle x_0^{a+b} x_1^{w_1} x_2^{w_2} \ldots x_n^{w_n}\rangle \tag{86}$$

by setting $x_0 = 0$ or 1. In other words, we know all threshold functions of n variables if and only if we know all of the distinct median-of-odd functions of $n+1$ or fewer variables (containing no constants). Every pure majority function is monotone and self-dual; thus we've seen the pure majority functions of four variables $\{w, x, y, z\}$ in column s_j of Table 2 on page 71, namely $\langle w\rangle$, $\langle wwxyz\rangle$, $\langle wyz\rangle$, $\langle wxyzz\rangle$, $\langle xyz\rangle$, $\langle z\rangle$, $\langle wxyyz\rangle$, $\langle y\rangle$, $\langle wxz\rangle$, $\langle wxxyz\rangle$, $\langle x\rangle$, $\langle wxy\rangle$. By setting $w = 0$ or 1, we obtain all the positive threshold functions $f(x, y, z)$ of three variables:

$$\langle 0\rangle, \langle 1\rangle, \langle 00xyz\rangle, \langle 11xyz\rangle, \langle 0yz\rangle, \langle 1yz\rangle, \langle 0xyzz\rangle, \langle 1xyzz\rangle, \langle xyz\rangle, \langle z\rangle,$$

$$\langle 0xyyz\rangle, \langle 1xyyz\rangle, \langle y\rangle, \langle 0xz\rangle, \langle 1xz\rangle, \langle 0xxyz\rangle, \langle 1xxyz\rangle, \langle x\rangle, \langle 0xy\rangle, \langle 1xy\rangle. \tag{87}$$

All 150 positive threshold functions of four variables can be obtained in a similar fashion from the self-dual majority functions in the answer to exercise 84.

There are infinitely many sequences of weights $(w_1, w_2, \ldots, w_n)$, but only finitely many threshold functions for any given value of n. So it is clear that many different weight sequences are equivalent. For example, consider the pure majority function

$$\langle x_1^2 x_2^3 x_3^5 x_4^7 x_5^{11} x_6^{13}\rangle,$$

in which prime numbers have been used as weights. A brute-force examination of 2^6 cases shows that

$$\langle x_1^2 x_2^3 x_3^5 x_4^7 x_5^{11} x_6^{13}\rangle = \langle x_1 x_2^2 x_3^2 x_4^3 x_5^4 x_6^5\rangle; \tag{88}$$

thus we can express the same function with substantially smaller weights. Similarly, the threshold function

$$[(x_1x_2\ldots x_{20})_2 \ge (01100100100001111110)_2] = \langle 1^{225028} x_1^{524288} x_2^{262144} \ldots x_{20}\rangle,$$

a special case of (80), turns out to be simply

$$\langle 1^{323} x_1^{764} x_2^{323} x_3^{323} x_4^{118} x_5^{118} x_6^{87} x_7^{31} x_8^{31} x_9^{25} x_{10}^6 x_{11}^6 x_{12}^6 x_{13}^6 x_{14} x_{15} x_{16} x_{17} x_{18} x_{19}\rangle. \tag{89}$$

Exercise 103 explains how to find a minimum set of weights without resorting to a huge brute-force search, using linear programming.

A nice indexing scheme by which a unique identifier can be assigned to any threshold function was discovered by C. K. Chow [*FOCS* **2** (1961), 34–38]. Given any Boolean function $f(x_1, \ldots, x_n)$, let $N(f)$ be the number of vectors $x = (x_1, \ldots, x_n)$ for which $f(x) = 1$, and let $\Sigma(f)$ be the sum of all those vectors. For example, if $f(x_1, x_2) = x_1 \lor x_2$, we have $N(f) = 3$ and $\Sigma(f) = (0, 1) + (1, 0) + (1, 1) = (2, 2)$.

Theorem T. *Let $f(x_1, \ldots, x_n)$ and $g(x_1, \ldots, x_n)$ be Boolean functions with $N(f) = N(g)$ and $\Sigma(f) = \Sigma(g)$, where f is a threshold function. Then $f = g$.*

Proof. Suppose there are exactly k vectors $x^{(1)}, \ldots, x^{(k)}$ such that $f(x^{(j)}) = 1$ and $g(x^{(j)}) = 0$. Since $N(f) = N(g)$, there must be exactly k vectors $y^{(1)}, \ldots, y^{(k)}$ such that $f(y^{(j)}) = 0$ and $g(y^{(j)}) = 1$. And since $\Sigma(f) = \Sigma(g)$, we must also have $x^{(1)} + \cdots + x^{(k)} = y^{(1)} + \cdots + y^{(k)}$.

Now suppose f is the threshold function (75); then we have $w \cdot x^{(j)} \geq t$ and $w \cdot y^{(j)} < t$ for $1 \leq j \leq k$. But if $f \neq g$ we have $k > 0$, and $w \cdot (x^{(1)} + \cdots + x^{(k)}) \geq kt > w \cdot (y^{(1)} + \cdots + y^{(k)})$, a contradiction. ∎

Threshold functions have many curious properties, some of which are explored in the exercises below. Their classical theory is well summarized in Saburo Muroga's book *Threshold Logic and its Applications* (Wiley, 1971).

Symmetric Boolean functions. A function $f(x_1, \ldots, x_n)$ is called *symmetric* if $f(x_1, \ldots, x_n)$ is equal to $f(x_{p(1)}, \ldots, x_{p(n)})$ for all permutations $p(1) \ldots p(n)$ of $\{1, \ldots, n\}$. When all the x_j are 0 or 1, this condition means that f depends only on the number of 1s that are present in the arguments, namely the "sideways sum" $\nu x = \nu(x_1, \ldots, x_n) = x_1 + \cdots + x_n$. The notation $S_{k_1, k_2, \ldots, k_r}(x_1, \ldots, x_n)$ is commonly used to stand for the Boolean function that is true if and only if νx is either k_1 or k_2 or $\cdots$ or k_r. For example, $S_{1,3,5}(v, w, x, y, z) = v \oplus w \oplus x \oplus y \oplus z$; $S_{3,4,5}(v, w, x, y, z) = \langle vwxyz \rangle$; $S_{4,5}(v, w, x, y, z) = \langle 00vwxyz \rangle$.

Many applications of symmetry involve the basic functions $S_k(x_1, \ldots, x_n)$ that are true only when $\nu x = k$. For example, $S_3(x_1, x_2, x_3, x_4, x_5, x_6)$ is true if and only if exactly half of the arguments $\{x_1, \ldots, x_6\}$ are true and the other half are false. In such cases we obviously have

$$S_k(x_1, \ldots, x_n) = S_{\geq k}(x_1, \ldots, x_n) \wedge \overline{S_{\geq k+1}(x_1, \ldots, x_n)}, \qquad (90)$$

where $S_{\geq k}(x_1, \ldots, x_n)$ is an abbreviation for $S_{k, k+1, \ldots, n}(x_1, \ldots, x_n)$. The functions $S_{\geq k}(x_1, \ldots, x_n)$ are, of course, the threshold functions $[x_1 + \cdots + x_n \geq k]$ that we have already studied.

More complicated cases can be treated as threshold functions of threshold functions. For example, we have

$$S_{2,3,6,8,9}(x_1, \ldots, x_{12}) = \left[\nu x \geq 2 + 4[\nu x \geq 4] + 2[\nu x \geq 7] + 5[\nu x \geq 10] \right]$$

$$= \langle 00x_1 \ldots x_{12} \langle 0^5 \bar{x}_1 \ldots \bar{x}_{12} \rangle^4 \langle 1\bar{x}_1 \ldots \bar{x}_{12} \rangle^2 \langle 1^7 \bar{x}_1 \ldots \bar{x}_{12} \rangle^5 \rangle, \qquad (91)$$

because the number of 1s in the outermost majority-of-25 turns out to be respectively $(11, 12, 13, 14, 11, 12, 13, 12, 13, 14, 10, 11, 12)$ when $x_1 + \cdots + x_{12} = (0, 1, \ldots, 12)$. A similar two-level scheme works in general [R. C. Minnick, *IRE Trans.* **EC-10** (1961), 6–16]; and with three or more levels of logic we can reduce the number of thresholding operations even further. (See exercise 113.)

A variety of ingenious tricks have been discovered for evaluating symmetric Boolean functions. For example, S. Muroga attributes the following remarkable sequence of formulas to F. Sasaki:

$$x_0 \oplus x_1 \oplus \cdots \oplus x_{2m} = \langle \bar{x}_0 s_1 s_2 \ldots s_{2m} \rangle,$$

$$\text{where} \quad s_j = \langle x_0 x_j x_{j+1} \ldots x_{j+m-1} \bar{x}_{j+m} \bar{x}_{j+m+1} \ldots \bar{x}_{j+2m-1} \rangle, \qquad (92)$$

if $m > 0$ and if we consider x_{2m+k} to be the same as x_k for $k \geq 1$. In particular, when $m = 1$ and $m = 2$ we have the identities

$$x_0 \oplus x_1 \oplus x_2 = \langle \bar{x}_0 \langle x_0 x_1 \bar{x}_2 \rangle \langle x_0 x_2 \bar{x}_1 \rangle \rangle; \tag{93}$$

$$x_0 \oplus \cdots \oplus x_4 = \langle \bar{x}_0 \langle x_0 x_1 x_2 \bar{x}_3 \bar{x}_4 \rangle \langle x_0 x_2 x_3 \bar{x}_4 \bar{x}_1 \rangle \langle x_0 x_3 x_4 \bar{x}_1 \bar{x}_2 \rangle \langle x_0 x_4 x_1 \bar{x}_2 \bar{x}_3 \rangle \rangle. \tag{94}$$

The right-hand sides are fully symmetric, but not obviously so! (See exercise 115.)

Canalizing functions. A Boolean function $f(x_1, \ldots, x_n)$ is said to be *canalizing* or "forcing" if we might be able to deduce its value by examining at most one of its variables. More precisely, f is canalizing if $n = 0$ or if there's a subscript j for which $f(x)$ either has a constant value when we set $x_j = 0$ or a constant value when we set $x_j = 1$. For example, $f(x, y, z) = (x \oplus z) \vee \bar{y}$ is canalizing because it always equals 1 when $y = 0$. (When $y = 1$ we don't know the value of f without examining also x and z; but half a loaf is better than none.) Such functions, introduced by Stuart Kauffman [*Lectures on Mathematics in the Life Sciences* **3** (1972), 63–116; *J. Theoretical Biology* **44** (1974), 167–190], have proved to be important in many applications, especially in chemistry and biology. Some of their properties are examined in exercises 125–129.

Quantitative considerations. We've been studying many different kinds of Boolean functions, so it's natural to ask: How many n-variable functions of each type actually exist? Tables 3, 4, and 5 provide the answers, at least for small values of n.

All functions are counted in Table 3. There are 2^{2^n} possibilities for each n, since there are 2^{2^n} possible truth tables. Some of these functions are self-dual, some are monotone; some are both monotone and self-dual, as in Theorem P. Some are Horn functions as in Theorem H; some are Krom functions as in Theorem S; and so on.

But in Table 4, two functions are considered identical if they differ only because the names of variables have changed. Thus only 12 different cases arise when $n = 2$, because (for example) $x \vee \bar{y}$ and $\bar{x} \vee y$ are essentially the same.

Table 5 goes a step further: It allows us to complement individual variables, and even to complement the entire function, without essentially changing it. From this perspective the 256 Boolean functions of (x, y, z) fall into only 14 different equivalence classes:

Representative	Class size	Representative	Class size	
0	2	$x \wedge (y \oplus z)$	24	
x	6	$x \oplus (y \wedge z)$	24	
$x \wedge y$	24	$(x \wedge y) \vee (\bar{x} \wedge z)$	24	
$x \oplus y$	6	$(x \vee y) \wedge (x \oplus z)$	48	(95)
$x \wedge y \wedge z$	16	$(x \oplus y) \vee (x \oplus z)$	8	
$x \oplus y \oplus z$	2	$\langle xyz \rangle$	8	
$x \wedge (y \vee z)$	48	$S_1(x, y, z)$	16	

We shall study ways to count and to list inequivalent combinatorial objects in Section 7.2.3.

Table 3

BOOLEAN FUNCTIONS OF n VARIABLES

	$n=0$	$n=1$	$n=2$	$n=3$	$n=4$	$n=5$	$n=6$
arbitrary	2	4	16	256	65,536	4,294,967,296	18,446,744,073,709,551,616
self-dual	0	2	4	16	256	65,536	4,294,967,296
monotone	2	3	6	20	168	7,581	7,828,354
both	0	1	2	4	12	81	2,646
Horn	2	4	14	122	4,960	2,771,104	151,947,502,948
Krom	2	4	16	166	4,170	224,716	24,445,368
threshold	2	4	14	104	1,882	94,572	15,028,134
symmetric	2	4	8	16	32	64	128
canalizing	2	4	14	120	3,514	1,292,276	103,071,426,294

Table 4

BOOLEAN FUNCTIONS DISTINCT UNDER PERMUTATION OF VARIABLES

	$n=0$	$n=1$	$n=2$	$n=3$	$n=4$	$n=5$	$n=6$
arbitrary	2	4	12	80	3,984	37,333,248	25,626,412,338,274,304
self-dual	0	2	2	8	32	1,088	6,385,408
monotone	2	3	5	10	30	210	16,353
both	0	1	1	2	3	7	30
Horn	2	4	10	38	368	29,328	216,591,692
Krom	2	4	12	48	308	3,028	49,490
threshold	2	4	10	34	178	1,720	590,440
canalizing	2	4	10	38	294	15,774	149,325,022

Table 5

BOOLEAN FUNCTIONS DISTINCT UNDER COMPLEMENTATION/PERMUTATION

	$n=0$	$n=1$	$n=2$	$n=3$	$n=4$	$n=5$	$n=6$
arbitrary	1	2	4	14	222	616,126	200,253,952,527,184
self-dual	0	1	1	3	7	83	109,950
threshold	1	2	3	6	15	63	567
both	0	1	1	2	3	7	21
canalizing	1	2	3	6	22	402	1,228,158

EXERCISES

1. [15] (Lewis Carroll.) Make sense of Tweedledee's comment, quoted near the beginning of this section. [*Hint:* See Table 1.]

2. [17] Logicians on the remote planet Pincus use the symbol 1 to represent "false" and 0 to represent "true." Thus, for example, they have a binary operation called "or" whose properties

$$1 \text{ or } 1 = 1, \qquad 1 \text{ or } 0 = 0, \qquad 0 \text{ or } 1 = 0, \qquad 0 \text{ or } 0 = 0$$

we associate with $\land$. What operations would we associate with the 16 logical operators that Pincusians respectively call "falsehood," "and," ..., "nand," "validity" (see Table 1)?

▶ **3.** [*13*] Suppose logical values were respectively -1 for falsehood and $+1$ for truth, instead of 0 and 1. What operations $\circ$ in Table 1 would then correspond to (a) $\max(x, y)$? (b) $\min(x, y)$? (c) $-x$? (d) $x \cdot y$?

4. [*24*] (H. M. Sheffer.) The purpose of this exercise is to show that all of the operations in Table 1 can be expressed in terms of NAND. (a) For each of the 16 operators $\circ$ in that table, find a formula equivalent to $x \circ y$ that uses only $\bar{\wedge}$ as an operator. Your formula should be as short as possible. For example, the answer for operation $\llcorner$ is simply "x", but the answer for $\bar{\llcorner}$ is "$x \bar{\wedge} x$". Do not use the constants 0 or 1 in your formulas. (b) Similarly, find 16 short formulas when constants *are* allowed. For example, $x \bar{\llcorner} y$ can now be expressed also as "$x \bar{\wedge} 1$".

5. [*24*] Consider exercise 4 with $\bar{\subset}$ as the basic operation instead of $\bar{\wedge}$.

6. [*21*] (E. Schröder.) (a) Which of the 16 operations in Table 1 are associative — in other words, which of them satisfy $x \circ (y \circ z) = (x \circ y) \circ z$? (b) Which of them satisfy the identity $(x \circ y) \circ (y \circ z) = x \circ z$?

7. [*20*] Which operations in Table 1 have the property that $x \circ y = z$ if and only if $y \circ z = x$?

8. [*24*] Which of the 16^2 pairs of operations $(\circ, \square)$ satisfy the left-distributive law $x \circ (y \square z) = (x \circ y) \square (x \circ z)$?

9. [*16*] True or false: (a) $(x \oplus y) \vee z = (x \vee z) \oplus (y \vee z)$; (b) $(w \oplus x \oplus y) \vee z = (w \vee z) \oplus (x \vee z) \oplus (y \vee z)$; (c) $(x \oplus y) \vee (y \oplus z) = (x \oplus z) \vee (y \oplus z)$.

10. [*17*] What is the multilinear representation of the "random" function (22)?

11. [*M25*] Is there an intuitive way to understand exactly when the multilinear representation of $f(x_1, \ldots, x_n)$ contains, say, the term $x_2 x_3 x_6 x_8$? (See (19).)

▶ **12.** [*M23*] The *integer multilinear representation* of a Boolean function extends representations like (19) to a polynomial $f(x_1, \ldots, x_n)$ with integer coefficients, in such a way that $f(x_1, \ldots, x_n)$ has the correct value (0 or 1) for all 2^n possible 0–1 vectors $(x_1, \ldots, x_n)$, *without* taking a remainder mod 2. For example, the integer multilinear representation corresponding to (19) is $1 - xy - xz - yz + 3xyz$.

    a) What is the integer multilinear representation of the "random" function (22)?

    b) How large can the coefficients of such a representation $f(x_1, \ldots, x_n)$ be?

    c) Show that, in every integer multilinear representation, $0 \le f(x_1, \ldots, x_n) \le 1$ whenever $x_1, \ldots, x_n$ are real numbers with $0 \le x_1, \ldots, x_n \le 1$.

    d) Similarly, if $f(x_1, \ldots, x_n) \le g(x_1, \ldots, x_n)$ whenever $\{x_1, \ldots, x_n\} \subseteq \{0, 1\}$, then $f(x_1, \ldots, x_n) \le g(x_1, \ldots, x_n)$ whenever $\{x_1, \ldots, x_n\} \subseteq [0 \ldots 1]$.

    e) If f is monotone and $0 \le x_j \le y_j \le 1$ for $1 \le j \le n$, prove that $f(x) \le f(y)$.

▶ **13.** [*20*] Consider a system that consists of n units, each of which may be "working" or "failing." If x_j represents the condition "unit j is working," then a Boolean function like $x_1 \wedge (\bar{x}_2 \vee \bar{x}_3)$ represents the statement "unit 1 is working, but either unit 2 or unit 3 is failing"; and $S_3(x_1, \ldots, x_n)$ means "exactly three units are working."

    Suppose each unit j is in working order with probability p_j, independent of the other units. Show that the Boolean function $f(x_1, \ldots, x_n)$ is true with probability $F(p_1, \ldots, p_n)$, where F is a polynomial in the variables $p_1, \ldots, p_n$.

14. [*20*] The probability function $F(p_1, \ldots, p_n)$ in exercise 13 is often called the *availability* of the system. Find the self-dual function $f(x_1, x_2, x_3)$ of maximum availability when the probabilities (p_1, p_2, p_3) are (a) $(.9, .8, .7)$; (b) $(.8, .6, .4)$; (c) $(.8, .6, .1)$.

▶ **15.** [*M20*] If $f(x_1, \ldots, x_n)$ is any Boolean function, show that there is a polynomial $F(x)$ with the property that $F(x)$ is an integer when x is an integer, and $f(x_1, \ldots, x_n) = F((x_n \ldots x_1)_2) \bmod 2$. *Hint:* Consider $\binom{x}{k} \bmod 2$.

16. [*13*] Can we replace each ∨ by ⊕ in a full disjunctive normal form?

17. [*10*] By De Morgan's laws, a general disjunctive normal form such as (25) is not only an OR of ANDs, it is a NAND of NANDs:

$$\overline{\overline{(u_{11} \wedge \cdots \wedge u_{1s_1})} \wedge \cdots \wedge \overline{(u_{m1} \wedge \cdots \wedge u_{ms_m})}}.$$

Both levels of logic can therefore be considered to be identical.

A student named J. H. Quick rewrote this expression in the form

$$(u_{11} \overline{\wedge} \cdots \overline{\wedge} u_{1s_1}) \overline{\wedge} \cdots \overline{\wedge} (u_{m1} \wedge \cdots \overline{\wedge} u_{ms_m}).$$

Was that a good idea?

▶ **18.** [*20*] Let $u_1 \wedge \cdots \wedge u_s$ be an implicant in a disjunctive normal form for a Boolean function f, and let $v_1 \vee \cdots \vee v_t$ be a clause in a conjunctive normal form for the same function. Prove that $u_i = v_j$ for some i and j.

19. [*20*] What is the conjunctive prime form of the "random" function in (22)?

20. [*M21*] True or false: Every prime implicant of $f \wedge g$ can be written $f' \wedge g'$, where f' is a prime implicant of f and g' is a prime implicant of g.

21. [*M20*] Prove that a nonconstant Boolean function is monotone if and only if it can be expressed entirely in terms of the operations ∧ and ∨.

22. [*20*] Suppose $f(x_1, \ldots, x_n) = g(x_1, \ldots, x_{n-1}) \oplus h(x_1, \ldots, x_{n-1}) \wedge x_n$ as in (16). What conditions on the functions g and h are necessary and sufficient for f to be monotone?

23. [*15*] What is the conjunctive prime form of $(v \wedge w \wedge x) \vee (v \wedge x \wedge z) \vee (x \wedge y \wedge z)$?

24. [*M20*] Consider the complete binary tree with 2^k leaves, illustrated here for $k = 3$. Operate alternately with ∧ or ∨ on each level, using ∧ at the root, obtaining for example $((x_0 \wedge x_1) \vee (x_2 \wedge x_3)) \wedge$ 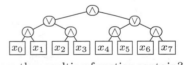 $((x_4 \wedge x_5) \vee (x_6 \wedge x_7))$. How many prime implicants does the resulting function contain?

25. [*M21*] How many prime implicants does $(x_1 \vee x_2) \wedge (x_2 \vee x_3) \wedge \cdots \wedge (x_{n-1} \vee x_n)$ have?

26. [*M23*] Let $\mathcal{F}$ and $\mathcal{G}$ be the families of index sets for the prime clauses and the prime implicants of a monotone CNF and a monotone DNF:

$$f(x) = \bigwedge_{I \in \mathcal{F}} \bigvee_{i \in I} x_i; \qquad g(x) = \bigvee_{J \in \mathcal{G}} \bigwedge_{j \in J} x_j.$$

Efficiently exhibit an x such that $f(x) \neq g(x)$ if any of the following conditions hold:
a) There is an $I \in \mathcal{F}$ and a $J \in \mathcal{G}$ with $I \cap J = \emptyset$.
b) $\bigcup_{I \in \mathcal{F}} I \neq \bigcup_{J \in \mathcal{G}} J$.
c) There's an $I \in \mathcal{F}$ with $|I| > |\mathcal{G}|$, or a $J \in \mathcal{G}$ with $|J| > |\mathcal{F}|$.
d) $\sum_{I \in \mathcal{F}} 2^{n-|I|} + \sum_{J \in \mathcal{G}} 2^{n-|J|} < 2^n$, where $n = |\bigcup_{I \in \mathcal{F}} I|$.

27. [*M31*] Continuing the previous exercise, consider the following algorithm $X(\mathcal{F}, \mathcal{G})$, which either returns a vector x with $f(x) \neq g(x)$, or returns Λ if $f = g$:

X1. [Check necessary conditions.] Return an appropriate value x if condition (a), (b), (c), or (d) in exercise 26 applies.

X2. [Done?] If $|\mathcal{F}||\mathcal{G}| \le 1$, return Λ.

X3. [Recurse.] Compute the following reduced families, for a "best" index k:

$$\mathcal{F}_1 = \{I \mid I \in \mathcal{F},\ k \notin I\}, \qquad \mathcal{F}_0 = \mathcal{F}_1 \cup \{I \mid k \notin I,\ I \cup \{k\} \in \mathcal{F}\};$$
$$\mathcal{G}_0 = \{J \mid J \in \mathcal{G},\ k \notin J\}, \qquad \mathcal{G}_1 = \mathcal{G}_0 \cup \{J \mid k \notin J,\ J \cup \{k\} \in \mathcal{G}\}.$$

Delete any member of $\mathcal{F}_0$ or $\mathcal{G}_1$ that contains another member of the same family. The index k should be chosen so that the ratio $\rho = \min(|\mathcal{F}_1|/|\mathcal{F}|, |\mathcal{G}_0|/|\mathcal{G}|)$ is as small as possible. If $X(\mathcal{F}_0, \mathcal{G}_0)$ returns a vector x, return the same vector extended with $x_k = 0$. Otherwise if $X(\mathcal{F}_1, \mathcal{G}_1)$ returns a vector x, return the same vector extended with $x_k = 1$. Otherwise return Λ. ▪

If $N = |\mathcal{F}| + |\mathcal{G}|$, prove that step X1 is executed at most $N^{O(\log N)^2}$ times. *Hint:* Show that we always have $\rho \le 1 - 1/\lg N$ in step X3.

28. [*21*] (W. V. Quine, 1952.) If $f(x_1, \dots, x_n)$ is a Boolean function with prime implicants $p_1, \dots, p_q$, let $g(y_1, \dots, y_q) = \bigwedge_{f(x)=1} \bigvee \{y_j \mid p_j(x) = 1\}$. For example, the "random" function (22) is true at the eight points (28), and it has five prime implicants given by (29) and (30); so $g(y_1, \dots, y_5)$ is

$$(y_1 \vee y_2) \wedge (y_1) \wedge (y_2 \vee y_3) \wedge (y_4) \wedge (y_3 \vee y_5) \wedge (y_5) \wedge (y_5) \wedge (y_4 \vee y_5)$$
$$= (y_1 \wedge y_2 \wedge y_4 \wedge y_5) \vee (y_1 \wedge y_3 \wedge y_4 \wedge y_5)$$

in this case. Prove that every shortest DNF expression for f corresponds to a prime implicant of the monotone function g.

29. [*22*] (The next several exercises are devoted to algorithms that deal with the implicants of Boolean functions by representing points of the n-cube as n-bit numbers $(b_{n-1} \dots b_1 b_0)_2$, rather than as bit strings $x_1 \dots x_n$.) Given a bit position j, and given n-bit values $v_0 < v_1 < \cdots < v_{m-1}$, explain how to find all pairs (k, k') such that $0 \le k < k' < m$ and $v_{k'} = v_k \oplus 2^j$, in increasing order of k. The running time of your procedure should be $O(m)$, if bitwise operations on n-bit words take constant time.

▶ **30.** [*27*] The text points out that an implicant of a Boolean function can be regarded as a subcube such as $01{*}0{*}$, contained in the set V of all points for which the function is true. Every subcube can be represented as a pair of binary numbers $a = (a_{n-1} \dots a_0)_2$ and $b = (b_{n-1} \dots b_0)_2$, where a records the positions of the asterisks and b records the bits in non-$*$ positions. For example, the numbers $a = (00101)_2$ and $b = (01000)_2$ represent the subcube $c = 01{*}0{*}$. We always have $a \mathbin{\&} b = 0$.

The "j-buddy" of a subcube is defined whenever $a_j = 0$, by changing b to $b \oplus 2^j$. For example, $01{*}0{*}$ has three buddies, namely its 4-buddy $11{*}0{*}$, its 3-buddy $00{*}0{*}$, and its 1-buddy $01{*}1{*}$. Every subcube $c \subseteq V$ can be assigned a tag value $(t_{n-1} \dots t_0)_2$, where $t_j = 1$ if and only if the j-buddy of c is defined and contained in V. With this definition, c represents a maximal subcube (hence a prime implicant) if and only if its tag is zero.

Use these concepts to design an algorithm that finds all maximal subcubes (a, b) of a given set V, where V is represented by the n-bit numbers $v_0 < v_1 < \cdots < v_{m-1}$.

▶ **31.** [*28*] The algorithm in exercise 30 requires a complete list of all points where a Boolean function is true, and that list may be quite long. Therefore we may prefer to work directly with subcubes, never going down to the level of explicit n-tuples unless necessary. The key to such higher-level methods is the notion of *consensus* between subcubes c and c', denoted by $c \sqcup c'$ and defined to be the largest subcube c'' such that

$$c'' \subseteq c \cup c', \qquad c'' \not\subseteq c, \quad \text{and} \quad c'' \not\subseteq c'.$$

Such a c'' does not always exist. For example, if $c = 000*$ and $c' = *111$, every subcube contained in $c \cup c'$ is contained either in c or in c'.

a) Prove that the consensus, when it exists, can be computed componentwise using the following formulas in each coordinate position:

$$x \sqcup x = x \sqcup * = * \sqcup x = x \quad \text{and} \quad x \sqcup \bar{x} = * \sqcup * = *, \qquad \text{for } x = 0 \text{ and } x = 1.$$

Furthermore, $c \sqcup c'$ exists if and only if the rule $x \sqcup \bar{x} = *$ has been used in exactly one component.

b) A subcube with k asterisks is called a k-cube. Show that, if c is a k-cube and c' is a k'-cube, and if the consensus $c'' = c \sqcup c'$ exists, then c'' is a k''-cube where $1 \leq k'' \leq \min(k, k') + 1$.

c) If C and C' are families of subcubes, let

$$C \sqcup C' = \{ c \sqcup c' \mid c \in C, \, c' \in C', \text{ and } c \sqcup c' \text{ exists} \}.$$

Explain why the following algorithm works.

Algorithm E (*Find maximal subcubes*). Given a family C of subcubes of the n-cube, this algorithm outputs the maximal subcubes of $V = \bigcup_{c \in C} c$, without actually computing the set V itself.

E1. [Initialize.] Set $j \leftarrow 0$. Delete any subcube c of C that is contained in another.

E2. [Done?] (At this point, every j-cube $\subseteq V$ is contained in some element of C, and C contains no k-cubes with $k < j$.) If C is empty, the algorithm terminates.

E3. [Take consensuses.] Set $C' \leftarrow C \sqcup C$, and remove all subcubes from C' that are k-cubes for $k \leq j$. While performing this computation, also output any j-cube $c \in C$ for which $c \sqcup C$ does not produce a $(j+1)$-cube of C'.

E4. [Advance.] Set $C \leftarrow C \cup C'$, but delete all j-cubes from this union. Then delete any subcube $c \in C$ that is contained in another. Set $j \leftarrow j+1$ and go to E2. ∎

(See exercise 7.1.3–142 for an efficient way to perform these computations.)

▸ **32.** [*M29*] Let $c_1, \ldots, c_m$ be subcubes of the n-cube.

a) Prove that $c_1 \cup \cdots \cup c_m$ contains at most one maximal subcube c that is not contained in $c_1 \cup \cdots \cup c_{j-1} \cup c_{j+1} \cup \cdots \cup c_m$ for any $j \in \{1, \ldots, m\}$. (If c exists, we call it the *generalized consensus* of $c_1, \ldots, c_m$, because $c = c_1 \sqcup c_2$ in the notation of exercise 31 when $m = 2$.)

b) Find a set of m subcubes for which each of the $2^m - 1$ nonempty subsets of $\{c_1, \ldots, c_m\}$ has a generalized consensus.

c) Prove that a DNF with m implicants has at most $2^m - 1$ prime implicants.

d) Find a DNF that has m implicants and $2^m - 1$ prime implicants.

33. [*M21*] Let $f(x_1, \ldots, x_n)$ be one of the $\binom{2^n}{m}$ Boolean functions that are true at exactly m points. If f is chosen at random, what is the probability that $x_1 \wedge \cdots \wedge x_k$ is (a) an implicant of f? (b) a prime implicant of f? [Give the answer to part (b) as a sum; but evaluate it in closed form when $k = n$.]

▶ **34.** [*HM37*] Continuing exercise 33, let $c(m, n)$ be the average total number of implicants, and let $p(m, n)$ be the average total number of prime implicants.

    a) If $0 \le m \le 2^n/n$, show that $m \le c(m, n) \le \frac{3}{2}m + O(m/n)$ and $p(m, n) \ge me^{-1} + O(m/n)$; hence $p(m, n) = \Theta(c(m, n))$ in this range.

    b) Now let $2^n/n \le m \le (1 - \epsilon)2^n$, where ϵ is a fixed positive constant. Define the numbers t and α_{mn} by the relations

$$n^{-4/3} \le \left(\frac{m}{2^n}\right)^{2^t} = \alpha_{mn} < n^{-2/3}, \qquad \text{integer } t.$$

    Express the asymptotic values of $c(m, n)$ and $p(m, n)$ in terms of n, t, and α_{mn}. [*Hint:* Show that almost all of the implicants have exactly $n-t$ or $n-t-1$ literals.]

    c) Estimate $c(m, n)/p(m, n)$ when $m = 2^{n-1}$ and $n = \lfloor (\ln t - \ln \ln t)2^{2^t} \rfloor$, integer t.

    d) Prove that $c(m, n)/p(m, n) = O(\log \log n / \log \log \log n)$ when $m \le (1 - \epsilon)2^n$.

▶ **35.** [*M25*] A DNF is called *orthogonal* if its implicants correspond to disjoint subcubes. Orthogonal disjunctive normal forms are particularly useful when the reliability polynomial of exercise 13 is being calculated or estimated.

    The full DNF of every function is obviously orthogonal, because its subcubes are single points. But we can often find an orthogonal DNF that has significantly fewer implicants, especially when the function is monotone. For example, the function $(x_1 \wedge x_2) \vee (x_2 \wedge x_3) \vee (x_3 \wedge x_4)$ is true at eight points, and it has the orthogonal DNF

$$(x_1 \wedge x_2) \vee (\bar{x}_1 \wedge x_2 \wedge x_3) \vee (\bar{x}_2 \wedge x_3 \wedge x_4).$$

In other words, the overlapping subcubes 11**, *11*, **11 can be replaced by the disjoint subcubes 11**, 011*, *011. Using the binary notation for subcubes in exercise 30, these subcubes have asterisk codes 0011, 0001, 1000 and bit codes 1100, 0110, 0011.

    Every monotone function can be defined by a list of bit codes $B_1, \ldots, B_p$, when the asterisk codes are respectively $\bar{B}_1, \ldots, \bar{B}_p$. Given such a list, let the "shadow" S_k of B_k be the bitwise OR of $B_j \mathbin{\&} \bar{B}_k$, for all $1 \le j < k$ such that $\nu(B_j \mathbin{\&} \bar{B}_k) = 1$:

$$S_k = \beta_{1k} \mid \cdots \mid \beta_{(k-1)k}, \qquad \beta_{jk} = ((B_j \mathbin{\&} \bar{B}_k) \oplus ((B_j \mathbin{\&} \bar{B}_k) - 1)) \mathbin{\dot{-}} ((B_j \mathbin{\&} \bar{B}_k) - 1).$$

For example, when the bit codes are $(B_1, B_2, B_3) = (1100, 0110, 0011)$, in that order, we get the shadow codes $(S_1, S_2, S_3) = (0000, 1000, 0100)$.

    a) Show that the asterisk codes $A'_j = \bar{B}_j - S_j$ and bit codes B_j define subcubes that cover the same points as the subcubes with asterisk codes $A_j = \bar{B}_j$.

    b) A list of bit codes $B_1, \ldots, B_p$ is called a *shelling* if $B_j \mathbin{\&} S_k$ is nonzero for all $1 \le j < k \le p$. For example, $(1100, 0110, 0011)$ is a shelling; but if we arrange those bit codes in the order $(1100, 0011, 0110)$ the shelling condition fails when $j = 1$ and $k = 2$, although we do have $S_3 = 1001$. Prove that the subcubes in part (a) are disjoint if and only if the list of bit codes is a shelling.

    c) According to Theorem Q, every prime implicant must appear among the B's when we represent a monotone Boolean function in this way. But sometimes we need to add additional implicants if we want the subcubes to be disjoint. For example, there is no shelling for the bit codes 1100 and 0011. Show that we can, however, obtain a shelling for this function $(x_1 \wedge x_2) \vee (x_3 \wedge x_4)$ by adding one more bit code. What is the resulting orthogonal DNF?

    d) Permute the bit codes $\{11000, 01100, 00110, 00011, 11010\}$ to obtain a shelling.

    e) Add two bit codes to the set $\{110000, 011000, 001100, 000110, 000011\}$ in order to make a shellable list.

36. [*M21*] Continuing exercise 35, let f be any monotone function, not identically 1. Show that the set of bit vectors

$$B = \{ x \mid f(x) = 1 \text{ and } f(x') = 0 \}, \qquad x' = x \,\&\, (x-1),$$

is always shellable when listed in decreasing lexicographic order. (The vector x' is obtained from x by zeroing out the rightmost 1.) For example, this method produces an orthogonal DNF for $(x_1 \wedge x_2) \vee (x_3 \wedge x_4)$ from the list $(1100, 1011, 0111, 0011)$.

▸ **37.** [*M31*] Find a shellable DNF for $(x_1 \wedge x_2) \vee (x_3 \wedge x_4) \vee \cdots \vee (x_{2n-1} \wedge x_{2n})$ that has $2^n - 1$ implicants, and prove that no orthogonal DNF for this function has fewer.

38. [*05*] Is it hard to test the satisfiability of functions in *disjunctive* normal form?

▸ **39.** [*25*] Let $f(x_1, \ldots, x_n)$ be a Boolean formula represented as an extended binary tree with $N > 0$ internal nodes and $N+1$ leaves. Each leaf is labeled with a variable x_k, and each internal node is labeled with one of the sixteen binary operators in Table 1; applying the operators from bottom to top yields $f(x_1, \ldots, x_n)$ as the value of the root.

Explain how to construct a formula $F(x_1, \ldots, x_n, y_1, \ldots, y_N)$ in 3CNF, having exactly $4N+1$ clauses, such that $f(x_1, \ldots, x_n) = \exists y_1 \ldots \exists y_N F(x_1, \ldots, x_n, y_1, \ldots, y_N)$. (Thus f is satisfiable if and only if F is satisfiable.)

40. [*23*] Given an undirected graph G, construct the following clauses on the Boolean variables $\{p_{uv} \mid u \neq v\} \cup \{q_{uvw} \mid u \neq v, u \neq w, v \neq w, u \not\!\!\!-\!\!\!- w\}$, where u, v, and w denote vertices of G:

$$A = \bigwedge \{ (p_{uv} \vee p_{vu}) \wedge (\bar{p}_{uv} \vee \bar{p}_{vu}) \mid u \neq v \};$$
$$B = \bigwedge \{ (\bar{p}_{uv} \vee \bar{p}_{vw} \vee p_{uw}) \mid u \neq v, u \neq w, v \neq w \};$$
$$C = \bigwedge \{ (\bar{q}_{uvw} \vee p_{uv}) \wedge (\bar{q}_{uvw} \vee p_{vw}) \wedge (q_{uvw} \vee \bar{p}_{uv} \vee \bar{p}_{vw}) \mid u \neq v, u \neq w, v \neq w, u \not\!\!\!-\!\!\!- w \};$$
$$D = \bigwedge \{ (\textstyle\bigvee_{v \notin \{u,w\}} (q_{uvw} \vee q_{wvu})) \mid u \neq w, u \not\!\!\!-\!\!\!- w \}.$$

Prove that the formula $A \wedge B \wedge C \wedge D$ is satisfiable if and only if G has a Hamiltonian path. *Hint:* Think of p_{uv} as the statement '$u < v$'.

41. [*20*] (*The pigeonhole principle.*) The island of San Serriffe contains m pigeons and n holes. Find a conjunctive normal form that is satisfiable if and only if each pigeon can be the sole occupant of at least one hole.

42. [*20*] Find a short, unsatisfiable CNF that is not totally trivial, although it consists entirely of Horn clauses that are also Krom clauses.

43. [*20*] Is there an efficient way to decide satisfiability of a conjunctive normal form that consists entirely of Horn clauses and/or Krom clauses (possibly mixed)?

44. [*M23*] Complete the proof of Theorem H by studying the implications of (33).

45. [*M20*] (a) Show that exactly half of the Horn functions of n variables are definite. (b) Also show that there are more Horn functions of n variables than monotone functions of n variables (unless $n = 0$).

46. [*20*] Which of the 11×11 character pairs **xy** can occur next to each other in the context-free grammar (34)?

47. [*20*] Given a sequence of relations $j \prec k$ with $1 \leq j, k \leq n$ as in Algorithm 2.2.3T (topological sorting), consider the clauses

$$x_{j_1} \wedge \cdots \wedge x_{j_t} \Rightarrow x_k \qquad \text{for } 1 \leq k \leq n,$$

where $\{j_1, \ldots, j_t\}$ is the set of elements such that $j_i \prec k$. Compare the behavior of Algorithm C on these clauses to the behavior of Algorithm 2.2.3T.

▶ **48.** [*21*] What's a good way to test an indefinite set of Horn clauses for satisfiability?

49. [*22*] Show that, if $f(x_1, \ldots, x_n)$ and $g(x_1, \ldots, x_n)$ are both defined by Horn clauses in CNF, there is an easy way to test if $f(x_1, \ldots, x_n) \le g(x_1, \ldots, x_n)$ for all $x_1, \ldots, x_n$.

50. [*HM42*] There are $(n+2)2^{n-1}$ possible Horn clauses on n variables. Select $c \cdot 2^n$ of them at random, with repetition permitted, where $c > 0$; and let $P_n(c)$ be the probability that all of the selected clauses are simultaneously satisfiable. Prove that

$$\lim_{n\to\infty} P_n(c) = 1 - (1-e^{-c})(1-e^{-2c})(1-e^{-4c})(1-e^{-8c})\ldots.$$

▶ **51.** [*22*] A great many two-player games can be defined by specifying a directed graph in which each vertex represents a game position. There are two players, Alice and Bob, who construct an oriented path by starting at a particular vertex and taking turns to extend the path, one arc at a time. Before the game starts, each vertex has either been marked A (meaning that Alice wins), or marked B (meaning that Bob wins), or marked C (meaning that the cat wins), or left unmarked.

When the path reaches a vertex v marked A or B, that player wins. The game stops without a winner if v has been visited before, with the same player to move. If v is marked C, the currently active player has the option of accepting a draw; otherwise he or she must choose an outgoing arc to extend the path, and the other player becomes active. (If v is an unmarked vertex with out-degree zero, the active player loses.)

Associating four propositional variables $A^+(v)$, $A^-(v)$, $B^+(v)$, and $B^-(v)$ with every vertex v of the graph, explain how to construct a set of definite Horn clauses such that $A^+(v)$ is in the core if and only if Alice can force a win when the path starts at v and she moves first; $A^-(v)$ is in the core if and only if Bob can force her to lose in that game; $B^+(v)$ and $B^-(v)$ are similar to $A^+(v)$ and $A^-(v)$, but with roles reversed.

52. [*25*] (*Boolean games.*) Any Boolean function $f(x_1, \ldots, x_n)$ leads to a game called "two steps forward or one step back," in the following way: There are two players, 0 and 1, who repeatedly assign values to the variables x_j; player y tries to make $f(x_1, \ldots, x_n)$ equal to y. Initially all variables are unassigned, and the position marker m is zero. Players take turns, and the currently active player either sets $m \leftarrow m+2$ (if $m+2 \le n$) or $m \leftarrow m-1$ (if $m-1 \ge 1$), then sets

$$\begin{cases} x_m \leftarrow 0 \text{ or } 1, & \text{if } x_m \text{ was not previously assigned;} \\ x_m \leftarrow \bar{x}_m, & \text{if } x_m \text{ was previously assigned.} \end{cases}$$

The game is over as soon as a value has been assigned to all variables; then $f(x_1, \ldots, x_n)$ is the winner. A draw is declared if the same state (including the value of m) is reached twice. Notice that at most four moves are possible at any time.

Study examples of this game when $2 \le n \le 9$, in the following four cases:

a) $f(x_1, \ldots, x_n) = [x_1 \ldots x_n < x_n \ldots x_1]$ (in lexicographic order);

b) $f(x_1, \ldots, x_n) = x_1 \oplus \cdots \oplus x_n$;

c) $f(x_1, \ldots, x_n) = [x_1 \ldots x_n \text{ contains no two consecutive 1s}]$;

d) $f(x_1, \ldots, x_n) = [(x_1 \ldots x_n)_2 \text{ is prime}]$.

53. [*23*] Show that the impossible comedy festival of (37) *can* be scheduled if a change is made to the requirements of only (a) Tomlin; (b) Unwin; (c) Vegas; (d) Xie; (e) Yankovic; (f) Zany.

54. [*20*] Let $S = \{u_1, u_2, \ldots, u_k\}$ be the set of literals in some strong component of a digraph that corresponds to a 2CNF formula as in Fig. 6. Show that S contains both a variable and its complement if and only if $u_j = \bar{u}_1$ for some j with $2 \le j \le k$.

▶ **55.** [*30*] Call $f(x_1, \ldots, x_n)$ a *renamed Horn function* if there are Boolean constants $y_1, \ldots, y_n$ such that $f(x_1 \oplus y_1, \ldots, x_n \oplus y_n)$ is a Horn function.
     a) Given $f(x_1, \ldots, x_n)$ in CNF, explain how to construct $g(y_1, \ldots, y_n)$ in 2CNF so that the clauses of $f(x_1 \oplus y_1, \ldots, x_n \oplus y_n)$ are Horn clauses if and only if $g(y_1, \ldots, y_n) = 1$.
     b) Design an algorithm that decides in $O(m)$ steps whether or not all clauses of a given CNF of length m can be converted into Horn clauses by complementing some subset of the variables.

▶ **56.** [*20*] The satisfiability problem for a Boolean function $f(x_1, x_2, \ldots, x_n)$ can be stated formally as the question of whether or not the quantified formula

$$\exists x_1 \exists x_2 \ldots \exists x_n \, f(x_1, x_2, \ldots, x_n)$$

is true; here '$\exists x_j \, \alpha$' means, "There exists a Boolean value x_j such that α holds."
     A much more general evaluation problem arises when we replace one or more of the existential quantifiers $\exists x_j$ by the universal quantifier $\forall x_j$, where '$\forall x_j \, \alpha$' means, "for all Boolean values x_j, α holds."
     Which of the eight quantified formulas $\exists x \, \exists y \, \exists z \, f(x, y, z)$, $\exists x \, \exists y \, \forall z \, f(x, y, z)$, $\ldots$, $\forall x \, \forall y \, \forall z \, f(x, y, z)$ are true when $f(x, y, z) = (x \vee y) \wedge (\bar{x} \vee z) \wedge (y \vee \bar{z})$?

▶ **57.** [*30*] (B. Aspvall, M. F. Plass, and R. E. Tarjan.) Continuing exercise 56, design an algorithm that decides in linear time whether or not a given fully quantified formula $f(x_1, \ldots, x_n)$ is true, when f is any formula in 2CNF (any conjunction of Krom clauses).

▶ **58.** [*37*] Continuing exercise 57, design an efficient algorithm that decides whether or not a given fully quantified conjunction of *Horn* clauses is true.

▶ **59.** [*M20*] (D. Pehoushek and R. Fraer, 1997.) If the truth table for $f(x_1, x_2, \ldots, x_n)$ has a 1 in exactly k places, show that exactly k of the fully quantified formulas $Q x_1 \, Q x_2 \, \ldots \, Q x_n \, f(x_1, x_2, \ldots, x_n)$ are true, when each Q is either $\exists$ or $\forall$.

60. [*12*] Which of the following expressions yield the median $\langle xyz \rangle$, as defined in (43)?
(a) $(x \wedge y) \oplus (y \wedge z) \oplus (x \wedge z)$. (b) $(x \vee y) \oplus (y \vee z) \oplus (x \vee z)$. (c) $(x \oplus y) \wedge (y \oplus z) \wedge (x \oplus z)$.
(d) $(x \equiv y) \oplus (y \equiv z) \oplus (x \equiv z)$. (e) $(x \bar\wedge y) \wedge (y \bar\wedge z) \wedge (x \bar\wedge z)$. (f) $(x \bar\wedge y) \vee (y \bar\wedge z) \vee (x \bar\wedge z)$.

61. [*13*] True or false: If $\circ$ is any one of the Boolean binary operations in Table 1, we have the distributive law $w \circ \langle xyz \rangle = \langle (w \circ x)(w \circ y)(w \circ z) \rangle$.

62. [*25*] (C. Schensted.) If $f(x_1, \ldots, x_n)$ is a monotone Boolean function and $n \geq 3$, prove the median expansion formula

$$f(x_1, \ldots, x_n) = \langle f(x_1, x_1, x_3, x_4, \ldots, x_n) \, f(x_1, x_2, x_2, x_4, \ldots, x_n) \, f(x_3, x_2, x_3, x_4, \ldots, x_n) \rangle.$$

63. [*20*] Equation (49) shows how to compute the median of five elements via medians of three. Conversely, can we compute $\langle xyz \rangle$ with a subroutine for medians of five?

64. [*23*] (S. B. Akers, Jr.) (a) Prove that a Boolean function $f(x_1, \ldots, x_n)$ is monotone and self-dual if and only if it satisfies the following condition:

For all $x = x_1 \ldots x_n$ and $y = y_1 \ldots y_n$ there exists k such that $f(x) = x_k$ and $f(y) = y_k$.

(b) Suppose f is undefined for certain values, but the stated condition holds whenever both $f(x)$ and $f(y)$ are defined. Show that there is a monotone self-dual Boolean function g for which $g(x) = f(x)$ whenever $f(x)$ is defined.

▶ **65.** [*M21*] Any subset X of $\{1, 2, \ldots, n\}$ corresponds to a binary vector $x = x_1 x_2 \ldots x_n$ via the rule $x_j = [j \in X]$. And any family $\mathcal{F}$ of such subsets corresponds to a Boolean function $f(x) = f(x_1, x_2, \ldots, x_n)$ of n variables, via the rule $f(x) = [X \in \mathcal{F}]$. Therefore every statement about families of subsets corresponds to a statement about Boolean functions, and vice versa.

A family $\mathcal{F}$ is called *intersecting* if $X \cap Y \neq \emptyset$ whenever $X, Y \in \mathcal{F}$. An intersecting family that loses this property whenever we try to add another subset is said to be *maximal*. Prove that $\mathcal{F}$ is a maximal intersecting family if and only if the corresponding Boolean function f is monotone and self-dual.

▶ **66.** [*M25*] A *coterie* of $\{1, \ldots, n\}$ is a family $\mathcal{C}$ of subsets called *quorums*, which have the following properties whenever $Q \in \mathcal{C}$ and $Q' \in \mathcal{C}$: (i) $Q \cap Q' \neq \emptyset$; (ii) $Q \subseteq Q'$ implies $Q = Q'$. Coterie $\mathcal{C}$ *dominates* coterie $\mathcal{C}'$ if $\mathcal{C} \neq \mathcal{C}'$ and if, for every $Q' \in \mathcal{C}'$, there is a $Q \in \mathcal{C}$ with $Q \subseteq Q'$. For example, the coterie $\{\{1,2\},\{2,3\}\}$ is dominated by $\{\{1,2\},\{1,3\},\{2,3\}\}$ and also by $\{\{2\}\}$. [Coteries were introduced in classic papers by L. Lamport, *CACM* **21** (1978), 558–565; H. Garcia-Molina and D. Barbara, *JACM* **32** (1985), 841–860. They have numerous applications to distributed system protocols, including mutual exclusion, data replication, and name servers. In these applications $\mathcal{C}$ is preferred to any coterie that it dominates.]

Prove that $\mathcal{C}$ is a nondominated coterie if and only if its quorums are the index sets of variables in the prime implicants of a monotone self-dual Boolean function $f(x_1, \ldots, x_n)$. (Thus Table 2 illustrates the nondominated coteries on $\{1, 2, 3, 4\}$.)

▶ **67.** [*M30*] (J. W. Milnor and C. Schensted.) A triangular grid of order n, illustrated here for $n = 3$, contains $(n+2)(n+1)/2$ points with nonnegative "barycentric coordinates" xyz, where $x+y+z = n$. Two points are adjacent if they differ by ± 1 in exactly two coordinate positions. A point is said to lie on the x side if its x coordinate is zero, on the y side if its y coordinate is zero, or on the z side if its z coordinate is zero; thus each side contains $n+1$ points. If $n > 0$, a point lies on two different sides if and only if it occupies one of the three corner positions.

A "Y" is a connected set of points with at least one point on each side. Suppose each vertex of a triangular grid is covered with a white stone or a black stone. For example, the 52 black stones in

contain a (somewhat distorted) Y; but if any of them is changed from black to white, there is a white Y instead. A moment's thought makes it intuitively clear that, in any placement, the black stones contain a Y if and only if the white stones do not.

We can represent the color of each stone by a Boolean variable, with 0 for white and 1 for black. Let $Y(t) = 1$ if and only if there's a black Y, where t is a triangular grid comprising all the Boolean variables. This function Y is clearly monotone; and the intuitive claim made in the preceding paragraph is equivalent to saying that Y is also self-dual. The purpose of this exercise is to prove the claim rigorously, using median algebra.

Given $a, b, c \geq 0$, let t_{abc} be the triangular subgrid containing all points whose coordinates xyz satisfy $x \geq a$, $y \geq b$, $z \geq c$. For example, t_{001} denotes all points except those on the z side (the bottom row). Notice that, if $a + b + c = n$, t_{abc} is the single point with coordinates abc; and in general, t_{abc} is a triangular grid of order $n - a - b - c$.

a) If $n > 0$, let t^* be the triangular grid of order $n - 1$ defined by the rule

$$t^*_{xyz} = \langle t_{(x+1)yz} t_{x(y+1)z} t_{xy(z+1)} \rangle, \qquad \text{for } x + y + z = n - 1.$$

Prove that $Y(t) = Y(t^*)$. [In other words, t^* condenses each small triangle of stones by taking the median of their colors. Repeating this process defines a *pyramid* of stones, with the top stone black if and only if there is a black Y at the bottom. It's fun to apply this condensation principle to the twisted Y above.]

b) Prove that, if $n > 0$, $Y(t) = \langle Y(t_{100}) Y(t_{010}) Y(t_{001}) \rangle$.

68. [*46*] The just-barely-Y configuration shown in the previous exercise has 52 black stones. What is the largest number of black stones possible in such a configuration? (That is, how many variables can there be in a prime implicant of the function $Y(t)$?)

▶ **69.** [*M26*] (C. Schensted.) Exercise 67 expresses the Y function in terms of medians. Conversely, let $f(x_1, \ldots, x_n)$ be any monotone self-dual Boolean function with $m + 1$ prime implicants $p_0, p_1, \ldots, p_m$. Prove that $f(x_1, \ldots, x_n) = Y(T)$, where T is any triangular grid of order $m - 1$ in which T_{abc} is a variable common to p_a and p_{a+b+1}, for $a + b + c = m - 1$. For example, when $f(w, x, y, z) = \langle xwywz \rangle$ we have $m = 3$ and

$$f(w, x, y, z) = (w \wedge x) \vee (w \wedge y) \vee (w \wedge z) \vee (x \wedge y \wedge z) = Y\left(\begin{smallmatrix} & & w & & \\ & w & & w & \\ x & & y & & z \end{smallmatrix} \right).$$

▶ **70.** [*M20*] (A. Meyerowitz, 1989.) Given any monotone self-dual Boolean function $f(x) = f(x_1, \ldots, x_n)$, choose any prime implicant $x_{j_1} \wedge \cdots \wedge x_{j_s}$ and let

$$g(x) = (f(x) \wedge [x \neq t]) \vee [x = \bar{t}],$$

where $t = t_1 \ldots t_n$ is the bit vector that has 1s in positions $\{j_1, \ldots, j_s\}$. Prove that $g(x)$ is also monotone and self-dual. (Notice that $g(x)$ is equal to $f(x)$ except at the two points t and $\bar{t}$.)

▶ **71.** [*M21*] Given the axioms (50), (51), and (52) of a median algebra, prove that the long distributive law (54) is a consequence of the shorter law (53).

72. [*M22*] Derive (58), (59), and (60) from the median laws (50)–(53).

73. [*M32*] (S. P. Avann.) Given a median algebra M, whose intervals are defined by (57) and whose corresponding median graph is defined by (61), let $d(u, v)$ denote the distance from u to v. Also let '$[uxv]$' stand for the statement "x lies on a shortest path from u to v."

a) Prove that $[uxv]$ holds if and only if $d(u, v) = d(u, x) + d(x, v)$.

b) Suppose $x \in [u \, .. \, v]$ and $u \in [x \, .. \, y]$, where $x \neq u$ and $y \,—\, v$ is an edge of the graph. Show that $x \,—\, u$ is also an edge.

c) If $x \in [u \, .. \, v]$, prove $[uxv]$, by induction on $d(u, v)$.

d) Conversely, prove that $[uxv]$ implies $x \in [u \, .. \, v]$.

74. [*M21*] In a median algebra, show that $w = \langle xyz \rangle$ whenever we have $w \in [x \, .. \, y]$, $w \in [x \, .. \, z]$, and $w \in [y \, .. \, z]$ according to definition (57).

▶ **75.** [*M36*] (M. Sholander, 1954.) Suppose M is a set of points with a betweenness relation "x lies between u and v," symbolized by $[uxv]$, which satisfies the following three axioms:

i) If $[uvu]$ then $u = v$.

ii) If $[uxv]$ and $[xyu]$ then $[vyu]$.

iii) Given x, y, and z, exactly one point $w = \langle xyz \rangle$ satisfies $[xwy]$, $[xwz]$, and $[ywz]$.

The object of this exercise is to prove that M is a median algebra.

a) Prove the majority law $\langle xxy \rangle = x$, Eq. (50).

b) Prove the commutative law $\langle xyz \rangle = \langle xzy \rangle = \cdots = \langle zyx \rangle$, Eq. (51).

c) Prove that $[uxv]$ if and only if $x = \langle uxv \rangle$.

d) If $[uxy]$ and $[uyv]$, prove that $[xyv]$.

e) If $[uxv]$ and $[uyz]$ and $[vyz]$, prove that $[xyz]$. *Hint:* Construct the points $w = \langle yuv \rangle$, $p = \langle wux \rangle$, $q = \langle wvx \rangle$, $r = \langle pxz \rangle$, $s = \langle qxz \rangle$, and $t = \langle rsz \rangle$.

f) Finally, deduce the short distributive law, Eq. (53): $\langle \langle xyz \rangle uv \rangle = \langle x \langle yuv \rangle \langle zuv \rangle \rangle$.

76. [*M33*] Derive the betweenness axioms (i), (ii), and (iii) of exercise 75, starting from the three median axioms (50), (51), and (52), letting $[uxv]$ be an abbreviation for "$x = \langle uxv \rangle$." Do not use the distributive law (53). *Hint:* See exercise 74.

77. [*M28*] Let G be a median graph containing the edge $r \mathbin{\rule[0.5ex]{1.2em}{0.4pt}} s$. For each edge $u \mathbin{\rule[0.5ex]{1.2em}{0.4pt}} v$, call u an *early neighbor* of v if and only if r is closer to u than to v. Partition the vertices into "left" and "right" parts, where left vertices are closer to r than to s and right vertices are closer to s than to r. Each right vertex v has a *rank*, which is the shortest distance from v to a left vertex. Similarly, each left vertex u has rank $1 - d$, where d is the shortest distance from u to a right vertex. Thus u has rank zero if it is adjacent to a right vertex, otherwise its rank is negative. Vertex r clearly has rank 0, and s has rank 1.

a) Show that every vertex of rank 1 is adjacent to exactly one vertex of rank 0.

b) Show that the set of all right vertices is convex.

c) Show that the set of all vertices with rank 1 is convex.

d) Prove that steps I3–I9 of Subroutine I correctly mark all vertices of ranks 1 and 2.

e) Prove that Algorithm H is correct.

▶ **78.** [*M26*] If the vertex v is examined k times in step I4 during the execution of Algorithm H, prove that the graph has at least 2^k vertices. *Hint:* There are k ways to start a shortest path from v to a; thus at least k 1s appear in $l(v)$.

▶ **79.** [*M27*] (R. L. Graham.) An induced *subgraph of a hypercube* is a graph whose vertices v can be labeled with bit strings $l(v)$ in such a way that $u \mathbin{\rule[0.5ex]{1.2em}{0.4pt}} v$ if and only if $l(u)$ and $l(v)$ differ in exactly one bit position. (Each label has the same length.)

a) One way to define an n-vertex subgraph of a hypercube is to let $l(v)$ be the binary representation of v, for $0 \le v < n$. Show that this subgraph has exactly $f(n) = \sum_{k=0}^{n-1} \nu(k)$ edges, where $\nu(k)$ is the sideways addition function.

b) Prove that $f(n) \le n \lceil \lg n \rceil / 2$.

c) Prove that no n-vertex subgraph of a hypercube has more than $f(n)$ edges.

80. [*27*] A *partial cube* is an "isometric" subgraph of a hypercube, namely a subgraph in which the distances between vertices are the same as they are in the full graph. The vertices of a partial cube can therefore be labeled in such a way that the distance from u to v is the "Hamming distance" between $l(u)$ and $l(v)$, namely $\nu(l(u) \oplus l(v))$. Algorithm H shows that every median graph is a partial cube.

a) Find an induced subgraph of the 4-cube that isn't a partial cube.

b) Give an example of a partial cube that isn't a median graph.

81. [*16*] Is every median graph bipartite?

82. [*25*] (*Incremental changes in service.*) Given a sequence of vertices $(v_0, v_1, \ldots, v_t)$ in a graph G, consider the problem of finding another sequence $(u_0, u_1, \ldots, u_t)$ for which $u_0 = v_0$ and the sum

$$\big(d(u_0, u_1) + d(u_1, u_2) + \cdots + d(u_{t-1}, u_t)\big) + \big(d(u_1, v_1) + d(u_2, v_2) + \cdots + d(u_t, v_t)\big)$$

is minimized, where $d(u, v)$ denotes the distance from u to v. (Each v_k can be regarded as a request for a resource needed at that vertex; a server moves to u_k as those requests are handled in sequence.) Prove that if G is a median graph, we get an optimum solution by choosing $u_k = \langle u_{k-1} v_k v_{k+1} \rangle$ for $0 < k < t$, and $u_t = v_t$.

▸ **83.** [*38*] Generalizing exercise 82, find an efficient way to minimize

$$(d(u_0, u_1) + d(u_1, u_2) + \cdots + d(u_{t-1}, u_t)) + \rho(d(u_1, v_1) + d(u_2, v_2) + \cdots + d(u_t, v_t))$$

in a median graph, given any positive ratio ρ.

84. [*30*] Write a program to find all monotone self-dual Boolean functions of five variables. What are the edges of the corresponding median graph? (Table 2 illustrates the four-variable case.)

▸ **85.** [*M22*] Theorem S tells us that every formula in 2CNF corresponds to a median set; therefore every antisymmetric digraph such as Fig. 6 also corresponds to a median set. Precisely which of those digraphs correspond to *reduced* median sets?

86. [*15*] If v, w, x, y, and z belong to a median set X, does their five-element median $\langle vwxyz \rangle$, computed componentwise, always belong to X?

87. [*24*] What CI-net does the proof of Theorem F construct for the free tree (63)?

88. [*M21*] We can use parallel computation to condense the network (74) into

by letting each module act at the earliest possible time. Prove that, although the network constructed in the proof of Theorem F may contain $\Omega(t^2)$ modules, it always requires at most $O(t \log t)$ levels of delay.

89. [*24*] When the construction (73) appends a new cluster of modules to enforce the condition $u \to v$, for some literals u and v, prove that it preserves all previously enforced conditions $u' \to v'$.

▸ **90.** [*21*] Construct a CI-net with input bits $x_1 \ldots x_t$ and output bits $y_1 \ldots y_t$, where $y_1 = \cdots = y_{t-1} = 0$ and $y_t = x_1 \oplus \cdots \oplus x_t$. Try for only $O(\log t)$ levels of delay.

91. [*46*] Can a retraction mapping for the labels of every median graph of dimension t be computed by a CI-net that has only $O(\log t)$ levels of delay? [This question is motivated by the existence of asymptotically optimum networks for the analogous problem of sorting; see M. Ajtai, J. Komlós, and E. Szemerédi, *Combinatorica* **3** (1983), 1–19.]

92. [*46*] Can a CI-net sort n Boolean inputs with fewer modules than a "pure" sorting network that has no inverters?

93. [*M20*] Prove that every retract X of a graph G is an isometric subgraph of G. (In other words, distances in X are the same as in G; see exercise 80.)

94. [*M21*] Prove that every retract X of a hypercube is a set of median labels, if we suppress coordinates that are constant for all $x \in X$.

95. [*M25*] True or false: The set of all outputs produced by a comparator-inverter network, when the inputs range over all possible bit strings, is always a median set.

96. [*HM25*] Instead of insisting that the constants w_1, w_2, $\ldots$, w_n, and t in (75) must be integers, we could allow them to be arbitrary real numbers. Would that increase the number of threshold functions?

97. [*10*] What median/majority functions arise in (8₁) when $n = 2$, $w_1 = w_2 = 1$, and $t = -1, 0, 1, 2, 3,$ or 4?

98. [*M23*] Prove that any self-dual threshold function can be expressed in the form

$$f(x_1, x_2, \ldots, x_n) = [v_1 y_1 + \cdots + v_n y_n > 0],$$

where each y_j is either x_j or $\bar{x}_j$. For example, $2x_1 + 3x_2 + 5x_3 + 7x_4 + 11x_5 + 13x_6 \geq 21$ if and only if $2x_1 + 3x_2 + 5x_3 - 7\bar{x}_4 + 11x_5 - 13\bar{x}_6 > 0$.

▶ **99.** [*20*] (J. E. Mezei, 1961.) Prove that

$$\langle\langle x_1 \ldots x_{2s-1}\rangle y_1 \ldots y_{2t-2}\rangle = \langle x_1 \ldots x_{2s-1} y_1^s \ldots y_{2t-2}^s\rangle.$$

100. [*20*] True or false: If $f(x_1, \ldots, x_n)$ is a threshold function, so are the functions $f(x_1, \ldots, x_n) \wedge x_{n+1}$ and $f(x_1, \ldots, x_n) \vee x_{n+1}$.

101. [*M23*] The *Fibonacci threshold function* $F_n(x_1, \ldots, x_n)$ is defined by the formula $\langle x_1^{F_1} x_2^{F_2} \ldots x_{n-1}^{F_{n-1}} x_n^{F_{n-2}}\rangle$ when $n \geq 3$; for example, $F_7(x_1, \ldots, x_7) = \langle x_1 x_2 x_3^2 x_4^3 x_5^5 x_6^8 x_7^5\rangle$.
   a) What are the prime implicants of $F_n(x_1, \ldots, x_n)$?
   b) Find an orthogonal DNF for $F_n(x_1, \ldots, x_n)$ (see exercise 35).
   c) Express $F_n(x_1, \ldots, x_n)$ in terms of the Y function (see exercises 67 and 69).

102. [*M21*] The *self-dualization* of a Boolean function is defined by the formulas

$$\hat{f}(x_0, x_1, \ldots, x_n) = (x_0 \wedge f(x_1, \ldots, x_n)) \vee (\bar{x}_0 \wedge \overline{f(\bar{x}_1, \ldots, \bar{x}_n)})$$
$$= (\bar{x}_0 \vee f(x_1, \ldots, x_n)) \wedge (x_0 \vee \overline{f(\bar{x}_1, \ldots, \bar{x}_n)}).$$

   a) If $f(x_1, \ldots, x_n)$ is any Boolean function, prove that $\hat{f}$ is self-dual.
   b) Prove that $\hat{f}$ is a threshold function if and only if f is a threshold function.

103. [*HM25*] Explain how to use linear programming to test whether or not a monotone, self-dual Boolean function is a threshold function, given a list of its prime implicants. Also, if it *is* a threshold function, explain how to minimize the size of its representation as a majority function $\langle x_1^{w_1} \ldots x_n^{w_n}\rangle$.

104. [*25*] Apply the method of exercise 103 to find the shortest representations of the following threshold functions as majority functions: (a) $\langle x_1^2 x_2^3 x_3^5 x_4^7 x_5^{11} x_6^{13} x_7^{17} x_8^{19}\rangle$; (b) $[(x_1 x_2 x_3 x_4)_2 \geq t]$, for $0 \leq t \leq 16$ (17 cases); (c) $\langle x_1^{29} x_2^{25} x_3^{19} x_4^{15} x_5^{12} x_6^8 x_7^7 x_8^3 x_9^3 x_{10}\rangle$.

105. [*M25*] Show that the Fibonacci threshold function in exercise 101 has no shorter representation as a majority function than the one used to define it.

▶ **106.** [*M25*] The median-of-three operation $\langle x\bar{y}\bar{z}\rangle$ is true if and only if $x \geq y + z$.
   a) Generalizing, show that we can test the condition $(x_1 x_2 \ldots x_n)_2 \geq (y_1 y_2 \ldots y_n)_2 + z$ by performing a median of $2^{n+1} - 1$ Boolean variables.
   b) Prove that no median of fewer than $2^{n+1} - 1$ will suffice for this problem.

107. [*17*] Calculate $N(f)$ and $\Sigma(f)$ for the 16 functions in Table 1. (See Theorem T.)

108. [*M21*] Let $g(x_0, x_1, \ldots, x_n)$ be a self-dual function; thus $N(g) = 2^n$ in the notation of Theorem T. Express $N(f)$ and $\Sigma(f)$ in terms of $\Sigma(g)$, when $f(x_1, \ldots, x_n)$ is (a) $g(0, x_1, \ldots, x_n)$; (b) $g(1, x_1, \ldots, x_n)$.

109. [*M25*] The binary string $\alpha = a_1 \ldots a_n$ is said to *majorize* the binary string $\beta = b_1 \ldots b_n$, written $\alpha \succeq \beta$ or $\beta \preceq \alpha$, if $a_1 + \cdots + a_k \geq b_1 + \cdots + b_k$ for $0 \leq k \leq n$.
   a) Let $\bar{\alpha} = \bar{a}_1 \ldots \bar{a}_n$. Show that $\alpha \succeq \beta$ if and only if $\bar{\beta} \succeq \bar{\alpha}$.

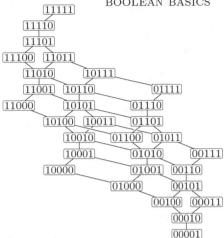

Fig. 8. The binary majorization lattice for strings of length 5. (See exercise 109.)

b) Show that any two binary strings of length n have a greatest lower bound $\alpha \wedge \beta$, which has the property that $\alpha \succeq \gamma$ and $\beta \succeq \gamma$ if and only if $\alpha \wedge \beta \succeq \gamma$. Explain how to compute $\alpha \wedge \beta$, given α and β.

c) Similarly, explain how to compute a least upper bound $\alpha \vee \beta$, with the property that $\gamma \succeq \alpha$ and $\gamma \succeq \beta$ if and only if $\gamma \succeq \alpha \vee \beta$.

d) True or false: $\alpha \wedge (\beta \vee \gamma) = (\alpha \wedge \beta) \vee (\alpha \wedge \gamma)$; $\alpha \vee (\beta \wedge \gamma) = (\alpha \vee \beta) \wedge (\alpha \vee \gamma)$.

e) Say that α *covers* β if $\alpha \succeq \beta$ and $\alpha \neq \beta$, and if $\alpha \succeq \gamma \succeq \beta$ implies that we have either $\gamma = \alpha$ or $\gamma = \beta$. For example, Fig. 8 illustrates the covering relations between binary strings of length 5. Find a simple way to describe the strings that are covered by a given binary string.

f) Show that every path $\alpha = \alpha_0, \alpha_1, \ldots, \alpha_r = 0 \ldots 0$ from a given string α to $0 \ldots 0$, where α_{j-1} covers α_j for $1 \leq j \leq r$, has the same length $r = r(\alpha)$.

g) Let $m(\alpha)$ be the number of strings β with $\beta \succeq \alpha$. Prove that $m(1\alpha) = m(\alpha)$ and $m(0\alpha) = m(\alpha) + m(\alpha')$, where α' is α with its leftmost 1 (if any) changed to 0.

h) How many strings α of length n satisfy $\bar{\alpha} \succeq \alpha$?

110. [*M23*] A Boolean function is called *regular* if $x \preceq y$ implies that $f(x) \leq f(y)$ for all vectors x and y, where $\preceq$ is the majorization relation in exercise 109. Prove or disprove the following statements:

a) Every regular function is monotone.

b) If f is a threshold function (75) for which $w_1 \geq w_2 \geq \cdots \geq w_n$, then f is regular.

c) If f is as in (b) and $\Sigma(f) = (s_1, \ldots, s_n)$, then $s_1 \geq s_2 \geq \cdots \geq s_n$.

d) Suppose f is a pure majority function, namely a threshold function of the form (86) with $a = b = 0$. Then $s_1 \geq s_2 \geq \cdots \geq s_n$ implies that $w_1 \geq w_2 \geq \cdots \geq w_n$.

111. [*M36*] An *optimum coterie* for a system with working probabilities $(p_1, \ldots, p_n)$ is a coterie that corresponds to a monotone self-dual function with maximum availability, among all monotone self-dual functions with n variables. (See exercises 14 and 66.)

a) Prove that if $1 \geq p_1 \geq \cdots \geq p_n \geq \frac{1}{2}$, at least one self-dual function with maximum availability is a regular function. Describe such a function.

b) Furthermore, it suffices to test the optimality of a regular self-dual function f at points y of the binary majorization lattice for which $f(y) = 1$ but $f(x) = 0$ for all x covered by y.

c) What coterie is optimum when some probabilities are $< \frac{1}{2}$?

▶ **112.** [*M37*] (J. Håstad.) If $f(x_1, x_2, \ldots, x_m)$ is a Boolean function, let $M(f)$ be its representation as a multilinear polynomial with integer coefficients (see exercise 12). Arrange the terms in this polynomial by using Chase's sequence $\alpha_0 = 00\ldots0$, $\alpha_1 = 10\ldots0$, $\ldots$, $\alpha_{2^m-1} = 11\ldots1$ to order the exponents; Chase's sequence, obtained by concatenating the sequences A_{m0}, $A_{(m-1)1}$, $\ldots$, A_{0m} of 7.2.1.3–(35), has the nice property that α_j is identical to α_{j+1} except for a slight change, either $0 \to 1$ or $01 \to 10$ or $001 \to 100$ or $10 \to 01$ or $100 \to 001$. For example, Chase's sequence is

$$0000, 1000, 0010, 0001, 0100, 1100, 1010, 1001, 0011, 0101, 0110, 1110, 1101, 1011, 0111, 1111$$

when $m = 4$, corresponding to the respective terms $1, x_1, x_3, x_4, x_2, x_1x_2, \ldots, x_2x_3x_4$, $x_1x_2x_3x_4$; so the relevant representation of, say, $((x_1 \oplus \bar{x}_2) \wedge x_3) \vee (x_1 \wedge \bar{x}_3 \wedge x_4)$ is

$$x_3 - x_1x_3 + x_1x_4 - x_2x_3 + 2x_1x_2x_3 - x_1x_3x_4$$

when the terms have been arranged in this order. Now let

$$F(f) = [\text{the most significant coefficient of } M(f) \text{ is positive}].$$

For example, the most significant (final) nonzero term of $((x_1 \oplus \bar{x}_2) \wedge x_3) \vee (x_1 \wedge \bar{x}_3 \wedge x_4)$ is $-x_1x_3x_4$ in Chase's ordering, so $F(f) = 0$ in this case.

    a) Determine $F(f)$ for each of the 16 functions in Table 1.

    b) Show that $F(f)$ is a threshold function of the $n = 2^m$ entries $\{f_{0\ldots00}, f_{0\ldots01}, \ldots, f_{1\ldots11}\}$ of the truth table for f. Write this function out explicitly when $m = 2$.

    c) Prove that, when m is large, all the weights in any threshold representation of F must be huge: Their absolute values must all exceed

$$\frac{3^{\binom{m}{3}} 7^{\binom{m}{4}} 15^{\binom{m}{5}} \cdots (2^{m-1}-1)^{\binom{m}{m}}}{n}(1 - O(n^{-1})) = 2^{mn/2 - n - 2(3/2)^m/\ln 2 + O((5/4)^m)}.$$

    Hint: Consider discrete Fourier transforms of the truth table entries.

113. [*24*] Show that the following three threshold operations suffice to evaluate the function $S_{2,3,6,8,9}(x_1, \ldots, x_{12})$ in (91):

$$g_1(x_1, \ldots, x_{12}) = [\nu x \geq 6] = \langle 1x_1 \ldots x_{12} \rangle;$$
$$g_2(x_1, \ldots, x_{12}) = [\nu x - 6g_1 \geq 2] = \langle 1^3 x_1 \ldots x_{12} \bar{g}_1^6 \rangle;$$
$$g_3(x_1, \ldots, x_{12}) = [-2\nu x + 13g_1 + 7g_2 \geq 1] = \langle 0^5 \bar{x}_1^2 \ldots \bar{x}_{12}^2 g_1^{13} g_2^7 \rangle.$$

Also find a four-threshold scheme that evaluates $S_{1,3,5,8}(x_1, \ldots, x_{12})$.

114. [*20*] (D. A. Huffman.) What is the function $S_{3,6}(x, x, x, x, y, y, z)$?

115. [*M22*] Explain why (92) correctly computes the parity function $x_0 \oplus x_1 \oplus \cdots \oplus x_{2m}$.

▶ **116.** [*HM28*] (B. Dunham and R. Fridshal, 1957.) By considering symmetric functions, one can prove that Boolean functions of n variables might have many prime implicants.

    a) Suppose $0 \leq j \leq k \leq n$. For which symmetric functions $f(x_1, \ldots, x_n)$ is the term $x_1 \wedge \cdots \wedge x_j \wedge \bar{x}_{j+1} \wedge \cdots \wedge \bar{x}_k$ a prime implicant?

    b) How many prime implicants does the function $S_{3,4,5,6}(x_1, \ldots, x_9)$ have?

    c) Let $\hat{b}(n)$ be the maximum number of prime implicants, over all symmetric Boolean functions of n variables. Find a recurrence formula for $\hat{b}(n)$, and compute $\hat{b}(9)$.

    d) Prove that $\hat{b}(n) = \Theta(3^n/n)$.

    e) Show that, furthermore, there are symmetric functions $f(x_1, \ldots, x_n)$ for which both f and $\bar{f}$ have $\Theta(2^{3n/2}/n)$ prime implicants.

117. [*M26*] A disjunctive normal form is called *irredundant* if none of its implicants implies another. Let $b^*(n)$ be the maximum number of implicants in an irredundant DNF, over all Boolean functions of n variables. Find a simple formula for $b^*(n)$, and determine its asymptotic value.

118. [*29*] How many Boolean functions $f(x_1, x_2, x_3, x_4)$ have exactly m prime implicants, for $m = 0, 1, \ldots$?

119. [*M48*] Continuing the previous exercises, let $b(n)$ be the maximum number of prime implicants in a Boolean function of n variables. Clearly $\hat{b}(n) \le b(n) < b^*(n)$; what is the asymptotic value of $b(n)$?

120. [*23*] What is the shortest DNF for the symmetric functions (a) $x_1 \oplus x_2 \oplus \cdots \oplus x_n$? (b) $S_{0,1,3,4,6,7}(x_1, \ldots, x_7)$? (c) Prove that every Boolean function of n variables can be expressed as a DNF with at most 2^{n-1} prime implicants.

▶ **121.** [*M23*] The function $\langle 1(x_1 \oplus x_2)y_1 y_2 y_3 \rangle$ is partially symmetric, since it is symmetric in $\{x_1, x_2\}$ and in $\{y_1, y_2, y_3\}$, but not in all five variables $\{x_1, x_2, y_1, y_2, y_3\}$.
  a) Exactly how many Boolean functions $f(x_1, \ldots, x_m, y_1, \ldots, y_n)$ are symmetric in $\{x_1, \ldots, x_m\}$ and $\{y_1, \ldots, y_n\}$?
  b) How many of those functions are monotone?
  c) How many of those functions are self-dual?
  d) How many of those functions are monotone and self-dual?

122. [*M25*] Continuing exercises 110 and 121, find all Boolean functions $f(x_1, x_2, x_3, y_1, y_2, y_3, y_4, y_5, y_6)$ that are simultaneously symmetric in $\{x_1, x_2, x_3\}$, symmetric in $\{y_1, y_2, \ldots, y_6\}$, self-dual, and regular. Which of them are threshold functions?

123. [*46*] Determine the exact number of self-dual Boolean functions of ten variables that are threshold functions.

124. [*20*] Find a Boolean function of four variables that is equivalent to 767 other functions, under the ground rules of Table 5.

125. [*18*] Which of the function classes in (95) are canalizing?

126. [*23*] (a) Show that a Boolean function is canalizing if and only if its sets of prime implicants and prime clauses have a certain simple property. (b) Show that a Boolean function is canalizing if and only if its Chow parameters $N(f)$ and $\Sigma(f)$ have a certain simple property (see Theorem T). (c) Define the Boolean vectors

$$\vee(f) = \bigvee \{x \mid f(x) = 1\} \quad \text{and} \quad \wedge(f) = \bigwedge \{x \mid f(x) = 1\};$$

by analogy with the integer vector $\Sigma(f)$. Show that it's possible to decide whether or not f is canalizing, given only the four vectors $\vee(f)$, $\vee(\bar{f})$, $\wedge(f)$, and $\wedge(\bar{f})$.

127. [*M25*] Which canalizing functions are (a) self-dual? (b) definite Horn functions?

▶ **128.** [*20*] Find a noncanalizing $f(x_1, \ldots, x_n)$ that is true at exactly two points.

129. [*M25*] How many different canalizing functions of n variables exist?

130. [*M21*] According to Table 3, there are 168 monotone Boolean functions of four variables. But some of them, like $x \wedge y$, depend on only three variables or fewer.
  a) How many 4-variable monotone Boolean functions actually involve each variable?
  b) How many of those functions are distinct under permutation, as in Table 4?

131. [*HM42*] Table 3 makes it clear that there are many more Horn functions than Krom functions. What is the asymptotic number, as $n \to \infty$?

▶ **132.** [*HM30*] The Boolean function $g(x) = g(x_1, \ldots, x_n)$ is called *affine* if it can be written in the form $y_0 \oplus (x_1 \wedge y_1) \oplus \cdots \oplus (x_n \wedge y_n) = (y_0 + x \cdot y) \bmod 2$ for some Boolean constants $y_0, y_1, \ldots, y_n$.

   a) Given any Boolean function $f(x)$, show that some affine function agrees with $f(x)$ at $2^{n-1} + 2^{n/2-1}$ or more points x. *Hint:* Let $s(y) = \sum_x (-1)^{f(x)+x \cdot y}$, and prove that $\sum_y s(y) s(y \oplus z) = 2^{2n}[z = 0 \ldots 0]$ for all n-bit vectors z.

   b) The Boolean function $f(x)$ is called *bent* if no affine function agrees with it at more than $2^{n-1} + 2^{n/2-1}$ points. Prove that

$$(x_1 \wedge x_2) \oplus (x_3 \wedge x_4) \oplus \cdots \oplus (x_{n-1} \wedge x_n) \oplus h(x_2, x_4, \ldots, x_n)$$

is a bent function, when n is even and $h(y_1, y_2, \ldots, y_{n/2})$ is arbitrary.

   c) Prove that $f(x)$ is a bent function if and only if

$$\sum_x (f(x) \oplus f(x \oplus y)) = 2^{n-1} \qquad \text{for all } y \neq 0 \ldots 0.$$

   d) If a bent function $f(x_1, \ldots, x_n)$ is represented by a multilinear polynomial mod 2 as in (19), show that it never contains the term $x_1 \ldots x_r$ when $r > n/2 > 1$.

▶ **133.** [*20*] (Mark A. Smith, 1990.) Suppose we flip n independent coins to get n random bits, where the kth coin produces bit 1 with probability p_k. Find a way to choose $(p_1, \ldots, p_n)$ so that $f(x_1, \ldots, x_n) = 1$ with probability $(t_0 t_1 \ldots t_{2^n-1})_2/(2^{2^n}-1)$, where $t_0 t_1 \ldots t_{2^n-1}$ is the truth table of the Boolean function f. (Thus, n suitable random coins can generate a probability with 2^n-bit precision.)

> *By and large the minimization of switching components*
> *outweighs all other engineering considerations*
> *in designing economical logic circuits.*
> — H. A. CURTIS, *A New Approach to the Design of Switching Circuits* (1962)

> *He must be a great calculator indeed who succeeds.*
> *Simplify, simplify.*
> — HENRY D. THOREAU, *Walden; or, Life in the Woods* (1854)

7.1.2. Boolean Evaluation

Our next goal is to study the efficient evaluation of Boolean functions, much as we studied the evaluation of polynomials in Section 4.6.4. One natural way to investigate this topic is to consider chains of basic operations, analogous to the polynomial chains discussed in that section.

A *Boolean chain*, for functions of n variables $(x_1, \ldots, x_n)$, is a sequence $(x_{n+1}, \ldots, x_{n+r})$ with the property that each step combines two of the preceding steps:

$$x_i = x_{j(i)} \circ_i x_{k(i)}, \qquad \text{for } n+1 \leq i \leq n+r, \tag{1}$$

where $1 \leq j(i) < i$ and $1 \leq k(i) < i$, and where $\circ_i$ is one of the sixteen binary operators of Table 7.1.1–1. For example, when $n = 3$ the two chains

$$
\begin{aligned}
x_4 &= x_1 \wedge x_2 \\
x_5 &= \bar{x}_1 \wedge x_3 \qquad \text{and} \\
x_6 &= x_4 \vee x_5
\end{aligned}
\qquad\qquad
\begin{aligned}
x_4 &= x_2 \oplus x_3 \\
x_5 &= x_1 \wedge x_4 \\
x_6 &= x_3 \oplus x_5
\end{aligned}
\tag{2}
$$

both evaluate the "mux" or "if-then-else" function $x_6 = (x_1? \, x_2 \colon x_3)$, which takes the value x_2 or x_3 depending on whether x_1 is 1 (true) or 0 (false).

(Notice that the left-hand example in (2) uses the simplified notation '$x_5 = \bar{x}_1 \wedge x_3$' to specify the NOTBUT operation, instead of the form '$x_5 = x_1 \bar{\subset} x_3$' that appears in Table 7.1.1–1. The main point is that, regardless of notation, every step of a Boolean chain is a Boolean combination of two prior results.)

Boolean chains correspond naturally to electronic circuits, with each step in the chain corresponding to a "gate" that has two inputs and one output. Electrical engineers traditionally represent the Boolean chains of (2) by circuit diagrams such as

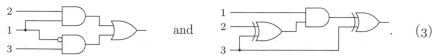

$$\text{and} \hspace{6em} . \hspace{2em} (3)$$

They need to design economical circuits that are subject to various technological constraints; for example, some gates might be more expensive than others, some outputs might need to be amplified if reused, the layout might need to be planar or nearly so, some paths might need to be short. But our chief concern in this book is software, not hardware, so we don't have to worry about such things. For our purposes, all gates have equal cost, and all outputs can be reused as often as desired. (Jargonwise, our Boolean chains boil down to circuits in which all gates have fanin 2 and unlimited fanout.)

Furthermore we shall depict Boolean chains as binary trees such as

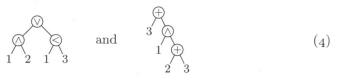

$$\text{and} \hspace{10em} (4)$$

instead of using circuit diagrams like (3). Such binary trees will have overlapping subtrees when intermediate steps of the chain are used more than once. Every internal node is labeled with a binary operator; external nodes are labeled with an integer k, representing the variable x_k. The label '$\ominus$' in the left tree of (4) stands for the NOTBUT operator, since $\bar{x} \wedge y = [x < y]$; similarly, the BUTNOT operator, $x \wedge \bar{y}$, can be represented by the node label '$\odot$'.

Several different Boolean chains might have the same tree diagram. For example, the left-hand tree of (4) also represents the chain

$$x_4 = \bar{x}_1 \wedge x_3, \hspace{2em} x_5 = x_1 \wedge x_2, \hspace{2em} x_6 = x_5 \vee x_4.$$

Any topological sorting of the tree nodes yields an equivalent chain.

Given a Boolean function f of n variables, we often want to find a Boolean chain such that $x_{n+r} = f(x_1, \ldots, x_n)$, where r is as small as possible. The *combinational complexity* $C(f)$ of a function f is the length of the shortest chain that computes it. To save excess verbiage, we will simply call $C(f)$ the "cost of f." The mux function in our examples above has cost 3, because one can show by exhaustive trials that it can't be produced by any Boolean chain of length 2.

The DNF and CNF representations of f, which we studied in Section 7.1.1, rarely tell us much about $C(f)$, since substantially more efficient schemes of calculation are usually possible. For example, in the discussion following 7.1.1–(30) we found that the more-or-less random function of four variables whose truth table is 1100 1001 0000 1111 has no DNF expression shorter than

$$(\bar{x}_1 \wedge \bar{x}_2 \wedge \bar{x}_3) \vee (\bar{x}_1 \wedge \bar{x}_3 \wedge \bar{x}_4) \vee (x_2 \wedge x_3 \wedge x_4) \vee (x_1 \wedge x_2). \qquad (5)$$

This formula corresponds to a Boolean chain of 10 steps. But that function can also be expressed more cleverly as

$$\big(((x_2 \wedge \bar{x}_4) \oplus \bar{x}_3) \wedge \bar{x}_1\big) \oplus x_2, \qquad (6)$$

so its complexity is at most 4.

How can nonobvious formulas like (6) be discovered? We will see that a computer can find the best chains for functions of four variables without doing an enormous amount of work. Still, the results can be quite startling, even for people who have had considerable experience with Boolean algebra. Typical examples of this phenomenon can be seen in Fig. 9, which illustrates the four-variable functions that are perhaps of greatest general interest, namely the functions that are symmetric under all permutations of their variables.

Consider, for example, the function $S_2(x_1, x_2, x_3, x_4)$, for which we have

x_1	0000 0000 1111 1111	
x_2	0000 1111 0000 1111	
x_3	0011 0011 0011 0011	
x_4	0101 0101 0101 0101	
$x_5 = x_1 \oplus x_3$	0011 0011 1100 1100	
$x_6 = x_1 \oplus x_2$	0000 1111 1111 0000	(7)
$x_7 = x_3 \oplus x_4$	0110 0110 0110 0110	
$x_8 = x_5 \vee x_6$	0011 1111 1111 1100	
$x_9 = x_6 \oplus x_7$	0110 1001 1001 0110	
$x_{10} = x_8 \wedge \bar{x}_9$	0001 0110 0110 1000	

according to Fig. 9. Truth tables are shown here so that we can easily verify each step of the calculation. Step x_8 yields a function that is true whenever $x_1 \neq x_2$ or $x_1 \neq x_3$; and $x_9 = x_1 \oplus x_2 \oplus x_3 \oplus x_4$ is the parity function $(x_1 + x_2 + x_3 + x_4)$ mod 2. Therefore the final result, x_{10}, is true precisely when exactly two of $\{x_1, x_2, x_3, x_4\}$ are 1; these are the cases that satisfy x_8 and have even parity.

Several of the other computational schemes of Fig. 9 can also be justified intuitively. But some of the chains, like the one for $S_{1,4}$, are quite amazing.

Notice that the intermediate result x_6 is used twice in (7). In fact, no six-step chain for the function $S_2(x_1, x_2, x_3, x_4)$ is possible without making double use of some intermediate subexpression; the shortest algebraic formulas for S_2, including nice symmetrical ones like

$$\big((x_1 \wedge x_2) \vee (x_3 \wedge x_4)\big) \oplus \big((x_1 \vee x_2) \wedge (x_3 \vee x_4)\big), \qquad (8)$$

all have cost 7. But Fig. 9 shows that the other symmetric functions of four variables can all be evaluated optimally via "pure" binary trees, without overlapping subtrees except at external nodes (which represent the variables).

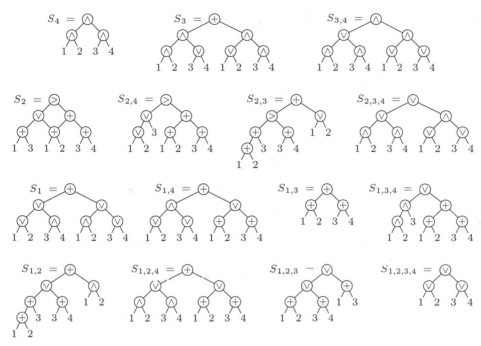

Fig. 9. Optimum Boolean chains for the symmetric functions of four variables.

In general, if $f(x_1, \ldots, x_n)$ is any Boolean function, we say that its *length* $L(f)$ is the number of binary operators in the shortest formula for f. Obviously $L(f) \geq C(f)$; and we can easily verify that $L(f) = C(f)$ whenever $n \leq 3$, by considering the fourteen basic types of 3-variable functions in 7.1.1–(95). But we have just seen that $L(S_2) = 7$ exceeds $C(S_2) = 6$ when $n = 4$, and in fact $L(f)$ is almost always substantially larger than $C(f)$ when n is large (see exercise 49).

The *depth* $D(f)$ of a Boolean function f is another important measure of its inherent complexity: We say that the depth of a Boolean chain is the length of the longest downward path in its tree diagram, and $D(f)$ is the minimum achievable depth when all Boolean chains for f are considered. All of the chains illustrated in Fig. 9 have not only the minimum cost but also the minimum depth — except in the cases $S_{2,3}$ and $S_{1,2}$, where we cannot simultaneously achieve cost 6 and depth 3. The formula

$$S_{2,3}(x_1, x_2, x_3, x_4) = \big((x_1 \wedge x_2) \oplus (x_3 \wedge x_4)\big) \vee \big((x_1 \vee x_2) \wedge (x_3 \oplus x_4)\big) \qquad (9)$$

shows that $D(S_{2,3}) = 3$, and a similar formula works for $S_{1,2}$.

Optimum chains for $n = 4$. Exhaustive computations for 4-variable functions are feasible because such functions have only $2^{16} = 65{,}536$ possible truth tables. In fact we need only consider half of those truth tables, because the complement $\bar{f}$ of any function f has the same cost, length, and depth as f itself.

Let's say that $f(x_1, \ldots, x_n)$ is *normal* if $f(0, \ldots, 0) = 0$, and in general that

$$f(x_1, \ldots, x_n) \oplus f(0, \ldots, 0) \tag{10}$$

is the "normalization" of f. Any Boolean chain can be normalized by normalizing each of its steps and by making appropriate changes to the operators; for if $(\hat{x}_1, \ldots, \hat{x}_{i-1})$ are the normalizations of $(x_1, \ldots, x_{i-1})$ and if $x_i = x_{j(i)} \circ_i x_{k(i)}$ as in (1), then $\hat{x}_i$ is clearly a binary function of $\hat{x}_{j(i)}$ and $\hat{x}_{k(i)}$. (Exercise 7 presents an example.) Therefore we can restrict consideration to normal Boolean chains, in which each step x_i is normal, without loss of generality.

Notice that a Boolean chain is normal if and only if each of its binary operators $\circ_i$ is normal. And there are only eight normal binary operators — three of which, namely $\perp$, L, and R, are trivial. So we can assume that all Boolean chains of interest are formed from the five operators $\wedge$, $\overline{\mathsf{C}}$, $\overline{\mathsf{D}}$, $\vee$, and $\oplus$, which are denoted respectively by $\langle\!\wedge\!\rangle$, $\langle\!\oslash\!\rangle$, $\langle\!\oslash\!\rangle$, $\langle\!\vee\!\rangle$, and $\oplus$ in Fig. 9. Furthermore we can assume that $j(i) < k(i)$ in each step.

There are $2^{15} = 32{,}768$ normal functions of four variables, and we can compute their lengths without difficulty by systematically enumerating all functions of length 0, 1, 2, etc. Indeed, $L(f) = r$ implies that $f = g \circ h$ for some g and h, where $L(g) + L(h) = r - 1$ and $\circ$ is one of the five nontrivial normal operators; so we can proceed as follows:

Algorithm L (*Find normal lengths*). This algorithm determines $L(f)$ for all normal truth tables $0 \le f < 2^{2^n - 1}$, by building lists of all nonzero normal functions of length r for $r \ge 0$.

L1. [Initialize.] Let $L(0) \leftarrow 0$ and $L(f) \leftarrow \infty$ for $1 \le f < 2^{2^n - 1}$. Then, for $1 \le k \le n$, set $L(x_k) \leftarrow 0$ and put x_k into list 0, where

$$x_k = (2^{2^n} - 1)/(2^{2^{n-k}} + 1) \tag{11}$$

is the truth table for x_k. (See exercise 8.) Finally, set $c \leftarrow 2^{2^n - 1} - n - 1$; c is the number of places where $L(f) = \infty$.

L2. [Loop on r.] Do step L3 for $r = 1, 2, \ldots$; eventually the algorithm will terminate when c becomes 0.

L3. [Loop on j and k.] Do step L4 for $j = 0, 1, \ldots$, and $k = r - 1 - j$, while $j \le k$.

L4. [Loop on g and h.] Do step L5 for all g in list j and all h in list k. (If $j = k$, it suffices to restrict h to functions that *follow* g in list k.)

L5. [Loop on f.] Do step L6 for $f = g \mathbin{\&} h$, $f = \bar{g} \mathbin{\&} h$, $f = g \mathbin{\&} \bar{h}$, $f = g \mid h$, and $f = g \oplus h$. (Here $g \mathbin{\&} h$ denotes the bitwise AND of the integers g and h; we are representing truth tables by integers in binary notation.)

L6. [Is f new?] If $L(f) = \infty$, set $L(f) \leftarrow r$, $c \leftarrow c - 1$, and put f in list r. Terminate the algorithm if $c = 0$. ∎

Exercise 10 shows that a similar procedure will compute all depths $D(f)$.

With a little more work, we can in fact modify Algorithm L so that it finds better upper bounds on $C(f)$, by computing a heuristic bit vector $\phi(f)$ called

Table 1

THE NUMBER OF FOUR-VARIABLE FUNCTIONS WITH GIVEN COMPLEXITY

$C(f)$	Classes	Functions	$L(f)$	Classes	Functions	$D(f)$	Classes	Functions
0	2	10	0	2	10	0	2	10
1	2	60	1	2	60	1	2	60
2	5	456	2	5	456	2	17	1458
3	20	2474	3	20	2474	3	179	56456
4	34	10624	4	34	10624	4	22	7552
5	75	24184	5	75	24184	5	0	0
6	72	25008	6	68	24640	6	0	0
7	12	2720	7	16	3088	7	0	0

the "footprint" of f. A normal Boolean chain can begin in only $5\binom{n}{2}$ different ways, since the first step x_{n+1} must be either $x_1 \wedge x_2$ or $\bar{x}_1 \wedge x_2$ or $x_1 \wedge \bar{x}_2$ or $x_1 \vee x_2$ or $x_1 \oplus x_2$ or $x_1 \wedge x_3$ or $\cdots$ or $x_{n-1} \oplus x_n$. Suppose $\phi(f)$ is a bit vector of length $5\binom{n}{2}$ and $U(f)$ is an upper bound on $C(f)$, with the following property: Every 1 bit in $\phi(f)$ corresponds to the first step of some Boolean chain that computes f in $U(f)$ steps.

Such pairs $(U(f), \phi(f))$ can be computed by extending the basic strategy of Algorithm L. Initially we set $U(f) \leftarrow 1$ and we set $\phi(f)$ to an appropriate vector $0\ldots010\ldots0$, for all functions f of cost 1. Then, for $r = 2, 3, \ldots$, we proceed to look for functions $f = g \circ h$ where $U(g) + U(h) = r - 1$, as before, but with two changes: (1) If the footprints of g and h have at least one element in common, namely if $\phi(g) \mathbin{\&} \phi(h) \neq 0$, then we know that $C(f) \leq r - 1$, so we can decrease $U(f)$ if it was $\geq r$. (2) If the cost of $g \circ h$ is equal to (but not less than) our current upper bound $U(f)$, we can set $\phi(f) \leftarrow \phi(f) \mid (\phi(g) \mid \phi(h))$ if $U(f) = r$, $\phi(f) \leftarrow \phi(f) \mid (\phi(g) \mathbin{\&} \phi(h))$ if $U(f) = r - 1$. Exercise 11 works out the details.

It turns out that this footprint heuristic is powerful enough to find chains of optimum cost $U(f) = C(f)$ for all functions f, when $n = 4$. Moreover, we'll see later that footprints also help us solve more complicated evaluation problems.

According to Table 7.1.1–5, the $2^{16} = 65{,}536$ functions of four variables belong to only 222 distinct classes when we ignore minor differences due to permutation of variables and/or complementation of values. Algorithm L and its variants lead to the overall statistics shown in Table 1.

*Evaluation with minimum memory. Suppose the Boolean values $x_1, \ldots, x_n$ appear in n registers, and we want to evaluate a function by performing a sequence of operations having the form

$$x_{j(i)} \leftarrow x_{j(i)} \circ_i x_{k(i)}, \qquad \text{for } 1 \leq i \leq r, \tag{12}$$

where $1 \leq j(i) \leq n$ and $1 \leq k(i) \leq n$ and $\circ_i$ is a binary operator. At the end of the computation, the desired function value should appear in one of the registers. When $n = 3$, for example, the four-step sequence

$$
\begin{aligned}
x_1 &\leftarrow x_1 \oplus x_2 \\
x_3 &\leftarrow x_3 \wedge x_1 \\
x_2 &\leftarrow x_2 \wedge \bar{x}_1 \\
x_3 &\leftarrow x_3 \vee x_2
\end{aligned}
\qquad
\begin{aligned}
&(x_1 = 00001111 \quad x_2 = 00110011 \quad x_3 = 01010101) \\
&(x_1 = 00111100 \quad x_2 = 00110011 \quad x_3 = 01010101) \\
&(x_1 = 00111100 \quad x_2 = 00110011 \quad x_3 = 00010100) \\
&(x_1 = 00111100 \quad x_2 = 00000011 \quad x_3 = 00010100) \\
&(x_1 = 00111100 \quad x_2 = 00000011 \quad x_3 = 00010111)
\end{aligned}
\tag{13}
$$

computes the median $\langle x_1 x_2 x_3 \rangle$ and puts it into the original position of x_3. (All eight possibilities for the register contents are shown here as truth tables, before and after each operation.)

In fact we can check the calculation by working with only one truth table at a time, instead of keeping track of all three, if we analyze the situation backwards. Let $f_l(x_1, \ldots, x_n)$ denote the function computed by steps $l, l+1, \ldots, r$ of the sequence, omitting the first $l-1$ steps; thus, in our example, $f_2(x_1, x_2, x_3)$ would be the result in x_3 after the three steps $x_3 \leftarrow x_3 \wedge x_1$, $x_2 \leftarrow x_2 \wedge \bar{x}_1$, $x_3 \leftarrow x_3 \vee x_2$. Then the function computed in register x_3 by all four steps is

$$f_1(x_1, x_2, x_3) = f_2(x_1 \oplus x_2, x_2, x_3). \qquad (14)$$

Similarly $f_2(x_1, x_2, x_3) = f_3(x_1, x_2, x_3 \wedge x_1)$, $f_3(x_1, x_2, x_3) = f_4(x_1, x_2 \wedge \bar{x}_1, x_3)$, $f_4(x_1, x_2, x_3) = f_5(x_1, x_2, x_3 \vee x_2)$, and $f_5(x_1, x_2, x_3) = x_3$. We can therefore go back from f_5 to f_4 to $\cdots$ to f_1 by operating on truth tables in an appropriate way.

For example, suppose $f(x_1, x_2, x_3)$ is a function whose truth table is

$$t = a_0 a_1 a_2 a_3 a_4 a_5 a_6 a_7;$$

then the truth table for $g(x_1, x_2, x_3) = f(x_1 \oplus x_2, x_2, x_3)$ is

$$u = a_0 a_1 a_6 a_7 a_4 a_5 a_2 a_3,$$

obtained by replacing a_x by $a_{x'}$, where

$$x = (x_1 x_2 x_3)_2 \qquad \text{implies} \qquad x' = ((x_1 \oplus x_2) x_2 x_3)_2.$$

Similarly the truth table for, say, $h(x_1, x_2, x_3) = f(x_1, x_2, x_3 \wedge x_1)$ is

$$v = a_0 a_0 a_2 a_2 a_4 a_5 a_6 a_7.$$

And we can use bitwise operations to compute u and v from t (see 7.1.3–(83)):

$$u = t \oplus \big((t \oplus (t \gg 4) \oplus (t \ll 4)) \,\&\, (00110011)_2\big); \qquad (15)$$
$$v = t \oplus \big((t \oplus (t \gg 1)) \,\&\, (01010000)_2\big). \qquad (16)$$

Let $C_m(f)$ be the length of a shortest minimum-memory computation for f. The backward-computation principle tells us that, if we know the truth tables of all functions f with $C_m(f) < r$, we can readily find all the truth tables of functions with $C_m(f) = r$. Namely, we can restrict consideration to normal functions as before. Then, for all normal g such that $C_m(g) = r - 1$, we can construct the $5n(n-1)$ truth tables for

$$g(x_1, \ldots, x_{j-1}, x_j \circ x_k, x_{j+1}, \ldots, x_n) \qquad (17)$$

and mark them with cost r if they haven't previously been marked. Exercise 14 shows that those truth tables can all be computed by performing simple bitwise operations on the truth table for g.

When $n = 4$, all but 13 of the 222 basic function types turn out to have $C_m(f) = C(f)$, so they can be evaluated in minimum memory without increasing the cost. In particular, all of the symmetric functions have this property — although that fact is not at all obvious from Fig. 9. Five classes of functions have $C(f) = 5$ but $C_m(f) = 6$; eight classes have $C(f) = 6$ but $C_m(f) = 7$. The most interesting example of the latter type is probably the function $(x_1 \vee x_2) \oplus (x_3 \vee x_4) \oplus (x_1 \wedge x_2 \wedge x_3 \wedge x_4)$, which has cost 6 because of the formula

$$x_1 \oplus (x_3 \vee x_4) \oplus \big(x_2 \wedge (\bar{x}_1 \vee (x_3 \wedge x_4))\big), \tag{18}$$

but it has no minimum-memory chain of length less than 7. (See exercise 15.)

*Determining the minimum cost. The exact value of $C(f)$ can be found by observing that all optimum Boolean chains $(x_{n+1}, \ldots, x_{n+r})$ for f obviously satisfy at least one of three conditions:

i) $x_{n+r} = x_j \circ x_k$, where x_j and x_k use no common intermediate results;

ii) $x_{n+1} = x_j \circ x_k$, where either x_j or x_k is not used in steps $x_{n+2}, \ldots, x_{n+r}$;

iii) Neither of the above, even when the intermediate steps are renumbered.

In case (i) we have $f = g \circ h$, where $C(g) + C(h) = r - 1$, and we can call this a "top-down" construction. In case (ii) we have $f(x_1, \ldots, x_n) = g(x_1, \ldots, x_{j-1}, x_j \circ x_k, x_{j+1}, \ldots, x_n)$, where $C(g) = r - 1$; we call this construction "bottom-up."

The best chains that recursively use only top-down constructions correspond to minimum formula length, $L(f)$. The best chains that recursively use only bottom-up constructions correspond to minimum-memory calculations, of length $C_m(f)$. We can do better yet, by mixing top-down constructions with bottom-up constructions; but we still won't know that we've found $C(f)$, because a special chain belonging to case (iii) might be shorter.

Fortunately such special chains are rare, because they must satisfy rather strong conditions, and they can be exhaustively listed when n and r aren't too large. For example, exercise 19 proves that no special chains exist when $r < n+2$; and when $n = 4$, $r = 6$, there are only 25 essentially different special chains that cannot be shortened in an obvious way:

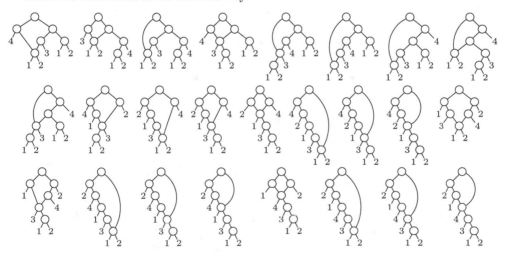

By systematically trying 5^r possibilities in every special chain, one for each way to assign a normal operator to the internal nodes of the tree, we will find at least one function f in every equivalence class for which the minimum cost $C(f)$ is achievable only in case (iii).

In fact, when $n = 4$ and $r = 6$, these $25 \cdot 5^6 = 390{,}625$ trials yield only one class of functions that can't be computed in 6 steps by any top-down-plus-bottom-up chain. The missing class, typified by the partially symmetric function $(\langle x_1 x_2 x_3 \rangle \vee x_4) \oplus (x_1 \wedge x_2 \wedge x_3)$, can be reached in six steps by appropriately specializing any of the first five chains illustrated above; for example, one way is

$$x_5 = x_1 \wedge x_2, \quad x_6 = x_1 \vee x_2, \quad x_7 = x_3 \oplus x_5,$$
$$x_8 = x_4 \wedge \bar{x}_5, \quad x_9 = x_6 \wedge x_7, \quad x_{10} = x_8 \vee x_9, \qquad (19)$$

corresponding to the first special chain. Since all other functions have $L(f) \le 7$, these trial calculations have established the true minimum cost in all cases.

Historical notes: The first concerted attempts to evaluate all Boolean functions $f(w, x, y, z)$ optimally were reported in *Annals of the Computation Laboratory of Harvard University* **27** (1951), where Howard Aiken's staff presented heuristic methods and extensive tables of the best switching circuits they were able to construct. Their cost measure $V(f)$ was different from the cost $C(f)$ that we've been considering, because it was based on "control grids" of vacuum tubes: They had four kinds of gates, $\text{NOT}(f)$, $\text{NAND}(f, g)$, $\text{OR}(f_1, \dots, f_k)$, and $\text{AND}(f_1, \dots, f_k)$, respectively costing 1, 2, k, and 0. Every input to NOT, NAND, or OR could be either a variable, or the complement of a variable, or the result of a previous gate; every input to AND had to be the output of either NOT or NAND that wasn't also used elsewhere.

With those cost criteria, a function might not have the same cost as its complement. One could, for instance, evaluate $x \wedge y$ as $\text{AND}\big(\text{NOT}(\bar{x}), \text{NOT}(\bar{y})\big)$, with cost 2; but the cost of $\bar{x} \vee (\bar{y} \wedge \bar{z}) = \text{NAND}(x, \text{OR}(y, z))$ was 4 while its complement $x \wedge (y \vee z) = \text{AND}\big(\text{NOT}(\bar{x}), \text{NAND}(\bar{y}, \bar{z})\big)$ cost only 3. Therefore the Harvard researchers needed to consider 402 essentially different classes of 4-variable functions instead of 222 (see the answer to exercise 7.1.1–125). Of course in those days they worked mostly by hand. They found $V(f) < 20$ in all cases, except for the 64 functions equivalent to $S_{0,1}(w, x, y, z) \vee \big(S_2(w, x, y) \wedge z\big)$, which they evaluated with 20 control grids as follows:

$$g_1 = \text{AND}(\text{NOT}(\bar{w}), \text{NOT}(\bar{x})), \quad g_2 = \text{NAND}(\bar{y}, z),$$
$$g_3 = \text{AND}(\text{NOT}(w), \text{NOT}(x));$$
$$f = \text{AND}\big(\text{NAND}(g_1, g_2), \text{NAND}(g_3, \text{AND}(\text{NOT}(\bar{y}), \text{NOT}(\bar{z}))),$$
$$\text{NOT}(\text{AND}(\text{NOT}(g_3), \text{NOT}(\bar{y}), \text{NOT}(z))),$$
$$\text{NOT}(\text{AND}(\text{NOT}(g_1), \text{NOT}(g_2), \text{NOT}(g_3)))\big). \qquad (20)$$

The first computer program to find provably optimum circuits was written by Leo Hellerman [*IEEE Transactions* **EC-12** (1963), 198–223], who determined the fewest NOR gates needed to evaluate any given function $f(x, y, z)$. He required every input of every gate to be either an uncomplemented variable or the output of a previous gate; fanin and fanout were limited to at most 3. When two circuits had the same gate count, he preferred the one with smallest sum-

Table 2
THE NUMBER OF FIVE-VARIABLE FUNCTIONS WITH GIVEN COMPLEXITY

$C(f)$	Classes	Functions	$L(f)$	Classes	Functions	$D(f)$	Classes	Functions
0	2	12	0	2	12	0	2	12
1	2	100	1	2	100	1	2	100
2	5	1140	2	5	1140	2	17	5350
3	20	11570	3	20	11570	3	1789	6702242
4	93	109826	4	93	109826	4	614316	4288259592
5	389	995240	5	366	936440	5	0	0
6	1988	8430800	6	1730	7236880	6	0	0
7	11382	63401728	7	8782	47739088	7	0	0
8	60713	383877392	8	40297	250674320	8	0	0
9	221541	1519125536	9	141422	955812256	9	0	0
10	293455	2123645248	10	273277	1945383936	10	0	0
11	26535	195366784	11	145707	1055912608	11	0	0
12	1	1920	12	4423	31149120	12	0	0

of-inputs. For example, he computed $\bar{x} = \text{NOR}(x)$ with cost 1; $x \lor y \lor z = \text{NOR}(\text{NOR}(x, y, z))$ with cost 2; $\langle xyz \rangle = \text{NOR}(\text{NOR}(x, y), \text{NOR}(x, z), \text{NOR}(y, z))$ with cost 4; $S_1(x, y, z) = \text{NOR}(\text{NOR}(x, y, z), \langle xyz \rangle)$ with cost 6; etc. Since he limited the fanout to 3, he found that every function of three variables could be evaluated with cost 7 or less, except for the parity function $x \oplus y \oplus z = (x \equiv y) \equiv z$, where $x \equiv y$ has cost 4 because it is $\text{NOR}(\text{NOR}(x, \text{NOR}(x, y)), \text{NOR}(y, \text{NOR}(x, y)))$.

Electrical engineers continued to explore other cost criteria; but four-variable functions seemed out of reach until 1977, when Frank M. Liang established the values of $C(f)$ shown in Table 1. Liang's unpublished derivation was based on a study of all chains that cannot be reduced by the bottom-up construction.

The case $n = 5$. There are 616,126 classes of essentially different functions $f(x_1, x_2, x_3, x_4, x_5)$, according to Table 7.1.1–5. Computers are now fast enough that this number is no longer frightening; so the author decided while writing this section to investigate $C(f)$ for all Boolean functions of five variables. Thanks to a bit of good luck, complete results could indeed be obtained, leading to the statistics shown in Table 2.

For this calculation Algorithm L and its variants were modified to deal with class representatives, instead of with the entire set of 2^{31} normal truth tables. The method of exercise 7.2.1.2–20 made it easy to generate all functions of a class, given any one of them, resulting in a thousand-fold speedup. The bottom-up method was enhanced slightly, allowing it to deduce for example that $f(x_1 \land x_2, x_1 \lor x_2, x_3, x_4, x_5)$ has cost $\leq r$ if $C(f) = r - 2$. After all classes of cost 10 had been found, the top-down and bottom-up methods were able to find chains of length ≤ 11 for all but seven classes of functions. Then the time-consuming part of the computation began, in which approximately 53 million special chains with $n = 5$ and $r = 11$ were generated; every such chain led to $5^{11} = 48,828,125$ functions, some of which would hopefully fall into the seven remaining mystery classes. But only six of those classes were found to have 11-step solutions. The lone survivor, whose truth table is 169ae443 in hexadecimal notation, is the unique class for which $C(f) = 12$, and it also has $L(f) = 12$.

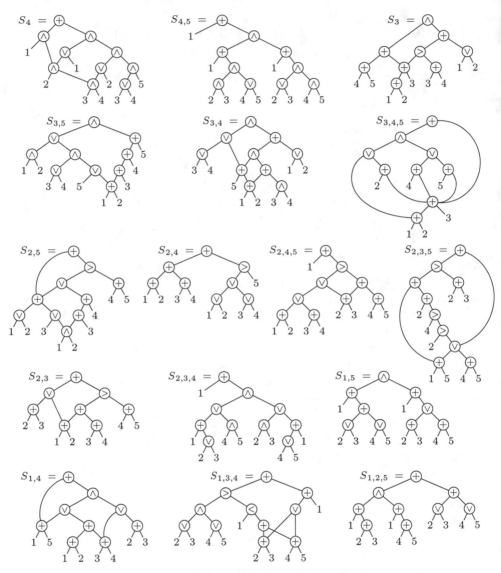

Fig. 10. Boolean chains of minimum cost
for symmetric functions of five variables.

The resulting constructions of symmetric functions are shown in Fig. 10. Some of them are astonishingly beautiful; some of them are beautifully simple; and others are simply astonishing. (Look, for example, at the 8-step computation of $S_{2,3}(x_1, x_2, x_3, x_4, x_5)$, or the elegant formula for $S_{2,3,4}$, or the nonmonotonic chains for $S_{4,5}$ and $S_{3,4,5}$.) Incidentally, Table 2 shows that all 5-variable functions have depth ≤ 4, but no attempt to minimize depth has been made in Fig. 10.

It turns out that all of these symmetric functions can be evaluated in minimum memory without increasing the cost. No simple reason is known.

Multiple outputs. We often want to evaluate several different Boolean functions $f_1(x_1, \ldots, x_n)$, $\ldots$, $f_m(x_1, \ldots, x_n)$ at the same input values x_1, $\ldots$, x_n; in other words, we often want to evaluate a multibit function $y = f(x)$, where $y = f_1 \ldots f_m$ is a binary vector of length m and $x = x_1 \ldots x_n$ is a binary vector of length n. With luck, much of the work involved in the computation of one component value $f_j(x_1, \ldots, x_n)$ can be shared with the operations that are needed to evaluate the other component values $f_k(x_1, \ldots, x_n)$.

Let $C(f) = C(f_1 \ldots f_m)$ be the length of a shortest Boolean chain that computes all of the nontrivial functions f_j. More precisely, the chain $(x_{n+1}, \ldots, x_{n+r})$ should have the property that, for $1 \le j \le m$, either $f_j(x_1, \ldots, x_n) = x_{l(j)}$ or $f_j(x_1, \ldots, x_n) = \bar{x}_{l(j)}$, for some $l(j)$ with $0 \le l(j) \le n+r$, where $x_0 = 0$. Clearly $C(f) \le C(f_1) + \cdots + C(f_m)$, but we might be able to do much better.

For example, suppose we want to compute the functions z_1 and z_0 defined by

$$(z_1 z_0)_2 = x_1 + x_2 + x_3, \tag{21}$$

the two-bit binary sum of three Boolean variables. We have

$$z_1 = \langle x_1 x_2 x_3 \rangle \quad \text{and} \quad z_0 = x_1 \oplus x_2 \oplus x_3, \tag{22}$$

so the individual costs are $C(z_1) = 4$ and $C(z_0) = 2$. But it's easy to see that the combined cost $C(z_1 z_0)$ is at most 5, because $x_1 \oplus x_2$ is a suitable first step in the evaluation of each bit z_j:

$$x_4 = x_1 \oplus x_2, \quad z_0 = x_5 = x_3 \oplus x_4;$$
$$x_6 = x_3 \wedge x_4, \quad x_7 = x_1 \wedge x_2, \quad z_1 = x_8 = x_6 \vee x_7. \tag{23}$$

Furthermore, exhaustive calculations show that $C(z_1 z_0) > 4$; hence $C(z_1 z_0) = 5$.

Electrical engineers traditionally call a circuit for (21) a *full adder*, because n such building blocks can be hooked together to add two n-bit numbers. The special case of (22) in which $x_3 = 0$ is also important, although it boils down simply to

$$z_1 = x_1 \wedge x_2 \quad \text{and} \quad z_0 = x_1 \oplus x_2 \tag{24}$$

and has complexity 2; engineers call it a "half adder" in spite of the fact that the cost of a full adder exceeds the cost of two half adders.

The general problem of radix-2 addition

$$\begin{array}{r} (x_{n-1} \ldots x_1 x_0)_2 \\ (y_{n-1} \ldots y_1 y_0)_2 \\ \hline (z_n z_{n-1} \ldots z_1 z_0)_2 \end{array} \tag{25}$$

is to compute $n + 1$ Boolean outputs $z_n \ldots z_1 z_0$ from the $2n$ Boolean inputs $x_{n-1} \ldots x_1 x_0 y_{n-1} \ldots y_1 y_0$; and it is readily solved by the formulas

$$c_{j+1} = \langle x_j y_j c_j \rangle, \quad z_j = x_j \oplus y_j \oplus c_j, \quad \text{for } 0 \le j < n, \tag{26}$$

where the c_j are "carry bits" and we have $c_0 = 0$, $z_n = c_n$. Therefore we can use a half adder to compute c_1 and z_0, followed by $n - 1$ full adders to compute the other c's and z's, accumulating a total cost of $5n - 3$. And in fact N. P. Red'kin [*Problemy Kibernetiki* **38** (1981), 181–216] has proved that $5n - 3$ steps are actually necessary, by constructing an elaborate 35-page proof by induction, which concludes with Case 2.2.2.3.1.2.3.2.4.3(!). But the depth of this circuit, $2n-1$, is far too large for practical parallel computation, so a great deal of effort has gone into the task of devising circuits for addition that have depth $O(\log n)$ as well as reasonable cost. (See exercises 41–44.)

Now let's extend (21) and try to compute a general "sideways sum"

$$(z_{\lfloor \lg n \rfloor} \dots z_1 z_0)_2 = x_1 + x_2 + \dots + x_n. \tag{27}$$

If $n = 2k+1$, we can use k full adders to reduce the sum to $(x_1 + \dots + x_n) \bmod 2$ plus k bits of weight 2, because each full adder decreases the number of weight-1 bits by 2. For example, if $n = 9$ and $k = 4$ the computation is

$$x_{10}=x_1 \oplus x_2 \oplus x_3, \quad x_{11}=x_4 \oplus x_5 \oplus x_6, \quad x_{12}=x_7 \oplus x_8 \oplus x_9, \quad x_{13}=x_{10} \oplus x_{11} \oplus x_{12},$$
$$y_1=\langle x_1 x_2 x_3 \rangle, \quad y_2=\langle x_4 x_5 x_6 \rangle, \quad y_3=\langle x_7 x_8 x_9 \rangle, \quad y_4=\langle x_{10} x_{11} x_{12} \rangle,$$

and we have $x_1 + \dots + x_9 = x_{13} + 2(y_1 + y_2 + y_3 + y_4)$. If $n = 2k$ is even, a similar reduction applies but with a half adder at the end. The bits of weight 2 can then be summed in the same way; so we obtain the recurrence

$$s(n) = 5\lfloor n/2 \rfloor - 3[n \text{ even}] + s(\lfloor n/2 \rfloor), \qquad s(0) = 0, \tag{28}$$

for the total number of gates that will compute $z_{\lfloor \lg n \rfloor} \dots z_1 z_0$. (A closed formula for $s(n)$ appears in exercise 30.) We have $s(n) < 5n$, and the first values

$$n = 1 \; 2 \; 3 \; 4 \; 5 \; \; 6 \; \; 7 \; \; 8 \; \; 9 \; \; 10 \; \; 11 \; \; 12 \; \; 13 \; \; 14 \; \; 15 \; \; 16 \; \; 17 \; \; 18 \; \; 19 \; \; 20$$
$$s(n) = 0 \; 2 \; 5 \; 9 \; 12 \; 17 \; 20 \; 26 \; 29 \; 34 \; 37 \; 44 \; 47 \; 52 \; 55 \; 63 \; 66 \; 71 \; 74 \; 81$$

show that the method is quite efficient even for small n. For example, when $n = 5$ it produces

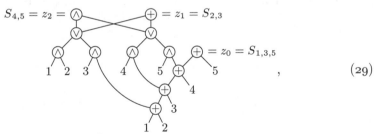

$$\tag{29}$$

which computes three different symmetric functions $z_2 = S_{4,5}(x_1, \dots, x_5)$, $z_1 = S_{2,3}(x_1, \dots, x_5)$, $z_0 = S_{1,3,5}(x_1, \dots, x_5)$ in just 12 steps. The 10-step computation of $S_{4,5}$ is optimum, according to Fig. 10; of course the 4-step computation of $S_{1,3,5}$ is also optimum. Furthermore, although $C(S_{2,3}) = 8$, the function $S_{2,3}$ is computed here in a clever 10-step way that shares all but one gate with $S_{4,5}$.

Notice that we can now compute *any* symmetric function efficiently, because every symmetric function of $\{x_1, \dots, x_n\}$ is a Boolean function of $z_{\lfloor \lg n \rfloor} \dots z_1 z_0$. We know, for example, that any Boolean function of four variables has complexity ≤ 7; therefore any symmetric function $S_{k_1, \dots, k_t}(x_1, \dots, x_{15})$ costs at most $s(15) + 7 = 62$. Surprise: The symmetric functions of n variables were among the hardest of all to evaluate, when n was small, but they're among the easiest when $n \ge 10$.

We can also compute *sets* of symmetric functions efficiently. If we want, say, to evaluate all $n + 1$ symmetric functions $S_k(x_1, \ldots, x_n)$ for $0 \le k \le n$ with a single Boolean chain, we simply need to evaluate the first $n+1$ *minterms* of z_0, z_1, $\ldots$, $z_{\lfloor \lg n \rfloor}$. For example, when $n = 5$ the minterms that give us all functions S_k are respectively $S_0 = \bar{z}_0 \wedge \bar{z}_1 \wedge \bar{z}_2$, $S_1 = z_0 \wedge \bar{z}_1 \wedge \bar{z}_2$, $\ldots$, $S_5 = z_0 \wedge \bar{z}_1 \wedge z_2$.

How hard is it to compute all 2^n minterms of n variables? Electrical engineers call this function an *n-to-2^n binary decoder*, because it converts n bits $x_1 \ldots x_n$ into a sequence of 2^n bits $d_0 d_1 \ldots d_{2^n-1}$, exactly one of which is 1. The principle of "divide and conquer" suggests that we first evaluate all minterms on the first $\lceil n/2 \rceil$ variables, as well as all minterms on the last $\lfloor n/2 \rfloor$; then 2^n AND gates will finish the job. The cost of this method is $t(n)$, where

$$t(0) = t(1) = 0; \qquad t(n) = 2^n + t(\lceil n/2 \rceil) + t(\lfloor n/2 \rfloor) \quad \text{for } n \ge 2. \tag{30}$$

So $t(n) = 2^n + O(2^{n/2})$; there's roughly one gate per minterm. (See exercise 32.)

Functions with multiple outputs often help us build larger functions with single outputs. For example, we've seen that the sideways adder (27) allows us to compute symmetric functions; and an n-to-2^n decoder also has many applications, in spite of the fact that 2^n can be huge when n is large. A case in point is the *2^m-way multiplexer* $M_m(x_1, \ldots, x_m; y_0, y_1, \ldots, y_{2^m-1})$, also known as the m-bit *storage access function*, which has $n = m + 2^m$ inputs and takes the value y_k when $(x_1 \ldots x_m)_2 = k$. By definition we have

$$M_m(x_1, \ldots, x_m; y_0, y_1, \ldots, y_{2^m-1}) = \bigvee_{k=0}^{2^m-1} (d_k \wedge y_k), \tag{31}$$

where d_k is the kth output of an m-to-2^m binary decoder; thus, by (30), we can evaluate M_m with $2^m + (2^m-1) + t(m) = 3n + O(\sqrt{n})$ gates. But exercise 39 shows that we can actually reduce the cost to only $2n + O(\sqrt{n})$. (See also exercise 78.)

Asymptotic facts. When the number of variables is small, our exhaustive-search methods have turned up lots of cases where Boolean functions can be evaluated with stunning efficiency. So it's natural to expect that, when more variables are present, even more opportunities for ingenious evaluations will arise. But the truth is exactly the opposite, at least from a statistical standpoint:

Theorem S. *The cost of almost every Boolean function $f(x_1, \ldots, x_n)$ exceeds $2^n/n$. More precisely, if $c(n, r)$ Boolean functions have complexity $\le r$, we have*

$$(r - 1)! \, c(n, r) \le 2^{2r+1}(n + r - 1)^{2r}. \tag{32}$$

Proof. If a function can be computed in $r - 1$ steps, it is also computable by an r-step chain. (This statement is obvious when $r = 1$; otherwise we can let $x_{n+r} = x_{n+r-1} \wedge x_{n+r-1}$.) We will show that there aren't very many r-step chains, hence we can't compute very many different functions with cost $\le r$.

Let π be a permutation of $\{1, \ldots, n + r\}$ that takes $1 \mapsto 1, \ldots, n \mapsto n$, and $n+r \mapsto n+r$; there are $(r-1)!$ such permutations. Suppose $(x_{n+1}, \ldots, x_{n+r})$ is a

Boolean chain in which each of the intermediate steps $x_{n+1}, \ldots, x_{n+r-1}$ is used in at least one subsequent step. Then the permuted chains defined by the rule

$$x_i = x_{j'(i)} \circ'_i x_{k'(i)} = x_{j(i\pi)\pi^-} \circ_{i\pi} x_{k(i\pi)\pi^-}, \qquad \text{for } n < i \le n+r, \qquad (33)$$

are distinct for different π. (If π takes $a \mapsto b$, we write $b = a\pi$ and $a = b\pi^-$.) For example, if π takes $5 \mapsto 6 \mapsto 7 \mapsto 8 \mapsto 9 \mapsto 5$, the chain (7) becomes

Original	Permuted
$x_5 = x_1 \oplus x_3,$	$x_5 = x_1 \oplus x_2,$
$x_6 = x_1 \oplus x_2,$	$x_6 = x_3 \oplus x_4,$
$x_7 = x_3 \oplus x_4,$	$x_7 = x_9 \vee x_5,$
$x_8 = x_5 \vee x_6,$	$x_8 = x_5 \oplus x_6,$
$x_9 = x_6 \oplus x_7,$	$x_9 = x_1 \oplus x_3,$
$x_{10} = x_8 \wedge \bar{x}_9;$	$x_{10} = x_7 \wedge \bar{x}_8.$

$$(34)$$

Notice that we might have $j'(i) \ge k'(i)$ or $j'(i) > i$ or $k'(i) > i$, contrary to our usual rules. But the permuted chain computes the same function x_{n+r} as before, and it doesn't have any cycles by which an entry is defined indirectly in terms of itself, because the permuted x_i is the original $x_{i\pi}$.

We can restrict consideration to *normal* Boolean chains, as remarked earlier. So the $c(n, r)/2$ normal Boolean functions of cost $\le r$ lead to $(r-1)!\, c(n, r)/2$ different permuted chains, where the operator $\circ_i$ in each step is either $\wedge$, $\vee$, $\bar{\supset}$, or $\oplus$. And there are at most $4^r(n+r-1)^{2r}$ such chains, because there are four choices for $\circ_i$ and $n+r-1$ choices for each of $j(i)$ and $k(i)$, for $n < i \le n+r$. Equation (32) follows; and we obtain the opening statement of the theorem by setting $r = \lfloor 2^n/n \rfloor$. (See exercise 46.) ∎

On the other hand, there's also good news for infinity-minded people: We can actually evaluate every Boolean function of n variables with only slightly more than $2^n/n$ steps of computation, even if we avoid $\oplus$ and $\equiv$, using a technique devised by C. E. Shannon and improved by O. B. Lupanov [*Bell System Tech. J.* **28** (1949), 59–98, Theorem 6; *Izvestiia VUZov, Radiofizika* **1** (1958), 120–140].

In fact, the Shannon–Lupanov approach leads to useful results even when n is small, so let's get acquainted with it by studying a small example. Consider

$$f(x_1, x_2, x_3, x_4, x_5, x_6) = \big[(x_1 x_2 x_3 x_4 x_5 x_6)_2 \text{ is prime}\big], \qquad (35)$$

a function that identifies all 6-bit prime numbers. Its truth table has $2^6 = 64$ bits, and we can work with it conveniently by using a 4×16 array to look at those bits instead of confining ourselves to one dimension:

$$
\begin{array}{l}
x_3 = 0\ 0\ 0\ 0\ 0\ 0\ 0\ 0\ 1\ 1\ 1\ 1\ 1\ 1\ 1\ 1 \\
x_4 = 0\ 0\ 0\ 0\ 1\ 1\ 1\ 1\ 0\ 0\ 0\ 0\ 1\ 1\ 1\ 1 \\
x_5 = 0\ 0\ 1\ 1\ 0\ 0\ 1\ 1\ 0\ 0\ 1\ 1\ 0\ 0\ 1\ 1 \\
x_6 = 0\ 1\ 0\ 1\ 0\ 1\ 0\ 1\ 0\ 1\ 0\ 1\ 0\ 1\ 0\ 1
\end{array}
$$

$x_1 x_2 = 00$	$0\ 0\ 1\ 1\ 0\ 1\ 0\ 1\ 0\ 0\ 0\ 1\ 0\ 1\ 0\ 0$	$\left.\vphantom{\begin{array}{c}a\\b\end{array}}\right\}$ Group 1
$x_1 x_2 = 01$	$0\ 1\ 0\ 1\ 0\ 0\ 0\ 1\ 0\ 0\ 0\ 0\ 0\ 1\ 0\ 1$	
$x_1 x_2 = 10$	$0\ 0\ 0\ 0\ 0\ 1\ 0\ 0\ 0\ 1\ 0\ 1\ 0\ 0\ 0\ 1$	$\left.\vphantom{\begin{array}{c}a\\b\end{array}}\right\}$ Group 2
$x_1 x_2 = 11$	$0\ 0\ 0\ 0\ 0\ 1\ 0\ 0\ 0\ 0\ 0\ 1\ 0\ 1\ 0\ 0$	

$$(36)$$

The rows have been divided into two groups of two rows each; and each group of rows has 16 columns, which are of four basic types, namely $\begin{smallmatrix}0\\0\end{smallmatrix}$, $\begin{smallmatrix}0\\1\end{smallmatrix}$, $\begin{smallmatrix}1\\0\end{smallmatrix}$, or $\begin{smallmatrix}1\\1\end{smallmatrix}$. Thus we see that the function can be expressed as

$$
\begin{aligned}
f(x_1,\ldots,x_6) \;=\; & \big([x_1x_2 \in \{00\}] & \wedge\,[x_3x_4x_5x_6 \in \{0010, 0101, 1011\}]\big) \\
\vee\; & \big([x_1x_2 \in \{01\}] & \wedge\,[x_3x_4x_5x_6 \in \{0001, 1111\}]\big) \\
\vee\; & \big([x_1x_2 \in \{00, 01\}] \wedge\,[x_3x_4x_5x_6 \in \{0011, 0111, 1101\}]\big) \\
\vee\; & \big([x_1x_2 \in \{10\}] & \wedge\,[x_3x_4x_5x_6 \in \{1001, 1111\}]\big) \\
\vee\; & \big([x_1x_2 \in \{11\}] & \wedge\,[x_3x_4x_5x_6 \in \{1101\}]\big) \\
\vee\; & \big([x_1x_2 \in \{10, 11\}] \wedge\,[x_3x_4x_5x_6 \in \{0101, 1011\}]\big). \quad (37)
\end{aligned}
$$

(The first line corresponds to group 1, type $\begin{smallmatrix}1\\0\end{smallmatrix}$, then comes group 1, type $\begin{smallmatrix}0\\1\end{smallmatrix}$, etc.; the last line corresponds to group 2 and type $\begin{smallmatrix}1\\1\end{smallmatrix}$.) A function like $[x_3x_4x_5x_6 \in \{0010, 0101, 1011\}]$ is the OR of three minterms of $\{x_3, x_4, x_5, x_6\}$.

In general we can view the truth table as a $2^k \times 2^{n-k}$ array, with l groups of rows having either $\lfloor 2^k/l \rfloor$ or $\lceil 2^k/l \rceil$ rows in each group. A group of size m will have columns of 2^m basic types. We form a conjunction $(g_{it}(x_1,\ldots,x_k) \wedge h_{it}(x_{k+1},\ldots,x_n))$ for each group i and each nonzero type t, where g_{it} is the OR of all minterms of $\{x_1,\ldots,x_k\}$ for the rows of the group where t has a 1, while h_{it} is the OR of all minterms of $\{x_{k+1},\ldots,x_n\}$ for the columns having type t in group i. The OR of all these conjunctions $(g_{it} \wedge h_{it})$ gives $f(x_1,\ldots,x_n)$.

Once we've chosen the parameters k and l, with $1 \le k \le n-2$ and $1 \le l \le 2^k$, the computation starts by computing all the minterms of $\{x_1,\ldots,x_k\}$ and all the minterms of $\{x_{k+1},\ldots,x_n\}$, in $t(k) + t(n - k)$ steps (see (30)). Then, for $1 \le i \le l$, we let group i consist of rows for the values of $(x_1,\ldots,x_k)$ such that $(i-1)2^k/l \le (x_1 \ldots x_k)_2 < i2^k/l$; it contains $m_i = \lceil i2^k/l \rceil - \lceil (i-1)2^k/l \rceil$ rows. We form all functions g_{it} for $t \in S_i$, the family of $2^{m_i} - 1$ nonempty subsets of those rows; $2^{m_i} - m_i - 1$ ORs of previously computed minterms will accomplish that task. We also form all functions h_{it} representing columns of nonzero type t; for this purpose we'll need at most 2^{n-k} OR operations in each group i, since we can OR each minterm into the h function of the appropriate type t. Finally we compute $f = \bigvee_{i=1}^{l} \bigvee_{t \in S_i}(g_{it} \wedge h_{it})$; each AND operation is compensated by an unnecessary first OR into h_{it}. So the total cost is at most

$$
t(k) + t(n-k) + (l-1) + \sum_{i=1}^{l}\big((2^{m_i} - m_i - 1) + 2^{n-k} + (2^{m_i} - 2)\big); \quad (38)
$$

we want to choose k and l so that this upper bound is minimized. Exercise 52 discusses the best choice when n is small. And when n is large, a good choice yields a provably near-optimum chain, at least for most functions:

Theorem L. *Let $C(n)$ denote the cost of the most expensive Boolean functions of n variables. Then as $n \to \infty$ we have*

$$
C(n) \;\ge\; \frac{2^n}{n}\Big(1 + \frac{\lg n}{n} + O\Big(\frac{1}{n}\Big)\Big); \quad (39)
$$

$$
C(n) \;\le\; \frac{2^n}{n}\Big(1 + 3\frac{\lg n}{n} + O\Big(\frac{1}{n}\Big)\Big). \quad (40)
$$

Proof. Exercise 48 shows that the lower bound (39) is a consequence of Theorem S. For the upper bound, we set $k = \lfloor 2 \lg n \rfloor$ and $l = \lceil 2^k/(n - 3 \lg n) \rceil$ in Lupanov's method; see exercise 53.   ∎

[An even better upper bound, replacing $3 \lg n$ by $\lg n + \lg \lg n$, has been proved by S. A. Lozhkin, *Moscow University Mathematics Bulletin* **77** (2022), 144–153.]

Synthesizing a good chain. Formula (37) isn't the best way to implement a 6-bit prime detector, but it does suggest a decent strategy. For example, we needn't let variables x_1 and x_2 govern the rows: Exercise 51 shows that a better chain results if the rows are based on x_5x_6 while the columns come from $x_1x_2x_3x_4$, and in general there are many ways to partition a truth table by playing k of the variables against the other $n - k$.

Furthermore, we can improve on (37) by using our complete knowledge of all 4-variable functions; there's no need to evaluate a function like $[x_3x_4x_5x_6 \in \{0010, 0101, 1011\}]$ by first computing the minterms of $\{x_3, x_4, x_5, x_6\}$, if we know the best way to evaluate every such function from scratch. On the other hand, we do need to evaluate several 4-variable functions simultaneously, so the minterm approach might not be such a bad idea after all. Can we really improve on it?

Let's try to find a good way to synthesize a Boolean chain that computes a given set of 4-variable functions. The six functions of $x_3x_4x_5x_6$ in (37) are rather tame (see exercise 54), so we'll learn more by considering a more interesting example chosen from everyday life.

A *seven-segment display* is a now-ubiquitous way to represent a 4-bit number $(x_1x_2x_3x_4)_2$ in terms of seven cleverly positioned segments that are either visible or invisible. The segments are traditionally named (a, b, c, d, e, f, g) as shown; we get a '0' by turning on segments (a, b, c, d, e, f), but a '1' uses only segments (b, c). (Incidentally, the idea for such displays was invented by F. W. Wood, *U.S. Patent 974943* (1910), although Wood's original design used eight segments because he thought that a '4' requires a diagonal stroke.) Seven-segment displays usually support only the decimal digits '0', '1', ..., '9'; but of course a computer scientist's digital watch should display also hexadecimal digits. So we shall design seven-segment logic that displays the sixteen digits

$$\textsf{0 1 2 3 4 5 6 7 8 9 A b c d E F} \tag{41}$$

when given the respective inputs $x_1x_2x_3x_4 = 0000, 0001, 0010, \ldots, 1111$.

In other words, we want to evaluate seven Boolean functions whose truth tables are respectively

$$
\begin{aligned}
a &= \texttt{1011 0111 1110 0011}, \\
b &= \texttt{1111 1001 1110 0100}, \\
c &= \texttt{1101 1111 1111 0100}, \\
d &= \texttt{1011 0110 1101 1110}, \\
e &= \texttt{1010 0010 1011 1111}, \\
f &= \texttt{1000 1111 1111 0011}, \\
g &= \texttt{0011 1110 1111 1111}.
\end{aligned}
\tag{42}
$$

If we simply wanted to evaluate each function separately, several methods that we've already discussed would tell us how to do it with minimum costs $C(a) = 5$, $C(b) = C(c) = C(d) = 6$, $C(e) = C(f) = 5$, and $C(g) = 4$; the total cost for all seven functions would then be 37. But we want to find a single Boolean chain that contains them all, and the shortest such chain is presumably much more efficient. How can we discover it?

Well, the task of finding a truly optimum chain for $\{a, b, c, d, e, f, g\}$ is probably infeasible from a computational standpoint. But a surprisingly good solution can be found with the help of the "footprint" idea explained earlier. Namely, we know how to compute not only a function's minimum cost, but also the set of all first steps consistent with that minimum cost in a normal chain. Function e, for example, has cost 5, but only if we evaluate it by starting with one of the instructions

$$x_5 = x_1 \oplus x_4 \qquad \text{or} \qquad x_5 = x_2 \wedge \bar{x}_3 \qquad \text{or} \qquad x_5 = x_2 \vee x_3.$$

Fortunately, one of the desirable first steps belongs to four of the seven footprints: Functions c, d, f, and g can all be evaluated optimally by starting with $x_5 = x_2 \oplus x_3$. So that is a natural choice; it essentially saves us three steps, because we know that at most 33 of the original 37 steps will be needed to finish.

Now we can recompute the costs and footprints of all 2^{16} functions, proceeding as before but also initializing the cost of the new function x_5 to zero. The costs of functions c, d, f, and g decrease by 1 as a result, and the footprints change too. For example, function a still has cost 5, but its footprint has increased from $\{x_1 \oplus x_3, x_2 \wedge x_3\}$ to $\{x_1 \oplus x_3, x_1 \wedge x_4, \bar{x}_1 \wedge x_4, x_2 \wedge x_3, \bar{x}_2 \wedge x_4, x_2 \oplus x_4, x_4 \wedge x_5, x_4 \oplus x_5\}$ when the function $x_5 = x_2 \oplus x_3$ is available for free.

In fact, $x_6 = \bar{x}_1 \wedge x_4$ is common to four of the new footprints, so again we have a natural way to proceed. And when everything is recalculated with zero cost given to both x_5 and x_6, the subsequent step $x_7 = x_3 \wedge \bar{x}_6$ turns out to be desirable in five of the newest footprints. Continuing in this "greedy" fashion, we aren't always so lucky, but a chain of 22 steps does emerge; and David Stevenson has shown that only 21 steps are actually needed if we choose x_{10} non-greedily:

$$
\begin{array}{lll}
x_5 = x_2 \oplus x_3, & x_{12} = x_1 \wedge x_2, & \bar{a} = x_{19} = x_{15} \oplus x_{18}, \\
x_6 = \bar{x}_1 \wedge x_4, & x_{13} = x_9 \wedge \bar{x}_{12}, & \bar{b} = x_{20} = x_{11} \wedge \bar{x}_{13}, \\
x_7 = x_3 \wedge \bar{x}_6, & x_{14} = \bar{x}_3 \wedge x_{13}, & \bar{c} = x_{21} = \bar{x}_8 \wedge x_{11}, \\
x_8 = x_1 \oplus x_2, & x_{15} = x_5 \oplus x_{14}, & \bar{d} = x_{22} = x_9 \wedge \bar{x}_{16}, \quad (43) \\
x_9 = x_4 \oplus x_5, & x_{16} = x_1 \oplus x_7, & \bar{e} = x_{23} = x_6 \vee x_{14}, \\
x_{10} = x_3 \vee x_9, & x_{17} = x_1 \vee x_5, & \bar{f} = x_{24} = \bar{x}_8 \wedge x_{15}, \\
x_{11} = x_6 \oplus x_{10}, & x_{18} = x_6 \oplus x_{13}, & g = x_{25} = x_7 \vee x_{17}.
\end{array}
$$

(This is a *normal* chain, so it contains the normalizations $\{\bar{a}, \bar{b}, \bar{c}, \bar{d}, \bar{e}, \bar{f}, g\}$ instead of $\{a, b, c, d, e, f, g\}$. Simple changes will produce the unnormalized functions without changing the cost.)

Partial functions. In practice the output value of a Boolean function is often specified only at certain inputs $x_1 \ldots x_n$, and the outputs in other cases don't really matter. We might know, for example, that some of the input combinations will never arise. In such cases, we place an asterisk into the corresponding positions of the truth table, instead of specifying 0 or 1 everywhere.

The seven-segment display provides a case in point, because most of its applications involve only the ten binary-coded decimal inputs for which we have $(x_1x_2x_3x_4)_2 \leq 9$. We don't care what segments are visible in the other six cases. So the truth tables of (42) actually become

$$
\begin{aligned}
a &= \text{1011 0111 11** ****,} \\
b &= \text{1111 1001 11** ****,} \\
c &= \text{1101 1111 11** ****,} \\
d &= \text{1011 0110 11** ****,} \\
e &= \text{1010 0010 10** ****,} \\
f &= \text{1000 111* 11** ****,} \\
g &= \text{0011 1110 11** ****.}
\end{aligned}
\tag{44}
$$

(Function f here has an asterisk also in position $x_1x_2x_3x_4 = 0111$, because a '7' can be displayed as either ⁊ or ⁊. Both of these styles appeared about equally often in the display units available to the author when this section was written. Truncated variants of the 6 and the 9 were sometimes seen in olden days, but they have thankfully disappeared.)

Asterisks in truth tables are generally known as *don't-cares* — a quaint term that could only have been invented by an electrical engineer. Table 3 shows that the freedom to choose arbitrary outputs is advantageous. For example, there are $\binom{16}{3}2^{13} = 4{,}587{,}520$ truth tables with 3 don't-cares; 69% of them cost 4 or less, even though only 21% of the asterisk-free truth tables permit such economy. On the other hand, don't-cares don't save us as much as we might hope; exercise 63 proves that a random function with, say, 30% don't-cares in its truth table tends to save only about 30% of the cost of a fully specified function.

What is the shortest Boolean chain that evaluates the seven partially specified functions in (44)? Our greedy-footprint method adapts itself readily to the presence of don't-cares, because we can OR together the footprints of all 2^d functions that match a pattern with d asterisks. The initial costs to evaluate each function separately are now reduced to $C(a) = 3$, $C(b) = C(c) = 2$, $C(d) = 5$, $C(e) = 2$, $C(f) = 3$, $C(g) = 4$, totalling just 21 instead of 37. Function g hasn't gotten cheaper, but it does have a larger footprint. Proceeding as before, but taking advantage of the don't-cares, we now can find a suitable chain of length only 11 — a chain with fewer than 1.6 operations per output(!):

$$
\begin{aligned}
x_5 &= x_1 \lor x_2, & \bar{d} = x_9 &= x_6 \oplus x_8, & \bar{c} = x_{13} &= \bar{x}_4 \land x_{10}, \\
x_6 &= x_3 \oplus x_5, & \bar{f} = x_{10} &= \bar{x}_5 \land x_8, & \bar{e} = x_{14} &= x_4 \lor x_9, \\
x_7 &= \bar{x}_2 \land x_6, & \bar{b} = x_{11} &= x_2 \land \bar{x}_9, & g = x_{15} &= x_6 \lor x_{11}. \\
x_8 &= x_4 \lor x_7, & \bar{a} = x_{12} &= \bar{x}_3 \land x_9,
\end{aligned}
\tag{45}
$$

This amazing chain, found by Corey Plover in 2011, chooses x_7 non-greedily.

Tic-tac-toe. Let's turn now to a slightly larger problem, based on a popular children's game. Two players take turns filling the cells of a 3×3 grid. One player writes ✗'s and the other writes ○'s, continuing until there either are three

Table 3

THE NUMBER OF 4-VARIABLE FUNCTIONS WITH d DON'T-CARES AND COST c

	$c=0$	$c=1$	$c=2$	$c=3$	$c=4$	$c=5$	$c=6$	$c=7$
$d=0$	10	60	456	2474	10624	24184	25008	2720
$d=1$	160	960	7296	35040	131904	227296	119072	2560
$d=2$	1200	7200	52736	221840	700512	816448	166144	
$d=3$	5600	33600	228992	831232	2045952	1381952	60192	
$d=4$	18200	108816	666528	2034408	3505344	1118128	3296	
$d=5$	43680	257472	1367776	3351488	3491648	433568	32	
$d=6$	80080	455616	2015072	3648608	1914800	86016		
$d=7$	114400	606944	2115648	2474688	533568	12032		
$d=8$	128660	604756	1528808	960080	71520	896		
$d=9$	114080	440960	707488	197632	4160			
$d=10$	78960	224144	189248	20160				
$d=11$	41440	72064	25472	800				
$d=12$	15480	12360	1280					
$d=13$	3680	800						
$d=14$	480							
$d=15$	32							
$d=16$	1							

X's or three O's in a straight line (in which case that player wins) or all nine cells are filled without a winner (in which case it's a "cat's game" or tie). For example, the game might proceed thus:

$$\tag{46}$$

X has won. Our goal is to design a machine that plays tic-tac-toe optimally — making a winning move from each position in which a forced victory is possible, and never making a losing move from a position in which defeat is avoidable.

More precisely, we will set things up so that there are 18 Boolean variables $x_1, \ldots, x_9, o_1, \ldots, o_9$, which govern lamps to illuminate cells of the current position. The cells are numbered $\begin{smallmatrix}1&2&3\\4&5&6\\7&8&9\end{smallmatrix}$ as on a telephone dial. Cell j displays an X if $x_j = 1$, an O if $o_j = 1$, or remains blank if $x_j = o_j = 0$.* We never have $x_j = o_j = 1$, because that would display '⊗'. We shall assume that the variables $x_1 \ldots x_9 o_1 \ldots o_9$ have been set to indicate a legal position in which nobody has won; the computer plays the X's, and it is the computer's turn to move. For this purpose we want to define nine functions $y_1, \ldots, y_9$, where y_j means "change x_j from 0 to 1." If the current position is a cat's game, we should make $y_1 = \cdots = y_9 = 0$; otherwise exactly one y_j should be equal to 1, and of course the output value $y_j = 1$ should occur only if $x_j = o_j = 0$.

With 18 variables, each of our nine functions y_j will have a truth table of size $2^{18} = 262{,}144$. It turns out that only 4520 legal inputs $x_1 \ldots x_9 o_1 \ldots o_9$ are

---

* This setup is based on an exhibit from the early 1950s at the Museum of Science and Industry in Chicago, where the author was first introduced to the magic of switching circuits. The machine in Chicago, designed circa 1940 by W. Keister at Bell Telephone Laboratories, allowed me to go first; yet I soon discovered that there was no way to defeat it. Therefore I decided to move as stupidly as possible, hoping that the designer had not anticipated such bizarre behavior. In fact I allowed the machine to reach a position where it had two winning moves; and it seized *both* of them! Moving twice is of course a flagrant violation of the rules, so I had won a moral victory even though the machine announced that I had lost.

I commenced an examination of a game called "tit-tat-to" ...
to ascertain what number of combinations were required
for all the possible variety of moves and situations.
I found this to be comparatively insignificant.
... A difficulty, however, arose of a novel kind.
When the automaton had to move, it might occur that there were
two different moves, each equally conducive to his winning the game.
... Unless, also, some provision were made,
the machine would attempt two contradictory motions.

— CHARLES BABBAGE, *Passages from the Life of a Philosopher* (1864)

possible, so those truth tables are 98.3% filled with don't-cares. Still, 4520 is uncomfortably large if we hope to design and understand a Boolean chain that makes sense intuitively. Section 7.1.4 will discuss alternative ways to represent Boolean functions, by which it is often possible to deal with hundreds of variables even though the associated truth tables are impossibly large.

Most functions of 18 variables require more than $2^{18}/18$ gates, but let's hope we can do better. Indeed, a plausible strategy for making suitable moves in tic-tac-toe suggests itself immediately, in terms of several conditions that aren't hard to recognize:

w_j, an ✗ in cell j will win, completing a line of ✗'s;
b_j, an ◯ in cell j would lose, completing a line of ◯'s;
f_j, an ✗ in cell j will give ✗ two ways to win;
d_j, an ◯ in cell j would give ◯ two ways to win.

For example, ✗'s move to the center in (46) was needed to block ◯, so it was of type b_5; fortunately it was also of type f_5, forcing a win on the next move.

Let $L = \{\{1,2,3\},\{4,5,6\},\{7,8,9\},\{1,4,7\},\{2,5,8\},\{3,6,9\},\{1,5,9\},\{3,5,7\}\}$ be the set of winning lines. Then we have

$$m_j = \bar{x}_j \wedge \bar{o}_j; \qquad\qquad\qquad \text{[moving in cell } j \text{ is legal]} \quad (47)$$

$$w_j = m_j \wedge \bigvee\nolimits_{\{i,j,k\}\in L}(x_i \wedge x_k); \qquad \text{[moving in cell } j \text{ wins]} \quad (48)$$

$$b_j = m_j \wedge \bigvee\nolimits_{\{i,j,k\}\in L}(o_i \wedge o_k); \qquad \text{[moving in cell } j \text{ blocks]} \quad (49)$$

$$f_j = m_j \wedge S_2\big(\{\alpha_{ik} \mid \{i,j,k\} \in L\}\big); \qquad \text{[moving in cell } j \text{ forks]} \quad (50)$$

$$d_j = m_j \wedge S_2\big(\{\beta_{ik} \mid \{i,j,k\} \in L\}\big); \qquad \text{[moving in cell } j \text{ defends]} \quad (51)$$

here α_{ik} and β_{ik} denote a single ✗ or ◯ together with a blank, namely

$$\alpha_{ik} = (x_i \wedge m_k) \vee (m_i \wedge x_k), \qquad \beta_{ik} = (o_i \wedge m_k) \vee (m_i \wedge o_k). \quad (52)$$

For example, $b_1 = m_1 \wedge \big((o_2 \wedge o_3) \vee (o_4 \wedge o_7) \vee (o_5 \wedge o_9)\big)$; $f_2 = m_2 \wedge S_2(\alpha_{13}, \alpha_{58}) = m_2 \wedge \alpha_{13} \wedge \alpha_{58}$; $d_5 = m_5 \wedge S_2(\beta_{19}, \beta_{28}, \beta_{37}, \beta_{46})$.

With these definitions we might try rank-ordering our moves thus:

$$\{w_1,\ldots,w_9\} > \{b_1,\ldots,b_9\} > \{f_1,\ldots,f_9\} > \{d_1,\ldots,d_9\} > \{m_1,\ldots,m_9\}. \quad (53)$$

"Win if you can; otherwise block if you can; otherwise fork if you can; otherwise defend if you can; otherwise make a legal move." Furthermore, when choosing between legal moves it seems sensible to use the ordering

$$m_5 > m_1 > m_3 > m_9 > m_7 > m_2 > m_6 > m_8 > m_4, \qquad (54)$$

because 5, the middle cell, occurs in four winning lines, while a corner move to 1, 3, 9, or 7 occurs in three, and a side cell 2, 6, 8, or 4 occurs in only two. We might as well adopt this ordering of subscripts within all five groups of moves $\{w_j\}$, $\{b_j\}$, $\{f_j\}$, $\{d_j\}$, and $\{m_j\}$ in (53).

To ensure that at most one move is chosen, we define w'_j, b'_j, f'_j, d'_j, m'_j to mean "a prior choice is better." Thus, $w'_5 = 0$, $w'_1 = w_5$, $w'_3 = w_1 \vee w'_1$, ..., $w'_4 = w_8 \vee w'_8$, $b'_5 = w_4 \vee w'_4$, $b'_1 = b_5 \vee b'_5$, ..., $m'_4 = m_8 \vee m'_8$. Then we can complete the definition of a tic-tac-toe automaton by letting

$$y_j = (w_j \wedge \overline{w'_j}) \vee (b_j \wedge \overline{b'_j}) \vee (f_j \wedge \overline{f'_j}) \vee (d_j \wedge \overline{d'_j}) \vee (m_j \wedge \overline{m'_j}), \quad \text{for } 1 \le j \le 9. \ (55)$$

So we've constructed 9 gates for the m's, 48 for the w's, 48 for the b's, 144 for the α's and β's, 35 for the f's (with the help of Fig. 9), 35 for the d's, 43 for the primed variables, and 80 for the y's. Furthermore we can use our knowledge of partial 4-variable functions to reduce the six operations in (52) to only four,

$$\alpha_{ik} = (x_i \oplus x_k) \wedge \overline{(o_i \oplus o_k)}, \qquad \beta_{ik} = \overline{(x_i \oplus x_k)} \wedge (o_i \oplus o_k). \qquad (56)$$

This trick saves 48 gates; so our design has cost 394 gates altogether.

The strategy for tic-tac-toe in (47)–(56) works fine in most cases, but it also has some glaring glitches. For example, it loses ignominiously in the game

$$\boxed{} \quad \boxed{} \quad \boxed{} \quad \boxed{} \quad \boxed{} \quad \boxed{} \quad \boxed{}; \qquad (57)$$

the second $\times$ move is d_3, defending against a fork by $\bigcirc$, yet it actually forces $\bigcirc$ to fork in the opposite corner! Another failure arises, for example, after position $\boxed{}$, when move m_5 leads to the cat's game $\boxed{}$, $\boxed{}$, $\boxed{}$, $\boxed{}$, $\boxed{}$, $\boxed{}$, $\boxed{}$, instead of to the victory for $\times$ that appeared in (46). Exercise 65 patches things up and obtains a fully correct Boolean tic-tac-toe player that needs just 445 gates.

*Functional decomposition. If the function $f(x_1, \ldots, x_n)$ can be written in the form $g(x_1, \ldots, x_k, h(x_{k+1}, \ldots, x_n))$, it's usually a good idea to evaluate $y = h(x_{k+1}, \ldots, x_n)$ first and then to compute $g(x_1, \ldots, x_k, y)$. Robert L. Ashenhurst inaugurated the study of such decompositions in 1952 [see *Annals Computation Lab. Harvard University* **29** (1957), 74–116], and observed that there's an easy way to recognize when f has this special property: If we write the truth table for f in a $2^k \times 2^{n-k}$ array as in (36), with rows for each setting of $x_1 \ldots x_k$ and columns for each setting of $x_{k+1} \ldots x_n$, then the desired subfunctions g and h exist if and only if the columns of this array have at most two different values. For example, the truth table for the function $\langle x_1 x_2 \langle x_3 x_4 x_5 \rangle \rangle$ is

$$\begin{matrix}
0 & 0 & 0 & 0 & 0 & 0 & 0 & 0 \\
0 & 0 & 0 & 1 & 0 & 1 & 1 & 1 \\
0 & 0 & 0 & 1 & 0 & 1 & 1 & 1 \\
1 & 1 & 1 & 1 & 1 & 1 & 1 & 1
\end{matrix}$$

when expressed in this two-dimensional form. One type of column corresponds to the case $h(x_{k+1}, \ldots, x_n) = 0$; the other corresponds to $h(x_{k+1}, \ldots, x_n) = 1$.

In general the variables $X = \{x_1, \ldots, x_n\}$ might be partitioned into any two disjoint subsets $Y = \{y_1, \ldots, y_k\}$ and $Z = \{z_1, \ldots, z_{n-k}\}$, and we might have $f(x) = g(y, h(z))$. We could test for a (Y, Z) decomposition by looking at the columns of the $2^k \times 2^{n-k}$ truth table whose rows correspond to values of y. But there are 2^n such ways to partition X; and all of them are potential winners, except for trivial cases when $|Y| = 0$ or $|Z| \le 1$. How can we avoid examining such a humongous number of possibilities?

A practical way to proceed was discovered by V. Y.-S. Shen, A. C. McKellar, and P. Weiner [*IEEE Transactions* **C-20** (1971), 304–309], whose method usually needs only $O(n^2)$ steps to identify any potentially useful partition (Y, Z) that may exist. The basic idea is simple: Suppose $x_i \in Z$, $x_j \in Z$, and $x_m \in Y$. Define eight binary vectors δ_l for $l = (l_1 l_2 l_3)_2$, where δ_l has (l_1, l_2, l_3) respectively in components (i, j, m), and zeros elsewhere. Consider any randomly chosen vector $x = x_1 \ldots x_n$, and evaluate $f_l = f(x \oplus \delta_l)$ for $0 \le l \le 7$. Then the four pairs

$$\binom{f_0}{f_1} \qquad \binom{f_2}{f_3} \qquad \binom{f_4}{f_5} \qquad \binom{f_6}{f_7} \tag{58}$$

will appear in a 2×4 submatrix of the $2^k \times 2^{n-k}$ truth table. So a decomposition is impossible if these pairs are distinct, or if they contain three different values.

Let's call the pairs "good" if they're all equal, or if they have only two different values. Otherwise they're "bad." If f has essentially random behavior, we'll soon find bad pairs if we do this experiment with several different randomly chosen vectors x, because only 88 of the 256 possibilities for $f_0 f_1 \ldots f_7$ correspond to a good set of pairs; the probability of finding good pairs ten times in a row is only $(\frac{88}{256})^{10} \approx .00002$. And when we do discover bad pairs, we can conclude that

$$x_i \in Z \quad \text{and} \quad x_j \in Z \implies x_m \in Z, \tag{59}$$

because the alternative $x_m \in Y$ is impossible.

Suppose, for example, that $n = 9$ and that f is the function whose truth table $11001001000011\ldots00101$ consists of the 512 most significant bits of π, in binary notation. (This is the "more-or-less random function" that we studied for $n = 4$ in (5) and (6) above.) Bad pairs for this π function are quickly found in each of the cases (i, j, m) for which $m \ne i < j \ne m$. Indeed, in the author's experiments, 170 of those 252 cases were decided immediately; the average number of random x vectors per case was only 1.52; and only one case needed as many as eight x's before bad pairs appeared. Thus (59) holds for all relevant (i, j, m), and the function is clearly indecomposable. In fact, exercise 73 points out that we needn't make 252 tests to establish the indecomposability of this π function; only $\binom{n}{2} = 36$ of them would have been sufficient.

Turning to a less random function, let $f(x_1, \ldots, x_9) = (\det X) \bmod 2$, where

$$X = \begin{pmatrix} x_1 & x_2 & x_3 \\ x_4 & x_5 & x_6 \\ x_7 & x_8 & x_9 \end{pmatrix}. \tag{60}$$

This function does not satisfy condition (59) when $i = 1$, $j = 2$, and $m = 3$, because there are no bad pairs in that case. But it does satisfy (59) for $4 \le m \le 9$ when $\{i, j\} = \{1, 2\}$. We can denote this behavior by the convenient abbreviation '$12 \Rightarrow 456789$'; the full set of implications, for all pairs $\{i, j\}$, is

$12 \Rightarrow 456789$	$18 \Rightarrow 34569$	$27 \Rightarrow 34569$	$37 \Rightarrow 24568$	$48 \Rightarrow 12369$	$67 \Rightarrow 12358$
$13 \Rightarrow 456789$	$19 \Rightarrow 24568$	$28 \Rightarrow 134679$	$38 \Rightarrow 14567$	$49 \Rightarrow 12358$	$68 \Rightarrow 12347$
$14 \Rightarrow 235689$	$23 \Rightarrow 456789$	$29 \Rightarrow 14567$	$39 \Rightarrow 124578$	$56 \Rightarrow 123789$	$69 \Rightarrow 124578$
$15 \Rightarrow 36789$	$24 \Rightarrow 36789$	$34 \Rightarrow 25789$	$45 \Rightarrow 123789$	$57 \Rightarrow 12369$	$78 \Rightarrow 123456$
$16 \Rightarrow 25789$	$25 \Rightarrow 134679$	$35 \Rightarrow 14789$	$46 \Rightarrow 123789$	$58 \Rightarrow 134679$	$79 \Rightarrow 123456$
$17 \Rightarrow 235689$	$26 \Rightarrow 14789$	$36 \Rightarrow 124578$	$47 \Rightarrow 235689$	$59 \Rightarrow 12347$	$89 \Rightarrow 123456$

(see exercise 69). Bad pairs are a little more difficult to find when we probe this function at random: The average number of x's needed in the author's experiments rose to about 3.6, when bad pairs did exist. And of course there was a need to limit the testing, by choosing a tolerance threshold t and then giving up when t consecutive trials failed to find any bad pairs. Choosing $t = 10$ would have found all but 8 of the 198 implications listed above.

Implications like (59) are Horn clauses, and we know from Section 7.1.1 that it's easy to make further deductions from Horn clauses. Indeed, the method of exercise 74 will deduce that the only possible partition with $|Z| > 1$ is the trivial one ($Y = \emptyset$, $Z = \{x_1, \ldots, x_9\}$), after looking at fewer than 50 cases (i, j, m).

Similar results occur when $f(x_1, \ldots, x_9) = [\operatorname{per} X > 0]$, where per denotes the *permanent* function. (In this case f tells us if there is a perfect matching in the bipartite subgraph of $K_{3,3}$ whose edges are specified by the variables $x_1 \ldots x_9$.) Now there are just 180 implications,

$12 \Rightarrow 456789$	$18 \Rightarrow 3459$	$27 \Rightarrow 3459$	$37 \Rightarrow 2468$	$48 \Rightarrow 1269$	$67 \Rightarrow 1358$
$13 \Rightarrow 456789$	$19 \Rightarrow 2468$	$28 \Rightarrow 134679$	$38 \Rightarrow 1567$	$49 \Rightarrow 1358$	$68 \Rightarrow 2347$
$14 \Rightarrow 235689$	$23 \Rightarrow 456789$	$29 \Rightarrow 1567$	$39 \Rightarrow 124578$	$56 \Rightarrow 123789$	$69 \Rightarrow 124578$
$15 \Rightarrow 3678$	$24 \Rightarrow 3678$	$34 \Rightarrow 2579$	$45 \Rightarrow 123789$	$57 \Rightarrow 1269$	$78 \Rightarrow 123456$
$16 \Rightarrow 2579$	$25 \Rightarrow 134679$	$35 \Rightarrow 1489$	$46 \Rightarrow 123789$	$58 \Rightarrow 134679$	$79 \Rightarrow 123456$
$17 \Rightarrow 235689$	$26 \Rightarrow 1489$	$36 \Rightarrow 124578$	$47 \Rightarrow 235689$	$59 \Rightarrow 2347$	$89 \Rightarrow 123456$,

only 122 of which would have been discovered with $t = 10$ as the cutoff threshold. (The best choice of t is not clear; perhaps it should vary dynamically.) Still, those 122 Horn clauses were more than enough to establish indecomposability.

What about a decomposable function? With $f = \langle x_2 x_3 x_6 x_9 \langle x_1 x_4 x_5 x_7 x_8 \rangle \rangle$ we get $i \wedge j \Rightarrow m$ for all $m \notin \{i, j\}$, except when $\{i, j\} \subseteq \{1, 4, 5, 7, 8\}$; in the latter case, m must also belong to $\{1, 4, 5, 7, 8\}$. Although only 185 of these 212 implications were discovered with tolerance $t = 10$, the partition $Y = \{x_2, x_3, x_6, x_9\}$, $Z = \{x_1, x_4, x_5, x_7, x_8\}$ emerged quickly as a strong possibility.

Whenever a potential decomposition is supported by the evidence, we need to verify that the corresponding $2^k \times 2^{n-k}$ truth table does indeed have only one or two distinct columns. But we're happy to spend 2^n units of time on that verification, because we've greatly simplified the evaluation of f.

The comparison function $f = \left[(x_1x_2x_3x_4)_2 \geq (x_5x_6x_7x_8)_2 + x_9\right]$ is another interesting case. Its 184 potentially deducible implications are

$12 \Rightarrow 3456789$	$18 \Rightarrow 2345679$	$27 \Rightarrow 34689$	$37 \Rightarrow 489$	$48 \Rightarrow 9$	$67 \Rightarrow 23489$
$13 \Rightarrow 2456789$	$19 \Rightarrow 2345678$	$28 \Rightarrow 34679$	$38 \Rightarrow 479$	$49 \Rightarrow 8$	$68 \Rightarrow 23479$
$14 \Rightarrow 2356789$	$23 \Rightarrow 46789$	$29 \Rightarrow 34678$	$39 \Rightarrow 478$	$56 \Rightarrow 1234789$	$69 \Rightarrow 23478$
$15 \Rightarrow 2346789$	$24 \Rightarrow 36789$	$34 \Rightarrow 789$	$45 \Rightarrow 1236789$	$57 \Rightarrow 1234689$	$78 \Rightarrow 349$
$16 \Rightarrow 2345789$	$25 \Rightarrow 1346789$	$35 \Rightarrow 1246789$	$46 \Rightarrow 23789$	$58 \Rightarrow 1234679$	$79 \Rightarrow 348$
$17 \Rightarrow 2345689$	$26 \Rightarrow 34789$	$36 \Rightarrow 24789$	$47 \Rightarrow 389$	$59 \Rightarrow 1234678$	$89 \Rightarrow 4,$

and 145 of them were found when $t = 10$. Three decompositions reveal themselves in this case, having $Z = \{x_4, x_8, x_9\}$, $Z = \{x_3, x_4, x_7, x_8, x_9\}$, and $Z = \{x_2, x_3, x_4, x_6, x_7, x_8, x_9\}$, respectively. Ashenhurst proved that we can reduce f immediately as soon as we find a nontrivial decomposition; the other decompositions will show up later, when we try to reduce the simpler functions g and h.

*Decomposition of partial functions. When the function f is only partially specified, a decomposition with partition (Y, Z) hinges on being able to assign values to the don't-cares so that at most two different columns appear in the corresponding $2^k \times 2^{n-k}$ truth table.

Two vectors $u_1 \ldots u_m$ and $v_1 \ldots v_m$ consisting of 0s, 1s, and *s are said to be *incompatible* if either $u_j = 0$ and $v_j = 1$ or $u_j = 1$ and $v_j = 0$, for some j — equivalently, if the subcubes of the m-cube specified by u and v have no points in common. Consider the graph whose vertices are the columns of a truth table with don't-cares, where $u \rule[0.4ex]{1em}{0.4pt} v$ if and only if u and v are incompatible. We can assign values to the *s to achieve at most two distinct columns if and only if this graph is *bipartite*. For if $u_1, \ldots, u_l$ are mutually compatible, their generalized consensus $u_1 \sqcup \cdots \sqcup u_l$, defined in exercise 7.1.1–32, is compatible with all of them. [See S. L. Hight, *IEEE Trans.* **C-22** (1973), 103–110; E. Boros, V. Gurvich, P. L. Hammer, T. Ibaraki, and A. Kogan, *Discrete Applied Math.* **62** (1995), 51–75.] Since a graph is bipartite if and only if it contains no odd cycles, we can easily test this condition with a depth-first search (see Section 7.4.1.2).

Consequently the method of Shen, McKellar, and Weiner works also when don't-cares are present: The four pairs in (58) are considered bad if and only if three of them are mutually incompatible. We can operate almost as before, although bad pairs will naturally be harder to find when there are lots of *s (see exercise 72). However, Ashenhurst's theorem no longer applies. When several decompositions exist, they all should be explored further, because they might use different settings of the don't-cares, and some might be better than the others.

Although most functions $f(x)$ have no simple decomposition $g(y, h(z))$, we needn't give up hope too quickly, because other forms like $g(y, h_1(z), h_2(z))$ might well lead to an efficient chain. If, for example, f is symmetric in three of its variables $\{z_1, z_2, z_3\}$, we can always write $f(x) = g\big(y, S_{1,2}(z_1, z_2, z_3), S_{1,3}(z_1, z_2, z_3)\big)$, since $S_{1,2}(z_1, z_2, z_3)$ and $S_{1,3}(z_1, z_2, z_3)$ characterize the value of $z_1 + z_2 + z_3$. (Notice that just four steps will suffice to compute both $S_{1,2}$ and $S_{1,3}$.)

In general, as observed by H. A. Curtis [*JACM* **8** (1961), 484–496], $f(x)$ can be expressed in the form $g(y, h_1(z), \ldots, h_r(z))$ if and only if the $2^k \times 2^{n-k}$ truth table corresponding to Y and Z has at most 2^r different columns. And when don't-cares are present, the same result holds if and only if the incompatibility graph for Y and Z can be colored with at most 2^r colors.

For example, the function $f(x) = (\det X) \bmod 2$ considered above turns out to have eight distinct columns when $Z = \{x_4, x_5, x_6, x_7, x_8, x_9\}$; that's a surprisingly small number, considering that the truth table has 8 rows and 64 columns. From this fact we might be led to discover how to expand a determinant by cofactors of the first row,

$$f(x) = x_1 {\wedge} h_1(x_4, \ldots, x_9) \oplus x_2 {\wedge} h_2(x_4, \ldots, x_9) \oplus x_3 {\wedge} h_3(x_4, \ldots, x_9),$$

if we didn't already know such a rule.

When there are $d \leq 2^r$ different columns, we can think of $f(x)$ as a function of y and $h(z)$, where h takes each binary vector $z_1 \ldots z_{n-k}$ into one of the values $\{0, 1, \ldots, d-1\}$. Thus $(h_1, \ldots, h_r)$ is essentially an encoding of the different column types, and we hope to find very simple functions $h_1, \ldots, h_r$ that provide such an encoding. Moreover, if d is strictly less than 2^r, the function $g(y, h_1, \ldots, h_r)$ will have many don't-cares that may well decrease its cost.

The distinct columns might also suggest a function g for which the h's have don't-cares. For example, we can use $g(y_1, y_2, h_1, h_2) = (y_1 \oplus (h_1 \wedge y_2)) \wedge h_2$ when all columns are either $(0, 0, 0, 0)^T$ or $(0, 0, 1, 1)^T$ or $(0, 1, 1, 0)^T$; then the value of $h_1(z)$ is arbitrary when z corresponds to an all-zero column. H. A. Curtis has explained how to exploit this idea when $|Y| = 1$ and $|Z| = n - 1$ [see *IEEE Transactions* **C-25** (1976), 1033–1044].

For a comprehensive discussion of decomposition techniques, see Richard M. Karp, *J. Society for Industrial and Applied Math.* **11** (1963), 291–335.

Larger values of n. We've been considering only rather tiny examples of Boolean functions. Theorem S tells us that large, random examples are inherently difficult; but practical examples might well be highly nonrandom. So it makes sense to search for simplifications using heuristic methods.

When n grows, the best ways currently known for dealing with Boolean functions generally start with a Boolean chain — not with a huge truth table — and they try to improve that chain via "local changes." The chain can be specified by a set of equations. Then, if an intermediate result is used in comparatively few subsequent steps, we can try to eliminate it, temporarily making those subsequent steps into functions of three variables, and reformulating those functions in order to make a better chain when possible.

For example, suppose the gate $x_i = x_j \circ x_k$ is used only once, in the gate $x_l = x_i \,\square\, x_m$, so that $x_l = (x_j \circ x_k) \,\square\, x_m$. Other gates might already exist, by which we have computed other functions of x_j, x_k, and x_m; and the definitions of x_j, x_k, and x_m may imply that some of the joint values of (x_j, x_k, x_m) are impossible. Thus we might be able to compute x_l from other gates by doing just one further operation. For example, if $x_i = x_j \wedge x_k$ and $x_l = x_i \vee x_m$, and if the values $x_j \vee x_m$ and $x_k \vee x_m$ appear elsewhere in the chain, we can set $x_l = (x_j {\vee} x_m) \wedge (x_k {\vee} x_m)$; this eliminates x_i and reduces the cost by 1. Or if, say, $x_j \wedge (x_k \oplus x_m)$ appears elsewhere and we know that $x_j x_k x_m \neq 101$, we can set $x_l = x_m \oplus (x_j \wedge (x_k \oplus x_m))$.

If x_i is used only in x_l and x_l is used only in x_p, then gate x_p depends on four variables, and we might be able to reduce the cost by using our total knowledge of four-variable functions, obtaining x_p in a better way while eliminating x_i and x_l. Similarly, if x_i appears only in x_l and x_p, we can eliminate x_i if we find a better way to evaluate two different functions of four variables, possibly with don't-cares and with other functions of those four variables available for free. Again, we know how to solve such problems, using the footprint method discussed above.

When no local changes are able to decrease the cost, we can also try local changes that preserve or even increase the cost, in order to discover different kinds of chains that might simplify in other ways. We shall discuss such local search methods extensively in Section 7.10.

Excellent surveys of techniques for Boolean optimization, which electrical engineers call the problem of "multilevel logic synthesis," have been published by R. K. Brayton, G. D. Hachtel, and A. L. Sangiovanni-Vincentelli, *Proceedings of the IEEE* **78** (1990), 264–300, and in the book *Synthesis and Optimization of Digital Circuits* by G. De Micheli (McGraw–Hill, 1994).

Lower bounds.   Theorem S tells us that nearly every Boolean function of $n \geq 12$ variables is hard to evaluate, requiring a chain whose length exceeds $2^n/n$. Yet modern computers, which are built from logic circuits involving electric signals that represent thousands of Boolean variables, happily evaluate zillions of Boolean functions every microsecond. Evidently there are plenty of important functions that can be evaluated quickly, in spite of Theorem S. Indeed, the proof of that theorem was indirect; we simply counted the cases of low cost, so we learned absolutely nothing about any particular examples that might arise in practice. When we want to compute a given function and we can only think of a laborious way to do the job, how can we be sure that there's no tricky shortcut?

The answer to that question is almost scandalous: After decades of concentrated research, computer scientists have been unable to find *any* explicit family of functions $f(x_1, \ldots, x_n)$ whose cost is inherently nonlinear, as n increases. The true behavior is $2^n/n$, but no lower bound as strong as $n \log \log \log n$ has yet been proved! Of course we could rig up artificial examples, such as "the lexicographically smallest truth table of length 2^n that isn't achievable by any Boolean chain of length $\lfloor 2^n/n \rfloor - 1$"; but such functions are surely not explicit. The truth table of an explicit function $f(x_1, \ldots, x_n)$ should be computable in at most, say, 2^{cn} units of time for some constant c; that is, the time needed to specify all of the function values should be polynomial in the length of the truth table. Under those ground rules, no family of single-output functions is currently known to have a combinational complexity that exceeds $3n + O(1)$ as $n \to \infty$. [See N. Blum, *Theoretical Computer Science* **28** (1984), 337–345.]

The picture is not totally bleak, because several interesting *linear* lower bounds have been proved for functions of practical importance. A basic way to obtain such results was introduced by N. P. Red'kin in 1970: Suppose we have an optimum chain of cost r for $f(x_1, \ldots, x_n)$. By setting $x_n \leftarrow 0$ or $x_n \leftarrow 1$, we obtain reduced chains for the functions $g(x_1, \ldots, x_{n-1}) = f(x_1, \ldots, x_{n-1}, 0)$ and $h(x_1, \ldots, x_{n-1}) = f(x_1, \ldots, x_{n-1}, 1)$, having cost $r - u$ if x_n was used as an input to u different gates. Moreover, if x_n is used in a "canalizing" gate $x_i = x_n \circ x_k$, where the operator $\circ$ is neither $\oplus$ nor $\equiv$, some setting of x_n will force x_i to be constant, thereby further reducing the chain for g or h. Lower bounds on g and/or h therefore lead to a lower bound on f. (See exercises 77–81.)

But where are the proofs of nonlinear lower bounds? Almost every problem with a yes-no answer can be formulated as a Boolean function, so there's no shortage of explicit functions that we don't know how to evaluate in linear time, or even in polynomial time. For example, any directed graph G with vertices $\{v_1, \ldots, v_m\}$ can be represented by its adjacency matrix X, where $x_{ij} = [v_i \to v_j]$; then

$$f(x_{12}, \ldots, x_{1m}, \ldots, x_{m1}, \ldots, x_{m(m-1)}) = [G \text{ has a Hamiltonian path}] \quad (61)$$

is a Boolean function of $n = m(m-1)$ variables. We would dearly love to be able to evaluate this function in, say, n^4 steps. We do know how to compute the truth table for f in $O(m!\, 2^n) = 2^{n+O(\sqrt{n} \log n)}$ steps, since only $m!$ potential Hamiltonian paths exist; thus f is indeed "explicit." But nobody knows how to evaluate f in polynomial time, or how to prove that there isn't a $4n$-step chain.

For all we know, short Boolean chains for f might exist, for each n. After all, Figs. 9 and 10 reveal the existence of fiendishly clever chains even in the cases of 4 and 5 variables. Efficient chains for all of the larger problems that we ever will need to solve might well be "out there" — yet totally beyond our grasp, because we don't have time to find them. Even if an omniscient being revealed the simple chains to us, we might find them incomprehensible, because the shortest proof of their correctness might be longer than the number of cells in our brains.

Theorem S rules out such a scenario for most Boolean functions. But fewer than 2^{100} Boolean functions will ever be of practical importance in the entire history of the world, and Theorem S tells us zilch about them.

In 1974, Larry Stockmeyer and Albert Meyer were, however, able to construct a Boolean function f whose complexity is provably huge. Their f isn't "explicit," in the precise sense described above, but it isn't artificial either; it arises naturally in mathematical logic. Consider symbolic statements such as

```
048+1015≠1063;                                                     (62)
∀m∃n(m<n+1);                                                       (63)
∀n∃m(m+1<n);                                                       (64)
∀a∀b(b≥a+2⇒∃ab(a<ab∧ab<b));                                        (65)
∀A∀B(A≡B⇔¬∃n(n∈A∧n∉B∨n∈B∧n∉A));                                    (66)
∀A(∃n(n∈A)⇒∃m(m∈A∧∀n(n∈A⇒m≤n)));                                   (67)
∀A(∃n(n∈A)⇒∃m(m∈A∧∀n(n∈A⇒m≥n)));                                   (68)
∃P∀a((a∈P⇔a+3∉P)⇔a<1000);                                          (69)
∀A∀B(∀C∀c(C≡A∧c=1∨C≡B∧c=0⇒(∀n(n∈C⇔n+1∈C)⇔c=1))⇒¬A≡B).             (70)
```

Stockmeyer and Meyer defined a language L by using the 63-character alphabet

∀∃¬()≡∈∉+∧∨≠⊕<≤=≠≥>abcdefghijklmnopqABCDEFGHIJKLMNOPQ0123456789

and giving conventional meanings to these symbols. Strings of lowercase letters within the sentences of L, like 'ab' in (65), represent numeric variables, restricted to nonnegative integers; strings of uppercase letters represent set variables, restricted to finite sets of such numbers. For example, (66) means, "For all finite sets A and B, we have $A = B$ if and only if there doesn't exist a number n that is in A but not in B, or in B but not in A." Some of these statements are true; others are false. (See exercise 82.)

All of the strings (62)–(70) belong to L, but the language is actually quite restricted: The only arithmetic operation allowed on a number is to add a constant; we can write 'a+13' but not 'a+b'. The only relation allowed between a number and a set is elementhood ($\in$ or $\notin$). The only relation allowed between sets is equality ($\equiv$). Furthermore all variables must be quantified by $\exists$ or $\forall$.*

Every sentence of L that has length $k \le n$ can be represented by a binary vector of length $6n$, with zeros in the last $6(n - k)$ bits. Let $f(x)$ be a Boolean function of $6n$ variables such that $f(x) = 1$ whenever x represents a true sentence of L, and $f(x) = 0$ whenever x represents a sentence that is false; the value of $f(x)$ is unspecified when x doesn't represent a meaningful sentence. The truth table for such a function f can be constructed in a finite number of steps, according to theorems of Büchi and Elgot [*Zeitschrift für math. Logik und Grundlagen der Math.* **6** (1960), 66–92; *Transactions of the Amer. Math. Soc.* **98** (1961), 21–51]. But "finite" does not mean "feasible": Stockmeyer and Meyer proved that

$$C(f) > 2^{r-5} \qquad \text{whenever } n \ge 460 + .302r + 5.08 \ln r \text{ and } r > 36. \qquad (71)$$

In particular, we have $C(f) > 2^{426} > 10^{128}$ when $n = 621$. *A Boolean chain with that many gates could never be built*, since 10^{128} is a generous upper bound on the number of protons in the universe. So this is a fairly small, finite problem that will never be solved.

Details of Stockmeyer and Meyer's proof appear in *JACM* **49** (2002), 753–784. The basic idea is that the language L, though limited, is rich enough to describe truth tables and the complexity of Boolean chains, using fairly short sentences; hence f has to deal with inputs that essentially refer to themselves.

*For further reading. Thousands of significant papers have been written about networks of Boolean gates, because such networks underlie so many aspects of theory and practice. We have focused in this section chiefly on topics that are relevant to computer programming for sequential machines. But other topics have also been extensively investigated, of primary relevance to parallel computation, such as the study of small-depth circuits in which gates can have any number of inputs ("unlimited fanin"). Ingo Wegener's book *The Complexity of*

---

* Technically speaking, the sentences of L belong to "weak second-order monadic logic with one successor." Weak second-order logic allows quantification over finite sets; monadic logic with k successors is the theory of unlabeled k-ary trees.

Boolean Functions (Teubner and Wiley, 1987) provides a good introduction to the entire subject.

We have mostly considered Boolean chains in which all binary operators have equal importance. For our purposes, gates such as $\oplus$ or $\overline{\subset}$ are neither more nor less desirable than gates such as $\wedge$ or $\vee$. But it's natural to wonder if we can get by with only the monotone operators $\wedge$ and $\vee$ when we are computing a monotone function. Alexander Razborov has developed striking proof techniques to show that, in fact, monotone operators by themselves have inherently limited capabilities. He proved, for example, that all AND-OR chains to determine whether the permanent of an $n \times n$ matrix of 0s and 1s is zero or nonzero must have cost $n^{\Omega(\log n)}$. [See *Doklady Akademii Nauk SSSR* **281** (1985), 798–801; *Matematicheskie Zametki* **37** (1985), 887–900.] By contrast, we will see in Section 7.5.1 that this problem, equivalent to "bipartite matching," is solvable in only $O(n^{2.5})$ steps. Furthermore, the efficient methods in that section can be implemented as Boolean chains of only slightly larger cost, when we allow negation or other Boolean operations in addition to $\wedge$ and $\vee$. (Vaughan Pratt has called this "the power of negative thinking.") An introduction to Razborov's methods appears in exercises 85 and 86.

EXERCISES

▸ **1.** [*24*] The "random" function in formula (6) corresponds to a Boolean chain of cost 4 and depth 4. Find a formula of depth 3 that has the same cost.

2. [*21*] Show how to compute (a) $w \oplus \langle xyz \rangle$ and (b) $w \wedge \langle xyz \rangle$ with formulas that have depth 3 and cost 5.

3. [*M23*] (B. I. Finikov, 1957.) If the Boolean function $f(x_1, \ldots, x_n)$ is true at exactly k points, prove that $L(f) < 2n + (k-2)2^{k-1}$. *Hint:* Think of $k = 3$ and $n = 10^6$.

4. [*M28*] Prove that the minimum depth and formula length of a Boolean function satisfy $\lg L(f) < D(f) < \alpha \lg L(f)$ when $L(f) > 1$, where $\alpha = 1/\lg \rho \approx 2.464965$ is related to the "plastic constant" ρ of Eq. 7.1.4–(90). *Hint:* If f contains a subformula g, we have $f = (g?\ f_1 : f_0)$ for suitable f_1 and f_0.

▸ **5.** [*21*] The Fibonacci threshold function $F_n(x_1, \ldots, x_n) = \langle x_1^{F_1} x_2^{F_2} \ldots x_{n-1}^{F_{n-1}} x_n^{F_{n-2}} \rangle$ was analyzed in exercise 7.1.1–101, when $n \geq 3$. Is there an efficient way to evaluate it?

6. [*20*] True or false: A Boolean function $f(x_1, \ldots, x_n)$ is normal if and only if it satisfies the general distributive law $f(x_1, \ldots, x_n) \wedge y = f(x_1 \wedge y, \ldots, x_n \wedge y)$.

7. [*20*] Convert the Boolean chain '$x_5 = x_1 \bar{\vee} x_4$, $x_6 = \bar{x}_2 \vee x_5$, $x_7 = \bar{x}_1 \wedge \bar{x}_3$, $x_8 = x_6 \equiv x_7$' to an equivalent chain $(\hat{x}_5, \hat{x}_6, \hat{x}_7, \hat{x}_8)$ in which every step is normal.

▸ **8.** [*20*] Explain why (11) is the truth table of variable x_k.

9. [*20*] Algorithm L determines the lengths of shortest formulas for all functions f, but it gives no further information. Extend the algorithm so that it also provides actual minimum-length formulas like (6).

▸ **10.** [*20*] Modify Algorithm L so that it computes $D(f)$ instead of $L(f)$.

▸ **11.** [*22*] Modify Algorithm L so that, instead of lengths $L(f)$, it computes upper bounds $U(f)$ and footprints $\phi(f)$ as described in the text.

12. [*15*] What Boolean chain is equivalent to the minimum-memory scheme (13)?

13. [*16*] What are the truth tables of f_1, f_2, f_3, f_4, and f_5 in example (13)?

14. [*22*] What's a convenient way to compute the $5n(n-1)$ truth tables of (17), given the truth table of g? (Use bitwise operations as in (15) and (16).)

15. [*28*] Find short-as-possible ways to evaluate the following Boolean functions using minimum memory: (a) $S_1(x_1, x_2, x_3)$; (b) $S_2(x_1, x_2, x_3, x_4)$; (c) $S_1(x_1, x_2, x_3, x_4)$; (d) the function in (18).

16. [*HM33*] Prove that fewer than 2^{118} of the 2^{128} Boolean functions $f(x_1, \ldots, x_7)$ are computable in minimum memory.

▶ **17.** [*25*] (M. S. Paterson, 1977.) Although Boolean functions $f(x_1, \ldots, x_n)$ cannot always be evaluated in n registers, prove that $n+1$ registers are always sufficient. In other words, show that there is always a sequence of operations like (13) to compute $f(x_1, \ldots, x_n)$ if we allow $0 \le j(i), k(i) \le n$.

▶ **18.** [*35*] Investigate optimum minimum-memory computations for $f(x_1, x_2, x_3, x_4, x_5)$: How many classes of five-variable functions have $C_m(f) = r$, for $r = 0, 1, 2, \ldots$?

19. [*M22*] If a Boolean chain uses n variables and has length $r < n+2$, prove that it must be either a "top-down" or a "bottom-up" construction.

▶ **20.** [*40*] (R. Schroeppel, 2004.) A Boolean chain is *canalizing* if it does not use the operators $\oplus$ or $\equiv$. Find the optimum cost, length, and depth of all 4-variable functions under this constraint. Does the footprint heuristic still give optimum results?

21. [*46*] For how many four-variable functions did the Harvard researchers discover an optimum vacuum-tube circuit in 1951?

22. [*21*] Explain the chain for S_3 in Fig. 10, by noting that it incorporates the chain for $S_{2,3}$ in Fig. 9. Find a similar chain for $S_2(x_1, x_2, x_3, x_4, x_5)$.

▶ **23.** [*23*] Figure 10 illustrates only 16 of the 64 symmetric functions on five elements. Explain how to write down optimum chains for the others.

24. [*47*] Does every symmetric function f have $C_m(f) = C(f)$?

▶ **25.** [*17*] Suppose we want a Boolean chain that includes *all* functions of n variables: Let $f_k(x_1, \ldots, x_n)$ be the function whose truth table is the binary representation of k, for $0 \le k < m = 2^{2^n}$. What is $C(f_0 f_1 \ldots f_{m-1})$?

26. [*25*] True or false: If $f(x_0, \ldots, x_n) = (x_0 \wedge g(x_1, \ldots, x_n)) \oplus h(x_1, \ldots, x_n)$, where g and h are nontrivial Boolean functions whose joint cost is $C(gh)$, then $C(f) = 2 + C(gh)$.

▶ **27.** [*23*] Can a full adder (22) be implemented in five steps using only minimum memory (that is, completely inside three one-bit registers)?

28. [*26*] Prove that $C(u'v') = C(u''v'') = 5$ for the two-output functions defined by

$$(u'v')_2 = (x + y - (uv)_2) \bmod 4, \qquad (u''v'')_2 = (-x - y - (uv)_2) \bmod 4.$$

Use these functions to evaluate $[(x_1 + \cdots + x_n) \bmod 4 = 0]$, in fewer than $2.5n$ steps.

29. [*M28*] Prove that the text's circuit for sideways addition (27) has depth $O(\log n)$.

30. [*M25*] Solve the binary recurrence (28) for the cost $s(n)$ of sideways addition.

31. [*21*] If $f(x_1, \ldots, x_n)$ is symmetric, prove that $C(f) \le 5n + O(n/\log n)$.

32. [*HM16*] Why does the solution to (30) satisfy $t(n) = 2^n + O(2^{n/2})$?

33. [*HM22*] True or false: If $1 \le N \le 2^n$, the first N minterms of $\{x_1, \ldots, x_n\}$ can all be evaluated in $N + O(\sqrt{N})$ steps, as $n \to \infty$ and $N \to \infty$.

▶ **34.** [*22*] A *priority encoder* has $n = 2^m - 1$ inputs $x_1 \ldots x_n$ and m outputs $y_1 \ldots y_m$, where $(y_1 \ldots y_m)_2 = k$ if and only if $k = \max\{j \mid j = 0 \text{ or } x_j = 1\}$. Design a priority encoder that has cost $O(n)$ and depth $O(m)$.

35. [*23*] If $n > 1$, show that the conjunctions $x_1 \wedge \cdots \wedge x_{k-1} \wedge x_{k+1} \wedge \cdots \wedge x_n$ for $1 \le k \le n$ can all be computed from $(x_1, \ldots, x_n)$ with total cost $\le 3n - 6$.

▶ **36.** [*M28*] (R. E. Ladner and M. J. Fischer, 1980.) Let y_k be the "prefix" $x_1 \wedge \cdots \wedge x_k$ for $1 \le k \le n$. Clearly $C(y_1 \ldots y_n) = n - 1$ and $D(y_1 \ldots y_n) = \lceil \lg n \rceil$; but we can't simultaneously minimize both cost and depth. Find a chain of optimum depth $\lceil \lg n \rceil$ that has cost $< 4n$.

37. [*M28*] (Marc Snir, 1986.) Given $n \ge m \ge 1$, consider the following algorithm:

S1. [Upward loop.] For $l \leftarrow 1, 2, \ldots, \lceil \lg m \rceil$, set $x_{\min(m, 2^t k)} \leftarrow x_{2^t(k-1/2)} \wedge x_{\min(m, 2^t k)}$ for $k \ge 1$ and $2^t(k - 1/2) < m$.

S2. [Downward loop.] For $t \leftarrow \lceil \lg m \rceil - 1, \lceil \lg m \rceil - 2, \ldots, 1$, set $x_{2^t(k+1/2)} \leftarrow x_{2^t k} \wedge x_{2^t(k+1/2)}$ for $k \ge 1$ and $2^t(k + 1/2) < m$.

S3. [Extension.] For $k \leftarrow m+1, m+2, \ldots, n$, set $x_k \leftarrow x_{k-1} \wedge x_k$. ∎

a) Prove that this algorithm solves the prefix problem of exercise 36: It transforms $(x_1, x_2, \ldots, x_n)$ into $(x_1, x_1 \wedge x_2, \ldots, x_1 \wedge x_2 \wedge \cdots \wedge x_n)$.

b) Let $c(m, n)$ and $d(m, n)$ be the cost and depth of the corresponding Boolean chain. Prove for fixed m that, if n is sufficiently large, $c(m, n) + d(m, n) = 2n - 2$.

c) Given $n > 1$, what is $d(n) = \min_{1 \le m \le n} d(m, n)$? Show that $d(n) < 2 \lg n$.

d) Prove that there's a Boolean chain of cost $2n - 2 - d$ and depth d for the prefix problem whenever $d(n) \le d < n$. (This cost is optimum, by exercise 81.)

38. [*25*] In Section 5.3.4 we studied *sorting networks*, by which $\hat{S}(n)$ comparator modules are able to sort n numbers $(x_1, x_2, \ldots, x_n)$ into ascending order. If the inputs x_j are 0s and 1s, each comparator module is equivalent to two gates $(x \wedge y, x \vee y)$; so a sorting network corresponds to a certain kind of Boolean chain, which evaluates n particular functions of $(x_1, x_2, \ldots, x_n)$.

a) What are the n functions $f_1 f_2 \ldots f_n$ that a sorting network computes?

b) Show that those functions $\{f_1, f_2, \ldots, f_n\}$ can be computed in $O(n)$ steps with a chain of depth $O(\log n)$. (Hence sorting networks aren't asymptotically optimal, Booleanwise.)

▶ **39.** [*M21*] (M. S. Paterson and P. Klein, 1980.) Implement the 2^m-way multiplexer $M_m(x_1, \ldots, x_m; y_0, y_1, \ldots, y_{2^m-1})$ of (31) with an efficient chain that simultaneously establishes the upper bounds $C(M_m) \le 2n + O(\sqrt{n})$ and $D(M_m) \le m + O(\log m)$.

40. [*25*] If $n \ge k \ge 1$, let $f_{nk}(x_1, \ldots, x_n)$ be the "k in a row" function,

$$(x_1 \wedge \cdots \wedge x_k) \vee (x_2 \wedge \cdots \wedge x_{k+1}) \vee \cdots \vee (x_{n+1-k} \wedge \cdots \wedge x_n).$$

Show that the cost $C(f_{nk})$ of this function is less than $4n - 3k$.

41. [*M23*] (*Conditional-sum adders.*) One way to accomplish binary addition (25) with depth $O(\log n)$ is based on the multiplexer trick of exercise 4: If $(xx')_2 + (yy')_2 = (zz')_2$, where $|x'| = |y'| = |z'|$, we have either $(x)_2 + (y)_2 = (z)_2$ and $(x')_2 + (y')_2 = (z')_2$, or $(x)_2 + (y)_2 + 1 = (z)_2$ and $(x')_2 + (y')_2 = (1z')_2$. To save time, we can compute *both* $(x)_2 + (y)_2$ and $(x)_2 + (y)_2 + 1$ simultaneously as we compute $(x')_2 + (y')_2$. Afterwards, when we know whether or not the less significant part $(x')_2 + (y')_2$ produces a carry, we can use multiplexers to select the correct bits for the most significant part.

If this method is used recursively to build $2n$-bit adders from n-bit adders, how many gates are needed when $n = 2^m$? What is the corresponding depth?

42. [*30*] In the binary addition (25), let $u_k = x_k \wedge y_k$ and $v_k = x_k \oplus y_k$ for $0 \le k < n$.

a) Show that $z_k = v_k \oplus c_k$, where the carry bits c_k satisfy

$$c_k = u_{k-1} \vee (v_{k-1} \wedge (u_{k-2} \vee (v_{k-2} \wedge (\cdots (v_1 \wedge u_0) \cdots)))).$$

b) Let $U_k^k = 0$, $V_k^k = 1$, and $U_j^{k+1} = u_k \vee (v_k \wedge U_j^k)$, $V_j^{k+1} = v_k \wedge V_j^k$, for $k \ge j$. Prove that $c_k = U_0^k$, and that $U_i^k = U_j^k \vee (V_j^k \wedge U_i^j)$, $V_i^k = V_j^k \wedge V_i^j$ for $i \le j \le k$.

c) Let $h(m) = 2^{m(m-1)/2}$. Show that when $n = h(m)$, the carries $c_1, \ldots, c_n$ can all be evaluated with depth $(m+1)m/2 \approx \lg n + \sqrt{2 \lg n}$ and with total cost $O(2^m n)$.

▶ **43.** [*28*] A *finite-state transducer* is an abstract machine with a finite input alphabet A, a finite output alphabet B, and a finite set of internal states Q. One of those states, q_0, is called the "initial state." Given a string $\alpha = a_1 \ldots a_n$, where each $a_j \in A$, the machine computes a string $\beta = b_1 \ldots b_n$, where each $b_j \in B$, as follows:

T1. [Initialize.] Set $j \leftarrow 1$ and $q \leftarrow q_0$.

T2. [Done?] Terminate the algorithm if $j > n$.

T3. [Output b_j.] Set $b_j \leftarrow c(q, a_j)$.

T4. [Advance j.] Set $q \leftarrow d(q, a_j)$, $j \leftarrow j + 1$, and return to step T2. ∎

The machine has built-in instructions that specify $c(q, a) \in B$ and $d(q, a) \in Q$ for every state $q \in Q$ and every character $a \in A$. The purpose of this exercise is to show that, if the alphabets A and B of any finite state transducer are encoded in binary, the string β can be computed from α by a Boolean chain of size $O(n)$ and depth $O(\log n)$.

a) Consider the problem of changing a binary vector $a_1 \ldots a_n$ to $b_1 \ldots b_n$ by setting

$$b_j \leftarrow a_j \oplus [a_j = a_{j-1} = \cdots = a_{j-k} = 1 \text{ and } a_{j-k-1} = 0, \text{ where } k \ge 1 \text{ is odd}],$$

assuming that $a_0 = 0$. For example, $\alpha = 110010010001111101101010 \mapsto \beta = 100010010010101001001010$. Prove that this transformation can be carried out by a finite state transducer with $|A| = |B| = |Q| = 2$.

b) Suppose a finite state transducer with $|Q| = 2$ is in state q_j after reading $a_1 \ldots a_{j-1}$. Explain how to compute the sequence $q_1 \ldots q_n$ with a Boolean chain of cost $O(n)$ and depth $O(\log n)$, using the construction of Ladner and Fischer in exercise 36. (From this sequence $q_1 \ldots q_n$ it is easy to compute $b_1 \ldots b_n$, since $b_j = c(q_j, a_j)$.)

c) Apply the method of (b) to the problem in (a).

▶ **44.** [*26*] (R. E. Ladner and M. J. Fischer, 1980.) Show that the problem of binary addition (25) can be viewed as a finite state transduction. Describe the Boolean chain that results from the construction of exercise 43 when $n = 2^m$, and compare it to the conditional-sum adder of exercise 41.

45. [*HM20*] Why doesn't the proof of Theorem S simply argue that the number of ways to choose $j(i)$ and $k(i)$ so that $1 \le j(i), k(i) < i$ is $n^2(n+1)^2 \ldots (n+r-1)^2$?

▶ **46.** [*HM21*] Let $\alpha(n) = c(n, \lfloor 2^n/n \rfloor)/2^{2^n}$ be the fraction of n-variable Boolean functions $f(x_1, \ldots, x_n)$ for which $C(f) \le 2^n/n$. Prove that $\alpha(n) \to 0$ rapidly as $n \to \infty$.

47. [*M23*] Extend Theorem S to functions with n inputs and m outputs.

48. [*HM23*] Find the smallest integer $r = r(n)$ such that $(r-1)! \, 2^{2^n} \le 2^{2r+1}(n+r-1)^{2r}$, (a) exactly when $1 \le n \le 16$; (b) asymptotically when $n \to \infty$.

49. [*HM25*] Prove that, as $n \to \infty$, almost all Boolean functions $f(x_1, \ldots, x_n)$ have minimum formula length $L(f) > 2^n/\lg n - 2^{n+2}/(\lg n)^2$.

50. [*24*] What are the prime implicants and prime clauses of the prime-number function (35)? Express that function in (a) DNF (b) CNF of minimum length.

51. [*20*] What representation of the prime-number detector replaces (37), if rows of the truth table are based on $x_5 x_6$ instead of $x_1 x_2$?

52. [*23*] What choices of k and l minimize the upper bound (38) when $5 \le n \le 16$?

53. [*HM22*] Estimate (38) when $k = \lfloor 2 \lg n \rfloor$ and $l = \lceil 2^k/(n - 3 \lg n) \rceil$ and $n \to \infty$.

54. [*29*] Find a short Boolean chain to evaluate all six of the functions $f_j(x) = [x_1 x_2 x_3 x_4 \in A_j]$, where $A_1 = \{0010, 0101, 1011\}$, $A_2 = \{0001, 1111\}$, $A_3 = \{0011, 0111, 1101\}$, $A_4 = \{1001, 1111\}$, $A_5 = \{1101\}$, $A_6 = \{0101, 1011\}$. (These six functions appear in the prime-number detector (37).) Compare your chain to the minterm-first evaluation scheme of Lupanov's general method.

55. [*34*] Show that the cost of the 6-bit prime-detecting function is at most 14.

▶ **56.** [*16*] Explain why all functions with 14 or more don't-cares in Table 3 have cost 0.

57. [*19*] What seven-segment "digits" are displayed when $(x_1 x_2 x_3 x_4)_2 > 9$ in (45)?

▶ **58.** [*30*] A 4×4-bit *S-box* is a permutation of the 4-bit vectors $\{0000, 0001, \ldots, 1111\}$; such permutations are used as components of well-known cryptographic systems such as the USSR All-Union standard GOST 28147 (1989). Every 4×4-bit S-box corresponds to a sequence of four functions $f_1(x_1, x_2, x_3, x_4), \ldots, f_4(x_1, x_2, x_3, x_4)$, which transform $x_1 x_2 x_3 x_4 \mapsto f_1 f_2 f_3 f_4$.

   Find all 4×4-bit S-boxes for which $C(f_1) = C(f_2) = C(f_3) = C(f_4) = 7$.

59. [*29*] One of the S-boxes satisfying the conditions of exercise 58 takes $(0, \ldots, \mathsf{f}) \mapsto (0, 6, 5, \mathsf{b}, 3, 9, \mathsf{f}, \mathsf{e}, \mathsf{c}, 4, 7, 8, \mathsf{d}, 2, \mathsf{a}, 1)$; in other words, the truth tables of (f_1, f_2, f_3, f_4) are respectively ($\mathsf{179a}, \mathsf{63e8}, \mathsf{5b26}, \mathsf{3e29}$). Find a Boolean chain that evaluates these four "maximally difficult" functions in fewer than 20 steps.

60. [*23*] (Frank Ruskey.) Suppose $z = (x + y) \bmod 3$, where $x = (x_1 x_2)_2$, $y = (y_1 y_2)_2$, $z = (z_1 z_2)_2$, and each two-bit value is required to be either 00, 01, or 10. Compute z_1 and z_2 from x_1, x_2, y_1, and y_2 in six Boolean steps.

61. [*34*] Continuing exercise 60, find a good way to compute $z = (x + y) \bmod 5$, using the three-bit values 000, 001, 010, 011, 100.

62. [*HM23*] Consider a random Boolean partial function of n variables that has $2^n c$ "cares" and $2^n d$ "don't-cares," where $c + d = 1$. Prove that the cost of almost all such partial functions exceeds $2^n c/n$.

63. [*HM35*] (L. A. Sholomov, 1969.) Continuing exercise 62, prove that all such functions have cost $\le 2^n c/n(1 + O(n^{-1} \log n))$. *Hint:* There is a set of $2^m(1 + k)$ vectors $x_1 \ldots x_k$ that intersects every $(k - m)$-dimensional subcube of the k-cube.

64. [*25*] (*Magic Fifteen.*) Two players alternately select digits from 1 to 9, using no digit twice; the winner, if any, is the first to get three digits that sum to 15. What's a good strategy for playing this game?

▶ **65.** [*35*] Modify the tic-tac-toe strategy of (47)–(56) so that it always plays correctly.

66. [*20*] Criticize the moves chosen in exercise 65. Are they always optimum?

▶ **67.** [*40*] Instead of simply finding one correct move for each position in tic-tac-toe, we might prefer to find them all. In other words, given $x_1 \ldots x_9 o_1 \ldots o_9$, we could try to compute nine outputs $g_1 \ldots g_9$, where $g_j = 1$ if and only if a move into cell j is legal and minimizes X's worst-case outcome. For example, exclamation marks indicate all of the right moves for X in the following typical positions:

▦; ▦; ▦; ▦; ▦; ▦; ▦; ▦; ▦; ▦; ▦; ▦; ▦; ▦; ▦; ▦.

A machine that chooses randomly among these possibilities is more fun to play against than a machine that has only one fixed strategy.

One attractive way to solve the all-good-moves problem is to use the fact that tic-tac-toe has eight symmetries. Imagine a chip that has 18 inputs $x_1 \ldots x_9 o_1 \ldots o_9$ and three outputs (c, s, m), for "corner," "side," and "middle," with the property that the desired functions g_j can be computed by hooking together eight of the chips appropriately:

$$g_1 = c(x_1 x_2 x_3 x_4 x_5 x_6 x_7 x_8 x_9 o_1 o_2 o_3 o_4 o_5 o_6 o_7 o_8 o_9)$$
$$\vee\, c(x_1 x_4 x_7 x_2 x_5 x_8 x_3 x_6 x_9 o_1 o_4 o_7 o_2 o_5 o_8 o_3 o_6 o_9),$$

$$g_2 = s(x_1 x_2 x_3 x_4 x_5 x_6 x_7 x_8 x_9 o_1 o_2 o_3 o_4 o_5 o_6 o_7 o_8 o_9)$$
$$\vee\, s(x_3 x_2 x_1 x_6 x_5 x_4 x_9 x_8 x_7 o_3 o_2 o_1 o_6 o_5 o_4 o_9 o_8 o_7),$$

$$g_3 = c(x_3 x_2 x_1 x_6 x_5 x_4 x_9 x_8 x_7 o_3 o_2 o_1 o_6 o_5 o_4 o_9 o_8 o_7)$$
$$\vee\, c(x_3 x_6 x_9 x_2 x_5 x_8 x_1 x_4 x_7 o_3 o_6 o_9 o_2 o_5 o_8 o_1 o_4 o_7),$$

$$g_4 = s(x_1 x_4 x_7 x_2 x_5 x_8 x_3 x_6 x_9 o_1 o_4 o_7 o_2 o_5 o_8 o_3 o_6 o_9)$$
$$\vee\, s(x_7 x_4 x_1 x_8 x_5 x_2 x_9 x_6 x_3 o_7 o_4 o_1 o_8 o_5 o_2 o_9 o_6 o_3), \qquad \ldots$$

$$g_9 = c(x_9 x_8 x_7 x_6 x_5 x_4 x_3 x_2 x_1 o_9 o_8 o_7 o_6 o_5 o_4 o_3 o_2 o_1)$$
$$\vee\, c(x_9 x_6 x_3 x_8 x_5 x_2 x_7 x_4 x_1 o_9 o_6 o_3 o_8 o_5 o_2 o_7 o_4 o_1),$$

and g_5 is the OR of the m outputs from all eight chips.

Design the logic for such a chip, using fewer than 2000 gates.

68. [*M25*] Consider the n-bit π function $\pi_n(x_1 \ldots x_n)$, whose value is the $(x_1 \ldots x_n)_2$th bit to the right of the most significant bit in the binary representation of π. Does the method of exercise 4.3.1–39, which describes an efficient way to compute arbitrary bits of π, prove that $C(\pi_n) < 2^n/n$ for sufficiently large n?

69. [*M24*] Let the multilinear representation of f be

$$\alpha_{000} \oplus \alpha_{001} x_m \oplus \alpha_{010} x_j \oplus \alpha_{011} x_j x_m \oplus \alpha_{100} x_i \oplus \alpha_{101} x_i x_m \oplus \alpha_{110} x_i x_j \oplus \alpha_{111} x_i x_j x_m,$$

where each coefficient α_l is a function of the variables $\{x_1, \ldots, x_n\} \setminus \{x_i, x_j, x_m\}$.

a) Prove that the pairs (58) are "good" if and only if the coefficients satisfy

$$\alpha_{010}\alpha_{101} = \alpha_{011}\alpha_{100}, \quad \alpha_{101}\alpha_{110} = \alpha_{100}\alpha_{111}, \quad \text{and} \quad \alpha_{110}\alpha_{011} = \alpha_{111}\alpha_{010}.$$

b) For which values (i, j, m) are the pairs bad, when $f = (\det X) \bmod 2$? (See (60).)

▶ **70.** [*M27*] Let X be the 3×3 Boolean matrix (60). Find efficient chains for the Boolean functions (a) $(\det X) \bmod 2$; (b) [per $X > 0$]; (c) [$\det X > 0$].

▶ **71.** [*M26*] Suppose $f(x)$ is equal to 0 with probability p at each point $x = x_1 \ldots x_n$, independent of its value at other points.

a) What is the probability that the pairs (58) are good?

b) What is the probability that bad pairs (58) exist?

c) What is the probability that bad pairs (58) are found in at most t random trials?

d) What is the expected time to test case (i, j, m), as a function of p, t, and n?

72. [*M24*] Extend the previous exercise to the case of partial functions, where $f(x) = 0$ with probability p, $f(x) = 1$ with probability q, and $f(x) = *$ with probability r.

▶ **73.** [*20*] If bad pairs (58) exist for all (i, j, m) with $m \neq i \neq j \neq m$, show that the indecomposability of f can be deduced after testing only $\binom{n}{2}$ well-chosen triples (i, j, m).

74. [*25*] Extend the idea in the previous exercise, suggesting a strategy for choosing successive triples (i, j, m) when using the method of Shen, McKellar, and Weiner.

75. [*20*] What happens when the text's decomposition procedure is applied to the "all-equal" function $S_{0,n}(x_1, \ldots, x_n)$?

▶ **76.** [*M26*] (D. Uhlig, 1974.) The purpose of this exercise is to prove the amazing fact that, for certain functions f, the best chain to evaluate the Boolean function

$$F(u_1, \ldots, u_n, v_1, \ldots, v_n) = f(u_1, \ldots, u_n) \vee f(v_1, \ldots, v_n)$$

costs *less* than $2C(f)$; hence functional decomposition is *not* always a good idea.

    We let $n = m + 2^m$ and write $f(i_1, \ldots, i_m, x_0, \ldots, x_{2^m-1}) = f_i(x)$, where i is regarded as the number $(i_1 \ldots i_m)_2$. Then $(u_1, \ldots, u_n) = (i_1, \ldots, i_m, x_0, \ldots, x_{2^m-1})$, $(v_1, \ldots, v_n) = (j_1, \ldots, j_m, y_0, \ldots, y_{2^m-1})$, and $F(u, v) = f_i(x) \vee f_j(y)$.

   a) Prove that a chain of cost $O(n^2)$ suffices to evaluate the $2^m + 1$ functions

$$z_l = x \oplus (([l \leq i] \oplus [i \leq j]) \wedge (x \oplus y)), \qquad 0 \leq l \leq 2^m,$$

    from given vectors i, j, x, and y; each z_l is a vector of length 2^m, and the one-bit quantity $([l \leq i] \oplus [i \leq j])$ is ANDed with each component of $x \oplus y$.

   b) Let $g_i(x) = f_i(x) \oplus f_{i-1}(x)$ for $0 \leq i \leq 2^m$, where $f_{-1}(x) = f_{2^m}(x) = 0$. Estimate the cost of computing the $2^m + 1$ values $c_l = g_l(z_l)$, given the vectors z_l, for $0 \leq l \leq 2^m$.

   c) Let $c'_l = c_l \wedge ([i \leq j] \equiv [l \leq i])$ and $c''_l = c_l \wedge ([i \leq j] \equiv [j > l])$. Prove that

$$f_i(x) = c'_0 \oplus c'_1 \oplus \cdots \oplus c'_{2^m}, \qquad f_j(y) = c''_0 \oplus c''_1 \oplus \cdots \oplus c''_{2^m}.$$

   d) Conclude that $C(F) \leq 2^n/n + O(2^n (\log n)/n^2)$. (When n is sufficiently large, this cost is definitely less than $2^{n+1}/n$, but functions f exist with $C(f) > 2^n/n$.)

   e) For clarity, write out the chain for F when $m = 1$ and $f(i, x_0, x_1) = (i \wedge x_0) \vee x_1$.

▶ **77.** [*35*] (N. P. Red'kin, 1970.) Suppose a Boolean chain uses only the operations AND, OR, or NOT; thus, every step is either $x_i = x_{j(i)} \wedge x_{k(i)}$ or $x_i = x_{j(i)} \vee x_{k(i)}$ or $x_i = \bar{x}_{j(i)}$. Prove that if such a chain computes either the "odd parity" function $f_n(x_1, \ldots, x_n) = x_1 \oplus \cdots \oplus x_n$ or the "even parity" function $\bar{f}_n(x_1, \ldots, x_n) = 1 \oplus x_1 \oplus \cdots \oplus x_n$, where $n \geq 2$, the length of the chain is at least $4(n - 1)$.

78. [*26*] (W. J. Paul, 1977.) Let $f(x_1, \ldots, x_m, y_0, \ldots, y_{2^m-1})$ be any Boolean function that equals y_k whenever $(x_1 \ldots x_m)_2 = k \in S$, for some given set $S \subseteq \{0, 1, \ldots, 2^m - 1\}$; we don't care about the value of f at other points. Show that $C(f) \geq 2|S| - 2$ whenever S is nonempty. (In particular, when $S = \{0, 1, \ldots, 2^m - 1\}$, the multiplexer chain of exercise 39 is asymptotically optimum.)

79. [*32*] (C. P. Schnorr, 1976.) Say that variables u and v are "mates" in a Boolean chain if there is exactly one simple path between them in the corresponding binary tree diagram. Two variables can be mates only if they are each used only once in the chain; but this necessary condition is not sufficient. For example, variables 2 and 4 are mates in the chain for $S_{1,2,3}$ in Fig. 9, but they are not mates in the chain for S_2.

   a) Prove that a Boolean chain on n variables with no mates has cost $\geq 2n - 2$.

   b) Prove that $C(f) = 2n - 3$ when f is the all-equal function $S_{0,n}(x_1, \ldots, x_n)$.

▶ **80.** [*M29*] (L. J. Stockmeyer, 1977.) Another notation for symmetric functions is sometimes convenient: If $\alpha = a_0 a_1 \ldots a_n$ is any binary string, let $S_\alpha(x) = a_{\nu x}$. For example, $\langle x_1 x_2 x_3 \rangle = S_{0011}$ and $x_1 \oplus x_2 \oplus x_3 = S_{0101}$ in this notation. Notice that $S_\alpha(0, x_2, \ldots, x_n) = S_{\alpha'}(x_2, \ldots, x_n)$ and $S_\alpha(1, x_2, \ldots, x_n) = S_{'\alpha}(x_2, \ldots, x_n)$, where α' and $'\alpha$ stand respectively for α with its last or first element deleted. Also,

$$S_\alpha(f(x_3, \ldots, x_n), \bar{f}(x_3, \ldots, x_n), x_3, \ldots, x_n) = S_{'\alpha'}(x_3, \ldots, x_n)$$

when f is any Boolean function of $n - 2$ variables.

a) A parity function has $a_0 \neq a_1 \neq a_2 \neq \cdots \neq a_n$. Assume that $n \geq 2$. Prove that if S_α is not a parity function and $S_{'\alpha'}$ isn't constant, then

$$C(S_\alpha) \geq \max(C(S_{\alpha'})+2,\, C(S_{'\alpha})+2,\, \min(C(S_{\alpha'})+3,\, C(S_{'\alpha})+3,\, C(S_{'\alpha'})+5)).$$

b) What lower bounds on $C(S_k)$ and $C(S_{\geq k})$ follow from this result, when $0 \leq k \leq n$?

81. [*23*] (M. Snir, 1986.) Show that any chain of cost c and depth d for the prefix problem of exercise 36 has $c + d \geq 2n - 2$.

▶ **82.** [*M23*] Explain the logical sentences (62)–(70). Which of them are true?

83. [*21*] If there's a Boolean chain for $f(x_1, \ldots, x_n)$ that contains p canalizing operations, show that $C(f) < (p+1)(n+p/2)$.

84. [*M20*] A *monotone Boolean chain* is a Boolean chain in which every operator $\circ_i$ is monotone. The length of a shortest monotone chain for f is denoted by $C^+(f)$. If there's a monotone Boolean chain for $f(x_1, \ldots, x_n)$ that contains p occurrences of $\wedge$ and q occurrences of $\vee$, show that $C^+(f) < \min((p+1)(n+p/2), (q+1)(n+q/2))$.

▶ **85.** [*M28*] Let M_n be the set of all monotone functions of n variables. If L is a family of functions contained in M_n, let

$$x \sqcup y = \bigwedge \{z \in L \mid z \supseteq x \vee y\} \qquad \text{and} \qquad x \sqcap y = \bigvee \{z \in L \mid z \subseteq x \wedge y\}.$$

We call L "legitimate" if it includes the constant functions 0 and 1 as well as the projection functions x_j for $1 \leq j \leq n$, and if $x \sqcup y \in L$, $x \sqcap y \in L$ whenever $x, y \in L$.

a) When $n = 3$ we can write $M_3 = \{$00, 01, 03, 05, 11, 07, 13, 15, 0f, 33, 55, 17, 1f, 37, 57, 3f, 5f, 77, 7f, ff$\}$, representing each function by its hexadecimal truth table. There are 2^{15} families L such that $\{$00, 0f, 33, 55, ff$\} \subseteq L \subseteq M_3$; how many of them are legitimate?

b) If A is a subset of $\{1, \ldots, n\}$, let $\lceil A \rceil = \bigvee_{a \in A} x_a$; also let $\lceil \infty \rceil = 1$. Suppose $\mathcal{A}$ is a family of subsets of $\{1, \ldots, n\}$ that contains all sets of size ≤ 1 and is closed under intersection; in other words, $A \cap B \in \mathcal{A}$ whenever $A \in \mathcal{A}$ and $B \in \mathcal{A}$. Prove that the family $L = \{\lceil A \rceil \mid A \in \mathcal{A} \cup \infty\}$ is legitimate.

c) Let $(x_{n+1}, \ldots, x_{n+r})$ be a monotone Boolean chain (1). Suppose $(\hat{x}_{n+1}, \ldots, \hat{x}_{n+r})$ is obtained from the same Boolean chain, but with every operator $\wedge$ changed to $\sqcap$ and with every operator $\vee$ changed to $\sqcup$, with respect to some legitimate family L. Prove that, for $n + 1 \leq l \leq n + r$, we must have

$$\hat{x}_l \subseteq x_l \vee \bigvee_{i=n+1}^{l} \{\hat{x}_i \oplus (\hat{x}_{j(i)} \vee \hat{x}_{k(i)}) \mid \circ_i = \vee\};$$

$$x_l \subseteq \hat{x}_l \vee \bigvee_{i=n+1}^{l} \{\hat{x}_i \oplus (\hat{x}_{j(i)} \wedge \hat{x}_{k(i)}) \mid \circ_i = \wedge\}.$$

86. [*HM37*] A graph G on vertices $\{1,\ldots,n\}$ can be defined by $N = \binom{n}{2}$ Boolean variables x_{uv} for $1 \le u < v \le n$, where $x_{uv} = [u \text{—} v \text{ in } G]$. Let f be the function $f(x) = [G \text{ contains a triangle}]$; for example, when $n = 4$, $f(x_{12}, x_{13}, x_{14}, x_{23}, x_{24}, x_{34}) = (x_{12} \wedge x_{13} \wedge x_{23}) \vee (x_{12} \wedge x_{14} \wedge x_{24}) \vee (x_{13} \wedge x_{14} \wedge x_{34}) \vee (x_{23} \wedge x_{24} \wedge x_{34})$. The purpose of this exercise is to prove that the monotone complexity $C^+(f)$ is $\Omega(n/\log n)^3$.

a) If $u_j \text{—} v_j$ for $1 \le j \le r$ in a graph G, call $S = \{\{u_1, v_1\}, \ldots, \{u_r, v_r\}\}$ an r-*family*, and let $\Delta(S) = \bigcup_{1 \le i < j \le r}(\{u_i, v_i\} \cap \{u_j, v_j\})$ be the elements of its pairwise intersections. Say that G is r-*closed* if we have $u \text{—} v$ whenever $\Delta(S) \subseteq \{u, v\}$ for some r-family S. It is *strongly* r-closed if, in addition, we have $|\Delta(S)| \ge 2$ for all r-families S. Prove that a strongly r-closed graph is also strongly $(r + 1)$-closed.

b) Prove that the complete bigraph $K_{m,n}$ is strongly r-closed when $r > \max(m, n)$.

c) Prove that a strongly r-closed graph has at most $(r-1)^2$ edges.

d) Let L be the family of functions $\{1\} \cup \{\lceil G \rceil \mid G \text{ is a strongly } r\text{-closed graph on } \{1, \ldots, n\}\}$. (See exercise 85(b); we regard G as a set of edges. For example, when the edges are $1 \text{—} 3$, $1 \text{—} 4$, $2 \text{—} 3$, $2 \text{—} 4$, we have $\lceil G \rceil = x_{13} \vee x_{14} \vee x_{23} \vee x_{24}$.) Is L legitimate?

e) Let $x_{N+1}, \ldots, x_{N+p+q} = f$ be a monotone Boolean chain with p $\wedge$-steps and q $\vee$-steps, and consider the modified chain $\hat{x}_{N+1}, \ldots, \hat{x}_{N+p+q} = \hat{f}$ based on the family L in (d). If $\hat{f} \ne 1$, show that $2(r-1)^3 p + (r-1)^2(n-2) \ge \binom{n}{3}$. *Hint:* Use the second formula in exercise 85(c).

f) Furthermore, if $\hat{f} = 1$ we must have $r^2 q \ge 2^{r+1}$. *Hint:* Now use the first formula.

g) Therefore $p = \Omega(n/\log n)^3$. *Hint:* Let $r \approx 6 \lg n$ and apply exercise 84.

87. [*M22*] Show that when nonmonotonic operations are permitted, the triangle function of exercise 86 has cost $C(f) = O(n^{\lg 7}(\log n)^2) = O(n^{2.81})$. *Hint:* A graph has a triangle if and only if the cube of its adjacency matrix has a nonzero diagonal.

88. [*40*] A *median chain* is analogous to a Boolean chain, but it uses median-of-three steps $x_i = \langle x_{j(i)} x_{k(i)} x_{l(i)} \rangle$ for $n+1 \le i \le n+r$, instead of the binary operations in (1).

Study the optimum length, depth, and cost of median chains, for all self-dual monotone Boolean functions of 7 variables. What is the shortest chain for $\langle x_1 x_2 x_3 x_4 x_5 x_6 x_7 \rangle$?

> Lady Caroline.   *Psha! that's such a hack!*
> Sir Simon.   *A hack, Lady Caroline, that the knowing ones have warranted sound.*
> — GEORGE COLMAN, *John Bull*, Act 3, Scene 1 (1803)

7.1.3. Bitwise Tricks and Techniques

Now comes the fun part: We get to use Boolean operations in our programs.

People are more familiar with arithmetic operations like addition, subtraction, and multiplication than they are with bitwise operations such as "and," "exclusive-or," and so on, because arithmetic has a very long history. But we will see that Boolean operations on binary numbers deserve to be much better known. Indeed, they're an important component of every good programmer's toolkit.

Early machine designers provided fullword bitwise operations in their computers primarily because such instructions could be included in a machine's repertoire almost for free. Binary logic seemed to be potentially useful, although only a few applications were originally foreseen. For example, the EDSAC computer, completed in 1949, included a "collate" command that essentially performed the operation $z \leftarrow z + (x \& y)$, where z was the accumulator, x was the multiplier register, and y was a specified word in memory; it was used for unpacking data. The Manchester Mark I computer, built at about the same time, included not only bitwise AND, but also OR and XOR. When Alan Turing wrote the first programming manual for the Mark I in 1950, he remarked that bitwise NOT can be obtained by using XOR (denoted '$\not\equiv$') in combination with a row of 1s. R. A. Brooker, who extended Turing's manual in 1952 when the Mark II computer was being designed, remarked further that OR could be used "to round off a number by forcing 1 into its least significant digit position." By this time the Mark II, which was to become the prototype of the Ferranti Mercury, had also acquired new instructions for sideways addition and for the position of the most significant 1.

Keith Tocher published an unusual application of AND and OR in 1954, which has subsequently been reinvented frequently (see exercise 85). And during the ensuing decades, programmers have gradually discovered that bitwise operations can be amazingly useful. Many of these tricks have remained part of the folklore; the time is now ripe to take advantage of what has been learned.

A *trick* is a clever idea that can be used once, while a *technique* is a mature trick that can be used at least twice. We will see in this section that tricks tend to evolve naturally into techniques.

Enriched arithmetic. Let's begin by officially defining bitwise operations on integers so that, if $x = (\ldots x_2 x_1 x_0)_2$, $y = (\ldots y_2 y_1 y_0)_2$, and $z = (\ldots z_2 z_1 z_0)_2$ in binary notation, we have

$$x \& y = z \iff x_k \wedge y_k = z_k, \qquad \text{for all } k \geq 0; \tag{1}$$

$$x \mid y = z \iff x_k \vee y_k = z_k, \qquad \text{for all } k \geq 0; \tag{2}$$

$$x \oplus y = z \iff x_k \oplus y_k = z_k, \qquad \text{for all } k \geq 0. \tag{3}$$

(It would be tempting to write '$x \wedge y$' instead of $x \& y$, and '$x \vee y$' instead of $x \mid y$; but when we study optimization problems we'll find it better to reserve the notations $x \wedge y$ and $x \vee y$ for $\min(x, y)$ and $\max(x, y)$, respectively.) Thus, for example,

$$5 \,\&\, 11 = 1, \qquad 5 \mid 11 = 15, \qquad \text{and} \qquad 5 \oplus 11 = 14,$$

since $5 = (0101)_2$, $11 = (1011)_2$, $1 = (0001)_2$, $15 = (1111)_2$, and $14 = (1110)_2$. Negative integers are to be thought of in this connection as infinite-precision numbers in two's complement notation, having infinitely many 1s at the left; for example, -5 is $(\ldots 1111011)_2$. Such infinite-precision numbers are a special case of *2-adic integers*, which are discussed in exercise 4.1–31, and in fact the operators $\&$, $\mid$, $\oplus$ make perfect sense when they are applied to arbitrary 2-adic numbers.

Mathematicians have never paid much attention to the properties of $\&$ and $\mid$ as operations on integers. But the third operation, $\oplus$, has a venerable history, because it describes a winning strategy in the game of nim (see exercises 8–16). For this reason $x \oplus y$ has often been called the "nim sum" of the integers x and y.

All three of the basic bitwise operations turn out to have many useful properties. For example, every relation between $\wedge$, $\vee$, and $\oplus$ that we studied in Section 7.1.1 is automatically inherited by $\&$, $|$, and $\oplus$ on integers, since the relation holds in every bit position. We might as well recap the main identities here:

$$x \,\&\, y = y \,\&\, x, \qquad x \mid y = y \mid x, \qquad x \oplus y = y \oplus x; \tag{4}$$

$$(x \,\&\, y) \,\&\, z = x \,\&\, (y \,\&\, z), \quad (x \mid y) \mid z = x \mid (y \mid z), \quad (x \oplus y) \oplus z = x \oplus (y \oplus z); \tag{5}$$

$$(x \mid y) \,\&\, z = (x \,\&\, z) \mid (y \,\&\, z), \qquad (x \,\&\, y) \mid z = (x \mid z) \,\&\, (y \mid z); \tag{6}$$

$$(x \oplus y) \,\&\, z = (x \,\&\, z) \oplus (y \,\&\, z); \tag{7}$$

$$(x \,\&\, y) \mid x = x, \qquad (x \mid y) \,\&\, x = x; \tag{8}$$

$$(x \,\&\, y) \oplus (x \mid y) = x \oplus y; \tag{9}$$

$$x \,\&\, 0 = 0, \qquad x \mid 0 = x, \qquad x \oplus 0 = x; \tag{10}$$

$$x \,\&\, x = x, \qquad x \mid x = x, \qquad x \oplus x = 0; \tag{11}$$

$$x \,\&\, -1 = x, \qquad x \mid -1 = -1, \qquad x \oplus -1 = \bar{x}; \tag{12}$$

$$x \,\&\, \bar{x} = 0, \qquad x \mid \bar{x} = -1, \qquad x \oplus \bar{x} = -1; \tag{13}$$

$$\overline{x \,\&\, y} = \bar{x} \mid \bar{y}, \qquad \overline{x \mid y} = \bar{x} \,\&\, \bar{y}, \qquad \overline{x \oplus y} = \bar{x} \oplus y = x \oplus \bar{y}. \tag{14}$$

The notation $\bar{x}$ in (12), (13), and (14) stands for bitwise *complementation* of x, namely $(\dots \bar{x}_2 \bar{x}_1 \bar{x}_0)_2$, also written $\sim x$. Notice that (12) and (13) aren't quite the same as 7.1.1–(10) and 7.1.1–(18); we must now use $-1 = (\dots 1111)_2$ instead of $1 = (\dots 0001)_2$ in order to make the formulas bitwise correct.

We say that x is *contained in* y, written $x \subseteq y$ or $y \supseteq x$, if the individual bits of x and y satisfy $x_k \leq y_k$ for all $k \geq 0$. Thus

$$x \subseteq y \quad \Longleftrightarrow \quad x \,\&\, y = x \quad \Longleftrightarrow \quad x \mid y = y \quad \Longleftrightarrow \quad x \,\&\, \bar{y} = 0. \tag{15}$$

Of course we needn't use bitwise operations only in connection with each other; we can combine them with all the ordinary operations of arithmetic. For example, from the relation $x + \bar{x} = (\dots 1111)_2 = -1$ we can deduce the formula

$$-x = \bar{x} + 1, \tag{16}$$

which turns out to be extremely important. Replacing x by $x - 1$ gives also

$$-x = \overline{x - 1}; \tag{17}$$

and in general we can reduce subtraction to complementation and addition:

$$\overline{x - y} = \bar{x} + y. \tag{18}$$

We often want to shift binary numbers to the left or right. These operations are equivalent to multiplication and division by powers of 2, with appropriate rounding, but it is convenient to have special notations for them:

$$x \ll k \;=\; x \text{ shifted left } k \text{ bits} \;\;=\; \lfloor 2^k x \rfloor; \tag{19}$$

$$x \gg k \;=\; x \text{ shifted right } k \text{ bits} \;=\; \lfloor 2^{-k} x \rfloor. \tag{20}$$

Here k can be any integer, possibly negative. In particular we have

$$x \ll (-k) = x \gg k \qquad \text{and} \qquad x \gg (-k) = x \ll k, \tag{21}$$

for every infinite-precision number x. Also $(x \mathbin{\&} y) \ll k = (x \ll k) \mathbin{\&} (y \ll k)$, etc.

When bitwise operations are combined with addition, subtraction, multiplication, and/or shifting, extremely intricate results can arise, even when the formulas are quite short. A taste of the possibilities can be seen, for example, in Fig. 11. Furthermore, such formulas do not merely produce purposeless, chaotic behavior: A famous chain of operations known as "Gosper's hack," first published in 1972, opened people's eyes to the fact that a large number of useful and nontrivial functions can be computed rapidly (see exercise 20). Our goal in this section is to explore how such efficient constructions might be discovered.

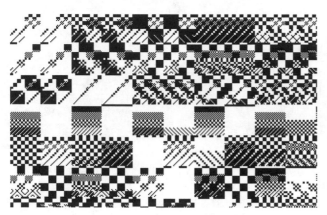

Fig. 11. A small portion of the patchwork quilt defined by the bitwise function $f(x,y) = ((x \oplus \bar{y}) \mathbin{\&} ((x - 350) \gg 3))^2$; the square cell in row x and column y is painted white or black according as the value of $((f(x,y) \gg 12) \mathbin{\&} 1)$ is 0 or 1. (Design by D. Sleator, 1976; see also exercise 18.)

Packing and unpacking. We studied algorithms for multiple-precision arithmetic in Section 4.3.1, dealing with situations where integers are too large to fit in a single word of memory or a single computer register. But the opposite situation, when integers are significantly *smaller* than the capacity of one computer word, is actually much more common; D. H. Lehmer called this "fractional precision." We can often deal with several integers at once, by packing them into a single word.

For example, a date x that consists of a year number y, a month number m, and a day number d, can be represented by using 4 bits for m and 5 bits for d:

$$x = (((y \ll 4) + m) \ll 5) + d. \tag{22}$$

We'll see below that many operations can be performed directly on dates in this packed form. For example, $x < x'$ when date x precedes date x'. But if necessary the individual components (y, m, d) can readily be unpacked when x is given:

$$d = x \bmod 32, \qquad m = (x \gg 5) \bmod 16, \qquad y = x \gg 9. \tag{23}$$

And these "mod" operations do not require division, because of the important law

$$x \bmod 2^n = x \mathbin{\&} (2^n - 1) \tag{24}$$

for any integer $n \geq 0$. We have, for instance, $d = x \mathbin{\&} 31$ in (22) and (23).

Such packing of data obviously saves space in memory, and it also saves time: We can more quickly move or copy items of data from one place to another when they've been packed together. Moreover, computers run considerably faster when they operate on numbers that fit into a cache memory of limited size.

The ultimate packing density is achieved when we have 1-bit items, because we can then cram 64 of them into a single 64-bit word. Suppose, for example, that we want a table of all odd prime numbers less than 1024, so that we can easily decide the primality of a small integer. No problem; only eight 64-bit numbers are required:

$P_0 = 0111011011010011001011010010011001011001010010001011011010000001,$
$P_1 = 0100110000110010010010011000011011000001000001011010011000000100,$
$P_2 = 1001001100101100001000000101101000000100100001101001000100100101,$
$P_3 = 0010001010001000011000011001010010001011010000010001010001010010,$
$P_4 = 0000110000000010010000100100110010000100100110010010110000010000,$
$P_5 = 1101001001100000101001000100001000100001000100100101000100101000,$
$P_6 = 1010000001000010000011000011011000010000001011010000001011010000,$
$P_7 = 0000010100010000100010100100100000010100100100010010000010100110.$

To test whether $2k + 1$ is prime, for $0 \le k < 512$, we simply compute

$$P_{\lfloor k/64 \rfloor} \ll (k \mathbin{\&} 63) \tag{25}$$

in a 64-bit register, and see if the leftmost bit is 1. For example, the following MMIX instructions will do the job, if register pbase holds the address of P_0:

SRU	$0,k,3	$0 \leftarrow \lfloor k/8 \rfloor$ (i.e., $k \gg 3$).	
LDOU	$1,pbase,$0	$1 \leftarrow P_{\lfloor \$0/8 \rfloor}$ (i.e., $P_{\lfloor k/64 \rfloor}$).	
AND	$0,k,#3f	$0 \leftarrow k \bmod 64$ (i.e., $k \mathbin{\&} {}^{\#}\mathtt{3f}$).	(26)
SLU	$1,$1,$0	$1 \leftarrow (\$1 \ll \$0) \bmod 2^{64}$.	
BN	$1,Prime	Branch to Prime if $s(\$1) < 0$. ∎	

Notice that the leftmost bit of a register is 1 if and only if the register contents are negative.

We could equally well pack the bits from right to left in each word:

$Q_0 = 1000000101101101000100101001101001100100101101001100101101101110,$
$Q_1 = 0010000110010110100000100000110110000110010010100100110000110010,$
$Q_2 = 1010010010001001011000010010000001011010000001000011010011001001,$
$Q_3 = 0100101000101000100000101101000100101001100001100001000101000100,$
$Q_4 = 0000100000110100100110010010000100110010010000100100000000110000,$
$Q_5 = 0001010010001010010010001000010001000100010010101000001100101001 1,$
$Q_6 = 0000101101000000101101000000100001101100001100000100001000000101,$
$Q_7 = 0110010100000100100010010010010100000010010010100010000100010100000;$

here $Q_j = P_j^R$. Instead of shifting left as in (25), we now shift right,

$$Q_{\lfloor k/64 \rfloor} \gg (k \mathbin{\&} 63), \tag{27}$$

and look at the *rightmost* bit of the result. The last two lines of (26) become

SRU	$1,$1,$0	$1 \leftarrow \$1 \gg \$0$.	
BOD	$1,Prime	Branch to Prime if $1 is odd. ∎	(28)

(And of course we use qbase instead of pbase.) Either way, the classic *sieve of Eratosthenes* will readily set up the basic table entries P_j or Q_j (see exercise 24).

Table 1

THE BIG-ENDIAN VIEW OF A 32-BYTE MEMORY

octa 0							
tetra 0				tetra 4			
wyde 0		wyde 2		wyde 4		wyde 6	
byte 0	byte 1	byte 2	byte 3	byte 4	byte 5	byte 6	byte 7
$a_0 \ldots a_7$	$a_8 \ldots a_{15}$	$a_{16} \ldots a_{23}$	$a_{24} \ldots a_{31}$	$a_{32} \ldots a_{39}$	$a_{40} \ldots a_{47}$	$a_{48} \ldots a_{55}$	$a_{56} \ldots a_{63}$

octa 8							
tetra 8				tetra 12			
wyde 8		wyde 10		wyde 12		wyde 14	
byte 8	byte 9	byte 10	byte 11	byte 12	byte 13	byte 14	byte 15
$a_{64} \ldots a_{71}$	$a_{72} \ldots a_{79}$	$a_{80} \ldots a_{87}$	$a_{88} \ldots a_{95}$	$a_{96} \ldots a_{103}$	$a_{104} \ldots a_{111}$	$a_{112} \ldots a_{119}$	$a_{120} \ldots a_{127}$

octa 16							
tetra 16				tetra 20			
wyde 16		wyde 18		wyde 20		wyde 22	
byte 16	byte 17	byte 18	byte 19	byte 20	byte 21	byte 22	byte 23
$a_{128} \ldots a_{135}$	$a_{136} \ldots a_{143}$	$a_{144} \ldots a_{151}$	$a_{152} \ldots a_{159}$	$a_{160} \ldots a_{167}$	$a_{168} \ldots a_{175}$	$a_{176} \ldots a_{183}$	$a_{184} \ldots a_{191}$

octa 24							
tetra 24				tetra 28			
wyde 24		wyde 26		wyde 28		wyde 30	
byte 24	byte 25	byte 26	byte 27	byte 28	byte 29	byte 30	byte 31
$a_{192} \ldots a_{199}$	$a_{200} \ldots a_{207}$	$a_{208} \ldots a_{215}$	$a_{216} \ldots a_{223}$	$a_{224} \ldots a_{231}$	$a_{232} \ldots a_{239}$	$a_{240} \ldots a_{247}$	$a_{248} \ldots a_{255}$

Big-endian and little-endian conventions. Whenever we pack bits or bytes into words, we must decide whether to place them from left to right or from right to left. The left-to-right convention is called "big-endian," because the initial items go into the most significant positions; thus they will have bigger significance than their successors, when numbers are compared. The right-to-left convention is called "little-endian"; it puts the first items where little numbers go.

A big-endian approach seems more natural in many cases, because we're accustomed to reading and writing from left to right. But a little-endian placement has advantages too. For example, let's consider the prime number problem again; let $a_k = [2k+1 \text{ is prime}]$. Our table entries $\{P_0, P_1, \ldots, P_7\}$ are big-endian, and we can regard them as the representation of a single multiple-precision integer that is 512 bits long:

$$(P_0 P_1 \ldots P_7)_{2^{64}} = (a_0 a_1 \ldots a_{511})_2. \tag{29}$$

Similarly, our little-endian table entries represent the multiprecise integer

$$(Q_7 \ldots Q_1 Q_0)_{2^{64}} = (a_{511} \ldots a_1 a_0)_2. \tag{30}$$

The latter integer is mathematically nicer than the former, because it is

$$\sum_{k=0}^{511} 2^k a_k = \sum_{k=0}^{511} 2^k [2k+1 \text{ is prime}] = \left(\sum_{k=0}^{\infty} 2^k [2k+1 \text{ is prime}] \right) \bmod 2^{512}. \tag{31}$$

Table 2

THE LITTLE-ENDIAN VIEW OF A 32-BYTE MEMORY

octa 24							
tetra 28				tetra 24			
wyde 30		wyde 28		wyde 26		wyde 24	
byte 31	byte 30	byte 29	byte 28	byte 27	byte 26	byte 25	byte 24
$a_{255}\ldots a_{248}$	$a_{247}\ldots a_{240}$	$a_{239}\ldots a_{232}$	$a_{231}\ldots a_{224}$	$a_{223}\ldots a_{216}$	$a_{215}\ldots a_{208}$	$a_{207}\ldots a_{200}$	$a_{199}\ldots a_{192}$

octa 16							
tetra 20				tetra 16			
wyde 22		wyde 20		wyde 18		wyde 16	
byte 23	byte 22	byte 21	byte 20	byte 19	byte 18	byte 17	byte 16
$a_{191}\ldots a_{184}$	$a_{183}\ldots a_{176}$	$a_{175}\ldots a_{168}$	$a_{167}\ldots a_{160}$	$a_{159}\ldots a_{152}$	$a_{151}\ldots a_{144}$	$a_{143}\ldots a_{136}$	$a_{135}\ldots a_{128}$

octa 8							
tetra 12				tetra 8			
wyde 14		wyde 12		wyde 10		wyde 8	
byte 15	byte 14	byte 13	byte 12	byte 11	byte 10	byte 9	byte 8
$a_{127}\ldots a_{120}$	$a_{119}\ldots a_{112}$	$a_{111}\ldots a_{104}$	$a_{103}\ldots a_{96}$	$a_{95}\ldots a_{88}$	$a_{87}\ldots a_{80}$	$a_{79}\ldots a_{72}$	$a_{71}\ldots a_{64}$

octa 0							
tetra 4				tetra 0			
wyde 6		wyde 4		wyde 2		wyde 0	
byte 7	byte 6	byte 5	byte 4	byte 3	byte 2	byte 1	byte 0
$a_{63}\ldots a_{56}$	$a_{55}\ldots a_{48}$	$a_{47}\ldots a_{40}$	$a_{39}\ldots a_{32}$	$a_{31}\ldots a_{24}$	$a_{23}\ldots a_{16}$	$a_{15}\ldots a_{8}$	$a_{7}\ldots a_{0}$

Notice, however, that we used $(Q_7 \ldots Q_1 Q_0)_{2^{64}}$ to get this simple result, not $(Q_0 Q_1 \ldots Q_7)_{2^{64}}$. The other number,

$$(Q_0 Q_1 \ldots Q_7)_{2^{64}} = (a_{63} \ldots a_1 a_0 a_{127} \ldots a_{65} a_{64} a_{191} \ldots a_{385} a_{384} a_{511} \ldots a_{449} a_{448})_2$$

is in fact quite weird, and it has no really nice formula. (See exercise 25.)

Endianness has important consequences, because most computers allow individual bytes of the memory to be addressed as well as register-sized units. MMIX has a big-endian architecture; therefore if register x contains the 64-bit number #0123456789abcdef, and if we use the commands 'STOU x,0; LDBU y,1' to store x into octabyte location 0 and read back the byte in location 1, the result in register y will be #23. On machines with a little-endian architecture, the analogous commands would set y ← #cd instead; #23 would be byte 6.

Tables 1 and 2 illustrate the competing "world views" of big-endian and little-endian aficionados. The big-endian approach is basically top-down, with bit 0 and byte 0 at the top left; the little-endian approach is basically bottom-up, with bit 0 and byte 0 at the bottom right. Because of this difference, great care is necessary when transmitting data from one kind of computer to another, or when writing programs that are supposed to give equivalent results in both cases. On the other hand, our example of the Q table for primes shows that we can perfectly well use a little-endian packing convention on a big-endian computer like MMIX, or vice versa. The difference is noticeable only when data is loaded and stored in different-sized chunks, or passed between machines.

Working with the rightmost bits. Big-endian and little-endian approaches aren't readily interchangeable in general, because the laws of arithmetic send signals leftward from the bits that are "least significant." Some of the most important bitwise manipulation techniques are based on this fact.

If x is almost any nonzero 2-adic integer, we can write its bits in the form

$$x = (\alpha\, 01^a 10^b)_2; \tag{32}$$

in other words, x consists of some arbitrary (but infinite) binary string α, followed by a 0, which is followed by $a + 1$ ones, and followed by b zeros, for some $a \geq 0$ and $b \geq 0$. (The exceptions occur when $x = -2^b$; then $a = \infty$.) Consequently

$$\bar{x} = (\bar{\alpha}\, 10^a 01^b)_2, \tag{33}$$
$$x - 1 = (\alpha\, 01^a 01^b)_2, \tag{34}$$
$$-x = (\bar{\alpha}\, 10^a 10^b)_2; \tag{35}$$

and we see that $\bar{x}+1 = -x = \overline{x - 1}$, in agreement with (16) and (17). With two operations we can therefore compute relatives of x in several useful ways:

$$x \,\&\, (x-1) = (\ \alpha\ 01^a 00^b)_2 \quad [\text{replace the rightmost 1 by 0}]; \tag{36}$$
$$x \,\&\, -x = (0^\infty 00^a 10^b)_2 \quad [\text{extract the rightmost 1}]; \tag{37}$$
$$x \mid -x = (1^\infty 11^a 10^b)_2 \quad [\text{smear the rightmost 1 to the left}]; \tag{38}$$
$$x \oplus -x = (1^\infty 11^a 00^b)_2 \quad [\text{zero it out and smear 1s to the left}]; \tag{39}$$
$$x \mid (x-1) = (\ \alpha\ 01^a 11^b)_2 \quad [\text{smear the rightmost 1 to the right}]; \tag{40}$$
$$x \oplus (x-1) = (0^\infty 00^a 11^b)_2 \quad [\text{extract it and smear 1s to the right}]; \tag{41}$$
$$\bar{x} \,\&\, (x-1) = (0^\infty 00^a 01^b)_2 \quad [\text{extract, zero, and smear it to the right}]. \tag{42}$$

And two further operations produce yet another variant:

$$((x \mid (x-1))+1) \,\&\, x = (\ \alpha\ 00^a 00^b)_2 \quad [\text{zero out the rightmost run of 1s}]. \tag{43}$$

When $x = 0$, five of these formulas produce 0, the other three give -1. [Formula (36) is due to Peter Wegner, *CACM* **3** (1960), 322; and (43) is due to H. Tim Gladwin, *CACM* **14** (1971), 407–408. See also Henry S. Warren, Jr., *CACM* **20** (1977), 439–441.]

The quantity b in these formulas, which specifies the number of trailing zeros in x, is called the *ruler function* of x and written ρx, because it is related to the lengths of the tick marks that are often used to indicate fractions of an inch: '⌐ᵀᵀᵀᵀᵀᵀᵀᵀᵀᵀᵀᵀ⌐'. In general, ρx is the largest integer k such that 2^k divides x, when $x \neq 0$; and we define $\rho 0 = \infty$. The recurrence relations

$$\rho(2y + 1) = 0, \qquad \rho(2y) = \rho(y) + 1 \tag{44}$$

also serve to define ρx for nonzero x. Another handy relation is worthy of note:

$$\rho(x - y) = \rho(x \oplus y). \tag{45}$$

The elegant formula $x \& -x$ in (37) allows us to *extract* the rightmost 1 bit very nicely, but we often want to identify exactly which bit it is. The ruler function can be computed in many ways, and the best method often depends heavily on the computer that is being used. For example, a two-instruction sequence due to J. Dallos does the job quickly and easily on MMIX (see (42)):

$$\text{SUBU t,x,1; SADD rho,t,x.} \qquad (46)$$

(See exercise 30 for the case $x = 0$.) We shall discuss here two approaches that do not rely on exotic commands like SADD; and later, after learning a few more techniques, we'll consider a third way.

The first general-purpose method makes use of "magic mask" constants μ_k that prove to be useful in many other applications, namely

$$\mu_0 = (\dots 10101010101010101010101010101010)_2 = -1/3,$$
$$\mu_1 = (\dots 10011001100110011001100110011001)_2 = -1/5, \qquad (47)$$
$$\mu_2 = (\dots 10000111100001111000011110000111)_2 = -1/17,$$

and so on. In general μ_k is the infinite 2-adic fraction $-1/(2^{2^k} + 1)$, because $(2^{2^k} + 1)\mu_k = (\mu_k \ll 2^k) + \mu_k = (\dots 11111)_2 = -1$. On a computer that has 2^d-bit registers we don't need infinite precision, of course, so we use the truncated constants

$$\mu_{d,k} = (2^{2^d} - 1)/(2^{2^k} + 1) \qquad \text{for } 0 \le k < d. \qquad (48)$$

These constants are familiar from our study of Boolean evaluation, because they are the truth tables of the projection functions x_{d-k} (see, for example, 7.1.2–(7)).

When x is a power of 2, we can use these masks to compute

$$\rho x = [x \& \mu_0 = 0] + 2[x \& \mu_1 = 0] + 4[x \& \mu_2 = 0] + 8[x \& \mu_3 = 0] + \cdots, \quad (49)$$

because $[2^j \& \mu_k = 0] = j_k$ when $j = (\dots j_3 j_2 j_1 j_0)_2$. Thus, on a 2^d-bit computer, we can start with $\rho \leftarrow 0$ and $y \leftarrow x \& -x$; then set $\rho \leftarrow \rho + 2^k$ if $y \& \mu_{d,k} = 0$, for $0 \le k < d$. This procedure gives $\rho = \rho x$ when $x \ne 0$. (It also gives $\rho 0 = 2^d - 1$, an anomalous value that may need to be corrected; see exercise 30.)

For example, the corresponding MMIX program might look like this:

```
m0 GREG #5555555555555555  ;m1 GREG #3333333333333333;
m2 GREG #0f0f0f0f0f0f0f0f  ;m3 GREG #00ff00ff00ff00ff;
m4 GREG #0000ffff0000ffff  ;m5 GREG #00000000ffffffff;
 NEGU y,x;  AND y,x,y;  AND q,y,m5; ZSZ rho,q,32;
 AND q,y,m4;  ADD t,rho,16;  CSZ rho,q,t;            (50)
 AND q,y,m3;  ADD t,rho,8;  CSZ rho,q,t;
 AND q,y,m2;  ADD t,rho,4;  CSZ rho,q,t;
 AND q,y,m1;  ADD t,rho,2;  CSZ rho,q,t;
 AND q,y,m0;  ADD t,rho,1;  CSZ rho,q,t;
```

total time $= 19\upsilon$. Or we could replace the last three lines by

$$\text{SRU y,y,rho; LDB t,rhotab,y; ADD rho,rho,t} \qquad (51)$$

where rhotab points to the beginning of an appropriate 129-byte table (only eight of whose entries are actually used). The total time would then be $\mu + 13\upsilon$.

The second general-purpose approach to the computation of ρx is quite different. On a 64-bit machine it starts as before, with $y \leftarrow x \,\&\, -x$; but then it simply sets

$$\rho \leftarrow decode\left[((a \cdot y) \bmod 2^{64}) \gg 58\right], \tag{52}$$

where a is a suitable multiplier and $decode$ is a suitable 64-byte table. The constant $a = (a_{63} \ldots a_1 a_0)_2$ must have the property that its 64 truncated shifts

$$a_{63} a_{62} \ldots a_{58}, \; a_{62} a_{61} \ldots a_{57}, \; \ldots, \; a_5 a_4 \ldots a_0, \; a_4 a_3 a_2 a_1 a_0 0, \; \ldots, \; a_0 00000$$

are distinct. Exercise 2.3.4.2–23 shows that many such "de Bruijn cycles" exist; for example, we can use M. H. Martin's constant #03f79d71b4ca8b09, which is discussed in exercise 3.2.2–17. The decoding table $decode[0], \ldots, decode[63]$ is then

$$\begin{aligned}
&00, 01, 56, 02, 57, 49, 28, 03, 61, 58, 42, 50, 38, 29, 17, 04,\\
&62, 47, 59, 36, 45, 43, 51, 22, 53, 39, 33, 30, 24, 18, 12, 05,\\
&63, 55, 48, 27, 60, 41, 37, 16, 46, 35, 44, 21, 52, 32, 23, 11,\\
&54, 26, 40, 15, 34, 20, 31, 10, 25, 14, 19, 09, 13, 08, 07, 06.
\end{aligned} \tag{53}$$

[This technique was devised in 1967 by Luther Woodrum of IBM's Systems Development Division (unpublished); many other programmers have subsequently discovered it independently.]

Working with the leftmost bits. The function $\lambda x = \lfloor \lg x \rfloor$, which is dual to ρx because it locates the *leftmost* 1 when $x > 0$, was introduced in Eq. 4.6.3–(6). It satisfies the recurrence

$$\lambda 1 = 0; \qquad \lambda(2x) = \lambda(2x+1) = \lambda(x) + 1 \quad \text{for } x > 0; \tag{54}$$

and it is undefined when x is not a positive integer. What is a good way to compute it? Once again MMIX provides a quick-but-tricky solution:

```
FLOTU y,ROUND_DOWN,x;  SUB y,y,fone;  SR lam,y,52      (55)
```

where fone = #3ff0000000000000 is the floating point representation of 1.0. (Total time $6v$.) This code floats x, then extracts the exponent.

But if floating point conversion is not readily available, a binary reduction strategy works fairly well on a 2^d-bit machine. We can start with $\lambda \leftarrow 0$ and $y \leftarrow x$; then we set $\lambda \leftarrow \lambda + 2^k$ and $y \leftarrow y \gg 2^k$ if $y \gg 2^k \neq 0$, for $k = d - 1$, $\ldots, 1, 0$ (or until k is reduced to the point where a short table can be used to finish up). The MMIX code analogous to (50) and (51) is now

```
SRU y,x,32;  ZSNZ lam,y,32;
ADD t,lam,16;  SRU y,x,t;  CSNZ lam,y,t;
ADD t,lam,8;  SRU y,x,t;  CSNZ lam,y,t;               (56)
SRU y,x,lam;  LDB t,lamtab,y;  ADD lam,lam,t;
```

and the total time is $\mu + 11v$. In this case table lamtab has 256 entries, namely λx for $0 \le x < 256$. Notice that the "conditional set" (CS) and "zero or set" (ZS) instructions have been used here and in (50) instead of branch instructions.

There appears to be no simple way to extract the leftmost 1 bit that appears in a register, analogous to the trick by which we extracted the rightmost 1 in (37). For this purpose we could compute $y \leftarrow \lambda x$ and then $1 \ll y$, if $x \neq 0$; but a binary "smearing right" method is somewhat shorter and faster:

$$\text{Set } y \leftarrow x, \text{ then } y \leftarrow y \mid (y \gg 2^k) \text{ for } 0 \le k < d. \tag{57}$$
$$\text{The leftmost 1 bit of } x \text{ is then } y - (y \gg 1).$$

[These non-floating-point methods have been suggested by H. S. Warren, Jr.]

Other operations at the left of a register, like removing the leftmost run of 1s, are harder yet; see exercise 39. But there is a remarkably simple, machine-independent way to determine whether or not $\lambda x = \lambda y$, given unsigned integers x and y, in spite of the fact that we can't compute λx or λy quickly:

$$\lambda x = \lambda y \qquad \text{if and only if} \qquad x \oplus y \le x \mathbin{\&} y. \tag{58}$$

[See exercise 40. This elegant relation was discovered by W. C. Lynch in 2006.] We will use (58) below, to devise another way to compute λx.

Sideways addition. Binary n-bit numbers $x = (x_{n-1} \dots x_1 x_0)_2$ are often used to represent subsets X of the n-element universe $\{0, 1, \dots, n-1\}$, with $k \in X$ if and only if $2^k \subseteq x$. The functions λx and ρx then represent the largest and smallest elements of X. The function

$$\nu x = x_{n-1} + \dots + x_1 + x_0, \tag{59}$$

which is called the "sideways sum" or "population count" of x, also has obvious importance in this connection, because it represents the cardinality $|X|$, namely the number of elements in X. This function, which we considered in 4.6.3–(7), satisfies the recurrence

$$\nu 0 = 0; \qquad \nu(2x) = \nu(x) \quad \text{and} \quad \nu(2x+1) = \nu(x) + 1, \quad \text{for } x \ge 0. \tag{60}$$

It also has an interesting connection with the ruler function (exercise 1.2.5–11),

$$\rho x = 1 + \nu(x-1) - \nu x; \qquad \text{equivalently,} \quad \sum_{k=1}^{n} \rho k = n - \nu n. \tag{61}$$

The first textbook on programming, *The Preparation of Programs for an Electronic Digital Computer* by Wilkes, Wheeler, and Gill, second edition (Reading, Mass.: Addison–Wesley, 1957), 155, 191–193, presented an interesting subroutine for sideways addition due to D. B. Gillies and J. C. P. Miller. Their method was devised for the 35-bit numbers of the EDSAC, but it is readily converted to the following 64-bit procedure for νx when $x = (x_{63} \dots x_1 x_0)_2$:

Set $y \leftarrow x - ((x \gg 1) \mathbin{\&} \mu_0)$. (Now $y = (u_{31} \dots u_1 u_0)_4$, where $u_j = x_{2j+1} + x_{2j}$.)
Set $y \leftarrow (y \mathbin{\&} \mu_1) + ((y \gg 2) \mathbin{\&} \mu_1)$. (Now $y = (v_{15} \dots v_1 v_0)_{16}$, $v_j = u_{2j+1} + u_{2j}$.)
Set $y \leftarrow (y + (y \gg 4)) \mathbin{\&} \mu_2$. (Now $y - (w_7 \dots w_1 w_0)_{256}$, $w_j = v_{2j+1} + v_{2j}$.)
Finally $\nu \leftarrow ((a \cdot y) \bmod 2^{64}) \gg 56$, where $a = (11111111)_{256}$. $\tag{62}$

The last step cleverly computes $y \bmod 255 = w_7 + \dots + w_1 + w_0$ via multiplication, using the fact that the sum fits comfortably in eight bits. [David Muller had programmed a similar method for the ILLIAC I machine in 1954.]

If x is expected to be "sparse," having at most a few 1-bits, we can use a faster method [P. Wegner, *CACM* **3** (1960), 322]:

Set $\nu \leftarrow 0$, $y \leftarrow x$. Then while $y \neq 0$, set $\nu \leftarrow \nu + 1$, $y \leftarrow y \,\&\, (y - 1)$.   (63)

A similar approach, using $y \leftarrow y \,|\, (y+1)$, works when x is expected to be "dense."

Bit reversal. For our next trick, let's change $x = (x_{63} \ldots x_1 x_0)_2$ to its left-right mirror image, $x^R = (x_0 x_1 \ldots x_{63})_2$. Anybody who has been following the developments so far, seeing methods like (50), (56), (57), and (62), will probably think, "Aha — once again we can divide by 2 and conquer! If we've already discovered how to reverse 32-bit numbers, we can reverse 64-bit numbers almost as fast, because $(xy)^R = y^R x^R$. All we have to do is apply the 32-bit method in parallel to both halves of the register, then swap the left half with the right half."
    Right. For example, we can reverse an 8-bit string in three easy steps:

$$
\begin{array}{lll}
\text{Given} & x_7 x_6 x_5 x_4 x_3 x_2 x_1 x_0 & \\
\text{Swap bits} & x_6 x_7 x_4 x_5 x_2 x_3 x_0 x_1 & \\
\text{Swap nyps} & x_4 x_5 x_6 x_7 x_0 x_1 x_2 x_3 & (64) \\
\text{Swap nybbles} & x_0 x_1 x_2 x_3 x_4 x_5 x_6 x_7 &
\end{array}
$$

And six such easy steps will reverse 64 bits. Fortunately, each of the swapping operations turns out to be quite simple with the help of the magic masks μ_k:

$$
\begin{array}{lll}
y \leftarrow (x \gg 1) \,\&\, \mu_0, & z \leftarrow (x \,\&\, \mu_0) \ll 1, & x \leftarrow y \,|\, z; \\
y \leftarrow (x \gg 2) \,\&\, \mu_1, & z \leftarrow (x \,\&\, \mu_1) \ll 2, & x \leftarrow y \,|\, z; \\
y \leftarrow (x \gg 4) \,\&\, \mu_2, & z \leftarrow (x \,\&\, \mu_2) \ll 4, & x \leftarrow y \,|\, z; \\
y \leftarrow (x \gg 8) \,\&\, \mu_3, & z \leftarrow (x \,\&\, \mu_3) \ll 8, & x \leftarrow y \,|\, z; \\
y \leftarrow (x \gg 16) \,\&\, \mu_4, & z \leftarrow (x \,\&\, \mu_4) \ll 16, & x \leftarrow y \,|\, z; \\
\end{array}
$$
$$
x \leftarrow (x \gg 32) \,|\, ((x \ll 32) \bmod 2^{64}). \qquad (65)
$$

[Christopher Strachey foresaw some aspects of this construction in *CACM* **4** (1961), 146, and a similar *ternary* method was devised in 1973 by Bruce Baumgart (see exercise 49). The mature algorithm (65) was presented by Henry S. Warren, Jr., in *Hacker's Delight* (Addison–Wesley, 2002), 102.]
    But MMIX is once again able to improve on this general-purpose technique, with less traditional commands that do the job much faster. Consider

        rev GREG #0102040810204080; MOR x,x,rev; MOR x,rev,x;   (66)

the first MOR instruction reverses the bytes of x from big-endian to little-endian or vice versa, while the second reverses the bits within each byte.

Bit swapping. Suppose we only want to interchange two bits within a register, $x_i \leftrightarrow x_j$, where $i > j$. What would be a good way to proceed? (Dear reader, please pause for a moment and solve this problem in your head, or with pencil and paper — without looking at the answer below.)
    Let $\delta = i - j$. Here is one solution (but don't peek until you're ready):

$$y \leftarrow (x \gg \delta) \,\&\, 2^j, \quad z \leftarrow (x \,\&\, 2^j) \ll \delta, \quad x \leftarrow (x \,\&\, m) \,|\, y \,|\, z, \quad \text{where } \overline{m} = 2^i \,|\, 2^j. \quad (67)$$

It uses two shifts and five bitwise Boolean operations, assuming that i and j are given constants. It is like each of the first lines of (65), except that a new mask m is needed because y and z don't account for all of the bits of x.

We can, however, do better, saving one operation and one constant:

$$y \leftarrow (x \oplus (x \gg \delta)) \mathbin{\&} 2^j, \qquad x \leftarrow x \oplus y \oplus (y \ll \delta). \tag{68}$$

The first assignment now puts $x_i \oplus x_j$ into position j; the second changes x_i to $x_i \oplus (x_i \oplus x_j)$ and x_j to $x_j \oplus (x_i \oplus x_j)$, as desired. In general it's often wise to convert a problem of the form "change x to $f(x)$" into a problem of the form "change x to $x \oplus g(x)$," since the bit-difference $g(x)$ might be easy to calculate.

On the other hand, there's a sense in which (67) might be preferable to (68), because the assignments to y and z in (67) can sometimes be performed simultaneously. When expressed as a circuit, (67) has a depth of 4 while (68) has depth 5.

Operation (68) can of course be used to swap several pairs of bits simultaneously, when we use a mask θ that's more general than 2^j:

$$y \leftarrow (x \oplus (x \gg \delta)) \mathbin{\&} \theta, \qquad x \leftarrow x \oplus y \oplus (y \ll \delta). \tag{69}$$

Let us call this operation a "δ-swap," because it allows us to swap any non-overlapping pairs of bits that are δ places apart. The mask θ has a 1 in the rightmost position of each pair that's supposed to be swapped. For example, (69) will swap the leftmost 25 bits of a 64-bit word with the rightmost 25 bits, while leaving the 14 middle bits untouched, if we let $\delta = 39$ and $\theta = 2^{25} - 1 = {}^{\#}\mathtt{1ffffff}$.

Indeed, there's an astonishing way to reverse 64 bits using δ-swaps, namely

$$\begin{aligned}
&y \leftarrow (x \gg 1) \mathbin{\&} \mu_0, \quad z \leftarrow (x \mathbin{\&} \mu_0) \ll 1, \quad x \leftarrow y \mid z, \\
&y \leftarrow (x \oplus (x \gg 4)) \mathbin{\&} {}^{\#}\mathtt{0300c0303030c303}, \quad x \leftarrow x \oplus y \oplus (y \ll 4), \\
&y \leftarrow (x \oplus (x \gg 8)) \mathbin{\&} {}^{\#}\mathtt{00c0300c03f0003f}, \quad x \leftarrow x \oplus y \oplus (y \ll 8), \\
&y \leftarrow (x \oplus (x \gg 20)) \mathbin{\&} {}^{\#}\mathtt{00000ffc00003fff}, \quad x \leftarrow x \oplus y \oplus (y \ll 20), \\
&x \leftarrow (x \gg 34) \mid ((x \ll 30) \bmod 2^{64}),
\end{aligned} \tag{70}$$

saving two of the bitwise operations in (65) even though (65) looks "optimum."

*Bit permutation in general. The methods we've just seen can be extended to obtain an *arbitrary* permutation of the bits in a register. In fact, there always exist masks $\theta_0, \ldots, \theta_5, \hat{\theta}_4, \ldots, \hat{\theta}_0$ such that the following operations transform $x = (x_{63} \ldots x_1 x_0)_2$ into any desired rearrangement $x^\pi = (x_{63\pi} \ldots x_{1\pi} x_{0\pi})_2$ of its bits:

$$\begin{aligned}
&x \leftarrow 2^k\text{-swap of } x \text{ with mask } \theta_k, \text{ for } k = 0, 1, 2, 3, 4, 5; \\
&x \leftarrow 2^k\text{-swap of } x \text{ with mask } \hat{\theta}_k, \text{ for } k = 4, 3, 2, 1, 0.
\end{aligned} \tag{71}$$

In general, a permutation of 2^d bits can be achieved with $2d - 1$ such steps, using appropriate masks θ_k and $\hat{\theta}_k$, where the swap distances are respectively 2^0, 2^1, $\ldots$, $2^{d-1}, \ldots, 2^1, 2^0$.

To prove this fact, we can use a special case of the permutation networks discovered independently by A. M. Duguid and J. Le Corre in 1959, based on earlier work of D. Slepian [see V. E. Beneš, *Mathematical Theory of Connecting Networks and Telephone Traffic* (New York: Academic Press, 1965), Section 3.3].

Figure 12 shows a permutation network $P(2n)$ for $2n$ elements constructed from two permutation networks for n elements, when $n = 4$. Each ' connection between two lines represents a *crossbar module* that either leaves the line contents unaltered or interchanges them, as the data flows from left to right. To start the recursion when $n = 1$, we let $P(2)$ consist of a single crossbar. Every setting of the individual crossbars clearly causes $P(2n)$ to produce a permutation of its inputs; conversely, we will show that any permutation of the $2n$ inputs can be achieved if we are clever enough to set the crossbars appropriately.

The construction of Fig. 12 is best understood by considering an example. Suppose we want to route the inputs $(0, 1, 2, 3, 4, 5, 6, 7)$ to $(3, 2, 4, 1, 6, 0, 5, 7)$, respectively. The first job is to determine the contents of the lines just after the first column of crossbars and just before the last column, since we can then use a similar method to set the crossbars in the inner $P(4)$'s. Thus, in the network

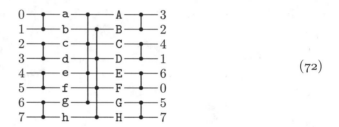

$$(72)$$

we want to find permutations abcdefgh and ABCDEFGH such that $\{a, b\} = \{0, 1\}$, $\{c, d\} = \{2, 3\}$, $\ldots$, $\{g, h\} = \{6, 7\}$, $\{a, c, e, g\} = \{A, C, E, G\}$, $\{b, d, f, h\} = \{B, D, F, H\}$, $\{A, B\} = \{3, 2\}$, $\{C, D\} = \{4, 1\}$, $\ldots$, $\{G, H\} = \{5, 7\}$. Starting at the bottom, let us choose $h = 7$, because we don't wish to disturb the contents of that line unless necessary. Then the following choices are *forced*:

$$H = 7; \ G = 5; \ e = 5; \ f = 4; \ D = 4; \ C = 1; \ a = 1; \ b = 0; \ F = 0; \ E = 6; \ g = 6. \quad (73)$$

If we had chosen $h = 6$, the forcing pattern would have been similar but reversed,

$$F = 6; \ E = 0; \ a = 0; \ b = 1; \ D = 1; \ C = 4; \ e = 4; \ f = 5; \ H = 5; \ G = 7; \ g = 7. \quad (74)$$

Options (73) and (74) can both be completed by choosing either $d = 3$ (hence $B = 3$, $A = 2$, $c = 2$) or $d = 2$ (hence $B = 2$, $A = 3$, $c = 3$).

In general the forcing pattern will go in cycles, no matter what permutation we begin with. To see this, consider the graph on eight vertices $\{ab, cd, ef, gh, AB, CD, EF, GH\}$ that has an edge from uv to UV whenever the pair of inputs connected to uv has an element in common with the pair of outputs connected to UV. Thus, in our example the edges are ab — EF, ab — CD, cd — AB, cd — AB, ef — CD, ef — GH, gh — EF, gh — GH. We have a "double bond" between cd and AB, since the inputs connected to c and d are exactly the outputs connected to A and B; subject to this slight bending of the strict definition of a graph, we see that each vertex is adjacent to exactly two other vertices, and lowercase vertices are always adjacent to uppercase ones. Therefore the graph

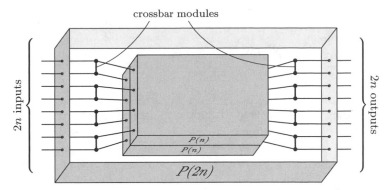

Fig. 12. The inside of a black box $P(2n)$ that permutes $2n$ elements in all possible ways, when $n > 1$. (Illustrated for $n = 4$.)

always consists of disjoint cycles of even length. In our example, the cycles are

$$\mathtt{ab} \overset{\text{EF} \;-\; \text{gh}}{\underset{\text{CD} \;-\; \text{ef}}{\diagdown \;\;\diagup}} \text{GH} \qquad \mathtt{cd} = \mathtt{AB}, \tag{75}$$

where the longer cycle corresponds to (73) and (74). If there are k different cycles, there will be 2^k different ways to specify the behavior of the first and last columns of crossbars.

To complete the network, we can process the inner 4-element permutations in the same way; and *any* 2^d-element permutation is achievable in this same recursive fashion. The resulting crossbar settings determine the masks θ_j and $\hat{\theta}_j$ of (71). Some choices of crossbars may lead to a mask that is entirely zero; then we can eliminate the corresponding stage of the computation.

If the input and output are identical on the bottom lines of the network, our construction shows how to ensure that none of the crossbars touching those lines are active. For example, the 64-bit algorithm in (71) could be used also with a 60-bit register, without needing the four extra bits for any intermediate results.

Of course we can often beat the general procedure of (71) in special cases. For example, exercise 52 shows that method (71) needs nine swapping steps to transpose an 8×8 matrix, but in fact three swaps suffice:

Given	7-swap	14-swap	28-swap
00 01 02 03 04 05 06 07	00 **10** 02 **12** 04 **14** 06 **16**	00 10 **20 30** 04 14 **24 34**	00 10 20 30 **40 50 60 70**
10 11 12 13 14 15 16 17	**01** 11 **03** 13 **05** 15 **07** 17	01 11 **21 31** 05 15 **25 35**	01 11 21 31 **41 51 61 71**
20 21 22 23 24 25 26 27	20 **30** 22 **32** 24 **34** 26 **36**	**02 12** 22 32 **06 16** 26 36	02 12 22 32 **42 52 62 72**
30 31 32 33 34 35 36 37	**21** 31 **23** 33 **25** 35 **27** 37	**03 13** 23 33 **07 17** 27 37	03 13 23 33 **43 53 63 73**
40 41 42 43 44 45 46 47	40 **50** 42 **52** 44 **54** 46 **56**	40 50 **60 70** 44 54 **64 74**	**04 14 24 34** 44 54 64 74
50 51 52 53 54 55 56 57	**41** 51 **43** 53 **45** 55 **47** 57	41 51 **61 71** 45 55 **65 75**	**05 15 25 35** 45 55 65 75
60 61 62 63 64 65 66 67	60 **70** 62 **72** 64 **74** 66 **76**	**42 52** 62 72 **46 56** 66 76	**06 16 26 36** 46 56 66 76
70 71 72 73 74 75 76 77	**61** 71 **63** 73 **65** 75 **67** 77	**43 53** 63 73 **47 57** 67 77	**07 17 27 37** 47 57 67 77

The "perfect shuffle" is another bit permutation that arises frequently in practice. If $x = (\dots x_2 x_1 x_0)_2$ and $y = (\dots y_2 y_1 y_0)_2$ are any 2-adic integers, we define $x \ddagger y$ ("x zip y," the *zipper function* of x and y) by interleaving their bits:

$$x \ddagger y = (\dots x_2 y_2 x_1 y_1 x_0 y_0)_2. \tag{76}$$

This operation has important applications to the representation of 2-dimensional data, because a small change in either x or y usually causes only a small change in $x \updownarrow y$ (see exercise 86). Notice also that the magic mask constants (47) satisfy

$$\mu_k \updownarrow \mu_k = \mu_{k+1}. \tag{77}$$

If x appears in the left half of a register and y appears in the right half, a perfect shuffle is the permutation that changes the register contents to $x \updownarrow y$.

A sequence of $d-1$ swapping steps will perfectly shuffle a 2^d-bit register; in fact, exercise 53 shows that there are several ways to achieve this. Once again, therefore, we are able to improve on the $(2d-1)$-step method of (71) and Fig. 12.

Conversely, suppose we're given the shuffled value $z = x \updownarrow y$ in a 2^d-bit register; is there an efficient way to extract the original value of y? Sure: If the $d-1$ swaps that do a perfect shuffle are performed in reverse order, they'll undo the shuffle and recover both x and y. But if only y is wanted, we can save half of the work: Start with $y \leftarrow z \mathbin{\&} \mu_0$; then set $y \leftarrow (y + (y \gg 2^{k-1})) \mathbin{\&} \mu_k$ for $k = 1$, $\ldots$, $d-1$. For example, when $d = 3$ this procedure goes $(0y_3 0y_2 0y_1 0y_0)_2 \mapsto (00y_3y_2 00y_1y_0)_2 \mapsto (0000y_3y_2y_1y_0)_2$. "Divide and conquer" conquers again.

Consider now a more general problem, where we want to extract and compress an *arbitrary* subset of a register's bits. Suppose we're given a 2^d-bit word $z = (z_{2^d-1} \ldots z_1 z_0)_2$ and a mask $\chi = (\chi_{2^d-1} \ldots \chi_1 \chi_0)_2$ that has s 1-bits; thus $\nu\chi = s$. The problem is to assemble the compact subword

$$y = (y_{s-1} \ldots y_1 y_0)_2 = (z_{j_{s-1}} \ldots z_{j_1} z_{j_0})_2, \tag{78}$$

where $j_{s-1} > \cdots > j_1 > j_0$ are the indices where $\chi_j = 1$. For example, if $d = 3$ and $\chi = (10110010)_2$, we want to transform $z = (y_3 x_3 y_2 y_1 x_2 x_1 y_0 x_0)_2$ into $y = (y_3 y_2 y_1 y_0)_2$. (The problem of going from $x \updownarrow y$ to y, considered above, is the special case $\chi = \mu_0$.) We know from (71) that y can be found by δ-swapping, at most $2d-1$ times; but in this problem the relevant data always moves to the right, so we can speed things up by doing *shifts* instead of swaps.

Let's say that a δ-shift of x with mask θ is the operation

$$x \leftarrow x \oplus \big((x \oplus (x \gg \delta)) \mathbin{\&} \theta\big), \tag{79}$$

which changes bit x_j to $x_{j+\delta}$ if θ has 1 in position j but leaves x_j unchanged otherwise. Guy Steele discovered that there always exist masks θ_0, θ_1, $\ldots$, θ_{d-1} so that the general extraction problem (78) can be solved with a few δ-shifts:

Start with $x \leftarrow z$; then do a 2^k-shift of x with mask θ_k,
for $k = 0, 1, \ldots, d-1$; finally set $y \leftarrow x$. $\hfill(80)$

In fact, the idea for finding appropriate masks is surprisingly simple. Every bit that wants to move a total of exactly $l = (l_{d-1} \ldots l_1 l_0)_2$ places to the right should be transported in the 2^k-shifts for which $l_k = 1$.

For example, suppose $d = 3$ and $\chi = (10110010)_2$. (We must assume that $\chi \neq 0$.) Remembering that some 0s need to be shifted in from the left, we can set $\theta_0 = (00011001)_2$, $\theta_1 = (00000110)_2$, $\theta_2 = (11111000)_2$; then (80) maps

$$(y_3 x_3 y_2 y_1 x_2 x_1 y_0 x_0)_2 \mapsto (y_3 x_3 y_2 y_2 y_1 x_1 y_0 y_0)_2 \mapsto (y_3 x_3 y_2 y_2 y_1 y_2 y_1 y_0)_2 \mapsto (0000 y_3 y_2 y_1 y_0)_2.$$

Exercise 69 proves that the bits being extracted will never interfere with each other during their journey. Furthermore, there's a slick way to compute suitable masks θ_k dynamically from χ, in $O(d^2)$ steps (see exercise 70).

A "sheep-and-goats" or "grouping" operation has been suggested for computer hardware, extending (78) to produce the general unshuffled word

$$(x_{r-1}\ldots x_1 x_0 y_{s-1}\ldots y_1 y_0)_2 = (z_{i_{r-1}}\ldots z_{i_1} z_{i_0} z_{j_{s-1}}\ldots z_{j_1} z_{j_0})_2; \qquad (81)$$

here $i_{r-1} > \cdots > i_1 > i_0$ are the indices where $\chi_i = 0$. But another operation called "gather-flip," which reverses the order of the unmasked bits and gives

$$(x_0 x_1 \ldots x_{r-1} y_{s-1} \ldots y_1 y_0)_2 = (z_{i_0} z_{i_1} \ldots z_{i_{r-1}} z_{j_{s-1}} \ldots z_{j_1} z_{j_0})_2, \qquad (81')$$

turns out to be more useful and easier to implement. Any permutation of 2^d bits is achievable by using either operation, at most d times (see exercises 72 and 73).

Shifting also allows us to go beyond permutations, to arbitrary *mappings* of bits within a register. Suppose we want to transform

$$x = (x_{2^d-1}\ldots x_1 x_0)_2 \quad \mapsto \quad x^\varphi = (x_{(2^d-1)\varphi}\ldots x_{1\varphi} x_{0\varphi})_2, \qquad (82)$$

where φ is any of the $(2^d)^{2^d}$ functions from the set $\{0, 1, \ldots, 2^d - 1\}$ into itself. K. M. Chung and C. K. Wong [*IEEE Transactions* **C-29** (1980), 1029–1032] introduced an attractive way to do this in $O(d)$ steps by using *cyclic δ-shifts*, which are like (79) except that we set

$$x \leftarrow x \oplus \big((x \oplus (x \gg \delta)) \oplus (x \ll (2^d - \delta))\big) \;\&\; \theta\big). \qquad (83)$$

Their idea is to let c_l be the number of indices j such that $j\varphi = l$, for $0 \le l < 2^d$. Then they find masks $\theta_0, \theta_1, \ldots, \theta_{d-1}$ with the property that a cyclic 2^k-shift of x with mask θ_k, done successively for $0 \le k < d$, will transform x into a number x' that contains exactly c_l copies of bit x_l for each l. Finally the general permutation procedure (71) can be used to change $x' \mapsto x^\varphi$.

For example, suppose $d = 3$ and $x^\varphi = (x_3 x_1 x_1 x_0 x_3 x_7 x_5 x_5)_2$. Then we have $(c_0, c_1, c_2, c_3, c_4, c_5, c_6, c_7) = (1, 2, 0, 2, 0, 2, 0, 1)$. Using masks $\theta_0 = (00011100)_2$, $\theta_1 = (00001000)_2$, and $\theta_2 = (01100000)_2$, three cyclic 2^k-shifts now take $x = (x_7 x_6 x_5 x_4 x_3 x_2 x_1 x_0)_2 \mapsto (x_7 x_6 x_5 x_5 x_4 x_3 x_1 x_0)_2 \mapsto (x_7 x_6 x_5 x_5 x_5 x_3 x_1 x_0)_2 \mapsto (x_7 x_3 x_1 x_5 x_5 x_3 x_1 x_0)_2 = x'$. Then, some δ-swaps: $x' \mapsto (x_3 x_7 x_5 x_1 x_3 x_5 x_1 x_0)_2 \mapsto (x_3 x_1 x_5 x_7 x_3 x_5 x_1 x_0)_2 \mapsto (x_3 x_1 x_1 x_0 x_3 x_5 x_5 x_7)_2 \mapsto (x_3 x_1 x_1 x_0 x_3 x_7 x_5 x_5)_2 = x^\varphi$; we're done! Of course any 8-bit mapping can be achieved more quickly by brute force, one bit at a time; the method of Chung and Wong becomes much more impressive in a 256-bit register. Even with MMIX's 64-bit registers it's pretty good, needing at most 96 cycles in the worst case.

To find θ_0, we use the fact that $\sum c_l = 2^d$, and we look at $\Sigma_{\text{even}} = \sum c_{2l}$ and $\Sigma_{\text{odd}} = \sum c_{2l+1}$. If $\Sigma_{\text{even}} = \Sigma_{\text{odd}} = 2^{d-1}$, we can set $\theta_0 = 0$ and omit the cyclic 1-shift. But if, say, $\Sigma_{\text{even}} < \Sigma_{\text{odd}}$, we find an even l with $c_l = 0$. Cyclically shifting into bits $l, l+1, \ldots, l+t$ (modulo 2^d) for some t will produce new counts $(c'_0, \ldots, c'_{2^d-1})$ for which $\Sigma'_{\text{even}} = \Sigma'_{\text{odd}} = 2^{d-1}$; so $\theta_0 = 2^l + \cdots + 2^{(l+t) \bmod 2^d}$. Then we can deal with the bits in even and odd positions separately, using the same method, until getting down to 1-bit subwords. Exercise 74 has the details.

Working with fragmented fields. Instead of extracting bits from various parts of a word and gathering them together, we can often manipulate those bits directly in their original positions.

For example, suppose we want to run through all subsets of a given set U, where (as usual) the set is specified by a mask χ such that $[k \in U] = (\chi \gg k) \mathbin{\&} 1$. If $x \subseteq \chi$ and $x \neq \chi$, there's an easy way to calculate the next largest subset of U in lexicographic order, namely the smallest integer $x' > x$ such that $x' \subseteq \chi$:

$$x' = (x - \chi) \mathbin{\&} \chi. \tag{84}$$

In the special case when $x = 0$ and $\chi \neq 0$, we've already seen in (37) that this formula produces the rightmost bit of χ, which corresponds to the lexicographically smallest nonempty subset of U.

Why does formula (84) work? Imagine adding 1 to the number $x \mid \bar\chi$, which has 1s wherever χ is 0. A carry will propagate through those 1s until it reaches the rightmost bit position where x has a 0 and χ has a 1; furthermore all bits to the right of that position will become zero. Therefore $x' = ((x \mid \bar\chi) + 1) \mathbin{\&} \chi$. But we have $(x \mid \bar\chi) + 1 = (x + \bar\chi) + 1 = x + (\bar\chi + 1) = x - \chi$ when $x \subseteq \chi$. QED.

Notice further that $x' = 0$ if and only if $x = \chi$. So we'll know when we've found the largest subset. Exercise 79 shows how to go back to x, given x'.

We might also want to run through all elements of a *subcube* — for example, to find all bit patterns that match a specification like *10*1*01, consisting of 0s, 1s, and *s (don't-cares). Such a specification can be represented by asterisk codes $a = (a_{n-1} \dots a_0)_2$ and bit codes $b = (b_{n-1} \dots b_0)_2$, as in exercise 7.1.1–30; our example corresponds to $a = (10010100)_2$, $b = (01001001)_2$. The problem of enumerating all subsets of a set is the special case where $a = \chi$ and $b = 0$. In the more general subcube problem, the successor of a given bit pattern x is

$$x' = ((x - (a + b)) \mathbin{\&} a) + b. \tag{85}$$

Suppose the bits of $z = (z_{n-1} \dots z_0)_2$ have been stitched together from two subwords $x = (x_{r-1} \dots x_0)_2$ and $y = (y_{s-1} \dots y_0)_2$, where $r + s = n$, using an arbitrary mask χ for which $\nu\chi = s$ to govern the stitching. For example, $z = (y_2 x_4 x_3 y_1 x_2 y_0 x_1 x_0)_2$ when $n = 8$ and $\chi = (10010100)_2$. We can think of z as a "scattered accumulator," in which alien bits x_i lurk among friendly bits y_j. From this viewpoint the problem of finding successive elements of a subcube is essentially the problem of computing $y + 1$ inside a scattered accumulator z, without changing the value of x. The sheep-and-goats operation (81) would untangle x and y; but it's expensive, and (85) shows that we can solve the problem without it. We can, in fact, compute $y + y'$ when $y' = (y'_{s-1} \dots y'_0)_2$ is *any* value inside a scattered accumulator z', if y and y' both appear in the positions specified by χ: Consider $t = z \mathbin{\&} \chi$ and $t' = z' \mathbin{\&} \chi$. If we form the sum $(t \mid \bar\chi) + t'$, all carries that occur in a normal addition $y + y'$ will propagate through the blocks of 1s in $\bar\chi$, just as if the scattered bits were adjacent. Thus

$$((z \mathbin{\&} \chi) + (z' \mid \bar\chi)) \mathbin{\&} \chi \tag{86}$$

is the sum of y and y', modulo 2^s, scattered according to the mask χ.

Tweaking several bytes at once. Instead of concentrating on the data in one field within a word, we often want to deal simultaneously with two or more sub-words, performing calculations on each of them in parallel. For example, many applications need to process long sequences of bytes, and we can gain speed by acting on eight bytes at a time; we might as well use all 64 bits that our machine provides. General multibyte techniques were introduced by Leslie Lamport in *CACM* **18** (1975), 471–475, and subsequently extended by many programmers.

Suppose first that we simply wish to take two sequences of bytes and find their sum, regarding them as coordinates of vectors, doing arithmetic modulo 256 in each byte. Algebraically speaking, we're given 8-byte vectors $x = (x_7 \ldots x_1 x_0)_{256}$ and $y = (y_7 \ldots y_1 y_0)_{256}$; we want to compute $z = (z_7 \ldots z_1 z_0)_{256}$, where $z_j = (x_j + y_j) \bmod 256$ for $0 \le j < 8$. Ordinary addition of x to y doesn't quite work, because we need to prevent carries from propagating between bytes. So we extract the high-order bits and deal with them separately:

$$z \leftarrow (x \oplus y) \mathbin{\&} h, \qquad \text{where } h = {}^\#8080808080808080;$$
$$z \leftarrow ((x \mathbin{\&} \bar{h}) + (y \mathbin{\&} \bar{h})) \oplus z. \tag{87}$$

The total time for MMIX to do this is 6υ, plus $3\mu + 3\upsilon$ if we also count the time to load x, load y, and store z. By contrast, eight one-byte additions (LDBU, LDBU, ADDU, and STBU, repeated eight times) would cost $8 \times (3\mu + 4\upsilon) = 24\mu + 32\upsilon$. Parallel *subtraction* of bytes is just as easy (see exercise 88).

We can also compute bytewise *averages*, with $z_j = \lfloor (x_j + y_j)/2 \rfloor$ for each j:

$$z \leftarrow ((x \oplus y) \mathbin{\&} \bar{l}) \gg 1, \qquad \text{where } l = {}^\#0101010101010101;$$
$$z \leftarrow (x \mathbin{\&} y) + z. \tag{88}$$

This elegant trick, suggested by H. G. Dietz, is based on the well-known formula

$$x + y = (x \oplus y) + ((x \mathbin{\&} y) \ll 1) \tag{89}$$

for radix-2 addition. (We can implement (88) with four MMIX instructions, not five, because a single MOR operation will change $x \oplus y$ to $((x \oplus y) \mathbin{\&} \bar{l}) \gg 1$.)

Exercises 88–93 and 100–104 develop these ideas further, showing how to do mixed-radix arithmetic, as well as such things as the addition and subtraction of vectors whose components are treated modulo m when m needn't be a power of 2.

In essence, we can regard the bits, bytes, or other subfields of a register as if they were elements of an array of independent microprocessors, acting independently on their own subproblems yet tightly synchronized, and communicating with each other via shift instructions and carry bits. Computer designers have been interested for many years in the development of parallel processors with a so-called SIMD architecture, namely a "Single Instruction stream with Multiple Data streams"; see, for example, S. H. Unger, *Proc. IRE* **46** (1958), 1744–1750. The increased availability of 64-bit registers has meant that programmers of ordinary sequential computers are now able to get a taste of SIMD processing. Indeed, computations such as (87), (88), and (89) are called SWAR methods — "SIMD Within A Register," a name coined by R. J. Fisher and H. G. Dietz [see *Lecture Notes in Computer Science* **1656** (1999), 290–305]. See also R. B. Lee, *IEEE Micro* **16**, 4 (August 1996), 51–59.

Of course bytes often contain alphabetic data as well as numbers, and one of the most common programming tasks is to search through a long string of characters in order to find the first appearance of some particular byte value. For example, strings are often represented as a sequence of nonzero bytes terminated by 0. In order to locate the end of a string quickly, we need a fast way to determine whether all eight bytes of a given word x are nonzero (because they usually are). Several fairly good solutions to this problem were found by Lamport and others; but Alan Mycroft discovered in 1987 that *three* instructions actually suffice:

$$t \leftarrow h \,\&\, (x - l) \,\&\, \bar{x}, \tag{90}$$

where h and l appear in (87) and (88). If each byte x_j is nonzero, t will be zero; for $(x_j - 1) \,\&\, \bar{x}_j$ will be $2^{\rho x_j} - 1$, which is always less than $\#80 = 2^7$. But if $x_j = 0$, while its right neighbors $x_{j-1}, \ldots, x_0$ (if any) are all nonzero, the subtraction $x - l$ will produce $\#\mathtt{ff}$ in byte j, and t will be nonzero. In fact, ρt will be $8j + 7$.

Caution: Although the computation in (90) pinpoints the *rightmost* zero byte of x, we cannot deduce the position of the *leftmost* zero byte from the value of t alone. (See exercise 94.) In this respect the little-endian convention proves to be preferable to the corresponding big-endian behavior. An application that needs to locate the leftmost zero byte can use (90) to skip quickly over nonzeros, but then it must fall back on a slower method when the search has been narrowed down to eight finalists. The following 4-operation formula produces a completely precise test value $t = (t_7 \ldots t_1 t_0)_{256}$, in which $t_j = 128[x_j = 0]$ for each j:

$$t \leftarrow h \,\&\, {\sim}(x \mid ((x \mid h) - l)). \tag{91}$$

The leftmost zero byte of x is now x_j, where $\lambda t = 8j + 7$.

Incidentally, the single MMIX instruction 'BDIF t,l,x' solves the zero-byte problem immediately by setting each byte t_j of t to $[x_j = 0]$, because $1 \mathbin{\dot{-}} x = [x = 0]$. But we are primarily interested here in fairly universal techniques that don't rely on exotic hardware; MMIX's special features will be discussed later.

Now that we know a fast way to find the first 0, we can use the same ideas to search for *any* desired byte value. For example, to test if any byte of x is the newline character ($\#\mathtt{a}$), we simply look for a zero byte in $x \oplus \#\mathtt{0a0a0a0a0a0a0a0a}$.

And these techniques also open up many other doors. Suppose, for instance, that we want to compute $z = (z_7 \ldots z_1 z_0)_{256}$ from x and y, where $z_j = x_j$ when $x_j = y_j$ but $z_j = {}$'$*$' when $x_j \neq y_j$. (Thus if $x = {}$"beaching" and $y = {}$"belching", we're supposed to set $z \leftarrow {}$"be*ching".) It's easy:

$$\begin{aligned} &t \leftarrow h \,\&\, ((x \oplus y) \mid (((x \oplus y) \mid h) - l)); \\ &m \leftarrow (t \ll 1) - (t \gg 7); \\ &z \leftarrow x \oplus ((x \oplus {}\texttt{"********"}) \,\&\, m). \end{aligned} \tag{92}$$

The first step uses a variant of (91) to flag the high-order bits in each byte where $x_j \neq y_j$. The next step creates a mask to highlight those bytes: $\#\mathtt{00}$ if $x_j = y_j$, otherwise $\#\mathtt{ff}$. And the last step, which could also be written $z \leftarrow (x \,\&\, \overline{m}) \mid ({}\texttt{"********"} \,\&\, m)$, sets $z_j \leftarrow x_j$ or $z_j \leftarrow {}$'$*$', depending on the mask.

Operations (90) and (91) were originally designed as tests for bytes that are zero; but a closer look reveals that we can more wisely regard them as tests for bytes that are less than 1. Indeed, if we replace l by $c \cdot l = (cccccccc)_{256}$ in either formula, where c is any positive constant ≤ 128, we can use (90) or (91) to see if x contains any bytes that are less than c. Furthermore the comparison values c need not be the same in every byte position; and with a bit more work we can also do bytewise comparison in the cases where $c > 128$. Here's a 6-step formula that sets $t_j \leftarrow 128[x_j < y_j]$ for each byte position j in the test word t:

$$t \leftarrow \left((\bar{x} \mathbin{\&} y) + (((\bar{x} \oplus y) \gg 1) \mathbin{\&} \bar{h})\right) \mathbin{\&} h. \tag{93}$$

(See exercise 96. This trick was discovered in 2013 by Norbert Juffa.) Notice that $((\bar{x} \oplus y) \gg 1) \mathbin{\&} \bar{h}$ is the same as the quantity $((\bar{x} \oplus y) \mathbin{\&} \bar{l}) \gg 1$ that we saw in (88).

Once we've found a nonzero t in (90) or (91) or (93), we might want to compute ρt or λt in order to discover the index j of the rightmost or leftmost byte that has been flagged. The problem of calculating ρ or λ is now simpler than before, since t can take on only 256 different values. Indeed, the operation

$$j \leftarrow table\left[((a \cdot t) \bmod 2^{64}) \gg 56\right], \quad \text{where } a = \frac{2^{56} - 1}{2^7 - 1}, \tag{94}$$

now suffices to compute j, given an appropriate 256-byte table. And the multiplication here can often be performed faster by doing three shift-and-add operations, "$t \leftarrow t + (t \ll 7)$, $t \leftarrow t + (t \ll 14)$, $t \leftarrow t + (t \ll 28)$," instead.

Broadword computing. We've now seen more than a dozen ways in which a computer's bitwise operations can produce astonishing results at high speed, and the exercises below contain many more such surprises.

Elwyn Berlekamp has remarked that computer chips containing N flip-flops continue to be built with ever larger values of N, yet in practice only $O(\log N)$ of those components are flipping or flopping at any given moment. The surprising effectiveness of bitwise operations suggests that computers of the future might make use of this untapped potential by having enhanced memory units that are able to do efficient n-bit computations for fairly large values of n. To prepare for that day, we ought to have a good name for the concept of manipulating "wide words." Lyle Ramshaw has suggested the pleasant term *broadword*, so that we can speak of n-bit quantities as broadwords of width n.

Many of the methods we've discussed are *2-adic*, in the sense that they work correctly with binary numbers that have arbitrary (even infinite) precision. For example, the operation $x \mathbin{\&} -x$ always extracts $2^{\rho x}$, the least significant 1 bit of any nonzero 2-adic integer x. But other methods have an inherently broadword nature, such as the methods that use $O(d)$ steps to perform sideways addition or bit permutation of 2^d-bit words. Broadword computing is the art of dealing with n-bit words, when n is a parameter that is not extremely small.

Some broadword algorithms are of theoretical interest only, because they are efficient only in an asymptotic sense when n exceeds the size of the universe. But others are eminently practical even when $n = 64$. And in general, a broadword mindset often suggests good techniques.

One fascinating-but-impractical fact about broadword operations is the discovery by M. L. Fredman and D. E. Willard that $O(1)$ broadword steps suffice to evaluate the function $\lambda x = \lfloor \lg x \rfloor$ for any nonzero n-bit number x, no matter how big n is. Here is their remarkable scheme, when $n = g^2$ and g is a power of 2:

$$t_1 \leftarrow h \mathrel{\&} (x \mid ((x \mid h) - l)), \quad \text{where } h = 2^{g-1}l \text{ and } l = (2^n - 1)/(2^g - 1);$$
$$y \leftarrow (((a \cdot t_1) \bmod 2^n) \gg (n - g)) \cdot l, \quad \text{where } a = (2^{n-g} - 1)/(2^{g-1} - 1);$$
$$t_2 \leftarrow h \mathrel{\&} (y \mid ((y \mid h) - b)), \quad \text{where } b = (2^{n+g} - 1)/(2^{g+1} - 1);$$
$$m \leftarrow (t_2 \ll 1) - (t_2 \gg (g - 1)), \ m \leftarrow m \oplus (m \gg g); \tag{95}$$
$$z \leftarrow (((l \cdot (x \mathrel{\&} m)) \bmod 2^n) \gg (n - g)) \cdot l;$$
$$t_3 \leftarrow h \mathrel{\&} (z \mid ((z \mid h) - b));$$
$$\lambda \leftarrow ((l \cdot ((t_2 \gg (2g - \lg g - 1)) + (t_3 \gg (2g - 1)))) \bmod 2^n) \gg (n - g).$$

(See exercise 106.) The method fails to be practical because five of these 29 steps are multiplications, so they aren't really "bitwise" operations. In fact, we'll prove later that multiplication by a constant requires at least $\Omega(\log n)$ bitwise steps.

A multiplication-free way to find λx, with only $O(\log \log n)$ bitwise broadword operations, was discovered in 1997 by Gerth Brodal, whose method is even more remarkable than (95). It is based on a formula analogous to (49),

$$\lambda x \;=\; [\lambda x = \lambda(x \mathrel{\&} \bar{\mu}_0)] + 2[\lambda x = \lambda(x \mathrel{\&} \bar{\mu}_1)] + 4[\lambda x = \lambda(x \mathrel{\&} \bar{\mu}_2)] + \cdots, \tag{96}$$

and the fact that the relation $\lambda x = \lambda y$ is easily tested (see (58)):

Algorithm B (*Binary logarithm*). This algorithm uses n-bit operations to compute $\lambda x = \lfloor \lg x \rfloor$, assuming that $0 < x < 2^n$ and $n = d \cdot 2^d$.

B1. [Scale down.] Set $\lambda \leftarrow 0$. Then set $\lambda \leftarrow \lambda + 2^k$ and $x \leftarrow x \gg 2^k$ if $x \geq 2^{2^k}$, for $k = \lceil \lg n \rceil - 1, \lceil \lg n \rceil - 2, \ldots, d$.

B2. [Replicate.] (At this point $0 < x < 2^{2^d}$; the remaining task is to increase λ by $\lfloor \lg x \rfloor$. We will replace x by d copies of itself, in 2^d-bit fields.) Set $x \leftarrow x \mid (x \ll 2^{d+k})$ for $0 \leq k < \lceil \lg d \rceil$.

B3. [Change leading bits.] Set $y \leftarrow x \mathrel{\&} \sim(\mu_{d,d-1} \cdots \mu_{d,1}\mu_{d,0})_{2^{2d}}$. (See (48).)

B4. [Compare all fields.] Set $t \leftarrow h \mathrel{\&} (y \mid ((y \mid h) - (x \oplus y)))$, where $h = (2^{2^d - 1} \ldots 2^{2^d - 1}2^{2^d - 1})_{2^{2d}}$.

B5. [Compress bits.] Set $t \leftarrow (t + (t \ll (2^{d+k} - 2^k))) \bmod 2^n$ for $0 \leq k < \lceil \lg d \rceil$.

B6. [Finish.] Finally, set $\lambda \leftarrow \lambda + (t \gg (n - d))$. $\blacksquare$

This algorithm is almost competitive with (56) when $n = 64$ (see exercise 107).

Another surprisingly efficient broadword algorithm was discovered in 2006 by M. S. Paterson and the author, who considered the problem of identifying all occurrences of the pattern 01^r in a given n-bit binary string. This problem, which is related to finding r contiguous free blocks when allocating storage, is equivalent to computing

$$q \;=\; \bar{x} \mathrel{\&} (x \ll 1) \mathrel{\&} (x \ll 2) \mathrel{\&} (x \ll 3) \mathrel{\&} \cdots \mathrel{\&} (x \ll r) \tag{97}$$

when $x = (x_{n-1} \ldots x_1 x_0)_2$ is given. For example, when $n = 16$, $r = 3$, and $x = (1110111101100111)_2$, we have $q = (0001000000001000)_2$. One might expect intuitively that $\Omega(\log r)$ bitwise operations would be needed. But in fact the following 20-step computation does the job for all $n > r > 0$: Let $s = \lceil r/2 \rceil$, $l = \sum_{k \geq 0} 2^{ks} \bmod 2^n$, $h = (2^{s-1}l) \bmod 2^n$, and $a = \left(\sum_{k \geq 0}(-1)^{k+1} 2^{2ks}\right) \bmod 2^n$.

$$
\begin{aligned}
&y \leftarrow h \mathbin{\&} x \mathbin{\&} ((x \mathbin{\&} \bar{h}) + l); \\
&t \leftarrow (x + y) \mathbin{\&} \bar{x} \mathbin{\&} -2^r; \\
&u \leftarrow t \mathbin{\&} a, \quad v \leftarrow t \mathbin{\&} \bar{a}; \\
&m \leftarrow (u - (u \gg r)) \mid (v - (v \gg r)); \\
&q \leftarrow t \mathbin{\&} ((x \mathbin{\&} m) + ((t \gg r) \mathbin{\&} {\sim}(m \ll 1))).
\end{aligned}
\tag{98}
$$

Exercise 111 explains why these machinations are valid. The method has little or no practical value; there's an easy way to evaluate (97) in $2\lceil \lg r \rceil + 2$ steps, so (98) is not advantageous until $r > 512$. But (98) is another indication of the unexpected power of broadword methods.

*__Lower bounds.__ Indeed, the existence of so many tricks and techniques makes it natural to wonder whether we've only been scratching the surface. Are there many more incredibly fast methods, still waiting to be discovered? A few theoretical results are known by which we can derive certain limitations on what is possible, although such studies are still in their infancy.

Let's say that a *2-adic chain* is a sequence $(x_0, x_1, \ldots, x_r)$ of 2-adic integers in which each element x_i for $i > 0$ is obtained from its predecessors via bitwise manipulation. More precisely, we want the steps of the chain to be defined by binary operations

$$
x_i = x_{j(i)} \circ_i x_{k(i)} \quad \text{or} \quad c_i \circ_i x_{k(i)} \quad \text{or} \quad x_{j(i)} \circ_i c_i,
\tag{99}
$$

where each $\circ_i$ is one of the operators $\{+, -, \mathbin{\&}, \mid, \oplus, \equiv, \subset, \supset, \overline{\subset}, \overline{\supset}, \wedge, \vee, \ll, \gg\}$ and each c_i is a constant. Furthermore, when the operator $\circ_i$ is a left shift or right shift, the amount of shift must be a positive integer constant; operations such as $x_{j(i)} \ll x_{k(i)}$ or $c_i \gg x_{k(i)}$ are *not* permitted. (Without the latter restriction we couldn't derive meaningful lower bounds, because *every* 0–1 valued function of a nonnegative integer x would be computable in two steps as "$(c \gg x) \mathbin{\&} 1$" for some constant c.)

Similarly, a *broadword chain* of width n, also called an n-bit broadword chain, is a sequence $(x_0, x_1, \ldots, x_r)$ of n-bit numbers subject to essentially the same restrictions, where n is a parameter and all operations are performed modulo 2^n. Broadword chains behave like 2-adic chains in many ways, but subtle differences can arise because of the information loss that occurs at the left of n-bit computations (see exercise 113).

Both types of chains compute a function $f(x) = x_r$ when we start them out with a given value $x = x_0$. Exercise 114 shows that an mn-bit broadword chain is able to do m essentially simultaneous evaluations of any function that is computable with an n-bit chain. Our goal is to study the *shortest* chains that are able to evaluate a given function f.

Any 2-adic or broadword chain $(x_0, x_1, \ldots, x_r)$ has a sequence of "shift sets" $(S_0, S_1, \ldots, S_r)$ and "bounds" $(B_0, B_1, \ldots, B_r)$, defined as follows: Start with $S_0 = \{0\}$ and $B_0 = 1$; then for $i \geq 1$, let

$$S_i = \begin{cases} S_{j(i)} \cup S_{k(i)}, \\ S_{k(i)}, \\ S_{j(i)}, \\ S_{j(i)} + c_i, \\ S_{j(i)} - c_i, \end{cases} \quad \text{and} \quad B_i = \begin{cases} M_i B_{j(i)} B_{k(i)}, & \text{if } x_i = x_{j(i)} \circ_i x_{k(i)}, \\ M_i B_{k(i)}, & \text{if } x_i = c_i \circ_i x_{k(i)}, \\ M_i B_{j(i)}, & \text{if } x_i = x_{j(i)} \circ_i c_i, \\ B_{j(i)}, & \text{if } x_i = x_{j(i)} \gg c_i, \\ B_{j(i)}, & \text{if } x_i = x_{j(i)} \ll c_i, \end{cases} \quad (100)$$

where $M_i = 2$ if $\circ_i \in \{+, -\}$ and $M_i = 1$ otherwise, and these formulas assume that $\circ_i \notin \{\ll, \gg\}$. For example, consider the following 7-step chain:

$$\begin{array}{ccc} x_i & S_i & B_i \\ x_0 = x & \{0\} & 1 \\ x_1 = x_0 \mathbin{\&} -2 & \{0\} & 1 \\ x_2 = x_1 + 2 & \{0\} & 2 \\ x_3 = x_2 \gg 1 & \{1\} & 2 \\ x_4 = x_2 + x_3 & \{0, 1\} & 8 \\ x_5 = x_4 \gg 4 & \{4, 5\} & 8 \\ x_6 = x_4 + x_5 & \{0, 1, 4, 5\} & 128 \\ x_7 = x_6 \gg 4 & \{4, 5, 8, 9\} & 128 \end{array} \quad (101)$$

(We encountered this chain in exercise 4.4–9, which proved that these operations will yield $x_7 = \lfloor x/10 \rfloor$ for $0 \leq x < 160$ when performed with 8-bit arithmetic.)

To begin a theory of lower bounds, let's notice first that the high-order bits of $x = x_0$ cannot influence any low-order bits unless we shift them to the right.

Lemma A. *Given a 2-adic or broadword chain, let the binary representation of x_i be $(\ldots x_{i2} x_{i1} x_{i0})_2$. Then bit x_{ip} can depend on bit x_{0q} only if $q \leq p + \max S_i$.*

Proof. By induction on i we can in fact show that, if $B_i = 1$, bit x_{ip} can depend on bit x_{0q} only if $q - p \in S_i$. Addition and subtraction, which force $B_i > 1$, allow any particular bit of their operands to affect all bits that lie to the left in the sum or difference, but not those that lie to the right. ∎

Corollary I. *The function $x \mathbin{\dot-} 1$ cannot be computed by a 2-adic chain, nor can any function for which at least one bit of $f(x)$ depends on an unbounded number of bits of x.* ∎

Corollary W. *An n-bit function $f(x)$ can be computed by an n-bit broadword chain without shifts if and only if $x \equiv y$ (modulo 2^p) implies $f(x) \equiv f(y)$ (modulo 2^p) for $0 \leq p < n$.*

Proof. If there are no shifts we have $S_i = \{0\}$ for all i. Thus bit x_{rp} cannot depend on bit x_{0q} unless $q \leq p$. In other words we must have $x_r \equiv y_r$ (modulo 2^p) whenever $x_0 \equiv y_0$ (modulo 2^p).

Conversely, all such functions are achievable by a sufficiently long chain. Exercise 119 gives shift-free n-bit chains for the functions

$$f_{py}(x) = 2^p [x \bmod 2^{p+1} = y], \quad \text{when } 0 \leq p < n \text{ and } 0 \leq y < 2^{p+1}, \quad (102)$$

from which all the relevant functions arise by addition. [H. S. Warren, Jr., generalized this result to functions of m variables in *CACM* **20** (1977), 439–441.] ∎

Shift sets S_i and bounds B_i are important chiefly because of a fundamental
lemma that is our principal tool for proving lower bounds:

Lemma B. *Let $X_{pqr} = \{x_r \,\&\, \lfloor 2^p - 2^q \rfloor \mid x_0 \in V_{pqr}\}$ in an n-bit broadword chain,
where*

$$V_{pqr} = \{x \mid x \,\&\, \lfloor 2^{p+s} - 2^{q+s} \rfloor = 0 \text{ for all } s \in S_r\} \qquad (103)$$

and $p > q$. Then $|X_{pqr}| \le B_r$. (Here p and q are integers, possibly negative.)
This lemma states that at most B_r different bit patterns $x_{r(p-1)} \dots x_{rq}$ can occur
within $f(x)$, when certain intervals of bits in x are constrained to be zero.

Proof. The result certainly holds when $r = 0$. Otherwise if, for example, $x_r =
x_j + x_k$, we know by induction that $|X_{pqj}| \le B_j$ and $|X_{pqk}| \le B_k$. Furthermore
$V_{pqr} = V_{pqj} \cap V_{pqk}$, since $S_r = S_j \cup S_k$. Thus at most $B_j B_k$ possibilities for
$(x_j + x_k) \,\&\, \lfloor 2^p - 2^q \rfloor$ arise when there's no carry into position q, and at most
$B_j B_k$ when there is a carry, making a grand total of at most $B_r = 2 B_j B_k$
possibilities altogether. Exercise 122 considers the other cases. ∎

We now can prove that the ruler function needs $\Omega(\log \log n)$ steps.

Theorem R. *If $n = d \cdot 2^d$, every n-bit broadword chain that computes ρx for
$0 < x < 2^n$ has more than $\lg d$ steps that are not shifts.*

Proof. If there are l nonshift steps, we have $|S_r| \le 2^l$ and $B_r \le 2^{2^l - 1}$. Apply
Lemma B with $p = d$ and $q = 0$, and suppose $|X_{d0r}| = 2^d - t$. Then there are t
values of $k < 2^d$ such that

$$\{2^k, \, 2^{k+2^d}, \, 2^{k+2 \cdot 2^d}, \, \dots, \, 2^{k+(d-1)2^d}\} \cap V_{d0r} = \emptyset.$$

But V_{d0r} excludes at most $2^l d$ of the n possible powers of 2; so $t \le 2^l$.

If $l \le \lg d$, Lemma B tells us that $2^d - t \le B_r \le 2^{d-1}$; hence $2^{d-1} \le t \le
2^l \le d$. But this is impossible unless $d \le 2$, when the theorem clearly holds. ∎

The same proof works also for the binary logarithm function:

Corollary L. *If $n = d \cdot 2^d > 2$, every n-bit broadword chain that computes λx
for $0 < x < 2^n$ has more than $\lg d$ steps that are not shifts.* ∎

By using Lemma B with $q > 0$ we can derive the stronger lower bound
$\Omega(\log n)$ for bit reversal, and hence for bit permutation in general.

Theorem P. *If $2 \le g \le n$, every n-bit broadword chain that computes the
g-bit reversal x^R for $0 \le x < 2^g$ has at least $\lfloor \frac{1}{3} \lg g \rfloor$ steps that are not shifts.*

Proof. Assume as above that there are l nonshifts. Let $h = \lfloor \sqrt[3]{g} \rfloor$ and suppose
that $l < \lfloor \lg(h+1) \rfloor$. Then S_r is a set of at most $2^l \le \frac{1}{2}(h+1)$ shift amounts s.
We shall apply Lemma B with $p = q + h$, where $p \le g$ and $q \ge 0$, thus in $g - h + 1$
cases altogether. The key observation is that $x^R \,\&\, \lfloor 2^p - 2^q \rfloor$ is independent of
$x \,\&\, \lfloor 2^{p+s} - 2^{q+s} \rfloor$ whenever there are no indices j and k such that $0 \le j, k < h$
and $g - 1 - q - j = q + s + k$. The number of "bad" choices of q for which such

indices exist is at most $\frac{1}{2}(h+1)h^2 \leq g-h$; therefore at least one "good" choice of q yields $|X_{pqr}| = 2^h$. But then Lemma B leads to a contradiction, because we obviously cannot have $2^h \leq B_r \leq 2^{(h-1)/2}$.   ∎

Corollary M. *Multiplication by certain constants, modulo 2^n, requires $\Omega(\log n)$ steps in an n-bit broadword chain.*

Proof. In Hack 167 of the classic memorandum HAKMEM (M.I.T. A.I. Laboratory, 1972), Richard Schroeppel observed that the operations

$$t \leftarrow ((ax) \bmod 2^n) \mathbin{\&} b, \quad y \leftarrow ((ct) \bmod 2^n) \gg (n-g) \qquad (104)$$

compute $y = x^R$ whenever $n = g^2$ and $0 \leq x < 2^g$, using the constants $a = (2^{n+g}-1)/(2^{g+1}-1)$, $b = 2^{g-1}(2^n-1)/(2^g-1)$, and $c = (2^{n-g}-1)/(2^{g-1}-1)$. (See exercise 123.)   ∎

At this point the reader might well be thinking, "Okay, I agree that broadword chains sometimes have to be asymptotically long. But programmers needn't be shackled by such chains; we can use other techniques, like conditional branches or references to precomputed tables, which go beyond those restrictions."

Right. And we're in luck, because broadword theory can also be extended to more general models of computation. Consider, for example, the following idealization of an abstract reduced-instruction-set computer, called a *basic RAM*: The machine has n-bit registers r_1, $\ldots$, r_l, and n-bit memory words $\{M[0], \ldots, M[2^m - 1]\}$. It can perform the instructions

$$r_i \leftarrow r_j \pm r_k, \quad r_i \leftarrow r_j \circ r_k, \quad r_i \leftarrow r_j \gg r_k, \quad r_i \leftarrow c,$$
$$r_i \leftarrow M[r_j \bmod 2^m], \quad M[r_j \bmod 2^m] \leftarrow r_i, \qquad (105)$$

where $\circ$ is any bitwise Boolean operator, and where r_k in the shift instruction is treated as a signed integer in two's complement notation. The machine is also able to branch if $r_i \leq r_j$, treating r_i and r_j as unsigned integers. Its *state* is the entire contents of all registers and memory, together with a "program counter" that points to the current instruction. Its program begins in a designated state, which may include precomputed tables in memory, and with an n-bit input value x in register r_1. This initial state is called $Q(x,0)$, and $Q(x,t)$ denotes the state after t instructions have been performed. When the machine stops, r_1 will contain some n-bit value $f(x)$. Given a function $f(x)$, we want to find a lower bound on the least t such that r_1 is equal to $f(x)$ in state $Q(x,t)$, for $0 \leq x < 2^n$.

Theorem R′. *Let $\epsilon = 2^{-e}$. A basic n-bit RAM with memory parameter $m \leq n^{1-\epsilon}$ requires at least $\lg \lg n - e$ steps to evaluate the ruler function ρx, as $n \to \infty$.*

Proof. Let $n = 2^{2^{e+f}}$, so that $m \leq 2^{2^{e+f}-2^f}$. Exercise 124 explains how an omniscient observer can construct a broadword chain from a certain class of inputs x, in such a way that each x causes the RAM to take the same branches, use the same shift amounts, and refer to the same memory locations. Our earlier methods can then be used to show that this chain has length $\geq f$.   ∎

A skeptical reader may still object that Theorem R′ has no practical value, because $\lg \lg n$ never exceeds 6 in the real world. To this argument there is no rebuttal. But the following result is slightly more relevant:

Theorem P′. *A basic n-bit RAM requires at least $\frac{1}{3}\lg g$ steps to compute the g-bit reversal x^R for $0 \leq x < 2^g$, if $g \leq n$ and*

$$\max(m, 1 + \lg n) < \frac{h+1}{2\lfloor \lg(h+1)\rfloor - 2}, \qquad h = \lfloor \sqrt[3]{g} \rfloor. \qquad (106)$$

Proof. An argument like the proof of Theorem R′ appears in exercise 125. ∎

Lemma B and Theorems R, P, R′, P′ and their corollaries are due to A. Brodnik, P. B. Miltersen, and J. I. Munro, *Lecture Notes in Comp. Sci.* **1272** (1997), 426–439, based on earlier work of Miltersen in *Lecture Notes in Comp. Sci.* **1099** (1996), 442–453.

Many unsolved questions remain (see exercises 126–130). For example, does sideways addition require $\Omega(\log n)$ steps in an n-bit broadword chain? Can the parity function $(\nu x) \bmod 2$, or the majority function $[\nu x > n/2]$, be computed substantially faster than νx itself, broadwordwise?

An application to directed graphs. Now let's use some of what we've learned, by implementing a simple algorithm. Given a digraph on a set of vertices V, we write $u \longrightarrow v$ when there's an arc from u to v. The *reachability problem* is to find all vertices that lie on oriented paths beginning in a specified set $Q \subseteq V$; in other words, we seek the set

$$R = \{v \mid u \longrightarrow^* v \text{ for some } u \in Q\}, \qquad (107)$$

where $u \longrightarrow^* v$ means that there is a sequence of t arcs

$$u = u_0 \longrightarrow u_1 \longrightarrow \cdots \longrightarrow u_t = v, \qquad \text{for some } t \geq 0. \qquad (108)$$

This problem arises frequently in practice. For example, we encountered it in Section 2.3.5 when marking all elements of Lists that are not "garbage."

If the number of vertices is small, say $|V| \leq 64$, we may want to approach the reachability problem in quite a different way than we did before, by working directly with subsets of vertices. Let

$$S[u] = \{v \mid u \longrightarrow v\} \qquad (109)$$

be the set of successors of vertex u, for all $u \in V$. Then the following algorithm is almost completely different from Algorithm 2.3.5E, yet it solves the same abstract problem:

Algorithm R (*Reachability*). Given a simple directed graph, represented by the successor sets $S[u]$ in (109), this algorithm computes the elements R that are reachable from a given set Q.

R1. [Initialize.] Set $R \leftarrow Q$ and $X \leftarrow \emptyset$. (In the following steps, X is the subset of vertices $u \in R$ for which we've looked at $S[u]$.)

R2. [Done?] If $X = R$, the algorithm terminates.

R3. [Examine another vertex.] Let u be an element of $R \setminus X$. Set $X \leftarrow X \cup u$, $R \leftarrow R \cup S[u]$, and return to step R2. ∎

The algorithm is correct because (i) every element placed into R is reachable; (ii) every reachable element u_j in (108) is present in R, by induction on j; and (iii) termination eventually occurs, because step R3 always increases $|X|$.

To implement Algorithm R we will assume that $V = \{0, 1, \ldots, n-1\}$, with $n \leq 64$. The set X is conveniently represented by the integer $\sigma(X) = \sum \{2^u \mid u \in X\}$, and the same convention works nicely for the other sets Q, R, and $S[u]$. Notice that the bits of $S[0]$, $S[1]$, $\ldots$, $S[n-1]$ are essentially the *adjacency matrix* of the given digraph, as explained in Section 7, but in little-endian order: The "diagonal" elements, which tell us whether or not $u \in S[u]$, go from right to left. For example, if $n = 3$ and the arcs are $\{0 \to 0, 0 \to 1, 1 \to 0, 2 \to 0\}$, we have $S[0] = (011)_2$ and $S[1] = S[2] = (001)_2$, while the adjacency matrix is $\left(\begin{smallmatrix}110\\100\\100\end{smallmatrix}\right)$.

Step R3 allows us to choose any element of $R \setminus X$, so we use the ruler function $u \leftarrow \rho(\sigma(R) - \sigma(X))$ to choose the smallest. The bitwise operations require no further trickery when we adapt the algorithm to MMIX:

Program R (*Reachability*). The input set Q is given in register q, and each successor set $S[u]$ appears in octabyte $M_8[\text{suc} + 8u]$. The output set R will appear in register r; other registers s, t, tt, u, and x hold intermediate results.

01	1H	SET	r,q	1	*R1. Initialize.* r $\leftarrow \sigma(Q)$.
02		SET	x,0	1	x $\leftarrow \sigma(\emptyset)$.
03		JMP	2F	1	To R2.
04	3H	SUBU	tt,t,1	$\|R\|$	*R3. Examine another vertex.* tt $\leftarrow$ t -1.
05		SADD	u,tt,t	$\|R\|$	u $\leftarrow \rho(\text{t})$ [see (46)].
06		SLU	s,u,3	$\|R\|$	s $\leftarrow 8u$.
07		LDOU	s,suc,s	$\|R\|$	s $\leftarrow \sigma(S[u])$.
08		ANDN	tt,t,tt	$\|R\|$	tt $\leftarrow$ t $\&$ $\sim$tt $= 2^u$.
09		OR	x,x,tt	$\|R\|$	$X \leftarrow X \cup u$; that is, x $\leftarrow$ x $\mid 2^u$, since x $= \sigma(X)$.
10		OR	r,r,s	$\|R\|$	$R \leftarrow R \cup S[u]$; that is, r $\leftarrow$ r $\mid$ s, since r $= \sigma(R)$.
11	2H	SUBU	t,r,x	$\|R\|+1$	*R2. Done?* t $\leftarrow$ r $-$ x $= \sigma(R \setminus X)$, since $X \subseteq R$.
12		PBNZ	t,3B	$\|R\|+1$	To R3 if $R \neq X$. ∎

The total running time is $(\mu + 9v)|R| + 7v$. By contrast, exercise 131 implements Algorithm R with linked lists; the overall execution time then grows to $(3S + 4|R| - 2|Q| + 1)\mu + (5S + 12|R| - 5|Q| + 4)v$, where $S = \sum_{u \in R} |S[u]|$. (But of course that program is also able to handle graphs with millions of vertices.)

Exercise 132 presents another instructive algorithm where bitwise operations work nicely on not-too-large graphs.

Application to data representation. Computers are binary, but (alas?) the world isn't. We often must find a way to encode nonbinary data into 0s and 1s. One of the most common problems of this sort is to choose an efficient representation for items that can be in exactly three different states.

Suppose we know that $x \in \{a, b, c\}$, and we want to represent x by two bits $x_l x_r$. We could, for example, map $a \mapsto 00$, $b \mapsto 01$, and $c \mapsto 10$. But there are many other possibilities—in fact, 4 choices for a, then 3 choices for b, and 2 for c, making 24 altogether. Some of these mappings might be much easier to deal with than others, depending on what we want to do with x.

Given two elements $x, y \in \{a, b, c\}$, we typically want to compute $z = x \circ y$, for some binary operation $\circ$. If $x = x_l x_r$ and $y = y_l y_r$ then $z = z_l z_r$, where

$$z_l = f_l(x_l, x_r, y_l, y_r) \qquad \text{and} \qquad z_r = f_r(x_l, x_r, y_l, y_r); \qquad (110)$$

these Boolean functions f_l and f_r of four variables depend on $\circ$ and the chosen representation. We seek a representation that makes f_l and f_r easy to compute.

Suppose, for example, that $\{a, b, c\} = \{-1, 0, +1\}$ and that $\circ$ is multiplication. If we decide to use the natural mapping $x \mapsto x \bmod 3$, namely

$$0 \mapsto 00, \qquad +1 \mapsto 01, \qquad -1 \mapsto 10, \tag{111}$$

so that $x = x_r - x_l$, then the truth tables for f_l and f_r are respectively

$$f_l \leftrightarrow 000{*}001{*}010{*}{*}{*}{*}{*} \qquad \text{and} \qquad f_r \leftrightarrow 000{*}010{*}001{*}{*}{*}{*}{*}. \tag{112}$$

(There are seven "don't-cares," for cases where $x_l x_r = 11$ and/or $y_l y_r = 11$.) The methods of Section 7.1.2 tell us how to compute z_l and z_r optimally, namely

$$z_l = (x_l \oplus y_l) \wedge (x_r \oplus y_r), \qquad z_r = (x_l \oplus y_r) \wedge (x_r \oplus y_l); \tag{113}$$

unfortunately the functions f_l and f_r in (112) are independent, in the sense that they cannot both be evaluated in fewer than $C(f_l) + C(f_r) = 6$ steps.

On the other hand the somewhat less natural mapping scheme

$$+1 \mapsto 00, \qquad 0 \mapsto 01, \qquad -1 \mapsto 10 \tag{114}$$

leads to the transformation functions

$$f_l \leftrightarrow 001{*}000{*}100{*}{*}{*}{*}{*} \qquad \text{and} \qquad f_r \leftrightarrow 010{*}111{*}010{*}{*}{*}{*}{*}, \tag{115}$$

and three operations now suffice to do the desired evaluation:

$$z_r = x_r \vee y_r, \qquad z_l = (x_l \oplus y_l) \wedge \bar{z}_r. \tag{116}$$

Is there an easy way to discover such improvements? Fortunately we don't need to try all 24 possibilities, because many of them are basically alike. For example, the mapping $x \mapsto x_r x_l$ is equivalent to $x \mapsto x_l x_r$, because the new representation $x_l' x_r' = x_r x_l$ obtained by swapping coordinates makes

$$f_l'(x_l', x_r', y_l', y_r') = z_l' = z_r = f_r(x_l, x_r, y_l, y_r);$$

the new transformation functions f_l' and f_r' defined by

$$f_l'(x_l, x_r, y_l, y_r) = f_r(x_r, x_l, y_r, y_l), \quad f_r'(x_l, x_r, y_l, y_r) = f_l(x_r, x_l, y_r, y_l) \tag{117}$$

have the same complexity as f_l and f_r. Similarly we can complement a coordinate, letting $x_l' x_r' = \bar{x}_l x_r$; then the transformation functions turn out to be

$$f_l'(x_l, x_r, y_l, y_r) = \bar{f}_l(\bar{x}_l, x_r, \bar{y}_l, y_r), \quad f_r'(x_l, x_r, y_l, y_r) = f_r(\bar{x}_l, x_r, \bar{y}_l, y_r), \tag{118}$$

and again the complexity is essentially unchanged.

Repeated use of swapping and/or complementation leads to eight mappings that are equivalent to any given one. So the 24 possibilities reduce to only three, which we shall call classes I, II, and III:

Class I	Class II	Class III

$a \mapsto$ 00 01 10 11 00 10 01 11 00 01 10 11 00 10 01 11 00 01 10 11 00 10 01 11;
$b \mapsto$ 01 00 11 10 10 00 11 01 01 00 11 10 10 00 11 01 11 10 01 00 11 01 10 00; (119)
$c \mapsto$ 10 11 00 01 01 11 00 10 11 10 01 00 11 01 10 00 01 00 11 10 10 00 11 01.

To choose a representation we need consider only one representative of each class. For example, if $a = +1$, $b = 0$, and $c = -1$, representation (111) belongs to class II, and (114) belongs to class I. Class III turns out to have cost 3, like class I. So it appears that representation (114) is as good as any, with z computed by (116), for the 3-element multiplication problem we've been studying.

Appearances can, however, be deceiving, because we need not map $\{a, b, c\}$ into *unique* two-bit codes. Consider the one-to-many mapping

$$+1 \mapsto 00, \qquad 0 \mapsto 01 \text{ or } 11, \qquad -1 \mapsto 10, \tag{120}$$

where both 01 and 11 are allowed as representations of zero. The truth tables for f_l and f_r are now quite different from (112) and (115), because all inputs are legal but some outputs can be arbitrary:

$$f_l \leftrightarrow 0*1*****1*0***** \qquad \text{and} \qquad f_r \leftrightarrow 0101111101011111. \tag{121}$$

And in fact, this approach needs just two operations, instead of the three in (116):

$$z_l = x_l \oplus y_l, \qquad z_r = x_r \vee y_r. \tag{122}$$

A moment's thought shows that indeed, these operations obviously yield the product $z = x \cdot y$ when the three elements $\{+1, 0, -1\}$ are represented as in (120).

Such nonunique mappings add 36 more possibilities to the 24 that we had before. But again, they reduce under "2-cube equivalence" to a small number of equivalence classes. First there are three classes that we call IV_a, IV_b, and IV_c, depending on which element has an ambiguous representation:

Class IV_a	Class IV_b	Class IV_c

$a \mapsto$ 0* 0* 1* 1* *0 *0 *1 *1 11 10 01 00 11 01 10 00 10 11 00 01 01 11 00 10;

$b \mapsto$ 10 11 00 01 01 11 00 10 0* 0* 1* 1* *0 *0 *1 *1 11 10 01 00 11 01 10 00; (123)

$c \mapsto$ 11 10 01 00 11 01 10 00 10 11 00 01 01 11 00 10 0* 0* 1* 1* *0 *0 *1 *1.

(Representation (120) belongs to class IV_b. Classes IV_a and IV_c don't work well for $z = x \cdot y$.) Then there are three further classes with only four mappings each:

Class V_a				Class V_b				Class V_c			
$a \mapsto$ tt	$t\bar{t}$	$t\bar{t}$	tt	10	11	00	01	01	00	11	10;
$b \mapsto$ 01	00	11	10	tt	$t\bar{t}$	$t\bar{t}$	tt	10	11	00	01;
$c \mapsto$ 10	11	00	01	01	00	11	10	tt	$t\bar{t}$	$t\bar{t}$	tt.

$$\tag{124}$$

These classes are a bit of a nuisance, because the indeterminacy in their truth tables cannot be expressed simply in terms of don't-cares as we did in (121). For example, if we try

$$+1 \mapsto 00 \text{ or } 11, \qquad 0 \mapsto 01, \qquad -1 \mapsto 10, \tag{125}$$

which is the first mapping in class V_a, there are binary variables $pqrst$ such that

$$f_l \leftrightarrow p01q000010r1s01t \qquad \text{and} \qquad f_r \leftrightarrow p10q111101r0s10t. \tag{126}$$

Furthermore, mappings of classes V_a, V_b, and V_c almost never turn out to be better than the mappings of the other six classes (see exercise 138). Still, representatives of all nine classes must be examined before we can be sure that an optimal mapping has been found.

In practice we often want to perform several different operations on ternary-valued variables, not just a single operation like multiplication. For example, we might want to compute $\max(x, y)$ as well as $x \cdot y$. With representation (120), the best we can do is $z_l = x_l \wedge y_l$, $z_r = (x_l \wedge y_r) \vee (x_r \wedge (y_l \vee y_r))$; but the "natural" mapping (111) now shines, with $z_l = x_l \wedge y_l$, $z_r = x_r \vee y_r$. Class III turns out to have cost 4; other classes are inferior. To choose between classes II, III, and IV$_b$ in this case, we need to know the relative frequencies of $x \cdot y$ and $\max(x, y)$. And if we add $\min(x, y)$ to the mix, classes II, III, and IV$_b$ compute it with the respective costs 2, 5, 5; hence (111) looks better yet.

The ternary max and min operations arise also in other contexts, such as the three-valued logic developed by Jan Łukasiewicz in 1917. [See his *Selected Works*, edited by L. Borkowski (1970), 84–88, 153–178.] Consider the logical values "true," "false," and "maybe," denoted respectively by 1, 0, and $*$. Łukasiewicz defined the three basic operations of conjunction, disjunction, and implication on these values by specifying the tables

$$
x \left\{
\begin{array}{c|ccc}
 & 0 & * & 1 \\
\hline
0 & 0 & 0 & 0 \\
* & 0 & * & * \\
1 & 0 & * & 1
\end{array}
\right. ,
\qquad
x \left\{
\begin{array}{c|ccc}
 & 0 & * & 1 \\
\hline
0 & 0 & * & 1 \\
* & * & * & 1 \\
1 & 1 & 1 & 1
\end{array}
\right. ,
\qquad
x \left\{
\begin{array}{c|ccc}
 & 0 & * & 1 \\
\hline
0 & 1 & 1 & 1 \\
* & * & 1 & 1 \\
1 & 0 & * & 1
\end{array}
\right. .
\qquad (127)
$$
$$
x \wedge y \qquad\qquad\qquad x \vee y \qquad\qquad\qquad x \Rightarrow y
$$

For these operations the methods above show that the binary representation

$$
0 \mapsto 00, \qquad * \mapsto 01, \qquad 1 \mapsto 11 \qquad (128)
$$

works well, because we can compute the logical operations thus:

$$
x_l x_r \wedge y_l y_r = (x_l \wedge y_l)(x_r \wedge y_r), \qquad x_l x_r \vee y_l y_r = (x_l \vee y_l)(x_r \vee y_r),
$$
$$
x_l x_r \Rightarrow y_l y_r = ((\bar{x}_l \vee y_l) \wedge (\bar{x}_r \vee y_r))(\bar{x}_l \vee y_r). \qquad (129)
$$

Of course x need not be an isolated ternary value in this discussion; we often want to deal with ternary *vectors* $x = x_1 x_2 \ldots x_n$, where each x_j is either a, b, or c. Such ternary vectors are conveniently represented by two binary vectors

$$
x_l = x_{1l} x_{2l} \ldots x_{nl} \qquad \text{and} \qquad x_r = x_{1r} x_{2r} \ldots x_{nr}, \qquad (130)
$$

where $x_j \mapsto x_{jl} x_{jr}$ as above. We could also pack the ternary values into two-bit fields of a single vector,

$$
x = x_{1l} x_{1r} x_{2l} x_{2r} \ldots x_{nl} x_{nr}; \qquad (131)
$$

that would work fine if, say, we're doing Łukasiewicz logic with the operations $\wedge$ and $\vee$ but not $\Rightarrow$. Usually, however, the two-vector approach of (130) is better, because it lets us do bitwise calculations without shifting and masking.

Applications to data structures. Bitwise operations offer many efficient ways to represent elements of data and the relationships between them. For example, chess-playing programs often use a "bit board" to represent the positions of pieces (see exercise 143).

In Chapter 8 we shall discuss an important data structure developed by Peter van Emde Boas for representing a dynamically changing subset of integers between 0 and N. Insertions, deletions, and other operations such as "find the largest element less than x" can be done in $O(\log \log N)$ steps with his methods; the general idea is to organize the full structure recursively as $\sqrt{N}$ substructures for subsets of intervals of size $\sqrt{N}$, together with an auxiliary structure that tells which of those intervals are occupied. [See *Information Processing Letters* **6** (1977), 80–82; also P. van Emde Boas, R. Kaas, and E. Zijlstra, *Math. Systems Theory* **10** (1977), 99–127.] Bitwise operations make those computations fast.

Hierarchical data can sometimes be arranged so that the links between elements are implicit rather than explicit. For example, we studied "heaps" in Section 5.2.3, where n elements of a sequential array implicitly have a binary tree structure like

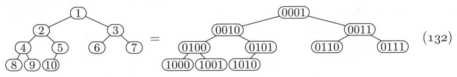

$$(132)$$

when, say, $n = 10$. (Node numbers are shown here both in decimal and binary notation.) There is no need to store pointers in memory to relate node j of a heap to its parent (which is node $j \gg 1$ if $j \neq 1$), or to its sibling (which is node $j \oplus 1$ if $j \neq 1$), or to its children (which are nodes $j \ll 1$ and $(j \ll 1) + 1$ if those numbers don't exceed n), because a simple calculation leads directly from j to any desired neighbor.

Similarly, a *sideways heap* provides implicit links for another useful family of n-node binary tree structures, typified by

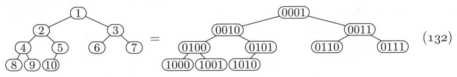

$$(133)$$

when $n = 10$. (We sometimes need to go beyond n when moving from a node to its parent, as in the path from 10 to 12 to 8 shown here.) Heaps and sideways heaps can both be regarded as nodes 1 to n of *infinite* binary tree structures: The heap with $n = \infty$ is rooted at node 1 and has no leaves; by contrast, the sideways heap with $n = \infty$ has infinitely many leaves $1, 3, 5, \ldots$, but no root(!).

The leaves of a sideways heap are the odd numbers, and their parents are the odd multiples of 2. The grandparents of leaves, similarly, are the odd multiples of 4; and so on. Thus the ruler function ρj tells how high node j is above leaf level.

The parent of node j in the infinite sideways heap is easily seen to be node

$$(j - k) \mid (k \ll 1), \qquad \text{where } k = j \,\&\, {-j}; \qquad (134)$$

this formula rounds j to the nearest odd multiple of $2^{1+\rho j}$. And the children are

$$j - (k \gg 1) \qquad \text{and} \qquad j + (k \gg 1) \tag{135}$$

when j is even. In general the descendants of node j form a closed interval

$$[j - 2^{\rho j} + 1 .. j + 2^{\rho j} - 1], \tag{136}$$

arranged as a complete binary tree of $2^{1+\rho j} - 1$ nodes. (These are the "inclusive" descendants, including j itself.) The ancestor of node j at height h is node

$$(j \mid (1 \ll h)) \mathbin{\&} -(1 \ll h) = ((j \gg h) \mid 1) \ll h \tag{137}$$

when $h \geq \rho j$. Notice that the symmetric order of the nodes, also called inorder, is just the natural order 1, 2, 3, ...

Dov Harel noted these properties in his Ph.D. thesis (U. of California, Irvine, 1980), and observed that the *nearest* common ancestor of any two nodes of a sideways heap can also be easily calculated. Indeed, if node l is the nearest common ancestor of nodes i and j, where $i \leq j$, there is a remarkable identity

$$\rho l = \max\{\rho x \mid i \leq x \leq j\} = \lambda(j \mathbin{\&} -i), \tag{138}$$

which relates the ρ and λ functions. (See exercise 146.) We can therefore use formula (137) with $h = \lambda(j \mathbin{\&} -i)$ to calculate l.

Subtle extensions of this approach lead to an asymptotically efficient algorithm that finds nearest common ancestors in *any* oriented forest whose arcs grow dynamically [D. Harel and R. E. Tarjan, *SICOMP* **13** (1984), 338–355]. Baruch Schieber and Uzi Vishkin [*SICOMP* **17** (1988), 1253–1262] subsequently discovered a much simpler way to compute nearest common ancestors in an arbitrary (but fixed) oriented forest, using an attractive and instructive blend of bitwise and algorithmic techniques that we shall consider next.

Recall that an oriented forest with m trees and n vertices is an acyclic digraph with $n - m$ arcs. There is at most one arc from each vertex; the vertices with out-degree zero are the roots of the trees. We say that v is the *parent* of u when $u \longrightarrow v$, and v is an (inclusive) *ancestor* of u when $u \longrightarrow^* v$. Two vertices have a common ancestor if and only if they belong to the same tree. Vertex w is called the nearest common ancestor of u and v when we have

$$u \longrightarrow^* z \text{ and } v \longrightarrow^* z \quad \text{if and only if} \quad w \longrightarrow^* z. \tag{139}$$

Schieber and Vishkin preprocess the given forest, mapping its vertices into a sideways heap S of size n by computing three quantities for each vertex v:

πv, the rank of v in preorder ($1 \leq \pi v \leq n$);
βv, a node of the sideways heap S ($1 \leq \beta v \leq n$);
αv, a $(1 + \lambda n)$-bit routing code ($1 \leq \alpha v < 2^{1+\lambda n}$).

If $u \longrightarrow v$ we have $\pi u > \pi v$ by the definition of preorder. Node βv is defined to be the nearest common ancestor of all sideways-heap nodes πu such that v is an ancestor of vertex u (always meaning an *inclusive* ancestor). And we define

$$\alpha v = \sum \{2^{\rho \beta w} \mid v \longrightarrow^* w\}. \tag{140}$$

For example, here's an oriented forest with ten vertices and two trees:

$$\text{(141)}$$

Each node has been labeled with its preorder rank, from which we can compute the β and α codes:

$$
\begin{array}{ccccccccccc}
v = & A & B & C & D & E & F & G & H & I & J \\
\pi v = & 0001 & 1000 & 0010 & 0100 & 1001 & 0011 & 0101 & 0111 & 1010 & 0110 \\
\beta v = & 0100 & 1000 & 0010 & 0100 & 1010 & 0011 & 0110 & 0111 & 1010 & 0110 \\
\alpha v = & 0100 & 1000 & 0110 & 0100 & 1010 & 0111 & 0110 & 0101 & 1010 & 0110
\end{array}
$$

Notice that, for instance, $\beta A = 4 = 0100$ because the preorder ranks of the descendants of A are $\{1,2,3,4,5,6,7\}$. And $\alpha H = 0101$ because the ancestors of H have β codes $\{\beta H, \beta D, \beta A\} = \{0111, 0100\}$. One can prove without difficulty that the mapping $v \mapsto \beta v$ satisfies the following key properties:

 i) If $u \longrightarrow v$ in the forest, then βu is a descendant of βv in S.

 ii) If several vertices have the same value of βv, they form a path in the forest.

Property (ii) holds because exactly one child u of v has $\beta u = \beta v$ when $\beta v \neq \pi v$.

Now let's imagine placing every vertex v of the forest into node βv of S:

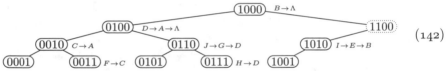

$$\text{(142)}$$

If k vertices map into node j, we can arrange them into a path

$$v_0 \longrightarrow v_1 \longrightarrow \cdots \longrightarrow v_{k-1} \longrightarrow v_k, \qquad \text{where } \beta v_0 = \beta v_1 = \cdots = \beta v_{k-1} = j. \quad \text{(143)}$$

These paths are illustrated in (142); for example, $J \longrightarrow G \longrightarrow D$ is a path in (141), and '$J \rightarrow G \rightarrow D$' appears with node $0110 = \beta J = \beta G$.

The preprocessing algorithm also computes a table τj for all nodes j of S, containing pointers to the vertices v_k at the tail ends of (143):

$$
\begin{array}{ccccccccccc}
j = & 0001 & 0010 & 0011 & 0100 & 0101 & 0110 & 0111 & 1000 & 1001 & 1010 \\
\tau j = & \Lambda & A & C & \Lambda & \Lambda & D & D & \Lambda & \Lambda & B
\end{array}
$$

Exercise 149 shows that all four tables πv, βv, αv, and τj can be prepared in $O(n)$ steps. And once those tables are ready, they contain just enough information to identify the nearest common ancestor of any two given vertices quickly:

Algorithm V (*Nearest common ancestors*). Suppose πv, βv, αv, and τj are known for all n vertices v of an oriented forest, and for $1 \leq j \leq n$. A dummy vertex Λ is also assumed to be present, with $\pi \Lambda = \beta \Lambda = \alpha \Lambda = 0$. This algorithm computes the nearest common ancestor z of any given vertices x and y, returning $z = \Lambda$ if x and y belong to different trees. We assume that the values $\lambda j = \lfloor \lg j \rfloor$ have been precomputed for $1 \leq j \leq n$, and that $\lambda 0 = \lambda n$.

V1. [Find common height.] If $\beta x \leq \beta y$, set $h \leftarrow \lambda(\beta y \ \& \ -\beta x)$; otherwise set $h \leftarrow \lambda(\beta x \ \& \ -\beta y)$. (See (138).)

V2. [Find true height.] Set $k \leftarrow \alpha x \ \& \ \alpha y \ \& \ -(1 \ll h)$, then $h \leftarrow \lambda(k \ \& \ -k)$.

V3. [Find βz.] Set $j \leftarrow ((\beta x \gg h) \mid 1) \ll h$. (Now $j = \beta z$, if $z \neq \Lambda$.)

V4. [Find $\hat{x}$ and $\hat{y}$.] (We now seek the lowest ancestors of x and y in node j.) If $j = \beta x$, set $\hat{x} \leftarrow x$; otherwise set $l \leftarrow \lambda(\alpha x \ \& \ ((1 \ll h) - 1))$ and $\hat{x} \leftarrow \tau(((\beta x \gg l) \mid 1) \ll l)$. Similarly, if $j = \beta y$, set $\hat{y} \leftarrow y$; otherwise set $l \leftarrow \lambda(\alpha y \ \& \ ((1 \ll h) - 1))$ and $\hat{y} \leftarrow \tau(((\beta y \gg l) \mid 1) \ll l)$.

V5. [Find z.] Set $z \leftarrow \hat{x}$ if $\pi \hat{x} \leq \pi \hat{y}$, otherwise $z \leftarrow \hat{y}$. ∎

These artful dodges obviously exploit (137); exercise 152 explains why they work.

Sideways heaps can also be used to implement an interesting type of priority queue that J. Katajainen and F. Vitale call a "navigation pile," illustrated here for $n = 10$:

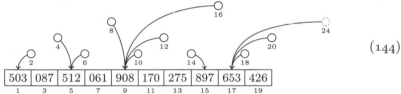

$$(144)$$

Data elements go into the leaf positions 1, 3, ..., $2n - 1$ of the sideways heap; they can be many bits wide, and they can appear in any order. By contrast, each branch position 2, 4, 6, ... contains a pointer to its largest descendant. And the novel point is that these pointers take up almost no extra space — fewer than two bits per item of data, on average — because only one bit is needed for pointers 2, 6, 10, ..., only two bits for pointers 4, 12, 20, ..., and only ρj for pointer j in general. (See exercise 153.) Thus the navigation pile requires very little memory, and it behaves nicely with respect to cache performance on a typical computer.

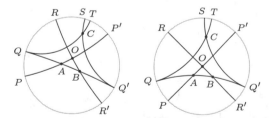

Fig. 13. Two views of five lines in the hyperbolic plane.

***Cells in the hyperbolic plane.** Hyperbolic geometry suggests an instructive implicit data structure that has a rather different flavor. The *hyperbolic plane* is a fascinating example of non-Euclidean geometry that is conveniently viewed by projecting its points into the interior of a circle. Its straight lines then become circular arcs, which meet the rim at right angles. For example, the lines PP', QQ', and RR' in Fig. 13 intersect at points O, A, B, and those points form a triangle. Lines SQ' and QQ' are *parallel*: They never touch, but their points get closer and closer together. Line QT is also parallel to QQ'.

We get different views by focusing on different center points. For example, the second view in Fig. 13 puts O smack in the center. Notice that if a line passes through the very center, it remains straight after being projected; such diameter-spanning chords are the special case of a "circular arc" whose radius is infinite.

Most of Euclid's axioms for plane geometry remain valid in the hyperbolic plane. For example, exactly one line passes through any two distinct points; and if point A lies on line PP' there's exactly one line QQ' such that angle PAQ has any given value θ, for $0 < \theta < 180°$. But Euclid's famous fifth postulate does *not* hold: If point C is *not* on line QQ', there always are exactly *two* lines through C that are parallel to QQ'. Furthermore there are many pairs of lines, like RR' and SQ' in Fig. 13, that are totally disjoint or *ultraparallel*, in the sense that their points never become arbitrarily close. [These properties of the hyperbolic plane were discovered by G. Saccheri in the early 1700s, and made rigorous by N. I. Lobachevsky, J. Bolyai, and C. F. Gauss a century later.]

Quantitatively speaking, when points are projected onto the unit disk $|z| < 1$, the arc that meets the circle at $e^{i\theta}$ and $e^{-i\theta}$ has center at $\sec\theta$ and radius $\tan\theta$. The actual distance between two points whose projections are z and z' is $d(z, z') = \ln(|1 - \bar{z}z'| + |z - z'|) - \ln(|1 - \bar{z}z'| - |z - z'|)$. Thus objects far from the center appear dramatically shrunken when we see them near the circle's rim.

The sum of the angles of a hyperbolic triangle is always *less* than 180°. For example, the angles at O, A, and B in Fig. 13 are respectively 90°, 45°, and 36°. Ten such 36°-45°-90° triangles can be placed together to make a regular pentagon with 90° angles at each corner. And four such pentagons fit snugly together at their corners, allowing us to tile the entire hyperbolic plane with right regular pentagons (see Fig. 14). The edges of these pentagons form an interesting family of lines, every two of which are either ultraparallel or perpendicular; so we have a grid structure analogous to the unit squares of the ordinary plane. We call it the *pentagrid*, because each cell now has five neighbors instead of four.

There's a nice way to navigate in the pentagrid using Fibonacci numbers, based on ideas of Maurice Margenstern [see F. Herrmann and M. Margenstern, *Theoretical Comp. Sci.* **296** (2003), 345–351]. Instead of the ordinary Fibonacci sequence $\langle F_n \rangle$, however, we shall use the *negaFibonacci* numbers $\langle F_{-n} \rangle$, namely

$$F_{-1} = 1, \ F_{-2} = -1, \ F_{-3} = 2, \ F_{-4} = -3, \ \ldots, \ F_{-n} = (-1)^{n-1}F_n. \tag{145}$$

Exercise 1.2.8–34 introduced the Fibonacci number system, in which every non-negative integer x can be written uniquely in the form

$$x = F_{k_1} + F_{k_2} + \cdots + F_{k_r}, \qquad \text{where } k_1 \ggg k_2 \ggg \cdots \ggg k_r \ggg 0; \tag{146}$$

here '$j \ggg k$' means '$j \geq k+2$'. But there's also a *negaFibonacci number system*, which suits our purposes better: *Every integer x, whether positive, negative, or zero, can be written uniquely in the form*

$$x = F_{k_1} + F_{k_2} + \cdots + F_{k_r}, \qquad \text{where } k_1 \lll k_2 \lll \cdots \lll k_r \lll 1. \tag{147}$$

For example, $4 = 5 - 1 = F_{-5} + F_{-2}$ and $-2 = -3 + 1 = F_{-4} + F_{-1}$. This representation can conveniently be expressed as a binary code $\alpha = \ldots a_3 a_2 a_1$,

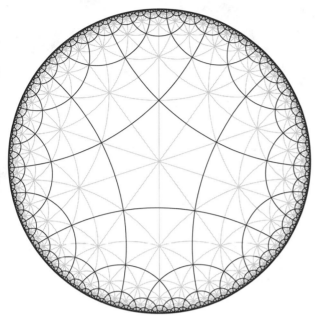

Fig. 14. The pentagrid,
in which identical pentagons
tile the hyperbolic plane.
[See H. A. Schwarz, *Crelle* **75**
(1873), page 318 and Tafel II
following page 348.]

A circular regular tiling, confined on all sides
by infinitely small shapes, is really wonderful.
— M. C. ESCHER, letter to George Escher (9 November 1958)

standing for $N(\alpha) = \sum_k a_k F_{-k}$, with no two 1s in a row. For example, here are
the negaFibonacci representation codes of all integers between -14 and $+15$:

$-14 = 10010100$	$-8 = 100000$	$-2 = 1001$	$4 = 10010$	$10 = 1001000$
$-13 = 10010101$	$-7 = 100001$	$-1 = 10$	$5 = 10000$	$11 = 1001001$
$-12 = 101010$	$-6 = 100100$	$0 = 0$	$6 = 10001$	$12 = 1000010$
$-11 = 101000$	$-5 = 100101$	$1 = 1$	$7 = 10100$	$13 = 1000000$
$-10 = 101001$	$-4 = 1010$	$2 = 100$	$8 = 10101$	$14 = 1000001$
$-9 = 100010$	$-3 = 1000$	$3 = 101$	$9 = 1001010$	$15 = 1000100$

As in the negadecimal system (see 4.1–(6) and (7)), we can tell whether x is
negative or not by seeing if its representation has an even or odd number of digits.

The predecessor $\alpha-$ and successor $\alpha+$ of any negaFibonacci binary code α
can be computed recursively by using the rules

$$(\alpha 01)- = \alpha 00, \quad (\alpha 000)- = \alpha 010, \quad (\alpha 100)- = \alpha 001, \quad (\alpha 10)- = (\alpha-)01,$$
$$(\alpha 10)+ = \alpha 00, \quad (\alpha 00)+ = \alpha 01, \quad (\alpha 1)+ = (\alpha-)0. \qquad (148)$$

(See exercise 157.) But ten elegant 2-adic steps do the calculation directly:

$$y \leftarrow x \oplus \bar{\mu}_0, \quad z \leftarrow y \oplus (y \pm 1), \quad \text{where } x = (\alpha)_2;$$
$$z \leftarrow z \mid (x \mathbin{\&} (z \ll 1)); \qquad (149)$$
$$w \leftarrow x \oplus z \oplus ((z+1) \gg 2); \quad \text{then } w = (\alpha\pm)_2.$$

We just use $y-1$ in the top line to get the predecessor, $y+1$ to get the successor.

And now here's the point: A negaFibonacci code can be assigned to each cell of the pentagrid in such a way that the codes of its five neighbors are easy to compute. Let's call the neighbors n, s, e, w, and o, for "north," "south," "east," "west," and "other." If α is the code assigned to a given cell, we define

$$\alpha_n = \alpha \gg 2, \quad \alpha_s = \alpha \ll 2, \quad \alpha_e = \alpha_s+, \quad \alpha_w = \alpha_s-; \tag{150}$$

thus $\alpha_{sn} = \alpha$, and also $\alpha_{en} = (\alpha 01)_n = \alpha$. The "other" direction is trickier:

$$\alpha_o = \begin{cases} \alpha_n+, & \text{if } \alpha \,\&\, 1 = 1; \\ \alpha_w-, & \text{if } \alpha \,\&\, 1 = 0. \end{cases} \tag{151}$$

For example, $1000_o = 101001$ and $101001_o = 1000$. This mysterious interloper lies between north and east when α ends with 1, but between north and west when α ends with 0.

If we choose any cell and label it with code 0, and if we also choose an orientation so that its neighbors are n, e, s, w, and o in clockwise order, rules (150) and (151) will assign consistent labels to every cell of the pentagrid. (See exercise 160.) For example, the vicinity of a cell labeled 1000 will look like this:

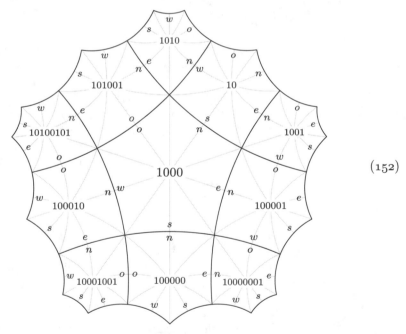

$$\tag{152}$$

The code labels do not, however, identify cells uniquely, because infinitely many cells receive the same label. (Indeed, we clearly have $0_n = 0_s = 0$ and $1_w = 1_o = 1$.) To get a unique identifier, we attach a second coordinate so that each cell's full name has the form (α, y), where y is an integer. When y is constant and α ranges over all negaFibonacci codes, the cells (α, y) form a more-or-less hook-shaped strip whose edges take a 90° turn next to cell $(0, y)$. In general, the five neighbors of (α, y) are $(\alpha, y)_n = (\alpha_n, y + \delta_n(\alpha))$, $(\alpha, y)_s = (\alpha_s, y + \delta_s(\alpha))$,

$(\alpha, y)_e = (\alpha_e, y + \delta_e(\alpha))$, $(\alpha, y)_w = (\alpha_w, y + \delta_w(\alpha))$, and $(\alpha, y)_o = (\alpha_o, y + \delta_o(\alpha))$, where

$$\delta_n(\alpha) = [\alpha = 0], \quad \delta_s(\alpha) = -[\alpha = 0], \quad \delta_e(\alpha) = 0, \quad \delta_w(\alpha) = -[\alpha = 1];$$

$$\delta_o(\alpha) = \begin{cases} \text{sign}(\alpha_o - \alpha_n)[\alpha_o \,\&\, \alpha_n = 0], & \text{if } \alpha \,\&\, 1 = 1; \\ \text{sign}(\alpha_o - \alpha_w)[\alpha_o \,\&\, \alpha_w = 0], & \text{if } \alpha \,\&\, 1 = 0. \end{cases} \tag{153}$$

(See the illustration below.) Bitwise operations now allow us to surf the entire hyperbolic plane with ease. On the other hand, we could also ignore the y coordinates as we move, thereby wrapping around a "hyperbolic cylinder" of pentagons; the α coordinates define an interesting multigraph on the set of all negaFibonacci codes, in which every vertex has degree 5.

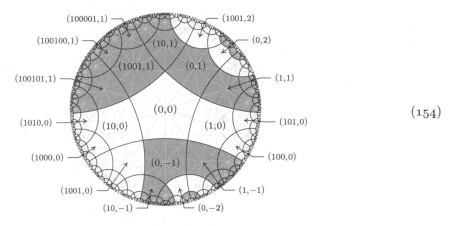

$$\tag{154}$$

Bitmap graphics. It's fun to write programs that deal with pictures and shapes, because they involve our left and right brains simultaneously. When image data is involved, the results can be engrossing even if there are bugs in our code.

The book you are now reading was typeset by software that treated each page as a gigantic matrix of 0s and 1s, called a "raster" or "bitmap," containing millions of square picture elements called "pixels." The rasters were transmitted to printing machines, causing tiny dots of ink to be placed wherever a 1 appeared in the matrix. Physical properties of ink and paper caused those small clusters of dots to look like smooth curves; but each pixel's basic squareness becomes evident if we enlarge the images tenfold, as in the letter 'A' shown in Fig. 15(a).

With bitwise operations we can achieve special effects like "custering," in which black pixels disappear when they're surrounded on all sides (Fig. 15(b)):

Fig. 15. The letter A, before and after custering.

This operation, introduced by R. A. Kirsch, L. Cahn, C. Ray, and G. H. Urban [*Proc. Eastern Joint Computer Conf.* **12** (1957), 221–229], can be expressed as

$$\text{custer}(X) \;=\; X \;\&\; {\sim}\big((X \vee\!\!\!\!\vee 1) \;\&\; (X \gg 1) \;\&\; (X \ll 1) \;\&\; (X \wedge\!\!\!\!\wedge 1)\big), \qquad (155)$$

where '$X \vee\!\!\!\!\vee 1$' and '$X \wedge\!\!\!\!\wedge 1$' stand respectively for the result of shifting the bitmap X down or up by one row. Let us write

$$X_{\mathrm{N}} = X \vee\!\!\!\!\vee 1, \quad X_{\mathrm{W}} = X \gg 1, \quad X_{\mathrm{E}} = X \ll 1, \quad X_{\mathrm{S}} = X \wedge\!\!\!\!\wedge 1 \qquad (156)$$

for the 1-pixel shifts of a bitmap X. Then, for example, the symbolic expression '$X_{\mathrm{N}} \;\&\; (X_{\mathrm{S}} \mid \overline{X_{\mathrm{E}}})$' evaluates to 1 in those pixel positions whose northern neighbor is black, and which also have either a black neighbor on the south side or a white neighbor to the east. With these abbreviations, (155) takes the form

$$\text{custer}(X) \;=\; X \;\&\; {\sim}(X_{\mathrm{N}} \;\&\; X_{\mathrm{W}} \;\&\; X_{\mathrm{E}} \;\&\; X_{\mathrm{S}}), \qquad (157)$$

which can also be expressed as $X \;\&\; (\overline{X_{\mathrm{N}}} \mid \overline{X_{\mathrm{W}}} \mid \overline{X_{\mathrm{E}}} \mid \overline{X_{\mathrm{S}}})$.

Every pixel has four "rook-neighbors," with which it shares an edge at the top, left, right, or bottom. It also has eight "king-neighbors," with which it shares at least one corner point. For example, the king-neighbors that lie to the northeast of all pixels in a bitmap X can be denoted by X_{NE}, which is equivalent to $(X_{\mathrm{N}})_{\mathrm{E}}$ in pixel algebra. Notice that we also have $X_{\mathrm{NE}} = (X_{\mathrm{E}})_{\mathrm{N}}$.

A 3×3 *cellular automaton* is an array of pixels that changes dynamically via a sequence of local transformations, all performed simultaneously: The state of each pixel at time $t + 1$ depends entirely on its state at time t and the states of its king-neighbors at that time. Thus the automaton defines a sequence of bitmaps $X^{(0)}, X^{(1)}, X^{(2)}, \ldots$ that begin with any given initial state $X^{(0)}$, where

$$X^{(t+1)} \;=\; f(X_{\mathrm{NW}}^{(t)}, X_{\mathrm{N}}^{(t)}, X_{\mathrm{NE}}^{(t)}, X_{\mathrm{W}}^{(t)}, X^{(t)}, X_{\mathrm{E}}^{(t)}, X_{\mathrm{SW}}^{(t)}, X_{\mathrm{S}}^{(t)}, X_{\mathrm{SE}}^{(t)}) \qquad (158)$$

and f is any bitwise Boolean function of nine variables. Fascinating patterns often emerge in this way. For example, after Martin Gardner introduced John Conway's game of Life to the world in 1970, more computer time was probably devoted to studying its implications than to any other computational task during the next several years — although the people paying the computer bills were rarely told! (See exercise 167.)

There are 2^{512} Boolean functions of nine variables, so there are 2^{512} different 3×3 cellular automata. Many of them are trivial, but most of them probably have such complicated behavior that they are humanly impossible to understand. Fortunately there also are many cases that do turn out to be useful in practice — and much easier to justify on economic grounds than the simulation of a game.

For example, algorithms for recognizing alphabetic characters, fingerprints, or similar patterns often make use of a "thinning" process, which removes excess black pixels and reduces each component of the image to an underlying skeleton that is comparatively simple to analyze. Several authors have proposed cellular automata for this problem, beginning with D. Rutovitz [*J. Royal Stat. Society* **A129** (1966), 512–513] who suggested a 4×4 scheme. But parallel algorithms are notoriously subtle, and flaws tended to turn up after various methods had been

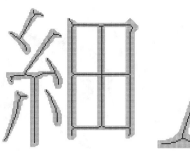 

Fig. 16. Example results of Guo and Hall's 3×3 automaton for thinning the components of a bitmap. ("Hollow" pixels were originally black.)

published. For example, one, two, or three of the black pixels in a component like ▦ should be removed, yet a symmetrical scheme will erroneously erase all four.

A satisfactory solution to the thinning problem was finally found by Z. Guo and R. W. Hall [*CACM* **32** (1989), 359–373, 759], using a 3×3 automaton that invokes alternate rules on odd and even steps. Consider the function

$$f(x_{\mathrm{NW}}, x_{\mathrm{N}}, x_{\mathrm{NE}}, x_{\mathrm{W}}, x, x_{\mathrm{E}}, x_{\mathrm{SW}}, x_{\mathrm{S}}, x_{\mathrm{SE}}) = x \wedge \neg g(x_{\mathrm{NW}}, \ldots, x_{\mathrm{W}}, x_{\mathrm{E}}, \ldots, x_{\mathrm{SE}}), \quad (159)$$

where $g = 1$ only in the following 37 configurations surrounding a black pixel:

Then we use (158), but with $f(x_{\mathrm{NW}}, x_{\mathrm{N}}, x_{\mathrm{NE}}, x_{\mathrm{W}}, x, x_{\mathrm{E}}, x_{\mathrm{SW}}, x_{\mathrm{S}}, x_{\mathrm{SE}})$ replaced by its 180° rotation $f(x_{\mathrm{SE}}, x_{\mathrm{S}}, x_{\mathrm{SW}}, x_{\mathrm{E}}, x, x_{\mathrm{W}}, x_{\mathrm{NE}}, x_{\mathrm{N}}, x_{\mathrm{NW}})$ on even-numbered steps. The process stops when two consecutive cycles make no change.

With this rule Guo and Hall proved that the 3×3 automaton will preserve the connectivity structure of the image, in a strong sense that we will discuss below. Furthermore their algorithm obviously leaves an image intact if it is already so thin that it contains no three pixels that are king-neighbors of each other. On the other hand it usually succeeds in "removing the meat off the bones" of each black component, as shown in Fig. 16. Slightly thinner thinning is obtained in certain cases if we add four additional configurations

$$\quad (160)$$

to the 37 listed above. In either case the function g can be evaluated with a Boolean chain of length 25. (See exercises 170–172.)

In general, the black pixels of an image can be grouped into segments or components that are *kingwise connected*, in the sense that any black pixel can be reached from any other pixel of its component by a sequence of king moves through black pixels. The white pixels also form components, which are *rookwise connected*: Any two white cells of a component are mutually reachable via rook moves that touch nothing black. It's best to use different kinds of connectedness for white and black, in order to preserve the topological concepts of "inside" and "outside" that are familiar from continuous geometry [see A. Rosenfeld, *JACM* **17** (1970), 146–160]. If we imagine that the corner points of a raster are black, an infinitely thin black curve can cross between pixels at a corner, but a white curve cannot. (We could also imagine white corner points, which would lead to rookwise connectivity for black and kingwise connectivity for white.)

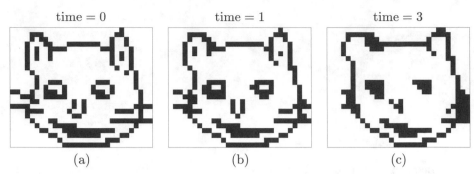

Fig. 17. The shrinking of a Cheshire cat

An amusing algorithm for shrinking a picture while preserving its connectivity, except that isolated black or white pixels disappear, was presented by S. Levialdi in *CACM* **15** (1972), 7–10; an equivalent algorithm, but with black and white reversed, had also appeared in T. Beyer's Ph.D. thesis (M.I.T., 1969). The idea is to use a cellular automaton with the simple transition function

$$f(x_{\mathrm{NW}}, x_{\mathrm{N}}, x_{\mathrm{NE}}, x_{\mathrm{W}}, x, x_{\mathrm{E}}, x_{\mathrm{SW}}, x_{\mathrm{S}}, x_{\mathrm{SE}}) = (x \wedge (x_{\mathrm{W}} \vee x_{\mathrm{SW}} \vee x_{\mathrm{S}})) \vee (x_{\mathrm{W}} \wedge x_{\mathrm{S}}) \quad (161)$$

at each step. This formula is actually a 2×2 rule, but we still need a 3×3 window if we want to keep track of the cases when a one-pixel component goes away.

For example, the 25×30 picture of a Cheshire cat in Fig. 17(a) has seven kingwise black components: the outline of its head, the two earholes, the two eyes, the nose, and the smile. The result after one application of (161) is shown in Fig. 17(b): Seven components remain, but there's an isolated point in one ear, and the other earhole will become isolated after the next step. Hence Fig. 17(c) has only five components. After six steps the cat loses its nose, and even the smile will be gone at time 14. Sadly, the last bit of cat will vanish during step 46.

At most $M + N - 1$ transitions will wipe out any $M \times N$ picture, because the lowest visible northwest-to-southeast diagonal line moves relentlessly upward each time. Exercises 176 and 177 prove that different components will never merge together and interfere with each other.

Of course this cubic-time cellular method isn't the fastest way to count or identify the components of a picture. We can actually do that job "online," while looking at a large image one row at a time, not bothering to keep all of the previously seen rows in memory if we don't wish to look at them again.

While we're analyzing the components we might as well also record the relationships between them. Let's assume that only finitely many black pixels are present. Then there's an infinite component of white pixels called the *background*. Black components adjacent to the background constitute the main *objects* of the image. And these objects may in turn have *holes*, which may serve as a background for another level of objects, and so on. Thus the connected components of any finite picture form a hierarchy — an oriented tree, rooted at the background. Black components appear at the odd-numbered levels of this tree, and white components at the even-numbered levels, alternating between

time = 5　　　　　　　　time = 10　　　　　　　time = 20

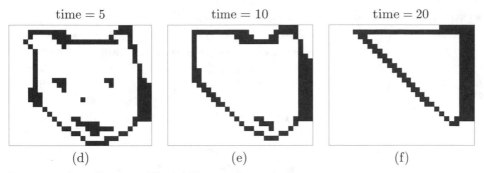

(d)　　　　　　　　　　(e)　　　　　　　　　　(f)

by repeated application of Levialdi's transformation.

kingwise and rookwise connectedness. Each component except the background is *surrounded* by its parent. Childless components are said to be *simply connected*.

For example, here are the Cheshire cat's components, labeled with digits for white pixels and letters for the black ones, and the corresponding oriented tree:

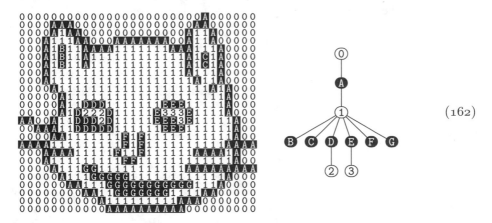

(162)

During the shrinking process of Fig. 17, components disappear in the order Ⓒ, {Ⓑ,②,③} (all at time 3), Ⓕ, Ⓔ, Ⓓ, Ⓖ, ①, Ⓐ.

Suppose we want to analyze the components of such a picture by reading one row at a time. After we've seen four rows the result-so-far will be

(163)

and we'll be ready to scan row five. A comparison of rows four and five will then show that Ⓑ and Ⓒ should merge into Ⓐ, but that new components Ⓑ and ③ should also be launched. Exercise 179 contains full details about an instructive algorithm that properly updates the current tree as new rows are input. Additional information can also be computed on the fly: For example, we could determine the area of each component, the locations of its first and last pixels, the smallest enclosing rectangle, and/or its center of gravity.

*Filling. Let's complete our quick tour of raster graphics by considering how to fill regions that are bounded by straight lines and/or simple curves. Particularly efficient algorithms are available when the curves are built up from "conic sections" — circles, ellipses, parabolas, or hyperbolas, as in classical geometry.

In keeping with geometric tradition, we shall adopt Cartesian coordinates (x, y) in the following discussion, instead of speaking about rows or columns of pixels: An increase of x will signify a move to the right, while an increase of y will move upward. More significantly, we will focus on the *edges* between square pixels, instead of on the pixels themselves. Edges run between integer points (x, y) and (x', y') of the plane when $|x - x'| + |y - y'| = 1$. Each pixel is bounded by the four edges (x, y) — $(x{-}1, y)$ — $(x{-}1, y{-}1)$ — $(x, y{-}1)$ — (x, y). Experience has shown that algorithms for filling contours become simpler and faster when we concentrate on the edge transitions between white and black, instead of on the black pixels of a custerized boundary. (See, for example, the discussion by B. D. Ackland and N. Weste in *IEEE Trans.* **C-30** (1981), 41–48.)

Consider a continuous curve $z(t) = \bigl(x(t), y(t)\bigr)$ that is traced out as t varies from 0 to 1. We assume that the curve doesn't intersect itself for $0 \le t < 1$, and that $z(0) = z(1)$. The famous Jordan curve theorem [C. Jordan, *Cours d'analyse* **3** (1887), 587–594; O. Veblen, *Trans. Amer. Math. Soc.* **6** (1905), 83–98] states that every such curve divides the plane into two regions, called the inside and the outside. We can "digitize" $z(t)$ by forcing it to travel along edges between pixels; then we obtain an approximation in which the inside pixels are black and the outside pixels are white. This digitization process essentially replaces the original curve by the sequence of integer points

$$\text{round}(z(t)) \;=\; \bigl(\lfloor x(t) + \tfrac{1}{2} \rfloor, \lfloor y(t) + \tfrac{1}{2} \rfloor\bigr), \qquad \text{for } 0 \le t \le 1. \qquad (164)$$

The curve can be perturbed slightly, if necessary, so that $z(t)$ never passes exactly through the center of a pixel. Then the digitized curve takes discrete steps along pixel edges as t grows; and a pixel lies inside the digitization if and only if its center lies inside the original continuous curve $\{z(t) \mid 0 \le t \le 1\}$.

For example, the equations $x(t) = 20 \cos 2\pi t$ and $y(t) = 10 \sin 2\pi t$ define an ellipse. Its digitization, $\text{round}(z(t))$, starts at $(20, 0)$ when $t = 0$, then jumps to $(20, 1)$ when $t \approx .008$ and $10 \sin 2\pi t = 0.5$. Then it proceeds to the points $(20, 2)$, $(19, 2)$, $(19, 3)$, $(19, 4)$, $(18, 4)$, ..., $(20, -1)$, $(20, 0)$, as t increases through the values .024, .036, .040, .057, .062, ..., .976, .992:

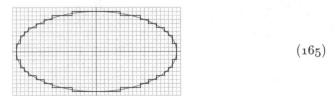

$$(165)$$

The horizontal edges of such a boundary are conveniently represented by bit vectors $H(y)$ for each y; for example, $H(10) = \ldots 00000011111111111000000 \ldots$ and $H(9) = \ldots 01111100000000000111110 \ldots$ in (165). If the ellipse is filled with black to obtain a bitmap B, the H vectors mark transitions between black and white, so we have the symbolic relation

$$H = B \oplus (B \wedge 1). \qquad (166)$$

Conversely, it's easy to obtain B when the H vectors are given:

$$B(y) = H(y_{\text{max}}) \oplus H(y_{\text{max}-1}) \oplus \cdots \oplus H(y+1)$$
$$= H(y_{\text{min}}) \oplus H(y_{\text{min}+1}) \oplus \cdots \oplus H(y). \qquad (167)$$

Notice that $H(y_{\text{min}}) \oplus H(y_{\text{min}+1}) \oplus \cdots \oplus H(y_{\text{max}})$ is the zero vector, because each bitmap is white at both top and bottom. Notice further that the analogous *vertical* edge vectors $V(x)$ are redundant: They satisfy the formulas $V = B \oplus (B \ll 1)$ and $B = V^\oplus$ (see exercise 36), but we need not bother to keep track of them.

Conic sections are easier to deal with than most other curves, because we can readily eliminate the parameter t. For example, the ellipse that led to (165) can be defined by the equation $(x/20)^2 + (y/10)^2 = 1$, instead of using sines and cosines. Therefore pixel (x, y) should be black if and only if its center point $(x-\frac{1}{2}, y-\frac{1}{2})$ lies inside the ellipse, if and only if $(x-\frac{1}{2})^2/400 + (y-\frac{1}{2})^2/100 - 1 < 0$.

In general, every conic section is the set of points for which $F(x, y) = 0$, when F is an appropriate quadratic form. Therefore there's a quadratic form

$$Q(x, y) = F(x - \tfrac{1}{2}, y - \tfrac{1}{2}) = ax^2 + bxy + cy^2 + dx + ey + f \qquad (168)$$

that is negative at the integer point (x, y) if and only if pixel (x, y) lies on a given side of the digitized curve.

For practical purposes we may assume that the coefficients $(a, b, \ldots, f)$ of Q are not-too-large integers. Then we're in luck, because the exact value of $Q(x, y)$ is easy to compute. In fact, as pointed out by M. L. V. Pitteway [*Comp. J.* **10** (1967), 282–289], there's a nice "three-register algorithm" by which we can quickly track the boundary points: Let x and y be integers, and suppose we've got the values of $Q(x, y)$, $Q_x(x, y)$, and $Q_y(x, y)$ in three registers (Q, Q_x, Q_y), where

$$Q_x(x, y) = 2ax + by + d \qquad \text{and} \qquad Q_y(x, y) = bx + 2cy + e \qquad (169)$$

are $\frac{\partial}{\partial x}Q$ and $\frac{\partial}{\partial y}Q$. We can then move to any adjacent integer point, because

$$Q(x\pm1, y) = Q(x, y)\pm Q_x(x, y)+a, \qquad Q(x, y\pm1) = Q(x, y)\pm Q_y(x, y)+c,$$
$$Q_x(x\pm1, y) = Q_x(x, y)\pm 2a, \qquad Q_x(x, y\pm1) = Q_x(x, y)\pm b,$$
$$Q_y(x\pm1, y) = Q_y(x, y)\pm b; \qquad Q_y(x, y\pm1) = Q_y(x, y)\pm 2c. \qquad (170)$$

Furthermore we can divide the contour into separate pieces, in each of which $x(t)$ and $y(t)$ are both monotonic. For example, when the ellipse (165) travels from $(20, 0)$ to $(0, 10)$, the value of x decreases while y increases; thus we need only move from (x, y) to $(x-1, y)$ or to $(x, y+1)$. If registers (Q, R, S) respectively hold $(Q, Q_x - a, Q_y + c)$, a move to $(x-1, y)$ simply sets $Q \leftarrow Q - R$, $R \leftarrow R - 2a$, and $S \leftarrow S - b$; a move to $(x, y+1)$ is just as quick. With care, this idea leads to a blindingly fast way to discover the correctly digitized edges of almost any conic curve.

For example, the quadratic form $Q(x, y)$ for ellipse (165) is $4x^2 + 16y^2 - (4x + 16y + 1595)$, when we integerize its coefficients. We have $Q(20, 0) = F(19.5, -0.5) = -75$ and $Q(21, 0) = +85$; therefore pixel $(20, 0)$, whose center is $(19.5, -0.5)$, is inside the ellipse, but pixel $(21, 0)$ isn't. Let's zoom in closer:

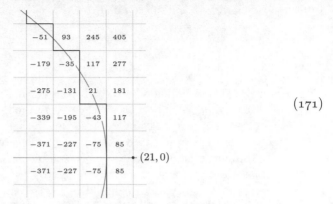

(171)

The boundary can be deduced without examining Q at very many points. In fact, we don't need to look at $Q(21, 0)$, because we know that all edges between $(20, 0)$ and $(0, 10)$ must go either upwards or to the left. First we test $Q(20, 1)$ and find it negative (-75); so we move up. Also $Q(20, 2)$ is negative (-43), so we go up again. Then we test $Q(20, 3)$, and find it positive (21); so we move left. And so on. Only the Q values -75, -43, 21, -131, -35, 93, -51, ... actually need to be examined, if we've set the three-register method up properly.

Algorithm T (*Three-register algorithm for conics*). Given two integer points (x, y) and (x', y'), and an integer quadratic form Q as in (168), this algorithm decides how to digitize a portion of the conic section defined by $F(x, y) = 0$, where $F(x, y) = Q(x + \frac{1}{2}, y + \frac{1}{2})$. It creates $|x' - x|$ horizontal edges and $|y' - y|$ vertical edges, which form a path from (x, y) to (x', y'). We assume that

  i) Real-valued points (ξ, η) and (ξ', η') exist such that $F(\xi, \eta) = F(\xi', \eta') = 0$.
 ii) The curve travels from (ξ, η) to (ξ', η') monotonically in both coordinates.
iii) $x = \lfloor \xi + \frac{1}{2} \rfloor$, $y = \lfloor \eta + \frac{1}{2} \rfloor$, $x' = \lfloor \xi' + \frac{1}{2} \rfloor$, and $y' = \lfloor \eta' + \frac{1}{2} \rfloor$.
 iv) If we traverse the curve from (ξ, η) to (ξ', η'), we see $F < 0$ on our left.
  v) No edge of the integer grid contains two roots of Q (see exercise 183).

  T1. [Initialize.] If $x = x'$, go to T11; if $y = y'$, go to T10. If $x < x'$ and $y < y'$, set $Q \leftarrow Q(x+1, y+1)$, $R \leftarrow Q_x(x+1, y+1)+a$, $S \leftarrow Q_y(x+1, y+1)+c$, and go to T2. If $x < x'$ and $y > y'$, set $Q \leftarrow Q(x+1, y)$, $R \leftarrow Q_x(x+1, y) + a$, $S \leftarrow Q_y(x+1, y) - c$, and go to T3. If $x > x'$ and $y < y'$, set $Q \leftarrow Q(x, y+1)$, $R \leftarrow Q_x(x, y+1) - a$, $S \leftarrow Q_y(x, y+1) + c$, and go to T4. If $x > x'$ and $y > y'$, set $Q \leftarrow Q(x, y)$, $R \leftarrow Q_x(x, y) - a$, $S \leftarrow Q_y(x, y) - c$, and go to T5.

  T2. [Right or up.] If $Q < 0$, do T9; otherwise do T6. Repeat until interrupted.

  T3. [Down or right.] If $Q < 0$, do T7; otherwise do T9. Repeat until interrupted.

T4. [Up or left.] If $Q < 0$, do T6; otherwise do T8. Repeat until interrupted.

T5. [Left or down.] If $Q < 0$, do T8; otherwise do T7. Repeat until interrupted.

T6. [Move up.] Create the edge $(x, y) - (x, y{+}1)$, then set $y \leftarrow y{+}1$. Interrupt to T10 if $y = y'$; otherwise set $Q \leftarrow Q + S$, $R \leftarrow R + b$, $S \leftarrow S + 2c$.

T7. [Move down.] Create the edge $(x, y) - (x, y{-}1)$, then set $y \leftarrow y - 1$. Interrupt to T10 if $y = y'$; otherwise set $Q \leftarrow Q{-}S$, $R \leftarrow R{-}b$, $S \leftarrow S{-}2c$.

T8. [Move left.] Create the edge $(x, y) - (x{-}1, y)$, then set $x \leftarrow x - 1$. Interrupt to T11 if $x = x'$; otherwise set $Q \leftarrow Q{-}R$, $R \leftarrow R{-}2a$, $S \leftarrow S{-}b$.

T9. [Move right.] Create the edge $(x, y) - (x{+}1, y)$, then set $x \leftarrow x + 1$. Interrupt to T11 if $x = x'$; otherwise set $Q \leftarrow Q{+}R$, $R \leftarrow R{+}2a$, $S \leftarrow S{+}b$.

T10. [Finish horizontally.] While $x < x'$, create the edge $(x, y) - (x{+}1, y)$ and set $x \leftarrow x + 1$. While $x > x'$, create the edge $(x, y) - (x{-}1, y)$ and set $x \leftarrow x - 1$. Terminate the algorithm.

T11. [Finish vertically.] While $y < y'$, create the edge $(x, y) - (x, y{+}1)$ and set $y \leftarrow y + 1$. While $y > y'$, create the edge $(x, y) - (x, y{-}1)$ and set $y \leftarrow y - 1$. Terminate the algorithm. ∎

For example, when this algorithm is invoked with $(x, y) = (20, 0)$, $(x', y') = (0, 10)$, and $Q(x, y) = 4x^2 + 16y^2 - 4x - 16y - 1595$, it will create the edges $(20, 0) - (20, 1) - (20, 2) - (19, 2) - (19, 3) - (19, 4) - (18, 4) - (18, 5) - (17, 5) - (17, 6) - \cdots - (6, 9) - (6, 10)$, then make a beeline for $(0, 10)$. (See (165) and (171).) Exercise 182 explains why it works.

Movement to the left in step T8 is conveniently implemented by setting $H(y) \leftarrow H(y) \oplus (1 \ll (x_{\max} - x))$, using the H vectors of (166) and (167). Movement to the right is similar, but we set $x \leftarrow x + 1$ first. Step T10 could set

$$H(y) \leftarrow H(y) \oplus ((1 \ll (x_{\max} - \min(x, x'))) - (1 \ll (x_{\max} - \max(x, x')))); \quad (172)$$

but one move at a time might be just as good, because $|x' - x|$ is often small. Movement up or down needs no action, because vertical edges are redundant.

Notice that the algorithm runs somewhat faster in the special case when $b = 0$; circles always belong to this case. The even more special case of straight lines, when $a = b = c = 0$, is of course faster yet; then we have a simple *one-register* algorithm (see exercise 185).

Fig. 18. Pixels change from white to black and back again, at the edges of digitized circles.

When many contours are filled in the same image, using H vectors, the pixel values change between black and white whenever we cross an odd number of edges. Figure 18 illustrates a tiling of the hyperbolic plane by equilateral 45°-45°-45° triangles, obtained by superimposing the results of several hundred applications of Algorithm T.

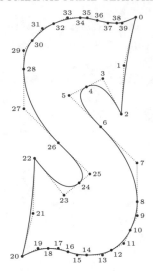

Fig. 19. Squines that define
the outline contour of an '**S**'.

Algorithm T applies only to conic curves. But that's not really a limitation in practice, because just about every shape we ever need to draw can be well approximated by "piecewise conics" called quadratic Bézier splines or *squines*. For example, Fig. 19 shows a typical squine curve with 40 points $(z_0, z_1, \ldots, z_{39}, z_{40})$, where $z_{40} = z_0$. The even-numbered points $(z_0, z_2, \ldots, z_{40})$ lie on the curve; the others, $(z_1, z_3, \ldots, z_{39})$, are called "control points," because they regulate local bending and flexing. Each section $S(z_{2j}, z_{2j+1}, z_{2j+2})$ begins at point z_{2j}, traveling in direction $z_{2j+1} - z_{2j}$. It ends at point z_{2j+2}, traveling in direction $z_{2j+2} - z_{2j+1}$. Thus if z_{2j} lies on the straight line from z_{2j-1} to z_{2j+1}, the squine passes smoothly through point z_{2j} without changing direction.

Exercise 186 defines $S(z_{2j}, z_{2j+1}, z_{2j+2})$ precisely, and exercise 187 explains how to digitize any squine curve using Algorithm T. The region inside the digitized edges can then be filled with black pixels.

Incidentally, the task of *drawing* lines and curves on a bitmap turns out to be much more difficult than the task of *filling* a digitized contour, because we want diagonal strokes to have the same apparent thickness as vertical and horizontal strokes do. An excellent solution to the line-drawing problem was found by John D. Hobby, *JACM* **36** (1989), 209–229.

*Branchless computation. Modern computers tend to slow down when a program contains conditional branch instructions, because an uncertain flow of control can interfere with predictive lookahead circuitry. Therefore we've used MMIX's conditional-set instructions like CSNZ in programs like (56). Indeed, four instructions such as 'ADD z,y,1; SR t,u,2; CSNZ x,q,z; CSNZ v,q,t' are probably faster than their three-instruction counterpart

$$\text{BZ q,@+12; ADD x,y,1; SR v,u,2} \tag{173}$$

when the actual running time is measured on a highly pipelined machine, even though the rule-of-thumb cost of (173) is only 3υ according to Table 1.3.1′–1.

Bitwise operations can help diminish the need for costly branching. For example, if MMIX didn't have a CSNZ instruction we could write

```
NEGU m,q;   OR m,m,q;   SR m,m,63;
ADD t,y,1;  XOR t,t,x;  AND t,t,m;  XOR x,x,t;      (174)
SR t,u,2;   XOR t,t,v;  AND t,t,m;  XOR v,v,t;
```

here the first line creates the mask $m = -[q \neq 0]$. On some computers these eleven branchless instructions would still run faster than the three instructions in (173).

The inner loop of a merge sort algorithm provides an instructive example. Suppose we want to do the following operations repeatedly:

> If $x_i < y_j$, set $z_k \leftarrow x_i$, $i \leftarrow i+1$, and go to *x_done* if $i = i_{\max}$.
> Otherwise set $z_k \leftarrow y_j$, $j \leftarrow j+1$, and go to *y_done* if $j = j_{\max}$.
> Then set $k \leftarrow k+1$ and go to *z_done* if $k = k_{\max}$.

If we implement them in the "obvious" way, four conditional branches are involved, three of which are active on each path through the loop:

```
1H CMP   t,xi,yj; BNN t,2F       Branch if xi ≥ yj.
   STO   xi,zbase,kk             zk ← xi.
   ADD   ii,ii,8                 i ← i+1.
   BZ    ii,X_Done               To x_done if i = imax.
   LDO   xi,xbase,ii             Load xi into register xi.
   JMP   3F                      Join the other branch.
2H STO   yj,zbase,kk             zk ← yj.
   ADD   jj,jj,8                 j ← j+1.
   BZ    jj,Y_Done               To y_done if j = jmax.
   LDO   yj,ybase,jj             Load yj into register yj.
3H ADD   kk,kk,8                 k ← k+1.
   PBNZ  kk,1B                   Repeat if k ≠ kmax.
   JMP   Z_Done                  To z_done.  ∎
```

(Here $ii = 8(i - i_{\max})$, $jj = 8(j - j_{\max})$, and $kk = 8(k - k_{\max})$; the factor of 8 is needed because x_i, y_j, and z_k are octabytes.) Those four branches can be reduced to just one:

```
1H CMP   t,xi,yj                 t ← sign(xi − yj).
   CSN   yj,t,xi                 yj ← min(xi,yj).
   STO   yj,zbase,kk             zk ← yj.
   AND   t,t,8                   t ← 8[xi < yj].
   ADD   ii,ii,t                 i ← i+[xi < yj].
   LDO   xi,xbase,ii             Load xi into register xi.
   XOR   t,t,8                   t ← t ⊕ 8.
   ADD   jj,jj,t                 j ← j+[xi ≥ yj].
   LDO   yj,ybase,jj             Load yj into register yj.
   ADD   kk,kk,8                 k ← k+1.
   AND   u,ii,jj; AND u,u,kk     u ← ii & jj & kk.
   PBN   u,1B                    Repeat if i<imax, j<jmax, and k<kmax.  ∎
```

When the loop stops in this version, we can readily decide whether to continue at *x_done*, *y_done*, or *z_done*. These instructions load both x_i and y_j from memory each time, but the redundant value will already be present in the cache.

*More applications of MOR and MXOR. Let's finish off our study of bitwise manipulation by taking a look at two operations that are specifically designed for 64-bit work. MMIX's instructions MOR and MXOR, which essentially carry out matrix multiplication on 8×8 Boolean matrices, turn out to be extremely flexible and powerful, both by themselves and in combination with other bitwise operations.

If $x = (x_7 \ldots x_1 x_0)_{256}$ is an octabyte and $a = (a_7 \ldots a_1 a_0)_2$ is a single byte, the instruction MOR t,x,a sets $t \leftarrow a_7 x_7 \mid \cdots \mid a_1 x_1 \mid a_0 x_0$, while MXOR t,x,a sets $t \leftarrow a_7 x_7 \oplus \cdots \oplus a_1 x_1 \oplus a_0 x_0$. For example, MOR t,x,2 and MXOR t,x,2 both set $t \leftarrow x_1$; MOR t,x,3 sets $t \leftarrow x_1 \mid x_0$; and MXOR t,x,3 sets $t \leftarrow x_1 \oplus x_0$.

In general, of course, MOR and MXOR are functions of octabytes. When $y = (y_7 \ldots y_1 y_0)_{256}$ is a general octabyte, the instruction MOR t,x,y produces the octabyte t whose jth byte t_j is the result of MOR applied to x and y_j.

Suppose $x = -1 = {}^\#\texttt{ffffffffffffffff}$. Then MOR t,x,y computes the mask t in which byte t_j is ${}^\#\texttt{ff}$ whenever $y_j \neq 0$, while t_j is zero when $y_j = 0$. This simple special case is quite useful, because it accomplishes in just one instruction what we previously needed seven operations to achieve in situations like (92).

We observed in (66) that two MORs will suffice to reverse the bits of any 64-bit word, and many other important bit permutations also become easy when MOR is in a computer's repertoire. Suppose π is a permutation of $\{0, 1, \ldots, 7\}$ that takes $0 \mapsto 0\pi$, $1 \mapsto 1\pi$, $\ldots$, $7 \mapsto 7\pi$. Then the octabyte $p = (2^{7\pi} \ldots 2^{1\pi} 2^{0\pi})_{256}$ corresponds to a permutation matrix that makes MOR do nice tricks: MOR t,x,p will *permute the bytes* of x, setting $t_j \leftarrow x_{j\pi}$. Furthermore, MOR u,p,y will *permute the bits* of each byte of y, according to the *inverse* permutation; it sets $u_j \leftarrow (a_7 \ldots a_1 a_0)_2$ when $y_j = (a_{7\pi} \ldots a_{1\pi} a_{0\pi})_2$.

With a little more skullduggery we can also expedite further permutations such as the perfect shuffle (76), which transforms a given octabyte $z = 2^{32}x + y = (x_{31} \ldots x_1 x_0 y_{31} \ldots y_1 y_0)_2$ into the "zippered" octabyte

$$ w = x \ddagger y = (x_{31} y_{31} \ldots x_1 y_1 x_0 y_0)_2. \tag{175} $$

With appropriate permutation matrices p, q, and r, the intermediate results

$$ t = (x_{31} x_{27} x_{30} x_{26} x_{29} x_{25} x_{28} x_{24} y_{31} y_{27} y_{30} y_{26} y_{29} y_{25} y_{28} y_{24} \cdots $$
$$ x_7 x_3 x_6 x_2 x_5 x_1 x_4 x_0 y_7 y_3 y_6 y_2 y_5 y_1 y_4 y_0)_2, \tag{176} $$
$$ u = (y_{27} y_{31} y_{26} y_{30} y_{25} y_{29} y_{24} y_{28} x_{27} x_{31} x_{26} x_{30} x_{25} x_{29} x_{24} x_{28} \cdots $$
$$ y_3 y_7 y_2 y_6 y_1 y_5 y_0 y_4 x_3 x_7 x_2 x_6 x_1 x_5 x_0 x_4)_2 \tag{177} $$

can be computed quickly via the four instructions

$$ \texttt{MOR t,z,p; \quad MOR t,q,t; \quad MOR u,t,r; \quad MOR u,r,u;} \tag{178} $$

see exercise 204. So there's a mask m for which 'PUT rM,m; MUX w,t,u' completes the perfect shuffle in just six cycles altogether. By contrast, the traditional method in exercise 53 requires 30 cycles (five δ-swaps).

The analogous instruction MXOR is especially useful when binary linear algebra is involved. For example, exercise 1.3.1′–37 shows that XOR and MXOR directly implement addition and multiplication in a finite field of 2^k elements, for $k \leq 8$.

The problem of *cyclic redundancy checking* provides an instructive example of another case where MXOR shines. Streams of data are often accompanied by "CRC bytes" in order to detect common types of transmission errors [see W. W. Peterson and D. T. Brown, *Proc. IRE* **49** (1961), 228–235]. One popular method, used for example in MP3 audio files, is to regard each byte $\alpha = (a_7 \dots a_1 a_0)_2$ as if it were the polynomial

$$\alpha(x) = (a_7 \dots a_1 a_0)_x = a_7 x^7 + \cdots + a_1 x + a_0. \tag{179}$$

When transmitting n bytes $\alpha_{n-1} \dots \alpha_1 \alpha_0$, we then compute the remainder

$$\beta = \left(\alpha_{n-1}(x) x^{8(n-1)} + \cdots + \alpha_1(x) x^8 + \alpha_0(x)\right) x^{16} \bmod p(x), \tag{180}$$

where $p(x) = x^{16} + x^{15} + x^2 + 1$, using polynomial arithmetic mod 2, and append the coefficients of β as a 16-bit redundancy check.

The usual way to compute β is to process one byte at a time, according to classical methods like Algorithm 4.6.1D. The basic idea is to define the partial result $\beta_m = \left(\alpha_{n-1}(x) x^{8(n-1-m)} + \cdots + \alpha_{m+1}(x) x^8 + \alpha_m(x)\right) x^{16} \bmod p(x)$ so that $\beta_n = 0$, and then to use the recursion

$$\beta_m = ((\beta_{m+1} \ll 8) \,\&\, {}^\#\mathtt{ff00}) \oplus crc\_table[(\beta_{m+1} \gg 8) \oplus \alpha_m] \tag{181}$$

to decrease m by 1 until $m = 0$. Here $crc\_table[\alpha]$ is a 16-bit table entry that holds the remainder of $\alpha(x) x^{16}$, modulo $p(x)$ and mod 2, for $0 \le \alpha < 256$. [See A. Perez, *IEEE Micro* **3**, 3 (June 1983), 40–50.]

But of course we'd prefer to process 64 bits at once instead of 8. The solution is to find 8×8 matrices A and B such that

$$\alpha(x) x^{64} \equiv (\alpha A)(x) + (\alpha B)(x) x^{-8} \quad (\text{modulo } p(x) \text{ and 2}), \tag{182}$$

for arbitrary bytes α, considering α to be a 1×8 vector of bits. Then we can pad the given data bytes $\alpha_{n-1} \dots \alpha_1 \alpha_0$ with leading zeros so that n is a multiple of 8, and use the following efficient reduction method:

> Begin with $c \leftarrow 0$, $n \leftarrow n - 8$, and $t \leftarrow (\alpha_{n+7} \dots \alpha_n)_{256}$.
> While $n > 0$, set $u \leftarrow t \cdot A$, $v \leftarrow t \cdot B$, $n \leftarrow n - 8$, $\qquad(183)$
> $\quad t \leftarrow (\alpha_{n+7} \dots \alpha_n)_{256} \oplus u \oplus (v \gg 8) \oplus (c \ll 56)$, and $c \leftarrow v \,\&\, {}^\#\mathtt{ff}$.

Here $t \cdot A$ and $t \cdot B$ denote matrix multiplication via MXOR. The desired CRC bytes, $(tx^{16} + cx^8) \bmod p(x)$, are then readily obtained from the 64-bit quantity t and the 8-bit quantity c. Exercise 213 contains full details; the total running time for n bytes comes to only $(\mu + 10v)n/8 + O(1)$.

The exercises below contain many more instances where MOR and MXOR lead to substantial economies. New tricks undoubtedly remain to be discovered.

For further reading. The book *Hacker's Delight* by Henry S. Warren, Jr. (Addison–Wesley, 2002) discusses bitwise operations in depth, emphasizing the great variety of options that are available on real-world computers that are not as ideal as MMIX.

EXERCISES

▶ **1.** [*15*] What is the net effect of setting $x \leftarrow x \oplus y$, $y \leftarrow y \oplus (x \mathbin{\&} m)$, $x \leftarrow x \oplus y$?

2. [*16*] (H. S. Warren, Jr.) Are any of the following relations valid for all integers x and y? (i) $x \oplus y \leq x \mid y$; (ii) $x \mathbin{\&} y \leq x \mid y$; (iii) $|x - y| \leq x \oplus y$.

3. [*M20*] If $x = (x_{n-1} \dots x_1 x_0)_2$ with $x_{n-1} = 1$, let $x^M = (\bar{x}_{n-1} \dots \bar{x}_1 \bar{x}_0)_2$. Thus we have 0^M, 1^M, 2^M, 3^M, $\dots = -1, 0, 1, 0, 3, 2, 1, 0, 7, 6, \dots$, if we let $0^M = -1$. Prove that $(x \oplus y)^M < |x - y| \leq x \oplus y$ for all $x, y \geq 0$.

▶ **4.** [*M16*] Let $x^C = \bar{x}$, $x^N = -x$, $x^S = x + 1$, and $x^P = x - 1$ denote the complement, the negative, the successor, and the predecessor of an infinite-precision integer x. Then we have $x^{CC} = x^{NN} = x^{SP} = x^{PS} = x$. What are x^{CN} and x^{NC}?

5. [*M21*] Prove or disprove the following conjectured laws concerning binary shifts:
a) $(x \ll j) \ll k = x \ll (j + k)$;
b) $(x \gg j) \mathbin{\&} (y \ll k) = ((x \gg (j + k)) \mathbin{\&} y) \ll k = (x \mathbin{\&} (y \ll (j + k))) \gg j$.

6. [*M22*] Find all integers x and y such that (a) $x \gg y = y \gg x$; (b) $x \ll y = y \ll x$.

7. [*M22*] (R. Schroeppel, 1972.) Find a fast way to convert the binary number $x = (\dots x_2 x_1 x_0)_2$ to its negabinary counterpart $x = (\dots x'_2 x'_1 x'_0)_{-2}$, and vice versa. *Hint:* Only two bitwise operations are needed!

▶ **8.** [*M22*] Given a finite set S of nonnegative integers, the "minimal excludant" of S is defined to be
$$\operatorname{mex}(S) = \min\{\, k \mid k \geq 0 \text{ and } k \notin S \,\}.$$
Let $x \oplus S$ denote the set $\{x \oplus y \mid y \in S\}$, and let $S \oplus y$ denote $\{x \oplus y \mid x \in S\}$. Prove that if $x = \operatorname{mex}(S)$ and $y = \operatorname{mex}(T)$ then $x \oplus y = \operatorname{mex}((S \oplus y) \cup (x \oplus T))$.

9. [*M26*] (*Nim.*) Two people play a game with k piles of sticks, where there are a_j sticks in pile j. If $a_1 = \dots = a_k = 0$ when it is a player's turn to move, that player loses; otherwise the player reduces one of the piles by any desired amount, throwing away the removed sticks, and it is the other player's turn. Prove that the player to move can force a victory if and only if $a_1 \oplus \dots \oplus a_k \neq 0$. [*Hint:* Use exercise 8.]

10. [*HM40*] (*Nimbers*, also known as *Conway's field.*) Continuing exercise 8, define the operation $x \otimes y$ of "nim multiplication" recursively by the formula
$$x \otimes y = \operatorname{mex}\{(x \otimes j) \oplus (i \otimes y) \oplus (i \otimes j) \mid 0 \leq i < x, 0 \leq j < y\}.$$
Prove that $\oplus$ and $\otimes$ define a *field* over the set of all nonnegative integers. Prove also that if $0 \leq x, y < 2^{2^n}$ then $x \otimes y < 2^{2^n}$, and $2^{2^n} \otimes y = 2^{2^n} y$. (In particular, this field contains subfields of size 2^{2^n} for all $n \geq 0$.) Explain how to compute $x \otimes y$ efficiently.

▶ **11.** [*M26*] (H. W. Lenstra, 1978.) Find a simple way to characterize all pairs of positive integers (m, n) for which $m \otimes n = mn$ in Conway's field.

12. [*M26*] Devise an algorithm for *division* of nimbers. *Hint:* If $x < 2^{2^{n+1}}$ then we have $x \otimes (x \oplus (x \gg 2^n)) < 2^{2^n}$.

13. [*M32*] (*Second-order nim.*) Extend the game of exercise 9 by allowing two kinds of moves: Either a_j is reduced for some j, as before; or a_j is reduced and a_i is replaced by an arbitrary nonnegative integer, for some $i < j$. Prove that the player to move can now force a victory if and only if the pile sizes satisfy either $a_2 \neq a_3 \oplus \dots \oplus a_k$ or $a_1 \neq a_3 \oplus (2 \otimes a_4) \oplus \dots \oplus ((k-2) \otimes a_k)$. For example, when $k = 4$ and $(a_1, a_2, a_3, a_4) = (7, 5, 0, 5)$, the only winning move is to $(7, 5, 6, 3)$.

14. [*M30*] Suppose each node of a complete, infinite binary tree has been labeled with 0 or 1. Such a labeling is conveniently represented as a sequence $T = (t, t_0, t_1, t_{00}, t_{01}, t_{10}, t_{11}, t_{000}, \ldots)$, with one bit t_α for every binary string α; the root is labeled t, the left subtree labels are $T_0 = (t_0, t_{00}, t_{01}, t_{000}, \ldots)$, and the right subtree labels are $T_1 = (t_1, t_{10}, t_{11}, t_{100}, \ldots)$. Any such labeling can be used to transform a 2-adic integer $x = (\ldots x_2 x_1 x_0)_2$ into the 2-adic integer $y = (\ldots y_2 y_1 y_0)_2 = T(x)$ by setting $y_0 = t$, $y_1 = t_{x_0}$, $y_2 = t_{x_0 x_1}$, etc., so that $T(x) = 2T_{x_0}(\lfloor x/2 \rfloor) + t$. (In other words, x defines an infinite path in the binary tree, and y corresponds to the labels on that path, from right to left in the bit strings as we proceed from top to bottom of the tree.)

A *branching function* is the mapping $x^T = x \oplus T(x)$ defined by such a labeling. For example, if $t_{01} = 1$ and all of the other t_α are 0, we have $x^T = x \oplus 4[x \bmod 4 = 2]$.

  a) Prove that every branching function is a permutation of the 2-adic integers.

  b) For which integers k is $x \oplus (x \ll k)$ a branching function?

  c) Let $x \mapsto x^T$ be a mapping from 2-adic integers into 2-adic integers. Prove that x^T is a branching function if and only if $\rho(x \oplus y) = \rho(x^T \oplus y^T)$ for all 2-adic x and y.

  d) Prove that compositions and inverses of branching functions are branching functions. (Thus the set $\mathcal{B}$ of all branching functions is a permutation group.)

  e) A branching function is *balanced* if the labels satisfy $t_\alpha = t_{\alpha 0} \oplus t_{\alpha 1}$ for all α. Show that the set of all balanced branching functions is a subgroup of $\mathcal{B}$.

▶ **15.** [*M26*] J. H. Quick noticed that $((x + 2) \oplus 3) - 2 = ((x - 2) \oplus 3) + 2$ for all x. Find all constants a and b such that $((x + a) \oplus b) - a = ((x - a) \oplus b) + a$ is an identity.

16. [*M31*] A function of x is called *animating* if it can be written in the form

$$((\ldots ((((x + a_1) \oplus b_1) + a_2) \oplus b_2) + \cdots) + a_m) \oplus b_m$$

for some integer constants $a_1, b_1, a_2, b_2, \ldots, a_m, b_m$, with $m > 0$.

  a) Prove that every animating function is a branching function (see exercise 14).

  b) Furthermore, prove that it is balanced if and only if $b_1 \oplus b_2 \oplus \cdots \oplus b_m = 0$. *Hint:* What binary tree labeling corresponds to the animating function $((x \oplus c) - 1) \oplus c$?

  c) Let $\lfloor x \rceil = x \oplus (x - 1) = 2^{\rho(x)+1} - 1$. Show that every balanced animating function can be written in the form

$$x \oplus \lfloor x \oplus p_1 \rceil \oplus \lfloor x \oplus p_2 \rceil \oplus \cdots \oplus \lfloor x \oplus p_l \rceil, \qquad p_1 < p_2 < \cdots < p_l,$$

    for some integers $\{p_1, p_2, \ldots, p_l\}$, where $l \geq 0$, and this representation is unique.

  d) Conversely, show that every such expression defines a balanced animating function.

17. [*HM36*] The results of exercise 16 make it possible to decide whether or not any two given animating functions are equal. Is there an algorithm that decides whether *any* given expression is identically zero, when that expression is constructed from a finite number of integer variables and constants using only the binary operations $+$ and $\oplus$? What if we also allow $\&$?

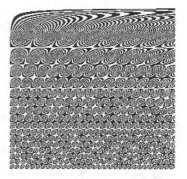

18. [*M25*] The curious pixel pattern shown here has $(x^2 y \gg 11) \& 1$ in row x and column y, for $1 \leq x, y \leq 256$. Is there any simple way to explain some of its major characteristics mathematically?

▶ **19.** [*M37*] (*Paley's rearrangement theorem.*) Given three vectors $A = (a_0, \ldots, a_{2^n-1})$, $B = (b_0, \ldots, b_{2^n-1})$, and $C = (c_0, \ldots, c_{2^n-1})$ of nonnegative numbers, let

$$f(A, B, C) = \sum_{j\oplus k\oplus l=0} a_j b_k c_l.$$

For example, if $n = 2$ we have $f(A, B, C) = a_0 b_0 c_0 + a_0 b_1 c_1 + a_0 b_2 c_2 + a_0 b_3 c_3 + a_1 b_0 c_1 + a_1 b_1 c_0 + a_1 b_2 c_3 + \cdots + a_3 b_3 c_0$; in general there are 2^{2n} terms, one for each choice of j and k. Our goal is to prove that $f(A, B, C) \le f(A^*, B^*, C^*)$, where A^* denotes the vector A sorted into nonincreasing order: $a_0^* \ge a_1^* \ge \cdots \ge a_{2^n-1}^*$.

a) Prove the result when all elements of A, B, and C are 0s and 1s.
b) Show that it is therefore true in general.
c) Similarly, $f(A, B, C, D) = \sum_{j\oplus k\oplus l\oplus m=0} a_j b_k c_l d_m \le f(A^*, B^*, C^*, D^*)$.

▶ **20.** [*21*] (*Gosper's hack.*) The following seven operations produce a useful function y of x, when x is a positive integer. Explain what this function is and why it is useful.

$$u \leftarrow x \mathbin{\&} -x; \qquad v \leftarrow x + u; \qquad y \leftarrow v + (((v \oplus x)/u) \gg 2).$$

21. [*22*] Construct the *reverse* of Gosper's hack: Show how to compute x from y.

22. [*21*] Implement Gosper's hack efficiently with MMIX code, assuming that $x < 2^{64}$, without using division.

▶ **23.** [*27*] A sequence of nested parentheses can be represented as a binary number by putting a 1 in the position of each right parenthesis. For example, '(())()' corresponds in this way to $(001101)_2$, the number 13. Call such a number a *parenthesis trace*.

a) What are the smallest and largest parenthesis traces that have exactly m 1s?
b) Suppose x is a parenthesis trace and y is the next larger parenthesis trace with the same number of 1s. Show that y can be computed from x with a short chain of operations analogous to Gosper's hack.
c) Implement your method on MMIX, assuming that $\nu x \le 32$.

▶ **24.** [*M30*] Program 1.3.2′P instructed MMIX to produce a table of the first five hundred prime numbers, using trial division to establish primality. Write an MMIX program that uses the "sieve of Eratosthenes" (exercise 4.5.4–8) to build a table of all odd primes that are less than N, packed into octabytes $Q_0, Q_1, \ldots, Q_{N/128-1}$ as in (27). Assume that $N \le 2^{32}$, and that it's a multiple of 128. What is the running time when $N = 3584$?

▶ **25.** [*15*] Four volumes sit side by side on a bookshelf. Each of them contains exactly 500 pages, printed in English on 250 sheets of paper 0.1 mm thick; each book also has a front and back cover whose thicknesses are 1 mm each. A bookworm gnaws its way from page 1 of Volume 1 to page 500 of Volume 4. How far does it travel while doing so?

26. [*22*] Suppose we want random access to a table of 12 million items of 5-bit data. We could pack 12 such items into one 64-bit word, thereby fitting the table into 8 megabytes of memory. But random access then seems to require division by 12, which is rather slow; we might therefore prefer to let each item occupy a full byte, thus using 12 megabytes altogether.

Show, however, that there's a memory-efficient approach that avoids division.

27. [*21*] In the notation of Eqs. (32)–(43), how would you compute (a) $(\alpha 10^a 01^b)_2$? (b) $(\alpha 10^a 11^b)_2$? (c) $(\alpha 00^a 01^b)_2$? (d) $(0^\infty 11^a 00^b)_2$? (e) $(0^\infty 01^a 00^b)_2$? (f) $(0^\infty 11^a 11^b)_2$?

28. [*16*] What does the operation $(x+1) \mathbin{\&} \bar x$ produce?

29. [*20*] (V. R. Pratt.) Express the magic mask μ_k of (47) in terms of μ_{k+1}.

30. [*20*] If $x = 0$, the MMIX instructions (46) will set $\rho \leftarrow 64$ (which is a close enough approximation to ∞). What changes to (50) and (51) will produce the same result?

▶ **31.** [*20*] A mathematician named Dr. L. I. Presume decided to calculate the ruler function with a simple loop as follows: "Set $\rho \leftarrow 0$; then while $x \mathbin{\&} 1 = 0$, set $\rho \leftarrow \rho + 1$ and $x \leftarrow x \gg 1$." He reasoned that, when x is a random integer, the average number of right shifts is the average value of ρ, which is 1; and the standard deviation is only $\sqrt{2}$, so the loop almost always terminates quickly. Criticize his decision.

32. [*20*] What is the execution time for ρx when (52) is programmed for MMIX?

▶ **33.** [*26*] (Leiserson, Prokop, and Randall, 1998.) Show that if '58' is replaced by '49' in (52), we can use that method to identify *both* bits of the number $y = 2^j + 2^k$ quickly, when $64 > j > k \geq 0$. (Altogether $\binom{64}{2} = 2016$ cases need to be distinguished.)

34. [*M23*] Let x and y be 2-adic integers. True or false: (a) $\rho(x \mathbin{\&} y) = \max(\rho x, \rho y)$; (b) $\rho(x \mid y) = \min(\rho x, \rho y)$; (c) $\rho x = \rho y$ if and only if $x \oplus y = (x - 1) \oplus (y - 1)$.

▶ **35.** [*M26*] According to Reitwiesner's theorem, exercise 4.1–34, every integer n has a unique representation $n = n^+ - n^-$ such that $n^+ \mathbin{\&} n^- = (n^+ \mid n^-) \mathbin{\&} ((n^+ \mid n^-) \gg 1) = 0$. Show that n^+ and n^- can be calculated quickly with bitwise operations. *Hint:* Prove the identity $(x \oplus 3x) \mathbin{\&} ((x \oplus 3x) \gg 1) = 0$.

36. [*20*] Given $x = (x_{63} \ldots x_1 x_0)_2$, suggest efficient ways to calculate the quantities
　　i) $x^\oplus = (x_{63}^\oplus \ldots x_1^\oplus x_0^\oplus)_2$, where $x_k^\oplus = x_k \oplus \cdots \oplus x_1 \oplus x_0$ for $0 \leq k < 64$;
　　ii) $x^\& = (x_{63}^\& \ldots x_1^\& x_0^\&)_2$, where $x_k^\& = x_k \wedge \cdots \wedge x_1 \wedge x_0$ for $0 \leq k < 64$.

37. [*16*] What changes to (55) and (56) will make $\lambda 0$ come out -1?

38. [*17*] How long does the leftmost-bit-extraction procedure (57) take when implemented on MMIX?

▶ **39.** [*20*] Formula (43) shows how to remove the rightmost run of 1 bits from a given number x. How would you remove the *leftmost* run of 1 bits?

▶ **40.** [*21*] Prove (58), and find a simple way to decide if $\lambda x < \lambda y$, given x and $y \geq 0$.

41. [*M22*] What are the generating functions of the integer sequences (a) ρn, (b) λn, and (c) νn?

42. [*M21*] If $n = 2^{e_1} + \cdots + 2^{e_r}$, with $e_1 > \cdots > e_r \geq 0$, express the sum $\sum_{k=0}^{n-1} \nu k$ in terms of the exponents $e_1, \ldots, e_r$.

▶ **43.** [*20*] How sparse should x be, to make (63) faster than (62) on MMIX?

▶ **44.** [*23*] (E. Freed, 1983.) What's a fast way to evaluate the *weighted* bit sum $\sum j x_j$?

▶ **45.** [*20*] (T. Rokicki, 1999.) Explain how to test if $x^R < y^R$, without reversing x and y.

46. [*22*] Method (68) uses six operations to interchange two bits $x_i \leftrightarrow x_j$ of a register. Show that this interchange can actually be done with only *three* MMIX instructions.

47. [*10*] Can the general δ-swap (69) also be done with a method like (67)?

48. [*M21*] How many different δ-swaps are possible in an n-bit register? (When $n = 4$, a δ-swap can transform 1234 into 1234, 1243, 1324, 1432, 2134, 2143, 3214, 3412, 4231.)

▶ **49.** [*M30*] Let $s(n)$ denote the fewest δ-swaps that suffice to reverse an n-bit number.
　　a) Prove that $s(n) \geq \lceil \log_3 n \rceil$ when n is odd, $s(n) \geq \lceil \log_3 3n/2 \rceil$ when n is even.
　　b) Evaluate $s(n)$ when $n = 3^m$, $2 \cdot 3^m$, $(3^m + 1)/2$, and $(3^m - 1)/2$.
　　c) What are $s(32)$ and $s(64)$? *Hint:* Show that $s(5n + 2) \leq s(n) + 2$.

50. [*M37*] Continuing exercise 49, prove that $s(n) = \log_3 n + O(\log \log n)$.

51. [*23*] Let c be a constant, $0 \le c < 2^d$. Find all sequences of masks $(\theta_0, \theta_1, \ldots, \theta_{d-1},$ $\hat{\theta}_{d-2}, \ldots, \hat{\theta}_1, \hat{\theta}_0)$ such that the general permutation scheme (71) takes $x \mapsto x^\pi$, where the bit permutation π is defined by either (a) $j\pi = j \oplus c$; or (b) $j\pi = (j + c) \bmod 2^d$. [The masks should satisfy $\theta_k \subseteq \mu_{d,k}$ and $\hat{\theta}_k \subseteq \mu_{d,k}$, so that (71) corresponds to Fig. 12; see (48). Notice that reversal, $x^\pi = x^R$, is the special case $c = 2^d - 1$ of part (a), while part (b) corresponds to the cyclic right shift $x^\pi = (x \gg c) + (x \ll (2^d - c))$.]

52. [*22*] Find hexadecimal constants $(\theta_0, \theta_1, \theta_2, \theta_3, \theta_4, \theta_5, \hat{\theta}_4, \hat{\theta}_3, \hat{\theta}_2, \hat{\theta}_1, \hat{\theta}_0)$ that cause (71) to produce the following important 64-bit permutations, based on the binary representation $j = (j_5 j_4 j_3 j_2 j_1 j_0)_2$: (a) $j\pi = (j_0 j_5 j_4 j_3 j_2 j_1)_2$; (b) $j\pi = (j_2 j_1 j_0 j_5 j_4 j_3)_2$; (c) $j\pi = (j_1 j_0 j_5 j_4 j_3 j_2)_2$; (d) $j\pi = (j_0 j_1 j_2 j_3 j_4 j_5)_2$. [Case (a) is the "perfect shuffle" (175) that takes $(x_{63} \ldots x_{33} x_{32} x_{31} \ldots x_1 x_0)_2$ into $(x_{63} x_{31} \ldots x_{33} x_1 x_{32} x_0)_2$; case (b) transposes an 8×8 matrix of bits; case (c), similarly, transposes a 4×16 matrix; and case (d) arises in connection with "fast Fourier transforms," see exercise 4.6.4–14.]

▶ **53.** [*M25*] The permutations in exercise 52 are said to be "induced by a permutation of index digits," because we obtain $j\pi$ by permuting the binary digits of j. Suppose $j\pi = (j_{(d-1)\psi} \ldots j_{1\psi} j_{0\psi})_2$, where ψ is a permutation of $\{0, 1, \ldots, d - 1\}$. Prove that if ψ has t cycles, the 2^d-bit permutation $x \mapsto x^\pi$ can be obtained with only $d - t$ swaps. In particular, show that this observation speeds up all four cases of exercise 52.

54. [*22*] (R. W. Gosper, 1985.) If an $m \times m$ bit matrix is stored in the rightmost m^2 bits of a register, show that it can be transposed by doing $(2^k(m-1))$-swaps for $0 \le k < \lceil \lg m \rceil$. Write out the method in detail when $m = 7$.

▶ **55.** [*26*] Suppose an $n \times n$ bit matrix is stored in the rightmost n^2 bits of an n^3-bit register. Prove that $18d + 2$ bitwise operations suffice to multiply two such matrices, when $n = 2^d$; the matrix multiplication can be either Boolean (like MOR) or mod 2 (like MXOR).

56. [*24*] Suggest a way to transpose a 7×9 bit matrix in a 64-bit register.

57. [*22*] The network $P(2^d)$ of Fig. 12 has a total of $(2d - 1)2^{d-1}$ crossbars. Prove that any permutation of 2^d elements can be realized by some setting in which at most $d 2^{d-1}$ of them are active.

▶ **58.** [*M32*] The first d columns of crossbar modules in the permutation network $P(2^d)$ perform a 1-swap, then a 2-swap, $\ldots$, and finally a 2^{d-1}-swap, when the network's wires are stretched into horizontal lines as shown here for $d = 3$. Let $N = 2^d$. These N lines, together with the $Nd/2$ crossbars, form a so-called "Omega router" or "inverse butterfly." The purpose of this exercise is to study the set Ω of all permutations φ such that we can obtain $(0\varphi, 1\varphi, \ldots, (N-1)\varphi)$ as outputs on the right of an Omega router when the inputs at the left are $(0, 1, \ldots, N - 1)$.

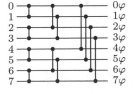

  a) Prove that $|\Omega| = 2^{Nd/2}$. (Thus $\lg |\Omega| = Nd/2 \sim \frac{1}{2} \lg N!$.)
  b) Prove that a permutation φ of $\{0, 1, \ldots, N - 1\}$ belongs to Ω if and only if

$$i \bmod 2^k = j \bmod 2^k \quad \text{and} \quad i\varphi \gg k = j\varphi \gg k \quad \text{implies} \quad i\varphi = j\varphi \qquad (*)$$

  for all $0 \le i, j < N$ and all $0 \le k \le d$.
  c) Simplify condition $(*)$ to the following, for all $0 \le i, j < N$:

$$\lambda(i\varphi \oplus j\varphi) < \rho(i \oplus j) \quad \text{implies} \quad i = j.$$

  d) Let T be the set of all permutations τ of $\{0, 1, \ldots, N - 1\}$ such that $\rho(i \oplus j) = \rho(i\tau \oplus j\tau)$ for all i and j. (This is the set of branching functions considered in exercise 14, modulo 2^d; so it has 2^{N-1} members, $2^{N/2+d-1}$ of which are the animating functions modulo 2^d.) Prove that $\varphi \in \Omega$ if and only if $\tau\varphi \in \Omega$ for all $\tau \in T$.

e) Suppose φ and ψ are permutations of Ω that operate on different elements; that is, $j\varphi \neq j$ implies $j\psi = j$, for $0 \leq j < N$. Prove that $\varphi\psi \in \Omega$.

f) Prove that the permutation $0\varphi \ldots (N-1)\varphi$ is Omega-routable if and only if it is sorted by Batcher's bitonic sorting network of order N. (See Section 5.3.4.)

59. [*M30*] Given $0 \leq a < b < N = 2^d$, how many Omega-routable permutations operate only on the interval $[a \mathinner{..} b]$? (Thus we want to count the number of $\varphi \in \Omega$ such that $j\varphi \neq j$ implies $a \leq j \leq b$. Exercise 58(a) is the special case $a = 0$, $b = N - 1$.)

60. [*HM28*] Given a random permutation of $\{0, 1, \ldots, 2n-1\}$, let p_{nk} be the probability that there are 2^k ways to set the crossbars in the first and last columns of the permutation network $P(2n)$ when realizing this permutation. In other words, p_{nk} is the probability that the associated graph has k cycles (see (75)). What is the generating function $\sum_{k \geq 0} p_{nk} z^k$? What are the mean and variance of 2^k?

61. [*46*] Is it NP-hard to decide whether a given permutation is realizable with at least one mask $\theta_j = 0$, using the recursive method of Fig. 12 as implemented in (71)?

▶ **62.** [*22*] Let $N = 2^d$. We can obviously represent a permutation π of $\{0, 1, \ldots, N-1\}$ by storing a table of N numbers, d bits each. With this representation we have instant access to $y = x\pi$, given x; but it takes $\Omega(N)$ steps to find $x = y\pi^-$ when y is given.

Show that, with the same amount of memory, we can represent an arbitrary permutation in such a way that $x\pi$ and $y\pi^-$ are both computable in $O(d)$ steps.

63. [*19*] For what integers w, x, y, and z does the zipper function satisfy (i) $x\ddagger y = y\ddagger x$? (ii) $(x\ddagger y) \gg z = (x \gg \lceil z/2 \rceil) \ddagger (y \gg \lfloor z/2 \rfloor)$? (iii) $(w \ddagger x) \mathbin{\&} (y \ddagger z) = (w \mathbin{\&} y) \ddagger (x \mathbin{\&} z)$?

64. [*22*] Find a "simple" expression for the zipper-of-sums $(x + x') \ddagger (y + y')$, as a function of $z = x \ddagger y$ and $z' = x' \ddagger y'$.

65. [*M16*] The binary polynomial $u(x) = u_0 + u_1 x + \cdots + u_{n-1} x^{n-1} \pmod 2$ can be represented by the integer $u = (u_{n-1} \ldots u_1 u_0)_2$. If $u(x)$ and $v(x)$ correspond to integers u and v in this way, what polynomial corresponds to $u \ddagger v$?

▶ **66.** [*M26*] Suppose the polynomial $u(x)$ has been represented as an n-bit integer u as in exercise 65, and let $v = u \oplus (u \ll \delta) \oplus (u \ll 2\delta) \oplus (u \ll 3\delta) \oplus \cdots$ for some integer δ.

a) What's a simple way to describe the polynomial $v(x)$?

b) Suppose n is large, and the bits of u have been packed into 64-bit words. How would you compute v when $\delta = 1$, using bitwise operations in 64-bit registers?

c) Consider the same question as (b), but when $\delta = 64$.

d) Consider the same question as (b), but when $\delta = 3$.

e) Consider the same question as (b), but when $\delta = 67$.

67. [*M31*] If $u(x)$ is a polynomial of degree $< n$, represented as in exercise 65, discuss the computation of $v(x) = u(x)^2 \bmod (x^n + x^m + 1)$, when $0 < m < n$ and both m and n are odd. *Hint:* This problem has an interesting connection with perfect shuffling.

68. [*20*] What three MMIX instructions implement the δ-shift operation, (79)?

69. [*25*] Prove that method (80) always extracts the proper bits when the masks θ_k have been set up properly: We never clobber any of the crucial bits y_j.

▶ **70.** [*31*] (Guy L. Steele Jr., 1994.) What's a good way to compute the masks θ_0, θ_1, $\ldots$, θ_{d-1} that are needed in the general compression procedure (80), given $\chi \neq 0$?

71. [*20*] Explain how to *reverse* the procedure of (80), going from the compact value $y = (y_{r-1} \ldots y_1 y_0)_2$ to a number $z = (z_{63} \ldots z_1 z_0)_2$ that has $z_{j_i} = y_i$ for $0 \leq i < r$.

72. [*25*] (Y. Hilewitz and R. B. Lee.) Prove that the gather-flip operation (81′) is Omega-routable in the sense of exercise 58.

73. [22] Prove that d well-chosen steps of (a) the sheep-and-goats operation (81) or (b) the gather-flip operation (81') will implement any desired 2^d-bit permutation.

74. [22] Given counts $(c_0, c_1, \ldots, c_{2^d-1})$ for the Chung–Wong procedure, explain why an appropriate cyclic 1-shift can always produce new counts $(c'_0, c'_1, \ldots, c'_{2^d-1})$ for which $\sum c'_{2l} = \sum c'_{2l+1}$, thus allowing the recursion to proceed.

▶ **75.** [32] The method of Chung and Wong replicates bit l of a register exactly c_l times, but it produces results in scrambled order. For example, the case $(c_0, \ldots, c_7) = (1, 2, 0, 2, 0, 2, 0, 1)$ illustrated in the text produces $(x_7 x_3 x_1 x_5 x_5 x_3 x_1 x_0)_2$. In some applications this can be a disadvantage; we might prefer to have the bits retain their original order, namely $(x_7 x_5 x_5 x_3 x_3 x_1 x_1 x_0)_2$ in that example.

Prove that the permutation network $P(2^d)$ of Fig. 12 can be modified to achieve this goal, given any sequence of counts $(c_0, c_1, \ldots, c_{2^d-1})$, if we replace the $d \cdot 2^{d-1}$ crossbar modules in the right-hand half by general 2×2 *mapping modules*. (A crossbar module with inputs (a, b) produces either (a, b) or (b, a) as output; a mapping module can also produce (a, a) or (b, b).)

76. [47] A *mapping network* is analogous to a sorting network or a permutation network, but it uses 2×2 mapping modules instead of comparators or crossbars, and it is supposed to be able to output all n^n possible mappings of its n inputs. Exercise 75, in conjunction with Fig. 12, shows that a mapping network for $n = 2^d$ exists with only $4d - 2$ levels of delay, and with $n/2$ modules on each level; furthermore, this construction needs general 2×2 mapping modules (instead of simple crossbars) in only d of those levels.

To within $O(n)$, what is the smallest number $G(n)$ of modules that are sufficient to implement a general n-element mapping network?

77. [26] (R. W. Floyd and V. R. Pratt.) Design an algorithm that tests whether or not a given standard n-network is a sorting network, as defined in the exercises of Section 5.3.4. When the given network has r comparator modules, your algorithm should use $O(r)$ bitwise operations on words of length 2^n.

78. [M27] (*Testing disjointness.*) Suppose the binary numbers x_1, x_2, $\ldots$, x_m each represent sets in a universe of $n - k$ elements, so that each x_j is less than 2^{n-k}. J. H. Quick (a student) decided to test whether the sets are disjoint by testing the condition

$$x_1 \mid x_2 \mid \cdots \mid x_m = (x_1 + x_2 + \cdots + x_m) \bmod 2^n.$$

Prove or disprove: Quick's test is valid if and only if $k \geq \lg(m - 1)$.

▶ **79.** [20] If $x \neq 0$ and $x \subseteq \chi$, what is an easy way to determine the largest integer $x_l < x$ such that $x_l \subseteq \chi$? (Thus $(x_l)' = (x')_l = x$, in connection with (84).)

80. [20] Suggest a fast way to find all maximal proper subsets of a set. More precisely, given χ with $\nu \chi = m$, we want to find all $x \subseteq \chi$ such that $\nu x = m - 1$.

81. [21] Find a formula for "scattered difference," to go with the "scattered sum" (86).

82. [21] Is it easy to shift a scattered accumulator to the left by 1, for example to change $(y_2 x_4 x_3 y_1 x_2 y_0 x_1 x_0)_2$ to $(y_1 x_4 x_3 y_0 x_2 0 x_1 x_0)_2$?

▶ **83.** [33] Continuing exercise 82, find a way to shift a scattered 2^d-bit accumulator to the *right* by 1, given z and χ, in $O(d)$ steps.

84. [25] Given n-bit numbers $z = (z_{n-1} \ldots z_1 z_0)_2$ and $\chi = (\chi_{n-1} \ldots \chi_1 \chi_0)_2$, explain how to calculate the "stretched" quantities $z \leftarrow \chi = (z_{(n-1) \leftarrow \chi} \ldots z_{1 \leftarrow \chi} z_{0 \leftarrow \chi})_2$ and

$z \to \chi = (z_{(n-1)\to\chi} \cdots z_{1\to\chi} z_{0\to\chi})_2$, where

$$j \gets \chi = \max\{k \mid k \le j \text{ and } \chi_k = 1\}, \qquad j \to \chi = \min\{k \mid k \ge j \text{ and } \chi_k = 1\};$$

we let $z_{j\gets\chi} = 0$ if $\chi_k = 0$ for $0 \le k \le j$, and $z_{j\to\chi} = 0$ if $\chi_k = 0$ for $n > k \ge j$. For example, if $n = 11$ and $\chi = (01101110010)_2$, then $z \gets \chi = (z_9 z_9 z_8 z_6 z_6 z_5 z_4 z_1 z_1 z_1 z_1 0)_2$ and $z \to \chi = (0 z_9 z_8 z_8 z_6 z_5 z_4 z_4 z_4 z_1 z_1)_2$.

85. [*22*] (K. D. Tocher, 1954.) Imagine that you have a vintage 1950s computer with a drum memory for storing data, and that you need to do some computations with a $32 \times 32 \times 32$ array $a[i, j, k]$, whose subscripts are 5-bit integers in the range $0 \le i, j, k < 32$. Unfortunately your machine has only a very small high-speed memory: You can access only 128 consecutive elements of the array in fast memory at any time. Since your application usually moves from $a[i, j, k]$ to a neighboring position $a[i', j', k']$, where $|i - i'| + |j - j'| + |k - k'| = 1$, you have decided to allocate the array so that, if $i = (i_4 i_3 i_2 i_1 i_0)_2$, $j = (j_4 j_3 j_2 j_1 j_0)_2$, and $k = (k_4 k_3 k_2 k_1 k_0)_2$, the array entry $a[i, j, k]$ is stored in drum location $(k_4 j_4 i_4 k_3 j_3 i_3 k_2 j_2 i_2 k_1 j_1 i_1 k_0 j_0 i_0)_2$. By interleaving the bits in this way, a small change to i, j, or k will cause only a small change in the address.

Discuss the implementation of this addressing function: (a) How does it change when i, j, or k changes by ± 1? (b) How would you handle a random access to $a[i, j, k]$, given i, j, and k? (c) How would you detect a "page fault" (namely, the condition that a new segment of 128 elements must be swapped into fast memory from the drum)?

86. [*M27*] An array of $2^p \times 2^q \times 2^r$ elements is to be allocated by putting $a[i, j, k]$ into a location whose bits are the $p + q + r$ bits of (i, j, k), permuted in some fashion. Furthermore, this array is to be stored in an external memory using pages of size 2^s. (Exercise 85 considers the case $p = q = r = 5$ and $s = 7$.) What allocation strategy of this kind minimizes the number of times that $a[i, j, k]$ is on a different page from $a[i', j', k']$, summed over all i, j, k, i', j', and k' such that $|i - i'| + |j - j'| + |k - k'| = 1$?

▶ **87.** [*20*] Suppose each byte of a 64-bit word x contains an ASCII code that represents either a letter, a digit, or a space. What three bitwise operations will convert all the lowercase letters to uppercase?

88. [*20*] Given $x = (x_7 \ldots x_0)_{256}$ and $y = (y_7 \ldots y_0)_{256}$, compute $z = (z_7 \ldots z_0)_{256}$, where $z_j = (x_j - y_j) \bmod 256$ for $0 \le j < 8$. (See the addition operation in (87).)

89. [*23*] Given $x = (x_{31} \ldots x_1 x_0)_4$ and $y = (y_{31} \ldots y_1 y_0)_4$, compute $z = (z_{31} \ldots z_1 z_0)_4$, where $z_j = \lfloor x_j / y_j \rfloor$ for $0 \le j < 32$, assuming that no y_j is zero.

90. [*20*] The bytewise averaging rule (88) always rounds downward when $x_j + y_j$ is odd. Make it less biased by rounding to the nearest odd integer in such cases.

▶ **91.** [*26*] (*Alpha channels.*) Recipe (88) is a good way to compute bytewise averages, but applications to computer graphics often require a more general blending of 8-bit values. Given three octabytes $x = (x_7 \ldots x_0)_{256}$, $y = (y_7 \ldots y_0)_{256}$, $\alpha = (a_7 \ldots a_0)_{256}$, show that bitwise operations allow us to compute $z = (z_7 \ldots z_0)_{256}$, where each byte z_j is a good approximation to $((255 - a_j)x_j + a_j y_j)/255$, *without* doing any multiplication. Implement your method with MMIX instructions.

▶ **92.** [*21*] What happens if the second line of (88) is changed to '$z \gets (x \mid y) - z$'?

93. [*18*] What basic formula for subtraction is analogous to formula (89) for addition?

94. [*21*] Let $x = (x_7 \ldots x_1 x_0)_{256}$ and $t = (t_7 \ldots t_1 t_0)_{256}$ in (90). Can t_j be nonzero when x_j is nonzero? Can t_j be zero when x_j is zero?

95. [*22*] What's a bitwise way to tell if all bytes of $x = (x_7 \ldots x_1 x_0)_{256}$ are distinct?

96. [*21*] Explain (93), and find a similar formula that sets test flags $t_j \leftarrow 128[x_j \leq y_j]$.

97. [*23*] Leslie Lamport's paper in 1975 presented the following "problem taken from an actual compiler optimization algorithm": Given octabytes $x = (x_7 \ldots x_0)_{256}$ and $y = (y_7 \ldots y_0)_{256}$, compute $t = (t_7 \ldots t_0)_{256}$ and $z = (z_7 \ldots z_0)_{256}$ so that $t_j \neq 0$ if and only if $x_j \neq 0$, $x_j \neq$ '*', and $x_j \neq y_j$; and $z_j = (x_j = 0?\ y_j: (x_j \neq$ '*' $\wedge x_j \neq y_j?$ '*': $x_j))$.

98. [*20*] Given $x = (x_7 \ldots x_0)_{256}$ and $y = (y_7 \ldots y_0)_{256}$, compute $z = (z_7 \ldots z_0)_{256}$ and $w = (w_7 \ldots w_0)_{256}$, where $z_j = \max(x_j, y_j)$ and $w_j = \min(x_j, y_j)$ for $0 \leq j < 8$.

▶ **99.** [*28*] Find hexadecimal constants a, b, c, d, e such that the six bitwise operations
$$y \leftarrow x \oplus a, \quad t \leftarrow ((((y \ \& \ b) + c) \mid y) \oplus d) \ \& \ e$$
will compute the flags $t = (f_7 \ldots f_1 f_0)_{256} \ll 7$ from any bytes $x = (x_7 \ldots x_1 x_0)_{256}$, where
$$f_0 = [x_0 = \text{'!'}], \ f_1 = [x_1 \neq \text{'*'}], \ f_2 = [x_2 < \text{'A'}], \ f_3 = [x_3 > \text{'z'}], \ f_4 = [x_4 \geq \text{'a'}],$$
$$f_5 = [x_5 \in \{\text{'0'}, \text{'1'}, \ldots, \text{'9'}\}], \ f_6 = [x_6 \leq 168], \ f_7 = [x_7 \in \{\text{'<'}, \text{'='}, \text{'>'}, \text{'?'}\}].$$

100. [*25*] Suppose $x = (x_{15} \ldots x_1 x_0)_{16}$ and $y = (y_{15} \ldots y_1 y_0)_{16}$ are *binary-coded decimal* numbers, where $0 \leq x_j, y_j < 10$ for each j. Explain how to compute their sum $u = (u_{15} \ldots u_1 u_0)_{16}$ and difference $v = (v_{15} \ldots v_1 v_0)_{16}$, where $0 \leq u_j, v_j < 10$ and
$$(u_{15} \ldots u_1 u_0)_{10} = ((x_{15} \ldots x_1 x_0)_{10} + (y_{15} \ldots y_1 y_0)_{10}) \bmod 10^{16},$$
$$(v_{15} \ldots v_1 v_0)_{10} = ((x_{15} \ldots x_1 x_0)_{10} - (y_{15} \ldots y_1 y_0)_{10}) \bmod 10^{16},$$
without bothering to do any radix conversion.

▶ **101.** [*22*] Two octabytes x and y contain amounts of time, represented in five fields that respectively signify days (3 bytes), hours (1 byte), minutes (1 byte), seconds (1 byte), and milliseconds (2 bytes). Can you add and subtract them quickly, without converting from this mixed-radix representation to binary and back again?

102. [*25*] Discuss routines for the addition and subtraction of polynomials modulo 5, when (a) 16 4-bit coefficients or (b) 21 3-bit coefficients are packed into a 64-bit word.

▶ **103.** [*22*] Sometimes it's convenient to represent small numbers in *unary* notation, so that $0, 1, 2, 3, \ldots, k$ appear respectively as $(0)_2, (1)_2, (11)_2, (111)_2, \ldots, 2^k - 1$ inside the computer. Then max and min are easily implemented as $\mid$ and $\&$.

Suppose the bytes of $x = (x_7 \ldots x_0)_{256}$ are such unary numbers, while the bytes of $y = (y_7 \ldots y_0)_{256}$ are all either 0 or 1. Explain how to "add" y to x or "subtract" y from x, giving $u = (u_7 \ldots u_0)_{256}$ and $v = (v_7 \ldots v_0)_{256}$ where
$$u_j = 2^{\min(8, \lg(x_j+1)+y_j)} - 1 \quad \text{and} \quad v_j = 2^{\max(0, \lg(x_j+1)-y_j)} - 1.$$

104. [*22*] Use bitwise operations to check the validity of a date represented in "year-month-day" fields (y, m, d) as in (22). You should compute a value t that is zero if and only if $1900 < y < 2100$, $1 \leq m \leq 12$, and $1 \leq d \leq max\_day(m)$, where month m has at most $max\_day(m)$ days. Can it be done in fewer than 20 operations?

105. [*30*] Given $x = (x_7 \ldots x_0)_{256}$ and $y = (y_7 \ldots y_0)_{256}$, discuss bitwise operations that will *sort* the bytes into order, so that $x_0 \leq y_0 \leq \cdots \leq x_7 \leq y_7$ afterwards.

106. [*27*] Explain the Fredman–Willard procedure (95). Also show that a simple modification of their method will compute $2^{\lambda x}$ without doing any left shifts.

▶ **107.** [*22*] Implement Algorithm B on MMIX when $d = 4$, and compare it with (56).

108. [*26*] Adapt Algorithm B to cases where n does not have the form $d \cdot 2^d$.

109. [20] Evaluate ρx for n-bit numbers x in $O(\log \log n)$ broadword steps.

▶ **110.** [30] Suppose $n = 2^{2^e}$ and $0 \le x < n$. Show how to compute $1 \ll x$ in $O(e)$ broadword steps, using only shift commands that shift by a constant amount. (Together with Algorithm B we can therefore extract the most significant bit of an n-bit number in $O(\log \log n)$ such steps.)

111. [23] Explain the 01^r pattern recognizer, (98).

112. [46] Can all occurrences of the pattern $1^r 0$ be identified in $O(1)$ broadword steps?

113. [23] A *strong broadword chain* is a broadword chain of a specified width n that is also a 2-adic chain, for all n-bit choices of x_0. For example, the 2-bit broadword chain (x_0, x_1) with $x_1 = x_0 + 1$ is not strong because $x_0 = (11)_2$ makes $x_1 = (00)_2$. But $(x_0, x_1, \ldots, x_4)$ is a strong broadword chain that computes $(x_0 + 1) \bmod 4$ for all $0 \le x_0 < 4$ if we set $x_1 = x_0 \oplus 1$, $x_2 = x_0 \mathbin{\&} 1$, $x_3 = x_2 \ll 1$, and $x_4 = x_1 \oplus x_3$.

Given a broadword chain $(x_0, x_1, \ldots, x_r)$ of width n, construct a strong broadword chain $(x'_0, x'_1, \ldots, x'_{r'})$ of the same width, such that $r' = O(r)$ and $(x_0, x_1, \ldots, x_r)$ is a subsequence of $(x'_0, x'_1, \ldots, x'_{r'})$.

114. [16] Suppose $(x_0, x_1, \ldots, x_r)$ is a strong broadword chain of width n that computes the value $f(x) = x_r$ whenever an n-bit number $x = x_0$ is given. Construct a broadword chain $(X_0, X_1, \ldots, X_r)$ of width mn that computes $X_r = (f(\xi_1) \ldots f(\xi_m))_{2^n}$ for any given mn-bit value $X_0 = (\xi_1 \ldots \xi_m)_{2^n}$, where $0 \le \xi_1, \ldots, \xi_m < 2^n$.

▶ **115.** [24] Given a 2-adic integer $x = (\ldots x_2 x_1 x_0)_2$, we might want to compute $y = (\ldots y_2 y_1 y_0)_2 = f(x)$ from x by zeroing out all blocks of consecutive 1s that (a) are not immediately followed by two 0s; or (b) are followed by an odd number of 0s before the next block of 1s begins; or (c) contain an odd number of 1s. For example, if x is $(\ldots 01110111001101000110)_2$ then y is (a) $(\ldots 00000111000001000110)_2$; (b) $(\ldots 00000111000000000110)_2$; (c) $(\ldots 00000000001100000110)_2$. (Infinitely many 0s are assumed to appear at the right of x_0. Thus, in case (a) we have

$$y_j = x_j \wedge ((\bar{x}_{j-1} \wedge \bar{x}_{j-2}) \vee (x_{j-1} \wedge \bar{x}_{j-2} \wedge \bar{x}_{j-3}) \vee (x_{j-1} \wedge x_{j-2} \wedge \bar{x}_{j-3} \wedge \bar{x}_{j-4}) \vee \cdots)$$

for all j, where $x_k = 0$ for $k < 0$.) Find 2-adic chains for y in each case.

116. [HM30] Suppose $x = (\ldots x_2 x_1 x_0)_2$ and $y = (\ldots y_2 y_1 y_0)_2 = f(x)$, where y is computable by a 2-adic chain having no shift operations. Let L be the set of all binary strings such that $y_j = [x_j \ldots x_1 x_0 \in L]$, and assume that all constants used in the chain are rational 2-adic numbers. Prove that L is a regular language. What languages L correspond to the functions in exercise 115(a) and 115(b)?

117. [HM46] Continuing exercise 116, is there any simple way to characterize the regular languages L that arise in shift-free 2-adic chains? (The language $L = 0^*(10^*10^*)^*$ does not seem to correspond to any such chain.)

118. [30] According to Lemma A, we cannot compute the function $x \gg 1$ for all n-bit numbers x by using only additions, subtractions, and bitwise Boolean operations (no shifts or branches). Show, however, that $O(n)$ such operations are necessary and sufficient if we include also the "monus" operator $y \mathbin{\dot-} z$ in our repertoire.

119. [20] Evaluate the function $f_{py}(x)$ in (102) with four broadword steps.

▶ **120.** [M25] There are $2^{n 2^{mn}}$ functions that take n-bit numbers $(x_1, \ldots, x_m)$ into an n-bit number $f(x_1, \ldots, x_m)$. How many of them can be implemented with addition, subtraction, multiplication, and nonshift bitwise Boolean operations (modulo 2^n)?

▶ **121.** [*M25*] By exercise 3.1–6, a function from $[0 .. 2^n)$ into itself is eventually periodic.

    a) Prove that if f is any n-bit broadword function that can be implemented without shift instructions, the lengths of its periods are always powers of 2.

    b) However, for every p between 1 and n, there's an n-bit broadword chain of length 3 that has a period of length p.

122. [*M22*] Complete the proof of Lemma B.

123. [*M23*] Let a_q be the constant $1 + 2^q + 2^{2q} + \cdots + 2^{(q-1)q} = (2^{q^2} - 1)/(2^q - 1)$. Using (104), show that there are infinitely many q such that the operation of multiplying by a_q, modulo 2^{q^2}, requires $\Omega(\log q)$ steps in any n-bit broadword chain with $n \geq q^2$.

124. [*M38*] Complete the proof of Theorem R' by defining an n-bit broadword chain $(x_0, x_1, \ldots, x_f)$ and sets $(U_0, U_1, \ldots, U_f)$ such that, for $0 \leq t \leq f$, all inputs $x \in U_t$ lead to an essentially similar state $Q(x, t)$, in the following sense: (i) The current instruction in $Q(x, t)$ does not depend on x. (ii) If register r_j has a known value in $Q(x, t)$, it holds $x_{j'}$ for some definite index $j' \leq t$. (iii) If memory location $M[z]$ has been changed, it holds $x_{z''}$ for some definite index $z'' \leq t$. (The values of j' and z'' depend on j, z, and t, but not on x.) Furthermore $|U_t| \geq n/2^{2^t - 1}$, and the program cannot guarantee that $r_1 = \rho x$ when $t < f$. *Hint:* Lemma B implies that a limited number of shift amounts and memory addresses need to be considered when t is small.

125. [*M33*] Prove Theorem P'. *Hint:* Lemma B remains true if we replace '= 0' by '= α_s' in (103), for any values α_s.

126. [*M46*] Does the operation of extracting the most significant bit, $2^{\lambda x}$, require $\Omega(\log \log n)$ steps in an n-bit basic RAM? (See exercise 110.)

127. [*HM40*] Prove that at least $\Omega(\log n/\log \log n)$ broadword steps are needed to compute the parity function, $(\nu x) \bmod 2$, using the theory of circuit complexity. [*Hint:* Every broadword operation is in complexity class AC_0.]

128. [*M46*] Can $(\nu x) \bmod 2$ be computed in $O(\log n/\log \log n)$ broadword steps?

129. [*M46*] Does sideways addition require $\Omega(\log n)$ broadword steps?

130. [*M46*] Is there an n-bit constant a such that the function $(a \ll x) \bmod 2^n$ requires $\Omega(\log n)$ n-bit broadword steps?

▶ **131.** [*23*] Write an `MMIX` program for Algorithm R when the graph is represented by arc lists. Vertex nodes have at least two fields, called `LINK` and `ARCS`, and arc nodes have `TIP` and `NEXT` fields, as explained in Section 7. Initially all `LINK` fields are zero, except in the given set of vertices Q, which is represented as a circular list. Your program should change that circular list so that it represents the set R of all reachable vertices.

▶ **132.** [*M27*] A *clique* in a graph is a set of mutually adjacent vertices; a clique is *maximal* if it's not contained in any other. The purpose of this exercise is to discuss an algorithm due to J. K. M. Moody and J. Hollis, which provides a convenient way to find every maximal clique of a not-too-large graph, using bitwise operations.

    Suppose G is a graph with n vertices $V = \{0, 1, \ldots, n-1\}$. Let $\rho_v = \sum \{2^u \mid u - v \text{ or } u = v\}$ be row v of G's reflexive adjacency matrix, and let $\delta_v = \sum \{2^u \mid u \neq v\} = 2^n - 1 - 2^v$. Every subset $U \subseteq V$ is representable as an n-bit integer $\sigma(U) = \sum_{u \in U} 2^u$; for example, $\delta_v = \sigma(V \setminus v)$. We also define the bitwise intersection

$$\tau(U) = \underset{0 \leq u < n}{\&} (u \in U? \ \rho_u : \delta_u).$$

For example, if $n = 5$ we have $\tau(\{0, 2\}) = \rho_0 \ \& \ \delta_1 \ \& \ \rho_2 \ \& \ \delta_3 \ \& \ \delta_4$.

a) Prove that U is a clique if and only if $\tau(U) = \sigma(U)$.

b) Show that if $\tau(U) = \sigma(T)$ then T is a clique.

c) For $1 \le k \le n$, consider the 2^k bitwise intersections

$$C_k = \left\{ \mathop{\&}_{0 \le u < k} (u \in U? \; \rho_u \colon \delta_u) \;\middle|\; U \subseteq \{0, 1, \dots, k-1\} \right\},$$

and let C_k^+ be the maximal elements of C_k. Prove that U is a maximal clique if and only if $\sigma(U) \in C_n^+$.

d) Explain how to compute C_k^+ from C_{k-1}^+, starting with $C_0^+ = \{2^n - 1\}$.

▶ **133.** [*20*] Given a graph G, how can the algorithm of exercise 132 be used to find (a) all maximal independent sets of vertices? (b) all minimal vertex covers (sets that hit every edge)?

134. [*15*] Nine classes of mappings for ternary values appear in (119), (123), and (124). To which class does the representation (128) belong, if $a = 0$, $b = *$, $c = 1$?

135. [*22*] Łukasiewicz included a few operations besides (127) in his three-valued logic: $\neg x$ (negation) interchanges 0 with 1 but leaves $*$ unchanged; $\diamond x$ (possibility) is defined as $\neg x \Rightarrow x$; $\square x$ (necessity) is defined as $\neg \diamond \neg x$; and $x \Leftrightarrow y$ (equivalence) is defined as $(x \Rightarrow y) \wedge (y \Rightarrow x)$. Explain how to perform these operations using representation (128).

136. [*29*] Suggest two-bit encodings for binary operations on the set $\{a, b, c\}$ that are defined by the following "multiplication tables":

$$\text{(a)} \begin{pmatrix} a & b & c \\ b & c & c \\ c & c & c \end{pmatrix}; \qquad \text{(b)} \begin{pmatrix} a & c & b \\ c & b & a \\ b & a & c \end{pmatrix}; \qquad \text{(c)} \begin{pmatrix} a & b & a \\ a & a & c \\ a & b & c \end{pmatrix}.$$

137. [*21*] Show that the operation in exercise 136(c) is simpler with packed vectors like (131) than with the unpacked form (130).

138. [*24*] Find an example of three-state-to-two-bit encoding where class V_a is best.

139. [*25*] If x and y are signed bits 0, $+1$, or -1, what 2-bit encoding is good for calculating their sum $(z_1 z_2)_3 = x + y$, where z_1 and z_2 are also required to be signed bits? (This is a "half adder" for balanced ternary numbers.)

140. [*27*] Design an economical *full adder* for balanced ternary numbers: Show how to compute signed bits u and v such that $3u + v = x + y + z$ when $x, y, z \in \{0, +1, -1\}$.

▶ **141.** [*30*] The *Ulam numbers* $\langle U_1, U_2, \dots \rangle = \langle 1, 2, 3, 4, 6, 8, 11, 13, 16, 18, 26, \dots \rangle$ are defined for $n \ge 3$ by letting U_n be the smallest integer $> U_{n-1}$ that has a *unique* representation $U_n = U_j + U_k$ for $0 < j < k < n$. Show that a million Ulam numbers can be computed rapidly with the help of bitwise techniques.

▶ **142.** [*33*] A subcube such as $*10*1*01$ can be represented by asterisk codes 10010100 and bit codes 01001001, as in (85); but many other encodings are also possible. What representation scheme for subcubes works best, for finding prime implicants by the consensus-based algorithm of exercise 7.1.1 31?

143. [*20*] Let x be a 64-bit number that represents an 8×8 chessboard, with a 1 bit in every position where a knight is present. Find a formula for the 64-bit number $f(x)$ that has a 1 in every position reachable in one move by a knight of x. For example, the white knights at the start of a game correspond to $x = {}^\#42$; then $f(x) = {}^\#\text{a51800}$.

144. [*16*] What node is the sibling of node j in a sideways heap? (See (134).)

145. [*17*] Interpret (137) when h is *less* than the height of j.

▶ **146.** [*M20*] Prove Eq. (138), which relates the ρ and λ functions.

▶ **147.** [*M20*] What values of πv, βv, αv, and τj occur in Algorithm V when the forest is
  a) the empty digraph with vertices $\{v_1, \ldots, v_n\}$ and no arcs?
  b) the oriented path $v_n \longrightarrow \cdots \longrightarrow v_2 \longrightarrow v_1$?

148. [*M21*] When preprocessing for Algorithm V, is it possible to have $\beta x_3 \longrightarrow^*$
$\beta y_2 \longrightarrow^* \beta x_2 \longrightarrow^* \beta y_1 \longrightarrow^* \beta x_1$ in S when $x_3 \longrightarrow x_2 \longrightarrow x_1 \longrightarrow \Lambda$ and $y_2 \longrightarrow y_1 \longrightarrow \Lambda$ in
the forest? (If so, two different trees are "entangled" in S.)

▶ **149.** [*23*] Design a preprocessing procedure for Algorithm V.

▶ **150.** [*25*] Given an array of elements $A_1, \ldots, A_n$, the *range minimum query* problem
is to determine $k(i,j)$ such that $A_{k(i,j)} = \min(A_i, \ldots, A_j)$ for any given indices i and j
with $1 \le i \le j \le n$. Prove that Algorithm V will solve this problem, after $O(n)$ steps of
preprocessing on the array A have prepared the necessary tables $(\pi, \beta, \alpha, \tau)$. *Hint:* Consider the binary search tree constructed from the sequence of keys $(p(1), p(2), \ldots, p(n))$,
where p is a permutation of $\{1, 2, \ldots, n\}$ such that $A_{p(1)} \le A_{p(2)} \le \cdots \le A_{p(n)}$.

151. [*22*] Conversely, show that any algorithm for range minimum queries can be used
to find nearest common ancestors, with essentially the same efficiency.

152. [*M21*] Prove that Algorithm V is correct.

▶ **153.** [*M20*] The pointers in a navigation pile like (144) can be packed into a binary
string such as

0	1	0	0	1	0	0	0	0	0	1	0	1	0	0	0	0	0	0	0	0	0	0	0
2		4		6		8			10	12	14			16			18	20	22	24			

At what bit position (from the left) does the pointer for node j end?

154. [*20*] The gray lines in Fig. 14 show how each pentagon is composed of ten
triangles. What decomposition of the hyperbolic plane is defined by those gray lines
alone, without the black pentagon edges?

▶ **155.** [*M21*] Prove that $(x\phi) \bmod 1 = (\alpha 0)_{1/\phi}$ when α is the negaFibonacci code for x.

156. [*21*] Design algorithms (a) to convert a given integer x to its negaFibonacci
code α, and (b) to convert a given negaFibonacci code α to $x = N(\alpha)$.

157. [*M21*] Explain the recursion (148) for negaFibonacci predecessor and successor.

158. [*M26*] Let $\alpha = a_n \ldots a_1$ be the binary code for $F(\alpha 0) = a_n F_{n+1} + \cdots + a_1 F_2$
in the standard Fibonacci number system (146). Develop methods analogous to (148)
and (149) for incrementing and decrementing such codewords.

159. [*M34*] Exercise 7 shows that it's easy to convert between the negabinary and
binary number systems. Discuss conversion between negaFibonacci codewords and the
ordinary Fibonacci codes in exercise 158.

160. [*M29*] Prove that (150) and (151) yield consistent code labels for the pentagrid.

161. [*20*] The cells of a chessboard can be colored black and white, so that neighboring
cells have different colors. Does the pentagrid also have this property?

▶ **162.** [*HM37*] Explain how to draw the pentagrid, Fig. 14. What circles are present?

163. [*HM41*] Devise a way to navigate through the triangles in the tiling of Fig. 18.

164. [*23*] The original definition of custerization in 1957 was not (157) but

$$\text{custer}'(X) = X \mathbin{\&} \sim(X_{\text{NW}} \mathbin{\&} X_{\text{N}} \mathbin{\&} X_{\text{NE}} \mathbin{\&} X_{\text{W}} \mathbin{\&} X_{\text{E}} \mathbin{\&} X_{\text{SW}} \mathbin{\&} X_{\text{S}} \mathbin{\&} X_{\text{SE}}).$$

Why is (157) preferable?

165. [*21*] (R. A. Kirsch.) Discuss the computation of the 3×3 cellular automaton with

$$X^{(t+1)} = \text{custer}(\overline{X}^{(t)}) = {\sim}X^{(t)} \mathbin{\&} (X_{\text{N}}^{(t)} \mid X_{\text{W}}^{(t)} \mid X_{\text{E}}^{(t)} \mid X_{\text{S}}^{(t)}).$$

166. [*M23*] Let $f(M, N)$ be the maximum number of black pixels in an $M \times N$ bitmap X for which $X = \text{custer}(X)$. Prove that $f(M, N) = \frac{4}{5}MN + O(M+N)$.

167. [*24*] (*Life.*) If the bitmap X represents an array of cells that are either dead (0) or alive (1), the Boolean function

$$f(x_{\text{NW}}, \ldots, x, \ldots, x_{\text{SE}}) = [2 < x_{\text{NW}} + x_{\text{N}} + x_{\text{NE}} + x_{\text{W}} + \tfrac{1}{2}x + x_{\text{E}} + x_{\text{SW}} + x_{\text{S}} + x_{\text{SE}} < 4]$$

can lead to astonishing life histories when it governs a cellular automaton as in (158).

    a) Find a way to evaluate f with a Boolean chain of 26 steps or less.

    b) Let $X_j^{(t)}$ denote row j of X at time t. Show that $X_j^{(t+1)}$ can be evaluated in at most 23 broadword steps, as a function of the three rows $X_{j-1}^{(t)}$, $X_j^{(t)}$, and $X_{j+1}^{(t)}$.

▶ **168.** |*23*| To keep an image finite, we might insist that a 3×3 cellular automaton treats a $M \times N$ bitmap as a *torus*, wrapping around seamlessly between top and bottom and between left and right. The task of simulating its actions efficiently with bitwise operations is somewhat tricky: We want to minimize references to memory, yet each new pixel value depends on old values that lie on all sides. Furthermore the shifting of bits between neighboring words tends to be awkward, taxing the capacity of a register.

    Show that such difficulties can be surmounted by maintaining an array of n-bit words A_{jk} for $0 \le j \le M$ and $0 \le k \le N' = \lceil N/(n-2) \rceil$. If $j \ne M$ and $k \ne 0$, word A_{jk} should contain the pixels of row j and columns $(k-1)(n-2)$ through $k(n-2)+1$, inclusive; the other words A_{Mk} and A_{j0} provide auxiliary buffer space. (Notice that some bits of the raster appear twice.)

169. [*22*] Continuing the previous two exercises, what happens to the Cheshire cat of Fig. 17(a) when it is subjected to the vicissitudes of Life, in a 26×31 torus?

▶ **170.** [*21*] What result does the Guo–Hall thinning automaton produce when given a solid black rectangle of M rows and N columns? How long does it take?

171. [*24*] Find a Boolean chain of length ≤ 25 to evaluate the local thinning function $g(x_{\text{NW}}, x_{\text{N}}, x_{\text{NE}}, x_{\text{W}}, x_{\text{E}}, x_{\text{SW}}, x_{\text{S}}, x_{\text{SE}})$ of (159), with or without the extra cases in (160).

172. [*M29*] Prove or disprove: If a pattern contains three black pixels that are king-neighbors of each other, the Guo–Hall procedure extended by (160) will reduce it, unless none of those pixels can be removed without destroying the connectivity.

▶ **173.** [*M30*] Raster images often need to be cleaned up if they contain noisy data. For example, accidental specks of black or white may well spoil the results when a thinning algorithm is used for optical character recognition.

    Say that a bitmap X is *closed* if every white pixel is part of a 2×2 square of white pixels, and *open* if every black pixel is part of a 2×2 square of black pixels. Let

$$X^D = \bigcap \{Y \mid Y \supseteq X \text{ and } Y \text{ is closed}\}; \quad X^L = \bigcup \{Y \mid Y \subseteq X \text{ and } Y \text{ is open}\}.$$

A bitmap is called *clean* if it equals X^{DL} for some X. We might, for example, have

$$X = \text{■} ; \quad X^D = \text{■} ; \quad X^{DL} = \text{■} .$$

In general X^D is "darker" than X, while X^L is "lighter": $X^D \supseteq X \supseteq X^L$.

    a) Prove that $(X^{DL})^{DL} = X^{DL}$. *Hint:* $X \subseteq Y$ implies $X^D \subseteq Y^D$ and $X^L \subseteq Y^L$.

    b) Show that X^D can be computed with one step of a 3×3 cellular automaton.

174. [*M46*] (M. Minsky and S. Papert.) Is there a three-dimensional shrinking algorithm that preserves connectivity, analogous to (161)?

175. [*15*] How many *rookwise* connected black components does the Cheshire cat have?

176. [*M24*] Let G be the graph whose vertices are the black pixels of a given bitmap X, with $u \!-\! v$ when u and v are a king move apart. Let G' be the corresponding graph after the shrinking transformation (161) has been applied. The purpose of this exercise is to show that the number of connected components of G' is the number of components of G minus the number of isolated vertices of G.

Let $N_{(i,j)} = \{(i,j), (i{-}1,j), (i{-}1,j{+}1), (i,j{+}1)\}$ be pixel (i,j) together with its north and/or east neighbors. For each $v \in G$ let $S(v) = \{v' \in G' \mid v' \in N_v\}$.

a) Prove that $S(v)$ is empty if and only if v is isolated in G.

b) If $u \!-\! v$ in G, $u' \in S(u)$, and $v' \in S(v)$, prove that $u' \!-\!^* v'$ in G' (that is, they are in the same component).

c) For each $v' \in G'$ let $S'(v') = \{v \in G \mid v' \in N_v\}$. Is $S'(v')$ always nonempty?

d) If $u' \!-\! v'$ in G', $u \in S'(u')$, and $v \in S'(v')$, prove that $u \!-\!^* v$ in G.

e) Hence there's a one-to-one correspondence between the nontrivial components of G and the components of G'.

177. [*M22*] Continuing exercise 176, prove an analogous result for the white pixels.

178. [*20*] If X is an $M \times N$ bitmap, let X^* be the $M \times (2N+1)$ bitmap $X \ddagger (X \mid (X \ll 1))$. Show that the kingwise connected components of X^* are also rookwise connected, and that bitmap X^* has the same "surroundedness tree" (162) as X.

▶ **179.** [*34*] Design an algorithm that constructs the surroundedness tree of a given $M \times N$ bitmap, scanning the image one row at a time as discussed in the text. (See (162) and (163).)

▶ **180.** [*M24*] Digitize the hyperbola $y^2 = x^2 + 13$ by hand, for $0 < y \le 7$.

181. [*HM20*] Explain how to subdivide a general conic (168) with rational coefficients into monotonic parts so that Algorithm T applies.

182. [*M31*] Why does the three-register method (Algorithm T) digitize correctly?

▶ **183.** [*M29*] (G. Rote.) Explain why Algorithm T might fail if condition (v) is false.

▶ **184.** [*M22*] Find a quadratic form $Q'(x,y)$ so that, when Algorithm T is applied to (x',y'), (x,y), and Q', it produces exactly the same edges as it does from (x,y), (x',y'), and Q, but in the reverse order. *Hint:* There is a simple answer.

▶ **185.** [*23*] Design an algorithm that properly digitizes a straight line from (ξ, η) to (ξ', η'), when ξ, η, ξ', and η' are rational numbers, by simplifying Algorithm T.

186. [*HM22*] Given three complex numbers (z_0, z_1, z_2), consider the curve traced out by

$$B(t) = (1-t)^2 z_0 + 2(1-t)t z_1 + t^2 z_2, \qquad \text{for } 0 \le t \le 1.$$

a) What is the approximate behavior of $B(t)$ when t is near 0 or 1?

b) Let $S(z_0, z_1, z_2) = \{B(t) \mid 0 \le t \le 1\}$. Prove that all points of $S(z_0, z_1, z_2)$ lie on or inside the triangle whose vertices are z_0, z_1, and z_2.

c) True or false: $S(w + \zeta z_0, w + \zeta z_1, w + \zeta z_2) = w + \zeta S(z_0, z_1, z_2)$.

d) Prove that $S(z_0, z_1, z_2)$ is part of a straight line if and only if z_0, z_1, and z_2 are collinear; otherwise it is part of a parabola.

e) Prove that if $0 \le \theta \le 1$, we have the recurrence

$$S(z_0, z_1, z_2) \;=\; S\big(z_0, (1{-}\theta)z_0 + \theta z_1, B(\theta)\big) \cup S\big(B(\theta), (1{-}\theta)z_1 + \theta z_2, z_2\big).$$

187. [*M29*] Continuing exercise 186, show how to digitize $S(z_0, z_1, z_2)$ using the three-register method (Algorithm T). For best results, the digitizations of $S(z_2, z_1, z_0)$ and $S(z_0, z_1, z_2)$ should produce the same edges, but in reverse order.

▶ **188.** [*25*] Bitmap images can often be viewed conveniently using pixels that are *shades of gray* instead of just black or white. Such gray levels typically are 8-bit values that range from 0 (black) to 255 (white); notice that the black/white convention is traditionally *reversed* with respect to the 1-bit case. An $m \times n$ bitmap whose resolution is 600 dots per inch corresponds nicely to the $(m/8) \times (n/8)$ grayscale image with 75 pixels per inch that is obtained by mapping each 8×8 subarray of 1-bit pixels into the gray level $\lfloor 255(1 - k/64)^{1/\gamma} + \frac{1}{2} \rfloor$, where $\gamma = 1.3$ and k is the number of 1s in the subarray.

Write an `MMIX` routine that converts a given $m \times n$ array `BITMAP` into the corresponding $(m/8) \times (n/8)$ image `GRAYMAP`, assuming that $m = 8m'$ and $n = 64n'$.

189. [*25*] Given a 64×64 bitmap, what's a good way (a) to transpose it, or (b) to rotate it counterclockwise by $90°$, using operations on 64-bit numbers?

190. [*23*] A *parity pattern* of length m and width n is an $m \times n$ matrix of 0s and 1s with the property that each element is the sum of its rook-neighbors, mod 2. For example,

$$
\begin{matrix} 1\,1 \\ 0\,0, \\ 1\,1 \end{matrix}
\qquad
\begin{matrix} 0\,0\,1\,1 \\ 0\,1\,0\,0 \\ 1\,1\,0\,1, \\ 0\,1\,0\,1 \end{matrix}
\qquad
\begin{matrix} 0\,1\,0\,1\,0 \\ 1\,1\,0\,1\,1, \\ 0\,1\,0\,1\,0 \end{matrix}
\qquad
\begin{matrix} 1\,0\,0 \\ 1\,1\,0 \\ 1\,0\,1, \\ 0\,1\,1 \\ 0\,0\,1 \end{matrix}
\qquad \text{and} \qquad
\begin{matrix} 0\,1\,1\,1\,0 \\ 1\,0\,1\,0\,1 \\ 1\,1\,0\,1\,1 \\ 1\,0\,1\,0\,1 \\ 0\,1\,1\,1\,0 \end{matrix}
$$

are parity patterns of sizes 3×2, 4×4, 3×5, 5×3, and 5×5.

a) If the binary vectors $\alpha_1, \alpha_2, \ldots, \alpha_m$ are the rows of a parity pattern, show that $\alpha_2, \ldots, \alpha_m$ can all be computed from the top row α_1 by using bitwise operations. Thus at most one $m \times n$ parity pattern can begin with any given bit vector.

b) True or false: The sum (mod 2) of two $m \times n$ parity patterns is a parity pattern.

c) A parity pattern is called *perfect* if it contains no all-zero row or column. For example, three of the matrices above are perfect, but the 3×2 and 3×5 examples are not. Show that every $m \times n$ parity pattern contains a perfect parity pattern as a submatrix. Furthermore, all such submatrices have the same size, $m' \times n'$, where $m' + 1$ is a divisor of $m + 1$ and $n' + 1$ is a divisor $n + 1$.

d) There's a perfect parity pattern whose first row is 0011, but there is no such pattern beginning with 01010. Is there a simple way to decide whether a given binary vector is the top row of a perfect parity pattern?

e) Prove that there's a unique perfect parity pattern that begins with $1\overbrace{0\ldots0}^{n-1}$.

191. [*M30*] A *wraparound parity pattern* is analogous to the parity patterns of exercise 190, except that the leftmost and rightmost elements of each row are also neighbors.

a) Find a simple relation between the parity pattern of width n that begins with α and the wraparound parity pattern of width $2n + 2$ that begins with $0\alpha0\alpha^R$.

b) The Fibonacci polynomials $F_j(x)$ are defined by the recurrence

$$F_0(x) = 0, \qquad F_1(x) = 1, \qquad \text{and} \qquad F_{j+1}(x) = x F_j(x) + F_{j-1}(x) \quad \text{for } j \ge 1.$$

Show that there's a simple relation between the wraparound parity patterns that begin with $10\ldots0$ ($N{-}1$ zeros) and the Fibonacci polynomials modulo $x^N + 1$. *Hint:* Consider $F_j(x^{-1} + 1 + x)$, and do arithmetic mod 2 as well as mod $x^N + 1$.

c) If α is the binary string $a_1 \ldots a_n$, let $f_\alpha(x) = a_1 x + \cdots + a_n x^n$. Show that

$$f_{(\alpha_j 0 \alpha_j^R)}(x) = (f_\alpha(x) + f_\alpha(x^{-1}))F_j(x^{-1}+1+x) \bmod (x^N + 1) \text{ and mod } 2,$$

when $N = 2n + 2$ and α_j is row j of a width-n parity pattern that begins with α.

d) Consequently we can compute α_j from α in only $O(n^2 \log j)$ steps. *Hints:* See exercise 4.6.3–26; and use the identity $F_{m+n}(x) = F_m(x)F_{n+1}(x) + F_{m-1}(x)F_n(x)$, which generalizes Eq. 1.2.8–(6).

192. [*HM38*] The shortest parity pattern that begins with a given string can be quite long; for example, it turns out that the perfect pattern of width 120 whose first row is $10 \ldots 0$ has length 36,028,797,018,963,966(!). The purpose of this exercise is to consider how to calculate the interesting function

$$c(q) = 1 + \max\{ m \mid \text{there exists a perfect parity pattern of length } m \text{ and width } q-1 \},$$

whose initial values $(1, 3, 4, 6, 5, 24, 9, 12, 28)$ for $1 \le q \le 9$ are easy to compute by hand.

a) Characterize $c(q)$ algebraically, using the Fibonacci polynomials of exercise 191.

b) Explain how to calculate $c(q)$ if we know a number M such that $c(q)$ divides M, and if we also know the prime factors of M.

c) Prove that $c(2^e) = 3 \cdot 2^{e-1}$ when $e > 0$. *Hint:* $F_{2^e}(y)$ has a simple form, mod 2.

d) Prove that when q is odd and not a multiple of 3, $c(q)$ is a divisor of $2^{2e} - 1$, where e is the order of 2 modulo q. *Hint:* $F_{2^e-1}(y)$ has a simple form, mod 2.

e) What happens when q is an odd multiple of 3?

f) Finally, explain how to handle the case when q is even.

▶ **193.** [*M21*] If a perfect $m \times n$ parity pattern exists, when m and n are odd, show that there's also a perfect $(2m+1) \times (2n+1)$ parity pattern. (Intricate fractals arise when this observation is applied repeatedly; for example, the 5×5 pattern in exercise 190 leads to Fig. 20.)

194. [*M24*] Find all $n \le 383$ for which there exists a perfect $n \times n$ parity pattern with 8-fold symmetry, such as the example in Fig. 20. *Hint:* The diagonal elements of all such patterns must be zero.

Fig. 20. A perfect 383×383 parity pattern.

▶ **195.** [*HM25*] Let A be a binary matrix having rows $\alpha_1, \ldots, \alpha_m$ of length n. Explain how to use bitwise operations to compute the rank $m - r$ of A over the binary field $\{0, 1\}$, and to find linearly independent binary vectors $\theta_1, \ldots, \theta_r$ of length m such that $\theta_j A = 0 \ldots 0$ for $1 \le j \le r$. *Hint:* See the "triangularization" algorithm for null spaces, Algorithm 4.6.2N.

196. [*21*] (K. Thompson, 1992.) Integers in the range $0 \le x < 2^{31}$ can be encoded as a string of up to six bytes $\alpha(x) = \alpha_1 \ldots \alpha_l$ in the following way: If $x < 2^7$, set $l \leftarrow 1$ and $\alpha_1 \leftarrow x$. Otherwise let $x = (x_5 \ldots x_1 x_0)_{64}$; set $l \leftarrow \lceil (\lambda x)/5 \rceil$, $\alpha_1 \leftarrow 2^8 - 2^{8-l} + x_{l-1}$, and $\alpha_j \leftarrow 2^7 + x_{l-j}$ for $2 \le j \le l$. Notice that $\alpha(x)$ contains a zero byte if and only if $x = 0$.

a) What are the encodings of $^\#$a, $^\#$3a3, $^\#$7b97, and $^\#$1d141?

b) If $x \le x'$, prove that $\alpha(x) \le \alpha(x')$ in lexicographic order.

c) Suppose a sequence of values $x^{(1)} x^{(2)} \ldots x^{(n)}$ has been encoded as a byte string $\alpha(x^{(1)})\alpha(x^{(2)}) \ldots \alpha(x^{(n)})$, and let α_k be the kth byte in that string. Show that it's easy to determine the value $x^{(i)}$ from which α_k came, by looking at a few of the neighboring bytes if necessary.

197. [*22*] The Universal Character Set (UCS), also known as Unicode, is a standard mapping of characters to integer codepoints x in the range $0 \le x < 2^{20} + 2^{16}$. An encoding called UTF-16 represents such integers as one or two wydes $\beta(x) = \beta_1$ or $\beta(x) = \beta_1\beta_2$, in the following way: If $x < 2^{16}$ then $\beta(x) = x$; otherwise

$$\beta_1 = {}^\#\mathsf{d800} + \lfloor y/2^{10} \rfloor \text{ and } \beta_2 = {}^\#\mathsf{dc00} + (y \bmod 2^{10}), \text{ where } y = x - 2^{16}.$$

Answer questions (a), (b), and (c) of exercise 196 for this encoding.

▶ **198.** [*21*] Unicode characters are often represented as strings of bytes using a scheme called UTF-8, which is the encoding of exercise 196 restricted to integers in the range $0 \le x < 2^{20} + 2^{16}$. Notice that UTF-8 efficiently preserves the standard ASCII character set (the codepoints with $x < 2^7$), and that it is quite different from UTF-16.

Let α_1 be the first byte of a UTF-8 string $\alpha(x)$. Show that there are reasonably small integer constants a, b, and c such that only four bitwise operations

$$(a \gg ((\alpha_1 \gg b) \mathbin{\&} c)) \mathbin{\&} 3$$

suffice to determine the number $l - 1$ of bytes between α_1 and the end of $\alpha(x)$.

▶ **199.** [*23*] A person might try to encode $^\#\mathsf{a}$ as $^\#\mathsf{c08a}$ or $^\#\mathsf{e0808a}$ or $^\#\mathsf{f080808a}$ in UTF-8, because the obvious decoding algorithm produces the same result in each case. But such unnecessarily long forms are illegal, because they could lead to security holes.

Suppose α_1 and α_2 are bytes such that $\alpha_1 \ge {}^\#\mathsf{80}$ and $^\#\mathsf{80} \le \alpha_2 < {}^\#\mathsf{c0}$. Find a branchless way to decide whether α_1 and α_2 are the first two bytes of at least one legitimate UTF-8 string $\alpha(x)$.

200. [*20*] Interpret the contents of register \$3 after the following three MMIX instructions have been executed: MOR \$1,\$0,#94; MXOR \$2,\$0,#94; SUBU \$3,\$1,\$2.

201. [*20*] Suppose $x = (x_{15} \ldots x_1 x_0)_{16}$ has sixteen hexadecimal digits. What one MMIX instruction will change each nonzero digit to f, while leaving zeros untouched?

202. [*20*] What two instructions will change an octabyte's nonzero wydes to $^\#\mathsf{ffff}$?

203. [*22*] (József Dallos, 2018.) Suppose we want to convert a given tetrabyte $x = (x_7 \ldots x_1 x_0)_{16}$ to the octabyte $y = (y_7 \ldots y_1 y_0)_{256}$, where y_j is the ASCII code for the hexadecimal digit x_j. For example, if $x = {}^\#\mathsf{1234abcd}$, y should represent the 8-character string "1234abcd". What clever choices of five constants a, b, c, d, and e will make the following MMIX instructions do the job?

> MOR t,x,a; SLU s,t,4; MOR t,b,s
> ADD t,t,c; MOR s,d,t; ADD t,t,e; ADD y,t,s

▶ **204.** [*22*] What are the amazing constants p, q, r, m that achieve a perfect shuffle with just six MMIX commands? (See (175)–(178).)

▶ **205.** [*22*] How would you perfectly *unshuffle* on MMIX, going from w in (175) back to z?

206. [*20*] The perfect shuffle (175) is sometimes called an "outshuffle," by comparison with the "inshuffle" that takes $z \mapsto y \ddagger x = (y_{31}x_{31} \ldots y_1 x_1 y_0 x_0)_2$; the outshuffle preserves the leftmost and rightmost bits of z, but the inshuffle has no fixed points. Can an inshuffle be performed as efficiently as an outshuffle?

207. [*22*] Use MOR to perform a 3-way perfect shuffle or "triple zip," taking $(x_{63} \ldots x_0)_2$ to $(x_{21}x_{42}x_{63}x_{20} \ldots x_2x_{23}x_{44}x_1x_{22}x_{43}x_0)_2$, as well as the inverse of this shuffle.

▶ **208.** [*23*] What's a fast way for MMIX to transpose an 8×8 Boolean matrix?

▶ **209.** [*21*] Is the suffix parity operation $x^\oplus$ of exercise 36 easy to compute with MXOR?

210. [*22*] A puzzle: Register x contains a number $8j+k$, where $0 \le j, k < 8$. Registers a and b contain arbitrary octabytes $(a_7 \ldots a_1 a_0)_{256}$ and $(b_7 \ldots b_1 b_0)_{256}$. Find a sequence of four MMIX instructions that will put a_j & b_k into register x.

▶ **211.** [*M25*] The truth table of a Boolean function $f(x_1, \ldots, x_6)$ is essentially a 64-bit number $f = (f(0,0,0,0,0,0) \ldots f(1,1,1,1,1,0) f(1,1,1,1,1,1))_2$. Show that two MOR instructions will convert f to the truth table of the least monotone Boolean function, $\hat{f}$, that is greater than or equal to f at each point.

212. [*M32*] Suppose $a = (a_{63} \ldots a_1 a_0)_2$ represents the polynomial

$$a(x) = (a_{63} \ldots a_1 a_0)_x = a_{63} x^{63} + \cdots + a_1 x + a_0.$$

Discuss using MXOR to compute the product $c(x) = a(x)b(x)$, modulo x^{64} and mod 2.

▶ **213.** [*HM26*] Implement the CRC procedure (183) on MMIX.

▶ **214.** [*HM28*] (R. W. Gosper.) Find a short, branchless MMIX computation that computes the inverse of any given 8×8 matrix X of 0s and 1s, modulo 2, if $\det X$ is odd.

▶ **215.** [*21*] What's a quick way for MMIX to test if a 64-bit number is a multiple of 3?

▶ **216.** [*M26*] Given n-bit integers $x_1, \ldots, x_m \ge 0$, $n \ge \lambda m$, compute in $O(m)$ steps the least $y > 0$ such that $y \notin \{a_1 x_1 + \cdots + a_m x_m \mid a_1, \ldots, a_m \in \{0,1\}\}$, if λx takes unit time.

217. [*40*] Explore the processing of long strings of text by packing them in a "transposed" or "sliced" manner: Represent 64 consecutive characters as a sequence of eight octabytes $w_0 \ldots w_7$, where w_k contains all 64 of their kth bits.

▶ **218.** [*M30*] (Hans Petter Selasky, 2009.) For fixed $d \ge 3$, design an algorithm to compute $a \cdot x^y \bmod 2^d$, given integers a, x, and y, where x is odd, using $O(d)$ additions and bitwise operations together with a single multiplication by y.

▶ **219.** [*20*] What does this hack do? "While $x \& (x+1) \ne 0$, set $x \leftarrow x - ((x \& (x+1)) \gg 1)$."

> *In popular usage, the term **BDD** almost always refers to*
> *Reduced Ordered Binary Decision Diagram (ROBDD in the literature,*
> *used when the ordering and reduction aspects need to be emphasized).*
> — WIKIPEDIA, *The Free Encyclopedia* (7 July 2007)

7.1.4. Binary Decision Diagrams

Let's turn now to an important family of data structures that have rapidly become the method of choice for representing and manipulating Boolean functions inside a computer. The basic idea is a divide-and-conquer scheme somewhat like the binary tries of Section 6.3, but with several new twists.

Figure 21 shows the binary decision diagram for a simple Boolean function of three variables, the median function $\langle x_1 x_2 x_3 \rangle$ of Eq. 7.1.1–(43). We can understand it as follows: The node at the top is called the *root*. Every internal node $\textcircled{j}$, also called a *branch node*, is labeled with a name or index $j = V(\textcircled{j})$ that designates a variable; for example, the root node $\textcircled{1}$ in Fig. 21 designates x_1. Branch nodes have two successors, indicated by descending lines. One of the successors is drawn as a dashed line and called LO; the other is drawn as a solid line and called HI. These branch nodes define a path in the diagram for any values of the Boolean variables, if we start at the root and take the LO branch from node $\textcircled{j}$ when $x_j = 0$, the HI branch when $x_j = 1$. Eventually this path leads to a *sink node*, which is either $\boxed{\perp}$ (denoting FALSE) or $\boxed{\top}$ (denoting TRUE).

Fig. 21. The binary decision diagram (BDD) for the majority or median function $\langle x_1 x_2 x_3 \rangle$.

In Fig. 21 it's easy to verify that this process yields the function value FALSE when at least two of the variables $\{x_1, x_2, x_3\}$ are 0, otherwise it yields TRUE.

Many authors use $\boxed{0}$ and $\boxed{1}$ to denote the sink nodes. We use $\boxed{\perp}$ and $\boxed{\top}$ instead, hoping to avoid any confusion with the branch nodes $\textcircled{0}$ and $\textcircled{1}$.

Inside a computer, Fig. 21 would be represented as a set of four nodes in arbitrary memory locations, where each node has three fields $\boxed{\text{V} \mid \text{LO} \mid \text{HI}}$. The V field holds the index of a variable, while the LO and HI fields each point to another node or to a sink:

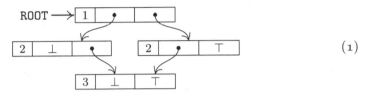

$$(1)$$

With 64-bit words, we might for example use 8 bits for V, then 28 bits for LO and the other 28 bits for HI.

Such a structure is called a "binary decision diagram," or BDD for short. Small BDDs can readily be drawn as actual diagrams on a piece of paper or a computer screen. But in essence each BDD is really an abstract set of linked nodes, which might more properly be called a "binary decision dag" — a binary tree with shared subtrees, a directed acyclic graph in which exactly two distinguished arcs emanate from every nonsink node.

We shall assume that every BDD obeys two important restrictions. First, it must be *ordered*: Whenever a LO or HI arc goes from branch node $\textcircled{i}$ to branch node $\textcircled{j}$, we must have $i < j$. Thus, in particular, no variable x_j will ever be queried twice when the function is evaluated. Second, a BDD must be *reduced*, in the sense that it doesn't waste space. This means that a branch node's LO and HI pointers must never be equal, and that no two nodes are allowed to have the same triple of values (V, LO, HI). Every node should also be accessible from the root. For example, the diagrams

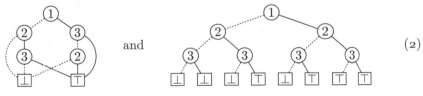

and $$(2)$$

are not BDDs, because the first one isn't ordered and the other one isn't reduced.

Many other flavors of decision diagrams have been invented, and the literature of computer science now contains a rich alphabet soup of acronyms like

EVBDD, FBDD, IBDD, OBDD, OFDD, OKFDD, PBDD, ..., ZDD. In this book we shall always use the unadorned code name "BDD" to denote a binary decision diagram that is ordered and reduced as described above, just as we generally use the word "tree" to denote an ordered (plane) tree, because such BDDs and such trees are the most common in practice.

Recall from Section 7.1.1 that every Boolean function $f(x_1, \ldots, x_n)$ corresponds to a *truth table*, which is the 2^n-bit binary string that starts with the function value $f(0, \ldots, 0)$ and continues with $f(0, \ldots, 0, 1)$, $f(0, \ldots, 0, 1, 0)$, $f(0, \ldots, 0, 1, 1)$, ..., $f(1, \ldots, 1, 1, 1)$. For example, the truth table of the median function $\langle x_1 x_2 x_3 \rangle$ is 00010111. Notice that this truth table is the same as the sequence of leaves in the unreduced decision tree of (2), with $0 \mapsto \boxed{\bot}$ and $1 \mapsto \boxed{\top}$. In fact, there's an important relationship between truth tables and BDDs, which is best understood in terms of a class of binary strings called "beads."

A truth table of order n is a binary string of length 2^n. A *bead* of order n is a truth table β of order n that is not a square; that is, β doesn't have the form $\alpha\alpha$ for any string α of length 2^{n-1}. (Mathematicians would say that a bead is a "primitive string of length 2^n.") There are two beads of order 0, namely 0 and 1; and there are two of order 1, namely 01 and 10. In general there are $2^{2^n} - 2^{2^{n-1}}$ beads of order n when $n > 0$, because there are 2^{2^n} binary strings of length 2^n and $2^{2^{n-1}}$ of them are squares. The $16 - 4 = 12$ beads of order 2 are

$$0001, 0010, 0011, 0100, 0110, 0111, 1000, 1001, 1011, 1100, 1101, 1110; \quad (3)$$

these are also the truth tables of all functions $f(x_1, x_2)$ that depend on x_1, in the sense that $f(0, x_2)$ is not the same function as $f(1, x_2)$.

Every truth table τ is a power of a unique bead, called its root. For if τ has length 2^n and isn't already a bead, it's the square of another truth table τ'; and by induction on the length of τ, we must have $\tau' = \beta^k$ for some root β. Hence $\tau = \beta^{2k}$, and β is the root of τ as well as τ'. (Of course k is a power of 2.)

A truth table τ of order $n > 0$ always has the form $\tau_0 \tau_1$, where τ_0 and τ_1 are truth tables of order $n - 1$. Clearly τ represents the function $f(x_1, x_2, \ldots, x_n)$ if and only if τ_0 represents $f(0, x_2, \ldots, x_n)$ and τ_1 represents $f(1, x_2, \ldots, x_n)$. These functions $f(0, x_2, \ldots, x_n)$ and $f(1, x_2, \ldots, x_n)$ are called *subfunctions* of f; and their truth tables, τ_0 and τ_1, are called *subtables* of τ.

Subtables of a subtable are also considered to be subtables, and a table is considered to be a subtable of itself. Thus, in general, a truth table of order n has 2^k subtables of order $n - k$, for $0 \le k \le n$, corresponding to 2^k possible settings of the first k variables $(x_1, \ldots, x_k)$. Many of these subtables often turn out to be identical; in such cases we're able to represent τ in a compressed form.

The *beads* of a Boolean function are the subtables of its truth table that happen to be beads. For example, let's consider again the median function $\langle x_1 x_2 x_3 \rangle$, with its truth table 00010111. The distinct subtables of this truth table are $\{00010111, 0001, 0111, 00, 01, 11, 0, 1\}$; and all of them except 00 and 11 are beads. Therefore the beads of $\langle x_1 x_2 x_3 \rangle$ are

$$\{00010111, 0001, 0111, 01, 0, 1\}. \quad (4)$$

And now we get to the point: *The nodes of a Boolean function's BDD are in one-to-one correspondence with its beads.* For example, we can redraw Fig. 21 by placing the relevant bead inside of each node:

$$(5)$$

In general, a function's truth tables of order $n + 1 - k$ correspond to its subfunctions $f(c_1, \ldots, c_{k-1}, x_k, \ldots, x_n)$ of that order; so its beads of order $n + 1 - k$ correspond to those subfunctions that depend on their first variable, x_k. Therefore every such bead corresponds to a branch node (k) in the BDD. And if (k) is a branch node corresponding to the truth table $\tau' = \tau'_0 \tau'_1$, its LO and HI branches point respectively to the nodes that correspond to the roots of τ'_0 and τ'_1.

This correspondence between beads and nodes proves that *every Boolean function has one and only one representation as a BDD.* The individual nodes of that BDD might, of course, be placed in different locations inside a computer.

If f is any Boolean function, let $B(f)$ denote the number of beads that it has. This is the size of its BDD — the total number of nodes, including the sinks. For example, $B(f) = 6$ when f is the median-of-three function, because (5) has size 6.

To fix the ideas, let's work out another example, the "more-or-less random" function of 7.1.1–(22) and 7.1.2–(6). Its truth table, 1100100100001111, is a bead, and so are the two subtables 11001001 and 00001111. Thus we know that the root of its BDD will be a (1) branch, and that the LO and HI nodes below the root will both be (2)s. The subtables of length 4 are $\{1100, 1001, 0000, 1111\}$; here the first two are beads, but the others are squares. To get to the next level, we break the beads in half and carry over the square roots of the nonbeads, identifying duplicates; this leaves us with $\{11, 00, 10, 01\}$. Again there are two beads, and a final step produces the desired BDD:

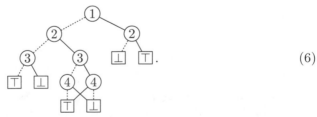

$$(6)$$

(In this diagram and others below, it's convenient to repeat the sink nodes $\boxed{\perp}$ and $\boxed{\top}$ in order to avoid excessively long connecting lines. Only one $\boxed{\perp}$ node and one $\boxed{\top}$ node are actually present; so the size of (6) is 9, not 13.)

An alert reader might well be thinking at this point, "Very nice, but what if the BDD is huge?" Indeed, functions can easily be constructed whose BDD is impossibly large; we'll study such cases later. But the wonderful thing is that a great many of the Boolean functions that are of practical importance turn out to have reasonably small values of $B(f)$. So we shall concentrate on the good

news first, postponing the bad news until we've seen why BDDs have proved to
be so popular.

BDD virtues. If $f(x) = f(x_1, \ldots, x_n)$ is a Boolean function whose BDD is
reasonably small, we can do many things quickly and easily. For example:

• We can *evaluate* $f(x)$ in at most n steps, given any input vector $x = x_1 \ldots x_n$,
by simply starting at the root and branching until we get to a sink.

• We can *find the lexicographically smallest* x such that $f(x) = 1$, by starting at the root and repeatedly taking the LO branch unless it goes directly
to $\boxed{\perp}$. The solution has $x_j = 1$ only when the HI branch was necessary at $\textcircled{j}$.
For example, this procedure gives $x_1x_2x_3 = 011$ in the BDD of Fig. 21, and
$x_1x_2x_3x_4 = 0000$ in (6). (It locates the value of x that corresponds to the
leftmost 1 in the truth table for f.) Only n steps are needed, because every
branch node corresponds to a nonzero bead; we can always find a downward
path to $\boxed{\top}$ without backing up. Of course this method fails when the root itself
is $\boxed{\perp}$. But that happens only when f is identically zero.

• We can *count the number of solutions* to the equation $f(x) = 1$, using
Algorithm C below. That algorithm does $B(f)$ operations on n-bit numbers; so
its running time is $O(nB(f))$ in the worst case.

• After Algorithm C has acted, we can speedily *generate random solutions*
to the equation $f(x) = 1$, in such a way that every solution is equally likely.

• We can also *generate all solutions* x to the equation $f(x) = 1$. The algorithm
in exercise 16 does this in $O(nN)$ steps when there are N solutions.

• We can *solve the linear Boolean programming problem*: Find x such that

$$w_1x_1 + \cdots + w_nx_n \text{ is maximum, subject to } f(x_1, \ldots, x_n) = 1, \qquad (7)$$

given constants $(w_1, \ldots, w_n)$. Algorithm B (below) does this in $O(n+B(f))$ steps.

• We can *compute the generating function* $a_0 + a_1z + \cdots + a_nz^n$, where there
are a_j solutions to $f(x_1, \ldots, x_n) = 1$ with $x_1 + \cdots + x_n = j$. (See exercise 25.)

• We can *calculate the reliability polynomial* $F(p_1, \ldots, p_n)$, which is the probability that $f(x_1, \ldots, x_n) = 1$ when each x_j is independently set to 1 with a
given probability p_j. Exercise 26 does this in $O(B(f))$ steps.

Moreover, we will see that BDDs can be combined and modified efficiently. For
example, it is not difficult to form the BDDs for $f(x_1, \ldots, x_n) \wedge g(x_1, \ldots, x_n)$
and $f(x_1, \ldots, x_{j-1}, g(x_1, \ldots, x_n), x_{j+1}, \ldots, x_n)$ from the BDDs for f and g.

Algorithms for solving basic problems with BDDs are often described most
easily if we assume that the BDD is given as a sequential list of branch instruc-
tions $I_{s-1}, I_{s-2}, \ldots, I_1, I_0$, where each I_k has the form $(\bar{v}_k? \, l_k : h_k)$. For example,
(6) might be represented as a list of $s = 9$ instructions

$$
\begin{array}{lll}
I_8 = (\bar{1}? \, 7{:}6), & I_5 = (\bar{3}? \, 1{:}0), & I_2 = (\bar{4}? \, 0{:}1), \\
I_7 = (\bar{2}? \, 5{:}4), & I_4 = (\bar{3}? \, 3{:}2), & I_1 = (\bar{5}? \, 1{:}1), \qquad (8) \\
I_6 = (\bar{2}? \, 0{:}1), & I_3 = (\bar{4}? \, 1{:}0), & I_0 = (\bar{5}? \, 0{:}0),
\end{array}
$$

with $v_8 = 1$, $l_8 = 7$, $h_8 = 6$, $v_7 = 2$, $l_7 = 5$, $h_7 = 4$, $\ldots$, $v_0 = 5$, $l_0 = h_0 = 0$. In
general the instruction '$(\bar{v}? \, l{:}h)$' means, "If $x_v = 0$, go to I_l, otherwise go to I_h,"

except that the last cases I_1 and I_0 are special. We require that the LO and HI branches l_k and h_k satisfy

$$l_k < k, \qquad h_k < k, \qquad v_{l_k} > v_k, \quad \text{and} \quad v_{h_k} > v_k, \qquad \text{for } s > k \geq 2; \qquad (9)$$

in other words, all branches move downward, to variables of greater index. But the sink nodes $\boxed{\top}$ and $\boxed{\bot}$ are represented by dummy instructions I_1 and I_0, in which $l_k = h_k = k$ and the "variable index" v_k has the impossible value $n+1$.

These instructions can be numbered in any way that respects the topological ordering of the BDD, as required by (9). The root node must correspond to I_{s-1}, and the sink nodes must correspond to I_1 and I_0, but the other index numbers aren't so rigidly prescribed. For example, (6) might also be expressed as

$$
\begin{aligned}
I_8' &= (\bar{1}?\,7{:}\,2), & I_5' &= (\bar{4}?\,0{:}\,1), & I_2' &= (\bar{2}?\,0{:}\,1), \\
I_7' &= (\bar{2}?\,4{:}\,6), & I_4' &= (\bar{3}?\,1{:}\,0), & I_1' &= (\bar{5}?\,1{:}\,1), & (10) \\
I_6' &= (\bar{3}?\,3{:}\,5), & I_3' &= (\bar{4}?\,1{:}\,0), & I_0' &= (\bar{5}?\,0{:}\,0),
\end{aligned}
$$

and in 46 other isomorphic ways. Inside a computer, the BDD need not actually appear in consecutive locations; we can readily traverse the nodes of any acyclic digraph in topological order, when the nodes are linked as in (1). But we will imagine that they've been arranged sequentially as in (8), so that various algorithms are easier to understand.

One technicality is worth noting: If $f(x) = 1$ for all x, so that the BDD is simply the sink node $\boxed{\top}$, we let $s = 2$ in this sequential representation. Otherwise s is the size of the BDD. Then the root is always represented by I_{s-1}.

Algorithm C (*Count solutions*). Given the BDD for a Boolean function $f(x) = f(x_1, \ldots, x_n)$, represented as a sequence $I_{s-1}, \ldots, I_0$ as described above, this algorithm determines $|f|$, the number of binary vectors $x = x_1 \ldots x_n$ such that $f(x) = 1$. It also computes the table $c_0, c_1, \ldots, c_{s-1}$, where c_k is the number of 1s in the bead that corresponds to I_k.

C1. [Loop over k.] Set $c_0 \leftarrow 0$, $c_1 \leftarrow 1$, and do step C2 for $k = 2, 3, \ldots, s-1$. Then return the answer $2^{v_{s-1}-1}c_{s-1}$.

C2. [Compute c_k.] Set $l \leftarrow l_k$, $h \leftarrow h_k$, and $c_k \leftarrow 2^{v_l - v_k - 1}c_l + 2^{v_h - v_k - 1}c_h$. ∎

For example, when presented with (8), this algorithm computes

$$c_2 \leftarrow 1, \; c_3 \leftarrow 1, \; c_4 \leftarrow 2, \; c_5 \leftarrow 2, \; c_6 \leftarrow 4, \; c_7 \leftarrow 4, \; c_8 \leftarrow 8;$$

the total number of solutions to $f(x_1, x_2, x_3, x_4) = 1$ is 8.

The integers c_k in Algorithm C satisfy

$$0 \leq c_k < 2^{n+1-v_k}, \qquad \text{for } 2 \leq k < s, \qquad (11)$$

and this upper bound is the best possible. Therefore multiprecision arithmetic may be needed when n is large. If extra storage space for high precision is problematic, one could use modular arithmetic instead, running the algorithm several times and computing $c_k \bmod p$ for various single-precision primes p; then the final answer would be deducible with the Chinese remainder algorithm, Eq. 4.3.2–(24). On the other hand, floating point arithmetic is usually sufficient in practice.

Let's look at some examples that are more interesting than (6):

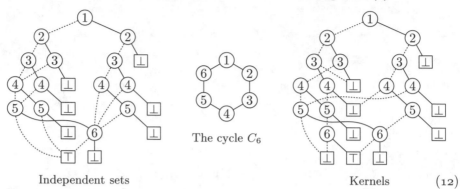

Independent sets   Kernels   (12)

These two BDDs represent functions of six variables that correspond to subsets of vertices in the cycle graph C_6. In this setup a vector such as $x_1 \ldots x_6 = 100110$ stands for the subset $\{1, 4, 5\}$; the vector 000000 stands for the empty subset; and so on. The left BDD makes $f(x) = 1$ when x is *independent* in C_6; on the right is the BDD for *maximal* independent subsets, also called the *kernels* of C_6 (see exercise 12). In general, the independent subsets of C_n correspond to arrangements of 0s and 1s in a circle of length n, with no two 1s in a row; the kernels correspond to such arrangements in which there also are no three consecutive 0s.

Algorithm C decorates a BDD with counts c_k, working from bottom to top, where c_k is the number of ways to go from node k to $\top$ by choosing values for $x_l \ldots x_n$, if l is the label of node k. When we apply that algorithm to the BDDs in (12) we get

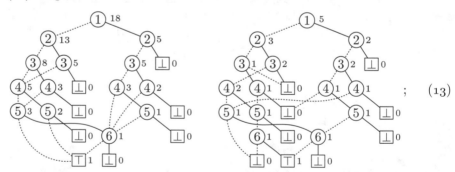

;   (13)

hence C_6 has 18 independent sets and 5 kernels.

These counts make it easy to generate uniformly *random* solutions. For example, to get a random independent set vector $x_1 \ldots x_6$, we know that 13 of the solutions in the left-hand BDD have $x_1 = 0$, while the other 5 have $x_1 = 1$. So, with probability 13/18, we set $x_1 \leftarrow 0$ and take the LO branch; otherwise we set $x_1 \leftarrow 1$ and take the HI branch. In the latter case, $x_1 = 1$ forces $x_2 \leftarrow 0$, but then x_3 could go either way.

Suppose we've chosen to set $x_1 \leftarrow 1$, $x_2 \leftarrow 0$, $x_3 \leftarrow 0$, and $x_4 \leftarrow 0$; this case occurs with probability $\frac{5}{18} \cdot \frac{5}{5} \cdot \frac{3}{5} \cdot \frac{2}{3} = \frac{2}{18}$. Then there's a branch from ④ to ⑥, so we flip a coin and set x_5 to a completely random value. In general, a branch from (i) to (j) means that the $j - i - 1$ intermediate bits $x_{i+1} \ldots x_{j-1}$ should independently become 0 or 1 with equal probability. Similarly, a branch from (i) to $\boxed{\top}$ should assign random values to $x_{i+1} \ldots x_n$.

Of course there are simpler ways to make a random choice between 18 solutions to a combinatorial problem. Moreover, the right-hand BDD in (13) is an embarrassingly complex way to represent the five kernels of C_6: We could simply have listed them, 001001, 010010, 010101, 100100, 101010! But the point is that this same method will yield the independent sets and kernels of C_n when n is much larger. For example, the 100-cycle C_{100} has 1,630,580,875,002 kernels, yet the BDD describing them has only 855 nodes. One hundred simple steps will therefore generate a fully random kernel from this vast collection.

Boolean programming and beyond. A bottom-up algorithm analogous to Algorithm C is also able to find optimum *weighted* solutions (7) to the Boolean equation $f(x) = 1$. The basic idea is that it's easy to deduce an optimum solution for any bead of f, once we know optimum solutions for the LO and HI beads that lie directly below it.

Algorithm B (*Solutions of maximum weight*). Let $I_{s-1}, \ldots, I_0$ be a sequence of branch instructions that represents the BDD for a Boolean function f, as in Algorithm C, and let $(w_1, \ldots, w_n)$ be an arbitrary sequence of integer weights. This algorithm finds a binary vector $x = x_1 \ldots x_n$ such that $w_1 x_1 + \cdots + w_n x_n$ is maximum, over all x with $f(x) = 1$. We assume that $s > 1$; otherwise $f(x)$ is identically 0. Auxiliary integer vectors $m_1 \ldots m_{s-1}$ and $W_1 \ldots W_{n+1}$ are used in the calculations, as well as an auxiliary bit vector $t_2 \ldots t_{s-1}$.

B1. [Initialize.] Set $W_{n+1} \leftarrow 0$ and $W_j \leftarrow W_{j+1} + \max(w_j, 0)$ for $n \geq j \geq 1$.

B2. [Loop on k.] Set $m_1 \leftarrow 0$ and do step B3 for $2 \leq k < s$. Then do step B4.

B3. [Process I_k.] Set $v \leftarrow v_k$, $l \leftarrow l_k$, $h \leftarrow h_k$, $t_k \leftarrow 0$. If $l \neq 0$, set $m_k \leftarrow m_l + W_{v+1} - W_{v_l}$. Then if $h \neq 0$, do the following: Compute $m \leftarrow m_h + W_{v+1} - W_{v_h} + w_v$; and if $l = 0$ or $m > m_k$, set $m_k \leftarrow m$ and $t_k \leftarrow 1$.

B4. [Compute the x's.] Set $j \leftarrow 0$, $k \leftarrow s - 1$, and do the following operations until $j = n$: While $j < v_k - 1$, set $j \leftarrow j + 1$ and $x_j \leftarrow [w_j > 0]$; if $k > 1$, set $j \leftarrow j + 1$ and $x_j \leftarrow t_k$ and $k \leftarrow (t_k = 0?\ l_k: h_k)$. ∎

A simple case of this algorithm is worked out in exercise 18. Step B3 does technical maneuvers that may look a bit scary, but their net effect is just to compute

$$m_k \leftarrow \max(m_l + W_{v+1} - W_{v_l}, m_h + W_{v+1} - W_{v_h} + w_v), \qquad (14)$$

and to record in t_k whether l or h is better. In fact, v_l and v_h are usually both equal to $v + 1$; then the calculation simply sets $m_k \leftarrow \max(m_l, m_h + w_v)$, corresponding to the cases $x_v = 0$ and $x_v = 1$. Technicalities arise only because we want to avoid fetching m_0, which is $-\infty$, and because v_l or v_h might exceed $v+1$.

With this algorithm we can, for example, quickly find an optimum set of kernel vertices in an n-cycle C_n, using weights based on the "Thue–Morse" sequence,

$$w_j = (-1)^{\nu j}; \qquad (15)$$

here νj denotes sideways addition, Eq. 7.1.3–(59). In other words, w_j is -1 or $+1$, depending on whether j has odd parity or even parity when expressed as a binary number. The maximum of $w_1 x_1 + \cdots + w_n x_n$ occurs when the even-parity vertices 3, 5, 6, 9, 10, 12, 15, ... most strongly outnumber the odd-parity vertices 1, 2, 4, 7, 8, 11, 13, ... that appear in a kernel. It turns out that

$$\{1, 3, 6, 9, 12, 15, 18, 20, 23, 25, 27, 30, 33, 36, 39, 41, 43, 46, 48,$$
$$51, 54, 57, 60, 63, 66, 68, 71, 73, 75, 78, 80, 83, 86, 89, 92, 95, 97, 99\} \quad (16)$$

is an optimum kernel in this sense when $n = 100$; only five vertices of odd parity, namely $\{1, 25, 41, 73, 97\}$, need to be included in this set of 38 to satisfy the kernel conditions, hence $\max(w_1 x_1 + \cdots + w_{100} x_{100}) = 28$. Thanks to Algorithm B, a few thousand computer instructions are sufficient to select (16) from more than a trillion possible kernels, because the BDD for all those kernels happens to be small.

Mathematically pristine problems related to combinatorial objects like cycle kernels could also be resolved efficiently with more traditional techniques, which are based on recurrences and induction. But the beauty of BDD methods is that they apply also to real-world problems that don't have any elegant structure. For example, let's consider the graph of 49 "united states" that appeared in 7–(17) and 7–(61). The Boolean function that represents all the maximal independent sets of that graph (all the kernels) has a BDD of size 780 that begins as follows:

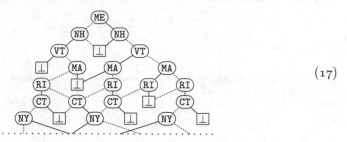

$$(17)$$

Algorithm B quickly discovers the following kernels of minimum and maximum weight, when each state vertex is simply weighted according to the sum of letters in its postal code ($w_{CA} = 3 + 1$, $w_{DC} = 4 + 3$, ..., $w_{WY} = 23 + 25$):

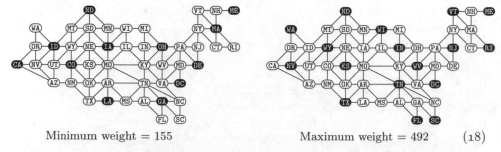

Minimum weight = 155   Maximum weight = 492   (18)

This graph has 266,137 kernels; but with Algorithm B, we needn't generate them all. In fact, the right-hand example in (18) could also be obtained with a smaller BDD of size 428, which characterizes the *independent sets*, because all weights are positive. (A kernel of maximum weight is the same thing as an independent set of maximum weight, in such cases.) There are 211,954,906 independent sets in this graph, many more than the number of kernels; yet we can find an independent set of maximum weight more quickly than a kernel of maximum weight, because the BDD is smaller.

Fig. 22. The grid $P_3 \,\square\, P_3$, and
a BDD for its connected subgraphs.

A quite different sort of graph-related BDD is shown in Fig. 22. This one is based on the 3×3 grid $P_3\square P_3$; it characterizes the sets of edges that connect all vertices of the grid together. Thus, it's a function $f(x_{12}, x_{13}, \ldots, x_{89})$ of the twelve edges $1 \!-\! 2$, $1 \!-\! 3$, $\ldots$, $8 \!-\! 9$ instead of the nine vertices $\{1, \ldots, 9\}$. Exercise 55 describes one way to construct it. When Algorithm C is applied to this BDD, it tells us that exactly 431 of the $2^{12} = 4096$ spanning subgraphs of $P_3 \,\square\, P_3$ are connected.

A straightforward extension of Algorithm C (see exercise 25) will refine this total and compute the *generating function* of these solutions, namely

$$G(z) = \sum_x z^{\nu x} f(x) = 192z^8 + 164z^9 + 62z^{10} + 12z^{11} + z^{12}. \qquad (19)$$

Thus $P_3 \,\square\, P_3$ has 192 spanning trees, plus 164 spanning subgraphs that are connected and have nine edges, and so on. Exercise 7.2.1.6–106(a) gives a formula for the number of spanning trees in $P_m \,\square\, P_n$ for general m and n; but the full generating function $G(z)$ contains considerably more information, and it probably has no simple formula unless $\min(m, n)$ is small.

Suppose each edge $u \!-\! v$ is present with probability p_{uv}, independent of all other edges of $P_3 \square P_3$. What is the probability that the resulting subgraph is connected? This is the *reliability polynomial*, which also goes by a variety of other names because it arises in many different applications. In general, as discussed in exercise 7.1.1–12, every Boolean function $f(x_1, \ldots, x_n)$ has a unique representation as a polynomial $F(x_1, \ldots, x_n)$ with the properties that

i) $F(x_1, \ldots, x_n) = f(x_1, \ldots, x_n)$ whenever each x_j is 0 or 1;

ii) $F(x_1, \ldots, x_n)$ is multilinear: Its degree in x_j is ≤ 1 for all j.

This polynomial F has integer coefficients and satisfies the basic recurrence

$$F(x_1, \ldots, x_n) = (1 - x_1)F_0(x_2, \ldots, x_n) + x_1 F_1(x_2, \ldots, x_n), \qquad (20)$$

where F_0 and F_1 are the integer multilinear representations of $f(0, x_2, \ldots, x_n)$ and $f(1, x_2, \ldots, x_n)$. Indeed, (20) is George Boole's "law of development."

Two important things follow from recurrence (20). First, F is precisely the reliability polynomial $F(p_1, \ldots, p_n)$ mentioned earlier, because the reliability polynomial obviously satisfies the same recurrence. Second, F is easily calculated from the BDD for f, working upward from the bottom and using (20) to compute the reliability of each bead. (See exercise 26.)

The connectedness function for an 8×8 grid $P_8 \square P_8$ is, of course, much more complicated than the one for $P_3 \square P_3$; it is a Boolean function of 112 variables and its BDD has 43790 nodes, compared to only 37 in Fig. 22. Still, computations with this BDD are quite feasible, and in a second or two we can compute

$$G(z) = 1262313229124985396825948816z^{63}$$
$$+ 10066111400354110626007613442z^{64}$$
$$+ \cdots + 6212z^{110} + 112z^{111} + z^{112},$$

as well as the probability $F(p)$ of connectedness and its derivative $F'(p)$, when each of the edges is present with probability p (see exercise 29):

$$F(p): \quad \text{[graph]} \quad ; \qquad\qquad F'(p): \quad \text{[graph]} \quad . \qquad (21)$$
$$\;\; 0 \quad p \quad 1 \qquad\qquad\qquad\qquad 0 \quad p \quad 1$$

*A sweeping generalization. Algorithms B and C and the algorithms we've been discussing for bottom-up BDD scanning are actually special cases of a much more general scheme that can be exploited in many additional ways. Consider an abstract algebra with two associative binary operators $\circ$ and $\bullet$, satisfying the distributive laws

$$\alpha \bullet (\beta \circ \gamma) = (\alpha \bullet \beta) \circ (\alpha \bullet \gamma), \qquad (\beta \circ \gamma) \bullet \alpha = (\beta \bullet \alpha) \circ (\gamma \bullet \alpha). \qquad (22)$$

Every Boolean function $f(x_1, \ldots, x_n)$ corresponds to a *fully elaborated truth table* involving the symbols $\circ$, $\bullet$, $\perp$, and $\top$, together with $\bar{x}_j$ and x_j for $1 \le j \le n$, in a way that's best understood by considering a small example: When $n = 2$ and when the ordinary truth table for f is 0010, the fully elaborated truth table is

$$(\bar{x}_1 \bullet \bar{x}_2 \bullet \perp) \circ (\bar{x}_1 \bullet x_2 \bullet \perp) \circ (x_1 \bullet \bar{x}_2 \bullet \top) \circ (x_1 \bullet x_2 \bullet \perp). \qquad (23)$$

The meaning of such an expression depends on the meanings that we attach to the symbols $\circ$, $\bullet$, $\perp$, $\top$, and to the literals $\bar{x}_j$ and x_j; but whatever the expression means, we can compute it directly from the BDD for f.

For example, let's return to Fig. 21, the BDD for $\langle x_1 x_2 x_3 \rangle$. The elaborations of nodes $\boxed{\perp}$ and $\boxed{\top}$ are $\alpha_\perp = \perp$ and $\alpha_\top = \top$, respectively. Then the elaboration of $\boxed{3}$ is $\alpha_3 = (\bar{x}_3 \bullet \alpha_\perp) \circ (x_3 \bullet \alpha_\top)$; the elaborations of the nodes labeled $\boxed{2}$ are $\alpha_2^l = (\bar{x}_2 \bullet (\bar{x}_3 \circ x_3) \bullet \alpha_\perp) \circ (x_2 \bullet \alpha_3)$ on the left and $\alpha_2^r = (\bar{x}_2 \bullet \alpha_3) \circ (x_2 \bullet (\bar{x}_3 \circ x_3) \bullet \alpha_\top)$ on the right; and the elaboration of node $\boxed{1}$ is $\alpha_1 = (\bar{x}_1 \bullet \alpha_2^l) \circ (x_1 \bullet \alpha_2^r)$. (Exercise 31 discusses the general procedure.) Expanding these formulas via the distributive laws (22) leads to a full elaboration with $2^n = 8$ "terms":

$$\alpha_1 = (\bar{x}_1 \bullet \bar{x}_2 \bullet \bar{x}_3 \bullet \perp) \circ (\bar{x}_1 \bullet \bar{x}_2 \bullet x_3 \bullet \perp) \circ (\bar{x}_1 \bullet x_2 \bullet \bar{x}_3 \bullet \perp) \circ (\bar{x}_1 \bullet x_2 \bullet x_3 \bullet \top)$$
$$\circ (x_1 \bullet \bar{x}_2 \bullet \bar{x}_3 \bullet \perp) \circ (x_1 \bullet \bar{x}_2 \bullet x_3 \bullet \top) \circ (x_1 \bullet x_2 \bullet \bar{x}_3 \bullet \top) \circ (x_1 \bullet x_2 \bullet x_3 \bullet \top). \qquad (24)$$

Algorithm C is the special case where 'o' is addition, '•' is multiplication, '⊥' is 0, 'T' is 1, '$\bar{x}_j$' is 1, and 'x_j' is also 1. Algorithm B arises when 'o' is the *maximum operator* and '•' is addition; the distributive laws

$$\alpha + \max(\beta, \gamma) = \max(\alpha+\beta, \alpha+\gamma), \quad \max(\beta, \gamma) + \alpha = \max(\beta+\alpha, \gamma+\alpha) \quad (25)$$

are easily checked. We interpret '⊥' as $-\infty$, 'T' as 0, '$\bar{x}_j$' as 0, and 'x_j' as w_j. Then, for example, (24) becomes

$$\max(-\infty, -\infty, -\infty, w_2 + w_3, -\infty, w_1 + w_3, w_1 + w_2, w_1 + w_2 + w_3);$$

and in general the full elaboration under this interpretation is equivalent to the expression $\max\{w_1 x_1 + \cdots + w_n x_n \mid f(x_1, \ldots, x_n) = 1\}$.

Friendly functions. Many families of functions are known to have BDDs of modest size. If f is, for example, a symmetric function of n variables, it's easy to see that $B(f) = O(n^2)$. Indeed, when $n = 5$ we can start with the triangular pattern

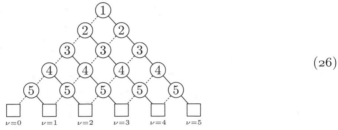

$$(26)$$

and set the leaves to ⊥ or T depending on the respective values of f when the value of $\nu x = x_1 + \cdots + x_5$ equals 0, 1, 2, 3, 4, or 5. Then we can remove redundant or equivalent nodes, always obtaining a BDD whose size is $\binom{n+1}{2} + 2$ or less.

Suppose we take any function $f(x_1, \ldots, x_n)$ and make two adjacent variables equal:

$$g(x_1, \ldots, x_n) = f(x_1, \ldots, x_{k-1}, x_k, x_k, x_{k+2}, \ldots, x_n). \quad (27)$$

Exercise 40 proves that $B(g) \le B(f)$. And by repeating this condensation process, we find that a function such as $f(x_1, x_1, x_3, x_3, x_3, x_6)$ has a small BDD whenever $B(f)$ is small. In particular, the threshold function $[2x_1 + 3x_3 + x_6 \ge t]$ must have a small BDD for any value of t, because it's a condensed version of the symmetric function $f(x_1, \ldots, x_6) = [x_1 + \cdots + x_6 \ge t]$. This argument shows that *any* threshold function with nonnegative integer weights,

$$f(x_1, x_2, \ldots, x_n) = [w_1 x_1 + w_2 x_2 + \cdots + w_n x_n \ge t], \quad (28)$$

can be obtained by condensing a symmetric function of $w_1 + w_2 + \cdots + w_n$ variables, so its BDD size is $O(w_1 + w_2 + \cdots + w_n)^2$.

Threshold functions often turn out to be easy even when the weights grow exponentially. For example, suppose $t = (t_1 t_2 \ldots t_n)_2$ and consider

$$f_t(x_1, x_2, \ldots, x_n) = [2^{n-1} x_1 + 2^{n-2} x_2 + \cdots + x_n \ge t]. \quad (29)$$

This function is true if and only if the binary string $x_1x_2\ldots x_n$ is lexicographically greater than or equal to $t_1t_2\ldots t_n$, and its BDD always has exactly $n+2$ nodes when $t_n = 1$. (See exercise 170.)

Another kind of function with small BDD is the 2^m-way multiplexer of Eq. 7.1.2–(31), a function of $n = m + 2^m$ variables:

$$M_m(x_1,\ldots,x_m;x_{m+1},\ldots,x_n) \;=\; x_{m+1+(x_1\ldots x_m)_2}. \tag{30}$$

Its BDD begins with 2^{k-1} branch nodes $\boxed{k}$ for $1 \le k \le m$. But below that complete binary tree, there's just one $\boxed{k}$ for each x_k in the main block of variables with $m < k \le n$. Hence $B(M_m) = 1+2+\cdots+2^{m-1}+2^m+2 = 2^{m+1}+1 < 2n$.

A linear network model of computation, illustrated in Fig. 23, helps to clarify the cases where a BDD is especially efficient. Consider an arrangement of computational modules M_1, M_2, $\ldots$, M_n, in which the Boolean variable x_k is input to module M_k; there also are wires between neighboring modules, each carrying a Boolean signal, with a_k wires from M_k to M_{k+1} and b_k wires from M_{k+1} to M_k for $1 \le k \le n$. A special wire out of M_n contains the output of the function, $f(x_1,\ldots,x_n)$. We define $a_0 = b_0 = b_n = 0$ and $a_n = 1$, so that module M_k has exactly $c_k = 1+a_{k-1}+b_k$ input ports and exactly $d_k = a_k+b_{k-1}$ output ports for each k. It computes d_k Boolean functions of its c_k inputs.

The individual functions computed by each module can be arbitrarily complicated, but they must be *well defined* in the sense that their joint values are completely determined by the x's: Every choice of $(x_1,\ldots,x_n)$ must lead to exactly one way to set the signals on all the wires, consistent with all of the given functions. Kenneth McMillan has discovered an interesting upper bound that holds whenever we can formulate a computation using this general setup.

Theorem M. *If f can be computed by such a network, then $B(f) \le \sum_{k=0}^{n} 2^{a_k 2^{b_k}}$.*

Proof. We will show that the BDD for f has at most $2^{a_{k-1}2^{b_{k-1}}}$ branch nodes $\boxed{k}$, for $1 \le k \le n$. This is clear if $b_{k-1} = 0$, because at most $2^{a_{k-1}}$ subfunctions are possible when x_1 through x_{k-1} have any given values. So we will show that any network that has a_{k-1} forward wires and b_{k-1} backward wires between M_{k-1} and M_k can be replaced by an equivalent network that has $a_{k-1}2^{b_{k-1}}$ forward wires and none that run backward.

For convenience, let's consider the case $k = 4$ in Fig. 23, with $a_3 = 4$ and $b_3 = 2$; we want to replace those 6 wires by 16 that run only forward. Suppose Alice is in charge of M_3 and Bob is in charge of M_4. Alice sends a 4-bit signal, a, to Bob while he sends a 2-bit signal, b, to her. More precisely, for any fixed value of $(x_1,\ldots,x_n)$, Alice computes a certain function A and Bob computes a function B, where

$$A(b) = a \qquad \text{and} \qquad B(a) = b. \tag{31}$$

Alice's function A depends on (x_1, x_2, x_3), so Bob doesn't know what it is; Bob's function B is, similarly, unknown to Alice, since it depends on $(x_4,\ldots,x_n)$. But those unknown functions have the key property that, for every choice of $(x_1,\ldots,x_n)$, there's exactly one solution (a,b) to the equations (31).

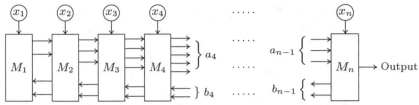

Fig. 23. A generic network of Boolean modules for which Theorem M is valid.

So Alice changes the behavior of module M_3: She sends Bob *four* 4-bit values, $A(00)$, $A(01)$, $A(10)$, and $A(11)$, thereby revealing her A function. And Bob changes the behavior of M_4: Instead of sending any feedback, he looks at those four values, together with his other inputs (namely x_4 and the b_4 bits received from M_5), and discovers the unique a and b that solve (31). His new module uses this value of a to compute the a_4 bits that he outputs to M_5. ∎

Theorem M says that the BDD size will be reasonably small if we can construct such a network with small values of a_k and b_k. Indeed, $B(f)$ will be $O(n)$ if the a's and b's are bounded, although the constant of proportionality might be huge. Let's work an example by considering the *three-in-a-row function*,

$$f(x_1, \ldots, x_n) = x_1 x_2 x_3 \lor x_2 x_3 x_4 \lor \cdots \lor x_{n-2} x_{n-1} x_n \lor x_{n-1} x_n x_1 \lor x_n x_1 x_2, \quad (32)$$

which is true if and only if a circular necklace labeled with bits $x_1, \ldots, x_n$ has three consecutive 1s. One way to implement it via Boolean modules is to give M_k three inputs (u_k, v_k, w_k) from M_{k-1} and two inputs (y_k, z_k) from M_{k+1}, where

$$u_k = x_{k-1}, \quad v_k = x_{k-2} x_{k-1}, \quad w_k = x_{n-1} x_n x_1 \lor \cdots \lor x_{k-3} x_{k-2} x_{k-1};$$
$$y_k = x_n, \quad z_k = x_{n-1} x_n. \quad (33)$$

Here subscripts are treated modulo n, and appropriate changes are made at the left or right when $k = 1$ or $k \geq n - 1$. Then M_k computes the functions

$$u_{k+1} = x_k, \quad v_{k+1} = u_k x_k, \quad w_{k+1} = w_k \lor v_k x_k, \quad y_{k-1} = y_k, \quad z_{k-1} = z_k \quad (34)$$

for nearly all values of k; exercise 45 has the details. With this construction we have $a_k \leq 3$ and $b_k \leq 2$ for all k, hence Theorem M tells us that $B(f) \leq 2^{12} n = 4096n$. In fact, the truth is much sweeter: $B(f)$ is actually $< 9n$ (see exercise 46).

Shared BDDs. We often want to deal with several Boolean functions at once, and related functions often have common subfunctions. In such cases we can work with the "BDD base" for $\{f_1(x_1, \ldots, x_n), \ldots, f_m(x_1, \ldots, x_n)\}$, which is a directed acyclic graph that contains one node for every bead that occurs within the truth tables of any of the functions. The BDD base also has m "root pointers," F_j, one for each function f_j; the BDD for f_j is then the set of all nodes reachable from node F_j. Notice that node F_j itself is reachable from node F_i if and only if f_j is a subfunction of f_i.

For example, consider the problem of computing the $n + 1$ bits of the sum of two n-bit numbers,

$$(f_{n+1} f_n f_{n-1} \ldots f_1)_2 = (x_1 x_3 \ldots x_{2n-1})_2 + (x_2 x_4 \ldots x_{2n})_2. \quad (35)$$

The BDD base for those $n + 1$ bits looks like this when $n = 4$:

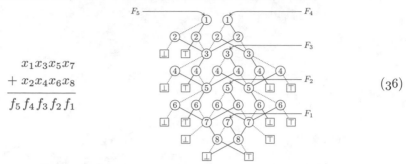

$$\dfrac{\begin{array}{c}x_1 x_3 x_5 x_7 \\ + \, x_2 x_4 x_6 x_8\end{array}}{f_5 \, f_4 \, f_3 \, f_2 \, f_1} \tag{36}$$

The way we've numbered the x's in (35) is important here (see exercise 51). In general there are exactly $B(f_1, \ldots, f_{n+1}) = 9n - 5$ nodes, when $n > 1$. The node just to the left of F_j, for $1 \le j \le n$, represents the subfunction for a *carry* c_j out of the jth bit position from the right; the node just to the right of F_j represents the complement of that carry, $\bar{c}_j$; and node F_{n+1} represents the final carry c_n.

Operations on BDDs. We've been talking about lots of things to do when a BDD is given. But how do we get a BDD into the computer in the first place?

One way is to start with an ordered binary decision diagram such as (26) or the right-hand example in (2), and to reduce it so that it becomes a true BDD. The following algorithm, based on ideas of D. Sieling and I. Wegener [*Information Processing Letters* **48** (1993), 139–144], shows that an arbitrary N-node binary decision diagram whose branches are properly ordered can be reduced to a BDD in $O(N + n)$ steps when there are n variables.

Of course we need some extra memory space in order to decide whether two nodes are equivalent, when doing such a reduction. Having only the three fields (V, LO, HI) in each node, as in (1), would give us no room to maneuver. Fortunately, only one additional pointer-size field, called AUX, is needed, together with two additional state bits. We will assume for convenience that the state bits are implicitly present in the *signs* of the LO and AUX fields, so that the algorithm needs to deal with only four fields: (V, LO, HI, AUX). The fact that the sign is preempted does mean that a 28-bit LO field will accommodate only 2^{27} nodes at most — about 134 million — instead of 2^{28}. (On a computer like MMIX, we might prefer to assume that all node addresses are even, and to add 1 to a field instead of complementing it as done here.)

Algorithm R (*Reduction to a BDD*). Given a binary decision diagram that is ordered but not necessarily reduced, this algorithm transforms it into a valid BDD by removing unnecessary nodes and rerouting all pointers appropriately. Each node is assumed to have four fields (V, LO, HI, AUX) as described above, and ROOT points to the diagram's top node. The AUX fields are initially irrelevant, except that they must be nonnegative; they will again be nonnegative at the end of the process. All deleted nodes are pushed onto a stack addressed by AVAIL, linked together by the HI fields of its nodes. (The LO fields of these nodes will be negative; their complements point to equivalent nodes that have *not* been deleted.)

The V fields of branch nodes are assumed to run from V(ROOT) up to v_{max}, in increasing order from the top downwards in the given dag. The sink nodes $\boxed{\bot}$ and $\boxed{\top}$ are assumed to be nodes 0 and 1, respectively, with nonnegative LO and HI fields. They are never deleted; in fact, they are left untouched except for their AUX fields. An auxiliary array of pointers, HEAD[v] for $V(ROOT) \leq v \leq v_{max}$, is used to create temporary lists of all nodes that have a given value of V.

R1. [Initialize.] Terminate immediately if $ROOT \leq 1$. Otherwise, set $AUX(0) \leftarrow AUX(1) \leftarrow AUX(ROOT) \leftarrow -1$, and $HEAD[v] \leftarrow -1$ for $V(ROOT) \leq v \leq v_{max}$. (We use the fact that $-1 = \sim 0$ is the bitwise complement of 0.) Then set $s \leftarrow ROOT$ and do the following operations while $s \neq 0$:

Set $p \leftarrow s$, $s \leftarrow \sim AUX(p)$, $AUX(p) \leftarrow HEAD[V(p)]$, $HEAD[V(p)] \leftarrow \sim p$.
If $AUX(LO(p)) \geq 0$, set $AUX(LO(p)) \leftarrow \sim s$ and $s \leftarrow LO(p)$.
If $AUX(HI(p)) \geq 0$, set $AUX(HI(p)) \leftarrow \sim s$ and $s \leftarrow HI(p)$.

(We've essentially done a depth-first search of the dag, temporarily marking all nodes reachable from ROOT by making their AUX fields negative.)

R2. [Loop on v.] Set $AUX(0) \leftarrow AUX(1) \leftarrow 0$, and $v \leftarrow v_{max}$.

R3. [Bucket sort.] (At this point all remaining nodes whose V field exceeds v have been properly reduced, and their AUX fields are nonnegative.) Set $p \leftarrow \sim HEAD[v]$, $s \leftarrow 0$, and do the following steps while $p \neq 0$:

Set $p' \leftarrow \sim AUX(p)$.
Set $q \leftarrow HI(p)$; if $LO(q) < 0$, set $HI(p) \leftarrow \sim LO(q)$.
Set $q \leftarrow LO(p)$; if $LO(q) < 0$, set $LO(p) \leftarrow \sim LO(q)$ and $q \leftarrow LO(q)$.
If $q = HI(p)$, set $LO(p) \leftarrow \sim q$, $HI(p) \leftarrow AVAIL$, $AUX(p) \leftarrow 0$, $AVAIL \leftarrow p$;
otherwise if $AUX(q) \geq 0$, set $AUX(p) \leftarrow s$, $s \leftarrow \sim q$, and $AUX(q) \leftarrow \sim p$;
otherwise set $AUX(p) \leftarrow AUX(\sim AUX(q))$ and $AUX(\sim AUX(q)) \leftarrow p$.
Then set $p \leftarrow p'$.

R4. [Clean up.] (Nodes with $LO = x \neq HI$ have now been linked together via their AUX fields, beginning with $\sim AUX(x)$.) Set $r \leftarrow \sim s$, $s \leftarrow 0$, and do the following while $r \geq 0$:

Set $q \leftarrow \sim AUX(r)$ and $AUX(r) \leftarrow 0$.
If $s = 0$ set $s \leftarrow q$; otherwise set $AUX(p) \leftarrow q$.
Set $p \leftarrow q$; then while $AUX(p) > 0$, set $p \leftarrow AUX(p)$.
Set $r \leftarrow \sim AUX(p)$.

R5. [Loop on p.] Set $p \leftarrow s$. Go to step R9 if $p = 0$. Otherwise set $q \leftarrow p$.

R6. [Examine a bucket.] Set $s \leftarrow LO(p)$. (At this point $p = q$.)

R7. [Remove duplicates.] Set $r \leftarrow HI(q)$. If $AUX(r) \geq 0$, set $AUX(r) \leftarrow \sim q$; otherwise set $LO(q) \leftarrow AUX(r)$, $HI(q) \leftarrow AVAIL$, and $AVAIL \leftarrow q$. Then set $q \leftarrow AUX(q)$. If $q \neq 0$ and $LO(q) = s$, repeat step R7.

R8. [Clean up again.] If $LO(p) \geq 0$, set $AUX(HI(p)) \leftarrow 0$. Then set $p \leftarrow AUX(p)$, and repeat step R8 until $p = q$.

R9. [Done?] If $p \neq 0$, return to R6. Otherwise, if $v > V(ROOT)$, set $v \leftarrow v - 1$ and return to R3. Otherwise, if $LO(ROOT) < 0$, set $ROOT \leftarrow \sim LO(ROOT)$. ∎

The intricate link manipulations of Algorithm R are easier to program than to explain, but they are highly instructive and not really difficult. The reader is urged to work through the example in exercise 53.

Algorithm R can also be used to compute the BDD for any *restriction* of a given function, namely for any function obtained by "hardwiring" one or more variables to a constant value. The idea is to do a little extra work between steps R1 and R2, setting HI(p) ← LO(p) if variable V(p) is supposed to be fixed at 0, or LO(p) ← HI(p) if V(p) is to be fixed at 1. We also need to recycle all nodes that become inaccessible after restriction. Exercise 57 fleshes out the details.

Synthesis of BDDs. We're ready now for the most important algorithm on binary decision diagrams, which takes the BDD for one function, f, and combines it with the BDD for another function, g, in order to obtain the BDD for further functions such as $f \wedge g$ or $f \oplus g$. Synthesis operations of this kind are the principal way to build up the BDDs for complex functions, and the fact that they can be done efficiently is the main reason why BDD data structures have become popular. We will discuss several approaches to the synthesis problem, beginning with a simple method and then speeding it up in various ways.

The basic notion that underlies synthesis is a product operation on BDD structures that we shall call *melding*. Suppose $\alpha = (v, l, h)$ and $\alpha' = (v', l', h')$ are BDD nodes, each containing the index of a variable together with LO and HI pointers. The "meld" of α and α', written $\alpha \diamond \alpha'$, is defined as follows when α and α' are not both sinks:

$$\alpha \diamond \alpha' = \begin{cases} (v, l \diamond l', h \diamond h'), & \text{if } v = v'; \\ (v, l \diamond \alpha', h \diamond \alpha'), & \text{if } v < v'; \\ (v', \alpha \diamond l', \alpha \diamond h'), & \text{if } v > v'. \end{cases} \tag{37}$$

For example, Fig. 24 shows how two small but typical BDDs are melded. The one on the left, with branch nodes $(\alpha, \beta, \gamma, \delta)$, represents $f(x_1, x_2, x_3, x_4) = (x_1 \vee x_2) \wedge (x_3 \vee x_4)$; the one in the middle, with branch nodes $(\omega, \psi, \chi, \varphi, \upsilon, \tau)$, represents $g(x_1, x_2, x_3, x_4) = (x_1 \oplus x_2) \vee (x_3 \oplus x_4)$. Nodes δ and τ are essentially the same, so we would have $\delta = \tau$ if f and g were part of a single BDD base; but melding can be applied also to BDDs that do not have common nodes. At the right of Fig. 24, $\alpha \diamond \omega$ is the root of a decision diagram that has eleven branch nodes, and it essentially represents the *ordered pair* (f, g).

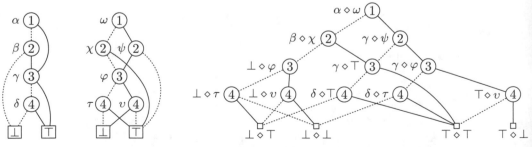

Fig. 24. Two BDDs can be melded together with the $\diamond$ operation (37).

An ordered pair of two Boolean functions can be visualized by placing the truth table of one above the truth table of the other. With this interpretation, $\alpha \diamond \omega$ stands for the ordered pair $\frac{0000011101110111}{0110111111110110}$, and $\beta \diamond \chi$ stands for $\frac{00000111}{01101111}$, etc. The melded BDD of Fig. 24 corresponds to the diagram

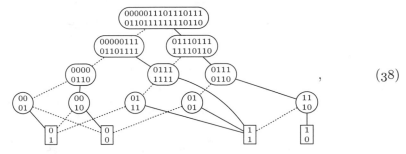

$$(38)$$

which is analogous to (5) except that each node denotes an ordered pair of functions instead of a single function. Beads and subtables are defined on ordered pairs just as before. But now we have four possible sinks instead of two, namely

$$\bot \diamond \bot, \qquad \bot \diamond \top, \qquad \top \diamond \bot, \qquad \text{and} \qquad \top \diamond \top, \tag{39}$$

corresponding to the ordered pairs $\frac{0}{0}$, $\frac{0}{1}$, $\frac{1}{0}$, and $\frac{1}{1}$.

To compute the conjunction $f \wedge g$, we AND together the truth tables of f and g. This operation corresponds to replacing $\frac{0}{0}$, $\frac{0}{1}$, $\frac{1}{0}$, and $\frac{1}{1}$ by 0, 0, 0, and 1, respectively; so we get the BDD for $f \wedge g$ from $f \diamond g$ by replacing the respective sink nodes of (39) by $\boxed{\bot}$, $\boxed{\bot}$, $\boxed{\bot}$, and $\boxed{\top}$, then reducing the result. Similarly, the BDD for $f \oplus g$ is obtained if we replace the sinks (39) by $\boxed{\bot}$, $\boxed{\top}$, $\boxed{\top}$, and $\boxed{\bot}$. (In this particular case $f \oplus g$ turns out to be the symmetric function $S_{1,4}(x_1, x_2, x_3, x_4)$, as computed in Fig. 9 of Section 7.1.2.) The melded diagram $f \diamond g$ contains all the information needed to compute *any* Boolean combination of f and g; and the BDD for every such combination has at most $B(f \diamond g)$ nodes.

Clearly $B(f \diamond g) \le B(f)B(g)$, because each node of $f \diamond g$ corresponds to a node of f and a node of g. Therefore the meld of small BDDs cannot be extremely large. Usually, in fact, melding produces a result that is considerably smaller than this worst-case upper bound, with something like $B(f) + B(g)$ nodes instead of $B(f)B(g)$. Exercise 60 discusses a sharper bound that sheds some light on why melds often turn out to be small. But exercises 59(b) and 63 present interesting examples where quadratic growth does occur.

Melding suggests a simple algorithm for synthesis: We can form an array of $B(f)B(g)$ nodes, with node $\alpha \diamond \alpha'$ in row α and column α' for every α in the BDD for f and every α' in the BDD for g. Then we can convert the four sink nodes (39) to $\boxed{\bot}$ or $\boxed{\top}$ as desired, and apply Algorithm R to the root node $f \diamond g$. Voilà — we've got the BDD for $f \wedge g$ or $f \oplus g$ or $f \vee \bar{g}$ or whatever.

The running time of this algorithm is clearly of order $B(f)B(g)$. We can reduce it to order $B(f \diamond g)$, because there's no need to fill in all of the matrix entries $\alpha \diamond \alpha'$; only the nodes that are reachable from $f \diamond g$ are relevant, and we can generate them on the fly when necessary. But even with this improvement in the running time, the simple algorithm is unsatisfactory because of the requirement for $B(f)B(g)$ nodes in memory. When we deal with BDDs, time is cheap but space is expensive: Attempts to solve large problems tend to fail more often because of "spaceout" than because of "timeout." That's why Algorithm R was careful to perform its machinations with only one auxiliary link field per node.

The following algorithm solves the synthesis problem with working space of order $B(f \diamond g)$; in fact, it needs only about sixteen bytes per element of the BDD for $f \diamond g$. The algorithm is designed to be used as the main engine of a "Boolean function calculator," which represents functions as BDDs in compressed form on a sequential stack. The stack is maintained at the lower end of a large array called the *pool*. Each BDD on the stack is a sequence of *nodes*, which each have three fields $(\text{V}, \text{LO}, \text{HI})$. The rest of the pool is available to hold temporary results called *templates*, which each have four fields $(\text{L}, \text{H}, \text{LEFT}, \text{RIGHT})$. A node typically occupies one octabyte of memory, while a template occupies two.

The purpose of Algorithm S is to examine the top two Boolean functions on the stack, f and g, and to replace them by the Boolean combination $f \circ g$, where $\circ$ is one of the 16 possible binary operators. This operator is identified by its 4-bit truth table, *op*. For example, Algorithm S will form the BDD for $f \oplus g$ when *op* is $(0110)_2 = 6$; it will deliver $f \wedge g$ when $op = 1$.

When the algorithm begins, operand f appears in locations $[f_0 .. g_0)$ of the pool, and operand g appears in locations $[g_0 .. \text{NTOP})$. All higher locations $[\text{NTOP} .. \text{POOLSIZE})$ are available for storing the templates that the algorithm needs. Those templates will appear in locations $[\text{TBOT} .. \text{POOLSIZE})$ at the high end of the pool; the boundary markers NTOP and TBOT will change dynamically as the algorithm proceeds. The resulting BDD for $f \circ g$ will eventually be placed in locations $[f_0 .. \text{NTOP})$, taking over the space formerly occupied by f and g. We assume that a template occupies the space of two nodes. Thus, the assignments "$t \leftarrow \text{TBOT} - 2, \text{TBOT} \leftarrow t$" allocate space for a new template, pointed to by t; the assignments "$p \leftarrow \text{NTOP}, \text{NTOP} \leftarrow p + 1$" allocate a new node p. For simplicity of exposition, Algorithm S does not check that the condition $\text{NTOP} \leq \text{TBOT}$ remains valid throughout the process; but of course such tests are essential in practice. Exercise 69 remedies this oversight.

The input functions f and g are specified to Algorithm S as sequences of instructions $(I_{s-1}, \ldots, I_1, I_0)$ and $(I'_{s'-1}, \ldots, I'_1, I'_0)$, as in Algorithms B and C above. The lengths of these sequences are $s = B^+(f)$ and $s' = B^+(g)$, where

$$B^+(f) = B(f) + [f \text{ is identically } 1] \tag{40}$$

is the number of BDD nodes when the sink $\boxed{\perp}$ is forced to be present. For example, the two BDDs at the left of Fig. 24 could be specified by the instructions

$$I_5 = (\bar{1}?\ 4{:}\ 3), \quad I_3 = (\bar{3}?\ 2{:}\ 1), \qquad I'_7 = (\bar{1}?\ 5{:}\ 6), \quad I'_4 = (\bar{3}?\ 2{:}\ 3),$$
$$\qquad\qquad\qquad\qquad\qquad\qquad\qquad\qquad\quad I'_6 = (\bar{2}?\ 1{:}\ 4), \quad I'_3 = (\bar{4}?\ 1{:}\ 0), \tag{41}$$
$$I_4 = (\bar{2}?\ 0{:}\ 3), \quad I_2 = (\bar{4}?\ 0{:}\ 1); \qquad I'_5 = (\bar{2}?\ 4{:}\ 1), \quad I'_2 = (\bar{4}?\ 0{:}\ 1);$$

as usual, I_1, I_0, I'_1, and I'_0 are the sinks. These instructions are packed into nodes, so that if $I_k = (\bar{v}_k?\ l_k{:}\ h_k)$ we have $\text{V}(f_0 + k) = v_k$, $\text{LO}(f_0 + k) = l_k$, and

$\mathtt{HI}(f_0 + k) = h_k$ for $2 \le k < s$ when Algorithm S begins. Similar conventions apply to the instructions I'_k that define g. Furthermore

$$\mathtt{V}(f_0) = \mathtt{V}(f_0 + 1) = \mathtt{V}(g_0) = \mathtt{V}(g_0 + 1) = v_{\max} + 1, \tag{42}$$

where we assume that f and g depend only on the variables x_v for $1 \le v \le v_{\max}$.

Like the simple but space-hungry algorithm described earlier, Algorithm S proceeds in two phases: First it builds the BDD for $f \diamond g$, constructing templates so that every important meld $\alpha \diamond \alpha'$ is represented as a template t for which

$$\mathtt{LEFT}(t) = \alpha, \quad \mathtt{RIGHT}(t) = \alpha', \quad \mathtt{L}(t) = \mathtt{LO}(\alpha \diamond \alpha'), \quad \mathtt{H}(t) = \mathtt{HI}(\alpha \diamond \alpha'). \tag{43}$$

(The L and H fields point to templates, not nodes.) Then the second phase reduces these templates, using a procedure similar to Algorithm R; it changes template t from (43) to

$$\begin{aligned} \mathtt{LEFT}(t) = {\sim}\kappa(t), \quad \mathtt{RIGHT}(t) = \tau(t), \\ \mathtt{L}(t) = \tau(\mathtt{LO}(\alpha \diamond \alpha')), \quad \mathtt{H}(t) = \tau(\mathtt{HI}(\alpha \diamond \alpha')), \end{aligned} \tag{44}$$

where $\tau(t)$ is the unique template to which t has been reduced, and where $\kappa(t)$ is the "clone" of t if $\tau(t) = t$. Every reduced template t corresponds to an instruction node in the BDD of $f \circ g$, and $\kappa(t)$ is the index of this node relative to position f_0 in the stack. (Setting $\mathtt{LEFT}(t)$ to ${\sim}\kappa(t)$ instead of $\kappa(t)$ is a sneaky trick that makes steps S7–S10 run faster.) Special overlapping templates are permanently reserved for sinks at the *bottom* of the pool, so that we always have

$$\mathtt{LEFT}(0) = {\sim}0, \quad \mathtt{RIGHT}(0) = 0, \quad \mathtt{LEFT}(1) = {\sim}1, \quad \mathtt{RIGHT}(1) = 1, \tag{45}$$

in accord with the conventions of (42) and (44).

We needn't make a template for $\alpha \diamond \alpha'$ when the value of $\alpha \circ \alpha'$ is obviously constant. For example, if we're computing $f \wedge g$, we know that $\alpha \diamond \alpha'$ will eventually reduce to $\boxed{\perp}$ if $\alpha = 0$ or $\alpha' = 0$. Such simplifications are discovered by a subroutine called $find\_level(f, g)$, which returns the positive integer j if the root of $f \diamond g$ begins with the branch (j), unless $f \circ g$ clearly has a constant value; in the latter case, $find\_level(f, g)$ returns the value $-(f \circ g)$, which is 0 or -1. The procedure is slightly technical, but simple, using the global truth table op:

Subroutine $find\_level(f, g)$, with local variable t:
If $f \le 1$ and $g \le 1$, return $-((op \gg (3 - 2f - g)) \mathbin{\&} 1)$, which is $-(f \circ g)$.
If $f \le 1$ and $g > 1$, set $t \leftarrow (f? \; op \mathbin{\&} 3: op \gg 2)$; return 0 if $t = 0$, -1 if $t = 3$.
If $f > 1$ and $g \le 1$, set $t \leftarrow (g? \; op: op \gg 1) \mathbin{\&} 5$; return 0 if $t = 0$, -1 if $t = 5$.
Otherwise return $\min(\mathtt{V}(f_0 + f), \mathtt{V}(g_0 + g))$. $\tag{46}$

The main difficulty that faces us, when generating a template for a descendant of $\alpha \diamond \alpha'$ according to (37), is to decide whether or not such a template already exists — and if so, to link to it. The best way to solve such problems is usually to use a hash table; but then we must decide where to put such a table, and how much extra space to devote to it. Alternatives such as binary search trees would be much easier to adapt to our purposes, but they would add an unwanted factor of $\log B(f \diamond g)$ to the running time. The synthesis problem can actually be solved in worst-case time and space $O(B(f \diamond g))$ by using a bucket sort method analogous to Algorithm R (see exercise 72); but that solution is complicated and somewhat awkward.

Fortunately there's a nice way out of this dilemma, requiring almost no extra memory and only modestly complex code, if we generate the templates one level at a time. Before generating the templates for level l, we'll know the number N_l of templates to be requested on that level. So we can temporarily allocate space for 2^b templates at the top of the currently free area, where $b = \lceil \lg N_l \rceil$, and put new templates there while hashing into the same area. The idea is to use chaining with separate lists, as in Fig. 38 of Section 6.4; the H and L fields of our templates and potential templates play the roles of heads and links in that illustration, while the keys appear in (LEFT, RIGHT). Here's the logic, in detail:

Subroutine $make\_template(f, g)$, with local variable t:
Set $h \leftarrow \text{HBASE} + 2(((314159257f + 271828171g) \bmod 2^d) \gg (d - b))$, where d is a convenient upper bound on the size of a pointer (usually $d = 32$). Then set $t \leftarrow \text{H}(h)$. While $t \neq \Lambda$ and either $\text{LEFT}(t) \neq f$ or $\text{RIGHT}(t) \neq g$, set $t \leftarrow \text{L}(t)$. If $t = \Lambda$, set $t \leftarrow \text{TBOT} - 2$, $\text{TBOT} \leftarrow t$, $\text{LEFT}(t) \leftarrow f$, $\text{RIGHT}(t) \leftarrow g$, $\text{L}(t) \leftarrow \text{H}(h)$, and $\text{H}(h) \leftarrow t$. Finally, return the value t.   (47)

The calling routine in steps S4 and S5 ensures that $\text{NTOP} \leq \text{HBASE} \leq \text{TBOT}$.

This breadth-first, level-at-a-time strategy for constructing the templates has an added payoff, because it promotes "locality of reference": Memory accesses tend to be confined to nearby locations that have recently been seen, hence controlled in such a way that cache misses and page faults are significantly reduced. Furthermore, the eventual BDD nodes placed on the stack will also appear in order, so that all branches on the same variable appear consecutively.

Algorithm S (*Breadth-first synthesis of BDDs*). This algorithm computes the BDD for $f \circ g$ as described above, using subroutines (46) and (47). Auxiliary arrays $\text{LSTART}[l]$, $\text{LCOUNT}[l]$, $\text{LLIST}[l]$, and $\text{HLIST}[l]$ are used for $0 \leq l \leq v_{\max}$.

S1. [Initialize.] Set $f \leftarrow g_0 - 1 - f_0$, $g \leftarrow \text{NTOP} - 1 - g_0$, and $l \leftarrow find\_level(f, g)$. See exercise 66 if $l \leq 0$. Otherwise set $\text{LSTART}[l - 1] \leftarrow \text{POOLSIZE}$, and $\text{LLIST}[k] \leftarrow \text{HLIST}[k] \leftarrow \Lambda$, $\text{LCOUNT}[k] \leftarrow 0$ for $l < k \leq v_{\max}$. Set $\text{TBOT} \leftarrow \text{POOLSIZE} - 2$, $\text{LEFT}(\text{TBOT}) \leftarrow f$, and $\text{RIGHT}(\text{TBOT}) \leftarrow g$.

S2. [Scan the level-l templates.] Set $\text{LSTART}[l] \leftarrow \text{TBOT}$ and $t \leftarrow \text{LSTART}[l - 1]$. While $t > \text{TBOT}$, schedule requests for future levels by doing the following:

Set $t \leftarrow t-2$, $f \leftarrow \text{LEFT}(t)$, $g \leftarrow \text{RIGHT}(t)$, $vf \leftarrow \text{V}(f_0+f)$, $vg \leftarrow \text{V}(g_0+g)$,
$ll \leftarrow find\_level((vf \leq vg? \ \text{LO}(f_0 + f): f), (vf \geq vg? \ \text{LO}(g_0 + g): g))$,
$lh \leftarrow find\_level((vf \leq vg? \ \text{HI}(f_0 + f): f), (vf \geq vg? \ \text{HI}(g_0 + g): g))$.

If $ll \leq 0$, set $\text{L}(t) \leftarrow -ll$; otherwise set $\text{L}(t) \leftarrow \text{LLIST}[ll]$, $\text{LLIST}[ll] \leftarrow t$, $\text{LCOUNT}[ll] \leftarrow \text{LCOUNT}[ll] + 1$. If $lh \leq 0$, set $\text{H}(t) \leftarrow -lh$; otherwise set $\text{H}(t) \leftarrow \text{HLIST}[lh]$, $\text{HLIST}[lh] \leftarrow t$, $\text{LCOUNT}[lh] \leftarrow \text{LCOUNT}[lh] + 1$.

S3. [Done with phase one?] Go to S6 if $l = v_{\max}$. Otherwise set $l \leftarrow l + 1$, and return to S2 if $\text{LCOUNT}[l] = 0$.

S4. [Initialize for hashing.] Set $b \leftarrow \lceil \lg \text{LCOUNT}[l] \rceil$, $\text{HBASE} \leftarrow \text{TBOT} - 2^{b+1}$, and $\text{H}(\text{HBASE} + 2k) \leftarrow \Lambda$ for $0 \leq k < 2^b$.

S5. [Make the level-l templates.] Set $t \leftarrow \text{LLIST}[l]$. While $t \neq \Lambda$, set $s \leftarrow \text{L}(t)$, $f \leftarrow \text{LEFT}(t)$, $g \leftarrow \text{RIGHT}(t)$, $vf \leftarrow \text{V}(f_0 + f)$, $vg \leftarrow \text{V}(g_0 + g)$, $\text{L}(t) \leftarrow \textit{make\_template}((vf \leq vg?\ \text{LO}(f_0+f):\ f),(vf \geq vg?\ \text{LO}(g_0+g):\ g))$, $t \leftarrow s$. (We're half done.) Then set $t \leftarrow \text{HLIST}[l]$. While $t \neq \Lambda$, set $s \leftarrow \text{H}(t)$, $f \leftarrow \text{LEFT}(t)$, $g \leftarrow \text{RIGHT}(t)$, $vf \leftarrow \text{V}(f_0 + f)$, $vg \leftarrow \text{V}(g_0 + g)$, $\text{H}(t) \leftarrow \textit{make\_template}((vf \leq vg?\ \text{HI}(f_0+f):\ f),(vf \geq vg?\ \text{HI}(g_0+g):\ g))$, $t \leftarrow s$. (Now the other half is done.) Go back to step S2.

S6. [Prepare for phase two.] (At this point it's safe to obliterate the nodes of f and g, because we've built all the templates (43). Now we'll convert them to form (44). Note that $\text{V}(f_0) = \text{V}(f_0 + 1) = v_{\max} + 1$.) Set $\text{NTOP} \leftarrow f_0 + 2$.

S7. [Bucket sort.] Set $t \leftarrow \text{LSTART}[l - 1]$. Do the following while $t > \text{LSTART}[l]$:

Set $t \leftarrow t - 2$, $\text{L}(t) \leftarrow \text{RIGHT}(\text{L}(t))$, and $\text{H}(t) \leftarrow \text{RIGHT}(\text{H}(t))$.
If $\text{L}(t) = \text{H}(t)$, set $\text{RIGHT}(t) \leftarrow \text{L}(t)$. (This branch is redundant.)
Otherwise set $\text{RIGHT}(t) \leftarrow -1$, $\text{LEFT}(t) \leftarrow \text{LEFT}(\text{L}(t))$, $\text{LEFT}(\text{L}(t)) \leftarrow t$.

S8. [Restore clone addresses.] If $t = \text{LSTART}[l - 1]$, set $t \leftarrow \text{LSTART}[l] - 2$ and go to S9. Otherwise, if $\text{LEFT}(t) < 0$, set $\text{LEFT}(\text{L}(t)) \leftarrow \text{LEFT}(t)$. Set $t \leftarrow t + 2$ and repeat step S8.

S9. [Done with level?] Set $t \leftarrow t+2$. If $t = \text{LSTART}[l - 1]$, go to S12. Otherwise, if $\text{RIGHT}(t) \geq 0$ repeat step S9.

S10. [Examine a bucket.] (Suppose $\text{L}(t_1) = \text{L}(t_2) = \text{L}(t_3)$, where $t_1 > t_2 > t_3 = t$ and no other templates on level l have this L value. Then at this point we have $\text{LEFT}(t_3) = t_2$, $\text{LEFT}(t_2) = t_1$, $\text{LEFT}(t_1) < 0$, and $\text{RIGHT}(t_1) = \text{RIGHT}(t_2) = \text{RIGHT}(t_3) = -1$.) Set $s \leftarrow t$. While $s > 0$, do the following: Set $r \leftarrow \text{H}(s)$, $\text{RIGHT}(s) \leftarrow \text{LEFT}(r)$; if $\text{LEFT}(r) < 0$, set $\text{LEFT}(r) \leftarrow s$; and set $s \leftarrow \text{LEFT}(s)$. Finally set $s \leftarrow t$ again.

S11. [Make clones.] If $s < 0$, go back to step S9. Otherwise if $\text{RIGHT}(s) \geq 0$, set $s \leftarrow \text{LEFT}(s)$. Otherwise set $r \leftarrow \text{LEFT}(s)$, $\text{LEFT}(\text{H}(s)) \leftarrow \text{RIGHT}(s)$, $\text{RIGHT}(s) \leftarrow s$, $q \leftarrow \text{NTOP}$, $\text{NTOP} \leftarrow q + 1$, $\text{LEFT}(s) \leftarrow \sim(q - f_0)$, $\text{LO}(q) \leftarrow \sim\text{LEFT}(\text{L}(s))$, $\text{HI}(q) \leftarrow \sim\text{LEFT}(\text{H}(s))$, $\text{V}(q) \leftarrow l$, $s \leftarrow r$. Repeat step S11.

S12. [Loop on l.] Set $l \leftarrow l - 1$. Return to S7 if $\text{LSTART}[l] < \text{POOLSIZE}$. Otherwise, if $\text{RIGHT}(\text{POOLSIZE} - 2) = 0$, set $\text{NTOP} \leftarrow \text{NTOP} - 1$ (because $f \circ g$ is identically 0). ∎

As usual, the best way to understand an algorithm like this is to trace through an example. Exercise 67 discusses what Algorithm S does when it is asked to compute $f \wedge g$, given the BDDs in (41).

Algorithm S can be used, for example, to construct the BDDs for interesting functions such as the "monotone-function function" $\mu_n(x_1, \ldots, x_{2^n})$, which is true if and only if $x_1 \ldots x_{2^n}$ is the truth table of a monotone function:

$$\mu_n(x_1, \ldots, x_{2^n}) = \bigwedge_{0 \leq i \subseteq j < 2^n} [x_{i+1} \leq x_{j+1}]. \tag{48}$$

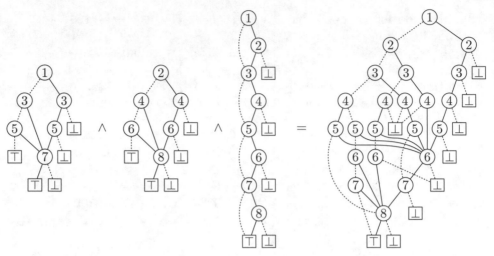

Fig. 25. $\mu_2(x_1, x_3, x_5, x_7) \wedge \mu_2(x_2, x_4, x_6, x_8) \wedge G_8(x_1, \ldots, x_8) = \mu_3(x_1, \ldots, x_8)$, as computed by Algorithm S.

Starting with $\mu_0(x_1) = 1$, this function satisfies the recursion relation

$$\mu_n(x_1, \ldots, x_{2^n}) =$$
$$\mu_{n-1}(x_1, x_3, \ldots, x_{2^n-1}) \wedge \mu_{n-1}(x_2, x_4, \ldots, x_{2^n}) \wedge G_{2^n}(x_1, \ldots, x_{2^n}), \quad (49)$$

where $G_{2^n}(x_1, \ldots, x_{2^n}) = [x_1 \leq x_2] \wedge [x_3 \leq x_4] \wedge \cdots \wedge [x_{2^n-1} \leq x_{2^n}]$. So its BDD is easy to obtain with a BDD calculator like Algorithm S: The BDDs for $\mu_{n-1}(x_1, x_3, \ldots, x_{2^n-1})$ and $\mu_{n-1}(x_2, x_4, \ldots, x_{2^n})$ are simple variants of the one for $\mu_{n-1}(x_1, x_2, \ldots, x_{2^n-1})$, and G_{2^n} has an extremely simple BDD (see Fig. 25).

Repeating this process six times will produce the BDD for μ_6, which has 103,924 nodes. There are exactly 7,828,354 monotone Boolean functions of six variables (see exercise 5.3.4–31); this BDD nicely characterizes them all, and we need only about 4.8 million memory accesses to compute it with Algorithm S. Furthermore, 6.7 billion mems will suffice to compute the BDD for μ_7, which has 155,207,320 nodes and characterizes 2,414,682,040,998 monotone functions.

We must stop there, however; the size of the next case, $B(\mu_8)$, turns out to be a whopping 69,258,301,585,604 (see exercise 77).

Synthesis in a BDD base. Another approach is called for when we're dealing with many functions at once instead of computing a single BDD on the fly. The functions of a BDD base often share common subfunctions, as in (36). Algorithm S is designed to take disjoint BDDs and to combine them efficiently, afterwards destroying the originals; but in many cases we would rather form combinations of functions whose BDDs overlap. Furthermore, after forming a new function $f \wedge g$, say, we might want to keep f and g around for future use; indeed, the new function might well share nodes with f or g or both.

Let's therefore consider the design of a general-purpose toolkit for manipulating a collection of Boolean functions. BDDs are especially attractive for this purpose because most of the necessary operations have a simple recursive formulation. We know that every nonconstant Boolean function can be written

$$f(x_1, x_2, \ldots, x_n) = (\bar{x}_v?\ f_l\!:\ f_h), \tag{50}$$

where $v = f_o$ indexes the first variable on which f depends, and where we have

$$f_l = f(0, \ldots, 0, x_{v+1}, \ldots, x_n); \quad f_h = f(1, \ldots, 1, x_{v+1}, \ldots, x_n). \tag{51}$$

This rule corresponds to branch node $\textcircled{v}$ at the root of the BDD for f; and the rest of the BDD follows by using (50) and (51) recursively, until we reach constant functions that correspond to $\boxed{\bot}$ or $\boxed{\top}$. A similar recursion defines any combination of two functions, $f \circ g$: For if f and g aren't both constant, we have

$$f(x_1, \ldots, x_n) = (\bar{x}_v?\ f_l\!:\ f_h) \quad \text{and} \quad g(x_1, \ldots, x_n) = (\bar{x}_v?\ g_l\!:\ g_h), \tag{52}$$

where $v = \min(f_o, g_o)$ and where f_l, f_h, g_l, g_h are given by (51). Then, presto,

$$f \circ g = (\bar{x}_v?\ f_l \circ g_l\!:\ f_h \circ g_h). \tag{53}$$

This important formula is another way of stating the rule by which we defined melding, Eq. (37).

Caution: The notations above need to be understood carefully, because the subfunctions f_l and f_h in (50) might not be the same as the f_l and f_h in (52). Suppose, for example, that $f = x_2 \lor x_3$ while $g = x_1 \oplus x_3$. Then Eq. (50) holds with $f_o = 2$ and $f = (\bar{x}_2?\ f_l\!:\ f_h)$, where $f_l = x_3$ and $f_h = 1$. We also have $g_o = 1$ and $g = (\bar{x}_1?\ x_3\!:\ \bar{x}_3)$. But in (52) we use the same branch variable x_v for both functions, and $v = \min(f_o, g_o) = 1$ in our example; so Eq. (52) holds with $f = (\bar{x}_1?\ f_l\!:\ f_h)$ and $f_l = f_h = x_2 \lor x_3$.

Every node of a BDD base represents a Boolean function. Furthermore, a BDD base is reduced; therefore two of its functions or subfunctions are equal if and only if they correspond to exactly the same node. (This convenient uniqueness property was *not* true in Algorithm S.)

Formulas (51)–(53) immediately suggest a recursive way to compute $f \land g$:

$$\text{AND}(f, g) = \begin{cases} \text{If } f \land g \text{ has an obvious value, return it.} \\ \text{Otherwise represent } f \text{ and } g \text{ as in (52);} \\ \text{compute } r_l \leftarrow \text{AND}(f_l, g_l) \text{ and } r_h \leftarrow \text{AND}(f_h, g_h); \\ \text{return the function } (\bar{x}_v?\ r_l\!:\ r_h). \end{cases} \tag{54}$$

(Recursions always need to terminate when a sufficiently simple case arises. The "obvious" values in the first line correspond to the terminal cases $f \land 1 = f$, $1 \land g = g$, $f \land 0 = 0 \land g = 0$, and $f \land g = f$ when $f = g$.) When f and g are the functions in our example above, (54) reduces $f \land g$ to the computation of $(x_2 \lor x_3) \land x_3$ and $(x_2 \lor x_3) \land \bar{x}_3$. Then $(x_2 \lor x_3) \land x_3$ reduces to $x_3 \land x_3$ and $1 \land x_3$; etc.

But (54) is problematic if we simply implement it as stated, because every nonterminal step launches two more instances of the recursion. The computation explodes, with 2^k instances of AND when we're k levels deep!

Fortunately there's a good way to avoid that blowup. Since f has only $B(f)$ different subfunctions, at most $B(f)B(g)$ distinctly different calls of AND can arise. To keep a lid on the computations, we just need to remember what we've done before, by making a *memo* of the fact that $f \wedge g = r$ just before returning r as the computed value. Then when the same subproblem occurs later, we can retrieve the memo and say, "Hey, we've already been there and done that." Previously solved cases thereby become terminal; only distinct subproblems can generate new ones. (Chapter 8 will discuss this memoization technique in detail.)

The algorithm in (54) also glosses over another problem: It's not so easy to "return the function $(\bar{x}_v?\ r_l\colon r_h)$," because we must keep the BDD base reduced. If $r_l = r_h$, we should return the node r_l; and if $r_l \neq r_h$, we need to decide whether the branch node $(\bar{x}_v?\ r_l\colon r_h)$ already exists, before creating a new one.

Thus we need to maintain additional information, besides the BDD nodes themselves. We need to keep memos of problems already solved; we also need to be able to find a node by its content, instead of by its address. The search algorithms of Chapter 6 now come to our rescue by telling us how to do both of these things, for example by hashing. To record a memo that $f \wedge g = r$, we can hash the key '$(f, \wedge, g)$' and associate it with the value r; to record the existence of an existing node (V, LO, HI), we can hash the key '(V, LO, HI)' and associate it with that node's memory address.

The dictionary of all existing nodes (V, LO, HI) in a BDD base is traditionally called the *unique table*, because we use it to enforce the all-important uniqueness criterion that forbids duplication. Instead of putting all that information into one giant dictionary, however, it turns out to be better to maintain a collection of smaller unique tables, one for each variable V. With such separate tables we can efficiently find all nodes that branch on a particular variable.

The memos are handy, but they aren't as crucial as the unique table entries. If we happen to forget the isolated fact that $f \wedge g = r$, we can always recompute it again later. Exponential blowup won't be worrisome, if the answers to the subproblems $f_l \wedge g_l$ and $f_h \wedge g_h$ are still remembered with high probability. Therefore we can use a less expensive method to store memos, designed to do a pretty-good-but-not-perfect job of retrieval: After hashing the key '$(f, \wedge, g)$' to a table position p, we need look for a memo only in that one position, not bothering to consider collisions with other keys. If several keys all share the same hash address, position p will record only the most recent relevant memo. This simplified scheme will still be adequate in practice, as long as the hash table is large enough. We shall call such a near-perfect table the *memo cache*, because it is analogous to the hardware caches by which a computer tries to remember significant values that it has dealt with in relatively slow storage units.

Okay, let's flesh out algorithm (54) by explicitly stating how it interacts with the unique tables and the memo cache:

$$\text{AND}(f, g) = \begin{cases} \text{If } f \wedge g \text{ has an obvious value, return it.} \\ \text{Otherwise, if } f \wedge g = r \text{ is in the memo cache, return } r. \\ \text{Otherwise represent } f \text{ and } g \text{ as in (52);} \\ \text{compute } r_l \leftarrow \text{AND}(f_l, g_l) \text{ and } r_h \leftarrow \text{AND}(f_h, g_h); \\ \text{set } r \leftarrow \text{UNIQUE}(v, r_l, r_h), \text{ using Algorithm U;} \\ \text{put } `f \wedge g = r\text{' into the memo cache, and return } r. \end{cases} \quad (55)$$

Algorithm U (*Unique table lookup*). Given (v, p, q), where v is an integer while p and q point to nodes of a BDD base with variable rank $> v$, this algorithm returns a pointer to a node $\text{UNIQUE}(v, p, q)$ that represents the function $(\bar{x}_v? \; p\colon q)$. A new node is added to the base if that function wasn't already present.

U1. [Easy case?] If $p = q$, return p.

U2. [Check the table.] Search variable x_v's unique table using the key (p, q). If the search successfully finds the value r, return r.

U3. [Create a node.] Allocate a new node r, and set $\text{V}(r) \leftarrow v$, $\text{LO}(r) \leftarrow p$, $\text{HI}(r) \leftarrow q$. Put r into x_v's unique table using the key (p, q). Return r.   ∎

Notice that we needn't zero out the memo cache after finishing a top-level computation of $\text{AND}(f, g)$. Each memo that we have made states a relationship between nodes of the structure; those facts are still valid, and they might be useful later when we want to compute $\text{AND}(f, g)$ for new functions f and g.

A refinement of (55) will enhance that method further, namely to swap $f \leftrightarrow g$ if we discover that $f > g$ when $f \wedge g$ isn't obvious. Then we won't have to waste time computing $f \wedge g$ when we've already computed $g \wedge f$.

With simple changes to (55), the other binary operators $\text{OR}(f, g)$, $\text{XOR}(f, g)$, $\text{BUTNOT}(f, g)$, $\text{NOR}(f, g)$, ... can also be computed readily; see exercise 81.

The combination of (55) and Algorithm U looks considerably simpler than Algorithm S. Thus one might well ask, why should anybody bother to learn the other method? Its breadth-first approach seems quite complex by comparison with the "depth-first" order of computation in the recursive structure of (55); yet Algorithm S is able to deal only with BDDs that are disjoint, while Algorithm U and recursions like (55) apply to any BDD base.

Appearances can, however, be deceiving: Algorithm S has been described at a low level, with every change to every element of its data structures spelled out explicitly. By contrast, the high-level descriptions in (55) and Algorithm U assume that a substantial infrastructure exists behind the scenes. The memo cache and the unique tables need to be set up, and their sizes need to be carefully adjusted as the BDD base grows or contracts. When all is said and done, the total length of a program that implements Algorithms (55) and U properly "from scratch" is roughly ten times the length of a similar program for Algorithm S.

Indeed, the maintenance of a BDD base involves interesting questions of dynamic storage allocation, because we want to free up memory space when nodes are no longer accessible. Algorithm S solves this problem in a last-in-first-out manner, by simply keeping its nodes and templates on sequential stacks, and by making do with a single small hash table that can easily be integrated with the other data. A general BDD base, however, requires a more intricate system.

The best way to maintain a dynamic BDD base is probably to use *reference counters*, as discussed in Section 2.3.5, because BDDs are acyclic by definition. Therefore let's assume that every BDD node has a REF field, in addition to V, LO, and HI. The REF field tells us how many references exist to this node, either from LO or HI pointers in other nodes or from external root pointers F_j as in (36). For example, the REF fields for the nodes labeled ③ in (36) are respectively 4,

1, and 2; and all of the nodes labeled ② or ④ or ⑥ in that example have REF = 1. Exercise 82 discusses the somewhat tricky issue of how to increase and decrease REF counts properly in the midst of a recursive computation.

A node becomes *dead* when its reference count becomes zero. When that happens, we should decrease the REF fields of the two nodes below it; and then they too might die in the same manner, recursively spreading the plague.

But a dead node needn't be removed from memory immediately. It still represents a potentially useful Boolean function, and we might discover that we need that function again as our computation proceeds. For example, we might find a dead node in step U2, because pointers from the unique table don't get counted as references. Likewise, in (55), we might accidentally stumble across a cache memo telling us that $f \wedge g = r$, when r is currently dead. In such cases, node r comes back to life. (And we must increase the REF counts of its LO and HI descendants, possibly resurrecting them recursively in the same fashion.)

Periodically, however, we will want to reclaim memory space by removing the deadbeats. Then we must do two things: We must purge all memos from the cache for which either f, g, or r is dead; and we must remove all dead nodes from memory and from their unique tables. See exercise 84 for typical heuristic strategies by which an automated system might decide when to invoke such cleanups and when to resize the tables dynamically.

Because of the extra machinery that is needed to support a BDD base, Algorithm U and top-down recursions like (55) cannot be expected to match the efficiency of Algorithm S on one-shot examples such as the monotone-function function μ_n in (49). The running time is approximately quadrupled when the more general approach is applied to this example, and the memory requirement grows by a factor of about 2.4.

But a BDD base really begins to shine in numerous other applications. Suppose, for example, that we want the formulas for each bit of the product of two binary numbers,

$$(z_1 \ldots z_{m+n})_2 = (x_1 \ldots x_m)_2 \times (y_1 \ldots y_n)_2. \tag{56}$$

Clearly $z_1 \ldots z_m = 0 \ldots 0$ when $n = 0$, and the simple recurrence

$$(x_1 \ldots x_m)_2 \times (y_1 \ldots y_n y_{n+1})_2 = (z_1 \ldots z_{m+n}0)_2 + (x_1 \ldots x_m)_2 y_{n+1} \tag{57}$$

allows us to increase n by 1. This recurrence is easy to code for a BDD base. Here's what we get when $m = n = 3$, with subscripts chosen to match the analogous diagram for binary addition in (36):

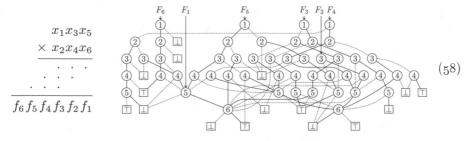

Clearly multiplication is much more complicated than addition, bitwise. (Indeed, if it weren't, factorization wouldn't be so hard.) The corresponding BDD base for binary multiplication when $m = n = 16$ is huge, with $B(f_1, \ldots, f_{32}) = 136{,}398{,}751$ nodes. It can be found after doing about 56 gigamems of calculation with Algorithm U, in 6.3 gigabytes of memory — including some 1.9 billion invocations of recursive subroutines, with hundreds of dynamic resizings of the unique tables and the memo cache, plus dozens of timely garbage collections. A similar calculation with Algorithm S would be almost unthinkable, although the individual functions in this particular example do not share many common subfunctions: It turns out that $B(f_1) + \cdots + B(f_{32}) = 168{,}640{,}131$, with the maximum occurring at the "middle bit," $B(f_{16}) = 38{,}174{,}143$.

*Ternary operations. Given three Boolean functions $f = f(x_1, \ldots, x_n)$, $g = g(x_1, \ldots, x_n)$, and $h = h(x_1, \ldots, x_n)$, not all constant, we can generalize (52) to

$$f = (\bar{x}_v?\ f_l\colon f_h) \quad \text{and} \quad g = (\bar{x}_v?\ g_l\colon g_h) \quad \text{and} \quad h = (\bar{x}_v?\ h_l\colon h_h), \tag{59}$$

by taking $v = \min(f_o, g_o, h_o)$. Then, for example, (53) generalizes to

$$\langle fgh \rangle = (\bar{x}_v?\ \langle f_l g_l h_l \rangle \colon \langle f_h g_h h_h \rangle); \tag{60}$$

and similar formulas hold for *any* ternary operation on f, g, and h, including

$$(\bar{f}?\ g\colon h) = (\bar{x}_v?\ (\bar{f}_l?\ g_l\colon h_l)\colon (\bar{f}_h?\ g_h\colon h_h)). \tag{61}$$

(The reader of these formulas will please forgive the two meanings of 'h' in 'h_h'.)

Now it's easy to generalize (55) to ternary combinations like multiplexing:

$$\text{MUX}(f, g, h) = \begin{cases} \text{If } (\bar{f}?\ g\colon h) \text{ has an obvious value, return it.} \\ \text{Otherwise, if } (\bar{f}?\ g\colon h) = r \text{ is in the memo cache, return } r. \\ \text{Otherwise represent } f,\ g, \text{ and } h \text{ as in (59);} \\ \text{compute } r_l \leftarrow \text{MUX}(f_l, g_l, h_l) \text{ and } r_h \leftarrow \text{MUX}(f_h, g_h, h_h); \\ \text{set } r \leftarrow \text{UNIQUE}(v, r_l, r_h), \text{ using Algorithm U;} \\ \text{put } '(\bar{f}?\ g\colon h) = r' \text{ into the memo cache, and return } r. \end{cases} \tag{62}$$

(See exercises 86 and 87.) The running time is $O\big(B(f)B(g)B(h)\big)$. The memo cache must now be consulted with a more complex key than before, including *three* pointers (f, g, h) instead of two, together with a code for the relevant operation. But each memo (op, f, g, h, r) can still be represented conveniently in, say, two octabytes, if the number of distinct pointer addresses is at most 2^{31}.

The ternary operation $f \wedge g \wedge h$ is an interesting special case. We could compute it with two invocations of (55), either as $\text{AND}(f, \text{AND}(g, h))$ or as $\text{AND}(g, \text{AND}(h, f))$ or as $\text{AND}(h, \text{AND}(f, g))$; or we could use a ternary subroutine, $\text{ANDAND}(f, g, h)$, analogous to (62). This ternary routine first sorts the operands so that the pointers satisfy $f \le g \le h$. Then if $f = 0$, it returns 0; if $f = 1$ or $f = g$, it returns $\text{AND}(g, h)$; if $g = h$ it returns $\text{AND}(f, g)$; otherwise $1 < f < g < h$ and the operation remains ternary at the current level of recursion. Suppose, for example, that $f = \mu_5(x_1, x_3, \ldots, x_{63})$, $g = \mu_5(x_2, x_4, \ldots, x_{64})$, and $h = G_{64}(x_1, \ldots, x_{64})$, as in Eq. (49). The computation $\text{AND}(f, \text{AND}(g, h))$

costs $0.2 + 6.8 = 7.0$ megamems in the author's experimental implementation; $\text{AND}(g, \text{AND}(h, f))$ costs $0.1 + 7.0 = 7.1$; $\text{AND}(h, \text{AND}(f, g))$ costs $24.4 + 5.6 = 30.0$ (!); and $\text{ANDAND}(f, g, h)$ costs 7.5. So in this instance the all-binary approach wins, if we don't choose a bad order of computation. But sometimes ternary ANDAND beats all three of its binary competitors (see exercise 88).

*Quantifiers. If $f = f(x_1, \ldots, x_n)$ is a Boolean function and $1 \le j \le n$, logicians traditionally define *existential and universal quantification* by the formulas

$$\exists x_j \, f(x_1, \ldots, x_n) = f_0 \lor f_1 \quad \text{and} \quad \forall x_j \, f(x_1, \ldots, x_n) = f_0 \land f_1, \quad (63)$$

where $f_c = f(x_1, \ldots, x_{j-1}, c, x_{j+1}, \ldots, x_n)$. Thus the quantifier '$\exists x_j$', pronounced "there exists x_j," changes f to the function of the remaining variables $(x_1, \ldots, x_{j-1}, x_{j+1}, \ldots, x_n)$ that is true if and only if at least one value of x_j satisfies $f(x_1, \ldots, x_n)$; the quantifier '$\forall x_j$', pronounced "for all x_j," changes f to the function that is true if and only if *both* values of x_j satisfy f.

Several quantifiers are often applied simultaneously. For example, the formula $\exists x_2 \exists x_3 \exists x_6 \, f(x_1, \ldots, x_n)$ stands for the OR of eight terms, representing the eight functions of $(x_1, x_4, x_5, x_7, \ldots, x_n)$ that are obtained when we plug the values 0 or 1 into the variables x_2, x_3, and x_6 in all possible ways. Similarly, $\forall x_2 \forall x_3 \forall x_6 \, f(x_1, \ldots, x_n)$ stands for the AND of those same eight terms.

One common application arises when the function $f(i_1, \ldots, i_l; j_1, \ldots, j_m)$ denotes the value in row $(i_1 \ldots i_l)_2$ and column $(j_1 \ldots j_m)_2$ of a $2^l \times 2^m$ Boolean matrix F. Then the function $h(i_1, \ldots, i_l; k_1, \ldots, k_n)$ given by

$$\exists j_1 \ldots \exists j_m \left(f(i_1, \ldots, i_l; j_1, \ldots, j_m) \land g(j_1, \ldots, j_m; k_1, \ldots, k_n) \right) \quad (64)$$

represents the matrix H that is the Boolean product $F \, G$.

A convenient way to implement multiple quantification in a BDD base has been suggested by R. L. Rudell: Let $g = x_{j_1} \land \cdots \land x_{j_m}$ be a conjunction of positive literals. Then we can regard $\exists x_{j_1} \ldots \exists x_{j_m} f$ as the binary operation $f \mathrel{E} g$, implemented by the following variant of (55):

$$\text{EXISTS}(f, g) = \begin{cases} \text{If } f \mathrel{E} g \text{ has an obvious value, return it.} \\ \text{Otherwise represent } f \text{ and } g \text{ as in (52);} \\ \text{if } v \ne f_o, \text{ return EXISTS}(f, g_h). \\ \text{Otherwise, if } f \mathrel{E} g = r \text{ is in the memo cache, return } r. \\ \text{Otherwise, } r_l \leftarrow \text{EXISTS}(f_l, g_h) \text{ and } r_h \leftarrow \text{EXISTS}(f_h, g_h); \\ \text{if } v \ne g_o, \text{ set } r \leftarrow \text{UNIQUE}(v, r_l, r_h) \text{ using Algorithm U,} \\ \text{otherwise compute } r \leftarrow \text{OR}(r_l, r_h); \\ \text{put '} f \mathrel{E} g = r \text{' into the memo cache, and return } r. \end{cases} \quad (65)$$

(See exercise 94.) The E operation is undefined when g does *not* have the stated form. Notice how the memo cache nicely remembers existential computations that have gone before.

The running time of (65) is highly variable — not like (55) where we know that $O(B(f)B(g))$ is the worst possible case — because m OR operations are invoked when g specifies m-fold quantification. The worst case now can be as bad as order $B(f)2^{2^m}$, if all of the quantification occurs near the root of the BDD for f; this is only $O(B(f)^2)$ if $m = 1$, but it might become unbearably large as m grows. On the other hand, if all of the quantification occurs near the sinks, the running time is simply $O(B(f))$, regardless of the size of m. (See exercise 97.)

Several other quantifiers are worthy of note, and equally easy, although they aren't as famous as $\exists$ and $\forall$. The *Boolean difference* and the *yes/no quantifiers* are defined by formulas analogous to (63):

$$\mathbb{C}x_j\, f = f_0 \oplus f_1; \qquad \mathsf{A}x_j\, f = \bar{f}_0 \wedge f_1; \qquad \mathsf{N}x_j\, f = f_0 \wedge \bar{f}_1. \qquad (66)$$

The Boolean difference, $\mathbb{C}$, is the most important of these: $\mathbb{C}x_j\, f$ is true for all values of $\{x_1, \ldots, x_{j-1}, x_{j+1}, \ldots, x_n\}$ such that f depends on x_j. If the multilinear representation of f is $f = (x_j g + h) \bmod 2$, where g and h are multilinear polynomials in $\{x_1, \ldots, x_{j-1}, x_{j+1}, \ldots, x_n\}$, then $\mathbb{C}x_j\, f = g \bmod 2$. (See Eq. 7.1.1–(19).) Thus $\mathbb{C}$ acts like a derivative in calculus, over a finite field.

A Boolean function $f(x_1, \ldots, x_n)$ is monotone (nondecreasing) if and only if $\bigvee_{j=1}^{n} \mathsf{N}x_j\, f = 0$, which is the same as saying that $\mathsf{N}x_j\, f = 0$ for all j. However, exercise 105 presents a faster way to test a BDD for monotonicity.

Let's consider now a detailed example of existential quantification that is particularly instructive. If G is any graph, we can form Boolean functions $\mathrm{IND}(x)$ and $\mathrm{KER}(x)$ for its independent sets and kernels as follows, where x is a bit vector with one entry x_v for each vertex v of G:

$$\mathrm{IND}(x) = \neg \bigvee_{u - v} (x_u \wedge x_v); \qquad (67)$$

$$\mathrm{KER}(x) = \mathrm{IND}(x) \wedge \bigwedge_v \Big(x_v \vee \bigvee_{u-v} x_u\Big). \qquad (68)$$

We can form a new graph $\mathcal{G}$ whose vertices are the kernels of G, namely the vectors x such that $\mathrm{KER}(x) = 1$. Let's say that two kernels x and y are *adjacent* in $\mathcal{G}$ if they differ in just the two entries for u and v, where $(x_u, x_v) = (1, 0)$ and $(y_u, y_v) = (0, 1)$, in which case we'll also have $u - v$. Kernels can be considered as certain ways to place markers on vertices of G; moving a marker from one vertex to a neighboring vertex produces an adjacent kernel. Formally we define

$$\mathrm{ADJ}(x, y) = [\nu(x \oplus y) = 2] \wedge \mathrm{KER}(x) \wedge \mathrm{KER}(y). \qquad (69)$$

Then $x - y$ in $\mathcal{G}$ if and only if $\mathrm{ADJ}(x, y) = 1$.

Notice that, if $x = x_1 \ldots x_n$, the function $[\nu(x) = 2]$ is the symmetric function $S_2(x_1, \ldots, x_n)$. Furthermore $f(x \oplus y)$ has at most 3 times as many nodes as $f(x)$, if we interleave the variables zipperwise so that the branching order is $(x_1, y_1, \ldots, x_n, y_n)$. So $B(\mathrm{ADJ})$ won't be extremely large unless $B(\mathrm{KER})$ is large.

Quantification now makes it easy to express the condition that x is an *isolated vertex* of $\mathcal{G}$ (a vertex of degree 0, a kernel without neighbors):

$$\mathrm{ISO}(x) = \mathrm{KER}(x) \wedge \neg \exists y\, \mathrm{ADJ}(x, y). \qquad (70)$$

For example, suppose G is the graph of contiguous states in the USA, as in (18). Then each kernel vector x has 49 entries x_v for $v \in \{\mathrm{ME}, \mathrm{NH}, \ldots, \mathrm{CA}\}$.

The graph $\mathcal{G}$ has 266,137 vertices, and we have observed earlier that the BDD sizes for $\mathrm{IND}(x)$ and $\mathrm{KER}(x)$ are respectively 428 and 780 (see (17)). In this case $\mathrm{ADJ}(x, y)$ in (69) has a BDD of only 7260 nodes, even though it's a function of 98 Boolean variables. The BDD for $\exists y\, \mathrm{ADJ}(x, y)$, which describes all kernels x of G that have at least one neighbor, turns out to have 842 nodes; and the one for $\mathrm{ISO}(x)$ has only 77. We find that G has exactly three isolated kernels, namely

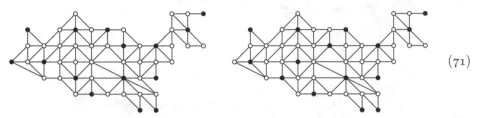

$$(71)$$

and another that is a blend of these two. Using the algorithms above, this entire calculation, starting from a list of the vertices and edges of G (not $\mathcal{G}$), can be carried out with a total cost of about 4 megamems, in about 1.6 megabytes of memory; that's only about 15 memory accesses per kernel of G.

In a similar fashion we can use BDDs to work with other "implicit graphs," which have more vertices than could possibly be represented in memory, if those vertices can be characterized as the solution vectors of Boolean functions. When the functions aren't too complicated, we can answer queries about those graphs that could never be answered by representing the vertices and arcs explicitly.

*Functional composition. The *pièce de résistance* of recursive BDD algorithms is a general procedure to compute $f(g_1, g_2, \ldots, g_n)$, where f is a given function of $\{x_1, x_2, \ldots, x_n\}$ and so is each argument g_j. Suppose we know a number $m \geq 0$ such that $g_j = x_j$ for $m < j \leq n$; then the procedure can be expressed as follows:

$$\mathrm{COMPOSE}(f, g_1, \ldots, g_n) = \begin{cases} \text{If } f = 0 \text{ or } f = 1, \text{ return } f. \\ \text{Otherwise suppose } f = (\bar{x}_v?\ f_l\text{: } f_h), \text{ as in } (50); \\ \text{if } v > m, \text{ return } f; \text{ otherwise, if } f(g_1, \ldots, g_n) = r \\ \quad \text{is in the memo cache, return } r. \\ \text{Compute } r_l \leftarrow \mathrm{COMPOSE}(f_l, g_1, \ldots, g_n) \\ \quad \text{and } r_h \leftarrow \mathrm{COMPOSE}(f_h, g_1, \ldots, g_n); \\ \text{set } r \leftarrow \mathrm{MUX}(g_v, r_l, r_h) \text{ using } (62); \\ \text{put '}f(g_1, \ldots, g_n) = r\text{' into the cache, and return } r. \end{cases} \quad (72)$$

The representation of cache memos like '$f(g_1, \ldots, g_n) = r$' in this algorithm is a bit tricky; we will discuss it momentarily.

Although the computations here look basically the same as those we've been seeing in previous recursions, there is in fact a huge difference: The functions r_l and r_h in (72) can now involve *all* variables $\{x_1, \ldots, x_n\}$, not just the x's near the bottom of the BDDs. So the running time of (72) might actually be huge. But there also are many cases when everything works together harmoniously and efficiently. For example, the computation of $[\nu(x \oplus y) = 2]$ in (69) is no problem.

The key of a memo like '$f(g_1, \ldots, g_n) = r$' should not be a completely detailed specification of $(f, g_1, \ldots, g_n)$, because we want to hash it efficiently. Therefore we store only '$f[G] = r$', where G is an identification number for the sequence of functions $(g_1, \ldots, g_n)$. Whenever that sequence changes, we can use a new number G; and we can remember the G's for special sequences of functions that occur repeatedly in a particular computation, as long as the individual functions g_j don't die. (See also the alternative scheme in exercise 102.)

Let's return to the graph of contiguous states for one more example. That graph is planar; suppose we want to color it with four colors. Since the colors can be given 2-bit codes $\{00, 01, 10, 11\}$, it's easy to express the valid colorings as a Boolean function of 98 variables that is true if and only if the color codes ab are different for each pair of adjacent states:

$$\mathrm{COLOR}(a_{\mathrm{ME}}, b_{\mathrm{ME}}, \ldots, a_{\mathrm{CA}}, b_{\mathrm{CA}}) =$$
$$\mathrm{IND}(a_{\mathrm{ME}} \wedge b_{\mathrm{ME}}, \ldots, a_{\mathrm{CA}} \wedge b_{\mathrm{CA}}) \wedge \mathrm{IND}(a_{\mathrm{ME}} \wedge \bar{b}_{\mathrm{ME}}, \ldots, a_{\mathrm{CA}} \wedge \bar{b}_{\mathrm{CA}}) \qquad (73)$$
$$\wedge \mathrm{IND}(\bar{a}_{\mathrm{ME}} \wedge b_{\mathrm{ME}}, \ldots, \bar{a}_{\mathrm{CA}} \wedge b_{\mathrm{CA}}) \wedge \mathrm{IND}(\bar{a}_{\mathrm{ME}} \wedge \bar{b}_{\mathrm{ME}}, \ldots, \bar{a}_{\mathrm{CA}} \wedge \bar{b}_{\mathrm{CA}}).$$

Each of the four INDs has a BDD of 854 nodes, which can be computed via (72) with a cost of about 70 kilomems. The COLOR function turns out to have only 25579 BDD nodes. Algorithm C now quickly establishes that the total number of ways to 4-color this graph is exactly 25,623,183,458,304 — or, if we divide by 4! to remove symmetries, about 1.1 trillion. The total time needed for this computation, starting from a description of the graph, is less than 3.5 megamems, in 2.2 megabytes of memory. (We can also find *random* 4-colorings, etc.)

Nasty functions. Of course there also are functions of 98 variables that aren't nearly so nice as COLOR. Indeed, the total number of 98-variable functions is $2^{2^{98}}$; exercise 108 proves that at most $2^{2^{46}}$ of them have a BDD size less than a trillion, and that almost all Boolean functions of 98 variables actually have $B(f) \approx 2^{98}/98 \approx 3.2 \times 10^{27}$. There's just no way to compress 2^{98} bits of data into a small space, unless that data happens to be highly redundant.

What's the worst case? If f is a Boolean function of n variables, how large can $B(f)$ be? The answer isn't hard to discover, if we consider the *profile* of a given BDD, which is the sequence $(b_0, \ldots, b_{n-1}, b_n)$ when there are b_k nodes that branch on variable x_{k+1} and b_n sinks. Clearly

$$B(f) = b_0 + \cdots + b_{n-1} + b_n. \qquad (74)$$

We also have $b_0 \leq 1$, $b_1 \leq 2$, $b_2 \leq 4$, $b_3 \leq 8$, and in general

$$b_k \leq 2^k, \qquad (75)$$

because each node has only two branches. Furthermore $b_n = 2$ whenever f isn't constant; and $b_{n-1} \leq 2$, because there are only two legal choices for the LO and HI branches of (n). Indeed, we know that b_k is the number of *beads* of order $n - k$ in the truth table for f, namely the number of distinct subfunctions of $(x_{k+1}, \ldots, x_n)$ that depend on x_{k+1} after the values of $(x_1, \ldots, x_k)$ have been specified. Only $2^{2^m} - 2^{2^{m-1}}$ beads of order m are possible, so we must have

$$b_k \leq 2^{2^{n-k}} - 2^{2^{n-k-1}}, \qquad \text{for } 0 \leq k < n. \qquad (76)$$

When $n = 11$, for instance, (75) and (76) tell us that $(b_0, \ldots, b_{11})$ is at most

$$(1, 2, 4, 8, 16, 32, 64, 128, 240, 12, 2, 2). \tag{77}$$

Thus $B(f) \leq 1 + 2 + \cdots + 128 + 240 + \cdots + 2 = 255 + 256 = 511$ when $n = 11$. This upper bound is in fact obtained with the truth table

$$00000000 \ 00000001 \ 00000010 \ \ldots \ 11111110 \ 11111111, \tag{78}$$

or with any string of length 2^{11} that is a permutation of the 256 possible 8-bit bytes, because all of the 8-bit beads are clearly present, and because all of the subtables of lengths 16, 32, $\ldots$, 2^{11} are clearly beads. Similar examples can be constructed for all n (see exercise 110). Therefore the worst case is known:

Theorem U. *Every Boolean function $f(x_1, \ldots, x_n)$ has $B(f) \leq U_n$, where*

$$U_n = 2 + \sum_{k=0}^{n-1} \min(2^k, 2^{2^{n-k}} - 2^{2^{n-k-1}}) = 2^{n-\lambda(n-\lambda n)} + 2^{2^{\lambda(n-\lambda n)}} - 1. \tag{79}$$

Furthermore, explicit functions f_n with $B(f_n) = U_n$ exist for all n. ∎

If we replace λ by lg, the right-hand side of (79) becomes $2^n/(n - \lg n) + 2^n/n - 1$. In general, U_n is u_n times $2^n/n$, where the factor u_n lies between 1 and $2 + O(\frac{\log n}{n})$. A BDD with about $2^{n+1}/n$ nodes needs about $n + 1 - \lg n$ bits for each of two pointers in every node, plus $\lg n$ bits to indicate the variable for branching. So the total amount of memory space taken up by the BDD for any function $f(x_1, \ldots, x_n)$ is never more than about 2^{n+2} bits, which is four times the number of bits in its truth table, even if f happens to be one of the worst possible functions from the standpoint of BDD representation.

The average case turns out to be almost the same as the worst case, if we choose the truth table for f at random from among all 2^{2^n} possibilities. Again the calculations are straightforward: The average number of (k+1) nodes is exactly

$$\hat{b}_k = \left(2^{2^{n-k}} - 2^{2^{n-k-1}}\right)\left(2^{2^n} - \left(2^{2^{n-k}} - 1\right)^{2^k}\right)/2^{2^n}, \tag{80}$$

because there are $2^{2^{n-k}} - 2^{2^{n-k-1}}$ beads of order $n - k$ and $\left(2^{2^{n-k}} - 1\right)^{2^k}$ truth tables in which any particular bead does not occur. Exercise 112 shows that this complicated-looking quantity $\hat{b}_k$ always lies extremely close to the worst-case estimate $\min(2^k, 2^{2^{n-k}} - 2^{2^{n-k-1}})$, except for two values of k. The exceptional levels occur when $k \approx 2^{n-k}$ and the "min" has little effect. For example, the average profile $(\hat{b}_0, \ldots, \hat{b}_{n-1}, \hat{b}_n)$ when $n = 11$ is approximately

$$(1.0, 2.0, 4.0, 8.0, 16.0, 32.0, 64.0, 127.4, 151.9, 12.0, 2.0, 2.0) \tag{81}$$

when rounded to one decimal place, and these values are virtually indistinguishable from the worst case (77) except when $k = 7$ or 8.

A related concept called a *quasi-BDD*, or "QDD," is also important. Every function has a unique QDD, which is similar to its BDD except that the root node is always (1), and every (k) node for $k < n$ branches to two (k+1) nodes; thus every path from the root to a sink has length n. To make this possible, we allow the LO and HI pointers of a QDD node to be identical. But the QDD must still be reduced, in the sense that different nodes cannot have the same two pointers (LO, HI). For example, the QDD for $\langle x_1 x_2 x_3 \rangle$ is

$$(82)$$

it has two more nodes than the corresponding BDD in Fig. 21. Notice that the V fields are redundant in a QDD, so they needn't be present in memory.

The *quasi-profile* of a function is $(q_0, \ldots, q_{n-1}, q_n)$, where q_{k-1} is the number of (k) nodes in the QDD. It's easy to see that q_k is also the number of distinct *subtables* of order $n - k$ in the truth table, just as b_k is the number of distinct beads. Every bead is a subtable, so we have

$$q_k \geq b_k, \qquad \text{for } 0 \leq k \leq n. \tag{83}$$

Furthermore, exercise 115 proves that

$$q_k \leq 1 + b_0 + \cdots + b_{k-1} \text{ and } q_k \leq b_k + \cdots + b_n, \quad \text{for } 0 \leq k \leq n. \tag{84}$$

Consequently each element of the quasi-profile is a lower bound on the BDD size:

$$B(f) \geq 2q_k - 1, \qquad \text{for } 0 \leq k \leq n. \tag{85}$$

Let $Q(f) = q_0 + \cdots + q_{n-1} + q_n$ be the total size of the QDD for f. We obviously have $Q(f) \geq B(f)$, by (83). On the other hand $Q(f)$ can't be too much bigger than $B(f)$, because (85) implies that

$$Q(f) \leq \frac{n+1}{2}(B(f) + 1). \tag{86}$$

Exercises 116 and 117 explore other basic properties of quasi-profiles.

The worst-case truth table (78) actually corresponds to a familiar function that we've already seen, the 8-way multiplexer

$$M_3(x_9, x_{10}, x_{11}; x_1, \ldots, x_8) = x_{1+(x_9 x_{10} x_{11})_2}. \tag{87}$$

But we've renumbered the variables perversely so that the multiplexing now occurs with respect to the *last* three variables (x_9, x_{10}, x_{11}), instead of the first three as in Eq. (30). This simple change to the ordering of the variables raises the BDD size of M_3 from 17 to 511; and an analogous change when $n = 2^m + m$ would cause $B(M_m)$ to make a colossal leap from $2n - 2m + 1$ to $2^{n-m+1} - 1$.

R. E. Bryant has introduced an interesting "navel-gazing" multiplexer called the *hidden weighted bit function*, defined as follows:

$$h_n(x_1, \ldots, x_n) = x_{x_1 + \cdots + x_n} = x_{\nu x}, \tag{88}$$

with the understanding that $x_0 = 0$. For example, $h_4(x_1, x_2, x_3, x_4)$ has the truth table 0000 0111 1001 1011. He proved [*IEEE Trans.* **C-40** (1991), 208–210] that h_n has a large BDD, regardless of how we might try to renumber its variables.

With the standard ordering of variables, the profile $(b_0, \ldots, b_{11})$ of h_{11} is

$$(1, 2, 4, 8, 15, 27, 46, 40, 18, 7, 2, 2); \tag{89}$$

hence $B(h_{11}) = 172$. The first half of this profile is actually the Fibonacci sequence in slight disguise, with $b_k = F_{k+4} - k - 2$. In general, h_n always has this value of b_k for $k < n/2$; thus its initial profile counts grow with order ϕ^k instead of the worst-case rate of 2^k. This growth rate slackens after k surpasses $n/2$, so that, for example, $B(h_{32})$ is only a modest 86,636. But exponential growth eventually takes over, and $B(h_{100})$ is out of sight: 17,530,618,296,680. (When $n = 100$, the maximum profile element is $b_{59} = 2,947,635,944,748$, which dwarfs $b_0 + \cdots + b_{49} = 139,583,861,115$.) Exercise 125 proves that $B(h_n)$ is asymptotically $c\rho^n + O(n^2)$, where

$$\rho = \frac{\sqrt[3]{27 - \sqrt{621}} + \sqrt[3]{27 + \sqrt{621}}}{\sqrt[3]{54}}$$

$$= 1.32471\ 79572\ 44746\ 02596\ 09088\ 54478\ 09734\ 07344+ \tag{90}$$

is the so-called "plastic constant," the positive root of $\rho^3 = \rho + 1$, and the coefficient c is $7\rho - 1 + 14/(3 + 2\rho) \approx 10.75115$.

On the other hand we can do substantially better if we change the order in which the variables are tested in the BDD. If $f(x_1, \ldots, x_n)$ is any Boolean function and if π is any permutation of $\{1, \ldots, n\}$, let us write

$$f^\pi(x_1, \ldots, x_n) = f(x_{1\pi}, \ldots, x_{n\pi}). \tag{91}$$

For example, if $f(x_1, x_2, x_3, x_4) = (x_3 \vee (x_1 \wedge x_4)) \wedge (\bar{x}_2 \vee \bar{x}_4)$ and if $(1\pi, 2\pi, 3\pi, 4\pi) = (3, 2, 4, 1)$, then $f^\pi(x_1, x_2, x_3, x_4) = (x_4 \vee (x_3 \wedge x_1)) \wedge (\bar{x}_2 \vee \bar{x}_1)$; and we have $B(f) = 10$, $B(f^\pi) = 6$ because the BDDs are

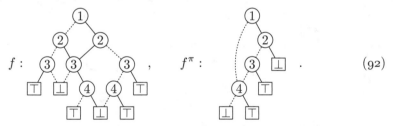

$$\tag{92}$$

The BDD for f^π corresponds to a BDD for f that has a nonstandard ordering, in which a branch is permitted from $\textcircled{i}$ to $\textcircled{j}$ only if $i\pi < j\pi$:

$$\tag{93}$$

The root is $\textcircled{i}$, where $i = 1\pi^-$ is the index for which $i\pi = 1$. When the branch variables are listed from the top down, we have $(4\pi, 2\pi, 1\pi, 3\pi) = (1, 2, 3, 4)$.

Applying these ideas to the hidden weighted bit function, we have

$$h_n^\pi(x_1, \ldots, x_n) = x_{(x_1 + \cdots + x_n)\pi}, \tag{94}$$

with the understanding that $0\pi = 0$ and $x_0 = 0$. For example, $h_3^\pi(0, 0, 1) = 1$ if $(1\pi, 2\pi, 3\pi) = (3, 1, 2)$, because $x_{(x_1 + x_2 + x_3)\pi} = x_3 = 1$. (See exercise 120.)

Element q_k of the quasi-profile counts the number of distinct subfunctions that arise when the values of x_1 through x_k are known. Using (94), we can represent all such subfunctions by means of a *slate of options* $[r_0, \ldots, r_{n-k}]$, where r_j is the result of the subfunction when $x_{k+1} + \cdots + x_n = j$. Suppose $x_1 = c_1, \ldots, x_k = c_k$, and let $s = c_1 + \cdots + c_k$. Then $r_j = c_{(s+j)\pi}$ if $(s+j)\pi \le k$; otherwise $r_j = x_{(s+j)\pi}$. However, we set $r_0 \leftarrow 0$ if $s\pi > k$, and $r_{n-k} \leftarrow 1$ if $(s + n - k)\pi > k$, so that the first and last options of every slate are constant.

For example, calculations show that the following permutation $1\pi \ldots 100\pi$ reduces the BDD size of h_{100} from 17.5 trillion to $B(h_{100}^\pi) = 1{,}124{,}432{,}105$:

```
 2   4   6   8  10  12  14  16  18  20  97  57  77  37  87  47  67  27  92  52
72  32  82  42  62  22 100  60  80  40  90  50  70  30  95  55  75  35  85  45
65  25  98  58  78  38  88  48  68  28  93  53  73  33  83  43  63  23  99  59   (95)
79  39  89  49  69  29  94  54  74  34  84  44  64  24  96  56  76  36  86  46
66  26  91  51  71  31  81  41  61  21  19  17  15  13  11   9   7   5   3   1
```

Such calculations can be based on an enumeration of all slates that can arise, for $0 \le s \le k \le n$. Suppose we've tested $x_1, \ldots, x_{83}$ and found that $x_j = [j \le 42]$, say, for $1 \le j \le 83$. Then $s = 42$; and the subfunction of the remaining 17 variables $(x_{84}, \ldots, x_{100})$ is given by the slate $[r_0, \ldots, r_{17}] = [c_{25}, x_{98}, c_{58}, c_{78}, c_{38}, x_{88}, c_{48}, c_{68}, c_{28}, x_{93}, c_{53}, c_{73}, c_{33}, c_{83}, c_{43}, c_{63}, c_{23}, x_{99}]$, which reduces to

$$[1, x_{98}, 0, 0, 1, x_{88}, 0, 0, 1, x_{93}, 0, 0, 1, 0, 0, 0, 1, 1]. \tag{96}$$

This is one of the 2^{14} subfunctions counted by q_{83} when $s = 42$. Exercise 124 explains how to deal similarly with the other values of k and s.

We're ready now to prove Bryant's theorem:

Theorem B. *The BDD size of h_n^π exceeds $2^{\lfloor n/5 \rfloor}$, for all permutations π.*

Proof. Observe first that two subfunctions of h_n^π are equal if and only if they have the same slate. For if $[r_0, \ldots, r_{n-k}] \ne [r_0', \ldots, r_{n-k}']$, suppose $r_j \ne r_j'$. If both r_j and r_j' are constant, the subfunctions differ when $x_{k+1} + \cdots + x_n = j$. If r_j is constant but $r_j' = x_i$, we have $0 < j < n - k$; the subfunctions differ because $x_{k+1} + \cdots + x_n$ can equal j with $x_i \ne r_j$. And if $r_j = x_i$ but $r_j' = x_{i'}$ with $i \ne i'$, we can have $x_{k+1} + \cdots + x_n = j$ with $x_i \ne x_{i'}$. (The latter case can arise only when the slates correspond to different offsets s and s'.)

Therefore q_k is the number of different slates $[r_0, \ldots, r_{n-k}]$. Exercise 123 proves that this number, for any given k, n, and s as described above, is exactly

$$\binom{w}{w-s} + \binom{w}{w-s+1} + \cdots + \binom{w}{k-s} = \binom{w}{s+w-k} + \cdots + \binom{w}{s-1} + \binom{w}{s}, \tag{97}$$

where w is the number of indices j such that $s \le j \le s + n - k$ and $j\pi \le k$.

Now consider the case $k = \lfloor 3n/5 \rfloor + 1$, and let $s = k - \lceil n/2 \rceil$, $s' = \lfloor n/2 \rfloor + 1$. (Think of $n = 100$, $k = 61$, $s = 11$, $s' = 51$. We may assume that $n \ge 10$.) Then

$w + w' = k - w''$, where w'' counts the indices with $j\pi \leq k$ and either $j < s$ or $j > s' + n - k$. Since $w'' \leq (s-1) + (k - s') = 2k - 2 - n$, we must have $w + w' \geq n + 2 - k = \lceil 2n/5 \rceil + 1$. Hence either $w > \lfloor n/5 \rfloor$ or $w' > \lfloor n/5 \rfloor$; and in both cases (97) exceeds $2^{\lfloor n/5 \rfloor - 1}$. The theorem follows from (85). ∎

Conversely, there's always a permutation π such that $B(h_n^\pi) = O(2^{0.2029n})$, although the constant hidden by O-notation is quite large. This result was proved by B. Bollig, M. Löbbing, M. Sauerhoff, and I. Wegener, *Theoretical Informatics and Applications* **33** (1999), 103–115, using a permutation like (95): The first indices, with $j\pi \leq n/5$, come alternately from $j > 9n/10$ and $j \leq n/10$; the others are ordered by reading the binary representation of $9n/10 - j$ from right to left (*colex order*).

Let's also look briefly at a much simpler example, the *permutation function* $P_m(x_1, \ldots, x_{m^2})$, which equals 1 if and only if the binary matrix with $x_{(i-1)m+j}$ in row i and column j is a permutation matrix:

$$P_m(x_1, \ldots, x_{m^2}) = \bigwedge_{i=1}^{m} S_1(x_{(i-1)m+1}, x_{(i-1)m+2}, \ldots, x_{(i-1)m+m})$$

$$\wedge \bigwedge_{j=1}^{m} S_1(x_j, x_{m+j}, \ldots, x_{m^2-m+j}). \quad (98)$$

In spite of its simplicity, this function cannot be represented with a small BDD, under any reordering of its variables:

Theorem K. *The BDD size of P_m^π exceeds $m2^{m-1}$, for all permutations π.*

Proof. [See I. Wegener, *Branching Programs and Binary Decision Diagrams* (SIAM, 2000), Theorem 4.12.3.] Given the BDD for P_m^π, notice that each of the $m!$ vectors x such that $P_m^\pi(x) = 1$ traces a path of length $n = m^2$ from the root to $\boxed{\top}$; every variable must be tested. Let $v_k(x)$ be the node from which the path for x takes its kth HI branch. This node branches on the value in row i and column j of the given matrix, for some pair $(i, j) = (i_k(x), j_k(x))$.

Suppose $v_k(x) = v_{k'}(x')$, where $x \neq x'$. Construct x'' by letting it agree with x up to $v_k(x)$ and with x' thereafter. Then $P_m^\pi(x'') = 1$; consequently we must have $k = k'$. In fact, this argument shows that we must also have

$$\{i_1(x), i_2(x), \ldots, i_{k-1}(x)\} = \{i_1(x'), i_2(x'), \ldots, i_{k-1}(x')\}$$

$$\text{and } \{j_1(x), j_2(x), \ldots, j_{k-1}(x)\} = \{j_1(x'), j_2(x'), \ldots, j_{k-1}(x')\}. \quad (99)$$

Imagine m colors of tickets, with $m!$ tickets of each color. Place a ticket of color k on node $v_k(x)$, for all k and all x. Then no node gets tickets of different colors; and no node of color k gets more than $(k-1)!(m-k)!$ tickets altogether, by Eq. (99). Therefore at least $m!/((k-1)!(m-k)!) = k\binom{m}{k}$ different nodes must receive tickets of color k. Summing over k gives $m2^{m-1}$ non-sink nodes. ∎

Exercise 184 shows that $B(P_m)$ is less than $m2^{m+1}$, so the lower bound in Theorem K is nearly optimum except for a factor of 4. Although the size grows exponentially, the behavior isn't hopelessly bad, because $m = \sqrt{n}$. For example, $B(P_{20})$ is only 38,797,317, even though P_{20} is a Boolean function of 400 variables.

*Optimizing the order. Let $B_{\min}(f)$ and $B_{\max}(f)$ denote the smallest and largest values of $B(f^\pi)$, taken over all permutations π that can prescribe an ordering of the variables. We've seen several cases where $B_{\min}$ and $B_{\max}$ are dramatically different; for example, the 2^m-way multiplexer has $B_{\min}(M_m) \approx 2n$ and $B_{\max}(M_m) \approx 2^n/n$, when $n = 2^m + m$. And indeed, simple functions for which a good ordering is crucial are not at all unusual. Consider, for instance,

$$f(x_1, x_2, \ldots, x_n) = (\bar{x}_1 \vee x_2) \wedge (\bar{x}_3 \vee x_4) \wedge \cdots \wedge (\bar{x}_{n-1} \vee x_n), \quad n \text{ even}; \quad (100)$$

this is the important *subset function* $[x_1 x_3 \ldots x_{n-1} \subseteq x_2 x_4 \ldots x_n]$, and we have $B(f) = B_{\min}(f) = n + 2$. But the BDD size explodes to $B(f^\pi) = B_{\max}(f) = 2^{n/2+1}$ when π is "organ-pipe order," namely the ordering for which

$$f^\pi(x_1, x_2, \ldots, x_n) = (\bar{x}_1 \vee x_n) \wedge (\bar{x}_2 \vee x_{n-1}) \wedge \cdots \wedge (\bar{x}_{n/2} \vee x_{n/2+1}). \quad (101)$$

And the same bad behavior occurs for the ordering $[x_1 \ldots x_{n/2} \subseteq x_{n/2+1} \ldots x_n]$. In these orderings the BDD must "remember" the states of $n/2$ variables, while the original formulation (100) needs very little memory.

Every Boolean function f has a *master profile chart*, which encapsulates the set of all its possible sizes $B(f^\pi)$. If f has n variables, this chart has 2^n vertices, one for each subset of the variables; and it has $n2^{n-1}$ edges, one for each pair of subsets that differ in just one element. For example, the master profile chart for the function in (92) and (93) is

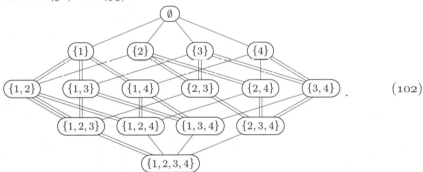

$$(102)$$

Every edge has a weight, illustrated here by the number of lines; for example, the weight between $\{1,2\}$ and $\{1,2,3\}$ is 3. The chart has the following interpretation: *If X is a subset of k variables, and if $x \notin X$, then the weight between X and $X \cup x$ is the number of subfunctions of f that depend on x when the variables of X have been replaced by constants in all 2^k possible ways.* For example, if $X = \{1, 2\}$, we have $f(0, 0, x_3, x_4) = x_3$, $f(0, 1, x_3, x_4) = f(1, 1, x_3, x_4) = x_3 \wedge \bar{x}_4$, and $f(1, 0, x_3, x_4) = x_3 \vee x_4$; all three of these subfunctions depend on x_3, but only two of them depend on x_4, as shown in the weights below $\{1, 2\}$.

There are $n!$ paths of length n from $\emptyset$ to $\{1, \ldots, n\}$, and we can let the path $\emptyset \to \{a_1\} \to \{a_1, a_2\} \to \cdots \to \{a_1, \ldots, a_n\}$ correspond to the permutation π if $a_1\pi = 1$, $a_2\pi = 2$, $\ldots$, $a_n\pi = n$. Then the sum of the weights on path π is $B(f^\pi)$, if we add 2 for the sink nodes. For example, the path $\emptyset \to \{4\} \to \{2, 4\} \to \{1, 2, 4\} \to \{1, 2, 3, 4\}$ yields the only way to achieve $B(f^\pi) = 6$ as in (93).

Notice that the master profile chart is a familiar graph, the n-cube, whose edges have been decorated so that they count the number of beads in various sets of subfunctions. The graph has exponential size, $n2^{n-1}$; yet it is much smaller than the total number of permutations, $n!$. When n is, say, 25 or less, exercise 138 shows that the entire chart can be computed without great difficulty, and we can find an optimum permutation for any given function. For example, the hidden weighted bit function turns out to have $B_{\min}(h_{25}) = 2090$ and $B_{\max}(h_{25}) = 35441$; the minimum is achieved with $(1\pi, \ldots, 25\pi) = (3, 5, 7, 9, 11, 13, 15, 17, 25, 24, 23, 22, 21, 20, 19, 18, 16, 14, 12, 10, 8, 6, 4, 2, 1)$, while the maximum results from a strange permutation $(22, 19, 17, 25, 15, 13, 11, 10, 9, 8, 7, 24, 6, 5, 4, 3, 2, 12, 1, 14, 23, 16, 18, 20, 21)$ that tests many "middle" variables first.

Instead of computing the entire master profile chart, we can sometimes save time by learning just enough about it to determine a path of least weight. (See exercise 140.) But when n grows and functions get more weird, we are unlikely to be able to determine $B_{\min}(f)$ exactly, because the problem of finding the best ordering is NP-complete (see exercise 137).

We've defined the profile and quasi-profile of a single Boolean function f, but the same ideas apply also to an arbitrary BDD base that contains m functions $\{f_1, \ldots, f_m\}$. Namely, the profile is $(b_0, \ldots, b_n)$ when there are b_k nodes on level k, and the quasi-profile is $(q_0, \ldots, q_n)$ when there are q_k nodes on level k of the corresponding QDD base; the truth tables of the functions have b_k different beads of order $n - k$, and q_k different subtables. For example, the profile of the $(4+4)$-bit addition functions $\{f_1, f_2, f_3, f_4, f_5\}$ in (36) is $(2, 4, 3, 6, 3, 6, 3, 2, 2)$, and the quasi-profile is worked out in exercise 144. Similarly, the concept of master profile chart applies to m functions whose variables are reordered simultaneously; and we can use it to find $B_{\min}(f_1, \ldots, f_m)$ and $B_{\max}(f_1, \ldots, f_m)$, the minimum and maximum of $b_0 + \cdots + b_n$ taken over all profiles.

*Local reordering. What happens to a BDD base when we decide to branch on x_2 first, then on x_1, x_3, $\ldots$, x_n? Figure 26 shows that the structure of the top two levels can change dramatically, but all other levels remain the same.

A closer analysis reveals, in fact, that this level-swapping process isn't difficult to understand or to implement. The ① nodes before swapping can be divided into two kinds, "tangled" and "solitary," depending on whether they have ② nodes as descendants; for example, there are three tangled nodes at the left of Fig. 26, pointed to by s_1, s_2, and s_3, while s_4 points to a solitary node. Similarly, the ② nodes before swapping are either "visible" or "hidden," depending on whether they are independent source functions or accessible only from ① nodes; all four of the ② nodes at the left of Fig. 26 are hidden.

After swapping, the solitary ① nodes simply move down one level; but the tangled nodes are transmogrified into ② s, according to a process that we shall explain shortly. The hidden ② nodes disappear, if any, and the visible ones simply move up to the top level. Additional nodes might also arise during the transmogrification process; such nodes, labeled ① , are called "newbies." For example, two newbies appear above t_2 at the right of Fig. 26. This process decreases the total number of nodes if and only if the hidden nodes outnumber the newbies.

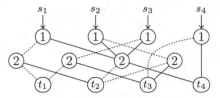 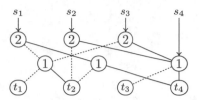

Fig. 26. Interchanging the top two levels of a BDD base. Here (s_1, s_2, s_3, s_4) are source functions; (t_1, t_2, t_3, t_4) are target nodes, representing subfunctions at lower levels.

The reverse of a swap is, of course, the same as a swap, but with the roles of ① and ② interchanged. If we begin with the diagram at the right of Fig. 26, we see that it has three tangled nodes (labeled ②) and one that's visible (labeled ①); two of its nodes are hidden, none are solitary. The swapping process in general sends (tangled, solitary, visible, hidden) nodes into (tangled, visible, solitary, newbie) nodes, respectively — after which newbies would become hidden in a reverse swap, and the originally hidden nodes would reappear as newbies.

Transmogrification is easiest to understand if we treat all nodes below the top two levels as if they were sinks, having constant values. Then every source function $f(x_1, x_2)$ depends only on x_1 and x_2; hence it takes on four values $a = f(0,0)$, $b = f(0,1)$, $c = f(1,0)$, and $d = f(1,1)$, where a, b, c, and d represent sinks. We may suppose that there are q sinks, $\boxed{1}$, $\boxed{2}$, ..., $\boxed{q}$, and that $1 \le a, b, c, d \le q$. Then $f(x_1, x_2)$ is fully described by its *extended truth table*, $f(0,0)f(0,1)f(1,0)f(1,1) = abcd$. And after swapping, we're left with $f(x_2, x_1)$, which has the extended truth table $acbd$. For example, Fig. 26 can be redrawn as follows, using extended truth tables to label its nodes:

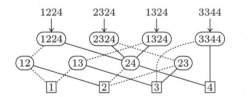 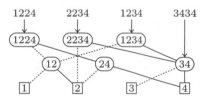

Fig. 27. Another way to represent the transformations in Fig. 26.

In these terms, the source function $abcd$ points to a solitary node when $a = b \ne c = d$, and to a visible node when $a = c \ne b = d$; otherwise it points to a tangled node (unless $a = b = c = d$, when it points directly to a sink). The tangled node $abcd$ usually has LO $= ab$ and HI $= cd$, unless $a = b$ or $c = d$; in the exceptional cases, LO or HI is a sink. After transmogrification it will have LO $= ac$ and HI $= bd$ in a similar way, where latter nodes will be either newbies or visibles or sinks (but not both sinks). One interesting case is 1224, whose children 12 and 24 on the left are hidden nodes, while the 12 and 24 on the right are newbies.

Exercise 147 discusses an efficient implementation of this transformation, which was introduced by Richard Rudell in *IEEE/ACM International Conf. Computer-Aided Design* **CAD-93** (1993), 42–47. It has the important property that no pointers need to change, except within the nodes on the top two levels:

All source nodes s_j still point to the same place in computer memory, and all sinks retain their previous identity. We have described it as a swap between ①s and ②s, but in fact the same transformation will swap ⓙs and ⓚs whenever the variables x_j and x_k correspond to branching on adjacent levels. The reason is that the upper levels of any BDD base essentially define source functions for the lower levels, which constitute a BDD base in their own right.

We know from our study of sorting that *any* reordering of the variables of a BDD base can be produced by a sequence of swaps between adjacent levels. In particular, we can use adjacent swaps to do a "jump-up" transformation, which brings a given variable x_k to the top level without disturbing the relative order of the other variables. It's easy, for instance, to jump x_4 up to the top: We simply swap ④ ↔ ③, then ④ ↔ ②, then ④ ↔ ①, because x_4 will be adjacent to x_1 after it has jumped past x_2.

Since repeated swaps can produce any ordering, they are sometimes able to make a BDD base grow until it is too big to handle. How bad can a single swap be? If exactly (s, t, v, h, ν) nodes are solitary, tangled, visible, hidden, and newbie, the top two levels end up with $s + t + v + \nu$ nodes; and this is at most $m + \nu \leq m + 2t$ when there are m source functions, because $m \geq s + t + v$. Thus the new size of those levels can't exceed twice the original, plus the number of sources.

If a single swap can double the size, a jump-up for x_k threatens to increase the size exponentially, because it does $k - 1$ swaps. Fortunately, however, jump-ups are no worse than single swaps in this regard:

Theorem J⁺. $B(f_1^\pi, \ldots, f_m^\pi) < m + 2B(f_1, \ldots, f_m)$ after a *jump-up operation.*

Proof. Let $a_1 a_2 \ldots a_{2^k-1} a_{2^k}$ be the extended truth table for a source function $f(x_1, \ldots, x_k)$, with lower-level nodes regarded as sinks. After the jump-up, the extended truth table for $f^\pi(x_1, \ldots, x_k) = f(x_{1\pi}, \ldots, x_{k\pi}) = f(x_2, \ldots, x_k, x_1)$ is $a_1 a_3 \ldots a_{2^k-1} a_2 a_4 \ldots a_{2^k}$. Thus we can see that each bead on level j of f^π is derived from some bead on level $j - 1$ of f, for $1 \leq j < k$; but every bead on level $j - 1$ of f spawns at most two beads, of half the size, in f^π. Therefore, if the respective profiles of $\{f_1, \ldots, f_m\}$ and $\{f_1^\pi, \ldots, f_m^\pi\}$ are $(b_0, \ldots, b_n)$ and $(b_0', \ldots, b_n')$, we must have $b_0' \leq m$, $b_1' \leq 2b_0$, $\ldots$, $b_{k-1}' \leq 2b_{k-2}$, $b_k' = b_k$, $\ldots$, $b_n' = b_n$. The total is therefore $\leq m + B(f_1, \ldots, f_m) + b_0 + \cdots + b_{k-2} - b_{k-1}$. ∎

The opposite of a jump-up is a "jump-down," which demotes the topmost variable by $k - 1$ levels. As before, this operation can be implemented with $k - 1$ swaps. But we have to settle for a much weaker upper bound on the resulting size:

Theorem J⁻. $B(f_1^\pi, \ldots, f_m^\pi) < B(f_1, \ldots, f_m)^2$ after a *jump-down operation.*

Proof. Now the extended truth table in the previous proof changes from $a_1 \ldots a_{2^k}$ to $a_1 \ldots a_{2^{k-1}} \ddagger a_{2^{k-1}+1} \ldots a_{2^k} = a_1 a_{2^{k-1}+1} \ldots a_{2^{k-1}} a_{2^k}$, the "zipper function" 7.1.3–(76). In this case we can identify every bead after the jump with an ordered pair of original subfunctions, as in the melding operation (37) and (38). For example, when $k = 3$ the truth table 12345678 becomes 15263748, whose bead 1526 can be regarded as the meld $12 \diamond 56$. ∎

This proof indicates why quadratic growth might occur. If, for example,

$$f(x_1, \ldots, x_n) \;=\; x_1?\; M_m(x_2, \ldots, x_{m+1}; x_{2m+2}, \ldots, x_n):$$
$$M_m(x_{m+2}, \ldots, x_{2m+1}; \bar{x}_{2m+2}, \ldots, \bar{x}_n), \quad (103)$$

where $n = 1 + 2m + 2^m$, a jump-down of $2m$ levels changes $B(f) = 4n - 8m - 3$ to $B(f^\pi) = 2n^2 - 8m(n-m) - 2(n-2m) + 1 \approx B(f)^2/8$.

Since jump-up and jump-down are inverse operations, we can also use Theorems J^+ and J^- in reverse: *A jump-up operation might conceivably decrease the BDD size to something like its square root, but a jump-down cannot reduce the size to less than about half.* That's bad news for fans of jump-down, although they can take comfort from the knowledge that jump-downs are sometimes the only decent way to get from a given ordering to an optimum one.

Theorems J^+ and J^- are due to B. Bollig, M. Löbbing, and I. Wegener, *Inf. Processing Letters* **59** (1996), 233–239. (See also exercise 149.)

*Dynamic reordering. In practice, a natural way to order the variables often suggests itself, based on the modules-in-a-row perspective of Fig. 23 and Theorem M. But sometimes no suitable ordering is apparent, and we can only hope to be lucky; perhaps the computer will come to our rescue and find one. Furthermore, even if we do know a good way to begin a computation, the ordering of variables that works best in the first stages of the work might turn out to be unsatisfactory in later stages. Therefore we can get better results if we don't insist on a fixed ordering. Instead, we can try to tune up the current order of branching whenever a BDD base becomes unwieldy.

For example, we might try to swap $x_{j-1} \leftrightarrow x_j$ in the order, for $1 < j \le n$, undoing the swap if it increases the total number of nodes but letting it ride otherwise; we could keep this up until no such swap makes an improvement. That method is easy to implement, but unfortunately it's too weak; it doesn't give much of a reduction. A much better reordering technique was proposed by Richard Rudell at the same time as he introduced the swap-in-place algorithm of exercise 147. His method, called "sifting," has proved to be quite successful. The idea is simply to take a variable x_k and to try jumping it up or down to all other levels — that is, essentially to remove x_k from the ordering and then to insert it again, choosing a place for insertion that keeps the BDD size as small as possible. All of the necessary work can be done with a sequence of elementary swaps:

Algorithm J (*Sifting a variable*). This algorithm moves variable x_k into an optimum position with respect to the current ordering of the other variables $\{x_1, \ldots, x_{k-1}, x_{k+1}, \ldots, x_n\}$ in a given BDD base. It works by repeatedly calling the procedure of exercise 147 to swap adjacent variables $x_{j-1} \leftrightarrow x_j$. Throughout this algorithm, S denotes the current size of the BDD base (the total number of nodes); the swapping operation usually changes S.

J1. [Initialize.] Set $p \leftarrow 0$, $j \leftarrow k$, and $s \leftarrow S$. If $k > n/2$, go to J5.

J2. [Sift up.] While $j > 1$, swap $x_{j-1} \leftrightarrow x_j$ and set $j \leftarrow j - 1$, $s \leftarrow \min(S, s)$.

J3. [End the pass.] If $p = 1$, go to J4. Otherwise, while $j \neq k$, set $j \leftarrow j+1$ and swap $x_{j-1} \leftrightarrow x_j$; then set $p \leftarrow 1$ and go to J5.

J4. [Finish downward.] While $s \neq S$, set $j \leftarrow j+1$ and swap $x_{j-1} \leftrightarrow x_j$. Stop.

J5. [Sift down.] While $j < n$, set $j \leftarrow j+1$, swap $x_{j-1} \leftrightarrow x_j$, and set $s \leftarrow \min(S, s)$.

J6. [End the pass.] If $p = 1$, go to J7. Otherwise, while $j \neq k$, swap $x_{j-1} \leftrightarrow x_j$ and set $j \leftarrow j - 1$; then set $p \leftarrow 1$ and go to J2.

J7. [Finish upward.] While $s \neq S$, swap $x_{j-1} \leftrightarrow x_j$ and set $j \leftarrow j - 1$. Stop. ∎

Whenever Algorithm J swaps $x_{j-1} \leftrightarrow x_j$, the original variable x_k is currently called either x_{j-1} or x_j. The total number of swaps varies from about n to about $2.5n$, depending on k and the optimum final position of x_k. But we can improve the running time substantially, without seriously affecting the outcome, if steps J2 and J5 are modified to proceed immediately to J3 and J6, respectively, whenever S becomes larger than, say, $1.2s$ or even $1.1s$ or even $1.05s$. In such cases, further sifting in the same direction is unlikely to decrease s.

Rudell's sifting procedure applies Algorithm J exactly n times, once for each variable that is present; see exercise 151. We could continue sifting again and again until there is no more improvement; but the additional gain is usually not worth the extra effort.

Let's look at a detailed example, in order to make these ideas concrete. We've observed that when the contiguous United States are arranged in the order

$$\begin{array}{l} \text{ME NH VT MA RI CT NY NJ PA DE MD DC VA NC SC GA FL AL TN KY WV OH MI IN} \\ \text{IL WI MN IA MO AR MS LA TX OK KS NE SD ND MT WY CO NM AZ UT ID WA OR NV CA} \end{array} \quad (104)$$

as in (17), they lead to a BDD of size 428 for the independent-set function

$$\neg\big((x_{\text{AL}} \wedge x_{\text{FL}}) \vee (x_{\text{AL}} \wedge x_{\text{GA}}) \vee (x_{\text{AL}} \wedge x_{\text{MS}}) \vee \cdots \vee (x_{\text{UT}} \wedge x_{\text{WY}}) \vee (x_{\text{VA}} \wedge x_{\text{WV}})\big). \quad (105)$$

The author chose the ordering (104) by hand, starting with the historical/geographical listing of states that he had been taught as a child, then trying to minimize the size of the boundary between states-already-listed and states-to-come, so that the BDD for (105) would not need to "remember" too many partial results at any level. The resulting size, 428, is pretty good for a function of 49 variables; but sifting is able to make it even better. For example, consider WV: Some of the possibilities for altering its position, with varying sizes S, are

$$\begin{array}{cccccccccccccccccccc} |\text{RI}|&\text{CT}|&\text{NY}|&\text{NJ}|&\text{PA}|&\text{DE}|&\text{MD}|&\text{DC}|&\text{VA}|&\text{NC}|&\text{SC}|&\text{GA}|&\text{FL}|&\text{AL}|&\text{TN}|&\text{KY}|&\text{OH}|&\text{MI}|&\text{IN}|&\text{IL}| \\ 424&422&417&415&414&412&411&410&412&412&415&420&421&426&425&427&428&428&436&442&453 \end{array}$$

so we can save $428 - 410 = 18$ nodes by jumping WV up to a position between MD and DC. By using Algorithm J to sift on all the variables — first on ME, then on NH, then ..., then on CA — we end up with the ordering

$$\begin{array}{l} \text{VT MA ME NH CT RI NY NJ DE PA MD WV VA DC KY OH NC GA SC AL FL MS TN IN} \\ \text{IL MI AR TX LA OK MO IA WI MN CO NE KS MT ND WY SD UT AZ NM ID CA OR WA NV} \end{array} \quad (106)$$

and the BDD size has been reduced to 345(!). That sifting process involves a total of 4663 swaps, requiring less than 4 megamems of computation altogether.

Instead of choosing an ordering carefully, let's consider a lazier alternative: We might begin with the states in alphabetic order

$$\begin{array}{l}\text{AL AR AZ CA CO CT DC DE FL GA IA ID IL IN KS KY LA MA MD ME MI MN MO MS}\\ \text{MT NC ND NE NH NJ NM NV NY OH OK OR PA RI SC SD TN TX UT VA VT WA WI WV WY}\end{array} \quad (107)$$

and proceed from there. Then the BDD for (105) turns out to have 306,214 nodes; it can be computed either via Algorithm S (with about 380 megamems of machine time) or via (55) and Algorithm U (with about 565 megamems). In this case sifting makes a dramatic difference: Those 306,214 nodes become only 2871, at a cost of 430 additional megamems. Furthermore, the sifting cost goes down from 430 Mμ to 210 Mμ if the loops of Algorithm J are aborted when $S > 1.1s$. (The more radical choice of aborting when $S > 1.05s$ would reduce the cost of sifting to 155 Mμ; but the BDD size would be reduced only to 2946 in that case.)

And we can actually do much, much better, if we sift the variables *while* evaluating (105), instead of waiting until that whole long sequence of disjunctions has been entirely computed. For example, suppose we invoke sifting automatically whenever the BDD size surpasses twice the number of nodes that were present after the previous sift. Then the evaluation of (105), starting from the alphabetic ordering (107), runs like a breeze: It automatically churns out a BDD that has only 419 nodes, after only about 60 megamems of calculation! Neither human ingenuity nor "geometric understanding" are needed to discover the ordering

$$\begin{array}{l}\text{NV OR ID WA AZ CA UT NM WY CO MT OK TX NE MO KS LA AR MS TN IA ND MN SD}\\ \text{GA FL AL NC SC KY WI MI IL OH IN WV MD VA DC PA NJ DE NY CT RI NH ME VT MA}\end{array} \quad (108)$$

which beats the author's (104). For this one, the computer just decided to invoke autosifting 39 times, on smaller BDDs.

What is the *best* ordering of states for the function (105)? The answer to that question will probably never be known for sure, but we can make a pretty good guess. First of all, a few more sifts of (108) will yield a still-better ordering

$$\begin{array}{l}\text{OR ID NV WA AZ CA UT NM WY CO MT SD MN ND IA NE OK KS TX MO LA AR MS TN}\\ \text{GA FL AL NC SC KY WI MI IL OH IN WV MD DC VA PA NJ DE NY CT RI NH ME VT MA}\end{array} \quad (109)$$

with BDD size 354. Sifting will not improve (109) further; but sifting has only limited power, because it explores only $(n-1)^2$ alternative orderings, out of $n!$ possibilities. (Indeed, exercise 134 exhibits a function of only four variables whose BDD cannot be improved by sifting, even though the ordering of its variables is not optimum.) There is, however, another arrow in our quiver: We can use *master profile charts* to optimize every window of, say, 16 consecutive levels in the BDD. There are 34 such windows; and the algorithm of exercise 139 optimizes each of them rather quickly. After about 9.6 gigamems of computation, that algorithm discovers a new champion

$$\begin{array}{l}\text{OR ID NV WA AZ CA UT NM WY CO MT SD MN ND IA NE OK KS TX MO LA AR MS WI}\\ \text{KY MI IN IL AL TN FL NC SC GA WV OH MD DC VA PA NJ DE NY CT RI NH ME VT MA}\end{array} \quad (110)$$

by cleverly rearranging 16 states within (109). This ordering, for which the BDD size is only 339, might well be optimum, because it cannot be improved either by sifting or by optimizing any window of width 25. However, such a conjecture rests on shaky ground: The ordering

$$
\begin{array}{l}
\text{AL GA FL TN NC SC VA MS AR TX LA OK KY MO NM WV MD DC PA NJ DE OH IL MI} \\
\text{IN IA NE KS WI SD WY ND MN MT UT CO ID CA AZ OR WA NV NY CT RI NH ME VT MA}
\end{array} \quad (111)
$$

also happens to be unimprovable by sifting and by width-25 window optimization, yet its BDD has 606 nodes and is far from optimum.

With the improved ordering (110), the 98-variable COLOR function of (73)
needs only 22037 BDD nodes, instead of 25579. Sifting reduces it to 16098.

*Read-once functions. Boolean functions such as $(x_1 \supset x_2) \oplus ((x_3 \equiv x_4) \wedge x_5)$,
which can be expressed as formulas in which each variable occurs exactly once,
form an important class for which optimum orderings of variables can easily be
computed. Formally, let us say that $f(x_1, \ldots, x_n)$ is a *read-once function* if either
(i) $n = 1$ and $f(x_1) = x_1$; or (ii) $f(x_1, \ldots, x_n) = g(x_1, \ldots, x_k) \circ h(x_{k+1}, \ldots, x_n)$,
where $\circ$ is one of the binary operators $\{\wedge, \vee, \bar{\wedge}, \bar{\vee}, \supset, \subset, \bar{\supset}, \bar{\subset}, \oplus, \equiv\}$ and where
both g and h are read-once functions. In case (i) we obviously have $B(f) = 3$.
And in case (ii), exercise 163 proves that

$$
B(f) = \begin{cases} B(g) + B(h) - 2, & \text{if } \circ \in \{\wedge, \vee, \bar{\wedge}, \bar{\vee}, \supset, \subset, \bar{\supset}, \bar{\subset}\}; \\ B(g) + B(h, \bar{h}) - 2, & \text{if } \circ \in \{\oplus, \equiv\}. \end{cases} \quad (112)
$$

In order to get a recurrence, we also need the similar formulas

$$
B(f, \bar{f}) = \begin{cases} 4, & \text{if } n = 1; \\ 2B(g) + B(h, \bar{h}) - 4, & \text{if } \circ \in \{\wedge, \vee, \bar{\wedge}, \bar{\vee}, \supset, \subset, \bar{\supset}, \bar{\subset}\}; \\ B(g, \bar{g}) + B(h, \bar{h}) - 2, & \text{if } \circ \in \{\oplus, \equiv\}. \end{cases} \quad (113)
$$

A particularly interesting family of read-once functions arises when we define

$$
\begin{aligned}
u_{m+1}(x_1, \ldots, x_{2m+1}) &= v_m(x_1, \ldots, x_{2m}) \wedge v_m(x_{2m+1}, \ldots, x_{2m+1}), \\
v_{m+1}(x_1, \ldots, x_{2m+1}) &= u_m(x_1, \ldots, x_{2m}) \oplus u_m(x_{2m+1}, \ldots, x_{2m+1}),
\end{aligned} \quad (114)
$$

and $u_0(x_1) = v_0(x_1) = x_1$; for example, $u_3(x_1, \ldots, x_8) = ((x_1 \wedge x_2) \oplus (x_3 \wedge x_4)) \wedge ((x_5 \wedge x_6) \oplus (x_7 \wedge x_8))$. Exercise 165 shows that the BDD sizes for these functions,
calculated via (112) and (113), involve Fibonacci numbers:

$$
\begin{aligned}
B(u_{2m}) &= 2^m F_{2m+2} + 2, & B(u_{2m+1}) &= 2^{m+1} F_{2m+2} + 2; \\
B(v_{2m}) &= 2^m F_{2m+2} + 2, & B(v_{2m+1}) &= 2^m F_{2m+4} + 2.
\end{aligned} \quad (115)
$$

Thus u_m and v_m are functions of $n = 2^m$ variables whose BDD sizes grow as

$$
\Theta(2^{m/2} \phi^m) = \Theta(n^\beta), \qquad \text{where } \beta = 1/2 + \lg \phi \approx 1.19424. \quad (116)
$$

In fact, the BDD sizes in (115) are optimum for the u and v functions,
under all permutations of the variables, because of a fundamental result due to
M. Sauerhoff, I. Wegener, and R. Werchner:

Theorem W. *If $f(x_1, \ldots, x_n) = g(x_1, \ldots, x_k) \circ h(x_{k+1}, \ldots, x_n)$ is a read-
once function, there is a permutation π that minimizes $B(f^\pi)$ and $B(f^\pi, \bar{f}^\pi)$
simultaneously, and in which the variables $\{x_1, \ldots, x_k\}$ occur either first or last.*

Proof. Any permutation $(1\pi, \ldots, n\pi)$ leads naturally to an "unshuffled" per-mutation $(1\sigma, \ldots, n\sigma)$ in which the first k elements are $\{1, \ldots, k\}$ and the last $n - k$ elements are $\{k+1, \ldots, n\}$, retaining the π order within each group. For example, if $k = 7$, $n = 9$, and $(1\pi, \ldots, 9\pi) = (3,1,4,5,9,2,6,8,7)$, we have $(1\sigma, \ldots, 9\sigma) = (3,1,4,5,2,6,7,9,8)$. Exercise 166 proves that, in appropriate circumstances, we have $B(f^\sigma) \leq B(f^\pi)$ and $B(f^\sigma, \bar{f}^\sigma) \leq B(f^\pi, \bar{f}^\pi)$. ∎

Using this theorem together with (112) and (113), we can readily optimize the ordering of variables for the BDD of any given read-once function. Consider, for example, $(x_1 \vee x_2) \oplus (x_3 \wedge x_4 \wedge x_5) = g(x_1, x_2) \oplus h(x_3, x_4, x_5)$. We have $B(g) = 4$ and $B(g, \bar{g}) = 6$; $B(h) = 5$ and $B(h, \bar{h}) = 8$. For the overall formula $f = g \oplus h$, Theorem W says that there are two candidates for a best ordering $(1\pi, \ldots, 5\pi)$, namely $(1,2,3,4,5)$ and $(4,5,1,2,3)$. The first of these gives $B(f^\pi) = B(g) + B(h, \bar{h}) - 2 = 10$; the other one excels, with $B(f^\pi) = B(h) + B(g, \bar{g}) - 2 = 9$.

The algorithm in exercise 167 finds an optimum π for any read-once function $f(x_1, \ldots, x_n)$ in $O(n)$ steps. Moreover, a careful analysis proves that $B(f^\pi) = O(n^\beta)$ in the best ordering, where β is the constant in (116). (See exercise 168.)

*Multiplication. Some of the most interesting Boolean functions, from a mathematical standpoint, are the $m + n$ bits that arise when an m-bit number is multiplied by an n-bit number:

$$(x_m \ldots x_2 x_1)_2 \times (y_n \ldots y_2 y_1)_2 = (z_{m+n} \ldots z_2 z_1)_2. \qquad (117)$$

In particular, the "leading bit" z_{m+n}, and the "middle bit" z_n when $m = n$, are especially noteworthy. To remove the dependence of this notation on m and n, we can imagine that $m = n = \infty$ by letting $x_i = y_j = 0$ for all $i > m$ and $j > n$; then each z_k is a function of $2k$ variables, $z_k = Z_k(x_1, \ldots, x_k; y_1, \ldots, y_k)$, namely the middle bit of the product $(x_k \ldots x_1)_2 \times (y_k \ldots y_1)_2$.

The middle bit turns out to be difficult, BDDwise, even when y is constant. Let $Z_{n,a}(x_1, \ldots, x_n) = Z_n(x_1, \ldots, x_n; a_1, \ldots, a_n)$, where $a = (a_n \ldots a_1)_2$.

Theorem X. *There is a constant a such that $B_{\min}(Z_{n,a}) > \frac{5}{288} \cdot 2^{\lfloor n/2 \rfloor} - 2$.*

Proof. [P. Woelfel, *J. Computer and System Sci.* **71** (2005), 520–534.] We may assume that $n = 2t$ is even, since $Z_{2t+1,2a} = Z_{2t,a}$. Let $x = (x_n \ldots x_1)_2$ and $m = ([n\pi \leq t] \ldots [1\pi \leq t])_2$. Then $x = p + q$, where $q = x \,\&\, m$ represents the "known" bits of x after t branches have been taken in a BDD for $Z_{n,a}$ with the ordering π, and $p = x \,\&\, \bar{m}$ represents the bits yet unknown. Let

$$P = \{x \,\&\, \bar{m} \mid 0 \leq x < 2^n\} \quad \text{and} \quad Q = \{x \,\&\, m \mid 0 \leq x < 2^n\}. \qquad (118)$$

For any fixed a, the function $Z_{n,a}$ has 2^t subfunctions

$$f_q(p) = ((pa + qa) \gg (n-1)) \,\&\, 1, \qquad q \in Q. \qquad (119)$$

We want to show that some n-bit number a will make many of these subfunctions differ; in other words we want to find a large subset $Q^* \subseteq Q$ such that

$$q \in Q^* \text{ and } q' \in Q^* \text{ and } q \neq q' \text{ implies } f_q(p) \neq f_{q'}(p) \text{ for some } p \in P. \qquad (120)$$

Exercise 176 shows in detail how this can be done. ∎

Table 1
BEST AND WORST ORDERINGS FOR THE MIDDLE BIT z_n OF MULTIPLICATION

$$x_{11}x_{10}x_9x_7x_8x_6x_{13}x_{15}$$
$$\times\ x_{16}x_{14}x_{12}x_5x_4x_3x_2x_1$$
$$B_{\min}(Z_8) = 756$$

$$x_{10}x_{11}x_9x_8x_7x_{16}x_6x_{15}$$
$$\times\ x_5x_4x_3x_{12}x_{13}x_2x_1x_{14}$$
$$B_{\max}(Z_8) = 6791$$

$$x_{24}x_{20}x_{18}x_{16}x_9x_8x_{10}x_{11}x_7x_{12}x_{14}x_{21}$$
$$\times\ x_{22}x_{19}x_{17}x_{15}x_6x_5x_4x_3x_2x_1x_{13}x_{23}$$
$$B_{\min}(Z_{12}) = 21931$$

$$x_{16}x_{17}x_{15}x_{14}x_{24}x_{13}x_{12}x_{11}x_{20}x_{10}x_9x_{23}$$
$$\times\ x_8x_7x_6x_5x_{18}x_4x_{22}x_3x_2x_{19}x_1x_{21}$$
$$B_{\max}(Z_{12}) = 866283$$

Table 2
BEST AND WORST ORDERINGS FOR ALL BITS $\{z_1, \ldots, z_{m+n}\}$ OF MULTIPLICATION

$$x_{11}x_{16}x_{15}x_{14}x_{13}x_{12}x_{10}x_9$$
$$\times\ x_8x_7x_6x_5x_4x_3x_2x_1$$
$$B_{\min}(Z_{8,8}^{(1)}, \ldots, Z_{8,8}^{(16)}) = 9700$$

$$x_{10}x_8x_9x_{13}x_2x_1x_{11}x_7$$
$$\times\ x_{16}x_5x_{15}x_6x_4x_{14}x_3x_{12}$$
$$B_{\max}(Z_{8,8}^{(1)}, \ldots, Z_{8,8}^{(16)}) = 28678$$

$$x_{15}x_{17}x_{24}x_{23}x_{22}x_{21}x_{20}x_{19}x_{18}x_{16}x_{14}x_{13}$$
$$\times\ x_1x_2x_3x_4x_5x_6x_7x_8x_9x_{10}x_{11}x_{12}$$
$$B_{\min}(Z_{12,12}^{(1)}, \ldots, Z_{12,12}^{(24)}) = 648957$$

$$x_{17}x_{22}x_{14}x_{13}x_{16}x_{10}x_{20}x_3x_2x_1x_{19}x_{12}$$
$$\times\ x_{24}x_{15}x_9x_8x_{21}x_7x_6x_{11}x_{23}x_5x_4x_{18}$$
$$B_{\max}(Z_{12,12}^{(1)}, \ldots, Z_{12,12}^{(24)}) = 4224195$$

$$x_{17}x_{16}x_{10}x_9x_{11}x_{12}\ldots x_{15}x_{18}x_{19}x_{24}x_{23}\ldots x_{20}$$
$$\times\ x_1x_2x_3x_4x_5x_6x_7x_8$$
$$B_{\min}(Z_{16,8}^{(1)}, \ldots, Z_{16,8}^{(24)}) = 157061$$

$$x_{13}x_{14}x_{12}x_{15}x_{16}x_{17}x_{22}x_{10}x_8x_7x_{18}x_9x_2x_1x_{19}x_6$$
$$\times\ x_{24}x_{11}x_{21}x_5x_4x_{23}x_3x_{20}$$
$$B_{\max}(Z_{16,8}^{(1)}, \ldots, Z_{16,8}^{(24)}) = 1236251$$

A good upper bound for the BDD size of the middle bit function when neither operand is constant has been found by K. Amano and A. Maruoka, *Discrete Applied Math.* **155** (2007), 1224–1232:

Theorem A. *Let* $f(x_1, \ldots, x_{2n}) = Z_n(x_1, x_3, \ldots, x_{2n-1}; x_2, x_4, \ldots, x_{2n})$. *Then*

$$B(f) \leq Q(f) < \tfrac{19}{7} 2^{\lceil 6n/5 \rceil}. \tag{121}$$

Proof. Consider two n-bit numbers $x = 2^k x_h + x_l$ and $y = 2^k y_h + y_l$, with $n - k$ unknown bits in each of their high parts (x_h, y_h), while their k-bit low parts (x_l, y_l) are both known. Then the middle bit of xy is determined by adding together three $(n - k)$-bit quantities when $k \geq n/2$, namely $x_h y_l \bmod 2^{n-k}$, $x_l y_h \bmod 2^{n-k}$, and $(x_l y_l \gg k) \bmod 2^{n-k}$. Hence level $2k$ of the QDD needs to "remember" only the least significant $n - k$ bits of each of the prior quantities x_l, y_l, and $x_l y_l \gg k$, a total of $3n - 3k$ bits, and we have $q_{2k} \leq 2^{3n-3k}$ in f's quasi-profile. Exercise 177 completes the proof. ∎

Amano and Maruoka also discovered another important upper bound. Let $Z_{m,n}^{(p)}(x_1, \ldots, x_m; y_1, \ldots, y_n)$ denote the pth bit z_p of the product (117).

Theorem Y. *For all constants* $(a_m \ldots a_1)_2$ *and for all* p, *the BDD and QDD for the function* $Z_{m,n}^{(p)}(a_1, \ldots, a_m; x_1, \ldots, x_n)$ *have fewer than* $3 \cdot 2^{(n+1)/2}$ *nodes.*

Proof. Exercise 180 proves that $q_k \leq 2^{n+1-k}$ for this function. The theorem follows when we combine that result with the obvious upper bound $q_k \leq 2^k$. ∎

Theorem Y shows that the lower bound of Theorem X is best possible, except for a constant factor. It also shows that the BDD base for all $m + n$ product functions $Z_{m,n}^{(p)}(x_1, \ldots, x_m; x_{m+1}, \ldots, x_{m+n})$ is not nearly as large as $\Theta(2^{m+n})$, which we get for almost all instances of $m + n$ functions of $m + n$ variables:

Corollary Y. *If $m \leq n$, $B(Z_{m,n}^{(1)}, \ldots, Z_{m,n}^{(m+n)}) < 3(m + n)2^{m+(n+1)/2}$.* ∎

The best orderings of variables for the middle-bit function Z_n and for the complete BDD base remain mysterious, but empirical results for small m and n give reason to conjecture that the upper bounds of Theorem A and Corollary Y are not far from the truth; see Tables 1 and 2. Here, for example, are the optimum results of Z_n when $n \leq 12$:

$n =$	1	2	3	4	5	6	7	8	9	10	11	12
$B_{\min}(Z_n) =$	4	8	14	31	63	136	315	756	1717	4026	9654	21931
$2^{6n/5} \approx$	2	5	12	28	64	147	338	776	1783	4096	9410	21619

The ratios $B_{\max}/B_{\min}$ with respect to the full BDD base $\{Z_{m,n}^{(1)}, \ldots, Z_{m,n}^{(m+n)}\}$ are surprisingly small in Table 2. Therefore all orderings for that problem might turn out to be roughly equivalent.

Zero-suppressed BDDs: A combinatorial alternative. When BDDs are applied to combinatorial problems, a glance at the data in memory often reveals that most of the HI fields simply point to ⊥. In such cases, we're better off using a variant data structure called a *zero-suppressed binary decision diagram*, or "ZDD" for short, introduced by Shin-ichi Minato [*ACM/IEEE Design Automation Conf.* **30** (1993), 272–277]. A ZDD has nodes like a BDD, but its nodes are interpreted differently: When an (i) node's HI points to a (j) node for $j > i+1$, it means that the Boolean function is false unless $x_{i+1} = \cdots = x_{j-1} = 0$.

For example, the BDDs for independent sets and kernels in (12) have many nodes with HI = ⊥. Those nodes go away in the corresponding ZDDs, although a few new nodes must also be added:

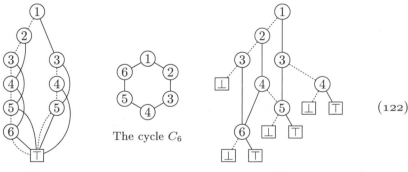

The cycle C_6

Independent sets   Kernels   (122)

Notice that we might have LO = HI in a ZDD, because of the new conventions. Furthermore, the example on the left shows that a ZDD need not contain ⊥ at all! About 40% of the nodes in (12) have been eliminated from each diagram.

One good way to understand a ZDD is to regard it as a condensed representation of a *family of sets*. Indeed, the ZDDs in (122) represent respectively the families of all independent sets and all kernels of C_6. The root node of a ZDD names the smallest element that appears in at least one of the sets; its HI and LO branches represent the residual subfamilies that do and don't contain that element; and so on. At the bottom, $\boxed{\bot}$ represents the empty family '$\emptyset$', and $\boxed{\top}$ represents '$\{\emptyset\}$'. For example, the rightmost ZDD in (122) represents the family $\{\{1,3,5\}, \{1,4\}, \{2,4,6\}, \{2,5\}, \{3,6\}\}$, because the HI branch of the root represents $\{\{3,5\}, \{4\}\}$ and the LO branch represents $\{\{2,4,6\}, \{2,5\}, \{3,6\}\}$.

Every Boolean function $f(x_1,\ldots,x_n)$ is, of course, equivalent to a family of subsets of $\{1,\ldots,n\}$, and vice versa. But the family concept gives us a different perspective from the function concept. For example, the family $\{\{1,3\}, \{2\}, \{2,5\}\}$ has the same ZDD for all $n \geq 5$; but if, say, $n = 7$, the BDD for the function $f(x_1,\ldots,x_7)$ that defines this family needs additional nodes to ensure that $x_4 = x_6 = x_7 = 0$ when $f(x) = 1$.

Almost every notion that we've discussed for BDDs has a counterpart in the theory of ZDDs, although the actual data structures are often strikingly different. We can, for example, take the truth table for any given function $f(x_1,\ldots,x_n)$ and construct its unique ZDD in a straightforward way, analogous to the construction of its BDD as illustrated in (5). We know that the BDD nodes for f correspond to the "beads" of f's truth table; the ZDD nodes, similarly, correspond to *zeads*, which are binary strings of the form $\alpha\beta$ with $|\alpha| = |\beta|$ and $\beta \neq 0\ldots0$, or with $|\alpha| = |\beta| - 1$. Any binary string corresponds to a unique zead, obtained by lopping off the right half repeatedly, if necessary, until the string either has odd length or its right half is nonzero.

Dear reader, please take a moment now to work exercise 187. (Really.)

The *z-profile* of $f(x_1,\ldots,x_n)$ is $(z_0,\ldots,z_n)$, where z_k is the number of zeads of order $n-k$ in f's truth table, for $0 \leq k < n$, namely the number of $\boxed{k+1}$ nodes in the ZDD; also z_n is the number of sinks. We write $Z(f) = z_0 + \cdots + z_n$ for the total number of nodes. For example, the functions in (122) have z-profiles $(1,1,2,2,2,1,1)$ and $(1,1,2,2,1,1,2)$, respectively, so $Z(f) = 10$ in each case.

The basic relations (83)–(85) between profiles and quasi-profiles hold true also for z-profiles, but with q'_k counting only *nonzero* subtables of order $n - k$:

$$q'_k \geq z_k, \qquad \text{for } 0 \leq k < n; \tag{123}$$

$$q'_k \leq 1 + z_0 + \cdots + z_{k-1} \text{ and } q'_k \leq z_k + \cdots + z_n, \quad \text{for } 0 \leq k \leq n; \tag{124}$$

$$Z(f) \geq 2q'_k - 1, \qquad \text{for } 0 \leq k \leq n. \tag{125}$$

Consequently the BDD size and the ZDD size can never be wildly different:

$$Z(f) \leq \frac{n}{2}\big(B(f)+1\big)+1 \qquad \text{and} \qquad B(f) \leq \frac{n}{2}\big(Z(f)+1\big)+2. \tag{126}$$

On the other hand, a factor of 50 when $n = 100$ is nothing to sneeze at.

When ZDDs are used to find independent sets and kernels of the contiguous USA, using the original order of (17), the BDD sizes of 428 and 780 go down to 177 and 385, respectively. Sifting reduces these ZDD sizes to 160 and 335. Is anybody sneezing? That's amazingly good, for complicated functions of 49 variables.

When we know the ZDDs for f and g, we can synthesize them to obtain the ZDDs for $f \wedge g$, $f \vee g$, $f \oplus g$, etc., using algorithms that are very much like the methods we've used for BDDs. Furthermore we can count and/or optimize the solutions of f, with analogs of Algorithms C and B; in fact, ZDD-based techniques for counting and optimization turn out to be a bit easier than the corresponding BDD-based algorithms are. With slight modifications of BDD methods, we can also do dynamic variable reordering via sifting. Exercises 197–209 discuss the nuts and bolts of all the basic ZDD procedures.

In general, a ZDD tends to be better than a BDD when we're dealing with functions whose solutions are *sparse*, in the sense that νx tends to be small when $f(x) = 1$. And if $f(x)$ itself happens to be sparse, in the sense that it has comparatively few solutions, so much the better.

For example, ZDDs are well suited to *exact cover problems*, defined by an $m \times n$ matrix of 0s and 1s: We want to find all ways to choose rows that sum to $(1, 1, \ldots, 1)$. Our goal might be, say, to cover a chessboard with 32 dominoes, like

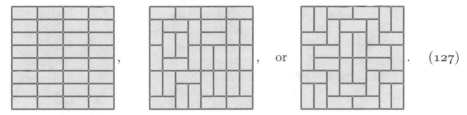

$$, \qquad , \quad \text{or} \quad . \qquad (127)$$

This is an exact cover problem whose matrix has $8 \times 8 = 64$ columns, one for each cell; there are $2 \times 7 \times 8 = 112$ rows, one for each pair of adjacent cells:

$$\begin{pmatrix}
1\,1\,0\,0\,0\,0\,0\,0\,0\,0\,0\,0\ldots0\,0\,0\,0\,0\,0\,0\,0\,0\,0\,0 \\
1\,0\,0\,0\,0\,0\,0\,0\,1\,0\,0\,0\ldots0\,0\,0\,0\,0\,0\,0\,0\,0\,0\,0 \\
0\,1\,1\,0\,0\,0\,0\,0\,0\,0\,0\,0\ldots0\,0\,0\,0\,0\,0\,0\,0\,0\,0\,0 \\
0\,1\,0\,0\,0\,0\,0\,0\,0\,1\,0\,0\ldots0\,0\,0\,0\,0\,0\,0\,0\,0\,0\,0 \\
\vdots \qquad\qquad\qquad \vdots \\
0\,0\,0\,0\,0\,0\,0\,0\,0\,0\,0\,0\ldots0\,0\,0\,0\,0\,0\,0\,1\,1\,0\,0 \\
0\,0\,0\,0\,0\,0\,0\,0\,0\,0\,0\,0\ldots0\,0\,0\,0\,0\,0\,0\,0\,1\,1\,0 \\
0\,0\,0\,0\,0\,0\,0\,0\,0\,0\,0\,0\ldots0\,0\,0\,0\,0\,0\,0\,0\,0\,1\,1
\end{pmatrix}. \qquad (128)$$

Let variable x_j represent the choice (or not) of row j. Thus the three solutions in (127) have $(x_1, x_2, x_3, x_4, \ldots, x_{110}, x_{111}, x_{112}) = (1, 0, 0, 0, \ldots, 1, 0, 1)$, $(1, 0, 0, 0, \ldots, 1, 0, 1)$, and $(0, 1, 0, 1, \ldots, 1, 0, 0)$, respectively. In general, the solutions to an exact cover problem are represented by the function

$$f(x_1, \ldots, x_m) = \bigwedge_{j=1}^{n} S_1(X_j) = \bigwedge_{j=1}^{n} [\nu X_j = 1], \qquad (129)$$

where $X_j = \{x_i \mid a_{ij} = 1\}$ and (a_{ij}) is the given matrix.

The dominoes-on-a-chessboard ZDD turns out to have only $Z(f) = 2300$ nodes, even though f has $m = 112$ variables in this case. We can use it to prove that there are exactly 12,988,816 coverings such as (127).

Similarly, we can investigate more exotic kinds of covering. In

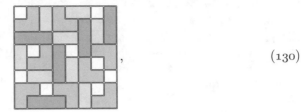

$$(130)$$

for instance, a chessboard has been covered with monominoes, dominoes, and/or trominoes — that is, with rookwise-connected pieces that each have either one, two, or three cells. There are exactly 92,109,458,286,284,989,468,604 ways to do this(!); and we can compute that number almost instantly, doing only about 75 megamems of calculation, by forming a ZDD of size 512,227 on 468 variables.

A special algorithm could be devised to find the ZDD for any given exact cover problem; or we can synthesize the result using (129). See exercise 212.

Incidentally, the problem of domino covering as in (127) is equivalent to finding the perfect matchings of the grid graph $P_8 \square P_8$, which is bipartite. We will see in Section 7.5.1 that efficient algorithms are available by which perfect matchings can be studied on graphs that are far too large to be treated with BDD/ZDD techniques. In fact, there's even an explicit formula for the number of domino coverings of an $m \times n$ grid. By contrast, general coverings such as (130) fall into a wider category of hypergraph problems for which polynomial-time methods are unlikely to be helpful as $m, n \to \infty$.

An amusing variant of domino covering called the "mutilated chessboard" was considered by Max Black in his book *Critical Thinking* (1946), pages 142 and 394: Suppose we remove opposite corners of the chessboard, and try to cover the remaining cells with 31 dominoes. It's easy to place 30 of them, for example as shown here; but then we're stuck. Indeed, if we consider the corresponding 108×62 exact cover problem, but leave out the last 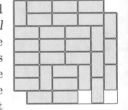 two constraints of (129), we obtain a ZDD with 1224 nodes from which we can deduce that there are 324,480 ways to choose rows that sum to $(1, 1, \ldots, 1, 1, *, *)$. But each of those solutions has at least two 1s in column 61; therefore the ZDD reduces to $\boxed{\perp}$ after we AND in the constraint $[\nu X_{61} = 1]$. ("Critical thinking" explains why; see exercise 213.) This example reminds us that (i) the size of the final ZDD or BDD in a calculation can be much smaller than the time needed to compute it; and (ii) using our brains can save oodles of computer cycles.

ZDDs as dictionaries. Let's switch gears now, to note that ZDDs are advantageous also in applications that have an entirely different flavor. We can use them, for instance, to represent the *five-letter words of English*, the set WORDS(5757) from the Stanford GraphBase that is discussed near the beginning of this chapter. One way to do this is to consider the function $f(x_1, \ldots, x_{25})$ that is defined to be 1 if and only if the five numbers $(x_1 \ldots x_5)_2$, $(x_6 \ldots x_{10})_2$, $\ldots$, $(x_{21} \ldots x_{25})_2$ encode the letters of an English word, where $\mathtt{a} = (00001)_2$, $\ldots$, $\mathtt{z} = (11010)_2$.

For example, $f(0, 0, 1, 1, 1, 0, 1, 1, 1, 1, 0, 1, 1, 1, 1, 0, 0, 1, 1, 0, 1, 1, 0, 0, x_{25}) = x_{25}$. This function of 25 variables has $Z(f) = 6233$ nodes — which isn't bad, since it represents 5757 words.

Of course we've studied many other ways to represent 5757 words, in Chapter 6. The ZDD approach is no match for binary trees or tries or hash tables, when we merely want to do simple searches. But with ZDDs we can also retrieve data that is only partially specified, or data that is only supposed to match a key approximately; many complex queries can be handled with ease.

Furthermore, we don't need to worry very much about having lots of variables when ZDDs are being used. Instead of working with the 25 variables x_j considered above, we can also represent those five-letter words as a sparse function $F(a_1, \ldots, z_1, a_2, \ldots, z_2, \ldots, a_5, \ldots, z_5)$ that has $26 \times 5 = 130$ variables, where variable a_2 (for example) controls whether the second letter is 'a'. To indicate that crazy is a word, we make F true when $c_1 = r_2 = a_3 = z_4 = y_5 = 1$ and all other variables are 0. Equivalently, we consider F to be a family consisting of the 5757 subsets $\{w_1, h_2, i_3, c_4, h_5\}$, $\{t_1, h_2, e_3, r_4, e_5\}$, etc. With these 130 variables the ZDD size $Z(F)$ turns out to be only 5020 instead of 6233.

Incidentally, $B(F)$ is 46,189 — more than nine times as large as $Z(F)$. But $B(f)/Z(f)$ is only $8870/6233 \approx 1.4$ in the 25-variable case. The ZDD world is different from the BDD world in many ways, in spite of having similar algorithms and a similar theory.

One consequence of this difference is a need for new primitive operations by which complex families of subsets can readily be constructed from elementary families. Notice that the simple subset $\{f_1, u_2, n_3, n_4, y_5\}$ is actually an extremely long-winded Boolean function:

$$\bar{a}_1 \wedge \cdots \wedge \bar{e}_1 \wedge f_1 \wedge \bar{g}_1 \wedge \cdots \wedge \bar{t}_2 \wedge u_2 \wedge \bar{v}_2 \wedge \cdots \wedge \bar{x}_5 \wedge y_5 \wedge \bar{z}_5, \qquad (131)$$

a minterm of 130 Boolean variables. Exercise 203 discusses an important *family algebra*, by which that subset is expressed more naturally as '$f_1 \sqcup u_2 \sqcup n_3 \sqcup n_4 \sqcup y_5$'. With family algebra we can readily describe and compute many interesting collections of words and word fragments (see exercise 222).

ZDDs to represent simple paths. An important connection between arbitrary directed, acyclic graphs (dags) and a special class of ZDDs is illustrated in Fig. 28. When every source vertex of the dag has out-degree 1 and every sink vertex has in-degree 1, the ZDD for all oriented paths from a source to a sink has essentially the same "shape" as the original dag. The variables in this ZDD are the *arcs* of the dag, in a suitable topological order. (See exercise 224.)

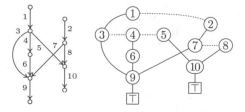

Fig. 28. A dag, and the ZDD for its source-to-sink paths. Arcs of the dag correspond to vertices of the ZDD. All branches to $\boxed{\bot}$ have been omitted from this ZDD diagram in order to show the structural similarities more clearly.

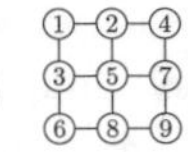

We can also use ZDDs to represent simple paths in an *undirected* graph. For example, there are 12 ways to go from the upper left corner of a 3×3 grid to the lower right corner, without visiting any point twice:

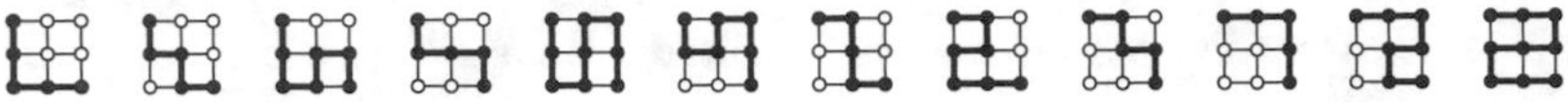

(132)

These paths can be represented by the ZDD shown at the right, which characterizes all sets of suitable edges. For example, we get the first path by taking the HI branches at (13), (36), (68), and (89) of the ZDD. (As in Fig. 28, this diagram has been simplified by omitting all of the uninteresting LO branches that merely go to $\boxed{\bot}$.) Of course this ZDD isn't a truly great way to represent (132), because that family of paths has only 12 members. But on the larger grid $P_8 \,\square\, P_8$, the number of simple paths from corner to corner turns out to be 789,360,053,252; and they can all be represented by a ZDD that has at most 33580 nodes. Exercise 225 explains how to construct such a ZDD quickly.

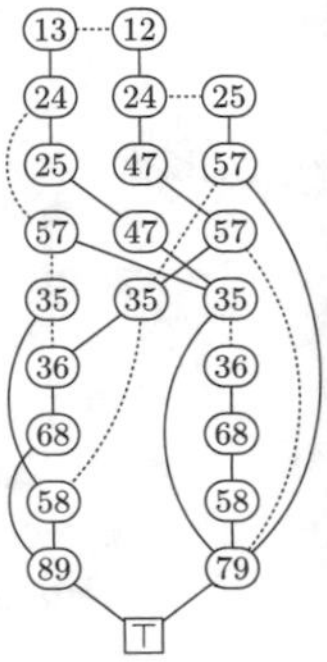

A similar algorithm, discussed in exercise 226, constructs a ZDD that represents all *cycles* of a given graph. With a ZDD of size 22275, we can deduce that $P_8 \,\square\, P_8$ has exactly 603,841,648,931 simple cycles. This ZDD may well provide the best way to represent all of those cycles within a computer, and the best way to generate them systematically if desired.

The same ideas work well with graphs from the "real world" that don't have a neat mathematical structure. For example, we can use them to answer a question posed to the author in 2008 by Randal Bryant: "Suppose I wanted to take a driving tour of the Continental U.S., visiting all of the state capitols, and passing through each state only once. What route should I take to minimize the total distance?" The following diagram shows the shortest distances between neighboring capital cities, when restricted to local itineraries that each cross only one state boundary:

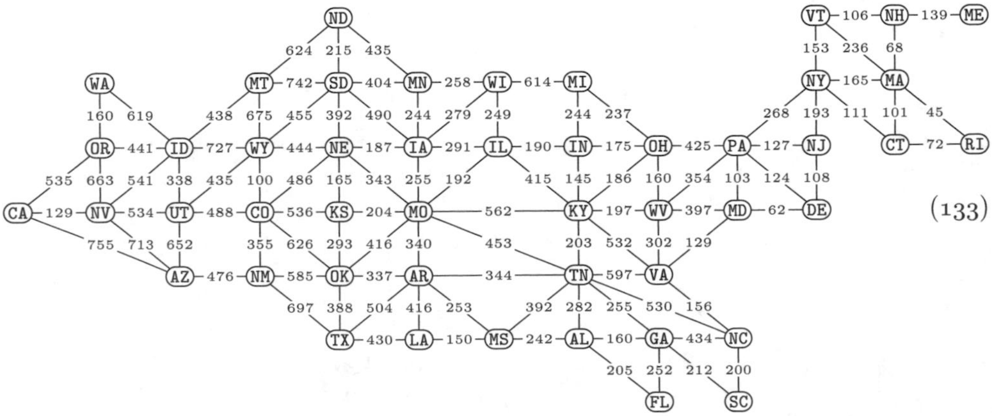

(133)

The problem is to choose a subset of these edges that form a Hamiltonian path of smallest total length.

Every Hamiltonian path in this graph must clearly either start or end at Augusta, Maine (ME). Suppose we start in Sacramento, California (CA). Proceeding as above, we can find a ZDD that characterizes all paths from CA to ME; this ZDD turns out to have only 7850 nodes, and it quickly tells us that exactly 437,525,772,584 simple paths from CA to ME are possible. In fact, the generating function by number of edges turns out to be

$$4z^{11} + 124z^{12} + 1539z^{13} + \cdots + 33385461z^{46} + 2707075z^{47}; \qquad (134)$$

so the longest such paths are Hamiltonian, and there are exactly 2,707,075 of them. Furthermore, exercise 227 shows how to construct a smaller ZDD, of size 4726, which describes just the Hamiltonian paths from CA to ME.

We could repeat this experiment for each of the states in place of California. (Well, the starting point had better be outside of New England, if we are going to get past New York, which is an articulation point of this graph.) For example, there are 483,194 Hamiltonian paths from NJ to ME. But exercise 228 shows how to construct a *single* ZDD of size 28808 for the family of all Hamiltonian paths from ME to *any* other final state — of which there are 68,656,026. The answer to Bryant's problem now pops out immediately, via Algorithm B. (The reader may like to try finding a minimum route by hand, before turning to exercise 230 and discovering the absolutely optimum answer.)

*ZDDs and prime implicants. Finally, let's look at an instructive application in which BDDs and ZDDs are both used simultaneously.

According to Theorem 7.1.1Q, every monotone Boolean function f has a unique shortest two-level representation as an OR of ANDs, called its "disjunctive prime form" — the disjunction of all of its prime implicants. The prime implicants correspond to the minimal points where $f(x) = 1$, namely the binary vectors x for which we have $f(x') = 1$ and $x' \subseteq x$ if and only if $x' = x$. If

$$f(x_1, x_2, x_3) = x_1 \lor (x_2 \land x_3), \qquad (135)$$

for example, the prime implicants of f are x_1 and $x_2 \land x_3$, while the minimal solutions are $x_1 x_2 x_3 = 100$ and 011. These minimal solutions can also be expressed conveniently as e_1 and $e_2 \sqcup e_3$, using family algebra (see exercise 203).

In general, $x_{i_1} \land \cdots \land x_{i_s}$ is a prime implicant of a monotone function f if and only if $e_{i_1} \sqcup \cdots \sqcup e_{i_s}$ is a minimal solution of f. Thus we can consider f's prime implicants PI(f) to be its family of minimal solutions. Notice, however, that $x_{i_1} \land \cdots \land x_{i_s} \subseteq x_{j_1} \land \cdots \land x_{j_t}$ if and only if $e_{i_1} \sqcup \cdots \sqcup e_{i_s} \supseteq e_{j_1} \sqcup \cdots \sqcup e_{j_t}$; so it's confusing to say that one prime implicant "contains" another. Instead, we say that the shorter one "absorbs" the longer one.

A curious phenomenon shows up in example (135): The diagram is not only the BDD for f, it's also the ZDD for PI(f)! Similarly, Fig. 21 at the beginning of this section illustrates not only the BDD for $\langle x_1 x_2 x_3 \rangle$ but also the ZDD for PI($\langle x_1 x_2 x_3 \rangle$). On the other hand, let $g = (x_1 \land x_3) \lor x_2$. Then the BDD for g is but the ZDD for PI(g) is . What's going on here?

The key to resolving this mystery lies in the recursive structure on which BDDs and ZDDs are based. Every Boolean function can be represented as

$$f(x_1, \ldots, x_n) = (\bar{x}_1?\ f_0\colon f_1) = (\bar{x}_1 \wedge f_0) \vee (x_1 \wedge f_1), \qquad (136)$$

where f_c is the value of f when x_1 is replaced by c. When f is monotone we also have $f = f_0 \vee (x_1 \wedge f_1)$, because $f_0 \subseteq f_1$. If $f_0 \neq f_1$, the BDD for f is obtained by creating a node ① whose LO and HI branches point to the BDDs for f_0 and f_1. Similarly, it's not difficult to see that the prime implicants of f are

$$\mathrm{PI}(f) = \mathrm{PI}(f_0) \cup \left(e_1 \sqcup (\mathrm{PI}(f_1) \setminus \mathrm{PI}(f_0))\right). \qquad (137)$$

(See exercise 253.) This is the recursion that defines the ZDD for $\mathrm{PI}(f)$, when we add the termination conditions for constant functions: The ZDDs for $\mathrm{PI}(0)$ and $\mathrm{PI}(1)$ are $\boxed{\perp}$ and $\boxed{\top}$.

Let's say that a Boolean function f is *sweet* if it is monotone and if the ZDD for $\mathrm{PI}(f)$ is exactly the same as the BDD for f. Constant functions are clearly sweet. And nonconstant sweetness is easily characterized:

Theorem S. *A Boolean function that depends on x_1 is sweet if and only if its prime implicants are $P \cup (e_1 \sqcup Q)$, where P and Q are sweet and independent of x_1, and every member of P is absorbed by some member of Q.*

Proof. See exercise 246. (To say that "P and Q are sweet" means that they each are families of prime implicants that define a sweet Boolean function.) ∎

Corollary S. *The connectedness function of any graph is sweet.*

Proof. The prime implicants of the connectedness function f are the spanning trees of the graph. Every spanning tree that does not include arc x_1 has at least one subforest that will be spanning when arc x_1 is added to it. Furthermore, all subfunctions of f are the connectedness functions of smaller graphs. ∎

Thus, for example, the BDD in Fig. 22, which defines all 431 of the connected subgraphs of $P_3 \square P_3$, also is the ZDD that defines all 192 of its spanning trees.

Whether f is sweet or not, we can use (137) to compute the ZDD for $\mathrm{PI}(f)$ whenever f is monotone. When we do this we can actually let the BDD nodes and the ZDD nodes *coexist* in the same big base of data: Two nodes with identical (V, LO, HI) fields might as well appear only once in memory, even though they might have completely different meanings in different contexts. We use one routine to synthesize $f \wedge \bar{g}$ when f and g point to BDDs, and another routine to form $f \setminus g$ when f and g point to ZDDs; no trouble will arise if these routines happen to share nodes, as long as the variables aren't being reordered. (Of course the cache memos must distinguish BDD facts from ZDD facts when we do this.)

For example, exercise 7.1.1–67 defines an interesting class of self-dual functions called the Y functions, and the BDD for Y_{12} (which is a function of 91 variables) has 748,416 nodes. This function has 2,178,889,774 prime implicants; yet $Z(\mathrm{PI}(Y_{12}))$ is only 217,388. (We can find this ZDD with a computational cost of about 13 gigamems and 660 megabytes.)

A brief history. The seeds of binary decision diagrams were implicitly planted by Claude Shannon [*Trans. Amer. Inst. Electrical Engineers* **57** (1938), 713–723], in his illustrations of relay-contact networks. Section 4 of that paper showed that any symmetric Boolean function of n variables has a BDD with at most $\binom{n+1}{2}$ branch nodes. Shannon preferred to work with Boolean algebra; but C. Y. Lee, in *Bell System Tech. J.* **38** (1959), 985–999, pointed out several advantages of what he called "binary-decision programs," because any n-variable function could be evaluated by executing at most n branch instructions in such a program.

S. Akers coined the name "binary decision diagrams" and pursued the ideas further in *IEEE Trans.* **C-27** (1978), 509–516. He showed how to obtain a BDD from a truth table by working bottom-up, or from algebraic subfunctions by working top-down. He explained how to count the paths from a root to $\boxed{\top}$ or $\boxed{\bot}$, and observed that these paths partition the n-cube into disjoint subcubes.

Meanwhile a very similar model of Boolean computation arose in theoretical studies of automata. For example, A. Cobham [*FOCS* **7** (1966), 78–87] related the minimum sizes of branching programs for a sequence of functions $f_n(x_1, \ldots, x_n)$ to the space complexity of nonuniform Turing machines that compute this sequence. More significantly, S. Fortune, J. Hopcroft, and E. M. Schmidt [*Lecture Notes in Comp. Sci.* **62** (1978), 227–240] considered "free B-schemes," now known as FBDDs, in which no Boolean variable is tested twice on any path (see exercise 35). Among other results, they gave a polynomial-time algorithm to test whether $f = g$, given FBDDs for f and g, provided that at least one of those FBDDs is ordered consistently as in a BDD. The theory of finite-state automata, which has intimate connections to BDD structure, was also being developed; thus several researchers worked on problems that are equivalent to analyzing the size, $B(f)$, for various functions f. (See exercise 261.)

All of this work was conceptual, not implemented in computer programs, although programmers had found good uses for binary tries and Patricia trees — which are similar to BDDs except that they are trees instead of dags (see Section 6.3). But then Randal E. Bryant discovered that binary decision diagrams are significantly important in practice when they are required to be both *reduced* and *ordered*. His introduction to the subject [*IEEE Trans.* **C-35** (1986), 677–691] became for many years the most cited paper in all of computer science, because it revolutionized the data structures used to represent Boolean functions.

In his paper, Bryant pointed out that the BDD for any function is essentially unique under his conventions, and that most of the functions encountered in practice had BDDs of reasonable size. He presented efficient algorithms to synthesize the BDDs for $f \wedge g$ and $f \oplus g$, etc., from the BDDs for f and g. He also showed how to compute the lexicographically least x such that $f(x) = 1$, etc.

Lee, Akers, and Bryant all noted that many functions can profitably co-exist in a BDD base, sharing their common subfunctions. A high-performance "package" for BDD base operations, developed by K. S. Brace, R. L. Rudell, and R. E. Bryant [*ACM/IEEE Design Automation Conf.* **27** (1990), 40–45], has strongly influenced all subsequent implementations of BDD toolkits. Bryant summarized the early uses of BDDs in *Computing Surveys* **24** (1992), 293–318.

Shin-ichi Minato introduced ZDDs in 1993, as noted above, to improve performance in combinatorial work. He gave a retrospective account of early ZDD applications in *Software Tools for Technology Transfer* **3** (2001), 156–170.

The use of Boolean methods in graph theory was pioneered by K. Maghout [*Comptes Rendus Acad. Sci.* **248** (Paris, 1959), 3522–3523], who showed how to express the maximal independent sets and the minimal dominating sets of any graph or digraph as the prime implicants of a monotone function. Then R. Fortet [*Cahiers du Centre d'Etudes de Recherche Operationelle* **1**, 4 (1959), 5–36] considered Boolean approaches to a variety of other problems; for example, he introduced the idea of 4-coloring a graph by assigning two Boolean variables to each vertex, as we have done in (73). P. Camion, in that same journal [**2** (1960), 234–289], transformed integer programming problems into equivalent problems in Boolean algebra, hoping to resolve them via techniques of symbolic logic. This work was extended by others, notably P. L. Hammer and S. Rudeanu, whose book *Boolean Methods in Operations Research* (Springer, 1968) summarized the ideas. Unfortunately, however, their approach foundered, because no good techniques for Boolean calculation were available at the time. The proponents of Boolean methods had to wait until the advent of BDDs before the general Boolean programming problem (7) could be resolved, thanks to Algorithm B. The special case of Algorithm B in which all weights are nonnegative was introduced by B. Lin and F. Somenzi [*International Conf. Computer-Aided Design* **CAD-90** (IEEE, 1990), 88–91]. S. Minato [*Formal Methods in System Design* **10** (1997), 221–242] developed software that automatically converts linear inequalities between integer variables into BDDs that can be manipulated conveniently, somewhat as the researchers of the 1960s had hoped would be possible.

The classic problem of finding a minimum size DNF for a given function also became spectacularly simpler when BDD methods became understood. The latest techniques for that problem are beyond the scope of this book, but Olivier Coudert has given an excellent overview in *Integration* **17** (1994), 97–140.

A fine book by Ingo Wegener, *Branching Programs and Binary Decision Diagrams* (SIAM, 2000), surveys the vast literature of the subject, develops the mathematical foundations carefully, and discusses many ways in which the basic ideas have been generalized and extended.

Caveat. We've seen dozens of examples in which the use of BDDs and/or ZDDs has made it possible to solve a wide variety of combinatorial problems with amazing efficiency, and the exercises below contain dozens of additional examples where such methods shine. But BDD and ZDD structures are by no means a panacea; they're only two of the weapons in our arsenal. They apply chiefly to problems that have more solutions than can readily be examined one by one, problems whose solutions have a local structure that allows our algorithms to deal with only relatively few subproblems at a time. In later sections of *The Art of Computer Programming* we shall be studying additional techniques by which other kinds of combinatorial problems can be tamed.

EXERCISES

▶ **1.** [*20*] Draw the BDDs for all 16 Boolean functions $f(x_1, x_2)$. What are their sizes?

▶ **2.** [*21*] Draw a planar dag with sixteen vertices, each of which is the root of one of the 16 BDDs in exercise 1.

3. [*16*] How many Boolean functions $f(x_1, \ldots, x_n)$ have BDD size 3 or less?

4. [*21*] Suppose three fields $\boxed{\text{V} \mid \text{LO} \mid \text{HI}}$ have been packed into a 64-bit word x, where V occupies 8 bits and the other two fields occupy 28 bits each. Show that five bitwise instructions will transform $x \mapsto x'$, where x' is equal to x except that a LO or HI value of 0 is changed to 1 and vice versa. (Repeating this operation on every branch node x of a BDD for f will produce the BDD for the complementary function, $\bar{f}$.)

5. [*20*] If you take the BDD for $f(x_1, \ldots, x_n)$ and interchange the LO and HI pointers of every node, and if you also swap the two sinks $\boxed{\perp} \leftrightarrow \boxed{\top}$, what do you get?

6. [*10*] Let $g(x_1, x_2, x_3, x_4) = f(x_4, x_3, x_2, x_1)$, where f has the BDD in (6). What is the truth table of g, and what are its beads?

7. [*21*] Given a Boolean function $f(x_1, \ldots, x_n)$, let

$$g_k(x_0, x_1, \ldots, x_n) = f(x_0, \ldots, x_{k-2}, x_{k-1} \lor x_k, x_{k+1}, \ldots, x_n) \qquad \text{for } 1 \le k \le n.$$

Find a simple relation between (a) the truth tables and (b) the BDDs of f and g_k.

8. [*22*] Solve exercise 7 with $x_{k-1} \oplus x_k$ in place of $x_{k-1} \lor x_k$.

9. [*16*] Given the BDD for a function $f(x) = f(x_1, \ldots, x_n)$, represented sequentially as in (8), explain how to determine the lexicographically largest x such that $f(x) = 0$.

▶ **10.** [*21*] Given two BDDs that define Boolean functions f and f', represented sequentially as in (8) and (10), design an algorithm that tests $f = f'$.

11. [*20*] Does Algorithm C give the correct answer if it is applied to a binary decision diagram that is (a) ordered but not reduced? (b) reduced but not ordered?

▶ **12.** [*M21*] A *kernel* of a digraph is a set of vertices K such that

$$v \in K \quad \text{implies} \quad v \nrightarrow u \text{ for all } u \in K;$$
$$v \notin K \quad \text{implies} \quad v \longrightarrow u \text{ for some } u \in K.$$

  a) Show that when the digraph is an ordinary graph (that is, when $u \longrightarrow v$ if and only if $v \longrightarrow u$), a kernel is the same as a maximal independent set.
  b) Describe the kernels of the *oriented* cycle $\vec{C_n}$.
  c) Prove that an acyclic digraph has a *unique* kernel.

13. [*M15*] How is the concept of a graph kernel related to the concept of (a) a maximal clique? (b) a minimal vertex cover?

14. [*M24*] How big, exactly, are the BDDs for (a) all independent sets of the cycle graph C_n, and (b) all kernels of C_n, when $n \ge 3$? (Number the vertices as in (12).)

15. [*M23*] How many (a) independent sets and (b) kernels does C_n have, when $n \ge 3$?

▶ **16.** [*22*] Design an algorithm that successively generates all vectors $x_1 \ldots x_n$ for which $f(x_1, \ldots, x_n) = 1$, when a BDD for f is given.

17. [*32*] If possible, improve the algorithm of exercise 16 so that its running time is $O(B(f)) + O(N)$ when there are N solutions.

18. [*13*] Play through Algorithm B with the BDD (8) and $(w_1, \ldots, w_4) = (1, -2, -3, 4)$.

19. [*20*] What are the largest and smallest possible values of variable m_k in Algorithm B, based only on the weights $(w_1, \ldots, w_n)$, not on any details of the function f?

20. [*15*] Devise a fast way to compute the Thue–Morse weights (15) for $1 \le j \le n$.

21. [*05*] Can Algorithm B *minimize* $w_1 x_1 + \cdots + w_n x_n$, instead of maximizing it?

▶ **22.** [*M21*] Suppose step B3 has been simplified so that '$W_{v+1} - W_{v_l}$' and '$W_{v+1} - W_{v_h}$' are eliminated from the formulas. Prove that the algorithm will still work, when applied to BDDs that represent kernels of graphs.

▶ **23.** [*M20*] All paths from the root of the BDD in Fig. 22 to $\boxed{\top}$ have exactly eight solid arcs. Why is this not a coincidence?

24. [*M22*] Suppose twelve weights $(w_{12}, w_{13}, \ldots, w_{89})$ have been assigned to the edges of the grid in Fig. 22. Explain how to find a minimum spanning tree in that graph (namely, a spanning tree whose edges have minimum total weight), by applying Algorithm B to the BDD shown there.

25. [*M20*] Modify Algorithm C so that it computes the generating function for the solutions to $f(x_1, \ldots, x_n) = 1$, namely $G(z) = \sum_{x_1=0}^{1} \cdots \sum_{x_n=0}^{1} z^{x_1 + \cdots + x_n} f(x_1, \ldots, x_n)$.

26. [*M20*] Modify Algorithm C so that it computes the reliability polynomial for given probabilities, namely

$$F(p_1, \ldots, p_n) = \sum_{x_1=0}^{1} \cdots \sum_{x_n=0}^{1} (1 - p_1)^{1-x_1} p_1^{x_1} \ldots (1 - p_n)^{1-x_n} p_n^{x_n} f(x_1, \ldots, x_n).$$

▶ **27.** [*M26*] Suppose $F(p_1, \ldots, p_n)$ and $G(p_1, \ldots, p_n)$ are the reliability polynomials for Boolean functions $f(x_1, \ldots, x_n)$ and $g(x_1, \ldots, x_n)$, where $f \ne g$. Let q be a prime number, and choose independent random integers $q_1, \ldots, q_n$, uniformly distributed in the range $0 \le q_k < q$. Prove that $F(q_1, \ldots, q_n) \bmod q \ne G(q_1, \ldots, q_n) \bmod q$ with probability $\ge (1 - 1/q)^n$. (In particular, if $n = 1000$ and $q = 2^{31} - 1$, different functions lead to different "hash values" under this scheme with probability at least 0.9999995.)

28. [*M16*] Let $F(p)$ be the value of the reliability polynomial $F(p_1, \ldots, p_n)$ when $p_1 = \cdots = p_n = p$. Show that it's easy to compute $F(p)$ from the generating function $G(z)$.

29. [*HM20*] Modify Algorithm C so that it computes the reliability polynomial $F(p)$ of exercise 28 and also its derivative $F'(p)$, given p and the BDD for f.

▶ **30.** [*M21*] The reliability polynomial is the sum, over all solutions to $f(x_1, \ldots, x_n) = 1$, of contributions from all "minterms" $(1 - p_1)^{1-x_1} p_1^{x_1} \ldots (1 - p_n)^{1-x_n} p_n^{x_n}$. Explain how to find a solution $x_1 \ldots x_n$ whose contribution to the total reliability is maximum, given a BDD for f and a sequence of probabilities $(p_1, \ldots, p_n)$.

31. [*M21*] Modify Algorithm C so that it computes the fully elaborated truth table of f, formalizing the procedure by which (24) was obtained from Fig. 21.

▶ **32.** [*M20*] What interpretations of '$\circ$', '$\bullet$', '$\bot$', '$\top$', '$\bar{x}_j$', and 'x_j' will make the general algorithm of exercise 31 specialize to the algorithms of exercises 25, 26, 29, and 30?

▶ **33.** [*M22*] Specialize exercise 31 so that we can efficiently compute

$$\sum_{f(x)=1} (w_1 x_1 + \cdots + w_n x_n) \qquad \text{and} \qquad \sum_{f(x)=1} (w_1 x_1 + \cdots + w_n x_n)^2$$

from the BDD of a Boolean function $f(x) = f(x_1, \ldots, x_n)$.

34. [*M25*] Specialize exercise 31 so that we can efficiently compute

$$\max\{\max_{1\le k\le n}(w_1x_1+\cdots+w_{k-1}x_{k-1}+w'_kx_k+w_{k+1}x_{k+1}+\cdots+w_nx_n+w''_k)\mid f(x)=1\}$$

from the BDD of f, given $3n$ arbitrary weights $(w_1,\ldots,w_n,w'_1,\ldots,w'_n,w''_1,\ldots,w''_n)$.

▶ **35.** [*22*] A *free binary decision diagram* (FBDD) is a binary decision diagram such as

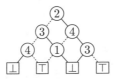

where the branch variables needn't appear in any particular order, but no variable is allowed to occur more than once on any downward path from the root. (An FBDD is "free" in the sense that every path in the dag is possible: No branch constrains another.)
a) Design an algorithm to verify that a supposed FBDD is really free.
b) Show that it's easy to compute the reliability polynomial $F(p_1,\ldots,p_n)$ of a Boolean function $f(x_1,\ldots,x_n)$, given $(p_1,\ldots,p_n)$ and an FBDD that defines f, and to compute the number of solutions to $f(x_1,\ldots,x_n)=1$.

36. [*25*] By extending exercise 31, explain how to compute the elaborated truth table for any given FBDD, if the abstract operators ∘ and • are commutative as well as distributive and associative. (Thus we can find optimum solutions as in Algorithm B, or solve problems such as those in exercises 30 and 33, with FBDDs as well as with BDDs.)

37. [*M20*] (R. L. Rivest and J. Vuillemin, 1976.) A Boolean function $f(x_1,\ldots,x_n)$ is called *evasive* if every FBDD for f contains a downward path of length n. Let $G(z)$ be the generating function for f, as in exercise 25. Prove that f is evasive if $G(-1)\ne 0$.

▶ **38.** [*27*] Let $I_{s-1},\ \ldots,\ I_0$ be branch instructions that define a nonconstant Boolean function $f(x_1,\ldots,x_n)$ as in (8) and (10). Design an algorithm that computes the status variables $t_1\ldots t_n$, where

$$t_j = \begin{cases} +1, & \text{if } f(x_1,\ldots,x_n)=1 \text{ whenever } x_j=1; \\ -1, & \text{if } f(x_1,\ldots,x_n)=1 \text{ whenever } x_j=0; \\ 0, & \text{otherwise.} \end{cases}$$

(If $t_1\ldots t_n\ne 0\ldots 0$, the function f is therefore *canalizing* as defined in Section 7.1.1.) The running time of your algorithm should be $O(n+s)$.

39. [*M20*] What is the size of the BDD for the threshold function $[x_1+\cdots+x_n\ge k]$?

▶ **40.** [*22*] Let g be the "condensation" of f obtained by setting $x_{k+1}\leftarrow x_k$ as in (27).
a) Prove that $B(g)\le B(f)$. [*Hint:* Consider subtables and beads.]
b) Suppose h is obtained from f by setting $x_{k+2}\leftarrow x_k$. Is $B(h)\le B(f)$?

41. [*M25*] Assuming that $n\ge 4$, find the BDD size of the Fibonacci threshold functions (a) $\langle x_1^{F_1}x_2^{F_2}\ldots x_{n-2}^{F_{n-2}}x_{n-1}^{F_{n-1}}x_n^{F_{n-2}}\rangle$ and (b) $\langle x_n^{F_1}x_{n-1}^{F_2}\ldots x_3^{F_{n-2}}x_2^{F_{n-1}}x_1^{F_{n-2}}\rangle$.

42. [*22*] Draw the BDD base for all symmetric Boolean functions of 3 variables.

▶ **43.** [*22*] What is $B(f)$ when (a) $f(x_1,\ldots,x_{2n})=[x_1+\cdots+x_n=x_{n+1}+\cdots+x_{2n}]$? (b) $f(x_1,\ldots,x_{2n})=[x_1+x_3+\cdots+x_{2n-1}=x_2+x_4+\cdots+x_{2n}]$?

▶ **44.** [*M32*] Determine the maximum possible size, Σ_n, of $B(f)$ when f is a symmetric Boolean function of n variables.

45. [*22*] Give precise specifications for the Boolean modules that compute the three-in-a-row function as in (33) and (34), and show that the network is well defined.

46. [*M23*] What is the true BDD size of the three-in-a-row function?

47. [*M21*] Devise and prove a *converse* of Theorem M: Every Boolean function f with a small BDD can be implemented by an efficient network of modules.

48. [*M22*] Implement the hidden weighted bit function with a network of modules like Fig. 23, using $a_k = 2 + \lambda k$ and $b_k = 1 + \lambda(n - k)$ connecting wires for $1 \le k < n$. Conclude from Theorem B that the upper bound in Theorem M cannot be improved to $\sum_{k=0}^{n} 2^{p(a_k, b_k)}$ for any polynomial p.

49. [*20*] Draw the BDD base for the following sets of symmetric Boolean functions: (a) $\{S_{\ge k}(x_1, x_2, x_3, x_4) \mid 1 \le k \le 4\}$; (b) $\{S_k(x_1, x_2, x_3, x_4) \mid 0 \le k \le 4\}$.

50. [*22*] Draw the BDD base for the functions of the ⧠-segment display (7.1.2–(42)).

51. [*22*] Describe the BDD base for binary addition when the input bits are numbered from right to left, namely $(f_{n+1} f_n f_{n-1} \dots f_1)_2 = (x_{2n-1} \dots x_3 x_1)_2 + (x_{2n} \dots x_4 x_2)_2$, instead of from left to right as in (35) and (36).

52. [*20*] There's a sense in which the BDD base for m functions $\{f_1, \dots, f_m\}$ isn't really very different from a BDD with just one root: Consider the *junction function* $J(u_1, \dots, u_n; v_1, \dots, v_n) = (u_1? \ v_1\colon u_2? \ v_2\colon \cdots u_n? \ v_n\colon 0)$, and let

$$f(t_1, \dots, t_{m+1}, x_1, \dots, x_n) = J(t_1, \dots, t_{m+1}; f_1(x_1, \dots, x_n), \dots, f_m(x_1, \dots, x_n), 1),$$

where $(t_1, \dots, t_{m+1})$ are new "dummy" variables, placed ahead of $(x_1, \dots, x_n)$ in the ordering. Show that $B(f)$ is almost the same as the size of the BDD base for $\{f_1, \dots, f_m\}$.

▶ **53.** [*23*] Play through Algorithm R, when it is applied to the binary decision diagram with seven branch nodes in (2).

54. [*17*] Construct the BDD of $f(x_1, \dots, x_n)$ from f's truth table, in $O(2^n)$ steps.

55. [*M30*] Explain how to construct the "connectedness BDD" of a graph (like Fig. 22).

56. [*20*] Modify Algorithm R so that, instead of pushing any unnecessary nodes onto an `AVAIL` stack, it creates a brand new BDD, consisting of consecutive instructions $I_{s-1}, \dots, I_1, I_0$ that have the compact form $(\bar{v}_k? \ l_k\colon h_k)$ assumed in Algorithms B and C. (The original nodes input to the algorithm can then all be recycled en masse.)

57. [*25*] Specify additional actions to be taken between steps R1 and R2 when Algorithm R is extended to compute the restriction of a function. Assume that $\texttt{FIX}[v] = t \in \{0, 1\}$ if variable v is to be given the fixed value t; otherwise $\texttt{FIX}[v] < 0$.

58. [*20*] Prove that the "melded" diagram defined by recursive use of (37) is reduced.

▶ **59.** [*M28*] Let $h(x_1, \dots, x_n)$ be a Boolean function. Describe the melded BDD $f \diamond g$ in terms of the BDD for h, when (a) $f(x_1, \dots, x_{2n}) = h(x_1, \dots, x_n)$ and $g(x_1, \dots, x_{2n}) = h(x_{n+1}, \dots, x_{2n})$; (b) $f(x_1, x_2, \dots, x_{2n}) = h(x_1, x_3, \dots, x_{2n-1})$ and $g(x_1, x_2, \dots, x_{2n}) = h(x_2, x_4, \dots, x_{2n})$. [In both cases we obviously have $B(f) = B(g) = B(h)$.]

60. [*22*] Suppose $f(x_1, \dots, x_n)$ and $g(x_1, \dots, x_n)$ have the profiles $(b_0, \dots, b_n)$ and $(b_0', \dots, b_n')$, respectively, and let their respective quasi-profiles be $(q_0, \dots, q_n)$ and $(q_0', \dots, q_n')$. Show that their meld $f \diamond g$ has $B(f \diamond g) \le \sum_{j=0}^{n} (q_j b_j' + b_j q_j' - b_j b_j')$ nodes.

▶ **61.** [*M27*] If α and β are nodes of the respective BDDs for f and g, prove that

$$\text{in-degree}(\alpha \diamond \beta) \ \le \ \text{in-degree}(\alpha) \cdot \text{in-degree}(\beta)$$

in the melded BDD $f \diamond g$. (Imagine that the root of a BDD has in-degree 1.)

▶ **62.** [*M21*] If $f(x) = \bigvee_{j=1}^{\lfloor n/2 \rfloor}(x_{2j-1} \wedge x_{2j})$ and $g(x) = (x_1 \wedge x_n) \vee \bigvee_{j=1}^{\lceil n/2 \rceil - 1}(x_{2j} \wedge x_{2j+1})$, what are the asymptotic values of $B(f)$, $B(g)$, $B(f \diamond g)$, and $B(f \vee g)$ as $n \to \infty$?

63. [*M27*] Let $f(x_1, \ldots, x_n) = M_m(x_1 \oplus x_2, x_3 \oplus x_4, \ldots, x_{2m-1} \oplus x_{2m}; x_{2m+1}, \ldots, x_n)$ and $g(x_1, \ldots, x_n) = M_m(x_2 \oplus x_3, \ldots, x_{2m-2} \oplus x_{2m-1}, x_{2m}; \bar{x}_{2m+1}, \ldots, \bar{x}_n)$, where $n = 2m + 2^m$. What are $B(f)$, $B(g)$, and $B(f \wedge g)$?

64. [*M21*] We can compute the median $\langle f_1 f_2 f_3 \rangle$ of three Boolean functions by forming

$$f_4 = f_1 \vee f_2, \quad f_5 = f_1 \wedge f_2, \quad f_6 = f_3 \wedge f_4, \quad f_7 = f_5 \vee f_6.$$

Then $B(f_4) = O(B(f_1)B(f_2))$, $B(f_5) = O(B(f_1)B(f_2))$, $B(f_6) = O(B(f_3)B(f_4)) = O(B(f_1)B(f_2)B(f_3))$; therefore $B(f_7) = O(B(f_5)B(f_6)) = O(B(f_1)^2 B(f_2)^2 B(f_3))$. Prove, however, that $B(f_7)$ is actually only $O(B(f_1)B(f_2)B(f_3))$, and the running time to compute it from f_5 and f_6 is also $O(B(f_1)B(f_2)B(f_3))$.

▶ **65.** [*M25*] If $h(x_1, \ldots, x_n) = f(x_1, \ldots, x_{j-1}, g(x_1, \ldots, x_n), x_{j+1}, \ldots, x_n)$, prove that $B(h) = O(B(f)^2 B(g))$. Can this upper bound be improved to $O(B(f)B(g))$ in general?

66. [*20*] Complete Algorithm S by explaining what to do in step S1 if $f \circ g$ turns out to be trivially constant.

67. [*24*] Sketch the actions of Algorithm S when (41) defines f and g, and $op = 1$.

68. [*20*] Speed up step S10 by streamlining the common case when LEFT(t) < 0.

69. [*21*] Algorithm S ought to have one or more precautionary instructions such as "if NTOP > TBOT, terminate the algorithm unsuccessfully," in case it runs out of room. Where are the best places to insert them?

70. [*21*] Discuss setting b to $\lfloor \lg$ LCOUNT[l] $\rfloor$ instead of $\lceil \lg$ LCOUNT[l] $\rceil$ in step S4.

71. [*20*] Discuss how to extend Algorithm S to ternary operators.

72. [*25*] Explain how to eliminate hashing from Algorithm S.

▶ **73.** [*25*] Discuss the use of "virtual addresses" instead of actual addresses as the links of a BDD: Each pointer p has the form $\pi(p)2^e + \sigma(p)$, where $\pi(p) = p \gg e$ is p's "page" and $\sigma(p) = p \bmod 2^e$ is p's "slot"; the parameter e can be chosen for convenience. Show that, with this approach, only two fields (LO, HI) are needed in BDD nodes, because the variable identifier $V(p)$ can be deduced from the virtual address p itself.

▶ **74.** [*M23*] Explain how to count the number of *self-dual* monotone Boolean functions of n variables, by modifying (49).

75. [*M20*] Let $\rho_n(x_1, \ldots, x_{2^n})$ be the Boolean function that is true if and only if $x_1 \ldots x_{2^n}$ is the truth table of a *regular* function (see exercise 7.1.1–110). Show that the BDD for ρ_n can be computed by a procedure similar to that of μ_n in (49).

▶ **76.** [*M22*] A "clutter" is a family S of mutually incomparable sets; in other words, $S \not\subseteq S'$ whenever S and S' are distinct members of S. Every set $S \subseteq \{0, 1, \ldots, n-1\}$ can be represented as an n-bit integer $s = \sum \{2^e \mid e \in S\}$; so every family of subsets of $\{0, 1, \ldots, n-1\}$ corresponds to a binary vector $x_0 x_1 \ldots x_{2^n-1}$, with $x_s = 1$ if and only if s represents a set of the family.

    Show that the BDD for the function '[$x_0 x_1 \ldots x_{2^n-1}$ corresponds to a clutter]' has a simple relation to the BDD for the monotone-function function $\mu_n(x_1, \ldots, x_{2^n})$.

▶ **77.** [*M35*] Show that there's an infinite sequence $(b_0, b_1, b_2, \ldots) = (1, 2, 3, 5, 6, \ldots)$ such that the profile of the BDD for μ_n is $(b_0, b_1, \ldots, b_{2^{n-1}-1}, b_{2^{n-1}-1}, \ldots, b_1, b_0, 2)$. (See Fig. 25.) How many branch nodes of that BDD have LO = $\boxed{\perp}$?

▶ **78.** [*25*] Use BDDs to determine the number of graphs on 12 labeled vertices for which the maximum vertex degree is d, for $0 \le d \le 11$.

79. [*20*] For $0 \le d \le 11$, compute the probability that a graph on vertices $\{1, \dots, 12\}$ has maximum degree d, if each edge is present with probability $1/3$.

80. [*23*] The recursive algorithm (55) computes $f \wedge g$ in a depth-first manner, while Algorithm S does its computation breadth-first. Do both algorithms encounter the same subproblems $f' \wedge g'$ as they proceed (but in a different order), or does one algorithm consider fewer cases than the other?

▶ **81.** [*20*] By modifying (55), explain how to compute $f \oplus g$ in a BDD base.

▶ **82.** [*25*] When the nodes of a BDD base have been endowed with REF fields, explain how those fields should be adjusted within (55) and within Algorithm U.

83. [*M20*] Prove that if f and g both have reference count 1, we needn't consult the memo cache when computing $\text{AND}(f, g)$ by (55).

84. [*24*] Suggest strategies for choosing the size of the memo cache and the sizes of the unique tables, when implementing algorithms for BDD bases. What is a good way to schedule periodic garbage collections?

85. [*16*] Compare the size of a BDD base for the 32 functions of 16×16-bit binary multiplication with the alternative of just storing a complete table of all possible products.

▶ **86.** [*21*] The routine MUX in (62) refers to "obvious" values. What are they?

87. [*20*] If the median operator $\langle fgh \rangle$ is implemented with a recursive subroutine analogous to (62), what are its "obvious" values?

▶ **88.** [*M25*] Find functions f, g, and h for which the recursive ternary computation of $f \wedge g \wedge h$ outperforms any of the binary computations $(f \wedge g) \wedge h$, $(g \wedge h) \wedge f$, $(h \wedge f) \wedge g$.

89. [*15*] Are the following quantified formulas true or false? (a) $\exists x_1 \exists x_2 f = \exists x_2 \exists x_1 f$. (b) $\forall x_1 \forall x_2 f = \forall x_2 \forall x_1 f$. (c) $\forall x_1 \exists x_2 f \le \exists x_2 \forall x_1 f$. (d) $\forall x_1 \exists x_2 f \ge \exists x_2 \forall x_1 f$.

90. [*M20*] When $l = m = n = 3$, Eq. (64) corresponds to the MOR operation of MMIX. Is there an analogous formula that corresponds to MXOR (matrix multiplication mod 2)?

▶ **91.** [*26*] In practice we often want to simplify a Boolean function f with respect to a "care set" g, by finding a function $\hat{f}$ with small $B(\hat{f})$ such that

$$f(x) \wedge g(x) \;\le\; \hat{f}(x) \;\le\; f(x) \vee \bar{g}(x) \qquad \text{for all } x.$$

In other words, $\hat{f}(x)$ must agree with $f(x)$ whenever x satisfies $g(x) = 1$, but we don't care what value $\hat{f}(x)$ assumes when $g(x) = 0$. An appealing candidate for such an $\hat{f}$ is provided by the function $f \downarrow g$, "f constrained by g," defined as follows: If $g(x)$ is identically 0, $f \downarrow g = 0$. Otherwise $(f \downarrow g)(x) = f(y)$, where y is the first element of the sequence x, $x \oplus 1$, $x \oplus 2$, $\dots$, such that $g(y) = 1$. (Here we think of x and y as n-bit numbers $(x_1 \dots x_n)_2$ and $(y_1 \dots y_n)_2$. Thus $x \oplus 1 = x \oplus 0 \dots 01 = x_1 \dots x_{n-1} \bar{x}_n$; $x \oplus 2 = x \oplus 0 \dots 010 = x_1 \dots x_{n-2} \bar{x}_{n-1} x_n$; etc.)

a) What are $f \downarrow 1$, $f \downarrow x_j$, and $f \downarrow \bar{x}_j$?
b) Prove that $(f \wedge f') \downarrow g = (f \downarrow g) \wedge (f' \downarrow g)$.
c) True or false: $\bar{f} \downarrow g = \overline{f \downarrow g}$.
d) Simplify the formula $f(x_1, \dots, x_n) \downarrow (x_2 \wedge \bar{x}_3 \wedge \bar{x}_5 \wedge x_6)$.
e) Simplify the formula $f(x_1, \dots, x_n) \downarrow (x_1 \oplus x_2 \oplus \cdots \oplus x_n)$.
f) Simplify the formula $f(x_1, \dots, x_n) \downarrow ((x_1 \wedge \cdots \wedge x_n) \vee (\bar{x}_1 \wedge \cdots \wedge \bar{x}_n))$.
g) Simplify the formula $f(x_1, \dots, x_n) \downarrow (x_1 \wedge g(x_2, \dots, x_n))$.

h) Find functions $f(x_1, x_2)$ and $g(x_1, x_2)$ such that $B(f \downarrow g) > B(f)$.

i) Devise a recursive way to compute $f \downarrow g$, analogous to (55).

92. [*M27*] The operation $f \downarrow g$ in exercise 91 sometimes depends on the ordering of the variables. Given $g = g(x_1, \ldots, x_n)$, prove that $(f^\pi \downarrow g^\pi) = (f \downarrow g)^\pi$ for all permutations π of $\{1, \ldots, n\}$ and for all functions $f = f(x_1, \ldots, x_n)$ if and only if $g = 0$ or g is a subcube (a conjunction of literals).

93. [*36*] Given a graph G on the vertices $\{1, \ldots, n\}$, construct Boolean functions f and g with the property that an approximating function $\hat{f}$ exists as in exercise 91 with small $B(\hat{f})$ if and only if G can be 3-colored. (Hence the task of minimizing $B(\hat{f})$ is NP-complete.)

94. [*21*] Explain why (65) performs existential quantification correctly.

▶ **95.** [*20*] Improve on (65) by testing if $r_l = 1$ before computing r_h.

96. [*20*] Show how to achieve (a) universal quantification $\forall x_{j_1} \ldots \forall x_{j_m} f = f \mathbin{A} g$, and (b) differential quantification $\mathbb{G} x_{j_1} \ldots \mathbb{G} x_{j_m} f = f \mathbin{D} g$, by modifying (65).

97. [*M20*] Prove that it's possible to compute arbitrary bottom-of-the-BDD quantifications such as $\exists x_{n-5} \forall x_{n-4} \mathbb{G} x_{n-3} \exists x_{n-2} \mathbin{\wedge} x_{n-1} \forall x_n f(x_1, \ldots, x_n)$ in $O(B(f))$ steps.

▶ **98.** [*22*] In addition to (70), explain how to define the vertices $\mathrm{ENDPT}(x)$ of $\mathcal{G}$ that have degree ≤ 1. Also characterize $\mathrm{PAIR}(x, y)$, the components of size 2.

99. [*20*] (R. E. Bryant, 1984.) Every 4-coloring of the US map considered in the text corresponds to 24 solutions of the COLOR function (73), under permutation of colors. What's a good way to remove this redundancy?

▶ **100.** [*24*] In how many ways is it possible to 4-color the contiguous USA with exactly 12 states of each color? (Eliminate DC from the graph.)

101. [*20*] Continuing exercise 100, with colors $\{1, 2, 3, 4\}$, find such a coloring that maximizes $\sum$ (state weight) $\times$ (state color), where states are weighted as in (18).

102. [*23*] Design a method to cache the results of functional composition using the following conventions: The system maintains at all times an array of functions $[g_1, \ldots, g_n]$, one for each variable x_j. Initially g_j is simply the projection function x_j, for $1 \leq j \leq n$. This array can be changed only by the subroutine $\mathrm{NEWG}(j, g)$, which replaces g_j by g. The subroutine $\mathrm{COMPOSE}(f)$ always performs functional composition with respect to the current array of replacement functions.

▶ **103.** [*20*] Mr. B. C. Dull wanted to evaluate the formula

$$\exists y_1 \ldots \exists y_m ((y_1 = f_1(x_1, \ldots, x_n)) \wedge \cdots \wedge (y_m = f_m(x_1, \ldots, x_n)) \wedge g(y_1, \ldots, y_m)),$$

for certain functions $f_1, \ldots, f_m$, and g. But his fellow student, J. H. Quick, found a much simpler formula for the same problem. What was Quick's idea?

▶ **104.** [*21*] Devise an efficient way to decide whether $f \leq g$ or $f \geq g$ or $f \parallel g$, where $f \parallel g$ means that f and g are incomparable, given the BDDs for f and g.

105. [*25*] A Boolean function $f(x_1, \ldots, x_n)$ is called *unate* with polarities $(y_1, \ldots, y_n)$ if the function $h(x_1, \ldots, x_n) = f(x_1 \oplus y_1, \ldots, x_n \oplus y_n)$ is monotone.

a) Show that f can be tested for unateness by using the $\wedge$ and N quantifiers.

b) Design a recursive algorithm to test unateness in at most $O(B(f)^2)$ steps, given the BDD for f. If f is unate, your algorithm should also find appropriate polarities.

106. [*25*] Let $f\$g\$h$ denote the relation "$f(x) = g(y) = 1$ implies $h(x \wedge y) = 1$, for all x and y." Show that this relation can be evaluated in at most $O(B(f)B(g)B(h))$ steps. [*Motivation:* Theorem 7.1.1H states that f is a Horn function if and only if $f\$f\$f$; thus we can test Horn-ness in $O(B(f)^3)$ steps.]

107. [*26*] Continuing exercise 106, show that it's possible to determine whether or not f is a Krom function in $O(B(f)^4)$ steps. [*Hint:* See Theorem 7.1.1S.]

108. [*HM24*] Let $b(n, s)$ be the number of n-variable Boolean functions with $B(f) \le s$. Prove that $(s - 3)!\,b(n, s) \le (n(s - 1)^2)^{s-2}$ when $s \ge 3$, and explore the ramifications of this inequality when $s = \lfloor 2^n/(n + 1/\ln 2) \rfloor$. [*Hint:* See the proof of Theorem 7.1.2S.]

▶ **109.** [*HM17*] Continuing exercise 108, show that almost all Boolean functions of n variables have $B(f^\pi) > 2^n/(n + 1/\ln 2)$, for all permutations π of $\{1, \ldots, n\}$, as $n \to \infty$.

110. [*25*] Construct explicit worst-case functions f_n with $B(f_n) = U_n$ in Theorem U.

111. [*M22*] Verify the summation formula (79) in Theorem U.

112. [*HM23*] Prove that $\min(2^k, 2^{2^{n-k}} - 2^{2^{n-k-1}}) - \hat{b}_k$ is very small, where $\hat{b}_k$ is the number defined in (80), except when $n - \lg n - 1 < k < n - \lg n + 1$.

113. [*20*] Instead of having two sink nodes, one for each Boolean constant, we could have 2^{16} sinks, one for each Boolean function of four variables. Then a BDD could stop four levels earlier, after branching on x_{n-4}. Would this be a good idea?

114. [*20*] Is there a function with profile $(1, 1, 1, 1, 1, 2)$ and quasi-profile $(1, 2, 3, 4, 3, 2)$?

▶ **115.** [*M22*] Prove the quasi-profile inequalities (84) and (124).

116. [*M21*] What is the (a) worst case (b) average case of a random quasi-profile?

117. [*M20*] Compare $Q(f)$ to $B(f)$ when $f = M_m(x_1, \ldots, x_m; x_{m+1}, \ldots, x_{m+2^m})$.

118. [*M23*] Show that, from the perspective of Section 7.1.2, the hidden weighted bit function has cost $C(h_n) = O(n)$. What is the exact value of $C(h_4)$?

119. [*20*] True or false: Every symmetric Boolean function of n variables is a special case of h_{2n+1}. (For example, $x_1 \oplus x_2 = h_5(0, 1, 0, x_1, x_2)$.)

120. [*18*] Explain the hidden-permuted-weighted-bit formula (94).

▶ **121.** [*M22*] If $f(x_1, \ldots, x_n)$ is any Boolean function, its *dual* f^D is $\bar{f}(\bar{x}_1, \ldots, \bar{x}_n)$, and its *reflection* f^R is $f(x_n \ldots, x_1)$. Notice that $f^{DD} = f^{RR} = f$ and $f^{DR} = f^{RD}$.

  a) Show that $h_n^{DR}(x_1, \ldots, x_n) = h_n(x_2, \ldots, x_n, x_1)$.

  b) Furthermore, the hidden weighted bit function satisfies the recurrence

  $$h_1(x_1) = x_1, \quad h_{n+1}(x_1, \ldots, x_{n+1}) = (x_{n+1}?\ h_n(x_2, \ldots, x_n, x_1): h_n(x_1, \ldots, x_n)).$$

  c) Define $x\psi$, a permutation on the set of all binary strings x, by the recursive rules

  $$\epsilon\psi = \epsilon, \quad (x_1 \ldots x_n 0)\psi = (x_1 \ldots x_n\psi)0, \quad (x_1 \ldots x_n 1)\psi = (x_2 \ldots x_n x_1)\psi 1.$$

  For example, $1101\psi = (101\psi)1 = (01\psi)11 = (0\psi)111 = (\psi)0111 = 0111$; and we also have $0111\psi = 1101$. Is ψ an involution?

  d) Show that $h_n(x) = \hat{h}_n(x\psi)$, where the function $\hat{h}_n$ has a very small BDD.

122. [*27*] Construct an FBDD for h_n that has fewer than n^2 nodes, when $n > 1$.

123. [*M20*] Prove formula (97), which enumerates all slates of offset s.

▶ **124.** [*27*] Design an efficient algorithm to compute the profile and quasi-profile of h_n^π, given a permutation π. [*Hint:* When does the slate $[r_0, \ldots, r_{n-k}]$ correspond to a bead?

▶ **125.** [*HM34*] Prove that $B(h_n)$ can be expressed exactly in terms of the sequences

$$A_n = \sum_{k=0}^{n} \binom{n-k}{2k}, \qquad B_n = \sum_{k=0}^{n} \binom{n-k}{2k+1}.$$

126. [*HM42*] Analyze $B(h_n^\pi)$ for the organ-pipe permutation $\pi = (2, 4, \ldots, n, \ldots, 3, 1)$.

127. [*46*] Find a permutation π that minimizes $B(h_{100}^\pi)$.

▶ **128.** [*25*] Given a permutation π of $\{1, \ldots, m + 2^m\}$, explain how to compute the profile and quasi-profile of the permuted 2^m-way multiplexer

$$M_m^\pi(x_1, \ldots, x_m; x_{m+1}, \ldots, x_{m+2^m}) = M_m(x_{1\pi}, \ldots, x_{m\pi}; x_{(m+1)\pi}, \ldots, x_{(m+2^m)\pi}).$$

129. [*M25*] Define $Q_m(x_1, \ldots, x_{m^2})$ to be 1 if and only if the 0–1 matrix $(x_{(i-1)m+j})$ has no all-zero row and no all-zero column. Prove that $B(Q_m^\pi) = \Omega(2^m/m^2)$ for all π.

130. [*HM31*] The adjacency matrix of an undirected graph G on vertices $\{1, \ldots, m\}$ consists of $\binom{m}{2}$ variable entries $x_{uv} = [u \!-\! v$ in $G]$, for $1 \le u < v \le m$. Let $C_{m,k}$ be the Boolean function [G has a k-clique], for some ordering of those $\binom{m}{2}$ variables.

   a) If $1 < k \le \sqrt{m}$, prove that $B(C_{m,k}) \ge \binom{s+t}{s}$, where $s = \binom{k}{2} - 1$ and $t = m + 2 - k^2$.

   b) Consequently $B(C_{m,\lceil m/2 \rceil}) = \Omega(2^{m/3 - O(\sqrt{m})})$, regardless of the variable ordering.

131. [*M28*] (*The covering function.*) The Boolean function

$$C(x_1, x_2, \ldots, x_p; y_{11}, y_{12}, \ldots, y_{1q}, y_{21}, \ldots, y_{2q}, \ldots, y_{p1}, y_{p2}, \ldots, y_{pq})$$
$$= ((x_1 {\wedge} y_{11}) {\vee} (x_2 {\wedge} y_{21}) {\vee} \cdots {\vee} (x_p {\wedge} y_{p1})) \wedge \cdots \wedge ((x_1 {\wedge} y_{1q}) {\vee} (x_2 {\wedge} y_{2q}) {\vee} \cdots {\vee} (x_p {\wedge} y_{pq}))$$

is true if and only if all columns of the matrix product

$$x \cdot Y = (x_1 x_2 \ldots x_p) \begin{pmatrix} y_{11} & y_{12} & \cdots & y_{1q} \\ y_{21} & y_{22} & \cdots & y_{2q} \\ \vdots & \vdots & \ddots & \vdots \\ y_{p1} & y_{p2} & \cdots & y_{pq} \end{pmatrix}$$

are positive, i.e., when the rows of Y selected by x "cover" every column of that matrix. The reliability polynomial of C is important in the analysis of fault-tolerant systems.

   a) When a BDD for C tests the variables in the order

$$x_1, y_{11}, y_{12}, \ldots, y_{1q}, x_2, y_{21}, y_{22}, \ldots, y_{2q}, \ldots, x_p, y_{p1}, y_{p2}, \ldots, y_{pq},$$

   show that the number of nodes is asymptotically $pq2^{q-1}$ for fixed q as $p \to \infty$.

   b) Find an ordering for which the size is asymptotically $pq2^{p-1}$ for fixed p as $q \to \infty$.

   c) Prove that $B_{\min}(C) = \Omega(2^{\min(p,q)/2})$ in general.

132. [*32*] What Boolean functions $f(x_1, x_2, x_3, x_4, x_5)$ have the largest $B_{\min}(f)$?

133. [*20*] Explain how to compute $B_{\min}(f)$ and $B_{\max}(f)$ from f's master profile chart.

134. [*24*] Construct the master profile chart, analogous to (102), for the Boolean function $x_1 \oplus ((x_2 \oplus (x_1 \vee (\bar{x}_2 \wedge x_3))) \wedge (x_3 \oplus x_4))$. What are $B_{\min}(f)$ and $B_{\max}(f)$? *Hint:* The identity $f(x_1, x_2, x_3, x_4) = f(x_1, x_2, \bar{x}_4, \bar{x}_3)$ saves about half the work.

135. [*M27*] For all $n \ge 4$, find a Boolean function $\theta_n(x_1, \ldots, x_n)$ that is *uniquely thin*, in the sense that $B(\theta_n^\pi) = n + 2$ for exactly one permutation π. (See (93) and (102).)

▶ **136.** [*M34*] What is the master profile chart of the median-of-medians function

$$\langle\langle x_{11}x_{12}\dots x_{1n}\rangle\langle x_{21}x_{22}\dots x_{2n}\rangle\dots\langle x_{m1}x_{m2}\dots x_{mn}\rangle\rangle,$$

when m and n are odd integers? What is the best ordering? (There are mn variables.)

137. [*M38*] Given a graph, the *optimum linear arrangement problem* asks for a permutation π of the vertices that minimizes $\sum_{u \,-\, v}|u\pi - v\pi|$. Construct a Boolean function f for which this minimum value is characterized by the optimum BDD size $B_{\min}(f)$.

▶ **138.** [*M36*] The purpose of this exercise is to develop an attractive algorithm that computes the master profile chart for a function f, given f's QDD (not its BDD).

   a) Explain how to find $\binom{n+1}{2}$ weights of the master profile chart from a single QDD.

   b) Show that the jump-up operation can be performed easily in a QDD, without garbage collection or hashing. *Hint:* See the "bucket sort" in Algorithm R.

   c) Consider the 2^{n-1} orderings of variables in which the $(i + 1)$st is obtained from the ith by a jump-up from depth $\rho i + \nu i$ to depth $\nu i - 1$. For example, we get

12345 21345 32145 31245 43125 41325 42135 42315 54231 52431 53241 53421 51342 51432 51243 51234

   when $n = 5$. Show that every k-element subset of $\{1, \dots, n\}$ occurs at the top k levels of one of these orderings.

   d) Combine these ideas to design the desired chart-construction algorithm.

   e) Analyze the space and time requirements of your algorithm.

139. [*22*] Generalize the algorithm of exercise 138 so that (i) it computes a common profile chart for all functions of a BDD base, instead of a single function; and (ii) it restricts the chart to variables $\{x_a, x_{a+1}, \dots, x_b\}$, preserving $\{x_1, \dots, x_{a-1}\}$ at the top and $\{x_{b+1}, \dots, x_n\}$ at the bottom.

140. [*27*] Explain how to find $B_{\min}(f)$ without knowing all of f's master profile chart.

141. [*30*] True or false: If $X_1, X_2, \dots, X_m$ are disjoint sets of variables, then an optimum BDD ordering for the variables of $g(h_1(X_1), h_2(X_2), \dots, h_m(X_m))$ can be found by restricting consideration to cases where the variables of each X_j are consecutive.

▶ **142.** [*HM32*] The representation of threshold functions by BDDs is surprisingly mysterious. Consider the self-dual function $f(x) = \langle x_1^{w_1} \dots x_n^{w_n}\rangle$, where each w_j is a positive integer and $w_1 + \dots + w_n$ is odd. We observed in (28) that $B(f) = O(w_1 + \dots + w_n)^2$; and $B(f)$ is often $O(n)$ even when the weights grow exponentially, as in (29) or exercise 41.

   a) Prove that when $w_1 = 1$, $w_k = 2^{k-2}$ for $1 < k \le m$, and $w_k = 2^m - 2^{n-k}$ for $m < k \le 2m = n$, $B(f)$ grows exponentially as $n \to \infty$, but $B_{\min}(f) = O(n^2)$.

   b) Find weights $\{w_1, \dots, w_n\}$ for which $B_{\min}(f) = \Omega(2^{\sqrt{n}/2})$.

143. [*24*] Continuing exercise 142(a), find an optimum ordering of variables for the function $\langle x_1 x_2 x_3^2 x_4^4 x_5^8 x_6^{16} x_7^{32} x_8^{64} x_9^{128} x_{10}^{256} x_{11}^{512} x_{12}^{768} x_{13}^{896} x_{14}^{960} x_{15}^{992} x_{16}^{1008} x_{17}^{1016} x_{18}^{1020} x_{19}^{1022} x_{20}^{1023}\rangle$.

144. [*16*] What is the quasi-profile of the addition functions $\{f_1, f_2, f_3, f_4, f_5\}$ in (36)?

145. [*24*] Find $B_{\min}(f_1, f_2, f_3, f_4, f_5)$ and $B_{\max}(f_1, f_2, f_3, f_4, f_5)$ of those functions.

▶ **146.** [*M22*] Let $(b_0, \dots, b_n)$ and $(q_0, \dots, q_n)$ be a BDD base profile and quasi-profile.

   a) Prove that $b_0 \le \min(q_0, (b_1 + q_2)(b_1 + q_2 - 1))$, $b_1 \le \min(b_0 + q_0, q_2(q_2 - 1))$, and $b_0 + b_1 \ge q_0 - q_2$.

   b) Conversely, if b_0, b_1, q_0, and q_2 are nonnegative integers that satisfy those inequalities, there is a BDD base with such a profile and quasi-profile.

▶ **147.** [*27*] Flesh out the details of Rudell's swap-in-place algorithm, using the conventions of Algorithm U and the reference counters of exercise 82.

148. [*M21*] True or false: $B(f_1^\pi, \ldots, f_m^\pi) \leq 2B(f_1, \ldots, f_m)$, after swapping ① ↔ ②.

149. [*M20*] (Bollig, Löbbing, and Wegener.) Show that, in addition to Theorem J⁻, we also have $B(f_1^\pi, \ldots, f_m^\pi) \leq (2^k - 2)b_0 + B(f_1, \ldots, f_m)$ after a jump-down operation of $k - 1$ levels, when $(b_0, \ldots, b_n)$ is the profile of $\{f_1, \ldots, f_m\}$.

150. [*30*] When repeated swaps are used to implement jump-up or jump-down, the intermediate results might be much larger than the initial or final BDD. Show that variable jumps can actually be done more directly, with a method whose worst-case running time is $O\big(B(f_1, \ldots, f_m) + B(f_1^\pi, \ldots, f_m^\pi)\big)$.

151. [*20*] Suggest a way to invoke Algorithm J so that each variable is sifted just once.

152. [*25*] The hidden weighted bit function h_{100} has more than 17.5 trillion nodes in its BDD. By how much does sifting reduce this number? *Hint:* Use exercise 124, instead of actually constructing the diagrams.

153. [*30*] Put the tic-tac-toe functions $\{y_1, \ldots, y_9\}$ of exercise 7.1.2–65 into a BDD base. How many nodes are present when variables are tested in the order $x_1, x_2, \ldots, x_9$, $o_1, o_2, \ldots, o_9$, from top to bottom? What is $B_{\min}(y_1, \ldots, y_9)$?

154. [*20*] By comparing (104) to (106), can you tell how far each state was moved when it was sifted?

▶ **155.** [*25*] Let f_1 be the independent-set function (105) of the contiguous USA, and let f_2 be the corresponding kernel function (see (68)). Find orderings π of the states so that (a) $B(f_2^\pi)$ and (b) $B(f_1^\pi, f_2^\pi)$ are as small as you can make them. (Note that the ordering (110) gives $B(f_1^\pi) = 339$, $B(f_2^\pi) = 795$, and $B(f_1^\pi, f_2^\pi) = 1129$.)

156. [*30*] Theorems J⁺ and J⁻ suggest that we could save reordering time by only jumping up when sifting, not bothering to jump down. Then we could eliminate steps J3, J5, J6, and J7 of Algorithm J. Would that be wise?

157. [*M24*] Show that if the $m + 2^m$ variables of the 2^m-way multiplexer M_m are arranged in any order such that $B(M_m^\pi) > 2^{m+1} + 1$, then sifting will reduce the BDD size.

158. [*M24*] When a Boolean function $f(x_1, \ldots, x_n)$ is symmetrical in the variables $\{x_1, \ldots, x_p\}$, it's natural to expect that those variables will appear consecutively in at least one of the reorderings $f^\pi(x_1, \ldots, x_n)$ that minimize $B(f^\pi)$. Show, however, that if

$$f(x_1, \ldots, x_n) = [x_1 + \cdots + x_p = \lfloor p/3 \rfloor] + [x_1 + \cdots + x_p = \lceil 2p/3 \rceil] \, g(x_{p+1}, \ldots, x_{p+m}),$$

where $p = n - m$ and $g(y_1, \ldots, y_m)$ is any nonconstant Boolean function, then $B(f^\pi) = \frac{1}{3}n^2 + O(n)$ as $n \to \infty$ when $\{x_1, \ldots, x_p\}$ are consecutive in π, but $B(f^\pi) = \frac{1}{4}n^2 + O(n)$ when π places about half of those variables at the beginning and half at the end.

159. [*20*] John Conway's basic rule for Life, exercise 7.1.3–167, is a Boolean function $L(x_{\mathrm{NW}}, x_{\mathrm{N}}, x_{\mathrm{NE}}, x_{\mathrm{W}}, x, x_{\mathrm{E}}, x_{\mathrm{SW}}, x_{\mathrm{S}}, x_{\mathrm{SE}})$. What ordering of those nine variables will make the BDD as small as possible?

▶ **160.** [*24*] (*Chess Life.*) Consider an 8×8 matrix $X = (x_{ij})$ of 0s and 1s, bordered by infinitely many 0s on all sides. Let $L_{ij}(X) = L(x_{(i-1)(j-1)}, \ldots, x_{ij}, \ldots, x_{(i+1)(j+1)})$ be Conway's basic rule at position (i, j). Call X "tame" if $L_{ij}(X) = 0$ whenever $i \notin [1 \, . . \, 8]$ or $j \notin [1 \, . . \, 8]$; otherwise X is "wild," because it activates cells outside the matrix.

　　a) How many tame configurations X vanish in one Life step, making all $L_{ij}(X) = 0$?
　　b) What is the maximum weight $\sum_{i=1}^{8} \sum_{j=1}^{8} x_{ij}$ among all such solutions?
　　c) How many wild configurations vanish *within* the matrix after one Life step?
　　d) What are the minimum and maximum weight, among all such solutions?
　　e) How many configurations X make $L_{ij}(X) = 1$ for $1 \leq i, j \leq 8$?

f) Investigate the tame 8×8 predecessors of the following patterns:

(1) (2) ▣ (3) ▦ (4) (5) ▨

(Here, as in Section 7.1.3, black cells denote 1s in the matrix.)

161. [*28*] Continuing exercise 160, write $L(X) = Y = (y_{ij})$ if X is a tame matrix such that $L_{ij}(X) = y_{ij}$ for $1 \le i, j \le 8$.

a) How many X's satisfy $L(X) = X$ ("still Life")?

b) Find an 8×8 still Life with weight 35.

c) A "flip-flop" is a pair of distinct matrices with $L(X)=Y$, $L(Y)=X$. Count them.

d) Find a flip-flop for which X and Y both have weight 28.

▶ **162.** [*30*] (*Caged Life.*) If X and $L(X)$ are tame but $L(L(X))$ is wild, we say that X "escapes" its cage after three steps. How many 6×6 matrices escape their 6×6 cage after exactly k steps, for $k = 1, 2, \ldots$?

163. [*23*] Prove formulas (112) and (113) for the BDD sizes of read-once functions.

▶ **164.** [*M27*] What is the maximum of $B(f)$, over all read-once functions $f(x_1, \ldots, x_n)$?

165. [*M21*] Verify the Fibonacci-based formulas (115) for $B(u_m)$ and $B(v_m)$.

166. [*M29*] Complete the proof of Theorem W.

167. [*21*] Design an efficient algorithm that computes a permutation π for which both $B(f^{\pi})$ and $B(f^{\pi}, \bar{f}^{\pi})$ are minimized, given any read-once function $f(x_1, \ldots, x_n)$.

▶ **168.** [*HM40*] Consider the following binary operations on ordered pairs $z = (x, y)$:

$$z \circ z' = (x, y) \circ (x', y') = (x + x', \min(x + y', x' + y));$$
$$z \bullet z' = (x, y) \bullet (x', y') = (x + x' + \min(y, y'), \max(y, y')).$$

(These operations are associative and commutative.) Let $S_1 = \{(1, 0)\}$, and

$$S_n = \bigcup_{k=1}^{n-1} \{z \circ z' \mid z \in S_k, \ z' \in S_{n-k}\} \cup \bigcup_{k=1}^{n-1} \{z \bullet z' \mid z \in S_k, \ z' \in S_{n-k}\} \text{ for } n > 1.$$

Thus $S_2 = \{(2, 0), (2, 1)\}$; $S_3 = \{(3, 0), (3, 1), (3, 2)\}$; $S_4 = \{(4, 0), \ldots, (4, 3), (5, 1)\}$; etc.

a) Prove that there exists a read-once function $f(x_1, \ldots, x_n)$ for which we have $\min_{\pi} B(f^{\pi}) = c$ and $\min_{\pi} B(f^{\pi}, \bar{f}^{\pi}) = c'$ if and only if $(\frac{1}{2}c' - 1, c - \frac{1}{2}c' - 1) \in S_n$.

b) True or false: $0 \le y < x$ for all $(x, y) \in S_n$.

c) If $z^T = (x + y, x - y)/\sqrt{2}$, show that $z^T \circ z'^T = (z \bullet z')^T$ and $z^T \bullet z'^T = (z \circ z')^T$.

d) Prove that $x^2 + y^2 \le n^{2\beta}$ for all $(x, y) \in S_n$, if β is the constant in (116). *Hints:* Let $|z|^2 = x^2 + y^2$; it suffices to prove that $|z \bullet z'| \le 2^{\beta} = \sqrt{2}\phi$ whenever $0 \le y \le x$, $0 \le y' \le x'$, $|z| = r = (1-\delta)^{\beta}$, $|z'| = r' = (1+\delta)^{\beta}$, and $0 \le \delta \le 1$. If also $y = y'$, $z \bullet z'$ lies inside the ellipse $(a \cos \theta + b \sin \theta, b \sin \theta)$, where $a = r + r'$ and $b = \sqrt{rr'}$.

169. [*M46*] Is $\min_{\pi} B(f^{\pi}) \le B(v_{2m+1})$ for every read-once function f of 2^{2m+1} variables?

▶ **170.** [*M25*] Let's say that a Boolean function is "skinny" if its BDD involves all the variables in the simplest possible way: A skinny BDD has exactly one branch node ⓙ for each variable x_j, and either LO or HI is a sink node at every branch.

a) How many Boolean functions $f(x_1, \ldots, x_n)$ are skinny in this sense?

b) How many of them are monotone?

c) Show that $f_t(x_1, \ldots, x_n) = [(x_1 \ldots x_n)_2 \ge t]$ is skinny when $0 < t < 2^n$ and t is odd.

d) What is the *dual* of the function f_t in part (c)?

e) Explain how to find the shortest CNF and DNF formulas for f_t, given t.

171. [*M26*] Continuing exercise 170, show that a function is *read-once* and *regular* if and only if it is skinny and monotone.

172. [*M28*] How many skinny functions $f(x_1, \ldots, x_n)$ are also Horn functions? How many of them have the property that f and $\bar{f}$ *both* satisfy Horn's condition?

▶ **173.** [*HM33*] Exactly how many Boolean functions $f(x_1, \ldots, x_n)$ are skinny after some reordering of the variables, $f(x_{1\pi}, \ldots, x_{n\pi})$?

▶ **174.** [*M39*] Let S_n be the number of Boolean functions $f(x_1, \ldots, x_n)$ whose BDD is "thin" in the sense that it has exactly one node labeled (j) for $1 \le j \le n$. Show that S_n is also the number of combinatorial objects of the following types:

a) *Dellac permutations of order $2n$* (namely, permutations $p_1 p_2 \ldots p_{2n}$ such that $\lceil k/2 \rceil \le p_k \le n + \lceil k/2 \rceil$ for $1 \le k \le 2n$).

b) *Genocchi derangements of order $2n+2$* (namely, permutations $q_1 q_2 \ldots q_{2n+2}$ such that $q_k > k$ if and only if k is odd, for $1 \le k \le 2n+2$; also $q_k \ne k$ in a derangement).

c) *Irreducible Dumont pistols of order $2n+2$* (namely, sequences $r_1 r_2 \ldots r_{2n+2}$ such that $k \le r_k \le 2n+2$ for $1 \le k \le 2n+2$ and $\{r_1, r_2, \ldots, r_{2n+2}\} = \{2, 4, 6, \ldots, 2n, 2n+2\}$, with the special property that $2k \in \{r_1, \ldots, r_{2k-1}\}$ for $1 \le k \le n$).

d) Paths from $(1,0)$ to $(2n+2, 0)$ in the directed graph

$$
\begin{array}{ccccccccc}
& & & & & & (7,3) & \rightarrow & (8,3) \rightarrow \cdots \\
& & & & & & \uparrow & & \downarrow \\
& & (5,2) & \rightarrow & (6,2) & \rightarrow & (7,2) & \rightarrow & (8,2) \rightarrow \cdots \\
& & \uparrow & & \downarrow & & \uparrow & & \downarrow \\
(3,1) \rightarrow & (4,1) & \rightarrow & (5,1) & \rightarrow & (6,1) & \rightarrow & (7,1) & \rightarrow (8,1) \rightarrow \cdots \\
\uparrow & & \downarrow & & \uparrow & & \downarrow & & \downarrow \\
(1,0) \rightarrow (2,0) \rightarrow & (3,0) & \rightarrow & (4,0) \rightarrow (5,0) & \rightarrow & (6,0) \rightarrow (7,0) & \rightarrow (8,0) \rightarrow \cdots
\end{array}
$$

(Notice that objects of type (d) are very easy to count.)

175. [*M30*] Continuing exercise 174, find a way to enumerate the Boolean functions whose BDD contains exactly b_{j-1} nodes labeled (j), given a profile $(b_0, \ldots, b_{n-1}, b_n)$.

176. [*M35*] To complete the proof of Theorem X, we will use exercise 6.4–78, which states that $\{h_{a,b} \mid a \in A \text{ and } b \in B\}$ is a universal family of hash functions from n bits to l bits, when $h_{a,b}(x) = ((ax+b) \gg (n-l)) \bmod 2^l$, $A = \{a \mid 0 < a < 2^n, a \text{ odd}\}$, $B = \{b \mid 0 \le b < 2^{n-l}\}$, and $0 \le l \le n$. Let $I = \{h_{a,b}(p) \mid p \in P\}$ and $J = \{h_{a,b}(q) \mid q \in Q\}$.

a) Show that if $2^l - 1 \le 2^{t-1}\epsilon/(1-\epsilon)$, there are constants $a \in A$ and $b \in B$ for which $|I| \ge (1-\epsilon)2^l$ and $|J| \ge (1-\epsilon)2^l$.

b) Given such an a, let $J = \{j_1, \ldots, j_{|J|}\}$ where $0 = j_1 < \cdots < j_{|J|}$, and choose $Q' = \{q_1, \ldots, q_{|J|}\} \subseteq Q$ so that $h_{a,b}(q_k) = j_k$ for $1 \le k \le |J|$. Let $g(q)$ denote the middle $l-1$ bits of aq, namely $(aq \gg (n-l+1)) \bmod 2^{l-1}$. Prove that $g(q) \ne g(q')$ whenever q and q' are distinct elements of the set $Q'' = \{q_1, q_3, \ldots, q_{2\lceil |J|/2\rceil - 1}\}$.

c) Prove that the following set Q^* satisfies condition (120), when $l \ge 3$ and $y = a$:

$$Q^* = \{q \mid q \in Q'', g(q) \text{ is even, and } g(p) + g(q) = 2^{l-1} \text{ for some } p \in P\}.$$

d) Finally, show that $|Q^*|$ is large enough to prove Theorem X.

177. [*M22*] Complete the proof of Theorem A by bounding the entire quasi-profile.

178. [*M24*] (Amano and Maruoka.) Improve the constant in (121) by using a better variable ordering: $Z_n(x_{2n-1}, x_1, x_3, \ldots, x_{2n-3}; x_{2n}, x_2, x_4, \ldots, x_{2n-2})$.

179. [*M47*] Does the middle bit of multiplication satisfy $B_{\min}(Z_n) = \Theta(2^{6n/5})$?

180. [*M27*] Prove Theorem Y, using the hint given in the text.

181. [*M21*] Let $L_{m,n}$ be the *leading bit function* $Z_{m,n}^{(m+n)}(x_1, \ldots, x_m; y_1, \ldots, y_n)$. Prove that $B_{\min}(L_{m,n}) = O(2^m n)$ when $m \le n$.

182. [*M38*] (I. Wegener.) Does $B_{\min}(L_{n,n})$ grow exponentially as $n \to \infty$?

▶ **183.** [*M25*] Draw the first few levels of the BDD for the "limiting leading bit function"

$$[(.x_1 x_3 x_5 \ldots)_2 \cdot (.x_2 x_4 x_6 \ldots)_2 \ge \tfrac{1}{2}],$$

which has infinitely many Boolean variables. How many nodes b_k are there on level k? (We don't allow $(.x_1 x_3 x_5 \ldots)_2$ or $(.x_2 x_4 x_6 \ldots)_2$ to end with infinitely many 1s.)

184. [*M23*] What are the BDD and ZDD profiles of the permutation function P_m?

185. [*M25*] How large can $Z(f)$ be, when f is a symmetric Boolean function of n variables? (See exercise 44.)

186. [*10*] What Boolean function of $\{x_1, x_2, x_3, x_4, x_5, x_6\}$ has the ZDD '⊕'?

▶ **187.** [*20*] Draw the ZDDs for all 16 Boolean functions $f(x_1, x_2)$ of two variables. [*Hint:* Just as a BDD is obtained from a QDD by removing nodes with HI = LO, a ZDD is obtained by removing nodes with HI = $\perp$.]

188. [*16*] Express the 16 Boolean functions $f(x_1, x_2)$ as families of subsets of $\{1, 2\}$.

189. [*18*] What functions $f(x_1, \ldots, x_n)$ have a ZDD equal to their BDD?

190. [*20*] Describe all functions f for which (a) $Q(f) = B(f)$; (b) $Q(f) = Z(f)$.

▶ **191.** [*HM25*] How many functions $f(x_1, \ldots, x_n)$ have no $\boxed{\perp}$ in their ZDD?

192. [*M20*] Define the *Z-transform* of binary strings as follows: $\epsilon^Z = \epsilon$, $0^Z = 0$, $1^Z = 1$, and

$$(\alpha\beta)^Z = \begin{cases} \alpha^Z \alpha^Z, & \text{if } |\alpha| = n \text{ and } \beta = 0^n; \\ \alpha^Z 0^n, & \text{if } |\alpha| = n \text{ and } \beta = \alpha; \\ \alpha^Z \beta^Z, & \text{if } |\alpha| = |\beta| - 1, \text{ or if } |\alpha| = |\beta| = n \text{ and } \alpha \ne \beta \ne 0^n. \end{cases}$$

a) What is 11001001000011111^Z?

b) True or false: $(\tau^Z)^Z = \tau$ for all binary strings τ.

c) If $f(x_1, \ldots, x_n)$ is a Boolean function with truth table τ, let $f^Z(x_1, \ldots, x_n)$ be the Boolean function whose truth table is τ^Z. Show that the profile of f is almost identical to the z-profile of f^Z, and vice versa. (Therefore Theorem U holds for ZDDs as well as for BDDs, and statistics such as (80) are valid also for z-profiles.)

193. [*M21*] Continuing exercise 192, what is $S_k^Z(x_1, \ldots, x_n)$ when $0 \le k \le n$?

194. [*M25*] How many $f(x_1, \ldots, x_n)$ have the z-profile $(1, \ldots, 1)$? (See exercise 174.)

195. [*24*] Find $Z(M_2)$, $Z_{\min}(M_2)$, and $Z_{\max}(M_2)$, where M_2 is the 4-way multiplexer.

196. [*M21*] Find a function $f(x_1, \ldots, x_n)$ for which $Z(f) = O(n)$ and $Z(\bar{f}) = \Omega(n^2)$.

197. [*25*] Modify the algorithm of exercise 138 so that it computes the "master z-profile chart" of f. (Then $Z_{\min}(f)$ and $Z_{\max}(f)$ can be found as in exercise 133.)

▶ **198.** [*23*] Explain how to compute AND(f, g) with ZDDs instead of BDDs (see (55)).

199. [*21*] Similarly, implement (a) OR(f, g), (b) XOR(f, g), (c) BUTNOT(f, g).

200. [*21*] And similarly, implement MUX(f, g, h) for ZDDs (see (62)).

201. [*22*] The projection functions x_j each have a simple 3-node BDD, but their ZDD representations are more complicated. What's a good way to implement these functions in a general-purpose ZDD toolkit?

202. [*24*] What changes are needed to the swap-in-place algorithm of exercise 147, when levels $(u) \leftrightarrow (v)$ are being interchanged in a ZDD base instead of a BDD base?

▶ **203.** [*M24*] (*Family algebra.*) The following algebraic conventions are useful for dealing with finite families of finite subsets of positive integers, and with their representation as ZDDs. The simplest such families are the *empty family*, denoted by $\emptyset$ and represented by $\boxed{\perp}$; the *unit family* $\{\emptyset\}$, denoted by ϵ and represented by $\boxed{\top}$; and the *elementary families* $\{\{j\}\}$ for $j \geq 1$, denoted by e_j and represented by a branch node (j) with LO $= \boxed{\perp}$ and HI $= \boxed{\top}$. (Exercise 186 illustrates the ZDD for e_3.)

Two families f and g can be combined with the usual set operations:
- The *union* $f \cup g = \{\alpha \mid \alpha \in f \text{ or } \alpha \in g\}$ is implemented by $\text{OR}(f, g)$;
- The *intersection* $f \cap g = \{\alpha \mid \alpha \in f \text{ and } \alpha \in g\}$ is implemented by $\text{AND}(f, g)$;
- The *difference* $f \setminus g = \{\alpha \mid \alpha \in f \text{ and } \alpha \notin g\}$ is implemented by $\text{BUTNOT}(f, g)$;
- The *symmetric difference* $f \oplus g = (f \setminus g) \cup (g \setminus f)$ is implemented by $\text{XOR}(f, g)$.

And we also define three new ways to construct families of subsets:
- The *join* $f \sqcup g = \{\alpha \cup \beta \mid \alpha \in f \text{ and } \beta \in g\}$, sometimes written just fg;
- The *meet* $f \sqcap g = \{\alpha \cap \beta \mid \alpha \in f \text{ and } \beta \in g\}$;
- The *delta* $f \boxplus g = \{\alpha \oplus \beta \mid \alpha \in f \text{ and } \beta \in g\}$.

All three are commutative and associative: $f \sqcup g = g \sqcup f$, $f \sqcup (g \sqcup h) = (f \sqcup g) \sqcup h$, etc.

a) Suppose $f = \{\emptyset, \{1, 2\}, \{1, 3\}\} = \epsilon \cup (e_1 \sqcup (e_2 \cup e_3))$ and $g = \{\{1, 2\}, \{3\}\} = (e_1 \sqcup e_2) \cup e_3$. What are $f \sqcup g$ and $(f \sqcap g) \setminus (f \boxplus e_1)$?

b) Any family f can also be regarded as a Boolean function $f(x_1, x_2, \dots)$, where $\alpha \in f \iff f([1 \in \alpha], [2 \in \alpha], \dots) = 1$. Describe the operations $\sqcup$, $\sqcap$, and $\boxplus$ in terms of Boolean logical formulas.

c) Which of the following formulas hold for all families f, g, and h? (i) $f \sqcup (g \cup h) = (f \sqcup g) \cup (f \sqcup h)$; (ii) $f \sqcap (g \cup h) = (f \sqcap g) \cup (f \sqcap h)$; (iii) $f \sqcup (g \cap h) = (f \sqcup g) \cap (f \sqcup h)$; (iv) $f \cup (g \sqcup h) = (f \cup g) \sqcup (f \cup h)$; (v) $f \boxplus \emptyset = \emptyset \sqcap g = h \sqcup \emptyset$; (vi) $f \sqcap \epsilon = \epsilon$.

d) We say that f and g are *orthogonal*, written $f \perp g$, if $\alpha \cap \beta = \emptyset$ for all $\alpha \in f$ and all $\beta \in g$. Which of the following statements is true for all families f and g? (i) $f \perp g \iff f \sqcap g = \epsilon$; (ii) $f \perp g \implies |f \sqcup g| = |f||g|$; (iii) $|f \sqcup g| = |f||g| \implies f \perp g$; (iv) $f \perp g \iff f \sqcup g = f \boxplus g$.

e) Describe all families f for which the following statements hold: (i) $f \cup g = g$ for all g; (ii) $f \sqcup g = g$ for all g; (iii) $f \sqcap g = g$ for all g; (iv) $f \sqcup (e_1 \sqcup e_2) = f$; (v) $f \sqcup (e_1 \cup e_2) = f$; (vi) $f \boxplus ((e_1 \sqcup e_2) \cup e_3) = f$; (vii) $f \boxplus f = \epsilon$; (viii) $f \sqcap f = f$.

▶ **204.** [*M25*] Continuing exercise 203, two further operations are also important:
- the *quotient* $f/g = \{\alpha \mid \alpha \cup \beta \in f \text{ and } \alpha \cap \beta = \emptyset, \text{ for all } \beta \in g\}$.
- the *remainder* $f \bmod g = f \setminus (g \sqcup (f/g))$.

The quotient is sometimes also called the "cofactor" of f with respect to g.

a) Prove that $f/(g \cup h) = (f/g) \cap (f/h)$.

b) Suppose $f = \{\{1, 2\}, \{1, 3\}, \{2\}, \{3\}, \{4\}\}$. What are f/e_2 and $f/(f/e_2)$?

c) Simplify the expressions $f/\emptyset$, f/ϵ, f/f, and $(f \bmod g)/g$, for arbitrary f and g.

d) Show that $f/g = f/(f/(f/g))$. *Hint:* Start with the relation $g \subseteq f/(f/g)$.

e) Prove that f/g can also be defined as $\bigcup \{h \mid g \sqcup h \subseteq f \text{ and } g \perp h\}$.

f) Given f and j, show that f has a unique representation $(e_j \sqcup g) \cup h$ with $e_j \perp (g \cup h)$.

g) True or false: $(f \sqcup g) \bmod e_j = (f \bmod e_j) \sqcup (g \bmod e_j)$; $(f \sqcap g)/e_j = (f/e_j) \sqcap (g/e_j)$.

205. [*M25*] Implement the five basic operations of family algebra, namely (a) $f \sqcup g$, (b) $f \sqcap g$, (c) $f \boxplus g$, (d) f/g, and (e) $f \bmod g$, using the conventions of exercise 198.

206. [*M46*] What are the worst-case running times of the algorithms in exercise 205?

▶ **207.** [*M25*] When one or more projection functions x_j are needed in applications, as in exercise 201, the following "symmetrizing" operation turns out to be very handy:

$$(e_{i_1} \cup e_{i_2} \cup \cdots \cup e_{i_l}) \S k = S_k(x_{i_1}, x_{i_2}, \ldots, x_{i_l}), \qquad \text{integer } k \geq 0.$$

For example, $e_j \S 1 = x_j$; $e_j \S 0 = \bar{x}_j$; $(e_i \cup e_j) \S 1 = x_i \oplus x_j$; $(e_2 \cup e_3 \cup e_5) \S 2 = (x_2 \wedge x_3 \wedge \bar{x}_5) \vee (x_2 \wedge \bar{x}_3 \wedge x_5) \vee (\bar{x}_2 \wedge x_3 \wedge x_5)$. Show that it's easy to implement this operation. (Notice that $e_{i_1} \cup \cdots \cup e_{i_l}$ has a very simple ZDD of size $l + 2$, when $l > 0$.)

▶ **208.** [*16*] By modifying Algorithm C, show that all solutions of a Boolean function can readily be counted when its ZDD is given instead of its BDD.

209. [*M21*] Explain how to compute the fully elaborated truth table of a Boolean function from its ZDD representation. (See exercise 31.)

▶ **210.** [*23*] Given the ZDD for f, show how to construct the ZDD for the function

$$g(x) = [f(x) = 1 \text{ and } \nu x = \max\{\nu y \mid f(y) = 1\}].$$

211. [*M20*] When f describes the solutions to an exact cover problem, is $Z(f) \leq B(f)$?

▶ **212.** [*25*] What's a good way to compute the ZDD for an exact cover problem?

213. [*16*] Why can't the mutilated chessboard be perfectly covered with dominoes?

▶ **214.** [*21*] When some shape is covered by dominoes, we say that the covering is *faultfree* if every straight line that passes through the interior of the shape also passes through the interior of some domino. For example, the right-hand covering in (127) is faultfree, but the middle one isn't; and the left-hand one has faults galore.

How many domino coverings of a chessboard are faultfree?

215. [*21*] Japanese tatami mats are 1×2 rectangles that are traditionally used to cover rectangular floors in such a way that no four mats meet at any corner. For example, Fig. 29(a) shows a 6×5 pattern from the 1641 edition of Mitsuyoshi Yoshida's *Jinkōki*, a book first published in 1627.

Find all domino coverings of a chessboard that are also tatami tilings.

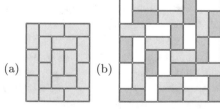

Fig. 29. Two nice examples:
(a) A 17th-century tatami tiling;   (a)
(b) a tricolored domino covering.

▶ **216.** [*30*] Figure 29(b) shows a chessboard covered with red, white, and blue dominoes, in such a way that no two dominoes of the same color are next to each other.

a) In how many ways can this be done?
b) How many of the 12,988,816 domino coverings are 3-colorable?

217. [*29*] The monomino/domino/tromino covering illustrated in (130) happens to satisfy an additional constraint: *No two congruent pieces are adjacent.* How many of the 92 sextillion coverings mentioned in the text are "separated," in this sense?

▶ **218.** [*24*] Apply BDD and ZDD techniques to the problem of Langford pairs, discussed at the beginning of this chapter.

219. [*20*] What is $Z(F)$ when F is the family (a) WORDS(1000); ...; (e) WORDS(5000)?

▶ **220.** [*21*] The z-profile of the 5757 SGB words, represented with 130 variables $a_1 \mathinner{.\,.} z_5$ as discussed in (131), is $(1, 1, 1, \ldots, 1, 1, 1, 23, 3, \ldots, 6, 2, 0, 3, 2, 1, 1, 2)$.

   a) Explain the entries 23 and 3, which correspond to the variables a_2 and b_2.

   b) Explain the final entries 0, 3, 2, 1, 1, 2, which correspond to v_5, w_5, x_5, etc.

▶ **221.** [*M27*] Only 5020 nodes are needed to represent the 5757 most common five-letter words of English, using the 130-variable representation, because of special linguistic properties. But there are $26^5 = 11{,}881{,}376$ possible five-letter words. Suppose we choose 5757 of them at random; how big will the ZDD be then, on average?

▶ **222.** [*27*] When family algebra is applied to five-letter words as in (131), the 130 variables are called a_1, b_1, ..., z_5 instead of x_1, x_2, ..., x_{130}; and the corresponding elementary families are denoted by the symbols a_1, b_1, ..., z_5 instead of e_1, e_2, ..., e_{130}. Thus the family $F = \mathtt{WORDS}(5757)$ can be constructed by synthesizing the formula

$$F = (\mathsf{w}_1 \sqcup \mathsf{h}_2 \sqcup \mathsf{i}_3 \sqcup \mathsf{c}_4 \sqcup \mathsf{h}_5) \cup \cdots \cup (\mathsf{f}_1 \sqcup \mathsf{u}_2 \sqcup \mathsf{n}_3 \sqcup \mathsf{n}_4 \sqcup \mathsf{y}_5) \cup \cdots \cup (\mathsf{p}_1 \sqcup \mathsf{u}_2 \sqcup \mathsf{p}_3 \sqcup \mathsf{a}_4 \sqcup \mathsf{l}_5).$$

   a) Let $\wp$ denote the *universal family* of all subsets of $\{a_1, \ldots, z_5\}$, also called the "power set." What does the formula $F \sqcap \wp$ signify?

   b) Let $X = X_1 \sqcup \cdots \sqcup X_5$, where $X_j = \{\mathsf{a}_j, \mathsf{b}_j, \ldots, \mathsf{z}_j\}$. Interpret the formula $F \sqcap X$.

   c) Find a simple formula for all words of F that match the pattern t*u*h.

   d) Find a formula for all SGB words that contain exactly k vowels, for $0 \le k \le 5$ (considering only a, e, i, o, and u to be vowels). Let $V_j = \mathsf{a}_j \cup \mathsf{e}_j \cup \mathsf{i}_j \cup \mathsf{o}_j \cup \mathsf{u}_j$.

   e) How many patterns in which exactly three letters are specified are matched by at least one SGB word? (For example, m*tc* is such a pattern.) Give a formula.

   f) How many of those patterns are matched at least twice (e.g., *atc*)?

   g) Express all words that remain words when a 'b' is changed to 'o'.

   h) What's the significance of the formula F/V_2?

   i) Contrast $(X_1 \sqcup V_2 \sqcup V_3 \sqcup V_4 \sqcup X_5) \cap F$ with $(X_1 \sqcup X_5) \setminus ((\wp \setminus F)/(V_2 \sqcup V_3 \sqcup V_4))$.

223. [*28*] A "median word" is a five-letter word $\mu = \mu_1 \ldots \mu_5$ that can be obtained from three words $\alpha = \alpha_1 \ldots \alpha_5$, $\beta = \beta_1 \ldots \beta_5$, $\gamma = \gamma_1 \ldots \gamma_5$ by the rule $[\alpha_i = \mu_i] + [\beta_i = \mu_i] + [\gamma_i = \mu_i] = 2$ for $1 \le i \le 5$. For example, mixed is a median of the words {fixed, mixer, mound}, and also of {mated, mixup, nixed}. But noted is not a median of {notes, voted, naked}, because each of those words has e in position 4.

   a) Show that $\{d(\alpha, \mu), d(\beta, \mu), d(\gamma, \mu)\}$ is either $\{1, 1, 3\}$ or $\{1, 2, 2\}$ whenever μ is a median of $\{\alpha, \beta, \gamma\}$. (Here d denotes Hamming distance.)

   b) How many medians can be obtained from WORDS(n), when $n = 100$? 1000? 5757?

   c) How many of those medians belong to WORDS(m), when $m = 100$? 1000? 5757?

▶ **224.** [*20*] Suppose we form the ZDD for all source-to-sink paths in a dag, as in Fig. 28, when the dag happens to be a forest; that is, assume that every non-source vertex of the dag has in-degree 1. Show that the corresponding ZDD is essentially the same as the binary tree that represents the forest under the "natural correspondence between forests and binary trees," Eqs. 2.3.2–(1) through 2.3.2–(3).

▶ **225.** [*30*] Design an algorithm SIMPATH that produces a ZDD for all sets of edges that form a simple path from s to t, given a graph and two distinct vertices $\{s, t\}$.

▶ **226.** [*20*] Modify the algorithm of exercise 225 so that it yields a ZDD for all of the simple *cycles* in a given graph.

227. [*20*] Similarly, modify it so that it considers only *Hamiltonian paths* from s to t.

228. [*21*] And mutate it once more, for Hamiltonian paths from s to *any* other vertex.

229. [*15*] There are 587,218,421,488 paths from CA to ME in the graphs (18), but only 437,525,772,584 such paths in (133). Explain the discrepancy.

230. [*25*] Find the Hamiltonian paths of (133) that have minimum and maximum total length. What is the *average* length, if all Hamiltonian paths are equally likely?

231. [*23*] In how many ways can a king travel from one corner of a chessboard to the opposite corner, never occupying the same cell twice? (These are the simple paths from corner to corner of the graph $P_8 \boxtimes P_8$.)

▸ **232.** [*23*] Continuing exercise 231, a *king's tour* of the chessboard is an oriented Hamiltonian cycle of $P_8 \boxtimes P_8$. Determine the exact number of king's tours. What is the longest possible king's tour, in terms of Euclidean distance traveled?

▸ **233.** [*25*] Design an algorithm that builds a ZDD for the family of all *oriented cycles* of a given digraph. (See exercise 226.)

234. [*22*] Apply the algorithm of exercise 233 to the directed graph on the 49 postal codes AL, AR, ..., WY of (18), with XY $\longrightarrow$ YZ as in exercise 7–54(b). For example, one such oriented cycle is NC $\longrightarrow$ CT $\longrightarrow$ TN $\longrightarrow$ NC. How many oriented cycles are possible? What are the minimum and maximum cycle lengths?

235. [*22*] Form a digraph on the five-letter words of English by saying that $x \longrightarrow y$ when the last three letters of x match the first three letters of y (e.g., crown $\longrightarrow$ owner). How many oriented cycles does this digraph have? What are the longest and shortest?

▸ **236.** [*M25*] Many extensions to the family algebra of exercise 203 suggest themselves when ZDDs are applied to combinatorial problems, including the following five operations on families of sets:

- The *maximal elements* $f^\uparrow = \{\alpha \in f \mid \beta \in f$ and $\alpha \subseteq \beta$ implies $\alpha = \beta\}$;
- The *minimal elements* $f^\downarrow = \{\alpha \in f \mid \beta \in f$ and $\alpha \supseteq \beta$ implies $\alpha = \beta\}$;
- The *nonsubsets* $f \nearrow g = \{\alpha \in f \mid \beta \in g$ implies $\alpha \not\subseteq \beta\}$;
- The *nonsupersets* $f \searrow g = \{\alpha \in f \mid \beta \in g$ implies $\alpha \not\supseteq \beta\}$;
- The *minimal hitting sets* $f^\sharp = \{\alpha \mid \beta \in f$ implies $\alpha \cap \beta \neq \emptyset\}^\downarrow$.

For example, when f and g are the families of exercise 203(a) we have $f^\uparrow = e_1 \sqcup (e_2 \cup e_3)$, $f^\downarrow = \epsilon$, $f^\sharp = \emptyset$, $g^\uparrow = g^\downarrow = g$, $g^\sharp = (e_1 \cup e_2) \sqcup e_3$, $f \nearrow g = e_1 \sqcup e_3$, $f \searrow g = \epsilon$, $g \nearrow f = g \searrow f = \emptyset$.

a) Prove that $f \nearrow g = f \setminus (f \sqcap g)$, and give a similar formula for $f \searrow g$.

b) Let $f^C = \{\bar{\alpha} \mid \alpha \in f\} = f \boxplus U$, where $U = e_1 \sqcup e_2 \sqcup \cdots$ is the "universal set." Clearly $f^{CC} = f$, $(f \cup g)^C = f^C \cup g^C$, $(f \cap g)^C = f^C \cap g^C$, $(f \setminus g)^C = f^C \setminus g^C$. Show that we also have the duality laws $f^{\uparrow C} = f^{C \downarrow}$, $f^{\downarrow C} = f^{C \uparrow}$; $(f \sqcup g)^C = f^C \sqcap g^C$, $(f \sqcap g)^C = f^C \sqcup g^C$; $(f \nearrow g)^C = f^C \searrow g^C$, $(f \searrow g)^C = f^C \nearrow g^C$; $f^\sharp = (\wp \nearrow f^C)^\downarrow$.

c) True or false: (i) $x_1^\downarrow = e_1$; (ii) $x_1^\uparrow = e_1$; (iii) $x_1^\sharp = e_1$; (iv) $(x_1 \vee x_2)^\downarrow = e_1 \sqcup e_2$; (v) $(x_1 \wedge x_2)^\downarrow = e_1 \sqcup e_2$.

d) Which of the following formulas hold for all families f, g, and h? (i) $f^{\uparrow\uparrow} = f^\uparrow$; (ii) $f^{\uparrow\downarrow} = f^\downarrow$; (iii) $f^{\uparrow\downarrow} = f^\uparrow$; (iv) $f^{\downarrow\uparrow} = f^\downarrow$; (v) $f^{\sharp\sharp} = f^\sharp$; (vi) $f^{\sharp\uparrow} = f^\sharp$; (vii) $f^{\downarrow\sharp} = f^\sharp$; (viii) $f^{\uparrow\sharp} = f^\sharp$; (ix) $f^{\sharp\sharp} = f^\sharp$; (x) $f \nearrow (g \cup h) = (f \nearrow g) \cap (f \nearrow h)$; (xi) $f \searrow (g \cup h) = (f \searrow g) \cap (f \searrow h)$; (xii) $f \searrow (g \cup h) = (f \searrow g) \searrow h$; (xiii) $f \nearrow g^\uparrow = f \nearrow g$; (xiv) $f \searrow g^\uparrow = f \searrow g$; (xv) $(f \sqcup g)^\sharp = (f^\sharp \sqcup g^\sharp)^\downarrow$; (xvi) $(f \cup g)^\sharp = (f^\sharp \sqcup g^\sharp)^\downarrow$.

e) Suppose $g = \bigcup_{u-v}(e_u \sqcup e_v)$ is the family of all edges in a graph, and let f be the family of all the independent sets. Using the operations of extended family algebra, find simple formulas that express (i) f in terms of g; (ii) g in terms of f.

237. [25] Implement the five operations of exercise 236, in the style of exercise 205.

▶ **238.** [22] Use ZDDs to compute the *maximal induced bipartite subgraphs* of the contiguous-USA graph G in (18), namely the maximal subsets U such that $G \mid U$ has no cycles of odd length. How many such sets U exist? Give examples of the smallest and largest. Consider also the maximal induced *tripartite* (3-colorable) subgraphs.

▶ **239.** [21] Explain how to compute the *maximal cliques* of a graph G using family algebra, when G is specified by its edges g as in exercise 236(e). Find the maximal sets of vertices that can be covered by k cliques, for $k = 1, 2, \ldots$, when G is the graph (18).

▶ **240.** [22] A set of vertices U is called a *dominating set* of a graph if every vertex is at most one step away from U.
   a) Prove that every kernel of a graph is a minimal dominating set.
   b) How many minimal dominating sets does the USA graph (18) have?
   c) Find seven vertices of (18) that dominate 36 of the others.

▶ **241.** [28] The *queen graph* Q_8 consists of the 64 squares of a chessboard, with $u \!-\! v$ when squares u and v lie in the same row, column, or diagonal. How large are the ZDDs for its (a) kernels? (b) maximal cliques? (c) minimal dominating sets? (d) minimal dominating sets that are also cliques? (e) maximal induced bipartite subgraphs?
   Illustrate each of these five categories by exhibiting smallest and largest examples.

242. [24] Find all of the maximal ways to choose points on an 8×8 grid so that no three points lie on a straight line of any slope.

243. [M23] The *closure* $f^\cap$ of a family f of sets is the family of all sets that can be obtained by intersecting one or more members of f.
   a) Prove that $f^\cap = \{\alpha \mid \alpha = \bigcap\{\beta \mid \beta \in f \text{ and } \beta \supseteq \alpha\}\}$.
   b) What's a good way to compute the ZDD for $f^\cap$, given the ZDD for f?
   c) Find the generating function for $F^\cap$ when $F = \text{WORDS}(5757)$ as in exercise 222.

244. [25] What is the ZDD for the connectedness function of $P_3 \square P_3$ (Fig. 22)? What is the BDD for the spanning tree function of the same graph? (See Corollary S.)

▶ **245.** [M22] Show that the *prime clauses* of a monotone function f are $\text{PI}(f)^\sharp$.

246. [M21] Prove Theorem S, assuming that (137) is true.

▶ **247.** [M27] Determine the number of sweet Boolean functions of n variables for $n \leq 7$.

248. [M22] True or false: If f and g are sweet, so is $f(x_1, \ldots, x_n) \wedge g(x_1, \ldots, x_n)$.

249. [HM31] The connectedness function of a graph is "ultrasweet," in the sense that it is sweet under all permutations of its variables. Is there a nice way to characterize ultrasweet Boolean functions?

250. [28] There are 7581 monotone Boolean functions $f(x_1, x_2, x_3, x_4, x_5)$. What are the average values of $B(f)$ and $Z(\text{PI}(f))$ when one of them is chosen at random? What is the probability that $Z(\text{PI}(f)) > B(f)$? What is the maximum of $Z(\text{PI}(f))/B(f)$?

251. [M46] Is $Z(\text{PI}(f)) = O(B(f))$ for all monotone Boolean functions f?

252. [M30] When a Boolean function isn't monotone, its prime implicants involve negative literals; for example, the prime implicants of $(x_1? \; x_2 \colon x_3)$ are $x_1 \wedge x_2$, $\bar{x}_1 \wedge x_3$, and $x_2 \wedge x_3$. In such cases we can conveniently represent them with ZDDs if we consider them to be words in the $2n$-letter alphabet $\{e_1, e_1', \ldots, e_n, e_n'\}$. A "subcube" such as $01{*}0{*}$ is then $e_1' \sqcup e_2 \sqcup e_4'$ in family algebra (see 7.1.1–(29)); and $\text{PI}(x_1? \; x_2 \colon x_3) = (e_1 \sqcup e_2) \cup (e_1' \sqcup e_3) \cup (e_2 \sqcup e_3)$.

Exercise 7.1.1–116 shows that symmetric functions of n variables might have $\Omega(3^n/n)$ prime implicants. How large can $Z(\mathrm{PI}(f))$ be when f is symmetric?

▶ **253.** [*M26*] Continuing exercise 252, prove that if $f = (\bar{x}_1 \wedge f_0) \vee (x_1 \wedge f_1)$ we have $\mathrm{PI}(f) = A \cup (e'_1 \sqcup B) \cup (e_1 \sqcup C)$, where $A = \mathrm{PI}(f_0 \wedge f_1)$, $B = \mathrm{PI}(f_0) \setminus A$, and $C = \mathrm{PI}(f_1) \setminus A$. (Equation (137) is the special case when f is monotone.)

▶ **254.** [*M23*] Let the functions f and g of (52) be monotone, with $f \subseteq g$. Prove that

$$\mathrm{PI}(g) \setminus \mathrm{PI}(f) = (\mathrm{PI}(g_l) \setminus \mathrm{PI}(f_l)) \cup (\mathrm{PI}(g_h) \setminus \mathrm{PI}(f_h \cup g_l)).$$

▶ **255.** [*25*] A *multifamily* of sets, in which members of f are allowed to occur more than once, can be represented as a sequence of ZDDs $(f_0, f_1, f_2, \dots)$ in which f_k is the family of sets that occur $(\dots a_2 a_1 a_0)_2$ times in f where $a_k = 1$. For example, if α appears exactly $9 = (1001)_2$ times in the multifamily, α would be in f_3 and f_0.

a) Explain how to insert and delete items from this representation of a multifamily.

b) Implement the multiset union $h = f \uplus g$ for multifamilies.

256. [*M32*] Any nonnegative integer x can be represented as a family of subsets of the binary powers $U = \{2^{2^k} \mid k \geq 0\} = \{2^1, 2^2, 2^4, 2^8, \dots\}$, in the following way: If $x = 2^{e_1} + \dots + 2^{e_t}$, where $e_1 > \dots > e_t \geq 0$ and $t \geq 0$, the corresponding family has t sets $E_j \subseteq U$, where $2^{e_j} = \prod\{u \mid u \in E_j\}$. Conversely, every finite family of finite subsets of U corresponds in this way to a nonnegative integer x. For example, the number $41 = 2^5 + 2^3 + 1$ corresponds to the family $\{\{2^1, 2^4\}, \{2^1, 2^2\}, \emptyset\}$.

a) Find a simple connection between the binary representation of x and the truth table of the Boolean function that corresponds to the family for x.

b) Let $Z(x)$ be the size of the ZDD for the family that represents x, when the elements of U are tested in reverse order $\dots, 2^4, 2^2, 2^1$ (with highest exponents nearest to the root); for example, $Z(41) = 5$. Show that $Z(x) = O(\log x / \log\log x)$.

c) The integer x is called "sparse" if $Z(x)$ is substantially smaller than the upper bound in (b). Prove that the sum of sparse integers is sparse, in the sense that $Z(x + y) = O(Z(x)Z(y))$.

d) Is the saturating difference of sparse integers, $x \mathbin{\dot-} y$, always sparse?

e) Is the product of sparse integers always sparse?

257. [*40*] (S. Minato.) Explore the use of ZDDs to represent polynomials with nonnegative integer coefficients. *Hint:* Any such polynomial in x, y, and z can be regarded as a family of subsets of $\{2, 2^2, 2^4, \dots, x, x^2, x^4, \dots, y, y^2, y^4, \dots, z, z^2, z^4, \dots\}$; for example, $x^3 + 3xy + 2z$ corresponds naturally to the family $\{\{x, x^2\}, \{x, y\}, \{2, x, y\}, \{2, z\}\}$.

▶ **258.** [*25*] Given a positive integer n, what is the minimum size of a BDD that has exactly n solutions? Answer this question also for a ZDD of minimum size.

▶ **259.** [*25*] A sequence of *parentheses* can be encoded as a binary string by letting 0 represent '(' and 1 represent ')'. For example, ())(() is encoded as 011001.

Every forest of n nodes corresponds to a sequence of $2n$ parentheses that are properly *nested*, in the sense that left and right parentheses match in the normal way. (See, for example, 2.3.3–(2) or 7.2.1.6–(1).) Let

$$N_n(x_1, \dots, x_{2n}) = [x_1 \dots x_{2n} \text{ represents properly nested parentheses}].$$

For example, $N_3(0, 1, 1, 0, 0, 1) = 0$ and $N_3(0, 0, 1, 0, 1, 1) = 1$; in general, N_n has $C_n \approx 4^n/(\sqrt{\pi} n^{3/2})$ solutions, where C_n is a Catalan number. What are $B(N_n)$ and $Z(N_n)$?

▶ **260.** [*M27*] We will see in Section 7.2.1.5 that every partition of $\{1, \ldots, n\}$ into disjoint subsets corresponds to a "restricted growth string" $a_1 \ldots a_n$, which is a sequence of nonnegative integers with

$$a_1 = 0 \quad \text{and} \quad a_{j+1} \leq 1 + \max(a_1, \ldots, a_j) \text{ for } 1 \leq j < n.$$

Elements j and k belong to the same subset of the partition if and only if $a_j = a_k$.

a) Let $x_{j,k} = [a_j = k]$ for $0 \leq k < j \leq n$, and let R_n be the function of these $\binom{n+1}{2}$ variables that is true if and only if $a_1 \ldots a_n$ is a restricted growth string. (By studying this Boolean function we can study the family of all set partitions, and by placing further restrictions on R_n we can study set partitions with special properties. There are $\varpi_{100} \approx 5 \times 10^{115}$ set partitions when $n = 100$.) Calculate $B(R_{100})$ and $Z(R_{100})$. Approximately how large are $B(R_n)$ and $Z(R_n)$ as $n \to \infty$?

b) Show that, with a proper ordering of the variables $x_{j,k}$, the BDD base for $\{R_1, \ldots, R_n\}$ has the same number of nodes as the BDD for R_n alone.

c) We can also use fewer variables, approximately $n \lg n$ instead of $\binom{n+1}{2}$, if we represent each a_k as a binary integer with $\lceil \lg k \rceil$ bits. How large are the BDD and ZDD bases in *this* representation of set partitions?

261. [*HM21*] "The deterministic finite-state automaton with fewest states that accepts any given regular language is unique." What is the connection between this famous theorem of automata theory and the theory of binary decision diagrams?

262. [*M26*] The determination of optimum Boolean chains in Section 7.1.2 was greatly accelerated by restricting consideration to Boolean functions that are *normal*, in the sense that $f(0, \ldots, 0) = 0$. (See Eq. 7.1.2–(10).) Similarly, we could restrict BDDs so that each of their nodes denotes a normal function.

a) Explain how to do this by introducing "complement links," which point to the complement of a subfunction instead of to the subfunction itself.

b) Show that every Boolean function has a unique normalized BDD.

c) Draw the normalized BDDs for the 16 functions in exercise 1.

d) Let $B^0(f)$ be the size of the normalized BDD for f. Find the average and worst case of $B^0(f)$, and compare $B^0(f)$ to $B(f)$. (See (80) and Theorem U.)

e) The BDD base for 3×3 multiplication in (58) has $B(F_1, \ldots, F_6) = 52$ nodes. What is $B^0(F_1, \ldots, F_6)$?

f) How do (54) and (55) change, when AND is implemented with complement links?

263. [*HM25*] A *linear block code* is the set of binary column vectors $x = (x_1, \ldots, x_n)^T$ such that $Hx = 0$, where H is a given $m \times n$ "parity check matrix."

a) The linear block code with $n = 2^m - 1$, whose columns are the nonzero binary m-tuples from $(0, \ldots, 0, 1)^T$ to $(1, \ldots, 1, 1)^T$, is called the *Hamming code*. Prove that the Hamming code is 1-error correcting in the sense of exercise 7–23.

b) Let $f(x) = [Hx = 0]$, where H is an $m \times n$ matrix with no all-zero columns. Show that the BDD profile of f has a simple relation to the ranks of submatrices of H mod 2, and compute $B(f)$ for the Hamming code.

c) In general we can let $f(x) = [x$ is a codeword$]$ define *any* block code. Suppose some codeword $x = x_1 \ldots x_n$ has been transmitted through a possibly noisy channel, and that we've received the bits $y = y_1 \ldots y_n$, where the channel delivers $y_k = x_k$ with probability p_k for each k independently. Explain how to determine the most likely codeword x, given y, p_1, $\ldots$, p_n, and the BDD for f.

264. [*M46*] The text's "sweeping generalization" of Algorithms B and C, based on (22), embraces many important applications; but it does not appear to include quantities such as

$$\max_{f(x)=1}\left(\sum_{k=1}^{n} w_k x_k + \sum_{k=1}^{n-1} w_k' x_k x_{k+1}\right) \quad \text{or} \quad \max_{f(x)=1}\sum_{j=0}^{n-1}\left(w_j \sum_{k=1}^{n-j} x_k \dots x_{k+j}\right),$$

which also can be computed efficiently from the BDD or ZDD for f.

Develop a generalization that is even more sweeping.

▶ **265.** [*21*] Devise an algorithm that finds the mth smallest solution to $f(x) = 1$ in lexicographic order of $x_1 \dots x_n$, given m and the BDD for a Boolean function f of n variables. Your algorithm should take $O(nB(f) + n^2)$ steps.

▶ **266.** [*20*] Every forest F whose nodes are numbered $\{1, \dots, n\}$ in preorder defines two families of sets

$$a(F) = \{\text{anc}(1), \dots, \text{anc}(n)\} \quad \text{and} \quad d(F) = \{\text{dec}(1), \dots, \text{dec}(n)\},$$

where anc(k) and dec(k) are the inclusive ancestors and descendants of node k. For example, if F is

then $a(F) = \{\{1\}, \{1,2\}, \{3\}, \{3,4\}, \{3,5\}\}$ and $d(F) = \{\{1,2\}, \{2\}, \{3,4,5\}, \{4\}, \{5\}\}$. Conversely, F can be reconstructed from either $a(F)$ or $d(F)$.

Prove that the ZDD for the family $a(F)$ has exactly $n + 2$ nodes.

267. [*HM32*] Continuing exercise 266, find the minimum, maximum, and average size of the ZDD for the family $d(F)$, as F ranges over all forests on n nodes.

We dare not lengthen this book much more,
lest it be out of due proportion,
and repel men by its size.

— ÆLFRIC, *Catholic Homilies II* (c. 1000)

There are a thousand hacking at the branches of evil
to one who is striking at the root.

— HENRY D. THOREAU, *Walden; or, Life in the Woods* (1854)

7.2. GENERATING ALL POSSIBILITIES

All present or accounted for, sir.
— Traditional American military saying

All present and correct, sir.
— Traditional British military saying

7.2.1. Generating Basic Combinatorial Patterns

OUR GOAL in this section is to study methods for running through all of the possibilities in some combinatorial universe, because we often face problems in which an exhaustive examination of all cases is necessary or desirable. For example, we might want to look at all permutations of a given set.

Some authors call this the task of *enumerating* all of the possibilities; but that's not quite the right word, because "enumeration" most often means that we merely want to *count* the total number of cases, not that we actually want to look at them all. If somebody asks you to enumerate the permutations of $\{1, 2, 3\}$, you are quite justified in replying that the answer is $3! = 6$; you needn't give the more complete answer $\{123, 132, 213, 231, 312, 321\}$.

Other authors speak of *listing* all the possibilities; but that's not such a great word either. No sensible person would want to make a list of the $10! = 3{,}628{,}800$ permutations of $\{0, 1, 2, 3, 4, 5, 6, 7, 8, 9\}$ by printing them out on thousands of sheets of paper, nor even by writing them all in a computer file. All we really want is to have them present momentarily in some data structure, so that a program can examine each permutation one at a time.

So we will speak of *generating* all of the combinatorial objects that we need, and *visiting* each object in turn. Just as we studied algorithms for tree traversal in Section 2.3.1, where the goal was to visit every node of a tree, we turn now to algorithms that systematically traverse a combinatorial space of possibilities.

He's got 'em on the list —
he's got 'em on the list;
And they'll none of 'em be missed —
they'll none of 'em be missed.
— WILLIAM S. GILBERT, *The Mikado* (1885)

7.2.1.1. Generating all n-tuples. Let's start small, by considering how to run through all 2^n strings that consist of n binary digits. Equivalently, we want to visit all n-tuples $(a_1, \ldots, a_n)$ where each a_j is either 0 or 1. This task is also, in essence, equivalent to examining all subsets of a given set $\{x_1, \ldots, x_n\}$, because we can say that x_j is in the subset if and only if $a_j = 1$.

Of course such a problem has an absurdly simple solution. All we need to do is start with the binary number $(0 \ldots 00)_2 = 0$ and repeatedly add 1 until we reach $(1 \ldots 11)_2 = 2^n - 1$. We will see, however, that even this utterly trivial problem has astonishing points of interest when we look into it more deeply. And our study of n-tuples will pay off later when we turn to the generation of more difficult kinds of patterns.

In the first place, we can see that the binary-notation trick extends to other kinds of n-tuples. If we want, for example, to generate all $(a_1, \ldots, a_n)$ in which each a_j is one of the decimal digits $\{0, 1, 2, 3, 4, 5, 6, 7, 8, 9\}$, we can simply count from $(0 \ldots 00)_{10} = 0$ to $(9 \ldots 99)_{10} = 10^n - 1$ in the decimal number system. And if we want more generally to run through all cases in which

$$0 \le a_j < m_j \qquad \text{for } 1 \le j \le n, \tag{1}$$

where the upper limits m_j might be different in different components of the vector $(a_1, \ldots, a_n)$, the task is essentially the same as repeatedly adding unity to the number

$$\begin{bmatrix} a_1, & a_2, & \ldots, & a_n \\ m_1, & m_2, & \ldots, & m_n \end{bmatrix} \tag{2}$$

in a mixed-radix number system; see Eq. 4.1–(9) and exercise 4.3.1–9.

We might as well pause to describe the process more formally:

Algorithm M (*Mixed-radix generation*). This algorithm visits all n-tuples that satisfy (1), by repeatedly adding 1 to the mixed-radix number in (2) until overflow occurs. Auxiliary variables a_0 and m_0 are introduced for convenience.

M1. [Initialize.] Set $a_j \leftarrow 0$ for $0 \le j \le n$, and set $m_0 \leftarrow 2$.

M2. [Visit.] Visit the n-tuple $(a_1, \ldots, a_n)$. (The program that wants to examine all n-tuples now does its thing.)

M3. [Prepare to add one.] Set $j \leftarrow n$.

M4. [Carry if necessary.] If $a_j = m_j - 1$, set $a_j \leftarrow 0$, $j \leftarrow j - 1$, and repeat this step.

M5. [Increase, unless done.] If $j = 0$, terminate the algorithm. Otherwise set $a_j \leftarrow a_j + 1$ and go back to step M2. ∎

Algorithm M is simple and straightforward, but we shouldn't forget that nested loops are even simpler, when n is a fairly small constant. When $n = 4$, we could for example write out the following instructions:

> For $a_1 = 0, 1, \ldots, m_1 - 1$ (in this order) do the following:
>   For $a_2 = 0, 1, \ldots, m_2 - 1$ (in this order) do the following:
>   For $a_3 = 0, 1, \ldots, m_3 - 1$ (in this order) do the following: (3)
>   For $a_4 = 0, 1, \ldots, m_4 - 1$ (in this order) do the following:
>   Visit (a_1, a_2, a_3, a_4).

These instructions are equivalent to Algorithm M, and they are easily expressed in any programming language.

Gray binary code. Algorithm M runs through all $(a_1, \ldots, a_n)$ in lexicographic order, as in a dictionary. But there are many situations in which we prefer to visit those n-tuples in some other order. The most famous alternative arrangement is the so-called Gray binary code, which lists all 2^n strings of n bits in such a way

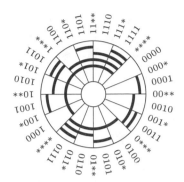   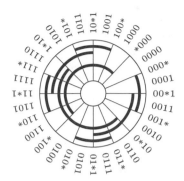

Fig. 30. (a) Lexicographic binary code.   (b) Gray binary code.

that only one bit changes each time, in a simple and regular way. For example, the Gray binary code for $n = 4$ is

$$0000, 0001, 0011, 0010, 0110, 0111, 0101, 0100,$$
$$1100, 1101, 1111, 1110, 1010, 1011, 1001, 1000. \tag{4}$$

Such codes are especially important in applications where analog information is being converted to digital or vice versa. For example, suppose we want to identify our current position on a rotating mechanical disk that has been divided into 16 sectors, using four fixed optical sensors that each distinguish black from white. If we use lexicographic order to mark the tracks from 0000 to 1111, as in Fig. 30(a), wildly inaccurate measurements can occur at the boundaries between sectors; but the code in Fig. 30(b) never gives a bad reading.

Gray binary code can be defined in many equivalent ways. For example, if Γ_n stands for the Gray binary sequence of n-bit strings, we can define Γ_n recursively by the two rules

$$\Gamma_0 = \epsilon;$$
$$\Gamma_{n+1} = 0\Gamma_n, \ 1\Gamma_n^R. \tag{5}$$

Here ϵ denotes the empty string, $0\Gamma_n$ denotes the sequence Γ_n with 0 prefixed to each string, and $1\Gamma_n^R$ denotes the sequence Γ_n in *reverse order* with 1 prefixed to each string. Since the last string of Γ_n equals the first string of Γ_n^R, it is clear from (5) that exactly one bit changes in every step of Γ_{n+1} if Γ_n enjoys the same property.

Another way to define the sequence $\Gamma_n = g(0), g(1), \ldots, g(2^n - 1)$ is to give an explicit formula for its individual elements $g(k)$. Indeed, since Γ_{n+1} begins with $0\Gamma_n$, the infinite sequence

$$\Gamma_\infty = g(0), g(1), g(2), g(3), g(4), \ldots$$
$$= (0)_2, (1)_2, (11)_2, (10)_2, (110)_2, \ldots \tag{6}$$

is a permutation of all the nonnegative integers, if we regard each string of 0s and 1s as a binary integer with optional leading 0s. Then Γ_n consists of the first 2^n elements of (6), converted to n-bit strings by inserting 0s at the left if needed.

When $k = 2^n + r$, where $0 \le r < 2^n$, relation (5) tells us that $g(k)$ is equal to $2^n + g(2^n - 1 - r)$. Therefore we can prove by induction on n that the integer k whose binary representation is $(\ldots b_2 b_1 b_0)_2$ has a Gray binary equivalent $g(k)$ with the representation $(\ldots a_2 a_1 a_0)_2$, where

$$a_j = b_j \oplus b_{j+1}, \qquad \text{for } j \ge 0. \tag{7}$$

(See exercise 6.) For example, $g\big((111001000011)_2\big) = (100101100010)_2$. Conversely, if $g(k) = (\ldots a_2 a_1 a_0)_2$ is given, we can find $k = (\ldots b_2 b_1 b_0)_2$ by inverting the system of equations (7), obtaining

$$b_j = a_j \oplus a_{j+1} \oplus a_{j+2} \oplus \cdots, \qquad \text{for } j \ge 0; \tag{8}$$

this infinite sum is really finite because $a_{j+t} = 0$ for all large t.

One of the many pleasant consequences of Eq. (7) is that $g(k)$ can be computed very easily with bitwise arithmetic:

$$g(k) = k \oplus \lfloor k/2 \rfloor. \tag{9}$$

Similarly, the inverse function in (8) satisfies

$$g^{[-1]}(l) = l \oplus \lfloor l/2 \rfloor \oplus \lfloor l/4 \rfloor \oplus \cdots; \tag{10}$$

this function, however, requires more computation (see exercise 7.1.3–8). We can also deduce from (7) that, if k and k' are any nonnegative integers,

$$g(k \oplus k') = g(k) \oplus g(k'). \tag{11}$$

Yet another consequence is that the $(n+1)$-bit Gray binary code can be written

$$\Gamma_{n+1} = 0\Gamma_n, \ (0\Gamma_n) \oplus 110 \ldots 0;$$

this pattern is evident, for example, in (4). Comparing with (5), we see that reversing the order of Gray binary code is equivalent to complementing the first bit:

$$\Gamma_n^R = \Gamma_n \oplus \overbrace{10 \ldots 0}^{n-1}, \text{ also written } \Gamma_n \oplus 10^{n-1}. \tag{12}$$

The exercises below show that the function $g(k)$ defined in (7), and its inverse $g^{[-1]}$ defined in (8), have many further properties and applications of interest. Sometimes we think of these as functions taking binary strings to binary strings; at other times we regard them as functions from integers to integers, via binary notation, with leading zeros irrelevant.

Gray binary code is named after Frank Gray, a physicist who became famous for helping to devise the method long used for compatible color television broadcasting [*Bell System Tech. J.* **13** (1934), 464–515]. He invented Γ_n for applications to pulse code modulation, a method for analog transmission of digital signals [see *Bell System Tech. J.* **30** (1951), 38–40; *U.S. Patent 2632058* (17 March 1953); W. R. Bennett, *Introduction to Signal Transmission* (1971), 238–240]. But the idea of "Gray binary code" was known long before he worked on it; for example, it appeared in *U.S. Patent 2307868* by George Stibitz (12 January 1943). More significantly, Γ_5 was used in a telegraph machine demonstrated in 1878 by Émile Baudot, after whom the term "baud" was later named. At about the same time, a similar but less systematic code for telegraphy was independently devised by Otto Schäffler [see *Journal Télégraphique* **4** (1878), 252–253; *Annales Télégraphiques* **6** (1879), 361, 382–383].*

In fact, Gray binary code is implicitly present in a classic toy that has fascinated people for centuries, now generally known as the "Chinese ring puzzle" in English, although Englishmen used to call it "tarrying irons" or "tiring irons." Figure 31 shows a seven-ring example. The challenge is to remove the rings from the bar, and the rings are interlocked in such a way that only two basic types of move are possible (although this may not be immediately apparent):

  a) The rightmost ring can be removed or replaced at any time;
  b) Any other ring can be removed or replaced if and only if the ring to its right is on the bar and all rings to the right of that one are off.

We can represent the current state of the puzzle in binary notation, writing 1 if a ring is on the bar and 0 if it is off; thus Fig. 31 shows the rings in state 1011000. (The second ring from the left is encoded as 0, because it lies entirely above the bar.)

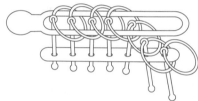

Fig. 31.
The Chinese ring puzzle.

A French magistrate named Louis Gros demonstrated an explicit connection between Chinese rings and binary numbers, in a booklet called *Théorie du Bague-nodier* [sic] (Lyon: Aimé Vingtrinier, 1872) that was published anonymously. If the rings are in state $a_{n-1} \ldots a_0$, and if we define the binary number $k = (b_{n-1} \ldots b_0)_2$ by Eq. (8), he showed that exactly k more steps are necessary and sufficient to solve the puzzle. Thus Gros is the true inventor of Gray binary code.

> *Certainly no home should be without*
> *this fascinating, historic, and instructive puzzle.*
> — HENRY E. DUDENEY (1901)

When the rings are in any state other than $00\ldots0$ or $10\ldots0$, exactly two moves are possible, one of type (a) and one of type (b). Only one of these moves advances toward the desired goal; the other is a step backward that will need to be undone. A type (a) move changes k to $k \oplus 1$; thus we want to do it when k is odd, since this will decrease k. A type (b) move from a position that ends in $(10^{j-1})_2$ for $1 \leq j < n$ changes k to $k \oplus (1^{j+1})_2 = k \oplus (2^{j+1} - 1)$. [In this formula '$1^{j+1}$' stands for $j + 1$ repetitions of '1', but '2^{j+1}' denotes a power of 2.] When

---

* Some authors have asserted that Gray code was invented by Elisha Gray, who developed a printing telegraph machine at the same time as Baudot and Schäffler. Such claims are untrue, although Elisha did get a raw deal with respect to priority for inventing the telephone [see L. W. Taylor, *Amer. Physics Teacher* **5** (1937), 243–251].

k is even, we want $k \oplus (2^{j+1} - 1)$ to equal $k - 1$, which means that k must be a multiple of 2^j but not a multiple of 2^{j+1}; in other words,

$$j = \rho(k), \tag{13}$$

where ρ is the "ruler function" of Eq. 7.1.3–(44). Therefore the rings follow a nice pattern when the puzzle is solved properly: If we number them $0, 1, \ldots, n-1$ (starting at the free end), the sequence of ring moves on or off the bar is the sequence of numbers that ends with $\ldots, \rho(4), \rho(3), \rho(2), \rho(1)$.

Going backwards, starting with $00\ldots0$ and successively putting rings on or off until we reach the ultimate state $10\ldots0$ (which, as John Wallis observed in 1693, is more difficult to reach than the supposedly harder state $11\ldots1$), yields an algorithm for counting in Gray binary code:

Algorithm G (*Gray binary generation*). This algorithm visits all binary n-tuples $(a_{n-1}, \ldots, a_1, a_0)$ by starting with $(0, \ldots, 0, 0)$ and changing only one bit at a time, also maintaining an even parity bit a_{-1} (as suggested by G. Rote) such that

$$a_{-1} = a_{n-1} \oplus \cdots \oplus a_1 \oplus a_0. \tag{14}$$

It successively complements bits $\rho(1), \rho(2), \rho(3), \ldots, \rho(2^n - 1)$ and then stops.

G1. [Initialize.] Set $a_j \leftarrow 0$ for $-1 \le j < n$.

G2. [Visit.] Visit the n-tuple $(a_{n-1}, \ldots, a_1, a_0)$.

G3. [Change parity.] Set $a_{-1} \leftarrow 1 - a_{-1}$.

G4. [Choose j.] Let $j \ge 0$ be minimum such that $a_{j-1} = 1$. (After the kth time we have performed this step, $j = \rho(k)$.)

G5. [Complement coordinate j.] Terminate if $j = n$; otherwise set $a_j \leftarrow 1 - a_j$ and return to G2. ▮

The parity bit a_{-1} comes in handy if we are computing a sum like

$$X_{000} - X_{001} - X_{010} + X_{011} - X_{100} + X_{101} + X_{110} - X_{111}$$

or

$$X_\emptyset - X_a - X_b + X_{ab} - X_c + X_{ac} + X_{bc} - X_{abc},$$

where the sign depends on the parity of a binary string or the number of elements in a subset. Such sums arise frequently in "inclusion-exclusion" formulas such as Eq. 1.3.3–(29). The parity bit is also necessary, for efficiency: Without it we could not easily choose between the two ways of determining j, which correspond to performing a type (a) or type (b) move in the Chinese ring puzzle. But the most important feature of Algorithm G is that step G5 makes only a single coordinate change. Therefore only a simple change is usually needed to the terms X that we are summing, or to whatever other structures we are concerned with as we visit each n-tuple.

> It is impossible, of course, to remove all ambiguity in the lowest-order digit
> except by a scheme like one the Irish railways are said to have used
> of removing the last car of every train
> because it is too susceptible to collision damage.
> — G. R. STIBITZ and J. A. LARRIVEE, *Mathematics and Computers* (1957)

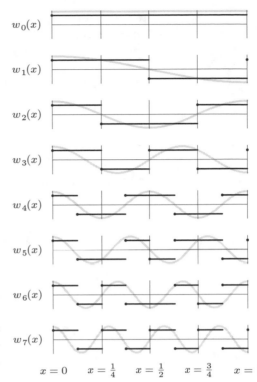

$$w_0(x)$$
$$w_1(x)$$
$$w_2(x)$$
$$w_3(x)$$
$$w_4(x)$$
$$w_5(x)$$
$$w_6(x)$$

Fig. 32. Walsh functions $w_k(x)$ for $0 \le k < 8$, with the analogous trigonometric functions $\sqrt{2}\cos k\pi x$ shown in gray for comparison.

$$w_7(x)$$

$x = 0 \qquad x = \frac{1}{4} \qquad x = \frac{1}{2} \qquad x = \frac{3}{4} \qquad x = 1$

Another key property of Gray binary code was discovered by J. L. Walsh in connection with an important sequence of functions now known as *Walsh functions* [see *Amer. J. Math.* **45** (1923), 5–24]. Let $w_0(x) = 1$ for all real numbers x, and

$$w_k(x) = (-1)^{\lfloor 2x \rfloor \lceil k/2 \rceil} w_{\lfloor k/2 \rfloor}(2x), \qquad \text{for } k > 0. \tag{15}$$

For example, $w_1(x) = (-1)^{\lfloor 2x \rfloor}$ changes sign whenever x is an integer or an integer plus $\frac{1}{2}$. It follows that $w_k(x) = w_k(x+1)$ for all k, and that $w_k(x) = \pm 1$ for all x. More significantly, $w_k(0) = 1$ and $w_k(x)$ has *exactly k sign changes in the interval* $(0 \mathinner{.\,.} 1)$, so that it approaches $(-1)^k$ as x approaches 1 from the left. Therefore $w_k(x)$ behaves rather like a trigonometric function $\cos k\pi x$ or $\sin k\pi x$, and we can represent other functions as a linear combination of Walsh functions in much the same way as they are traditionally represented as Fourier series. This fact, together with the simple discrete nature of $w_k(x)$, makes Walsh functions extremely useful in computer calculations related to information transmission, image processing, and many other applications.

Figure 32 shows the first eight Walsh functions together with their trigonometric cousins. Engineers commonly call $w_k(x)$ the Walsh function of *sequency* k, by analogy with the fact that $\cos k\pi x$ and $\sin k\pi x$ have *frequency* $k/2$. [See, for example, the book *Sequency Theory: Foundations and Applications* (New York: Academic Press, 1977), by H. F. Harmuth.]

Although Eq. (15) may look formidable at first glance, it actually provides an easy way to see by induction why $w_k(x)$ has exactly k sign changes as claimed. If k is even, say $k = 2l$, we have $w_{2l}(x) = w_l(2x)$ for $0 \le x < \frac{1}{2}$; the effect is simply to compress the function $w_l(x)$ into half the space, so $w_{2l}(x)$ has accumulated l sign changes so far. Then $w_{2l}(x) = (-1)^l w_l(2x) = (-1)^l w_l(2x - 1)$ in the range $\frac{1}{2} \le x < 1$; this concatenates another copy of $w_l(2x)$, flipping the sign if necessary to avoid a sign change at $x = \frac{1}{2}$. The function $w_{2l+1}(x)$ is similar, but it *forces* a sign change when $x = \frac{1}{2}$.

What does this have to do with Gray binary code? Walsh discovered that his functions could all be expressed neatly in terms of simpler functions called *Rademacher functions* [Hans Rademacher, *Math. Annalen* **87** (1922), 112–138],

$$r_k(x) = (-1)^{\lfloor 2^k x \rfloor}, \tag{16}$$

which take the value $(-1)^{c_{-k}}$ when $(\ldots c_2 c_1 c_0 . c_{-1} c_{-2} \ldots)_2$ is the binary representation of x. Indeed, we have $w_1(x) = r_1(x)$, $w_2(x) = r_1(x) r_2(x)$, $w_3(x) = r_2(x)$, and in general

$$w_k(x) = \prod_{j \ge 0} r_{j+1}(x)^{b_j \oplus b_{j+1}} \qquad \text{when } k = (\ldots b_2 b_1 b_0)_2. \tag{17}$$

(See exercise 33.) Thus the exponent of $r_{j+1}(x)$ in $w_k(x)$ is the jth bit of the Gray binary number $g(k)$, according to (7), and we have

$$w_k(x) = r_{\rho(k)+1}(x) w_{k-1}(x), \qquad \text{for } k > 0. \tag{18}$$

Equation (17) implies the handy formula

$$w_k(x) w_{k'}(x) = w_{k \oplus k'}(x), \tag{19}$$

which is much simpler than the corresponding product formulas for sines and cosines. This identity follows easily because $r_j(x)^2 = 1$ for all j and x, hence $r_j(x)^{a \oplus b} = r_j(x)^{a+b}$. It implies in particular that $w_k(x)$ is *orthogonal* to $w_{k'}(x)$ when $k \ne k'$, in the sense that the average value of $w_k(x) w_{k'}(x)$ is zero. We also can use (17) to define $w_k(x)$ for fractional values of k like $1/2$ or $13/8$.

The *Walsh transform* of 2^n numbers $(X_0, \ldots, X_{2^n-1})$ is the vector defined by the equation $(x_0, \ldots, x_{2^n-1})^T = W_n(X_0, \ldots, X_{2^n-1})^T$, where W_n is the $2^n \times 2^n$ matrix having $w_j(k/2^n)$ in row j and column k, for $0 \le j, k < 2^n$. For example, Fig. 32 tells us that the Walsh transform when $n = 3$ is

$$
\begin{pmatrix} x_{000} \\ x_{001} \\ x_{010} \\ x_{011} \\ x_{100} \\ x_{101} \\ x_{110} \\ x_{111} \end{pmatrix}
=
\begin{pmatrix}
1 & 1 & 1 & 1 & 1 & 1 & 1 & 1 \\
1 & 1 & 1 & 1 & \bar{1} & \bar{1} & \bar{1} & \bar{1} \\
1 & 1 & \bar{1} & \bar{1} & \bar{1} & \bar{1} & 1 & 1 \\
1 & 1 & \bar{1} & \bar{1} & 1 & 1 & \bar{1} & \bar{1} \\
1 & \bar{1} & \bar{1} & 1 & 1 & \bar{1} & \bar{1} & 1 \\
1 & \bar{1} & \bar{1} & 1 & \bar{1} & 1 & 1 & \bar{1} \\
1 & \bar{1} & 1 & \bar{1} & \bar{1} & 1 & \bar{1} & 1 \\
1 & \bar{1} & 1 & \bar{1} & 1 & \bar{1} & 1 & \bar{1}
\end{pmatrix}
\begin{pmatrix} X_{000} \\ X_{001} \\ X_{010} \\ X_{011} \\ X_{100} \\ X_{101} \\ X_{110} \\ X_{111} \end{pmatrix} . \tag{20}
$$

(Here $\bar{1}$ stands for -1, and the subscripts are conveniently regarded as binary strings 000–111 instead of as the integers 0–7.) The *Hadamard transform* is defined similarly, but with the matrix H_n in place of W_n, where H_n has $(-1)^{j \cdot k}$ in row j and column k; here '$j \cdot k$' denotes the dot product $a_{n-1}b_{n-1} + \cdots + a_0 b_0$ of the binary representations $j = (a_{n-1} \ldots a_0)_2$ and $k = (b_{n-1} \ldots b_0)_2$. For example, the Hadamard transform for $n = 3$ is

$$
\begin{pmatrix} x'_{000} \\ x'_{001} \\ x'_{010} \\ x'_{011} \\ x'_{100} \\ x'_{101} \\ x'_{110} \\ x'_{111} \end{pmatrix}
=
\begin{pmatrix}
1 & 1 & 1 & 1 & 1 & 1 & 1 & 1 \\
1 & \bar{1} & 1 & \bar{1} & 1 & \bar{1} & 1 & \bar{1} \\
1 & 1 & \bar{1} & \bar{1} & 1 & 1 & \bar{1} & \bar{1} \\
1 & \bar{1} & \bar{1} & 1 & 1 & \bar{1} & \bar{1} & 1 \\
1 & 1 & 1 & 1 & \bar{1} & \bar{1} & \bar{1} & \bar{1} \\
1 & \bar{1} & 1 & \bar{1} & \bar{1} & 1 & \bar{1} & 1 \\
1 & 1 & \bar{1} & \bar{1} & \bar{1} & \bar{1} & 1 & 1 \\
1 & \bar{1} & \bar{1} & 1 & \bar{1} & 1 & 1 & \bar{1}
\end{pmatrix}
\begin{pmatrix} X_{000} \\ X_{001} \\ X_{010} \\ X_{011} \\ X_{100} \\ X_{101} \\ X_{110} \\ X_{111} \end{pmatrix}.
\tag{21}
$$

This is the same as the discrete Fourier transform on an n-dimensional cube, Eq. 4.6.4–(38), and we can evaluate it quickly "in place" by adapting the method of Yates discussed in Section 4.6.4:

Given	First step	Second step	Third step
X_{000}	$X_{000}+X_{001}$	$X_{000}+X_{001}+X_{010}+X_{011}$	$X_{000}+X_{001}+X_{010}+X_{011}+X_{100}+X_{101}+X_{110}+X_{111}$
X_{001}	$X_{000}-X_{001}$	$X_{000}-X_{001}+X_{010}-X_{011}$	$X_{000}-X_{001}+X_{010}-X_{011}+X_{100}-X_{101}+X_{110}-X_{111}$
X_{010}	$X_{010}+X_{011}$	$X_{000}+X_{001}-X_{010}-X_{011}$	$X_{000}+X_{001}-X_{010}-X_{011}+X_{100}+X_{101}-X_{110}-X_{111}$
X_{011}	$X_{010}-X_{011}$	$X_{000}-X_{001}-X_{010}+X_{011}$	$X_{000}-X_{001}-X_{010}+X_{011}+X_{100}-X_{101}-X_{110}+X_{111}$
X_{100}	$X_{100}+X_{101}$	$X_{100}+X_{101}+X_{110}+X_{111}$	$X_{000}+X_{001}+X_{010}+X_{011}-X_{100}-X_{101}-X_{110}-X_{111}$
X_{101}	$X_{100}-X_{101}$	$X_{100}-X_{101}+X_{110}-X_{111}$	$X_{000}-X_{001}+X_{010}-X_{011}-X_{100}+X_{101}-X_{110}+X_{111}$
X_{110}	$X_{110}+X_{111}$	$X_{100}+X_{101}-X_{110}-X_{111}$	$X_{000}+X_{001}-X_{010}-X_{011}-X_{100}-X_{101}+X_{110}+X_{111}$
X_{111}	$X_{110}-X_{111}$	$X_{100}-X_{101}-X_{110}+X_{111}$	$X_{000}-X_{001}-X_{010}+X_{011}-X_{100}+X_{101}+X_{110}-X_{111}$

Notice that the rows of H_3 are a permutation of the rows of W_3. This is true in general, so we can obtain the Walsh transform by permuting the elements of the Hadamard transform. Exercise 36 discusses the details.

Going faster. When we're running through 2^n possibilities, we usually want to reduce the computation time as much as possible. Algorithm G needs to complement only one bit a_j per visit to $(a_{n-1}, \ldots, a_0)$, but it loops in step G4 while choosing an appropriate value of j. Another approach has been suggested by Gideon Ehrlich [*JACM* **20** (1973), 500–513], who introduced the notion of *loopless* combinatorial generation: With a loopless algorithm, the number of operations performed between successive visits is required to be bounded in advance, so there never is a long wait before a new pattern has been generated.

We learned some tricks in Section 7.1.3 about quick ways to determine the number of leading or trailing 0s in a binary number. Those methods could be used in step G4 to make Algorithm G loopless, assuming that n isn't unreasonably large. But Ehrlich's method is quite different, and much more versatile, so it provides us with a new weapon in our arsenal of techniques for efficient computation. Here is how his approach can be used to generate binary n-tuples [see Bitner, Ehrlich, and Reingold, *CACM* **19** (1976), 517–521]:

Algorithm L (*Loopless Gray binary generation*). This algorithm, like Algorithm G, visits all binary n-tuples $(a_{n-1}, \ldots, a_0)$ in the order of the Gray binary code. But instead of maintaining a parity bit, it uses an array of "focus pointers" $(f_n, \ldots, f_0)$, whose significance is discussed below.

L1. [Initialize.] Set $a_j \leftarrow 0$ and $f_j \leftarrow j$ for $0 \le j < n$; also set $f_n \leftarrow n$. (A loopless algorithm is allowed to have loops in its initialization step, as long as the initial setup is reasonably efficient; after all, every program needs to be loaded and launched.)

L2. [Visit.] Visit the n-tuple $(a_{n-1}, \ldots, a_1, a_0)$.

L3. [Choose j.] Set $j \leftarrow f_0$, $f_0 \leftarrow 0$. (If this is the kth time we are performing the present step, j is now equal to $\rho(k)$.) Terminate if $j = n$; otherwise set $f_j \leftarrow f_{j+1}$ and $f_{j+1} \leftarrow j+1$.

L4. [Complement coordinate j.] Set $a_j \leftarrow 1 - a_j$ and return to L2. ▌

For example, the computation proceeds as follows when $n = 4$. Elements a_j have been underlined in this table if the corresponding bit b_j is 1 in the binary string $b_3 b_2 b_1 b_0$ such that $a_3 a_2 a_1 a_0 = g(b_3 b_2 b_1 b_0)$:

a_3	0	0	0	0	0	0	0	0	1	1	1	1	1	1	1	1
a_2	0	0	0	0	1	1	1	1	1	1	1	1	0	0	0	0
a_1	0	0	1	1	1	1	0	0	0	0	1	1	1	1	0	0
a_0	0	1	1	0	0	1	1	0	0	1	1	0	0	1	1	0
f_3	3	3	3	3	3	3	3	3	4	4	4	4	3	3	3	3
f_2	2	2	2	2	3	3	2	2	2	2	2	2	4	4	2	2
f_1	1	1	2	1	1	1	3	1	1	1	2	1	1	1	4	1
f_0	0	1	0	2	0	1	0	3	0	1	0	2	0	1	0	4

Although the binary number $k = (b_{n-1} \ldots b_0)_2$ never appears explicitly in Algorithm L, the focus pointers f_j represent it implicitly in a clever way, so that we can repeatedly form $g(k) = (a_{n-1} \ldots a_0)_2$ by complementing bit $a_{\rho(k)}$ as we should. Let's say that a_j is *passive* when it is underlined, *active* otherwise. Then the focus pointers satisfy the following invariant relations:

1) If a_j is passive and a_{j-1} is active, then f_j is the smallest index $j' > j$ such that $a_{j'}$ is active. (Bits a_n and a_{-1} are considered to be active for purposes of this rule, although they aren't really present in the algorithm.)
2) Otherwise $f_j = j$.

Thus, the rightmost element a_j of a block of passive elements $a_{i-1} \ldots a_{j+1} a_j$, with decreasing subscripts, has a focus f_j that points to the element a_i just to the left of that block. All other elements a_j have f_j pointing to themselves.

In these terms, the first two operations '$j \leftarrow f_0$, $f_0 \leftarrow 0$' in step L3 are equivalent to saying, "Set j to the index of the rightmost active element, and activate all elements to the right of a_j." Notice that if $f_0 = 0$, the operation $f_0 \leftarrow 0$ is redundant; but it doesn't do any harm. The other two operations of L3, '$f_j \leftarrow f_{j+1}$, $f_{j+1} \leftarrow j+1$', are equivalent to saying, "Make a_j passive," because we know that a_j and a_{j-1} are both active at this point in the computation.

(Again the operation $f_{j+1} \leftarrow j + 1$ might be harmlessly redundant.) The net effect of activation and passivation is therefore equivalent to counting in binary notation, as in Algorithm M, with 1-bits passive and 0-bits active.

Algorithm L is almost blindingly fast, because it does only five assignment operations and one test for termination between each visit to a generated n-tuple. But we can do even better. In order to see how, let's consider an application to recreational linguistics: Rudolph Castown, in *Word Ways* **1** (1968), 165–169, noted that all 16 of the ways to intermix the letters of `sins` with the corresponding letters of `fate` produce words that are found in a sufficiently large dictionary of English: `sine`, `sits`, `site`, etc.; and all but three of those words (namely `fane`, `fite`, and `sats`) are sufficiently common as to be unquestionably part of standard English. Therefore it is natural to ask the analogous question for five-letter words: What two strings of five letters will produce the maximum number of words in the Stanford GraphBase, when letters in corresponding positions are swapped in all 32 possible ways?

To answer this question, we need not examine all $\binom{26}{2}^5 = 3{,}625{,}908{,}203{,}125$ essentially different pairs of strings; it suffices to look at all $\binom{5757}{2} = 16{,}568{,}646$ pairs of words in the GraphBase, provided that at least one of those pairs produces at least 17 words, because every set of 17 or more five-letter words obtainable from two five-letter strings must contain two that are "antipodal" (with no corresponding letters in common). For every antipodal pair, we want to determine as rapidly as possible whether the 32 possible subset-swaps produce a significant number of English words.

Every 5-letter word can be represented as a 25-bit number using 5 bits per letter, from `"a"` $= 00000$ to `"z"` $= 11001$. A table of 2^{25} bits or bytes will then determine quickly whether a given five-letter string is a word. So the problem is reduced to generating the bit patterns of the 32 potential words obtainable by mixing the letters of two given words, and looking those patterns up in the table. We can proceed as follows, for each pair of 25-bit words w and w':

W1. [Check the difference.] Set $z \leftarrow w \oplus w'$. Reject the word pair (w, w') if m' & $(z - m)$ & $\bar{z} \neq 0$, where $m = 2^{20} + 2^{15} + 2^{10} + 2^5 + 1$ and $m' = 2^4 m$; this test eliminates cases where w and w' have a common letter in some position. (See 7.1.3–(90). It turns out that 10,614,085 of the 16,568,646 word pairs have no such common letters.)

W2. [Form individual masks.] Set $m_0 \leftarrow z$ & $(2^5 - 1)$, $m_1 \leftarrow z$ & $(2^{10} - 2^5)$, $m_2 \leftarrow z$ & $(2^{15} - 2^{10})$, $m_3 \leftarrow z$ & $(2^{20} - 2^{15})$, and $m_4 \leftarrow z$ & $(2^{25} - 2^{20})$, in preparation for the next step.

W3. [Count words.] Set $l \leftarrow 1$ and $A_0 \leftarrow w$; the variable l will count how many words starting with w we have found so far. Then perform the operations $swap(4)$ defined below.

W4. [Print a record-setting solution.] If l exceeds or equals the current maximum, print A_j for $0 \leq j < l$. ∎

The heart of this high-speed method is the sequence of operations $swap(4)$, which should be expanded inline (for example with a macro-processor) to eliminate all unnecessary overhead. It is defined in terms of the basic operation

$sw(j)$: Set $w \leftarrow w \oplus m_j$. Then if w is a word, set $A_l \leftarrow w$ and $l \leftarrow l + 1$.

Given $sw(j)$, which flips the letters in position j, we define

$$
\begin{aligned}
swap(0) &= sw(0); \\
swap(1) &= swap(0), sw(1), swap(0); \\
swap(2) &= swap(1), sw(2), swap(1); \\
swap(3) &= swap(2), sw(3), swap(2); \\
swap(4) &= swap(3), sw(4), swap(3).
\end{aligned}
\tag{22}
$$

Thus $swap(4)$ expands into a sequence of 31 steps $sw(0)$, $sw(1)$, $sw(0)$, $sw(2)$, $\ldots$, $sw(0) = sw(\rho(1))$, $sw(\rho(2))$, $\ldots$, $sw(\rho(31))$; these steps will be used 10 million times. We clearly gain speed by embedding the ruler function values $\rho(k)$ directly into our program, instead of recomputing them repeatedly for each word pair via Algorithm M, G, or L.

The winning pair of words generates a set of 21, namely

$$
\begin{aligned}
&\text{ducks, ducky, duces, dunes, dunks, dinks, dinky,} \\
&\text{dines, dices, dicey, dicky, dicks, picks, picky,} \tag{23} \\
&\text{pines, piney, pinky, pinks, punks, punky, pucks.}
\end{aligned}
$$

If, for example, $w = \text{ducks}$ and $w' = \text{piney}$, then $m_0 = \text{s} \oplus \text{y}$, so the first operation $sw(0)$ changes ducks to ducky, which is seen to be a word. The next operation $sw(1)$ applies m_1, which is $\text{k} \oplus \text{e}$ in the next-to-last letter position, so it produces the nonword ducey. Another application of $sw(0)$ changes ducey to duces (a legal term generally followed by the word tecum). And so on. All word pairs can be processed by this method in at most a few seconds.

Further streamlining is also possible. For example, once we have found a pair that yields k words, we can reject later pairs as soon as they generate $33 - k$ nonwords. But the method we've discussed is already quite fast, and it demonstrates the fact that even the loopless Algorithm L can be beaten.

Fans of Algorithm L may, of course, complain that we have speeded up the process only in the small special case $n = 5$, while Algorithm L solves the generation problem for n in general. A similar idea does, however, work also for general values of $n > 5$: We can expand out a program so that it rapidly generates all 32 settings of the rightmost bits $a_4 a_3 a_2 a_1 a_0$, as above; then we can apply Algorithm L after every 32 steps, using it to generate successive changes to the other bits $a_{n-1} \ldots a_5$. This approach reduces the amount of work done by Algorithm L by nearly a factor of 32.

Other binary Gray codes. The Gray binary code $g(0)$, $g(1)$, $\ldots$, $g(2^n - 1)$ is only one of many ways to traverse all possible n-bit strings while changing only a single bit at each step. Let us say that, in general, a "Gray cycle" on binary n-tuples is *any* sequence $(v_0, v_1, \ldots, v_{2^n-1})$ that includes every n-tuple and has the property that v_k differs from $v_{(k+1) \bmod 2^n}$ in just one bit position. Thus, in the terminology of graph theory, a Gray cycle is an oriented Hamiltonian

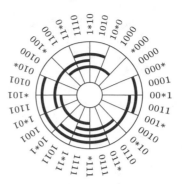

Fig. 33. (a) Complementary Gray code.   (b) Balanced Gray code.

cycle on the n-cube. We can assume that subscripts have been chosen so that $v_0 = 0 \ldots 0$.

If we think of the v's as binary numbers, there are integers $\delta_0 \ldots \delta_{2^n-1}$ such that

$$v_{(k+1) \bmod 2^n} = v_k \oplus 2^{\delta_k}, \qquad \text{for } 0 \le k < 2^n; \qquad (24)$$

this so-called "delta sequence" is another way to describe a Gray cycle. For example, the delta sequence for standard Gray binary when $n = 3$ is 01020102; it is essentially the ruler function $\delta_k = \rho(k+1)$ of (13), but the final value δ_{2^n-1} is $n-1$ instead of n, so that the cycle closes. The individual elements δ_k always lie in the range $0 \le \delta_k < n$, and they are called "coordinates."

Let $d(n)$ be the number of different delta sequences that define an n-bit Gray cycle, and let $c(n)$ be the number of "canonical" delta sequences in which each coordinate k appears before the first appearance of $k+1$. Then $d(n) = n!\, c(n)$, because every permutation of the coordinate numbers in a delta sequence obviously produces another delta sequence. The only possible canonical delta sequences for $n \le 3$ are easily seen to be

$$00; \qquad 0101; \qquad 01020102 \quad \text{and} \quad 01210121. \qquad (25)$$

Therefore $c(1) = c(2) = 1$, $c(3) = 2$; $d(1) = 1$, $d(2) = 2$, and $d(3) = 12$. A straightforward computer calculation, using techniques for the enumeration of Hamiltonian cycles that we will study later, establishes the next values,

$$\begin{aligned} c(4) &= 112; & d(4) &= 2688; \\ c(5) &= 15{,}109{,}096; & d(5) &= 1{,}813{,}091{,}520. \end{aligned} \qquad (26)$$

No simple pattern is evident, and the numbers grow quite rapidly (see exercise 47); therefore it's a fairly safe bet that nobody will ever know the exact values of $c(8)$ and $d(8)$.

Since the number of possibilities is so huge, people have been encouraged to look for Gray cycles that have additional useful properties. For example, Fig. 33(a) shows a 4-bit Gray cycle in which every string $a_3 a_2 a_1 a_0$ is diametrically opposite to its complement $\bar{a}_3 \bar{a}_2 \bar{a}_1 \bar{a}_0$. Such coding schemes are possible whenever the number of bits is even (see exercise 49).

An even more interesting Gray cycle, found by G. C. Tootill [*Proc. IEE* **103**, Part B Supplement (1956), 435], is shown in Fig. 33(b). This one has the same number of changes in each of the four coordinate tracks, hence all coordinates share equally in the activities. Gray cycles that are balanced in a similar way can in fact be constructed for all larger values of n, by using the following versatile method to extend a cycle from n bits to $n+2$ bits:

Theorem D. *Let $\alpha_1 j_1 \alpha_2 j_2 \ldots \alpha_l j_l$ be a delta sequence for an n-bit Gray cycle, where each j_k is a single coordinate, each α_k is a possibly empty sequence of coordinates, and l is odd. Then*

$$\alpha_1(n+1)\alpha_1^R n \alpha_1$$
$$j_1 \alpha_2 n \alpha_2^R (n+1)\alpha_2 \; j_2 \alpha_3 (n+1)\alpha_3^R n \alpha_3 \; \ldots \; j_{l-1}\alpha_l(n+1)\alpha_l^R n \alpha_l \quad (27)$$
$$(n+1)\alpha_l^R j_{l-1} \alpha_{l-1}^R \ldots \alpha_2^R j_1 \alpha_1^R n$$

is the delta sequence of an $(n+2)$-bit Gray cycle.

For example, if we start with the sequence $0102010\underline{2}$ for $n=3$ and let the three underlined elements be j_1, j_2, j_3, the new sequence (27) for a 5-bit cycle is

$$0141030102013102420104340102010103. \quad (28)$$

Proof. Let α_k have length m_k and let v_{kt} be the vertex reached if we start at $0\ldots0$ and apply the coordinate changes $\alpha_1 j_1 \ldots \alpha_{k-1} j_{k-1}$ and the first t of α_k. We need to prove that all vertices $00v_{kt}$, $01v_{kt}$, $10v_{kt}$, and $11v_{kt}$ occur when (27) is used, for $1 \le k \le l$ and $0 \le t \le m_k$. (The leftmost coordinate is $n+1$.)

Starting with $000\ldots0 = 00v_{10}$, we proceed to obtain the vertices

$$00v_{11}, \ldots, 00v_{1m_1}, 10v_{1m_1}, \ldots, 10v_{10}, 11v_{10}, \ldots, 11v_{1m_1};$$

then j_1 yields $11v_{20}$, which is followed by

$$11v_{21}, \ldots, 11v_{2m_2}, 10v_{2m_2}, \ldots, 10v_{20}, 00v_{20}, \ldots, 00v_{2m_2};$$

then comes $00v_{30}$, etc., and we eventually reach $11v_{lm_l}$. The glorious finale then uses the third line of (27) to generate all the missing vertices $01v_{lm_l}, \ldots, 01v_{10}$ and take us back to $000\ldots0$. ∎

The *transition counts* $(c_0, \ldots, c_{n-1})$ of a delta sequence are defined by letting c_j be the number of times $\delta_k = j$. For example, (28) has transition counts $(12, 8, 4, 4, 4)$, and it arose from a sequence with transition counts $(4, 2, 2)$. If we choose the original delta sequence carefully and underline appropriate elements j_k, we can obtain transition counts that are as equal as possible:

Corollary B. *For all $n \ge 1$, there is an n-bit Gray cycle with transition counts $(c_0, c_1, \ldots, c_{n-1})$ that satisfy the condition*

$$|c_j - c_k| \le 2 \qquad \text{for } 0 \le j < k < n. \quad (29)$$

(This is the best possible balance condition, because each c_j must be an even number, and we must have $c_0 + c_1 + \cdots + c_{n-1} = 2^n$. Indeed, condition (29) holds if and only if $n - r$ of the counts are equal to $2q$ and r are equal to $2q + 2$, where $q = \lfloor 2^{n-1}/n \rfloor$ and $r = 2^{n-1} \bmod n$.)

Proof. Given a delta sequence for an n-bit Gray cycle with transition counts $(c_0, \ldots, c_{n-1})$, the counts for cycle (27) are obtained by starting with the values $(c'_0, \ldots, c'_{n-1}, c'_n, c'_{n+1}) = (4c_0, \ldots, 4c_{n-1}, l+1, l+1)$, then subtracting 2 from c'_{j_k} for $1 \le k < l$ and subtracting 4 from c'_{j_l}. For example, when $n = 3$ we can obtain a balanced 5-bit Gray cycle having transition counts $(8 - 2, 16 - 10, 8, 6, 6) = (6, 6, 8, 6, 6)$ if we apply Theorem D to the delta sequence $0\underline{1}2\underline{1}0\underline{1}2\underline{1}$. Exercise 51 works out the details for other values of n. ∎

Another important class of n-bit Gray cycles in which each of the coordinate tracks has equal responsibility arises when we consider *run lengths*, namely the distances between consecutive appearances of the same δ value. Standard Gray binary code has run length 2 in the least significant position, and this can lead to a loss of accuracy when precise measurements need to be made [see, for example, the discussion by G. M. Lawrence and W. E. McClintock, *Proc. SPIE* **2831** (1996), 104–111]. But all runs have length 4 or more in the remarkable 5-bit Gray cycle whose delta sequence is

$$(0123042103210423)^2. \tag{30}$$

Let $r(n)$ be the maximum value r such that an n-bit Gray cycle can be found in which all runs have length $\ge r$. Clearly $r(1) = 1$, and $r(2) = r(3) = r(4) = 2$; and it is easy to see that $r(n)$ must be less than n when $n > 2$, hence (30) proves that $r(5) = 4$. Exhaustive computer searches establish the values $r(6) = 4$ and $r(7) = 5$. Indeed, a fairly straightforward backtrack calculation for the case $n = 7$ needs a tree of only about 60 million nodes to determine that $r(7) < 6$, and exercise 61(a) constructs a 7-bit cycle with no run shorter than 5. The exact values of $r(n)$ are unknown for $n \ge 8$; but $r(10)$ is almost certainly 8, and interesting constructions are known by which we can prove that $r(n) = n - O(\log n)$ as $n \to \infty$. (See exercises 60–64.)

*Binary Gray paths. We have defined an n-bit Gray cycle as a way to arrange all binary n-tuples into a sequence $(v_0, v_1, \ldots, v_{2^n-1})$ with the property that v_k is adjacent to v_{k+1} in the n-cube for $0 \le k < 2^n - 1$, and such that v_{2^n-1} is also adjacent to v_0. The cyclic property is nice, but not always essential; sometimes we can do better without it. Therefore we say that an n-bit *Gray path*, also commonly called a *Gray code*, is any sequence that satisfies the conditions of a Gray cycle except that the last element need not be adjacent to the first. In other words, a Gray cycle is a Hamiltonian *cycle* on the vertices of the n-cube, but a Gray code is simply a Hamiltonian *path* on that graph.

The most important binary Gray paths that are not also Gray cycles are n-bit sequences $(v_0, v_1, \ldots, v_{2^n-1})$ that are *monotonic*, in the sense that

$$\nu(v_k) \le \nu(v_{k+2}) \qquad \text{for } 0 \le k < 2^n - 2. \tag{31}$$

(Here, as elsewhere, we use ν to denote the "weight" or the "sideways sum" of a binary string, namely the number of 1s that it has.) Trial and error shows that

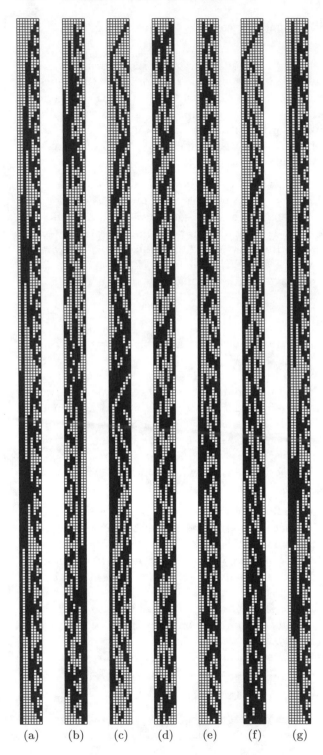

(a)   (b)   (c)   (d)   (e)   (f)   (g)

Fig. 34. Examples of
8-bit Gray codes:

    a) standard;
    b) balanced;
    c) complementary;
    d) long-run;
    e) nonlocal;
    f) monotonic;
    g) trend-free.

there are essentially only two monotonic n-bit Gray codes for each $n \le 4$, one starting with 0^n and the other starting with $0^{n-1}1$. The two for $n = 3$ are

$$000, \ 001, \ 011, \ 010, \ 110, \ 100, \ 101, \ 111; \tag{32}$$

$$001, \ 000, \ 010, \ 110, \ 100, \ 101, \ 111, \ 011. \tag{33}$$

The two for $n = 4$ are slightly less obvious, but not really difficult to discover.

Since $\nu(v_{k+1}) = \nu(v_k) \pm 1$ whenever v_k is adjacent to v_{k+1}, we obviously can't strengthen (31) to the requirement that all n-tuples be strictly sorted by weight. But relation (31) is strong enough to determine the weight of each v_k, given k and the weight of v_0, because we know that exactly $\binom{n}{j}$ of the n-tuples have weight j.

Figure 34 summarizes our discussions so far, by illustrating seven of the zillions of Gray codes that make a grand tour through all 256 of the possible 8-bit bytes. Black squares represent ones and white squares represent zeros. Figure 34(a) is the standard Gray binary code, while Fig. 34(b) is balanced with exactly $256/8 = 32$ transitions in each coordinate position. Figure 34(c) is a Gray code analogous to Fig. 33(a), in which the bottom 128 codes are complements of the top 128. In Fig. 34(d), the transitions in each coordinate position never occur closer than five steps apart; in other words, all run lengths are at least 5. The cycle in Fig. 34(e) is *nonlocal* in the sense of exercise 59. A monotonic path for $n = 8$ appears in Fig. 34(f); notice how black it gets near the bottom. Finally, Fig. 34(g) illustrates a Gray code that is totally nonmonotonic, in the sense that the center of gravity of the black squares lies exactly at the halfway point in each column. Standard Gray binary code has this property in seven of the coordinate positions, but Fig. 34(g) achieves perfect black-white weight balance in all eight. Such codes are called *trend-free*; they are important in the design of agricultural and other experiments (see exercises 75 and 76).

Carla Savage and Peter Winkler [*J. Combinatorial Theory* **A70** (1995), 230–248] found an elegant way to construct monotonic binary Gray codes for all $n > 0$. Such paths are necessarily built from subpaths P_{nj} in which all transitions are between n-tuples of weights j and $j + 1$. Savage and Winkler defined suitable subpaths recursively by letting $P_{10} = 0, 1$ and, for all $n > 0$,

$$P_{(n+1)j} = 1 P^{\pi_n}_{n(j-1)}, \ 0 P_{nj}; \tag{34}$$

$$P_{nj} = \emptyset \quad \text{if } j < 0 \text{ or } j \ge n. \tag{35}$$

Here π_n is a permutation of the coordinates that we will specify later, and the notation P^{π} means that every element $a_{n-1} \ldots a_1 a_0$ of the sequence P is replaced by $b_{n-1} \ldots b_1 b_0$, where $b_{j\pi} = a_j$. (We don't define P^{π} by letting $b_j = a_{j\pi}$, because we want $(2^j)^{\pi}$ to be $2^{j\pi}$.) It follows, for example, that

$$P_{20} = 0 P_{10} = 00, \ 01 \tag{36}$$

because $P_{1(-1)}$ is vacuous; also

$$P_{21} = 1 P^{\pi_1}_{10} = 10, \ 11 \tag{37}$$

because P_{11} is vacuous and π_1 must be the identity permutation. In general, P_{nj} is a sequence of n-bit strings containing exactly $\binom{n-1}{j}$ strings of weight j interleaved with $\binom{n-1}{j}$ strings of weight $j+1$.

Let α_{nj} and ω_{nj} be the first and last elements of P_{nj}. Then we easily find

$$\omega_{nj} = 0^{n-j-1}1^{j+1}, \qquad \text{for } 0 \le j < n; \tag{38}$$

$$\alpha_{n0} = 0^n, \qquad \text{for } n > 0; \tag{39}$$

$$\alpha_{nj} = 1\alpha_{(n-1)(j-1)}^{\pi_{n-1}}, \qquad \text{for } 1 \le j < n. \tag{40}$$

In particular, α_{nj} always has weight j, and ω_{nj} always has weight $j+1$. We will define permutations π_n of $\{0, 1, \ldots, n-1\}$ so that both of the sequences

$$P_{n0}, \; P_{n1}^R, \; P_{n2}, \; P_{n3}^R, \; \ldots \tag{41}$$

$$\text{and } P_{n0}^R, \; P_{n1}, \; P_{n2}^R, \; P_{n3}, \; \ldots \tag{42}$$

are monotonic binary Gray paths for $n = 1, 2, 3, \ldots$. In fact, the monotonicity is clear, so only the Grayness is in doubt; and the sequences (41), (42) link up nicely because the adjacencies

$$\alpha_{n0} \text{ —— } \alpha_{n1} \text{ —— } \cdots \text{ —— } \alpha_{n(n-1)}, \qquad \omega_{n0} \text{ —— } \omega_{n1} \text{ —— } \cdots \text{ —— } \omega_{n(n-1)} \tag{43}$$

follow immediately from (34), regardless of the permutations π_n. Thus the crucial point is the transition at the comma in formula (34), which makes $P_{(n+1)j}$ a Gray subpath if and only if

$$\omega_{n(j-1)}^{\pi_n} = \alpha_{nj} \qquad \text{for } 0 < j < n. \tag{44}$$

For example, when $n = 2$ and $j = 1$ we need $(01)^{\pi_2} = \alpha_{21} = 10$, by (38)–(40); hence π_2 must transpose coordinates 0 and 1. The general formula (see exercise 71) turns out to be

$$\pi_n = \sigma_n \pi_{n-1}^2, \tag{45}$$

where σ_n is the n-cycle $(n-1 \; \ldots \; 1 \; 0)$. The first few cases are therefore

$$\pi_1 = (0), \qquad\qquad \pi_4 = (0\,3),$$
$$\pi_2 = (0\,1), \qquad\qquad \pi_5 = (0\,4\,3\,2\,1),$$
$$\pi_3 = (0\,2\,1), \qquad\qquad \pi_6 = (0\,5\,2\,4\,1\,3);$$

no simple "closed form" for the magic permutations π_n is apparent. Exercise 73 shows that the Savage–Winkler codes can be generated efficiently.

Nonbinary Gray codes. We have studied the case of binary n-tuples in great detail, because it is the simplest, most classical, most applicable, and most thoroughly explored part of the subject. But of course there are numerous applications in which we want to generate $(a_1, \ldots, a_n)$ with integer components in the more general ranges $0 \le a_j < m_j$, as in Algorithm M. Gray codes apply nicely to this case as well.

Consider, for example, decimal digits, where we want $0 \le a_j < 10$ for each j. Is there a decimal way to count that is analogous to the Gray binary code, changing only one digit at a time? Yes; in fact, *two* natural schemes are available. In the first, called *reflected Gray decimal*, the digits change by ± 1 and the sequence for counting up to a thousand with 3-digit strings has the form

$$000, 001, \ldots, 009, 019, 018, \ldots, 011, 010, 020, 021, \ldots, 091, 090, 190, 191, \ldots, 900,$$

with each component moving alternately from 0 up to 9 and then back down from 9 to 0. In the second, called *modular Gray decimal*, the digits always increase by 1 mod 10, therefore they "wrap around" from 9 to 0:

$$000, 001, \ldots, 009, 019, 010, \ldots, 017, 018, 028, 029, \ldots, 099, 090, 190, 191, \ldots, 900.$$

In both cases the digit that changes on step k is determined by the radix-ten ruler function $\rho_{10}(k)$, the largest power of 10 that divides k. Therefore each n-tuple of digits occurs exactly once: We generate 10^j different settings of the rightmost j digits before changing any of the others, for $1 \le j \le n$.

In general, the reflected Gray code in any mixed-radix system can be regarded as a permutation of the nonnegative integers, a function that maps an ordinary mixed-radix number

$$k = \begin{bmatrix} b_{n-1}, & \ldots, & b_1, & b_0 \\ m_{n-1}, & \ldots, & m_1, & m_0 \end{bmatrix} = b_{n-1}m_{n-2}\ldots m_1 m_0 + \cdots + b_1 m_0 + b_0 \qquad (46)$$

into its reflected-Gray equivalent

$$\hat{g}(k) = \begin{bmatrix} a_{n-1}, & \ldots, & a_1, & a_0 \\ m_{n-1}, & \ldots, & m_1, & m_0 \end{bmatrix} = a_{n-1}m_{n-2}\ldots m_1 m_0 + \cdots + a_1 m_0 + a_0, \qquad (47)$$

just as (7) does this in the special case of binary numbers. Let

$$A_j = \begin{bmatrix} a_{n-1}, & \ldots, & a_j \\ m_{n-1}, & \ldots, & m_j \end{bmatrix}, \qquad B_j = \begin{bmatrix} b_{n-1}, & \ldots, & b_j \\ m_{n-1}, & \ldots, & m_j \end{bmatrix}, \qquad (48)$$

with $A_n = B_n = 0$, so that when $0 \le j < n$ we have

$$A_j = m_j A_{j+1} + a_j \qquad \text{and} \qquad B_j = m_j B_{j+1} + b_j. \qquad (49)$$

The rule connecting the a's and b's is not difficult to derive by induction on $n - j$:

$$a_j = \begin{cases} b_j, & \text{if } B_{j+1} \text{ is even;} \\ m_j - 1 - b_j, & \text{if } B_{j+1} \text{ is odd.} \end{cases} \qquad (50)$$

(Here we are numbering the coordinates of the n-tuples $(a_{n-1}, \ldots, a_1, a_0)$ and $(b_{n-1}, \ldots, b_1, b_0)$ from right to left, for consistency with (7) and the conventions of mixed-radix notation in Eq. 4.1–(9). Readers who prefer notations like $(a_1, \ldots, a_n)$ can change j to $n - j$ in all the formulas if they wish.) Going the other way, we have

$$b_j = \begin{cases} a_j, & \text{if } a_{j+1} + a_{j+2} + \cdots \text{ is even;} \\ m_j - 1 - a_j, & \text{if } a_{j+1} + a_{j+2} + \cdots \text{ is odd.} \end{cases} \qquad (51)$$

Curiously, rule (50) and its inverse in (51) are exactly the same when all of the radices m_j are odd. In Gray ternary code, for example, when $m_0 = m_1 = \cdots = 3$, we have $\hat{g}((10010211012)_3) = (12210211010)_3$ and also $\hat{g}((12210211010)_3) =$

$(10010211012)_3$. Exercise 78 proves (50) and (51), and discusses similar formulas that hold in the modular case.

We can in fact generate such Gray sequences looplessly, generalizing Algorithms M and L:

Algorithm H (*Loopless reflected mixed-radix Gray generation*). This algorithm visits all n-tuples $(a_{n-1}, \ldots, a_0)$ such that $0 \le a_j < m_j$ for $0 \le j < n$, changing only one component by ± 1 at each step. It maintains an array of focus pointers $(f_n, \ldots, f_0)$ to control the actions as in Algorithm L, together with an array of directions $(o_{n-1}, \ldots, o_0)$. We assume that each radix m_j is ≥ 2.

H1. [Initialize.] Set $a_j \leftarrow 0$, $f_j \leftarrow j$, and $o_j \leftarrow 1$, for $0 \le j < n$; also set $f_n \leftarrow n$.

H2. [Visit.] Visit the n-tuple $(a_{n-1}, \ldots, a_1, a_0)$.

H3. [Choose j.] Set $j \leftarrow f_0$ and $f_0 \leftarrow 0$. (As in Algorithm L, j was the rightmost active coordinate; all elements to its right have now been reactivated.)

H4. [Change coordinate j.] Terminate if $j = n$; otherwise set $a_j \leftarrow a_j + o_j$.

H5. [Reflect?] If $a_j = 0$ or $a_j = m_j - 1$, set $o_j \leftarrow -o_j$, $f_j \leftarrow f_{j+1}$, and $f_{j+1} \leftarrow j + 1$. (Coordinate j has thus become passive.) Return to H2. ∎

A similar algorithm generates the modular variation (see exercise 77).

*Subforests. An interesting and instructive generalization of Algorithm H, discovered by Y. Koda and F. Ruskey [*J. Algorithms* **15** (1993), 324–340], sheds further light on the subject of Gray codes and loopless generation. Suppose we have a forest of n nodes, and we want to visit all of its "principal subforests," namely all subsets of nodes S such that if x is in S and x is not a root, the parent of x is also in S. For example, the 7-node forest has 33 such subsets, corresponding to the black nodes in the following 33 diagrams:

$$(52)$$

Notice that if we read the top row from left to right, the middle row from right to left, and the bottom row from left to right, the status of exactly one node changes at each step.

If the given forest consists of degenerate nonbranching trees, the principal subforests are equivalent to mixed-radix numbers. For example, a forest like

has $3 \times 2 \times 4 \times 2$ principal subforests, corresponding to 4-tuples (x_1, x_2, x_3, x_4) such that $0 \le x_1 < 3$, $0 \le x_2 < 2$, $0 \le x_3 < 4$, and $0 \le x_4 < 2$; the value of x_j is the number of nodes selected in the jth tree. When the algorithm of Koda and

Ruskey is applied to such a forest, it will visit the subforests in the same order
as the reflected Gray code on radices $(3, 2, 4, 2)$.

Algorithm K (*Loopless reflected subforest generation*). Given a forest whose
nodes are $(1, \ldots, n)$ when arranged in postorder, this algorithm visits all binary
n-tuples $(a_1, \ldots, a_n)$ such that $a_p \geq a_q$ whenever p is a parent of q. (Thus,
$a_p = 1$ means that p is a node in the current subforest.) Exactly one bit a_j
changes between one visit and the next. Focus pointers $(f_0, f_1, \ldots, f_n)$ analogous
to those of Algorithm L are used together with additional arrays of pointers
$(l_0, l_1, \ldots, l_n)$ and $(r_0, r_1, \ldots, r_n)$, which represent a doubly linked list called the
"current fringe." The current fringe contains all nodes of the current subforest
and their children; r_0 points to its leftmost node and l_0 to its rightmost.

An auxiliary array $(c_0, c_1, \ldots, c_n)$ defines the forest as follows: If p has no
children, $c_p = 0$; otherwise c_p is the leftmost (smallest) child of p. Also c_0 is the
leftmost root of the forest itself. When the algorithm begins, we assume that
$r_p = q$ and $l_q = p$ whenever p and q are consecutive children of the same family.
Thus, for example, the forest in (52) has the postorder numbering

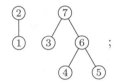

therefore we should have $(c_0, \ldots, c_7) = (2, 0, 1, 0, 0, 0, 4, 3)$ and $r_2 = 7$, $l_7 = 2$,
$r_3 = 6$, $l_6 = 3$, $r_4 = 5$, and $l_5 = 4$ at the beginning of step K1 in this case.

K1. [Initialize.] Set $a_j \leftarrow 0$ and $f_j \leftarrow j$ for $1 \leq j \leq n$, thereby making the initial
subforest empty and all nodes active. Set $f_0 \leftarrow 0$, $l_0 \leftarrow n$, $r_n \leftarrow 0$, $r_0 \leftarrow c_0$,
and $l_{c_0} \leftarrow 0$, thereby putting all roots into the current fringe.

K2. [Visit.] Visit the subforest defined by $(a_1, \ldots, a_n)$.

K3. [Choose p.] Set $q \leftarrow l_0$, $p \leftarrow f_q$. (Now p is the rightmost active node of the
fringe.) Also set $f_q \leftarrow q$ (thereby activating all nodes to p's right).

K4. [Check a_p.] Terminate the algorithm if $p = 0$. Otherwise go to K6 if $a_p = 1$.

K5. [Insert p's children.] Set $a_p \leftarrow 1$. Then, if $c_p \neq 0$, set $q \leftarrow r_p$, $l_q \leftarrow p - 1$,
$r_{p-1} \leftarrow q$, $r_p \leftarrow c_p$, $l_{c_p} \leftarrow p$ (thereby putting p's children to the right of p
in the fringe). Go to K7.

K6. [Delete p's children.] Set $a_p \leftarrow 0$. Then, if $c_p \neq 0$, set $q \leftarrow r_{p-1}$, $r_p \leftarrow q$,
$l_q \leftarrow p$ (thereby removing p's children from the fringe).

K7. [Make p passive.] (At this point we know that p is active.) Set $f_p \leftarrow f_{l_p}$
and $f_{l_p} \leftarrow l_p$. Return to K2. ∎

The reader is encouraged to play through this algorithm on examples like (52),
in order to understand the beautiful mechanism by which the fringe grows and
shrinks at just the right times.

*Shift register sequences. A completely different way to generate all n-tuples of m-ary digits is also possible: We can generate one digit at a time, and repeatedly work with the n most recently generated digits, thus passing from one n-tuple $(x_0, x_1, \ldots, x_{n-1})$ to another one $(x_1, \ldots, x_{n-1}, x_n)$ by shifting an appropriate new digit in at the right. For example, Fig. 35 shows how all 5-bit numbers can be obtained as blocks of 5 consecutive bits in a certain cyclic pattern of length 32. This general idea has already been discussed in some of the exercises of Sections 2.3.4.2 and 3.2.2, and we now are ready to explore it further.

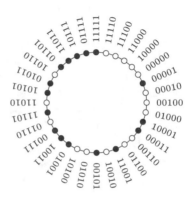

Fig. 35.

A de Bruijn cycle
for 5-bit numbers.

Algorithm S (*Generic shift register generation*). This algorithm visits all n-tuples $(a_1, \ldots, a_n)$ such that $0 \le a_j < m$ for $1 \le j \le n$, provided that a suitable function f is used in step S3.

S1. [Initialize.] Set $a_j \leftarrow 0$ for $-n < j \le 0$ and $k \leftarrow 1$.

S2. [Visit.] Visit the n-tuple $(a_{k-n}, \ldots, a_{k-1})$. Terminate if $k = m^n$.

S3. [Advance.] Set $a_k \leftarrow f(a_{k-n}, \ldots, a_{k-1})$, $k \leftarrow k + 1$, and return to S2. ∎

Every function f that makes Algorithm S valid corresponds to a cycle of m^n radix-m digits such that every combination of n digits occurs consecutively in the cycle. For example, the case $m = 2$ and $n = 5$ illustrated in Fig. 35 corresponds to the binary cycle

$$00000100011001010011101011011111; \tag{53}$$

and the first m^2 digits of the infinite sequence

$$00110212203132330413233041424344\ldots \tag{54}$$

yield an appropriate cycle for $n = 2$ and arbitrary m. Such cycles are commonly called m-ary *de Bruijn cycles*, because N. G. de Bruijn treated the binary case for arbitrary n in *Indagationes Mathematicæ* **8** (1946), 461–467.

Exercise 2.3.4.2–23 proves that exactly $m!^{m^{n-1}}/m^n$ functions f have the required properties. That's a huge number, but only a few of those functions are known to be efficiently computable. We will discuss three kinds of f that appear to be the most useful.

Table 1

PARAMETERS FOR ALGORITHM A

$3:1$	$8:1,5$	$13:1,3$	$18:7$	$23:5$	$28:3$
$4:1$	$9:4$	$14:1,11$	$19:1,5$	$24:1,3$	$29:2$
$5:2$	$10:3$	$15:1$	$20:3$	$25:3$	$30:1,15$
$6:1$	$11:2$	$16:2,3$	$21:2$	$26:1,7$	$31:3$
$7:1$	$12:3,4$	$17:3$	$22:1$	$27:1,7$	$32:1,27$

The entries '$n:s$' or '$n:s,t$' mean that the polynomials $x^n + x^s + 1$ or $x^n + (x^s + 1)(x^t + 1)$ are primitive modulo 2. Additional values up to $n = 168$ have been tabulated by W. Stahnke, *Math. Comp.* **27** (1973), 977–980.

The first important case occurs when m is a prime number, and f is the almost linear recurrence

$$
f(x_1, \ldots, x_n) = \begin{cases} c_1, & \text{if } (x_1, x_2, \ldots, x_n) = (0, 0, \ldots, 0); \\ 0, & \text{if } (x_1, x_2, \ldots, x_n) = (1, 0, \ldots, 0); \\ (c_1 x_1 + c_2 x_2 + \cdots + c_n x_n) \bmod m, & \text{otherwise.} \end{cases} \tag{55}
$$

Here the coefficients $(c_1, \ldots, c_n)$ must be such that

$$
x^n - c_n x^{n-1} - \cdots - c_2 x - c_1 \tag{56}
$$

is a primitive polynomial modulo m, in the sense discussed following Eq. 3.2.2–(9). The number of such polynomials is $\varphi(m^n - 1)/n$, large enough to allow us to find one in which only a few of the c's are nonzero. [This construction goes back to a pioneering paper of Willem Mantel, *Nieuw Archief voor Wiskunde* (2) **1** (1897), 172–184.]

For example, suppose $m = 2$. We can generate binary n-tuples with a very simple loopless procedure:

Algorithm A (*Almost linear bit-shift generation*). This algorithm visits all n-bit vectors, by using either a special offset s [Case 1] or two special offsets s and t [Case 2], as found in Table 1.

A1. [Initialize.] Set $(x_0, x_1, \ldots, x_{n-1}) \leftarrow (1, 0, \ldots, 0)$ and $k \leftarrow 0$, $j \leftarrow s$. In Case 2, also set $i \leftarrow t$ and $h \leftarrow s + t$.

A2. [Visit.] Visit the n-tuple $(x_{k-1}, \ldots, x_0, x_{n-1}, \ldots, x_{k+1}, x_k)$.

A3. [Test for end.] If $x_k \neq 0$, set $r \leftarrow 0$; otherwise set $r \leftarrow r + 1$, and go to A6 if $r = n - 1$. (We have just seen r consecutive zeros.)

A4. [Shift.] Set $k \leftarrow (k - 1) \bmod n$ and $j \leftarrow (j - 1) \bmod n$. In Case 2 also set $i \leftarrow (i - 1) \bmod n$ and $h \leftarrow (h - 1) \bmod n$.

A5. [Compute a new bit.] Set $x_k \leftarrow x_k \oplus x_j$ [Case 1] or $x_k \leftarrow x_k \oplus x_j \oplus x_i \oplus x_h$ [Case 2]. Return to A2.

A6. [Finish.] Visit $(0, \ldots, 0)$ and terminate. ∎

Appropriate offset parameters s and possibly t almost certainly exist for all n, because primitive polynomials are so abundant; for example, eight different choices of (s, t) would work when $n = 32$, and Table 1 merely lists the smallest.

However, a rigorous proof of existence in all cases lies well beyond the present state of mathematical knowledge.

Our first construction of de Bruijn cycles, in (55), was algebraic, relying for its validity on the theory of finite fields. A similar method that works when m is not a prime number appears in exercise 3.2.2–21. Our next construction, by contrast, will be purely combinatorial. In fact, it is strongly related to the idea of modular Gray m-ary codes.

Algorithm R (*Recursive de Bruijn cycle generation*). Suppose $f()$ is a coroutine that will output the successive digits of an m-ary de Bruijn cycle of length m^n, beginning with n zeros, when it is invoked repeatedly. This algorithm is a similar coroutine that outputs a cycle of length m^{n+1}, provided that $n \geq 2$. It maintains three private variables x, y, and t; variable x should initially be zero.

R1. [Output.] Output x. Go to R3 if $x \neq 0$ and $t \geq n$.

R2. [Invoke f.] Set $y \leftarrow f()$.

R3. [Count ones.] If $y = 1$, set $t \leftarrow t + 1$; otherwise set $t \leftarrow 0$.

R4. [Skip one?] If $t = n$ and $x \neq 0$, go back to R2.

R5. [Adjust x.] Set $x \leftarrow (x + y) \bmod m$ and return to R1.   ∎

For example, let $m = 3$ and $n = 2$. If $f()$ produces the infinite 9-cycle

$$001102122\ 001102122\ 0\ldots, \tag{57}$$

then Algorithm R will produce the following infinite 27-cycle at step R1:

$$
\begin{aligned}
y &= \ 001021220011110212200102122\ 001\ldots\\
t &= \ 001001000012340010000100100\ 001\ldots\\
x &= 000110102220120020211122121\ 0001\ldots
\end{aligned}
$$

The proof that Algorithm R works correctly is interesting and instructive (see exercise 93). And the proof of the next algorithm, which *doubles* the window size n, is even more so (see exercise 95).

Algorithm D (*Doubly recursive de Bruijn cycle generation*). Suppose $f()$ and $f'()$ are coroutines that each will output the successive digits of an m-ary de Bruijn cycle of length m^n when invoked repeatedly, beginning with $n \geq 2$ zeros. (The two cycles must be identical; but they are to be generated by independent coroutines, because we will consume their values at different rates.) This algorithm is a similar coroutine that outputs a cycle of length m^{2n}. It maintains six private variables x, y, t, x', y', and t'; variables x and x' should initially be m.

The special parameter r must be set to a constant value such that

$$1 \leq r \leq m \qquad \text{and} \qquad \gcd(m^n - r, m^n + r) = 2. \tag{58}$$

The best choice is usually $r = 1$ when m is odd and $r = 2$ when m is even.

D1. [Possibly invoke f.] If $t \neq n$ or $x \geq r$, set $y \leftarrow f()$.

D2. [Count repeats.] If $x \neq y$, set $x \leftarrow y$ and $t \leftarrow 1$. Otherwise set $t \leftarrow t + 1$.

D3. [Output from f.] Output the current value of x.

D4. [Invoke f'.] Set $y' \leftarrow f'()$.

D5. [Count repeats.] If $x' \neq y'$, set $x' \leftarrow y'$ and $t' \leftarrow 1$. Otherwise set $t' \leftarrow t'+1$.

D6. [Possibly reject f'.] If $t' = n$ and $x' < r$ and either $t < n$ or $x' < x$, go to D4. If $t' = n$ and $x' < r$ and $x' = x$, go to D3.

D7. [Output from f'.] Output the current value of x'. Return to D3 if $t' = n$ and $x' < r$; otherwise return to D1. ∎

The basic idea of Algorithm D is to output from $f()$ and $f'()$ alternately, making special adjustments when either sequence generates n consecutive x's for $x < r$. For example, when $f()$ and $f'()$ produce the 9-cycle (57), we take $r = 1$ and get

t in step D2: 12 31211112 12312111 12123121 11121231 21111212 ...
x in step D3: 00001102122 00011021 22000110 21220001 102122000 ...
t' in step D5: 121211112121211112121211112121211112121211112121 ...
x' in step D7: 0 11021220 11021220 11021220 11021220 11021220 1 ...;

so the 81-cycle produced in steps D3 and **D7** is $00001011012\ldots2222\,00001\ldots$.

The case $m = 2$ of Algorithm R was discovered by Abraham Lempel [*IEEE Trans.* **C-19** (1970), 1204–1209]; Algorithm D was not discovered until more than 25 years later [C. J. Mitchell, T. Etzion, and K. G. Paterson, *IEEE Trans.* **IT-42** (1996), 1472–1478]. By using them together, starting with simple coroutines for $n = 2$ based on (54), we can build up an interesting family of cooperating coroutines that will generate a de Bruijn cycle of length m^n for any desired $m \geq 2$ and $n \geq 2$, using only $O(\log n)$ simple computations for each digit of output. (See exercise 96.) Furthermore, in the simplest case $m = 2$, this combination "R&D method" has the property that its kth output can be computed directly, as a function of k, by doing $O(n \log n)$ simple operations on n-bit numbers. Conversely, given any n-bit pattern β, the position of β in the cycle can also be computed in $O(n \log n)$ steps. (See exercises 97–99.) No other family of binary de Bruijn cycles is presently known to have the latter property.

Our third construction of de Bruijn cycles is based on the theory of prime strings, which will be of great importance to us when we study pattern matching in Chapter 9. Suppose $\gamma = \alpha\beta$ is the concatenation of two strings; we say that α is a *prefix* of γ and β is a *suffix*. A prefix or suffix of γ is called *proper* if its length is positive but less than the length of γ. Thus β is a proper suffix of $\alpha\beta$ if and only if $\alpha \neq \epsilon$ and $\beta \neq \epsilon$.

Definition P. *A string is* prime *if it is nonempty and (lexicographically) less than all of its proper suffixes.* ∎

For example, 01101 is not prime, because it is greater than 01; but 01102 is prime, because it is less than 1102, 102, 02, and 2. (We assume that strings are composed of letters, digits, or other symbols from a linearly ordered alphabet. Lexicographic or dictionary order is the normal way to compare strings, so we write $\alpha < \beta$ and say that α is less than β when α is lexicographically less than β. In particular, we always have $\alpha \leq \alpha\beta$, and $\alpha < \alpha\beta$ if and only if $\beta \neq \epsilon$.)

Prime strings have often been called *Lyndon words*, because they were introduced by R. C. Lyndon [*Trans. Amer. Math. Soc.* **77** (1954), 202–215]; Lyndon called them "standard sequences." The simpler term "prime" is justified because of the fundamental factorization theorem in exercise 101. We will, however, continue to pay respect to Lyndon implicitly by often using the letter λ to denote strings that are prime.

Several of the most important properties of prime strings were derived by Chen, Fox, and Lyndon in an important paper on group theory [*Annals of Math.* (2) **68** (1958), 81–95], including the following easy but basic result:

Theorem P. *A nonempty string that is less than all its cyclic shifts is prime.*

(The cyclic shifts of $a_1 \ldots a_n$ are $a_2 \ldots a_n a_1$, $a_3 \ldots a_n a_1 a_2$, $\ldots$, $a_n a_1 \ldots a_{n-1}$.)

Proof. Suppose $\gamma = \alpha\beta$ is not prime, because $\alpha \neq \epsilon$ and $\gamma \geq \beta \neq \epsilon$; but suppose γ is also less than its cyclic shift $\beta\alpha$. Then the conditions $\beta \leq \gamma < \beta\alpha$ imply that $\gamma = \beta\theta$ for some string $\theta < \alpha$. Therefore, if γ is also less than its cyclic shift $\theta\beta$, we have $\theta < \alpha < \alpha\beta < \theta\beta$. But that is impossible, because α and θ have the same length. ∎

Let $L_m(n)$ be the number of m-ary primes of length n. Every string $a_1 \ldots a_n$, together with its cyclic shifts, yields d distinct strings for some divisor d of n, corresponding to exactly one prime of length d. For example, from 010010 we get also 100100 and 001001 by cyclic shifting, and the smallest of the periodic parts $\{010, 100, 001\}$ is the prime 001. Therefore we must have

$$\sum_{d\backslash n} dL_m(d) = m^n, \qquad \text{for all } m, n \geq 1. \tag{59}$$

This family of equations can be solved for $L_m(n)$, using the Möbius function and exercise 4.5.3–28(a); we obtain

$$L_m(n) = \frac{1}{n} \sum_{d\backslash n} \mu(d) m^{n/d}. \tag{60}$$

During the 1970s, Harold Fredricksen and James Maiorana discovered a beautifully simple way to generate all of the m-ary primes of length n or less, in increasing order [*Discrete Math.* **23** (1978), 207–210]. Before we are ready to understand their algorithm, we need to consider the *n-extension* of a nonempty string λ, namely the first n characters of the infinite string $\lambda\lambda\lambda\ldots$. For example, the 10-extension of 123 is 1231231231. In general if $|\lambda| = k$, its n-extension is $\lambda^{\lfloor n/k \rfloor} \lambda'$, where λ' is the prefix of λ whose length is $n \bmod k$.

Definition Q. *A string is preprime if it is a nonempty prefix of a prime, on some alphabet.* ∎

Theorem Q. *A string of length $n > 0$ is preprime if and only if it is the n-extension of a prime string λ of length $k \leq n$. This prime string is uniquely determined.*

Proof. See exercise 105. ∎

Theorem Q states, in essence, that there is a one-to-one correspondence between primes of length $\leq n$ and preprimes of length n. The following algorithm generates all of the m-ary instances, in increasing order.

Algorithm F (*Prime and preprime string generation*). This algorithm visits all m-ary n-tuples $(a_1, \ldots, a_n)$ such that the string $a_1 \ldots a_n$ is preprime. It also identifies the index j such that $a_1 \ldots a_n$ is the n-extension of the prime $a_1 \ldots a_j$.

F1. [Initialize.] Set $a_1 \leftarrow \cdots \leftarrow a_n \leftarrow 0$ and $j \leftarrow 1$; also set $a_0 \leftarrow -1$.

F2. [Visit.] Visit $(a_1, \ldots, a_n)$ with index j.

F3. [Prepare to increase.] Set $j \leftarrow n$. Then if $a_j = m - 1$, decrease j until finding $a_j < m - 1$.

F4. [Add one.] Terminate if $j = 0$. Otherwise set $a_j \leftarrow a_j + 1$. (Now $a_1 \ldots a_j$ is prime, by exercise 105(a).)

F5. [Make n-extension.] For $k \leftarrow j + 1$, $\ldots$, n (in this order) set $a_k \leftarrow a_{k-j}$. Return to F2. ∎

For example, Algorithm F visits 32 ternary preprimes when $m = 3$ and $n = 4$:

$$
\begin{array}{llllllll}
0000 & 0011 & 0022 & 0111 & 0122 & 0212 & 1111 & 1212 \\
0001 & 0012 & 0101 & 0112 & 0202 & 0220 & 1112 & 1221 \\
0002 & 0020 & 0102 & 0120 & 0210 & 0221 & 1121 & 1222 \\
0010 & 0021 & 0110 & 0121 & 0211 & 0222 & 1122 & 2222
\end{array}
\tag{61}
$$

(The digits preceding '$_\wedge$' are the prime strings 0, 0001, 0002, 001, 0011, $\ldots$, 2.)

Theorem Q explains why this algorithm is correct, because steps F3 and F4 obviously find the smallest m-ary prime of length $\leq n$ that exceeds the previous preprime $a_1 \ldots a_n$. Notice that after a_1 increases from 0 to 1, the algorithm proceeds to visit all the $(m - 1)$-ary primes and preprimes, increased by $1 \ldots 1$.

Algorithm F is quite beautiful, but what does it have to do with de Bruijn cycles? Here now comes the punch line: If we output the digits a_1, $\ldots$, a_j in step F2 whenever j is a divisor of n, the sequence of all such digits forms a de Bruijn cycle! For example, in the case $m = 3$ and $n = 4$, the following 81 digits are output:

$$0\,0001\,0002\,0011\,0012\,0021\,0022\,01\,0102\,0111\,0112$$
$$0121\,0122\,02\,0211\,0212\,0221\,0222\,1\,1112\,1122\,12\,1222\,2. \tag{62}$$

(We omit the primes 001, 002, 011, $\ldots$, 122 of (61) because their length does not divide 4.) The reasons underlying this almost magical property are explored in exercise 108. Notice that the cycle has the correct length, by (59).

There is a sense in which the outputs of this procedure are actually equivalent to the "granddaddy" of all de Bruijn cycle constructions that work for all m and n, namely the construction first published by M. H. Martin in *Bull. Amer. Math. Soc.* **40** (1934), 859–864: Martin's original cycle for $m = 3$ and $n = 4$ was $2222122202211 \ldots 10000$, the twos' complement of (62). In fact, Fredricksen and Maiorana discovered Algorithm F almost by accident while looking for a simple way to generate Martin's sequence. The explicit connection between their algorithm and preprime strings was not noticed until many years later, when Ruskey, Savage, and Wang carried out a careful analysis of the running time [*J. Algorithms* **13** (1992), 414–430]. The principal results of that analysis appear in exercise 107, namely

i) The average value of $n - j$ in steps F3 and F5 is approximately $1/(m-1)$.

ii) The total running time to produce a de Bruijn cycle like (62) is $O(m^n)$.

EXERCISES

   1. [*10*] Explain how to generate all n-tuples $(a_1, \ldots, a_n)$ in which $l_j \le a_j \le u_j$, given lower bounds l_j and upper bounds u_j for each component. (Assume that $l_j \le u_j$.)

   2. [*15*] What is the 1000000th n-tuple visited by Algorithm M if $n = 10$ and $m_j = j$ for $1 \le j \le n$? *Hint:* $\left[\begin{smallmatrix} 0, & 0, & 1, & 2, & 3, & 0, & 2, & 7, & 1, & 0 \\ 1, & 2, & 3, & 4, & 5, & 6, & 7, & 8, & 9, & 10 \end{smallmatrix} \right] = 1000000$.

▶ **3.** [*M20*] How many times does Algorithm M perform step M4?

▶ **4.** [*18*] On most computers it is faster to count down to 0 rather than up to m. Revise Algorithm M so that it visits all n-tuples in the opposite order, starting with $(m_1 - 1, \ldots, m_n - 1)$ and finishing with $(0, \ldots, 0)$.

▶ **5.** [*22*] Algorithms such as the "fast Fourier transform" (exercise 4.6.4–14) often end with an array of answers in bit-reflected order, having $A[(b_0 \ldots b_{n-1})_2]$ in the place where $A[(b_{n-1} \ldots b_0)_2]$ is desired. What is a good way to rearrange the answers into proper order? [*Hint:* Reflect Algorithm M.]

   6. [*M17*] Prove (7), the basic formula for Gray binary code.

   7. [*20*] Figure 30(b) shows the Gray binary code for a disk that is divided into 16 sectors. What would be a good Gray-like code to use if the number of sectors were 12 or 60 (for hours or minutes on a clock), or 360 (for degrees in a circle)?

   8. [*15*] What's an easy way to run through all n-bit strings of even parity, changing only two bits at each step?

   9. [*16*] What move should follow Fig. 31, when solving the Chinese ring puzzle?

▶ **10.** [*M21*] Find a simple formula for the total number of steps A_n or B_n in which a ring is (a) removed or (b) replaced, in the shortest procedure for removing n Chinese rings. For example, $A_3 = 4$ and $B_3 = 1$.

   11. [*M22*] (H. J. Purkiss, 1865.) The two smallest rings of the Chinese ring puzzle can actually be taken on or off the bar simultaneously. How many steps does the puzzle require when such accelerated moves are permitted?

▶ **12.** [*25*] The *compositions* of n are the sequences of positive integers that sum to n. For example, the compositions of 4 are 1111, 112, 121, 13, 211, 22, 31, and 4. An integer n has exactly 2^{n-1} compositions, corresponding to all subsets of the points $\{1, \ldots, n-1\}$ that might be used to break the interval $(0 .. n)$ into integer-sized subintervals.

   a) Design a loopless algorithm to generate all compositions of n, representing each composition as a sequential array of integers $s_1 s_2 \ldots s_t$.

   b) Similarly, design a loopless algorithm that represents the compositions implicitly in an array of pointers $q_0 q_1 \ldots q_t$, where the elements of the composition are $(q_0 - q_1)(q_1 - q_2) \ldots (q_{t-1} - q_t)$ and we have $q_0 = n$, $q_t = 0$. For example, the composition 211 would be represented under this scheme by the pointers $q_0 = 4$, $q_1 = 2$, $q_2 = 1$, $q_3 = 0$, and with $t = 3$.

13. [*21*] Continuing the previous exercise, compute also the multinomial coefficient $C = \binom{n}{s_1,\dots,s_t}$ for use as the composition $s_1 \dots s_t$ is being visited.

14. [*20*] Design an algorithm to generate all strings $a_1 \dots a_j$ such that $0 \le j \le n$ and $0 \le a_i < m_i$ for $1 \le i \le j$, in lexicographic order. For example, if $m_1 = m_2 = n = 2$, your algorithm should successively visit ϵ, 0, 00, 01, 1, 10, 11.

▶ **15.** [*25*] Design a *loopless* algorithm to generate the strings of the previous exercise. All strings of the same length should be visited in lexicographic order as before, but strings of different lengths can be intermixed in any convenient way. For example, 0, 00, 01, ϵ, 10, 11, 1 is an acceptable order when $m_1 = m_2 = n = 2$.

16. [*23*] A loopless algorithm obviously cannot generate all binary vectors $(a_1, \dots, a_n)$ in lexicographic order, because the number of components a_j that need to change between successive visits is not bounded. Show, however, that loopless lexicographic generation does become possible if a *linked* representation is used instead of a sequential one: Suppose there are $2n + 1$ nodes $\{0, 1, \dots, 2n\}$, each containing a LINK field. The binary n-tuple $(a_1, \dots, a_n)$ is represented by letting

> LINK$(0) = 1 + na_1$;
>
> LINK$(j - 1 + na_{j-1}) = j + na_j$,   for $1 < j \le n$;
>
> LINK$(n + na_n) = 0$;

the other n LINK fields can have any convenient values.

17. [*20*] A well-known construction called the *Karnaugh map* [M. Karnaugh, *Amer. Inst. Elect. Eng. Trans.* **72**, part I (1953), 593–599] uses Gray binary code in two dimensions to display all 4-bit numbers in a 4×4 torus:

0000	0001	0011	0010
0100	0101	0111	0110
1100	1101	1111	1110
1000	1001	1011	1010

(The entries of a torus "wrap around" at the left and right and also at the top and bottom — just as if they were tiles, replicated infinitely often in a plane.) Show that, similarly, all 6-bit numbers can be arranged in an 8×8 torus so that only one coordinate position changes when we move north, south, east, or west from any point.

▶ **18.** [*20*] The *Lee weight* of a vector $u = (u_1, \dots, u_n)$, where each component satisfies $0 \le u_j < m_j$, is defined to be

$$\nu_L(u) = \sum_{j=1}^{n} \min(u_j, m_j - u_j);$$

and the *Lee distance* between two such vectors u and v is

$$d_L(u, v) = \nu_L(u - v), \qquad \text{where } u - v = ((u_1 - v_1) \bmod m_1, \dots, (u_n - v_n) \bmod m_n).$$

(This is the minimum number of steps needed to change u to v if we adjust some component u_j by ± 1 (modulo m_j) in each step.)

A quaternary vector has $m_j = 4$ for $1 \le j \le n$, and a binary vector has all $m_j = 2$. Find a simple one-to-one correspondence between quaternary vectors $u = (u_1, \dots, u_n)$ and binary vectors $u' = (u'_1, \dots, u'_{2n})$, with the property that $\nu_L(u) = \nu(u')$ and $d_L(u, v) = \nu(u' \oplus v')$.

19. [23] (*The octacode.*) Let $g(x) = x^3 + 2x^2 + x - 1$.

a) Use one of the algorithms in this section to evaluate $\sum z_{u_0} z_{u_1} z_{u_2} z_{u_3} z_{u_4} z_{u_5} z_{u_6} z_{u_\infty}$, a polynomial in the variables z_0, z_1, z_2, and z_3, summed over all 256 polynomials

$$(v_0 + v_1 x + v_2 x^2 + v_3 x^3) g(x) \bmod 4 = u_0 + u_1 x + u_2 x^2 + u_3 x^3 + u_4 x^4 + u_5 x^5 + u_6 x^6$$

for $0 \le v_0, v_1, v_2, v_3 < 4$, where u_∞ is chosen so that $0 \le u_\infty < 4$ and $(u_0 + u_1 + u_2 + u_3 + u_4 + u_5 + u_6 + u_\infty) \bmod 4 = 0$.

b) Construct a set of 256 16-bit numbers that differ from each other in at least six different bit positions. (Such a set, first discovered by Nordstrom and Robinson [*Information and Control* **11** (1967), 613–616], is essentially unique.)

20. [M36] The 16-bit codewords in the previous exercise can be used to transmit 8 bits of information, allowing transmission errors to be corrected if any one or two bits are corrupted; furthermore, mistakes will be detected (but not necessarily correctable) if any three bits are received incorrectly. Devise an algorithm that either finds the nearest codeword to a given 16-bit number u' or determines that at least three bits of u' are erroneous. How does your algorithm decode the number $(1100100100001111)_2$? [*Hint:* Use the facts that $x^7 \equiv 1$ (modulo $g(x)$ and 4), and that every quaternary polynomial of degree < 3 is congruent to $x^j + 2x^k$ (modulo $g(x)$ and 4) for some $j, k \in \{0, 1, 2, 3, 4, 5, 6, \infty\}$, where $x^\infty = 0$.]

21. [M30] A t-subcube of an n-cube can be represented by a string like $**10**0*$, containing t asterisks and $n - t$ specified bits. If all 2^n binary n-tuples are written in lexicographic order, the elements belonging to such a subcube appear in $2^{t'}$ clusters of consecutive entries, where t' is the number of asterisks that lie to the left of the rightmost specified bit. (In the example given, $n = 8$, $t = 5$, and $t' = 4$.) But if the n-tuples are written in Gray binary order, the number of clusters might be reduced. For example, the $(n-1)$-subcubes $*\dots*0$ and $*\dots*1$ occur in only $2^{n-2}+1$ and 2^{n-2} clusters, respectively, when Gray binary order is used, not in 2^{n-1} of them.

a) Explain how to compute $C(\alpha)$, the number of Gray binary clusters of the subcube defined by a given string α of asterisks, 0s, and 1s. What is $C(**10**0*)$?

b) Prove that $C(\alpha)$ always lies between $2^{t'-1}$ and $2^{t'}$, inclusive.

c) What is the average value of $C(\alpha)$, over all $2^{n-t}\binom{n}{t}$ possible t-subcubes?

▶ **22.** [22] A "right subcube" is a subcube such as $0110**$ in which all the asterisks appear after all the specified digits. Any binary trie (Section 6.3) can be regarded as a way to partition a cube into disjoint right subcubes, as in Fig. 36(a). If we interchange the left and right subtries of every right subtrie, proceeding downward from the root, we obtain a *Gray binary trie*, as in Fig. 36(b).

Prove that if the "lieves" of a Gray binary trie are traversed in order, from left to right, consecutive lieves correspond to adjacent subcubes. (Subcubes are adjacent if they contain adjacent vertices. For example, $00**$ is adjacent to $011*$ because the first contains 0010 and the second contains 0110; but $011*$ is not adjacent to $10**$.)

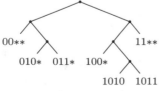   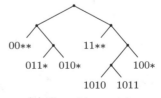

Fig. 36.   (a) Normal binary trie.   (b) Gray binary trie.

23. [20] Suppose $g(k) \oplus 2^j = g(l)$. What is a simple way to find l, given j and k?

24. [M21] Consider extending the Gray binary function g to all 2-adic integers (see Section 7.1.3). What is the corresponding inverse function $g^{[-1]}$?

▸ **25.** [M25] Prove that if $g(k)$ and $g(l)$ differ in $t > 0$ bits, and if $0 \le k, l < 2^n$, then $\lceil 2^t/3 \rceil \le |k - l| \le 2^n - \lceil 2^t/3 \rceil$.

26. [25] (Frank Ruskey.) For which integers N is it possible to generate all of the nonnegative integers less than N in such a way that only one bit of the binary representation changes at each step?

▸ **27.** [20] Let $S_0 = \{1\}$ and $S_{n+1} = 1/(2 + S_n) \cup 1/(2 - S_n)$; thus, for example,

$$S_2 = \left\{ \cfrac{1}{2 + \cfrac{1}{2+1}}, \cfrac{1}{2 + \cfrac{1}{2-1}}, \cfrac{1}{2 - \cfrac{1}{2+1}}, \cfrac{1}{2 - \cfrac{1}{2-1}} \right\} = \left\{ \frac{3}{7}, \frac{1}{3}, \frac{3}{5}, 1 \right\},$$

and S_n has 2^n elements that lie between $\frac{1}{3}$ and 1. Compute the 10^{10}th smallest element of S_{100}.

28. [M27] A *median* of n-bit strings $\{\alpha_1, \ldots, \alpha_t\}$, where α_k has the binary representation $\alpha_k = a_{k(n-1)} \ldots a_{k0}$, is a string $\hat{\alpha} = a_{n-1} \ldots a_0$ whose bits a_j for $0 \le j < n$ agree with the majority of the bits a_{kj} for $1 \le k \le t$. (If t is even and the bits a_{kj} are half 0 and half 1, the median bit a_j can be either 0 or 1.) For example, the strings $\{0010, 0100, 0101, 1110\}$ have two medians, 0100 and 0110, which we can denote by 01∗0.

a) Find a simple way to describe the medians of $G_t = \{g(0), \ldots, g(t-1)\}$, the first t Gray binary strings, when $0 < t \le 2^n$.

b) Prove that if $\alpha = a_{n-1} \ldots a_0$ is such a median, and if $2^{n-1} < t < 2^n$, then the string β obtained from α by complementing any bit a_j is also an element of G_t.

29. [M24] If integer values k are transmitted as n-bit Gray binary codes $g(k)$ and received with errors described by a bit pattern $p = (p_{n-1} \ldots p_0)_2$, the average numerical error is

$$\frac{1}{2^n} \sum_{k=0}^{2^n-1} \left| g^{[-1]}(g(k) \oplus p) - k \right|,$$

assuming that all values of k are equally likely. Show that this sum is equal to $\sum_{k=0}^{2^n-1} |(k \oplus p) - k|/2^n$, just as if Gray binary code were not used, and evaluate it explicitly.

▸ **30.** [M27] (*Gray permutation.*) Design a one-pass algorithm to replace the array elements $(X_0, X_1, X_2, \ldots, X_{2^n-1})$ by $(X_{g(0)}, X_{g(1)}, X_{g(2)}, \ldots, X_{g(2^n-1)})$, using only a constant amount of auxiliary storage. *Hint:* Considering the function $g(n)$ as a permutation of all nonnegative integers, show that the set

$$L = \{0, 1, (10)_2, (100)_2, (100*)_2, (100*0)_2, (100*0*)_2, \ldots\}$$

is the set of *cycle leaders* (the smallest elements of the cycles).

31. [HM35] (*Gray fields.*) Let $f_n(x) = g(r_n(x))$ denote the operation of reflecting the bits of an n-bit binary string as in exercise 5 and then converting to Gray binary code. For example, the operation $f_3(x)$ takes $(001)_2 \mapsto (110)_2 \mapsto (010)_2 \mapsto (011)_2 \mapsto (101)_2 \mapsto (111)_2 \mapsto (100)_2 \mapsto (001)_2$, hence all of the nonzero possibilities appear in a single cycle. Therefore we can use f_3 to define a field of 8 elements, with $\oplus$ as the addition operator and with multiplication defined by the rule

$$f_3^{[j]}(1) \times f_3^{[k]}(1) = f_3^{[j+k]}(1) = f_3^{[j]}(f_3^{[k]}(1)).$$

The functions f_2, f_5, and f_6 have the same nice property. But f_4 does not, because $f_4((1011)_2) = (1011)_2$.

Find all $n \leq 100$ for which f_n defines a field of 2^n elements.

32. [*M20*] True or false: Walsh functions satisfy $w_k(-x) = (-1)^k w_k(x)$.

▶ **33.** [*M20*] Prove the Rademacher-to-Walsh law (17).

34. [*M21*] The *Paley functions* $p_k(x)$ are defined by

$$p_0(x) = 1 \qquad \text{and} \qquad p_k(x) = (-1)^{\lfloor 2x \rfloor k} p_{\lfloor k/2 \rfloor}(2x).$$

Show that $p_k(x)$ has a simple expression in terms of Rademacher functions, analogous to (17), and relate Paley functions to Walsh functions.

35. [*HM23*] The $2^n \times 2^n$ Paley matrix P_n is obtained from Paley functions just as the Walsh matrix W_n is obtained from Walsh functions. (See (20).) Find interesting relations between P_n, W_n, and the Hadamard matrix H_n. Prove that all three matrices are symmetric.

36. [*21*] Spell out the details of an efficient algorithm to compute the Walsh transform $(x_0, \ldots, x_{2^n-1})$ of a given vector $(X_0, \ldots, X_{2^n-1})$.

37. [*HM23*] Let z_{kl} be the location of the lth sign change in $w_k(x)$, for $1 \leq l \leq k$ and $0 < z_{kl} < 1$. Prove that $|z_{kl} - l/(k+1)| = O((\log k)/k)$.

▶ **38.** [*M25*] Devise a ternary generalization of Walsh functions.

▶ **39.** [*HM30*] (J. J. Sylvester.) The rows of $\left(\begin{smallmatrix} a & b \\ b & -a \end{smallmatrix}\right)$ are orthogonal to each other and have the same magnitude; therefore the matrix identity

$$(A\ B)\begin{pmatrix} a^2+b^2 & 0 \\ 0 & a^2+b^2 \end{pmatrix}\begin{pmatrix} A \\ B \end{pmatrix} = (A\ B)\begin{pmatrix} a & b \\ b & -a \end{pmatrix}\begin{pmatrix} a & b \\ b & -a \end{pmatrix}\begin{pmatrix} A \\ B \end{pmatrix}$$

$$= (Aa + Bb\ \ Ab - Ba)\begin{pmatrix} aA + bB \\ bA - aB \end{pmatrix}$$

implies the sum-of-two-squares identity $(a^2+b^2)(A^2+B^2) = (aA+bB)^2 + (bA-aB)^2$. Similarly, the matrix

$$\begin{pmatrix} a & b & c & d \\ b & -a & d & -c \\ d & c & -b & -a \\ c & -d & -a & b \end{pmatrix}$$

leads to the sum-of-four-squares identity

$$(a^2+b^2+c^2+d^2)(A^2+B^2+C^2+D^2) = (aA+bB+cC+dD)^2 + (bA-aB+dC-cD)^2$$
$$+ (dA + cB - bC - aD)^2 + (cA - dB - aC + bD)^2.$$

a) Attach the signs of the matrix H_3 in (21) to the symbols $\{a, b, c, d, e, f, g, h\}$, obtaining a matrix with orthogonal rows and a sum-of-eight-squares identity.

b) Generalize to H_4 and higher-order matrices.

▶ **40.** [*21*] Would the text's five-letter word pairing scheme produce correct answers also if the masks in step W2 were computed as $m_j = z\ \&\ (2^{5j+5} - 1)$ for $0 \leq j < 5$?

41. [*25*] If we use only the 3000 most common five-letter words — thereby omitting ducky, duces, dunks, dinks, dinky, dices, dicey, dicky, dicks, picky, pinky, punky, and pucks from (23) — how many valid words can still be generated from a single pair?

42. [*35*] (M. L. Fredman.) Algorithm L uses $\Theta(n \log n)$ bits of auxiliary memory for focus pointers as it chooses the Gray binary bit a_j to complement next. Step L3 examines $\Theta(\log n)$ of the auxiliary bits, and it occasionally changes $\Omega(\log n)$ of them.

Show that, from a theoretical standpoint, we can do better: The n-bit Gray binary code can be generated by changing at most 2 auxiliary bits between visits. (We still allow ourselves to examine $O(\log n)$ of the auxiliary bits on each step, so that we know which of them should be changed.)

43. [*41*] Determine $d(6)$, the number of 6-bit Gray cycles. (See (26).)

44. [*M20*] Show that $d(n) \le \binom{M(n)}{2}$, if the n-cube has $M(n)$ perfect matchings.

45. [*M40*] (T. Feder and C. Subi, 2009.) This exercise constructs a large number of Gray cycles in the $(4r+2)$-cube $G = G_4 \square G_3 \square G_2 \square G_1 \square G_0 \square G_{-1}$, where G_i is an r-cube for $i > 0$ and $G_0 = G_{-1} = P_2$. The vertices v are $(4r+2)$-bit strings $v_4 \ldots v_0 v_{-1}$, where v_i has r bits for $i > 0$ and 1 bit for $i \le 0$. The "signature" of v is the 4-bit string $\sigma(v) = s_4 s_3 s_2 (s_1 \oplus v_0)$, where s_i is the parity of v_i. We treat bit strings as binary numbers.

For $1 \le l \le 4$, let $\mathcal{M}_l(v)$ be a perfect matching in G with $v \text{---} v' = v_4' \ldots v_0' v_{-1}'$ and $v_i' = v_i$ for $i \ne l$. (Note that $\mathcal{M}_l(v') = v$.) Also define $\mathcal{M}_0(v) = v \oplus 2$. Consider the cycles formed by the edges $v \text{---} \mathcal{M}_{l(v)}(v)$, where $l(v)$ depends on v's signature:

$$\sigma(v) = \quad 0000 \; 0001 \; 0011 \; 0010 \; 0110 \; 0111 \; 0101 \; 0100 \; 1100 \; 1101 \; 1111 \; 1110 \; 1010 \; 1011 \; 1001 \; 1000$$
$$l(v) = \quad\; 0 \quad\; 2 \quad\; 0 \quad\; 3 \quad\; 1 \quad\; 2 \quad\; 0 \quad\; 4 \quad\; 1 \quad\; 2 \quad\; 1 \quad\; 3 \quad\; 1 \quad\; 2 \quad\; 0 \quad\; 4$$

a) Suppose $r = 2$ and $\mathcal{M}_l(v) = v \oplus 2^{2l + s_{l-1}}$ for $l > 1$ and $\mathcal{M}_1(v) = v \oplus 2^{2 + (v_0 \oplus v_{-1})}$. What cycle contains vertex $0 \ldots 0$ in this case?

b) A vertex whose signature is a power of 2 is called a "ground vertex." Four vertices with the same $v_4 \ldots v_1$ are called "siblings." Define $u \equiv v$ if u and v are in the same cycle, or if u and v are sibling ground vertices, or if a chain of such equivalences leads from u to v. Explain how to construct cycles in G for each equivalence class.

c) Furthermore, if u and v are sibling ground vertices, there is such a cycle that retains the edges $\{u \oplus 2 \text{---} u, v \oplus 2 \text{---} v\}$ of the original cycles.

d) Finally, show how to convert the cycles of (b) and (c) into a single cycle.

e) When $\mathcal{M}_1, \ldots, \mathcal{M}_4$ vary, how many different Hamiltonian cycles do we get?

46. [*M23*] Extend exercise 45 to the $(kr + 2)$-cube, for k even.

47. [*HM24*] What asymptotic estimates do exercises 44 and 46 give for $d(n)^{1/2^n}$?

48. [*HM48*] Determine the asymptotic behavior of $d(n)^{1/2^n}$ as $n \to \infty$.

49. [*20*] Prove that for all $n \ge 1$ there is a $2n$-bit Gray cycle in which $v_{k+2^{2n-1}}$ is the complement of v_k, for all $k \ge 0$.

▶ **50.** [*21*] Find a construction like that of Theorem D but with l even.

51. [*M24*] (*Balanced Gray cycles.*) Complete the proof of Corollary B to Theorem D.

52. [*M20*] Prove that if the transition counts of an n-bit Gray cycle satisfy $c_0 \le c_1 \le \cdots \le c_{n-1}$, we must have $c_0 + \cdots + c_{j-1} \ge 2^j$, with equality when $j = n$.

53. [*M46*] If the numbers $(c_0, \ldots, c_{n-1})$ are even and satisfy the condition of the previous exercise, is there always an n-bit Gray cycle with these transition counts?

54. [*M20*] (H. S. Shapiro, 1953.) Show that if a sequence of integers $(a_1, \ldots, a_{2^n})$ contains only n distinct values, then there is a subsequence whose product $a_{k+1} a_{k+2} \ldots a_l$ is a perfect square, for some $0 \le k < l \le 2^n$. However, this conclusion might not be true if we disallow the case $l = 2^n$.

▶ **55.** [*35*] (F. Ruskey and C. Savage, 1993.) If $(v_0, \ldots, v_{2^n-1})$ is an n-bit Gray cycle, the pairs $\{\{v_{2k}, v_{2k+1}\} \mid 0 \le k < 2^{n-1}\}$ form a perfect matching between the vertices of even and odd parity in the n-cube. Conversely, does every such perfect matching arise as "half" of some n-bit Gray cycle?

56. [*M30*] (E. N. Gilbert, 1958.) Say that two Gray cycles are equivalent if their delta sequences can be made equal by permuting the coordinate names, or by reversing the cycle and/or starting the cycle at a different place. Show that the 2688 different 4-bit Gray cycles fall into just 9 equivalence classes.

57. [*32*] Consider a graph whose vertices are the 2688 possible 4-bit Gray cycles, where two such cycles are adjacent if they are related by one of the following simple transformations:

Before   After Type 1   After Type 2   After Type 3   After Type 4

(Type 1 changes arise when the cycle can be broken into two parts and reassembled with one part reversed. Types 2, 3, and 4 arise when the cycle can be broken into three parts and reassembled after reversing 0, 1, or 2 of the parts. The parts need not have equal size. Such transformations of Hamiltonian cycles are often possible.)

Write a program to discover which 4-bit Gray cycles are transformable into each other, by finding the connected components of the graph; restrict consideration to only one of the four types at a time.

▶ **58.** [*21*] Let α be the delta sequence of an n-bit Gray cycle, and obtain β from α by changing q occurrences of 0 to n, where q is odd. Prove that $\beta\beta$ is the delta sequence of an $(n+1)$-bit Gray cycle.

59. [*22*] The 5-bit Gray cycle of (30) is *nonlocal* in the sense that no 2^t consecutive elements belong to a single t-subcube, for $1 < t < n$. Prove that nonlocal n-bit Gray cycles exist for all $n \geq 5$. [*Hint:* See the previous exercise.]

60. [*20*] Show that the run-length-bound function satisfies $r(n+1) \geq r(n)$.

61. [*M30*] Show that $r(m+n) \geq r(m) + r(n) - 1$ if (a) $m = 2$ and $2 < r(n) < 8$; or (b) $m \leq n$ and $r(n) \leq 2^{m-3}$.

62. [*46*] Does $r(8) = 6$?

63. [*30*] (Luis Goddyn.) Prove that $r(10) \geq 8$.

▶ **64.** [*HM35*] (L. Goddyn and P. Gvozdjak.) An n-bit *Gray stream* is a sequence of permutations $(\sigma_0, \sigma_1, \ldots, \sigma_{l-1})$ where each σ_k is a permutation of the vertices of the n-cube, taking every vertex to one of its neighbors.

a) Suppose $(u_0, \ldots, u_{2^m-1})$ is an m-bit Gray cycle and $(\sigma_0, \sigma_1, \ldots, \sigma_{2^m-1})$ is an n-bit Gray stream. Let $v_0 = 0\ldots0$ and $v_{k+1} = v_k\sigma_k$, where $\sigma_k = \sigma_{k \bmod 2^m}$ if $k \geq 2^m$. Under what conditions is the sequence

$$W = \left(u_0 v_0,\ u_0 v_1,\ u_1 v_1,\ u_1 v_2,\ \ldots,\ u_{2^{m+n-1}-1} v_{2^{m+n-1}-1},\ u_{2^{m+n-1}-1} v_{2^{m+n-1}}\right)$$

an $(m+n)$-bit Gray cycle?

b) Show that if m is sufficiently large, there is an n-bit Gray stream satisfying the conditions of (a) for which all run lengths of the sequence $(v_0, v_1, \ldots)$ are $\geq n-2$.

c) Apply these results to prove that $r(n) \geq n - O(\log n)$.

65. [*30*] (Brett Stevens.) In Samuel Beckett's play *Quad*, the stage begins and ends empty; n actors enter and exit one at a time, running through all 2^n possible subsets, and the actor who leaves is always the one whose previous entrance was earliest. When

$n = 4$, as in the actual play, some subsets are necessarily repeated. Show, however, that there is a perfect pattern with exactly 2^n entrances and exits when $n = 5$.

66. [*40*] Is there a perfect Beckett–Gray pattern for 8 actors?

67. [*20*] Sometimes it is desirable to run through all n-bit binary strings by changing as *many* bits as possible from one step to the next, for example when testing a physical circuit for reliable behavior in worst-case conditions. Explain how to traverse all binary n-tuples in such a way that each step changes n or $n - 1$ bits, alternately.

68. [*21*] Rufus Q. Perverse decided to construct an *anti-Gray* ternary code, in which each n-trit number differs from its neighbors in *every* digit position. Is such a code possible for all n?

▶ **69.** [*M25*] Modify the definition of Gray binary code (7) by letting

$$h(k) = (\ldots (b_6 \oplus b_5)(b_5 \oplus b_4)(b_4 \oplus b_3 \oplus b_2 \oplus b_0)(b_3 \oplus b_0)(b_2 \oplus b_1 \oplus b_0)b_1)_2,$$

when $k = (\ldots b_5 b_4 b_3 b_2 b_1 b_0)_2$.
   a) Show that the sequence $h(0)$, $h(1)$, $\ldots$, $h(2^n - 1)$ runs through all n-bit numbers in such a way that exactly 3 bits change each time, when $n > 3$.
   b) Generalize this rule to obtain sequences in which exactly t bits change at each step, when t is odd and $n > t$.

70. [*21*] How many monotonic n-bit Gray codes exist for $n = 5$ and $n = 6$?

71. [*M22*] Derive (45), the recurrence that defines the Savage–Winkler permutations.

72. [*20*] What is the Savage–Winkler code from 00000 to 11111?

▶ **73.** [*32*] Design an efficient algorithm to construct the delta sequence of an n-bit monotonic Gray code.

74. [*HM25*] (Savage and Winkler.) Prove that adjacent vertices of the n-cube cannot be separated by more than $O(2^n/\sqrt{n})$ positions in a monotonic Gray code.

75. [*32*] Find all 5-bit Gray paths v_0, $\ldots$, v_{31} that are *trend-free*, in the sense that $\sum_{k=0}^{31} k(-1)^{v_{kj}} = 0$ in each coordinate position j.

76. [*M25*] Prove that trend-free n-bit Gray codes exist for all $n \geq 5$.

77. [*21*] Modify Algorithm H in order to visit mixed-radix n-tuples in *modular* Gray order.

78. [*M26*] Prove the conversion formulas (50) and (51) for reflected mixed-radix Gray codes, and derive analogous formulas for the modular case.

▶ **79.** [*M22*] When is the last n-tuple of the (a) reflected (b) modular mixed-radix Gray code adjacent to the first?

80. [*M20*] Explain how to run through all divisors of a number, given its prime factorization $p_1^{e_1} \ldots p_t^{e_t}$, repeatedly multiplying or dividing by a single prime at each step.

81. [*M21*] Let (a_0, b_0), (a_1, b_1), $\ldots$, (a_{m^2-1}, b_{m^2-1}) be the 2-digit m-ary modular Gray code. Show that, if $m > 2$, every edge $(x, y) \!-\! (x, (y + 1) \bmod m)$ and $(x, y) \!-\! ((x + 1) \bmod m, y)$ occurs in one of the two cycles

$$(a_0, b_0) \!-\! (a_1, b_1) \!-\! \cdots \!-\! (a_{m^2-1}, b_{m^2-1}) \!-\! (a_0, b_0),$$
$$(b_0, a_0) \!-\! (b_1, a_1) \!-\! \cdots \!-\! (b_{m^2-1}, a_{m^2-1}) \!-\! (b_0, a_0).$$

▶ **82.** [*M25*] (G. Ringel, 1956.) Use the previous exercise to deduce that there exist four 8-bit Gray cycles that, together, cover all edges of the 8-cube.

83. [*41*] Can four *balanced* 8-bit Gray cycles cover all edges of the 8-cube?

▶ **84.** [*25*] (Howard L. Dyckman.) Figure 37 shows a fascinating puzzle called Loony Loop or the Gordian Knot, in which the object is to remove a flexible cord from the rigid loops that surround it. Show that the solution to this puzzle is inherently related to the reflected Gray ternary code.

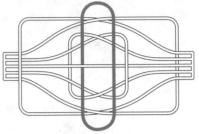

Fig. 37. The Loony Loop puzzle.

▶ **85.** [*M25*] (Dana Richards.) If $\Gamma = (\alpha_0, \ldots, \alpha_{t-1})$ is any sequence of t strings and $\Gamma' = (\alpha'_0, \ldots, \alpha'_{t'-1})$ is any sequence of t' strings, the *boustrophedon product* $\Gamma \wr \Gamma'$ is the sequence of tt' strings that begins

$$(\alpha_0\alpha'_0, \ldots, \alpha_0\alpha'_{t'-1}, \alpha_1\alpha'_{t'-1}, \ldots, \alpha_1\alpha'_0, \alpha_2\alpha'_0, \ldots, \alpha_2\alpha'_{t'-1}, \alpha_3\alpha'_{t'-1}, \ldots)$$

and ends with $\alpha_{t-1}\alpha'_0$ if t is even, $\alpha_{t-1}\alpha'_{t'-1}$ if t is odd. For example, the basic definition of Gray binary code in (5) can be expressed in this notation as $\Gamma_n = (0,1) \wr \Gamma_{n-1}$ when $n > 0$. Prove that the operation $\wr$ is associative, hence $\Gamma_{m+n} = \Gamma_m \wr \Gamma_n$.

▶ **86.** [*26*] Define an infinite Gray code that runs through all possible nonnegative integer n-tuples $(a_1, \ldots, a_n)$ in such a way that $\max(a_1, \ldots, a_n) \leq \max(a'_1, \ldots, a'_n)$ when $(a_1, \ldots, a_n)$ is followed by $(a'_1, \ldots, a'_n)$.

87. [*27*] Continuing the previous exercise, define an infinite Gray code that runs through *all* integer n-tuples $(a_1, \ldots, a_n)$, in such a way that $\max(|a_1|, \ldots, |a_n|) \leq \max(|a'_1|, \ldots, |a'_n|)$ when $(a_1, \ldots, a_n)$ is followed by $(a'_1, \ldots, a'_n)$.

▶ **88.** [*25*] After Algorithm K has terminated in step K4, what would happen if we immediately restarted it in step K2?

▶ **89.** [*25*] (*Gray code for Morse code.*) The Morse code words of length n (exercise 4.5.3–32) are strings of dots and dashes, where n is the number of dots plus twice the number of dashes.

    a) Show that it is possible to generate all Morse code words of length n by successively changing a dash to two dots or vice versa. For example, the path for $n = 3$ must be •—, •••, —• or its reverse.

    b) What string follows •——••——•—• in your sequence for $n = 15$?

90. [*26*] For what values of n can the Morse code words be arranged in a *cycle*, under the ground rules of exercise 89? [*Hint:* The number of code words is F_{n+1}.]

▶ **91.** [*34*] Design a loopless algorithm to visit all binary n-tuples $(a_1, \ldots, a_n)$ such that $a_1 \leq a_2 \geq a_3 \leq a_4 \geq \cdots$. [The number of such n-tuples is F_{n+2}.]

92. [*M30*] Is there an infinite sequence Φ_n whose first m^n elements form an m-ary de Bruijn cycle, for all m? [The case $n = 2$ is solved in (54).]

▶ **93.** [*M28*] Prove that Algorithm R outputs a de Bruijn cycle as advertised.

94. [*22*] What is the output of Algorithm D when $m = 5$, $n = 1$, and $r = 3$, if the coroutines $f()$ and $f'()$ generate the trivial cycles 01234 01234 01...?

▶ **95.** [*M24*] Suppose an infinite sequence $a_0 a_1 a_2 \ldots$ of period p is interleaved with an infinite sequence $b_0 b_1 b_2 \ldots$ of period q to form the infinite cyclic sequence

$$c_0 c_1 c_2 c_3 c_4 c_5 \ldots = a_0 b_0 a_1 b_1 a_2 b_2 \ldots.$$

    a) Under what circumstances does $c_0 c_1 c_2 \ldots$ have period pq? (The "period" of a sequence $a_0 a_1 a_2 \ldots$, for the purposes of this exercise, is the smallest integer $p > 0$ such that $a_k = a_{k+p}$ for all $k \geq 0$.)

    b) Which $2n$-tuples would occur as consecutive outputs of Algorithm D if step D6 were changed to say simply "If $t' = n$ and $x' < r$, go to D4"?

    c) Prove that Algorithm D outputs a de Bruijn cycle as advertised.

▶ **96.** [*M28*] Suppose a family of coroutines has been set up to generate a de Bruijn cycle of length m^n using Algorithms R and D, based recursively on simple coroutines like Algorithm S for the base case $n = 2$, and using Algorithm D when $n > 2$ is even.

    a) How many coroutines (R_n, D_n, S_n) of each type will there be?

    b) What is the maximum number of coroutine activations needed to get one top-level digit of output?

97. [*M29*] The purpose of this exercise is to analyze the de Bruijn cycles constructed by Algorithms R and D in the important special case $m = 2$. Let $f_n(k)$ be the $(k+1)$st bit of the 2^n-cycle, so that $f_n(k) = 0$ for $0 \leq k < n$. Also let j_n be the index such that $0 \leq j_n < 2^n$ and $f_n(k) = 1$ for $j_n \leq k < j_n + n$.

    a) Write out the cycles $(f_n(0) \ldots f_n(2^n - 1))$ for $n = 2$, 3, 4, and 5.

    b) Prove that, for all even values of n, there is a number $\delta_n = \pm 1$ such that we have

$$f_{n+1}(k) \equiv \begin{cases} \Sigma f_n(k), & \text{if } 0 < k \leq j_n \text{ or } 2^n + j_n < k \leq 2^{n+1}, \\ 1 + \Sigma f_n(k + \delta_n), & \text{if } j_n < k \leq 2^n + j_n, \end{cases}$$

where the congruence is modulo 2. (In this formula Σf stands for the summation function $\Sigma f(k) = \sum_{j=0}^{k-1} f(j)$.) Hence $j_{n+1} = 2^n - \delta_n$ when n is even.

    c) Let $(c_n(0) c_n(1) \ldots c_n(2^{2n} - 5))$ be the cycle produced when the simplified version of Algorithm D in exercise 95(b) is applied to $f_n()$. Where do the $(2n - 1)$-tuples 1^{2n-1} and $(01)^{n-1}0$ occur in this cycle?

    d) Use the results of (c) to express $f_{2n}(k)$ in terms of $f_n()$.

    e) Find a (somewhat) simple formula for j_n as a function of n.

98. [*M34*] Continuing the previous exercise, design an efficient algorithm to compute $f_n(k)$, given $n \geq 2$ and $k \geq 0$.

▶ **99.** [*M23*] Exploit the technology of the previous exercises to design an efficient algorithm that locates any given n-bit string in the cycle $(f_n(0) f_n(1) \ldots f_n(2^n - 1))$.

100. [*40*] Do the de Bruijn cycles of exercise 97 provide a useful source of pseudo-random bits when n is large?

▶ **101.** [*M30*] (*Unique factorization of strings into nonincreasing primes.*)

    a) Prove that if λ and λ' are prime, then $\lambda \lambda'$ is prime if $\lambda < \lambda'$.

    b) Consequently every string α can be written in the form

$$\alpha = \lambda_1 \lambda_2 \ldots \lambda_t, \qquad \lambda_1 \geq \lambda_2 \geq \cdots \geq \lambda_t, \qquad \text{where each } \lambda_j \text{ is prime.}$$

    c) In fact, only one such factorization is possible. *Hint:* Show that λ_t must be the lexicographically smallest nonempty suffix of α.

    d) True or false: λ_1 is the longest prime prefix of α.

    e) What are the prime factors of 31415926535897932384626433832795028841197?

102. [*HM28*] Deduce the number of m-ary primes of length n from the unique factorization theorem in the previous exercise.

103. [*M20*] Use Eq. (59) to prove Fermat's theorem that $m^p \equiv m$ (modulo p).

104. [*17*] According to formula (60), about $1/n$ of all n-letter words are prime. How many of the 5757 five-letter GraphBase words are prime? Which of them is the smallest nonprime? The largest prime?

105. [*M31*] Let α be a preprime string of length n on an infinite alphabet.

  a) Show that if the final letter of α is increased, the resulting string is prime.
  b) If α has been factored as in exercise 101, show that it is the n-extension of λ_1.
  c) Furthermore α cannot be the n-extension of two different primes.

▶ **106.** [*M30*] By reverse-engineering Algorithm F, design an algorithm that visits all m-ary primes and preprimes in *decreasing* order.

107. [*HM30*] Analyze the running time of Algorithm F, for fixed m as $n \to \infty$.

108. [*M35*] Let $\lambda_1 < \cdots < \lambda_t$ be the m-ary prime strings whose lengths divide n, and let $a_1 \ldots a_n$ be any m-ary string. The object of this exercise is to prove that $a_1 \ldots a_n$ appears in $\lambda_1 \ldots \lambda_t \lambda_1 \lambda_2$; hence $\lambda_1 \ldots \lambda_t$ is a de Bruijn cycle (since it has length m^n). For convenience we may assume that $m = 10$ and that strings correspond to decimal numbers; the same arguments will apply for arbitrary $m \geq 2$.

  a) Show that if $a_1 \ldots a_n = \alpha\beta$ is distinct from all its cyclic shifts, and if $\beta\alpha = \lambda_k$ is prime, then $\alpha\beta$ is a substring of $\lambda_k \lambda_{k+1}$, unless $\alpha = 9^j$ for some $j \geq 1$.
  b) Where does $\alpha\beta$ appear in $\lambda_1 \ldots \lambda_t$ if $\beta\alpha$ is prime and α consists of all 9s? *Hint:* Show that if $a_{n+1-l} \ldots a_n = 9^l$ in step F2 for some $l > 0$, and if j is not a divisor of n, the previous step F2 had $a_{n-l} \ldots a_n = 9^{l+1}$.
  c) Now consider n-tuples of the form $(\alpha\beta)^d$, where $d > 1$ is a divisor of n and $\beta\alpha = \lambda_k$ is prime.
  d) Where do 899135, 997879, 913131, 090909, 909090, and 911911 occur when $n=6$?
  e) Is $\lambda_1 \ldots \lambda_t$ the lexicographically least m-ary de Bruijn cycle of length m^n?

109. [*M22*] An m-ary de Bruijn torus of size $m^2 \times m^2$ for 2×2 windows is a matrix of m-ary digits d_{ij} such that each of the m^4 submatrices

$$\begin{pmatrix} d_{ij} & d_{i(j+1)} \\ d_{(i+1)j} & d_{(i+1)(j+1)} \end{pmatrix}, \qquad 0 \leq i, j < m^2$$

is different, where subscripts wrap around modulo m^2. Thus every possible m-ary 2×2 submatrix occurs exactly once; Ian Stewart [*Game, Set, and Math* (Oxford: Blackwell, 1989), Chapter 4] has therefore called it an m-ary *ourotorus*. For example,

$$\begin{pmatrix} 0 & 0 & 1 & 0 \\ 0 & 0 & 0 & 1 \\ 0 & 1 & 1 & 1 \\ 1 & 0 & 1 & 1 \end{pmatrix}$$

is a binary ourotorus; indeed, it is essentially the only such matrix when $m = 2$, except for shifting and/or transposition.

Consider the infinite matrix D whose entry in row $i = (\ldots a_2 a_1 a_0)_2$ and column $j = (\ldots b_2 b_1 b_0)_2$ is $d_{ij} = (\ldots c_2 c_1 c_0)_2$, where

$$c_0 = (a_0 \oplus b_0)(a_1 \oplus b_1) \oplus b_1;$$
$$c_k = (a_{2k} a_0 \oplus b_{2k}) b_0 \oplus (a_{2k+1} a_0 \oplus b_{2k+1})(b_0 \oplus 1), \quad \text{for } k > 0.$$

Show that the upper left $2^{2n} \times 2^{2n}$ submatrix of D is a 2^n-ary ourotorus for all $n \geq 0$.

110. [*M25*] Continuing the previous exercise, construct m-ary ourotoruses for all m.

111. [*20*] We can obtain the number 100 in twelve ways by inserting $+$ and $-$ signs into the sequence 123456789; for example, $100 = 1 + 23 - 4 + 5 + 6 + 78 - 9 = 123 - 45 - 67 + 89 = -1 + 2 - 3 + 4 + 5 + 6 + 78 + 9$.

    a) What is the smallest positive integer that cannot be represented in such a way?

    b) Consider also inserting signs into the 10-digit sequence 9876543210.

▶ **112.** [*25*] Continuing the previous exercise, how far can we go by inserting signs into 12345678987654321? For example, $100 = -1234 - 5 - 6 + 7898 - 7 - 6543 - 2 - 1$.

7.2.1.2. Generating all permutations.

After n-tuples, the next most important item on nearly everybody's wish list for combinatorial generation is the task of visiting all *permutations* of some given set or multiset. Many different ways have been devised to solve this problem. In fact, almost as many different algorithms have been published for unsorting as for sorting! We will study the most important permutation generators in this section, beginning with a classical method that is both simple and flexible:

Algorithm L (*Lexicographic permutation generation*). Given a sequence of n elements $a_1 a_2 \ldots a_n$, initially sorted so that

$$a_1 \leq a_2 \leq \cdots \leq a_n, \tag{1}$$

this algorithm generates all permutations of $\{a_1, a_2, \ldots, a_n\}$, visiting them in lexicographic order. (For example, the permutations of $\{1, 2, 2, 3\}$ are

    1223, 1232, 1322, 2123, 2132, 2213, 2231, 2312, 2321, 3122, 3212, 3221,

ordered lexicographically.) An auxiliary element a_0 is assumed to be present for convenience; a_0 must be strictly less than the largest element a_n.

L1. [Visit.] Visit the permutation $a_1 a_2 \ldots a_n$.

L2. [Find j.] Set $j \leftarrow n - 1$. If $a_j \geq a_{j+1}$, decrease j by 1 repeatedly until $a_j < a_{j+1}$. Terminate the algorithm if $j = 0$. (At this point j is the smallest subscript such that we've already visited all permutations beginning with $a_1 \ldots a_j$. So the lexicographically next permutation will make a_j larger.)

L3. [Increase a_j.] Set $l \leftarrow n$. If $a_j \geq a_l$, decrease l by 1 repeatedly until $a_j < a_l$. Then interchange $a_j \leftrightarrow a_l$. (Since $a_{j+1} \geq \cdots \geq a_n$, element a_l is the smallest element greater than a_j that can legitimately follow $a_1 \ldots a_{j-1}$ in a permutation. Before the interchange we had $a_{j+1} \geq \cdots \geq a_{l-1} \geq a_l > a_j \geq a_{l+1} \geq \cdots \geq a_n$; after the interchange, we have $a_{j+1} \geq \cdots \geq a_{l-1} \geq a_j > a_l \geq a_{l+1} \geq \cdots \geq a_n$.)

L4. [Reverse $a_{j+1} \ldots a_n$.] Set $k \leftarrow j + 1$ and $l \leftarrow n$. Then, while $k < l$, interchange $a_k \leftrightarrow a_l$ and set $k \leftarrow k + 1$, $l \leftarrow l - 1$. Return to L1. ∎

This algorithm goes back to Nārāyaṇa Paṇḍita in 14th-century India (see Section 7.2.1.7); it also appeared in C. F. Hindenburg's preface to *Specimen Analyticum de Lineis Curvis Secundi Ordinis* by C. F. Rüdiger (Leipzig: 1784), xlvi–xlvii; and it has been frequently rediscovered ever since. The parenthetical remarks in steps L2 and L3 explain why it works.

Tin tan din dan bim bam bom bo —
tan tin din dan bam bim bo bom —
tin tan dan din bim bam bom bo —
tan tin dan din bam bim bo bom —
tan dan tin bam din bo bim bom —
. . . . Tin tan din dan bim bam bom bo.

— DOROTHY L. SAYERS, *The Nine Tailors* (1934)

A permutation on the ten decimal digits is simply a 10 digit decimal number
in which all digits are distinct. Hence all we need to do is to produce
all 10 digit numbers and select only those whose digits are distinct.
Isn't it wonderful how high speed computing saves us from
the drudgery of thinking! We simply program $k + 1 \to k$
and examine the digits of k for undesirable equalities.
This gives us the permutations in dictionary order too!
On second sober thought . . . we do need to think of something else.

— D. H. LEHMER (1957)

In general, the lexicographic successor of any combinatorial pattern $a_1 \ldots a_n$ is obtainable by a three-step procedure:

1) Find the largest j such that a_j can be increased.
2) Increase a_j by the smallest feasible amount.
3) Find the lexicographically least way to extend the new $a_1 \ldots a_j$ to a complete pattern.

Algorithm L follows this general procedure in the case of permutation generation, just as Algorithm 7.2.1.1M followed it in the case of n-tuple generation; we will see numerous further instances later, as we consider other kinds of combinatorial patterns. Notice that we have $a_{j+1} \geq \cdots \geq a_n$ at the beginning of step L4. Therefore the first permutation beginning with the current prefix $a_1 \ldots a_j$ is $a_1 \ldots a_j a_n \ldots a_{j+1}$, and step L4 produces it by doing $\lfloor (n - j)/2 \rfloor$ interchanges.

In practice, step L2 finds $j = n - 1$ half of the time when the elements are distinct, because exactly $n!/2$ of the $n!$ permutations have $a_{n-1} < a_n$. Therefore Algorithm L can be speeded up by recognizing this special case, without making it significantly more complicated. (See exercise 1.) Similarly, the probability that $j \leq n - t$ is only $1/t!$ when the a's are distinct; hence the loops in steps L2–L4 usually go very fast. Exercise 6 analyzes the running time in general, showing that Algorithm L is reasonably efficient even when equal elements are present, unless some values appear much more often than others do in the multiset $\{a_1, a_2, \ldots, a_n\}$.

Adjacent interchanges. We saw in Section 7.2.1.1 that Gray codes are advantageous for generating n-tuples, and similar considerations apply when we want to generate permutations. The simplest possible change to a permutation is to interchange adjacent elements, and we know from Chapter 5 that any permutation can be sorted into order if we make a suitable sequence of such interchanges. (For example, Algorithm 5.2.2B works in this way.) Hence we can

go backward and obtain any desired permutation, by starting with all elements
in order and then exchanging appropriate pairs of adjacent elements.

A natural question now arises: Is it possible to run through *all* permutations
of a given multiset in such a way that only two adjacent elements change places
at every step? If so, the overall program that is examining all permutations will
often be simpler and faster, because it will only need to calculate the effect of
an exchange instead of to reprocess an entirely new array $a_1 \ldots a_n$ each time.

Alas, when the multiset has repeated elements, we can't always find such
a Gray-like sequence. For example, the six permutations of $\{1,1,2,2\}$ are connected to each other in the following way by adjacent interchanges:

$$1122 \;\text{---}\; 1212 \begin{array}{c} \diagup\; 2112 \;\diagdown \\ \diagdown\; 1221 \;\diagup \end{array} 2121 \;\text{---}\; 2211; \qquad (2)$$

this graph has no Hamiltonian path.

But most applications deal with permutations of *distinct* elements, and for
this case there is good news: A simple algorithm makes it possible to generate
all $n!$ permutations by making just $n! - 1$ adjacent interchanges. Furthermore,
another such interchange returns to the starting point, so we have a Hamiltonian
cycle analogous to Gray binary code.

The idea is to take such a sequence for $\{1, \ldots, n - 1\}$ and to insert the
number n into each permutation in all ways. For example, if $n = 4$ the sequence
$(123, 132, 312, 321, 231, 213)$ leads to the columns of the array

$$\begin{array}{cccccc}
1234 & 1324 & 3124 & 3214 & 2314 & 2134 \\
1243 & 1342 & 3142 & 3241 & 2341 & 2143 \\
1423 & 1432 & 3412 & 3421 & 2431 & 2413 \\
4123 & 4132 & 4312 & 4321 & 4231 & 4213
\end{array} \qquad (3)$$

when 4 is inserted in all four possible positions. Now we obtain the desired
sequence by reading downwards in the first column, upwards in the second, downwards in the third, ..., upwards in the last: $(1234, 1243, 1423, 4123, 4132, 1432,$
$1342, 1324, 3124, 3142, \ldots, 2143, 2134)$.

In Section 5.1.1 we studied the inversions of a permutation, namely the pairs
of elements (not necessarily adjacent) that are out of order. Every interchange
of adjacent elements changes the total number of inversions by ± 1. In fact, when
we consider the so-called inversion table $c_1 \ldots c_n$ of exercise 5.1.1–7, where c_j is
the number of elements lying to the right of j that are less than j, we find that
the permutations in (3) have the following inversion tables:

$$\begin{array}{cccccc}
0000 & 0010 & 0020 & 0120 & 0110 & 0100 \\
0001 & 0011 & 0021 & 0121 & 0111 & 0101 \\
0002 & 0012 & 0022 & 0122 & 0112 & 0102 \\
0003 & 0013 & 0023 & 0123 & 0113 & 0103
\end{array} \qquad (4)$$

And if we read these columns alternately down and up as before, we obtain
precisely the reflected Gray code for mixed radices $(1, 2, 3, 4)$, as in Eqs. (46)–(51)

of Section 7.2.1.1. The same property holds for all n, as noticed by E. W. Dijkstra [*Acta Informatica* **6** (1976), 357–359], and it leads us to the following formulation:

Algorithm P (*Plain changes*). Given a sequence $a_1 a_2 \ldots a_n$ of n distinct elements, this algorithm generates all of their permutations by repeatedly interchanging adjacent pairs. It uses an auxiliary array $c_1 c_2 \ldots c_n$, which represents inversions as described above, running through all sequences of integers such that

$$0 \le c_j < j \qquad \text{for } 1 \le j \le n. \tag{5}$$

Another array $o_1 o_2 \ldots o_n$ governs the directions by which the entries c_j change.

P1. [Initialize.] Set $c_j \leftarrow 0$ and $o_j \leftarrow 1$ for $1 \le j \le n$.

P2. [Visit.] Visit the permutation $a_1 a_2 \ldots a_n$.

P3. [Prepare for change.] Set $j \leftarrow n$ and $s \leftarrow 0$. (The following steps determine the coordinate j for which c_j is about to change, preserving (5); variable s is the number of indices $k > j$ such that $c_k = k - 1$.)

P4. [Ready to change?] Set $q \leftarrow c_j + o_j$. If $q < 0$, go to P7; if $q = j$, go to P6.

P5. [Change.] Interchange $a_{j-c_j+s} \leftrightarrow a_{j-q+s}$. Then set $c_j \leftarrow q$ and return to P2.

P6. [Increase s.] Terminate if $j = 1$; otherwise set $s \leftarrow s + 1$.

P7. [Switch direction.] Set $o_j \leftarrow -o_j$, $j \leftarrow j - 1$, and go back to P4. ∎

This procedure, which clearly works for all $n \ge 1$, originated in 17th-century England, when bell ringers began the delightful custom of ringing a set of bells in all possible permutations. They called Algorithm P the method of *plain changes*. Figure 38(a) illustrates the "Cambridge Forty-Eight," an irregular and ad hoc sequence of 48 permutations on 5 bells that had been used in the early 1600s, before the plain-change principle revealed how to achieve all $5! = 120$ possibilities. The venerable history of Algorithm P has been traced to a manuscript by Peter Mundy now in the Bodleian Library, written about 1653 and transcribed by Ernest Morris in *The History and Art of Change Ringing* (1931), 29–30. Shortly afterwards, a famous book called *Tintinnalogia*, published anonymously in 1668 but now known to have been written by Richard Duckworth and Fabian Stedman, devoted its first 60 pages to a detailed description of plain changes, working up from $n = 3$ to the case of arbitrarily large n.

> Cambridge Forty-eight, *for many years,*
> *was the greatest* Peal *that was* Rang *or invented; but now,*
> *neither* Forty-eight, *nor a* Hundred, *nor* Seven-hundred and twenty,
> *nor any* Number *can confine us; for we can* Ring Changes, Ad infinitum.
> *... On four* Bells, *there are* Twenty four several Changes,
> *in* Ringing *of which, there is one* Bell called the Hunt,
> *and the other three are* Extream Bells;
> *the* Hunt *moves, and hunts* up and down continually *...;*
> *two of the* Extream Bells makes a Change
> *every time the* Hunt *comes before or behind them.*
> — R. DUCKWORTH and F. STEDMAN, *Tintinnalogia* (1668)

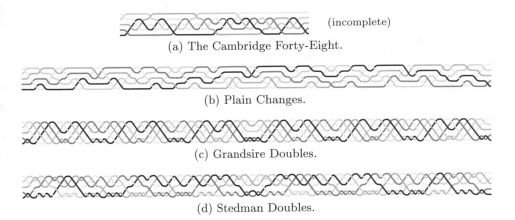

(a) The Cambridge Forty-Eight. (incomplete)

(b) Plain Changes.

(c) Grandsire Doubles.

(d) Stedman Doubles.

Fig. 38. Four patterns that were used in 17th-century England to ring permutations of five different church-bells. Pattern (b) corresponds to Algorithm P.

British bellringing enthusiasts soon went on to develop more complicated schemes in which two or more pairs of bells change places simultaneously. For example, they devised the pattern in Fig. 38(c) known as Grandsire Doubles, "the best and most ingenious Peal that ever was composed, to be rang on five bells" [*Tintinnalogia*, page 95]. Such fancier methods are more interesting than Algorithm P from a musical standpoint, but they are less useful in computer applications, so we shall not dwell on them here. Interested readers can learn more by reading W. G. Wilson's book, *Change Ringing* (1965); see also A. T. White, *AMM* **103** (1996), 771–778.

H. F. Trotter published the first computer implementation of plain changes in *CACM* **5** (1962), 434–435. The algorithm is quite efficient, especially when it is streamlined as in exercise 16, because $n - 1$ out of every n permutations are generated without using steps P6 and P7. By contrast, Algorithm L enjoys its best case only about half of the time.

The fact that Algorithm P does exactly one interchange per visit means that the permutations it generates are alternately even and odd (see exercise 5.1.1–13). Therefore we can generate all the even permutations by simply bypassing the odd ones. In fact, the c and o tables make it easy to keep track of the current total number of inversions, $c_1 + \cdots + c_n$, as we go.

Many programs need to generate the same permutations repeatedly, and in such cases we needn't run through the steps of Algorithm P each time. We can simply prepare a list of suitable transitions, using the following method:

Algorithm T (*Plain change transitions*). This algorithm computes a table $t[1]$, $t[2]$, ..., $t[n! - 1]$ such that the actions of Algorithm P are equivalent to the successive interchanges $a_{t[k]} \leftrightarrow a_{t[k]+1}$ for $1 \le k < n!$. We assume that $n \ge 2$.

T1. [Initialize.] Set $N \leftarrow n!$, $d \leftarrow N/2$, $t[d] \leftarrow 1$, and $m \leftarrow 2$.

T2. [Loop on m.] Terminate if $m = n$. Otherwise set $m \leftarrow m + 1$, $d \leftarrow d/m$, and $k \leftarrow 0$. (We maintain the condition $d = n!/m!$.)

T3. [Hunt down.] Set $k \leftarrow k + d$ and $j \leftarrow m - 1$. Then while $j > 0$, set $t[k] \leftarrow j$, $k \leftarrow k + d$, and $j \leftarrow j - 1$.

T4. [Offset.] Set $t[k] \leftarrow t[k] + 1$.

T5. [Hunt up.] Set $k \leftarrow k + d$, $j \leftarrow 1$. While $j < m$, set $t[k] \leftarrow j$, $k \leftarrow k + d$, $j \leftarrow j + 1$. Then return to T3 if $k < N$, otherwise return to T2. ∎

For example, if $n = 4$ we get the table $(t[1], t[2], \ldots, t[23]) = (3, 2, 1, 3, 1, 2, 3, 1, 3, 2, 1, 3, 1, 2, 3, 1, 3, 2, 1, 3, 1, 2, 3)$.

Alphametics. Now let's consider a simple kind of puzzle in which permutations are useful: How can the pattern

$$
\begin{array}{r}
\text{SEND} \\
+ \text{MORE} \\
\hline
\text{MONEY}
\end{array}
\qquad (6)
$$

represent a correct sum, if every letter stands for a different decimal digit? [H. E. Dudeney, *Strand* **68** (1924), 97, 214.] Such puzzles are often called "alphametics," a word coined by J. A. H. Hunter [*Globe and Mail* (Toronto: 27 October 1955), 27]; another term, "cryptarithm," has also been suggested by S. Vatriquant [*Sphinx* **1** (May 1931), 50].

The classic alphametic (6) can easily be solved by hand (see exercise 21). But let's suppose we want to deal with a large set of complicated alphametics, some of which may be unsolvable while others may have dozens of solutions. Then we can save time by programming a computer to try out all permutations of digits that match a given pattern, seeing which permutations yield a correct sum. [Early computer programs for solving alphametics were published by R. M. Burstall, *Comp. J.* **12** (1969), 48–51; John Beidler, *Creative Computing* **4**, 6 (November–December 1978), 110–113.]

We might as well raise our sights slightly and consider additive alphametics in general, dealing not only with simple sums like (6) but also with examples like

$$\text{VIOLIN} + \text{VIOLIN} + \text{VIOLA} = \text{TRIO} + \text{SONATA}.$$

Equivalently, we want to solve puzzles such as

$$2(\text{VIOLIN}) + \text{VIOLA} - \text{TRIO} - \text{SONATA} = 0, \qquad (7)$$

where a sum of terms with integer coefficients is given and the goal is to obtain zero by substituting distinct decimal digits for the different letters. Each letter in such a problem has a "signature" obtained by substituting 1 for that letter and 0 for the others; for example, the signature for I in (7) is

$$2(010010) + 01000 - 0010 - 000000,$$

namely 21010. If we arbitrarily assign the codes $(1, 2, \ldots, 10)$ to the letters $(\text{V}, \text{I}, \text{O}, \text{L}, \text{N}, \text{A}, \text{T}, \text{R}, \text{S}, \text{X})$, the respective signatures corresponding to (7) are

$$
\begin{aligned}
&s_1 = 210000, \quad s_2 = 21010, \quad s_3 = -7901, \quad s_4 = 210, \quad s_5 = -998, \\
&s_6 = -100, \quad s_7 = -1010, \quad s_8 = -100, \quad s_9 = -100000, \quad s_{10} = 0.
\end{aligned}
\qquad (8)
$$

(An additional letter, X, has been added because we need ten of them.) The problem now is to find all permutations $a_1 \ldots a_{10}$ of $\{0, 1, \ldots, 9\}$ such that

$$a \cdot s = \sum_{j=1}^{10} a_j s_j = 0. \tag{9}$$

There also is a side condition, because the numbers in alphametics should not have zero as a leading digit. For example, the sums

7316		5731		6524		2817
+ 0823	and	+ 0647	and	+ 0735	and	+ 0368
08139		06378		07259		03185

and numerous others are *not* considered to be valid solutions of (6). In general there is a set F of first letters such that we must have

$$a_j \neq 0 \quad \text{for all } j \in F; \tag{10}$$

the set F corresponding to (7) and (8) is $\{1, 7, 9\}$.

One way to tackle a family of additive alphametics is to start by using Algorithm T to prepare a table of $10! - 1$ transitions $t[k]$. Then, for each problem defined by a signature sequence $(s_1, \ldots, s_{10})$ and a first-letter set F, we can exhaustively look for solutions as follows:

A1. [Initialize.] Set $a_1 a_2 \ldots a_{10} \leftarrow 01 \ldots 9$, $v \leftarrow \sum_{j=1}^{10}(j-1)s_j$, $k \leftarrow 1$, and $\delta_j \leftarrow s_{j+1} - s_j$ for $1 \leq j < 10$.

A2. [Test.] If $v = 0$ and if (10) holds, output the solution $a_1 \ldots a_{10}$.

A3. [Swap.] Stop if $k = 10!$. Otherwise set $j \leftarrow t[k]$, $v \leftarrow v - (a_{j+1} - a_j)\delta_j$, $a_{j+1} \leftrightarrow a_j$, $k \leftarrow k + 1$, and return to A2. ∎

Step A3 is justified by the fact that swapping a_j with a_{j+1} simply decreases $a \cdot s$ by $(a_{j+1} - a_j)(s_{j+1} - s_j)$. Even though 10! is 3,628,800, a fairly large number, the operations in step A3 are so simple that the whole job takes only a fraction of a second on a modern computer.

An alphametic is said to be *pure* if it has a unique solution. Unfortunately (7) is not pure; the permutations 1764802539 and 3546281970 both solve (9) and (10), hence we have both

$$176478 + 176478 + 17640 = 2576 + 368020$$

and

$$354652 + 354652 + 35468 = 1954 + 742818.$$

Furthermore $s_6 = s_8$ in (8), so we can obtain two more solutions by interchanging the digits assigned to A and R.

On the other hand (6) *is* pure, yet the method we have described will find two different permutations that solve it. The reason is that (6) involves only eight distinct letters, hence we will set it up for solution by using two dummy signatures $s_9 = s_{10} = 0$. In general, an alphametic with m distinct letters will have $10 - m$ dummy signatures $s_{m+1} = \cdots = s_{10} = 0$, and each of its solutions will be found $(10 - m)!$ times unless we insist that, say, $a_{m+1} < \cdots < a_{10}$.

A general framework. A great many algorithms have been proposed for generating permutations of distinct objects, and the best way to understand them is to apply the multiplicative properties of permutations that we studied in Section 1.3.3. For this purpose we will change our notation slightly, by using 0-origin indexing and writing $a_0 a_1 \ldots a_{n-1}$ for permutations of $\{0, 1, \ldots, n-1\}$ instead of writing $a_1 a_2 \ldots a_n$ for permutations of $\{1, 2, \ldots, n\}$. More importantly, we will consider schemes for generating permutations in which most of the action takes place at the *left*, so that all permutations of $\{0, 1, \ldots, k-1\}$ will be generated during the first $k!$ steps, for $1 \le k \le n$. For example, one such scheme for $n = 4$ is

$$0123, 1023, 0213, 2013, 1203, 2103, 0132, 1032, 0312, 3012, 1302, 3102,$$
$$0231, 2031, 0321, 3021, 2301, 3201, 1230, 2130, 1320, 3120, 2310, 3210; \quad (11)$$

this is called "reverse colex order," because if we reflect the strings from right to left we get 3210, 3201, 3120, ..., 0123, the reverse of lexicographic order. Another way to think of (11) is to view the entries as $(n-a_n)\ldots(n-a_2)(n-a_1)$, where $a_1 a_2 \ldots a_n$ runs lexicographically through the permutations of $\{1, 2, \ldots, n\}$.

Let's recall from Section 1.3.3 that a permutation like $\alpha = 250143$ can be written either in the two-line form

$$\alpha = \begin{pmatrix} 012345 \\ 250143 \end{pmatrix}$$

or in the more compact cycle form

$$\alpha = (0\ 2)(1\ 5\ 3),$$

with the meaning that α takes $0 \mapsto 2$, $1 \mapsto 5$, $2 \mapsto 0$, $3 \mapsto 1$, $4 \mapsto 4$, and $5 \mapsto 3$; a 1-cycle like '(4)' need not be indicated. Since 4 is a fixed point of this permutation we say that "α fixes 4." We also write $0\alpha = 2$, $1\alpha = 5$, and so on, saying that "$j\alpha$ is the image of j under α." Multiplication of permutations, like α times β where $\beta = 543210$, is readily carried out either in the two-line form

$$\alpha\beta = \begin{pmatrix} 012345 \\ 250143 \end{pmatrix}\begin{pmatrix} 012345 \\ 543210 \end{pmatrix} = \begin{pmatrix} 012345 \\ 250143 \end{pmatrix}\begin{pmatrix} 250143 \\ 305412 \end{pmatrix} = \begin{pmatrix} 012345 \\ 305412 \end{pmatrix}$$

or in the cycle form

$$\alpha\beta = (0\ 2)(1\ 5\ 3) \cdot (0\ 5)(1\ 4)(2\ 3) = (0\ 3\ 4\ 1)(2\ 5).$$

Notice that the image of 1 under $\alpha\beta$ is $1(\alpha\beta) = (1\alpha)\beta = 5\beta = 0$, etc. *Warning:* About half of all books that deal with permutations multiply them the other way (from right to left), imagining that $\alpha\beta$ means that β should be applied before α. The reason is that traditional functional notation, in which one writes $\alpha(1) = 5$, makes it natural to think that $\alpha\beta(1)$ should mean $\alpha(\beta(1)) = \alpha(4) = 4$. However, the present book subscribes to the other philosophy, and we shall always multiply permutations from left to right.

The order of multiplication needs to be understood carefully when permutations are represented by arrays of numbers. For example, if we "apply" the reflection $\beta = 543210$ to the permutation $\alpha = 250143$, the result 341052 is not $\alpha\beta$

but $\beta\alpha$. In general, the operation of replacing a permutation $\alpha = a_0 a_1 \ldots a_{n-1}$ by some rearrangement $a_{0\beta} a_{1\beta} \ldots a_{(n-1)\beta}$ takes $k \mapsto a_{k\beta} = k\beta\alpha$. Permuting the *positions* by β corresponds to *premultiplication* by β, changing α to $\beta\alpha$; permuting the *values* by β corresponds to *postmultiplication* by β, changing α to $\alpha\beta$. Thus, for example, a permutation generator that interchanges $a_1 \leftrightarrow a_2$ is premultiplying the current permutation by $(1\ 2)$, postmultiplying it by $(a_1\ a_2)$.

Following a proposal made by Évariste Galois in 1830, a nonempty set G of permutations is said to form a *group* if it is closed under multiplication, that is, if the product $\alpha\beta$ is in G whenever α and β are elements of G [see *Écrits et Mémoires Mathématiques d'Évariste Galois* (Paris: 1962), 47]. Consider, for example, the 4-cube represented as a 4×4 torus

$$\begin{matrix} 0 & 1 & 3 & 2 \\ 4 & 5 & 7 & 6 \\ c & d & f & e \\ 8 & 9 & b & a \end{matrix} \tag{12}$$

as in exercise 7.2.1.1–17, and let G be the set of all permutations of the vertices $\{0, 1, \ldots, f\}$ that preserve adjacency: A permutation α is in G if and only if $u \relbar v$ implies $u\alpha \relbar v\alpha$ in the 4-cube. (Here we are using hexadecimal digits $(0, 1, \ldots, f)$ to stand for the integers $(0, 1, \ldots, 15)$. The labels in (12) are chosen so that $u \relbar v$ if and only if u and v differ in only one bit position.) This set G is obviously a group, and its elements are called the symmetries or "automorphisms" of the 4-cube.

Groups of permutations G are conveniently represented inside a computer by means of a *Sims table*, introduced by Charles C. Sims [*Computational Problems in Abstract Algebra* (Oxford: Pergamon, 1970), 169–183], which is a family of subsets $S_1, S_2, \ldots$ of G having the following property: S_k contains exactly one permutation σ_{kj} that takes $k \mapsto j$ and fixes the values of all elements greater than k, whenever G contains such a permutation. We let σ_{kk} be the identity permutation, which is always present in G; but when $0 \le j < k$, any suitable permutation can be selected to play the role of σ_{kj}. The main advantage of a Sims table is that it provides a convenient representation of the entire group:

Lemma S. *Let $S_1, S_2, \ldots, S_{n-1}$ be a Sims table for a group G of permutations on $\{0, 1, \ldots, n-1\}$. Then every element α of G has a unique representation*

$$\alpha = \sigma_1 \sigma_2 \ldots \sigma_{n-1}, \qquad \text{where } \sigma_k \in S_k \text{ for } 1 \le k < n. \tag{13}$$

Proof. If α has such a representation and if σ_{n-1} is the permutation $\sigma_{(n-1)j} \in S_{n-1}$, then α takes $n-1 \mapsto j$, because all elements of $S_1 \cup \cdots \cup S_{n-2}$ fix the value of $n-1$. Conversely, if α takes $n-1 \mapsto j$ we have $\alpha = \alpha' \sigma_{(n-1)j}$, where

$$\alpha' = \alpha \sigma^-_{(n-1)j}$$

is a permutation of G that fixes $n-1$. (As in Section 1.3.3, σ^- denotes the inverse of σ.) The set G' of all such permutations is a group, and $S_1, \ldots, S_{n-2}$ is a Sims table for G'; therefore the result follows by induction on n. ∎

For example, a bit of calculation shows that one possible Sims table for the automorphism group of the 4-cube is

$$S_f = \{(), (01)(23)(45)(67)(89)(ab)(cd)(ef), \ldots,$$
$$(0f)(1e)(2d)(3c)(4b)(5a)(69)(78)\};$$
$$S_e = \{(), (12)(56)(9a)(de), (14)(36)(9c)(be), (18)(3a)(5c)(7e)\};$$
$$S_d = \{(), (24)(35)(ac)(bd), (28)(39)(6c)(7d)\}; \tag{14}$$
$$S_c = \{()\};$$
$$S_b = \{(), (48)(59)(6a)(7b)\};$$
$$S_a = S_9 = \cdots = S_1 = \{()\};$$

here S_f contains 16 permutations σ_{fj} for $0 \le j \le 15$, which respectively take $i \mapsto i \oplus (15 - j)$ for $0 \le i \le 15$. The set S_e contains only four permutations, because an automorphism that fixes f must take e into a neighbor of f; thus the image of e must be either e or d or b or 7. The set S_c contains only the identity permutation, because an automorphism that fixes f, e, and d must also fix c. Most groups have $S_k = \{()\}$ for all small values of k, as in this example; hence a Sims table usually needs to contain only a fairly small number of permutations although the group itself might be quite large.

The Sims representation (13) makes it easy to test if a given permutation α lies in G: First we determine $\sigma_{n-1} = \sigma_{(n-1)j}$, where α takes $n - 1 \mapsto j$, and we let $\alpha' = \alpha\sigma_{n-1}^-$; then we determine $\sigma_{n-2} = \sigma_{(n-2)j'}$, where α' takes $n - 2 \mapsto j'$, and we let $\alpha'' = \alpha'\sigma_{n-2}^-$; and so on. If at any stage the required σ_{kj} does not exist in S_k, the original permutation α does not belong to G. In the case of (14), this process must reduce α to the identity after finding σ_f, σ_e, σ_d, σ_c, and σ_b.

For example, let α be the permutation $(14)(28)(3c)(69)(7d)(be)$, which corresponds to transposing (12) about its main diagonal $\{0, 5, f, a\}$. Since α fixes f, σ_f will be the identity permutation (), and $\alpha' = \alpha$. Then σ_e is the member of S_e that takes $e \mapsto b$, namely $(14)(36)(9c)(be)$, and we find $\alpha'' = (28)(39)(6c)(7d)$. This permutation belongs to S_d, so α is indeed an automorphism of the 4-cube.

Conversely, (13) also makes it easy to generate all elements of the corresponding group. We simply run through all permutations of the form

$$\sigma(1, c_1)\sigma(2, c_2)\ldots\sigma(n - 1, c_{n-1}),$$

where $\sigma(k, c_k)$ is the $(c_k + 1)$st element of S_k for $0 \le c_k < s_k = |S_k|$ and $1 \le k < n$, using any algorithm of Section 7.2.1.1 that runs through all $(n - 1)$-tuples $(c_1, \ldots, c_{n-1})$ for the respective radices $(s_1, \ldots, s_{n-1})$.

Using the general framework. Our chief concern is the group of *all* permutations on $\{0, 1, \ldots, n-1\}$, and in this case every set S_k of a Sims table will contain $k+1$ elements $\{\sigma(k, 0), \sigma(k, 1), \ldots, \sigma(k, k)\}$, where $\sigma(k, 0)$ is the identity and the others take k to the values $\{0, \ldots, k-1\}$ in some order. (The permutation $\sigma(k, j)$ need not be the same as σ_{kj}, and it usually is different.) Every such Sims table leads to a permutation generator, according to the following outline:

Algorithm G (*General permutation generator*). Given a Sims table $(S_1, S_2, \ldots, S_{n-1})$ where each S_k has $k+1$ elements $\sigma(k, j)$ as just described, this algorithm generates all permutations $a_0 a_1 \ldots a_{n-1}$ of $\{0, 1, \ldots, n-1\}$, using an auxiliary control table $c_n \ldots c_2 c_1$.

G1. [Initialize.] Set $a_j \leftarrow j$ and $c_{j+1} \leftarrow 0$ for $0 \le j < n$.

G2. [Visit.] (At this point the mixed-radix number $\left[\begin{smallmatrix} c_{n-1}, & \ldots, & c_2, & c_1 \\ n, & \ldots, & 3, & 2 \end{smallmatrix}\right]$ is the number of permutations visited so far.) Visit the permutation $a_0 a_1 \ldots a_{n-1}$.

G3. [Add 1 to $c_n \ldots c_2 c_1$.] Set $k \leftarrow 1$. While $c_k = k$, set $c_k \leftarrow 0$ and $k \leftarrow k+1$. Terminate the algorithm if $k = n$; otherwise set $c_k \leftarrow c_k + 1$.

G4. [Permute.] Apply the permutation $\tau(k, c_k) \omega(k-1)^-$ to $a_0 a_1 \ldots a_{n-1}$, as explained below, and return to G2. ∎

Applying a permutation π to $a_0 a_1 \ldots a_{n-1}$ means replacing a_j by $a_{j\pi}$ for $0 \le j < n$; this corresponds to premultiplication by π as explained earlier. Let us define

$$\tau(k, j) = \sigma(k, j) \sigma(k, j-1)^-, \qquad \text{for } 1 \le j \le k; \tag{15}$$

$$\omega(k) = \sigma(1, 1) \ldots \sigma(k, k). \tag{16}$$

Then steps G3 and G4 maintain the property that

$$a_0 a_1 \ldots a_{n-1} \text{ is the permutation } \sigma(1, c_1) \sigma(2, c_2) \ldots \sigma(n-1, c_{n-1}), \tag{17}$$

and Lemma S proves that every permutation is visited exactly once.

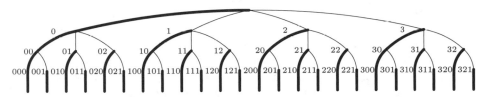

Fig. 39. Algorithm G implicitly traverses this tree when $n = 4$.

The tree in Fig. 39 illustrates Algorithm G in the case $n = 4$. According to (17), every permutation $a_0 a_1 a_2 a_3$ of $\{0, 1, 2, 3\}$ corresponds to a three-digit control string $c_3 c_2 c_1$, with $0 \le c_3 \le 3$, $0 \le c_2 \le 2$, and $0 \le c_1 \le 1$. Some nodes of the tree are labeled by a single digit c_3; these correspond to the permutations $\sigma(3, c_3)$ of the Sims table being used. Other nodes, labeled with two digits $c_3 c_2$, correspond to the permutations $\sigma(2, c_2) \sigma(3, c_3)$. A heavy line connects node c_3 to node $c_3 0$ and node $c_3 c_2$ to node $c_3 c_2 0$, because $\sigma(2, 0)$ and $\sigma(1, 0)$ are the identity permutation and these nodes are essentially equivalent. Adding 1 to the mixed-radix number $c_3 c_2 c_1$ in step G3 corresponds to moving from one node of Fig. 39 to its successor in preorder, and the transformation in step G4 changes the permutations accordingly. For example, when $c_3 c_2 c_1$ changes from 121 to 200, step G4 premultiplies the current permutation by

$$\tau(3, 2) \omega(2)^- = \tau(3, 2) \sigma(2, 2)^- \sigma(1, 1)^-;$$

premultiplying by $\sigma(1,1)^-$ takes us from node 121 to node 12, premultiplying by $\sigma(2,2)^-$ takes us from node 12 to node 1, and premultiplying by $\tau(3,2) = \sigma(3,2)\sigma(3,1)^-$ takes us from node 1 to node $2 \equiv 200$, which is the preorder successor of node 121. Stating this another way, premultiplication by $\tau(3,2)w(2)^-$ is exactly what is needed to change $\sigma(1,1)\sigma(2,2)\sigma(3,1)$ to $\sigma(1,0)\sigma(2,0)\sigma(3,2)$, preserving (17).

Algorithm G defines a huge number of permutation generators (see exercise 37), so it is no wonder that many of its special cases have appeared in the literature. Of course some of its variants are much more efficient than others, and we want to find examples where the operations are particularly well suited to the computer we are using.

We can, for instance, obtain permutations in reverse colex order as a special case of Algorithm G (see (11)), by letting $\sigma(k,j)$ be the $(j+1)$-cycle

$$\sigma(k,j) \;=\; (k{-}j \ \ k{-}j{+}1 \ \ \ldots \ \ k). \tag{18}$$

The reason is that $\sigma(k,j)$ should be the permutation that corresponds to $c_n \ldots c_1$ in reverse colex order when $c_k = j$ and $c_i = 0$ for $i \neq k$, and this permutation $a_0 a_1 \ldots a_{n-1}$ is $01 \ldots (k{-}j{-}1)(k{-}j{+}1) \ldots (k)(k{-}j)(k{+}1) \ldots (n{-}1)$. For example, when $n = 8$ and $c_n \ldots c_1 = 00030000$ the corresponding reverse colex permutation is 01345267, which is $(2\,3\,4\,5)$ in cycle form. When $\sigma(k,j)$ is given by (18), Eqs. (15) and (16) lead to the formulas

$$\tau(k,j) = (k{-}j \ \ k); \tag{19}$$
$$w(k) = (0\,1)(0\,1\,2) \ldots (0\,1 \ \ldots \ k) = (0\,k)(1\,k{-}1)(2\,k{-}2) \ldots = \phi(k); \tag{20}$$

here $\phi(k)$ is the "$(k{+}1)$-flip" that changes $a_0 \ldots a_k$ to $a_k \ldots a_0$. In this case $w(k)$ turns out to be the same as $w(k)^-$, because $\phi(k)^2 = ()$.

Equations (19) and (20) are implicitly present behind the scenes in Algorithm L and in its reverse colex equivalent (exercise 2), where step L3 essentially applies a transposition and step L4 does a flip. Step G4 actually does the flip first; but the identity

$$(k{-}j \ \ k)\phi(k-1) \;=\; \phi(k-1)(j{-}1 \ \ k) \tag{21}$$

shows that a flip followed by a transposition is the same as a (different) transposition followed by the flip.

In fact, equation (21) is a special case of the important identity

$$\pi^-(j_1 \ j_2 \ \ldots \ j_t)\pi \;=\; (j_1\pi \ j_2\pi \ \ldots \ j_t\pi), \tag{22}$$

which is valid for *any* permutation π and any t-cycle $(j_1 \ j_2 \ \ldots \ j_t)$. On the left of (22) we have, for example, $j_1\pi \mapsto j_1 \mapsto j_2 \mapsto j_2\pi$, in agreement with the cycle on the right. Therefore if α and π are any permutations whatsoever, the permutation $\pi^-\alpha\pi$ (called the *conjugate* of α by π) has exactly the same cycle structure as α; we simply replace each element j in each cycle by $j\pi$.

Another significant special case of Algorithm G was introduced by R. J. Ord-Smith [*CACM* **10** (1967), 452; **12** (1969), 638; see also *Comp. J.* **14** (1971),

136–139], whose algorithm is obtained by setting

$$\sigma(k, j) = (k \ \ldots \ 1 \ 0)^j. \tag{23}$$

Now it is clear from (15) that

$$\tau(k, j) = (k \ \ldots \ 1 \ 0); \tag{24}$$

and once again we have

$$\omega(k) = (0 \ k)(1 \ k{-}1)(2 \ k{-}2) \ldots = \phi(k), \tag{25}$$

because $\sigma(k, k) = (0 \ 1 \ \ldots \ k)$ is the same as before. The nice thing about this method is that the permutation needed in step G4, namely $\tau(k, c_k)\omega(k-1)^-$, does not depend on c_k:

$$\tau(k, j)\,\omega(k-1)^- = (k \ \ldots \ 1 \ 0)\phi(k-1)^- = \phi(k). \tag{26}$$

Thus, Ord-Smith's algorithm is the special case of Algorithm G in which step G4 simply interchanges $a_0 \leftrightarrow a_k$, $a_1 \leftrightarrow a_{k-1}$, $\ldots$; this operation is usually quick, because k is small, and it saves some of the work of Algorithm L. (See exercise 38 and the reference to G. S. Klügel in Section 7.2.1.7.)

We can do even better by rigging things so that step G4 needs to do only a single transposition each time, somewhat as in Algorithm P but not necessarily on adjacent elements. Many such schemes are possible. The best is probably to let

$$\tau(k, j)\,\omega(k-1)^- = \begin{cases} (k \ 0), & \text{if } k \text{ is even,} \\ (k \ j{-}1), & \text{if } k \text{ is odd,} \end{cases} \tag{27}$$

as suggested by B. R. Heap [*Comp. J.* **6** (1963), 293–294]. Notice that Heap's method always transposes $a_k \leftrightarrow a_0$ except when $k = 3, 5, \ldots$; and the value of k, in 5 of every 6 steps, is either 1 or 2. Exercise 40 proves that Heap's method does indeed generate all permutations.

Bypassing unwanted blocks. One noteworthy advantage of Algorithm G is that it runs through all permutations of $a_0 \ldots a_{k-1}$ before touching a_k; then it performs another $k!$ cycles before changing a_k again, and so on. Therefore if at any time we reach a setting of the final elements $a_k \ldots a_{n-1}$ that is unimportant to the problem we're working on, we can skip quickly over all permutations that end with the undesirable suffix. More precisely, we could replace step G2 by the following substeps:

G2.0. [Acceptable?] If $a_k \ldots a_{n-1}$ is not an acceptable suffix, go to G2.1. Otherwise set $k \leftarrow k - 1$. Then if $k > 0$, repeat this step; if $k = 0$, proceed to step G2.2.

G2.1. [Skip this suffix.] While $c_k = k$, apply $\sigma(k, k)^-$ to $a_0 \ldots a_{n-1}$ and set $c_k \leftarrow 0$, $k \leftarrow k + 1$. Terminate if $k = n$; otherwise set $c_k \leftarrow c_k + 1$, apply $\tau(k, c_k)$ to $a_0 \ldots a_{n-1}$, and return to G2.0.

G2.2. [Visit.] Visit the permutation $a_0 \ldots a_{n-1}$. ∎

Step G1 should also set $k \leftarrow n - 1$. Notice that the new steps are careful to preserve condition (17). The algorithm has become more complicated, because we need to know the permutations $\tau(k, j)$ and $\sigma(k, k)$ in addition to the permutations $\tau(k, j)\omega(k-1)^-$ that appear in G4. But the additional complications are often worth the effort, because the resulting program might run significantly faster.

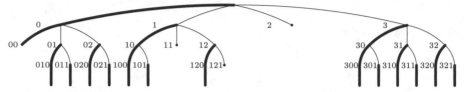

Fig. 40. Unwanted branches can be pruned from the tree of Fig. 39, if Algorithm G is suitably extended.

For example, Fig. 40 shows what happens to the tree of Fig. 39 when the suffixes of $a_0 a_1 a_2 a_3$ that correspond to nodes 00, 11, 121, and 2 are not acceptable. (Each suffix $a_k \ldots a_{n-1}$ of the permutation $a_0 \ldots a_{n-1}$ corresponds to a *prefix* $c_n \ldots c_k$ of the control string $c_n \ldots c_1$, because the permutations $\sigma(1, c_1) \ldots \sigma(k-1, c_{k-1})$ do not affect $a_k \ldots a_{n-1}$.) Step G2.1 premultiplies by $\tau(k, j)$ to move from node $c_{n-1} \ldots c_{k+1}(j-1)$ to its right sibling $c_{n-1} \ldots c_{k+1} j$, and it premultiplies by $\sigma(k, k)^-$ to move up from node $c_{n-1} \ldots c_{k+1} k$ to its parent $c_{n-1} \ldots c_{k+1}$. Thus, to get from the rejected prefix 121 to its preorder successor, the algorithm premultiplies by $\sigma(1, 1)^-$, $\sigma(2, 2)^-$, and $\tau(3, 2)$, thereby moving from node 121 to 12 to 1 to 2. (This is a somewhat exceptional case, because a prefix with $k = 1$ is rejected only if we don't want to visit the unique permutation $a_0 a_1 \ldots a_{n-1}$ that has suffix $a_1 \ldots a_{n-1}$.) After node 2 is rejected, $\tau(3, 3)$ takes us to node 3, etc.

Notice, incidentally, that bypassing a suffix $a_k \ldots a_{n-1}$ in this extension of Algorithm G is essentially the same as bypassing a prefix $a_1 \ldots a_j$ in our original notation, if we go back to the idea of generating permutations $a_1 \ldots a_n$ of $\{1, \ldots, n\}$ and doing most of the work at the right-hand end. Our original notation corresponds to choosing a_1 first, then a_2, $\ldots$, then a_n; the notation in Algorithm G essentially chooses a_{n-1} first, then a_{n-2}, $\ldots$, then a_0. Algorithm G's conventions may seem backward, but they make the formulas for Sims table manipulation a lot simpler. A good programmer soon learns to switch without difficulty from one viewpoint to another.

We can apply these ideas to alphametics, because it is clear for example that most choices of the values for the letters D, E, and Y will make it impossible for SEND plus MORE to equal MONEY: We need to have $(D + E - Y) \bmod 10 = 0$ in that problem. Therefore many permutations can be eliminated from consideration.

In general, if r_k is the maximum power of 10 that divides the signature value s_k, we can sort the letters and assign codes $\{0, 1, \ldots, 9\}$ so that $r_0 \geq r_1 \geq \cdots \geq r_9$. For example, to solve the trio sonata problem (7), we could use $(0, 1, \ldots, 9)$ respectively for (X, S, V, A, R, I, L, T, O, N), obtaining the signatures

$$s_0 = 0, \quad s_1 = -100000, \quad s_2 = 210000, \quad s_3 = -100, \quad s_4 = -100,$$
$$s_5 = 21010, \quad s_6 = 210, \quad s_7 = -1010, \quad s_8 = -7901, \quad s_9 = -998;$$

hence $(r_0, \ldots, r_9) = (\infty, 5, 4, 2, 2, 1, 1, 1, 0, 0)$. Now if we get to step G2.0 for a value of k with $r_{k-1} \neq r_k$, we can say that the suffix $a_k \ldots a_9$ is unacceptable unless $a_k s_k + \cdots + a_9 s_9$ is a multiple of $10^{r_{k-1}}$. Also, (10) tells us that $a_k \ldots a_9$ is unacceptable if $a_k = 0$ and $k \in F$; the first-letter set F is now $\{1, 2, 7\}$.

Our previous approach to alphametics with steps A1–A3 above used brute force to run through 10! possibilities. It operated rather fast under the circumstances, since the adjacent-transposition method allowed it to get by with only 6 memory references per permutation; but still, 10! is 3,628,800, so the entire process cost almost 22 megamems, regardless of the alphametic being solved. By contrast, the extended Algorithm G with Heap's method and the cutoffs just described will find all four solutions to (7) with fewer than 128 *kilo*mems! Thus the suffix-skipping technique runs more than 170 times faster than the previous method, which simply blasted away blindly.

Most of the 128 kilomems in the new approach are spent applying $\tau(k, c_k)$ in step G2.1. The other memory references come primarily from applications of $\sigma(k, k)^-$ in that step, but τ is needed 7812 times while σ^- is needed only 2162 times. The reason is easy to understand from Fig. 40, because the "shortcut move" $\tau(k, c_k)\omega(k-1)^-$ in step G4 hardly ever applies; in this case it is used only four times, once for each solution. Thus, preorder traversal of the tree is accomplished almost entirely by τ steps that move to the right and σ^- steps that move upward. The τ steps dominate in a problem like this, where very few complete permutations are actually visited, because each step $\sigma(k, k)^-$ is preceded by k steps $\tau(k, 1), \tau(k, 2), \ldots, \tau(k, k)$.

This analysis reveals that Heap's method — which goes to great lengths to optimize the permutations $\tau(k, j)\omega(k-1)^-$ so that each transition in step G4 is a simple transposition — is *not* especially good for the extended Algorithm G unless comparatively few suffixes are rejected in step G2.0. The simpler reverse colex order, for which $\tau(k, j)$ itself is always a simple transposition, is now much more attractive (see (19)). Indeed, Algorithm G with reverse colex order solves the alphametic (7) with only 97 kilomems.

Similar results occur with respect to other alphametic problems. For example, if we apply the extended Algorithm G to the alphametics in exercise 24, parts (a) through (h), the computations involve respectively

$$(551, 110, 14, 8, 350, 84, 153, 1598) \text{ kilomems with Heap's method;}$$
$$(429, 84, 10, 5, 256, 63, 117, 1189) \text{ kilomems with reverse colex.} \tag{28}$$

The speedup factor for reverse colex in these examples, compared to brute force with Algorithm T, ranges from 18 in case (h) to 4200 in case (d), and it is about 80 on the average; Heap's method gives an average speedup of about 60.

We know from Algorithm L, however, that lexicographic order is easily handled *without* the complication of the control table $c_n \ldots c_1$ used by Algorithm G. And a closer look at Algorithm L shows that we can improve its behavior when permutations are frequently being skipped, by using a linked list instead of a sequential array. The improved algorithm is well-suited to a wide variety of algorithms that wish to generate restricted classes of permutations:

Algorithm X (*Lexicographic permutations with restricted prefixes*). This algorithm generates all permutations $a_1 a_2 \ldots a_n$ of $\{1, 2, \ldots, n\}$ that pass a given sequence of tests

$$t_1(a_1), \quad t_2(a_1, a_2), \quad \ldots, \quad t_n(a_1, a_2, \ldots, a_n),$$

visiting them in lexicographic order. It uses an auxiliary table of links l_0, l_1, $\ldots$, l_n to maintain a cyclic list of unused elements, so that if the currently available elements are

$$\{1, \ldots, n\} \setminus \{a_1, \ldots, a_k\} = \{b_1, \ldots, b_{n-k}\}, \qquad \text{where } b_1 < \cdots < b_{n-k}, \quad (29)$$

then we have

$$l_0 = b_1, \quad l_{b_j} = b_{j+1} \quad \text{for } 1 \le j < n - k, \quad \text{and} \quad l_{b_{n-k}} = 0. \tag{30}$$

It also uses an auxiliary table $u_1 \ldots u_n$ to undo operations that have been performed on the l array.

X1. [Initialize.] Set $l_k \leftarrow k + 1$ for $0 \le k < n$, and $l_n \leftarrow 0$. Then set $k \leftarrow 1$.

X2. [Enter level k.] Set $p \leftarrow 0$, $q \leftarrow l_0$.

X3. [Test $a_1 \ldots a_k$.] Set $a_k \leftarrow q$. If $t_k(a_1, \ldots, a_k)$ is false, go to X5. Otherwise, if $k = n$, visit $a_1 \ldots a_n$ and go to X6.

X4. [Increase k.] Set $u_k \leftarrow p$, $l_p \leftarrow l_q$, $k \leftarrow k + 1$, and return to X2.

X5. [Increase a_k.] Set $p \leftarrow q$, $q \leftarrow l_p$. If $q \ne 0$ return to X3.

X6. [Decrease k.] Set $k \leftarrow k - 1$, and terminate if $k = 0$. Otherwise set $p \leftarrow u_k$, $q \leftarrow a_k$, $l_p \leftarrow q$, and go to X5. ∎

The basic idea of this elegant algorithm is due to J. S. Rohl [*Inf. Proc. Letters* **17** (1983), 231–233]. We can apply it to alphametics by changing notation slightly, obtaining permutations $a_0 \ldots a_9$ of $\{0, \ldots, 9\}$ and letting l_{10} play the former role of l_0. The resulting algorithm needs only 49 kilomems to solve the trio-sonata problem (7), and it solves the alphametics of exercise 24(a)–(h) in

$$(248, 38, 4, 3, 122, 30, 55, 553) \text{ kilomems}, \tag{31}$$

respectively. Thus it runs about 165 times faster than the brute-force approach.

Another way to apply Algorithm X to alphametics is often faster yet (see exercise 49).

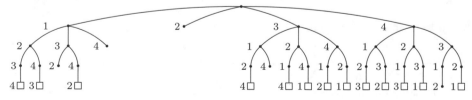

Fig. 41. The tree implicitly traversed by Algorithm X when $n = 4$, if all permutations are visited except those beginning with 132, 14, 2, 314, or 4312.

*Dual methods. If $S_1, \ldots, S_{n-1}$ is a Sims table for a permutation group G, we learned in Lemma S that every element of G can be expressed uniquely as a product $\sigma_1 \ldots \sigma_{n-1}$, where $\sigma_k \in S_k$; see (13). Exercise 50 shows that every element α can also be expressed uniquely in the dual form

$$\alpha = \sigma_{n-1}^- \ldots \sigma_2^- \sigma_1^-, \qquad \text{where } \sigma_k \in S_k \text{ for } 1 \le k < n, \tag{32}$$

and this fact leads to another large family of permutation generators. In particular, when G is the group of all $n!$ permutations, every permutation can be written

$$\sigma(n-1, c_{n-1})^- \ldots \sigma(2, c_2)^- \sigma(1, c_1)^-, \tag{33}$$

where $0 \le c_k \le k$ for $1 \le k < n$ and the permutations $\sigma(k, j)$ are the same as in Algorithm G. Now, however, we want to vary c_{n-1} most rapidly and c_1 least rapidly, so we arrive at an algorithm of a different kind:

Algorithm H (*Dual permutation generator*). Given a Sims table as in Algorithm G, this algorithm generates all permutations $a_0 \ldots a_{n-1}$ of $\{0, \ldots, n-1\}$, using an auxiliary table $c_0 \ldots c_{n-1}$.

H1. [Initialize.] Set $a_j \leftarrow j$ and $c_j \leftarrow 0$ for $0 \le j < n$.

H2. [Visit.] (At this point the mixed-radix number $\begin{bmatrix} c_1, & c_2, & \ldots, & c_{n-1} \\ 2, & 3, & \ldots, & n \end{bmatrix}$ is the number of permutations visited so far.) Visit the permutation $a_0 a_1 \ldots a_{n-1}$.

H3. [Add 1 to $c_0 c_1 \ldots c_{n-1}$.] Set $k \leftarrow n-1$. If $c_k = k$, set $c_k \leftarrow 0$, $k \leftarrow k-1$, and repeat until $k = 0$ or $c_k < k$. Terminate the algorithm if $k = 0$; otherwise set $c_k \leftarrow c_k + 1$.

H4. [Permute.] Apply the permutation $\tau(k, c_k) \omega(k+1)^-$ to $a_0 a_1 \ldots a_{n-1}$, as explained below, and return to H2. ∎

Although this algorithm looks almost identical to Algorithm G, the permutations τ and ω that it needs in step H4 are quite different from those needed in step G4. The new rules, which replace (15) and (16), are

$$\tau(k, j) = \sigma(k, j)^- \sigma(k, j-1), \qquad \text{for } 1 \le j \le k; \tag{34}$$

$$\omega(k) = \sigma(n-1, n-1)^- \sigma(n-2, n-2)^- \ldots \sigma(k, k)^-. \tag{35}$$

The number of possibilities is just as vast as it was for Algorithm G, so we will confine our attention to a few cases that have special merit. One natural case to try is, of course, the Sims table that makes Algorithm G produce reverse colex order, namely

$$\sigma(k, j) \;=\; (k{-}j \;\; k{-}j{+}1 \;\; \ldots \;\; k) \tag{36}$$

as in (18). The resulting permutation generator turns out to be very nearly the same as the method of plain changes; so we can say that Algorithms L and P are essentially dual to each other. (See exercise 52.)

Another natural idea is to construct a Sims table for which step H4 always makes a single transposition of two elements, by analogy with the construction of (27) that achieves maximum efficiency in step G4. But such a mission now turns out to be impossible: We cannot achieve it even when $n = 4$. For if we start with the identity permutation $a_0 a_1 a_2 a_3 = 0123$, the transitions that take us from control table $c_0 c_1 c_2 c_3 = 0000$ to 0001 to 0002 to 0003 must move the 3; so, if they are transpositions, they must be $(3\,a)$, $(a\,b)$, and $(b\,c)$ for some permutation abc of $\{0, 1, 2\}$. The permutation corresponding to $c_0 c_1 c_2 c_3 = 0003$ is now $\sigma(3,3)^- = (b\,c)(a\,b)(3\,a) = (3\,a\,b\,c)$; and the next permutation, which corresponds to $c_0 c_1 c_2 c_3 = 0010$, will be $\sigma(2,1)^-$, which must fix the element 3. The only suitable transposition is $(3\,c)$, hence $\sigma(2,1)^-$ must be $(3\,c)(3\,a\,b\,c) = (a\,b\,c)$. Similarly we find that $\sigma(2,2)^-$ must be $(a\,c\,b)$, and the permutation corresponding to $c_0 c_1 c_2 c_3 = 0023$ will be $(3\,a\,b\,c)(a\,c\,b) = (3\,c)$. Step H4 is now supposed to convert this to the permutation $\sigma(1,1)^-$, which corresponds to the control table 0100 that follows 0023. But the only transposition that will convert $(3\,c)$ into a permutation that fixes 2 and 3 is $(3\,c)$; and the resulting permutation also fixes 1, so it cannot be $\sigma(1,1)^-$.

The proof in the preceding paragraph shows that we cannot use Algorithm H to generate all permutations with the minimum number of transpositions. But it also suggests a simple generation scheme that comes very close to the minimum, and the resulting algorithm is quite attractive because it needs to do extra work only once per $n(n-1)$ steps. (See exercise 53.)

Finally, let's consider the dual of Ord-Smith's method, when

$$\sigma(k, j) = (k\ \ldots\ 1\ 0)^j \tag{37}$$

as in (23). Once again the value of $\tau(k, j)$ is independent of j,

$$\tau(k, j) = (0\ 1\ \ldots\ k), \tag{38}$$

and this fact is particularly advantageous in Algorithm H because it allows us to dispense with the control table $c_0 c_1 \ldots c_{n-1}$. The reason is that $c_{n-1} = 0$ in step H3 if and only if $a_{n-1} = n - 1$, because of (33); and indeed, when $c_j = 0$ for $k < j < n$ in step H3 we have $c_k = 0$ if and only if $a_k = k$. Therefore we can reformulate this variant of Algorithm H as follows.

Algorithm C (*Permutation generation by cyclic shifts*). This algorithm visits all permutations $a_1 \ldots a_n$ of the distinct elements $\{x_1, \ldots, x_n\}$.

C1. [Initialize.] Set $a_j \leftarrow x_j$ for $1 \le j \le n$.

C2. [Visit.] Visit the permutation $a_1 \ldots a_n$, and set $k \leftarrow n$.

C3. [Shift.] Replace $a_1 a_2 \ldots a_k$ by the cyclic shift $a_2 \ldots a_k a_1$, and return to C2 if $a_k \ne x_k$.

C4. [Decrease k.] Set $k \leftarrow k - 1$, and go back to C3 if $k > 1$; otherwise stop. ∎

For example, the successive permutations of $\{1, 2, 3, 4\}$ generated when $n = 4$ are

$$1234,\ 2341,\ 3412,\ 4123,\ (1234),$$
$$2314,\ 3142,\ 1423,\ 4231,\ (2314),$$
$$3124,\ 1243,\ 2431,\ 4312,\ (3124),\ (1234),$$
$$2134,\ 1342,\ 3421,\ 4213,\ (2134),$$
$$1324,\ 3241,\ 2413,\ 4132,\ (1324),$$
$$3214,\ 2143,\ 1432,\ 4321,\ (3214),\ (2134),\ (1234),$$

with unvisited intermediate permutations shown in parentheses. This algorithm
may well be the simplest permutation generator of all, in terms of minimum
program length. It is due to G. G. Langdon, Jr. [*CACM* **10** (1967), 298–299;
11 (1968), 392]; similar methods had been published previously by C. Tompkins
[*Proc. Symp. Applied Math.* **6** (1956), 202–205] and, more explicitly, by R. Seitz
[*Unternehmensforschung* **6** (1962), 2–15]. The procedure is particularly well
suited to applications in which cyclic shifting is efficient, for example when successive permutations are being kept in a machine register instead of in an array.

The main disadvantage of dual methods is that they usually do not adapt
well to situations where large blocks of permutations need to be skipped, because the set of all permutations with a given value of the first control entries
$c_0 c_1 \ldots c_{k-1}$ is usually not of importance. The special case (36) is, however,
sometimes an exception, because the $n!/k!$ permutations with $c_0 c_1 \ldots c_{k-1} =$
$00 \ldots 0$ in that case are precisely those $a_0 a_1 \ldots a_{n-1}$ in which 0 precedes 1,
1 precedes 2, $\ldots$, and $k-2$ precedes $k-1$.

*Ehrlich's swap method. Gideon Ehrlich has discovered a completely different
approach to permutation generation, based on yet another way to use a control
table $c_1 \ldots c_{n-1}$. His method obtains each permutation from its predecessor by
interchanging the leftmost element with another:

Algorithm E (*Ehrlich swaps*). This algorithm generates all permutations of the
distinct elements $a_0 \ldots a_{n-1}$ by using auxiliary tables $b_0 \ldots b_{n-1}$ and $c_1 \ldots c_n$.

E1. [Initialize.] Set $b_j \leftarrow j$ and $c_{j+1} \leftarrow 0$ for $0 \leq j < n$.

E2. [Visit.] Visit the permutation $a_0 \ldots a_{n-1}$.

E3. [Find k.] Set $k \leftarrow 1$. Then while $c_k = k$, set $c_k \leftarrow 0$ and $k \leftarrow k+1$.
  Terminate if $k = n$, otherwise set $c_k \leftarrow c_k + 1$.

E4. [Swap.] Interchange $a_0 \leftrightarrow a_{b_k}$.

E5. [Flip.] Set $j \leftarrow 1$, $k \leftarrow k-1$. While $j < k$, interchange $b_j \leftrightarrow b_k$ and set
  $j \leftarrow j+1$, $k \leftarrow k-1$. Return to E2. ∎

Notice that steps E2 and E3 are identical to steps G2 and G3 of Algorithm G.
The most amazing thing about this algorithm, which Ehrlich communicated to
Martin Gardner in 1987, is that it works; exercise 55 contains a proof. A similar
method, which simplifies the operations of step E5, can be validated in the same
way (see exercise 56). The average number of interchanges performed in step E5
is less than 0.18 (see exercise 57).

As it stands, Algorithm E isn't faster than other methods we have seen. But
it has the nice property that it changes each permutation in a minimal way, using
only $n-1$ different kinds of transpositions. Whereas Algorithm P used adjacent
interchanges, $a_{t-1} \leftrightarrow a_t$, Algorithm E uses first-element swaps, $a_0 \leftrightarrow a_t$, also
called *star transpositions*, for some well-chosen sequence of indices $t[1]$, $t[2]$, $\ldots$,
$t[n! - 1]$. And if we are generating permutations repeatedly for the same fairly
small value of n, we can precompute this sequence, as we did in Algorithm T

for the index sequence of Algorithm P. Notice that star transpositions have an advantage over adjacent interchanges, because we always know the value of a_0 from the previous swap; we need not read it from memory.

Let E_n be the sequence of $n! - 1$ indices t such that Algorithm E swaps a_0 with a_t in step E4. Since E_{n+1} begins with E_n, we can regard E_n as the first $n! - 1$ elements of an infinite sequence

$$E_\infty = 121213212123121213212124313132131312\ldots. \qquad (39)$$

For example, if $n = 4$ and $a_0 a_1 a_2 a_3 = 1234$, the permutations visited by Algorithm E are

$$\begin{array}{cccccc}
1234, & 2134, & 3124, & 1324, & 2314, & 3214, \\
4213, & 1243, & 2143, & 4123, & 1423, & 2413, \\
3412, & 4312, & 1342, & 3142, & 4132, & 1432, \\
2431, & 3421, & 4321, & 2341, & 3241, & 4231.
\end{array} \qquad (40)$$

*Using fewer generators. After seeing Algorithms P and E, we might naturally ask whether all permutations can be obtained by using just *two* basic operations, instead of $n - 1$. For example, Nijenhuis and Wilf [*Combinatorial Algorithms* (1975), Exercise 6] noticed that all permutations can be generated for $n = 4$ if we replace $a_1 a_2 a_3 \ldots a_n$ at each step by either $a_2 a_3 \ldots a_n a_1$ or $a_2 a_1 a_3 \ldots a_n$, and they wondered whether such a method exists for all n.

In general, if G is any group of permutations and if $\alpha_1, \ldots, \alpha_k$ are elements of G, the *Cayley graph* for G with generators $(\alpha_1, \ldots, \alpha_k)$ is the directed graph whose vertices are the permutations π of G and whose arcs go from π to $\alpha_1 \pi, \ldots, \alpha_k \pi$. [Arthur Cayley, *American J. Math.* **1** (1878), 174–176.] The question of Nijenhuis and Wilf is equivalent to asking whether the Cayley graph for all permutations of $\{1, 2, \ldots, n\}$, with generators σ and τ where σ is the cyclic permutation $(1 \ 2 \ \ldots \ n)$ and τ is the transposition $(1 \ 2)$, has a Hamiltonian path.

A basic theorem due to R. A. Rankin [*Proc. Cambridge Philos. Soc.* **44** (1948), 17–25] allows us to conclude in many cases that Cayley graphs with two generators do not have a Hamiltonian cycle:

Theorem R. *Let G be a group consisting of g permutations. If the Cayley graph for G with generators (α, β) has a Hamiltonian cycle, and if the permutations $(\alpha, \beta, \alpha\beta^-)$ are respectively of order (a, b, c), then either c is even or g/a and g/b are odd.*

(The *order* of a permutation α is the least positive integer a such that α^a is the identity.)

Proof. See exercise 73. ▮

In particular, when $\alpha = \sigma$ and $\beta = \tau$ as above, we have $g = n!$, $a = n$, $b = 2$, and $c = n - 1$, because $\sigma\tau^- = (2 \ \ldots \ n)$. Therefore we conclude that no Hamiltonian cycle is possible when $n \geq 4$ is even. However, a Hamiltonian *path* is easy to construct when $n = 4$, because we can join up the 12-cycles

$$\begin{aligned} 1234 &\rightarrow 2341 \rightarrow 3412 \rightarrow 4312 \rightarrow 3124 \rightarrow 1243 \rightarrow 2431 \\ &\rightarrow 4231 \rightarrow 2314 \rightarrow 3142 \rightarrow 1423 \rightarrow 4123 \rightarrow 1234, \\ 2134 &\rightarrow 1342 \rightarrow 3421 \rightarrow 4321 \rightarrow 3214 \rightarrow 2143 \rightarrow 1432 \\ &\rightarrow 4132 \rightarrow 1324 \rightarrow 3241 \rightarrow 2413 \rightarrow 4213 \rightarrow 2134, \end{aligned} \tag{41}$$

by starting at 2341 and jumping from 1234 to 2134, ending at 4213.

Ruskey, Jiang, and Weston [*Discrete Applied Math.* **57** (1995), 75–83] undertook an exhaustive search in the σ–τ graph for $n = 5$ and discovered that it has five essentially distinct Hamiltonian cycles, one of which (the "most beautiful") is illustrated in Fig. 42(a). They also found a Hamiltonian path for $n = 6$; this was a difficult feat, because it is the outcome of a 720-stage binary decision tree. Unfortunately the solution they discovered has no apparent logical structure. A somewhat less complex path is described in exercise 70, but even that path cannot be called simple. Therefore a σ–τ approach will probably not be of practical interest for larger values of n unless a new construction is discovered. R. C. Compton and S. G. Williamson [*Linear and Multilinear Algebra* **35** (1993), 237–293] have proved that Hamiltonian cycles exist for all n if the three generators σ, σ^-, and τ are allowed instead of just σ and τ; their cycles have the interesting property that every nth transformation is τ, and the intervening $n - 1$ transformations are either all σ or all σ^-. But their method is too complicated to explain in a short space.

Exercise 69 describes a general permutation algorithm that is reasonably simple and needs only three generators, each of order 2. Figure 42(b) illustrates the case $n = 5$ of this method, which was motivated by examples of bell-ringing.

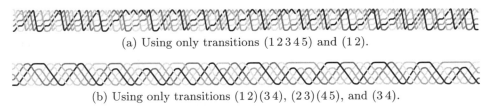

(a) Using only transitions $(1\,2\,3\,4\,5)$ and $(1\,2)$.

(b) Using only transitions $(1\,2)(3\,4)$, $(2\,3)(4\,5)$, and $(3\,4)$.

Fig. 42. Hamiltonian cycles for 5! permutations.

Faster, faster. What is the fastest way to generate permutations? This question has often been raised in computer publications, because people who examine $n!$ possibilities want to keep the running time as small as possible. But the answers have generally been contradictory, because there are many different ways to formulate the question. Let's try to understand the related issues by studying how permutations might be generated most rapidly on the MMIX computer.

Suppose first that our goal is to produce permutations in an array of n consecutive memory words (octabytes). The fastest way to do this, of all those we've seen in this section, is to streamline Heap's method (27), as suggested by R. Sedgewick [*Computing Surveys* **9** (1977), 157–160].

The key idea is to optimize the code for the most common cases of steps G2 and G3, namely the cases in which all activity occurs at the beginning of the array. If registers u, v, and w contain the contents of the first three words, and if the next six permutations to be generated involve permuting those words in all six possible ways, we can clearly do the job as follows:

$$
\begin{array}{lll}
\text{PUSHJ 0,Visit} \\
\text{STO v,A0;} & \text{STO u,A1;} & \text{PUSHJ 0,Visit} \\
\text{STO w,A0;} & \text{STO v,A2;} & \text{PUSHJ 0,Visit} \\
\text{STO u,A0;} & \text{STO w,A1;} & \text{PUSHJ 0,Visit} \\
\text{STO v,A0;} & \text{STO u,A2;} & \text{PUSHJ 0,Visit} \\
\text{STO w,A0;} & \text{STO v,A1;} & \text{PUSHJ 0,Visit}
\end{array}
\tag{42}
$$

(Here A0 is the address of octabyte a_0, etc.) A complete permutation program, which takes care of getting the right things into u, v, and w, appears in exercise 77, but the other instructions are less important because they need to be performed only $\frac{1}{6}$ of the time. The total cost per permutation, not counting the $4v$ needed for PUSHJ and POP on each call to Visit, comes to approximately $2.77\mu + 5.69v$ with this approach. If we use four registers u, v, w, x, and if we expand (42) to 24 calls on Visit, the running time per permutation drops to about $2.19\mu + 3.07v$. And with r registers and $r!$ Visits, exercise 78 shows that the cost is $(2 + O(1/r!))(\mu + v)$, which is very nearly the cost of two STO instructions.

The latter is, of course, the minimum possible time for any method that generates all permutations in a sequential array. ... Or is it? We have assumed that the visiting routine wants to see permutations in consecutive locations, but perhaps that routine is able to read the permutations from different starting points. Then we can arrange to keep a_{n-1} fixed and to keep two copies of the other elements in its vicinity:

$$
a_0 a_1 \ldots a_{n-2} a_{n-1} a_0 a_1 \ldots a_{n-2}.
\tag{43}
$$

If we now let $a_0 a_1 \ldots a_{n-2}$ run through $(n-1)!$ permutations, always changing both copies simultaneously by doing two STO commands instead of one, we can let every call to Visit look at the n permutations

$$
a_0 a_1 \ldots a_{n-1}, \quad a_1 \ldots a_{n-1} a_0, \quad \ldots, \quad a_{n-1} a_0 \ldots a_{n-2},
\tag{44}
$$

which all appear consecutively. The cost per permutation is now reduced to the cost of three simple instructions like ADD, CMP, PBNZ, plus $O(1/n)$. [See Varol and Rotem, *Comp. J.* **24** (1981), 173–176.]

Furthermore, we might not want to waste time storing permutations into memory at all. Suppose, for example, that our goal is to generate all permutations of $\{0, 1, \ldots, n-1\}$. The value of n will probably be at most 16, because $16! = 20{,}922{,}789{,}888{,}000$ and $17! = 355{,}687{,}428{,}096{,}000$. Therefore an entire permutation will fit in the 16 nybbles of an octabyte, and we can keep it in a single register. This will be advantageous only if the visiting routine doesn't need to unpack the individual nybbles; but let's suppose that it doesn't. How fast can we generate permutations in the nybbles of a 64-bit register?

One idea, suggested by a technique due to A. J. Goldstein [*U.S. Patent 3383661* (14 May 1968)], is to precompute the table $(t[1], \ldots, t[5039])$ of plain-change transitions for seven elements, using Algorithm T. These numbers $t[k]$ lie between 1 and 6, so we can pack 20 of them into a 64-bit word. It is convenient to put the number $\sum_{k=1}^{20} 2^{3k-1} t[20j + k]$ into word j of an auxiliary table, for $0 \le j < 252$, with $t[5040] = 1$; for example, the table begins with the codeword

00 001 010 011 100 101 110 100 110 101 100 011 010 001 110 001 010 011 100 101 110 00.

The following program reads such codes efficiently:

```
Perm   ⟨Set register a to the first permutation⟩
0H     LDA   p,T        p ← address of first codeword.
       JMP   3F
1H     ⟨Visit the permutation in register a⟩
       ⟨Swap the nybbles of a that lie t bits from the right⟩
       SRU   c,c,3      c ← c ≫ 3.
2H     AND   t,c,#1c    t ← c & (11100)₂.
       PBNZ  t,1B       Branch if t ≠ 0.
       ADD   p,p,8
3H     LDO   c,p,0      c ← next codeword.
       PBNZ  c,2B       (The final codeword is followed by 0.)
       ⟨If not done, advance the leading n − 7 nybbles and return to 0B⟩
```

$$(45)$$

Exercise 79 shows how to ⟨Swap the nybbles ... ⟩ with seven instructions, using bit manipulation operations that are found on most computers. Therefore the cost per permutation is just a bit more than $10v$. (The instructions that fetch new codewords cost only $(\mu + 5v)/20$; and the instructions that advance the leading $n-7$ nybbles are even more negligible since their cost is divided by 5040.) Notice that there is now no need for PUSHJ and POP as there was with (42); we ignored those instructions before, but they did cost $4v$.

We can, however, do even better by adapting Langdon's cyclic-shift method, Algorithm C. Suppose we start with the lexicographically largest permutation and operate as follows:

```
       GREG  @
0H     OCTA  #fedcba9876543210&(1<<(4*N)-1)
Perm   LDOU  a,0B                              Set a ← # ...3210.
       JMP   2F
1H     SRU   a,a,4*(16-N)                      a ← ⌊a/16^(16-n)⌋.
       OR    a,a,t                             a ← a | t.
2H     ⟨Visit the permutation in register a⟩
       SRU   t,a,4*(N-1)                       t ← ⌊a/16^(n-1)⌋.
       SLU   a,a,4*(17-N)                      a ← 16^(17-n)a mod 16^16.
       PBNZ  t,1B                              To 1B if t ≠ 0
       ⟨Continue with Langdon's method⟩
```

$$(46)$$

The running time per permutation is now only $5v + O(1/n)$, again without the need for PUSHJ and POP. See exercise 81 for an interesting way to extend (46) to a complete program, obtaining a remarkably short and fast routine.

Fast permutation generators are amusing, but in practice we can usually save more time by streamlining the visiting routine than by speeding up the generator.

Topological sorting. Instead of working with all $n!$ permutations of $\{1, \ldots, n\}$, we often want to look only at permutations that obey certain restrictions. For example, we might be interested only in permutations for which 1 precedes 3, 2 precedes 3, and 2 precedes 4; there are five such permutations of $\{1, 2, 3, 4\}$, namely

$$1234, \quad 1243, \quad 2134, \quad 2143, \quad 2413. \tag{47}$$

The problem of *topological sorting*, which we studied in Section 2.2.3 as a first example of nontrivial data structures, is the general problem of finding a permutation that satisfies m such conditions $x_1 \prec y_1, \ldots, x_m \prec y_m$, where $x \prec y$ means that x should precede y in the permutation. This problem arises frequently in practice, so it has several different names; for example, it is often called the *linear embedding* problem, because we want to arrange objects in a line while preserving certain order relationships. It is also the problem of extending a partial ordering to a total ordering, also called a linear ordering (see exercise 2.2.3–14).

Our goal in Section 2.2.3 was to find a *single* permutation that satisfies all the relations. But now we want rather to find *all* such permutations, all topological sorts. Indeed, we will assume in the present section that the elements x and y on which the relations are defined are integers between 1 and n, and that we have $x < y$ whenever $x \prec y$. Consequently the permutation $12 \ldots n$ will always be topologically correct. (If this simplifying assumption is not met, we can preprocess the data by using Algorithm 2.2.3T to rename the objects appropriately.)

Many important classes of permutations are special cases of this topological ordering problem. For example, the permutations of $\{1, \ldots, 8\}$ such that

$$1 \prec 2, \quad 2 \prec 3, \quad 3 \prec 4, \quad 6 \prec 7, \quad 7 \prec 8$$

are equivalent to permutations of the multiset $\{1, 1, 1, 1, 2, 3, 3, 3\}$, because we can map $\{1, 2, 3, 4\} \mapsto 1$, $5 \mapsto 2$, and $\{6, 7, 8\} \mapsto 3$. We know how to generate permutations of a multiset using Algorithm L, but now we will learn another way.

Notice that x precedes y in a permutation $a_1 \ldots a_n$ if and only if $a'_x < a'_y$ in the inverse permutation $a'_1 \ldots a'_n$. Therefore the algorithm we are about to study will also find all permutations $a'_1 \ldots a'_n$ such that $a'_j < a'_k$ whenever $j \prec k$. For example, we learned in Section 5.1.4 that a Young tableau is an arrangement of $\{1, \ldots, n\}$ in rows and columns so that each row is increasing from left to right and each column is increasing from top to bottom. The problem of generating all 3×3 Young tableaux is therefore equivalent to generating all $a'_1 \ldots a'_9$ such that

$$\begin{aligned}
a'_1 < a'_2 < a'_3, \quad a'_4 < a'_5 < a'_6, \quad a'_7 < a'_8 < a'_9, \\
a'_1 < a'_4 < a'_7, \quad a'_2 < a'_5 < a'_8, \quad a'_3 < a'_6 < a'_9,
\end{aligned} \tag{48}$$

and this is a special kind of topological sorting.

We might also want to find all *perfect matchings* of $2n$ elements, namely all ways to partition $\{1, \ldots, 2n\}$ into n pairs. There are $(2n - 1)(2n - 3) \ldots (1) = (2n)!/(2^n n!)$ ways to do this, and they correspond to permutations that satisfy

$$a_1' < a_2', \quad a_3' < a_4', \quad \ldots, \quad a_{2n-1}' < a_{2n}', \qquad a_1' < a_3' < \cdots < a_{2n-1}'. \qquad (49)$$

An elegant algorithm for exhaustive topological sorting was discovered by Y. L. Varol and D. Rotem [*Comp. J.* **24** (1981), 83–84], who realized that a method analogous to plain changes (Algorithm P) can be used. Suppose we have found a way to arrange $\{1, \ldots, n - 1\}$ topologically, so that $a_1 \ldots a_{n-1}$ satisfies all the conditions that do not involve n. Then we can easily write down all the allowable ways to insert the final element n without changing the relative order of $a_1 \ldots a_{n-1}$: We simply start with $a_1 \ldots a_{n-1} n$, then shift n left one step at a time, until it cannot move further. Applying this idea recursively yields the following straightforward procedure.

Algorithm V (*All topological sorts*). Given a relation $\prec$ on $\{1, \ldots, n\}$ with the property that $x \prec y$ implies $x < y$, this algorithm generates all permutations $a_1 \ldots a_n$ and their inverses $a_1' \ldots a_n'$ with the property that $a_j' < a_k'$ whenever $j \prec k$. We assume for convenience that $a_0 = a_0' = 0$ and that $0 \prec k$ for $1 \le k \le n$.

V1. [Initialize.] Set $a_j \leftarrow j$ and $a_j' \leftarrow j$ for $0 \le j \le n$.

V2. [Visit.] Visit the permutation $a_1 \ldots a_n$ and its inverse $a_1' \ldots a_n'$. Then set $k \leftarrow n$.

V3. [Can k move left?] Set $j \leftarrow a_k'$ and $l \leftarrow a_{j-1}$. If $l \prec k$, go to V5.

V4. [Yes, move it.] Set $a_{j-1} \leftarrow k$, $a_j \leftarrow l$, $a_k' \leftarrow j - 1$, and $a_l' \leftarrow j$. Go to V2.

V5. [No, put k back.] While $j < k$, set $l \leftarrow a_{j+1}$, $a_j \leftarrow l$, $a_l' \leftarrow j$, and $j \leftarrow j+1$. Then set $a_k \leftarrow a_k' \leftarrow k$. Decrease k by 1 and return to V3 if $k > 0$. ∎

For example, Theorem 5.1.4H tells us that there are exactly 42 Young tableaux of size 3×3. If we apply Algorithm V to the relations (48) and write the inverse permutation in array form

$$\begin{array}{|ccc|} a_1' & a_2' & a_3' \\ a_4' & a_5' & a_6' \\ a_7' & a_8' & a_9' \end{array}, \qquad (50)$$

we get the following 42 results:

123	123	123	123	123	124	124	124	124	124	125	125	125	125
456	457	458	467	468	356	357	358	367	368	367	368	346	347
789	689	679	589	579	789	689	679	589	579	489	479	789	689

125	126	126	127	126	126	127	134	134	134	134	134	135	135
348	347	348	348	357	358	358	256	257	258	267	268	267	268
679	589	579	569	489	479	469	789	689	679	589	579	489	479

145	145	135	135	135	136	136	137	136	136	137	146	146	147
267	268	246	247	248	247	248	248	257	258	258	257	258	258
389	379	789	689	679	589	579	569	489	479	469	389	379	369

Let t_r be the number of topological sorts for which the final $n - r$ elements are in their initial position $a_j = j$ for $r < j \leq n$. Equivalently, t_r is the number of topological sorts $a_1 \ldots a_r$ of $\{1, \ldots, r\}$, when we ignore the relations involving elements greater than r. Then the recursive mechanism underlying Algorithm V shows that step V2 is performed N times and step V3 is performed M times, where

$$M = t_n + \cdots + t_1 \quad \text{and} \quad N = t_n. \tag{51}$$

Also, step V4 and the loop operations of V5 are performed $N - 1$ times; the rest of step V5 is done $M - N + 1$ times. Therefore the total running time of the algorithm is a linear combination of M, N, and n.

If the element labels are chosen poorly, M might be much larger than N. For example, if the constraints input to Algorithm V are

$$2 \prec 3, \quad 3 \prec 4, \quad \ldots, \quad n - 1 \prec n, \tag{52}$$

then $t_j = j$ for $1 \leq j \leq n$ and we have $M = \frac{1}{2}(n^2 + n)$, $N = n$. But those constraints are also equivalent to

$$1 \prec 2, \quad 2 \prec 3, \quad \ldots, \quad n - 2 \prec n - 1, \tag{53}$$

under renaming of the elements; then M is reduced to $2n - 1 = 2N - 1$.

Exercise 89 shows that a simple preprocessing step will find element labels so that a slight modification of Algorithm V is able to generate all topological sorts in $O(N + n)$ steps. Thus topological sorting can always be done efficiently.

Think twice before you permute. We have seen several attractive algorithms for permutation generation in this section, but many algorithms are known by which permutations that are optimum for particular purposes can be found *without* running through all possibilities. For example, Theorem 6.1S showed that we can find the best way to arrange records on a sequential storage simply by sorting them with respect to a certain cost criterion, and this process takes only $O(n \log n)$ steps. In Section 7.5.2 we will study the *assignment problem*, which asks how to permute the columns of a square matrix so that the sum of the diagonal elements is maximized. That problem can be solved in at most $O(n^3)$ operations, so it would be foolish to use a method of order $n!$ unless n is extremely small. Even in cases like the traveling salesrep problem, when no efficient algorithm is known, we can usually find a much better approach than to examine every possible solution. Permutation generation is best used when there is good reason to look at each permutation individually.

EXERCISES

▶ **1.** [*20*] Explain how to make Algorithm L run faster, by streamlining its operations when the value of j is near n.

2. [*20*] Rewrite Algorithm L so that it produces all permutations of $a_1 \ldots a_n$ in reverse colex order. (In other words, the values of the reflections $a_n \ldots a_1$ should be lexicographically decreasing, as in (11). This form of the algorithm is often simpler and faster than the original, because fewer calculations depend on the value of n.)

▶ **3.** [*M21*] The *rank* of a combinatorial arrangement X with respect to a generation algorithm is the number of other arrangements that the algorithm visits prior to X. Explain how to compute the rank of a given permutation $a_1 \ldots a_n$ with respect to Algorithm L, if $\{a_1, \ldots, a_n\} = \{1, \ldots, n\}$. What is the rank of 314592687?

4. [*M23*] Generalizing exercise 3, explain how to compute the rank of $a_1 \ldots a_n$ with respect to Algorithm L when $\{a_1, \ldots, a_n\}$ is the multiset $\{n_1 \cdot x_1, \ldots, n_t \cdot x_t\}$; here $n_1 + \cdots + n_t = n$ and $x_1 < \cdots < x_t$. (The total number of permutations is, of course, the multinomial coefficient

$$\binom{n}{n_1, \ldots, n_t} = \frac{n!}{n_1! \ldots n_t!};$$

see Eq. 5.1.2–(3).) What is the rank of 314159265?

5. [*HM25*] Compute the mean and variance of the number of comparisons made by Algorithm L in (a) step L2, (b) step L3, when the elements $\{a_1, \ldots, a_n\}$ are distinct.

6. [*HM34*] Derive generating functions for the mean number of comparisons made by Algorithm L in (a) step L2, (b) step L3, when $\{a_1, \ldots, a_n\}$ is a general multiset as in exercise 4. Also give the results in closed form when $\{a_1, \ldots, a_n\}$ is the binary multiset $\{s \cdot 0, (n \ s) \cdot 1\}$.

7. [*HM35*] What is the limit as $t \to \infty$ of the average number of comparisons made per permutation in step L2 when Algorithm L is being applied to the multiset (a) $\{2 \cdot 1, 2 \cdot 2, \ldots, 2 \cdot t\}$? (b) $\{1 \cdot 1, 2 \cdot 2, \ldots, t \cdot t\}$? (c) $\{2 \cdot 1, 4 \cdot 2, \ldots, 2^t \cdot t\}$?

▶ **8.** [*21*] The *variations* of a multiset are the permutations of all its submultisets. For example, the variations of $\{1, 2, 2, 3\}$ are

ϵ, 1, 12, 122, 1223, 123, 1232, 13, 132, 1322,

2, 21, 212, 2123, 213, 2132, 22, 221, 2213, 223, 2231, 23, 231, 2312, 232, 2321,

3, 31, 312, 3122, 32, 321, 3212, 322, 3221.

Show that simple changes to Algorithm L will generate all variations of a given multiset $\{a_1, a_2, \ldots, a_n\}$.

9. [*22*] Continuing the previous exercise, design an algorithm to generate all r-variations of a given multiset $\{a_1, a_2, \ldots, a_n\}$, also called its r-permutations, namely all permutations of its r-element submultisets. (For example, the solution to an alphametic with r distinct letters is an r-variation of $\{0, 1, \ldots, 9\}$.)

10. [*20*] What are the values of $a_1 a_2 \ldots a_n$, $c_1 c_2 \ldots c_n$, and $o_1 o_2 \ldots o_n$ at the end of Algorithm P, if $a_1 a_2 \ldots a_n = 12 \ldots n$ at the beginning?

11. [*M22*] How many times is each step of Algorithm P performed? (Assume that $n \geq 2$.)

▶ **12.** [*M23*] What is the 1000000th permutation visited by (a) Algorithm L, (b) Algorithm P, (c) Algorithm C, if $\{a_1, \ldots, a_n\} = \{0, \ldots, 9\}$? *Hint:* In mixed-radix notation we have $1000000 = \left[\begin{smallmatrix} 2, & 6, & 6, & 2, & 5, & 1, & 2, & 2, & 0, & 0 \\ 10, & 9, & 8, & 7, & 6, & 5, & 4, & 3, & 2, & 1 \end{smallmatrix}\right] = \left[\begin{smallmatrix} 0, & 0, & 1, & 2, & 3, & 0, & 2, & 7, & 1, & 0 \\ 1, & 2, & 3, & 4, & 5, & 6, & 7, & 8, & 9, & 10 \end{smallmatrix}\right]$.

13. [*M21*] (Martin Gardner, 1974.) True or false: If $a_1 a_2 \ldots a_n$ is initially $12 \ldots n$, Algorithm P begins by visiting all $n!/2$ permutations in which 1 precedes 2; then the next permutation is $n \ldots 21$.

14. [*M22*] True or false: If $a_1 a_2 \ldots a_n$ is initially $x_1 x_2 \ldots x_n$ in Algorithm P, we always have $a_{j-c_j+s} = x_j$ at the beginning of step P5.

15. [*M23*] (Selmer Johnson, 1963.) Show that the offset variable s never exceeds 2 in Algorithm P.

16. [*21*] Explain how to make Algorithm P run faster, by streamlining its operations when the value of j is near n. (This problem is analogous to exercise 1.)

▶ **17.** [*20*] Extend Algorithm P so that the *inverse permutation* $a'_1 \ldots a'_n$ is available for processing when $a_1 \ldots a_n$ is visited in step P2. (The inverse satisfies $a'_k = j$ if and only if $a_j = k$.)

18. [*21*] (*Rosary permutations.*) Devise an efficient way to generate $(n-1)!/2$ permutations that represent all possible undirected cycles on the vertices $\{1, \ldots, n\}$; that is, no cyclic shift of $a_1 \ldots a_n$ or $a_n \ldots a_1$ will be generated if $a_1 \ldots a_n$ is generated. The permutations (1234, 1324, 3124) could, for example, be used when $n = 4$.

19. [*25*] Construct an algorithm that generates all permutations of n distinct elements *looplessly* in the spirit of Algorithm 7.2.1.1L.

▶ **20.** [*20*] The n-cube has $2^n n!$ symmetries, one for each way to permute and/or complement the coordinates. Such a symmetry is conveniently represented as a *signed permutation*, namely a permutation with optional signs attached to the elements. For example, $23\bar{1}$ is a signed permutation that transforms the vertices of the 3-cube by changing $x_1 x_2 x_3$ to $x_2 x_3 \bar{x}_1$, so that $000 \mapsto 001$, $001 \mapsto 011$, $\ldots$, $111 \mapsto 110$. Design a simple algorithm that generates all signed permutations of $\{1, 2, \ldots, n\}$, where each step either interchanges two adjacent elements or negates the first element.

21. [*M21*] (E. P. McCravy, 1971.) How many solutions does the alphametic (6) have in radix b?

22. [*M15*] True or false: If an alphametic has a solution in radix b, it has a solution in radix $b + 1$.

23. [*M20*] True or false: A pure alphametic cannot have two identical signatures $s_j = s_k \neq 0$ when $j \neq k$.

24. [*25*] Solve the following alphametics by hand or by computer:
   a) SEND + A + TAD + MORE = MONEY.
   b) ZEROES + ONES = BINARY.   (Peter MacDonald, 1977)
   c) DCLIX + DLXVI = MCCXXV.   (Willy Enggren, 1972)
   d) COUPLE + COUPLE = QUARTET.   (Michael R. W. Buckley, 1977)
   e) FISH + N + CHIPS = SUPPER.   (Bob Vinnicombe, 1978)
   f) SATURN + URANUS + NEPTUNE + PLUTO = PLANETS.   (Willy Enggren, 1968)
   g) EARTH + AIR + FIRE + WATER = NATURE.   (Herman Nijon, 1977)
   h) AN + ACCELERATING + INFERENTIAL + ENGINEERING + TALE + ELITE + GRANT + FEE + ET + CETERA = ARTIFICIAL + INTELLIGENCE.
   i) HARDY + NESTS = NASTY + HERDS.

▶ **25.** [*M21*] Devise a fast way to compute $\min(a \cdot s)$ and $\max(a \cdot s)$ over all valid permutations $a_1 \ldots a_{10}$ of $\{0, \ldots, 9\}$, given the signature vector $s = (s_1, \ldots, s_{10})$ and the first-letter set F of an alphametic problem. (Such a procedure makes it possible to rule out many cases quickly when a large family of alphametics is being considered, as in several of the exercises that follow, because a solution can exist only when $\min(a \cdot s) \leq 0 \leq \max(a \cdot s)$.)

26. [*25*] What is the unique alphametic solution to

$$\text{NIIHAU} \pm \text{KAUAI} \pm \text{OAHU} \pm \text{MOLOKAI} \pm \text{LANAI} \pm \text{MAUI} \pm \text{HAWAII} = 0?$$

27. [*30*] Construct pure additive alphametics in which all words have five letters.

28. [*M25*] A *partition* of the integer n is an expression of the form $n = n_1 + \cdots + n_t$ with $n_1 \geq \cdots \geq n_t > 0$. Such a partition is called *doubly true* if $\alpha(n) = \alpha(n_1) + \cdots + \alpha(n_t)$ is also a pure alphametic, where $\alpha(n)$ is the "name" of n in some language. Doubly true partitions were introduced by Alan Wayne in *AMM* **54** (1947), 38, 412–414, where he suggested solving TWENTY = SEVEN + SEVEN + SIX and a few others.

   a) Find all partitions that are doubly true in English when $1 \leq n \leq 20$.

   b) Wayne also gave the example EIGHTY = FIFTY + TWENTY + NINE + ONE. Find all doubly true partitions for $1 \leq n \leq 100$ in which the parts are *distinct*, using the names ONE, TWO, ..., NINETYNINE, ONEHUNDRED.

▸ **29.** [*M25*] Continuing the previous exercise, find all equations of the form $n_1 + \cdots + n_t = n'_1 + \cdots + n'_{t'}$ that are both mathematically and alphametically true in English, when $\{n_1, \ldots, n_t, n'_1, \ldots, n'_{t'}\}$ are distinct positive integers less than 20. For example,

$$\text{TWELVE} + \text{NINE} + \text{TWO} = \text{ELEVEN} + \text{SEVEN} + \text{FIVE};$$

the alphametics should all be pure.

30. [*25*] Solve these multiplicative alphametics by hand or by computer:

   a) TWO × TWO = SQUARE.   (H. E. Dudeney, 1929)

   b) HIP × HIP = HURRAY.   (Willy Enggren, 1970)

   c) PI × R × R = AREA.   (Brian Barwell, 1981)

   d) NORTH/SOUTH = EAST/WEST.   (Nob Yoshigahara, 1995)

   e) NAUGHT × NAUGHT = ZERO × ZERO × ZERO.   (Alan Wayne, 2003)

31. [*M22*] (Nob Yoshigahara.) (a) What is the unique solution to A/BC+D/EF+G/HI = 1, when $\{A, \ldots, I\} = \{1, \ldots, 9\}$? (b) Similarly, make AB mod 2 = 0, ABC mod 3 = 0, etc.

32. [*M25*] (H. E. Dudeney, 1901.) Find all ways to represent 100 by inserting a plus sign and a slash into a permutation of the digits $\{1, \ldots, 9\}$. For example, $100 = 91 + 5742/638$. The plus sign should precede the slash.

33. [*25*] Continuing the previous exercise, find all positive integers less than 150 that (a) cannot be represented in such a fashion; (b) have a unique representation.

34. [*M26*] Make the equation EVEN + ODD + PRIME = x doubly true when (a) x is a perfect 5th power; (b) x is a perfect 7th power.

▸ **35.** [*M20*] The automorphisms of a 4-cube have many different Sims tables, only one of which is shown in (14). How many different Sims tables are possible for that group, when the vertices are numbered as in (12)?

36. [*M23*] Find a Sims table for the group of all automorphisms of the 4×4 tic-tac-toe board

$$\begin{array}{|cccc|}
\hline
0 & 1 & 2 & 3 \\
4 & 5 & 6 & 7 \\
8 & 9 & a & b \\
c & d & e & f \\
\hline
\end{array},$$

namely the permutations that take lines into lines, where a "line" is a set of four elements that belong to a row, column, or diagonal.

▸ **37.** [*HM22*] How many Sims tables can be used with Algorithms G or H? Estimate the logarithm of this number as $n \to \infty$.

38. [*HM21*] Prove that the average number of transpositions per permutation when using Ord-Smith's algorithm (26) is approximately $\sinh 1 \approx 1.175$.

39. [*16*] Write down the 24 permutations generated for $n = 4$ by (a) Ord-Smith's method (26); (b) Heap's method (27).

40. [*M23*] Show that Heap's method (27) corresponds to a valid Sims table.

▶ **41.** [*M33*] Design an algorithm that generates all r-variations of $\{0, 1, \ldots, n-1\}$ by interchanging just two elements when going from one variation to the next. (See exercise 9.) *Hint:* Generalize Heap's method (27), obtaining the results in positions $a_{n-r} \ldots a_{n-1}$ of an array $a_0 \ldots a_{n-1}$. For example, one solution when $n = 5$ and $r = 2$ uses the final two elements of the respective permutations 01234, 31204, 30214, 30124, 40123, 20143, 24103, 24013, 34012, 14032, 13042, 13402, 23401, 03421, 02431, 02341, 12340, 42310, 41320, 41230.

42. [*M20*] Construct a Sims table for all permutations in which every $\sigma(k, j)$ and every $\tau(k, j)$ for $1 \leq j \leq k$ is a cycle of length ≤ 3.

43. [*M24*] Construct a Sims table for all permutations in which every $\sigma(k, k)$, $\omega(k)$, and $\tau(k, j)\omega(k-1)^-$ for $1 \leq j \leq k$ is a cycle of length ≤ 3.

44. [*20*] When blocks of unwanted permutations are being skipped by the extended Algorithm G, is the Sims table of Ord-Smith's method (23) superior to the Sims table of the reverse colex method (18)?

45. [*20*] (a) What are the indices $u_1 \ldots u_9$ when Algorithm X visits the permutation 314592687? (b) What permutation is visited when $u_1 \ldots u_9 = 161800000$?

46. [*20*] True or false: When Algorithm X visits $a_1 \ldots a_n$, we have $u_k > u_{k+1}$ if and only if $a_k > a_{k+1}$, for $1 \leq k < n$.

▶ **47.** [*M21*] Express the number of times that each step of Algorithm X is performed in terms of the numbers N_0, N_1, ..., N_n, where N_k is the number of prefixes $a_1 \ldots a_k$ that satisfy $t_j(a_1, \ldots, a_j)$ for $1 \leq j \leq k$.

▶ **48.** [*M25*] Compare the running times of Algorithm X and Algorithm L, in the case when the tests $t_1(a_1)$, $t_2(a_1, a_2)$, ..., $t_n(a_1, a_2, \ldots, a_n)$ always are true.

▶ **49.** [*28*] The text's suggested method for solving additive alphametics with Algorithm X essentially chooses digits from right to left; in other words, it assigns tentative values to the least significant digits before considering digits that correspond to higher powers of 10.

Explore an alternative approach that chooses digits from left to right. For example, such a method will deduce immediately that M = 1 when SEND + MORE = MONEY. *Hint:* See exercise 25.

50. [*M15*] Explain why the dual formula (32) follows from (13).

51. [*M16*] True or false: If the sets $S_k = \{\sigma(k, 0), \ldots, \sigma(k, k)\}$ form a Sims table for the group of all permutations, so also do the sets $S_k^- = \{\sigma(k, 0)^-, \ldots, \sigma(k, k)^-\}$.

▶ **52.** [*M22*] What permutations $\tau(k, j)$ and $\omega(k)$ arise when Algorithm H is used with the Sims table (36)? Compare the resulting generator with Algorithm P.

▶ **53.** [*M26*] (F. M. Ives.) Construct a Sims table for which Algorithm H will generate all permutations by making only $n! + O((n-2)!)$ transpositions.

54. [*20*] Would Algorithm C work properly if step C3 did a right-cyclic shift, setting $a_1 \ldots a_{k-1}a_k \leftarrow a_k a_1 \ldots a_{k-1}$, instead of a left-cyclic shift?

55. [*M27*] Consider the *factorial ruler function*

$$\rho_!(m) = \max\{k \mid m \bmod k! = 0\}.$$

Let σ_k and τ_k be permutations of the nonnegative integers such that $\sigma_j \tau_k = \tau_k \sigma_j$ whenever $j \le k$. Let α_0 and β_0 be the identity permutation, and for $m > 0$ define

$$\alpha_m = \beta_{m-1}^- \tau_{\rho!(m)} \beta_{m-1} \alpha_{m-1}, \qquad \beta_m = \sigma_{\rho!(m)} \beta_{m-1}.$$

For example, if σ_k is the flip operation $(1\ k-1)(2\ k-2)\ldots = (0\ k)\phi(k)$ and if $\tau_k = (0\ k)$, and if Algorithm E is started with $a_j = j$ for $0 \le j < n$, then α_m and β_m are the contents of $a_0 \ldots a_{n-1}$ and $b_0 \ldots b_{n-1}$ after step E5 has been performed m times.

a) Prove that $\beta_{(n+1)!} \alpha_{(n+1)!} = \sigma_{n+1} \sigma_n^- \tau_{n+1} \tau_n^- (\beta_{n!} \alpha_{n!})^{n+1}$.

b) Use the result of (a) to establish the validity of Algorithm E.

56. [*M22*] Prove that Algorithm E remains valid if step E5 is replaced by

E5′. [Transpose pairs.] If $k > 2$, interchange $b_{j+1} \leftrightarrow b_j$ for $j = k-2,\ k-4,\ \ldots,$ (2 or 1). Return to E2. ∎

57. [*HM22*] What is the average number of interchanges made in step E5?

58. [*M21*] True or false: If Algorithm E begins with $a_0 \ldots a_{n-1} = x_1 \ldots x_n$ then the final permutation visited begins with $a_0 = x_n$.

59. [*M20*] Some authors define the arcs of a Cayley graph as running from π to $\pi \alpha_j$ instead of from π to $\alpha_j \pi$. Are the two definitions essentially different?

▶ **60.** [*21*] A *Gray cycle for permutations* is a cycle $(\pi_0, \pi_1, \ldots, \pi_{n!-1})$ that includes every permutation of $\{1, 2, \ldots, n\}$ and has the property that π_k differs from $\pi_{(k+1) \bmod n!}$ by an adjacent transposition. It can also be described as a Hamiltonian cycle on the Cayley graph for the group of all permutations on $\{1, 2, \ldots, n\}$, with the $n-1$ generators $((1\ 2), (2\ 3), \ldots, (n-1\ n))$. The *delta sequence* of such a Gray cycle is the sequence of integers $\delta_0 \delta_1 \ldots \delta_{n!-1}$ such that

$$\pi_{(k+1) \bmod n!} = (\delta_k\ \delta_k+1)\, \pi_k.$$

(See 7.2.1.1–(24), which describes the analogous situation for binary n-tuples.) For example, Fig. 43 illustrates the Gray cycle defined by plain changes when $n = 4$; its delta sequence is $(32131231)^3$.

a) Find all Gray cycles for permutations of $\{1, 2, 3, 4\}$.

b) Two Gray cycles are considered to be equivalent if their delta sequences can be obtained from each other by cyclic shifting $(\delta_k \ldots \delta_{n!-1} \delta_0 \ldots \delta_{k-1})$ and/or reversal $(\delta_{n!-1} \ldots \delta_1 \delta_0)$ and/or complementation $((n-\delta_0)(n-\delta_1) \ldots (n-\delta_{n!-1}))$. Which of the Gray cycles in (a) are equivalent?

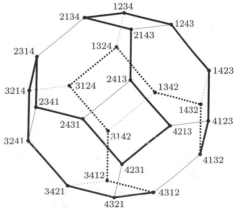

Fig. 43. Algorithm P traces out this Hamiltonian cycle on the truncated octahedron of Fig. 5–1 in Section 5.1.1.

61. [*21*] Continuing the previous exercise, a *Gray code for permutations* is like a Gray cycle except that the final permutation $\pi_{n!-1}$ is not required to be adjacent to the initial permutation π_0. Study the set of all Gray codes for $n = 4$ that start with 1234.

▸ **62.** [*M23*] What permutations can be reached as the final element of a Gray code that starts at $12\ldots n$?

63. [*M25*] Estimate the total number of Gray cycles for permutations of $\{1, 2, 3, 4, 5\}$.

64. [*23*] A "doubly Gray" code for permutations is a Gray cycle with the additional property that $\delta_{k+1} = \delta_k \pm 1$ for all k. Compton and Williamson have proved that such codes exist for all $n \geq 3$. How many doubly Gray codes exist for $n = 5$?

65. [*M25*] For which integers N is there a Gray path through the N lexicographically smallest permutations of $\{1, \ldots, n\}$? (Exercise 7.2.1.1–26 solves the analogous problem for binary n-tuples.)

66. [*22*] Ehrlich's swap method suggests another type of Gray cycle for permutations, in which the $n - 1$ generators are the star transpositions $(1\ 2)$, $(1\ 3)$, $\ldots$, $(1\ n)$. For example, Fig. 44 shows the relevant graph when $n = 4$. Analyze the Hamiltonian cycles of this graph.

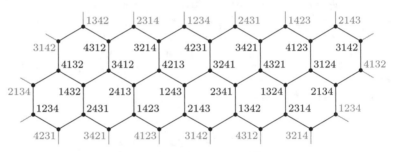

Fig. 44. The Cayley graph for permutations of $\{1, 2, 3, 4\}$, generated by the star transpositions $(1\,2)$, $(1\,3)$, and $(1\,4)$, drawn as a twisted torus.

67. [*26*] Continuing the previous exercise, find a first-element-swap Gray cycle for $n = 5$ in which each star transposition $(1\ j)$ occurs 30 times, for $2 \leq j \leq 5$.

68. [*M30*] (V. L. Kompel'makher and V. A. Liskovets, 1975.) Let G be the Cayley graph for all permutations of $\{1, \ldots, n\}$, with generators $(\alpha_1, \ldots, \alpha_k)$ where each α_j is a transposition $(u_j\ v_j)$; also let A be the graph with vertices $\{1, \ldots, n\}$ and edges $u_j \relbar v_j$ for $1 \leq j \leq k$. Prove that G has a Hamiltonian cycle if and only if A is connected. (Figure 43 is the special case when A is a path; Figure 44 is the special case when A is a "star.")

▸ **69.** [*28*] If $n \geq 4$, the following algorithm generates all permutations $A_1 A_2 A_3 \ldots A_n$ of $\{1, 2, 3, \ldots, n\}$ using only three transformations,

$$\rho = (1\,2)(3\,4)(5\,6)\ldots, \qquad \sigma = (2\,3)(4\,5)(6\,7)\ldots, \qquad \tau = (3\,4)(5\,6)(7\,8)\ldots,$$

never applying ρ and τ next to each other. Explain why it works.

Z1. [Initialize.] Set $A_j \leftarrow j$ for $1 \leq j \leq n$. Also set $a_j \leftarrow 2j$ for $1 \leq j \leq n/2$ and $a_{n-j} \leftarrow 2j+1$ for $1 \leq j < n/2$. Then invoke Algorithm P, but with parameter $n - 1$ instead of n. We will treat that algorithm as a coroutine, which should return control to us whenever it "visits" $a_1 \ldots a_{n-1}$ in step P2. We will also share its variables (except n).

Z2. [Set x and y.]   Invoke Algorithm P again, obtaining a new permutation $a_1 \ldots a_{n-1}$ and a new value of j. If $j = 2$, interchange $a_{1+s} \leftrightarrow a_{2+s}$ (thereby undoing the effect of step P5) and repeat this step; in such a case we are at the halfway point of Algorithm P. If $j = 1$ (so that Algorithm P has terminated), set $x \leftarrow y \leftarrow 0$ and go to Z3. Otherwise set

$$x \leftarrow a_{j-c_j+s+[o_j=+1]}, \qquad y \leftarrow a_{j-c_j+s-[o_j=-1]};$$

these are the two elements most recently interchanged in step P5.

Z3. [Visit.] Visit the permutation $A_1 \ldots A_n$. Then go to Z5 if $A_1 = x$ and $A_2 = y$.

Z4. [Apply ρ, then σ.] Interchange $A_1 \leftrightarrow A_2$, $A_3 \leftrightarrow A_4$, $A_5 \leftrightarrow A_6$, …. Visit $A_1 \ldots A_n$. Then interchange $A_2 \leftrightarrow A_3$, $A_4 \leftrightarrow A_5$, $A_6 \leftrightarrow A_7$, …. Terminate if $A_1 \ldots A_n = 1 \ldots n$, otherwise return to Z3.

Z5. [Apply τ, then σ.] Interchange $A_3 \leftrightarrow A_4$, $A_5 \leftrightarrow A_6$, $A_7 \leftrightarrow A_8$, …. Visit $A_1 \ldots A_n$. Then interchange $A_2 \leftrightarrow A_3$, $A_4 \leftrightarrow A_5$, $A_6 \leftrightarrow A_7$, …, and return to Z2. ∎

Hint: Show first that the algorithm works if modified so that $A_j \leftarrow n + 1 - j$ and $a_j \leftarrow j$ in step Z1, and if the "flip" permutations

$$\rho' = (1 \ n)(2 \ n{-}1)\ldots, \qquad \sigma' = (2 \ n)(3 \ n{-}1)\ldots, \qquad \tau' = (2 \ n{-}1)(3 \ n{-}2)\ldots$$

are used instead of ρ, σ, τ in steps Z4 and Z5. In this modification, step Z3 should go to Z5 if $A_1 = x$ and $A_n = y$; step Z4 should terminate when $A_1 \ldots A_n = n \ldots 1$.

▶ **70.** [*M33*] The two 12-cycles ($_4^1$) can be regarded as σ–τ cycles for the twelve permutations of $\{1, 1, 3, 4\}$:

$$1134 \to 1341 \to 3411 \to 4311 \to 3114 \to 1143 \to 1431$$
$$\to 4131 \to 1314 \to 3141 \to 1413 \to 4113 \to 1134.$$

Replacing $\{1, 1\}$ by $\{1, 2\}$ yields disjoint cycles, and we obtained a Hamiltonian path by jumping from one to the other. Can a σ–τ path for all permutations of 6 elements be formed in a similar way, based on a 360-cycle for the permutations of $\{1, 1, 3, 4, 5, 6\}$?

71. [*41*] Does the Cayley graph with generators $\sigma = (1\,2\,\ldots\,n)$ and $\tau = (1\,2)$ have a Hamiltonian cycle whenever $n \geq 3$ is odd?

72. [*M21*] Given a Cayley graph with generators $(\alpha_1, \ldots, \alpha_k)$, assume that each α_j takes $x \mapsto y$. (For example, both σ and τ in exercise 71 take $1 \mapsto 2$.) Prove that any Hamiltonian path starting at $12\ldots n$ in G must end at a permutation that takes $y \mapsto x$.

▶ **73.** [*M30*] Let α, β, and σ be permutations of a set X, where $X = A \cup B$. Assume that $x\sigma = x\alpha$ when $x \in A$ and $x\sigma = x\beta$ when $x \in B$, and that the order of $\alpha\beta^-$ is odd.

a) Prove that all three permutations α, β, σ have the same sign; that is, they are all even or all odd. *Hint:* A permutation has odd order if and only if its cycles all have odd length.

b) Derive Theorem R from part (a).

74. [*M30*] (R. A. Rankin.) Assuming that $\alpha\beta = \beta\alpha$ in Theorem R, prove that a Hamiltonian cycle exists in the Cayley graph for G if and only if there is a number k such that $0 \leq k \leq g/c$ and $t + k \perp c$, where $\beta^{g/c} = \gamma^t$, $\gamma = \alpha\beta^-$. *Hint:* Represent elements of the group in the form $\beta^j \gamma^k$.

75. [*M26*] The directed torus $C_m^{\rightarrow} \times C_n^{\rightarrow}$ has mn vertices (x, y) for $0 \le x < m$, $0 \le y < n$, and arcs $(x, y) \longrightarrow (x, y)\alpha = ((x + 1) \bmod m, y)$, $(x, y) \longrightarrow (x, y)\beta = (x, (y + 1) \bmod n)$. Prove that, if $m > 1$ and $n > 1$, the number of Hamiltonian cycles of this digraph is

$$\sum_{k=1}^{d-1} \binom{d}{k} [\gcd((d - k)m, kn) = d], \qquad d = \gcd(m, n).$$

76. [*M31*] The cells numbered 0, 1, ..., 63 in Fig. 45 illustrate a *northeasterly knight's tour* on an 8×8 torus: If k appears in cell (x_k, y_k), then $(x_{k+1}, y_{k+1}) \equiv (x_k + 2, y_k + 1)$ or $(x_k + 1, y_k + 2)$, modulo 8, and $(x_{64}, y_{64}) = (x_0, y_0)$. How many such tours are possible on an $m \times n$ torus, when $m, n \ge 3$?

29	24	19	14	49	44	39	34
58	53	48	43	38	9	4	63
23	18	13	8	3	62	33	28
52	47	42	37	32	27	22	57
17	12	7	2	61	56	51	46
6	41	36	31	26	21	16	11
35	30	1	60	55	50	45	40
0	59	54	25	20	15	10	5

Fig. 45. A northeasterly knight's tour.

▶ **77.** [*22*] Complete the MMIX program whose inner loop appears in (42), using Heap's method (27).

78. [*M23*] Analyze the running time of the program in exercise 77, generalizing it so that the inner loop does $r!$ visits (with $a_0 \ldots a_{r-1}$ in global registers).

79. [*20*] What seven MMIX instructions will ⟨Swap the nybbles ...⟩ as (45) requires? For example, if register t contains the value 4 and register a contains the nybbles #12345678, register a should change to #12345687.

80. [*21*] Solve the previous exercise with only five MMIX instructions. *Hint:* Use MXOR.

▶ **81.** [*22*] Complete the MMIX program (46) by specifying how to ⟨Continue with Langdon's method⟩.

82. [*M21*] Analyze the running time of the program in exercise 81.

83. [*22*] Use the σ–τ path of exercise 70 to design an MMIX routine analogous to (42) that generates all permutations of #123456 in register a.

84. [*20*] Suggest a good way to generate all $n!$ permutations of $\{1, \ldots, n\}$ on p processors that are running in parallel.

▶ **85.** [*25*] Assume that n is small enough that $n!$ fits in a computer word. What's a good way to convert a given permutation $\alpha = a_1 \ldots a_n$ of $\{1, \ldots, n\}$ into an integer $k = r(\alpha)$ in the range $0 \le k < n!$? Both functions $k = r(\alpha)$ and $\alpha = r^{[-1]}(k)$ should be computable in only $O(n)$ steps.

86. [*20*] A partial order relation is supposed to be transitive; that is, $x \prec y$ and $y \prec z$ should imply $x \prec z$. But Algorithm V does not require its input relation to satisfy this condition.

Show that if $x \prec y$ and $y \prec z$, Algorithm V will produce identical results whether or not $x \prec z$.

87. [*20*] (F. Ruskey.) Consider the inversion tables $c_1 \ldots c_n$ of the permutations visited by Algorithm V. What noteworthy property do they have? (Compare with the inversion tables (4) in Algorithm P.)

88. [*21*] Show that Algorithm V can be used to generate all ways to partition the digits $\{0, 1, \ldots, 9\}$ into two 3-element sets and two 2-element sets.

▶ **89.** [*M30*] Consider the numbers $t_0, t_1, \ldots, t_n$ defined before (51). Clearly $t_0 = t_1 = 1$.
  a) Say that index j is "trivial" if $t_j = t_{j-1}$. For example, 9 is trivial with respect to the Young tableau relations (48). Explain how to modify Algorithm V so that the variable k takes on only nontrivial values.
  b) Analyze the running time of the modified algorithm. What formulas replace (51)?
  c) Say that the interval $[j \mathbin{.\,.} k]$ is not a chain if there is an index l such that $j \le l < k$ and we do not have $l \prec l + 1$. Prove that in such a case $t_k \ge 2t_{j-1}$.
  d) Every inverse topological sort $a'_1 \ldots a'_n$ defines a labeling that corresponds to relations $a'_{j_1} \prec a'_{k_1}, \ldots, a'_{j_m} \prec a'_{k_m}$, which are equivalent to the original relations $j_1 \prec k_1, \ldots, j_m \prec k_m$. Explain how to find a labeling such that $[j \mathbin{.\,.} k]$ is not a chain when j and k are consecutive nontrivial indices.
  e) Prove that with such a labeling, $M < 4N$ in the formulas of part (b).

90. [*M21*] Algorithm V can be used to produce all permutations that are h-*ordered* for all h in a given set, namely all $a'_1 \ldots a'_n$ such that $a'_j < a'_{j+h}$ for $1 \le j \le n - h$ (see Section 5.2.1). Analyze the running time of Algorithm V when it generates all permutations that are both 2-ordered and 3-ordered.

91. [*HM21*] Analyze the running time of Algorithm V when it is used with the relations (49) to find perfect matchings.

92. [*M18*] How many permutations is Algorithm V likely to visit, in a "random" case? Let P_n be the number of partial orderings on $\{1, \ldots, n\}$, namely the number of relations that are reflexive, antisymmetric, and transitive. Let Q_n be the number of such relations with the additional property that $j < k$ whenever $j \prec k$. Express the expected number of ways to sort n elements topologically, averaged over all partial orderings, in terms of P_n and Q_n.

93. [*35*] Prove that all topological sorts can be generated in such a way that only one or two adjacent transpositions are made at each step. (The example $1 \prec 2$, $3 \prec 4$ shows that a single transposition per step cannot always be achieved, even if we allow nonadjacent swaps, because only two of the six relevant permutations are odd.)

▶ **94.** [*25*] Show that in the case of perfect matchings, using the relations in (49), all topological sorts can be generated with just one transposition per step.

95. [*21*] Discuss how to generate all *up-down permutations* of $\{1, \ldots, n\}$, namely those $a_1 \ldots a_n$ such that $a_1 < a_2 > a_3 < a_4 > \cdots$.

96. [*21*] Discuss how to generate all *cyclic permutations* of $\{1, \ldots, n\}$, namely those $a_1 \ldots a_n$ whose cycle representation consists of a single n-cycle.

97. [*21*] Discuss how to generate all *derangements* of $\{1, \ldots, n\}$, namely those $a_1 \ldots a_n$ such that $a_1 \ne 1$, $a_2 \ne 2$, $a_3 \ne 3$, $\ldots$.

98. [*HM23*] Analyze the asymptotic running time of the method in the previous exercise.

99. [*M30*] Given $n \ge 3$, show that all derangements of $\{1, \ldots, n\}$ can be generated by making at most two transpositions between visits.

100. [*21*] Discuss how to generate all of the *indecomposable* permutations of $\{1, \ldots, n\}$, namely those $a_1 \ldots a_n$ such that $\{a_1, \ldots, a_j\} \ne \{1, \ldots, j\}$ for $1 \le j < n$.

101. [*28*] Discuss how to generate all *involutions* of $\{1, \ldots, n\}$, namely those permutations $a_1 \ldots a_n$ with $a_{a_1} \ldots a_{a_n} = 1 \ldots n$.

102. [*M30*] Show that all involutions of $\{1,\ldots,n\}$ can be generated by making at most two transpositions between visits.

103. [*M32*] Show that all even permutations of $\{1,\ldots,n\}$ can be generated by successive *rotations of three consecutive elements*.

▶ **104.** [*M22*] A permutation $a_1 \ldots a_n$ of $\{1,\ldots,n\}$ is *well-balanced* if

$$\sum_{k=1}^{n} k a_k = \sum_{k=1}^{n} (n+1-k)a_k.$$

For example, 3142 is well-balanced when $n = 4$.
  a) Prove that no permutation is well-balanced when $n \bmod 4 = 2$.
  b) Prove that if $a_1 \ldots a_n$ is well-balanced, so are its reversal $a_n \ldots a_1$, its complement $(n{+}1{-}a_1)\ldots(n{+}1{-}a_n)$, and its inverse $a_1' \ldots a_n'$.
  c) Determine the number of well-balanced permutations for small values of n.

▶ **105.** [*26*] A *weak order* is a relation $\preceq$ that is transitive ($x \preceq y$ and $y \preceq z$ implies $x \preceq z$) and complete ($x \preceq y$ or $y \preceq x$ always holds). We can write $x \equiv y$ if $x \preceq y$ and $y \preceq x$; $x \prec y$ if $x \preceq y$ and $y \npreceq x$. There are thirteen weak orders on three elements $\{1,2,3\}$, namely

$$1 \equiv 2 \equiv 3, \quad 1 \equiv 2 \prec 3, \quad 1 \prec 2 \equiv 3, \quad 1 \prec 2 \prec 3, \quad 1 \equiv 3 \prec 2, \quad 1 \prec 3 \prec 2,$$
$$2 \prec 1 \equiv 3, \quad 2 \prec 1 \prec 3, \quad 2 \equiv 3 \prec 1, \quad 2 \prec 3 \prec 1, \quad 3 \prec 1 \equiv 2, \quad 3 \prec 1 \prec 2, \quad 3 \prec 2 \prec 1.$$

  a) Explain how to generate all weak orders of $\{1,\ldots,n\}$ systematically, as sequences of digits separated by the symbols $\equiv$ or $\prec$.
  b) A weak order can also be represented as a sequence $a_1 \ldots a_n$ where $a_j = k$ if j is preceded by $k \prec$ signs. For example, the thirteen weak orders on $\{1,2,3\}$ are respectively 000, 001, 011, 012, 010, 021, 101, 102, 100, 201, 110, 120, 210 in this form. Find a simple way to generate all such sequences of length n.

106. [*M40*] Can exercise 105(b) be solved with a Gray-like code?

▶ **107.** [*30*] (John H. Conway, 1973.) To play the solitaire game of "topswops," start by shuffling a pack of n cards labeled $\{1,\ldots,n\}$ and place them face up in a pile. Then if the top card is $k > 1$, deal out the top k cards and put them back on top of the pile, thereby changing the permutation from $a_1 \ldots a_n$ to $a_k \ldots a_1 a_{k+1} \ldots a_n$. Continue until the top card is 1. For example, the 7-step sequence

$$31452 \to 41352 \to 53142 \to 24135 \to 42135 \to 31245 \to 21345 \to 12345$$

might occur when $n = 5$. What is the longest sequence possible when $n = 13$?

108. [*M27*] If the longest n-card game of topswops has length $f(n)$, prove that $f(n) \le F_{n+1} - 1$.

109. [*M47*] Find good upper and lower bounds on the topswops function $f(n)$.

▶ **110.** [*25*] Find all permutations $a_0 \ldots a_9$ of $\{0,\ldots,9\}$ such that

$$\{a_0, a_2, a_3, a_7\} = \{2,5,7,8\}, \qquad \{a_1, a_4, a_5\} = \{0,3,6\},$$
$$\{a_1, a_3, a_7, a_8\} = \{3,4,5,7\}, \qquad \{a_0, a_3, a_4\} = \{0,7,8\}.$$

Also suggest an algorithm for solving large problems of this type.

▶ **111.** [*M25*] Several permutation-oriented analogs of de Bruijn cycles have been proposed. The simplest and nicest of these is the notion of a *universal cycle of permutations*, introduced by B. W. Jackson in *Discrete Math.* **117** (1993), 141–150, namely a cycle of $n!$ digits such that each permutation of $\{1,\ldots,n\}$ occurs exactly once as a block of $n-1$ consecutive digits (with its redundant final element suppressed). For example, (121323) is a universal cycle of permutations for $n = 3$, and it is essentially unique.

Prove that universal cycles of permutations exist for all $n \geq 2$. What is the lexicographically smallest one when $n = 4$?

▶ **112.** [*M30*] (A. Williams, 2007.) Continuing exercise 111, construct *explicit* cycles:
　　a) Show that a universal cycle of permutations is equivalent to a Hamiltonian cycle on the Cayley graph with two generators $\rho = (1\ 2\ \ldots\ n{-}1)$ and $\sigma = (1\ 2\ \ldots\ n)$.
　　b) Prove that any Hamiltonian path in that graph is actually a Hamiltonian cycle.
　　c) Find such a path of the form $\sigma^2 \rho^{n-3}\alpha_1 \ldots \sigma^2 \rho^{n-3}\alpha_{(n-1)!}$, $\alpha_j \in \{\rho, \sigma\}$, for $n \geq 3$.

113. [*HM43*] Exactly how many universal cycles exist, for permutations of ≤ 9 objects?

7.2.1.3. Generating all combinations. Combinatorial mathematics is often described as "the study of permutations, combinations, etc.," so we turn our attention now to combinations. A *combination of n things, taken t at a time*, often called simply a *t-combination of n things*, is a way to select a subset of size t from a given set of size n. We know from Eq. 1.2.6–(2) that there are exactly $\binom{n}{t}$ ways to do this; and we learned in Section 3.4.2 how to choose t-combinations at random.

Selecting t of n objects is equivalent to choosing the $n - t$ elements not selected. We will emphasize this symmetry by letting

$$n = s + t \tag{1}$$

throughout our discussion, and we will often refer to a t-combination of n things as an "(s, t)-combination." Thus, an (s, t)-combination is a way to subdivide $s + t$ objects into two collections of sizes s and t.

> *If I ask how many combinations of 21 can be taken out of 25,*
> *I do in effect ask how many combinations of 4 may be taken.*
> *For there are just as many ways of taking 21 as there are of leaving 4.*
> — AUGUSTUS DE MORGAN, *An Essay on Probabilities* (1838)

There are two main ways to represent (s, t)-combinations: We can list the elements $c_t \ldots c_2 c_1$ that have been selected, or we can work with binary strings $a_{n-1} \ldots a_1 a_0$ for which

$$a_{n-1} + \cdots + a_1 + a_0 = t. \tag{2}$$

The string representation has s 0s and t 1s, corresponding to elements that are unselected or selected. The list representation $c_t \ldots c_2 c_1$ tends to work out best if we let the elements be members of the set $\{0, 1, \ldots, n - 1\}$ and if we list them in *decreasing* order:

$$n > c_t > \cdots > c_2 > c_1 \geq 0. \tag{3}$$

Binary notation connects these two representations nicely, because the item list $c_t \ldots c_2 c_1$ corresponds to the sum

$$2^{c_t} + \cdots + 2^{c_2} + 2^{c_1} = \sum_{k=0}^{n-1} a_k 2^k = (a_{n-1} \ldots a_1 a_0)_2. \tag{4}$$

Of course we could also list the positions $b_s \ldots b_2 b_1$ of the 0s in $a_{n-1} \ldots a_1 a_0$, where

$$n > b_s > \cdots > b_2 > b_1 \geq 0. \tag{5}$$

Combinations are important not only because subsets are omnipresent in mathematics but also because they are equivalent to many other configurations. For example, every (s,t)-combination corresponds to a combination of $s+1$ things taken t at a time *with repetitions permitted*, also called a *multicombination* of $s+1$ things, namely a sequence of integers $d_t \ldots d_2 d_1$ with

$$s \geq d_t \geq \cdots \geq d_2 \geq d_1 \geq 0. \tag{6}$$

One reason is that $d_t \ldots d_2 d_1$ solves (6) if and only if $c_t \ldots c_2 c_1$ solves (3), where

$$c_t = d_t + t - 1, \quad \ldots, \quad c_2 = d_2 + 1, \quad c_1 = d_1 \tag{7}$$

(see exercise 1.2.6–60). And there is another useful way to relate combinations with repetition to ordinary combinations, suggested by Solomon Golomb [*AMM* **75** (1968), 530–531], namely to define

$$e_j = \begin{cases} c_j, & \text{if } c_j \leq s; \\ e_{c_j - s}, & \text{if } c_j > s. \end{cases} \tag{8}$$

In this form the numbers $e_t \ldots e_1$ don't necessarily appear in descending order, but the multiset $\{e_1, e_2, \ldots, e_t\}$ is equal to $\{c_1, c_2, \ldots, c_t\}$ if and only if $\{e_1, e_2, \ldots, e_t\}$ is a set. (See Table 1 and exercise 1.)

An (s,t)-combination is also equivalent to a *composition* of $n+1$ into $t+1$ parts, namely an ordered sum

$$n + 1 = p_t + \cdots + p_1 + p_0, \quad \text{where } p_t, \ldots, p_1, p_0 \geq 1. \tag{9}$$

The connection with (3) is now

$$p_t = n - c_t, \quad p_{t-1} = c_t - c_{t-1}, \quad \ldots, \quad p_1 = c_2 - c_1, \quad p_0 = c_1 + 1. \tag{10}$$

Equivalently, if $q_j = p_j - 1$, we have

$$s = q_t + \cdots + q_1 + q_0, \quad \text{where } q_t, \ldots, q_1, q_0 \geq 0, \tag{11}$$

a composition of s into $t+1$ *nonnegative* parts, related to (6) by setting

$$q_t = s - d_t, \quad q_{t-1} = d_t - d_{t-1}, \quad \ldots, \quad q_1 = d_2 - d_1, \quad q_0 = d_1. \tag{12}$$

Furthermore it is easy to see that an (s,t)-combination is equivalent to a path of length $s+t$ from corner to corner of an $s \times t$ grid, because such a path contains s vertical steps and t horizontal steps.

Thus, combinations can be studied in at least eight different guises. Table 1 illustrates all $\binom{6}{3} = 20$ possibilities in the case $s = t = 3$.

These cousins of combinations might seem rather bewildering at first glance, but most of them can be understood directly from the binary representation $a_{n-1} \ldots a_1 a_0$. Consider, for example, the "random" bit string

$$a_{23} \ldots a_1 a_0 = 011001001000011111101101, \tag{13}$$

Table 1

THE $(3,3)$-COMBINATIONS AND THEIR EQUIVALENTS

$a_5a_4a_3a_2a_1a_0$	$b_3b_2b_1$	$c_3c_2c_1$	$d_3d_2d_1$	$e_3e_2e_1$	$p_3p_2p_1p_0$	$q_3q_2q_1q_0$	path
000111	543	210	000	210	4111	3000	
001011	542	310	100	310	3211	2100	
001101	541	320	110	320	3121	2010	
001110	540	321	111	321	3112	2001	
010011	532	410	200	010	2311	1200	
010101	531	420	210	020	2221	1110	
010110	530	421	211	121	2212	1101	
011001	521	430	220	030	2131	1020	
011010	520	431	221	131	2122	1011	
011100	510	432	222	232	2113	1002	
100011	432	510	300	110	1411	0300	
100101	431	520	310	220	1321	0210	
100110	430	521	311	221	1312	0201	
101001	421	530	320	330	1231	0120	
101010	420	531	321	331	1222	0111	
101100	410	532	322	332	1213	0102	
110001	321	540	330	000	1141	0030	
110010	320	541	331	111	1132	0021	
110100	310	542	332	222	1123	0012	
111000	210	543	333	333	1114	0003	

which has $s = 11$ zeros and $t = 13$ ones, hence $n = 24$. The dual combination $b_s \ldots b_1$ lists the positions (subscripts) of the zeros, namely

$$23\ 20\ 19\ 17\ 16\ 14\ 13\ 12\ 11\ 4\ 1,$$

because the leftmost position in (13) is $n - 1$ and the rightmost is 0. The primal combination $c_t \ldots c_1$ lists the positions of the ones, namely

$$22\ 21\ 18\ 15\ 10\ 9\ 8\ 7\ 6\ 5\ 3\ 2\ 0.$$

The corresponding multicombination $d_t \ldots d_1$ lists the number of 0s to the right of each 1:

$$10\ 10\ 8\ 6\ 2\ 2\ 2\ 2\ 2\ 2\ 1\ 1\ 0.$$

The composition $p_t \ldots p_0$ lists the distances between consecutive 1s, if we imagine additional 1s at the left and the right:

$$2\ 1\ 3\ 3\ 5\ 1\ 1\ 1\ 1\ 1\ 2\ 1\ 2\ 1.$$

And the nonnegative composition $q_t \ldots q_0$ counts how many 0s appear between "fenceposts" represented by 1s:

$$1\ 0\ 2\ 2\ 4\ 0\ 0\ 0\ 0\ 0\ 1\ 0\ 1\ 0;$$

thus we have

$$a_{n-1} \ldots a_1 a_0 = 0^{q_t} 1 0^{q_{t-1}} 1 \ldots 1 0^{q_1} 1 0^{q_0}. \qquad (14)$$

The paths in Table 1 also have a simple interpretation (see exercise 2).

Lexicographic generation. Table 1 shows combinations $a_{n-1} \ldots a_1 a_0$ and $c_t \ldots c_1$ in lexicographic order, which is also the lexicographic order of $d_t \ldots d_1$. Notice that the dual combinations $b_s \ldots b_1$ and the corresponding compositions $p_t \ldots p_0$, $q_t \ldots q_0$ then appear in *reverse* lexicographic order.

Lexicographic order usually suggests the most convenient way to generate combinatorial configurations. Indeed, Algorithm 7.2.1.2L already solves the problem for combinations in the form $a_{n-1} \ldots a_1 a_0$, since (s, t)-combinations in bitstring form are the same as permutations of the multiset $\{s \cdot 0, t \cdot 1\}$. That general-purpose algorithm can be streamlined in obvious ways when it is applied to this special case. (See also exercise 7.1.3–20, which presents a remarkable sequence of seven bitwise operations that will convert any given binary number $(a_{n-1} \ldots a_1 a_0)_2$ to the lexicographically next t-combination, assuming that n does not exceed the computer's word length.)

Let's focus, however, on generating combinations in the other principal form $c_t \ldots c_2 c_1$, which is more directly relevant to the ways in which combinations are often needed, and which is more compact than the bit strings when t is small compared to n. In the first place we should keep in mind that a simple sequence of nested loops will do the job nicely when t is very small. For example, when $t = 3$ the following instructions suffice:

$$
\begin{aligned}
&\text{For } c_3 = 2, 3, \ldots, n - 1 \text{ (in this order) do the following:}\\
&\quad \text{For } c_2 = 1, 2, \ldots, c_3 - 1 \text{ (in this order) do the following:}\\
&\qquad \text{For } c_1 = 0, 1, \ldots, c_2 - 1 \text{ (in this order) do the following:}\\
&\qquad\quad \text{Visit the combination } c_3 c_2 c_1.
\end{aligned}
\tag{15}
$$

(See the analogous situation in 7.2.1.1–(3).)

On the other hand when t is variable or not so small, we can generate combinations lexicographically by following the general recipe discussed after Algorithm 7.2.1.2L, namely to find the rightmost element c_j that can be increased and then to set the subsequent elements $c_{j-1} \ldots c_1$ to their smallest possible values:

Algorithm L (*Lexicographic combinations*). This algorithm visits all t-combinations $c_t \ldots c_2 c_1$ of the n numbers $\{0, 1, \ldots, n - 1\}$, given $n \geq t \geq 0$, in lexicographic order. Additional variables c_{t+1} and c_{t+2} are used as sentinels.

L1. [Initialize.] Set $c_j \leftarrow j - 1$ for $1 \leq j \leq t$; also set $c_{t+1} \leftarrow n$ and $c_{t+2} \leftarrow 0$.

L2. [Visit.] Visit the combination $c_t \ldots c_2 c_1$.

L3. [Find j.] Set $j \leftarrow 1$. Then, while $c_j + 1 = c_{j+1}$, set $c_j \leftarrow j - 1$ and $j \leftarrow j + 1$; eventually the condition $c_j + 1 \neq c_{j+1}$ will occur.

L4. [Done?] Terminate the algorithm if $j > t$.

L5. [Increase c_j.] Set $c_j \leftarrow c_j + 1$ and return to L2. ∎

The running time of this algorithm is not difficult to analyze: Step L3 sets $c_j \leftarrow j - 1$ just after visiting a combination for which $c_{j+1} = c_1 + j$; and the number of such combinations is the number of solutions to the inequalities

$$
n > c_t > \cdots > c_{j+1} \geq j.
\tag{16}
$$

But this formula is equivalent to a $(t-j)$-combination of the $n-j$ objects $\{n-1, \ldots, j\}$, so the assignment $c_j \leftarrow j-1$ occurs exactly $\binom{n-j}{t-j}$ times. Summing for $1 \le j \le t$ tells us that the loop in step L3 is performed

$$\binom{n-1}{t-1} + \binom{n-2}{t-2} + \cdots + \binom{n-t}{0} = \binom{n-1}{s} + \binom{n-2}{s} + \cdots + \binom{s}{s} = \binom{n}{s+1} \quad (17)$$

times altogether, or an average of

$$\binom{n}{s+1} \Big/ \binom{n}{t} = \frac{n!}{(s+1)!\,(t-1)!} \Big/ \frac{n!}{s!\,t!} = \frac{t}{s+1} \quad (18)$$

times per visit. This ratio is less than 1 when $t \le s$, so Algorithm L is quite efficient in such cases.

But the quantity $t/(s+1)$ can be embarrassingly large when t is near n and s is small. Indeed, Algorithm L occasionally sets $c_j \leftarrow j-1$ needlessly, at times when c_j already equals $j-1$. Further scrutiny reveals that we need not always search for the index j that is needed in steps L4 and L5, since the correct value of j can often be predicted from the actions just taken. For example, after we have increased c_4 and reset $c_3 c_2 c_1$ to their starting values 210, the next combination will inevitably increase c_3. These observations lead to a tuned-up version of the algorithm:

Algorithm T (*Lexicographic combinations*). This algorithm is like Algorithm L, but faster. It also assumes, for convenience, that $0 < t < n$.

T1. [Initialize.] Set $c_j \leftarrow j-1$ for $1 \le j \le t$; then set $c_{t+1} \leftarrow n$, $c_{t+2} \leftarrow 0$, and $j \leftarrow t$.

T2. [Visit.] (At this point j is the smallest index such that $c_{j+1} > j$.) Visit the combination $c_t \ldots c_2 c_1$. Then, if $j > 0$, set $x \leftarrow j$ and go to step T6.

T3. [Easy case?] If $c_1 + 1 < c_2$, set $c_1 \leftarrow c_1 + 1$ and return to T2. Otherwise set $j \leftarrow 2$.

T4. [Find j.] Set $c_{j-1} \leftarrow j-2$ and $x \leftarrow c_j + 1$. If $x = c_{j+1}$, set $j \leftarrow j+1$ and repeat step T4.

T5. [Done?] Terminate the algorithm if $j > t$.

T6. [Increase c_j.] Set $c_j \leftarrow x$, $j \leftarrow j-1$, and return to T2. ∎

Now $j = 0$ in step T2 if and only if $c_1 > 0$, so the assignments in step T4 are never redundant. Exercise 6 carries out a complete analysis of Algorithm T.

Notice that the parameter n appears only in the initialization steps L1 and T1, not in the principal parts of Algorithms L and T. Thus we can think of the process as generating the first $\binom{n}{t}$ combinations of an *infinite* list, which depends only on t. This simplification arises because the list of t-combinations for $n+1$ things begins with the list for n things, under our conventions; we have been using lexicographic order on the decreasing sequences $c_t \ldots c_1$ for this very reason, instead of working with the increasing sequences $c_1 \ldots c_t$.

Derrick Lehmer noticed another pleasant property of Algorithms L and T [*Applied Combinatorial Mathematics*, edited by E. F. Beckenbach (1964), 27–30]:

Theorem L. *The combination $c_t \ldots c_2 c_1$ is visited after exactly*

$$\binom{c_t}{t} + \cdots + \binom{c_2}{2} + \binom{c_1}{1} \tag{19}$$

other combinations have been visited.

Proof. There are $\binom{c_k}{k}$ combinations $c'_t \ldots c'_2 c'_1$ with $c'_j = c_j$ for $t \geq j > k$ and $c'_k < c_k$, namely $c_t \ldots c_{k+1}$ followed by the k-combinations of $\{0, \ldots, c_k - 1\}$. ∎

When $t = 3$, for example, the numbers

$$\binom{2}{3} + \binom{1}{2} + \binom{0}{1}, \ \binom{3}{3} + \binom{1}{2} + \binom{0}{1}, \ \binom{3}{3} + \binom{2}{2} + \binom{0}{1}, \ \ldots, \ \binom{5}{3} + \binom{4}{2} + \binom{3}{1}$$

that correspond to the combinations $c_3 c_2 c_1$ in Table 1 simply run through the sequence 0, 1, 2, ..., 19. Theorem L gives us a nice way to understand the *combinatorial number system* of degree t, which represents every nonnegative integer N uniquely in the form

$$N = \binom{n_t}{t} + \cdots + \binom{n_2}{2} + \binom{n_1}{1}, \qquad n_t > \cdots > n_2 > n_1 \geq 0. \tag{20}$$

[See Ernesto Pascal, *Giornale di Matematiche* **25** (1887), 45–49.]

Binomial trees. The family of trees T_n defined by

$$T_0 = \bullet \,, \qquad T_n = \begin{array}{c} \text{tree with root edges } 0, 1, \ldots, n-1 \\ T_0 \quad T_1 \quad \cdots \quad T_{n-1} \end{array} \qquad \text{for } n > 0, \tag{21}$$

arises in several important contexts and sheds further light on combination generation. For example, T_4 is

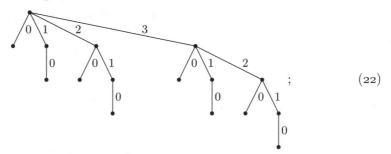

$$; \tag{22}$$

and T_5, rendered more artistically, appears as the frontispiece to Volume 1 of this series of books.

Notice that T_n is like T_{n-1}, except for an additional copy of T_{n-1}; therefore T_n has 2^n nodes altogether. Furthermore, the number of nodes on level t is the binomial coefficient $\binom{n}{t}$; this fact accounts for the name "binomial tree." Indeed, the sequence of labels encountered on the path from the root to each node on level t defines a combination $c_t \ldots c_1$, and all combinations occur in lexicographic order from left to right. Thus, Algorithms L and T can be regarded as procedures to traverse the nodes on level t of the binomial tree T_n.

The infinite binomial tree T_∞ is obtained by letting $n \to \infty$ in (21). The root of this tree has infinitely many branches, but every node except for the overall root at level 0 is the root of a finite binomial subtree. All possible t-combinations appear in lexicographic order on level t of T_∞.

Let's get more familiar with binomial trees by considering all possible ways to pack a rucksack. More precisely, suppose we have n items that take up respectively $w_{n-1}, \ldots, w_1, w_0$ units of capacity, where

$$w_{n-1} \geq \cdots \geq w_1 \geq w_0 \geq 0; \tag{23}$$

we want to generate all binary vectors $a_{n-1} \ldots a_1 a_0$ such that

$$a \cdot w = a_{n-1}w_{n-1} + \cdots + a_1 w_1 + a_0 w_0 \leq N, \tag{24}$$

where N is the total capacity of a rucksack. Equivalently, we want to find all subsets C of $\{0, 1, \ldots, n-1\}$ such that $w(C) = \sum_{c \in C} w_c \leq N$; such subsets will be called *feasible*. We will write a feasible subset as $c_1 \ldots c_t$, where $c_1 > \cdots > c_t \geq 0$, numbering the subscripts differently from the convention of (3) above because t is variable in this problem.

Every feasible subset corresponds to a node of T_n, and our goal is to visit each feasible node. Clearly the parent of every feasible node is feasible, and so is the left sibling, if any; therefore a simple tree exploration procedure works well:

Algorithm F (*Filling a rucksack*). This algorithm visits all feasible ways $c_1 \ldots c_t$ to fill a rucksack, given $w_{n-1}, \ldots, w_1, w_0$, and N. We let $\delta_j = w_j - w_{j-1}$ for $1 \leq j < n$.

F1. [Initialize.] Set $t \leftarrow 0$, $c_0 \leftarrow n$, and $r \leftarrow N$.

F2. [Visit.] Visit the combination $c_1 \ldots c_t$, which uses $N - r$ units of capacity.

F3. [Try to add w_0.] If $c_t > 0$ and $r \geq w_0$, set $t \leftarrow t + 1$, $c_t \leftarrow 0$, $r \leftarrow r - w_0$, and return to F2.

F4. [Try to increase c_t.] Terminate if $t = 0$. Otherwise, if $c_{t-1} > c_t + 1$ and $r \geq \delta_{c_t+1}$, set $c_t \leftarrow c_t + 1$, $r \leftarrow r - \delta_{c_t}$, and return to F2.

F5. [Remove c_t.] Set $r \leftarrow r + w_{c_t}$, $t \leftarrow t - 1$, and return to F4. ∎

Notice that the algorithm implicitly visits nodes of T_n in preorder, skipping over unfeasible subtrees. An element $c > 0$ is placed in the rucksack, if it fits, just after the procedure has explored all possibilities using element $c - 1$ in its place. The running time is proportional to the number of feasible combinations visited (see exercise 20).

Incidentally, the classical "knapsack problem" of operations research is different: It asks for a feasible subset C such that $v(C) = \sum_{c \in C} v(c)$ is maximum, where each item c has been assigned a value $v(c)$. Algorithm F is not a particularly good way to solve that problem, because it often considers cases that could be ruled out. For example, if C and C' are subsets of $\{1, \ldots, n-1\}$ with $w(C) \leq w(C') \leq N - w_0$ and $v(C) \geq v(C')$, Algorithm F will examine both $C \cup 0$ and $C' \cup 0$, but the latter subset will never improve the maximum. We will consider methods for the classical knapsack problem later; Algorithm F is intended only for situations when *all* of the feasible possibilities are potentially relevant.

Gray codes for combinations. Instead of merely generating all combinations, we often prefer to visit them in such a way that each one is obtained by making only a small change to its predecessor.

For example, we can ask for what Nijenhuis and Wilf have called a "revolving-door algorithm": Imagine two rooms that contain respectively s and t people, with a revolving door between them. Whenever a person 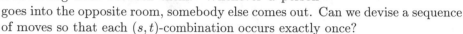 goes into the opposite room, somebody else comes out. Can we devise a sequence of moves so that each (s, t)-combination occurs exactly once?

The answer is yes, and in fact a huge number of such patterns exist. For example, it turns out that if we examine all n-bit strings $a_{n-1} \dots a_1 a_0$ in the well-known order of Gray binary code (Section 7.2.1.1), but select only those that have exactly s 0s and t 1s, the resulting strings form a revolving-door code.

Here's the proof: Gray binary code is defined by the recurrence $\Gamma_n = 0\Gamma_{n-1}$, $1\Gamma_{n-1}^R$ of 7.2.1.1–(5), so its (s, t) subsequence satisfies the recurrence

$$\Gamma_{st} = 0\Gamma_{(s-1)t}, \quad 1\Gamma_{s(t-1)}^R \tag{25}$$

when $st > 0$. We also have $\Gamma_{s0} = 0^s$ and $\Gamma_{0t} = 1^t$. Therefore it is clear by induction that Γ_{st} begins with $0^s 1^t$ and ends with $10^s 1^{t-1}$ when $st > 0$. The transition at the comma in (25) is from the last element of $0\Gamma_{(s-1)t}$ to the last element of $1\Gamma_{s(t-1)}$, namely from $010^{s-1}1^{t-1} = 010^{s-1}11^{t-2}$ to $110^s 1^{t-2} = 110^{s-1}01^{t-2}$ when $t \geq 2$, and this satisfies the revolving-door constraint. The case $t = 1$ also checks out. For example, Γ_{33} is given by the columns of

000111	011010	110001	101010
001101	011100	110010	101100
001110	010101	110100	100101
001011	010110	111000	100110
011001	010011	101001	100011

$\tag{26}$

and Γ_{23} can be found in the first two columns of this array. One more turn of the door takes the last element into the first. [These properties of Γ_{st} were discovered by J. E. Miller in her Ph.D. thesis (Columbia University, 1971), then independently by D. T. Tang and C. N. Liu, *IEEE Trans.* **C-22** (1973), 176–180. A loopless implementation was presented by J. R. Bitner, G. Ehrlich, and E. M. Reingold, *CACM* **19** (1976), 517–521.]

When we convert the bit strings $a_5 a_4 a_3 a_2 a_1 a_0$ in (26) to the corresponding index-list forms $c_3 c_2 c_1$, a striking pattern becomes evident:

210	431	540	531
320	432	541	532
321	420	542	520
310	421	543	521
430	410	530	510

$\tag{27}$

The first components c_3 occur in nondecreasing order; but for each fixed value of c_3, the values of c_2 occur in non*increasing* order. And for fixed $c_3 c_2$, the values of c_1 are again nondecreasing. The same is true in general: *All combinations*

$c_t \dots c_2 c_1$ appear *in lexicographic order of*

$$(c_t, \ -c_{t-1}, \ c_{t-2}, \ \dots, \ (-1)^{t-1} c_1) \tag{28}$$

in the revolving-door Gray code Γ_{st}. This property follows by induction, because (25) becomes

$$\Gamma_{st} \ = \ \Gamma_{(s-1)t}, \ (s+t-1)\Gamma^R_{s(t-1)} \tag{29}$$

for $st > 0$ when we use index-list notation instead of bitstring notation. Consequently the sequence can be generated efficiently by the following algorithm due to W. H. Payne [see *ACM Trans. Math. Software* **5** (1979), 163–172]:

Algorithm R (*Revolving-door combinations*). This algorithm generates all t-combinations $c_t \dots c_2 c_1$ of $\{0, 1, \dots, n-1\}$ in lexicographic order of the alternating sequence (28), assuming that $n \geq t > 1$. An auxiliary variable c_{t+1} is used. Step R3 has two variants, depending on whether t is even or odd.

R1. [Initialize.] Set $c_j \leftarrow j - 1$ for $t \geq j \geq 1$, and $c_{t+1} \leftarrow n$.

R2. [Visit.] Visit the combination $c_t \dots c_2 c_1$.

R3. [Easy case?] If t is odd: If $c_1 + 1 < c_2$, increase c_1 by 1 and return to R2, otherwise set $j \leftarrow 2$ and go to R4. If t is even: If $c_1 > 0$, decrease c_1 by 1 and return to R2, otherwise set $j \leftarrow 2$ and go to R5.

R4. [Try to decrease c_j.] (At this point $c_{j-1} = c_j - 1$.) If $c_j \geq j$, set $c_j \leftarrow c_{j-1}$, $c_{j-1} \leftarrow j - 2$, and return to R2. Otherwise increase j by 1.

R5. [Try to increase c_j.] (At this point $c_{j-1} = j - 2$.) If $c_j + 1 < c_{j+1}$, set $c_{j-1} \leftarrow c_j$, $c_j \leftarrow c_j + 1$, and return to R2. Otherwise increase j by 1, and go to R4 if $j \leq t$. Otherwise the algorithm terminates. ∎

Exercises 21–25 explore further properties of this interesting sequence. One of them is a nice companion to Theorem L: *The combination $c_t c_{t-1} \dots c_2 c_1$ is visited by Algorithm R after exactly*

$$N = \binom{c_t+1}{t} - \binom{c_{t-1}+1}{t-1} + \cdots + (-1)^t \binom{c_2+1}{2} - (-1)^t \binom{c_1+1}{1} - [t \text{ odd}] \tag{30}$$

other combinations have been visited. We may call this the representation of N in the "alternating combinatorial number system" of degree t; one consequence, for example, is that every positive integer has a unique representation of the form $N = \binom{a}{3} - \binom{b}{2} + \binom{c}{1}$ with $a > b > c > 0$. Algorithm R tells us how to add 1 to N in this system.

Although the strings of (26) and (27) are not in lexicographic order, they are examples of a more general concept called *genlex order*, a name coined by Timothy Walsh. A sequence of strings $\alpha_1, \dots, \alpha_N$ is said to be in genlex order when all strings with a common prefix occur consecutively. For example, all 3-combinations that begin with 53 appear together in (27).

Genlex order means that the strings can be arranged in a trie structure, as in Fig. 31 of Section 6.3, but with the children of each node ordered arbitrarily. When a trie is traversed in any order such that each node is visited just before or just after its descendants, all nodes with a common prefix — that is, all nodes of

a subtrie — appear consecutively. This principle corresponds to recursive generation schemes, so it makes genlex order convenient. Many of the algorithms we've
seen for generating n-tuples have therefore produced their results in some version
of genlex order; similarly, the method of "plain changes" (Algorithm 7.2.1.2P)
visits permutations in a genlex order of the corresponding inversion tables.

The revolving-door method of Algorithm R is a genlex routine that changes
only one element of the combination at each step. But it isn't totally satisfactory,
because it frequently must change two of the indices c_j simultaneously, in order
to preserve the condition $c_t > \cdots > c_2 > c_1$. For example, Algorithm R changes
210 into 320, and (27) includes nine such "crossing" moves.

The source of this defect can be traced to our proof that (25) satisfies the
revolving-door property: We observed that the string $010^{s-1}11^{t-2}$ is followed
by $110^{s-1}01^{t-2}$ when $t \geq 2$. Hence the recursive construction Γ_{st} involves
transitions of the form $110^a0 \leftrightarrow 010^a1$, when a substring like 11000 is changed
to 01001 or vice versa; the two 1s cross each other.

A Gray path for combinations is said to be *homogeneous* if it changes only
one of the indices c_j at each step. A homogeneous scheme is characterized
in bitstring form by having only transitions of the forms $10^a \leftrightarrow 0^a1$ within
strings, for $a \geq 1$, when we pass from one string
to the next. With a homogeneous scheme we can,
for example, play all t-note chords on an n-note
keyboard by moving only one finger at a time.

A slight modification of (25) yields a genlex
scheme for (s, t)-combinations that is pleasantly
homogeneous. The basic idea is to construct a
sequence that begins with 0^s1^t and ends with 1^t0^s, and the following recursion
suggests itself almost immediately: Let $K_{s0} = 0^s$, $K_{0t} = 1^t$, $K_{s(-1)} = \emptyset$, and

$$K_{st} = 0K_{(s-1)t}, \; 10K^R_{(s-1)(t-1)}, \; 11K_{s(t-2)} \quad \text{for } st > 0. \tag{31}$$

At the commas of this sequence we have 01^t0^{s-1} followed by $101^{t-1}0^{s-1}$, and
10^s1^{t-1} followed by 110^s1^{t-2}; both of these transitions are homogeneous, although the second one requires the 1 to jump across s 0s. The combinations K_{33}
for $s = t = 3$ are

000111	010101	101100	100011
001011	010011	101001	110001
001101	011001	101010	110010
001110	011010	100110	110100
010110	011100	100101	111000

$$\tag{32}$$

in bitstring form, and the corresponding "finger patterns" are

210	420	532	510
310	410	530	540
320	430	531	541
321	431	521	542
421	432	520	543.

$$\tag{33}$$

When a homogeneous scheme for ordinary combinations $c_t \ldots c_1$ is converted to the corresponding scheme (6) for combinations with repetitions $d_t \ldots d_1$, it retains the property that only one of the indices d_j changes at each step. And when it is converted to the corresponding schemes (9) or (11) for compositions $p_t \ldots p_0$ or $q_t \ldots q_0$, only two (adjacent) parts change when c_j changes.

Near-perfect schemes. But we can do even better! All (s,t)-combinations can be generated by a sequence of strongly homogeneous transitions that are either $01 \leftrightarrow 10$ or $001 \leftrightarrow 100$. In other words, we can insist that each step causes a single index c_j to change by at most 2. Let's call such generation schemes *near-perfect*.

Imposing such strong conditions actually makes it fairly easy to discover near-perfect schemes, because comparatively few choices are available. Indeed, if we restrict ourselves to *genlex* methods that are near-perfect on n-bit strings, T. A. Jenkyns and D. McCarthy observed that all such methods can be easily characterized [*Ars Combinatoria* **40** (1995), 153–159]:

Theorem N. *If $st > 0$, there are exactly $2s$ near-perfect ways to list all (s,t)-combinations in a genlex order. In fact, when $1 \leq a \leq s$, there is exactly one such listing, N_{sta}, that begins with $1^t 0^s$ and ends with $0^a 1^t 0^{s-a}$; the other s possibilities are the reverse lists, N_{sta}^R.*

Proof. The result certainly holds when $s = t = 1$; otherwise we use induction on $s+t$. The listing N_{sta}, if it exists, must have the form $1X_{s(t-1)}, 0Y_{(s-1)t}$ for some near-perfect genlex listings $X_{s(t-1)}$ and $Y_{(s-1)t}$. If $t = 1$, $X_{s(t-1)}$ is the single string 0^s; hence $Y_{(s-1)t}$ must be $N_{(s-1)1(a-1)}$ if $a > 1$, and it must be $N_{(s-1)11}^R$ if $a = 1$. On the other hand if $t > 1$, the near-perfect condition implies that the last string of $X_{s(t-1)}$ cannot begin with 1; hence $X_{s(t-1)} = N_{s(t-1)b}$ for some b. If $a > 1$, $Y_{(s-1)t}$ must be $N_{(s-1)t(a-1)}$, hence b must be 1; similarly, b must be 1 if $s = 1$. Otherwise we have $a = 1 < s$, and this forces $Y_{(s-1)t} = N_{(s-1)tc}^R$ for some c. The transition from $10^b 1^{t-1} 0^{s-b}$ to $0^{c+1} 1^t 0^{s-1-c}$ is near-perfect only if $c = 1$ and $b = 2$. ∎

The proof of Theorem N yields the following recursive formulas when $st > 0$:

$$N_{sta} = \begin{cases} 1N_{s(t-1)1}, \ 0N_{(s-1)t(a-1)}, & \text{if } 1 < a \leq s; \\ 1N_{s(t-1)2}, \ 0N_{(s-1)t1}^R, & \text{if } 1 = a < s; \\ 1N_{1(t-1)1}, \ 01^t, & \text{if } 1 = a = s. \end{cases} \qquad (34)$$

Also, of course, $N_{s0a} = 0^s$.

Let us set $A_{st} = N_{st1}$ and $B_{st} = N_{st2}$. These near-perfect listings, discovered by Phillip J. Chase in 1976, have the net effect of shifting a leftmost block of 1s to the right by one or two positions, respectively, and they satisfy the following mutual recursions:

$$A_{st} = 1B_{s(t-1)}, \ 0A_{(s-1)t}^R; \qquad\qquad B_{st} = 1A_{s(t-1)}, \ 0A_{(s-1)t}. \qquad (35)$$

"To take one step forward, take two steps forward, then one step backward; to take two steps forward, take one step forward, then another." These equations

Table 2
CHASE'S SEQUENCES FOR $(3,3)$-COMBINATIONS

$A_{33} = \widehat{C}_{33}^R$					$B_{33} = C_{33}$			
543	531	321	420		543	520	432	410
541	530	320	421		542	510	430	210
540	510	310	431		540	530	431	310
542	520	210	430		541	531	421	320
532	521	410	432		521	532	420	321

hold for all integer values of s and t, if we define A_{st} and B_{st} to be $\emptyset$ when s or t is negative, except that $A_{00} = B_{00} = \epsilon$ (the empty string). Thus A_{st} actually takes $\min(s, 1)$ forward steps, and B_{st} actually takes $\min(s, 2)$. For example, Table 2 shows the relevant listings for $s = t = 3$, using an equivalent index-list form $c_3 c_2 c_1$ instead of the bit strings $a_5 a_4 a_3 a_2 a_1 a_0$.

Chase noticed that a computer implementation of these sequences becomes simpler if we define

$$C_{st} = \begin{cases} A_{st}, & \text{if } s + t \text{ is odd}; \\ B_{st}, & \text{if } s + t \text{ is even}; \end{cases} \qquad \widehat{C}_{st} = \begin{cases} A_{st}^R, & \text{if } s + t \text{ is even}; \\ B_{st}^R, & \text{if } s + t \text{ is odd}. \end{cases} \tag{36}$$

[See *Congressus Numerantium* **69** (1989), 215–242.] Then we have

$$C_{st} = \begin{cases} 1 C_{s(t-1)}, \; 0 \widehat{C}_{(s-1)t}, & \text{if } s + t \text{ is odd}; \\ 1 C_{s(t-1)}, \; 0 C_{(s-1)t}, & \text{if } s + t \text{ is even}; \end{cases} \tag{37}$$

$$\widehat{C}_{st} = \begin{cases} 0 C_{(s-1)t}, \; 1 \widehat{C}_{s(t-1)}, & \text{if } s + t \text{ is even}; \\ 0 \widehat{C}_{(s-1)t}, \; 1 \widehat{C}_{s(t-1)}, & \text{if } s + t \text{ is odd}. \end{cases} \tag{38}$$

When bit a_j is ready to change, we can tell where we are in the recursion by testing whether j is even or odd.

Indeed, the sequence C_{st} can be generated by a surprisingly simple algorithm, based on general ideas that apply to *any* genlex scheme. Let us say that bit a_j is *active* in a genlex algorithm if it is supposed to change before anything to its left is altered. (In other words, the node for an active bit in the corresponding trie is not the rightmost child of its parent.) Suppose we have an auxiliary table $w_n \ldots w_1 w_0$, where $w_j = 1$ if and only if either a_j is active or $j < r$, where r is the least subscript such that $a_r \neq a_0$; we also let $w_n = 1$. Then the following method will find the successor of $a_{n-1} \ldots a_1 a_0$:

> Set $j \leftarrow r$. If $w_j = 0$, set $w_j \leftarrow 1$, $j \leftarrow j + 1$, and repeat until $w_j = 1$. Terminate if $j = n$; otherwise set $w_j \leftarrow 0$. Change a_j to $1 - a_j$, and make any other changes to $a_{j-1} \ldots a_0$ and r that apply to the particular genlex scheme being used. $\tag{39}$

The beauty of this approach comes from the fact that the loop is guaranteed to be efficient: We can prove that the operation $j \leftarrow j + 1$ will be performed less than once per generation step, on the average (see exercise 36).

By analyzing the transitions that occur when bits change in (37) and (38), we can readily flesh out the remaining details:

Algorithm C (*Chase's sequence*). This algorithm visits all (s,t)-combinations $a_{n-1}\ldots a_1 a_0$, where $n = s+t$, in the near-perfect order of Chase's sequence C_{st}.

C1. [Initialize.] Set $a_j \leftarrow 0$ for $0 \le j < s$, $a_j \leftarrow 1$ for $s \le j < n$, and $w_j \leftarrow 1$ for $0 \le j \le n$. If $s > 0$, set $r \leftarrow s$; otherwise set $r \leftarrow t$.

C2. [Visit.] Visit the combination $a_{n-1}\ldots a_1 a_0$.

C3. [Find j and branch.] Set $j \leftarrow r$. While $w_j = 0$, set $w_j \leftarrow 1$ and $j \leftarrow j+1$. Terminate if $j = n$; otherwise set $w_j \leftarrow 0$ and make a four-way branch: Go to C4 if j is odd and $a_j \ne 0$, to C5 if j is even and $a_j \ne 0$, to C6 if j is even and $a_j = 0$, to C7 if j is odd and $a_j = 0$.

C4. [Move right one.] Set $a_{j-1} \leftarrow 1$, $a_j \leftarrow 0$. If $r = j$ and $j > 1$, set $r \leftarrow j-1$; otherwise if $r = j-1$ set $r \leftarrow j$. Return to C2.

C5. [Move right two.] If $a_{j-2} \ne 0$, go to C4. Otherwise set $a_{j-2} \leftarrow 1$, $a_j \leftarrow 0$. If $r = j$, set $r \leftarrow \max(j-2, 1)$; otherwise if $r = j-2$, set $r \leftarrow j-1$. Return to C2.

C6. [Move left one.] Set $a_j \leftarrow 1$, $a_{j-1} \leftarrow 0$. If $r = j$ and $j > 1$, set $r \leftarrow j-1$; otherwise if $r = j-1$ set $r \leftarrow j$. Return to C2.

C7. [Move left two.] If $a_{j-1} \ne 0$, go to C6. Otherwise set $a_j \leftarrow 1$, $a_{j-2} \leftarrow 0$. If $r = j-2$, set $r \leftarrow j$; otherwise if $r = j-1$, set $r \leftarrow j-2$. Return to C2. ∎

*Analysis of Chase's sequence. The magical properties of Algorithm C cry out for further exploration, and a closer look turns out to be quite instructive. Given a bit string $a_{n-1}\ldots a_1 a_0$, let us define $a_n = 1$, $u_n = n \bmod 2$, and

$$u_j = (1 - u_{j+1})a_{j+1}, \quad v_j = (u_j + j) \bmod 2, \quad w_j = (v_j + a_j) \bmod 2, \quad (40)$$

for $n > j \ge 0$. For example, we might have $n = 26$ and

$$
\begin{aligned}
a_{25}\ldots a_1 a_0 &= 11001001000011111101101010, \\
u_{25}\ldots u_1 u_0 &= 10100100100001010100100101, \\
v_{25}\ldots v_1 v_0 &= 00001110001011111110001111, \\
w_{25}\ldots w_1 w_0 &= 11000111001000000011100101.
\end{aligned}
\quad (41)
$$

With these definitions we can prove by induction that $v_j = 0$ if and only if bit a_j is being "controlled" by C rather than by $\widehat{C}$ in the recursions (37)–(38) that generate $a_{n-1}\ldots a_1 a_0$, except when a_j is part of the final run of 0s or 1s at the right end. Therefore w_j agrees with the value computed by Algorithm C at the moment when $a_{n-1}\ldots a_1 a_0$ is visited, for $r \le j < n$. These formulas can be used to determine exactly where a given combination appears in Chase's sequence (see exercise 39).

If we want to work with the index-list form $c_t \ldots c_2 c_1$ instead of the bit strings $a_{n-1}\ldots a_1 u_0$, it is convenient to change the notation slightly, writing

$C_t(n)$ for C_{st} and $\widehat{C}_t(n)$ for $\widehat{C}_{st}$ when $s + t = n$. Then $C_0(n) = \widehat{C}_0(n) = \epsilon$, and the recursions for $t \geq 0$ take the form

$$C_{t+1}(n+1) = \begin{cases} nC_t(n),\ \widehat{C}_{t+1}(n), & \text{if } n \text{ is even}; \\ nC_t(n),\ C_{t+1}(n), & \text{if } n \text{ is odd}; \end{cases} \tag{42}$$

$$\widehat{C}_{t+1}(n+1) = \begin{cases} C_{t+1}(n),\ n\widehat{C}_t(n), & \text{if } n \text{ is odd}; \\ \widehat{C}_{t+1}(n),\ n\widehat{C}_t(n), & \text{if } n \text{ is even}. \end{cases} \tag{43}$$

These new equations can be expanded to tell us, for example, that

$$
\begin{aligned}
C_{t+1}(9) &= 8C_t(8),\ 6C_t(6),\ 4C_t(4),\ \ldots,\ 3\widehat{C}_t(3),\ 5\widehat{C}_t(5),\ 7\widehat{C}_t(7); \\
C_{t+1}(8) &= 7C_t(7),\ 6C_t(6),\ 4C_t(4),\ \ldots,\ 3\widehat{C}_t(3),\ 5\widehat{C}_t(5); \\
\widehat{C}_{t+1}(9) &= 6C_t(6),\ 4C_t(4),\ \ldots,\ 3\widehat{C}_t(3),\ 5\widehat{C}_t(5),\ 7\widehat{C}_t(7),\ 8\widehat{C}_t(8); \\
\widehat{C}_{t+1}(8) &= 6C_t(6),\ 4C_t(4),\ \ldots,\ 3\widehat{C}_t(3),\ 5\widehat{C}_t(5),\ 7\widehat{C}_t(7);
\end{aligned}
\tag{44}
$$

notice that the same pattern predominates in all four sequences. The meaning of "$\ldots$" in the middle depends on the value of t: We simply omit all terms $nC_t(n)$ and $n\widehat{C}_t(n)$ where $n < t$.

Except for edge effects at the very beginning or end, all of the expansions in (44) are based on the infinite progression

$$\ldots,\ 10,\ 8,\ 6,\ 4,\ 2,\ 0,\ 1,\ 3,\ 5,\ 7,\ 9,\ \ldots, \tag{45}$$

which is a natural way to arrange the nonnegative integers into a doubly infinite sequence. If we omit all terms of (45) that are $< t$, given any integer $t \geq 0$, the remaining terms retain the property that adjacent elements differ by either 1 or 2. Richard Stanley has suggested the name *endo-order* for this sequence, because we can remember it by thinking "even numbers decreasing, odd $\ldots$". (Notice that if we retain only the terms less than N and complement with respect to N, endo-order becomes organ-pipe order; see exercise 6.1–18.)

We could program the recursions of (42) and (43) directly, but it is interesting to unwind them using (44), thus obtaining an iterative algorithm analogous to Algorithm C. The result needs only $O(t)$ memory locations, and it is especially efficient when t is relatively small compared to n. Exercise 45 contains the details.

*Near-perfect multiset permutations. Chase's sequences lead in a natural way to an algorithm that will generate permutations of any desired multiset $\{s_0 \cdot 0, s_1 \cdot 1, \ldots, s_d \cdot d\}$ in a near-perfect manner, meaning that

i) every transition is either $a_{j+1}a_j \leftrightarrow a_j a_{j+1}$ or $a_{j+1}a_j a_{j-1} \leftrightarrow a_{j-1}a_j a_{j+1}$;

ii) transitions of the second kind have $a_j = \min(a_{j-1}, a_{j+1})$.

Algorithm C tells us how to do this when $d = 1$, and we can extend it to larger values of d by the following recursive construction [*CACM* **13** (1970), 368–369, 376]: Suppose

$$\alpha_0,\ \alpha_1,\ \ldots,\ \alpha_{N-1}$$

is any near-perfect listing of the permutations of $\{s_1 \cdot 1, \ldots, s_d \cdot d\}$. Then Algorithm C, with $s = s_0$ and $t = s_1 + \cdots + s_d$, tells us how to generate a listing

$$\Lambda_j = \alpha_j 0^s, \ldots, 0^a \alpha_j 0^{s-a} \tag{46}$$

in which all transitions are $0x \leftrightarrow x0$ or $00x \leftrightarrow x00$; the final entry has $a = 1$ or 2 leading zeros, depending on s and t. Therefore all transitions of the sequence

$$\Lambda_0, \Lambda_1^R, \Lambda_2, \ldots, (\Lambda_{N-1} \text{ or } \Lambda_{N-1}^R) \tag{47}$$

are near-perfect; and this list clearly contains all the permutations.

For example, the permutations of $\{0, 0, 0, 1, 1, 2\}$ generated in this way are

211000, 210100, 210001, 210010, 200110, 200101, 200011, 201001, 201010, 201100,
021100, 021001, 021010, 020110, 020101, 020011, 000211, 002011, 002101, 002110,
001120, 001102, 001012, 000112, 010012, 010102, 010120, 011020, 011002, 011200,
101200, 101020, 101002, 100012, 100102, 100120, 110020, 110002, 110200, 112000,
121000, 120100, 120001, 120010, 100210, 100201, 100021, 102001, 102010, 102100,
012100, 012001, 012010, 010210, 010201, 010021, 000121, 001021, 001201, 001210.

*Perfect schemes. Why should we settle for a near-perfect generator like C_{st}, instead of insisting that all transitions have the simplest possible form $01 \leftrightarrow 10$?

One reason is that perfect schemes don't always exist. For example, we observed in 7.2.1.2–(2) that there is no way to generate all six permutations of $\{1, 1, 2, 2\}$ with adjacent interchanges; thus there is no perfect scheme for $(2, 2)$-combinations. In fact, our chances of achieving perfection are only about 1 in 4:

Theorem P. *The generation of all (s, t)-combinations $a_{s+t-1} \ldots a_1 a_0$ by adjacent interchanges $01 \leftrightarrow 10$ is possible if and only if $s \le 1$ or $t \le 1$ or st is odd.*

Proof. Consider all permutations of the multiset $\{s \cdot 0, t \cdot 1\}$. We learned in exercise 5.1.2–16 that the number m_k of such permutations having k inversions is the coefficient of z^k in the z-nomial coefficient

$$\binom{s+t}{t}_z = \prod_{k=s+1}^{s+t} (1 + z + \cdots + z^{k-1}) \Big/ \prod_{k=1}^{t} (1 + z + \cdots + z^{k-1}). \tag{48}$$

Every adjacent interchange changes the number of inversions by ± 1, so a perfect generation scheme is possible only if approximately half of all the permutations have an odd number of inversions. More precisely, the value of $\binom{s+t}{t}_{-1} = m_0 - m_1 + m_2 - \cdots$ must be 0 or ± 1. But exercise 49 shows that

$$\binom{s+t}{t}_{-1} = \binom{\lfloor (s+t)/2 \rfloor}{\lfloor t/2 \rfloor} [st \text{ is even}], \tag{49}$$

and this quantity exceeds 1 unless $s \le 1$ or $t \le 1$ or st is odd.

Conversely, perfect schemes are easy with $s \le 1$ or $t \le 1$, and they turn out to be possible also whenever st is odd. The first nontrivial case occurs for $s = t = 3$, when there are four essentially different solutions; the most symmetrical of these is

210 — 310 — 410 — 510 — 520 — 521 — 531 — 532 — 432 — 431 —
　421 — 321 — 320 — 420 — 430 — 530 — 540 — 541 — 542 — 543 　(50)

(see exercise 51). Several authors have constructed Hamiltonian paths in the relevant graph for arbitrary odd numbers s and t; for example, the method of Eades, Hickey, and Read [*JACM* **31** (1984), 19–29] makes an interesting exercise in programming with recursive coroutines. Unfortunately, however, none of the known constructions are sufficiently simple to describe in a short space, or to implement with reasonable efficiency. Perfect combination generators have therefore not yet proved to be of practical importance. ▮

In summary, then, we have seen that the study of (s, t)-combinations leads to many fascinating patterns, some of which are of great practical importance and some of which are merely elegant and/or beautiful. Figure 46 illustrates the principal options that are available in the case $s = t = 5$, when $\binom{10}{5} = 252$ combinations arise. Lexicographic order (Algorithm L), the revolving-door Gray code (Algorithm R), the homogeneous scheme K_{55} of (31), and Chase's near-perfect scheme (Algorithm C) are shown in parts (a), (b), (c), and (d) of the illustration. Part (e) shows the near-perfect scheme that is as close to perfection as possible while still being in genlex order of the c array (see exercise 34), while part (f) is the perfect scheme of Eades, Hickey, and Read. Finally, Figs. 46(g) and 46(h) are listings that proceed by rotating $a_j a_{j-1} \dots a_0 \leftarrow a_{j-1} \dots a_0 a_j$ or by swapping $a_j \leftrightarrow a_0$, akin to Algorithms 7.2.1.2C and 7.2.1.2E (see exercises 55 and 56).

Combinations of a multiset. If multisets can have permutations, they can have combinations too. For example, consider the multiset $\{b, b, b, b, g, g, g, r, r, r, w, w\}$, representing a sack that contains four blue balls and three that are green, three red, two white. There are 37 ways to choose five balls from this sack; in lexicographic order (but descending in each combination) they are

$$gbbbb,\ ggbbb,\ gggbb,\ rbbbb,\ rgbbb,\ rggbb,\ rgggb,\ rrbbb,\ rrgbb,\ rrggb,$$
$$rrggg,\ rrrbb,\ rrrgb,\ rrrgg,\ wbbbb,\ wgbbb,\ wggbb,\ wgggb,\ wrbbb,\ wrgbb,$$
$$wrggb,\ wrggg,\ wrrbb,\ wrrgb,\ wrrgg,\ wrrrb,\ wrrrg,\ wwbbb,\ wwgbb,\ wwggb,$$
$$wwggg,\ wwrbb,\ wwrgb,\ wwrgg,\ wwrrb,\ wwrrg,\ wwrrr. \tag{51}$$

This fact might seem frivolous and/or esoteric, yet we will see in Theorem W below that the lexicographic generation of multiset combinations yields optimal solutions to significant combinatorial problems.

James Bernoulli observed in his *Ars Conjectandi* (1713), 119–123, that we can enumerate such combinations by looking at the coefficient of z^5 in the product $(1+z+z^2)(1+z+z^2+z^3)^2(1+z+z^2+z^3+z^4)$. Indeed, his observation is easy to understand, because we get all possible selections from the sack if we multiply out the polynomials

$$(1 + w + ww)(1 + r + rr + rrr)(1 + g + gg + ggg)(1 + b + bb + bbb + bbbb).$$

Multiset combinations are also equivalent to *bounded compositions*, namely to compositions in which the individual parts are bounded. For example, the 37 multicombinations listed in (51) correspond to 37 solutions of

$$5 = r_3 + r_2 + r_1 + r_0, \quad 0 \le r_3 \le 2, \quad 0 \le r_2, r_1 \le 3, \quad 0 \le r_0 \le 4,$$

namely $5 = 0+0+1+4 = 0+0+2+3 = 0+0+3+2 = 0+1+0+4 = \cdots = 2+3+0+0$.

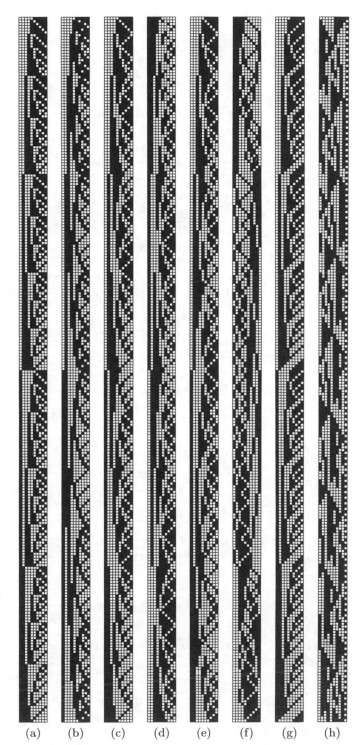

Fig. 46. Examples
of (5, 5)-combinations:

  a) lexicographic;
  b) revolving-door;
  c) homogeneous;
  d) near-perfect;
  e) nearer-perfect;
  f) perfect;
  g) suffix-rotated;
  h) right-swapped.

(a)   (b)   (c)   (d)   (e)   (f)   (g)   (h)

Bounded compositions, in turn, are special cases of *contingency tables*, which are of great importance in statistics. And all of these combinatorial configurations can be generated with Gray-like codes as well as in lexicographic order. Exercises 60–63 explore some of the basic ideas involved.

*Shadows. Sets of combinations appear frequently in mathematics. For example, a set of 2-combinations (namely a set of pairs) is essentially a graph, and a set of t-combinations for general t is called a uniform hypergraph. If the vertices of a convex polyhedron are perturbed slightly, so that no three are collinear, no four lie in a plane, and in general no $t + 1$ lie in a $(t - 1)$-dimensional hyperplane, the resulting $(t - 1)$-dimensional faces are "simplexes" whose vertices have great significance in computer applications. Researchers have learned that such sets of combinations have important properties related to lexicographic generation.

If α is any t-combination $c_t \ldots c_2 c_1$, its *shadow* $\partial \alpha$ is the set of all its $(t - 1)$-element subsets $c_{t-1} \ldots c_2 c_1, \ldots, c_t \ldots c_3 c_1, c_t \ldots c_3 c_2$. For example, $\partial 5310 = \{310, 510, 530, 531\}$. We can also represent a t-combination as a bit string $a_{n-1} \ldots a_1 a_0$, in which case $\partial \alpha$ is the set of all strings obtained by changing a 1 to a 0: $\partial 101011 = \{001011, 100011, 101001, 101010\}$. If A is any set of t-combinations, we define its shadow

$$\partial A = \bigcup \{ \partial \alpha \mid \alpha \in A \} \tag{52}$$

to be the set of all $(t - 1)$-combinations in the shadows of its members. For example, $\partial \partial 5310 = \{10, 30, 31, 50, 51, 53\}$.

These definitions apply also to combinations with repetitions, namely to multicombinations: $\partial 5330 = \{330, 530, 533\}$ and $\partial \partial 5330 = \{30, 33, 50, 53\}$. In general, when A is a set of t-element multisets, ∂A is a set of $(t - 1)$-element multisets. Notice, however, that ∂A never has repeated elements itself.

The *upper shadow* $\varrho \alpha$ with respect to a universe U is defined similarly, but it goes from t-combinations to $(t + 1)$-combinations:

$$\varrho \alpha = \{ \beta \subseteq U \mid \alpha \in \partial \beta \}, \qquad \text{for } \alpha \in U; \tag{53}$$
$$\varrho A = \bigcup \{ \varrho \alpha \mid \alpha \in A \}, \qquad \text{for } A \subseteq U. \tag{54}$$

If, for example, $U = \{0, 1, 2, 3, 4, 5, 6\}$, we have $\varrho 5310 = \{53210, 54310, 65310\}$; on the other hand, if $U = \{\infty \cdot 0, \infty \cdot 1, \ldots, \infty \cdot 6\}$, we have $\varrho 5310 = \{53100, 53110, 53210, 53310, 54310, 55310, 65310\}$.

The following fundamental theorems, which have many applications in various branches of mathematics and computer science, tell us how small a set's shadows can be:

Theorem K. *If A is a set of N t-combinations contained in $U = \{0, 1, \ldots, n-1\}$, then*

$$|\partial A| \geq |\partial P_{Nt}| \qquad \text{and} \qquad |\varrho A| \geq |\varrho Q_{Nnt}|, \tag{55}$$

where P_{Nt} denotes the first N combinations generated by Algorithm L, namely the N lexicographically smallest combinations $c_t \ldots c_2 c_1$ that satisfy (3), and Q_{Nnt} denotes the N lexicographically largest. ∎

Theorem M. *If A is a set of N t-multicombinations contained in the multiset $U = \{\infty \cdot 0, \infty \cdot 1, \ldots, \infty \cdot s\}$, then*

$$|\partial A| \geq |\partial \widehat{P}_{Nt}| \quad \text{and} \quad |\varrho A| \geq |\varrho \widehat{Q}_{Nst}|, \tag{56}$$

where $\widehat{P}_{Nt}$ denotes the N lexicographically smallest multicombinations $d_t \ldots d_2 d_1$ that satisfy (6), and $\widehat{Q}_{Nst}$ denotes the N lexicographically largest. ∎

Both of these theorems are consequences of a stronger result that we shall prove later. Theorem K is generally called the Kruskal–Katona theorem, because it was discovered by J. B. Kruskal [*Math. Optimization Techniques*, edited by R. Bellman (1963), 251–278] and rediscovered by G. Katona [*Theory of Graphs*, Tihany 1966, edited by Erdős and Katona (Academic Press, 1968), 187–207]; M. P. Schützenberger had previously stated it in a less-well-known publication, with incomplete proof [*RLE Quarterly Progress Report* **55** (1959), 117–118]. Theorem M goes back to F. S. Macaulay, many years earlier [*Proc. London Math. Soc.* (2) **26** (1927), 531–555].

Before proving (55) and (56), let's take a closer look at what those formulas mean. We know from Theorem L that the first N of all t-combinations visited by Algorithm L are those that precede $n_t \ldots n_2 n_1$, where

$$N = \binom{n_t}{t} + \cdots + \binom{n_2}{2} + \binom{n_1}{1}, \qquad n_t > \cdots > n_2 > n_1 \geq 0$$

is the degree-t combinatorial representation of N. Sometimes this representation has fewer than t nonzero terms, because n_j can be equal to $j - 1$; let's suppress the zeros, and write

$$N = \binom{n_t}{t} + \binom{n_{t-1}}{t-1} + \cdots + \binom{n_v}{v}, \qquad n_t > n_{t-1} > \cdots > n_v \geq v \geq 1. \tag{57}$$

Now the first $\binom{n_t}{t}$ combinations $c_t \ldots c_1$ are the t-combinations of $\{0, \ldots, n_t - 1\}$; the next $\binom{n_{t-1}}{t-1}$ are those in which $c_t = n_t$ and $c_{t-1} \ldots c_1$ is a $(t-1)$-combination of $\{0, \ldots, n_{t-1} - 1\}$; and so on. For example, if $t = 5$ and $N = \binom{9}{5} + \binom{7}{4} + \binom{4}{3}$, the first N combinations are

$$P_{N5} = \{43210, \ldots, 87654\} \cup \{93210, \ldots, 96543\} \cup \{97210, \ldots, 97321\}. \tag{58}$$

The shadow of this set P_{N5} is, fortunately, easy to understand: It is

$$\partial P_{N5} = \{3210, \ldots, 8765\} \cup \{9210, \ldots, 9654\} \cup \{9710, \ldots, 9732\}, \tag{59}$$

namely the first $\binom{9}{4} + \binom{7}{3} + \binom{4}{2}$ combinations in lexicographic order when $t = 4$.

In other words, if we define Kruskal's function κ_t by the formula

$$\kappa_t N = \binom{n_t}{t-1} + \binom{n_{t-1}}{t-2} + \cdots + \binom{n_v}{v-1} \tag{60}$$

when N has the unique representation (57), with $\kappa_t 0 = 0$, we have

$$\partial P_{Nt} = P_{(\kappa_t N)(t-1)}. \tag{61}$$

Theorem K tells us, for example, that a graph with a million edges can contain at most

$$\binom{1414}{3} + \binom{1009}{2} = 470{,}700{,}300$$

triangles, that is, at most 470,700,300 sets of vertices $\{u, v, w\}$ with $u \!-\! v \!-\! w \!-\! u$. The reason is that $1000000 = \binom{1414}{2} + \binom{1009}{1}$ by exercise 17, and the edges $P_{(1000000)2}$ do support $\binom{1414}{3} + \binom{1009}{2}$ triangles; but if there were more, the graph would necessarily have at least $\kappa_3 470700301 = \binom{1414}{2} + \binom{1009}{1} + \binom{1}{0} = 1000001$ edges in their shadow.

Kruskal defined the companion function

$$\lambda_t N = \binom{n_t}{t+1} + \binom{n_{t-1}}{t} + \cdots + \binom{n_v}{v+1} \tag{62}$$

to deal with questions such as this. The κ and λ functions are related by an interesting law proved in exercise 72:

$$M + N = \binom{s+t}{t} \quad \text{implies} \quad \kappa_s M + \lambda_t N = \binom{s+t}{t+1}, \quad \text{if } st > 0. \tag{63}$$

Turning to Theorem M, the sizes of $\partial \widehat{P}_{Nt}$ and $\varrho \widehat{Q}_{Nst}$ turn out to be

$$|\partial \widehat{P}_{Nt}| = \mu_t N \quad \text{and} \quad |\varrho \widehat{Q}_{Nst}| = N + \kappa_s N \tag{64}$$

(see exercise 81), where the function μ_t satisfies

$$\mu_t N = \binom{n_t - 1}{t - 1} + \binom{n_{t-1} - 1}{t - 2} + \cdots + \binom{n_v - 1}{v - 1} \tag{65}$$

when N has the combinatorial representation (57).

Table 3 shows how these functions $\kappa_t N$, $\lambda_t N$, and $\mu_t N$ behave for small values of t and N. When t and N are large, they can be well approximated in terms of a remarkable function $\tau(x)$ introduced by Teiji Takagi in 1903; see Fig. 47 and exercises 82–85.

Theorems K and M are corollaries of a much more general theorem of discrete geometry, discovered by Da-Lun Wang and Ping Wang [*SIAM J. Applied Math.* **33** (1977), 55–59], which we shall now proceed to investigate. Consider the *discrete n-dimensional torus* $T(m_1, \ldots, m_n)$ whose elements are integer vectors $x = (x_1, \ldots, x_n)$ with $0 \le x_1 < m_1, \ldots, 0 \le x_n < m_n$. We define the sum and difference of two such vectors x and y as in Eqs. 4.3.2–(2) and 4.3.2–(3):

$$x + y = ((x_1 + y_1) \bmod m_1, \ldots, (x_n + y_n) \bmod m_n), \tag{66}$$
$$x - y = ((x_1 - y_1) \bmod m_1, \ldots, (x_n - y_n) \bmod m_n). \tag{67}$$

We also define the so-called *cross order* on such vectors by saying that $x \preceq y$ if and only if

$$\nu x < \nu y \quad \text{or} \quad (\nu x = \nu y \text{ and } x \ge y \text{ lexicographically}); \tag{68}$$

here, as usual, $\nu(x_1, \ldots, x_n) = x_1 + \cdots + x_n$. For example, when $m_1 = m_2 = 2$ and $m_3 = 3$, the 12 vectors $x_1 x_2 x_3$ in increasing cross order are

$$000, \ 100, \ 010, \ 001, \ 110, \ 101, \ 011, \ 002, \ 111, \ 102, \ 012, \ 112, \tag{69}$$

Table 3

EXAMPLES OF THE KRUSKAL–MACAULAY FUNCTIONS κ, λ, AND μ

$N =$	0	1	2	3	4	5	6	7	8	9	10	11	12	13	14	15	16	17	18	19	20
$\kappa_1 N =$	0	1	1	1	1	1	1	1	1	1	1	1	1	1	1	1	1	1	1	1	1
$\kappa_2 N =$	0	2	3	3	4	4	4	5	5	5	5	6	6	6	6	6	7	7	7	7	7
$\kappa_3 N =$	0	3	5	6	6	8	9	9	10	10	10	12	13	13	14	14	14	15	15	15	15
$\kappa_4 N =$	0	4	7	9	10	10	13	15	16	16	18	19	19	20	20	20	23	25	26	26	28
$\kappa_5 N =$	0	5	9	12	14	15	15	19	22	24	25	25	28	30	31	31	33	34	34	35	35
$\lambda_1 N =$	0	0	1	3	6	10	15	21	28	36	45	55	66	78	91	105	120	136	153	171	190
$\lambda_2 N =$	0	0	0	1	1	2	4	4	5	7	10	10	11	13	16	20	20	21	23	26	30
$\lambda_3 N =$	0	0	0	0	1	1	1	2	2	3	5	5	5	6	6	7	9	9	10	12	15
$\lambda_4 N =$	0	0	0	0	0	1	1	1	1	2	2	2	3	3	4	6	6	6	6	7	7
$\lambda_5 N =$	0	0	0	0	0	0	1	1	1	1	1	2	2	2	2	3	3	3	4	4	5
$\mu_1 N =$	0	1	1	1	1	1	1	1	1	1	1	1	1	1	1	1	1	1	1	1	1
$\mu_2 N =$	0	1	2	2	3	3	3	4	4	4	4	5	5	5	5	5	6	6	6	6	6
$\mu_3 N =$	0	1	2	3	3	4	5	5	6	6	6	7	8	8	9	9	9	10	10	10	10
$\mu_4 N =$	0	1	2	3	4	4	5	6	7	7	8	9	9	10	10	10	11	12	13	13	14
$\mu_5 N =$	0	1	2	3	4	5	5	6	7	8	9	9	10	11	12	12	13	14	14	15	15

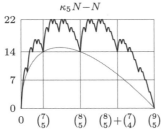
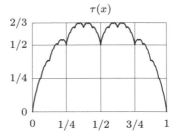

Fig. 47. Approximating a Kruskal function with the Takagi function. (The smooth curve in the left-hand graph is the lower bound $\underline{\kappa}_5 N - N$ of exercise 80.)

omitting parentheses and commas for convenience. The *complement* of a vector in $T(m_1, \ldots, m_n)$ is

$$\bar{x} = (m_1 - 1 - x_1, \ldots, m_n - 1 - x_n). \tag{70}$$

Notice that $x \preceq y$ holds if and only if $\bar{x} \succeq \bar{y}$. Therefore we have

$$\operatorname{rank}(x) + \operatorname{rank}(\bar{x}) = T - 1, \qquad \text{where } T = m_1 \ldots m_n, \tag{71}$$

if $\operatorname{rank}(x)$ denotes the number of vectors that precede x in cross order.

We will find it convenient to call the vectors "points" and to name the points $e_0, e_1, \ldots, e_{T-1}$ in increasing cross order. Thus we have $e_7 = 002$ in (69), and $\bar{e}_r = e_{T-1-r}$ in general. Notice that

$$e_1 = 100 \ldots 00, \qquad e_2 = 010 \ldots 00, \qquad \ldots, \qquad e_n = 000 \ldots 01; \tag{72}$$

these are the so-called *unit vectors*. The set

$$S_N = \{e_0, e_1, \ldots, e_{N-1}\} \tag{73}$$

consisting of the smallest N points is called a *standard set*, and in the special case $N = n + 1$ we write

$$E = \{e_0, e_1, \ldots, e_n\} = \{000\ldots00, 100\ldots00, 010\ldots00, \ldots, 000\ldots01\}. \tag{74}$$

Any set of points X has a *spread* X^+, a *core* X°, and a *dual* $X^\sim$, defined by the rules

$$X^+ = \{\, x \in S_T \mid x \in X \text{ or } x - e_1 \in X \text{ or } \cdots \text{ or } x - e_n \in X \,\}; \tag{75}$$
$$X^\circ = \{\, x \in S_T \mid x \in X \text{ and } x + e_1 \in X \text{ and } \cdots \text{ and } x + e_n \in X \,\}; \tag{76}$$
$$X^\sim = \{\, x \in S_T \mid \bar{x} \notin X \,\}. \tag{77}$$

We can also define the spread of X algebraically, writing

$$X^+ = X + E, \tag{78}$$

where $X + Y$ denotes $\{\, x + y \mid x \in X \text{ and } y \in Y \,\}$. Clearly

$$X^+ \subseteq Y \qquad \text{if and only if} \qquad X \subseteq Y^\circ. \tag{79}$$

These notions can be illustrated in the two-dimensional case $m_1 = 4$, $m_2 = 6$, by the more-or-less random toroidal arrangement $X = \{00, 12, 13, 14, 15, 21, 22, 25\}$ for which we have, pictorially,

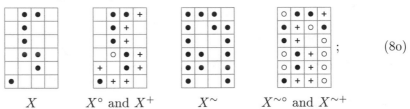

$$\tag{80}$$

$$\begin{array}{cccc} X & X^\circ \text{ and } X^+ & X^\sim & X^{\sim\circ} \text{ and } X^{\sim+} \end{array}$$

here X in the first two diagrams consists of points marked $\bullet$ or $\circ$, X° comprises just the $\circ$s, and X^+ consists of $+$s plus $\bullet$s plus $\circ$s. Notice that if we rotate the diagram for $X^{\sim\circ}$ and $X^{\sim+}$ by $180°$, we obtain the diagram for X° and X^+, but with $(\bullet, \circ, +, \ )$ respectively changed to $(+, \ , \bullet, \circ)$; and in fact the identities

$$X^\circ = X^{\sim+\sim}, \qquad X^+ = X^{\sim\circ\sim} \tag{81}$$

hold in general (see exercise 86).

Now we are ready to state the theorem of Wang and Wang:

Theorem W. *Let X be any set of N points in the discrete torus $T(m_1, \ldots, m_n)$, where $m_1 \le \cdots \le m_n$. Then $|X^+| \ge |S_N^+|$ and $|X^\circ| \le |S_N^\circ|$.*

Proof. In other words, the standard sets S_N have the smallest spread and largest core, among all N-point sets. We will prove this result by following a general approach first used by F. W. J. Whipple to prove Theorem M [*Proc. London Math. Soc.* (2) **28** (1928), 431–437]. The first step is to prove that the spread and the core of standard sets are standard:

Lemma S. *There are functions α and β such that $S_N^+ = S_{\alpha N}$ and $S_N^\circ = S_{\beta N}$.*

Proof. We may assume that $N > 0$. Let r be maximum with $e_r \in S_N^+$, and let $\alpha N = r + 1$; we must prove that $e_q \in S_N^+$ for $0 \le q < r$. Suppose $e_q = x = (x_1, \ldots, x_n)$ and $e_r = y = (y_1, \ldots, y_n)$, and let k be the largest subscript with $x_k > 0$. Since $y \in S_N^+$, there is a subscript j such that $y - e_j \in S_N$. It suffices to prove that $x - e_k \preceq y - e_j$, and exercise 88 does this.

The second part follows from (81), with $\beta N = T - \alpha(T - N)$, because $S_N^\sim = S_{T-N}$. ∎

Theorem W is obviously true when $n = 1$, so we assume by induction that it has been proved in $n - 1$ dimensions. The next step is to *compress* the given set X in the kth coordinate position, by partitioning it into disjoint sets

$$X_k(a) = \{\, x \in X \mid x_k = a \,\} \tag{82}$$

for $0 \le a < m_k$ and replacing each $X_k(a)$ by

$$X_k'(a) = \{\, (s_1, \ldots, s_{k-1}, a, s_k, \ldots, s_{n-1}) \mid (s_1, \ldots, s_{n-1}) \in S_{|X_k(a)|} \,\}, \tag{83}$$

a set with the same number of elements. The sets S used in (83) are standard in the $(n-1)$-dimensional torus $T(m_1, \ldots, m_{k-1}, m_{k+1}, \ldots, m_n)$. Notice that we have $(x_1, \ldots, x_{k-1}, a, x_{k+1}, \ldots, x_n) \preceq (y_1, \ldots, y_{k-1}, a, y_{k+1}, \ldots, y_n)$ if and only if $(x_1, \ldots, x_{k-1}, x_{k+1}, \ldots, x_n) \preceq (y_1, \ldots, y_{k-1}, y_{k+1}, \ldots, y_n)$; therefore $X_k'(a) = X_k(a)$ if and only if the $(n-1)$-dimensional points $(x_1, \ldots, x_{k-1}, x_{k+1}, \ldots, x_n)$ with $(x_1, \ldots, x_{k-1}, a, x_{k+1}, \ldots, x_n) \in X$ are as small as possible when projected onto the $(n-1)$-dimensional torus. We let

$$C_k X = X_k'(0) \cup X_k'(1) \cup \cdots \cup X_k'(m_k - 1) \tag{84}$$

be the compression of X in position k. Exercise 90 proves the basic fact that compression does not increase the size of the spread:

$$|X^+| \ge |(C_k X)^+|, \qquad \text{for } 1 \le k \le n. \tag{85}$$

Furthermore, if compression changes X, it replaces some of the elements by other elements of lower rank. Therefore we need to prove Theorem W only for sets X that are totally compressed, having $X = C_k X$ for all k.

Consider, for example, the case $n = 2$. A totally compressed set in two dimensions has all points moved to the left of their rows and the bottom of their columns, as in the eleven-point sets

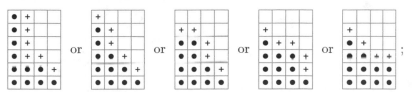

the rightmost of these is standard, and has the smallest spread. Exercise 91 completes the proof of Theorem W in two dimensions.

When $n > 2$, suppose $x = (x_1, \ldots, x_n) \in X$ and $x_j > 0$. The condition $C_k X = X$ implies that, if $0 \leq i < j$ and $i \neq k \neq j$, we have $x + e_i - e_j \in X$. Applying this fact for three values of k tells us that $x + e_i - e_j \in X$ whenever $0 \leq i < j$. Consequently

$$X_n(a) + E_n(0) \subseteq X_n(a-1) + e_n \quad \text{for } 0 < a < m, \tag{86}$$

where $m = m_n$ and $E_n(0)$ is a clever abbreviation for the set $\{e_0, \ldots, e_{n-1}\}$.

Let $X_n(a)$ have N_a elements, so that $N = |X| = N_0 + N_1 + \cdots + N_{m-1}$, and let $Y = X^+$. Then

$$Y_n(a) = \big(X_n((a-1) \bmod m) + e_n\big) \cup \big(X_n(a) + E_n(0)\big)$$

is standard in $n - 1$ dimensions, and (86) tells us that

$$N_{m-1} \leq \beta N_{m-2} \leq N_{m-2} \leq \cdots \leq N_1 \leq \beta N_0 \leq N_0 \leq \alpha N_0,$$

where α and β refer to coordinates 1 through $n - 1$. Therefore

$$\begin{aligned}
|Y| &= |Y_n(0)| + |Y_n(1)| + |Y_n(2)| + \cdots + |Y_n(m-1)| \\
&= \alpha N_0 + N_0 + N_1 + \cdots + N_{m-2} = \alpha N_0 + N - N_{m-1}.
\end{aligned}$$

The proof of Theorem W now has a beautiful conclusion. Let $Z = S_N$, and suppose $|Z_n(a)| = M_a$. We want to prove that $|X^+| \geq |Z^+|$, namely that

$$\alpha N_0 + N - N_{m-1} \geq \alpha M_0 + N - M_{m-1}, \tag{87}$$

because the arguments of the previous paragraph apply to Z as well as to X. We will prove (87) by showing that $N_{m-1} \leq M_{m-1}$ and $N_0 \geq M_0$.

Using the $(n-1)$-dimensional α and β functions, let us define

$$N'_{m-1} = N_{m-1}, \ N'_{m-2} = \alpha N'_{m-1}, \ \ldots, \ N'_1 = \alpha N'_2, \ N'_0 = \alpha N'_1; \tag{88}$$

$$N''_0 = N_0, \ N''_1 = \beta N''_0, \ N''_2 = \beta N''_1, \ \ldots, \ N''_{m-1} = \beta N''_{m-2}. \tag{89}$$

Then we have $N'_a \leq N_a \leq N''_a$ for $0 \leq a < m$, and it follows that

$$N' = N'_0 + N'_1 + \cdots + N'_{m-1} \leq N \leq N'' = N''_0 + N''_1 + \cdots + N''_{m-1}. \tag{90}$$

Exercise 92 proves that the standard set $Z' = S_{N'}$ has exactly N'_a elements with nth coordinate equal to a, for each a; and by the duality between α and β, the standard set $Z'' = S_{N''}$ likewise has exactly N''_a elements with nth coordinate a. Finally, therefore,

$$M_{m-1} = |Z_n(m-1)| \geq |Z'_n(m-1)| = N_{m-1},$$
$$M_0 = |Z_n(0)| \leq |Z''_n(0)| = N_0,$$

because $Z' \subseteq Z \subseteq Z''$ by (90). By (81) we also have $|X^\circ| \leq |Z^\circ|$. ∎

Now we are ready to prove Theorems K and M, which are in fact special cases of a substantially more general theorem of Clements and Lindström that applies to arbitrary multisets [*J. Combinatorial Theory* **7** (1969), 230–238]:

Corollary C. *If A is a set of N t-multicombinations contained in the multiset $U = \{s_0 \cdot 0, s_1 \cdot 1, \ldots, s_d \cdot d\}$, where $s_0 \geq s_1 \geq \cdots \geq s_d$, then*

$$|\partial A| \geq |\partial P_{Nt}| \qquad \text{and} \qquad |\varrho A| \geq |\varrho Q_{Nt}|, \tag{91}$$

where P_{Nt} denotes the N lexicographically smallest multicombinations $d_t \ldots d_2 d_1$ of U, and Q_{Nt} denotes the N lexicographically largest.

Proof. Multicombinations of U can be represented as points $x_1 \ldots x_n$ of the torus $T(m_1, \ldots, m_n)$, where $n = d + 1$ and $m_j = s_{n-j} + 1$; we let x_j be the number of occurrences of $n - j$. This correspondence preserves lexicographic order. For example, if $U = \{0, 0, 0, 1, 1, 2, 3\}$, its 3-multicombinations are

$$000, \ 100, \ 110, \ 200, \ 210, \ 211, \ 300, \ 310, \ 311, \ 320, \ 321, \tag{92}$$

in lexicographic order, and the corresponding points $x_1 x_2 x_3 x_4$ are

$$0003, 0012, 0021, 0102, 0111, 0120, 1002, 1011, 1020, 1101, 1110. \tag{93}$$

Let T_w be the points of the torus that have weight $x_1 + \cdots + x_n = w$. Then every allowable set A of t-multicombinations is a subset of T_t. Furthermore — and this is the main point — the spread of $T_0 \cup T_1 \cup \cdots \cup T_{t-1} \cup A$ is

$$
\begin{aligned}
(T_0 \cup T_1 \cup \cdots \cup T_{t-1} \cup A)^+ &= T_0^+ \cup T_1^+ \cup \cdots \cup T_{t-1}^+ \cup A^+ \\
&= T_0 \cup T_1 \cup \cdots \cup T_t \cup \varrho A. \tag{94}
\end{aligned}
$$

Thus the upper shadow ϱA is simply $(T_0 \cup T_1 \cup \cdots \cup T_{t-1} \cup A)^+ \cap T_{t+1}$, and Theorem W tells us in essence that $|A| = N$ implies $|\varrho A| \geq |\varrho(S_{M+N} \cap T_t)|$, where $M = |T_0 \cup \cdots \cup T_{t-1}|$. Hence, by the definition of cross order, $S_{M+N} \cap T_t$ consists of the lexicographically largest N t-multicombinations, namely Q_{Nt}.

The proof that $|\partial A| \geq |\partial P_{Nt}|$ now follows by complementation (see exercise 94). ∎

EXERCISES

1. [*M23*] Explain why Golomb's rule (8) makes all sets $\{c_1, \ldots, c_t\} \subseteq \{0, \ldots, n-1\}$ correspond uniquely to multisets $\{e_1, \ldots, e_t\} \subseteq \{\infty \cdot 0, \ldots, \infty \cdot (n-t)\}$.

2. [*16*] What path in an 11×13 grid corresponds to the bit string (13)?

▶ **3.** [*21*] (R. R. Fenichel, 1968.) Show that the compositions $q_t + \cdots + q_1 + q_0$ of s into $t + 1$ nonnegative parts can be generated in lexicographic order by a simple loopless algorithm.

4. [*16*] Show that every composition $q_t \ldots q_0$ of s into $t + 1$ nonnegative parts corresponds to a composition $r_s \ldots r_0$ of t into $s + 1$ nonnegative parts. What composition corresponds to 10224000001010 under this correspondence?

▶ **5.** [*20*] What is a good way to generate all of the integer solutions to the following systems of inequalities?
   a) $n > x_t \geq x_{t-1} > x_{t-2} \geq x_{t-3} > \cdots > x_1 \geq 0$, when t is odd.
   b) $n \gg x_t \gg x_{t-1} \gg \cdots \gg x_2 \gg x_1 \gg 0$, where $a \gg b$ means $a \geq b + 2$.

6. [*M22*] How often is each step of Algorithm T performed?

7. [*22*] Design an algorithm that runs through the "dual" combinations $b_s \ldots b_2 b_1$ in *decreasing* lexicographic order (see (5) and Table 1). Like Algorithm T, your algorithm should avoid redundant assignments and unnecessary searching.

8. [*M23*] Design an algorithm that generates all (s,t)-combinations $a_{n-1} \ldots a_1 a_0$ lexicographically in bitstring form. The total running time should be $O(\binom{n}{t})$, assuming that $st > 0$.

9. [*M26*] When all (s,t)-combinations $a_{n-1} \ldots a_1 a_0$ are listed in lexicographic order, let $2A_{st}$ be the total number of bit changes between adjacent strings. For example, $A_{33} = 25$ because there are respectively

$$2 + 2 + 2 + 4 + 2 + 2 + 4 + 2 + 2 + 6 + 2 + 2 + 4 + 2 + 2 + 4 + 2 + 2 + 2 = 50$$

bit changes between the 20 strings in Table 1.

a) Show that $A_{st} = \min(s,t) + A_{(s-1)t} + A_{s(t-1)}$ when $st > 0$; $A_{st} = 0$ when $st = 0$.

b) Prove that $A_{st} < 2\binom{s+t}{t}$.

▶ **10.** [*21*] The "World Series" of baseball is traditionally a competition in which the American League champion (A) plays the National League champion (N) until one of them has beaten the other four times. What is a good way to list all possible scenarios AAAA, AAANA, AAANNA, ..., NNNN? What is a simple way to assign consecutive integers to those scenarios?

11. [*19*] Which of the scenarios in exercise 10 occurred most often during the 1900s? Which of them never occurred? [*Hint:* World Series scores are easily found on the Internet.]

12. [*HM32*] A set V of n-bit vectors that is closed under addition modulo 2 is called a *binary vector space*.

a) Prove that every such V contains 2^t elements, for some integer t, and can be represented as the set $\{x_1\alpha_1 \oplus \cdots \oplus x_t\alpha_t \mid 0 \le x_1, \ldots, x_t \le 1\}$ where the vectors $\alpha_1, \ldots, \alpha_t$ form a "canonical basis" with the following property: There is a t-combination $c_t \ldots c_2 c_1$ of $\{0, 1, \ldots, n-1\}$ such that, if α_k is the binary vector $a_{k(n-1)} \ldots a_{k1} a_{k0}$, we have

$$a_{kc_j} = [j=k] \quad \text{for } 1 \le j, k \le t; \qquad\qquad a_{kl} = 0 \quad \text{for } 0 \le l < c_k, 1 \le k \le t.$$

For example, the canonical bases with $n = 9$, $t = 4$, and $c_4 c_3 c_2 c_1 = 7641$ have the general form

$$
\begin{aligned}
\alpha_1 &= {*}\,0\,0\,{*}\,0\,{*}\,{*}\,1\,0, \\
\alpha_2 &= {*}\,0\,0\,{*}\,1\,0\,0\,0\,0, \\
\alpha_3 &= {*}\,0\,1\,0\,0\,0\,0\,0\,0, \\
\alpha_4 &= {*}\,1\,0\,0\,0\,0\,0\,0\,0;
\end{aligned}
$$

there are 2^8 ways to replace the eight asterisks by 0s and/or 1s, and each of these defines a canonical basis. We call t the dimension of V.

b) How many t-dimensional spaces are possible with n-bit vectors?

c) Design an algorithm to generate all canonical bases $(\alpha_1, \ldots, \alpha_t)$ of dimension t. *Hint:* Let the associated combinations $c_t \ldots c_1$ increase lexicographically as in Algorithm L.

d) What is the 1000000th basis visited by your algorithm when $n = 9$ and $t = 4$?

13. [*25*] A one-dimensional *Ising configuration* of length n, weight t, and energy r, is a binary string $a_{n-1} \ldots a_0$ such that $\sum_{j=0}^{n-1} a_j = t$ and $\sum_{j=1}^{n-1} b_j = r$, where $b_j =$

$a_j \oplus a_{j-1}$. For example, $a_{12} \ldots a_0 = 1100100100011$ has weight 6 and energy 6, since $b_{12} \ldots b_1 = 010110110010$.

Design an algorithm to generate all such configurations, given n, t, and r.

14. [*26*] When the binary strings $a_{n-1} \ldots a_1 a_0$ of (s,t)-combinations are generated in lexicographic order, we sometimes need to change $2 \min(s,t)$ bits to get from one combination to the next. For example, 011100 is followed by 100011 in Table 1. Therefore we apparently cannot hope to generate all combinations with a loopless algorithm unless we visit them in some other order.

Show, however, that there actually is a way to compute the lexicographic successor of a given combination in $O(1)$ steps, if each combination is represented indirectly in a doubly linked list as follows: There are arrays $l[0], \ldots, l[n]$ and $r[0], \ldots, r[n]$ such that $l[r[j]] = j$ for $0 \le j \le n$. If $x_0 = l[0]$ and $x_j = l[x_{j-1}]$ for $0 < j < n$, then $a_j = [x_j > s]$ for $0 \le j < n$.

15. [*M22*] Use the fact that dual combinations $b_s \ldots b_2 b_1$ occur in reverse lexicographic order to prove that the sum $\binom{b_s}{s} + \cdots + \binom{b_2}{2} + \binom{b_1}{1}$ has a simple relation to the sum $\binom{c_t}{t} + \cdots + \binom{c_2}{2} + \binom{c_1}{1}$.

16. [*M21*] What is the millionth combination generated by Algorithm L when t is (a) 2? (b) 3? (c) 4? (d) 5? (e) 1000000?

17. [*HM25*] Given N and t, what is a good way to compute the combinatorial representation (20)?

▶ **18.** [*20*] What binary tree do we get when the binomial tree T_n is represented by "right child" and "left sibling" pointers as in exercise 2.3.2–5?

19. [*21*] Instead of labeling the branches of the binomial tree T_4 as shown in (22), we could label each node with the bit string of its corresponding combination:

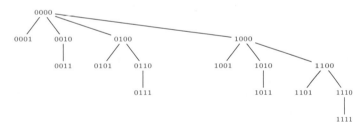

If T_∞ has been labeled in this way, suppressing leading zeros, preorder is the same as the ordinary increasing order of binary notation; so the millionth node turns out to be 11110100001000111111. But what is the millionth node of T_∞ in *postorder*?

20. [*M20*] Devise generating functions g and h such that Algorithm F finds exactly $[z^N] g(z)$ feasible combinations and sets $t \leftarrow t + 1$ exactly $[z^N] h(z)$ times.

21. [*M22*] (Joan E. Miller, 1971.) Prove the alternating combination law (30).

22. [*M23*] What is the millionth revolving-door combination visited by Algorithm R when t is (a) 2? (b) 3? (c) 4? (d) 5? (e) 1000000?

23. [*M24*] Suppose we augment Algorithm R by setting $j \leftarrow t + 1$ in step R1, and $j \leftarrow 1$ if R3 goes directly to R2. Find the probability distribution of j, and its average value. What does this imply about the running time of the algorithm?

▶ **24.** [*M25*] (W. H. Payne, 1974.) Continuing the previous exercise, let j_k be the value of j on the kth visit by Algorithm R. Show that $|j_{k+1} - j_k| \le 2$, and explain how to make the algorithm loopless by exploiting this property.

25. [*M35*] Let $c_t \ldots c_2 c_1$ and $c'_t \ldots c'_2 c'_1$ be the Nth and N'th combinations generated by the revolving-door method, Algorithm R. If the set $C = \{c_t, \ldots, c_2, c_1\}$ has $m > 0$ elements not in $C' = \{c'_t, \ldots, c'_2, c'_1\}$, prove that $|N - N'| > \sum_{k=1}^{m-1} \binom{2k}{k-1}$.

26. [*26*] Do elements of the *ternary* reflected Gray code have properties similar to the revolving-door Gray code Γ_{st}, if we extract only the n-tuples $a_{n-1} \ldots a_1 a_0$ such that (a) $a_{n-1} + \cdots + a_1 + a_0 = t$? (b) $\{a_{n-1}, \ldots, a_1, a_0\} = \{r \cdot 0, s \cdot 1, t \cdot 2\}$?

▶ **27.** [*25*] Show that there is a simple way to generate all combinations of *at most* t elements of $\{0, 1, \ldots, n-1\}$, using only Gray-code-like transitions $0 \leftrightarrow 1$ and $01 \leftrightarrow 10$. (In other words, each step should either insert a new element, delete an element, or shift an element by ± 1.) For example,

$$0000, \ 0001, \ 0011, \ 0010, \ 0110, \ 0101, \ 0100, \ 1100, \ 1010, \ 1001, \ 1000$$

is one such sequence when $n = 4$ and $t = 2$. *Hint:* Think of Chinese rings.

28. [*M21*] True or false: A listing of (s, t)-combinations $a_{n-1} \ldots a_1 a_0$ in bitstring form is in genlex order if and only if the corresponding index-form listings $b_s \ldots b_2 b_1$ (for the 0s) and $c_t \ldots c_2 c_1$ (for the 1s) are both in genlex order.

▶ **29.** [*M28*] (P. J. Chase.) Given a string on the symbols +, -, and 0, say that an *R-block* is a substring of the form $-^{k+1}$ that is preceded by 0 and not followed by -; an *L-block* is a substring of the form $+-^k$ that is followed by 0; in both cases $k \ge 0$. For example, the string +00++-++-000- has two L-blocks and one R-block, shown in gray. Notice that blocks cannot overlap.

We form the *successor* of such a string as follows, whenever at least one block is present: Replace the rightmost $0-^{k+1}$ by $-+^k 0$, if the rightmost block is an R-block; otherwise replace the rightmost $+-^k 0$ by $0+^{k+1}$. Also negate the first sign, if any, that appears to the right of the block that has been changed. For example,

$$-+00++- \ \to \ -0+0-+- \ \to \ -0+-0-- \ \to \ -0+--+0 \ \to \ -0+--0+ \ \to \ -00+++-,$$

where the notation $\alpha \to \beta$ means that β is the successor of α.

a) What strings have no blocks (and therefore no successor)?

b) Can there be a cycle of strings with $\alpha_0 \to \alpha_1 \to \cdots \to \alpha_{k-1} \to \alpha_0$?

c) Prove that if $\alpha \to \beta$ then $-\beta \to -\alpha$, where "$-$" means "negate all the signs." (Therefore every string has at most one predecessor.)

d) Show that if $\alpha_0 \to \alpha_1 \to \cdots \to \alpha_k$ and $k > 0$, the strings α_0 and α_k do not have all their 0s in the same positions. (Therefore, if α_0 has s signs and t zeros, k must be less than $\binom{s+t}{t}$.)

e) Prove that every string α with s signs and t zeros belongs to exactly one chain $\alpha_0 \to \alpha_1 \to \cdots \to \alpha_{\binom{s+t}{t}-1}$.

30. [*M32*] The previous exercise defines 2^s ways to generate all combinations of s 0s and t 1s, via the mapping $+ \mapsto 0$, $- \mapsto 0$, and $0 \mapsto 1$. Show that each of these ways is a homogeneous genlex sequence, definable by an appropriate recurrence. Is Chase's sequence (37) a special case of this general construction?

31. [*M23*] How many genlex listings of (s, t)-combinations are possible in (a) bitstring form $a_{n-1} \ldots a_1 a_0$? (b) index-list form $c_t \ldots c_2 c_1$?

▶ **32.** [*M32*] How many of the genlex listings of (s,t)-combination strings $a_{n-1} \ldots a_1 a_0$ (a) have the revolving-door property? (b) are homogeneous?

33. [*HM33*] How many of the genlex listings in exercise 31(b) are near-perfect?

34. [*M32*] Continuing exercise 33, explain how to find such schemes that are as near as possible to perfection, in the sense that the number of "imperfect" transitions $c_j \leftarrow c_j \pm 2$ is minimized, when s and t are not too large.

35. [*M26*] How many steps of Chase's sequence C_{st} use an imperfect transition?

▶ **36.** [*M21*] Prove that method (39) performs the operation $j \leftarrow j+1$ a total of exactly $\binom{s+t}{t} - 1$ times as it generates all (s,t)-combinations $a_{n-1} \ldots a_1 a_0$, given any genlex scheme for combinations in bitstring form.

▶ **37.** [*27*] What algorithm results when the general genlex method (39) is used to produce (s,t)-combinations $a_{n-1} \ldots a_1 a_0$ in (a) lexicographic order? (b) the revolving-door order of Algorithm R? (c) the homogeneous order of (31)?

38. [*26*] Design a genlex algorithm like Algorithm C for the *reverse* sequence C_{st}^R.

39. [*M21*] When $s = 12$ and $t = 14$, how many combinations precede the bit string 11001001000011111101101010 in Chase's sequence C_{st}? (See (41).)

40. [*M22*] What is the millionth combination in Chase's sequence C_{st}, when $s = 12$ and $t = 14$?

41. [*M27*] Show that there is a permutation $c(0)$, $c(1)$, $c(2)$, $\ldots$ of the nonnegative integers such that the elements of Chase's sequence C_{st} are obtained by complementing the least significant $s + t$ bits of the elements $c(k)$ for $0 \le k < 2^{s+t}$ that have weight $\nu(c(k)) = s$. (Thus the sequence $\bar{c}(0)$, $\ldots$, $\bar{c}(2^n - 1)$ contains, as subsequences, all of the C_{st} for which $s + t = n$, just as Gray binary code $g(0)$, $\ldots$, $g(2^n - 1)$ contains all the revolving-door sequences Γ_{st}.) Explain how to compute the binary representation $c(k) = (\ldots a_2 a_1 a_0)_2$ from the binary representation $k = (\ldots b_2 b_1 b_0)_2$.

42. [*HM34*] Use generating functions of the form $\sum_{s,t} g_{st} w^s z^t$ to analyze each step of Algorithm C.

43. [*20*] Prove or disprove: If $s(x)$ and $p(x)$ denote respectively the successor and predecessor of x in endo-order, then $s(x + 1) = p(x) + 1$.

▶ **44.** [*M21*] Let $C_t(n) - 1$ denote the sequence obtained from $C_t(n)$ by striking out all combinations with $c_1 = 0$, then replacing $c_t \ldots c_1$ by $(c_t - 1) \ldots (c_1 - 1)$ in the combinations that remain. Show that $C_t(n) - 1$ is near-perfect.

45. [*32*] Exploit endo-order and the expansions sketched in (44) to generate the combinations $c_t \ldots c_2 c_1$ of Chase's sequence $C_t(n)$ with a nonrecursive procedure.

▶ **46.** [*33*] Construct a nonrecursive algorithm for the dual combinations $b_s \ldots b_2 b_1$ of Chase's sequence C_{st}, namely for the positions of the zeros in $a_{n-1} \ldots a_1 a_0$.

47. [*26*] Implement the near-perfect multiset permutation method of (46) and (47).

48. [*M21*] Suppose $\alpha_0, \alpha_1, \ldots, \alpha_{N-1}$ is any listing of the permutations of the multiset $\{s_1 \cdot 1, \ldots, s_d \cdot d\}$, where α_k differs from α_{k+1} by the interchange of two elements. Let $\beta_0, \ldots, \beta_{M-1}$ be any revolving-door listing for (s,t)-combinations, where $s = s_0$, $t = s_1 + \cdots + s_d$, and $M = \binom{s+t}{t}$. Then let Λ_j be the list of M elements obtained by starting with $\alpha_j \uparrow \beta_0$ and applying the revolving-door exchanges; here $\alpha \uparrow \beta$ denotes the string obtained by substituting the elements of α for the 1s in β, preserving left-right order. For example, if $\beta_0, \ldots, \beta_{M-1}$ is 0110, 0101, 1100, 1001, 0011, 1010, and if $\alpha_j = 12$, then Λ_j is 0120, 0102, 1200, 1002, 0012, 1020. (The revolving-door listing need *not* be homogeneous.)

Prove that the list (47) contains all permutations of $\{s_0 \cdot 0, s_1 \cdot 1, \ldots, s_d \cdot d\}$, and that adjacent permutations differ from each other by the interchange of two elements.

49. [*HM23*] If q is a primitive mth root of unity, such as $e^{2\pi i/m}$, show that

$$\binom{n}{k}_q = \binom{\lfloor n/m \rfloor}{\lfloor k/m \rfloor}\binom{n \bmod m}{k \bmod m}_q.$$

▶ **50.** [*HM25*] Extend the formula of the previous exercise to *q-multinomial* coefficients

$$\binom{n_1 + \cdots + n_t}{n_1, \ldots, n_t}_q.$$

51. [*25*] Find all Hamiltonian paths in the graph whose vertices are permutations of $\{0,0,0,1,1,1\}$ related by adjacent transposition. Which of those paths are equivalent under the operations of interchanging 0s with 1s and/or left-right reflection?

52. [*M37*] Generalizing Theorem P, find a necessary and sufficient condition that all permutations of the multiset $\{s_0 \cdot 0, \ldots, s_d \cdot d\}$ can be generated by adjacent transpositions $a_j a_{j-1} \leftrightarrow a_{j-1} a_j$.

53. [*M46*] (D. H. Lehmer, 1965.) Suppose the N permutations of $\{s_0 \cdot 0, \ldots, s_d \cdot d\}$ cannot be generated by a perfect scheme, because $(N + x)/2$ of them have an even number of inversions, where $x \geq 2$. Is it possible to generate them all with a sequence of $N + x - 2$ adjacent interchanges $a_{\delta_k} \leftrightarrow a_{\delta_k - 1}$ for $1 \leq k < N + x - 1$, where $x - 1$ cases are "spurs" with $\delta_k = \delta_{k-1}$ that take us back to the permutation we've just seen? For example, a suitable sequence $\delta_1 \ldots \delta_{94}$ for the 90 permutations of $\{0,0,1,1,2,2\}$, where $x = \binom{2+2+2}{2,2,2}_{-1} = 6$, is $234535432523451\alpha 42\alpha^R 51\alpha 42\alpha^R 51\alpha 4$, where $\alpha = 45352542345355$, if we start with $a_5 a_4 a_3 a_2 a_1 a_0 = 221100$.

54. [*M40*] For what values of s and t can all (s,t)-combinations be generated if we allow end-around swaps $a_{n-1} \leftrightarrow a_0$ in addition to adjacent interchanges $a_j \leftrightarrow a_{j-1}$?

▶ **55.** [*33*] (Frank Ruskey, 2004.) (a) Show that all (s,t)-combinations $a_{s+t-1} \ldots a_1 a_0$ can be generated efficiently by doing successive rotations $a_j a_{j-1} \ldots a_0 \leftarrow a_{j-1} \ldots a_0 a_j$. (b) What MMIX instructions will take $(a_{s+t-1} \ldots a_1 a_0)_2$ to its successor, when $s+t < 64$?

56. [*M41*] (Buck and Wiedemann, 1984.) Can all (t,t)-combinations $a_{2t-1} \ldots a_1 a_0$ be generated by repeatedly swapping a_0 with some other element?

▶ **57.** [*22*] (Frank Ruskey.) Can a piano player run through all possible 4-note chords that span at most one octave, changing only one finger at a time? This is the problem of generating all combinations $c_t \ldots c_1$ such that $n > c_t > \cdots > c_1 \geq 0$ and $c_t - c_1 < m$, where $t = 4$ and (a) $m = 8$, $n = 52$ if we consider only the white notes of a piano keyboard; (b) $m = 13$, $n = 88$ if we consider also the black notes.

58. [*20*] Consider the piano player's problem of exercise 57 with the additional condition that the chords don't involve adjacent notes. (In other words, $c_{j+1} > c_j + 1$ for $t > j \geq 1$. Such chords tend to be more harmonious.)

59. [*M25*] Is there a *perfect* solution to the 4-note piano player's problem, in which each step moves a finger to an *adjacent* key?

60. [*23*] Design an algorithm to generate all *bounded* compositions

$$t = r_s + \cdots + r_1 + r_0, \qquad \text{where } 0 \leq r_j \leq m_j \text{ for } s \geq j \geq 0.$$

61. [*32*] Show that all bounded compositions can be generated by changing only two of the parts at each step.

▶ **62.** [*M27*] A *contingency table* is an $m \times n$ matrix of nonnegative integers (a_{ij}) having given row sums $r_i = \sum_{j=1}^{n} a_{ij}$ and column sums $c_j = \sum_{i=1}^{m} a_{ij}$, where $r_1 + \cdots + r_m = c_1 + \cdots + c_n$.

a) Show that $2 \times n$ contingency tables are equivalent to bounded compositions.

b) What is the lexicographically largest contingency table for $(r_1, \ldots, r_m; c_1, \ldots, c_n)$, when matrix entries are read row-wise from left to right and top to bottom, namely in the order $(a_{11}, a_{12}, \ldots, a_{1n}, a_{21}, a_{22}, \ldots, a_{2n}, \ldots, a_{m1}, a_{m2}, \ldots, a_{mn})$?

c) What is the lexicographically largest contingency table for $(r_1, \ldots, r_m; c_1, \ldots, c_n)$, when matrix entries are read column-wise from top to bottom and left to right, namely in the order $(a_{11}, a_{21}, \ldots, a_{m1}, a_{12}, a_{22}, \ldots, a_{m2}, \ldots, a_{1n}, a_{2n}, \ldots, a_{mn})$?

d) What is the lexicographically smallest contingency table for $(r_1, \ldots, r_m; c_1, \ldots, c_n)$, in the row-wise and column-wise senses?

e) Explain how to generate all contingency tables for $(r_1, \ldots, r_m; c_1, \ldots, c_n)$ in lexicographic order.

63. [*M41*] Show that all contingency tables for $(r_1, \ldots, r_m; c_1, \ldots, c_n)$ can be generated by changing exactly four entries of the matrix at each step.

▶ **64.** [*M30*] Construct a genlex Gray cycle for all of the $2^s \binom{s+t}{t}$ *subcubes* that have s digits and t asterisks, using only the transformations $*0 \leftrightarrow 0*$, $*1 \leftrightarrow 1*$, $0 \leftrightarrow 1$. For example, one such cycle when $s = t = 2$ is

$$(00**, 01**, 0*1*, 0**1, 0**0, 0*0*, *00*, *01*, *0*1, *0*0, **00, **01,$$
$$**11, **10, *1*0, *1*1, *11*, *10*, 1*0*, 1**0, 1**1, 1*1*, 11**, 10**).$$

65. [*M40*] Enumerate the total number of genlex Gray paths on subcubes that use only the transformations allowed in exercise 64. How many of those paths are cycles?

▶ **66.** [*22*] Given $n \geq t \geq 0$, show that there is a Gray path through all of the canonical bases $(\alpha_1, \ldots, \alpha_t)$ of exercise 12, changing just one bit at each step. For example, one such path when $n = 3$ and $t = 2$ is

$$\frac{001}{010}, \quad \frac{101}{010}, \quad \frac{101}{110}, \quad \frac{001}{110}, \quad \frac{001}{100}, \quad \frac{011}{100}, \quad \frac{010}{100}.$$

67. [*46*] Consider the Ising configurations of exercise 13 for which $a_0 = 0$. Given n, t, and r, is there a Gray cycle for these configurations in which all transitions have the forms $0^k 1 \leftrightarrow 10^k$ or $01^k \leftrightarrow 1^k 0$? For example, in the case $n = 9$, $t = 5$, $r = 6$, there is a unique cycle

$$(010101110, 010110110, 011010110, 011011010, 011101010, 010111010).$$

68. [*M01*] If α is a t-combination, what is (a) $\partial^t \alpha$? (b) $\partial^{t+1} \alpha$?

▶ **69.** [*M22*] How large is the smallest set A of t-combinations for which $|\partial A| < |A|$?

70. [*M25*] What is the maximum value of $\kappa_t N - N$, for $N \geq 0$?

71. [*M20*] How many t-cliques can a million-edge graph have?

▶ **72.** [*M22*] Show that if N has the degree-t combinatorial representation (57), there is an easy way to find the degree-s combinatorial representation of the complementary number $M = \binom{s+t}{t} - N$, whenever $N < \binom{s+t}{t}$. Derive (63) as a consequence.

73. [*M23*] (A. J. W. Hilton, 1976.) Let A be a set of s-combinations and B a set of t-combinations, both contained in $U = \{0, \ldots, n-1\}$ where $n \geq s + t$. Show that if A and B are *cross-intersecting*, in the sense that $\alpha \cap \beta \neq \emptyset$ for all $\alpha \in A$ and $\beta \in B$, then so are the sets Q_{Mns} and Q_{Nnt} defined in Theorem K, where $M = |A|$ and $N = |B|$.

74. [*M21*] What are $|\varrho P_{Nt}|$ and $|\varrho Q_{Nnt}|$ in Theorem K?

75. [*M20*] The right-hand side of (60) is not always the degree-$(t-1)$ combinatorial representation of $\kappa_t N$, because $v-1$ might be zero. Show, however, that a positive integer N has at most two representations if we allow $v=0$ in (57), and both of them yield the same value $\kappa_t N$ according to (60). Therefore

$$\kappa_k \kappa_{k+1} \ldots \kappa_t N = \binom{n_t}{k-1} + \binom{n_{t-1}}{k-2} + \cdots + \binom{n_v}{k-1+v-t} \qquad \text{for } 1 \le k \le t.$$

76. [*M20*] Find a simple formula for $\kappa_t(N+1) - \kappa_t N$.

▶ **77.** [*M26*] Prove the following properties of the κ functions by manipulating binomial coefficients, without assuming Theorem K:

    a) $\kappa_t(M+N) \le \kappa_t M + \kappa_t N$.

    b) $\kappa_t(M+N) \le \max(\kappa_t M, N) + \kappa_{t-1}N$.

Hint: $\binom{m_t}{t} + \cdots + \binom{m_1}{1} + \binom{n_t}{t} + \cdots + \binom{n_1}{1}$ is equal to $\binom{m_t \vee n_t}{t} + \cdots + \binom{m_1 \vee n_1}{1} + \binom{m_t \wedge n_t}{t} + \cdots + \binom{m_1 \wedge n_1}{1}$, where $\vee$ and $\wedge$ denote max and min.

78. [*M22*] Show that Theorem K follows easily from inequality (b) in the previous exercise. Conversely, both inequalities are simple consequences of Theorem K. *Hint:* Any set A of t-combinations can be written $A = A_1 + A_0 0$, where $A_1 = \{\alpha \in A \mid 0 \notin \alpha\}$.

79. [*M23*] Prove that if $t \ge 2$, we have $M \ge \mu_t N$ if and only if $M + \lambda_{t-1}M \ge N$.

80. [*HM26*] (L. Lovász, 1979.) The function $\binom{x}{t}$ increases monotonically from 0 to ∞ as x increases from $t-1$ to ∞; hence we can define

$$\underline{\kappa}_t N = \binom{x}{t-1}, \qquad \text{if } N = \binom{x}{t} \text{ and } x \ge t-1.$$

Prove that $\kappa_t N \ge \underline{\kappa}_t N$ for all integers $t \ge 1$ and $N \ge 0$. *Hint:* Equality holds when x is an integer.

▶ **81.** [*M27*] Show that the minimum shadow sizes in Theorem M are given by (64).

82. [*HM31*] The Takagi function of Fig. 47 is defined for $0 \le x \le 1$ by the formula

$$\tau(x) = \sum_{k=1}^{\infty} \int_0^x r_k(t)\,dt,$$

where $r_k(t) = (-1)^{\lfloor 2^k t \rfloor}$ is the Rademacher function of Eq. 7.2.1.1–(16).

    a) Prove that $\tau(x)$ is continuous in the interval $[0 .. 1]$, but its derivative does not exist at any point.

    b) Show that $\tau(x)$ is the only continuous function that satisfies

$$\tau(\tfrac{1}{2}x) = \tau(1 - \tfrac{1}{2}x) = \tfrac{1}{2}x + \tfrac{1}{2}\tau(x) \qquad \text{for } 0 \le x \le 1.$$

    c) What is the asymptotic value of $\tau(\epsilon)$ when ϵ is small?

    d) Prove that $\tau(x)$ is rational when x is rational.

    e) Find all roots of the equation $\tau(x) = 1/2$.

    f) Find all roots of the equation $\tau(x) = \max_{0 \le x \le 1} \tau(x)$.

83. [*HM46*] Determine the set R of all rational numbers r such that the equation $\tau(x) = r$ has uncountably many solutions. If $\tau(x)$ is rational and x is irrational, is it true that $\tau(x) \in R$? (*Warning:* This problem can be addictive.)

84. [*HM27*] If $T = \binom{2t-1}{t}$, prove the asymptotic formula

$$\kappa_t N - N = \frac{T}{t}\left(\tau\left(\frac{N}{T}\right) + O\left(\frac{(\log t)^3}{t}\right)\right) \qquad \text{for } 0 \le N \le T.$$

85. [*HM21*] Relate the functions $\lambda_t N$ and $\mu_t N$ to the Takagi function $\tau(x)$.

86. [*M20*] Prove the law of spread/core duality, $X^{\sim+} = X^{\circ\sim}$.

87. [*M21*] True or false: (a) $X \subseteq Y^\circ$ if and only if $Y^\sim \subseteq X^{\sim\circ}$; (b) $X^{\circ+\circ} = X^\circ$; (c) $\alpha M \leq N$ if and only if $M \leq \beta N$.

88. [*M20*] Explain why cross order is useful, by completing the proof of Lemma S.

89. [*16*] Compute the α and β functions for the $2 \times 2 \times 3$ torus (69).

90. [*M22*] Prove the basic compression lemma, (85).

91. [*M24*] Prove Theorem W for two-dimensional toruses $T(l, m)$, $l \leq m$.

92. [*M28*] Let $x = x_1 \ldots x_{n-1}$ be the Nth element of the torus $T(m_1, \ldots, m_{n-1})$, and let S be the set of all elements of $T(m_1, \ldots, m_{n-1}, m)$ that are $\preceq x_1 \ldots x_{n-1}(m-1)$ in cross order. If N_a elements of S have final component a, for $0 \leq a < m$, prove that $N_{m-1} = N$ and $N_{a-1} = \alpha N_a$ for $1 \leq a < m$, where α is the spread function for standard sets in $T(m_1, \ldots, m_{n-1})$.

93. [*M25*] (a) Find an N for which the conclusion of Theorem W is false when the parameters m_1, m_2, $\ldots$, m_n have not been sorted into nondecreasing order. (b) Where does the proof of that theorem use the hypothesis that $m_1 \leq m_2 \leq \cdots \leq m_n$?

94. [*M20*] Show that the ∂ half of Corollary C follows from the ϱ half. *Hint:* The complements of the multicombinations (92) with respect to U are 3211, 3210, 3200, 3110, 3100, 3000, 2110, 2100, 2000, 1100, 1000.

95. [*17*] Explain why Theorems K and M follow from Corollary C.

▶ **96.** [*M22*] If S is an infinite sequence $(s_0, s_1, s_2, \ldots)$ of positive integers, let

$$\binom{S(n)}{k} = [z^k] \prod_{j=0}^{n-1} (1 + z + \cdots + z^{s_j});$$

thus $\binom{S(n)}{k}$ is the ordinary binomial coefficient $\binom{n}{k}$ if $s_0 = s_1 = s_2 = \cdots = 1$.

Generalizing the combinatorial number system, show that every nonnegative integer N has a unique representation

$$N = \binom{S(n_t)}{t} + \binom{S(n_{t-1})}{t-1} + \cdots + \binom{S(n_1)}{1}$$

where $n_t \geq n_{t-1} \geq \cdots \geq n_1 \geq 0$ and $\{n_t, n_{t-1}, \ldots, n_1\} \subseteq \{s_0 \cdot 0, s_1 \cdot 1, s_2 \cdot 2, \ldots\}$. Use this representation to give a simple formula for the numbers $|\partial P_{Nt}|$ in Corollary C.

▶ **97.** [*M26*] The text remarked that the vertices of a convex polyhedron can be perturbed slightly so that all of its faces are simplexes. In general, any set of combinations that contains the shadows of all its elements is called a *simplicial complex*; thus C is a simplicial complex if and only if $\alpha \subseteq \beta$ and $\beta \in C$ implies that $\alpha \in C$, if and only if C is an order ideal with respect to set inclusion.

The *size vector* of a simplicial complex C on n vertices is $(N_0, N_1, \ldots, N_n)$ when C contains exactly N_t combinations of size t.

a) What are the size vectors of the five regular solids (the tetrahedron, cube, octahedron, dodecahedron, and icosahedron), when their vertices are slightly tweaked?

b) Construct a simplicial complex with size vector $(1, 4, 5, 2, 0)$.

c) Find a necessary and sufficient condition that a given size vector $(N_0, N_1, \ldots, N_n)$ is feasible.

d) Prove that $(N_0, \ldots, N_n)$ is feasible if and only if its "dual" vector $(\overline{N}_0, \ldots, \overline{N}_n)$ is feasible, where we define $\overline{N}_t = \binom{n}{t} - N_{n-t}$.

e) List all feasible size vectors $(N_0, N_1, N_2, N_3, N_4)$ and their duals. Which of them are self-dual?

98. [*30*] Continuing exercise 97, find an efficient way to count the feasible size vectors $(N_0, N_1, \ldots, N_n)$ when $n \leq 100$.

99. [*M25*] A *clutter* is a set C of combinations that are incomparable, in the sense that $\alpha \subseteq \beta$ and $\alpha, \beta \in C$ implies $\alpha = \beta$. The size vector of a clutter is defined as in exercise 97.

a) Find a necessary and sufficient condition that $(M_0, M_1, \ldots, M_n)$ is the size vector of a clutter.

b) List all such size vectors in the case $n = 4$.

▶ **100.** [*M30*] (Clements and Lindström.) Let A be a "simplicial multicomplex," a set of submultisets of the multiset U in Corollary C with the property that $\partial A \subseteq A$. How large can the total weight $\nu A = \sum \{|\alpha| \mid \alpha \in A\}$ be when $|A| = N$?

101. [*M25*] If $f(x_1, \ldots, x_n)$ is a Boolean formula, let $F(p)$ be the probability that $f(x_1, \ldots, x_n) = 1$ when each variable x_j independently is 1 with probability p.

a) Calculate $G(p)$ and $H(p)$ for the Boolean formulas $g(w, x, y, z) = wxz \vee wyz \vee xy\bar{z}$, $h(w, x, y, z) = \bar{w}yz \vee xyz$.

b) Show that there is a *monotone* Boolean function $f(w, x, y, z)$ such that $F(p) = G(p)$, but there is no such function with $F(p) = H(p)$. Explain how to test this condition in general.

102. [*HM35*] (F. S. Macaulay, 1927.) A *polynomial ideal I* in the variables $\{x_1 \ldots, x_s\}$ is a set of polynomials closed under the operations of addition, multiplication by a constant, and multiplication by any of the variables. It is called *homogeneous* if it consists of all linear combinations of a set of homogeneous polynomials, namely of polynomials like $xy + z^2$ whose terms all have the same degree. Let N_t be the maximum number of linearly independent elements of degree t in I. For example, if $s = 2$, the set of all $\alpha(x_0, x_1, x_2)(x_0 x_1^2 - 2x_1 x_2^2) + \beta(x_0, x_1, x_2)x_0 x_1 x_2^2$, where α and β run through all possible polynomials in $\{x_0, x_1, x_2\}$, is a homogeneous polynomial ideal with $N_0 = N_1 = N_2 = 0$, $N_3 = 1$, $N_4 = 4$, $N_5 = 9$, $N_6 = 15, \ldots$.

a) Prove that for any such ideal I there is another ideal I' in which all homogeneous polynomials of degree t are linear combinations of N_t independent *monomials*. (A monomial is a product of variables, like $x_1^3 x_2 x_5^4$.)

b) Use Theorem M and (64) to prove that $N_{t+1} \geq N_t + \kappa_s N_t$ for all $t \geq 0$.

c) Show that $N_{t+1} > N_t + \kappa_s N_t$ occurs for only finitely many t. (This statement is equivalent to "Hilbert's basis theorem," proved by David Hilbert in *Göttinger Nachrichten* (1888), 450–457; *Math. Annalen* **36** (1890), 473–534.)

▶ **103.** [*M38*] The shadow of a subcube $a_1 \ldots a_n$, where each a_j is either 0 or 1 or $*$, is obtained by replacing some $*$ by 0 or 1. For example,

$$\partial 0*11*0 = \{0011*0, 0111*0, 0*1100, 0*1110\}.$$

Find a set P_{Nst} such that, if A is any set of N subcubes $a_1 \ldots a_n$ having s digits and t asterisks, $|\partial A| \geq |P_{Nst}|$.

104. [*M41*] The shadow of a binary string $a_1 \ldots a_n$ is obtained by deleting one of its bits. For example,

$$\partial 110010010 = \{10010010, 11010010, 11000010, 11001000, 11001010, 11001001\}.$$

Find a set P_{Nn} such that, if A is any set of N binary strings $a_1 \ldots a_n$, $|\partial A| \geq |P_{Nn}|$.

105. [*M20*] A *universal cycle of t-combinations* for $\{0, 1, \ldots, n-1\}$ is a cycle of $\binom{n}{t}$ numbers whose blocks of t consecutive elements run through every t-combination $\{c_1, \ldots, c_t\}$. For example,

$$(0214506132051624315263042536410 3546)$$

is a universal cycle when $t = 3$ and $n = 7$.

Prove that no such cycle is possible unless $\binom{n}{t}$ is a multiple of n.

106. [*M21*] (L. Poinsot, 1809.) Find a "nice" universal cycle of 2-combinations for $\{0, 1, \ldots, 2m\}$. *Hint:* Consider the differences of consecutive elements, mod $(2m + 1)$.

107. [*22*] (O. Terquem, 1849.) Poinsot's theorem implies that all 28 dominoes of a traditional "double-six" set can be arranged in a cycle so that the spots of adjacent dominoes match each other:

How many such cycles are possible?

108. [*M31*] Find universal cycles of 3-combinations for the sets $\{0, \ldots, n-1\}$ when $n \bmod 3 \neq 0$.

109. [*M31*] Find universal cycles of 3-*multicombinations* for $\{0, 1, \ldots, n-1\}$ when $n \bmod 3 \neq 0$ (namely for combinations $d_1 d_2 d_3$ with repetitions permitted). For example,

$$(0001224111233022234413334002444 0113)$$

is such a cycle when $n = 5$.

▶ **110.** [*26*] *Cribbage* is a game played with 52 cards, where each card has a suit (♣, ◇, ♡, or ♠) and a face value (A, 2, 3, 4, 5, 6, 7, 8, 9, 10, J, Q, or K). Its players must become adept at computing the score of a 5-card combination $C = \{c_1, c_2, c_3, c_4, c_5\}$, where a player holds $\{c_1, c_2, c_3, c_4\}$ and card c_5 is called the *starter*. The score is the sum of points computed as follows, for each subset S of C: Let $|S| = s$.

   i) Fifteens: If $\sum \{v(c) \mid c \in S\} = 15$, where $(v(A), v(2), v(3), \ldots, v(9), v(10), v(J), v(Q), v(K)) = (1, 2, 3, \ldots, 9, 10, 10, 10, 10)$, score two points.

   ii) Pairs: If $s = 2$ and both cards have the same face value, score two points.

   iii) Runs: If $s \geq 3$ and the face values are consecutive, and if C does not contain a run of length $s + 1$, score s points.

   iv) Flushes: If $S = \{c_1, c_2, c_3, c_4\}$ and all cards of S have the same suit, score $4 +$ [c_5 has the same suit as the others].

   v) Nobs: If $s = 1$ and $c_5 \notin S$, score 1 if the card is J of the same suit as c_5.

For example, if you hold $\{J♣, 5♣, 5◇, 6♡\}$ and if 4♣ is the starter, you score 4×2 for fifteens, 2 for a pair, 2×3 for runs, plus 1 for nobs, totalling 17.

Exactly how many combinations lead to a score of x points, for $x = 0, 1, 2, \ldots$?

▶ **111.** [*M26*] (P. Erdős, C. Ko, and R. Rado.) Suppose A is a set of r-combinations of an n-set, with $\alpha \cap \beta \neq \emptyset$ whenever $\alpha, \beta \in A$. Show that $|A| \leq \binom{n-1}{r-1}$, if $r \leq n/2$. *Hint:* Consider $\partial^{n-2r} B$, where B is the set of complements of A.

7.2.1.4. Generating all partitions. Richard Stanley's magnificent book *Enumerative Combinatorics* (1986) begins by discussing The Twelvefold Way, a $2 \times 2 \times 3$ array of basic combinatorial problems that arise frequently in practice (see Table 1), based on a series of lectures by Gian-Carlo Rota. All twelve of these basic problems can be described in terms of the ways that a given number of balls can be placed into a given number of urns. For example, there are nine ways to put 2 balls into 3 urns if the balls and urns are labeled:

(The order of balls *within* an urn is ignored.) But if the balls are unlabeled, some of these arrangements are indistinguishable, so only six different ways are possible:

$$ \tag{1} $$

If the urns are unlabeled, arrangements like ① ② and ② ① are essentially the same, hence only two of the original nine arrangements are distinguishable. And if we have three labeled balls, the only distinct ways to place them into three unlabeled urns are

$$ \tag{2} $$

Finally, if neither balls nor urns are labeled, these five possibilities reduce to only three:

$$ \tag{3} $$

The Twelvefold Way considers all arrangements that are possible when balls and urns are labeled or unlabeled, and when the urns may optionally be required to contain at least one ball or at most one ball.

Table 1
THE TWELVEFOLD WAY

balls per urn	unrestricted	≤ 1	≥ 1
n labeled balls, m labeled urns	n-tuples of m things	n-permutations of m things	partitions of $\{1, \ldots, n\}$ into m ordered parts
n unlabeled balls, m labeled urns	n-multicombinations of m things	n-combinations of m things	compositions of n into m parts
n labeled balls, m unlabeled urns	partitions of $\{1, \ldots, n\}$ into $\leq m$ parts	n pigeons into m holes	partitions of $\{1, \ldots, n\}$ into m parts
n unlabeled balls, m unlabeled urns	partitions of n into $\leq m$ parts	n pigeons into m holes	partitions of n into m parts

We've learned about n-tuples, permutations, combinations, and compositions in previous sections of this chapter; and two of the twelve entries in Table 1 are trivial (namely the ones related to "pigeons"). So we can complete our study of classical combinatorial mathematics by learning about the remaining five entries in the table, which all involve *partitions*.

> *Let us begin by acknowledging that the word "partition"*
> *has numerous meanings in mathematics.*
> *Any time a division of some object into subobjects is undertaken,*
> *the word partition is likely to pop up.*
> — GEORGE ANDREWS, *The Theory of Partitions* (1976)

Two quite different concepts share the same name: The *partitions of a set* are the ways to subdivide it into nonempty, disjoint subsets; thus (2) illustrates the five partitions of $\{1, 2, 3\}$, namely

$$\{1, 2, 3\}, \qquad \{1, 2\}\{3\}, \qquad \{1, 3\}\{2\}, \qquad \{1\}\{2, 3\}, \qquad \{1\}\{2\}\{3\}. \qquad (4)$$

And the *partitions of an integer* are the ways to write it as a sum of positive integers, disregarding order; thus (3) illustrates the three partitions of 3, namely

$$3, \qquad 2 + 1, \qquad 1 + 1 + 1. \qquad (5)$$

We shall follow the common practice of referring to integer partitions as simply "partitions," without any qualifying adjective; the other kind will be called "set partitions" in what follows, to make the distinction clear. Both kinds of partitions are important, so we'll study each of them in turn.

Generating all partitions of an integer. A partition of n can be defined formally as a sequence of nonnegative integers $a_1 \geq a_2 \geq \cdots$ such that $n = a_1 + a_2 + \cdots$; for example, one partition of 7 has $a_1 = a_2 = 3$, $a_3 = 1$, and $a_4 = a_5 = \cdots = 0$. The number of nonzero terms is called the number of *parts*, and the zero terms are usually suppressed. Thus we write $7 = 3 + 3 + 1$, or simply 331 to save space when the context is clear.

The simplest way to generate all partitions, and one of the fastest, is to visit them in reverse lexicographic order, starting with 'n' and ending with '$11\ldots1$'. For example, the partitions of 8 are

$$8, 71, 62, 611, 53, 521, 5111, 44, 431, 422, 4211, 41111, 332, 3311,$$
$$3221, 32111, 311111, 2222, 22211, 221111, 2111111, 11111111, \qquad (6)$$

when listed in this order.

If a partition isn't all 1s, it ends with $(x{+}1)$ followed by zero or more 1s, for some $x \geq 1$; therefore the next smallest partition in lexicographic order is obtained by replacing the suffix $(x{+}1)1\ldots1$ by $x\ldots xr$ for some appropriate remainder $r \leq x$. The process is quite efficient if we keep track of the largest subscript q such that $a_q \neq 1$, as suggested by J. K. S. McKay [*CACM* **13** (1970), 52], and pad the array with 1s as suggested by A. Zoghbi and I. Stojmenović [*International Journal of Computer Math.* **70** (1998), 319–332]:

Algorithm P (*Partitions of n in reverse lexicographic order*). Given an integer $n \geq 1$, this algorithm generates all partitions $a_1 \geq a_2 \geq \cdots \geq a_m \geq 1$ with $a_1 + a_2 + \cdots + a_m = n$ and $1 \leq m \leq n$. The value of a_0 is also set to zero.

P1. [Initialize.] Set $a_m \leftarrow 1$ for $n \geq m > 1$. Then set $m \leftarrow 1$ and $a_0 \leftarrow 0$.

P2. [Store the final part.] Set $a_m \leftarrow n$ and $q \leftarrow m - [n=1]$.

P3. [Visit.] Visit the partition $a_1 a_2 \ldots a_m$. Then go to P5 if $a_q \neq 2$.

P4. [Change 2 to 1+1.] Set $a_q \leftarrow 1$, $q \leftarrow q - 1$, $m \leftarrow m + 1$, and return to P3. (At this point we have $a_k = 1$ for $q < k \leq n$.)

P5. [Decrease a_q.] Terminate the algorithm if $q = 0$. Otherwise set $x \leftarrow a_q - 1$, $a_q \leftarrow x$, $n \leftarrow m - q + 1$, and $m \leftarrow q + 1$.

P6. [Copy x if necessary.] If $n \leq x$, return to step P2. Otherwise set $a_m \leftarrow x$, $m \leftarrow m + 1$, $n \leftarrow n - x$, and repeat this step.   ∎

Notice that the operation of going from one partition to the next is particularly easy if a 2 is present; then step P4 simply changes the rightmost 2 to a 1 and appends another 1 at the right. This happy situation is, fortunately, the most common case. For example, nearly 79% of all partitions contain a 2 when $n = 100$.

Another simple algorithm is available when we want to generate all partitions of n into a fixed number of parts. The following method, which was featured in C. F. Hindenburg's 18th-century dissertation [*Infinitinomii Dignitatum Exponentis Indeterminati* (Göttingen, 1779), 73–91], visits the partitions in *colex* order, namely in lexicographic order of the reflected sequence $a_m \ldots a_2 a_1$:

Algorithm H (*Partitions of n into m parts*). Given integers $n \geq m \geq 2$, this algorithm generates all integer m-tuples $a_1 \ldots a_m$ such that $a_1 \geq \cdots \geq a_m \geq 1$ and $a_1 + \cdots + a_m = n$. A sentinel value is stored in a_{m+1}.

H1. [Initialize.] Set $a_1 \leftarrow n - m + 1$ and $a_j \leftarrow 1$ for $1 < j \leq m$. Also set $a_{m+1} \leftarrow -1$.

H2. [Visit.] Visit the partition $a_1 \ldots a_m$. Then go to H4 if $a_2 \geq a_1 - 1$.

H3. [Tweak a_1 and a_2.] Set $a_1 \leftarrow a_1 - 1$, $a_2 \leftarrow a_2 + 1$, and return to H2.

H4. [Find j.] Set $j \leftarrow 3$ and $s \leftarrow a_1 + a_2 - 1$. Then, while $a_j \geq a_1 - 1$, set $s \leftarrow s + a_j$ and $j \leftarrow j + 1$. (Now $s = a_1 + \cdots + a_{j-1} - 1$ and $a_j < a_1 - 1$.)

H5. [Increase a_j.] Terminate if $j > m$. Otherwise set $x \leftarrow a_j + 1$, $a_j \leftarrow x$, $j \leftarrow j - 1$.

H6. [Tweak $a_1 \ldots a_j$.] While $j > 1$, set $a_j \leftarrow x$, $s \leftarrow s - x$, and $j \leftarrow j - 1$. Finally set $a_1 \leftarrow s$ and return to H2.   ∎

For example, when $n = 11$ and $m = 4$ the successive partitions visited are

$$8111, \ 7211, \ 6311, \ 5411, \ 6221, \ 5321, \ 4421, \ 4331, \ 5222, \ 4322, \ 3332. \qquad (7)$$

The basic idea is that colex order goes from one partition $a_1 \ldots a_m$ to the next by finding the smallest j such that a_j can be increased without changing $a_{j+1} \ldots a_m$. The new partition $a'_1 \ldots a'_m$ will have $a'_1 \geq \cdots \geq a'_j = a_j + 1$ and $a'_1 + \cdots + a'_j =$

$a_1 + \cdots + a_j$, and these conditions are achievable if and only if $a_j < a_1 - 1$. Furthermore, the smallest such partition $a_1' \ldots a_m'$ in colex order has $a_2' = \cdots = a_j' = a_j + 1$.

Step H3 handles the simple case $j = 2$, which is by far the most common. And indeed, the value of j almost always turns out to be quite small; we will prove later that the total running time of Algorithm H is at most a small constant times the number of partitions visited, plus $O(m)$.

Other representations of partitions. We've defined a partition as a sequence of nonnegative integers $a_1 a_2 \ldots$ with $a_1 \geq a_2 \geq \cdots$ and $a_1 + a_2 + \cdots = n$, but we can also regard it as an n-tuple of nonnegative integers $c_1 c_2 \ldots c_n$ such that

$$c_1 + 2c_2 + \cdots + nc_n = n. \tag{8}$$

Here c_j is the number of times the integer j appears in the sequence $a_1 a_2 \ldots$; for example, the partition 331 corresponds to the counts $c_1 = 1$, $c_2 = 0$, $c_3 = 2$, $c_4 = c_5 = c_6 = c_7 = 0$. The number of parts is then $c_1 + c_2 + \cdots + c_n$. A procedure analogous to Algorithm P can readily be devised to generate partitions in part-count form; see exercise 5.

We have already seen the part-count representation implicitly in formulas like Eq. 1.2.9–(38), which expresses the symmetric function

$$h_n = \sum_{N \geq d_n \geq \cdots \geq d_2 \geq d_1 \geq 1} x_{d_1} x_{d_2} \ldots x_{d_n} \tag{9}$$

as

$$\sum_{\substack{c_1, c_2, \ldots, c_n \geq 0 \\ c_1 + 2c_2 + \cdots + nc_n = n}} \frac{S_1^{c_1}}{1^{c_1} c_1!} \frac{S_2^{c_2}}{2^{c_2} c_2!} \cdots \frac{S_n^{c_n}}{n^{c_n} c_n!}, \tag{10}$$

where S_j is the symmetric function $x_1^j + x_2^j + \cdots + x_N^j$. The sum in (9) is essentially taken over all n-multicombinations of N things, while the sum in (10) is taken over all partitions of n. Thus, for example, $h_3 = \frac{1}{6} S_1^3 + \frac{1}{2} S_1 S_2 + \frac{1}{3} S_3$, and when $N = 2$ we have

$$x^3 + x^2 y + xy^2 + y^3 = \tfrac{1}{6}(x+y)^3 + \tfrac{1}{2}(x+y)(x^2+y^2) + \tfrac{1}{3}(x^3+y^3).$$

Other sums over partitions appear in exercises 1.2.5–21, 1.2.9–10, 1.2.9–11, 1.2.10–12, etc.; for this reason partitions are of central importance in the study of symmetric functions, a class of functions that pervades mathematics in general. [Chapter 7 of Richard Stanley's *Enumerative Combinatorics* **2** (1999) is an excellent introduction to advanced aspects of symmetric function theory.]

Partitions can be visualized in an appealing way by considering an array of n dots, having a_1 dots in the top row and a_2 in the next row, etc. Such an arrangement of dots is called the *Ferrers diagram* of the partition, in honor of N. M. Ferrers [see *Philosophical Mag.* (4) **5** (1853), 199–202]; and the largest square subarray of dots that it contains is called the *Durfee square*, after W. P. Durfee [see *Johns Hopkins Univ. Circular* **2** (December 1882), 23]. For example, the Ferrers diagram of 8887211 is shown with its 4×4 Durfee square in Fig. 48(a).

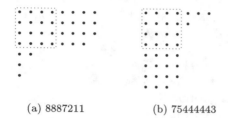

Fig. 48. The Ferrers diagrams and Durfee squares of two conjugate partitions.

(a) 8887211   (b) 75444443

The Durfee square contains k^2 dots when k is the largest subscript such that $a_k \geq k$; we may call k the *trace* of the partition.

If α is any partition $a_1 a_2 \ldots$, its *conjugate* $\alpha^T = b_1 b_2 \ldots$ is obtained by transposing its Ferrers diagram — that is, by reflecting the diagram about the main diagonal. For example, Fig. 48(b) shows that $(8887211)^T = 75444443$. When $\beta = \alpha^T$ we obviously have $\alpha = \beta^T$; the partition β has a_1 parts and α has b_1 parts. Indeed, there's a simple relation between the part-count representation $c_1 \ldots c_n$ of α and the conjugate partition $b_1 b_2 \ldots$, namely

$$b_j - b_{j+1} = c_j \qquad \text{for all } j \geq 1. \tag{11}$$

This relation makes it easy to compute the conjugate of a given partition, or to write it down by inspection (see exercise 6).

The notion of conjugation often explains properties of partitions that would otherwise be quite mysterious. For example, now that we know the definition of α^T, we can easily see that the value of $j - 1$ in step H5 of Algorithm H is just the second-smallest part of the conjugate partition $(a_1 \ldots a_m)^T$, if $m < n$. Therefore the average amount of work that needs to be done in steps H4 and H6 is essentially proportional to the average size of the second-smallest part of a random partition whose largest part is m. And we will see below that the second-smallest part is almost always quite small.

Moreover, *Algorithm H produces partitions in lexicographic order of their conjugates.* For example, the respective conjugates of (7) are

$$41111111, \; 4211111, \; 422111, \; 42221, \; 431111,$$
$$43211, \; 4322, \; 4331, \; 44111, \; 4421, \; 443; \tag{12}$$

these are the partitions of $n = 11$ with largest part 4. One way to generate all partitions of n is to start with the trivial partition 'n', then run Algorithm H for $m = 2, 3, \ldots, n$ in turn; this process yields all α in lexicographic order of α^T (see exercise 7). Thus Algorithm H can be regarded as a dual of Algorithm P.

There is at least one more useful way to represent partitions, called the *rim representation* [see S. Comét, *Numer. Math.* **1** (1959), 90–109]. Suppose we replace the dots of a Ferrers diagram by boxes, thereby obtaining a tableau shape as we did in Section 5.1.4; for example, the partition 8887211 of Fig. 48(a) becomes

$$. \tag{13}$$

The right-hand boundary of this shape can be regarded as a path of length $2n$ from the lower left corner to the upper right corner of an $n \times n$ square, and we know from Table 7.2.1.3–1 that such a path corresponds to an (n, n)-combination.

For example, (13) corresponds to the 70-bit string

$$0\ldots 01001011111010001\ldots 1 \ = \ 0^{28}1^10^21^10^11^50^11^10^31^{27}, \tag{14}$$

where we place enough 0s at the beginning and 1s at the end to make exactly n of each. The 0s represent upward steps of the path, and the 1s represent rightward steps. It is easy to see that the bit string defined in this way has exactly n inversions; conversely, every permutation of the multiset $\{n \cdot 0, \ n \cdot 1\}$ that has exactly n inversions corresponds to a partition of n. When the number of distinct parts of a partition is equal to t, its bit string can be written in the form

$$0^{n-q_1-q_2-\cdots-q_t}1^{p_1}0^{q_1}1^{p_2}0^{q_2}\ldots 1^{p_t}0^{q_t}1^{n-p_1-p_2-\cdots-p_t}, \tag{15}$$

where the exponents p_j and q_j are positive integers. Then the partition's standard representation is

$$a_1a_2\ldots \ = \ (p_1+\cdots+p_t)^{q_t}(p_1+\cdots+p_{t-1})^{q_{t-1}}\ldots(p_1)^{q_1}, \tag{16}$$

namely $(1+1+5+1)^3(1+1+5)^1(1+1)^1(1)^2 = 8887211$ in our example.

The number of partitions. Inspired by a question that was posed to him by Philippe Naudé in 1740, Leonhard Euler wrote two fundamental papers in which he counted partitions of various kinds by studying their generating functions [*Commentarii Academiæ Scientiarum Petropolitanæ* **13** (1741), 64–93; *Novi Comment. Acad. Sci. Pet.* **3** (1750), 125–169]. He observed that the coefficient of z^n in the infinite product

$$(1+z+z^2+\cdots+z^j+\cdots)(1+z^2+z^4+\cdots+z^{2k}+\cdots)(1+z^3+z^6+\cdots+z^{3l}+\cdots)\ldots$$

is the number of nonnegative integer solutions to the equation $j+2k+3l+\cdots = n$; and $1 + z^m + z^{2m} + \cdots$ is $1/(1 - z^m)$. Therefore if we write

$$P(z) \ = \ \prod_{m=1}^{\infty} \frac{1}{1 - z^m} \ = \ \sum_{n=0}^{\infty} p(n)z^n, \tag{17}$$

the number of partitions of n is $p(n)$. This function $P(z)$ turns out to have an amazing number of subtle mathematical properties.

For example, Euler discovered that massive cancellation occurs when the denominator of $P(z)$ is multiplied out:

$$(1-z)(1-z^2)(1-z^3)\ldots = 1 - z - z^2 + z^5 + z^7 - z^{12} - z^{15} + z^{22} + z^{26} - \cdots$$

$$= \sum_{-\infty<n<\infty} (-1)^n z^{(3n^2+n)/2}. \tag{18}$$

A combinatorial proof of this remarkable identity, based on Ferrers diagrams, appears in exercise 5.1.1–14; we can also prove it by setting $u = z$ and $v = z^2$ in the even more remarkable identity that Jacobi published in 1829,

$$\prod_{k=1}^{\infty}(1 - u^k v^{k-1})(1 - u^{k-1} v^k)(1 - u^k v^k) = \sum_{n=-\infty}^{\infty}(-1)^n u^{\binom{n}{2}} v^{\binom{-n}{2}}, \qquad (19)$$

because the left-hand side becomes $\prod_{k=1}^{\infty}(1 - z^{3k-2})(1 - z^{3k-1})(1 - z^{3k})$; see exercise 5.1.1–20. Euler pointed out that, because of (18), the partition numbers for $n > 0$ satisfy the unusual recurrence

$$p(n) = p(n-1) + p(n-2) - p(n-5) - p(n-7) + p(n-12) + p(n-15) - \cdots, \quad (20)$$

with $p(k) = 0$ when $k < 0$; this recurrence allows us to compute their values more rapidly than by performing the power series calculations in (17):

$n =$	0	1	2	3	4	5	6	7	8	9	10	11	12	13	14	15
$p(n) =$	1	1	2	3	5	7	11	15	22	30	42	56	77	101	135	176

We know from Section 1.2.8 that solutions to the Fibonacci recurrence $f(n) = f(n-1) + f(n-2)$ grow exponentially, with $f(n) = \Theta(\phi^n)$ when $f(0)$ and $f(1)$ are positive. The additional terms '$- p(n-5) - p(n-7)$' in (20) have a dampening effect on partition numbers, however; in fact, if we were to stop the recurrence there, the resulting sequence would oscillate between positive and negative values. Further terms '$+p(n-12)+p(n-15)$' reinstate exponential growth.

The actual growth rate of $p(n)$ turns out to be of order $A^{\sqrt{n}}/n$ for a certain constant A. For example, exercise 33 proves directly that $p(n)$ grows at least as fast as $e^{2\sqrt{n}}/n$. And one fairly easy way to obtain a decent *upper* bound is to take logarithms in (17),

$$\ln P(z) = \sum_{m=1}^{\infty} \ln \frac{1}{1 - z^m} = \sum_{m=1}^{\infty}\sum_{n=1}^{\infty} \frac{z^{mn}}{n}, \qquad (21)$$

and then to look at the behavior near $z = 1$ by setting $z = e^{-t}$ with $t > 0$:

$$\ln P(e^{-t}) = \sum_{m,n\geq 1} \frac{e^{-mnt}}{n} = \sum_{n\geq 1}\frac{1}{n}\frac{1}{e^{tn} - 1} < \sum_{n\geq 1}\frac{1}{n^2 t} = \frac{\zeta(2)}{t}. \qquad (22)$$

Consequently, since $p(n) \leq p(n+1) < p(n+2) < \cdots$ and $e^t > 1$, we have

$$\frac{p(n)}{1 - e^{-t}} = \sum_{k=n}^{\infty} p(n)e^{(n-k)t} < \sum_{k=0}^{\infty} p(k)e^{(n-k)t} = e^{nt}P(e^{-t}) < e^{nt+\zeta(2)/t} \qquad (23)$$

for all $t > 0$. Setting $t = \sqrt{\zeta(2)/n}$ gives

$$p(n) < Ce^{2C\sqrt{n}}/\sqrt{n}, \qquad \text{where } C = \sqrt{\zeta(2)} = \pi/\sqrt{6}. \qquad (24)$$

We can obtain more accurate information about the size of $\ln P(e^{-t})$ by using Euler's summation formula (Section 1.2.11.2) or Mellin transforms (Section 5.2.2); see exercise 25. But the methods we have seen so far aren't powerful enough to deduce the precise behavior of $P(e^{-t})$, so it is time for us to add a new weapon to our arsenal of techniques.

Euler's generating function $P(z)$ is ideally suited to the *Poisson summation formula* [*J. École Royale Polytechnique* **12** (1823), 404–509, §63], according to which

$$\sum_{n=-\infty}^{\infty} f(n + \theta) \;=\; \lim_{M \to \infty} \sum_{m=-M}^{M} e^{2\pi m i \theta} \int_{-\infty}^{\infty} e^{-2\pi m i y} f(y)\, dy, \qquad (25)$$

whenever f is a "well-behaved" function. This formula is based on the fact that the left-hand side is a periodic function of θ, and the right-hand side is the expansion of that function as a Fourier series. The function f is sufficiently nice if, for example, $\int_{-\infty}^{\infty} |f(y)|\, dy < \infty$ and either

i) $f(n + \theta)$ is an analytic function of the complex variable θ in the region $|\Im\theta| \le \epsilon$ for some $\epsilon > 0$ and $0 \le \Re\theta \le 1$ and every n, and the left-hand side of (25) converges uniformly for $|\Im\theta| \le \epsilon$; or

ii) $f(\theta) = \frac{1}{2}\lim_{\epsilon\to 0}\big(f(\theta - \epsilon) + f(\theta + \epsilon)\big) = g(\theta) - h(\theta)$ for all real numbers θ, where g and h are monotone increasing and $g(\pm\infty)$, $h(\pm\infty)$ are finite.

[See Peter Henrici, *Applied and Computational Complex Analysis* **2** (New York: Wiley, 1977), Theorem 10.6e.] Poisson's formula is not a panacea for summation problems of every kind; but when it does apply the results can be spectacular, as we will see.

Let us multiply Euler's formula (18) by $z^{1/24}$ in order to "complete the square":

$$\frac{z^{1/24}}{P(z)} \;=\; \sum_{n=-\infty}^{\infty} (-1)^n\, z^{\frac{3}{2}(n+\frac{1}{6})^2}. \qquad (26)$$

Then for all $t > 0$ we have $e^{-t/24}/P(e^{-t}) = \sum_{n=-\infty}^{\infty} f(n)$, where

$$f(y) \;=\; e^{-\frac{3}{2}t(y+\frac{1}{6})^2 + \pi i y}; \qquad (27)$$

and this function f qualifies for Poisson's summation formula under both of the criteria (i) and (ii) stated above. Therefore we try to integrate $e^{-2\pi m i y} f(y)$, and that integral turns out to be easy for all m (see exercise 27):

$$\int_{-\infty}^{\infty} e^{-a(y+b)^2 + 2ciy}\, dy \;=\; \sqrt{\frac{\pi}{a}}\, e^{-c^2/a - 2bci} \qquad \text{when } a > 0. \qquad (28)$$

Plugging in to (25), with $\theta = 0$, $a = \frac{3}{2}t$, $b = \frac{1}{6}$, and $c = (\frac{1}{2} - m)\pi$, yields

$$\sum_{n=-\infty}^{\infty} f(n) = \sum_{m=-\infty}^{\infty} g(m), \qquad g(m) = \sqrt{\frac{2\pi}{3t}}\, e^{-2(m-\frac{1}{2})^2 \pi^2/(3t) + \frac{1-2m}{6}\pi i}. \qquad (29)$$

These terms combine and cancel beautifully, as shown in exercise 27, giving

$$\frac{e^{-t/24}}{P(e^{-t})} \;=\; \sqrt{\frac{2\pi}{t}} \sum_{n=-\infty}^{\infty} (-1)^n e^{-6\pi^2(n+\frac{1}{6})^2/t} \;=\; \sqrt{\frac{2\pi}{t}}\, \frac{e^{-\zeta(2)/t}}{P(e^{-4\pi^2/t})}. \qquad (30)$$

Surprise! We have proved another remarkable fact about $P(z)$:

Theorem D. *The generating function* (17) *for partitions satisfies the functional relation*

$$\ln P(e^{-t}) = \frac{\zeta(2)}{t} + \frac{1}{2}\ln\frac{t}{2\pi} - \frac{t}{24} + \ln P(e^{-4\pi^2/t}) \tag{31}$$

when $\Re t > 0$. ∎

This theorem was discovered by Richard Dedekind [*Crelle* **83** (1877), 265–292, §6], who wrote $\eta(\tau)$ for the function $z^{1/24}/P(z)$ when $z = e^{2\pi i\tau}$; his proof was based on a much more complicated theory of elliptic functions. Notice that when t is a small positive number, $\ln P(e^{-4\pi^2/t})$ is *extremely* tiny; for example, when $t = 0.1$ we have $\exp(-4\pi^2/t) \approx 3.5 \times 10^{-172}$. Therefore Theorem D tells us essentially everything we need to know about the value of $P(z)$ when z is near 1.

G. H. Hardy and S. Ramanujan used this knowledge to deduce the asymptotic behavior of $p(n)$ for large n, and their work was extended many years later by Hans Rademacher, who discovered a series that is not only asymptotic but convergent [*Proc. London Math. Soc.* (2) **17** (1918), 75–115; **43** (1937), 241–254]. The Hardy–Ramanujan–Rademacher formula for $p(n)$ is surely one of the most astonishing identities ever discovered; it states that

$$p(n) = \frac{\pi}{2^{5/4}3^{3/4}(n - 1/24)^{3/4}} \sum_{k=1}^{\infty} \frac{A_k(n)}{k} I_{3/2}\left(\sqrt{\frac{2}{3}}\frac{\pi}{k}\sqrt{n - 1/24}\right). \tag{32}$$

Here $I_{3/2}$ denotes the modified spherical Bessel function

$$I_{3/2}(z) = \left(\frac{z}{2}\right)^{3/2} \sum_{k=0}^{\infty} \frac{1}{\Gamma(k + 5/2)}\frac{(z^2/4)^k}{k!} = \sqrt{\frac{2z}{\pi}}\left(\frac{\cosh z}{z} - \frac{\sinh z}{z^2}\right); \tag{33}$$

and the coefficient $A_k(n)$ is defined by the formula

$$A_k(n) = \sum_{h=0}^{k-1} [h \perp k] \exp\left(2\pi i\left(\frac{\sigma(h, k, 0)}{24} - \frac{nh}{k}\right)\right) \tag{34}$$

where $\sigma(h, k, 0)$ is the Dedekind sum defined in Eq. 3.3.3–(16). We have

$$A_1(n) = 1, \qquad A_2(n) = (-1)^n, \qquad A_3(n) = 2\cos\frac{(24n + 1)\pi}{18}, \tag{35}$$

and in general $A_k(n)$ lies between $-k$ and k.

A proof of (32) would take us far afield, but the basic idea is to use the "saddle point method" discussed in Section 7.2.1.5. The term for $k = 1$ is derived from the behavior of $P(z)$ when z is near 1; and the next term is derived from the behavior when z is near -1, where a transformation similar to (31) can be applied. In general, the kth term of (32) takes account of the way $P(z)$ behaves when z approaches $e^{2\pi ih/k}$ for irreducible fractions h/k with denominator k; every kth root of unity is a pole of each of the factors $1/(1 - z^k)$, $1/(1 - z^{2k})$, $1/(1 - z^{3k})$, ... in the infinite product for $P(z)$.

The leading term of (32) can be simplified greatly, if we merely want a rough approximation:

$$p(n) = \frac{e^{\pi\sqrt{2n/3}}}{4n\sqrt{3}}\left(1 + O(n^{-1/2})\right). \tag{36}$$

Or, if we choose to retain a few more details,

$$p(n) = \frac{e^{\pi\sqrt{2n'/3}}}{4n'\sqrt{3}}\left(1 - \frac{1}{\pi}\sqrt{\frac{3}{2n'}}\right)\left(1 + O(e^{-\pi\sqrt{n/6}})\right), \quad n' = n - \frac{1}{24}. \tag{37}$$

For example, $p(100)$ has the exact value 190,569,292; formula (36) tells us that $p(100) \approx 1.993 \times 10^8$, while (37) gives the far better estimate 190,568,944.783.

Andrew Odlyzko has observed that, when n is large, the Hardy–Ramanujan–Rademacher formula actually gives a near-optimum way to compute the precise value of $p(n)$, because the arithmetic operations can be carried out in nearly $O(\log p(n)) = O(n^{1/2})$ steps. [See *Handbook of Combinatorics* **2** (MIT Press, 1995), 1068–1069.] The first few terms of (32) give the main contribution; then the series settles down to terms that are of order $k^{-3/2}$ and usually of order k^{-2}. Furthermore, about half of the coefficients $A_k(n)$ turn out to be zero (see exercise 28). For example, when $n = 10^6$, the terms for $k = 1$, 2, and 3 are $\approx 1.47 \times 10^{1107}$, 1.23×10^{550}, and -1.23×10^{364}, respectively. The sum of the first 250 terms is $\approx 1471684986\ldots73818.01$, while the true value is $1471684986\ldots73818$; and 123 of those 250 terms are zero.

The number of parts. It is convenient to introduce the notation

$$\left|\begin{matrix} n \\ m \end{matrix}\right| \tag{38}$$

for the number of partitions of n that have exactly m parts. Then the recurrence

$$\left|\begin{matrix} n \\ m \end{matrix}\right| = \left|\begin{matrix} n-1 \\ m-1 \end{matrix}\right| + \left|\begin{matrix} n-m \\ m \end{matrix}\right| \tag{39}$$

holds for all integers m and n, because $\left|\begin{smallmatrix} n-1 \\ m-1 \end{smallmatrix}\right|$ counts the partitions whose smallest part is 1 and $\left|\begin{smallmatrix} n-m \\ m \end{smallmatrix}\right|$ counts the others. (If the smallest part is 2 or more, we can subtract 1 from each part and get a partition of $n - m$ into m parts.) By similar reasoning we can conclude that $\left|\begin{smallmatrix} m+n \\ m \end{smallmatrix}\right|$ is the number of partitions of n into *at most* m parts, namely into m nonnegative summands. We also know, by transposing Ferrers diagrams, that $\left|\begin{smallmatrix} n \\ m \end{smallmatrix}\right|$ is the number of partitions of n whose *largest* part is m. Thus $\left|\begin{smallmatrix} n \\ m \end{smallmatrix}\right|$ is a good number to know. The boundary conditions

$$\left|\begin{matrix} n \\ 0 \end{matrix}\right| = \delta_{n0} \quad \text{and} \quad \left|\begin{matrix} n \\ m \end{matrix}\right| = 0 \quad \text{for } m < 0 \text{ or } n < 0 \tag{40}$$

make it easy to tabulate $\left|\begin{smallmatrix} n \\ m \end{smallmatrix}\right|$ for small values of the parameters, and we obtain an array of numbers analogous to the familiar triangles for $\binom{n}{m}$, $\left[\begin{smallmatrix} n \\ m \end{smallmatrix}\right]$, $\left\{\begin{smallmatrix} n \\ m \end{smallmatrix}\right\}$, and $\left\langle\begin{smallmatrix} n \\ m \end{smallmatrix}\right\rangle$ that we've seen before; see Table 2. The generating function is

$$\sum_n \left|\begin{matrix} n \\ m \end{matrix}\right| z^n = \frac{z^m}{(1-z)(1-z^2)\ldots(1-z^m)}. \tag{41}$$

Table 2
PARTITION NUMBERS

n	$\left\lvert\begin{smallmatrix}n\\0\end{smallmatrix}\right\rvert$	$\left\lvert\begin{smallmatrix}n\\1\end{smallmatrix}\right\rvert$	$\left\lvert\begin{smallmatrix}n\\2\end{smallmatrix}\right\rvert$	$\left\lvert\begin{smallmatrix}n\\3\end{smallmatrix}\right\rvert$	$\left\lvert\begin{smallmatrix}n\\4\end{smallmatrix}\right\rvert$	$\left\lvert\begin{smallmatrix}n\\5\end{smallmatrix}\right\rvert$	$\left\lvert\begin{smallmatrix}n\\6\end{smallmatrix}\right\rvert$	$\left\lvert\begin{smallmatrix}n\\7\end{smallmatrix}\right\rvert$	$\left\lvert\begin{smallmatrix}n\\8\end{smallmatrix}\right\rvert$	$\left\lvert\begin{smallmatrix}n\\9\end{smallmatrix}\right\rvert$	$\left\lvert\begin{smallmatrix}n\\10\end{smallmatrix}\right\rvert$	$\left\lvert\begin{smallmatrix}n\\11\end{smallmatrix}\right\rvert$
0	1	0	0	0	0	0	0	0	0	0	0	0
1	0	1	0	0	0	0	0	0	0	0	0	0
2	0	1	1	0	0	0	0	0	0	0	0	0
3	0	1	1	1	0	0	0	0	0	0	0	0
4	0	1	2	1	1	0	0	0	0	0	0	0
5	0	1	2	2	1	1	0	0	0	0	0	0
6	0	1	3	3	2	1	1	0	0	0	0	0
7	0	1	3	4	3	2	1	1	0	0	0	0
8	0	1	4	5	5	3	2	1	1	0	0	0
9	0	1	4	7	6	5	3	2	1	1	0	0
10	0	1	5	8	9	7	5	3	2	1	1	0
11	0	1	5	10	11	10	7	5	3	2	1	1

Almost all partitions of n have $\Theta(\sqrt{n}\log n)$ parts. This fact, discovered by P. Erdős and J. Lehner [*Duke Math. J.* **8** (1941), 335–345], has a very instructive proof:

Theorem E. *Let $C = \pi/\sqrt{6}$ and $m = \frac{1}{2C}\sqrt{n}\ln n + x\sqrt{n} + O(1)$. Then*

$$\frac{1}{p(n)}\left\lvert\begin{matrix}m+n\\m\end{matrix}\right\rvert = F(x)\bigl(1 + O(n^{-1/2+\epsilon})\bigr) \tag{42}$$

for all $\epsilon > 0$ and all fixed x as $n \to \infty$, where

$$F(x) = e^{-e^{-Cx}/C}. \tag{43}$$

The function $F(x)$ in (43) approaches 0 quite rapidly when $x \to -\infty$, and it rapidly increases to 1 when $x \to +\infty$; so it is a probability distribution function. Figure 49(b) shows that the corresponding density function $f(x) = F'(x)$ is largely concentrated in the region $-2 \le x \le 4$. (See exercise 35.)

The values of $\left\lvert\begin{smallmatrix}n\\m\end{smallmatrix}\right\rvert = \left\lvert\begin{smallmatrix}m+n\\m\end{smallmatrix}\right\rvert - \left\lvert\begin{smallmatrix}m-1+n\\m-1\end{smallmatrix}\right\rvert$ are shown in Fig. 49(a) for comparison when $n = 100$; in this case $\frac{1}{2C}\sqrt{n}\ln n \approx 18$.

Proof. We will use the fact that $\left\lvert\begin{smallmatrix}m+n\\m\end{smallmatrix}\right\rvert$ is the number of partitions of n whose largest part is $\le m$. Then, by the principle of inclusion and exclusion, Eq. 1.3.3–(29), we have

$$\left\lvert\begin{matrix}m+n\\m\end{matrix}\right\rvert = p(n) - \sum_{j>m} p(n-j) + \sum_{j_2>j_1>m} p(n-j_1-j_2) - \sum_{j_3>j_2>j_1>m} p(n-j_1-j_2-j_3) + \cdots,$$

because $p(n - j_1 - \cdots - j_r)$ is the number of partitions of n that use each of the parts $\{j_1, \ldots, j_r\}$ at least once. Let us write this as

$$\frac{1}{p(n)}\left\lvert\begin{matrix}m+n\\m\end{matrix}\right\rvert = 1 - \Sigma_1 + \Sigma_2 - \Sigma_3 + \cdots, \qquad \Sigma_r = \sum_{j_r>\cdots>j_1>m} \frac{p(n-j_1-\cdots-j_r)}{p(n)}. \tag{44}$$

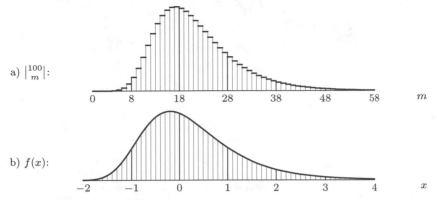

Fig. 49. Partitions of n with m parts, when (a) $n = 100$; (b) $n \to \infty$. (See Theorem E.)

In order to evaluate Σ_r we need to have a good estimate of the ratio $p(n-t)/p(n)$. And we're in luck, because Eq. (36) implies that

$$\frac{p(n-t)}{p(n)} = \exp\bigl(2C\sqrt{n-t} - \ln(n-t) + O\bigl((n-t)^{-1/2}\bigr) - 2C\sqrt{n} + \ln n\bigr)$$

$$= \exp\bigl(-Ctn^{-1/2} + O(n^{-1/2+2\epsilon})\bigr) \qquad \text{if } 0 \le t \le n^{1/2+\epsilon}. \qquad (45)$$

Furthermore, if $t \ge n^{1/2+\epsilon}$ we have $p(n-t)/p(n) \le p(n-n^{1/2+\epsilon})/p(n) \approx \exp(-Cn^\epsilon)$, a value that is asymptotically smaller than any power of n. Therefore we may safely use the approximation

$$\frac{p(n-t)}{p(n)} \approx \alpha^t, \qquad \alpha = \exp(-Cn^{-1/2}), \qquad (46)$$

for all values of $t \ge 0$. For example, we have

$$\Sigma_1 = \sum_{j>m} \frac{p(n-j)}{p(n)} = \frac{\alpha^{m+1}}{1-\alpha}\bigl(1 + O(n^{-1/2+2\epsilon})\bigr) + \sum_{n \ge j > n^{1/2+\epsilon}} \frac{p(n-j)}{p(n)}$$

$$= \frac{e^{-Cx}}{C}\bigl(1 + O(n^{-1/2+2\epsilon})\bigr) + O(ne^{-Cn^\epsilon}),$$

because $\alpha/(1-\alpha) = n^{1/2}/C + O(1)$ and $\alpha^m = n^{-1/2}e^{-Cx} + O(n^{-1})$. A similar argument (see exercise 36) proves that, if $r = O(\log n)$,

$$\Sigma_r = \frac{e^{-Crx}}{C^r r!}\bigl(1 + O(n^{-1/2+2\epsilon})\bigr) + O(e^{-n^{\epsilon/2}}). \qquad (47)$$

Finally — and this is a wonderful property of the inclusion-exclusion principle in general — the partial sums of (44) always "bracket" the true value, in the sense that

$$1 - \Sigma_1 + \Sigma_2 - \cdots - \Sigma_{2r-1} \le \frac{1}{p(n)}\left|\begin{matrix} m+n \\ m \end{matrix}\right| \le 1 - \Sigma_1 + \Sigma_2 - \cdots - \Sigma_{2r-1} + \Sigma_{2r} \quad (48)$$

for all r. (See exercise 37.) When $2r$ is near $\ln n$ and n is large, the term Σ_{2r} is extremely tiny; therefore we obtain (42), except with 2ϵ in place of ϵ. ∎

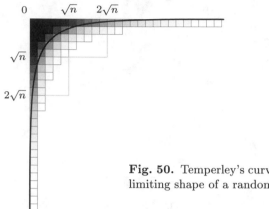

Fig. 50. Temperley's curve (49) for the limiting shape of a random partition.

Theorem E tells us that the largest part of a random partition almost always is $\frac{1}{2C}\sqrt{n}\ln n + O(\sqrt{n}\log\log\log n)$, and when n is reasonably large the other parts tend to be predictable as well. Suppose, for example, that we take all the partitions of 25 and superimpose their Ferrers diagrams, changing dots to boxes as in the rim representation. Which cells are occupied most often? Figure 50 shows the result: A random partition tends to have a typical shape that approaches a limiting curve as $n \to \infty$.

H. N. V. Temperley [*Proc. Cambridge Philos. Soc.* **48** (1952), 683–697] gave heuristic reasons to believe that most parts a_k of a large random partition $a_1 \ldots a_m$ will satisfy the approximate law

$$e^{-Ck/\sqrt{n}} + e^{-Ca_k/\sqrt{n}} \approx 1, \tag{49}$$

and his formula has subsequently been verified in a strong form. For example, a theorem of Boris Pittel [*Advances in Applied Math.* **18** (1997), 432–488] allows us to conclude that the trace of a random partition is almost always $\frac{\ln 2}{C}\sqrt{n} \approx 0.54\sqrt{n}$, in accordance with (49), with an error of at most $O(\sqrt{n}\ln n)^{1/2}$; thus about 29% of all the Ferrers dots tend to lie in the Durfee square.

If, on the other hand, we look only at partitions of n with m parts, where m is fixed, the limiting shape is rather different: Almost all such partitions have

$$a_k \approx \frac{n}{m}\ln\frac{m}{k}, \tag{50}$$

if m and n are reasonably large. Figure 51 illustrates the case $n = 50$, $m = 5$. In fact, the same limit holds when m grows with n, but at a slower rate than $\sqrt{n}$ [see Vershik and Yakubovich, *Moscow Math. J.* **1** (2001), 457–468].

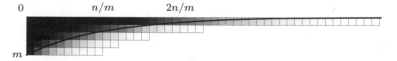

Fig. 51. The limiting shape (50) when there are m parts.

The rim representation of partitions gives us further information about partitions that are *doubly* bounded, in the sense that we not only restrict the number of parts but also the size of each part. A partition that has at most m parts, each of size at most l, fits inside an $m \times l$ box. All such partitions correspond to permutations of the multiset $\{m \cdot 0, \, l \cdot 1\}$ that have exactly n inversions, and we have studied the inversions of multiset permutations in exercise 5.1.2–16. In particular, that exercise derives a nonobvious formula for the number of ways n inversions can happen:

Theorem C. *The number of partitions of n that have no more than m parts and no part larger than l is*

$$[z^n] \binom{l+m}{m}_z = [z^n] \frac{(1-z^{l+1})}{(1-z)} \frac{(1-z^{l+2})}{(1-z^2)} \cdots \frac{(1-z^{l+m})}{(1-z^m)}. \tag{51}$$

This result is due to A. Cauchy, *Comptes Rendus Acad. Sci.* **17** (Paris, 1843), 523–531. Notice that when $l \to \infty$ the numerator becomes simply 1. An interesting combinatorial proof of a more general result appears in exercise 40 below. ∎

Analysis of the algorithms. Now we know more than enough about the quantitative aspects of partitions to deduce the behavior of Algorithm P quite precisely. Suppose steps P1, ..., P6 of that algorithm are executed respectively $T_1(n), \ldots, T_6(n)$ times. We obviously have $T_1(n) = 1$ and $T_3(n) = p(n)$; furthermore Kirchhoff's law tells us that $T_2(n) = T_5(n)$ and $T_4(n) + T_5(n) = T_3(n)$. We get to step P4 once for each partition that contains a 2; and this is clearly $p(n-2)$.

Thus the only possible mystery about the running time of Algorithm P is the number of times we must perform step P6, which loops back to itself. A moment's thought, however, reveals that the algorithm stores a value ≥ 2 into the array $a_1 a_2 \ldots$ only in step P2 or when we'll soon test $n \leq x$ in P6; and every such value is eventually decreased by 1, either in step P4 or step P5. Therefore

$$T_2''(n) + T_6(n) = p(n) - 1, \tag{52}$$

where $T_2''(n)$ is the number of times step P2 sets a_m to a value ≥ 2. Let $T_2(n) = T_2'(n) + T_2''(n)$, so that $T_2'(n)$ is the number of times step P2 sets $a_m \leftarrow 1$. Then $T_2'(n) + T_4(n)$ is the number of partitions that end in 1, hence

$$T_2'(n) + T_4(n) = p(n-1). \tag{53}$$

Aha! We've found enough equations to determine all of the required quantities:

$$\begin{aligned}
&\bigl(T_1(n), \ldots, T_6(n)\bigr) = \\
&\qquad \bigl(1, \; p(n) - p(n-2), \; p(n), \; p(n-2), \; p(n) - p(n-2), \; p(n-1) - 1\bigr). \tag{54}
\end{aligned}$$

And from the asymptotics of $p(n)$ we also know the average amount of computation per partition:

$$\left(\frac{T_1(n)}{p(n)}, \ldots, \frac{T_6(n)}{p(n)}\right) = \left(0, \; \frac{2C}{\sqrt{n}}, \; 1, \; 1 - \frac{2C}{\sqrt{n}}, \; \frac{2C}{\sqrt{n}}, \; 1 - \frac{C}{\sqrt{n}}\right) + O\left(\frac{1}{n}\right), \tag{55}$$

where $C = \pi/\sqrt{6} \approx 1.283$. (See exercise 45.) The total number of memory accesses per partition therefore comes to only $3 + C/\sqrt{n} + O(1/n)$.

> *Whoever wants to go about generating all partitions*
> *not only immerses himself in immense labor,*
> *but also must take pains to keep fully attentive,*
> *so as not to be grossly deceived.*
>
> — LEONHARD EULER, *De Partitione Numerorum* (1750)

Algorithm H is more difficult to analyze, but we can at least prove a decent upper bound on its running time. The key quantity is the value of j, the smallest subscript for which $a_j < a_1 - 1$. The successive values of j when $m = 4$ and $n = 11$ are $(2, 2, 2, 3, 2, 2, 3, 4, 2, 3, 5)$, and we have observed that $j = b_{l-1} + 1$ when $b_1 \ldots b_l$ is the conjugate partition $(a_1 \ldots a_m)^T$ and $m < n$. (See (7) and (12).) Step H3 singles out the case $j = 2$, because this case is not only the most common, it is also especially easy to handle.

Let $c_m(n)$ be the accumulated total value of $j - 1$, summed over all of the $\left|{n \atop m}\right|$ partitions generated by Algorithm H. For example, $c_4(11) = 1 + 1 + 1 + 2 + 1 + 1 + 2 + 3 + 1 + 2 + 4 = 19$. We can regard $c_m(n)/\left|{n \atop m}\right|$ as a good indication of the running time per partition, because the time to perform the most costly steps, H4 and H6, is roughly proportional to $j - 2$. This ratio $c_m(n)/\left|{n \atop m}\right|$ is *not* bounded, because $c_m(m) = m$ while $\left|{m \atop m}\right| = 1$. But the following theorem shows that Algorithm H is efficient nonetheless:

Theorem H. *The cost measure $c_m(n)$ for Algorithm H is at most $3\left|{n \atop m}\right| + m$.*

Proof. We can readily verify that $c_m(n)$ satisfies the same recurrence as $\left|{n \atop m}\right|$, namely

$$c_m(n) = c_{m-1}(n-1) + c_m(n-m), \qquad \text{for } m, n \geq 1, \tag{56}$$

if we artificially define $c_m(n) = 1$ when $1 \leq n < m$; see (39). But the boundary conditions are now different:

$$c_m(0) = [m > 0]; \qquad\qquad c_0(n) = 0. \tag{57}$$

Table 3 shows how $c_m(n)$ behaves when m and n are small.

To prove the theorem, we will actually prove a stronger result,

$$c_m(n) \leq 3\left|{n \atop m}\right| + 2m - n - 1 \qquad \text{for } n \geq m \geq 2. \tag{58}$$

Exercise 50 shows that this inequality holds when $m \leq n \leq 2m$, so the proof will be complete if we can prove it when $n > 2m$. In the latter case we have

$$
\begin{aligned}
c_m(n) &= c_1(n-m) + c_2(n-m) + c_3(n-m) + \cdots + c_m(n-m) \\
&\leq 1 + \left(3\left|{n-m \atop 2}\right| + 3 - n + m\right) + \left(3\left|{n-m \atop 3}\right| + 5 - n + m\right) + \cdots \\
&\qquad\qquad\qquad\qquad + \left(3\left|{n-m \atop m}\right| + 2m - 1 - n + m\right) \\
&= 3\left|{n-m \atop 1}\right| + 3\left|{n-m \atop 2}\right| + \cdots + 3\left|{n-m \atop m}\right| - 3 + m^2 - (m-1)(n-m) \\
&= 3\left|{n \atop m}\right| + 2m^2 - m - (m-1)n - 3
\end{aligned}
$$

by induction; and $2m^2 - m - (m-1)n - 3 \leq 2m - n - 1$ because $n \geq 2m + 1$. ∎

Table 3

COSTS IN ALGORITHM H

n	$c_0(n)$	$c_1(n)$	$c_2(n)$	$c_3(n)$	$c_4(n)$	$c_5(n)$	$c_6(n)$	$c_7(n)$	$c_8(n)$	$c_9(n)$	$c_{10}(n)$	$c_{11}(n)$
0	0	1	1	1	1	1	1	1	1	1	1	1
1	0	1	1	1	1	1	1	1	1	1	1	1
2	0	1	2	1	1	1	1	1	1	1	1	1
3	0	1	2	3	1	1	1	1	1	1	1	1
4	0	1	3	3	4	1	1	1	1	1	1	1
5	0	1	3	4	4	5	1	1	1	1	1	1
6	0	1	4	6	5	5	6	1	1	1	1	1
7	0	1	4	7	7	6	6	7	1	1	1	1
8	0	1	5	8	11	8	7	7	8	1	1	1
9	0	1	5	11	12	12	9	8	8	9	1	1
10	0	1	6	12	16	17	13	10	9	9	10	1
11	0	1	6	14	19	21	18	14	11	10	10	11

*A Gray code for partitions. When partitions are generated in part-count form $c_1 \ldots c_n$ as in exercise 5, at most four of the c_j values change at each step. But we might prefer to minimize the changes to the individual parts, generating partitions in such a way that the successor of $a_1 a_2 \ldots$ is always obtained by simply setting $a_j \leftarrow a_j + 1$ and $a_k \leftarrow a_k - 1$ for some j and k, as in the "revolving-door" algorithms of Section 7.2.1.3. It turns out that this is always possible; in fact, there is a unique way to do it when $n = 6$:

$$111111, \ 21111, \ 3111, \ 2211, \ 222, \ 321, \ 33, \ 42, \ 411, \ 51, \ 6. \tag{59}$$

And in general, the $\left|{m+n \atop m}\right|$ partitions of n into at most m parts can always be generated by a suitable Gray path.

Notice that $\alpha \to \beta$ is an allowable transition from one partition to another if and only if we get the Ferrers diagram for β by moving just one dot in the Ferrers diagram for α. Therefore $\alpha^T \to \beta^T$ is also an allowable transition. It follows that every Gray code for partitions into at most m parts corresponds to a Gray code for partitions into parts that do not exceed m. We shall work with the latter constraint.

The total number of Gray codes for partitions is vast: There are 52 when $n = 7$, and 652 when $n = 8$; there are 298,896 when $n = 9$, and 2,291,100,484 when $n = 10$. But no really simple construction is known. The reason is probably that a few partitions have only two neighbors, namely the partitions $d^{n/d}$ when $1 < d < n$ and d is a divisor of n. Such partitions must be preceded and followed by $\{(d+1)d^{n/d-2}(d-1), \ d^{n/d-1}(d-1)1\}$, and this requirement seems to rule out any simple recursive approach.

Carla D. Savage [*J. Algorithms* **10** (1989), 577–595] found a way to surmount the difficulties with only a modest amount of complexity. Let

$$\mu(m, n) = \overbrace{m \ m \ \ldots \ m}^{\lfloor n/m \rfloor} \ (n \bmod m) \tag{60}$$

be the lexicographically largest partition of n with parts $\le m$; our goal will be to construct recursively defined Gray paths $L(m,n)$ and $M(m,n)$ from the partition 1^n to $\mu(m,n)$, where $L(m,n)$ runs through all partitions whose parts are bounded by m while $M(m,n)$ runs through those partitions and a few more: $M(m,n)$ also includes partitions whose largest part is $m+1$, provided that the other parts are all strictly less than m. For example, $L(3,8)$ is 11111111, 2111111, 311111, 221111, 22211, 2222, 3221, 32111, 3311, 332, while $M(3,8)$ is

$$11111111,\ 2111111,\ 221111,\ 22211,\ 2222,\ 3221,$$
$$3311,\ 32111,\ 311111,\ 41111,\ 4211,\ 422,\ 332; \tag{61}$$

the additional partitions starting with 4 will give us "wiggle room" in other parts of the recursion. We will define $L(m,n)$ for all $n \ge 0$, but $M(m,n)$ only for $n > 2m$.

The following construction, illustrated for $m = 5$ to simplify the notation, *almost* works:

$$L(5) = \begin{Bmatrix} L(3) \\ 4L(\infty)^R \\ 5L(\infty) \end{Bmatrix} \text{ if } n \le 7; \quad \begin{Bmatrix} L(3) \\ 4L(2)^R \\ 5L(2) \\ 431 \\ 44 \\ 53 \end{Bmatrix} \text{ if } n = 8; \quad \begin{Bmatrix} M(4) \\ 54L(4)^R \\ 55L(5) \end{Bmatrix} \text{ if } n \ge 9; \tag{62}$$

$$M(5) = \begin{Bmatrix} L(4) \\ 5L(4)^R \\ 6L(3) \\ 64L(\infty)^R \\ 55L(\infty) \end{Bmatrix} \text{ if } 11 \le n \le 13; \quad \begin{Bmatrix} L(4) \\ 5M(4)^R \\ 6L(4) \\ 554L(4)^R \\ 555L(5) \end{Bmatrix} \text{ if } n \ge 14. \tag{63}$$

Here the parameter n in $L(m,n)$ and $M(m,n)$ has been omitted because it can be deduced from the context; each L or M is supposed to generate partitions of whatever amount remains after previous parts have been subtracted. Thus, for example, (63) specifies that

$$M(5,14) \ = \ L(4,14),\ 5M(4,9)^R,\ 6L(4,8),\ 554L(4,0)^R,\ 555L(5,-1);$$

the sequence $L(5,-1)$ is actually empty, and $L(4,0)$ is the empty string, so the final partition of $M(5,14)$ is $554 = \mu(5,14)$ as it should be. The notation $L(\infty)$ stands for $L(\infty, n) = L(n,n)$, the Gray path of all partitions of n, starting with 1^n and ending with n^1.

In general, $L(m)$ and $M(m)$ are defined for all $m \ge 3$ by essentially the same rules, if we replace the digits 2, 3, 4, 5, and 6 in (62) and (63) by $m-3$, $m-2$, $m-1$, m, and $m+1$, respectively. The ranges $n \le 7$, $n = 8$, $n \ge 9$ become $n \le 2m-3$, $n = 2m-2$, $n \ge 2m-1$; the ranges $11 \le n \le 13$ and $n \ge 14$ become $2m+1 \le n \le 3m-2$ and $n \ge 3m-1$. The sequences $L(0)$, $L(1)$, $L(2)$ have obvious definitions because the paths are unique when $m \le 2$. The sequence $M(2)$ is 1^n, 21^{n-2}, 31^{n-3}, 221^{n-4}, 2221^{n-6}, ..., $\mu(2,n)$ for $n \ge 5$.

Theorem S. *Gray paths $L'(m,n)$ for $m, n \geq 0$ and $M'(m,n)$ for $n \geq 2m+1 \geq 5$ exist for all partitions with the properties described above, except in the case $L'(4,6)$. Furthermore, L' and M' obey the mutual recursions (62) and (63) except in a few cases.*

Proof. We noted above that (62) and (63) *almost* work; the reader may verify that the only glitch occurs in the case $L(4,6)$, when (62) gives

$$L(4,6) = L(2,6), \; 3L(1,3)^R, \; 4L(1,2), \; 321, \; 33, \; 42$$
$$= 111111, \; 21111, \; 2211, \; 222, \; 3111, \; 411, \; 321, \; 33, \; 42. \qquad (64)$$

If $m > 4$, we're OK because the transition from the end of $L(m{-}2, 2m{-}2)$ to the beginning of $(m{-}1)L(m{-}3, m{-}1)^R$ is from $(m{-}2)(m{-}2)2$ to $(m{-}1)(m{-}3)2$. There is no satisfactory path $L(4,6)$, because all Gray codes through those nine partitions must end with either 411, 33, 3111, 222, or 2211.

In order to neutralize this anomaly we need to patch the definitions of $L(m,n)$ and $M(m,n)$ at eight places where the "buggy subroutine" $L(4,6)$ is invoked. One simple way is to make the following definitions:

$$L'(4,6) = 111111, 21111, 3111, 411, 321, 33, 42;$$
$$L'(3,5) = 11111, 2111, 221, 311, 32. \qquad (65)$$

Thus, we omit 222 and 2211 from $L(4,6)$; we also reprogram $L(3,5)$ so that 2111 is adjacent to 221. Then exercise 60 shows that it is always easy to "splice in" the two partitions that are missing from $L(4,6)$. ∎

EXERCISES

▶ **1.** [*M21*] Give formulas for the total number of possibilities in each problem of The Twelvefold Way. For example, the number of n-tuples of m things is m^n. (Use the notation (38) when appropriate, and be careful to make your formulas correct even when $m = 0$ or $n = 0$.)

▶ **2.** [*20*] Show that a small change to step H1 yields an algorithm that will generate all partitions of n into *at most* m parts.

3. [*M17*] A partition $a_1 + \cdots + a_m$ of n into m parts $a_1 \geq \cdots \geq a_m$ is *optimally balanced* if $|a_i - a_j| \leq 1$ for $1 \leq i, j \leq m$. Prove that there is exactly one such partition, whenever $n \geq m \geq 1$, and give a simple formula that expresses the jth part a_j as a function of j, m, and n.

4. [*M22*] (Gideon Ehrlich, 1974.) What is the lexicographically smallest partition of n in which all parts are $\geq r$? For example, when $n = 19$ and $r = 5$ the answer is 766.

▶ **5.** [*23*] Design an algorithm that generates all partitions of n in the part-count form $c_1 \ldots c_n$ of (8). Generate them in colex order, namely in the lexicographic order of $c_n \ldots c_1$, which is equivalent to lexicographic order of the corresponding partitions $a_1 a_2 \ldots$. For efficiency, maintain also a table of links $l_0 l_1 \ldots l_n$ so that, if the distinct values of k for which $c_k > 0$ are $k_1 < \cdots < k_t$, we have

$$l_0 = k_1, \quad l_{k_1} = k_2, \quad \ldots, \quad l_{k_{t-1}} = k_t, \quad l_{k_t} = 0.$$

(Thus the partition 331 would be represented by $c_1 \ldots c_7 = 1020000$, $l_0 = 1$, $l_1 = 3$, and $l_3 = 0$; the other links l_2, l_4, l_5, l_6, l_7 can be set to any convenient values.)

6. [*20*] Design an algorithm to compute $b_1 b_2 \ldots = (a_1 a_2 \ldots)^T$, given $a_1 a_2 \ldots$.

7. [*M20*] Suppose $a_1 \ldots a_n$ and $a'_1 \ldots a'_n$ are partitions of n with $a_1 \geq \cdots \geq a_n \geq 0$ and $a'_1 \geq \cdots \geq a'_n \geq 0$, and let their respective conjugates be $b_1 \ldots b_n = (a_1 \ldots a_n)^T$, $b'_1 \ldots b'_n = (a'_1 \ldots a'_n)^T$. Show that $b_1 \ldots b_n < b'_1 \ldots b'_n$ if and only if $a_n \ldots a_1 < a'_n \ldots a'_1$.

8. [*15*] When $(p_1 \ldots p_t, q_1 \ldots q_t)$ yields the rim representation of a partition $a_1 a_2 \ldots$ as in (15) and (16), what's the rim representation of the conjugate partition $(a_1 a_2 \ldots)^T$?

9. [*22*] If $a_1 a_2 \ldots a_m$ and $b_1 b_2 \ldots b_m = (a_1 a_2 \ldots a_m)^T$ are conjugate partitions, show that the multisets $\{a_1+1, a_2+2, \ldots, a_m+m\}$ and $\{b_1+1, b_2+2, \ldots, b_m+m\}$ are equal.

10. [*21*] Two simple kinds of binary trees are sometimes helpful for reasoning about partitions: (a) a tree that includes all partitions of all integers, and (b) a tree that includes all partitions of a given integer n, illustrated here for $n = 8$:

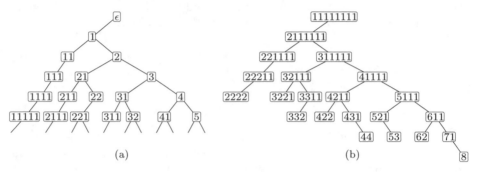

(a)   (b)

Deduce the general rules underlying these constructions. What order of tree traversal corresponds to lexicographic order of the partitions?

11. [*M22*] How many ways are there to pay one euro, using coins worth 1, 2, 5, 10, 20, 50, and/or 100 cents? What if you are allowed to use at most two of each coin?

▶ **12.** [*M21*] (L. Euler, 1750.) Use generating functions to prove that the number of ways to partition n into *distinct* parts is the number of ways to partition n into *odd* parts. For example, $5 = 4+1 = 3+2$; $5 = 3+1+1 = 1+1+1+1+1$.

[*Note:* The next two exercises use combinatorial techniques to prove extensions of this famous theorem.]

▶ **13.** [*M23*] (F. Franklin, 1882.) Find a one-to-one correspondence $\alpha \leftrightarrow \beta$ between partitions of n such that α has exactly k parts repeated more than once if and only if β has exactly k even parts. (For example, the partition 64421111 has two repeated parts $\{4, 1\}$ and three even parts $\{6, 4, 2\}$. The case $k = 0$ corresponds to Euler's result.)

▶ **14.** [*M28*] (J. J. Sylvester, 1882.) Find a one-to-one correspondence between partitions of n into distinct parts $a_1 > a_2 > \cdots > a_m$ that have exactly k "gaps" where $a_j > a_{j+1} + 1$, and partitions of n into odd parts that have exactly $k + 1$ different values. (For example, when $k = 0$ this construction proves that the number of ways to write n as a sum of consecutive integers is the number of odd divisors of n.)

15. [*M20*] (J. J. Sylvester.) Find a generating function for the number of partitions that are *self-conjugate* (namely, partitions such that $\alpha = \alpha^T$).

16. [*M21*] Find a formula for $\sum_{m,n} p(k, m, n) w^m z^n$, where $p(k, m, n)$ is the number of partitions of n that have m parts and trace k. Sum it on k to obtain a nontrivial identity.

17. [*M26*] A *joint partition* of n is a pair of sequences $(a_1, \ldots, a_r; b_1, \ldots, b_s)$ of positive integers for which we have

$$a_1 \geq \cdots \geq a_r, \quad b_1 > \cdots > b_s, \quad \text{and} \quad a_1 + \cdots + a_r + b_1 + \cdots + b_s = n.$$

Thus it is an ordinary partition if $s = 0$, and a partition into distinct parts if $r = 0$.

   a) Find a simple formula for the generating function $\sum u^{r+s} v^s z^n$, summed over all joint partitions of n with r ordinary parts a_i and s distinct parts b_j.

   b) Similarly, find a simple formula for $\sum v^s z^n$ when the sum is over all joint partitions that have exactly $r + s = t$ total parts, given the value of t. For example, the answer when $t = 2$ is $(1 + v)(1 + vz)z^2/((1 - z)(1 - z^2))$.

   c) What identity do you deduce?

▶ **18.** [*M23*] (Doron Zeilberger.) Show that there is a one-to-one correspondence between pairs of integer sequences $(a_1, a_2, \ldots, a_r; b_1, b_2, \ldots, b_s)$ such that

$$a_1 \geq a_2 \geq \cdots \geq a_r, \quad b_1 > b_2 > \cdots > b_s,$$

and pairs of integer sequences $(c_1, c_2, \ldots, c_{r+s}; d_1, d_2, \ldots, d_{r+s})$ such that

$$c_1 \geq c_2 \geq \cdots \geq c_{r+s}, \quad d_j \in \{0, 1\} \quad \text{for } 1 \leq j \leq r + s,$$

related by the multiset equations

$$\{a_1, a_2, \ldots, a_r\} = \{c_j \mid d_j = 0\} \quad \text{and} \quad \{b_1, b_2, \ldots, b_s\} = \{c_j + r + s - j \mid d_j = 1\}.$$

Consequently we obtain the interesting identity

$$\sum_{\substack{a_1 \geq \cdots \geq a_r > 0, \, r \geq 0 \\ b_1 > \cdots > b_s > 0, \, s \geq 0}} u^{r+s} v^s z^{a_1 + \cdots + a_r + b_1 + \cdots + b_s} = \sum_{\substack{c_1 \geq \cdots \geq c_t > 0, \, t \geq 0 \\ d_1, \ldots, d_t \in \{0, 1\}}} u^t v^{d_1 + \cdots + d_t} z^{c_1 + \cdots + c_t + (t-1)d_1 + \cdots + d_{t-1}}.$$

19. [*M22*] (E. Heine, 1847.) Prove the four-parameter identity

$$\prod_{m=1}^{\infty} \frac{(1 - wxz^m)(1 - wyz^m)}{(1 - wz^m)(1 - wxyz^m)} = \sum_{k=0}^{\infty} \frac{w^k (x-1)(x-z) \ldots (x - z^{k-1})(y-1)(y-z) \ldots (y - z^{k-1}) z^k}{(1-z)(1-z^2) \ldots (1-z^k)(1-wz)(1-wz^2) \ldots (1-wz^k)}.$$

Hint: Carry out the sum over either k or l in the formula

$$\sum_{k,l \geq 0} u^k v^l z^{kl} \frac{(z - az)(z - az^2) \ldots (z - az^k)}{(1-z)(1-z^2) \ldots (1-z^k)} \frac{(z - bz)(z - bz^2) \ldots (z - bz^l)}{(1-z)(1-z^2) \ldots (1-z^l)}$$

and consider the simplifications that occur when $b = auz$.

▶ **20.** [*M21*] Approximately how long does it take to compute a table of the partition numbers $p(n)$ for $1 \leq n \leq N$, using Euler's recurrence (20)?

21. [*M21*] (L. Euler.) Let $q(n)$ be the number of partitions of n into distinct parts. What is a good way to compute $q(n)$ if you already know the values of $p(1), \ldots, p(n)$?

22. [*HM21*] (L. Euler.) Let $\sigma(n)$ be the sum of all positive divisors of the positive integer n. Thus, $\sigma(n) = n + 1$ when n is prime, and $\sigma(n)$ can be significantly larger than n when n is highly composite. Prove that, in spite of this rather chaotic behavior, $\sigma(n)$ satisfies almost the same recurrence (20) as the partition numbers:

$$\sigma(n) = \sigma(n-1) + \sigma(n-2) - \sigma(n-5) - \sigma(n-7) + \sigma(n-12) + \sigma(n-15) - \cdots$$

for $n \geq 1$, except that when a term on the right is '$\sigma(0)$' the value 'n' is used instead. For example, $\sigma(11) = 1 + 11 = \sigma(10) + \sigma(9) - \sigma(6) - \sigma(4) = 18 + 13 - 12 - 7$; $\sigma(12) = 1 + 2 + 3 + 4 + 6 + 12 = \sigma(11) + \sigma(10) - \sigma(7) - \sigma(5) + 12 = 12 + 18 - 8 - 6 + 12$.

23. [*HM25*] Use Jacobi's triple product identity (19) to prove another formula that he discovered:

$$\prod_{k=1}^{\infty}(1-z^k)^3 = 1 - 3z + 5z^3 - 7z^6 + 9z^{10} - \cdots = \sum_{n=0}^{\infty}(-1)^n(2n+1)z^{\binom{n+1}{2}}.$$

24. [*M26*] (S. Ramanujan, 1919.) Let $A(z) = \prod_{k=1}^{\infty}(1-z^k)^4$.

a) Prove that $[z^n]\,A(z)$ is a multiple of 5 when $n \bmod 5 = 4$.

b) Prove that $[z^n]\,A(z)B(z)^5$ has the same property, if B is any power series with integer coefficients.

c) Therefore $p(n)$ is a multiple of 5 when $n \bmod 5 = 4$.

25. [*HM27*] Improve on (22) by using (a) Euler's summation formula and (b) Mellin transforms to estimate $\ln P(e^{-t})$. *Hint:* The dilogarithm function $\text{Li}_2(x) = x/1^2 + x^2/2^2 + x^3/3^2 + \cdots$ satisfies $\text{Li}_2(x) + \text{Li}_2(1-x) = \zeta(2) - (\ln x)\ln(1-x)$.

26. [*HM22*] In exercises 5.2.2–44 and 5.2.2–51 we studied two ways to prove that

$$\sum_{k=1}^{\infty}e^{-k^2/n} = \frac{1}{2}(\sqrt{\pi n} - 1) + O(n^{-M}) \qquad \text{for all } M > 0.$$

Show that Poisson's summation formula gives a much stronger result.

27. [*HM21*] Prove (28) and complete the calculations leading to Theorem D.

28. [*HM42*] (D. H. Lehmer.) Show that the Hardy–Ramanujan–Rademacher coefficients $A_k(n)$ defined in (34) have the following remarkable properties:

a) If k is odd, then $A_{2k}(km + 4n + (k^2-1)/8) = A_2(m)\,A_k(n)$.

b) If p is prime, $p^e > 2$, and $k \perp 2p$, then

$$A_{p^e k}(k^2 m + p^{2e}n - (k^2 + p^{2e} - 1)/24) = (-1)^{[p^e=4]}A_{p^e}(m)\,A_k(n).$$

In this formula $k^2 + p^{2e} - 1$ is a multiple of 24 if p or k is divisible by 2 or 3; otherwise division by 24 should be done modulo $p^e k$.

c) If p is prime, $|A_{p^e}(n)| < 2^{[p>2]}p^{e/2}$.

d) If p is prime, $A_{p^e}(n) \neq 0$ if and only if $1 - 24n$ is a quadratic residue modulo p and either $e = 1$ or $24n \bmod p \neq 1$.

e) The probability that $A_k(n) = 0$, when k is divisible by exactly t primes ≥ 5 and n is a random integer, is approximately $1 - 2^{-t}$.

▶ **29.** [*M16*] Generalizing (41), evaluate the sum $\sum_{a_1 \geq a_2 \geq \cdots \geq a_m \geq 1} z_1^{a_1} z_2^{a_2} \cdots z_m^{a_m}$.

30. [*M17*] Find closed forms for the sums

$$\text{(a)} \ \sum_{k\geq 0}\left|{n - km \atop m - 1}\right| \qquad \text{and} \qquad \text{(b)} \ \sum_{k\geq 0}\left|{n \atop m - k}\right|$$

(which are finite, because the terms being summed are zero when k is large).

31. [*M24*] (A. De Morgan, 1843.) Show that $\left|{n \atop 2}\right| = \lfloor n/2 \rfloor$ and $\left|{n \atop 3}\right| = \lfloor (n^2 + 6)/12 \rfloor$; find a similar formula for $\left|{n \atop 4}\right|$.

32. [*M15*] Prove that $\left|{n \atop m}\right| \leq p(n - m)$ for all $m, n \geq 0$. When does equality hold?

33. [*HM20*] Use the fact that there are exactly $\binom{n-1}{m-1}$ *compositions* of n into m parts, Eq. 7.2.1.3–(9), to prove a lower bound on $\left|{n \atop m}\right|$. Then set $m = \lfloor\sqrt{n}\rfloor$ to obtain an elementary lower bound on $p(n)$.

▸ **34.** [*HM21*] Show that $\left|{n - m(m-1)/2 \atop m}\right|$ is the number of partitions of n into m distinct parts. Consequently

$$\left|{n \atop m}\right| = \frac{n^{m-1}}{m!\,(m-1)!}\left(1 + O\left(\frac{m^3}{n}\right)\right) \qquad \text{when } m \le n^{1/3}.$$

35. [*HM21*] In the Erdős–Lehner probability distribution (43), what value of x is (a) most probable? (b) the median? (c) the mean? (d) What is the standard deviation?

36. [*HM24*] Prove the key estimate (47) that is needed in Theorem E.

37. [*M22*] Prove the inclusion-exclusion bracketing lemma (48), by analyzing how many times a partition that has exactly q different parts exceeding m is counted in the rth partial sum.

38. [*M20*] Given positive integers l and m, what generating function enumerates partitions that have exactly m parts, and largest part l? (See Eq. (51).)

39. [*M20*] (A. Cauchy.) Continuing exercise 38, what is the generating function for the number of partitions into m parts, all *distinct* and less than l?

▸ **40.** [*M25*] (F. Franklin.) Generalizing Theorem C, show that, for $0 \le k \le m$,

$$[z^n]\,\frac{(1 - z^{l+1})\ldots(1 - z^{l+k})}{(1 - z)(1 - z^2)\ldots(1 - z^m)}$$

is the number of partitions $a_1 a_2 \ldots$ of n into m or fewer parts with the property that $a_1 \le a_{k+1} + l$.

41. [*HM42*] Extend the Hardy–Ramanujan–Rademacher formula (32) to obtain a convergent series for partitions of n into at most m parts, with no part exceeding l.

42. [*HM42*] Find the limiting shape, analogous to (49), for random partitions of n into at most $\theta\sqrt{n}$ parts, with no part exceeding $\varphi\sqrt{n}$, assuming that $\theta\varphi > 1$.

43. [*M18*] Given n and k, how many partitions of n have $a_1 > a_2 > \cdots > a_k$?

▸ **44.** [*M22*] How many partitions of n have their two smallest parts equal?

45. [*HM21*] Compute the asymptotic value of $p(n-1)/p(n)$, with relative error $O(n^{-2})$.

46. [*M20*] In the text's analysis of Algorithm P, which is larger, $T_2'(n)$ or $T_2''(n)$?

▸ **47.** [*HM22*] (A. Nijenhuis and H. S. Wilf, 1975.) The following simple algorithm, based on a table of the partition numbers $p(0)$, $p(1)$, $\ldots$, $p(n)$, generates a random partition of n using the part-count representation $c_1 \ldots c_n$ of (8). Prove that it produces each partition with equal probability.

> **N1.** [Initialize.] Set $m \leftarrow n$ and $c_1 \ldots c_n \leftarrow 0 \ldots 0$.
>
> **N2.** [Done?] Terminate if $m = 0$.
>
> **N3.** [Generate.] Generate a random integer M in the range $0 \le M < mp(m)$.
>
> **N4.** [Choose parts.] Set $s \leftarrow 0$. Then for $j = 1, 2, \ldots$, and for $k = 1, 2, \ldots, \lfloor m/j \rfloor$, repeatedly set $s \leftarrow s + kp(m - jk)$ until $s > M$.
>
> **N5.** [Update.] Set $c_k \leftarrow c_k + j$, $m \leftarrow m - jk$, and return to N2. ▌

Hint: Step N4, which is based on the identity

$$\sum_{j=1}^{\infty} \sum_{k=1}^{\lfloor m/j \rfloor} kp(m - jk) = mp(m),$$

chooses each particular pair of values (j, k) with probability $kp(m - jk)/(mp(m))$.

48. [*HM40*] Analyze the running time of the algorithm in the previous exercise.

▶ **49.** [*HM26*] (a) What is the generating function $F(z)$ for the sum of the smallest parts of all partitions of n? (The series begins $z + 3z^2 + 5z^3 + 9z^4 + 12z^5 + \cdots$.)

(b) Find the asymptotic value of $[z^n] F(z)$, with relative error $O(n^{-1})$.

50. [*HM33*] Let $c(m) = c_m(2m)$ in the recurrence (56), (57).

a) Prove that $c_m(m + k) = m - k + c(k)$ for $0 \le k \le m$.

b) Consequently (58) holds for $m \le n \le 2m$, if $c(m) < 3p(m)$ for all $m \ge 0$.

c) Show that $c(m) - m$ is the sum of the second-smallest parts of all partitions of m.

d) Find a one-to-one correspondence between all partitions of n with second-smallest part k and all partitions of numbers $\le n$ with smallest part $k + 1$.

e) Describe the generating function $\sum_{m \ge 0} c(m) z^m$.

f) Conclude that $c(m) < 3p(m)$ for all $m \ge 0$.

51. [*M46*] Make a detailed analysis of Algorithm H.

▶ **52.** [*M21*] What is the millionth partition generated by Algorithm P when $n = 64$? *Hint:* $p(64) = 1741630 = 1000000 + \left|{77 \atop 13}\right| + \left|{60 \atop 10}\right| + \left|{47 \atop 8}\right| + \left|{35 \atop 5}\right| + \left|{27 \atop 3}\right| + \left|{22 \atop 2}\right| + \left|{18 \atop 1}\right| + \left|{15 \atop 0}\right|$.

▶ **53.** [*M21*] What is the millionth partition generated by Algorithm H when $m = 32$ and $n = 100$? *Hint:* $999999 = \left|{80 \atop 12}\right| + \left|{66 \atop 11}\right| + \left|{50 \atop 7}\right| + \left|{41 \atop 6}\right| + \left|{33 \atop 5}\right| + \left|{26 \atop 4}\right| + \left|{21 \atop 4}\right|$.

▶ **54.** [*M30*] Let $\alpha = a_1 a_2 \ldots$ and $\beta = b_1 b_2 \ldots$ be partitions of n. We say that α *majorizes* β, written $\alpha \succeq \beta$ or $\beta \preceq \alpha$, if $a_1 + \cdots + a_k \ge b_1 + \cdots + b_k$ for all $k \ge 0$.

a) True or false: $\alpha \succeq \beta$ implies $\alpha \ge \beta$ (lexicographically).

b) True or false: $\alpha \succeq \beta$ implies $\beta^T \succeq \alpha^T$.

c) Show that any two partitions of n have a greatest lower bound $\alpha \wedge \beta$ such that $\alpha \succeq \gamma$ and $\beta \succeq \gamma$ if and only if $\alpha \wedge \beta \succeq \gamma$. Explain how to compute $\alpha \wedge \beta$.

d) Similarly, explain how to compute a least upper bound $\alpha \vee \beta$ such that $\gamma \succeq \alpha$ and $\gamma \succeq \beta$ if and only if $\gamma \succeq \alpha \vee \beta$.

e) If α has l parts and β has m parts, how many parts do $\alpha \wedge \beta$ and $\alpha \vee \beta$ have?

f) True or false: If α has distinct parts and β has distinct parts, then so do $\alpha \wedge \beta$ and $\alpha \vee \beta$.

▶ **55.** [*M37*] Continuing the previous exercise, say that α *covers* β if $\alpha \succeq \beta$ and $\alpha \ne \beta$, and if $\alpha \succeq \gamma \succeq \beta$ implies that $\gamma = \alpha$ or $\gamma = \beta$. For example, Fig. 52 illustrates the covering relations between partitions of the number 12.

a) Let us write $\alpha \vartriangleright \beta$ if $\alpha = a_1 a_2 \ldots$ and $\beta = b_1 b_2 \ldots$ are partitions for which $b_k = a_k - [k = l] + [k = l + 1]$ for all $k \ge 1$ and some $l \ge 1$. Prove that α covers β if and only if $\alpha \vartriangleright \beta$ or $\beta^T \vartriangleright \alpha^T$.

b) Show that there is an easy way to tell if α covers β by looking at the rim representations of α and β.

c) Let $n = \binom{n_2}{2} + \binom{n_1}{1}$ where $n_2 > n_1 \ge 0$ and $n_2 > 2$. Show that no partition of n covers more than $n_2 - 2$ partitions.

d) Say that the partition μ is *minimal* if there is no partition λ with $\mu \vartriangleright \lambda$. Prove that μ is minimal if and only if μ^T has distinct parts.

e) Suppose $\alpha = \alpha_0 \vartriangleright \alpha_1 \vartriangleright \cdots \vartriangleright \alpha_k$ and $\alpha = \alpha'_0 \vartriangleright \alpha'_1 \vartriangleright \cdots \vartriangleright \alpha'_{k'}$, where α_k and $\alpha'_{k'}$ are minimal partitions. Prove that $k = k'$ and $\alpha_k = \alpha'_{k'}$.

f) Explain how to compute the lexicographically smallest partition into distinct parts that majorizes a given partition α.

g) Describe λ_n, the lexicographically smallest partition of n into distinct parts. What is the length of all paths $n^1 = \alpha_0 \vartriangleright \alpha_1 \vartriangleright \cdots \vartriangleright \lambda_n^T$?

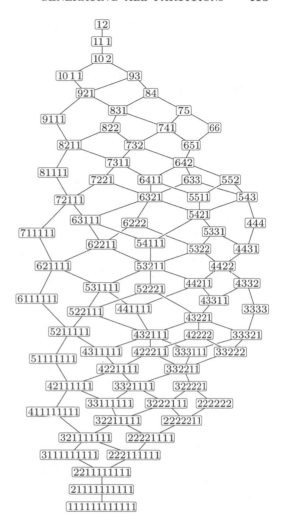

Fig. 52. The majorization lattice for partitions of 12. (See exercises 54–58.)

h) What are the lengths of the longest and shortest paths of the form $n^1 = \alpha_0, \alpha_1, \ldots, \alpha_l = 1^n$, where α_j covers α_{j+1} for $0 \leq j < l$?

▶ **56.** [*M32*] Design an algorithm to generate all partitions α such that $\lambda \preceq \alpha \preceq \mu$, given partitions λ and μ with $\lambda \preceq \mu$.

Note: Such an algorithm has numerous applications. For example, to generate all partitions that have m parts and no part exceeding l, we can let λ be the smallest such partition, namely $\lceil n/m \rceil \ldots \lfloor n/m \rfloor$ as in exercise 3, and let μ be the largest, namely $((n-m+1)1^{m-1}) \wedge (l^{\lfloor n/l \rfloor}(n \bmod l))$. Similarly, according to a well-known theorem of H. G. Landau [*Bull. Math. Biophysics* **15** (1953), 143–148], the partitions of $\binom{m}{2}$ such that

$$\left\lfloor \frac{m}{2} \right\rfloor^{\lfloor m/2 \rfloor} \left\lfloor \frac{m-1}{2} \right\rfloor^{\lceil m/2 \rceil} \preceq \alpha \preceq (m-1)(m-2)\ldots 21$$

are the possible "score vectors" of a round-robin tournament, namely the partitions $a_1 \ldots a_m$ such that the jth strongest player wins a_j games.

57. [*M22*] Suppose a matrix (a_{ij}) of 0s and 1s has row sums $r_i = \sum_j a_{ij}$ and column sums $c_j = \sum_i a_{ij}$. By permuting rows and columns we can assume that $r_1 \geq r_2 \geq \cdots$ and $c_1 \geq c_2 \geq \cdots$. Then $\lambda = r_1 r_2 \ldots$ and $\mu = c_1 c_2 \ldots$ are partitions of $n = \sum_{i,j} a_{ij}$. Prove that such a matrix exists if and only if $\lambda \preceq \mu^T$.

58. [*M23*] (*Symmetrical means.*) Let $\alpha = a_1 \ldots a_m$ and $\beta = b_1 \ldots b_m$ be partitions of n. Prove that the inequality

$$\frac{1}{m!} \sum x_{p_1}^{a_1} \ldots x_{p_m}^{a_m} \geq \frac{1}{m!} \sum x_{p_1}^{b_1} \ldots x_{p_m}^{b_m}$$

holds for all nonnegative values of the variables $(x_1, \ldots, x_m)$, where the sums range over all $m!$ permutations of $\{1, \ldots, m\}$, if and only if $\alpha \succeq \beta$. (For example, this inequality reduces to $(y_1 + \cdots + y_n)/n \geq (y_1 \ldots y_n)^{1/n}$, "the arithmetic mean dominates the geometric mean," in the special case $m = n$, $\alpha = n0 \ldots 0$, $\beta = 11 \ldots 1$, $x_j = y_j^{1/n}$.)

59. [*M22*] The Gray path (59) is symmetrical in the sense that the reversed sequence 6, 51, ..., 111111 is the same as the conjugate sequence $(111111)^T$, $(21111)^T$, ..., $(6)^T$. Find all Gray paths $\alpha_1, \ldots, \alpha_{p(n)}$ that are symmetrical in this way.

60. [*23*] Complete the proof of Theorem S by modifying the definitions of $L(m, n)$ and $M(m, n)$ in all places where $L(4, 6)$ is called in (62) and (63).

61. [*26*] Implement a partition-generation scheme based on Theorem S, always specifying the two parts that have changed between visits.

62. [*46*] Prove or disprove: For all sufficiently large integers n and $3 \leq m < n$ such that $n \bmod m \neq 0$, and for all partitions α of n with $a_1 \leq m$, there is a Gray path for all partitions with parts $\leq m$, beginning at 1^n and ending at α, unless $\alpha = 1^n$ or $\alpha = 21^{n-2}$.

63. [*47*] For which partitions λ and μ is there a Gray code through all partitions α such that $\lambda \preceq \alpha \preceq \mu$?

▶ **64.** [*32*] (*Binary partitions.*) Design a loopless algorithm that visits all partitions of n into powers of 2, where each step replaces $2^k + 2^k$ by 2^{k+1} or vice versa.

65. [*23*] It is well known that every commutative group of m elements can be represented as a discrete torus $T(m_1, \ldots, m_n)$ with the addition operation of 7.2.1.3–(66), where $m = m_1 \ldots m_n$ and m_j is a multiple of m_{j+1} for $1 \leq j < n$. For example, when $m = 360 = 2^3 \cdot 3^2 \cdot 5^1$ there are six such groups, corresponding to the factorizations $(m_1, m_2, m_3) = (30, 6, 2)$, $(60, 6, 1)$, $(90, 2, 2)$, $(120, 3, 1)$, $(180, 2, 1)$, and $(360, 1, 1)$.

Explain how to generate all such factorizations systematically with an algorithm that changes exactly two of the factors m_j at each step.

▶ **66.** [*M25*] (*P-partitions.*) Instead of insisting that $a_1 \geq a_2 \geq \cdots$, suppose we want to consider all nonnegative compositions of n that satisfy a given *partial* order. For example, P. A. MacMahon observed that all solutions to the "up-down" inequalities $a_4 \leq a_2 \geq a_3 \leq a_1$ can be divided into five nonoverlapping types:

$$a_1 \geq a_2 \geq a_3 \geq a_4; \quad a_1 \geq a_2 \geq a_4 > a_3;$$
$$a_2 > a_1 \geq a_3 \geq a_4; \quad a_2 > a_1 \geq a_4 > a_3; \quad a_2 \geq a_4 > a_1 \geq a_3.$$

Each of these types is easily enumerated since, for example, $a_2 > a_1 \geq a_4 > a_3$ is equivalent to $a_2 - 2 \geq a_1 - 1 \geq a_4 - 1 \geq a_3$; the number of solutions with $a_3 \geq 0$ and $a_1 + a_2 + a_3 + a_4 = n$ is the number of partitions of $n - 1 - 2 - 0 - 1$ into at most four parts.

Explain how to solve a general problem of this kind: Given any partial order relation $\prec$ on m elements, consider all m-tuples $a_1 \ldots a_m$ with the property that $a_j \geq a_k$

when $j \prec k$. Assuming that the subscripts have been chosen so that $j \prec k$ implies $j \leq k$, show that all of the desired m-tuples fall into exactly N classes, one for each of the outputs of the topological sorting algorithm 7.2.1.2V. What is the generating function for all such $a_1 \ldots a_m$ that are nonnegative and sum to n? How could you generate them all?

67. [*M25*] (P. A. MacMahon, 1886.) A *perfect partition* of n is a multiset that has exactly $n+1$ submultisets, and these multisets are partitions of the integers $0, 1, \ldots, n$. For example, the multisets $\{1,1,1,1,1\}$, $\{2,2,1\}$, and $\{3,1,1\}$ are perfect partitions of 5.

Explain how to construct the perfect partitions of n that have fewest elements.

68. [*M23*] What partition of n into m parts has the largest product $a_1 \ldots a_m$, when (a) m is given; (b) m is arbitrary?

69. [*M30*] Find all $n < 10^9$ such that the equation $x_1 + x_2 + \cdots + x_n = x_1 x_2 \ldots x_n$ has only one solution in positive integers $x_1 \geq x_2 \geq \cdots \geq x_n$. (There is, for example, only one solution when $n = 2$, 3, or 4; but $5 + 2 + 1 + 1 + 1 = 5 \cdot 2 \cdot 1 \cdot 1 \cdot 1$ and $3 + 3 + 1 + 1 + 1 = 3 \cdot 3 \cdot 1 \cdot 1 \cdot 1$ and $2 + 2 + 2 + 1 + 1 = 2 \cdot 2 \cdot 2 \cdot 1 \cdot 1$.)

70. [*M30*] ("Bulgarian solitaire.") Take n cards and divide them arbitrarily into one or more piles. Then repeatedly remove one card from each pile and form a new pile.

Show that if $n = 1 + 2 + \cdots + m$, this process always reaches a self-repeating state with piles of sizes $\{m, m-1, \ldots, 1\}$. For example, if $n = 10$ and if we start with piles whose sizes are $\{3, 3, 2, 2\}$, we get the sequence of partitions

$$3322 \rightarrow 42211 \rightarrow 5311 \rightarrow 442 \rightarrow 3331 \rightarrow 4222 \rightarrow 43111 \rightarrow 532 \rightarrow 4321 \rightarrow 4321 \rightarrow \cdots.$$

What cycles of states are possible for other values of n?

71. [*M46*] Continuing the previous problem, what is the maximum number of steps that can occur before n-card Bulgarian solitaire reaches a cyclic state?

72. [*M30*] How many partitions of n have no predecessor in Bulgarian solitaire?

73. [*M25*] Suppose we write down all partitions of n, for example

$$6, \quad 51, \quad 42, \quad 411, \quad 33, \quad 321, \quad 3111, \quad 222, \quad 2211, \quad 21111, \quad 111111$$

when $n = 6$, and change each jth occurrence of k to j in each one:

$$1, \quad 11, \quad 11, \quad 112, \quad 12, \quad 111, \quad 1123, \quad 123, \quad 1212, \quad 11234, \quad 123456.$$

a) Prove that this operation yields a permutation of the individual elements.
b) How many times does the element k appear altogether?

7.2.1.5. Generating all set partitions.

Now let's shift gears and concentrate on a rather different kind of partition. The *partitions of a set* are the ways to regard that set as a union of nonempty, disjoint subsets called *blocks*. For example, we listed the five essentially different partitions of $\{1, 2, 3\}$ at the beginning of the previous section, in 7.2.1.4–(2) and 7.2.1.4–(4). Those five partitions can also be written more compactly in the form

$$123, \quad 12|3, \quad 13|2, \quad 1|23, \quad 1|2|3, \tag{1}$$

using a vertical line to separate one block from another. In this list the elements of each block could have been written in any order, and so could the blocks themselves, because '13|2' and '31|2' and '2|13' and '2|31' all represent the same partition. But we can standardize the representation by agreeing, for example, to list the elements of each block in increasing order, and to arrange the blocks in increasing order of their smallest elements. With this convention the partitions of $\{1,2,3,4\}$ are

$$1234, \ 123|4, \ 124|3, \ 12|34, \ 12|3|4, \ 134|2, \ 13|24, \ 13|2|4,$$
$$14|23, \ 1|234, \ 1|23|4, \ 14|2|3, \ 1|24|3, \ 1|2|34, \ 1|2|3|4, \tag{2}$$

obtained by placing 4 among the blocks of (1) in all possible ways.

Set partitions arise in many different contexts. Political scientists and economists, for example, often see them as "coalitions"; computer system designers may consider them to be "cache hit patterns" for memory accesses; poets know them as "rhyme schemes" (see exercises 34–37). We saw in Section 2.3.3 that any *equivalence relation* between objects — namely any binary relation that is reflexive, symmetric, and transitive — defines a partition of those objects into so-called "equivalence classes." Conversely, every set partition defines an equivalence relation: If Π is a partition of $\{1,2,\ldots,n\}$ we can write

$$j \equiv k \quad (\text{modulo } \Pi) \tag{3}$$

whenever j and k belong to the same block of Π.

One of the most convenient ways to represent a set partition inside a computer is to encode it as a *restricted growth string*, namely as a string $a_1 a_2 \ldots a_n$ of nonnegative integers in which we have

$$a_1 = 0 \quad \text{and} \quad a_{j+1} \le 1 + \max(a_1, \ldots, a_j) \text{ for } 1 \le j < n. \tag{4}$$

The idea is to set $a_j = a_k$ if and only if $j \equiv k$, and to choose the smallest available number for a_j whenever j is smallest in its block. For example, the restricted growth strings for the fifteen partitions in (2) are respectively

$$0000, \ 0001, \ 0010, \ 0011, \ 0012, \ 0100, \ 0101, \ 0102,$$
$$0110, \ 0111, \ 0112, \ 0120, \ 0121, \ 0122, \ 0123. \tag{5}$$

This convention suggests the following simple generation scheme, due to George Hutchinson [*CACM* **6** (1963), 613–614]:

Algorithm H (*Restricted growth strings in lexicographic order*). Given $n \ge 2$, this algorithm generates all partitions of $\{1,2,\ldots,n\}$ by visiting all strings $a_1 a_2 \ldots a_n$ that satisfy the restricted growth condition (4). We maintain an auxiliary array $b_1 b_2 \ldots b_n$, where $b_{j+1} = 1 + \max(a_1, \ldots, a_j)$; the value of b_n is actually kept in a separate variable, m, for efficiency.

H1. [Initialize.] Set $a_1 \ldots a_n \leftarrow 0 \ldots 0$, $b_1 \ldots b_{n-1} \leftarrow 1 \ldots 1$, and $m \leftarrow 1$.

H2. [Visit.] Visit the restricted growth string $a_1 \ldots a_n$, which represents a partition into $m + [a_n = m]$ blocks. Then go to H4 if $a_n = m$.

H3. [Increase a_n.] Set $a_n \leftarrow a_n + 1$ and return to H2.

H4. [Find j.] Set $j \leftarrow n - 1$; then, while $a_j = b_j$, set $j \leftarrow j - 1$.

H5. [Increase a_j.] Terminate if $j = 1$. Otherwise set $a_j \leftarrow a_j + 1$.

H6. [Zero out $a_{j+1} \ldots a_n$.] Set $m \leftarrow b_j + [a_j = b_j]$ and $j \leftarrow j + 1$. Then, while $j < n$, set $a_j \leftarrow 0$, $b_j \leftarrow m$, and $j \leftarrow j + 1$. Finally set $a_n \leftarrow 0$ and go back to H2. ∎

Exercise 47 proves that steps H4–H6 are rarely necessary, and that the loops in H4 and H6 are almost always short. A linked-list variant of this algorithm appears in exercise 2.

Gray codes for set partitions. One way to pass quickly through all set partitions is to change just one digit of the restricted growth string $a_1 \ldots a_n$ at each step, because a change to a_j simply means that element j moves from one block to another. An elegant way to arrange such a list was proposed by Gideon Ehrlich [*JACM* **20** (1973), 507–508]: We can successively append the digits

$$0, \ m, \ m-1, \ \ldots, \ 1 \qquad \text{or} \qquad 1, \ \ldots, \ m-1, \ m, \ 0 \qquad (6)$$

to each string $a_1 \ldots a_{n-1}$ in the list for partitions of $n - 1$ elements, where $m = 1 + \max(a_1, \ldots, a_{n-1})$, alternating between the two cases. Thus the list '00, 01' for $n = 2$ becomes '000, 001, 011, 012, 010' for $n = 3$; and that list becomes

$$0000, \ 0001, \ 0011, \ 0012, \ 0010, \ 0110, \ 0112, \ 0111,$$
$$0121, \ 0122, \ 0123, \ 0120, \ 0100, \ 0102, \ 0101 \qquad (7)$$

when we extend it to the case $n = 4$. Exercise 14 shows that Ehrlich's scheme leads to a simple algorithm that achieves this Gray-code order without doing much more work than Algorithm H.

Suppose, however, that we aren't interested in *all* of the partitions; we might want only the ones that have exactly m blocks. Can we run through this smaller collection of restricted growth strings, still changing only one digit at a time? Yes; a very pretty way to generate such a list has been discovered by Frank Ruskey [*Lecture Notes in Comp. Sci.* **762** (1993), 205–206]. He defined two such sequences, A_{mn} and A'_{mn}, both of which start with the lexicographically smallest m-block string $0^{n-m}01 \ldots (m-1)$. The difference between them, if $n > m + 1$, is that A_{mn} ends with $01 \ldots (m-1)0^{n-m}$ while A'_{mn} ends with $0^{n-m-1}01 \ldots (m-1)0$. Here are Ruskey's recursive rules, when $1 < m < n$:

$$A_{m(n+1)} = \begin{cases} A_{(m-1)n}(m-1), A^R_{mn}(m-1), \ldots, A^R_{mn}1, A_{mn}0, & \text{if } m \text{ is even}; \\ A'_{(m-1)n}(m-1), A_{mn}(m-1), \ldots, A^R_{mn}1, A_{mn}0, & \text{if } m \text{ is odd}; \end{cases} \qquad (8)$$

$$A'_{m(n+1)} = \begin{cases} A'_{(m-1)n}(m-1), A_{mn}(m-1), \ldots, A_{mn}1, A^R_{mn}0, & \text{if } m \text{ is even}; \\ A_{(m-1)n}(m-1), A^R_{mn}(m-1), \ldots, A_{mn}1, A^R_{mn}0, & \text{if } m \text{ is odd}. \end{cases} \qquad (9)$$

(In other words, we begin with either $A_{(m-1)n}(m-1)$ or $A'_{(m-1)n}(m-1)$ and then use either $A^R_{mn}j$ or $A_{mn}j$, alternately, as j decreases from $m - 1$ to 0.) Of course the base cases are simply one-element lists,

$$A_{1n} = A'_{1n} = \{0^n\} \qquad \text{and} \qquad A_{nn} = \{01 \ldots (n-1)\}. \qquad (10)$$

With these definitions the ${5 \brace 3} = 25$ partitions of $\{1,2,3,4,5\}$ into three blocks are

$$00012,\ 00112,\ 01112,\ 01012,\ 01002,\ 01102,\ 00102,$$
$$00122,\ 01122,\ 01022,\ 01222,\ 01212,\ 01202,$$
$$01201,\ 01211,\ 01221,\ 01021,\ 01121,\ 00121,$$
$$00120,\ 01120,\ 01020,\ 01220,\ 01210,\ 01200.$$

(11)

(See exercise 17 for an efficient implementation.)

In Ehrlich's scheme (7) the rightmost digits of $a_1 \ldots a_n$ vary most rapidly, but in Ruskey's scheme most of the changes occur near the left. In both cases, however, each step affects just one digit a_j, and the changes are quite simple: Either a_j changes by ± 1, or it jumps between the two extreme values 0 and $1 + \max(a_1, \ldots, a_{j-1})$. Under the same constraints, the sequence A'_{1n}, A'_{2n}, $\ldots$, A'_{nn} runs through *all* partitions, in increasing order of the number of blocks.

The number of set partitions.   We've seen that there are 5 partitions of $\{1,2,3\}$ and 15 of $\{1,2,3,4\}$.   A quick way to compute these counts was discovered by C. S. Peirce, who presented the following triangle of numbers in the *American Journal of Mathematics* **3** (1880), page 48:

$$
\begin{array}{cccccc}
1 \\
2 & 1 \\
5 & 3 & 2 \\
15 & 10 & 7 & 5 \\
52 & 37 & 27 & 20 & 15 \\
203 & 151 & 114 & 87 & 67 & 52
\end{array}
$$

(12)

Here the entries ϖ_{n1}, ϖ_{n2}, $\ldots$, ϖ_{nn} of the nth row obey the simple recurrence

$$\varpi_{nk} = \varpi_{(n-1)k} + \varpi_{n(k+1)}, \ \text{if } 1 \le k < n; \qquad \varpi_{nn} = \varpi_{(n-1)1}, \ \text{if } n > 1; \quad (13)$$

and $\varpi_{11} = 1$. Peirce's triangle has many remarkable properties, some of which are surveyed in exercises 26–31 and 33.   For example, ϖ_{nk} is the number of partitions of $\{1, 2, \ldots, n\}$ in which k is the smallest of its block.

The entries on the diagonal and in the first column of Peirce's triangle, which tell us the total number of set partitions, are commonly known as *Bell numbers*, because E. T. Bell wrote several influential papers about them [*AMM* **41** (1934), 411–419; *Annals of Math.* (2) **35** (1934), 258–277; **39** (1938), 539–557].   We shall denote Bell numbers by ϖ_n, following the lead of Louis Comtet, in order to avoid confusion with the Bernoulli numbers B_n.   The first few cases are

$$n = 0\ 1\ 2\ 3\ \ 4\ \ 5\ \ \ 6\ \ \ \ 7\ \ \ \ \ 8\ \ \ \ \ \ \ 9\ \ \ \ \ \ \ 10\ \ \ \ \ \ \ \ 11\ \ \ \ \ \ \ \ \ \ 12$$
$$\varpi_n = 1\ 1\ 2\ 5\ 15\ 52\ 203\ 877\ 4140\ 21147\ 115975\ 678570\ 4213597$$

Notice that this sequence grows rapidly, but not as fast as $n!$; we will prove below that $\varpi_n = \big(\Theta(n/\ln n)\big)^n$.

The Bell numbers $\varpi_n = \varpi_{n1}$ for $n \ge 0$ must satisfy the recurrence formula

$$\varpi_{n+1} = \varpi_n + \binom{n}{1}\varpi_{n-1} + \binom{n}{2}\varpi_{n-2} + \cdots = \sum_k \binom{n}{k}\varpi_{n-k}, \qquad (14)$$

because every partition of $\{1, \ldots, n+1\}$ is obtained by choosing k elements of $\{1, \ldots, n\}$ to put in the block containing $n+1$ and by partitioning the remaining elements in ϖ_{n-k} ways, for some k. This recurrence, found by Yoshisuke Matsunaga in the 18th century (see Section 7.2.1.7), leads to a nice generating function,

$$\Pi(z) = \sum_{n=0}^{\infty} \varpi_n \frac{z^n}{n!} = e^{e^z - 1}, \tag{15}$$

discovered by W. A. Whitworth [*Choice and Chance*, 3rd edition (1878), 3.XXIV]. For if we multiply both sides of (14) by $z^n/n!$ and sum on n we get

$$\Pi'(z) = \sum_{n=0}^{\infty} \varpi_{n+1} \frac{z^n}{n!} = \left(\sum_{k=0}^{\infty} \frac{z^k}{k!} \right) \left(\sum_{m=0}^{\infty} \varpi_m \frac{z^m}{m!} \right) = e^z \Pi(z),$$

and (15) is the solution to this differential equation with $\Pi(0) = 1$.

The numbers ϖ_n had been studied for many years because of their curious properties related to this formula, long before Whitworth pointed out their combinatorial connection with set partitions. For example, we have

$$\varpi_n = \frac{n!}{e} [z^n] e^{e^z} = \frac{n!}{e} [z^n] \sum_{k=0}^{\infty} \frac{e^{kz}}{k!} = \frac{1}{e} \sum_{k=0}^{\infty} \frac{k^n}{k!} \tag{16}$$

[*Mat. Sbornik* **3** (1868), 62; **4** (1869), 39; G. Dobiński, *Archiv der Math. und Physik* **61** (1877), 333–336; **63** (1879), 108–110]. Christian Kramp discussed the expansion of e^{e^z} in *Der polynomische Lehrsatz*, ed. by C. F. Hindenburg (Leipzig: 1796), 112–113; he mentioned two ways to compute the coefficients, namely either to use (14) or to use a summation of $p(n)$ terms, one for each ordinary partition of n. (See Arbogast's formula, exercise 1.2.5–21. Kramp, who came close to discovering that formula, seemed to prefer his partition-based method, not realizing that it would require more than polynomial time as n got larger and larger; and he computed 116015, not 115975, for the coefficient of z^{10}.)

*Asymptotic estimates. We can learn how fast ϖ_n grows by using one of the most basic principles of complex residue theory: If the power series $\sum_{k=0}^{\infty} a_k z^k$ converges whenever $|z| < r$, then

$$a_{n-1} = \frac{1}{2\pi i} \oint \frac{a_0 + a_1 z + a_2 z^2 + \cdots}{z^n} \, dz, \tag{17}$$

if the integral is taken along a simple closed path that goes counterclockwise around the origin and stays inside the circle $|z| = r$. Let $f(z) = \sum_{k=0}^{\infty} a_k z^{k-n}$ be the integrand. We're free to choose any such path; but special techniques often apply when the path goes through a point z_0 at which the derivative $f'(z_0)$ is zero, because we have

$$f(z_0 + \epsilon e^{i\theta}) = f(z_0) + \frac{f''(z_0)}{2} \epsilon^2 e^{2i\theta} + O(\epsilon^3) \tag{18}$$

in the vicinity of such a point. If, for example, $f(z_0)$ and $f''(z_0)$ are real and positive, say $f(z_0) = u$ and $f''(z_0) = 2v$, this formula says that the value of

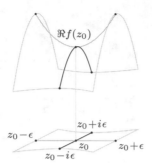

Fig. 53. The behavior of an analytic function near a saddle point.

$f(z_0 \pm \epsilon)$ is approximately $u + v\epsilon^2$ while $f(z_0 \pm i\epsilon)$ is approximately $u - v\epsilon^2$. If z moves from $z_0 - i\epsilon$ to $z_0 + i\epsilon$, the value of $f(z)$ rises to a maximum value u, then falls again; but the larger value $u + v\epsilon^2$ occurs both to the left and to the right of this path. In other words, a mountaineer who goes hiking on the complex plane, when the altitude at point z is $\Re f(z)$, encounters a "pass" at z_0; the terrain looks like a saddle at that point. The overall integral of $f(z)$ will be the same if taken around any path, but a path that doesn't go through the pass won't be as nice because it will have to cancel out some higher values of $f(z)$ that could have been avoided. Therefore we tend to get best results by choosing a path that goes through z_0, in the direction of increasing imaginary part. This important technique, due to P. Debye [*Math. Annalen* **67** (1909), 535–558], is called the "saddle point method."

Let's get familiar with the saddle point method by starting with an example for which we already know the answer:

$$\frac{1}{(n-1)!} = \frac{1}{2\pi i} \oint \frac{e^z}{z^n} \, dz. \tag{19}$$

Our goal is to find a good approximation for the value of the integral on the right when n is large. It will be convenient to deal with $f(z) = e^z/z^n$ by writing it as $e^{g(z)}$ where $g(z) = z - n \ln z$; then the saddle point occurs where $g'(z_0) = 1 - n/z_0$ is zero, namely at $z_0 = n$. If $z = n + it$ we have

$$g(z) = g(n) + \sum_{k=2}^{\infty} \frac{g^{(k)}(n)}{k!} (it)^k$$

$$= n - n \ln n - \frac{t^2}{2n} + \frac{it^3}{3n^2} + \frac{t^4}{4n^3} - \frac{it^5}{5n^4} + \cdots$$

because $g^{(k)}(z) = (-1)^k (k-1)! \, n/z^k$ when $k \geq 2$. Let's integrate $f(z)$ on a rectangular path from $n - im$ to $n + im$ to $-n + im$ to $-n - im$ to $n - im$:

$$\frac{1}{2\pi i} \oint \frac{e^z}{z^n} \, dz = \frac{1}{2\pi} \int_{-m}^{m} f(n + it) \, dt + \frac{1}{2\pi i} \int_{n}^{-n} f(t + im) \, dt$$

$$+ \frac{1}{2\pi} \int_{m}^{-m} f(-n + it) \, dt + \frac{1}{2\pi i} \int_{-n}^{n} f(t - im) \, dt.$$

Clearly $|f(z)| \le 2^{-n} f(n)$ on the last three sides of this path if we choose $m = 2n$, because $|e^z| = e^{\Re z}$ and $|z| \ge \max(|\Re z|, |\Im z|)$; so we're left with

$$\frac{1}{2\pi i} \oint \frac{e^z}{z^n} \, dz = \frac{1}{2\pi} \int_{-m}^{m} e^{g(n+it)} \, dt + O\!\left(\frac{ne^n}{2^n n^n}\right).$$

Now we fall back on a technique that we've used several times before— for example to derive Eq. 5.1.4–(53): If $\hat{f}(t)$ is a good approximation to $f(t)$ when $t \in A$, and if the sums $\sum_{t \in B} |f(t)|$ and $\sum_{t \in C} |\hat{f}(t)|$ are both small, then $\sum_{t \in A \cup C} \hat{f}(t)$ is a good approximation to $\sum_{t \in A \cup B} f(t)$. The same idea applies to integrals as well as sums. [This general method, introduced by Laplace in 1782, is often called "trading tails"; see *CMath* §9.4.] If $|t| \le n^{1/2+\epsilon}$ we have

$$\begin{aligned}
e^{g(n+it)} &= \exp\!\left(g(n) - \frac{t^2}{2n} + \frac{it^3}{3n^2} + \cdots\right) \\
&= \frac{e^n}{n^n} \exp\!\left(-\frac{t^2}{2n} + \frac{it^3}{3n^2} + \frac{t^4}{4n^3} + O(n^{5\epsilon - 3/2})\right) \\
&= \frac{e^n}{n^n} e^{-t^2/(2n)}\left(1 + \frac{it^3}{3n^2} + \frac{t^4}{4n^3} - \frac{t^6}{18n^4} + O(n^{9\epsilon - 3/2})\right).
\end{aligned}$$

And when $|t| > n^{1/2+\epsilon}$ we have

$$|e^{g(n+it)}| < |f(n + in^{1/2+\epsilon})| = \frac{e^n}{n^n} \exp\!\left(-\frac{n}{2}\ln(1 + n^{2\epsilon - 1})\right) = O\!\left(\frac{e^{n - n^{2\epsilon}/2}}{n^n}\right).$$

Furthermore the incomplete gamma function

$$\int_{n^{1/2+\epsilon}}^{\infty} e^{-t^2/(2n)} t^k \, dt = 2^{(k-1)/2} n^{(k+1)/2} \Gamma\!\left(\frac{k+1}{2}, \frac{n^{2\epsilon}}{2}\right) = O(n^{O(1)} e^{-n^{2\epsilon}/2})$$

is negligible. Thus we can trade tails and obtain the approximation

$$\begin{aligned}
\frac{1}{2\pi i} \oint \frac{e^z}{z^n} \, dz &= \frac{e^n}{2\pi n^n} \int_{-\infty}^{\infty} e^{-t^2/(2n)}\left(1 + \frac{it^3}{3n^2} + \frac{t^4}{4n^3} - \frac{t^6}{18n^4} + O(n^{9\epsilon - 3/2})\right) dt \\
&= \frac{e^n}{2\pi n^n}\left(I_0 + \frac{i}{3n^2} I_3 + \frac{1}{4n^3} I_4 - \frac{1}{18n^4} I_6 + O(n^{9\epsilon - 3/2})\right),
\end{aligned}$$

where $I_k = \int_{-\infty}^{\infty} e^{-t^2/(2n)} t^k \, dt$. Of course $I_k = 0$ when k is odd. Otherwise we can evaluate I_k by using the well-known fact that

$$\int_{-\infty}^{\infty} e^{-at^2} t^{2l} \, dt = \frac{\Gamma\big((2l+1)/2\big)}{a^{(2l+1)/2}} = \frac{\sqrt{2\pi}}{(2a)^{(2l+1)/2}} \prod_{j=1}^{l} (2j - 1) \qquad (20)$$

when $a > 0$; see exercise 39. Putting everything together gives us, for all $\epsilon > 0$, the asymptotic estimate

$$\frac{1}{(n-1)!} = \frac{e^n}{\sqrt{2\pi} n^{n-1/2}}\left(1 + 0 + \frac{3}{4n} - \frac{15}{18n} + O(n^{9\epsilon - 2})\right); \qquad (21)$$

this result agrees perfectly with Stirling's approximation, which we derived by quite different methods in 1.2.11.2–(19). Further terms in the expansion of

$g(n+it)$ would allow us to prove that the true error in (21) is only $O(n^{-2})$, because the same procedure yields an asymptotic series of the general form $e^n/(\sqrt{2\pi}n^{n-1/2})(1+c_1/n+c_2/n^2+\cdots+c_m/n^m+O(n^{-m-1}))$ for all m.

Our derivation of this result has glossed over an important technicality: The function $\ln z$ is not single-valued along the path of integration, because it grows by $2\pi i$ when we loop around the origin. Indeed, this fact underlies the basic mechanism that makes the residue theorem work. But our reasoning was valid because the ambiguity of the logarithm does not affect the integrand $f(z) = e^z/z^n$ when n is an integer. Furthermore, if n were not an integer, we could have adapted the argument and kept it rigorous by choosing to carry out the integral (19) along a path that starts at $-\infty$, circles the origin counterclockwise and returns to $-\infty$. That would have given us Hankel's integral for the gamma function, Eq. 1.2.5–(17); we could thereby have derived the asymptotic formula

$$\frac{1}{\Gamma(x)} = \frac{1}{2\pi i}\oint \frac{e^z}{z^x}\,dz = \frac{e^x}{\sqrt{2\pi}\,x^{x-1/2}}\left(1-\frac{1}{12x}+O(x^{-2})\right), \tag{22}$$

valid for all real x as $x\to\infty$.

So the saddle point method seems to work — although it isn't the simplest way to get this particular result. Let's apply it now to deduce the approximate size of the Bell numbers:

$$\frac{\varpi_{n-1}}{(n-1)!} = \frac{1}{2\pi i e}\oint e^{g(z)}\,dz, \qquad g(z) = e^z - n\ln z. \tag{23}$$

A saddle point for the new integrand occurs at the point $z_0 = \xi > 0$, where

$$\xi e^\xi = n. \tag{24}$$

(We should actually write $\xi(n)$ to indicate that ξ depends on n; but that would clutter up the formulas below.) Let's assume for the moment that a little bird has told us the value of ξ. Then we want to integrate on a path where $z = \xi+it$, and we have

$$g(\xi+it) = e^\xi - n\left(\ln\xi - \frac{(it)^2}{2!}\frac{\xi+1}{\xi^2} - \frac{(it)^3}{3!}\frac{\xi^2-2!}{\xi^3} - \frac{(it)^4}{4!}\frac{\xi^3+3!}{\xi^4} + \cdots\right).$$

By integrating on a suitable rectangular path, we can prove as above that the integral in (23) is well approximated by

$$\int_{-n^{\epsilon-1/2}}^{n^{\epsilon-1/2}} e^{g(\xi)-na_2t^2-nia_3t^3+na_4t^4+\cdots}\,dt, \qquad a_k = \frac{\xi^{k-1}+(-1)^k(k-1)!}{k!\,\xi^k}; \tag{25}$$

see exercise 43. Noting that $a_k t^k$ is $O(n^{k\epsilon-k/2})$ inside this integral, we obtain an asymptotic expansion of the form

$$\varpi_{n-1} = \frac{e^{e^\xi-1}(n-1)!}{\xi^{n-1}\sqrt{2\pi n(\xi+1)}}\left(1+\frac{b_1}{n}+\frac{b_2}{n^2}+\cdots+\frac{b_m}{n^m}+O\left(\frac{\log n}{n}\right)^{m+1}\right), \tag{26}$$

where $(\xi + 1)^{3k} b_k$ is a polynomial of degree $4k$ in ξ. (See exercise 44.) For example,

$$b_1 = -\frac{2\xi^4 - 3\xi^3 - 20\xi^2 - 18\xi + 2}{24(\xi+1)^3}; \tag{27}$$

$$b_2 = \frac{4\xi^8 - 156\xi^7 - 695\xi^6 - 696\xi^5 + 1092\xi^4 + 2916\xi^3 + 1972\xi^2 - 72\xi + 4}{1152(\xi+1)^6}. \tag{28}$$

Stirling's approximation (21) can be used in (26) to prove that

$$\varpi_{n-1} = \exp\left(n\left(\xi - 1 + \frac{1}{\xi}\right) - \xi - \frac{1}{2}\ln(\xi+1) - 1 - \frac{\xi}{12n} + O\left(\frac{\log n}{n}\right)^2\right); \tag{29}$$

and exercise 45 proves the similar formula

$$\varpi_n = \exp\left(n\left(\xi - 1 + \frac{1}{\xi}\right) - \frac{1}{2}\ln(\xi+1) - 1 - \frac{\xi}{12n} + O\left(\frac{\log n}{n}\right)^2\right). \tag{30}$$

Consequently we have $\varpi_n/\varpi_{n-1} \approx e^\xi = n/\xi$. More precisely,

$$\frac{\varpi_{n-1}}{\varpi_n} = \frac{\xi}{n}\left(1 + O\left(\frac{1}{n}\right)\right). \tag{31}$$

But what is the asymptotic value of ξ? The definition (24) implies that

$$\xi = \ln n - \ln \xi = \ln n - \ln(\ln n - \ln \xi)$$

$$= \ln n - \ln \ln n + O\left(\frac{\log \log n}{\log n}\right); \tag{32}$$

and we can go on in this vein, as shown in exercise 49. But the asymptotic series for ξ developed in this way never gives better accuracy than $O(1/(\log n)^m)$ for larger and larger m; so it is hugely inaccurate when multiplied by n in formula (29) for ϖ_{n-1} or formula (30) for ϖ_n.

Thus if we want to use (29) or (30) to calculate good numerical approximations to Bell numbers, our best strategy is to start by computing a good numerical value for ξ, without using a slowly convergent series. Newton's rootfinding method, discussed in the remarks preceding Algorithm 4.7N, yields the efficient iterative scheme

$$\xi_0 = \ln n, \qquad \xi_{k+1} = \frac{\xi_k}{\xi_k + 1}(1 + \xi_0 - \ln \xi_k), \tag{33}$$

which converges rapidly to the correct value. For example, when $n = 100$ the fifth iterate

$$\xi_5 = 3.38563\,01402\,90050\,18488\,82443\,64529\,72686\,74917- \tag{34}$$

is already correct to 40 decimal places. Using this value in (26) gives us successive approximations

$$(1.6176088053\ldots, 1.6187421339\ldots, 1.6187065391\ldots, 1.6187060254\ldots) \times 10^{114}$$

when we take terms up to 1, b_1/n, b_2/n^2, b_3/n^3 into account; the true value of ϖ_{99} is the 115-digit integer $16187060274460\ldots20741$.

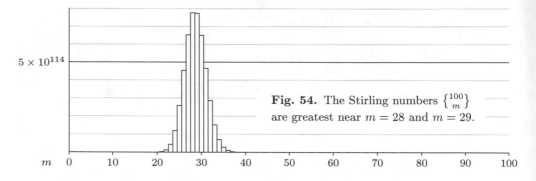

5×10^{114}

Fig. 54. The Stirling numbers $\left\{{100 \atop m}\right\}$ are greatest near $m = 28$ and $m = 29$.

m 0   10   20   30   40   50   60   70   80   90   100

Now that we know the number of set partitions ϖ_n, let's try to figure out how many of them have exactly m blocks. It turns out that nearly all partitions of $\{1, \ldots, n\}$ have roughly $n/\xi = e^\xi$ blocks, with about ξ elements per block. For example, Fig. 54 shows a histogram of the Stirling numbers $\left\{{n \atop m}\right\}$ when $n = 100$; in that case $e^\xi \approx 29.54$.

We can investigate the size of $\left\{{n \atop m}\right\}$ by applying the saddle point method to formula 1.2.9–(23), which states that

$$\left\{{n \atop m}\right\} = \frac{n!}{m!} \, [z^n] \, (e^z - 1)^m = \frac{n!}{m!} \frac{1}{2\pi i} \oint e^{m \ln(e^z - 1) - (n+1)\ln z} \, dz. \qquad (35)$$

Let $\alpha = (n+1)/m$. The function $g(z) = \alpha^{-1} \ln(e^z - 1) - \ln z$ has a saddle point at $\sigma > 0$ when

$$\frac{\sigma}{1 - e^{-\sigma}} = \alpha. \qquad (36)$$

Notice that $\alpha > 1$ for $1 \leq m \leq n$. This special value σ is given by

$$\sigma = \alpha - \beta, \qquad \beta = T(\alpha e^{-\alpha}), \qquad (37)$$

where T is the tree function of Eq. 2.3.4.4–(30). Indeed, β is the value between 0 and 1 for which we have

$$\beta e^{-\beta} = \alpha e^{-\alpha}; \qquad (38)$$

the function $x e^{-x}$ increases from 0 to e^{-1} when x increases from 0 to 1, then it decreases to 0 again. Therefore β is uniquely defined, and we have

$$e^\sigma = \frac{\alpha}{\beta}. \qquad (39)$$

All such pairs α and β are obtainable by using the inverse formulas

$$\alpha = \frac{\sigma e^\sigma}{e^\sigma - 1}, \qquad \beta = \frac{\sigma}{e^\sigma - 1}; \qquad (40)$$

for example, the values $\alpha = \ln 4$ and $\beta = \ln 2$ correspond to $\sigma = \ln 2$.

We can show as above that the integral in (35) is asymptotically equivalent to an integral of $e^{(n+1)g(z)} \, dz$ over the path $z = \sigma + it$. (See exercise 58.) Exercise 56 proves that the Taylor series about $z = \sigma$,

$$g(\sigma + it) = g(\sigma) - \frac{t^2(1 - \beta)}{2\sigma^2} - \sum_{k=3}^{\infty} \frac{(it)^k}{k!} g^{(k)}(\sigma), \qquad (41)$$

has the property that

$$|g^{(k)}(\sigma)| < 2(k - 1)! (1 - \beta)/\sigma^k \qquad \text{for all } k > 0. \qquad (42)$$

Therefore we can conveniently remove a factor of $N = (n + 1)(1 - \beta)$ from the power series $(n + 1)g(z)$, and the saddle point method leads to the formula

$$\left\{ {n \atop m} \right\} = \frac{n!}{m!} \frac{1}{(\alpha - \beta)^{n-m}\beta^m \sqrt{2\pi N}} \left(1 + \frac{b_1}{N} + \frac{b_2}{N^2} + \cdots + \frac{b_l}{N^l} + O\left(\frac{1}{N^{l+1}}\right) \right) \quad (43)$$

as $N \to \infty$, where $(1 - \beta)^{2k}b_k$ is a polynomial in α and β. (The quantity $(\alpha - \beta)^{n-m}\beta^m$ in the denominator comes from the fact that $(e^\sigma - 1)^m/\sigma^n = (\alpha/\beta - 1)^m/(\alpha - \beta)^n$, by (37) and (39).) For example,

$$b_1 = \frac{6 - \beta^3 - 4\alpha\beta^2 - \alpha^2\beta}{8(1 - \beta)} - \frac{5(2 - \beta^2 - \alpha\beta)^2}{24(1 - \beta)^2}. \qquad (44)$$

Exercise 57 proves that $N \to \infty$ if and only if $n - m \to \infty$. An asymptotic expansion for $\left\{ {n \atop m} \right\}$ similar to (43), but somewhat more complicated, was first obtained by Leo Moser and Max Wyman, *Duke Math. J.* **25** (1958), 29–43.

Formula (43) looks a bit scary because it is designed to apply over the entire range of block counts m. Significant simplifications are possible when m is relatively small or relatively large (see exercises 60 and 61); but the simplified formulas don't give accurate results in the important cases when $\left\{ {n \atop m} \right\}$ is largest. Let's look at those crucial cases more closely now, so that we can account for the sharp peak illustrated in Fig. 54.

Let $\xi e^\xi = n$ as in (24), and suppose $m = \exp(\xi + r/\sqrt{n}) = ne^{r/\sqrt{n}}/\xi$; we will assume that $|r| \leq n^\epsilon$, so that m is near e^ξ. The leading term of (43) can be rewritten

$$\frac{n!}{m!} \frac{1}{(\alpha - \beta)^{n-m}\beta^m \sqrt{2\pi(n + 1)(1 - \beta)}} =$$

$$\frac{m^n}{m!} \frac{(n + 1)!}{(n + 1)^{n+1}} \frac{e^{n+1}}{\sqrt{2\pi(n + 1)}} \left(1 - \frac{\beta}{\alpha} \right)^{m-n} \frac{e^{-\beta m}}{\sqrt{1 - \beta}}, \qquad (45)$$

and Stirling's approximation for $(n + 1)!$ is evidently ripe for cancellation in the midst of this expression. With the help of computer algebra we find

$$\frac{m^n}{m!} = \frac{1}{\sqrt{2\pi}} \exp\left(n\left(\xi - 1 + \frac{1}{\xi} \right) - \frac{1}{2}\left(\xi + r^2 + \frac{r^2}{\xi} \right) \right.$$

$$\left. - \left(\frac{r}{2} + \frac{r^3}{6} + \frac{r^3}{3\xi} \right) \frac{1}{\sqrt{n}} + O(n^{4\epsilon-1}) \right);$$

and the relevant quantities related to α and β are

$$\frac{\beta}{\alpha} = \frac{\xi}{n} + \frac{r\xi^2}{n\sqrt{n}} + O(\xi^3 n^{2\epsilon-2});$$

$$e^{-\beta m} = \exp\left(-\xi - \frac{r\xi^2}{\sqrt{n}} + O(\xi^3 n^{2\epsilon-1})\right);$$

$$\left(1 - \frac{\beta}{\alpha}\right)^{m-n} = \exp\left(\xi - 1 + \frac{r(\xi^2 - \xi - 1)}{\sqrt{n}} + O(\xi^3 n^{2\epsilon-1})\right).$$

Therefore the overall result is

$$\left\{\begin{matrix} n \\ e^{\xi+r/\sqrt{n}} \end{matrix}\right\} = \frac{1}{\sqrt{2\pi}} \exp\left(n\left(\xi - 1 + \frac{1}{\xi}\right) - \frac{\xi}{2} - 1\right.$$

$$\left. - \frac{\xi+1}{2\xi}\left(r + \frac{3\xi(2\xi+3) + (\xi+2)r^2}{6(\xi+1)\sqrt{n}}\right)^2 + O(\xi^3 n^{4\epsilon-1})\right). \quad (46)$$

The squared expression on the last line is zero when

$$r = -\frac{\xi(2\xi+3)}{2(\xi+1)\sqrt{n}} + O(\xi^2 n^{-3/2});$$

thus the maximum occurs when the number of blocks is

$$m = \frac{n}{\xi} - \frac{3+2\xi}{2+2\xi} + O\left(\frac{\xi}{n}\right). \quad (47)$$

By comparing (46) to (30) we see that the largest Stirling number $\left\{\begin{smallmatrix} n \\ m \end{smallmatrix}\right\}$ for a given value of n is approximately equal to $\xi\varpi_n/\sqrt{2\pi n}$.

The saddle point method applies to problems that are considerably more difficult than the ones we have considered here. Excellent expositions of advanced techniques can be found in several books: N. G. de Bruijn, *Asymptotic Methods in Analysis* (1958), Chapters 5 and 6; F. W. J. Olver, *Asymptotics and Special Functions* (1974), Chapter 4; R. Wong, *Asymptotic Approximations of Integrals* (2001), Chapters 2 and 7.

*Random set partitions. The sizes of blocks in a partition of $\{1, \ldots, n\}$ constitute by themselves an ordinary partition of the number n. Therefore we might wonder what sort of partition they are likely to be. Figure 50 in Section 7.2.1.4 showed the result of superimposing the Ferrers diagrams of all $p(25) = 1958$ partitions of 25; those partitions tended to follow the symmetrical curve of Eq. 7.2.1.4–(49). By contrast, Fig. 55 shows what happens when we superimpose the corresponding diagrams of all $\varpi_{25} \approx 4.6386 \times 10^{18}$ partitions of the set $\{1, \ldots, 25\}$. Evidently the "shape" of a random set partition is quite different from the shape of a random integer partition.

This change is due to the fact that some integer partitions occur only a few times as block sizes of set partitions, while others are extremely common. For example, the partition $n = 1 + 1 + \cdots + 1$ arises in only one way, but if n is

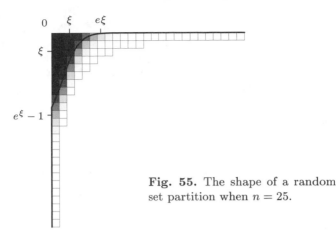

Fig. 55. The shape of a random set partition when $n = 25$.

even the partition $n = 2 + 2 + \cdots + 2$ arises in $(n-1)(n-3)\ldots(1)$ ways. When $n = 25$, the integer partition

$$25 = 4 + 4 + 3 + 3 + 3 + 2 + 2 + 2 + 1 + 1$$

actually occurs in more than 2% of all possible set partitions. (This particular partition turns out to be most common in the case $n = 25$. The answer to exercise 1.2.5–21 explains that exactly

$$\frac{n!}{c_1!\,1!^{c_1}\,c_2!\,2!^{c_2}\ldots c_n!\,n!^{c_n}} \tag{48}$$

set partitions correspond to the integer partition $n = c_1 \cdot 1 + c_2 \cdot 2 + \cdots + c_n \cdot n$.)

We can easily determine the average number of k-blocks in a random partition of $\{1, \ldots, n\}$: If we write out all ϖ_n of the possibilities, every particular k-element block occurs exactly ϖ_{n-k} times. Therefore the average number is

$$\binom{n}{k}\frac{\varpi_{n-k}}{\varpi_n}. \tag{49}$$

An extension of Eq. (31) above, proved in exercise 64, shows moreover that

$$\frac{\varpi_{n-k}}{\varpi_n} = \left(\frac{\xi}{n}\right)^k\left(1 + \frac{k\xi(k\xi + k + 1)}{2(\xi+1)^2 n} + O\left(\frac{k^3}{n^2}\right)\right) \qquad \text{if } k \leq n^{2/3}, \tag{50}$$

where ξ is defined in (24). Therefore if, say, $k \leq n^\epsilon$, formula (49) simplifies to

$$\frac{n^k}{k!}\left(\frac{\xi}{n}\right)^k\left(1 + O\left(\frac{1}{n}\right)\right) = \frac{\xi^k}{k!}\left(1 + O(n^{2\epsilon-1})\right). \tag{51}$$

There are, on average, about ξ blocks of size 1, and $\xi^2/2!$ blocks of size 2, etc.

The variance of these quantities is small (see exercise 65), and it turns out that a random partition behaves essentially as if the number of k-blocks were a Poisson deviate with mean $\xi^k/k!$. The smooth curve shown in Fig. 55 runs through the points $(f(k), k)$ in Ferrers-like coordinates, where

$$f(k) = \xi^{k+1}/(k+1)! + \xi^{k+2}/(k+2)! + \xi^{k+3}/(k+3)! + \cdots \tag{52}$$

The largest block tends to contain approximately $e\xi$ elements. Furthermore, the probability that the block containing element 1 has size less than $\xi + a\sqrt{\xi}$ approaches the probability that a normal deviate is less than a. [See John Haigh, *J. Combinatorial Theory* **A13** (1972), 287–295; V. N. Sachkov, *Probabilistic Methods in Combinatorial Analysis* (1997), Chapter 4, translated from a Russian book published in 1978; Yu. Yakubovich, *J. Mathematical Sciences* **87** (1997), 4124–4137, translated from a Russian paper published in 1995; B. Pittel, *J. Combinatorial Theory* **A79** (1997), 326–359.]

An interesting way to generate random partitions of $\{1, 2, \ldots, n\}$ was introduced by A. J. Stam in the *Journal of Combinatorial Theory* **A35** (1983), 231–240: Let M be a random integer that takes the value m with probability

$$p_m = \frac{m^n}{e\,m!\,\varpi_n}; \qquad (53)$$

these probabilities sum to 1 because of (16). Once M has been chosen, generate a random n-tuple $X_1 X_2 \ldots X_n$, where each X_j is uniformly and independently distributed between 0 and $M - 1$. Then let $i \equiv j$ in the partition if and only if $X_i = X_j$. This procedure works because each set partition that has k blocks is obtained with probability $\sum_{m\geq 0}(m^k/m^n)p_m = 1/\varpi_n$. We can generate M by using 3.4.1–(3); it tends to be approximately $n/\xi = e^\xi$ (see exercise 67).

There's also an all-integer method, based on Peirce's triangle:

Algorithm P (*Uniformly random set partitions*). Given $N \geq 1$, this algorithm generates the blocks of a random partition of $\{1, \ldots, N\}$, using ideas explained in exercise 26. Three auxiliary stacks, S, T, and B, hold auxiliary data.

P1. [Initialize.] Set $n \leftarrow N$, $k \leftarrow 1$, $S \leftarrow \{1, \ldots, N\}$, and $T \leftarrow B \leftarrow \emptyset$.

P2. [Begin a block.] Pop $x \Leftarrow S$ and push $B \Leftarrow x$. (See 2.2.1–(2) and 2.2.1–(1).)

P3. [Done with block?] If $n = k$, output B as a block of the partition, and set $n \leftarrow n - 1$, $k \leftarrow 1$, $S \leftarrow T$, $T \leftarrow B \leftarrow \emptyset$; terminate if $n = 0$, else go to P2.

P4. [Add to block?] Pop $x \Leftarrow S$ and let U be a random integer, $0 \leq U < \varpi_{nk}$. If $U < \varpi_{(n-1)k}$, push $B \Leftarrow x$ and set $n \leftarrow n - 1$; otherwise push $T \Leftarrow x$ and set $k \leftarrow k + 1$. Return to P3. ∎

*Partitions of a multiset. The partitions of an integer and the partitions of a set are just the extreme cases of a far more general problem, the partitions of a multiset. Indeed, the partitions of n are essentially the same as the partitions of $\{1, 1, \ldots, 1\}$, where there are n 1s.

From this standpoint there are essentially $p(n)$ types of multisets with n elements. For example, five different cases of multiset partitions arise when $n = 4$:

$$1234, \ 123|4, \ 124|3, \ 12|34, \ 12|3|4, \ 134|2, \ 13|24, \ 13|2|4,$$
$$14|23, \ 14|2|3, \ 1|234, \ 1|23|4, \ 1|24|3, \ 1|2|34, \ 1|2|3|4;$$
$$1123, \ 112|3, \ 113|2, \ 11|23, \ 11|2|3, \ 123|1, \ 12|13, \ 12|1|3, \ 13|1|2, \ 1|1|23, \ 1|1|2|3;$$
$$1122, \ 112|2, \ 11|22, \ 11|2|2, \ 122|1, \ 12|12, \ 12|1|2, \ 1|1|22, \ 1|1|2|2;$$
$$1112, \ 111|2, \ 112|1, \ 11|12, \ 11|1|2, \ 12|1|1, \ 1|1|1|2;$$
$$1111, \ 111|1, \ 11|11, \ 11|1|1, \ 1|1|1|1. \qquad (54)$$

When the multiset contains m distinct elements, with n_1 of one kind, n_2 of another, ..., and n_m of the last, we write $p(n_1, n_2, \ldots, n_m)$ for the total number of partitions. Thus the examples in (54) show that

$$p(1,1,1,1) = 15, \quad p(2,1,1) = 11, \quad p(2,2) = 9, \quad p(3,1) = 7, \quad p(4) = 5. \quad (55)$$

Partitions with $m = 2$ are often called "bipartitions"; those with $m = 3$ are "tripartitions"; and in general these combinatorial objects are known as *multi-partitions*. The study of multipartitions was inaugurated long ago by P. A. MacMahon [*Philosophical Transactions* **181** (1890), 481–536; **217** (1917), 81–113; *Proc. Cambridge Philos. Soc.* **22** (1925), 951–963]; but the subject is so vast that many unsolved problems remain. In the remainder of this section and in the exercises below we shall take a glimpse at some of the most interesting and instructive aspects of the theory that have been discovered so far.

In the first place it is important to notice that multipartitions are essentially the partitions of *vectors* with nonnegative integer components, namely the ways to decompose such a vector as a sum of such vectors. For example, the nine partitions of $\{1, 1, 2, 2\}$ listed in (54) are the same as the nine partitions of the bipartite column vector $\frac{2}{2}$, namely

$$\frac{2}{2}, \quad \frac{2\,0}{1\,1}, \quad \frac{2\,0}{0\,2}, \quad \frac{2\,0\,0}{0\,1\,1}, \quad \frac{1\,1}{2\,0}, \quad \frac{1\,1}{1\,1}, \quad \frac{1\,1\,0}{1\,0\,1}, \quad \frac{1\,1\,0}{0\,0\,2}, \quad \frac{1\,1\,0\,0}{0\,0\,1\,1}. \quad (56)$$

(We drop the $+$ signs for brevity, as in the case of one-dimensional integer partitions.) Each partition can be written in canonical form if we list its parts in nonincreasing lexicographic order.

A fairly simple algorithm suffices to generate the partitions of any given multiset. In the following procedure we represent partitions on a stack that contains triples of elements (c, u, v), where c denotes a component number, $u > 0$ denotes the yet-unpartitioned amount remaining in component c, and v denotes the c component of the current part, where $0 \le v \le u$. Triples are actually kept in three arrays $(c_0, c_1, \ldots)$, $(u_0, u_1, \ldots)$, and $(v_0, v_1, \ldots)$ for convenience, and a "stack frame" array $(f_0, f_1, \ldots)$ is also maintained so that the $(l+1)$st vector of the partition consists of elements f_l through $f_{l+1} - 1$ in the c, u, and v arrays. For example, the following arrays would represent the bipartition $\frac{3\,2\,2\,1\,1\,0\,0}{1\,2\,0\,1\,1\,3\,1}$:

j	0	1	2	3	4	5	6	7	8	9	10	11
c_j	1	2	1	2	1	2	1	2	1	2	2	2
u_j	9	9	6	8	4	6	2	6	1	5	4	1
v_j	3	1	2	2	2	0	1	1	1	1	3	1

$$f_0 = 0 \quad f_1 = 2 \quad f_2 = 4 \quad f_3 = 6 \quad f_4 = 8 \quad f_5 = 10 \quad f_6 = 11 \quad f_7 = 12 \quad (57)$$

Algorithm M (*Multipartitions in decreasing lexicographic order*). Given a multiset $\{n_1 \cdot 1, \ldots, n_m \cdot m\}$, this algorithm visits all of its partitions using arrays $f_0 f_1 \ldots f_n$, $c_0 c_1 \ldots c_{mn}$, $u_0 u_1 \ldots u_{mn}$, and $v_0 v_1 \ldots v_{mn}$ as described above, where $n = n_1 + \cdots + n_m$. We assume that $m > 0$ and $n_1, \ldots, n_m > 0$.

M1. [Initialize.] Set $c_j \leftarrow j+1$ and $u_j \leftarrow v_j \leftarrow n_{j+1}$ for $0 \le j < m$; also set $f_0 \leftarrow a \leftarrow l \leftarrow 0$ and $f_1 \leftarrow b \leftarrow m$. (In the following steps, the current stack frame runs from a to $b-1$, inclusive.)

M2. [Subtract v from u.] (At this point we want to find all partitions of the vector u in the current frame, into parts that are lexicographically $\le v$. First we will use v itself.) Set $j \leftarrow a$, $k \leftarrow b$, and $x \leftarrow 0$. Then while $j < b$ do the following: Set $u_k \leftarrow u_j - v_j$. If $u_k = 0$, just set $x \leftarrow 1$ and $j \leftarrow j+1$. Otherwise if $x = 0$, set $c_k \leftarrow c_j$, $v_k \leftarrow \min(v_j, u_k)$, $x \leftarrow [u_k < v_j]$, $k \leftarrow k+1$, $j \leftarrow j+1$. Otherwise set $c_k \leftarrow c_j$, $v_k \leftarrow u_k$, $k \leftarrow k+1$, $j \leftarrow j+1$. (Notice that $x = [v$ has changed].)

M3. [Push if nonzero.] If $k > b$, set $a \leftarrow b$, $b \leftarrow k$, $l \leftarrow l+1$, $f_{l+1} \leftarrow b$, and return to M2.

M4. [Visit a partition.] Visit the partition represented by the $l+1$ vectors currently in the stack. (For $0 \le k \le l$, the vector has v_j in component c_j, for $f_k \le j < f_{k+1}$.)

M5. [Decrease v.] Set $j \leftarrow b-1$; while $v_j = 0$, set $j \leftarrow j-1$. Then if $j = a$ and $v_j = 1$, go to M6. Otherwise set $v_j \leftarrow v_j - 1$, and $v_k \leftarrow u_k$ for $j < k < b$. Return to M2.

M6. [Backtrack.] Terminate if $l = 0$. Otherwise set $l \leftarrow l-1$, $b \leftarrow a$, $a \leftarrow f_l$, and return to M5. ▌

The key to this algorithm is step M2, which decreases the current residual vector, u, by the largest permissible part, v; that step also decreases v, if necessary, to the lexicographically largest vector $\le v$ that is less than or equal to the new residual amount in every component. (See exercise 68.)

Let us conclude this section by discussing an amusing connection between multipartitions and the least-significant-digit-first procedure for radix sorting (Algorithm 5.2.5R). The idea is best understood by considering an example. See Table 1, where Step (0) shows nine 4-partite column vectors in lexicographic order. Serial numbers ①–⑨ have been attached at the bottom for identification. Step (1) performs a stable sort of the vectors, bringing their fourth (least significant) entries into decreasing order; similarly, Steps (2), (3), and (4) do a stable sort on the third, second, and top rows. The theory of radix sorting tells us that the original lexicographic order is thereby restored.

Suppose the serial number sequences after these stable sorting operations are respectively α_4, $\alpha_3\alpha_4$, $\alpha_2\alpha_3\alpha_4$, and $\alpha_1\alpha_2\alpha_3\alpha_4$, where the α's are permutations; Table 1 shows the values of α_4, α_3, α_2, and α_1 in parentheses. And now comes the point: Wherever the permutation α_j has a descent, the numbers in row j after sorting must also have a descent, because the sorting is stable. (These descents are indicated by caret marks in the table.) For example, where α_3 has 8 followed by 7, we have 5 followed by 3 in row 3. Therefore the entries $a_1 \ldots a_9$ in row 3 after Step (2) are not an arbitrary partition of their sum; they must satisfy

$$a_1 \ge a_2 \ge a_3 \ge a_4 > a_5 \ge a_6 > a_7 \ge a_8 \ge a_9. \tag{58}$$

Table 1

RADIX SORTING AND MULTIPARTITIONS

Step (0): Original partition	Step (1): Sort row 4	Step (2): Sort row 3
6 5 5 4 3 2 1 0 0	0 6 4 3 5 0 5 2 1	0 6 5 2 5 1 4 3 0
3 2 1 0 4 5 6 4 2	2 3 0 4 2 4 1 5 6	2 3 2 5 1 6 0 4 4
6 6 3 1 1 5 2 0 7	7 6 1 1 6 0 3 5 2	7 6 6 5$_\wedge$3 2$_\wedge$1 1 0
4 2 1 3 3 1 1 2 5	5$_\wedge$4 3 3$_\wedge$2 2$_\wedge$1 1 1	5 4 2 1 1 1 3 3 2
①②③④⑤⑥⑦⑧⑨	⑨①④⑤②⑧③⑥⑦	⑨①②⑥③⑦④⑤⑧

$$\alpha_4 = (\ 9_\wedge 1\ 4\ 5_\wedge 2\ 8_\wedge 3\ 6\ 7\ ) \qquad \alpha_3 = (\ 1\ 2\ 5\ 8_\wedge 7\ 9_\wedge 3\ 4\ 6\ )$$

Step (3): Sort row 2	Step (4): Sort row 1
1 2 3 0 6 0 5 5 4	6 5 5 4$_\wedge$3$_\wedge$2$_\wedge$1 0 0
6$_\wedge$5 4 4$_\wedge$3$_\wedge$2 2 1 0	3 2 1 0 4 5 6 4 2
2 5 1 0 6 7 6 3 1	6 6 3 1 1 5 2 0 7
1 1 3 2 4 5 2 1 3	4 2 1 3 3 1 1 2 5
⑦⑥⑤⑧①⑨②③④	①②③④⑤⑥⑦⑧⑨

$$\alpha_2 = (\ 6_\wedge 4\ 8\ 9_\wedge 2_\wedge 1\ 3\ 5\ 7\ ) \qquad \alpha_1 = (\ 5\ 7\ 8\ 9_\wedge 3_\wedge 2_\wedge 1\ 4\ 6\ )$$

But the numbers $(a_1-2, a_2-2, a_3-2, a_4-2, a_5-1, a_6-1, a_7, a_8, a_9)$ do form an essentially arbitrary partition of the original sum, minus $(4+6)$. The amount of decrease, $4+6$, is the sum of the indices where descents occur; this number is what we called ind α_3, the "index" of α_3, in Section 5.1.1.

Thus we see that any given partition of an m-partite number into at most r parts, with extra zeros added so that the number of columns is exactly r, can be encoded as a sequence of permutations $\alpha_1, \ldots, \alpha_m$ of $\{1, \ldots, r\}$ such that the product $\alpha_1 \ldots \alpha_m$ is the identity, together with a sequence of ordinary one-dimensional partitions of the numbers $(n_1 - \text{ind}\,\alpha_1, \ldots, n_m - \text{ind}\,\alpha_m)$ into at most r parts. For example, the vectors in Table 1 represent a partition of $(26, 27, 31, 22)$ into 9 parts; the permutations $\alpha_1, \ldots, \alpha_4$ appear in the table, and we have $(\text{ind}\,\alpha_1, \ldots, \text{ind}\,\alpha_4) = (15, 10, 10, 11)$; the partitions are respectively

$$26-15 = (322111100), \qquad 27-10 = (332222210),$$
$$31-10 = (544321110), \qquad 22-11 = (221111111).$$

Conversely, any such permutations and partitions will yield a multipartition of $(n_1, \ldots, n_m)$. If r and m are small, it can be helpful to consider these $r!^{m-1}$ sequences of one-dimensional partitions when listing or reasoning about multipartitions, especially in the bipartite case. [This construction is due to Basil Gordon, *J. London Math. Soc.* (2) **38** (1963), 459–464.]

A good summary of early work on multipartitions, including studies of partitions into distinct parts and/or strictly positive parts, appears in a paper by M. S. Cheema and T. S. Motzkin, *Proc. Symp. Pure Math.* **19** (Amer. Math. Soc., 1971), 39–70.

EXERCISES

1. [*20*] (G. Hutchinson.) Show that a simple modification to Algorithm H will generate all partitions of $\{1, \ldots, n\}$ into *at most* r blocks, given n and $r \geq 2$.

▶ **2.** [*22*] When set partitions are used in practice, we often want to link the elements of each block together. Thus it is convenient to have an array of links $l_1 \ldots l_n$ and an array of headers $h_1 \ldots h_t$ so that the elements of the jth block of a t-block partition are $i_1 > \cdots > i_k$, where

$$i_1 = h_j, \quad i_2 = l_{i_1}, \quad \ldots, \quad i_k = l_{i_{k-1}}, \quad \text{and} \quad l_{i_k} = 0.$$

For example, the representation of 137|25|489|6 would have $t = 4$, $l_1 \ldots l_9 = 001020348$, and $h_1 \ldots h_4 = 7596$.

Design a variant of Algorithm H that generates partitions using this representation.

3. [*M23*] What is the millionth partition of $\{1, \ldots, 12\}$ generated by Algorithm H?

▶ **4.** [*21*] If $x_1 \ldots x_n$ is any string, let $\rho(x_1 \ldots x_n)$ be the restricted growth string that corresponds to the equivalence relation $j \equiv k \iff x_j = x_k$. Classify each of the five-letter English words in the Stanford GraphBase by applying this ρ function; for example, $\rho(\text{tooth}) = 01102$. How many of the 52 set partitions of five elements are representable by English words in this way? What's the most common word of each type?

5. [*22*] Guess the next elements of the following two sequences: (a) 0, 1, 1, 1, 12, 12, 12, 12, 12, 12, 100, 121, 122, 123, 123, …; (b) 0, 1, 12, 100, 112, 121, 122, 123, ….

▶ **6.** [*25*] Suggest an algorithm to generate all partitions of $\{1, \ldots, n\}$ in which there are exactly c_1 blocks of size 1, c_2 blocks of size 2, etc.

7. [*M20*] How many permutations $a_1 \ldots a_n$ of $\{1, \ldots, n\}$ have the property that $a_{k-1} > a_k > a_j$ implies $j > k$?

8. [*20*] Suggest a way to generate all permutations of $\{1, \ldots, n\}$ that have exactly m left-to-right minima.

9. [*M20*] How many restricted growth strings $a_1 \ldots a_n$ contain exactly k_j occurrences of j, given the integers $k_0, k_1, \ldots, k_{n-1}$?

10. [*25*] A *semilabeled tree* is an oriented tree in which the leaves are labeled with the integers $\{1, \ldots, k\}$, but the other nodes are unlabeled. Thus there are 15 semilabeled trees with 5 vertices:

Find a one-to-one correspondence between partitions of $\{1, \ldots, n\}$ and semilabeled trees with $n + 1$ vertices.

▶ **11.** [*28*] We observed in Section 7.2.1.2 that Dudeney's famous problem send+more = money is a "pure" alphametic, namely an alphametic with a unique solution. His puzzle corresponds to a set partition on 13 digit positions, for which the restricted growth string $\rho(\text{sendmoremoney})$ is 0123456145217; and we might wonder how lucky he had to be in order to come up with such a construction. How many restricted growth strings of length 13 define pure alphametics of the form $a_1 a_2 a_3 a_4 + a_5 a_6 a_7 a_8 = a_9 a_{10} a_{11} a_{12} a_{13}$?

12. [*M31*] (*The partition lattice.*) If Π and Π' are partitions of the same set, we write $\Pi \preceq \Pi'$ if $x \equiv y$ (modulo Π) whenever $x \equiv y$ (modulo Π'). In other words, $\Pi \preceq \Pi'$ means that Π' is a "refinement" of Π, obtained by partitioning zero or more of the latter's blocks; and Π is a "crudification" or *coalescence* of Π', obtained by merging zero or more blocks together. This partial ordering is easily seen to be a lattice, with

$\Pi \vee \Pi'$ the greatest common refinement of Π and Π', and with $\Pi \wedge \Pi'$ their least common coalescence. For example, the lattice of partitions of $\{1, 2, 3, 4\}$ is

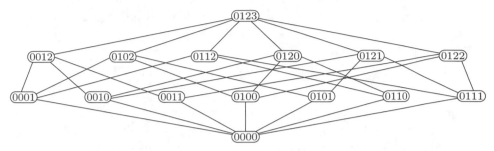

if we represent partitions by restricted growth strings $a_1 a_2 a_3 a_4$; upward paths in this diagram take each partition into its refinements. Partitions with t blocks appear on level t from the bottom, and their descendants form the partition lattice of $\{1, \ldots, t\}$.

a) Explain how to compute $\Pi \vee \Pi'$, given $a_1 \ldots a_n$ and $a'_1 \ldots a'_n$.

b) Explain how to compute $\Pi \wedge \Pi'$, given $a_1 \ldots a_n$ and $a'_1 \ldots a'_n$.

c) When does Π' cover Π in this lattice? (See exercise 7.2.1.4–55.)

d) If Π has t blocks of sizes $s_1, \ldots, s_t$, how many partitions does it cover?

e) If Π has t blocks of sizes $s_1, \ldots, s_t$, how many partitions cover it?

f) True or false: If $\Pi \vee \Pi'$ covers Π, then Π' covers $\Pi \wedge \Pi'$.

g) True or false: If Π' covers $\Pi \wedge \Pi'$, then $\Pi \vee \Pi'$ covers Π.

h) Let $b(\Pi)$ denote the number of blocks of Π. Prove that

$$b(\Pi) + b(\Pi') \;\le\; b(\Pi \vee \Pi') + b(\Pi \wedge \Pi').$$

13. [*M28*] (Stephen C. Milne, 1977.) If A is a set of partitions of $\{1, \ldots, n\}$, its *shadow* ∂A is the set of all partitions Π' such that Π covers Π' for some $\Pi \in A$. (We considered the analogous concept for the subset lattice in 7.2.1.3–(54).)

Let $\Pi_1, \Pi_2, \ldots$ be the partitions of $\{1, \ldots, n\}$ into t blocks, in lexicographic order of their restricted growth strings; and let $\Pi'_1, \Pi'_2, \ldots$ be the $(t-1)$-block partitions, also in lexicographic order. Prove that there is a function $f_{nt}(N)$ such that

$$\partial\{\Pi_1, \ldots, \Pi_N\} = \{\Pi'_1, \ldots, \Pi'_{f_{nt}(N)}\} \qquad \text{for } 0 \le N \le \left\{ {n \atop t} \right\}.$$

Hint: The diagram in exercise 12 shows that $(f_{43}(0), \ldots, f_{43}(6)) = (0, 3, 5, 7, 7, 7, 7)$.

14. [*23*] Design an algorithm to generate set partitions in Gray-code order like (7).

15. [*M21*] What is the final partition generated by the algorithm of exercise 14?

16. [*16*] The list (11) is Ruskey's A_{35}; what is A'_{35}?

17. [*26*] Implement Ruskey's Gray code (8) for all m-block partitions of $\{1, \ldots, n\}$.

18. [*M46*] For which n is it possible to generate all restricted growth strings $a_1 \ldots a_n$ in such a way that some a_j changes by ± 1 at each step?

19. [*28*] Prove that there's a Gray code for restricted growth strings in which, at each step, some a_j changes by either ± 1 or ± 2, when (a) we want to generate all ϖ_n strings $a_1 \ldots a_n$; or (b) we want to generate only the $\left\{ {n \atop m} \right\}$ cases with $\max(a_1, \ldots, a_n) = m - 1$.

20. [*17*] If Π is a partition of $\{1, \ldots, n\}$, its conjugate Π^T is defined by the rule

$$j \equiv k \pmod{\Pi^T} \qquad \Longleftrightarrow \qquad n + 1 - j \equiv n + 1 - k \pmod{\Pi}.$$

Suppose Π has the restricted growth string 001010202013; what is the restricted growth string of Π^T?

21. [*M27*] How many partitions of $\{1, \ldots, n\}$ are self-conjugate?

22. [*M23*] If X is a random variable with a given distribution, the expected value of X^n is called the nth *moment* of that distribution. What is the nth moment when X is (a) a Poisson deviate with mean 1 (Eq. 3.4.1–(40))? (b) the number of fixed points of a random permutation of $\{1, \ldots, m\}$, when $m \geq n$ (Eq. 1.3.3–(27))?

23. [*HM30*] If $f(x) = \sum a_k x^k$ is a polynomial, let $f(\varpi)$ stand for $\sum a_k \varpi_k$.

a) Prove the symbolic formula $f(\varpi + 1) = \varpi f(\varpi)$. (For example, if $f(x)$ is the polynomial x^2, this formula states that $\varpi_2 + 2\varpi_1 + \varpi_0 = \varpi_3$.)

b) Similarly, prove that $f(\varpi + k) = \varpi^k f(\varpi)$ for all positive integers k.

c) If p is prime, prove that $\varpi_{n+p} \equiv \varpi_n + \varpi_{n+1} \pmod{p}$. *Hint:* Show first that $x^{\underline{p}} \equiv x^p - x$.

d) Consequently $\varpi_{n+N} \equiv \varpi_n \pmod{p}$ when $N = p^{p-1} + p^{p-2} + \cdots + p + 1$.

24. [*HM35*] Continuing the previous exercise, prove that the Bell numbers satisfy the periodic law $\varpi_{n+p^e-1 N} \equiv \varpi_n \pmod{p^e}$, if p is an odd prime. *Hint:* Show that

$$x^{\underline{p^e}} \equiv g_e(x) + 1 \pmod{p^e, \ p^{e-1} g_1(x), \ \ldots, \ \text{and} \ p g_{e-1}(x)}, \ \text{where} \ g_j(x) = (x^p - x - 1)^{p^j}.$$

25. [*M27*] Prove that $\varpi_n / \varpi_{n-1} \leq \varpi_{n+1} / \varpi_n \leq \varpi_n / \varpi_{n-1} + 1$.

▶ **26.** [*M22*] According to the recurrence equations (13), the numbers ϖ_{nk} in Peirce's triangle count the paths from $\textcircled{nk}$ to $\textcircled{11}$ in the infinite directed graph

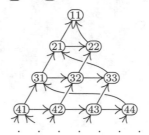

Explain why each path from $\textcircled{n1}$ to $\textcircled{11}$ corresponds to a partition of $\{1, \ldots, n\}$.

▶ **27.** [*M35*] A "vacillating tableau loop" of order n is a sequence of integer partitions $\lambda_k = a_{k1} a_{k2} a_{k3} \ldots$ with $a_{k1} \geq a_{k2} \geq a_{k3} \geq \cdots$ for $0 \leq k \leq 2n$, such that $\lambda_0 = \lambda_{2n} = e_0$ and $\lambda_k = \lambda_{k-1} + (-1)^k e_{t_k}$ for $1 \leq k \leq 2n$ and for some t_k with $0 \leq t_k \leq n$; here e_t denotes the unit vector $0^{t-1} 1 0^{n-t}$ when $0 < t \leq n$, and e_0 is all zeros.

a) List all the vacillating tableau loops of order 4. [*Hint:* There are 15 altogether.]

b) Prove that exactly ϖ_{nk} vacillating tableau loops of order n have $t_{2k-1} = 0$.

▶ **28.** [*M25*] (*Generalized rook polynomials.*) Consider an arrangement of $a_1 + \cdots + a_m$ square cells in rows and columns, where row k contains cells in columns $1, \ldots, a_k$. Place zero or more "rooks" into the cells, with at most one rook in each row and at most one in each column. An empty cell is called "free" if there is no rook to its right and no rook below. For example, Fig. 56 shows two such placements, one with four rooks in rows of lengths $(3,1,4,1,5,9,2,6,5)$, and another with nine on a 9×9 square board. Rooks are indicated by solid circles; hollow circles have been placed above and to the left of each rook, thereby leaving the free cells blank.

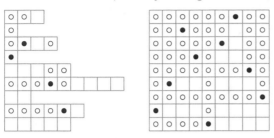

Fig. 56. Rook placements and free cells.

Let $R(a_1, \ldots, a_m)$ be the polynomial in x and y obtained by summing $x^r y^f$ over all legal rook placements, where r is the number of rooks and f is the number of free cells; for example, the left-hand placement in Fig. 56 contributes $x^4 y^{17}$ to the polynomial $R(3, 1, 4, 1, 5, 9, 2, 6, 5)$.

a) Prove that we have $R(a_1, \ldots, a_m) = R(a_1, \ldots, a_{j-1}, a_{j+1}, a_j, a_{j+2}, \ldots, a_m)$; in other words, the order of the row lengths is irrelevant, and we can assume that $a_1 \geq \cdots \geq a_m$ as in a tableau shape like 7.2.1.4–(13).

b) If $a_1 \geq \cdots \geq a_m$ and if $b_1 \ldots b_n = (a_1 \ldots a_m)^T$ is the conjugate partition, prove that $R(a_1, \ldots, a_m) = R(b_1, \ldots, b_n)$.

c) Find a recurrence for evaluating $R(a_1, \ldots, a_m)$ and use it to compute $R(3, 2, 1)$.

d) Generalize Peirce's triangle (12) by changing the addition rule (13) to

$$\varpi_{nk}(x, y) = x\varpi_{(n-1)k}(x, y) + y\varpi_{n(k+1)}(x, y), \qquad 1 \leq k < n.$$

Thus $\varpi_{21}(x, y) = x+y$, $\varpi_{32}(x, y) = x+xy+y^2$, $\varpi_{31}(x, y) = x^2+2xy+xy^2+y^3$, etc. Prove that the resulting quantity $\varpi_{nk}(x, y)$ is the rook polynomial $R(a_1, \ldots, a_{n-1})$ where $a_j = n - j - [j < k]$.

e) The polynomial $\varpi_{n1}(x, y)$ in part (d) can be regarded as a generalized Bell number $\varpi_n(x, y)$, representing paths from $\textcircled{n1}$ to $\textcircled{11}$ in the digraph of exercise 26 that have a given number of "x steps" to the northeast and a given number of "y steps" to the east. Prove that

$$\varpi_n(x, y) = \sum_{a_1 \ldots a_n} x^{n-1-\max(a_1, \ldots, a_n)} y^{a_1 + \cdots + a_n}$$

summed over all restricted growth strings $a_1 \ldots a_n$ of length n.

29. [*M26*] Continuing the previous exercise, let $R_r(a_1, \ldots, a_m) = [x^r] R(a_1, \ldots, a_m)$ be the polynomial in y that enumerates free cells when r rooks are placed.

a) Show that the number of ways to place n rooks on an $n \times n$ board, leaving f cells free, is the number of permutations of $\{1, \ldots, n\}$ that have f inversions. Thus, by Eq. 5.1.1–(8) and exercise 5.1.2–16, we have

$$R_n(\overbrace{n, \ldots, n}^{n}) = n!_y = \prod_{k=1}^{n}(1 + y + \cdots + y^{k-1}).$$

b) What is $R_r(\overbrace{n, \ldots, n}^{m})$, the generating function for r rooks on an $m \times n$ board?

c) If $a_1 \geq \cdots \geq a_m \geq 0$ and t is a nonnegative integer, prove the general formula

$$\prod_{j=1}^{m} \frac{1 - y^{a_j+j-m+t}}{1 - y} = \sum_{k=0}^{m} \frac{t!_y}{(t-k)!_y} R_{m-k}(a_1, \ldots, a_m).$$

[*Note:* The quantity $t!_y/(t-k)!_y = \prod_{j=0}^{k-1}((1-y^{t-j})/(1-y))$ is zero when $k > t \geq 0$. Thus, for example, when $t = 0$ the right-hand side reduces to $R_m(a_1, \ldots, a_m)$. We can compute R_m, R_{m-1}, $\ldots$, R_0 by successively setting $t = 0$, 1, $\ldots$, m.]

d) If $a_1 \geq a_2 \geq \cdots \geq a_m \geq 0$ and $a'_1 \geq a'_2 \geq \cdots \geq a'_m \geq 0$, show that we have $R(a_1, a_2 \ldots, a_m) = R(a'_1, a'_2, \ldots, a'_m)$ if and only if the associated multisets $\{a_1+1, a_2+2, \ldots, a_m+m\}$ and $\{a'_1+1, a'_2+2, \ldots, a'_m+m\}$ are the same.

30. [*HM30*] The generalized Stirling number $\left\{ {n \atop m} \right\}_q$ is defined by the recurrence

$$\left\{ {n+1 \atop m} \right\}_q = (1+q+\cdots+q^{m-1})\left\{ {n \atop m} \right\}_q + \left\{ {n \atop m-1} \right\}_q; \qquad \left\{ {0 \atop m} \right\}_q = \delta_{m0}.$$

Thus $\left\{ {n \atop m} \right\}_q$ is a polynomial in q; and $\left\{ {n \atop m} \right\}_1$ is the ordinary Stirling number $\left\{ {n \atop m} \right\}$, because it satisfies the recurrence relation in Eq. 1.2.6–(46).

a) Prove that the generalized Bell number $\varpi_n(x, y) = R(n-1, \ldots, 1)$ of exercise 28(e) has the explicit form

$$\varpi_n(x, y) = \sum_{m=0}^{n} x^{n-m} y^{\binom{m}{2}} \left\{ {n \atop m} \right\}_y.$$

b) Show that generalized Stirling numbers also obey the recurrence

$$q^m \left\{ {n+1 \atop m+1} \right\}_q = q^n \left\{ {n \atop m} \right\}_q + \binom{n}{1} q^{n-1} \left\{ {n-1 \atop m} \right\}_q + \cdots = \sum_k \binom{n}{k} q^k \left\{ {k \atop m} \right\}_q.$$

c) Find generating functions for $\left\{ {n \atop m} \right\}_q$, generalizing 1.2.9–(23) and 1.2.9–(28).

31. [*HM23*] Generalizing (15), show that the elements of Peirce's triangle have a simple generating function, if we compute the sum

$$\sum_{n,k} \varpi_{nk} \frac{w^{n-k}}{(n-k)!} \frac{z^{k-1}}{(k-1)!}.$$

32. [*M22*] Let δ_n be the number of restricted growth strings $a_1 \ldots a_n$ for which the sum $a_1 + \cdots + a_n$ is even minus the number for which $a_1 + \cdots + a_n$ is odd. Prove that

$$\delta_n = (1, 0, -1, -1, 0, 1) \qquad \text{when} \qquad n \bmod 6 = (1, 2, 3, 4, 5, 0).$$

Hint: See exercise 28(e).

33. [*M21*] How many partitions of $\{1, 2, \ldots, n\}$ have $1 \not\equiv 2$, $2 \not\equiv 3$, $\ldots$, $k-1 \not\equiv k$?

34. [*34*] Many poetic forms involve *rhyme schemes*, which are partitions of the lines of a stanza with the property that $j \equiv k$ if and only if line j rhymes with line k. For example, a "limerick" is generally a 5-line poem with certain rhythmic constraints and with a rhyme scheme described by the restricted growth string 00110.

What rhyme schemes were used in the classical *sonnets* by (a) Guittone d'Arezzo (c. 1270)? (b) Petrarch (c. 1350)? (c) Spenser (1595)? (d) Shakespeare (1609)? (e) Elizabeth Barrett Browning (1850)?

35. [*M21*] Let ϖ'_n be the number of schemes for n-line poems that are "completely rhymed," in the sense that every line rhymes with at least one other. Thus we have $\langle \varpi'_0, \varpi'_1, \varpi'_2, \ldots \rangle = \langle 1, 0, 1, 1, 4, 11, 41, \ldots \rangle$. Give a combinatorial proof of the fact that $\varpi'_n + \varpi'_{n+1} = \varpi_n$.

36. [*M22*] Continuing exercise 35, what is the generating function $\sum_n \varpi'_n z^n/n!$?

37. [*M18*] Alexander Pushkin adopted an elaborate structure in his poetic novel *Eugene Onegin* (1833), based not only on "masculine" rhymes in which the sounds of accented final syllables agree with each other (pain–gain, form–warm, pun–fun, bucks–crux), but also on "feminine" rhymes in which one or two unstressed syllables also participate (humor–tumor, tetrameter–pentameter, lecture–conjecture, iguana–piranha). Every stanza of *Eugene Onegin* is a sonnet with the strict scheme 01012233455477, where the rhyme is feminine or masculine according as the digit is even or odd. Several modern translators of Pushkin's novel have also succeeded in retaining the same form in English and German.

> *How do I justify this stanza? / These feminine rhymes? My wrinkled muse?*
> *This whole passé extravaganza? / How can I (careless of time) use*
> *The dusty bread molds of Onegin / In the brave bakery of Reagan?*
> *The loaves will surely fail to rise / Or else go stale before my eyes.*
> *The truth is, I can't justify it. / But as no shroud of critical terms*
> *Can save my corpse from boring worms, / I may as well have fun and try it.*
> *If it works, good; and if not, well, / A theory won't postpone its knell.*
> — VIKRAM SETH, *The Golden Gate* (1986)

A 14-line poem might have any of $\varpi'_{14} = 24{,}011{,}157$ complete rhyme schemes, according to exercise 35. But how many schemes are possible if we are allowed to specify, for each block, whether its rhyme is to be feminine or masculine?

▶ **38.** [*M30*] Let σ_k be the cyclic permutation $(1, 2, \ldots, k)$. The object of this exercise is to study the sequences $k_1 k_2 \ldots k_n$, called σ-*cycles*, for which $\sigma_{k_1} \sigma_{k_2} \ldots \sigma_{k_n}$ is the identity permutation. For example, when $n = 4$ there are exactly 15 σ-cycles, namely

$$1111, 1122, 1212, 1221, 1333, 2112, 2121, 2211, 2222, 2323, 3133, 3232, 3313, 3331, 4444.$$

a) Find a one-to-one correspondence between partitions of $\{1, 2, \ldots, n\}$ and σ-cycles of length n.
b) How many σ-cycles of length n have $1 \le k_1, \ldots, k_n \le m$, given m and n?
c) How many σ-cycles of length n have $k_i = j$, given i, j, and n?
d) How many σ-cycles of length n have $k_1, \ldots, k_n \ge 2$?
e) How many partitions of $\{1, \ldots, n\}$ have $1 \not\equiv 2$, $2 \not\equiv 3$, $\ldots$, $n - 1 \not\equiv n$, and $n \not\equiv 1$?

39. [*HM16*] Evaluate $\int_0^\infty e^{-t^{p+1}} t^q \, dt$ when p and q are nonnegative integers. *Hint:* See exercise 1.2.5–20.

40. [*HM20*] Suppose the saddle point method is used to estimate $[z^{n-1}] e^{cz}$. The text's derivation of (21) from (19) deals with the case $c = 1$; how should that derivation change if c is an arbitrary positive constant?

41. [*HM21*] Solve the previous exercise when $c = -1$.

42. [*HM23*] Use the saddle point method to estimate $[z^{n-1}] e^{z^2}$ with relative error $O(1/n^2)$.

43. [*HM22*] Justify replacing the integral in (23) by (25).

44. [*HM22*] Explain how to compute $b_1, b_2, \ldots$ in (26) from $a_2, a_3, \ldots$ in (25).

▶ **45.** [*HM23*] Show that, in addition to (26), we also have the expansion

$$\varpi_n = \frac{e^{e^\xi - 1} n!}{\xi^n \sqrt{2\pi n(\xi + 1)}} \left(1 + \frac{b'_1}{n} + \frac{b'_2}{n^2} + \cdots + \frac{b'_m}{n^m} + O\left(\frac{1}{n^{m+1}}\right) \right),$$

where $b'_1 = -(2\xi^4 + 9\xi^3 + 16\xi^2 + 6\xi + 2)/(24(\xi + 1)^3)$.

46. [*HM25*] Estimate the value of ϖ_{nk} in Peirce's triangle when $n \to \infty$.

47. [*M21*] Analyze the running time of Algorithm H.

48. [*HM25*] If n is not an integer, the integral in (23) can be taken over a Hankel contour to define a generalized Bell number ϖ_x for all real $x > 0$. Show that, as in (16),

$$\varpi_x = \frac{1}{e} \sum_{k=0}^{\infty} \frac{k^x}{k!}.$$

▶ **49.** [*HM35*] Prove that, for large n, the number ξ defined in Eq. (24) is equal to

$$\ln n - \ln \ln n + \sum_{j,k \geq 0} \begin{bmatrix} j+k \\ j+1 \end{bmatrix} \alpha^j \frac{\beta^k}{k!}, \qquad \alpha = -\frac{1}{\ln n}, \qquad \beta = \frac{\ln \ln n}{\ln n}.$$

▶ **50.** [*HM21*] If $\xi(n) e^{\xi(n)} = n$ and $\xi(n) > 0$, how does $\xi(n+k)$ relate to $\xi(n)$?

51. [*HM27*] Use the saddle point method to estimate $t_n = n! [z^n] e^{z+z^2/2}$, the number of *involutions* on n elements (aka partitions of $\{1, \ldots, n\}$ into blocks of sizes ≤ 2).

52. [*HM22*] The *cumulants* of a probability distribution are defined in Eq. 1.2.10–(23). What are the cumulants, when the probability that a random integer equals k is (a) $e^{1-e^\xi} \varpi_k \xi^k / k!$? (b) $\sum_j \begin{Bmatrix} k \\ j \end{Bmatrix} e e^{-1-j} / k!$?

▶ **53.** [*HM30*] Let $G(z) = \sum_{k=0}^{\infty} p_k z^k$ be the generating function for a discrete probability distribution, converging for $|z| < 1 + \delta$; thus the coefficients p_k are nonnegative, $G(1) = 1$, and the mean and variance are respectively $\mu = G'(1)$ and $\sigma^2 = G''(1) + G'(1) - G'(1)^2$. If $X_1, \ldots, X_n$ are independent random variables having this distribution, the probability that $X_1 + \cdots + X_n = m$ is $[z^m] G(z)^n$, and we often want to estimate this probability when m is near the mean value μn.

Assume that $p_0 \neq 0$ and that no integer $d > 1$ is a common divisor of all subscripts k with $p_k \neq 0$; this assumption means that m does not have to satisfy any special congruence conditions mod d when n is large. Prove that

$$[z^{\mu n + r}] G(z)^n = \frac{e^{-r^2/(2\sigma^2 n)}}{\sigma \sqrt{2\pi n}} + O\left(\frac{1}{n}\right) \qquad \text{as } n \to \infty,$$

when $\mu n + r$ is an integer. *Hint:* Integrate $G(z)^n / z^{\mu n + r}$ on the circle $|z| = 1$.

54. [*HM20*] If α and β are defined by (40), show that their arithmetic and geometric means are respectively $\frac{\alpha+\beta}{2} = s \coth s$ and $\sqrt{\alpha\beta} = s \operatorname{csch} s$, where $s = \sigma/2$.

55. [*HM20*] Suggest a good way to compute the number β needed in (43).

▶ **56.** [*HM26*] Let $g(z) = \alpha^{-1} \ln(e^z - 1) - \ln z$ and $\sigma = \alpha - \beta$ as in (37).

a) Prove that $(-\sigma)^{n+1} g^{(n+1)}(\sigma) = n! - \sum_{k=0}^{n} \left\langle {n \atop k} \right\rangle \alpha^k \beta^{n-k}$, where the Eulerian numbers $\left\langle {n \atop k} \right\rangle$ are defined in Section 5.1.3.

b) Prove that $\frac{\beta}{\alpha} n! < \sum_{k=0}^{n} \left\langle {n \atop k} \right\rangle \alpha^k \beta^{n-k} < n!$ for all $\sigma > 0$. *Hint:* See exercise 5.1.3–25.

c) Now verify the inequality (42).

57. [*HM22*] In the notation of (43), prove that (a) $n+1-m < 2N$; (b) $N < 2(n+1-m)$.

58. [*HM31*] Complete the proof of (43) as follows.

a) Show that for all $\sigma > 0$ there is a number $\tau \geq 2\sigma$ such that τ is a multiple of 2π and $|e^{\sigma+it} - 1|/|\sigma + it|$ is monotone decreasing for $0 \leq t \leq \tau$.

b) Prove that $\int_{-\tau}^{\tau} \exp((n+1)g(\sigma + it)) \, dt$ leads to (43).

c) Show that the corresponding integrals over the straight-line paths $z = t \pm i\tau$ for $-n \leq t \leq \sigma$ and $z = -n \pm it$ for $-\tau \leq t \leq \tau$ are negligible.

▶ **59.** [*HM23*] What does (43) predict for the approximate value of $\{{}^n_n\}$?

60. [*HM25*] (a) Show that the partial sums in the identity

$$\left\{{n \atop m}\right\} = \frac{m^n}{m!} - \frac{(m-1)^n}{1!\,(m-1)!} + \frac{(m-2)^n}{2!\,(m-2)!} - \cdots + (-1)^m \frac{0^n}{m!\,0!}$$

alternately overestimate and underestimate the final value. (b) Conclude that

$$\left\{{n \atop m}\right\} = \frac{m^n}{m!}\left(1 - O(ne^{-n^\epsilon})\right) \qquad \text{when } m \le n^{1-\epsilon}.$$

(c) Derive a similar result from (43).

61. [*HM26*] Prove that if $m = n - r$ where $r \le n^\epsilon$ and $\epsilon \le n^{1/2}$, Eq. (43) yields

$$\left\{{n \atop n-r}\right\} = \frac{n^{2r}}{2^r\,r!}\left(1 + O(n^{2\epsilon-1}) + O\!\left(\frac{1}{r}\right)\right).$$

62. [*HM40*] Prove rigorously that if $\xi e^\xi = n$, the maximum $\{{}^n_m\}$ occurs either when $m = \lfloor e^\xi - 1 \rfloor$ or when $m = \lceil e^\xi - 1 \rceil$.

▶ **63.** [*M35*] (J. Pitman.) Prove that there is an elementary way to locate the maximum Stirling numbers, and many similar quantities, as follows: Suppose $0 \le p_j \le 1$.

   a) Let $f(z) = (1+p_1(z-1))\ldots(1+p_n(z-1))$ and $a_k = [z^k]\,f(z)$; thus a_k is the probability that k heads turn up after n independent coin flips with the respective probabilities $p_1, \ldots, p_n$. Prove that $a_{k-1} < a_k$ whenever $k \le \mu = p_1 + \cdots + p_n$, $a_k \ne 0$.

   b) Similarly, prove that $a_{k+1} < a_k$ whenever $k \ge \mu$ and $a_k \ne 0$.

   c) If $f(x) = a_0 + a_1 x + \cdots + a_n x^n$ is any nonzero polynomial with nonnegative coefficients and with n real roots, prove that $a_{k-1} < a_k$ when $k \le \mu$ and $a_{k+1} < a_k$ when $k \ge \mu$, where $\mu = f'(1)/f(1)$. Therefore if $a_m = \max(a_0, \ldots, a_n)$ we must have either $m = \lfloor \mu \rfloor$ or $m = \lceil \mu \rceil$.

   d) Under the hypotheses of (c), and with $a_j = 0$ when $j < 0$ or $j > n$, show that there are indices $s \le t$, such that $a_{k+1} - a_k < a_k - a_{k-1}$ if and only if $s \le k \le t$. (Thus, a histogram of the sequence $(a_0, a_1, \ldots, a_n)$ is always "bell-shaped.")

   e) What do these results tell us about Stirling numbers?

64. [*HM21*] Prove the approximate ratio (50), using (30) and exercise 50.

▶ **65.** [*HM22*] What is the variance of the number of blocks of size k in a random partition of $\{1, \ldots, n\}$?

66. [*M46*] What partition of n leads to the most partitions of $\{1, \ldots, n\}$?

67. [*HM20*] What are the mean and variance of M in Stam's method (53)?

68. [*21*] How large can variables l and b get in Algorithm M, when that algorithm is generating all $p(n_1, \ldots, n_m)$ partitions of $\{n_1 \cdot 1, \ldots, n_m \cdot m\}$?

▶ **69.** [*22*] Modify Algorithm M so that it produces only partitions into at most r parts.

▶ **70.** [*M22*] Analyze the number of r-block partitions possible in the n-element multisets (a) $\{0, \ldots, 0, 1\}$; (b) $\{1, 2, \ldots, n-1, n-1\}$. What is the total, summed over r?

71. [*M20*] How many partitions of $\{n_1 \cdot 1, \ldots, n_m \cdot m\}$ have exactly 2 parts?

72. [*M26*] Can $p(n, n)$ be evaluated in polynomial time?

▶ **73.** [*M32*] Can $p(2, \ldots, 2)$ be evaluated in polynomial time when there are n 2s?

74. [*M46*] Can $p(n, \ldots, n)$ be evaluated in polynomial time when there are n ns?

75. [*HM41*] Find the asymptotic value of $p(n, n)$.

76. [*HM36*] Find the asymptotic value of $p(2, \ldots, 2)$ when there are n 2s.

77. [*HM46*] Find the asymptotic value of $p(n, \ldots, n)$ when there are n ns.

78. [*20*] What partition of $(15, 10, 10, 11)$ leads to the permutations α_1, α_2, α_3, and α_4 shown in Table 1?

79. [*22*] A sequence u_1, u_2, u_3, ... is called *universal* for partitions of $\{1, \ldots, n\}$ if its subsequences $(u_{m+1}, u_{m+2}, \ldots, u_{m+n})$ for $0 \le m < \varpi_n$ represent all possible set partitions under the convention "$j \equiv k$ if and only if $u_{m+j} = u_{m+k}$." For example, $(0, 0, 0, 1, 0, 2, 2)$ is a universal sequence for partitions of $\{1, 2, 3\}$.

Write a program to find all universal sequences for partitions of $\{1, 2, 3, 4\}$ with the properties that (i) $u_1 = u_2 = u_3 = u_4 = 0$; (ii) the sequence has restricted growth; (iii) $0 \le u_j \le 3$; and (iv) $u_{16} = u_{17} = u_{18} = 0$ (hence the sequence is essentially *cyclic*).

80. [*M28*] Prove that universal cycles for partitions of $\{1, 2, \ldots, n\}$ exist in the sense of the previous exercise whenever $n \ge 4$.

81. [*29*] Find a way to arrange an ordinary deck of 52 playing cards so that the following trick is possible: Five players each cut the deck (applying a cyclic permutation) as often as they like. Then each player takes a card from the top. A magician tells them to look at their cards and to form affinity groups, joining with others who hold the same suit: Everybody with clubs gets together, everybody with diamonds forms another group, and so on. (The Jack of Spades is, however, considered to be a "joker"; its holder, if any, should remain aloof.)

Observing the affinity groups, but not being told any of the suits, the magician can name all five cards, if the cards were suitably arranged in the first place.

82. [*22*] In how many ways can the following 15 dominoes, optionally rotated, be partitioned into three sets of five having the same sum when regarded as fractions?

$$\frac{\bullet}{\bullet\bullet} + \frac{\bullet}{\bullet} + \frac{\bullet\bullet}{\bullet\bullet} + \frac{\bullet}{\bullet\bullet} + \frac{\bullet}{\bullet\bullet\bullet} = \frac{\bullet\bullet}{\bullet} + \frac{\bullet\bullet}{\bullet\bullet} + \frac{\bullet}{\bullet} + \frac{\bullet\bullet}{\bullet\bullet} + \frac{\bullet}{\bullet\bullet} = \frac{\bullet\bullet}{\bullet\bullet} + \frac{\bullet\bullet}{\bullet} + \frac{\bullet}{\bullet\bullet} + \frac{\bullet\bullet\bullet}{\bullet\bullet} + \frac{\bullet\bullet\bullet}{\bullet\bullet\bullet}$$

> *Just as in a single body there are pairs of individual members,*
> *called by the same name but distinguished as right and left,*
> *so when my speeches had postulated the notion of madness,*
> *as a single generic aspect of human nature,*
> *the speech that divided the left-hand portion*
> *repeatedly broke it down into smaller and smaller parts.*
> — SOCRATES, *in Phædrus 266A* (c. 370 B.C.)

7.2.1.6. Generating all trees.

We've now completed our study of the classical concepts of combinatorics: tuples, permutations, combinations, and partitions. But computer scientists have added another fundamental class of patterns to the traditional repertoire, namely the hierarchical arrangements known as trees. Trees sprout up just about everywhere in computer science, as we've seen in Section 2.3 and in nearly every subsequent section of *The Art of Computer Programming*. Therefore we turn now to the study of simple algorithms by which trees of various species can be explored exhaustively.

First let's review the basic connection between nested parentheses and forests of trees. For example,

$$
\begin{array}{c}
\text{1 2}\quad\text{3 4 5}\quad\text{6 7 8}\quad\text{9 a}\quad\text{b}\quad\text{c d}\quad\text{e f} \\
\text{(( )) ((( )) ((( ) ( ))) ( )) (( ) (( )))} \\
\text{1 2}\quad\quad\text{3 4}\quad\quad\text{5}\quad\text{6 7 8}\quad\text{9 a}\quad\text{b}\quad\text{c d e f}
\end{array}
\tag{1}
$$

illustrates a string containing fifteen left parens '(' labeled 1, 2, ..., f, and fifteen right parens ')' also labeled 1 through f; gray lines beneath the string show how the parentheses match up to form fifteen pairs 12, 21, 3f, 44, 53, 6a, 78, 85, 97, a6, b9, ce, db, ed, and fc. This string corresponds to the forest

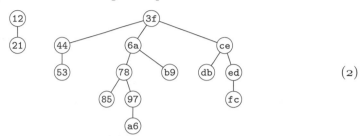

$$(2)$$

in which the nodes are ⑫, ㉑, ③f, ..., ⓕc in preorder (sorted by first coordinates) and ㉑, ⑫, ㌀, ..., ③f in postorder (sorted by second coordinates). If we imagine a worm that crawls around the periphery of the forest,

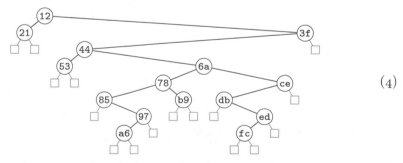

$$(3)$$

seeing a '(' whenever it passes the left edge of a node and a ')' whenever it passes a node's right edge, that worm will have reconstructed the original string (1).

The forest in (2) corresponds, in turn, to the binary tree

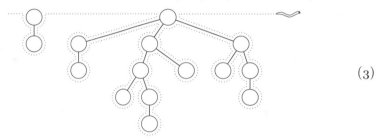

$$(4)$$

via the "natural correspondence" discussed in Section 2.3.2; here the nodes are ㉑, ⑫, ㌀, ..., ③f in *symmetric* order, also known as inorder. The left subtree of node $\textcircled{x}$ in the binary tree is the leftmost child of $\textcircled{x}$ in the forest, or it is an "external node" □ if $\textcircled{x}$ is childless. The right subtree of $\textcircled{x}$ in the binary tree is its right sibling in the forest, or □ if $\textcircled{x}$ is the rightmost child in its family. Roots of the trees in the forest are considered to be siblings, and the leftmost root of the forest is the root of the binary tree.

Table 1

NESTED PARENTHESES AND RELATED OBJECTS WHEN $n = 4$

$a_1a_2\ldots a_8$	forest	binary tree	$d_1d_2d_3d_4$	$z_1z_2z_3z_4$	$p_1p_2p_3p_4$	$c_1c_2c_3c_4$	matching
()()()()			1111	1357	1234	0000	
()()(())			1102	1356	1243	0001	
()(())()			1021	1347	1324	0010	
()(()())			1012	1346	1342	0011	
()((()))			1003	1345	1432	0012	
(())()()			0211	1257	2134	0100	
(())(())			0202	1256	2143	0101	
(()())()			0121	1247	2314	0110	
(()()())			0112	1246	2341	0111	
(()(()))			0103	1245	2431	0112	
((()))()			0031	1237	3214	0120	
((())())			0022	1236	3241	0121	
((()()))			0013	1235	3421	0122	
(((())))			0004	1234	4321	0123	

A string $a_1a_2\ldots a_{2n}$ of parentheses is properly nested if and only if it contains n occurrences of '(' and n occurrences of ')', where the kth '(' precedes the kth ')' for $1 \le k \le n$. The easiest way to explore all strings of nested parentheses is to visit them in lexicographic order. The following algorithm, which considers ')' to be lexicographically smaller than '(', includes some refinements for efficiency suggested by I. Semba [*Inf. Processing Letters* **12** (1981), 188–192]:

Algorithm P (*Nested parentheses in lexicographic order*). Given an integer $n \geq 2$, this algorithm visits all strings $a_1 a_2 \ldots a_{2n}$ of nested parentheses.

P1. [Initialize.] Set $a_{2k-1} \leftarrow$ '(' and $a_{2k} \leftarrow$ ')' for $1 \leq k \leq n$; also set $a_0 \leftarrow$ ')' and $m \leftarrow 2n - 1$. (We use a_0 as a sentinel in step P4.)

P2. [Visit.] Visit the nested string $a_1 a_2 \ldots a_{2n}$. (At this point $a_m =$ '(', and $a_k =$ ')' for $m < k \leq 2n$.)

P3. [Easy case?] Set $a_m \leftarrow$ ')'. Then if $a_{m-1} =$ ')', set $a_{m-1} \leftarrow$ '(', $m \leftarrow m - 1$, and return to P2.

P4. [Find j.] Set $j \leftarrow m - 1$ and $k \leftarrow 2n - 1$. While $a_j =$ '(', set $a_j \leftarrow$ ')', $a_k \leftarrow$ '(', $j \leftarrow j - 1$, and $k \leftarrow k - 2$.

P5. [Increase a_j.] Terminate the algorithm if $j = 0$. Otherwise set $a_j \leftarrow$ '(', $m \leftarrow 2n - 1$, and go back to P2. ∎

We will see later that the loop in step P4 is almost always short: The operation $a_j \leftarrow$ ')' is performed only about $\frac{1}{3}$ times per nested string visited, on the average.

Why does Algorithm P work? Let A_{pq} be the sequence of all strings α that contain p left parentheses and $q \geq p$ right parentheses, where $({}^{q-p}\alpha$ is properly nested, listed in lexicographic order. Then Algorithm P is supposed to generate A_{nn}, where it is easy to see that A_{pq} obeys the recursive rules

$$A_{pq} \;=\;)\, A_{p(q-1)}, \; (\, A_{(p-1)q}, \quad \text{if } 0 \leq p \leq q \neq 0; \qquad A_{00} = \epsilon; \qquad (5)$$

also A_{pq} is empty if $p < 0$ or $p > q$. The first element of A_{pq} is $)^{q-p}() \ldots ()$, where there are p pairs '()'; the last element is $({}^{p})^{q}$. Thus the lexicographic generation process scans from the right until finding a trailing string of the form $a_j \ldots a_{2n} =)\, ({}^{p+1})^{q}$, and replaces it by $()^{q+1-p}() \ldots ()$. Steps P4 and P5 do this efficiently, while step P3 handles the simple case $p = 0$.

Table 1 illustrates the output of Algorithm P when $n = 4$, together with the corresponding forest and binary tree as in (2) and (4). Several other equivalent combinatorial objects also appear in Table 1: For example, a string of nested parentheses can be run-length encoded as

$$()^{d_1} ()^{d_2} \ldots ()^{d_n}, \qquad (6)$$

where the nonnegative integers $d_1 d_2 \ldots d_n$ are characterized by the constraints

$$d_1 + d_2 + \cdots + d_k \leq k \quad \text{for } 1 \leq k < n; \qquad d_1 + d_2 + \cdots + d_n = n. \qquad (7)$$

We can also represent nested parentheses by the sequence $z_1 z_2 \ldots z_n$, which specifies the indices where the left parentheses appear. In essence, $z_1 z_2 \ldots z_n$ is one of the $\binom{2n}{n}$ combinations of n things from the set $\{1, 2, \ldots, 2n\}$, subject to the special constraints

$$z_{k-1} < z_k < 2k \qquad \text{for } 1 < k \leq n, \qquad (8)$$

if we assume that $z_0 = 0$. The z's are of course related to the d's:

$$d_k \;=\; z_{k+1} - z_k - 1 \qquad \text{for } 1 \leq k < n. \qquad (9)$$

Algorithm P becomes particularly simple when it is rewritten to generate the combinations $z_1 z_2 \ldots z_n$ instead of the strings $a_1 a_2 \ldots a_{2n}$. (See exercise 2.)

A parenthesis string can also be represented by the permutation $p_1 p_2 \ldots p_n$, where the kth right parenthesis matches the p_kth left parenthesis; in other words, the kth node of the associated forest in postorder is the p_kth node in preorder. By exercise 2.3.2–20, node j is a (proper) descendant of node k in the forest if and only if $j < k$ and $p_j > p_k$, when we label the nodes in postorder. The inversion table $c_1 c_2 \ldots c_n$ characterizes this permutation by the rule that exactly c_k elements to the right of k are less than k (see exercise 5.1.1–7); allowable inversion tables have $c_1 = 0$ and

$$0 \leq c_{k+1} \leq c_k + 1 \qquad \text{for } 1 \leq k < n. \tag{10}$$

Moreover, exercise 3 proves that c_k is the level of the forest's kth node in preorder (the depth of the kth left parenthesis), a fact that is equivalent to the formula

$$c_k = 2k - 1 - z_k. \tag{11}$$

Table 1 and exercise 6 also illustrate a special kind of *matching*, by which $2n$ people at a circular table can simultaneously shake hands without interference.

Thus Algorithm P can be useful indeed. But if our goal is to generate all binary trees, represented by left links $l_1 l_2 \ldots l_n$ and right links $r_1 r_2 \ldots r_n$, the lexicographic sequence in Table 1 is rather awkward; the data we need to get from one tree to its successor is not readily available. Fortunately, an ingenious alternative scheme for direct generation of all linked binary trees is also available:

Algorithm B (*Binary trees*). Given $n \geq 1$, this algorithm visits all binary trees with n internal nodes, representing them via left links $l_1 l_2 \ldots l_n$ and right links $r_1 r_2 \ldots r_n$, with nodes labeled in preorder. (Thus, for example, node 1 is always the root, and l_k is either $k+1$ or 0; if $l_1 = 0$ and $n > 1$ then $r_1 = 2$.)

B1. [Initialize.] Set $l_k \leftarrow k+1$ and $r_k \leftarrow 0$ for $1 \leq k < n$; also set $l_n \leftarrow r_n \leftarrow 0$, and set $l_{n+1} \leftarrow 1$ (for convenience in step B3).

B2. [Visit.] Visit the binary tree represented by $l_1 l_2 \ldots l_n$ and $r_1 r_2 \ldots r_n$.

B3. [Find j.] Set $j \leftarrow 1$. While $l_j = 0$, set $r_j \leftarrow 0$, $l_j \leftarrow j+1$, and $j \leftarrow j+1$. Then terminate the algorithm if $j > n$.

B4. [Find k and y.] Set $y \leftarrow l_j$ and $k \leftarrow 0$. While $r_y > 0$, set $k \leftarrow y$ and $y \leftarrow r_y$.

B5. [Promote y.] If $k > 0$, set $r_k \leftarrow 0$; otherwise set $l_j \leftarrow 0$. Then set $r_y \leftarrow r_j$, $r_j \leftarrow y$, and return to B2. ∎

[See W. Skarbek, *Theoretical Computer Science* **57** (1988), 153–159; step B3 uses an idea of J. Korsh.] Exercise 44 proves that the loops in steps B3 and B4 both tend to be very short. Indeed, fewer than 9 memory references are needed, on the average, to transform a linked binary tree into its successor.

Table 2 shows the fourteen binary trees that are generated when $n = 4$, together with their corresponding forests and with two related sequences: Arrays $e_1 e_2 \ldots e_n$ and $s_1 s_2 \ldots s_n$ are defined by the property that node k in preorder has e_k children and s_k descendants in the associated forest. (Thus s_k is the size of k's left subtree in the binary tree; also, $s_k + 1$ is the length of the SCOPE link in the sense of 2.3.3–(5).) The next column repeats the fourteen forests of Table 1 in the lexicographic ordering of Algorithm P, but mirror-reversed from left to right.

Table 2

LINKED BINARY TREES AND RELATED OBJECTS WHEN $n = 4$

$l_1l_2l_3l_4$	$r_1r_2r_3r_4$	binary tree	forest	$e_1e_2e_3e_4$	$s_1s_2s_3s_4$	colex forest	lsib/rchild
2340	0000			1110	3210		
0340	2000			0110	0210		
2040	0300			2010	3010		
2040	3000			1010	1010		
0040	2300			0010	0010		
2300	0040			1200	3200		
0300	2040			0200	0200		
2300	0400			2100	3100		
2300	4000			1100	2100		
0300	2400			0100	0100		
2000	0340			3000	3000		
2000	4300			2000	2000		
2000	3040			1000	1000		
0000	2340			0000	0000		

And the final column shows the binary tree that represents the colex forest; it also happens to represent the forest in column 4, but by links to left sibling and right child instead of to left child and right sibling. This final column provides an interesting connection between nested parentheses and binary trees, so it gives us some insight into why Algorithm B is valid (see exercise 19).

*Gray codes for trees. Our previous experiences with other combinatorial patterns suggest that we can probably generate parentheses and trees by making only small perturbations to get from one instance to another. And indeed, there are at least three very nice ways to achieve this goal.

Consider first the case of nested parentheses, which we can represent by the sequences $z_1 z_2 \ldots z_n$ that satisfy condition (8). A "near-perfect" way to generate all such combinations, in the sense of Section 7.2.1.3, is one in which we run through all possibilities in such a way that some component z_j changes by ± 1 or ± 2 at each step; this means that we get from each string of parentheses to its successor by simply changing either () $\leftrightarrow$)(or ()) $\leftrightarrow$))(in the vicinity of the jth left parenthesis. Here's one way to do the job when $n = 4$:

$$1357, 1356, 1346, 1345, 1347, 1247, 1245, 1246, 1236, 1234, 1235, 1237, 1257, 1256.$$

And we can extend any solution for $n-1$ to a solution for n, by taking each pattern $z_1 z_2 \ldots z_{n-1}$ and letting z_n run through all of its legal values using *endo-order* or its reverse as in 7.2.1.3–(45), proceeding downward from $2n-2$ and then up to $2n-1$ or vice versa, and omitting all elements that are $\leq z_{n-1}$.

Algorithm N (*Near-perfect nested parentheses*). This algorithm visits all n-combinations $z_1 \ldots z_n$ of $\{1, \ldots, 2n\}$ that represent the indices of left parentheses in a nested string, changing only one index at a time. The process is controlled by an auxiliary array $g_1 \ldots g_n$ that represents temporary goals.

N1. [Initialize.] Set $z_j \leftarrow 2j - 1$ and $g_j \leftarrow 2j - 2$ for $1 \leq j \leq n$.

N2. [Visit.] Visit the n-combination $z_1 \ldots z_n$. Then set $j \leftarrow n$.

N3. [Find j.] If $z_j = g_j$, set $g_j \leftarrow g_j \oplus 1$ (thereby complementing the least significant bit), $j \leftarrow j - 1$, and repeat this step.

N4. [Home stretch?] If $g_j - z_j$ is even, set $z_j \leftarrow z_j + 2$ and return to N2.

N5. [Decrease or turn.] Set $t \leftarrow z_j - 2$. If $t < 0$, terminate the algorithm. Otherwise, if $t \leq z_{j-1}$, set $t \leftarrow t + 2[t < z_{j-1}] + 1$. Finally set $z_j \leftarrow t$ and go back to N2. ∎

[A somewhat similar algorithm was introduced by D. Rœlants van Baronaigien in *J. Algorithms* **35** (2000), 100–107; see also Xiang, Ushijima, and Tang, *Inf. Proc. Letters* **76** (2000), 169–174. F. Ruskey and A. Proskurowski, in *J. Algorithms* **11** (1990), 68–84, had previously shown how to construct *perfect* Gray codes for all tables $z_1 \ldots z_n$ when $n \geq 4$ is even, thus changing some z_j by only ± 1 at every step; but their construction was quite complex, and no known perfect scheme is simple enough to be of practical use. Exercise 48 shows that perfection is impossible when $n \geq 5$ is odd.]

If our goal is to generate linked tree structures instead of strings of parentheses, perfection of the z-index changes is not good enough, because simple swaps like () $\leftrightarrow$)(don't necessarily correspond to simple link manipulations. A far better approach can be based on the "rotation" algorithms by which we were

able to keep search trees balanced in Section 6.2.3. *Rotation to the left* changes
a binary tree

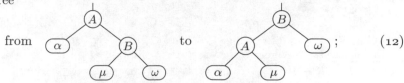

from   to   ;   (12)

thus the corresponding forest is changed

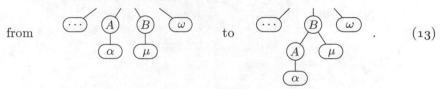

from   to   .   (13)

"Node $\textcircled{A}$ becomes the leftmost child of its right sibling." *Rotation to the right*
is, of course, the opposite transformation: "The leftmost child of $\textcircled{B}$ becomes
its left sibling." The vertical line in (12) stands for a connection to the overall
context, either a left link or a right link or the pointer to the root. Any or all
of the subtrees α, μ, or ω may be empty. The '$\cdots$' in (13), which represents
additional siblings at the left of the family containing $\textcircled{B}$, might also be empty.

The nice thing about rotations is that only three links change: The right
link from $\textcircled{A}$, the left link from $\textcircled{B}$, and the pointer from above. Rotations
preserve inorder of the binary tree and postorder of the forest. (Notice also that
the binary-tree form of a rotation corresponds in a natural way to an application
of the *associative law*

$$(\alpha\mu)\omega \;=\; \alpha(\mu\omega) \tag{14}$$

in the midst of an algebraic formula.)

A simple scheme very much like the classical reflected Gray code for n-tuples
(Algorithm 7.2.1.1H) and the method of plain changes for permutations (Algorithm 7.2.1.2P) can be used to generate all binary trees or forests via rotations.
Consider any forest on $n-1$ nodes, with k roots $\textcircled{A_1}$, ..., $\textcircled{A_k}$. Then there are
$k+1$ forests on n nodes that have the same postorder sequence on the first $n-1$
nodes but with node $\textcircled{n}$ last; for example, when $k=3$ they are

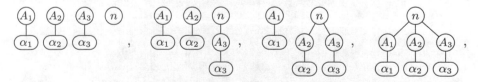

obtained by successively rotating $\textcircled{A_3}$, $\textcircled{A_2}$, and $\textcircled{A_1}$ to the left. Moreover, at
the extremes when $\textcircled{n}$ is either at the right or at the top, we can perform
any desired rotation on the other $n-1$ nodes, because node $\textcircled{n}$ isn't in the
way. Therefore, as observed by J. M. Lucas, D. Rœlants van Baronaigien, and
F. Ruskey [*J. Algorithms* **15** (1993), 343–366], we can extend any list of the
$(n-1)$-node trees to a list of all n-node trees by simply letting node $\textcircled{n}$ roam

back and forth. A careful attention to low-level details makes it possible in fact to do the job with remarkable efficiency:

Algorithm L (*Linked binary trees by rotations*). This algorithm generates all pairs of arrays $l_0 l_1 \ldots l_n$ and $r_1 \ldots r_n$ that represent left links and right links of n-node binary trees, where l_0 is the root of the tree and the links (l_j, r_j) point respectively to the left and right subtrees of the jth node in symmetric order. Equivalently, it generates all n-node forests, where l_j and r_j denote the left child and right sibling of the jth node in postorder. Each tree is obtained from its predecessor by doing a single rotation. Two auxiliary arrays $k_1 \ldots k_n$ and $o_0 o_1 \ldots o_n$, representing backpointers and directions, are used to control the process.

L1. [Initialize.] Set $l_j \leftarrow 0$, $r_j \leftarrow j + 1$, $k_j \leftarrow j - 1$, and $o_j \leftarrow -1$ for $1 \leq j < n$; also set $l_0 \leftarrow o_0 \leftarrow 1$, $l_n \leftarrow r_n \leftarrow 0$, $k_n \leftarrow n - 1$, and $o_n \leftarrow -1$.

L2. [Visit.] Visit the binary tree or forest represented by $l_0 l_1 \ldots l_n$ and $r_1 \ldots r_n$. Then set $j \leftarrow n$ and $p \leftarrow 0$.

L3. [Find j.] If $o_j > 0$, set $m \leftarrow l_j$ and go to L5 if $m \neq 0$. If $o_j < 0$, set $m \leftarrow k_j$; then go to L4 if $m \neq 0$, otherwise set $p \leftarrow j$. If $m = 0$ in either case, set $o_j \leftarrow -o_j$, $j \leftarrow j - 1$, and repeat this step.

L4. [Rotate left.] Set $r_m \leftarrow l_j$, $l_j \leftarrow m$, $x \leftarrow k_m$, and $k_j \leftarrow x$. If $x = 0$, set $l_p \leftarrow j$, otherwise set $r_x \leftarrow j$. Return to L2.

L5. [Rotate right.] Terminate if $j = 0$. Otherwise set $l_j \leftarrow r_m$, $r_m \leftarrow j$, $k_j \leftarrow m$, $x \leftarrow k_m$. If $x = 0$, set $l_p \leftarrow m$, otherwise set $r_x \leftarrow m$. Go back to L2. ∎

Exercise 38 proves that Algorithm L needs only about 9 memory references per tree generated; thus it is almost as fast as Algorithm B. (In fact, two memory references per step could be saved by keeping the three quantities o_n, l_n, and k_n in registers. But of course Algorithm B can be speeded up too.)

Table 3 shows the sequence of binary trees and forests visited by Algorithm L when $n = 4$, with some auxiliary tables that shed further light on the process. The permutation $q_1 q_2 q_3 q_4$ lists the nodes in preorder, when they have been numbered in postorder of the forest (symmetric order of the binary tree); it is the inverse of the permutation $p_1 p_2 p_3 p_4$ in Table 1. The "coforest" is the conjugate (right-to-left reflection) of the forest; and the numbers $u_1 u_2 u_3 u_4$ are its scope coordinates, analogous to $s_1 s_2 s_3 s_4$ in Table 2. A final column shows the so-called "dual forest." The significance of these associated quantities is explored in exercises 11–13, 19, 24, 26, and 27.

The links $l_0 l_1 \ldots l_n$ and $r_1 \ldots r_n$ in Algorithm L and Table 3 are *not* comparable to the links $l_1 \ldots l_n$ and $r_1 \ldots r_n$ in Algorithm B and Table 2, because Algorithm L preserves inorder/postorder while Algorithm B preserves preorder. Node k in Algorithm L is the kth node from left to right in the binary tree, so l_0 is needed to identify the root; but node k in Algorithm B is the kth node in preorder, so the root is always node 1 in that case.

Algorithm L has the desired property that only three links change per step; but we can actually do even better in this respect if we stick to the preorder convention of Algorithm B. Exercise 25 presents an algorithm that generates

Table 3

BINARY TREES AND FORESTS GENERATED BY ROTATIONS WHEN $n = 4$

$l_0l_1l_2l_3l_4$	$r_1r_2r_3r_4$	$k_1k_2k_3k_4$	binary tree	forest	$q_1q_2q_3q_4$	coforest	$u_1u_2u_3u_4$	dual
10000	2340	0123			1234		0000	
10003	2400	0122			1243		1000	
10002	4300	0121			1423		2000	
40001	2300	0120			4123		3000	
40021	3000	0110			4132		3100	
10023	4000	0111			1432		2100	
10020	3040	0113			1324		0100	
30010	2040	0103			3124		0200	
40013	2000	0100			4312		3200	
40123	0000	0000			4321		3210	
30120	0040	0003			3214		0210	
20100	0340	0023			2134		0010	
20103	0400	0022			2143		1010	
40102	0300	0020			4213		3010	

all linked binary trees or forests by changing just two links per step, preserving preorder. One link becomes zero while another becomes nonzero. This prune-and-graft algorithm, which is the third of the three "very nice Gray codes for trees" promised above, has only one downside: Its controlling mechanism is a bit trickier than that of Algorithm L, so it needs about 40% more time to do the calculations when we include the cost of deciding what links to change at each step.

The number of trees. There's a simple formula for the total number of outputs that are generated by Algorithms P, B, N, and L, namely

$$C_n = \frac{1}{n+1}\binom{2n}{n} = \binom{2n}{n} - \binom{2n}{n-1}; \qquad (15)$$

we proved this fact in Eq. 2.3.4.4–(14). The first few values are

$$n = 0\ 1\ 2\ 3\ 4\ 5\ 6\ 7\ 8\ 9\ 10\ 11\ 12\ 13$$
$$C_n = 1\ 1\ 2\ 5\ 14\ 42\ 132\ 429\ 1430\ 4862\ 16796\ 58786\ 208012\ 742900$$

and they are called *Catalan numbers* because of some influential papers written by Eugène Catalan [*Journal de math.* **3** (1838), 508–516; **4** (1839), 95–99]. Stirling's approximation tells us the asymptotic value,

$$C_n = \frac{4^n}{\sqrt{\pi}\,n^{3/2}}\left(1 - \frac{9}{8n} + \frac{145}{128n^2} - \frac{1155}{1024n^3} + \frac{36939}{32768n^4} + O(n^{-5})\right); \qquad (16)$$

in particular we can conclude that

$$\frac{C_{n-k}}{C_n} = \frac{1}{4^k}\left(1 + \frac{3k}{2n} + O\left(\frac{k^2}{n^2}\right)\right) \qquad \text{when } |k| \le \frac{n}{2}. \qquad (17)$$

(And of course C_{n-1}/C_n is equal to $(n+1)/(4n-2)$, exactly, by (15).) In Section 2.3.4.4 we also derived the generating function

$$C(z) = C_0 + C_1 z + C_2 z^2 + C_3 z^3 + \cdots = \frac{1 - \sqrt{1-4z}}{2z} \qquad (18)$$

and proved the important formula

$$[z^n]\, C(z)^r = \frac{r}{n+r}\binom{2n+r-1}{n} = \binom{2n+r-1}{n} - \binom{2n+r-1}{n-1}; \qquad (19)$$

see the answer to exercise 2.3.4.4–33, and *CMath* equation (5.70).

These facts give us more than enough information to analyze Algorithm P, our algorithm for lexicographic generation of nested parentheses. Step P2 is obviously performed C_n times; then P3 usually makes a simple change and goes back to P2. How often do we need to go on to step P4? Easy: It's the number of times that step P2 finds $m = 2n - 1$. And m is the location of the rightmost '(', so we have $m = 2n - 1$ in exactly C_{n-1} cases. Thus the probability that P3 sets $m \leftarrow m - 1$ and returns immediately to P2 is $(C_n - C_{n-1})/C_n \approx 3/4$, by (17). On the other hand when we do get to step P4, suppose we need to set $a_j \leftarrow$ ')' and $a_k \leftarrow$ '(' exactly $h - 1$ times in that step. The number of cases with $h > x$ is the number of nested strings of length $2n$ that end with x trivial pairs () ... (), namely C_{n-x}. Therefore the total number of times the algorithm changes a_j and a_k in step P4 is

$$C_{n-1} + C_{n-2} + \cdots + C_1 = C_n\left(\frac{C_{n-1}}{C_n} + \frac{C_{n-2}}{C_n} + \cdots + \frac{C_1}{C_n}\right)$$
$$= \frac{1}{3}C_n\left(1 + \frac{2}{n} + O\left(\frac{1}{n^2}\right)\right), \qquad (20)$$

by (17); we have proved the claim for efficiency made earlier.

For a deeper understanding it is helpful to study the recursive structure underlying Algorithm P, as expressed in (5). The sequences A_{pq} in that formula have C_{pq} elements, where

$$C_{pq} = C_{p(q-1)} + C_{(p-1)q}, \quad \text{if } 0 \le p \le q \ne 0; \qquad C_{00} = 1; \qquad (21)$$

and $C_{pq} = 0$ if $p < 0$ or $p > q$. Thus we can form the triangular array

$$
\begin{array}{llllll}
C_{00} \\
C_{01} & C_{11} \\
C_{02} & C_{12} & C_{22} \\
C_{03} & C_{13} & C_{23} & C_{33} \\
C_{04} & C_{14} & C_{24} & C_{34} & C_{44} \\
C_{05} & C_{15} & C_{25} & C_{35} & C_{45} & C_{55} \\
C_{06} & C_{16} & C_{26} & C_{36} & C_{46} & C_{56} & C_{66}
\end{array}
\quad = \quad
\begin{array}{lllllll}
1 \\
1 & 1 \\
1 & 2 & 2 \\
1 & 3 & 5 & 5 \\
1 & 4 & 9 & 14 & 14 \\
1 & 5 & 14 & 28 & 42 & 42 \\
1 & 6 & 20 & 48 & 90 & 132 & 132
\end{array}
\qquad (22)
$$

in which every entry is the sum of its nearest neighbors above and to the left; the Catalan numbers $C_n = C_{nn}$ appear on the diagonal. The elements of this triangle, which themselves have a venerable pedigree going back to de Moivre in 1711, are called "ballot numbers," because they represent sequences of $p + q$ ballots for which a running tabulation never favors a candidate with p votes over an opponent who receives q votes. The general formula

$$C_{pq} = \frac{q-p+1}{q+1}\binom{p+q}{p} = \binom{p+q}{p} - \binom{p+q}{p-1} \qquad (23)$$

can be proved by induction or in a variety of more interesting ways; see exercise 39 and the answer to exercise 2.2.1–4. Notice that, because of (19), we have

$$C_{pq} = [z^p]\,C(z)^{q-p+1}. \qquad (24)$$

When $n = 4$, Algorithm P essentially describes the recursion tree

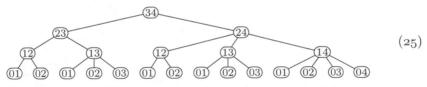

$$(25)$$

because the specification (5) implies that $A_{nn} = (\,A_{(n-1)n}$ and that

$$A_{pq} =)^{q-p}(\,A_{(p-1)p}, \quad)^{q-p-1}(\,A_{(p-1)(p+1)}, \quad)^{q-p-2}(\,A_{(p-1)(p+2)},$$
$$\dots, \ (\,A_{(p-1)q} \qquad \text{when } 0 \le p < q. \quad (26)$$

The number of leaves below node $\textcircled{pq}$ in this recursion tree is C_{pq}, and node $\textcircled{pq}$ appears exactly $C_{(n-q)(n-1-p)}$ times on level $n - 1 - p$; therefore we must have

$$\sum_q C_{(n-q)(n-1-p)}\,C_{pq} = C_n, \qquad \text{for } 0 \le p < n. \qquad (27)$$

The fourteen leaves of (25), from left to right, correspond to the fourteen rows of Table 1, from top to bottom. Notice that the entries in column $c_1 c_2 c_3 c_4$ of that table assign the respective numbers 0000, 0001, 0010, ..., 0123 to the leaves of (25), in accord with "Dewey decimal notation" for tree nodes (but with indices starting at 0 instead of 1, and with an extra 0 tacked on at the beginning).

A worm that crawls from one leaf to the next, around the bottom of the recursion tree, will ascend and descend h levels when h of the coordinates $c_1 \dots c_n$ are changed, namely when Algorithm P resets the values of h (s and h)s. This observation makes it easy to understand our previous conclusion that the condition $h > x$ occurs exactly C_{n-x} times during a complete crawl.

Yet another way to understand Algorithm P arises when we contemplate an infinite directed graph that is suggested by the recursion (21):

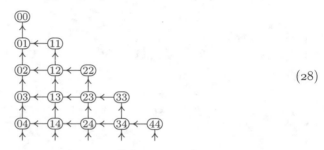

$$(28)$$

Clearly C_{pq} is the number of paths from (pq) to (00) in this digraph, because of (21). And indeed, every string of parentheses in A_{pq} corresponds directly to such a path, with '(' signifying a step to the left and ')' signifying a step upward. Algorithm P explores all such paths systematically by trying first to go upward when extending a partial path.

Therefore it is easy to determine the Nth string of nested parentheses that is visited by Algorithm P, by starting at node (nn) and doing the following calculation when at node (pq): If $p = q = 0$, stop; otherwise, if $N \leq C_{p(q-1)}$, emit ')', set $q \leftarrow q - 1$, and continue; otherwise set $N \leftarrow N - C_{p(q-1)}$, emit '(', set $p \leftarrow p - 1$, and continue. The following algorithm [Frank Ruskey, Ph.D. thesis (University of California at San Diego, 1978), 16–24] avoids the need to precompute the Catalan triangle by evaluating C_{pq} on the fly as it goes:

Algorithm U (*Unrank a string of nested parentheses*). Given n and N, where $1 \leq N \leq C_n$, this algorithm computes the Nth output $a_1 \dots a_{2n}$ of Algorithm P.

U1. [Initialize.] Set $q \leftarrow n$ and $m \leftarrow p \leftarrow c \leftarrow 1$. While $p < n$, set $p \leftarrow p + 1$ and $c \leftarrow ((4p - 2)c)/(p + 1)$.

U2. [Done?] Terminate the algorithm if $q = 0$.

U3. [Go up?] Set $c' \leftarrow ((q+1)(q-p)c)/((q+p)(q-p+1))$. (At this point we have $1 \leq N \leq c = C_{pq}$ and $c' = C_{p(q-1)}$.) If $N \leq c'$, set $q \leftarrow q - 1$, $c \leftarrow c'$, $a_m \leftarrow$ ')', $m \leftarrow m + 1$, and return to U2.

U4. [Go left.] Set $p \leftarrow p - 1$, $c \leftarrow c - c'$, $N \leftarrow N - c'$, $a_m \leftarrow$ '(', $m \leftarrow m + 1$, and return to U3. ∎

Random trees. We could choose a string $a_1 a_2 \dots a_{2n}$ of nested parentheses at random by simply applying Algorithm U to a random integer N between 1 and C_n. But that idea isn't really very good, when n is bigger than 32 or so, because C_n can be quite large. A simpler and better way, proposed by D. B. Arnold and M. R. Sleep [*ACM Trans. Prog. Languages and Systems* **2** (1980), 122–128], is to generate a random "worm walk" by starting at ⓝⓝ in (28) and repeatedly taking leftward or upward branches with the appropriate probabilities. The resulting algorithm is almost the same as Algorithm U, but it deals only with nonnegative integers less than $n^2 + n + 1$:

Algorithm W (*Uniformly random strings of nested parentheses*). This algorithm generates a random string $a_1 a_2 \ldots a_{2n}$ of properly nested (s and)s.

W1. [Initialize.] Set $p \leftarrow q \leftarrow n$ and $m \leftarrow 1$.

W2. [Done?] Terminate the algorithm if $q = 0$.

W3. [Go up?] Let X be a random integer in the range $0 \le X < (q+p)(q-p+1)$. If $X < (q+1)(q-p)$, set $q \leftarrow q - 1$, $a_m \leftarrow$ ')', $m \leftarrow m + 1$, and return to W2.

W4. [Go left.] Set $p \leftarrow p - 1$, $a_m \leftarrow$ '(', $m \leftarrow m + 1$, and return to W3. ∎

A worm's walk can be regarded as a sequence $w_0 w_1 \ldots w_{2n}$, where w_m is the worm's current depth after m steps. Thus, $w_0 = 0$; $w_m = w_{m-1} + 1$ when $a_m =$ '('; $w_m = w_{m-1} - 1$ when $a_m =$ ')'; and we have $w_m \ge 0$, $w_{2n} = 0$. The sequence $w_0 w_1 \ldots w_{30}$ corresponding to (1) and (2) is 012101232123434543232123234
3210. At step W3 of Algorithm W we have $q + p = 2n + 1 - m$ and $q - p = w_{m-1}$.

Let's say that the *outline* of a forest is the path that runs through the points $(m, -w_m)$ in the plane, for $0 \le m \le 2n$, where $w_0 w_1 \ldots w_{2n}$ is the worm walk corresponding to the associated string $a_1 \ldots a_{2n}$ of nested parentheses. Figure 57 shows what happens if we plot the outlines of all 50-node forests and darken each point according to the number of forests that lie above it. For example, w_1 is always 1, so the triangular region at the upper left of Fig. 57 is solid black. But w_2 is either 0 or 2, and 0 occurs in $C_{49} \approx C_{50}/4$ cases; so the adjacent diamond-shaped area is a 75% shade of gray. Thus Fig. 57 illustrates the shape of a random forest, analogous to the shapes of random partitions that we've seen in Figs. 50, 51, and 55 of Sections 7.2.1.4 and 7.2.1.5.

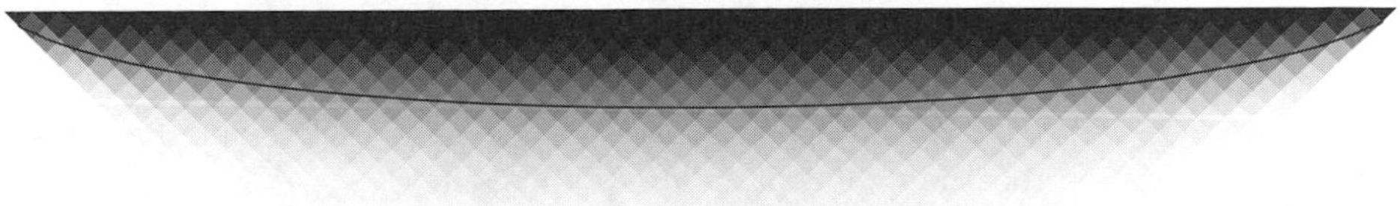

Fig. 57. The shape of a random 50-node forest.

Of course we can't really draw the outlines of all those forests, since there are $C_{50} = 1{,}978{,}261{,}657{,}756{,}160{,}653{,}623{,}774{,}456$ of them. But with the help of mathematics we can pretend that we've done so. The probability that $w_{2m} = 2k$ is $C_{(m-k)(m+k)} C_{(n-m-k)(n-m+k)} / C_n$, because there are $C_{(m-k)(m+k)}$ ways to start with $m + k$ (s and $m - k$)s, and $C_{(n-m-k)(n-m+k)}$ ways to finish with

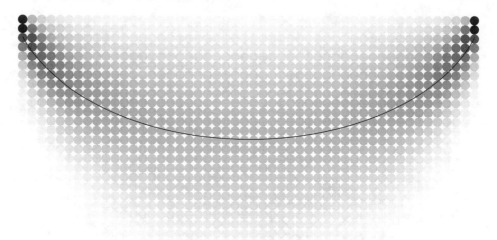

Fig. 58. Locations of the internal nodes in a random 50-node binary tree.

$n - (m + k)$ (s and $n - (m - k)$)s. By (23) and Stirling's approximation, this probability is

$$\frac{(2k+1)^2(n+1)}{(m+k+1)(n-m+k+1)}\binom{2m}{m-k}\binom{2n-2m}{n-m+k}\Big/\binom{2n}{n}$$

$$= \frac{(2k+1)^2}{\sqrt{\pi}\,\big(\theta(1-\theta)n\big)^{3/2}}\, e^{-k^2/(\theta(1-\theta)n)}\Big(1+O\Big(\frac{k+1}{n}\Big)+O\Big(\frac{k^3}{n^2}\Big)\Big) \qquad (29)$$

when $m = \theta n$ and $n \to \infty$, for $0 < \theta < 1$. The average value of w_{2m} is worked out in exercise 57; it comes to

$$\frac{(4m(n-m)+n)\binom{2m}{m}\binom{2n-2m}{n-m}}{n\binom{2n}{n}} - 1 = 4\sqrt{\frac{\theta(1-\theta)n}{\pi}} - 1 + O\Big(\frac{1}{\sqrt{n}}\Big), \quad (30)$$

and it is illustrated for $n = 50$ as a curved line in Fig. 57.

When n is large, worm walks approach the so-called "Brownian excursion," which is an important concept in probability theory. See, for example, Paul Lévy, *Processus Stochastiques et Mouvement Brownien* (1948), 225–237; Guy Louchard, *J. Applied Prob.* **21** (1984), 479–499, and *BIT* **26** (1986), 17–34; David Aldous, *Electronic Communications in Probability* **3** (1998), 79–90; Jon Warren, *Electronic Communications in Probability* **4** (1999), 25–29; J.-F. Marckert, *Random Structures & Algorithms* **24** (2004), 118–132.

What is the shape of a random *binary* tree? This question was investigated by Frank Ruskey in *SIAM J. Algebraic and Discrete Methods* **1** (1980), 43–50, and the answer turns out to be quite interesting. Suppose we draw a binary tree

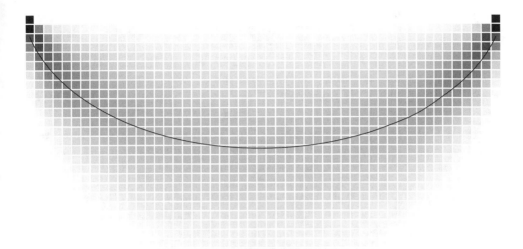

Fig. 59. Locations of the external nodes in a random 50-node binary tree.

as in (4), with the mth internal node at horizontal position m when the nodes are numbered in symmetric order. If all of the 50-node binary trees are drawn in this way and superimposed on each other, we get the distribution of node positions shown in Fig. 58. Similarly, if we number the *external* nodes from 0 to n in symmetric order and place them at horizontal positions $.5, 1.5, \ldots, n+.5$, the "fringes" of all 50-node binary trees form the distribution shown in Fig. 59. Notice that the root node is most likely to be either number 1 or number n, at the extreme left or right; it is least likely to be either $\lfloor (n+1)/2 \rfloor$ or $\lceil (n+1)/2 \rceil$, in the middle.

As in Fig. 57, the smooth curves in Figs. 58 and 59 show the average node depths; exact formulas are derived in exercises 58 and 59. Asymptotically, the average depth of external node m is

$$8\sqrt{\frac{\theta(1-\theta)n}{\pi}} - 1 + O\Big(\frac{1}{\sqrt{n}}\Big), \qquad \text{when } m = \theta n \text{ and } n \to \infty, \qquad (31)$$

for all fixed ratios θ with $0 < \theta < 1$, curiously like (30); and the average depth of *internal* node m is asymptotically the same, but with '-1' replaced by '-3'. Thus we can say that *the average shape of a random binary tree is approximately the lower half of an ellipse, n units wide and $4\sqrt{n/\pi}$ levels deep.*

Three other noteworthy ways to generate random encodings of forests are discussed in exercises 60, 61, and 62. They are less direct than Algorithm W, yet they have substantial combinatorial interest. The first one begins with an arbitrary random string containing n (s and n)s, not necessarily nested; each of the $\binom{2n}{n}$ possibilities is equally likely. It then proceeds to convert every such string into a sequence that is properly nested, in such a way that exactly $n + 1$

strings map into each final outcome. The second method is similar, but it starts
with a sequence of $n + 1$ 0s and n 2s, mapping them in such a way that exactly
$2n + 1$ original strings produce each possible result. And the third method
produces each output from exactly n of the bit strings that contain exactly
$n - 1$ 1s and $n + 1$ 0s. In other words, the three methods provide combinatorial
proofs of the fact that C_n is simultaneously equal to $\binom{2n}{n}/(n+1)$, $\binom{2n+1}{n}/(2n+1)$,
and $\binom{2n}{n-1}/n$. For example, when $n = 4$ we have $14 = 70/5 = 126/9 = 56/4$.

If we want to generate random binary trees directly in linked form, we can
use a beautiful method suggested by J. L. Rémy [*RAIRO Informatique Théorique*
19 (1985), 179–195]. His approach is particularly instructive because it shows
how random Catalan trees might actually occur "in nature," using a deliciously
simple mechanism based on a classical idea of Olinde Rodrigues [*J. de Math.*
3 (1838), 549]. Let us suppose that our goal is to obtain not only an ordinary
n-node binary tree, but a *decorated* binary tree, namely an extended binary tree
in which the external nodes have been labeled with the numbers 0 to n in some
order. There are $(n + 1)!$ ways to decorate any given binary tree; so the total
number of decorated binary trees with n internal nodes is

$$D_n = (n + 1)! \, C_n = \frac{(2n)!}{n!} = (4n - 2) D_{n-1}. \tag{32}$$

Rémy observed that there are $4n - 2$ easy ways to build a decorated tree of
order n from a given decorated tree of order $n - 1$: We simply choose any one
of the $2n - 1$ nodes (internal or external) in the given tree, say x, and replace it
by either

$$\tag{33}$$

thus inserting a new internal node and a new leaf while moving x and its
descendants (if any) down one level.

For example, here's one way to construct a decorated tree of order 6:

$$\tag{34}$$

Notice that every decorated tree is obtained by this process in exactly one way,
because the predecessor of each tree must be the tree we get by striking out the
highest-numbered leaf. Therefore Rémy's construction produces decorated trees
that are uniformly random; and if we ignore the external nodes, we get random
binary trees of the ordinary, undecorated variety.

One appealing way to implement Rémy's procedure is to maintain a table of
links $L_0 L_1 \ldots L_{2n}$ where external (leaf) nodes have even numbers and internal
(branch) nodes have odd numbers. The root is node number L_0; the left and
right children of branch node $2k-1$ are respectively the nodes that are numbered
L_{2k-1} and L_{2k}, for $1 \le k \le n$. Then the program is short and sweet:

Algorithm R (*Growing a random binary tree*). This algorithm constructs the linked representation $L_0 L_1 \ldots L_{2N}$ of a uniformly random binary tree with N internal nodes, using the conventions explained above.

R1. [Initialize.] Set $n \leftarrow 0$ and $L_0 \leftarrow 0$.

R2. [Done?] (At this point the links $L_0 L_1 \ldots L_{2n}$ represent a random n-node binary tree.) Terminate the algorithm if $n = N$.

R3. [Advance n.] Let X be a random integer between 0 and $4n + 1$, inclusive. Set $n \leftarrow n + 1$, $b \leftarrow X \bmod 2$, $k \leftarrow \lfloor X/2 \rfloor$, $L_{2n-b} \leftarrow 2n$, $L_{2n-1+b} \leftarrow L_k$, $L_k \leftarrow 2n - 1$, and return to R2. (Here L_k corresponds to x in (33).) ∎

*Chains of subsets. Now that we've got trees and parentheses firmly in mind, it's a good time to discuss the *Christmas tree pattern*,* which is a remarkable way to arrange the set of all 2^n bit strings of length n into $\binom{n}{\lfloor n/2 \rfloor}$ rows and $n+1$ columns, discovered by de Bruijn, van Ebbenhorst Tengbergen, and Kruyswijk [*Nieuw Archief voor Wiskunde* (2) **23** (1951), 191–193].

The Christmas tree pattern of order 1 is the single row '0 1'; and the pattern of order 2 is

$$\begin{matrix} & 10 & \\ 00 & 01 & 11 \end{matrix} \quad . \tag{35}$$

In general we get the Christmas tree pattern of order $n + 1$ by taking every row '$\sigma_1 \; \sigma_2 \; \ldots \; \sigma_s$' of the order-$n$ pattern and replacing it by the two rows

$$\begin{matrix} \sigma_2 0 & \ldots & \sigma_s 0 & \\ \sigma_1 0 & \sigma_1 1 & \ldots & \sigma_{s-1} 1 & \sigma_s 1 \end{matrix} \quad . \tag{36}$$

(The first of these rows is omitted when $s = 1$.)

Proceeding in this way, we obtain for example the pattern of order 8 that appears in Table 4 on the next page. It is easy to verify by induction that

  i) Each of the 2^n bit strings appears exactly once in the pattern.
 ii) The bit strings with k 1s all appear in the same column.
iii) Within each row, consecutive bit strings differ by changing a 0 to a 1.

If we think of the bit strings as representing subsets of $\{1, \ldots, n\}$, with 1-bits to indicate the members of a set, property (iii) says that each row represents a *chain* in which each subset is covered by its successor. In symbols, using the notation of Section 7.1.3, every row $\sigma_1 \; \sigma_2 \; \ldots \; \sigma_s$ has the property that $\sigma_j \subseteq \sigma_{j+1}$ and $\nu(\sigma_{j+1}) = \nu(\sigma_j) + 1$ for $1 \le j < s$.

Properties (i) and (ii) tell us that there are exactly $\binom{n}{k}$ elements in column k, if we number the columns from 0 to n. This observation, together with the fact that each row is centered among the columns, proves that the total number of rows is $\max_{0 \le k \le n} \binom{n}{k} = \binom{n}{\lfloor n/2 \rfloor}$, as claimed. Let us call this number M_n.

---

* This name was chosen for sentimental reasons, because the pattern has a general shape not unlike that of a festive tree, and because it was the subject of the author's ninth annual "Christmas Tree Lecture" at Stanford University in December 2002.

Table 4

THE CHRISTMAS TREE PATTERN OF ORDER 8

				10101010				
			10101000	10101001	10101011			
				10101100				
			10100100	10100101	10101101			
			10100010	10100110	10101110			
		10100000	10100001	10100011	10100111	10101111		
				10110010				
			10110000	10110001	10110011			
				10110100				
			10010100	10010101	10110101			
			10010010	10010110	10110110			
		10010000	10010001	10010011	10010111	10110111		
				10111000				
			10011000	10011001	10111001			
			10001010	10011010	10111010			
		10001000	10001001	10001011	10011011	10111011		
			10001100	10011100	10111100			
		10000100	10000101	10001101	10011101	10111101		
		10000010	10000110	10001110	10011110	10111110		
	10000000	10000001	10000011	10000111	10001111	10011111	10111111	
				11001010				
			11001000	11001001	11001011			
				11001100				
			11000100	11000101	11001101			
			11000010	11000110	11001110			
		11000000	11000001	11000011	11000111	11001111		
				11010010				
			11010000	11010001	11010011			
				11010100				
			01010100	01010101	11010101			
			01010010	01010110	11010110			
		01010000	01010001	01010011	01010111	11010111		
				11011000				
			01011000	01011001	11011001			
			01001010	01011010	11011010			
		01001000	01001001	01001011	01011011	11011011		
			01001100	01011100	11011100			
		01000100	01000101	01001101	01011101	11011101		
		01000010	01000110	01001110	01011110	11011110		
	01000000	01000001	01000011	01000111	01001111	01011111	11011111	
				11100010				
			11100000	11100001	11100011			
				11100100				
			01100100	01100101	11100101			
			01100010	01100110	11100110			
		01100000	01100001	01100011	01100111	11100111		
				11101000				
			01101000	01101001	11101001			
			00101010	01101010	11101010			
		00101000	00101001	00101011	01101011	11101011		
			00101100	01101100	11101100			
		00100100	00100101	00101101	01101101	11101101		
		00100010	00100110	00101110	01101110	11101110		
	00100000	00100001	00100011	00100111	00101111	01101111	11101111	
				11110000				
			01110000	01110001	11110001			
			00110010	01110010	11110010			
		00110000	00110001	00110011	01110011	11110011		
			00110100	01110100	11110100			
		00010100	00010101	00110101	01110101	11110101		
		00010010	00010110	00110110	01110110	11110110		
	00010000	00010001	00010011	00010111	00110111	01110111	11110111	
			00111000	01111000	11111000			
		00011000	00011001	00111001	01111001	11111001		
		00001010	00011010	00111010	01111010	11111010		
	00001000	00001001	00001011	00011011	00111011	01111011	11111011	
		00001100	00011100	00111100	01111100	11111100		
	00000100	00000101	00001101	00011101	00111101	01111101	11111101	
	00000010	00000110	00001110	00011110	00111110	01111110	11111110	
00000000	00000001	00000011	00000111	00001111	00011111	00111111	01111111	11111111

A set C of bit strings is called a *clutter*, or an "antichain of subsets," if its bit strings are incomparable in the sense that $\sigma \not\subseteq \tau$ whenever σ and τ are distinct elements of C. A famous theorem of Emanuel Sperner [*Math. Zeitschrift* **27** (1928), 544–548] asserts that no clutter on $\{1, \ldots, n\}$ can have more than M_n elements; and the Christmas tree pattern provides a simple proof, because no clutter can contain more than one element of each row.

Indeed, the Christmas tree pattern can be used to show that much more is true. Let's note first that exactly $\binom{n}{k} - \binom{n}{k-1}$ rows of length $n + 1 - 2k$ are present, for $0 \le k \le n/2$, because there are exactly $\binom{n}{k}$ elements in column k. For example, Table 4 has one row of length 9, namely the bottom row; it also has $\binom{8}{1} - \binom{8}{0} = 7$ rows of length 7, $\binom{8}{2} - \binom{8}{1} = 20$ rows of length 5, $\binom{8}{3} - \binom{8}{2} = 28$ of length 3, and $\binom{8}{4} - \binom{8}{3} = 14$ of length 1. Moreover, these numbers $\binom{n}{k} - \binom{n}{k-1}$ appear in the Catalan triangle (22), because they're equal to $C_{k(n-k)}$ according to Eq. (23).

Further study reveals that this Catalan connection is not simply a coincidence; nested parentheses are, in fact, the key to a deeper understanding of the Christmas tree pattern, because the theory of parentheses tells us where an arbitrary bit string fits into the array. Suppose we use the symbols (and) instead of 1 and 0, respectively. Any string of parentheses, nested or not, can be written uniquely in the form

$$\alpha_0) \ldots \alpha_{p-1}) \alpha_p (\alpha_{p+1} \ldots (\alpha_q \qquad (37)$$

for some p and q with $0 \le p \le q$, where the substrings $\alpha_0, \ldots, \alpha_q$ are properly nested and possibly empty; exactly p of the right parentheses and $q - p$ of the left parentheses are "free" in the sense that they have no mate. For example, the string

$$) (( )) ( )) ( )))) (((((( ) ( ) ( ) ( ) ((( )) \qquad (38)$$

has $p = 5$, $q = 12$, $\alpha_0 = \epsilon$, $\alpha_1 = (( )) ( )$, $\alpha_2 = ( )$, $\alpha_3 = \epsilon, \ldots, \alpha_{12} = (( ))$. In general, the string (37) is part of a chain of length $q + 1$,

$$\alpha_0) \ldots \alpha_{q-1}) \alpha_q, \quad \alpha_0) \ldots \alpha_{q-2}) \alpha_{q-1} (\alpha_q, \quad \ldots, \quad \alpha_0 (\alpha_1 \ldots (\alpha_q, \qquad (39)$$

in which we start with q free)s and change them one by one into free (s. Every row of the Christmas tree pattern is obtained in exactly this manner, but using 1 and 0 instead of (and); for if the chain $\sigma_1 \ldots \sigma_s$ corresponds to the nested strings $\alpha_0, \ldots, \alpha_{s-1}$, its successor chains in (36) correspond respectively to $\alpha_0, \ldots, \alpha_{s-3}, \alpha_{s-2} (\alpha_{s-1})$ and to $\alpha_0, \ldots, \alpha_{s-3}, \alpha_{s-2}, \alpha_{s-1}, \epsilon$. [See Curtis Greene and Daniel J. Kleitman, *J. Combinatorial Theory* **A20** (1976), 80–88.]

Notice furthermore that the rightmost elements in each row of the pattern — such as 10101010, 10101011, 10101100, 10101101, $\ldots$, 11111110, 11111111 in the case $n = 8$ — are in lexicographic order. Thus, for example, the fourteen rows of length 1 in Table 4 correspond precisely to the fourteen strings of nested parentheses in Table 1. This observation makes it easy to generate the rows of Table 4 sequentially from bottom to top, with a method analogous to Algorithm P; see exercise 77.

Let $f(x_1, \ldots, x_n)$ be any monotone Boolean function of n variables. If $\sigma = a_1 \ldots a_n$ is any bit string of length n, we can write $f(\sigma) = f(a_1, \ldots, a_n)$ for convenience. Any row $\sigma_1 \ldots \sigma_s$ of the Christmas tree pattern forms a chain, so we have

$$0 \leq f(\sigma_1) \leq \cdots \leq f(\sigma_s) \leq 1. \tag{40}$$

In other words, there is an index t such that $f(\sigma_j) = 0$ for $j < t$ and $f(\sigma_j) = 1$ for $j \geq t$; we will know the value of $f(\sigma)$ for all 2^n bit strings σ if we know the indices t for each row of the pattern.

Georges Hansel [*Comptes Rendus Acad. Sci.* (A) **262** (Paris, 1966), 1088–1090] noticed that the Christmas tree pattern has another important property: If σ_{j-1}, σ_j, and σ_{j+1} are three consecutive entries of any row, the bit string

$$\sigma'_j = \sigma_{j-1} \oplus \sigma_j \oplus \sigma_{j+1} \tag{41}$$

lies in a *previous* row. In fact, σ'_j lies in the same column as σ_j, and it satisfies

$$\sigma_{j-1} \subseteq \sigma'_j \subseteq \sigma_{j+1}; \tag{42}$$

it is called the relative complement of σ_j in the interval $(\sigma_{j-1} .. \sigma_{j+1})$. Hansel's observation is easy to prove by induction, because of the recursive rule (36) that defines the Christmas tree pattern. He used it to show that we can deduce the values of $f(\sigma)$ for all σ by actually evaluating the function at relatively few well-chosen places; for if we know the value of $f(\sigma'_j)$, we will know either $f(\sigma_{j-1})$ or $f(\sigma_{j+1})$ because of relation (42).

Algorithm H (*Learning a monotone Boolean function*). Let $f(x_1, \ldots, x_n)$ be a Boolean function that is nondecreasing in each Boolean variable, but otherwise unknown. Given a bit string σ of length n, let $r(\sigma)$ be the number of the row in which σ appears in the Christmas tree pattern, where $1 \leq r(\sigma) \leq M_n$. If $1 \leq m \leq M_n$, let $s(m)$ be the number of bit strings in row m; also let $\chi(m, k)$ be the bit string in column k of that row, for $(n+1-s(m))/2 \leq k \leq (n-1+s(m))/2$. This algorithm determines the sequence of threshold values $t(1)$, $t(2)$, $\ldots$, $t(M_n)$ such that

$$f(\sigma) = 1 \quad \Longleftrightarrow \quad \nu(\sigma) \geq t(r(\sigma)), \tag{43}$$

by evaluating f at no more than two points per row.

H1. [Loop on m.] Perform steps H2 through H4 for $m = 1$, $\ldots$, M_n; then stop.

H2. [Begin row m.] Set $a \leftarrow (n+1-s(m))/2$ and $z \leftarrow (n-1+s(m))/2$.

H3. [Do a binary search.] If $z \leq a+1$, go to H4. Otherwise set $k \leftarrow \lfloor (a+z)/2 \rfloor$, and

$$\sigma \leftarrow \chi(m, k-1) \oplus \chi(m, k) \oplus \chi(m, k+1). \tag{44}$$

If $k \geq t(r(\sigma))$, set $z \leftarrow k$; otherwise set $a \leftarrow k$. Repeat step H3.

H4. [Evaluate.] If $f(\chi(m, a)) = 1$, set $t(m) \leftarrow a$; otherwise, if $a = z$, set $t(m) \leftarrow a+1$; otherwise set $t(m) \leftarrow z+1-f(\chi(m, z))$. ∎

Hansel's algorithm is *optimum*, in the sense that it evaluates f at the fewest possible points in the worst case. For if f happens to be the threshold function

$$f(\sigma) = [\nu(\sigma) > n/2], \tag{45}$$

any valid algorithm that learns f on the first m rows of the Christmas tree pattern must evaluate $f(\sigma)$ in column $\lfloor n/2 \rfloor$ of each row, and in column $\lfloor n/2 \rfloor + 1$ of each row that has size greater than 1. Otherwise we could not distinguish f from a function that differs from it only at an unexamined point. [See V. K. Korobkov, *Problemy Kibernetiki* **13** (1965), 5–28, Theorem 5.]

P. Gregor, O. Mička, and T. Mütze have found a nice way to reorder the rows of the Christmas tree pattern so that we obtain a Gray code for all binary n-tuples by reading alternately left-to-right and right-to-left. (See arXiv:1912.01566 [math.CO] (2019), 33 pages.)

Oriented trees and forests. Let's turn now to another kind of tree, in which the parent-child relationship is important but the order of children in each family is not. An *oriented forest* of n nodes can be defined by a sequence of pointers $p_1 \ldots p_n$, where p_j is the parent of node j (or $p_j = 0$ if j is a root); the directed graph on vertices $\{0, 1, \ldots, n\}$ with arcs $\{j \to p_j \mid 1 \le j \le n\}$ will have no oriented cycles. An *oriented tree* is an oriented forest with exactly one root. (See Section 2.3.4.2.) Every n-node oriented forest is equivalent to an $(n + 1)$-node oriented tree, because the root of that tree can be regarded as the parent of all the roots of the forest. We saw in Section 2.3.4.4 that there are A_n oriented trees with n nodes, where the first few values are

$$
\begin{array}{rccccccccccccccc}
n = & 1 & 2 & 3 & 4 & 5 & 6 & 7 & 8 & 9 & 10 & 11 & 12 & 13 & 14 \\
A_n = & 1 & 1 & 2 & 4 & 9 & 20 & 48 & 115 & 286 & 719 & 1842 & 4766 & 12486 & 32973
\end{array} \; ; \quad (46)
$$

asymptotically, $A_n = c\alpha^n n^{-3/2} + O(\alpha^n n^{-5/2})$ where $\alpha \approx 2.9558$ and $c \approx 0.4399$. Thus, for example, only 9 of the 14 forests in Table 1 are distinct when we ignore the horizontal left-to-right ordering and consider only the vertical orientation.

Every oriented forest corresponds to a unique ordered forest if we sort the members of each family appropriately, using an ordering on trees introduced by H. I. Scoins [*Machine Intelligence* **3** (1968), 43–60]: Recall from (11) that ordered forests can be characterized by their level codes $c_1 \ldots c_n$, where node j in preorder appears on level c_j. An ordered forest is called *canonical* if the level code sequences for the subtrees in each family are in nonincreasing lexicographic order. For example, the canonical forests in Table 1 are those whose level codes $c_1 c_2 c_3 c_4$ are 0000, 0100, 0101, 0110, 0111, 0120, 0121, 0122, and 0123. The level sequence 0112 is not canonical, because the subtrees of the root have respective level codes 1 and 12; the string 1 is lexicographically less than 12. We can readily verify by induction that *the canonical level codes are lexicographically largest, among all ways of reordering the subtrees of a given oriented forest.*

T. Beyer and S. M. Hedetniemi [*SICOMP* **9** (1980), 706–712] noticed that there is a remarkably simple way to generate oriented forests if we visit them in *decreasing* lexicographic order of the canonical level codes. Suppose $c_1 \ldots c_n$ is canonical, where $c_k > 0$ and $c_{k+1} = \cdots = c_n = 0$. The next smallest sequence is obtained by decreasing c_k, then increasing $c_{k+1} \ldots c_n$ to the largest levels consistent with canonicity; and those levels are easy to compute. For if $j = p_k$ is the parent of node k, we have $c_j = c_k - 1 < c_l$ for $j < l \le k$, hence the levels $c_j \ldots c_k$

represent the subtree currently rooted at node j. To get the largest sequence of levels less than $c_1 \ldots c_n$ we therefore replace $c_k \ldots c_n$ by the first $n+1-k$ elements of the infinite sequence $(c_j \ldots c_{k-1})^\infty = c_j \ldots c_{k-1} c_j \ldots c_{k-1} c_j \ldots$. (The effect is to remove k from its current position as the rightmost child of j, then to append new subtrees that are siblings of j, by cloning j and its descendants as often as possible. This cloning process may terminate in the midst of the sequence $c_j \ldots c_{k-1}$, but that causes no difficulty because every prefix of a canonical level sequence is canonical.) For example, to obtain the successor of any sequence of canonical codes that ends with 23443433000000000, we replace the final 3000000000 by 2344343234.

Algorithm O (*Oriented forests*). This algorithm generates all oriented forests on n nodes, by visiting all canonical n-node forests in decreasing lexicographic order of their level codes $c_1 \ldots c_n$. The level codes are not computed explicitly, however; each canonical forest is represented directly by its sequence of parent pointers $p_1 \ldots p_n$, in preorder of the nodes. To generate all oriented trees on $n+1$ nodes, we can imagine that node 0 is the root. The algorithm sets $p_0 \leftarrow -1$.

O1. [Initialize.] Set $p_k \leftarrow k - 1$ for $0 \le k \le n$. (In particular, this step makes p_0 nonzero, for use in termination testing; see step O4.)

O2. [Visit.] Visit the forest represented by parent pointers $p_1 \ldots p_n$.

O3. [Easy case?] If $p_n > 0$, set $p_n \leftarrow p_{p_n}$ and return to step O2.

O4. [Find j and k.] Find the largest $k < n$ such that $p_k \ne 0$. Terminate the algorithm if $k = 0$; otherwise set $j \leftarrow p_k$ and $d \leftarrow k - j$.

O5. [Clone.] If $p_{k-d} = p_j$, set $p_k \leftarrow p_j$; otherwise set $p_k \leftarrow p_{k-d} + d$. Return to step O2 if $k = n$; otherwise set $k \leftarrow k + 1$ and repeat this step. ∎

As in other algorithms we've been seeing, the loops in steps O4 and O5 tend to be quite short; see exercise 88. Exercise 90 proves that slight changes to this algorithm suffice to generate all arrangements of edges that form *free* trees.

E. F. Harding [*Advances in Appl. Prob.* **3** (1971), 44–77] has shown how to generate the kth oriented *binary* tree with n vertices (see exercise 2.3.4.4–6).

Spanning trees. Now let's consider the minimal subgraphs that "span" a given graph. If G is a connected graph on n vertices, the *spanning trees* of G are the subsets of $n - 1$ edges that contain no cycles; equivalently, they are the subsets of edges that form a free tree connecting all the vertices. Spanning trees are important in many applications, especially in the study of networks, so the problem of generating all spanning trees has been treated by many authors. In fact, systematic ways to list them all were developed early in the 20th century by Wilhelm Feussner [*Annalen der Physik* (4) **9** (1902), 1304–1329], long before anybody thought about generating other kinds of trees.

In the following discussion we will allow graphs to have any number of edges between two vertices; but we disallow loops from a vertex to itself, because self-loops cannot be part of a tree. Feussner's basic idea was very simple, yet eminently suited for calculation: If e is any edge of G, a spanning tree either contains e or it doesn't. Suppose e joins vertex u to vertex v, and suppose it is part of a spanning tree; then the other $n - 2$ edges of that tree span the graph G / e that we obtain by regarding u and v as identical. In other words, the spanning trees that contain e are essentially the same as the spanning trees of the contracted graph G / e that results when we shrink e down to a single point. On the other hand the spanning trees that do *not* contain e are spanning trees of the reduced graph $G \setminus e$ that results when we eliminate edge e. Symbolically, therefore, the set $S(G)$ of all spanning trees of G satisfies

$$S(G) = e\,S(G / e) \cup S(G \setminus e). \tag{47}$$

Malcolm J. Smith, in his Master's thesis at the University of Victoria (1997), introduced a nice way to carry out the recursion (47) by finding all spanning trees in a "revolving-door Gray code" order: Each tree in his scheme is obtained from its predecessor by simply removing one edge and substituting another. Such orderings are not difficult to find, but the trick is to do the job efficiently.

The basic idea of Smith's algorithm is to generate $S(G)$ in such a way that the first spanning tree includes a given *near tree*, namely a set of $n - 2$ edges containing no cycle. This task is trivial if $n = 2$; we simply list all the edges. If $n > 2$ and if the given near tree is $\{e_1, \ldots, e_{n-2}\}$, we proceed as follows: Assume that G is connected; otherwise there are no spanning trees. Form G / e_1 and append e_1 to each of its spanning trees, beginning with one that contains $\{e_2, \ldots, e_{n-2}\}$; notice that $\{e_2, \ldots, e_{n-2}\}$ is a near tree of G / e_1, so this recursion makes sense. If the last spanning tree found in this way for G / e_1 is $f_1 \ldots f_{n-2}$, complete the task by listing all spanning trees for $G \setminus e_1$, beginning with one that contains the near tree $\{f_1, \ldots, f_{n-2}\}$.

For example, suppose G is the graph

$$G \;=\; \tag{48}$$

with four vertices and five edges $\{p, q, r, s, t\}$. Starting with the near tree $\{p, q\}$, Smith's procedure first forms the contracted graph

$$G / p \;=\; \tag{49}$$

and lists its spanning trees, beginning with one that contains $\{q\}$. This list might be qs, qt, ts, tr, rs; thus the trees pqs, pqt, pts, ptr, and prs span G. The remaining task is to list the spanning trees of

$$G \setminus p \;=\; \qquad, \tag{50}$$

starting with one that contains $\{r, s\}$; they are rsq, rqt, qts.

A detailed implementation of Smith's algorithm turns out to be quite instructive. As usual we represent the graph by letting two arcs $u \longrightarrow v$ and $v \longrightarrow u$ correspond to each edge $u \relbar v$, and we maintain lists of "arc nodes" to represent the arcs that leave each vertex. We'll need to shrink and unshrink the graph's edges, so we will make these lists doubly linked. If a points to an arc node that represents $u \longrightarrow v$, then we arrange everything in memory so that

$a \oplus 1$ points to the "mate" of a, which represents $v \longrightarrow u$;

$\quad t_a$ is the "tip" of a, namely v (hence $t_{a \oplus 1} = u$);

$\quad i_a$ is an optional name that identifies this edge (and equals $i_{a \oplus 1}$);

$\quad n_a$ points to the next element of u's arc list;

$\quad p_a$ points to the previous element of u's arc list;

and l_a is a link used for undeleting arcs as explained below.

The vertices are represented by integers $\{1, \ldots, n\}$; and arc number $v - 1$ is a header node for vertex v's doubly linked arc list. A header node a is recognizable by the fact that its tip, t_a, is 0. We let d_v be the degree of vertex v. Thus, for example, the graph (48) might be represented by $(d_1, d_2, d_3, d_4) = (2, 3, 3, 2)$ and by the following fourteen nodes of arc data:

$$
\begin{array}{rccccccccccccccc}
a = & 0 & 1 & 2 & 3 & 4 & 5 & 6 & 7 & 8 & 9 & 10 & 11 & 12 & 13 \\
t_a = & 0 & 0 & 0 & 0 & 1 & 2 & 1 & 3 & 2 & 3 & 2 & 4 & 3 & 4 \\
i_a = & & & & & p & p & q & q & r & r & s & s & t & t \\
n_a = & 5 & 4 & 6 & 10 & 9 & 7 & 8 & 0 & 13 & 11 & 12 & 1 & 3 & 2 \\
p_a = & 7 & 11 & 13 & 12 & 1 & 0 & 2 & 5 & 6 & 4 & 3 & 9 & 10 & 8 \\
\end{array}
$$

The implicit recursion of Smith's algorithm can be controlled conveniently by using an array of arc pointers $a_1 \ldots a_{n-1}$. At level l of the process, arcs $a_1 \ldots a_{l-1}$ denote edges that have been included in the current spanning tree; a_l is ignored; and arcs $a_{l+1} \ldots a_{n-1}$ denote edges of a near tree on the contracted graph $(\ldots (G/a_1) \ldots)/a_{l-1}$ that should be part of the next spanning tree visited.

There's also another array of arc pointers $s_1 \ldots s_{n-2}$, representing stacks of arcs that have been temporarily removed from the current graph. The top element of the stack for level l is s_l, and each arc a links to its successor, l_a (which is 0 at the bottom of the stack).

An edge whose removal would disconnect a connected graph is called a *bridge*. One of the key points in the algorithm that follows is the fact that we want to keep the current graph connected; therefore we don't set $G \leftarrow G \setminus e$ when e is a bridge.

Algorithm S (*All spanning trees*). Given a connected graph represented with the data structures explained above, this algorithm visits all of its spanning trees.

A technique called "dancing links," which we will discuss extensively in Section 7.2.2.1, is used here to remove and restore items from and to doubly linked lists. The abbreviation "delete(a)" in the steps below is shorthand for the pair of operations

$$ n_{p_a} \leftarrow n_a, \quad p_{n_a} \leftarrow p_a; \tag{51} $$

similarly, "undelete(a)" stands for

$$ p_{n_a} \leftarrow a, \quad n_{p_a} \leftarrow a. \tag{52} $$

S1. [Initialize.] Set $a_1 \ldots a_{n-1}$ to a spanning tree of the graph. (See exercise 94.) Also set $x \leftarrow 0$, $l \leftarrow 1$, and $s_1 \leftarrow 0$. If $n = 2$, set $v \leftarrow 1$, $e \leftarrow n_0$, and go to S5.

S2. [Enter level l.] Set $e \leftarrow a_{l+1}$, $u \leftarrow t_e$, and $v \leftarrow t_{e \oplus 1}$. If $d_u > d_v$, interchange $v \leftrightarrow u$ and set $e \leftarrow e \oplus 1$.

S3. [Shrink e.] (Now we will make u identical to v by inserting u's adjacency list into v's. We also must delete all former edges between u and v, including e itself, because such edges would otherwise become loops. Deleted edges are linked together so that we can restore them later in step S7.) Set $k \leftarrow d_u + d_v$, $f \leftarrow n_{u-1}$, and $g \leftarrow 0$. While $t_f \neq 0$, do the following: If $t_f = v$, delete(f), delete($f \oplus 1$), and set $k \leftarrow k - 2$, $l_f \leftarrow g$, $g \leftarrow f$; otherwise set $t_{f \oplus 1} \leftarrow v$. Then set $f \leftarrow n_f$ and repeat these operations until $t_f = 0$. Finally set $l_e \leftarrow g$, $d_v \leftarrow k$, $g \leftarrow v - 1$, $n_{p_f} \leftarrow n_g$, $p_{n_g} \leftarrow p_f$, $p_{n_f} \leftarrow g$, $n_g \leftarrow n_f$, and $a_l \leftarrow e$.

S4. [Advance l.] Set $l \leftarrow l + 1$. If $l < n - 1$, set $s_l \leftarrow 0$ and return to S2. Otherwise set $e \leftarrow n_{v-1}$.

S5. [Visit.] (The current graph now has only two vertices, one of which is v.) Set $a_{n-1} \leftarrow e$ and visit the spanning tree $a_1 \ldots a_{n-1}$. (If $x = 0$, this is the first spanning tree to be visited; otherwise it differs from its predecessor by deleting x and inserting e.) Set $x \leftarrow e$ and $e \leftarrow n_e$. Repeat step S5 if $t_e \neq 0$.

S6. [Decrease l.] Set $l \leftarrow l - 1$. Terminate the algorithm if $l = 0$; otherwise set $e \leftarrow a_l$, $u \leftarrow t_e$, and $v \leftarrow t_{e \oplus 1}$.

S7. [Unshrink e.] Set $f \leftarrow u - 1$, $g \leftarrow v - 1$, $n_g \leftarrow n_{p_f}$, $p_{n_g} \leftarrow g$, $n_{p_f} \leftarrow f$, $p_{n_f} \leftarrow f$, and $f \leftarrow p_f$. While $t_f \neq 0$, set $t_{f \oplus 1} \leftarrow u$ and $f \leftarrow p_f$. Then set $f \leftarrow l_e$, $k \leftarrow d_v$; while $f \neq 0$ set $k \leftarrow k + 2$, undelete($f \oplus 1$), undelete(f), and set $f \leftarrow l_f$. Finally set $d_v \leftarrow k - d_u$.

S8. [Test for bridge.] If e is a bridge, go to S9. (See exercise 95 for one way to perform this test.) Otherwise set $x \leftarrow e$, $l_e \leftarrow s_l$, $s_l \leftarrow e$; delete(e) and delete($e \oplus 1$). Set $d_u \leftarrow d_u - 1$, $d_v \leftarrow d_v - 1$, and go to S2.

S9. [Undo level l deletions.] Set $e \leftarrow s_l$. While $e \neq 0$, set $u \leftarrow t_e$, $v \leftarrow t_{e \oplus 1}$, $d_u \leftarrow d_u + 1$, $d_v \leftarrow d_v + 1$, undelete($e \oplus 1$), undelete(e), and $e \leftarrow l_e$. Return to S6. ∎

The reader is encouraged to play through the steps of this algorithm on a small graph such as (48). Notice that a subtle case arises in steps S3 and S7, if u's adjacency list happens to become empty. Notice also that several shortcuts would be possible, at the expense of a more complicated algorithm; we will discuss such improvements later in this section.

*Series-parallel graphs. The task of finding all spanning trees becomes especially simple when the given graph has a serial and/or parallel decomposition. A *series-parallel graph between s and t* is a graph G with two designated vertices, s and t, whose edges can be built up recursively as follows: Either G consists of a single edge, s — t; or G is a *serial superedge* consisting of $k \geq 2$ series-parallel subgraphs G_j between s_j and t_j, joined in series with $s = s_1$ and $t_j = s_{j+1}$ for

$1 \leq j < k$ and $t_k = t$; or G is a *parallel superedge* consisting of $k \geq 2$ series-parallel subgraphs G_j between s and t joined in parallel. This decomposition is essentially unique, given s and t, if we require that the subgraphs G_j for serial superedges are not themselves serial superedges, and that the subgraphs G_j for parallel superedges are not themselves parallel.

Any series-parallel graph can be represented conveniently as a tree, with no nodes of degree 1. The leaf nodes of this tree represent edges, and the branch nodes represent superedges, alternating between serial and parallel from level to level. For example, the tree

$$\begin{array}{c}\\\\\\\end{array}\qquad\qquad (53)$$

corresponds to the series-parallel graphs and subgraphs

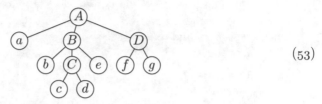

$$ (54) $$

if the top node A is taken to be parallel. Edges are named in (54), but not vertices, because edges are of prime importance with respect to spanning trees.

Let's say that a *near tree* of a series-parallel graph between s and t is a set of $n - 2$ cycle-free edges that do not connect s to t. The spanning trees and near trees of a series-parallel graph are easy to describe recursively, as follows: (1) A spanning tree of a serial superedge corresponds to spanning trees of all its principal subgraphs G_j; a near tree corresponds to spanning trees in all but one of the G_j, and a near tree in the other. (2) A near tree of a parallel superedge corresponds to near trees of all its principal subgraphs G_j; a spanning tree corresponds to near trees in all but one of the G_j, and a spanning tree in the other.

Rules (1) and (2) suggest the following data structures for listing the spanning trees and/or near trees of series-parallel graphs. Let p point to a node in a tree like (53). Then we define

> $t_p = 1$ for serial superedges, 0 otherwise (the "type" of p);
> $v_p = 1$ if we have a spanning tree for p, 0 if we have a near tree;
> $l_p = $ pointer to p's leftmost child, or 0 if p is a leaf;
> $r_p = $ pointer to p's right sibling, wrapping around cyclically;
> $d_p = $ pointer to a designated child of p, or 0 if p is a leaf.

If q points to the rightmost child of p, its "right sibling" r_q equals l_p. And if q points to *any* child of p, rules (1) and (2) state that

$$ v_q = \begin{cases} v_p, & \text{if } q = d_p; \\ t_p, & \text{if } q \neq d_p. \end{cases} \qquad (55) $$

(For example, if p is a branch node that represents a serial superedge, we must have $v_q = 1$ for all but one of p's children; the only exception is the designated child d_p. Thus we must have a spanning tree for all of the subgraphs that were joined serially to form p, except for one designated subgraph in the case that we have a near tree for p.)

Given any setting of the designated-child pointers d_p, and given any value 0 or 1 for v_p at the root of the tree, Eq. (55) tells us how to propagate values down to all of the leaves. For example, if we set $v_A \leftarrow 1$ in the tree (53), and if we designate the leftmost child of each branch node (so that $d_A = a$, $d_B = b$, $d_C = c$, and $d_D = f$), we find successively

$$v_a = 1,\ v_B = 0,\ v_b = 0,\ v_C = 1,\ v_c = 1,\ v_d = 0,\ v_e = 1,\ v_D = 0,\ v_f = 0,\ v_g = 1. \quad (56)$$

A leaf node q is present in the spanning tree if and only if $v_q = 1$; hence (56) specifies the spanning tree $aceg$ of the series-parallel graph A in (54).

For convenience, let's say that the *configs* of p are its spanning trees if $v_p = 1$, its near trees if $v_p = 0$. We would like to generate all configs of the root. A branch node p is called "easy" if $v_p = t_p$; that is, a serial node is easy if its configs are spanning trees, and a parallel node is easy if its configs are near trees. If p is easy, its configs are the Cartesian product of the configs of its children, namely all k-tuples of the children's configs, varying independently; the designated child d_p is immaterial in the easy case. But if p is uneasy, its configs are the union of such Cartesian k-tuples, taken over all possible choices of d_p.

As luck would have it, easy nodes are relatively rare: At most one child of an uneasy node (namely the designated child) can be easy, and all children of an easy node are uneasy unless they are leaves.

Even so, the tree representation of a series-parallel graph makes the recursive generation of all its spanning trees and/or near trees quite straightforward and efficient. The operations of Algorithm S — shrinking and unshrinking, deleting and undeleting, bridge detection — are not needed when we deal with series-parallel graphs. Furthermore, exercise 99 shows that there is a pleasant way to obtain the spanning trees or near trees in a revolving-door Gray code order, by using focus pointers as in several algorithms that we've seen earlier.

*Refinements of Algorithm S. Although Algorithm S provides us with a simple and reasonably effective way to visit all spanning trees of a general graph, its author Malcolm Smith realized that the properties of series-parallel graphs can be used to make it even better. For example, if a graph has two or more edges that run between the same vertices u and v, we can combine them into a superedge; the spanning trees of the original graph can then be obtained readily from those of the simpler, reduced graph. And if a graph has a vertex v of degree 2, so that the only edges touching v are $u - v$ and $v - w$, we can eliminate v and replace those edges by a single superedge between u and w. Furthermore, any vertex of degree 1 can effectively be eliminated, together with its adjacent edge, by simply including that edge in every spanning tree.

After the reductions in the preceding paragraph have been applied to a given graph G, we obtain a reduced graph $\hat{G}$ having no parallel edges and no vertices of degrees 1 or 2, together with a set of $m \geq 0$ series-parallel graphs $S_1, \ldots, S_m$, representing edges (or superedges) that must be included in all spanning trees of G. Every remaining edge $u \,\text{---}\, v$ of $\hat{G}$ corresponds, in fact, to a series-parallel graph S_{uv} between vertices u and v. *The spanning trees of G are then obtained as the union, taken over all spanning trees T of $\hat{G}$, of the Cartesian product of the spanning trees of $S_1, \ldots, S_m$ and the spanning trees of all S_{uv} for edges $u \,\text{---}\, v$ in T, together with the near trees of all S_{uv} for edges $u \,\text{---}\, v$ that are in $\hat{G}$ but not in T.* And all spanning trees T of $\hat{G}$ can be obtained by using the strategy of Algorithm S.

In fact, when Algorithm S is extended in this way, its operations of replacing the current graph G by $G \,/\, e$ or $G \,\backslash\, e$ typically trigger further reductions, as new parallel edges appear or as the degree of a vertex drops below 3. Therefore it turns out that the "stopping state" of the implicit recursion in Algorithm S, namely the case when only two vertices are left (step S5), never actually arises: A reduced graph $\hat{G}$ either has only a single vertex and no edges, or it has at least four vertices and six edges.

The resulting algorithm retains the desirable revolving-door property of Algorithm S, and it is quite pretty (although about four times as long as the original); see exercise 100. Smith proved that it has the best possible asymptotic running time: If G has n vertices, m edges, and N spanning trees, the algorithm visits them all in $O(m + n + N)$ steps.

The performance of Algorithm S and of its souped-up version Algorithm S' can best be appreciated by considering the number of memory accesses that those algorithms actually make when they generate the spanning trees of typical graphs, as shown in Table 5. The bottom line of that table corresponds to the graph *plane_miles*$(16, 0, 0, 1, 0, 0, 0)$ from the Stanford GraphBase, which serves as an "organic" antidote to the purely mathematical examples on the previous lines. The random multigraph on the penultimate line, also from the Stanford GraphBase, can be described more precisely by its official name *random_graph*$(16, 37, 1, 0, 0, 0, 0, 0, 0, 0)$. Although the 4×4 torus is isomorphic to the 4-cube (see exercise 7.2.1.1–17), those isomorphic graphs yield slightly different running times because their vertices and edges are encountered differently when the algorithms are run.

In general we can say that Algorithm S is not too bad on small examples, except when the graph is quite sparse; but Algorithm S' begins to shine when many spanning trees are present. Once Algorithm S' gets warmed up, it tends to crank out a new tree after every 18 or 19 mems go by.

Table 5 also indicates that a mathematically-defined graph often has a surprisingly "round" number of spanning trees. For example, D. M. Cvetković [*Srpska Akademija Nauka, Matematicheski Institut* **11** (Belgrade: 1971), 135–141] discovered, among other things, that the n-cube has exactly

$$2^{2^n - n - 1} \, 1^{\binom{n}{1}} \, 2^{\binom{n}{2}} \ldots n^{\binom{n}{n}} \tag{57}$$

of them. Exercises 104–109 explore some of the reasons why that happens.

Table 5

RUNNING TIME IN MEMS NEEDED TO GENERATE ALL SPANNING TREES

	m	n	N	Algorithm S	Algorithm S'	μ per tree	
path P_{10}	9	10	1	794 μ	473 μ	794.0	473.0
path P_{100}	99	100	1	9,974 μ	5,063 μ	9974.0	5063.0
cycle C_{10}	10	10	10	3,480 μ	998 μ	348.0	99.8
cycle C_{100}	100	100	100	355,605 μ	10,538 μ	3556.1	105.4
complete graph K_4	6	4	16	1,213 μ	1,336 μ	75.8	83.5
complete graph K_{10}	45	10	100,000,000	3,759.58 Mμ	1,860.95 Mμ	37.6	18.6
complete bigraph $K_{5,5}$	25	10	390,625	23.43 Mμ	8.88 Mμ	60.0	22.7
4×4 grid $P_4\square P_4$	24	16	100,352	12.01 Mμ	1.87 Mμ	119.7	18.7
5×5 grid $P_5\square P_5$	40	25	557,568,000	54.68 Gμ	10.20 Gμ	98.1	18.3
4×4 cylinder $P_4\square C_4$	28	16	2,558,976	230.96 Mμ	49.09 Mμ	90.3	19.2
5×5 cylinder $P_5\square C_5$	45	25	38,720,000,000	3,165.31 Gμ	711.69 Gμ	81.7	18.4
4×4 torus $C_4\square C_4$	32	16	42,467,328	3,168.15 Mμ	823.08 Mμ	74.6	19.4
4-cube $P_2\square P_2\square P_2\square P_2$	32	16	42,467,328	3,172.19 Mμ	823.38 Mμ	74.7	19.4
random multigraph	37	16	59,933,756	3,818.19 Mμ	995.91 Mμ	63.7	16.6
16 cities	37	16	179,678,881	11,772.11 Mμ	3,267.43 Mμ	65.5	18.2

A general quasi-Gray code. Let's close this section by discussing something completely different, yet still related to trees. Consider the following hybrid variants of the two standard ways to traverse a nonempty forest:

Prepostorder traversal	Postpreorder traversal
Visit the root of the first tree	Traverse the subtrees of the first
Traverse the subtrees of the first	tree, in prepostorder
tree, in postpreorder	Visit the root of the first tree
Traverse the remaining trees,	Traverse the remaining trees,
in prepostorder	in postpreorder

In the first case, every tree of the forest is traversed in prepostorder, with its root first; but the subtrees of those roots are traversed in postpreorder, with roots coming last. The second variant is similar but with 'pre' and 'post' interchanged. And in general, prepostorder visits roots first on every even-numbered level of the forest, but visits them last on the odd-numbered levels. For example, the forest in (2) becomes

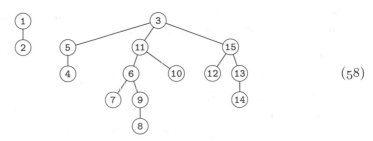 (58)

when we label its nodes in prepostorder.

Prepostorder and postpreorder are not merely curiosities; they're actually useful. The reason is that adjacent nodes, in either of these orders, are always near each other in the forest. For example, nodes k and $k+1$ are adjacent in (58) for $k = 1, 4, 6, 8, 10, 13$; they are separated by only one node when $k = 3, 12, 14$; and they're three steps apart when $k = 2, 5, 7, 9, 11$ (if we imagine an invisible super-parent at the top of the forest). A moment's thought proves inductively that at most two nodes can possibly intervene between prepostorder neighbors or postpreorder neighbors — because postpreorder(F) always begins with the root of the first tree or its leftmost child, and prepostorder(F) always ends with the root of the last tree or its rightmost child.

Suppose we want to generate all combinatorial patterns of some kind, and we want to visit them in a Gray-code-like manner so that consecutive patterns are always "close" to each other. We can form, at least conceptually, the graph of all possible patterns p, with edges $p \!\!-\!\! q$ for all pairs of patterns that are close to each other. The following theorem, due to Milan Sekanina [*Spisy Přírodovědecké Fakulty University v Brně*, No. 412 (1960), 137–140], proves that a pretty good Gray code is always possible, provided only that we can get from any pattern to any other in a sequence of short steps:

Theorem S. *The vertices of any connected graph can be listed in a cyclic order* $(v_0, v_1, \ldots, v_{n-1})$ *so that the distance between* v_k *and* $v_{(k+1) \bmod n}$ *is at most 3, for* $0 \le k < n$.

Proof. Find a spanning tree in the graph, and traverse it in prepostorder. ∎

Graph theorists traditionally say that the kth power of a graph G is the graph G^k whose vertices are those of G, with $u \!\!-\!\! v$ in G^k if and only if there's a path of length k or less from u to v in G. Thus they can state Theorem S much more succinctly, when $n > 2$: *The cube of a connected graph is Hamiltonian.*

Prepostorder traversal is also useful when we want to visit the nodes of a tree in loopless fashion, with a bounded number of steps between stops:

Algorithm Q (*Prepostorder successor in a triply linked forest*). If P points to a node in a forest represented by links PARENT, CHILD, and SIB, corresponding to each node's parent, leftmost child, and right sibling, this algorithm computes P's successor node, Q, in prepostorder. We assume that we know the level L at which P appears in the forest; the value of L is updated to be the level of Q. If P happens to be the final node in prepostorder, the algorithm sets Q ← Λ and L ← −1.

Q1. [Pre or post?] If L is even, go to step Q4.

Q2. [Continue postpreorder.] Set Q ← SIB(P). Go to Q6 if Q ≠ Λ.

Q3. [Move up.] Set P ← PARENT(P) and L ← L − 1. Go to Q7.

Q4. [Continue prepostorder.] If CHILD(P) = Λ, go to Q7.

Q5. [Move down.] Set Q ← CHILD(P) and L ← L + 1.

Q6. [Move down if possible.] If CHILD(Q) ≠ Λ, set Q ← CHILD(Q) and L ← L+1. Terminate the algorithm.

Q7. [Move right or up.] If $\mathtt{SIB(P)} \neq \Lambda$, set $\mathtt{Q} \leftarrow \mathtt{SIB(P)}$; otherwise set $\mathtt{Q} \leftarrow$ $\mathtt{PARENT(P)}$ and $\mathtt{L} \leftarrow \mathtt{L} - 1$. Terminate the algorithm. ▮

Notice that, as in Algorithm 2.4C, the link $\mathtt{PARENT(P)}$ is examined only if $\mathtt{SIB(P)} = \Lambda$. A complete traversal is really a worm walk around the forest, like (3): The worm "sees" the nodes on even-numbered levels when it passes them on the left, and it sees the odd-level nodes when it passes them on the right.

EXERCISES

1. [*15*] If a worm crawls around the binary tree (4), how could it easily reconstruct the parentheses of (1)?

2. [*20*] (S. Zaks, 1980.) Modify Algorithm P so that it produces the combinations $z_1 z_2 \ldots z_n$ of (8) instead of the parenthesis strings $a_1 a_2 \ldots a_{2n}$.

▶ **3.** [*23*] Prove that (11) converts $z_1 z_2 \ldots z_n$ to the inversion table $c_1 c_2 \ldots c_n$.

4. [*20*] True or false: If the strings $a_1 \ldots a_{2n}$ are generated in lexicographic order, so are the corresponding strings $d_1 \ldots d_n$, $z_1 \ldots z_n$, $p_1 \ldots p_n$, and $c_1 \ldots c_n$.

5. [*15*] What tables $d_1 \ldots d_n$, $z_1 \ldots z_n$, $p_1 \ldots p_n$, and $c_1 \ldots c_n$ correspond to the nested parenthesis string (1)?

▶ **6.** [*20*] What *matching* corresponds to (1)? (See the final column of Table 1.)

7. [*16*] (a) What is the state of the string $a_1 a_2 \ldots a_{2n}$ when Algorithm P terminates? (b) What do the arrays $l_1 l_2 \ldots l_n$ and $r_1 r_2 \ldots r_n$ contain when Algorithm B terminates?

8. [*15*] What tables $l_1 \ldots l_n$, $r_1 \ldots r_n$, $e_1 \ldots e_n$, and $s_1 \ldots s_n$ correspond to the example forest (2)?

9. [*M20*] Show that the tables $c_1 \ldots c_n$ and $s_1 \ldots s_n$ are related by the law

$$c_k = [s_1 \geq k - 1] + [s_2 \geq k - 2] + \cdots + [s_{k-1} \geq 1].$$

10. [*M20*] (*Worm walks.*) Given a string of nested parentheses $a_1 a_2 \ldots a_{2n}$, let w_j be the excess of left parentheses over right parentheses in $a_1 a_2 \ldots a_j$, for $0 \leq j \leq 2n$. Prove that $w_0 + w_1 + \cdots + w_{2n} = 2(c_1 + \cdots + c_n) + n$.

11. [*11*] If F is a forest, its *conjugate* F^R is obtained by left-to-right mirror reflection. For example, the fourteen forests in Table 1 are

$$\cdots , \; \cdots\mathtt{!} , \; \cdot\mathtt{!}\cdot , \; \cdot\wedge , \; \cdot\mathtt{!} , \mathtt{!}\cdots , \; \mathtt{!}\,\mathtt{!} , \wedge\cdot , \; \wedge , \wedge , \mathtt{!}\cdot , \wedge , \lambda , \mathtt{!}$$

and their conjugates are respectively

$$\cdots , \; \mathtt{!}\cdots , \; \cdot\mathtt{!}\cdot , \wedge\cdot , \; \mathtt{!}\cdot , \; \cdots\mathtt{!} , \mathtt{!}\,\mathtt{!} , \; \cdot\wedge , \wedge , \wedge , \; \cdot\mathtt{!} , \wedge , \lambda , \mathtt{!}$$

as in the colex forests of Table 2. If F corresponds to the nested parentheses $a_1 a_2 \ldots a_{2n}$, what string of parentheses corresponds to F^R?

12. [*15*] If F is a forest, its *transpose* F^T is the forest whose binary tree is obtained by interchanging left and right links in the binary tree representing F. For example, the transposes of the fourteen forests in Table 1 are respectively

$$\mathtt{!} , \lambda , \wedge , \wedge , \wedge , \mathtt{!}\cdot , \wedge\cdot , \mathtt{!}\,\mathtt{!} , \; \cdot\mathtt{!} , \; \cdot\wedge , \mathtt{!}\cdots , \; \cdot\mathtt{!}\cdot , \; \cdots\mathtt{!} , \cdots .$$

What is the transpose of the forest (2)?

13. [*20*] Continuing exercises 11 and 12, how do the preorder and postorder of a labeled forest F relate to the preorder and postorder of (a) F^R? (b) F^T?

▶ **14.** [*21*] Find all labeled forests F such that $F^{RT} = F^{TR}$.

15. [*20*] Suppose B is the binary tree obtained from a forest F by linking each node to its left sibling and its rightmost child, as in exercise 2.3.2–5 and the last column of Table 2. Let F' be the forest that corresponds to B in the normal way, via left-child and right-sibling links. Prove that $F' = F^{RT}$, in the notation of exercises 11 and 12.

16. [*20*] If F and G are forests, let FG be the forest obtained by placing the trees of F to the left of the trees of G; also let $F \mid G = (G^T F^T)^T$. Give an intuitive explanation of the operator $\mid$, and prove that it is associative.

17. [*M46*] Characterize all *unlabeled* forests F such that $F^{RT} = F^{TR}$. (See exercise 14.)

18. [*30*] Two forests are said to be *cognate* if one can be obtained from the other by repeated operations of taking the conjugate and/or the transpose. The examples in exercises 11 and 12 show that all forests on 4 nodes belong to one of three cognate classes:

$$\cdots \asymp \, {\textstyle\substack{\bullet\\\bullet}} \, ; \qquad \lambda \asymp \, {}^{\bullet\bullet}{\textstyle\substack{\bullet}} \asymp {\textstyle\substack{\bullet}}{}^{\bullet\bullet} \asymp {\textstyle\substack{\bullet\\\bullet}}{}^{\bullet} \asymp {}^{\bullet}{\textstyle\substack{\bullet\\\bullet}} \asymp \wedge \, ;$$

$$ {\textstyle\substack{\bullet\\\bullet}} {\textstyle\substack{\bullet\\\bullet}} \asymp \wedge {}^{\bullet} \asymp {}^{\bullet}\wedge \asymp {\textstyle\substack{\wedge\\\bullet}} \asymp {\textstyle\substack{\bullet\\\wedge}} \asymp {}^{\bullet}{\textstyle\substack{\bullet\\\bullet}}{}^{\bullet}.$$

Study the set of all forests with 15 nodes. How many equivalence classes of cognate forests do they form? What is the largest class? What is the smallest class? What is the size of the class containing (2)?

19. [*28*] Let F_1, F_2, $\ldots$, F_N be the sequence of unlabeled forests that correspond to the nested parentheses generated by Algorithm P, and let G_1, G_2, $\ldots$, G_N be the sequence of unlabeled forests that correspond to the binary trees generated by Algorithm B. Prove that $G_k = F_k^{RTR}$, in the notation of exercises 11 and 12. (The forest F^{RTR} is called the *dual* of F; it is denoted by F^D in several exercises below.)

20. [*25*] Recall from Section 2.3 that the *degree* of a node in a tree is the number of children it has, and that an extended binary tree is characterized by the property that every node has degree either 0 or 2. In the extended binary tree (4), the sequence of node degrees is 22002220022202200020022022002000000 in preorder; this string of 0s and 2s is identical to the sequence of parentheses in (1), except that each '(' has been replaced by 2, each ')' has been replaced by 0, and an additional 0 has been appended.

  a) Prove that a sequence of nonnegative integers $b_1 b_2 \ldots b_N$ is the preorder degree sequence of a forest if and only if it satisfies the following property for $0 \le k \le N$:

$$b_1 + b_2 + \cdots + b_k + f > k \qquad \text{if and only if} \qquad k < N.$$

Here $f = N - b_1 - b_2 - \cdots - b_N$ is the number of trees in the forest.

  b) Recall from exercise 2.3.4.5–6 that an *extended ternary tree* is characterized by the property that every node has degree 0 or 3; an extended ternary tree with n internal nodes has $2n + 1$ external nodes, hence $N = 3n + 1$ nodes altogether. Design an algorithm to generate all ternary trees with n internal nodes, by generating the associated sequences $b_1 b_2 \ldots b_N$ in lexicographic order.

▶ **21.** [*26*] (S. Zaks and D. Richards, 1979.) Continuing exercise 20, explain how to generate the preorder degree sequences of all forests that have $N = n_0 + \cdots + n_t$ nodes, with exactly n_j nodes of degree j. *Example:* When $n_0 = 4$, $n_1 = n_2 = n_3 = 1$, and $t = 3$, the valid sequences $b_1 b_2 b_3 b_4 b_5 b_6 b_7$ are

1203000, 1230000, 1300200, 1302000, 1320000, 2013000, 2030010, 2030100, 2031000, 2103000, 2130000, 2300010, 2300100, 2301000, 2310000, 3001200, 3002010, 3002100, 3010200, 3012000, 3020010, 3020100, 3021000, 3100200, 3102000, 3120000, 3200010, 3200100, 3201000, 3210000.

▶ **22.** [*30*] (J. Korsh, 2004.) As an alternative to Algorithm B, show that binary trees can also be generated directly and efficiently in linked form if we produce them in *colex* order of the numbers $d_1 \ldots d_{n-1}$ defined in (9). (The actual values of $d_1 \ldots d_{n-1}$ should not be computed explicitly; but the links $l_1 \ldots l_n$ and $r_1 \ldots r_n$ should be manipulated in such a way that we get the binary trees corresponding successively to $d_1 d_2 \ldots d_{n-1} = 000 \ldots 0,\ 100 \ldots 0,\ 010 \ldots 0,\ 110 \ldots 0,\ 020 \ldots 0,\ 001 \ldots 0,\ \ldots,\ 000 \ldots (n{-}1).$)

▶ **23.** [*25*] (a) What is the last string visited by Algorithm N? (b) What is the last binary tree or forest visited by Algorithm L? *Hint:* See exercise 40 below.

24. [*22*] Using the notation of Table 3, what sequences $l_0 l_1 \ldots l_{15}$, $r_1 \ldots r_{15}$, $k_1 \ldots k_{15}$, $q_1 \ldots q_{15}$, and $u_1 \ldots u_{15}$ correspond to the binary tree (4) and the forest (2)?

▶ **25.** [*30*] (*Pruning and grafting.*) Representing binary trees as in Algorithm B, design an algorithm that visits all link tables $l_1 \ldots l_n$ and $r_1 \ldots r_n$ in such a way that, between visits, exactly one link changes from j to 0 and another from 0 to j, for some index j. (In other words, every step removes some subtree j from the binary tree and places it elsewhere, preserving preorder.)

26. [*M31*] (*The Kreweras lattice.*) Let F and F' be n-node forests with their nodes numbered 1 to n in preorder. We write $F \prec F'$ ("F coalesces F'") if j and k are siblings in F whenever they are siblings in F', for $1 \le j < k \le n$. Figure 60 illustrates this partial ordering in the case $n = 4$; each forest is encoded by the sequence $c_1 \ldots c_n$ of (10) and (11), which specifies the depth of each node. (With this encoding, j and k are siblings if and only if $c_j = c_k \le c_{j+1}, \ldots, c_{k-1}$.)

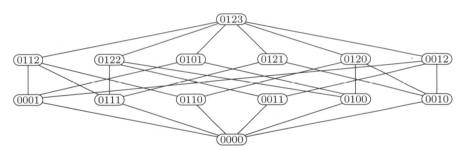

Fig. 60. The Kreweras lattice of order 4. Each forest is represented by its sequence of node depths $c_1 c_2 c_3 c_4$ in preorder. (See exercises 26–28.)

a) Let Π be a partition of $\{1, \ldots, n\}$. Show that there exists a forest F, with nodes labeled $(1, \ldots, n)$ in preorder and with

$$j \equiv k \ (\text{modulo } \Pi) \iff j \text{ is a sibling of } k \text{ in } F,$$

if and only if Π satisfies the *noncrossing* property

$$i < j < k < l \text{ and } i \equiv k \text{ and } j \equiv l \ (\text{modulo } \Pi) \quad \text{implies} \quad i \equiv j \equiv k \equiv l \ (\text{modulo } \Pi).$$

b) Given any two n-node forests F and F', explain how to compute their least upper bound $F \vee F'$, the element such that $F \prec G$ and $F' \prec G$ if and only if $F \vee F' \prec G$.

c) When does F' cover F with respect to the relation $\prec$? (See exercise 7.2.1.4–55.)

d) Show that if F' covers F, it has exactly one less leaf than F.

e) How many forests cover F, when node k has e_k children for $1 \le k \le n$?

f) Using the definition of duality in exercise 19, what is the dual of the forest (2)?

g) Prove that $F \ltimes F'$ holds if and only if $F'^D \ltimes F^D$. (Because of this property, dual elements have been placed symmetrically about the center of Fig. 60.)

h) Given any two n-node forests F and F', explain how to compute their greatest lower bound $F \curlywedge F'$; that is, $G \ltimes F$ and $G \ltimes F'$ if and only if $G \ltimes F \curlywedge F'$.

i) Does this lattice satisfy a semimodular law analogous to exercise 7.2.1.5–12(f)?

▶ **27.** [*M33*] (*The Tamari lattice.*) Continuing exercise 26, let us write $F \dashv F'$ if the jth node in preorder has at least as many descendants in F' as it does in F, for all j. In other words, if F and F' are characterized by their scope sequences $s_1 \ldots s_n$ and $s'_1 \ldots s'_n$ as in Table 2, we have $F \dashv F'$ if and only if $s_j \le s'_j$ for $1 \le j \le n$. (See Fig. 61.)

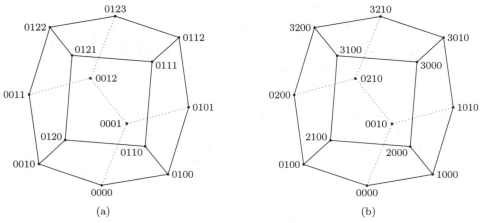

Fig. 61. The Tamari lattice of order 4. Each forest is represented by its sequences of (a) node depths $c_1c_2c_3c_4$ and (b) descendant counts $s_1s_2s_3s_4$, in preorder. (See exercises 26–28.)

a) Show that the scope coordinates $\min(s_1, s'_1)\min(s_2, s'_2)\ldots\min(s_n, s'_n)$ define a forest that is the greatest lower bound of F and F'. (We denote it by $F \perp F'$.) *Hint:* Prove that $s_1 \ldots s_n$ corresponds to a forest if and only if $0 \le k \le s_j$ implies $s_{j+k} + k \le s_j$, for $0 \le j \le n$, if we define $s_0 = n$.

b) When does F' cover F in this partial ordering?

c) Prove that $F \dashv F'$ if and only if $F'^D \dashv F^D$. (Compare with exercise 26(g).)

d) Explain how to compute a least upper bound, $F \top F'$, given F and F'.

e) Prove that $F \ltimes F'$ in the Kreweras lattice implies $F \dashv F'$ in the Tamari lattice.

f) True or false: $F \curlywedge F' \dashv F \perp F'$.

g) True or false: $F \curlyvee F' \ltimes F \top F'$.

h) What are the longest and shortest paths from the top of the Tamari lattice to the bottom, when each forest of the path covers its successor? (Such paths are called *maximal chains* in the lattice; compare with exercise 7.2.1.4–55(h).)

28. [*M26*] (*The Stanley lattice.*) Continuing exercises 26 and 27, let us define yet another partial ordering on n-node forests, saying that $F \subseteq F'$ whenever the depth coordinates $c_1 \ldots c_n$ and $c'_1 \ldots c'_n$ satisfy $c_j \le c'_j$ for $1 \le j \le n$. (See Fig. 62.)

a) Prove that this partial ordering is a lattice, by explaining how to compute the greatest lower bound $F \cap F'$ and least upper bound $F \cup F'$ of any two given forests.

b) Show that Stanley's lattice satisfies the distributive laws

$$F \cap (G \cup H) = (F \cap G) \cup (F \cap H), \qquad F \cup (G \cap H) = (F \cup G) \cap (F \cup H).$$

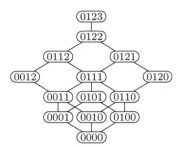

Fig. 62. The Stanley lattice of order 4. Each forest is represented by its sequence of node depths $c_1c_2c_3c_4$ in preorder. (See exercises 26–28.)

c) When does F' cover F in this lattice?

d) True or false: $F \subseteq G$ if and only if $F^R \subseteq G^R$.

e) Prove that $F \subseteq F'$ in the Stanley lattice whenever $F \dashv F'$ in the Tamari lattice.

29. [*HM31*] The covering graph of a Tamari lattice is sometimes known as an "associahedron," because of its connection with the associative law (14), proved in exercise 27(b). The associahedron of order 4, depicted in Fig. 61, looks like it has three square faces and six faces that are regular pentagons. (Compare with Fig. 43 in exercise 7.2.1.2–60, which shows the "permutahedron" of order 4, a well-known Archimedean solid.) Why doesn't Fig. 61 show up in classical lists of uniform polyhedra?

30. [*M33*] The *canopy* of a forest is the bit string $f_1 \ldots f_{n-1}$ defined by

$$f_j = [\text{node } j \text{ in preorder is not a leaf}].$$

a) If F has canopy $f_1 \ldots f_{n-1}$, what is the canopy of F^D? (See exercises 26 and 27.)

b) How many forests have the canopy 1010110111111000010101000101100?

c) Prove that $f_j = [d_j = 0]$, for $1 \le j < n$, in the notation of (6).

d) Two elements of a lattice are called *complementary* if their greatest lower bound is the bottom element while their least upper bound is the top element. Show that F and F' are complementary in the Tamari lattice if and only if their canopies are complementary, in the sense that $f'_1 \ldots f'_{n-1} = \bar{f}_1 \ldots \bar{f}_{n-1}$.

▶ **31.** [*M28*] A binary tree with n internal nodes is called *degenerate* if it has height n.

a) How many n-node binary trees are degenerate?

b) We've seen in Tables 1, 2, and 3 that binary trees and forests can be encoded by various n-tuples of numbers. For each of the encodings $c_1 \ldots c_n$, $d_1 \ldots d_n$, $e_1 \ldots e_n$, $k_1 \ldots k_n$, $p_1 \ldots p_n$, $s_1 \ldots s_n$, $u_1 \ldots u_n$, and $z_1 \ldots z_n$, explain how to see at a glance if the corresponding binary tree is degenerate.

c) True or false: If F is degenerate, so is F^D.

d) Prove that if F and F' are degenerate, so are $F \barwedge F' = F \perp F'$ and $F \vee F' = F \top F'$.

▶ **32.** [*M30*] Prove that if $F \dashv F'$, there is a forest F'' such that for all G we have

$$F' \perp G = F \quad \text{if and only if} \quad F \dashv G \dashv F''.$$

Consequently the *semidistributive laws* hold in the Tamari lattice:

$$F \perp G = F \perp H \quad \text{implies} \quad F \perp (G \top H) = F \perp G;$$
$$F \top G = F \top H \quad \text{implies} \quad F \top (G \perp H) = F \top G.$$

▶ **33.** [*M27*] (*Permutation representation of trees.*) Let σ be the cycle (1 2 ... n).

a) Given any binary tree whose nodes are numbered 1 to n in symmetric order, prove that there is a unique permutation λ of $\{1,\ldots,n\}$ such that, for $1 \le k \le n$,

$$\texttt{LLINK}[k] = \begin{cases} k\lambda, & \text{if } k\lambda < k; \\ 0, & \text{otherwise}; \end{cases} \qquad \texttt{RLINK}[k] = \begin{cases} k\sigma\lambda, & \text{if } k\sigma\lambda > k; \\ 0, & \text{otherwise}. \end{cases}$$

Thus λ neatly packs $2n$ link fields into a single n-element array.

b) Show that this permutation λ is particularly easy to describe in cycle form when the binary tree is the left-sibling/right-child representation of a forest F. What is the cycle form of $\lambda(F)$ when F is the forest in (2)?

c) Find a simple relation between $\lambda(F)$ and the dual permutation $\lambda(F^D)$.

d) Prove that, in exercise 26, F' covers F if and only if $\lambda(F') = (j\,k)\,\lambda(F)$, where j and k are siblings in F.

e) Consequently the number of maximal chains in the Kreweras lattice of order n is the number of ways to factor an n-cycle as a product of $n-1$ transpositions. Evaluate this number. *Hint:* See Eq. 1.2.6–(16).

34. [*M25*] (R. P. Stanley.) Show that the number of maximal chains in the Stanley lattice of order n is $(n(n-1)/2)!/(1^{n-1}3^{n-2}\ldots(2n-5)^2(2n-3)^1)$.

35. [*HM37*] (D. B. Tyler and D. R. Hickerson.) Explain why the denominators of the asymptotic formula (16) are all powers of 2.

▶ **36.** [*M25*] Analyze the ternary tree generation algorithm of exercise 20(b). *Hint:* There are $(2n+1)^{-1}\binom{3n}{n}$ ternary trees with n internal nodes, by exercise 2.3.4.4–11.

▶ **37.** [*M40*] Analyze the Zaks–Richards algorithm for generating all trees with a given distribution $n_0, n_1, n_2, \ldots, n_t$ of degrees (exercise 21). *Hint:* See exercise 2.3.4.4–32.

38. [*M22*] What is the total number of memory references performed by Algorithm L, as a function of n?

39. [*22*] Prove formula (23) by showing that the elements of A_{pq} in (5) correspond to Young tableaux with two rows.

40. [*M22*] (a) Prove that C_{pq} is odd if and only if $p\ \&\ (q+1) = 0$, in the sense that the binary representations of p and $q+1$ have no bits in common. (b) Therefore C_n is odd if and only if $n+1$ is a power of 2.

41. [*M21*] Show that the ballot numbers have a simple generating function $\sum C_{pq}w^p z^q$.

▶ **42.** [*M22*] How many unlabeled forests with n nodes are (a) self-conjugate? (b) self-transpose? (c) self-dual? (See exercises 11, 12, 19, and 26.)

43. [*M21*] Express C_{pq} in terms of the Catalan numbers $\langle C_0, C_1, C_2, \ldots \rangle$, aiming for a formula that is simple when $q - p$ is small. (For example, $C_{(q-2)q} = C_q - C_{q-1}$.)

▶ **44.** [*M27*] Prove that Algorithm B makes only $8\frac{2}{3}+O(n^{-1})$ references to memory per binary tree visited.

45. [*M26*] Analyze the memory references made by the algorithm in exercise 22. How does it compare to Algorithm B?

46. [*M30*] (*Generalized Catalan numbers.*) Generalize (21) by defining

$$C_{pq}(x) = C_{p(q-1)}(x) + x^{q-p}C_{(p-1)q}(x), \quad \text{if } 0 \le p \le q \ne 0; \qquad C_{00}(x) = 1;$$

and $C_{pq}(x) = 0$ if $p < 0$ or $p > q$; thus $C_{pq} = C_{pq}(1)$. Also let $C_n(x) = C_{nn}(x)$, so that

$$\langle C_0(x), C_1(x), \ldots \rangle = \langle 1, 1, 1+x, 1+2x+x^2+x^3, 1+3x+3x^2+3x^3+2x^4+x^5+x^6, \ldots \rangle.$$

a) Show that $[x^k] C_{pq}(x)$ is the number of paths from ⓟⓠ to ⓪⓪ in (28) that have area k, where the "area" of a path is the number of rectangular cells above it. (Thus an L-shaped path has the maximum possible area, $p(q-p) + \binom{p}{2}$.)

b) Prove that $C_n(x) = \sum_F x^{c_1 + \cdots + c_n} = \sum_F x^{\text{internal path length}(F)}$, summed over all n-node forests F.

c) If $C(x, z) = \sum_{n=0}^{\infty} C_n(x) z^n$, show that $C(x, z) = 1 + zC(x, z)C(x, xz)$.

d) Furthermore, $C(x, z)C(x, xz) \ldots C(x, x^r z) = \sum_{p=0}^{\infty} C_{p(p+r)}(x) z^p$.

47. [*M27*] Continuing the previous exercise, generalize the identity (27).

48. [*M28*] (F. Ruskey and A. Proskurowski.) Evaluate $C_{pq}(x)$ when $x = -1$, and use this result to show that no "perfect" Gray code for nested parentheses is possible when $n \geq 5$ is odd.

49. [*17*] What is the lexicographically millionth string of 15 nested parenthesis pairs?

50. [*20*] Design the inverse of Algorithm U: Given a string $a_1 \ldots a_{2n}$ of nested parentheses, determine its rank $N - 1$ in lexicographic order. What is the rank of (1)?

51. [*M22*] Let $\bar{z}_1 \bar{z}_2 \ldots \bar{z}_n$ be the complement of $z_1 z_2 \ldots z_n$ with respect to $2n$; in other words, $\bar{z}_j = 2n - z_j$, where z_j is defined in (8). Show that if $\bar{z}_1 \bar{z}_2 \ldots \bar{z}_n$ is the $(N+1)$st n-combination of $\{0, 1, \ldots, 2n - 1\}$ generated by Algorithm 7.2.1.3L, then $z_1 z_2 \ldots z_n$ is the $(N - \kappa_n N + 1)$st n-combination of $\{1, 2, \ldots, 2n\}$ generated by the algorithm of exercise 2. (Here κ_n denotes the nth Kruskal function, defined in 7.2.1.3–(60).)

52. [*M23*] Find the mean and variance of the quantity d_n in Table 1, when nested parentheses $a_1 \ldots a_{2n}$ are chosen at random.

53. [*M28*] Let X be the distance from the root of an extended binary tree to the leftmost external node. (a) What is the expected value of X, when all binary trees with n nodes are equally likely? (b) What is the expected value of X in a random *binary search tree*, constructed by Algorithm 6.2.2T from a random permutation $K_1 \ldots K_n$? (c) What is the expected value of X in a random *degenerate* binary tree, in the sense of exercise 31? (d) What is the expected value of 2^X in all three cases?

54. [*HM29*] What are the mean and variance of $c_1 + \cdots + c_n$? (See exercise 46.)

55. [*HM33*] Evaluate $C'_{pq}(1)$, the total area of all the paths in exercise 46(a).

56. [*M23*] (Renzo Sprugnoli, 1990.) Prove the summation formula

$$\sum_{k=0}^{m-1} C_k C_{n-1-k} = \frac{1}{2} C_n + \frac{2m - n}{2n(n+1)} \binom{2m}{m} \binom{2n - 2m}{n - m}, \qquad \text{for } 0 \leq m \leq n.$$

57. [*M28*] Express the sums $S_p(a, b) = \sum_{k \geq 0} \binom{2a}{a-k} \binom{2b}{b-k} k^p$ in closed form for $p = 0$, 1, 2, 3, and use these formulas to prove (30).

58. [*HM34*] Let t_{lmn} be the number of n-node binary trees in which external node m appears at level l when the external nodes are numbered from 0 to n in symmetric order. Also let $t_{mn} = \sum_{l=1}^{n} l t_{lmn}$, so that t_{mn}/C_n is the average level of external node m; and let $t(w, z)$ be the super generating function

$$\sum_{m,n} t_{mn} w^m z^n = (1+w)z + (3+4w+3w^2)z^2 + (9+13w+13w^2+9w^3)z^3 + \cdots.$$

Prove that $t(w, z) = (C(z) - wC(wz))/(1 - w) - 1 + zC(z)t(w, z) + wzC(wz)t(w, z)$, and deduce a simple formula for the numbers t_{mn}.

59. [*HM29*] Similarly, let T_{lmn} count all n-node binary trees in which *internal* node m appears at level l. Find a simple formula for $T_{mn} = \sum_{l=1}^{n} l T_{lmn}$.

▶ **60.** [*M26*] (*Balanced strings.*) A string α of nested parentheses is *atomic* if it has the form (α') where α' is nested; every nested string can be represented uniquely as a product of atoms $\alpha_1 \dots \alpha_r$. A string with equal numbers of left and right parentheses is called *balanced*; every balanced string can be represented uniquely as $\beta_1 \dots \beta_r$ where each β_j is either an atom or a *co-atom* (the reverse of an atom). The *defect* of a balanced string is half the length of its co-atoms. For example, the balanced string

$$(( )) ((( ))))) ( ) (( )) ((( )) (( )$$

has the factored form $\beta_1\beta_2\beta_3\beta_4\beta_5\beta_6\beta_7\beta_8 = \alpha_1\alpha_2^R\alpha_3\alpha_4^R\alpha_5^R\alpha_6\alpha_7^R\alpha_8$, with four atoms and four co-atoms; its defect is $|\alpha_2\alpha_4\alpha_5\alpha_7|/2 = 9$.

a) Prove that the defect of a balanced string is the number of indices k for which the kth right parenthesis *precedes* the kth left parenthesis.

b) If $\beta_1 \dots \beta_r$ is balanced, we can map it into a nested string by simply reversing its co-atoms. But the following mapping is more interesting, because it produces unbiased (uniformly random) nested strings from unbiased balanced strings: Let there be s co-atoms $\beta_{i_1} = \alpha_{i_1}^R, \dots, \beta_{i_s} = \alpha_{i_s}^R$. Replace each co-atom by (; then append the string $)\alpha'_{i_s} \dots)\alpha'_{i_1}$, where $\alpha_j = (\alpha'_j)$. For example, the string above is mapped into $\alpha_1(\alpha_3((\alpha_6(\alpha_8)\alpha_7)\alpha_5')\alpha_4')\alpha_2'$, which just happens to equal the string (1) illustrated at the beginning of this section. Design an algorithm that applies this mapping to a given balanced string $b_1 \dots b_{2n}$.

c) Also design an algorithm for the inverse mapping: Given a nested string $\alpha = a_1 \dots a_{2n}$ and an integer l with $0 \le l \le n$, compute a balanced string $\beta = b_1 \dots b_{2n}$ of defect l for which $\beta \mapsto \alpha$. What balanced string of defect 11 maps into (1)?

▶ **61.** [*M26*] (*Raney's Cycle Lemma.*) Let $b_1 b_2 \dots b_N$ be a string of nonnegative integers such that $f = N - b_1 - b_2 - \cdots - b_N > 0$.

a) Prove that exactly f of the cyclic shifts $b_{j+1} \dots b_N b_1 \dots b_j$ for $1 \le j \le N$ satisfy the preorder degree sequence property in exercise 20.

b) Design an efficient algorithm to determine all such j, given $b_1 b_2 \dots b_N$.

c) Explain how to generate a random forest that has $N = n_0 + \cdots + n_t$ nodes, with exactly n_j nodes of degree j. (For example, we obtain random n-node t-ary trees as a special case of this general procedure when $N = tn + 1$, $n_0 = (t-1)n + 1$, $n_1 = \cdots = n_{t-1} = 0$, and $n_t = n$.)

62. [*22*] A binary tree can also be represented by bit strings $(l_1 \dots l_n, r_1 \dots r_n)$, where l_j and r_j tell whether the left and right subtrees of node j in preorder are nonempty. (See Theorem 2.3.1A.) Prove that if $l_1 \dots l_n$ and $r_1 \dots r_n$ are arbitrary bit strings with $l_1 + \cdots + l_n + r_1 + \cdots + r_n = n - 1$, exactly one cyclic shift $(l_{j+1} \dots l_n l_1 \dots l_j, r_{j+1} \dots r_n r_1 \dots r_j)$ yields a valid binary tree representation, and explain how to find it.

63. [*16*] If the first two iterations of Rémy's algorithm have produced , what decorated binary trees are possible after the next iteration?

64. [*20*] What sequence of X values in Algorithm R corresponds to the decorated trees of (34), and what are the final values of $L_0 L_1 \dots L_{12}$?

65. [*38*] Generalize Rémy's algorithm (Algorithm R) to t-ary trees.

66. [*21*] A *Schröder tree* is a binary tree in which every nonnull right link is colored either white or black. The number S_n of n-node Schröder trees is

$n =$	0	1	2	3	4	5	6	7	8	9	10	11	12
$S_n =$	1	1	3	11	45	197	903	4279	20793	103049	518859	2646723	13648869

for small n. For example, $S_3 = 11$ because the possibilities are

(White links are "hollow"; external nodes have also been attached.)

a) Find a simple correspondence between Schröder trees with n internal nodes and ordinary trees with $n + 1$ leaves and no nodes of degree one.

b) Devise a Gray code for Schröder trees.

67. [*M22*] What is the generating function $S(z) = \sum_n S_n z^n$ for Schröder numbers?

68. [*10*] What is the Christmas tree pattern of order 0?

69. [*20*] Are the Christmas tree patterns of orders 6 and 7 visible in Table 4, possibly in slight disguise?

▶ **70.** [*20*] Find a simple rule that defines, for every bit string σ, another bit string σ' called its *mate*, with the following properties: (i) $\sigma'' = \sigma$; (ii) $|\sigma'| = |\sigma|$; (iii) either $\sigma \subseteq \sigma'$ or $\sigma' \subseteq \sigma$; (iv) $\nu(\sigma) + \nu(\sigma') = |\sigma|$.

71. [*M21*] Let $M_{t,n}$ be the size of the largest possible set S of n-bit strings with the property that, if σ and τ are members of S with $\sigma \subseteq \tau$, then $\nu(\tau) < \nu(\sigma) + t$. (Thus, for example, $M_{1,n} = M_n$ by Sperner's theorem.) Find a formula for $M_{t,n}$.

▶ **72.** [*M28*] If you start with a single row $\sigma_1 \sigma_2 \ldots \sigma_s$ of length s and apply the growth rule (36) repeatedly n times, how many rows do you obtain?

73. [*15*] In the Christmas tree pattern of order 30, what are the first and last elements of the row that contains the bit string 011001001000011111101101011100?

74. [*M26*] Continuing the previous exercise, how many rows precede that row?

▶ **75.** [*HM23*] Let $(r_1^{(n)}, r_2^{(n)}, \ldots, r_{n-1}^{(n)})$ be the row numbers in which the Christmas tree pattern of order n has $n - 1$ entries; for example, Table 4 tells us that $(r_1^{(8)}, \ldots, r_7^{(8)}) = (20, 40, 54, 62, 66, 68, 69)$. Find formulas for $r_{j+1}^{(n)} - r_j^{(n)}$ and for $\lim_{n \to \infty} r_j^{(n)} / M_n$.

76. [*HM46*] Study the limiting shape of the Christmas tree patterns as $n \to \infty$. Does it, for example, have a fractal dimension under some appropriate scaling?

77. [*21*] Design an algorithm to generate the sequence of rightmost elements $a_1 \ldots a_n$ in the rows of the Christmas tree pattern, given n. *Hint:* These bit strings are characterized by the property that $a_1 + \cdots + a_k \geq k/2$ for $0 \leq k \leq n$.

78. [*20*] True or false: If $\sigma_1 \ldots \sigma_s$ is a row of the Christmas tree pattern, so is $\bar{\sigma}_s^R \ldots \bar{\sigma}_1^R$ (the reverse sequence of reverse complements).

79. [*M26*] The number of permutations $p_1 \ldots p_n$ that have exactly one "descent" where $p_k > p_{k+1}$ is the Eulerian number $\left\langle {n \atop 1} \right\rangle = 2^n - n - 1$, according to Eq. 5.1.3–(12). The number of entries in the Christmas tree pattern, above the bottom row, is the same.

a) Find a combinatorial explanation of this coincidence, by giving a one-to-one correspondence between one-descent permutations and unsorted bit strings.

b) Show that two unsorted bit strings belong to the same row of the Christmas tree pattern if and only if they correspond to permutations that define the same P tableau under the Robinson–Schensted correspondence (Theorem 5.1.4A).

80. [*30*] Say that two bit strings are *concordant* if we can obtain one from the other via the transformations 010 ↔ 100 or 101 ↔ 110 on substrings. For example, the strings

$$011100 \leftrightarrow 011010 \leftrightarrow 010110 \leftrightarrow 010101 \leftrightarrow 011001$$
$$\updownarrow \qquad\qquad \updownarrow$$
$$100110 \leftrightarrow 100101 \leftrightarrow 101001 \leftrightarrow 110001$$

are mutually concordant, but no other string is concordant with any of them.

Prove that strings are concordant if and only if they belong to the same column of the Christmas tree pattern and to rows of the same length in that pattern.

81. [*M30*] A *biclutter* of order (n, n') is a family S of bit string pairs (σ, σ'), where $|\sigma| = n$ and $|\sigma'| = n'$, with the property that distinct members (σ, σ') and (τ, τ') of S are allowed to satisfy $\sigma \subseteq \tau$ and $\sigma' \subseteq \tau'$ only if $\sigma \neq \tau$ and $\sigma' \neq \tau'$.

Use Christmas tree patterns to prove that S contains at most $M_{n+n'}$ string pairs.

▶ **82.** [*M26*] Let $E(f)$ be the number of times Algorithm H evaluates the function f.
  a) Show that $M_n \leq E(f) \leq M_{n+1}$, with equality when f is constant.
  b) Among all f such that $E(f) = M_n$, which one minimizes $\sum_\sigma f(\sigma)$?
  c) Among all f such that $E(f) = M_{n+1}$, which one maximizes $\sum_\sigma f(\sigma)$?

83. [*M20*] (G. Hansel.) Show that there are at most 3^{M_n} monotone Boolean functions $f(x_1, \ldots, x_n)$ of n Boolean variables.

▶ **84.** [*HM27*] (D. Kleitman.) Let A be an $m \times n$ matrix of real numbers in which every column v has length $\|v\| \geq 1$, and let b be an m-dimensional column vector. Prove that at most M_n column vectors $x = (a_1, \ldots, a_n)^T$, with components $a_j = 0$ or 1, satisfy $\|Ax - b\| < \frac{1}{2}$. *Hint:* Use a construction analogous to the Christmas tree pattern.

85. [*HM30*] (Philippe Golle.) Let V be any vector space contained in the set of all real n-dimensional vectors, but containing none of the unit vectors $(1, 0, \ldots, 0)$, $(0, 1, 0, \ldots, 0)$, ..., $(0, \ldots, 0, 1)$. Prove that V contains at most M_n vectors whose components are all 0 or 1; furthermore the upper bound M_n is achievable.

86. [*15*] If (2) is regarded as an *oriented forest* instead of an ordered forest, what canonical forest corresponds to it? Specify that forest both by its level codes $c_1 \ldots c_{15}$ and its parent pointers $p_1 \ldots p_{15}$.

87. [*M20*] Let F be an ordered forest in which the kth node in preorder appears on level c_k and has parent p_k, where $p_k = 0$ if that node is a root.
  a) How many forests satisfy the condition $c_k = p_k$ for $1 \leq k \leq n$?
  b) Suppose F and F' have level codes $c_1 \ldots c_n$ and $c'_1 \ldots c'_n$, respectively, as well as parent links $p_1 \ldots p_n$ and $p'_1 \ldots p'_n$. Prove that, lexicographically, $c_1 \ldots c_n \leq c'_1 \ldots c'_n$ if and only if $p_1 \ldots p_n \leq p'_1 \ldots p'_n$.

88. [*M20*] Analyze Algorithm O: How often is step O4 performed? What is the total number of times p_k is changed in step O5?

89. [*M46*] How often does step O5 set $p_k \leftarrow p_j$?

▶ **90.** [*M27*] If $p_1 \ldots p_n$ is a canonical sequence of parent pointers for an oriented forest, the graph with vertices $\{0, 1, \ldots, n\}$ and edges $\{k \text{---} p_k \mid 1 \leq k \leq n\}$ is a *free tree*, namely a connected graph with no cycles. (See Theorem 2.3.4.1A.) Conversely, every free tree corresponds to at least one oriented forest in this way. But the parent pointers 011 and 000 both yield the same free tree $\succ$; similarly, 012 and 010 both yield ———.

The purpose of this exercise is to restrict the sequences $p_1 \ldots p_n$ further so that each free tree is obtained exactly once. We proved in 2.3.4.4–(9) that the number of structurally different free trees on $n+1$ vertices has a fairly simple generating function, by showing that a free tree always has at least one *centroid*.

    a) Show that a canonical n-node forest corresponds to a free tree with a single centroid if and only if no tree in the forest has more than $\lfloor n/2 \rfloor$ nodes.

    b) Modify Algorithm O so that it generates all sequences $p_1 \ldots p_n$ that satisfy (a).

    c) Explain how to find all $p_1 \ldots p_n$ for free trees that have *two* centroids.

91. [*M37*] (Nijenhuis and Wilf.) Show that a random oriented tree can be generated with a procedure analogous to the random partition algorithm of exercise 7.2.1.4–47.

92. [*15*] Are the first and last spanning trees visited by Algorithm S adjacent, in the sense that they have $n-2$ edges in common?

93. [*20*] When Algorithm S terminates, has it restored the graph to its original state?

94. [*22*] Algorithm S needs to "prime the pump" by finding an initial spanning tree in step S1. Explain how to do that task.

95. [*26*] Complete Algorithm S by implementing the bridge test in step S8.

▶ **96.** [*28*] Analyze the approximate running time of Algorithm S when the given graph is simply (a) a path P_n of length $n-1$; (b) a cycle C_n of length n.

97. [*15*] Is (48) a series-parallel graph?

98. [*16*] What series-parallel graph corresponds to (53) if A is taken to be *serial*?

▶ **99.** [*30*] Consider a series-parallel graph represented by a tree as in (53), together with node values that satisfy (55). These values define a spanning tree or a near tree, according as v_p is 1 or 0 at the root p. Show that the following method will generate all of the other configs of the root:

    i) Begin with all uneasy nodes active, other nodes passive.

    ii) Select the rightmost active node, p, in preorder; but terminate if all nodes are passive.

    iii) Change $d_p \leftarrow r_{d_p}$, update all values in the tree, and visit the new config.

    iv) Activate all uneasy nodes to the right of p.

    v) If d_p has run through all children of p since p last became active, make node p passive. Return to (ii).

Also explain how to perform these steps efficiently. *Hints:* To implement step (v), introduce a pointer z_p; make node p passive when d_p becomes equal to z_p, and at such times also reset z_p to the previous value of d_p. To implement steps (ii) and (iv), use focus pointers f_p analogous to those in Algorithms 7.2.1.1L and 7.2.1.1K.

100. [*40*] Implement the text's "Algorithm S′" for revolving-door generation of all spanning trees, by combining Algorithm S with the ideas of exercise 99.

101. [*46*] Is there a simple revolving-door way to list all n^{n-2} spanning trees of the complete graph K_n? (The order produced by Algorithm S is quite complicated.)

102. [*46*] An *oriented spanning tree* of a directed graph D on n vertices, also known as a "spanning arborescence," is an oriented subtree of D containing $n-1$ arcs. The matrix tree theorem (exercise 2.3.4.2–19) tells us that the oriented subtrees having a given root can readily be counted by evaluating an $(n-1) \times (n-1)$ determinant.

    Can those oriented subtrees be listed in a revolving-door order, always removing one arc and replacing it with another?

▶ **103.** [*HM39*] (*Sandpiles.*) Consider any digraph D on vertices $V_0, V_1, \ldots, V_n$ with e_{ij} arcs from V_i to V_j, where $e_{ii} = 0$. Assume that D has at least one oriented spanning tree rooted at V_0; this assumption means that, if we number the vertices appropriately, we have $e_{i0} + \cdots + e_{i(i-1)} > 0$ for $1 \leq i \leq n$. Let $d_i = e_{i0} + \cdots + e_{in}$ be the total out-degree of V_i. Put x_i grains of sand on vertex V_i for $0 \leq i \leq n$, and play the following game: If $x_i \geq d_i$ for any $i \geq 1$, decrease x_i by d_i and set $x_j \leftarrow x_j + e_{ij}$ for all $j \neq i$. (In other words, pass one grain of sand from V_i through each of its outgoing arcs, whenever possible, except when $i = 0$. This operation is called "toppling" V_i, and a sequence of topplings is called an "avalanche." Vertex V_0 is special; instead of toppling, it collects particles of sand that essentially leave the system.) Continue until $x_i < d_i$ for $1 \leq i \leq n$. Such a state $x = (x_1, \ldots, x_n)$ is called *stable*.

a) Prove that every avalanche terminates in a stable state after a finite number of topplings. Furthermore, the final state depends only on the initial state, not on the order in which toppling is performed.

b) Let $\sigma(x)$ be the stable state that results from initial state x. A stable state is called *recurrent* if it is $\sigma(x)$ for some x with $x_i \geq d_i$ for $1 \leq i \leq n$. (Recurrent states correspond to sandpiles that have evolved over a long period of time, after new grains of sand are repeatedly introduced at random.) Find the recurrent states in the special case when $n = 4$ and when the only arcs of D are

$$V_1 \to V_0, \ V_1 \to V_2, \ V_2 \to V_0, \ V_2 \to V_1, \ V_3 \to V_0, \ V_3 \to V_4, \ V_4 \to V_0, \ V_4 \to V_3.$$

c) Let $d = (d_1, \ldots, d_n)$. Prove that x is recurrent if and only if $x = \sigma(x + t)$, where t is the vector $d - \sigma(d)$.

d) Let a_i be the vector $(-e_{i1}, \ldots, -e_{i(i-1)}, d_i, -e_{i(i+1)}, \ldots, -e_{in})$, for $1 \leq i \leq n$; thus, toppling V_i corresponds to changing the state vector $x = (x_1, \ldots, x_n)$ to $x - a_i$. Say that two states x and x' are *congruent*, written $x \equiv x'$, if $x - x' = m_1 a_1 + \cdots + m_n a_n$ for some integers $m_1, \ldots, m_n$. Prove that there are exactly as many equivalence classes of congruent states as there are oriented spanning trees in D, rooted at V_0. *Hint:* See the matrix tree theorem, exercise 2.3.4.2–19.

e) If $x \equiv x'$ and if both x and x' are recurrent, prove that $x = x'$.

f) Prove that every congruence class contains a unique recurrent state.

g) If D is *balanced*, in the sense that the in-degree of each vertex equals its out-degree, prove that x is recurrent if and only if $x = \sigma(x + a)$, where $a = (e_{01}, \ldots, e_{0n})$.

h) Illustrate these concepts when D is a "wheel" with n spokes: Let there be $3n$ arcs, $V_j \to V_0$ and $V_j \leftrightarrow V_{j+1}$ for $1 \leq j \leq n$, regarding V_{n+1} as identical to V_1. Find a one-to-one correspondence between the oriented spanning trees of this digraph and the recurrent states of its sandpiles.

i) Similarly, analyze the recurrent sandpiles when D is the *complete* graph on $n+1$ vertices, namely when $e_{ij} = [i \neq j]$ for $0 \leq i, j \leq n$. *Hint:* See exercise 6.4–31.

▶ **104.** [*HM21*] If G is a graph on n vertices $\{V_1, \ldots, V_n\}$, with e_{ij} edges between V_i and V_j, let $C(G)$ be the matrix with entries $c_{ij} = -e_{ij} + \delta_{ij} d_i$, where $d_i = e_{i1} + \cdots + e_{in}$ is the degree of V_i. Let us say that the *aspects* of G are the eigenvalues of $C(G)$, namely the roots $\alpha_0, \ldots, \alpha_{n-1}$ of the equation $\det(\alpha I - C(G)) = 0$. Since $C(G)$ is a symmetric matrix, its eigenvalues are real numbers, and we can assume that $\alpha_0 \leq \alpha_1 \leq \cdots \leq \alpha_{n-1}$. [This important matrix is called the *Laplacian* of G; see answer 2.3.4.2–19.]

a) Prove that $\alpha_0 = 0$.

b) Prove that G has exactly $c(G) = \alpha_1 \ldots \alpha_{n-1}/n$ spanning trees.

c) What are the aspects of the complete graph K_n?

105. [*HM38*] Continuing exercise 104, we wish to prove that there is often an easy way to determine the aspects of G when G has been constructed from other graphs whose aspects are known. Suppose G' has aspects $\alpha'_0, \ldots, \alpha'_{n'-1}$ and G'' has aspects $\alpha''_0, \ldots, \alpha''_{n''-1}$; what are the aspects of G in the following cases?

a) $G = \overline{G'}$ is the complement of G'. (Assume that $e'_{ij} \leq [i \neq j]$ in this case.)

b) $G = G' \oplus G''$ is the direct sum (juxtaposition) of G' and G''.

c) $G = G' \!-\! G''$ is the join of G' and G''.

d) $G = G' \,\square\, G''$ is the Cartesian product of G' and G''.

e) $G = L(G')$ is the line graph of G', when G' is a regular graph of degree d' (namely when all vertices of G' have exactly d' neighbors, and there are no self-loops).

f) $G = G' \otimes G''$ is the direct product (conjunction) of G' and G'', when G' is regular of degree d' and G'' is regular of degree d''.

g) $G = G' \boxtimes G''$ is the strong product of regular graphs G' and G''.

h) $G = G' \triangle G''$ is the odd product of regular graphs G' and G''.

i) $G = G' \circ G''$ is the lexicographic product of regular graphs G' and G''.

▶ **106.** [*HM37*] Find the total number of spanning trees in (a) an $m \times n$ grid $P_m \,\square\, P_n$; (b) an $m \times n$ cylinder $P_m \,\square\, C_n$; (c) an $m \times n$ torus $C_m \,\square\, C_n$. Why do these numbers tend to have only small prime factors? *Hint:* Show that the aspects of P_n and C_n can be expressed in terms of the numbers $\sigma_{kn} = 4\sin^2\frac{k\pi}{2n}$.

107. [*M24*] Determine the aspects of all connected graphs that have $n \leq 5$ vertices and no self-loops or parallel edges.

108. [*HM40*] Extend the results of exercises 104–106 to directed graphs.

109. [*M46*] Find a combinatorial explanation for the fact that (57) is the number of spanning trees in the n-cube.

▶ **110.** [*M27*] Prove that if G is any connected multigraph without self-loops, it has

$$c(G) > \sqrt{(d_1 - 1) \ldots (d_n - 1)}$$

spanning trees, where d_j is the degree of vertex j.

111. [*05*] List the nodes of the tree (58) in postpreorder.

112. [*15*] If node p of a forest precedes node q in prepostorder and follows it in postpreorder, what can you say about p and q?

▶ **113.** [*20*] How do prepostorder and postpreorder of a forest F relate to prepostorder and postpreorder of the conjugate forest F^R? (See exercise 13.)

114. [*15*] If we want to traverse an entire forest in prepostorder using Algorithm Q, how should we begin the process?

115. [*20*] Analyze Algorithm Q: How often is each step performed, during the complete traversal of a forest?

▶ **116.** [*28*] If the nodes of a forest F are labeled 1 to n in prepostorder, say that node k is *lucky* if it is adjacent to node $k+1$ in F, *unlucky* if it is three steps away, and *ordinary* otherwise, for $1 \leq k \leq n$; in this definition, node $n+1$ is an imaginary super-root considered to be the parent of each root.

a) Prove that lucky nodes occur only on even-numbered levels; unlucky nodes occur only on odd-numbered levels.

b) Show that the number of lucky nodes is exactly one greater than the number of unlucky nodes, unless $n = 0$.

117. [*21*] Continuing exercise 116, how many n-node forests contain no unlucky nodes?

118. [*M28*] How many lucky nodes are present in (a) the complete t-ary tree with $(t^k - 1)/(t - 1)$ internal nodes? (b) the Fibonacci tree of order k, with $F_{k+1} - 1$ internal nodes? (See 2.3.4.5–(6) and Fig. 8 in Section 6.2.1.)

119. [*21*] The *twisted binomial tree* $\tilde{T}_n$ of order n is defined recursively by the rules

$$\tilde{T}_0 = \bullet \,, \qquad \tilde{T}_n = \qquad \text{for } n > 0.$$

(Compare with 7.2.1.3–(21); we reverse the order of children on alternate levels.) Show that prepostorder traversal of $\tilde{T}_n$ has a simple connection with Gray binary code.

120. [*22*] True or false: The square of a graph is Hamiltonian if the graph is connected and has no bridges.

121. [*M34*] (F. Neuman, 1964.) The *derivative* of a graph G is the graph $G^{(\prime)}$ obtained by removing all vertices of degree 1 and the edges touching them. Prove that, when T is a free tree, its square T^2 contains a Hamiltonian path if and only if its derivative has no vertex of degree greater than 4 and the following two additional conditions hold:
  i) All vertices of degree 3 or 4 in $T^{(\prime)}$ lie on a single path.
  ii) Between any two vertices of degree 4 in $T^{(\prime)}$, there is at least one vertex that has degree 2 in T.

▶ **122.** [*31*] (*Dudeney's Digital Century puzzle.*) There are many curious ways to obtain the number 100 by inserting arithmetical operators and possibly also parentheses into the sequence 123456789. For example,

$$100 = 1 + 2 \times 3 + 4 \times 5 - 6 + 7 + 8 \times 9 = (1 + 2 - 3 - 4) \times (5 - 6 - 7 - 8 - 9)$$
$$= ((1/((2 + 3)/4 - 5 + 6)) \times 7 + 8) \times 9 \,.$$

a) How many such representations of 100 are possible? To make this question precise, in view of the associative law and other algebraic properties, assume that expressions are written in canonical form according to the following syntax:

$\langle\,\text{expression}\,\rangle \to \langle\,\text{number}\,\rangle \mid \langle\,\text{sum}\,\rangle \mid \langle\,\text{product}\,\rangle \mid \langle\,\text{quotient}\,\rangle$
$\langle\,\text{sum}\,\rangle \to \langle\,\text{term}\,\rangle + \langle\,\text{term}\,\rangle \mid \langle\,\text{term}\,\rangle - \langle\,\text{term}\,\rangle \mid \langle\,\text{sum}\,\rangle + \langle\,\text{term}\,\rangle \mid \langle\,\text{sum}\,\rangle - \langle\,\text{term}\,\rangle$
$\langle\,\text{term}\,\rangle \to \langle\,\text{number}\,\rangle \mid \langle\,\text{product}\,\rangle \mid \langle\,\text{quotient}\,\rangle$
$\langle\,\text{product}\,\rangle \to \langle\,\text{factor}\,\rangle \times \langle\,\text{factor}\,\rangle \mid \langle\,\text{product}\,\rangle \times \langle\,\text{factor}\,\rangle \mid (\langle\,\text{quotient}\,\rangle) \times \langle\,\text{factor}\,\rangle$
$\langle\,\text{quotient}\,\rangle \to \langle\,\text{factor}\,\rangle/\langle\,\text{factor}\,\rangle \mid \langle\,\text{product}\,\rangle/\langle\,\text{factor}\,\rangle \mid (\langle\,\text{quotient}\,\rangle)/\langle\,\text{factor}\,\rangle$
$\langle\,\text{factor}\,\rangle \to \langle\,\text{number}\,\rangle \mid (\langle\,\text{sum}\,\rangle)$
$\langle\,\text{number}\,\rangle \to \langle\,\text{digit}\,\rangle$

The digits used must be 1 through 9, in that order.

b) Extend problem (a) by allowing multidigit numbers, with the syntax

$$\langle\,\text{number}\,\rangle \to \langle\,\text{digit}\,\rangle \mid \langle\,\text{number}\,\rangle\langle\,\text{digit}\,\rangle$$

For example, $100 = (1/(2 - 3 + 4)) \times 567 - 89$. What is the shortest such representation? What is the longest?

c) Extend problem (b) by also allowing decimal points:

$$\langle\,\text{number}\,\rangle \to \langle\,\text{digit string}\,\rangle \mid .\langle\,\text{digit string}\,\rangle$$
$$\langle\,\text{digit string}\,\rangle \to \langle\,\text{digit}\,\rangle \mid \langle\,\text{digit string}\,\rangle\langle\,\text{digit}\,\rangle$$

For example, $100 = (.1 - 2 - 34 \times .5)/(.6 - .789)$, amazingly enough.

123. [*21*] Continuing the previous exercise, what are the smallest positive integers that *cannot* be represented using conventions (a), (b), (c)?

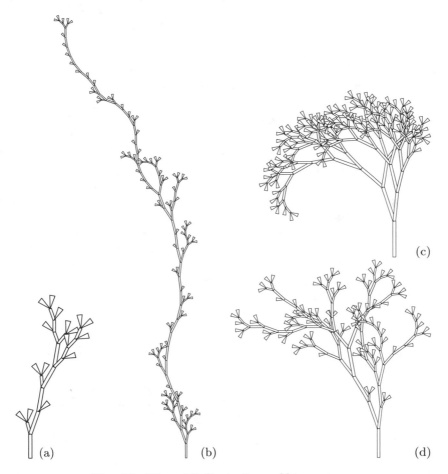

Fig. 63. "Organic" illustrations of binary trees.

▶ **124.** [*40*] Experiment with methods for drawing extended binary trees that are inspired by simple models from nature. For example, we can assign a value $v(x)$ to each node x, called its *Horton–Strahler number*, as follows: Each external (leaf) node has $v(x) = 0$; an internal node with children (l, r) has $v(x) = \max(v(l), v(r)) + [v(l) = v(r)]$. The edge from internal node x to its parent can be drawn as a rectangle with height $h(v(x))$ and width $w(v(x))$, and the edge rectangles with children (l, r) can be offset by angles $\theta(v(l(x)), v(r(x)))$, $-\theta(v(r(x)), v(l(x)))$, for certain functions h, w, and θ. The examples in Fig. 63 show typical results when we choose $w(k) = 3 + k$, $h(k) = 18k$, $\theta(k, k) = 30°$, $\theta(j, k) = ((k + 1)/j) \times 20°$ for $0 \le k < j$, and $\theta(j, k) = ((k - j)/k) \times 30°$ for $0 \le j < k$; the roots appear at the bottom. Part (a) of Fig. 63 is the binary tree (4); part (b) is a random 100-node tree generated by Algorithm R; part (c) is the Fibonacci tree of order 11, which has 143 nodes; and part (d) is a random 100-node binary search tree. (The trees in parts (b), (c), and (d) clearly belong to different species.)

[This subject] has a relation
to almost every species of useful knowledge
that the mind of man can be employed upon.

— JAMES BERNOULLI, *Ars Conjectandi* (1713)

7.2.1.7. History and further references. Early work on the generation of combinatorial patterns began as civilization itself was taking shape. The story is quite fascinating, and we will see that it spans many cultures in many parts of the world, with ties to poetry, music, and religion. There is space here to discuss only some of the principal highlights; but perhaps a few glimpses into the past will stimulate the reader to dig deeper into the roots of the subject, as the world gets ever smaller and as global scholarship continues to advance.

Lists of binary n-tuples can be traced back thousands of years to ancient China, India, and Greece. The most notable source — because it still is a best-selling book in modern translations — is the Chinese *I Ching* or *Yijing*, whose name means "the Bible of Changes." This book, which is one of the five classics of Confucian wisdom, consists essentially of $2^6 = 64$ chapters; and each chapter is symbolized by a hexagram formed from six lines, each of which is either -- ("yin") or — ("yang"). For example, hexagram 1 is pure yang, ☰; hexagram 2 is pure yin, ☷; and hexagram 64 intermixes yin and yang, with yang on top: ䷿. Here is the complete list:

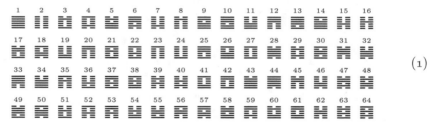

$$(1)$$

This arrangement of the 64 possibilities is called King Wen's ordering, because the basic text of the *I Ching* has traditionally been ascribed to King Wen (c. 1100 B.C.), the legendary progenitor of the Chou dynasty. Ancient texts are, however, notoriously difficult to date reliably, and modern historians have found no solid evidence that anyone actually compiled such a list of hexagrams before the third century B.C.

Notice that the hexagrams of (1) occur in pairs: Those with odd numbers are immediately followed by their top-to-bottom reflections, except when reflection would make no change; and the eight symmetrical diagrams are paired with their complements ($1 = \bar{2}$, $27 = \bar{28}$, $29 = \bar{30}$, $61 = \bar{62}$). Hexagrams that are composed from two trigrams that represent the four basic elements heaven (☰), earth (☷), fire (☲), and water (☵) have also been placed judiciously. Otherwise the arrangement appears to be essentially random, as if a person untrained in mathematics kept listing different possibilities until being unable to come up with any more. A few intriguing patterns do exist between the pairs, but no more than are present by coincidence in the digits of π (see 3.3–(1)).

Yin and yang represent complementary aspects of the elementary forces of nature, always in tension, always changing. The *I Ching* is somewhat analogous to a thesaurus in which the hexagrams serve as an index to accumulated wisdom about fundamental concepts like giving (☰), receiving (☷), modesty (☶), joy (☱), fellowship (☲), withdrawal (☴), peace (☷), conflict (☰), organization (☵), corruption (☶), immaturity (☶), elegance (☲), etc. One can choose a pair of hexagrams at random, obtaining the second from the first by, say, independently changing each yin to yang (or vice versa) with probability $1/4$; this technique yields 4096 ways to ponder existential mysteries, as well as a Markov process by which change itself might perhaps give meaning to life.

A strictly logical way to arrange the hexagrams was eventually introduced about A.D. 1060 by Shao Yung. His ordering, which proceeded lexicographically from ☷ to ☴ to ☵ to ☶ to ☲ to $\cdots$ to ☱ to ☰ (reading each hexagram from bottom to top), was much more user-friendly than the King Wen order, because a random pattern could now be found quickly. When G. W. Leibniz learned about Shao Yung's sequence of hexagrams in 1703, he was mistakenly led to believe that Chinese mathematicians had once been familiar with binary arithmetic. [See Frank Swetz, *Mathematics Magazine* **76** (2003), 276–291. Further details about the *I Ching* can be found, for example, in Joseph Needham's *Science and Civilisation in China* **2** (Cambridge University Press, 1956), 304–345; R. J. Lynn, *The Classic of Changes* (New York: Columbia University Press, 1994).]

Another ancient Chinese philosopher, Yang Hsiung, proposed a system based on 81 ternary tetragrams instead of 64 binary hexagrams. His *Canon of Supreme Mystery*, written c. 2 B.C., has recently been translated into English by Michael Nylan (Albany, New York: 1993). Yang described a complete, hierarchical ternary tree structure in which there are 3 regions, with 3 provinces in each region, 3 departments in each province, 3 families in each department, and 9 short poems called "appraisals" for each family, hence 729 appraisals in all — making almost exactly 2 appraisals for every day in the year. His tetragrams were arranged in strict lexicographic order when read top-to-bottom: ≡, ≡, ≡, ≡, ≡, ≡, ≡, ..., ≣. In fact, as explained on page 28 of Nylan's book, Yang presented a simple way to compute the rank of each tetragram, as if using a radix-3 number system. Thus he would not have been surprised or impressed by Shao Yung's systematic ordering of binary hexagrams, although Shao lived more than 1000 years later.

Indian prosody. Binary n-tuples were studied in a completely different context by pundits in ancient India, who investigated the poetic meters of sacred Vedic chants. Syllables in Sanskrit are either short (ı) or long (ऽ), and the study of syllable patterns is called "prosody." Modern writers use the symbols $\smile$ and $-$ instead of ı and ऽ. A typical Vedic verse consists of four lines with n syllables per line, for some $n \geq 8$; prosodists therefore sought a way to classify all 2^n possibilities. The classic work *Chandaḥśāstra* by Piṅgala, written before A.D. 400 and probably much earlier (the exact date is quite uncertain), described procedures by which one could readily find the index k of any given pattern of $\smile$s and $-$s, as well as to find the kth pattern, given k. In other words, Piṅgala explained how to *rank* any given pattern as well as to *unrank* any given index;

thus he went beyond the work of Yang Hsiung, who had considered ranking but not unranking. Piṅgala's methods were also related to exponentiation, as we have noted earlier in connection with Algorithm 4.6.3A.

The next important step was taken by a prosodist named Kedāra in his work *Vṛttaratnākara*, thought to have been written in the 8th century. Kedāra gave a step-by-step procedure for listing all the n-tuples from $---\ldots-$ to $\smile--\ldots-$ to $-\smile-\ldots-$ to $\smile\smile-\ldots-$ to $--\smile\ldots-$ to $\smile-\smile\ldots-$ to $\cdots$ to $\smile\smile\smile\ldots\smile$, essentially Algorithm 7.2.1.1M in the case of radix 2. His method may well have been the first-ever explicit algorithm for combinatorial sequence generation. [See B. van Nooten, *J. Indian Philos.* **21** (1993), 31–50.]

Poetic meters can also be regarded as rhythms, with one beat for each $\smile$ and two beats for each $-$. An n-syllable pattern can involve between n and $2n$ beats, but musical rhythms suitable for marching or dancing generally are based on a fixed number of beats. Therefore it was natural to consider the set of all sequences of $\smile$s and $-$s that have exactly m beats, for fixed m. Such patterns are now called Morse code sequences of length m, and we know from exercise 4.5.3–32 that there are exactly F_{m+1} of them. For example, the 21 sequences when $m = 7$ are

$$\smile---, \ -\smile--, \ \smile\smile\smile--, \ ---\smile-, \ \smile\smile-\smile-,$$
$$\smile-\smile\smile-, \ -\smile\smile\smile-, \ \smile\smile\smile\smile\smile-, \ ---\smile\smile,$$
$$\smile\smile--\smile, \ \smile-\smile-\smile, \ -\smile\smile-\smile, \ \smile\smile\smile\smile-\smile, \quad (2)$$
$$\smile--\smile\smile, \ -\smile-\smile\smile, \ \smile\smile\smile-\smile\smile, \ --\smile\smile\smile,$$
$$\smile\smile-\smile\smile\smile, \ \smile-\smile\smile\smile\smile, \ -\smile\smile\smile\smile\smile, \ \smile\smile\smile\smile\smile\smile\smile.$$

In this way Indian prosodists were led to discover the Fibonacci sequence, as we have observed in Section 1.2.8.

Moreover, the anonymous author of *Prākṛta Paiṅgala* (c. 1320) discovered elegant algorithms for ranking and unranking with respect to m-beat rhythms. To find the kth pattern, one starts by writing down m $\smile$s, then expresses the difference $d = F_{m+1} - k$ as a sum of Fibonacci numbers $F_{j_1} + \cdots + F_{j_t}$; here F_{j_1} is the largest Fibonacci number that is $\leq d$ and F_{j_2} is the largest $\leq d - F_{j_1}$, etc., continuing until the remainder is zero. Then beats $j - 1$ and j are to be changed from $\smile\smile$ to $-$, for $j = j_1, \ldots, j_t$. For example, to get the 5th element of (2) we compute $21 - 5 = 16 = 13 + 3 = F_7 + F_4$; the answer is $\smile\smile-\smile-$.

A few years later, Nārāyaṇa Paṇḍita treated the more general problem of finding all compositions of m whose parts are $\leq q$, where q is *any* given positive integer. As a consequence he discovered the qth-order Fibonacci sequence 5.4.2–(4), which was destined to be used 600 years later in polyphase sorting; he also developed the corresponding ranking and unranking algorithms. [See Parmanand Singh, *Historia Mathematica* **12** (1985), 229–244, and exercise 16.]

Piṅgala gave special code names to all the three-syllable meters,

$$
\begin{array}{llll}
--- = \text{म (m)}, & \qquad & --\smile = \text{त (t)}, & \\
\smile-- = \text{य (y)}, & \qquad & \smile-\smile = \text{ज (j)}, & \\
-\smile- = \text{र (r)}, & \qquad & -\smile\smile = \text{भ (bh)}, & \quad (3) \\
\smile\smile- = \text{स (s)}, & \qquad & \smile\smile\smile = \text{न (n)}, &
\end{array}
$$

and students of Sanskrit have been expected to memorize them ever since. Somebody long ago devised a clever way to recall these codes, by inventing the nonsense word *yamātārājabhānasalagām* (यमातारājभानसलगाम्); the point is that the ten syllables of this word can be written

$$\text{ya mā tā rā ja bhā na sa la gām} \atop \smile - - - \smile - \smile \smile \smile - \tag{4}$$

and each three-syllable pattern occurs just after its code name. The origin of yamā...lagām is obscure, but Subhash Kak [*Indian J. History of Science* **35** (2000), 123–127] has traced it back at least to C. P. Brown's *Sanskrit Prosody* (1869), page 28; thus it qualifies as the earliest known appearance of a "de Bruijn cycle" that encodes binary n-tuples.

Meanwhile, in Europe. In a similar way, classic Greek poetry was based on groups of short and/or long syllables called "metrical feet," analogous to bars of music. Each basic type of foot acquired a Greek name; for example, two short syllables '$\smile\smile$' were called a *pyrrhic*, and two long syllables '$--$' were called a *spondee*, because those rhythms were used respectively in a song of war (πυρρίχη) or a song of peace (σπονδαί). Greek names for metric feet were soon assimilated into Latin and eventually into modern languages, including English:

$\smile$	arsis	$\smile\smile\smile\smile$	proceleusmatic	
$-$	thesis	$\smile\smile\smile-$	fourth pæon	
		$\smile\smile-\smile$	third pæon	
$\smile\smile$	pyrrhic	$\smile\smile--$	minor ionic	
$\smile-$	iambus	$\smile-\smile\smile$	second pæon	
$-\smile$	trochee	$\smile-\smile-$	diiambus	
$--$	spondee	$\smile--\smile$	antispast	
		$\smile---$	first epitrite	(5)
$\smile\smile\smile$	tribrach	$-\smile\smile\smile$	first pæon	
$\smile\smile-$	anapest	$-\smile\smile-$	choriambus	
$\smile-\smile$	amphibrach	$-\smile-\smile$	ditrochee	
$\smile--$	bacchius	$-\smile--$	second epitrite	
$-\smile\smile$	dactyl	$--\smile\smile$	major ionic	
$-\smile-$	amphimacer	$--\smile-$	third epitrite	
$--\smile$	palimbacchius	$---\smile$	fourth epitrite	
$---$	molossus	$----$	dispondee	

Alternative names, like "choree" instead of "trochee," or "cretic" instead of "amphimacer," were also in common use. Moreover, by the time Diomedes wrote his Latin grammar (approximately A.D. 375), each of the 32 *five*-syllable feet had acquired at least one name. Diomedes also pointed out the relation between complementary patterns; he stated for example that tribrach and molossus are "*contrarius*," as are amphibrach and amphimacer. But he also regarded dactyl as the contrary of anapest, and bacchius as the contrary of palimbacchius, although the literal meaning of *palimbacchius* is actually "reverse bacchius." Greek prosodists had no standard order in which to list the individual possibilities, and the form of the names makes it clear that no connection to a radix-two number system was contemplated. [See H. Keil, *Grammatici Latini* **1** (1857), 474–482; W. von Christ, *Metrik der Griechen und Römer* (1879), 78–79.]

Surviving fragments of a work by Aristoxenus called *Elements of Rhythm* (c. 325 B.C.) show that the same terminology was applied also to music. And indeed, the same traditions lived on after the Renaissance; for example, we find

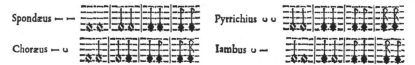

on page 32 of Athanasius Kircher's *Musurgia Universalis* **2** (Rome: 1650), and Kircher went on to describe all of the three-note and four-note rhythms of (5).

Early lists of permutations. We've traced the history of formulas for counting permutations in Section 5.1.2; but nontrivial *lists* of permutations were not published until hundreds of years after the formula $n!$ was discovered. The first such tabulation currently known was compiled by the Italian physician Shabbetai Donnolo in his commentary Ḥakhmoni on the kabbalistic *Sefer Yetzirah*, written in A.D. 946. Table 1 shows his list for $n = 5$ as it was subsequently printed in Warsaw (1884). (The Hebrew letters in this table are typeset in a rabbinical font traditionally used for commentaries; notice that the letter מ changes its shape to ם when it appears at the left end of a word.) Donnolo went on to list 120 permutations of the six-letter word שכתבנו, all beginning with shin (ש); then he noted that 120 more could be obtained with each of the other five letters in front, making 720 in all. His lists involved groupings of six permutations, but in a haphazard fashion that led him into error (see exercise 4). He knew how many permutations there were supposed to be, and sketched a "rolling" method that would extend his list to the 5040 that arise with seven letters.

Table 1

A MEDIEVAL LIST OF PERMUTATIONS

דברים, דבירם, דבימר, דבמיר, דבמרי, דברמי, דרבים, דרבמי, דלבמי, דלימב, דלריבס, דלרמבי, דלרמיב,

דיברס, דירבם, דירמב, דיברמ, דימרב, דיומבר, דימביר, דמביר, דמברי, דמרבי, דמריב, דמיבר, דמירב,

בדימר, בדירס, בדרמי, בדרים, בדמרי, בדמיר, בידרם, בידרס, בירדם, בירמד, בימדר, בימרד, בידמר,

במדרי, במדיר, במריד, במרדי, במדיר, במידר, בדמיר, בדמרי, בדרלמי, בדרים, בדימר, בדירס,

רימדב, רימבד, רידבס, רידמב, ריבדם, ריבדס, ריבמד, ריבמ, רדבמי, רדבמי, רדימב, רדיבס, רדמיב,

רבמדי, רבדמי, רבדיס, רביום, רבימד, רבמיד, רבמדי, רמיבד, רמידב, רמיבד, רמיבד, רמבדי, רמבדי,

ימדרב, ימרדב, ימברד, ימבדר, ימברד, יומברד, יומדבר, יומדבר, ידרבס, ידרבמ, ידמבר, ידרמב, ידמרב,

יבדרם, יבדמר, יבדרס, יברמד, יברמד, יברמד, יברמד, יברמד, ירמבד, ירמבד, ירבדס, ירדמב,

מדברי, מדבריר, מדביר, מדברד, מדיבר, מדירב, מדברד, מדביד, מבירד, מבריד, מבירד, מבדרי, מבדרי,

מרדבי, מרבדי, מרדיב, מריבד, מרביד, מריבד, מריבד, מרדיב, מרדיב, מידרב, מידבר, מיבדר, מידבר, מירבד

A complete list of all 720 permutations of $\{a, b, c, d, e, f\}$ appeared on pages 668–671 of Jeremias Drexel's *Orbis Phaëthon* (Munich: 1629; also on pages 526–531 of the Cologne edition in 1631). He offered it as proof that a man with six guests could seat them differently at lunch and dinner every day for a year—

altogether 360 days, because there were five days of fasting during Holy Week. Shortly afterwards, Marin Mersenne exhibited all 720 permutations of the six tones {ut, re, mi, fa, sol, la}, on pages 111–115 of his *Traitez de la Voix et des Chants* (Volume 2 of *Harmonie Universelle*, 1636); then on pages 117–128 he presented the same data in musical notation:

Drexel's table was organized lexicographically by columns; Mersenne's tables were lexicographic with respect to the order ut < re < mi < fa < sol < la, beginning with "ut,re,mi,fa,sol,la" and ending with "la,sol,fa,mi,re,ut." Mersenne also prepared a "grand et immense" manuscript that listed all 40,320 permutations of *eight* notes on 672 folio pages, followed by ranking and unranking algorithms [Bibliothèque nationale de France, Fonds Français, no. 24256].

We saw in Section 7.2.1.2 that the important idea of plain changes, Algorithm 7.2.1.2P, was invented in England a few years later.

Methods for listing all permutations of a multiset with *repeated* elements were often misunderstood by early authors. For example, when Bhāskara exhibited the permutations of {4, 5, 5, 5, 8} in section 271 of his *Līlāvatī* (c. 1150), he gave them in the following order:

$$
\begin{array}{ccccc}
\text{४८५५५} & \text{५४५५५} & \text{५४८५५} & \text{५८४५५} & \text{५५४८५} \\
\text{५५८४५} & \text{५५५४८} & \text{५५५८४} & \text{८५४५५} & \text{८५५४५} \\
\text{८५५५४} & \text{५८५४५} & \text{५८५५४} & \text{५५८५४} & \text{४५८५५} \\
\text{५८५४५} & \text{५५५४८} & \text{५५८४५} & \text{४५५५८} & \text{५८५५४}
\end{array}
\tag{6}
$$

Mersenne used a slightly more sensible but not completely systematic order on page 131 of his book when he listed sixty anagrams of the Latin name IESVS. When Athanasius Kircher wanted to illustrate the 30 permutations of a five-note melody on pages 10 and 11 of *Musurgia Universalis* **2** (1650), this lack of a system got him into trouble (see exercise 5):

$$\tag{7}$$

But John Wallis knew better. On page 117 of his *Discourse of Combinations* (1685) he correctly listed the 60 anagrams of "messes" in lexicographic order, if we let m < e < s; and on page 126 he recommended respecting alphabetic order "that we may be the more sure, not to miss any."

We will see later that the Indian pundits Śārṅgadeva and Nārāyaṇa had already developed a theory of permutation generation in the 13th and 14th centuries, although their work was ahead of its time and remained obscure.

Seki's list. Takakazu Seki (1642–1708) was a charismatic teacher and researcher who revolutionized the study of mathematics in 17th-century Japan. While he was studying the elimination of variables from simultaneous homogeneous equations, he was led to expressions such as $a_1b_2 - a_2b_1$ and $a_1b_2c_3 - a_1b_3c_2 + a_2b_3c_1 - a_2b_1c_3 + a_3b_1c_2 - a_3b_2c_1$, which we now recognize as *determinants*. In 1683 he published a booklet about this discovery, introducing an ingenious scheme for listing all permutations in such a way that half of them were "alive" (even) and the other half were "dead" (odd). Starting with the case $n = 2$, when '12' was alive and '21' was dead, he formulated the following rules for $n > 2$:

1) Take every live permutation for $n-1$, increase all its elements by 1, and insert 1 in front. This rule produces $(n-1)!/2$ "basic permutations" of $\{1, \ldots, n\}$.

2) From each basic permutation, form $2n$ others by rotation and reflection:

$$a_1a_2 \ldots a_{n-1}a_n, \ a_2 \ldots a_{n-1}a_na_1, \ \ldots, \ a_na_1a_2 \ldots a_{n-1}; \tag{8}$$

$$a_na_{n-1} \ldots a_2a_1, \ a_1a_na_{n-1} \ldots a_2, \ \ldots, \ a_{n-1} \ldots a_2a_1a_n. \tag{9}$$

If n is odd, those in the first row are alive and those in the second are dead; if n is even, those in each row are alternately alive, dead, ..., alive, dead. For example, when $n = 3$ the only basic permutation is 123. Thus 123, 231, 312 are alive while 321, 132, 213 are dead, and we've successfully generated the six terms of a 3×3 determinant. The basic permutations for $n = 4$ are 1234, 1342, 1423; and from, say, 1342 we get a set of eight, namely

$$+ 1342 - 3421 + 4213 - 2134 + 2431 - 1243 + 3124 - 4312, \tag{10}$$

alternately alive $(+)$ and dead $(-)$. A 4×4 determinant therefore includes the terms $a_1b_3c_4d_2 - a_3b_4c_2d_1 + \cdots - a_4b_3c_1d_2$ and sixteen others.

Seki's rule for permutation generation is quite pretty, but unfortunately it has a serious problem: It doesn't work when $n > 4$. His error seems to have gone unrecognized for hundreds of years. [See Y. Mikami, *The Development of Mathematics in China and Japan* (1913), 191–199; *Takakazu Seki's Collected Works* (Osaka: 1974), 18–20, 八五———四—; and exercises 7–8.]

Lists of combinations. The earliest exhaustive list of *combinations* known to have survived the ravages of time appears in the last book of Suśruta's well-known Sanskrit treatise on medicine, Chapter 63, written before A.D. 600 and perhaps much earlier. Noting that medicine can be sweet, sour, salty, peppery, bitter, and/or astringent, Suśruta's book diligently listed the $(15, 20, 15, 6, 1, 6)$ cases that arise when those qualities occur two, three, four, five, six, and one at a time.

Bhāskara repeated this example in sections 110–114 of *Līlāvatī*, and observed that the same reasoning applies to six-syllable poetic meters with a given number of long syllables. But he simply mentioned the totals, $(6, 15, 20, 15, 6, 1)$, without listing the combinations themselves. In sections 274 and 275, he observed that the numbers $(n(n - 1) \ldots (n - k + 1))/(k(k - 1) \ldots (1))$ enumerate *compositions* (that is, ordered partitions) as well as combinations; again he gave no list.

> *To avoid prolixity this is treated in a brief manner;*
> *for the science of calculation is an ocean without bounds.*
> — BHĀSKARA (c. 1150)

An isolated but interesting list of combinations appeared in the remarkable algebra text *Al-Bāhir fi'l-ḥisāb* (*The Shining Book of Calculation*), written by al-Samaw'al of Baghdad when he was only 19 years old (1144). In the closing part of that work he presented a list of $\binom{10}{6} = 210$ simultaneous linear equations in 10 unknowns:

Al-Samaw'al's Arabic original				Equivalent modern notation	
٦٥	٦٥٤٣٢١	ا		(1)　$x_1 + x_2 + x_3 + x_4 + x_5 + x_6 = 65$	
٧٠	٧٥٤٣٢١	ب		(2)　$x_1 + x_2 + x_3 + x_4 + x_5 + x_7 = 70$	
٧٥	٨٥٤٣٢١	ج		(3)　$x_1 + x_2 + x_3 + x_4 + x_5 + x_8 = 75$	(11)
⋮	⋮			⋮	
٩١	١٠٩٨٧٦٤	ر ط		(209)　$x_4 + x_6 + x_7 + x_8 + x_9 + x_{10} = 91$	
١٠٠	١٠٩٨٧٦٥	ر ي		(210)　$x_5 + x_6 + x_7 + x_8 + x_9 + x_{10} = 100$	

Each combination of ten things taken six at a time yielded one of his equations. His purpose was evidently to demonstrate that over-determined equations can still have a unique solution—which in this case was $(x_1, x_2, \ldots, x_{10}) = (1, 4, 9, 16, 25, 10, 15, 20, 25, 5)$. [Salah Ahmad and Roshdi Rashed, *Al-Bāhir en Algèbre d'As-Samaw'al* (Damascus: 1972), 77–82, ٢٤٨–٢٣١.]

Rolling dice. Some glimmerings of elementary combinatorics arose also in medieval Europe, especially in connection with the question of listing all possible outcomes when three dice are thrown. There are, of course, $\binom{8}{3} = 56$ ways to choose 3 things from 6 when repetitions are allowed. Gambling was officially prohibited; yet these 56 ways became rather well known. In about A.D. 965, Bishop Wibold of Cambrai in northern France devised a game called Ludus Clericalis, so that members of the clergy could enjoy rolling dice while remaining pious. His idea was to associate each possible roll with one of 56 virtues, according to the following table:

Virtue	Virtue	Virtue	Virtue
love	perseverance	hospitality	mortification
faith	kindness	economy	innocence
hope	modesty	patience	contrition
justice	resignation	zeal	confession
prudence	gentleness	poverty	maturity
temperance	generosity	softness	solicitude
courage	wisdom	virginity	constancy
peace	remorse	respect	intelligence
chastity	joy	piety	sighing
mercy	sobriety	indulgence	weeping
obedience	satisfaction	prayer	cheerfulness
fear	sweetness	affection	compassion
foresight	cleverness	judgment	self-control
discretion	simplicity	vigilance	humility

Players took turns, and the first to roll each virtue acquired it. After all possibilities had arisen, the most virtuous player won. Wibold noted that love (*caritas*) is the best virtue of all. He gave a complicated scoring system by which two virtues could be combined if the sum of pips on all six of their dice was 21; for example, love + humility or chastity + intelligence could be paired in this way, and such combinations ranked above any individual virtue. He also considered more complex variants of the game in which vowels appeared on the dice instead of spots, so that virtues could be claimed if their vowels were thrown.

Wibold's table of virtues was presented in lexicographic order, as above, when it was first described by Baldéric in his *Chronicon Cameracense*, about 150 years later. [*Patrologia Latina* **134** (Paris: 1884), 1007–1016.] But another medieval manuscript presented the possible dice rolls in quite a different order:

$$(12)$$

In this case the author knew how to deal with repeated values, but had a very complicated, ad hoc way to handle the cases in which all dice were different. [See D. R. Bellhouse, *International Statistical Review* **68** (2000), 123–136.]

An amusing poem entitled "Chaunce of the Dyse," attributed to John Lydgate, was written in the early 1400s for use at parties. Its opening verses invite each person to throw three dice; then the remaining verses, which are indexed in decreasing lexicographic order from ⚅⚅⚅ to ⚅⚅⚄ to ⋯ to ⚀⚀⚀, give 56 character sketches that light-heartedly describe the thrower. [The full text was published by E. P. Hammond in *Englische Studien* **59** (1925), 1–16; a translation into modern English would be desirable.]

> *I pray to god that euery wight may caste*
> *Vpon three dyse ryght as is in hys herte*
> *Whether he be rechelesse or stedfaste*
> *So moote he lawghen outher elles smerte*
> *He that is gilty his lyfe to converte*
> *They that in trouthe haue suffred many a throwe*
> *Moote ther chaunce fal as they moote be knowe.*
>
> — *The Chaunce of the Dyse* (c. 1410)

Ramon Llull. Significant ripples of combinatorial concepts also emanated from an energetic and quixotic Catalan poet, novelist, encyclopedist, educator, mystic, and missionary named Ramon Llull (c. 1232–1316). Llull's approach to knowledge was essentially to identify basic principles and then to contemplate combining them in all possible ways.

For example, one chapter in his *Ars Compendiosa Inveniendi Veritatem* (c. 1274) began by enumerating sixteen attributes of God: Goodness, greatness, eternity, power, wisdom, love, virtue, truth, glory, perfection, justice, generosity, mercy, humility, sovereignty, and patience. Then Llull wrote $\binom{16}{2} = 120$ short essays of about 80 words each, considering God's goodness as related to greatness,

God's goodness as related to eternity, and so on, ending with God's sovereignty as related to patience. In another chapter he considered seven virtues (faith, hope, charity, justice, prudence, fortitude, temperance) and seven vices (gluttony, lust, greed, sloth, pride, envy, anger), with $\binom{14}{2} = 91$ subchapters to deal with each pair in turn. Other chapters were systematically divided in a similar way, into $\binom{8}{2} = 28$, $\binom{15}{2} = 105$, $\binom{4}{2} = 6$, and $\binom{16}{2} = 120$ subsections. (One wonders what might have happened if he had been familiar with Wibold's list of 56 virtues; would he have produced commentaries on all $\binom{56}{2} = 1540$ of their pairs?)

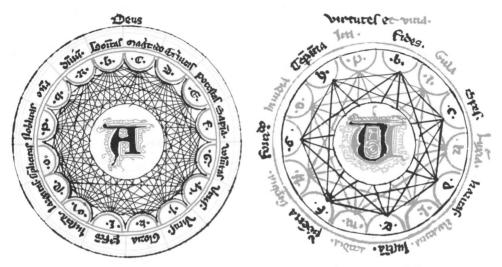

Fig. 64. Illustrations in a manuscript presented by Ramon Llull to the doge of Venice in 1280. [From his *Ars Demonstrativa*, Biblioteca Marciana, VI 200, folio 3^{v}.]

Llull illustrated his methodology by drawing circular diagrams like those in Figure 64. The left-hand circle in this illustration, *Deus*, names sixteen divine attributes — essentially the same sixteen listed earlier, except that love (*amor*) was now called will (*voluntas*), and the final four were now simplicity, rank, mercy, and sovereignty, in that order. Each attribute was assigned a code letter, and the illustration depicts their interrelations as the complete graph K_{16} on vertices (B, C, D, E, F, G, H, I, K, L, M, N, O, P, Q, R). The right-hand figure, *virtutes et vitia*, shows the seven virtues (b, c, d, e, f, g, h) interleaved with the seven vices (i, k, l, m, n, o, p); in the original manuscript virtues appeared in blue ink while vices appeared in red. Notice that in this case his illustration depicted two independent complete graphs K_7, one of each color. (He no longer bothered to compare each individual virtue with each individual vice, since every virtue was clearly better than every vice.)

Llull used the same approach to write about medicine: Instead of juxtaposing theological concepts, his *Liber Principiorum Medicinæ* (c. 1275) considered combinations of symptoms and treatments. And he also wrote books

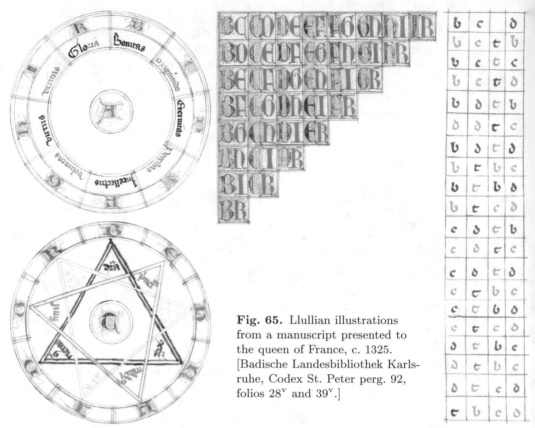

Fig. 65. Llullian illustrations from a manuscript presented to the queen of France, c. 1325. [Badische Landesbibliothek Karlsruhe, Codex St. Peter perg. 92, folios 28^{v} and 39^{v}.]

on philosophy, logic, jurisprudence, astrology, zoology, geometry, rhetoric, and chivalry — more than 200 works in all. It must be admitted, however, that much of this material was highly repetitive; modern data compression techniques would probably reduce Llull's output to a size much less than that of, say, Aristotle.

He eventually decided to simplify his system by working primarily with groups of nine things. See, for example, Fig. 65, where circle A now lists only the first nine of God's attributes (B, C, D, E, F, G, H, I, K). The $\binom{9}{2} = 36$ associated pairs (BC, BD, . . . , IK) appear in the stairstep chart at the right of that circle. By adding two more virtues, namely patience and compassion — as well as two more vices, namely lying and inconsistency — he could treat virtues vis-à-vis virtues and vices vis-à-vis vices with the same chart. He also proposed using the same chart to carry out an interesting scheme for voting, in an election with nine candidates [see I. McLean and J. London, *Studia Lulliana* **32** (1992), 21–37].

The encircled triangles at the lower left of Fig. 65 illustrate another key aspect of Llull's approach. Triangle (B, C, D) stands for (difference, concordance, contrariness); triangle (E, F, G) stands for (beginning, middle, ending); and triangle (H, I, K) stands for (greater, equal, less). These three interleaved appearances of K_3 represent three kinds of three-valued logic. Llull had experimented earlier with other such triplets, notably '(true, unknown, false)'. We can get an idea of how he used the triangles by considering how he dealt with combinations of the four basic elements (earth, air, fire, water): All four elements are different; earth is concordant with fire, which concords with air, which concords with water, which concords with earth; earth is contrary to air, and fire is contrary to water; these considerations complete an analysis with respect to triangle (B, C, D). Turning to triangle (E, F, G), he noted that various processes in nature begin with one element dominating another; then a transition or middle state occurs, until a goal is reached, like air becoming warm. For triangle (H, I, K) he said that in general we have fire > air > water > earth with respect to their "spheres," their "velocities," and their "nobilities"; nevertheless we also have, for example, air > fire with respect to supporting life, while air and fire have equal value when they are working together.

Llull provided the vertical table at the right of Fig. 65 as a further aid. (See exercise 11 below.) He also introduced movable concentric wheels, labeled with the letters $(B, C, D, E, F, G, H, I, K)$ and with other names, so that many things could be contemplated simultaneously. In this way a faithful practitioner of the Llullian art could be sure to have all the bases covered. [Llull may have seen similar wheels that were used in nearby Jewish communities; see M. Idel, *J. Warburg and Courtauld Institutes* **51** (1988), 170–174 and plates 16–17.]

Several centuries later, Athanasius Kircher published an extension of Llull's system as part of a large tome entitled *Ars Magna Sciendi sive Combinatoria* (Amsterdam: 1669), with five movable wheels accompanying page 173 of that book. Kircher also extended Llull's repertoire of complete graphs K_n by providing illustrations of complete *bipartite* graphs $K_{m,n}$; for example, Fig. 66 is taken from page 171 of Kircher's book, and his page 170 contains a glorious picture of $K_{18,18}$.

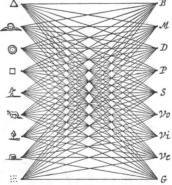

Fig. 66. $K_{9,9}$ as presented by Athanasius Kircher in 1669.

> *It is an investigative and inventive art.*
> *When ideas are combined in all possible ways,*
> *the new combinations start the mind thinking along novel channels*
> *and one is led to discover fresh truths and arguments.*
> — MARTIN GARDNER, *Logic Machines and Diagrams* (1958)

The most extensive modern development of Llull-like methods is perhaps *The Schillinger System of Musical Composition* by Joseph Schillinger (New York:

Carl Fischer, 1946), a remarkable two-volume work that presents theories of rhythm, melody, harmony, counterpoint, composition, orchestration, etc., from a combinatorial perspective. On page 56, for example, Schillinger lists the 24 permutations of $\{a, b, c, d\}$ in the Gray-code order of plain changes (Algorithm 7.2.1.2P); then on page 57 he applies them not to pitches but rather to rhythms, to the durations of notes. On page 364 he exhibits the symmetrical cycle

$$(2, 0, 3, 4, 2, 5, 6, 4, 0, 1, 6, 2, 3, 1, 4, 5, 3, 6, 0, 5, 1), \tag{13}$$

a universal cycle of 2-combinations for the seven objects $\{0, 1, 2, 3, 4, 5, 6\}$; in other words, (13) is an Eulerian trail in K_7: All $\binom{7}{2} = 21$ pairs of digits occur exactly once. Such patterns are grist for a composer's mill. But we can be grateful that Schillinger's better students (like George Gershwin) did not commit themselves entirely to a strictly mathematical sense of aesthetics.

Tacquet, van Schooten, and Izquierdo. Three additional books related to our story were published during the 1650s. André Tacquet wrote a popular text, *Arithmeticæ Theoria et Praxis* (Louvain: 1656), that was reprinted and revised often during the next fifty years. Near the end, on pages 376 and 377, he gave a procedure for listing combinations two at a time, then three at a time, etc.

Frans van Schooten's *Exercitationes Mathematicæ* (Leiden: 1657) was more advanced. On page 373 he listed all combinations in an appealing layout

$$\frac{\begin{array}{c} a \\ \hline b.\ ab \\ \hline c.\ ac.\ bc.\ abc \\ \hline \end{array}}{d.\ ad.\ bd.\ abd.\ cd.\ acd.\ bcd.\ abcd} \tag{14}$$

and he proceeded on the next few pages to extend this pattern to the letters e, f, g, h, i, k, "et sic in infinitum." On page 376 he observed that one can replace (a, b, c, d) by $(2, 3, 5, 7)$ in (14) to get the divisors of 210 that exceed unity:

$$\frac{\begin{array}{c} 2 \\ \hline 3\ \ 6 \\ \hline 5\ \ 10\ \ 15\ \ 30 \\ \hline \end{array}}{7\ \ 14\ \ 21\ \ 42\ \ 35\ \ 70\ \ 105\ \ 210} \tag{15}$$

And on the following page he extended the idea to

$$\frac{\begin{array}{c} a \\ \hline a.\ aa \\ \hline b.\ ab.\ aab \\ \hline \end{array}}{c.\ ac.\ aac.\ bc.\ abc.\ aabc} \tag{16}$$

thereby allowing two a's. He didn't really understand this extension, though; his next example

$$\frac{\begin{array}{c} a \\ \hline a.\ aa \\ \hline a.\ aaa \\ \hline b.\ ab.\ aab.\ aaab \\ \hline \end{array}}{b.\ bb.\ abb.\ aabb.\ aaabb} \tag{17}$$

was botched, indicating the limits of his knowledge at the time. (See exercise 13.)

On page 411 van Schooten observed that the weights $(a, b, c, d) = (1, 2, 4, 8)$ could be assigned in (14), leading to

$$\frac{\dfrac{\dfrac{1}{2 \quad 3}}{4 \quad 5 \quad 6 \quad 7}}{8 \quad 9 \quad 10 \quad 11 \quad 12 \quad 13 \quad 14 \quad 15} \tag{18}$$

after addition. But he didn't see the connection with radix-2 numbers.

Sebastián Izquierdo's two-volume work *Pharus Scientiarum* (Lyon: 1659), "The Lighthouse of Science," included a nicely organized discussion of combinatorics entitled Disputatio 29, *De Combinatione*. He gave a detailed discussion of four key parts of Stanley's Twelvefold Way, namely the n-tuples, n-variations, n-multicombinations, and n-combinations of m objects that appear in the first two rows and the first two columns of Table 7.2.1.4–1.

In Sections 81–84 of *De Combinatione* he listed all combinations of m letters taken n at a time, for $2 \le n \le 5$ and $n \le m \le 9$, always in lexicographic order; he also tabulated them for $m = 10$ and 20 in the cases $n = 2$ and 3. But when he listed the $m^{\underline{n}}$ *variations* of m things taken n at a time, he chose a more complicated ordering (see exercise 14).

Izquierdo was first to discover the formula $\binom{m+n-1}{n}$ for combinations of m things taken n at a time with unlimited repetition; this rule appeared in §48–§51 of his work. But in §105, when he attempted to list all such combinations in the case $n = 3$, he didn't know that there was a simple way to do it. In fact, his listing of the 56 cases for $m = 6$ was rather like the old, awkward ordering of (12).

Combinations with repetition were not well understood until James Bernoulli's *Ars Conjectandi*, "The Art of Guessing," came out in 1713. In Part 2, Chapter 5, Bernoulli simply listed the possibilities in lexicographic order, and showed that the formula $\binom{m+n-1}{n}$ follows by induction as an easy consequence. [Niccolò Tartaglia had, incidentally, come close to discovering this formula in his *General trattato di numeri, et misure* **2** (Venice: 1556), 17^{r} and 69^{v}; so had the Maghrebi mathematician Ibn Mun'im in his 13th-century *Fiqh al-Ḥisāb*.]

The null case. Before we conclude our discussion of early work on combinations, we should not forget a small yet noble step taken by John Wallis on page 110 of his *Discourse of Combinations* (1685), where he specifically considered the combination of m things taken 0 at a time: "It is manifest, That, if we would *take None*, that is, if we would *leave All*; there can be but one case thereof, what ever be the Number of things exposed." Furthermore, on page 113, he knew that $\binom{0}{0} = 1$: "(for, here, to take all, or to leave all, is but one and the same case)."

However, when he gave a table of $n!$ for $n \le 24$, he did not go so far as to point out that $0! = 1$, or that there is exactly one permutation of the empty set.

The work of Nārāyaṇa. A remarkable monograph entitled *Gaṇita Kaumudī* ("Lotus Delight of Calculation"), written by Nārāyaṇa Paṇḍita in 1356, has recently become known in detail to scholars outside of India for the first time, thanks to an English translation by Parmanand Singh [*Gaṇita Bhāratī* **20** (1998), 25–82; **21** (1999), 10–73; **22** (2000), 19–85; **23** (2001), 18–82; **24** (2002), 35–98];

see also the Ph.D. thesis of Takanori Kusuba, Brown University (1993). Chapter 13 of Nārāyaṇa's work, subtitled *Aṅka Pāśa* ("Concatenation of Numbers"), was devoted to combinatorial generation. Indeed, although the 97 "sutras" of this chapter were rather cryptic, they presented a comprehensive theory of the subject that anticipated developments in the rest of the world by several hundred years.

For example, Nārāyaṇa dealt with permutation generation in sutras 49–55a, where he gave algorithms to list all permutations of a set in decreasing colex order, together with algorithms to rank a given permutation and to unrank a given serial number. These algorithms had appeared more than a century earlier in the well-known work *Saṅgītaratnākara* ("Jewel-Mine of Music") by Śārṅgadeva, §1.4.60–71, who thereby had essentially discovered the factorial representation of positive integers. Nārāyaṇa went on in sutras 57–60 to extend Śārṅgadeva's algorithms so that general multisets could readily be permuted; for example, he listed the permutations of $\{1, 1, 2, 4\}$ as

$$1124, 1214, 2114, 1142, 1412, 4112, 1241, 2141, 1421, 4121, 2411, 4211,$$

again in decreasing colex order.

Nārāyaṇa's sutras 88–92 dealt with systematic generation of combinations. Besides illustrating the combinations of $\{1, \ldots, 8\}$ taken 3 at a time, namely

$$(678, 578, 478, \ldots, 134, 124, 123),$$

he also considered a bit-string representation of these combinations in the reverse order (*increasing* colex), extending a 10th-century method of Bhaṭṭotpala:

$$(11100000, 11010000, 10110000, \ldots, 00010011, 00001011, 00000111).$$

He almost, but not quite, discovered Theorem 7.2.1.3L.

Permutable poetry. Let's turn now to a curious question that attracted the attention of several prominent mathematicians in the seventeenth century, because it sheds considerable light on the state of combinatorial knowledge in Europe at that time. A Jesuit priest named Bernard Bauhuis had composed a famous one-line tribute to the Virgin Mary, in Latin hexameter:

Tot tibi sunt dotes, Virgo, quot sidera cælo.   (19)

["Thou hast as many virtues, O Virgin, as there are stars in heaven"; see his *Epigrammatum Libri V* (Cologne: 1615), 49.] His verse inspired Erycius Puteanus, a professor at the University of Louvain, to write a book entitled *Pietatis Thaumata* (Antwerp: 1617), presenting 1022 permutations of Bauhuis's words. For example, Puteanus wrote

... 107	Tot dotes tibi, quot cælo sunt sidera, Virgo.	
... 270	Dotes tot, cælo sunt sidera quot, tibi Virgo.	
... 329	Dotes, cælo sunt quot sidera, Virgo tibi tot.	
... 384	Sidera quot cælo, tot sunt Virgo tibi dotes.	(20)
... 725	Quot cælo sunt sidera, tot Virgo tibi dotes.	
... 949	Sunt dotes Virgo, quot sidera, tot tibi cælo.	
... 1022	Sunt cælo tot Virgo tibi, quot sidera, dotes.	

He stopped at 1022, because 1022 was the number of visible stars in Ptolemy's well-known catalog of the heavens.

The idea of permuting words in this way was well known at the time; such wordplay was what Julius Scaliger had called "Proteus verses" in his *Poetices Libri Septem* (Lyon: 1561), Book 2, Chapter 30. The Latin language lends itself to permutations like (20), because Latin word endings tend to define the function of each noun, making the relative word order much less important to the meaning of a sentence than it is in English. Puteanus did state, however, that he had specifically avoided unsuitable permutations such as

$$\text{Sidera tot cælo, Virgo, quot sunt tibi dotes,} \tag{21}$$

because they would place an *upper* bound on the Virgin's virtues rather than a lower bound. [See pages 12 and 103 of his book.]

Of course there are $8! = 40{,}320$ ways to permute the words of (19). But that wasn't the point; most of those ways don't "scan." Each of Puteanus's 1022 verses obeyed the strict rules of classical *hexameter*, the rules that had been followed by Greek and Latin poets since the days of Homer and Vergil, namely:

i) Each word consists of syllables that are either long ($-$) or short ($\smile$).

ii) The syllables of each line belong to one of 32 patterns,

$$\left\{{-\smile\smile \atop --}\right\}\left\{{-\smile\smile \atop --}\right\}\left\{{-\smile\smile \atop --}\right\}\left\{{-\smile\smile \atop --}\right\} -\smile\smile \left\{{-\smile \atop --}\right\}. \tag{22}$$

In other words there are six metrical feet, where each of the first four is either a dactyl or a spondee in the terminology of (5); the fifth foot should be a dactyl; and the last is either trochee or spondee.

The rules for long versus short syllables in Latin poetry are somewhat tricky in general, but the eight words of Bauhuis's verse can be characterized by the following patterns:

$$\text{tot} = -, \quad \text{tibi} = \left\{{\smile\smile \atop \smile-}\right\}, \quad \text{sunt} = -, \quad \text{dotes} = --,$$

$$\text{Virgo} = \left\{{-\smile \atop --}\right\}, \quad \text{quot} = -, \quad \text{sidera} = -\smile\smile, \quad \text{cælo} = --. \tag{23}$$

Notice that poets had two choices when they used the words 'tibi' or 'Virgo'. Thus, for example, (19) fits the hexameter pattern

$$\begin{array}{cccccc} - \; \smile\smile & - \; - & - \; - & - \; - & - \; \smile\smile & - \; - \\ \text{Tot ti- bi} & \text{sunt do-} & \text{tes, Vir-} & \text{go, quot} & \text{si-de-ra} & \text{cæ-lo.} \end{array} \tag{24}$$

(Dactyl, spondee, spondee, spondee, dactyl, spondee; "dum-diddy dum-dum dum, dum dum, dum dum-diddy dum-dum." The commas represent slight pauses, called "cæsuras," when the words are read; they don't concern us here, although Puteanus inserted them carefully into each of his 1022 permutations.)

A natural question now arises: If we permute Bauhuis's words at random, what are the odds that they scan? In other words, how many of the permutations obey rules (i) and (ii), given the syllable patterns in (23)? G. W. Leibniz raised this question, among others, in his *Dissertatio de Arte Combinatoria* (1666), a work published when he was applying for a position at the University of Leipzig. At this time Leibniz was just 19 years old, largely self-taught, and his understanding of combinatorics was quite limited; for example, he believed that there are 600 permutations of $\{$ut, ut, re, mi, fa, sol$\}$ and 480 of $\{$ut, ut, re, re, mi, fa$\}$, and he even stated that (22) represents 76 possibilities instead of 32. [See §5 and §8 in his Problem 6.]

But Leibniz did realize that it would be worthwhile to develop general methods for counting all permutations that are "useful," in situations when many permutations are "useless." He considered several examples of Proteus verses, enumerating some of the simpler ones correctly but making many errors when the words were complicated. Although he mentioned Puteanus's work, he didn't attempt to enumerate the scannable permutations of (19).

A much more successful approach was introduced a few years later by Jean Prestet in his *Élémens des Mathématiques* (Paris: 1675), 342–438. Prestet gave a clear exposition leading to the conclusion that exactly 2196 permutations of Bauhuis's verse would yield a proper hexameter. However, he soon realized that he had forgotten to count quite a few cases — including those numbered 270, 384, and 725 in (20). So he completely rewrote this material when he published *Nouveaux Élémens des Mathématiques* in 1689. Pages 127–133 of Prestet's new book were devoted to showing that the true number of scannable permutations was 3276, almost 50% larger than his previous total.

Meanwhile John Wallis had treated the problem in his *Discourse of Combinations* (London: 1685), 118–119, published as a supplement to his *Treatise of Algebra*. After explaining why he believed the correct number to be 3096, Wallis admitted that he may have overlooked some possibilities and/or counted some cases more than once; "but I do not, at present, discern either the one and other."

An anonymous reviewer of Wallis's work remarked that the true number of metrically correct permutations was actually 2580 — but he gave no proof [*Acta Eruditorum* **5** (1686), 289]. The reviewer was almost certainly G. W. Leibniz himself, although no clue to the reasoning behind the number 2580 has been found among Leibniz's voluminous unpublished notes.

Finally James Bernoulli entered the picture. In his inaugural lecture as Dean of Philosophy at the University of Basel, 1692, he mentioned the tottibi enumeration problem and stated that a careful analysis is necessary to obtain the correct answer — which, he said, was 3312(!). His proof appeared posthumously in the first edition of his *Ars Conjectandi* (1713), 79–81. [Bernoulli didn't actually intend to publish those pages in this now-famous book; but the proofreader who found them among his notes decided to include the full details, in order "to gratify curiosity." See *Die Werke von Jakob Bernoulli* **3** (Basel: Birkhäuser, 1975), 78, 98–106, 108, 154–155.]

So who was right? Are there 2196 scannable permutations, or 3276, or 3096, or 2580, or 3312? W. A. Whitworth and W. E. Hartley considered the question anew in *The Mathematical Gazette* **2** (1902), 227–228, where they each presented elegant arguments and concluded that the true total was in fact none of the above. Their joint answer, 2880, represented the first time that any two mathematicians had independently come to the same conclusion about this problem.

But exercises 21 and 22, below, reveal the truth: Bernoulli is vindicated, and everybody else was wrong. Moreover, a study of Bernoulli's systematic and carefully indented 3-page derivation indicates that he was successful chiefly because he adhered faithfully to a discipline that we now call the *backtrack method*. We shall study the backtrack method thoroughly in Section 7.2.2, where we will also see that the tot-tibi question is readily solved as a special case of the *exact cover problem*.

> *Even the wisest and most prudent people often suffer from*
> *what Logicians call insufficient enumeration of cases.*
>
> — JAMES BERNOULLI (1692)

Set partitions. The partitions of a set seem to have been studied first in Japan, where a parlor game called *genji-ko* ("Genji incense") became popular among upperclass people about A.D. 1500. The host of a gathering would secretly select five packets of incense, some of which might be identical, and he would burn them one at a time. The guests would try to discern which of the scents were the same and which were different; in other words, they would try to guess which of the $\varpi_5 = 52$ partitions of $\{1, 2, 3, 4, 5\}$ had been chosen by their host.

Fig. 67. Diagrams used to represent set partitions in 16th century Japan. [From a copy in the collection of Tamaki Yano at Saitama University.]

Soon it became customary to represent the 52 possible outcomes by diagrams like those in Fig. 67. For example, the uppermost diagram of that illustration, when read from right to left, would indicate that the first two scents are identical and so are the last three; thus the partition is $12|345$. The other two diagrams, similarly, are pictorial ways to represent the respective partitions $124|35$ and $1|24|35$. As an aid to memory, each of the 52 patterns was named after a chapter of Lady Murasaki's famous 11th-century *Tale of Genji*, according to the following sequence [*Encyclopedia Japonicæ* (Tokyo: Sanseido, 1910), 1299]:

$$\tag{25}$$

(Once again, as we've seen in many other examples, the possibilities were not arranged in any particularly logical order.)

The appealing nature of these genji-ko patterns led many families to adopt them as heraldic crests. For example, the following stylized variants of (25) were found in standard catalogs of kimono patterns early in the 20th century:

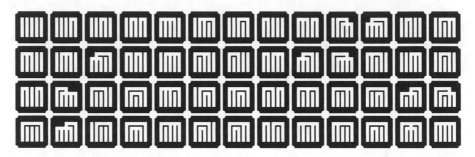

[See Fumie Adachi, *Japanese Design Motifs* (New York: Dover, 1972), 150–153.]

Early in the 1700s, Takakazu Seki and his students began to investigate the number of set partitions ϖ_n for arbitrary n, inspired by the known result that $\varpi_5 = 52$. Yoshisuke Matsunaga found formulas for the number of set partitions when there are k_j subsets of size n_j for $1 \le j \le t$, with $k_1 n_1 + \cdots + k_t n_t = n$ (see the answer to exercise 1.2.5–21). He also discovered the basic recurrence relation 7.2.1.5–(14), namely

$$\varpi_{n+1} = \binom{n}{0}\varpi_n + \binom{n}{1}\varpi_{n-1} + \binom{n}{2}\varpi_{n-2} + \cdots + \binom{n}{n}\varpi_0, \qquad (26)$$

by which the values of ϖ_n can readily be computed.

Matsunaga's discoveries remained unpublished until Yoriyuki Arima's five-volume *Shūki Sanpō* came out in 1769. The problem on pages 32–35 of volume 2 asked the reader to solve the equation "$\varpi_n = 678570$" for n; and Arima's answer, worked out in detail (with credit duly given to Matsunaga), was $n = 11$.

Shortly afterwards, Masanobu Saka studied the number $\left\{{n \atop k}\right\}$ of ways that an n-set can be partitioned into k subsets, in his work *Sanpō-Gakkai* (1782). He discovered the recurrence formula

$$\left\{{n+1 \atop k}\right\} = k\left\{{n \atop k}\right\} + \left\{{n \atop k-1}\right\}, \qquad (27)$$

and tabulated the results for $n \le 11$. James Stirling, in his *Methodus Differentialis* (1730), had discovered the numbers $\left\{{n \atop k}\right\}$ in a purely algebraic context; thus Saka was the first person to realize their combinatorial significance.

An interesting algorithm for listing set partitions was subsequently devised by Toshiaki Honda (see exercise 24). Further details about genji-ko and its relation to the history of mathematics can be found in Japanese articles by Tamaki Yano, *Sugaku Seminar* **34**, 11 (Nov. 1995), 58–61; **34**, 12 (Dec. 1995), 56–60.

Set partitions remained virtually unknown in Europe until much later, except for three isolated incidents. First, George and/or Richard Puttenham published *The Arte of English Poesie* in 1589, and pages 70–72 of that book contain diagrams similar to those of genji-ko. For example, the seven diagrams

$$\equiv \!\!\supset \quad \equiv \!\!\supset \quad \equiv \!\!\supset \quad \equiv \!\!\supset \quad \equiv \!\!\supset \quad \equiv \!\!\supset \quad \equiv \!\!\supset \qquad (28)$$

were used to illustrate possible rhyme schemes for 5-line poems, "whereof some of them be harsher and unpleasaunter to the eare then other some be." But this visually appealing list was incomplete (see exercise 25).

Second, an unpublished manuscript of G. W. Leibniz from the late 1600s shows that he had tried to count the number of ways to partition $\{1, \ldots, n\}$ into three or four subsets, but with almost no success. He enumerated $\left\{\begin{smallmatrix} n \\ 2 \end{smallmatrix}\right\}$ by a very cumbersome method, which would not have led him to see readily that $\left\{\begin{smallmatrix} n \\ 2 \end{smallmatrix}\right\} = 2^{n-1} - 1$. He attempted to compute $\left\{\begin{smallmatrix} n \\ 3 \end{smallmatrix}\right\}$ and $\left\{\begin{smallmatrix} n \\ 4 \end{smallmatrix}\right\}$ only for $n \leq 5$, and made several numerical slips leading to incorrect answers. [See E. Knobloch, *Studia Leibnitiana Supplementa* **11** (1973), 229–233; **16** (1976), 316–321.]

The third European appearance of set partitions had a completely different character. John Wallis devoted the third chapter of his *Discourse of Combinations* (1685) to questions about "aliquot parts," the proper divisors of numbers, and in particular he studied the set of all ways to factorize a given integer. This question is equivalent to the study of *multiset* partitions; for example, the factorizations of $p^3 q^2 r$ are essentially the same as the partitions of $\{p, p, p, q, q, r\}$, when p, q, and r are prime numbers. Wallis devised an excellent algorithm for listing all factorizations of a given integer n, essentially anticipating Algorithm 7.2.1.5M (see exercise 28). But he didn't investigate the important special cases that arise when n is the power of a prime (equivalent to integer partitions) or when n is squarefree (equivalent to set partitions). Thus, although Wallis was able to solve the more general problem, its complexities paradoxically deflected him from discovering partition numbers, Bell numbers, or Stirling subset numbers, or from devising simple algorithms that would generate integer partitions or set partitions.

Integer partitions. Partitions of integers arrived on the scene even more slowly. We saw above that Bishop Wibold (c. 965) knew the partitions of n into exactly three parts ≤ 6. So did Galileo, who wrote a memo about them (c. 1627) and also studied their frequency of occurrence as rolls of three dice. ["Sopra le scoperte de i dadi," in Galileo's *Opere*, Volume 8, 591–594; he listed partitions in decreasing lexicographic order.] Thomas Harriot, in unpublished work a few years earlier, had considered up to six dice [see J. Stedall, *Historia Math.* **34** (2007), 398].

Mersenne listed the partitions of 9 into any number of parts, on page 130 of his *Traitez de la Voix et des Chants* (1636). With each partition $9 = a_1 + \cdots + a_k$ he also computed the multinomial coefficient $9!/(a_1! \ldots a_k!)$; as we've seen earlier, he was interested in counting various melodies, and he knew for example that there are $9!/(3!\,3!\,3!) = 1680$ melodies on the nine notes $\{a, a, a, b, b, b, c, c, c\}$. But he failed to mention the cases $8 + 1$ and $3 + 2 + 1 + 1 + 1 + 1$, probably because he hadn't listed the possibilities in any systematic way.

Leibniz considered two-part partitions in Problem 3 of his *Dissertatio de Arte Combinatoria* (1666), and his unpublished notes show that he subsequently spent considerable time trying to enumerate the partitions that have three or more summands. He called them "discerptions," or (less frequently) "divulsions" — in Latin of course — or sometimes "sections" or "dispersions" or even "partitions." He was interested in them primarily because of their connection with the monomial symmetric functions $\sum x_{i_1}^{a_1} x_{i_2}^{a_2} \ldots$. But his many attempts led to almost total failure, except in the case of three summands, when he almost (but not quite) discovered the formula for $\left|{n \atop 3}\right|$ in exercise 7.2.1.4–31. For example, he carelessly counted only 21 partitions of 8, forgetting the case $2+2+2+1+1$; and he got only 26 for $p(9)$, after missing $3 + 2 + 2 + 2$, $3 + 2 + 2 + 1 + 1$, $2 + 2 + 2 + 1 + 1 + 1$, and $2 + 2 + 1 + 1 + 1 + 1 + 1$ — in spite of the fact that he was trying to list partitions systematically in decreasing lexicographic order. [See E. Knobloch, *Studia Leibnitiana Supplementa* **11** (1973), 91–258; **16** (1976), 255–337; *Historia Mathematica* **1** (1974), 409–430.]

Abraham de Moivre had the first real success with partitions, in his paper "A Method of Raising an infinite Multinomial to any given Power, or Extracting any given Root of the same" [*Philosophical Transactions* **19** (1697), 619–625 and Fig. 5]. He proved that the coefficient of z^{m+n} in $(az + bz^2 + cz^3 + \cdots)^m$ has one term for each partition of n; for example, the coefficient of z^{m+6} is

$$\binom{m}{6} a^{m-6} b^6 + 5\binom{m}{5} a^{m-5} b^4 c + 4\binom{m}{4} a^{m-4} b^3 d + 6\binom{m}{4} a^{m-4} b^2 c^2$$
$$+ 3\binom{m}{3} a^{m-3} b^2 e + 6\binom{m}{3} a^{m-3} bcd + 2\binom{m}{2} a^{m-2} bf + \binom{m}{3} a^{m-3} c^3$$
$$+ 2\binom{m}{2} a^{m-2} ce + \binom{m}{2} a^{m-2} d^2 + \binom{m}{1} a^{m-1} g. \qquad (29)$$

If we set $a = 1$, the term with exponents $b^i c^j d^k e^l \ldots$ corresponds to the partition with i 1s, j 2s, k 3s, l 4s, etc. Thus, for example, when $n = 6$ he essentially presented the partitions in the order

$$111111, \quad 11112, \quad 1113, \quad 1122, \quad 114, \quad 123, \quad 15, \quad 222, \quad 24, \quad 33, \quad 6. \qquad (30)$$

He explained how to list the partitions recursively, as follows (but in different language related to his own notation): For $k = 1, 2, \ldots, n$, start with k and append the (previously listed) partitions of $n - k$ whose smallest part is $\geq k$.

> *[My solution] was ordered to be published in the Transactions,*
> *not so much as a matter relating to Play,*
> *but as containing some general Speculations*
> *not unworthy to be considered by the Lovers of Truth.*
> — ABRAHAM DE MOIVRE (1717)

P. R. de Montmort tabulated all partitions of numbers ≤ 9 into ≤ 6 parts in his *Essay d'Analyse sur les Jeux de Hazard* (1708), in connection with dice problems. His partitions were listed in a different order from (30); for example,

$$111111, \quad 21111, \quad 2211, \quad 222, \quad 3111, \quad 321, \quad 33, \quad 411, \quad 42, \quad 51, \quad 6. \qquad (31)$$

He probably was unaware of de Moivre's prior work.

So far almost none of the authors we've been discussing actually bothered to describe the procedures by which they generated combinatorial patterns. We can only infer their methods, or lack thereof, by studying the lists that they actually published. Furthermore, in rare cases such as de Moivre's paper where a tabulation method *was* explicitly described, the author assumed that all patterns for the first cases 1, 2, ..., $n-1$ had been listed before it was time to tackle the case of order n. No method for generating patterns "on the fly," moving directly from one pattern to its successor without looking at auxiliary tables, was actually explained by any of the authors we have encountered, except for Kedāra and Nārāyaṇa. Today's computer programmers naturally prefer methods that are more direct and need little memory.

Roger Joseph Boscovich published the first direct algorithm for partition generation in *Giornale de' Letterati* (Rome, 1747), on pages 393–404 together with two foldout tables facing page 404. His method, which produces for $n=6$ the respective outputs

$$111111, \quad 11112, \quad 1122, \quad 222, \quad 1113, \quad 123, \quad 33, \quad 114, \quad 24, \quad 15, \quad 6, \qquad (32)$$

generates partitions in precisely the reverse order from which they are visited by Algorithm 7.2.1.4P; and his method would indeed have been featured in Section 7.2.1.4, except for the fact that the reverse order turns out to be slightly easier and faster than the order that he had chosen.

Boscovich published sequels in *Giornale de' Letterati* (Rome, 1748), 12–27 and 84–99, extending his algorithm in two ways. First, he considered generating only partitions whose parts belong to a given set S, so that symbolic multinomials with sparse coefficients could be raised to the mth power. (He said that the gcd of all elements of S should be 1; in fact, however, his method could fail if $1 \notin S$.) Second, he introduced an algorithm for generating partitions of n into m parts, given m and n. Again he was unlucky: A slightly better way to do that task, Algorithm 7.2.1.4H, was found subsequently, diminishing his chances for fame.

Hindenburg's hype. The inventor of Algorithm 7.2.1.4H was Carl Friedrich Hindenburg, who also rediscovered Nārāyaṇa's Algorithm 7.2.1.2L, a winning technique for generating multiset permutations. Unfortunately, these small successes led him to believe that he had made revolutionary advances in mathematics — although he did condescend to remark that other people such as de Moivre, Euler, and Lambert had come close to making similar discoveries.

Hindenburg was a prototypical overachiever, extremely energetic if not inspired. He founded or cofounded Germany's first professional journals of mathematics (published 1786–1789 and 1794–1800), and contributed long articles to each. He served several times as academic dean at the University of Leipzig, where he was also the Rector in 1792. If he had been a better mathematician, German mathematics might well have flourished more in Leipzig than in Berlin or Göttingen.

But his first mathematical work, *Beschreibung einer ganz neuen Art, nach einem bekannten Gesetze fortgehende Zahlen, durch Abzählen oder Abmessen bequem und sicher zu finden* (Leipzig: 1776), amply foreshadowed what was to come: His "ganz neue" (completely new) idea in that booklet was simply to give combinatorial significance to the digits of numbers written in decimal notation. Incredibly, he concluded his monograph with large foldout sheets that contained a table of the numbers 0000 through 9999 — followed by two other tables that listed the even numbers and odd numbers separately(!).

Hindenburg published letters from people who praised his work, and invited them to contribute to his journals. In 1796 he edited *Sammlung combinatorisch-analytischer Abhandlungen*, whose subtitle stated (in German) that de Moivre's multinomial theorem was "the most important proposition in all of mathematical analysis." About a dozen people joined forces to form what became known as Hindenburg's Combinatorial School, and they published thousands of pages filled with esoteric symbolism that must have impressed many nonmathematicians.

The work of this School was not completely trivial from the standpoint of computer science. For example, H. A. Rothe, who was Hindenburg's best student, noticed that there is a simple way to go from a Morse code sequence to its lexicographic successor or predecessor. Another student, J. K. Burckhardt, observed that Morse code sequences of length n could also be generated easily by first considering those with no dashes, then one dash, then two, etc. Their motivation was not to tabulate poetic meters of n beats, as it had been in India, but rather to list the terms of the continuant polynomials $K(x_1, x_2, \ldots, x_n)$, Eq. 4.5.3–(4). [See *Archiv der reinen und angewandten Mathematik* **1** (1794), 154–195.] Furthermore, on page 53 of Hindenburg's 1796 *Sammlung* cited above, G. S. Klügel introduced a way to list all permutations that has subsequently become known as Ord-Smith's algorithm; see Eqs. (23)–(26) in Section 7.2.1.2.

Hindenburg believed that his methods deserved equal time with algebra, geometry, and calculus in the standard curriculum. But he and his disciples were combinatorialists who only made combinatorial lists. Burying themselves in formulas and formalisms, they rarely discovered any new mathematics of real interest. Eugen Netto has admirably summarized their work in M. Cantor's *Geschichte der Mathematik* **4** (1908), 201–219: "For a while they controlled the German market; however, most of what they dug up soon sank into a not-entirely-deserved oblivion."

The sad outcome was that combinatorial studies in general got a bad name. Gösta Mittag-Leffler, who assembled a magnificent library of mathematical literature about 100 years after Hindenburg's death, decided to place all such work on a special shelf marked "Dekadenter." And this category still persists in the library of Sweden's Institut Mittag-Leffler today, even as that institute attracts world-class combinatorial mathematicians whose research is anything but decadent.

Looking on the bright side, we may note that at least one good book did emerge from all of this activity. Andreas von Ettingshausen's *Die combina-torische Analysis* (Vienna: 1826) is noteworthy as the first text to discuss combinatorial generation methods in a perspicuous way. He discussed the general principles of lexicographic generation in §8, and applied them to construct good ways to list all permutations (§11), combinations (§30), and partitions (§41–§44).

Where were the trees? We've now seen that lists of tuples, permutations, combinations, and partitions were compiled rather early in human history, by interested and interesting researchers. Thus we've accounted for the evolution of the topics studied in Sections 7.2.1.1 through 7.2.1.5, and our story will be complete if we can trace the origins of tree generation, Section 7.2.1.6.

But the historical record of that topic before the advent of computers is virtually a blank page, with the exception of a few 19th-century papers by Arthur Cayley. Cayley's major work on trees, originally published in 1875 and reprinted on pages 427–460 of his *Collected Mathematical Papers*, Volume 9, was climaxed by a large foldout illustration that exhibited all the free trees with 9 or fewer unlabeled vertices. Earlier in that paper he had also illustrated the nine *oriented* trees with 5 vertices. The methods he used to produce those lists were quite complicated, completely different from Algorithm 7.2.1.6O and exercise 7.2.1.6–90. All free trees with up to 10 vertices were listed many years later by F. Harary and G. Prins [*Acta Math.* **101** (1958), 158–162], who also went up to $n = 12$ in the cases of free trees with no nodes of degree 2 or with no symmetries.

The trees most dearly beloved by computer scientists — binary trees or the equivalent ordered forests or nested parentheses — are however strangely absent from the literature. We saw in Section 2.3.4.5 that many mathematicians of the 1700s and 1800s had learned how to count binary trees, and we also know that the Catalan numbers C_n enumerate dozens of different kinds of combinatorial objects. Yet nobody seems to have published an actual *list* of the $C_4 = 14$ objects of order 4 in *any* of these guises, much less the $C_5 = 42$ objects of order 5, before 1950. (Except indirectly: The 42 genji-ko diagrams in (25) that have no intersecting lines turn out to be equivalent to the 5-node binary trees and forests. But this fact was not learned until the 20th century.)

There are a few isolated instances where authors of yore did prepare lists of $C_3 = 5$ Catalan-related objects. Cayley, again, was first; he illustrated the binary trees with 3 internal nodes and 4 leaves as follows in *Philosophical Magazine* (4) **18** (1859), 374–378:

$$\tag{33}$$

(That same paper also illustrated another species of tree, equivalent to so-called weak orderings.) Then, in 1901, E. Netto listed the five ways to insert parentheses into the expression '$a + b + c + d$':

$$(a+b)+(c+d), \quad [(a+b)+c]+d, \quad [a+(b+c)]+d, \quad a+[(b+c)+d], \quad a+[b+(c+d)]. \tag{34}$$

[*Lehrbuch der Combinatorik*, §122.] And the five permutations of $\{+1, +1, +1, -1, -1, -1\}$ whose partial sums are nonnegative were listed in the following way by Paul Erdős and Irving Kaplansky [*Scripta Math.* **12** (1946), 73–75]:

$$1+1+1-1-1-1, \quad 1+1-1+1-1-1, \quad 1+1-1-1+1-1,$$
$$1-1+1+1-1-1, \quad 1-1+1-1+1-1. \tag{35}$$

Even though only five objects are involved, we can see that the orderings in (33) and (34) were basically catch-as-catch-can; only (35), which matches Algorithm 7.2.1.6P, was systematic and lexicographic.

We should also note briefly the work of Walther von Dyck, since many recent papers use the term "Dyck words" to refer to strings of nested parentheses. Dyck was an educator known for co-founding the Deutsches Museum in Munich, among other things. He wrote two pioneering papers about the theory of free groups [*Math. Annalen* **20** (1882), 1–44; **22** (1883), 70–108]. Yet the so-called Dyck words have at best a tenuous connection to his actual research: He studied the words on $\{x_1, x_1^{-1}, \ldots, x_k, x_k^{-1}\}$ that reduce to the empty string after repeatedly erasing adjacent letter-pairs of the forms $x_i x_i^{-1}$ or $x_i^{-1} x_i$; the connection with parentheses and trees arises only when we limit erasures to the first case, $x_i x_i^{-1}$.

Thus we may conclude that, although an explosion of interest in binary trees and their cousins occurred after 1950, such trees represent the only aspect of our story whose historical roots are rather shallow.

After 1950. Of course the arrival of electronic computers changed everything. The first computer-oriented publication about combinatorial generation methods was a note by C. B. Tompkins, "Machine attacks on problems whose variables are permutations" [*Proc. Symp. Applied Math.* **6** (1956), 202–205]. Thousands more were destined to follow.

Several articles by D. H. Lehmer, especially his "Teaching combinatorial tricks to a computer" in *Proc. Symp. Applied Math.* **10** (1960), 179–193, proved to be extremely influential in the early days. [See also *Proc. 1957 Canadian Math. Congress* (1959), 160–173; *Proc. IBM Scientific Computing Symposium on Combinatorial Problems* (1964), 23–30; and Chapter 1 of *Applied Combinatorial Mathematics*, edited by E. F. Beckenbach (Wiley, 1964), 5–31.] Lehmer represented an important link to previous generations. For example, Stanford's library records show that he had checked out Netto's *Lehrbuch der Combinatorik* in January of 1932.

The main publications relevant to particular algorithms that we've studied have already been cited in previous sections, so there is no need to repeat them here. But textbooks and monographs that first put pieces of the subject together in a coherent framework were also of great importance. Three books, in particular, were especially noteworthy with respect to establishing general principles:

- *Elements of Combinatorial Computing* by Mark B. Wells (Pergamon Press, 1971), especially Chapter 5.
- *Combinatorial Algorithms* by Albert Nijenhuis and Herbert S. Wilf (Academic Press, 1975). A second edition was published in 1978, containing additional material, and Wilf subsequently wrote *Combinatorial Algorithms: An Update* (Philadelphia: SIAM, 1989).
- *Combinatorial Algorithms: Theory and Practice* by Edward M. Reingold, Jurg Nievergelt, and Narsingh Deo (Prentice–Hall, 1977), especially the material in Chapter 5.

Robert Sedgewick compiled the first extensive survey of permutation generation methods in *Computing Surveys* **9** (1977), 137–164, 314. Carla Savage's survey article about Gray codes in *SIAM Review* **39** (1997), 605–629, was another milestone.

We noted above that algorithms to generate Catalan-counted objects were not invented until computer programmers developed an appetite for them. The first such algorithms to be published were not cited in Section 7.2.1.6 because they have been superseded by better techniques; but it is appropriate to list them here. First, H. I. Scoins gave two recursive algorithms for ordered tree generation, in the same paper we have cited with respect to the generation of *oriented* trees [*Machine Intelligence* **3** (1968), 43–60]. His algorithms dealt with binary trees represented as bit strings that were essentially equivalent to Polish prefix notation or to nested parentheses. Then Mark Wells, in Section 5.5.4 of his book cited above, generated binary trees by representing them as noncrossing set partitions. And Gary Knott [*CACM* **20** (1977), 113–115] gave recursive ranking and unranking algorithms for binary trees, representing them via the inorder-to-preorder permutations $q_1 \ldots q_n$ of Table 7.2.1.6–3.

Algorithms to generate all spanning trees of a given graph have been published by numerous authors ever since the 1950s, motivated originally by the study of electrical networks. Among the earliest such papers were works of N. Nakagawa, *IRE Trans.* **CT-5** (1958), 122–127; W. Mayeda, *IRE Trans.* **CT-6** (1959), 136–137, 394; H. Watanabe, *IRE Trans.* **CT-7** (1960), 296–302; S. Hakimi, *J. Franklin Institute* **272** (1961), 347–359.

A recent introduction to the entire subject can be found in Chapters 2 and 3 of *Combinatorial Algorithms: Generation, Enumeration, and Search* by Donald L. Kreher and Douglas R. Stinson (CRC Press, 1999).

Frank Ruskey is preparing a book entitled *Combinatorial Generation* that will contain a thorough treatment and a comprehensive bibliography. He has made working drafts of several chapters available on the Internet.

EXERCISES

Many of the exercises below ask a modern reader to find and/or to correct errors in the literature of bygone days. The point is not to gloat over how smart we are in the 21st century; the point is rather to understand that even the pioneers of a subject can stumble. One good way to learn that a set of ideas is not really as simple as it might seem to today's computer scientists and mathematicians is to observe that some of the world's leading thinkers had to struggle with the concepts when they were new.

1. [*15*] Does the notion of "computing" arise in the *I Ching*?

▶ **2.** [*M30*] (*The genetic code.*) DNA molecules are strings of "nucleotides" on the 4-letter alphabet $\{T, C, A, G\}$, and most protein molecules are strings of "amino acids" on the 20-letter alphabet $\{A, C, D, E, F, G, H, I, K, L, M, N, P, Q, R, S, T, V, W, Y\}$. Three consecutive nucleotides xyz form a "codon," and a strand $x_1y_1z_1x_2y_2z_2\ldots$ of DNA specifies the protein $f(x_1, y_1, z_1)f(x_2, y_2, z_2)\ldots$, where $f(x, y, z)$ is the element in row z and column y of matrix x in the array

$$\begin{pmatrix} F & S & Y & C \\ F & S & Y & C \\ L & S & - & - \\ L & S & - & W \end{pmatrix} \begin{pmatrix} L & P & H & R \\ L & P & H & R \\ L & P & Q & R \\ L & P & Q & R \end{pmatrix} \begin{pmatrix} I & T & N & S \\ I & T & N & S \\ I & T & K & R \\ M & T & K & R \end{pmatrix} \begin{pmatrix} V & A & D & G \\ V & A & D & G \\ V & A & E & G \\ V & A & E & G \end{pmatrix}.$$

(Here $(T, C, A, G) = (1, 2, 3, 4)$; for example, $f(\text{CAT})$ is the element in row 1 and column 3 of matrix 2, namely H.) Encoding proceeds until a codon leads to the stopper '$-$'.

a) Show that there is a simple way to map each codon into a hexagram of the *I Ching*, with the property that the 21 possible outcomes $\{A, C, D, \ldots, W, Y, -\}$ correspond to 21 *consecutive* hexagrams of the King Wen ordering (1).

b) Is that a sensational discovery?

3. [*20*] What is the millionth meter that has 30 beats, in colex ordering analogous to (2)? What is the rank of ⌣⌣⌣−⌣−−⌣⌣⌣⌣−−⌣⌣⌣⌣⌣⌣−⌣−?

4. [*19*] Analyze the imperfections of Donnolo's list of permutations in Table 1.

5. [*16*] What's wrong with Kircher's list of five-note permutations in (7)?

6. [*25*] Mersenne published a table of the first 64 factorials on pages 108–110 of his *Traitez de la Voix et des Chants* (1636). His value for 64! was $\approx 2.2 \times 10^{89}$; but it should have been $\approx 1.3 \times 10^{89}$. Find a copy of his book and try to figure out where he erred.

7. [*20*] What permutations of $\{1, 2, 3, 4, 5\}$ are "alive" and "dead" according to Seki's rules (8) and (9)?

▶ **8.** [*M27*] Make a patch to (9) so that Seki's procedure will be correct.

9. [*15*] From (11), deduce the Arabic way to write the Arabic numerals $(0, 1, \ldots, 9)$.

▶ **10.** [*HM27*] In Ludus Clericalis, what is the expected number of times the three dice are rolled before all possible virtues are acquired?

11. [*21*] Decipher Llull's vertical table at the right of Fig. 65. What 20 combinatorial objects does it represent? *Hint:* Don't be misled by typographical errors.

12. [*M20*] Relate Schillinger's universal cycle (13) to the universal cycle of Poinsot in exercise 7.2.1.3–106.

13. [*21*] What should van Schooten have written, instead of (17)? Give also the corresponding tableau for combinations of the multiset $\{a, a, a, b, b, c\}$.

▶ **14.** [*20*] Complete the following sequence, from §95 of Izquierdo's *De Combinatione*:

$$\text{ABC ABD ABE ACD ACE ACB ADE ADB ADC AEB \ldots.}$$

15. [*15*] If all n-combinations $x_1 \ldots x_n$ of $\{1, \ldots, m\}$ with repetition are listed in lexicographic order, with $x_1 \le \cdots \le x_n$, how many of them begin with the number j?

16. [*20*] (Nārāyaṇa Paṇḍita, 1356.) Design an algorithm to generate all compositions of n into parts $\le q$, namely all ordered partitions $n = a_1 + \cdots + a_t$, where $1 \le a_j \le q$ for $1 \le j \le t$ and t is arbitrary. Illustrate your method when $n = 7$ and $q = 3$.

17. [*HM27*] Analyze the algorithm of exercise 16.

18. [*10*] Trick question: Leibniz published his *Dissertatio de Arte Combinatoria* in 1666. Why was that a particularly auspicious year, permutationwise?

19. [*17*] In which of Puteanus's verses (20) is 'tibi' treated as ⌣− instead of ⌣⌣?

20. [*M25*] To commemorate the visit of three illustrious noblemen to Dresden in 1617, a poet published 1617 permutations of the hexameter verse

$$\text{Dant tria jam Dresdæ, ceu sol dat, lumina lucem.}$$

"Three give now to Dresden, as the sun gives, lights to light." [Gregor Kleppis, *Proteus Poeticus* (Leipzig: 1617).] How many permutations of those words would actually scan properly? *Hint:* The verse has dactyls in the first and fifth feet, spondees elsewhere.

21. [*HM30*] Let $f(p, q, r; s, t)$ be the number of ways to make (o^p, o^q, o^r) by concatenating the strings $\{s \cdot o, t \cdot oo\}$, when $p + q + r = s + 2t$. For example, $f(2, 3, 2; 3, 2) = 5$ because the five ways are

$$(o|o, o|oo, oo), \quad (o|o, oo|o, oo), \quad (oo, o|o|o, oo), \quad (oo, o|oo, o|o), \quad (oo, oo|o, o|o).$$

a) Show that $f(p, q, r; s, t) = [u^p v^q w^r z^s] \, 1/((1 - zu - u^2)(1 - zv - v^2)(1 - zw - w^2))$.
b) Use the function f to enumerate the scannable permutations of (19), subject to the additional condition that the fifth foot doesn't begin in the middle of a word.
c) Now enumerate the remaining cases.

▶ **22.** [*M40*] Look up the original discussions of the tot-tibi problem that were published by Prestet, Wallis, Whitworth, and Hartley. What errors did they make?

23. [*20*] What order of the 52 genji-ko diagrams corresponds to Algorithm 7.2.1.5H?

▶ **24.** [*23*] Early in the 1800s, Toshiaki Honda gave a recursive rule for generating all partitions of $\{1, \ldots, n\}$. His algorithm produced them in the following order when $n = 4$:

Can you guess the corresponding order for $n = 5$? *Hint:* See (26).

25. [*15*] The 16th-century author of *The Arte of English Poesie* was interested only in rhyme schemes that are "complete" in the sense of exercise 7.2.1.5–35; in other words, every line should rhyme with at least one other. Furthermore, the scheme should be "indecomposable" in the sense of exercise 7.2.1.2–100: A partition like $12|345$ decomposes into a 2-line poem followed by a 3-line poem. And the scheme shouldn't consist trivially of lines that all rhyme with each other. Under these conditions, is (28) a complete list of 5-line rhyme schemes?

▶ **26.** [*HM25*] How many n-line rhyme schemes satisfy the constraints of exercise 25?

▶ **27.** [*HM31*] The set partition $14|25|36$ can be represented by a genji-ko diagram such as ; but every such diagram for this partition must have at least three places where lines cross, and crossings are sometimes considered undesirable. How many partitions of $\{1, \ldots, n\}$ have a genji-ko diagram in which the lines cross at most once?

▶ **28.** [*25*] Let a, b, and c be prime numbers. John Wallis listed all possible factorizations of $a^3 b^2 c$ as follows: $cbbaaa$, $cbbaa \cdot a$, $cbaaa \cdot b$, $bbaaa \cdot c$, $cbba \cdot aa$, $cbba \cdot a \cdot a$, $cbaa \cdot ba$, $cbaa \cdot b \cdot a$, $bbaa \cdot ca$, $bbaa \cdot c \cdot a$, $caaa \cdot bb$, $caaa \cdot b \cdot b$, $baaa \cdot cb$, $baaa \cdot c \cdot b$, $cbb \cdot aaa$, $cbb \cdot aa \cdot a$, $cbb \cdot a \cdot a \cdot a$, $cba \cdot baa$, $cba \cdot ba \cdot a$, $cba \cdot aa \cdot b$, $cba \cdot b \cdot a \cdot a$, $bba \cdot caa$, $bba \cdot ca \cdot a$, $bba \cdot aa \cdot c$, $bba \cdot c \cdot a \cdot a$, $caa \cdot bb \cdot a$, $caa \cdot ba \cdot b$, $caa \cdot b \cdot b \cdot a$, $baa \cdot cb \cdot a$, $baa \cdot ca \cdot b$, $baa \cdot ba \cdot c$, $baa \cdot c \cdot b \cdot a$, $aaa \cdot cb \cdot b$, $aaa \cdot bb \cdot c$, $aaa \cdot c \cdot b \cdot b$, $cb \cdot ba \cdot aa$, $cb \cdot ba \cdot a \cdot a$, $cb \cdot aa \cdot b \cdot a$, $cb \cdot b \cdot a \cdot a \cdot a$, $bb \cdot ca \cdot aa$, $bb \cdot ca \cdot a \cdot a$, $bb \cdot aa \cdot c \cdot a$, $bb \cdot c \cdot a \cdot a \cdot a$, $ca \cdot ba \cdot ba$, $ca \cdot ba \cdot b \cdot a$, $ca \cdot aa \cdot b \cdot b$, $ca \cdot b \cdot b \cdot a \cdot a$, $ba \cdot ba \cdot c \cdot a$, $ba \cdot aa \cdot c \cdot b$, $ba \cdot c \cdot b \cdot a \cdot a$, $aa \cdot c \cdot b \cdot b \cdot a$, $c \cdot b \cdot b \cdot a \cdot a \cdot a$. What algorithm did he use to generate them in this order?

▶ **29.** [*24*] In what order would Wallis have generated all factorizations of the number $abcde = 5 \cdot 7 \cdot 11 \cdot 13 \cdot 17$? Give your answer as a sequence of genji-ko diagrams.

30. [*M20*] What is the coefficient of $a_1^{i_1} a_2^{i_2} \ldots z^{m+n}$ in $(a_0 z + a_1 z^2 + a_2 z^3 + \cdots)^m$? (See (29).)

31. [*20*] Compare de Moivre's and de Montmort's orders for partitions, (30) and (31), with Algorithm 7.2.1.4P.

32. [*21*] (R. J. Boscovich, 1748.) List all partitions of 20 for which all parts are 1, 7, or 10. Also design an algorithm that lists all such partitions of any given integer $n > 0$.

ANSWERS TO EXERCISES

Answer not a fool according to his folly,
lest thou also be like unto him.
— Proverbs 26:4

NOTES ON THE EXERCISES

1. A moderately easy problem for a mathematically inclined reader.

2. The author will reward you if you are first to report an error in the statement of an exercise or in its answer, assuming that he or she is suitably sagacious.

3. See H. Poincaré, *Rendiconti del Circolo Matematico di Palermo* **18** (1904), 45–110; R. H. Bing, *Annals of Math.* (2) **68** (1958), 17–37; G. Perelman, arXiv:math/0211159 [math.DG] (2002), 39 pages; 0303109 and 0307245 [math.DG] (2003), 22+7 pages.

SECTION 7

1. Following the hint, we'll want the second '$4m-4$' to be immediately followed by the first '$2m-1$'. The desired arrangements can be deduced from the first four examples, given in hexadecimal notation: 231213, 46171435623725, 86a31b1368597a425b2479, ca8e531f1358ac7db9e6427f2469bd. [R. O. Davies, *Math. Gazette* **43** (1959), 253–255.]

2. Such arrangements exist if and only if $n \bmod 4 = 0$ or 1. This condition is necessary because there must be an even number of odd items. And it is sufficient because we can place '00' in front of the solutions in the previous exercise.

> *Notes:* This question was first raised by Marshall Hall in 1951, and solved the following year by F. T. Leahy, Jr., in unpublished work [Armed Forces Security Agency report 343 (28 January 1952)]. It was independently posed and resolved by T. Skolem and T. Bang, *Math. Scandinavica* **5** (1957), 57–58. For other intervals of numbers, see the complete solution by J. E. Simpson, *Discrete Math.* **44** (1983), 97–104.

3. Yes. For example, the cycle (0072362435714165) can't be broken up.

4. The kth occurrence of b is in position $\lfloor k\phi \rfloor$ from the left, and the kth occurrence of a is in position $\lfloor k\phi^2 \rfloor$. Clearly $\lfloor k\phi^2 \rfloor - \lfloor k\phi \rfloor = k$, because $\phi^2 = \phi + 1$. (The integers $\lfloor k\phi \rfloor$ form the "spectrum" of ϕ; see exercise 3.13 of *CMath*.)

5. $2n - k - 1$ of the $\binom{2n}{2}$ equally likely pairs of positions satisfy the stated condition. If these probabilities were independent (but they aren't), the value of $2L_n$ would be

$$\binom{2n}{2,2,\ldots,2} \prod_{k=1}^{n} ((2n-1-k)/\binom{2n}{2})) = \frac{(2n)!^2 n(n-1)}{n!(2n)^{n+1}(2n-1)^{n+1}}$$

$$= \exp\left(n \ln \frac{4n}{e^3} + \ln \sqrt{\frac{\pi e n}{2}} + O(n^{-1})\right).$$

514

6. (a) When the products are expanded, we obtain a polynomial of $(2n-2)!/(n-2)!$ terms, each of degree $4n$. There's a term $x_1^2 \ldots x_{2n}^2$ for each Langford pairing; every other term has at least one variable of degree 1. Summing over $x_1, \ldots, x_{2n} \in \{-1, +1\}$ therefore cancels out all the bad terms, but gives 2^{2n} for the good terms. An extra factor of 2 arises because there are $2L_n$ Langford pairings (including left-right reversals).

(b) Let $f_k = \sum_{j=1}^{2n-k-1} x_j x_{j+k+1}$ be the main part of the kth factor. We can run through all 4^n cases $x_1, \ldots, x_{2n} \in \{-1, +1\}$ in Gray-code order (Algorithm 7.2.1.1L), negating only one of the x_j each time. A change in x_j causes at most two adjustments to each f_k; so each Gray-code step costs $O(n)$.

We needn't compute the sum exactly; it suffices to work mod 2^N, where 2^N comfortably exceeds $2^{2n+1} L_n$. Even better, when $n = 24$, would be to do the computations mod $2^{60} - 1$, or mod both $2^{30} - 1$ and $2^{30} + 1$, because $2^{49} \perp 2^{60} - 1$. One can also save $\lceil n/2 \rceil$ bits of precision by exploiting the fact that $f_k \equiv k + 1$ (modulo 2).

(c) The third equality is actually valid only when $n \bmod 4 = 0$ or 3; but those are the interesting n's. The sum can be carried out in n phases, where phase p for $p < n$ involves the cases where $x_{n-1} = x_{n+2}$, $x_{n-2} = x_{n+3}$, $\ldots$, $x_{n-p+1} = x_{n+p}$, $x_{n-p} = x_n = x_{n+1} = +1$, and $x_{n+p+1} = -1$; it has an outer loop that chooses $(x_{n-p+1}, \ldots, x_{n-1})$ in all 2^{p-1} ways, and an inner loop that chooses $(x_1, \ldots, x_{n-p-1}, x_{n+p+2}, \ldots, x_{2n})$ in all $2^{2n-2p-2}$ ways. (The inner loop uses Gray binary code, preferably with "organ-pipe order" to prioritize the subscripts so that x_1 and x_{2n} vary most rapidly. The outer loop need not be especially efficient.) Phase n covers the 2^{n-1} palindromic cases with $x_j = x_{2n+1-j}$ for $1 \le j < n$ and $x_n = x_{n+1} = +1$. If s_p denotes the sum in phase p, then $s_1 + \cdots + s_{n-1} + \frac{1}{2} s_n = 2^{2n-2} L_n$.

A substantial fraction of the terms turn out be zero. For example, when $n = 16$, zeros appear about 76% of the time (in 408,838,754 cases out of $2^{29} + 2^{14}$). This fact can be used to avoid many multiplications in the inner loop. (Only $f_1, f_3, \ldots$ can be zero.)

7. Let d_k be the number of incomplete pairs after k characters have been read; thus $d_0 = d_{2n} = 0$, and $d_k = d_{k-1} \pm 1$ for $1 \le k \le 2n$. The largest such sequence in which d_k never exceeds 6 is $(d_0, d_1, \ldots, d_{2n}) = (0, 1, 2, 3, 4, 5, 6, 5, 6, \ldots, 5, 6, 5, 4, 3, 2, 1, 0)$, which has $\sum_{k=1}^{2n} d_k = 11n - 30$. But $\sum_{k=1}^{2n} d_k = \sum_{k=1}^{n}(k+1) = \binom{n+1}{2} + n$ in any Langford pairing. Hence $\binom{n+1}{2} + n \le 11n - 30$, and $n \le 15$. (In fact, width 6 is also impossible when $n = 15$. The largest and smallest possible width are unknown in general.)

8. There are no solutions when $n = 4$ or $n = 7$. When $n = 8$ there are four:

1317538642572468; 1418634753268257; 4275248635713168; 5286235743681417.

(This problem makes a pleasant mechanical puzzle, using gadgets of width $k + 1$ and height $\lceil k/2 \rceil$ for piece k. In his original note [*Math. Gazette* **42** (1958), 228], C. Dudley Langford illustrated similar pieces, and exhibited a planar solution for $n = 12$. The question can be cast as an exact cover problem, with nonprimary items representing places where two gadgets are not allowed to intersect; see exercise 7.2.2.1–27. Jean Brette has devised a somewhat similar puzzle, based on the problem of exercise 2 and using width instead of planarity; he gave a copy to David Singmaster in 1992.)

9. Just three ways: 18191526728529647538463 9743, 191218246279458634753968357, 19161825726925847635493 8743 (and their reversals). [First found in 1969 by G. Baron; see *Combinatorial Theory and Its Applications* (Budapest: 1970), 81–92. The "dancing links" method of Section 7.2.2.1 resolves this question by traversing a search tree that has only 360 nodes, given an exact cover problem with 132 options.]

10. For example, let $A = 12$, $K = 8$, $Q = 4$, $J = 0$, $\spadesuit = 4$, $\heartsuit = 3$, $\diamondsuit = 2$, $\clubsuit = 1$; add.

[In this connection, orthogonal latin squares equivalent to Fig. 1 were implicitly present already in medieval Islamic talismans illustrated by Ibn al-Hajj in his *Kitab Shumus al-Anwar* (Cairo: 1322); he also gave a 5×5 example. See E. Doutté, *Magie et Religion dans l'Afrique du Nord* (Algiers: 1909), 193–194, 214, 247; W. Ahrens, *Der Islam* **7** (1917), 228–238. See also Lars D. Andersen's excellent history of latin squares in *Combinatorics: Ancient and Modern* (Oxford University Press, 2013), Chapter 11.]

11. $\begin{pmatrix} d\gamma\aleph & a\delta\beth & b\beta\gimel & c\alpha\daleth \\ c\beta\gimel & b\alpha\aleph & a\gamma\daleth & d\delta\beth \\ a\alpha\beth & d\beta\daleth & c\delta\aleph & b\gamma\gimel \\ b\delta\daleth & c\gamma\beth & d\alpha\gimel & a\beta\aleph \end{pmatrix}$.   [Joseph Sauveur presented the earliest known example of such squares in *Mémoires de l'Académie Royale des Sciences* (Paris, 1710), 92–138, §83.]

12. If n is odd, we can let $M_{ij} = (i - j) \bmod n$. But if n is even, there are no transversals: For if $\{(t_0+0) \bmod n, \ldots, (t_{n-1}+n-1) \bmod n\}$ is a transversal, we have $\sum_{k=0}^{n-1} t_k \equiv \sum_{k=0}^{n-1}(t_k + k)$ (modulo n), hence $\sum_{k=0}^{n-1} k = \frac{1}{2}n(n-1)$ is a multiple of n.

13. Replace each element l by $\lfloor l/5 \rfloor$ to get a matrix of 0s and 1s. Let the four quarters be named $\left(\begin{smallmatrix} A & B \\ C & D \end{smallmatrix} \right)$; then A and D each contain exactly k 1s, while B and C each contain exactly k 0s. Suppose the original matrix has ten disjoint transversals. If $k \le 2$, at most four of them go through a 1 in A or D, and at most four go through a 0 in B or C. Thus at least two of them hit only 0s in A and D, only 1s in B and C. But such a transversal has an even number of 0s (not five), because it intersects A and D equally often.

Similarly, a latin square of order $4m + 2$ with an orthogonal mate must have more than m intruders in each of its $(2m + 1) \times (2m + 1)$ submatrices, under all renamings of the elements. [H. B. Mann, *Bull. Amer. Math. Soc.* (2) **50** (1944), 249–257.]

14. Cases (b) and (d) have no mates. Cases (a), (c), and (e) have respectively 2, 6, and 12265168(!), of which the lexicographically first and last are

(a)	(a)	(c)	(c)	(e)	(e)
0456987213	0691534782	0362498571	0986271435	0214365897	0987645321
1305629847	1308257964	1408327695	1354068792	1025973468	1795402638
2043798165	2169340578	2673519408	2741853960	2690587143	2506913874
3289176504	3250879416	3521970846	3572690814	3857694201	3154067289
4518263790	4587902631	4890253167	4630789251	4168730925	4231850967
5167432089	5412763890	5736841920	5218947306	5473829016	5348276190
6894015372	6945081327	6259784013	6095324178	6942158730	6820394715
7920341658	7836425109	7915602384	7869512043	7309216584	7069128543
8731504926	8723196045	8147036259	8407136529	8531402679	8412739056
9672850431	9074618253	9084165732	9123405687	9786041352	9673581402

Notes: Squares (a), (b), (c), and (d) were obtained from the decimal digits of π, e, γ, and ϕ, by discarding each digit that is inconsistent with a completed latin square. Although they aren't truly random, they're probably typical of 10×10 latin squares in general, roughly half of which appear to have orthogonal mates. Parker constructed square (e) in order to obtain an unusually large number of transversals; it has 5504 of them. (Euler had studied a similar example of order 6, therefore "just missing" the discovery of a 10×10 pair.)

15. Parker was dismayed to discover that none of the mates of square 14(e) are orthogonal to each other. With J. W. Brown and A. S. Hedayat [*J. Combinatorics, Inf. and System Sci.* **18** (1993), 113–115], he later found two 10×10s that have four disjoint common transversals (but not ten). [See also B. Ganter, R. Mathon, and A. Rosa,

Congressus Numerantium **20** (1978), 383–398; **22** (1979), 181–204.] While pursuing an idea of L. Weisner [*Canadian Math. Bull.* **6** (1963), 61–63], the author accidentally noticed some squares that come even closer to a mutually orthogonal trio: The square below is orthogonal to its transpose; and it has five diagonally symmetric transversals, in cells $(0, p_0)$, ..., $(9, p_9)$ for $p_0 \ldots p_9 = 0132674598$, 2301457689, 3210896745, 4897065312, and 6528410937, which are *almost* disjoint: They cover 49 cells.

$$L = \begin{pmatrix} 0234567891 \\ 3192708546 \\ 6528139407 \\ 8753241960 \\ 1689473025 \\ 4970852613 \\ 5047986132 \\ 9416320758 \\ 7361095284 \\ 2805614379 \end{pmatrix} \perp \begin{pmatrix} 0368145972 \\ 2157690438 \\ 3925874160 \\ 4283907615 \\ 5712489306 \\ 6034758291 \\ 7891326054 \\ 8549061723 \\ 9406213587 \\ 1670532849 \end{pmatrix} = L^T.$$

Extensive computations by B. D. McKay, A. Meynert, and W. Myrvold [*J. Comb. Designs* **15** (2007), 98–119] prove that no 10×10 latin square with nontrivial symmetry has two mates orthogonal to each other. Three mutually orthogonal latin squares are known to exist for all orders $n > 10$ [see S. M. P. Wang and R. M. Wilson, *Congressus Numerantium* **21** (1978), 688; D. T. Todorov, *Ars Combinatoria* **20** (1985), 45–47].

16. See R. A. Brualdi and H. J. Ryser, *Combinatorial Matrix Theory* (Cambridge University Press, 1991), §8.2.

17. (a) Let there be $3n$ vertices r_j, c_j, v_j for $0 \le j < n$, and n^2 hyperedges; hyperedge (i, j) consists of the three vertices $\{r_i, c_j, v_l\}$, where $l = L_{ij}$, for $0 \le i, j < n$.

(b) Let there be $4n^2$ vertices r_{ij}, c_{ij}, x_{ij}, y_{ij} for $0 \le i, j < n$, and $n^3 - n^2 + n$ hyperedges; hyperedge (i, j, k) consists of the four vertices $\{r_{ik}, c_{jk}, x_{ij}, y_{lk}\}$, where $l = L_{ij}$, for $0 \le i, j, k < n$ and ($i = k$ or $j > 0$).

18. Given an orthogonal array A with rows A_i for $1 \le i \le m$, define latin square $L_i = (L_{ijk})$ for $1 \le i \le m - 2$ by setting $L_{ijk} = A_{iq}$ when $A_{(m-1)q} = j$ and $A_{mq} = k$, for $0 \le j, k < n$. (The value of q is uniquely determined by the values of j and k.) Permuting the columns of the array does not change the corresponding latin squares.

This construction can also be reversed, to produce orthogonal arrays of order n from mutually orthogonal latin squares of order n. In exercise 11, for example, we can let $a = \alpha = \aleph = 0$, $b = \beta = \beth = 1$, $c = \gamma = \gimel = 2$, and $d = \delta = \daleth = 3$, obtaining

$$A = \begin{pmatrix} 3012210303211230 \\ 2310102301323201 \\ 0123103223013210 \\ 0000111122223333 \\ 0123012301230123 \end{pmatrix}.$$

(The concept of an orthogonal array is mathematically "cleaner" than the concept of orthogonal latin squares, because it accounts better for the underlying symmetries. Notice, for example, that an $n \times n$ matrix L with entries in $\{1, 2, \ldots, n\}$ is a latin square if and only if it is orthogonal to two particular non-latin squares, namely

$$L \perp \begin{pmatrix} 1 & 1 & \cdots & 1 \\ 2 & 2 & \cdots & 2 \\ \vdots & \vdots & \ddots & \vdots \\ n & n & \cdots & n \end{pmatrix} \quad \text{and} \quad L \perp \begin{pmatrix} 1 & 2 & \cdots & n \\ 1 & 2 & \cdots & n \\ \vdots & \vdots & \ddots & \vdots \\ 1 & 2 & \cdots & n \end{pmatrix}.$$

Therefore Latin squares, Græco-Latin squares, Hebraic-Græco-Latin squares, etc., are equivalent to orthogonal arrays of depth 3, 4, 5, ... Moreover, the orthogonal arrays considered here are merely the special case $t = 2$ and $\lambda = 1$ of a more general concept of n-ary $m \times \lambda n^t$ arrays having "strength t" and "index λ," introduced by C. R. Rao in *Proc. Edinburgh Math. Soc.* **8** (1949), 119–125; see the book *Orthogonal Arrays* by A. S. Hedayat, N. J. A. Sloane, and J. Stufken (Springer, 1999).)

19. We can rearrange the columns so that the first row is $0^n 1^n \dots (n-1)^n$. Then we can renumber the elements of the other rows so that they begin with $01 \dots (n-1)$. The elements in each remaining column must then be distinct, in all rows but the first.

To achieve the upper bound when $n = p$, let each column be indexed by two numbers x and y, where $0 \le x, y < p$, and put the numbers y, x, $(x + y) \bmod p$, $(x + 2y) \bmod p$, ..., $(x + (p-1)y) \bmod p$ into that column. For example, when $p = 5$ we get the following orthogonal array, equivalent to four mutually orthogonal latin squares:

$$\begin{pmatrix} 0000011111222223333344444 \\ 0123401234012340123401234 \\ 0123412340234013401240123 \\ 0123423401401231234034012 \\ 0123434012123404012323401 \\ 0123440123340122340112340 \end{pmatrix}.$$

[Essentially the same idea works when n is a prime power, using the finite field $\mathrm{GF}(p^e)$; see E. H. Moore, *American Journal of Mathematics* **18** (1896), 264–303, §15(1). These arrays are equivalent to finite *projective planes*; see Marshall Hall, Jr., *Combinatorial Theory* (Blaisdell, 1967), Chapters 12 and 13.]

20. Let $\omega = e^{2\pi i/n}$, and suppose $a_1 \dots a_{n^2}$ and $b_1 \dots b_{n^2}$ are the vectors in different rows. Then $a_1 b_1 + \dots + a_{n^2} b_{n^2} = \sum_{0 \le j,k < n} \omega^{j+k} = 0$ because $\sum_{k=0}^{n-1} \omega^k = 0$.

21. (a) To show that equality-or-parallelism is an equivalence relation, we need to verify the transitive law: If $L \parallel M$ and $M \parallel N$ and $L \ne N$, then we must have $L \parallel N$. Otherwise there would be a point p with $L \cap N = \{p\}$, by (ii); and p would lie on two different lines parallel to M, contradicting (iii).

(b) Let $\{L_1, \dots, L_n\}$ be a class of parallel lines, and assume that M is a line of another class. Then each L_j intersects M in a unique point p_j; and every point of M is encountered in this way, because every point of the geometry lies on exactly one line of each class, by (iii). Thus M contains exactly n points.

(c) We've already observed that every point belongs to m lines when there are m classes. If lines L, M, and N belong to three different classes, then M and N have the same number of points as the number of lines in L's class. So there's a common line size n, and in fact the total number of points is n^2. (Of course n might be infinite.)

22. Given an orthogonal array A of order n and depth m, define a geometric net with n^2 points and m classes of parallel lines by regarding the columns of A as points; line j of class k is the set of columns where symbol j appears in row k of A.

All finite geometric nets with $m \ge 3$ classes arise in this way. But a geometric net with only one class is trivially a partition of the points into disjoint subsets. A geometric net with $m = 2$ classes has nn' points (x, x'), where there are n lines 'x = constant' in one class and n' lines 'x' = constant' in the other. [For further information, see R. H. Bruck, *Canadian J. Math.* **3** (1951), 94–107; *Pacific J. Math.* **13** (1963), 421–457.]

23. (a) If $d(x, y) \le t$ and $d(x', y) \le t$ and $x \ne x'$, then $d(x, x') \le 2t$. Thus a code with distance $> 2t$ between codewords allows the correction of up to t errors — at least in principle, although the computations might be complex. Conversely, if $d(x, x') \leq 2t$ and $x \neq x'$, there's an element y with $d(x, y) \leq t$ and $d(x', y) \leq t$; hence we can't reconstruct x uniquely when y is received.

(b, c) Let $m = r + 2$, and observe that a set of b^2 b-ary m-tuples has Hamming distance $\geq m - 1$ between all pairs of elements if and only if it forms the columns of a b-ary orthogonal array of depth m. [See S. W. Golomb and E. C. Posner, *IEEE Trans.* **IT-10** (1964), 196–208. The literature of coding theory often denotes a code $C(b, n, r)$ of distance d by the symbol $(n + r, b^n, d)_b$. Thus, a b-ary orthogonal array of depth m is essentially an $(m, b^2, m - 1)_b$ code.]

24. (a) Suppose $x_j \neq x'_j$ for $1 \leq j \leq l$ and $x_j = x'_j$ for $l < j \leq N$. We have $x = x'$ if $l = 0$. Otherwise consider the parity bits that correspond to the m lines through point 1. At most $l - 1$ of those bits correspond to lines that touch the points $\{2, \dots, l\}$. Hence x' has at least $m - (l-1)$ parity changes, and $d(x, x') \geq l + (m - (l-1)) = m + 1$.

(b) Let $l_{p1}, \dots, l_{pm}$ be the index numbers of the lines through point p. After receiving a message $y_1 \dots y_{N+R}$, compute x_p for $1 \leq p \leq N$ by taking the majority value of the $m + 1$ "witness bits" $\{y_{p0}, \dots, y_{pm}\}$, where $y_{p0} = y_p$ and

$$y_{pk} = (y_{N+l_{pk}} + \sum\{y_j \mid j \neq p \text{ and point } j \text{ lies on line } l_{pk}\}) \bmod 2, \quad \text{for } 1 \leq k < m.$$

This method works because each received bit y_j affects at most one of the witness bits.

For example, in the 25-point geometry of exercise 19, suppose the parity bit $x_{26+5i+j}$ of each codeword corresponds to line j of row i, for $0 \leq i \leq 5$ and $0 \leq j < 5$; thus $x_{26} = x_1 \oplus x_2 \oplus x_3 \oplus x_4 \oplus x_5$, $x_{27} = x_6 \oplus x_7 \oplus x_8 \oplus x_9 \oplus x_{10}$, ..., $x_{55} = x_5 \oplus x_6 \oplus x_{12} \oplus x_{18} \oplus x_{24}$. Given message $y_1 \dots y_{55}$, we decode bit x_1 (say) by computing the majority of the seven bits y_1, $y_{26} \oplus y_2 \oplus y_3 \oplus y_4 \oplus y_5$, $y_{31} \oplus y_6 \oplus y_{11} \oplus y_{16} \oplus y_{21}$, $y_{36} \oplus y_{10} \oplus y_{14} \oplus y_{18} \oplus y_{22}$, $y_{41} \oplus y_9 \oplus y_{12} \oplus y_{20} \oplus y_{23}$, $y_{46} \oplus y_8 \oplus y_{15} \oplus y_{17} \oplus y_{24}$, $y_{51} \oplus y_7 \oplus y_{13} \oplus y_{19} \oplus y_{25}$. [Section 7.1.2 explains how to calculate majority functions efficiently. Notice that we can eliminate the last 10 bits if we only wish to correct up to two errors, and the last 20 if single-error correction is sufficient. See M. Y. Hsiao, D. C. Bossen, and R. T. Chien, *IBM J. Research and Development* **14** (1970), 390–394.]

25. By considering anagrams of $\{1, e, a, s, t\}$ (see exercise 5–21), we're led to the square

```
stela
telas
elast ,
laste
astel
```

and the cyclic rotations of its rows. Here `telas` are Spanish fabrics; `elast` is a prefix meaning flexible; and `laste` is an imperative Chaucerian verb. (Of course just about every pronounceable combination of five letters has been used to spell or misspell something somewhere, at some point in history.)

26. "`every night, young video buffs catch rerun fever forty years after those great shows first aired.`" [Robert Leighton, *GAMES* **16**, 6 (December 1992), 34, 47.]

27. $(0, 4, 163, 1756, 3834)$ for $k = (1, 2, 3, 4, 5)$; `mamma` and `esses` give a "full house."

28. Yes, 38 pairs altogether. The "most common" solution is `needs` (rank 180) and `offer` (rank 384). Only three cases differ consistently by +1 (`adder beefs`, `sheer tiffs`, `sneer toffs`). Other memorable examples are `ghost hints` and `strut rusts`. One word of the pair ends with the letter s except in four cases, such as `robed spade`. [See Leonard J. Gordon, *Word Ways* **23** (1990), 59–61.]

29. There are 18 palindromes, from `level` (rank 184) to `dewed` (rank 5688). Some of the 34 mirror pairs are 'devil lived', 'knits stink', 'smart trams', 'faced decaf'.

30. Among 105 such words in the SGB, `first`, `below`, `floor`, `begin`, `cells`, `empty`, and `hills` are the most common; `abbey` and `pssst` are lexicographically first and last. (If you don't like `pssst`, the next-to-last is `mossy`.) Only 37 words, from `mecca` to `zoned`, have their letters in *reverse* order; but they are, of course, `wrong` answers.

31. The middle word is the average of the other two, so the extreme words must be congruent mod 2; this observation reduces the number of dictionary lookups by a factor of about 32. There are 119 such triples in `WORDS`(5757), but only two in `WORDS`(2000): `marry, photo, solve`; `risky, tempo, vague`. [*Word Ways* **25** (1992), 13–15.]

32. The only reasonably common example seems to be `peopleless`.

33. `chief`, `fight`, `right`, `which`, `ouija`, `jokes`, `ankle`, `films`, `hymns`, `known`, `crops`, `pique`, `quart`, `first`, `first`, `study`, `mauve`, `vowel`, `waxes`, `proxy`, `crazy`, `pizza`. (The idea is to find the most common word in which x is followed by $(x+1) \bmod 26$, for $x = \texttt{a}$ (0), $x = \texttt{b}$ (1), ..., $x = \texttt{z}$ (25). We also minimize the intervening distance, thus preferring `bacon` to the more common word `black`. In the one case where no such word exists, `crazy` seems most rational. See *OMNI* **16**, 8 (May 1994), 94.)

34. The top two (and total number) in each category are: `pssst` and `pffft` (2), `schwa` and `schmo` (2), `threw` and `throw` (36), `three` and `spree` (5), `which` and `think` (709), `there` and `these` (234), `their` and `great` (291), `whooo` and `wheee` (3), `words` and `first` (628), `large` and `since` (376), `water` and `never` (1313), `value` and `radio` (84), `would` and `could` (460), `house` and `voice` (101), `quiet` and `queen` (25), `queue` only (1), `ahhhh` and `ankhs` (4), `angle` and `extra` (20), `other` and `after` (227), `agree` and `issue` (20), `along` and `using` (124), `above` and `alone` (92), `about` and `again` (58), `adieu` and `aquae` (2), `earth` and `eight` (16), `eagle` and `ounce` (8), `outer` and `eaten` (42), `eerie` and `audio` (4), (0), `ouija` and `aioli` (2), (0), (0); `years` and `every` are the most common of the 868 omitted words. [To fill the three holes, Internet usage suggests `ooops`, `ooooh`, and `ooooo`. See P. M. Cohen, *Word Ways* **10** (1977), 221–223.]

35. Consider the collection `WORDS`(n) for $n = 1, 2, \ldots, 5757$. The illustrated trie, rooted at `s`, first becomes possible when n reaches 978 (the rank of `stalk`). The next root letter to support such a trie is `c`, which acquires enough branching in its descendants when $n = 2503$ (the rank of `craze`). Subsequent breakthroughs occur when $n = 2730$ (`bulks`), 3999 (`ducky`), 4230 (`panty`), 4459 (`minis`), 4709 (`whooo`), 4782 (`lardy`), 4824 (`herem`), 4840 (`firma`), 4924 (`ridgy`), 5343 (`taxol`).

(A breakthrough occurs when a top-level trie acquires Horton–Strahler number 4; see exercise 7.2.1.6–124. Amusing sets of words, suggestive of a new kind of poetry, arise also when the branching is right-to-left instead of left-to-right: `black`, `slack`, `crack`, `track`, `click`, `slick`, `brick`, `trick`, `blank`, `plank`, `crank`, `drank`, `blink`, `clink`, `brink`, `drink`. In fact, right-to-left branching yields a complete *ternary* trie with 81 leaves: `males`, `sales`, `tales`, `files`, `miles`, `piles`, `holes`, ..., `tests`, `costs`, `hosts`, `posts`.)

36. Denoting the elements of the cube by a_{ijk} for $1 \le i, j, k \le 5$, the symmetry condition is $a_{ijk} = a_{ikj} = a_{jik} = a_{jki} = a_{kij} = a_{kji}$. In general an $n \times n \times n$ cube has $3n^2$ words, obtained by fixing two coordinates and letting the third range from 1 to n; but the symmetry condition means that we need only $\binom{n+1}{2}$ words. Hence when $n = 5$ the number of necessary words is reduced from 75 to 15. [Jeff Grant was able to find 75 suitable words in the *Oxford English Dictionary*; see *Word Ways* **11** (1978), 156–157.]

Changing (`stove`, `event`) to (`store`, `erect`) or (`stole`, `elect`) gives two more.

37. The densest part of the graph, which we might call its "bare core," contains the vertices named `bares` and `cores`, which each have degree 25.

38. tears → raise → aisle → smile; the second word might also be reals. [Going from tears to smile as in (11) was one of Lewis Carroll's first five-letter examples. He would have been delighted to learn that the directed rule makes it more difficult to go from smile to tears, because *four* steps are needed in that direction.]

39. Always spanning, never induced.

40. (a) 2^e, (b) 2^n, one for each subset of E or V.

41. (a) $n = 1$ and $n = 2$; P_0 is undefined. (b) $n = 0$ and $n = 3$.

42. G has $65/2$ edges (hence it doesn't exist).

43. Yes: The first three are isomorphic to Fig. 2(e). [The left-hand diagram is, in fact, identical to the earliest known appearance of the Petersen graph in print: See A. B. Kempe, *Philosophical Transactions* **177** (1886), 1–70, especially Fig. 13 in §59.] But the right-hand graph is definitely different; it is planar, Hamiltonian, and has girth 3.

44. Any automorphism must take a corner point into a corner point, because three distinct paths of length 2 can be found only between certain pairs of non-corner points. Therefore the graph has only the eight symmetries of C_4.

45. All edges of this graph connect vertices of the same row or adjacent rows. Therefore we can use the colors 0 and 2 alternately in even-numbered rows, 1 and 3 alternately in odd-numbered rows. The neighbors of NV form a 5-cycle, hence four colors are necessary.

46. (a) Every vertex has degree ≥ 2, and its neighbors have a well-defined cyclic order corresponding to the incoming lines. If $u \,\text{---}\, v$ and $u \,\text{---}\, w$, where v and w are cyclically consecutive neighbors of u, we must have $v \,\text{---}\, w$. Thus all points in the vicinity of any vertex u belong to a unique triangular region.

    (b) The formula holds when $n = 3$. If $n > 3$, shrink any edge to a point; this transformation removes one vertex and three edges. (If $u \,\text{---}\, v$ shrinks, suppose it was part of the triangles $x \,\text{---}\, u \,\text{---}\, v \,\text{---}\, x$ and $y \,\text{---}\, u \,\text{---}\, v \,\text{---}\, y$. We lose vertex v and edges $\{x \,\text{---}\, v, u \,\text{---}\, v, y \,\text{---}\, v\}$; all other edges of the form $w \,\text{---}\, v$ become $w \,\text{---}\, u$.)

47. A planar diagram would divide the plane into regions, with either 4 or 6 vertices in the boundary of each region (because $K_{3,3}$ has no odd cycles). If there are f_4 and f_6 of each kind, we must have $4f_4 + 6f_6 = 18$, since there are 9 edges; hence $(f_4, f_6) = (3, 1)$ or $(0, 3)$. We could also triangulate the graph by adding $f_4 + 3f_6$ more edges; but then it would have at least 15 edges, contradicting exercise 46.

    [W. Blaschke and G. Bol called $K_{3,3}$ "Thomsen's three corners" in *Geometrie der Gewebe* (1938). The fact that it is nonplanar goes back to a puzzle about connecting three houses to three utilities (water, gas, and electricity), without crossing pipes. Its origin is unknown; H. E. Dudeney called it "ancient" in *Strand* **46** (1913), 110.]

48. If u, v, w are vertices and $u \,\text{---}\, v$, we must have $d(w, u) \not\equiv d(w, v)$ (modulo 2); otherwise shortest paths from w to u and from w to v would yield an odd cycle. After w is colored 0, the procedure therefore assigns the color $d(w, v) \bmod 2$ to each new uncolored vertex v that is adjacent to a colored vertex u; and every vertex v with $d(w, v) < \infty$ is colored before a new w is chosen.

49. There are only three: K_4, $K_{3,3}$, and ⬡ (which is $\overline{C}_6$ and $K_2 \mathbin{\square} K_3$).

50. The graph must be connected, because the number of 3-colorings is divisible by 3^r when there are r components. It must also be contained in a complete bipartite graph $K_{m,n}$, which can be 3-colored in $3(2^m + 2^n - 2)$ ways. Deleting edges from $K_{m,n}$ does not decrease the number of colorings; hence $2^m + 2^n - 2 \leq 8$, and we have $\{m, n\} = \{1, 1\}$, $\{1, 2\}$, $\{1, 3\}$, or $\{2, 2\}$. So only the claw $K_{1,3}$ and the path P_4 are possible.

51. A 4-cycle $p_1 - L_1 - p_2 - L_2 - p_1$ would correspond to two distinct lines $\{L_1, L_2\}$ with two common points $\{p_1, p_2\}$, contradicting (ii). So the girth is at least 6.

If there's only one class of parallel lines, the girth is ∞; if there are two classes, with $n \leq n'$ members, it is 8, or ∞ if $n = 1$. (See answer 22.) Otherwise we can find a 6-cycle by making a triangle from three lines that are chosen from different classes.

52. If the diameter is d and the girth is g, then $d \geq \lfloor g/2 \rfloor$, unless $g = \infty$.

53. `happy` (which is connected to `tears` and `sweat`, but not to `world`).

54. (a) It's a single, highly connected component. (Incidentally, this graph is the *line graph* of the bipartite graph in which one part corresponds to the initial letters $\{\mathtt{A}, \mathtt{C}, \mathtt{D}, \mathtt{F}, \mathtt{G}, \ldots, \mathtt{W}\}$ and the other to the final letters $\{\mathtt{A}, \mathtt{C}, \mathtt{D}, \mathtt{E}, \mathtt{H}, \ldots, \mathtt{Z}\}$.)

(b) Vertex `WY` is isolated. The other vertices with in-degree zero, namely `FL`, `GA`, `PA`, `UT`, `WA`, `WI`, and `WV`, form strong components by themselves; they all precede a giant strong component, which is followed by each of the remaining single-vertex strong components with out-degree zero: `AZ`, `DE`, `KY`, `ME`, `NE`, `NH`, `NJ`, `NY`, `OH`, `TX`.

(c) Now the strong component $\{\mathtt{GU}\}$ precedes $\{\mathtt{UT}\}$; `NH`, `OH`, `PA`, `WA`, `WI`, and `WV` join the giant strong component; $\{\mathtt{FM}\}$ precedes it; $\{\mathtt{AE}\}$ and $\{\mathtt{WY}\}$ follow it.

[This digraph was first considered by Darryl Francis and Philip Cohen in *Word Ways* **9** (1976), 241; **10** (1977), 46–47.]

55. $\binom{N}{2} - \binom{n_1}{2} - \cdots - \binom{n_k}{2}$, or $(N^2 - n_1^2 - \cdots - n_k^2)/2$, where $N = n_1 + \cdots + n_k$.

56. True. Note that J_n is simple, but it doesn't correspond to any multigraph.

57. False, in the connected digraph $u \longrightarrow w \longleftarrow v$. (But u and v are in the same *strongly connected* component if and only if $d(u, v) < \infty$ and $d(v, u) < \infty$; see Section 2.3.4.2.)

58. Each component is a cycle whose order is at least (a) 3 (b) 1.

59. (a) By induction on n, we can use straight insertion sorting: Suppose $v_1 \longrightarrow \cdots \longrightarrow v_{n-1}$. Then either $v_n \longrightarrow v_1$ or $v_{n-1} \longrightarrow v_n$ or $v_{k-1} \longrightarrow v_n \longrightarrow v_k$, where k is minimum such that $v_n \longrightarrow v_k$. [L. Rédei, *Acta litterarum ac scientiarum* **7** (Szeged, 1934), 39–43.]

(b) 15: 01234, 02341, 02413, and their cyclic shifts. [The number of such oriented paths is always odd; see T. Szele, *Matematikai és Fizikai Lapok* **50** (1943), 223–256.]

(c) Yes. (By induction: If there's only one place to insert v_n as in part (a), the tournament is transitive.)

60. Let $A = \{x \mid u \longrightarrow x\}$, $B = \{x \mid x \longrightarrow v\}$, $C = \{x \mid v \longrightarrow x\}$. If $v \notin A$ and $A \cap B = \emptyset$ we have $|A| + |B| = |A \cup B| \leq n - 2$, because $u \notin A \cup B$ and $v \notin A \cup B$. But $|B| + |C| = n - 1$; hence $|A| < |C|$. [H. G. Landau, *Bull. Math. Biophysics* **15** (1953), 148.]

61. $1 \longrightarrow 1$, $1 \longrightarrow 2$, $2 \longrightarrow 2$; then $A = \begin{pmatrix} 1 & 1 \\ 0 & 1 \end{pmatrix}$ and $A^k = \begin{pmatrix} 1 & k \\ 0 & 1 \end{pmatrix}$ for all integers k.

62. (a) Suppose the vertices are $\{1, \ldots, n\}$. Each of the $n!$ terms $a_{1p_1} \ldots a_{np_n}$ in the expansion of the permanent is the number of spanning permutation digraphs that have arcs $j \longrightarrow p_j$. (b) A similar argument shows that $\det A$ is the number of even spanning permutation digraphs minus the number of odd ones. [See F. Harary, *SIAM Review* **4** (1962), 202–210, where permutation digraphs are called "linear subgraphs."]

63. Let v be any vertex. If $g = 2t+1$, at least $d(d-1)^{k-1}$ vertices x satisfy $d(v, x) = k$, for $1 \leq k \leq t$. If $g = 2t + 2$ and v' is any neighbor of v, there also are at least $(d-1)^t$ vertices x for which $d(v, x) = t + 1$ and $d(v', x) = t$.

64. To achieve the lower bound in answer 63, *every* vertex v must have degree d, and the d neighbors of v must all be adjacent to the remaining $d - 1$ vertices. This graph is, in fact, $K_{d,d}$.

65. (a) By answer 63, G must be regular of degree d, and there must be exactly one path of length ≤ 2 between any two distinct vertices.

(b) We may take $\lambda_1 = d$, with $x_1 = (1 \ldots 1)^T$. All other eigenvectors satisfy $Jx_j = (0 \ldots 0)^T$; hence $\lambda_j^2 + \lambda_j = d - 1$ for $1 < j \leq N$.

(c) If $\lambda_2 = \cdots = \lambda_m = (-1 + \sqrt{4d-3})/2$ and $\lambda_{m+1} = \cdots = \lambda_N = (-1 - \sqrt{4d-3})/2$, we must have $m - 1 = N - m$. With this value we find $\lambda_1 + \cdots + \lambda_N = d - d^2/2$.

(d) If $4d - 3 = s^2$ and m is as in (c), the eigenvalues sum to

$$\frac{s^2 + 3}{4} + (m - 1)\frac{s - 1}{2} - \left(\frac{(s^2 + 3)^2}{16} + 1 - m\right)\frac{s + 1}{2},$$

which is $15/32$ plus a multiple of s. Hence s must be a divisor of 15.

[These results are due to A. J. Hoffman and R. R. Singleton, *IBM J. Research and Development* **4** (1960), 497–504, who also proved that the graph for $d = 7$ is unique.]

66. Denote the 50 vertices by $[a, b]$ and (a, b) for $0 \leq a, b < 5$, and define three kinds of edges, using arithmetic mod 5:

$$[a, b] \text{---} [a + 1, b]; \qquad (a, b) \text{---} (a + 2, b); \qquad (a, b) \text{---} [a + bc, c] \quad \text{for } 0 \leq a, b, c < 5.$$

[See W. G. Brown, *Canadian J. Math.* **19** (1967), 644–648; *J. London Math. Soc.* (2) **42** (1967), 514–520. Without the edges of the first two kinds, the graph has girth 6 and corresponds to a geometric net as in exercise 51, using the orthogonal array in answer 19.]

67. Certain possibilities have been ruled out by Michael Aschbacher in *Journal of Algebra* **19** (1971), 538–540.

68. If G has s automorphisms, it has $n!/s$ adjacency matrices, because there are s permutation matrices P such that $P^-AP = A$.

69. First set `IDEG`$(v) \leftarrow 0$ for all vertices v. Then perform (31) for all v, also setting $u \leftarrow$ `TIP`(a) and `IDEG`$(u) \leftarrow$ `IDEG`$(u) + 1$ in the second line of that mini-algorithm.

To do something "for all v" using the SGB format, first set $v \leftarrow$ `VERTICES`(g); then while $v <$ `VERTICES`$(g) +$ `N`(g), do the operation and set $v \leftarrow v + 1$.

70. Step B1 is performed once (but it takes $O(n)$ units of time). Steps (B2, B3, $\ldots$, B8) are performed respectively $(n + 1, n, n, m + n, m, m, n)$ times, each with $O(1)$ cost.

71. Many choices are possible. Here we use 32-bit pointers, all relative to a symbolic address `Pool`, which lies in the `Data_Segment`. The following declarations provide one way to establish conventions for dealing with basic SGB data structures.

```
VSIZE IS 32 ;ASIZE IS 20            Node sizes in bytes
ARCS IS 0 ;COLOR IS 8 ;LINK IS 12   Offsets of vertex fields
TIP IS 0 ;NEXT IS 4                 Offsets of arc fields

arcs GREG Pool+ARCS ;color GREG Pool+COLOR ;link GREG Pool+LINK
tip GREG Pool+TIP ;next GREG Pool+NEXT
u GREG ;v GREG ;w GREG ;s GREG ;a GREG ;mone GREG -1
```

```
AlgB    BZ      n,Success           Exit if the graph is null.
        MUL     $0,n,VSIZE          B1. Initialize.
        ADDU    v,v0,$0             v ← v0 + n.
        SET     w,v0                w ← v0.
1H      STT     mone,color,w        COLOR(w) ← −1.
        ADDU    w,w,VSIZE           w ← w + 1.
        CMP     $0,w,v
        PBNZ    $0,1B               Repeat until w = v.
```

	OH	SUBU	w,w,VSIZE	$w \leftarrow w - 1$.
	3H	LDT	$0,color,w	B3. *Color w if necessary.*
		PBNN	$0,2F	To B2 if COLOR(w) ≥ 0.
		STCO	0,link,w	COLOR(w) $\leftarrow 0$, LINK(w) $\leftarrow \Lambda$.
		SET	s,w	$s \leftarrow w$.
	4H	SET	u,s	B4. *Stack $\Rightarrow u$.* Set $u \leftarrow s$.
		LDTU	s,link,s	$s \leftarrow$ LINK(s).
		LDT	$1,color,u	
		NEG	$1,1,$1	$\$1 \leftarrow 1 -$ COLOR(u).
		LDTU	a,arcs,u	$a \leftarrow$ ARCS(u).
	5H	BZ	a,8F	B5. *Done with u?* To B8 if $a = \Lambda$.
	5H	LDTU	v,tip,a	$v \leftarrow$ TIP(a).
	6H	LDT	$0,color,v	B6. *Process v.*
		CMP	$2,$0,$1	(Here the program is slightly clever)
		PBZ	$2,7F	To B7 if COLOR(v) $= 1 -$ COLOR(u).
		BNN	$0,Failure	Fail if COLOR(v) $=$ COLOR(u).
		STT	$1,color,v	COLOR(v) $\leftarrow 1 -$ COLOR(u).
		STTU	s,link,v	LINK(v) $\leftarrow s$.
		SET	s,v	$s \leftarrow v$.
	7H	LDTU	a,next,a	B7. *Loop on a.* Set $a \leftarrow$ NEXT(a).
		PBNZ	a,5B	To B5 if $a \neq \Lambda$.
	8H	PBNZ	s,4B	B8. *Stack nonempty?* To B4 if $s \neq \Lambda$.
	2H	CMP	$0,w,v0	B2. *Done?*
		PBNZ	$0,0B	If $w \neq v_0$, decrease w and go to B3.
	Success LOC	@		(Successful termination) ▮

72. (a) This condition clearly remains invariant as vertices enter or leave the stack.

(b) Vertex v has been colored but not yet explored, because the neighbors of every explored vertex have the proper color.

(c) Just before setting $s \leftarrow v$ in step B6, set PARENT(v) $\leftarrow u$, where PARENT is a new utility field. And just before terminating unsuccessfully in that step, do the following: "Repeatedly output NAME(u) and set $u \leftarrow$ PARENT(u), until $u =$ PARENT(v); then output NAME(u) and NAME(v)."

73. K_{10}. (And *random_graph*$(10, 100, 0, 1, 1, 0, 0, 0, 0, 0)$ is J_{10}.)

74. badness has out-degree 22; no other vertices have out-degree > 20.

75. Let the parameters $(n_1, n_2, n_3, n_4, p, w, o)$ be respectively (a) $(n, 0, 0, 0, -1, 0, 0)$; (b) $(n, 0, 0, 0, 1, 0, 0)$; (c) $(n, 0, 0, 0, 1, 1, 0)$; (d) $(n, 0, 0, 0, -1, 0, 1)$; (e) $(n, 0, 0, 0, 1, 0, 1)$; (f) $(n, 0, 0, 0, 1, 1, 1)$; (g) $(m, n, 0, 0, 1, 0, 0)$; (h) $(m, n, 0, 0, 1, 2, 0)$; (i) $(m, n, 0, 0, 1, 3, 0)$; (j) $(m, n, 0, 0, -1, 0, 0)$; (k) $(m, n, 0, 0, 1, 3, 1)$; (l) $(n, 0, 0, 0, 2, 0, 0)$; (m) $(2, -n, 0, 0, 1, 0, 0)$.

76. Yes, for example from C_1 and C_2 in answer 75(c). (But no self-loops can occur when $p < 0$, because arcs $x \longrightarrow y = x + k\delta$ are generated for $k = 1, 2, \ldots$ until y is out of range or $y = x$.)

77. Suppose x and y are vertices with $d(x, y) > 2$. Thus $x \not\!\!- y$; and if v is any other vertex we must have either $v \not\!\!- x$ or $v \not\!\!- y$. These facts yield a path of length at most 3 in $\overline{G}$ between any two vertices u and v.

78. (a) The number of edges, $\binom{n}{2}/2$, must be an integer. The smallest examples are K_0, K_1, P_4, C_5, and ⥾ (called the "bull").

(b) If q is any odd number, we have $u \!-\! v$ if and only if $\varphi^q(u) \not\!-\! \varphi^q(v)$. Therefore φ^q cannot have two fixed points, nor can it contain a 2-cycle.

(c) Such a permutation of V also defines a permutation $\widehat{\varphi}$ of the edges of K_n, taking $\{u,v\} \mapsto \widehat{\varphi}(\{u,v\}) = \{\varphi(u), \varphi(v)\}$, and it's easy to see that the cycle lengths of $\widehat{\varphi}$ are all even. If $\widehat{\varphi}$ has t cycles, we obtain 2^t self-complementary graphs by painting the edges of each cycle with alternating colors.

(d) In this case φ has a unique fixed point v, and $G' = G \setminus v$ is self-complementary. Suppose φ has r cycles in addition to (v); then $\widehat{\varphi}$ has r cycles involving the edges that touch vertex v, and there are 2^r ways to extend G' to a graph G.

[*References:* H. Sachs, *Publicationes Mathematicæ* **9** (Debrecen, 1962), 270–288; G. Ringel, *Archiv der Mathematik* **14** (1963), 354–358.]

79. Solution 1, by H. Sachs, with $\varphi = (1\,2\,\ldots\,4k)$: Let $u \!-\! v$ when $u > v > 0$ and $u + v \bmod 4 \le 1$; also $0 \!-\! v$ when $v \bmod 2 = 0$.

Solution 2, with $\varphi = (a_1\,b_1\,c_1\,d_1)\ldots(a_k\,b_k\,c_k\,d_k)$, where $a_j = 4j - 3$, $b_j = 4j - 2$, $c_j = 4j - 1$, and $d_j = 4j$: Let $0 \!-\! b_j \!-\! a_j \!-\! c_j \!-\! d_j \!-\! 0$ for $1 \le j \le k$, and $a_i \!-\! a_j \!-\! b_i \!-\! d_j \!-\! c_i \!-\! c_j \!-\! d_i \!-\! b_j \!-\! a_i$, for $1 \le i < j \le k$.

80. (Solution by G. Ringel.) Let φ be as in answer 79, solution 2. Let E_0 be the $3k$ edges $b_j \!-\! a_j \!-\! c_j \!-\! d_j$ for $1 \le j \le k$; let E_1 be the $8\binom{k}{2}$ edges between $\{a_i, b_i, c_i, d_i\}$ and $\{b_j, d_j\}$ for $1 \le i < j \le k$; let E_2 be the $8\binom{k}{2}$ edges between $\{a_i, b_i, c_i, d_i\}$ and $\{a_j, c_j\}$ for $1 \le i < j \le k$. In case (a), $E_0 \cup E_1$ gives diameter 2; $E_0 \cup E_2$ gives diameter 3. Case (b) is similar, but we add $2k$ edges $b_j \!-\! 0 \!-\! d_j$ to E_1, $a_j \!-\! 0 \!-\! c_j$ to E_2.

81. $\vec{C_3}$, $\vec{K_3}$, $D = \circ\!\!-\!\!\!\!\curvearrowright\!\!\!\curvearrowright\!\!\!\circ$, and $D^T = \circ\!\!\!\curvearrowleft\!\!\!-\!\!\!\curvearrowleft\!\!\!\circ$. (The *converse* D^T of a digraph D is obtained by reversing the direction of its arcs. There are 16 nonisomorphic simple digraphs of order 3 without loops, 10 of which are self-converse, including $\vec{C_3}$ and $\vec{K_3}$.)

82. (a) True, by definition. (b) True: If every vertex has d neighbors, every edge $u \!-\! v$ has $d - 1$ neighbors $u \!-\! w$ and $d - 1$ neighbors $w \!-\! v$. (c) True: $\{a_i, b_j\}$ has $m + n - 2$ neighbors, for $0 \le i < m$ and $0 \le j < n$. (d) False: $L(K_{1,1,2})$ has 5 vertices and 8 edges. (e) True. (f) True: The only nonadjacent edges are $\{0,1\} \not\!-\! \{2,3\}$, $\{0,2\} \not\!-\! \{1,3\}$, $\{0,3\} \not\!-\! \{1,2\}$. (g) True, for all $n > 0$. (h) False, unless G has no isolated vertices.

83. It is the Petersen graph. [A. Kowalewski, *Sitzungsberichte der Akademie der Wissenschaften in Wien*, Mathematisch-Nat. Klasse, Abteilung IIa, **126** (1917), 67–90.]

84. Yes: Let $\varphi(\{a_u, b_v\}) = \{a_{(u+v) \bmod 3}, b_{(u-v) \bmod 3}\}$ for $0 \le u, v < 3$.

85. Let the vertex degrees be $\{d_1, \ldots, d_n\}$. Then G has $\frac{1}{2}(d_1 + \cdots + d_n)$ edges, and $L(G)$ has $\frac{1}{2}(d_1(d_1 - 1) + \cdots + d_n(d_n - 1))$. Thus G and $L(G)$ both have exactly n edges if and only if $(d_1 - 2)^2 + \cdots + (d_n - 2)^2 = 0$. Consequently exercise 58 gives the answer. [See V. V. Menon, *Canadian Math. Bull.* **8** (1965), 7–15.]

86. If $G = \scriptsize\bigwedge$ then $\overline{G} = \scriptsize\triangle = L(G)$.

87. (a) Yes, easily. [In fact, R. L. Brooks has proved that *every* connected graph with maximum vertex degree $d > 2$ is d-colorable, except for the complete graph K_{d+1}; see *Proc. Cambridge Phil. Soc.* **37** (1941), 194–197.]

(b) No. There's essentially only one way to 3-color the edges of the outer 5-cycle in Fig. 2(e); this forces a conflict on the inner 5-cycle. [Petersen proved this in 1898.]

88. One cycle that doesn't use the center vertex, plus $n(n-1)$ cycles that do (namely, one for every ordered pair of distinct vertices on the rim). Just $n + 1$ are induced.

89. Both sides equal $\begin{pmatrix} A & O & O \\ O & B & O \\ O & O & C \end{pmatrix}$, $\begin{pmatrix} A & J & J \\ J & B & J \\ J & J & C \end{pmatrix}$, $\begin{pmatrix} A & J & J \\ O & B & J \\ O & O & C \end{pmatrix}$, $\begin{pmatrix} A & O & O \\ J & B & O \\ J & J & C \end{pmatrix}$, respectively.

90. K_4 and $\overline{K_4}$; $K_{1,1,2}$ and $\overline{K_{1,1,2}}$; $K_{2,2} = C_4$ and $\overline{K_{2,2}}$; $K_{1,3}$ and $\overline{K_{1,3}}$; $K_1 \oplus K_{1,2}$ and its complement; all graphs K_α are cographs by (39). Missing is $P_4 = \overline{P_4}$. (All connected subgraphs of a cograph have diameter ≤ 2; W_4 is a cograph, but not W_5.)

91. (a) ⬜; (b) ✕; (c) ⊠; (d) ⬜; (e) ⊠; (f) ⎸⎸; (g) ✕.   (In general we have $K_2 \triangle H = (K_2 \square H) \cup (K_2 \otimes \overline{H})$, and $K_2 \circ H = H \relbar H$. Thus the coincidences $K_2 \triangle H = K_2 \square H$ and $K_2 \circ H = K_2 \boxtimes H$ occur if and only if H is a complete graph.)

Mnemonics: Our notations $G \square H$ and $G \boxtimes H$ nicely match diagrams (a) and (c), as suggested by J. Nešetřil, *Lecture Notes in Comp. Sci.* **118** (1981), 94–102. His analogous recommendation to write $G \times H$ for (b) is also tempting; but it wasn't adopted here, because hundreds of authors have used $G \times H$ to denote $G \square H$.

92. (a) ⬚; (b) ⟋; (c) ◩; (d) ⬙; (e) ⊠.

93. $K_m \boxtimes K_n = K_m \circ K_n \cong K_{mn}$.

94. No; they're induced subgraphs of $K_{26} \square K_{26} \square K_{26} \square K_{26} \square K_{26}$.

95. (a) $d_u + d_v$. (b) $d_u d_v$. (c) $d_u d_v + d_u + d_v$. (d) $d_u(n - d_v) + (m - d_u)d_v$. (e) $d_u n + d_v$.

96. (a) $A \square B = A \otimes I + I \otimes B$. (b) $A \boxtimes B = A \square B + A \otimes B$. (c) $A \triangle B = A \otimes J + J \otimes B - 2A \otimes B$. (d) $A \circ B = A \otimes J + I \otimes B$. (Formulas (a), (b), and (d) define graph products of arbitrary digraphs and multigraphs. Formula (c) is valid in general for simple digraphs; but negative entries can occur when A and B contain values > 1.)

Historical notes: The direct product of matrices is often called the Kronecker product, because K. Hensel [*Crelle* **105** (1889), 329–344] said he had heard it in Kronecker's lectures; however, Kronecker never actually published anything about it. Its first known appearance was in a paper by J. G. Zehfuss [*Zeitschrift für Math. und Physik* **3** (1858), 298–301], who proved that $\det(A \otimes B) = (\det A)^n (\det B)^m$ when $m = m'$ and $n = n'$. The basic formulas $(A \otimes B)^T = A^T \otimes B^T$, $(A \otimes B)(A' \otimes B') = AA' \otimes BB'$, and $(A \otimes B)^{-1} = A^{-1} \otimes B^{-1}$ are due to A. Hurwitz [*Math. Annalen* **45** (1894), 381–404].

97. Operations on adjacency matrices prove that $(G \oplus G') \square H = (G \square H) \oplus (G' \square H)$; $(G \oplus G') \boxtimes H = (G \boxtimes H) \oplus (G' \boxtimes H)$; $(G \oplus G') \circ H = (G \circ H) \oplus (G' \circ H)$. Since $G \square H \cong H \square G$, $G \otimes H \cong H \otimes G$, and $G \boxtimes H \cong H \boxtimes G$, we also have right-distributive laws $G \square (H \oplus H') \cong (G \square H) \oplus (G \square H')$; $G \otimes (H \oplus H') \cong (G \otimes H) \oplus (G \otimes H')$; $G \boxtimes (H \oplus H') \cong (G \boxtimes H) \oplus (G \boxtimes H')$. The lexicographic product satisfies $\overline{G \circ H} = \overline{G} \circ \overline{H}$; also $K_m \circ H = H \relbar \cdots \relbar H$, hence $K_m \circ \overline{K_n} = K_{n,\dots,n}$. Furthermore $G \circ K_n = G \boxtimes K_n$; $K_m \square K_n = \overline{K_m} \otimes \overline{K_n} = L(K_{m,n})$.

98. There are kl components (because of the distributive laws in the previous exercise, and the facts that $G \square H$ and $G \boxtimes H$ are connected when G and H are connected).

99. Every path from (u, v) to (u', v') in $G \square H$ must use at least $d_G(u, u')$ "G-steps" and at least $d_H(v, v')$ "H-steps"; and that minimum is achievable. Similar reasoning shows that $d_{G \boxtimes H}((u, v), (u', v')) = \max(d_G(u, u'), d_H(v, v'))$.

100. If G and H are connected, and if each of them has at least two vertices, $G \otimes H$ is disconnected if and only if G and H are bipartite. The "if" part is easy; conversely, if there's an odd cycle in G, we can get from (u, v) to (u', v') as follows: First go to (u'', v'), where u'' is any vertex of G that happens to be expedient. Then walk an even number of steps in G from u'' to u', while alternating in H between v' and one of its neighbors. [P. M. Weichsel, *Proc. Amer. Math. Soc.* **13** (1962), 47–52.]

101. Choose vertices u and v with maximum degree. Then $d_u + d_v = d_u d_v$ by exercise 95; so either $G = H = K_1$, or $d_u = d_v = 2$. In the latter case, $G = P_m$ or C_m, and $H = P_n$ or C_n. But $G \square H$ is connected, so G or H must be nonbipartite, say G. Then $G \square H$ is nonbipartite, so H must also be nonbipartite; thus $G = C_m$ and $H = C_n$, with m and n both odd. The shortest odd cycle in $C_m \square C_n$ has length $\min(m, n)$; in $C_m \otimes C_n$ it has length $\max(m, n)$; hence $m = n$. Conversely, if $n \geq 3$ is odd, we have $C_n \square C_n \cong C_n \otimes C_n$, under the isomorphism that takes $(u, v) \mapsto ((u + v) \bmod n, (u - v) \bmod n)$ for $0 \leq u, v < n$. [D. J. Miller, *Canadian J. Math.* **20** (1968), 1511–1521.]

102. $P_m \boxtimes P_n$. (It is planar only when $\min(m, n) \leq 2$ or $m = n = 3$.)

103.

1	2	3	4	5	7				1	2	3	4	5	6	7	8	9
2	1	3	4	6	8				2	1	3	4	6	8	9		
3	1	2	5	6	8				3	1	2	5	6	8	9		
4	1	2	5	6					4	1	2	5	7				
5	3	4	1	7					5	3	4	1	7				
6	2	3	4						6	2	3	1	7				
7	5	1							7	4	5	6	1				
8	2	3							8	2	3	1	9				
									9	8	2	3	1				

104. Edges must be created in a somewhat circuitous order, to maintain the tableau shape. Variables i and r delimit the available rows in column t. For example, the second part of exercise 103 begins with $i \leftarrow 1$, $t \leftarrow 8$, $r \leftarrow 1$; then $9 — 1$, $i \leftarrow 2$, $t \leftarrow 6$, $r \leftarrow 3$; then $9 — 3$, $9 — 2$, $i \leftarrow 4$, $t \leftarrow 4$, $r \leftarrow 8$; then $9 — 8$.

105. Notice that $d_k \geq k$ if and only if $c_k \geq k$. When $d_k \geq k$ we have

$$c_1 + \cdots + c_k = k^2 + \min(k, d_{k+1}) + \min(k, d_{k+2}) + \cdots + \min(k, d_n);$$

therefore the condition $d_1 + \cdots + d_k \leq c_1 + \cdots + c_k - k$ is equivalent to

$$d_1 + \cdots + d_k \leq f(k), \quad \text{where } f(k) = k(k-1) + \min(k, d_{k+1}) + \cdots + \min(k, d_n). \quad (*)$$

If $k \geq s$ we have $f(k + 1) - f(k) = 2k - d_{k+1} \geq d_{k+1}$; hence $(*)$ holds for $1 \leq k \leq n$ if and only if it holds for $1 \leq k \leq s$. Condition $(*)$ was discovered by P. Erdős and T. Gallai [*Matematikai Lapok* **11** (1960), 264–274]. It is obviously necessary, if we consider the edges between $\{1, \ldots, k\}$ and $\{k+1, \ldots, n\}$.

Let $a_k = d_1 + \cdots + d_k - c_1 - \cdots - c_k + k$, and suppose that we reach $a_k > 0$ in step H2 for some $k \leq s$. Let A_j, C_j, D_j, N, and S be the numbers that correspond to a_j, c_j, d_j, n, and s *before* steps H3 and H4; thus $N = n + 1$, $D_j = d_j + (0 \text{ or } 1)$, etc. We want to prove that $A_K > 0$ for some $K \leq S$.

Steps H3 and H4 have removed row N and the bottommost remaining q cells in column t, for some $t \geq S$ and $q > 0$, together with the rightmost cells in rows 1 through p. If $p > 0$ we have $C_{t+1} = p$. Let $r = D_N = p + q$, and $u = C_t$. Notice that $D_j = t$ for $p < j \leq u$, and $C_j = N$ for $1 \leq j \leq r$; also $A_j = a_j$ for $1 \leq j \leq p$.

If k is minimal we have $1 \leq a_k \leq d_k - c_k + 1$, hence $c_k \leq d_k$. If $D_k > t$ then $k \leq p$ and $A_k = a_k$. If $D_k < t$ it follows that $A_k = a_k + r - \min(k, r) \geq a_k$, because $k \leq D_k$. Thus we may assume that $D_k = t$.

Suppose $t > S$; hence $u \leq S$. For $k < j \leq u$ we have $d_j \geq D_j - 1 = t - 1 \geq d_k - 1 \geq c_k - 1 \geq c_j - 1$. Thus $a_u \geq a_k > 0$. But $A_u = a_u$, because $r \leq u \leq S < t$. We may therefore assume that $t = S$. Suppose $k < t$; then $c_k = d_k = t$, because $S \leq c_k \leq d_k \leq t$. But $r = t$ leads to $c_k = N - 1$ and a contradiction; and $r < t$ leads to $u = t$, from which it follows that $A_t > A_{t-1} = a_{t-1} - 1 \geq 0$.

(Deep breath.) OK; we've reduced the problem to cases with $k = t = S$. Hence $t = s \leq c_t \leq d_t \leq D_t = t$, and we have $a_t = a_{t-1} + 1$. Consequently $a_{t-1} = 0$.

In fact we can show by induction on $t - j$ that $a_j = 0$ for $p \leq j < t$: If $a_{j+1} = 0$ then $0 \geq a_j = c_{j+1} - t - 1 \geq q - 1 \geq 0$, because $c_{j+1} \geq t + q$ when $p \leq j < t - 1$.

If $p < t - 1$, this argument proves that $q = 1$ and $c_r = N - 1 = t + 1$. We conclude that, regardless of p, we must have $q = 1$, $N = t + 2$, $D_j = t + 1$ for $1 \leq j \leq p$, $D_j = t$ for $p < j \leq t + 1$, and $D_N = p + 1$. Algorithm H does actually change this "good" sequence into a "bad" one; but $D_1 + \cdots + D_N = 2p + t(t + 1) + 1$ is odd.

106. False in the trivial cases when $d \leq 1$ and $n \geq d + 2$. Otherwise true: In fact, the first $n - 1$ edges generated in step H4 contain no cycles, so they form a spanning tree.

107. The permutation φ of exercise 78 takes a vertex of degree d into a vertex of degree $n - 1 - d$. And φ^2 is an automorphism that pairs up two vertices of equal degree, except for a possible fixed point of degree $(n - 1)/2$.

(Conversely, a somewhat intricate extension of Algorithm H will construct a self-complementary graph from every graphical sequence that satisfies these conditions, provided that $d_{(n-1)/2} = (n - 1)/2$ when n is odd. See C. R. J. Clapham and D. J. Kleitman, *J. Combinatorial Theory* **B20** (1976), 67–74.)

108. We may assume that $d_1^+ \geq \cdots \geq d_n^+$; the in-degrees d_k^- need not be in any particular order. Apply Algorithm H to the sequence $d_1 \ldots d_n = d_1^+ \ldots d_n^+$, but with the following changes: Step H2 becomes "[Done?] Terminate successfully if $d_1 = n = 0$; terminate unsuccessfully if $d_1 > n$." In step H3, change "$j \leftarrow d_n$" to "$j \leftarrow d_n^-$," and terminate unsuccessfully if $j > c_1$. In step H4, change "Set ... and set" to "If $j > 0$, set $m \leftarrow c_t$, create the arc $m \longrightarrow n$, and set"; and set $n \leftarrow n - 1$ just before returning to H2. An argument like Lemma M and Corollary H justifies this approach.

(Exercise 7.2.1.4–57 proves that such digraphs exist if and only if $d_1^- + \cdots + d_n^- = d_1^+ + \cdots + d_n^+$ and $d_1^- \ldots d_n^- = \{d_1', \ldots, d_n'\}$, where $d_1' \geq \cdots \geq d_n'$ and $d_1' \ldots d_n'$ is majorized by the conjugate partition $c_1 \ldots c_n = (d_1^+ \ldots d_n^+)^T$. The variant where loops $v \longrightarrow v$ are forbidden is harder; see D. R. Fulkerson, *Pacific J. Math.* **10** (1960), 831–836.)

109. It's the same as exercise 108, if we put $d_k^+ = d_k[k \leq m]$ and $d_k^- = d_k[k > m]$.

110. There are p vertices of degree $d = d_1$ and q vertices of degree $d - 1$, where $p + q = n$.

Case 1, $d = 2k + 1$. Make $u - v$ whenever $(u - v) \bmod n \in \{2, 3, \ldots, k + 1, n - k - 1, \ldots, n - 3, n - 2\}$; also add the $p/2$ edges $1 - 2$, $3 - 4$, $\ldots$, $(p-1) - p$.

Case 2, $d = 2k > 0$. Make $u - v$ whenever $(u - v) \bmod n \in \{2, 3, \ldots, k, n - k, \ldots, n - 3, n - 2\}$; also add the edges $1 - 2$, $\ldots$, $(q-1) - q$, as well as the path or cycle $(q = 0? n : q) - (q+1) - \cdots - (n-1) - n$. [D. L. Wang and D. J. Kleitman, in *Networks* **3** (1973), 225–239, have proved that such graphs are highly connected.]

111. Suppose $N = n + n'$ and $V' = \{n + 1, \ldots, N\}$. We want to construct $e_k = d - d_k$ edges between k and V', and additional edges within V', so that each vertex of V' has degree d. Let $s = e_1 + \cdots + e_n$. This task is possible only if (i) $n' \geq \max(e_1, \ldots, e_n)$; (ii) $n'd \geq s$; (iii) $n'd \leq s + n'(n' - 1)$; and (iv) $(n + n')d$ is even.

Such edges do exist whenever n' satisfies (i)–(iv): First, s suitable edges between V and V' can be created by cyclically choosing endpoints $(n+1, n+2, \ldots, n+n', n+1, \ldots)$, because of (i). This process assigns either $\lfloor s/n' \rfloor$ or $\lceil s/n' \rceil$ edges to each vertex of V'; we have $\lceil s/n' \rceil \leq d$ by (ii), and $d - \lfloor s/n' \rfloor \leq n' - 1$ by (iii). Therefore the additional edges needed inside V' are constructible by exercise 110 and (iv).

The choice $n' = n$ always works. Conversely, if $G = K_n(V) \setminus \{1 - 2\}$, condition (iii) requires $n' \geq n$ when $n \geq 4$. [P. Erdős and P. Kelly, *AMM* **70** (1963), 1074–1075.]

112. The uniquely best triangle in the *miles* data is

$$\text{Saint Louis, MO} \overset{748}{\text{---}} \text{Toronto, ON} \overset{746}{\text{---}} \text{Winston-Salem, NC} \overset{748}{\text{---}} \text{Saint Louis, MO}.$$

113. By Murphy's Law, it has n rows and m columns; so it's $n \times m$, not $m \times n$.

114. A loop in a multigraph is an edge $\{a, a\}$ with repeated vertices, and a multigraph is a 2-uniform hypergraph. Thus we should allow the incidence matrix of a general hypergraph to have entries greater than 1 when an edge contains a vertex more than once. (A pedant would probably call this a "multihypergraph.") With these considerations in mind, the incidence matrix and bipartite multigraph corresponding to (26) are

$$\begin{pmatrix} 210000 \\ 011100 \\ 001122 \end{pmatrix};$$

115. The element in row e and column f of B^TB is $\sum_v b_{ve}b_{vf}$; so B^TB is $2I$ plus the adjacency matrix of $L(G)$. Similarly, BB^T is D plus the adjacency matrix of G, where D is the diagonal matrix with $d_{vv} = $ degree of v. (See exercises 2.3.4.2–18, 19, and 20.)

116. $\overline{K_{m,n}^{(r)}} = K_m^{(r)} \oplus K_n^{(r)}$, generalizing (38), for all $r \geq 1$.

117. The nonisomorphic multisets of singleton edges for $m = 4$ and $V = \{0, 1, 2\}$ are $\{\{0\}, \{0\}, \{0\}, \{0\}\}$, $\{\{0\}, \{0\}, \{0\}, \{1\}\}$, $\{\{0\}, \{0\}, \{1\}, \{1\}\}$, and $\{\{0\}, \{0\}, \{1\}, \{2\}\}$. The answer in general is the number of partitions of m into at most n parts, namely $\left|\begin{smallmatrix} m+n \\ n \end{smallmatrix}\right|$, using the notation explained in Section 7.2.1.4. (Of course, there's little reason to think of partitions as 1-uniform hypergraphs, except when answering strange exercises.)

118. Let d be the sum of the vertex degrees. The corresponding bipartite graph is a forest with $m + n$ vertices, d edges, and p components. Hence $d = m + n - p$, by Theorem 2.3.4.1A.

119. Then there's an additional edge, containing all seven vertices.

120. We could say that (hyper)arcs are arbitrary sequences of vertices, or sequences of distinct vertices. But most authors seem to define hyperarcs to be $A \longrightarrow v$, where A is an unordered set of vertices. When the best definition is found, it will probably be the one that has the most important practical applications.

121. $\chi(H) = |F| - \alpha(I(H)^T)$ is the size of a minimum cover of V by sets of F.

122. (a) One can verify that there are just seven 3-element covers, namely the vertices of an edge; so there are seven 4-element independent sets, namely the complements of an edge. We can't two-color the hypergraph, because one color would need to be used 4 times and the other three vertices would be an edge. (Hypergraph (56) is essentially the projective plane with seven points and seven lines.)

(b) Since we're dualizing, let's call the vertices and edges of the Petersen graph "points" and "lines"; then the vertices and edges of the dual are lines and points, respectively. Color red the five lines that join an outer point to an inner point. The other ten lines are independent (they don't contain all three of the lines touching any point); so they can be colored green. No set of eleven lines can be independent, because no four lines can touch all ten points. (Thus the Petersen dual is a bipartite hypergraph, in spite of the fact that it contains cycles of length 5.)

123. They correspond to $n \times n$ latin squares, whose entries are the vertex colors.

124. Four colors easily suffice. If it were 3-colorable, there must be four vertices of each color, since no five vertices are independent. Then two opposite corners must have the same color, and a contradiction arises quickly.

125. The Chvátal graph is the smallest such graph with $g = 4$. G. Brinkmann found the smallest with $g = 5$: It has 21 vertices a_j, b_j, c_j for $0 \le j < 7$, with edges $a_j - a_{j+2}$, $a_j - b_j$, $a_j - b_{j+1}$, $b_j - c_j$, $b_j - c_{j+2}$, $c_j - c_{j+3}$ and subscripts mod 7. M. Meringer showed that there must be at least 35 vertices if $g > 5$. B. Grünbaum conjectured that g can be arbitrarily large; but no further constructions are known. [See *AMM* **77** (1970), 1088–1092; *Graph Theory Notes of New York* **32** (1997), 40–41.]

126. When m and n are even, both C_m and C_n are bipartite, and 4-coloring is easy. Otherwise a 4-coloring is impossible. When $m = n = 3$, a 9-coloring is optimum by exercise 93. When $m = 3$ and $n = 4$ or 5, at most two vertices are independent; it's easy to find an optimum 6- or 8-coloring. Otherwise we obtain a 5-coloring by painting vertex (j, k) with $(a_j + 2b_k) \bmod 5$, where periodic sequences $\langle a_j \rangle$ and $\langle b_k \rangle$ exist with period lengths m and n, respectively, such that $a_j - a_{j+1} \equiv \pm 1$ and $b_k - b_{k+1} \equiv \pm 1$ for all j and k. [K. Vesztergombi, *Acta Cybernetica* **4** (1979), 207–212.]

127. (a) The result is true when $n = 1$. Otherwise let $H = G \backslash v$, where v is any vertex. Then $\overline{H} = \overline{G} \backslash v$, and we have $\chi(H) + \chi(\overline{H}) \le n$ by induction. Clearly $\chi(G) \le \chi(H) + 1$ and $\chi(\overline{G}) \le \chi(\overline{H}) + 1$; so there's no problem unless equality holds in all three cases. But that can't happen; it implies that $\chi(H) \le d$ and $\chi(\overline{H}) \le n - 1 - d$, where d is the degree of v in G. [E. A. Nordhaus and J. W. Gaddum, *AMM* **63** (1956), 175–177.]

To get equality, let $G = K_a \oplus \overline{K_b}$, where $ab > 0$ and $a + b = n$. Then we have $\overline{G} = \overline{K_a} - K_b$, $\chi(G) = a$, and $\chi(\overline{G}) = b + 1$. [All graphs for which equality holds have been found by H.-J. Finck, *Wiss. Zeit. der Tech. Hochschule Ilmenau* **12** (1966), 243–246.]

(b) A k-coloring of G has at least $\lceil n/k \rceil$ vertices of some color; those vertices form a clique in $\overline{G}$. Hence $\chi(G) \chi(\overline{G}) \ge \chi(G) \lceil n/\chi(G) \rceil \ge n$. Equality holds when $G = K_n$.

(From (a) and (b) we deduce that $\chi(G) + \chi(\overline{G}) \ge 2\sqrt{n}$ and $\chi(G) \chi(\overline{G}) \le \frac{1}{4}(n+1)^2$.)

128. $\chi(G \square H) = \max(\chi(G), \chi(H))$. This many colors is clearly necessary. And if the functions $a(u)$ and $b(v)$ color G and H with the colors $\{0, 1, \ldots, k-1\}$, we can color $G \square H$ with $c(u, v) = (a(u) + b(v)) \bmod k$.

129. A complete row or column (16 cases); a complete diagonal of length 4 or more (18 cases); a 5-cell pattern $\{(x, y), (x-a, y-a), (x-a, y+a), (x+a, y-a), (x+a, y+a)\}$ for $a \in \{1, 2, 3\}$ ($36 + 16 + 4$ cases); a 5-cell pattern $\{(x, y), (x-a, y), (x+a, y), (x, y-a), (x, y+a)\}$ for $a \in \{1, 2, 3\}$ ($36 + 16 + 4$ cases); a pattern containing four of those five cells, when the fifth lies off the board ($24 + 32 + 24$ cases); or a 4-cell pattern $\{(x, y), (x+a, y), (x, y+a), (x+a, y+a)\}$ for $a \in \{1, 3, 5, 7\}$ ($49 + 25 + 9 + 1$ cases). Altogether 310 maximal cliques, with respectively $(168, 116, 4, 4, 18)$ of size $(4, 5, 6, 7, 8)$.

130. If graph G has p maximal cliques and graph H has q, then the join $G - H$ has pq, because the cliques of $G - H$ are simply the unions of cliques from G and H. Furthermore, the empty graph $\overline{K_n}$ has n maximal cliques (namely its singleton sets).

Thus the complete k-partite graph with part sizes $\{n_1, \ldots, n_k\}$, being the join of empty graphs of those sizes, has $n_1 \ldots n_k$ maximal cliques.

131. Assume that $n > 1$. In a complete k-partite graph, the number $n_1 \ldots n_k$ is maximized when each part has size 3, except perhaps for one or two parts of size 2. (See exercise 7.2.1.4–68(b).) So we must prove that $N(n)$ cannot be larger than this in *any* graph.

Let $m(v)$ be the number of maximal cliques that contain vertex v. If $u \not\mkern-1mu- v$ and $m(u) \le m(v)$, construct the graph G' that is like G except that u is now adjacent to all the neighbors of v instead of to its former neighbors. Every maximal clique U in either graph belongs to one of three classes:

i) $u \in U$; there are $m(u)$ of these in G and $m(v)$ of them in G'.

ii) $v \in U$; there are $m(v)$ of these in G and also in G'.

iii) $u \notin U$ and $v \notin U$; such maximal cliques in G are also maximal in G'.

Therefore G' has at least as many maximal cliques as G. And we can obtain a complete k-partite graph by appropriately repeating the process.

[This argument, due to Paul Erdős, was presented by J. W. Moon and L. Moser in *Israel J. Math.* **3** (1965), 23–25.]

132. The strong product of cliques in G and H is a clique in $G \boxtimes H$, by exercise 93; hence $\omega(G \boxtimes H) \geq \omega(G)\omega(H) = \chi(G)\chi(H)$. On the other hand, colorings $a(u)$ and $b(v)$ of G and H lead to the coloring $c(u,v) = (a(u), b(v))$ of $G \boxtimes H$; hence $\chi(G \boxtimes H) \leq \chi(G)\chi(H)$. And $\omega(G \boxtimes H) \leq \chi(G \boxtimes H)$.

133. (a) 24; (b) 60; (c) 3; (d) 6; (e) 6; (f) 4; (g) 5; (h) 4; (i) $K_2 \boxtimes C_{12}$; (j) 18; (k) 12. (l) Yes, of degree 5. (m) No. [In fact, Markus Chimani used branch-and-cut methods in 2009 to prove that it cannot be drawn with fewer than 12 crossings.] (n) Yes; in fact, it is 4-connected (see Section 7.4.1.3). (o) Yes; we consider *every* graph to be directed, with two arcs for each edge. (p) Of course not. (q) Yes, easily.

[The musical graph represents simple modulations between key signatures. It appears on page 73 of *Graphs* by R. J. Wilson and J. J. Watkins (1990).]

134. By rotating and/or swapping the inner and outer vertices, we can find an automorphism that takes any vertex into C. If C is fixed, we can interchange the inner and outer vertices of any subset of the remaining 11 pairs, and/or do a left-right reflection. Therefore there are $24 \times 2^{11} \times 2 = 98{,}304$ automorphisms altogether.

135. Let $\omega = e^{2\pi i/12}$, and define the matrices $Q = (q_{ij})$, $S = (s_{ij})$, where $q_{ij} = [j = (i+1) \bmod 12]$ and $s_{ij} = \omega^{ij}$, for $0 \leq i, j < 12$. By exercise 96(b), the adjacency matrix of the musical graph $K_2 \boxtimes C_{12}$ is $A = \binom{1\,1}{1\,1} \otimes (I + Q + Q^-) - I$. Let T be the matrix $\binom{1\ \ 1}{1\ -1} \otimes S$; then T^-AT is a diagonal matrix D whose first 12 entries are $1 + 4\cos\frac{j\pi}{6}$ for $0 \leq j < 12$, and whose other 12 entries are -1. Therefore $A^{2m} = TD^{2m}T^-$, and it follows that the number of $2m$-step walks from C to $(C, G, D, A, E, B, F^\sharp)$ respectively is

$$C_m = \tfrac{1}{24}(25^m + 2(13 + 4\sqrt{3})^m + 3^{2m+1} + 2(13 - 4\sqrt{3})^m + 16);$$
$$G_m = \tfrac{1}{24}(25^m + \sqrt{3}(13 + 4\sqrt{3})^m - \sqrt{3}(13 - 4\sqrt{3})^m - 1);$$
$$D_m = \tfrac{1}{24}(25^m + (13 + 4\sqrt{3})^m + (13 - 4\sqrt{3})^m - 3);$$
$$A_m = \tfrac{1}{24}(25^m - 3^{2m+1} + 2);$$
$$E_m = \tfrac{1}{24}(25^m - (13 + 4\sqrt{3})^m - (13 - 4\sqrt{3})^m + 1);$$
$$B_m = \tfrac{1}{24}(25^m - \sqrt{3}(13 + 4\sqrt{3})^m + \sqrt{3}(13 - 4\sqrt{3})^m - 1);$$
$$F^\sharp_m = \tfrac{1}{24}(25^m - 2(13 + 4\sqrt{3})^m + 3^{2m+1} - 2(13 - 4\sqrt{3})^m);$$

also $a_m = C_m - 1$, $d_m = F_m = e_m = G_m$, etc. In particular, $(C_6, G_6, D_6, A_6, E_6, B_6, F^\sharp_6) = (15462617, 14689116, 12784356, 10106096, 7560696, 5655936, 5015296)$, so the desired probability is $15462617/5^{12} \approx 6.33\%$. As $m \to \infty$, the probabilities are all $\frac{1}{24} + O(0.8^m)$.

136. No. Only two Cayley graphs of order 10 are cubic, namely $K_2 \sqcup C_5$ (whose vertices can be written $\{e, \alpha, \alpha^2, \alpha^3, \alpha^4, \beta, \beta\alpha, \beta\alpha^2, \beta\alpha^3, \beta\alpha^4\}$ where $\alpha^5 = \beta^2 = (\alpha\beta)^2 = e$) and the graph with vertices $\{0, 1, \ldots, 9\}$ and arcs $v \to (v\pm 1) \bmod 10$, $v \to (v+5) \bmod 10$. [See D. A. Holton and J. Sheehan, *The Petersen Graph* (1993), exercise 9.10. Incidentally, the SGB graphs *raman*$(p, q, t, 0)$ are Cayley graphs.]

137. Let $[x, y]$ denote the label of (x, y); we want $[x, y] = [x + a, y + b] = [x + c, y + d]$ for all x and y. If A is the matrix $\left(\begin{smallmatrix} a & b \\ c & d \end{smallmatrix}\right)$, the operation of adding t times the bottom row of A to the top row changes A to the matrix $A' = \left(\begin{smallmatrix} 1 & t \\ 0 & 1 \end{smallmatrix}\right)A = \left(\begin{smallmatrix} a' & b' \\ c' & d' \end{smallmatrix}\right)$, where $a' = a + tc$, $b' = b + td$, $c' = c$, $d' = d$. The new condition $[x, y] = [x + a', y + b'] = [x + c', y + d']$ is equivalent to the old; and $\gcd(a', b', c', d') = \gcd(a, b, c, d)$. Similarly we can premultiply A by $\left(\begin{smallmatrix} 1 & 0 \\ t & 1 \end{smallmatrix}\right)$ without really changing the problem.

We can also operate on columns, replacing A by $A'' = A\left(\begin{smallmatrix} 1 & t \\ 0 & 1 \end{smallmatrix}\right) = \left(\begin{smallmatrix} a'' & b'' \\ c'' & d'' \end{smallmatrix}\right)$, where $a'' = a$, $b'' = ta + b$, $c'' = c$, $d'' = tc + d$. This operation does alter the problem, but only slightly: If we find a labeling that satisfies $[\![x, y]\!] = [\![x + a'', y + b'']\!] = [\![x + c'', y + d'']\!]$ for all x and y, then we'll have $[x, y] = [x + a, y + b] = [x + c, x + d]$ if $[x, y] = [\![x, y + tx]\!]$. Similarly we can postmultiply A by $\left(\begin{smallmatrix} 1 & 0 \\ t & 1 \end{smallmatrix}\right)$; the problem remains almost the same.

A series of such row and column operations will reduce A to the simple form $UAV = \left(\begin{smallmatrix} 1 & 0 \\ 0 & n \end{smallmatrix}\right)$, where U and V are integer matrices with $\det U = \det V = 1$. Furthermore, if we have $V = \left(\begin{smallmatrix} \alpha & \beta \\ \gamma & \delta \end{smallmatrix}\right)$, a labeling for the reduced problem that satisfies the simple conditions $[\![x, y]\!] = [\![x + 1, y]\!] = [\![x, y + n]\!]$ will provide a solution to the original labeling problem if we define $[x, y] = [\![\alpha x + \gamma y, \beta x + \delta y]\!]$.

Finally, the reduced labeling problem is easy: We let $[\![x, y]\!] = y \bmod n$. Thus the desired answer is to set $p = \beta$, $q = \delta$.

138. Proceeding as before, but with a $k \times k$ matrix A, row and column operations will reduce the problem to a diagonal matrix UAV. The diagonal entries $(d_1, \ldots, d_k)$ are characterized by the condition that $d_1 \ldots d_j$ is the greatest common divisor of the determinants of all $j \times j$ submatrices of A. [This is "Smith normal form"; see H. J. S. Smith, *Philosophical Transactions* **151** (1861), 293–326, §14.] If the labeling $[\![x]\!]$ satisfies the reduced problem, the original problem is satisfied by $[x] = [\![xV]\!]$. The number of elements in the generalized torus is $n = \det A = d_1 \ldots d_k$.

The reduced problem has a simple solution as before if $d_1 = \cdots = d_{k-1} = 1$. But in general the reduced labeling will be an r-dimensional ordinary torus of dimensions $(d_{k-r+1}, \ldots, d_k)$, where $d_{k-r+1} > d_{k-r} = 1$. (Here $d_0 = 1$; we might have $r = k$.)

In the requested example, we find $d_1 = 1$, $d_2 = 2$, $d_3 = 10$, $n = 20$; indeed,

$$UAV = \begin{pmatrix} 1 & -2 & 0 \\ 0 & 1 & -1 \\ -1 & -1 & 4 \end{pmatrix} \begin{pmatrix} 3 & 1 & 1 \\ 1 & 3 & 1 \\ 1 & 1 & 3 \end{pmatrix} \begin{pmatrix} 1 & 5 & 6 \\ 0 & 1 & 1 \\ 0 & 0 & 1 \end{pmatrix} = \begin{pmatrix} 1 & 0 & 0 \\ 0 & 2 & 0 \\ 0 & 0 & 10 \end{pmatrix}.$$

Each point (x, y, z) now receives a two-dimensional label $(u, v) = ((5x + y) \bmod 2, (6x + y + z) \bmod 10)$. The six neighbors of (u, v) are then $((u \pm 1) \bmod 2, (v \pm 6) \bmod 10)$, $((u \pm 1) \bmod 2, (v \pm 1) \bmod 10)$, $(u, (v \pm 1) \bmod 10)$. One consequence is that 3D space can be "tiled" with interesting 20-element subsets of a $3 \times 3 \times 3$ cube.

[Generalized toruses are essentially the Cayley graphs of Abelian groups; see exercise 136. They have been proposed as convenient interconnection networks, in which case it is desirable to minimize the diameter when k and n are given. See C. K. Wong and D. Coppersmith, *JACM* **21** (1974), 392–402; C. M. Fiduccia, R. W. Forcade, and J. S. Zito, *SIAM J. Discrete Math.* **11** (1998), 157–167.]

139. (This exercise helps clarify the distinction between labeled graphs G, in which the vertices have definite names, and unlabeled graphs H such as those in Fig. 2.) If N_H is the number of labeled graphs on $\{1, 2, \ldots, h\}$ that are isomorphic to H, and if U is any h-element subset of V, the probability that $G \mid U$ is isomorphic to H is $N_H/2^{h(h-1)/2}$. Therefore the answer is $\binom{n}{h} N_H/2^{h(h-1)/2}$. We need only figure out the value of N_H, which is: (a) 1; (b) $h!/2$; (c) $(h - 1)!/2$; (d) $h!/a$, where H has a automorphisms.

140. (a) $\#(K_3{:}W_n) = n$ and $\#(P_3{:}W_n) = \binom{n}{2}$ for $n \geq 4$; also $\#(\overline{K_3}{:}W_7) = 7$.

(b) G is proportional if and only if $\#(K_3{:}G) = \#(\overline{K_3}{:}G) = \frac{1}{8}\binom{n}{3}$ and $\#(P_3{:}G) = \#(\overline{P_3}{:}G) = \frac{3}{8}\binom{n}{3}$. If G has e edges, we have $(n-2)e = 3\#(K_3{:}G)+2\#(P_3{:}G)+\#(\overline{P_3}{:}G)$, because every pair of vertices appears in $n-2$ induced subgraphs. If G has degree sequence $d_1 \ldots d_n$, we have $d_1 + \cdots + d_n = 2e$, $\binom{d_1}{2} + \cdots + \binom{d_n}{2} = 3\#(K_3{:}G)+\#(P_3{:}G)$, and $d_1(n-1-d_1)+\cdots+d_n(n-1-d_n) = 2\#(P_3{:}G)+2\#(\overline{P_3}{:}G)$. Therefore a proportional graph satisfies $(*)$ — unless $n = 2$. (The exercise should have excluded that case.)

Conversely, if G satisfies $(*)$ and has the correct $\#(K_3{:}G)$, it also has the correct $\#(P_3{:}G)$, $\#(\overline{P_3}{:}G)$, and $\#(\overline{K_3}{:}G)$.

[*References:* S. Janson and J. Kratochvíl, *Random Structures & Algorithms* **2** (1991), 209–224. In *J. Combinatorial Theory* **B47** (1989), 125–145, A. D. Barbour, M. Karoński, and A. Ruciński had shown that the variance of $\#(H{:}G)$ is proportional to either n^{2h-2}, n^{2h-3}, or n^{2h-4}, where the first case occurs when H does not have $\frac{1}{2}\binom{h}{2}$ edges, and the third case occurs when H is a proportional graph.]

141. Only 8 degree sequences $d_1 \ldots d_8$ satisfy $(*)$: 73333333 $(1/2)$, 65433322 $(26/64)$, 64444222 $(2/10)$, 64443331 $(8/22)$, 55543222 $(8/20)$, 55533331 $(2/10)$, 55444321 $(26/64)$, and 44444440 $(1/2)$. Each degree sequence is shown here with statistics (N_1/N), where N nonisomorphic graphs have that sequence and N_1 of them are proportional. The last three cases are complements of the first three. No graph of order 8 is both proportional and self-complementary. Maximally symmetric examples of the first five cases are W_8,

, , ,   and   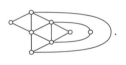 .

142. The hint follows as in answer 140; $(n-3)\#(\overline{K_3}{:}G)$ and $(n-3)\#(P_3{:}G)$ can also be expressed in terms of four-vertex counts. Furthermore, a graph with e edges has $\binom{e}{2} = \#(P_3 \subseteq G)+\#(K_2 \oplus K_2 \subseteq G)$, because any two edges form either P_3 or $K_2 \oplus K_2$; in this formula, $\#(P_3 \subseteq G)$ counts not-necessarily-induced subgraphs.

We have $\#(P_3 \subseteq G) = \#(P_3{:}G) + 3\#(K_3{:}G)$, and a similar formula expresses $\#(K_2 \oplus K_2 \subseteq G)$ in terms of induced counts. Thus an extraproportional graph must be proportional and satisfy $e = \frac{1}{2}\binom{n}{2}$, $\#(P_3 \subseteq G) = \frac{3}{4}\binom{n}{3}$, $\#(K_2 \oplus K_2 \subseteq G) = \frac{3}{4}\binom{n}{4}$. But these values contradict the formula for $\binom{e}{2}$.

143. Consider the graph whose vertices are the rows of A, and whose edges $u \rule[0.5ex]{1.5em}{0.4pt} v$ signify that rows u and v agree except in one column, j. Label such an edge j.

If the graph contains a cycle, delete any edge of the cycle, and repeat the process until no cycles remain. Notice that the label on every deleted edge appears elsewhere in its cycle; hence the deletions don't affect the set of edge labels. But we're left with fewer than $m \leq n$ edges, by Theorem 2.3.4.1A; so there are fewer than n different labels. [See J. A. Bondy, *J. Combinatorial Theory* **B12** (1972), 201–202.]

144. Let G be the graph on vertices $\{1, \ldots, m\}$, with edges $i \rule[0.5ex]{1.5em}{0.4pt} j$ if and only if $* \neq x_{il} \neq x_{jl} \neq *$ for some l. This graph is k-colorable if and only if there is a completion with at most k distinct rows. Conversely, if G is a graph on vertices $\{1, \ldots, n\}$, with adjacency matrix A, the $n \times n$ matrix $X = A + *(J - I - A)$ has the property that $i \rule[0.5ex]{1.5em}{0.4pt} j$ if and only if $* \neq x_{il} \neq x_{jl} \neq *$ for some l. [See M. Sauerhoff and I. Wegener, *IEEE Trans.* **CAD-15** (1996), 1435–1437.]

145. Set $c \leftarrow 0$ and repeat the following operations for $1 \leq j \leq n$: If $c = 0$, set $x \leftarrow a_j$ and $c \leftarrow 1$; otherwise if $x = a_j$, set $c \leftarrow c + 1$; otherwise set $c \leftarrow c - 1$. Then x is the answer. The idea is to keep track of a possible majority element x, which occurs c times in nondiscarded elements; we discard a_j and one x whenever finding $x \neq a_j$. [See *Automated Reasoning* (Kluwer, 1991), 105–117. Extensions to find all elements that occur more than n/k times, in $O(n \log k)$ steps, have been discussed by J. Misra and D. Gries, *Science of Computer Programming* **2** (1982), 143–152. See also the analysis by Alonso and Reingold, *Information Processing Letters* **113** (2013), 495–497.]

SECTION 7.1.1

1. (Solution by C. Sartena.) He was describing the implication $x \Rightarrow y$, with "it" standing respectively for y, x, x, y, y, x. (Other solutions are possible.)

2. The Earth operation corresponding to the Pincusian $x \circ y$ is $\overline{\bar{x} \circ \bar{y}}$; its truth table is therefore the reverse of the complement of the truth table for $\circ$. Hence the respective answers are $\top, \vee, \subset, \mathsf{L}, \supset, \mathsf{R}, \equiv, \wedge, \bar{\wedge}, \oplus, \bar{\mathsf{R}}, \bar{\supset}, \bar{\mathsf{L}}, \bar{\subset}, \bar{\vee}, \bot$. (Any identity involving the 16 operations of Table 1 implies a corresponding dual identity obtained by substituting the Pincusian equivalents. For example, each of De Morgan's laws (11) and (12) is the dual of the other, as are the identities (3), (4) relating $\equiv$ and $\oplus$. In this sense $\equiv$ can be considered to be just as useful as its dual, $\oplus$.)

3. (a) $\vee$; (b) $\wedge$; (c) $\bar{\mathsf{L}}$; (d) $\equiv$. [Many formulas actually work out better if we use -1 for truth and $+1$ for falsehood, even though this convention seems a bit immoral; then $x \cdot y$ corresponds to $\oplus$. Notice that $\langle xyz \rangle = \text{sign}(x + y + z)$, with either convention.]

4. [*Trans. Amer. Math. Soc.* **14** (1913), 481–488.] (a) Start with the truth tables for L and R; then compute truth table $\alpha \bar{\wedge} \beta$ bitwise from each known pair of truth tables α and β, generating the results in order of the length of each formula and writing down a shortest formula that leads to each new 4-bit table:

$\bot : (x \bar{\wedge} (x \bar{\wedge} x)) \bar{\wedge} (x \bar{\wedge} (x \bar{\wedge} x))$

$\wedge : (x \bar{\wedge} y) \bar{\wedge} (x \bar{\wedge} y)$

$\supset : (x \bar{\wedge} (x \bar{\wedge} y)) \bar{\wedge} (x \bar{\wedge} (x \bar{\wedge} y))$

$\mathsf{L} : x$

$\bar{\subset} : (y \bar{\wedge} (x \bar{\wedge} x)) \bar{\wedge} (y \bar{\wedge} (x \bar{\wedge} x))$

$\mathsf{R} : y$

$\oplus : (y \bar{\wedge} (x \bar{\wedge} x)) \bar{\wedge} (x \bar{\wedge} (x \bar{\wedge} y))$

$\vee : (y \bar{\wedge} y) \bar{\wedge} (x \bar{\wedge} x)$

$\bar{\vee} : (x \bar{\wedge} (x \bar{\wedge} x)) \bar{\wedge} ((y \bar{\wedge} y) \bar{\wedge} (x \bar{\wedge} x))$

$\equiv : (x \bar{\wedge} y) \bar{\wedge} ((y \bar{\wedge} y) \bar{\wedge} (x \bar{\wedge} x))$

$\bar{\mathsf{R}} : y \bar{\wedge} y$

$\subset : y \bar{\wedge} (x \bar{\wedge} x)$

$\bar{\mathsf{L}} : x \bar{\wedge} x$

$\supset : x \bar{\wedge} (x \bar{\wedge} y)$

$\bar{\wedge} : x \bar{\wedge} y$

$\top : x \bar{\wedge} (x \bar{\wedge} x)$

(b) In this case we start with four tables $\bot, \top, \mathsf{L}, \mathsf{R}$, and we prefer formulas with fewer occurrences of variables whenever there's a choice between formulas of a given length:

$\bot : 0$

$\wedge : (x \bar{\wedge} y) \bar{\wedge} 1$

$\supset : ((y \bar{\wedge} 1) \bar{\wedge} x) \bar{\wedge} 1$

$\mathsf{L} : x$

$\bar{\subset} : (y \bar{\wedge} (x \bar{\wedge} 1)) \bar{\wedge} 1$

$\mathsf{R} : y$

$\oplus : (y \bar{\wedge} (x \bar{\wedge} 1)) \bar{\wedge} ((y \bar{\wedge} 1) \bar{\wedge} x)$

$\vee : (y \bar{\wedge} 1) \bar{\wedge} (x \bar{\wedge} 1)$

$\bar{\vee} : 1 \bar{\wedge} ((y \bar{\wedge} 1) \bar{\wedge} (x \bar{\wedge} 1))$

$\equiv : (x \bar{\wedge} y) \bar{\wedge} ((y \bar{\wedge} 1) \bar{\wedge} (x \bar{\wedge} 1))$

$\bar{\mathsf{R}} : y \bar{\wedge} 1$

$\subset : y \bar{\wedge} (x \bar{\wedge} 1)$

$\bar{\mathsf{L}} : x \bar{\wedge} 1$

$\supset : (y \bar{\wedge} 1) \bar{\wedge} x$

$\bar{\wedge} : x \bar{\wedge} y$

$\top : 1$

5. (a) $\bot$: $x\,\bar{\subset}\,x$; $\wedge$: $(x\,\bar{\subset}\,y)\,\bar{\subset}\,y$; $\supset$: $y\,\bar{\subset}\,x$; L: x; $\bar{\mathsf{C}}$: $x\,\bar{\subset}\,y$; R: y;   the other 10 cannot be expressed.   (b) With constants, however, all 16 are possible:

$\bot$: 0

$\wedge$: $(y\,\bar{\subset}\,1)\,\bar{\subset}\,x$

$\supset$: $y\,\bar{\subset}\,x$

L: x

$\bar{\mathsf{C}}$: $x\,\bar{\subset}\,y$

R: y

$\oplus$: $((y\,\bar{\subset}\,x)\,\bar{\subset}\,((x\,\bar{\subset}\,y)\,\bar{\subset}\,1))\,\bar{\subset}\,1$

$\vee$: $(y\,\bar{\subset}\,(x\,\bar{\subset}\,1))\,\bar{\subset}\,1$

$\bar{\vee}$: $y\,\bar{\subset}\,(x\,\bar{\subset}\,1)$

$\equiv$: $(y\,\bar{\subset}\,x)\,\bar{\subset}\,((x\,\bar{\subset}\,y)\,\bar{\subset}\,1)$

$\bar{\mathsf{R}}$: $y\,\bar{\subset}\,1$

C: $(x\,\bar{\subset}\,y)\,\bar{\subset}\,1$

$\bar{\mathsf{L}}$: $x\,\bar{\subset}\,1$

$\supset$: $(y\,\bar{\subset}\,x)\,\bar{\subset}\,1$

$\bar{\wedge}$: $((y\,\bar{\subset}\,1)\,\bar{\subset}\,x)\,\bar{\subset}\,1$

$\top$: 1

[B. A. Bernstein, *University of California Publications in Mathematics* **1** (1914), 87–96.]

6. (a) $\bot, \wedge, \mathsf{L}, \mathsf{R}, \oplus, \vee, \equiv, \top$.   (b) $\bot, \mathsf{L}, \mathsf{R}, \oplus, \equiv, \top$. [Notice that all of these operators are associative. In fact, the stated identity implies the associative law in general: First we have (i) $(x \circ y) \circ ((z \circ y) \circ w) = ((x \circ z) \circ (z \circ y)) \circ ((z \circ y) \circ w) = (x \circ z) \circ w$, and similarly (ii) $(x \circ (y \circ z)) \circ (y \circ w) = x \circ (z \circ w)$. Furthermore (iii) $(x \circ y) \circ (z \circ w) = (x \circ y) \circ ((z \circ y) \circ (y \circ w)) = (x \circ z) \circ (y \circ w)$ by (i). Thus $(x \circ z) \circ w = (x \circ z) \circ ((z \circ z) \circ w) = (x \circ (z \circ z)) \circ (z \circ w) = x \circ (z \circ w)$ by (i), (iii), (ii). The free system generated by $\{x_1, \ldots, x_n\}$ has exactly $n + 2^n n^2$ distinct elements, namely $\{x_j \mid 1 \le j \le n\}$ and $\{x_i \circ x_{j_1} \circ \cdots \circ x_{j_r} \circ x_k \mid r \ge 0 \text{ and } 1 \le i, k \le n \text{ and } 1 \le j_1 < \cdots < j_r \le n\}$.]

7. Equivalently, we want the identity $y \circ (x \circ y) = x$, which holds only for $\oplus$ and $\equiv$. [Jevons noticed this property of $\oplus$ in *Pure Logic* §151, but he did not pursue the matter. We will investigate general systems of this nature, called "gropes," in Section 7.2.2.1.]

8. $(\{\bot, \wedge, \bar{\mathsf{C}}\}, S_0)$, $(\{\top, \vee, \supset\}, S_1)$, $(\{\mathsf{L}, \bar{\mathsf{L}}\}, S_0 \cap S_1)$, $(\{\oplus, \equiv, \bar{\mathsf{R}}\}, S_2)$, $(\{\supset, \bar{\vee}\}, S_0 \cap S_2)$, $(\{\mathsf{C}, \bar{\wedge}\}, S_1 \cap S_2)$, and (R, any), where $S_0 = \{\square \mid 0 \square 0 = 0\}$, $S_1 = \{\square \mid 1 \square 1 = 1\}$, and $S_2 = \{\square \mid \bar{x} \square \bar{y} = \overline{x \square y}\} = \{\mathsf{L}, \mathsf{R}, \bar{\mathsf{L}}, \bar{\mathsf{R}}\}$. Thus 92 of the 256 pairs are left-distributive. [This problem and those of exercise 6 were first treated by E. Schröder in §55 of his posthumously published *Vorlesungen über die Algebra der Logik* **2**, 2 (1905). He expressed the answer by saying in essence that the respective truth tables $(pqrs, wxyz)$ of $(\circ, \square)$ must satisfy the relation $((pq \vee rs) \wedge \bar{z}) \vee ((\bar{p}\bar{q} \vee \bar{r}\bar{s}) \wedge w) \vee ((p\bar{q} \vee r\bar{s}) \wedge ((w \equiv z) \vee (x \equiv y))) = 0$.]

9. (a) False; $(x \oplus y) \vee z = (x \vee z) \oplus (y \vee z) \oplus z$. (b) True, because the identity obviously holds when $z = 0$ and when $z = 1$. (c) True; it's also $(x \oplus y) \vee (x \oplus z) = 1 - [x = y = z]$.

10. The first stage of decomposition (16) yields the functions with truth tables $g = 10100011$ and $h = 10100011 \oplus 10010011 = 00110000$; and the process continues in a similar way, yielding $1 + y + xz + w + wy + wx + wxz$ (modulo 2).

11. The stated term is present if and only if $f(x_1, \ldots, x_n)$ is true an odd number of times when $x_1 = x_4 = x_5 = x_7 = x_9 = x_{10} = \cdots = 0$. (There are 2^k such cases when we set all but k variables to zero.) In other words the multilinear representation can be expressed in a suggestive notation like

$$f(x, y, z) = (f_{000} + f_{00*}z + f_{0*0}y + f_{0**}yz + f_{*00}x + f_{*0*}xz + f_{**0}xy + f_{***}xyz) \bmod 2$$

illustrated here for $n = 3$, where $f_{**0} = f(1, 1, 0) \oplus f(1, 0, 0) \oplus f(0, 1, 0) \oplus f(0, 0, 0)$, etc.

12. (a) Substitute $1 - w$ for $\bar{w}$, etc., in (23), getting $1 - y - xz + 2xyz - w + wy + wx + wxz - 2wxyz$. [Some authors have called this the "Zhegalkin polynomial"; but I. I. Zhegalkin himself always worked modulo 2. Other names in the literature are "availability polynomial," "reliability polynomial," "characteristic polynomial."]

(b) The corresponding coefficients for an arbitrary n-ary function can be as large as 2^{n-1} in absolute value (and this, by induction, is the maximum). For example, the integer multilinear representation of $x_1 \oplus \cdots \oplus x_n$ over the integers turns out to be $e_1 - 2e_2 + 4e_3 - \cdots + (-2)^{n-1}e_n$, where e_k is the kth elementary symmetric function of $\{x_1, \ldots, x_n\}$. The formula in the previous answer becomes

$$f(x, y, z) = f_{000} + f_{00*}z + f_{0*0}y + f_{0**}yz + f_{*00}x + f_{*0*}xz + f_{**0}xy + f_{***}xyz$$

over the integers, where we now have $f_{**0} = f(1, 1, 0) - f(1, 0, 0) - f(0, 1, 0) + f(0, 0, 0)$, etc. The latter, with k *'s, is a k-variable Hadamard transform, Eq. 4.6.4–(38).

(c, d) The polynomial is the sum of its minterms like $x_1(1 - x_2)(1 - x_3)x_4$. Each minterm is nonnegative for $0 \le x_1, \ldots, x_n \le 1$, and the sum of all minterms is 1.

(e) $\partial f / \partial x_j = h(x) - g(x)$, where $h(x) \ge g(x)$ by (d). (See exercise 21.)

13. In fact, F is precisely the integer multilinear representation (see exercise 12).

14. Let $r_j = p_j / (1 - p_j)$. We want $f(0, 0, 0) = 0$ and $f(1, 1, 1) = 1 \Leftrightarrow r_1 r_2 r_3 > 1$, $f(0, 0, 1) = 0$ and $f(1, 1, 0) = 1 \Leftrightarrow r_1 r_2 > r_3$, $f(0, 1, 0) = 0$ and $f(1, 0, 1) = 1 \Leftrightarrow r_1 r_3 > r_2$, $f(0, 1, 1) = 0$ and $f(1, 0, 0) = 1 \Leftrightarrow r_1 > r_2 r_3$. So we get (a) $\langle x_1 x_2 x_3 \rangle$; (b) x_1; (c) $\bar{x}_3$.

15. Exercise 1.2.6–10 tells us that $\binom{x}{k} \bmod 2 = [x \;\&\; k = k]$. Hence, for example, $\binom{x}{11} \equiv x_4 \wedge x_2 \wedge x_1$ (modulo 2) when $x = (x_n \ldots x_1)_2$; and we can obtain every term in a multilinear representation like (19) in this way. Moreover, we needn't work mod 2, because the interpolating polynomial $\binom{x}{11}\binom{15-x}{4}$ represents $x_4 \wedge \bar{x}_3 \wedge x_2 \wedge x_1$ exactly.

16. Yes, or even by $+$, because different minterms can't be simultaneously true. (But we can't do that in ordinary disjunctive normal forms like (25). See exercise 35.)

17. The binary operation $\bar{\wedge}$ is not associative, so an expression like $x \bar{\wedge} y \bar{\wedge} z$ must be interpreted as a *ternary* operation. Quick's notation is fine if one understands NAND to be an n-ary operation, being careful to note that the NAND of a *single* variable x is $\bar{x}$.

18. If not, we could set $u_1 \leftarrow \cdots \leftarrow u_s \leftarrow 1$ and $v_1 \leftarrow \cdots \leftarrow v_t \leftarrow 0$, making f both true and false. (And if we consider applying the distributive law (2) repeatedly to a DNF until it becomes a CNF, we find that the converse is also true: The disjunction $v_1 \vee \cdots \vee v_t$ is implied by f if and only if it has a literal in common with every implicant of f, if and only if it has a literal in common with every prime implicant of f, if and only if it has a literal in common with every implicant of some DNF for f.)

19. The maximal subcubes contained in 0010, 0011, 0101, 0110, 1000, 1001, 1010, and 1011 are 0*10, 0101, *01*, and 10**; so the answer is $(w \vee \bar{y} \vee z) \wedge (w \vee \bar{x} \vee y \vee \bar{z}) \wedge (x \vee \bar{y}) \wedge (\bar{w} \vee x)$. (This CNF is also shortest.)

20. True. The corresponding maximal subcube is contained in some maximal subcubes f' and g', and their intersection can't be larger. (This observation is due to Samson and Mills, whose paper is cited in answer 31 below.)

21. By Boole's law (20), we see that an n-ary function f is monotone if and only if its $(n-1)$-ary projections g and h are monotone and satisfy $g \le h$. Therefore

$$f = (g \wedge \bar{x}_n) \vee (h \wedge x_n) = (g \wedge \bar{x}_n) \vee (g \wedge x_n) \vee (h \wedge x_n) = g \vee (h \wedge x_n),$$

so we can do without complementation. The constants 0 and 1 disappear unless the function is identically constant. Conversely, any expression built up from $\wedge$ and $\vee$ is obviously monotone.

Note on terminology: Strictly speaking, we should say "monotone nondecreasing" instead of simply "monotone," if we want to preserve the language of classical mathematics, because a decreasing function of a real variable is also said to be monotonic.

(See, for example, the "run test" in Section 3.3.2G.) But "nondecreasing" is quite a mouthful; so researchers who work extensively on Boolean functions have almost unanimously opted to assume that "monotone" automatically implies nondecreasing, in a Boolean context. Similarly, the mathematical term "positive function" normally refers to a function whose value exceeds zero; but authors who write about "positive Boolean functions" are referring to the functions that we are calling monotone. Since a monotone function is order-preserving, some authors have adopted the term *isotone*; but that word has already been coopted by physicists, chemists, and musicologists.

A Boolean function like $\bar{x} \vee y$, which becomes monotone if some subset of its variables is complemented, is called *unate*. Theorem Q obviously applies to unate functions.

22. Both g and $g \oplus h$ must be monotone, and $g(x) \wedge h(x) = 0$.

23. $x \wedge (v \vee y) \wedge (v \vee z) \wedge (w \vee z)$. (Corollary Q applies also to *conjunctive* prime forms of monotone functions. Therefore, to solve any problem of this kind, we need only apply the distributive law (2) until no $\wedge$ occurs within a $\vee$, then remove any clause that contains all the variables of another.)

24. By induction on k, the similar tree with $\vee$ at the root gives a function with $2^{2^{\lceil k/2 \rceil}-1}$ prime implicants of length $2^{\lfloor k/2 \rfloor}$, while the tree with $\wedge$ gives $4^{2^{\lfloor k/2 \rfloor}-1}$ of length $2^{\lceil k/2 \rceil}$. When $k = 6$, for example, the $4^7 = 2^{14}$ prime implicants in the $\wedge$ case have the form

$$x_{(0t_0 0t_{00} 0t_{000})_2} \wedge x_{(0t_0 0t_{00} 1t_{001})_2} \wedge x_{(0t_0 1t_{01} 0t_{010})_2} \wedge x_{(0t_0 1t_{01} 1t_{011})_2}$$

$$\wedge x_{(1t_1 0t_{10} 0t_{100})_2} \wedge x_{(1t_1 0t_{10} 1t_{101})_2} \wedge x_{(1t_1 1t_{11} 0t_{110})_2} \wedge x_{(1t_1 1t_{11} 1t_{111})_2},$$

with the t's either 0 or 1. [For further information about such Boolean functions, see D. E. Knuth and R. W. Moore, *Artificial Intelligence* **6** (1975), 293–326; V. Gurvich and L. Khachiyan, *Discrete Mathematics* **169** (1997), 245–248.]

25. Let a_n be the answer. Then $a_2 = a_3 = 2$, $a_4 = 3$, and $a_n = a_{n-2} + a_{n-3}$ for $n > 4$, because the prime implicants when $n > 4$ are either $p_{n-2} \wedge x_{n-1}$ or $p_{n-3} \wedge x_{n-2} \wedge x_n$ for some prime implicant p_k in the k-variable case. (These prime implicants correspond to minimal vertex covers of the path graph P_n. They are *shellable*, in the sense of exercise 35, when listed in lexicographic order. We have $a_n = (7P_n + 10P_{n+1} + P_{n+2})/23$ when P_n is the Perrin number of exercise 7.1.4–15.)

26. (a) Let $x_j = [j \in J]$. Then $f(x) = 0$ and $g(x) = 1$. (This fact was exercise 18.)

(b) Suppose, for example, that $k \in J \in \mathcal{G}$ and $k \notin \bigcup_{I \in \mathcal{F}} I$, and assume that test (a) has been passed. Let $x_j = [j \in J \text{ and } j \neq k]$. Then $f(x) = 1$; and $g(x) = 0$, because every $J' \in \mathcal{G}$ with $J' \neq J$ contains an element $\notin J$.

(c) Again assume that condition (a) has been ruled out. If, say, $|J| > |\mathcal{F}|$, let $x_j = [j \text{ is the smallest element of } I \cap J, \text{ for some } I \in \mathcal{F}]$. Then $f(x) = 1$, $g(x) = 0$.

(d) Now we assume that $\bigcup_{I \in \mathcal{F}} I = \bigcup_{J \in \mathcal{G}} J$. Each $I \in \mathcal{F}$ stands for $2^{n-|I|}$ vectors where $f(x) = 0$; similarly, each $J \in \mathcal{G}$ stands for $2^{n-|J|}$ vectors where $g(x) = 1$. If the sum s is less than 2^n, we can compute $s = s_0 + s_1$, where s_0 counts the contributions to s when $x_n = 0$. If $s_0 < 2^{n-1}$, set $x_n \leftarrow 0$; otherwise $s_1 < 2^{n-1}$, so we set $x_n \leftarrow 1$. Then we set $n \leftarrow n - 1$; eventually all x_j are known, and $f(x) = 1$, $g(x) = 0$.

27. Let $m = \min(\{|I| \mid I \in \mathcal{F}\} \cup \{|J| \mid J \in \mathcal{G}\})$ be the length of the shortest prime clause or implicant. Then $N \cdot 2^{n-m} \geq \sum_{I \in \mathcal{F}} 2^{n-|I|} + \sum_{J \in \mathcal{G}} 2^{n-|J|} \geq 2^n$; so we have $m \leq \lg N$. If, say, $|I| = m$, some index k must appear in at least $1/m$ of the members $J \in \mathcal{G}$, because each J intersects I. This observation proves the hint.

Now let $A(0) = A(1) = 1$ and $A(v) = 1 + A(v-1) + A(\lfloor \rho v \rfloor)$ for $v > 1$. Then $A(|\mathcal{F}||\mathcal{G}|)$ is an upper bound on the number of recursive calls (the number of times X1 is performed). Letting $B(v) = A(v) + 1$, we have $B(v) = B(v-1) + B(\lfloor \rho v \rfloor)$ for $v > 1$, hence $B(v) \leq B(v-k) + kB(\lfloor \rho v \rfloor)$ for $v > k$. Taking $k = v - \lfloor \rho v \rfloor$ shows that $B(v) \leq ((1-\rho)v + 2)B(\lfloor \rho v \rfloor)$; hence $B(v) = O(((1-\rho)v + 2)^t)$ when $\rho^t v \leq 1$, namely when $t \geq \ln v / \ln(1/\rho) = \Theta((\log v)(\log N))$. Consequently $A(|\mathcal{F}||\mathcal{G}|) \leq A(N^2/4) = N^{O(\log N)^2}$.

In practice the algorithm will run much faster than the pessimistic bounds just derived. Since the prime clauses of a function are the prime implicants of its dual, this problem is essentially the same as verifying that one given DNF is the dual of another. Moreover, if we start with $f(x) = 0$ and repeatedly find minimal x's where $f(x) = g(\bar{x}) = 0$, we can "grow" f until we've obtained the dual of g.

The ideas presented here are due to M. L. Fredman and L. Khachiyan, *J. Algorithms* **21** (1996), 618–628, who also presented refinements that reduce the running time to $N^{O(\log N / \log \log N)}$. No polynomial-time algorithm is known; yet the problem is unlikely to be NP-complete, because we can solve it in less-than-exponential time.

28. This result is obvious once understood, but the notations and terminology can make it confusing; so let's consider a concrete example: If, say, $y_1 = y_4 = y_6 = 1$ and the other y_k are zero, the function g is true if and only if the prime implicants p_1, p_4, and p_6 cover all the places where f is true. Thus we see that there is a one-to-one correspondence between every implicant of g and every DNF for f that contains only prime implicants p_j. In this correspondence, the prime implicants of g correspond to the "irredundant" DNFs in which no p_j can be left out.

Numerous refinements of this principle have been discussed by R. B. Cutler and S. Muroga, *IEEE Transactions* **C-36** (1987), 277–292.

29. **B1.** [Initialize.] Set $k \leftarrow k' \leftarrow 0$. (Similar methods are discussed in exercise 5–19.)

   B2. [Find a zero.] Increase k zero or more times, until either $k = m$ (terminate) or $v_k \,\&\, 2^j = 0$.

   B3. [Make $k' > k$.] If $k' \leq k$, set $k' \leftarrow k + 1$.

   B4. [Advance k'.] Increase k' zero or more times, until either $k' = m$ (terminate) or $v_{k'} \geq v_k + 2^j$.

   B5. [Skip past a big mismatch.] If $v_k \oplus v_{k'} \geq 2^{j+1}$, set $k \leftarrow k'$ and return to B2.

   B6. [Record a match.] If $v_{k'} = v_k + 2^j$, output (k, k').

   B7. [Advance k.] Set $k \leftarrow k + 1$ and return to B2. ▮

(Steps B3 and B5 are optional, but recommended.)

30. The following algorithm keeps variable-length, sorted lists in a stack S whose size will never exceed $2m + n$. When the topmost entry of the stack is $S_t = s$, the topmost list is the ordered set $S_s < S_{s+1} < \cdots < S_{t-1}$. Tag bits are maintained in another stack T, having the same size as S (after the initialization step).

   P1. [Initialize.] Set $T_k \leftarrow 0$ for $0 \leq k < m$. Then for $0 \leq j < n$, apply the j-buddy scan algorithm of exercise 29, and set $T_k \leftarrow T_k + 2^j$, $T_{k'} \leftarrow T_{k'} + 2^j$ for all pairs (k, k') found. Then set $s \leftarrow t \leftarrow 0$ and repeat the following operations until $s = m$: If $T_s = 0$, output the subcube $(0, v_s)$ and set $s \leftarrow s+1$; otherwise set $S_t \leftarrow v_s$, $T_t \leftarrow T_s$, $t \leftarrow t+1$, $s \leftarrow s+1$. Finally set $A \leftarrow 0$ and $S_t \leftarrow 0$.

   P2. [Advance A.] (At this point stack S contains $\nu(A) + 1$ lists of subcubes. Namely, if $A = 2^{e_1} + \cdots + 2^{e_r}$ with $e_1 > \cdots > e_r \geq 0$, the stack contains the b-values of all subcubes $(a, b) \subseteq V$ whose a-values are respectively 0, 2^{e_1}, $2^{e_1} + 2^{e_2}, \ldots, A$, except that subcubes whose tags are zero do not appear. All of these lists are nonempty, except possibly the last. We will now increase A to the next relevant value.) Set $j \leftarrow 0$. If $S_t = t$ (that is, if the topmost list is empty), increase j zero or more times until $j \geq n$ or $A \,\&\, 2^j \neq 0$. Then while $j < n$ and $A \,\&\, 2^j \neq 0$, set $t \leftarrow S_t - 1$, $A \leftarrow A - 2^j$, and $j \leftarrow j + 1$. Terminate the algorithm if $j \geq n$; otherwise set $A \leftarrow A + 2^j$.

P3. [Generate list A.] Set $r \leftarrow t$, $s \leftarrow S_t$, and apply the j-buddy scan algorithm of exercise 29 to the $r - s$ numbers $S_s < \cdots < S_{r-1}$. For all pairs (k, k') found, set $x \leftarrow (T_k \,\&\, T_{k'}) - 2^j$; and if $x = 0$, output the subcube (A, S_k), otherwise set $t \leftarrow t + 1$, $S_t \leftarrow S_k$, $T_t \leftarrow x$. Finally set $t \leftarrow t + 1$, $S_t \leftarrow r + 1$, and go back to step P2. ∎

This algorithm is based in part on ideas of Eugenio Morreale [*IEEE Trans.* **EC-16** (1967), 611–620; *Proc. ACM Nat. Conf.* **23** (1968), 355–365]. The running time is at most proportional to mn (for step P1) plus n times the total number of subcubes contained in V. If $m \leq 2^n(1 - \epsilon)$, and if V is chosen at random with size m, exercise 34 shows that the average total number of subcubes is at most $O(\log \log n / \log \log \log n)$ times the average number of maximal subcubes; hence the average running time in most cases will be nearly proportional to the average amount of output produced. On the other hand, exercises 32 and 116 show that the amount of output might be huge.

31. (a) Let $c = c_{n-1} \ldots c_0$, $c' = c'_{n-1} \ldots c'_0$, $c'' = c''_{n-1} \ldots c''_0$. There must be some j with $c_j \neq *$ and $c_j \neq c''_j$; otherwise $c'' \subseteq c$. Similarly there must be some k with $c'_k \neq *$ and $c'_k \neq c''_k$. If $j \neq k$, there would be a point $x_{n-1} \ldots x_0 \in c''$ that is in neither c nor c', because we could let $x_j = \bar{c}_j$ and $x_k = \bar{c}'_k$. Hence $j = k$, and the value of j is uniquely determined. Furthermore it's easy to see that $c'_j = \bar{c}_j$. And if $i \neq j$, we have either $c_i = *$ or $c_i = c''_i$, and either $c'_i = *$ or $c'_i = c''_i$.

(b) This statement is an obvious consequence of (a).

(c) First we prove that the parenthesized remark in step E2 is true whenever that step is encountered. It's clearly true when $j = 0$. Otherwise, let $c \subseteq V$ be a j-cube, and suppose $c = c_0 \cup c_1$ where c_0 and c_1 are $(j-1)$-cubes. On the preceding execution of step E2 we had $c_0 \subseteq c'_0 \in C$ and $c_1 \subseteq c'_1 \in C$ for some c'_0 and c'_1; hence either $c \subseteq c'_0 \sqcup c'_1$ or $c \subseteq c'_0$ or $c \subseteq c'_1$. In each case, c is now contained in some element of C.

Secondly, we prove that the outputs in step E3 are precisely the maximal j-cubes contained in V: Let $c \subseteq V$ be any k-cube. If c is maximal, then c will be in C when we reach step E3 with $j = k$, and it will be output. If c isn't maximal, it has a buddy $c' \subseteq V$, which is a k-cube contained in some subcube $c'' \in C$ when we reach E3. Since $c \not\subseteq c''$, the consensus $c \sqcup c''$ will be a $(j+1)$-cube of C', and c will not be output.

References: The notion of consensus was first defined (under the name "syllogistic result") by Archie Blake on page 25 of his Ph.D. dissertation, *Canonical Expressions in Boolean Algebra* (University of Chicago, 1937); see *J. Symbolic Logic* **3** (1938), 93, 112–113. It was independently rediscovered by Edward W. Samson and Burton E. Mills [Air Force Cambridge Research Center Tech. Report 54-21 (Cambridge, Mass.: April 1954), 54 pp.] and by W. V. Quine [*AMM* **62** (1955), 627–631]. The operation is also sometimes called the *resolvent*, since J. A. Robinson used it in a more general form (but with respect to clauses rather than implicants) as the basis of his "resolution principle" for theorem proving [*JACM* **12** (1965), 23–41]. Algorithm E is due to Ann C. Ewing, J. Paul Roth, and Eric G. Wagner, *AIEE Transactions*, Part 1, **80** (1961), 450–458.

32. (a) Change the definition of $\sqcup$ in exercise 31 to the following associative and commutative operation on the four symbols $A = \{0, 1, *, \bullet\}$, for all $a \in A$ and $x \in \{0, 1\}$:

$$* \sqcup a = a \sqcup * = a, \qquad \bullet \sqcup a = a \sqcup \bullet = x \sqcup \bar{x} = \bullet, \qquad \text{and} \qquad x \sqcup x = x.$$

Also let $h(0) = 0$, $h(1) = 1$, $h(*) = *$, and $h(\bullet) = *$. Then $c = h(c_1 \sqcup \cdots \sqcup c_m)$, computed componentwise, is the only subcube that could possibly be a generalized consensus. [See P. Tison, *IEEE Transactions* **EC-16** (1967), 446–456.]

(b) For example, let $c_j = *^{j-1}1*^{m-j}1^{j-1}0*^{m-j}$. [The final component is superfluous. All solutions have been characterized by R. H. Sloan, B. Szörényi, and G. Turán, in *SIAM J. Discrete Math.* **21** (2008), 987–998.]

(c) By (a), every prime implicant corresponds uniquely to the subset of implicants that it "meets." [A. K. Chandra and G. Markowsky, *Discrete Math.* **24** (1978), 7–11.]

(d) For example, $(y_1 \wedge \bar{x}_1) \vee (y_2 \wedge x_1 \wedge \bar{x}_2) \vee \cdots \vee (y_m \wedge x_1 \wedge \cdots \wedge x_{m-1} \wedge \bar{x}_m)$ as in (b). [J.-M. Laborde, *Discrete Math.* **32** (1980), 209–212.]

33. (a) $\binom{2^n - 2^{n-k}}{m - 2^{n-k}} / \binom{2^n}{m}$. (b) We must exclude the cases when $x_1 \wedge \cdots \wedge x_{j-1} \wedge \bar{x}_j \wedge x_{j+1} \wedge \cdots \wedge x_k$ is also an implicant. By the inclusion-exclusion principle, the answer is

$$\sum_l \binom{k}{l}(-1)^l \binom{2^n - (l+1)2^{n-k}}{m - (l+1)2^{n-k}} / \binom{2^n}{m}.$$

It simplifies to $\binom{2^n - n - 1}{m-1} / \binom{2^n}{m}$ when $k = n$; see, for example, Eq. 1.2.6–(24).

34. (a) We have $c(m, n) = \sum c_j(m, n)$, where $c_j(m, n) = 2^{n-j}\binom{n}{j}\binom{2^n - 2^j}{m - 2^j} / \binom{2^n}{m}$ is the average number of implicants with $n - j$ literals (the average number of subcubes of dimension j in the terminology of exercise 30). Clearly $c_0(m, n) = m$, and

$$c_1(m, n) = \frac{nm(m - 1)}{2(2^n - 1)} \leq \frac{mn}{2}\left(\frac{m}{2^n}\right) \leq \frac{1}{2}m;$$

similarly $c_j(m, n) \leq m/(2^j j! n^{2^j - 1 - j})$. Also $p(m, n) = \sum_j p_j(m, n)$, where we have

$$p_0(m, n) = 2^n \binom{2^n - n - 1}{m - 1} / \binom{2^n}{m} = m\frac{(2^n - n - 1)^{\underline{m-1}}}{(2^n - 1)^{\underline{m-1}}} \geq m\frac{(2^n - n - m)^{m-1}}{(2^n - m)^{m-1}}$$

$$\geq m\left(1 - \frac{n}{2^n - m}\right)^m \geq m\left(1 - \frac{n}{2^n - 2^n/n}\right)^{2^n/n} = m \exp\left(\frac{2^n}{n}\ln\left(1 - \frac{n^2}{2^n(n-1)}\right)\right).$$

(b) Notice that $t = \lfloor \lg\lg n - \lg\lg(2^n/m) + \lg(4/3) \rfloor \leq \lg\lg n + O(1)$ is quite small. We will repeatedly use the fact that $\binom{2^n - j \cdot 2^t}{m - j \cdot 2^t} / \binom{2^n}{m} < \alpha_{mn}^j$, and indeed that

$$\binom{2^n - j \cdot 2^t}{m - j \cdot 2^t} / \binom{2^n}{m} = \alpha_{mn}^j(1 + O(j^2 2^{2t}/m))$$

is an extremely good approximation when j isn't too large. To establish the hint, note that $\sum_{j < t} c_j(m, n)/c_t(m, n) = O(tc_{t-1}(m, n)/c_t(m, n)) = O(t^2/(n\sqrt{\alpha_{mn}})) = O((\log\log n)^2/n^{1/3})$; and $c_{t+j}(m, n)/c_t(m, n) = O((n/(2t))^j \alpha_{mn}^{2^j - 1})$. Consequently we have $c(m, n)/c_t(m, n) \approx 1 + \frac{1}{2}\left(\frac{n-t}{t+1}\right)\alpha_{mn}$, where the second term dominates when α_{mn} is in the upper part of its range. Furthermore

$$\sum_l \binom{n-t}{l}(-1)^l \alpha_{mn}^l\left(1 + O\left(\frac{l^2 2^{2t}}{m}\right)\right) = (1 - \alpha_{mn})^{n-t} + O(n^2 \alpha_{mn}(1 + \alpha_{mn})^n 2^{2t}/m)$$

has an exponentially small error term, because $(1 + \alpha_{mn})^n = O(e^{n^{1/3}}) \ll m$. Therefore $p(m, n)/c_t(m, n)$ is asymptotically $e^{-n\alpha_{mn}} + \frac{1}{2}\left(\frac{n-t}{t+1}\right)\alpha_{mn} e^{-n\alpha_{mn}^2}$.

(c) Here $\alpha_{mn} = 2^{-2^t} \approx n^{-1}\ln(t/\ln t)$; so $c(m,n)/c_t(m,n) = 1 + O(t^{-1}\log t)$, $p(m,n)/c_t(m,n) = t^{-1}\ln t + \frac{1}{2}t^{-1}\ln t + O(t^{-1}\log\log t)$. We conclude that, in this case,

$$\frac{c(m,n)}{p(m,n)} = \frac{2}{3}\frac{\lg\lg n}{\ln\lg\lg n}\left(1 + O\left(\frac{\log\log\log\log n}{\log\log\log n}\right)\right).$$

(d) If $n\alpha_{mn} \le \ln t - \ln\ln t$, we have $p(m,n)/c(m,n) \ge p_t(m,n)/c(m,n) \ge t^{-1}\ln t + O(t^{-1}\log t)^2$. On the other hand if $n\alpha_{mn} \ge \ln t - \ln\ln t$, we have $p(m,n)/c(m,n) \ge p_{t+1}(m,n)/c(m,n) \ge \frac{1}{2}t^{-1}\ln t + O(t^{-1}\log\log t)$.

[The means $c(m,n)$ and $p(m,n)$, and the variance of $c(m,n)$, were first studied by F. Mileto and G. Putzolu, *IEEE Trans.* **EC-13** (1964), 87–92; *JACM* **12** (1965), 364–375. Detailed asymptotic information about implicants, prime implicants, and irredundant DNFs of random Boolean functions, when each value $f(x_1,\ldots,x_n)$ is independently equal to 1 with probability $p(n)$, has been derived by Karl Weber, *Elektronische Informationsverarbeitung und Kybernetik* **19** (1983), 365–374, 449–458, 529–534.]

35. (a) By rearranging coordinates we can assume that the pth subcube is $0^k 1^u *^v$, so that $B_p = 0^k 1^u 0^v$ and $S_p = 1^k 0^{u+v}$. Then all points of $*^k 1^u *^v$ are still covered, by induction on p, because all points of $*^{j-1}1*^{k-j}1^u*^v$ have been covered for $1 \le j \le k$.

(b) The jth and kth subcubes differ in every coordinate position where $B_j \& S_k$ is nonzero. On the other hand if $B_j \& S_k$ is zero, the point $\bar{S}_k$ of subcube k lies in a previous subcube, by (a), because we have $\bar{S}_k \supseteq B_j$.

(c) From the list 1100, 1011, 0011 (with the bits of each S_k underlined) we obtain the orthogonal DNF $(x_1 \wedge x_2) \vee (x_1 \wedge \bar{x}_2 \wedge x_3 \wedge x_4) \vee (\bar{x}_1 \wedge x_3 \wedge x_4)$.

(d) There are eight solutions; for example, (01100, 00110, 00011, 11010, 11000).

(e) (001100, 011000, 000110, 110010, 110000, 010011, 000011) is a symmetrical solution. And there are many more possibilities; for example, 42 permutations of the bit codes $\{110000, 011000, 001100, 000110, 000011, 110010, 011010\}$ are shellings.

[The concept of a shelling for monotone Boolean functions was introduced by Michael O. Ball and J. Scott Provan, *Operations Research* **36** (1988), 703–715, who discussed many significant applications.]

36. If $j < k$ we have $B_j = \alpha 1\beta$ and $B_k = \alpha 0\gamma$ for some strings α, β, γ. Form the sequence $x_0 = \alpha 1\gamma$, $x_1 = x'_0$, ..., $x_l = x'_{l-1}$, where $x_l = \alpha 00^{|\gamma|}$. We have $f(x_0) = 1$ since $x_0 \supseteq B_k$, but $f(x_l) = 0$ since $x_l \subseteq B'_j$. So the string x_i, where $f(x_i) = 1$ and $f(x_{i+1}) = \cdots = f(x_l) = 0$, is in B. It precedes B_k and proves that $B_j \& S_k \supseteq 0^{|\alpha|}10^{|\beta|}$.

[This construction and parts of exercise 35 are due to E. Boros, Y. Crama, O. Ekin, P. L. Hammer, T. Ibaraki, and A. Kogan, *SIAM J. Discrete Math.* **13** (2000), 212–226.]

37. The shelling order (000011, 001101, 001100, 110101, 110100, 110001, 110000) generalizes to all n. There also are interesting solutions not based on shelling, like the cyclically symmetrical (110***, 1110**, **110*, **1110, 0***11, 10**11, 111111).

For the lower bound, assign the weight $w_x = -\prod_{j=1}^n (x_{2j-1} + x_{2j} - 3x_{2j-1}x_{2j})$ to each point x, and notice that the sum of w_x over all x in any subcube is 0 or ± 1. (It suffices to verify this curious fact for each of the nine possible subcubes when $n = 1$.) Now choose a set of disjoint subcubes that partition the set $F = \{x \mid f(x) = 1\}$; we have

$$\sum_{C \text{ chosen}} 1 \ge \sum_{C \text{ chosen}} \sum_{x \in C} w_x = \sum_{x \in F} w_x \sum_{C \text{ chosen}} [x \in C] = \sum_{x \in F} w_x.$$

There are $\binom{n}{k} 2^{n-k}$ vectors x with exactly k pairs $x_{2j-1}x_{2j} = 1$ and nonzero weight. Their weight is $(-1)^{k-1}$, and they lie in F except when $k = 0$. Hence $\sum_{x \in F} w_x = \sum_{k>0} \binom{n}{k} 2^{n-k}(-1)^{k-1} = 2^n - (2-1)^n$.

[See M. O. Ball and G. L. Nemhauser, *Mathematics of Operations Research* **4** (1979), 132–143.]

38. Certainly not; a DNF is satisfiable if and only if it has at least one implicant. The hard problem for a DNF is to decide whether or not it is a *tautology* (always true).

39. Associate variables $y_1, \ldots, y_N$ with each internal node in preorder, so that every tree node corresponds to exactly one variable of F. For each internal node y, with children (l, r) and labeled with the binary operator $\circ$, construct four 3CNF clauses $c_{00} \wedge c_{01} \wedge c_{10} \wedge c_{11}$, where

$$c_{pq} = (y^{\bar{p \circ q}} \vee l^p \vee r^q)$$

and x^p denotes $[x = p]$, so that $x^0 = \bar{x}$ and $x^1 = x$. These clauses state in effect that $y = l \circ r$; for example, if $\circ$ is $\wedge$, the four clauses are $(y \vee \bar{l} \vee \bar{r}) \wedge (\bar{y} \vee \bar{l} \vee r) \wedge (\bar{y} \vee l \vee \bar{r}) \wedge (\bar{y} \vee l \vee r)$. Finally, add one more clause, $(y_1 \vee y_1 \vee y_1)$, to force $f = 1$.

> *Every higher number can be formed by mere complications of threes.*
> *... Take the quadruple fact that A sells B to C for the price D.*
> *This is a compound of two facts:*
> *first, that A makes with C a certain transaction, which we may name E;*
> *and second, that this transaction E is a sale of B for the price D.*
> — CHARLES S. PEIRCE, *A Guess at the Riddle* (1887)

40. Following the hint, A says '$u < v \oplus v < u$' and B says '$u < v \wedge v < w \Rightarrow u < w$'. So $A \wedge B$ says that there's a linear ordering of the vertices, $u_1 < u_2 < \cdots < u_n$. (There are $n!$ ways to satisfy $A \wedge B$.) Now C says that q_{uvw} is equivalent to $u < v < w$; so D says that u and w are not consecutive in the ordering, when $u \not\!\!- w$. Thus $A \wedge B \wedge C \wedge D$ is satisfiable if and only if there is a linear ordering in which all nonadjacent vertices are nonconsecutive (that is, in which all consecutive vertices are adjacent).

41. Solution 0: '$[m \leq n]$' is such a formula, but it is not in the spirit of this exercise.

Solution 1: Let x_{jk} mean that pigeon j occupies hole k. Then the clauses are $(x_{j1} \vee \cdots \vee x_{jn})$ for $1 \leq j \leq m$ and $(\bar{x}_{ik} \vee \bar{x}_{jk})$ for $1 \leq i < j \leq m$ and $1 \leq k \leq n$. [See S. A. Cook and R. A. Reckhow, *J. Symbolic Logic* **44** (1979), 36–50; A. Haken, *Theoretical Comp. Sci.* **39** (1985), 297–308.]

Solution 2: Assume that $n = 2^t$ and let pigeon j occupy hole $(x_{j1} \ldots x_{jt})_2$. The clauses $((x_{i1} \oplus x_{j1}) \vee \cdots \vee (x_{it} \oplus x_{jt}))$ for $1 \leq i < j \leq m$ can be put into the CNF form $(y_{ij1} \vee \cdots \vee y_{ijt})$ as in exercise 39, by introducing auxiliary clauses $(\bar{y}_{ijk} \vee x_{ik} \vee x_{jk}) \wedge (y_{ijk} \vee x_{ik} \vee \bar{x}_{jk}) \wedge (y_{ijk} \vee \bar{x}_{ik} \vee x_{jk}) \wedge (\bar{y}_{ijk} \vee \bar{x}_{ik} \vee \bar{x}_{jk})$. (Only the first and last of these four clauses are actually needed.) The total size of this CNF is $\Theta(m^2 \log n)$, compared to $\Theta(m^2 n)$ in Solution 1. If n is not a power of 2, $O(m \log n)$ additional clauses of size $O(\log n)$ will rule out inappropriate values.

42. $(\bar{x} \vee y) \wedge (\bar{z} \vee x) \wedge (\bar{y} \vee z) \wedge (z \vee z)$.

43. Probably not, because every 3SAT problem can be converted to this form. For example, the clause $(x_1 \vee x_2 \vee \bar{x}_3)$ can be replaced by $(x_1 \vee \bar{y} \vee \bar{x}_3) \wedge (\bar{y} \vee \bar{x}_2) \wedge (y \vee x_2)$, where y is a new variable (essentially equivalent to $\bar{x}_2$).

44. Suppose $f(x) = f(y) = 1$ implies $f(x \& y) = 1$ and also that, say, $c = x_1 \vee x_2 \vee \bar{x}_3 \vee \bar{x}_4$ is a prime clause of f. Then $c' = \bar{x}_1 \vee x_2 \vee \bar{x}_3 \vee \bar{x}_4$ is *not* a clause; otherwise $c \wedge c' = x_2 \vee \bar{x}_3 \vee \bar{x}_4$ would also be a clause, contradicting primality. So there's a vector y with $f(y) = 1$ and $y_1 = 1$, $y_2 = 0$, $y_3 = y_4 = 1$. Similarly, there's a z with $f(z) = 1$ and $z_1 = 0$, $z_2 = 1$, $z_3 = z_4 = 1$. But then $f(y \& z) = 1$, and c isn't a clause. The same argument works for a clause c that has a different number of literals, as long as at least two of the literals aren't complemented.

45. (a) A Horn function $f(x_1, \ldots, x_n)$ is indefinite if and only if it is unequal to the definite Horn function $g(x_1, \ldots, x_n) = f(x_1, \ldots, x_n) \vee (x_1 \wedge \cdots \wedge x_n)$. So $f \leftrightarrow g$ is a one-to-one correspondence between indefinite and definite Horn functions. (b) If f is monotone, its complement $\bar{f}$ is either identically 1 or an indefinite Horn function.

46. Algorithm C puts 88 pairs xy in the core: When x = a, b, c, 0, or 1, the following character y can be anything but (. When x = (, *, /, +, -, we can have y = (, a, b, c, 0, 1; also y = - when x = (, +, or -. Finally, the legitimate pairs beginning with x =) are)+,)-,)*,)/,)).

47. The order in which Algorithm C brings vertices into the core is a topological sort, since all predecessors of k are asserted before the algorithm sets TRUTH$(x_k) \leftarrow 1$. But Algorithm 2.2.3T uses a queue instead of a stack, so the ordering it actually produces is usually different from that of Algorithm C.

48. Let $\bot$ be a new variable, and change every indefinite Horn clause to a definite one by ORing in this new variable. (For example, '$\bar{w} \vee \bar{y}$' becomes '$\bar{w} \vee \bar{y} \vee \bot$', namely '$w \wedge y \Rightarrow \bot$'; definite Horn clauses stay unchanged.) Then apply Algorithm C. The original clauses are unsatisfiable if and only if $\bot$ is in the core of the new clauses. The algorithm can therefore be terminated as soon as it is about to set TRUTH$(\bot) \leftarrow 1$.

(J. H. Quick thought of another solution: We could apply Algorithm C to the function g constructed in the answer to exercise 45(a), because f is unsatisfiable if and only if *every* variable x_j is in the core of g. However, indefinite clauses of f such as $\bar{w} \vee \bar{y}$ become many different clauses $(\bar{w} \vee \bar{y} \vee z) \wedge (\bar{w} \vee \bar{y} \vee x) \wedge (\bar{w} \vee \bar{y} \vee v) \wedge (\bar{w} \vee \bar{y} \vee u) \wedge \cdots$ of g, one for each variable not in the original clause. So Quick's suggestion, which might sound elegant at first blush, could increase the number of clauses by a factor of $\Omega(n)$.)

49. We have $f \leq g$ if and only if $f \wedge \bar{g}$ is unsatisfiable, if and only if $f \wedge \bar{c}$ is unsatisfiable for every clause c of g. But $\bar{c}$ is an AND of literals, so we can apply exercise 48. [See H. Kleine Büning and T. Lettmann, *Aussagenlogik: Deduktion und Algorithmen* (1994), §5.6, for further results including an efficient way to test if g is a "renaming" of f, namely to determine whether or not there exist constants $(y_1, \ldots, y_n)$ such that $f(x_1, \ldots, x_n) = g(x_1 \oplus y_1, \ldots, x_n \oplus y_n)$.]

50. See Gabriel Istrate, *Random Structures & Algorithms* **20** (2002), 483–506.

51. If vertex v is marked A, introduce the clauses $\Rightarrow A^+(v)$ and $\Rightarrow B^-(v)$; if it is marked B, introduce $\Rightarrow A^-(v)$ and $\Rightarrow B^+(v)$. Otherwise let v have k outgoing arcs $v \rightarrow u_1, \ldots, v \rightarrow u_k$. Introduce the clauses $A^-(u_j) \Rightarrow B^+(v)$ and $B^-(u_j) \Rightarrow A^+(v)$ for $1 \leq j \leq k$. Also, if v is not marked C, introduce the clauses $A^+(u_1) \wedge \cdots \wedge A^+(u_k) \Rightarrow B^-(v)$ and $B^+(u_1) \wedge \cdots \wedge B^+(u_k) \Rightarrow A^-(v)$. All forcing strategies are consequences of these clauses. Exercise 2.2.3–28 and its answer provide further information.

Notice that, in principle, Algorithm C can therefore be used to decide whether or not the game of chess is a forced victory for the white pieces — except for the annoying detail that the corresponding digraph is larger than the physical universe.

52. With best play, the results (see exercise 51) are:

n	(a)	(b)	(c)	(d)
2	0 wins	second player wins	1 wins	second player wins
3	0 wins	first player wins	first player wins	first player wins
4	first player wins	first player wins	first player wins	first player wins
5	second player wins	draw	draw	1 loses if first
6	second player wins	second player wins	1 loses if first	1 loses if first
7	1 loses if first	second player wins	1 loses if first	1 loses if first
8	draw	draw	draw	1 loses if first
9	draw	draw	draw	1 loses if first

(Here "1 loses if first" means that the game is a draw if player 0 plays first, otherwise 0 can win.) *Comments:* In (a), player 1 has a slight disadvantage, because $f(x) = 0$ when $x_1 \ldots x_n$ is a palindrome. This small difference affects the result even when $n = 7$. Although player 1 would seem to be better off playing 0s in the left half of the board, it turns out that his/her first move when $n = 4$ must be to *1**; the alternative, *0**, draws. Game (b) is essentially a race to see who can eliminate the last *. In game (c), a random choice of $x_1 \ldots x_n$ makes $f(x) = 1$ with probability $F_{n+2}/2^n = \Theta((\phi/2)^n)$; in game (d), this probability approaches zero more slowly, as $\Theta(1/\log n)$. Still, player 1 does better in (c) than in (d) when $n = 2, 5, 8$, and 9; no worse in the other cases.

53. (a) She should switch either day 1 or day 2 to day 3.

(b, f) Several possibilities; for example, change day 2 to day 3.

(c) This case is illustrated in Fig. 6; change either Desert or Excalibur to Aladdin.

(d) Change either Caesars or Excalibur to Aladdin.

(e) Change either Bellagio or Desert to Aladdin.

Of course Williams, who doesn't appear in the cycle (42), bears no responsibility whatever for the conflicts.

54. If x and $\bar{x}$ are both in S, then $u \in S \implies \bar{u} \in S$, because the existence of paths from x to u and u to x implies the existence of paths from $\bar{u}$ to $\bar{x}$ and $\bar{x}$ to $\bar{u}$. Similarly, $\bar{u} \in S \implies u \in S$.

55. (a) Necessary and sufficient conditions for successfully renaming a clause such as $x_1 \vee \bar{x}_2 \vee x_3 \vee \bar{x}_4$ are $(y_1 \vee \bar{y}_2) \wedge (y_1 \vee y_3) \wedge (y_1 \vee \bar{y}_4) \wedge (\bar{y}_2 \vee y_3) \wedge (\bar{y}_2 \vee \bar{y}_4) \wedge (y_3 \vee \bar{y}_4)$. A similar set of $\binom{k}{2}$ clauses of length 2 in the variables $\{y_1, \ldots, y_n\}$ corresponds to any clause of length k in $\{x_1, \ldots, x_n\}$. [H. R. Lewis, *JACM* **25** (1978), 134–135.]

(b) A given clause of length $k > 3$ in $\{x_1, \ldots, x_n\}$ can be converted into $3(k - 2)$ clauses of length 2, instead of the $\binom{k}{2}$ clauses above, by introducing $k - 3$ new variables $\{t_2, \ldots, t_{k-2}\}$, illustrated here for the clause $x_1 \vee x_2 \vee x_3 \vee x_4 \vee x_5$:

$$(y_1 \vee y_2) \wedge (y_1 \vee t_2) \wedge (y_2 \vee t_2) \wedge (\bar{t}_2 \vee y_3) \wedge (\bar{t}_2 \vee t_3) \wedge (y_3 \vee t_3) \wedge (\bar{t}_3 \vee y_4) \wedge (\bar{t}_3 \vee y_5) \wedge (y_4 \vee y_5).$$

In general, the clauses from $x_1 \vee \cdots \vee x_k$ are $(\bar{t}_{j-1} \vee y_j) \wedge (\bar{t}_{j-1} \vee t_j) \wedge (y_j \vee t_j)$ for $1 < j < k$, but with t_1 replaced by $\bar{y}_1$ and t_{k-1} replaced by y_k; change y_j to $\bar{y}_j$ if $\bar{x}_j$ appears instead of x_j. Do this for each given clause, using different auxiliary variables t_j for different clauses; the result is a formula in 2CNF that has length $< 3m$ and is satisfiable if and only if Horn renaming is possible. Now apply Theorem K. (The number of t variables can be reduced, as in exercise 7.2.2.2–12.)

[See B. Aspvall, *J. Algorithms* **1** (1980), 97–103. One consequence, noted by H. Kleine Büning and T. Lettmann in *Aussagenlogik: Deduktion und Algorithmen* (1994), Theorem 5.2.4, is that any satisfiable formula in 2CNF can be renamed to Horn clauses. Notice that two CNFs for the same function may give different outcomes; for example, $(x \lor y \lor z) \land (\bar{x} \lor \bar{y} \lor \bar{z}) \land (\bar{x} \lor z) \land (\bar{y} \lor z)$ is actually a Horn function, but the clauses in this representation cannot be converted to Horn form by complementation.]

56. Here $f(x, y, z)$ corresponds to the digraph shown below (analogous to Fig. 6), and it can also be simplified to $y \land (\bar{x} \lor z)$. Each vertex is a strong component. So the formula is true with respect to the quantifiers $\exists\exists\exists$, $\exists\exists\forall$, $\forall\exists\exists$; false in the other cases $\forall\exists\forall$, (any)$\forall$(any). In general the eight possibilities can be arranged at the corners of a cube, with each change from $\exists$ to $\forall$ making the formula more likely to be false.

57. Forming the digraph as in Theorem K, we can prove that the quantified formula holds if and only if (i) no strong component contains both x and $\bar{x}$; (ii) there is no path from one universal variable x to another universal variable y or to its complement $\bar{y}$; (iii) no strong component containing a universal variable x also contains an existential variable v or its complement $\bar{v}$, when '$\exists v$' appears to the left of '$\forall x$'. These three conditions are clearly necessary, and they are readily tested as the strong components are being found.

To show that they are sufficient, notice first that if S is a strong component with only existential literals, condition (i) allows us to set them all equal as in Theorem K. Otherwise S has exactly one universal literal, $u_j = x_j$ or $u_j = \bar{x}_j$; all other literals in S are existential and declared to the right of x_j, so we can equate them to u_j. And all paths into S in such a case come from purely existential strong components, whose value can be set to 0 because the complements of such strong components cannot also lead into S; for if v and $\bar{v}$ imply u_j, then $\bar{u}_j$ implies $\bar{v}$ and v.

[*Information Proc. Letters* **8** (1979), 121–123. By contrast, M. Krom had proved in *J. Symbolic Logic* **35** (1970), 210–216, that an analogous problem in first-order predicate calculus (where parameterized predicates take the place of simple Boolean variables, and quantification is over the parameters) is actually unsolvable in general.]

58. We can assume that each clause is definite, by introducing '$\perp$' as in exercise 48 and placing '$\forall\perp$' at the left. Call the universal variables $x_0, x_1, \ldots, x_m$ (where x_0 is $\perp$) and call the existential variables $y_1, \ldots, y_n$. Let '$u \prec v$' mean that variable u appears to the left of variable v in the list of quantifiers. Remove $\bar{x}_j$ from any clause whose unbarred literal is y_k when $y_k \prec x_j$. Then, for $0 \le j \le m$, let C_j be the core of the Horn clauses when the additional clauses $(x_0) \land \cdots \land (x_{j-1}) \land (x_{j+1}) \land \cdots \land (x_m) \land \bigwedge\{(y_k) \mid y_k \prec x_j$ and $y_k \in C_0\}$ are appended. (In other words, C_j tells us what can be deduced when all the x's except x_j are assumed to be true.) We claim that the given formula is true if and only if $x_j \notin C_j$, for $0 \le j \le m$.

To prove this claim, note first that the formula is certainly false if $x_j \in C_j$ for some j. (When $y_k \in C_0$ and $y_k \prec x_j$ and $x_i = 1$ for $i \ne j$ we must set $y_k \leftarrow 1$.) Otherwise we can choose each y_k to make the formula true, as follows: If $y_k \notin C_0$, set $y_k \leftarrow 0$; otherwise set $y_k \leftarrow \bigwedge\{x_j \mid y_k \notin C_j\}$. Notice that y_k depends on x_j only when $x_j \prec y_k$. Each clause c with unbarred literal x_j is now true: For if $x_j = 0$, some $\bar{y}_k$ appears in c for which $y_k \notin C_j$, because $x_j \notin C_j$; hence $y_k = 0$. And each clause c with unbarred literal y_k is also true: If $y_k = 0$, we either have $y_k \notin C_0$, in which case some $\bar{y}_l$ in c is $\notin C_0$, hence $y_l = 0$; or $y_k \in C_0 \setminus C_j$ for some j, in which case some $x_j = 0$ and either $\bar{x}_j$ appears in c or some $\bar{y}_l$ appears in c where $y_l \notin C_j$, making $y_l = 0$.

[This solution is due to T. Dahlheimer. See M. Karpinski, H. Kleine Büning, and P. H. Schmitt, *Lecture Notes in Comp. Sci.* **329** (1988), 129–137; H. Kleine Büning, K. Subramani, and X. Zhao, *Lecture Notes in Comp. Sci.* **2919** (2004), 93–104.]

59. By induction on n: Suppose $f(0, x_2, \ldots, x_n)$ leads to the quantified results $y_1, \ldots, y_{2^{n-1}}$, while $f(1, x_2, \ldots, x_n)$ leads similarly to $z_1, \ldots, z_{2^{n-1}}$. Then $\exists x_1 f(x_1, x_2, \ldots, x_n)$ leads to $y_1 \vee z_1, \ldots, y_{2^{n-1}} \vee z_{2^{n-1}}$, and $\forall x_1 f(x_1, x_2, \ldots, x_n)$ leads to $y_1 \wedge z_1, \ldots, y_{2^{n-1}} \wedge z_{2^{n-1}}$. Now use the fact that $(y \vee z) + (y \wedge z) = y + z$. [See *Proc. Mini-Workshop on Quantified Boolean Formulas* **2** (QBF-02) (Cincinnati: May 2002), 1–16.]

60. Both (a) and (b). But (c) is always 0; (d) is always 1; (e) is $\overline{\langle xyz \rangle}$; (f) is $\bar{x} \vee \bar{y} \vee \bar{z}$.

61. True — indeed obviously so, when $w = 0$, and when $w = 1$.

62. Since $\{x_1, x_2, x_3\} \subseteq \{0, 1\}$, we can assume by symmetry that x_1 equals x_2. Then either $f(x_1, x_1, x_3, x_4, \ldots, x_n) = f(x_1, x_1, x_1, x_4, \ldots, x_n)$ or $f(x_1, x_1, x_3, x_4, \ldots, x_n) = f(x_3, x_1, x_3, x_4, \ldots, x_n)$, assuming only that f is monotone in its first three variables.

63. $\langle xyz \rangle = \langle xxyyz \rangle$. *Note:* Emil Post proved, in fact, that a single subroutine for *any* nontrivial monotone self-dual function will suffice to compute them all. (By induction on n, at least one appropriate way to call such an n-ary subroutine will yield $\langle xyz \rangle$.)

64. [*FOCS* **3** (1962), 149–157.] (a) If f is monotone and self-dual, Theorem P says that $f(x) = x_k$ or $f(x) = \langle f_1(x) f_2(x) f_3(x) \rangle$. The condition therefore holds either immediately or by induction. Conversely, if the condition holds it implies that f is monotone (when x and y differ in just one bit) and self-dual (when they differ in all bits).

(b) We merely need to show that it is possible to define f at one new point without introducing a conflict. Let x be the lexicographically smallest point where $f(x)$ is undefined. If $f(\bar{x})$ is defined, set $f(x) = \overline{f(\bar{x})}$. Otherwise if $f(x') = 1$ for some $x' \subseteq x$, set $f(x) = 1$; otherwise set $f(x) = 0$. Then the condition still holds.

65. If $\mathcal{F}$ is maximal intersecting, we have (i) $X \in \mathcal{F} \implies \bar{X} \notin \mathcal{F}$, where $\bar{X}$ is the complementary set $\{1, 2, \ldots, n\} \setminus X$; (ii) $X \in \mathcal{F}$ and $X \subseteq Y \implies Y \in \mathcal{F}$, because $\mathcal{F} \cup \{Y\}$ is intersecting; and (iii) $X \notin \mathcal{F} \implies \bar{X} \in \mathcal{F}$, because $\mathcal{F} \cup \{X\}$ must contain an element $Y \subseteq \bar{X}$. Conversely, one can prove without difficulty that any family $\mathcal{F}$ satisfying (i) and (ii) is intersecting, and maximal if it also satisfies (iii).

Punch line: All three statements are simple, in the language of Boolean functions: (i) $f(x) = 1 \implies f(\bar{x}) = 0$; (ii) $x \subseteq y \implies f(x) \leq f(y)$; (iii) $f(x) = 0 \implies f(\bar{x}) = 1$.

66. [T. Ibaraki and T. Kameda, *IEEE Transactions on Parallel and Distributed Systems* **4** (1993), 779–794.] Every family with the property that $Q \subseteq Q'$ implies $Q = Q'$ clearly corresponds to the prime implicants of a monotone Boolean function f. The further condition that $Q \cap Q' \neq \emptyset$ corresponds to the further relation $f(\bar{x}) \leq \overline{f(x)}$, because $f(\bar{x}) = f(x) = 1$ holds if and only if x and $\bar{x}$ both make prime implicants true.

If coteries $\mathcal{C}$ and $\mathcal{C}'$ correspond in this way to functions f and f', then $\mathcal{C}$ dominates $\mathcal{C}'$ if and only if $f \neq f'$ and $f'(x) \leq f(x)$ for all x. Then f' is not self-dual, because there is an x with $f'(\bar{x}) = 0$, $f(\bar{x}) = 1$; and we have $f(x) = 0$, hence $f'(x) = 0$.

Conversely, if f' is not self-dual, there's a y with $f'(y) = f'(\bar{y}) = 0$. If $y = 0 \ldots 0$, coterie $\mathcal{C}'$ is empty, and dominated by every other coterie. Otherwise define $f(x) = f'(x) \vee [x \supseteq y]$. Then f is monotone, and $f(\bar{x}) \leq \overline{f(x)}$ for all x; so it corresponds to a coterie that dominates $\mathcal{C}'$.

67. (a) A black Y in t forces a black Y in t^*, because adjacent black stones $a - b - c$ in t yield two adjacent black stones in t^*. Similarly, a black Y in t^* forces a black Y in t.

(b) This formula follows from (a) and the fact that $(t_{abc})_{def} = t_{(a+d)(b+e)(c+f)} = (t_{def})_{abc}$. [Schensted stated the results of this exercise, and those of exercises 62 and 69, in a 28-page letter sent to Martin Gardner on 21 January 1979. Milnor had written to Gardner on 26 March 1957 about a corresponding game called "Triangle."]

68. Here is one of the 258,594 solutions for $n = 15$ that has 59 black stones: (The answers for $1 \le n \le 15$ are respectively 2, 3, 4, 6, 8, 11, 14, 18, 23, 27, 33, 39, 45, 52, 59. The prime implicants for these functions can be represented by fairly small ZDDs; see Section 7.1.4.)

69. The proof of Theorem P shows that we need only prove $Y(T) \le f(x)$. A Y in T means that we've got at least one variable in each p_j. Therefore $f(\bar{x}_1, \ldots, \bar{x}_n) = 0$, and $f(x_1, \ldots, x_n) = 1$.

70. Self-duality of g is obvious for arbitrary t when f is self-dual: $\overline{g(\bar{x})} = (\overline{f(\bar{x})} \vee [\bar{x} = t]) \wedge [\bar{x} \ne \bar{t}] = (f(x) \vee [x = \bar{t}]) \wedge [x \ne t] = (f(x) \wedge [x \ne t]) \vee ([x = \bar{t}] \wedge [x \ne t]) = g(x)$.

Let $x = x_1 \ldots x_{j-1} 0 x_{j+1} \ldots x_n$ and $y = x_1 \ldots x_{j-1} 1 x_{j+1} \ldots x_n$; for monotonicity we must prove that $g(x) \le g(y)$. If $x = t$ or $y = t$, we have $g(x) = 0$; if $x = \bar{t}$ or $y = \bar{t}$, we have $g(y) = 1$; otherwise $g(x) = f(x) \le f(y) = g(y)$. [*European J. Combinatorics* **16** (1995), 491–501; discovered independently by J. C. Bioch and T. Ibaraki, *IEEE Transactions on Parallel and Distributed Systems* **6** (1995), 905–914.]

71. $\langle\langle xyz\rangle uv\rangle = \langle\langle\langle xyz\rangle uv\rangle uv\rangle = \langle\langle\langle yuv\rangle x\langle zuv\rangle\rangle uv\rangle = \langle\langle yuv\rangle\langle xuv\rangle\langle\langle zuv\rangle uv\rangle\rangle = \langle\langle xuv\rangle\langle yuv\rangle\langle zuv\rangle\rangle$.

72. For (58), $v = \langle uvu\rangle = u$. For (59), $\langle uyv\rangle = \langle vu\langle xuy\rangle\rangle = \langle\langle vux\rangle uy\rangle = \langle xuy\rangle = y$. And for (60), $\langle xyz\rangle = \langle\langle xuv\rangle yz\rangle = \langle x\langle uyz\rangle\langle vyz\rangle\rangle = \langle xyy\rangle = y$.

73. (a) If $d(u, v) = d(u, x) + d(x, v)$, we obviously obtain a shortest path of the form $u \,\text{---}\, \cdots \,\text{---}\, x \,\text{---}\, \cdots \,\text{---}\, v$. Conversely, if $[uxv]$, let $u \,\text{---}\, \cdots \,\text{---}\, x \,\text{---}\, \cdots \,\text{---}\, v$ be a shortest path, with l steps to x followed by m steps to v. Then $d(u, v) = l + m \ge d(u, x) + d(x, v) \ge d(u, v)$.

(b) For all z, $\langle zxu\rangle = \langle z\langle vux\rangle\langle yux\rangle\rangle = \langle\langle zvy\rangle ux\rangle \in \{\langle yux\rangle, \langle vux\rangle\} = \{u, x\}$.

(c) We can assume that $d(x, u) \ge d(x, v) > 0$. Let $u \,\text{---}\, \cdots \,\text{---}\, y \,\text{---}\, v$ be a shortest path, and let $w = \langle xuy\rangle$. Then $\langle vxw\rangle = \langle v\langle vux\rangle\langle wux\rangle\rangle = \langle\langle vvw\rangle ux\rangle = \langle vux\rangle = x$, so $x \in [w \mathinner{.\,.} v]$. We have $[uwy]$, because $d(u, y) < d(u, v)$ and $w \in [u \mathinner{.\,.} y]$. If $w \ne u$ we have $d(w, v) < d(u, v)$; hence $[wxv]$, hence $[uxv]$. If $w = u$ we have $x \,\text{---}\, u$ by (b). But $d(x, u) \ge d(x, v)$; therefore $x \,\text{---}\, v$, and $[uxv]$.

(d) Let $y = \langle uxv\rangle$. Since $y \in [u \mathinner{.\,.} x]$, we have $d(u, x) = d(u, y) + d(y, x)$ by (a) and (c). Similarly, $d(u, v) = d(u, y) + d(y, v)$ and $d(x, v) = d(x, y) + d(y, v)$. But these three equations, together with $d(u, v) = d(u, x) + d(x, v)$, yield $d(x, y) = 0$. [*Proc. Amer. Math. Soc.* **12** (1961), 407–414.]

74. $w = \langle yxw\rangle = \langle yx\langle zxw\rangle\rangle = \langle yx\langle zx\langle yzw\rangle\rangle\rangle = \langle\langle yxz\rangle x\langle yzw\rangle\rangle = \langle x\langle xyz\rangle\langle wyz\rangle\rangle = \langle\langle xxw\rangle yz\rangle = \langle xyz\rangle$ by (55), (55), (55), (52), (51), (53), and (50).

75. (a) If $w = \langle xxy\rangle$ we have $[xwx]$ by (iii), hence $w = x$ by (i).

(b) Axiom (iii) and part (a) tell us that $[xxy]$ is always true. So we can set $y = x$ in (ii) to conclude that $[uxv] \iff [vxu]$. The definition of $\langle xyz\rangle$ in (iii) is therefore perfectly symmetrical between x, y, and z.

(c) By the definition of $\langle uxv\rangle$ in (iii), we have $x = \langle uxv\rangle$ if and only if $[uxx]$, $[uxv]$, and $[xxv]$. But we know that $[uxx]$ and $[xxv]$ are always true.

(d) In this step and subsequent steps, we will construct one or more auxiliary points of M and then use Algorithm C to derive every consequence of the betweenness relations that are known. (The axioms have the convenient form of Horn clauses.) For example, here we define $z = \langle xyv \rangle$, so that we know $[uxy]$, $[uyv]$, $[xzy]$, $[xzv]$, and $[yzv]$. From these hypotheses we deduce $[uzy]$ and $[uzv]$. So $z = \langle uyv \rangle = y$.

(e) The hinted construction implies, among other things, $[utv]$, $[utz]$, $[vtz]$, $[uwv]$, $[uwz]$, $[vwz]$; hence $t = w$. (A computer program is helpful here.) Adding the hypotheses $[rws]$, $[rwz]$, $[swz]$ now yields $[xyz]$ as desired; it also turns out that $r = p$ and $s = q$.

(f) Let $r = \langle yuv \rangle$, $s = \langle zuv \rangle$, $t = \langle xyz \rangle$, $p = \langle xrs \rangle$, $q = \langle tuv \rangle$; then $[pqp]$ flows out. [*Proc. Amer. Math. Soc.* **5** (1954), 801–807. For early studies of betweenness axioms, see E. V. Huntington and J. R. Kline, *Trans. Amer. Math. Soc.* **18** (1917), 301–325.]

76. Axiom (i) obviously holds, and axiom (ii) follows from commutativity and (52). The answer to exercise 74 derives (iii) from the identity $\langle xyz \rangle = \langle x \langle xyz \rangle \langle wyz \rangle \rangle$; so we need only verify that formula: $\langle x \langle xyz \rangle \langle wyz \rangle \rangle = \langle \langle yxz \rangle x \langle wyz \rangle \rangle = \langle \langle \langle yxz \rangle xz \rangle x \langle wyz \rangle \rangle = \langle \langle yxz \rangle x \langle zx \langle wyz \rangle \rangle \rangle = \langle x \langle xyz \rangle \langle z \langle xyz \rangle w \rangle \rangle = \langle \langle x \langle xyz \rangle z \rangle \langle xyz \rangle w \rangle = \langle \langle xyz \rangle \langle xyz \rangle w \rangle$.

Notes: The original treatment of median algebra by Birkhoff and Kiss in *Bull. Amer. Math. Soc.* **53** (1947), 749–752, assumed (50), (51), and the short distributive law (53). The fact that associativity (52) actually implies distributivity was not realized until many years later; M. Kolibiar and T. Marcisová, *Matematický Časopis* **24** (1974), 179–185, proved it via Sholander's axioms as in this exercise. A mechanical derivation of (53) from (50)–(52) was found in 2005 by R. Veroff and W. McCune, using an extension of the Otter theorem prover.

77. (a) In coordinate $r \longrightarrow s$ of the labels, suppose $l(r)$ has a 0 and $l(s)$ has a 1; then the left vertices have 0 in that coordinate. If $u \longrightarrow v \longrightarrow u'$, where u and u' are on the left but v is on the right, $\langle uu'v \rangle$ lies on the left. But $[u..v] \cap [u'..v] = \{v\}$, unless $u = u'$.

(b) This statement is obvious, by Corollary C.

(c) Suppose $u \longrightarrow v$ and $u' \longrightarrow v'$, where u and u' are on the left, v and v' are on the right. Let $v = v_0 \longrightarrow \cdots \longrightarrow v_k = v'$ be a shortest path, and let $u_0 = u$, $u_k = u'$. All vertices v_j lie on the right, by (b). The left vertex $u_1 = \langle u_0 v_1 u_k \rangle$ must be a common neighbor of u_0 and v_1, since the distance $d(u_0, v_1) = 2$. (We cannot have $u_1 = u_0$, because that would imply the existence of a shortest path from v to v' going through the left vertex u.) Therefore v_1 has rank 1; and so do v_2, ..., v_{k-1}, by the same argument. [L. Nebeský, *Commentationes Mathematicæ Universitatis Carolinæ* **12** (1971), 317–325; M. Mulder, *Discrete Math.* **24** (1978), 197–204.]

(d) These steps visit all vertices v of rank 1 in order of their distance $d(v, s)$ from s. If such a v has a late neighbor u not yet seen, the rank of u must be 1 or 2. If the rank is 1, u will have at least two early neighbors, namely v and the future MATE(u). Step I8 bases its decision on an arbitrary early neighbor w of u such that $w \neq v$. The vertex $x = \langle svw \rangle$ has rank 1 by (c). If $x = v$, then u has rank 2 unless w has rank 0. Otherwise $d(x, s) < d(v, s)$, and the rank of w was correctly determined when x was visited. If w has rank 1, u lies on a shortest path from v to w; if w has rank 2, w lies on a shortest path from u to s. In both cases u and w have the same rank, by (c).

(e) The algorithm removes all edges equivalent to $r \longrightarrow s$, by (a) and (d). Their removal clearly disconnects the graph; the two pieces that remain are convex by (b), so they are connected and in fact they are median graphs. Step I7 records all of the relevant relations between the two pieces, because all 4-cycles that disappear are examined there. By induction on the number of vertices, each piece is properly labeled.

78. Every time v appears in step I4, it loses one of its neighbors u_j. Each of these edges v —— u_j corresponds to a different coordinate of the labels, so we can assume that $l(v)$ has the form $\alpha 1^k$ for some binary string α. The labels for $u_1, u_2, \ldots, u_k$ are then $\alpha 01^{k-1}$, $\alpha 101^{k-2}$, $\ldots$, $\alpha 1^{k-1}0$. By taking componentwise medians, we can now prove that all 2^k labels of the form $\alpha\beta$ occur for vertices in the graph, since $\langle(\alpha\beta)(\alpha\beta')(0\ldots0)\rangle$ is the bit string $\alpha(\beta \,\&\, \beta')$.

79. (a) If $l(v) = k$, exactly $\nu(k)$ smaller vertices are neighbors of v.

(b) At most $\lfloor n/2\rfloor$ 1s appear in bit position j, for $0 \le j < \lceil \lg n\rceil$.

(c) Suppose exactly k vertices have labels beginning with 0. At most $\min(k, n-k)$ edges correspond to that bit position, and at most $f(k) + f(n-k)$ other edges are present. But
$$f(n) = \max_{0\le k\le n}\big(\min(k, n-k) + f(k) + f(n-k)\big),$$
because the function $g(m,n) = f(m+n) - m - f(m) - f(n)$ satisfies the recurrence
$$g(2m + a, 2n + b) = ab + g(m + a, n) + g(m, n + b) \qquad \text{for } 0 \le a, b \le 1.$$
It follows by induction that $g(m,m) = g(m, m+1) = 0$, and that $q(m,n) \ge 0$ when $m \le n$. [*Annals of the New York Academy of Sciences* **175** (1970), 170–186; D. E. Knuth, *Proc. IFIP Congress 1971* (1972), 24.]

80. (a) (Solution by W. Imrich.) The graph with vertex labels 0000, 0001, 0010, 0011, 0100, 0110, 0111, 1100, 1101, 1110, 1111 cannot be labeled in any essentially different way; but the distance from 0001 to 1101 is 4, not 2.

(b) The cycle C_{2m} is a partial cube, because its vertices can be labeled $l(k) = 1^k 0^{m-k}$, $l(m+k) = 0^k 1^{m-k}$ for $0 \le k < m$. But the bitwise median of $l(0)$, $l(m-1)$, and $l(m+1)$ is $01^{m-2}0$; and indeed those vertices don't have a median, when $m > 2$.

81. Yes. A median graph is an induced subgraph of a hypercube, which is bipartite.

82. The general case reduces to the simple case where G has only two vertices $\{0,1\}$, because we can operate componentwise on the median labels, and because $d(u,v)$ is the Hamming distance between $l(u)$ and $l(v)$.

In the simple case, the stated rule sets $u_k \leftarrow v_k$ except when $u_{k-1} = v_{k-1} = v_{k+1} \neq v_k$, and it is readily proved optimum. (Other optimum possibilities do exist, however; for example, if $v_0 v_1 v_2 v_3 = 0110$, we could set $u_0 u_1 u_2 u_3 = 0000$.)

[This problem was motivated by the study of self-organizing data structures. F. R. K. Chung, R. L. Graham, and M. E. Saks, in *Discrete Algorithms and Complexity* (Academic Press, 1987), 351–387, have proved that median graphs are the *only* graphs for which u_k can always be chosen optimally as a function of $(v_0, v_1, \ldots, v_{k+1})$, regardless of the subsequent values $(v_{k+2}, \ldots, v_t)$. They have also characterized all cases for which a given finite amount of lookahead will suffice, in *Combinatorica* **9** (1989), 111–131.]

83. Consider first the Boolean (two-vertex) case, and let an optimum solution be obtainable by the recursive rules $u_0 \leftarrow v_0$ and $u_j \leftarrow f_{t+2-j}(u_{j-1}, v_j, \ldots, v_t)$ for $1 \le j \le t$, where each f_k is a suitable Boolean function of k variables. The first function $f_{t+1}(v_0, v_1, \ldots, v_t)$ actually depends on its "most remote" variable v_t, because we must have $f_{2k+1}(0, 1, 0, 1, 0, 1, \ldots, 0, 1, 0, x) = x$ when $\rho = 1 - \epsilon$ and $k \ge 2$.

One suitable function f_{t+1} can be obtained as follows: Let $f_{t+1}(0, v_1, \ldots, v_t) = 0$ if $v_1 = 0$. Otherwise let the "runs" of the input sequence be
$$v_0 v_1 \ldots v_t = 01^{a_k}0^{a_{k-1}}\ldots 1^{a_2}0^{a_1} \qquad \text{or} \qquad 01^{a_k}0^{a_{k-1}}\ldots 1^{a_3}0^{a_2}1^{a_1},$$

where $a_k, \ldots, a_1 \geq 1$, and let $\alpha_j = 2 \dot{-} a_j\rho = \max(0, 2 - a_j\rho)$ for $1 \leq j \leq k$. Then

$$f_{t+1}(0, v_1, \ldots, v_t) = [\alpha_k \dot{-} (\alpha_{k-1} \dot{-} (\cdots \dot{-} (\alpha_2 \dot{-} (1 \dot{-} a_1\rho)) \cdots)) = 0].$$

Also let $f_{t+1}(1, v_1, \ldots, v_t) = \bar{f}_{t+1}(0, \bar{v}_1, \ldots, \bar{v}_t)$, so that f_{t+1} is self-dual.

With a somewhat delicate proof one can show that f_{t+1} is also monotone.

Therefore, by Theorem P, we can apply f_{t+1} componentwise to the labels of an arbitrary median graph, always staying within the graph.

84. There are 81 such functions, each of which can be represented as the median of an odd number of elements. Seven types of vertices occur:

Type	Typical vertex	Cases	Adjacent to	Degree
1	$\langle z \rangle$	5	$\langle vwxyzzz \rangle$	1
2	$\langle vwxyzzz \rangle$	5	$\langle z \rangle, \langle wxyzz \rangle$	5
3	$\langle wxyzz \rangle$	20	$\langle vwxyzzz \rangle, \langle vwxxyyzzz \rangle$	4
4	$\langle vwxxyyzzz \rangle$	30	$\langle xyz \rangle, \langle wxyzz \rangle, \langle vwxyyzz \rangle$	5
5	$\langle vwxyyzz \rangle$	10	$\langle vwxxyyzzz \rangle, \langle vwxyz \rangle$	7
6	$\langle vwxyz \rangle$	1	$\langle vwxyyzz \rangle$	10
7	$\langle xyz \rangle$	10	$\langle vwxxyyzzz \rangle$	3

[Von Neumann and Morgenstern enumerated these seven types in their book *Theory of Games and Economic Behavior* (1944), §52.5, in connection with the study of an equivalent problem about systems of winning coalitions that they called *simple games*. The graph for six-variable functions, which has 2646 vertices of 30 types, appears in the paper by Meyerowitz cited in exercise 70. Only 21 of those types can be represented as a simple median-of-odd; a vertex like $\langle \langle abd \rangle \langle ace \rangle \langle bcf \rangle \rangle$, for example, has no such representation. Let the corresponding graph for n variables have M_n vertices. P. Erdös and N. Hindman, in *Discrete Math.* **48** (1984), 61–65, showed that $\lg M_n$ is asymptotic to $\binom{n-1}{\lfloor n/2 \rfloor}$. D. Kleitman, in *J. Combin. Theory* **1** (1966), 153–155, showed that the vertices for distinct projection functions like x and y are always furthest apart in this graph.]

85. Every strong component must consist of a single vertex; otherwise two coordinates would always be equal, or always complementary. Thus the digraph must be acyclic.

Furthermore, there must be no path from a vertex to its complement; otherwise a coordinate would be constant.

When these two conditions are satisfied, we can prove that no vertex x is redundant, by assigning the value 0 to all vertices that precede x or $\bar{x}$, assigning 1 to all vertices that follow, and giving appropriate values to all other vertices.

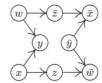

(Consequently we obtain a completely different way to represent a median graph. For example, the digraph shown corresponds to the median graph whose labels are $\{0000, 0001, 0010, 0011, 0111, 1010\}$.)

86. Yes. By Theorem P, *any* monotone self-dual function maps elements of X into X.

87. Here the topological ordering $7\,6\,5\,4\,3\,2\,1\,\bar{1}\,\bar{2}\,\bar{3}\,\bar{4}\,\bar{5}\,\bar{6}\,\bar{7}$ can replace (72); we get

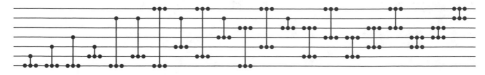

(Consecutive inverters on the same line can, of course, be canceled out.)

88. A given value of d contributes at most $6\lceil t/d\rceil$ units of delay (for $2\lceil t/d\rceil$ clusters). (Actually $O(t)$ delay suffices, as observed by Omid Etesami, if we rearrange clusters having the same d, since those can each be done in ≤ 9 units.)

89. Suppose first that the new condition is $i \to j$ while the old was $i' \to j'$, where $i < j$ and $i' < j'$ and there are no complemented literals. The new module changes $x_1 \ldots x_t$ to $y_1 \ldots y_t$, where $y_i = x_i \wedge x_j$, $y_j = x_i \vee x_j$, and $y_k = x_k$ otherwise. We certainly have $y_{i'} \leq y_{j'}$ when $\{i', j'\} \cap \{i, j\} = \emptyset$. And there is no problem if $i = i'$, since $y_{i'} = y_i \leq x_i = x_{i'} \leq x_{j'} = y_{j'}$. But the case $i = j'$ is trickier: Here the relations $i' \to i$ and $i \to j$ imply also $i' \to j$; and this relation has been enforced by *previous* modules, because modules have been appended in order of decreasing distance d in the topological ordering $u_1 \ldots u_{2t}$. Therefore $y_{i'} = x_{i'} \leq x_j$ and $y_{i'} \leq x_{j'} = x_i$, hence $y_{i'} \leq x_i \wedge x_j = y_i = y_{j'}$. A similar proof works when $j = i'$ or $j = j'$.

Finally, with complemented literals, the construction cleverly reduces the general case to the uncomplemented case by inverting and un-inverting the bits.

90. When $t = 2$, ▭▭ does the job. The general case follows recursively from this building block by reducing t to $\lceil t/2\rceil$.

[The study of CI-nets, and other networks of greater generality, was initiated by E. W. Mayr and A. Subramanian, *J. Computer and System Sci.* **44** (1992), 302–323.]

91. The answer does not yet seem to be known even in the special case when the median graph is a free tree (with $t + 1$ vertices), or in the monotone case when it is a distributive lattice as in Corollary F. In the latter case, inverters may be unnecessary.

93. Let $d_X(u, v)$ be the number of edges on a shortest path between u and v, when the path lies entirely within X. Clearly $d_X(u, v) \geq d_G(u, v)$. And if $u = u_0 \,—\, u_1 \,—\, \cdots \,—\, u_k = v$ is a shortest path in G, the path $u = f(u_0) \,—\, f(u_1) \,—\, \cdots \,—\, f(u_k) = v$ lies in X when f is a retraction from G to X; hence $d_X(u, v) \leq d_G(u, v)$.

94. If f is a retraction of the t-cube onto X, two different coordinate positions cannot always be equal or always complementary for all $x \in X$, unless they are constant. For if, say, all elements of X have the forms $00*\ldots*$ or $11*\ldots*$, there would be no path between vertices of those two types, contradicting the fact that X is an isometric subgraph (hence connected).

Given $x, y, z \in X$, let $w = \langle xyz\rangle$ be their median in the t-cube. Then $f(w) \in [x \mathbin{..} y] \cap [x \mathbin{..} z] \cap [y \mathbin{..} z]$, because (for example) $f(w)$ lies on a shortest path from x to y in X. So $f(w) = w$, and we have proved that $w \in X$. [This result and its considerably more subtle converse are due to H. J. Bandelt, *J. Graph Theory* **8** (1984), 501–510.]

95. False (although the author was hoping otherwise); the network at the right takes $0001 \mapsto 0000$, $0010 \mapsto 0011$, $1101 \mapsto 0110$, but nothing $\mapsto 0010$. (The set of all possible outputs appears to have no easy characterization, even when no inverters are used. For example, the pure-comparator network at the left, constructed by Tomás Feder, takes $000000 \mapsto 000000$, $010101 \mapsto 010101$, and $101010 \mapsto 011001$, but nothing $\mapsto 010001$. See also exercises 5.3.4–50, 5.3.4–52.)

96. No. If f is a threshold function based on real parameters $w = (w_1, \ldots, w_n)$ and t, let $\max\{w \cdot x \mid f(x) = 0\} = t - \epsilon$. Then $\epsilon > 0$, and f is defined by the 2^n inequalities $w \cdot x - t \geq 0$ when $f(x) = 1$, $t - w \cdot x - \epsilon \geq 0$ when $f(x) = 0$. If A is any $M \times N$ matrix of integers for which the system of linear inequalities $Av \geq (0, \ldots, 0)^T$ has a real-valued solution $v = (v_1, \ldots, v_N)^T$ with $v_N > 0$, there also is such a solution in integers. (Proof by induction on N.) So we can assume that $w_1, \ldots, w_n$, t, and ϵ are integers.

[A closer analysis using Hadamard's inequality (see Eq. 4.6.1–(25)) proves in fact that integer weights of magnitude at most $(n + 1)^{(n+1)/2}/2^n$ will suffice; see S. Muroga, I. Toda, and S. Takasu, *J. Franklin Inst.* **271** (1961), 376–418, Theorem 16. Furthermore, exercise 112 shows that weights nearly that large are sometimes needed.]

97. $\langle 11111x_1x_2 \rangle$, $\langle 111x_1x_2 \rangle$, $\langle 1x_1x_2 \rangle$, $\langle 0x_1x_2 \rangle$, $\langle 000x_1x_2 \rangle$, $\langle 00000x_1x_2 \rangle$.

98. We may assume that $f(x_1, \ldots, x_n) = \langle y_1^{w_1} \ldots y_n^{w_n} \rangle$, with positive integer weights w_j and with $w_1 + \cdots + w_n$ odd. Let δ be the minimum positive value of the 2^n sums $\pm w_1 \pm \cdots \pm w_n$, with n independently varying signs. Renumber all subscripts so that $w_1 + \cdots + w_k - w_{k+1} - \cdots - w_n = \delta$. Then $w_1 y_1 + \cdots + w_n y_n > \frac{1}{2}(w_1 + \cdots + w_n) \iff$ $w_1(y_1 - \frac{1}{2}) + \cdots + w_n(y_n - \frac{1}{2}) > 0 \iff w_1(y_1 - \frac{1}{2}) + \cdots + w_n(y_n - \frac{1}{2}) > -\delta/2 \iff$ $w_1 y_1 + \cdots + w_n y_n > \frac{1}{2}(w_1 + \cdots + w_n - (w_1 + \cdots + w_k - w_{k+1} - \cdots - w_n)) = w_{k+1} + \cdots + w_n \iff w_1 y_1 + \cdots + w_k y_k - w_{k+1} \bar{y}_{k+1} - \cdots - w_n \bar{y}_n > 0$.

99. We have $[x_1 + \cdots + x_{2s-1} + s(y_1 + \cdots + y_{2t-2}) \geq st] = [\lfloor(x_1 + \cdots + x_{2s-1})/s\rfloor + y_1 + \cdots + y_{2t-2} \geq t]$; and $\lfloor(x_1 + \cdots + x_{2s-1})/s\rfloor = [x_1 + \cdots + x_{2s-1} \geq s]$.

(For example, $\langle\langle xyz \rangle uv \rangle = \langle xyzu^2v^2 \rangle$, a quantity that we also know is equal to $\langle x\langle yuv \rangle\langle zuv \rangle\rangle$ and $\langle\langle xuv \rangle\langle yuv \rangle\langle zuv \rangle\rangle$ by Eqs. (53) and (54). *Reference:* C. C. Elgot, *FOCS* **2** (1961), 238.)

100. True, because of the preceding exercise and (45).

101. (a) When $n = 7$ they are $x_7 \wedge x_6$, $x_6 \wedge x_5$, $x_7 \wedge x_5 \wedge x_4$, $x_6 \wedge x_4 \wedge x_3$, $x_7 \wedge x_5 \wedge x_3 \wedge x_2$, $x_6 \wedge x_4 \wedge x_2 \wedge x_1$, $x_7 \wedge x_5 \wedge x_3 \wedge x_1$; and in general there are n prime implicants, forming a similar pattern. (We have either $x_n = x_{n-1}$ or $x_n = \bar{x}_{n-1}$. In the first case, $x_n \wedge x_{n-1}$ is obviously a prime implicant. In the second case, $F_n(x_1, \ldots, x_{n-1}, \bar{x}_{n-1}) = F_{n-1}(x_1, \ldots, x_{n-1})$; so we use the prime implicants of the latter, and insert x_n when x_{n-1} does not appear.)

(b) The shelling pattern (0000011, 0000110, 0001101, 0011010, 0110101, 1101010, 1010101) for $n = 7$ works for all n.

(c) Two of several possibilities for $n = 7$ illustrate the general case:

$$F_7(x_1, \ldots, x_7) = Y \begin{pmatrix} x_6 \\ x_7 \; x_5 \\ x_6 \; x_6 \; x_4 \\ x_7 \; x_5 \; x_7 \; x_3 \\ x_6 \; x_6 \; x_4 \; x_6 \; x_2 \\ x_7 \; x_5 \; x_7 \; x_3 \; x_7 \; x_1 \end{pmatrix} = Y \begin{pmatrix} x_6 \\ x_7 \; x_5 \\ x_6 \; x_6 \; x_4 \\ x_7 \; x_5 \; x_5 \; x_3 \\ x_6 \; x_6 \; x_4 \; x_4 \; x_2 \\ x_7 \; x_5 \; x_5 \; x_3 \; x_3 \; x_1 \end{pmatrix}.$$

[The Fibonacci threshold functions were introduced by S. Muroga, who also discovered the optimality result in exercise 105; see *IEEE Transactions* **EC-14** (1965), 136–148.]

102. (a) By (11) and (12), $\hat{f}(\bar{x}_0, \bar{x}_1, \ldots, \bar{x}_n)$ is the complement of $\hat{f}(x_0, x_1, \ldots, x_n)$.

(b) If f is given by (75), $\hat{f}$ is $[(w + 1 - 2t)x_0 + w_1x_1 + \cdots + w_nx_n \geq w + 1 - t]$, where $w = w_1 + \cdots + w_n$. Conversely, if $\hat{f}$ is a threshold function, so is $f(x_1, \ldots, x_n) = \hat{f}(1, x_1, \ldots, x_n)$. [E. Goto and H. Takahasi, *Proc. IFIP Congress* (1962), 747–752.]

103. [See R. C. Minnick, *IRE Transactions* **EC-10** (1961), 6–16.] We want to minimize $w_1 + \cdots + w_n$ subject to the constraints $w_j \geq 0$ for $1 \leq j \leq n$ and $(2e_1 - 1)w_1 + \cdots + (2e_n - 1)w_n \geq 1$ for each prime implicant $x_1^{e_1} \wedge \cdots \wedge x_n^{e_n}$. For example, if $n = 6$, the prime implicant $x_2 \wedge x_5 \wedge x_6$ would lead to the constraint $-w_1 + w_2 - w_3 - w_4 + w_5 + w_6 \geq 1$. If the minimum is $+\infty$, the given function is not a threshold function. (The answer to exercise 84 gives one of the simplest examples of such a case.) Otherwise, if the solution $(w_1, \ldots, w_n)$ involves only integers, it minimizes the desired size. When noninteger solutions arise, additional constraints must be added until the best solution is found, as in part (c) of the following exercise.

104. First we need an algorithm to generate the prime implicants $x_1^{e_1} \wedge \cdots \wedge x_n^{e_n}$ of a given majority function $\langle x_1^{w_1} \ldots x_n^{w_n} \rangle$, when $w_1 \geq \cdots \geq w_n$ and $w_1 + \cdots + w_n$ is odd:

K1. [Initialize.] Set $t \leftarrow 0$. Then for $j = n, n-1, \ldots, 1$ (in this order), set $a_j \leftarrow t, t \leftarrow t + w_j, e_j \leftarrow 0$. Finally set $t \leftarrow (t+1)/2$, $s_1 \leftarrow 0$, and $l \leftarrow 0$.

K2. [Enter level l.] Set $l \leftarrow l+1$, $e_l \leftarrow 1$, $s_{l+1} \leftarrow s_l + w_l$.

K3. [Below threshold?] If $s_{l+1} < t$, return to K2.

K4. [Visit a prime implicant.] Visit the exponents $(e_1, \ldots, e_n)$.

K5. [Downsize.] Set $e_l \leftarrow 0$. Then if $s_l + a_l \geq t$, set $s_{l+1} \leftarrow s_l$ and go to K2.

K6. [Backtrack.] Set $l \leftarrow l-1$. Terminate if $l = 0$; otherwise go to K5 if $e_l = 1$; otherwise repeat this step. ∎

(a) $\langle x_1 x_2^2 x_3^3 x_4^5 x_5^6 x_6^8 x_7^{10} x_8^{12} \rangle$ (21 prime implicants).

(b) The optimum weights for $\langle x_0^{16-2t} x_1^8 x_2^4 x_3^2 x_4 \rangle$ are $w_0 w_1 w_2 w_3 w_4 = 10000, 31111,$ $21110, 32211, 11100, 23211, 12110, 13111, 01000$, for $0 \leq t \leq 8$; the other cases are dual.

(c) Here the optimum weights $(w_1, \ldots, w_{10})$ are $(29, 25, 19, 15, 12, 8, 8, 3, 3, 0)/2$; so we learn that x_{10} is irrelevant, and we must deal with fractional weights. Constraining $w_8 \geq 2$ gives integer weights $(15, 13, 10, 8, 6, 4, 4, 2, 1, 0)$, which must be optimum because their sum exceeds the previous sum by 2. (Only two of the 175,428 self-dual threshold functions on nine variables have nonintegral weights minimizing $w_1 + \cdots + w_n$; the other one is $\langle x_1^{17} x_2^{15} x_3^{11} x_4^9 x_5^7 x_6^5 x_7^4 x_8^2 x_9 \rangle$. The largest w_1 in a minimum representation occurs in $\langle x_1^{42} x_2^{22} x_3^{18} x_4^{15} x_5^{13} x_6^{10} x_7^8 x_8^4 x_9^3 \rangle$; the largest $w_1 + \cdots + w_9$ occurs uniquely in $\langle x_1^{34} x_2^{32} x_3^{28} x_4^{27} x_5^{24} x_6^{20} x_7^{18} x_8^{15} x_9^{11} \rangle$, which is also an example of the largest w_9. See S. Muroga, T. Tsuboi, and C. R. Baugh, *IEEE Transactions* **C-19** (1970), 818–825.)

105. When $n = 7$, the inequalities generated in exercise 103 are $w_7 + w_6 - w_5 - w_4 - w_3 - w_2 - w_1 \geq 1$, $-w_7 + w_6 + w_5 - w_4 - w_3 - w_2 - w_1 \geq 1$, $w_7 - w_6 + w_5 + w_4 - w_3 - w_2 - w_1 \geq 1$, $-w_7 + w_6 - w_5 + w_4 + w_3 - w_2 - w_1 \geq 1$, $w_7 - w_6 + w_5 - w_4 + w_3 + w_2 - w_1 \geq 1$, $-w_7 + w_6 - w_5 + w_4 - w_3 + w_2 + w_1 \geq 1$, $w_7 - w_6 + w_5 - w_4 + w_3 - w_2 + w_1 \geq 1$. Multiply them respectively by 1, 1, 2, 3, 5, 8, 5 to get $w_1 + \cdots + w_7 \geq 1 + 1 + 2 + 3 + 5 + 8 + 5$. The same idea works for all $n \geq 3$.

106. (a) $\langle x_1^{2^{n-1}} x_2^{2^{n-2}} \ldots x_n \, \bar{y}_1^{2^{n-1}} \bar{y}_2^{2^{n-2}} \ldots \bar{y}_n \bar{z} \rangle$. (By exercise 99, we could also perform n medians-of-three: $\langle\langle \ldots \langle x_n \bar{y}_n \bar{z} \rangle \ldots x_2 \bar{y}_2 \rangle x_1 \bar{y}_1 \rangle$.)

(b) If $\langle x_1^{u_1} x_2^{u_2} \ldots x_n^{u_n} \bar{y}_1^{v_1} \bar{y}_2^{v_2} \ldots \bar{y}_n^{v_n} \bar{z}^w \rangle$ solves the problem, $2^{n+1} - 1$ basic inequalities need to hold; for example, when $n = 2$ they are $u_1 + u_2 - v_1 + v_2 - w \geq 1$, $u_1 + u_2 - v_1 - v_2 + w \geq 1$, $u_1 - u_2 + v_1 - v_2 - w \geq 1$, $u_1 - u_2 - v_1 + v_2 + w \geq 1$, $-u_1 + u_2 + v_1 + v_2 - w \geq 1$, $-u_1 + u_2 + v_1 - v_2 + w \geq 1$, $-u_1 - u_2 + v_1 + v_2 + w \geq 1$. Add them all up to get $u_1 + u_2 + \cdots + u_n + v_1 + v_2 + \cdots + v_n + w \geq 2^{n+1} - 1$.

107.

f	$N(f)$	$\Sigma(f)$	f	$N(f)$	$\Sigma(f)$	f	$N(f)$	$\Sigma(f)$	f	$N(f)$	$\Sigma(f)$
⊥	0	(0,0)	$\bar{\subset}$	1	(0,1)	▽	1	(0,0)	⌐	2	(0,1)
∧	1	(1,1)	R	2	(1,2)	=	2	(1,1)	⊃	3	(1,2)
⊃̄	1	(1,0)	⊕	2	(1,1)	$\bar{R}$	2	(1,0)	⊼	3	(1,1)
∟	2	(2,1)	∨	3	(2,2)	⊂	3	(2,1)	⊤	4	(2,2)

Notice that $\oplus$ and $\equiv$ have the same parameters $N(f)$ and $\Sigma(f)$; they are the only Boolean binary operations that aren't threshold functions.

108. If $\Sigma(g) = (s_0, s_1, \ldots, s_n)$, the value of g is 1 in s_0 cases when $x_0 = 1$ and in $2^n - s_0$ cases when $x_0 = 0$. We also have $\Sigma(f_0) + \Sigma(f_1) = (s_1, \ldots, s_n)$, and

$$\Sigma(f_0) = \sum_{x_1=0}^{1} \cdots \sum_{x_n=0}^{1} (\bar{x}_1, \ldots, \bar{x}_n) g(0, \bar{x}_1, \ldots, \bar{x}_n)$$

$$= \sum_{x_1=0}^{1} \cdots \sum_{x_n=0}^{1} ((1, \ldots, 1) - (x_1, \ldots, x_n))(1 - g(1, x_1, \ldots, x_n))$$

$$= (2^{n-1} - s_0, \ldots, 2^{n-1} - s_0) + \Sigma(f_1).$$

So the answers, for $n > 0$, are (a) $N(f_0) = 2^n - s_0$, $\Sigma(f_0) = \frac{1}{2}(s_1 - s_0 + 2^{n-1}, \ldots, s_n - s_0 + 2^{n-1})$; (b) $N(f_1) = s_0$, $\Sigma(f_1) = \frac{1}{2}(s_1 + s_0 - 2^{n-1}, \ldots, s_n + s_0 - 2^{n-1})$. [Equivalent results were presented by E. Goto in lectures at MIT in 1963.]

109. (a) $a_1 + \cdots + a_k \geq b_1 + \cdots + b_k$ if and only if $k - a_1 - \cdots - a_k \leq k - b_1 - \cdots - b_k$.

(b) Let $\alpha^+ = (a_1, a_1 + a_2, \ldots, a_1 + \cdots + a_n)$. Then the vector $(c_1, \ldots, c_n)$ obtained by componentwise minimization of α^+ and β^+ is $(\alpha \wedge \beta)^+$. (Clearly $c_j = c_{j-1} + a_j$ or b_j.)

(c) Proceed as in (b) but with componentwise *maximization*; or take $\bar{\alpha} \wedge \bar{\beta}$.

(d) True, because max and min satisfy these distributive laws. (In fact, we obtain a distributive *mixed-radix majorization lattice* in a similar way from the set of all n-tuples $a_1 \ldots a_n$ with $0 \leq a_j < m_j$ for $1 \leq j \leq n$. R. P. Stanley has observed that Fig. 8 is also the lattice of order ideals of the triangular grid shown here.)

(e) $\alpha 1$ covers $\alpha 0$ and $\alpha 10\beta$ covers $\alpha 01\beta$. [This characterization is due to R. O. Winder, *IEEE Trans.* **EC-14** (1965), 315–325, but he didn't prove the lattice property. The lattice is often called $M(n)$; see B. Lindström, *Nordisk Mat. Tidskrift* **17** (1969), 61–70; R. P. Stanley, *SIAM J. Algebraic and Discrete Methods* **1** (1980), 177–179.]

(f) Because of (e) we have $r(\alpha) = na_1 + (n-1)a_2 + \cdots + a_n$.

(g) The point is that $0\beta \succeq 0\alpha$ if and only if $\beta \succeq \alpha$ and that $1\beta \succeq 0\alpha$ if and only if $1\beta \succeq 10 \ldots 0 \vee 0\alpha = 1\alpha'$.

(h) That is, how many $a_1 \ldots a_n$ have the property that $a_1 \ldots a_k$ contains no more 1s than 0s? The answer is $\binom{n}{\lfloor n/2 \rfloor}$; see, for example, exercise 2.2.1–4 or 7.2.1.6–42(a).

110. (a) If $x \subseteq y$ then $x \preceq y$, hence $f(x) \leq f(y)$; QED.

(b) No; a threshold function need not be monotone (see (79)). But we *can* show that f is regular if we also require $w_n \geq 0$: For if $f(x) = 1$ and y covers x we then have $w \cdot y \geq w \cdot x$.

(c) Whenever $f(x) = 1$ and $x_j < x_{j+1}$, we have $f(y) = 1$ when y covers x with $x_j \leftrightarrow x_{j+1}$; hence $s_j \geq s_{j+1}$. (This argument holds even when $w_n < 0$.)

(d) No; consider, for example, $\langle x_1 x_2^2 x_3^2 \rangle$, which equals $\langle x_1 x_2 x_3 \rangle$. Counterexamples can arise even when the weights minimize $w_1 + \cdots + w_n$, because the solution to the linear program in exercise 103 is not always unique. One such case, found by Muroga, Tsuboi, and Baugh, is $\langle x_1^{17} x_2^9 x_3^8 x_4^6 x_5^7 x_6^5 x_7^3 x_8^2 x_9^2 \rangle$, a function that is actually symmetric in x_4 and x_5. But if $s_j > s_{j+1}$ we must have $w_j > w_{j+1}$, because of (c).

111. (a) Find an optimum self-dual function f pointwise as in exercise 14; in case of ties, choose $f(x_1, \ldots, x_n) = x_1$. Thus $f(x_1, \ldots, x_n) = [r_1^{x_1} \ldots r_n^{x_n} \geq \sqrt{r_1 \ldots r_n}]$, except that '$\geq$' becomes '$>$' when $x_1 = 0$. This function is regular when $r_1 \geq \cdots \geq r_n \geq 1$.

(b) Let g be the regular, self-dual function constructed in (a). If f is a given regular, self-dual function, we want to verify that $f(x) \leq g(x)$ for all vectors x; this will imply that $f = g$, because both functions are self-dual.

Suppose $f(x) = 1$, and let $y \preceq x$ be minimal such that $f(y) = 1$. If we have verified that $g(y) = 1$, then indeed $g(x) = 1$, as desired. [See K. Makino and T. Kameda, *SIAM Journal on Discrete Mathematics* **14** (2001), 381–407.]

For example, there are only seven self-dual regular Boolean functions when $n = 5$, generated by the following minimal elements in Fig. 8: 10000; 01111, 10001; 01110, 10010; 01101, 10011, 10100; 01100; 01011, 11000; 00111. So an optimum coterie can be found by examining only a few function values.

(c) Suppose $1 > p_1 \geq \cdots \geq p_r \geq \frac{1}{2} > p_{r+1} \geq \cdots \geq p_n > 0$. Let $f_k(x_1, \ldots, x_n)$ be the kth monotone, self-dual function and $F_k(x_1, \ldots, x_n)$ its integer multilinear representation. We want to find the optimum availability $G(p_1, \ldots, p_n) = \max_k F_k(p_1, \ldots, p_n)$. If $p_1 \leq p_1'$, ..., $p_n \leq p_n'$, we have $F_k(p_1, \ldots, p_n) \leq F_k(p_1', \ldots, p_n')$ by exercise 12(e); hence $G(p_1, \ldots, p_n) \leq G(p_1', \ldots, p_n')$.

Therefore if $0 < r < n$ we have

$$G(p_1, \ldots, p_n) \leq G(p_1, \ldots, p_r, \tfrac{1}{2}, \ldots, \tfrac{1}{2}).$$

And the latter is $F(p_1, \ldots, p_r, \tfrac{1}{2}, \ldots, \tfrac{1}{2})$, derived from these larger probabilities as in part (a). This function does not depend on $(x_{r+1}, \ldots, x_n)$, so it gives the optimum.

If $r = 0$ the problem seems to be deeper. We have $G(p_1, \ldots, p_n) \leq G(p_1, \ldots, p_1)$; so we can conclude that the optimum coterie is $f(x_1, \ldots, x_n) = x_1$ in this case if we can show that $F_k(p, \ldots, p) \leq p$ for all k whenever $p < \frac{1}{2}$. In general $F_k(p, \ldots, p) = \sum_m c_m p^m (1-p)^{n-m}$, where c_m is the number of vectors x such that $f_k(x) = 1$ and $\nu x = m$. Since f_k is self-dual we have $c_m + c_{n-m} = \binom{n}{m}$, for all k. And the Erdős–Ko–Rado theorem (exercise 7.2.1.3–111) tells us that we have $c_m \leq \binom{n-1}{m-1}$ for any intersecting family of m-sets when $m \leq n/2$. The result follows.

[See Y. Amir and A. Wool, *Information Processing Letters* **65** (1998), 223–228.]

112. (a) The leading terms are respectively 0, $+xy$, $-xy$, $+x$, $-xy$, $+y$, $-2xy$, $-xy$, $+xy$, $+2xy$, $-y$, $+xy$, $-x$, $+xy$, $-xy$, 1; so $F(f) = 1$ when f is $\wedge$, L, R, $\bar{\vee}$, $\equiv$, $\subset$, $\supset$, T.

(b) The coefficient corresponding to exponents 01101, say, is f_{0**0*} in the notation of answer 12; it is a linear combination of truth table entries, always lying in the range $\lceil -2^{k-1} \rceil \leq f_{0**0*} \leq \lceil 2^{k-1} \rceil$ when there are k asterisks. Thus the leading coefficient is positive if and only if the mixed-radix number

$$\begin{bmatrix} f_{**\ldots*}, & f_{0*\ldots*}, & \cdots, & f_{*0\ldots0}, & f_{00\ldots0} \\ 2^m+1, & 2^{m-1}+1, & \cdots, & 2^1+1, & 2^0+1 \end{bmatrix}$$

is positive, where the f's are arranged in reverse order of Chase's sequence and the radix $2^k + 1$ corresponds to an f with k asterisks. For example, when $m = 2$ we have $F(f) = 1$ if and only if the sum $18f_{**} + 6f_{0*} + 2f_{*0} + f_{00} = 18(f_{11} - f_{01} - f_{10} + f_{00}) + 6(f_{01} - f_{00}) + 2(f_{10} - f_{00}) + f_{00} = 18f_{11} - 12f_{01} - 16f_{10} + 11f_{00}$ is positive; so the threshold function can be written $\langle f_{11}^{18} \bar{f}_{01}^{12} \bar{f}_{10}^{16} f_{00}^{11} \rangle$.

(In this particular case the much simpler expression $\langle f_{11}f_{11}\bar{f}_{01}\bar{f}_{10}f_{00} \rangle$ is actually valid. But part (c) will show that when m is large we can't do a great deal better.)

(c) Suppose $F(f) = [\sum_\alpha v_\alpha(f_\alpha - \frac{1}{2}) > 0]$, where the sum is over all $n = 2^m$ binary strings α of length m and where each v_α is an integer weight. Define

$$w_\alpha = \sum_\beta (-1)^{\nu(\alpha \,\dot-\, \beta)} v_\beta \quad \text{and} \quad F_\alpha = \sum_\beta (-1)^{\nu(\alpha \,\dot-\, \beta)} f_\beta - 2^{m-1}[\alpha = 00\ldots0];$$

thus, for example, $w_{01} = -v_{00} + v_{01} - v_{10} + v_{11}$ and $F_{11} = f_{00} - f_{01} - f_{10} + f_{11}$. One can show that $F_{1^k0^l} = 2^l f_{*^k0^l}$, if $F_\alpha = 0$ whenever $\nu(\alpha) > k > 0$; therefore the signs of the transformed truth coefficients F_α determine the sign of the leading coefficient in the multilinear representation. Furthermore, we now have $F(f) = [\sum_\alpha w_\alpha F_\alpha > 0]$.

The general idea of the proof is to choose test functions f from which we can derive properties of the transformed weights w_α. For example, if $k \geq 0$ and $f(x_1, \ldots, x_m) = x_1 \oplus \cdots \oplus x_k \oplus [k\text{ even}]$, we find $F_\alpha = 0$ for all α except that $F_{1^k 0^{m-k}} = 2^{m-1}$. The multilinear representation of that function has leading term $[2^{k-1}]x_1 \ldots x_k$; hence we can conclude that $w_{1^k 0^{m-k}} > 0$, and in a similar way that $w_\alpha > 0$ for all α. In general if m changes to $m+1$ but f does not depend on x_{m+1}, we have $F_{\alpha 0} = 2F_\alpha$ and $F_{\alpha 1} = 0$.

The test function $x_2 \oplus \cdots \oplus x_m \oplus x_1 \bar{x}_2 \ldots \bar{x}_m$ proves that

$$w_{1^m} > (2^{m-1}-1)w_{01^{m-1}} + \sum_{k=1}^{m-1} w_{1^k 01^{m-1-k}} + \text{smaller terms},$$

where the smaller terms involve only w_α with $\nu(\alpha) \leq m - 2$. In particular, $w_{11} > w_{01} + w_{10} + w_{00}$. The test function $x_1 \oplus \cdots \oplus x_{m-1} \oplus \bar{x}_1 \ldots \bar{x}_{m-2}(x_{m-1} \oplus \bar{x}_m)$ proves

$$w_{1^{m-2}01} > (2^{m-2}-1)w_{1^{m-2}10} + \sum_{k=0}^{m-3}(w_{1^k 01^{m-3-k}10} + w_{1^k 01^{m-3-k}01}) + \text{smaller terms},$$

where the smaller terms this time have $\nu(\alpha) \leq m - 3$. In particular, $w_{101} > w_{110} + w_{010} + w_{001}$. By permuting subscripts, we obtain similar inequalities leading to

$$w_{\alpha_j} > (2^{\nu(\alpha_j)-1} - 1)w_{\alpha_{j-1}} \qquad \text{for } 0 < j < 2^m,$$

because the w's begin to grow rapidly. But we have $v_\alpha = \sum_\beta (-1)^{\nu(\beta \dot{-} \alpha)} w_\beta / n$; hence $|v_\alpha| = w_{11\ldots1}/n + O(w_{11\ldots1}/n^2)$. [SIAM J. Discrete Math. **7** (1994), 484–492. Important generalizations of this result have been obtained by N. Alon and V. H. Vũ, J. Combinatorial Theory **A79** (1997), 133–160.]

113. The stated g_3 is $S_{2,3,6,8,9}$ because the stated g_2 is $S_{2,3,4,5,8,9,10,11,12}$.

For the more difficult function $S_{1,3,5,8}$, let $g_1 = [\nu x \geq 6]$; $g_2 = [\nu x \geq 3]$; $g_3 = [\nu x - 5g_1 - 2g_2 \geq 2] = S_{2,4,5,9,10,11,12}$; $g_4 = [2\nu x - 15g_1 - 9g_3 \geq 1] = S_{1,3,5,8}$. [See M. A. Fischler and M. Tannenbaum, IEEE Transactions **C-17** (1968), 273–279.]

114. $[4x + 2y + z \in \{3, 6\}] = (\bar{x} \wedge y \wedge z) \vee (x \wedge y \wedge \bar{z})$. In the same way, any Boolean function of n variables is a special case of a symmetric function of $2^n - 1$ variables. [See W. H. Kautz, IRE Transactions **EC-10** (1961), 378.]

115. Both sides are self-dual, so we may assume that $x_0 = 0$. Then

$$s_j = [x_j + \cdots + x_{j+m-1} > x_{j+m} + \cdots + x_{j+2m-1}].$$

If $x_1 + \cdots + x_{2m}$ is odd, we have $s_j = \bar{s}_{j+m}$; hence $s_1 + \cdots + s_{2m} = m$ and the result is 1. But if $x_1 + \cdots + x_{2m}$ is even, the difference $x_j + \cdots + x_{j+m-1} - x_{j+m} - \cdots - x_{j+2m-1}$ will be zero for at least one $j \leq m$; that makes $s_j = s_{j+m} = 0$, so we will have $s_1 + \cdots + s_{2m} < m$.

116. (a) It's an implicant if and only if $f(x) = 1$ whenever $j \leq \nu x \leq n - k + j$. It's a prime implicant if and only if we also have $f(x) = 0$ when $\nu x = j-1$ or $\nu x = n-k+j+1$.

(b) Consider the string $v = v_0 v_1 \ldots v_n$ such that $f(x) = v_{\nu x}$. By part (a), there are $\binom{a+b+c}{a,b,c}$ prime implicants when $v = 0^a 1^{b+1} 0^c$. In the stated case, $a = b = c = 3$, so there are 1680 prime implicants.

(c) For a general symmetric function, we add together the prime implicants for each run of 1s in v. Clearly there are more for $v = 0^{a+1}1^{b+1}0^{c-1}$ than for $v = 0^a 1^{b+1} 0^c$ when $a < c - 1$; so v contains no two consecutive 0s when the maximum is reached.

Let $\hat{b}(m, n)$ be the maximum number of prime implicants possible when $v_m = 1$ and $v_j = 0$ for $m < j \le n$. Then when $m \le \frac{1}{2}n$ we have

$$\hat{b}(m, n) = \max_{0 \le k \le m} \left(\binom{n}{k, m-k, n-m} + \hat{b}(k-2, n) \right)$$
$$= \binom{n}{\lceil m/2 \rceil, \lfloor m/2 \rfloor, n-m} + \hat{b}(\lceil m/2 \rceil - 2, n),$$

with $\hat{b}(-2, n) = \hat{b}(-1, n) = 0$. And the overall maximum is

$$\hat{b}(n) = \binom{n}{n_0, n_1, n_2} + \hat{b}(n_1 - 2, n) + \hat{b}(n_2 - 2, n), \qquad n_j = \left\lfloor \frac{n+j}{3} \right\rfloor.$$

In particular we have $\hat{b}(9) = 1698$, with the maximum occurring for $v = 1101111011$.

(d) By Stirling's approximation, $\hat{b}(n) = 3^{n+3/2}/(2\pi n) + O(3^n/n^2)$.

(e) In this case the appropriate recurrence for $m < \lceil n/2 \rceil$ is

$$\tilde{b}(m, n) = \max_{0 \le k \le m} \left(\binom{n}{k, m-k, n-m} + \binom{n}{k-1, 0, n-k+1} + \tilde{b}(k-2, n) \right)$$
$$= \binom{n}{\lceil m/2 \rceil, \lfloor m/2 \rfloor, n-m} + \binom{n}{\lceil m/2 \rceil - 1} + \tilde{b}(\lceil m/2 \rceil - 2, n)$$

and $\tilde{b}(n) = \tilde{b}(\lceil n/2 \rceil - 1, n)$ maximizes $\min(\text{prime implicants}(f), \text{prime implicants}(\bar{f}))$. We have $(\tilde{b}(1), \tilde{b}(2), \dots) = (1, 1, 4, 5, 21, 31, 113, 177, 766, 1271, 4687, 7999, 34412, \dots)$; for example, $\tilde{b}(9) = 766$ corresponds to $S_{0,2,3,4,8}(x_1, \dots, x_9)$. Asymptotically, $\tilde{b}(n) = 2^{(3n+3+(n \bmod 2))/2}/(2\pi n) + O(2^{3n/2}/n^2)$.

References: Summaries, Summer Inst. for Symbolic Logic (Dept. of Math., Cornell Univ., 1957), 211–212; B. Dunham and R. Fridshal, *J. Symbolic Logic* **24** (1959), 17–19; A. P. Vikulin, *Problemy Kibernetiki* **29** (1974), 151–166, which reports on work done in 1960; Y. Igarashi, *Transactions of the IEICE of Japan* **E62** (1979), 389–394.

117. The maximum number of subcubes of the n-cube, with none contained in another, is obtained when we choose all subcubes of dimension $\lfloor n/3 \rfloor$. (It is also obtained by choosing all subcubes of dimension $\lfloor (n+1)/3 \rfloor$; for example, when $n = 2$ we can choose either $\{0*, 1*, *0, *1\}$ or $\{00, 01, 10, 11\}$.) Hence $b^*(n) = \binom{n}{\lfloor n/3 \rfloor} 2^{n - \lfloor n/3 \rfloor} = 3^{n+1}/\sqrt{4\pi n} + O(3^n/n^{3/2})$. [See the paper of Vikulin in the previous answer, pages 164–166; A. K. Chandra and G. Markowsky, *Discrete Math.* **24** (1978), 7–11; N. Metropolis and G. C. Rota, *SIAM J. Applied Math.* **35** (1978), 689–694.]

118. Consider two functions equivalent if we can obtain one from the other by complementing and/or permuting variables, but not complementing the function value itself. Such functions clearly have the same number of prime implicants; this equivalence relation is studied further in answer 125 below. A computer program based on exercise 30 produces the following results:

m	Classes	Functions	m	Classes	Functions	m	Classes	Functions
0	1	1	5	87	17472	10	7	632
1	5	81	6	70	12696	11	1	96
2	18	1324	7	43	7408	12	2	24
3	46	6608	8	24	3346	13	1	16
4	87	14536	9	10	1296	14	0	0

And here are the corresponding statistics for functions of five variables:

m	Classes	Functions	m	Classes	Functions	m	Classes	Functions
0	1	1	11	186447	666555696	22	338	608240
1	6	243	12	165460	590192224	23	130	197440
2	37	14516	13	129381	459299440	24	71	75720
3	244	318520	14	91026	319496560	25	37	28800
4	1527	3319580	15	57612	199792832	26	15	10560
5	6997	19627904	16	33590	113183894	27	6	2880
6	23434	73795768	17	17948	58653984	28	4	1040
7	57048	190814016	18	8880	27429320	29	2	640
8	105207	362973410	19	3986	11597760	30	2	48
9	152763	538238660	20	1795	4548568	31	2	64
10	183441	652555480	21	720	1633472	32	1	16

119. Several authors have conjectured that $b(n) = \hat{b}(n)$; M. M. Gadzhiev has proved that equality holds for $n \leq 6$ [*Diskretnyĭ Analiz* **18** (1971), 3–24].

120. (a) Every prime implicant is a minterm, since no adjacent points of the n-cube have the same parity. So the full disjunctive form is the only decent DNF in this case.

(b) Now all prime implicants consist of two adjacent points. We must include the 14 subcubes $0^j * 0^{6-j}$ and $1^j * 1^{6-j}$ for $0 \leq j \leq 6$, in order to cover the points with $\nu x = 1$ and $\nu x = 6$. The other $\binom{7}{3} + \binom{7}{4} = 70$ points can be covered by 35 well-chosen prime implicants (see, for example, exercise 6.5–1, or the "Christmas tree pattern" in Section 7.2.1.6). Thus the shortest DNF has length 49. [An ingeniously plausible but fallacious argument that 70 prime implicants are necessary was presented by S. B. Yablonsky in *Problemy Kibernetiki* **7** (1962), 229–230.]

(c) For each of 2^{n-1} choices of $(x_1, \ldots, x_{n-1})$ we need at most one implicant to account for the behavior of the function with respect to x_n.

[Asymptotically, almost all Boolean functions of n variables have a shortest DNF with $\Theta(2^n/(\log n \log \log n))$ prime implicants. See R. G. Nigmatullin, *Diskretnyĭ Analiz* **10** (1967), 69–89; V. V. Glagolev, *Problemy Kibernetiki* **19** (1967), 75–94; A. D. Korshunov, *Metody Diskretnogo Analiza* **37** (1981), 9–41; N. Pippenger, *Random Structures & Algorithms* **22** (2003), 161–186.]

121. (a) Let $x = x_1 \ldots x_m$ and $y = y_1 \ldots y_n$. Since f is a function of $(\nu x, \nu y)$, there are altogether $2^{(m+1)(n+1)}$ possibilities.

(b) In this case $\nu x \leq \nu x'$ and $\nu y \leq \nu y'$ implies $f(x, y) \leq f(x', y')$. Every such function corresponds to a zigzag path from $a_0 = (-\frac{1}{2}, n+\frac{1}{2})$ to $a_{m+n+2} = (m+\frac{1}{2}, -\frac{1}{2})$, with $a_j = a_{j-1} + (1,0)$ or $a_j = a_{j-1} - (0,1)$ for $1 \leq j \leq m+n+2$; we have $f(x,y) = 1$ if and only if the point $(\nu x, \nu y)$ lies above the path. So the number of possibilities is the number of such paths, namely $\binom{m+n+2}{m+1}$.

(c) Complementing x and y changes νx to $m - \nu x$ and νy to $n - \nu y$. So there are no such functions when m and n are both even; otherwise there are $2^{(m+1)(n+1)/2}$.

(d) The path in (b) must now satisfy $a_j + a_{m+n+2-j} = (m, n)$ for $0 \leq j \leq m+n+2$. Hence there are $\binom{\lceil m/2 \rceil + \lceil n/2 \rceil}{\lceil m/2 \rceil}$ [m odd or n odd] such functions. For example, the following ten cases arise when $m = 3$ and $n = 6$:

122. A function of this kind is regular with the x's to the left of the y's if and only if the zigzag path does not contain two points (x, y) and $(x + 2, y)$ with $0 < y < n$; it is regular with the y's left of the x's if and only if the zigzag path does not contain both $(x, y + 2)$ and (x, y) with $0 < x < m$. It is a threshold function if and only if there is a straight line through the point $(m/2, n/2)$ with the property that (s, t) is above the line if and only if (s, t) is above the path, for $0 \le s \le m$ and $0 \le t \le n$. So cases 5 and 8, illustrated in the previous answer, fail to be regular; cases 1, 2, 3, 7, 9, and 10 are threshold functions. The regular non-threshold functions that remain can also be expressed as follows: $((x_1 \vee x_2 \vee x_3) \wedge \langle x_1 x_2 x_3 y_1 y_2 y_3 y_4 y_5 y_6 \rangle) \vee (x_1 \wedge x_2 \wedge x_3)$ (case 4); $\langle 00 x_1 x_2 x_3 y_1 y_2 y_3 y_4 y_5 y_6 \rangle \vee (\langle x_1 x_2 x_3 \rangle \wedge \langle 11 x_1 x_2 x_3 y_1 y_2 y_3 y_4 y_5 y_6 \rangle)$ (case 6).

123. Self-dual *regular* functions are relatively easy to list, for small n, but the numbers grow rapidly: When $n = 9$ there are 319,124 of them, found by Muroga, Tsuboi, and Baugh in 1967, and when $n = 10$ there are 1,214,554,343 (see exercise 7.1.4–75). The corresponding numbers for $n \le 6$ appear in Table 5, because all such functions are threshold functions when $n < 9$; there are 135 when $n = 7$, and 2470 when $n = 8$.

The threshold condition can be tested quickly for any such function by improving on the method of exercise 103, because constraints are needed only for the *minimal* vectors x (with respect to majorization) such that $f(x) = 1$.

The number θ_n of n-variable threshold functions is known to satisfy $\lg \theta_n = n^2 - O(n^2 / \log n)$; see Yu. A. Zuev, *Matematicheskie Voprosy Kibernetiki* **5** (1994), 5–61.

124. The 222 equivalence classes listed in Table 5 include 24 classes of size $2^{n+1} n! = 768$; so there are $24 \times 768 = 18432$ answers to this problem. One of them is the function $(w \wedge (x \vee (y \wedge z))) \oplus z$.

125. 0; x; $x \wedge y$; $x \wedge y \wedge z$; $x \wedge (y \vee z)$; $x \wedge (y \oplus z)$. (These functions are $x \wedge f(y, z)$, where f runs through the equivalence classes of two-variable functions under permutation and/or complementation of variables but *not* of the function values. In general, let $f \simeq g$ mean that f is equivalent to g in that weaker sense, but write $f \cong g$ if they are equivalent in the sense of Table 5. Then $x \wedge f \cong x \wedge g$ if and only if $f \simeq g$, assuming that f and g are independent of the variable x. For it's easy to see that $(x \wedge f) \simeq (\bar{x} \vee \bar{g})$ is impossible. And if $(x \wedge f) \simeq (x \wedge g)$, we can prove that $f \simeq g$ by showing that, if σ is a signed permutation of $\{x_0, \ldots, x_n\}$ and if $x = x_1 \ldots x_n$, then the identity $x_0 \wedge f(x) = (x_0 \sigma) \wedge g(x\sigma)$ implies $f(x) = g(x\sigma\tau)$, where τ interchanges $x_0 \leftrightarrow x_0\sigma$. Consequently the bottom line of Table 5 enumerates equivalence classes under $\simeq$, but with n increased by 1; there are, for example, 402 such classes of 4-variable functions.)

126. (a) The function is canalizing if and only if it has a prime implicant with at most one literal, or a prime clause with at most one literal.

(b) The function is canalizing if and only if at least one of the components of $\Sigma(f)$ is equal to 0, 2^{n-1}, $N(f)$, or $N(f) - 2^{n-1}$. [See I. Shmulevich, H. Lähdesmäki, and K. Egiazarian, *IEEE Signal Processing Letters* **11** (2004), 289–292, Proposition 6.]

(c) If, say, $\vee(f) = y_1 \ldots y_n$ with $y_j = 0$, then $f(x) = 0$ whenever $x_j = 1$. Therefore f is canalizing if and only if we don't have $\vee(f) = \vee(\bar{f}) = 1 \ldots 1$ and $\wedge(f) = \wedge(\bar{f}) = 0 \ldots 0$. With this test one can prove that many functions are noncanalizing when their value is known at only a few points.

127. (a) Since a self-dual function $f(x_1, \ldots, x_n)$ is true at exactly 2^{n-1} points, it is canalizing with respect to the variable x_j if and only if $f(x_1, \ldots, x_n) = x_j$ or $\bar{x}_j$.

(b) A definite Horn function is clearly canalizing if (i) it contains any clause with a single literal, or (ii) some literal occurs in every clause. Otherwise it is not canalizing. For we have $f(0, \ldots, 0) = f(1, \ldots, 1) = 1$, because (i) is false; and if x_j is any variable, there is a clause C_0 not containing $\bar{x}_j$ and a clause C_1 not containing x_j, because (ii) is false. By choosing appropriate values of the other variables, we can make $C_0 \wedge C_1$ false when $x_j = 0$ and also when $x_j = 1$.

128. For example, $(x_1 \wedge \cdots \wedge x_n) \vee (\bar{x}_1 \wedge \cdots \wedge \bar{x}_n)$.

129. $\sum_{k=1}^{n}(-1)^{k+1}\binom{n}{k}2^{2^{n-k}+k+1} - 2(n-1) - 4(n \bmod 2) = n2^{2^{n-1}+2} + O(n^2 2^{2^{n-2}})$. [See W. Just, I. Shmulevich, and J. Konvalina, *Physica* **D197** (2004), 211–221.]

130. (a) If there are a_n functions of n or fewer variables, but b_n functions of exactly n variables, we have $a_n = \sum_k \binom{n}{k}b_k$. Therefore $b_n = \sum_k(-1)^{n-k}\binom{n}{k}a_k$. (This rule, noted by C. E. Shannon in *Trans. Amer. Inst. Electrical Engineers* **57** (1938), 713–723, §4, applies to all rows of Table 3, *except* for the case of symmetric functions.) In particular, the answer sought here is $168 - 4 \cdot 20 + 6 \cdot 6 - 4 \cdot 3 + 2 = 114$.

(b) If there are a'_n essentially distinct functions of n or fewer variables, and b'_n of exactly n variables, we have $a'_n = \sum_{k=0}^{n} b'_k$. Hence $b'_n = a'_n - a'_{n-1}$, and the answer in this case is $30 - 10 = 20$.

131. Let there be $h(n)$ Horn functions and $k(n)$ Krom functions. Clearly $\lg h(n) \geq \binom{n}{\lfloor n/2 \rfloor}$ and $\lg k(n) \geq \binom{n}{2}$. V. B. Alekseyev [*Diskretnaía Matematika* **1** (1989), 129–136] has proved that $\lg h(n) = \binom{n}{\lfloor n/2 \rfloor}(1 + O(n^{-1/4}\log n))$. B. Bollobás, G. Brightwell, and I. Leader [*Israel J. Math.* **133** (2003), 45–60] have proved that $\lg k(n) \sim \frac{1}{2}n^2$.

132. (a) The hint is true because $\sum_y s(y)s(y \oplus z) = \sum_{w,x,y}(-1)^{f(w)+w \cdot y + f(x)+x \cdot (y+z)} = 2^n \sum_{w,x}(-1)^{f(w)+f(x)+x \cdot z}[x = w]$. Now suppose that $f(x) = g(x)$ for $2^{n-1} + k$ values of x; then $f(x) = g(x) \oplus 1$ for $2^{n-1} - k$ values of x. But if $|k| < 2^{n/2-1}$ for all affine g, we would have $|s(y)| < 2^{n/2}$ for all y, contradicting the hint when $z = 0$.

(b) Given $y_0, y_1, \ldots, y_n$, there are exactly $2^{n/2}((y_1y_2 + y_3y_4 + \cdots + y_{n-1}y_n + 1 + y_0 + h(y_1, y_3, \ldots, y_{n-1}))\bmod 2)$ solutions to $f(x) = (y_0 + x \cdot y)\bmod 2$ when $x_{2k} = y_{2k-1}$ for $1 \leq k \leq n/2$, and there are $2^{n/2-1}$ solutions for each of the other $2^{n/2} - 1$ values of $(x_2, x_4, \ldots, x_n)$. So there are $2^{n-1} \pm 2^{n/2-1}$ solutions altogether. (This argument proves, in fact, that $(g(x_1, x_3, \ldots, x_{2n-1}) \cdot (x_2, x_4, \ldots, x_{2n}) + h(x_2, x_4, \ldots, x_{2n}))\bmod 2$ is bent whenever $g(x_1, x_3, \ldots, x_{2n-1})$ is a permutation of all $2^{n/2}$-bit vectors.)

(c) The argument in part (a) proves that $f(x)$ is bent if and only if $s(y) = 2^{n/2}(-1)^{g(y)}$ for some Boolean function $g(y)$. This function g, the Fourier/Hadamard transform of f, is also bent, because $\sum_y(-1)^{g(y)+w \cdot y} = 2^{-n/2}\sum_{x,y}(-1)^{f(x)+x \cdot y + w \cdot y} = 2^{n/2}\sum_x(-1)^{f(x)}[x = w] = 2^{n/2}(-1)^{f(w)}$ for all w. The hint now tells us that we have $\sum_y(-1)^{g(y)+g(y \oplus z)} = 0$ for all nonzero z, and the same holds for f.

Conversely, assume that $f(x)$ satisfies the stated condition. Then, for all y,
$$s(y)^2 = \sum_{x,t}(-1)^{f(x)+x \cdot y + f(x \oplus t)+(x \oplus t) \cdot y} = \sum_t(-1)^{t \cdot y}\sum_x(-1)^{f(x)+f(x \oplus t)} = 2^n.$$

(d) By exercise 11, the term $x_1 \ldots x_r$ is present if and only if the equation $f(x_1, \ldots, x_r, 0, \ldots, 0) = 1$ has an odd number of solutions, and an equivalent condition is $(\sum_{x_1, \ldots, x_r}(-1)^{f(x_1, \ldots, x_r, 0, \ldots, 0)})\bmod 4 = 2$. We've seen in part (c) that this sum is
$$2^{-n}\sum_{x_1, \ldots, x_r, y} s(y)(-1)^{x_1y_1 + \cdots + x_ry_r} = 2^{r-n}\sum_{y_{r+1}, \ldots, y_n} s(0, \ldots, 0, y_{r+1}, \ldots, y_n).$$
If $r = n$, the latter sum is $\pm 2^{n/2}$; otherwise it contains an even number of summands, each of which is $\pm 2^{r-n/2}$. So the result is a multiple of 4.

[Bent functions were introduced by O. S. Rothaus in 1966; his privately circulated paper was eventually published in *J. Combinatorial Theory* **A20** (1976), 300–305.

J. F. Dillon, *Congressus Numerantium* **14** (1975), 237–249, discovered additional families of bent functions, and many other examples have subsequently been found when $n \geq 8$ and n is even. Bent functions don't exist when n is odd, but a function like $g(x_1, \ldots, x_{n-1}) \oplus x_n \wedge h(x_1, \ldots, x_{n-1})$ has distance $2^{n-1} - 2^{(n-1)/2}$ from all affine functions when g and $g \oplus h$ are bent. A better construction for the case $n = 15$ was found by N. J. Patterson and D. H. Wiedemann, *IEEE Transactions* **IT-29** (1983), 354–356, **IT-36** (1990), 443, achieving distance $2^{14} - 108$. S. Kavut and M. Diker Yücel, *Information and Computation* **208** (2010), 341–350, have achieved distance $2^8 - 14$ when $n = 9$. See K.-U. Schmidt, *J. Combinatorial Theory* **A164** (2019), 50–59, for asymptotically optimum results as $n \to \infty$ through odd values.]

133. Let $p_k = 1/(2^{2^{n-k}} + 1)$, so that $\bar{p}_k = 2^{2^{n-k}}/(2^{2^{n-k}} + 1)$. [Ph.D. thesis (MIT, 1994).]

SECTION 7.1.2

1. $((x_1 \vee x_4) \wedge x_2) \equiv (x_1 \vee x_3)$.

2. (a) $(w \oplus (x \wedge y)) \oplus ((x \oplus y) \wedge z)$; (b) $(w \wedge (x \vee y)) \wedge ((x \wedge y) \vee z)$.

3. [*Doklady Akademii Nauk SSSR* **115** (1957), 247–248.] Construct a $k \times n$ matrix whose rows are the vectors x where $f(x) = 1$. By permuting and/or complementing variables, we may assume that the top row is $1 \ldots 1$ and that the columns are sorted. Suppose there are l distinct columns. Then $f = g \wedge h$, where g is the AND of the expressions $(x_{j-1} \equiv x_j)$ over all $1 < j \leq n$ such that column $j - 1$ equals column j, and h is the OR of k minterms of length l, using one variable from each group of equal columns. For example, if $n = 8$ and if f is 1 at the $k = 3$ points 11111111, 00001111, 00110111, then $l = 4$ and $f(x)$ equals $(x_1 \equiv x_2) \wedge (x_3 \equiv x_4) \wedge (x_6 \equiv x_7) \wedge (x_7 \equiv x_8) \wedge ((x_1 \wedge x_3 \wedge x_5 \wedge x_6) \vee (\bar{x}_1 \wedge \bar{x}_3 \wedge x_5 \wedge x_6) \vee (\bar{x}_1 \wedge x_3 \wedge \bar{x}_5 \wedge x_6))$. The length of this formula in general is $2n + (k - 2)l - 1$, and we have $l \leq 2^{k-1}$.

Notice that, if k is large, we get shorter formulas by writing $f(x)$ as a disjunction $f_1(x) \vee \cdots \vee f_r(x)$, where each f_j has at most $\lceil k/r \rceil$ 1s. Thus

$$L(f) \leq \min_{r \geq 1}(r - 1 + (2n + \lceil k/r - 2 \rceil 2^{\lceil k/r - 1 \rceil})r).$$

4. The first inequality is obvious, because a binary tree of depth d has at most $1 + 2 + \cdots + 2^{d-1} = 2^d - 1$ internal nodes.

The hint follows when we let f_t be the formula of size $L(f) - L(g) - 1$ that arises when g is replaced by t. For $1 \leq k < L(f)$ let g_k be a minimal subformula of size $\geq k$. Then g_k? f_{k1}: f_{k0} is obtained from a tree that has g_k, f_{k1}, and f_{k0} on level 2.

Let $d_r = \max\{D(f) \mid L(f) = r\}$. Since the children of g_k appear on level 3 and have size $< k$, we have $d_r \leq \min_{k=1}^{r-1} \max(3 + d_{k-1}, 2 + d_{r-k-1})$ for $r \geq 3$. By induction on r it follows that $d_r \leq l$ when $r \leq b_l$, where $b_l = l$ for $0 \leq l \leq 2$ and $b_l = b_{l-2} + b_{l-3} + 2$ for $l \geq 3$. We also have $b_l + 2 = (8P_l + 18P_{l+1} + 11P_{l+2})/23 = c\rho^l + O(0.87^l)$ in terms of the Perrin numbers of exercise 7.1.4–15, where $c = (2 + 4\rho + 3\rho^2)/(3 + 2\rho) \approx 2.224$. Hence $d_r < \alpha \lg r$ when $r > 1$. [See P. M. Spira, *Hawaii Int. Conf. Syst. Sci.* **4** (1971), 525–527; R. Brent, D. Kuck, and K. Maruyama, *IEEE* **C-22** (1973), 532–534. In *JACM* **23** (1976), 534–543, D. E. Muller and F. P. Preparata proved that $D(f) \leq \beta \lg L(f) + O(1)$, where $\beta = 1/\lg z \approx 2.0807$, $z^4 = 2z + 1$. Is β optimum?]

5. Let $g_0 = 0$, $g_1 = x_1$, and $g_j = x_j \wedge (x_{j-1} \vee g_{j-2})$ for $j \geq 2$. Then $F_n = g_n \vee g_{n-1}$, with cost $2n - 2$ and depth n. [These functions g_j also play a prominent role in binary addition; see exercises 42 and 44 for ways to compute them with depth $O(\log n)$.]

6. True: Consider the cases $y = 0$ and $y = 1$.

7. $\hat{x}_5 = x_1 \vee x_4$, $\hat{x}_6 = x_2 \wedge \hat{x}_5$, $\hat{x}_7 = x_1 \vee x_3$, $\hat{x}_8 = \hat{x}_6 \oplus \hat{x}_7$. (The original chain computes the "random" function (6); see exercise 1. The new chain computes the normalization of that function, namely its complement.)

8. The desired truth table consists of blocks of 2^{n-k} 0s alternating with blocks of 2^{n-k} 1s, as in (7). Therefore, if we multiply by $2^{2^{n-k}} + 1$ we get $x_k + (x_k \ll 2^{n-k})$, which is all 1s.

9. When finding $L(f) = \infty$ in step L6, we can store g and h in a record associated with f. Then a recursive procedure will be able to construct a minimum-length formula for f from the respective formulas for g and h.

10. In step L3, use $k = r - 1$ instead of $k = r - 1 - j$. Also change L to D everywhere.

11. The only subtle point is that j should *decrease* in step U3; then we'll never have $\phi(g) \,\&\, \phi(h) \neq 0$ when $j = 0$, so all cases of cost $r - 1$ will be discovered before we begin to look at list $r - 1$.

> **U1.** [Initialize.] Set $U(0) \leftarrow \phi(0) \leftarrow 0$ and $U(f) \leftarrow \infty$ for $1 \leq f < 2^{2^n - 1}$. Then set $U(x_k) \leftarrow \phi(x_k) \leftarrow 0$ and put x_k into list 0, as in step L1. Also set $U(x_j \circ x_k) \leftarrow 1$, set $\phi(x_j \circ x_k)$ to its unique footprint vector (which contains exactly one 1), and put $x_j \circ x_k$ into list 1, for $1 \leq j < k \leq n$ and all five normal operators $\circ$. Finally set $c \leftarrow 2^{2^n - 1} - 5\binom{n}{2} - n - 1$.
>
> **U2.** [Loop on r.] Do step U3 for $r = 2, 3, \ldots$, while $c > 0$.
>
> **U3.** [Loop on j and k.] Do step U4 for $j = \lfloor (r-1)/2 \rfloor$, $\lfloor (r-1)/2 \rfloor - 1$, $\ldots$, and $k = r - 1 - j$, while $j \geq 0$.
>
> **U4.** [Loop on g and h.] Do step U5 for all g in list j and all h in list k; if $j = k$, restrict h to functions that *follow* g in list k.
>
> **U5.** [Loop on f.] If $\phi(g) \,\&\, \phi(h) \neq 0$, set $u \leftarrow r - 1$ and $v \leftarrow \phi(g) \,\&\, \phi(h)$; otherwise set $u \leftarrow r$ and $v \leftarrow \phi(g) \mid \phi(h)$. Then do step U6 for $f = g \,\&\, h$, $f = \bar{g} \,\&\, h$, $f = g \,\&\, \bar{h}$, $f = g \mid h$, and $f = g \oplus h$.
>
> **U6.** [Update $U(f)$ and $\phi(f)$.] If $U(f) = \infty$, set $c \leftarrow c - 1$, $\phi(f) \leftarrow v$, $U(f) \leftarrow u$, and put f into list u. Otherwise if $U(f) > u$, move f from list $U(f)$ to list u and set $\phi(f) \leftarrow v$, $U(f) \leftarrow u$. Otherwise if $U(f) = u$, set $\phi(f) \leftarrow \phi(f) \mid v$. ∎

12. $x_4 = x_1 \oplus x_2$, $x_5 = x_3 \wedge x_4$, $x_6 = x_2 \wedge \bar{x}_4$, $x_7 = x_5 \vee x_6$.

13. $f_5 = 01010101 \ (x_3)$; $f_4 = 01110111 \ (x_2 \vee x_3)$; $f_3 = 01110101 \ ((\bar{x}_1 \wedge x_2) \vee x_3)$; $f_2 = 00110101 \ (x_1? \ x_3: x_2)$; $f_1 = 00010111 \ (\langle x_1 x_2 x_3 \rangle)$.

14. For $1 \leq j \leq n$, first compute $t \leftarrow (g \oplus (g \gg 2^{n-j})) \,\&\, x_j$, $t \leftarrow t \oplus (t \ll 2^{n-j})$, where x_j is the truth table (11); then for $1 \leq k \leq n$ and $k \neq j$, the desired truth table corresponding to $x_j \leftarrow x_j \circ x_k$ is $g \oplus (t \,\&\, ((x_j \circ x_k) \oplus x_j))$.

(The $5n(n-1)$ masks $(x_j \circ x_k) \oplus x_j$ are independent of g and can be computed in advance. The same idea applies if we allow more general computations of the form $x_{j(i)} \leftarrow x_{k(i)} \circ_i x_{l(i)}$, with $5n^2(n-1)$ masks $(x_k \circ x_l) \oplus x_j$.)

15. Remarkably asymmetrical ways to compute symmetrical functions:

(a) $x_1 \leftarrow x_1 \oplus x_2$,
 $x_1 \leftarrow x_1 \oplus x_3$,
 $x_2 \leftarrow x_2 \wedge x_3$,
 $x_1 \leftarrow x_1 \wedge \bar{x}_2$.

(b) $x_1 \leftarrow x_1 \oplus x_2$,
 $x_3 \leftarrow x_3 \oplus x_4$,
 $x_1 \leftarrow x_1 \oplus x_3$,
 $x_2 \leftarrow x_2 \oplus x_4$,
 $x_3 \leftarrow x_3 \vee x_2$,
 $x_3 \leftarrow x_3 \wedge \bar{x}_1$.

(c) $x_1 \leftarrow x_1 \oplus x_2$,
 $x_2 \leftarrow x_2 \wedge \bar{x}_1$,
 $x_3 \leftarrow x_3 \oplus x_4$,
 $x_4 \leftarrow x_4 \wedge x_1$,
 $x_2 \leftarrow \bar{x}_2 \wedge x_3$,
 $x_2 \leftarrow x_2 \oplus x_1$,
 $x_2 \leftarrow x_2 \wedge \bar{x}_4$.

(d) $x_1 \leftarrow x_1 \oplus x_2$,
 $x_2 \leftarrow x_2 \oplus x_3$,
 $x_2 \leftarrow x_2 \vee x_1$,
 $x_1 \leftarrow x_1 \oplus x_4$,
 $x_1 \leftarrow x_1 \wedge x_3$,
 $x_2 \leftarrow x_2 \wedge \bar{x}_1$,
 $x_2 \leftarrow x_2 \oplus x_4$.

16. A computation that uses only $\oplus$ and complementation produces nothing but affine functions (see exercise 7.1.1–132). Suppose $f(x) = f(x_1, \dots, x_n)$ is a non-affine function computable in minimum memory. Then $f(x)$ has the form $g(Ax + c)$ where $g(y_1, y_2, \dots, y_n) = g(y_1 \wedge y_2, y_2, \dots, y_n)$, for some nonsingular $n \times n$ matrix A of 0s and 1s, where x and c are column vectors and the vector operations are performed modulo 2; in this formula the matrix A and vector c account for all operations $x_i \leftarrow x_i \oplus x_j$ and/or permutations and complementations of coordinates that occur after the most recent non-affine operation that was performed. (See (14).) We will exploit the fact that $g(0, 0, y_3, \dots, y_n) = g(1, 0, y_3, \dots, y_n)$.

Let α and β be the first two rows of A; also let a and b be the first two elements of c. Then if $Ax + c \equiv y$ (modulo 2) we have $y_1 = y_2 = 0$ if and only if $\alpha \cdot x \equiv a$ and $\beta \cdot x \equiv b$. Exactly 2^{n-2} vectors x satisfy this condition, and for all such vectors we have $f(x) = f(x \oplus w)$, where $Aw \equiv (1, 0, \dots, 0)^T$.

Given α, β, a, b, and w, with $\alpha \neq (0, \dots, 0)$, $\beta \neq (0, \dots, 0)$, $\alpha \neq \beta$, and $\alpha \cdot w \equiv 1$ (modulo 2), there are $2^{2^n - 2^{n-2}}$ functions f with the property that $f(x) = f(x \oplus w)$ whenever $\alpha \cdot x \bmod 2 = a$ and $\beta \cdot x \bmod 2 = b$. Therefore the total number of functions computable in minimum memory is at most 2^{n+1} (for affine functions) plus

$$(2^n - 1)(2^n - 2)2^2(2^{n-1})(2^{2^n - 2^{n-2}}) < 2^{2^n - 2^{n-2} + 3n + 1}.$$

17. Let $f(x_1, \dots, x_n) = g(x_1, \dots, x_{n-1}) \oplus (h(x_1, \dots, x_{n-1}) \wedge x_n)$ as in 7.1.1–(16). Representing h in CNF, form the clauses one by one in x_0 and AND them into x_n, obtaining $h \wedge x_n$. Representing g as a sum (mod 2) of conjunctions, form the successive conjunctions in x_0 and XOR them into x_n when ready.

(It appears to be impossible to evaluate all functions inside of $n + 1$ registers if we disallow the non-canalizing operators $\oplus$ and $\equiv$. But $n + 2$ registers clearly do suffice, even if we restrict ourselves to the single operator $\bar\wedge$.)

18. As mentioned in answer 14, we should extend the text's definition of minimum-memory computation to allow also steps like $x_{j(i)} \leftarrow x_{k(i)} \circ_i x_{l(i)}$, with $k(i) \neq j(i)$ and $l(i) \neq j(i)$, because that will give better results for certain functions that depend on only four of the five variables. Then we find $C_m(f) = (0, 1, \dots, 13, 14)$ for respectively $(2, 2, 5, 20, 93, 389, 1960, 10459, 47604, 135990, 198092, 123590, 21540, 472, 0)$ classes of functions ... leaving 75,908 classes (and 575,963,136 functions) for which $C_m(f) = \infty$ because they cannot be evaluated *at all* in minimum memory. The most interesting function of that kind is probably

$$(x_1 \wedge x_2) \vee (x_2 \wedge x_3) \vee (x_3 \wedge x_4) \vee (x_4 \wedge x_5) \vee (x_5 \wedge x_1),$$

which has $C(f) = 7$ but $C_m(f) = \infty$. Another interesting case is $(((x_1 \vee x_2) \oplus x_3) \vee ((x_2 \vee \bar{x}_4) \wedge x_5)) \wedge ((x_1 \equiv x_2) \vee x_3 \vee x_4)$, for which $C(f) = 8$ and $C_m(f) = 13$. One way to evaluate that function in eight steps is $x_6 = x_1 \vee x_2$, $x_7 = x_1 \vee x_4$, $x_8 = x_2 \oplus x_7$, $x_9 = x_3 \oplus x_6$, $x_{10} = x_4 \oplus x_9$, $x_{11} = x_5 \vee x_9$, $x_{12} = x_8 \wedge x_{10}$, $x_{13} = x_{11} \wedge \bar{x}_{12}$.

19. If not, the left and right subtrees of the root must overlap, since case (i) fails. Each variable must occur at least once as a leaf, by hypothesis. At least two variables must occur at least twice as leaves, since case (ii) fails. But we can't have $n + 2$ leaves with $r \leq n + 1$ internal nodes, unless the subtrees fail to overlap.

20. Now Algorithm L (with '$f = g \oplus h$' omitted in step L5) shows that some formulas must have length 15; and even the footprint method of exercise 11 does no better than 14. To get truly minimum chains, the 25 special chains for $r = 6$ in the text must be supplemented by five others that can no longer be ruled out, namely

     ;

and when $r = (7, 8, 9)$ we must also consider respectively $(653, 12387, 225660)$ additional potential chains that are not special cases of the top-down and bottom-up constructions. Here are the resulting statistics, for comparison with Table 1:

$C_c(f)$	Class-es	Func-tions	$U_c(f)$	Class-es	Func-tions	$L_c(f)$	Class-es	Func-tions	$D_c(f)$	Class-es	Func-tions
0	2	10	0	2	10	0	2	10	0	2	10
1	1	48	1	1	48	1	1	48	1	1	48
2	2	256	2	2	256	2	2	256	2	7	684
3	7	940	3	7	940	3	7	940	3	59	17064
4	9	2336	4	9	2336	4	7	2048	4	151	47634
5	24	6464	5	21	6112	5	20	5248	5	2	96
6	30	10616	6	28	9664	6	23	8672	6	0	0
7	61	18984	7	45	15128	7	37	11768	7	0	0
8	45	17680	8	40	14296	8	27	10592	8	0	0
9	37	7882	9	23	8568	9	33	11536	9	0	0
10	4	320	10	28	5920	10	16	5472	10	0	0
11	0	0	11	6	1504	11	30	6304	11	0	0
12	0	0	12	5	576	12	3	960	12	0	0
13	0	0	13	3	144	13	8	1472	13	0	0
14	0	0	14	2	34	14	2	96	14	0	0
15	0	0	15	0	0	15	4	114	15	0	0

The two function classes of depth 5 are represented by $S_{2,4}(x_1, x_2, x_3, x_4)$ and $x_1 \oplus S_2(x_2, x_3, x_4)$; and those two functions, together with $S_2(x_1, x_2, x_3, x_4)$ and the parity function $S_{1,3}(x_1, x_2, x_3, x_4) = x_1 \oplus x_2 \oplus x_3 \oplus x_4$, have length 15. Also $U_c(S_{2,4}) = U_c(S_{1,3}) = 14$. The four classes of cost 10 are represented by $S_{1,4}(x_1, x_2, x_3, x_4)$, $S_{2,4}(x_1, x_2, x_3, x_4)$, $(x_4? \ x_1 \oplus x_2 \oplus x_3 : \langle x_1 x_2 x_3 \rangle)$, and $[(x_1 x_2 x_3 x_4)_2 \in \{0, 1, 4, 7, 10, 13\}]$. (The third of these, incidentally, is equivalent to (20), "Harvard's hardest case.")

21. (The authors stated that their table entries "should be regarded only as the most economical operators known to the present writers.") David Stevenson discovered in 2013 that 16 grids always suffice(!). In particular, $V(f) \leq 16$ for the f in (20), because

$$f = \text{AND}\big(\text{NOT}\big(\text{AND}\big(\text{NOT}(g), \text{NAND}(\bar{w}, z), \text{NAND}(\bar{x}, \bar{z})\big)\big), \text{NAND}(g, h)\big)$$

where $g = x \oplus y = \text{AND}\big(\text{NAND}(x, y), \text{NAND}(\bar{x}, \bar{y})\big)$ and $h = w \oplus z$ is similar. Although they failed to find this particular construction, the Harvard researchers did remarkably well, in some cases beating the footprint heuristic by as many as 6 grids.

22. $\nu(x_1 x_2 x_3 x_4 x_5) = 3$ if and only if $\nu(x_1 x_2 x_3 x_4) \in \{2, 3\}$ and $\nu(x_1 x_2 x_3 x_4 x_5)$ is odd. Similarly, $S_2(x_1, x_2, x_3, x_4, x_5) = S_3(\bar{x}_1, \bar{x}_2, \bar{x}_3, \bar{x}_4, \bar{x}_5)$ incorporates $S_{1,2}(x_1, x_2, x_3, x_4)$:

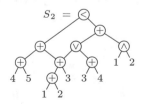

23. We need only consider the 32 normal cases, as in Fig. 9, since the complement of a symmetric function is symmetric. Then we can use reflection, like $S_{1,2}(x) = S_{3,4}(\bar{x})$, possibly together with complementation, like $S_{2,3,4,5}(x) = \bar{S}_{0,1}(x) = \bar{S}_{4,5}(\bar{x})$, to deduce most of the remaining cases. Of course S_5, $S_{1,3,5}$, and $S_{1,2,3,4,5}$ trivially have cost 4. That leaves only $S_{1,2,3,4}(x_1, x_2, x_3, x_4, x_5) = (x_1 \oplus x_2) \vee (x_2 \oplus x_3) \vee (x_3 \oplus x_4) \vee (x_4 \oplus x_5)$, which is discussed for general n in exercise 79.

24. As noted in the text, this conjecture holds for $n \leq 5$.

25. It is $2^{2^n - 1} - n - 1$, the number of nontrivial normal functions. (In any normal chain of length r that doesn't include all of these functions, $x_j \circ x_k$ will be a new function for some j and k in the range $1 \leq j, k \leq n + r$ and some normal binary operator $\circ$; so we can compute a new function with every new step, until we've got them all.)

26. False. For example, if $g = S_{1,3}(x_1, x_2, x_3)$ and $h = S_{2,3}(x_1, x_2, x_3)$, then $C(gh) = 5$ is the cost of a full adder; but $f = S_{2,3}(x_0, x_1, x_2, x_3)$ has cost 6 by Fig. 9.

27. Yes: The operations '$x_2 \leftarrow x_2 \oplus x_1$, $x_1 \leftarrow x_1 \oplus x_3$, $x_1 \leftarrow x_1 \wedge \bar{x}_2$, $x_1 \leftarrow x_1 \oplus x_3$, $x_2 \leftarrow x_2 \oplus x_3$' transform (x_1, x_2, x_3) into (z_1, z_0, x_3).

28. Let $v' = v'' = v \oplus (x \oplus y)$; $u' = ((v \oplus y) \,\overline{\supset}\, (x \oplus y)) \oplus u$, $u'' = ((v \oplus y) \vee (x \oplus y)) \oplus u$. Thus we can set $u_0 \leftarrow 0$, $v_0 \leftarrow x_1$, $u_j \leftarrow ((v_{j-1} \oplus x_{2j+1}) \vee (x_{2j} \oplus x_{2j+1})) \oplus u_{j-1}$ if j is odd, $u_j \leftarrow ((v_{j-1} \oplus x_{2j+1}) \,\overline{\supset}\, (x_{2j} \oplus x_{2j+1})) \oplus u_{j-1}$ if j is even, and $v_j \leftarrow v_{j-1} \oplus (x_{2j} \oplus x_{2j+1})$, giving $(u_j v_j)_2 = (-1)^j (x_1 + \cdots + x_{2j+1}) \bmod 4$ for $0 \leq j \leq \lfloor n/2 \rfloor$. Set $x_{n+1} \leftarrow 0$ if n is even. Thus $[(x_1 + \cdots + x_n) \bmod 4 = 0] = \bar{u}_{\lfloor n/2 \rfloor} \wedge \bar{v}_{\lfloor n/2 \rfloor}$ is computed in $\lfloor 5n/2 \rfloor - 2$ steps.

This construction is due to L. J. Stockmeyer, who proved that it is nearly optimal. In fact, the result of exercise 80 together with Figs. 9 and 10 shows that it is at most one step longer than a best possible chain, for all $n \geq 5$.

Incidentally, the analogous formula $u''' = ((v \oplus y) \wedge (x \oplus y)) \oplus u$ yields $(u''' v')_2 = ((uv)_2 + x - y) \bmod 4$. The simpler-looking function $((uv)_2 + x + y) \bmod 4$ costs 6, not 5.

29. To get an upper bound, assume that each full adder or half adder increases the depth by 3. If there are a_{jd} bits of weight 2^j and depth $3d$, we schedule at most $\lceil a_{jd}/3 \rceil$ subsequent bits of weights $\{2^j, 2^{j+1}\}$ and depth $3(d+1)$. It follows by induction that $a_{jd} \leq \binom{d}{j} 3^{-d} n + 4$. Hence $a_{jd} \leq 4$ when $d \geq l = \lceil \log_{3/2} n \rceil$. It follows that $a_{j(j+l+3)} = 0$ for $0 \leq j \leq \lg n$, giving total depth $\leq 3(l + \lg n + 2)$. (The actual depth turns out to be exactly 101 when $n = 10^7$, 118 when $n = 10^8$, 133 when $n = 10^9$.)

30. As usual, let νn denote the sideways addition of the bits in the binary representation of n itself. Then $s(n) = 5n - 2\nu n - 3\lfloor \lg n \rfloor - 3$.

31. After sideways addition in $s(n) < 5n$ steps, any function of $(z_{\lfloor \lg n \rfloor}, \ldots, z_0)$ can be evaluated in $\sim 2n/\lg n$ steps at most, by Theorem L. [See O. B. Lupanov, *Doklady Akademii Nauk SSSR* **140** (1961), 322–325. Exercise 7.2.2.2–481 improves $5n$ to $4.5n$.]

32. Bootstrap: First prove by induction on n that $t(n) \leq 2^{n+1}$.

33. False, on a technicality: If, say, $N = \sqrt{n}$, at least n steps are needed. A correct asymptotic formula $N + O(\sqrt{N}) + O(n)$ can, however, be proved by first noting that the text's method gives $N + O(\sqrt{N})$ when $N \geq 2^{n-1}$; otherwise, if $\lfloor \lg N \rfloor = n - k - 1$, we can use $O(n)$ operations to AND the quantity $\bar{x}_1 \wedge \cdots \wedge \bar{x}_k$ to the other variables $x_{k+1}, \ldots, x_n$, then proceed with n reduced by k.

(One consequence is that we can compute the symmetric functions $\{S_1, S_2, \ldots, S_n\}$ with cost $s(n) + n + O(\sqrt{n}) = 6n + O(\sqrt{n})$ and depth $O(\log n)$.)

34. Say that an *extended* priority encoder has $n + 1 = 2^m$ inputs $x_0 x_1 \ldots x_n$ and $m + 1$ outputs $y_0 y_1 \ldots y_m$, where $y_0 = x_0 \vee x_1 \vee \cdots \vee x_n$. If Q'_m and Q''_m are extended encoders for $x'_0 \ldots x'_n$ and $x''_0 \ldots x''_n$, then Q_{m+1} works for $x'_0 \ldots x'_n x''_0 \ldots x''_n$ if we define

$y_0 = y_0' \vee y_0''$, $y_1 = y_0''$, $y_2 = y_1?\ y_1'': y_1'$, $\ldots$, $y_{m+1} = y_1?\ y_m'': y_m'$. If P_m' is an ordinary priority encoder for $x_1' \ldots x_n'$, we get P_{m+1} for $x_1' \ldots x_n' x_0'' \ldots x_n''$ in a similar way.

Starting with $m = 2$ and $y_2 = x_3 \vee (x_1 \wedge \bar{x}_2)$, $y_1 = x_2 \vee x_3$, $y_0 = x_0 \vee x_1 \vee y_1$, this construction yields P_m and Q_m of costs p_m and q_m, where $p_2 = 3$, $q_2 = 5$, and $p_{m+1} = 3m + p_m + q_m$, $q_{m+1} = 3m + 1 + 2q_m$ for $m \geq 2$. Consequently $p_m = q_m - m$ and $q_m = 15 \cdot 2^{m-2} - 3m - 4 \approx 3.75n$.

35. If $n = 2m$, compute $x_1 \wedge x_2$, $\ldots$, $x_{n-1} \wedge x_n$, then recursively form $x_1 \wedge \cdots \wedge x_{2k-2} \wedge x_{2k+1} \wedge \cdots \wedge x_n$ for $1 \leq k \leq m$, and finish in n more steps. If $n = 2m - 1$, use this chain for $n + 1$ elements; three steps can be eliminated by setting $x_{n+1} \leftarrow 1$. [I. Wegener, *The Complexity of Boolean Functions* (1987), exercise 3.25. The same idea can be used with *any* associative and commutative operator in place of $\wedge$.]

36. Recursively construct $P_n(x_1, \ldots, x_n)$ and $Q_n(x_1, \ldots, x_n)$ as follows, where P_n has $D(y_j) \leq \lceil \lg n \rceil$ for $1 \leq j \leq n$ and Q_n has $D(y_j) \leq \lceil \lg n \rceil + [j \neq n]$: The case $n = 1$ is trivial; otherwise P_n is obtained from $Q_r'(x_1, \ldots, x_r)$ and $P_s''(x_{r+1}, \ldots, x_n)$, where $r = \lceil n/2 \rceil$ and $s = \lfloor n/2 \rfloor$, by setting $y_j \leftarrow y_j'$ for $1 \leq j \leq r$, $y_j \leftarrow y_r' \wedge y_{j-r}''$ for $r < j \leq n$. And Q_n is obtained from either $P_r'(x_1 \wedge x_2, \ldots, x_{n-1} \wedge x_n)$ or $P_r'(x_1 \wedge x_2, \ldots, x_{n-2} \wedge x_{n-1}, x_n)$ by setting $y_1 \leftarrow x_1$, $y_{2j} \leftarrow y_j'$, $y_{2j+1} \leftarrow y_j' \wedge x_{2j+1}$ for $1 \leq j < s$, and $y_{2s} \leftarrow y_s'$, $y_n \leftarrow y_r'$.

These calculations can be performed in *minimum memory*, setting $x_{k(i)} \leftarrow x_{j(i)} \wedge x_{k(i)}$ at step i for some indices $j(i) < k(i)$. Thus we can illustrate the construction with diagrams analogous to the diagrams for sorting networks. For example,

$$P_8 = \quad \begin{matrix} \text{(delay 0)} \\ \text{(delay 1)} \\ \text{(delay 2)} \\ \text{(delay 2)} \\ \text{(delay 3)} \\ \text{(delay 3)} \\ \text{(delay 3)} \\ \text{(delay 3)} \end{matrix} \ ; \qquad Q_8 = \quad \begin{matrix} \text{(delay 0)} \\ \text{(delay 1)} \\ \text{(delay 2)} \\ \text{(delay 2)} \\ \text{(delay 3)} \\ \text{(delay 3)} \\ \text{(delay 4)} \\ \text{(delay 3)} \end{matrix} \ .$$

The costs p_n and q_n satisfy $p_n = \lfloor n/2 \rfloor + q_{\lceil n/2 \rceil} + p_{\lfloor n/2 \rfloor}$, $q_n = 2\lfloor n/2 \rfloor - 1 + p_{\lceil n/2 \rceil}$ when $n > 1$; for example, $(p_1, \ldots, p_7) = (q_1, \ldots, q_7) = (0, 1, 2, 4, 5, 7, 9)$. Setting $\bar{p}_n = 4n - p_n$ and $\bar{q}_n = 3n - q_n$ leads to simpler formulas, which prove that $p_n < 4n$ and $q_n < 3n$: $\bar{q}_n = \bar{p}_{\lceil n/2 \rceil} + [n \text{ even}]$; $\bar{p}_{4n} = \bar{p}_{2n} + \bar{p}_n + 1$, $\bar{p}_{4n+1} = \bar{p}_{2n} + \bar{p}_{n+1} + 1$, $\bar{p}_{4n+2} = \bar{p}_{2n+1} + \bar{p}_{n+1}$, $\bar{p}_{4n+3} = \bar{p}_{4n+2} + 2$. In particular, $1 + \bar{p}_{2m} = F_{m+5}$ is a Fibonacci number. [See *JACM* **27** (1980), 831–834. Slightly better chains are obtained if we replace Q_{2n+1} by $(Q_{2n}$ and $y_{2n+1} = y_{2n} \wedge x_{2n+1})$ when n is a power of 2, if we replace P_5 and P_6 by Q_5 and Q_6, and if we then replace $(P_9, P_{10}, P_{11}, P_{17})$ by $(Q_9, Q_{10}, Q_{11}, Q_{17})$.]

Notice that this construction works in general if we replace '$\wedge$' by *any* associative operator. In particular, the sequence of prefixes $x_1 \oplus \cdots \oplus x_k$ for $1 \leq k \leq n$ defines the conversion from Gray binary code to radix-2 integers, Eq. 7.2.1.1–(10).

37. The case $m = 15$, $n = 16$ is illustrated at the right.

(a) Let $x_{i..j}$ denote the original value of $x_i \wedge \cdots \wedge x_j$. Whenever the algorithm sets $x_k \leftarrow x_j \wedge x_k$, one can show that the previous value of x_k was $x_{j+1..k}$. After step S1, x_k is $x_{f(k)+1..k}$ where $f(k) = k \ \& \ (k - 1)$ for $1 \leq k < m$ and $f(m) = 0$. After step S2, x_k is $x_{1..k}$ for $1 \leq k \leq m$.

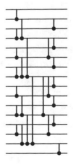

(b) The cost of S1 is $m - 1$, the cost of S2 is $m - 1 - \lceil \lg m \rceil$, and the cost of S3 is $n - m$. The final delay of x_k is $\lfloor \lg k \rfloor + \nu k - 1$ for $1 \leq k < m$, and it is $\lceil \lg m \rceil + k - m$ for $m \leq k \leq n$. So the maximum delay for $\{x_1, \ldots, x_{m-1}\}$ turns out to be $g(m) = m - 1$ for $m < 4$, $g(m) = \lfloor \lg m \rfloor + \lfloor \lg \frac{m}{3} \rfloor$ for $m \geq 4$. We have $c(m, n) = m + n - 2 - \lceil \lg m \rceil$, $d(m, n) = \max(g(m), \lceil \lg m \rceil + n - m)$. Hence $c(m, n) + d(m, n) = 2n - 2$

whenever $n \geq m + g(m) - \lceil \lg m \rceil$.

(c) A table of values reveals that $d(n) = \lceil \lg n \rceil$ for $n < 8$, and $d(n) = \lfloor \lg(n - \lfloor \lg n \rfloor + 3) \rfloor + \lfloor \lg \frac{2}{3}(n - \lfloor \lg n \rfloor + 3) \rfloor - 1$ for $n \geq 8$. Stating this another way, we have $d(n) > d(n - 1)$ and $n > 2$ if and only if $n = 2^k + k - 3$ or $2^k + 2^{k-1} + k - 3$ for some $k > 1$. The minimum with minimal cost occurs for $m = n$ when $n < 8$; otherwise it occurs for $m = n - \lfloor \lg \frac{2}{3}(n - \lfloor \lg n \rfloor + 3) \rfloor + 2 - [n = 2^k + k - 3$ for some $k]$.

(d) Set $m \leftarrow m(n, d)$, where $m(n, d(n))$ is defined in the previous sentence and $m(n, d) = m(n - 1, d - 1)$ when $d > d(n)$. [See $J.$ $Algorithms$ **7** (1986), 185–201.]

38. (a) From top to bottom, $f_k(x_1, \ldots, x_n)$ is an elementary symmetric function also called the threshold function $S_{\geq k}(x_1, \ldots, x_n)$. (See exercise 5.3.4–28, Eq. 7.1.1–(90).)

(b) After calculating $\{S_1, \ldots, S_n\}$ in $\approx 6n$ steps as in answer 33, we can apply the method of exercise 37 to finish in $2n$ further steps.

But it is more interesting to design a Boolean chain specifically for the computation of the $2^m + 1$ threshold functions $g_k(x_1, \ldots, x_m) = [(x_1 \ldots x_m)_2 \geq k]$ for $0 \leq k \leq 2^m$. Since $[(x'x'')_2 \geq (y'y'')_2] = [(x')_2 \geq (y')_2 + 1] \vee ([(x')_2 \geq (y')_2] \wedge [(x'')_2 \geq (y'')_2])$, a divide-and-conquer construction analogous to a binary decoder solves this problem with a cost at most $2t(m)$.

Furthermore, if $2^{m-1} \leq n < 2^m$, the cost $u(n)$ of computing $\{g_1, \ldots, g_n\}$ by this method turns out to be $2n + O(\sqrt{n})$, and it is quite reasonable when n is small:

$$n = 1\ \ 2\ \ 3\ \ 4\ \ 5\ \ 6\ \ 7\ \ 8\ \ \ 9\ \ 10\ \ 11\ \ 12\ \ 13\ \ 14\ \ 15\ \ 16\ \ 17\ \ 18\ \ 19\ \ 20$$
$$u(n) = 0\ \ 1\ \ 2\ \ 4\ \ 7\ \ 7\ \ 8\ \ 12\ \ 15\ \ 17\ \ 19\ \ 19\ \ 20\ \ 21\ \ 22\ \ 27\ \ 32\ \ 34\ \ 36\ \ 36$$

Starting with sideways addition, we can sort n Boolean values in $s(n) + u(n) \approx 7n$ steps. A sorting network, which costs $2\hat{S}(n)$, is better when $n = 4$ but loses when $n \geq 8$. [See 5.3.4–(11); D. E. Muller and F. P. Preparata, $JACM$ **22** (1975), 195–201.]

39. [$IEEE$ $Transactions$ **C-29** (1980), 737–738.] The identity

$$M_{r+s}(x_1, \ldots, x_r, x_{r+1}, \ldots, x_{r+s}; y_0, \ldots, y_{2^{r+s}-1}) = M_r(x_1, \ldots, x_r; y_0', \ldots, y_{2^r-1}'),$$

where $y_j' = \bigvee_{k=0}^{2^s-1}(d_k \wedge y_{2^s j + k})$ and d_k is the kth output of an s-to-2^s decoder applied to $(x_{r+1}, \ldots, x_{r+s})$, shows that $C(M_{r+s}) \leq C(M_r) + 2^{r+s} + 2^r(2^s - 1) + t(s)$, where $t(s)$ is the cost (30) of the decoder. The depth is $D(M_{r+s}) = \max(D_x(M_{r+s}), D_y(M_{r+s}))$, where D_x and D_y denote the maximum depth of the x and y variables; we have $D_x(M_{r+s}) \leq \max(D_x(M_r), 1 + s + \lceil \lg s \rceil + D_y(M_r))$ and $D_y(M_{r+s}) \leq 1 + s + D_y(M_r)$.

Taking $r = \lceil m/2 \rceil$ and $s = \lfloor m/2 \rfloor$ yields $C(M_m) \leq 2^{m+1} + O(2^{m/2})$, $D_y(M_m) \leq m + 1 + \lceil \lg m \rceil$, and $D_x(M_m) \leq D_y(M_m) + \lceil \lg m \rceil$.

40. We can, for example, let $f_{nk}(x) = \bigvee_{j=1}^{n+1-k}(l_j(x) \wedge r_{j+k-1}(x))$, where

$$l_j(x) = \begin{cases} x_j, & \text{if } j \bmod k = 0, \\ x_j \wedge l_{j+1}(x), & \text{if } j \bmod k \neq 0, \end{cases} \quad \text{for } 1 \leq j \leq n - (n \bmod k);$$

$$r_j(x) = \begin{cases} 1, & \text{if } j \bmod k = 0, \\ x_j \wedge r_{j-1}(x), & \text{if } j \bmod k \neq 0, \end{cases} \quad \text{for } k \leq j \leq n.$$

The cost is $4n - 3k - 3\lfloor \frac{n}{k} \rfloor - \lfloor \frac{n-1}{k} \rfloor + 2 - (n \bmod k)$.

A recursive solution is preferable when n is small or k is small: Observe that

$$f_{nk}(x) = \begin{cases} x_{n-k+1} \wedge \cdots \wedge x_k \wedge \\ \quad f_{(2n-2k)(n-k)}(x_1, \ldots, x_{n-k}, x_{k+1}, \ldots, x_n), & \text{for } k < n < 2k; \\ f_{\lfloor (n+k)/2 \rfloor k}(x_1, \ldots, x_{\lfloor (n+k)/2 \rfloor}) \vee \\ \quad f_{\lfloor (n+k-1)/2 \rfloor k}(x_{\lfloor (n-k)/2 \rfloor + 1}, \ldots, x_n), & \text{for } n \geq 2k. \end{cases}$$

The cost of this solution can be shown to equal $n - 1 + \sum_{j=1}^{n-k} \lfloor \lg j \rfloor$ when $k \leq n < 2k$, and it lies asymptotically between $(m + \alpha_k - 1)n + O(km)$ and $(m + 2 - 2/\alpha_k)n + O(km)$ as $n \to \infty$, where $m = \lfloor \lg k \rfloor$ and $1 < \alpha_k = (k+1)/2^m \leq 2$.

A marriage of these methods is better yet; the optimum cost is unknown.

41. Let $c(m)$ be the cost of computing both $(x)_2 + (y)_2$ and $(x)_2 + (y)_2 + 1$ by the conditional-sum method when x and y have $n = 2^m$ bits, and let $c'(m)$ be the cost of the simpler problem of computing just $(x)_2 + (y)_2$. Then $c(m+1) = 2c(m) + 6 \cdot 2^m + 2$, $c'(m + 1) = c(m) + c'(m) + 3 \cdot 2^m + 1$. (Bit z_n of the sum costs 1; but bits z_k for $n < k \leq 2n + 1$ cost 3, because they have the form $c? a_k: b_k$ where c is a carry bit.) If we start with $n = 1$ and $c(0) = 3$, $c'(0) = 2$, the solution is $c(m) = (3m + 5)2^m - 2$, $c'(m) = (3m + 2)2^m - m$. But improved constructions for the case $n = 2$ allow us to start with $c(1) = 11$ and $c'(1) = 7$; then the solution is $c(m) = (3m + \frac{7}{2})2^m - 2$, $c'(m) = (3m + \frac{1}{2})2^m - m + 1$. In either case the depth is $2m + 1$. [See J. Sklansky, *IRE Transactions* **EC-9** (1960), 226–231.]

42. (a) Since $\langle x_k y_k c_k \rangle = u_k \vee (v_k \wedge c_k)$, we can use (26) and induction.

(b) Notice that $U_k^{k+1} = u_k$ and $V_k^{k+1} = v_k$; use induction on $j - i$. [See A. Weinberger and J. L. Smith, *IRE Transactions* **EC-5** (1956), 65–73; R. P. Brent and H. T. Kung, *IEEE Transactions* **C-31** (1982), 260–264.]

(c) First, for $l = 1, 2, \ldots, m-1$, and for $1 \leq k \leq n$, compute V_i^k for all multiples i of $h(l)$ in the range $k_l \geq i \geq k_{l+1}$, where $k_l = h(l)\lfloor (k - 1)/h(l) \rfloor$ denotes the largest multiple of $h(l)$ that is less than k. For example, when $l = 3$ and $k = 99$, we compute V_{96}^{99}, $V_{88}^{99} = V_{96}^{99} \wedge V_{88}^{96}$, $V_{80}^{99} = V_{88}^{99} \wedge V_{80}^{88}$, $\ldots$, $V_{64}^{99} = V_{72}^{99} \wedge V_{64}^{72}$; this is a prefix computation using the values V_{96}^{99}, V_{88}^{96}, V_{80}^{88}, $\ldots$, V_{64}^{72} that were computed when $l = 2$. Using the method of exercise 36, step l adds at most l levels to the depth, and it requires a total of $(p_1 + p_2 + \cdots + p_{2l})n/2^l = O(2^l n)$ gates.

Then, again for $l = 1, 2, \ldots, m - 1$, and for $1 \leq k \leq n$, compute U_i^k for $i = k_{l+1}$, using the "unrolled" formula

$$U_{k_{l+1}}^k = U_{k_l}^k \vee \bigvee_{\substack{k_l > j \geq k_{l+1} \\ h(l) \backslash j}} (V_{j+h(l)}^k \wedge U_j^{j+h(l)}).$$

For example, the unrolled formula when $l = 3$ and $k = 99$ is

$$U_{64}^{99} = U_{96}^{99} \vee (V_{96}^{99} \wedge U_{88}^{96}) \vee (V_{88}^{99} \wedge U_{80}^{88}) \vee (V_{80}^{99} \wedge U_{72}^{80}) \vee (V_{72}^{99} \wedge U_{64}^{72}).$$

Every such U_i^k is a union of at most 2^l terms, so it can be computed with depth $\leq l$ in addition to the depth of each term. The total cost of this phase for $1 \leq k \leq n$ is $(0 + 2 + 4 + \cdots + (2^l - 2))n/2^l = O(2^l n)$.

The overall cost to compute all necessary U's and V's is therefore $\sum_{l=1}^{m-1} O(2^l n) = O(2^m n)$. (Furthermore the quantities V_0^k aren't actually needed, so we save the cost of $\sum_{l=1}^{m-1} h(l)p_{2l}$ gates.) For example, when $m = (2, 3, 4, 5)$ we obtain Boolean chains for the addition of $(2, 8, 64, 1024)$-bit numbers, respectively, with overall depths $(3, 7, 11, 16)$ and costs $(7, 64, 1254, 48470)$.

[This construction is due to V. M. Khrapchenko, *Problemy Kibernetiki* **19** (1967), 107–122, who also showed how to combine it with other methods so that the overall cost will be $O(n)$ while still achieving depth $\lg n + O(\sqrt{\log n})$. However, his combined method is purely of theoretical interest, because it requires $n > 2^{64}$ before the depth becomes less than $2 \lg n$. Another way to achieve small depth using the recurrences in (b) can be based on the Fibonacci numbers: The Fibonacci method computes the carries with depth $\log_\phi n + O(1) \approx 1.44 \lg n$ and cost $O(n \log n)$. For example, it yields chains for binary addition with the following characteristics:

$n =$	4	8	16	32	64	128	256	512	1024
depth	6	7	9	10	12	13	15	16	18
cost		24	71	186	467	1125	2648	6102	13775	30861

See D. E. Knuth, *The Stanford GraphBase* (1994), 276–279.

Charles Babbage found an ingenious mechanical solution to the analogous problem for addition in radix 10, claiming that his design would be able to add numbers of arbitrary precision in constant time; for this to work he would have needed idealized, rigid components with vanishing clearances. See H. P. Babbage, *Babbage's Calculating Engines* (1889), 334–335. Curiously, an equivalent idea works fine with physical transistors, although it cannot be expressed in terms of Boolean chains; see P. M. Fenwick, *Comp. J.* **30** (1987), 77–79.]

43. (a) Let $A = B = Q = \{0,1\}$ and $q_0 = 0$. Define $c(q, a) = d(q, a) = \bar{q} \wedge a$.

(b) The key idea is to construct the functions $d_1(q) \ldots d_{n-1}(q)$, where $d_1(q) = d(q, a_1)$ and $d_j(q) = d(d_{j-1}(q), a_j)$. In other words, $d_1 = d^{(a_1)}$ and $d_j = d_{j-1} \circ d^{(a_j)}$, where $d^{(a)}$ is the function that takes $q \mapsto d(q, a)$ and where $\circ$ denotes composition of functions. Each function d_j can be encoded in binary notation, and $\circ$ is an associative operation on these binary representations. Hence the functions $d_1 d_2 \ldots d_{n-1}$ are the prefixes $d^{(a_1)}$, $d^{(a_1)} \circ d^{(a_2)}$, ..., $d^{(a_1)} \circ \cdots \circ d^{(a_{n-1})}$; and $q_1 q_2 \ldots q_n = q_0 d_1(q_0) \ldots d_{n-1}(q_0)$.

(c) Represent a function $f(q)$ by its truth table $f_0 f_1$. Then the composition $f_0 f_1 \circ g_0 g_1$ is $h_0 h_1$, where the functions $h_0 = f_0$? g_1: g_0 and $h_1 = f_1$? g_1: g_0 are muxes that can each be computed with cost 3 and depth 2. (The combined cost $C(h_0 h_1)$ is only 5, but we are trying to keep the depth small.) The truth table for $d^{(a)}$ is $a0$. Using exercise 36, we can therefore compute the truth tables $d_{10} d_{11} d_{20} d_{21} \ldots d_{(n-1)0} d_{(n-1)1}$ with cost $\leq 6p_{n-1} < 24n$ and depth $\leq 2\lceil \lg(n-1) \rceil$; then $b_1 = a_1$, and $b_j = \bar{q}_j \wedge a_j = \bar{d}_{(j-1)0} \wedge a_j$ for $j > 1$. (These cost estimates are quite conservative; substantial simplifications arise because of the 0s in the initial truth tables of $d^{(a_j)}$ and because many of the intermediate values d_{j1} are never used. For example, when $n = 5$ the actual cost is only 10, not $6p_{n-1} + (n-1) = 28$; the actual depth is 4, not $2\lceil \lg(n-1) \rceil + 1 = 5$. Notice that the straightforward chain $b_j = a_j \wedge \bar{b}_{j-1}$ for $1 < j \leq n$ also solves problem (a); it wins on cost, but has depth $n-1$.)

44. The inputs may be regarded as the string $x_0 y_0\, x_1 y_1 \ldots x_{n-1} y_{n-1}$ whose elements belong to the four-letter alphabet $A = \{00, 01, 10, 11\}$; there are two states $Q = \{0,1\}$, representing a possible carry bit, with $q_0 = 0$; the output alphabet is $B = \{0,1\}$; and we have $c(q, xy) = q \oplus x \oplus y$, $d(q, xy) = \langle qxy \rangle$. In this case, therefore, the finite state transducer is essentially described by a full adder.

Only three of the four possible functions of q occur when we compose the mappings $d^{(xy)}$. We can encode them as $u \vee (q \wedge v)$. The initial functions $d^{(xy)}$ have $u = x \wedge y$, $v = x \oplus y$; and the composition $(uv) \circ (u'v')$ is $u''v''$, where $u'' = u' \vee (v' \wedge u)$ and $v'' = v \wedge v'$.

When $n = 4$, for example, the chain has the following form, using the notation of exercise 42: $U_k^{k+1} = x_k \wedge y_k$, $V_k^{k+1} = x_k \oplus y_k$, for $0 \leq k < 4$; $U_0^2 = U_1^2 \vee (V_1^2 \wedge U_0^1)$, $U_2^4 = U_3^4 \vee (V_3^4 \wedge U_2^3)$, $V_2^4 = V_2^3 \wedge V_3^4$; $U_0^3 = U_2^3 \vee (V_2^3 \wedge U_0^2)$, $U_0^4 = U_2^4 \vee (V_2^4 \wedge U_0^2)$; $z_0 = V_0^1$, $z_1 = U_0^1 \oplus V_1^2$, $z_2 = U_0^2 \oplus V_2^3$, $z_3 = U_0^3 \oplus V_3^4$, $z_4 = U_0^4$. The total cost is 20; the maximum depth, 6, occurs in the computation of z_3.

In general the cost will be $2n+3p_n$ in the notation of exercise 36, because we need $2n$ gates for the initial u's and v's, then $3p_n$ gates for the prefix computation; the $n-1$ additional gates needed to form z_j for $0 < j < n$ are compensated by the fact that we need not compute V_0^j for $1 < j \le n$. Therefore the total cost is $14 \cdot 2^m - 3F_{m+5} + 3$, superior to the conditional-sum method (which however has depth $2m+1$, not $2m+2$):

$n =$	2	4	8	16	32	64	128	256	512	1024
cost of conditional-sum chain	7	25	74	197	492	1179	2746	6265	14072	31223
cost of Ladner–Fischer chain	7	20	52	125	286	632	1363	2888	6040	12509

[George Boole introduced his Algebra in order to show that logic can be understood in terms of arithmetic. Eventually logic became so well understood, the situation was reversed: People like Shannon and Zuse began in the 1930s to design circuits for arithmetic in terms of logic, and since then many approaches to the problem of parallel addition have been discovered. The first Boolean chains of cost $O(n)$ and depth $O(\log n)$ were devised by Yu. P. Ofman, *Doklady Akademii Nauk SSSR* **145** (1962), 48–51. His chains were similar to the construction above, but the depth was approximately $4m$.]

45. That argument would indeed be simpler, but it wouldn't be strong enough to prove the desired result. (Many chains with steps of fanout 0 inflate the simpler estimate.) The text's permutation-enhanced proof technique was introduced by J. E. Savage in his book *The Complexity of Computing* (New York: Wiley, 1976), Theorem 3.4.1.

46. When $r = 2^n/n + O(1)$ we have $\ln(2^{2r+1}(n+r-1)^{2r}/(r-1)!) = r \ln r + (1 + \ln 4)r + O(n) = (2^n/n)(n \ln 2 - \ln n + 1 + \ln 4) + O(n)$. So $\alpha(n) \le (n/(4e))^{-2^n/n + O(n/\log n)}$, which approaches zero quite rapidly indeed when $n > 4e$.

(In fact, (32) gives $\alpha(11) < 7.6 \times 10^7$, $\alpha(12) < 4.2 \times 10^{-6}$, $\alpha(13) < 1.2 \times 10^{-38}$.)

47. Restrict permutations to the $(r - m)!$ cases where $i\pi = i$ for $1 \le i \le n$ and $(n+r+1-k)\pi$ is the kth output. Then we get $(r - m)! \, c(m, n, r) \le 2^{2r+1}(n+r-1)^{2r}$ in place of (32). Hence, as in exercise 46, almost all such functions have cost exceeding $2^n m/(n + \lg m)$ when $m = O(2^n/n^2)$.

48. (a) Not surprisingly, this lower bound on $C(n)$ is rather crude when n is small:

$n =$	1	2	3	4	5	6	7	8	9	10	11	12	13	14	15	16
$r(n) =$	1	1	2	3	5	9	16	29	54	99	184	343	639	1196	2246	4229

(b) The bootstrap method (see *Concrete Mathematics* §9.4) yields

$$r(n) = \frac{2^n}{n}\left(1 + \frac{\lg n - 2 - 1/\ln 2}{n} + O\left(\frac{\log n}{n^2}\right)\right).$$

49. The number of normal Boolean functions that can be represented by a formula of length $\le r$ is at most $5^r n^{r+1} g_r$, where g_r is the number of oriented binary trees with r internal nodes. Set $r = 2^n/\lg n - 2^{n+2}/(\lg n)^2$ in this formula and divide by 2^{2^n-1} to get an upper bound on the fraction of functions with $L(f) \le r$. The result rapidly approaches zero, by exercise 2.3.4.4–7, because it is $O((5\alpha/16)^{2^n/\lg n})$ where $\alpha \approx 2.483$.

[J. Riordan and C. E. Shannon obtained a similar lower bound for series-parallel switching networks in *J. Math. and Physics* **21** (1942), 83–93; such networks are equivalent to formulas in which only canalizing operators are used. R. E. Krichevsky obtained more general results in *Problemy Kibernetiki* **2** (1959), 123–138, and O. B. Lupanov gave an asymptotically matching upper bound in *Prob. Kibernetiki* **3** (1960), 61–80.]

50. (a) Using subcube notation as in exercise 7.1.1–30, the prime implicants are $00001*$, $(0001*1)$, $0100*1$, $0111*1$, $1010*1$, $101*11$, $00*011$, $00*101$, $(01*111)$, $11*101$,

$(0*1101)$, $(1*0101)$, $1*1011$, $0*0*11$, $*00101$, $(*01011)$, $(*11101)$, where the parenthesized subcubes are omitted in a shortest DNF. (b) Similarly, the prime clauses and a shortest CNF are given by $00111*$, $01010*$, $10110*$, $0110**$, $00*00*$, $11*00*$, $11*11*$, $(0*100*)$, $(1*00**)$, $1*0*1*$, $(1****0)$, $*0000*$, $(*1100*)$, $*1***0$, $**1**0$, $***1*0$, and $(****00)$. (Thus the CNF is $(x_1 \lor x_2 \lor \bar{x}_3 \lor \bar{x}_4 \lor \bar{x}_5) \land (x_1 \lor \bar{x}_2 \lor x_3 \lor \bar{x}_4 \lor x_5) \land \cdots \land (\bar{x}_4 \lor x_6)$.)

51. $f = ([x_5 x_6 \in \{01\}] \land [(x_1 x_2 x_3 x_4)_2 \in \{1, 3, 4, 7, 9, 10, 13, 15\}]) \lor ([x_5 x_6 \in \{10, 11\}] \land [x_1 x_2 x_3 x_4 = 0000]) \lor ([x_5 x_6 \in \{11\}] \land [(x_1 x_2 x_3 x_4)_2 \in \{1, 2, 4, 5, 7, 10, 11, 14\}])$.

52. The small-n results are quite different from those that work asymptotically:

n k l (38)	n k l (38)	n k l (38)	n k l (38)
5 2 2 39	8 3 2 175	11 4 4 803	14 5 5 4045
6 2 2 67	9 3 2 279	12 4 3 1329	15 5 5 7141
7 2 1 109	10 4 4 471	13 5 6 2355	16 5 4 12431

(These upper bounds are quite weak when n is small. For example, we know that $C(n) = (0, 1, 4, 7, 12)$ when $n = (1, 2, 3, 4, 5)$; and Eq. 7.1.1–(16) gives $C(n + 1) \leq 2C(n) + 2$, so that $C(6) \leq 26$, $C(7) \leq 54$, etc.)

53. First note that $2^k/l \leq n - 3 \lg n$, hence $m_i \leq n - 3 \lg n + 1$ and $2^{m_i} = O(2^n/n^3)$. Also $l = O(n)$ and $t(n - k) = O(2^n/n^2)$. So (38) reduces to $l \cdot 2^{n-k} + O(2^n/n^2) = 2^n/(n - 3 \lg n) + O(2^n/n^2)$.

54. The greedy-footprint heuristic gives a chain of length 14:

$$x_5 = x_1 \oplus x_3, \qquad x_{10} = x_4 \land \bar{x}_5, \qquad f_3 = x_{15} = \bar{x}_8 \land x_9,$$
$$x_6 = x_2 \oplus x_3, \qquad x_{11} = x_4 \oplus x_5, \qquad f_4 = x_{16} = x_4 \land x_8,$$
$$x_7 = x_1 \land x_2, \qquad x_{12} = x_6 \land x_{11}, \qquad f_5 = x_{17} = x_7 \land x_9,$$
$$x_8 = x_1 \land \bar{x}_6, \qquad f_1 = x_{13} = \bar{x}_7 \land x_{12}, \qquad f_6 = x_{19} = x_6 \land x_{10}.$$
$$x_9 = x_4 \land x_5, \qquad f_2 = x_{14} = \bar{x}_6 \land x_{10},$$

The minterm-first method corresponds to a chain of length 22, after we remove steps that are never used:

$$x_5 = \bar{x}_1 \land \bar{x}_2, \qquad x_{13} = x_5 \land x_{10}, \qquad x_{20} = x_8 \land x_{11},$$
$$x_6 = \bar{x}_1 \land x_2, \qquad x_{14} = x_5 \land x_{11}, \qquad f_6 = x_{21} = x_{15} \lor x_{18},$$
$$x_7 = x_1 \land \bar{x}_2, \qquad x_{15} = x_6 \land x_9, \qquad f_1 = x_{22} = x_{13} \lor x_{21},$$
$$x_8 = x_1 \land x_2, \qquad x_{16} = x_6 \land x_{11}, \qquad f_2 = x_{23} = x_{12} \lor x_{20},$$
$$x_9 = \bar{x}_3 \land x_4, \qquad x_{17} = x_7 \land x_9, \qquad x_{24} = x_{14} \lor x_{16},$$
$$x_{10} = x_3 \land \bar{x}_4, \qquad x_{18} = x_7 \land x_{11}, \qquad f_3 = x_{25} = x_{24} \lor x_{19},$$
$$x_{11} = x_3 \land x_4, \qquad f_5 = x_{19} = x_8 \land x_9, \qquad f_4 = x_{26} = x_{17} \lor x_{20}.$$
$$x_{12} = x_5 \land x_9,$$

(The distributive law could replace the computation of x_{14}, x_{16}, and x_{24} by two steps.)

Incidentally, the three functions in the answer to exercise 51 can be computed in only ten steps:

$$x_5 = x_2 \lor x_4, \qquad f_3 = x_9 = x_6 \oplus x_8, \qquad x_{12} = x_2 \oplus x_3,$$
$$x_6 = \bar{x}_1 \land x_5, \qquad x_{10} = x_1 \odot x_8, \qquad x_{13} = \bar{x}_{10} \land x_{12},$$
$$x_7 = x_2 \land x_4, \qquad \bar{f}_2 = x_{11} = x_9 \lor x_{10}, \qquad f_1 = x_{14} = x_4 \oplus x_{13}.$$
$$x_8 = x_3 \land \bar{x}_7,$$

55. The optimum two-level DNF and CNF representations in answer 50 cost 53 and 43, respectively. Formula (37) costs 29, when optimized as in exercise 54. The alternative in exercise 51 costs only 17. But the catalog of optimum five-variable chains suggests

$$
\begin{aligned}
&x_7 = \bar{x}_1 \wedge x_2, & &x_{11} = x_5 \wedge x_{10}, & &x_{15} = x_{13} \oplus x_{14}, & &x_{18} = \bar{x}_4 \wedge x_{17}, \\
&x_8 = x_3 \oplus x_7, & &x_{12} = x_5 \vee x_{10}, & &x_{16} = x_5 \wedge \bar{x}_{10}, & &x_{19} = x_6 \wedge x_{15}, \\
&x_9 = x_2 \wedge x_8, & &x_{13} = x_4 \wedge \bar{x}_{11}, & &x_{17} = \bar{x}_3 \wedge x_{16}, & &x_{20} = x_{18} \vee x_{19}, \\
&x_{10} = x_1 \oplus x_9, & &x_{14} = x_8 \wedge x_{12}, & & & &
\end{aligned}
$$

for this six-variable function. Is there a better way?

56. If we care about at most two values, the function can be either constant or x_j or $\bar{x}_j$.

57. The truth tables for x_5 through x_{15}, in hexadecimal notation, are respectively 0fff, 3ccc, 30c0, 75d5, 4919, 7000, 0606, 4808, 2000, 5d5d, 3ece. So we get

$$1010 \mapsto \text{0}, \quad 1011 \mapsto \text{7}, \quad 1100 \mapsto \text{4}, \quad 1101 \mapsto \text{5}, \quad 1110 \mapsto \text{6}, \quad 1111 \mapsto \text{7}.$$

[Corey Plover, believing that it might be better to have a solution in which nondigits never masquerade as digits, has discovered a 12-step chain (with non-greedy x_7)

$$
\begin{aligned}
&x_5 = x_1 \oplus x_2, & &x_9 = x_2 \oplus x_3, & &\bar{b} = x_{13} = x_2 \wedge \bar{x}_{11}, \\
&x_6 = x_3 \wedge \bar{x}_4, & &g = x_{10} = x_7 \vee x_9, & &\bar{c} = x_{14} = x_7 \wedge x_9, \\
&x_7 = x_1 \oplus x_6, & &\bar{d} = x_{11} = x_8 \oplus x_{10}, & &\bar{e} = x_{15} = x_4 \vee x_{12}, \\
&x_8 = x_4 \vee x_7, & &\bar{a} = x_{12} = \bar{x}_3 \wedge x_{11}, & &\bar{f} = x_{16} = \bar{x}_5 \wedge x_8,
\end{aligned}
$$

for which $a, \ldots, g$ have the truth tables b7ff, f9f0, dfe3, b6df, a2aa, 8ff2, 3efd, and

$$1010 \mapsto \text{A}, \quad 1011 \mapsto \text{0}, \quad 1100 \mapsto \text{c}, \quad 1101 \mapsto \text{-}, \quad 1110 \mapsto \text{L}, \quad 1111 \mapsto \text{-}.$$

He has also shown that all 11-step solutions to (44) map the nondigits into either $(\text{0},\text{7},\text{4},\text{5},\text{6},\text{7})$, $(\text{0},\text{7},\text{6},\text{!},\text{9},\text{5})$, $(\text{0},\text{7},\text{6},\text{!},\text{A},\text{5})$, $(\text{2},\text{3},\text{6},\text{7},\text{6},\text{7})$, $(\text{2},\text{!},\text{6},\text{7},\text{4},\text{5})$, or $(\text{2},\text{'},\text{6},\text{7},\text{4},\text{5})$.]

58. The truth tables of all cost-7 functions with exactly eight 1s in their truth tables are equivalent to either 0779, 169b, or 179a. Combining these in all possible ways yields 9656 solutions that are distinct under permutation and/or complementation of $\{x_1, x_2, x_3, x_4\}$ as well as under permutation and/or complementation of $\{f_1, f_2, f_3, f_4\}$.

59. The greedy-footprint heuristic produces the following 17-step chain:

$$
\begin{aligned}
&x_5 = x_2 \oplus x_3, & &x_{11} = x_2 \vee x_7, & &x_{17} = \bar{x}_6 \wedge x_8, \\
&x_6 = x_1 \oplus x_4, & &x_{12} = x_2 \wedge \bar{x}_6, & &f_1 = x_{18} = x_{11} \oplus x_{17}, \\
&x_7 = x_1 \oplus x_3, & &x_{13} = x_3 \wedge x_4, & &f_2 = x_{19} = x_{10} \wedge \bar{x}_{14}, \\
&x_8 = x_4 \vee x_5, & &x_{14} = x_4 \wedge x_5, & &f_3 = x_{20} = x_9 \oplus x_{16}, \\
&x_9 = x_6 \wedge x_8, & &x_{15} = x_5 \wedge x_{10}, & &f_4 = x_{21} = x_{12} \oplus x_{15}. \\
&x_{10} = x_7 \vee x_9, & &x_{16} = x_2 \wedge \bar{x}_{13}, & &
\end{aligned}
$$

The initial functions all have large footprints, so we can't achieve $C(f_1 f_2 f_3 f_4) = 28$; but a slightly more difficult S-box probably does exist.

60. One way is $u_1 = x_1 \oplus y_1$, $u_2 = x_2 \oplus y_2$, $v_1 = y_2 \oplus u_1$, $v_2 = y_1 \oplus u_2$, $z_1 = v_1 \wedge \bar{u}_2$, $z_2 = v_2 \wedge \bar{u}_1$.

61. The following 17-gate solution by David Stevenson generalizes to $8m + 1$ gates for addition mod $2^m + 1$: $u_0 = x_0 \wedge y_0$, $v_0 = x_0 \oplus y_0$, $u_1 = x_1 \wedge y_1$, $v_1 = x_1 \oplus y_1$, $t_1 = v_1 \wedge u_0$, $t_2 = v_1 \oplus u_0$, $c_2 = u_1 \vee t_1$; $u_2 = x_2 \wedge y_2$, $t_3 = x_2 \vee y_2$, $t_4 = t_3 \vee c_2$; $t_5 = t_2 \vee v_0$, $t_6 = t_5 \wedge t_4$, $t_7 = t_6 \vee u_2$; $t_8 = t_7 \wedge \bar{v}_0$, $z_0 = t_7 \oplus v_0$, $z_1 = t_2 \oplus t_8$; $z_2 = t_4 \oplus t_7$. (Notice that $(x_2 x_1 x_0)_2 + (y_2 y_1 y_0)_2 = (u_2 t_4 t_2 v_0)_2 - 4[x = y = 4]$. Gilbert Lee has found another 17-step solution if the inputs are represented by 000, 001, 011, 101, and 111.)

62. There are $\binom{2^n}{2^n d} 2^{2^n c}$ such functions, at most $\binom{2^n}{2^n d} c(n,r)$ of which have cost $\leq r$. So we can argue as in exercise 46 to conclude from (32) that the fraction with cost $\leq r = \lfloor 2^n c/n \rfloor$ is at most $2^{2r+1-2^n c}(n+r-1)^{2r}/(r-1)! = 2^{-r \lg n + O(r)}$.

63. [*Problemy Kibernetiki* **21** (1969), 215–226.] Put the truth table in a $2^k \times 2^{n-k}$ array as in Lupanov's method, and suppose there are c_j cares in column j, for $0 \leq j < 2^{n-k}$. Break that column into $\lfloor c_j/m \rfloor$ subcolumns that each have m cares, plus a possibly empty subcolumn at the bottom that contains fewer than m of them. The hint tells us that at most 2^{m+k} column vectors suffice to match the 0s and 1s of every subcolumn that has a specified top row i_0 and bottom row i_1. With $O(m2^{m+3k})$ operations we can therefore construct $O(2^{m+3k})$ functions $g_t(x_1, \ldots, x_k)$ from the minterms of $\{x_1, \ldots, x_k\}$, so that every subcolumn matches some type t. And for every type t we can construct functions $h_t(x_{k+1}, \ldots, x_n)$ from the minterms of $\{x_{k+1}, \ldots, x_n\}$, specifying the columns that match t; the cost is at most $\sum_j (\lfloor c_j/m \rfloor + 1) \leq 2^n c/m + 2^{n-k}$. Finally, $f = \bigvee_t (g_t \wedge h_t)$ requires $O(2^{m+3k})$ additional steps. Choosing $k = \lfloor 2 \lg n \rfloor$ and $m = \lceil n - 9 \lg n \rceil$ makes the total cost at most $(2^n c/n)(1 + 9n^{-1} \lg n + O(n^{-1}))$.

Of course we need to prove the hint, which is due to E. I. Nechiporuk [*Doklady Akad. Nauk SSSR* **163** (1965), 40–42]. In fact, $2^m(1 + \lceil k \ln 2 \rceil)$ vectors suffice (see S. K. Stein, *J. Combinatorial Theory* **A16** (1974), 391–397): If we choose $q = 2^m \lceil k \ln 2 \rceil$ vectors at random, not necessarily distinct, the expected number of untouched subcubes is $\binom{k}{m} 2^m (1 - 2^{-m})^q < \binom{k}{m} 2^m e^{-q2^{-m}} < 2^m$. (An explicit construction would be nicer.)

For extensive generalizations — tolerating a percentage of errors and specifying the density of 1s — see N. Pippenger, *Mathematical Systems Theory* **10** (1977), 129–167.

64. It's exactly the game of tic-tac-toe, if we number the cells $\begin{smallmatrix}6&1&8\\7&5&3\\2&9&4\end{smallmatrix}$ as in an ancient Chinese magic square. [Berlekamp, Conway, and Guy use this numbering scheme to present a complete analysis of tic-tac-toe in their book *Winning Ways* **3** (2003), 732–736.]

65. One solution is to replace the "defending" moves d_j by "attacking" moves a_j and "counterattacking" moves c_j, and to include them only for corner cells $j \in \{1, 3, 9, 7\}$. Let $j \cdot k = (jk) \bmod 10$; then

$$\begin{matrix} j \cdot 1 & j \cdot 2 & j \cdot 3 \\ j \cdot 4 & j \cdot 5 & j \cdot 6 \\ j \cdot 7 & j \cdot 8 & j \cdot 9 \end{matrix}$$

gives us another way to look at the tic-tac-toe diagram, when j is a corner, because $j \perp 10$. The precise definition of a_j and c_j is then

$$a_j = m_j \wedge \big((x_{j\cdot3} \wedge \beta_{(j\cdot8)(j\cdot9)} \wedge (o_{j\cdot4} \oplus o_{j\cdot6})) \vee (x_{j\cdot7} \wedge \beta_{(j\cdot6)(j\cdot9)} \wedge (o_{j\cdot2} \oplus o_{j\cdot8}))$$
$$\vee \big(m_{j\cdot9} \wedge ((m_{j\cdot8} \wedge x_{j\cdot2} \wedge \overline{(o_{j\cdot3} \oplus o_{j\cdot6})}) \vee (m_{j\cdot6} \wedge x_{j\cdot4} \wedge \overline{(o_{j\cdot7} \oplus o_{j\cdot8}))})) \big) \big);$$
$$c_j = d_j \wedge \overline{(x_{j\cdot6} \wedge o_{j\cdot7})} \wedge \overline{(x_{j\cdot8} \wedge o_{j\cdot3})} \wedge \bar{d}_{j\cdot9};$$

here $d_j = m_j \wedge \beta_{(j\cdot2)(j\cdot3)} \wedge \beta_{(j\cdot4)(j\cdot7)}$ takes the place of (51). We also define

$$u = (x_1 \oplus x_3) \oplus (x_7 \oplus x_9),$$
$$v = (o_1 \oplus o_3) \oplus (o_7 \oplus o_9),$$
$$t = m_2 \wedge m_6 \wedge m_8 \wedge m_4 \wedge (u \vee \bar{v}),$$
$$z_j = \begin{cases} m_j \wedge \bar{t}, & \text{if } j = 5, \\ m_j \wedge \bar{d}_{j\cdot9}, & \text{if } j \in \{1, 3, 9, 7\}, \\ m_j, & \text{if } j \in \{2, 6, 8, 4\}, \end{cases}$$

in order to cover a few more exceptional cases. Finally the sequence of rank-ordered moves $d_5 d_1 d_3 d_9 d_7 d_2 d_6 d_8 d_4 m_5 m_1 m_3 m_9 m_7 m_2 m_6 m_8 m_4$ in (53) is replaced by the sequence $a_1 a_3 a_9 a_7 c_1 c_3 c_9 c_7 z_5 z_1 z_3 z_9 z_7 z_2 z_6 z_8 z_4$; and we replace $(d_j \wedge \bar{d}'_j) \vee (m_j \wedge \bar{m}'_j)$ in (55) by $(a_j \wedge \bar{a}'_j) \vee (c_j \wedge \bar{c}'_j) \vee (z_j \wedge \bar{z}'_j)$ when j is a corner cell, otherwise simply by $(z_j \wedge \bar{z}'_j)$.

(Notice that this machine is required to move correctly from *all* legal positions, even when those positions couldn't arise after the machine had made X's earlier moves. We essentially allow humans to play the game until they ask the machine for advice. Otherwise great simplifications would be possible. For example, if X always goes first, it could grab the center cell and eliminate a huge number of future possibilities; fewer than $8 \times 6 \times 4 \times 2 = 384$ games could arise. Even if O goes first, there are fewer than $9 \times 7 \times 5 \times 3 = 945$ possible scenarios against a fixed strategy. In fact, the actual number of different games with the strategy defined here turns out to be $76 + 457$, of which $72 + 328$ are won by the machine and the rest belong to the cat.)

66. The Boolean chain in the previous answer fulfills its mission of making correct moves from all 4520 legal positions, where correctness was essentially defined to mean that the worst-case final outcome is maximized. But a truly great tic-tac-toe player would do things differently. For example, from position ⊞ the machine takes the center, ⊞, and O probably draws by playing in a corner. But moving to ⊞ or ⊞ would give O only two chances to avoid defeat. [See Martin Gardner, *Hexaflexagons and Other Mathematical Diversions*, Chapter 4.]

Furthermore the best move from a position like ⊞ is to ⊞ instead of winning immediately; then if the reply is ⊞, move to ⊞. That way you still win, but without humiliating your opponent so badly.

Finally, even the concept of a single "best move" is flawed, because a good player will choose different moves in different games (as Babbage observed).

> *It might be thought that programing a digital computer to play ticktacktoe,*
> *or designing special circuits for a ticktacktoe machine,*
> *would be simple. This is true unless your aim is to construct a master robot*
> *that will win the maximum number of games against inexperienced players.*
>
> — MARTIN GARDNER, *The Scientific American Book of*
> *Mathematical Puzzles & Diversions* (1959)

67. The best solution known so far, due to David Stevenson in 2010, uses a total of 818 gates (472 AND, 327 OR, 13 NOR, 6 BUTNOT); see

> http://www-cs-faculty.stanford.edu/~knuth/818-gate-solution

for the details. After taking care of moves such as w_j and b_j, and cleverly optimizing don't-cares, Stevenson essentially ORs together about 200 special positions (such as ⊞) that make $c = 1$, about 200 others (such as ⊞) that make $s = 1$, and about 50 (such as ⊞) that make $m = 1$; then he saves gates by finding common subexpressions among the ANDs that define special positions, and by using the distributive law, etc.

[This exercise was inspired by a discussion in John Wakerly's book *Digital Design* (Prentice–Hall, 3rd edition, 2000), §6.2.7. Incidentally, Babbage planned to choose among k possible moves by looking at $N \bmod k$, where N was the number of games won so far; he didn't realize that successive moves would tend to be highly correlated until N changed. Much better would have been to let N be the number of *moves made* so far.]

68. No. That method yields a "uniform" chain with a comprehensible structure, but its cost is $\Omega(n2^n)$. A circuit with approximately $2^n/n$ gates, constructed by Theorem L, exists but is more difficult to fabricate. (Incidentally, $C(\pi_5) = 10$.)

69. (a) One can, for example, verify this result by trying all 64 cases.

(b) If x_m lies in the same row or column as x_i, and also in the same row or column as x_j, we have $\alpha_{111} = \alpha_{101} = \alpha_{011} = 0$, so the pairs are good. Otherwise there are essentially three different possibilities, all bad: If $(i, j, m) = (1, 2, 4)$ then $\alpha_{101} = 0$,

$\alpha_{100} = x_5 x_9 \oplus x_6 x_8$, $\alpha_{011} = x_9$; if $(i, j, m) = (1, 2, 6)$ then $\alpha_{010} = x_4 x_9$, $\alpha_{011} = x_7$, $\alpha_{100} = x_5 x_9$, $\alpha_{101} = x_8$; if $(i, j, m) = (1, 5, 9)$ then $\alpha_{111} = 1$, $\alpha_{110} = 0$, $\alpha_{010} = x_3 x_7$.

70. (a) $x_1 \wedge ((x_5 \wedge x_9) \oplus (x_6 \wedge x_8)) \oplus x_2 \wedge ((x_6 \wedge x_7) \oplus (x_4 \wedge x_9)) \oplus x_3 \wedge ((x_4 \wedge x_8) \oplus (x_5 \wedge x_7))$.

(b) $x_1 \wedge ((x_5 \wedge x_9) \vee (x_6 \wedge x_8)) \vee x_2 \wedge ((x_6 \wedge x_7) \vee (x_4 \wedge x_9)) \vee x_3 \wedge ((x_4 \wedge x_8) \vee (x_5 \wedge x_7))$.

(c) Let $y_1 = x_1 \wedge x_5 \wedge x_9$, $y_2 = x_1 \wedge x_6 \wedge x_8$, $y_3 = x_2 \wedge x_6 \wedge x_7$, $y_4 = x_2 \wedge x_4 \wedge x_9$, $y_5 = x_3 \wedge x_4 \wedge x_8$, $y_6 = x_3 \wedge x_5 \wedge x_7$. The function $f(y_1, \ldots, y_6) = [y_1 + y_2 + y_3 > y_4 + y_5 + y_6]$ can be evaluated in 15 further steps with two full adders and a comparator; but there is a 14-step solution: Let $z_1 = (y_1 \oplus y_2) \oplus y_3$, $z_2 = (y_1 \oplus y_2) \vee (y_1 \oplus y_3)$, $z_3 = (y_4 \oplus y_5) \oplus y_6$, $z_4 = (y_4 \oplus y_5) \vee (y_4 \oplus y_6)$. Then $f = (z_1 \oplus (z_2 \wedge (\bar{z}_4 \oplus (z_1 \vee z_3)))) \wedge (\bar{z}_3 \vee z_4)$. Furthermore $y_1 y_2 y_3 = 111 \iff y_4 y_5 y_6 = 111$; so there are don't-cares, leading to an 11-step solution: $f = ((\bar{z}_1 \wedge z_3) \vee \bar{z}_4) \wedge z_2$. The total cost is $12 + 11 = 23$.

(The author knows of no way by which a computer could discover such an efficient chain in a reasonable amount of time, given only the truth table of f. But perhaps an even better chain exists.)

71. (a) $P(p) = 1 - 12p^2 + 24p^3 + 12p^4 - 96p^5 + 144p^6 - 96p^7 + 24p^8$, which is $\frac{11}{32} + \frac{9}{2}\epsilon^2 - 3\epsilon^4 - 24\epsilon^6 + 24\epsilon^8$ when $p = \frac{1}{2} + \epsilon$.

(b) There are $N = 2^{n-3}$ sets of eight values $(f_0, \ldots, f_7)$, each of which yields good pairs with probability $P(p)$. So the answer is $1 - P(p)^N$.

(c) The probability is $\binom{N}{r} P(p)^r (1 - P(p))^{N-r}$ that exactly r sets succeed; and in such a case t trials will find good pairs with probability $(r/N)^t$. The answer is therefore $1 - \sum_{r=0}^{N} \binom{N}{r} P(p)^r (1 - P(p))^{N-r} (r/N)^t = 1 - P(p)^t + O(t^2/N)$.

(d) $\sum_{r=0}^{N} \binom{N}{r} P(p)^r (1-P(p))^{N-r} \sum_{j=0}^{t-1} (r/N)^j = (1 - P(p)^t)/(1-P(p)) + O(t^3/N)$.

72. The probability in exercise 71(a) becomes $P(p) + (72p^3 - 264p^4 + 432p^5 - 336p^6 + 96p^7)r + (60p^2 - 240p^3 + 456p^4 - 432p^5 + 144p^6)r^2 + (-48p^2 + 144p^3 - 216p^4 + 96p^5)r^3 + (-36p^2 + 24p^3 + 12p^4)r^4 + (48p^2 - 24p^3)r^5 - 12p^2 r^6$. If $p = q = (1 - r)/2$, this is $(11 + 48r + 36r^2 - 144r^3 - 30r^4 + 336r^5 - 348r^6 + 144r^7 - 21r^8)/32$; for example, it's $7739/8192 \approx 0.94$ when $r = 1/2$.

73. Consider the Horn clauses $1 \wedge 2 \Rightarrow 3$, $1 \wedge 3 \Rightarrow 4$, $\ldots$, $1 \wedge (n-1) \Rightarrow n$, $1 \wedge n \Rightarrow 2$, and $i \wedge j \Rightarrow 1$ for $1 < i < j \leq n$. Suppose $|Z| > 1$ in a decomposition, and let i be minimum such that $x_i \in Z$. Also let j be minimum such that $j > i$ and $x_j \in Z$. We cannot have $i > 1$, since $i \wedge j \Rightarrow 1$ in that case. Thus $i = 1$, and $x_j \in Z$ for $2 \leq j \leq n$.

74. Suppose we know that no nontrivial decomposition exists with $x_1 \in Z$ or $\cdots$ or $x_{i-1} \in Z$; initially $i = 1$. We hope to rule out $x_i \in Z$ too, by choosing j and m cleverly. The Horn clauses $i \wedge j \Rightarrow m$ reduce to Krom clauses $j \Rightarrow m$ when i is asserted. So we essentially want to use Tarjan's depth-first search for strong components, in a digraph with arcs $j \Rightarrow m$ that may or may not exist.

When exploring from vertex j, first try $m = 1$, $\ldots$, $m = i - 1$; if any such implication $i \wedge j \Rightarrow m$ succeeds, we can eliminate j and all its predecessors from the digraph for i. Otherwise, test if $j \Rightarrow m$ for any such eliminated vertex m. Otherwise test unexplored vertices m. Otherwise try vertices m that have already been seen, favoring those near the root of the depth-first tree.

In the example $f(x) = (\det X) \bmod 2$, we would successively find $1 \wedge 2 \not\Rightarrow 3$, $1 \wedge 2 \Rightarrow 4$, $1 \wedge 4 \Rightarrow 3$, $1 \wedge 3 \Rightarrow 5$, $1 \wedge 5 \Rightarrow 6$, $1 \wedge 6 \Rightarrow 7$, $1 \wedge 7 \Rightarrow 8$, $1 \wedge 8 \Rightarrow 9$, $1 \wedge 9 \Rightarrow 2$ (now $i \leftarrow 2$); $2 \wedge 3 \not\Rightarrow 1$, $2 \wedge 3 \Rightarrow 4$, $2 \wedge 4 \not\Rightarrow 1$, $2 \wedge 4 \not\Rightarrow 5$, $2 \wedge 4 \Rightarrow 6$, $2 \wedge 6 \Rightarrow 1$ (now 3, 4, and 6 are eliminated from the digraph for 2), $2 \wedge 5 \Rightarrow 1$ (and 5 is eliminated), $2 \wedge 7 \not\Rightarrow 1$, $2 \wedge 7 \Rightarrow 3$ (7 is eliminated), $2 \wedge 8 \Rightarrow 1$, $2 \wedge 9 \Rightarrow 1$ (now $i \leftarrow 3$); $3 \wedge 4 \not\Rightarrow 1$, $3 \wedge 4 \Rightarrow 2$, $3 \wedge 5 \Rightarrow 1$, etc.

75. This function is 1 at only two points, which are complementary. So it is inde-composable; yet the pairs (58) are *never* bad when $n > 3$. Every partition (Y, Z) will therefore be a candidate for decomposition.

Similarly, if f is decomposable with respect to (Y, Z), the indecomposable function $f(x) \oplus S_{0,n}(x)$ will act essentially like f in the tests. (A method to deal with *approximately decomposable functions* should probably be provided in a general-purpose decomposability tester.)

76. (a) Let $a_l = [i \geq l]$ for $0 \leq l \leq 2^m$. The cost is $\leq 2t(m)$, as observed in answer 38(b); and in fact, the cost can be reduced to $2^{m+1} - 2m - 2$ with $\Theta(m)$ depth. Furthermore the function $[i \leq j] = (\bar{\imath}_1 \wedge j_1) \vee ((i_1 \equiv j_1) \wedge [i_2 \ldots i_m \leq j_2 \ldots j_m])$ can be evaluated with $4m - 3$ gates. After computing $x \oplus y$, each z_l costs $2^{m+1} + 1 = O(n)$.

(b) Here the cost is at most $C(g_0) + \cdots + C(g_{2^m}) \leq (2^m + 1)(2^{2^m}/(2^m - O(m)))$ by Theorem L, because each g_l is a function of 2^m inputs.

(c) If $i \leq j$ we have $z_l = x$ for $l \leq i$ and $z_l = y$ for $l > i$; hence $f_i(x) = c_0 \oplus \cdots \oplus c_i$ and $f_j(y) = c_{j+1} \oplus \cdots \oplus c_{2^m}$. If $i > j$ we have $z_l = y$ for $l \leq i$ and $z_l = x$ for $l > i$; hence $f_j(y) = c_0 \oplus \cdots \oplus c_j$ and $f_i(x) = c_{i+1} \oplus \cdots \oplus c_{2^m}$.

(d) The functions $b_l = [j < l]$ can be computed for $0 \leq l \leq 2^m$ in $O(2^m)$ steps, as in (a). So we can compute F from $(c_0, \ldots, c_{2^m})$ with $O(2^m)$ further gates. Step (b) therefore dominates the cost, for large m.

(e) $a_0 = 1$, $a_1 = i$, $a_2 = 0$; $b_0 = 0$, $b_1 = j$, $b_2 = 1$; $d = [i \leq j] = \bar{\imath} \vee j$; $m_l = a_l \oplus d$, $z_{l0} = x_0 \oplus (m_l \wedge (x_0 \oplus y_0))$, $z_{l1} = x_1 \oplus (m_l \wedge (x_1 \oplus y_1))$, for $l = 0, 1, 2$; $c_0 = z_{01}$; $c_1 = z_{10} \wedge \bar{z}_{11}$; $c_2 = z_{20} \vee z_{21}$; $c'_l = c_l \wedge (d \equiv a_l)$, $c''_l = c_l \wedge (d \equiv b_l)$, for $l = 0, 1, 2$; and finally $F = (c'_0 \oplus c'_1 \oplus c'_2) \vee (c''_0 \oplus c''_1 \oplus c''_2)$.

The net cost (29 after obvious simplifications) is, of course, outrageous in such a small example. But one wonders if a state-of-the-art automatic optimizer would be able to reduce this chain to just 5 gates.

[This result is a special case of more general theorems in *Matematicheskie Zametki* **15** (1974), 937–944; *London Math. Soc. Lecture Note Series* **169** (1992), 165–173.]

77. Given a shortest such chain for f_n or $\bar{f}_n$, let $U_l = \{i \mid l = j(i) \text{ or } l = k(i)\}$ be the "uses" of x_l, and let $u_l = |U_l|$. Let $t_i = 1$ if $x_i = x_{j(i)} \vee x_{k(i)}$, otherwise $t_i = 0$. We will show that there's a chain of length $\leq r - 4$ that computes either f_{n-1} or $\bar{f}_{n-1}$, by using the following idea: If variable x_m is set to 0 or 1, for any m, we can obtain a chain for f_{n-1} or $\bar{f}_{n-1}$ by deleting all steps of U_m and modifying other steps appropriately. Furthermore, if $x_i = x_{j(i)} \circ x_{k(i)}$ and if either $x_{j(i)}$ or $x_{k(i)}$ is known to equal t_i when x_m has been set to 0 or 1, then we can also delete the steps U_i. (Throughout this argument, the letter m will stand for an index in the range $1 \leq m \leq n$.)

Case 1: $u_m = 1$ for some m. This case cannot occur in a shortest chain. For if the only use of x_m is $x_i = \bar{x}_m$, eliminating this step would change $f_n \leftrightarrow \bar{f}_n$; and otherwise we could set the values of $x_1, \ldots, x_{m-1}, x_{m+1}, \ldots, x_n$ to make x_i independent of x_m, contradicting $x_{n+r} = f_n$ or $\bar{f}_n$. Thus every variable must be used at least twice.

Case 2: $x_l = \bar{x}_m$ for some l and m, where $u_m > 1$. Then $x_i = x_l \circ x_k$ for some i and k, and we can set $x_m \leftarrow \bar{t}_i$ to make x_i independent of x_k. Eliminating steps U_m, U_l, and U_i then removes at least 4 steps, except when $u_l = u_i = 1$ and $u_m = 2$ and $x_j = x_m \circ x_i$; but in that case we can also eliminate U_j.

Case 3: $u_m \geq 3$ for some m, and not Case 2. If $i, j, k \in U_m$ and $i < j < k$, set $x_m \leftarrow t_k$ and remove steps i, j, k, U_k.

Case 4: $u_1 = u_2 = \cdots = u_n = 2$, and not Case 2. We may assume that the first step is $x_{n+1} = x_1 \circ x_2$, and that $x_l = x_1 \circ x_k$ for some $k < l$.

Case 4.1: $k > n$. Then $k > n+1$. If $u_k = 1$, set $x_1 \leftarrow t_l$ and remove steps $n+1$, k, l, U_l. Otherwise set $x_2 \leftarrow t_{n+1}$; this forces $x_k = \bar{t}_l$, and we can remove $n+1$, k, l, U_k.

Case 4.2: $x_l = x_1 \circ x_m$. Then we must have $m = 2$; for if $m > 2$ we could set $x_2 \leftarrow t_{n+1}$, $x_m \leftarrow t_l$, and make x_{n+r} independent of x_1. Hence we may assume that $x_{n+1} = x_1 \wedge x_2$, $x_{n+2} = x_1 \vee x_2$. Setting $x_1 \leftarrow 0$ allows us to remove U_1 and U_{n+1}; setting $x_1 \leftarrow 1$ allows us to remove U_1 and U_{n+2}. Thus we're done unless $u_{n+1} = u_{n+2} = 1$.

If $x_p = \bar{x}_{n+1}$, set $x_1 \leftarrow 0$ and remove $n+1$, $n+2$, p, U_p; if $x_q = \bar{x}_{n+2}$, set $x_1 \leftarrow 1$ and remove $n+1$, $n+2$, q, U_q. Otherwise $x_p = x_{n+1} \circ x_u$ and $x_q = x_{n+2} \circ x_v$, where x_u and x_v do not depend on x_1 or x_2. But that's impossible; it would allow us to set $x_3, \ldots, x_n$ to make $x_u = t_p$, then $x_2 \leftarrow 1$ to make x_{n+r} independent of x_1.

[*Problemy Kibernetiki* **23** (1970), 83–101; **28** (1974), 4. With similar proofs, Red'kin showed that the shortest AND-OR-NOT chains for the functions $[x_1 \ldots x_n < y_1 \ldots y_n]$ and $[x_1 \ldots x_n = y_1 \ldots y_n]$ have lengths $5n - 3$ and $5n - 1$, respectively.]

78. [*SICOMP* **6** (1977), 427–430.] Say that y_k is *active* if $k \in S$. We may assume that the chain is normal and that $|S| > 1$; the proof is like Red'kin's in answer 77:

Case 1: Some active y_k is used more than once. Setting $y_k \leftarrow 0$ saves at least two steps and yields a chain for a function with $|S| - 1$ active values.

Case 2: Some active y_k appears only in an AND gate. Setting $y_k \leftarrow 0$ eliminates at least two steps, unless this AND is the final step. But it can't be the final step, because $y_k = 0$ makes the result independent of every other active y_j.

Case 3: Like Case 2 but with an OR or NOTBUT or BUTNOT gate. Setting $y_k \leftarrow c$ for some appropriate constant c has the desired effect.

Case 4: Like Case 2 but with XOR. The gate can't be final, since the result should be independent of y_k when $(x_1 \ldots x_m)_2$ addresses a different active value y_j. So we can eliminate two steps by setting y_k to the function defined by the *other* input to XOR.

79. (a) Suppose the cost is $r < 2n - 2$; then $n > 1$. If each variable is used exactly once, two leaves must be mates. Therefore some variable is used at least twice. Pruning it away produces a chain of cost $\leq r - 2$ on $n - 1$ variables, having no mates.

(Incidentally, the cost is at least $2n - 1$ if every variable is used at least twice, because at least $2n$ uses of variables must be connected together in the chain.)

(b) Notice that $S_{0,n} = \bigwedge_{u - v} (u \equiv v)$ whenever the edges $u - v$ form a free tree on $\{x_1, \ldots, x_n\}$. So there are many ways to achieve cost $2n - 3$.

Any chain of cost $r < 2n - 3$ must have $n > 2$ and must contain mates u and v. By renaming and possibly complementing intermediate results, we can assume that $u = 1$, $v = 2$, and that $f(x_1, \ldots, x_n) = g(x_1 \circ h(x_3, \ldots, x_n), x_2, \ldots, x_n)$, where $\circ$ is $\wedge$ or $\oplus$.

Case 1: $\circ$ is AND. We must have $h(0, \ldots, 0) = h(1, \ldots, 1) = 1$, for otherwise $f(x_1, x_2, y, \ldots, y)$ wouldn't depend on x_1. Therefore $f(x_1, \ldots, x_n) = h(x_3, \ldots, x_n) \wedge g(x_1, x_2, \ldots, x_n)$ can be computed by a chain of the same cost in which 1 and 2 are mates and in which the path between them has gotten shorter.

Case 2: $\circ$ is XOR. Then $f = f_0 \vee f_1$, where $f_0(x_1, \ldots, x_n) = (x_1 \equiv h(x_3, \ldots, x_n)) \wedge g(0, x_2, \ldots, x_n)$ and $f_1(x_1, \ldots, x_n) = (x_1 \oplus h(x_3, \ldots, x_n)) \wedge g(1, x_2, \ldots, x_n)$. But $f = S_{0,n}$ has only two prime implicants; so there are only four possibilities:

Case 2a: $f_0 = f$. Then we can replace $x_1 \oplus h$ by 0, to get a chain of cost $\leq r - 2$ for the function $g(0, x_2, \ldots, x_n) = S_{0,n-1}(x_2, \ldots, x_n)$.

Case 2b: $f_1 = f$. Similar to Case 2a.

Case 2c: $f_0(x) = x_1 \wedge \cdots \wedge x_n$ and $f_1(x) = \bar{x}_1 \wedge \cdots \wedge \bar{x}_n$. In this case we must have $g(0, x_2, \ldots, x_n) = x_2 \wedge \cdots \wedge x_n$ and $g(1, x_2, \ldots, x_n) = \bar{x}_2 \wedge \cdots \wedge \bar{x}_n$. Replacing h by 1 therefore yields a chain that computes f in $< r$ steps.

Case 2d: $f_0(x) = \bar{x}_1 \wedge \cdots \wedge \bar{x}_n$ and $f_1(x) = x_1 \wedge \cdots \wedge x_n$. Similar to Case 2c.

Applying these reductions repeatedly will lead to a contradiction. Similarly, one can show that $C(S_0 S_n) = 2n - 2$. [*Theoretical Computer Science* **1** (1976), 289–295.]

80. (a) Without loss of generality, $a_0 = 0$ and the chain is normal. Define U_l and u_l as in answer 77. We may assume by symmetry that $u_1 = \max(u_1, \ldots, u_n)$.

We must have $u_1 \geq 2$. For if $u_1 = 1$, we could assume further that $x_{n+1} = x_1 \circ x_2$; hence two of the three functions $S_\alpha(0, 0, x_3, \ldots, x_n) = S_{\alpha''}$, $S_\alpha(0, 1, x_3, \ldots, x_n) = S_{'\alpha'}$, $S_\alpha(1, 1, x_3, \ldots, x_n) = S_{''\alpha}$ would be equal. But then S_α would be a parity function, or $S_{'\alpha'}$ would be constant.

Therefore setting $x_1 \leftarrow 0$ allows us to eliminate the gates of U_1, giving a chain for $S_{\alpha'}$ with at least 2 fewer gates. It follows that $C(S_\alpha) \geq C(S_{\alpha'}) + 2$. Similarly, setting $x_1 \leftarrow 1$ proves that $C(S_\alpha) \geq C(S_{'\alpha}) + 2$.

Three cases arise when we explore the situation further:

Case 1: $u_1 \geq 3$. Setting $x_1 \leftarrow 0$ proves that $C(S_\alpha) \geq C(S_{\alpha'}) + 3$.

Case 2: $U_1 = \{i, j\}$ and operator $\circ_j$ is canalizing (namely, AND, BUTNOT, NOTBUT, or OR). Setting x_1 to an appropriate constant forces the value of x_j and allows us to eliminate $U_1 \cup U_j$; notice that $i \notin U_j$ in an optimum chain. So either $C(S_\alpha) \geq C(S_{\alpha'}) + 3$ or $C(S_\alpha) \geq C(S_{'\alpha}) + 3$.

Case 3: $U_1 = \{i, j\}$ and $\circ_i = \circ_j = \oplus$. We may assume that $x_i = x_1 \oplus x_2$ and $x_j = x_1 \oplus x_k$. If $u_j = 1$ and $x_l = x_j \oplus x_p$, we can restructure the chain by letting $x_j = x_k \oplus x_p$, $x_l = x_1 \oplus x_j$; therefore we can assume that either $u_j \neq 1$ or $x_l = x_j \circ x_p$ for some canalizing operator $\circ$. If $U_2 = \{i, j'\}$, we can assume similarly that $x_{j'} = x_2 \oplus x_{k'}$ and that either $u_{j'} \neq 1$ or $x_{l'} = x_{j'} \circ' x_{p'}$ for some canalizing operator $\circ'$. Furthermore we can assume by symmetry that x_j does not depend on $x_{j'}$.

If x_k does not depend on x_i, let $f(x_3, \ldots, x_n) = x_k$; otherwise let $f(x_3, \ldots, x_n)$ be the value of x_k when $x_i = 1$. By setting $x_1 \leftarrow f(x_3, \ldots, x_n)$ and $x_2 \leftarrow \bar{f}(x_3, \ldots, x_n)$, or vice versa, we make x_i and x_j constant, and we obtain a chain for the nonconstant function $S_{'\alpha'}$. We can, in fact, ensure that x_l is constant in the case $u_j = 1$. We claim that at least five gates of this chain (including x_i and x_j) can be eliminated; hence $C(S_\alpha) \geq C(S_{'\alpha'}) + 5$. The claim is clearly true if $|U_i \cup U_j| \geq 3$.

We must have $|U_i \cup U_j| > 1$. Otherwise we'd have $p = i$, and x_k would not depend on x_i, so S_α would be independent of x_1 with our choice of x_2. Therefore $|U_i \cup U_j| = 2$.

Case 3a: $U_j = \{l\}$. Then x_l is constant; we can eliminate x_i, x_j, and $U_i \cup U_j \cup U_l$. If the latter set contains only two elements, then $x_q = x_i \circ x_l$ is also constant and we eliminate U_q. Since $S_{'\alpha'}$ isn't constant, we won't eliminate the output gate.

Case 3b: $U_i \subseteq U_j$, $|U_j| = 2$. Then $x_q = x_i \circ x_j$ for some q; we can eliminate x_i, x_j, and $U_j \cup U_q$. The claim has been proved.

(b) By induction, $C(S_k) \geq 2n + \min(k, n - k) - 3 - [n = 2k]$, for $0 < k < n$; $C(S_{\geq k}) \geq 2n + \min(k, n + 1 - k) - 4$, for $1 < k < n$. The easy cases are $C(S_0) = C(S_n) = C(S_{\geq 1}) = C(S_{\geq n}) = n - 1$; $C(S_{\geq 0}) = 0$.

Reference: Mathematical Systems Theory **10** (1977), 323–336.

(A nice unpublished idea of L. Adleman, circa 1978, proves that $C(S_{\geq 2}) = 2n + O(\sqrt{n})$: Given m^2 elements x_{ij}, compute $c \vee r$, where $c = S_{\geq 2}(\bigvee_{i=1}^m x_{i1}, \ldots, \bigvee_{i=1}^m x_{im})$ and $r = S_{\geq 2}(\bigvee_{j=1}^m x_{1j}, \ldots, \bigvee_{j=1}^m x_{mj})$ each cost $< m^2 + 3m$ using just $\vee$ and $\wedge$.)

81. If some variable is used more than once, we can set it to a constant, decreasing n by 1 and decreasing c by ≥ 2. Otherwise the first operation must involve x_1, because $y_1 = x_1$ is the only output that doesn't need computation; making x_1 constant decreases n by 1, c by ≥ 1, and d by ≥ 1. [*J. Algorithms* **7** (1986), 185–201.]

82. (62) is false.

(63) reads, "For all numbers m there's a number n such that $m < n + 1$"; it is true because we can take $m = n$.

(64) fails when $n = 0$ or $n = 1$, because the numbers in these formulas are required to be nonnegative integers.

(65) says that, if b exceeds a by 2 or more, there's a number ab between them. Of course it's true, because we can let $ab = a + 1$.

(66) was explained in the text, and it too is true. Notice that '$\wedge$' takes precedence over '$\vee$' and '$\equiv$' takes precedence over '$\Leftrightarrow$', just as '$+$' takes precedence over '$\geq$' and '$<$' over '$\wedge$' in (65); these conventions reduce the need for parentheses in sentences of L.

(67) says that, if A contains at least one element n, it must contain a minimum element m (an element that's less than or equal to all of its elements). True.

(68) is similar, but m is now a maximum element. Again true, because all sets are assumed to be finite.

(69) asks for a set P with the property that $[0 \in P] = [3 \notin P]$, $[1 \in P] = [4 \notin P]$, $\ldots$, $[999 \in P] = [1002 \notin P]$, $[1000 \in P] \neq [1003 \notin P]$, $[1001 \in P] \neq [1004 \notin P]$, etc. It's true if (and only if) $P = \{x \mid x \bmod 6 \in \{1, 2, 3\}$ and $0 \leq x < 1000\}$.

Finally, the subformula $\forall n\, (n \in C \Leftrightarrow n + 1 \in C)$ in (70) is another way of saying that $C = \emptyset$, because C is finite. Hence the parenthesized formula after $\forall A \forall B$ is a tricky way to say that $A = \emptyset$ and $B \neq \emptyset$. (Stockmeyer and Meyer used this trick to abbreviate statements in L that involve long subformulas more than once.) Statement (70) is true because an empty set doesn't equal a nonempty set.

83. We can assume that the chain is normal. Let the canalizing steps be $y_1, \ldots, y_p$. Then $y_k = \alpha_k \circ \beta_k$ and $f = \alpha_{p+1}$, where α_k and β_k are $\oplus$'s of some subsets of $\{x_1, \ldots, x_n, y_1, \ldots, y_{k-1}\}$; at most $n + k - 2$ $\oplus$'s are needed to compute them, combining common terms first. Hence $C(f) \leq p + \sum_{k=1}^{p+1}(n + k - 2) = (p+1)(n + p/2) - 1$.

84. Argue as in the previous answer, with $\vee$ or $\wedge$ in place of $\oplus$. [N. Alon and R. B. Boppana, *Combinatorica* **7** (1987), 15–16.]

85. (a) A simple computer program shows that 13744 are legitimate and 19024 aren't. (An illegitimate family of this kind has at least 8 members; one such is $\{00, 0f, 33, 55,$ $ff, 15, 3f, 77\}$. Indeed, if the functions $x_1 \vee x_2$ (3f), $x_2 \vee x_3$ (77), and $(x_1 \vee x_2) \wedge x_3$ (15) are present in a legitimate family L, then $x_2 \sqcup 15 = 33 \mid 15 = 37$ must also be in L.)

(b) The projection and constant functions are obviously present. Define $A^* = \bigcap \{B \mid B \supseteq A$ and $B \in \mathcal{A}\}$, or $A^* = \infty$ if no such set B exists. Then we have $\lceil A \rceil \sqcap \lceil B \rceil = \lceil A \cap B \rceil$ and $\lceil A \rceil \sqcup \lceil B \rceil = \lceil (A \cup B)^* \rceil$.

(c) Abbreviate the formulas as $\hat{x}_l \subseteq x_l \vee \bigvee_{i=n+1}^{l} \delta_i$, $x_l \subseteq \hat{x}_l \vee \bigvee_{i=n+1}^{l} \epsilon_i$, and argue by induction: If step l is an AND step, $\hat{x}_l = \hat{x}_j \sqcap \hat{x}_k \subseteq \hat{x}_j \wedge \hat{x}_k \subseteq (x_j \vee \bigvee_{i=n+1}^{l} \delta_i) \wedge (x_k \vee \bigvee_{i=n+1}^{l} \delta_i) = x_l \vee \bigvee_{i=n+1}^{l} \delta_i$; $x_l = x_j \wedge x_k \subseteq (\hat{x}_j \vee \bigvee_{i=n+1}^{l-1} \epsilon_i) \wedge (\hat{x}_k \vee \bigvee_{i=n+1}^{l-1} \epsilon_i) = (\hat{x}_j \wedge \hat{x}_k) \vee \bigvee_{i=n+1}^{l-1} \epsilon_i$, and $\hat{x}_j \wedge \hat{x}_k = \hat{x}_l \vee \epsilon_l$. Argue similarly if step l is an OR step.

86. (a) If S is an r-family contained in the $(r+1)$-family S', clearly $\Delta(S) \subseteq \Delta(S')$.

(b) By the pigeonhole principle, $\Delta(S)$ contains elements u and v of each part, whenever S is an r-family. And if $\Delta(S) = \{u, v\}$, we certainly have $u \!-\! v$.

(c) The result is obvious when $r = 1$. There are at most $r - 1$ edges containing any given vertex u, by the "strong" property. And if $u \!-\! v$, the edges *disjoint* from $\{u, v\}$ are strongly $(r-1)$-closed; so there are at most $(r-2)^2$ of them, by induction. Thus there are at most $1 + 2(r - 2) + (r - 2)^2$ edges altogether.

(d) Yes, by exercise 85(b), if $r > 1$, because strongly r-closed graphs are closed under intersection. All graphs with ≤ 1 edges are strongly r-closed when $r > 1$, because they have no r-families containing distinct edges.

(e) There are $\binom{n}{3}$ triangles $x_{ij} \wedge x_{ik} \wedge x_{jk}$, only $n - 2$ of which are contained in any term x_{uv} of $\hat{f}$. Hence the minterms for at most $(r - 1)^2(n - 2)$ triangles are contained in $\hat{f}$, and the others must be contained in the union of the terms $\epsilon_i = \hat{x}_i \oplus (\hat{x}_{j(i)} \wedge \hat{x}_{k(i)})$ for the p AND steps. Such a term has the form

$$T = (\lceil G \rceil \sqcap \lceil H \rceil) \oplus (\lceil G \rceil \wedge \lceil H \rceil) = (\lceil G \rceil \wedge \lceil H \rceil) \wedge \overline{\lceil G \cap H \rceil},$$

where G and H are strongly r-closed; but T contains at most $2(r - 1)^3$ triangles.

Why? Because a triangle $x_{ij} \wedge x_{ik} \wedge x_{jk}$ in T must involve some variable (say x_{ij}) of $\lceil G \rceil$ and some variable (say x_{ik}) of $\lceil H \rceil$, but no variable of $\lceil G \cap H \rceil$. There are at most $(r - 1)^2$ choices for ij; and then there are at most $2(r - 1)$ choices for k, since H has at most $r - 1$ edges touching i and at most $r - 1$ edges touching j.

(f) There are 2^{n-1} complete bigraphs obtained by coloring 1 red, coloring other vertices either red or blue, and letting $u \text{ --- } v$ if and only if u and v have opposite colors. By the first formula in exercise 85(c), every such graph's minterms B must be contained within the terms

$$T = \delta_i = \hat{x}_i \oplus (\hat{x}_{j(i)} \vee \hat{x}_{k(i)}) = \lceil (G \cup H)^* \rceil \wedge \overline{\lceil G \cup H \rceil}.$$

(For example, if $n = 4$ and if vertices $(2, 3, 4)$ are (red, blue, blue), then $B = \bar{x}_{12} \wedge x_{13} \wedge x_{14} \wedge x_{23} \wedge x_{24} \wedge \bar{x}_{34}$.) A minterm B is contained in T if and only if, in the coloring for B, some edge of $(G \cup H)^*$ has vertices of opposite colors, but all edges of $G \cup H$ are monochromatic. We will prove that each term T includes at most $2^{n-2-r}r^2$ such B, hence $2^{n-2-r}r^2 q \geq 2^{n-1}$.

We can compute $G^* = G_t$ from any given graph G by the following (inefficient) algorithm: Set $G_0 \leftarrow G$, $t \leftarrow 0$. If G_t has an r-family S with $|\Delta(S)| < 2$, set $t \leftarrow t+1$, $G_t \leftarrow \infty$, and stop. Otherwise, if $\Delta(S) = \{u, v\}$ and $u \not\!\!- v$, set $t \leftarrow t+1$, $G_t \leftarrow (G_{t-1}$ plus the edge $u \text{ --- } v)$ and repeat. Otherwise stop.

There are 2^{n-1-r} bipartite minterms B with monochromatic $\{u_j, v_j\}$ for $1 \leq j \leq r$ when $|\Delta(S)| < 2$. And when $\Delta(S) = \{u, v\}$ there are 2^{n-2-r} with monochromatic $\{u_j, v_j\}$ and bichromatic $\{u, v\}$. Hence

$$T = \lceil G^* \rceil \setminus \lceil G \rceil = (\lceil G_t \rceil \setminus \lceil G_{t-1} \rceil) \vee \cdots \vee (\lceil G_1 \rceil \setminus \lceil G_0 \rceil)$$

contains $2^{n-2-r}(t + [G^* = \infty])$ minterms B. And the algorithm stops with $t \leq (r-1)^2$.

(g) Exercise 84 tells us that $q < \binom{p}{2} + (p+1)\binom{n}{2}$. Thus we have either $2(r-1)^3 p \geq \binom{n}{3} - (r-1)^2(n-2)$ or $\binom{p}{2} + (p+1)\binom{n}{2} > 2^{r+1}/r^2$. Both lower bounds for p are

$$\geq \frac{1}{6}\left(\frac{n}{6\lg n}\right)^3 \left(1 + O\left(\frac{\log\log n}{\log n}\right)\right) \quad \text{when} \quad r = \left\lceil \lg\left(\frac{n^6}{746496(\lg n)^4}\right) \right\rceil.$$

[Noga Alon and Ravi B. Boppana, *Combinatorica* **7** (1987), 1–22, proceeded in this way to prove, among other things, the lower bound $\Omega(n/\log n)^s$ for the number of $\wedge$'s in any monotone chain that decides whether or not G has a clique of fixed size $s \geq 3$.]

87. The entries of X^3 are at most n^2 when X is a 0–1 matrix. A Boolean chain with $O(n^{\lg 7}(\log n)^2)$ gates can implement Strassen's matrix multiplication algorithm 4.6.4–(36), on integers modulo $2^{\lfloor \lg n^2 \rfloor + 1}$.

88. There are 1,422,564 such functions, in 716 classes with respect to permutation of variables. Algorithm L and the other methods of this section extend readily to ternary operations, and we obtain the following results for optimum median-only computation:

$C(f)$	Classes	Functions	$C_m(f)$	Classes	Functions	$L(f)$	Classes	Functions	$D(f)$	Classes	Functions
0	1	7	0	1	7	0	1	7	0	1	7
1	1	35	1	1	35	1	1	35	1	1	35
2	2	350	2	2	350	2	2	350	2	13	5670
3	9	3885	3	9	3885	3	8	3745	3	700	1416822
4	48	42483	4	48	42483	4	38	35203	4	1	30
5	201	406945	5	188	391384	5	139	270830	5	0	0
6	354	799946	6	253	622909	6	313	699377	6	0	0
7	98	168631	7	69	134337	7	176	367542	7	0	0
8	2	282	8	2	2520	8	34	43135	8	0	0
9	0	0	9	0	0	9	3	2310	9	0	0
10	0	0	10	0	0	10	0	0	10	0	0
11	0	0	∞	143	224654	11	1	30	11	0	0

(These results for $C(f)$ were corrected and independently verified by E. Testa in 2019.)
S. Amarel, G. E. Cooke, and R. O. Winder [*IEEE Trans.* **EC-13** (1964), 4–13, Fig. 5b]
conjectured that the 9-operation formula

$$\langle x_1 x_2 x_3 x_4 x_5 x_6 x_7 \rangle = \langle x_1 \langle\langle x_2 x_3 x_5 \rangle \langle x_2 x_4 x_6 \rangle \langle x_3 x_4 x_7 \rangle\rangle\langle\langle x_2 x_5 x_6 \rangle \langle x_3 x_5 x_7 \rangle \langle x_4 x_6 x_7 \rangle\rangle\rangle$$

is the best way to compute medians-of-7 via medians-of-3. But the "magic" formula

$$\langle x_1 \langle x_2 \langle x_3 x_4 x_5 \rangle \langle x_3 x_6 x_7 \rangle\rangle\langle x_4 \langle x_2 x_6 x_7 \rangle \langle x_3 x_5 \langle x_5 x_6 x_7 \rangle\rangle\rangle\rangle$$

needs only 8 operations; and in fact the shortest chain needs just seven steps:

$$\langle x_1 x_2 x_3 x_4 x_5 x_6 x_7 \rangle = \langle x_1 \langle x_2 \langle x_5 x_6 x_7 \rangle \langle x_3 \langle x_5 x_6 x_7 \rangle x_4 \rangle\rangle\langle x_5 \langle x_2 x_3 x_4 \rangle \langle x_6 \langle x_2 x_3 x_4 \rangle x_7 \rangle\rangle\rangle.$$

The interesting function $f(x_1, \ldots, x_7) = (x_1 \wedge x_2 \wedge x_4) \vee (x_2 \wedge x_3 \wedge x_5) \vee (x_3 \wedge x_4 \wedge x_6) \vee (x_4 \wedge x_5 \wedge x_7) \vee (x_5 \wedge x_6 \wedge x_1) \vee (x_6 \wedge x_7 \wedge x_2) \vee (x_7 \wedge x_1 \wedge x_3)$, whose prime implicants correspond to the projective plane with 7 points, is the toughest of all: Its minimum length $L(f) = 11$ and minimum depth $D(f) = 4$ are achieved by the remarkable formula

$$\langle\langle x_1 x_4 \langle x_4 x_5 x_6 \rangle\rangle\langle x_3 x_6 \langle x_1 \langle x_2 x_3 x_7 \rangle \langle x_2 x_5 x_6 \rangle\rangle\rangle\langle x_2 x_7 \langle x_1 \langle x_5 x_2 x_4 \rangle \langle x_5 x_3 x_7 \rangle\rangle\rangle\rangle.$$

And the following even more astonishing chain computes it optimally:

$$x_8 = \langle x_1 x_2 x_3 \rangle, \quad x_9 = \langle x_1 x_4 x_6 \rangle, \quad x_{10} = \langle x_1 x_5 x_8 \rangle, \quad x_{11} = \langle x_2 x_7 x_8 \rangle,$$
$$x_{12} = \langle x_3 x_9 x_{10} \rangle, \quad x_{13} = \langle x_4 x_5 x_{12} \rangle, \quad x_{14} = \langle x_6 x_{11} x_{12} \rangle, \quad x_{15} = \langle x_7 x_{13} x_{14} \rangle.$$

SECTION 7.1.3

1. These operations interchange the bits of x and y in positions where m is 1. (In particular, if $m = -1$, the step '$y \leftarrow y \oplus (x \& m)$' becomes just '$y \leftarrow y \oplus x$', and the three assignments will swap $x \leftrightarrow y$ without needing an auxiliary register. H. S. Warren, Jr., has located this trick in vintage-1961 IBM programming course notes.)

2. All three hold when x and y are nonnegative, or if we regard x and y as "unsigned 2-adic integers" in which $0 < 1 < 2 < \cdots < -3 < -2 < -1$. But if negative integers are less than nonnegative integers, (i) fails if and only if $x < 0$ and $y < 0$; (ii) and (iii) fail if and only if $x \oplus y < 0$, namely, if and only if $x < 0$ and $y \geq 0$ or $x \geq 0$ and $y < 0$.

3. Note that $x - y = (x \oplus y) - 2(\bar{x} \& y)$ (see exercise 93). By removing bits common to x and y at the left, we may assume that $x_{n-1} = 1$ and $y_{n-1} = 0$. Then $2(\bar{x} \& y) \leq 2((x \oplus y) - 2^{n-1}) = (x \oplus y) - (x \oplus y)^M - 1$.

4. $x^{CN} = x + 1 = x^S$, by (16). Hence $x^{NC} = x^{NCSP} = x^{NCCNP} = x^{NNP} = x^P$.

5. (a) Disproof: Let $x = (\ldots x_2 x_1 x_0)_2$. Then bit l of $x \ll k$ is $x_{l-k}[l \geq k]$. So bit l of the left-hand side is $x_{l-k-j}[l \geq k][l - k \geq j]$, while bit l of the right-hand side is $x_{l-j-k}[l \geq j + k]$. These expressions agree if $j \geq 0$ or $k \leq 0$. But if $j < 0 < k$, they differ when $l = \max(0, j + k)$ and $x_{l-j-k} = 1$.

(We do, however, have $(x \ll j) \ll k \subseteq x \ll (j + k)$ in all cases.)

(b) Proof: Bit l in all three formulas is $x_{l+j}[l \geq -j] \wedge y_{l-k}[l \geq k]$.

6. Since $x \ll y \geq 0$ if and only if $x \geq 0$, we must have $x \geq 0$ if and only if $y \geq 0$. Obviously $x = y$ is always a solution. The solutions with $x > y$ are (a) $x = -1$ and $y = -2$, or $2^y > x > y > 0$; (b) $x = 2$ and $y = 1$, or $2^{-x} \geq -y > -x > 0$.

7. Set $x' \leftarrow (x + \bar{\mu}_0) \oplus \bar{\mu}_0$, where μ_0 is the constant in (47). Then $x' = (\ldots x_2' x_1' x_0')_2$, since $(x' \oplus \bar{\mu}_0) - \bar{\mu}_0 = (\ldots \bar{x}_3' x_2' \bar{x}_1' x_0')_2 - (\ldots 1010)_2 = (\ldots 0 x_2' 0 x_0')_2 - (\ldots x_3' 0 x_1' 0)_2 = x$.

[This is Hack 128 in HAKMEM; see answer 20 below. An alternative formula, $x' \leftarrow (\mu_0 - x) \oplus \mu_0$, has also been suggested by D. P. Agrawal, *IEEE Trans.* **C-29** (1980), 1032–1035. The results are correct modulo 2^n for all n, but overflow or underflow can occur. For example, two's complement binary numbers in an n-bit register range from -2^{n-1} to $2^{n-1} - 1$, inclusive, but negabinary numbers range from $-\frac{2}{3}(2^n - 1)$ to $\frac{1}{3}(2^n - 1)$ when n is even. In general the formula $x' \leftarrow (x + \mu) \oplus \mu$ converts from binary notation to the general number system with binary basis $\langle 2^n(-1)^{mn} \rangle$ discussed in exercise 4.1–30(c), when $\mu = (\ldots m_2 m_1 m_0)_2$.]

8. First, $x \oplus y \notin (S \oplus y) \cup (x \oplus T)$. Second, suppose that $0 \leq k < x \oplus y$, and let $x \oplus y = (\alpha 1 \alpha')_2$, $k = (\alpha 0 \alpha'')_2$, where α, α', and α'' are strings of 0s and 1s with $|\alpha'| = |\alpha''|$. Assume by symmetry that $x = (\beta 1 \beta')_2$ and $y = (\gamma 0 \gamma')_2$, where $|\alpha'| = |\beta'| = |\gamma'|$. Then $k \oplus y = (\beta 0 \gamma'')_2$ is less than x. Hence $k \oplus y \in S$, and $k = (k \oplus y) \oplus y \in S \oplus y$. [See R. P. Sprague, *Tôhoku Math. J.* **41** (1936), 438–444; P. M. Grundy, *Eureka* **2** (1939), 6–8.]

9. The Sprague–Grundy theorem in the previous exercise shows that two piles of x and y sticks are equivalent in play to a single pile of $x \oplus y$ sticks. (There is a nonnegative integer $k < x \oplus y$ if and only if there either is a nonnegative $i < x$ with $i \oplus y < x \oplus y$ or a nonnegative $j < y$ with $x \oplus j < x \oplus y$.) So the k piles are equivalent to a single pile of size $a_1 \oplus \cdots \oplus a_k$. [See C. L. Bouton, *Annals of Math.* (2) **3** (1901–1902), 35–39.]

10. For clarity and brevity we shall write simply xy for $x \otimes y$ and $x + y$ for $x \oplus y$, *in parts (i) through (iv) of this answer only.*

(i) Clearly $0y = 0$ and $x + y = y + x$ and $xy = yx$. Also $1y = y$, by induction on y.

(ii) If $x \neq x'$ and $y \neq y'$ then $xy + xy' + x'y + x'y' \neq 0$, because the definition of xy says that $xy' + x'y + x'y' \neq xy$ when $0 \leq x' < x$ and $0 \leq y' < y$. In particular, if $x \neq 0$ and $y \neq 0$ then $xy \neq 0$. Another consequence is that, if $x = \text{mex}(S)$ and $y = \text{mex}(T)$ for arbitrary finite sets S and T, we have $xy = \text{mex}\{xj + iy + ij \mid i \in S, j \in T\}$.

(iii) Consequently, by induction on the (ordinary) sum of x, y, and z, $(x + y)z$ is

$$\text{mex}\{(x + y)z' + (x' + y)z + (x' + y)z', (x + y)z' + (x + y')z + (x + y')z' \\ \mid 0 \leq x' < x, \ 0 \leq y' < y, \ 0 \leq z' < z\},$$

which is $\text{mex}\{xz' + x'z + x'z' + yz, xz + yz' + y'z + y'z'\} = xz + yz$. In particular, there's a cancellation law: If $xz = yz$ then $(x + y)z = 0$, so $x = y$ or $z = 0$.

(iv) By a similar induction, $(xy)z = \text{mex}\{(xy)z' + (xy' + x'y + x'y')(z + z')\} = \text{mex}\{(xy)z' + (xy')z + (xy')z' + \cdots\} = \text{mex}\{x(yz') + x(y'z) + x(y'z') + \cdots\} = \text{mex}\{(x + x')(yz' + y'z + y'z') + x'(yz)\} = x(yz)$.

(v) If $0 \leq x, y < 2^{2^n}$ we shall prove that $x \otimes y < 2^{2^n}$, $2^{2^n} \otimes y = 2^{2^n}y$, and $2^{2^n} \otimes 2^{2^n} = \frac{3}{2} 2^{2^n}$. By the distributive law (iii) it suffices to consider the case $x = 2^a$

and $y = 2^b$ for $0 \le a, b < 2^n$. Let $a = 2^p + a'$ and $b = 2^q + b'$, where $0 \le a' < 2^p$ and $0 \le b' < 2^q$; then $x = 2^{2^p} \otimes 2^{a'}$ and $y = 2^{2^q} \otimes 2^{b'}$, by induction on n.

If $p < n-1$ and $q < n-1$ we've already proved that $x \otimes y < 2^{2^{n-1}}$. If $p < q = n-1$, then $x \otimes 2^{b'} < 2^{2^q}$, hence $x \otimes y < 2^{2^n}$. And if $p = q = n - 1$, we have $x \otimes y = 2^{2^p} \otimes 2^{2^p} \otimes 2^{a'} \otimes 2^{b'} = (\frac{3}{2}2^{2^p}) \otimes z$, where $z < 2^{2^p}$. Thus $x \otimes y < 2^{2^n}$ in all cases.

By the cancellation law, the nonnegative integers less than 2^{2^n} form a subfield. Hence in the formula

$$2^{2^n} \otimes y = \text{mex}\{2^{2^n}y' \oplus x' \otimes (y \oplus y') \mid 0 \le x' < 2^{2^n}, 0 \le y' < y\}$$

we can choose x' for each y' to exclude all numbers between $2^{2^n}y'$ and $2^{2^n}(y' + 1) - 1$; but $2^{2^n}y$ is never excluded.

Finally in $2^{2^n} \otimes 2^{2^n} = \text{mex}\{2^{2^n}(x' \oplus y') \oplus (x' \otimes y') \mid 0 \le x', y' < 2^{2^n}\}$, choosing $x' = y'$ will exclude all numbers up to and including $2^{2^n} - 1$, since $x \otimes x = y \otimes y$ implies that $(x \oplus y) \otimes (x \oplus y) = 0$, hence $x = y$. Choosing $x' = y' \oplus 1$ excludes numbers from 2^{2^n} to $\frac{3}{2}2^{2^n} - 1$, since $(x \otimes x) \oplus x = (y \otimes y) \oplus y$ implies that $x = y$ or $x = y \oplus 1$, and since the most significant bit of $x \otimes x$ is the same as that of x. This same observation shows that $\frac{3}{2}2^{2^n}$ is *not* excluded. QED.

Consider, for example, the subfield $\{0, 1, \ldots, 15\}$. By the distributive law we can reduce $x \otimes y$ to a sum of $x \otimes 1$, $x \otimes 2$, $x \otimes 4$, and/or $x \otimes 8$. We have $2 \otimes 2 = 3$, $2 \otimes 4 = 8$, $4 \otimes 4 = 6$; and multiplication by 8 can be done by multiplying first by 2 and then by 4 or vice versa, because $8 = 2 \otimes 4$. Thus $2 \otimes 8 = 12$, $4 \otimes 8 = 11$, $8 \otimes 8 = 13$.

In general, for $n > 0$, let $n = 2^m + r$ where $0 \le r < 2^m$. There is a $2^{m+1} \times 2^{m+1}$ matrix Q_n such that multiplication by 2^n is equivalent to applying Q_n to blocks of 2^{m+1} bits and working mod 2. For example, $Q_1 = \left(\begin{smallmatrix} 1 & 1 \\ 1 & 0 \end{smallmatrix}\right)$, and $(\ldots x_4 x_3 x_2 x_1 x_0)_2 \otimes 2^1 = (\ldots y_4 y_3 y_2 y_1 y_0)_2$, where $y_0 = x_1$, $y_1 = x_1 \oplus x_0$, $y_2 = x_3$, $y_3 = x_3 \oplus x_2$, $y_4 = x_5$, etc. The matrices are formed recursively as follows: Let $Q_0 = R_0 = (1)$ and

$$Q_{2^m + r} = \begin{pmatrix} I & R_m \\ I & 0 \end{pmatrix} \begin{pmatrix} Q_r & & 0 \\ & \ddots & \\ 0 & & Q_r \end{pmatrix}, \qquad R_{m+1} = \begin{pmatrix} R_m & R_m^2 \\ R_m & 0 \end{pmatrix} = Q_{2^{m+1} - 1},$$

where Q_r is replicated enough times to make 2^{m+1} rows and columns. For example,

$$Q_2 = \begin{pmatrix} 1 & 0 & 1 & 1 \\ 0 & 1 & 1 & 0 \\ 1 & 0 & 0 & 0 \\ 0 & 1 & 0 & 0 \end{pmatrix}; \qquad Q_3 = Q_2 \begin{pmatrix} Q_1 & 0 \\ 0 & Q_1 \end{pmatrix} = \begin{pmatrix} 1 & 1 & 0 & 1 \\ 1 & 0 & 1 & 1 \\ 1 & 1 & 0 & 0 \\ 1 & 0 & 0 & 0 \end{pmatrix} = R_2.$$

If register x holds any 64-bit number, and if $0 \le j \le 7$, the MMIX instruction MXOR y, q_j, x will compute $y = x \otimes 2^j$, given the hexadecimal matrix constants

$q_0 = $ 8040201008040201, $q_3 = $ d0b0c0800d0b0c08,
$q_1 = $ c08030200c080302, $q_4 = $ 8d4b2c1880402010, $q_6 = $ b9678d4bb0608040,
$q_2 = $ b06080400b060804, $q_5 = $ c68d342cc0803020, $q_7 = $ deb9c68dd0b0c080.

[J. H. Conway, *On Numbers and Games* (1976), Chapter 6, shows that these definitions actually yield an algebraically closed field over the ordinal numbers.]

11. Let $m = 2^{a_s} + \cdots + 2^{a_1}$ with $a_s > \cdots > a_1 \ge 0$ and $n = 2^{b_t} + \cdots + 2^{b_1}$ with $b_t > \cdots > b_1 \ge 0$. Then $m \otimes n = mn$ if and only if $(a_s \mid \cdots \mid a_1) \& (b_t \mid \cdots \mid b_1) = 0$.

12. If $x = 2^{2^n}a + b$ where $0 \le a, b < 2^{2^n}$, let $x' = x \otimes (x \oplus a)$. Then

$$x' = ((2^{2^n} \otimes a) \oplus b) \otimes ((2^{2^n} \otimes a) \oplus a \oplus b) = (2^{2^n - 1} \otimes a \otimes a) \oplus (b \otimes (a \oplus b)) < 2^{2^n}.$$

To nim-divide by x we can therefore nim-divide by x' and multiply by $x \oplus a$. [This algorithm is due to H. W. Lenstra, Jr.; see *Séminaire de Théorie des Nombres* (Université de Bordeaux, 1977–1978), exposé 11, exercise 5.]

13. If $a_2 \oplus \cdots \oplus a_k = a_1 \oplus a_3 \oplus \cdots \oplus ((k-2) \otimes a_k) = 0$, every move breaks this condition; we can't have $(a \otimes x) \oplus (b \otimes y) = (a \otimes x') \oplus (b \otimes y')$ when $x \oplus y = x' \oplus y'$ and $a \neq b$ unless $(x, y) = (x', y')$.

Conversely, if $a_2 \oplus \cdots \oplus a_k \neq 0$ we can reduce some a_j with $j \geq 2$ to make this sum zero; then a_1 can be set to $a_3 \oplus \cdots \oplus ((k-2) \otimes a_k)$. If $a_2 \oplus \cdots \oplus a_k = 0$ and $a_1 \neq a_3 \oplus \cdots \oplus ((k-2) \otimes a_k)$, we simply reduce a_1 if it is too large. Otherwise there's a $j \geq 3$ such that equality will occur if $(j-2) \otimes a_j$ is replaced by an appropriate smaller value $((j-2) \otimes a_j') \oplus ((i-2) \otimes (a_j \oplus a_j'))$, for some $2 \leq i < j$ and $0 \leq a_j' < a_j$, because of the definition of nim multiplication; hence both of the desired equalities are achieved by setting $a_j \leftarrow a_j'$ and $a_i \leftarrow a_i \oplus a_j \oplus a_j'$. [This game was introduced in *Winning Ways* by Berlekamp, Conway, and Guy, at the end of Chapter 14.]

14. (a) Each $y = (\ldots y_2 y_1 y_0)_2 = x^T$ determines $x = (\ldots x_2 x_1 x_0)_2$ uniquely, since $x_0 = y_0 \oplus t$ and $\lfloor y/2 \rfloor = \lfloor x/2 \rfloor^{T_{x_0}}$.

(b) When $k > 0$, it is a branching function with labels $t_{\alpha a \beta} = a$ for $|\beta| = k - 1$, and $t_\alpha = 0$ for $|\alpha| < k$. But when $k \leq 0$, the mapping is not a permutation; in fact, it sends 2^{-k} different 2-adic integers into 0, when $k < 0$.

[The case $k = 1$ is particularly interesting: Then x^T takes nonnegative integers into nonnegative integers of even parity, negative integers into nonnegative integers of odd parity, and $-1/3 \mapsto -1$. Furthermore $\lfloor x^T/2 \rfloor$ is "Gray binary code," 7.2.1.1–(9).]

(c) If $\rho(x \oplus y) = k$ we have $T(x) \equiv T(y)$ and $x \equiv y + 2^k$ (modulo 2^{k+1}). Hence $\rho(x^T \oplus y^T) = \rho(x \oplus y \oplus T(x) \oplus T(y)) = k$. Conversely, if $\rho(x^T \oplus y^T) = k$ whenever $y = x + 2^k$, we obtain a suitable bit labeling by letting $t_\alpha = (x^T \gg |\alpha|) \bmod 2$ when $x = (\alpha^R)_2$.

(d) This statement follows immediately from (a) and (c). For if we always have $\rho(x \oplus y) = \rho(x^U \oplus y^U) = \rho(x^V \oplus y^V)$, then $\rho(x \oplus y) = \rho(x^U \oplus y^U) = \rho(x^{UV} \oplus y^{UV})$. And if $x^{TU} = x$ for all x, $\rho(x^U \oplus y^U) = \rho(x \oplus y)$ is equivalent to $\rho(x \oplus y) = \rho(x^T \oplus y^T)$.

We can also construct the labelings explicitly: If $W = UV$, note that when $a, b, c \in \{0, 1\}$ we have $W_a = U_a V_{a'}$, $W_{ab} = U_{ab} V_{a'b'}$, and $W_{abc} = U_{abc} V_{a'b'c'}$, where $a' = a \oplus u$, $b' = b \oplus u_a$, $c' = c \oplus u_{ab}$, and so on; hence $w = u \oplus v$, $w_a = u_a \oplus v_{a'}$, $w_{ab} = u_{ab} \oplus v_{a'b'}$, etc. The labeling T inverse to U is obtained by swapping left and right subtrees of all nodes labeled 1; thus $t = u$, $t_{a'} = u_a$, $t_{a'b'} = u_{ab}$, etc.

(e) The explicit constructions in (d) demonstrate that the balance condition is preserved by compositions and inverses, because $\{0', 1'\} = \{0, 1\}$ at each level.

Notes: Hendrik Lenstra observes that branching functions can profitably be viewed as the *isometries* (distance-preserving permutations) of the 2-adic integers, when we use the formula $1/2^{\rho(x \oplus y)}$ to define the "distance" between 2-adic integers x and y. Moreover, the branching functions mod 2^d turn out to be the Sylow 2-subgroup of the group of all permutations of $\{0, 1, \ldots, 2^d - 1\}$, namely the unique (up to isomorphism) subgroup that has maximum power-of-2 order among all subgroups of that group. They also are equivalent to the automorphisms of the complete binary tree with 2^d leaves.

15. Equivalently, $(x + 2a) \oplus b = (x \oplus b) + 2a$; so we might as well find all b and c such that $(x \oplus b) + c = (x + c) \oplus b$. Setting $x = 0$ and $x = -c$ implies that $b + c = b \oplus c$ and $b - c = b \oplus (-c)$; hence $b \& c = b \& (-c) = 0$ by (89), and we have $b < 2^{\rho c}$. This condition is also sufficient. Thus $0 \leq b < 2^{\rho a + 1}$ is necessary and sufficient for the original problem.

16. (a) If $\rho(x \oplus y) = k$ we have $x \equiv y + 2^k$ (modulo 2^{k+1}); hence $x + a \equiv y + a + 2^k$ and $\rho((x + a) \oplus (y + a)) = k$. And $\rho((x \oplus b) \oplus (y \oplus b))$ is obviously k.

(b) The hinted labeling, call it $P(c)$, has 1s on the path corresponding to c, and 0s elsewhere; thus it is balanced. The general animating function can be written

$$x^{P(c_0)^{-a_1} P(c_1)^{-a_2} \ldots P(c_{m-1})^{-a_m}} \oplus c_m, \qquad \text{where } c_j = b_1 \oplus \cdots \oplus b_j;$$

so it is balanced if and only if $c_m = 0$.

[Incidentally, the set $S = \{P(0)\} \cup \{P(k) \oplus P(k + 2^e) \mid k \geq 0 \text{ and } 2^e > k\}$ provides an interesting *basis* for all possible balanced labelings: A labeling is balanced if and only if it is $\bigoplus \{q \mid q \in Q\}$ for some $Q \subseteq S$. This exclusive-or operation is well defined even though Q might be infinite, because only finitely many 1s appear at each node.]

(c) The function $P(c)$ in (b) has this form, because $x^{P(c)} = x \oplus \lfloor x \oplus c \rfloor$. Its inverse, $x^{S(c)} = ((x \oplus c) + 1) \oplus c$, is $x \oplus \lfloor x \oplus \bar{c} \rfloor = x^{P(\bar{c})}$. Furthermore we have $x^{P(c)P(d)} = x^{P(c)} \oplus \lfloor x^{P(c)} \oplus d \rfloor = x \oplus \lfloor x \oplus c \rfloor \oplus \lfloor x \oplus d^{S(c)} \rfloor$, because $\lfloor x \oplus y \rfloor = \lfloor x^T \oplus y^T \rfloor$ for any branching function x^T. Similarly $x^{P(c)P(d)P(e)} = x \oplus \lfloor x \oplus c \rfloor \oplus \lfloor x \oplus d^{S(c)} \rfloor \oplus \lfloor x \oplus e^{S(d)S(c)} \rfloor$, etc. After discarding equal terms we obtain the desired form. The resulting numbers p_j are unique because they are the only values of x at which the function changes sign.

(d) We have, for example, $x \oplus \lfloor x \oplus a \rfloor \oplus \lfloor x \oplus b \rfloor \oplus \lfloor x \oplus c \rfloor = x^{P(a')P(b')P(c')}$ where $a' = a$, $b' = b^{P(a')}$, and $c' = c^{P(a')P(b')}$.

[The theory of animating functions was developed by J. H. Conway in Chapter 13 of his book *On Numbers and Games* (1976), inspired by previous work of C. P. Welter in *Indagationes Math.* **14** (1952), 304–314; **16** (1954), 194–200.]

17. (Solution by M. Slanina.) Such equations are decidable even if we also allow operations such as $x \& y$, $\bar{x}$, $x \ll 1$, $x \gg 1$, $2^{\rho x}$, and $2^{\lambda x}$, and even if we allow Boolean combinations of statements and quantifications over integer variables, by translating them into formulas of second-order monadic logic with one successor (S1S). Each 2-adic variable $x = (\ldots x_2 x_1 x_0)_2$ corresponds to an S1S set variable X, where $j \in X$ means $x_j = 1$:

$$
\begin{array}{lll}
z = \bar{x} & \text{becomes} & \forall t (t \in Z \Leftrightarrow t \notin X); \\
z = x \& y & \text{becomes} & \forall t (t \in Z \Leftrightarrow (t \in X \wedge t \in Y)); \\
z = 2^{\rho x} & \text{becomes} & \forall t (t \in Z \Leftrightarrow (t \in X \wedge \forall s (s < t \Rightarrow s \notin X))); \\
z = x + y & \text{becomes} & \exists C \forall t (0 \notin C \ \wedge \ (t \in Z \Leftrightarrow (t{\in}X) \oplus (t{\in}Y) \oplus (t{\in}C)) \\
& & \qquad\qquad \wedge \ (t{+}1 \in C \Leftrightarrow \langle (t{\in}X)(t{\in}Y)(t{\in}C) \rangle)).
\end{array}
$$

An identity such as $x \& (-x) = 2^{\rho x}$ is equivalent to the translation of

$$\forall X \forall Y \forall Z ((\text{integer}(X) \ \wedge \ 0 = x + y \ \wedge \ z = x \& y) \ \Rightarrow \ z = 2^{\rho x}),$$

where $\text{integer}(X)$ stands for $\exists t \forall s (s > t \Rightarrow (s \in X \Leftrightarrow t \in X))$. We can also include 2-adic constants if they are, say, ratios of integers; for example, $z = \mu_0$ is equivalent to the formula $0 \in Z \wedge \forall t (t \in Z \Leftrightarrow t + 1 \notin Z)$. But of course we cannot include arbitrary (uncomputable) constants.

J. R. Büchi proved that all formulas of S1S are decidable, in *Logic, Methodology, and Philosophy of Science: Proceedings* (Stanford, 1960), 1–11. If we restrict attention to equations, one can show in fact that exponential time suffices.

On the other hand M. Hamburg has shown that the problem would be unsolvable if ρx, λx, or $1 \ll x$ were added to the repertoire; multiplication could then be encoded.

Incidentally, many nontrivial identities exist, even if we use only the operations $x \oplus y$ and $x + 1$. For example, C. P. Welter noticed in 1952 that

$$((x \oplus (y + 1)) + 1) \oplus (x + 1) \ = \ ((((x + 1) \oplus y) + 1) \oplus x) + 1.$$

18. Of course row x is entirely blank when x is a multiple of 64. The fine details of this image are apparently "chaotic" and complex, but there is a fairly easy way to understand what happens near the points where the straight lines $x = 64\sqrt{j}$ intersect the hyperbolas $xy = 2^{11}k$, for integers $j, k \geq 1$ that aren't too large.

Indeed, when x and y are integers, the value of $x^2y \gg 11$ is odd if and only if $x^2y/2^{12} \bmod 1 \geq \frac{1}{2}$. Thus, if $x = 64\sqrt{j} + \delta$ and $xy = 2^{11}(k + \epsilon)$ we have

$$\frac{x^2y}{2^{12}} \bmod 1 = \left(\frac{128\sqrt{j}\delta + \delta^2}{4096}\right)y \bmod 1 = \left(\frac{2\delta x - \delta^2}{4096}\right)y \bmod 1 = \left((k+\epsilon)\delta - \frac{\delta^2 y}{4096}\right) \bmod 1,$$

and this quantity has a known relation to $\frac{1}{2}$ when, say, δ is close to a small integer. [See C. A. Pickover and A. Lakhtakia, *J. Recreational Math.* **21** (1989), 166–169.]

19. (a) When $n = 1$, $f(A, B, C)$ has the same value under all arrangements except when $a_0 \neq a_1$, $b_0 \neq b_1$, and $c_0 \neq c_1$; and then it cannot exceed 1. For larger values of n we argue by induction, assuming that $n = 3$ in order to avoid cumbersome notation. Let $A_0 = (a_0, a_1, a_2, a_3)$, $A_1 = (a_4, a_5, a_6, a_7)$, ..., $C_1 = (c_4, c_5, c_6, c_7)$. Then $f(A, B, C) = \sum_{j \oplus k \oplus l = 0} f(A_j, B_k, C_l) \leq \sum_{j \oplus k \oplus l = 0} f(A_j^*, B_k^*, C_l^*)$ by induction. Thus we can assume that $a_0 \geq a_1 \geq a_2 \geq a_3$, $a_4 \geq a_5 \geq a_6 \geq a_7$, ..., $c_4 \geq c_5 \geq c_6 \geq c_7$. We can also sort the subvectors $A_0' = (a_0, a_1, a_4, a_5)$, $A_1' = (a_2, a_3, a_6, a_7)$, ..., $C_1' = (c_2, c_3, c_6, c_7)$ in a similar way. Finally, we can sort $A_0'' = (a_0, a_1, a_6, a_7)$, $A_1'' = (a_2, a_3, a_4, a_5)$, ..., $C_1'' = (c_2, c_3, c_4, c_5)$, because in each term $a_j b_k c_l$ the number of subscripts $\{j, k, l\}$ with leading bits 01, 10, and 11 must satisfy $s_{01} \equiv s_{10} \equiv s_{11}$ (modulo 2). And these three sorting operations leave A, B, C fully sorted, by exercise 5.3.4–48. (Exactly three sorts on subvectors of length 2^{n-1} are needed, for all $n \geq 2$.)

(b) Suppose $A = A^*$, $B = B^*$, and $C = C^*$. Then we have $a_j = \sum_{t=0}^{2^n - 1} \alpha_t[j \leq t]$, where $\alpha_j = a_j - a_{j+1} \geq 0$ and we set $a_{2^n} = 0$; similar formulas hold for b_k and c_l. Let $A_{(p)}$ denote the vector $(a_{p(0)}, \ldots, a_{p(2^n - 1)})$ when p is a permutation of $\{0, 1, \ldots, 2^n - 1\}$. Then by part (a) we have

$$f(A_{(p)}, B_{(q)}, C_{(r)}) = \sum_{j \oplus k \oplus l = 0} \sum_{t,u,v} \alpha_t \beta_u \gamma_v [p(j) \leq t][q(k) \leq u][r(l) \leq v]$$
$$\leq \sum_{j \oplus k \oplus l = 0} \sum_{t,u,v} \alpha_t \beta_u \gamma_v [j \leq t][k \leq u][l \leq v] = f(A, B, C).$$

[This proof is due to Hardy, Littlewood, and Pólya, *Inequalities* (1934), §10.3.]

(c) The same proof technique extends to any number of vectors. [R. E. A. C. Paley, *Proc. London Math. Soc.* (2) **34** (1932), 265–279, Theorem 15.]

20. The given steps compute the least integer y greater than x such that $\nu y = \nu x$. They're useful for generating all combinations of n objects, taken m at a time (that is, all m-element subsets of an n-element set, with elements represented by 1 bits).

[This tidbit is Hack 175 in HAKMEM, Massachusetts Institute of Technology Artificial Intelligence Laboratory Memo No. 239 (29 February 1972).]

21. Set $t \leftarrow y + 1$, $u \leftarrow t \oplus y$, $v \leftarrow t \& y$, $x \leftarrow v - (v \& -v)/(u + 1)$. If $y = 2^m - 1$ is the *first* m-combination, these eight operations set x to zero. (The fact that $x = \bar{f}(\bar{y})$ does not seem to yield any shorter scheme.)

22. Sideways addition avoids the division: SUBU t,x,1; ANDN u,x,t; SADD k,t,x; ADDU v,x,u; XOR t,v,x; ADDU k,k,2; SRU t,t,k; ADDU y,v,t. But we can actually save a step by judiciously using the constant mone $= -1$: SUBU t,x,1; XOR u,t,x; ADDU y,x,u; SADD k,t,y; ANDN y,y,u; SLU t,mone,k; ORN y,y,t.

23. (a) $(0\ldots01\ldots1)_2 = 2^m - 1$ and $(0101\ldots01)_2 = (2^{2m} - 1)/3$.

(b) This solution uses the 2-adic constant $\mu_0 = (\ldots 010101)_2 = -1/3$:

$$t \leftarrow x \oplus \mu_0, \quad u \leftarrow (t-1) \oplus t, \quad v \leftarrow x \mid u, \quad w \leftarrow v+1, \quad y \leftarrow w + \left\lfloor \frac{v \,\&\, \overline{w}}{\sqrt{u+1}} \right\rfloor.$$

If $x = (2^{2m} - 1)/3$, the operations produce a strange result because $u = 2^{2m+1} - 1$.

(c) `XOR t,x,m0; SUBU u,t,1; XOR u,t,u; OR v,x,u; SADD y,u,m0; ADDU w,v,1;`
`ANDN t,v,w; SRU y,t,y; ADDU y,w,y.` [This exercise was inspired by Jörg Arndt.]

24. It's expedient to "prime the pump" by initializing the array to the state that it should have after all multiples of 3, 5, 7, and 11 have been sieved out. We can combine 3 with 11 and 5 with 7, as suggested by E. Wada:

```
      LOC Data_Segment
qbase GREG @ ;N IS 3584 ;n GREG N ;one GREG 1
Q     OCTA #816d129a64b4cb6e                              Q₀ (little-endian)
      LOC Q+N/16
qtop  GREG @                                              End of the Q table
Init  OCTA #9249249249249249|#4008010020040080           Multiples of 3 or 11 in [129..255]
      OCTA #8421084210842108|#0408102040810204           Multiples of 5 or 7
t IS $255 ;x33 IS $0 ;x35 IS $1 ;j IS $4
      LOC #100
Main  LDOU x33,Init; LDOU x35,Init+8
      LDA j,qbase,8; SUB j,j,qtop                         Prepare to set Q₁.
1H    NOR t,x33,x33; ANDN t,t,x35; STOU t,qtop,j          Initialize 64 sieve bits.
      SLU t,x33,2; SRU x33,x33,31; OR x33,x33,t           Prepare for the next 64 values.
      SLU t,x35,6; SRU x35,x35,29; OR x35,x35,t
      ADD j,j,8; PBN j,1B                                 Repeat until reaching qtop.  ∎
```

Then we cast out nonprimes p^2, $p^2 + 2p$, …, for $p = 13, 17, \ldots$, until $p^2 > N$:

```
p IS $0 ;pp IS $1 ;m IS $2 ;mm IS $3 ;q IS $4 ;s IS $5
      LDOU q,qbase,0; LDA pp,qbase,8
      SET p,13; NEG m,13*13,n; SRU q,q,6                  Begin with p = 13.
1H    SR m,m,1                                            m ← ⌊(p² − N)/2⌋.
2H    SR mm,m,3; LDOU s,qtop,mm; AND t,m,#3f;
      SLU t,one,t; ANDN s,s,t; STOU s,qtop,mm             Zero out a bit.
      ADD m,m,p; PBN m,2B                                 Advance by p bits.
      SRU q,q,1; PBNZ q,3F                                Move to next potential prime.
2H    LDOU q,pp,0; INCL pp,8                              Read in another batch
      OR p,p,#7f; PBNZ q,3F                                 of potential primes.
      ADD p,p,2; JMP 2B                                   Skip past 128 nonprimes.
2H    SRU q,q,1
3H    ADD p,p,2; PBEV q,2B                                Set p ← p + 2 until p is prime.
      MUL m,p,p; SUB m,m,n; PBN m,1B                      Repeat until p² > N.  ∎
```

The running time, $1172\mu + 5166v$, is of course much less than the time needed for steps P1–P8 of Program 1.3.2′P, namely $10037\mu + 641543v$ (improved to $10096\mu + 215351v$ in exercise 1.3.2′–14). [See P. Pritchard, *Science of Computer Programming* **0** (1987), 17–35, for several instructive variations. In practice, a program like this one tends to slow down dramatically when the sieve is too big for the computer's cache. Better results are obtained by working with a segmented sieve, which contains bits for numbers between $N_0 + k\delta$ and $N_0 + (k+1)\delta$, as suggested by L. J. Lander and T. R. Parkin,

Math. Comp. **21** (1967), 483–488; C. Bays and R. H. Hudson, *BIT* **17** (1977), 121–127. Here N_0 can be quite large, but δ is limited by the cache size; calculations are done separately for $k = 0, 1, \ldots$. Segmented sieves have become highly developed; see, for example, T. R. Nicely, *Math. Comp.* **68** (1999), 1311–1315, and the references cited there. The author used such a program in 2006 to discover an unusually large gap of length 1370 between 418032645936712127 and the next larger prime.]

25. $(1 + 1 + 25 + 1 + 1 + 25 + 1 + 1 = 56)$ mm; the worm never sees pages 2–500 of Volume 1 or 1–499 of Volume 4. (Unless the books have been placed in little-endian fashion on the bookshelf; then the answer would be 106 mm.) This classic brain-teaser can be found in Sam Loyd's *Cyclopedia* (New York: 1914), pages 327 and 383.

26. We could multiply by $^{\#}$`aa...ab` instead of dividing by 12 (see exercise 1.3.1′–17); but multiplication is slow too. Or we could deal with a "flat" sequence of 12000000×5 consecutive bits ($= 7.5$ megabytes), ignoring the boundaries between words. Another possibility is to use a scheme that is neither big-endian nor little-endian but *transposed*: Put item k into octabyte $8(k \bmod 2^{20})$, where it is shifted left by $5\lfloor k/2^{20} \rfloor$. Since $k < 12000000$, the amount of shift is always less than 60. The MMIX code to put item k into register $1 is `AND $0,k,[#fffff]`; `SLU $0,$0,3`; `LDOU $1,base,$0`; `SRU $0,k,20`; `4ADDU $0,$0,$0`; `SRU $1,$1,$0`; `AND $1,$1,#1f`.

[This solution uses 8 large megabytes (2^{23} bytes). *Any* convenient scheme for converting item numbers to octabyte addresses and shift amounts will work, as long as the same method is used consistently. Of course, just '`LDBU $1,base,k`' would be faster.]

27. (a) $((x-1) \oplus x) + x$. [This exercise is based on an idea of Luther Woodrum, who noticed that $((x-1) \,|\, x) + 1 = (x \,\&\, -x) + x$.]

(b) $(y + x) \,|\, y$, where $y = (x-1) \oplus x$.

(c, d, e) $((z \oplus x) + x) \,\&\, z$, $((z \oplus x) + x) \oplus z$, and $\overline{((z \oplus x) + x)} \,\&\, z$, where $z = x - 1$.

(f) $x \oplus (a)$; alternatively, $t \oplus (t+1)$, where $t = x \,|\, (x-1)$. [The number $(0^\infty 01^a 11^b)_2$ looks simpler, but it apparently requires *five* operations: $((t + 1) \,\&\, \bar{t}) - 1$.]

These constructions all give sensible results in the exceptional cases when $x = -2^b$.

28. A 1 bit indicates x's rightmost 0 (for example, $(101011)_2 \mapsto (000100)_2$); $-1 \mapsto 0$.

29. $\mu_k = \mu_{k+1} \oplus (\mu_{k+1} \ll 2^k)$ [see *STOC* **6** (1974), 125]. This relation holds also for the constants $\mu_{d,k}$ of (48), when $0 \le k < d$, if we start with $\mu_{d,d} = 2^{2^d} - 1$. (There is, however, no easy way to go from μ_k to μ_{k+1}, unless we use the "zip" operation; see (77).)

30. Append '`CSZ rho,x,64`' to (50), thereby adding 1υ to its execution time; or replace the last two lines by `SRU t,y,rho`; `SLU t,t,2`; `SRU t,[#300020104],t`; `AND t,t,#f`; `ADD rho,rho,t`, saving 1υ. For (51), we simply need to make sure that $rhotab[0] = 8$.

31. In the first place, his code loops forever when $x = 0$. But even after that bug is patched, his assumption that x is a random integer is highly questionable. In many applications when we want to compute ρx for a nonzero 64-bit number x, a more reasonable assumption would be that each of the outcomes $\{0, 1, \ldots, 63\}$ is equally likely. The average and standard deviation then become 31.5 and ≈ 18.5.

32. '`NEGU y,x`; `AND y,x,y`; `MULU y,debruijn,y`; `SRU y,y,58`; `LDB rho,decode,y`' has estimated cost $\mu + 14\upsilon$, although multiplication by a power of 2 might well be faster than a typical multiplication. Add 1υ for the correction in answer 30.

33. In fact, an exhaustive calculation shows that exactly 94727 suitable constants a yield a "perfect hash function" for this problem, 90970 of which also identify the power-of-two cases $y = 2^j$; 90918 of those also distinguish the case $y = 0$. The multiplier

$^\#$208b2430c8c82129 is uniquely best, in the sense that it doesn't need to refer to table entries above $decode\,[32400]$ when y is known to be a valid input.

34. Identity (a) fails when $x = 5$, $y = 6$; but (b) is true, also when $xy = 0$. Proof of (c) by Liviu Lalescu: $x \oplus y = (x-1) \oplus (y-1)$ if and only if $x \oplus (x-1) = y \oplus (y-1)$; and $x \oplus (x-1) = 2^{1+\rho x} - 1$ by Eq. (41).

35. Let $f(x) = x \oplus 3x$. Clearly $f(2x) = 2f(x)$, and $f(4x+1) = 4f(x)+2$. We also have $f(4x-1) = 4f(x)+2$, by exercise 34(c). The hinted identity follows.

Given n, set $u \leftarrow n \gg 1$, $v \leftarrow u + n$, $t \leftarrow u \oplus v$, $n^+ \leftarrow v \mathbin{\&} t$, and $n^- \leftarrow u \mathbin{\&} t$. Clearly $u = \lfloor n/2 \rfloor$ and $v = \lfloor 3n/2 \rfloor$, so $n^+ - n^- = v - u = n$. And this is Reitwiesner's representation, because $n^+ \,|\, n^-$ has no consecutive 1s. [H. Prodinger, *Integers* **0** (2000), A8:1–A8:14. Incidentally we also have $f(-x) = f(x)$.]

36. (i) The commands $x \leftarrow x \oplus (x \ll 1)$, $x \leftarrow x \oplus (x \ll 2)$, $x \leftarrow x \oplus (x \ll 4)$, $x \leftarrow x \oplus (x \ll 8)$, $x \leftarrow x \oplus (x \ll 16)$, $x \leftarrow x \oplus (x \ll 32)$ change x to $x^\oplus$. (ii) $x^{\&} = x \mathbin{\&} \sim(x+1)$. (See exercises 66 and 70 for applications of $x^\oplus$; see also exercises 128 and 209.)

37. Insert 'CSZ y,x,half' after the FLOTU in (55), where half $= {}^\#$3fe0000000000000; note that (55) says 'SR' (not 'SRU'). No change is needed to (56), if $lamtab[0] = -1$.

38. 'SRU t,x,1; OR y,x,t; SRU t,y,2; OR y,y,t; SRU t,y,4; OR y,y,t; ...; SRU t,y,32; OR y,y,t; SRU t,y,1; SUBU y,y,t' takes 14υ.

[But J. Dallos needs only 5υ! Do 'MOR y,a,x; SRU y,y,1; MOR y,a,y; MOR y,y,b; ANDN y,x,y', where $a = {}^\#$ff7f3f1f0f070301, $b = {}^\#$80c0e0f0f8fcfeff. And to extract leading bits in each byte, we can use 'MOR y,c,x; ANDN y,x,y', where $c = a \ll 8$.]

39. (Solution by H. S. Warren, Jr.) Let $\sigma(x)$ denote the result of smearing x to the right, as in the first line of (57). Compute $x \mathbin{\&} \sigma((x \gg 1) \mathbin{\&} \bar{x})$.

40. Suppose $\lambda x = \lambda y = k$. If $x = y = 0$, (58) certainly holds, regardless of how we define $\lambda 0$. Otherwise $x = (1\alpha)_2$ and $y = (1\beta)_2$, for some binary strings α and β with $|\alpha| = |\beta| = k$; and $x \oplus y < 2^k \le x \mathbin{\&} y$. On the other hand if $\lambda x < \lambda y = k$, we have $x \oplus y \ge 2^k > x \mathbin{\&} y$. And H. S. Warren, Jr., notes that $\lambda x < \lambda y$ if and only if $x < y \mathbin{\&} \bar{x}$.

41. (a) $\sum_{n=1}^{\infty}(\rho n)z^n = \sum_{k=1}^{\infty} z^{2^k}/(1 - z^{2^k}) = \sum_{k=1}^{\infty} k z^{2^k}/(1 - z^{2^{k+1}}) = z/(1 - z) - \sum_{k=0}^{\infty} z^{2^k}/(1 + z^{2^k})$. The Dirichlet generating function is simpler: $\sum_{n=1}^{\infty}(\rho n)/n^z = \zeta(z)/(2^z - 1)$.

(b) $\sum_{n=1}^{\infty}(\lambda n)z^n = \sum_{k=1}^{\infty} z^{2^k}/(1 - z)$.

(c) $\sum_{n=1}^{\infty}(\nu n)z^n = \sum_{k=0}^{\infty} z^{2^k}/((1 - z)(1 + z^{2^k})) = \sum_{k=0}^{\infty} z^{2^k}\mu_k(z)$, where $\mu_k(z) = (1 + z + \cdots + z^{2^k-1})/(1 - z^{2^{k+1}})$. (The "magic masks" of (47) correspond to $\mu_k(2)$.)

[See *Automatic Sequences* by J.-P. Allouche and J. Shallit (2003), Chapter 3, for further information about the functions ρ and ν, which they denote by ν_2 and s_2.]

42. $e_1 2^{e_1-1} + (e_2+2)2^{e_2-1} + \cdots + (e_r + 2r - 2)2^{e_r-1}$, by induction on r. [D. E. Knuth, *Proc. IFIP Congress* (1971), **1**, 19–27. The fractal aspects of this sum are illustrated in Figs. 3.1 and 3.2 of the book by Allouche and Shallit.] Consider also $S'_n(1)$ where

$$S_n(z) = \sum_{k=0}^{n-1} z^{\nu k} = (1 + z)^{e_1} + z(1 + z)^{e_2} + \cdots + z^{r-1}(1 + z)^{e_r}.$$

43. The straightforward implementation of (63), 'SET nu,0; SET y,x; BZ y,Done; 1H ADD nu,nu,1; SUBU t,y,1; AND y,y,t; PBNZ y,1B' costs $(5 + 4\nu x)\upsilon$, it beats the implementation of (62) when $\nu x < 4$, ties when $\nu x = 4$, and loses when $\nu x > 4$.

But we can save 4υ from the implementation of (62) if we replace the final multiplication-and-shift by '$y \leftarrow y + (y \gg 8)$, $y \leftarrow y + (y \gg 16)$, $y \leftarrow y + (y \gg 32)$, $\nu \leftarrow y \mathbin{\&} {}^\#$ff'. [Of course, MMIX's single instruction 'SADD nu,x,0' is much better.]

44. Let this sum be $\nu^{(2)}x$. If we can solve the problem for 2^d-bit numbers, we can solve it for 2^{d+1}-bit numbers, because $\nu^{(2)}(2^{2^d}x+x') = \nu^{(2)}x+\nu^{(2)}x'+2^d\nu x$. Therefore a solution analogous to (62) suggests itself, on a 64-bit machine:

Set $z \leftarrow (x \gg 1)$ & μ_0 and $y \leftarrow x - z$.
Set $z \leftarrow ((z + (z \gg 2))$ & $\mu_1) + ((y$ & $\bar{\mu}_1) \gg 1)$ and $y \leftarrow (y$ & $\mu_1) + ((y \gg 2)$ & $\mu_1)$.
Set $z \leftarrow ((z + (z \gg 4))$ & $\mu_2) + ((y$ & $\bar{\mu}_2) \gg 2)$ and $y \leftarrow (y + (y \gg 4))$ & μ_2.
Finally $\nu^{(2)} \leftarrow (((Az) \bmod 2^{64}) \gg 56) + ((((By) \bmod 2^{64}) \gg 56) \ll 3)$,
    where $A = (11111111)_{256}$ and $B = (01234567)_{256}$.

But on MMIX, which has sideways addition built in, there's a better solution by J. Dallos:

SADD nu2,x,m5	SADD t,x,m3	2ADDU nu2,nu2,t	SADD t,x,m0
SADD t,x,m4	2ADDU nu2,nu2,t	SADD t,x,m1	2ADDU nu2,nu2,t ∎
2ADDU nu2,nu2,t	SADD t,x,m2	2ADDU nu2,nu2,t	

[In general, $\nu^{(2)}x = \sum_k 2^k\nu(x$ & $\bar{\mu}_k)$. See *Dr. Dobb's Journal* **8**, 4 (April 1983), 24–37.]

45. Let $d = (x - y)$ & $(y - x)$; test if d & $y \neq 0$. [Rokicki found that this idea, which is called *colex ordering*, can be used with node addresses to near-randomize binary search trees or Cartesian trees as if they were treaps, without needing an additional random "priority key" in each node. See *U.S. Patent 6347318* (12 February 2002).]

46. SADD t,x,m; NXOR y,x,m; CSOD x,t,y; the mask m is ~(1<<i|1<<j). (In general, these instructions complement the bits specified by $\bar{m}$ if those bits have odd parity.)

47. $y \leftarrow (x \gg \delta)$ & θ, $z \leftarrow (x$ & $\theta) \ll \delta$, $x \leftarrow (x$ & $m) \mid y \mid z$, where $\bar{m} = \theta \mid (\theta \ll \delta)$.

48. Given δ, there are $s_\delta = \prod_{j=0}^{\delta-1} F_{\lfloor(n+j)/\delta\rfloor+1}$ different δ-swaps, including the identity permutation. (See exercise 4.5.3–32.) Summing over δ gives $1+\sum_{\delta=1}^{n-1}(s_\delta-1)$ altogether.

49. (a) The set $S = \{a_1\delta_1+\cdots+a_m\delta_m \mid \{a_1,\ldots,a_m\} \subseteq \{-1,0,+1\}\}$ for displacements $\delta_1, \ldots, \delta_m$ must contain $\{n-1,n-3,\ldots,1-n\}$, because the kth bit must be exchanged with the $(n+1-k)$th bit for $1 \leq k \leq n$. Hence $|S| \geq n$. And S contains at most 3^m numbers, at most $2 \cdot 3^{m-1}$ of which are odd.

(b) Clearly $s(mn) \leq s(m) + s(n)$, because we can reverse m fields of n bits each. Thus $s(3^m) \leq m$ and $s(2 \cdot 3^m) \leq m + 1$. Furthermore the reversal of 3^m bits uses only δ-swaps with even values of δ; the corresponding $(\delta/2)$-swaps prove that we have $s((3^m \pm 1)/2) \leq m$. These upper bounds match the lower bounds of (a) when $m > 1$.

(c) The string $\alpha a\beta\theta\psi z\omega$ with $|\alpha| = |\beta| = |\theta| = |\psi| = |\omega| = n$ can be changed to $\omega z\psi\theta\beta a\alpha$ with a $(3n+1)$-swap followed by an $(n+1)$-swap. Then $s(n)$ further swaps reverse all. Hence $s(32) \leq s(6) + 2 = 4$, and $s(64) \leq 5$. Again, equality holds by (a).

Incidentally, $s(63) = 4$ because $s(7) = s(9) = 2$. The lower bound in (a) turns out to be the exact value of $s(n)$ for $1 \leq n \leq 22$, except that $s(16) = 4$.

50. Express $n = (t_m \ldots t_1t_0)_3$ in balanced ternary notation. Let $n_j = (t_m \ldots t_j)_3$ and $\delta_j = 2n_j + t_{j-1}$, so that $n_{j-1} - \delta_j = n_j$ and $2\delta_j - n_{j-1} = n_j + t_{j-1}$ for $1 \leq j \leq m$. Let $E_0 = \{0\}$ and $E_{j+1} = E_j \cup \{t_j - x \mid x \in E_j\}$ for $0 \leq j < m$. (Thus, for example, $E_1 = \{0,t_0\}$ and $E_2 = \{0,t_0,t_1,t_1 - t_0\}$.) Notice that $\varepsilon \in E_j$ implies $|\varepsilon| \leq j$.

Assume by induction on j that δ-swaps for $\delta = \delta_1, \ldots, \delta_j$ have changed the n-bit word $\alpha_1 \ldots \alpha_{3j}$ to $\alpha_{3j} \ldots \alpha_1$, where each subword α_k has length $n_j+\varepsilon_k$ for some $\varepsilon_k \in E_j$. If $n_{j+1} > j$, a δ_{j+1}-swap within each subword will preserve this assumption. Otherwise each subword α_k has $|\alpha_k| \leq n_j+j \leq 3n_{j+1}+1+j \leq 4j+1 < 4m$. Therefore 2^k-swaps for $\lfloor\lg 4m\rfloor \geq k \geq 0$ will reverse them all. (Note that a 2^k-swap on a subword of size t, where $2^k < t \leq 2^{k+1}$, reduces it to three subwords of sizes $t - 2^k$, $2^{k+1} - t$, $t - 2^k$.)

51. (a) If $c = (c_{d-1} \ldots c_0)_2$, we must have $\theta_{d-1} = c_{d-1}\mu_{d,d-1}$. But for $0 \le k < d-1$ we can take $\theta_k = c_k\mu_{d,k} \oplus \hat{\theta}_k$, where $\hat{\theta}_k$ is *any* mask $\subseteq \mu_{d,k}$.

(b) Let $\Theta(d,c)$ be the set of all such mask sequences. Clearly $\Theta(1,c) = \{c\}$. When $d > 1$ we will have, recursively,

$$\Theta(d,c) = \{(\theta_0, \ldots, \theta_{d-2}, \hat{\theta}_{d-2}, \ldots, \hat{\theta}_0) \mid \theta_k = \theta'_{k-1} \ddagger \theta''_{k-1}, \ \hat{\theta}_k = \hat{\theta}'_{k-1} \ddagger \hat{\theta}''_{k-1}\},$$

by "zipping together" two sequences $(\theta'_0, \ldots, \theta'_{d-3}, \theta'_{d-2}, \hat{\theta}'_{d-3}, \ldots, \hat{\theta}'_0) \in \Theta(d-1, c')$ and $(\theta''_0, \ldots, \theta''_{d-3}, \theta''_{d-2}, \hat{\theta}''_{d-3}, \ldots, \hat{\theta}''_0) \in \Theta(d-1, c'')$ for some appropriate θ_0, $\hat{\theta}_0$, c', and c''.

When c is odd, the bigraph corresponding to (75) has only one cycle; so $(\theta_0, \hat{\theta}_0, c', c'')$ is either $(\mu_{d,0}, 0, \lceil c/2 \rceil, \lfloor c/2 \rfloor)$ or $(0, \mu_{d,0}, \lfloor c/2 \rfloor, \lceil c/2 \rceil)$. But when c is even, the bigraph has 2^{d-1} double bonds; so $\theta_0 = \hat{\theta}_0$ is any mask $\subseteq \mu_{d,0}$, and $c' = c'' = c/2$. [Incidentally, $\lg |\Theta(d,c)| = 2^{d-1}(d-1) - \sum_{k=1}^{d-1}(2^{d-k} - 1)(2^{k-1} - |2^{k-1} - c \bmod 2^k|)$.]

In both cases we can therefore let $\hat{\theta}_{d-2} = \cdots = \hat{\theta}_0 = 0$ and omit the second half of (71) entirely. Of course in case (b) we would do the cyclic shift directly, instead of using (71) at all. But exercise 58 proves that many other useful permutations, such as selective reversal followed by cyclic shift, can also be handled by (71) with $\hat{\theta}_k = 0$ for all k. The *inverses* of those permutations can be handled with $\theta_k = 0$ for $0 \le k < d-1$.

52. The following solutions make $\hat{\theta}_j = 0$ whenever possible. We shall express the θ masks in terms of the μ's, for example by writing $\mu_{6,5} \ \& \ \mu_0$ instead of stating the requested hexadecimal form $^{\#}55555555$; the μ form is shorter and more instructive.

(a) $\theta_k = \mu_{6,k} \ \& \ \mu_5$ and $\hat{\theta}_k = \mu_{6,k} \ \& \ (\mu_{k+1} \oplus \mu_{k-1})$ for $0 \le k < 5$; $\theta_5 = \theta_4$. (Here $\mu_{-1} = 0$. To get the "other" perfect shuffle, $(x_{31}x_{63} \ldots x_1 x_{33} x_0 x_{32})_2$, let $\hat{\theta}_0 = \mu_{6,0} \& \bar{\mu}_1$.)

(b) $\theta_0 = \theta_3 = \hat{\theta}_0 = \mu_{6,0} \ \& \ \mu_3$; $\theta_1 = \theta_4 = \hat{\theta}_1 = \mu_{6,1} \ \& \ \mu_4$; $\theta_2 = \theta_5 = \hat{\theta}_2 = \mu_{6,2} \ \& \ \mu_5$; $\hat{\theta}_3 = \hat{\theta}_4 = 0$. [See J. Lenfant, *IEEE Trans.* **C-27** (1978), 637–647, for a general theory.]

(c) $\theta_0 = \mu_{6,0} \ \& \ \mu_4$; $\theta_1 = \mu_{6,1} \ \& \ \mu_5$; $\theta_2 = \theta_4 = \mu_{6,2} \ \& \ \mu_4$; $\theta_3 = \theta_5 = \mu_{6,3} \ \& \ \mu_5$; $\hat{\theta}_0 = \mu_{6,0} \ \& \ \mu_2$; $\hat{\theta}_1 = \mu_{6,1} \ \& \ \mu_3$; $\hat{\theta}_2 = \hat{\theta}_0 \oplus \theta_2$; $\hat{\theta}_3 = \hat{\theta}_1 \oplus \theta_3$; $\hat{\theta}_4 = 0$.

(d) $\theta_k = \mu_{6,k} \ \& \ \mu_{5-k}$ for $0 \le k \le 5$; $\hat{\theta}_k = \theta_k$ for $0 \le k \le 2$; $\hat{\theta}_3 = \hat{\theta}_4 = 0$.

53. We can write ψ as a product of $d - t$ transpositions, $(u_1 v_1) \ldots (u_{d-t} v_{d-t})$ (see exercise 5.2.2–2). The permutation induced by a single transposition (uv) on the index digits, when $u < v$, corresponds to a $(2^v - 2^u)$-swap with mask $\mu_{d,v} \ \& \ \bar{\mu}_u$. We should do such a swap for $(u_1 v_1)$ first, $\ldots$, $(u_{d-t} v_{d-t})$ last.

In particular, the perfect shuffle in a 2^d-bit register corresponds to the case where $\psi = (01 \ldots (d-1))$ is a one-cycle; so it can be achieved by doing such $(2^v - 2^u)$-swaps for $(u,v) = (0,1)$, $\ldots$, $(0, d-1)$. For example, when $d = 3$ the two-step procedure is $12345678 \mapsto 13245768 \mapsto 15263748$. [Guy Steele suggests an alternative $(d-1)$-step procedure: We can do a 2^k-swap with mask $\mu_{d,k+1} \ \& \ \bar{\mu}_k$ for $d-1 > k \ge 0$. When $d = 3$ his method takes $12345678 \mapsto 12563478 \mapsto 15263748$.]

The matrix transposition in exercise 52(b) corresponds to $d = 6$ and $(u,v) = (0,3)$, $(1,4)$, $(2,5)$. These operations are the 7-swap, 14-swap, and 28-swap steps for 8×8 matrix transposition illustrated in the text; they can be done in any order.

For exercise 52(c), use $d = 6$ and $(u,v) = (0,2)$, $(1,3)$, $(0,4)$, $(1,5)$. Exercise 52(d) is as easy as 52(b), with $(u,v) = (0,5)$, $(1,4)$, $(2,3)$.

54. Transposition amounts to reversing the bits of the minor diagonals. Successive elements of those diagonals are $m - 1$ apart in the register. Simultaneous reversal of all diagonals corresponds to simultaneous reversal of subwords of sizes $1, \ldots, m$, which can be done with 2^k-swaps for $0 \le k < \lceil \lg m \rceil$ (because such transposition is easy when m is a power of 2, as illustrated in the text). Here's the procedure for $m = 7$:

Given	6-swap	12-swap	24-swap
00 01 02 03 04 05 06	00 **10** 02 **12** 04 **14** 06	00 **10 20 30** 04 **14 24**	00 **10 20 30 40 50 60**
10 11 12 13 14 15 16	**01 11 03** 13 **05 15 25**	01 11 **21 31** 05 15 25	01 11 21 31 **41 51 61**
20 21 22 23 24 25 26	20 **30** 22 **32** 24 **16** 26	**02 12** 22 32 **06** 16 26	02 12 22 32 **42 52 62**
30 31 32 33 34 35 36	**21 31 23** 33 **43 35 45**	**03 13** 23 33 43 **53 63**	03 13 23 33 43 53 63
40 41 42 43 44 45 46	40 **50** 42 **34** 44 **36** 46	40 50 **60** 34 44 **54 64**	**04 14 24** 34 44 54 64
50 51 52 53 54 55 56	**41 51 61** 53 **63** 55 **65**	41 51 61 **35 45** 55 65	**05 15 25** 35 45 55 65
60 61 62 63 64 65 66	60 **52** 62 **54** 64 **56** 66	42 52 62 **36 46** 56 66	**06 16 26** 36 46 56 66

55. Given x and y, first set $x \leftarrow x \,|\, (x \ll 2^k)$ and $y \leftarrow y \,|\, (y \ll 2^k)$ for $2d \le k < 3d$. Then set $x \leftarrow (2^{2d+k} - 2^k)$-swap of x with mask $\mu_{2d+k} \,\&\, \bar{\mu}_k$ and $y \leftarrow (2^{2d+k} - 2^{d+k})$-swap of y with mask $\mu_{2d+k} \,\&\, \bar{\mu}_{d+k}$ for $0 \le k < d$. Finally set $z \leftarrow x \,\& \, y$, then either $z \leftarrow z \,|\, (z \gg 2^k)$ or $z \leftarrow z \oplus (z \gg 2^k)$ for $2d \le k < 3d$, and $z \leftarrow z \,\& \, (2^{n^2} - 1)$. [The idea is to form two $n \times n \times n$ arrays $x = (x_{000} \ldots x_{(n-1)(n-1)(n-1)})_2$ and $y = (y_{000} \ldots y_{(n-1)(n-1)(n-1)})_2$ with $x_{ijk} = a_{jk}$ and $y_{ijk} = b_{jk}$, then transpose coordinates so that $x_{ijk} = a_{ji}$ and $y_{ijk} = b_{ik}$; now $x \,\& \, y$ does all n^3 bitwise multiplications at once. This method is due to V. R. Pratt and L. J. Stockmeyer, *J. Computer and System Sci.* **12** (1976), 210–213.]

56. Use (71) with $\theta_0 = \hat{\theta}_0 = 0$, $\theta_1 = {}^\#0010201122113231$, $\theta_2 = {}^\#00080e0400080c06$, $\theta_3 = {}^\#00000092008100a2$, $\theta_4 = {}^\#0000000000000f16$, $\theta_5 = {}^\#0000000003199c26$, $\hat{\theta}_4 = {}^\#00000c9f0000901a$, $\hat{\theta}_3 = {}^\#003a00b50015002b$, $\hat{\theta}_2 = {}^\#000103080c0d0f0c$, and $\hat{\theta}_1 = {}^\#0020032033233333$.

57. The two choices for each cycle when $d > 1$ have complementary settings. So we can choose a setting in which at least half of the crossbars are inactive, except in the middle column. (See exercise 5.3.4–55 for more about permutation networks.)

58. (a) Every different setting of the crossbars gives a different permutation, because there is exactly one path from input line i to output line j for all $0 \le i, j < N$. (A network with that property is called a "banyan.") The unique such path carries input i on line $l(i, j, k) = ((i \gg k) \ll k) + (j \bmod 2^k)$ after k swapping steps have been made.

(b) We have $l(i\varphi, i, k) = l(j\varphi, j, k)$ if and only if $i \bmod 2^k = j \bmod 2^k$ and $i\varphi \gg k = j\varphi \gg k$; so $(*)$ is necessary. And it is also sufficient, because a mapping φ that satisfies $(*)$ can always be routed in such a way that $j\varphi$ appears on line $l = l(j\varphi, j, k)$ after k steps: If $k > 0$, $j\varphi$ will appear on line $l(j\varphi, j, k-1)$, which is one of the inputs to l. Condition $(*)$ says that we can route it to l without conflict, even if l is $l(i\varphi, i, k)$.

[In *IEEE Transactions* **C-24** (1975), 1145–1155, Duncan Lawrie proved that condition $(*)$ is necessary and sufficient for an arbitrary *mapping* φ of the set $\{0, 1, \ldots, N-1\}$ into itself, when the crossbar modules are allowed to be general 2×2 mapping modules as in exercise 75. Furthermore the mapping φ might be only partially specified, with $j\varphi = *$ ("wildcard" or "don't-care") for some values of j. The proof that appears in the previous paragraph actually demonstrates Lawrie's more general theorem.]

(c) $i \bmod 2^k = j \bmod 2^k$ if and only if $k \le \rho(i \oplus j)$; $i \gg k = j \gg k$ if and only if $k > \lambda(i \oplus j)$; and $i\varphi = j\varphi$ if and only if $i = j$, when φ is a permutation.

(d) $\lambda(i\varphi \oplus j\varphi) \ge \rho(i \oplus j)$ for all $i \ne j$ if and only if $\lambda(i\tau\varphi \oplus j\tau\varphi) \ge \rho(i\tau \oplus j\tau) = \rho(i \oplus j)$ for all $i \ne j$, because τ is a permutation. [Note that the notation can be confusing: Bit $j\tau\varphi$ appears in bit position j if permutation φ is applied first, *then* τ. The Sylow group T includes many interesting and important permutations, including bit reversal and cyclic shifts. It corresponds to settings of the Omega network where crossbars of length 2^j that are congruent mod 2^{j+1} all switch or all pass, as a unit.]

(e) Since $l(j, j, k) = j$ for $0 \le k \le d$, a permutation of Ω fixes j if and only if each of its swaps fixes j. Thus the swaps performed by φ and by ψ operate on disjoint elements. The union of these swaps gives $\varphi\psi$.

(f) Any setting of the crossbars corresponds to a permutation that makes Batcher's comparator modules do the equivalent switching.

59. It is $2^{M_d(a,b)}$, where $M_d(a, b)$ is the number of crossbars that have both endpoints in $[a \mathinner{.\,.} b]$. To count them, let $k = \lambda(a \oplus b)$, $a' = a \bmod 2^k$, and $b' = b \bmod 2^k$; notice that $b - a = 2^k + b' - a'$, and $M_d(a, b) = M_{k+1}(a', 2^k + b')$. Counting the crossbars in the top half and bottom half, plus those that jump between halves, gives $M_{k+1}(a', 2^k + b') = M_k(a', 2^k - 1) + M_k(0, b') + ((b' + 1) \mathbin{\dot-} a')$. Finally, we have $M_k(0, b') = S(b' + 1)$; and $M_k(a', 2^k - 1) = M_k(0, 2^k - 1 - a') = S(2^k - a') = k2^{k-1} - ka' + S(a')$, where $S(n)$ is evaluated in exercise 42.

60. A cycle of length $2l$ corresponds to a pattern $u_0 \leftarrow v_0 \leftrightarrow v_1 \to u_1 \leftrightarrow u_2 \leftarrow v_2 \leftrightarrow \cdots \leftrightarrow v_{2l-1} \to u_{2l-1} \leftrightarrow u_{2l}$, where $u_{2l} = u_0$ and '$u \leftarrow v$' or '$v \to u$' means that the permutation sends u to v, '$x \leftrightarrow y$' means that $x = y \oplus 1$.

We can generate a random permutation as follows: Given u_0, there are $2n$ choices for v_0, then $2n - 1$ choices for u_1 only one of which causes $u_2 = u_0$, then $2n - 2$ choices for v_2, then $2n - 3$ choices for u_3 only one of which closes a cycle, etc.

Consequently the generating function is $G(z) = \prod_{j=1}^{n} \frac{2n - 2j + z}{2n - 2j + 1}$. The expected number of cycles, k, is $G'(1) = H_{2n} - \frac{1}{2}H_n = \frac{1}{2}\ln n + \ln 2 + \frac{1}{2}\gamma + O(n^{-1})$. The mean of 2^k is

$$G(2) = (2^n n!)^2 / (2n)! = \sqrt{\pi n} + O(n^{-1/2});$$

and the variance is $G(4) - G(2)^2 = (n + 1 - G(2))G(2) = \sqrt{\pi} n^{3/2} + O(n)$.

62. The crossbar settings in $P(2^d)$ can be stored in $(2d - 1)2^{d-1} = Nd - \frac{1}{2}N$ bits. To get the inverse permutation proceed from right to left. [See P. Heckel and R. Schroeppel, *Electronic Design* **28**, 8 (12 April 1980), 148–152. Note that *any* way to represent an arbitrary permutation requires at least $\lg N! > Nd - N/\ln 2$ bits of memory; so this representation is nearly optimum, spacewise.]

63. (i) $x = y$. (ii) Either z is even or $x \oplus y < 2^{\max(0, (z-1)/2)}$. (When z is odd we have $(x \ddagger y) \gg z = (y \gg \lceil z/2 \rceil) \ddagger (x \gg \lfloor z/2 \rfloor)$, even when $z < 0$.) (iii) This identity holds for all w, x, y, and z (and also with any other bitwise Boolean operator in place of $\&$).

64. $(((z \,\&\, \mu_0) + (z' \mid \bar\mu_0)) \,\&\, \mu_0) \mid (((z \,\&\, \bar\mu_0) + (z' \mid \mu_0)) \,\&\, \bar\mu_0)$. (See (86).)

65. $x u(x^2) + v(x^2) = x u(x)^2 + v(x)^2$.

66. (a) $v(x) = (u(x)/(1 + x^\delta)) \bmod x^n$; it's the unique polynomial of degree less than n such that $(1 + x^\delta) v(x) \equiv u(x)$ (modulo x^n). (Equivalently, v is the unique n-bit integer such that $(v \oplus (v \ll \delta)) \bmod 2^n = u$.)

(b) We may as well assume that $n = 64m$, and that $u = (u_{m-1} \ldots u_1 u_0)_{2^{64}}$, $v = (v_{m-1} \ldots v_1 v_0)_{2^{64}}$. Set $c \leftarrow 0$; then, using exercise 36, set $v_j \leftarrow u_j^{\oplus} \oplus (-c)$ and $c \leftarrow v_j \gg 63$ for $j = 0, 1, \ldots, m - 1$.

(c) Set $c \leftarrow v_0 \leftarrow u_0$; then $v_j \leftarrow u_j \oplus c$ and $c \leftarrow v_j$, for $j = 1, 2, \ldots, m - 1$.

(d) Start with $c \leftarrow 0$ and do the following for $j = 0, 1, \ldots, m - 1$: Set $t \leftarrow u_j$, $t \leftarrow t \oplus (t \ll 3)$, $t \leftarrow t \oplus (t \ll 6)$, $t \leftarrow t \oplus (t \ll 12)$, $t \leftarrow t \oplus (t \ll 24)$, $t \leftarrow t \oplus (t \ll 48)$, $v_j \leftarrow t \oplus c$, $c \leftarrow (t \gg 61) \times {}^\#9249249249249249$.

(e) Start with $v \leftarrow u$. Then, for $j = 1, 2, \ldots, m - 1$, set $v_j \leftarrow v_j \oplus (v_{j-1} \ll 3)$ and (if $j < m - 1$) $v_{j+1} \leftarrow v_{j+1} \oplus (v_{j-1} \gg 61)$.

67. Let $n = 2l - 1$ and $m = n - 2d$. If $\frac{1}{2}n < k < n$ we have $x^{2k} \equiv x^{m+t} + x^t$ (modulo $x^n + x^m + 1$), where $t = 2k - n$ is odd. Consequently, if $v = (v_{n-1} \ldots v_1 v_0)_2$, the number

$$w = u \oplus (((u \gg d) \oplus (u \gg 2d) \oplus (u \gg 3d) \oplus \cdots) \& -2^{l-d})$$

turns out to equal $(v_{n-2} \ldots v_3 v_1 v_{n-1} \ldots v_2 v_0)_2$. For example, when $l = 4$ and $d = 2$, the square of $u_6 x^6 + \cdots + u_1 x + u_0$ modulo $(x^7 + x^3 + 1)$ is $u_6 x^5 + u_5 x^3 + (u_6 \oplus u_4) x^1 + (u_5 \oplus u_3) x^6 + (u_6 \oplus u_4 \oplus u_2) x^4 + u_1 x^2 + u_0$. To compute v, we therefore do a perfect shuffle, $v = \lfloor w/2^l \rfloor \ddagger (w \bmod 2^l)$. The number w can be calculated by methods like those of the previous exercise. [See R. P. Brent, S. Larvala, and P. Zimmermann, *Math. Comp.* **72** (2003), 1443–1452; **74** (2005), 1001–1002.]

68. SRU t,x,delta; PUT rM,theta; MUX x,t,x.

69. Notice that the procedure might fail if we attempt to do the 2^{d-1}-shift first instead of last. The key to proving that a small-shift-first strategy works correctly is to watch the spaces *between* selected bits; we will prove that the lengths of these spaces are multiples of 2^{k+1} after the 2^k-shift.

Consider the infinite string $\chi_k = \ldots 1^{t_4} 0^{2^k} 1^{t_3} 0^{2^k} 1^{t_2} 0^{2^k} 1^{t_1} 0^{2^k} 1^{t_0}$, which represents the situation where $t_l \geq 0$ items need to move $2^k l$ places to the right. A 2^k-shift with any mask of the form $\theta_k = \ldots 0^{t_4} *^{2^{k+1}} 1^{t_3} 0^{t_2} *^{2^{k+1}} 1^{t_1} 0^{t_0}$ leaves us with the situation represented by the string $\chi_{k+1} = \ldots 1^{T_2} 0^{2^{k+1}} 1^{T_1} 0^{2^{k+1}} 1^{T_0}$, where exactly $T_l = t_{2l} + t_{2l+1}$ items need to move right $2^{k+1} l$ places. So the claim holds by induction on k.

70. Let $\psi_k = \theta_k \oplus (\theta_k \ll 1)$, so that $\theta_k = \psi_k^\oplus$ in the notation of exercise 36. If we take $*^{2^{k+1}} = 0^{2^k} 1^{2^k}$ in the previous answer, we have $\psi_0 = \bar{\chi}$ and $\psi_{k+1} = (\psi_k \& \bar{\theta}_k) \gg 2^k$. Therefore we can proceed as follows:

Set $\psi \leftarrow \bar{\chi}$, $k \leftarrow 0$, and repeat the following steps while $\psi \neq 0$: Set $x \leftarrow \psi$, then $x \leftarrow x \oplus (x \ll 2^l)$ for $0 \leq l < d$, then $\theta_k \leftarrow x$, $\psi \leftarrow (\psi \& \bar{x}) \gg 2^k$, and $k \leftarrow k + 1$.

The computation ends with $k = \lambda \nu \bar{\chi} + 1$; the remaining masks $\theta_k, \ldots, \theta_{d-1}$, if any, are zero and those steps can be omitted from (80). "Minimal" masks, for which $*^{2^{k+1}} = 0^{2^{k+1}}$ in answer 69, are obtained if the operations '$\theta_k \leftarrow x$, $\psi \leftarrow (\psi \& \bar{x}) \gg 2^k$' are replaced by '$\psi \leftarrow (\psi \& \bar{x}) \gg 2^k$, $\theta_k \leftarrow x \& (x + \psi)$' in the loop above.

[See *compress* in H. S. Warren, Jr., *Hacker's Delight* (Addison–Wesley, 2002), §7–4; also G. L. Steele Jr., *U.S. Patent 6715066* (30 March 2004). The BESM-6 computer, designed in 1965, implemented *compress* under the name «сборка» ("gather" or "pack"). Its «разборка» command ("scatter" or "unpack") went the other way.]

71. Start with $x \leftarrow y$. Do a (-2^k)-shift of x with mask $\theta_k \ll 2^k$, for $k = d-1, \ldots, 1, 0$, using exercise 70's masks. Finally set $z \leftarrow x$ (or $z \leftarrow x \& \chi$, if you want a "clean" result).

72. Assume that the leftmost mask bit, χ_{N-1}, is zero, since it is immaterial. Then the result $(z_{(N-1)\varphi} \ldots z_{1\varphi} z_{0\varphi})_2$ of any gather-flip corresponds to a permutation with $0\varphi < \cdots < k\varphi > \cdots > (N-1)\varphi$, where $k = \nu \chi$. For example, if $N = 8$ and $\chi = (00101100)_2$, the result is $(z_0 z_1 z_4 z_6 z_7 z_5 z_3 z_2)_2$. So $\varphi \in \Omega$ by exercises 5.3.4–11 and 58(f).

Moreover, the masks $\theta_0, \theta_1, \ldots, \theta_{d-1}$ for the 1-swap, 2-swap, $\ldots$, 2^{d-1}-swap can be computed as follows: The permutation $\psi = \varphi^-$ satisfies $j\psi = (N-1-j)\bar{\chi}_j + s_j$, where $s_j = \chi_{j-1} + \cdots + \chi_1 + \chi_0$ counts the 1s following mask bit χ_j. Let $\psi_0 = \psi$ and $\theta_k = (\lfloor \psi_k/2^k \rfloor \bmod 2) \& \mu_k$, where ψ_{k+1} is the 2^k-swap of ψ_k with mask θ_k. (In our example, $s_7 \ldots s_1 s_0 = 33221000$ and $(0\bar{\chi}_7) \ldots (6\bar{\chi}_1)(7\bar{\chi}_0) = 01030067$; hence $\psi_0 = (7\psi) \ldots (1\psi)(0\psi) = 33221000 + 01030067 = 34251067$. Then $\theta_0 = (10011001)_2 \& \mu_0 = (00010001)_2$; $\psi_1 = 34521076$; $\theta_1 = (10010011)_2 \& \mu_1 = (00010011)_2$; $\psi_2 = 32547610$; $\theta_2 = (00111100)_2 \& \mu_2 = (00001100)_2$. In general $j\psi_k \equiv j$ (modulo 2^k).) Represent each permutation ψ_k as a set of d bit vectors, namely as the "bit slices" $\psi_k \bmod 2$, $\lfloor \psi_k/2 \rfloor \bmod 2$, etc. Then $O(d^2)$ bitwise operations suffice for this computation.

The *scatter-flip* operation, which undoes the effect of gather-flip, is obtained via the same crossbar network but from right to left (first a 2^{d-1}-swap, ending with a 1-swap). [See *Journal of Signal Processing Systems* **53** (2008), 145–169.]

73. (a) Equivalently, d sheep-and-goats operations must be able to transform the word $x^\pi = (x_{(2^d-1)\pi} \ldots x_{1\pi} x_{0\pi})_2$ into $(x_{2^d-1} \ldots x_1 x_0)_2$, for any permutation π of $\{0, 1, \ldots, 2^d-1\}$. And this can be done by radix-2 sorting (Algorithm 5.2.5R): First bring the odd-numbered bits to the left, then bring the bits j for odd $\lfloor j/2 \rfloor$ left, and so on. For example, when $d = 3$ and $x^\pi = (x_3 x_1 x_0 x_7 x_5 x_2 x_6 x_4)_2$, the three operations yield successively $(x_3 x_1 x_7 x_5 x_0 x_2 x_6 x_4)_2$, $(x_3 x_7 x_2 x_6 x_1 x_5 x_0 x_4)_2$, $(x_7 x_6 x_5 x_4 x_3 x_2 x_1 x_0)_2$. [See Z. Shi and R. Lee, *Proc. IEEE Conf. ASAP'00* (IEEE CS Press, 2000), 138–148.]

(b) With gather-flip, the same strategy always yields $(x_{g(2^d-1)} \ldots x_{g(1)} x_{g(0)})_2$, where $g(k)$ is Gray binary code, 7.2.1.1–(9). For instance, the example of (a) is now $(x_5 x_7 x_1 x_3 x_0 x_2 x_6 x_4)_2$, $(x_6 x_2 x_3 x_7 x_5 x_1 x_0 x_4)_2$, $(x_4 x_5 x_7 x_6 x_2 x_3 x_1 x_0)_2$.

74. If $|\sum c_{2l} - \sum c_{2l+1}| = 2\Delta > 0$, we must rob Δ from the rich half and give it to the poor. There's a position l in the poor half with $c_l = 0$; otherwise that half would sum to at least 2^{d-1}. A cyclic 1-shift that modifies positions l through $(l + t) \bmod 2^d$ makes $c'_{l+k} = c_{l+k+1}$ for $0 \leq k < t$, $c'_{l+t} = c_{l+t+1} - \delta$, $c'_{l+t+1} = \delta$, and $c'_{l+k} = c_{l+k}$ for all other k; here δ can be any desired value in the range $0 \leq \delta \leq c_{l+t+1}$. (We've treated all subscripts modulo 2^d in these formulas.) So we can use the smallest even t such that $c_{l+1} + c_{l+3} + \cdots + c_{l+t+1} = c_l + c_{l+2} + \cdots + c_{l+t} + \Delta + \delta$ for some $\delta \geq 0$.

(The 1-shift need not be cyclic, if we allow ourselves to shift left instead of right. But the cyclic property may be needed in subsequent steps.)

75. Equivalently, given indices $0 \leq i_0 < i_1 < \cdots < i_{s-1} < i_s = 2^d$ and $0 = j_0 < j_1 < \cdots < j_{s-1} < j_s = 2^d$, we want to map $(x_{2^d-1} \ldots x_1 x_0)_2 \mapsto (x_{(2^d-1)\varphi} \ldots x_{1\varphi} x_{0\varphi})_2$, where $j\varphi = i_r$ for $j_r \leq j < j_{r+1}$ and $0 \leq r < s$. If $d = 1$, a mapping module does this.

When $d > 1$, we can set the left-hand crossbars so that they route input i_r to line $i_r \oplus ((i_r + r) \bmod 2)$. If s is even, we recursively ask one of the networks $P(2^{d-1})$ inside $P(2^d)$ to solve the problem for indices $\lfloor \{i_0, i_2, \ldots, i_s\}/2 \rfloor$ and $\lfloor \{j_0, j_2, \ldots, j_s\}/2 \rfloor$, while the other solves it for $\lfloor \{i_1, i_3, \ldots, i_{s-1}, 2^d\}/2 \rfloor$ and $\lceil \{j_0, j_2, \ldots, j_s\}/2 \rceil$. At the right of $P(2^d)$, one can now check that when $j_r \leq j < j_{r+1}$, the mapping module for lines j and $j \oplus 1$ has input i_r on line j if $j \equiv r$ (modulo 2), otherwise i_r is on line $j \oplus 1$. A similar proof works when s is odd. For example, if $(i_0, \ldots, i_5) = (j_0, \ldots, j_5) = (0, 1, 3, 5, 7, 8)$, the subproblems have $i = j = (0, 1, 3, 4)$ and $(0, 2, 4)$; $x_7 \ldots x_0 \mapsto x_6 x_7 x_5 x_4 x_2 x_3 x_1 x_0 \mapsto \cdots \mapsto x_5 x_7 x_5 x_3 x_1 x_3 x_1 x_0 \mapsto x_7 x_5 x_5 x_3 x_3 x_1 x_1 x_0$.

Notes: This network is a slight improvement over a construction by Yu. P. Ofman, *Trudy Mosk. Mat. Obshchestva* **14** (1965), 186–199. We can implement the corresponding network by substituting a "δ-map" for a δ-swap; instead of (69), we use two masks and do seven operations instead of six: $y \leftarrow x \oplus (x \gg \delta)$, $x \leftarrow x \oplus (y \& \theta) \oplus ((y \& \theta') \ll \delta)$. This extension of (71) therefore takes only d additional units of time.

76. When a mapping network realizes a permutation, all of its modules must act as crossbars; hence $G(n) \geq \lg n!$. Ofman proved that $G(n) \leq 2.5n \lg n$, and remarked in a footnote that the constant 2.5 could be improved (without giving any details). We have seen that in fact $G(n) \leq 2n \lg n$. Note that $G(3) = 3$.

77. Represent an n-network by $(x_{2^n-1} \ldots x_1 x_0)_2$, where $x_k = $ [the binary representation of k is a possible configuration of 0s and 1s when the network has been applied to all 2^n sequences of 0s and 1s], for $0 \le k < 2^n$. Thus the empty network is represented by $2^{2^n} - 1$, and a sorting network for $n = 3$ is represented by $(10001011)_2$. In general, x represents a sorting network for n elements if and only if it represents an n-network and $\nu x = n + 1$, if and only if $x = 2^0 + 2^1 + 2^3 + 2^7 + \cdots + 2^{2^n - 1}$.

If x represents α according to these conventions, the representation of $\alpha[i{:}j]$ is $(x \oplus y) \mid (y \gg (2^{n-i} - 2^{n-j}))$, where $y = x \mathbin{\&} \bar\mu_{n-i} \mathbin{\&} \mu_{n-j}$.

[See V. R. Pratt, M. O. Rabin, and L. J. Stockmeyer, *STOC* **6** (1974), 122–126.]

78. If $k \ge \lg(m - 1)$ the test is valid, because we always have $x_1 + x_2 + \cdots + x_m \ge x_1 \mid x_2 \mid \cdots \mid x_m$, with equality if and only if the sets are disjoint. Moreover, we have $(x_1 + \cdots + x_m) - (x_1 \mid \cdots \mid x_m) \le (m-1)(2^{n-k-1} + \cdots + 1) < (m-1)2^{n-k} \le 2^n$.

Conversely, if $m \ge 2^k + 2$ and $n > 2k$, the test is invalid. We might have, for example, $x_1 + \cdots + x_m = (2^k + 1)(2^{n-k} - 2^{n-2k-1}) + 2^{n-k-1} = 2^n + (2^{n-k} - 2^{n-2k-1})$.

But if $n \le 2k$ the test is still valid when $m = 2^k + 2$, because our proof shows that $x_1 + \cdots + x_m - (x_1 \mid \cdots \mid x_m) \le (2^k + 1)(2^{n-k} - 1) < 2^n$ in that case.

79. $x_{\scriptscriptstyle\prime} = (x - 1) \mathbin{\&} \chi$. (And the formula $x_{\scriptscriptstyle\prime} = ((x - b - 1) \mathbin{\&} a) + b$ corresponds to (85).) These recipes for x' and $x_{\scriptscriptstyle\prime}$ are part of Jörg Arndt's "bit wizardry" routines (2001); their origin is unknown.

80. Perhaps the nicest way is to start with $x \leftarrow \chi - 1$ as a signed number; then while $x \ge 0$, set $x \leftarrow x \mathbin{\&} \chi$, visit x, and set $x \leftarrow 2x - \chi$. (The operation $2x - \chi$ can in fact be performed with a single `MMIX` instruction, '`2ADDU x,x,minuschi`'.)

But that trick fails if χ is so large as to be *already* "negative." A slightly slower but more general method starts with $x \leftarrow \chi$ and does the following while $x \ne 0$: Set $t \leftarrow x \mathbin{\&} -x$, visit $\chi - t$, and set $x \leftarrow x - t$.

81. $((z \mathbin{\&} \chi) - (z' \mathbin{\&} \chi)) \mathbin{\&} \chi$. (One way to verify this formula is to use (18).)

82. Yes, by letting $z = z'$ in (86): $w \mid (z \mathbin{\&} \bar\chi)$, where $w = ((z \mathbin{\&} \chi) + (z \mid \bar\chi)) \mathbin{\&} \chi$.

83. (The following iteration propagates bits of y to the right, in the gaps of a scattered accumulator t. Auxiliary variables u and v respectively mark the left and right of each gap; they double in size until being wiped out by w.) Set $t \leftarrow z \mathbin{\&} \chi$, $u' \leftarrow (\chi \gg 1) \mathbin{\&} \bar\chi$, $v \leftarrow ((\chi \ll 1) + 1) \mathbin{\&} \bar\chi$, $w \leftarrow 3(u' \mathbin{\&} v)$, $u \leftarrow 3u'$, $v \leftarrow 3v$, and $k \leftarrow 1$. Then, while $u \ne 0$, do the following steps: $t \leftarrow t \mid ((t \gg k) \mathbin{\&} u')$, $k \leftarrow k \ll 1$, $u \leftarrow u \mathbin{\&} \bar w$, $v \leftarrow v \mathbin{\&} \bar w$, $w \leftarrow ((v \mathbin{\&} (u \gg 1) \mathbin{\&} \bar u) \ll (k+1)) - ((u \mathbin{\&} (v \ll 1) \mathbin{\&} \bar v) \gg k)$, $u' \leftarrow (u \mathbin{\&} \bar v) \gg k$, $v \leftarrow v + ((v \mathbin{\&} \bar u) \ll k)$, $u \leftarrow u + u'$. Finally return the answer $((t \gg 1) \mathbin{\&} \chi) \mid (z \mathbin{\&} \bar\chi)$.

84. $z \leftarrow \chi = w - (z \mathbin{\&} \chi)$, where $w = (((z \mathbin{\&} \chi) \ll 1) + \bar\chi) \mathbin{\&} \chi$ appears in answer 82; $z \to \chi$ is the quantity t computed (with more difficulty) in the answer to exercise 83.

85. (a) If $x = \mathtt{LOC}(a[i, j, k])$ is the drum location corresponding to interleaved bits as stated, then $\mathtt{LOC}(a[i + 1, j, k]) = x \oplus ((x \oplus ((x \mathbin{\&} \chi) - \chi)) \mathbin{\&} \chi)$ and $\mathtt{LOC}(a[i - 1, j, k]) = x \oplus ((x \oplus ((x \mathbin{\&} \chi) - 1)) \mathbin{\&} \chi)$, where $\chi = (11111)_8$, by (84) and answer 79. The formulas for $\mathtt{LOC}(a[i, j \pm 1, k])$ and $\mathtt{LOC}(a[i, j, k \pm 1])$ are similar, with masks 2χ and 4χ.

(b) For random access, let's hope there is room for a table of length 32 giving $f[(i_4 i_3 i_2 i_1 i_0)_2] = (i_4 i_3 i_2 i_1 i_0)_8$. Then $\mathtt{LOC}(a[i, j, k]) = (((f[k] \ll 1) + f[j]) \ll 1) + f[i]$. (On a vintage machine, bitwise computation of f would be much worse than table lookup, because register operations used to be as slow as fetches from memory.)

(c) Let p be the location of the page currently in fast memory, and let $z = -128$. When accessing location x, if $x \mathbin{\&} z \ne p$ it is necessary to read 128 words from drum location $x \mathbin{\&} z$ (after saving the current data to drum location p if it has changed); then set $p \leftarrow x \mathbin{\&} z$. [See *J. Royal Stat. Soc.* **B-16** (1954), 53–55. This scheme of array allocation for external storage was devised independently by E. W. Dijkstra, circa 1960, who called it the "zip-fastener" method. It has often been rediscovered, for example in 1966 by G. M. Morton and later by developers of quadtrees; see Hanan Samet, *Applications of Spatial Data Structures* (Addison–Wesley, 1990). See also R. Raman and D. S. Wise, *IEEE Trans.* **C57** (2008), 567–573, for a contemporary perspective. Georg Cantor had considered interleaving the digits of decimal fractions in *Crelle* **84** (1878), 242–258, §7; but he observed that this idea does *not* lead to an easy one-to-one correspondence between the unit interval $[0 . . 1]$ and the unit square $[0 . . 1] \times [0 . . 1]$.]

86. If (p', q', r') rightmost bits and (p'', q'', r'') other bits of (i, j, k) are in the part of the address that does not affect the page number, the total number of page faults is $2((2^{p-p'}-1)2^{q+r}+(2^{q-q'}-1)2^{p+r}+(2^{r-r'}-1)2^{p+q})$. Hence we want to minimize $2^{-p'} + 2^{-q'} + 2^{-r'}$ over nonnegative integers $(p', q', r', p'', q'', r'')$ with $p'+p'' \leq p$, $q'+q'' \leq q$, $r'+r'' \leq r$, $p'+q'+r'+p''+q''+r'' = s$. Since $2^a+2^b > 2^{a-1}+2^{b+1}$ when a and b are integers with $a > b+1$, the minimum (for all s) occurs when we select bits from right to left cyclically until running out. For example, when $(p, q, r) = (2, 6, 3)$ the addressing function would be $(j_5 j_4 j_3 k_2 j_2 k_1 j_1 i_1 k_0 j_0 i_0)_2$. In particular, Tocher's scheme is optimal.

[But such a mapping is not necessarily best when the page size isn't a power of 2. For example, consider a 16×16 matrix; the addressing function $(j_3 i_3 i_2 i_1 i_0 j_2 j_1 j_0)_2$ is better than $(j_3 i_3 j_2 i_2 j_1 i_1 j_0 i_0)_2$ for all page sizes from 17 to 62, except for size 32 when they are equally good.]

87. Set $x \leftarrow x \& \sim((x \& \texttt{"@@@@@@@@"}) \gg 1)$; each byte $(a_7 \ldots a_0)_2$ is thereby changed to $(a_7 a_6 (a_5 \wedge \bar{a}_6) a_4 \ldots a_0)_2$. The same transformation works also on 30 additional letters in the Latin-1 supplement to ASCII (for example, æ $\mapsto$ Æ); but there's one glitch, ÿ $\mapsto$ ß.

[Don Woods used this trick in his original program for the game of Adventure (1976), uppercasing the user's input words before looking them up in a dictionary. On **MMIX**, J. Dallos saves one instruction: 'MOR y,m,x; ANDN x,x,y', where $m = 1 \ll 53$.]

88. Set $z \leftarrow (x \oplus \bar{y}) \& h$, then $z \leftarrow ((x \mid h) - (y \& \bar{h})) \oplus z$.

89. $t \leftarrow x \mid \bar{y}$, $t \leftarrow t \& (t \gg 1)$, $z \leftarrow (x \& \bar{y} \& \bar{\mu}_0) \mid (t \& \mu_0)$. [From the "**nasty**" test program for H. G. Dietz and R. J. Fisher's SWARC compiler (1998), optimized by T. Dahlheimer.]

90. Insert '$z \leftarrow z \mid ((x \oplus y) \& l)$' either before or after '$z \leftarrow (x \& y) + z$'. (The ordering makes no difference, because $x+y \equiv x \oplus y$ (modulo 4) when $x+y$ is odd. Therefore **MMIX** can round to odd at no additional cost, using **MOR**. Rounding to even in the ambiguous cases is more difficult, and with fixed point arithmetic it is not advantageous.)

91. If $\frac{1}{2}[x, y]$ denotes the average as in (88), the desired result is obtained by repeating the following operations seven times, then concluding with $z \leftarrow \frac{1}{2}[x, y]$ once more:

$$z \leftarrow \tfrac{1}{2}[x, y], \quad t \leftarrow \alpha \& h, \quad m \leftarrow (t \ll 1) - (t \gg 7),$$
$$x \leftarrow (m \& z) \mid (\overline{m} \& x), \quad y \leftarrow (\overline{m} \& z) \mid (m \& y), \quad \alpha \leftarrow \alpha \ll 1.$$

Although rounding errors accumulate through eight levels, the resulting absolute error never exceeds $807/255$. Moreover, it is ≈ 1.13 if we average over all 256^3 cases, and it is less than 2 with probability $\approx 94.2\%$. If we round to odd as in exercise 90, the maximum and average error are reduced to $616/255$ and ≈ 0.58; the probability of error < 2 rises to $\approx 99.9\%$. Therefore the following **MMIX** code uses such unbiased rounding:

```
x GREG ;y GREG ;z GREG              XOR   t,x,y      MOR  m,ffhi,alf
alf GREG ;m GREG ;t IS $255         MOR   z,rodd,t   PUT  rM,m
                    repeat seven times: AND t,x,y    MUX  x,z,x
rodd GREG #4020100804020101         ADDU  z,z,t      MUX  y,y,z
ffhi GREG -1<<56                                     SLU  alf,alf,1
```

but omit the final SLU, then repeat the first four instructions again. The total time for eight α-blends ($66v$) is less than the cost of eight multiplications.

92. We get $z_j = \lceil (x_j + y_j)/2 \rceil$ for each j. (This fact, noticed by H. S. Warren, Jr., follows from the identity $x + y = ((x \mid y) \ll 1) - (x \oplus y)$. See also the next exercise.)

93. $x - y = (x \oplus y) - ((\bar{x} \,\&\, y) \ll 1)$. ("Borrows" instead of "carries.")

94. $(x - l)_j = (x_j - 1 - b_j) \bmod 256$, where b_j is the "borrow" from fields to the right. So t_j is nonzero if and only if $(x_j \ldots x_0)_{256} < (1 \ldots 1)_{256} = (256^{j+1} - 1)/255$. (The answers to the stated questions are therefore "yes" and "no.")

In general if the constant l is allowed to have *any* value $(l_7 \ldots l_1 l_0)_{256}$, operation (90) makes $t_j \neq 0$ if and only if $(x_j \ldots x_0)_{256} < (l_j \ldots l_0)_{256}$ and $x_j < 128$.

95. Use (90): Test if $h \,\&\, \big(t(x \oplus ((x \gg 8) + (x \ll 56))) \mid t(x \oplus ((x \gg 16) + (x \ll 48))) \mid t(x \oplus ((x \gg 24) + (x \ll 40))) \mid t(x \oplus ((x \gg 32) + (x \ll 32)))\big) = 0$, where $t(x) = (x - l) \,\&\, \bar{x}$. (These 28 steps reduce to 20 if cyclic shift is available, or to 11 with MXOR and BDIF.)

96. If $0 \le x, y < 256$, we have $x < y \iff \bar{x} + y \ge 256 \iff \lfloor (\bar{x} + y)/2 \rfloor \ge 128$. Thus we can use (88), replacing x by $\bar{x}$.

To get a similar test function for $[x_j \le y_j] = 1 - [y_j < x_j]$, we just interchange $x \leftrightarrow y$ and take the complement. The result, after noting that $\bar{y} \oplus x = \bar{x} \oplus y$ and $\overline{u + v} = \bar{u} - v$ and $\overline{\bar{y} \,\&\, x} = \bar{x} \mid y$, is analogous to (93):

$$t \leftarrow ((\bar{x} \mid y) - (((\bar{x} \oplus y) \gg 1) \,\&\, \bar{h})) \,\&\, h.$$

Before the final '$\&h$', N. Juffa observes that we have $\lfloor (\bar{x}_j + y_j + 1)/2 \rfloor$ in each byte, a bytewise average that is rounded up instead of down when $x_j + y_j$ is odd.

97. Set $x' \leftarrow x \oplus \text{"********"}$, $y' \leftarrow x \oplus y$, $t \leftarrow h \,\&\, (x \mid ((x \mid h) - l)) \,\&\, (y' \mid ((y' \mid h) - l))$, $m \leftarrow (t \ll 1) - (t \gg 7)$, $t \leftarrow t \,\&\, (x' \mid ((x' \mid h) - l))$, $z \leftarrow (m \,\&\, \text{"********"}) \mid (\bar{m} \,\&\, y)$. (20 steps.)

98. Set $t \leftarrow ((\bar{x} \,\&\, y) + (((\bar{x} \oplus y) \gg 1) \,\&\, \bar{h})) \,\&\, h$, $t \leftarrow (t - (t \gg 1)) + t$, $v \leftarrow (x \oplus y) \,\&\, t$, $z \leftarrow x \oplus v$, $w \leftarrow y \oplus v$. [This 13-step procedure uses (93) to find the bytes in which we want to swap $x_j \leftrightarrow y_y$. Of course the MMIX solution is much quicker, if available, because $\min(x, y) = x - (x \dot- y)$: BDIF t,x,y; ADDU z,y,t; SUBU w,x,t.]

99. In this potpourri, each of the eight bytes appears to be solving a different kind of problem; we must recast the conditions so that they fit into a common framework: $f_0 = [x_0 \oplus \text{'!'} \le 0]$, $f_1 = [x_1 \oplus \text{'*'} > 0]$, $f_2 = [x_2 \le \text{'A'} - 1]$, $f_3 = [x_3 > \text{'z'}]$, $f_4 = [x_4 > \text{'a'} - 1]$, $f_5 = [x_5 \oplus \text{'0'} \le 9]$, $f_6 = [x_6 \oplus 255 > 86]$, $f_7 = [x_7 \oplus \text{'?'} \le 3]$. Aha! We can use formulas analogous to (91), adjusting d to switch between $\le$ and $>$ as needed: $a = (\text{'?'}(255)\text{'0'}000\text{'*''}!\text{'})_{256} = {}^\#\text{3fff300000002a21}$; $b = \bar{h} = {}^\#\text{7f7f7f7f7f7f7f7f}$; $c = \bar{h} \,\&\, {\sim}(3(86)9(\text{'a'} - 1)\text{'z'}(\text{'A'} - 1)00)_{256} = {}^\#\text{7c29761f053f7f7f}$ (the hardest one); $d = {}^\#\text{8000800000800080}$; and $e = h = {}^\#\text{8080808080808080}$.

100. We want $u_j = x_j + y_j + c_j - 10c_{j+1}$ and $v_j = x_j - y_j - b_j + 10b_{j+1}$, where c_j and b_j are the "carry" and "borrow" into digit position j. Set $u' \leftarrow (x + y + (6 \ldots 66)_{16}) \bmod 2^{64}$ and $v' \leftarrow (x - y) \bmod 2^{64}$. Then we find $u'_j = x_j + y_j + c_j + 6 - 16c_{j+1}$ and $v'_j = x_j - y_j - b_j + 16b_{j+1}$ for $0 \le j < 16$, by induction on j. Hence u' and v' have the same pattern of carries and borrows as if we were working in radix 10, and we have $u = u' - 6(\bar{c}_{16} \ldots \bar{c}_2 \bar{c}_1)_{16}$, $v = v' - 6(b_{16} \ldots b_2 b_1)_{16}$. The following computation schemes therefore provide the desired results (10 operations for addition, 9 for subtraction):

$$\begin{aligned} &y' \leftarrow y + (6 \ldots 66)_{16}, \quad u' \leftarrow x + y', && v' \leftarrow x - y, \\ &t \leftarrow \langle \bar{x}\bar{y}'u' \rangle \,\&\, (8 \ldots 88)_{16}, && t \leftarrow \langle \bar{x}yv' \rangle \,\&\, (8 \ldots 88)_{16}, \\ &u \leftarrow u' - t + (t \gg 2); && v \leftarrow v' - t + (t \gg 2). \end{aligned}$$

101. For subtraction, set $z \leftarrow x - y$; for addition, set $z \leftarrow x + y + \#\mathtt{e8c4c4fc18}$, where this constant is built from $256 - 24 = \#\mathtt{e8}$, $256 - 60 = \#\mathtt{c4}$, and $65536 - 1000 = \#\mathtt{fc18}$. Borrows and carries will occur between fields as if mixed-radix subtraction or addition were being performed. The remaining task is to correct for cases in which borrows occurred or carries did not; we can do this easily by inspecting individual digits, because the radices are less than half of the field sizes: Set $t \leftarrow z \,\&\, \#\mathtt{8080808000}$, $t \leftarrow (t \ll 1) - (t \gg 7) - ((t \gg 15) \,\&\, 1)$, $z \leftarrow z - (t \,\&\, \#\mathtt{e8c4c4fc18})$. [See Stephen Soule, *CACM* **18** (1975), 344–346. We're lucky that the 'c' in 'fc18' is even.]

102. (a) We assume that $x = (x_{15} \ldots x_0)_{16}$ and $y = (y_{15} \ldots y_0)_{16}$, with $0 \le x_j, y_j < 5$; the goal is to compute $u = (u_{15} \ldots u_0)_{16}$ and $v = (v_{15} \ldots v_0)_{16}$, with components $u_j = (x_j + y_j) \bmod 5$ and $v_j = (x_j - y_j) \bmod 5$. Here's how:

$$
\begin{aligned}
&u \leftarrow x + y, &\qquad &v \leftarrow x - y + 5l, \\
&t \leftarrow (u + 3l) \,\&\, h, &\qquad &t \leftarrow (v + 3l) \,\&\, h, \\
&u \leftarrow u - ((t - (t \gg 3)) \,\&\, 5l); &\qquad &v \leftarrow v - ((t - (t \gg 3)) \,\&\, 5l).
\end{aligned}
$$

Here $l = (1 \ldots 1)_{16} = (2^{64} - 1)/15$, $h = 8l$. (Addition in 7 operations, subtraction in 8.)

    (b) Now $x = (x_{20} \ldots x_0)_8$, etc., and we must be more careful to confine carries:

$$
\begin{aligned}
&t \leftarrow x + \bar{h}, &\qquad &z \leftarrow (x \mid h) - (y \,\&\, \bar{h}), \\
&z \leftarrow (t \,\&\, \bar{h}) + (y \,\&\, \bar{h}), &\qquad &t \leftarrow (y \mid \bar{z}) \,\&\, \bar{x} \,\&\, h, \\
&t \leftarrow (y \mid z) \,\&\, t \,\&\, h, &\qquad &v \leftarrow x - y + t + (t \gg 2). \\
&u \leftarrow x + y - (t + (t \gg 2));
\end{aligned}
$$

Here $h = (4 \ldots 4)_8 = (2^{65} - 4)/7$. (Addition in 11 operations, subtraction in 10.)

    Similar procedures work, of course, for other moduli. In fact we can do multibyte arithmetic on the coordinates of toruses in general, with different moduli in each component (see 7.2.1.3–(66)).

103. Let h and l be the constants in (87) and (88). Addition is easy: $u \leftarrow x \mid ((x \,\&\, \bar{h}) + y)$. For subtraction, take away 1 and add $x_j \,\&\, (1 - y_j)$: $t \leftarrow (x \,\&\, \bar{l}) \gg 1$, $v \leftarrow t \mid (t + (x \,\&\, (y \oplus l)))$.

104. Yes, in 19: Let $a = (((1901 \ll 4) + 1) \ll 5) + 1$, $b = (((2099 \ll 4) + 12) \ll 5) + 28$. Set $m \leftarrow (x \gg 5) \,\&\, \#\mathtt{f}$ (the month), $c \leftarrow \#\mathtt{10} \,\&\, {\sim}((x \mid (x \gg 1)) \gg 5)$ (the leap year correction), $u \leftarrow b + \#\mathtt{3} \,\&\, ((\#\mathtt{3bbeecc} + c) \gg (m + m))$ (the *max_day* adjustment), and $t \leftarrow ((x \oplus a \oplus (x - a)) \mid (x \oplus u \oplus (u - x))) \,\&\, \#\mathtt{1000220}$ (the test for unwanted carries).

105. Exercise 98 explains how to compute bytewise min and max; a simple modification will compute min in some byte positions and max in others. Thus we can "sort by perfect shuffles" as in Section 5.3.4, Fig. 57, if we can permute bytes between x and y appropriately. And such permutation is easy, by exercise 1. [Of course there are much simpler and faster ways to sort 16 bytes. But see S. Albers and T. Hagerup, *Inf. and Computation* **136** (1997), 25–51, and M. Thorup, *J. Algorithms* **42** (2002), 205–230, for asymptotic implications of this approach.]

106. The n bits are regarded as g fields of g bits each. First the nonzero fields are detected (t_1), and we form a word y that has $(y_{g-1} \ldots y_0)_2$ in each g-bit field, where $y_j = [\text{field } j \text{ of } x \text{ is nonzero}]$. Then we compare each field with the constants 2^{g-1}, $\ldots$, 2^0 (t_2), and form a mask m that identifies the most significant nonzero field of x. After putting g copies of that field into z, we test z as we tested y (t_3). Finally an appropriate sideways addition of t_2 and t_3 (g-bit-wise) yields λ. (Try the case $g = 4$, $n = 16$.)

    To compute 2^λ without shifting left, replace '$t_2 \ll 1$' by '$t_2 + t_2$', and replace the final line by $w \leftarrow (((a \cdot (t_3 \oplus (t_3 \gg g))) \bmod 2^n) \gg (n - g)) \cdot l$; then $w \,\&\, m$ is $2^{\lambda x}$.

107.

```
107. h   GREG #8000800080008000        SLU  q,t,16         OR   t,t,y
     ms  GREG #00ff0f0f33335555        ADDU t,t,q          AND  t,t,h
     1H  SRU  q,x,32                   SLU  q,t,32    5H SLU  q,t,15
         ZSNZ lam,q,32                 ADDU t,t,q             ADDU t,t,q
         ADD  t,lam,16             3H ANDN y,t,ms            SLU  q,t,30
         SRU  q,x,t                4H XOR  t,t,y             ADDU t,t,q
         CSNZ lam,q,t                  OR   q,y,h    6H SRU  q,t,60
     2H  SRU  t,x,lam                  SUBU t,q,t             ADDU lam,lam,q  ∎
```

The total time is $22v$ (and no mems). [There's also a mem-less version of (56), costing only $16v$, if its last line is replaced by ADD t,lam,4; SRU y,x,t; CSNZ lam,y,t; SRU y,x,lam; SLU t,y,1; SRU t,[#ffffaa50],t; AND t,t,3; ADD lam,lam,t.]

108. For example, let e be minimum so that $n \le 2^e \cdot 2^{2^e}$. If n is a multiple of 2^e, we can use 2^e fields of size $n/2^e$, with e reductions in step B1; otherwise we can use 2^e fields of size $2^{\lceil \lg n\rceil - e - 1}$, with $e + 1$ reductions in step B1. In either case there are e iterations in steps B2 and B5, so the total running time is $O(e) = O(\log \log n)$.

109. Start with $x \leftarrow x \mathbin{\&} -x$ and apply Algorithm B. (Step B4 of that algorithm can be slightly simplified in this special case, using a constant l instead of $x \oplus y$.)

110. Let $s = 2^d$ where $d = 2^e - e$. We will use s-bit fields in n-bit words.

K1. [Stretch x mod s.] Set $y \leftarrow x \mathbin{\&} (s - 1)$. Then set $t \leftarrow y \mathbin{\&} \bar{\mu}_j$ and $y \leftarrow y \oplus t \oplus (t \ll 2^j (s - 1))$ for $e > j \ge 0$. Finally set $y \leftarrow (y \ll s) - y$. [If $x = (x_{2^e - 1} \ldots x_0)_2$ we now have $y = (y_{2^e - 1} \ldots y_0)_{2^s}$, where $y_j = (2^s - 1) x_j [j < d]$.]

K2. [Set up minterms.] Set $y \leftarrow y \oplus (a_{2^e - 1} \ldots a_0)_{2^s}$, where $a_j = \mu_{d,j}$ for $0 \le j < d$ and $a_j = 2^s - 1$ for $d \le j < 2^e$.

K3. [Compress.] Set $y \leftarrow y \mathbin{\&} (y \gg 2^j s)$ for $e > j \ge 0$. [Now $y = 1 \ll (x \bmod s)$. This is the key point that makes the algorithm work.]

K4. [Finish.] Set $y \leftarrow y \mid (y \ll 2^j s)$ for $0 \le j < e$. Finally set $y \leftarrow y \mathbin{\&} (\mu_{2^e, j} \oplus -((x \gg j) \mathbin{\&} 1))$ for $d \le j < 2^e$. ∎

111. The n bits are divided into fields of s bits each, although the leftmost field might be shorter. First y is set to flag the all-1 fields. Then $t = (\ldots t_1 t_0)_{2^s}$ contains candidate bits for q, including "false drops" for certain patterns 01^k with $s \le k < r$. We always have $v t_j \le 1$, and $t_j \ne 0$ implies $t_{j-1} = 0$. The bits of u and v subdivide t into two parts so that we can safely compute $m = (t \gg 1) \mid (t \gg 2) \mid \cdots \mid (t \gg r)$, before making a final test to eliminate the false drops.

112. Notice that if $q = x \mathbin{\&} (x \ll 1) \mathbin{\&} \cdots \mathbin{\&} (x \ll (r - 1)) \mathbin{\&} {\sim}(x \ll r)$ then we have $x \mathbin{\&} \overline{x + q} = x \mathbin{\&} (x \ll 1) \mathbin{\&} \cdots \mathbin{\&} (x \ll (r - 1))$.

If we can solve the stated problem in $O(1)$ steps, we can also extract the most significant bit of an r-bit number in $O(1)$ steps: Apply the case $n = 2r$ to the number $2^n - 1 - x$. Conversely, a solution to the extraction problem can be shown to yield a solution to the $1^r 0$ problem. Exercise 110 therefore implies a solution in $O(\log \log r)$ steps.

113. Let $0' = 0$, $x'_0 = x_0$, and construct $x'_{i'} = x_i$ for $1 \le i \le r$ as follows: If $x_i = a \circ_i b$ and $\circ_i \notin \{+, -, \ll\}$, let $i' = (i - 1)' + 1$ and $x'_{i'} = a' \circ_i b'$, where $a' = x'_{j'}$ if $a = x_j$ and $a' = a$ if $a = c_i$. If $x_i = a \ll c$, let $i' = (i - 1)' + 2$ and $(x'_{i'-1}, x'_{i'}) = (a' \mathbin{\&} (\lceil 2^{n-c}\rceil - 1), x'_{i'-1} \ll c)$. If $x_i = a + b$, let $i' = (i-1)' + 6$ and let $(x'_{(i-1)'+1}, \ldots, x'_{i'})$ compute $((a' \mathbin{\&} \bar{h}) + (b' \mathbin{\&} \bar{h})) \oplus ((a' \oplus b') \mathbin{\&} h)$, where $h = 2^{n-1}$. And if $x_i = a - b$, do the similar computation $((a' \mid h) - (b' \mathbin{\&} \bar{h})) \oplus ((a' \equiv b') \mathbin{\&} h)$. Clearly $r' \le 6r$.

114. Simply let $X_i = X_{j(i)} \circ_i X_{k(i)}$ when $x_i = x_{j(i)} \circ_i x_{k(i)}$, $X_i = C_i \circ_i X_{k(i)}$ when $x_i = c_i \circ_i x_{k(i)}$, and $X_i = X_{j(i)} \circ_i C_i$ when $x_i = x_{j(i)} \circ_i c_i$, where $C_i = c_i$ when c_i is a shift amount, otherwise $C_i = (c_i \ldots c_i)_{2^n} = (2^{mn} - 1)c_i/(2^n - 1)$. This construction is possible thanks to the fact that variable-length shifts are prohibited.

[Notice that if $m = 2^d$, we can use this idea to simulate 2^d instances of $f(x, y_i)$; then $O(d)$ further operations allow "quantification."]

115. (a) $z \leftarrow (\bar{x} \ll 1) \mathbin{\&} (x \ll 2)$, $y \leftarrow x \mathbin{\&} (x + z)$. [This problem was posed to the author by Vaughan Pratt in 1977.]

(b) First find $x_l \leftarrow (x \ll 1) \mathbin{\&} \bar{x}$ and $x_r \leftarrow x \mathbin{\&} (\bar{x} \ll 1)$, the left and right ends of x's blocks; and set $x'_r \leftarrow x_r \mathbin{\&} (x_r - 1)$. Then $z_e \leftarrow x'_r \mathbin{\&} (x'_r - (x_l \mathbin{\&} \bar{\mu}_0))$ and $z_o \leftarrow x'_r \mathbin{\&} (x'_r - (x_l \mathbin{\&} \mu_0))$ are the right ends that are followed by a left end in even or odd position, respectively. The answer is $y \leftarrow x \mathbin{\&} (x + (z_e \mathbin{\&} \bar{\mu}_0) + (z_o \mathbin{\&} \mu_0))$; it can be simplified to $y \leftarrow x \mathbin{\&} (x + (z_e \oplus (x'_r \mathbin{\&} \mu_0)))$.

(c) This case is impossible, by Corollary I.

116. The language L is well defined, by Lemma A (except that the presence or absence of the empty string is irrelevant). A language is regular if and only if it can be defined by a finite-state automaton, and a 2-adic integer is rational if and only if it can be defined by a finite-state automaton that ignores its inputs. The identity function corresponds to the language $L = 1(0 \cup 1)^*$, and a simple construction will define an automaton that corresponds to the sum, difference, or Boolean combination of the numbers defined by any two given automata acting on the sequence $x_0 x_1 x_2 \ldots$. Hence L is regular.

In exercise 115, L is (a) $11^*(000^*1(0 \cup 1)^* \cup 0^*)$; (b) $11^*(00(00)^*1(0 \cup 1)^* \cup 0^*)$.

117. Incidentally, the stated language L corresponds to an inverse Gray binary code: It defines a function with the property that $f(2x) = {\sim}f(2x + 1)$, and $g(f(2x)) = g(f(2x+1)) = x$, where $g(x) = x \oplus (x \gg 1)$ (see Eq. 7.2.1.1–(9)).

118. If $x = (x_{n-1} \ldots x_1 x_0)_2$ and $0 \le a_j \le 2^j$ for $0 \le j < n$, we have $\sum_{j=0}^{n-1} a_j x_j = \sum_{j=0}^{n-1}(a_j \mathbin{\dot-} (\bar{x} \mathbin{\&} 2^j))$. Take $a_j = \lfloor 2^{j-1} \rfloor$ to get $x \gg 1$.

Conversely, the following argument by M. S. Paterson proves that monus must be used at least $n - 1$ times: Consider any chain for $f(x)$ that uses addition, subtraction, bitwise Booleans, and k occurrences of the "underflow" operation $y \triangleleft z = (2^n - 1)[y < z]$. If $k < n-1$ there must be two n-bit numbers x' and x'' such that $x' \bmod 2 = x'' \bmod 2 = 0$ and such that all k of the $\triangleleft$'s yield the same result for both x' and x''. Then $f(x') \bmod 2^j = f(x'') \bmod 2^j$ when $j = \rho(x' \oplus x'')$. So $f(x)$ is not the function $x \gg 1$.

119. $z \leftarrow x \oplus y$, $f \leftarrow 2^p \mathbin{\&} \bar{z} \mathbin{\&} (z - 1)$. (See (90).)

120. Generalizing Corollary W, these are the functions such that $f(x_1, \ldots, x_m) \equiv f(y_1, \ldots, y_m)$ (modulo 2^k) whenever $x_j \equiv y_j$ (modulo 2^k) for $1 \le j \le m$, for $0 \le k \le n$. The least significant bit is a binary function of m variables, so it has 2^{2^m} possibilities. The next-to-least is a binary function of $2m$ variables, namely the bits of $(x_1 \bmod 4, \ldots, x_m \bmod 4)$, so it has $2^{2^{2m}}$; and so on. Thus the answer is $2^{2^m + 2^{2m} + \cdots + 2^{nm}}$.

121. (a) If f has a period of length pq, where $q > 1$ is odd, its p-fold iteration $f^{[p]}$ has a period of length q, say $y_0 \mapsto y_1 \mapsto \cdots \mapsto y_q = y_0$ where $y_{j+1} = f^{[p]}(y_j)$ and $y_1 \ne y_0$. But then, by Corollary W, we must have $y_0 \bmod 2^{n-1} \mapsto y_1 \bmod 2^{n-1} \mapsto \cdots \mapsto y_q \bmod 2^{n-1}$ in the corresponding $(n-1)$-bit chain. Consequently $y_1 \equiv y_0$ (modulo 2^{n-1}), by induction on n. Hence $y_1 = y_0 \oplus 2^{n-1}$, and $y_2 = y_0$, etc., a contradiction.

(b) $x_1 = x_0 + x_0$, $x_2 = x_0 \gg (p - 1)$, $x_3 = x_1 \mid x_2$; a period of length p starts with the value $x_0 = (1 + 2^p + 2^{2p} + \cdots) \bmod 2^n$.

122. Subtraction is analogous to addition; Boolean operations are even simpler; and constants have only one bit pattern. The only remaining case is $x_r = x_j \gg c$, where we have $S_r = S_j + c$; the shift goes left when $c < 0$. Then $V_{pqr} = V_{(p+c)(q+c)j}$, and

$$x_r \,\&\, \lfloor 2^p - 2^q \rfloor \;=\; ((x_j \,\&\, \lfloor 2^{p+c} - 2^{q+c} \rfloor) \gg c) \,\&\, (2^n - 1).$$

Hence $|X_{pqr}| \le |X_{(p+c)(q+c)j}| \le B_j = B_r$ by induction.

123. If $x = (x_{g-1} \ldots x_0)_2$, note first that $t = 2^{g-1}(x_0 \ldots x_{g-1})_{2^g}$ in (104); hence $y = (x_0 \ldots x_{g-1})_2$ as claimed. Theorem P now implies that $\lfloor \frac{1}{3} \lg g \rfloor$ broadword steps are needed to multiply by a_{g+1} and by a_{g-1}. At least one of those multiplications must require $\lfloor \frac{1}{6} \lg g \rfloor$ or more steps.

124. Initially $t \leftarrow 0$, $x_0 = x$, $U_0 = \{2^0, 2^1, \ldots, 2^{n-1}\}$, and $1' \leftarrow 0$. When advancing $t \leftarrow t+1$, if the current instruction is $r_i \leftarrow r_j \pm r_k$ we simply define $x_t = x_{j'} \pm x_{k'}$ and $i' \leftarrow t$. The cases $r_i \leftarrow r_j \circ r_k$ and $r_i \leftarrow c$ are similar.

If the current instruction branches when $r_i \le r_j$, define $x_t = x_{t-1}$ and let $V_1 = \{x \in U_{t-1} \mid x_{i'} \le x_{j'}\}$, $V_0 = U_{t-1} \setminus V_1$. Let U_t be the larger of V_0 and V_1; branch if $U_t = V_1$. Notice that $|U_t| \ge |U_{t-1}|/2$ in this case.

If the current instruction is $r_i \leftarrow r_j \gg r_k$, let $W = \{x \in U_{t-1} \mid x \,\&\, \lfloor 2^{\lg n+s} - 2^s \rfloor \ne 0$ for some $s \in S_{k'}\}$, and note that $|W| \le |S_{k'}| \lg n \le 2^{t-1+e+f}$. Let $V_c = \{x \in U_{t-1} \setminus W \mid x_{k'} = c\}$ for $|c| < n$, and $V_n = U_{t-1} \setminus W \setminus \bigcup_{|c|<n} V_c$. Lemma B tells us that at most $B_{k'} + 1 \le 2^{2^{t-1}-1} + 1$ of the sets V_c are nonempty. Let U_t be the largest; and if it is V_c, define $x_t = x_{j'} \gg c$, $i' \leftarrow t$. In this case $|U_t| \ge (|U_{t-1}| - 2^{t-1+e+f})/(2^{2^{t-1}-1} + 1)$.

Similarly for $r_i \leftarrow M[r_j \bmod 2^m]$ or $M[r_j \bmod 2^m] \leftarrow r_i$, let $W = \{x \in U_{t-1} \mid x \,\&\, \lfloor 2^{m+s} - 2^s \rfloor \ne 0$ for some $s \in S_{j'}\}$, and $V_z = \{x \in U_{t-1} \setminus W \mid x_{j'} \bmod 2^m = z\}$, for $0 \le z < 2^m$. By Lemma B, at most $B_{j'} \le 2^{2^{t-1}-1}$ of the sets V_z are nonempty; let $U_t = V_z$ be the largest. To write r_i in $M[z]$, define $x_t = x_{t-1}$, $z'' \leftarrow i'$; to read r_i from $M[z]$, set $i' \leftarrow t$ and put $x_t = x_{z''}$ if z'' is defined, otherwise let x_t be the precomputed constant $M[z]$. In both cases $|U_t| \ge (|U_{t-1}| - 2^{t-1}m)/2^{2^{t-1}-1}$ is sufficiently large.

If $t < f$ we cannot be sure that $r_1 = \rho x$. The reason is that the set $W = \{x \in U_t \mid x \,\&\, \lfloor 2^{\lg n+s} - 2^s \rfloor \ne 0$ for some $s \in S_{1'}\}$ has size $|W| \le |S_{1'}| \lg n \le 2^{t+e+f}$, and $|U_t \setminus W| \ge 2^{2^{e+f}-2^t+1} - 2^{t+e+f} > 2^{2^t-1} \ge |\{x_{1'} \,\&\, \lfloor 2^{\lg n} - 1 \rfloor \mid x_0 \in U_t \setminus W\}|$. Two elements of $U_t \setminus W$ cannot have the same value of $\rho x = x_{1'} \,\&\, \lfloor 2^{\lg n} - 1 \rfloor$.

[The same lower bound applies even if we allow the RAM to make arbitrary $2^{2^{t-1}}$-way branches based on the contents of $(r_1, \ldots, r_l)$ at time t.]

125. Start as in answer 124, but with $U_0 = [0 \mathinner{\ldotp\ldotp} 2^g)$. Simplifying that argument by eliminating the sets W will yield sets such that $|U_t| \ge 2^g / \max(2^m, 2n)^t$; for example, at most $2n$ different shift instructions can occur.

Suppose we can stop at time $t < \lfloor \lg(h+1) \rfloor$. The proof of Theorem P yields p and q with $x^R \,\&\, \lfloor 2^p - 2^q \rfloor$ independent of $x \,\&\, \lfloor 2^{p+s} - 2^{q+s} \rfloor$. Hence the hinted extension of Lemma B shows that x^R takes on at most $2^{2^t-1} \le 2^{(h-1)/2}$ different values, for every setting of the other bits $\{x \,\&\, \lfloor 2^{p+s} - 2^{q+s} \rfloor \mid s \in S_t\}$. So $r_1 = x_{1'}$ can be the correct value of x^R for at most $2^{(h-1)/2+g-h}$ values of x. But $2^{(h-1)/2+g-h} < |U_t|$, by (106).

126. M. S. Paterson has proposed a related (but different) conjecture: For every 2-adic chain with k addition-subtraction operations, there is a (possibly huge) integer x with $\nu x = k+1$ such that the chain does not calculate $2^{\lambda x}$.

127. Johan Håstad [*Advances in Computing Research* **5** (1989), 143–170] has shown that every polynomial-size circuit that computes the parity function from the inputs $\{x_1, \ldots, x_n, \bar{x}_1, \ldots, \bar{x}_n\}$ with AND and OR gates of unlimited fanin must have depth $\Omega(\log n / \log \log n)$.

128. (Note also that the suffix parity function $x^\oplus$ is considered in exercises 36 and 66.)

130. If the answer is "no," the analogous question with *variable* a suggests itself.

131. This program does a typical "breadth-first search," keeping $\texttt{LINK(q)} = \texttt{r}$. Register $\texttt{u}$ is the vertex currently being examined; $\texttt{v}$ is one of its successors.

OH	LDOU r,q,link	1	$\texttt{r} \leftarrow \texttt{LINK(q)}$.	STOU v,q,link	$\|R\|-\|Q\|$	$\texttt{LINK(q)} \leftarrow \texttt{v}$.
	SET u,r	1	$\texttt{u} \leftarrow \texttt{r}$.	STOU r,v,link	$\|R\|-\|Q\|$	$\texttt{LINK(v)} \leftarrow \texttt{r}$.
1H	LDOU a,u,arcs	$\|R\|$	$\texttt{a} \leftarrow \texttt{ARCS(u)}$.	SET q,v	$\|R\|-\|Q\|$	$\texttt{q} \leftarrow \texttt{v}$.
	BZ a,4F	$\|R\|$	Is $S[u] = \emptyset$?	3H PBNZ a,2B	S	Loop on $\texttt{a}$.
2H	LDOU v,a,tip	S	$\texttt{v} \leftarrow \texttt{TIP(a)}$.	4H LDOU u,u,link	$\|R\|$	$\texttt{u} \leftarrow \texttt{LINK(u)}$.
	LDOU a,a,next	S	$\texttt{a} \leftarrow \texttt{NEXT(a)}$.	CMPU t,u,r	$\|R\|$	Is $\texttt{u} \neq \texttt{r}$?
	LDOU t,v,link	S	$\texttt{t} \leftarrow \texttt{LINK(v)}$.	PBNZ t,1B	$\|R\|$	If so, continue.
	PBNZ t,3F	S	Is $\texttt{v} \subset R$?			∎

132. (a) We always have $\tau(U) \subseteq \&_{u \notin U}\, \delta_u = \sigma(U)$. And equality holds if and only if $2^u \subseteq \rho(u')$ for all $u \in U$ and $u' \in U$.

    (b) We've proved that $\tau(U) \subseteq \sigma(U)$; hence $T \subseteq U$. And if $t \in T$ we have $2^t \subseteq \rho_u$ for all $u \in U$. Therefore $\sigma(T) \subseteq \tau(T)$.

    (c) Parts (a) and (b) prove that the elements of C_n represent the cliques.

    (d) If $u \subseteq v$ then $u \& \rho_k \subseteq v \& \rho_k$ and $u \& \delta_k \subseteq v \& \delta_k$; so we can work entirely with maximal entries. The following algorithm uses cache-friendly sequential (rather than linked) allocation, in a manner analogous to radix exchange sort (Algorithm 5.2.2R).

    We assume that $w_1 \ldots w_s$ is a workspace of s unsigned words, bounded by $w_0 = 0$ and $w_{s+1} = 2^n - 1$. The elements of C_{k-1}^+ appear initially in positions $w_1 \ldots w_m$, and our goal is to replace them by the elements of C_k^+.

    M1. [Initialize.] Terminate if $\rho_k = 2^n - 1$. Otherwise set $v \leftarrow 2^k$, $i \leftarrow 1$, $j \leftarrow m$.

    M2. [Partition on v.] While $w_i \& v = 0$, set $i \leftarrow i + 1$. While $w_j \& v \neq 0$, set $j \leftarrow j - 1$. Then if $i > j$, go to M3; otherwise swap $w_i \leftrightarrow w_j$, set $i \leftarrow i+1$, $j \leftarrow j - 1$, and repeat this step.

    M3. [Split $w_i \ldots w_m$.] Set $l \leftarrow j$, $p \leftarrow s + 1$. While $i \leq m$, do subroutine Q with $u = w_i$ and set $i \leftarrow i + 1$.

    M4. [Combine maximal elements.] Set $m \leftarrow l$. While $p \leq s$, set $m \leftarrow m + 1$, $w_m \leftarrow w_p$, and $p \leftarrow p + 1$. ∎

Subroutine Q uses global variables j, k, l, p, and v. It essentially replaces the word u by $u' = u \& \rho_k$ and $u'' = u \& \delta_k$, retaining them if they are still maximal. If so, u' goes into the upper workspace $w_p \ldots w_s$ but u'' stays below.

    Q1. [Examine u'.] Set $w \leftarrow u \& \rho_k$ and $q \leftarrow s$. If $w = u$, go to Q4.

    Q2. [Is it comparable?] If $q < p$, go to Q3. Otherwise if $w \& w_q = w$, go to Q7. Otherwise if $w \& w_q = w_q$, go to Q4. Otherwise set $q \leftarrow q - 1$ and repeat Q2.

    Q3. [Tentatively accept u'.] Set $p \leftarrow p - 1$ and $w_p \leftarrow w$. Memory overflow occurs if $p \leq m + 1$. Otherwise go to Q7.

    Q4. [Prepare for loop.] Set $r \leftarrow p$ and $w_{p-1} \leftarrow 0$.

    Q5. [Remove nonmaximals.] While $w \mid w_q \neq w$, set $q \leftarrow q - 1$. While $w \mid w_r = w$, set $r \leftarrow r + 1$. Then if $q < r$, go to Q6; otherwise set $w_q \leftarrow w_r$, $w_r \leftarrow 0$, $q \leftarrow q - 1$, $r \leftarrow r + 1$, and repeat this step.

    Q6. [Reset p.] Set $w_q \leftarrow w$ and $p \leftarrow q$. Terminate the subroutine if $w = u$.

Q7. [Examine u''.] Set $w \leftarrow u \,\&\, \bar{v}$. If $w = w_q$ for some q in the range $1 \leq q \leq j$, do nothing. Otherwise set $l \leftarrow l + 1$ and $w_l \leftarrow w$. ∎

In practice this algorithm performs reasonably well; for example, when it is applied to the 8×8 queen graph (exercise 7–129), it finds the 310 maximal cliques after 306,513 mems of computation, using 397 words of workspace. It finds the 10188 maximal independent sets of that same graph after about 310 megamems, using 15090 words; there are respectively $(728, 6912, 2456, 92)$ such sets of sizes $(5, 6, 7, 8)$, including the 92 famous solutions to the eight queens problem.

Reference: N. Jardine and R. Sibson, *Mathematical Taxonomy* (Wiley, 1971), Appendix 5. Many other algorithms for listing maximal cliques have also been published. See, for example, W. Knödel, *Computing* **3** (1968), 239–240, **4** (1969), 75; C. Bron and J. Kerbosch, *CACM* **16** (1973), 575–577; S. Tsukiyama, M. Ide, H. Ariyoshi, and I. Shirakawa, *SICOMP* **6** (1977), 505–517; E. Loukakis, *Computers and Math. with Appl.* **9** (1983), 583–589; D. S. Johnson, M. Yannakakis, and C. H. Papadimitriou, *Inf. Proc. Letters* **27** (1988), 119–123. See also exercise 5–23.

133. (a) An independent set is a clique of $\overline{G}$; so complement G. (b) A vertex cover is the complement of an independent set; so complement G, then complement the outputs.

134. $a \mapsto 00$, $b \mapsto 01$, $c \mapsto 11$ is the first mapping of class II.

135. The unary operators are simple: $\neg(x_l x_r) = \bar{x}_r \bar{x}_l$; $\diamond(x_l x_r) = x_r x_r$; $\square(x_l x_r) = x_l x_l$. And $x_l x_r \Leftrightarrow y_l y_r = (z_l \wedge z_r)(z_l \vee z_r)$, where $z_l = (x_l \equiv y_l)$ and $z_r = (x_r \equiv y_r)$.

136. (a) Classes II, III, IV$_a$, and IV$_c$ all have the optimum cost 4. Curiously the functions $z_l = x_l \vee y_l \vee (x_r \wedge y_r)$, $z_r = x_r \vee y_r$ work for the mapping $(a, b, c) \mapsto (00, 01, 11)$ of class II as well as for the mapping $(a, b, c) \mapsto (00, 01, 1*)$ of class IV$_c$. [This operation is equivalent to saturating addition, when $a = 0$, $b = 1$, and c stands for "more than 1."]

(b) The symmetry between a, b, and c implies that we need only try classes I, IV$_a$, and V$_a$; and those classes turn out to cost 6, 7, and 8. One winner for class I, with $(a, b, c) \mapsto (00, 01, 10)$, is $z_l = v_r \wedge \bar{u}_l$, $z_r = v_l \wedge \bar{u}_r$, where $u_l = x_l \oplus y_l$, $u_r = x_r \oplus y_r$, $v_l = y_r \oplus u_l$, and $v_r = y_l \oplus u_r$. [See exercise 7.1.2–60, which gives the same answer but with $z_l \leftrightarrow z_r$. The reason is that we have $(x + y + z) \bmod 3 = 0$ in this problem but $(x + y - z) \bmod 3 = 0$ in that one; and $z_l \leftrightarrow z_r$ is equivalent to negation. The binary operation $z = x \circ y$ in this case can also be characterized by the fact that the elements (x, y, z) are all the same or all different; thus it is familiar to people who play the game of SET. It is the only binary operation on n-element sets that has $n!$ automorphisms and differs from the trivial examples $x \circ y = x$ or $x \circ y = y$.]

(c) Cost 3 is achieved only with class I: Let $(a, b, c) \mapsto (00, 01, 10)$ and $z_l = (x_l \vee x_r) \wedge y_l$, $z_r = \bar{x}_r \wedge y_r$.

137. In fact, $z = (x + 1) \,\&\, y$ when $(a, b, c) \mapsto (00, 01, 10)$. [It's a contrived example.]

138. The simplest case known to the author requires the calculation of *two* binary operations, such as

$$\begin{pmatrix} a & b & b \\ a & b & b \\ c & a & a \end{pmatrix} \quad \text{and} \quad \begin{pmatrix} a & b & a \\ a & b & a \\ c & a & c \end{pmatrix};$$

each has cost 2 in class V$_a$, but the costs are $(3, 2)$ and $(2, 3)$ in classes I and II.

139. The calculation of z_2 is essentially equivalent to exercise 136(b); so the natural representation (111) wins. Fortunately this representation also is good for z_1, with $z_{1l} = x_l \wedge y_l$, $z_{1r} = x_r \wedge y_r$.

140. With representation (111), first use full binary adders to compute $(a_1 a_0)_2 = x_l + y_l + z_l$ and $(b_1 b_0)_2 = x_r + y_r + z_r$ in $5 + 5 = 10$ steps. Now the "greedy footprint" method shows how to compute the four desired functions of (a_1, a_0, b_1, b_0) in eight further steps: $u_l = a_1 \wedge \bar{b}_0$, $u_r = a_0 \wedge \bar{b}_1$; $t_1 = a_1 \oplus b_0$, $t_2 = a_0 \oplus b_1$, $t_3 = a_1 \oplus t_2$, $t_4 = a_0 \oplus t_1$, $v_l = t_3 \wedge \bar{t}_1$, $v_r = t_4 \wedge \bar{t}_2$. [Is this method optimum?]

141. Suppose we've computed bits $a = a_0 a_1 \ldots a_{2m-1}$ and $b = b_0 b_1 \ldots b_{2m-1}$ such that

$$a_s = [s = 1 \text{ or } s = 2 \text{ or } s \text{ is a sum of distinct Ulam numbers} \leq m \text{ in exactly one way}],$$

$$b_s = [s \text{ is a sum of distinct Ulam numbers} \leq m \text{ in more than one way}],$$

for some integer $m = U_n \geq 2$. For example, when $m = n = 2$ we have $a = 0111$ and $b = 0000$. Then $\{s \mid s \leq m \text{ and } a_s = 1\} = \{U_1, \ldots, U_n\}$; and $U_{n+1} = \min\{s \mid s > m$ and $a_s = 1\}$. (Notice that $a_s = 1$ when $s = U_{n-1} + U_n$.) The following simple bitwise operations preserve these conditions: $n \leftarrow n + 1$, $m \leftarrow U_n$, and

$$(a_m \ldots a_{2m-1}, b_m \ldots b_{2m-1}) \leftarrow ((a_m \ldots a_{2m-1} \oplus a_0 \ldots a_{m-1}) \mathbin{\&} \overline{b_m \ldots b_{2m-1}},$$
$$(a_m \ldots a_{2m-1} \mathbin{\&} a_0 \ldots a_{m-1}) \mid b_m \ldots b_{2m-1}),$$

where $a_s = b_s = 0$ for $2U_{n-1} \leq s < 2U_n$ on the right side of this assignment.

[See M. C. Wunderlich, *BIT* **11** (1971), 217–224; *Computers in Number Theory* (1971), 249–257. These mysterious numbers, which were first defined by S. Ulam in *SIAM Review* **6** (1964), 348, have baffled number theorists for many years. The ratio U_n/n appears to converge to $\rho \approx 13.52$; for example, $U_{10000000} = 135160791$ and $U_{1000000000} = 13517631473$. D. W. Wilson noticed that the numbers form quasi-periodic "clusters" whose centers differ by multiples of $\delta \approx 21.6016$; then S. Steinerberger discovered empirically that $U_n \bmod \lambda$ almost always lies in $[\frac{1}{3}\lambda \, .. \, \frac{2}{3}\lambda]$, where $\lambda \approx 2.443443$ [Report DCS/TR-1508 (Yale University, 2015)]. By exploiting that amazing property, P. Gibbs [viXra:1508.0085 (2015)] found that roughly $O(N)$ time and $O(N)$ space suffice to compute the first N Ulam numbers. He and Jud McCranie calculated more than 25 billion Ulam numbers in 2015, discovering large gaps such as $U_{23647775834} - U_{23647775833} = 319654122989 - 319654121875 = 1114$. The smallest gap $U_n - U_{n-1} = 1$ apparently occurs only when $U_n \in \{2, 3, 4, 48\}$; certain small gaps like 6, 11, 14, and 16 have never yet been observed.]

142. Algorithm E in that exercise performs the following operations on subcubes: (i) Count the $*$s in a given subcube c. (ii) Given c and c', test if $c \subseteq c'$. (iii) Given c and c', compute $c \sqcup c'$ (if it exists). Operation (i) is simple with sideways addition; let's see which of the nine classes of two-bit encodings (119), (123), (124) works best for (ii) and (iii). Suppose $a = 0$, $b = 1$, $c = *$; the symmetry between 0 and 1 means that we need only examine classes I, III, IV$_a$, IV$_c$, V$_a$, and V$_c$.

For the asterisks-and-bits mapping $(0, 1, *) \mapsto (00, 01, 10)$, which belongs to class I, the truth table for $c \not\subseteq c'$ is $010*100*110*****$ in each component. (For example, $0 \subseteq *$ and $* \not\subseteq 1$. The $*$s in this truth table are don't-cares for the unused codes 11.) The methods of Section 7.1.2 tell us that the cheapest such functions have cost 3; for example, $c \subseteq c'$ if and only if $((b \oplus b') \mid a) \mathbin{\&} \bar{a}' = 0$. Furthermore the consensus $c \sqcup c' = c''$ exists if and only if $\nu z = 1$, where $z = (b \oplus b') \mathbin{\&} \sim(a \oplus a')$. And in that case, $a'' = (a \oplus b \oplus b') \mathbin{\&} \sim(a \oplus a')$, $b'' = (b \mid b') \mathbin{\&} \bar{z}$. [The asterisk and bit codes were used for this purpose by M. A. Breuer in *Proc. ACM Nat. Conf.* **23** (1968), 241–250.]

But class III works out better, with $(0, 1, *) \mapsto (01, 10, 00)$. Then $c \subseteq c'$ if and only if $(\bar{c}_l \mathbin{\&} c'_l) \mid (\bar{c}_r \mathbin{\&} c'_r) = 0$; $c \sqcup c' = c''$ exists if and only if $\nu z = 1$ where $z = x \mathbin{\&} y$, $x = c_l \mid c'_l$, $y = c_r \mid c'_r$; and $c''_l = x \oplus z$, $c''_r = y \oplus z$. We save two operations for each consensus, with respect to class I, compensating for an extra step when counting asterisks.

Classes IV$_a$, V$_a$, and V$_c$ turn out to be far inferior. Class IV$_c$ has some merit, but class III is best.

143. $f(x) = ((x \& m_1) \ll 17) | ((x \gg 17) \& m_1) | ((x \& m_2) \ll 15) | ((x \gg 15) \& m_2) | ((x \& m_3) \ll$
$10) | ((x \gg 10) \& m_3) | ((x \& m_4) \ll 6) | ((x \gg 6) \& m_4)$, where $m_1 = {}^\#\mathtt{7f7f7f7f7f7f7f}$,
$m_2 = {}^\#\mathtt{fefefefefefe}$, $m_3 = {}^\#\mathtt{3f3f3f3f3f3f3f3f}$, $m_4 = {}^\#\mathtt{fcfcfcfcfcfcfc}$. [See, for
example, *Chess Skill in Man and Machine*, edited by Peter W. Frey (1977), page 59.
Five steps suffice to compute $f(x)$ on MMIX (four MOR operations and one OR), since
$f(x) = q \cdot x \cdot q' | q' \cdot x \cdot q$ with $q = {}^\#\mathtt{40a05028140a0502}$ and $q' = {}^\#\mathtt{2010884422110804}$.]

144. Node $j \oplus (k \ll 1)$, where $k = j \& -j$.

145. It names the ancestor of the leaf node $j | 1$ at height h.

146. By (136) we want to show that $\lambda(j \& -i) = \rho l$ when $l - 2^{\rho l} < i \le l \le j < l + 2^{\rho l}$.
The desired result follows from (35) because $-l \le -i < -l + 2^{\rho l}$.

147. (a) $\pi v_j = \beta v_j = j$, $\alpha v_j = 1 \ll \rho j$, and $\tau j = \Lambda$, for $1 \le j \le n$.

(b) Suppose $n = 2^{e_1} + \cdots + 2^{e_t}$ where $e_1 > \cdots > e_t \ge 0$, and let $n_k = 2^{e_1} + \cdots + 2^{e_k}$
for $0 \le k \le t$. Then $\pi v_j = j$ and $\beta v_j = \alpha v_j = n_k$ for $n_{k-1} < j \le n_k$. Also $\tau n_k = v_{n_{k-1}}$
for $1 \le k \le t$, where $v_0 = \Lambda$; all other $\tau j = \Lambda$.

148. Yes, if $\pi y_1 = 010000$, $\pi y_2 = 010100$, $\pi x_1 = 010101$, $\pi x_2 = 010110$, $\pi x_3 = 010111$,
$\beta x_3 = 010111$, $\beta y_2 = 010100$, $\beta x_2 = 011000$, $\beta y_1 = 010000$, and $\beta x_1 = 100000$.

149. We assume that $\mathtt{CHILD}(v) = \mathtt{SIB}(v) = \mathtt{PARENT}(v) = \Lambda$ initially for all vertices v
(including $v = \Lambda$), and that there is at least one nonnull vertex.

> **S1.** [Make triply linked tree.] For each of the n arcs $u \longrightarrow v$ (perhaps $v = \Lambda$), set
> $\mathtt{SIB}(u) \leftarrow \mathtt{CHILD}(v)$, $\mathtt{CHILD}(v) \leftarrow u$, $\mathtt{PARENT}(u) \leftarrow v$. (See exercise 2.3.3–6.)
>
> **S2.** [Begin first traversal.] Set $p \leftarrow \mathtt{CHILD}(\Lambda)$, $n \leftarrow 0$, and $\lambda 0 \leftarrow -1$.
>
> **S3.** [Compute β in the easy case.] Set $n \leftarrow n + 1$, $\pi p \leftarrow n$, $\tau n \leftarrow \Lambda$, and
> $\lambda n \leftarrow 1 + \lambda(n \gg 1)$. If $\mathtt{CHILD}(p) \ne \Lambda$, set $p \leftarrow \mathtt{CHILD}(p)$ and repeat this step;
> otherwise set $\beta p \leftarrow n$.
>
> **S4.** [Compute τ, bottom-up.] Set $\tau \beta p \leftarrow \mathtt{PARENT}(p)$. Then if $\mathtt{SIB}(p) \ne \Lambda$, set
> $p \leftarrow \mathtt{SIB}(p)$ and return to S3; otherwise set $p \leftarrow \mathtt{PARENT}(p)$.
>
> **S5.** [Compute β in the hard case.] If $p \ne \Lambda$, set $h \leftarrow \lambda(n \& -\pi p)$, then $\beta p \leftarrow$
> $((n \gg h) | 1) \ll h$, and go back to S4.
>
> **S6.** [Begin second traversal.] Set $p \leftarrow \mathtt{CHILD}(\Lambda)$, $\lambda 0 \leftarrow \lambda n$, $\pi \Lambda \leftarrow \beta \Lambda \leftarrow \alpha \Lambda \leftarrow 0$.
>
> **S7.** [Compute α, top-down.] Set $\alpha p \leftarrow \alpha(\mathtt{PARENT}(p)) | (\beta p \& -\beta p)$. Then if
> $\mathtt{CHILD}(p) \ne \Lambda$, set $p \leftarrow \mathtt{CHILD}(p)$ and repeat this step.
>
> **S8.** [Continue to traverse.] If $\mathtt{SIB}(p) \ne \Lambda$, set $p \leftarrow \mathtt{SIB}(p)$ and go to S7.
> Otherwise set $p \leftarrow \mathtt{PARENT}(p)$, and repeat step S8 if $p \ne \Lambda$. ∎

150. We may assume that the elements A_j are distinct, by regarding them as ordered
pairs (A_j, j). The hinted binary search tree, which is a special case of the "Cartesian
trees" introduced by Jean Vuillemin [*CACM* **23** (1980), 229–239], has the property that
$k(i, j)$ is the nearest common ancestor of i and j. Indeed, the ancestors of any given
node j are precisely the nodes k such that A_k is a right-to-left minimum of $A_1 \ldots A_j$
or A_k is a left-to-right minimum of $A_j \ldots A_n$.

The algorithm of the preceding answer does the desired preprocessing, except
that we need to set up a triply linked tree differently on the nodes $\{0, 1, \ldots, n\}$. Start
as before with $\mathtt{CHILD}(v) = \mathtt{SIB}(v) = \mathtt{PARENT}(v) = 0$ for $0 \le v \le n$, and let $\Lambda = 0$.
Assume that $A_0 \le A_j$ for $1 \le j \le n$. Set $t \leftarrow 0$ and do the following steps for $v = n$,
$n - 1$, ..., 1: Set $u \leftarrow 0$; then while $A_v < A_t$ set $u \leftarrow t$ and $t \leftarrow \mathtt{PARENT}(t)$. If $u \ne 0$,
set $\mathtt{SIB}(v) \leftarrow \mathtt{SIB}(u)$, $\mathtt{SIB}(u) \leftarrow 0$, $\mathtt{PARENT}(u) \leftarrow v$, $\mathtt{CHILD}(v) \leftarrow u$; otherwise simply
set $\mathtt{SIB}(v) \leftarrow \mathtt{CHILD}(t)$. Also set $\mathtt{CHILD}(t) \leftarrow v$, $\mathtt{PARENT}(v) \leftarrow t$, $t \leftarrow v$.

Continue with step S2 after the tree has been built. The running time is $O(n)$, because the operation $t \leftarrow \texttt{PARENT}(t)$ is performed at most once for each node t. [This beautiful way to reduce the range minimum query problem to the nearest common ancestor problem was discovered by H. N. Gabow, J. L. Bentley, and R. E. Tarjan, *STOC* **16** (1984), 137–138, who also suggested the following exercise.]

151. For node v with k children $u_1, \ldots, u_k$, define the node sequence $S(v) = v$ if $k = 0$; $S(v) = vS(u_1)$ if $k = 1$; and $S(v) = S(u_1)v \ldots vS(u_k)$ if $k > 1$. (Consequently v appears exactly $\max(k-1, 1)$ times in $S(v)$.) If there are k trees in the forest, rooted at $u_1, \ldots, u_k$, write down the node sequence $S(u_1)\Lambda \ldots \Lambda S(u_k) = V_1 \ldots V_N$. (The length of this sequence will satisfy $n \leq N < 2n$.) Let A_j be the depth of node V_j, for $1 \leq j \leq N$, where Λ has depth 0. (For example, consider the forest (141), but add another child $K \longrightarrow D$ and an isolated node L. Then $V_1 \ldots V_{15} = CFAGJDHDK\Lambda BEI\Lambda L$ and $A_1 \ldots A_{15} = 231342323012301$.) The nearest common ancestor of u and v, when $u = V_i$ and $v = V_j$, is then $V_{k(i,j)}$ in the range minimum query problem. [See J. Fischer and V. Heun, *Lecture Notes in Comp. Sci.* **4009** (2006), 36–48.]

152. Step V1 finds the level above which αx and αy have bits that apply to both of their ancestors. (See exercise 148.) Step V2 increases h, if necessary, to the level where they have a common ancestor, or to the top level λn if they don't (namely if $k = 0$). If $\beta x \neq \beta z$, step V4 finds the topmost level among x's ancestors that leads to level h; hence it knows the lowest ancestor $\hat{x}$ for which $\beta \hat{x} = \beta z$ (or $\hat{x} = \Lambda$). Finally in V5, preorder tells us which of $\hat{x}$ or $\hat{y}$ is an ancestor of the other.

153. That pointer has ρj bits, so it ends after $\rho 1 + \rho 2 + \cdots + \rho j = j - \nu j$ bits of the packed string, by (61). [Here j is even. Navigation piles were introduced in *Nordic Journal of Computing* **10** (2003), 238–262; see also O. Darwish, A. Elmasry, and J. Katajainen, *ACM Transactions on Algorithms* **17** (2021), 18:1–18:19.]

154. The gray lines define $36°$-$36°$-$90°$ triangles, ten of which make a pentagon with $72°$ angles at each vertex. These pentagons tile the hyperbolic plane in such a way that *five* of them meet at each vertex.

155. Observe first that $0 \leq (\alpha 0)_{1/\phi} < \phi^{-1} + \phi^{-3} + \phi^{-5} + \cdots = 1$, since there are no consecutive 1s. Observe next that $F_{-n}\phi \equiv \phi^{-n}$ (modulo 1), by exercise 1.2.8–11. Now add $F_{k_1}\phi + \cdots + F_{k_r}\phi$. For example, $(4\phi) \bmod 1 = \phi^{-5} + \phi^{-2}$; $(-2\phi) \bmod 1 = \phi^{-4} + \phi^{-1}$.

This argument also proves the interesting formula $\lfloor N(\alpha)\phi \rfloor = -N(\alpha 0)$.

156. (a) Start with $y \leftarrow 0$, and with k large enough that $|x| < F_{k+1}$. If $x < 0$, set $k \leftarrow (k-1) \mid 1$, and while $x + F_k > 0$ set $k \leftarrow k - 2$; then set $y \leftarrow y + (1 \ll k)$, $x \leftarrow x + F_{k+1}$; repeat. Otherwise if $x > 1$, set $k \leftarrow k \mathbin{\&} -2$, and while $x - F_k \leq 0$ set $k \leftarrow k - 2$; then set $y \leftarrow y + (1 \ll k)$, $x \leftarrow x - F_{k+1}$; repeat. Otherwise set $y \leftarrow y + x$ and terminate with $y = (\alpha)_2$.

(b) The operations $x_1 \leftarrow a_1$, $y_1 \leftarrow -a_1$, $x_k \leftarrow y_{k-1} + a_k$, $y_k \leftarrow x_{k-1} - x_k$ compute $x_k = N(a_1 \ldots a_k)$ and $y_k = N(a_1 \ldots a_k 0)$. [Does *every* broadword chain for $N(a_1 \ldots a_n)$ require $\Omega(n)$ steps?]

157. The laws are obvious except for the two cases involving $(\alpha-)$. For those we have $N((\alpha-)0^k) = N(\alpha 0^k) + F_{-k-2}$ for all $k \geq 0$, because decrementation never "borrows" at the right. (But the analogous formula $N((\alpha+)0^k) = N(\alpha 0^k) + F_{-k-1}$ does *not* hold.)

158. Incrementation satisfies the rules $(\alpha 00)+ = \alpha 01$, $(\alpha 10)+ = (\alpha+)00$, $(\alpha 1)+ = (\alpha+)0$. It can be achieved with six 2-adic operations on the integer $x = (\alpha)_2$ by setting $y \leftarrow x \mid (x \gg 1)$, $z \leftarrow y \mathbin{\&} \sim(y+1)$, $x \leftarrow (x \mid z) + 1$.

Decrementation of a nonzero codeword is more difficult. It satisfies $(\alpha 10^{2k})- = \alpha 0(10)^k$, $(\alpha 10^{2k+1})- = \alpha(01)^{k+1}$; hence by Corollary I it cannot be computed by a 2-adic chain. Yet seven operations suffice, if we allow monus: $y \leftarrow x - 1$, $z \leftarrow y \,\&\, \bar{x}$, $w \leftarrow z \,\&\, \mu_0$, $x \leftarrow y - w + (w \,\dot{-}\, (z - w))$.

159. Besides the Fibonacci number system (146) and the negaFibonacci number system (147), there's also an *odd Fibonacci number system*: *Every positive integer x can be written uniquely in the form*

$$x = F_{l_1} + F_{l_2} + \cdots + F_{l_s}, \qquad \text{where } l_1 \ggg l_2 \ggg \cdots \ggg l_s > 0 \text{ and } l_s \text{ is odd.}$$

Given a negaFibonacci code α, the following 19-step 2-adic chain converts $x = (\alpha)_2$ to $y = (\beta)_2$ to $z = (\gamma)_2$, where β is the odd codeword with $N(\alpha) = F(\beta)$ and γ is the standard codeword with $F(\beta) = F(\gamma 0)$: $x^+ \leftarrow x \,\&\, \mu_0$, $x^- \leftarrow x \oplus x^+$; $d \leftarrow x^+ - x^-$; $t \leftarrow d \mid x^-$, $t \leftarrow t \,\&\, {\sim}(t \ll 1)$; $y \leftarrow (d \,\&\, \bar{\mu}_0) \oplus t \oplus ((t \,\&\, x^-) \gg 1)$; $z \leftarrow (y+1) \gg 1$; $w \leftarrow z \oplus (4\mu_0)$; $t \leftarrow w \,\&\, {\sim}(w+1)$; $z \leftarrow (z \mid t) - (t \gg 1)$.

Corresponding negaFibonacci and odd representations satisfy the remarkable law

$$F_{k_1+m} + \cdots + F_{k_r+m} = (-1)^m (F_{l_1-m} + \cdots + F_{l_s-m}), \qquad \text{for all integers } m.$$

For example, if $N(\alpha) < 0$ the steps above will convert $x = (\alpha 0)_2$ to $y = (\beta)_2$, where $F((\beta \gg 2)0) = -N(\alpha)$. Furthermore β is the odd code for negaFibonacci α if and only if α^R is the odd code for negaFibonacci β^R, when $|\alpha| = |\beta|$ is odd and $N(\alpha) > 0$.

No finite 2-adic chain will go the other way, by Corollary I, because the Fibonacci code 10^k corresponds to negaFibonacci 10^{k+1} when k is odd, $(10)^{k/2}1$ when k is even. But if γ is a standard Fibonacci codeword we can compute $y = (\beta)_2$ from $z = (\gamma)_2$ by setting $y \leftarrow z \ll 1$, $t \leftarrow y \,\&\, -y \,\&\, \bar{\mu}_0$, $y \leftarrow (t{=}0?\ y : y - 1 - ((t-1) \,\&\, \bar{\mu}_0))$. And the method above will compute α^R from β^R. The overall running time for conversion from standard to negaFibonacci form will then be of order $\log |\gamma|$, for two string reversals.

160. The text's rules are actually incomplete: They should also define the orientation of each neighbor. Let us stipulate that $\alpha_{sn} = \alpha$; $\alpha_{en} = \alpha$; $(\alpha 0)_{wn} = \alpha 0$, $(\alpha 1)_{wo} = \alpha 1$; $(\alpha 00)_{ns} = \alpha 00$, $(\alpha 10)_{nw} = \alpha 10$, $(\alpha 1)_{ne} = \alpha 1$; $(\alpha 0)_{oo} = \alpha 0$, $(\alpha 101)_{oo} = \alpha 101$, $(\alpha 1001)_{oo} = \alpha 1001$, $(\alpha 0001)_{ow} = \alpha 0001$. Then a case analysis proves that all cells within d steps of the starting cell have a consistent labeling and orientation, by induction on the graph distance d. (Note the identity $\alpha+ = ((\alpha 0)-) \gg 1$.) Furthermore the labeling remains consistent when we attach y coordinates and move when necessary from one strip to another via the δ-rules of (153).

161. Yes, it is bipartite, because all of its edges are defined by the boundary lines. (The hyperbolic *cylinder* can't be bicolored; but two adjacent strips, y mod 2, can.)

162. It's convenient to view the hyperbolic plane through another lens, by mapping its points to the upper halfplane $\Im z > 0$. Then the "straight lines" become semicircles centered on the x-axis, together with vertical halflines as a limiting case. In this representation, the edges $|z-1| = \sqrt{2}$, $|z| = r$, and $\Re z = 0$ define a 36°-45°-90° triangle if $r^2 = \phi + \sqrt{\phi}$. Every triangle ABC has three neighbors CBA', ACB', and BAC', obtained by "reflecting" two of its edges about the third, where the reflection of $|z - c'| = r'$ about $|z - c| = r$ is $|z - c - \frac{1}{2}(x_1 + x_2)| = \frac{1}{2}|x_1 - x_2|$, $x_j = r^2/(c' \pm r' - c)$.

The mapping $z \mapsto (z - z_0)/(z - \bar{z}_0)$ takes the upper halfplane into the unit circle; when $z_0 = \frac{1}{2}(\sqrt{\phi} - 1/\phi)(1 + 5^{1/4}i)$ the central pentagon will be symmetric. Repeated reflections of the initial triangle, using breadth-first search until reaching triangles that are invisible, will lead to Fig. 14. To get just the pentagons (without the gray lines), one can begin with just the central cell and perform reflections about *its* edges, etc.

163. (This figure can be drawn as in exercise 162, starting with vertices that project to the three points ir, $ir\omega$, and $ir\omega^2$, where $r^2 = \frac{1}{2}(1+\sqrt{2})(4-\sqrt{2}-\sqrt{6})$ and $\omega = e^{2\pi i/3}$. Using a notation devised by L. Schläfli in 1852, it can be described as the infinite tiling with parameters $\{3, 8\}$, meaning that eight triangles meet at every vertex; see Schläfli's *Gesammelte Mathematische Abhandlungen* **1** (1950), 212. Similarly, the pentagrid and the tiling of exercise 154 have Schläfli symbols $\{5, 4\}$ and $\{5, 5\}$, respectively.)

164. The original definition requires more computation, even though it can be factored:

$$\text{custer}'(X) = X \mathbin{\&} \sim(Y_{\text{N}} \mathbin{\&} Y \mathbin{\&} Y_{\text{S}}), \qquad Y = X_{\text{W}} \mathbin{\&} X \mathbin{\&} X_{\text{E}}.$$

But the main reason for preferring (157) is that it produces a thinner, kingwise connected border. The rookwise connected border that results from the 1957 definition is less attractive, because it's noticeably darker when the border travels diagonally than when it travels horizontally or vertically. (Try some experiments and you'll see.)

165. The first image $X^{(1)}$ is the "outer" border of the original black pixels. Fingerprint-like whorls are formed thereafter. For example, starting with Fig. 15(a) we get

in a 120×120 bitmap, eventually alternating endlessly between two bizarre patterns. (Does *every* nonempty $M \times N$ bitmap lead to such a 2-cycle?)

166. If $X = \text{custer}(X)$, the sum of the elements of $X + (X \mathbin{\wedge} 1) + (X \ll 1) + (X \gg 1) + (X \mathbin{\vee} 1)$ is at most $4MN + 2M + 2N$, since it is at most 4 in each cell of the rectangle and at most 1 in the adjacent cells. This sum is also five times the number of black pixels. Hence $f(M, N) \le \frac{4}{5}MN + \frac{2}{5}M + \frac{2}{5}N$. Conversely we get $f(M, N) \ge \frac{4}{5}MN - \frac{2}{5}$ by letting the pixel in row i and column j be black unless $(i + 2j) \bmod 5 = 2$. (This problem is equivalent to finding a minimum dominating set of the $M \times N$ grid.)

167. (a) With 17 steps we can construct a half adder and three full adders (see 7.1.2–(23)) so that $(z_1 z_2)_2 = x_{\text{NW}} + x_{\text{W}} + x_{\text{SW}}$, $(z_3 z_4)_2 = x_{\text{N}} + x_{\text{S}}$, $(z_5 z_6)_2 = x_{\text{NE}} + x_{\text{E}} + x_{\text{SE}}$, and $(z_7 z_8)_2 = z_2 + z_4 + z_6$. Then $f = S_1(z_1, z_3, z_5, z_7) \wedge (x \vee z_8)$, where the symmetric function S_1 needs seven operations by Fig. 9 in Section 7.1.2. [This solution is based on ideas of W. F. Mann and D. Sleator.]

(b) Given $x^- = X_{j-1}^{(t)}$, $x = X_j^{(t)}$, and $x^+ = X_{j+1}^{(t)}$, compute $a \leftarrow x^- \mathbin{\&} x^+ (= z_3)$, $b \leftarrow x^- \oplus x^+ (= z_4)$, $c \leftarrow x \mathbin{\&} b$, $d \leftarrow c \gg 1 (= z_6)$, $c \leftarrow c \ll 1 (= z_2)$, $e \leftarrow c \oplus d$, $c \leftarrow c \mathbin{\&} d$, $f \leftarrow b \mathbin{\&} e$, $f \leftarrow f \mid c (= z_7)$, $e \leftarrow b \oplus e (= z_8)$, $c \leftarrow x \mathbin{\&} b$, $c \leftarrow c \mid a$, $b \leftarrow c \ll 1 (= z_5)$, $c \leftarrow c \gg 1 (= z_1)$, $d \leftarrow b \mathbin{\&} c$, $c \leftarrow b \mid c$, $b \leftarrow a \mathbin{\&} f$, $f \leftarrow a \mid f$, $f \leftarrow d \mid f$, $c \leftarrow b \mid c$, $f \leftarrow f \oplus c (= S_1(z_1, z_3, z_5, z_7))$, $e \leftarrow e \mid x$, $f \leftarrow f \mathbin{\&} e$.

> *At last I've got what I wanted — an apparently unpredictable law of genetics.*
> *... Overpopulation, like underpopulation, tends to kill.*
> *A healthy society is neither too dense nor too sparse.*
> — JOHN H. CONWAY, letter to Martin Gardner (March 1970)

[For excellent summaries of the joys and passions of Life, including a proof that any Turing machine can be simulated, see Martin Gardner, *Wheels, Life and Other*

Mathematical Amusements (1983), Chapters 20–22; E. R. Berlekamp, J. H. Conway, and R. K. Guy, *Winning Ways 4* (A K Peters, 2004), Chapter 25.]

168. The following algorithm, which uses four n-bit registers x^-, x, x^+, and y, works properly even when $M = 1$ or $N = 1$. It needs only about two reads and two writes per raster word to transform $X^{(t)}$ to $X^{(t+1)}$ in (158):

C1. [Loop on k.] Set $A_{j0} \leftarrow 0$ for $0 \le j < M$. Then do step C2 for $k = 1, 2, \ldots,$ N'. Then go to C5.

C2. [Loop on j.] Set $x \leftarrow A_{(M-1)k}$, $x^+ \leftarrow A_{0k}$, and $A_{Mk} \leftarrow x^+$. Then perform steps C3 and C4 for $j = 0, 1, \ldots, M - 1$.

C3. [Move down.] Set $x^- \leftarrow x$, $x \leftarrow x^+$, and $x^+ \leftarrow A_{(j+1)k}$. (Now $x = A_{jk}$, and x^- holds the former value of $A_{(j-1)k}$.) Compute the bitwise function values $y \leftarrow f(x^- \gg 1, x^-, x^- \ll 1, x \gg 1, x, x \ll 1, x^+ \gg 1, x^+, x^+ \ll 1)$.

C4. [Update A_{jk}.] Set $x^- \leftarrow A_{j(k-1)} \,\&\, -2$, $y \leftarrow y \,\&\, (2^{n-1} - 1)$, $A_{j(k-1)} \leftarrow x^- + (y \gg (n-2))$, $A_{jk} \leftarrow y + (x^- \ll (n-2))$.

C5. [Wrap around.] For $0 \le j < M$, set $x \leftarrow A_{jN'} \,\&\, -2^{n-1-d}$, $A_{jN'} \leftarrow x + (A_{j1} \gg d)$, and $A_{j1} \leftarrow A_{j1} + (x \ll d)$, where $d = 1 + (N-1) \bmod (n-2)$. ∎

[In many cases, like (157) and (159) and even (161), an $M \times N$ torus is equivalent to an $(M-1) \times (N-1)$ array surrounded by zeros. For exercise 173 we can clean an $(M-2) \times (N-2)$ array that is bordered by two rows and columns of zeros. But Life images (exercise 167) can grow without bound; they can't safely be confined to a torus.]

169. It quickly morphs into a rabbit, which proceeds to explode. Beginning at time 278, all activity stabilizes to a two-cycle formed from a set of traffic lights and three additional blinkers, together with three still lifes (tub, boat, and bee hive).

170. If $M \ge 2$ and $N \ge 2$, the first step blanks out the top row and the rightmost column. Then if $M \ge 3$ and $N \ge 3$, the next step blanks out the bottom row and the leftmost column. So in general we're left after $t = \min(M, N) - 1$ steps with a single row or column of black pixels: The first $\lceil t/2 \rceil$ rows, the last $\lceil t/2 \rceil$ columns, the last $\lfloor t/2 \rfloor$ rows, and the first $\lfloor t/2 \rfloor$ columns have been set to zero. The automaton will stop after making two more (nonproductive) cycles.

171. Without (160): $x_1 \leftarrow x_{\rm SE} \,\&\, \bar{x}_{\rm N}$, $x_2 \leftarrow x_{\rm N} \,\&\, \bar{x}_{\rm SE}$, $x_3 \leftarrow x_{\rm E} \,\&\, \bar{x}_1$, $x_4 \leftarrow x_{\rm NE} \,\&\, \bar{x}_2$, $x_5 \leftarrow x_3 \mid x_4$, $x_6 \leftarrow x_{\rm W} \,\&\, \bar{x}_5$, $x_7 \leftarrow x_1 \,\&\, \bar{x}_{\rm NE}$, $x_8 \leftarrow x_7 \,\&\, \bar{x}_{\rm NW}$, $x_9 \leftarrow x_{\rm E} \mid x_{\rm SW}$, $x_{10} \leftarrow x_8 \,\&\, x_9$, $x_{11} \leftarrow x_{10} \mid x_6$, $x_{12} \leftarrow x_{\rm S} \,\&\, x_{11}$, $x_{13} \leftarrow x_2 \,\&\, \bar{x}_{\rm E}$, $x_{14} \leftarrow x_{13} \,\&\, x_{\rm W}$, $x_{15} \leftarrow x_{\rm N} \,\&\, x_{\rm NE}$, $x_{16} \leftarrow x_{\rm SW} \,\&\, x_{\rm W}$, $x_{17} \leftarrow x_{15} \mid x_{16}$, $x_{18} \leftarrow x_{\rm NE} \,\&\, x_{\rm SW}$, $x_{19} \leftarrow x_{17} \,\&\, \bar{x}_{18}$, $x_{20} \leftarrow x_{\rm E} \mid x_{\rm SE}$, $x_{21} \leftarrow x_{20} \mid x_{\rm S}$, $x_{22} \leftarrow x_{\rm NW} \,\&\, \bar{x}_{21}$, $x_{23} \leftarrow x_{22} \,\&\, x_{19}$, $x_{24} \leftarrow x_{12} \mid x_{14}$, $g \leftarrow x_{23} \mid x_{24}$. With (160), set $x_4 \leftarrow x_{\rm NE} \,\&\, \bar{x}_{\rm N}$ and leave everything else the same.

172. The statement isn't quite true; consider the following examples:

The 'I' and 'H' at the left show that pixels are sometimes left intact where paths join, and that rotating by 90° can make a difference. The next two examples illustrate a quirky influence of left-right reflection. The diamond example demonstrates that very thick images can be unthinnable; none of its black pixels can be removed without changing the number of holes. The final examples, one of which was inspired by the answer to exercise 166, were processed first without (160), in which case they are unchanged by the transformation. But with (160) they're thinned dramatically.

173. (a) The hint is readily verified. Notice that if X and Y are closed, $X \& Y$ is closed; if X and Y are open, $X \mid Y$ is open. Thus X^D is closed and X^L is open; $X^{DD} = X^D$ and $X^{LL} = X^L$. (In fact we have $X^L = \sim(\sim X)^D$, because the definitions are dual, obtained by swapping black with white.) Now $X^{DL} \subseteq X^D$, so $X^{DLD} \subseteq X^{DD} = X^D$. And dually, $X^L \subseteq X^{LDL}$. We conclude that there's no reason to launder a clean picture: $X^{DLDL} = (X^{DLD})^L \subseteq X^{DL} \subseteq (X^D)^{LDL} = X^{DLDL}$.

(b) We have $X^D = (X \mid X_{\mathrm{W}} \mid X_{\mathrm{NW}} \mid X_{\mathrm{N}}) \& (X \mid X_{\mathrm{N}} \mid X_{\mathrm{NE}} \mid X_{\mathrm{E}}) \& (X \mid X_{\mathrm{E}} \mid X_{\mathrm{SE}} \mid X_{\mathrm{S}}) \& (X \mid X_{\mathrm{S}} \mid X_{\mathrm{SW}} \mid X_{\mathrm{W}})$. Furthermore, in analogy with answer 167(b), this function can be computed from x^-, x, and x^+ in ten broadword steps: $f \leftarrow x \mid (x \gg 1) \mid ((x^- \mid (x^- \gg 1)) \& (x^+ \mid (x^+ \gg 1)))$, $f \leftarrow f \& (f \ll 1)$. [This answer incorporates ideas of D. R. Fuchs.]

To get X^L, just interchange $\mid$ and $\&$. [For further discussion, see C. Van Wyk and D. E. Knuth, Report STAN-CS-79-707 (Stanford Univ., 1979), 15–36. See also J. Serra, *Image Analysis and Mathematical Morphology* (1982).]

174. Three-dimensional digital topology has been studied by R. Malgouyres, *Theoretical Computer Science* **186** (1997), 1–41.

175. There are 25 in the outline, $2 + 3$ in the eyes, $1 + 1$ in the ears, 4 in the nose, and 1 in the smile, totalling 37. (All white pixels are connected kingwise to the background.)

176. (a) If v isn't isolated, there are eight easy cases to consider, depending on what kind of neighbor v has in G.

(b) Some $w' \in G'$ is adjacent or equal to each vertex of $N_u \cup N_v$. (Four cases.)

(c) Yes. In fact, by definition (161), we always have $|S'(v')| \geq 2$.

(d) Let $N'_{v'} = \{v \mid v' \in N_v\}$. If v' is the east neighbor of u', call it u'_{E}, either $u' \in G$ or $u'_{\mathrm{S}} \in G$; this element is equal-or-adjacent to every vertex of $N'_{u'} \cup N'_{v'}$. A similar argument applies when $v' = u'_{\mathrm{N}}$. If $v' = u'_{\mathrm{NE}}$, there's no problem if $u' \in G$. Otherwise $u'_{\mathrm{W}} \in G$, $u'_{\mathrm{S}} \in G$, and either $u'_{\mathrm{N}} \in G$ or $u'_{\mathrm{E}} \in G$; hence $N'_{u'} \cup N'_{v'}$ is connected in G. Finally if $v' = u'_{\mathrm{SE}}$, the proof is easy if $u'_{\mathrm{S}} \in G$; otherwise $u' \in G$ and $v' \in G$.

(e) Given a nontrivial component C of G, with $v \in C$ and $v' \in S(v)$, let C' be the component of G' that contains v'. This component C' is well defined, by (a) and (b). Given a component C' of G', with $v' \in C'$ and $v \in S'(v')$, let C be the component of G that contains v. This component C is nontrivial and well defined, by (c) and (d). Finally, the correspondence $C \leftrightarrow C'$ is one-to-one.

177. Now the vertices of G are the *white* pixels, adjacent when they are *rook*-neighbors. So we define $N_{(i,j)} = \{(i,j), (i-1,j), (i,j+1)\}$. Arguments like those of answer 176, but simpler, establish a one-to-one correspondence between the nontrivial components of G and the components of G'.

178. Observe that in adjacent rows of X^*, two pixels of the same value are kingwise neighbors only if they are rookwise connected.

179. The pixels $x_1 \ldots x_N$ of each row can be "runlength encoded" as a sequence of integers $0 = c_0 < c_1 < \cdots < c_{2m+1} = N+2$ so that $x_j = 0$ for $j \in [c_0 \mathinner{.\,.} c_1) \cup [c_2 \mathinner{.\,.} c_3) \cup \cdots \cup [c_{2m} \mathinner{.\,.} c_{2m+1})$ and $x_j = 1$ for $j \in [c_1 \mathinner{.\,.} c_2) \cup \cdots \cup [c_{2m-1} \mathinner{.\,.} c_{2m})$. (The number of runs per row tends to be reasonably small in most images. Notice that the background condition $x_0 = x_{N+1} = 0$ is implicitly assumed.)

The algorithm below uses a modified encoding with $a_j = 2c_j - (j \bmod 2)$ for $0 \leq j \leq 2m+1$. For example, the second row of the Cheshire cat has $(c_1, c_2, c_3, c_4, c_5) = (5, 8, 23, 25, 32)$; we will use $(a_1, a_2, a_3, a_4, a_5) = (9, 16, 45, 50, 63)$ instead. The reason is that white runs of adjacent rows are rookwise adjacent if and only if the corresponding

intervals $[a_j \, . \, . \, a_{j+1})$ and $[b_k \, . \, . \, b_{k+1})$ overlap, and exactly the same condition characterizes when black runs of adjacent rows are kingwise adjacent. Thus the modified
encoding nicely unifies both cases (see exercise 178).

We construct a triply linked tree of current components, where each node has
several fields: CHILD, SIB, and PARENT (tree links); DORMANT (a circular list, via SIB
links, of all former children that aren't connected to the current row); HEIR (a node
that has absorbed this one); ROW and COL (location of the first pixel); and AREA (the
total number of pixels in the component).

The algorithm traverses the tree in *double order* (see exercise 2.3.1–18), using
pairs of pointers (P, P'), where $P' = P$ when P is traversed the first time, $P' = $ PARENT(P)
when P is traversed the second time. The successor of (P, P') is $(Q, Q') = $ next(P, P'),
determined as follows: If $P = P'$, then $Q \leftarrow Q' \leftarrow $ CHILD(P) if CHILD(P) $\neq \Lambda$, otherwise
$Q \leftarrow P$ and $Q' \leftarrow $ PARENT(Q). If $P \neq P'$, then $Q \leftarrow Q' \leftarrow $ SIB(P) if SIB(P) $\neq \Lambda$, otherwise
$Q \leftarrow $ PARENT(P) and $Q' \leftarrow $ PARENT(Q).

When there are m black runs, the tree will have $m + 1$ nodes, not counting nodes
that are dormant or have been absorbed. Moreover, the primed pointers $P'_1, \ldots, P'_{2m+1}$
of the double traversal $(P_1, P'_1), \ldots, (P_{2m+1}, P'_{2m+1})$ are precisely the components of
the current row, in left-to-right order. For example, in (163) we have $m = 5$; and
$(P'_1, \ldots, P'_{11})$ point respectively to ⓪, Ⓑ, ①, Ⓑ, ⓪, Ⓒ, ⓪, Ⓐ, ②, Ⓐ, ⓪.

I1. [Initialize.] Set $t \leftarrow 1$, ROOT $\leftarrow$ LOC(NODE(0)), CHILD(ROOT) $\leftarrow$ SIB(ROOT) $\leftarrow$
PARENT(ROOT) $\leftarrow$ DORMANT(ROOT) $\leftarrow$ HEIR(ROOT) $\leftarrow \Lambda$. Also set ROW(ROOT) $\leftarrow$
COL(ROOT) $\leftarrow 0$, AREA(ROOT) $\leftarrow N + 2$, $s \leftarrow 0$, $a_0 \leftarrow b_0 \leftarrow 0$, $a_1 \leftarrow 2N + 3$.

I2. [Input a new row.] Terminate if $s > M$. Otherwise set $b_k \leftarrow a_k$ for $k = 1, 2,$
$\ldots$, until $b_k = 2N + 3$; then set $b_{k+1} \leftarrow b_k$ as a "stopper." Set $s \leftarrow s + 1$. If
$s > M$, set $a_1 \leftarrow 2N + 3$; otherwise let $a_1, \ldots, a_{2m+1}$ be the modified runlength
encoding of row s as discussed above. (This encoding can be obtained with the
help of the ρ function; see (43).) Set $j \leftarrow k \leftarrow 1$ and P $\leftarrow$ P' $\leftarrow$ ROOT.

I3. [Gobble up short b's.] If $b_{k+1} \geq a_j$, go to I9. Otherwise set $(Q, Q') \leftarrow$ next(P, P'),
$(R, R') \leftarrow$ next(Q, Q'), and do a four-way branch to (I4, I5, I6, I7) according as
$2[Q \neq Q'] + [R \neq R'] = (0, 1, 2, 3)$.

I4. [Case 0.] (Now $Q = Q'$ is a child of P', and $R = R'$ is the first child of Q'. Node Q
will remain a child of P', but it will be preceded by any children of R.) Absorb
R into P' (see below). Set CHILD(Q) $\leftarrow$ SIB(R) and $Q' \leftarrow$ CHILD(R). If $Q' \neq \Lambda$,
set $R \leftarrow Q'$, and while $R \neq \Lambda$ set PARENT(R) $\leftarrow P'$, $R \leftarrow$ SIB(R); then SIB(R) $\leftarrow Q$,
$Q \leftarrow Q'$. If $P = P'$, set CHILD(P) $\leftarrow Q$; otherwise SIB(P) $\leftarrow Q$. Go to I8.

I5. [Case 1.] (Now component $Q = R$ is surrounded by $P' = R'$.) If $P = P'$, set
CHILD(P) $\leftarrow$ SIB(Q); otherwise set SIB(P) $\leftarrow$ SIB(Q). Set $R \leftarrow$ DORMANT(R').
Then if $R = \Lambda$, set DORMANT(R') $\leftarrow$ SIB(Q) $\leftarrow Q$; otherwise SIB(Q) $\leftarrow$ SIB(R) and
SIB(R) $\leftarrow Q$. Go to I8.

I6. [Case 2.] (Now Q' is the parent of both P' and R. Either $P = P'$ is childless, or
P is the last child of P'.) Absorb R into P' (see below). Set SIB(P') $\leftarrow$ SIB(R)
and $R \leftarrow$ CHILD(R). If $P = P'$, set CHILD(P) $\leftarrow$ R; otherwise SIB(P) $\leftarrow$ R. While
$R \neq \Lambda$, set PARENT(R) $\leftarrow P'$ and $R \leftarrow$ SIB(R). Go to I8.

I7. [Case 3.] (Node $P' = Q$ is the last child of $Q' = R$, which is a child of R'.) Absorb P'
into R' (see below). If $P = P'$, set P $\leftarrow$ R. Otherwise set $P' \leftarrow$ CHILD(P'), and while
$P' \neq \Lambda$ set PARENT(P') $\leftarrow R'$, $P' \leftarrow$ SIB(P'); also set SIB(P) $\leftarrow$ SIB(Q'), SIB(Q') $\leftarrow$

CHILD(Q). If Q = CHILD(R), set CHILD(R) ← Λ. Otherwise set R ← CHILD(R), then R ← SIB(R) until SIB(R) = Q, then SIB(R) ← Λ. Finally set P' ← R'.

I8. [Advance k.] Set $k \leftarrow k + 2$ and return to step I3.

I9. [Update the area.] Set AREA(P') ← AREA(P') + $\lceil a_j/2 \rceil - \lceil a_{j-1}/2 \rceil$. Then go back to I2 if $a_j = 2N + 3$.

I10. [Gobble up short a.] If $a_{j+1} \geq b_k$, go to I11. Otherwise set Q ← LOC(NODE(t)) and $t \leftarrow t + 1$. Set PARENT(Q) ← P', DORMANT(Q) ← HEIR(Q) ← Λ; also ROW(Q) ← s, COL(Q) ← $\lceil a_j/2 \rceil$, AREA(Q) ← $\lceil a_{j+1}/2 \rceil - \lceil a_j/2 \rceil$. If P = P', set SIB(Q) ← CHILD(P) and CHILD(P) ← Q; otherwise set SIB(Q) ← SIB(P) and SIB(P) ← Q. Finally set P ← Q, $j \leftarrow j + 2$, and return to I3.

I11. [Move on.] Set $j \leftarrow j + 1$, $k \leftarrow k + 1$, (P, P') ← next(P, P'), and go to I3. ∎

To "absorb P into Q" means to do the following things: If (ROW(P), COL(P)) is less than (ROW(Q), COL(Q)), set (ROW(Q), COL(Q)) ← (ROW(P), COL(P)). Set AREA(Q) ← AREA(P) + AREA(Q). If DORMANT(Q) = Λ, set DORMANT(Q) ← DORMANT(P); otherwise if DORMANT(P) ≠ Λ, swap SIB(DORMANT(P)) ↔ SIB(DORMANT(Q)). Finally, set HEIR(P) ← Q. (The HEIR links could be used on a second pass to identify the final component of each pixel. Notice that the PARENT links of dormant nodes are not kept up to date.)

[A similar algorithm was given by R. K. Lutz in *Comp. J.* **23** (1980), 262–269.]

180. Let $F(x, y) = x^2 - y^2 + 13$ and $Q(x, y) = F(x - \frac{1}{2}, y - \frac{1}{2}) = x^2 - y^2 - x + y + 13$. Apply Algorithm T to digitize the hyperbola from $(\xi, \eta) = (-6, 7)$ to $(\xi', \eta') = (0, \sqrt{13})$; hence $x = -6$, $y = 7$, $x' = 0$, $y' = 4$. The resulting edges are $(-6, 7) \!-\! (-5, 7) \!-\! (-5, 6) \!-\! (-4, 6) \!-\! (-4, 5) \!-\! (-3, 5) \!-\! (-3, 4) \!-\! \cdots \!-\! (0, 4)$. Then apply it again with $\xi = 0$, $\eta = \sqrt{13}$, $\xi' = 6$, $\eta' = 7$, $x = 0$, $y = 4$, $x' = 6$, $y' = 7$; the same edges are found (in reverse order), but with negated x coordinates.

181. Subdivide at points (ξ, η) where $F_x(\xi, \eta) = 0$ or $F_y(\xi, \eta) = 0$, namely at the real roots of $\{Q(-(b(\eta + \frac{1}{2}) + d)/(2a), \eta + \frac{1}{2}) = 0, \ \xi = -(b(\eta + \frac{1}{2}) + d)/(2a) - \frac{1}{2}\}$ or of $\{Q(\xi + \frac{1}{2}, -(b(\xi + \frac{1}{2}) + e)/(2c)) = 0, \ \eta = -(b(\xi + \frac{1}{2}) + e)/(2c) - \frac{1}{2}\}$, if they exist.

182. By induction on $|x' - x| + |y' - y|$. Consider, for example, the case $x > x'$ and $y < y'$. We know from (iii) that (ξ, η) lies in the box $x - \frac{1}{2} \leq \xi < x + \frac{1}{2}$ and $y - \frac{1}{2} \leq \eta < y + \frac{1}{2}$, and from (ii) that the curve travels monotonically as it moves from (ξ, η) to (ξ', η'). It must therefore exit the box at the edge $(x - \frac{1}{2}, y - \frac{1}{2}) \!-\! (x - \frac{1}{2}, y + \frac{1}{2})$ or $(x - \frac{1}{2}, y + \frac{1}{2}) \!-\! (x + \frac{1}{2}, y + \frac{1}{2})$. The latter holds if and only if $F(x - \frac{1}{2}, y + \frac{1}{2}) < 0$, because the curve can't intersect that edge twice when $x' < x$. And $F(x - \frac{1}{2}, y + \frac{1}{2})$ is the value $Q(x, y + 1)$ that is tested in step T4, because of the initialization in step T1. (We assume that the curve doesn't go *exactly* through $(x - \frac{1}{2}, y + \frac{1}{2})$, by implicitly adding a tiny positive amount to the function F behind the scenes.)

183. Consider, for example, the ellipse defined by $F(x - \frac{1}{2}, y - \frac{1}{2}) = Q(x, y) = 13x^2 + 7xy + y^2 - 2 = 0$; this ellipse is a cigar-shaped curve that extends roughly between $(-2, 5)$ and $(1, -6)$. Suppose we want to digitize its upper right boundary. Hypotheses (i)–(iv) of Algorithm T hold with

$$\xi = \sqrt{\frac{8}{3}} - \frac{1}{2}, \quad \eta = -\sqrt{\frac{98}{3}} - \frac{1}{2}, \quad \xi' = -\sqrt{\frac{98}{39}} - \frac{1}{2}, \quad \eta' = \sqrt{\frac{104}{3}} - \frac{1}{2},$$

$x = 1$, $y = -6$, $x' = -2$, $y' = 5$. Step T1 sets Q ← $Q(1, -5) = 1$, which causes step T4 to move left (L); in fact, the resulting path is L^3U^{11}, while the correct digitization according to (164) is $\text{U}^3\text{LU}^4\text{LU}^3\text{LU}$. Failure occurred because $Q(x, y) = 0$ has two roots on the edge $(1, -5) \!-\! (2, -5)$, namely $((35 \pm -\sqrt{29})/26, -5)$, causing $Q(1, -5)$

to have the same sign as $Q(2, -5)$. (One of those roots is on the boundary we are *not* trying to draw, but it's still there.) Similar failure occurs with the parabola defined by $Q(x, y) = 9x^2 + 6xy + y^2 - y = 0$, $\xi = -5/12$, $\eta = -1/4$, $\xi' = -5/2$, $\eta' = -19/2$, $x = 0$, $y = 0$, $x' = -2$, $y' = 9$. Hyperbolas can fail too (consider $6x^2 + 5xy + y^2 = 1$).

Algorithms for discrete geometry are notoriously delicate; unusual cases tend to drive them berserk. Algorithm T works properly for portions of any ellipse or parabola whose maximum curvature is less than 2. The maximum curvature of an ellipse with semiaxes $\alpha \geq \beta$ is α/β^2; the cigar-shaped example has maximum curvature ≈ 42.5. The maximum curvature of the parabola $y = \alpha x^2$ is $\alpha/2$; the anomalous parabola above has maximum curvature ≈ 5.27. "Reasonable" conics don't make such sharp turns.

To make Algorithm T work correctly *without* hypothesis (v), we need to slow it down a bit, by changing the tests '$Q < 0$' to '$Q < 0$ or X', where X is a test on the sign of a derivative. Namely, X is respectively '$S > c$', '$R > a$', '$R < -a$', '$S < -c$', in steps T2, T3, T4, T5.

184. Let $Q'(x, y) = -1 - Q(x, y)$. The key point is that $Q(x, y) < 0$ if and only if $Q'(x, y) \geq 0$. (Curiously the algorithm makes the same decisions, backwards, although it probes the values of Q' and Q in different places.)

185. Find a positive integer h so that $d = (\eta - \eta')h$ and $e = (\xi' - \xi)h$ are integers and $d + e$ is even. Then carry out Algorithm T with $x = \lfloor \xi + \frac{1}{2} \rfloor$, $y = \lfloor \eta + \frac{1}{2} \rfloor$, $x' = \lfloor \xi' + \frac{1}{2} \rfloor$, $y' = \lfloor \eta' + \frac{1}{2} \rfloor$, and $Q(x, y) = d(x - \frac{1}{2}) + e(y - \frac{1}{2}) + f$, where

$$f = \lfloor (\eta'\xi - \xi'\eta)h \rfloor - [d > 0 \text{ and } (\eta'\xi - \xi'\eta)h \text{ is an integer}].$$

(The '$d > 0$' term ensures that the opposite straight line, from (ξ', η') back to (ξ, η), will have precisely the same edges; see exercise 184.) Steps T1 and T6–T9 become much simpler than they were in the general case, because $R = d$ and $S = e$ are constant.

(F. G. Stockton [*CACM* **6** (1963), 161, 450] and J. E. Bresenham [*IBM Systems Journal* **4** (1965), 25–30] gave similar algorithms, but with diagonal edges permitted.)

186. (a) $B(\epsilon) = z_0 + 2\epsilon(z_1 - z_0) + O(\epsilon^2)$; $B(1 - \epsilon) = z_2 - 2\epsilon(z_2 - z_1) + O(\epsilon^2)$.

(b) Every point of $S(z_0, z_1, z_2)$ is a convex combination of z_0, z_1, and z_2.

(c) Obviously true, since $(1 - t)^2 + 2(1 - t)t + t^2 = 1$.

(d) The collinear condition follows from (b). Otherwise, by (c), we need only consider the case $z_0 = 0$ and $z_2 - 2z_1 = 1$, where $z_1 = x_1 + iy_1$ and $y_1 \neq 0$. In that case all points lie on the parabola $4x = (y/y_1)^2 + 4yx_1/y_1$.

(e) Note that $B(u\theta) = (1-u)^2 z_0 + 2u(1-u)((1-\theta)z_0 + \theta z_1) + u^2 B(\theta)$ for $0 \leq u \leq 1$.

[S. N. Bernshteĭn introduced $B_n(z_0, z_1, \ldots, z_n; t) = \sum_k \binom{n}{k}(1 - t)^{n-k} t^k z_k$ in *Soobshcheniiâ Khar'kovskoe matematicheskoe obshchestvo* (2) **13** (1912), 1–2.]

187. We can assume that $z_0 = (x_0, y_0)$, $z_1 = (x_1, y_1)$, and $z_2 = (x_2, y_2)$, where the coordinates are (say) fixed-point numbers represented as 16-bit integers divided by 32.

If z_0, z_1, and z_2 are collinear, use the method of exercise 185 to draw a straight line from z_0 to z_2. (If z_1 doesn't lie between z_0 and z_2, the other edges will cancel out, because edges are implicitly XORed by a filling algorithm.) This case occurs if and only if $D = x_0 y_1 + x_1 y_2 + x_2 y_0 - x_1 y_0 - x_2 y_1 - x_0 y_2 = 0$.

Otherwise the points (x, y) of $S(z_0, z_1, z_2)$ satisfy $F(x, y) = 0$, where

$$F(x, y) = ((x - x_0)(y_2 - 2y_1 + y_0) - (y - y_0)(x_2 - 2x_1 + x_0))^2$$
$$- 4D((x_1 - x_0)(y - y_0) - (y_1 - y_0)(x - x_0))$$

and D is defined above. We multiply by 32^4 to obtain integer coefficients; then negate this formula and subtract 1, if $D < 0$, to satisfy condition (iv) of Algorithm T and the reverse-order condition. (See exercise 184.)

The monotonicity condition (ii) holds if and only if $(x_1 - x_0)(x_2 - x_1) \geq 0$ and $(y_1 - y_0)(y_2 - y_1) \geq 0$. If necessary, we can use the recurrence of exercise 186(e) to break $S(z_0, z_1, z_2)$ into at most three monotonic subsquines; for example, setting $\theta = (x_0 - x_1)/(x_0 - 2x_1 + x_2)$ will achieve monotonicity in x. (A slight rounding error may occur during this fixed point arithmetic, but the recurrence can be performed in such a way that the subsquines are definitely monotonic.)

Notes: When z_0, z_1, and z_2 are near each other, a simpler and faster method based on exercise 186(e) with $\theta = \frac{1}{2}$ is adequate for most practical purposes, if one doesn't care about making the exactly correct choice between local edge sequences like "up-then-left" versus "left-then-up." In the late 1980s, Sampo Kaasila chose to use squines as the basic method of shape specification in the TrueType font format, because they can be digitized so rapidly. The METAFONT system achieves greater flexibility with cubic Bézier splines [see D. E. Knuth, *METAFONT: The Program* (Addison–Wesley, 1986)], but at the cost of extra processing time. A fairly fast "six-register algorithm" for the resulting cubic curves was, however, developed subsequently by John Hobby [*ACM Trans. on Graphics* **9** (1990), 262–277]. Vaughan Pratt introduced *conic splines*, which are sort of midway between squines and Bézier cubics, in *Computer Graphics* **19**, 3 (July 1985), 151–159. Conic spline segments can be elliptical and hyperbolic as well as parabolic, hence they require fewer intermediate points and control points than squines; furthermore, they can be handled by Algorithm T.

188. The following big-endian program assumes that $n \leq 74880$.

```
        LOC   Data_Segment                LDO   k,Initk
BITMAP  LOC   @+M*N/8            0H  SET   s,N/64
base    GREG  @                 1H  SET   a,h         A trick (see below)
GRAYMAP LOC   @+M*N/64              SET   r,8
GTAB    BYTE  255,252,249,246,243  2H  LDOU  t,base,k
        BYTE  240,236,233,230,227      MOR   u,c1,t
        BYTE  224,221,217,214,211      SUBU  t,t,u       (Nypwise sums)
        BYTE  208,204,201,198,194      MOR   u,c2,t
        BYTE  191,188,184,181,178      AND   t,t,mu1
        BYTE  174,171,167,164,160      ADDU  t,t,u       (Nybblewise sums)
        BYTE  157,153,150,146,142      MOR   u,c3,t
        BYTE  139,135,131,128,124      AND   t,t,mu2
        BYTE  120,116,112,108,104      ADDU  t,t,u       (Bytewise sums)
        BYTE  100,96,92,88,84          ADDU  a,a,t
        BYTE  79,75,70,66,61           INCL  k,N/8       Move to next row.
        BYTE  56,52,46,41,36           SUB   r,r,1
        BYTE  30,24,18,10,0            PBNZ  r,2B        Repeat 8 times.
Initk   OCTA  BITMAP-GRAYMAP    3H  SRU   t,a,56
corr    GREG  N-8                   LDBU  t,gtab,t
c1      GREG  #4000100004000100      SLU   a,a,8
c2      GREG  #2010000002010000      STBU  t,z,0
c3      GREG  #0804020100000000      INCL  z,1
mu1     GREG  #3333333333333333      PBN   a,3B        (The trick)
mu2     GREG  #0f0f0f0f0f0f0f0f      SUB   k,k,corr
h       GREG  #8080808080808080      SUB   s,s,1
gtab    GREG  GTAB-#80               PBNZ  s,1B        Loop on columns.
        LOC   #100                   INCL  k,7*N/8     Loop on groups
MakeGray LDA   z,GRAYMAP             PBN   k,0B        of 8 rows. ∎
```

[Inspired by Neil Hunt's DVIPAGE, the author used such graymaps extensively when preparing new editions of *The Art of Computer Programming* in 1992–1998.]

189. If the rows of the bitmap are $(X_0, X_1, \ldots, X_{63})$, do the following operations for $k = 0, 1, \ldots, 5$: For all i such that $0 \le i < 64$ and $i \,\&\, 2^k = 0$, let $j = i + 2^k$ and either (a) set $t \leftarrow (X_i \oplus (X_j \gg 2^k)) \,\&\, \mu_{6,k}$, $X_i \leftarrow X_i \oplus t$, $X_j \leftarrow X_j \oplus (t \ll 2^k)$; or (b) set $t \leftarrow X_i \,\&\, \bar{\mu}_{6,k}$, $u \leftarrow X_j \,\&\, \mu_{6,k}$, $X_i \leftarrow ((X_i \ll 2^k) \,\&\, \bar{\mu}_{6,k}) \mid u$, $X_j \leftarrow ((X_j \gg 2^k) \,\&\, \mu_{6,k}) \mid t$.

[The basic idea is to transform $2^k \times 2^k$ submatrices for increasing k, as in exercise 5–12. Speedups are possible with MMIX, using MOR and MUX as in exercise 208, and using LDTU/STTU when $k = 5$. See L. J. Guibas and J. Stolfi, *ACM Transactions on Graphics* **1** (1982), 204–207; M. Thorup, *J. Algorithms* **42** (2002), 217. Incidentally, Theorem P and answer 54 show that $\Omega(n \log n)$ operations on n-bit numbers are needed to transpose an $n \times n$ bit matrix. An application that needs frequent transpositions might therefore be better off using a redundant representation, maintaining its matrices in both normal and transposed form.]

190. (a) We must have $\alpha_{j+1} = f(\alpha_j) \oplus \alpha_{j-1}$ for $j \ge 1$, where $\alpha_0 = 0 \ldots 0$ and $f(\alpha) = ((\alpha \ll 1) \,\&\, 1 \ldots 1) \oplus \alpha \oplus (\alpha \gg 1)$. The elements of the bottom row α_m satisfy the parity condition if and only if this rule makes α_{m+1} entirely zero.

(b) True. The parity condition on matrix entries a_{ij} is $a_{ij} = a_{(i-1)j} \oplus a_{i(j-1)} \oplus a_{i(j+1)} \oplus a_{(i+1)j}$, where $a_{ij} = 0$ if $i = 0$ or $i = m + 1$ or $j = 0$ or $j = n + 1$. If two matrices (a_{ij}) and (b_{ij}) satisfy this condition, so does (c_{ij}) when $c_{ij} = a_{ij} \oplus b_{ij}$.

(c) The upper left submatrix consisting of all rows that precede the first all-zero row (if any) and all columns that precede the first all-zero column (if any) is perfect. And this submatrix determines the entire matrix, because the pattern on the other side of a row or column of zeros is the top/bottom or left/right reflection of its neighbor. For example, if $\alpha_{m'+1}$ is zero, then $\alpha_{m'+1+j} = \alpha_{m'+1-j}$ for $1 \le j \le m'$.

(d) Starting with a given vector α_1 and using the rule in (a) will always lead to a row with $\alpha_{m+1} = 0 \ldots 0$. Proof: We must have $(\alpha_j, \alpha_{j+1}) = (\alpha_k, \alpha_{k+1})$ for some $0 \le j < k \le 2^{2n}$, by the pigeonhole principle. If $j > 0$ we also have $(\alpha_{j-1}, \alpha_j) = (\alpha_{k-1}, \alpha_k)$, because $\alpha_{j-1} = f(\alpha_j) \oplus \alpha_{j+1} = f(\alpha_k) \oplus \alpha_{k+1} = \alpha_{k-1}$. Therefore the first repeated pair begins with a row α_k of zeros. Furthermore we have $\alpha_i = \alpha_{k-i}$ for $0 \le i \le k$; hence the first all-zero row α_{m+1} occurs when m is $k - 1$ or $k/2 - 1$.

Rows $\alpha_1, \ldots, \alpha_m$ will form a perfect pattern unless there is a column of 0s. There are $t > 0$ such columns if and only if $t + 1$ is a divisor of $n + 1$ and α_1 has the form $\alpha 0 \alpha^R 0 \ldots 0 \alpha$ (t even) or $\alpha 0 \alpha^R 0 \ldots 0 \alpha^R$ (t odd), where $|\alpha| + 1 = (n + 1)/(t + 1)$.

(e) This starting vector does not have the form forbidden in (d).

191. (a) The former is $\alpha_1, \alpha_2, \ldots$ if and only if the latter is $0 \alpha_1 0 \alpha_1^R$, $0 \alpha_2 0 \alpha_2^R, \ldots$.

(b) Let the binary string $a_0 a_1 \ldots a_{N-1}$ correspond to the polynomial $a_0 + a_1 x + \cdots + a_{N-1} x^{N-1}$, and let $y = x^{-1} + 1 + x$. Then $\alpha_0 = 0 \ldots 0$ corresponds to $F_0(y)$; $\alpha_1 = 10 \ldots 0$ corresponds to $F_1(y)$; and by induction α_j corresponds to $F_j(y)$, mod $x^N + 1$ and mod 2. For example, when $N = 6$ we have $\alpha_2 = 110001 \leftrightarrow 1 + x + x^5$ because $x^{-1} \bmod (x^6 + 1) = x^5$, etc.

(c) Again, induction on j.

(d) The identity in the hint holds by induction on m, because it is clearly true when $m = 1$ and $m = 2$. Working mod 2, this identity yields the simple equations

$$F_{2k}(y) = y F_k(y)^2; \qquad F_{2k-1}(y) = (F_{k-1}(y) + F_k(y))^2.$$

So we can go from the pair $P_k = (F_{k-1}(y) \bmod (x^N + 1), F_k(y) \bmod (x^N + 1))$ to the pair P_{k+1} in $O(n)$ steps, and to the pair P_{2k} in $O(n^2)$ steps. We can therefore compute

$F_j(y) \bmod (x^N + 1)$ after $O(\log j)$ iterations. Multiplying by $f_a(x) + f_a(x^{-1})$ and reducing mod $x^N + 1$ then allows us to read off the value of α_j.

Incidentally, $F_{n+1}(x)$ is the special case $K_n(x, x, \ldots, x)$ of a continuant polynomial; see Eq. 4.5.3–(4). We have $F_{n+1}(x) = \sum_{k=0}^{n} \binom{n-k}{k} x^{n-2k} = i^{-n} U_n(ix/2)$, where U_n is the classical Chebyshev polynomial defined by $U_n(\cos\theta) = \sin((n+1)\theta)/\sin\theta$.

192. (a) By exercise 191(c), $c(q)$ is the least $j > 0$ such that $(x+x^{-1})F_j(x^{-1}+1+x) \equiv 0$ (modulo $x^{2q} + 1$), using polynomial arithmetic mod 2. Equivalently, it's the smallest positive j for which $F_j(y)$ is a multiple of $(x^{2q} + 1)/(x^2 + 1) = (1 + x + \cdots + x^{q-1})^2$, when $y = x^{-1}+1+x$.

(b) Use the method of exercise 191(d) to evaluate $((x + x^{-1})F_j(y)) \bmod (x^{2q} + 1)$ when $j = M/p$, for all prime divisors p of M. If the result is zero, set $M \leftarrow M/p$ and repeat the process. If no such result is zero, $c(q) = M$.

(c) We want to show that $c(2^e)$ is a divisor of $3 \cdot 2^{e-1}$ but not of $3 \cdot 2^{e-2}$ or 2^{e-1}. The latter holds because $F_{2^e-1}(y) = y^{2^{e-1}-1}$ is relatively prime to $x^{2^{e+1}} + 1$. The former holds because

$$F_{3 \cdot 2^e - 1}(y) = y^{2^{e-1}-1} F_3(y)^{2^{e-1}} = y^{2^{e-1}-1}(1 + y)^{2^e} = y^{2^{e-1}-1}(x^{-1}+x)^{2^e},$$

which is $\equiv 0$ modulo $x^{2^{e+1}} + 1$ but not modulo $x^{2^{e+2}} + 1$.

(d) $F_{2^e-1}(y) = \sum_{k=1}^{e} y^{2^e - 2^k}$. Since $y = x^{-1}(1+x+x^2)$ is relatively prime to $x^q + 1$, we have $y^{-1} \equiv a_0 + a_1 x + \cdots + a_{q-1}x^{q-1}$ (modulo $x^q + 1$) for some coefficients a_i; hence

$$y^{-2^k} \equiv a_0 + a_1 x^{2^k} + \cdots + a_{q-1}x^{2^k(q-1)} \equiv a_0 + a_1 x^{2^{k+e}} + \cdots + a_{q-1}x^{2^{k+e}(q-1)} \equiv y^{-2^{k+e}}$$

(modulo $x^q + 1$) for $0 \le k < e$, and it follows that $F_{2^{2e}-1}(y)$ is a multiple of $x^{2q} + 1$.

(e) In this case $c(q)$ divides $4(2^{2e} - 1)$. Proof: Let $x^q + 1 = f_1(x)f_2(x)\ldots f_r(x)$ where $f_1(x) = x + 1$, $f_2(x) = x^2 + x + 1$, and each $f_i(x)$ is irreducible mod 2. Since q is odd, these factors are distinct. Therefore, in the finite field of polynomials mod $f_j(x)$ for $j \ge 3$, we have $y^{-2^k} = y^{-2^{k+e}}$ as in (d). Consequently $F_{2^{2e}-1}(y)$ is a multiple of $f_3(x)\ldots f_r(x) = (x^q + 1)/(x^3 + 1)$. So $F_{4(2^{2e}-1)}(y) = y^3 F_{2^{2e}-1}(y)^4$ is a multiple of $(x^{2q} + 1)/(x^2 + 1) = f_2(x)^2 f_3(x)^2 \ldots f_r(x)^2$ as desired.

(f) If $F_{c(q)}(y)$ is a multiple of $x^{2q}+1$, it's easy to see that $c(2q) = 2c(q)$. Otherwise $F_{3c(q)}(y)$ is a multiple of $F_3(y) = (1 + y)^2 = x^{-2}(1+x)^4$; hence $F_{6c(q)}(y)$ is a multiple of $x^{4q} + 1$ and $c(2q)$ divides $6c(q)$. The latter case can happen only when q is odd.

Notes: Parity patterns are related to a popular puzzle called "Lights Out," which was invented in the early 1980s by Dario Uri, also invented independently about the same time by László Mérő and called ✗LƎ⊇. [See David Singmaster's *Cubic Circular*, issues 7&8 (Summer 1985), 39–42; Dieter Gebhardt, *Cubism For Fun 69* (March 2006), 23–25.] Klaus Sutner has pursued further aspects of this theory in *Theoretical Computer Science* **230** (2000), 49–73.

193. Let $b_{(2i)(2j)} = a_{ij}$, $b_{(2i+1)(2j)} = a_{ij} \oplus a_{(i+1)j}$, $b_{(2i)(2j+1)} = a_{ij} \oplus a_{i(j+1)}$, and $b_{(2i+1)(2j+1)} = 0$, for $0 \le i \le m$ and $0 \le j \le n$, where we regard $a_{ij} = 0$ when $i = 0$ or $i = m+1$ or $j = 0$ or $j = n+1$. We don't have $(b_{(2i)1}, b_{(2i)2}, \ldots, b_{(2i)(2n+1)}) = (0, 0, \ldots, 0)$ because $(a_{i1}, \ldots, a_{in}) \ne (0, \ldots, 0)$ for $1 \le i \le m$. And we don't have $(b_{(2i+1)1}, b_{(2i+1)2}, \ldots, b_{(2i+1)(2n+1)}) = (0, 0, \ldots, 0)$ because adjacent rows $(a_{i1}, \ldots, a_{in})$ and $(a_{(i+1)1}, \ldots, a_{(i+1)n})$ always differ for $0 \le i \le m$ when m is odd.

194. Set $\beta_i \leftarrow (1 \ll (n-i)) \mid (1 \ll (i-1))$ for $1 \le i \le m$, where $m = \lceil n/2 \rceil$. Also set $\gamma_i \leftarrow (\beta_1 \& \alpha_{i1}) + (\beta_2 \& \alpha_{i2}) + \cdots + (\beta_m \& \alpha_{im})$, where α_{ij} is the jth row of the parity pattern that begins with β_i; vector γ_i records the diagonal elements of such a matrix. Then set $r \leftarrow 0$ and apply subroutine N of answer 195 for $i = 1, 2, \ldots, m$. The resulting vectors $\theta_1, \ldots, \theta_r$ are a basis for all $n \times n$ parity patterns with 8-fold symmetry.

To test if any such pattern is perfect, let the pattern starting with θ_i first be zero in row c_i. If any $c_i = n + 1$, the answer is yes. If $\operatorname{lcm}(c_1, \ldots, c_r) \leq n$, the answer is no. If neither of these conditions decides the matter, we can resort to brute-force examination of $2^r - 1$ nonzero linear combinations of the θ vectors.

For example, when $n = 9$ we find $\gamma_1 = 111101111$, $\gamma_2 = \gamma_3 = 010101010$, $\gamma_4 = 000000000$, $\gamma_5 = 001010100$; then $r = 0$, $\theta_1 = 011000110$, $\theta_2 = 000101000$, $c_1 = c_2 = 5$. So there is no perfect solution.

In the author's experiments for $n \leq 3000$, "brute force" was needed only when $n = 1709$. Then $r = 21$ and the values of c_i were all equal to 171 or 855 except that $c_{21} = 342$. The solution $\theta_1 \oplus \theta_{21}$ was found immediately.

The answers for $1 \leq n \leq 383$ are 4, 5, 11, 16, 23, 29, 30, 32, 47, 59, 62, 64, 65, 84, 95, 101, 119, 125, 126, 128, 131, 154, 164, 170, 185, 191, 203, 204, 239, 251, 254, 256, 257, 263, 314, 329, 340, 341, 371, 383.

[A fractal similar to Fig. 20, called the "mikado pattern," appears in a paper by H. Eriksson, K. Eriksson, and J. Sjöstrand, *Advances in Applied Math.* **27** (2001), 365. See also S. Wolfram, *A New Kind of Science* (2002), rule 150R on page 439.]

195. Set $\beta_i \leftarrow 1 \ll (m - i)$ and $\gamma_i \leftarrow \alpha_i$ for $1 \leq i \leq m$; also set $r \leftarrow 0$. Then perform the following subroutine for $i = 1, 2, \ldots, m$:

N1. [Extract low bit.] Set $x \leftarrow \gamma_i \ \& -\gamma_i$. If $x = 0$, go to N4.

N2. [Find j.] Find the smallest $j \geq 1$ such that $\gamma_j \ \& \ x \neq 0$ and $\gamma_j \ \& \ (x - 1) = 0$.

N3. [Dependent?] If $j < i$, set $\gamma_i \leftarrow \gamma_i \oplus \gamma_j$, $\beta_i \leftarrow \beta_i \oplus \beta_j$, and return to N1. (These operations preserve the matrix equation $C = BA$.) Otherwise terminate the subroutine (because γ_i is linearly independent from $\gamma_1, \ldots, \gamma_{i-1}$).

N4. [Record a solution.] Set $r \leftarrow r + 1$ and $\theta_r \leftarrow \beta_i$. ∎

At the conclusion, the $m - r$ nonzero vectors γ_i are a basis for the vector space of all linear combinations of $\alpha_1, \ldots, \alpha_m$; they're characterized by their low bits.

196. (a) $^\#$0a; $^\#$cea3; $^\#$e7ae97; $^\#$f09d8581.

(b) If $\lambda x = \lambda x'$, the result is clear because $l = l'$. Otherwise we have either $\alpha_1 < \alpha_1'$ or $(\alpha_1 = \alpha_1'$ and $\alpha_2 < \alpha_2')$; the latter case can occur only when $x \geq 2^{16}$.

(c) Set $j \leftarrow k$; while $\alpha_j \oplus {}^\#80 < {}^\#40$, set $j \leftarrow j - 1$. Then $\alpha(x^{(i)})$ begins with α_j.

197. (a) $^\#$000a; $^\#$03a3; $^\#$7b97; $^\#$d834dd41.

(b) Lexicographic order is *not* preserved when, say, $x = {}^\#$ffff and $x' = {}^\#$10000.

(c) To answer this question properly one needs to know that the 2048 integers in the range $^\#$d800 $\leq x < {}^\#$e000 are not legal codepoints of UCS; they are called *surrogates*. With this understanding, $\beta(x^{(i)})$ begins at β_k if $\beta_k \oplus {}^\#$dc00 $\geq {}^\#$0400, otherwise it begins at β_{k-1}.

198. $a = {}^\#$e50000, $b = 3$, $c = {}^\#$16. (We could let $b = 0$, but then a would be huge. This trick was suggested by P. Raynaud-Richard in 1997. The stated constants, suggested by R. Pournader in 2008, are the smallest possible.)

199. We want $\alpha_1 > {}^\#$c1; $2^8 \alpha_1 + \alpha_2 < {}^\#$f490; and either $(\alpha_1 \ \& -\alpha_1) + \alpha_1 < {}^\#$100 or $\alpha_1 + \alpha_2 > {}^\#$17f. These conditions hold if and only if

$$({}^\#\text{c1} - \alpha_1) \ \& \ (2^8 \alpha_1 + \alpha_2 - {}^\#\text{f490}) \ \& \ (((\alpha_1 \ \& -\alpha_1) + \alpha_1 - {}^\#\text{100}) \mid ({}^\#\text{17f} - \alpha_1 - \alpha_2)) < 0.$$

Markus Kuhn suggests adding the further clause '& $(^\#20 - ((2^8\alpha_1 + \alpha_2) \oplus ^\#\text{eda0}))$', to ensure that $\alpha_1\alpha_2$ doesn't begin the encoding of a surrogate.

200. If $\$0 = (x_7 \ldots x_1x_0)_{256}$ then $\$3$ is set to the symmetric function $S_2(x_7, x_4, x_2)$.

201. MOR x,c,x, where $c = ^\#\text{f0f0f0f00f0f0f0f}$.

202. MOR x,x,c, where $c = ^\#\text{c0c030300c0c0303}$; then MOR x,mone,x. (See answer 209.)

203. $a = ^\#0008000400020001$, $b = ^\#0804020108040201f$, $c = ^\#0606060606060606$, $d = ^\#0000002700000000$, $e = ^\#2a2a2a2a2a2a2a2a$. (The ASCII code for 0 is $6 + ^\#2a$; the ASCII code for a is $6 + ^\#2a + 10 + ^\#27$.)

204. $p = ^\#8008400420021001$, $q = ^\#8020080240100401$ (the transpose of p), $r = ^\#4080102004080102$ (a symmetric matrix), and $m = ^\#\text{aa55aa55aa55aa55}$.

205. Shuffle, but with $p \leftrightarrow q$, $r = ^\#0804020180402010$, $m = ^\#\text{f0f0f0f00f0f0f0f}$.

206. Just change p to $^\#0880044002200110$. (Incidentally, these shuffles can also be defined as permutations on $z = (z_{63} \ldots z_1z_0)_2$ in another way: The outshuffle maps $z_j \mapsto z_{(2j) \bmod 63}$, for $0 \leq j < 63$, while the inshuffle maps $z_j \mapsto z_{(2j+1) \bmod 65}$.)

207. Do MOR y,p,x; MOR y,y,p; MOR t,y,q; PUT rM,m1; MUX y,y,t; MOR t,t,q; PUT rM,m2; MUX y,y,t. In both cases $p = ^\#2004801002400801$; for triple zip, $q = ^\#4020100804020180$, $m_1 = ^\#4949494949494949$, $m_2 = ^\#\text{dbdbdbdbdbdbdbdb}$; for the inverse, $q = ^\#0402018040201008$, $m_1 = ^\#0707070707070707$, $m_2 = ^\#\text{3f3f3f3f3f3f3f3f}$.

208. (Solution by H. S. Warren, Jr.) The text's 7-swap, 14-swap, 28-swap method can be implemented with only 12 instructions:

```
MOR t,x,c1;  MOR t,c1,t;  PUT rM,m1;  MUX y,x,t;
MOR t,y,c2;  MOR t,c2,t;  PUT rM,m2;  MUX y,y,t;
MOR t,y,c3;  MOR t,c3,t;  PUT rM,m3;  MUX y,y,t;
```

here $c_1 = ^\#4080102004080102$, $c_2 = ^\#2010804002010804$, $c_3 = ^\#0804020180402010$, $m_1 = ^\#\text{aa55aa55aa55aa55}$, $m_2 = ^\#\text{cccc3333cccc3333}$, $m_3 = ^\#\text{f0f0f0f00f0f0f0f}$.

209. Four instructions suffice: MXOR y,p,x; MXOR x,mone,x; MXOR x,x,q; XOR x,x,y; here $p = ^\#80\text{c0e0f0f8fcfeff}} = \bar{q}$, and register mone $= -1$.

210. SLU x,one,x; MOR x,b,x; AND x,x,a; MOR x,x,#ff; here register one $= 1$.

211. In general, element ij of the Boolean matrix product AXB is $\bigvee\{x_{kl} \mid a_{ik}b_{lj} = 1\}$. For this problem we choose $a_{ik} = [i \supseteq k]$ and $b_{lj} = [l \subseteq j]$; the answer is 'MOR t,f,a; MOR t,b,t' where $a = ^\#80\text{c0a0f088ccaaff}}$ and $b = ^\#\text{ff5533110f050301} = a^T$.

(Notice that this trick gives a simple test $[f = \hat{f}]$ for monotonicity. Furthermore, the 64-bit result $(t_{63} \ldots t_1t_0)_2$ gives the coefficients of the multilinear representation

$$f(x_1, \ldots, x_6) = (t_{63} + t_{62}x_6 + \cdots + t_1x_1x_2x_3x_4x_5 + t_0x_1x_2x_3x_4x_5x_6) \bmod 2,$$

if we substitute MXOR for MOR, by the result of exercise 7.1.1–11.)

212. If $\cdot$ denotes MXOR as in (183) and $b = (\beta_7 \ldots \beta_1\beta_0)_{256}$ has bytes β_j, we can evaluate

$$c = (a \cdot B_0^L) \oplus ((a \ll 8) \cdot (B_1^L + B_0^U)) \oplus ((a \ll 16) \cdot (B_2^L + B_1^U)) \oplus \cdots \oplus ((a \ll 56) \cdot (B_7^L + B_6^U)),$$

where $B_j^U = (q\beta_j) \& m$, $B_j^L = (((q\beta_j) \ll 8) + \beta_j) \& \bar{m}$, $q = ^\#0080402010080402$, and $m = ^\#\text{7f3f1f0f07030100}$. (Here $q\beta_j$ denotes *ordinary* multiplication of integers.)

213. In this big-endian computation, register nn holds $-n$, and register data points to the octabyte following the given bytes $\alpha_{n-1} \ldots \alpha_1 \alpha_0$ in memory (with α_{n-1} first). The constants aa = #8381808080402010 and bb = #339bcf6530180c06 correspond to matrices A and B, found by computing the remainders $x^k \bmod p(x)$ for $72 \le k < 80$.

	SET	c,0	$c \leftarrow 0$.		LDOU	t,data,nn	$t \leftarrow$ next octa.
	LDOU	t,data,nn	$t \leftarrow$ next octa.		XOR	u,u,c	$u \leftarrow u \oplus c$.
	ADD	nn,nn,8	$n \leftarrow n - 8$.		SLU	c,v,56	$c \leftarrow v \ll 56$.
	BZ	nn,2F	Done if $n = 0$.		SRU	v,v,8	$v \leftarrow v \gg 8$.
1H	MXOR	u,aa,t	$u \leftarrow t \cdot A$.		XOR	u,u,v	$u \leftarrow u \oplus v$.
	MXOR	v,bb,t	$v \leftarrow t \cdot B$.		XOR	t,t,u	$t \leftarrow t \oplus u$.
	ADD	nn,nn,8	$n \leftarrow n - 8$.		PBN	nn,1B	Repeat if $n > 0$. ∎

A similar method finishes the job, with no auxiliary table needed:

2H	SET	nn,8	$n \leftarrow 8$.		SRU	v,v,8	$v \leftarrow v \gg 8$.
3H	AND	x,t,ffooo	$x \leftarrow$ high byte.		XOR	t,t,v	$t \leftarrow t \oplus v$.
	MXOR	u,aaa,x	$u \leftarrow x \cdot A'$.		SUB	nn,nn,1	$n \leftarrow n - 1$.
	MXOR	v,bbb,x	$v \leftarrow x \cdot B'$.		PBP	nn,3B	Repeat if $n > 0$.
	SLU	t,t,8	$t \leftarrow t \ll 8$.		XOR	t,t,c	$t \leftarrow t \oplus c$.
	XOR	t,t,u	$t \leftarrow t \oplus u$.		SRU	crc,t,48	Return $t \gg 48$. ∎

Here aaa = #8381808080808080, bbb = #0383c363331b0f05, and ffooo = #ff00...00.

The Books of the Big-Endians *have been long forbidden.*
— LEMUEL GULLIVER, *Travels Into Several Remote Nations of the World* (1726)

214. (Solution by Adam P. Goucher.) By considering the irreducible factors of X's characteristic polynomial, we must have $X^{n-1} = I$ or $X^n = I$, where $n = 2^3 \cdot 3^2 \cdot 5 \cdot 7 \cdot 17 \cdot 31 = 1328040$, since $n \bmod 127 = 1$. Hence the following sequence of 28 instructions, based on an addition chain of length $l(n-2) = 25$, will compute $Y = X^{-1}$:
MXOR \$1,x,x; MXOR \$2,\$1,x; MXOR y,\$2,\$1; S^3; MXOR \$1,y,x; MXOR y,\$1,y; S^6;
MXOR y,y,\$2; S^6; MXOR y,y,\$1; S; MXOR y,y,x; S; MXOR \$1,y,x; CMPU \$2,\$1,i;
CSNZ y,\$2,\$1;   here S stands for 'MXOR y,y,y' and i = #8040201008040201 is the identity matrix. To test if X is nonsingular, do MXOR \$1,y,x and compare \$1 to i.

215. SADD \$0,x,0; SADD \$1,x,a; NEG \$0,32,\$0; 2ADDU \$1,\$1,\$0; SLU \$0,b,\$1; then BN \$0,Yes; here a = #aaaaaaaaaaaaaaaa and b = #2492492492492492.

216. Start with $s_k \leftarrow 0$ and $t_k \leftarrow -1$ for $0 \le k < m$. Then do the following for $1 \le k \le m$: If $x_k \ne 0$ and $x_k < 2^m$, set $l \leftarrow \lambda x_k$ and $s_l \leftarrow s_l + x_k$; if $t_l < 0$ or $t_l > x_k$, also set $t_l \leftarrow x_k$. Finally, set $y \leftarrow 1$ and $k \leftarrow 0$; while $y \ge t_k$ and $k < m$, set $y \leftarrow y + s_k$ and $k \leftarrow k + 1$. Double-precision n-bit arithmetic is sufficient for y and s_k. [This pleasant algorithm appeared in D. Eppstein's blog, 2008.03.22.]

217. See R. D. Cameron, *U.S. Patent 7400271* (15 July 2008); *Proc. ACM Symp. Principles and Practice of Parallel Programming* **13** (2008), 91–98.

218. Let b be any integer with $b \bmod 8 = 5$. Then $x = b^{L(x)} \bmod 2^d$ for some integer $L(x)$, depending on b, whenever $0 < x < 2^d$ and $x \bmod 4 = 1$ (see Section 3.2.1.2). The following algorithm computes $s = 4L(x)$, given a table of the numbers $t_k = -4L(2^k+1)$ for $1 < k < d$, and assuming that $t_k = 2^k$ for $k \ge d/2$: Set $s \leftarrow 0$, $j \leftarrow 1$; then while $j < d/2 - 1$, set $j \leftarrow j + 1$, and if $x \mathbin{\&} (1 \ll j) \ne 0$ also set $x \leftarrow (x + (x \ll j)) \bmod 2^d$, $s \leftarrow (s + t_j) \bmod 2^d$. Finally set $s \leftarrow (s + 1 - x) \bmod 2^d$.

Now to compute $a \cdot x^y$ we can proceed as follows (with all arithmetic done mod 2^d): If $x \mathbin{\&} 2 \ne 0$, set $x \leftarrow -x$ and $a \leftarrow (-1)^{y \mathbin{\&} 1} a$. (Now $x \bmod 4 = 1$.) Set $s \leftarrow 4L(x) \cdot y$, using the algorithm above, and $j \leftarrow 1$; then while $s \neq 0$, set $j \leftarrow j + 1$, and if $s \mathbin{\&} (1 \ll j) \neq 0$ also set $s \leftarrow s + t_j$, $a \leftarrow a + (a \ll j)$. The desired answer is then a. (With another multiplication we could return $(1 - s)a$ as soon as $j \geq d/2$.)

Suitable numbers t_k can be computed by setting $t_k \leftarrow 1 \ll k$ for $d - 1 \geq k \geq d/2$ and proceeding as follows for the remaining ks, in decreasing order: Set $x \leftarrow 1 + (1 \ll k)$, $x \leftarrow x + (x \ll k)$, $s \leftarrow 0$, $j \leftarrow k$; then while $j < d/2 - 1$ set $j \leftarrow j + 1$, and if $x \mathbin{\&} (1 \ll j) \neq 0$ also set $x \leftarrow x + (x \ll j)$, $s \leftarrow s - t_j$; finally $t_k \leftarrow (s + x - 1) \gg 1$. For example, when $d = 32$ we get $t_{15} = {}^\#\texttt{20008000}$, $t_{14} = {}^\#\texttt{18004000}$, $t_{13} = {}^\#\texttt{0e002000}$, $t_{12} = {}^\#\texttt{07801000}$, $t_{11} = {}^\#\texttt{03e00800}$, $t_{10} = {}^\#\texttt{41f80400}$, $t_9 = {}^\#\texttt{18fe0200}$, $t_8 = {}^\#\texttt{0b7f8100}$, $t_7 = {}^\#\texttt{319fe080}$, $t_6 = {}^\#\texttt{5e8bf840}$, $t_5 = {}^\#\texttt{4a617e20}$, $t_4 = {}^\#\texttt{17c26f90}$, $t_3 = {}^\#\texttt{6119d1e8}$, $t_2 = {}^\#\texttt{2c30267c}$. (This procedure finds the L's for *some* integer b, without revealing the actual value of b itself!)

[The methods of this exercise have interesting connections to the algorithms of Briggs and Feynman for *real*-valued logarithm and exponential in exercises 1.2.2–25 and 1.2.2–28. Our broadword procedure for x^y works also for calculating the inverse of x, modulo 2^d, when $y = -1$; but there's a direct algorithm available for that: Set $z \leftarrow 1$, $j \leftarrow 0$; while $x \neq 1$ set $j \leftarrow j + 1$, and if $x \mathbin{\&} (1 \ll j) \neq 0$, also set $z \leftarrow (z + (z \ll j)) \bmod 2^d$, $x \leftarrow (x + (x \ll j)) \bmod 2^d$. The final z is the inverse of the original odd number x.]

219. It "sorts" the bits, changing x to $2^{\nu x} - 1$.

SECTION 7.1.4

1. Here are the BDDs for truth tables 0000, 0001, ..., 1111, showing the sizes below:

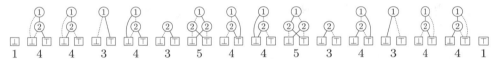

| 1 | 4 | 4 | 3 | 4 | 3 | 5 | 4 | 4 | 5 | 3 | 4 | 3 | 4 | 4 | 1 |

2. (The ordering property determines the direction of each arc.)

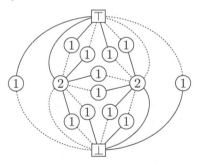

3. There are two with size 1 (namely the two constant functions); none with size 2 (because two sinks cannot both be reachable unless there's also a branch node); and $2n$ with size 3 (namely x_j and $\bar{x}_j$ for $1 \leq j \leq n$).

4. Set $y \leftarrow {}^\#\texttt{0ffffffefffffffe} \mathbin{\&} \bar{x} + {}^\#\texttt{20000002}$, $y \leftarrow (y \gg 28) \mathbin{\&} {}^\#\texttt{10000001}$, $x' \leftarrow x \oplus y$.

5. You get $\overline{f(\bar{x}_1, \ldots, \bar{x}_n)} = f^D(x_1, \ldots, x_n)$, the *dual* of f (see exercise 7.1.1–2).

6. The largest subtables of 1011000110010011, namely 10110001, 10010011, 1011, 0001, 1001, 0011, are all distinct beads; squares and duplicates don't appear until we look at the subtables $\{10, 11, 00, 01\}$ of length 2. So g has size 11.

7. (a) If the truth table of f is $\alpha_0 \alpha_1 \ldots \alpha_{2^k - 1}$, where each α_j is a binary string of length 2^{n-k}, the truth table of g_k is $\beta_0 \beta_2 \ldots \beta_{2^k - 2}$, where $\beta_{2j} = \alpha_{2j} \alpha_{2j+1} \alpha_{2j+1} \alpha_{2j+1}$.

(b) Thus the beads of f and g_k are closely related. We get the BDD for g_k from the BDD for f by changing (j) to $\boxed{j-1}$ for $1 \le j < k$, and replacing (k) by $\boxed{k-1}$.

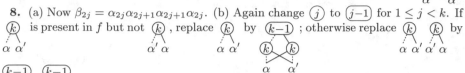

8. (a) Now $\beta_{2j} = \alpha_{2j}\alpha_{2j+1}\alpha_{2j+1}\alpha_{2j}$. (b) Again change (j) to $\boxed{j-1}$ for $1 \le j < k$. If (k) is present in f but not (k), replace (k) by $\boxed{k-1}$; otherwise replace (k) (k) by

. [E. Dubrova and L. Macchiarulo, *IEEE Trans.* **C-49** (2000), 1290–1292.]

9. There is no solution if $s = 1$. Otherwise set $k \leftarrow s-1$, $j \leftarrow 1$, and do the following steps repeatedly: (i) While $j < v_k$, set $x_j \leftarrow 1$ and $j \leftarrow j+1$; (ii) stop if $k = 0$; (iii) if $h_k \ne 1$, set $x_j \leftarrow 1$ and $k \leftarrow h_k$, otherwise set $x_j \leftarrow 0$ and $k \leftarrow l_k$; (iv) set $j \leftarrow j+1$.

10. Let $I_k = (\bar{v}_k ? \, l_k \colon h_k)$ for $0 \le k < s$ and $I'_k = (\bar{v}'_k ? \, l'_k \colon h'_k)$ for $0 \le k < s'$. We may assume that $s = s'$; otherwise $f \ne f'$. The following algorithm either finds indices $(t_0, \ldots, t_{s-1})$ such that I_k corresponds to I'_{t_k}, or concludes that $f \ne f'$:

I1. [Initialize and loop.] Set $t_{s-1} \leftarrow s - 1$, $t_1 \leftarrow 1$, $t_0 \leftarrow 0$, and $t_k \leftarrow -1$ for $2 \le k \le s - 2$. Do steps I2–I4 for $k = s - 1$, $s - 2$, $\ldots$, 2 (in this order). If those steps "quit" at any point, we have $f \ne f'$; otherwise $f = f'$.

I2. [Test v_k.] Set $t \leftarrow t_k$. (Now $t \ge 0$; otherwise I_k would have no predecessor.) Quit if $v'_t \ne v_k$.

I3. [Test l_k.] Set $l \leftarrow l_k$. If $t_l < 0$, set $t_l \leftarrow l'_t$; otherwise quit if $l'_t \ne t_l$.

I4. [Test h_k.] Set $h \leftarrow h_k$. If $t_h < 0$, set $t_h \leftarrow h'_t$; otherwise quit if $h'_t \ne t_h$. ∎

11. (a) Yes, since c_k correctly counts the number of settings of $x_{v_k} \ldots x_n$ that lead from node k to node 1. (In fact, many BDD algorithms will run correctly — but more slowly — in the presence of equivalent nodes or redundant branches. But reduction is important when, say, we want to test quickly if $f = f'$ as in exercise 10.)

(b) No. For example, suppose $I_3 = (\bar{1}? \, 2 \colon 1)$, $I_2 = (\bar{1}? \, 0 \colon 1)$, $I_1 = (\bar{2}? \, 1 \colon 1)$, $I_0 = (\bar{2}? \, 0 \colon 0)$; then the algorithm sets $c_2 \leftarrow 1$, $c_3 \leftarrow \frac{3}{2}$. (But see exercise 35(b).)

12. (a) The first condition makes K independent; the second makes it maximally so.

(b) None when n is odd; otherwise there are two sets of alternate vertices.

(c) A vertex is in the kernel if and only if it is a sink vertex or in the kernel of the graph obtained by deleting all sink vertices and their immediate predecessors.

[Kernels represent winning positions in nim-like games, and they also arise in n-person games. See J. von Neumann and O. Morgenstern, *Theory of Games and Economic Behavior* (1944), §30.1; C. Berge, *Graphs and Hypergraphs* (1973), Chapter 14.]

13. (a) A maximal clique of G is a kernel of $\bar{G}$, and vice versa. (b) A minimal vertex cover U is the complement $V \setminus W$ of a kernel W, and vice versa (see 7–(61)).

14. (a) The size is $4(n - 2) + 2[n = 3]$. When $n \ge 6$ these BDDs form a pattern in which there are four branch nodes for variables 4, 5, $\ldots$, $n - 2$, together with a fixed pattern at the top and bottom. The four branches are essentially

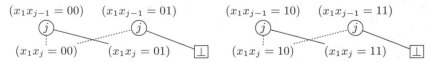

(b) Here the numbers for $3 \le n \le 10$ are $(7, 9, 14, 17, 22, 30, 37, 45)$; then a fixed pattern at the top and bottom develops as in (a), with nine branch nodes for each variable in the middle, and the total size comes to $9(n-5)$. The nine nodes on each middle level fall into three groups of three,

with one group for $x_1 x_2 = 00$, one for $x_1 x_2 = 01$, and one for $x_1 = 1$.

15. Both cases lead by induction to well known sequences of numbers: (a) The Lucas numbers $L_n = F_{n+1} + F_{n-1} = \phi^n + \hat{\phi}^n$ [see E. Lucas, *Théorie des Nombres* (1891), Chapter 18]. (b) The Perrin numbers, defined by $P_3 = 3$, $P_4 = 2$, $P_5 = 5$, $P_n = P_{n-2} + P_{n-3} = \rho^n + \hat{\rho}^n + \overline{\hat{\rho}}^n$. [See E. Lucas, *Association Française pour l'Avancement des Sciences*, Compte-rendu **5** (1876), 62; R. Perrin, *L'Intermédiaire des Mathématiciens* **6** (1899), 76–77; Z. Füredi, *Journal of Graph Theory* **11** (1987), 463.]

16. When the BDD isn't $\boxed{\perp}$, all solutions are generated by calling $List(1, \text{root})$, where $List(j, p)$ is the following recursive procedure: If $v(p) > j$, set $x_j \leftarrow 0$, call $List(j+1, p)$, set $x_j \leftarrow 1$, and call $List(j+1, p)$. Otherwise if p is the sink node $\boxed{\top}$, visit the solution $x_1 \ldots x_n$. (The idea of "visiting" a combinatorial object while generating them all is discussed at the beginning of Section 7.2.1.) Otherwise set $x_j \leftarrow 0$; call $List(j+1, \text{LO}(p))$ if $\text{LO}(p) \ne \boxed{\perp}$; set $x_j \leftarrow 1$; and call $List(j+1, \text{HI}(p))$ if $\text{HI}(p) \ne \boxed{\perp}$.

The solutions are generated in lexicographic order. Suppose there are N of them. If the kth solution agrees with the $(k-1)$st solution in positions $x_1 \ldots x_{j-1}$ but not in x_j, let $c(k) = n - j$; and let $c(1) = n$. Then the running time is proportional to $\sum_{k=1}^{N} c(k)$, which is $O(nN)$ in general. (This bound holds because every branch node of a BDD leads to at least one solution. In fact, the running time is usually $O(N)$ in practice.)

17. That mission is impossible, because there's a function with $N = 2^{2^k}$ and $B(f) = O(2^{2^k})$ for which every two solutions differ in more than 2^{k-1} bit positions. The running time for any algorithm that generates all solutions for such a function must be $\Omega(2^{3k})$, because $\Omega(2^k)$ operations are needed between solutions. To construct f, first let

$$g(x_1, \ldots, x_k, y_0, \ldots, y_{2^k-1}) = \left[y_{(t_1 \ldots t_k)_2} = x_1 t_1 \oplus \cdots \oplus x_k t_k \text{ for } 0 \le t_1, \ldots, t_k \le 1 \right].$$

(In other words, g asserts that $y_0 \ldots y_{2^k-1}$ is row $(x_1 \ldots x_k)_2$ of an Hadamard matrix; see Eq. 4.6.4–(38).) Now we let $f(x_1, \ldots, x_k, y_0, \ldots, y_{2^k-1}, x'_1, \ldots, x'_k, y'_0, \ldots, y'_{2^k-1}) = g(x_1, \ldots, x_k, y_0, \ldots, y_{2^k-1}) \wedge g(x'_1, \ldots, x'_k, y'_0, \ldots, y'_{2^k-1})$. Clearly $B(f) = O(2^{2^k})$ when the variables are ordered in this way. Indeed, T. Dahlheimer observes that $B(f) = 2B(g) - 2$, where $B(g) = 2^k + 1 + \sum_{j=1}^{2^k} 2^{\min(k, 1 + \lceil \lg j \rceil)} = \frac{5}{3} 2^{2k-1} + 2^k + \frac{5}{3}$.

18. First, $(W_1, \ldots, W_5) = (5, 4, 4, 4, 0)$. Then $m_2 = w_4 = 4$ and $t_2 = 1$; $m_3 = t_3 = 0$; $m_4 = \max(m_3, m_2 + w_3) = 1$, $t_4 = 1$; $m_5 = W_4 - W_5 = 4$, $t_5 = 0$; $m_6 = w_2 + W_3 - W_5 = 2$, $t_6 = 1$; $m_7 = \max(m_5, m_4 + w_2) = 4$, $t_7 = 0$; $m_8 = \max(m_7, m_6 + w_1) = 4$, $t_8 = 0$. Solution $x_1 x_2 x_3 x_4 = 0001$.

19. $\sum_{j=1}^{n} \min(w_j, 0) \le \sum_{j=v_k}^{n} \min(w_j, 0) \le m_k \le \sum_{j=v_k}^{n} \max(w_j, 0) = W_{v_k} \le W_1$.

20. Set $w_1 \leftarrow -1$, then $w_{2j} \leftarrow w_j$ and $w_{2j+1} \leftarrow -w_j$ for $1 \le j \le n/2$. [This method may also compute w_{n+1}. The sequence is named for works of A. Thue, *Skrifter udgivne af Videnskabs-Selskabet i Christiania*, Mathematisk-Naturvidenskabelig Klasse (1912), No. 1, §7, and H. M. Morse, *Trans. Amer. Math. Soc.* **22** (1921), 84–100, §14.]

21. Yes; we just have to change the sign of each weight w_j. (Or we could reverse the roles of LO and HI at each vertex.)

22. If $f(x) = f(x') = 1$ when f represents a graph kernel, the Hamming distance $\nu(x \oplus x')$ cannot be 1. In such cases $v_l = v + 1$ when $l \neq 0$ and $v_h = v + 1$ when $h \neq 0$.

23. The BDD for the connectedness function of any connected graph will have exactly $n - 1$ solid arcs on every root-to-$\boxed{\top}$ path, because that many edges are needed to connect n vertices, and because a BDD has no redundant branches. (See also Theorem S.)

24. Apply Algorithm B with weights $(w'_{12}, \ldots, w'_{89}) = (-w_{12}-x, \ldots, -w_{89}-x)$, where x is large enough to make all of these new weights w'_{uv} negative. The maximum of $\sum w'_{uv}x_{uv}$ will then occur with $\sum x_{uv} = 8$, and those edges will form a spanning tree with minimum $\sum w_{uv}x_{uv}$. (We've seen a better algorithm for minimum spanning trees in exercise 2.3.4.1–11, and other methods will be studied in Section 7.5.4. However, this exercise indicates that a BDD can compactly represent the set of *all* spanning trees.)

25. The answer in step C1 becomes $(1 + z)^{v_s-1-1}c_{s-1}$; the value of c_k in step C2 becomes $(1 + z)^{v_l-v_k-1}c_l + (1 + z)^{v_h-v_k-1}zc_h$.

26. In this case the answer in step C1 is simply c_{s-1}; and the value of c_k in step C2 is simply $(1 - p_{v_k})c_l + p_{v_k}c_h$.

27. The multilinear polynomial $H(x_1, \ldots, x_n) = F(x_1, \ldots, x_n) - G(x_1, \ldots, x_n)$ is nonzero modulo q, because it is ± 1 for some choice of integers with each $x_k \in \{0, 1\}$. If it has degree d (modulo q), we can prove that there are at least $(q - 1)^d q^{n-d}$ sets of values $(q_1, \ldots, q_n)$ with $0 \leq q_k < q$ such that $H(q_1, \ldots, q_n) \bmod q \neq 0$. This statement is clear when $d = 0$. And if x_k is a variable that appears in a term of degree $d > 0$, the coefficient of x_k is a polynomial of degree $d - 1$, which by induction on d is nonzero for at least $(q - 1)^{d-1}q^{n-d}$ choices of $(q_1, \ldots, q_{k-1}, q_{k+1}, \ldots, q_n)$; for each of those choices there are $q - 1$ values of q_k such that $H(q_1, \ldots, q_n) \bmod q \neq 0$.

Hence the stated probability is $\geq (1 - 1/q)^d \geq (1 - 1/q)^n$. [See M. Blum, A. K. Chandra, and M. N. Wegman, *Information Processing Letters* **10** (1980), 80–82.]

28. $F(p) = (1 - p)^n G(p/(1 - p))$. Similarly, $G(z) = (1 + z)^n F(z/(1 + z))$.

29. In step C1, also set $c'_0 \leftarrow 0$, $c'_1 \leftarrow 0$; return c_{s-1} and c'_{s-1}. In step C2, set $c_k \leftarrow (1 - p)c_l + pc_h$ and $c'_k \leftarrow (1 - p)c'_l - c_l + pc'_h + c_h$.

30. The following analog of Algorithm B does the job (assuming exact arithmetic):

A1. [Initialize.] Set $P_{n+1} \leftarrow 1$ and $P_j \leftarrow P_{j+1}\max(1 - p_j, p_j)$ for $n \geq j \geq 1$.

A2. [Loop on k.] Set $m_1 \leftarrow 1$ and do step A3 for $2 \leq k < s$. Then do step A4.

A3. [Process I_k.] Set $v \leftarrow v_k$, $l \leftarrow l_k$, $h \leftarrow h_k$, $t_k \leftarrow 0$. If $l \neq 0$, set $m_k \leftarrow m_l(1 - p_v)P_{v+1}/P_{v_l}$. Then if $h \neq 0$, compute $m \leftarrow m_h p_v P_{v+1}/P_{v_h}$; and if $l = 0$ or $m > m_k$, set $m_k \leftarrow m$ and $t_k \leftarrow 1$.

A4. [Compute the x's.] Set $j \leftarrow 0$, $k \leftarrow s - 1$, and do the following operations until $j = n$: While $j < v_k - 1$, set $j \leftarrow j + 1$ and $x_j \leftarrow [p_j > \frac{1}{2}]$; if $k > 1$, set $j \leftarrow j + 1$ and $x_j \leftarrow t_k$ and $k \leftarrow (t_k = 0?\ l_k : h_k)$. ∎

31. **C1′.** [Loop over k.] Set $\alpha_0 \leftarrow \bot$, $\alpha_1 \leftarrow \top$, and do step C2′ for $k = 2, 3, \ldots, s - 1$. Then go to C3′.

C2′. [Compute α_k.] Set $v \leftarrow v_k$, $l \leftarrow l_k$, and $h \leftarrow h_k$. Set $\beta \leftarrow \alpha_l$ and $j \leftarrow v_l - 1$; then while $j > v$ set $\beta \leftarrow (\bar{x}_j \circ x_j) \bullet \beta$ and $j \leftarrow j - 1$. Set $\gamma \leftarrow \alpha_h$ and $j \leftarrow v_h - 1$; then while $j > v$ set $\gamma \leftarrow (\bar{x}_j \circ x_j) \bullet \gamma$ and $j \leftarrow j - 1$. Finally set $\alpha_k \leftarrow (\bar{x}_v \bullet \beta) \circ (x_v \bullet \gamma)$.

C3′. [Finish.] Set $\alpha \leftarrow \alpha_{s-1}$ and $j \leftarrow v_{s-1}-1$; then while $j > 0$ set $\alpha \leftarrow (\bar{x}_j \circ x_j) \bullet \alpha$ and $j \leftarrow j - 1$. Return the answer α. $\blacksquare$

This algorithm performs $\circ$ and $\bullet$ operations at most $O(nB(f))$ times. The upper bound can often be lowered to $O(n) + O(B(f))$; but shortcuts like the calculation of W_k in step B1 aren't always available. [See O. Coudert and J. C. Madre, *Proc. Reliability and Maint. Conf.* (IEEE, 1993), 240–245, §4; O. Coudert, *Integration* **17** (1994), 126–127.]

32. For exercise 25, '$\circ$' is addition, '$\bullet$' is multiplication, '$\perp$' is 0, '$\top$' is 1, '$\bar{x}_j$' is 1, 'x_j' is z. Exercise 26 is similar, but '$\bar{x}_j$' is $1 - p_j$ and 'x_j' is p_j.

In exercise 29 the objects of the algebra are pairs (c, c'), and we have $(a, a') \circ (b, b') = (a + b, a' + b')$, $(a, a') \bullet (b, b') = (ab, ab' + a'b)$. Also '$\perp$' is $(0, 0)$, '$\top$' is $(1, 0)$, '$\bar{x}_j$' is $(1-p, -1)$, and 'x_j' is $(p, 1)$.

In exercise 30, '$\circ$' is max, '$\bullet$' is multiplication, '$\perp$' is $-\infty$, '$\top$' is 1, '$\bar{x}_j$' is $1 - p_j$, 'x_j' is p_j. Multiplication distributes over max in this case because the quantities are either nonnegative or $-\infty$; we must define $0 \bullet (-\infty) = -\infty$ in order to satisfy (22).

(Additional possibilities abound, because associative and distributive operators are ubiquitous in mathematics. The algebraic objects need not be numbers or polynomials or pairs; they can be strings, matrices, functions, sets of numbers, sets of strings, sets or multisets of matrices of pairs of functions of strings, etc., etc. We will see many further examples in Section 7.3. The min-plus algebra, with $\circ = \min$ and $\bullet = +$, is particularly important, and we could have used it in exercise 21 or 24. It is often called *tropical*, implicitly honoring the Brazilian mathematician Imre Simon.)

33. Operate on triples (c, c', c''), with $(a, a', a'') \circ (b, b', b'') = (a + b, a' + b', a'' + b'')$ and $(a, a', a'') \bullet (b, b', b'') = (ab, a'b + b'a, a''b + 2a'b' + ab'')$. Interpret '$\perp$' as $(0, 0, 0)$, '$\top$' as $(1, 0, 0)$, '$\bar{x}_j$' as $(1, 0, 0)$, and 'x_j' as $(1, w_j, w_j^2)$.

34. Let $x \vee y = \max(x, y)$. Operate on pairs (c, c'), with $(a, a') \circ (b, b') = (a \vee b, a' \vee b')$ and $(a, a') \bullet (b, b') = (a + b, (a' + b) \vee (a + b'))$. Interpret '$\perp$' as $(-\infty, -\infty)$, '$\top$' as $(0, -\infty)$, '$\bar{x}_j$' as $(0, w_j'')$, and 'x_j' as $(w_j, w_j' + w_j'')$. The first component of the result will agree with Algorithm B; the second component is the desired maximum.

35. (a) The supposed FBDD can be represented by instructions $I_{s-1}, \ldots, I_0$ as in Algorithm C. Start with $R_0 \leftarrow R_1 \leftarrow \emptyset$, then do the following for $k = 2, \ldots, s - 1$: Report failure if $v_k \in R_{l_k} \cup R_{h_k}$; otherwise set $R_k \leftarrow \{v_k\} \cup R_{l_k} \cup R_{h_k}$. (The set R_k identifies all variables that are reachable from I_k.)

(b) The reliability polynomial can be calculated just as in answer 26. To count solutions, we essentially set $p_1 = \cdots = p_n = \frac{1}{2}$ and multiply by 2^n: Start with $c_0 \leftarrow 0$ and $c_1 \leftarrow 2^n$, then set $c_k \leftarrow (c_{l_k} + c_{h_k})/2$ for $1 < k < s$. The answer is c_{s-1}.

36. Compute the sets R_k as in answer 35(a). Instead of looping on j as stated in step C2′ of answer 31, set $\beta \leftarrow \alpha_l$ and then $\beta \leftarrow (\bar{x}_j \circ x_j) \bullet \beta$ for all $j \in R_k \setminus R_l \setminus \{v\}$; treat γ in the same manner. Similarly, in step C3′ set $\alpha \leftarrow (\bar{x}_j \circ x_j) \bullet \alpha$ for all $j \notin R_{s-1}$.

37. Given any FBDD for f, the function $G(z)$ is the sum of $(1+z)^{n-\text{length}\,P} z^{\text{solid arcs in } P}$ over all paths P from the root to $\boxed{\top}$. [See *Theoretical Comp. Sci.* **3** (1976), 371–384.]

38. The key fact is that $x_j = 1$ forces $f = 1$ if and only if we have (i) $h_k = 1$ whenever $v_k = j$; (ii) $v_k = j$ in at least one step k; (iii) there are no steps with ($v_k < j < v_{l_k}$ and $l_k \neq 1$) or ($v_k < j < v_{h_k}$ and $h_k \neq 1$).

    K1. [Initialize.] Set $t_j \leftarrow 2$ and $p_j \leftarrow 0$ for $1 \leq j \leq n$.

    K2. [Examine all branches.] Do the following operations for $2 \leq k < s$: Set $j \leftarrow v_k$ and $q \leftarrow 0$. If $l_k = 1$, set $q \leftarrow -1$; otherwise set $p_j \leftarrow \max(p_j, v_{l_k})$. If $h_k = 1$, set $q \leftarrow +1$; otherwise set $p_j \leftarrow \max(p_j, v_{h_k})$. If $t_j = 2$, set $t_j \leftarrow q$; otherwise if $t_j \neq q$ set $t_j \leftarrow 0$.

K3. [Finish up.] Set $m \leftarrow v_{s-1}$, and do the following for $j = 1, 2, \ldots, n$: If $j < m$, set $t_j \leftarrow 0$; then if $p_j > m$, set $m \leftarrow p_j$. ∎

[See S.-W. Jeong and F. Somenzi, in *Logic Synthesis and Optimization* (1993), 154–156.]

39. $k(n + 1 - k) + 2$, for $1 \leq k \leq n$. (See (26).)

40. (a) Suppose the BDDs for f and g have respectively a_j and b_j branch nodes $\textcircled{j}$, for $1 \leq j \leq n$. Each subtable of f of order $n + 1 - k$ has the form $\alpha\beta\gamma\delta$, where α, β, γ, and δ are subtables of order $n - 1 - k$. The corresponding subtables of g are $\alpha\alpha\delta\delta$; hence they are beads if and only if $\alpha \neq \delta$, in which case either $\alpha\beta\gamma\delta$ is a bead or $\alpha\beta = \gamma\delta$ is a bead. Consequently $b_k \leq a_k + a_{k+1}$, and $b_{k+1} = 0$. We also have $b_j \leq a_j$ for $1 \leq j < k$, because every bead of g of order $> n+1-k$ is "condensed" from at least one such bead of f. And $b_j \leq a_j$ for $j > k+1$, because the subtables on $(x_{k+2}, \ldots, x_n)$ are identical although they might not appear in g.

(b) Not always, although $B(h) < 2B(f)$. The simplest counterexample is $f(x_1, x_2, x_3, x_4) = x_2 \wedge (x_3 \vee x_4)$, $h(x_1, x_2, x_1, x_4) = x_2 \wedge (x_1 \vee x_4)$, when $B(f) = 5$ and $B(h) = 6$.

41. (a) $3n - 3$; (b) $2n$. (The general patterns are illustrated here for $n = 6$. One can also show that the "organ-pipe ordering" $\langle x_n^{F_1} x_1^{F_2} x_{n-1}^{F_3} x_2^{F_4} \cdots x_{\lfloor n/2 \rfloor + [n \text{ even}]}^{F_{n-1}} x_{\lceil n/2 \rceil}^{F_{n-2}} \rangle$ produces the profile $1, 2, 4, \ldots, 2\lceil n/2 \rceil - 2$, $2\lfloor n/2 \rfloor - 1, \ldots, 5, 3, 1, 2$, giving the total BDD size $\binom{n}{2} + 3$; this ordering appears to be the worst for the Fibonacci weights.)

The functions $[F_n x_1 + \cdots + F_1 x_n \geq t]$ have been studied by J. T. Butler and T. Sasao, *Fibonacci Quart.* **34** (1996), 413–422.

42. (Compare with exercise 2.) The sixteen roots are the $\textcircled{1}$ nodes and the two sinks:

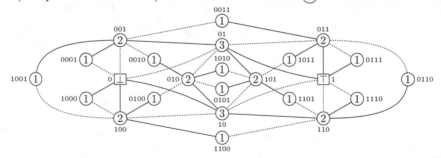

43. (a) Since $f(x_1, \ldots, x_{2n})$ is the symmetric function $S_n(x_1, \ldots, x_n, \bar{x}_{n+1}, \ldots, \bar{x}_{2n})$, we have $B(f) = 1 + 2 + \cdots + (n+1) + \cdots + 3 + 2 + 2 = n^2 + 2n + 2$.

(b) By symmetry, the size is the same for $[\sum\{x_i \mid i \in I\} = \sum\{x_i \mid i \notin I\}]$, $|I| = n$.

44. There are at most $\min(k, 2^{n+2-k} - 2)$ nodes labeled $\textcircled{k}$, for $1 \leq k \leq n$, because there are $2^{n+2-k} - 2$ symmetric functions of $(x_k, \ldots, x_n)$ that aren't constant. Thus Σ_n is at most $2 + \sum_{k=1}^{n} \min(k, 2^{n+2-k} - 2)$, which can be expressed in closed form as $(n+2-b_n)(n+1-b_n)/2 + 2(2^{b_n} - b_n)$, where $b_n = \lambda(n+4 - \lambda(n+4))$ and $\lambda n = \lfloor \lg n \rfloor$.

A symmetric function that attains this worst-case bound can be constructed in the following way (related to the de Bruijn cycles constructed in exercise 3.2.2–7): Let $p(x) = x^d + a_1 x^{d-1} + \cdots + a_d$ be a primitive polynomial modulo 2. Set $t_k \leftarrow 1$

for $0 \le k < d$; $t_k \leftarrow (a_1 t_{k-1} + \cdots + a_d t_{k-d}) \bmod 2$ for $d \le k < 2^d + d - 2$; $t_k \leftarrow (1 + a_1 t_{k-1} + \cdots + a_d t_{k-d}) \bmod 2$ for $2^d + d - 2 \le k < 2^{d+1} + d - 3$; and $t_{2^{d+1}+d-3} \leftarrow 1$. For example, when $p(x) = x^3 + x + 1$ we get $t_0 \ldots t_{16} = 11100101101000111$.

Then (i) the sequence $t_1 \ldots t_{2^d+d-3}$ contains all d-tuples except 0^d and 1^d as substrings; (ii) the sequence $t_{2^d+d-2} \ldots t_{2^{d+1}+d-4}$ is a cyclic shift of $\bar{t}_0 \ldots \bar{t}_{2^d-2}$; and (iii) $t_k = 1$ for $2^d - 1 \le k \le 2^d + d - 3$ and $2^{d+1} - 2 \le k \le 2^{d+1} + d - 3$. Consequently the sequence $t_0 \ldots t_{2^{d+1}+d-3}$ contains all $(d+1)$-tuples except 0^{d+1} and 1^{d+1} as substrings. Set $f(x) = t_{\nu x}$ to maximize $B(f)$ when $2^d + d - 4 < n \le 2^{d+1} + d - 3$.

Asymptotically, $\Sigma_n = \frac{1}{2}n^2 - n \lg n + O(n)$. [See I. Wegener, *Information and Control* **62** (1984), 129–143; M. Heap, *J. Electronic Testing* **4** (1993), 191–195.]

45. Module M_1 has only three inputs (x_1, y_1, z_1), and only three outputs $u_2 = x_1$, $v_2 = y_1 x_1$, $w_2 = z_1 x_1$. Module M_{n-1} is almost normal, but it has no input port for z_{n-1}, and it doesn't output u_n; it sets $z_{n-2} = x_{n-1} y_{n-1}$. Module M_n has only three inputs (v_n, w_n, x_n), and one output $y_{n-1} = x_n$ together with the main output, $w_n \vee v_n x_n$. With these definitions the dependencies between ports form an acyclic digraph.

(Modules could be constructed with all $b_k = 0$ and $a_k \le 5$, or even with $a_k \le 4$ as we'll see in exercise 47. But (33) and (34) are intended to illustrate backward signals in a simple example, not to demonstrate the tightest possible construction.)

46. For $6 \le k \le n - 3$ there are nine branches on (k), corresponding to three cases $(\bar{x}_1, x_1 \bar{x}_2, x_1 x_2)$ times three cases $(\bar{x}_{k-1}, \bar{x}_{k-2} x_{k-1}, \bar{x}_{k-3} x_{k-2} x_{k-1})$. The total BDD size turns out to be exactly $9n - 38$, if $n \ge 6$.

47. Suppose f has q_k subtables of order $n-k$, so that its QDD has q_k nodes that branch on x_{k+1}. We can encode them in $a_k = \lceil \lg q_k \rceil$ bits, and construct a module M_{k+1} with $b_k = b_{k+1} = 0$ that mimics the behavior of those q_k branch nodes. Thus by (86),

$$\sum_{k=0}^{n} 2^{a_k 2^{b_k}} = \sum_{k=0}^{n} 2^{\lceil \lg q_k \rceil} \le \sum_{k=0}^{n} (2q_k - 1) = 2Q(f) - (n+1) \le (n+1)B(f).$$

(The 2^m-way multiplexer shows that the additional factor of $(n+1)$ is necessary; indeed, Theorem M actually gives an upper bound on $Q(f)$.)

48. The sums $u_k = x_1 + \cdots + x_k$ and $v_k = x_{k+1} + \cdots + x_n$ can be represented on $1 + \lambda k$ and $1 + \lambda(n - k)$ wires, respectively. Let $t_k = x_k \wedge [u_k + v_k = k]$ and $w_k = t_1 \vee \cdots \vee t_k$. We can construct modules M_k having inputs u_{k-1} and w_{k-1} from M_{k-1} together with inputs v_k from M_{k+1}; module M_k outputs $u_k = u_{k-1} + x_k$ and $w_k = w_{k-1} \vee t_k$ to M_{k+1} as well as $v_{k-1} = v_k + x_k$ to M_{k-1}.

If p is a polynomial, $\sum_{k=0}^{n} 2^{p(a_k, b_k)} = 2^{(\log n)^{O(1)}}$ is asymptotically less than $2^{\Omega(n)}$. [See K. L. McMillan, *Symbolic Model Checking* (1993), §3.5, where Theorem M was introduced, with extensions to nonlinear layouts. The special case $b_1 = \cdots = b_n = 0$ had been noted previously by C. L. Berman, *IEEE Trans.* **CAD-10** (1991), 1059–1066.]

49.

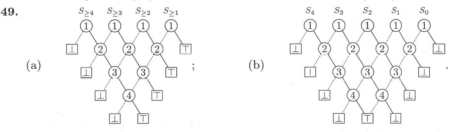

[See I. Semba and S. Yajima, *Trans. Inf. Proc. Soc. Japan* **35** (1994), 1663–1665.]

50.

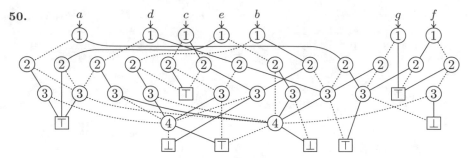

51. In this case $B(f_j) = 3j+2$ for $1 \le j \le n$, and $B(f_{n+1}) = 3n+1$; so the individual BDDs are only about $1/3$ as big as they are within (36). But almost no nodes are shared — only the sinks and one branch. So the total BDD size comes to $(3n^2 + 9n)/2$.

52. If the BDD base for $\{f_1, \ldots, f_m\}$ has s nodes, then $B(f) = s + m + 1 + [s\,{=}\,1]$.

53. Call the branch nodes a, b, c, d, e, f, g, with $\texttt{ROOT} = a$. After step R1 we have $\texttt{HEAD}[1] = {\sim}a$, $\texttt{AUX}(a) = {\sim}0$; $\texttt{HEAD}[2] = {\sim}b$, $\texttt{AUX}(b) = {\sim}c$, $\texttt{AUX}(c) = {\sim}0$; $\texttt{HEAD}[3] = {\sim}d$, $\texttt{AUX}(d) = {\sim}e$, $\texttt{AUX}(e) = {\sim}f$, $\texttt{AUX}(f) = {\sim}g$, $\texttt{AUX}(g) = {\sim}0$.

After R3 with $v = 3$ we have $s = {\sim}0$, $\texttt{AUX}(0) = {\sim}e$, $\texttt{AUX}(e) = f$, $\texttt{AUX}(f) = 0$; also $\texttt{AVAIL} = g$, $\texttt{LO}(g) = {\sim}1$, $\texttt{HI}(g) = d$, $\texttt{LO}(d) = {\sim}0$, and $\texttt{HI}(d) = \alpha$, where α was the initial value of $\texttt{AVAIL}$. (Nodes g and d have been recycled in favor of 1 and 0.) Then R4 sets $s \leftarrow e$ and $\texttt{AUX}(0) \leftarrow 0$. (The remaining nodes with $\texttt{V} = v$ start at s, linked via $\texttt{AUX}$.)

Now R7, starting with $p = q = e$ and $s = 0$, sets $\texttt{AUX}(1) \leftarrow {\sim}e$, $\texttt{LO}(f) \leftarrow {\sim}e$, $\texttt{HI}(f) \leftarrow g$, $\texttt{AVAIL} \leftarrow f$; and R8 resets $\texttt{AUX}(1) \leftarrow 0$.

Then step R3 with $v = 2$ sets $\texttt{LO}(b) \leftarrow 0$, $\texttt{LO}(c) \leftarrow e$, and $\texttt{HI}(c) \leftarrow 1$. No further changes of importance take place, although some $\texttt{AUX}$ fields temporarily become negative. We end up with Fig. 21.

54. Create nodes j for $1 < j \le 2^{n-1}$ by setting $\texttt{V}(j) \leftarrow \lceil \lg j \rceil$, $\texttt{LO}(j) \leftarrow 2j - 1$, and $\texttt{HI}(j) \leftarrow 2j$; also for $2^{n-1} < j \le 2^n$ by setting $\texttt{V}(j) \leftarrow n$, $\texttt{LO}(j) \leftarrow f(x_1, \ldots, x_{n-1}, 0)$, and $\texttt{HI}(j) \leftarrow f(x_1, \ldots, x_{n-1}, 1)$ when $j = (1x_1 \ldots x_{n-1})_2 + 1$. Then apply Algorithm R with $\texttt{ROOT} = 2$. (We can bypass step R1 by first setting $\texttt{AUX}(j) \leftarrow -j$ for $4 \le j \le 2^n$, then $\texttt{HEAD}[k] \leftarrow {\sim}(2^k)$ and $\texttt{AUX}(2^{k-1} + 1) \leftarrow -1$ for $1 \le k \le n$.)

55. It suffices to construct an unreduced diagram, since Algorithm R will then finish the job. Number the vertices $1, \ldots, n$ in such a way that no vertex except 1 appears before all of its neighbors. Represent the edges by arcs $a_1, \ldots, a_e$, where a_k is $u_k \longrightarrow v_k$ for some $u_k < v_k$, and where the arcs having $u_k = j$ are consecutive, with $s_j \le k < s_{j+1}$ and $1 = s_1 \le \cdots \le s_n = s_{n+1} = e + 1$. Define the "frontier" $V_k = \{1, v_1, \ldots, v_k\} \cap \{u_k, \ldots, n\}$ for $1 \le k \le e$, and let $V_0 = \{1\}$. The unreduced decision diagram will have branches on arc a_k for all partitions of V_{k-1} that correspond to connectedness relations that have arisen because of previous branches.

For example, consider $P_3 \,\square\, P_3$, where $(s_1, \ldots, s_{10}) = (1, 3, 5, 7, 8, 10, 11, 12, 13, 13)$ and $V_0 = \{1\}$, $V_1 = \{1, 2\}$, $V_2 = \{1, 2, 3\}$, $V_3 = \{2, 3, 4\}$, $\ldots$, $V_{12} = \{8, 9\}$. The branch on a_1 goes from the trivial partition 1 of V_0 to the partition $1|2$ of V_1 if $1 \not\!\!- 2$, or to the partition 12 if $1 - 2$. (The notation '$1|2$' stands for the set partition $\{1\} \cup \{2\}$, as in Section 7.2.1.5.) From $1|2$, the branch on a_2 goes to the partition $1|2|3$ of V_2 if $1 \not\!\!- 3$, otherwise to $13|2$; from 12, the branches go respectively to partitions $12|3$ and 123. Then from $1|2|3$, both branches on a_3 go to $\boxed{\perp}$, because vertex 1 can no longer be connected to the others. And so on. Eventually the partitions of $V_e = V_{12}$ are all identified with $\boxed{\perp}$, except for the trivial one-set partition, which corresponds to $\boxed{\top}$.

56. Start with $m \leftarrow 2$ in step R1, and $v_0 \leftarrow v_1 \leftarrow v_{\max} + 1$, $l_0 \leftarrow h_0 \leftarrow 0$, $l_1 \leftarrow h_1 \leftarrow 1$ as in (8). Assume that $\mathtt{HI}(0) = 0$ and $\mathtt{HI}(1) = 1$. Omit the assignments that involve $\mathtt{AVAIL}$ in steps R3 and R7. After setting $\mathtt{AUX(HI}(p)) \leftarrow 0$ in step R8, also set $v_m \leftarrow v$, $l_m \leftarrow \mathtt{HI(LO}(p))$, $h_m \leftarrow \mathtt{HI(HI}(p))$, $\mathtt{HI}(p) \leftarrow m$, and $m \leftarrow m + 1$. At the end of step R9, set $s \leftarrow m - [\mathtt{ROOT} = 0]$.

57. Set $\mathtt{LO(ROOT)} \leftarrow {\sim}\mathtt{LO(ROOT)}$. (We briefly complement the $\mathtt{LO}$ field of nodes that are still accessible after restriction.) Then for $v = \mathtt{V(ROOT)}, \ldots, v_{\max}$, set $p \leftarrow {\sim}\mathtt{HEAD}[v]$, $\mathtt{HEAD}[v] \leftarrow {\sim}0$, and do the following while $p \neq 0$: (i) Set $p' \leftarrow {\sim}\mathtt{AUX}(p)$. (ii) If $\mathtt{LO}(p) \geq 0$, set $\mathtt{HI}(p) \leftarrow \mathtt{AVAIL}$, $\mathtt{AUX}(p) \leftarrow 0$, and $\mathtt{AVAIL} \leftarrow p$ (node p can no longer be reached). Otherwise set $\mathtt{LO}(p) \leftarrow {\sim}\mathtt{LO}(p)$; if $\mathtt{FIX}[v] = 0$, set $\mathtt{HI}(p) \leftarrow \mathtt{LO}(p)$; if $\mathtt{FIX}[v] = 1$, set $\mathtt{LO}(p) \leftarrow \mathtt{HI}(p)$; if $\mathtt{LO(LO}(p)) \geq 0$, set $\mathtt{LO(LO}(p)) \leftarrow {\sim}\mathtt{LO(LO}(p))$; if $\mathtt{LO(HI}(p)) \geq 0$, set $\mathtt{LO(HI}(p)) \leftarrow {\sim}\mathtt{LO(HI}(p))$; and set $\mathtt{AUX}(p) \leftarrow \mathtt{HEAD}[v]$, $\mathtt{HEAD}[v] \leftarrow {\sim}p$. (iii) Set $p \leftarrow p'$. Finally, after finishing the loop on v, restore $\mathtt{LO}(0) \leftarrow 0$, $\mathtt{LO}(1) \leftarrow 1$.

58. Since $l \neq h$ and $l' \neq h'$, we have $l \diamond l' \neq h \diamond h'$, $l \diamond \alpha' \neq h \diamond \alpha'$, and $\alpha \diamond l' \neq \alpha \diamond h'$.

Suppose $\alpha \diamond \alpha' = \beta \diamond \beta'$, where $\beta = (v'', l'', h'')$ and $\beta' = (v''', l''', h''')$. If $v'' = v'''$ we have $v = v''$, $l \diamond l' = l'' \diamond l'''$, and $h \diamond h' = h'' \diamond h'''$. If $v'' < v'''$ we have $v = v''$, $l \diamond \alpha' = l'' \diamond \beta'$, and $h \diamond \alpha' = h'' \diamond \beta'$. Otherwise we have $v' = v'''$, $\alpha \diamond l' = \beta \diamond l'''$, and $\alpha \diamond h' = \beta \diamond h'''$. By induction, therefore, we have $\alpha = \beta$ and $\alpha' = \beta'$ in all cases.

59. (a) If h isn't constant we have $B(f \diamond g) = 3B(h) - 2$, essentially obtained by taking a copy of the BDD for h and replacing its sink nodes by two other copies.

(b) Suppose the profile and quasi-profile of h are $(b_0, \ldots, b_n)$ and $(q_0, \ldots, q_n)$, where $b_n = q_n = 2$. Then there are $b_k q_k$ branches on x_{2k+1} in $f \diamond g$, and $q_k b_{k-1}$ branches on x_{2k}, corresponding to ordered pairs of beads and subtables of h. When the BDD for h contains a branch from α to β and from α' to β', where $\mathtt{V}(\alpha) = j$, $\mathtt{V}(\beta) = k$, $\mathtt{V}(\alpha') = j'$, and $\mathtt{V}(\beta') = k'$, the BDD for $f \diamond g$ contains a corresponding branch with $\mathtt{V}(\alpha \diamond \alpha') = 2j - 1$ from $\alpha \diamond \alpha'$ to $\beta \diamond \alpha'$ when $j \leq j' < k$, and with $\mathtt{V}(\alpha \diamond \alpha') = 2j'$ from $\alpha \diamond \alpha'$ to $\alpha \diamond \beta'$ when $j' < j \leq k'$.

60. Every bead of order $n - j$ of the ordered pair (f, g) is either one of the $b_j b_j'$ ordered pairs of beads of f and g, or one of the $b_j(q_j' - b_j') + (q_j - b_j)b_j'$ ordered pairs that have the form (bead, nonbead) or (nonbead, bead). [This upper bound is achieved in the examples of exercises 59(b) and 63.]

61. Assume that $v = V(\alpha) \leq V(\beta)$. Let $\alpha_1, \ldots, \alpha_k$ be the nodes that point to α, and let $\beta_1, \ldots, \beta_l$ be the nodes with $V(\beta_j) < v$ that point to β; an imaginary node is assumed to point to each root. (Thus $k = $ in-degree(α) and $l \leq $ in-degree(β).) Then the melded nodes that point to $\alpha \diamond \beta$ are of three types: (i) $\alpha_i \diamond \beta_j$, where $V(\alpha_i) = V(\beta_j)$ and either $(\mathtt{LO}(\alpha_i) = \alpha$ and $\mathtt{LO}(\beta_j) = \beta)$ or $(\mathtt{HI}(\alpha_i) = \alpha$ and $\mathtt{HI}(\beta_j) = \beta)$; (ii) $\alpha \diamond \beta_j$, where $V(\alpha_i) < V(\beta_j)$ for some i; or (iii) $\alpha_i \diamond \beta$, where $V(\alpha_i) > V(\beta_j)$ for some j.

62. The BDD for f has one node on each level, and the BDD for g has two, except at the top and bottom. The BDD for $f \vee g$ has four nodes on nearly every level, by exercise 14(a). The BDD for $f \diamond g$ has seven nodes $\textcircled{j}$ when $5 \leq j \leq n - 3$, corresponding to ordered pairs of subtables of (f, g) that depend on x_j when $(x_1, \ldots, x_{j-1})$ have fixed values. Thus $B(f) = n + O(1)$, $B(g) = 2n + O(1)$, $B(f \diamond g) = 7n + O(1)$, and $B(f \vee g) = 4n + O(1)$. (Also $B(f \wedge g) = 7n + O(1)$, $B(f \oplus g) = 7n + O(1)$.)

63. The profiles of f and g are respectively $(1, 2, 2, \ldots, 2^{m-1}, 2^{m-1}, 2^m, 1, 1, \ldots, 1, 2)$ and $(0, 1, 2, 2, \ldots, 2^{m-1}, 2^{m-1}, 1, 1, \ldots, 1, 2)$; so $B(f) = 2^{m+2} - 1 \approx 4n$ and $B(g) = 2^{m+1} + 2^m - 1 \approx 3n$. The profile of $f \wedge g$ begins with $(1, 2, 4, \ldots, 2^{2m-2}, 2^{2m-1} - 2^{m-1})$, because there's a unique solution $x_1 \ldots x_{2m}$ to the equations

$$((x_1 \oplus x_2)(x_3 \oplus x_4) \ldots (x_{2m-1} \oplus x_{2m}))_2 = p, \ ((x_2 \oplus x_3) \ldots (x_{2m-2} \oplus x_{2m-1})x_{2m})_2 = q$$

for $0 \le p, q < 2^m$, and $p = q$ if and only if $x_1 = x_3 = \cdots = x_{2m-1} = 0$. After that the profile continues $(2^{m+1} - 2, 2^{m+1} - 2, 2^{m+1} - 4, 2^{m+1} - 6, \ldots, 4, 2, 2)$; the subfunctions are $x_{2m+j} \wedge \bar{x}_{2m+k}$ or $\bar{x}_{2m+j} \wedge x_{2m+k}$ for $1 \le j < k \le 2^m$, together with x_{2m+j} and $\bar{x}_{2m+j}$ for $2 \le j \le 2^m$. All in all, we have $B(f \wedge g) = 2^{2m+1} + 2^{m-1} - 1 \approx 2n^2$.

64. The BDD for *any* Boolean combination of f_1, f_2, and f_3 is contained in the meld $f_1 \diamond f_2 \diamond f_3$, whose size is at most $B(f_1)B(f_2)B(f_3)$.

65. $h = g$? f_1: f_0, where f_c is the restriction of f obtained by setting $x_j \leftarrow c$. The first upper bound follows as in answer 64, because $B(f_c) \le B(f)$. The second bound fails when, for example, $n = 2^m + 3m$ and $h = M_m(x;y)$? $M_m(x';y)$: $M_m(x'';y)$, where $x = (x_1, \ldots, x_m)$, $x' = (x'_1, \ldots, x'_m)$, $x'' = (x''_1, \ldots, x''_m)$, and $y = (y_0, \ldots, y_{2^m-1})$; but such failures appear to be rare. [See R. E. Bryant, *IEEE Trans.* **C-35** (1986), 685; J. Jain, K. Mohanram, D. Moundanos, I. Wegener, and Y. Lu, *ACM/IEEE Design Automation Conf.* **37** (2000), 681–686.]

66. Set NTOP $\leftarrow f_0 + 1 - l$ and terminate the algorithm.

67. Let t_k denote template location POOLSIZE $- 2k$. Step S1 sets LEFT$(t_1) \leftarrow 5$, RIGHT$(t_1) \leftarrow 7$, $l \leftarrow 1$. Step S2 for $l = 1$ puts t_1 into both LLIST[2] and HLIST[2]. Step S5 for $l = 2$ sets LEFT$(t_2) \leftarrow 4$, RIGHT$(t_2) \leftarrow 5$, L$(t_1) \leftarrow t_2$; LEFT$(t_3) \leftarrow 3$, RIGHT$(t_3) \leftarrow 6$, H$(t_1) \leftarrow t_3$. Step S2 for $l = 2$ sets L$(t_2) \leftarrow 0$ and puts t_2 in HLIST[3]; then it puts t_3 into LLIST[3] and HLIST[3]. And so on. Phase 1 ends with $(\text{LSTART}[0], \ldots, \text{LSTART}[4]) = (t_0, t_1, t_3, t_5, t_8)$ and

k	LEFT(t_k)	RIGHT(t_k)	L(t_k)	H(t_k)		k	LEFT(t_k)	RIGHT(t_k)	L(t_k)	H(t_k)
1	5 $[\alpha]$	7 $[\omega]$	t_2	t_3		5	3 $[\gamma]$	4 $[\varphi]$	t_6	t_8
2	4 $[\beta]$	5 $[\chi]$	0	t_4		6	2 $[\delta]$	2 $[\tau]$	0	1
3	3 $[\gamma]$	6 $[\psi]$	t_4	t_5		7	2 $[\delta]$	1 $[\top]$	0	1
4	3 $[\gamma]$	1 $[\top]$	t_7	1		8	1 $[\top]$	3 $[\upsilon]$	1	0

representing the meld $\alpha \diamond \omega$ in Fig. 24 but with $\bot \diamond x = x \diamond \bot = \bot$ and $\top \diamond \top = \top$.

Let $f_k = f_0 + k$. In phase 2, step S7 for $l = 4$ sets LEFT$(t_6) \leftarrow {\sim}0$, LEFT$(t_7) \leftarrow t_6$, LEFT$(t_8) \leftarrow {\sim}1$, and RIGHT$(t_6) \leftarrow$ RIGHT$(t_7) \leftarrow$ RIGHT$(t_8) \leftarrow -1$. Step S8 undoes the changes made to LEFT(0) and LEFT(1). Step S11 with $s = t_8$ sets LEFT$(t_8) \leftarrow {\sim}2$, RIGHT$(t_8) \leftarrow t_8$, V$(f_2) \leftarrow 4$, LO$(f_2) \leftarrow 1$, HI$(f_2) \leftarrow 0$. With $s = t_7$ that step sets LEFT$(t_7) \leftarrow {\sim}3$, RIGHT$(t_7) \leftarrow t_7$, V$(f_3) \leftarrow 4$, LO$(f_3) \leftarrow 0$, HI$(f_3) \leftarrow 1$; meanwhile step S10 has set RIGHT$(t_6) \leftarrow t_7$. Eventually the templates will be transformed to

k	LEFT(t_k)	RIGHT(t_k)	L(t_k)	H(t_k)		k	LEFT(t_k)	RIGHT(t_k)	L(t_k)	H(t_k)
1	${\sim}8$	t_1	t_2	t_3		5	${\sim}4$	t_5	t_7	t_8
2	${\sim}7$	t_2	0	t_4		6	${\sim}0$	t_7	0	1
3	${\sim}6$	t_3	t_4	t_5		7	${\sim}3$	t_7	0	1
4	${\sim}5$	t_4	t_7	1		8	${\sim}2$	t_8	1	0

(but they can then be discarded). The resulting BDD for $f \wedge g$ is

k	V(f_k)	LO(f_k)	HI(f_k)		k	V(f_k)	LO(f_k)	HI(f_k)
2	4	1	0		6	2	5	4
3	4	0	1		7	2	0	5
4	3	3	2		8	1	7	6.
5	3	3	1					

68. If LEFT$(t) < 0$ at the beginning of step S10, set RIGHT$(t) \leftarrow t$, $q \leftarrow$ NTOP, NTOP $\leftarrow$ $q + 1$, LEFT$(t) \leftarrow \sim(q - f_0)$, LO$(q) \leftarrow \sim$LEFT$(L(t))$, HI$(q) \leftarrow \sim$LEFT$(H(t))$, V$(q) \leftarrow l$, and return to S9.

69. Make sure that NTOP $\leq$ TBOT at the end of step S1 and when going from S11 to S9. (It's *not* necessary to make this test inside the loop of S11.) Also make sure that NTOP $\leq$ HBASE just after setting HBASE in step S4.

70. This choice would make the hash table a bit smaller; memory overflow would therefore be slightly less likely, at the expense of slightly more collisions. But it also would slow down the action, because *make_template* would have to check that NTOP $\leq$ TBOT whenever TBOT decreases.

71. Add a new field, EXTRA$(t) = \alpha''$, to each template t (see (43)).

72. In place of steps S4 and S5, use the approach of Algorithm R to bucket-sort the elements of the linked lists that begin at LLIST$[l]$ and HLIST$[l]$. This is possible if an extra one-bit hint is used within the pointers to distinguish links in the L fields from links in the H fields, because we can then determine the LO and HI parameters of t's descendants as a function of t and its "parity."

73. If the BDD profile is $(b_0, \ldots, b_n)$, we can assign $p_j = \lceil b_{j-1}/2^e \rceil$ pages to branches on x_j. Auxiliary tables of $p_1 + \cdots + p_{n+1} \leq \lceil B(f)/2^e \rceil + n$ short integers allow us to compute $V(p) = T[\pi(p)]$, LO$(p) =$ LO$(M[\pi(p)] + \sigma(p))$, HI$(p) =$ HI$(M[\pi(p)] + \sigma(p))$.

For example, if $e = 12$ and $n < 2^{16}$, we can represent arbitrary BDDs of up to $2^{32} - 2^{28} + 2^{16} + 2^{12}$ nodes with 32-bit virtual LO and HI pointers. Each BDD requires appropriate auxiliary T and M tables of size $\leq 2^{20}$, constructible from its profile.

[This method can significantly improve caching behavior. It was inspired by the paper of P. Ashar and M. Cheong, *IEEE/ACM Internat. Conf. Computer-Aided Design* **CAD-94** (1994), 622–627, which also introduced algorithms similar to Algorithm S.]

74. The required condition is now $\mu_n(x_1, \ldots, x_{2^n}) \wedge [\bar{x}_1 = x_{2^n}] \wedge \cdots \wedge [\bar{x}_{2^{n-1}} = x_{2^{n-1}+1}]$. If we set $y_1 = x_1$, $y_2 = x_3$, $\ldots$, $y_{2^{n-2}} = x_{2^{n-1}-1}$, $y_{2^{n-2}+1} = \bar{x}_{2^{n-1}}$, $y_{2^{n-2}+2} = \bar{x}_{2^{n-1}-2}$, $\ldots$, $y_{2^{n-1}} = \bar{x}_2$, (49) yields the equivalent condition $\mu_{n-1}(y_1, \ldots, y_{2^{n-1}}) \wedge [y_{2^{n-2}} \leq \bar{y}_{2^{n-2}+1}] \wedge [y_{2^{n-2}-1} \leq y_{2^{n-2}+2}] \wedge \cdots \wedge [y_1 \leq \bar{y}_{2^{n-1}}]$, which is eminently suitable for evaluation by Algorithm S. (The evaluation should be from left to right; right-to-left would generate enormous intermediate results.)

With this approach we find that there are respectively 1, 2, 4, 12, 81, 2646, 1422564, 229809982112 monotone self-dual functions of 1, 2, $\ldots$, 8 variables. (See Table 7.1.1–3 and answer 7.1.2–88.) The 8-variable functions are characterized by a BDD of 130,305,082 nodes; Algorithm S needs about 204 gigamems to compute it.

75. Begin with $\rho_1(x_1, x_2) = [x_1 \leq x_2]$, and replace $G_{2^n}(x_1, \ldots, x_{2^n})$ in (49) by the function $H_{2^n}(x_1, \ldots, x_{2^n}) = [x_1 \leq x_2 \leq x_3 \leq x_4] \wedge \cdots \wedge [x_{2^n-3} \leq x_{2^n-2} \leq x_{2^n-1} \leq x_{2^n}]$.

(It turns out that $B(\rho_9) = 3{,}683{,}424$; about 170 megamems suffice to compute that BDD, and ρ_{10} is almost within reach. Algorithm C now quickly yields the exact numbers of regular n-variable Boolean functions for $1 \leq n \leq 9$, namely 3, 5, 10, 27, 119, 1173, 44315, 16175190, 284432730176. Similarly, we can count the self-dual ones, as in exercise 74; those numbers, whose early history is discussed in answer 7.1.1–123, are 1, 1, 2, 3, 7, 21, 135, 2470, 319124, 1214554343, for $1 \leq n \leq 10$.)

76. Say that $x_0 \ldots x_{j-1}$ *forces* x_j if $x_i = 1$ for some $i \subseteq j$ with $0 \leq i < j$. Then $x_0 x_1 \ldots x_{2^n-1}$ corresponds to a clutter if and only if $x_j = 0$ whenever $x_0 \ldots x_{j-1}$ forces x_j, for $0 \leq j < 2^n$. And $\mu_n(x_0, \ldots, x_{2^n-1}) = 1$ if and only if $x_j = 1$ whenever $x_0 \ldots x_{j-1}$ forces x_j. So we get the desired BDD from that of $\mu_n(x_1, \ldots, x_{2^n})$ by (i) changing each branch (j) to $(j-1)$, and (ii) interchanging the LO and HI branches at every branch node that has LO $= \boxed{\perp}$. (Notice that, by Corollary 7.1.1Q, the prime implicants of every monotone Boolean function correspond to clutters.)

77. Continuing the previous answer, say that the bit vector $x_0 \ldots x_{k-1}$ is *consistent* if we have $x_j = 1$ whenever $x_0 \ldots x_{j-1}$ forces x_j, for $0 < j < k$. Let b_k be the number of consistent vectors of length k. For example, $b_4 = 6$ because of the vectors $\{0000, 0001, 0011, 0101, 0111, 1111\}$. Notice that exactly $c_k = b_{k+1} - b_k$ clutters $\mathcal{S}$ have the property that k represents their "largest" set, $\max\{s \mid s \text{ represents a set of } \mathcal{S}\}$. We have $(c_0, c_1, c_2, \ldots) = (1, 1, 2, 1, 5, 3, 5, 1, 19, 14, 25, 6, 50, 14, 19, 1, 167, 148, 282, 84, \ldots)$.

The BDD for $\mu_n(x_1, \ldots, x_{2^n})$ has b_{k-1} branch nodes (k) when $1 \le k \le 2^{n-1}$. Proof: Every subfunction defined by $x_1, \ldots, x_{k-1}$ is either identically false or defines a consistent vector $x_1 \ldots x_{k-1}$. In the latter case the subfunction is a bead, because it takes different values under certain settings of $x_{k+1}, \ldots, x_{2^n}$. Indeed, if $x_1 \ldots x_{k-1}$ forces x_k, we set $x_{k+1} \leftarrow \cdots \leftarrow x_{2^n} \leftarrow 1$; otherwise we set $x_j \leftarrow y_j$ for $k < j \le 2^n$, where

$$y_{j+1} = [x_{i+1} = 1 \text{ for some } i \subseteq j \text{ with } i + 1 < k],$$

noting that $y_{2^{n-1}+k} = 0$.

On the other hand there are $b_{k'}$ branches (k) when $k = 2^n - k'$ and $0 \le k' < 2^{n-1}$. In this case the nonconstant subfunctions arising from $x_1, \ldots, x_{k-1}$ lead to values y_j as above, where the vector $\bar{y}_{0'} \bar{y}_{1'} \ldots \bar{y}_{k'}$ is consistent. (Here $0' = 2^n$, $1' = 2^n - 1$, etc.) Conversely, every such consistent vector describes such a subfunction; we can, for example, set $x_j \leftarrow 0$ when $j < k - 2^{n-1}$ or $2^{n-1} \le j < k$, otherwise $x_j \leftarrow y_{2^{n-1}+j}$. This subfunction is a bead if and only if $y_{k'} = 1$ or $\bar{y}_{0'} \ldots \bar{y}_{(k-1)'}$ forces $\bar{y}_{k'}$. Thus the beads correspond to consistent vectors of length k'; and different vectors define different beads.

This argument shows that there are $b_{k-1} - c_{k-1}$ branches (k) with LO $= \boxed{\perp}$ when $1 \le k \le 2^{n-1}$ and c_{2^n-k} such branches when $2^{n-1} < k \le 2^n$. Hence exactly half of the $B(\mu_n) - 2$ branch nodes have LO $= \boxed{\perp}$.

78. To count graphs on n labeled vertices with maximum degree $\le d$, construct the Boolean function of the $\binom{n}{2}$ variables in its adjacency matrix, namely $\bigwedge_{k=1}^{n} S_{\le d}(X_k)$, where X_k is the set of variables in row k of the matrix. For example, when $n = 5$ there are 10 variables, and the function is $S_{\le d}(x_1, x_2, x_3, x_4) \wedge S_{\le d}(x_1, x_5, x_6, x_7) \wedge S_{\le d}(x_2, x_5, x_8, x_9) \wedge S_{\le d}(x_3, x_6, x_8, x_{10}) \wedge S_{\le d}(x_4, x_7, x_9, x_{10})$. When $n = 12$ the BDDs for $d = (1, 2, \ldots, 10)$ have respectively (5960, 137477, 1255813, 5295204, 10159484, 11885884, 9190884, 4117151, 771673, 28666) nodes, so they are readily computed with Algorithm S. To count solutions with maximum degree d, subtract the number of solutions for degree $\le d-1$ from the number for degree $\le d$; the answers for $0 \le d \le 11$ are:

1	3038643940889754	29271277569846191555
140151	211677202624318662	17880057008325613629
3568119351	3617003021179405538	4489497643961740521
8616774658305	17884378201906645374	430038382710483623

[In general there are $t_n - 1$ graphs on n labeled vertices with maximum degree 1, where t_n is the number of involutions, Eq. 5.1.4–(40).]

The methods of Section 7.2.3 are superior to BDDs for enumerations such as these, when n is large, because labeled graphs have $n!$ symmetries. But when n has a moderate size, BDDs produce answers quickly, and nicely characterize all the solutions.

79. In the following counts, obtained from the BDDs in the previous answer, each graph with k edges is weighted by 2^{66-k}. Divide by 3^{66} to get probabilities.

$$73786976294838206464 \qquad 11646725483430295546484263747584$$
$$55315674993080529074112 \qquad 77677416878709243055475188803968$$
$$598535502868315236548476928 \qquad 25144575345589759186086668688384$$
$$6837983522058455011716759520 \qquad 4527336156360899392181934039044$$
$$138035892756457768347923329432 \qquad 4596863773888180534154567736$$
$$7024096376298397076969081536512 \qquad 2093195580480313818292294985$$

80. If the original functions f and g have no BDD nodes in common, both algorithms encounter almost exactly the same subproblems: Algorithm S deals with all nodes of $f \diamond g$ that aren't descended from nodes of the forms $\alpha \diamond \boxed{\perp}$ or $\boxed{\perp} \diamond \beta$, while (55) also avoids nodes that descend from the forms $\alpha \diamond \boxed{\top}$ or $\boxed{\top} \diamond \beta$. Furthermore, (55) takes shortcuts when it meets nontrivial subproblems $\text{AND}(f', g')$ with $f' = g'$; Algorithm S cannot recognize the fact that such cases are easy. And (55) can also win if it happens to stumble across a relevant memo left over from a previous computation.

81. Just change 'AND' to 'XOR' and '$\wedge$' to '$\oplus$' throughout. The simple cases are now $f \oplus 0 = f$, $0 \oplus g = g$, and $f \oplus g = 0$ if $f = g$. We should also swap $f \leftrightarrow g$ if $f > g \neq 0$.

  Notes: The author experimentally inserted further memos '$f \oplus r = g$' and '$g \oplus r = f$' in the bottom line; but these additional cache entries seemed to do more harm than good. Considering other binary operators, there's no need to implement both $\text{BUTNOT}(f,g) = f \wedge \bar{g}$ and $\text{NOTBUT}(f,g) = \bar{f} \wedge g$, since the latter is $\text{BUTNOT}(g,f)$. Also, $\text{XOR}(1, \text{OR}(f,g))$ may be better than an implementation of $\text{NOR}(f,g) = \neg(f \vee g)$.

82. A top-level computation of $F \leftarrow \text{AND}(f,g)$ begins with f and g in computer registers, but $\text{REF}(f)$ and $\text{REF}(g)$ do not include "references" such as those. (We do, however, assume that f and g are both alive.)

  If (55) discovers that $f \wedge g$ is obviously r, it increases $\text{REF}(r)$ by 1.

  If (55) finds $f \wedge g = r$ in the memo cache, it increases $\text{REF}(r)$, and recursively increases $\text{REF}(\text{LO}(r))$ and $\text{REF}(\text{HI}(r))$ in the same way if r was dead.

  If step U1 finds $p = q$, it *decreases* $\text{REF}(p)$ by 1 (believe it or not); this won't kill p.

  If step U2 finds r, there are two cases: If r was alive, it sets $\text{REF}(r) \leftarrow \text{REF}(r) + 1$, $\text{REF}(p) \leftarrow \text{REF}(p) - 1$, $\text{REF}(q) \leftarrow \text{REF}(q) - 1$. Otherwise it simply sets $\text{REF}(r) \leftarrow 1$.

  When step U3 creates a new node r, it sets $\text{REF}(r) \leftarrow 1$.

  Finally, after the top-level AND returns a value r that we wish to assign to F, we must first *dereference* F, if $F \neq \Lambda$; this means setting $\text{REF}(F) \leftarrow \text{REF}(F) - 1$, and recursively dereferencing $\text{LO}(F)$ and $\text{HI}(F)$ if $\text{REF}(F)$ has become 0. Then we set $F \leftarrow r$ (without adjusting $\text{REF}(r)$).

  [Furthermore, in a quantification routine such as (65) or in the composition routine (72), both r_l and r_h should be dereferenced after the OR or MUX has computed r.]

83. Exercise 61 shows that the subproblem $f \wedge g$ occurs at most once per top-level call, when $\text{REF}(f) = \text{REF}(g) = 1$. [This idea is due to F. Somenzi; see the paper cited in answer 84. Many nodes have reference count 1, because the average count is approximately 2, and because the sinks usually have large counts. However, such cache-avoidance did not improve the overall performance in the author's experiments, possibly because of the examples investigated, or possibly because "accidental" cache hits in other top-level operations can be useful.]

84. Many possibilities exist, and no simple technique appears to be a clear winner. The cache and table sizes should be powers of 2, to facilitate calculating the hash functions. The size of the unique table for x_v should be roughly proportional to the number of nodes that currently branch on x_v (alive or dead). It's necessary to rehash everything when a table is downsized or upsized.

In the author's experiments while writing this section, the cache size was doubled whenever the number of insertions since the beginning of the most recent top-level command exceeded ln 2 times the current cache size. (At that point a random hash function will have filled about half of the slots.) After garbage collection, the cache was downsized, if necessary, so that it either had 256 slots or was at least $1/4$ full.

It's easy to keep track of the current number of dead nodes; hence we know at all times how much memory a garbage collection will reclaim. The author obtained satisfactory results by inserting a new step $U2\frac{1}{2}$ between U2 and U3: "Increase C by 1, where C is a global counter. If $C \bmod 1024 = 0$, and if at least $1/8$ of all current nodes are dead, collect garbage."

[See F. Somenzi, *Software Tools for Technology Transfer* **3** (2001), 171–181 for numerous further suggestions based on extensive experience.]

85. The complete table would have 2^{32} entries of 32 bits each, for a total of 2^{34} bytes ($\approx$ 17.2 gigabytes). The BDD base discussed after (58), with about 136 million nodes using zip-ordered bits, can be stored in about 1.1 gigabyte; the one discussed in Corollary Y, which ranks all of the multiplier bits first, needs only about 400 megabytes.

86. If $f = 0$ or $g = h$, return g. If $f = 1$, return h. If $g = 0$ or $f = g$, return AND(f, h). If $h = 1$ or $f = h$, return OR(f, g). If $g = 1$, return IMPLIES(f, h); if $h = 0$, return BUTNOT(g, f). (If binary IMPLIES and/or BUTNOT aren't implemented directly, it's OK to let the corresponding cases propagate in ternary guise.)

87. Sort the given pointer values f, g, h so that $f \le g \le h$. If $f = 0$, return AND(g, h). If $f = 1$, return OR(g, h). If $f = g$ or $g = h$, return g.

88. The trio of functions $(f, g, h) = (R_0, R_1, R_2)$ makes an amusing example, when

$$R_a(x_1, \ldots, x_n) = [(x_n \ldots x_1)_2 \bmod 3 \ne a] = R_{(2a+x_1) \bmod 3}(x_2, \ldots, x_n).$$

Thanks to the memos, the ternary recursion finds $f \wedge g \wedge h = 0$ by examining only one case at each level; the binary computation of, say, $f \wedge g = \bar{h}$ definitely takes longer.

More dramatically, let $f = x_1 \wedge (x_2?\ F{:}\ G)$, $g = x_2 \wedge (x_1?\ G{:}\ F)$, and $h = x_1?\ \bar{x}_2 \wedge F{:}\ x_2 \wedge G$, where F and G are functions of $(x_3, \ldots, x_n)$ such that $B(F \wedge G) = \Theta(B(F)B(G))$ as in exercise 63. Then $f \wedge g$, $g \wedge h$, and $h \wedge f$ all have large BDDs, but the ternary recursion immediately discovers that $f \wedge g \wedge h = 0$.

89. (a) True; the left side is $(f_{00} \vee f_{01}) \vee (f_{10} \vee f_{11})$, the right side is $(f_{00} \vee f_{10}) \vee (f_{01} \vee f_{11})$.
(b) Similarly true. (And $\u$'s are commutative too.)
(c) Usually false; see part (d).
(d) $\forall x_1 \exists x_2 f = (f_{00} \vee f_{01}) \wedge (f_{10} \vee f_{11}) = (\exists x_2 \forall x_1 f) \vee (f_{00} \wedge f_{11}) \vee (f_{01} \wedge f_{10})$.

90. Change $\exists j_1 \ldots \exists j_m$ to $\u j_1 \ldots \u j_m$.

91. (a) $f \downarrow 1 = f$, $f \downarrow x_j = f_1$, and $f \downarrow \bar{x}_j = f_0$, in the notation of (63).
(b) This distributive law is obvious, by the definition of $\downarrow$. (Also true for $\vee$, $\oplus$, etc.)
(c) True if and only if g is not identically zero. (Consequently the value of $f(x_1, \ldots, x_n) \downarrow g$ for $g \ne 0$ is determined solely by the values of $x_j \downarrow g$ for $1 \le j \le n$.)
(d) $f(x_1, 1, 0, x_4, 0, 1, x_7, \ldots, x_n)$. This is the restriction of f with respect to $x_2 = 1$, $x_3 = 0$, $x_5 = 0$, $x_6 = 1$ (see exercise 57), also called the *cofactor* of f with respect to the subcube g. (A similar result holds when g is any product of literals.)
(e) $f(x_1, \ldots, x_{n-1}, x_1 \oplus \cdots \oplus x_{n-1} \oplus 1)$. (Consider the case $f = x_j$, for $1 \le j \le n$.)
(f) $x_1?\ f(1, \ldots, 1){:}\ f(0, \ldots, 0)$.
(g) $f(1, x_2, \ldots, x_n) \downarrow g(x_2, \ldots, x_n)$.
(h) If $f = x_2$ and $g = x_1 \vee x_2$ we have $f \downarrow g = \bar{x}_1 \vee x_2$.

(i) CONSTRAIN$(f, g) =$ "If $f \downarrow g$ has an obvious value, return it. Otherwise, if $f \downarrow g = r$ is in the memo cache, return r. Otherwise represent f and g as in (52); set $r \leftarrow$ CONSTRAIN(f_h, g_h) if $g_l = 0$, $r \leftarrow$ CONSTRAIN(f_l, g_l) if $g_h = 0$, otherwise $r \leftarrow$ UNIQUE$(v, \text{CONSTRAIN}(f_l, g_l), \text{CONSTRAIN}(f_h, g_h))$; put '$f \downarrow g = r$' into the memo cache, and return r." Here the obvious values are $f \downarrow 0 = 0 \downarrow g = 0$; $f \downarrow 1 = f$; $1 \downarrow g = g \downarrow g = [g \neq 0]$.

[The operator $f \downarrow g$ was introduced in 1989 by O. Coudert, C. Berthet, and J. C. Madre. Examples such as the functions in (h) led them to propose also the modified operator $f \Downarrow g$, "f restricted to g," which has a similar recursion except that it uses $f \Downarrow (\exists x_v g)$ instead of $(\bar{x}_v? f_l \Downarrow g_l: f_h \Downarrow g_h)$ when $f_l = f_h$. See *Lecture Notes in Computer Science* **407** (1989), 365–373.]

92. See answer 91(d) for the "if" part. Notice also that (i) $x_1 \downarrow g = x_1$ if and only if $g_0 \neq 0$ and $g_1 \neq 0$, where $g_c = g(c, x_2, \ldots, x_n)$; (ii) $x_n \downarrow g = x_n$ if and only if $\partial x_n g = 0$ and $g \neq 0$.

　　Suppose $f^\pi \downarrow g^\pi = (f \downarrow g)^\pi$ for all f and π. If $g \neq 0$ isn't a subcube, there's an index j such that $g_0 \neq 0$ and $g_1 \neq 0$ and $\partial x_j g \neq 0$, where $g_c = g(x_1, \ldots, x_{j-1}, c, x_{j+1}, \ldots, x_n)$. By the previous paragraph, we have (i) $x_j \downarrow g = x_j$ and (ii) $x_j \downarrow g \neq x_j$, a contradiction.

93. Let $f = J(x_1, \ldots, x_n; f_1, \ldots, f_n)$ and $g = J(x_1, \ldots, x_n; g_1, \ldots, g_n)$, where

$$f_v = x_{n+1} \vee \cdots \vee x_{5n} \vee J(x_{5n+1}, \ldots, x_{6n}; [v-1], \ldots, [v-n]),$$
$$g_v = x_{n+1} \vee \cdots \vee x_{5n} \vee J(x_{5n+1}, \ldots, x_{6n}; [v=1]+[v-1], \ldots, [v=n]+[v-n]),$$

and J is the junction function of exercise 52.

　　If G can be 3-colored, let $\hat{f} = J(x_1, \ldots, x_n; \hat{f}_1, \ldots, \hat{f}_n)$, where

$$\hat{f}_v = x_{n+1} \vee \cdots \vee x_{5n} \vee J(x_{5n+1}, \ldots, x_{6n}; \hat{f}_{v1}, \ldots, \hat{f}_{vn}),$$

and $\hat{f}_{vw} = [v$ and w have different colors]. Then $B(\hat{f}) < n + 3(5n) + 2$.

　　Conversely, suppose there's an approximating $\hat{f}$ such that $B(\hat{f}) < 16n + 2$, and let $\hat{f}_v$ be the subfunction with $x_1 = [v=1]$, ..., $x_n = [v=n]$. At most three of these subfunctions are distinct, because every distinct $\hat{f}_v$ must branch on each of x_{n+1}, ..., x_{5n}. Color the vertices so that u and v get the same color if and only if $\hat{f}_u = \hat{f}_v$; this can happen only if $u \not\!\!- v$, so the coloring is legitimate. [M. Sauerhoff and I. Wegener, *IEEE Transactions* **CAD-15** (1996), 1435–1437.]

94. *Case 1:* $v \neq g_o$. Then we aren't quantifying over x_v; hence $g = g_h$, and $f \,E\, g = \bar{x}_v? f_l \,E\, g: f_h \,E\, g$.

　　Case 2: $v = g_o$. Then $g = x_v \wedge g_h$ and $f \,E\, g = (f_l \,E\, g_h) \vee (f_h \,E\, g_h) = r_l \vee r_h$. In the subcase $v \neq f_o$, we have $f_l = f_h = f$; hence $r_l = r_h$, and we can directly reduce $f \,E\, g$ to $f \,E\, g_h$ (an instance of "tail recursion").

　　[Rudell observes that the order of quantification in (65) corresponds to bottom-up order of the variables. That order is convenient, but not always best; sometimes it's better to remove the $\exists$s one by one in another order, based on knowledge of the functions involved.]

95. If $r_l = 1$ and $v = y_o$, we can set $r \leftarrow 1$ and forget about r_h. (This change led to a 100-fold speedup in some of the author's experiments.)

96. For $\forall$, just change E to A and OR to AND. For ∂, change E to D and OR to XOR; also, if $v \neq f_o$, return 0. [Routines for the yes/no quantifiers $\curlywedge$ and N are analogous to ∂. Yes/no quantifiers should be used only when $m = 1$; otherwise they make little sense.]

97. Proceeding bottom-up, the amount of work on each level is at worst proportional to the number of nodes on that level.

98. The function $\mathrm{NOTEND}(x) = \exists y \exists z (\mathrm{ADJ}(x,y) \wedge \mathrm{ADJ}(x,z) \wedge [y \neq z])$ identifies all vertices of degree ≥ 2. Hence $\mathrm{ENDPT}(x) = \mathrm{KER}(x) \wedge \neg \mathrm{NOTEND}(x)$. And $\mathrm{PAIR}(x,y) = \mathrm{ENDPT}(x) \wedge \mathrm{ENDPT}(y) \wedge \mathrm{ADJ}(x,y)$.

[For example, when G is the contiguous-USA graph, with the states ordered as in (104), we have $B(\mathrm{NOTEND}) = 992$, $B(\mathrm{ENDPT}) = 264$, and $B(\mathrm{PAIR}) = 203$. Before applying $\exists y \exists z$ the BDD size is 50511. There are exactly 49 kernels of degree 1. The nine components of size 2 are obtained by mixing the following three solutions:

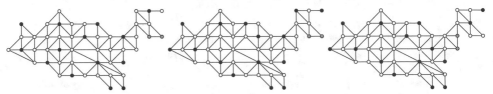

The total cost of this calculation, using the stated algorithms, is about 14 megamems, in 6.3 megabytes of memory — only about 52 memory references per kernel.]

99. Find a triangle of mutually adjacent states, and fix their colors. The BDD size also decreases substantially if we choose states of high degree in the "middle" levels. For example, by setting $a_{\mathrm{MO}} = b_{\mathrm{MO}} = a_{\mathrm{TN}} = \bar{b}_{\mathrm{TN}} = \bar{a}_{\mathrm{AR}} = b_{\mathrm{AR}} = 1$ we reduce the 25579 nodes to only 4642 (and the total execution time also drops below 2 megamems).

[Bryant's original manuscript about BDDs discussed graph coloring in detail, but he decided to substitute other material when his paper was published in 1986.]

100. Replace $\mathrm{IND}(x_{\mathrm{ME}}, \ldots, x_{\mathrm{CA}})$ by $\mathrm{IND}(x_{\mathrm{ME}}, \ldots, x_{\mathrm{CA}}) \wedge S_{12}(x_{\mathrm{ME}}, \ldots, x_{\mathrm{CA}})$, to get the 12-node independent sets; this BDD has size 1964. Then use (73) as before, and the trick of answer 99, getting a COLOR function with 184,260 nodes and 12,554,677,864 solutions. (The running time is approximately 26 megamems.)

101. If a state's weight is w, assign $2w$ and w as the respective weights of its a and b variables, and use Algorithm B. (For example, variable a_{WY} gets weight $2(23 + 25) = 96$.) The solution, shown here with color codes ①②❸❹, is unique.

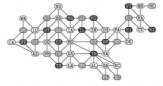

102. The main idea is that, when g_j changes, all results in the cache for functions with $f_o > j$ remain valid. To exploit this principle we can maintain an array of "time stamps" $G_1 \geq G_2 \geq \cdots \geq G_n \geq 0$, one for each variable. There's a master clock time $G \geq G_1$, representing the number of distinct compositions done or prepared; another variable G' records whether G has changed since COMPOSE was last invoked. Initially $G = G' = G_1 = \cdots = G_n = 0$. The subroutine $\mathrm{NEWG}(j,g)$ is implemented as follows:

N1. [Easy case?] If $g_j = g$, exit the subroutine. Otherwise set $g_j \leftarrow g$.

N2. [Can we reset?] If $g \neq x_j$, or if $j < n$ and $G_{j+1} > 0$, go to N4.

N3. [Reset stamps.] While $j > 0$ and $g_j = x_j$, set $G_j \leftarrow 0$ and $j \leftarrow j - 1$. Then if $j = 0$, set $G \leftarrow G - G'$, $G' \leftarrow 0$, and exit.

N4. [Update G?] If $G' = 0$, set $G \leftarrow G + 1$ and $G' \leftarrow 1$.

N5. [New stamps.] While $j > 0$ and $G_j \neq G$, set $G_j \leftarrow G$ and $j \leftarrow j - 1$. Exit. ∎

(Reference counts also need to be maintained appropriately.) Before launching a top-level call of COMPOSE, set $G' \leftarrow 0$. Change the COMPOSE routine (72) to use $f[G_v]$ in references to the cache, where $v = f_o$; the test '$v > m$' becomes '$G_v = 0$'.

103. The equivalent formula $g(f_1(x_1, \ldots, x_n), \ldots, f_m(x_1, \ldots, x_n))$ can be implemented with the COMPOSE operation (72). (However, Dull was vindicated when it turned out that his formula could be evaluated more than a hundred times faster than Quick's, in spite of the fact that it uses twice as many variables! In his application, the computation of $(y_1 = f_1(x_1, \ldots, x_n)) \wedge \cdots \wedge (y_m = f_m(x_1, \ldots, x_n)) \wedge g(y_1, \ldots, y_m)$ turned out to be much easier than COMPOSE's computation of $g_j(f_1, \ldots, f_m)$ for every subfunction g_j of g; see, for example, exercise 162.)

104. The following recursive algorithm COMPARE(f, g) needs at most $O(B(f)B(g))$ steps when used with a memo cache: If $f = g$, return '$=$'. Otherwise, if $f = 0$ or $g = 1$, return '$<$'; if $f = 1$ or $g = 0$, return '$>$'. Otherwise represent f and g as in (52); compute $r_l \leftarrow$ COMPARE(f_l, g_l). If r_l is '$\|$', return '$\|$'; otherwise compute $r_h \leftarrow$ COMPARE(f_h, g_h). If r_h is '$\|$', return '$\|$'. Otherwise if r_l is '$=$', return r_h; if r_h is '$=$', return r_l; if $r_l = r_h$, return r_l. Otherwise return '$\|$'.

105. (a) A unate function with polarities $(y_1, \ldots, y_n)$ has $\wedge x_j f = 0$ when $y_j = 1$ and $\mathsf{N} x_j f = 0$ when $y_j = 0$, for $1 \le j \le n$. Conversely, f is unate if these conditions hold for all j. (Notice that $\wedge x_j f = \mathsf{N} x_j f = 0$ if and only if $\exists x_j f = 0$, if and only if f doesn't depend on x_j. In such cases y_j is irrelevant; otherwise y_j is uniquely determined.)

(b) The following algorithm maintains global variables $(p_1, \ldots, p_n)$, initially zero, with the property that $p_j = +1$ if y_j must be 0 and $p_j = -1$ if y_j must be 1; p_j will remain zero if f doesn't depend on x_j. With this understanding, UNATE(f) is defined as follows: If f is constant, return *true*. Otherwise represent f as in (50). Return *false* if either UNATE(f_l) or UNATE(f_h) is *false*; otherwise set $r \leftarrow$ COMPARE(f_l, f_h) using exercise 104. If r is '$\|$', return *false*. If r is '$<$', return *false* if $p_v < 0$, otherwise set $p_v \leftarrow +1$ and return *true*. If r is '$>$', return *false* if $p_v > 0$, otherwise set $p_v \leftarrow -1$ and return *true*.

This algorithm often terminates quickly. It relies on the fact that $f(x) \le g(x)$ for all x if and only if $f(x \oplus y) \le g(x \oplus y)$ for all x, when y is fixed. If we simply want to test whether or not f is monotone, the p variables should be initialized to $+1$ instead of 0.

106. Define HORN(f, g, h) thus: If $f > g$, interchange $f \leftrightarrow g$. Then if $f = 0$ or $h = 1$, return *true*. Otherwise if $g = 1$ or $h = 0$, return *false*. Otherwise represent f, g, and h as in (59). Return *true* if HORN(f_l, g_l, h_l), HORN(f_l, g_h, h_l), HORN(f_h, g_l, h_l), and HORN(f_h, g_h, h_h) are all *true*; otherwise return *false*. [This algorithm is due to T. Horiyama and T. Ibaraki, *Artificial Intelligence* **136** (2002), 189–213, who also introduced an algorithm similar to that of answer 105(b).]

107. Let $e\$f\$g\$h$ mean that $e(x) = f(y) = g(z) = 1$ implies $h(\langle xyz \rangle) = 1$. Then f is a Krom function if and only if $f\$f\$f\$f$, and we can use the following recursive algorithm KROM(e, f, g, h): Rearrange $\{e, f, g\}$ so that $e \le f \le g$. Then if $e = 0$ or $h = 1$, return *true*. Otherwise if $f = 1$ or $h = 0$, return *false*. Otherwise represent e, f, g, h with the quaternary analog of (59). Return *true* if KROM(e_l, f_l, g_l, h_l), KROM(e_l, f_l, g_h, h_l), KROM(e_l, f_h, g_l, h_l), KROM(e_l, f_h, g_h, h_h), KROM(e_h, f_l, g_l, h_l), KROM(e_h, f_l, g_h, h_h), KROM(e_h, f_h, g_l, h_h), and KROM(e_h, f_h, g_h, h_h) are all *true*; otherwise return *false*.

108. Label the nodes $\{1, \ldots, s\}$ with root 1 and sinks $\{s-1, s\}$, then $(s-3)!$ permutations of the other labels give different dags for the same function. The stated inequality follows because each instruction $(\bar{v}_k? \; l_k: h_k)$ has at most $n(s-1)^2$ possibilities, for $1 \le k \le s-2$. (In fact, it holds also for arbitrary *branching programs*, namely for binary decision diagrams in general, whether or not they are ordered and/or reduced.)

Since $1/(s-3)! < (s-1)^3/s!$ and $s! > (s/e)^s$, we have (generously) $b(n,s) < (nse)^s$. Let $s_n = 2^n/(n+\theta)$, where $\theta = \lg e = 1/\ln 2$; then $\lg b(n, s_n) < s_n \lg(n s_n e) = 2^n(1 - (\lg(1 + \theta/n))/(n + \theta)) = 2^n - \Omega(2^n/n^2)$. So the probability that a random n-variable Boolean function has $B(f) \le s_n$ is at most $1/2^{\Omega(2^n/n^2)}$. And that is really tiny.

109. $1/2^{\Omega(2^n/n^2)}$ is really tiny even when multiplied by $n!$.

110. Let $f_n = M_m(x_{n-m+1}, \ldots, x_n; 0, \ldots, 0, x_1, \ldots, x_{n-m}) \vee (\bar{x}_{n-m+1} \wedge \cdots \wedge \bar{x}_n \wedge [0 \ldots 0 x_1 \ldots x_{n-m}$ is a square$])$, when $2^{m-1} + m - 1 < n < 2^m + m$. Each term of this formula has $2^m + m - n$ zeros; the second term destroys all of the 2^m-bit squares. [See H.-T. Liaw and C.-S. Lin, *IEEE Transactions* **C-41** (1992), 661–664; Y. Breitbart, H. Hunt III, and D. Rosenkrantz, *Theoretical Comp. Sci.* **145** (1995), 45–69.]

111. Let $\mu n = \lambda(n - \lambda n)$, and notice that $\mu n = m$ if and only if $2^m + m \le n < 2^{m+1} + m + 1$. The sum for $0 \le k < n - \mu n$ is $2^{n - \mu n} - 1$; the other terms sum to $2^{2^{\mu n}}$.

112. Suppose $k = n - \lg n + \lg \alpha$. Then

$$\frac{(2^{2^{n-k}} - 1)^{2^k}}{2^{2^n}} = \exp\left(\frac{2^n \alpha}{n} \ln\left(1 - \frac{1}{2^{n/\alpha}}\right)\right) = \exp\left(-\frac{2^{n-n/\alpha}\alpha}{n}\left(1 + O\left(\frac{1}{2^{n/\alpha}}\right)\right)\right).$$

If $\alpha \le \frac{1}{2}$ we have $2^{n - n/\alpha}\alpha/n \le 1/(n2^{n+1})$; hence $\hat{b}_k = (2^{n/\alpha} - 2^{n/(2\alpha)})(2^{n-n/\alpha}\alpha/n) \times (1 + O(2^{-n/\alpha})) = 2^k(1 - O(2^{-n/(2\alpha)}))$. And if $\alpha \ge 2$ we have $2^{n-n/\alpha}\alpha/n \ge 2^{n/2+1}/n$; thus $\hat{b}_k = (2^{2^{n-k}} - 2^{2^{n-k-1}})(1 + O(\exp(-2^{n/2}/n)))$.

[For the variance of b_k, see I. Wegener, *IEEE Trans.* **C-43** (1994), 1262–1269.]

113. The idea looks attractive at first glance, but loses its luster when examined closely. Comparatively few nodes of a BDD base appear on the lower levels, by Theorem U; and algorithms like Algorithm S spend comparatively little of their time dealing with those levels. Furthermore, nonconstant sink nodes would make several algorithms more complicated, especially those for reordering.

114. For example, the truth table might be 01010101 00110011 00001111 00001111.

115. Let $N_k = b_0 + \cdots + b_{k-1}$ be the number of nodes $\boxed{j}$ of the BDD for which $j \le k$. The sum of the in-degrees of those nodes is at least N_k; the sum of the out-degrees is $2N_k$; and there's an external pointer to the root. Thus at most $N_k + 1$ branches can cross from the upper k levels to lower levels. Every subtable of order $n - k$ corresponds to some such branch. Therefore $q_k \le N_k + 1$.

Moreover, we must have $q_k \le b_k + \cdots + b_n$, because every subtable of order $n - k$ corresponds to a unique bead of order $\le n - k$.

For (124), change 'BDD' to 'ZDD', 'b_k' to 'z_k', 'bead' to 'zead', and 'q_k' to 'q'_k'.

116. (a) Let $v_k = 2^{2^k} + 2^{2^{k-1}} + \cdots + 2^{2^0}$. Then $Q(f) \le \sum_{k=1}^{n+1} \min(2^{k-1}, 2^{2^{n+1-k}}) = U_n + v_{\lambda(n - \lambda n) - 1}$. Examples like (78) show that this upper bound cannot be improved.

(b) $\hat{q}_k/\hat{b}_k = 2^{2^{n-k}}/(2^{2^{n-k}} - 2^{2^{n-k-1}})$ for $0 \le k < n$; $\hat{q}_n = \hat{b}_n$.

117. $q_k = 2^k$ for $0 \le k \le m$, and $q_{m+k} = 2^m + 2 - k$ for $1 \le k \le 2^m$. Hence $Q(f) = 2^{2m-1} + 7 \cdot 2^{m-1} - 1 \approx B(f)^2/8$. (Such f's make QDDs unattractive in practice.)

118. If $n = 2^m - 1$ we have $h_n(x_1, \ldots, x_n) = M_m(z_{m-1}, \ldots, z_0; 0, x_1, \ldots, x_n)$, where $(z_{m-1} \ldots z_0)_2 = x_1 + \cdots + x_n$ is computable in $5n - 5m$ steps by exercise 7.1.2–30, and M_m takes another $2n + O(\sqrt{n})$ by exercise 7.1.2–39. Since $h_n(x_1, \ldots, x_n) = h_{n+k}(x_1, \ldots, x_n, 0, \ldots, 0)$, we have $C(h_n) \le 14n + O(\sqrt{n})$ for all n. (A little more work will bring this down to $7n + O(\sqrt{n}\log n)$; can the reader do better?)

The cost of h_4 is $6 = L(h_4)$, and $x_2 \oplus ((x_1 \oplus (x_2 \wedge \bar{x}_4)) \wedge (\bar{x}_3 \oplus (\bar{x}_2 \wedge x_4)))$ is a formula of shortest length. (Also $C(h_5) = 10$ and $L(h_5) = 11$.)

119. True. For example, $S_{2,3,5}(x_1, \ldots, x_6) = h_{13}(x_1, x_2, 0, 0, 1, 1, 0, 1, 0, x_3, x_4, x_5, x_6)$.

120. We have $h_n^\pi(x_1, \ldots, x_n) = h_n(y_1, \ldots, y_n)$, where $y_j = x_{j\pi}$ for $1 \le j \le n$. And $h_n(y_1, \ldots, y_n) = y_{y_1 + \cdots + y_n} = y_{x_1 + \cdots + x_n} = x_{(x_1 + \cdots + x_n)\pi}$.

121. (a) If $y_k = \bar{x}_{n+1-k}$ we have $h_n(y_1, \ldots, y_n) = y_{\nu y} = y_{n-\nu x} = \bar{x}_{n+1-(n-\nu x)} = \bar{x}_{\nu x + 1}$.

    (b) If $x = (x_1, \ldots, x_n)$ and $t \in \{0, 1\}$ we have $h_{n+1}(x, t) = (t? \ x_{\nu x+1} : x_{\nu x})$.

    (c) No. For example, ψ sends $0^k 11 \mapsto 0^{k-1} 101 \mapsto 0^{k-2} 10^2 1 \mapsto \cdots \mapsto 10^k 1 \mapsto 0^k 11$. (In spite of its simple definition, ψ has remarkable properties, including fixed points such as $10011010000101011000111001011$ and $1110111101100101110111101111$.)

    (d) In fact, $\hat{h}_n(x_1 \ldots x_n) = x_1(!)$, by induction using recurrence (b).

    (If $f(x_1, \ldots, x_n)$ is *any* Boolean function and τ is *any* permutation of the binary vectors $x_1 \ldots x_n$, we can write $f(x) = \hat{f}(x\tau)$, and the transformed function $\hat{f}$ may well be much easier to work with. Since $f(x) \wedge g(x) = \hat{f}(x\tau) \wedge \hat{g}(x\tau)$, the transform of the AND of two functions is the AND of their transforms, etc. The vector permutations $(x_1 \ldots x_n)\pi = x_{1\pi} \ldots x_{n\pi}$ that merely transform the indices, as considered in the text, are a simple special case of this general principle. But the principle is, in a sense, *too* general, because every function f trivially has at least one τ for which $\hat{f}$ is skinny in the sense of exercise 170; all the complexity of f can be transferred to τ. Even simple transformations like ψ have limited utility, because they don't compose well; for example, $\psi\psi$ is not a transformation of the same type. But linear transformations, which take $x \mapsto xT$ for some nonsingular binary matrix T, have proved to be useful ways to simplify BDDs. [See S. Aborhey, *IEEE Trans.* **C-37** (1988), 1461–1465; J. Bern, C. Meinel, and A. Slobodová, *ACM/IEEE Design Automation Conf.* **32** (1995), 408–413; C. Meinel, F. Somenzi, and T. Theobald, *IEEE Trans.* **CAD-19** (2000), 521–533.])

122. For example, when $n = 7$ the recurrence in answer 121(b) gives

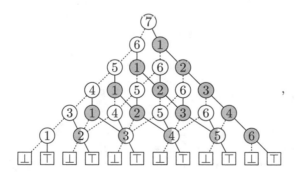

 ,

where shaded nodes compute the subfunction h^{DR} on the variables that haven't yet been tested. Simplifications occur at the bottom, because $h_2(x_1, x_2) = x_1$ and $h_2^{DR}(x_1, x_2) = x_2$. [See D. Sieling and I. Wegener, *Theoretical Comp. Sci.* **141** (1995), 283–310.]

123. Let $t = k - s = \bar{x}_1 + \cdots + \bar{x}_k$. There's a slate for every combination of s' 1s and t' 0s such that $s' + t' = w$, $s' \le s$, and $t' \le t$. The sum of $\binom{w}{s'} = \binom{w}{t'}$ over all such (s', t') is (97). (Notice furthermore that it equals 2^w if and only if $w \le \min(s, t)$.)

124. Let $m = n - k$. Each slate $[r_0, \ldots, r_m]$ corresponds to a function of $(x_{k+1}, \ldots, x_n)$, whose truth table is a bead except in four cases: (i) $[0, \ldots, 0] = 0$; (ii) $[1, \ldots, 1] = 1$; (iii) $[0, x_n, 1] = x_n$ (which doesn't depend on x_{n-1}); (iv) $[1, \ldots, 1, x_{k+1}, 0, \ldots, 0]$, where there are p 1s so that $x_{k+1} = r_p$, is $S_{<p}(x_{k+2}, \ldots, x_n)$.

The following polynomial-time algorithm computes $q_k = q$ and $b_k = q - q'$ by counting all slates. A subtle aspect arises when the entries of $[r_0, \ldots, r_m]$ are all 0 or 1, because such slates can occur for different values of s; we don't want to count them twice. The solution is to maintain four sets

$$C_{ab} = \{r_1 + \cdots + r_{m-1} \mid r_0 = a \text{ and } r_m = b \text{ in some slate}\}.$$

The value of 0π should be artificially set to $n+1$, not 0. Assume that $0 \le k < n$.

H1. [Initialize.] Set $m \leftarrow n - k$, $q \leftarrow q' \leftarrow s \leftarrow 0$, $C_{00} \leftarrow C_{01} \leftarrow C_{10} \leftarrow C_{11} \leftarrow \emptyset$.

H2. [Find v and w.] Set $v \leftarrow \sum_{j=1}^{m-1}[(s+j)\pi \le k]$ and $w \leftarrow v + [s\pi \le k] + [(s+m)\pi \le k]$. If $v = m - 1$, go to step H5.

H3. [Check for nonbeads.] Set $p \leftarrow -1$. If $v \ne m - 2$, go to H4. Otherwise, if $m = 2$ and $(s+1)\pi = n$, set $p \leftarrow [(s+2)\pi \le k]$. Otherwise, if $w = m$ and $(s+j)\pi = k+1$ for some $j \in [1 \ldots m-1]$, set $p \leftarrow j$.

H4. [Add binomials.] For all s' and t' such that $s' + t' = w$, $0 \le s' \le s$, and $0 \le t' \le k - s$, set $q \leftarrow q + \binom{w}{s'}$ and $q' \leftarrow q' + [s' = p]$. Then go to H6.

H5. [Remember 0–1 slates.] Do the following for all s' and t' as in step H4: If $(s+m)\pi \le k$, set $C_{00} \leftarrow C_{00} \cup s'$ and $C_{01} \leftarrow C_{01} \cup (s'-1)$; otherwise set $C_{01} \leftarrow C_{01} \cup s'$. If $s\pi \le k$ and $(s+m)\pi \le k$, set $C_{10} \leftarrow C_{10} \cup (s'-1)$ and $C_{11} \leftarrow C_{11} \cup (s'-2)$. If $s\pi \le k$ and $(s+m)\pi > k$, set $C_{11} \leftarrow C_{11} \cup (s'-1)$.

H6. [Loop on s.] If $s < k$, set $s \leftarrow s + 1$ and return to H2.

H7. [Finish.] For $ab = 00$, 01, 10, and 11, set $q \leftarrow q + \binom{m-1}{r}$ for all $r \in C_{ab}$. Also set $q' \leftarrow q' + [0 \in C_{00}] + [m-1 \in C_{11}]$. ∎

125. Let $S(n, m) = \binom{n}{0} + \cdots + \binom{n}{m}$. There are $S(k+1-s, s) - 1$ nonconstant slates when $0 < s \le k$ and $s \ge 2k - n + 2$. The only other nonconstant slates, one each, arise when $s = 0$ and $k < (n-1)/2$. The constant slates are trickier to count, but there usually are $S(n+1-k, 2k+1-n)$ of them, appearing when $s = 2k - n$ or $s = 2k+1-n$. Taking account of nitpicky boundary conditions and nonbeads, we find

$$b_k = S(n-k, 2k-n) + \sum_{s=0}^{n-k} S(n-k-s, \, 2k+1-n+s)$$

$$- \min(k, n-k) - [n = 2k] - [3k \ge 2n - 1] - 1$$

for $0 \le k < n$. Although $S(n, m)$ has no simple form, we can express $\sum_{k=0}^{n-1} b_k$ as $B_{n/2} + \sum_{0 \le m \le n-2k \le n}(n + 3 - m - 2k)\binom{k}{m} + $ (small change) when n is even, and the same expression works when n is odd if we replace $B_{n/2}$ by $A_{(n+1)/2}$. The double sum can be reduced by summing first on k, since $(k+1)\binom{k}{m} = (m+1)\binom{k+1}{m+1}$:

$$\sum_{m=0}^{n}\left((n+5-m)\binom{\lfloor(n-m+2)/2\rfloor}{m+1} - (2m+2)\binom{\lfloor(n-m+4)/2\rfloor}{m+2}\right).$$

And the remaining sum can be tackled by breaking it into four parts, depending on whether m and/or n is odd. Generating functions are helpful: Let $A(z) = \sum_{k \le n}\binom{n-k}{2k}z^n$ and $B(z) = \sum_{k \le n}\binom{n-k}{2k+1}z^n$. Then $A(z) = 1 + \sum_{k<n}\binom{n-k-1}{2k}z^n + \sum_{k<n}\binom{n-k-1}{2k-1}z^n = 1 + \sum_{k \le n}\binom{n-k}{2k}z^{n+1} + \sum_{k \le n}\binom{n-k}{2k+1}z^{n+2} = 1 + zA(z) + z^2 B(z)$. A similar derivation proves that $B(z) = zB(z) + zA(z)$. Consequently

$$A(z) = \frac{1-z}{1-2z+z^2-z^3} = \frac{1-z^2}{1-z-z^2-z^4}, \qquad B(z) = \frac{z}{1-2z+z^2-z^3} = \frac{z+z^2}{1-z-z^2-z^4}.$$

Thus $A_n = 2A_{n-1} - A_{n-2} + A_{n-3} = A_{n-1} + A_{n-2} + A_{n-4}$ for $n \geq 4$, and B_n satisfies the same recurrences. In fact, we have $A_n = (3P_{2n+1} + 7P_{2n} - 2P_{2n-1})/23$ and $B_n = (3P_{2n+2} + 7P_{2n+1} - 2P_{2n})/23$, using the Perrin numbers of exercise 15.

Furthermore, setting $A^*(z) = \sum_{k \leq n} k\binom{n-k}{2k}z^n$ and $B^*(z) = \sum_{k \leq n} k\binom{n-k}{2k+1}z^n$, we find $A^*(z) = z^2 A(z)B(z)$ and $B^*(z) = z^2 B(z)^2$. Putting it all together now yields the remarkable exact formula

$$B(h_n) = \frac{56P_{n+2} + 77P_{n+1} + 47P_n}{23} - \left\lfloor \frac{n^2}{4} \right\rfloor - \left\lfloor \frac{7n+1}{3} \right\rfloor + (n \bmod 2) - 10.$$

Historical notes: The sequence $\langle A_n \rangle$ was apparently first studied by R. Austin and R. K. Guy, *Fibonacci Quarterly* **16** (1978), 84–86; it counts binary $x_1 \ldots x_{n-1}$ with each 1 next to another. The plastic constant ρ was shown by C. L. Siegel to be the smallest "Pisot number," namely the smallest algebraic integer > 1 whose conjugates all lie inside the unit circle; see *Duke Math. J.* **11** (1944), 597–602.

126. When $n \geq 6$, we have $b_k = F_{\lfloor(k+7)/2\rfloor} + F_{\lceil(k+7)/2\rceil} - 4$ for $1 \leq k < 2n/3$, and $b_k = 2^{n-k+2} - 6 - [k = n - 2]$ for $4n/5 \leq k < n$. But the main contributions to $B(h_n^\pi)$ come from the $2n/15$ profile elements between those two regions, and the methods of answer 125 can be extended to deal with them. The interesting sequences

$$A_n = \sum_{k=0}^{\lfloor n/2 \rfloor} \binom{n-2k}{3k}, \qquad B_n = \sum_{k=0}^{\lfloor n/2 \rfloor} \binom{n-2k}{3k+1}, \qquad C_n = \sum_{k=0}^{\lfloor n/2 \rfloor} \binom{n-2k}{3k+2}$$

have respective generating functions $(1-z)^2/p(z)$, $(1-z)z/p(z)$, $z^2/p(z)$, where $p(z) = (1-z)^3 - z^5$. These sequences arise in this problem because $\sum_{k=0}^{n} \binom{\lfloor n-2k/3 \rfloor}{k} = A_n + B_{n-1} + C_{n-2}$. They grow as α^n, where $\alpha \approx 1.7016$ is the real root of $(\alpha-1)^3\alpha^2 = 1$.

The BDD size can't be expressed in closed form, but there is a closed form in terms of $A_{\lfloor n/3 \rfloor}$ through $A_{\lfloor n/3 \rfloor + 4}$ that is accurate to $O(2^{n/4}/\sqrt{n})$. Thus $B(h_n^\pi) = \Theta(\alpha^{n/3})$.

127. (The permutation $\pi = (3, 5, 7, \ldots, 2n' - 1, n, n - 1, n - 2, \ldots, 2n', 2n' - 2, \ldots, 4, 2, 1)$, $n' = \lfloor 2n/5 \rfloor$, turns out to be optimum for h_n when $12 < n \leq 24$; but it gives $B(h_{100}^\pi) = 1{,}366{,}282{,}025$. Sifting does much better, as shown in answer 152; but still better permutations almost surely exist.)

128. Consider, for example, $M_3(x_4, x_2, x_7; x_6, x_1, x_8, x_3, x_9, x_{11}, x_5, x_{10})$. The first m variables $\{x_4, x_2, x_7\}$ are called "address bits"; the other 2^m are called "targets." The subfunctions corresponding to $x_1 = c_1, \ldots, x_k = c_k$ can be described by slates of options analogous to (96). For example, when $k = 2$ there are three slates $[x_6, 0, x_9, x_{11}]$, $[x_6, 1, x_9, x_{11}]$, $[x_8, x_3, x_5, x_{10}]$, where the result is obtained by using $(x_4x_7)_2$ to select the appropriate component. Only the third of these depends on x_3; hence $q_2 = 3$ and $b_2 = 1$. When $k = 6$ the slates are $[0, 0]$, $[0, 1]$, $[1, 0]$, $[1, 1]$, $[x_8, 0]$, $[x_8, 1]$, $[x_9, x_{11}]$, $[0, x_{10}]$, and $[1, x_{10}]$, with components selected by x_7; hence $q_6 = 9$ and $b_6 = 7$.

In general, if the variables $\{x_1, \ldots, x_k\}$ include a address bits and t targets, the slates will have $A = 2^{m-a}$ entries. Divide the set of all 2^m targets into 2^a subsets, depending on the known address bits, and suppose s_j of those subsets contain j known targets. (Thus $s_0 + s_1 + \cdots + s_A = 2^a$ and $s_1 + 2s_2 + \cdots + As_A = t$. We have $(s_0, \ldots, s_4) = (1, 1, 0, 0, 0)$ when $k - 2$ and $a - t - 1$ in the example above; and $(s_0, s_1, s_2) = (1, 2, 1)$ when $k = 6$, $a = 2$, $t = 4$.) Then the total number of slates, q_k, is $2^0s_0 + 2^1s_1 + \cdots + 2^{A-1}s_{A-1} + 2^A[s_A > 0]$. If x_{k+1} is an address bit, the number b_k of slates that depend on x_{k+1} is $q_k - 2^{A/2}[s_A > 0]$. Otherwise $b_k = 2^c$, where c is the number of constants that appear in the slates containing target x_{k+1}.

129. (Solution by M. Sauerhoff; see I. Wegener, *Branching Programs* (2000), Theorem 6.2.13.) Since $P_m(x_1, \ldots, x_{m^2}) = Q_m(x_1, \ldots, x_{m^2}) \wedge S_m(x_1, \ldots, x_{m^2})$ and $B(S_m) = m^3 + 2$, we have $B(P_m^\pi) \le (m^3 + 2)B(Q_m^\pi)$. Apply Theorem K.

(A stronger lower bound should be possible, because Q_m seems to have *larger* BDDs than P_m. For example, when $m = 5$ the permutation $(1\pi, \ldots, 25\pi) = (3, 1, 5, 7, 9, 2, 4, 6, 8, 10, 11, 12, 13, 14, 15, 16, 20, 23, 17, 21, 19, 18, 22, 24, 25)$ is optimum for Q_5; but $B(Q_5^\pi) = 535$, while $B(P_5) = 229$.)

130. (a) Each path that starts at the root of the BDD and takes s HI branches and t LO branches defines a subfunction that corresponds to graphs in which s adjacencies are forced and t are forbidden. We shall show that these $\binom{s+t}{s}$ subfunctions are distinct.

If subfunctions g and h correspond to different paths, we can find k vertices W with the following properties: (i) W contains vertices w and w' with $w - w'$ forced in g and forbidden in h. (ii) No adjacencies between vertices of W are forced in h or forbidden in g. (iii) If $u \in W$ and $v \notin W$ and $u - v$ is forced in h, then $u = w$ or $u = w'$. (These conditions make at most $2s + t = m - k$ vertices ineligible to be in W.)

We can set the remaining variables so that $u - v$ if and only if $\{u, v\} \subseteq W$, whenever adjacency is neither forced nor forbidden. This assignment makes $g = 1$, $h = 0$.

(b) Consider the subfunction of $C_{m, \lceil m/2 \rceil}$ in which vertices $\{1, \ldots, k\}$ are required to be isolated, but $u - v$ whenever $k < u \le \lceil m/2 \rceil < v \le m$. Then a k-clique on the $\lfloor m/2 \rfloor$ vertices $\{\lceil m/2 \rceil + 1, \ldots, m\}$ is equivalent to an $\lceil m/2 \rceil$-clique on $\{1, \ldots, m\}$. In other words, this subfunction of $C_{m, \lceil m/2 \rceil}$ is $C_{\lfloor m/2 \rfloor, k}$.

Now chose $k \approx \sqrt{m/3}$ and apply (a). [I. Wegener, *JACM* **35** (1988), 461–471.]

131. (a) The profile can be shown to be $(1, 1, 2, 4, \ldots, 2^{q-1}, (p-2) \times (2^q - 1, q \times 2^{q-1}), 2^q - 1, 2^{q-1}, \ldots, 4, 2, 1, 2)$, where $r \times b$ denotes the r-fold repetition of b. Hence the total size is $(pq + 2p - 2q + 2)2^{q-1} - p + 2$.

(b) With the ordering $x_1, x_2, \ldots, x_p, y_{11}, y_{21}, \ldots, y_{p1}, \ldots, y_{1q}, y_{2q}, \ldots, y_{pq}$, the profile comes to $(1, 2, 4, \ldots, 2^{p-1}, (q-1)p \times (2^{p-1}), 2^{p-1}, \ldots, 4, 2, 1, 2)$, making the total size $(pq - p + 4)2^{p-1}$.

(c) Suppose exactly $m = \lfloor \min(p, q)/2 \rfloor$ x's occur among the first k variables in some ordering; we may assume that they are $\{x_1, \ldots, x_m\}$. Consider the 2^m paths in the QDD for C such that $x_j = \bar{x}_{m+j}$ for $1 \le j \le p - m$ and $y_{ij} = [i = j$ or $i = j+m$ or $j > m]$. These paths must pass through distinct nodes on level k. Hence $q_k \ge 2^m$; use (85). [See M. Nikolskaia and L. Nikolskaia, *Theor. Comp. Sci.* **255** (2001), 615–625.]

Optimum orderings for $(p, q) = (4, 4)$, $(4, 5)$, and $(5, 4)$, via exercise 138, are:

$$x_1 y_{11} x_2 y_{21} x_3 y_{31} y_{41} y_{12} y_{22} y_{32} y_{42} y_{13} y_{23} y_{33} y_{43} y_{14} y_{24} y_{34} y_{44} x_4 \text{ (size 108)};$$
$$x_1 y_{11} x_2 y_{21} x_3 y_{31} y_{41} y_{12} y_{22} y_{32} y_{42} y_{13} y_{23} y_{33} y_{43} y_{14} y_{24} y_{34} y_{44} y_{15} y_{25} y_{35} y_{45} x_4 \text{ (size 140)};$$
$$x_1 y_{11} x_2 y_{21} y_{12} y_{22} y_{13} y_{23} y_{14} y_{24} x_3 y_{31} y_{32} y_{33} y_{34} x_4 y_{41} y_{42} y_{51} y_{52} y_{43} y_{53} y_{44} y_{54} x_5 \text{ (size 167)}.$$

132. There are 616,126 essentially different classes of 5-variable functions, by Table 7.1.1–5. The maximum $B_{\min}(f)$, 17, is attained by 38 of those classes. Three classes have the property that $B(f^\pi) = 17$ for *all* permutations π; one such example, $((x_2 \oplus x_4 \oplus (x_1 \wedge (x_3 \vee \bar{x}_4))) \wedge ((x_2 \oplus x_5) \vee (x_3 \oplus x_4))) \oplus (x_5 \wedge (x_3 \oplus (x_1 \vee \bar{x}_2)))$, has the interesting symmetries $f(x_1, x_2, x_3, x_4, x_5) = f(\bar{x}_2, \bar{x}_3, \bar{x}_4, \bar{x}_1, \bar{x}_5) = f(x_2, \bar{x}_5, x_1, x_3, \bar{x}_4)$.

Incidentally, the maximum difference $B_{\max}(f) - B_{\min}(f) = 10$ occurs only in the "junction function" class $x_1? x_2: x_3? x_4: x_5$, when $B_{\min} = 7$ and $B_{\max} = 17$.

(When $n = 4$ there are 222 classes; and $B_{\min}(f) = 10$ in 25 of them, including S_2 and $S_{2,4}$. The class exemplified by truth table 16ad is uniquely hardest, in the sense that $B_{\min}(f) = 10$ and most of the 24 permutations give $B(f^\pi) = 11$.)

133. Represent each subset $X \subseteq \{1, \ldots, n\}$ by the n-bit integer $i(X) = \sum_{x \in X} 2^{x-1}$, and let $b_{i(X),x}$ be the weight of the edge between X and $X \cup x$. Set $c_0 \leftarrow 0$, and for $1 \leq i < 2^n$ set $c_i \leftarrow \min\{c_{i \oplus j} + b_{i \oplus j, x} \mid 1 \leq x \leq n,\ j = 2^{x-1},$ and $i \,\&\, j \neq 0\}$. Then $B_{\min}(f) = c_{2^n - 1} + 2$, and an optimum ordering can be found by remembering which $x = x(i)$ minimizes each c_i. For $B_{\max}$, replace 'min' by 'max' in this recipe.

134.

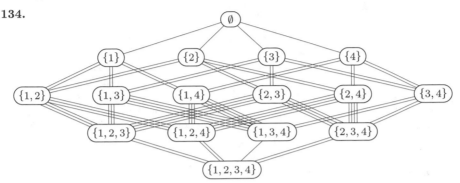

The maximum profile, $(1, 2, 4, 2, 2)$, occurs on paths such as $\emptyset \to \{2\} \to \{2, 3\} \to \{2, 3, 4\} \to \{1, 2, 3, 4\}$. The minimum profile, $(1, 2, 2, 1, 2)$, occurs only on the paths $\emptyset \to (\{3\} \text{ or } \{4\}) \to \{3, 4\} \to \{1, 3, 4\} \to \{1, 2, 3, 4\}$. (Five of the 24 possible paths have the profile $(1, 2, 3, 2, 2)$ and are unimprovable by sifting on any variable.)

135. Let $\theta_0 = 1$, $\theta_1 = x_1$, $\theta_2 = x_1 \wedge x_2$, and $\theta_n = x_n?\ \theta_{n-1}: \theta_{n-3}$ for $n \geq 3$. One can prove that, when $n \geq 4$, $B(\theta_n^\pi) = n + 2$ if and only if $(n\pi, \ldots, 1\pi) = (1, \ldots, n)$. The key fact is that if $k < n$ and $n \geq 5$, the subfunctions obtained by setting $x_k \leftarrow 0$ or $x_k \leftarrow 1$ are distinct, and they both depend on the variables $\{x_1, \ldots, x_{k-1}, x_{k+1}, \ldots, x_n\}$, except that the subfunction for $x_{n-1} \leftarrow 0$ does not depend on x_{n-2}. Thus the weights $\{x_k\} \to \{x_k, x_l\}$ in the master profile chart are 2 except when $k = n$ or $(k, l) = (n-1, n-2)$. Below $\{x_{n-1}, x_{n-2}\}$ there are three subfunctions, namely $x_n?\ \theta_{n-4}: \theta_{n-3}$, $x_n?\ \theta_{n-5}: \theta_{n-3}$, and θ_{n-3}; all of them depend on $\{x_1, \ldots, x_{n-3}\}$, and two of them on x_n.

136. Let $n = 2n' - 1$ and $m = 2m' - 1$. The inputs form an $m \times n$ matrix, and we're computing the median of m row-medians. Let V_i be the variables in row i. If X is a subset of the mn variables, let $X_i = X \cap V_i$ and $r_i = |X_i|$. Subfunctions of type $(s_1, \ldots, s_m)$ arise when exactly s_i elements of X_i are set to 1; these subfunctions are

$$\langle S_1 S_2 \ldots S_m \rangle, \qquad \text{where } S_i = S_{\geq n' - s_i}(V_i \setminus X_i) \text{ and } 0 \leq s_i \leq r_i \text{ for } 1 \leq i \leq m.$$

When $x \notin X$, we want to count how many of these subfunctions depend on x. By symmetry we may assume that $x = x_{mn}$. Notice that the symmetric threshold function $S_{\geq t}(x_1, \ldots, x_n)$ equals 0 if $t > n$, or 1 if $t \leq 0$; it depends on all n variables if $1 \leq t \leq n$. In particular, S_m depends on x for exactly $r_m \$ n = \min(r_m + 1, n - r_m)$ choices of s_m.

Let $a_j = \sum_{i=1}^{m-1} [r_i = j]$ for $0 \leq j \leq n$. Then a_n of the functions $\{S_1, \ldots, S_{m-1}\}$ are constant, and $a_{n-1} + \cdots + a_{n'}$ of them might or might not be constant. Choosing c_i to be nonconstant gives us $(r_m \$ n)((a_n + a_{n-1} + \cdots + a_{n'} - c_{n-1} - \cdots - c_{n'}) \$ m)$ times

$$\binom{a_{n-1}}{c_{n-1}} \cdots \binom{a_{n'}}{c_{n'}} 1^{a_0} 2^{a_1} \ldots (n')^{a_{n'} - 1} (n' - 1)^{c_{n'}} (n' - 2)^{c_{n'} + 1} \ldots 1^{c_{n-1}}$$

distinct subfunctions that depend on x. Summing over $\{c_{n-1}, \ldots, c_{n'}\}$ gives the answer.

When variables have the natural row-by-row order, these formulas apply with $r_m = k \bmod n$, $a_n = \lfloor k/n \rfloor$, $a_0 = m - 1 - a_n$. The profile element b_k for $0 \le k < mn$ is therefore $(\lfloor k/n \rfloor \$m)((k \bmod n)\$n)$, and we have $\sum_{k=0}^{mn} b_k = (m'n')^2 + 2$. This ordering is optimum, although no easy proof is apparent; for example, some orderings can decrease b_{n+2} or b_{2n-2} from 4 to 3 while increasing b_k for other k.

Every path from top to bottom of the master chart can be represented as $\alpha_0 \to \alpha_1 \to \cdots \to \alpha_{mn}$, where each α_j is a string $r_{j1} \dots r_{jm}$ with $0 \le r_{j1} \le \cdots \le r_{jm} \le n$, $r_{j1} + \cdots + r_{jm} = j$, one coordinate increasing at each step. For example, one path when $m = 5$ and $n = 3$ is $00000 \to 00001 \to 00011 \to 00111 \to 00112 \to 00122 \to 00123 \to 01123 \to 11123 \to 11223 \to 12223 \to 12233 \to 12333 \to 22333 \to 23333 \to 33333$. We can convert this path to the "natural" path by a series of steps that don't increase the total edge weight, as follows: In the initial segment up to the first time $r_{jm} = n$, do all transitions on the rightmost coordinate first. (Thus the first steps of the example path would become $00000 \to 00001 \to 00002 \to 00003 \to 00013 \to 00113 \to 00123$.) Then in the final segment after the last time $r_{j1} = 0$, do all transitions on the leftmost coordinate last. (The final steps would thereby become $01123 \to 01223 \to 02223 \to 02233 \to 02333 \to 03333 \to 13333 \to 23333 \to 33333$.) Then, after the first n steps, normalize the second-last coordinates in a similar fashion ($00003 \to 00013 \to 00023 \to 00033 \to 00133 \to 01133 \to 01233 \to 02233$); and before the last n steps, normalize the second coordinates ($00133 \to 00233 \to 00333 \to 01333 \to 02333 \to 03333$). Et cetera.

[This back-and-forth proof technique was inspired by the paper of Bollig and Wegener cited below. Can every nonoptimal ordering be improved by merely sifting?]

137. If we add a clique of c new vertices and $\binom{c}{2}$ new edges, the cost of the optimum arrangement increases by $\binom{c+1}{3}$. So we may assume that the given graph has m edges and n vertices $\{1, \dots, n\}$, where m and n are odd and sufficiently large. The corresponding function f, which depends on $mn + m + 1$ variables x_{ij} and s_k for $1 \le i \le m$, $1 \le j \le n$, and $0 \le k \le m$, is $J(s_0, s_1, \dots, s_m; h, g_1, \dots, g_m)$, where $g_i = (x_{iu_i} \oplus x_{iv_i}) \wedge \bigwedge \{x_{iw} \mid w \notin \{u_i, v_i\}\}$ when the ith edge is $u_i \text{ --- } v_i$, and where $h = \langle \langle x_{11} \dots x_{m1} \rangle \dots \langle x_{1n} \dots x_{mn} \rangle \rangle$ is the transpose of the function in exercise 136.

One can show that $B_{\min}(f) = \min_\pi \sum_{u-v} |u\pi - v\pi| + (\frac{m+1}{2})^2 (\frac{n+1}{2})^2 + mn + m + 2$; the optimum ordering uses $(\frac{m+1}{2})^2 (\frac{n+1}{2})^2$ nodes for h, $n + |u_i\pi - v_i\pi|$ nodes for g_i, one node for each s_k, and two sink nodes, minus one node that is shared between h and some g_i. [See B. Bollig and I. Wegener, *IEEE Trans.* **C-45** (1996), 993–1002.]

138. (a) Let $X_k = \{x_1, \dots, x_k\}$. The QDD nodes at depth k represent the subfunctions that can arise when constants replace the variables of X_k. We can add an n-bit field DEP to each node, to specify exactly which variables of $X_n \setminus X_k$ it depends on. For example, the QDD for f in (92) has the following subfunctions and DEPs:

> depth 0: 0011001001110010 [1111];
> depth 1: 00110010 [0111], 01110010 [0111];
> depth 2: 0010 [0011], 0011 [0010], 0111 [0011];
> depth 3: 00 [0000], 01 [0001], 10 [0001], 11 [0000].

An examination of all DEP fields at depth k tells us the master profile weights between X_k and $X_k \cup x_l$, for $0 \le k < l \le n$.

(b) Represent the nodes at depth k as triples $N_{kp} = (l_{kp}, h_{kp}, d_{kp})$ for $0 \le p < q_k$, where (l_{kp}, h_{kp}) are the (LO, HI) pointers and d_{kp} records the DEP bits. If $k < n$, these nodes branch on x_{k+1}, so we have $0 \le l_{kp}, h_{kp} < q_{k+1}$; but if $k = n$, we have

$l_{n0} = h_{n0} = 0$ and $l_{n1} = h_{n1} = 1$ to represent $\boxed{\perp}$ and $\boxed{\top}$. We define

$$d_{kp} = \sum \{2^{t-k-1} \mid N_{kp} \text{ depends on } x_t\};$$

hence $0 \le d_{kp} < 2^{n-k}$. For example, the QDD (82) is equivalent to $N_{00} = (0, 1, 7)$; $N_{10} = (0, 1, 3)$, $N_{11} = (1, 2, 3)$; $N_{20} = (0, 0, 0)$, $N_{21} = (0, 1, 1)$, $N_{22} = (1, 1, 0)$; $N_{30} = (0, 0, 0)$, $N_{31} = (1, 1, 0)$.

To jump up from depth b to depth a, we essentially make two copies of the nodes at depths $b - 1$, $b - 2$, $\ldots$, a, one for the case $x_{b+1} = 0$ and one for the case $x_{b+1} = 1$. Those copies are moved down to depths b, $b - 1$, $\ldots$, $a + 1$, and reduced to eliminate duplicates. Then every original node at depth a is replaced by a node that branches on x_{b+1}; its LO and HI fields point respectively to the 0-copy and the 1-copy of the original.

This process involves some simple (but cool) list processing to update DEPs while bucket sorting: Nodes are unpacked into a work area consisting of auxiliary arrays r, s, t, u, and v, initially zero. Instead of using l_{kp} and h_{kp} for LO and HI, we store HI in cell u_p of the work area, and we let v_p link to the previous node (if any) with the same LO field; furthermore we make s_l point to the last node (if any) for which LO $= l$. The algorithm below uses UNPACK(p, l, h) as an abbreviation for "$u_p \leftarrow h$, $v_p \leftarrow s_l$, $s_l \leftarrow p+1$."

When nodes of depth k have been unpacked in this way to arrays s, u, and v, the following subroutine ELIM(k) packs them back into the main QDD structure with duplicates eliminated. It also sets r_p to the new address of node p.

E1. [Loop on l.] Set $q \leftarrow 0$ and $t_h \leftarrow 0$ for $0 \le h < q_{k+1}$. Do step E2 for $0 \le l < q_{k+1}$. Then set $q_k \leftarrow q$ and terminate.

E2. [Loop on p.] Set $p \leftarrow s_l$ and $s_l \leftarrow 0$. While $p > 0$, do step E3 and set $p \leftarrow v_{p-1}$. Then resume step E1.

E3. [Pack node $p - 1$.] Set $h \leftarrow u_{p-1}$. (The unpacked node has (LO, HI) $= (l, h)$.) If $t_h \ne 0$ and $l_{k(t_h - 1)} = l$, set $r_{p-1} \leftarrow t_h - 1$. Otherwise set $l_{kq} \leftarrow l$, $h_{kq} \leftarrow h$, $d_{kq} \leftarrow ((d_{(k+1)l} \mid d_{(k+1)h}) \ll 1) + [l \ne h]$, $r_{p-1} \leftarrow q$, $q \leftarrow q+1$, $t_h \leftarrow q$. Resume step E2. ∎

We can now use ELIM to jump up from b to a. (i) For $k = b - 1$, $b - 2$, $\ldots$, a, do the following steps: For $0 \le p < q_k$, set $l \leftarrow l_{kp}$, $h \leftarrow h_{kp}$; if $k = b - 1$, UNPACK$(2p, l_{bl}, h_{bl})$ and UNPACK$(2p+1, l_{bh}, h_{bh})$, otherwise UNPACK$(2p, r_{2l}, r_{2h})$ and UNPACK$(2p + 1, r_{2l+1}, r_{2h+1})$ (thereby making two copies of N_{kp} in the work area). Then ELIM$(k + 1)$. (ii) For $0 \le p < q_a$, UNPACK(p, r_{2p}, r_{2p+1}). Then ELIM(a). (iii) If $a > 0$, set $l \leftarrow l_{(a-1)p}$, $h \leftarrow h_{(a-1)p}$, $l_{(a-1)p} \leftarrow r_l$, $h_{(a-1)p} \leftarrow r_h$, for $0 \le p < q_{a-1}$.

This jump-up procedure garbles the DEP fields above depth a, because the variables have been reordered. But we'll use it only when those fields are no longer needed.

(c) By induction, the first 2^{n-2} steps account for all subsets that do not contain n; then comes a jump-up from $n - 1$ to 0, and the remaining steps account for all subsets that do contain n.

(d) Start by setting $y_k \leftarrow k$ and $w_k \leftarrow 2^k - 1$ for $0 \le k < n$. In the following algorithm, the y array represents the current variable ordering, and the bitmap $w_k = \sum \{2^{y_j} \mid 0 \le j < k\}$ represents the set of variables on the top k levels.

We augment the subroutine ELIM(k) so that it also computes the desired edge weights of the master profile: Counters c_j are initially 0 for $0 \le j < n - k$; after setting d_{kq} in step E3, we set $c_j \leftarrow c_j + 1$ for each j such that $2^j \subseteq d_{kq}$; finally we set $b_{w_k, y_{k+j}+1} \leftarrow c_j$ for $0 \le j < n - k$, using the notation of answer 133. [To speed this up, we could count bytes not bits, increasing $c_{j, (d_{kq} \gg 8j) \& \#ff}$ by 1 for $0 \le j < (n - k)/8$.]

We initialize the DEP fields by doing the following for $k = n - 1, n - 2, \ldots, 0$: UNPACK$(p, l_{kp}, h_{kp})$ for $0 \le p < q_k$; ELIM(k); if $k > 0$, set $l \leftarrow l_{(k-1)p}$, $h \leftarrow h_{(k-1)p}$, $l_{(k-1)p} \leftarrow r_l$, and $h_{(k-1)p} \leftarrow r_h$, for $0 \le p < q_{k-1}$.

The main loop of the algorithm now does the following for $1 \le i < 2^{n-1}$: Set $a \leftarrow \nu i - 1$ and $b \leftarrow \nu i + \rho i$. Set $(y_a, \ldots, y_b) \leftarrow (y_b, y_a, \ldots, y_{b-1})$ and $(w_{a+1}, \ldots, w_b) \leftarrow (2^{y_b} + w_a, \ldots, 2^{y_b} + w_{b-1})$. Jump up from b to a with the procedure of part (b); but use the original (non-augmented) ELIM routine for ELIM(a) in step (ii).

(e) The space required for nodes at depth k is at most $Q_k = \min(2^k, 2^{2^{n-k}})$; we also need space for $2\max(Q_1, \ldots, Q_n)$ elements in arrays r, u, v, plus $\max(Q_1, \ldots, Q_n)$ elements in arrays s and t. So the total is dominated by $O(2^n n)$ for the outputs $b_{w,x}$.

Subroutine ELIM(k) is called $\binom{n}{k}$ times in augmented form, for $0 \le k < n$, and $\binom{n-1}{k+1}$ times non-augmented. Its running time in either case is $O(q_k(n-k))$. Thus the total comes to $O(\sum_k \binom{n}{k} 2^k (n-k)) = O(3^n n)$, and it will be substantially less if the QDD never gets large. (For example, it's $O((1+\sqrt{2})^n n)$ for the function h_n.)

[The first exact algorithm to determine optimum variable ordering in a BDD was introduced by S. J. Friedman and K. J. Supowit, *IEEE Trans.* **C-39** (1990), 710–713. They used extended truth tables instead of QDDs, obtaining a method that required $\Theta(3^n/\sqrt{n})$ space and $\Theta(3^n n^2)$ time, improvable to $\Theta(3^n n)$.]

139. The same algorithm applies, almost unchanged: Consider all QDD nodes that branch on x_a to be at level 0, and all nodes that branch on x_{b+1} to be sinks. Thus we do 2^{b-a} jump-ups, not 2^{n-1}. (The algorithm doesn't rely on the assumptions that $q_0 = 1$ and $q_n = 2$, except in the space and time analyses of part (e).)

140. We can find shortest paths in a network without knowing the network in advance, by generating vertices and arcs "on the fly" as needed. Section 7.3 points out that the distance $d(X, Y)$ of each arc $X \to Y$ can be changed to $d'(X, Y) = d(X, Y) - l(X) + l(Y)$ for any function $l(X)$, without changing the shortest paths. If the revised distances d' are nonnegative, $l(X)$ is a lower bound on the distance from X to the goal; the trick is to find a good lower bound that focuses the search yet isn't difficult to compute.

If $|X| = l$, and if a QDD for f with X on its top l levels has q nonconstant nodes on the next level, then $l(X) = \max(q, n - l)$ is a suitable lower bound for the $B_{\min}$ problem. [See R. Drechsler, N. Drechsler, and W. Günther, *ACM/IEEE Design Automation Conf.* **35** (1998), 200–205.] However, a stronger lower bound is needed to make this approach competitive with the algorithm of exercise 138, unless f has a relatively short BDD that cannot be attained in very many ways.

141. False. Consider $g(x_1 \vee \cdots \vee x_6, x_7 \vee \cdots \vee x_{12}, (x_{13} \vee \cdots \vee x_{16}) \oplus x_{18}, x_{17}, x_{19} \vee \cdots \vee x_{22})$, where $g(y_1, \ldots, y_5) = ((((\bar{y}_1 \vee y_5) \wedge y_4) \oplus y_3) \wedge ((y_1 \wedge y_2) \oplus y_4 \oplus y_5)) \oplus y_5$. Then $B(g) = 40 = B_{\min}(g)$ can't be achieved with $\{x_{13}, \ldots, x_{16}, x_{18}\}$ consecutive. [M. Teslenko, A. Martinelli, and E. Dubrova, *IEEE Trans.* **C-54** (2005), 236–237.]

142. (a) Suppose m is odd. The subfunctions that arise after $(x_1, \ldots, x_{m+1})$ are known are $[w_{m+2}x_{m+2} + \cdots + w_n x_n > 2^{m-1}m - 2^{m-2} - t]$, where $0 \le t \le 2^m$. The subcases $x_{m+2} + \cdots + x_n = (m-1)/2$ show that at least $\binom{m-1}{(m-1)/2}$ of these subfunctions differ.

But organ-pipe order, $\langle x_1 x_2^{2^m-1} x_3^1 x_4^{2^m-2} x_5^2 \ldots x_{n-2}^{2^m-2} x_{n-1}^{2^{m-2}} x_n^{2^{m-1}} \rangle$, is much better: Let $t_k = x_1 + (2^m - 1)x_2 + x_3 + \cdots + (2^m - 2^{k-1})x_{2k} + 2^{k-1}x_{2k+1}$, for $1 \le k < m-1$. The remaining subfunction depends on at most $2k + 2$ different values, $\lceil t_k/2^k \rceil$.

(b) Let $n = 1 + 4m^2$. The variables are x_0 and x_{ij} for $0 \le i, j < 2m$; the weights are $w_0 = 1$ and $w_{ij} = 2^i + 2^{2m+1+j}m$. Let X_l be the first l variables in some ordering, and suppose X_l includes elements in i_l rows and j_l columns of the matrix (x_{ij}). If $\max(i_l, j_l) = m$, we will prove that $q_l \geq 2^m$; hence $B(f) > 2^m$ by (85).

Let I and J be subsets of $\{1, \ldots, 2m\}$ with $|I| = |J| = m$ and $X_l \subseteq x_0 \cup \{x_{ij} \mid i \in I,\ j \in J\}$; let I' and J' be the complementary subsets. Choose m elements $X' \subseteq X_l \setminus x_0$, in different rows (or, if $i_l < m$, in different columns). Consider 2^m paths in the QDD defined as follows: $x_0 = 0$, and $x_{ij} = 0$ if $x_{ij} \in X_l \setminus X'$; also $x_{i'j} = x_{ij'} = \bar{x}_{i'j'} = \bar{x}_{ij}$ for $i \in I$, $j \in J$, where $i \leftrightarrow i'$ and $j \leftrightarrow j'$ are matchings between $I \leftrightarrow I'$ and $J \leftrightarrow J'$. Then there are 2^m distinct values $t = \sum_{i \in I, j \in J} w_{ij} x_{ij}$; but $\sum_{0 \leq i,j < 2m} w_{ij} x_{ij} = (2^{2m} - 1)(1 + 2^{2m+1} m)$ on each path. The paths must pass through distinct nodes on level l. Otherwise, if $t \neq t'$, one of the lower subpaths would lead to $\boxed{\bot}$, the other to $\boxed{\top}$.

[These results are due to K. Hosaka, Y. Takenaga, T. Kaneda, and S. Yajima, *Theoretical Comp. Sci.* **180** (1997), 47–60, who also proved that $|Q(f) - Q(f^R)| < n$. Do self-dual threshold functions always satisfy also $|B(f) - B(f^R)| < n$?]

143. In fact, the algorithm of exercises 133 and 138 proves that organ-pipe order is best for these weights: (1, 1023, 1, 1022, 2, 1020, 4, 1016, 8, 1008, 16, 992, 32, 960, 64, 896, 128, 768, 256, 512) gives the profile (1, 2, 2, 4, 3, 6, 4, 8, 5, 10, 4, 8, 3, 6, 2, 4, 1, 2, 2, 1, 2) and $B(f) = 80$. The worst ordering, (1022, 896, 512, 64, 8, 1, 4, 32, 1008, 1020, 768, 992, 1016, 1023, 960, 256, 128, 16, 2, 1), makes $B(f) = 1913$.

(One might think that properties of binary notation are crucial to this example. But $\langle x_1 x_2 x_3^2 x_4^4 x_5^8 x_6^{16} x_7^{31} x_8^{60} x_9^{116} x_{10}^{224} x_{11}^{224} x_{12}^{448} x_{13}^{564} x_{14}^{620} x_{15}^{649} x_{16}^{664} x_{17}^{672} x_{18}^{676} x_{19}^{678} x_{20}^{679} \rangle$ is actually the same function, by exercise 7.1.1–103(!).)

144. $(5, 7, 7, 10, 6, 9, 5, 4, 2)$; the QDD-not-BDD nodes correspond to f_1, f_2, f_3, 0, 1.

145. $B_{\min} = 31$ is attained in (36). The worst ordering for $(x_3 x_2 x_1 x_0)_2 + (y_3 y_2 y_1 y_0)_2$ is y_0, y_1, y_2, y_3, x_2, x_1, x_0, x_3, making $B_{\max} = 107$. Incidentally, the worst ordering for the 24 inputs of 12-bit addition, $(x_{11} \ldots x_0)_2 + (y_{11} \ldots y_0)_2$, turns out to be y_0, y_1, $\ldots$, y_{11}, x_{10}, x_8, x_6, x_4, x_3, x_5, x_2, x_7, x_1, x_9, x_0, x_{11}, yielding $B_{\max} = 39111$.

[B. Bollig, N. Range, and I. Wegener, *Lecture Notes in Comp. Sci.* **4910** (2008), 174–185, have proved that $B_{\min} = 9n - 5$ for addition of two n-bit numbers whenever $n > 1$, and also that $B_{\min}(M_m) = 2n - 2m + 1$ for the 2^m-way multiplexer.]

146. (a) Obviously $b_0 \leq q_0$; and if $q_0 = b_0 + a_0$, then $b_1 \leq 2b_0 + a_0 = b_0 + q_0$. Also $q_0 - b_0 = a_0 \leq b_1 + q_2 \leq q_2^2$, the number of strings of length 2 on a q_2-letter alphabet; similarly $b_0 + b_1 + q_2 \leq (b_1 + q_2)^2$. (The same relations hold between q_k, q_{k+2}, b_k, and b_{k+1}.)

(b) Let the subfunctions at level 2 have truth tables α_j for $1 \leq j \leq q_2$, and use them to construct beads $\beta_1, \ldots, \beta_{b_1}$ at level 1. Let $(\gamma_1, \ldots, \gamma_{q_2 + b_1})$ be the truth tables $(\alpha_1 \alpha_1, \ldots, \alpha_{q_2} \alpha_{q_2}, \beta_1, \ldots, \beta_{b_1})$. If $b_0 \leq b_1/2$, let the functions at level 0 have truth tables $\{\beta_{2i-1} \beta_{2i} \mid 1 \leq i \leq b_0\} \cup \{\beta_j \beta_j \mid 2b_0 < j \leq b_1\} \cup \{\gamma_j \gamma_j \mid 1 \leq j \leq b_0 + q_0 - b_1\}$. Otherwise it's not difficult to define b_0 beads that include all the β's, and use them at level 0 together with the nonbeads $\{\gamma_j \gamma_j \mid 1 \leq j \leq q_0 - b_0\}$.

147. Before doing any reordering, we clear the cache and collect all garbage. The following algorithm interchanges levels $\textcircled{u} \leftrightarrow \textcircled{v}$ when $v = u + 1$. It works by creating linked lists of solitary, tangled, and hidden nodes, pointed to by variables S, T, and H (initially Λ), using auxiliary LINK fields that can be borrowed temporarily from the hash-table algorithm of the unique lists as they are being rebuilt.

T1. [Build S and T.] For each $\textcircled{u}$-node p, set $q \leftarrow \text{LO}(p)$, $r \leftarrow \text{HI}(p)$, and delete p from its hash table. If $\text{V}(q) \neq v$ and $\text{V}(r) \neq v$ (p is solitary), set $\text{LINK}(p) \leftarrow S$ and

$S \leftarrow p$. Otherwise (p is tangled), set $\text{REF}(q) \leftarrow \text{REF}(q) - 1$, $\text{REF}(r) \leftarrow \text{REF}(r) - 1$, $\text{LINK}(p) \leftarrow T$, and $T \leftarrow p$.

T2. [Build H and move the visible nodes.] For each $\textcircled{v}$-node p, set $q \leftarrow \text{LO}(p)$, $r \leftarrow \text{HI}(p)$, and delete p from its hash table. If $\text{REF}(p) = 0$ (p is hidden), set $\text{REF}(q) \leftarrow \text{REF}(q) - 1$, $\text{REF}(r) \leftarrow \text{REF}(r) - 1$, $\text{LINK}(p) \leftarrow H$, and $H \leftarrow p$; otherwise (p is visible) set $\text{V}(p) \leftarrow u$ and $\text{INSERT}(u, p)$.

T3. [Move the solitary nodes.] While $S \neq \Lambda$, set $p \leftarrow S$, $S \leftarrow \text{LINK}(p)$, $\text{V}(p) \leftarrow v$, and $\text{INSERT}(v, p)$.

T4. [Transmogrify the tangled nodes.] While $T \neq \Lambda$, set $p \leftarrow T$, $T \leftarrow \text{LINK}(p)$, and do the following: Set $q \leftarrow \text{LO}(p)$, $r \leftarrow \text{HI}(p)$. If $\text{V}(q) > v$, set $q_0 \leftarrow q_1 \leftarrow q$; otherwise set $q_0 \leftarrow \text{LO}(q)$ and $q_1 \leftarrow \text{HI}(q)$. If $\text{V}(r) > v$, set $r_0 \leftarrow r_1 \leftarrow r$; otherwise set $r_0 \leftarrow \text{LO}(r)$ and $r_1 \leftarrow \text{HI}(r)$. Then set $\text{LO}(p) \leftarrow \text{UNIQUE}(v, q_0, r_0)$, $\text{HI}(p) \leftarrow \text{UNIQUE}(v, q_1, r_1)$, and $\text{INSERT}(u, p)$.

T5. [Kill the hidden nodes.] While $H \neq \Lambda$, set $p \leftarrow H$, $H \leftarrow \text{LINK}(p)$, and recycle node p. (All of the remaining nodes are alive.) ▮

The subroutine $\text{INSERT}(v, p)$ simply puts node p into x_v's unique table, using the key $(\text{LO}(p), \text{HI}(p))$; this key will not already be present. The subroutine UNIQUE in step T4 is like Algorithm U, but instead of using answer 82 it treats reference counts quite differently in steps U1 and U2: If U1 finds $p = q$, it *increases* $\text{REF}(p)$ by 1; if U2 finds r, it simply sets $\text{REF}(r) \leftarrow \text{REF}(r) + 1$.

Internally, the branch variables retain their natural order $1, 2, \ldots, n$ from top to bottom. Mapping tables ρ and π represent the current permutation from the external user's point of view, with $\rho = \pi^-$; thus the user's variable x_v appears on level $v\pi - 1$, and node $\text{UNIQUE}(v, p, q)$ on level $v - 1$ represents the user's function $(\bar{x}_{v\rho}? \, p: q)$. To maintain these mappings, set $j \leftarrow u\rho$, $k \leftarrow v\rho$, $u\rho \leftarrow k$, $v\rho \leftarrow j$, $j\pi \leftarrow v$, $k\pi \leftarrow u$.

148. False. For example, consider six sinks and nine source functions, with extended truth tables 1156, 2256, 3356, 4456, 5611, 5622, 5633, 5644, 5656. Eight of the nodes are tangled and one is visible, but none are hidden or solitary. There are 16 newbies: 15, 16, 25, 26, 35, 36, 45, 46, 51, 61, 52, 62, 53, 63, 54, 64. So the swap takes 15 nodes into 31. (We can use the nodes of $B(x_3 \oplus x_4, x_3 \oplus \bar{x}_4)$ for the sinks.)

149. The successive profiles are bounded by $(b_0, b_1, \ldots, b_n)$, $(b_0 + b_1, 2b_0, b_2, \ldots, b_n)$, $(b_0 + b_1, 2b_0 + b_2, 4b_0, b_3, \ldots, b_n)$, $\ldots$, $(2^0 b_0 + b_1, \ldots, 2^{k-2} b_0 + b_{k-1}, 2^{k-1} b_0, b_k, \ldots, b_n)$.

Similarly, we also have $B(f_1^\pi, \ldots, f_m^\pi) \leq B(f_1, \ldots, f_m) + 2(b_0 + \cdots + b_{k-1})$ in addition to Theorem J$^+$, because swaps contribute at most $2b_{k-1}, 2b_{k-2}, \ldots, 2b_0$ new nodes.

150. We may assume that $m = 1$, as in exercise 52. Suppose we want to jump x_k to the position that is jth in the ordering, where $j \neq k$. First compute the restrictions of f when $x_k = 0$ and $x_k = 1$ (see exercise 57); call them g and h. Then renumber the remaining variables: If $j < k$, change $(x_j, \ldots, x_{k-1})$ to $(x_{j+1}, \ldots, x_k)$; otherwise change $(x_{k+1}, \ldots, x_j)$ to $(x_k, \ldots, x_{j-1})$. Then compute $f \leftarrow (\bar{x}_j \wedge g) \vee (x_j \wedge h)$, using the linear-time variant of Algorithm S in exercise 72.

To show that this method has the desired running time, it suffices to prove the following: *Let $g(x_1, \ldots, x_n)$ and $h(x_1, \ldots, x_n)$ be functions such that $g(x) = 1$ implies $x_j = 0$ and $h(x) = 1$ implies $x_j = 1$. Then the meld $g \diamond h$ has at most twice as many nodes as $g \vee h$.* But this is almost obvious, when truth tables are considered: For example, if $n = 3$ and $j = 2$, the truth tables for g and h have the respective forms $ab00cd00$ and $00st00uv$. The beads β of $g \vee h$ on levels $< j$ correspond uniquely to the beads $\beta' \diamond \beta''$ of $g \diamond h$ on those levels, because $\beta = \beta' \vee \beta''$ can be "factored" in only one way by putting 0s in the appropriate places. And the beads β of $g \vee h$ on levels $\geq j$ correspond to at most two beads of $g \diamond h$, namely to $\beta \diamond \boxed{\perp}$ and/or $\boxed{\perp} \diamond \beta$.

[See P. Savický and I. Wegener, *Acta Informatica* **34** (1997), 245–256, Theorem 1.]

151. Set $t_k \leftarrow 0$ for $1 \leq k \leq n$, and make the swapping operation $x_{j-1} \leftrightarrow x_j$ also swap $t_{j-1} \leftrightarrow t_j$. Then set $k \leftarrow 1$ and do the following until $k > n$: If $t_k = 1$ set $k \leftarrow k + 1$; otherwise set $t_k \leftarrow 1$ and sift x_k.

(This method repeatedly sifts on the topmost variable that hasn't yet been sifted. Researchers have tried fancier strategies, such as to sift the largest level first; but no such method has turned out to dominate the simple-minded approach proposed here.)

152. Applying Algorithm J as in answer 151 yields $B(h_{100}^\pi) = 1{,}382{,}685{,}050$ after 17,179 swaps, which is almost as good as the result of the "hand-tuned" permutation (95). Another sift brings the size down to 300,451,396; and further repetitions converge down to just 231,376,264 nodes, after a total of 232,951 swaps.

If the loops of steps J2 and J5 are aborted when $S > 1.05s$, the results are even better(!), although fewer swaps are made: 1,342,191,700 nodes after one sift reduce eventually to 208,478,228 after 139,245 total swaps. Moreover, Filip Stappers used sifting together with random swapping in September 2010 to get the value of $B(h_{100}^\pi)$ down to only 198,961,868, with the following "current champion" permutation π:

```
 3  4  6  8 10 12 14 16 18 20 22 24 27 28 30 32 35 37 39 41
43 45 47 49 51 53 54 83 85 98 99 100 79 77 81 75 73 95 71 97
69 96 57 91 67 59 65 60 63 62 64 61 66 87 58 68 56 94 93 70
92 72 90 74 76 78 80 89 88 86 84 82 55 52 50 48 46 44 42 40
38 36 34 33 31 29 26 25 23 21 19 17 15 13 11  9  7  5  1  2
```

Incidentally, if we sift the variables of h_{100} in order of profile size, so that x_{60} is sifted first, then x_{59}, x_{61}, x_{58}, x_{57}, x_{62}, x_{56}, etc. (wherever they currently happen to be), the resulting BDD turns out to have 2,196,768,534 nodes.

Simple "downhill swapping" instead of full sifting is of no use whatever for h_{100}: The $\binom{100}{2}$ swaps $x_1 \leftrightarrow x_2$, $x_3 \leftrightarrow x_1$, $x_3 \leftrightarrow x_2$, ..., $x_{100} \leftrightarrow x_1$, ..., $x_{100} \leftrightarrow x_{99}$ completely reverse the order of all variables without changing the BDD size at any step.

153. Each gate is easily synthesized using recursions like (55). About 1 megabyte of memory and 3.5 megamems of computation suffice to construct the entire BDD base of 8242 nodes. Using exercise 138 we may conclude that the ordering x_7, x_3, x_9, x_1, o_9, o_1, o_3, o_7, x_4, x_6, o_6, o_4, o_2, o_8, x_2, x_8, o_5, x_5 is optimum, and that $B_{\min}(y_1, \ldots, y_9) = 5308$.

Reordering of variables is *not* advisable for a problem such as this, since there are only 18 variables. For example, autosifting whenever the size doubles would require more than 100 megamems of work, just to reduce 8242 nodes to about 6400.

154. Yes: CA was moved between ID and OR at the last sifting step, and we can work backwards all the way to deduce that the first sift moved ME between MA and RI.

155. The author's best attempt for (a) is

```
ME NH VT MA CT RI NY DE NJ MD PA DC VA OH WV KY NC SC GA FL AL IN MI IA
IL MO TN AR MS TX LA CO WI KS SD ND NE OK WY MN ID MT NM AZ OR CA WA UT NV
```

giving $B(f_1^\pi) = 403$, $B(f_2^\pi) = 677$, $B(f_1^\pi, f_2^\pi) = 1073$; and for (b) the ordering

```
NH ME MA VT CT RI NY DE NJ MD PA VA DC OH WV KY TN NC SC GA FL AL IN MI
IL IA AR MO MS TX LA CO KS OK WI SD NE ND MN WY ID MT AZ NM UT OR CA WA NV
```

gives $B(f_1^\pi) = 352$, $B(f_2^\pi) = 702$, $B(f_1^\pi, f_2^\pi) = 1046$.

156. One might expect two "siftups" to be at least as good as a single sifting process that goes both up and down. But in fact, benchmark tests by R. Rudell show that siftup alone is definitely unsatisfactory. Occasional jump-downs are needed to compensate for variables that temporarily jump up, although their optimum final position lies below.

157. A careful study of answer 128 shows that we always improve the size when the first address bit that follows a target bit is jumped up past all targets. [But simple swaps are too weak. For example, $M_2(x_1, x_6; x_2, x_3, x_4, x_5)$ and $M_3(x_1, x_{10}, x_{11}; x_2, x_3, \ldots, x_9)$ are locally optimal under the swapping of $x_{j-1} \leftrightarrow x_j$ for any j.]

158. Consider first the case when $m = 1$ and $n = 3t - 1 \geq 5$. Then if $n\pi = k$, the number of nodes that branch on j is a_j if $j\pi < k$, b_j if $j\pi = k$, and a_{n+2-j} if $j\pi > k$, where

$$a_j = j - 3\max(j - 2t, 0), \qquad b_j = \min(j, t, n + 1 - j).$$

The cases with $\{x_1, \ldots, x_{n-1}\}$ consecutive are $k = 1$ and $B(f^\pi) = 3t^2 + 2$; $k = n$ and $B(f^\pi) = 3t^2 + 1$. But when $k = \lceil n/2 \rceil$ we have $B(f^\pi) = \lfloor 3t/2 \rfloor (\lceil 3t/2 \rceil - 1) + n - \lfloor t/2 \rfloor + 2$.

Similar calculations apply when $m > 1$: We have $B(f^\pi) > 6\binom{p/3}{2} + B(g^\pi)$ when π makes $\{x_1, \ldots, x_p\}$ consecutive, but

$$B(f^\pi) \approx 2\binom{p/2}{2} + \tfrac{p}{3}B(g^\pi)$$

when π puts $\{x_{p+1}, \ldots, x_{p+m}\}$ in the middle. Since g is fixed, $pB(g^\pi) = O(n)$ as $n \to \infty$.

[If g is a function of the same kind, we obtain examples where symmetric variables within g are best split up, and so on. But no Boolean functions are known for which the optimum $B(f^\pi)$ is less than 3/4 of the best that is obtainable under the constraint that no blocks of symmetric variables are split. See D. Sieling, *Random Structures & Algorithms* **13** (1998), 49–70.]

159. The function is almost symmetric, so there are only nine possibilities. When the center element x is placed in position $(1, 2, \ldots, 9)$ from the top, the BDD size is respectively $(43, 43, 42, 39, 36, 33, 30, 28, 28)$.

160. (a) Compute $\bigwedge_{i=0}^{9} \bigwedge_{j=0}^{9} (\neg L_{ij}(X))$, a Boolean function of 64 variables — for example, by applying COMPOSE to the relatively simple L function of exercise 159, 100 times. With the author's experimental programs, about 320 megamems and 35 megabytes are needed to find this BDD, which has 251,873 nodes with the normal ordering. Then Algorithm C quickly finds the desired answer: 21,929,490,122. (The number of 11×11 solutions, 5,530,201,631,127,973,447, can be found in the same way.)

(b) The generating function is $1 + 64z + 2016z^2 + 39740z^3 + \cdots + 80z^{45} + 8z^{46}$, and Algorithm B rapidly finds the eight solutions of weight 46. Three of them are distinct under chessboard symmetry; the most symmetric solution is shown as (A0) below.

(c) The BDD for $\bigwedge_{i=1}^{8} \bigwedge_{j=1}^{8} (\neg L_{ij}(X))$ has 305,507 nodes and 21,942,036,750 solutions. So there must be 12,546,628 wild ones.

(d) Now the generating function is $40z^{14} + 936z^{15} + 10500z^{16} + \cdots + 16z^{55} + z^{56}$; examples of weight 14 and 56 appear below as (A1) and (A2).

(e) Exactly 28 of weight 27 and 54 of weight 28, all tame; see (A3).

(f) There are respectively $(26260, 5, 347, 0, 122216)$ solutions, found with about $(228, 3, 32, 1, 283)$ megamems of calculation. Among the lightest and heaviest solutions to (1) are (A4) and (A5); the nicest solution to (2) is (A6); (A7) and (A9) solve (3) lightly and (5) heavily. Pattern (4), which is based on the binary representation of π, has no 8×8 predecessor; but it does, for example, have the 9×10 in (A8):

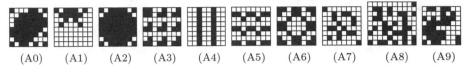

  (A0)   (A1)   (A2)   (A3)   (A4)   (A5)   (A6)   (A7)   (A8)   (A9)

161. (a) With the normal row-by-row ordering $(x_{11}, x_{12}, \ldots, x_{n(n-1)}, x_{nn})$, the BDD has 380,727 nodes and characterizes 4,782,725 solutions. The computational cost is about 2 gigamems, in 100 megabytes. (Similarly, the 29,305,144,137 still Lifes of size 10×10 can be enumerated with 14,492,923 nodes, after fewer than 50 gigamems.)

(b) This solution is essentially unique; see (B1) below. There's also a unique (and obvious) solution of weight 36.

(c) Now the BDD has 128 variables, with the ordering $(x_{11}, y_{11}, \ldots, x_{nn}, y_{nn})$. We could first set up BDDs for $[L(X) = Y]$ and $[L(Y) = X]$, then intersect them; but that turns out to be a bad idea, requiring some 36 million nodes even in the 7×7 case. Much better is to apply the constraints $L_{ij}(X) = y_{ij}$ and $L_{ij}(Y) = x_{ij}$ row by row, and also to add the lexicographic constraint $X < Y$ so that still Lifes are ruled out early. The computation can then be completed with about 20 gigamems and 1.6 gigabytes; there are 978,563 nodes and 582,769 solutions.

(d) Again the solution is unique, up to rotation; see the "spark plug" (B2) $\leftrightarrow$ (B3). (And (B4) $\leftrightarrow$ (B5) is the unique 7×7 flip-flop of constant weight 26. Life is astonishing.)

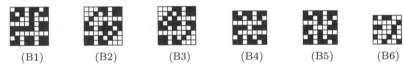

    (B1)   (B2)   (B3)   (B4)   (B5)   (B6)

162. Let $T(X) = [X \text{ is tame}]$ and $E_k(X) = [X \text{ escapes after } k \text{ steps}]$. We can compute the BDD for each E_k by using the recurrence

$$E_1(X) = \neg T(X); \qquad E_{k+1}(X) = \exists Y (T(X) \wedge [L(X) = Y] \wedge E_k(Y)).$$

(Here $\exists Y$ stands for $\exists y_{11} \exists y_{12} \cdots \exists y_{66}$. As noted in answer 103, this recurrence turns out to be much more efficient than the rule $E_{k+1} = T(X) \wedge E_k(L_{11}(X), \ldots, L_{66}(X))$, although the latter looks more "elegant.") The number of solutions, $|E_k|$, is found to be $(806544 \cdot 2^{16}$, $657527179 \cdot 2^4$, 2105885159, 763710262, 331054880, 201618308, 126169394, 86820176, 63027572, 41338572, 30298840, 17474640, 9797472, 5258660, 3058696, 1416132, 523776, 204192, 176520, 62456, 13648, 2776, 2256, 440, 104, 0) for $k = (1, 2, \ldots, 26)$; thus $\sum_{k=1}^{25} |E_k| = 67,166,017,379$ of the $2^{36} = 68,719,476,736$ possible configurations eventually escape from the 6×6 cage. (One of the 104 procrastinators in E_{25} is shown in (B6) above.)

BDD techniques are excellent for this problem when k is small; for example, $B(E_1) = 101$ and $B(E_2) = 14441$. But E_k eventually becomes a complicated "nonlocal" function: The size peaks at $B(E_6) = 28,696,866$, after which the number of solutions gets small enough to keep the size down. More than 80 million nodes are present in the formula $T(X) \wedge [L(X) = Y] \wedge E_5(Y)$ before quantification; this stretches memory limits. Indeed, the BDD for $\bigvee_{k=1}^{25} E_k(X)$ takes up more space than its 2^{33}-byte truth table. Therefore a "forward" method for this exercise would be preferable to the use of BDDs.

(Cages larger than 6×6 appear to be impossibly difficult, by *any* known method.)

163. Suppose first that $\circ$ is $\wedge$. We obtain the BDD for $f = g \wedge h$ by taking the BDD for g and replacing its $\boxed{\top}$ sink by the root of the BDD for h. To represent also $\bar{f}$, make a separate copy of the BDD for g, and use a BDD base for both h and $\bar{h}$; replace the $\boxed{\bot}$ in the copy by $\boxed{\top}$, and replace the $\boxed{\top}$ in the copy by the root of the BDD for $\bar{h}$. This decision diagram is reduced because h isn't constant.

Similarly, if $\circ$ is $\oplus$, we obtain a BDD for $f = g \oplus h$ (and possibly $\bar{f}$) from the BDD for g (and possibly $\bar{g}$) after replacing $\boxed{\bot}$ and $\boxed{\top}$ by the roots of BDDs for h and $\bar{h}$.

The other binary operations $\circ$ are essentially the same, because $B(f) = B(\bar{f})$. For example, if $f = g \supset h = \overline{g \wedge \bar{h}}$, we have $B(f) = B(\bar{f}) = B(g) + B(\bar{h}) - 2 = B(g) + B(h) - 2$.

164. Let $U_1(x_1) = V_1(x_1) = x_1$, $U_{n+1}(x_1, \ldots, x_{n+1}) = x_1 \oplus V_n(x_2, \ldots, x_{n+1})$, and $V_{n+1}(x_1, \ldots, x_{n+1}) = U_n(x_1, \ldots, x_n) \wedge x_{n+1}$. Then one can show by induction that $B(f) \leq B(U_n) = 2^{\lceil (n+1)/2 \rceil} + 2^{\lfloor (n+1)/2 \rfloor} - 1$ for all read-once f, and also that we always have $B(f, \bar{f}) \leq B(V_n, \overline{V_n}) = 2^{\lceil n/2 \rceil + 1} + 2^{\lfloor n/2 \rfloor + 1} - 2$. (But an optimum ordering reduces these sizes dramatically, to $B(U_n^\pi) = \lfloor \frac{3}{2}n + 2 \rfloor$ and $B(V_n^\pi, \overline{V_n^\pi}) = 2n + 2$.)

165. By induction, we prove also that $B(u_{2m}, \bar{u}_{2m}) = 2^m F_{2m+3} + 2$, $B(u_{2m+1}, \bar{u}_{2m+1}) = 2^{m+1} F_{2m+3} + 2$, $B(v_{2m}, \bar{v}_{2m}) = 2^{m+1} F_{2m+1} + 2$, $B(v_{2m+1}, \bar{v}_{2m+1}) = 2^{m+1} F_{2m+3} + 2$.

166. We may assume as in answer 163 that $\circ$ is either $\wedge$ or $\oplus$. By renumbering, we can also assume that $j\sigma = j$ for $1 \leq j \leq n$, hence $f^\sigma = f$. Let $(b_0, \ldots, b_n)$ be the profile of f, and $(b'_0, \ldots, b'_n)$ the profile of $(f, \bar{f})$; let $(c_{1\pi}, \ldots, c_{(n+1)\pi})$ and $(c'_{1\pi}, \ldots, c'_{(n+1)\pi})$ be the profiles of f^π and $(f^\pi, \bar{f}^\pi)$, where $(n+1)\pi = n+1$. Then $c_{j\pi}$ is the number of subfunctions of $f^\pi = g^\pi \circ h^\pi$ that depend on $x_{j\pi}$ after setting the variables $\{x_{1\pi}, \ldots, x_{(j-1)\pi}\}$ to fixed values. Similarly, $c'_{j\pi}$ is the number of such subfunctions of f^π or $\bar{f}^\pi$. We will try to prove that $b_{j\pi-1} \leq c_{j\pi}$ and $b'_{j\pi-1} \leq c'_{j\pi}$ for all j.

Case 1: $\circ$ is $\wedge$. We may assume that $n\pi = n$, since $\wedge$ is commutative. *Case 1a: $1 \leq j\pi \leq k$.* Then $b_{j\pi-1}$ and $b'_{j\pi-1}$ count subfunctions in which only the variables $x_{i\pi}$ with $1 \leq i < j$ and $1 \leq i\pi \leq k$ are specified. These subfunctions of $g \wedge h$ or $\bar{g} \vee \bar{h}$ have counterparts that are counted in $c_{j\pi}$ and $c'_{j\pi}$, because h^π is not constant in any subfunction when $n\pi = n$. *Case 1b: $k < j\pi \leq n$.* Then $b_{j\pi-1}$ and $b'_{j\pi-1}$ count subfunctions of h or $\bar{h}$, which have counterparts counted in $c_{j\pi}$ and $c'_{j\pi}$.

Case 2: $\circ$ is $\oplus$. We may assume that $1\pi = 1$, since $\oplus$ is commutative. Then an argument analogous to Case 1 applies. [*Discrete Applied Math.* **103** (2000), 237–258.]

167. Let $f = f_{1n}$; proceed recursively to compute $c_{ij} = B_{\min}(f_{ij})$, $c'_{ij} = B_{\min}(f_{ij}, \bar{f}_{ij})$, and a permutation π_{ij} of $\{i, \ldots, j\}$ for each subfunction $f_{ij}(x_i, \ldots, x_j)$ as follows: If $i = j$, we have $f_{ij}(x_i) = x_i$; let $c_{ij} = 3$, $c'_{ij} = 4$, $\pi_{ij} = i$. Otherwise $i < j$, and we have $f_{ij}(x_i, \ldots, x_j) = f_{ik}(x_i, \ldots, x_k) \circ f_{(k+1)j}(x_{k+1}, \ldots, x_j)$ for some k and some operator $\circ$. If $\circ$ is like $\wedge$, let $c_{ij} = c_{ik} + c_{(k+1)j} - 2$, and either $(c'_{ij} = 2c_{ik} + c'_{(k+1)j} - 4$, $\pi_{ij} = \pi_{ik}\pi_{(k+1)j})$ or $(c'_{ij} = 2c_{(k+1)j} + c'_{ik} - 4$, $\pi_{ij} = \pi_{(k+1)j}\pi_{ik})$, whichever minimizes c'_{ij}. If $\circ$ is like $\oplus$, let $c'_{ij} = c'_{ik} + c'_{(k+1)j} - 2$, and either $(c_{ij} = c_{ik} + c'_{(k+1)j} - 2$, $\pi_{ij} = \pi_{ik}\pi_{(k+1)j})$ or $(c_{ij} = c_{(k+1)j} + c'_{ik} - 2$, $\pi_{ij} = \pi_{(k+1)j}\pi_{ik})$, whichever minimizes c_{ij}.

(The permutations π_{ij} represented as strings in this description would be represented as linked lists inside a computer. We could also construct an optimum BDD for f recursively in $O(B_{\min}(f))$ steps, using answer 163.)

168. (a) This statement transforms and simplifies the recurrences (112) and (113).

(b) True by induction; also $x \geq n$.

(c) Easily verified. Notice that T is a reflection about the $22\frac{1}{2}°$ line $y = (\sqrt{2} - 1)x$.

(d) If $z \in S_k$ and $z' \in S_{n-k}$ we have $|z| = q^\beta$ and $|z'| = q'^\beta$, where $q \leq k$ and $q' \leq n - k$ by induction. By symmetry we may let $q = (1 - \delta)t$ and $q' = (1 + \delta)t$, where $t = \frac{1}{2}(q + q') \leq \frac{1}{2}n$. Then if the first hint is true, we have $|z \bullet z'| \leq (2t)^\beta \leq n^\beta$. And we also will have $|z \circ z'| \leq n^\beta$, by (c), since $|z^T| = |z|$.

To prove the first hint, we note that the maximum $|z \bullet z'|$ occurs when $y = y'$. For when $y \geq y'$ we have $|z \bullet z'|^2 = (x + x' + y')^2 + y^2 = r^2 + 2(x' + y')x + (x' + y')^2$; the largest value, given z', occurs when $y = y'$. A similar argument applies when $y' \geq y$.

Now when $y = y'$ we have $y = \sqrt{rr'}\sin\theta$ for some θ; and one can show that $x + x' \leq (r + r')\cos\theta$. Thus $z \bullet z' = (x + x' + y, y)$ lies in the ellipse of the second hint. On that ellipse we have $(a\cos\theta + b\sin\theta)^2 + (b\sin\theta)^2 = a^2/2 + b^2 + u\sin 2\theta + v\cos 2\theta = a^2/2 + b^2 + w\sin(2\theta + \tau)$, where $u = ab$, $v = \frac{1}{2}a^2 - b^2$, $w^2 = u^2 + v^2$, and $\cos\tau = u/w$. Hence $|z\bullet z'|^2 \leq \frac{1}{2}a^2 + b^2 + w$. And $4w^2 = (r + r')^4 + 4(rr')^2 \leq (r^2 + (2\sqrt{5} - 2)rr' + r'^2)^2$, so

$$|z \bullet z'|^2 \leq r^2 + (\sqrt{5} + 1)rr' + r'^2, \qquad r = (1 - \delta)^\beta, \; r' = (1 + \delta)^\beta.$$

The remaining task is to prove that this quantity is at most $2^{2\beta} = 2\phi^2$; equivalently, $f_t(2) \leq f_t(2\beta)$, where $f_t(\alpha) = (e^{t/\alpha} + e^{-t/\alpha})^\alpha - 2^\alpha$ and $t = \beta\ln((1 - \delta)/(1 + \delta))$. One can show, in fact, that f_t is an increasing function of α when $\alpha \geq 2$. [See G. Bennett, *AMM* **117** (2010), 334–351. The $O(n^\beta)$ bound on S_n seems to require a delicate analysis; an earlier attempt by Sauerhoff, Wegener, and Werchner was flawed. The proof given here is due to A. X. Chang and V. I. Spitkovsky in 2007.]

169. This conjecture has been verified for $m \leq 7$. [Many other curious properties also remain unexplained.]

170. (a) 2^{2n-1}. There are four choices at $\text{\textcircled{$j$}}$ when $1 \leq j < n$, namely $\text{LO} = \boxed{\bot}$ or $\text{LO} = \boxed{\top}$ or $\text{HI} = \boxed{\bot}$ or $\text{HI} = \boxed{\top}$; and there are two choices for $\text{\textcircled{$n$}}$.

(b) 2^{n-1}, since half the choices at each branch are ruled out.

(c) Indeed, if $t = (t_1 \ldots t_n)_2$ we have $\text{LO} = \boxed{\bot}$ at $\text{\textcircled{$j$}}$ when $t_j = 1$ and $\text{HI} = \boxed{\top}$ at $\text{\textcircled{$j$}}$ when $t_j = 0$. (This idea was applied to random bit generation in exercise 3.4.1–25. Since there are 2^{n-1} such values of t, we've shown that every monotone, skinny function is a threshold function, with weights $\{2^{n-1}, \ldots, 2, 1\}$. The other skinny functions are obtained by complementing individual variables.)

(d) $\bar{f}_t(\bar{x}) = [(\bar{x})_2 < t] = [(x)_2 > \bar{t}] = [(x)_2 > 2^n - 1 - t] = f_{2^n - t}(x)$.

(e) By Theorem 7.1.1Q, the shortest DNF is the OR of the prime implicants, and its general pattern is exhibited by the case $n = 10$ and $t = (1100010111)_2$: $(x_1 \wedge x_2 \wedge x_3) \vee (x_1 \wedge x_2 \wedge x_4) \vee (x_1 \wedge x_2 \wedge x_5) \vee (x_1 \wedge x_2 \wedge x_6 \wedge x_7) \vee (x_1 \wedge x_2 \wedge x_6 \wedge x_8 \wedge x_9 \wedge x_{10})$. (One term for each 0 in t, and one more.) The shortest CNF is the dual of the shortest DNF of the dual, which corresponds to $2^n - t = (0011101001)_2$: $(x_1) \wedge (x_2) \wedge (x_3 \vee x_4 \vee x_5 \vee x_6) \wedge (x_3 \vee x_4 \vee x_5 \vee x_7 \vee x_8) \wedge (x_3 \vee x_4 \vee x_5 \vee x_7 \vee x_9) \wedge (x_3 \vee x_4 \vee x_5 \vee x_7 \vee x_{10})$.

171. Note that the classes of read-once, regular, skinny, and monotone functions are each closed under the operations of taking duals and restrictions. A skinny function is clearly read-once; a monotone threshold function with $w_1 \geq \cdots \geq w_n$ is regular; and a regular function is monotone. We must show that a regular read-once function is skinny.

Suppose $f(x_1, \ldots, x_n) = g(x_{i_1}, \ldots, x_{i_k}) \circ h(x_{j_1}, \ldots, x_{j_l})$, where g and h are read-once and regular and $\circ$ is a nontrivial binary operator, and where we have $i_1 < \cdots < i_k$, $j_1 < \cdots < j_l$, $k + l = n$, and $\{i_1, \ldots, i_k, j_1, \ldots, j_l\} = \{1, \ldots, n\}$. (This condition is weaker than being "read-once.") We can assume that $i_1 = 1$. By taking restrictions and using induction, both g and h are skinny and monotone; thus their prime implicants have the special form in exercise 170(e). The operator $\circ$ must be monotone, so it is either $\vee$ or $\wedge$. By duality we can assume that $\circ$ is $\vee$.

Case 1: f has a prime implicant of length 1. Then x_1 is a prime implicant of f, by regularity. Hence $f(x_1, \ldots, x_n) = x_1 \vee f(0, x_2, \ldots, x_n)$, and we can use induction.

Case 2: All prime implicants of g and h have length > 1. Then $x_{j_1} \wedge \cdots \wedge x_{j_p}$ is a prime implicant, for some $p \geq 2$, but $x_{j_1-1} \wedge x_{j_2} \wedge \cdots \wedge x_{j_p}$ is not, contradicting regularity. [See T. Eiter, T. Ibaraki, and K. Makino, *Theor. Comp. Sci.* **270** (2002), 493–524.]

172. By examining the CNF for f_t in exercise 170(e), we see that when $t = (t_1 \ldots t_n)_2$ the number of Horn functions obtainable by complementing variables is one more than the number for $(t_2 \ldots t_n)_2$ when $t_1 = 0$, but twice that number when $t_1 = 1$. Thus the example $t = (1100010111)_2$ corresponds to $2 \times (2 \times (1 + (1 + (1 + (2 \times (1 + (2 \times (2 \times 2)))))))))$ Horn functions. Summing over all t gives s_n where $s_n = (2^{n-2} + s_{n-1}) + 2s_{n-1}$, where $s_1 = 2$; and the solution to this recurrence is $3^n - 2^{n-1}$.

To make both f and $\bar{f}$ Horn functions, assume (by duality) that $t \bmod 4 = 3$. Then we must complement x_j if and only if $t_j = 0$, except for the string of 1s at the right of t. For example, when $t = (1100010111)_2$, we should complement x_3, x_4, x_5, x_7, and then at most one of $\{x_8, x_9, x_{10}\}$. This gives $\rho(t+1) + 1 \geq 3$ choices related to f_t. Summing over all t with $t \bmod 4 = 3$ gives $2^n - 1$; so the answer is $2^{n+1} - 2$.

173. Consider monotone functions first. We can write $t = (0^{a_1} 1^{a_2} \ldots 0^{a_{2k-1}} 1^{a_{2k}})_2$, where $a_1 + \cdots + a_{2k} = n$, $a_1 \geq 0$, $a_j \geq 1$ for $1 < j < 2k$, and $a_{2k} \geq 2$ when $t \bmod 4 = 3$. When $t \bmod 4 = 1$, $2^n - t$ has this form. Then f_t has $a_1! a_2! \ldots a_{2k}!$ automorphisms, so it is equivalent to $n!/(a_1! a_2! \ldots a_{2k}!) - 1$ others, none of which are skinny. Summing over all t gives $2(P_n - nP_{n-1})$ monotone Boolean functions that are reorderable to skinny form, when $n \geq 2$, where P_n is the number of weak orderings (exercise 5.3.1–3). [See J. S. Beissinger and U. N. Peled, *Graphs and Combinatorics* **3** (1987), 213–219.]

Every such monotone function corresponds to 2^n different unate functions that are equally skinny, when variables are complemented. (These are the functions with the property that all of their restrictions are canalizing, known also as "unate cascades," "1-decision list functions," or "generalized read-once threshold functions.")

174. (a) Assign the numbers $0, \ldots, n-1, n, n+1$ to nodes ①, $\ldots$, ⓝ, ⊤, ⊥; and let the (LO, HI) branches from node k go to nodes (a_{2k+1}, a_{2k+2}) for $0 \leq k < n$. Then define p_k as follows, for $1 \leq k \leq 2n$: Let $l = \lfloor (k-1)/2 \rfloor$ and $P_l = \{p_1, \ldots, p_{2l}\}$. Set $p_k \leftarrow a_k$ if $a_k \notin P_l$; otherwise, if a_k is the mth smallest element of $P_l \cap \{l+1, \ldots, n+1\}$, set p_k to the mth smallest element of $\{n+2, \ldots, n+l+1\} \setminus P_l$. (This construction is due to T. Dahlheimer.)

(b) The inverse $p_1^{-1} \ldots p_{2n}^{-1}$ of a Dellac permutation satisfies $2(k-n) - 1 \leq p_k^{-1} \leq 2k$. It corresponds to a Genocchi derangement $q_1 \ldots q_{2n+2}$ when $q_2 = 1$, $q_{2n+1} = 2n+2$, and $q_{2k+2} = 1 + p_k^{-1}$, $q_{2k-1} = 1 + p_{k+n}^{-1}$ for $1 \leq k \leq n$.

(c) Given a permutation $q_1 \ldots q_{2n+2}$, let r_k be the first element of the sequence q_k^{-1}, $q_{q_k^{-1}}^{-1}$, $\ldots$ that is $\geq k$. This transformation takes Genocchi permutations into Dumont pistols, and has the property that $q_k = k$ if and only if $r_k = k \notin \{r_1, \ldots, r_{k-1}\}$.

(d) Each node (j, k) represents a set of strings $r_1 \ldots r_j$, where $(1, 0) = \{1\}$ and the other sets are defined by the following transition rules: Suppose $r_1 \ldots r_j \in (j, k)$, and let $l = 2k$. If $k = 0$ then $(j+1, k)$ contains $1r_1^+ \ldots r_j^+$ when j is even, $2r_1^+ \ldots r_j^+$ when j is odd, where r^+ denotes $r + 1$. If $k > 0$ then $(j+1, k)$ contains $r_1^+ \ldots r_l^+ (l+1) r_{l+1}^+ \ldots r_j^+$ when j is even, $r_1^\pm \ldots r_{l-1}^\pm (l) r_l^\pm \ldots r_j^\pm$ when j is odd, where $r^\pm$ denotes $r + 1$ when $r \geq l$, $r - 1$ when $r < l$. Going vertically, if $l \leq j - 3$ and j is odd, $(j, k+1)$ contains $r_1 \ldots r_l r_{l+2} r_{l+3} (l+3) r_{l+4} \ldots r_j$. On the other hand if $k = 1$ and j is even, $(j, 0)$ contains $r_2 r_1 r_3 \ldots r_j$. Finally if $k > 1$ and j is even, $(j, k-1)$ contains the string $r_1' \ldots r_{l-3}' (l-2) r_{l-2}' r_{l-1}' r_{l+1}' \ldots r_j'$, where r' denotes l when $r = l - 2$, otherwise $r' = r$. (One can show that the elements of $(2j, k)$ are the Dumont pistols for Genocchi permutations of order $2j$ whose largest fixed point is $2k$.)

All of these constructions are invertible. For example, the path $(1,0) \to (2,0) \to$ $(3,0) \to (3,1) \to (4,1) \to (5,1) \to (6,1) \to (7,1) \to (7,2) \to (7,3) \to (8,3) \to (8,2) \to$ $(8,1) \to (8,0)$ corresponds to the pistols $1 \to 22 \to 133 \to 333 \to 4244 \to 53355 \to$ $624466 \to 7335577 \to 7355577 \to 7355777 \to 82448688 \to 82646888 \to 82466888 \to$ 28466888. The latter pistol, which can be represented by the diagram ⌊•⸳•⸳⸳⸳⌋ , corresponds to the Genocchi derangement $q_1 \ldots q_8 = 61537482$. And this derangement corresponds to $p_1^{-1} \ldots p_6^{-1} = 231546$ and the Dellac permutation $p_1 \ldots p_6 = 312546$. That permutation, in turn, corresponds to $a_1 \ldots a_6 = 312343$, which stands for the thin BDD

$$①-②\cdots③-\boxed{⊤}\ \boxed{⊥}.$$

Let d_{jk} be the number of pistols in (j,k), which is also the number of directed paths from $(1,0)$ to (j,k). These numbers are readily found by addition, beginning with

```
                                              38227    38227   ···
                                    2073  2073 38227    76454   ···
                           155  155 2073  4146 36154   112608   ···
                    17  17 155  310 1918  6064 32008   144616   ···
              3  3  17  34 138  448 1608  7672 25944   170560   ···
        1  1  3  6  14  48 104  552 1160  8832 18272   188832   ···
  1  1  1  2  2  8  8  56  56 608  608  9440 9440    198272   ···  ;
```

and the column totals $D_j = \sum_k d_{jk}$ are $(D_1, D_2, \ldots) = (1, 1, 2, 3, 8, 17, 56, 155, 608, 2073, 9440, 38227, 198272, 929569, \ldots)$. The even-numbered elements of this sequence, D_{2n}, have long been known as the Genocchi numbers G_{2n+2}. The odd-numbered elements, D_{2n+1}, have therefore been called "median Genocchi numbers." The number S_n of thin BDDs is $d_{(2n+2)0} = D_{2n+1}$.

References: L. Euler discussed the Genocchi numbers in the second volume of his *Institutiones Calculi Differentialis* (1755), Chapter 7, where he showed that the odd integers G_{2n} are expressible in terms of the Bernoulli numbers: In fact, $G_{2n} = (2^{2n+1} - 2)|B_{2n}|$, and $z \tan \frac{z}{2} = \sum_{n=1}^{\infty} G_{2n} z^{2n}/(2n)!$. A. Genocchi examined these numbers further in *Annali di Scienze Matematiche e Fisiche* **3** (1852), 395–405; and L. Seidel, in *Sitzungsberichte math.-phys. Classe, Akademie Wissen. München* **7** (1877), 157–187, discovered that they could be computed additively via the numbers d_{jk}. Their combinatorial significance was not discovered until much later; see D. Dumont, *Duke Math. J.* **41** (1974), 305–318; D. Dumont and A. Randrianarivony, *Discrete Math.* **132** (1994), 37–49. Meanwhile H. Dellac had proposed an apparently unrelated problem, equivalent to enumerating what we have called Dellac permutations; see L'*Intermédiaire des Math.* **7** (1900), 9–10, 328; *Annales de la Faculté sci. Marseille* **11** (1901), 141–164.

There's also a *direct* connection between thin BDDs and the paths of (d), discovered in 2007 by Thorsten Dahlheimer. Notice first that unrestricted Dumont pistols of order $2n + 2$ correspond to thin BDDs that are ordered but not necessarily reduced, because we can let $r_1 \ldots r_{2n} r_{2n+1} r_{2n+2} = (2a_1) \ldots (2a_{2n})(2n+2)(2n+2)$. The number of such pistols in which $\min\{i \mid r_{2i-1} = r_{2i}\} = l$ turns out to be $d_{(2n+2)(n+1-l)}$.

To prove this, we can use new transition rules instead of those in answer (d): Suppose $r_1 \ldots r_j \in (j,k)$, and let $l = j - 2k$. Then $(j+1, k)$ contains $r_1^+ \ldots r_l^+ r_l^\dagger \ldots r_j^+$ when j is odd, $r_1^\pm \ldots r_{l-1}^\pm (l-1) r_l^\pm \ldots r_j^\pm$ when j is even. If j is odd, $(j, k+1)$ contains $1 r_1 r_3 \ldots r_j$ when $l = 3$, and when $l > 3$ it contains $r_1' \ldots r_{l-4}' (l-4) r_{l-3}' r_{l-2}' r_l' \ldots r_j'$, where $r' = r + 2[r = l - 4]$. Finally, if j is even and $k > 0$, $(j, k-1)$ contains $r_1 \ldots r_{l-1} q r_{l+2} r_{l+2} \ldots r_j$, where $q = l$ if $r_l = r_{l+1}$, otherwise $q = r_{l+1}$.

With these magic transitions the path above corresponds to $1 \to 22 \to 313 \to 133 \to 2244 \to 31355 \to 424466 \to 5153577 \to 5135577 \to 1535577 \to 22646688 \to 26446688 \to 26466688 \to 26466888$; so $a_1 \ldots a_6 = 132334$.

175. This problem seems to require a different approach from the methods that worked when $b_0 = \cdots = b_{n-1} = 1$. Suppose we have a BDD base of N nodes including the two sinks $\boxed{\bot}$ and $\boxed{\top}$ together with various branches labeled $\textcircled{2}, \ldots, \textcircled{n}$, and assume that exactly s of the nodes are sources (having in-degree zero). Let $c(b, s, t, N)$ be the number of ways to introduce b additional nodes labeled $\textcircled{1}$, in such a way that exactly $s+b-t$ source nodes remain. (Thus $0 \le t \le 2b$; exactly t of the old source nodes are now reachable from a $\textcircled{1}$ branch.) Then the number of nonconstant Boolean functions $f(x_1, \ldots, x_n)$ having the BDD profile $(b_0, \ldots, b_n)$ is equal to $T(b_0, \ldots, b_{n-1}; 1)$, where

$$T(b_0; s) = 2[s = b_0 = 1] + [s = 2][b_0 = 0] + [s = 2][b_0 = 2];$$

$$T(b_0, \ldots, b_{n-1}; s) = \sum_{t = \max(0, b_0 - s)}^{2b_0} c(b_0, s+t-b_0, t, b_1 + \cdots + b_{n-1} + 2)\, T(b_1, \ldots, b_{n-1}; s+t-b_0).$$

One can show that $c(b, s, t, N) = \sum_{r=0}^{2b} a_{rb} p_{tr}(s, N)/b!$, where we have $(N(N-1))^{\underline{b}} = \sum_{r=0}^{2b} a_{rb} N^r$ and $p_{tr}(s, N) = \sum_k \binom{r}{k} \{ {k \atop t} \} s^{\underline{t}} (N-s)^{r-k} = \sum_k \{ {r \atop k} \} \binom{k}{t} s^{\underline{t}} (N-s)^{\underline{k-t}} = r! [w^t z^r] e^{(N-s)z} (we^z - w + 1)^s$.

176. (a) If $p \ne p'$ we have $\sum_{a \in A, b \in B} [h_{a,b}(p) = h_{a,b}(p')] \le |A||B|/2^l$, by the definition of universal hashing. Let $r_i(a, b)$ be the number of $p \in P$ such that $h_{a,b}(p) = i$. Then

$$\sum_{a \in A, b \in B} \sum_{0 \le i < 2^l} r_i(a, b)^2 = \sum_{a \in A, b \in B} \sum_{p \in P} \sum_{p' \in P} [h_{a,b}(p) = h_{a,b}(p')]$$

$$\le |P||A||B| + \sum_{p \in P} \sum_{p' \in P} [p \ne p'] \frac{|A||B|}{2^l} = 2^t |A||B| \left(1 + \frac{2^t - 1}{2^l} \right).$$

On the other hand $\sum_{i=0}^{2^l - 1} r_i(a, b)^2 = \sum_{i=0}^{2^l - 1} (r_i(a, b) - 2^t/|I|)^2 + 2^{2t}/|I| \ge 2^{2t}/|I|$, for any a and b. Similar formulas apply when there are $s_j(a, b)$ solutions to $h_{a,b}(q) = j$. So there must be $a \in A$ and $b \in B$ such that

$$\frac{2^{2t}}{|I|} + \frac{2^{2t}}{|J|} \le \sum_{i \in I} r_i(a, b)^2 + \sum_{j \in J} s_j(a, b)^2 \le 2^{t+1} \left(1 + \frac{2^t - 1}{2^l} \right) \le \frac{2^{2t}}{2^l} + \frac{2^{2t}}{(1 - \epsilon)2^l}.$$

(b) The middle l bits of $aq_k + b$ and $aq_{k+2} + b$ differ by at least 2, so the middle $l - 1$ bits of aq_k and aq_{k+2} must be different.

(c) Let q and q' be different elements of Q^* with $(g(q') - g(q)) \bmod 2^{l-1} \ge 2^{l-2}$. (Otherwise we can swap $q \leftrightarrow q'$.) If $l \ge 3$, the condition $g(p) + g(q) = 2^{l-1}$ implies that $f_q(p) = 0$. Now we have $(g(p) + g(q')) \bmod 2^{l-1} = (g(q') - g(q)) \bmod 2^{l-1}$; furthermore $g(q')$ and $g(p)$ are both even. Therefore no carry can propagate to change the middle bit, and we have $f_{q'}(p) = 1$.

(d) The set Q'' has at least $(1-\epsilon)2^{l-1}$ elements, and so does the analogous set P''. At most 2^{l-2} elements of Q'' have $g(q)$ odd; and at most $2^{l-2} + 1 - |P''|$ of the elements with $g(q)$ even are not in Q^*. Thus $|Q^*| \ge (1 - \epsilon)2^{l-1} - 2^{l-2} - 2^{l-1} - 1 + (1 - \epsilon)2^{l-1} = (1 - 4\epsilon)2^{l-2} - 1$, and we have $B_{\min}(Z_{n,a}) \ge (1 - 4\epsilon)2^{l-1} - 2$ by (85).

Finally, choose $l = t - 4$ and $\epsilon = 1/9$. The theorem is obvious when $n < 14$.

177. Suppose $k \ge n/2$ and $x = 2^{k+1}x_h + x_l$, $y = 2^k y_h + y_l$. Then $(xy \gg k) \bmod 2^{n-k}$ depends on $2x_h y_l$, $x_l y_h$, and $x_l y_l \gg k$, modulo 2^{n-k}, so $q_{2k+1} \le 2^{n-k-1+n-k+n-k}$.

Summing up, we get $\sum_{k=0}^{2n} q_k \le \sum_{0 \le k \le 6n/5} 2^k + \sum_{6n/5 < k \le 2n} 2^{3n - 2\lfloor k/2 \rfloor - \lceil k/2 \rceil}$.

If $n = 5t + (0, 1, 2, 3, 4)$ the total comes to exactly $(2^{\lceil 6n/5 \rceil} \cdot (19, 10, 12, 13, 17) - 12)/7$. [M. Sauerhoff, in *Discrete Applied Math.* **158** (2010), 1195–1204, has proved the lower bound $\Omega(2^{6n/5})$ for this ordering.]

178. We can write $x = 2^k x_h + x_l$ as in the proof of Theorem A; but now $x_l = \hat{x}_l + (x \bmod 2)$, where $\hat{x}_l$ is even and $x \bmod 2$ is not yet known. Similarly $y = 2^k y_h + y_l = 2^k y_h + \hat{y}_l + (y \bmod 2)$. Let $\hat{z}_l = \hat{x}_l \hat{y}_l \bmod 2^k$. At level $2k - 2$, for $n/2 \le k < n$, we need only "remember" three $(n - k)$-bit numbers $\hat{x}_l \bmod 2^{n-k}$, $\hat{y}_l \bmod 2^{n-k}$, $(\hat{x}_l \hat{y}_l \gg k) \bmod 2^{n-k}$, and three "carries" $c_1 = (\hat{x}_l + \hat{z}_l) \gg k$, $c_2 = (\hat{y}_l + \hat{z}_l) \gg k$, $c_3 = (\hat{x}_l + \hat{y}_l + \hat{z}_l) \gg k$. These six quantities tell us the middle bit, once x_h, y_h, $x \bmod 2$, and $y \bmod 2$ are known.

There are only six possibilities for the carries: $c_1 c_2 c_3 = 000$, 001, 011, 101, 111, or 112. Thus $q_{2k-2} \le 6 \cdot 2^{(n-k-1)+(n-k-1)+(n-k)}$. Similarly, when $n/2 \le k < n - 1$, we have $q_{2k-1} \le 6 \cdot 2^{(n-k-2)+(n-k-1)+(n-k)}$. With these estimates, together with $q_k \le 2^k$, we get $\sum_{k=0}^{2n-4} q_k \le (2^{6t} \cdot (37, 86, 184, 464, 1024) - 268)/28$ when $n = 5t + (0, 1, 2, 3, 4)$.

The actual BDD sizes, for the function f of Theorem A and the function g of this exercise, are $B(f) = (169, 381, 928, 2188, 5248, 12373, 29400, 68777, 162768, 377359, 879709)$ and $B(g) = (165, 352, 806, 1802, 4195, 9774, 22454, 52714, 121198, 278223, 650188)$ for $6 \le n \le 16$; so this variant appears to save about 25%. A slightly better ordering is obtained by testing (lo-bit(x), hi-bit(y), hi-bit(x), lo-bit(y)) on the last four levels, giving $B(h) = B(g) - 20$ for $n \ge 6$. Then $B(h)/B_{\min}(f) \approx (1.07, 1.05, 1.04, 1.04, 1.04, 1.01, 1.02)$ for $6 \le n \le 12$, so this ordering may be close to optimal as $n \to \infty$.

180. By letting $a_{m+1} = a_{m+2} = \cdots = 0$, we may assume that $m \ge p$. Let $a = (a_p \ldots a_1)_2$, and write $x = 2^k x_h + x_l$ as in the proof of Theorem A. If $p \le n$, we have $q_k \le 2^{p-k}$ for $0 \le k < p$, because the given function $f = Z_{m,n}^{(p)}(a; x)$ depends only on a, x_h, and $(ax_l \gg k) \bmod 2^{p-k}$. We may therefore assume that $p > n$.

Consider the multiset $A = \{2^k x_h a \bmod 2^{p-1} \mid 0 \le x_h < 2^{n-k}\}$. Write $A = \{2^{p-1} - \alpha_1, \ldots, 2^{p-1} - \alpha_s\}$, where $s = 2^{n-k}$ and $0 < \alpha_1 \le \cdots \le \alpha_s \le 2^{p-1}$, and let $\alpha_{s+i} = \alpha_i + 2^{p-1}$ for $0 \le i \le s$. Then $q_k \le 2s$, because f depends only on a, x_h, and the index $i \in [0 .. 2s]$ such that $\alpha_i \le ax_l \bmod 2^p < \alpha_{i+1}$.

Consequently $\sum_{k=0}^{n} q_k \le \sum_{k=0}^{n} \min(2^k, 2^{n+1-k}) = 2^{\lfloor n/2 \rfloor + 1} + 2^{\lceil n/2 \rceil + 1} - 3$.

181. For every $(x_1, \ldots, x_m)$ only $O(n)$ further nodes are needed, by exercise 170.

182. Yes; B. Bollig [*Lecture Notes in Comp. Sci.* **4978** (2008), 306–317] has shown that it is $\Omega(2^{n/432})$. Incidentally, $B_{\min}(L_{12,12}) = 1158$ is obtained with the strange ordering $L_{12,12}(x_{18}, x_{17}, x_{16}, x_{15}, x_{14}, x_{12}, x_{10}, x_8, x_6, x_4, x_2, x_1; x_{19}, x_{20}, x_{21}, x_{22}, x_{23}, x_{13}, x_{11}, x_9, x_7, x_5, x_3, x_{24})$; and $B_{\max}(L_{12,12}) = 9302$ arises with $L_{12,12}(x_{24}, x_{23}, x_{20}, x_{19}, x_{22}, x_{11}, x_6, x_7, x_8, x_9, x_{10}, x_{13}; x_1, x_2, x_3, x_4, x_5, x_{21}, x_{18}, x_{17}, x_{16}, x_{15}, x_{14}, x_{12})$. Similarly $B_{\min}(L_{8,16}) = 606$ and $B_{\max}(L_{8,16}) = 3415$ aren't terribly far apart. Could $B_{\min}(L_{m,n})$ and $B_{\max}(L_{m,n})$ both conceivably be $\Theta(2^{\min(m,n)})$?

183. The profile $(b_0, b_1, \ldots)$ begins $(1, 1, 1, 2, 3, 5, 7, 11, 15, 23, 31, 47, 63, 95, \ldots)$. When $k > 1$ there's a node on level $2k$ for every pair of integers (a, b) such that $2^{k-1} \le a, b < 2^k$ and $ab < 2^{2k-1} < (a + 1)(b + 1)$; this node represents the function $[((a + x)/2^k)((b + y)/2^k) \ge \frac{1}{2}]$. When b is given, in the appropriate range, there are $\lceil 2^{2k-1}/b \rceil - \lfloor 2^{2k-1}/(b + 1) \rfloor$ choices for a; hence $b_{2k} = \sum_{2^{k-1} \le b < 2^k} (\lceil 2^{2k-1}/b \rceil - \lfloor 2^{2k-1}/(b + 1) \rfloor)$,

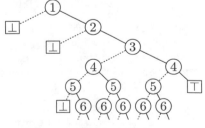

which telescopes to $2^k - 1$. A similar argument shows that $b_{2k+1} = 2^k + 2^{k-1} - 1$.

184. Two kinds of beads contribute to $b_{m(i-1)+j-1}$: One for every choice of i columns, at least one of which is $< j$; and one for every choice of $i-1$ columns, missing at least one element $\geq j$. Thus $b_{m(i-1)+j-1} = \left(\binom{m}{i} - \binom{m+1-j}{i}\right) + \left(\binom{m}{i-1} - \binom{j-1}{m+1-i}\right)$. Summing over $1 \leq i, j \leq m$ gives $B(P_m) = (2m-3)2^m + 5$. (Incidentally, $q_k = b_k + 1$ for $2 \leq k < m^2$.)

The ZDD has simply $z_{m(i-1)+j-1} = \binom{m-1}{i-1}$ for $1 \leq i, j \leq m$, one for every choice of $i-1$ columns $\neq j$; hence $Z(P_m) = m2^{m-1} + 2 \approx \frac{1}{4}B(P_m)$. (The lower bound of Theorem K applies also to ZDD nodes, because only such nodes get tickets; therefore the natural ordering of variables is optimum for ZDDs. The natural ordering might be optimum also for BDDs; this conjecture is known to be true for $m \leq 5$.)

185. Suppose $f(x) = t_{\nu x}$ for some binary vector $t_0 \ldots t_n$. Then the subfunctions of order $d > 0$ correspond to the distinct substrings $t_i \ldots t_{i+d}$. Such substrings τ correspond to beads if and only if $\tau \neq 0^{d+1}$ and $\tau \neq 1^{d+1}$; they correspond to zeads if and only if $\tau \neq 0^{d+1}$ and $\tau \neq 10^d$.

Thus the maximum $Z(f)$ is the function S_n of answer 44. To attain this worst case we need a binary vector of length $2^{d+1} + d - 2$ that contains all $(d+1)$-tuples except 0^{d+1} and 10^d as substrings; such vectors can be characterized as the first $2^{d+1} + d - 2$ elements of any de Bruijn cycle of period 2^{d+1}, beginning with $0^d 1$.

186. $\bar{x}_1 \wedge \bar{x}_2 \wedge x_3 \wedge \bar{x}_4 \wedge \bar{x}_5 \wedge \bar{x}_6$.

187. (These diagrams should be compared with the answer to exercise 1.)

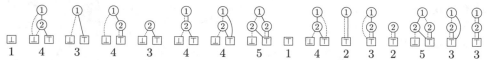

188. To avoid nested braces, let ϵ, a, b, and ab stand for the subsets $\emptyset$, $\{1\}$, $\{2\}$, and $\{1,2\}$. The families are then $\emptyset$, $\{ab\}$, $\{a\}$, $\{a, ab\}$, $\{b\}$, $\{b, ab\}$, $\{a, b\}$, $\{a, b, ab\}$, $\{\epsilon\}$, $\{\epsilon, ab\}$, $\{\epsilon, a\}$, $\{\epsilon, a, ab\}$, $\{\epsilon, b\}$, $\{\epsilon, b, ab\}$, $\{\epsilon, a, b\}$, $\{\epsilon, a, b, ab\}$, in truth-table order.

189. When $n = 0$, only the constant functions; when $n > 0$, only 0 and $x_1 \wedge \cdots \wedge x_n$. (But there are many functions, such as $x_2 \wedge (x_1 \vee \bar{x}_3)$, with $(b_0, \ldots, b_n) = (z_0, \ldots, z_n)$.)

190. (a) Only $x_1 \oplus \cdots \oplus x_n$ and $1 \oplus x_1 \oplus \cdots \oplus x_n$, for $n \geq 0$. (b) This condition holds if and only if all subtables of order 1 are either 01 or 11. So there are $2^{2^{n-1}}$ solutions when $n > 0$, namely all functions such that $f(x_1, \ldots, x_{n-1}, 1) = 1$.

191. The language L_n of truth tables for all such functions has the context-free grammar $L_0 \to 1$; $L_{n+1} \to L_n L_n \mid L_n 0^{2^n}$. The desired number $l_n = |L_n|$ therefore satisfies $l_0 = 1$, $l_{n+1} = l_n(l_n + 1)$; so $(l_0, l_1, l_2, \ldots)$ is the sequence $(1, 2, 6, 42, 1806, 3263442, 10650056950806, \ldots)$. Asymptotically, $l_n = \theta^{2^n} - \frac{1}{2} - \epsilon$, where $0 < \epsilon < \theta^{-2^n}/8$ and

$$\theta = 1.59791\,02180\,31873\,17833\,80701\,18157\,45531\,23622+.$$

[See *CMath* exercises 4.37 and 4.59, where $l_n + 1$ is called e_{n+1} (a "Euclid number") and θ is called E^2. The numbers $l_n + 1$ were introduced by J. J. Sylvester in connection with his study of Egyptian fractions, *Amer. J. Math.* **3** (1880), 388. Notice that a monotone decreasing function, like a function representing independent sets, always has $z_n = 1$.]

192. (a) 10101101000010110.

(b) True, by induction on $|\tau|$, because $\alpha \neq \beta \neq 0^n$ if and only if $\alpha^Z \neq \beta^Z \neq 0^n$.

(c) The beads of f of order k are the zeads of f^Z of order k, for $0 < k \leq n$. Hence the beads of f^Z are also the zeads of $(f^Z)^Z = f$. Therefore, if $(b_0, \ldots, b_n)$ and

$(z_0, \ldots, z_n)$ are the profile and z-profile of f while $(b'_0, \ldots, b'_n)$ and $(z'_0, \ldots, z'_n)$ are the profile and z-profile of f^Z, we have $b_k = z'_k$ and $z_k = b'_k$ for $0 \le k < n$.

(We also have $z_n = z'_n$, but they might both be 1 instead of 2. The *quasi-profiles* of f and f^Z may differ, but only by at most 1 at each level, because of all-0 subtables.)

193. $S_{\ge k}(x_1, \ldots, x_n)$, by induction on n. (Hence we also have $S^Z_{\ge k}(x_1, \ldots, x_n) = S_k(x_1, \ldots, x_n)$. Exercise 249 gives similar examples.)

194. Define $a_1 \ldots a_{2n}$ as in answer 174, but use the ZDD instead of the BDD. Then $(1, \ldots, 1)$ is the z-profile if and only if $(2a_1) \ldots (2a_{2n})$ is an unrestricted Dumont pistol of order $2n$. So the answer is the Genocchi number G_{2n+2}.

195. The z-profile is $(1, 2, 4, 4, 3, 2, 2)$. We get an optimum z-profile $(1, 2, 3, 2, 3, 2, 2)$ from $M_2(x_4, x_2; x_5, x_6, x_3, x_1)$, and a pessimum z-profile $(1, 2, 4, 8, 12, 2, 2)$ comes from $M_2(x_5, x_6; x_1, x_2, x_3, x_4)$ as in (78). (Incidentally, the algorithm of exercise 197 can be used to show that $Z_{\min}(M_4) = 116$ is obtained with the strikingly peculiar ordering $M_4(x_8, x_5, x_{17}, x_2; x_{20}, x_{19}, x_{18}, x_{16}, x_{15}, x_{13}, x_{14}, x_{12}, x_{11}, x_9, x_{10}, x_4, x_7, x_6, x_3, x_1)$!)

196. For example, $M_m(x_1, \ldots, x_m; e_{m+1}, \ldots, e_n)$, where $n = m + 2^m$ and e_j is the elementary function of exercise 203. Then we have $Z(f) = 2(n - m) + 1$ and $Z(\bar{f}) = (n - m + 7)(n - m)/2 - 2$.

197. The key idea is to change the significance of the DEP fields so that d_{kp} is now $\sum\{2^{t-k-1} \mid N_{kp} \text{ supports } x_t\}$, where we say that $g(x_1, \ldots, x_m)$ *supports* x_j if there is a solution to $g(x_1, \ldots, x_m) = 1$ with $x_j = 1$.

To implement this change, we introduce an auxiliary array $(\zeta_0, \ldots, \zeta_n)$, where we will have $\zeta_k = q$ if N_{kq} denotes the subfunction 0 and $\zeta_k = -1$ if that subfunction does not appear on level k. Initially $\zeta_n \leftarrow 0$, and we set $\zeta_k \leftarrow -1$ at the beginning of step E1. In step E3, the operation of setting d_{kq} should become the following: "If $d_{(k+1)h} \ne \zeta_{k+1}$, set $d_{kq} \leftarrow ((d_{(k+1)l} \mid d_{(k+1)h}) \ll 1) + 1$; otherwise set $d_{kq} \leftarrow d_{(k+1)l} \ll 1$. Also set $\zeta_k \leftarrow q$ if $d_{(k+1)l} = d_{(k+1)h} = \zeta_{k+1}$."

(The master z-profile chart can be used as before to minimize $z_0 + \cdots + z_{n-1}$; but additional work is needed to consider z_n if the *absolute* minimum is important.)

198. Reinterpreting (50), we represent an arbitrary family of sets f as $(\bar{x}_v? f_l: f_h)$, where $v = f_o$ indexes the first variable that f *supports*; see answer 197. Thus f_l is the subfamily of f that doesn't support x_v, and f_h is the subfamily that does (but with x_v deleted). We also let $f_o = \infty$ if f has no support (i.e., if f is either $\emptyset$ or $\{\emptyset\}$, represented internally by $\boxed{\perp}$ or $\boxed{\top}$; see answer 200). In (52), $v = \min(f_o, g_o)$ now indexes the first variable *supported* by either f or g; thus $f_h = \emptyset$ if $f_o > g_o$, and $g_h = \emptyset$ if $f_o < g_o$.

Subroutine AND(f, g), ZDD-style, is now the following instead of (55): "Represent f and g as in (52). While $f_o \ne g_o$, return $\emptyset$ if either $f = \emptyset$ or $g = \emptyset$; otherwise set $f \leftarrow f_l$ if $f_o < g_o$, set $g \leftarrow g_l$ if $f_o > g_o$. Swap $f \leftrightarrow g$ if $f > g$. Return f if $f = g$ or $f = \emptyset$. Otherwise, if $f \wedge g = r$ is in the memo cache, return r. Otherwise compute $r_l \leftarrow \text{AND}(f_l, g_l)$ and $r_h \leftarrow \text{AND}(f_h, g_h)$; set $r \leftarrow \text{ZUNIQUE}(v, r_l, r_h)$, using an algorithm like Algorithm U except that the first step returns p when $q = \emptyset$ instead of when $q = p$; put '$f \wedge g = r$' into the memo cache, and return r." (See also the suggestion in answer 200.)

Reference counts are updated as in exercise 82, with slight changes; for example, step U1 will now decrease the reference count of $\boxed{\perp}$ (and only of this node), when $q = \emptyset$. It is important to write a "sanity check" routine that double-checks all reference counts and other redundancies in the entire BDD/ZDD base, so that subtle errors are nipped in the bud. The sanity checker should be invoked frequently until all subroutines have been thoroughly tested.

199. (a) If $f = g$, return f. If $f > g$, swap $f \leftrightarrow g$. If $f = \emptyset$, return g. If $f \vee g = r$ is in the memo cache, return r. Otherwise

$$\begin{array}{ll}
\text{set } v \leftarrow f_o, \ r_l \leftarrow \text{OR}(f_l, g_l), \ r_h \leftarrow \text{OR}(f_h, g_h), & \text{if } f_o = g_o; \\
\text{set } v \leftarrow f_o, \ r_l \leftarrow \text{OR}(f_l, g), \ r_h \leftarrow f_h, \text{ increase REF}(f_h) \text{ by } 1, & \text{if } f_o < g_o; \\
\text{set } v \leftarrow g_o, \ r_l \leftarrow \text{OR}(f, g_l), \ r_h \leftarrow g_h, \text{ increase REF}(g_h) \text{ by } 1, & \text{if } f_o > g_o.
\end{array}$$

Then set $r \leftarrow \text{ZUNIQUE}(v, r_l, r_h)$; cache it and return it as in answer 198.

(b) If $f = g$, return $\emptyset$. Otherwise proceed as in (a), but use $(\oplus, \text{XOR})$ not $(\vee, \text{OR})$.

(c) If $f = \emptyset$ or $f = g$, return $\emptyset$. If $g = \emptyset$, return f. Otherwise, if $g_o < f_o$, set $g \leftarrow g_l$ and begin again. Otherwise

$$\begin{array}{ll}
\text{set } r_l \leftarrow \text{BUTNOT}(f_l, g_l), \ r_h \leftarrow \text{BUTNOT}(f_h, g_h), & \text{if } f_o = g_o; \\
\text{set } r_l \leftarrow \text{BUTNOT}(f_l, g), \ r_h \leftarrow f_h, \text{ increase REF}(f_h) \text{ by } 1, & \text{if } f_o < g_o.
\end{array}$$

Then set $r \leftarrow \text{ZUNIQUE}(f_o, r_l, r_h)$ and finish as usual.

200. If $f = \emptyset$, return g. If $f = h$, return $\text{OR}(f, g)$. If $g = h$, return g. If $g = \emptyset$ or $f = g$, return $\text{AND}(f, h)$. If $h = \emptyset$, return $\text{BUTNOT}(g, f)$. If $f_o < g_o$ and $f_o < h_o$, set $f \leftarrow f_l$ and start over. If $h_o < f_o$ and $h_o < g_o$, set $h \leftarrow h_l$ and start over. Otherwise check the cache and proceed recursively as usual.

201. In applications of ZDDs where projection functions and/or the complementation operation are permitted, it's best to fix the set of Boolean variables at the beginning, when everything is being initialized. Otherwise, *every* external function in a ZDD base must change whenever a new variable enters the fray.

Suppose therefore that we've decided to deal with functions of $(x_1, \ldots, x_N)$, where N is prespecified. In answer 198, we let $f_o = N + 1$, not ∞, when $f = \emptyset$ or $f = \{\emptyset\}$. Then the tautology function $1 = \wp$ has the $(N+1)$-node ZDD $\text{①}\text{②}\cdots\text{Ⓝ}\text{⊤}$, which we construct as soon as N is known. Let t_j be node ⓙ of this structure, with $t_{N+1} = \text{⊤}$. The ZDD for x_j is now $\text{①}\cdots\text{ⓙ}\text{—}t_{j+1}\text{⊥}$; thus the ZDD base for the set of all x_j will occupy $\binom{N+1}{2}$ nodes in addition to the representations of $\emptyset$ and $\wp$.

If N is small, all N projection functions can be prepared in advance. But N is large in many applications of ZDDs; and projection functions are rarely needed when "family algebra" is used to build the structures as in exercises 203–207. So it's generally best to wait until a projection function is actually required, before creating it.

Incidentally, the partial-tautology functions t_j can be used to speed up the synthesis operations of exercises 198–199: If $v = f_o \leq g_o$ and $f = t_v$, we have $\text{AND}(f, g) = g$, $\text{OR}(f, g) = f$, and (if $v \leq h_o$) also $\text{MUX}(f, g, h) = h$, $\text{MUX}(g, h, f) = \text{OR}(g, h)$.

202. In the transmogrification step T4, change '$q_0 \leftarrow q_1 \leftarrow q$' to '$q_0 \leftarrow q, q_1 \leftarrow \emptyset$' and '$r_0 \leftarrow r_1 \leftarrow r$' to '$r_0 \leftarrow r, r_1 \leftarrow \emptyset$'. Also use ZUNIQUE instead of UNIQUE; within T4, this subroutine increases REF(p) by 1 if step U1 finds $q = \emptyset$.

A subtler change is needed to keep the partial-tautology functions of answer 201 up to date, because of their special meaning. Correct behavior is to keep t_u unchanged and set $t_v \leftarrow \text{LO}(t_u)$.

203. (a) $f \sqcup g = \{\{1, 2\}, \{1, 3\}, \{1, 2, 3\}, \{3\}\} = (e_1 \sqcup ((e_2 \sqcup (e_3 \cup \epsilon)) \cup e_3)) \sqcup e_3$; the other is $(e_1 \sqcup e_2) \cup \epsilon$, because $f \sqcap g = (e_1 \sqcup (e_2 \cup \epsilon)) \cup e_3 \cup \epsilon$ and $f \boxplus e_1 = e_1 \cup e_2 \cup e_3$.

(b) $(f \sqcup g)(z) = \exists x \exists y (f(x) \wedge g(y) \wedge (z \equiv x \vee y))$; $(f \sqcap g)(z) = \exists x \exists y (f(x) \wedge g(y) \wedge (z \equiv x \wedge y))$; $(f \boxplus g)(z) = \exists x \exists y (f(x) \wedge g(y) \wedge (z \equiv x \oplus y))$. Another formula is $(f \boxplus g)(z) = \bigvee \{f(z \oplus y) \mid g(y) = 1\} = \bigvee \{g(z \oplus x) \mid f(x) = 1\}$.

(c) Both (i) and (ii) are true; also $f \boxplus (g \cup h) = (f \boxplus g) \cup (f \boxplus h)$. Formula (iii) fails in general, although we do have $f \sqcup (g \sqcap h) \subseteq (f \sqcup g) \sqcap (f \sqcup h)$. Formula (iv) makes little sense; the right-hand side is $(f \sqcup f) \cup (f \sqcup h) \cup (g \sqcup f) \cup (g \sqcup h)$, by (i). Formula (v) is true because all three parts are $\emptyset$. And (vi) is true if and only if $f \neq \emptyset$.

(d) Only (ii) is always true. For (i), the condition should be $f \sqcap g \subseteq \epsilon$, since $f \sqcap g = \emptyset$ implies $f \perp g$. For (iii), notice that $|f \sqcup g| = |f \sqcap g| = |f \boxplus g| = 1$ whenever $|f| = |g| = 1$. Finally, in statement (iv), we do have $f \perp g \implies f \sqcup g = f \boxplus g$; but the converse fails when, say, $f = g = e_1 \cup \epsilon$.

(e) $f = \emptyset$ in (i) and $f = \epsilon$ in (ii); also $\epsilon \boxplus g = g$ for all g. There's no solution to (iii), because f would have to be $\{\{1, 2, 3, \ldots\}\}$ and we are considering only finite sets. But in the finite universe of answer 201 we have $f = \{\{1, \ldots, N\}\}$. (This family U has the property that $(f \boxplus U) \sqcup (g \boxplus U) = (f \sqcap g) \boxplus U$.) The general solution to (iv) is $f = e_1 \sqcup e_2 \sqcup f'$, where f' is an arbitrary family; similarly, the general solution to (v) is $f = (e_1 \sqcup f') \cup (e_2 \sqcup f'') \cup (e_1 \sqcup e_2 \sqcup (f' \cup f'' \cup f'''))$, where f', f'', and f''' are arbitrary. In (vi), $f = ((((e_1 \sqcup e_2) \cup \epsilon) \sqcup f') \cup ((e_1 \cup e_2) \sqcup f'')) \sqcup (e_3 \cup \epsilon)$, where $f' \cup f'' \perp e_1 \cup e_2 \cup e_3$; this representation follows from exercise 204(f). In (vii), $|f| = 1$. Finally, (viii) characterizes Horn functions (Theorem 7.1.1H).

204. (a) This relation is obvious from the definition. (Also $(f \cup g)/h \supseteq (f/h) \cup (g/h)$.)

(b) $f/e_2 = \{\{1\}, \emptyset\} = e_1 \cup \epsilon$; $f/e_1 = e_2 \cup e_3$; $f/\epsilon = f$; hence $f/(e_1 \cup \epsilon) = e_2 \cup e_3$.

(c) Division by $\emptyset$ gives trouble, because *all* sets α belong to $f/\emptyset$. (But if we restrict consideration to families of subsets of $\{1, \ldots, N\}$, as in exercises 201 and 207, we have $f/\emptyset = \wp$; also $\wp/\wp = \epsilon$, and $f/\wp = \emptyset$ when $f \neq \wp$.) Clearly $f/\epsilon = f$. And $f/f = \epsilon$ when $f \neq \emptyset$. Finally, $(f \bmod g)/g = \emptyset$ when $g \neq \emptyset$, because $\alpha \in (f \bmod g)/g$ and $\beta \in g$ implies that $\alpha \cup \beta \in f$, $\alpha \in f/g$, and $\alpha \cup \beta \notin (f/g) \sqcup g$ — a contradiction.

(d) If $\beta \in g$, we have $\beta \cup \alpha \in f$ and $\beta \cap \alpha = \emptyset$ for all $\alpha \in f/g$; this proves the hint. Hence $f/g \subseteq f/(f/(f/g))$. Also $f/h \subseteq f/g$ when $h \supseteq g$, by (a); let $h = f/(f/g)$.

(e) Let $f/\!/g$ be the family in the new definition. Then $f/g \subseteq f/\!/g$, because $g \sqcup (f/g) \subseteq f$ and $g \perp (f/g)$. Conversely, if $\alpha \in f/\!/g$ and $\beta \in g$, we have $\alpha \in h$ for some h with $g \sqcup h \subseteq f$ and $g \perp h$; consequently $\alpha \cup \beta \in f$ and $\alpha \cap \beta = \emptyset$.

(f) If f has such a representation, we must have $g = f/e_j$ and $h = f \bmod e_j$. Conversely, those families satisfy $e_j \perp g \sqcup h$. (This law is the fundamental recursive principle underlying ZDDs — just as the unique representation $f = (x_j? g: h)$, with g and h independent of x_j, underlies BDDs.)

(g) Both true. (To prove them, represent f and g as in part (f).)

[R. K. Brayton and C. McMullen introduced the quotient and remainder operations in *Proc. Int. Symp. Circuits and Systems* (IEEE, 1982), 49–54, but in a slightly different context: They dealt with families of incomparable sets of subcubes.]

205. In all cases we construct a recursion based on exercise 204(f). For example, if $f_o = g_o = v$, we have $f \sqcup g = (\bar{v}? \, f_l \sqcup g_l: (f_l \sqcup g_h) \cup (f_h \sqcup g_l) \cup (f_h \sqcup g_h))$; $f \sqcap g = (\bar{v}? \, (f_l \sqcap g_l) \cup (f_l \sqcap g_h) \cup (f_h \sqcap g_l): f_h \sqcap g_h)$; $f \boxplus g = (\bar{v}? \, (f_l \boxplus g_l) \cup (f_h \boxplus g_h): (f_h \boxplus g_l) \cup (f_l \boxplus g_h))$.

(a) If $f_o < g_o$ or ($f_o = g_o$ and $f > g$), swap $f \leftrightarrow g$. If $f = \emptyset$, return f; if $f = \epsilon$, return g. If $f \sqcup g = r$ is in the memo cache, return r. If $f_o > g_o$, set $r_l \leftarrow \text{JOIN}(f, g_l)$ and $r_h \leftarrow \text{JOIN}(f, g_h)$; otherwise set $r_l \leftarrow \text{JOIN}(f_l, g_l)$, $r_{lh} \leftarrow \text{JOIN}(f_l, g_h)$, $r_{hl} \leftarrow \text{JOIN}(f_h, g_l)$, $r_{hh} \leftarrow \text{JOIN}(f_h, g_h)$, $r_h \leftarrow \text{OROR}(r_{lh}, r_{hl}, r_{hh})$, and dereference r_{lh}, r_{hl}, r_{hh}. Finish with $r \leftarrow \text{ZUNIQUE}(g_o, r_l, r_h)$; cache it and return it as in exercise 198.

(We could also compute r_h via the formula $\text{OR}(r_{lh}, \text{JOIN}(f_h, \text{OR}(g_l, g_h)))$, or via $\text{OR}(r_{hl}, \text{JOIN}(\text{OR}(f_l, f_h), g_h))$. Sometimes one way is much better than the other two.)

The DISJOIN operation, which produces the family of *disjoint* unions $\{\alpha \cup \beta \mid \alpha \in f, \beta \in g, \alpha \cap \beta = \emptyset\}$, is similar but with r_{hh} omitted.

(b) If $f_o < g_o$ or ($f_o = g_o$ and $f > g$), swap $f \leftrightarrow g$. If $f \leq \epsilon$, return f. (We consider $\emptyset < \epsilon$ and $\epsilon <$ all others.) Otherwise, if MEET(f, g) hasn't been cached, there are two cases. If $f_o > g_o$, set $r_h \leftarrow$ OR(g_l, g_h), $r \leftarrow$ MEET(f, r_h), and dereference r_h; otherwise proceed analogously to (a) but with $l \leftrightarrow h$. Cache and return r as usual.

(c) This operation is similar to (a), but $r_l \leftarrow$ OR(r_{ll}, r_{hh}) and $r_h \leftarrow$ OR(r_{lh}, r_{hl}).

(d) First we implement the important simple cases f/e_v and $f \bmod e_v$:

$$\text{EZDIV}(f, v) = \begin{cases} \text{If } f_o = v, \text{ return } f_h; \text{ if } f_o > v, \text{ return } \emptyset. \text{ Otherwise look for} \\ f/e_v = r \text{ in the cache; if it isn't present, compute it via} \\ r \leftarrow \text{ZUNIQUE}(f_o, \text{EZDIV}(f_l, v), \text{EZDIV}(f_h, v)). \end{cases}$$

$$\text{EZMOD}(f, v) = \begin{cases} \text{If } f_o = v, \text{ return } f_l; \text{ if } f_o > v, \text{ return } f. \text{ Otherwise look for} \\ f \bmod e_v = r \text{ in the cache; if it isn't present, compute it via} \\ r \leftarrow \text{ZUNIQUE}(f_o, \text{EZMOD}(f_l, v), \text{EZMOD}(f_h, v)). \end{cases}$$

Now DIV$(f, g) =$ "If $g = \emptyset$, see below; if $g = \epsilon$, return f. Otherwise, if $f \leq \epsilon$, return $\emptyset$; if $f = g$, return ϵ. If $g_l = \emptyset$ and $g_h = \epsilon$, return EZDIV(f, g_o). Otherwise, if $f/g = r$ is in the memo cache, return r. Otherwise set $r_l \leftarrow$ EZDIV(f, g_o), $r \leftarrow$ DIV(r_l, g_h), and dereference r_l. If $r \neq \emptyset$ and $g_l \neq \emptyset$, set $r_h \leftarrow$ EZMOD(f, g_o) and $r_l \leftarrow$ DIV(r_h, g_l), dereference r_h, set $r_h \leftarrow r$ and $r \leftarrow$ AND(r_l, r_h), dereference r_l and r_h. Insert '$f/g = r$' in the memo cache and return r." Division by $\emptyset$ returns $\wp$ if there is a fixed universe $\{1, \ldots, N\}$ as in exercise 201. Otherwise it's an error (because the universal family $\wp$ doesn't exist).

(e) If $g = \emptyset$, return f. If $g = \epsilon$, return $\emptyset$. If $(g_l, g_h) = (\emptyset, \epsilon)$, return EZMOD$(f, g_o)$. If $f \bmod g = r$ is cached, return it. Otherwise set $r \leftarrow$ DIV(f, g) and $r_h \leftarrow$ JOIN(r, g), dereference r, set $r \leftarrow$ BUTNOT(f, r_h), and dereference r_h. Cache and return r.

[S. Minato gave EZDIV(f, v), EZREM(f, v), and DELTA(f, e_v) in his original paper on ZDDs. His algorithms for JOIN(f, g) and DIV(f, g) appeared in the sequel, *ACM/IEEE Design Automation Conf.* **31** (1994), 420–424.]

206. The upper bound $O(Z(f)^3 Z(g)^3)$ is not difficult to prove for cases (a) and (b), as well as $O(Z(f)^2 Z(g)^2)$ for case (c). But are there examples that take such a long time? And can the running time for (d) be exponential? All five routines seem to be reasonably fast in practice.

207. If $f = e_{i_1} \cup \cdots \cup e_{i_l}$ and $k \geq 0$, let SYM(f, v, k) be the Boolean function that is true if and only if exactly k of the variables $\{x_{i_1}, \ldots, x_{i_l}\} \cap \{x_v, x_{v+1}, \ldots\}$ are 1 and $x_1 = \cdots = x_{v-1} = 0$. We compute $(e_{i_1} \cup \cdots \cup e_{i_l}) \S k$ by calling SYM$(f, 1, k)$.

SYM$(f, v, k) =$ "While $f_o < v$, set $f \leftarrow f_l$. If $f_o = N + 1$ and $k > 0$, return $\emptyset$. If $f_o = N + 1$ and $k = 0$, return the partial-tautology function t_v (see answer 201). If $f \S v \S k = r$ is in the cache, return r. Otherwise set $r \leftarrow$ SYM$(f, f_o + 1, k)$. If $k > 0$, set $q \leftarrow$ SYM$(f_l, f_o + 1, k - 1)$ and $r \leftarrow$ ZUNIQUE(f_o, r, q). While $f_o > v$, set $f_o \leftarrow f_o - 1$, increase REF(r) by 1, and set $r \leftarrow$ ZUNIQUE(f_o, r, r). Put '$f \S v \S k = r$' in the cache, and return r." The running time is $O((k + 1)N)$. Notice that $\emptyset \S 0 = \wp$.

208. Just omit the factors $2^{v_s - 1 - 1}$, $2^{v_l - v_k - 1}$, and $2^{v_h - v_k - 1}$ from steps C1 and C2. (And we get the generating function by setting $c_k \leftarrow c_l + z c_h$ in step C2; see exercise 25.) *The number of solutions equals the number of paths in the ZDD from the root to* $\boxed{\top}$.

209. Initially compute $\delta_n \leftarrow \bot$ and $\delta_j \leftarrow (\bar{x}_{j+1} \circ x_{j+1}) \bullet \delta_{j+1}$ for $n > j \geq 1$. Then, where answer 31 says '$\alpha \leftarrow (\bar{x}_j \circ x_j) \bullet \alpha$', change it to '$\alpha \leftarrow (\bar{x}_j \bullet \alpha) \circ (x_j \bullet \delta_j)$'. Also make the analogous changes with β and γ in place of α.

210. In fact, when $x = x_1 \ldots x_n$ we can replace νx in the definition of g by any linear function $c(x) = c_1 x_1 + \cdots + c_n x_n$, thus characterizing all of the optimal solutions to the general Boolean programming problem treated by Algorithm B.

For each branch node x of the ZDD, with fields $\mathtt{V}(x)$, $\mathtt{LO}(x)$, $\mathtt{HI}(x)$, we can compute its optimum value $\mathtt{M}(x)$ and new links $\mathtt{L}(x)$, $\mathtt{H}(x)$ as follows: Let $m_l = \mathtt{M}(\mathtt{LO}(x))$ and $m_h = c_{\mathtt{V}(x)} + \mathtt{M}(\mathtt{HI}(x))$, where $\mathtt{M}(\boxed{\perp}) = -\infty$ and $\mathtt{M}(\boxed{\top}) = 0$. Then $\mathtt{L}(x) \leftarrow \mathtt{LO}(x)$ if $m_l \geq m_h$, otherwise $\mathtt{L}(x) \leftarrow \boxed{\perp}$; $\mathtt{H}(x) \leftarrow \mathtt{HI}(x)$ if $m_l \leq m_h$, otherwise $\mathtt{H}(x) \leftarrow \boxed{\perp}$. The ZDD for g is obtained by reducing the $\mathtt{L}$ and $\mathtt{H}$ links accessible from the root. Notice that $Z(g) \leq Z(f)$, and the entire computation takes $O(Z(f))$ steps. (This nice property of ZDDs was pointed out by O. Coudert; see answer 237.)

211. Yes, unless the matrix has all-zero rows. Without such rows, in fact, the profile and z-profile of f satisfy $b_k \geq q_k - 1 \geq z_k$ for $0 \leq k < n$, because the only level-k subfunction independent of x_{k+1} is the constant 0.

212. The best alternative in the author's experiments was to make ZDDs for each term $T_j = S_1(X_j)$ in (129), using the algorithm of exercise 207, and then to AND them together. For example, in problem (128) we have $X_1 = \{x_1, x_2\}$, $X_2 = \{x_1, x_3, x_4\}$, $\ldots$, $X_{64} = \{x_{105}, x_{112}\}$; to make the term $S_1(X_2) = S_1(x_1, x_3, x_4)$, whose ZDD has 115 nodes, just form the 5-node ZDD for $e_1 \cup (e_3 \cup e_4)$ and compute $T_2 \leftarrow (e_1 \cup e_3 \cup e_4) \S 1$.

But in what order should the ANDs be done, after we've got the individual terms $T_1, \ldots, T_n$ of (129)? Consider problem (128). *Method 1:* $T_1 \leftarrow T_1 \wedge T_2$, $T_1 \leftarrow T_1 \wedge T_3$, $\ldots$, $T_1 \leftarrow T_1 \wedge T_{64}$. This "top-down" method fills in the upper levels first, and takes about 6.2 megamems. *Method 2:* $T_{64} \leftarrow T_{64} \wedge T_{63}$, $T_{64} \leftarrow T_{64} \wedge T_{62}$, $\ldots$, $T_{64} \leftarrow T_{64} \wedge T_1$. By filling in the lower levels first ("bottom-up"), the time goes down to about 1.75 megamems. *Method 3:* $T_2 \leftarrow T_2 \wedge T_1$, $T_4 \leftarrow T_4 \wedge T_3$, $\ldots$, $T_{64} \leftarrow T_{64} \wedge T_{63}$; $T_4 \leftarrow T_4 \wedge T_2$, $T_8 \leftarrow T_8 \wedge T_6$, $\ldots$, $T_{64} \leftarrow T_{64} \wedge T_{62}$; $T_8 \leftarrow T_8 \wedge T_4$, $T_{16} \leftarrow T_{16} \wedge T_{12}$, $\ldots$, $T_{64} \leftarrow T_{64} \wedge T_{60}$; $\ldots$; $T_{64} \leftarrow T_{64} \wedge T_{32}$. This "balanced" approach also takes about 1.75 megamems. *Method 4:* $T_{33} \leftarrow T_{33} \wedge T_1$, $T_{34} \leftarrow T_{34} \wedge T_2$, $\ldots$, $T_{64} \leftarrow T_{64} \wedge T_{32}$; $T_{49} \leftarrow T_{49} \wedge T_{33}$, $T_{50} \leftarrow T_{50} \wedge T_{34}$, $\ldots$, $T_{64} \leftarrow T_{64} \wedge T_{48}$; $T_{57} \leftarrow T_{57} \wedge T_{49}$, $T_{58} \leftarrow T_{58} \wedge T_{50}$, $\ldots$, $T_{64} \leftarrow T_{64} \wedge T_{56}$; $\ldots$; $T_{64} \leftarrow T_{64} \wedge T_{63}$. This is a much better way to balance the work, needing only about 850 kilomems. *Method 5:* An analogous balancing strategy that uses the ternary ANDAND operation turns out to be still better, costing just 675 kilomems. (In all five cases, add 190 kilomems for the time to form the 64 initial terms T_j.)

Incidentally, we can reduce the ZDD size from 2300 to 1995 by insisting that $x_1 = 0$ and $x_2 = 1$ in (128) and (129), because the "transpose" of every covering is another covering. This idea does not, however, reduce the running time substantially.

The rows of (128) appear in decreasing lexicographic order, and that may not be ideal. But dynamic variable ordering is unhelpful when so many variables are present. (Sifting reduces the size from 2300 to 1887, but takes a *long* time.)

Further study, with a variety of exact cover problems, would clearly be desirable.

213. It is a bipartite graph with 30 vertices in one part and 32 in the other. (Think of a chessboard as a *checkerboard*: Every domino joins a white square to a black square, and we've removed two black squares.) A row sum of $(1, \ldots, 1, 1, *, *)$ has 1s in at least 31 "white" positions, so its last two coordinates must be either $(2, 1)$ or $(3, 2)$.

214. Add further constraints to the covering condition (128), namely $\bigwedge_{j=1}^{14} S_{\geq 1}(Y_j)$, where Y_j is the set of x_i that cross the jth potential fault line. (For example, $Y_1 = \{x_2, x_4, x_6, x_8, x_{10}, x_{12}, x_{14}, x_{15}\}$ is the set of ways to place a domino vertically in the top two rows of the board; each $|Y_j| = 8$.) The resulting ZDD has 9812 nodes, and characterizes 25,506 solutions. Incidentally, the BDD size is 26,622. [Faultfree domino tilings of $m \times n$ boards exist if and only if mn is even, $m \geq 5$, $n \geq 5$, and $(m, n) \neq (6, 6)$; see R. L. Graham, *The Mathematical Gardner* (Wadsworth International, 1981), 120–126. The solution in (127) is the only 8×8 example that is symmetric under both horizontal and vertical reflection; see Fig. 29(b) for symmetry under $90°$ rotation.]

215. This time we add the constraints $\bigwedge_{j=1}^{49} S_{\geq 1}(Z_j)$, where Z_j is the set of four place-ments x_i that surround an internal corner point. (For example, $Z_1 = \{x_1, x_2, x_4, x_{16}\}$.) These constraints reduce the ZDD size to 66. There are just two solutions, one the transpose of the other, and they can readily be found by hand. [See Y. Kotani, *Puzzlers' Tribute* (A K Peters, 2002), 413–420. The set of all tatami tilings has been characterized by Dean Hickerson; the corresponding generating functions have been obtained by Frank Ruskey and Jennifer Woodcock, *Electronic J. Combinatorics* **16**, 1 (2009), #R126, 1–20.]

216. (a) Assign three variables (a_i, b_i, c_i) to each row of (128), corresponding to the domino's color if row i is chosen. Every branch node of the ZDD for f in (129) now becomes three branch nodes. We can take advantage of symmetry under transposition by replacing f by $f \wedge x_2$; this reduces the ZDD size from 2300 to 1995, which grows to 5981 when each branch node is triplicated.

Now we AND in the adjacency constraints, for all 682 cases $\{i, i'\}$ where rows i and i' are adjacent domino positions. Such constraints have the form $\neg((a_i \wedge a_{i'}) \vee (b_i \wedge b_{i'}) \vee (c_i \wedge c_{i'}))$, and we apply them bottom-up as in Method 2 of answer 212. This computation inflates the ZDD until it reaches more than 800 thousand nodes; but eventually it settles down and ends up with size 584,205.

The desired answer turns out to be 13,343,246,232 (which, of course, is a multiple of $3! = 6$, because each permutation of the three colors yields a different solution).

(b) This question is distinct from part (a), because many coverings (including Fig. 29(b)) can be 3-colored in several ways; we want to count them only once.

Suppose $f(a_1, b_1, c_1, \ldots, a_m, b_m, c_m) = f(x_1, \ldots, x_{3m})$ is a function with $a_i = x_{3i-2}$, $b_i = x_{3i-1}$, and $c_i = x_{3i}$, such that $f(x_1, \ldots, x_{3m}) = 1$ implies $a_i + b_i + c_i \leq 1$ for $1 \leq i \leq m$. Let's define the *uncoloring* $\$f$ of f to be

$$\$f(x_1, \ldots, x_m) = \exists y_1 \cdots \exists y_{3m} \left(f(y_1, \ldots, y_{3m}) \right.$$
$$\left. \wedge (x_1 = y_1 + y_2 + y_3) \wedge \cdots \wedge (x_m = y_{3m-2} + y_{3m-1} + y_{3m}) \right).$$

A straightforward recursive subroutine will compute the ZDD for $\$f$ from the ZDD for f. This process transforms the 584,205 nodes obtained in part (a) into a ZDD of size 33,731, from which we deduce the answer: 3,272,232.

(The running time is 1.2 gigamems for part (a), plus 1.3 gigamems to uncolor; the total memory requirement is about 44 megabytes. A similar computation based on BDDs instead of ZDDs cost $13.6 + 1.5$ gigamems and occupied 185 megabytes.)

217. The separation condition adds 4198 further constraints of the form $\neg(x_i \wedge x_{i'})$, where rows i and i' specify adjacent placements of congruent pieces. Applying these constraints while also evaluating the conjunction $\bigwedge_{j=1}^{468} S_1(X_j)$ turned out to be a bad idea, in the author's experiments; even worse was an attempt to construct a separate ZDD for the new constraints alone. Much better was to build the 512,227-node ZDD as before, then to incorporate the new constraints one by one, first constraining the variables at the lowest levels. The resulting ZDD of size 31,300,699 was finally com-pleted after 286 gigamems of work, proving that exactly 7,099,053,234,102 separated solutions exist.

We might also ask for *strongly* separated solutions, where congruent pieces are not allowed to touch even at their corners; this requirement adds 1948 more constraints. There are 554,626,216 strongly separated coverings, findable after 245 gigamems with a ZDD of size 4,785,236. (But standard backtracking finds them faster and uses negligible memory.)

218. This is an exact cover problem. For example, the incidence matrix when $n = 3$ is

$$
\begin{array}{ll}
001001010 & (--2--2) \\
010001001 & (-3---3) \\
010010010 & (-2--2-) \\
010100100 & (-1-1--) \\
100010001 & (3---3-) \\
100100010 & (2--2--) \\
101000100 & (1-1---) \\
\end{array}
$$

and in general there are $3n$ columns and $\binom{2n-1}{2} - \binom{n}{2}$ rows. Consider the case $n = 12$: The ZDD on 187 variables has 192,636 nodes. It can be found with a cost of 300 megamems, using Method 4 of answer 212 (binary balancing); Method 5 turns out to be 25% slower than Method 4 in this case. The BDD is much larger (2,198,195 nodes) and it costs more than 900 megamems.

Thus the ZDD is clearly preferable to the BDD for this problem, and it identifies the $L_{12} = 108,144$ solutions with reasonable efficiency. (However, the "dancing links" technique of Section 7.2.2.1 is about four times faster, and it needs far less memory.)

219. (a) 1267; (b) 2174; (c) 2958; (d) 3721; (e) 4502. (To form the ZDD for WORDS(n) we do $n - 1$ ORs of the 7-node ZDDs for $w_1 \sqcup h_2 \sqcup i_3 \sqcup c_4 \sqcup h_5$, $t_1 \sqcup h_2 \sqcup e_3 \sqcup r_4 \sqcup e_5$, etc.)

220. (a) There is one a_2 node for the descendants of each initial letter that can be followed by a in the second position (aargh, babel, ..., zappy); 23 letters qualify, all except q, u, and x. And there's one b_2 node for each initial letter that can be followed by b (abbey, ebony, oboes). However, the actual rule isn't so simple; for example, there are three z_2 nodes, not four, because of sharing between czars and tzars.

(b) There's no v_5 because no five-letter word ends with v. (The SGB collection doesn't include arxiv or webtv.) The three nodes for w_5 arise because one stands for cases where the letters $< w_5$ must be followed by w (aglo and many others); another node stands for cases where either w or y must follow (stra, or resa, or when we've seen allo but not allot); and there's also a w_5 node for the case when unse is not followed by e or t, because it must then be followed by either w or x. Similarly, the two nodes for x_5 represent the cases where x is forced, or where the last letter must be either x or y (following rela). There's only one y_5 node, because no four letters can be followed by both y and z. Of course there's just one z_5 node, and two sinks.

221. We compute, for every possible zead ζ, the probability that ζ will occur, and sum over all ζ. For definiteness, consider a zead that corresponds to branching on r_3, and suppose it represents a subfamily of 10 three-letter suffixes. There are exactly $\binom{6084}{10} - \binom{5408}{10} \approx 1.3 \times 10^{31}$ such zeads, and by the principle of inclusion and exclusion they each arise with probability $\sum_{k \geq 1} \binom{676}{k} (-1)^{k+1} \binom{11881376 - 6084k}{5757 - 10k} / \binom{11881376}{5757} \approx 2.5 \times 10^{-32}$. [*Hint:* $|\{r, s, t, u, v, w, x, y, z\}| = 9$, $676 = 26^2$, and $6084 = 9 \times 26^2$.] Thus such zeads contribute about 0.33 to the total. The r_3-zeads for subfamilies of sizes 1, 2, 3, 4, 5, ..., contribute approximately 11.5, 32.3, 45.1, 41.9, 29.3, ..., by a similar analysis;

so we expect about 188.8 branches on r_3 altogether, on average. The grand total

$$\sum_{l=1}^{5}\sum_{j=1}^{26}\sum_{s=1}^{5757}\left(\binom{26^{5-l}(27-j)}{s} - \binom{26^{5-l}(26-j)}{s}\right)$$

$$\times \sum_{k=1}^{\infty}\binom{26^{l-1}}{k}(-1)^{k+1}\binom{26^5 - 26^{5-l}(27-j)k}{5757-sk}\bigg/\binom{26^5}{5757},$$

plus 2 for the sinks, comes to ≈ 7151.986. The average z-profile is $\approx (1.00, \ldots, 1.00;$ $25.99, \ldots, 25.99; 188.86, \ldots, 171.43; 86.31, \ldots, 27.32; 3.53, \ldots, 1.00; 2.00)$.

222. (a) It's the set of all subsets of the words of F. (There are 50,569 such subwords, out of $27^5 = 14{,}348{,}907$ possibilities. They are described by a ZDD of size 18,784, constructed from F and $\wp$ via answer 205(b) at a cost of about 15 megamems.)

(b) This formula gives the same result as $F \sqcap \wp$, because every member of F contains exactly one element of each X_j. But the computation turns out to be much slower — about 370 megamems — in spite of the fact that $Z(X) = 132$ is almost as small as $Z(\wp) = 131$. (Notice that $|\wp| = 2^{130}$ while $|X| = 26^5 \approx 2^{23.5}$.)

(c) $(F/P) \sqcup P$, where $P = t_1 \sqcup u_3 \sqcup h_5$ is the pattern. (The words are touch, tough, truth. This computation costs about 3000 mems with the algorithms of answer 205.) Other contenders for simple formulas are $F \cap Q$, where Q describes the admissible words. If we set $Q = t_1 \sqcup X_2 \sqcup u_3 \sqcup X_4 \sqcup h_5$, we have $Z(Q) = 57$ and the cost once again is $\approx 3000\mu$. With $Q = (t_1 \cup u_3 \cup h_5)\,\S\,3$, on the other hand, we have $Z(Q) = 132$ and the cost rises to about 9000 mems. (Here $|Q|$ is 26^2 in the first case, but 2^{127} in the second — *reversing* any intuition gained from (a) and (b)! Go figure.)

(d) $F \cap ((V_1 \cup \cdots \cup V_5)\,\S\,k)$. The number of such words is $(24, 1974, 3307, 443, 9, 0)$ for $k = (0, \ldots, 5)$, respectively, from ZDDs of sizes $(70, 1888, 3048, 686, 34, 1)$. ("See exercise 7–34 for the words F mod y_1 mod y_2 mod $\cdots$ mod y_5," said the author wryly.)

(e) The desired patterns satisfy $P = (F \sqcap \wp) \cap Q$, where $Q = ((X_1 \cup \cdots \cup X_5)\,\S\,3)$. We have $Z(Q) = 386$, $Z(P) = 14221$, and $|P| = 19907$.

(f) The formula for this case is trickier. First, $P_2 = F \sqcap F$ gives F together with all patterns satisfied by two distinct words; we have $Z(P_2) = 11289$, $|P_2| = 21234$, and $|P_2 \cap Q| = 7753$. But $P_2 \cap Q$ is *not* the answer; for example, it omits the pattern *atc*, which occurs eight times but only in the context *atch*. The correct answer is given by $P_2' \cap Q$, where $P_2' = (P_2 \backslash F) \sqcap \wp$. Then $Z(P_2') = 8947$, $Z(P_2' \cap Q) = 7525$, $|P_2' \cap Q| = 10472$.

(g) $G_1 \cup \cdots \cup G_5$, where $G_j = (F/(b_j \cup o_j)) \sqcup b_j$. The answers are bared, bases, basis, baths, bobby, bring, busts, herbs, limbs, tribs.

(h) Patterns that admit all vowels in second place: b*lls, b*nds, m*tes, p*cks.

(i) The first gives all words whose middle three letters are vowels. The second gives all patterns with first and last letter specified, for which there's at least one match with three vowels inserted. There are 30 solutions to the first, but only 27 to the second (because, e.g., louis and luaus yield the same pattern). Incidentally, the complementary family $\wp \backslash F$ has $2^{130} - 5757$ members, and 46316 nodes in its ZDD.

223. (a) $d(\alpha, \mu) + d(\beta, \mu) + d(\gamma, \mu) = 5$, since $d(\alpha, \mu) = [\alpha_1 \neq \mu_1] + \cdots + [\alpha_5 \neq \mu_5]$.

(b) Given families f, g, h, the family $\{\mu \mid \mu = \langle \alpha\beta\gamma \rangle$ for some $\alpha \in f$, $\beta \in g$, $\gamma \in h$ with $\alpha \neq \mu$, $\beta \neq \mu$, $\gamma \neq \mu$, and $\alpha \cap \beta \cap \gamma = \emptyset\}$ can be defined recursively to allow ZDD computation, if we consider eight variants in which subsets of the inequality constraints are relaxed. In the author's experimental system, the ZDDs for medians of WORDS(n) for $n = (100, 1000, 5757)$ have respectively $(595, 14389, 71261)$ nodes and characterize $(47, 7310, 86153)$ five-letter solutions. Among the 86153 medians when $n = 5757$ are chads, stent, blogs, ditzy, phish, bling, and tetch; in fact, tetch = ⟨fetch teach total⟩ arises already when $n = 1000$. (The running times of about (.01, 2, 700) gigamems, respectively, were not especially impressive; ZDDs are probably not the best tool for this problem. Still, the programming was instructive.)

(c) When $n = 100$, exactly (1, 14, 47) medians of WORDS(n) belong to WORDS(100), WORDS(1000), and WORDS(5757), respectively; the solution with most common words is while = ⟨white whole still⟩. When $n = 1000$, the corresponding numbers are (38, 365, 1276); and when $n = 5757$ they are (78, 655, 4480). The most common English words that *aren't* medians of three other English words are their, first, and right.

224. Every arc $u \longrightarrow v$ of the dag corresponds to a vertex v of the forest. The ZDD has exactly one branch node for every arc. The LO pointer of that node leads to the right sibling of the corresponding vertex v, or to $\boxed{\perp}$ if v has no right sibling. The HI pointer leads to the left child of v, or to $\boxed{\top}$ if v is a leaf. The arcs can be ordered in many ways (e.g., preorder, postorder, level order), without changing this ZDD.

225. As in exercise 55, we try to number the vertices in such a way that the "frontier" between early and late vertices remains fairly small; then we needn't remember too much about what decisions were made on the early vertices. In the present case we also want the source vertex s to be number 1.

In answer 55, the relevant state from previous branches corresponded to an equivalence relation (a set partition); but now we express it by a table $mate[i]$ for $j \le i \le l$, where $j = u_k$ is the smaller vertex of the current edge $u_k \relbar v_k$ and where $l = \max\{v_1, \ldots, v_{k-1}\}$. Let $mate[i] = i$ if vertex i is untouched so far; let $mate[i] = 0$ if vertex i has been touched twice already. Otherwise $mate[i] = r$ and $mate[r] = i$, if previous edges form a simple path with endpoints $\{i, r\}$. Initially we set $mate[i] \leftarrow i$ for $1 \le i \le n$, except that $mate[1] \leftarrow t$ and $mate[t] \leftarrow 1$. (If $t > l$, the value of $mate[t]$ need not be stored, because it can be determined from the values of $mate[i]$ for $j \le i \le l$.)

Let $j' = u_{k+1}$ and $l' = \max\{v_1, \ldots, v_k\}$ be the values of j and l after edge k has been considered; and suppose $u_k = j$, $v_k = m$, $mate[j] = \hat{\jmath}$, $mate[m] = \hat{m}$. We cannot choose edge $j \relbar m$ if $\hat{\jmath} = 0$ or $\hat{m} = 0$. Otherwise, if $\hat{\jmath} \ne m$, the new $mate$ table after choosing edge $j \relbar m$ can be computed by doing the assignments $mate[j] \leftarrow 0$, $mate[m] \leftarrow 0$, $mate[\hat{\jmath}] \leftarrow \hat{m}$, $mate[\hat{m}] \leftarrow \hat{\jmath}$ (in that order).

Otherwise we have $\hat{\jmath} = m$ and $\hat{m} = j$; we must contemplate the endgame. Let i be the smallest integer such that $i > j$, $i \ne m$, and either $i > l'$ or $mate[i] \ne 0$ and $mate[i] \ne i$. The new state after choosing edge $j \relbar m$ is $\emptyset$ if $i \le l'$, otherwise it is ϵ.

Whether or not the edge is chosen, the new state will be $\emptyset$ if $mate[i] \ne 0$ and $mate[i] \ne i$ for some i in the range $j \le i < j'$.

For example, here are the first steps for paths from 1 to 9 in a 3×3 grid (see (132)):

k	j	l	m	$mate[1] \ldots mate[9]$	$\hat{\jmath}$	$\hat{m}$	$mate'[1] \ldots mate'[9]$
1	1	1	2	9 2 3 4 5 6 7 8 1	9	2	0 9 3 4 5 6 7 8 2
2	1	2	3	9 2 3 4 5 6 7 8 1	9	3	0 2 9 4 5 6 7 8 3
2	1	2	3	0 9 3 4 5 6 7 8 2	0	3	—
3	2	3	4	0 2 9 4 5 6 7 8 3	2	4	0 4 9 2 5 6 7 8 3
3	2	3	4	0 9 3 4 5 6 7 8 2	9	4	0 0 3 9 5 6 7 8 4

where $mate'$ describes the next state if edge $j \relbar m$ is chosen. The state transitions $mate_{j..l} \mapsto mate'_{j'..l'}$ are $9 \mapsto (\overline{12}? \; 92 : 09)$; $92 \mapsto (\overline{13}? \; \emptyset : 29)$; $09 \mapsto (\overline{13}? \; 93 : \emptyset)$; $29 \mapsto (\overline{24}? \; 294 : 492)$; $93 \mapsto (\overline{24}? \; 934 : 039)$.

After all reachable states have been found, the ZDD can be obtained by reducing equivalent states, using a procedure like Algorithm R. (In the 3×3 grid problem,

57 branch nodes are reduced to 28, plus two sinks. The 22-branch ZDD illustrated in the text was obtained by subsequently optimizing with exercise 197.)

226. Just omit the initial assignments '$mate[1] \leftarrow t$, $mate[t] \leftarrow 1$.'

227. Change the test '$mate[i] \neq 0$ and $mate[i] \neq i$' to just '$mate[i] \neq 0$' in two places. Also, change '$i \leq l''$' to '$i \leq n$'.

228. Use the previous answer with the following further changes: Add a dummy vertex $d = n+1$, with new edges $v - d$ for all $v \neq s$; accepting this new edge will mean "end at v." Initialize the $mate$ table with $mate[1] \leftarrow d$, $mate[d] \leftarrow 1$. Leave d out of the maximization when calculating l and l'. When beginning to examine a stored $mate$ table, start with $mate[d] \leftarrow 0$ and then, if encountering $mate[i] = d$, set $mate[d] \leftarrow i$.

229. 149,692,648,904 of the latter paths go from VA to MD; graph (133) omits DC. (However, the graphs of (18) have fewer *Hamiltonian* paths than (133), because (133) has 1,782,199 Hamiltonian paths from CA to ME that do not go from VA to MD.)

230. The unique minimum and maximum routes from ME both end at WA:

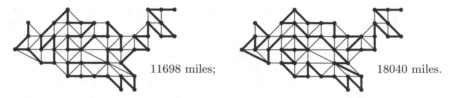

11698 miles;   18040 miles.

Let $g(z) = \sum z^{miles(r)}$, summed over all routes r. The average cost, $g'(1)/g(1) = 1022014257375/68656026 \approx 14886.01$, can be computed rapidly as in answer 29.
  (Similarly, $g''(1) = 15243164303013274$, so the standard deviation is ≈ 666.2.)

231. The algorithm of answer 225 gives a proto-ZDD with 8,062,831 branch nodes; it reduces to a ZDD with 3,024,214 branches. The number of solutions, via answer 208, is 50,819,542,770,311,581,606,906,543.

232. With answer 227 we find $h = 721,613,446,615,109,970,767$ Hamiltonian paths from a corner to its horizontal neighbor, and $d = 480,257,285,722,344,701,834$ of them to its diagonal neighbor; in both cases the relevant ZDD has about 1.3 million nodes. The number of oriented Hamiltonian cycles is $2h + d = 1,923,484,178,952,564,643,368$. (Divide by 2 to get the number of *undirected* Hamiltonian cycles.)

Essentially only two king's tours, shown here, achieve the maximal length $8 + 56\sqrt{2}$. [Nikolai Beluhov has proved that the longest $n \times n$ king's tours, when n is even, have length $n + n(n - 1)\sqrt{2}$. See the Bulgarian journal *Matematika Plyus* **14**, 4 (October–December 2006), 61–64.]

233. A similar procedure can be used but with $mate[i] = r$ and $mate[r] = -i$ when the previous choices define an oriented path from i to r. Process all arcs $u_k \longrightarrow v_k$ and $u_k \longleftarrow v_k$ consecutively when $u_k = j < v_k = m$. Define $\hat{\jmath} = -j$ if $mate[j] = j$, otherwise $\hat{\jmath} = mate[j]$. Choosing $j \longrightarrow m$ is illegal if $\hat{\jmath} \geq 0$ or $\hat{m} \leq 0$. The updating rule for that choice, when legal, is: $mate[j] \leftarrow 0$, $mate[m] \leftarrow 0$, $mate[-\hat{\jmath}] \leftarrow \hat{m}$, $mate[\hat{m}] \leftarrow \hat{\jmath}$.

234. The 437 oriented cycles can be represented by a ZDD of ≈ 800 nodes. The shortest are, of course, AL $\longrightarrow$ LA $\longrightarrow$ AL and MN $\longrightarrow$ NM $\longrightarrow$ MN. There are 37 of length 17 (the maximum), such as (ALARINVTNMIDCOKSC) — i.e., AL $\longrightarrow$ LA $\longrightarrow \cdots \longrightarrow$ SC $\longrightarrow$ CA $\longrightarrow$ AL.

Incidentally, the directed graph in question is the arc digraph D^* of the digraph D on 26 vertices $\{\texttt{A}, \texttt{B}, \ldots, \texttt{Z}\}$ whose 49 arcs are $\texttt{A} \longrightarrow \texttt{L}$, $\texttt{A} \longrightarrow \texttt{R}$, $\ldots$, $\texttt{W} \longrightarrow \texttt{Y}$. Every oriented walk of D^* is an oriented walk of D, and conversely (see exercise 2.3.4.2–21); but the oriented *cycles* of D^* are not necessarily simple in D. In fact, D has only 37 oriented cycles, the longest of which is unique: (`ARINMOKSDC`).

If we extend consideration to the 62 postal codes in exercise 7–54(c), the number of oriented cycles rises to 38336, including the unique 1-cycle (`A`), as well as 192 that have length 23, such as (`APRIALASCTNMNVINCOKSDCA`). About 17000 ZDD nodes suffice to characterize the entire family of oriented cycles in this case.

235. The digraph has 7912 arcs; but we can prune them dramatically by removing arcs from vertices of in-degree zero, or arcs to vertices of out-degree zero. For example, `owner` $\longrightarrow$ `nerdy` goes away, because `nerdy` is a dead end; in fact, all successors of `owner` are likewise eliminated, so `crown` is out too. Eventually we're left with only 112 arcs among 85 words, and the problem can basically be done by hand.

There are just 74 oriented cycles. The unique shortest one, `slant` $\longrightarrow$ `antes` $\longrightarrow$ `tesla` $\longrightarrow$ `slant`, can be abbreviated to '(`slante`)' as in the previous answer. The two longest are $(\alpha\omega)$ and $(\beta\omega)$, where $\alpha = $ `picastepsomaco`, $\beta = $ `pointrotherema`, and $\omega = $ `nicadrearedidoserumoreliciteslabsitaresetuplenactoricedarerunichesto`.

236. (a) Suppose $\alpha \in f$ and $\beta \in g$. If $\alpha \subseteq \beta$, then $\alpha \in f \sqcap g$. If $\alpha \cap \beta \in f$, then $\alpha \cap \beta \notin f \nearrow g$. A similar argument, or the use of part (b), shows that $f \searrow g = f \setminus (f \sqcup g)$.

Notes: The complementary operations "$f \diagdown g = f \setminus (f \searrow g) = \{\alpha \in f \mid \alpha \supseteq \beta$ for some $\beta \in g\}$" for supersets, and "$f \diagup g = f \setminus (f \nearrow g) = \{\alpha \in f \mid \alpha \subseteq \beta$ for some $\beta \in g\}$" for subsets, are also important in applications. They were omitted from this exercise only because five operations are already rather intimidating. The superset operation was introduced by O. Coudert, J. C. Madre, and H. Fraisse [*ACM/IEEE Design Automation Conference* **30** (1993), 625–630]. The identity $f \diagdown g = f \cap (f \sqcup g)$ was noted by H. G. Okuno, S. Minato, and H. Isozaki [*Information Processing Letters* **66** (1998), 195–199], who also listed several of the laws in (d).

(b) Elementary set theory suffices. (The first six identities appear in pairs, each of which is equivalent to its mate. Strictly speaking, f^C involves infinite sets, and U is the AND of infinitely many variables; but the formulas hold in any finite universe. Notice that, when cast in the language of Boolean functions, $f^C(x) = f(\bar{x})$ is the complement of f^D, the Boolean dual; see exercise 7.1.1–2. Is there any use for the dual of $f^\sharp$, namely $\{\alpha \mid \beta \in f$ implies $\alpha \cup \beta \neq U\}^\uparrow$? If so, we might denote it by $f^\flat$.)

(c) All true except (ii), which should have said that $x_1^\uparrow = x_1^{C \downarrow C} = \bar{x}_1^{\downarrow C} = \epsilon^C = U$.

(d) The "identities" to cross out here are (ii), (viii), (ix), (xiv), and (xvi); the others are worth remembering. Regarding (ii)–(vi), notice that $f = f^\uparrow$ if and only if $f = f^\downarrow$, if and only if f is a clutter. Formula (xiv) should be $f \searrow g^\downarrow = f \searrow g$, the dual of (xiii). Formula (xvi) is almost right; it fails only when $f = \emptyset$ or $g = \emptyset$. Formula (ix) is perhaps the most interesting: We actually have $f^{\sharp\sharp} = f$ if and only if f is a clutter.

(e) Assuming that the universe of all vertices is finite, we have (i) $f = \wp \searrow g$ and (ii) $g = (\wp \setminus f)^\downarrow$, where $\wp$ is the universal family of exercises 201 and 222, because g is the family of minimal dependent sets. (Purists should substitute $\wp_V = \bigsqcup_{v \in V} (\epsilon \cup e_v)$ for $\wp$ in these formulas. The same relations hold in any hypergraph for which no edge is contained in another.)

237. MAXMAL$(f) = $ "If $f = \emptyset$ or $f = \epsilon$, return f. If $f^\uparrow = r$ is cached, return r. Otherwise set $r \leftarrow$ MAXMAL(f_l), $r_h \leftarrow$ MAXMAL(f_h), $r_l \leftarrow$ NONSUB(r, r_h), dereference r, and $r \leftarrow$ ZUNIQUE(f_o, r_l, r_h); cache and return r."

MINMAL(f) = "If $f = \emptyset$ or $f = \epsilon$, return f. If $f^{\downarrow} = r$ is cached, return r. Otherwise set $r_l \leftarrow$ MINMAL(f_l), $r \leftarrow$ MINMAL(f_h), $r_h \leftarrow$ NONSUP(r, r_l), dereference r, and $r \leftarrow$ ZUNIQUE(f_o, r_l, r_h); cache and return r."

NONSUB(f, g) = "If $g = \emptyset$, return f. If $f = \emptyset$ or $f = \epsilon$ or $f = g$, return $\emptyset$. If $f \nearrow g = r$ is cached, return r. Otherwise represent f and g as explained in answer 198. If $f_o > g_o$, cache and return AND(NONSUB(f, g_l), NONSUB(f, g_h)). Otherwise set $v \leftarrow f_o$. If $v < g_o$, set $r_l \leftarrow$ NONSUB(f_l, g), $r_h \leftarrow f_h$, and increase REF(f_h) by 1; otherwise set $r_h \leftarrow$ NONSUB(f_l, g_l), $r \leftarrow$ NONSUB(f_l, g_h), $r_l \leftarrow$ AND(r, r_h), dereference r and r_h, and set $r_h \leftarrow$ NONSUB(f_h, g_h). Finally $r \leftarrow$ ZUNIQUE(v, r_l, r_h); cache and return r."

NONSUP(f, g) = "If $g = \emptyset$, return f. If $f = \emptyset$ or $g = \epsilon$ or $f = g$, return $\emptyset$. If $f_o > g_o$, return NONSUP(f, g_l). If $f \searrow g = r$ is cached, return r. Otherwise set $v = f_o$. If $v < g_o$, set $r_l \leftarrow$ NONSUP(f_l, g) and $r_h \leftarrow$ NONSUP(f_h, g); otherwise set $r_l \leftarrow$ NONSUP(f_h, g_h), $r \leftarrow$ NONSUP(f_h, g_l), $r_h \leftarrow$ AND(r, r_l), dereference r and r_l, and set $r_l \leftarrow$ NONSUP(f_l, g_l). Finally $r \leftarrow$ ZUNIQUE(v, r_l, r_h); cache and return r."

MINHIT(f) = "If $f = \emptyset$, return ϵ. If $f = \epsilon$, return $\emptyset$. If $f^{\sharp} = r$ is cached, return r. Otherwise set $r \leftarrow$ OR(f_l, f_h), $r_l \leftarrow$ MINHIT(r), dereference r, $r \leftarrow$ MINHIT(f_l), $r_h \leftarrow$ BUTNOT(r, r_l), dereference r, and $r \leftarrow$ ZUNIQUE(f_o, r_l, r_h); cache and return r."

As in exercise 206, the worst-case running times of these routines are unknown. Although NONSUB and NONSUP can be computed via JOIN or MEET and BUTNOT, by exercise 236(a), this direct implementation tends to be faster. It may be preferable to replace '$f = \epsilon$' by '$\epsilon \in f$' in MINMAL and MINHIT; also '$g = \epsilon$' by '$\epsilon \in g$' in NONSUP.

[Olivier Coudert introduced and implemented the operators $f^{\uparrow}$, $f \nearrow g$, and $f \searrow g$ in *Proc. Europ. Design and Test Conf.* (IEEE, 1997), 224–228. He also gave a recursive implementation of the interesting operator $f \odot g = (f \sqcup g)^{\uparrow}$; however, in the author's experiments, much better results have been obtained without it. For example, if f is the 177-node ZDD for the independent sets of the contiguous USA, the operation $g \leftarrow$ JOIN(f, f) costs about 350 kilomems and $h \leftarrow$ MAXMAL(g) costs about 3.6 megamems; but more than 69 *giga*mems are needed to compute $h \leftarrow$ MAXJOIN(f, f) all at once. Improved caching and garbage-collection strategies may, of course, change the picture.]

238. We can compute the 177-node ZDD for the family f of independent sets, using the ordering (104), in two ways: With Boolean algebra (67), $f = \neg \bigvee_{u - v}(x_u \wedge x_v)$; the cost is about 1.1 megamems with the algorithms of answers 198–201. With family algebra, on the other hand, we have $f = \wp \searrow \bigcup_{u - v}(e_u \sqcup e_v)$ by exercise 236(e); the cost, via answer 237, is less than 175 kilomems.

The subsets that give 2-colorable and 3-colorable subgraphs are $g = f \sqcup f$ and $h = g \sqcup f$, respectively; the maximal ones are $g^{\uparrow}$ and $h^{\uparrow}$. We have $Z(g) = 1009$, $Z(g^{\uparrow}) = 3040$, $Z(h) = 179$, $Z(h^{\uparrow}) = 183$, $|g| = 9{,}028{,}058{,}789{,}780$, $|g^{\uparrow}| = 2{,}949{,}441$, $|h| = 543{,}871{,}144{,}820{,}736$, and $|h^{\uparrow}| = 384$. The successive costs of computing g, $g^{\uparrow}$, h, and $h^{\uparrow}$ are approximately 350 Kμ (kilomems), 3.6 Mμ, 1.1 Mμ, and 230 Kμ. (We could compute $h^{\uparrow}$ by, say, $(g^{\uparrow} \sqcup f)^{\uparrow}$; but that turns out to be a bad idea.)

The maximal induced bipartite and tripartite subgraphs have the respective generating functions $7654z^{25} + \cdots + 9040z^{33} + 689z^{34}$ and $128z^{43} + 84z^{44} + 112z^{45} + 36z^{46} + 24z^{47}$. Here are typical examples of the smallest and largest:

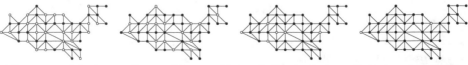

(Compare with the smallest and largest "1-partite" subgraphs in 7–(61) and 7–(62).)

Notice that the families g and h tell us exactly which induced subgraphs can be 2-colored and 3-colored, but they *don't* tell us how to color them.

239. Since $h = ((e_1 \cup \cdots \cup e_{49}) \S 2) \setminus g$ is the set of nonedges of G, the cliques are $f = \wp \setminus h$, and the maximal cliques are $f^\uparrow$. For example, we have $Z(f) = 144$ for the 214 cliques of the USA graph, and $Z(f^\uparrow) = 130$ for the 60 maximal ones. In this case the maximal cliques consist of 57 triangles (which are easily visible in (18)), together with three edges that aren't part of any triangle: AZ — NM, WI — MI, NH — ME.

Let f_k describe the sets coverable by k cliques. Then $f_1 = f$, and $f_{k+1} = f_k \sqcup f$ for $k \geq 1$. (It's not a good idea to compute f_{16} as $f_8 \sqcup f_8$; much faster is to do each join separately, even if the intermediate results are not of interest.)

The maxim*um* elements of f_k in the USA graph have sizes 3, 6, 9, ..., 36, 39, 41, 43, 45, 47, 48, 49 for $1 \leq k \leq 19$; these maxima can readily be determined by hand, in a small graph such as this. But the question of maxim*al* elements is much more subtle, and ZDDs are probably the best tool for investigating them. The ZDDs for $f_1, \ldots, f_{19}$ are quickly found after about 30 megamems of calculation, and they aren't large: $\max Z(f_k) = Z(f_{11}) = 9547$. Another 400 megamems produces the ZDDs for $f_1^\uparrow, \ldots, f_{19}^\uparrow$, which likewise are small: $\max Z(f_k^\uparrow) = Z(f_{11}^\uparrow) = 9458$.

We find, for example, that the generating function for $f_{18}^\uparrow$ is $12z^{47} + 13z^{48}$; eighteen cliques suffice to cover all but one of the 49 vertices, if we leave out CA, DC, FL, IL, LA, MI, MN, MT, SC, TN, UT, WA, or WV. There also are twelve cases where we can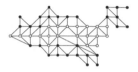
maximally cover 47 vertices; for example, if all but NE and NM are covered by 18 cliques, then neither of those states are covered. An unusual example of maximal clique covering is illustrated here: If the 29 "black" states are covered by 12 cliques, none of the "white" states will also be covered.

240. (a) In fact, the subformula $f(x) = \bigwedge_v (x_v \vee \bigvee_{u-v} x_u)$ of (68) precisely characterizes the dominating sets x. And if any element of a kernel is removed, it isn't dominated by the others. [C. Berge, *Théorie des graphes et ses applications* (1958), 44.]

(b) The Boolean formula of part (a) yields a ZDD with $Z(f) = 888$ after about 1.5 Mμ of computation; then another 1.5 Mμ with the MINMAL algorithm of answer 237 gives the minimal elements, with $Z(f^\downarrow) = 2082$.

A more clever way is to start with $h = \bigcup_v (e_v \sqcup \bigsqcup_{u-v} e_u)$, and then to compute $h^\sharp$, because $h^\sharp = f^\downarrow$. However, cleverness doesn't pay in this case: About 80 Kμ suffice to compute h, but the computation of $h^\sharp$ by the MINHIT algorithm costs about 350 Mμ.

Either way, we deduce that there are exactly 7,798,658 minimal dominating sets. More precisely, the generating function has the form $192z^{11} + 58855z^{12} + \cdots + 4170z^{18} + 40z^{19}$ (which can be compared to $80z^{11} + 7851z^{12} + \cdots + 441z^{18} + 18z^{19}$ for kernels).

(c) Proceeding as in answer 239, we can determine the sets of vertices d_k that are dominated by subsets of size $k = 1, 2, 3, \ldots$, because $d_{k+1} = d_k \sqcup d_1$. Here it's much faster to start with $d_1 = \wp \sqcap h$ instead of $d_1 = h$, even though $Z(\wp \sqcap h) = 313$ while $Z(h) = 213$, because we aren't interested in details about the small-cardinality members of d_k. Using the fact that the generating function for d_7 is $\cdots + 61z^{42} + z^{43}$, one can verify that the illustrated solution is unique. (Total cost ≈ 300 Mμ.)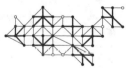

241. Let g be the family of all 728 edges. Then, as in previous exercises, $f = \wp \setminus g$ is the family of independent sets, and the cliques are $c = \wp \setminus (((\bigcup_v e_v) \S 2) \setminus g)$. We have $Z(g) = 699$, $Z(f) = 20244$, $Z(c) = 1882$.

(a) Among $|f| = 118969$ independent sets, there are $|f^\uparrow| = 10188$ kernels, with $Z(f^\uparrow) = 8577$ and generating function $728z^5 + 6912z^6 + 2456z^7 + 92z^8$. The 92 maximum independent sets are the famous solutions to the classic 8 queens problem, which we shall study in Section 7.2.2; example (C1) is the only solution with no three queens in a straight line, as noted by Sam Loyd in the *Brooklyn Daily Eagle* (20 December 1896). The $728 = 91 \times 8$ minimum kernels were first listed by C. F. de Jaenisch, *Traité des applications de l'analyse math. au jeu des échecs* **3** (1863), 255–259, who ascribed them to "M^r de R∗∗∗." The upper left queen in (C0) can be replaced by king, bishop, or pawn, still dominating every open square [H. E. Dudeney, *The Weekly Dispatch* (3 Dec 1899)].

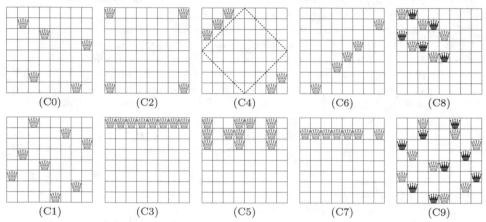

(C0)   (C2)   (C4)   (C6)   (C8)

(C1)   (C3)   (C5)   (C7)   (C9)

(b) Here $Z(c^\uparrow) = 866$; the 310 maximal cliques are described in exercise 7–129.

(c) These subsets are computationally more difficult: The ZDD for all dominating sets d has $Z(d) = 12,663,505$, $|d| = 18,446,595,708,474,987,957$; the minimal ones have $Z(d^\downarrow) = 11,363,849$, $|d^\downarrow| = 28,281,838$, and generating function $4860z^5 + 1075580z^6 + 14338028z^7 + 11978518z^8 + 873200z^9 + 11616z^{10} + 36z^{11}$. One can compute the ZDD for d in 1.5 Gμ by Boolean algebra, and then the ZDD for $d^\downarrow$ in another 680 Gμ; alternatively, the "clever" approach of answer 240 obtains $d^\downarrow$ in 775 Gμ without computing d. The 11-queen arrangement in (C5) is the only such minimal dominating set that is confined to three rows. H. E. Dudeney presented (C4), the only 5-queen solution that avoids the central diamond, in *Tit-Bits* **33** (1 January 1898), 257. All 4860 minimum solutions were first enumerated by K. von Szily [*Deutsche Schachzeitung* **57** (1902), 199]; his complete list appears in W. Ahrens, *Math. Unterhaltungen und Spiele* **1** (1910), 313–318.

(d) Here it suffices to compute $(c \cap d)^\downarrow$ instead of $c \cap (d^\downarrow)$, if we don't already know $d^\downarrow$, because $c \sqcap \wp = c$. We have $Z(c \sqcap d^\downarrow) = 342$ and $|c \sqcap d^\downarrow| = 92$, with generating function $20z^5 + 56z^6 + 16z^7$. See (C6) and (C7). Once again, Dudeney was first to discover all 20 of the 5-queen solutions [*The Weekly Dispatch* (30 July 1899)].

(e) We have $Z(f \sqcup f) = 91,780,989$ at a cost of 24 Gμ; then $Z((f \sqcup f)^\uparrow) = 11,808,436$ after another 290 Gμ. There are 27,567,390 maximal induced bipartite subgraphs, with generating function $109894z^{10} + 2561492z^{11} + 13833474z^{12} + 9162232z^{13} + 1799264z^{14} + 99408z^{15} + 1626z^{16}$. Any 8 independent queens can be combined with their mirror reflection to obtain a 16-queen solution, as (C1) yields (C9). But the disjoint union of minimum kernels is not always a maximal induced bipartite subgraph; for example, consider the union of (C0) with its reflection:

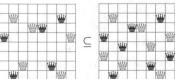

Parts (a), (b), (d), and possibly (c) can be solved just as well without the use of ZDDs; see, for example, exercise 7.1.3–132 for (a) and (b). But the ZDD approach seems best for (e). And the computation of all the maximal *tripartite* subgraphs of Q_8 may be beyond the reach of *any* feasible algorithm.

[In larger queen graphs Q_n, the smallest kernels and the minimum dominating sets are each known to have sizes either $\lceil n/2 \rceil$ or $\lceil n/2 \rceil + 1$ for $12 \le n \le 120$. See P. R. J. Östergård and W. D. Weakley, *Electronic J. Combinatorics* **8**, 1 (2001), #R29, 1–19 and corrigenda; D. Finozhenok and W. D. Weakley, *Australasian J. Combinatorics* **37** (2007), 295–300. The largest minimal dominating sets have been investigated by A. P. Burger, E. J. Cockayne, and C. M. Mynhardt, *Discrete Math.* **163** (1997), 47–66.]

242. These are the kernels of an interesting 3-uniform hypergraph with 1544 edges. Its 4,113,975,079 independent subsets f (that is, its subsets with no three collinear points) have $Z(f) = 52,322,105$, computable with about 12 gigamems using family algebra as in answer 236(e). Another 575 Gμ will compute the kernels $f^{\uparrow}$, for which we have $Z(f^{\uparrow}) = 31,438,750$ and $|f^{\uparrow}| = 66,509,584$; the generating function is $228z^8 + 8240z^9 + 728956z^{10} + 9888900z^{11} + 32215908z^{12} + 20739920z^{13} + 2853164z^{14} + 73888z^{15} + 380z^{16}$.

```
○○○○●●○○    ○○●○○○●○    ○○○○○○○○    ○○○○○○○○    ○○○○○○○○○○
○○○○●●○○    ○○●○○○●○    ○○●○○●○○    ○○●●○○●○    ○●○○○●●○○●
●●○○○○○○    ●●○○○○○○    ○○●○○●○○    ○●○○●○○○    ●○●○○○○○○○
●●○○○○○○    ○●○○●○○○    ○○●○○●○○    ○○○●●○○○    ○●○○●○○○○○
○○○○○○●●    ○○○○○○●●    ○○○●●○○○    ○○●○○●○○    ○○○●○○○○○○
○○○○○○●●    ○●○○●○○○    ○○○●●○○○    ○○○○○○○○    ○●○○○●○○○●
○○●●○○○○    ●○○●○○○○    ○○●○○●○○    ○○○○○○○○    ○○○○●○●○○○
○○●●○○○○    ○○○○○●○●    ○○○○○○○○    ○○○○○○○○    ○○○○○○○○○○
```

[The problem of finding an independent set of size 16 was first posed by H. E. Dudeney in *The Weekly Dispatch* (29 Apr 1900 and 13 May 1900), where he gave the leftmost pattern shown above. Later, in the London *Tribune* (7 Nov 1906), Dudeney asked puzzlists to find the second pattern, which has two points in the center. The full set of maximum kernels, including 57 that are distinct under symmetry, was found by M. A. Adena, D. A. Holton, and P. A. Kelly, *Lecture Notes in Math.* **403** (1974), 6–17, who also noted the existence of 8-point kernels. The middle pattern above is the only such kernel with all points in the central 4×4. The other two patterns yield kernels that have respectively $(8, 8, 10, 10, 12, 12, 12)$ points in $n \times n$ grids for $n = (8, 9, \ldots, 14)$; they were found by S. Ainley and described in a letter to Martin Gardner, 27 Oct 1976.]

243. (a) This result is readily verified even for infinite sets. (Notice that, as a Boolean function, $f^{\cap}$ is the least Horn function that is $\supseteq f$, by Theorem 7.1.1H.)

(b) We could form $f^{(2)} = f \sqcap f$, then $f^{(4)} = f^{(2)} \sqcap f^{(2)}$, $\ldots$, until $f^{(2^{k+1})} = f^{(2^k)}$, using exercise 205. But it's faster to devise a recurrence that goes to the limit all at once. If $f = f_0 \cup (e_1 \sqcup f_1)$ we have $f^{\cap} = f' \cup (e_1 \sqcup f_1^{\cap})$, where $f' = f_0^{\cap} \cup (f_0^{\cap} \sqcap f_1^{\cap})$. [An alternative formula is $f' = (f_0 \cup f_1)^{\cap} \setminus (f_1^{\cap} \nearrow f_0)$; see S. Minato and H. Arimura, *Transactions of the Japanese Society for Artificial Intelligence* **22** (2007), 165–172.]

(c) With the first suggestion of (b), the computation of $F^{(2)}$, $F^{(4)}$, and $F^{(8)} = F^{(4)}$ costs about $(610 + 450 + 460)$ megamems. In this example it turns out that $F^{(4)} = F^{(3)}$, and that just three patterns belong to $F^{(3)} \setminus F^{(2)}$, namely c***f, *k*t*, and ***sp. (The words that match ***sp are clasp, crisp, and grasp.) A direct computation of $F^{\cap}$ using the recurrence based on $f_0^{\cap'} \sqcap f_1^{\cap}$ costs only 320 Mμ; and in this example the alternative recurrence based on $(f_0 \cup f_1)^{\cap}$ costs 470 Mμ. The generating function is $1 + 124z + 2782z^2 + 7753z^3 + 4820z^4 + 5757z^5$.

244. To convert Fig. 22 from a BDD to a ZDD, we add appropriate nodes with LO = HI where links jump levels, obtaining the z-profile $(1, 2, 2, 4, 4, 5, 5, 5, 5, 5, 2, 2, 2)$.

To convert it from a ZDD to a BDD, we add nodes in the same places, but with HI = $\boxed{\perp}$, obtaining the profile $(1, 2, 2, 4, 4, 5, 5, 5, 5, 5, 2, 2, 2)$. (In fact, the connectedness function and the spanning tree function are Z-transforms of each other; see exercise 192.)

245. See exercise 7.1.1–26. (It should be interesting to compare the performance of the Fredman–Khachiyan algorithm in exercise 7.1.1–27 with the ZDD-based algorithm MINHIT in answer 237, on a variety of different functions.)

246. If a nonconstant function doesn't depend on x_1, we can replace x_1 in the formulas by x_v, as in (50). Let P and Q be the prime implicants of functions p and q. (For example, if $P = e_2 \cup (e_3 \sqcup e_4)$ then $p = x_2 \vee (x_3 \wedge x_4)$.) By (137) and induction on $|f|$, the function f described in the theorem is sweet if and only if p and q are sweet and $\mathrm{PI}(f_0) \cap \mathrm{PI}(f_1) = \emptyset$. The latter equality holds if and only if $p \subseteq q$.

247. We can characterize them with BDDs as in (49) and exercise 75; but this time

$$\sigma_n(x_1, \ldots, x_{2^n}) = \sigma_{n-1}(x_1, \ldots, x_{2^n-1}) \wedge$$
$$\left((\bar{x}_2 \wedge \cdots \wedge \bar{x}_{2^n}) \vee \left(\sigma_{n-1}(x_2, \ldots, x_{2^n}) \wedge \bigwedge_{j=0}^{2^{k-1}} \left(\bar{x}_{2j+1} \vee \bigvee_{i \subset j} x_{2i+2} \right) \right) \right).$$

The answers $|\sigma_n|$ for $0 \leq n \leq 7$ are $(2, 3, 6, 18, 106, 2102, 456774, 7108935325)$. (This computation builds a BDD of size $B(\sigma_7) = 7{,}701{,}683$, using about 900 megamems and 725 megabytes altogether.)

248. False; for example, $(x_1 \vee x_2) \wedge (x_2 \vee x_3)$ isn't sweet. (But the conjunction *is* sweet if f and g depend on disjoint sets of variables, or if x_1 is the only variable on which they both depend.)

249. (Solution by Shaddin Dughmi and Ian Post.)   A nonzero monotone Boolean function is ultrasweet if and only if its prime implicants are the bases of a matroid; see Section 7.6.1. By extending answer 247 we can determine the number of ultrasweet functions $f(x_1, \ldots, x_n)$ for $0 \leq n \leq 7$: $(2, 3, 6, 17, 69, 407, 3808, 75165)$.

250. Exhaustive analysis shows that ave $B(f) = 76726/7581 \approx 10.1$; ave $Z(\mathrm{PI}(f)) = 71513/7581 \approx 9.4$; $\Pr(Z(\mathrm{PI}(f)) > B(f)) = 151/7581 \approx .02$; and max $Z(\mathrm{PI}(f))/B(f) = 8/7$ occurs uniquely when f is $(x_1 \wedge x_4) \vee (x_1 \wedge x_5) \vee (x_2 \wedge x_3 \wedge x_4) \vee (x_2 \wedge x_5)$.

251. More strongly, could it be that $\limsup Z(\mathrm{PI}(f))/B(f) = 1$?

252. The ZDD should describe all words on $\{e_1, e_1', \ldots, e_n, e_n'\}$ that have exactly j unprimed letters and $k - j$ primed letters, and no occurrences of both e_i and e_i' in the same word, for some set of pairs (j, k). For example, if $n = 9$ and $f(x) = v_{vx}$, where $v = 110111011$, the pairs are $(0, 8)$, $(3, 6)$, and $(8, 8)$. Regardless of the set of pairs, the z-profile elements will all be $O(n^2)$, hence $Z(\mathrm{PI}(f)) = O(n^3)$. (We order the variables so that x_i and x_i' are adjacent.) And $f(x) = S_{\lfloor n/3 \rfloor, \ldots, \lfloor 2n/3 \rfloor}(x)$ has $Z(\mathrm{PI}(f)) = \Omega(n^3)$.

253. Let $\mathrm{I}(f)$ be the family of all *implicants* of f; then $\mathrm{PI}(f) = \mathrm{I}(f)^{\downarrow}$. The formula $\mathrm{I}(f) = \mathrm{I}(f_0 \wedge f_1) \cup (e_1' \sqcup \mathrm{I}(f_0)) \cup (e_1 \sqcup \mathrm{I}(f_1))$ is easy to verify. Thus $\mathrm{I}(f)^{\downarrow} = A \cup (e_1' \sqcup (\mathrm{PI}(f_0) \searrow A)) \cup (e_1 \sqcup (\mathrm{PI}(f_1) \searrow A))$, as in exercise 237. But $\mathrm{PI}(f_0) \searrow A = \mathrm{PI}(f_0) \setminus A$, since $A \subseteq \mathrm{I}(f)$.

   [This recurrence for prime implicants is due to O. Coudert and J. C. Madre, *ACM/IEEE Design Automation Conf.* **29** (1992), 36–39. Partial results had previously been formulated by B. Reusch, *IEEE Trans.* **C-24** (1975), 924–930.]

254. By (53) and (137), we need to show that $\text{PI}(g_h) \setminus \text{PI}(f_h \cup g_l) = (\text{PI}(g_h) \setminus \text{PI}(g_l)) \setminus (\text{PI}(f_h) \setminus \text{PI}(f_l))$. But both of these are equal to $\text{PI}(g_h) \setminus (\text{PI}(f_h) \cup \text{PI}(g_l))$, because $f_l \subseteq f_h \subseteq g_h$ and $f_l \subseteq g_l \subseteq g_h$.

[This recurrence produces a ZDD directly from the BDDs for f and g, and it yields $\text{PI}(g)$ when $f = 0$. Thus it is easier to implement than (137), which requires also the set-difference operator on ZDDs. And it sometimes runs much faster in practice.]

255. (a) A typical item α like $e_2 \sqcup e_5 \sqcup e_6$ has a very simple ZDD. We can readily devise a BUMP routine that sets $g \leftarrow g \oplus \alpha$ and returns $[\alpha \in g]$, given ZDDs g and α.

To insert α into the multifamily f, start with $k \leftarrow c \leftarrow 0$; then while $c = 0$, set $c \leftarrow \text{BUMP}(f_k)$ and $k \leftarrow k + 1$. To delete α, assuming that it is present, start with $k \leftarrow 0$ and $c \leftarrow 1$; while $c = 1$, set $c \leftarrow \text{BUMP}(f_k)$ and $k \leftarrow k + 1$.

(b) Suppose f_k and g_k are $\emptyset$ for $k \geq m$. Set $k \leftarrow 0$ and $t \leftarrow \emptyset$ (the ZDD $\boxed{\perp}$). While $k < m$, set $h_k \leftarrow f_k \oplus g_k \oplus t$ and $t \leftarrow \langle f_k g_k t \rangle$. Finally set $h_m \leftarrow t$.

[This representation and its insertion algorithm are due to S. Minato and H. Arimura, *Proc. Workshop, Web Information Retrieval and Integration* (IEEE, 2005), 4–11.]

256. (a) Reflect the binary representation from left to right, and append 0s until the number of bits is 2^n for some n. The result is the truth table of the corresponding Boolean function $f(x_1, \ldots, x_n)$, with x_k corresponding to $2^{2^{n-k}} \in U$. When $x = 41$, for example, 10010100 is the truth table of $(x_1 \wedge \bar{x}_2 \wedge x_3) \vee (\bar{x}_1 \wedge x_2 \wedge x_3) \vee (\bar{x}_1 \wedge \bar{x}_2 \wedge \bar{x}_3)$.

(b) If $x < 2^{2^n}$, we have $Z(x) \leq U_n = O(2^n/n)$, by (79) and exercise 192.

(c) There's a simple recursive routine $\text{ADD}(x, y, c)$, which takes a "carry bit" c and pointers to the ZDDs for x and y and returns a pointer to the ZDD for $x + y + c$. This routine is invoked at most $4Z(x)Z(y)$ times.

(d) We cannot claim that $Z(x \dotdiv y) = O(Z(x)Z(y))$, because $Z(x \dotdiv y) = n + 1$ and $Z(x) = 3$ and $Z(y) = 1$ when $x = 2^{2^n}$ and $y = 1$. But by computing $x \dotdiv y = (x + 1 + ((2^{2^n} - 1) \oplus y)) - 2^{2^n}$ when $y \leq x < 2^{2^n}$, we can show that $Z(x \dotdiv y) = O(Z(x)Z(y) \log \log x)$. (See the ZDD nodes t_j in answer 201.) So the answer is "yes."

(e) No. For example, if $x = (2^{2^{2^k+k}} - 1)/(2^{2^k} - 1)$, we have $Z(x) = 2^k + 1$ but $Z(x^2) = 3 \cdot (2^{2^k} - 1) = U_{2^k+k+1} - 2$, where U_{2^k+k+1} is the largest possible ZDD size for numbers with $\lg \lg x^2 < 2^k + k + 1$ (see part (b)).

[This exercise was inspired by Jean Vuillemin, who began to experiment with such sparse integers about 1993. Unfortunately the numbers that are of greatest importance in combinatorial calculations, such as Fibonacci numbers, factorials, binomial coefficients, etc., rarely turn out to be sparse in practice.]

257. See *Proc. Europ. Design and Test Conf.* (IEEE, 1995), 449–454. With signed coefficients one can use $\{-2, 4, -8, \ldots\}$ instead of $\{2, 4, 8, \ldots\}$, as in negabinary arithmetic.

[In the special case where the degree is at most 1 in each variable and where addition is done modulo 2, the polynomials of this exercise are equivalent to the multilinear representations of Boolean functions (see 7.1.1–(19)), and the ZDDs are equivalent to "binary moment diagrams" (BMDs). See R. E. Bryant and Y.-A. Chen, *ACM/IEEE Design Automation Conf.* **32** (1995), 535–541.]

258. If n is odd, the BDD must depend on all its variables, and there must be at least $\lceil \lg n \rceil$ of them. Thus $B(f) \geq \lceil \lg n \rceil + 2$ when $n > 1$, and the skinny functions of exercise 170(c) achieve this bound. If n is even, add an unused variable to the solution for $n/2$.

The ZDD question is easily seen to be equivalent to finding a shortest addition chain, as in Section 4.6.3. Thus the smallest $Z(f)$ for $|f| = n$ is $l(n) + 1$, including $\boxed{\top}$.

259. The theory of nested parentheses (see, for example, exercise 2.2.1–3) tells us that $N_n(x) = 1$ if and only if $\bar{x}_1 + \cdots + \bar{x}_k \geq x_1 + \cdots + x_k$ for $0 \leq k \leq 2n$, with equality when $k = 2n$. Equivalently, $k - n \leq x_1 + \cdots + x_k \leq k/2$ for $0 \leq k \leq 2n$. So the BDD for N_n is rather like the BDD for $S_n(x)$, but simpler; in fact, the profile elements are $b_k = \lfloor k/2 \rfloor + 1$ for $0 \leq k \leq n$ and $b_k = n + 1 - \lceil k/2 \rceil$ for $n \leq k < 2n$. Hence $B(N_n) = b_0 + \cdots + b_{2n-1} + 2 = \binom{n+2}{2} + 1$. The z-profile has $z_k = b_k - [k \text{ even}]$ for $0 \leq k < 2n$, because of HI branches to $\boxed{\perp}$ on even levels; hence $Z(N_n) = B(N_n) - n$.

[An interesting BDD base for the $n+1$ Boolean functions that correspond to C_{nn}, $C_{(n-1)(n+1)}, \ldots, C_{0(2n)}$ in 7.2.1.6–(21) can be constructed by analogy with exercise 49.]

260. (a, b) Arrange the variables $x_{n,0}$, $x_{n,1}$, $\ldots$, $x_{n,n-1}$, $x_{n-1,0}$, $\ldots$, $x_{1,0}$, from top to bottom. Then the HI branch from the ZDD root of R_n is the ZDD root of R_{n-1}. (This ordering actually turns out to minimize $Z(R_n)$ for $n \leq 6$, probably also for all n.) The z-profile is $1, \ldots, 1; n - 2, \ldots, 2, 1, 1; n - 3, \ldots, 2, 1, 1; \ldots$; hence $Z(R_n) = \binom{n}{3} + 2n + 1 \approx \frac{1}{6}n^3$ and $Z(R_{100}) = 161{,}901$. The ordinary profile is $1, 2, 2, 3, 4, \ldots, n-1; n-1, 2n-4, 2n-5, \ldots, n-1; n-2, 2n-6, \ldots, n-2; \ldots$; altogether $B(R_n) = 3\binom{n}{3} + \binom{n+1}{2} + 3$ for $n \geq 2$, and $B(R_{100}) = 490{,}153$.

[See I. Semba and S. Yajima, *Trans. Inf. Proc. Soc. Japan* **35** (1994), 1666–1667. Incidentally, the method of exercise 7.2.1.5–26 leads to a ZDD for set partitions that has only $\binom{n}{2}$ variables and $\binom{n}{2} + 1$ nodes. But the connection between that representation and the partitions themselves is less direct, thus harder to restrict in a natural way.]

(c) Now there are 573 variables instead of 5050 when $n = 100$; the number of variables in general is $nl - 2^l + 1$, where $l = \lceil \lg n \rceil$, by Eq. 5.3.1–(3). We examine the bits of a_n, a_{n-1}, $\ldots$, with the most significant bit first. Then $B(R'_{100}) = 31{,}861$, and one can show that $B(R'_n) = \binom{n}{2}l - \frac{1}{6}4^l - \frac{1}{2}2^l - \nu(n-1) + l + \frac{8}{3}$ for $n > 2$. The ZDD size is more complicated, and appears to be roughly 60% larger; we have $Z(R'_{100}) = 50{,}154$.

261. Given a Boolean function $f(x_1, \ldots, x_n)$, the set of all binary strings $x_1 \ldots x_n$ such that $f(x_1, \ldots, x_n) = 1$ is a finite language, so it is regular. The minimum-state deterministic automaton $\mathcal{A}$ for this language is the QDD for f. (In general, when L is regular, the state of $\mathcal{A}$ after reading $x_1 \ldots x_k$ accepts the language $\{\alpha \mid x_1 \ldots x_k \alpha \in L\}$.)

[The quoted theorem was discovered in a more general context by D. A. Huffman, *Journal of the Franklin Institute* **257** (1954), 161–190, and independently by E. F. Moore, *Annals of Mathematics Studies* **34** (1956), 129–153.]

An interesting example of the connection between this theory and the theory of BDDs can be found in early work by Yuri Breitbart that is summarized in *Doklady Akad. Nauk SSSR* **180** (1968), 1053–1055. Lemma 7 of Breitbart's paper states, in essence, that $B_{\min}(\psi) = \Omega(2^{n/4})$, where ψ is the function of $2n$ variables $x = (x_1, \ldots, x_n)$ and $y = (y_1, \ldots, y_n)$ defined by $\psi(x, y) = x_{\nu y} \oplus y_{\nu x}$, with the understanding that $x_0 = y_0 = 0$. (Notice that ψ is sort of a "two-sided" hidden weighted bit function.)

262. (a) If a denotes the function or subfunction f, we can for example let $C(a) = a \oplus 1$ denote $\bar{f}$, assuming that each node occupies an even number of bytes. Then $C(C(a)) = a$, and a link to a denotes a nonnormal function if and only if a is odd; $a \ \& -2$ always points to a node, which always represents a normal function.

The LO pointer of every node is even, because a normal function remains normal when we replace any variable by 0. But the HI pointer of any node might be complemented, and an external root pointer to any function of a normalized BDD base might also be complemented. Notice that the $\boxed{\top}$ sink is now impossible.

(b) Uniqueness is obvious because of the relation to truth tables: A bead is either normal (i.e., begins with 0) or the complement of a normal bead.

(c) In diagrams, each complement link is conveniently indicated by a dot:

1   3   3   2   3   2   3   3   3   3   2   3   2   3   3   1

(d) There are $2^{2^m-1} - 2^{2^{m-1}-1}$ normal beads of order m. The worst case, $B^0(f) \le B^0(f_n) = 1 + \sum_{k=0}^{n-1} \min(2^k, 2^{2^{n-k}-1} - 2^{2^{n-k-1}-1}) = (U_{n+1} - 1)/2$, occurs with the functions of answer 110. For the average normalized profile, change $2^{2^{n-k}} - 1$ in (80) to $2^{2^{n-k}} - 2$, and divide the whole formula by 2; again the average case is very close to the worst case. For example, instead of (81) we have

$$(1.0, 2.0, 4.0, 8.0, 16.0, 32.0, 64.0, 127.3, 103.9, 6.0, 1.0, 1.0).$$

(e) We save $\boxed{\top}$, one $\textcircled{6}$, two $\textcircled{5}$s, and three $\textcircled{4}$s, leaving 45 normalized nodes.

(f) It's probably best to have subroutines AND, OR, BUTNOT for the case where f and g are known to be normal, together with a subroutine GAND for the general case. The routine $\mathrm{GAND}(f, g)$ returns $\mathrm{AND}(f, g)$ if f and g are even, $\mathrm{BUTNOT}(f, C(g))$ if f is even but g is odd, $\mathrm{BUTNOT}(g, C(f))$ if g is even but f is odd, $C(\mathrm{OR}(C(f), C(g)))$ if f and g are odd. The routine $\mathrm{AND}(f, g)$ is like (55) except that $r_h \leftarrow \mathrm{GAND}(f_h, y_h)$; only the cases $f = 0$, $g = 0$, and $f = g$ need be tested as "obvious" values.

Notes: Complement links were proposed by S. Akers in 1978, and independently by J. P. Billon in 1987. Although such links are used by all the major BDD packages, they are hard to recommend because the computer programs become much more complicated. The memory saving is usually negligible, and never better than a factor of 2; furthermore, the author's experiments show little gain in running time.

With ZDDs instead of BDDs, a "normal family" of functions is a family that doesn't contain the empty set. Shin-ichi Minato has suggested using $C(f)$ to denote the family $f \oplus \epsilon$, instead of $\bar{f}$, in ZDD work.

263. (a) If $Hx = 0$ and $x \ne 0$, we can't have $\nu x = 1$ or 2 because the columns of H are nonzero and distinct. [R. W. Hamming, *Bell System Tech. J.* **29** (1950), 147–160.]

(b) Let r_k be the rank of the first k columns of H, and s_k the rank of the last k columns. Then $b_k = 2^{r_k + s_{n-k} - r_n}$ for $0 \le k < n$, because this is the number of elements in the intersection of the vector spaces spanned by the first k and last $n - k$ columns. In the Hamming code, $r_k = 1 + \lambda k$ and $s_k = \min(m, 2 + \lambda(k-1))$ for $k > 1$; so we find $B(f) = (n^2 + 5)/2$. [See G. D. Forney, Jr., *IEEE Trans.* **IT-34** (1988), 1184–1187.]

(c) Let $q_k = 1 - p_k$. Maximizing $\prod_{k=1}^{n} p_k^{[x_k = y_k]} q_k^{[x_k \ne y_k]}$ is the same as maximizing $\sum_{k=1}^{n} w_k x_k$, where $w_k = (2y_k - 1)\log(p_k/q_k)$, so we can use Algorithm B.

Notes: Coding theorists, beginning with unpublished work of Forney in 1967, have developed the idea of a code's so-called *trellis*. In the binary case, the trellis is the same as the QDD for f, but with all nodes for the constant subfunction 0 eliminated. (Useful codes have distance > 1; then the trellis is also the BDD for f, but with $\boxed{\bot}$ eliminated.) Forney's original motivation was to show that the decoding algorithm of A. Viterbi [*IEEE Trans.* **IT-13** (1967), 260–269] is optimum for convolutional codes. A few years later, L. R. Bahl, J. Cocke, F. Jelinek, and J. Raviv [*IEEE Trans.* **IT-20** (1974), 284–287] extended trellis structure to linear block codes and presented further optimization algorithms. See also G. B. Horn and F. R. Kschischang [*IEEE Trans.* **IT-42** (1996), 2042–2048]; J. Lafferty and A. Vardy [*IEEE Trans.* **C-48** (1999), 971–986].

264. There may, for example, be a good way to combine the "bottom-up" methods of Algorithm B with "top-down" methods that optimize over predecessors of a node.

265. Compute counts c_j bottom-up as in Algorithm C, using n-bit arithmetic. Then proceed top-down, by starting with $k \leftarrow s - 1$, $j \leftarrow 1$, $m \leftarrow m - 1$, and repeating the following steps (during which we will have $0 \leq m < 2^{v_k - j} c_k$): If $v_k > j$, set $x_j \leftarrow \lfloor m/2^{v_k - j - 1} c_k \rfloor$, $m \leftarrow m \bmod 2^{v_k - j - 1} c_k$, $j \leftarrow j + 1$; otherwise if $k = 1$, terminate; otherwise set $l \leftarrow l_k$, $h \leftarrow h_k$, and if $m < 2^{v_l - v_k - 1} c_l$ set $x_j \leftarrow 0$, $k \leftarrow l$, $j \leftarrow j + 1$; otherwise set $x_j \leftarrow 1$, $m \leftarrow m - 2^{v_l - v_k - 1} c_l$, $k \leftarrow h$, $j \leftarrow j + 1$.

266. In fact, the ZDD is obtained directly from the standard "left child, right sibling" binary tree for F (see 7.2.1.6–(4)) if we use the left child link for HI and the right sibling link for LO; null links are changed to point to $\boxed{\top}$, except that the LO link of the root of the rightmost tree (the final node in postorder) should point to $\boxed{\bot}$.

267. The ZDD size of $d(F)$ can be computed as follows, using an auxiliary function $\zeta(T)$ defined recursively on trees: If $|T| = 1$ (that is, if T has only one node), $\zeta(T) = 1$. Otherwise T consists of a root together with $k \geq 1$ subtrees, $T_1, \ldots, T_k$, and we define $\zeta(T) = 1 + \zeta(T_1) + \cdots + \zeta(T_k) + |T| - |T_k|$. Then if F consists of $k \geq 1$ trees $T_1, \ldots, T_k$, we have $Z(d(F)) = 1 + \zeta(T_1) + \cdots + \zeta(T_k) + [|T_k| = 1]$.

The minimum size, n, clearly occurs when F consists of n one-node trees. The maximum size, $\lfloor n^2/4 \rfloor + 2n + 1$, occurs for $n = 2m - 1$ in a tree for which node k has two children, $k + 1$ and $k + m$ for $1 \leq k < m$; the case $n = 2m$ is similar.

For the average size, consider the generating function $Z(w, z) = \sum w^{\zeta(T)} z^{|T|}$, summed over all trees T. The definition of ζ yields the functional equation $Z(w, z) = wz + w^2 z Z(w, z)/(1 - Z(w, wz))$. Differentiation with respect to w and to z, then setting $w = 1$, tells us that $Z(1, z) = (1 - s)/2$, $Z_w(1, z) = z/s + z/s^2$, and $Z_z(1, z) = 1/s$, where $s = \sqrt{1 - 4z}$. The generating function $\sum_F w^{Z(d(F))} z^{|F|}$, summed over all nonempty forests F, is $(wZ(w, z) + w^3 z - w^2 z)/(1 - Z(w, z))$. Differentiating with respect to w and setting $w \leftarrow 1$, we obtain $z/(1 - 4z) + 2z/\sqrt{1 - 4z}$; hence the average of $Z(d(F))$ is

$$(4^{n-1} + 2nC_{n-1})/C_n = \tfrac{1}{4}\sqrt{\pi} n^{3/2} + \tfrac{n}{2} + O(n^{1/2}),$$

where C_n is the Catalan number 7.2.1.6–(15).

SECTION 7.2.1.1

1. Let $m_j = u_j - l_j + 1$, and visit $(a_1 + l_1, \ldots, a_n + l_n)$ instead of visiting $(a_1, \ldots, a_n)$ in Algorithm M. Or, change '$a_j \leftarrow 0$' to '$a_j \leftarrow l_j$' and '$a_j = m_j - 1$' to '$a_j = u_j$' in that algorithm, and set $l_0 \leftarrow 0$, $u_0 \leftarrow 1$ in step M1.

2. $(0, 0, 1, 2, 3, 0, 2, 7, 0, 9)$.

3. Step M4 is performed $m_1 m_2 \ldots m_k$ times when $j = k$; therefore the total is $\sum_{k=0}^{n} \prod_{j=1}^{k} m_j = m_1 \ldots m_n(1 + 1/m_n + 1/m_n m_{n-1} + \cdots + 1/m_n \ldots m_1)$. If all m_j are 2 or more, this is less than $2m_1 \ldots m_n$. [Thus, we should keep in mind that fancy Gray-code methods, which change only one digit per visit, actually reduce the total number of digit changes by at most a factor of 2.]

4. N1. [Initialize.] Set $a_j \leftarrow m_j - 1$ for $0 \leq j \leq n$, where $m_0 = 2$.

    N2. [Visit.] Visit the n-tuple $(a_1, \ldots, a_n)$.

    N3. [Prepare to subtract one.] Set $j \leftarrow n$.

    N4. [Borrow if needed.] If $a_j = 0$, set $a_j \leftarrow m_j - 1$, $j \leftarrow j - 1$, and repeat this step.

    N5. [Decrease, unless done.] If $j = 0$, terminate the algorithm. Otherwise set $a_j \leftarrow a_j - 1$ and go back to step N2. ∎

5. Bit reflection is easy on a machine like MMIX, but on other computers we can proceed as follows:

Z1. [Initialize.] Set $j \leftarrow k \leftarrow 0$.

Z2. [Swap.] Interchange $A[j+1] \leftrightarrow A[k+2^{n-1}]$. Also, if $j < k$, interchange $A[j] \leftrightarrow A[k]$ and $A[j+2^{n-1}+1] \leftrightarrow A[k+2^{n-1}+1]$.

Z3. [Advance k.] Set $k \leftarrow k+2$, and terminate if $k \geq 2^{n-1}$.

Z4. [Advance j.] Set $h \leftarrow 2^{n-2}$. If $j \geq h$, repeatedly set $j \leftarrow j - h$ and $h \leftarrow h/2$ until $j < h$. Then set $j \leftarrow j+h$. (Now $j = (b_0 \ldots b_{n-1})_2$ if $k = (b_{n-1} \ldots b_0)_2$.) Return to Z2. ∎

6. If $g((0b_{n-1} \ldots b_1 b_0)_2) = (0(b_{n-1}) \ldots (b_2 \oplus b_1)(b_1 \oplus b_0))_2$ then $g((1b_{n-1} \ldots b_1 b_0)_2) = 2^n + g((0\bar{b}_{n-1} \ldots \bar{b}_1 \bar{b}_0)_2) = (1(\bar{b}_{n-1}) \ldots (\bar{b}_2 \oplus \bar{b}_1)(\bar{b}_1 \oplus \bar{b}_0))_2$, where $\bar{b} = b \oplus 1$.

7. To accommodate $2r$ sectors one can use $g(k)$ for $2^n - r \leq k < 2^n + r$, where $n = \lceil \lg r \rceil$, because $g(2^n - r) \oplus g(2^n + r - 1) = 2^n$ by (5). [G. C. Tootill, *Proc. IEE* **103**, Part B Supplement (1956), 434.] See also exercise 26.

8. Use Algorithm G with $n \leftarrow n-1$ and include the parity bit a_{-1} at the right. (This yields $g(0)$, $g(2)$, $g(4)$, $g(6)$, ...)

9. Replace the rightmost ring, since $\nu(1011000)$ is odd.

10. $A_n + B_n = g^{[-1]}(2^n - 1) = \lfloor 2^{n+1}/3 \rfloor$ and $A_n = B_n + n$. Hence $A_n = \lfloor 2^n/3 + n/2 \rfloor$ and $B_n = \lfloor 2^n/3 - n/2 \rfloor$.

Historical notes: The early Japanese mathematician Yoriyuki Arima (1714–1783) treated this problem in his *Shūki Sanpō* **2** (1769), 20–21, observing that the n-ring puzzle reduces to an $(n-1)$-ring puzzle after a suitable number of steps. Let $C_n = A_n - A_{n-1} = B_n - B_{n-1} + 1$ be the number of rings removed during this reduction. Arima noticed that $C_n = 2C_{n-1} - [n \text{ even}]$; thus he could compute $A_n = C_1 + C_2 + \cdots + C_n$ for $n = 9$ without actually knowing the formula $C_n = \lceil 2^{n-1}/3 \rceil$.

A. M. Hinz has discovered that the German physicist G. C. Lichtenberg published similar results in *Göttingische Anzeigen von gemeinnützigen Sachen* **1** (1769), 637–640.

L. Pacioli explained how to solve the ring puzzle in Chapter 107 of *De Viribus Quantitatis* (unpublished, c. 1500). Then G. Cardano mentioned it in Book 15 of his *De Subtilitate Libri XXI* (Nuremberg: 1550), calling it "useless but admirably subtle." With the trick of exercise 11, he explained how to make a 95-move tour of every relevant configuration of seven rings. J. Wallis devoted seven pages to these "complicati annuli" in the Latin edition of his *Algebra* **2** (Oxford: 1693), Chapter 111, presenting detailed methods for the nine-ring case. He included the operation of sliding a ring through the bar as well as putting it on or off, but hinted that shortcuts were available. [See A. Heeffer and A. M. Hinz, *Recreational Math. Magazine* **4**, 8 (December 2017), 5–23.]

11. The solution to $S_n = S_{n-2} + 1 + S_{n-2} + S_{n-1}$ when $S_1 = S_2 = 1$ is $S_n = 2^{n-1} - [n \text{ even}]$. [*Math. Quest. Educational Times* **3** (1865), 66–67.]

12. (a) The theory of $n - 1$ Chinese rings proves that Gray binary code yields the compositions in a convenient order (4, 31, 211, 22, 112, 1111, 121, 13):

C1. [Initialize.] Set $t \leftarrow 1$, $s_1 \leftarrow n$. (We assume that $n > 1$.)

C2. [Visit.] Visit $s_1 \ldots s_t$. Then go to C4 if t is even.

C3. [Odd step.] If $s_t > 1$, set $s_t \leftarrow s_t - 1$, $s_{t+1} \leftarrow 1$, $t \leftarrow t + 1$; otherwise set $t \leftarrow t - 1$ and $s_t \leftarrow s_t + 1$. Return to C2.

C4. [Even step.] If $s_{t-1} > 1$, set $s_{t-1} \leftarrow s_{t-1} - 1$, $s_{t+1} \leftarrow s_t$, $s_t \leftarrow 1$, $t \leftarrow t + 1$; otherwise set $t \leftarrow t - 1$, $s_t \leftarrow s_{t+1}$, $s_{t-1} \leftarrow s_{t-1} + 1$ (but terminate if t has become 1). Return to C2. ∎

(b) Now $q_1, \ldots, q_{t-1}$ represent rings on the bar:

B1. [Initialize.] Set $t \leftarrow 1$, $q_0 \leftarrow n$. (We assume that $n > 1$.)

B2. [Visit.] Set $q_t \leftarrow 0$ and visit $(q_0 - q_1) \ldots (q_{t-1} - q_t)$. Go to B4 if t is even.

B3. [Odd step.] If $q_{t-1} > 1$, set $q_t \leftarrow 1$ and $t \leftarrow t + 1$; otherwise set $t \leftarrow t - 1$. Return to step B2.

B4. [Even step.] If $q_{t-2} > q_{t-1} + 1$, set $q_t \leftarrow q_{t-1}$, $q_{t-1} \leftarrow q_t + 1$, $t \leftarrow t + 1$; otherwise set $q_{t-2} \leftarrow q_{t-1}$ and $t \leftarrow t - 1$ (but terminate if t has become 1). Return to B2. ∎

These essentially equivalent algorithms [see J. Misra, *ACM Transactions on Mathematical Software* **1** (1975), 285] are loopless even in their initialization steps.

13. In step C1, also set $C \leftarrow 1$. In step C3, set $C \leftarrow s_t C$ if $s_t > 1$, otherwise $C \leftarrow C/(s_{t-1}+1)$. In step C4, set $C \leftarrow s_{t-1}C$ if $s_{t-1} > 1$, otherwise $C \leftarrow C/(s_{t-2}+1)$. Similar modifications apply to steps B1, B3, B4. Sufficient precision is needed to accommodate the value $C = n!$ for the composition $1 \ldots 1$; we are stretching the definition of looplessness by assuming that arithmetic operations take unit time.

14. V1. [Initialize.] Set $j \leftarrow 0$.

V2. [Visit.] Visit the string $a_1 \ldots a_j$.

V3. [Lengthen.] If $j < n$, set $j \leftarrow j + 1$, $a_j \leftarrow 0$, and return to V2.

V4. [Increase.] If $a_j < m_j - 1$, set $a_j \leftarrow a_j + 1$ and return to V2.

V5. [Shorten.] Set $j \leftarrow j - 1$, and return to V4 if $j > 0$. ∎

15. J1. [Initialize.] Set $j \leftarrow 0$.

J2. [Even visit.] If j is even, visit the string $a_1 \ldots a_j$.

J3. [Lengthen.] If $j < n$, set $j \leftarrow j + 1$, $a_j \leftarrow 0$, and return to J2.

J4. [Odd visit.] If j is odd, visit the string $a_1 \ldots a_j$.

J5. [Increase.] If $a_j < m_j - 1$, set $a_j \leftarrow a_j + 1$ and return to J2.

J6. [Shorten.] Set $j \leftarrow j - 1$, and return to J4 if $j > 0$. ∎

This algorithm is loopless, although it may appear at first glance to contain loops; at most four steps separate consecutive visits. The basic idea is related to exercise 2.3.1–5 and to "prepostorder" traversal (Algorithm 7.2.1.6Q).

16. Suppose $\mathrm{LINK}(j-1) = j + n b_j$ for $1 \leq j \leq n$ and $\mathrm{LINK}(j-1+n) = j + n(1-b_j)$ for $1 < j \leq n$. These links represent $(a_1, \ldots, a_n)$ if and only if $g(a_1 \ldots a_n) = b_1 \ldots b_n$, so we can use a loopless Gray binary generator to achieve the desired result.

17. Put the concatenation of 3-bit codes $(g(j), g(k))$ in row j and column k, for $0 \leq j, k < 8$. [It is not difficult to prove that this is essentially the *only* solution, except for permuting and/or complementing coordinate positions and/or rotating rows, because the coordinate that changes when moving north or south depends only on the row, and a similar statement applies to columns. Karnaugh's isomorphism between the 4-cube and the 4×4 torus can be traced back to *The Design of Switching Circuits* by W. Keister, A. E. Ritchie, and S. H. Washburn (1951), page 174. Incidentally, Keister went on to design an ingenious variant of Chinese rings called SpinOut, and a generalization called The Hexadecimal Puzzle, *U.S. Patents 3637215–3637216* (1972).]

18. Use 2-bit Gray code to represent the digits $u_j = (0, 1, 2, 3)$ respectively as the bit pairs $u'_{2j-1} u'_{2j} = (00, 01, 11, 10)$. [C. Y. Lee introduced his metric in *IRE Trans.* **IT-4** (1958), 77–82. A similar $m/2$-bit encoding works for even values of m; for example, when $m = 8$ we can represent $(0, 1, 2, 3, 4, 5, 6, 7)$ by $(0000, 0001, 0011, 0111, 1111, 1110,$ $1100, 1000)$. But such a scheme leaves out some of the binary patterns when $m > 4$.]

19. (a) A modular Gray quaternary algorithm needs slightly less computation than Algorithm M, but it doesn't matter because 256 is so small. The result is $z_0^8 + z_1^8 + z_2^8 + z_3^8 + 14(z_0^4 z_2^4 + z_1^4 z_3^4) + 56 z_0 z_1 z_2 z_3 (z_0^2 + z_2^2)(z_1^2 + z_3^2)$.

(b) Replacing (z_0, z_1, z_2, z_3) by $(1, z, z^2, z)$ gives $1 + 112 z^6 + 30 z^8 + 112 z^{10} + z^{16}$; thus all of the nonzero Lee weights are ≥ 6. Now use the construction in the previous exercise to convert each $(u_0, u_1, u_2, u_3, u_4, u_5, u_6, u_\infty)$ into a 16-bit number.

20. Recover the quaternary vector $(u_0, u_1, u_2, u_3, u_4, u_5, u_6, u_\infty)$ from u', and use Algorithm 4.6.1D to find the remainder of $u_0 + u_1 x + \cdots + u_6 x^6$ divided by $g(x)$, mod 4; that algorithm can be used in spite of the fact that the coefficients do not belong to a field, because $g(x)$ is monic. Express the remainder as $x^j + 2x^k$ (modulo $g(x)$ and 4), and let $d = (k - j) \bmod 7$, $s = (u_0 + \cdots + u_6 + u_\infty) \bmod 4$.

Case 1: $s = 1$. If $k = \infty$, the error was x^j (in other words, the correct vector has $u_j \leftarrow (u_j - 1) \bmod 4$); otherwise there were three or more errors.

Case 2: $s = 3$. If $j = k$ the error was $-x^j$; otherwise ≥ 3 errors occurred.

Case 3: $s = 0$. If $j = k = \infty$, no errors were made; if $j = \infty$ and $k < \infty$, at least four errors were made. Otherwise the errors were $x^a - x^b$, where $a = (j + (\infty, 6, 5, 2, 3, 1, 4, 0)) \bmod 7$ according as $d = (0, 1, 2, 3, 4, 5, 6, \infty)$, and $b = (j+2d) \bmod 7$.

Case 4: $s = 2$. If $j = \infty$ the errors were $2x^k$. Otherwise the errors were

$$x^j + x^\infty, \text{ if } k = \infty;$$
$$-x^j - x^\infty, \text{ if } d = 0;$$
$$x^a + x^b, \text{ if } d \in \{1, 2, 4\}, \ a = (j - 3d) \bmod 7, \ b = (j - 2d) \bmod 7;$$
$$-x^a - x^b, \text{ if } d \in \{3, 5, 6\}, \ a = (j - 3d) \bmod 7, \ b = (j - d) \bmod 7.$$

Given $u' = (1100100100001111)_2$, we have $u = (2, 0, 3, 1, 0, 0, 2, 2)$ and $2 + 3x^2 + x^3 + 2x^6 \equiv 1 + 3x + 3x^2 \equiv x^5 + 2x^6$; also $s = 2$. Thus the errors are $x^2 + x^3$, and the nearest errorfree codeword is $(2, 0, 2, 0, 0, 0, 2, 2)$. Algorithm 4.6.1D tells us that $2 + 2x^2 + 2x^6 \equiv (2 + 2x + 2x^3) g(x)$ (modulo 4); so the eight information bits correspond to $(v_0, v_1, v_2, v_3) = (2, 2, 0, 2)$. [A more intelligent algorithm would also say, "Aha: The first 16 bits of π."]

For generalizations to other efficient coding schemes based on quaternary vectors, see the classic paper by Hammons, Kumar, Calderbank, Sloane, and Solé, *IEEE Trans.* **IT-40** (1994), 301–319.

21. (a) $C(\epsilon) = 1$, $C(0\alpha) = C(1\alpha) = C(\alpha)$, and $C(*\alpha) = 2C(\alpha) - [10\ldots0 \in \alpha]$. Iterating this recurrence gives $C(\alpha) = 2^t - 2^{t-1} e_t - 2^{t-2} e_{t-1} - \cdots - 2^0 e_1$, where $e_j = [10\ldots0 \in \alpha_j]$ and α_j is the suffix of α following the jth asterisk. In the example we have $\alpha_1 = *10**0*$, $\alpha_2 = 10**0*$, $\ldots$, $\alpha_5 = \epsilon$; thus $e_1 = 0$, $e_2 = 1$, $e_3 = 1$, $e_4 = 0$, and $e_5 = 1$ (by convention), hence $C(**10**0*) = 2^5 - 2^4 - 2^2 - 2^1 = 10$.

(b) We may remove trailing asterisks so that $t = t'$. Then $e_t = 1$ implies $e_{t-1} = \cdots = e_1 = 0$. [The case $C(\alpha) = 2^{t'-1}$ occurs if and only if α ends in $10^j *^k$.]

(c) To compute the sum of $C(\alpha)$ over all t-subcubes, note that $\binom{n}{t}$ clusters begin at the n-tuple $0\ldots0$, and $\binom{n-1}{t}$ begin at each succeeding n-tuple (namely one cluster for each t-subcube containing that n-tuple and specifying the bit that changed). Thus the average is $\left(\binom{n}{t} + (2^n - 1)\binom{n-1}{t}\right)/2^{n-t}\binom{n}{t} = 2^t(1 - t/n) + 2^{t-n}(t/n)$. [The formula in (c) holds for *any* n-bit Gray path, but (a) and (b) are specific to the reflected Gray binary code. These results are due to C. Faloutsos, *IEEE Trans.* **SE-14** (1988), 1381–1393.]

22. Let $\alpha*^j$ and $\beta*^k$ be consecutive lieves of a Gray binary trie, where α and β are binary strings and $j \le k$. Then the last $k - j$ bits of α are a string α' such that α and $\beta\alpha'$ are consecutive elements of Gray binary code, hence adjacent. [Interesting applications of this property to cube-connected message-passing concurrent computers are discussed in *A VLSI Architecture for Concurrent Data Structures* by William J. Dally (Kluwer, 1987), Chapter 3.]

23. $2^j = g(k) \oplus g(l) = g(k \oplus l)$ implies that $l = k \oplus g^{[-1]}(2^j) = k \oplus (2^{j+1} - 1)$. In other words, if $k = (b_{n-1} \ldots b_0)_2$ we have $l = (b_{n-1} \ldots b_{j+1}\bar{b}_j \ldots \bar{b}_0)_2$.

24. Defining $g(k) = k \oplus \lfloor k/2 \rfloor$ as usual, we find $g(k) = g(-1-k)$; hence there are *two* 2-adic integers k such that $g(k)$ has a given 2-adic value l. One of them is even, the other is odd. We can conveniently define $g^{[-1]}$ to be the solution that is even; then (8) is replaced by $b_j = a_{j-1} \oplus \cdots \oplus a_0$, for $j \ge 0$. For example, $g^{[-1]}(1) = -2$ by this definition; when l is a normal integer, the "sign" of $g^{[-1]}(l)$ is the parity of l.

25. Let $p = k \oplus l$; exercise 7.1.3–3 tells us that $2^{\lfloor \lg p \rfloor + 1} - p \le |k - l| \le p$. We have $\nu(g(p)) = \nu(g(k) \oplus g(l)) = t$ if and only if there are positive integers $j_1, \ldots, j_t$ such that $p = (1^{j_1} 0^{j_2} 1^{j_3} \ldots (0 \text{ or } 1)^{j_t})_2$. The largest possible $p < 2^n$ occurs when $j_1 = n + 1 - t$ and $j_2 = \cdots = j_t = 1$, yielding $p = 2^n - \lceil 2^t/3 \rceil$. The smallest possible $q = 2^{\lfloor \lg p \rfloor + 1} - p = (1^{j_2} 0^{j_3} \ldots (1 \text{ or } 0)^{j_t})_2 + 1$ occurs when $j_2 = \cdots = j_t = 1$, yielding $q = \lceil 2^t/3 \rceil$. [C. K. Yuen, *IEEE Trans.* **IT-20** (1974), 668; S. R. Cavior, *IEEE Trans.* **IT-21** (1975), 596. The analogous bound for the modular m-ary Gray code is $\lceil m^t/(m^2 - 1) \rceil$, and this formula holds also for the reflected m-ary Gray code when m is even; see van Zanten and Suparta, *IEEE Trans.* **IT-49** (2003), 485–487; *Proc. South East Asian Math. Soc. Conf.* (Yogyakarta: Gadjah Mada University, 2003), 98–105.]

26. Let $N = 2^{n_t} + \cdots + 2^{n_1}$ where $n_t > \cdots > n_1 \ge 0$; also, let Γ_n be any Gray code for $\{0, 1, \ldots, 2^n - 1\}$ that begins at 0 and ends at 1, except that Γ_0 is simply 0. Use

$$\Gamma_{n_t}^R, \; 2^{n_t} + \Gamma_{n_{t-1}}, \; \ldots, \; 2^{n_t} + \cdots + 2^{n_3} + \Gamma_{n_2}^R, \; 2^{n_t} + \cdots + 2^{n_2} + \Gamma_{n_1}, \text{ if } t \text{ is even;}$$

$$\Gamma_{n_t}, \; 2^{n_t} + \Gamma_{n_{t-1}}^R, \; \ldots, \; 2^{n_t} + \cdots + 2^{n_3} + \Gamma_{n_2}^R, \; 2^{n_t} + \cdots + 2^{n_2} + \Gamma_{n_1}, \text{ if } t \text{ is odd.}$$

27. In general, if $k = (b_{n-1} \ldots b_0)_2$, the $(k+1)$st largest element of S_n is equal to

$$1/(2 - (-1)^{a_{n-1}}/(2 - \cdots /(2 - (-1)^{a_1}/(2 - (-1)^{a_0}))\ldots)),$$

corresponding to the sign pattern $g(k) = (a_{n-1} \ldots a_0)_2$. Thus we can compute any element of S_n in $O(n)$ steps, given its rank. Setting $k = 2^{100} - 10^{10}$ and $n = 100$ yields the answer $373065177/1113604409$. [Whenever $f(x)$ is a positive and monotonic function, the 2^n elements $f(\pm f(\ldots \pm f(\pm x) \ldots))$ are ordered according to Gray binary code, as observed by H. E. Salzer, *CACM* **16** (1973), 180. In this particular case there is, however, another way to get the answer, because we also have

$$S_n = /\!/2, \pm 2, \ldots, \pm 2, \pm 1/\!/$$

using the notation of Section 4.5.3; continued fractions in this form are ordered by complementing alternate bits of k.]

28. (a) As $t = 1, 2, \ldots$, bit a_j of median(G_t) runs through the periodic sequence

$$0, \ldots, 0, *, 1, \ldots, 1, *, 0, \ldots, 0, *, \ldots$$

with asterisks at every 2^{1+j}th step. Thus the strings that correspond to the binary representations of $\lfloor (t-1)/2 \rfloor$ and $\lfloor t/2 \rfloor$ are medians. And those strings are in fact "extreme" cases, in the sense that all medians agree with the common bits of $\lfloor (t-1)/2 \rfloor$

and $\lfloor t/2 \rfloor$, hence asterisks appear where they disagree. For example, when $t = 100 = (01100100)_2$ and $n = 8$, we have median$(G_{100}) = 001100**$.

(b) Since $G_{2t} = 2G_t \cup (2G_t + 1)$, we may assume that $t = (a_{n-2} \ldots a_1 a_0 1)_2$ is odd. If α is $g(p)$ and β is $g(q)$ in Gray binary, we have $p = (p_{n-1} \ldots p_0)_2$ and $q = (p_{n-1} \ldots p_{j+1} \bar{p}_j \ldots \bar{p}_0)_2$; and $a_{n-1} a_{n-2} = 01 = p_{n-1} p_{n-2}$. We cannot have $p < t \le q$, because this would imply that $j = n - 1$ and $p_{n-3} = p_{n-4} = \cdots = p_0 = 1$. [See A. J. Bernstein, K. Steiglitz, and J. E. Hopcroft, *IEEE Trans.* **IT-12** (1966), 425–430.]

29. Assuming that $p \ne 0$, let $l = \lfloor \lg p \rfloor$ and $S_a = \{s \mid 2^l a \le s < 2^l(a+1)\}$ for $0 \le a < 2^{n-l}$. Then $(k \oplus p) - k$ has a constant sign for all $k \in S_a$, and

$$\sum_{k \in S_a} \left| (k \oplus p) - k \right| = 2^l |S_a| = 2^{2l}.$$

Also $g^{[-1]}(g(k) \oplus p) = k \oplus g^{[-1]}(p)$, and $\lfloor \lg g^{[-1]}(p) \rfloor = \lfloor \lg p \rfloor$. Therefore

$$\frac{1}{2^n} \sum_{k=0}^{2^n - 1} \left| g^{[-1]}(g(k) \oplus p) - k \right| = \frac{1}{2^n} \sum_{a=0}^{2^{n-l}-1} \sum_{k \in S_a} \left| (k \oplus g^{[-1]}(p)) - k \right| = \frac{1}{2^n} \sum_{a=0}^{2^{n-l}-1} 2^{2l} = 2^l.$$

[See Morgan M. Buchner, Jr., *Bell System Tech. J.* **48** (1969), 3113–3130.]

30. The cycle containing $k > 1$ has length $2^{\lfloor \lg \lg k \rfloor + 1}$, because it is easy to show from Eq. (7) that if $k = (b_{n-1} \ldots b_0)_2$ we have

$$g^{[2^l]}(k) = (c_{n-1} \ldots c_0)_2, \qquad \text{where } c_j = b_j \oplus b_{j+2^l}.$$

To permute all elements k such that $\lfloor \lg k \rfloor = t$, there are two cases: If t is a power of 2, the cycle containing $2\lfloor k/2 \rfloor$ also contains $2\lfloor k/2 \rfloor + 1$, so we must double the cycle leaders for $t - 1$. Otherwise the cycle containing $2\lfloor k/2 \rfloor$ is disjoint from the cycle containing $2\lfloor k/2 \rfloor + 1$, so $L_t = (2L_{t-1}) \cup (2L_{t-1} + 1) = (L_{t-1}*)_2$. This argument, discovered by Jörg Arndt in 2001, establishes the hint and yields the following algorithm:

P1. [Initialize.] Set $l \leftarrow 1$, $m \leftarrow 0$. (We may assume that $n \ge 2$.)

P2. [Loop through leaders.] Set $r \leftarrow m$. Perform Algorithm Q with $k = 2^t + r$; then if $r > 0$, set $r \leftarrow (r-1) \,\&\, m$ and repeat until $r = 0$. [See exercise 7.1.3–79.]

P3. [Increase lg k.] Set $t \leftarrow t + 1$. Terminate if t is now equal to n; otherwise set $m \leftarrow 2m + [t \,\&\, (t-1) \ne 0]$ and return to P2. ∎

Q1. [Begin a cycle.] Set $s \leftarrow X_k$, $l \leftarrow k$, $j \leftarrow l \oplus \lfloor l/2 \rfloor$.

Q2. [Follow the cycle.] While $j \ne k$, set $X_l \leftarrow X_j$, $l \leftarrow j$, and $j \leftarrow l \oplus \lfloor l/2 \rfloor$. Then set $X_l \leftarrow s$. ∎

31. We get a field from f_n if and only if we get one from $f_n^{[2]}$, which takes $(a_{n-1} \ldots a_0)_2$ to $((a_{n-1} \oplus a_{n-2})(a_{n-1} \oplus a_{n-3})(a_{n-2} \oplus a_{n-4}) \ldots (a_2 \oplus a_0)(a_1))_2$. Let $c_n(x)$ be the characteristic polynomial of the matrix A defining this transformation, mod 2; then $c_1(x) = x + 1$, $c_2(x) = x^2 + x + 1$, and $c_{j+1}(x) = x c_j(x) + c_{j-1}(x)$. Since $c_n(A)$ is the zero matrix, by the Cayley–Hamilton theorem, a field is obtained if and only if $c_n(x)$ is a primitive polynomial, and this condition can be tested as in Section 3.2.2. The first such values of n are 1, 2, 3, 5, 6, 9, 11, 14, 23, 26, 29, 30, 33, 35, 39, 41, 51, 53, 65, 69, 74, 81, 83, 86, 89, 90, 95.

[Running the recurrence backwards shows that $c_{-j-1}(x) = c_j(x)$, hence $c_j(x)$ divides $c_{(2j+1)k+j}(x)$; for example, $c_{3k+1}(x)$ is always a multiple of $x+1$. All numbers n of the form $2jk + j + k$ are therefore excluded when $j > 0$ and $k > 0$. The polynomials $c_{18}(x)$, $c_{50}(x)$, $c_{98}(x)$, and $c_{99}(x)$ are irreducible but not primitive.]

32. Mostly true, but false at the points where $w_k(x)$ changes sign. (Walsh originally suggested that $w_k(x)$ should be zero at such points; but the convention adopted here is better, because it makes simple formulas like (15)–(19) valid for all x.)

33. By induction on k, we have

$$w_k(x) = w_{\lfloor k/2 \rfloor}(2x) = r_1(2x)^{b_1+b_2} r_2(2x)^{b_2+b_3} \ldots = r_1(x)^{b_0+b_1} r_2(x)^{b_1+b_2} r_3(x)^{b_2+b_3} \ldots$$

for $0 \le x < \frac{1}{2}$, because $r_1(x) = 1$ in this range and $r_j(2x) = r_{j+1}(x)$ for all x. On the other hand when $\frac{1}{2} \le x < 1$,

$$w_k(x) = (-1)^{\lceil k/2 \rceil} w_{\lfloor k/2 \rfloor}(2x) = (-1)^{\lceil k/2 \rceil} r_1(2x)^{b_1+b_2} r_2(2x)^{b_2+b_3} \ldots$$
$$= r_1(x)^{b_0+b_1} r_2(x)^{b_1+b_2} r_3(x)^{b_2+b_3} \ldots$$

because $\lceil k/2 \rceil \equiv b_0 + b_1$ (modulo 2) and $r_1(x) = -1$ in this range.

(Incidentally, the Rademacher functions had been discovered independently by Felix Hausdorff in 1915 but not published; see his *Gesammelte Werke* **5** (2006), 757–758.)

34. $p_k(x) = \prod_{j \ge 0} r_{j+1}^{b_j}(x)$; hence $w_k(x) = p_k(x) p_{\lfloor k/2 \rfloor}(x) = p_{g(k)}(x)$. [R. E. A. C. Paley, *Proc. London Math. Soc.* (2) **34** (1932), 241–279.]

35. If $j = (a_{n-1} \ldots a_0)_2$ and $k = (b_{n-1} \ldots b_0)_2$, the element in row j and column k is $(-1)^{f(j,k)}$, where $f(j,k)$ is the sum of all $a_r b_s$ such that: $r = s$ (Hadamard); $r+s = n-1$ (Paley); $r + s = n$ or $n - 1$ (Walsh).

Let R_n, F_n, and G_n be permutation matrices for the permutations that take $j = (a_{n-1} \ldots a_0)_2$ to $k = (a_0 \ldots a_{n-1})_2$, $k = 2^n - 1 - j = (\bar{a}_{n-1} \ldots \bar{a}_0)_2$, and $k = g^{[-1]}(j) = ((a_{n-1}) \ldots (a_{n-1} \oplus \cdots \oplus a_0))_2$, respectively. Then, using the direct product of matrices, we have the recursive formulas

$$R_{n+1} = \begin{pmatrix} R_n \otimes (1\ 0) \\ R_n \otimes (0\ 1) \end{pmatrix}, \qquad F_{n+1} = F_n \otimes \begin{pmatrix} 0 & 1 \\ 1 & 0 \end{pmatrix}, \qquad G_{n+1} = \begin{pmatrix} G_n & 0 \\ 0 & G_n F_n \end{pmatrix},$$

$$H_{n+1} = H_n \otimes \begin{pmatrix} 1 & 1 \\ 1 & \bar{1} \end{pmatrix}, \qquad P_{n+1} = \begin{pmatrix} P_n \otimes (1\ 1) \\ P_n \otimes (1\ \bar{1}) \end{pmatrix}, \qquad W_{n+1} = \begin{pmatrix} W_n \otimes (1\ 1) \\ F_n W_n \otimes (1\ \bar{1}) \end{pmatrix}.$$

Thus $W_n = G_n^T P_n = P_n G_n$; $H_n = P_n R_n = R_n P_n$; and $P_n = W_n G_n^T = G_n W_n = H_n R_n = R_n H_n$.

36. T1. [Hadamard transform.] For $k = 0, 1, \ldots, n - 1$, replace the pair (X_j, X_{j+2^k}) by $(X_j + X_{j+2^k}, X_j - X_{j+2^k})$ for all j with $\lfloor j/2^k \rfloor$ even, $0 \le j < 2^n$. (These operations effectively set $X^T \leftarrow H_n X^T$.)

T2. [Bit reversal.] Apply the algorithm of exercise 5 to the vector X. (These operations effectively set $X^T \leftarrow R_n X^T$, in the notation of exercise 35.)

T3. [Gray binary permutation.] Apply the algorithm of exercise 30 to the vector X. (These operations effectively set $X^T \leftarrow G_n^T X^T$.) ∎

If n has one of the special values in exercise 31, it may be faster to combine steps T2 and T3 into a single permutation step.

37. If $k = 2^{e_1} + \cdots + 2^{e_t}$ with $e_1 > \cdots > e_t \ge 0$, the sign changes occur at $S_{e_1} \cup \cdots \cup S_{e_t}$, where

$$S_0 = \left\{ \frac{1}{2} \right\}, \qquad S_1 = \left\{ \frac{1}{4}, \frac{3}{4} \right\}, \qquad \ldots, \qquad S_e = \left\{ \frac{2j+1}{2^{e+1}} \,\middle|\, 0 \le j < 2^e \right\}.$$

Therefore the number of sign changes in $(0 .. x)$ is $\sum_{j=1}^{t} \lfloor 2^{e_j} x + \frac{1}{2} \rfloor$. Setting $x = l/(k+1)$ gives $l+O(t)$ changes; so the lth is at a distance of at most $O(\nu(k))/2^{\lfloor \lg k \rfloor}$ from $l/(k+1)$.

[This argument makes it plausible that infinitely many pairs (k, l) exist with $|z_{kl} - l/(k+1)| = \Omega((\log k)/k)$. But no explicit construction of such "bad" pairs is immediately apparent.]

38. Let $t_0(x) = 1$ and $t_k(x) = \omega^{\lfloor 3x \rfloor \lceil 2k/3 \rceil} t_{\lfloor k/3 \rfloor}(3x)$, where $\omega = e^{2\pi i/3}$. Then $t_k(x)$ winds around the origin $\frac{2}{3}k$ times as x increases from 0 to 1. If $s_k(x) = \omega^{\lfloor 3^k x \rfloor}$ is the ternary analog of the Rademacher function $r_k(x)$, we have $t_k(x) = \prod_{j \ge 0} s_{j+1}(x)^{b_j - b_{j+1}}$ when $k = (b_{n-1} \ldots b_0)_3$, as in the modular ternary Gray code.

39. (a) Let's call the symbols $\{x_0, x_1, \ldots, x_7\}$ instead of $\{a, b, c, d, e, f, g, h\}$. We want to find a permutation p of $\{0, 1, \ldots, 7\}$ such that the matrix with $(-1)^{j \cdot k} x_{p(j) \oplus k}$ in row j and column k has orthogonal rows; this condition is equivalent to requiring that

$$(j \oplus j') \cdot (p(j) \oplus p(j')) \equiv 1 \pmod{2}, \qquad \text{for } 0 \le j < j' < 8.$$

One solution is $p(0) \ldots p(7) = 0\,1\,7\,2\,5\,6\,3\,4$, yielding the identity $(a^2 + b^2 + c^2 + d^2 + e^2 + f^2 + g^2 + h^2)(A^2 + B^2 + C^2 + D^2 + E^2 + F^2 + G^2 + H^2) = \mathcal{A}^2 + \mathcal{B}^2 + \mathcal{C}^2 + \mathcal{D}^2 + \mathcal{E}^2 + \mathcal{F}^2 + \mathcal{G}^2 + \mathcal{H}^2$, where

$$
\begin{pmatrix} \mathcal{A} \\ \mathcal{B} \\ \mathcal{C} \\ \mathcal{D} \\ \mathcal{E} \\ \mathcal{F} \\ \mathcal{G} \\ \mathcal{H} \end{pmatrix} = \begin{pmatrix} a & b & c & d & e & f & g & h \\ b & -a & d & -c & f & -e & h & -y \\ h & g & -f & -e & d & c & -b & -a \\ c & -d & -a & b & g & -h & -e & f \\ f & e & h & g & -b & -a & -d & -c \\ g & -h & e & -f & -c & d & -a & b \\ d & c & -b & -a & -h & -g & f & e \\ e & -f & -g & h & -a & b & c & -d \end{pmatrix} \begin{pmatrix} A \\ B \\ C \\ D \\ E \\ F \\ G \\ H \end{pmatrix}.
$$

[This identity was discovered by C. F. Degen, *Mémoires de l'Acad. Sci. St. Petersbourg* (5) **8** (1818), 207–219. The related octonions are discussed in an interesting survey by J. C. Baez, *Bull. Amer. Math. Soc.* **39** (2002), 145–205; **42** (2005), 213, 229–243. See also J. H. Conway and D. A. Smith, *On Quaternions and Octonions* (2003).]

(b) There *is* no 16×16 solution. The closest one can come is

$$p(0) \ldots p(15) = 0\ 1\ 11\ 2\ 14\ 15\ 13\ 4\ 9\ 10\ 7\ 12\ 5\ 6\ 3\ 8,$$

which fails if and only if $j \oplus j' = 5$. (See *Philos. Mag.* (4) **34** (1867), 461–475. In §9, §10, §11, and §13 of this paper, Sylvester stated and proved the basic results about what has somehow come to be known as the Hadamard transform — although Hadamard himself gave credit to Sylvester [*Bull. des Sciences Mathématiques* (2) **17** (1893), 240–246]. Moreover, Sylvester introduced transforms of m^n elements in §14, using mth roots of unity. See also the prior work of T. P. Kirkman, *Philosophical Mag.* (3) **33** (1848), 447–459, 494–509; **35** (1850), 292–301.)

40. Yes; this change would in fact run through the swapped subsets in lexicographic binary order rather than in Gray binary order. (Any 5×5 matrix of 0s and 1s that is nonsingular mod 2 will generate all 32 possibilities when we run through all linear combinations of its rows.) The most important thing is the appearance of the ruler function, or some other Gray code delta sequence, not the fact that only one a_j changes per step, in cases like this where any number of the a_j can be changed simultaneously at the same cost.

41. At most 16; for example, `fired`, `fires`, `finds`, `fines`, `fined`, `fares`, `fared`, `wares`, `wards`, `wands`, `wanes`, `waned`, `wines`, `winds`, `wires`, `wired`. We also get 16 from `paced`/`links` and `paled`/`mints`; perhaps also from a word mixed with an antipodal nonword.

42. Suppose $n \leq 2^{2^r} + r + 1$, and let $s = 2^r$. We use an auxiliary table of 2^{r+s} bits f_{jk} for $0 \leq j < 2^s$ and $0 \leq k < s$, representing focus pointers as in Algorithm L, together with an auxiliary s-bit "register" $j = (j_{s-1} \ldots j_0)_2$ and an $(r+2)$-bit "program counter" $p = (p_{r+1} \ldots p_0)_2$. At each step we examine the program counter and possibly the j register and one of the f bits; then, based on the bits seen, we complement a bit of the Gray code, complement a bit of the program counter, and possibly change a j or f bit, thereby emulating step L3 with respect to the most significant $n - r - 2$ bits.

For example, here is the construction when $r = 1$:

$p_2 p_1 p_0$	Change	Set			$p_2 p_1 p_0$	Change	Set	
0 0 0	a_0, p_0	$j_0 \leftarrow f_{00}$	$\left.\right\}$ $j \leftarrow f_0$		1 1 0	a_0, p_0	$f_{j0} \leftarrow f_{(j+1)0}$	$\left.\right\}$ $f_j \leftarrow f_{j+1}$
0 0 1	a_1, p_1	$j_1 \leftarrow f_{01}$			1 1 1	a_1, p_1	$f_{j1} \leftarrow f_{(j+1)1}$	
0 1 1	a_0, p_0	$f_{00} \leftarrow 0$	$\left.\right\}$ $f_0 \leftarrow 0$		1 0 1	a_0, p_0	$f_{(j+1)0} \leftarrow (j+1)_0$	$\left.\right\}$ $f_{j+1} \leftarrow j+1$
0 1 0	a_2, p_2	$f_{01} \leftarrow 0$			1 0 0	a_{j+3}, p_2	$f_{(j+1)1} \leftarrow (j+1)_1$	

The process stops when it attempts to change bit a_n.

[In fact, we need change only *one* auxiliary bit per step if we allow ourselves to examine some Gray binary bits as well as the auxiliary bits, because $p_r \ldots p_0 = a_r \ldots a_0$, and we can set $f_0 \leftarrow 0$ in a more clever way when j doesn't have its final value $2^s - 1$. This construction, suggested by Fredman in 2001, improves on another that he had published in *SICOMP* **7** (1978), 134–146. With a more elaborate construction it is possible to reduce the number of auxiliary bits to $O(n)$.]

43. This number was estimated by Silverman, Vickers, and Sampson [*IEEE Trans.* **IT-29** (1983), 894–901] to be about 7×10^{22}. And indeed, H. Haanpää and P. R. J. Östergård found the exact value $d(6) = 71{,}676{,}427{,}445{,}141{,}767{,}741{,}440$ in 2011, by using symmetry and "gluing together" disjoint paths whose endpoints x have $\nu x = 3$ and whose interior vertices have $\nu x \leq 3$. [*Math. Comp.* **83** (2014), 979–995.]

44. Every n-bit Gray cycle defines a pair of perfect matchings (see exercise 55).

45. (a) (000 002 012 010 090 094 0b4 ... 112 102 100), in hexadecimal, 32 elements in all. Notice that the signatures of elements in each cycle run through the Gray code Γ_4.

(b) A ground vertex v is preceded in its cycle by its sibling $v \oplus 2$. If v is a ground vertex in a different cycle from its sibling $u = v \oplus 1$, we can join the cycles by deleting $\{u \oplus 2 \text{---} u, v \oplus 2 \text{---} v\}$ and inserting $\{u \text{---} v, u \oplus 2 \text{---} v \oplus 2\}$. Repeat for all ground v.

(c) Consider the multigraph G' whose vertices are the cycles and whose edges go from the cycle of v to the cycle of $v + 1$ for all even ground vertices v. Every vertex of G' has even degree, so the edges are a union of cycles in G'. Thus any edge of G' can be deleted without changing the connected components.

(d) It's not difficult to construct a path $P = v^{(0)} \text{---} v^{(1)} \text{---} v^{(2)} \text{---} \cdots$ through vertices of G with $v_0 = v_{-1} = 0$ that passes through all such v with $\sigma(v) \leq 1$, and such that $\sigma(v^{(i)}) \in \{0, 1, 2, 4, 8\}$ for all i. Take the cycle from (b) that contains $v^{(0)}$ and call it the "working cycle" W; then do the following for $i = 1, 2, \ldots$, until W includes all vertices: If $v = v^{(i)} \notin W$, suppose $u = v^{(i-1)}$ has $u_l \neq v_l$. *Case 1:* $u \oplus c \text{---} u$ is an edge of W, for $c = 1$ or $c = 2$. Take a cycle for the equivalence class of v that has the edge $v \oplus c \text{---} v$. Delete those edges and insert $\{u \text{---} v, u \oplus c \text{---} v \oplus c\}$. *Case 2:* Otherwise Case 1 must have applied to $w = v^{(i-2)}$ and u on the previous step. If $c = 1$ then W contains the edge $u \oplus 2 \text{---} u \oplus 3$. We can find a cycle with $v \oplus 2 \text{---} v \oplus 3$, and replace those edges by $\{u \oplus 2 \text{---} v \oplus 3, u \oplus 3 \text{---} v \oplus 3\}$. A similar edge-swap works when $c = 2$.

(e) The final cycle W allows us to reconstruct $\mathcal{M}_{l(v)}(v)$. When $l(v) \neq 0$ the function $\mathcal{M}_{l(v)}$ is equivalent to $t = 2^{3r-1}$ independent matchings of the r-cube, because there are t ways to choose the v_i for $i \neq l$ having the correct signature. So the number of different cycles is at least $M(r)^{12t}$ (see exercise 44).

46. There are k-bit signatures $\sigma(v)$. When $\sigma(v) = g(j)$ in Gray binary code, $l(v) = (\rho(j+1) + [j \neq 2^k - 1])[j+2$ is not a power of 2]. At least $M(r)^{(2^k-k)t}$ cycles arise, where $t = 2^{(k-1)(r-1)+2}$. [*Information Processing Letters* **109** (2009), 267–272.]

47. The bounds $\left(\frac{r}{e}\right)^{2^{r-1}} < 2^{r-1}!/(2^{r-1}/r)^{2^{r-1}} \leq M(r) \leq r!^{2^{r-1}/r} = \left(\frac{r}{e} + O(\log r)\right)^{2^{r-1}}$ are proved in Section 7.5.1. Hence $d(n)^{1/2^n} \leq n/e + O(\log n)$ by exercise 44.

The lower bound from exercise 46, if we let G_j be an r_j-cube, is

$$\left(M(r_1)^{2^{n-r_1-k+1}}\right)^{2^{k-1}-k} \cdot \left(M(r_2)^{2^{n-r_2-k+1}}\right)^{2^{k-2}} \cdot \left(M(r_3)^{2^{n-r_3-k+1}}\right)^{2^{k-3}}$$
$$\cdot \ldots \cdot \left(M(r_{k-1})^{2^{n-r_{k-1}-k+1}}\right)^2 \cdot \left(M(r_k)^{2^{n-r_k-k+1}}\right)^2;$$

and it's better to choose $r_j \approx (n-2)/2^{j-[j=k]}$ for $1 \leq j \leq k$ instead of using cubes of roughly the same size. Let $\alpha_j = r_j/e$ be a lower bound on $M(r_j)^{2^{1-r_j}}$. The lower bound on $d(n)^{1/2^n}$ simplifies to

$$\alpha_1^{1/2} \alpha_2^{k/2^k} \alpha_3^{1/4} \alpha_3^{1/8} \ldots \alpha_{k-1}^{1/2^{k-1}} \alpha_k^{1/2^{k-1}} = 2^{-2+(k-4)/2^k} \left(\frac{n-2}{c}\right)^{1-k/2^k} \left(1 + O\left(\frac{k}{n}\right)\right),$$

and this is $n/(4e) + O(\log n)^2$ when $k = \lg n + O(1)$.

49. Take any Hamiltonian path P from $0\ldots0$ to $1\ldots1$ in the $(2n-1)$-cube, such as the Savage–Winkler code, and use $0P$, $1\overline{P}$. (All such cycles are obtained by this construction when $n = 1$ or $n = 2$, but many more possibilities exist when $n > 2$.)

50. $\alpha_1(n+1)\alpha_1^R n \alpha_1 j_1 \alpha_2 n \alpha_2^R (n+1)\alpha_2 \ldots j_{l-1} \alpha_l n \alpha_l^R (n+1)\alpha_l n \alpha_l^R j_{l-1} \ldots j_1 \alpha_1^R n$.

51. Let $c_j = 2\lfloor (2^{n-1}+j)/n \rfloor$ and $c_j' = 2\lfloor (2^{n+1}+j)/(n+2) \rfloor$. If $n \neq 3$, it is not difficult to verify that $4c_j \geq 8\lfloor 2^{n-1}/n \rfloor > 2\lceil 2^{n+1}/(n+2) \rceil \geq c_k'$ for $0 \leq j < n$ and $0 \leq k < n+2$. Therefore we can apply Theorem D to any n-bit Gray cycle with transition counts c_j, underlining b_j copies of j and putting an underlined digit 0 last, where $b_j = 2c_j - \frac{1}{2}c_{(j+2+d) \bmod (n+2)}' - [j=0]$ and d is chosen so that $c_d' = c_{d+1}'$. This construction works because $l = b_0 + \cdots + b_{n-1} = 2(c_0 + \cdots + c_{n-1}) - \frac{1}{2}(c_0' + \cdots + c_{n+1}' - c_d' - c_{d+1}') - 1 = c_d' - 1$ is odd. [Corollary B was discovered by T. Bakos in the 1950s, and proved in detail by A. Ádám in *Truth Functions* (Budapest: 1968), 28–37. Ádám's book also presents a proof by G. Pollák that, in fact, $c_0' = c_1'$ for all n; hence we may take $d = 0$. See also J. P. Robinson and M. Cohn, *IEEE Trans.* **C-30** (1981), 17–23.]

52. The number of different code patterns in the smallest j coordinate positions is at most $c_0 + \cdots + c_{j-1}$.

53. Theorem D produces only cycles with $c_j = c_{j+1}$ for some j, so it can't produce the counts $(2, 4, 6, 8, 12)$. The extension in exercise 50 gives also $c_j = c_{j+1} - 2$, but it can't produce $(6, 10, 14, 18, 22, 26, 32)$. The sets of numbers satisfying the conditions of exercise 52 are precisely those obtainable by starting with $\{2, 2, 4, \ldots, 2^{n-1}\}$ and repeatedly replacing some pair $\{c_j, c_k\}$ for which $c_j < c_k$ by the pair $\{c_j + 2, c_k - 2\}$.

54. Suppose the values are $\{p_1, \ldots, p_n\}$, and let x_{jk} be the number of times p_j occurs in $(a_1, \ldots, a_k)$. We must have $(x_{1k}, \ldots, x_{nk}) \equiv (x_{1l}, \ldots, x_{nl})$ (modulo 2) for some $k < l$. But if the p's are prime numbers, varying as the delta sequence of an n-bit Gray cycle, the only solution is $k = 0$ and $l = 2^n$. [*AMM* **60** (1953), 418; **83** (1976), 54.]

55. In fact, given any perfect matching Q of K_{2^n}, one can find in $O(2^n)$ steps a perfect matching R of the n-cube such that $Q \cup R$ is a Hamiltonian cycle of K_{2^n}. [See J. Fink, *J. Comb. Theory* **B97** (2007), 1074–1076; *Elect. Notes Disc. Math.* **29** (2007), 345–351.]

56. [*Bell System Tech. J.* **37** (1958), 815–826.] The 112 canonical delta sequences yield

Class	Example	t	Class	Example	t	Class	Example	t
A	0102101302012023	2	D	0102013201020132	4	G	0102030201020302	8
B	0102303132101232	2	E	0102032021202302	4	H	0102101301021013	8
C	0102030130321013	2	F	0102013102010232	4	I	0102013121012132	1

Here B is the balanced code (Fig. 33(b)), G is standard Gray binary (Fig. 30(b)), and H is the complementary code (Fig. 33(a)). Class H is also equivalent to the modular $(4, 4)$ Gray code under the correspondence of exercise 18. A class with t automorphisms corresponds to $32 \times 24/t$ of the 2688 different delta sequences $\delta_0 \delta_1 \ldots \delta_{15}$.

Similarly (see exercise 7.2.3–00), the 5-bit Gray cycles fall into 237,675 different equivalence classes.

57. With Type 1 only, 480 vertices are isolated, namely those of classes D, F, G in the previous answer. With Type 2 only, the graph has 384 components, 288 of which are isolated vertices of classes F and G. There are 64 components of size 9, each containing 3 vertices from E and 6 from A; 16 components of size 30, each with 6 from H and 24 from C; and 16 components of size 84, each with 12 from D, 24 from B, 48 from I. With Type 3 (or Type 4) only, the entire graph is connected. [Similarly, all 91,392 of the 4-bit Gray *paths* are connected if path $\alpha\beta$ is considered adjacent to path $\alpha^R \beta$. Vickers and Silverman, *IEEE Trans.* **C-29** (1980), 329–331, have conjectured that Type 3 changes will suffice to connect the graph of n-bit Gray cycles for all $n \geq 3$.]

58. If some nonempty substring of $\beta\beta$ involves each coordinate an even number of times, that substring cannot have length $|\beta|$, so some cyclic shift of β has a prefix γ with the same evenness property. But then α doesn't define a Gray cycle, because we could change each n of γ back to 0.

59. If α is nonlocal in exercise 58, so is $\beta\beta$, provided that $q > 1$ and that 0 occurs more than $q + 1$ times in α. Therefore, starting with the α of (30) but with 0 and 1 interchanged, we obtain nonlocal cycles for $n \geq 5$ in which coordinate 0 changes exactly 6 times. [Mark Ramras, *Discrete Math.* **85** (1990), 329–331.] On the other hand, a 4-bit Gray cycle cannot be nonlocal because it always has a run of length 2; if $\delta_k = \delta_{k+2}$, elements $\{v_k, v_{k+1}, v_{k+2}, v_{k+3}\}$ form a 2-subcube.

60. Use the construction of exercise 58 with $q = 1$.

61. The idea is to interleave an m-bit cycle $U = (u_0, u_1, u_2, \ldots)$ with an n-bit cycle $V = (v_0, v_1, v_2, \ldots)$, by forming concatenations

$$W = (u_{i_0} v_{j_0}, \; u_{i_1} v_{j_1}, \; u_{i_2} v_{j_2}, \; \ldots), \qquad i_k = \bar{a}_0 + \cdots + \bar{a}_{k-1}, \quad j_k = a_0 + \cdots + a_{k-1},$$

where $a_0 a_1 a_2 \ldots$ is a periodic string of control bits $\alpha\alpha\alpha\ldots$; we advance to the next element of U when $a_k = 0$, otherwise to the next element of V.

If α is any string of length $2^m \leq 2^n$, containing s bits that are 0 and $t = 2^m - s$ bits that are 1, W will be an $(m + n)$-bit Gray cycle if s and t are odd. For we have $i_{k+l} \equiv i_k$ (modulo 2^m) and $j_{k+l} \equiv j_k$ (modulo 2^n) only if l is a multiple of 2^m, since $i_k + j_k = k$. Suppose $l = 2^m c$; then $j_{k+l} = j_k + tc$, so c is a multiple of 2^n.

(a) Let $\alpha = 0111$; then runs of length 8 occur in the left 2 bits and runs of length $\geq \lfloor \frac{4}{3} r(n) \rfloor$ occur in the right n bits.

(b) Let s be the largest odd number $\leq 2^m r(m)/(r(m) + r(n))$. Also let $t = 2^m - s$ and $a_k = \lfloor (k + 1)t/2^m \rfloor - \lfloor kt/2^m \rfloor$, so that $i_k = \lceil ks/2^m \rceil$ and $j_k = \lfloor kt/2^m \rfloor$. If a run of length l occurs in the left m bits, we have $i_{k+l+1} \geq i_k + r(m) + 1$, hence

$l+1 > 2^m r(m)/s \ge r(m)+r(n)$. And if it occurs in the right n bits we have $j_{k+l+1} \ge j_k + r(n) + 1$, hence

$$l+1 > 2^m r(n)/t > 2^m r(n)/(2^m r(n)/(r(m)+r(n))+2)$$

$$= r(m) + r(n) - \frac{2(r(m)+r(n))^2}{2^m r(n) + 2(r(m)+r(n))} > r(m) + r(n) - 1$$

because $r(m) \le r(n)$.

The construction often works also in less restricted cases. See the paper that introduced the study of Gray-code runs: L. Goddyn, G. M. Lawrence, and E. Nemeth, *Utilitas Math.* **34** (1988), 179–192.

63. Set $a_k \leftarrow k \bmod 4$ for $0 \le k < 2^{10}$, except that $a_k = 4$ when $k \bmod 16 = 15$ or $k \bmod 64 = 42$ or $k \bmod 256 = 133$. Also set $(j_0, j_1, j_2, j_3, j_4) \leftarrow (0,2,4,6,8)$. Then for $k = 0, 1, \ldots, 1023$, set $\delta_k \leftarrow j_{a_k}$ and $j_{a_k} \leftarrow 1 + 4a_k - j_{a_k}$. (This construction generalizes the method of exercise 61.)

64. (a) Each element u_k appears together with $\{v_k, v_{k+2^m}, \ldots, v_{k+2^m(2^{n-1}-1)}\}$ and $\{v_{k+1}, v_{k+1+2^m}, \ldots, v_{k+1+2^m(2^{n-1}-1)}\}$. Thus the permutation $\sigma_0 \ldots \sigma_{2^m-1}$ must be a 2^{n-1}-cycle containing the n-bit vertices of even parity, times an arbitrary permutation of the other vertices. This condition is also sufficient.

(b) Let τ_j be the permutation that takes $v \mapsto v \oplus 2^j$, and let $\pi_j(u,w)$ be the permutation $(uw)\tau_j$. If $u \oplus w = 2^i + 2^j$ then $\pi_j(u,w)$ takes $u \mapsto u \oplus 2^i$ and $w \mapsto w \oplus 2^i$, while $v \mapsto v \oplus 2^j$ for all other vertices v, so it takes each vertex to a neighbor.

If S is any set $\subseteq \{0, \ldots, n-1\}$, let $\sigma(S)$ be the stream of all permutations τ_j for all $j \in \{0, \ldots, n-1\} \setminus S$, in increasing order of j, repeated twice; for example, if $n = 5$ we have $\sigma(\{1,2\}) = \tau_0 \tau_3 \tau_4 \tau_0 \tau_3 \tau_4$. Then the Gray stream

$$\Sigma(i,j,u) = \sigma(\{i,j\})\pi_j(u, u \oplus 2^i \oplus 2^j)\sigma(\{i,j\})\tau_j\sigma(\{j\})$$

consists of $6n - 8$ permutations whose product is the transposition $(u \; u \oplus 2^i \oplus 2^j)$. Moreover, when this stream is applied to any n-bit vertex v, its runs all have length $n - 2$ or more.

We may assume that $n \ge 5$. Let $\delta_0 \ldots \delta_{2^n-1}$ be the delta sequence for an n-bit Gray cycle $(v_0, v_1, \ldots, v_{2^n-1})$ with all runs of length 3 or more. Then the product of all permutations in

$$\Sigma = \prod_{k=1}^{2^{n-1}-1} \left(\Sigma(\delta_{2k-1}, \delta_{2k}, v_{2k-1}) \Sigma(\delta_{2k}, \delta_{2k+1}, v_{2k}) \right)$$

is $(v_1 v_3)(v_2 v_4) \ldots (v_{2^n-3} v_{2^n-1})(v_{2^n-2} v_0) = (v_{2^n-1} \ldots v_1)(v_{2^n-2} \ldots v_0)$, so it satisfies the cycle condition of (a).

Moreover, all powers $(\sigma(\emptyset)\Sigma)^t$ produce runs of length $\ge n - 2$ when applied to any vertex v. By repeating individual factors $\sigma(\{i,j\})$ or $\sigma(\{j\})$ in Σ as many times as we wish, we can adjust the length of $\sigma(\emptyset)\Sigma$, obtaining $2n + (2^{n-1} - 1)(12n - 16) + 2(n-2)a + 2(n-1)b$ for any integers $a, b \ge 0$; thus we can increase its length to exactly 2^m, provided that $2^m \ge 2n + (2^{n-1}-1)(12n-16) + 2(n^2 - 5n+6)$, by exercise 5.2.1–21.

(c) The bound $r(n) \ge n - 4\lg n + 8$ can be proved for $n \ge 5$ as follows. First we observe that it holds for $5 \le n < 33$ by the methods of exercises 60–63. Then we observe that every integer $N \ge 33$ can be written as $N = m + n$ or $N = m + n + 1$, for some $m \ge 20$, where

$$n = m - \lfloor 4 \lg m \rfloor + 10.$$

If $m \geq 20$, 2^m is sufficiently large for the construction in part (b) to be valid; hence

$$r(N) \geq r(m+n) \geq 2\min(r(m), n-2) \geq 2(m - \lfloor 4\lg m\rfloor + 8)$$
$$= m + n + 1 - \lfloor 4\lg N - 1 + \epsilon\rfloor + 8$$
$$\geq N - 4\lg N + 8$$

where $\epsilon = 4\lg(2m/N) < 1 + [N = m+n]$. [*Electronic Journal of Combinatorics* **10** (2003), #R27, 1–10.] Recursive use of (b) gives, in fact, $r(1024) \geq 1000$.

65. A computer search reveals that eight essentially different patterns (and their reverses) are possible. One of them has the delta sequence 01020314203024041234 214103234103, and it is close to two of the others.

66. (Solution by Mark Cooke.) One suitable delta sequence is 012345607012132435 6576071021353462670153741236256701731426206570134214656057310 2464537 5710204353761407363046427370356402713275054121027564150240365 4250136 0254161560431257603257204315762432176045204175163547670356475 7062543 72421326241615234175143671431 64314. (Solutions for $n > 8$ are still unknown.)

67. Let $v_{2k+1} = \bar{v}_{2k}$ and $v_{2k} = 0u_k$, where $(u_0, u_1, \dots, u_{2^{n-1}-1})$ is any $(n-1)$-bit Gray cycle. [See Robinson and Cohn, *IEEE Trans.* **C-30** (1981), 17–23.]

68. Yes. The simplest way is probably to take the $(n-1)$-trit modular Gray ternary code and add $0\dots0$, $1\dots1$, $2\dots2$ to each string (modulo 3). For example, when $n = 3$ the code is 000, 111, 222, 001, 112, 220, 002, 110, 221, 012, 120, 201, $\dots$, 020, 101, 212.

69. (a) We need only verify the change in h when bits $b_{j-1}\dots b_0$ are simultaneously complemented, for $j = 1, 2, \dots$; and these changes are respectively $(1110)_2$, $(1101)_2$, $(0111)_2$, $(1011)_2$, $(10011)_2$, $(100011)_2$, $\dots$. To prove that every n-tuple occurs, note that $0 \leq h(k) < 2^n$ when $0 \leq k < 2^n$ and $n > 3$; also $h^{[-1]}((a_{n-1}\dots a_0)_2) = (b_{n-1}\dots b_0)_2$, where $b_0 = a_0 \oplus a_1 \oplus a_2 \oplus \cdots$, $b_1 = a_0$, $b_2 = a_2 \oplus a_3 \oplus a_4 \oplus \cdots$, $b_3 = a_0 \oplus a_1 \oplus a_3 \oplus \cdots$, and $b_j = a_j \oplus a_{j+1} \oplus \cdots$ for $j \geq 4$.

(b) Let $h(k) = (\dots a_2 a_1 a_0)_2$ where $a_j = b_j \oplus b_{j+1} \oplus b_0[j \leq t] \oplus b_{t-1}[t-1 \leq j \leq t]$.

70. As in (32) and (33), we can remove a factor of $n!$ by assuming that the strings of weight 1 occur in order. Then there are 14 solutions for $n = 5$ starting with 00000, and 21 starting with 00001. When $n = 6$ there are 46,935 of each type (related by reversal and complementation). When $n = 7$ the number is much, much larger, yet very small by comparison with the total number of 7-bit Gray codes.

71. Suppose that $\alpha_{n(j+1)}$ differs from α_{nj} in coordinate t_j, for $0 \leq j < n-1$. Then $t_j = j\pi_n$, by (44) and (38). Now Eq. (34) tells us that $t_0 = n-1$; and if $0 < j < n-1$ we have $t_j = ((j-1)\pi_{n-1})\pi_{n-1}$ by (40). Thus $t_j = j\sigma_n\pi_{n-1}^2$ for $0 \leq j < n-1$, and the value of $(n-1)\pi_n$ is whatever is left. (Notations for permutations are notoriously confusing, so it is always wise to check a few small cases carefully.)

72. The delta sequence is 01021324302012340123130410 21323.

73. Let $Q_{nj} = P_{nj}^R$ and denote the sequences (41), (42) by S_n and T_n. Thus $S_n = P_{n0}Q_{n1}P_{n2}\dots$ and $T_n = Q_{n0}P_{n1}Q_{n2}\dots$, if we omit the commas; and we have

$$S_{n+1} = 0P_{n0}\ 0Q_{n1}\ 1Q_{n0}^\pi\ 1P_{n1}^\pi\ 0P_{n2}\ 0Q_{n3}\ 1Q_{n2}^\pi\ 1P_{n3}^\pi\ 0P_{n4}\ \cdots,$$
$$T_{n+1} = 0Q_{n0}\ 1P_{n0}^\pi\ 0P_{n1}\ 0Q_{n2}\ 1Q_{n1}^\pi\ 1P_{n2}^\pi\ 0P_{n3}\ 0Q_{n4}\ 1Q_{n3}^\pi\ \cdots,$$

where $\pi = \pi_n$, revealing a reasonably simple joint recursion between the delta sequences Δ_n and E_n of S_n and T_n. Namely, if we write

$$\Delta_n = \phi_1\ a_1\ \phi_2\ a_2\dots\phi_{n-1}\ a_{n-1}\ \phi_n, \qquad E_n = \psi_1\ b_1\ \psi_2\ b_2\dots\psi_{n-1}\ b_{n-1}\ \psi_n,$$

where each ϕ_j and ψ_j is a string of length $2\binom{n-1}{j-1} - 1$, the next sequences are

$$\Delta_{n+1} = \phi_1 \, a_1 \, \phi_2 \, n \, \psi_1\pi \, b_1\pi \, \psi_2\pi \, n \, \phi_3 \, a_3 \, \phi_4 \, n \, \psi_3\pi \, b_3\pi \, \psi_4\pi \, n \, \ldots$$
$$E_{n+1} = \psi_1 \, n \, \phi_1\pi \, n \, \psi_2 \, b_2 \, \psi_3 \, n \, \phi_2\pi \, a_2\pi \, \phi_3\pi \, n \, \psi_4 \, b_4 \, \psi_5 \, n \, \phi_4\pi \, a_4\pi \, \phi_5\pi \, n \, \ldots$$

For example, we have $\Delta_3 = 010 2 1 0 1$ and $E_3 = 0 2 1 2 0 2 1$, if we underline the a's and b's to distinguish them from the ϕ's and ψ's; and

$$\Delta_4 = 0 \; 1 \; 0 \; 2 \; 1 \; 3 \; 0\pi \; 2\pi \; 1\pi \; 2\pi \; 0\pi \; 3 \; 1 \; 3 \; 1\pi = 0 \; \underline{1} \; 0 \; 2 \; 1 \; 3 \; 2 \; \underline{1} \; 0 \; 1 \; 2 \; 3 \; 1 \; \underline{3} \; 0,$$
$$E_4 = 0 \; 3 \; 0\pi \; 3 \; 1 \; 2 \; 0 \; 2 \; 1 \; 3 \; 0\pi \; 2\pi \; 1\pi \; 0\pi \; 1\pi = 0 \; \underline{3} \; 2 \; 3 \; 1 \; 2 \; 0 \; \underline{2} \; 1 \; 3 \; 2 \; 1 \; 0 \; \underline{2} \; 0;$$

here $a_3\phi_4$ and $b_3\psi_4$ are empty. Elements have been underlined for the next step.

Thus we can compute the delta sequences in memory as follows. Here $p[j] = j\pi_n$ for $1 \le j < n$; $s_k = \delta_k$, $t_k = \varepsilon_k$, and $u_k = [\delta_k$ and ε_k are underlined$]$, for $0 \le k < 2^n - 1$.

X1. [Initialize.] Set $n \leftarrow 1$, $p[0] \leftarrow 0$, $s_0 \leftarrow t_0 \leftarrow u_0 \leftarrow 0$.

X2. [Advance n.] Perform Algorithm Y below, which computes the arrays s', t', and u' for the next value of n; then set $n \leftarrow n + 1$.

X3. [Ready?] If n is sufficiently large, the desired delta sequence Δ_n is in array s'; terminate. Otherwise keep going.

X4. [Compute π_n.] Set $p'[0] \leftarrow n - 1$, and $p'[j] \leftarrow p[p[j-1]]$ for $1 \le j < n$.

X5. [Prepare to advance.] Set $p[j] \leftarrow p'[j]$ for $0 \le j < n$; set $s_k \leftarrow s'_k$, $t_k \leftarrow t'_k$, and $u_k \leftarrow u'_k$ for $0 \le k < 2^n - 1$. Return to X2. ∎

In the following steps, "Transmit stuff(l,j) while $u_j = 0$" is an abbreviation for "If $u_j = 0$, repeatedly stuff(l,j), $l \leftarrow l + 1$, $j \leftarrow j + 1$, until $u_j \ne 0$."

Y1. [Prepare to compute Δ_{n+1}.] Set $j \leftarrow k \leftarrow l \leftarrow 0$ and $u_{2^n - 1} \leftarrow -1$.

Y2. [Advance j.] Transmit $s'_l \leftarrow s_j$ and $u'_l \leftarrow 0$ while $u_j = 0$. Then go to Y5 if $u_j < 0$.

Y3. [Advance j and k.] Set $s'_l \leftarrow s_j$, $u'_l \leftarrow 1$, $l \leftarrow l + 1$, $j \leftarrow j + 1$. Then transmit $s'_l \leftarrow s_j$ and $u'_l \leftarrow 0$ while $u_j = 0$. Then set $s'_l \leftarrow n$, $u'_l \leftarrow 0$, $l \leftarrow l + 1$. Then transmit $s'_l \leftarrow p[t_k]$ and $u'_l \leftarrow 0$ while $u_k = 0$. Then set $s'_l \leftarrow p[t_k]$, $u'_l \leftarrow 1$, $l \leftarrow l + 1$, $k \leftarrow k + 1$. And once again transmit $s'_l \leftarrow p[t_k]$ and $u'_l \leftarrow 0$ while $u_k = 0$.

Y4. [Done with Δ_{n+1}?] If $u_k < 0$, go to Y6. Otherwise set $s'_l \leftarrow n$, $u'_l \leftarrow 0$, $l \leftarrow l + 1$, $j \leftarrow j + 1$, $k \leftarrow k + 1$, and return to Y2.

Y5. [Finish Δ_{n+1}.] Set $s'_l \leftarrow n$, $u'_l \leftarrow 1$, $l \leftarrow l + 1$. Then transmit $s'_l \leftarrow p[t[k]]$ and $u'_l \leftarrow 0$ while $u_k = 0$.

Y6. [Prepare to compute E_{n+1}.] Set $j \leftarrow k \leftarrow l \leftarrow 0$. Transmit $t'_l \leftarrow t_k$ while $u_k = 0$. Then set $t'_l \leftarrow n$, $l \leftarrow l + 1$.

Y7. [Advance j.] Transmit $t'_l \leftarrow p[s_j]$ while $u_j = 0$. Then terminate if $u_j < 0$; otherwise set $t'_l \leftarrow n$, $l \leftarrow l + 1$, $j \leftarrow j + 1$, $k \leftarrow k + 1$.

Y8. [Advance k.] Transmit $t'_l \leftarrow t_k$ while $u_k = 0$. Then go to Y10 if $u_k < 0$.

Y9. [Advance k and j.] Set $t'_l \leftarrow t_k$, $l \leftarrow l + 1$, $k \leftarrow k + 1$. Then transmit $t'_l \leftarrow t_k$ while $u_k = 0$. Then set $t'_l \leftarrow n$, $l \leftarrow l + 1$. Then transmit $t'_l \leftarrow p[s_j]$ while $u_j = 0$. Then set $t'_l \leftarrow p[s_j]$, $l \leftarrow l + 1$, $j \leftarrow j + 1$. Return to Y7.

Y10. [Finish E_{n+1}.] Set $t'_l \leftarrow n$, $l \leftarrow l + 1$. Then transmit $t'_l \leftarrow p[s_j]$ while $u_j = 0$. ∎

To generate the monotonic Savage–Winkler code for fairly large n, one can first generate Δ_{10} and E_{10}, say, or even Δ_{20} and E_{20}. Using these tables, a suitable recursive procedure will then be able to reach higher values of n with very little computational overhead per step, on the average.

74. If the monotonic path is $v_0, \ldots, v_{2^n-1}$ and if v_k has weight j, we have

$$2\sum_{t>0}\binom{n}{j-2t} + ((j+\nu(v_0)) \bmod 2) \le k \le 2\sum_{t\ge0}\binom{n}{j-2t} + ((j+\nu(v_0)) \bmod 2) - 2.$$

Therefore the maximum distance between vertices of respective weights j and $j+1$ is $\le 2(\binom{n-1}{j-1} + \binom{n-1}{j} + \binom{n-1}{j+1}) - 1$. The maximum value, approximately $3 \cdot 2^{n+1}/\sqrt{2\pi n}$, occurs when j is approximately $n/2$. [This is only about three times the smallest value achievable in *any* ordering of the vertices, which is $\sum_{j=0}^{n-1}\binom{j}{\lfloor j/2\rfloor}$ by exercise 7.5.6–00.]

75. The trend-free canonical delta sequences all turn out to yield Gray *cycles*:

$$0\,1\,2\,3\,0\,1\,2\,4\,2\,1\,0\,3\,2\,1\,0\,1\,2\,1\,0\,3\,2\,1\,0\,4\,0\,1\,2\,3\,0\,1\,2\,(1)$$
$$0\,1\,2\,3\,0\,1\,2\,4\,2\,1\,0\,3\,2\,1\,0\,1\,3\,0\,1\,2\,3\,0\,1\,4\,1\,0\,3\,2\,1\,0\,3\,(1)$$
$$0\,1\,2\,3\,0\,1\,2\,4\,2\,1\,0\,3\,2\,1\,0\,2\,0\,3\,2\,1\,0\,3\,2\,4\,2\,3\,0\,1\,2\,3\,0\,(2)$$
$$0\,1\,2\,3\,0\,1\,2\,4\,2\,1\,0\,3\,2\,1\,0\,2\,1\,2\,3\,0\,1\,2\,3\,4\,3\,2\,1\,0\,3\,2\,1\,(2)$$
$$0\,1\,2\,3\,0\,1\,2\,4\,2\,3\,0\,1\,2\,3\,0\,2\,0\,1\,2\,3\,0\,1\,2\,4\,2\,3\,0\,1\,2\,3\,0\,(2)$$
$$0\,1\,2\,3\,4\,1\,0\,1\,2\,1\,0\,3\,0\,1\,4\,3\,2\,1\,0\,3\,0\,1\,4\,1\,0\,1\,2\,3\,4\,1\,0\,(3)$$

(The second and fourth of these are cyclically equivalent.)

76. If $v_0, \ldots, v_{2^n-1}$ is trend-free, so is the $(n+1)$-bit cycle $0v_0, 1v_0, 1v_1, 0v_1, 0v_2, 1v_2, \ldots, 1v_{2^n-1}, 0v_{2^n-1}$. Figure 34(g) shows a somewhat more interesting construction, which generalizes the first solution of exercise 75 to an $(n+2)$-bit cycle

$$00\Gamma''^R,\ 01\Gamma'^R,\ 11\Gamma',\ 10\Gamma'',\ 10\Gamma,\ 11\Gamma''',\ 01\Gamma'''^R,\ 00\Gamma^R,$$

where Γ is the n-bit sequence $g(1), \ldots, g(2^{n-1})$ and $\Gamma' = \Gamma \oplus g(1)$, $\Gamma'' = \Gamma \oplus g(2^{n-1})$, $\Gamma''' = \Gamma \oplus g(2^{n-1}+1)$. [An n-bit trend-free design that is *almost* a Gray code, having just four steps in which $\nu(v_k \oplus v_{k+1}) = 2$, was found for all $n \ge 3$ by C. S. Cheng, *Proc. Berkeley Conf. Neyman and Kiefer* **2** (Hayward, Calif.: Inst. of Math. Statistics, 1985), 619–633.]

77. Replace the array $(o_{n-1}, \ldots, o_0)$ by an array of sentinel values $(s_{n-1}, \ldots, s_0)$, with $s_j \leftarrow m_j - 1$ in step H1. Set $a_j \leftarrow (a_j + 1) \bmod m_j$ in step H4. If $a_j = s_j$ in step H5, set $s_j \leftarrow (s_j - 1) \bmod m_j$, $f_j \leftarrow f_{j+1}$, $f_{j+1} \leftarrow j+1$.

78. For (50), notice that B_{j+1} is the number of times reflection has occurred in coordinate j, because we bypass coordinate j on steps that are multiples of $m_j \ldots m_0$. Hence, if $b_j < m_j - 1$, an increase of b_j by 1 causes a_j to increase or decrease by 1 as appropriate. Furthermore, if $b_i = m_i - 1$ for $0 \le i < j$, changing all these b_i to 0 when incrementing b_j will increase each of $B_0, \ldots, B_j$ by 1, thereby leaving the values $a_0, \ldots, a_{j-1}$ unchanged in (50).

For (51), note that $B_j = m_j B_{j+1} + b_j \equiv m_j B_{j+1} + a_j + (m_j - 1)B_{j+1} \equiv a_j + B_{j+1}$ (modulo 2); hence $B_j \equiv a_j + a_{j+1} + \cdots$, and (51) is obviously equivalent to (50).

In the modular Gray code for general radices $(m_{n-1}, \ldots, m_0)$, let

$$\bar{g}(k) = \begin{bmatrix} a_{n-1}, & \ldots, & a_2, & a_1, & a_0 \\ m_{n-1}, & \ldots, & m_2, & m_1, & m_0 \end{bmatrix}$$

when k is given by (46). Then $a_j = (b_j - B_{j+1}) \bmod m_j$, because coordinate j has increased modulo m_j exactly $B_j - B_{j+1}$ times if we start at $(0, \ldots, 0)$. The inverse function, which determines the b's from the modular Gray a's, is $b_j = (a_j + a_{j+1} + a_{j+2} + \cdots) \bmod m_j$ in the special case that each m_j is a divisor of m_{j+1} (for example, if all m_j are equal). But the inverse has no simple form in general; it can be computed by using the recurrences $b_j = (a_j + B_{j+1}) \bmod m_j$, $B_j = m_j B_{j+1} + b_j$ for $j = n - 1$, $\ldots$, 0, starting with $B_n = 0$.

[Reflected Gray codes for radix $m > 2$ were introduced by Ivan Flores in *IRE Trans.* **EC-5** (1956), 79–82; he derived (50) and (51) in the case that all m_j are equal. Modular Gray codes with general mixed radices were implicitly discussed by Joseph Rosenbaum in *AMM* **45** (1938), 694–696, but without the conversion formulas; conversion formulas when all m_j have a common value m were published by Martin Cohn, *Information and Control* **6** (1963), 70–78.]

79. (a) The last n-tuple always has $a_{n-1} = m_{n-1} - 1$, so it is one step from $(0, \ldots, 0)$ only if $m_{n-1} = 2$. And this condition suffices to make the final n-tuple $(1, 0, \ldots, 0)$. [Similarly, the final subforest output by Algorithm K is adjacent to the initial one if and only if the leftmost tree is an isolated vertex.]

(b) The last n-tuple is $(m_{n-1} - 1, 0, \ldots, 0)$ if and only if $m_{n-1} \ldots m_{j+1} \bmod m_j = 0$ for $0 \le j < n - 1$, because $b_j = m_j - 1$ and $B_j = m_{n-1} \ldots m_j - 1$.

80. Run through $p_1^{a_1} \ldots p_t^{a_t}$ using reflected Gray code with radices $m_j = e_j + 1$.

81. The first cycle contains the edge from (x, y) to $(x, (y + 1) \bmod m)$ if and only if $(x + y) \bmod m \ne m - 1$ if and only if the second cycle contains the edge from (x, y) to $((x + 1) \bmod m, y)$.

82. There are two 4-bit Gray cycles $(u_0, \ldots, u_{15})$ and $(v_0, \ldots, v_{15})$ that cover all edges of the 4-cube. (Indeed, the non-edges of classes A, B, D, H, and I in exercise 56 form Gray cycles, in the same classes as their complements.) Therefore with 16-ary modular Gray code we can form the four desired cycles $(u_0 u_0, u_0 u_1, \ldots, u_0 u_{15}, u_1 u_{15}, \ldots, u_{15} u_0)$, $(u_0 u_0, u_1 u_0, \ldots, u_{15} u_0, u_{15} u_1, \ldots, u_0 u_{15})$, $(v_0 v_0, \ldots, v_{15} v_0)$, $(v_0 v_0, \ldots, v_0 v_{15})$.

In a similar way we can show that $n/2$ edge-disjoint n-bit Gray cycles exist when n is 16, 32, 64, etc. [*Abhandlungen Math. Sem. Hamburg* **20** (1956), 13–16.] J. Aubert and B. Schneider [*Discrete Math.* **38** (1982), 7–16] have proved that the same property holds for *all* even values of $n \ge 4$, but no simple construction is known.

83. Mark Cooke found the following totally unsymmetric solution in December, 2002:

(1) 27374650573202656123165467436105251060520424163143721451014421737
2506246064173213107351607103156205713172463452102434643207054702
4147356146737625047350745130620656415073123731427376432561240264
3016735467532402524637475217640270736065105215106073575463253105;

(2) 0616713417232175171671540460247164742473202531621673531632736052
67101415030473135706154536276232411426465272021632075363710750740
3157674761545652756510451024023107353424651230406545306213710537
262050175245340670343734353150260246304562764152752406021610434;

(3) 3701063751507131236243765735103012042353747207410473621617247324
6505132565057121565024570473247421427640231034362703262764130574
0560620341745613151756314702721725205613212604053506260460173642
671764174351340124536024173063654506156302741453676432625745051;

(4) 6706546435672147236210405432054510737405170532145431636430504673
45606212064162013207423736272045064731401710205141261074523436 72
13204527523534105154263706013635673071054201631512105350617312 36
4272537165617217542510760215462375452674257037346403647376271657.

(Each of these delta sequences should start from the same vertex of the cube.) Is there a symmetrical way to do the job?

84. Calling the initial position $(2,2)$, the 8-step solution in Fig. A–1 shows how the sequence progresses down to $(0,0)$. In the first move, for example, the front half of the cord passes around and behind the right comb, then through the large right loop. The middle line should be read from right to left. The generalization to n pairs of loops would, similarly, take $3^n - 1$ steps.

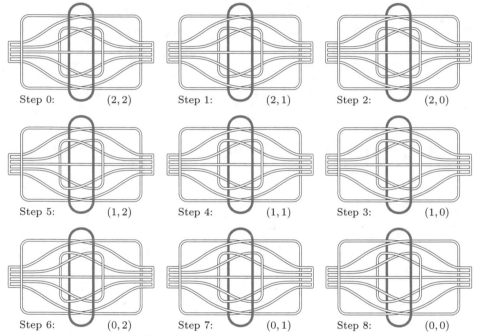

Fig. A–1. Freeing the Loony Loop.

[The origin of this delightful puzzle is obscure. *The Book of Ingenious & Diabolical Puzzles* by Jerry Slocum and Jack Botermans (1994) shows a 2-loop version carved from horn, probably made in China about 1850 [page 101], and a modern 6-loop version made in Malaysia about 1988 [page 93]. Slocum also owns a 4-loop version made from bamboo in England about 1884. He has found it listed in Henry Novra's *Catalogue of Conjuring Tricks and Puzzles* (1858 or 1859) and W. H. Cremer's *Games, Amusements, Pastimes and Magic* (1867), as well as in Hamley's catalog of 1895, under the name "Marvellous Canoe Puzzle." See also *U.S. Patents 2091191* (1937), *D172310* (1954), *3758114* (1973), *D406866* (1999). Dyckman noted its connection to reflected Gray ternary in a letter to Martin Gardner, dated 2 August 1972.]

85. By (50), element $\begin{bmatrix} b, & b' \\ t, & t' \end{bmatrix}$ of $\Gamma \wr \Gamma'$ is $\alpha_a \alpha'_{a'}$ if $\hat{g}(\begin{bmatrix} b, & b' \\ t, & t' \end{bmatrix}) = \begin{bmatrix} a, & a' \\ t, & t' \end{bmatrix}$ in the reflected Gray code for radices (t, t'). We can now show that element $\begin{bmatrix} b, & b', & b'' \\ t, & t', & t'' \end{bmatrix}$ of both $(\Gamma \wr \Gamma') \wr \Gamma''$

and $\Gamma \wr (\Gamma' \wr \Gamma'')$ is $\alpha_a \alpha'_{a'} \alpha''_{a''}$ if $\hat{g}([{}^{b,\ b',\ b''}_{t,\ t',\ t''}]) = [{}^{a,\ a',\ a''}_{t,\ t',\ t''}]$ in the reflected Gray code for radices (t, t', t''). See exercise 4.1–10, and note also the mixed-radix law

$$m_1 \ldots m_n - 1 - \begin{bmatrix} x_1, & \ldots, & x_n \\ m_1, & \ldots, & m_n \end{bmatrix} = \begin{bmatrix} m_1 - 1 - x_1, & \ldots, & m_n - 1 - x_n \\ m_1, & \ldots, & m_n \end{bmatrix}.$$

In general, the reflected Gray code for radices $(m_1, \ldots, m_n)$ is $(0, \ldots, m_1 - 1) \wr \cdots \wr (0, \ldots, m_n - 1)$. [*Information Processing Letters* **22** (1986), 201–205.]

86. Let Γ_{mn} be the reflected m-ary Gray code, which can be defined by $\Gamma_{m0} = \epsilon$ and

$$\Gamma_{m(n+1)} = (0, 1, \ldots, m - 1) \wr \Gamma_{mn}, \qquad n \geq 0.$$

This path runs from $(0, 0, \ldots, 0)$ to $(m-1, 0, \ldots, 0)$ when m is even. Consider the Gray path Π_{mn} defined by $\Pi_{m0} = \emptyset$ and

$$\Pi_{m(n+1)} = \begin{cases} (0, 1, \ldots, m - 1) \wr \Pi_{mn}, \ m\Gamma^R_{(m+1)n}, & \text{if } m \text{ is odd}; \\ (0, 1, \ldots, m) \wr \Pi_{mn}, \ m\Gamma^R_{mn}, & \text{if } m \text{ is even}. \end{cases}$$

This path traverses all of the $(m + 1)^n - m^n$ nonnegative integer n-tuples for which $\max(a_1, \ldots, a_n) = m$, starting with $(0, \ldots, 0, m)$ and ending with $(m, 0, \ldots, 0)$. The desired infinite Gray path is $\Pi_{0n}, \Pi^R_{1n}, \Pi_{2n}, \Pi^R_{3n}, \ldots$.

87. This is impossible when n is odd, because the n-tuples with $\max(|a_1|, \ldots, |a_n|) = 1$ include $\frac{1}{2}(3^n + 1)$ with odd parity and $\frac{1}{2}(3^n - 3)$ with even parity. When $n = 2$ we can use a spiral $\Sigma_0, \Sigma_1, \Sigma_2, \ldots$, where Σ_m winds counterclockwise from $(m, 1 - m)$ to $(m, -m)$ when $m > 0$. For even values of $n \geq 2$, if T_m is a path of n-tuples from $(m, 1 - m, m - 1, 1 - m, \ldots, m - 1, 1 - m)$ to $(m, -m, m, -m, \ldots, m, -m)$, we can use $\Sigma_m \wr (T_0, \ldots, T_{m-1})^R, (\Sigma_0, \ldots, \Sigma_m)^R \wr T_m$ for $(n + 2)$-tuples with the same property, where $\wr$ is the dual operation

$$\Gamma \bar{\wr} \Gamma' = (\alpha_0 \alpha'_0, \ldots, \alpha_{t-1} \alpha'_0, \alpha_{t-1} \alpha'_1, \ldots, \alpha_0 \alpha'_1, \alpha_0 \alpha'_2, \ldots, \alpha_{t-1} \alpha'_2, \alpha_{t-1} \alpha'_3, \ldots).$$

[Infinite n-dimensional Gray codes *without* the magnitude constraint were first constructed by E. Vázsonyi, *Acta Litterarum ac Scientiarum*, sectio Scientiarum Mathematicarum **9** (Szeged: 1938), 163–173.]

88. It would visit all the subforests again, but in reverse order, ending with $(0, \ldots, 0)$ and returning to the state it had after the initialization step K1. (This reflection principle is, in fact, the key to understanding how Algorithm K works.)

89. (a) Let $M_0 = \epsilon$, $M_1 = \bullet$, and $M_{n+2} = \bullet M^R_{n+1}, -M^R_n$. This construction works because the last element of M^R_{n+1} is the first element of M_{n+1}, namely a dot followed by the first element of M^R_n.

(b) Given a string $d_1 \ldots d_l$ where each d_j is $\bullet$ or $-$, we can find its successor by letting $k = l - [d_l = \bullet]$ and proceeding as follows: If k is odd and $d_k = \bullet$, change $d_k d_{k+1}$ to $-$; if k is even and $d_k = -$, change d_k to $\bullet\bullet$; otherwise decrease k by 1 and repeat until either making a change or reaching $k = 0$. The successor of the given word is $\bullet - \bullet\bullet\bullet - \bullet - \bullet$.

90. A cycle can exist only when the number of code words is even, since the number of dashes changes by ± 1 at each step. Thus we must have $n \bmod 3 = 2$. The Gray paths M_n of exercise 89 are not suitable; they begin with $(\bullet -)^{\lfloor n/3 \rfloor} \bullet^{n \bmod 3}$ and end with $(-\bullet)^{\lfloor n/3 \rfloor} \bullet^{[n \bmod 3 = 1]} -^{[n \bmod 3 = 2]}$. But $M_{3k+1} \bullet, M^R_{3k} -$ is a Hamiltonian cycle in the Morse code graph when $n = 3k + 2$.

91. Equivalently, the n-tuples $a_1 \bar{a}_2 a_3 \bar{a}_4 \ldots$ have no two consecutive 1s. Such n-tuples correspond to Morse code sequences of length $n + 1$, if we append 0 and then represent • and − respectively by 0 and 10. Under this correspondence we can convert the path M_{n+1} of exercise 89 into a procedure like Algorithm K, with the fringe containing the indices where each dot or dash begins (except for a final dot):

U1. [Initialize.] Set $a_j \leftarrow \lfloor ((j-1) \bmod 6)/3 \rfloor$ and $f_j \leftarrow j$ for $1 \le j \le n$. Also set $f_0 \leftarrow 0$, $r_0 \leftarrow 1$, $l_1 \leftarrow 0$, $r_j \leftarrow j + (j \bmod 3)$ and $l_{j+(j \bmod 3)} \leftarrow j$ for $1 \le j \le n$, except if $j + (j \bmod 3) > n$ set $r_j \leftarrow 0$ and $l_0 \leftarrow j$. (The "fringe" now contains 1, 2, 4, 5, 7, 8, ...)

U2. [Visit.] Visit the n-tuple $(a_1, \ldots, a_n)$.

U3. [Choose p.] Set $q \leftarrow l_0$, $p \leftarrow f_q$, $f_q \leftarrow q$.

U4. [Check a_p.] Terminate the algorithm if $p = 0$. Otherwise set $a_p \leftarrow 1 - a_p$ and go to U6 if $a_p + p$ is now even.

U5. [Insert $p+1$.] If $p < n$, set $q \leftarrow r_p$, $l_q \leftarrow p+1$, $r_{p+1} \leftarrow q$, $r_p \leftarrow p+1$, $l_{p+1} \leftarrow p$. Go to U7.

U6. [Delete $p+1$.] If $p < n$, set $q \leftarrow r_{p+1}$, $r_p \leftarrow q$, $l_q \leftarrow p$.

U7. [Make p passive.] Set $f_p \leftarrow f_{l_p}$ and $f_{l_p} \leftarrow l_p$. Return to U2. ∎

This algorithm can also be derived as a special case of a considerably more general method due to Gang Li, Frank Ruskey, and D. E. Knuth, which extends Algorithm K by allowing the user to specify either $a_p \ge a_q$ or $a_p \le a_q$ for each (parent, child) pair (p, q). [See Knuth and Ruskey, *Lecture Notes in Computer Science* **2635** (2004), 183–204.] A generalization in another direction, which produces all strings of length n that do not contain certain substrings, has been discovered by M. B. Squire, *Electronic J. Combinatorics* **3**, 1 (1996), #R17, 1–29.

Incidentally, it is amusing to note that the mapping $k \mapsto g(2k)$ is a one-to-one correspondence between all binary n-tuples with no consecutive 1s and all binary $(n+1)$-tuples with no odd-length runs.

92. Yes, because the digraph of all $(n-1)$-tuples $(x_1, \ldots, x_{n-1})$ with $x_1, \ldots, x_{n-1} \le m$ and with arcs $(x_1, \ldots, x_{n-1}) \to (x_2, \ldots, x_n)$ whenever $\max(x_1, \ldots, x_n) = m$ is connected and balanced; see Theorem 2.3.4.2G. Indeed, we get such a sequence from Algorithm F if we note that the final k^n elements of the prime strings of length dividing n, when subtracted from $m - 1$, are the same for all $m \ge k$. When $n = 4$, for example, the first 81 digits of the sequence Φ_4 are $2 - \alpha^R = 0\,0001\,01\,0011\ldots$, where α is the string (62). [There also are infinite m-ary sequences whose first m^n elements are de Bruijn cycles for all n, given any fixed $m \ge 3$. See L. J. Cummings and D. Wiedemann, *Cong. Numerantium* **53** (1986), 155–160.]

93. The cycle generated by $f()$ is a cyclic permutation of $\alpha 1$, where α has length $m^n - 1$ and ends with 1^{n-1}. The cycle generated by Algorithm R is a cyclic permutation of $\gamma = c_0 \ldots c_{m^{n+1}-1}$, where $c_k = (c_0 + b_0 + \cdots + b_{k-1}) \bmod m$ and $b_0 \ldots b_{m^{n+1}-1} = \beta = \alpha^m 1^m$.

If $x_0 \ldots x_n$ occurs in γ, say $x_j = c_{k+j}$ for $0 \le j \le n$, then $y_j = b_{k+j}$ for $0 \le j < n$, where $y_j = (x_{j+1} - x_j) \bmod m$. [This is the connection with modular m-ary Gray code; see exercise 78.] Now if $y_0 \ldots y_{n-1} = 1^n$ we have $m^{n+1} - m - n < k \le m^{n+1} - n$; otherwise there is an index k' such that $-n < k' < m^n - n$ and $y_0 \ldots y_{n-1}$ occurs in β at positions $k = (k' + r(m^n - 1)) \bmod m^{n+1}$ for $0 \le r < m$. In both cases the m choices of k have different values of x_0, because the sum of all elements in α is $m - 1$ (modulo m) when $n \ge 2$. [Algorithm R is valid also for $n = 1$ if $m \bmod 4 \ne 2$, because $m \perp \sum \alpha$ in that case.]

94. $00\underline{1}0\underline{2}0\underline{3}0\underline{4}1\underline{1}21\underline{3}14\underline{2}2\underline{3}24\underline{3}344$. (The underlined digits are effectively inserted into the interleaving of 00112234 with 34 as in answer 95. Algorithm D can be used in general when $n = 1$ and $r = m - 2 \geq 0$; but it is pointless to do so, in view of (54).)

95. (a) Let $c_0 c_1 c_2 \ldots$ have period r. If r is odd we have $p = q = r$, so $r = pq$ only in the trivial case when $p = q = 1$ and $a_0 = b_0$. Otherwise $r/2 = \mathrm{lcm}(p, q) = pq/\gcd(p, q)$ by 4.5.2–(10), hence $\gcd(p, q) = 2$. In the latter case the $2n$-tuples $c_l c_{l+1} \ldots c_{l+2n-1}$ that occur are $a_j b_k \ldots a_{j+n-1} b_{k+n-1}$ for $0 \leq j < p$, $0 \leq k < q$, $j \equiv k$ (modulo 2), and $b_k a_j \ldots b_{k+n-1} a_{j+n-1}$ for $0 \leq j < p$, $0 \leq k < q$, $j \not\equiv k$ (modulo 2).

(b) The output would interleave two sequences $a_0 a_1 \ldots$ and $b_0 b_1 \ldots$ whose periods are respectively $m^n + r$ and $m^n - r$; the a's are the cycle of $f()$ and $f'()$ with x^n changed to x^{n+1} and the b's are the same cycle with x^n changed to x^{n-1}, for $0 \leq x < r$. Hence we have $b_k \ldots b_{k+n-1} = a_{k+\delta_k} \ldots a_{k+n-1+\delta_k}$ for all k, where δ_k is even. By (58) and part (a), the period length is $m^{2n} - r^2$, and every $2n$-tuple occurs with the exception of $(xy)^n$ for $0 \leq x, y < r$.

(c) The real step D6 alters the behavior of (b) by going to D3 when $t \geq n$, $t' = n$, and $0 \leq x' = x < r$; this change emits an extra x at the time when x^{2n-1} has just been output and b is about to be emitted, where b is the digit following x^n in the cycle. D6 also allows control to pass to D7 and then D3 with $t' = n$ in the case that $l \geq n$ and $x < x' < r$; this behavior emits an extra $x'x$ at the time when $(xx')^{n-1}x$ has just been output and b will be next. These r^2 extra digits provide the r^2 missing $2n$-tuples of (b).

96. (a) For example, when $n = 5$ the top-level coroutine of type R invokes a coroutine of type D for $n = 4$, which invokes two of type S for $n = 2$; hence $R_5 = D_5 = 1$ and $S_5 = 2$. The recurrences $R_2 = 0$, $R_{2n+1} = 1 + R_{2n}$, $R_{2n} = 2R_n$, $D_2 = 0$, $D_{2n+1} = D_{2n} = 1 + 2D_n$, $S_2 = 1$, $S_{2n+1} = S_{2n} = 2S_n$ have the solution $R_n = n - 2S_n$, $D_n = S_n - 1$, $S_n = 2^{\lfloor \lg n \rfloor - 1}$. Thus $R_n + D_n + S_n = n - 1$.

(b) Each top-level output usually involves $\lfloor \lg n \rfloor - 1$ D-activations and $\nu(n) - 1$ R-activations, plus one basic activation at the bottom level. But there are exceptions: Algorithm R might invoke its $f()$ twice, if the first activation completed a sequence 1^n; and sometimes Algorithm R doesn't need to invoke $f()$ at all. Algorithm D might invoke its $f'()$ twice, if the first activation completed a sequence $(x')^n$ for $x' < r$; but sometimes Algorithm D doesn't need to invoke either $f()$ or $f'()$.

Algorithm R completes a sequence x^{n+1} if and only if its child $f()$ has just completed a sequence 0^n. Algorithm D completes a sequence x^{2n} for $x < r$ if and only if it has just jumped from D6 to D3 without invoking any child.

From these observations we can conclude that no exceptions arise at any level when the coroutine for an m^n-cycle produces the final digit of a run x^n, or the first digit following such a run. Hence the worst case occurs when the top-level coroutine activates a subcoroutine twice, making $2\lfloor \lg n \rfloor + 2\nu(n) - 3$ activations altogether.

97. (a) (0011), (00011101), (0000101001111011), and $(00000110001011011111$
$001110101001)$. Thus $j_2 = 2$, $j_3 = 3$, $j_4 = 9$, $j_5 = 15$.

(b) We obviously have $f_{n+1}(k) = \Sigma f_n(k) \bmod 2$ for $0 \leq k < j_n + n$. The next value, $f_{n+1}(j_n + n)$, depends on whether step R4 jumps to R2 after computing $y = f_n(j_n + n - 1)$. If it does (namely, if $f_{n+1}(j_n + n - 1) \neq 0$), we have $f_{n+1}(k) = 1 + \Sigma f_n(k+1)$ for $j_n + n \leq k < 2^n + j_n + n$; otherwise we have $f_{n+1}(k) \equiv 1 + \Sigma f_n(k-1)$ for those values of k. In particular, $f_{n+1}(k) = 1$ when $2^n \leq k + \delta_n \leq 2^n + n$. The stated formula, which has simpler ranges for the index k, holds because $1 + \Sigma f_n(k\pm 1) \equiv \Sigma f_n(k)$ when $j_n < k < j_n + n$ or $2^n + j_n < k < 2^n + j_n + n$.

(c) The interleaved cycle has $c_n(2k) = f_n^+(k)$ and $c_n(2k+1) = f_n^-(k)$, where

$$f_n^+(k) = \begin{cases} f_n(k-1), & \text{if } 0 < k \le j_n+1; \\ f_n(k-2), & \text{if } j_n+1 < k \le 2^n+2; \end{cases} \qquad f_n^-(k) = \begin{cases} f_n(k+1), & \text{if } 0 \le k < j_n; \\ f_n(k+2), & \text{if } j_n \le k < 2^n-2; \end{cases}$$

$f_n^+(k) = f_n^+(k \bmod (2^n+2))$, $f_n^-(k) = f_n^-(k \bmod (2^n-2))$. Therefore the subsequence 1^{2n-1} begins at position $k_n = (2^{n-1}-2)(2^n+2) + 2j_n+2$ in the c_n cycle; this will make j_{2n} odd. The subsequence $(01)^{n-1}0$ begins at position $l_n = (2^{n-1}+1)(j_n-1)$ if $j_n \bmod 4 = 1$, at $l_n = (2^{n-1}+1)(2^n+j_n-3)$ if $j_n \bmod 4 = 3$. Also $k_2 = 6$, $l_2 = 2$.

(d) Algorithm D inserts four elements into the c_n cycle; hence

when $j_n \bmod 4 < 3$ $(l_n < k_n)$:

$$f_{2n}(k) = \begin{cases} c_n(k-1), & \text{if } 0 < k \le l_n+2; \\ c_n(k-3), & \text{if } l_n+2 < k \le k_n+3; \\ c_n(k-4), & \text{if } k_n+3 < k \le 2^{2n}; \end{cases}$$

when $j_n \bmod 4 = 3$ $(k_n < l_n)$:

$$= \begin{cases} c_n(k-1), & \text{if } 0 < k \le k_n+1; \\ c_n(k-2), & \text{if } k_n+1 < k \le l_n+3; \\ c_n(k-4), & \text{if } l_n+3 < k \le 2^{2n}. \end{cases}$$

(e) Consequently $j_{2n} = k_n + 1 + 2[j_n \bmod 4 < 3]$. Indeed, the elements preceding 1^{2n} consist of $2^{n-2}-1$ complete periods of $f_n^+()$ interleaved with 2^{n-2} complete periods of $f_n^-()$, with one 0 inserted and also with 10 inserted if $l_n < k_n$, followed by $f_n(1)f_n(1)f_n(2)f_n(2)\ldots f_n(j_n-1)f_n(j_n-1)$. The sum of all these elements is odd, unless $l_n < k_n$; therefore $\delta_{2n} = 1 - 2[j_n \bmod 4 = 3]$.

Let $n = 2^t q$, where q is odd and $n > 2$. The recurrences imply that, if $q = 1$, we have $j_n = 2^{n-1} + b_t$ where $b_t = 2^t/3 - (-1)^t/3$. And if $q > 1$ we have $j_n = 2^{n-1} \pm b_{t+2}$, where the $+$ sign is chosen if and only if $\lfloor \lg q \rfloor + \lfloor \lfloor 4q/2^{\lfloor \lg q \rfloor} \rfloor = 5 \rfloor$ is even.

98. If $f(k) = g(k)$ when k lies in a certain range, there's a constant C such that $\Sigma f(k) = C + \Sigma g(k)$ for k in that range. We can therefore continue almost mindlessly to derive additional recurrences: If $n > 1$ we have

$\Sigma f_{2n}(k)$, when $j_n \bmod 4 < 3$ $(l_n < k_n)$:

$$\equiv \begin{cases} \Sigma c_n(k-1), & \text{if } 0 < k \le l_n+2; \\ 1 + \Sigma c_n(k-3), & \text{if } l_n+2 < k \le k_n+3; \\ \Sigma c_n(k-4), & \text{if } k_n+3 < k \le 2^{2n}; \end{cases}$$

when $j_n \bmod 4 = 3$ $(k_n < l_n)$:

$$\equiv \begin{cases} \Sigma c_n(k-1), & \text{if } 0 < k \le k_n+1; \\ 1 + \Sigma c_n(k-2), & \text{if } k_n+1 < k \le l_n+3; \\ \Sigma c_n(k-4), & \text{if } l_n+3 < k \le 2^{2n}. \end{cases}$$

$$\Sigma c_n(k) \equiv \Sigma f_n^+(\lceil k/2 \rceil) + \Sigma f_n^-(\lfloor k/2 \rfloor).$$

$$\Sigma f_n^+(k) \equiv \begin{cases} \Sigma f_n(k-1), & \text{if } 0 < k \le j_n+1; \\ 1 + \Sigma f_n(k-2), & \text{if } j_n+1 < k \le 2^n+2; \end{cases} \qquad \Sigma f_n^-(k) \equiv \begin{cases} \Sigma f_n(k+1), & \text{if } 0 \le k < j_n; \\ 1 + \Sigma f_n(k+2), & \text{if } j_n \le k < 2^n-2; \end{cases}$$

$$\Sigma f_n^\pm(k) \equiv \lfloor k/(2^n \pm 2) \rfloor + \Sigma f_n^\pm(k \bmod (2^n \pm 2)); \qquad \Sigma f_n(k) \equiv \Sigma f_n(k \bmod 2^n).$$

$$\Sigma f_{2n+1}(k) \equiv \begin{cases} \Sigma\Sigma f_{2n}(k), & \text{if } 0 < k \le j_{2n} \text{ or } 2^{2n} + j_{2n} < k \le 2^{2n+1}; \\ 1 + k + \Sigma\Sigma f_{2n}(k + \delta_{2n}), & \text{if } j_{2n} < k \le 2^{2n} + j_{2n}. \end{cases}$$

$\Sigma\Sigma f_{2n}(k)$, when $j_n \bmod 4 < 3$ $(l_n < k_n)$:

$$\equiv \begin{cases} \Sigma\Sigma c_n(k-1), & \text{if } 0 < k \le l_n+2; \\ 1 + k + \Sigma\Sigma c_n(k-3), & \text{if } l_n+2 < k \le k_n+3; \\ \Sigma\Sigma c_n(k-4), & \text{if } k_n+3 < k \le 2^{2n}; \end{cases}$$

when $j_n \bmod 4 = 3$ $(k_n < l_n)$:

$$\equiv \begin{cases} \Sigma\Sigma c_n(k-1), & \text{if } 0 < k \le k_n+1; \\ 1 + k + \Sigma\Sigma c_n(k-2), & \text{if } k_n+1 < k \le l_n+3; \\ 1 + \Sigma\Sigma c_n(k-4), & \text{if } l_n+3 < k \le 2^{2n}. \end{cases}$$

$$\Sigma\Sigma f_{2n}(k) \equiv [j_n \bmod 4 < 3]\lfloor k/2^{2n} \rfloor + \Sigma\Sigma f_{2n}(k \bmod 2^{2n}).$$

And then, aha, there is closure:

$$\Sigma\Sigma c_n(2k) = \Sigma f_n^+(k), \qquad \Sigma\Sigma c_n(2k+1) = \Sigma f_n^-(k).$$

If $n = 2^t q$ where q is odd, the running time to evaluate $f_n(k)$ by this system of recursive formulas is $O(t + S(q))$, where $S(1) = 1$, $S(2k) = 1 + 2S(k)$, and $S(2k+1) = 1 + S(k)$. Clearly $S(k) < 2k$, so the evaluations involve at most $O(n)$ simple operations on n-bit numbers. In fact, the method is often significantly faster: If we average $S(k)$ over all k with $\lfloor \lg k \rfloor = s$ we get $(3^{s+1} - 2^{s+1})/2^s$, which is less than $3k^{\lg(3/2)} < 3k^{0.59}$. (Incidentally, if $k = 2^{s+1} - 1 - (2^{s-e_1} + 2^{s-e_2} + \cdots + 2^{s-e_t})$ where $0 < e_1 < \cdots < e_t$, we have $S(k) = s + 1 + e_t + 2e_{t-1} + 4e_{t-2} + \cdots + 2^{t-1}e_1$.)

99. A string that starts at position k in $f_n()$ starts at position $k^+ = k+1+[k>j_n]$ in $f_n^+()$ and at position $k^- = k - 1 - [k>j_n]$ in $f_n^-()$, except that 0^n and 1^n occur twice in $f_n^+()$ but not at all in $f_n^-()$.

To find $\gamma = a_0 b_0 \ldots a_{n-1} b_{n-1}$ in the cycle $f_{2n}()$, let $\alpha = a_0 \ldots a_{n-1}$ and $\beta = b_0 \ldots b_{n-1}$. Suppose α starts at position j and β at position k in $f_n()$, and assume that neither α nor β is 0^n or 1^n. If $j^+ \equiv k^-$ (modulo 2), let $l/2$ be a solution to the equation $j^+ + (2^n+2)x = k^- + (2^n-2)y$; we may take $l/2 = k^- + (2^n - 2)(2^{n-3}(j^+ - k^-))$ $\bmod (2^{n-1}+1))$ if $j^+ \geq k^-$, otherwise $l/2 = j^+ + (2^n+2)(2^{n-3}(k^- - j^+) \bmod (2^{n-1}-1))$. Otherwise let $(l+1)/2 = k^+ + (2^n+2)x = j^- + 1 + (2^n - 2)y$ in a similar way. Then γ starts at position l in the cycle $c_n()$; hence it starts at position $l+1+[l \geq k_n] + 2[l \geq l_n]$ in the cycle $f_{2n}()$. Similar formulas hold when $\alpha \in \{0^n, 1^n\}$ or $\beta \in \{0^n, 1^n\}$ (but not both). Finally, 0^{2n}, 1^{2n}, $(01)^n$, and $(10)^n$ start respectively in positions 0, j_{2n}, $l_n + 1 + [k_n < l_n]$, and $l_n + 2 + [k_n < l_n]$.

To find $\beta = b_0 b_1 \ldots b_n$ in $f_{n+1}()$ when n is even, suppose the n-bit string $(b_0 \oplus b_1) \ldots (b_{n-1} \oplus b_n)$ starts at position j in $f_n()$. Then β starts at position $k = j - \delta_n [j \geq j_n] + 2^n [j = j_n][\delta_n = 1]$ if $f_{n+1}(k) = b_0$, otherwise at position $k + (2^n - \delta_n, \delta_n, 2^n + \delta_n)$ according as $(j<j_n, j=j_n, j>j_n)$.

The running time of this recursion satisfies $T(n) = O(n) + 2T(\lfloor n/2 \rfloor)$, so it is $O(n \log n)$. [Exercises 97–99 are based on the work of J. Tuliani, who also has developed methods for certain larger values of m; see *Discrete Math.* **226** (2001), 313–336.]

100. No obvious defects are apparent, but extensive testing should be done before any sequence can be recommended. By contrast, the de Bruijn cycle produced implicitly by Algorithm F is a terrible source of supposedly random bits, even though it is n-distributed in the sense of Definition 3.5D, because 0s predominate at the beginning. Indeed, when n is prime, bits $tn + 1$ of that sequence are zero for $0 \leq t < (2^n - 2)/n$.

101. (a) Let β be a proper suffix of $\lambda\lambda'$ with $\beta \leq \lambda\lambda'$. Either β is a suffix of λ', whence $\lambda < \lambda' \leq \beta$, or $\beta = \alpha\lambda'$ and we have $\lambda < \alpha < \beta$.

Now $\lambda < \beta \leq \lambda\lambda'$ implies that $\beta = \lambda\gamma$ for some $\gamma \leq \lambda'$. But γ is a suffix of β with $1 \leq |\gamma| = |\beta| - |\lambda| < |\lambda'|$; hence γ is a proper suffix of λ', and $\lambda' < \gamma$. Contradiction.

(b) Any string of length 1 is prime. Combine adjacent primes by (a), in any order, until no further combination is possible. [See the more general results of M. P. Schützenberger, *Proc. Amer. Math. Soc.* **16** (1965), 21–24.]

(c) If $t \neq 0$, let λ be the smallest suffix of $\lambda_1 \ldots \lambda_t$. Then λ is prime by definition, and it has the form $\beta\gamma$ where β is a nonempty suffix of some λ_j. Therefore $\lambda_t \leq \lambda_j \leq \beta \leq \beta\gamma = \lambda \leq \lambda_t$, so we must have $\lambda = \lambda_t$. Remove λ_t and repeat until $t = 0$.

(d) True. For if we had $\alpha = \lambda\beta$ for some prime λ with $|\lambda| > |\lambda_1|$, we could append the factors of β to obtain another factorization of α.

(e) $3 \cdot 14159265358979323846264338327 95 \cdot 02884197$. (An efficient algorithm appears in exercise 106. Knowing more digits of π would not change the first two factors. The infinite decimal expansion of any number that is "normal" in the sense of Borel (see Section 3.5) factors into primes of finite length.)

102. We must have $1/(1 - mz) = 1/\prod_{n=1}^{\infty}(1 - z^n)^{L_m(n)}$. This implies (60) as in exercise 4.6.2–4.

103. When $n = p$ is prime, (59) tells us that $L_m(1) + pL_m(p) = m^p$, and we also have $L_m(1) = m$. [This combinatorial proof provides an interesting contrast to the traditional algebraic proof of Theorem 1.2.4F.]

104. The 4483 nonprimes are `abaca`, `agora`, `ahead`, $\ldots$; the 1274 primes are $\ldots$, `rusts`, `rusty`, `rutty`. (Since `prime` isn't prime, we should perhaps call prime strings `lowly`.)

105. (a) Let α' be α with its last letter increased, and suppose $\alpha' = \beta\gamma'$ where $\alpha = \beta\gamma$ and $\beta \neq \epsilon$, $\gamma \neq \epsilon$. Let θ be the prefix of α with $|\theta| = |\gamma|$. By hypothesis there is a string ω such that $\alpha\omega$ is prime; hence $\theta \leq \alpha\omega < \gamma\omega$, so we must have $\theta \leq \gamma$. Consequently $\theta < \gamma'$, and we have $\alpha' < \gamma'$.

(b) Let $\alpha = \lambda_1\beta = a_1 \ldots a_n$ where $\lambda_1\beta\omega$ is prime and $|\lambda_1| = r$. If $a_j \neq a_{j+r}$ for some j, we must have $a_j < a_{j+r}$ for the smallest such j, because $\lambda_1\beta\omega < \beta\omega$. But then α would begin with a prime longer than λ_1, contradicting exercise 101(d).

(c) If α is the n-extension of both λ and λ', where $|\lambda| > |\lambda'|$, we must have $\lambda = (\lambda')^q\theta$ where θ is a nonempty prefix of λ'. But then $\theta \leq \lambda' < \lambda < \theta$.

106. **E1.** [Initialize.] Set $a_1 \leftarrow \cdots \leftarrow a_n \leftarrow m - 1$, $a_{n+1} \leftarrow -1$, and $j \leftarrow 1$.

E2. [Visit.] Visit $(a_1, \ldots, a_n)$ with index j.

E3. [Subtract one.] Terminate if $a_j = 0$. Otherwise set $a_j \leftarrow a_j - 1$, and $a_k \leftarrow m - 1$ for $j < k \leq n$.

E4. [Prepare to factor.] (According to exercise 105(b), we now want to find the first prime factor λ_1 of $a_1 \ldots a_n$.) Set $j \leftarrow 1$ and $k \leftarrow 2$.

E5. [Find the new j.] (Now $a_1 \ldots a_{k-1}$ is the $(k - 1)$-extension of the prime $a_1 \ldots a_j$.) If $a_{k-j} > a_k$, return to E2. Otherwise, if $a_{k-j} < a_k$, set $j \leftarrow k$. Then increase k by 1 and repeat this step. ∎

The efficient factoring algorithm in steps E4 and E5 is due to J. P. Duval, *J. Algorithms* **4** (1983), 363–381. For further information, see Cattell, Ruskey, Sawada, Serra, and Miers, *J. Algorithms* **37** (2000), 267–282.

107. The number of n-tuples visited is $P_m(n) = \sum_{j=1}^{n} L_m(j)$. Since $L_m(n) = \frac{1}{n}m^n + O(m^{n/2}/n)$, we have $P_m(n) = Q(m, n) + O(Q(\sqrt{m}, n))$, where

$$Q(m, n) = \sum_{k=1}^{n} \frac{m^k}{k} = \frac{m^n}{n} R(m, n);$$

$$R(m, n) = \sum_{k=0}^{n-1} \frac{m^{-k}}{1 - k/n} = \sum_{k=0}^{n/2} \frac{m^{-k}}{1 - k/n} + O(nm^{-n/2})$$

$$= \frac{m}{m - 1} \sum_{j=0}^{t-1} \frac{1}{n^j} \sum_{l} \left\{ {j \atop l} \right\} \frac{l!}{(m - 1)^l} + O(n^{-t}), \quad \text{for all } t.$$

Thus $P_m(n) \sim m^{n+1}/((m - 1)n)$. The main contributions to the running time come from the loops in steps F3 and F5, which cost $n - j$ for each prime of length j, hence a total of $nP_m(n) - \sum_{j=1}^{n} jL_m(j) = m^{n+1}(1/((m - 1)^2 n) + O(1/(mn^2)))$. This is less than the time needed to output the m^n individual digits of the de Bruijn cycle.

108. (a) If $\alpha \ne 9 \ldots 9$, we have $\beta\alpha < \lambda_{k+1} \le \beta 9^{|\alpha|}$, because the latter is prime.

(b) We can assume that β is not all 0s, since $9^j 0^{n-j}$ is a substring of $\lambda_{t-1}\lambda_t\lambda_1\lambda_2 = 89^n 0^n 1$. Let k be minimal with $\beta \le \lambda_k$; then $\lambda_k \le \beta\alpha$, so β is a prefix of λ_k. Since β is a preprime, it is the $|\beta|$-extension of some prime $\beta' \le \beta$. The preprime visited by Algorithm F just before β' is $(\beta' - 1)9^{n-|\beta'|}$, by exercise 106, where $\beta' - 1$ denotes the decimal number that is one less than β'. Thus, if β' is not λ_{k-1}, the hint (which also follows from exercise 106) implies that λ_{k-1} ends with at least $n - |\beta'| \ge n - |\beta|$ 9s, and α is a suffix of λ_{k-1}. On the other hand if $\beta' = \lambda_{k-1}$, α is a suffix of λ_{k-2} because $|\beta'| \le n/2$, and β is a prefix of $\lambda_{k-1}\lambda_k$.

(c) If $\alpha \ne 9 \ldots 9$, we have $\lambda_{k+1} \le (\beta\alpha)^{d-1}\beta 9^{|\alpha|}$, because the latter is prime. Otherwise λ_{k-1} ends with at least $(d-1)|\beta\alpha|$ 9s, and $\lambda_{k+1} \le (\beta\alpha)^{d-1}9^{|\beta\alpha|}$, so $(\alpha\beta)^d$ is a substring of $\lambda_{k-1}\lambda_k\lambda_{k+1}$.

(d) Within the primes $135899\,135914$, $787899\,787979$, $129999\,13\,131314$, $09\,090911$, $089999\,09\,090911$, $118999\,119\,119122$.

(e) Yes: In all cases, the position of $a_1 \ldots a_n$ precedes the position of the substring $a_1 \ldots a_{n-1}(a_n + 1)$, if $0 \le a_n < 9$ (and if we assume that strings like $9^j 0^{n-j}$ occur at the beginning). Furthermore $9^j 0^{n-j-1}$ occurs only after $9^{j-1}0^{n-j}a$ has appeared for $1 \le a \le 9$, so we must not place 0 after $9^j 0^{n-j-1}$. [See E. Moreno and D. Perrin, *Advances in Applied Mathematics* **33** (2004), 413–415; **62** (2015), 184–187.]

109. Suppose we want to locate the submatrix

$$\begin{pmatrix} (w_{n-1} \ldots w_1 w_0)_2 & (x_{n-1} \ldots x_1 x_0)_2 \\ (y_{n-1} \ldots y_1 y_0)_2 & (z_{n-1} \ldots z_1 z_0)_2 \end{pmatrix}.$$

The binary case $n = 1$ is the given example, and if $n > 1$ we can assume by induction that we only need to determine the leading bits a_{2n-1}, a_{2n-2}, b_{2n-1}, and b_{2n-2}. The case $n = 3$ is typical: We must solve

$$\begin{array}{llll} b_5 = w_2, & b_4 = x_2, & a_5 \oplus b_5 = y_2, & a_4 \oplus b_4 = z_2, & \text{if } a_0 = 0, b_0 = 0; \\ b_4 = w_2, & b_5' = x_2, & a_4 \oplus b_4 = y_2, & a_5 \oplus b_5' = z_2, & \text{if } a_0 = 0, b_0 = 1; \\ a_5 \oplus b_5 = w_2, & a_4 \oplus b_4 = x_2, & b_5 = y_2, & b_4 = z_2, & \text{if } a_0 = 1, b_0 = 0; \\ a_4 \oplus b_4 = w_2, & a_5 \oplus b_5' = x_2, & b_4 = y_2, & b_5' = z_2, & \text{if } a_0 = 1, b_0 = 1; \end{array}$$

here $b_5' = b_5 \oplus b_4 b_3 b_2 b_1$ takes account of carrying when j becomes $j + 1$.

[Binary examples were first considered by I. S. Reed and R. M. Stewart, *IRE Trans.* **IT-8** (1962), 10–12, who called them "perfect maps"; they allowed also certain generalized toruses as in exercise 7–137. Many subsequent authors decided to support only the $2^{mn} - 1$ *nonzero* settings of $m \times n$ windows; see F. J. MacWilliams and N. J. A. Sloane, *Proc. IEEE* **64** (1976), 1715–1729.]

110. Let $a_0 a_1 \ldots a_{m^2-1}$ be an m-ary de Bruijn cycle, such as the first m^2 elements of (54). If m is odd, let $d_{ij} = a_j$ when i is even, $d_{ij} = a_{(j+(i+1)/2) \bmod m^2}$ when i is odd, for $0 \le i, j < m^2$. [The first of many people to discover this construction seems to have been John C. Cock, who also constructed de Bruijn toruses of other shapes and sizes in *Discrete Math.* **70** (1988), 209–210.]

If $m = m'm''$ where $m' \perp m''$, we use the Chinese remainder algorithm to define

$$d_{ij} \equiv d_{ij}' \pmod{m'} \quad \text{and} \quad d_{ij} \equiv d_{ij}'' \pmod{m''}$$

in terms of matrices that solve the problem for m' and m''. Thus the previous exercise leads to a solution for arbitrary m.

Another interesting solution for even values of m was found by Antal Iványi and Zoltán Tóth [*2nd Conf. Automata, Languages, and Programming Systems* (1988), 165–172; see also Hurlbert and Isaak, *Contemp. Math.* **178** (1994), 153–160]. The first m^2 elements a_j of the infinite sequence

0011 021331203223 04152435534251405445 0617263746577564...07667 08...

define a de Bruijn cycle with the property that the distance between the appearances of ab and ba is always even. Then we can let $d_{ij} = a_j$ if $i + j$ is even, $d_{ij} = a_i$ if $i + j$ is odd. For example, when $m = 4$ we have

$$
\begin{pmatrix}
0010021220302232 \\
0001020320212223 \\
0111031321312333 \\
1011121330313233 \\
0010021220302232 \\
0203000122232021 \\
0111031321312333 \\
1213101132333031 \\
0010021220302232 \\
2021222300010203 \\
0111031321312333 \\
3031323310111213 \\
0010021220302232 \\
2223202102030001 \\
0111031321312333 \\
3233303112131011
\end{pmatrix}
\text{(exercise 109);}
\quad
\begin{pmatrix}
0010001030203020 \\
0001020301000203 \\
0111011131213121 \\
1011121311101213 \\
0010001030203020 \\
2021222321202223 \\
0111011131213121 \\
3031323331303233 \\
0313031333233323 \\
1011121311101213 \\
0212021232223222 \\
0001020301000203 \\
0313031333233323 \\
2021222321202223 \\
0212021232223222 \\
3031323331303233
\end{pmatrix}
\text{(Tóth).}
$$

111. (a) Let $d_j = j$ and $0 \le a_j < 3$ for $1 \le j \le 9$, $a_9 \ne 0$. Form sequences s_j, t_j by the rules $s_1 = 0$, $t_1 = d_1$; $t_{j+1} = d_{j+1} + 10t_j[a_j = 0]$ for $1 \le j < 9$; $s_{j+1} = s_j + (0, t_j, -t_j)$ for $a_j = (0, 1, 2)$ and $1 \le j \le 9$. Then s_{10} is a possible result; we need only remember the smallish values that occur. More than half the work is saved by disallowing $a_k = 2$ when $s_k = 0$, then using $|s_{10}|$ instead of s_{10}. Since fewer than $3^8 = 6561$ possibilities need to be tried, brute force via the ternary version of Algorithm M works well; fewer than 24,000 mems and 1600 multiplications are needed to deduce that all integers less than 211 are representable, but 211 is not.

Another approach, using Gray code to vary the signs after breaking the digits into blocks in 2^8 possible ways, reduces the number of multiplications to 255, but at the cost of about 500 additional mems. Therefore Gray code is not advantageous in this application.

(b) Now (with 73,000 mems and 4900 multiplications) we can reach all numbers less than 241, but not 241. There are 46 ways to represent 100, including the remarkable $9 - 87 + 6 + 5 - 43 + 210$.

[H. E. Dudeney introduced his "century" problem in *The Weekly Dispatch* (4 and 18 June 1899). See also *The Numerology of Dr. Matrix* by Martin Gardner, Chapter 6; Steven Kahan, *J. Recreational Math.* **23** (1991), 19–25; and exercise 7.2.1.6–122.]

112. The method of exercise 111 now needs more than 167 million mems and 10 million multiplications, because 3^{16} is so much larger than 3^8. We can do much better (10.4 million mems, 1100 mults) by first tabulating the possibilities obtainable from the first k and last k digits, for $1 \le k < 9$, then considering all blocks of digits that use the 9. There are 60,318 ways to represent 100, and the first unreachable number is 16,040.

SECTION 7.2.1.2

1. [J. P. N. Phillips, *Comp. J.* **10** (1967), 311.] Assuming that $n \ge 3$, we can replace steps L2–L4 by:

L2′. [Easiest case?] Set $y \leftarrow a_{n-1}$ and $z \leftarrow a_n$. If $y < z$, set $a_{n-1} \leftarrow z$, $a_n \leftarrow y$, and return to L1.

L2.1'. [Next easiest case?] Set $x \leftarrow a_{n-2}$. If $x \geq y$, go on to step L2.2'. Otherwise set $(a_{n-2}, a_{n-1}, a_n) \leftarrow (z, x, y)$ if $x < z$, (y, z, x) if $x \geq z$. Return to L1.

L2.2'. [Find j.] Set $j \leftarrow n - 3$ and $y \leftarrow a_j$. While $y \geq x$, set $j \leftarrow j - 1$, $x \leftarrow y$, and $y \leftarrow a_j$. Terminate if $j = 0$.

L3'. [Easy increase?] If $y < z$, set $a_j \leftarrow z$, $a_{j+1} \leftarrow y$, $a_n \leftarrow x$, and go to L4.1'.

L3.1'. [Increase a_j.] Set $l \leftarrow n - 1$; if $y \geq a_l$, repeatedly decrease l by 1 until $y < a_l$. Then set $a_j \leftarrow a_l$ and $a_l \leftarrow y$.

L4'. [Begin to reverse.] Set $a_n \leftarrow a_{j+1}$ and $a_{j+1} \leftarrow z$.

L4.1'. [Reverse $a_{j+2} \ldots a_{n-1}$.] Set $k \leftarrow j + 2$ and $l \leftarrow n - 1$. Then, while $k < l$, interchange $a_k \leftrightarrow a_l$ and set $k \leftarrow k + 1$, $l \leftarrow l - 1$. Return to L1. ∎

The program might run still faster if a_t is stored in memory location $A[n - t]$ for $0 \leq t \leq n$, or if reverse colex order is used as in the following exercise.

2. Again we assume that $a_1 \leq a_2 \leq \cdots \leq a_n$ initially; the permutations generated from $\{1, 2, 2, 3\}$ will, however, be 1223, 2123, 2213, ..., 2321, 3221. Let a_{n+1} be an auxiliary element, *larger* than a_n.

M1. [Visit.] Visit the permutation $a_1 a_2 \ldots a_n$.

M2. [Find j.] Set $j \leftarrow 2$. If $a_{j-1} \geq a_j$, increase j by 1 until $a_{j-1} < a_j$. Terminate if $j > n$.

M3. [Decrease a_j.] Set $l \leftarrow 1$. If $a_l \geq a_j$, increase l until $a_l < a_j$. Then swap $a_l \leftrightarrow a_j$.

M4. [Reverse $a_1 \ldots a_{j-1}$.] Set $k \leftarrow 1$ and $l \leftarrow j - 1$. Then, if $k < l$, swap $a_k \leftrightarrow a_l$, set $k \leftarrow k + 1$, $l \leftarrow l - 1$, and repeat until $k \geq l$. Return to M1. ∎

3. Let $C_1 \ldots C_n = c_{a_1} \ldots c_{a_n}$ be the inversion table, as in exercise 5.1.1–7. Then $\text{rank}(a_1 \ldots a_n)$ is the mixed-radix number $\left[\begin{smallmatrix} C_1, & \ldots, & C_{n-1}, & C_n \\ n, & \ldots, & 2, & 1 \end{smallmatrix} \right]$. [See H. A. Rothe, *Sammlung combinatorisch-analytischer Abhandlungen* **2** (1800), 263–264; and see also the pioneering work of Śārṅgadeva and Nārāyaṇa cited in Section 7.2.1.7.] For example, 314592687 has rank $\left[\begin{smallmatrix} 2, & 0, & 1, & 1, & 4, & 0, & 0, & 1, & 0 \\ 9, & 8, & 7, & 6, & 5, & 4, & 3, & 2, & 1 \end{smallmatrix} \right] = 2 \cdot 8! + 6! + 5! + 4 \cdot 4! + 1! = 81577$; this is the factorial number system featured in Eq. 4.1–(10).

4. Use the recurrence $\text{rank}(a_1 \ldots a_n) = \frac{1}{n} \sum_{j=1}^{t} n_j [x_j < a_1] \binom{n}{n_1, \ldots, n_t} + \text{rank}(a_2 \ldots a_n)$. For example, $\text{rank}(314159265)$ is

$$\tfrac{3}{9} \binom{9}{2,1,1,1,2,1,1} + 0 + \tfrac{2}{7} \binom{7}{1,1,1,2,1,1} + 0 + \tfrac{1}{5} \binom{5}{1,2,1,1} + \tfrac{3}{4} \binom{4}{1,1,1,1} + 0 + \tfrac{1}{2} \binom{2}{1,1} = 30991.$$

5. (a) Step L2 is performed $n!$ times. The probability that exactly k comparisons are made is $q_k - q_{k+1}$, where q_t is the probability that $a_{n-t+1} > \cdots > a_n$, namely $[t \leq n]/t!$. Therefore the mean is $\sum k(q_k - q_{k+1}) = q_1 + \cdots + q_n = \lfloor n! e \rfloor / n! - 1 \approx e - 1 \approx 1.718$, and the variance is

$$\sum k^2 (q_k - q_{k+1}) - \text{mean}^2 = q_1 + 3q_2 + \cdots + (2n-1)q_n - (q_1 + \cdots + q_n)^2 \approx e(3-e) \approx 0.766.$$

[For higher moments, see R. Kemp, *Acta Informatica* **35** (1998), 17–89, Theorem 4.]

Incidentally, the average number of interchange operations in step L4 is therefore $\sum \lfloor k/2 \rfloor (q_k - q_{k+1}) = q_2 + q_4 + \cdots \approx \cosh 1 - 1 = (e + e^{-1} - 2)/2 \approx 0.543$, a result due to R. J. Ord-Smith [*Comp. J.* **13** (1970), 152–155].

(b) Step L3 is performed only $n! - 1$ times, but we will assume for convenience that it occurs once more (with 0 comparisons). Then the probability that exactly k

comparisons are made is $\sum_{j=k+1}^{n} 1/j!$ for $1 \le k < n$ and $1/n!$ for $k = 0$. Hence the mean is $\frac{1}{2}\sum_{j=0}^{n-2} 1/j! \approx e/2 \approx 1.359$; exercise 1 reduces this number by $\frac{2}{3}$. The variance is $\frac{1}{3}\sum_{j=0}^{n-3} 1/j! + \frac{1}{2}\sum_{j=0}^{n-2} 1/j! - \text{mean}^2 \approx \frac{5}{6}e - \frac{1}{4}e^2 \approx 0.418$.

6. (a) Let $e_n(z) = \sum_{k=0}^{n} z^k/k!$; then the number of different prefixes $a_1 \ldots a_j$ is $j! [z^j] e_{n_1}(z) \ldots e_{n_t}(z)$. This is $N = \binom{n}{n_1,\ldots,n_t}$ times the probability q_{n-j} that at least $n-j$ comparisons are made in step L2. Therefore the mean is $\frac{1}{N}w(e_{n_1}(z) \ldots e_{n_t}(z)) - 1$, where $w(\sum x_k z^k/k!) = \sum x_k$. In the binary case the mean is $M/\binom{n}{s} - 1$, where $M = \sum_{l=0}^{s} \sum_{k=l}^{n-s+l} \binom{k}{l} = \sum_{l=0}^{s}\binom{n-s+l+1}{l+1} = \binom{n+2}{s+1} - 1 = \binom{n}{s}(2 + \frac{s}{n-s+1} + \frac{n-s}{s+1}) - 1$.

(b) If $\{a_1,\ldots,a_j\} = \{n_1' \cdot x_1, \ldots, n_t' \cdot x_t\}$, the prefix $a_1 \ldots a_j$ contributes altogether $\sum_{1 \le k < l \le t}(n_k - n_k')[n_l > n_l']$ to the total number of comparisons made in step L3. Thus the mean is $\frac{1}{N}\sum_{1 \le k < l \le t} w(f_{kl}(z))$, where

$$f_{kl}(z) = \left(\prod_{\substack{1 \le m \le t \\ m \ne k,\, m \ne l}} e_{n_m}(z) \right)\left(\sum_{r=0}^{n_k}(n_k - r)\frac{z^r}{r!} \right) e_{n_l - 1}(z)$$

$$= e_{n_1}(z) \ldots e_{n_t}(z)(n_k - z r_k(z)) r_l(z), \qquad \text{where } r_k(z) = \frac{e_{n_k - 1}(z)}{e_{n_k}(z)}.$$

In the two-valued case this formula reduces to $\frac{1}{N}w((se_s(z) - ze_{s-1}(z))e_{n-s-1}(z)) = \frac{s}{N}(\binom{n+1}{s+1} - 1) - \frac{1}{N}(\binom{n+1}{s+1}(s - \frac{s+1}{n-s+1}) + 1) = \frac{1}{N}(-s - 1 + \binom{n+1}{s}) = \frac{n+1}{n-s+1} - \frac{s+1}{N}$.

7. In the notation of the previous answer, the quantity $\frac{1}{N}w(e_{n_1}(z) \ldots e_{n_t}(z)) - 1$ is

$$\frac{n_1 + \cdots + n_t}{n} + \frac{(n_1 n_2 + n_1 n_3 + \cdots + n_{t-1} n_t) + n_1(n_1 - 1) + \cdots + n_t(n_t - 1)}{n(n-1)} + \cdots.$$

One can show using Eq. 1.2.9–(38) that the limit is $-1 + \exp \sum_{k \ge 1} r_k/k$, where $r_k = \lim_{t \to \infty}(n_1^k + \cdots + n_t^k)/(n_1 + \cdots + n_t)^k$. In cases (a) and (b) we have $r_k = [k{=}1]$, so the limit is $e - 1 \approx 1.71828$. In case (c) we have $r_k = 1/(2^k - 1)$, so the limit is $-1 + \exp \sum_{k \ge 1} 1/(k(2^k - 1)) \approx 2.46275$.

8. Assume that j is initially zero, and change step L1 to

L1'. [Visit.] Visit the variation $a_1 \ldots a_j$. If $j < n$, set $j \leftarrow j + 1$ and repeat this step. ∎

This algorithm is due to L. J. Fischer and K. C. Krause, *Lehrbuch der Combinationslehre und der Arithmetik* (Dresden: 1812), 55–57.

Incidentally, the total number of variations is $w(e_{n_1}(z) \ldots e_{n_t}(z))$ in the notation of answer 6. This counting problem was first treated by James Bernoulli in *Ars Conjectandi* (1713), Part 2, Chapter 9.

9. Assume that $r > 0$ and that we begin with $a_0 < a_1 \le a_2 \le \cdots \le a_n$.

R1. [Visit.] Visit the variation $a_1 \ldots a_r$. (At this point $a_{r+1} \le \cdots \le a_n$.)

R2. [Easy case?] If $a_r < a_n$, interchange $a_r \leftrightarrow a_j$ where j is the smallest subscript such that $j > r$ and $a_j > a_r$, and return to R1.

R3. [Reverse.] Set $(a_{r+1},\ldots,a_n) \leftarrow (a_n,\ldots,a_{r+1})$ as in step L4.

R4. [Find j.] Set $j \leftarrow r - 1$. If $a_j \ge a_{j+1}$, decrease j by 1 repeatedly until $a_j < a_{j+1}$. Terminate if $j = 0$.

R5. [Increase a_j.] Set $l \leftarrow n$. If $a_j \ge a_l$, decrease l by 1 repeatedly until $a_j < a_l$. Then interchange $a_j \leftrightarrow a_l$.

R6. [Reverse again.] Set $(a_{j+1}, \ldots, a_n) \leftarrow (a_n, \ldots, a_{j+1})$ as in step L4, and return to R1. ∎

The number of outputs is $r!\,[z^r]\,e_{n_1}(z)\ldots e_{n_t}(z)$; this is, of course, $n^{\underline{r}}$ when the elements are distinct.

10. $a_1 a_2 \ldots a_n = 213 \ldots n$, $c_1 c_2 \ldots c_n = 010 \ldots 0$, $o_1 o_2 \ldots o_n = 1(-1)1 \ldots 1$, if $n \geq 2$.

11. Step (P1, ..., P7) is performed $(1, n!, n!, n! + x_n, n! - 1, (x_n + 3)/2, x_n)$ times, where $x_n = \sum_{k=1}^{n-1} k!$, because P7 is performed $(j-1)!$ times when $2 \leq j \leq n$.

12. We want the permutation of rank 999999. The answers are (a) 2783915460, by exercise 3; (b) 8750426319, because the reflected mixed-radix number corresponding to $\begin{bmatrix} 0, & 0, & 1, & 2, & 3, & 0, & 2, & 7, & 0, & 9 \\ 1, & 2, & 3, & 4, & 5, & 6, & 7, & 8, & 9, & 10 \end{bmatrix}$ is $\begin{bmatrix} 0, & 0, & 1, & 3-2, & 3, & 5-0, & 2, & 7, & 8-0, & 9-9 \\ 1, & 2, & 3, & 4, & 5, & 6, & 7, & 8, & 9, & 10 \end{bmatrix}$ by 7.2.1.1–(50); (c) the product $(0\ 1\ \ldots\ 9)^9 (0\ 1\ \ldots\ 8)^0 (0\ 1\ \ldots\ 7)^7 (0\ 1\ \ldots\ 6)^2 \ldots (0\ 1\ 2)^1$, namely 9703156248.

13. The first statement is true for all $n \geq 2$. But when 2 crosses 1, namely when c_2 changes from 0 to 1, we have $c_3 = 2$, $c_4 = 3$, $c_5 = \cdots = c_n = 0$, and the next permutation when $n \geq 5$ is $432156 \ldots n$. [See *Time Travel* (1988), page 74.]

14. True at the beginning of steps P4, P5, and P6, because exactly $j - 1 - c_j + s$ elements lie to the left of x_j, namely $j - 1 - c_j$ from $\{x_1, \ldots, x_{j-1}\}$ and s from $\{x_{j+1}, \ldots, x_n\}$. (In a sense, this formula is the main point of Algorithm P.)

15. If $\begin{bmatrix} b_{n-1}, & \ldots, & b_0 \\ 1, & \ldots, & n \end{bmatrix}$ corresponds to the reflected Gray code $\begin{bmatrix} c_1, & \ldots, & c_n \\ 1, & \ldots, & n \end{bmatrix}$, we get to step P6 if and only if $b_{n-k} = k - 1$ for $j \leq k \leq n$ and B_{n-j+1} is even, by 7.2.1.1–(50). But $b_{n-k} = k - 1$ for $j \leq k \leq n$ implies that B_{n-k} is odd for $j < k \leq n$. Therefore $s = [c_{j+1} = j] + [c_{j+2} = j + 1] = [o_{j+1} < 0] + [o_{j+2} < 0]$ in step P5. [See *Math. Comp.* **17** (1963), 282–285.]

16. P1'. [Initialize.] Set $c_j \leftarrow j$ and $o_j \leftarrow -1$ for $1 \leq j < n$; also set $z \leftarrow a_n$.

P2'. [Visit.] Visit $a_1 \ldots a_n$. Then go to P3.5' if $a_1 = z$.

P3'. [Hunt down.] For $j \leftarrow n - 1, n - 2, \ldots, 1$ (in this order), set $a_{j+1} \leftarrow a_j$, $a_j \leftarrow z$, and visit $a_1 \ldots a_n$. Then set $j \leftarrow n - 1$, $s \leftarrow 1$, and go to P4'.

P3.5'. [Hunt up.] For $j \leftarrow 1, 2, \ldots, n - 1$ (in this order), set $a_j \leftarrow a_{j+1}$, $a_{j+1} \leftarrow z$, and visit $a_1 \ldots a_n$. Then set $j \leftarrow n - 1$, $s \leftarrow 0$.

P4'. [Ready to change?] Set $q \leftarrow c_j + o_j$. If $q = 0$, go to P6'; if $q > j$, go to P7'.

P5'. [Change.] Interchange $a_{c_j + s} \leftrightarrow a_{q+s}$. Then set $c_j \leftarrow q$ and return to P2'.

P6'. [Increase s.] Terminate if $j = 1$; otherwise set $s \leftarrow s + 1$.

P7'. [Switch direction.] Set $o_j \leftarrow -o_j$, $j \leftarrow j - 1$, and go back to P4'. ∎

17. Initially $a_j \leftarrow a_j' \leftarrow j$ for $1 \leq j \leq n$. Step P5 should now set $t \leftarrow j - c_j + s$, $u \leftarrow j - q + s$, $v \leftarrow a_u$, $a_t \leftarrow v$, $a_v' \leftarrow t$, $a_u \leftarrow j$, $a_j' \leftarrow u$, $c_j \leftarrow q$. (See exercise 14.)

But with the inverse required and available we can actually simplify the algorithm significantly, avoiding the offset variable s and letting the control table $c_1 \ldots c_n$ count only downwards, as noted by G. Ehrlich [*JACM* **20** (1973), 505–506]:

Q1. [Initialize.] Set $a_j \leftarrow a_j' \leftarrow j$, $c_j \leftarrow j - 1$, and $o_j \leftarrow -1$ for $1 \leq j \leq n$. Also set $c_0 \leftarrow -1$.

Q2. [Visit.] Visit the permutation $u_1 \ldots a_n$ and its inverse $a_1' \ldots a_n'$.

Q3. [Find k.] Set $k \leftarrow n$. Then, while $c_k = 0$, set $c_k \leftarrow k - 1$, $o_k \leftarrow -o_k$, and $k \leftarrow k - 1$. Terminate if $k = 0$.

Q4. [Change.] Set $c_k \leftarrow c_k - 1$, $j \leftarrow a_k'$, and $i \leftarrow j + o_k$. Then set $t \leftarrow a_i$, $a_i \leftarrow k$, $a_j \leftarrow t$, $a_t' \leftarrow j$, $a_k' \leftarrow i$, and return to Q2. ∎

18. Set $a_n \leftarrow n$, and use $(n-1)!/2$ iterations of Algorithm P to generate all permutations of $\{1, \ldots, n-1\}$ such that 1 precedes 2. [M. K. Roy, *CACM* **16** (1973), 312–313; see also exercise 13.]

19. For example, we can use the idea of Algorithm P, with the n-tuples $c_1 \ldots c_n$ changing as in Algorithm 7.2.1.1H with respect to the radices $(1, 2, \ldots, n)$. That algorithm maintains the directions correctly, although it numbers subscripts differently. The offset s needed by Algorithm P can be computed as in answer 15, or the inverse permutation can be maintained as in exercise 17. [See G. Ehrlich, *CACM* **16** (1973), 690–691.] Other algorithms, like that of Heap, can also be implemented looplessly.

(*Note:* In most applications of permutation generation we are interested in minimizing the *total* running time, not the maximum time between successive visits; from this standpoint looplessness is usually undesirable, except on a parallel computer. Yet there's something intellectually satisfying about the fact that a loopless algorithm exists, whether practical or not.)

20. For example, when $n = 3$ we can begin 123, 132, 312, $\bar{3}12$, $1\bar{3}2$, $12\bar{3}$, $21\bar{3}$, ..., 213, $\bar{2}13$, ... If the delta sequence for n is $(\delta_1 \delta_2 \ldots \delta_{2^n n!})$, the corresponding sequence for $n+1$ is $(\Delta_n \delta_1 \Delta_n \delta_2 \ldots \Delta_n \delta_{2^n n!})$, where Δ_n is the sequence of $2n+1$ operations n $n-1$ $\ldots$ 1 $-$ 1 $\ldots$ $n-1$ n; here $\delta_k = j$ means $a_j \leftrightarrow a_{j+1}$ and $\delta_k = -$ means $a_1 \leftarrow -a_1$.

(Signed permutations appear in another guise in exercises 5.1.4–43 and 44. The set of all signed permutations is called the hyperoctahedral group $\mathcal{B}_n$.)

21. Clearly $\mathtt{M} = 1$, hence $\mathtt{O}$ must be 0 and $\mathtt{S}$ must be $b-1$. Then $\mathtt{N} = \mathtt{E} + 1$, $\mathtt{R} = b-2$, and $\mathtt{D} + \mathtt{E} = b + \mathtt{Y}$. This leaves exactly $\max(0, b-7-k)$ choices for $\mathtt{E}$ when $\mathtt{Y} = k \geq 2$, hence a total of $\sum_{k=2}^{b-7}(b-7-k) = \binom{b-8}{2}$ solutions when $b \geq 8$. [*Math. Mag.* **45** (1972), 48–49. Incidentally, D. Eppstein has proved that the task of solving alphametics with a given radix is NP-complete; see *SIGACT News* **18**, 3 (1987), 38–40.]

22. $(\mathtt{X})_b + (\mathtt{X})_b = (\mathtt{XY})_b$ is solvable only when $b = 2$.

23. Almost true, because the number of solutions will be even, *unless* $[j \in F] \neq [k \in F]$. (Consider the ternary alphametic $\mathtt{X} + (\mathtt{XX})_3 + (\mathtt{YY})_3 + (\mathtt{XZ})_3 = (\mathtt{XYX})_3$.)

24. (a) $9283 + 7 + 473 + 1062 = 10825$. (b) $698392 + 3192 = 701584$. (c) $63952 + 69275 = 133227$. (d) $653924 + 653924 = 1307848$. (e) $5718 + 3 + 98741 = 104462$. (f) $127503 + 502351 + 3947539 + 46578 = 4623971$. (g) $67432 + 704 + 8046 + 97364 = 173546$. (h) $59 + 577404251698 + 69342491650 + 49869442698 + 1504 + 40614 + 82591 + 344 + 41 + 741425 = 5216367650 + 691400684974$. [All solutions are unique. References for (b)–(g): *J. Recreational Math.* **10** (1977), 115; **5** (1972), 296; **10** (1977), 41; **10** (1978), 274; **12** (1979), 133–134; **9** (1977), 207.]

(i) In this case there are $\frac{8}{10} 10! = 2903040$ solutions, because *every* permutation of $\{0, 1, \ldots, 9\}$ works except those that assign $\mathtt{H}$ or $\mathtt{N}$ to 0. (A well-written general additive alphametic solver will be careful to reduce the amount of output in such cases.)

25. We may assume that $s_1 \leq \cdots \leq s_{10}$. Let i be the least index $\notin F$, and set $a_i \leftarrow 0$; then set the remaining elements a_j in order of increasing j. A proof like that of Theorem 6.1S shows that this procedure maximizes $a \cdot s$. A similar procedure yields the minimum, because $\min(a \cdot s) = -\max(a \cdot (-s))$.

26. $400739 + 63930 - 2379 - 1252630 + 53430 - 1390 + 738300$.

27. Readers can probably improve upon the following examples: $\mathtt{BLOOD} + \mathtt{SWEAT} + \mathtt{TEARS} = \mathtt{LATER}$; $\mathtt{EARTH} + \mathtt{WATER} + \mathtt{WRATH} = \mathtt{HELLO} + \mathtt{WORLD}$; $\mathtt{AWAIT} + \mathtt{ROBOT} + \mathtt{ERROR} = \mathtt{SOBER} + \mathtt{WORDS}$; $\mathtt{CHILD} + \mathtt{THEME} + \mathtt{PEACE} + \mathtt{ETHIC} = \mathtt{IDEAL} + \mathtt{ALPHA} + \mathtt{METIC}$. (This

exercise was inspired by WHERE + SEDGE + GRASS + GROWS = MARSH [A. W. Johnson,
Jr., *J. Recr. Math.* **15** (1982), 51], which would be marvelously pure except that D
and O have the same signature.) J. A. Brown, J. Szabó, and T. J. Trowbridge suggest
GREAT + GREAT = LARGE and GREAT + GREAT = SMALL. F. Stappers has found WRITE +
WRITE + WRITE + WRITE + WRITE + WRITE = BOOKS; NOTES + SOUND + TONES = MUSIC.

28. (a) $11 = 3 + 3 + 2 + 2 + 1$, $20 = 11 + 3 + 3 + 3$, $20 = 11 + 3 + 3 + 2 + 1$,
$20 = 11+3+3+1+1+1$, $20 = 8+8+2+1+1$, $20 = 7+7+6$, $20 = 7+7+2+2+2$,
$20 = 7+7+2+1+1+1+1$, $20 = 7+5+5+2+1$, $20 = 7+5+2+2+2+1+1$, $20 =$
$7+5+2+2+1+1+1+1$, $20 = 7+3+3+2+2+1+1+1$, $20 = 7+3+3+1+1+1+1+1+1+1$,
$20 = 5+3+3+3+3+3$. [These fourteen solutions were first computed by Roy Childs
in 1999. The next doubly partitionable values of n are 30 (in 20 ways), then 40 (in 94
ways), 41 (in 67), 42 (in 57), 50 (in 190 ways, including $50 = 2+2+\cdots+2$), etc.]
  (b) $51 = 20 + 15 + 14 + 2$, $51 = 15 + 14 + 10 + 9 + 3$, $61 = 19 + 16 + 11 + 9 + 6$,
$65 = 17 + 16 + 15 + 9 + 7 + 1$, $66 = 20 + 19 + 16 + 6 + 5$, $69 = 18 + 17 + 16 + 10 + 8$,
$70 = 30 + 20 + 10 + 7 + 3$, $70 = 20 + 16 + 12 + 9 + 7 + 6$, $70 = 20 + 15 + 12 + 11 + 7 + 5$,
$80 = 50+20+9+1$, $90 = 50+12+11+9+5+2+1$, $91 = 45+19+11+10+5+1$. [The
two 51s are due to Steven Kahan; see his book *Have Some Sums To Solve* (Farmingdale,
New York: Baywood, 1978), 36–37, 84, 112. Amazing examples with seventeen distinct
terms in Italian and fifty-eight distinct terms in Roman numerals have been found by
Giulio Cesare, *J. Recr. Math.* **30** (1999), 63.]
  Notes: The beautiful example THREE = TWO+ONE+ZERO [Richard L. Breisch, *Recreational Math. Magazine* **12** (December 1962), 24] is unfortunately ruled out by our conventions. The total number of doubly true partitions into distinct parts is probably finite, in English, although nomenclature for arbitrarily large integers is not standard. Is
there an example bigger than NINETYNINENONILLIONNINETYNINESEXTILLIONSIXTYONE =
NINETYNINENONILLIONNINETYNINESEXTILLIONNINETEEN+SIXTEEN+ELEVEN+NINE+SIX
(suggested by G. González-Morris)?

29. $10 + 7 + 1 = 9 + 6 + 3$, $11 + 10 = 8 + 7 + 6$, $12 + 7 + 6 + 5 = 11 + 10 + 9$, $\ldots$,
$19 + 10 + 3 = 14 + 13 + 4 + 1$ (31 examples in all).

30. (a) $567^2 = 321489$, $807^2 = 651249$, or $854^2 = 729316$. (b) $958^2 = 917764$. (c) $96 \times$
$7^2 = 4704$. (d) $51304/61904 = 7260/8760$. (e) $328509^2 = 4761^3$. [*Strand* **78** (1929),
91, 208; *J. Recr. Math.* **3** (1970), 43; **13** (1981), 212; **27** (1995), 137; **31** (2003),
133. The solutions to (b), (c), (d), and (e) are unique. With a right-to-left approach
based on Algorithm X, the answers are found in (14, 13, 11, 3423, 42) kilomems,
respectively. Nob also noticed that NORTH/SOUTH = WEST/EAST has the unique solution
$67104/27504 = 9320/3820$.]

31. (a) $5/34 + 7/68 + 9/12(!)$. One can verify uniqueness with Algorithm X using the
side condition A < D < G, in about 265 Kμ. [*Quark Visual Science Magazine*, No. 136
(Tokyo: Kodansha, October 1993).] Curiously, a similar puzzle also has a unique solution: $1/(3 \times 6)+5/(8 \times 9)+7/(2 \times 4) = 1$ [Scot Morris, *Omni* **17**, 4 (January 1995), 97].
  (b) ABCDEFGHI $= 381654729$, via Algorithm X in 10 Kμ.

32. There are eleven ways, of which the most surprising is $3 + 69258/714$. [See *The
Weekly Dispatch* (9 and 23 June 1901); *Amusements in Mathematics* (1917), 158–159.]

33. (a) 1, 2, 3, 4, 15, 18, 118, 146. (b) 6, 9, 16, 20, 27, 126, 127, 129, 136, 145. [*The
Weekly Dispatch* (11 and 30 November, 1902); *Amusements in Math.* (1917), 159.]
  In this case one suitable strategy is to find all variations where $a_k \ldots a_{l-1}/a_l \ldots a_9$
is an integer, then to record solutions for all permutations of $a_1 \ldots a_{k-1}$. There are

exactly 164959 integers with a unique solution, the largest being 9876533. There are solutions for all years in the 21st century except 2091. The most solutions (389) occur when $n = 12221$; the longest stretch of representable n's is $5109 < n < 7060$. Dudeney was able to get the correct answers by hand for small n by "casting out nines."

34. (a) $x = 10^5$, $7378 + 155 + 92467 = 7178 + 355 + 92467 = 1016 + 733 + 98251 = 1014 + 255 + 98731 = 100000$.

(b) $x = 4^7$, $3036 + 455 + 12893 = 16384$ is unique. The fastest way to resolve this problem is probably to start with a list of the 2529 primes that consist of five distinct digits (namely 10243, 10247, ..., 98731) and to permute the five remaining digits.

Incidentally, the unrestricted alphametic EVEN + ODD = PRIME has ten solutions; both ODD and PRIME are prime in just one of them. [See M. Arisawa, *J. Recr. Math.* **8** (1975), 153.]

35. In general, if $s_k = |S_k|$ for $1 \le k < n$, there are $s_1 \ldots s_{k-1}$ ways to choose each of the nonidentity elements of S_k. Hence the answer is $\prod_{k=1}^{n-1}(\prod_{j=1}^{k-1} s_j^{s_k-1})$, which in this case is $2^2 \cdot 6^3 \cdot 24^{15} = 43619669247402383612313 6$.

(But if the vertices are renumbered, the s_k values may change. For example, if vertices $(0,3,5)$ of (12) are interchanged with (e,d,c), we have $s_{14} = 1$, $s_{13} = 6$, $s_{12} = 4$, $s_{11} = 1$, and $4^5 \cdot 24^{15}$ Sims tables.)

36. Since each of $\{0,3,5,6,9,a,c,f\}$ lies on three lines, but every other element lies on only two, it is clear that we may let $S_f = \{(), \sigma, \sigma^2, \sigma^3, \alpha, \alpha\sigma, \alpha\sigma^2, \alpha\sigma^3\}$, where $\sigma = (03fc)(17e8)(2bd4)(56a9)$ is a $90°$ rotation and $\alpha = (05)(14)(27)(36)(8d)(9c)(af)(be)$ is an inside-out twist. Also $S_e = \{(), \beta, \gamma, \beta\gamma\}$, where $\beta = (14)(28)(3c)(69)(7d)(be)$ is a transposition and $\gamma = (12)(48)(5a)(69)(7b)(de)$ is another twist; $S_d = \cdots = S_1 = \{()\}$. (There are $4^7 - 1$ alternative answers.)

37. The set S_k can be chosen in $k!^k$ ways (see exercise 35), and its nonidentity elements can be assigned to $\sigma(k,1), \ldots, \sigma(k,k)$ in $k!$ further ways. So the answer is $A_n = \prod_{k=1}^{n-1} k!^{k+1} = n!^{\binom{n+1}{2}} / \prod_{k=1}^{n} k^{\binom{k+1}{2}}$. For example, $A_{10} \approx 1.148 \times 10^{170}$. We have

$$\sum_{k=1}^{n-1} \binom{k}{2} \ln k = \frac{1}{2} \int_1^n x(x-1)\ln x\, dx + O(n^2 \log n) = \frac{1}{6} n^3 \ln n + O(n^3)$$

by Euler's summation formula; thus $\ln A_n = \frac{1}{3} n^3 \ln n + O(n^3)$.

38. The probability that $\phi(k)$ is needed in step G4 is $1/k! - 1/(k+1)!$, for $1 \le k < n$; the probability is $1/n!$ that we don't get to step G4 at all. Since $\phi(k)$ does $\lceil k/2 \rceil$ transpositions, the average is $\sum_{k=1}^{n-1}(1/k! - 1/(k+1)!)\lceil k/2 \rceil = \sum_{k=1}^{n-1}(\lceil k/2 \rceil - \lceil (k-1)/2 \rceil)/k! - \lceil (n-1)/2 \rceil/n! = \sum_{k \text{ odd}} 1/k! + O(1/(n-1)!)$.

39. (a) 0123, 1023, 2013, 0213, 1203, 2103, 3012, 0312, 1302, 3102, 0132, 1032, 2301, 3201, 0231, 2031, 3021, 0321, 1230, 2130, 3120, 1320, 2310, 3210; (b) 0123, 1023, 2013, 0213, 1203, 2103, 3102, 1302, 0312, 3012, 1032, 0132, 0231, 2031, 3021, 0321, 2301, 3201, 3210, 2310, 1320, 3120, 2130, 1230.

40. By induction we find $\sigma(1,1) = (0\ 1)$, $\sigma(2,2) = (0\ 1\ 2)$,

$$\sigma(k,k) = \begin{cases} (0\ k)(k{-}1\ k{-}2\ \ldots\ 1), & \text{if } k \ge 3 \text{ is odd,} \\ (0\ k{-}1\ k{-}2\ 1\ \ldots\ k{-}3\ k), & \text{if } k \ge 4 \text{ is even;} \end{cases}$$

also $\omega(k) = (0\ k)$ when k is even, $\omega(k) = (0\ k{-}2\ \ldots\ 1\ k{-}1\ k)$ when $k \ge 3$ is odd. Thus when $k \ge 3$ is odd, $\sigma(k,1) = (k\ k{-}1\ 0)$ and $\sigma(k,j)$ takes $k \mapsto j-1$ for $1 < j < k$; when $k \ge 4$ is even, $\sigma(k,j) = (0\ k\ k{-}3\ \ldots\ 1\ k{-}2\ k{-}1)^j$ for $1 \le j \le k$.

Notes: The first scheme that causes Algorithm G to generate all permutations by single transpositions was devised by Mark Wells [*Math. Comp.* **15** (1961), 192–195], but it was considerably more complicated. W. Lipski, Jr., studied such schemes in general and found a variety of additional methods [*Computing* **23** (1979), 357–365].

41. We may assume that $r < n$. Algorithm G will generate r-variations for any Sims table if we simply change '$k \leftarrow 1$' to '$k \leftarrow n - r$' in step G3, provided that we redefine $w(k)$ to be $\sigma(n-r, n-r)\ldots\sigma(k, k)$ instead of using (16).

If $n - r$ is odd, the method of (27) is still valid, although the formulas in answer 40 need to be revised when $k < n - r + 2$. The new formulas are $\sigma(k, j) = (k\ j{-}1\ \ldots\ 1\ 0)$ and $w(k) = (k\ \ldots\ 1\ 0)$ when $k = n - r$; $\sigma(k, j) = (k\ \ldots\ 1\ 0)^j$ when $k = n - r + 1$.

If $n - r$ is even, we can use (27) with even and odd reversed, if $r \leq 3$. But when $r \geq 4$ a more complex scheme is needed, because a fixed transposition like $(k\ 0)$ can be used for odd k only if $w(k - 1)$ is a k-cycle, which means that $w(k - 1)$ must be an even permutation; but $w(k)$ is odd for $k \geq n - r + 2$.

The following scheme works when $n - r$ is even: Let $\tau(k, j)w(k - 1)^- = (k\ k{-}j)$ for $1 \leq j \leq k = n - r$, and use (27) when $k > n - r$. Then, when $k = n - r + 1$, we have $w(k - 1) = (0\ 1\ \ldots\ k{-}1)$, hence $\sigma(k, j)$ takes $k \mapsto (2j - 1) \bmod k$ for $1 \leq j \leq k$, and $\sigma(k, k) = (k\ k{-}1\ k{-}3\ \ldots\ 0\ k{-}2\ \ldots\ 1)$, $w(k) = (k\ \ldots\ 1\ 0)$, $\sigma(k+1, j) = (k{+}1\ \ldots\ 0)^j$.

42. If $\sigma(k, j) = (k\ j{-}1)$ we have $\tau(k, 1) = (k\ 0)$ and $\tau(k, j) = (k\ j{-}1)(k\ j{-}2) = (k\ j{-}1\ j{-}2)$ for $2 \leq j \leq k$.

43. Of course $w(1) = \sigma(1, 1) = \tau(1, 1) = (0\ 1)$. The following construction makes $w(k) = (k{-}2\ k{-}1\ k)$ for all $k \geq 2$: Let $\alpha(k, j) = \tau(k, j)w(k-1)^-$, where $\alpha(2, 1) = (2\ 0)$, $\alpha(2, 2) = (2\ 0\ 1)$, $\alpha(3, 1) = \alpha(3, 3) = (3\ 1)$, $\alpha(3, 2) = (3\ 1\ 0)$; this makes $\sigma(2, 2) = (0\ 2)$, $\sigma(3, 3) = (0\ 3\ 1)$. Then for $k \geq 4$, let $\alpha(k, 1) = (k\ k{-}4)$, $\alpha(k, j) = (k\ k{-}3{-}j\ k{-}2{-}j)$ for $1 < j < k - 2$, and

	$k \bmod 3 = 0$		$k \bmod 3 = 1$		$k \bmod 3 = 2$
$\alpha(k, k{-}2) =$	$(k\ k{-}2\ 0)$	or	$(k\ k{-}3\ 0)$	or	$(k\ k{-}1\ 0)$,
$\alpha(k, k{-}1) =$	$(k\ k{-}2\ k{-}3)$	or	$(k\ k{-}3)$	or	$(k\ k{-}1\ k{-}3)$,
$\alpha(k, k) =$	$(k\ k{-}2)$	or	$(k\ k{-}3\ k{-}2)$	or	$(k\ k{-}2)$;

this makes $\sigma(k, k) = (k{-}3\ k\ k{-}2)$ as required.

44. No, because $\tau(k, j)$ is a $(k + 1)$-cycle, not a transposition. (See (19) and (24).)

45. (a) 202280070, since $u_k = \max\left(\{0, 1, \ldots, a_k - 1\} \setminus \{a_1, \ldots, a_{k-1}\}\right)$. (Actually u_n is never set by the algorithm, but we can assume that it is zero.) (b) 273914568.

46. True (assuming that $u_n = 0$). If either $u_k > u_{k+1}$ or $a_k > a_{k+1}$ we must have $a_k > u_k \geq a_{k+1} > u_{k+1}$.

47. Steps $(X1, X2, \ldots, X6)$ are performed respectively $(1, A, B, A-1, B-N_n, A)$ times, where $A = N_0 + \cdots + N_{n-1}$ and $B = nN_0 + (n - 1)N_1 + \cdots + 1N_{n-1}$.

48. Steps $(X2, X3, X4, X5, X6)$ are performed respectively $A_n + (1, n!, 0, 0, 1)$ times, where $A_n = \sum_{k=1}^{n-1} n^{\underline{k}} = n! \sum_{k=1}^{n-1} 1/k! \approx n!\,(e - 1)$. Assuming that they cost respectively $(1, 1, 3, 1, 3)$ mems, for operations involving a_j, l_j, or u_j, the total cost is about $9e - 8 \approx 16.46$ mems per permutation.

Algorithm L uses approximately $(e, 2 + e/2, 2e + 2e^{-1} - 4)$ mems per permutation in steps $(L2, L3, L4)$, for a total of $3.5e + 2e^{-1} - 2 \approx 8.25$ (see exercise 5).

Algorithm X could be tuned up for this case by streamlining the code when k is near n. But so can Algorithm L, as shown in exercise 1.

49. Order the signatures so that $|s_0| \geq \cdots \geq |s_9|$; also prepare tables $w_0 \ldots w_9$, $x_0 \ldots x_9$, $y_0 \ldots y_9$, so that the signatures $\{s_k, \ldots, s_9\}$ are $w_{x_k} \leq \cdots \leq w_{y_k}$. For example, when SEND + MORE = MONEY we have $(s_0, \ldots, s_9) = (-9000, 1000, -900, 91, -90, 10, 1, -1, 0, 0)$ for the respective letters (M, S, O, E, N, R, D, Y, A, B); also $(w_0, \ldots, w_9) = (-9000, -900, -90, -1, 0, 0, 1, 10, 91, 1000)$, and $x_0 \ldots x_9 = 0112233344$, $y_0 \ldots y_9 = 9988776554$. Yet another table $f_0 \ldots f_9$ has $f_j = 1$ if the digit corresponding to w_j cannot be zero; in this case $f_0 \ldots f_9 = 1000000001$. These tables make it easy to compute the largest and smallest values of

$$s_k a_k + \cdots + s_9 a_9$$

over all choices $a_k \ldots a_9$ of the remaining digits, using the method of exercise 25, since the links l_j tell us those digits in increasing order.

   This method requires a rather expensive computation at each node of the search tree, but it often succeeds in keeping that tree small. For example, it solves the first eight alphametics of exercise 24 with costs of only 7, 13, 7, 9, 5, 343, 44, and 89 kilomems; this is a substantial improvement in cases (a), (b), (e), and (h), although case (f) comes out significantly worse. Another bad case is the 'CHILD' example of answer 27, where left-to-right needs 2947 kilomems compared to 588 for the right-to-left approach. Left-to-right does, however, fare better on BLOOD + SWEAT + TEARS (73 versus 360) and HELLO + WORLD (340 versus 410).

50. If α is in a permutation group, so are all its powers α^2, α^3, $\ldots$, including $\alpha^{m-1} = \alpha^-$, where m is the order of α (the least common multiple of its cycle lengths). And (32) is equivalent to $\alpha^- = \sigma_1 \sigma_2 \ldots \sigma_{n-1}$.

51. False. For example, $\sigma(k, i)^-$ and $\sigma(k, j)^-$ might both take $k \mapsto 0$.

52. $\tau(k, j) = (k-j \ \ k-j+1)$ is an adjacent interchange, and

$$\omega(k) = (n-1 \ \ \ldots \ \ 0)(n-2 \ \ \ldots \ \ 0) \ldots (k \ \ \ldots \ \ 0) = \phi(n-1)\phi(k-1)$$

is a k-flip followed by an n-flip. The permutation corresponding to control table $c_0 \ldots c_{n-1}$ in Algorithm H has c_j elements to the right of j that are less than j, for $0 \leq j < n$; so it is the same as the permutation corresponding to $c_1 \ldots c_n$ in Algorithm P, except that subscripts are shifted by 1.

   The only essential difference between Algorithm P and this version of Algorithm H is that Algorithm P uses a reflected Gray code to run through all possibilities of its control table, while Algorithm H runs through those mixed-radix numbers in ascending (lexicographic) order.

   Indeed, Gray code can be used with any Sims table, by modifying either Algorithm G or Algorithm H. Then all transitions are by $\tau(k, j)$ or by $\tau(k, j)^-$, and the permutations $\omega(k)$ are irrelevant.

53. The text's proof that $n! - 1$ transpositions cannot be achieved for $n = 4$ also shows that we can reduce the problem from n to $n - 2$ at the cost of a single transposition $(n-1 \ \ n-2)$, which was called '(3c)' in the notation of that proof.

   Thus we can generate all permutations by making the following transformation in step H4: If $k = n - 1$ or $k = n - 2$, transpose $a_{j \bmod n} \leftrightarrow a_{(j-1) \bmod n}$, where $j = c_{n-1} - 1$. If $k = n - 3$ or $k = n - 4$, transpose $a_{n-1} \leftrightarrow a_{n-2}$ and also $a_{j \bmod (n-2)} \leftrightarrow a_{(j-1) \bmod (n-2)}$, where $j = c_{n-3} - 1$. And in general if $k = n - 2t - 1$ or $k = n - 2t - 2$, transpose $a_{n-2i+1} \leftrightarrow a_{n-2i}$ for $1 \leq i \leq t$ and also $a_{j \bmod (n-2t)} \leftrightarrow a_{(j-1) \bmod (n-2t)}$, where $j = c_{n-2t-1} - 1$. [See *CACM* **19** (1976), 68–72.]

The corresponding Sims table permutations can be written down as follows, although they don't appear explicitly in the algorithm itself:

$$\sigma(k,j)^- = \begin{cases} (0\ 1\ \ldots\ j{-}1\ k), & \text{if } n - k \text{ is odd}; \\ (0\ 1\ \ldots\ k)^j, & \text{if } n - k \text{ is even}. \end{cases}$$

The value of $a_{j \bmod (n-2t)}$ will be $n - 2t - 1$ after the interchange. For efficiency we can also use the fact that k usually equals $n - 1$. The total number of transpositions is $\sum_{t=0}^{\lfloor n/2 \rfloor}(n - 2t)! - \lfloor n/2 \rfloor - 1$.

54. Yes; the transformation can be any k-cycle on positions $\{1, \ldots, k\}$.

55. (a) Since $\rho_!(m) = \rho_!(m \bmod n!)$ when $n > \rho_!(m)$, we have $\rho_!(n! + m) = \rho_!(m)$ for $0 < m < n \cdot n! = (n + 1)! - n!$. Therefore $\beta_{n!+m} = \sigma_{\rho_!(n!+m)} \cdots \sigma_{\rho_!(n!+1)}\beta_{n!} = \sigma_{\rho_!(m)} \cdots \sigma_{\rho_!(1)}\beta_{n!} = \beta_m\beta_{n!}$ for $0 \le m < n \cdot n!$, and we have in particular

$$\beta_{(n+1)!} = \sigma_{n+1}\beta_{(n+1)!-1} = \sigma_{n+1}\beta_{n!-1}\beta_{n!}^n = \sigma_{n+1}\sigma_n^-\beta_{n!}^{n+1}.$$

Similarly $\alpha_{n!+m} = \beta_{n!}^-\alpha_m\beta_{n!}\alpha_{n!}$ for $0 \le m < n \cdot n!$.

Since $\beta_{n!}$ commutes with τ_n and τ_{n+1} we find $\alpha_{n!} = \tau_n\alpha_{n!-1}$, and

$$\alpha_{(n+1)!} = \tau_{n+1}\alpha_{(n+1)!-1} = \tau_{n+1}\beta_{n!}^-\alpha_{(n+1)!-1-n!}\beta_{n!}\alpha_{n!} = \cdots$$

$$= \tau_{n+1}\beta_{n!}^{-n}\alpha_{n!-1}(\beta_{n!}\alpha_{n!})^n$$

$$= \beta_{n!}^{-n-1}\tau_{n+1}\tau_n^-(\beta_{n!}\alpha_{n!})^{n+1}$$

$$= \beta_{(n+1)!}^-\sigma_{n+1}\sigma_n^-\tau_{n+1}\tau_n^-(\beta_{n!}\alpha_{n!})^{n+1}.$$

(b) In this case $\sigma_{n+1}\sigma_n^- = (n\ n{-}1\ \ldots\ 1)$ and $\tau_{n+1}\tau_n^- = (n{+}1\ n\ 0)$, and we have $\beta_{(n+1)!}\alpha_{(n+1)!} = (n{+}1\ n\ \ldots\ 0)$ by induction. Therefore $\alpha_{jn!+m} = \beta_{n!}^{-j}\alpha_m(n\ \ldots\ 0)^j$ for $0 \le j \le n$ and $0 \le m < n!$. All permutations of $\{0, \ldots, n\}$ are achieved because α_m fixes n, $\beta_{n!}$ fixes n, and $(n\ \ldots\ 0)^j$ takes $n \mapsto n - j$.

56. If we set $\sigma_k = (k{-}1\ k{-}2)(k{-}3\ k{-}4)\ldots$ in the previous exercise, we find by induction that $\beta_{n!}\alpha_{n!}$ is the $(n+1)$-cycle $(0\ n\ n{-}1\ n{-}3\ \ldots\ (2 \text{ or } 1)\ (1 \text{ or } 2)\ \ldots\ n{-}4\ n{-}2)$.

57. Arguing as in answer 5, we obtain $\sum_{k=2}^{n-1}[k \text{ odd}]/k! - (\lfloor n/2 \rfloor - 1)/n! = \sinh 1 - 1 - O(1/(n-1)!)$.

58. True. By the formulas of exercise 55 we have $\alpha_{n!-1} = (0\ n)\beta_{n!}^-(n\ \ldots\ 0)$, and this takes $0 \mapsto n - 1$ because $\beta_{n!}$ fixes n. (Consequently Algorithm E will define a Hamiltonian *cycle* on the graph of exercise 66 if and only if $\beta_{n!} = (n{-}1\ \ldots\ 2\ 1)$, and this holds if and only if the length of every cycle of $\beta_{(n-1)!}$ is a divisor of n. The latter is true for $n = 2, 3, 4, 6, 12, 20,$ and 40, but for no other $n \le 250{,}000$.)

59. The Cayley graph with generators $(\alpha_1, \ldots, \alpha_k)$ in the text's definition is isomorphic to the Cayley graph with generators $(\alpha_1^-, \ldots, \alpha_k^-)$ in the alternative definition, since $\pi \to \alpha_j\pi$ in the former if and only if $\pi^- \to \pi^-\alpha_j^-$ in the latter.

60. (a, b) There are 88 delta sequences, which reduce to four classes: $P = (32131231)^3$ (plain changes, represented by 8 different delta sequences); $Q = (32121232)^3$ (a doubly Gray variant of plain changes, with 8 representatives); $R = (121232321232)^2$ (a doubly Gray code with 24 representatives); $S = 2\alpha3\alpha^R$, $\alpha = 12321312121$ (48 representatives). Classes P and Q are cyclic shifts of their complements; classes P, Q, and S are shifts of their reversals; class R is a shifted reversal of its complement. [See A. L. Leigh Silver, *Math. Gazette* **48** (1964), 1–16.]

61. There are respectively $(26, 36, 20, 26, 28, 40, 40, 20, 26, 28, 28, 26)$ such paths ending at $(1243, 1324, 1432, 2134, 2341, 2413, 3142, 3214, 3421, 4123, 4231, 4312)$.

62. There are only two paths when $n = 3$, ending respectively at 132 and 213. But when $n \geq 4$ there are Gray codes leading from $12 \ldots n$ to any odd permutation $a_1 a_2 \ldots a_n$. Exercise 61 establishes this when $n = 4$, and we can prove it by induction for $n > 4$ as follows.

Let $A(j)$ be the set of all permutations that begin with j, and let $A(j, k)$ be those that begin with jk. If $(\alpha_0, \alpha_1, \ldots, \alpha_n)$ are any odd permutations such that $\alpha_j \in A(x_j, x_{j+1})$, then $(1\,2)\alpha_j$ is an even permutation in $A(x_{j+1}, x_j)$. Consequently, if $x_1 x_2 \ldots x_n$ is a permutation of $\{1, 2, \ldots, n\}$, there is at least one Hamiltonian path of the form

$$(1\,2)\alpha_0 \longrightarrow \cdots \longrightarrow \alpha_1 \longrightarrow (1\,2)\alpha_1 \longrightarrow \cdots \longrightarrow \alpha_2 \longrightarrow \cdots \longrightarrow (1\,2)\alpha_{n-1} \longrightarrow \cdots \longrightarrow \alpha_n;$$

the subpath from $(1\,2)\alpha_{j-1}$ to α_j includes all elements of $A(x_j)$.

This construction solves the problem in at least $(n-2)!^n / 2^{n-1}$ distinct ways when $a_1 \neq 1$, because we can take $\alpha_0 = 21 \ldots n$ and $\alpha_n = a_1 a_2 \ldots a_n$; there are $(n-2)!$ ways to choose $x_2 \ldots x_{n-1}$, and $(n-2)!/2$ ways to choose each of $\alpha_1, \ldots, \alpha_{n-1}$.

Finally, if $a_1 = 1$, take any path $12 \ldots n \longrightarrow \cdots \longrightarrow a_1 a_2 \ldots a_n$ that runs through all of $A(1)$, and choose any step $\alpha \longrightarrow \alpha'$ with $\alpha \in A(1, j)$ and $\alpha' \in A(1, j')$ for some $j \neq j'$. Replace that step by

$$\alpha \longrightarrow (1\,2)\alpha_1 \longrightarrow \cdots \longrightarrow \alpha_2 \longrightarrow \cdots \longrightarrow (1\,2)\alpha_{n-1} \longrightarrow \cdots \longrightarrow \alpha_n \longrightarrow \alpha',$$

using a construction like the Hamiltonian path above but now with $\alpha_1 = \alpha$, $\alpha_n = (1\,2)\alpha'$, $x_1 = 1$, $x_2 = j$, $x_n = j'$, and $x_{n+1} = 1$. (In this case the permutations $\alpha_1, \ldots, \alpha_n$ might all be even.)

63. Monte Carlo estimates using the techniques of Section 7.2.3 suggest that the total number of equivalence classes will be roughly 1.2×10^{21}; most of those classes will contain 480 Gray cycles.

64. Exactly 2,005,200 delta sequences have the doubly Gray property; they belong to 4206 equivalence classes under cyclic shift, reversal, and/or complementation. Nine classes, such as the code $2\alpha 2\alpha^R$ where

$$\alpha = 12343234321232121232321232121234343212123432123432121232321,$$

are shifts of their reversal; 48 classes are composed of repeated 60-cycles. One of the most interesting of the latter type is $\alpha\alpha$ where

$$\alpha = \beta 2\beta 4\beta 4\beta 4\beta 4, \qquad \beta = 32121232123.$$

65. Such a path exists for any given $N \leq n!$: Let the Nth permutation be $\alpha = a_1 \ldots a_n$, and let $j = a_1$. Also let Π_k be the set of all permutations $\beta = b_1 \ldots b_n$ for which $b_1 = k$ and $\beta \leq \alpha$. By induction on N there is a Gray path P_1 for Π_j. We can then construct Gray paths P_k for $\Pi_j \cup \Pi_1 \cup \cdots \cup \Pi_{k-1}$ for $2 \leq k \leq j$, successively combining P_{k-1} with a Gray cycle for Π_{k-1}. (See the "absorption" construction of answer 62. In fact, P_j will be a Gray *cycle* when N is a multiple of 6.)

66. Defining the delta sequence by the rule $\pi_{(k+1) \bmod n!} = (1\,\delta_k)\pi_k$, we find exactly 36 such sequences, all of which are cyclic shifts of a pattern like $(xyzyzyxzyzyz)^2$. (The next case, $n = 5$, probably has about 10^{18} solutions that are inequivalent with respect to cyclic shifting, reversal, and permutation of coordinates, thus about 6×10^{21} different delta sequences.) Incidentally, Igor Pak has shown that the Cayley graph generated by star transpositions is an $(n-2)$-dimensional torus in general.

67. If we let π be equivalent to $\pi(12345)$, we get a reduced graph on 24 vertices that has 40768 Hamiltonian cycles, 240 of which lead to delta sequences of the form α^5 in which α uses each transposition 6 times (for example, $\alpha = 35423253423453245 4352452$). The total number of solutions to this problem is probably about 10^{16}.

68. If A isn't connected, neither is G. If A is connected, we can assume that it is a free tree. Moreover, in this case we can prove a generalization of the result in exercise 62: For $n \geq 4$ there is a Hamiltonian path in G from the identity permutation to any odd permutation. For we can assume without loss of generality that A contains the edge $1 — 2$ where 1 is a leaf of the tree, and a proof like that of exercise 62 applies.

[This elegant construction is due to M. Tchuente, *Ars Combinatoria* **14** (1982), 115–122. Extensive generalizations have been discussed by Ruskey and Savage in *SIAM J. Discrete Math.* **6** (1993), 152–166. See also the original Russian publication in *Kibernetika* **11**, 3 (1975), 17–21; English translation, *Cybernetics* **11** (1975), 362–366.]

69. Following the hint, the modified algorithm behaves like this when $n = 5$:

```
1234   1243   1423   4123   4132   1432   1342   1324   3124   3142   3412   4312

 ↓      ↑      ↓      ↑      ↓      ↑      ↓      ↑      ↓      ↑      ↓      ↑
54321  24351  24153  54123  14523  14325  24315  24513  54213  14253  14352  54312
12345  15342  35142  32145  32541  52341  51342  31542  31245  35241  25341  21345
15432  12435  32415  35412←31452  51432  52431  32451←35421  31425  21435  25431
23451  53421  51423  21453→25413  23415  13425  15423→12453  52413  53412  13452
21543  51243  53241  23541  23145  25143  15243  13245  13542  53142  52143  12543
34512  34215  14235  14532  54132  34152  34251  54231  24531  24135  34125  34521
32154→35124  15324→12354  52314  32514←31524  51324  21354→25314  35214→31254
45123←42153  42351←45321  41325  41523→42513  42315  45312←41352  41253←45213
43215  43512←41532  41235  45231→43251  43152→45132  42135  42531←43521  43125
51234  21534→23514  53214  13254←15234  25134←23154  53124  13524→12534  52134

 ↓      ↑      ↓      ↑      ↓      ↑      ↓      ↑      ↓      ↑      ↓      ↑
```

Here the columns represent sets of permutations that are cyclically rotated and/or reflected in all $2n$ ways; therefore each column contains exactly one "rosary permutation" (exercise 18). We can use Algorithm P to run through the rosary permutations systematically, knowing that the pair xy will occur before yx in its column, at which time τ' instead of ρ' will move us to the right or to the left. Step Z2 omits the interchange $a_1 \leftrightarrow a_2$, thereby causing the permutations $a_1 \ldots a_{n-1}$ to repeat themselves going backwards. (We implicitly use the fact that $t[k] = t[n! - k]$ in the output of Algorithm T.)

Now if we replace $1 \ldots n$ by $24 \ldots 31$ and change $A_1 \ldots A_n$ to $A_1 A_n A_2 A_{n-1} \ldots$, we get the unmodified algorithm whose results are shown in Fig. 42(b).

This method was inspired by a (nonconstructive) theorem of E. S. Rapaport, *Scripta Math.* **24** (1959), 51–58. It illustrates a more general fact observed by Carla Savage in 1989, namely that the Cayley graph for *any* group generated by three involutions ρ, σ, τ has a Hamiltonian cycle when $\rho\tau = \tau\rho$. [See I. Pak and R. Radoičić, *Discrete Math.* **309** (2009), 5501–5508.]

70. No; the longest cycle in that digraph has length 358. But there do exist pairs of disjoint 180-cycles from which a Hamiltonian path of length 720 can be derived. For example, consider the cycles $\alpha\sigma\beta\sigma$ and $\gamma\sigma\sigma$ where

$$\alpha = \tau\sigma^5\tau\sigma^5\tau\sigma^3\tau\sigma^2\tau\sigma^5\tau\sigma^3\tau\sigma^2\tau\sigma^5\tau\sigma^5\tau\sigma^2\tau\sigma^3\tau\sigma^1\tau\sigma^5\tau\sigma^5\tau\sigma^3\tau\sigma^1\tau\sigma^3\tau\sigma^2\tau\sigma^1\tau\sigma^1;$$

$$\beta = \sigma^3\tau\sigma^5\tau\sigma^2\tau\sigma^2\tau\sigma^5\tau\sigma^2\tau\sigma^3\tau\sigma^1\tau\sigma^1\tau\sigma^5\tau\sigma^1\tau\sigma^3\tau\sigma^5\tau\sigma^5\tau\sigma^3\tau\sigma^2\tau\sigma^1\tau\sigma^2\tau\sigma^3\tau\sigma^1\tau\sigma^1\tau\sigma^3\tau\sigma^2\tau\sigma^4;$$

$$\gamma = \sigma\tau\sigma^5\tau\sigma^5\tau\sigma^3\tau\sigma^1\tau\sigma^1\tau\sigma^3\tau\sigma^2\tau\sigma^2\tau\sigma^5\tau\sigma^2\tau\sigma^3\tau\sigma^5\tau\sigma^5\tau\sigma^1\tau\sigma^5\tau\sigma^3\tau\sigma^2\tau\sigma^1\tau\sigma^2\tau\sigma^3\tau\sigma^1\tau\sigma^1\tau\sigma^3\tau\sigma^2\tau\sigma^2$$
$$\tau\sigma^5\tau\sigma^5\tau\sigma^5\tau\sigma^3\tau\sigma^5\tau\sigma^2\tau\sigma^5\tau\sigma^2\tau\sigma^3\tau\sigma^1\tau\sigma^1\tau\sigma^1\tau\sigma^5\tau\sigma^1\tau\sigma^3\tau\sigma^3\tau\sigma^5\tau\sigma^5\tau\sigma^1\tau\sigma^5\tau\sigma^2\tau\sigma^3\tau\sigma^1\tau\sigma^2.$$

If we start with 134526 and follow $\alpha\sigma\beta\tau$ we reach 163452; then follow $\gamma\sigma\tau$ and reach 126345; then follow $\sigma\gamma\tau$ and reach 152634; then follow $\beta\sigma\alpha$, ending at 415263.

71. Yes — including one that has a reasonably simple succession rule. See J. Sawada and A. Williams, *ACM Transactions on Algorithms* **16** (2020), #11.1–#11.17.

72. Any Hamiltonian path includes $(n-1)!$ vertices that take $y \mapsto x$, each of which (if not the last) is followed by a vertex that takes $x \mapsto x$. So one must be last; otherwise $(n-1)! + 1$ vertices would take $x \mapsto x$.

73. (a) Assume first that β is the identity permutation (). Then every cycle of α that contains an element of A lies entirely within A. Hence the cycles of σ are obtained by omitting all cycles of α that contain no element of A. All remaining cycles have odd length, so σ is an even permutation.

  If β is not the identity, we apply this argument to $\alpha' = \alpha\beta^-$, $\beta' = ()$, and $\sigma' = \sigma\beta^-$, concluding that σ' is an even permutation; thus σ and β have the same sign.

  Similarly, σ and α have the same sign, because $\beta\alpha^- = (\alpha\beta^-)^-$ has the same order as $\alpha\beta^-$.

  (b) Let X be the vertices of the Cayley graph in Theorem R, and let $\hat{\alpha}$ be the permutation of X that takes a vertex π into $\alpha\pi$; this permutation has g/a cycles of length a. Define the permutation $\hat{\beta}$ similarly. Then $\hat{\alpha}\hat{\beta}^-$ has g/c cycles of length c. If c is odd, any Hamiltonian cycle in the graph defines a cycle $\hat{\sigma}$ that contains all the vertices and satisfies the hypotheses of (a). Therefore $\hat{\alpha}$ and $\hat{\beta}$ have an odd number of cycles, because the sign of a permutation on n elements with r cycles is $(-1)^{n-r}$ (see exercise 5.2.2–2).

  [This proof, which shows that X cannot be the union of any odd number of cycles, was presented by Rankin in *Proc. Cambridge Phil. Soc.* **62** (1966), 15–16.]

74. The representation $\beta^j\gamma^k$ is unique if we require $0 \le j < g/c$ and $0 \le k < c$. For if we had $\beta^j = \gamma^k$ for some j with $0 < j < g/c$, the group would have at most jc elements. It follows that $\beta^{g/c} = \gamma^t$ for some t.

  Let $\hat{\sigma}$ be a Hamiltonian cycle, as in the previous answer, and let $\hat{\gamma} = \hat{\alpha}\hat{\beta}^-$. If $\pi\hat{\sigma} = \pi\hat{\alpha}$ then $\pi\hat{\gamma}\hat{\sigma}$ must be $\pi\hat{\gamma}\hat{\alpha}$, because $\pi\hat{\gamma}\hat{\beta} = \pi\hat{\alpha}$. And if $\pi\hat{\sigma} = \pi\hat{\beta}$ then $\pi\hat{\gamma}\hat{\sigma}$ cannot be $\pi\hat{\gamma}\hat{\alpha}$, because that would imply $\pi\hat{\gamma}^2\hat{\sigma} = \pi\hat{\gamma}^2\hat{\alpha}, \ldots, \pi\hat{\gamma}^c\hat{\sigma} = \pi\hat{\gamma}^c\hat{\alpha}$. Thus the elements π, $\pi\hat{\gamma}$, $\pi\hat{\gamma}^2$, $\ldots$, all have equivalent behavior with respect to their successors in $\hat{\sigma}$.

  When the path $\pi \longrightarrow \pi\hat{\sigma} \longrightarrow \cdots \longrightarrow \pi\hat{\sigma}^j$ has $k(j)$ steps of type $\hat{\alpha}$, we have $\pi\hat{\sigma}^j = \pi\hat{\beta}^j\hat{\gamma}^{k(j)}$. Thus $\pi\hat{\sigma}^{g/c} = \pi\hat{\gamma}^{t+k(g/c)}$, and we have $k(j+g/c) = k(j)$ for $j \ge 0$. The path returns to π for the first time in g steps if and only if $t + k(g/c)$ is relatively prime to c.

75. Apply the previous exercise with $g = mn$, $a = m$, $b = n$, $c = mn/d$. The number t satisfies $t \equiv 0$ (modulo m), $t + d \equiv 0$ (modulo n); and it follows that $k + t \perp c$ if and only if $(d-k)m/d \perp kn/d$.

  Notes: The modular Gray code of exercise 7.2.1.1–78 is a Hamiltonian path from $(0,0)$ to $(m-1, (-m) \bmod n)$, so it is a Hamiltonian cycle if and only if m is a multiple of n. It is natural to conjecture (falsely) that at least one Hamiltonian cycle exists whenever $d > 1$. But P. Erdős and W. T. Trotter have observed [*J. Graph Theory* **2**

(1978), 137–142] that if p and $2p+1$ are odd prime numbers, no suitable k exists when $m = p(2p+1)(3p+1)$ and $n = (3p+1)\prod_{q=1}^{3p} q^{[q \text{ is prime}][q\neq p][q\neq 2p+1]}$.

See J. A. Gallian, *Mathematical Intelligencer* **13**,3 (Summer 1991), 40–43, for interesting facts about other kinds of cycles in $C\vec{}_m \times C\vec{}_n$.

76. We may assume that the tour begins in the lower left corner. There are no solutions when m and n are both divisible by 3, because 2/3 of the cells are unreachable in that case. Otherwise, letting $d = \gcd(m,n)$ and arguing as in the previous exercise but with $(x,y)\alpha = ((x+2) \bmod m, (y+1) \bmod n)$ and $(x,y)\beta = ((x+1) \bmod m, (y+2) \bmod n)$, we find the answer

$$\sum_{k=0}^{d} \binom{d}{k}[\gcd((2d-k)m,(k+d)n) = d \ \text{ or } \ (mn \perp 3 \text{ and } \gcd((2d-k)m,(k+d)n) = 3d)].$$

77.

01		*	Permutation	generator à la Heap	
02	N	IS	10	The value of n (3 or more, not large)	
03	t	IS	$255		
04	j	IS	$0	$8j$	
05	k	IS	$1	$8k$	
06	ak	IS	$2		
07	aj	IS	$3		
08		LOC	Data_Segment		
09	a	GREG	@	Base address for $a_0 \ldots a_{n-1}$	
10	A0	IS	@		
11	A1	IS	@+8		
12	A2	IS	@+16		
13		LOC	@+8*N	Space for $a_0 \ldots a_{n-1}$	
14	c	GREG	@-8*3	Location of $8c_0$	
15		LOC	@-8*3+8*N	$8c_3 \ldots 8c_{n-1}$, initially zero	
16		OCTA	-1	$8c_n = -1$, a convenient sentinel	
17	u	GREG	0	Contents of a_0, except in inner loop	
18	v	GREG	0	Contents of a_1, except in inner loop	
19	w	GREG	0	Contents of a_2, except in inner loop	
20		LOC	#100		
21	1H	STCO	0,c,k	$B - A$	$c_k \leftarrow 0$.
22		INCL	k,8	$B - A$	$k \leftarrow k + 1$.
23	0H	LDO	j,c,k	B	$j \leftarrow c_k$.
24		CMP	t,j,k	B	
25		BZ	t,1B	B	Loop if $c_k = k$.
26		BN	j,Done	A	Terminate if $c_k < 0$ $(k = n)$.
27		LDO	ak,a,k	$A - 1$	Fetch a_k.
28		ADD	t,j,8	$A - 1$	
29		STO	t,c,k	$A - 1$	$c_k \leftarrow j + 1$.
30		AND	t,k,#8	$A - 1$	
31		CSZ	j,t,0	$A - 1$	Set $j \leftarrow 0$ if k is even.
32		LDO	aj,a,j	$A - 1$	Fetch a_j.
33		STO	ak,a,j	$A - 1$	Replace it by a_k.
34		CSZ	u,j,ak	$A - 1$	Set $u \leftarrow a_k$ if $j = 0$.
35		SUB	j,j,8	$A - 1$	$j \leftarrow j - 1$.
36		CSZ	v,j,ak	$A - 1$	Set $v \leftarrow a_k$ if $j = 0$.

37		SUB	j,j,8	$A-1$	$j \leftarrow j - 1$.
38		CSZ	w,j,ak	$A-1$	Set $w \leftarrow a_k$ if $j = 0$.
39		STO	aj,a,k	$A-1$	Replace a_k by what was a_j.
40	Inner	PUSHJ	0,Visit	A	
		...			(See (42))
55		PUSHJ	0,Visit	A	
56		SET	t,u	A	Swap $u \leftrightarrow w$.
57		SET	u,w	A	
58		SET	w,t	A	
59		SET	k,8*3	A	$k \leftarrow 3$.
60		JMP	0B	A	
61	Main	LDO	u,A0	1	
62		LDO	v,A1	1	
63		LDO	w,A2	1	
64		JMP	Inner	1	∎

78. Lines 31–38 become $2r - 1$ instructions, lines 61–63 become r, and lines 56–58 become $3 + (r-2)[r \text{ even}]$ instructions (see $\omega(r-1)$ in answer 40). The total running time is therefore $((2r!+2)A+2B+r-5)\mu+((2r!+2r+7+(r-2)[r\text{ even}])A+7B-r-4)v$, where $A = n!/r!$ and $B = n!(1/r! + \cdots + 1/n!)$.

79. SLU u,[#f],t; SLU t,a,4; XOR t,t,a; AND t,t,u; SRU u,t,4; OR t,t,u; XOR a,a,t; here, as in the answer to exercise 1.3.1′–34, the notation '[#f]' denotes a register that contains the constant value $^\#\text{f}$. (See the similar code in 7.1.3–(69).)

80. SLU u,a,t; MXOR u,[#8844221188442211],u; AND u,u,[#ff000000]; SRU u,u,t; XOR a,a,u. This cheats, since it transforms $^\#$12345678 to $^\#$13245678 when $t = 4$, but (45) still works.

Even faster and trickier would be a routine analogous to (42): Consider

PUSHJ 0,Visit; MXOR a,a,c1; PUSHJ 0,Visit; ... MXOR a,a,c5; PUSHJ 0,Visit

where c1, ..., c5 are constants that would cause $^\#$12345678 to become successively $^\#$12783456, $^\#$12567834, $^\#$12563478, $^\#$12785634, $^\#$12347856. Other instructions, executed only 1/6 or 1/24 as often, can take care of shuffling nybbles within and between bytes. Very clever, but it doesn't beat (46) in view of the PUSHJ/POP overhead.

81.
```
   k   IS   $0 ;kk IS $1 ;c IS $2 ;d IS $3
       SET  k,1      k ← 1.
   3H SRU   d,a,60   d ← leftmost nybble.
      SLU   a,a,4    a ← 16a mod 16¹⁶.
      CMP   c,d,k
      SLU   kk,k,2
      SLU   d,d,kk
      OR    t,t,d    t ← t + 16ᵏd.
      PBNZ  c,1B     Return to main loop if d ≠ k.
      INCL  k,1      k ← k + 1.
      PBNZ  a,3B     Return to second loop if k < n.  ∎
```

82. $\mu + (5n! + 11A - (n-1)! + 6)v = ((5 + 10/n)v + O(n^{-2}))n!$, plus the visiting time, where $A = \sum_{k=1}^{n-1} k!$ is the number of times the loop at 3H is used.

83. With suitable initialization and a 13-octabyte table, only about a dozen MMIX instructions are needed:

```
magic   GREG #8844221188442211
OH      ⟨Visit the permutation in register a⟩
        PBN  c,Sigma
Tau     MXOR t,magic,a; ANDNL t,#ffff; JMP 1F
Sigma   SRU  t,a,20; SLU a,a,4; ANDNML a,#f00
1H      XOR  a,a,t; SLU c,c,1
2H      PBNZ c,0B; INCL p,8
3H      LDOU c,p,0; PBNZ c,0B                     ▌
```

84. Assuming that the processors all have essentially the same speed, we can let the kth processor generate all permutations of rank r for $(k-1)n!/p \leq r < kn!/p$, using any method based on control tables $c_1 \ldots c_n$. The starting and ending control tables are easily computed by converting their ranks to mixed-radix notation (exercise 12).

85. We can use a technique like that of Algorithm 3.4.2P: To compute $k = r(\alpha)$, first set $a'_{a_j} \leftarrow j$ for $1 \leq j \leq n$ (the inverse permutation). Then set $k \leftarrow 0$, and for $j = n$, $n-1, \ldots, 2$ (in this order) set $t \leftarrow a'_j$, $k \leftarrow kj + t - 1$, $a_t \leftarrow a_j$, $a'_{a_j} \leftarrow t$. To compute $r^{[-1]}(k)$, start with $a_1 \leftarrow 1$. Then for $j = 2, \ldots, n-1, n$ (in this order) set $t \leftarrow (k \bmod j) + 1$, $a_j \leftarrow a_t$, $a_t \leftarrow j$, $k \leftarrow \lfloor k/j \rfloor$. [See S. Pleszczyński, *Inf. Proc. Letters* **3** (1975), 180–183; W. Myrvold and F. Ruskey, *Inf. Proc. Letters* **79** (2001), 281–284.]

Another method is preferable if we want to rank and unrank only the $n^{\underline{m}}$ *variations* $a_1 \ldots a_m$ of $\{1, \ldots, n\}$: To compute $k = r(a_1 \ldots a_m)$, start with $b_1 \ldots b_n \leftarrow b'_1 \ldots b'_n \leftarrow 1 \ldots n$; then for $j = 1, \ldots, m$ (in this order) set $t \leftarrow b'_{a_j}$, $b_t \leftarrow b_{n+1-j}$, and $b'_{b_t} \leftarrow t$; finally set $k \leftarrow 0$ and for $j = m, \ldots, 1$ (in this order) set $k \leftarrow k \times (n+1-j) + b'_{a_j} - 1$. To compute $r^{[-1]}(k)$, start with $b_1 \ldots b_n \leftarrow 1 \ldots n$; then for $j = 1, \ldots, m$ (in this order) set $t \leftarrow (k \bmod (n+1-j)) + 1$, $a_j \leftarrow b_t$, $b_t \leftarrow b_{n+1-j}$, $k \leftarrow \lfloor k/(n+1-j) \rfloor$. (See exercise 3.4.2–15 for cases with large n and small m.)

86. If $x \prec y$ and $y \prec z$, the algorithm will never move y to the left of x, nor z to the left of y, so it will never test x versus z.

87. They appear in lexicographic order; Algorithm P used a reflected Gray order.

88. Generate inverse permutations with $a'_0 < a'_1 < a'_2$, $a'_3 < a'_4 < a'_5$, $a'_6 < a'_7$, $a'_8 < a'_9$, $a'_0 < a'_3$, $a'_6 < a'_8$.

89. (a) Let $d_k = \max\{j \mid 0 \leq j \leq k$ and j is nontrivial$\}$, where 0 is considered nontrivial. This table is easily precomputed, because j is trivial if and only if it must follow $\{1, \ldots, j-1\}$. Set $k \leftarrow d_n$ in step V2 and $k \leftarrow d_{k-1}$ in step V5. (Assume $d_n > 0$.)

(b) Now $M = \sum_{j=1}^{n} t_j [j$ is nontrivial$]$.

(c) There are at least two topological sorts $a_j \ldots a_k$ of the set $\{j, \ldots, k\}$, and either of them can be placed after any topological sort $a_1 \ldots a_{j-1}$ of $\{1, \ldots, j-1\}$.

(d) Algorithm 2.2.3T repeatedly outputs minimal elements (elements with no predecessors), removing them from the relation graph. We use it in reverse, repeatedly removing and giving the highest labels to *maximal* elements (elements with no successors). If only one maximal element exists, it is trivial. If k and l are both maximal, they both are output before any element x with $x \prec k$ or $x \prec l$, because steps T5 and T7 keep maximal elements in a queue (not a stack). Thus if k is nontrivial and output first, element l might become trivial, but the next nontrivial element j will not be output before l; and k is unrelated to l.

[But when applied to (48), this procedure actually *increases* the value of M in (b).]

(e) Let the nontrivial t's be $s_1 < s_2 < \cdots < s_r = N$. Then we have $s_j \geq 2s_{j-2}$, by (c). Consequently $M = s_2 + \cdots + s_r \leq s_r(1 + \frac{1}{2} + \frac{1}{4} + \cdots) + s_{r-1}(1 + \frac{1}{2} + \frac{1}{4} + \cdots) < 4s_r$.

(A sharper estimate actually holds, as observed by M. Peczarski: Let $s_0 = 1$, let the nontrivial indices be $0 = k_1 < k_2 < \cdots < k_r$, and let $k'_j = \max\{k \mid 1 \leq k < k_j, k \not\prec k_j\}$ for $j > 1$. Then $k'_{j+1} \geq k_j$, because $[k_j .. k_{j+1}]$ is not a chain. There are s_j topological sorts of $\{1, \ldots, k_{j+1}\}$ that end with k_{j+1}; and there are at least s_{j-1} that end with k'_{j+1}, since each of the s_{j-1} topological sorts of $\{1, \ldots, k_j - 1\}$ can be extended. Hence

$$s_{j+1} \geq s_j + s_{j-1} \qquad \text{for } 1 \leq j < r.$$

Now let $y_0 = 0$, $y_1 = F_2 + \cdots + F_r$, and $y_j = y_{j-2} + y_{j-1} - F_{r+1}$ for $1 < j < r$. Then

$$F_{r+1}(s_1 + \cdots + s_r) + \sum_{j=1}^{r-1} y_j (s_{r+1-j} - s_{r-j} - s_{r-1-j}) = (F_2 + \cdots + F_{r+1})s_r,$$

and each $y_j = F_{r+1} - 2F_j - (-1)^j F_{r+1-j}$ is nonnegative. Hence $s_1 + \cdots + s_r \leq ((F_2 + \cdots + F_{r+1})/F_{r+1})s_r \approx 2.6 s_r$. The following exercise shows that this bound is best possible.)

90. The number N of such permutations is F_{n+1} by exercise 5.2.1–25. Therefore $M = F_{n+1} + \cdots + F_2 = F_{n+3} - 2 \approx \phi^2 N$. Notice incidentally that all such permutations satisfy $a_1 \ldots a_n = a'_1 \ldots a'_n$. They can be arranged in a Gray path (exercise 7.2.1.1–89).

91. Since $t_j = (j - 1)(j - 3) \ldots (2 \text{ or } 1)$, we find $M = (1 + 2/\sqrt{\pi n} + O(1/n))N$.

Note: The inversion tables $c_1 \ldots c_{2n}$ for permutations satisfying (49) are characterized by the conditions $c_1 = 0$, $0 \leq c_{2k} \leq c_{2k-1}$, $0 \leq c_{2k+1} \leq c_{2k-1} + 1$.

92. The total number of pairs (R, S), where R is a partial ordering and S is a linear ordering that includes R, is equal to P_n times the expected number of topological sorts; it is also Q_n times $n!$. So the answer is $n! Q_n/P_n$.

We will discuss the computation of P_n and Q_n in Section 7.2.3. For $1 \leq n \leq 12$ the expectation turns out to be approximately

$$(1, 1.33, 2.21, 4.38, 10.1, 26.7, 79.3, 262, 950, 3760, 16200, 74800).$$

Asymptotic values as $n \to \infty$ have been deduced by Brightwell, Prömel, and Steger [*J. Combinatorial Theory* **A73** (1996), 193–206], but the limiting behavior is quite different from what happens when n is in a practical range. The values of Q_n were first determined for $n \leq 5$ by S. P. Avann [*Æquationes Math.* **8** (1972), 95–102].

93. The basic idea is to introduce dummy elements $n + 1$ and $n + 2$ with $j \prec n + 1$ and $j \prec n + 2$ for $1 \leq j \leq n$, and to find all topological sorts of such an extended relation via adjacent interchanges; then take every *second* permutation, suppressing the dummy elements. An algorithm similar to Algorithm V can be used, but with a recursion that reduces n to $n - 2$ by inserting $n - 1$ and n among $a_1 \ldots a_{n-2}$ in all possible ways, assuming that $n - 1 \not\prec n$, occasionally swapping $n + 1$ with $n + 2$. [See G. Pruesse and F. Ruskey, *SICOMP* **23** (1994), 373–386. A loopless implementation has been described by Canfield and Williamson, *Order* **12** (1995), 57–75.]

94. The case $n = 3$ illustrates the general idea of a pattern that begins with $1 \ldots (2n)$ and ends with $1(2n)2(2n-1) \ldots n(n+1)$: 123456, 123546, 123645, 132645, 132546, 132456, 142356, 142536, 142635, 152634, 152436, 152346, 162345, 162435, 162534.

Perfect matchings can also be regarded as involutions of $\{1, \ldots, 2n\}$ that have n cycles. With that representation this pattern involves two transpositions per step.

Notice that the C inversion tables of the permutations just listed are respectively 000000, 000100, 000200, 010200, 010100, 010000, 020000, 020100, 020200, 030200, 030100, 030000, 040000, 040100, 040200. In general, $C_1 = C_3 = \cdots = C_{2n-1} = 0$ and the n-tuples $(C_2, C_4, \ldots, C_{2n})$ run through a reflected Gray code on the radices

$(2n - 1, 2n - 3, \ldots, 1)$. Thus the generation process can easily be made loopless if desired. [See Timothy Walsh, *J. Combinatorial Math. and Combinatorial Computing* **36** (2001), 95–118, Section 1.]

Note: Algorithms to generate all perfect matchings go back to J. F. Pfaff [*Abhandlungen Akad. Wissenschaften* (Berlin: 1814–1815), 124–125], who described two such procedures: His first method was lexicographic, which also corresponds to lexicographic order of the C inversion tables; his second method corresponds to *colex* order of those tables. Even and odd permutations alternate in both cases.

95. Using Algorithm V with the relations $1 \prec n \succ 2 \prec n - 1 \succ \cdots$, visit the up-down permutations $a_1' a_n' a_2' a_{n-1}' \ldots$. (See exercise 5.1.4–23 for the number of solutions.)

96. For example, we can start with $a_1 \ldots a_{n-1} a_n = 2 \ldots n1$ and $b_1 b_2 \ldots b_n b_{n+1} = 12 \ldots n1$, and use Algorithm P to generate the $(n - 1)!$ permutations $b_2 \ldots b_n$ of $\{2, \ldots, n\}$. Just after that algorithm swaps $b_i \leftrightarrow b_{i+1}$, we set $a_{b_{i-1}} \leftarrow b_i$, $a_{b_i} \leftarrow b_{i+1}$, $a_{b_{i+1}} \leftarrow b_{i+2}$, and visit $a_1 \ldots a_n$.

97. Use Algorithm X, with $t_k(a_1, \ldots, a_k) = {}'a_k \neq k'$.

98. Using the notation of exercise 47, we have $N_k = \sum \binom{k}{j}(-1)^j (n - j)^{\underline{k-j}}$ by the method of inclusion and exclusion (exercise 1.3.3–26). If $k = O(\log n)$ then $N_{n-k} = (n! e^{-1}/k!)(1 + O(\log n)^2/n)$; hence $A/n! \approx (e - 1)/e$ and $B/n! \approx 1$. The number of memory references, under the assumptions of answer 48, is therefore $\approx A + B + 3A + B - N_n + 3A \approx n!(9 - \frac{8}{e}) \approx 6.06n!$, about 16.5 per derangement. [See S. G. Akl, *BIT* **20** (1980), 2–7, for a similar method.]

99. Suppose L_n generates $D_n \cup D_{n-1}$, beginning with $(1\,2\,\ldots\,n)$, then $(2\,1\,\ldots\,n)$, and ending with $(1\,\ldots\,n-1)$; for example, $L_3 = (1\,2\,3), (2\,1\,3), (1\,2)$. Then we can generate D_{n+1} as $K_{nn}, \ldots, K_{n2}, K_{n1}$, where $K_{nk} = (1\,2\,\ldots\,n)^{-k}(n\ n+1)L_n(1\,2\,\ldots\,n)^k$; for example, D_4 is

$(1\,2\,3\,4), (2\,1\,3\,4), (1\,2)(3\,4), (3\,1\,2\,4), (1\,3\,2\,4), (3\,1)(2\,4), (2\,3\,1\,4), (3\,2\,1\,4), (2\,3)(1\,4)$.

Notice that K_{nk} begins with the cycle $(k+1\ \ldots\ n\ 1\ \ldots\ k\ n+1)$ and ends with $(k+1\ \ldots\ n\ 1\ \ldots\ k-1)(k\ n+1)$; so premultiplication by $(k\ 1\ k)$ takes us from K_{nk} to $K_{n(k-1)}$. Also, premultiplication by $(1\ n)$ will return from the last element of D_{n+1} to the first. Premultiplication by $(1\ 2\ n+1)$ takes us from the last element of D_{n+1} to $(2\,1\,3\,\ldots\,n)$, from which we can return to $(1\,2\,\ldots\,n)$ by following the cycle for D_n backwards, thereby completing the list L_{n+1} as desired.

100. Use Algorithm X, with $t_k(a_1, \ldots, a_k) = {}'p > 0$ or $l_q \neq k + 1'$.

Notes: The number of indecomposable permutations is $[z^n]\left(1 - 1/\sum_{k=0}^{\infty} k!\,z^k\right)$; see L. Comtet, *Comptes Rendus Acad. Sci.* **A275** (Paris, 1972), 569–572.

A. D. King [*Discrete Math.* **306** (2006), 508–516] has shown that indecomposable permutations can be generated efficiently by making only a single transposition at each step. In fact, *adjacent* transpositions may well suffice; for example, when $n = 4$ the indecomposable permutations are 3142, 3412, 3421, 3241, 2341, 2431, 4231, 4321, 4312, 4132, 4123, 4213, 2413.

101. Here is a lexicographic involution generator analogous to Algorithm X.

Y1. [Initialize.] Set $a_k \leftarrow k$ and $l_{k-1} \leftarrow k$ for $1 \leq k \leq n$. Then set $l_n \leftarrow 0$, $k \leftarrow 1$.

Y2. [Enter level k.] If $k > n$, visit $a_1 \ldots a_n$ and go to Y3. Otherwise set $p \leftarrow l_0$, $u_k \leftarrow p$, $l_0 \leftarrow l_p$, $k \leftarrow k + 1$, and repeat this step. (We have decided to let $a_p = p$.)

Y3. [Decrease k.] Set $k \leftarrow k - 1$, and terminate if $k = 0$. Otherwise set $q \leftarrow u_k$, $p \leftarrow a_q$, and $r \leftarrow l_q$. If $p = q$, set $q \leftarrow 0$ and $k \leftarrow k + 1$ (preparing to make $a_p > p$). Otherwise set $l_{u_{k-1}} \leftarrow q$ (preparing to make $a_p > q$).

Y4. [Increase a_p.] If $r = 0$ go to Y5. Otherwise set $l_q \leftarrow l_r$, $u_{k-1} \leftarrow q$, $u_k \leftarrow r$, $a_p \leftarrow r$, $a_q \leftarrow q$, $a_r \leftarrow p$, $k \leftarrow k + 1$, and go to Y2.

Y5. [Restore a_p.] Set $l_0 \leftarrow p$, $a_p \leftarrow p$, $a_q \leftarrow q$, $k \leftarrow k - 1$, and return to Y3. $\blacksquare$

Let $t_{n+1} = t_n + nt_{n-1}$, $a_{n+1} = 1 + a_n + na_{n-1}$, $t_0 = t_1 = 1$, $a_0 = 0$, $a_1 = 1$. (See Eq. 5.1.4–(40).) Step Y2 is performed t_n times with $k > n$ and a_n times with $k \le n$. Step Y3 is performed a_n times with $p = q$ and $a_n + t_n$ times altogether. Step Y4 is performed $t_n - 1$ times; step Y5, a_n times. The total number of mems for all t_n outputs is therefore approximately $9a_n + 12t_n$. It can be shown that $\sum a_n z^n/n! = e^z(z/1 + z^3/(1\cdot3) + z^5/(1\cdot3\cdot5) + \cdots)$, and that $a_n \sim \sqrt{\pi/2}\, t_n$.

102. We construct a list L_n that begins with $()$ and ends with $(n{-}1\ n)$, starting with $L_3 = ()$, $(1\ 2)$, $(1\ 3)$, $(2\ 3)$. If n is odd, L_{n+1} is L_n, K_{n1}^R, K_{n2}, $\ldots$, K_{nn}^R, where $K_{nk} = (k\ \ldots\ n)^- L_{n-1}(k\ \ldots n)(k\ n{+}1)$. For example,

$$L_4 = (),\ (1\ 2),\ (1\ 3),\ (2\ 3),\ (2\ 3)(1\ 4),\ (1\ 4),\ (2\ 4),\ (1\ 3)(2\ 4),\ (1\ 2)(3\ 4),\ (3\ 4).$$

If n is even, L_{n+1} is L_n, $K_{n(n-1)}$, $K_{n(n-2)}^R$, $\ldots$, K_{n1}, $(1\ n{-}2)L_{n-1}^R(1\ n{-}2)(n\ n{+}1)$.

For further developments, see the article by Walsh cited in answer 94.

103. The following elegant solution by Carla Savage needs only $n - 2$ different operations ρ_j, for $1 < j < n$, where ρ_j replaces $a_{j-1}a_ja_{j+1}$ by $a_{j+1}a_{j-1}a_j$ when j is even, $a_ja_{j+1}a_{j-1}$ when j is odd. We may assume that $n \ge 4$; let $A_4 = (\rho_3\rho_2\rho_2\rho_3)^3$. In general A_n will begin and end with ρ_{n-1}, and it will contain $2n-2$ occurrences of ρ_{n-1} altogether. To get A_{n+1}, replace the kth ρ_{n-1} of A_n by $\rho_n A_n' \rho_n$, where $k = 1, 2, 4, \ldots$, $2n-2$ if n is even and $k = 1, 3, \ldots, 2n-3, 2n-2$ if n is odd, and where A_n' is A_n with its first or last element deleted. Then, if we begin with $a_1 \ldots a_n = 1 \ldots n$, the operations ρ_{n-1} of A_n will cause position a_n to run through the successive values $n \to p_1 \to n \to p_2 \to \cdots \to p_{n-1} \to n$, where $p_1 \ldots p_{n-1} = (n{-}1{-}[n\,\text{even}]) \ldots 4213 \ldots (n{-}1{-}[n\,\text{odd}])$; the final permutation will again be $1 \ldots n$.

104. (a) A well-balanced permutation has $\sum_{k=1}^n ka_k = n(n+1)^2/4$, an integer.

(b) Replace k by a_k when summing over k.

(c) A fairly fast way to count, when n is not too large, can be based on the streamlined plain-change algorithm of exercise 16, because the quantity $\sum ka_k$ changes in a simple way with each adjacent interchange, and because $n - 1$ of every n steps are "hunts" that can be done rapidly. We can save half the work by considering only permutations in which 1 precedes 2. The values for $1 \le n \le 15$ are 1, 0, 0, 2, 6, 0, 184, 936, 6688, 0, 420480, 4298664, 44405142, 0, 6732621476.

[See E. I. Marshall, *Sankhyā* **B56** (1994), 59–66.]

105. (a) For each permutation $a_1 \ldots a_n$, insert $\prec$ between a_j and a_{j+1} if $a_j > a_{j+1}$; insert either $\equiv$ or $\prec$ between them if $a_j < a_{j+1}$. (A permutation with k "ascents" therefore yields 2^k weak orders.) Weak orders are sometimes called "preferential arrangements"; exercise 5.3.1–4 shows that there are approximately $n!/(2(\ln 2)^{n+1})$ of them. A Gray code for weak orders, in which each step changes $\prec \leftrightarrow \equiv$ and/or $a_j \leftrightarrow a_{j+1}$, can be obtained by combining Algorithm P with Gray binary code at the ascents.

(b) Start with $a_1 \ldots a_n a_{n+1} = 0 \ldots 00$ and $a_0 = -1$. Perform Algorithm L until it stops with $j = 0$. Find k such that $a_1 > \cdots > a_k = a_{k+1}$, and terminate if $k = n$. Otherwise set $a_l \leftarrow a_{k+1} + 1$ for $1 \le l \le k$ and go to step L4. [See M. Mor and A. S. Fraenkel, *Discrete Math.* **48** (1984), 101–112. Weak ordering sequences are characterized by the property that, if k appears and $k > 0$, then $k - 1$ also appears.]

106. All weak ordering sequences can be obtained by a sequence of elementary operations $a_i \leftrightarrow a_j$ or $a_i \leftarrow a_j$. (Perhaps one could actually restrict the transformations further, allowing only $a_j \leftrightarrow a_{j+1}$ or $a_j \leftarrow a_{j+1}$ for $1 \leq j < n$.)

107. Every step increases the quantity $\sum_{k=1}^{n} 2^k [a_k = k]$, as noted by H. S. Wilf, so the game must terminate. At least three approaches to the solution are plausible: one bad, one good, and one better. The bad one is to play the game on all 13! shuffles and to record the longest. This method does produce the correct answer; but 13! is 6,227,020,800, and the average game lasts ≈ 8.728 steps.

The good one [A. Pepperdine, *Math. Gazette* **73** (1989), 131–133] is to play backwards, starting with the final position $1*\ldots*$ where $*$ denotes a card that is face down; we will turn a card up only when its value becomes relevant. To move backward from a given position $a_1 \ldots a_n$, consider all $k > 1$ such that either $a_k = k$ or $a_k = *$ and k has not yet turned up. Thus the next-to-last positions are $21*\ldots*$, $3*1*\ldots*$, $\ldots$, $n*\ldots*1$. Some positions (like $6**213$ for $n = 6$) have no predecessors, even though we haven't turned all the cards up. It is easy to explore the tree of potential backwards games systematically, and one can in fact show that the number of nodes with t $*$'s is exactly $(n-1)!/t!$. Hence the total number of nodes considered is exactly $\lfloor (n-1)! e \rfloor$. When $n = 13$ this is 1,302,061,345.

The better one is to play forwards, starting with initial position $*\ldots*$ and turning over the top card when it is face down, running through all $(n-1)!$ permutations of $\{2, \ldots, n\}$ as cards are turned. If the bottom $n - m$ cards are known to be equal to $(m+1)(m+2)\ldots n$, in that order, at most $f(m)$ further moves are possible; thus we need not pursue a line of play any further if it cannot last long enough to be interesting. A permutation generator like Algorithm X allows us to share the computation for all permutations with the same prefix and to reject unimportant prefixes. The card in position j need not take the value j when it is turned. When $n = 13$ this method needs to consider only respectively $(1, 11, 940, 6960, 44745, 245083, 1118216, 4112676, 11798207, 26541611, 44380227, 37417359)$ branches at levels $(1, 2, \ldots, 12)$ and to make a total of only 482,663,902 forward moves. Although it repeats some lines of play, the early cutoffs of unprofitable branches make it run more than 11 times faster than the backward method when $n = 13$.

The unique way to attain length 80 is to start with 2 9 4 5 11 12 10 1 8 13 3 6 7.

108. This result holds for any game in which

$$a_1 \ldots a_n \to a_k a_{p(k,2)} \ldots a_{p(k,k-1)} a_1 a_{k+1} \ldots a_n$$

when $a_1 = k$, where $p(k,2)\ldots p(k,k-1)$ is an arbitrary permutation of $\{2, \ldots, k-1\}$. Suppose a_1 takes on exactly m distinct values $d(1) < \cdots < d(m)$ during a play of the game; we will prove that at most F_{m+1} permutations occur, including the initial shuffle. This assertion is obvious when $m = 1$.

Let $d(j)$ be the initial value of $a_{d(m)}$, where $j < m$, and suppose $a_{d(m)}$ changes on step r. If $d(j) = 1$, there are $r+1 \leq F_m+1 \leq F_{m+1}$ permutations. Otherwise $r \leq F_{m-1}$, and at most F_m further permutations follow step r. [*SIAM Review* **19** (1977), 739–741.]

The values of $f(n)$ for $1 \leq n \leq 16$ are $(0, 1, 2, 4, 7, 10, 16, 22, 30, 38, 51, 65, 80, 101, 113, 139)$, and they are attainable in respectively $(1, 1, 2, 2, 1, 5, 2, 1, 1, 1, 1, 1, 1, 4, 6, 1)$ ways. The unique longest-winded permutation for $n = 16$ is

9 12 6 7 2 14 8 1 11 13 5 4 15 16 10 3.

109. An ingenious construction by I. H. Sudborough and L. Morales [*Theoretical Comp. Sci.* **411** (2010), 3965–3970] proves that $f(n) \geq \frac{19}{128}n^2 + O(1)$.

110. For $0 \leq j \leq 9$ construct the bit vectors $A_j = [a_j \in S_1]\ldots[a_j \in S_m]$ and $B_j = [j \in S_1]\ldots[j \in S_m]$. Then the number of j such that $A_j = v$ must equal the number of k such that $B_k = v$, for all bit vectors v. And if so, the values $\{a_j \mid A_j = v\}$ should be assigned to permutations of $\{k \mid B_k = v\}$ in all possible ways.

For example, the bit vectors in the given problem are

$$(A_0,\ldots,A_9) = (9,6,8,\mathsf{b},5,4,0,\mathsf{a},2,0), \qquad (B_0,\ldots,B_9) = (5,0,8,6,2,\mathsf{a},4,\mathsf{b},9,0),$$

in hexadecimal notation; hence $a_0\ldots a_9 = 8327061549$ or 8327069541.

In a larger problem we would keep the bit vectors in a hash table. It would be better to give the answer in terms of equivalence classes, not permutations; indeed, this problem has comparatively little to do with permutations.

111. In the directed graph with $n!/2$ vertices $a_1\ldots a_{n-2}$ and $n!$ arcs $a_1\ldots a_{n-2} \to a_2\ldots a_{n-1}$ (one for each permutation $a_1\ldots a_n$), each vertex has in-degree 2 and out-degree 2. Furthermore, from paths like $a_1\ldots a_{n-2} \to a_2\ldots a_{n-1} \to a_3\ldots a_n \to a_4\ldots a_n a_2 \to a_5\ldots a_n a_2 a_1 \to \cdots \to a_2 a_1 a_3\ldots a_{n-2}$, we can see that any vertex is reachable from any other. Therefore an Eulerian trail exists by Theorem 2.3.4.2G, and such a trail clearly is equivalent to a universal cycle of permutations. The lexicographically smallest example when $n = 4$ is $(123124132134214324314234)$.

[*Notes:* C. Bachet presented a similar idea for $n = 4$ already in his *Problemes plaisans et delectables* (Lyon: 1612), 123, but with two half-cycles instead of a full cycle. G. Hurlbert and G. Isaak, in *Discrete Math.* **149** (1996), 123–129, have suggested another appealing approach: Let's say that a *modular universal cycle of permutations* is a cycle of $n!$ digits $\{0,\ldots,n\}$ with the property that each permutation $a_1\ldots a_n$ of $\{1,\ldots,n\}$ arises from consecutive digits $u_1\ldots u_n$ by letting $a_j = (u_j - c) \bmod (n+1)$, where c is the "missing" digit in $\{u_1,\ldots,u_n\}$. For example, the modular universal cycle (012032) is essentially unique for $n = 3$; and the lexicographically smallest for $n = 4$ is $(0123014201320143214301430243)$. If vertices $a_1\ldots a_{n-2}$ and $a'_1\ldots a'_{n-2}$ in the digraph of the previous paragraph are considered equivalent when $a_1 - a'_1 \equiv \cdots \equiv a_{n-2} - a'_{n-2}$ (modulo n), we get a digraph of $(n-1)!/2$ vertices whose Eulerian trails correspond to the modular universal cycles of permutations for $\{1,\ldots,n-1\}$.]

112. (a) If the cycle is $a_1 a_2 \ldots$, use σ at step j if the subsequence $a_j a_{j+1}\ldots a_{j+n-1}$ is a permutation; otherwise use ρ.

(b) This statement follows immediately from exercise 72.

(c) Let $\Omega_2 = \sigma^2$, and obtain Ω_{n+1} from Ω_n by substituting $\sigma \mapsto \sigma^2 \rho^{n-1}$ and $\rho \mapsto \sigma^2 \rho^{n-2}\sigma$. For example, $\Omega_3 = (\sigma^2\rho)^2$ and $\Omega_4 = ((\sigma^2\rho)^2\sigma^2\rho\sigma)^2$. Generate permutations by starting with $n\ldots 21$ and applying the successive elements of Ω_n; for example, the sequence when $n = 4$ is

$$4321, 3214, 2143, 1423, 4213, 2134, 1342, 3412, 4132, 1324, 3241, 2431,$$
$$4312, 3124, 1243, 2413, 4123, 1234, 2341, 3421, 4231, 2314, 3142, 1432,$$

and the corresponding universal cycle is $(432142134132431241234231)$. Notice that n moves cyclically in this sequence of permutations; and the permutations that begin with n correspond to the sequence obtained from Ω_{n-1}.

[See F. Ruskey and A. Williams, *ACM Transactions on Algorithms* **6** (2010), 45:1–45:12. Similar methods are said to be known to bell-ringers. Universal cycles can also be constructed explicitly for permutations of an arbitrary *multiset*, with a method analogous to 7.2.1.1–(62); see A. Williams, Ph.D. thesis (Univ. of Victoria, 2009).]

113. By exercise 2.3.4.2–22 it suffices to count the oriented trees rooted at $12\ldots(n-2)$, in the digraph of the preceding answer; and those trees can be counted by exercise 2.3.4.2–19. For $n \le 6$ the numbers U_n turn out to be tantalizingly simple: $U_2 = 1$, $U_3 = 3$, $U_4 = 2^7 \cdot 3$, $U_5 = 2^{33} \cdot 3^8 \cdot 5^3$, $U_6 = 2^{190} \cdot 3^{49} \cdot 5^{33}$. (Here we consider (121323) to be the same cycle as (213231), but different from (131232).)

Mark Cooke has discovered the following instructive way to compute these values efficiently: Consider the $n! \times n!$ matrix $M = 2I - R - S$, where $R_{\pi\pi'} = [\pi' = \pi\rho]$ and $S_{\pi\pi'} = [\pi' = \pi\sigma]$. There is a matrix H such that $H^- RH$ and $H^- SH$ each have block diagonal form consisting of k_λ copies of $k_\lambda \times k_\lambda$ matrices R_λ and S_λ, for each partition λ of n, where k_λ is $n!$ divided by the product of the hook lengths of shape λ (Theorem 5.1.4H), and where R_λ and S_λ are matrix representations of ρ and σ based on Young tableaux. [A proof can be found in Bruce Sagan, *The Symmetric Group* (Pacific Grove, Calif.: Wadsworth & Brooks/Cole, 1991).] For example, when $n = 3$ we have

$$R = \begin{pmatrix} 0 & 0 & 0 & 1 & 0 & 0 \\ 0 & 0 & 0 & 0 & 0 & 1 \\ 0 & 0 & 0 & 0 & 1 & 0 \\ 1 & 0 & 0 & 0 & 0 & 0 \\ 0 & 0 & 1 & 0 & 0 & 0 \\ 0 & 1 & 0 & 0 & 0 & 0 \end{pmatrix}, \quad S = \begin{pmatrix} 0 & 1 & 0 & 0 & 0 & 0 \\ 0 & 0 & 1 & 0 & 0 & 0 \\ 1 & 0 & 0 & 0 & 0 & 0 \\ 0 & 0 & 0 & 0 & 1 & 0 \\ 0 & 0 & 0 & 0 & 0 & 1 \\ 0 & 0 & 0 & 1 & 0 & 0 \end{pmatrix}, \quad H = \begin{pmatrix} 1 & 1 & 1 & -1 & 1 & 0 \\ 1 & 1 & -1 & 0 & 0 & -1 \\ 1 & 1 & 0 & 1 & -1 & 1 \\ 1 & -1 & -1 & 1 & 0 & 1 \\ 1 & -1 & 1 & 0 & 1 & -1 \\ 1 & -1 & 0 & -1 & -1 & 0 \end{pmatrix},$$

$$H^- RH = \begin{pmatrix} 1 & 0 & 0 & 0 & 0 & 0 \\ 0 & -1 & 0 & 0 & 0 & 0 \\ 0 & 0 & 0 & 1 & 0 & 0 \\ 0 & 0 & 1 & 0 & 0 & 0 \\ 0 & 0 & 0 & 0 & 0 & 1 \\ 0 & 0 & 0 & 0 & 1 & 0 \end{pmatrix}, \quad H^- SH = \begin{pmatrix} 1 & 0 & 0 & 0 & 0 & 0 \\ 0 & 1 & 0 & 0 & 0 & 0 \\ 0 & 0 & 0 & -1 & 0 & 0 \\ 0 & 0 & 1 & -1 & 0 & 0 \\ 0 & 0 & 0 & 0 & 0 & -1 \\ 0 & 0 & 0 & 0 & 1 & -1 \end{pmatrix}$$

when rows and columns are indexed by the respective permutations 1, σ, σ^2, ρ, $\rho\sigma$, $\rho\sigma^2$; here $k_3 = k_{111} = 1$ and $k_{21} = 2$. Therefore the eigenvalues of M are the union, over λ, of k_λ-fold repeated eigenvalues of the $k_\lambda \times k_\lambda$ matrices $2I - R_\lambda - S_\lambda$. In the example, the eigenvalues of (0), (2), and $\left(\begin{smallmatrix} 2 & 0 \\ -2 & 3 \end{smallmatrix}\right)$ twice are $\{0\}$, $\{2\}$, and $\{2, 3\}$ twice.

The eigenvalues of M are directly related to those of the matrix A in exercise 2.3.4.2–19. Indeed, each eigenvector of A yields an eigenvector of M, if we equate the components for permutations π and $\pi\rho\sigma^-$, because rows π and $\pi\rho\sigma^-$ of $R + S$ are equal. For example,

$$A = \begin{pmatrix} 2 & -1 & -1 \\ -1 & 2 & -1 \\ -1 & -1 & 2 \end{pmatrix} \text{ has eigenvectors } \begin{pmatrix} 1 \\ 1 \\ 1 \end{pmatrix}, \begin{pmatrix} 1 \\ -1 \\ 0 \end{pmatrix}, \begin{pmatrix} 1 \\ 0 \\ -1 \end{pmatrix} \text{ for eigenvalues } 0, 3, 3,$$

yielding the eigenvectors $(1, 1, 1, 1, 1, 1)^T$, $(1, -1, 0, 0, -1, 1)^T$, $(1, 0, -1, -1, 0, 1)^T$ of M for the same eigenvalues. And M has $n!/2$ additional eigenvectors, with all components zero except those indexed by π and $\pi\sigma^-\rho$ for some π, because only rows $\pi\rho^-$ and $\pi\sigma^-$ of $R+S$ have nonzero entries in columns π and $\pi\sigma^-\rho$; such vectors yield $n!/2$ additional eigenvalues, all equal to 2.

Therefore U_n, which is $2/n!$ times the product of the nonzero eigenvalues of A, is $2^{1-n!/2}/n!$ times the product of the nonzero eigenvalues of M.

Unfortunately the small-prime-factor phenomenon does not continue; U_7 equals $2^{1217} 3^{123} 5^{119} 7^5 11^{28} 43^{35} 73^{20} 79^{21} 109^{35}$, and U_9 is divisible by 59229013196333^{168}.

SECTION 7.2.1.3

1. Given a multiset, form the sequence $e_t \ldots e_2 e_1$ from right to left by first listing its distinct elements (in increasing order), then those that appear twice, then those that appear thrice, etc. Let us set $e_{-j} \leftarrow s - j$ for $0 \leq j \leq s = n - t$, so that every element e_j for $1 \leq j \leq t$ is equal to some element to its right in the sequence $e_t \ldots e_1 e_0 \ldots e_{-s}$. If the first such element is $e_{c_j - s}$, we obtain a solution to (3). Conversely, every solution to (3) yields a unique multiset $\{e_1, \ldots, e_t\}$, because $c_j < s + j$ for $1 \leq j \leq t$.

[A similar correspondence was proposed by E. Catalan: If $0 \leq e_1 \leq \cdots \leq e_t \leq s$, let

$$\{c_1, \ldots, c_t\} = \{e_1, \ldots, e_t\} \cup \{s + j \mid 1 \leq j < t \text{ and } e_j = e_{j+1}\}.$$

See *Mémoires de la Soc. roy. des Sciences de Liège* (2) **12** (1885), *Mélanges Math.*, 3.]

2. Start at the bottom left corner; then go up for each 0, go right for each 1. The result is [figure]. Conversely, we can easily "read off" the representations a_i, b_i, c_i, d_i, p_i, or q_i of (2)–(11) from any given path from $(0,0)$ to (s,t).

3. In this algorithm, variable r is the least positive index such that $q_r > 0$.

N1. [Initialize.] Set $q_j \leftarrow 0$ for $1 \leq j \leq t$, and $q_0 \leftarrow s$. (We assume that $st > 0$.)

N2. [Visit.] Visit the composition $q_t \ldots q_0$. Go to N4 if $q_0 = 0$.

N3. [Easy case.] Set $q_0 \leftarrow q_0 - 1$, $r \leftarrow 1$, and go to N5.

N4. [Tricky case.] Terminate if $r = t$. Otherwise set $q_0 \leftarrow q_r - 1$, $q_r \leftarrow 0$, $r \leftarrow r + 1$.

N5. [Increase q_r.] Set $q_r \leftarrow q_r + 1$ and return to N2. ∎

[See *CACM* **11** (1968), 430; **12** (1969), 187. The task of generating such compositions in *decreasing* lexicographic order is more difficult.]

4. We can reverse the roles of 0 and 1 in (14), so that $0^{q_t} 10^{q_{t-1}} 1 \ldots 10^{q_1} 10^{q_0} = 1^{r_s} 01^{r_s - 1} 0 \ldots 01^{r_1} 01^{r_0}$. This gives $0^1 10^0 10^2 10^2 10^4 10^0 10^0 10^0 10^0 10^1 10^0 10^1 10^0 = 1^0 01^2 01^0 01^1 01^0 01^1 01^0 01^0 01^0 01^6 01^2 01^1$. Lexicographic order of $a_{n-1} \ldots a_1 a_0$ corresponds to lexicographic order of $r_s \ldots r_1 r_0$.

Incidentally, there's also a multiset connection: $\{d_t, \ldots, d_1\} = \{r_s \cdot s, \ldots, r_0 \cdot 0\}$. For example, $\{10, 10, 8, 6, 2, 2, 2, 2, 2, 1, 1, 0\} = \{0 \cdot 11, 2 \cdot 10, 0 \cdot 9, 1 \cdot 8, 0 \cdot 7, 1 \cdot 6, 0 \cdot 5, 0 \cdot 4, 0 \cdot 3, 6 \cdot 2, 2 \cdot 1, 1 \cdot 0\}$.

5. (a) Set $x_j = c_j - \lfloor (j-1)/2 \rfloor$ in each t-combination of $n + \lfloor t/2 \rfloor$. (b) Set $x_j = c_j + j + 1$ in each t-combination of $n - t - 2$.

(A similar approach finds all solutions $(x_t, \ldots, x_1)$ to the inequalities $x_{j+1} \geq x_j + \delta_j$ for $0 \leq j \leq t$, given the values of x_{t+1}, $(\delta_t, \ldots, \delta_0)$, and x_0.)

6. Assume that $t > 0$. We get to T3 when $c_1 > 0$; to T5 when $c_2 = c_1 + 1 > 1$; to T4 for $2 \leq j \leq t+1$ when $c_j = c_1 + j - 1 \geq j$. So the counts are: T1, 1; T2, $\binom{n}{t}$; T3, $\binom{n-1}{t}$; T4, $\binom{n-2}{t-1} + \binom{n-3}{t-2} + \cdots + \binom{n-t-1}{0} = \binom{n-1}{t-1}$; T5, $\binom{n-2}{t-1}$; T6, $\binom{n-1}{t-1} + \binom{n-2}{t-1} - 1$.

7. A procedure slightly simpler than Algorithm T suffices: Assume that $s < n$.

S1. [Initialize.] Set $b_j \leftarrow j + n - s - 1$ for $1 \leq j \leq s$; then set $j \leftarrow 1$.

S2. [Visit.] Visit the combination $b_s \ldots b_2 b_1$. Terminate if $j > s$.

S3. [Decrease b_j.] Set $b_j \leftarrow b_j - 1$. If $b_j < j$, set $j \leftarrow j + 1$ and return to S2.

S4. [Reset $b_{j-1} \ldots b_1$.] While $j > 1$, set $b_{j-1} \leftarrow b_j - 1$ and $j \leftarrow j - 1$. Go to S2. ∎

(See S. Dvořák, *Comp. J.* **33** (1990), 188. Notice that if $x_k = n - b_k$ for $1 \le k \le s$, this algorithm runs through all combinations $x_s \ldots x_2 x_1$ of $\{1, 2, \ldots, n\}$ with $1 \le x_s < \cdots < x_2 < x_1 \le n$, in *increasing* lexicographic order.)

8. A1. [Initialize.] Set $a_n \ldots a_0 \leftarrow 0^{s+1} 1^t$, $q \leftarrow t$, $r \leftarrow 0$. (We assume that $0 < t < n$.)

A2. [Visit.] Visit the combination $a_{n-1} \ldots a_1 a_0$. Go to A4 if $q = 0$.

A3. [Replace $\ldots 01^q$ by $\ldots 101^{q-1}$.] Set $a_q \leftarrow 1$, $a_{q-1} \leftarrow 0$, $q \leftarrow q - 1$; then if $q = 0$, set $r \leftarrow 1$. Return to A2.

A4. [Shift block of 1s.] Set $a_r \leftarrow 0$ and $r \leftarrow r + 1$. Then if $a_r = 1$, set $a_q \leftarrow 1$, $q \leftarrow q + 1$, and repeat step A4.

A5. [Carry to left.] Terminate if $r = n$; otherwise set $a_r \leftarrow 1$.

A6. [Odd?] If $q > 0$, set $r \leftarrow 0$. Return to A2. ∎

In step A2, q and r point respectively to the rightmost 0 and 1 in $a_{n-1} \ldots a_0$. Steps A1, ..., A6 are executed with frequency 1, $\binom{n}{t}$, $\binom{n-1}{t-1}$, $\binom{n}{t} - 1$, $\binom{n-1}{t}$, $\binom{n-1}{t} - 1$.

9. (a) The first $\binom{n-1}{t}$ strings begin with 0 and have $2A_{(s-1)t}$ bit changes; the other $\binom{n-1}{t-1}$ begin with 1 and have $2A_{s(t-1)}$. And $\nu(01^t 0^{s-1} \oplus 10^s 1^{t-1}) = 2 \min(s, t)$.

(b) Solution 1 (direct): Let $B_{st} = A_{st} + \min(s, t) + 1$. Then

$$B_{st} = B_{(s-1)t} + B_{s(t-1)} + [s = t] \quad \text{when } st > 0; \qquad B_{st} = 1 \quad \text{when } st = 0.$$

Consequently $B_{st} = \sum_{k=0}^{\min(s,t)} \binom{s+t-2k}{s-k}$. If $s \le t$ this is $\le \sum_{k=0}^{s} \binom{s+t-k}{s-k} = \binom{s+t+1}{s} = \binom{s+t}{s} \frac{s+t+1}{t+1} < 2 \binom{s+t}{t}$.

Solution 2 (indirect): The algorithm in answer 8 makes $2(x + y)$ bit changes when steps (A3, A4) are executed (x, y) times. Thus $A_{st} \le \binom{n-1}{t-1} + \binom{n}{t} - 1 < 2 \binom{n}{t}$.

[The comment in answer 7.2.1.1–3 therefore applies to combinations as well.]

10. Each scenario corresponds to a $(4, 4)$-combination $b_4 b_3 b_2 b_1$ or $c_4 c_3 c_2 c_1$ in which A wins games $\{8 - b_4, 8 - b_3, 8 - b_2, 8 - b_1\}$ and N wins games $\{8 - c_4, 8 - c_3, 8 - c_2, 8 - c_1\}$, because we can assume that the losing team wins the remaining games in a series of 8. (Equivalently, we can generate all permutations of $\{A, A, A, A, N, N, N, N\}$ and omit the trailing run of As or Ns.) The American League wins if and only if $b_1 \ne 0$, if and only if $c_1 = 0$. The formula $\binom{c_4}{4} + \binom{c_3}{3} + \binom{c_2}{2} + \binom{c_1}{1}$ assigns a unique integer between 0 and 69 to each scenario.

For example, ANANAA $\Longleftrightarrow a_7 \ldots a_1 a_0 = 01010011 \Longleftrightarrow b_4 b_3 b_2 b_1 = 7532 \Longleftrightarrow c_4 c_3 c_2 c_1 = 6410$, and this is the scenario of rank $\binom{6}{4} + \binom{4}{3} + \binom{1}{2} + \binom{0}{1} = 19$ in lexicographic order. (The term $\binom{c_j}{j}$ will be zero if and only if it corresponds to a trailing N.)

11. AAAA (9 times), NNNN (8), and ANAAA (7) were most common. Exactly 27 of the 70 failed to occur, including all four beginning with NNNA. (We disregard the games that were tied because of darkness, in 1907, 1912, and 1922. The case ANNAAAA should perhaps be excluded too, because it occurred only in 1920 as part of ANNAAAAA in a best-of-nine series. The scenario NNAAANN occurred for the first time in 2001.)

12. (a) Let V_j be the subspace $\{a_{n-1} \ldots a_0 \in V \mid a_k = 0 \text{ for } 0 \le k < j\}$, so that $\{0 \ldots 0\} = V_n \subseteq V_{n-1} \subseteq \cdots \subseteq V_0 = V$. Then $\{c_1, \ldots, c_t\} = \{c \mid V_c \ne V_{c+1}\}$, and α_k is the unique element $a_{n-1} \ldots a_0$ of V with $a_{c_j} = [j = k]$ for $1 \le j \le t$.

Incidentally, the $t \times n$ matrix corresponding to a canonical basis is said to be in *reduced row-echelon form*. It can be found by a standard "triangulation" algorithm (see exercise 4.6.1–19 and Algorithm 4.6.2N).

(b) The 2-nomial coefficient $\binom{n}{t}_2 = 2^t \binom{n-1}{t}_2 + \binom{n-1}{t-1}_2$ of exercise 1.2.6–58 has the right properties, because $2^t \binom{n-1}{t}_2$ binary vector spaces have $c_t < n-1$ and $\binom{n-1}{t-1}_2$ have $c_t = n-1$. [In general the number of canonical bases with r asterisks is the number of partitions of r into at most t parts, with no part exceeding $n-t$, and this is $[z^r]\binom{n}{t}_z$ by Eq. 7.2.1.4–(51). See D. E. Knuth, *J. Combinatorial Theory* **A10** (1971), 178–180.]

(c) The following algorithm assumes that $n > t > 0$ and that $a_{(t+1)j} = 0$ for $t \le j \le n$.

V1. [Initialize.] Set $a_{kj} \leftarrow [j = k - 1]$ for $1 \le k \le t$ and $0 \le j < n$. Also set $q \leftarrow t$, $r \leftarrow 0$.

V2. [Visit.] (At this point we have $a_{k(k-1)} = 1$ for $1 \le k \le q$, $a_{(q+1)q} = 0$, and $a_{1r} = 1$.) Visit the canonical basis $(a_{1(n-1)} \ldots a_{11}a_{10}, \ldots, a_{t(n-1)} \ldots a_{t1}a_{t0})$. Go to V4 if $q > 0$.

V3. [Find block of 1s.] Set $q \leftarrow 1, 2, \ldots$, until $a_{(q+1)(q+r)} = 0$. Terminate if $q + r = n$.

V4. [Add 1 to column $q + r$.] Set $k \leftarrow 1$. While $a_{k(q+r)} = 1$, set $a_{k(q+r)} \leftarrow 0$ and $k \leftarrow k + 1$. Then if $k \le q$, set $a_{k(q+r)} \leftarrow 1$; otherwise set $a_{q(q+r)} \leftarrow 1$, $a_{q(q+r-1)} \leftarrow 0$, $q \leftarrow q - 1$.

V5. [Shift block right.] If $q = 0$, set $r \leftarrow r+1$. Otherwise, if $r > 0$, set $a_{k(k-1)} \leftarrow 1$ and $a_{k(r+k-1)} \leftarrow 0$ for $1 \le k \le q$, then set $r \leftarrow 0$. Go to V2. ∎

Step V2 finds $q > 0$ with probability $1 - (2^{n-t} - 1)/(2^n - 1) \approx 1 - 2^{-t}$, so we could save time by treating this case separately.

(d) Since $999999 = 4\binom{8}{4}_2 + 16\binom{7}{4}_2 + 5\binom{6}{3}_2 + 5\binom{5}{3}_2 + 8\binom{4}{3}_2 + 0\binom{3}{2}_2 + 4\binom{2}{2}_2 + 1\binom{1}{1}_2 + 2\binom{0}{1}_2$, the millionth output has binary columns 4, 16/2, 5, 5, 8/2, 0, 4/2, 1, 2/2, namely

$$\alpha_1 = 0\,0\,1\,1\,0\,0\,0\,1\,1,$$
$$\alpha_2 = 0\,0\,0\,0\,0\,0\,1\,0\,0,$$
$$\alpha_3 = 1\,0\,1\,1\,1\,0\,0\,0\,0,$$
$$\alpha_4 = 0\,1\,0\,0\,0\,0\,0\,0\,0.$$

[*Reference:* E. Calabi and H. S. Wilf, *J. Combinatorial Theory* **A22** (1977), 107–109.]

13. Let $n = s + t$. There are $\binom{s-1}{\lceil(r-1)/2\rceil}\binom{t-1}{\lfloor(r-1)/2\rfloor}$ configurations beginning with 0 and $\binom{s-1}{\lfloor(r-1)/2\rfloor}\binom{t-1}{\lceil(r-1)/2\rceil}$ beginning with 1, because an Ising configuration that begins with 0 corresponds to a composition of s 0s into $\lceil(r+1)/2\rceil$ parts and a composition of t 1s into $\lfloor(r+1)/2\rfloor$ parts. We can generate all such pairs of compositions and weave them into configurations. [See E. Ising, *Zeitschrift für Physik* **31** (1925), 253–258; J. M. S. Simões Pereira, *CACM* **12** (1969), 562.]

14. Start with $l[j] \leftarrow j - 1$ and $r[j - 1] \leftarrow j$ for $1 \le j \le n$; $l[0] \leftarrow n$, $r[n] \leftarrow 0$. To get the next combination, assuming that $t > 0$, set $p \leftarrow s$ if $l[0] > s$, otherwise $p \leftarrow r[n] - 1$. Terminate if $p \le 0$; otherwise set $q \leftarrow r[p]$, $l[q] \leftarrow l[p]$, and $r[l[p]] \leftarrow q$. Then if $r[q] > s$ and $p < s$, set $r[p] \leftarrow r[n]$, $l[r[n]] \leftarrow p$, $r[s] \leftarrow r[q]$, $l[r[q]] \leftarrow s$, $r[n] \leftarrow 0$, $l[0] \leftarrow n$; otherwise set $r[p] \leftarrow r[q]$, $l[r[q]] \leftarrow p$. Finally set $r[q] \leftarrow p$ and $l[p] \leftarrow q$.

[See Korsh and Lipschutz, *J. Algorithms* **25** (1997), 321–335, where the idea is extended to a loopless algorithm for multiset permutations. *Caution:* This exercise, like exercise 7.2.1.1–16, is more academic than practical, because the routine that visits the linked list might need a loop that nullifies any advantage of loopless generation.]

15. (The stated fact is true because lexicographic order of $c_t \ldots c_1$ corresponds to lexicographic order of $a_{n-1} \ldots a_0$, which is reverse lexicographic order of the complementary sequence $1 \ldots 1 \oplus a_{n-1} \ldots a_0$.) By Theorem L, the combination $c_t \ldots c_1$ is visited *before* exactly $\binom{b_s}{s} + \cdots + \binom{b_2}{2} + \binom{b_1}{1}$ others have been visited, and we must have

$$\binom{b_s}{s} + \cdots + \binom{b_1}{1} + \binom{c_t}{t} + \cdots + \binom{c_1}{1} = \binom{s+t}{t} - 1.$$

This general identity can be written

$$\sum_{j=0}^{n-1} x_j \binom{j}{x_0 + \cdots + x_j} + \sum_{j=0}^{n-1} \bar{x}_j \binom{j}{\bar{x}_0 + \cdots + \bar{x}_j} = \binom{n}{x_0 + \cdots + x_{n-1}} - 1$$

when each x_j is 0 or 1, and $\bar{x}_j = 1 - x_j$; it follows also from the equation

$$x_n \binom{n}{x_0 + \cdots + x_n} + \bar{x}_n \binom{n}{\bar{x}_0 + \cdots + \bar{x}_n} = \binom{n+1}{x_0 + \cdots + x_n} - \binom{n}{x_0 + \cdots + x_{n-1}}.$$

16. Since $999999 = \binom{1414}{2} + \binom{1008}{1} = \binom{182}{3} + \binom{153}{2} + \binom{111}{1} = \binom{71}{4} + \binom{56}{3} + \binom{36}{2} + \binom{14}{1} = \binom{43}{5} + \binom{32}{4} + \binom{21}{3} + \binom{15}{2} + \binom{6}{1}$, the answers are (a) 1414 1008; (b) 182 153 111; (c) 71 56 36 14; (d) 43 32 21 15 6; (e) 1000000 999999 ... 2 0.

17. By Theorem L, n_t is the largest integer such that $N \geq \binom{n_t}{t}$; the remaining terms are the degree-$(t-1)$ representation of $N - \binom{n_t}{t}$.

A simple sequential method for $t > 1$ starts with $x = 1$, $c = t$, and sets $c \leftarrow c + 1$, $x \leftarrow xc/(c-t)$ zero or more times until $x > N$; then we complete the first phase by setting $x \leftarrow x(c-t)/c$, $c \leftarrow c - 1$, at which point we have $x = \binom{c}{t} \leq N < \binom{c+1}{t}$. Set $n_t \leftarrow c$, $N \leftarrow N - x$; terminate with $n_1 \leftarrow N$ if $t = 2$; otherwise set $x \leftarrow xt/c$, $t \leftarrow t - 1$, $c \leftarrow c - 1$; while $x > N$ set $x \leftarrow x(c-t)/c$, $c \leftarrow c - 1$; repeat. This method requires $O(n)$ arithmetic operations if $N < \binom{n}{t}$, so it is suitable unless t is small and N is large.

When $t = 2$, exercise 1.2.4–41 tells us that $n_2 = \lfloor \sqrt{2N+2} + \frac{1}{2} \rfloor$. In general, n_t is $\lfloor x \rfloor$ where x is the largest root of $x^{\underline{t}} = t!\,N$; this root can be approximated by reverting the series $y = (x^{\underline{t}})^{1/t} = x - \frac{1}{2}(t-1) + \frac{1}{24}(t^2 - 1)x^{-1} + \cdots$ to get $x = y + \frac{1}{2}(t-1) + \frac{1}{24}(t^2 - 1)/y + O(y^{-3})$. Setting $y = (t!\,N)^{1/t}$ in this formula gives a good approximation, after which we can check that $\binom{\lfloor x \rfloor}{t} \leq N < \binom{\lfloor x \rfloor + 1}{t}$ or make a final adjustment. [See A. S. Fraenkel and M. Mor, *Comp. J.* **26** (1983), 336–343.]

18. A complete binary tree of $2^n - 1$ nodes is obtained, with an extra node at the top, like the "tree of losers" in replacement selection sorting (Fig. 63 in Section 5.4.1). Therefore explicit links aren't necessary; the right child of node k is node $2k + 1$, and the left sibling is node $2k$, for $1 \leq k < 2^{n-1}$.

This representation of a binomial tree has the curious property that node $k = (0^a 1\alpha)_2$ corresponds to the combination whose binary string is $0^a 1\alpha^R$.

19. It is 11110100001001000100, the binary representation of $\text{post}(1000000)$, where $\text{post}(2^{k+1} - 1) = 2^k$, and $\text{post}(n) = 2^k + \text{post}(n - 2^k + 1)$ if $2^k \leq n < 2^{k+1} - 1$, for $k \geq 0$. [Incidentally, the left-child/right-sibling representation of T_∞ is the sideways heap.]

20. $f(z) = (1 + z^{w_{n-1}}) \ldots (1 + z^{w_1})/(1 - z)$, $g(z) = (1 + z^{w_0})f(z)$, $h(z) = z^{w_0} f(z)$.

21. The rank of $c_t \ldots c_2 c_1$ is $\binom{c_t + 1}{t} - 1$ minus the rank of $c_{t-1} \ldots c_2 c_1$. [Page 40 of Miller's thesis; see also H. Lüneburg, *Abh. Math. Sem. Hamburg* **52** (1982), 208–227.]

22. Since $999999 = \binom{1415}{2} - \binom{406}{1} = \binom{183}{3} - \binom{98}{2} + \binom{21}{1} = \binom{72}{4} - \binom{57}{3} + \binom{32}{2} - \binom{27}{1} = \binom{44}{5} - \binom{40}{4} + \binom{33}{3} - \binom{13}{2} + \binom{3}{1}$, the answers are (a) 1414 405; (b) 182 97 21; (c) 71 56 31 26; (d) 43 39 32 12 3; (e) 1000000 999999 999998 999996 ... 0.

23. There are $\binom{n-r}{t-r}$ combinations with $j > r$, for $r = 1, 2, \ldots, t$. (If $t - r$ is even we have $j > r \iff c_r = r - 1$; otherwise $j > r \iff c_{r+1} = c_r + 1$ and $c_{r-1} = r - 2$, assuming that $c_0 = -1$.) Thus the mean is $(\binom{n}{t} + \binom{n-1}{t-1} + \cdots + \binom{n-t}{0})/\binom{n}{t} = \binom{n+1}{t}/\binom{n}{t} = (n+1)/(n+1-t)$. The average running time per step is approximately proportional to this quantity; thus the algorithm is quite fast when t is small, but slow if t is near n.

24. In fact $j_k - 2 \leq j_{k+1} \leq j_k + 1$ when $j_k \equiv t$ (modulo 2) and $j_k - 1 \leq j_{k+1} \leq j_k + 2$ when $j_k \not\equiv t$, because R5 is performed only when $c_i = i - 1$ for $1 \leq i < j$.

   Thus we could say, "If $j \geq 4$, set $j \leftarrow j-1-[j$ odd$]$ and go to R5" at the end of R2, if t is odd; "If $j \geq 3$, set $j \leftarrow j - 1 - [j$ even$]$ and go to R5" if t is even. The algorithm will then be loopless, since R4 and R5 will be performed at most twice per visit.

25. Assume that $N > N'$ and $N - N'$ is minimum; furthermore let t and c_t be minimum, subject to those assumptions. Then $c_t > c'_t$.

   If there is an element $x \notin C \cup C'$ with $0 \leq x < c_t$, map each t-combination of $C \cup C'$ by changing $j \mapsto j - 1$ for $j > x$; or, if there is an element $x \in C \cap C'$, map each t-combination that contains x into a $(t-1)$-combination by omitting x and changing $j \mapsto x - j$ for $j < x$. In either case the mapping preserves alternating lexicographic order; hence $N - N'$ must exceed the number of combinations between the images of C and C'. But c_t is minimum, so no such x can exist. Consequently $t = m$ and $c_t = 2m - 1$.

   Now if $c'_m < c_m - 1$, we could decrease $N - N'$ by increasing c'_m. Therefore $c'_m = 2m-2$, and the problem has been reduced to finding the *maximum* of $\text{rank}(c_{m-1} \ldots c_1) - \text{rank}(c'_{m-1} \ldots c'_1)$, where rank is calculated as in (30).

   Let $f(s,t) = \max(\text{rank}(b_s \ldots b_1) - \text{rank}(c_t \ldots c_1))$ over all $\{b_s, \ldots, b_1, c_t, \ldots, c_1\} = \{0, \ldots, s+t-1\}$. Then $f(s,t)$ satisfies the curious recurrence

$$f(s,0) = f(0,t) = 0; \qquad f(1,t) = t;$$
$$f(s,t) = \binom{s+t-1}{s} + \max(f(t-1, s-1), f(s-2, t)) \quad \text{if } st > 0 \text{ and } s > 1.$$

When $s + t = 2u + 2$ the solution turns out to be

$$f(s,t) = \binom{2u+1}{t-1} + \sum_{j=1}^{u-r} \binom{2u+1-2j}{r} + \sum_{j=0}^{r-1} \binom{2j+1}{j}, \qquad r = \min(s-2, t-1),$$

with the maximum occurring at $f(t-1, s-1)$ when $s \leq t$ and at $f(s-2, t)$ when $s \geq t+2$.

   Therefore the minimum $N - N'$ occurs for

$$C = \{2m - 1\} \cup \{2m - 2 - x \mid 1 \leq x \leq 2m - 2, \ x \bmod 4 \leq 1\},$$
$$C' = \{2m - 2\} \cup \{2m - 2 - x \mid 1 \leq x \leq 2m - 2, \ x \bmod 4 \geq 2\};$$

and it equals $\binom{2m-1}{m-1} - \sum_{k=0}^{m-2} \binom{2k+1}{k} = 1 + \sum_{k=1}^{m-1} \binom{2k}{k-1}$. [See A. J. van Zanten, *IEEE Trans.* **IT-37** (1991), 1229–1233.]

26. (a) Yes: The first is $0^{n - \lceil t/2 \rceil} 1^{t \bmod 2} 2^{\lfloor t/2 \rfloor}$ and the last is $2^{\lfloor t/2 \rfloor} 1^{t \bmod 2} 0^{n - \lceil t/2 \rceil}$; transitions are substrings of the forms $02^a 1 \leftrightarrow 12^a 0$, $02^a 2 \leftrightarrow 12^a 1$, $10^a 1 \leftrightarrow 20^a 0$, $10^a 2 \leftrightarrow 20^a 1$.

   (b) No: If $s = 0$ there is a big jump from $02^t 0^{r-1}$ to $20^r 2^{t-1}$.

27. The following procedure extracts all combinations $c_1 \ldots c_k$ of Γ_n that have weight $\leq t$: Begin with $k \leftarrow 0$ and $c_0 \leftarrow n$. Visit $c_1 \ldots c_k$. If k is even and $c_k = 0$, set $k \leftarrow k - 1$; if k is even and $c_k > 0$, set $c_k \leftarrow c_k - 1$ if $k = t$, otherwise $k \leftarrow k + 1$ and $c_k \leftarrow 0$. On the other hand if k is odd and $c_k + 1 = c_{k-1}$, set $k \leftarrow k - 1$ and

$c_k \leftarrow c_{k+1}$ (but terminate if $k = 0$); if k is odd and $c_k + 1 < c_{k-1}$, set $c_k \leftarrow c_k + 1$ if $k = t$, otherwise $k \leftarrow k + 1$, $c_k \leftarrow c_{k-1}$, $c_{k-1} \leftarrow c_k + 1$. Repeat.

(This loopless algorithm reduces to that of exercise 7.2.1.1–12(b) when $t = n$, with slight changes of notation.)

28. True. Bit strings $a_{n-1} \ldots a_0 = \alpha\beta$ and $a'_{n-1} \ldots a'_0 = \alpha\beta'$ correspond to index lists $(b_s \ldots b_1 = \theta\chi, c_t \ldots c_1 = \phi\psi)$ and $(b'_s \ldots b'_1 = \theta\chi', c'_t \ldots c'_1 = \phi\psi')$ such that everything between $\alpha\beta$ and $\alpha\beta'$ begins with α if and only if everything between $\theta\chi$ and $\theta\chi'$ begins with θ and everything between $\phi\psi$ and $\phi\psi'$ begins with ϕ. For example, if $n = 10$, the prefix $\alpha = 01101$ corresponds to prefixes $\theta = 96$ and $\phi = 875$.

(But just having $c_t \ldots c_1$ in genlex order is a much weaker condition. For example, *every* such sequence is genlex when $t = 1$.)

29. (a) $-^k 0^{l+1}$ or $-^k 0^{l+1} +\pm^m$ or $\pm^k$, for $k, l, m \geq 0$.

(b) No; the successor is always smaller in balanced ternary notation.

(c) For all α and all $k, l, m \geq 0$ we have $\alpha 0 -^{k+1} 0^l +\pm^m \to \alpha -+^k 0^{l+1} -\pm^m$ and $\alpha +-^k 0^{l+1} +\pm^m \to \alpha 0 +^{k+1} 0^l -\pm^m$; also $\alpha 0 -^{k+1} 0^l \to \alpha -+^k 0^{l+1}$ and $\alpha +-^k 0^{l+1} \to \alpha 0 +^{k+1} 0^l$.

(d) Let the jth sign of α_i be $(-1)^{a_{ij}}$, and let it be in position b_{ij}. Then we have $(-1)^{a_{ij} + b_{i(j-1)}} = (-1)^{a_{(i+1)j} + b_{(i+1)(j-1)}}$ for $0 \leq i < k$ and $1 \leq j \leq s$, if we let $b_{i0} = 0$.

(e) By parts (a), (b), and (c), α belongs to some chain $\alpha_0 \to \cdots \to \alpha_k$, where α_k is final (has no successor) and α_0 is initial (has no predecessor). By part (d), every such chain has at most $\binom{s+t}{t}$ elements. But there are 2^s final strings, by (a), and there are $2^s \binom{s+t}{t}$ strings with s signs and t zeros; so k must be $\binom{s+t}{t} - 1$.

Reference: SICOMP **2** (1973), 128–133.

30. Assume that $t > 0$. Initial strings are the negatives of final strings. Let σ_j be the initial string $0^t -\tau_j$ for $0 \leq j < 2^{s-1}$, where the kth character of τ_j for $1 \leq k < s$ is the sign of $(-1)^{a_k}$ when j is the binary number $(a_{s-1} \ldots a_1)_2$; thus $\sigma_0 = 0^t -++ \ldots +$, $\sigma_1 = 0^t --+ \ldots +$, $\ldots$, $\sigma_{2^{s-1}-1} = 0^t --- \ldots -$. Let ρ_j be the final string obtained by inserting -0^t after the first (possibly empty) run of minus signs in τ_j; thus $\rho_0 = -0^t ++ \ldots +$, $\rho_1 = --0^t + \ldots +$, $\ldots$, $\rho_{2^{s-1}-1} = -- \ldots -0^t$. We also let $\sigma_{2^s-1} = \sigma_0$ and $\rho_{2^s-1} = \rho_0$. Then we can prove by induction that the chain beginning with σ_j ends with ρ_j when t is even, with ρ_{j-1} when t is odd, for $1 \leq j \leq 2^{s-1}$. Therefore the chain beginning with $-\rho_j$ ends with $-\sigma_j$ or $-\sigma_{j+1}$.

Let $A_j(s,t)$ be the sequence of (s,t)-combinations derived by mapping the chain that starts with σ_j, and let $B_j(s,t)$ be the analogous sequence derived from $-\rho_j$. Then, for $1 \leq j \leq 2^{s-1}$, the reverse sequence $A_j(s,t)^R$ is $B_j(s,t)$ when t is even, $B_{j-1}(s,t)$ when t is odd. The corresponding recurrences when $st > 0$ are

$$A_j(s,t) = \begin{cases} 1A_j(s,t-1), \; 0A_{\lfloor(2^{s-1}-1-j)/2\rfloor}(s-1,t)^R, & \text{if } j+t \text{ is even;} \\ 1A_j(s,t-1), \; 0A_{\lfloor j/2\rfloor}(s-1,t), & \text{if } j+t \text{ is odd;} \end{cases}$$

and when $st > 0$ all 2^{s-1} of these sequences are distinct.

Chase's sequence C_{st} is $A_{\lfloor 2^s/3\rfloor}(s,t)$, and $\widehat{C}_{st}$ is $A_{\lfloor 2^s-1/3\rfloor}(s,t)^R$. Incidentally, the homogeneous sequence K_{st} of (31) is $A_{2^{s-1}-[t \text{ even}]}(s,t)^R$.

31. (a) $2^{\binom{s+t}{t}-1}$ solves the recurrence $f(s,t) = 2f(s-1,t)f(s,t-1)$ when $f(s,0) = f(0,t) = 1$. (b) Now $f(s,t) = (s+1)! \, f(s,t-1) \ldots f(0,t-1)$ has the solution

$$(s+1)!^t \, s!^{\binom{t}{2}} (s-1)!^{\binom{t+1}{3}} \ldots 2!^{\binom{s+t-2}{s}} = \prod_{r=1}^{s} (r+1)!^{\binom{s+t-1-r}{t-2}+[r=s]}.$$

32. (a) No simple formula seems to exist, but the listings can be counted for small s and t by systematically computing the number of genlex paths that run through all weight-t strings from a given starting point to a given ending point via revolving-door moves. The totals for $s+t \le 6$ are

$$\begin{array}{ccccccccccccc} &&&&&&1&&&&&& \\ &&&&&1&&1&&&&& \\ &&&&1&&2&&1&&&& \\ &&&1&&4&&4&&1&&& \\ &&1&&8&&20&&8&&1&& \\ &1&&16&&160&&160&&16&&1& \\ 1&&32&&2264&&17152&&2264&&32&&1 \end{array}$$

and $f(4,4) = 95{,}304{,}112{,}865{,}280$; $f(5,5) \approx 5.92646 \times 10^{48}$. [This class of combination generators was first studied by G. Ehrlich, *JACM* **20** (1973), 500–513, but he did not attempt to enumerate them.]

(b) By extending the proof of Theorem N, one can show that all such listings or their reversals must run from 1^t0^s to $0^a1^t0^{s-a}$ for some a, $1 \le a \le s$. Moreover, the number n_{sta} of possibilities, given s, t, and a with $st > 0$, satisfies $n_{1t1} = 1$ and

$$n_{sta} = \begin{cases} n_{s(t-1)1}\, n_{(s-1)t(a-1)}, & \text{if } a > 1; \\ n_{s(t-1)2}\, n_{(s-1)t1} + \cdots + n_{s(t-1)s}\, n_{(s-1)t(s-1)}, & \text{if } a = 1 < s. \end{cases}$$

This recurrence has the remarkable solution $n_{sta} = 2^{m(s,t,a)}$, where

$$m(s,t,a) = \begin{cases} \binom{s+t-3}{t} + \binom{s+t-5}{t-2} + \cdots + \binom{s-1}{2}, & \text{if } t \text{ is even;} \\ \binom{s+t-3}{t} + \binom{s+t-5}{t-2} + \cdots + \binom{s}{3} + s - a - [a<s], & \text{if } t \text{ is odd.} \end{cases}$$

33. Consider first the case $t = 1$: The number of near-perfect paths from i to $j > i$ is $f(j-i-[i>0]-[j<n-1])$, where $\sum_j f(j)z^j = 1/(1-z-z^3)$. (By coincidence, the same sequence $f(j)$ arises in Caron's polyphase merge on 6 tapes, Table 5.4.2–2.) The sum over $0 \le i < j < n$ is $3f(n) + f(n-1) + f(n-2) + 2 - n$; and we must double this, to cover cases with $j > i$.

When $t > 1$ we can construct $\binom{n}{t} \times \binom{n}{t}$ matrices that tell how many genlex listings begin and end with particular combinations. The entries of these matrices are sums of products of matrices for the case $t-1$, summed over all paths of the type considered for $t = 1$. The totals for $s + t \le 6$ turn out to be

$$\begin{array}{ccccccccccccc} &&&&&&1&&&&&& \\ &&&&&1&&1&&&&& \\ &&&&1&&2&&1&&&& \\ &&&1&&6&&2&&1&&& \\ &&1&&12&&10&&2&&1&& \\ &1&&20&&44&&10&&2&&1& \\ 1&&34&&238&&68&&10&&2&&1 \end{array} \qquad \begin{array}{ccccccccccccc} &&&&&&1&&&&&& \\ &&&&&1&&1&&&&& \\ &&&&1&&2&&1&&&& \\ &&&1&&2&&0&&1&&& \\ &&1&&2&&2&&0&&1&& \\ &1&&2&&0&&0&&0&&1& \\ 1&&2&&6&&0&&0&&0&&1 \end{array}$$

where the right-hand triangle shows the number of *cycles*, $g(s,t)$. Further values include $f(4,4) = 17736$; $f(5,5) = 9{,}900{,}888{,}879{,}984$; $g(4,4) = 96$; $g(5,5) = 30{,}961{,}456{,}320$.

There are exactly 10 such schemes when $s = 2$ and $n \ge 4$. For example, when $n = 7$ they run from 43210 to 65431 or 65432, or from 54321 to 65420 or 65430 or 65432, or the reverse.

34. The minimum can be computed as in the previous answer, but using min-plus matrix multiplication $c_{ij} = \min_k(a_{ik} + b_{kj})$ instead of ordinary matrix multiplication $c_{ij} = \sum_k a_{ik}b_{kj}$. (When $s = t = 5$, the genlex path in Fig. 46(e) with only 49 imperfect transitions is essentially unique. There is a genlex cycle for $s = t = 5$ that has only 55 imperfections.)

35. From the recurrences (35) we have $a_{st} = b_{s(t-1)} + [s>1][t>0] + a_{(s-1)t}$, $b_{st} = a_{s(t-1)} + a_{(s-1)t}$; consequently $a_{st} = b_{st} + [s>1][t\,\text{odd}]$ and $a_{st} = a_{s(t-1)} + a_{(s-1)t} + [s>1][t\,\text{odd}]$. The solution is

$$a_{st} = \sum_{k=0}^{t/2}\binom{s+t-2-2k}{s-2} - [s>1][t\,\text{even}];$$

this sum is approximately $s/(s+2t)$ times $\binom{s+t}{t}$.

36. Consider the binary tree with root node (s,t) and with recursively defined subtrees rooted at $(s-1,t)$ and $(s,t-1)$ whenever $st > 0$; the node (s,t) is a leaf if $st = 0$. Then the subtree rooted at (s,t) has $\binom{s+t}{t}$ leaves, corresponding to all (s,t)-combinations $a_{n-1}\dots a_1 a_0$. Nodes on level l correspond to prefixes $a_{n-1}\dots a_{n-l}$, and leaves on level l are combinations with $r = n - l$.

Any genlex algorithm for combinations $a_{n-1}\dots a_1 a_0$ corresponds to preorder traversal of such a tree, after the children of the $\binom{s+t}{t} - 1$ branch nodes have been ordered in any desired way; that, in fact, is why there are $2^{\binom{s+t}{t}-1}$ such genlex schemes (exercise 31(a)). And the operation $j \leftarrow j + 1$ is performed exactly once per branch node, namely after both children have been processed.

Incidentally, exercise 7.2.1.2–6(a) implies that the average value of r is $s/(t+1) + t/(s+1)$, which can be $\Omega(n)$; thus the extra time needed to keep track of r is worthwhile.

37. (a) In the lexicographic case we needn't maintain the w_j table, since a_j is active for $j \geq r$ if and only if $a_j = 0$. After setting $a_j \leftarrow 1$ and $a_{j-1} \leftarrow 0$ there are two cases to consider if $j > 1$: If $r = j$, set $r \leftarrow j - 1$; otherwise set $a_{j-2}\dots a_0 \leftarrow 0^r 1^{j-1-r}$ and $r \leftarrow j - 1 - r$ (or $r \leftarrow j$ if r was $j - 1$).

(b) Now the transitions to be handled when $j > 1$ are to change $a_j \dots a_0$ as follows: $01^r \rightarrow 1101^{r-2}$, $010^r \rightarrow 10^{r+1}$, $010^a 1^r \rightarrow 110^{a+1}1^{r-1}$, $10^r \rightarrow 010^{r-1}$, $110^r \rightarrow 010^{r-1}1$, $10^a 1^r \rightarrow 0^a 1^{r+1}$; these six cases are easily distinguished. The value of r should change appropriately.

(c) Again the case $j = 1$ is trivial. Otherwise $01^a 0^r \rightarrow 101^{a-1}0^r$; $0^a 1^r \rightarrow 10^a 1^{r-1}$; $101^a 0^r \rightarrow 01^{a+1}0^r$; $10^a 1^r \rightarrow 0^a 1^{r+1}$; and there is also an ambiguous case, which can occur only if $a_{n-1}\dots a_{j+1}$ contains at least one 0: Let $k > j$ be minimal with $a_k = 0$. Then $10^r \rightarrow 010^{r-1}$ if k is odd, $10^r \rightarrow 0^r 1$ if k is even.

38. The same algorithm works, except that (i) step C1 sets $a_{n-1}\dots a_0 \leftarrow 01^t 0^{s-1}$ if n is odd or $s = 1$, $a_{n-1}\dots a_0 \leftarrow 001^t 0^{s-2}$ if n is even and $s > 1$, with an appropriate value of r; (ii) step C3 interchanges the roles of even and odd; (iii) step C5 goes to C4 also if $j = 1$.

39. In general, start with $r \leftarrow 0$, $j \leftarrow s + t - 1$, and repeat the following steps until $st = 0$:

$$r \leftarrow r + \lfloor w_j = 0\rfloor\binom{j}{s-a_j}, \quad s \leftarrow s - [a_j = 0], \quad t \leftarrow t - [a_j = 1], \quad j \leftarrow j - 1.$$

Then r is the rank of $a_{n-1}\dots a_1 a_0$. So the rank of 110010010000111111101101010 is $\binom{23}{12} + \binom{22}{11} + \binom{21}{9} + \binom{17}{8} + \binom{16}{7} + \binom{14}{5} + \binom{13}{3} + \binom{12}{3} + \binom{11}{3} + \binom{10}{3} + \binom{9}{3} + \binom{8}{3} + \binom{4}{3} + \binom{3}{1} + \binom{1}{0} = 2390131$.

40. We start with $N \leftarrow 999999$, $v \leftarrow 0$, and repeat the following steps until $st = 0$: If $v = 0$, set $t \leftarrow t - 1$ and $a_{s+t} \leftarrow 1$ if $N < \binom{s+t-1}{s}$, otherwise set $N \leftarrow N - \binom{s+t-1}{s}$, $v \leftarrow (s+t) \bmod 2$, $s \leftarrow s - 1$, $a_{s+t} \leftarrow 0$. If $v = 1$, set $v \leftarrow (s+t) \bmod 2$, $s \leftarrow s - 1$, and $a_{s+t} \leftarrow 0$ if $N < \binom{s+t-1}{t}$, otherwise set $N \leftarrow N - \binom{s+t-1}{t}$, $t \leftarrow t - 1$, $a_{s+t} \leftarrow 1$. Finally if $s = 0$, set $a_{t-1} \dots a_0 \leftarrow 1^t$; if $t = 0$, set $a_{s-1} \dots a_0 \leftarrow 0^s$. The answer is $a_{25} \dots a_0 = 11101001111101010010000001$.

41. Let $c(0), \dots, c(2^n - 1) = C_n$ where $C_{2n} = 0C_{2n-1}, 1C_{2n-1}$; $C_{2n+1} = 0C_{2n}$, $1\widehat{C}_{2n}$; $\widehat{C}_{2n} = 1C_{2n-1}, 0\widehat{C}_{2n-1}$; $\widehat{C}_{2n+1} = 1\widehat{C}_{2n}, 0\widehat{C}_{2n}$; $C_0 = \widehat{C}_0 = \epsilon$. Then $a_j \oplus b_j = b_{j+1} \& (b_{j+2} \mid (b_{j+3} \& (b_{j+4} \mid \cdots)))$ if j is even, $b_{j+1} \mid (b_{j+2} \& (b_{j+3} \mid (b_{j+4} \& \cdots)))$ if j is odd. Curiously we also have the inverse relation $c((\dots a_4 \bar{a}_3 a_2 \bar{a}_1 a_0)_2) = (\dots b_4 \bar{b}_3 b_2 \bar{b}_1 b_0)_2$.

42. Equation (40) shows that the left context $a_{n-1} \dots a_{l+1}$ does not affect the behavior of the algorithm on $a_{l-1} \dots a_0$ if $a_l = 0$ and $l > r$. Therefore we can analyze Algorithm C by counting combinations that end with certain bit patterns, and it follows that the number of times each operation is performed can be represented as $[w^s z^t] p(w, z)/(1 - w^2)^2 (1 - z^2)^2 (1 - w - z)$ for an appropriate polynomial $p(w, z)$.

For example, the algorithm goes from C5 to C4 once for each combination that ends with $01^{2a+1} 01^{2b+1}$ or has the form $1^{a+1} 01^{2b+1}$, for integers $a, b \geq 0$; the corresponding generating functions are $w^2 z^2 / (1 - z^2)^2 (1 - w - z)$ and $w(z^2 + z^3)/(1 - z^2)^2$.

Here are the polynomials $p(w, z)$ for key operations. Let $W = 1 - w^2$, $Z = 1 - z^2$.

C3 → C4: $wzW(1+wz)(1-w-z^2)$;
C3 → C5: $wzW(w+z)(1-wz-z^2)$;
C3 → C6: $w^2z^2W(w+z)$;
C3 → C7: $w^2zW(1+wz)$;
C4($j = 1$): $wzW^2Z(1-w-z^2)$;
C4($r \leftarrow j-1$): $w^3zWZ(1-w-z^2)$;
C4($r \leftarrow j$): $wz^2W^2(1+z-2wz-z^2-z^3)$;
C5 → C4: $wz^2W^2(1-wz-z^2)$;
C5($r \leftarrow j-2$): $w^4zWZ(1-wz-z^2)$;

C5($r \leftarrow 1$): $w^2zW^2Z(1-wz-z^2)$;
C5($r \leftarrow j-1$): $w^2z^3W^2(1-wz-z^2)$;
C6($j = 1$): w^2zW^2Z;
C6($r \leftarrow j-1$): $w^2z^3W^2$;
C6($r \leftarrow j$): w^3z^2WZ;
C7 → C6: w^2zW^2;
C7($r \leftarrow j$): w^4zWZ;
C7($r \leftarrow j-2$): $w^3z^2W^2$.

The asymptotic value is $\binom{s+t}{t}(p(1 - x, x)/(2x - x^2)^2 (1 - x^2)^2 + O(n^{-1}))$, for fixed $0 < x < 1$, if $t = xn + O(1)$ as $n \to \infty$. Thus we find, for example, that the four-way branching in step C3 takes place with relative frequencies $x + x^2 - x^3 : 1 : x : 1 + x - x^2$.

Incidentally, the number of cases with j odd exceeds the number of cases with j even by

$$\sum_{k,l \geq 1} \binom{s+t-2k-2l}{s-2k} [2k + 2l \leq s + t] + [s \text{ odd}][t \text{ odd}],$$

in *any* genlex scheme that uses (39). This quantity has the interesting generating function $wz/(1 + w)(1 + z)(1 - w - z)$.

43. The identity is true for all nonnegative integers x, except when $x = 1$. (Incidentally, $s(x) = f(x) \oplus 1$ and $p(x) = f(x \oplus 1)$, where $f(x) = (x \dotminus 1) + ((x \& 1) \ll 1)$.)

44. In fact, $C_t(n) - 1 = \widehat{C}_t(n-1)^R$, and $\widehat{C}_t(n) - 1 = C_t(n-1)^R$. (Hence $C_t(n) - 2 = C_t(n-2)$, etc.)

45. In the following algorithm, r is the least subscript with $c_r \geq r$.

CC1. [Initialize.] Set $c_j \leftarrow n - t - 1 + j$ and $z_j \leftarrow 0$ for $1 \leq j \leq t + 1$. Also set $r \leftarrow 1$. (We assume that $0 < t < n$.)

CC2. [Visit.] Visit the combination $c_t \dots c_2 c_1$. Then set $j \leftarrow r$.

CC3. [Branch.] Go to CC5 if $z_j \neq 0$.

CC4. [Try to decrease c_j.] Set $x \leftarrow c_j + (c_j \bmod 2) - 2$. If $x \geq j$, set $c_j \leftarrow x$, $r \leftarrow 1$; otherwise if $c_j = j$, set $c_j \leftarrow j - 1$, $z_j \leftarrow c_{j+1} - ((c_{j+1} + 1) \bmod 2)$, $r \leftarrow j$; otherwise if $c_j < j$, set $c_j \leftarrow j$, $z_j \leftarrow c_{j+1} - ((c_{j+1} + 1) \bmod 2)$, $r \leftarrow \max(1, j - 1)$; otherwise set $c_j \leftarrow x$, $r \leftarrow j$. Return to CC2.

CC5. [Try to increase c_j.] Set $x \leftarrow c_j + 2$. If $x < z_j$, set $c_j \leftarrow x$; otherwise if $x = z_j$ and $z_{j+1} \neq 0$, set $c_j \leftarrow x - (c_{j+1} \bmod 2)$; otherwise set $z_j \leftarrow 0$, $j \leftarrow j + 1$, and go to CC3 (but terminate if $j > t$). If $c_1 > 0$, set $r \leftarrow 1$; otherwise set $r \leftarrow j - 1$. Return to CC2. ∎

46. Equation (40) implies that $u_k = (b_j + k + 1) \bmod 2$ when j is minimal with $b_j > k$. Then (37) and (38) yield the following algorithm, where we assume for convenience that $3 \leq s < n$.

CB1. [Initialize.] Set $b_j \leftarrow j - 1$ for $1 \leq j \leq s$; also set $z \leftarrow s + 1$, $b_z \leftarrow 1$. (When subsequent steps examine the value of z, it is the smallest index such that $b_z \neq z - 1$.)

CB2. [Visit.] Visit the dual combination $b_s \ldots b_2 b_1$.

CB3. [Branch.] If b_2 is odd: Go to CB4 if $b_2 \neq b_1 + 1$, otherwise to CB5 if $b_1 > 0$, otherwise to CB6 if b_z is odd. Go to CB9 if b_2 is even and $b_1 > 0$. Otherwise go to CB8 if $b_{z+1} = b_z + 1$, otherwise to CB7.

CB4. [Increase b_1.] Set $b_1 \leftarrow b_1 + 1$ and return to CB2.

CB5. [Slide b_1 and b_2.] If b_3 is odd, set $b_1 \leftarrow b_1 + 1$ and $b_2 \leftarrow b_2 + 1$; otherwise set $b_1 \leftarrow b_1 - 1$, $b_2 \leftarrow b_2 - 1$, $z \leftarrow 3$. Go to CB2.

CB6. [Slide left.] If z is odd, set $z \leftarrow z - 2$, $b_{z+1} \leftarrow z + 1$, $b_z \leftarrow z$; otherwise set $z \leftarrow z - 1$, $b_z \leftarrow z$. Go to CB2.

CB7. [Slide b_z.] If b_{z+1} is odd, set $b_z \leftarrow b_z + 1$ and terminate if $b_z \geq n$; otherwise set $b_z \leftarrow b_z - 1$, then if $b_z < z$ set $z \leftarrow z + 1$. Go to CB2.

CB8. [Slide b_z and b_{z+1}.] If b_{z+2} is odd, set $b_z \leftarrow b_{z+1}$, $b_{z+1} \leftarrow b_z + 1$, and terminate if $b_{z+1} \geq n$. Otherwise set $b_{z+1} \leftarrow b_z$, $b_z \leftarrow b_z - 1$, then if $b_z < z$ set $z \leftarrow z + 2$. Go to CB2.

CB9. [Decrease b_1.] Set $b_1 \leftarrow b_1 - 1$, $z \leftarrow 2$, and return to CB2. ∎

Notice that this algorithm is *loopless*. Chase gave a similar procedure for the sequence $\widehat{C}_{st}^R$ in *Cong. Num.* **69** (1989), 233–237. It is truly amazing that this algorithm defines precisely the complements of the indices $c_t \ldots c_1$ produced by the algorithm in the previous exercise.

47. We can, for example, use Algorithm C and its reverse (exercise 38), with w_j replaced by a d-bit number whose bits represent activity at different levels of the recursion. Separate pointers $r_0, r_1, \ldots, r_{d-1}$ are needed to keep track of the r-values on each level. (Many other solutions are possible.)

48. There are permutations $\pi_1, \ldots, \pi_M$ such that the kth element of Λ_j is $\pi_k \alpha_j \uparrow \beta_{k-1}$. And $\pi_k \alpha_j$ runs through all permutations of $\{s_1 \cdot 1, \ldots, s_d \cdot d\}$ as j varies from 0 to $N - 1$.

Historical note: The first publication of a homogeneous revolving-door scheme for (s, t)-combinations was by Éva Török, *Matematikai Lapok* **19** (1968), 143–146, who was motivated by the generation of multiset permutations. Many authors have subsequently relied on the homogeneity condition for similar constructions, but this exercise shows that homogeneity is not necessary.

49. We have $\lim_{z \to q}(z^{km+r} - 1)/(z^{lm+r} - 1) = 1$ when $0 < r < m$, and k/l when $r = 0$. So we can pair up factors of the numerator $\prod_{n-k<a\leq n}(z^a - 1)$ with factors of the denominator $\prod_{0<b\leq k}(z^b - 1)$ when $a \equiv b$ (modulo m).

Notes: This formula was discovered by G. Olive, *AMM* **72** (1965), 619. In the special case $m = 2$, $q = -1$, the second factor vanishes only when n is even and k is odd.

The formula $\binom{n}{k}_q = \binom{n}{n-k}_q$ holds for all $n \geq 0$, but $\binom{\lfloor n/m\rfloor}{\lfloor k/m\rfloor}$ is *not* always equal to $\binom{\lfloor n/m\rfloor}{\lfloor(n-k)/m\rfloor}$. The reason is that the second factor is zero unless $n \bmod m \geq k \bmod m$, and in that case we do have $\lfloor k/m\rfloor + \lfloor(n-k)/m\rfloor = \lfloor n/m\rfloor$.

50. The stated coefficient is zero when $n_1 \bmod m + \cdots + n_t \bmod m \geq m$. Otherwise it's

$$\binom{\lfloor(n_1 + \cdots + n_t)/m\rfloor}{\lfloor n_1/m\rfloor, \ldots, \lfloor n_t/m\rfloor}\binom{(n_1 + \cdots + n_t) \bmod m}{n_1 \bmod m, \ldots, n_t \bmod m}_q,$$

by Eq. 1.2.6–(43); here each upper index is the sum of the lower indices.

51. All paths clearly run between 000111 and 111000, since those vertices have degree 1. Fourteen total paths reduce to four under the stated equivalences. The path in (50), which is equivalent to itself under reflection-and-reversal, can be described by the delta sequence $A = 3452132523414354123$; the other three classes are $B = 3452541453414512543$, $C = 3452541453252154123$, $D = 3452134145341432543$. D. H. Lehmer found path C [*AMM* **72** (1965), Part II, 36–46]; D is essentially the path constructed by Eades, Hickey, and Read.

(Incidentally, perfect schemes aren't really rare, although they seem to be difficult to construct systematically. The case $(s, t) = (3, 5)$ has 4,050,046 of them.)

52. We may assume that each s_j is nonzero and that $d > 1$. Then the difference between permutations with an even and odd number of inversions is $\binom{\lfloor(s_0+\cdots+s_d)/2\rfloor}{\lfloor s_0/2\rfloor, \ldots, \lfloor s_d/2\rfloor} \geq 2$, by exercise 50, unless at least two of the multiplicities s_j are odd.

Conversely, if at least two multiplicities are odd, a general construction by G. Stachowiak [*SIAM J. Discrete Math.* **5** (1992), 199–206] shows that a perfect scheme exists. Indeed, his construction applies to a variety of topological sorting problems; in the special case of multisets it gives a Hamiltonian cycle in all cases with $d > 1$ and $s_0 s_1$ odd, except when $d = 2$, $s_0 = s_1 = 1$, and s_2 is even.

53. See *AMM* **72** (1965), Part II, 36–46, for solutions to some small cases. T. Verhoeff [*Designs, Codes and Cryptography* **84** (2017), 295–310] has found important structural information, which yields a general solution for $d = 1$ and probably for all d.

54. Assuming that $st \neq 0$, a Hamiltonian path exists if and only if s and t are not both even; a Hamiltonian cycle exists if and only if, in addition, ($s \neq 2$ and $t \neq 2$) or $n = 5$. [T. C. Enns, *Discrete Math.* **122** (1993), 153–165.]

55. (a) [Solution by Aaron Williams.] The sequence $0^s 1^t$, W_{st} has the right properties if

$$W_{st} = 0W_{(s-1)t}, \ 1W_{s(t-1)}, \ 10^s 1^{t-1}, \quad \text{for } st > 0; \qquad W_{0t} = W_{s0} = \emptyset.$$

And there is an amazingly efficient, *loopless* implementation: Assume that $t > 0$.

W1. [Initialize.] Set $n \leftarrow s + t$, $a_j \leftarrow 1$ for $0 \leq j < t$, and $a_j \leftarrow 0$ for $t \leq j \leq n$. Then set $j \leftarrow k \leftarrow t - 1$. (This is tricky, but it works.)

W2. [Visit.] Visit the (s, t)-combination $a_{n-1} \ldots a_1 a_0$.

W3. [Zero out a_j.] Set $a_j \leftarrow 0$ and $j \leftarrow j + 1$.

W4. [Easy case?] If $a_j = 1$, set $a_k \leftarrow 1$, $k \leftarrow k + 1$, and return to W2.

W5. [Wrap around.] Terminate if $j = n$. Otherwise set $a_j \leftarrow 1$. Then if $k > 0$, set $a_k \leftarrow 1$, $a_0 \leftarrow 0$, $j \leftarrow 1$, and $k \leftarrow 0$. Return to W2. ∎

After the second visit, j is the smallest index with $a_j a_{j-1} = 10$, and k is smallest with $a_k = 0$. The easy case occurs exactly $\binom{s+t-1}{s} - 1$ times; the condition $k = 0$ occurs in step W5 exactly $\binom{s+t-2}{t} + \delta_{t1}$ times. Curiously, if N has the combinatorial representation (57), the combination of rank N in Algorithm L has rank $N - t + \binom{n_v}{v-1} + v - 1$ in Algorithm W. [*Lecture Notes in Comp. Sci.* **3595** (2005), 570–576; see also A. Williams, *SODA* **20** (2009), 987–996, for a significant generalization by which the permutations of an arbitrary multiset can be generated looplessly by prefix rotations.]

(b) `SET bits,(1<<t)-1` (This program assumes that $s > 0$ and $0 < t \le 16$.)

```
1H PUSHJ $0,Visit                            Visit bits = (a_{s+t-1}...a_1a_0)_2.
   ADDU $0,bits,1; AND $0,$0,bits            Set $0 ← bits & (bits + 1).
   SUBU $1,$0,1; XOR $1,$0,$1                Set $1 ← $0 ⊕ ($0 − 1).
   ADDU $0,$1,1; AND $1,$1,bits              Set $0 ← $1 + 1, $1 ← $1 & bits.
   AND $0,$0,bits; ODIF $0,$0,1              Set $0 ← ($0 & bits) −̇ 1.
   SUBU $1,$1,$0; ADDU bits,bits,$1          Set bits ← bits + $1 − $0.
   SRU $0,bits,s+t; PBZ $0,1B                Repeat unless a_{s+t} = 1.    ∎
```

56. [*Discrete Mathematics* **48** (1984), 163–171.] Such a solution resolves the "middle levels conjecture" [I. Havel, *Teubner-Texte zur Mathematik* **59** (1983), 101–108], which states that there is a Gray path through all binary strings of length $2t - 1$ and weights $\{t - 1, t\}$. In fact, such strings can be generated by a delta sequence of the special form $\alpha_0 \alpha_1 \ldots \alpha_{2t-2}$, where the elements of α_k are those of α_0 shifted by k, modulo $2t-1$. For example, when $t = 3$ we can start with $a_5 a_4 a_3 a_2 a_1 a_0 = 000111$ and repeatedly swap $a_0 \leftrightarrow a_\delta$, where δ runs through the cycle $(4134\ 5245\ 1351\ 2412\ 3523)$. [See T. Mütze, *Proc. London Math. Soc.* (3) **112** (2016), 677–713; T. Mütze and J. Nummenpalo, *ACM Transactions on Algorithms* **14** (2018), 15:1–15:29; A. Merino, O. Mička, and T. Mütze, *SICOMP* **51** (2022), 379–423.]

57. Yes; there is a near-perfect genlex solution for all m, n, and t when $n \ge m > t$. One such scheme, in bitstring notation, is $1A_{(m-t)(t-1)}0^{n-m}$, $01A_{(m-t)(t-1)}0^{n-m-1}$, $\ldots$, $0^{n-m}1A_{(m-t)(t-1)}$, $0^{n-m+1}1A_{(m-1-t)(t-1)}$, $\ldots$, $0^{n-t}1A_{0(t-1)}$, using (35).

58. Solve the previous problem with m and n reduced by $t - 1$, then add $j - 1$ to each c_j. (Case (a), which is particularly simple, was probably known to Czerny.)

59. The generating function $G_{mnt}(z) = \sum g_{mntk} z^k$ for the number g_{mntk} of chords reachable in k steps from $0^{n-t}1^t$ satisfies $G_{mmt}(z) = \binom{m}{t}_z$ and $G_{m(n+1)t}(z) = G_{mnt}(z) + z^{tn-(t-1)m}\binom{m-1}{t-1}_z$, because the latter term accounts for cases with $c_t = n$ and $c_1 > n - m$. A perfect scheme is possible only if $|G_{mnt}(-1)| \le 1$. But if $n \ge m > t \ge 2$, this condition holds only when $m = t + 1$ or $(n - t)t$ is odd, by (49). So there is no perfect solution when $t = 4$ and $m > 5$. (Many chords have only two neighbors when $n = t + 2$, so one can easily rule out that case. All cases with $n \ge m > 5$ and $t = 3$ apparently do have perfect paths when n is even.)

60. The following solution uses lexicographic order, taking care to ensure that the average amount of computation per visit is bounded. We may assume that $stm_s \ldots m_0 \ne 0$ and $t \le m_s + \cdots + m_1 + m_0$.

Q1. [Initialize.] Set $q_j \leftarrow 0$ for $s \ge j \ge 1$, and $x \leftarrow t$.

Q2. [Distribute.] Set $j \leftarrow 0$. Then while $x > m_j$, set $q_j \leftarrow m_j$, $x \leftarrow x - m_j$, and $j \leftarrow j + 1$. Finally set $q_j \leftarrow x$.

Q3. [Visit.] Visit the bounded composition $q_s + \cdots + q_1 + q_0$.

Q4. [Pick up the rightmost units.] If $j = 0$, set $x \leftarrow q_0 - 1$, $j \leftarrow 1$. Otherwise if $q_0 = 0$, set $x \leftarrow q_j - 1$, $q_j \leftarrow 0$, and $j \leftarrow j + 1$. Otherwise go to Q7.

Q5. [Full?] Terminate if $j > s$. Otherwise if $q_j = m_j$, set $x \leftarrow x + m_j$, $q_j \leftarrow 0$, $j \leftarrow j + 1$, and repeat this step.

Q6. [Increase q_j.] Set $q_j \leftarrow q_j + 1$. Then if $x = 0$, set $q_0 \leftarrow 0$ and return to Q3. (In that case $q_{j-1} = \cdots = q_0 = 0$.) Otherwise go to Q2.

Q7. [Increase and decrease.] (Now $q_i = m_i$ for $j > i \geq 0$.) While $q_j = m_j$, set $j \leftarrow j + 1$ and repeat until $q_j < m_j$ (but terminate if $j > s$). Then set $q_j \leftarrow q_j + 1$, $j \leftarrow j - 1$, $q_j \leftarrow q_j - 1$. If $q_0 = 0$, set $j \leftarrow 1$. Return to Q3. ∎

For example, if $m_s = \cdots = m_0 = 9$, the successors of the composition $3+9+9+7+0+0$ are $4+0+0+6+9+9$, $4+0+0+7+8+9$, $4+0+0+7+9+8$, $4+0+0+8+7+9$, $\ldots$.

61. Let $F_s(t) = \emptyset$ if $t < 0$ or $t > m_s + \cdots + m_0$; otherwise let $F_0(t) = t$, and

$$F_s(t) = 0{+}F_{s-1}(t), \ 1{+}F_{s-1}(t-1)^R, \ 2{+}F_{s-1}(t-2), \ \ldots, \ m_s{+}F_{s-1}(t-m_s)^{R^{m_s}}$$

when $s > 0$. This sequence can be shown to have the required properties; it is, in fact, equivalent to the compositions defined by the homogeneous sequence K_{st} of (31) under the correspondence of exercise 4, when restricted to the subsequence defined by the bounds m_s, $\ldots$, m_0. [See T. Walsh, *J. Combinatorial Math. and Combinatorial Computing* **33** (2000), 323–345, who has implemented it looplessly.]

62. (a) A $2 \times n$ contingency table with row sums r and $c_1 + \cdots + c_n - r$ is equivalent to solving $r = a_1 + \cdots + a_n$ with $0 \leq a_1 \leq c_1$, $\ldots$, $0 \leq a_n \leq c_n$.

(b) We can compute it sequentially by setting $a_{ij} \leftarrow \min(r_i - a_{i1} - \cdots - a_{i(j-1)}, c_j - a_{1j} - \cdots - a_{(i-1)j})$ for $j = 1, \ldots, n$, for $i = 1, \ldots, m$. Alternatively, if $r_1 \leq c_1$, set $a_{11} \leftarrow r_1$, $a_{12} \leftarrow \cdots \leftarrow a_{1n} \leftarrow 0$, and do the remaining rows with c_1 decreased by r_1; if $r_1 > c_1$, set $a_{11} \leftarrow c_1$, $a_{21} \leftarrow \cdots \leftarrow a_{m1} \leftarrow 0$, and do the remaining columns with r_1 decreased by c_1. The second approach shows that at most $m + n - 1$ of the entries are nonzero. We can also write down the explicit formula

$$a_{ij} = \max(0, \min(r_i, c_j, r_1 + \cdots + r_i - c_1 - \cdots - c_{j-1}, c_1 + \cdots + c_j - r_1 - \cdots - r_{i-1})).$$

(c) The same matrix is obtained as in (b).

(d) Reverse left and right in (b) and (c); in both cases the answer is

$$a_{ij} = \max(0, \min(r_i, c_j, r_1 + \cdots + r_i - c_{j+1} - \cdots - c_n, c_j + \cdots + c_n - r_1 - \cdots - r_{i-1})).$$

(e) Here we choose, say, row-wise order: Generate the first row just as for bounded compositions of r_1, with bounds $(c_1, \ldots, c_n)$; and for each row $(a_{11}, \ldots, a_{1n})$, generate the remaining rows recursively in the same way, but with the column sums $(c_1 - a_{11}, \ldots, c_n - a_{1n})$. Most of the action takes place on the bottom two rows, but when a change is made to an earlier row the later rows must be re-initialized.

63. If a_{ij} and a_{kl} are positive, we obtain another contingency table by setting $a_{ij} \leftarrow a_{ij} - 1$, $a_{il} \leftarrow a_{il} + 1$, $a_{kj} \leftarrow a_{kj} + 1$, $a_{kl} \leftarrow a_{kl} - 1$. We want to show that the graph G whose vertices are the contingency tables for $(r_1, \ldots, r_m; c_1, \ldots, c_n)$, adjacent if they can be obtained from each other by such a transformation, has a Hamiltonian path.

When $m = n = 2$, G is a simple path. When $m = 2$ and $n = 3$, G has a two-dimensional structure from which we can see that every vertex is the starting point of at least two Hamiltonian paths, having distinct endpoints. When $m = 2$ and $n \geq 4$ we can show, inductively, that G actually has Hamiltonian paths from any vertex to any other.

When $m \geq 3$ and $n \geq 3$, we can reduce the problem from m to $m - 1$ as in answer 62(e), if we are careful not to "paint ourselves into a corner." Namely, we must avoid reaching a state where the nonzero entries of the bottom two rows have the form $\left(\begin{smallmatrix} 1 & a & 0 \\ 0 & b & c \end{smallmatrix}\right)$

for some a, b, $c > 0$ and a change to row $m - 2$ forces this to become $\left(\begin{smallmatrix} 0 & a & 1 \\ 0 & b & c \end{smallmatrix}\right)$. The previous round of changes to rows $m - 1$ and m can avoid such a trap unless $c = 1$ and it begins with $\left(\begin{smallmatrix} 0 & a+1 & 0 \\ 1 & b-1 & 1 \end{smallmatrix}\right)$ or $\left(\begin{smallmatrix} 1 & a-1 & 1 \\ 0 & b+1 & 0 \end{smallmatrix}\right)$. But that situation can be avoided too.

(A genlex method based on exercise 61 would be considerably simpler, and it almost always would make only four changes per step. But it would occasionally need to update $2\min(m,n)$ entries at a time.)

64. When $x_1 \ldots x_s$ is a binary string and A is a list of subcubes, let $A \oplus x_1 \ldots x_s$ denote replacing the digits $(a_1, \ldots, a_s)$ in each subcube of A by $(a_1 \oplus x_1, \ldots, a_s \oplus x_s)$, from left to right. For example, $0{*}1{*}{*}10 \oplus 1010 = 1{*}1{*}{*}00$. Then the following mutual recursions define a Gray cycle, because A_{st} gives a Gray path from $0^s {*}^t$ to $10^{s-1} {*}^t$ and B_{st} gives a Gray path from $0^s {*}^t$ to ${*}01^{s-1}{*}^{t-1}$, when $st > 0$:

$$A_{st} = 0B_{(s-1)t}, \; *A_{s(t-1)} \oplus 001^{s-2}, \; 1B^R_{(s-1)t};$$

$$B_{st} = 0A_{(s-1)t}, \; 1B_{(s-1)t} \oplus 010^{s-2}, \; *A_{s(t-1)} \oplus 1^s.$$

The strings 001^{s-2} and 010^{s-2} are simply 0^s when $s < 2$; A_{s0} is Gray binary code; $A_{0t} = B_{0t} = {*}^t$. (Incidentally, the somewhat simpler construction

$$G_{st} = *G_{s(t-1)}, \; a_t\, G_{(s-1)t}, \; a_{t-1}G^R_{(s-1)t}, \qquad a_t = t \bmod 2,$$

defines a pleasant Gray *path* from ${*}^t 0^s$ to $a_{t-1}{*}^t 0^{s-1}$.)

65. If a path P is considered equivalent to P^R and to $P \oplus x_1 \ldots x_s$, the total number can be computed systematically as in exercise 33, with the following results for $s+t \le 6$:

paths	cycles
1	1
1 1	1 1
1 2 1	1 1 1
1 3 3 1	1 1 1 1
1 5 10 4 1	1 2 1 1 1
1 6 36 35 5 1	1 2 3 1 1 1
1 9 310 4630 218 6 1	1 3 46 4 1 1 1

In general there are $t + 1$ paths when $s = 1$ and $\binom{\lceil s/2 \rceil + 2}{2} - (s \bmod 2)$ when $t = 1$. The cycles for $s \le 2$ are unique. When $s = t = 5$ there are approximately 6.869×10^{170} paths and 2.495×10^{70} cycles.

66. Let $G(n, 0) = \epsilon$; $G(n, t) = \emptyset$ when $n < t$; and for $1 \le t \le n$, let $G(n, t)$ be

$$\hat{g}(0)G(n-1, t), \; \hat{g}(1)G(n-1, t)^R, \; \ldots, \; \hat{g}(2^t - 1)G(n-1, t)^R, \; \hat{g}(2^t - 1)G(n-1, t-1),$$

where $\hat{g}(k)$ is a t-bit column containing the Gray binary number $g(k)$ with its least significant bit at the top. In this general formula we implicitly add a row of zeros below the bases of $G(n-1, t-1)$.

This remarkable rule gives ordinary Gray binary code when $t = 1$, omitting $0 \ldots 00$. A cyclic Gray code is impossible because $\binom{n}{t}_2$ is odd.

67. A Gray path for compositions corresponding to Algorithm C implies that there is a path in which all transitions are $0^k 1^l \leftrightarrow 1^l 0^k$ with $\min(k,l) \le 2$. Perhaps there is, in fact, a cycle with $\min(k,l) = 1$ in each transition.

68. (a) $\{\emptyset\}$; (b) $\emptyset$.

69. The least N with $\kappa_t N < N$ is $\binom{2t-1}{t} + \binom{2t-3}{t-1} + \cdots + \binom{1}{1} + 1 = \frac{1}{2}(\binom{2t}{t} + \binom{2t-2}{t-1} + \cdots + \binom{0}{0} + 1)$, because $\binom{n}{t-1} \le \binom{n}{t}$ if and only if $n \ge 2t - 1$.

70. Using the facts that $t \geq 3$ implies

$$\kappa_t\left(\binom{2t-3}{t}+N'\right)-\left(\binom{2t-3}{t}+N'\right) = \kappa_t\left(\binom{2t-2}{t}+N'\right)-\left(\binom{2t-2}{t}+N'\right) = \binom{2t-2}{t}\frac{1}{t-1}+\kappa_{t-1}N'-N'$$

when $N' < \binom{2t-3}{t}$, we conclude that the maximum is $\binom{2t-2}{t}\frac{1}{t-1}+\binom{2t-4}{t-1}\frac{1}{t-2}+\cdots+\binom{2}{2}\frac{1}{1}$, and it occurs at 2^{t-1} values of N when $t > 1$.

71. Let C_t be the t-cliques. The first $\binom{1414}{t} + \binom{1009}{t-1}$ t-combinations visited by Algorithm L define a graph on 1415 vertices with 1000000 edges. If $|C_t|$ were larger, $|\partial^{t-2}C_t|$ would exceed 1000000. Thus the single graph defined by $P_{(1000000)2}$ has the maximum number of t-cliques for all $t \geq 2$.

72. $M = \binom{m_s}{s} + \cdots + \binom{m_u}{u}$ for $m_s > \cdots > m_u \geq u \geq 1$, where $\{m_s,\ldots,m_u\} = \{s+t-1,\ldots,n_v\}\backslash\{n_t,\ldots,n_{v+1}\}$. (Compare with exercise 15, which gives $\binom{s+t}{t}-1-N$.)

   If $\alpha = a_{n-1}\ldots a_0$ is the bit string corresponding to the combination $n_t\ldots n_1$, then v is 1 plus the number of trailing 1s in α, and u is the length of the rightmost run of 0s. For example, when $\alpha = 1010001111$ we have $s = 4$, $t = 6$, $M = \binom{8}{4} + \binom{7}{3}$, $u = 3$, $N = \binom{9}{6} + \binom{7}{5}$, $v = 5$.

73. A and B are cross-intersecting $\Longleftrightarrow \alpha \nsubseteq U \backslash \beta$ for all $\alpha \in A$ and $\beta \in B \Longleftrightarrow A\cap\partial^{n-s-t}B^- = \emptyset$, where $B^- = \{U\backslash\beta \mid \beta \in B\}$ is a set of $(n-t)$-combinations. Since $Q^-_{Nnt} = P_{N(n-t)}$, we have $|\partial^{n-s-t}B^-| \geq |\partial^{n-s-t}P_{N(n-t)}|$, and $\partial^{n-s-t}P_{N(n-t)} = P_{N's}$ where $N' = \kappa_{s+1}\ldots\kappa_{n-t}N$. Thus if A and B are cross-intersecting we have $M + N' \leq |A| + |\partial^{n-s-t}B^-| \leq \binom{n}{s}$, and $Q_{Mns} \cap P_{N's} = \emptyset$.

   Conversely, if $Q_{Mns} \cap P_{N's} \neq \emptyset$ we have $\binom{n}{s} < M + N' \leq |A| + |\partial^{n-s-t}B^-|$, so A and B cannot be cross-intersecting.

74. $|\varrho Q_{Nnt}| = \kappa_{n-t}N$ (see exercise 94). Also, arguing as in (58) and (59), we find $\varrho P_{N5} = (n-1)P_{N5} \cup \cdots \cup 10P_{N5} \cup \{543210,\ldots,987654\}$ in that particular case; and $|\varrho P_{Nt}| = (n+1-n_t)N + \binom{n_t+1}{t+1}$ in general.

75. The identity $\binom{n+1}{k} = \binom{n}{k}+\binom{n-1}{k-1}+\cdots+\binom{n-k}{0}$, Eq. 1.2.6–(10), gives another representation if $n_v > v$. But (60) is unaffected, since $\binom{n+1}{k-1} = \binom{n}{k-1}+\binom{n-1}{k-2}+\cdots+\binom{n-k+1}{0}$.

76. Represent $N+1$ by adding $\binom{v-1}{v-1}$ to (57); then use the previous exercise to deduce that $\kappa_t(N+1) - \kappa_t N = \binom{v-1}{v-2} = v - 1$.

77. [D. E. Daykin, *Nanta Math.* **8**, 2 (1975), 78–83.] We work with extended representations $M = \binom{m_t}{t} + \cdots + \binom{m_u}{u}$ and $N = \binom{n_t}{t} + \cdots + \binom{n_v}{v}$ as in exercise 75, calling them *improper* if the final index u or v is zero. Call N *flexible* if it has both proper and improper representations, that is, if $n_v > v > 0$.

   (a) Given an integer S, find $M + N$ such that $M + N = S$ and $\kappa_t M + \kappa_t N$ is minimum, with M as large as possible. If $N = 0$, we're done. Otherwise the max-min operation preserves both $M + N$ and $\kappa_t M + \kappa_t N$, so we can assume that $v \geq u \geq 1$ in the proper representations of M and N. If N is inflexible, $\kappa_t(M+1) + \kappa_t(N-1) = (\kappa_t M + u - 1) + (\kappa_t N - v) < \kappa_t M + \kappa_t N$, by exercise 76; therefore N must be flexible. But then we can apply the max-min operation to M and the improper representation of N, increasing M: Contradiction.

   This proof shows that equality holds if and only if $MN = 0$, a fact that was noted in 1927 by F. S. Macaulay.

   (b) Now we try to minimize $\max(\kappa_t M, N) + \kappa_{t-1}N$ when $M + N = S$, this time representing N as $\binom{n_{t-1}}{t-1} + \cdots + \binom{n_v}{v}$. The max-min operation can still be used if $n_{t-1} < m_t$; leaving m_t unchanged, it preserves $M+N$ and $\kappa_t M + \kappa_{t-1}N$ as well as the relation $\kappa_t M > N$. We arrive at a contradiction as in (a) if $N \neq 0$, so we can assume that $n_{t-1} \geq m_t$.

If $n_{t-1} > m_t$ we have $N > \kappa_t M$ and also $\lambda_t N > M$; hence $M + N < \lambda_t N + N = \binom{n_{t-1}+1}{t} + \cdots + \binom{n_v+1}{v+1}$, and we have $\kappa_t(M + N) \leq \kappa_t(\lambda_t N + N) = N + \kappa_{t-1}N$.

Finally if $n_{t-1} = m_t = a$, let $M = \binom{a}{t} + M'$ and $N = \binom{a}{t-1} + N'$. Then $\kappa_t(M+N) = \binom{a+1}{t-1} + \kappa_{t-1}(M' + N')$, $\kappa_t M = \binom{a}{t-1} + \kappa_{t-1}M'$, and $\kappa_{t-1}N = \binom{a}{t-2} + \kappa_{t-2}N'$; the result follows by induction on t.

78. [J. Eckhoff and G. Wegner, *Periodica Math. Hung.* **6** (1975), 137–142; A. J. W. Hilton, *Periodica Math. Hung.* **10** (1979), 25–30.] Let $M = |A_1|$ and $N = |A_0|$; we can assume that $t > 0$ and $N > 0$. Then $|\partial A| = |\partial A_1 \cup A_0| + |\partial A_0| \geq \max(|\partial A_1|, |A_0|) + |\partial A_0| \geq \max(\kappa_t M, N) + \kappa_{t-1}N \geq \kappa_t(M + N) = |P_{|A|t}|$, by induction on $m + n + t$.

Conversely, let $A_1 = P_{Mt} + 1$ and $A_0 = P_{N(t-1)} + 1$; this notation means, for example, that $\{210, 320\} + 1 = \{321, 431\}$. Then $\kappa_t(M + N) \leq |\partial A| = |\partial A_1 \cup A_0| + |(\partial A_0)0| = \max(\kappa_t M, N) + \kappa_{t-1}N$, because $\partial A_1 = P_{(\kappa_t M)(t-1)} + 1$. [Schützenberger observed in 1959 that $\kappa_t(M + N) \leq \kappa_t M + \kappa_{t-1}N$ if and only if $\kappa_t M \geq N$.]

For the first inequality, let A and B be disjoint sets of t-combinations with $|A| = M$, $|\partial A| = \kappa_t M$, $|B| = N$, $|\partial B| = \kappa_t N$. Then $\kappa_t(M + N) = \kappa_t |A \cup B| \leq |\partial(A \cup B)| = |\partial A \cup \partial B| = |\partial A| + |\partial B| = \kappa_t M + \kappa_t N$.

79. In fact, $\mu_t(M + \lambda_{t-1}M) = M$, and $\mu_t N + \lambda_{t-1}\mu_t N = N + (n_2 - n_1)[v = 1]$ when N is given by (57).

80. If $N > 0$ and $t > 1$, represent N as in (57) and let $N = N_0 + N_1$, where

$$N_0 = \binom{n_t - 1}{t} + \cdots + \binom{n_v - 1}{v}, \qquad N_1 = \binom{n_t - 1}{t-1} + \cdots + \binom{n_v - 1}{v-1}.$$

Let $N_0 = \binom{y}{t}$ and $N_1 = \binom{z}{t-1}$. Then, by induction on t and $\lfloor x \rfloor$, we have $\binom{x}{t} = N_0 + \kappa_t N_0 \geq \binom{y}{t} + \binom{y}{t-1} = \binom{y+1}{t}$; $N_1 = \binom{x}{t} - \binom{y}{t} \geq \binom{x}{t} - \binom{x-1}{t} = \binom{x-1}{t-1}$; and $\kappa_t N = N_1 + \kappa_{t-1}N_1 \geq \binom{z}{t-1} + \binom{z}{t-2} = \binom{z+1}{t-1} \geq \binom{x}{t-1}$.

[Lovász actually proved a stronger result; see exercise 1.2.6–66. We have, similarly, $\mu_t N \geq \binom{x-1}{t-1}$; see Björner, Frankl, and Stanley, *Combinatorica* **7** (1987), 27 28.]

81. For example, if the largest element of $\widehat{P}_{N5}$ is 66433, we have

$$\widehat{P}_{N5} = \{00000, \ldots, 55555\} \cup \{60000, \ldots, 65555\} \cup \{66000, \ldots, 66333\} \cup \{66400, \ldots, 66433\};$$

so $N = \binom{10}{5} + \binom{9}{4} + \binom{6}{3} + \binom{5}{2}$. Its lower shadow is

$$\partial \widehat{P}_{N5} = \{0000, \ldots, 5555\} \cup \{6000, \ldots, 6555\} \cup \{6600, \ldots, 6633\} \cup \{6640, \ldots, 6643\},$$

of size $\binom{9}{4} + \binom{8}{3} + \binom{5}{2} + \binom{4}{1}$.

If the smallest element of Q_{N95} is 66433, we have

$$\widehat{Q}_{N95} = \{99999, \ldots, 70000\} \cup \{66666, \ldots, 66500\} \cup \{66444, \ldots, 66440\} \cup \{66433\};$$

so $N = \left(\binom{13}{9} + \binom{12}{8} + \binom{11}{7}\right) + \left(\binom{8}{6} + \binom{7}{5}\right) + \binom{5}{4} + \binom{3}{3}$. Its upper shadow is

$$\varrho \widehat{Q}_{N95} = \{999999, \ldots, 700000\} \cup \{666666, \ldots, 665000\}$$
$$\cup \{664444, \ldots, 664400\} \cup \{664333, \ldots, 664330\},$$

of size $\left(\binom{14}{9} + \binom{13}{8} + \binom{12}{7}\right) + \left(\binom{9}{6} + \binom{8}{5}\right) + \binom{6}{4} + \binom{4}{3} = N + \kappa_9 N$. The size, t, of each combination is essentially irrelevant, as long as $N \leq \binom{s+t}{t}$; for example, the smallest element of $\widehat{Q}_{N98}$ is 99966433 in the case we have considered.

82. (a) The derivative would have to be $\sum_{k>0} r_k(x)$, but that series diverges.

[Informally, the graph of $\tau(x)$ shows "pits" of relative magnitude 2^{-k} at all odd multiples of 2^{-k}. Takagi's original publication, in *Proc. Physico-Math. Soc. Japan* (2) **1** (1903), 176–177, has been translated into English in his *Collected Papers* (Iwanami Shoten, 1973).]

(b) Since $r_k(1-t) = (-1)^{\lceil 2^k t \rceil}$ when $k > 0$, we have $\int_0^{1-x} r_k(t)\,dt = \int_x^1 r_k(1-u)\,du = -\int_x^1 r_k(u)\,du = \int_0^x r_k(u)\,du$. The second equation follows from the fact that $r_k(\frac{1}{2}t) = r_{k-1}(t)$. Part (d) shows that these two equations suffice to define $\tau(x)$ when x is rational.

(c) Since $\tau(2^{-a}x) = a2^{-a}x + 2^{-a}\tau(x)$ for $0 \le x \le 1$, we have $\tau(\epsilon) = a\epsilon + O(\epsilon)$ when $2^{-a-1} \le \epsilon \le 2^{-a}$. Therefore $\tau(\epsilon) = \epsilon \lg \frac{1}{\epsilon} + O(\epsilon)$ for $0 < \epsilon \le 1$.

(d) Suppose $0 \le p/q \le 1$. If $p/q \le 1/2$ we have $\tau(p/q) = p/q + \tau(2p/q)/2$; otherwise $\tau(p/q) = (q-p)/q + \tau(2(q-p)/q)/2$. Therefore we can assume that q is odd. When q is odd, let $p' = p/2$ when p is even, $p' = (q-p)/2$ when p is odd. Then $\tau(p/q) = 2\tau(p'/q) - 2p'/q$ for $0 < p < q$; this system of $q-1$ equations has a unique solution. For example, the values for $q = 3, 4, 5, 6, 7$ are $2/3, 2/3$; $1/2, 1/2, 1/2$; $8/15, 2/3, 2/3, 8/15$; $1/2, 2/3, 1/2, 2/3, 1/2$; $22/49, 30/49, 32/49, 32/49, 30/49, 22/49$.

(e) The solutions $< \frac{1}{2}$ are $x = \frac{1}{4}, \frac{1}{4} - \frac{1}{16}, \frac{1}{4} - \frac{1}{16} - \frac{1}{64}, \frac{1}{4} - \frac{1}{16} - \frac{1}{64} - \frac{1}{256}, \ldots, \frac{1}{6}$.

(f) The value $\frac{2}{3}$ is achieved for $x = \frac{1}{2} \pm \frac{1}{8} \pm \frac{1}{32} \pm \frac{1}{128} \pm \cdots$, an uncountable set.

83. Given any integers $q > p > 0$, consider paths starting from 0 in the digraph

$$0 \leftarrow 1 \leftarrow 2 \leftarrow 3 \leftarrow 4 \leftarrow 5 \leftarrow \cdots$$
$$\updownarrow \quad \updownarrow \quad \updownarrow \quad \updownarrow \quad \updownarrow \quad \updownarrow$$
$$1 \rightarrow 2 \rightarrow 3 \rightarrow 4 \rightarrow 5 \rightarrow 6 \rightarrow \cdots$$

Compute an associated value v, starting with $v \leftarrow -p$; horizontal moves change $v \leftarrow 2v$, vertical moves from node a change $v \leftarrow 2(qa - v)$. The path stops if we reach a node twice with the same value v. Transitions are not allowed to upper node a if $v \le -q$ or $v \ge qa$ at that node; they are not allowed to lower node a with $v \le 0$ or $v \ge q(a+1)$. These restrictions force most steps of the path. (Node a in the upper row means, "Solve $\tau(x) = ax - v/q$"; in the lower row it means, "Solve $\tau(x) = v/q - ax$.") Empirical tests suggest that all such paths are finite. The equation $\tau(x) = p/q$ then has solutions $x = x_0$ defined by the sequence $x_0, x_1, x_2, \ldots$ where $x_k = \frac{1}{2}x_{k+1}$ on a horizontal step and $x_k = 1 - \frac{1}{2}x_{k+1}$ on a vertical step; eventually $x_k = x_j$ for some $j < k$. If $j > 0$ and if q is not a power of 2, these are all the solutions to $\tau(x) = p/q$ when $x > 1/2$.

For example, this procedure establishes that $\tau(x) = 1/5$ and $x > 1/2$ only when x is 83581/87040; the only path yields $x_0 = 1 - \frac{1}{2}x_1, x_1 = \frac{1}{2}x_2, \ldots, x_{18} = \frac{1}{2}x_{19}$, and $x_{19} = x_{11}$. There are, similarly, just two values $x > 1/2$ with $\tau(x) = 3/5$, having denominator $2^{46}(2^{56} - 1)/3$.

Moreover, it appears that all cycles in the digraph that pass through node 0 define values of p and q such that $\tau(x) = p/q$ has uncountably many solutions. Such values are, for example, $2/3, 8/15, 8/21$, corresponding to the cycles $(01), (0121), (012321)$. The value $32/63$ corresponds to (012121) and also to (012101234545454321), as well as to two other paths that do not return to 0.

84. [Frankl, Matsumoto, Ruzsa, and Tokushige, *J. Combinatorial Theory* **A69** (1995), 125–148.] If $a \le b$ we have

$$\binom{2t - 1 - b}{t - a} \bigg/ T = t^a (t-1)^{\frac{b-a}{}} / (2t-1)^b = 2^{-b}(1 + f(a,b)t^{-1} + O(b^4/t^2)),$$

where $f(a,b) = a(1+b) - a^2 - b(1+b)/4 = f(a+1,b) - b + 2a$. Therefore if N has the combinatorial representation (57), and if we set $n_j = 2t - 1 - b_j$, we have

$$\frac{t}{T}\left(\kappa_t N - N\right) = \frac{b_t}{2^{b_t}} + \frac{b_{t-1} - 2}{2^{b_{t-1}}} + \frac{b_{t-2} - 4}{2^{b_{t-2}}} + \cdots + \frac{O(\log t)^3}{t},$$

the terms being negligible when b_j exceeds $2\lg t$. And one can show that

$$\tau\left(\sum_{j=0}^{l} 2^{-e_j}\right) = \sum_{j=0}^{l} (e_j - 2j) 2^{-e_j}.$$

85. $N - \lambda_{t-1}N$ has the same asymptotic form as $\kappa_t N - N$, by (63), since $\tau(x) = \tau(1-x)$. So does $2\mu_t N - N$, up to $O(T(\log t)^3/t^2)$, because $\binom{2t-1-b}{t-a} = 2\binom{2t-2-b}{t-a}(1+O(\log t)/t)$ when $b < 2\lg t$.

86. $x \in X^{\circ\sim} \iff \bar{x} \notin X^{\circ} \iff \bar{x} \notin X$ or $\bar{x} \notin X + e_1$ or $\cdots$ or $\bar{x} \notin X + e_n \iff x \in X^{\sim}$ or $x \in X^{\sim} - e_1$ or $\cdots$ or $x \in X^{\sim} - e_n \iff x \in X^{\sim+}$.

87. All three are true, using the fact that $X \subseteq Y^{\circ}$ if and only if $X^+ \subseteq Y$: (a) $X \subseteq Y^{\circ} \iff X^{\sim} \supseteq Y^{\circ\sim} = Y^{\sim+} \iff Y^{\sim} \subseteq X^{\sim\circ}$. (b) $X^+ \subseteq X^+ \implies X \subseteq X^{+\circ}$; hence $X^{\circ} \subseteq X^{\circ+\circ}$. Also $X^{\circ} \subseteq X^{\circ} \implies X^{\circ+} \subseteq X$; hence $X^{\circ+\circ} \subseteq X^{\circ}$. (c) $\alpha M \le N \iff S_M^+ \subseteq S_N \iff S_M \subseteq S_N^{\circ} \iff M \le \beta N$.

88. If $\nu x < \nu y$ then $\nu(x - e_k) < \nu(y - e_j)$, so we can assume that $\nu x = \nu y$ and that $x > y$ in lexicographic order. We must have $y_j > 0$; otherwise $\nu(y - e_j)$ would exceed $\nu(x - e_k)$. If $x_i = y_i$ for $1 \le i \le j$, clearly $k > j$ and $x - e_k \prec y - e_j$. Otherwise $x_i > y_i$ for some $i \le j$; again we have $x - e_k \prec y - e_j$, unless $x - e_k = y - e_j$.

89. From the table

$j =$	0	1	2	3	4	5	6	7	8	9	10	11
$e_j + e_1 =$	e_1	e_0	e_4	e_5	e_2	e_3	e_8	e_9	e_6	e_7	e_{11}	e_{10}
$e_j + e_2 =$	e_2	e_4	e_0	e_6	e_1	e_8	e_3	e_{10}	e_5	e_{11}	e_7	e_9
$e_j + e_3 =$	e_3	e_5	e_6	e_7	e_8	e_9	e_{10}	e_0	e_{11}	e_1	e_2	e_4

we find $(\alpha 0, \alpha 1, \ldots, \alpha 12) = (0, 4, 6, 7, 8, 9, 10, 11, 11, 12, 12, 12, 12)$; $(\beta 0, \beta 1, \ldots, \beta 12) = (0, 0, 0, 0, 1, 1, 2, 3, 4, 5, 6, 8, 12)$.

90. Let $Y = X^+$ and $Z = C_k X$, and let $N_a = |X_k(a)|$ for $0 \le a < m_k$. Then

$$|Y| = \sum_{a=0}^{m_k-1} |Y_k(a)| = \sum_{a=0}^{m_k-1} |(X_k(a-1) + e_k) \cup (X_k(a) + E_k(0))|$$

$$\ge \sum_{a=0}^{m_k-1} \max(N_{a-1}, \alpha N_a),$$

where $a - 1$ stands for $(a-1) \bmod m_k$ and the α function comes from the $(n-1)$-dimensional torus, because $|X_k(a) + E_k(0)| \ge \alpha N_a$ by induction. Also

$$|Z^+| = \sum_{a=0}^{m_k-1} |Z_k^+(a)| = \sum_{a=0}^{m_k-1} |(Z_k(a-1) + e_k) \cup (Z_k(a) + E_k(0))|$$

$$= \sum_{a=0}^{m_k-1} \max(N_{a-1}, \alpha N_a),$$

because both $Z_k(a-1) + e_k$ and $Z_k(a) + E_k(0)$ are standard in $n - 1$ dimensions.

91. Let there be N_a points in row a of a totally compressed array, where row 0 is at the bottom; thus $l = N_{-1} \geq N_0 \geq \cdots \geq N_{m-1} \geq N_m = 0$. We show first that there is an optimum X for which the "bad" condition $N_a = N_{a+1}$ never occurs except when $N_a = 0$ or $N_a = l$. For if a is the smallest bad subscript, suppose $N_{a-1} > N_a = N_{a+1} = \cdots = N_{a+k} > N_{a+k+1}$. Then we can always decrease N_{a+k} by 1 and add 1 to some N_b for $b \leq a$ without increasing $|X^+|$, except in cases where $k = 1$ and $N_{a+2} = N_{a+1} - 1$ and $N_b = N_a + a - b < l$ for $0 \leq b \leq a$. Exploring such cases further, if $N_{c+1} < N_c = N_{c-1}$ for some $c > a + 1$, we can set $N_c \leftarrow N_c - 1$ and $N_a \leftarrow N_a + 1$, thereby either decreasing a or increasing N_0. Otherwise we can find a subscript d such that $N_c = N_{a+1} + a + 1 - c > 0$ for $a < c < d$, and either $N_d = 0$ or $N_d < N_{d-1} - 1$. Then it is OK to decrease N_c by 1 for $a < c < d$ and subsequently to increase N_b by 1 for $0 \leq b < d - a - 1$. (It is important to note that if $N_d = 0$ we have $N_0 \geq d - 1$; hence $d = m$ implies $l = m$.)

Repeating such transformations until $N_a > N_{a+1}$ whenever $N_a \neq l$ and $N_{a+1} \neq 0$, we reach situation (86), and the proof can be completed as in the text.

92. Let $x + k$ denote the lexicographically smallest element of $T(m_1, \ldots, m_{n-1})$ that exceeds x and has weight $\nu x + k$, if any such element exists. For example, if $m_1 = m_2 = m_3 = 4$ and $x = 211$, we have $x + 1 = 212$, $x + 2 = 213$, $x + 3 = 223$, $x + 4 = 233$, $x + 5 = 333$, and $x + 6$ does not exist; in general, $x + k + 1$ is obtained from $x + k$ by increasing the rightmost component that can be increased. If $x + k = (m_1 - 1, \ldots, m_{n-1} - 1)$, let us set $x + k + 1 = x + k$. Then if $S(k)$ is the set of all elements of $T(m_1, \ldots, m_{n-1})$ that are $\preceq x + k$, we have $S(k + 1) = S(k)^+$. Furthermore, the elements of S that end in a are those whose first $n - 1$ components are in $S(m - 1 - a)$.

The result of this exercise can be stated more intuitively: As we generate n-dimensional standard sets $S_1, S_2, \ldots$, the $(n - 1)$-dimensional standard sets on each layer become spreads of each other just after each point is added to layer $m - 1$. Similarly, they become cores of each other just before each point is added to layer 0.

93. (a) Suppose the parameters are $2 \leq m_1' \leq m_2' \leq \cdots \leq m_n'$ when sorted properly, and let k be minimal with $m_k \neq m_k'$. Then take $N = 1 + \text{rank}(0, \ldots, 0, m_k' - 1, 0, \ldots, 0)$. (We must assume that $\min(m_1, \ldots, m_n) \geq 2$, since parameters equal to 1 can be placed anywhere.)

(b) Only in the proof for $n = 2$, buried inside the answer to exercise 91. That proof is incorporated by induction when n is larger.

94. Complementation reverses lexicographic order and changes ϱ to ∂.

95. For Theorem K, let $d = n - 1$ and $s_0 = \cdots = s_d = 1$. For Theorem M, let $d = s$ and $s_0 = \cdots = s_d = t + 1$.

96. In such a representation, N is the number of t-multicombinations of $\{s_0 \cdot 0, s_1 \cdot 1, s_2 \cdot 2, \ldots\}$ that precede $n_t n_{t-1} \ldots n_1$ in lexicographic order, because the generalized coefficient $\binom{S(n)}{t}$ counts the multicombinations whose leftmost component is $< n$.

If we truncate the representation by stopping at the rightmost nonzero term $\binom{S(n_v)}{v}$, we obtain a nice generalization of (60):

$$|\partial P_{Nt}| = \binom{S(n_t)}{t-1} + \binom{S(n_{t-1})}{t-2} + \cdots + \binom{S(n_v)}{v-1}.$$

[See G. F. Clements, *J. Combinatorial Theory* **A37** (1984), 91–97. The inequalities $s_0 \geq s_1 \geq \cdots \geq s_d$ are needed for the validity of Corollary C, but not for the calculation of $|\partial P_{Nt}|$. Some terms $\binom{S(n_k)}{k}$ for $t \geq k > v$ may be zero. For example, when $N = 1$, $t = 4$, $s_0 = 3$, and $s_1 = 2$, we have $N = \binom{S(1)}{4} + \binom{S(1)}{3} = 0 + 1$.]

97. (a) The tetrahedron has four vertices, six edges, four faces: $(N_0, \ldots, N_4) =$ $(1, 4, 6, 4, 1)$. The octahedron, similarly, has $(N_0, \ldots, N_6) = (1, 6, 8, 8, 0, 0, 0)$, and the icosahedron has $(N_0, \ldots, N_{12}) = (1, 12, 30, 20, 0, \ldots, 0)$. The hexahedron, aka the 3-cube, has eight vertices, 12 edges, and six square faces; perturbation breaks each square face into two triangles and introduces new edges, so we have $(N_0, \ldots, N_8) =$ $(1, 8, 18, 12, 0, \ldots, 0)$. Finally, the perturbed pentagonal faces of the dodecahedron lead to $(N_0, \ldots, N_{20}) = (1, 20, 54, 36, 0, \ldots, 0)$.

(b) $\{210, 310\} \cup \{10, 20, 21, 30, 31\} \cup \{0, 1, 2, 3\} \cup \{\epsilon\}$.

(c) $0 \le N_t \le \binom{n}{t}$ for $0 \le t \le n$ and $N_{t-1} \ge \kappa_t N_t$ for $1 \le t \le n$. The second condition is equivalent to $\lambda_{t-1} N_{t-1} \ge N_t$ for $1 \le t \le n$, if we define $\lambda_0 1 = \infty$. These conditions are necessary for Theorem K, and sufficient if $A = \bigcup P_{N_t t}$.

(d) The complements of the elements not in a simplicial complex, namely the sets $\{\{0, \ldots, n-1\} \setminus \alpha \mid \alpha \notin C\}$, form a simplicial complex. (We can also verify that the necessary and sufficient condition holds: $N_{t-1} \ge \kappa_t N_t \iff \lambda_{t-1} N_{t-1} \ge N_t \iff$ $\kappa_{n-t+1} \overline{N}_{n-t+1} \le \overline{N}_{n-t}$, because $\kappa_{n-t} \overline{N}_{n-t+1} = \binom{n}{t} - \lambda_{t-1} N_{t-1}$ by exercise 94.)

(e) $00000 \leftrightarrow 14641$; $10000 \leftrightarrow 14640$; $11000 \leftrightarrow 14630$; $12000 \leftrightarrow 14620$; $13000 \leftrightarrow$ 14610; $14000 \leftrightarrow 14600$; $12100 \leftrightarrow 14520$; $13100 \leftrightarrow 14510$; $14100 \leftrightarrow 14500$; $13200 \leftrightarrow$ 14410; $14200 \leftrightarrow 14400$; $13300 \leftrightarrow 14310$; and the self-dual cases $14300, 13310$.

98. The following procedure by S. Linusson [*Combinatorica* **19** (1999), 255–266], who considered also the more general problem for multisets, is considerably faster than a more obvious approach. Let $L(n, h, l)$ count feasible vectors with $N_t = \binom{n}{t}$ for $0 \le t \le l$, $N_{t+1} < \binom{n}{t+1}$, and $N_t = 0$ for $t > h$. Then $L(n, h, l) = 0$ unless $-1 \le l \le h \le n$; also $L(n, h, h) = L(n, h, -1) = 1$, and $L(n, n, l) = L(n, n-1, l)$ for $l < n$. When $n > h \ge l \ge 0$ we can compute $L(n, h, l) = \sum_{j=l}^h L(n-1, h, j) L(n-1, j-1, l-1)$, a recurrence that follows from Theorem K. (Each size vector corresponds to the complex $\bigcup P_{N_t t}$, with $L(n-1, h, j)$ representing combinations that do not contain the maximum element $n-1$ and $L(n-1, j-1, l-1)$ representing those that do.) Finally the grand total is $L(n) = \sum_{l=1}^n L(n, n, l)$.

We have $L(0), L(1), L(2), \ldots = 2, 3, 5, 10, 26, 96, 553, 5461, 100709, 3718354,$ $289725509, \ldots$; $L(100) \approx 3.2299 \times 10^{1842}$.

99. The maximal elements of a simplicial complex form a clutter; conversely, the combinations contained in elements of a clutter form a simplicial complex. Thus the two concepts are essentially equivalent.

(a) If $(M_0, M_1, \ldots, M_n)$ is the size vector of a clutter, then $(N_0, N_1, \ldots, N_n)$ is the size vector of a simplicial complex if $N_n = M_n$ and $N_t = M_t + \kappa_{t+1} N_{t+1}$ for $0 \le t < n$. Conversely, every such $(N_0, \ldots, N_n)$ yields an $(M_0, \ldots, M_n)$ if we use the lexicographically first N_t t-combinations. [G. F. Clements extended this result to general multisets in *Discrete Math.* **4** (1973), 123–128.]

(b) In the order of answer 97(e) they are $00000, 00001, 10000, 00040, 01000, 00030,$ $02000, 00120, 03000, 00310, 04000, 00600, 00100, 00020, 01100, 00210, 02100, 00500,$ $00200, 00110, 01200, 00400, 00300, 01010, 01300, 00010$. Notice that $(M_0, \ldots, M_n)$ is feasible if and only if $(M_n, \ldots, M_0)$ is feasible, so we have a different sort of duality in this interpretation.

100. Represent A as a subset of $T(m_1, \ldots, m_n)$ as in the proof of Corollary C. Then the maximum value of νA is obtained when A consists of the N lexicographically smallest points $x_1 \ldots x_n$.

The proof starts by reducing to the case that A is compressed, in the sense that its t-multicombinations are $P_{|A \cap T_t|t}$ for each t. Then if y is the largest element $\in A$

and if x is the smallest element $\notin A$, we prove that $x < y$ implies $\nu x > \nu y$, hence $\nu(A \setminus y \cup x) > \nu A$. For if $\nu x = \nu y - k$ we could find an element of $\partial^k y$ that is greater than x, contradicting the assumption that A is compressed.

101. (a) In general, $F(p) = N_0 p^n + N_1 p^{n-1}(1-p) + \cdots + N_n(1-p)^n$ when $f(x_1, \ldots, x_n)$ is satisfied by exactly N_t binary strings $x_1 \ldots x_n$ of weight t. Thus we find $G(p) = p^4 + 3p^3(1-p) + p^2(1-p)^2$; $H(p) = p^4 + p^3(1-p) + p^2(1-p)^2$.

(b) A monotone formula f is equivalent to a simplicial complex C under the correspondence $f(x_1, \ldots, x_n) = 1 \iff \{j - 1 \mid x_j = 0\} \in C$. Therefore the functions $f(p)$ of monotone Boolean functions are those that satisfy the condition of exercise 97(c), and we obtain a suitable function by choosing the lexicographically last N_{n-t} t-combinations (which are complements of the first N_s s-combinations): $\{3210\}$, $\{321, 320, 310\}$, $\{32\}$ gives $f(w, x, y, z) = wxyz \vee xyz \vee wyz \vee wxz \vee yz = wxz \vee yz$.

M. P. Schützenberger observed that we can find the parameters N_t easily from $f(p)$ by noting that $f(1/(1+u)) = (N_0 + N_1 u + \cdots + N_n u^n)/(1+u)^n$. One can show that $H(p)$ is not equivalent to a monotone formula in any number of variables, because $(1 + u + u^2)/(1+u)^4 = (N_0 + N_1 u + \cdots + N_n u^n)/(1+u)^n$ implies that $N_1 = n - 3$, $N_2 = \binom{n-3}{2} + 1$, and $\kappa_2 N_2 = n - 2$.

But the task of deciding this question is not so simple in general. For example, the function $(1 + 5u + 5u^2 + 5u^3)/(1+u)^5$ does not match any monotone formula in five variables, because $\kappa_3 5 = 7$; but it equals $(1 + 6u + 10u^2 + 10u^3 + 5u^4)/(1+u)^6$, which works fine with six.

102. (a) Choose N_t linearly independent polynomials of degree t in I; order their terms lexicographically, and take linear combinations so that the lexicographically smallest terms are distinct monomials. Let I' consist of all multiples of those monomials.

(b) Each monomial of degree t in I' is essentially a t-multicombination; for example, $x_1^3 x_2 x_5^4$ corresponds to 55552111. If M_t is the set of independent monomials for degree t, the ideal property is equivalent to saying that $M_{t+1} \supseteq \varrho M_t$.

In the given example, $M_3 = \{x_0 x_1^2\}$; $M_4 = \varrho M_3 \cup \{x_0 x_1 x_2^2\}$; $M_5 = \varrho M_4 \cup \{x_1 x_2^4\}$, since $x_2^2(x_0 x_1^2 - 2x_1 x_2^2) - x_1(x_0 x_1 x_2^2) = -2x_1 x_2^4$; and $M_{t+1} = \varrho M_t$ thereafter.

(c) By Theorem M we can assume that $M_t = \widehat{Q}_{Mst}$. Let $N_t = \binom{n_{ts}}{s} + \cdots + \binom{n_{t2}}{2} + \binom{n_{t1}}{1}$, where $s + t \geq n_{ts} > \cdots > n_{t2} > n_{t1} \geq 0$; then $n_{ts} = s + t$ if and only if $n_{t(s-1)} = s - 2, \ldots, n_{t1} = 0$. Furthermore we have

$$N_{t+1} \geq N_t + \kappa_s N_t = \binom{n_{ts} + [n_{ts} \geq s]}{s} + \cdots + \binom{n_{t2} + [n_{t2} \geq 2]}{2} + \binom{n_{t1} + [n_{t1} \geq 1]}{1}.$$

Therefore the sequence $(n_{ts} - t - \infty[n_{ts} < s], \ldots, n_{t2} - t - \infty[n_{t2} < 2], n_{t1} - t - \infty[n_{t1} < 1])$ is lexicographically nondecreasing as t increases, where we insert '$-\infty$' in components that have $n_{tj} = j - 1$. Such a sequence cannot increase infinitely many times without exceeding the maximum value $(s, -\infty, \ldots, -\infty)$, by exercise 1.2.1–15(d).

103. Let P_{Nst} be the first N elements of a sequence determined as follows: For each binary string $x = x_{s+t-1} \ldots x_0$, in lexicographic order, write down $\binom{\nu x}{t}$ subcubes by changing t of the 1s to $*$s in all possible ways, in lexicographic order (considering $1 < *$). For example, if $x = 0101101$ and $t = 2$, we generate the subcubes $0101*0*$, $010*10*$, $010**01$, $0*0110*$, $0*01*01$, $0*0*101$.

[See B. Lindström, *Arkiv för Mat.* **8** (1971), 245–257; a generalization analogous to Corollary C appears in K. Engel, *Sperner Theory* (Cambridge Univ. Press, 1997), Theorem 8.1.1.]

104. The first N strings in cross order have the desired property. [T. N. Danh and D. E. Daykin, *J. London Math. Soc.* (2) **55** (1997), 417–426.]

Notes: Beginning with the observation that the "1-shadow" of the N lexicographically first strings of weight t (namely the strings obtained by deleting 1 bits only) consists of the first $\mu_t N$ strings of weight t, R. Ahlswede and N. Cai extended the Danh–Daykin theorem to allow insertion, deletion, and/or transposition of bits [*Combinatorica* **17** (1997), 11–29; *Applied Math. Letters* **11**, 5 (1998), 121–126]. Uwe Leck has proved that no total ordering of *ternary strings* has the analogous minimum-shadow property [Preprint 98/6 (Univ. Rostock, 1998), 6 pages].

105. Every number must occur the same number of times in the cycle. Equivalently, $\binom{n-1}{t-1}$ must be a multiple of t. This necessary condition appears to be sufficient as well, provided that n is not too small with respect to t; but such a result may well be true yet impossible to prove. [See Chung, Graham, and Diaconis, *Discrete Math.* **110** (1992), 55–57.]

The next few exercises consider the cases $t = 2$ and $t = 3$, for which elegant results are known. Similar but more complicated results have been derived for $t = 4$ and $t = 5$, and the case $t = 6$ has been partially resolved. The case $(n, t) = (12, 6)$ is currently the smallest for which the existence of a universal cycle is unknown.

106. Let the differences mod $(2m+1)$ be $1, 2, \ldots, m, 1, 2, \ldots, m, \ldots$, repeated $2m+1$ times; for example, the cycle for $m = 3$ is (013602561450346235124). This works because $1 + \cdots + m = \binom{m+1}{2}$ is relatively prime to $2m + 1$. [*J. École Polytechnique* **4**, Cahier 10 (1810), 16–48.]

107. The seven doubles ■■, ⬝⬝, $\ldots$, ⬞⬞ can be inserted in 3^7 ways into any universal cycle of 2-combinations for $\{0, 1, 2, 3, 4, 5, 6\}$. The number of such universal cycles is the number of Eulerian trails of the complete graph K_7, which can be shown to be 129,976,320 if we regard $(a_0 a_1 \ldots a_{20})$ as equivalent to $(a_1 \ldots a_{20} a_0)$ but not to the reverse-order cycle $(a_{20} \ldots a_1 a_0)$. So the answer is 284,258,211,840.

[This problem was first solved in 1859 by M. Reiss, whose method was so complicated that people doubted the result; see *Nouvelles Annales de Mathématiques* **8** (1849), 74; **11** (1852), 115; *Annali di Matematica Pura ed Applicata* (2) **5** (1871–1873), 63–120. A considerably simpler solution, confirming Reiss's claim, was found by P. Jolivald and G. Tarry, who also enumerated the Eulerian trails of K_9; see *Comptes Rendus Association Française pour l'Avancement des Sciences* **15**, part 2 (1886), 49–53; É. Lucas, *Récréations Mathématiques* **4** (1894), 123–151. Brendan D. McKay and Robert W. Robinson found an approach that is better still, enabling them to continue the enumeration through K_{21} by using the fact that the number of trails is

$$(m - 1)!^{2m+1} \, [z_0^{2m} z_1^{2m-2} \ldots z_{2m}^{2m-2}] \, \det(a_{jk}) \prod_{1 \le j < k \le 2m} (z_j^2 + z_k^2),$$

where $a_{jk} = -1/(z_j^2 + z_k^2)$ when $j \neq k$; $a_{jj} = -1/(2z_j^2) + \sum_{0 \le k \le 2m} 1/(z_j^2 + z_k^2)$; see *Combinatorics, Probability, and Computing* **7** (1998), 437–449.]

C. Flye Sainte-Marie, in *L'Intermédiaire des Mathématiciens* **1** (1894), 164–165, noted that the Eulerian trails of K_7 include 2×720 that have 7-fold symmetry under permutation of $\{0, 1, \ldots, 6\}$ (namely Poinsot's cycle and its reverse), plus 32×1680 with 3-fold symmetry, plus 25778×5040 cycles that are asymmetric.

108. No solution is possible for $n < 7$, except in the trivial case $n = 4$. When $n = 7$ there are $12,255,208 \times 7!$ universal cycles, not considering $(a_0 a_1 \ldots a_{34})$ to be the same as $(a_1 \ldots a_{34} a_0)$, including cases with 5-fold symmetry like the example cycle in exercise 105.

When $n \geq 8$ we can proceed systematically as suggested by B. Jackson in *Discrete Math.* **117** (1993), 141–150; see also G. Hurlbert, *SIAM J. Disc. Math.* **7** (1994), 598–604: Put each 3-combination into the "standard cyclic order" $c_1 c_2 c_3$ where $c_2 = (c_1 + \delta) \bmod n$, $c_3 = (c_2 + \delta') \bmod n$, $0 < \delta, \delta' < n/2$, and either $\delta = \delta'$ or $\max(\delta, \delta') < n - \delta - \delta' \neq (n-1)/2$ or $(1 < \delta < n/4$ and $\delta' = (n-1)/2)$ or $(\delta = (n-1)/2$ and $1 < \delta' < n/4)$. For example, when $n = 8$ the allowable values of (δ, δ') are $(1, 1)$, $(1, 2)$, $(1, 3)$, $(2, 1)$, $(2, 2)$, $(3, 1)$, $(3, 3)$; when $n = 11$ they are $(1, 1)$, $(1, 2)$, $(1, 3)$, $(1, 4)$, $(2, 1)$, $(2, 2)$, $(2, 3)$, $(2, 5)$, $(3, 1)$, $(3, 2)$, $(3, 3)$, $(4, 1)$, $(4, 4)$, $(5, 2)$, $(5, 5)$. Then construct the digraph with vertices (c, δ) for $0 \leq c < n$ and $1 \leq \delta < n/2$, and with arcs $(c_1, \delta) \to (c_2, \delta')$ for every combination $c_1 c_2 c_3$ in standard cyclic order. This digraph is connected and balanced, so it has an Eulerian trail by Theorem 2.3.4.2D. (The peculiar rules about $(n-1)/2$ make the digraph connected when n is odd. The Eulerian trail can be chosen to have n-fold symmetry when $n = 8$, but not when $n = 12$.)

109. When $n = 1$ the cycle (000) is trivial; when $n = 2$ there is no cycle; and there are essentially only two when $n = 4$, namely

$$(00011122223333022021313) \quad \text{and} \quad (00011120203332221313).$$

When $n \geq 5$, let the multicombination $d_1 d_2 d_3$ be in standard cyclic order if $d_2 = (d_1 + \delta - 1) \bmod n$, $d_3 = (d_2 + \delta' - 1) \bmod n$, and (δ, δ') is allowable for $n + 3$ in the previous answer. Construct the digraph with vertices (d, δ) for $0 \leq d < n$ and $1 \leq \delta < (n+3)/2$, and with arcs $(d_1, \delta) \to (d_2, \delta')$ for every multicombination $d_1 d_2 d_3$ in standard cyclic order; then find an Eulerian trail.

Perhaps a universal cycle of t-multicombinations exists for $\{0, 1, \ldots, n-1\}$ if and only if a universal cycle of t-combinations exists for $\{0, 1, \ldots, n+t-1\}$.

110. There are $5\binom{52}{5} = 52\binom{51}{4}$ cases, because each card of a 5-combination C can play the role of starter. A nice way to check for runs is to compute the numbers

$$b(S) = \sum \{2^{p(c)} \mid c \in S\},$$

where $(p(\mathtt{A}), \ldots, p(\mathtt{K})) = (1, \ldots, 13)$; then set $l \leftarrow b(S) \& {-}b(S)$ and check that $b(S) + l = l \ll s$, and also that $((l \ll s) \mid (l \gg 1)) \& a = 0$, where $a = 2^{p(c_1)} \mid \cdots \mid 2^{p(c_5)}$. The values of $b(S)$ and $\sum \{v(c) \mid c \in S\}$ are easily maintained as S runs through all 31 nonempty subsets in Gray-code order. The answers are (1009008, 99792, 2813796, 505008, 2855676, 697508, 1800268, 751324, 1137236, 361224, 388740, 51680, 317340, 19656, 90100, 9168, 58248, 11196, 2708, 0, 8068, 2496, 444, 356, 3680, 0, 0, 0, 76, 4) for $x = (0, \ldots, 29)$; thus the mean score is ≈ 4.769 and the variance is ≈ 9.768.

> *Hands without points are sometimes facetiously called* nineteen,
> *as that number cannot be made by the cards.*
> — G. H. DAVIDSON, *Dee's Hand-Book of Cribbage* (1839)

Note: A four-point flush is not counted in the so-called "crib hand." Then the distribution is a bit easier to compute, and it turns out to be (1022208, 99792, 2839800, 508908, 2868960, 703496, 1787176, 755320, 1118336, 358368, 378240, 43880, 310956, 16548, 88132, 9072, 57288, 11196, 2264, 0, 7828, 2472, 444, 356, 3680, 0, 0, 0, 76, 4); the mean and variance decrease to approximately 4.735 and 9.667.

111. $\partial^{n-2r} B$ is the set of all r-subsets of B; these subsets must not be in A. If $|A| = |B| = \binom{x}{n-r}$ for some real $x > n-1$, we would have $\binom{n}{r} \geq |A| + |\partial^{n-2r} B| \geq \binom{x}{n-r} + \binom{x}{r} > \binom{n-1}{n-r} + \binom{n-1}{r} = \binom{n}{r}$, by exercise 80. [See *Quart. J. Math. Oxford* **12** (1961), 313–320.]

SECTION 7.2.1.4

1.

m^n	$m^{\underline{n}}$	$m!\left\{{n\atop m}\right\}$
$\binom{m+n-1}{n}$	$\binom{m}{n}$	$\binom{n-1}{n-m}$
$\left\{{n\atop 0}\right\}+\cdots+\left\{{n\atop m}\right\}$	$[m\geq n]$	$\left\{{n\atop m}\right\}$
$\left\lvert{m+n\atop m}\right\rvert$	$[m\geq n]$	$\left\lvert{n\atop m}\right\rvert$

2. In general, given any integers $x_1 \geq \cdots \geq x_m$, we obtain all integer m-tuples $a_1 \ldots a_m$ such that $a_1 \geq \cdots \geq a_m$, $a_1+\cdots+a_m = x_1+\cdots+x_m$, and $a_m \ldots a_1 \geq x_m \ldots x_1$ by initializing $a_1 \ldots a_m \leftarrow x_1 \ldots x_m$ and $a_{m+1} \leftarrow x_m - 2$. In particular, if c is any integer constant, we obtain all integer m-tuples such that $a_1 \geq \cdots \geq a_m \geq c$ and $a_1 + \cdots + a_m = n$ by initializing $a_1 \leftarrow n - mc + c$, $a_j \leftarrow c$ for $1 < j \leq m$, and $a_{m+1} \leftarrow c - 2$, assuming that $n \geq cm$.

3. $a_j = \lfloor (n+m-j)/m \rfloor = \lceil (n+1-j)/m \rceil$, for $1 \leq j \leq m$; see *CMath* §3.4.

4. Assume that $1 \leq r \leq n$. We must have $a_m \geq a_1 - 1$; therefore $a_j = \lfloor (n+m-j)/m \rfloor$ for $1 \leq j \leq m$, where m is the largest integer with $\lfloor n/m \rfloor \geq r$, namely $m = \lfloor n/r \rfloor$.

5. [See Eugene M. Klimko, *BIT* **13** (1973), 38–49.]

    C1. [Initialize.] Set $c_0 \leftarrow 1$, $c_1 \leftarrow n$, $c_2 \ldots c_n \leftarrow 0 \ldots 0$, $l_0 \leftarrow 1$, $l_1 \leftarrow 0$. (We assume that $n > 0$.)

    C2. [Visit.] Visit the partition represented by part counts $c_1 \ldots c_n$ and links $l_0 l_1 \ldots l_n$.

    C3. [Branch.] Set $j \leftarrow l_0$ and $k \leftarrow l_j$. If $c_j = 1$, go to C6; otherwise, if $j > 1$, go to C5.

    C4. [Change 1+1 to 2.] Set $c_1 \leftarrow c_1 - 2$, $c_2 \leftarrow c_2 + 1$, and $l_{[c_1>0]} \leftarrow 2$. If $k \neq 2$, also set $l_2 \leftarrow k$. Return to C2.

    C5. [Change $j \cdot c_j$ to $(j+1) + 1 + \cdots + 1$.] Set $c_1 \leftarrow j(c_j - 1) - 1$ and go to C7.

    C6. [Change $k \cdot c_k + j$ to $(k+1) + 1 + \cdots + 1$.] Terminate if $k = 0$. Otherwise set $c_j \leftarrow 0$; then set $c_1 \leftarrow k(c_k - 1) + j - 1$, $j \leftarrow k$, and $k \leftarrow l_k$.

    C7. [Adjust links.] If $c_1 > 0$, set $l_0 \leftarrow 1$, $l_1 \leftarrow j + 1$; otherwise set $l_0 \leftarrow j + 1$. Then set $c_j \leftarrow 0$ and $c_{j+1} \leftarrow c_{j+1} + 1$. If $k \neq j + 1$, set $l_{j+1} \leftarrow k$. Return to C2. ∎

Notice that this algorithm is *loopless*; but it isn't really faster than Algorithm P. Steps C4, C5, and C6 are performed respectively $p(n-2)$, $2p(n) - p(n+1) - p(n-2)$, and $p(n+1) - p(n)$ times; thus step C4 is most important when n is large. (See exercise 45 and the detailed analysis by Fenner and Loizou in *Acta Inf.* **16** (1981), 237–252.)

6. Assume that each partition is followed by 0. Set $j \leftarrow 0$, $k \leftarrow a_1$, and $b_{k+1} \leftarrow 0$. Then, while $k > 0$, set $j \leftarrow j + 1$ and, while $k > a_{j+1}$, set $b_k \leftarrow j$ and $k \leftarrow k - 1$. (We have used (11) in the dual form $a_j - a_{j+1} = d_j$, where $d_1 \ldots d_n$ is the part-count representation of $b_1 b_2 \ldots$. This algorithm essentially walks along the rim of the Ferrers diagram; so its running time is roughly proportional to $a_1 + b_1$, the number of parts in the output plus the number of parts in the input.)

7. We have $b_1 \ldots b_n = n^{a_n} (n-1)^{a_{n-1}-a_n} \ldots 1^{a_1-a_2} 0^{n-a_1}$, by the dual of (11).

8. Transposing the Ferrers diagram corresponds to reflecting and complementing the bit string (15). So we simply interchange and reverse the p's and q's, getting the partition $(a_1 a_2 \ldots)^T = (q_t + \cdots + q_1)^{p_1} (q_t + \cdots + q_2)^{p_2} \ldots (q_t)^{p_t}$.

9. By induction: If $a_k = l - 1$ and $b_l = k - 1$, increasing a_k and b_l preserves equality.

10. (a) The left child of each node is obtained by appending '1'. The right child is obtained by increasing the rightmost digit; this child exists if and only if the parent node ends with unequal digits. All partitions of n appear on level n in lexicographic order.

(b) The left child is obtained by changing '11' to '2'; it exists if and only if the parent node contains at least two 1s. The right child is obtained by deleting a 1 and increasing the smallest part that exceeds 1; it exists if and only if there is at least one 1 and the smallest larger part appears exactly once. All partitions of n into m parts appear on level $n - m$ in lexicographic order; preorder of the entire tree gives lexicographic order of the whole. [T. I. Fenner and G. Loizou, *Comp. J.* **23** (1980), 332–337.]

11. $[z^{100}] \, 1/((1 - z)(1 - z^2)(1 - z^5)(1 - z^{10})(1 - z^{20})(1 - z^{50})(1 - z^{100})) = 4563$; and $[z^{100}] \, (1 + z + z^2)(1 + z^2 + z^4) \ldots (1 + z^{100} + z^{200}) = 7$. [See G. Pólya, *AMM* **63** (1956), 689–697.] In the infinite product $\prod_{k \geq 0} \prod_{r \in \{10^k, 2 \cdot 10^k, 5 \cdot 10^k\}} (1 + z^r + z^{2r})$, the coefficient of z^{10^n} is $2^{n+1} - 1$, and the coefficient of $z^{10^n - 1}$ is 2^n.

12. To prove that $(1 + z)(1 + z^2)(1 + z^3) \ldots = 1/((1 - z)(1 - z^3)(1 - z^5) \ldots)$, write the left-hand side as

$$\frac{(1 - z^2)}{(1 - z)} \, \frac{(1 - z^4)}{(1 - z^2)} \, \frac{(1 - z^6)}{(1 - z^3)} \cdots$$

and cancel common factors from numerator and denominator. Alternatively, replace z by z^1, z^3, z^5, $\ldots$ in the identity $(1 + z)(1 + z^2)(1 + z^4)(1 + z^8) \ldots = 1/(1 - z)$ and multiply the results together. [*Novi Comment. Acad. Sci. Pet.* **3** (1750), 125–169, §47.]

13. Map the partition $c_1 \cdot 1 + c_2 \cdot 2 + c_3 \cdot 3 + \cdots$ into $r_1 \cdot 1 + \lfloor c_1/2 \rfloor \cdot 2 + r_3 \cdot 3 + \lfloor c_2/2 \rfloor \cdot 4 + r_5 \cdot 5 + \lfloor c_3/2 \rfloor \cdot 6 + \cdots$, where $r_m = (c_m \bmod 2) + 2(c_{2m} \bmod 2) + 4(c_{4m} \bmod 2) + 8(c_{8m} \bmod 2) + \cdots$; $433222211 \mapsto 64421111 \mapsto 8332211$. [*Johns Hopkins Univ. Circular* **2** (1882), 72.]

14. Sylvester's correspondence is best understood as a diagram in which the dots of the odd parts are centered and the partition is divided into disjoint hooks. For example, the partition $17 + 15 + 15 + 9 + 9 + 9 + 9 + 5 + 5 + 3 + 3$, having five different odd parts, corresponds via the diagram

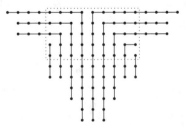

to the all-distinct partition $19 + 18 + 16 + 13 + 12 + 9 + 5 + 4 + 3$ with four gaps.

In general, when the "Durfee rectangle" (shown in the diagram) has t rows, suppose there are $a_1, \ldots, a_t$ extra dots at the right and $b_t, \ldots, b_1, \ldots, b_t$ extra dots below, where $a_1 \geq \cdots \geq a_t \geq 0$ and $b_1 \geq \cdots \geq b_t \geq 0$. Then the distinct parts obtained are $2t - 1 + a_1 + b_1$, $2t - 2 + a_1 + b_2$, $\ldots$, $2 + a_{t-1} + b_t$, $1 + a_t + b_t$, and (if it's nonzero) $0 + a_t$. Conversely, any partition with $2t$ distinct nonnegative parts can uniquely be written in this form.

The relevant odd-parts partitions when $n = 10$ are $9 + 1$, $7 + 3$, $7 + 1 + 1 + 1$, $5 + 5$, $5 + 3 + 1 + 1$, $5 + 1 + 1 + 1 + 1 + 1$, $3 + 3 + 3 + 1$, $3 + 3 + 1 + 1 + 1 + 1$, $3 + 1 + \cdots + 1$, $1 + \cdots + 1$, corresponding respectively to the distinct-parts partitions $6 + 4$, $5 + 4 + 1$,

$7 + 3, 4 + 3 + 2 + 1, 6 + 3 + 1, 8 + 2, 5 + 3 + 2, 7 + 2 + 1, 9 + 1, 10$. [See Sylvester's remarkable paper in *Amer. J. Math.* **5** (1882), 251–330; **6** (1883), 334–336.]

15. Every self-conjugate partition of trace k corresponds to a partition of n into k distinct odd parts ("hooks"). Therefore we can write the generating function either as the product $(1+z)(1+z^3)(1+z^5)\ldots$ or as the sum $1 + z^1/(1-z^2) + z^4/((1-z^2)(1-z^4)) + z^9/((1-z^2)(1-z^4)(1-z^6)) + \cdots$. [*Johns Hopkins Univ. Circular* **3** (1883), 42–43.]

16. The Durfee square contains k^2 dots, and the remaining dots correspond to two independent partitions with largest part $\le k$. Thus, if we use w to count parts and z to count dots, we find

$$\prod_{m=1}^{\infty} \frac{1}{1 - wz^m} = \sum_{k=0}^{\infty} \frac{w^k z^{k^2}}{(1-z)(1-z^2)\ldots(1-z^k)(1-wz)(1-wz^2)\ldots(1-wz^k)}.$$

[This impressive-looking formula turns out to be just the special case $x = y = 0$ of the even more impressive identity of exercise 19.]

17. (a) $((1 + uvz)(1 + uvz^2)(1 + uvz^3)\ldots)/((1 - uz)(1 - uz^2)(1 - uz^3)\ldots)$.

(b) A joint partition can be represented by a generalized Ferrers diagram in which all of the parts are merged together, with a_i above b_j if $a_i \ge b_j$, and with a mark on the rightmost dot of each b_j. For example, the joint partition $(8, 8, 5;\ 9, 7, 5, 2)$ has the diagram illustrated here, with marked dots shown as '$\blacklozenge$'. Marks appear only in corners; thus the transposed diagram corresponds to another joint partition, which in this case is $(7, 6, 6, 4, 3;\ 7, 6, 4, 1)$. [See J. T. Joichi and D. Stanton, *Pacific J. Math.* **127** (1987), 103–120; S. Corteel and J. Lovejoy, *Trans. Amer. Math. Soc.* **356** (2004), 1623–1635; Igor Pak, *The Ramanujan Journal* **12** (2006), 5–75.]

Every joint partition with $t > 0$ parts corresponds in this way to a "conjugate" in which the largest part is t. And the generating function for such joint partitions is $((1 + vz)\ldots(1 + vz^{t-1}))/((1 - z)\ldots(1 - z^t))$ times $(vz^t + z^t)$, where vz^t corresponds to the case that $b_1 = t$, and z^t corresponds to the case that $s = 0$ or $b_1 < t$.

(c) Thus we obtain a form of the general z-nomial theorem in answer 1.2.6 58:

$$\frac{(1 + uvz)}{(1 - uz)} \frac{(1 + uvz^2)}{(1 - uz^2)} \frac{(1 + uvz^3)}{(1 - uz^3)} \cdots = \sum_{t=0}^{\infty} \frac{(1 + v)}{(1 - z)} \frac{(1 + vz)}{(1 - z^2)} \cdots \frac{(1 + vz^{t-1})}{(1 - z^t)} u^t z^t.$$

18. The equations obviously determine the a's and b's when the c's and d's are given, so we want to show that the c's and d's are uniquely determined from the a's and b's. The following algorithm determines the c's and d's from right to left:

A1. [Initialize.] Set $i \leftarrow r$, $j \leftarrow s$, $k \leftarrow 0$, and $a_0 \leftarrow b_0 \leftarrow \infty$.

A2. [Branch.] Stop if $i + j = 0$. Otherwise go to A4 if $a_i \ge b_j - k$.

A3. [Absorb a_i.] Set $c_{i+j} \leftarrow a_i$, $d_{i+j} \leftarrow 0$, $i \leftarrow i - 1$, $k \leftarrow k + 1$, and return to A2.

A4. [Absorb b_j.] Set $c_{i+j} \leftarrow b_j - k$, $d_{i+j} \leftarrow 1$, $j \leftarrow j - 1$, $k \leftarrow k + 1$, and return to A2. $\blacksquare$

There's also a left-to-right method:

B1. [Initialize.] Set $i \leftarrow 1$, $j \leftarrow 1$, $k \leftarrow r + s$, and $a_{r+1} \leftarrow b_{s+1} \leftarrow -\infty$.

B2. [Branch.] Stop if $k = 0$. Otherwise set $k \leftarrow k - 1$, then go to B4 if $a_i \le b_j - k$.

B3. [Absorb a_i.] Set $c_{i+j-1} \leftarrow a_i$, $d_{i+j-1} \leftarrow 0$, $i \leftarrow i + 1$, and return to B2.

B4. [Absorb b_j.] Set $c_{i+j-1} \leftarrow b_j - k$, $d_{i+j-1} \leftarrow 1$, $j \leftarrow j + 1$, and return to B2. $\blacksquare$

In both cases the branching is forced and the resulting sequence satisfies $c_1 \geq \cdots \geq c_{r+s}$. Notice that $c_{r+s} = \min(a_r, b_s)$ and $c_1 = \max(a_1, b_1 - r - s + 1)$.

We have thereby proved the identity of exercise 17(c) in a different way. Extensions of this idea lead to a combinatorial proof of Ramanujan's "remarkable formula with many parameters,"

$$\sum_{n=-\infty}^{\infty} w^n \prod_{k=0}^{\infty} \frac{1 - bz^{k+n}}{1 - az^{k+n}} = \prod_{k=0}^{\infty} \frac{(1 - a^{-1}bz^k)(1 - a^{-1}w^{-1}z^{k+1})(1 - awz^k)(1 - z^{k+1})}{(1 - a^{-1}bw^{-1}z^k)(1 - a^{-1}z^{k+1})(1 - az^k)(1 - wz^k)}.$$

[*References:* G. H. Hardy, *Ramanujan* (1940), Eq. (12.12.2); D. Zeilberger, *Europ. J. Combinatorics* **8** (1987), 461–463; A. J. Yee, *J. Comb. Theory* **A105** (2004), 63–77.]

19. [*Crelle* **34** (1847), 285–328.] By exercise 17(c), the hinted sum over k is

$$\left(\sum_{l \geq 0} v^l \frac{(z - bz)\ldots(z - bz^l)}{(1 - z)\ldots(1 - z^l)} \frac{(1 - uz)\ldots(1 - uz^l)}{(1 - auz)\ldots(1 - auz^l)} \right) \cdot \prod_{m=1}^{\infty} \frac{1 - auz^m}{1 - uz^m} \, ;$$

and the sum over l is similar but with $u \leftrightarrow v$, $a \leftrightarrow b$, $k \leftrightarrow l$. Furthermore the sum over both k and l reduces to

$$\prod_{m=1}^{\infty} \frac{(1 - uvz^{m+1})(1 - auz^m)}{(1 - uz^m)(1 - vz^m)}$$

when $b = auz$. Now let $u = wxy$, $v = 1/(yz)$, $a = 1/x$, and $b = wyz$; equate this infinite product to the sum over l.

20. To get $p(n)$ we need to add or subtract approximately $\sqrt{8n/3}$ of the previous entries, and most of those entries are $\Theta(\sqrt{n})$ bits long. Therefore $p(n)$ is computed in $\Theta(n)$ steps and the total time is $\Theta(n^2)$.

(A straightforward use of (17) would take $\Theta(n^{5/2})$ steps.)

21. Since $\sum_{n=0}^{\infty} q(n)z^n = (1 + z)(1 + z^2)\ldots$ is equal to $(1 - z^2)(1 - z^4)\ldots P(z) = (1 - z^2 - z^4 + z^{10} + z^{14} - z^{24} - \cdots)P(z)$, we have

$$q(n) = p(n) - p(n - 2) - p(n - 4) + p(n - 10) + p(n - 14) - p(n - 24) - \cdots.$$

[There is also a "pure recurrence" in the q's alone, analogous to the recurrence for $\sigma(n)$ in the next exercise.]

22. From (21) we have $\sum_{n=1}^{\infty} \sigma(n)z^n = \sum_{m,n \geq 1} mz^{mn} = z\frac{d}{dz} \ln P(z) = (z + 2z^2 - 5z^5 - 7z^7 + \cdots)/(1 - z - z^2 + z^5 + z^7 + \cdots)$. [*Bibliothèque Impartiale* **3** (1751), 10–31.]

23. (Solution by Marc van Leeuwen.) Divide (19) by $1 - v$, to get

$$\prod_{k=1}^{\infty} (1 - u^k v^{k-1})(1 - u^k v^k)(1 - u^k v^{k+1}) = \sum_{n=0}^{\infty} (-1)^n u^{\binom{n+1}{2}} \left(\frac{v^{\binom{n}{2}} - v^{\binom{n+2}{2}}}{1 - v} \right)$$

$$= \sum_{n=0}^{\infty} (-1)^n u^{\binom{n+1}{2}} \sum_{k=0}^{2n} v^k;$$

now set $u = z$ and $v = 1$.

[See §57 of Sylvester's paper cited in answer 14. Jacobi's proof is in §66 of his monograph *Fundamenta Nova Theoriæ Functionum Ellipticarum* (1829).]

24. (a) By (18) and exercise 23, $[z^n] A(z) = \sum (-1)^{j+k}(2k+1)[3j^2 + j + k^2 + k = 2n]$, summed over all integers j and all nonnegative integers k. When $n \bmod 5 = 4$, the contributions all have $j \bmod 5 = 4$ and $k \bmod 5 = 2$; but then $(2k+1) \bmod 5 = 0$.

(b) $B(z)^p \equiv B(z^p)$ (modulo p) when p is prime, by Eq. 4.6.2–(5).

(c) Take $B(z) = P(z)$, since $A(z) = P(z)^{-4}$. [*Proc. Cambridge Philos. Soc.* **19** (1919), 207–210. A similar proof shows that $p(n)$ is a multiple of 7 when $n \bmod 7 = 5$. Ramanujan went on to obtain the beautiful formulas $p(5n+4)/5 = [z^n] P(z)^6/P(z^5)^5$; $p(7n+5)/7 = [z^n](P(z)^4/P(z^7)^3 + 7z P(z)^8/P(z^7)^7)$. Atkin and Swinnerton-Dyer, in *Proc. London Math. Soc.* (3) **4** (1954), 84–106, showed that the partitions of $5n+4$ and $7n+5$ can be divided into equal-size classes according to the respective values of (largest part $-$ number of parts) mod 5 or mod 7, as conjectured by F. Dyson. A slightly more complicated combinatorial statistic proves also that $p(n) \bmod 11 = 0$ when $n \bmod 11 = 6$; see F. G. Garvan, *Trans. Amer. Math. Soc.* **305** (1988), 47–77.]

25. [The hint can be proved by differentiating both sides of the stated identity. It is the special case $y = 1 - x$ of a beautiful formula discovered by N. H. Abel in 1826:

$$\text{Li}_2(x) + \text{Li}_2(y) = \text{Li}_2\left(\frac{x}{1-y}\right) + \text{Li}_2\left(\frac{y}{1-x}\right) - \text{Li}_2\left(\frac{xy}{(1-x)(1-y)}\right) - \ln(1-x)\ln(1-y).$$

See Abel's *Œuvres Complètes* **2** (Christiania: Grøndahl, 1881), 189–193.]

(a) Let $f(x) = \ln(1/(1 - e^{-xt}))$. Then $\int_1^x f(x)\,dx = -\text{Li}_2(e^{-tx})/t$ and $f^{(n)}(x) = (-t)^n e^{tx} \sum_k \binom{n-1}{k} e^{ktx}/(e^{tx} - 1)^n$, so Euler's summation formula gives $\text{Li}_2(e^{-t})/t + \frac{1}{2}\ln(1/(1 - e^{-t})) + O(1) = (\zeta(2) + t\ln(1 - e^{-t}) - \text{Li}_2(1 - e^{-t}))/t - \frac{1}{2}\ln t + O(1) = \zeta(2)/t + \frac{1}{2}\ln t + O(1)$, as $t \to 0$.

(b) We have $\sum_{m,n \geq 1} e^{-mnt}/n = \frac{1}{2\pi i} \sum_{m,n \geq 1} \int_{1-i\infty}^{1+i\infty} (mnt)^{-z}\Gamma(z)\,dz/n$, which sums to $\frac{1}{2\pi i} \int_{1-i\infty}^{1+i\infty} \zeta(z+1)\zeta(z)t^{-z}\Gamma(z)\,dz$. The pole at $z = 1$ gives $\zeta(2)/t$; the pole at $z = -1$ gives $-\zeta(-1)\zeta(0)t = -B_2 B_1 t/2 = -t/24$; the double pole at $z = 0$ gives $-\zeta(0)\ln t + \zeta'(0) = \frac{1}{2}\ln t - \frac{1}{2}\ln 2\pi$. Zeros of $\zeta(z+1)\zeta(z)$ cancel the other poles of $\Gamma(z)$, so the result is $\ln P(e^{-t}) = \zeta(2)/t + \frac{1}{2}\ln(t/2\pi) - t/24 + O(t^M)$ for arbitrarily large M.

26. Let $F(n) = \sum_{k=1}^{\infty} e^{-k^2/n}$. We can use (25) either with $f(x) = e^{-x^2/n}[x > 0] + \frac{1}{2}\delta_{x0}$, or with $f(x) = e^{-x^2/n}$ for all x because $2F(n) + 1 = \sum_{k=-\infty}^{\infty} e^{-k^2/n}$. Let's choose the latter alternative; then the right-hand side of (25), for $\theta = 0$, is the rapidly convergent

$$\lim_{M \to \infty} \sum_{m=-M}^{M} \int_{-\infty}^{\infty} e^{-2\pi m i y - y^2/n}\,dy = \sum_{m=-\infty}^{\infty} e^{-\pi^2 m^2 n} \int_{-\infty}^{\infty} e^{-u^2/n}\,du$$

if we substitute $u = y + \pi mni$; and the integral is $\sqrt{\pi n}$. [This result is formula (15) on page 420 of Poisson's original paper.]

27. First, $\int_{-\infty}^{\infty} e^{-a(y+b)^2 + 2ciy}\,dy = e^{-c^2/a - 2bci} \int_{-\infty}^{\infty} e^{-au^2}\,du$, by the substitution $u = y + b - ci/a$. And $\int_{-\infty}^{\infty} e^{-au^2}\,du = \int_0^{\infty} e^{-t}\,dt/\sqrt{at} = \Gamma(\frac{1}{2})/\sqrt{a} = \sqrt{\pi/a}$, by the substitution $t = au^2$ and exercises 1.2.5–20, 1.2.6–43.

Now (30) follows from (29) because we have, for all integers m,

$$g(3m+1) + g(-3m) = \sqrt{\frac{2\pi}{t}}(-1)^m e^{-6\pi^2(m+\frac{1}{6})^2/t}; \quad g(3m+2) + g(-3m-1) = 0.$$

[See M. I. Knopp, *Modular Functions in Analytic Number Theory* (1970), Chapter 3.]

28. (a, b, c, d) See *Trans. Amer. Math. Soc.* **43** (1938), 271–295. In fact, Lehmer found explicit formulas for $A_{p^e}(n)$, in terms of the Jacobi symbol of exercise 4.5.4–23:

$$A_{2^e}(n) = (-1)^e \left(\frac{-1}{m}\right) 2^{e/2} \sin \frac{4\pi m}{2^{e+3}}, \qquad \text{if } (3m)^2 \equiv 1 - 24n \text{ (modulo } 2^{e+3});$$

$$A_{3^e}(n) = (-1)^{e+1} \left(\frac{m}{3}\right) \frac{2}{\sqrt{3}} 3^{e/2} \sin \frac{4\pi m}{3^{e+1}}, \quad \text{if } (8m)^2 \equiv 1 - 24n \text{ (modulo } 3^{e+1});$$

$$A_{p^e}(n) = \begin{cases} 2\left(\dfrac{3}{p^e}\right) p^{e/2} \cos \dfrac{4\pi m}{p^e}, & \text{if } (24m)^2 \equiv 1 - 24n \text{ (modulo } p^e), \ p \geq 5, \\[4pt] & \text{and } 24n \bmod p \neq 1; \\[10pt] \left(\dfrac{3}{p^e}\right) p^{e/2} [e=1], & \text{if } 24n \bmod p = 1 \text{ and } p \geq 5. \end{cases}$$

(e) If $k = 2^a 3^b p_1^{e_1} \dots p_t^{e_t}$ for $3 < p_1 < \dots < p_t$ and $e_1 \dots e_t \neq 0$, the probability that $A_k(n) \neq 0$ is $2^{-t}(1 + (-1)^{[e_1 > 1]}/p_1) \dots (1 + (-1)^{[e_t > 1]}/p_t)$.

29. $z_1 z_2 \dots z_m / ((1 - z_1)(1 - z_1 z_2) \dots (1 - z_1 z_2 \dots z_m))$.

30. (a) $\left|{n+1 \atop m}\right|$ and (b) $\left|{m+n \atop m}\right|$, by (39).

31. *First solution* [Marshall Hall, Jr., *Combinatorial Theory* (1967), §4.1]: From the recurrence (39), we can show directly that, for $0 \leq r < k!$, there is a polynomial $f_{k,r}(n) = n^{k-1}/(k!(k-1)!) + O(n^{k-2})$ such that $\left|{n \atop k}\right| = f_{n,n \bmod k!}(n)$.

Second solution: Since $(1 - z) \dots (1 - z^m) = \prod_{p \perp q} (1 - e^{2\pi i p/q} z)^{\lfloor m/q \rfloor}$, where the product is over all reduced fractions p/q with $0 \leq p < q$, the coefficient of z^n in (41) can be expressed as a sum of roots of unity times polynomials in n, namely as $\sum_{p \perp q} e^{2\pi i p n/q} f_{p,q}(n)$ where $f_{p,q}(n)$ is a polynomial of degree less than $\lfloor m/q \rfloor$. Thus there exist constants such that $\left|{n \atop 2}\right| = a_1 n + a_2 + (-1)^n a_3$; $\left|{n \atop 3}\right| = b_1 n^2 + b_2 n + b_3 + (-1)^n b_4 + \omega^n b_5 + \omega^{-n} b_6$, where $\omega = e^{2\pi i/3}$; etc. The constants are determined by the values for small n, and the first two cases are

$$\left|{n \atop 2}\right| = \frac{1}{2} n - \frac{1}{4} + \frac{1}{4}(-1)^n; \qquad \left|{n \atop 3}\right| = \frac{1}{12} n^2 - \frac{7}{72} - \frac{1}{8}(-1)^n + \frac{1}{9}\omega^n + \frac{1}{9}\omega^{-n}.$$

It follows that $\left|{n \atop 3}\right|$ is the nearest integer to $n^2/12$. Similarly, $\left|{n \atop 4}\right|$ is the nearest integer to $(n^3 + 3n^2 - 9n [n \text{ odd}])/144$.

[Exact formulas for $\left|{n \atop 2}\right|, \left|{n \atop 3}\right|$, and $\left|{n \atop 4}\right|$, without the simplification of floor functions, were first found by G. F. Malfatti, *Memorie di Mat. e Fis. Società Italiana* **3** (1786), 571–663. W. J. A. Colman, in *Fibonacci Quarterly* **21** (1983), 272–284, showed that $\left|{n \atop 5}\right|$ is the nearest integer to $(n^4 + 10n^3 + 10n^2 - 75n - 45n(-1)^n)/2880$, and gave similar formulas for $\left|{n \atop 6}\right|$ and $\left|{n \atop 7}\right|$.]

32. Since $\left|{m+n \atop m}\right| \leq p(n)$, with equality if and only if $m \geq n$, we have $\left|{n \atop m}\right| \leq p(n - m)$ with equality if and only if $2m \geq n$.

33. A partition into m parts corresponds to at most $m!$ compositions; hence $\binom{n-1}{m-1} \leq m! \left|{n \atop m}\right|$. Consequently $p(n) \geq (n-1)!/((n-m)! \, m! \, (m-1)!)$, and when $m = \lfloor \sqrt{n} \rfloor$ Stirling's approximation proves that $\ln p(n) \geq 2\sqrt{n} - \ln n - \frac{1}{2} - \ln 2\pi$.

34. $a_1 > a_2 > \dots > a_m > 0$ if and only if $a_1 - m + 1 \geq a_2 - m + 2 \geq \dots \geq a_m \geq 1$. And partitions into m distinct parts correspond to $m!$ compositions. Thus, by the previous answer, we have

$$\frac{1}{m!}\binom{n-1}{m-1} \leq \left|{n \atop m}\right| \leq \frac{1}{m!}\binom{n + m(m-1)/2}{m-1}.$$

[See H. Gupta, *Proc. Indian Acad. Sci.* **A16** (1942), 101–102. A detailed asymptotic formula for $\left|\begin{smallmatrix}n\\m\end{smallmatrix}\right|$ when $n = \Theta(m^3)$ appears in exercise 3.3.2–30.]

35. (a) $x = \frac{1}{C}\ln\frac{1}{C} \approx -0.194$.

(b) $x = \frac{1}{C}\ln\frac{1}{C} - \frac{1}{C}\ln\ln 2 \approx 0.092$; in general we have $x = \frac{1}{C}\left(\ln\frac{1}{C} - \ln\ln\frac{1}{F(x)}\right)$.

(c) $\int_{-\infty}^{\infty} x\, dF(x) = \int_0^{\infty}(Cu)^{-2}(\ln u)e^{-1/(Cu)}\, du = -\frac{1}{C}\int_0^{\infty}(\ln C + \ln v)e^{-v}\, dv = (\gamma - \ln C)/C \approx 0.256$.

(d) Similarly, $\int_{-\infty}^{\infty} x^2 e^{-Cx}\exp(-e^{-Cx}/C)\, dx = (\gamma^2 + \zeta(2) - 2\gamma\ln C + (\ln C)^2)/C^2 \approx$ 1.0656. So the variance is $\zeta(2)/C^2 = 1$, exactly(!).

[The probability distribution $e^{-e^{(a-x)/b}}$ is commonly called the Fisher–Tippett distribution; see *Proc. Cambridge Phil. Soc.* **24** (1928), 180–190.]

36. The sum over $j_r - (m + r - 1) \geq \cdots \geq j_2 - (m + 1) \geq j_1 - m \geq 1$ gives

$$\Sigma_r = \sum_t \left|\begin{matrix} t - rm - r(r-1)/2 \\ r \end{matrix}\right| \frac{p(n-t)}{p(n)}$$

$$= \frac{\alpha}{1-\alpha}\frac{\alpha^2}{1-\alpha^2}\cdots\frac{\alpha^r}{1-\alpha^r}\alpha^{rm}(1 + O(n^{-1/2+2\epsilon})) + E$$

$$= \frac{n^{-1/2}}{\alpha^{-1}-1}\frac{n^{-1/2}}{\alpha^{-2}-1}\cdots\frac{n^{-1/2}}{\alpha^{-r}-1}\exp(-Crx + O(rn^{-1/2+2\epsilon})) + E,$$

where E is an error term that accounts for the cases $t > n^{1/2+\epsilon}$. The leading factor $n^{-1/2}/(\alpha^{-j}-1)$ is $\frac{1}{jC}(1+O(jn^{-1/2}))$. And it is easy to verify that $E = O(n^{\log n}e^{-Cn^\epsilon})$, even if we use the crude upper bound $\left|\begin{smallmatrix} t-rm-r(r-1)/2 \\ r \end{smallmatrix}\right| \leq t^r$, because

$$\sum_{t \geq xN} t^r e^{-t/N} = O\left(\int_{xN}^{\infty} t^r e^{-t/N}\, dt\right) = O(N^{r+1}x^r e^{-x}/(1 - r/x)),$$

where $N = \Theta(\sqrt{n})$, $x = \Theta(n^\epsilon)$, $r = O(\log n)$.

37. Such a partition is counted once in Σ_0, q times in Σ_1, $\binom{q}{2}$ times in Σ_2, $\ldots$; so it is counted exactly $\sum_{j=0}^r (-1)^j \binom{q}{j} = (-1)^r \binom{q-1}{r}$ times in the partial sum that ends with $(-1)^r\Sigma_r$. This count is at most δ_{q0} when r is odd, at least δ_{q0} when r is even. [A similar argument shows that the generalized principle of exercise 1.3.3–26 also has this bracketing property. *Reference:* C. Bonferroni, *Pubblicazioni del Reale Istituto Superiore di Scienze Economiche e Commerciali di Firenze* **8** (1936), 3–62.]

38. $z^{l+m-1}\binom{l+m-2}{m-1}_z = z^{l+m-1}(1-z^l)\ldots(1-z^{l+m-2})/((1-z)\ldots(1-z^{m-1}))$.

39. $[x^m](1 + zx)(1 + z^2 x)\ldots(1 + z^{l-1}x) = z^{m(m+1)/2}\binom{l-1}{m}_z$, by exercise 1.2.6–58; this is $(z - z^l)(z^2 - z^l)\ldots(z^m - z^l)/((1-z)(1-z^2)\ldots(1-z^m))$. The answer also follows from Theorem C: Replacing $a_1 \ldots a_m$ by $(a_1 - m)\ldots(a_m - 1)$ gives an equivalent partition of $n - m(m+1)/2$ into at most m parts, not exceeding $l - 1 - m$.

40. If $\alpha = a_1 \ldots a_m$ is a partition with at most m parts, let $f(\alpha) = \infty$ if $a_1 \leq l$, otherwise $f(\alpha) = \min\{j \mid a_1 > l + a_{j+1}\}$. Let g_k be the generating function for partitions with $f(\alpha) > k$. Partitions with $f(\alpha) = k < \infty$ are characterized by the inequalities

$$a_1 \geq a_2 \geq \cdots \geq a_k \geq a_1 - l > a_{k+1} \geq \cdots \geq a_{m+1} = 0.$$

Thus $a_1 a_2 \ldots a_m = (b_k + l + 1)(b_1 + 1)\ldots(b_{k-1}+1)b_{k+1}\ldots b_m$, where $f(b_1 \ldots b_m) \geq k$; and the converse is also true. It follows that $g_k = g_{k-1} - z^{l+k}g_{k-1}$.

[See *American J. Math.* **5** (1882), 254–257.]

41. See G. Almkvist and G. E. Andrews, *J. Number Theory* **38** (1991), 135–144.

42. A. Vershik [*Functional Anal. Applic.* **30** (1996), 90–105, Theorem 4.7] has stated the formula

$$\frac{1 - e^{-c\varphi}}{1 - e^{-c(\theta+\varphi)}} e^{-ck/\sqrt{n}} + \frac{1 - e^{-c\theta}}{1 - e^{-c(\theta+\varphi)}} e^{-ca_k/\sqrt{n}} \approx 1,$$

where the constant c must be chosen as a function of θ and φ so that the area of the shape is n. This constant c is negative if $\theta\varphi < 2$, positive if $\theta\varphi > 2$; the shape reduces to a straight line

$$\frac{k}{\theta\sqrt{n}} + \frac{a_k}{\varphi\sqrt{n}} \approx 1$$

when $\theta\varphi = 2$. If $\varphi = \infty$ we have $c = \sqrt{\text{Li}_2(t)}$ where t satisfies $\theta = (\ln\frac{1}{1-t})/\sqrt{\text{Li}_2(t)}$.

43. $p(n - k(k - 1)/2)$. (Change $a_1 a_2 \ldots a_k$ to $(a_1 - k + 1)(a_2 - k + 2)\ldots a_k$ to get an equivalent partition of $n - k(k - 1)/2$.)

44. Assume that $n > 0$. The number with smallest parts *unequal* (or with only one part) is $p(n+1) - p(n)$, the number of partitions of $n+1$ that don't end in 1, because we get the former from the latter by changing the smallest part. Therefore the answer is $2p(n) - p(n+1)$. [See R. J. Boscovich, *Giornale de' Letterati* (Rome, 1748), 15. The number of partitions whose smallest *three* parts are equal is $3p(n) - p(n+1) - 2p(n+2) + p(n+3)$; similar formulas can be derived for other constraints on the smallest parts.]

45. By Eq. (37) we have $p(n - j)/p(n) = 1 - Cjn^{-1/2} + (C^2 j^2 + 2j)/(2n) - (8C^3 j^3 + 60Cj^2 + Cj + 12C^{-1}j)/(48n^{3/2}) + O(j^4 n^{-2})$.

46. If $n > 1$, $T_2'(n) = p(n - 1) - p(n - 2) \le p(n) - p(n - 1) = T_2''(n)$, because $p(n) - p(n-1)$ is the number of partitions of n that don't end in 1; every such partition of $n - 1$ yields one for n if we increase the largest part. But the difference is rather small: $(T_2''(n) - T_2'(n))/p(n) = C^2/n + O(n^{-3/2})$.

47. The identity in the hint follows by differentiating (21); see exercise 22. The probability of obtaining the part-counts $c_1 \ldots c_n$ when $c_1 + 2c_2 + \cdots + nc_n = n$ is

$$\Pr(c_1 \ldots c_n) = \sum_{k=1}^{n} \sum_{j=1}^{c_k} \frac{kp(n - jk)}{np(n)} \Pr(c_1 \ldots c_{k-1}(c_k-j)c_{k+1} \ldots c_n)$$

$$= \sum_{k=1}^{n} \sum_{j=1}^{c_k} \frac{k}{np(n)} = \frac{1}{p(n)},$$

by induction on n. [*Combinatorial Algorithms* (Academic Press, 1975), Chapter 10.]

48. The probability that j has a particular fixed value in step N5 is $6/(\pi^2 j^2) + O(n^{-1/2})$, and the average value of jk is order $\sqrt{n}$. The average time spent in step N4 is $\Theta(n)$, so the average running time is of order $n^{3/2}$. (A more precise analysis would be desirable.)

49. (a) We have $F(z) = \sum_{k=1}^{\infty} F_k(z)$, where $F_k(z)$ is the generating function for all partitions whose smallest part is $\ge k$, namely $1/((1 - z^k)(1 - z^{k+1})\ldots) - 1$.

(b) Let $f_k(n) = [z^n] F_k(z)/p(n)$. Then $f_1(n) = 1$; $f_2(n) = 1 - p(n-1)/p(n) = Cn^{-1/2} + O(n^{-1})$; $f_3(n) = (p(n) - p(n - 1) - p(n - 2) + p(n - 3))/p(n) = 2C^2 n^{-1} + O(n^{-3/2})$; and $f_4(n) = 6C^3 n^{-3/2} + O(n^{-2})$. (See exercise 45.) It turns out that $f_{k+1}(n) = k! C^k n^{-k/2} + O(n^{-(k+1)/2})$; in particular, $f_5(n) = O(n^{-2})$. Hence $f_5(n) + \cdots + f_n(n) = O(n^{-1})$, because $f_{k+1}(n) \le f_k(n)$.

Adding everything up yields $[z^n] F(z) = p(n)(1 + C/\sqrt{n} + O(n^{-1}))$.

50. (a) $c_m(m+k) = c_{m-1}(m-1+k) + c_m(k) = m - 1 - k + c(k) + 1$ by induction when $0 \le k < m$.

(b) Because $\left|\begin{smallmatrix} m+k \\ m \end{smallmatrix}\right| = p(k)$ for $0 \le k \le m$.

(c) When $n = 2m$, Algorithm H essentially generates the partitions of m, and we know that $j - 1$ is the second-smallest part in the conjugate of the partition just generated — except when $j - 1 = m$, just after the partition $1 \ldots 1$ whose conjugate has only one part.

(d) If all parts of α exceed k, let $\alpha k^{q+1} j$ correspond to $\alpha(k+1)$.

(e) Continuing the previous exercise and its answer, the generating function $G_k(z)$ for all partitions whose second-smallest part is $\ge k$ is $F_{k+1}(z)/(1-z)$ by (d). Consequently $C(z) = (F(z) - F_1(z))/(1-z) + z/(1-z)^2$.

(f) We can show as in the previous exercise that $[z^n]\, G_k(n)/p(n) = O(n^{-k/2})$ for $k \le 5$; hence $c(m)/p(m) = 1 + O(m^{-1/2})$. The ratios $(c(m) + 1)/p(m)$, which are readily computed for small m, reach a maximum of 2.6 at $m = 7$ and decrease steadily thereafter. So a rigorous attention to asymptotic error bounds will complete the proof.

Note: B. Fristedt [*Trans. Amer. Math. Soc.* **337** (1993), 703–735] has proved, among other things, that the number of k's in a random partition of n is greater than $Cx\sqrt{n}$ with asymptotic probability e^{-x}.

52. In lexicographic order, $\left|\begin{smallmatrix} 64+13 \\ 13 \end{smallmatrix}\right|$ partitions of 64 have $a_1 \le 13$; $\left|\begin{smallmatrix} 50+10 \\ 10 \end{smallmatrix}\right|$ of them have $a_1 = 14$ and $a_2 \le 10$; etc. Therefore, by the hint, the partition $14\ 11\ 9\ 6\ 4\ 3\ 2\ 1^{15}$ is preceded by exactly $p(64) - 1000000$ partitions in lexicographic order, making it the millionth in *reverse* lexicographic order.

53. As in the previous answer, $\left|\begin{smallmatrix} 80 \\ 12 \end{smallmatrix}\right|$ partitions of 100 have $a_1 = 32$ and $a_2 \le 12$, etc.; so the lexicographically millionth partition in which $a_1 = 32$ is $32\ 13\ 12\ 8\ 7\ 6\ 5\ 5\ 1^{12}$. Algorithm H produces its conjugate, namely $20\ 8\ 8\ 8\ 8\ 6\ 5\ 4\ 3\ 3\ 3\ 2\ 1^{19}$.

54. (a) Obviously true. This question was just a warmup.

(b) True, but not so obvious. The Ferrers diagram shows us that

$$a'_1 + \cdots + a'_k = \sum_{j=1}^{\infty} \min(k, a_j);$$

thus we want to show that $\alpha \succeq \beta$ implies $\sum_{j=1}^{\infty} \min(k, a_j) \le \sum_{j=1}^{\infty} \min(k, b_j)$ for all $k \ge 0$. This inequality is clear when $k \ge b_1$; and if $b_l \ge k \ge b_{l+1}$ we have $\sum_{j=1}^{l} \min(k, a_j) \le \sum_{j=1}^{l} k + \sum_{j=l+1}^{\infty} a_j \le kl + \sum_{j=l+1}^{\infty} b_j = \sum_{j=1}^{\infty} \min(k, b_j)$.

(c) The recurrence $c_k = \min(a_1 + \cdots + a_k, \; b_1 + \cdots + b_k) - (c_1 + \cdots + c_{k-1})$ clearly defines a greatest lower bound, if $c_1 c_2 \ldots$ is a partition. And it is; for if $c_1 + \cdots + c_k = a_1 + \cdots + a_k$ we have $0 \le \min(a_{k+1}, b_{k+1}) \le \min(a_{k+1}, b_{k+1} + b_1 + \cdots + b_k - a_1 - \cdots - a_k) = c_{k+1} \le a_{k+1} \le a_k = c_k + (c_1 + \cdots + c_{k-1}) - (a_1 + \cdots + a_{k-1}) \le c_k$.

(d) $\alpha \vee \beta = (\alpha^T \wedge \beta^T)^T$. (Double conjugation is needed because a max-oriented recurrence analogous to the one in part (c) can fail.)

(e) $\alpha \wedge \beta$ has $\max(l, m)$ parts and $\alpha \vee \beta$ has $\min(l, m)$ parts. (Consider the first components of their conjugates.)

(f) True for $\alpha \wedge \beta$, by the derivation in part (c). False for $\alpha \vee \beta$; for example, $6321 \vee 543 = 633$ in Fig. 52.

Reference: T. Brylawski, *Discrete Mathematics* **6** (1973), 201–219.

55. (a) If $\alpha \vdash \beta$ and $\alpha \succeq \gamma \succeq \beta$, where $\gamma = c_1 c_2 \ldots$, we have $a_1 + \cdots + a_k = c_1 + \cdots + c_k = b_1 + \cdots + b_k$ for all k except $k = l$ and $k = l + 1$; thus α covers β. Therefore β^T covers α^T.

Conversely, if $\alpha \succeq \beta$ and $\alpha \ne \beta$ we can find $\gamma \succeq \beta$ such that $\alpha \vdash \gamma$ or $\gamma^T \vdash \alpha^T$, as follows: Find the smallest k with $a_k > b_k$, the smallest l with $a_k > a_{l+1}$, and the smallest m with $a_k - 1 > a_{m+1}$. (Note that $b_k > 0$.) If $a_m > a_{m+1} + 1$, define $\gamma = c_1 c_2 \ldots$ by $c_k = a_k - [k=m] + [k=m+1]$. Otherwise let $c_k = a_k - [k=l] + [k=m+1]$.

(b) Consider α and β to be strings of n 0s and n 1s, as in (15). Then $\alpha \succ \beta$ if and only if $\alpha \to \beta$, and $\beta^T \succ \alpha^T$ if and only if $\alpha \Rightarrow \beta$, where '$\to$' denotes replacing a substring of the form 011^q10 by 101^q01 and '$\Rightarrow$' denotes replacing a substring of the form 010^q10 by 100^q01, for some $q \geq 0$.

(c) A partition covers at most $[a_1 > a_2] + \cdots + [a_{m-1} > a_m] + [a_m \geq 2]$ others. The partition $\alpha = (n_2 + n_1 - 1)(n_2 - 2)(n_2 - 3) \ldots 21$ maximizes this quantity in the case $a_m = 1$; cases with $a_m \geq 2$ give no improvement. (The conjugate partition, namely $(n_2 - 1)(n_2 - 2) \ldots 21^{n_1 + 1}$, is just as good. Therefore both α and α^T are also *covered by* the maximum number of others.)

(d) Equivalently, consecutive parts of μ differ by at most 1, and the smallest part is 1; the rim representation has no consecutive 1s.

(e) Use rim representations and replace $\succ$ by the relation $\to$. If $\alpha \to \alpha_1$ and $\alpha \to \alpha'_1$ we can easily show the existence of a string β such that $\alpha_1 \to \beta$ and $\alpha'_1 \to \beta$; for example,

$$
\begin{array}{ccc}
& 101^q0111^r10 & \\
& \nearrow \qquad\qquad \searrow & \\
011^q1011^r10 & & 101^q1011^r01. \\
& \searrow \qquad\qquad \nearrow & \\
& 011^q1101^r01 &
\end{array}
$$

Let $\beta = \beta_2 \succ \cdots \succ \beta_m$ where β_m is minimal. Then, by induction on $\max(k, k')$, we have $k = m$ and $\alpha_k = \beta_m$; also $k' = m$ and $\alpha'_{k'} = \beta_m$.

(f) Set $\beta \leftarrow \alpha^T$; then repeatedly set $\beta \leftarrow \beta'$ until β is minimal, using any convenient partition β' such that $\beta \succ \beta'$. The desired partition is β^T.

Proof: Let $\mu(\alpha)$ be the common value $\alpha_k = \alpha'_{k'}$ in part (e); we must prove that $\alpha \succeq \beta$ implies $\mu(\alpha) \succeq \mu(\beta)$. There is a sequence $\alpha = \alpha_0, \ldots, \alpha_k = \beta$ where $\alpha_j \to \alpha_{j+1}$ or $\alpha_j \Rightarrow \alpha_{j+1}$ for $0 \leq j < k$. If $\alpha_0 \to \alpha_1$ we have $\mu(\alpha) = \mu(\alpha_1)$; thus it suffices to prove that $\alpha \Rightarrow \beta$ and $\alpha \to \alpha'$ implies $\alpha' \succeq \mu(\beta)$. But we have, for example,

$$
\begin{array}{ccc}
& 100^q0111^r10 & \\
& \nearrow \qquad\qquad \searrow & \\
010^q1011^r10 & & 100^q1011^r01 \\
& \searrow \qquad\qquad \nearrow & \\
& 010^q1101^r01 \to 010^{q-1}10011^r01 &
\end{array}
$$

because we may assume that $q > 0$; and the other cases are similar.

(g) The parts of λ_n are $a_k = n_2 + [k \leq n_1] - k$ for $1 \leq k < n_2$; the parts of λ_n^T are $b_k = n_2 - k + [n_2 - k < n_1]$ for $1 \leq k \leq n_2$. The algorithm of (f) reaches λ_n^T from n^1 after $\binom{n_2 + 1}{3} - \binom{n_2 - n_1}{2}$ steps, because each step increases $\sum k b_k = \sum \binom{a_k + 1}{2}$ by 1.

(h) The path n, $(n-1)1$, $(n-2)2$, $(n-2)11$, $(n-3)21$, $\ldots$, 321^{n-5}, 31^{n-3}, 221^{n-4}, 21^{n-2}, 1^n, of length $2n - 4$ when $n \geq 3$, is shortest.

It can be shown that the longest path has $m = 2\binom{n_2}{3} + n_1(n_2 - 1)$ steps. One such path has the form $\alpha_0, \ldots, \alpha_k, \ldots, \alpha_l, \ldots, \alpha_m$ where $\alpha_0 = n^1$; $\alpha_k = \lambda_n$; $\alpha_l = \lambda_n^T$; $\alpha_j \succ \alpha_{j+1}$ for $0 \leq j < l$; and $\alpha_{j+1}^T \succ \alpha_j^T$ for $k \leq j < m$.

Reference: C. Greene and D. J. Kleitman, *Europ. J. Combinatorics* **7** (1986), 1–10.

56. Suppose $\lambda = u_1 \ldots u_m$ and $\mu = v_1 \ldots v_m$. The following (unoptimized) algorithm applies the theory of exercise 54 to generate the partitions in colex order, maintaining $\alpha = a_1 a_2 \ldots a_m \preceq \mu$ as well as $\alpha^T = b_1 b_2 \ldots b_l \preceq \lambda^T$. To find the successor of α, we first find the largest j such that b_j can be increased. Then we have $\beta = b_1 \ldots b_{j-1}(b_j + 1)1 \ldots 1 \preceq \lambda^T$, hence the desired successor is $\beta^T \wedge \mu$. The algorithm maintains auxiliary tables $r_j = b_j + \cdots + b_l$, $s_j = v_1 + \cdots + v_j$, and $t_j = w_j + w_{j+1} + \cdots$, where $\lambda^T = w_1 w_2 \ldots$.

M1. [Initialize.] Set $q \leftarrow 0$, $k \leftarrow u_1$. For $j = 1, \ldots, m$, while $u_{j+1} < k$ set $t_k \leftarrow q \leftarrow q + j$ and $k \leftarrow k - 1$. Then set $q \leftarrow 0$ again, and for $j = 1, \ldots, m$ set $a_j \leftarrow v_j$, $s_j \leftarrow q \leftarrow q + a_j$. Then set $q \leftarrow 0$ yet again, and $k \leftarrow l \leftarrow a_1$. For $j = 1, \ldots, m$, while $a_{j+1} < k$ set $b_k \leftarrow j$, $r_k \leftarrow q \leftarrow q + j$, and $k \leftarrow k - 1$. Finally, set $t_1 \leftarrow 0$, $b_0 \leftarrow 0$, $b_{-1} \leftarrow -1$.

M2. [Visit.] Visit the partition $a_1 \ldots a_m$ and/or its conjugate $b_1 \ldots b_l$.

M3. [Find j.] Let j be the largest integer $< l$ such that $r_{j+1} > t_{j+1}$ and $b_j \neq b_{j-1}$. Terminate the algorithm if $j = 0$.

M4. [Increase b_j.] Set $x \leftarrow r_{j+1} - 1$, $k \leftarrow b_j$, $b_j \leftarrow k + 1$, and $a_{k+1} \leftarrow j$. (The previous value of a_{k+1} was $j - 1$. Now we're going to update $a_1 \ldots a_k$ using essentially the method of exercise 54(c) to distribute x dots into columns $j + 1, j + 2, \ldots$.)

M5. [Majorize.] Set $z \leftarrow 0$ and then do the following for $i = 1, \ldots, k$: Set $x \leftarrow x + j$, $y \leftarrow \min(x, s_i)$, $a_i \leftarrow y - z$, $z \leftarrow y$; if $i = 1$, set $l \leftarrow p \leftarrow a_1$ and $q \leftarrow 0$; if $i > 1$, while $p > a_i$ set $b_p \leftarrow i - 1$, $r_p \leftarrow q \leftarrow q + i - 1$, $p \leftarrow p - 1$. Finally, while $p > j$ set $b_p \leftarrow k$, $r_p \leftarrow q \leftarrow q + k$, $p \leftarrow p - 1$. Return to M2. ▌

57. If $\lambda = \mu^T$ there obviously is only one such matrix, essentially the Ferrers diagram of λ. And the condition $\lambda \preceq \mu^T$ is necessary, for if $\mu^T = b_1 b_2 \ldots$ we have $b_1 + \cdots + b_k = \min(c_1, k) + \min(c_2, k) + \cdots$, and this quantity must not be less than the number of 1s in the first k rows. Finally, if there is a matrix for λ and μ and if λ covers α, we can readily construct a matrix for α and μ by moving a 1 from any specified row to another that has fewer 1s.

Notes: This result is often called the Gale–Ryser theorem, because of well-known papers by D. Gale [*Pacific J. Math.* **7** (1957), 1073–1082] and H. J. Ryser [*Canadian J. Math.* **9** (1957), 371–377]. But the number of 0–1 matrices with row sums λ and column sums μ is the coefficient of the monomial symmetric function $\sum x_{i_1}^{c_1} x_{i_2}^{c_2} \ldots$ in the product of elementary symmetric functions $e_{r_1} e_{r_2} \ldots$, where

$$e_r = [z^r](1 + x_1 z)(1 + x_2 z)(1 + x_3 z) \ldots.$$

In this context the result has been known at least since the 1930s; see D. E. Littlewood's formula for $\prod_{m,n \geq 0}(1 + x_m y_n)$ in *Proc. London Math. Soc.* (2) **40** (1936), 49–70. [Cayley had shown much earlier, in *Philosophical Trans.* **147** (1857), 489–499, that the lexicographic condition $\lambda \leq \mu^T$ is necessary.] See also the algorithm in exercise 7–108.

58. [R. F. Muirhead, *Proc. Edinburgh Math. Soc.* **21** (1903), 144–157.] The condition $\alpha \succeq \beta$ is necessary, because we can set $x_1 = \cdots = x_k = x$ and $x_{k+1} = \cdots = x_n = 1$ and let $x \to \infty$. It is sufficient because we need only prove it when α covers β. Then if, say, parts (a_1, a_2) become $(a_1 - 1, a_2 + 1)$, the left-hand side is the right-hand side plus the nonnegative quantity

$$\frac{1}{2m!} \sum x_{p_1}^{a_3} x_{p_2}^{a_2} \ldots x_{p_m}^{a_m} (x_{p_1}^{a_1 - a_2 - 1} - x_{p_2}^{a_1 - a_2 - 1})(x_{p_1} - x_{p_2}).$$

[*Historical notes:* Muirhead's paper is the earliest known appearance of the concept now known as majorization; shortly afterward, an equivalent definition was given by M. O. Lorenz, *Quarterly Publ. Amer. Stat. Assoc.* **9** (1905), 209–219, who was interested in measuring nonuniform distribution of wealth. Yet another equivalent

concept was formulated by I. Schur in *Sitzungsberichte Berliner Math. Gesellschaft*
22 (1923), 9–20. "Majorization" was named by Hardy, Littlewood, and Pólya, who
established its most basic properties in *Messenger of Math.* **58** (1929), 145–152; see
exercise 2.3.4.5–17. An excellent book, *Inequalities* by A. W. Marshall and I. Olkin
(Academic Press, 1979), is entirely devoted to the subject.]

59. The unique paths for $n = 0$, 1, 2, 3, 4, and 6 must have the stated symmetry.
There is one such path for $n = 5$, namely 11111, 2111, 221, 311, 32, 41, 5. And there
are four for $n = 7$:

   1111111, 211111, 22111, 2221, 322, 3211, 31111, 4111, 511, 421, 331, 43, 52, 61, 7;
   1111111, 211111, 22111, 2221, 322, 421, 511, 4111, 31111, 3211, 331, 43, 52, 61, 7;
   1111111, 211111, 31111, 22111, 2221, 322, 3211, 4111, 421, 331, 43, 52, 511, 61, 7;
   1111111, 211111, 31111, 22111, 2221, 322, 421, 4111, 3211, 331, 43, 52, 511, 61, 7.

There are no others, because at least two self-conjugate partitions exist for all $n \geq 8$
(see exercise 15).

60. For $L(6,6)$, use (59); otherwise use $L'(4,6)$ and $L'(3,5)$ everywhere.
   In $M(4, 18)$, insert 444222, 4442211 between 443322 and 4432221.
   In $M(5, 11)$, insert 52211, 5222 between 62111 and 6221.
   In $M(5, 20)$, insert 5542211, 554222 between 5552111 and 555221.
   In $M(6, 13)$, insert 72211, 7222 between 62221 and 6322.
   In $L(4, 14)$, insert 44222, 442211 between 43322 and 432221.
   In $L(5, 15)$, insert 542211, 54222 between 552111 and 55221.
   In $L(7, 12)$, insert 62211, 6222 between 72111 and 7221.

62. The statement holds for $n = 7$, 8, and 9, except in two cases: $n = 8$, $m = 3$,
$\alpha = 3221$; $n = 9$, $m = 4$, $\alpha = 432$.

64. If $n = 2^k q$ where q is odd, let ω_n denote the partition $(2^k)^q$, namely q parts equal
to 2^k. The recursive rule

$$B(n) \;=\; B(n-1)^R 1,\; 2 \times B(n/2)$$

for $n > 0$, where $2 \times B(n/2)$ denotes doubling all parts of $B(n/2)$ (or the empty sequence
if n is odd), defines a pleasant Gray path that begins with $\omega_{n-1}1$ and ends with ω_n, if
we let $B(0)$ be the unique partition of 0. Thus,

$$B(1) = 1; \quad B(2) = 11, 2; \quad B(3) = 21, 111; \quad B(4) = 1111, 211, 22, 4.$$

Among the remarkable properties satisfied by this sequence is the fact that

$$B(n) = (2 \times B(0))1^n, \; (2 \times B(1))1^{n-2}, \; (2 \times B(2))1^{n-4}, \; \ldots, \; (2 \times B(n/2))1^0,$$

when n is even; for example,

$$B(8) = 11111111, 2111111, 221111, 41111, 4211, 22211, 2222, 422, 44, 8.$$

The following algorithm generates $B(n)$ looplessly when $n \geq 2$:

   K1. [Initialize.] Set $c_0 \leftarrow p_0 \leftarrow 0$, $p_1 \leftarrow 1$. If n is even, set $c_1 \leftarrow n$, $t \leftarrow 1$; otherwise let $n - 1 = 2^k q$ where q is odd and set $c_1 \leftarrow 1$, $c_2 \leftarrow q$, $p_2 \leftarrow 2^k$, $t \leftarrow 2$.

   K2. [Even visit.] Visit the partition $p_t^{c_t} \ldots p_1^{c_1}$. (Now $c_t + \cdots + c_1$ is even.)

   K3. [Change the largest part.] If $c_t = 1$, split the largest part: If $p_t \neq 2p_{t-1}$, set
   $c_t \leftarrow 2$, $p_t \leftarrow p_t/2$, otherwise set $c_{t-1} \leftarrow c_{t-1} + 2$, $t \leftarrow t - 1$. But if $c_t > 1$,
   merge two of the largest parts: If $c_t = 2$, set $c_t \leftarrow 1$, $p_t \leftarrow 2p_t$, otherwise set
   $c_t \leftarrow c_t - 2$, $c_{t+1} \leftarrow 1$, $p_{t+1} \leftarrow 2p_t$, $t \leftarrow t + 1$.

K4. [Odd visit.] Visit the partition $p_t^{c_t} \ldots p_1^{c_1}$. (Now $c_t + \cdots + c_1$ is odd.)

K5. [Change the next-largest part.] Now we wish to apply the following transformation: "Remove $c_t - [t$ is even$]$ of the largest parts temporarily, then apply step K3, then restore the removed parts." More precisely, there are nine cases: (1a) If c_t is odd and $t = 1$, terminate. (1b1) If c_t is odd, $c_{t-1} = 1$, and $p_{t-1} = 2p_{t-2}$, set $c_{t-2} \leftarrow c_{t-2} + 2$, $c_{t-1} \leftarrow c_t$, $p_{t-1} \leftarrow p_t$, $t \leftarrow t - 1$. (1b2) If c_t is odd, $c_{t-1} = 1$, and $p_{t-1} \neq 2p_{t-2}$, set $c_{t-1} \leftarrow 2$, $p_{t-1} \leftarrow p_{t-1}/2$. (1c1) If c_t is odd, $c_{t-1} = 2$, and $p_t = 2p_{t-1}$, set $c_{t-1} \leftarrow c_t + 1$, $p_{t-1} \leftarrow p_t$, $t \leftarrow t - 1$. (1c2) If c_t is odd, $c_{t-1} = 2$, and $p_t \neq 2p_{t-1}$, set $c_{t-1} \leftarrow 1$, $p_{t-1} \leftarrow 2p_{t-1}$. (1d1) If c_t is odd, $c_{t-1} > 2$, and $p_t = 2p_{t-1}$, set $c_{t-1} \leftarrow c_{t-1} - 2$, $c_t \leftarrow c_t + 1$. (1d2) If c_t is odd, $c_{t-1} > 2$, and $p_t \neq 2p_{t-1}$, set $c_{t+1} \leftarrow c_t$, $p_{t+1} \leftarrow p_t$, $c_t \leftarrow 1$, $p_t \leftarrow 2p_{t-1}$, $c_{t-1} \leftarrow c_{t-1} - 2$, $t \leftarrow t + 1$. (2a) If c_t is even and $p_t = 2p_{t-1}$, set $c_t \leftarrow c_t - 1$, $c_{t-1} \leftarrow c_{t-1} + 2$. (2b) If c_t is even and $p_t \neq 2p_{t-1}$, set $c_{t+1} \leftarrow c_t - 1$, $p_{t+1} \leftarrow p_t$, $c_t \leftarrow 2$, $p_t \leftarrow p_t/2$, $t \leftarrow t + 1$. Return to K2. ∎

[The transformations in K3 and K5 undo themselves when performed twice in a row. This construction is due to T. Colthurst and M. Kleber, arXiv:0907.3873 [math.CO] (2003), 6 pages. Euler had considered the number of such partitions in §50 of the fundamental paper on partitions that he wrote in 1750.]

65. If $p_1^{e_1} \ldots p_r^{e_r}$ is the prime factorization of m, the number of such factorizations is $p(e_1) \ldots p(e_r)$, and we can let $n = \max(e_1, \ldots, e_r)$. Indeed, for each r-tuple $(x_1, \ldots, x_r)$ with $0 \leq x_k < p(e_k)$ we can let $m_j = p_1^{a_{1j}} \ldots p_r^{a_{rj}}$, where $a_{k1} \ldots a_{kn}$ is the $(x_k + 1)$st partition of e_k. Thus we can use a reflected Gray code for r-tuples together with a Gray code for partitions.

66. Let $a_1 \ldots a_m$ be an m-tuple that satisfies the specified inequalities. We can sort it into nonincreasing order $a_{x_1} \geq \cdots \geq a_{x_m}$, where the permutation $x_1 \ldots x_m$ is uniquely determined if we require the sorting to be *stable*; see Eq. 5–(2).

If $j \prec k$, we have $a_j \geq a_k$, hence j appears to the left of k in the permutation $x_1 \ldots x_m$. Therefore $x_1 \ldots x_m$ is one of the permutations output by Algorithm 7.2.1.2V. Moreover, j will be left of k also when $a_j = a_k$ and $j < k$, by stability. Hence a_{x_i} is strictly greater than $a_{x_{i+1}}$ when $x_i > x_{i+1}$ is a "descent."

To generate all the relevant partitions of n, take each topological permutation $x_1 \ldots x_m$ and generate the partitions $y_1 \ldots y_m$ of $n - t$ where t is the *index* of $x_1 \ldots x_m$ (see Section 5.1.1). For $1 \leq j \leq m$ set $a_{x_j} \leftarrow y_j + t_j$, where t_j is the number of descents to the right of x_j in $x_1 \ldots x_m$.

For example, if $x_1 \ldots x_m = 314592687$ we want to generate all cases with $a_3 > a_1 \geq a_4 \geq a_5 \geq a_9 > a_2 \geq a_6 \geq a_8 > a_7$. In this case $t = 1 + 5 + 8 = 14$; so we set $a_1 \leftarrow y_2 + 2$, $a_2 \leftarrow y_6 + 1$, $a_3 \leftarrow y_1 + 3$, $a_4 \leftarrow y_3 + 2$, $a_5 \leftarrow y_4 + 2$, $a_6 \leftarrow y_7 + 1$, $a_7 \leftarrow y_9$, $a_8 \leftarrow y_8 + 1$, and $a_9 \leftarrow y_5 + 2$. The generalized generating function $\sum z_1^{a_1} \ldots z_9^{a_9}$ in the sense of exercise 29 is

$$\frac{z_1^2 z_2 z_3^3 z_4^2 z_5^2 z_6 z_8 z_9^2}{(1 - z_3)(1 - z_3 z_1)(1 - z_3 z_1 z_4)(1 - z_3 z_1 z_4 z_5) \ldots (1 - z_3 z_1 z_4 z_5 z_9 z_2 z_6 z_8 z_7)}.$$

When $\prec$ is any given partial ordering, the ordinary generating function for the number of all such partitions of n is therefore $\sum z^{\mathrm{ind}\,\alpha}/((1 - z)(1 - z^2) \ldots (1 - z^m))$, where the sum is over all outputs α of Algorithm 7.2.1.2V.

[See R. P. Stanley, *Memoirs Amer. Math. Soc.* **119** (1972), for significant extensions and applications of these ideas. See also L. Carlitz, *Studies in Foundations and Combinatorics* (New York: Academic Press, 1978), 101–129, for information about up-down partitions.]

67. If $n + 1 = q_1 \ldots q_r$, where the factors $q_1, \ldots, q_r$ are all ≥ 2, we get a perfect partition $\{(q_1-1) \cdot 1, (q_2-1) \cdot q_1, (q_3-1) \cdot q_1 q_2, \ldots, (q_r-1) \cdot q_1 \ldots q_{r-1}\}$ that corresponds in an obvious way to mixed radix notation. (The order of the factors q_j is significant.)

Conversely, all perfect partitions arise in this way. Suppose the multiset $M = \{k_1 \cdot p_1, \ldots, k_m \cdot p_m\}$ is a perfect partition, where $p_1 < \cdots < p_m$; then we must have $p_j = (k_1+1) \ldots (k_{j-1}+1)$ for $1 \leq j \leq m$, because p_j is the smallest sum of a submultiset of M that is not a submultiset of $\{k_1 \cdot p_1, \ldots, k_{j-1} \cdot p_{j-1}\}$.

The perfect partitions of n with fewest elements occur if and only if the q_j are all prime, because $pq - 1 > (p-1) + (q-1)$ whenever $p > 1$ and $q > 1$. Thus, for example, the minimal perfect partitions of 11 correspond to the ordered factorizations $2 \cdot 2 \cdot 3$, $2 \cdot 3 \cdot 2$, and $3 \cdot 2 \cdot 2$. *Reference: Quarterly Journal of Mathematics* **21** (1886), 367–373.

68. (a) If $a_i + 1 \leq a_j - 1$ for some i and j we can change $\{a_i, a_j\}$ to $\{a_i+1, a_j-1\}$, thereby increasing the product by $a_j - a_i - 1 > 0$. Thus the optimum occurs only in the optimally balanced partition of exercise 3. [L. Oettinger and J. Derbès, *Nouv. Ann. Math.* **18** (1859), 442; **19** (1860), 117–118.]

(b) Assume that $n > 1$. Then no part is 1; and if $a_j \geq 4$ we can change it to $2 + (a_j-2)$ without decreasing the product. Thus we can assume that all parts are 2 or 3. We get an improvement by changing $2 + 2 + 2$ to $3 + 3$, hence there are at most two 2s. The optimum therefore is $3^{n/3}$ when $n \bmod 3$ is 0; $4 \cdot 3^{(n-4)/3} = 3^{(n-4)/3} \cdot 2 \cdot 2 = (4/3^{4/3})3^{n/3}$ when $n \bmod 3$ is 1; $3^{(n-2)/3} \cdot 2 = (2/3^{2/3})3^{n/3}$ when $n \bmod 3$ is 2. [O. Meißner, *Mathematisch-naturwissenschaftliche Blätter* **4** (1907), 85.]

69. All $n > 2$ have the solution $(n, 2, 1, \ldots, 1)$. We can "sieve out" the other cases $\leq N$ by starting with $s_2 \ldots s_N \leftarrow 1 \ldots 1$ and then setting $s_{ak-b} \leftarrow 0$ whenever $ak - b \leq N$, where $a = x_1 \ldots x_t - 1$, $b = x_1 + \cdots + x_t - t - 1$, $k \geq x_1 \geq \cdots \geq x_t$, and $a > 1$, because $k + x_1 + \cdots + x_t + (ak - b - t - 1) = kx_1 \ldots x_t$. The sequence $(x_1, \ldots, x_t)$ needs to be considered only when $(x_1 \ldots x_t - 1)x_1 - (x_1 + \cdots + x_t) < N - t$; we can also continue to decrease N so that $s_N = 1$. In this way only $(32766, 1486539, 254887, 1511, 937, 478, 4)$ sequences $(x_1, \ldots, x_t)$ need to be tried when N is initially 2^{30}, and the only survivors turn out to be 2, 3, 4, 6, 24, 114, 174, and 444. [See E. Trost, *Elemente der Math.* **11** (1956), 135; M. Misiurewicz, *Elemente der Math.* **21** (1966), 90.]

Notes: No new survivors are likely as $N \to \infty$, but a new idea will be needed to rule them out. The simplest sequences $(x_1, \ldots, x_t) = (3)$ and $(2, 2)$ already exclude all $n > 5$ with $n \bmod 6 \neq 0$; this fact can be used to speed up the computation by a factor of 6. The sequences (6) and $(3, 2)$ exclude 40% of the remainder (namely all n of the forms $5k - 4$ and $5k - 2$); the sequences (8), $(4, 2)$, and $(2, 2, 2)$ exclude 3/7 of the remainder; the sequences with $t = 1$ imply that $n - 1$ must be prime; the sequences in which $x_1 \ldots x_t = 2^r$ exclude about $p(r)$ residues of $n \bmod (2^r - 1)$; sequences in which $x_1 \ldots x_t$ is the product of r distinct primes will exclude about ϖ_r residues of $n \bmod (x_1 \ldots x_t - 1)$.

70. Each step takes one partition of n into another, so we must eventually reach a repeating cycle. Many partitions simply perform a cyclic shift on each northeast-to-southwest diagonal of the Ferrers diagram, changing it

$$
\text{from}
\quad
\begin{matrix}
x_1 & x_2 & x_4 & x_7 & x_{11} & x_{16} \cdots \\
x_3 & x_5 & x_8 & x_{12} & x_{17} & x_{23} \cdots \\
x_6 & x_9 & x_{13} & x_{18} & x_{24} & x_{31} \cdots \\
x_{10} & x_{14} & x_{19} & x_{25} & x_{32} & x_{40} \cdots \\
x_{15} & x_{20} & x_{26} & x_{33} & x_{41} & x_{50} \cdots \\
x_{21} & x_{27} & x_{34} & x_{42} & x_{51} & x_{61} \cdots \\
\vdots & \vdots & \vdots & \vdots & \vdots & \vdots
\end{matrix}
\quad
\text{to}
\quad
\begin{matrix}
x_1 & x_3 & x_6 & x_{10} & x_{15} & x_{21} \cdots \\
x_2 & x_4 & x_7 & x_{11} & x_{16} & x_{22} \cdots \\
x_5 & x_8 & x_{12} & x_{17} & x_{23} & x_{30} \cdots \\
x_9 & x_{13} & x_{18} & x_{24} & x_{31} & x_{39} \cdots ; \\
x_{14} & x_{19} & x_{25} & x_{32} & x_{40} & x_{49} \cdots \\
x_{20} & x_{26} & x_{33} & x_{41} & x_{50} & x_{60} \cdots \\
\vdots & \vdots & \vdots & \vdots & \vdots & \vdots
\end{matrix}
$$

in other words, they apply the permutation $\rho = (1)(2\,3)(4\,5\,6)(7\,8\,9\,10)\dots$ to the cells. Exceptions occur only when ρ introduces an empty cell above a dot; for example, x_{10} might be empty when x_{11} isn't. But we can get the correct new diagram by moving the top row down, sorting it into its proper place after applying ρ in such cases. Such a move always reduces the number of occupied diagonals, so it cannot be part of a cycle. Thus every cycle consists entirely of permutations by ρ.

If any element of a diagonal is empty in a cyclic partition, all elements of the next diagonal must be empty. For if, say, x_5 is empty, repeated application of ρ will make x_5 adjacent to each of the cells x_7, x_8, x_9, x_{10} of the next diagonal. Therefore if $n = \binom{n_2}{2} + \binom{n_1}{1}$ with $n_2 > n_1 \geq 0$ the cyclic states are precisely those with $n_2 - 1$ completely filled diagonals and n_1 dots in the next. [This result is due to J. Brandt, *Proc. Amer. Math. Soc.* **85** (1982), 483–486. The problem reportedly stems from Russia via Bulgaria and Sweden. See also Martin Gardner, *The Last Recreations* (1997), Chapter 2.]

71. When $n = 1 + \cdots + m > 1$, the starting partition $(m-1)(m-1)(m-2)\dots211$ has distance $m(m-1)$ from the cyclic state, and this is maximum. [K. Igusa, *Math. Magazine* **58** (1985), 259–271; G. Etienne, *J. Combin. Theory* **A58** (1991), 181–197.] In the general case, Griggs and Ho [*Advances in Appl. Math.* **21** (1998), 205–227] have conjectured that the maximum distance to a cycle is $\max(2n+2-n_1(n_2+1), n+n_2+1, n_1(n_2+1)) - 2n_2$ for all $n > 1$; their conjecture has been verified for $n \leq 100$. Moreover, the worst-case starting partition appears to be unique when $n_2 = 2n_1 + \{-1, 0, 2\}$.

72. Thus $a_1 < m-1$ [B. Hopkins and J. A. Sellers, *Integers* **7**, 2 (2007), A19:1–A19:5].

73. (a) [R. Stanley, 1972 (unpublished).] Swap the jth occurrence of k in the partition $n = j \cdot k + \alpha$ with the kth occurrence of j in $k \cdot j + \alpha$, for every partition α of $n - jk$. For example, when $n = 6$ the swaps are

$$6,\ 51,\ 42,\ 411,\ 33,\ 321,\ 3111,\ 222,\ 2211,\ 21111,\ 111111.$$
$$\text{a\quad bl\quad fg\quad clg\quad hi\quad jkl\quad dlkh\quad n2i\quad m2ln\quad elmjf\quad ledcba}$$

(b) $p(n-k) + p(n-2k) + p(n-3k) + \cdots$. [A. H. M. Hoare, *AMM* **93** (1986), 475–476. This is a special case of considerably more general results proved by N. J. Fine in 1959; see R. A. Gilbert, *AMM* **122** (2015), 322–331.]

SECTION 7.2.1.5

1. Whenever m is set equal to r in step H6, change it back to $r - 1$.

2. **L1.** [Initialize.] Set $l_j \leftarrow j - 1$ and $a_j \leftarrow 0$ for $1 \leq j \leq n$. Also set $h_1 \leftarrow n$, $t \leftarrow 1$, and set l_0 to any convenient nonzero value.

    L2. [Visit.] Visit the t-block partition represented by $l_1 \dots l_n$ and $h_1 \dots h_t$. (The restricted growth string corresponding to this partition is $a_1 \dots a_n$.)

    L3. [Find j.] Set $j \leftarrow n$; then, while $l_j = 0$, set $j \leftarrow j - 1$ and $t \leftarrow t - 1$.

    L4. [Move j to the next block.] Terminate if $j = 0$. Otherwise set $k \leftarrow a_j + 1$, $h_k \leftarrow l_j$, $a_j \leftarrow k$. If $k = t$, set $t \leftarrow t + 1$ and $l_j \leftarrow 0$; otherwise set $l_j \leftarrow h_{k+1}$. Finally set $h_{k+1} \leftarrow j$.

    L5. [Move $j + 1$, $\dots$, n to block 1.] While $j < n$, set $j \leftarrow j + 1$, $l_j \leftarrow h_1$, $a_j \leftarrow 0$, and $h_1 \leftarrow j$. Return to L2. ∎

3. Let $\tau(k, n)$ be the number of strings $a_1 \dots a_n$ that satisfy the condition $0 \leq a_j \leq 1 + \max(k-1, a_1, \dots, a_{j-1})$ for $1 \leq j \leq n$; thus $\tau(k, 0) - 1 = \tau(0, n) = \varpi_n$, and $\tau(k, n) = k\tau(k, n-1) + \tau(k+1, n-1)$. [S. G. Williamson has called $\tau(k, n)$ a "tail coefficient"; see *SICOMP* **5** (1976), 602–617.] The number of strings that are generated by Algorithm H before a given restricted growth string $a_1 \dots a_n$ is $\sum_{j=1}^{n} a_j \tau(b_j, n - j)$, where $b_j = $

$1 + \max(a_1, \ldots, a_{j-1})$. Working backwards with the help of a precomputed table of the tail coefficients, we find that this formula yields 999999 when $a_1 \ldots a_{12} = 010220345041$.

4. The most common representatives of each type, subscripted by the number of corresponding occurrences in the GraphBase, are $\mathtt{zzzzz}_0$, $\mathtt{ooooh}_0$, $\mathtt{xxxix}_0$, $\mathtt{xxxii}_0$, $\mathtt{ooops}_0$, $\mathtt{llull}_0$, $\mathtt{llala}_0$, $\mathtt{eeler}_0$, $\mathtt{iitti}_0$, $\mathtt{xxiii}_0$, $\mathtt{ccxxv}_0$, $\mathtt{eerie}_1$, $\mathtt{llama}_1$, $\mathtt{xxvii}_0$, $\mathtt{oozed}_5$, $\mathtt{uhuuu}_0$, $\mathtt{mamma}_1$, $\mathtt{puppy}_{28}$, $\mathtt{anana}_0$, $\mathtt{hehee}_0$, $\mathtt{vivid}_{15}$, $\mathtt{rarer}_3$, $\mathtt{etext}_1$, $\mathtt{amass}_2$, $\mathtt{again}_{137}$, $\mathtt{ahhaa}_0$, $\mathtt{esses}_1$, $\mathtt{teeth}_{25}$, $\mathtt{yaaay}_0$, $\mathtt{ahhhh}_2$, $\mathtt{pssst}_2$, $\mathtt{seems}_7$, $\mathtt{added}_6$, $\mathtt{lxxii}_0$, $\mathtt{books}_{184}$, $\mathtt{swiss}_3$, $\mathtt{sense}_{10}$, $\mathtt{ended}_3$, $\mathtt{check}_{160}$, $\mathtt{level}_{18}$, $\mathtt{tepee}_4$, $\mathtt{slyly}_5$, $\mathtt{never}_{154}$, $\mathtt{sells}_6$, $\mathtt{motto}_{21}$, $\mathtt{whooo}_2$, $\mathtt{trees}_{384}$, $\mathtt{going}_{307}$, $\mathtt{which}_{151}$, $\mathtt{there}_{174}$, $\mathtt{three}_{100}$, $\mathtt{their}_{3834}$. (See S. Golomb, *Math. Mag.* **53** (1980), 219–221. Words with only two distinct letters are, of course, rare. The 18 representatives listed here with subscript 0 can be found in larger dictionaries or in English-language pages of the Internet.)

5. (a) $112 = \rho(0225)$. The sequence is $r(0)$, $r(1)$, $r(4)$, $r(9)$, $r(16)$, $\ldots$, where $r(n)$ is obtained by expressing n in decimal notation (with one or more leading zeros), applying the ρ function of exercise 4, then deleting the leading zeros. Notice that $n/9 \le r(n) \le n$.

(b) $1012 = r(45^2)$. The sequence is the same as (a), but sorted into order and with duplicates removed. (Who knew that $88^2 = 7744$, $212^2 = 44944$, and $264^2 = 69696$?)

6. Use the topological sorting approach of Algorithm 7.2.1.2V, with an appropriate partial ordering: Include c_j chains of length j, with their least elements ordered. For example, if $n = 20$, $c_2 = 3$, and $c_3 = c_4 = 2$, we use that algorithm to find all permutations $a_1 \ldots a_{20}$ of $\{1, \ldots, 20\}$ such that $1 \prec 2$, $3 \prec 4$, $5 \prec 6$, $1 \prec 3 \prec 5$, $7 \prec 8 \prec 9$, $10 \prec 11 \prec 12$, $7 \prec 10$, $13 \prec 14 \prec 15 \prec 16$, $17 \prec 18 \prec 19 \prec 20$, $13 \prec 17$, forming the restricted growth strings $\rho(f(a_1) \ldots f(a_{20}))$, where ρ is defined in exercise 4 and $(f(1), \ldots, f(20)) = (1, 1, 2, 2, 3, 3, 4, 4, 4, 5, 5, 5, 6, 6, 6, 6, 7, 7, 7, 7)$. The total number of outputs is, of course, given by (48).

7. Exactly ϖ_n. They are the permutations we get by reversing the left-right order of the blocks in (2) and dropping the '|' symbols: 1234, 4123, 3124, 3412, $\ldots$, 4321. [See A. Claesson, *European J. Combinatorics* **22** (2001), 961–971. S. Kitaev, in *Discrete Math.* **298** (2005), 212–229, has discovered a far-reaching generalization: Let π be a permutation of $\{0, \ldots, r\}$, let g_n be the number of permutations $a_1 \ldots a_n$ of $\{1, \ldots, n\}$ such that $a_{k-0\pi} > a_{k-1\pi} > \cdots > a_{k-r\pi} > a_j$ implies $j > k$, and let f_n be the number of permutations $a_1 \ldots a_n$ for which the pattern $a_{k-0\pi} > a_{k-1\pi} > \cdots > a_{k-r\pi}$ is avoided altogether for $r < k \le n$. Then $\sum_{n \ge 0} g_n z^n / n! = \exp(\sum_{n \ge 1} f_{n-1} z^n / n!)$.]

8. For each partition of $\{1, \ldots, n\}$ into m blocks, arrange the blocks in decreasing order of their smallest elements, and permute the non-smallest block elements in all possible ways. If $n = 9$ and $m = 3$, for example, the partition 126|38|4579 would yield 457938126 and eleven other cases obtained by permuting $\{5, 7, 9\}$ and $\{2, 6\}$ among themselves. (Essentially the same method generates all permutations that have exactly k cycles; see the "unusual correspondence" of Section 1.3.3.)

9. Among the permutations of the multiset $\{k_0 \cdot 0, k_1 \cdot 1, \ldots, k_{n-1} \cdot (n-1)\}$, exactly

$$\binom{k_0 + k_1 + \cdots + k_{n-1}}{k_0, k_1, \ldots, k_{n-1}} \frac{k_0}{(k_0 + k_1 + \cdots + k_{n-1})} \frac{k_1}{(k_1 + \cdots + k_{n-1})} \cdots \frac{k_{n-1}}{k_{n-1}}$$

have restricted growth, since $k_j/(k_j + \cdots + k_{n-1})$ is the probability that j precedes $\{j+1, \ldots, n-1\}$.

The average number of 0s, if $n > 0$, is $1 + (n-1)\varpi_{n-1}/\varpi_n = \Theta(\log n)$, because the total number of 0s among all ϖ_n cases is $\sum_{k=1}^n k \binom{n-1}{k-1} \varpi_{n-k} = \varpi_n + (n-1)\varpi_{n-1}$.

10. Given a partition of $\{1, \ldots, n\}$, construct an oriented tree on $\{0, 1, \ldots, n\}$ by letting $j - 1$ be the parent of all members of a block whose least member is j. Then relabel the leaves, preserving order, and erase the other labels. For example, the 15 partitions in (2) correspond respectively to

To reverse the process, take a semilabeled tree and assign new numbers to its nodes by considering the nodes first encountered on the path from the root to the smallest leaf, then on the path from the root to the second-smallest leaf, etc. The number of leaves is $n + 1$ minus the number of blocks. [This construction is closely related to exercise 2.3.4.4–18 and to many enumerations in that section. See P. L. Erdős and L. A. Székely, *Advances in Applied Math.* **10** (1989), 488–496.]

11. We get pure alphametics from 900 of the 64855 set partitions into at most 10 blocks for which $\rho(a_1 \ldots a_{13}) = \rho(a_5 \ldots a_8 a_1 \ldots a_4 a_9 \ldots a_{13})$, and from 563,527 of the 13,788,536 for which $\rho(a_1 \ldots a_{13}) < \rho(a_5 \ldots a_8 a_1 \ldots a_4 a_9 \ldots a_{13})$. The first examples are $\mathtt{aaaa} + \mathtt{aaaa} = \mathtt{baaac}$, $\mathtt{aaaa} + \mathtt{aaaa} = \mathtt{bbbbc}$, and $\mathtt{aaaa} + \mathtt{aaab} = \mathtt{baaac}$; the last are $\mathtt{abcd} + \mathtt{efgd} = \mathtt{dceab}$ ($\mathtt{goat} + \mathtt{newt} = \mathtt{tango}$) and $\mathtt{abcd} + \mathtt{efgd} = \mathtt{dceaf}$ ($\mathtt{clad} + \mathtt{nerd} = \mathtt{dance}$). [The idea of hooking a partition generator to an alphametic solver is due to Alan Sutcliffe.]

12. (a) Form $\rho((a_1 a'_1) \ldots (a_n a'_n))$, where ρ is defined in exercise 4, since we have $x \equiv y$ (modulo $\Pi \vee \Pi'$) if and only if $x \equiv y$ (modulo Π) and $x \equiv y$ (modulo Π').

(b) Represent Π by links as in exercise 2; represent Π' as in Algorithm 2.3.3E; and use that algorithm to make $j \equiv l_j$ whenever $l_j \neq 0$. (For efficiency, we can assume that Π has at least as many blocks as Π'.)

(c) When one block of Π has been split into two parts; that is, when two blocks of Π' have been merged together.

(d) $\binom{t}{2}$; (e) $(2^{s_1-1} - 1) + \cdots + (2^{s_t-1} - 1)$.

(f) True: Let $\Pi \vee \Pi'$ have blocks $B_1|B_2|\cdots|B_t$, where $\Pi = B_1 B_2 B_3 |\cdots|B_t$. Then Π' is essentially a partition of $\{B_1, \ldots, B_t\}$ with $B_1 \not\equiv B_2$, and $\Pi \wedge \Pi'$ is obtained by merging the block of Π' that contains B_1 with the block that contains B_2. [A finite lattice that satisfies this condition is called *lower semimodular*; see G. Birkhoff, *Lattice Theory* (1940), §I.8. The majorization lattice of exercise 7.2.1.4–54 does not have this property when, for example, $\alpha = 4111$ and $\alpha' = 331$.]

(g) False: For example, let $\Pi = 0011$, $\Pi' = 0101$.

(h) The blocks of Π and Π' are unions of the blocks of $\Pi \vee \Pi'$, so we can assume that $\Pi \vee \Pi' = \{1, \ldots, t\}$. As in part (b), merge j with l_j to get Π in r steps, when Π has $t - r$ blocks. These merges applied to Π' will each reduce the number of blocks by 0 or 1. Hence $b(\Pi') - b(\Pi \wedge \Pi') \leq r = b(\Pi \vee \Pi') - b(\Pi)$.

[In *Algebra Universalis* **10** (1980), 74–95, P. Pudlák and J. Tůma proved that *every* finite lattice is a sublattice of the partition lattice of $\{1, \ldots, n\}$, for suitably large n.]

13. [See *Advances in Math.* **26** (1977), 290–305.] If the j largest elements of a t-block partition appear in singleton blocks, but the next element $n - j$ does not, let us say that the partition has order $t - j$. Define the "Stirling string" Σ_{nt} to be the sequence of orders of the t-block partitions $\Pi_1, \Pi_2, \ldots$; for example, $\Sigma_{43} = 122333$. Then $\Sigma_{tt} = 0$, and we get $\Sigma_{(n+1)t}$ from Σ_{nt} by replacing each digit d in the latter by the string $d^d (d+1)^{d+1} \ldots t^t$ of length $\binom{t+1}{2} - \binom{d}{2}$; for example,

$$\Sigma_{53} = 122333223332233333333333.$$

The basic idea is to consider the lexicographic generation process of Algorithm H. Suppose $\Pi = a_1 \ldots a_n$ is a t-block partition of order j; then it is the lexicographically smallest t-block partition whose restricted growth string begins with $a_1 \ldots a_{n-t+j}$. The partitions covered by Π are, in lexicographic order, $\Pi_{12}, \Pi_{13}, \Pi_{23}, \Pi_{14}, \Pi_{24}, \Pi_{34},$ $\ldots, \Pi_{(t-1)t}$, where Π_{rs} means "coalesce blocks r and s of Π" (that is, "change all occurrences of $s - 1$ to $r - 1$ and then apply ρ to get a restricted growth string"). If Π' is any of the last $\binom{t}{2} - \binom{j}{2}$ of these, from $\Pi_{1(j+1)}$ onwards, then Π is the smallest t-block partition following Π'. For example, if $\Pi = 001012034$, then $n = 9$, $t = 5$, $j = 3$, and the relevant partitions Π' are $\rho(001012004)$, $\rho(001012014)$, $\rho(001012024)$, $\rho(001012030)$, $\rho(001012031)$, $\rho(001012032)$, $\rho(001012033)$.

Therefore $f_{nt}(N) = f_{nt}(N-1) + \binom{t}{2} - \binom{j}{2}$, where j is the Nth digit of Σ_{nt}.

14. E1. [Initialize.] Set $a_j \leftarrow 0$ and $b_j \leftarrow d_j \leftarrow 1$ for $1 \le j \le n$.

E2. [Visit.] Visit the restricted growth string $a_1 \ldots a_n$.

E3. [Find j.] Set $j \leftarrow n$; then, while $a_j = d_j$, set $d_j \leftarrow 1 - d_j$ and $j \leftarrow j - 1$.

E4. [Done?] Terminate if $j = 1$. Otherwise go to E6 if $d_j = 0$.

E5. [Move down.] If $a_j = 0$, set $a_j \leftarrow b_j$, $m \leftarrow a_j + 1$, and go to E7. Otherwise if $a_j = b_j$, set $a_j \leftarrow b_j - 1$, $m \leftarrow b_j$, and go to E7. Otherwise set $a_j \leftarrow a_j - 1$ and return to E2.

E6. [Move up.] If $a_j = b_j - 1$, set $a_j \leftarrow b_j$, $m \leftarrow a_j + 1$, and go to E7. Otherwise if $a_j = b_j$, set $a_j \leftarrow 0$, $m \leftarrow b_j$, and go to E7. Otherwise set $a_j \leftarrow a_j + 1$ and return to E2.

E7. [Fix $b_{j+1} \ldots b_n$.] Set $b_k \leftarrow m$ for $k = j + 1, \ldots, n$. Return to E2. ∎

[This algorithm can be extensively optimized because, as in Algorithm H, j is almost always equal to n.]

15. It corresponds to the first n digits of the infinite binary string $01011011011\ldots$, because ϖ_{n-1} is even if and only if $n \bmod 3 = 0$ (see exercise 23).

16. 00012, 01012, 01112, 00112, 00102, 01102, 01002, 01202, 01212, 01222, 01022, 01122, 00122, 00121, 01121, 01021, 01221, 01211, 01201, 01200, 01210, 01220, 01020, 01120, 00120.

17. The following solution uses two mutually recursive procedures, $f(\mu, \nu, \sigma)$ and $b(\mu, \nu, \sigma)$, for "forward" and "backward" generation of $A_{\mu\nu}$ when $\sigma = 0$ and of $A'_{\mu\nu}$ when $\sigma = 1$. To start the process, assuming that $1 < m < n$, first set $a_j \leftarrow 0$ for $1 \le j \le n - m$ and $a_{n-m+j} \leftarrow j - 1$ for $1 \le j \le m$, then call $f(m, n, 0)$.

Procedure $f(\mu, \nu, \sigma)$: If $\mu = 2$, visit $a_1 \ldots a_n$; otherwise call $f(\mu - 1, \nu - 1, (\mu+\sigma) \bmod 2)$. Then, if $\nu = \mu + 1$, do the following: Change a_μ from 0 to $\mu - 1$, and visit $a_1 \ldots a_n$; repeatedly set $a_\nu \leftarrow a_\nu - 1$ and visit $a_1 \ldots a_n$, until $a_\nu = 0$. But if $\nu > \mu + 1$, change $a_{\nu-1}$ (if $\mu+\sigma$ is odd) or a_μ (if $\mu+\sigma$ is even) from 0 to $\mu - 1$; then call $b(\mu, \nu-1, 0)$ if $a_\nu + \sigma$ is odd, $f(\mu, \nu-1, 0)$ if $a_\nu + \sigma$ is even; and while $a_\nu > 0$, set $a_\nu \leftarrow a_\nu - 1$ and call $b(\mu, \nu-1, 0)$ or $f(\mu, \nu-1, 0)$ again in the same way until $a_\nu = 0$.

Procedure $b(\mu, \nu, \sigma)$: If $\nu = \mu + 1$, first do the following: Repeatedly visit $a_1 \ldots a_n$ and set $a_\nu \leftarrow a_\nu + 1$, until $a_\nu = \mu - 1$; then visit $a_1 \ldots a_n$ and change a_μ from $\mu - 1$ to 0. But if $\nu > \mu + 1$, call $f(\mu, \nu-1, 0)$ if $a_\nu + \sigma$ is odd, $b(\mu, \nu-1, 0)$ if $a_\nu + \sigma$ is even; then while $a_\nu < \mu - 1$, set $a_\nu \leftarrow a_\nu + 1$ and call $f(\mu, \nu-1, 0)$ or $b(\mu, \nu-1, 0)$ again in the same way until $a_\nu = \mu - 1$; finally change $a_{\nu-1}$ (if $\mu+\sigma$ is odd) or a_μ (if $\mu+\sigma$ is even) from $\mu - 1$ to 0. And finally, in both cases, if $\mu = 2$ visit $a_1 \ldots a_n$, otherwise call $b(\mu - 1, \nu - 1, (\mu+\sigma) \bmod 2)$.

Most of the running time is actually spent handing the case $\mu = 2$; faster routines based on Gray binary code (and deviating from Ruskey's actual sequences) could be substituted for this case. A streamlined procedure could also be used when $\mu = \nu - 1$.

18. The sequence must begin (or end) with $01 \ldots (n-1)$. By exercise 32, no such Gray code can exist when $0 \neq \delta_n \neq (1)^{0+1+\cdots+(n-1)}$, namely when $n \bmod 12$ is 4, 6, 7, or 9.

The cases $n = 1, 2, 3$, are easily solved; and 1,927,683,326 solutions exist when $n = 5$. Thus there probably are zillions of solutions for all $n \geq 8$ except for the cases already excluded. Indeed, we can probably find such a Gray path through all ϖ_{nk} of the strings considered in answer 28(e) below, except when $n \equiv 2k + (2, 4, 5, 7)$ (modulo 12).

Note: The generalized Stirling number $\left\{{n \atop m}\right\}_{-1}$ in exercise 30 exceeds 1 for $2 < m < n$, so there can be no such Gray code for the partitions of $\{1, \ldots, n\}$ into m blocks.

19. (a) Change (6) to the pattern $0, 2, \ldots, m, \ldots, 3, 1$ or its reverse, as in endo-order (7.2.1.3–(45)). [See J. Kürschák, *Matematikai versenytételek* (Szeged: 1929), Problem 2 from the Eötvös Mathematical Competition of 1928.]

(b) We can generalize (8) and (9) to obtain sequences $A_{mn\alpha}$ and $A'_{mn\alpha}$ that begin with $0^{n-m}01 \ldots (m-1)$ and end with $01 \ldots (m-1)\alpha$ and $0^{n-m-1}01 \ldots (m-1)a$, respectively, where $0 \leq a \leq m-2$ and α is any string $a_1 \ldots a_{n-m}$ with $0 \leq a_j \leq m-2$. When $2 < m < n$ the new rules are

$$A_{m(n+1)(\alpha a)} = \begin{cases} A_{(m-1)n(b\beta)}x_1, A^R_{mn\beta}x_1, A_{mn\alpha}x_2, \ldots, A_{mn\alpha}x_m, & \text{if } m \text{ is even;} \\ A'_{(m-1)nb}x_1, A_{mn\alpha}x_1, A^R_{mn\alpha}x_2, \ldots, A_{mn\alpha}x_m, & \text{if } m \text{ is odd;} \end{cases}$$

$$A'_{m(n+1)a} = \begin{cases} A'_{(m-1)nb}x_1, A_{mn\beta}x_1, A^R_{mn\beta}x_2, \ldots, A^R_{mn\beta}x_m, & \text{if } m \text{ is even;} \\ A_{(m-1)n(b\beta)}x_1, A^R_{mn\beta}x_1, A_{mn\beta}x_2, \ldots, A^R_{mn\beta}x_m, & \text{if } m \text{ is odd;} \end{cases}$$

here $b = m - 3$, $\beta = b^{n-m}$, and $(x_1, \ldots, x_m)$ is a path from $x_1 = m - 1$ to $x_m = a$.

20. 012323212122; in general $(a_1 \ldots a_n)^T = \rho(a_n \ldots a_1)$, in the notation of exercise 4.

21. The numbers $\langle s_0, s_1, s_2, \ldots \rangle = \langle 1, 1, 2, 3, 7, 12, 31, 59, 164, 339, 999, \ldots \rangle$ satisfy the recurrences $s_{2n+1} = \sum_k \binom{n}{k} s_{2n-2k}$, $s_{2n+2} = \sum_k \binom{n}{k}(2^k + 1)s_{2n-2k}$, because of the way the middle elements relate to the others. Therefore $s_{2n} = n! \, [z^n] \exp\big((e^{2z}-1)/2+e^z-1\big)$ and $s_{2n+1} = n! \, [z^n] \exp\big((e^{2z} - 1)/2 + e^z + z - 1\big)$. By considering set partitions on the first half we also have $s_{2n} = \sum_k \left\{{n \atop k}\right\}x_k$ and $s_{2n+1} = \sum_k \left\{{n+1 \atop k}\right\}x_{k-1}$, where $x_n = 2x_{n-1} + (n-1)x_{n-2} = n! \, [z^n] \exp(2z + z^2/2)$. [T. S. Motzkin considered the sequence $\langle s_{2n} \rangle$ in *Proc. Symp. Pure Math.* **19** (1971), 173.]

22. (a) $\sum_{k=0}^{\infty} k^n \Pr(X=k) = e^{-1} \sum_{k=0}^{\infty} k^n/k! = \varpi_n$ by (16).

(b) $\sum_{k=0}^{\infty} k^n \Pr(X = k) = \sum_{k=0}^{\infty} k^n \sum_{j=0}^{m} \binom{j}{k}(-1)^{j-k}/j!$, and we can extend the inner sum to $j = \infty$ because $\sum_k \binom{j}{k}(-1)^k k^n = 0$ when $j > n$. Thus the nth moment turns out to be $\sum_{k=0}^{\infty}(k^n/k!) \sum_{l=0}^{\infty}(-1)^l/l! = \varpi_n$. [See J. O. Irwin, *J. Royal Stat. Soc.* **A118** (1955), 389–404; J. Pitman, *AMM* **104** (1997), 201–209.]

23. (a) The formula holds whenever $f(x) = x^n$, by (14), so it holds in general. (Thus we also have $\sum_{k=0}^{\infty} f(k)/k! = e f(\varpi)$, by (16).)

(b) Suppose we have proved the relation for k, and let $h(x) = (x-1)^k f(x)$, $g(x) = f(x+1)$. Then $f(\varpi + k + 1) = g(\varpi + k) = \varpi^k g(\varpi) = h(\varpi + 1) = \varpi h(\varpi) - \varpi^{k+1} f(\varpi)$. [See J. Touchard, *Ann. Soc. Sci. Bruxelles* **53** (1933), 21–31. This symbolic "umbral calculus," invented by John Blissard in *Quart. J. Pure and Applied Math.* **4** (1861), 279–305, is quite useful; but it must be handled carefully because $f(\varpi) = g(\varpi)$ does not imply that $f(\varpi)h(\varpi) = g(\varpi)h(\varpi)$.]

(c) The hint is a special case of exercise 4.6.2–16(c). Setting $f(x) = x^n$ and $k = p$ in (b) then yields $\varpi_n \equiv \varpi_{p+n} - \varpi_{1+n}$.

(d) Modulo p, the polynomial $x^N - 1$ is divisible by $g(x) = x^p - x - 1$, because $x^{p^k} \equiv x + k$ and $x^N \equiv x^{\bar{p}} \equiv x^{\underline{p}} \equiv x^p - x \equiv 1$ (modulo $g(x)$ and p). Thus if $h(x) = (x^N - 1)x^n/g(x)$ we have $h(\varpi) \equiv h(\varpi + p) = \varpi^p h(\varpi) \equiv (\varpi^p - \varpi)h(\varpi)$; and $0 \equiv g(\varpi)h(\varpi) = \varpi^{N+n} - \varpi^n$ (modulo p).

24. The hint follows by induction on e, because $x^{\underline{p^e}} = \prod_{k=0}^{p-1}(x - kp^{e-1})^{\underline{p^{e-1}}}$. We can also prove by induction on n that $x^n \equiv r_n(x)$ (modulo $g_1(x)$ and p) implies

$$x^{p^{e-1}n} \equiv r_n(x)^{p^{e-1}} \quad (\text{modulo } g_e(x), pg_{e-1}(x), \ldots, p^{e-1}g_1(x), \text{ and } p^e).$$

Hence $x^{p^{e-1}N} = 1 + h_0(x)g_e(x) + ph_1(x)g_{e-1}(x) + \cdots + p^{e-1}h_{e-1}(x)g_1(x) + p^e h_e(x)$ for certain polynomials $h_k(x)$ with integer coefficients. Modulo p^e we have $h_0(\varpi)\varpi^n \equiv h_0(\varpi + p^e)(\varpi + p^e)^n = \varpi^{\underline{p^e}} h_0(\varpi)\varpi^n \equiv (g_e(\varpi) + 1)h_0(\varpi)\varpi^n$; hence

$$\varpi^{p^{e-1}N+n} = \varpi^n + h_0(\varpi)g_e(\varpi)\varpi^n + ph_1(\varpi)g_{e-1}(\varpi)\varpi^n + \cdots \equiv \varpi^n.$$

[A similar derivation applies when $p = 2$, but we let $g_{j+1}(x) = g_j(x)^2 + 2[j\,{=}\,2]$, and we obtain $\varpi_n \equiv \varpi_{n+3 \cdot 2^e}$ (modulo 2^e). These results are due to Marshall Hall; see *Bull. Amer. Math. Soc.* **40** (1934), 387; *Amer. J. Math.* **70** (1948), 387–388. For further information see W. F. Lunnon, P. A. B. Pleasants, and N. M. Stephens, *Acta Arith.* **35** (1979), 1–16.]

25. The first inequality follows by applying a much more general principle to the tree of restricted growth strings: In any tree for which degree(p) $\geq$ degree(parent(p)) for all non-root nodes p, we have $w_k/w_{k-1} \leq w_{k+1}/w_k$ when w_k is the total number of nodes on level k. For if the $m = w_{k-1}$ nodes on level $k - 1$ have respectively $a_1, \ldots, a_m$ children, they have at least $a_1^2 + \cdots + a_m^2$ grandchildren; hence $w_{k-1}w_{k+1} \geq m(a_1^2 + \cdots + a_m^2) \geq (a_1 + \cdots + a_m)^2 = w_k^2$.

For the second inequality, note that $\varpi_{n+1} - \varpi_n = \sum_{k=0}^{n}\left(\binom{n}{k} - \binom{n-1}{k-1}\right)\varpi_{n-k}$; thus

$$\frac{\varpi_{n+1}}{\varpi_n} - 1 = \sum_{k=0}^{n-1}\binom{n-1}{k}\frac{\varpi_{n-k}}{\varpi_n} \leq \sum_{k=0}^{n-1}\binom{n-1}{k}\frac{\varpi_{n-k-1}}{\varpi_{n-1}} = \frac{\varpi_n}{\varpi_{n-1}}$$

because, for example, $\varpi_{n-3}/\varpi_n = (\varpi_{n-3}/\varpi_{n-2})(\varpi_{n-2}/\varpi_{n-1})(\varpi_{n-1}/\varpi_n)$ is less than or equal to $(\varpi_{n-4}/\varpi_{n-3})(\varpi_{n-3}/\varpi_{n-2})(\varpi_{n-2}/\varpi_{n-1}) = \varpi_{n-4}/\varpi_{n-1}$.

26. There are $\binom{n-1}{n-t}$ rightward paths from ⓝⓛ to ⓣⓣ; we can represent them by 0s and 1s, where 0 means "go right," 1 means "go up," and the positions of the 1s tell us which $n-t$ of the elements are in the block with 1. The next step, if $t > 1$, is to another vertex at the far left; so we continue with a path that defines a partition on the remaining $t-1$ elements. For example, the partition $14|2|3$ corresponds to the path 0010 under these conventions, where the respective bits mean that $1 \neq 2$, $1 \neq 3$, $1 \equiv 4$, $2 \neq 3$. [Many other interpretations are possible. The convention suggested here shows that ϖ_{nk} enumerates partitions with $1 \neq 2, \ldots, 1 \neq k$, a combinatorial property discovered by H. W. Becker; see *AMM* **51** (1944), 47, and *Mathematics Magazine* **22** (1948), 23–26.]

27. (a) In general, $\lambda_0 = \lambda_1 = \lambda_{2n-1} = \lambda_{2n} = 0$. The following list shows also the restricted growth strings that correspond to each loop via the algorithm of part (b):

0,0,0,0,0,0,0,0,0 0123	0,0,1,0,0,0,0,0,0 0012	0,0,1,1,1,0,0,0,0 0102
0,0,0,0,0,0,1,0,0 0122	0,0,1,0,0,0,1,0,0 0011	0,0,1,1,1,0,1,0,0 0100
0,0,0,0,1,0,0,0,0 0112	0,0,1,0,1,0,0,0,0 0001	0,0,1,1,1,1,1,0,0 0120
0,0,0,0,1,0,1,0,0 0111	0,0,1,0,1,0,1,0,0 0000	0,0,1,1,11,1,1,0,0 0101
0,0,0,0,1,1,1,0,0 0121	0,0,1,0,1,1,1,0,0 0010	0,0,1,1,2,1,1,0,0 0110

(b) The name "tableau" suggests a connection to Section 5.1.4, and indeed the theory developed there leads to an interesting one-to-one correspondence. We can represent set partitions on a triangular chessboard by putting a rook in column l_j of row $n + 1 - j$ whenever $l_j \neq 0$ in the linked list representation of exercise 2 (see the answer to exercise 5.1.3–19). For example, the rook representation of 135|27|489|6 is shown here. Equivalently, the nonzero links can be specified in a two-line array, such as $\binom{1\,2\,3\,4\,8}{3\,7\,5\,8\,9}$; see 5.1.4–(11).

Consider the path of length $2n$ that begins at the lower left corner of this triangular diagram and follows the right boundary edges, ending at the upper right corner: The points of this path are $z_k = (\lfloor k/2 \rfloor, \lceil k/2 \rceil)$ for $0 \leq k \leq 2n$. Moreover, the rectangle above and to the left of z_k contains precisely the rooks that contribute coordinate pairs $\frac{i}{j}$ to the two-line array when $i \leq \lfloor k/2 \rfloor$ and $j > \lceil k/2 \rceil$; in our example, there are just two such rooks when $9 \leq k \leq 12$, namely $\binom{2\,4}{7\,8}$. Theorem 5.1.4A tells us that such two-line arrays are equivalent to tableaux (P_k, Q_k), where the elements of P_k come from the lower line and the elements of Q_k come from the upper line, and where both P_k and Q_k have the same shape. It is advantageous to use decreasing order in the P tableaux but increasing order in the Q tableaux, so that in our example they are respectively

k	P_k	Q_k	k	P_k	Q_k	k	P_k	Q_k
2	3	1	7	7 5	2 3	12	8 / 7	2 / 4
3	3	1	8	8 5 / 7	2 3 / 4	13	8	4
4	7 / 3	1 / 2	9	8 / 7	2 / 4	14	8	4
5	7	2	10	8 / 7	2 / 4	15	·	·
6	7 5	2 3	11	8 / 7	2 / 4	16	9	8

while P_k and Q_k are empty for $k = 0$, 1, 17, and 18.

In this way every set partition leads to a vacillating tableau loop $\lambda_0, \lambda_1, \ldots, \lambda_{2n}$, if we let λ_k be the integer partition that specifies the common shape of P_k and Q_k. (The loop is 0, 0, 1, 1, 11, 1, 2, 2, 21, 11, 11, 11, 11, 1, 1, 0, 1, 0, 0 in our example.) Moreover, $t_{2k-1} = 0$ if and only if row $n + 1 - k$ contains no rook, if and only if k is smallest in its block.

Conversely, the elements of P_k and Q_k can be uniquely reconstructed from the sequence of shapes λ_k. Namely, $Q_k = Q_{k-1}$ if $t_k = 0$. Otherwise, if k is even, Q_k is Q_{k-1} with the number $k/2$ placed in a new cell at the right of row t_k; if k is odd, Q_k is obtained from Q_{k-1} by using Algorithm 5.1.4D to delete the rightmost entry of row t_k. A similar procedure defines P_k from the values of P_{k+1} and t_{k+1}, so we can work back from P_{2n} to P_0. Thus the sequence of shapes λ_k is enough to tell us where to place the rooks.

Vacillating tableau loops were introduced in a paper by W. Y. C. Chen, E. Y. P. Deng, R. R. X. Du, R. P. Stanley, and C. H. Yan [*Transactions of the Amer. Math. Soc.* **359** (2007), 1555–1575], who showed that the construction has significant (and surprising) consequences. For example, if the set partition $\varPi$ corresponds to the vacillating tableau loop $\lambda_0, \lambda_1, \ldots, \lambda_{2n}$, let's say that its *dual* $\varPi^D$ is the set partition that corresponds to the sequence of transposed shapes $\lambda_0^T, \lambda_1^T, \ldots, \lambda_{2n}^T$. Then, by exercise 5.1.4–7, $\varPi$ contains a "k-crossing at l," namely a sequence of indices with $i_1 < \cdots < i_k \leq l < j_1 < \cdots < j_k$ and $i_1 \equiv j_1, \ldots, i_k \equiv j_k$ (modulo $\varPi$), if and only if $\varPi^D$ contains a "k-nesting at l," which is a sequence of indices with $i_1' < \cdots < i_k' \leq l < j_k' < \cdots < j_1'$ and $i_1' \equiv j_1', \ldots, i_k' \equiv j_k'$ (modulo $\varPi^D$). Notice also that an involution is essentially a set partition in which all blocks have size 1 or 2; the dual of an involution is an involution having the same singleton sets. In particular, the dual of a perfect matching (when there are no singleton sets) is a perfect matching.

Furthermore, an analogous construction applies to rook placements in *any* Ferrers diagram, not only in the stairstep shapes that correspond to set partitions. Given a Ferrers diagram that has at most m parts, all of size $\leq n$, we simply consider the path $z_0 = (0,0), z_1, \ldots, z_{m+n} = (n, m)$ that hugs the right edge of the diagram, and stipulate that $\lambda_k = \lambda_{k-1} + e_{t_k}$ when $z_k = z_{k-1} + (1,0)$, $\lambda_k = \lambda_{k-1} - e_{t_k}$ when $z_k = z_{k-1} + (0,1)$. The proof we gave for stairstep shapes shows also that every placement of rooks in the Ferrers diagram, with at most one rook in each row and at most one in each column, corresponds to a unique tableau loop of this kind.

[And much more is true, besides! See A. Berele, *J. Combinatorial Theory* **A43** (1986), 320–328; S. Fomin, *J. Combinatorial Theory* **A72** (1995), 277–292; M. van Leeuwen, *Electronic J. Combinatorics* **3**, 2 (1996), #R15, 1–32.]

28. (a) Define a one-to-one correspondence between rook placements, by interchanging the positions of rooks in rows j and $j+1$ if and only if there's a rook in the "panhandle" of the longer row:

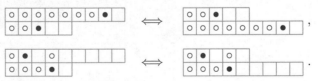

(b) This relation is obvious from the definition, by transposing all the rooks.

(c) Suppose $a_1 \geq a_2 \geq \cdots$ and $a_k > a_{k+1}$. Then we have

$$R(a_1, a_2, \ldots) = xR(a_1-1, \ldots, a_{k-1}-1, a_{k+1}, \ldots) + yR(a_1, \ldots, a_{k-1}, a_k-1, a_{k+1}, \ldots)$$

because the first term counts cases where a rook is in row k and column a_k. Also $R(0) = 1$ because of the empty placement. From these recurrences we find

$R(1) = x + y$; $R(2) = R(1,1) = x + xy + y^2$; $R(3) = R(1,1,1) = x + xy + xy^2 + y^3$;

$R(2,1) = x^2 + 2xy + xy^2 + y^3$;

$R(3,1) = R(2,2) = R(2,1,1) = x^2 + x^2y + xy + 2xy^2 + xy^3 + y^4$;

$R(3,1,1) = R(3,2) = R(2,2,1) = x^2 + 2x^2y + x^2y^2 + 2xy^2 + 2xy^3 + xy^4 + y^5$;

$R(3,2,1) = x^3 + 3x^2y + 3x^2y^2 + x^2y^3 + 3xy^3 + 2xy^4 + xy^5 + y^6$.

(d) For example, the formula $\varpi_{73}(x, y) = x\varpi_{63}(x, y) + y\varpi_{74}(x, y)$ is equivalent to $R(5, 4, 4, 3, 2, 1) = xR(4, 3, 3, 2, 1) + yR(5, 4, 3, 3, 2, 1)$, a special case of (c); and $\varpi_{nn}(x, y) = R(n - 2, \ldots, 0)$ is obviously equal to $\varpi_{(n-1)1}(x, y) = R(n - 2, \ldots, 1)$.

(e) In fact $y^{k-1}\varpi_{nk}(x, y)$ is the stated sum over all restricted growth strings $a_1 \ldots a_n$ for which $a_2 > 0, \ldots, a_k > 0$.

29. (a) If the rooks are respectively in columns $(c_1, \ldots, c_n)$, the number of free cells is the number of inversions of the permutation $(n+1-c_1) \ldots (n+1-c_n)$. [Rotate the right-hand example of Fig. 56 by $180°$ and compare the result to the illustration that follows Eq. 5.1.1–(5).]

(b) Each $r \times r$ configuration can be placed in, say, rows $i_1 < \cdots < i_r$ and columns $j_1 < \cdots < j_r$, yielding $(m-r)(n-r)$ free cells in the unchosen rows and columns; there are $(i_2-i_1+1) + 2(i_3-i_2-1) + \cdots + (r-1)(i_r-i_{r-1}-1) + r(m-i_r)$ in the unchosen rows and chosen columns, and a similar number in the chosen rows and unchosen columns. Furthermore

$$\sum_{1 \le i_1 < \cdots < i_r \le m} y^{(i_2-i_1+1)+2(i_3-i_2-1)+\cdots+(r-1)(i_r-i_{r-1}-1)+r(m-i_r)}$$

may be regarded as the sum of $y^{a_1+a_2+\cdots+a_m - r}$ over all partitions $r \ge a_1 \ge a_2 \ge \cdots \ge a_{m-r} \ge 0$, so it is $\binom{m}{r}_y$ by Theorem C. The polynomial $r!_y$ generates free cells for the chosen rows and columns, by (a). Therefore the answer is $y^{(m-r)(n-r)}\binom{m}{r}_y\binom{n}{r}_y r!_y = y^{(m-r)(n-r)} m!_y n!_y / ((m-r)!_y (n-r)!_y r!_y)$.

(c) The left-hand side is the generating function $R_m(t + a_1, \ldots, t + a_m)$ for the Ferrers diagram with t additional columns of height m. For there are $t + a_m$ ways to put a rook in row m, yielding $1 + y + \cdots + y^{t+a_m-1} = (1 - y^{t+a_m})/(1 - y)$ free cells with respect to those choices; then there are $t + a_{m-1} - 1$ available cells in row $m - 1$, etc.

The right-hand side, likewise, equals $R_m(t + a_1, \ldots, t + a_m)$. For if $m - k$ rooks are placed into columns $> t$, we must put k rooks into columns $\le t$ of the k unused rows; and we have seen that $t!_y/(t - k)!_y$ is the generating function for free cells when k rooks are placed on a $k \times t$ board.

Notes: The formula proved here can be regarded as a polynomial identity in the variables y and y^t; therefore it is valid for arbitrary t, although our proof assumed that t is a nonnegative integer. This result was discovered in the case $y = 1$ by J. Goldman, J. Joichi, and D. White, *Proc. Amer. Math. Soc.* **52** (1975), 485–492. The general case was established by A. M. Garsia and J. B. Remmel, *J. Combinatorial Theory* **A41** (1986), 246–275, who used a similar argument to prove the additional formula

$$\sum_{t=0}^{\infty} z^t \prod_{j=1}^{m} \frac{1 - y^{a_j+m-j+t}}{1 - y} = \sum_{k=0}^{n} k!_y \left(\frac{z}{1 - yz}\right) \cdots \left(\frac{z}{1 - y^k z}\right) R_{m-k}(a_1, \ldots, a_m).$$

(d) This statement, which follows immediately from (c), also implies that we have $R(a_1, \ldots, a_m) = R(a'_1, \ldots, a'_m)$ if and only if equality holds for all x and for any nonzero value of y. The Peirce polynomial $\varpi_{nk}(x, y)$ of exercise 28(d) is the rook polynomial for $\binom{n-1}{k-1}$ different Ferrers diagrams; for example, $\varpi_{63}(x, y)$ enumerates rook placements for the shapes 43321, 44221, 44311, 4432, 53221, 53311, 5332, 54211, 5422, and 5431.

30. (a) We have $\varpi_n(x, y) = \sum_m x^{n-m} A_{mn}$, where $A_{mn} = R_{n-m}(n-1, \ldots, 1)$ satisfies a simple law: If we don't place a rook in row 1 of the shape $(n - 1, \ldots, 1)$, that row has $m - 1$ free cells because of the $n - m$ rooks in other rows. But if we do put a rook there, we leave 0 or 1 or $\cdots$ or $m-1$ of its cells free. Hence $A_{mn} = y^{m-1}A_{(m-1)(n-1)} + (1+y+\cdots+y^{m-1})A_{m(n-1)}$, and it follows by induction that $A_{mn} = y^{m(m-1)/2}{n \brace m}_y$.

(b) The formula $\varpi_{n+1}(x,y) = \sum_k \binom{n}{k}x^{n-k}y^k\varpi_k(x,y)$ yields

$$A_{m(n+1)} = \sum_k \binom{n}{k}y^k A_{(m-1)k}.$$

(c) From (a) and (b) we have

$$\frac{z^n}{(1-z)(1-(1+q)z)\ldots(1-(1+q+\cdots+q^{n-1})z)} = \sum_k {k \brace n}_q z^k;$$

$$\sum_k \binom{n}{k}_q(-1)^k q^{\binom{k}{2}}e^{(1+q+\cdots+q^{n-k-1})z} = q^{\binom{n}{2}}n!_q \sum_k {k \brace n}_q \frac{z^k}{k!}.$$

[The second formula is proved by induction on n, because both sides satisfy the differential equation $G'_{n+1}(z) = (1+q+\cdots+q^n)e^z G_n(qz)$; exercise 1.2.6–58 proves equality when $z = 0$.]

   Historical note: Leonard Carlitz introduced q-Stirling numbers in *Transactions of the Amer. Math. Soc.* **33** (1933), 127–129. Then in *Duke Math. J.* **15** (1948), 987–1000, he derived (among other things) an appropriate generalization of Eq. 1.2.6–(45):

$$(1+q+\cdots+q^{m-1})^n = \sum_k {n \brace k}_q q^{\binom{k}{2}}\frac{m!_q}{(m-k)!_q}.$$

31. $\exp(e^{w+z}+w-1)$; therefore $\varpi_{nk} = (\varpi+1)^{n-k}\varpi^{k-1} = \varpi^{n+1-k}(\varpi-1)^{k-1}$ in the umbral notation of exercise 23. [L. Moser and M. Wyman, *Trans. Royal Soc. Canada* (3) **43** (1954), Section 3, 31–37.] In fact, the numbers $\varpi_{nk}(x,1)$ of exercise 28(d) are generated by $\exp((e^{xw+xz}-1)/x+xw)$.

32. We have $\delta_n = \varpi_n(1,-1)$, and a simple pattern is easily perceived in the generalized Peirce triangle of exercise 28(d) when $x = 1$ and $y = -1$: We have $|\varpi_{nk}(1,-1)| \leq 1$ and $\varpi_{n(k+1)}(1,-1) \equiv \varpi_{nk}(1,-1) + (-1)^n$ (modulo 3) for $1 \leq k < n$. [In *JACM* **20** (1973), 512–513, Gideon Ehrlich gave a combinatorial proof of an equivalent result.]

33. Representing set partitions by rook placements as in answer 27 leads to the answer ϖ_{nk}, by setting $x = y = 1$ in exercise 28(d). [The case $k = n$ was discovered by H. Prodinger, *Fibonacci Quarterly* **19** (1981), 463–465.]

34. (a) Guittone's *Sonetti* included 149 of scheme 01010101232323, 64 of scheme 01010101234234, two of scheme 01010101234342, seven with schemes used only once (like 01100110234432), and 29 poems that we would no longer consider to be sonnets because they do not have 14 lines.

   (b) Petrarch's *Canzoniere* included 115 sonnets of scheme 01100110234234, 109 of scheme 01100110232323, 66 of scheme 01100110234324, 7 of scheme 01100110232232, and 20 others of schemes like 01010101232323 used at most four times each.

   (c) In Spenser's *Amoretti*, 88 of 89 sonnets used the scheme 01011212232344; the exception (number 8) was "Shakespearean."

   (d) Shakespeare's 154 sonnets all used coalescences of the rather easy scheme 01012323454566, except that two of them (99 and 126) didn't have 14 lines.

   (e) Browning's 44 *Sonnets From the Portuguese* obeyed the Petrarchan scheme 01100110232323.

Sometimes the lines would rhyme (by chance?) even when they didn't need to; for example, Browning's final sonnet actually had the scheme 01100110121212.

Incidentally, the lengthy cantos in Dante's *Divine Comedy* used an interlocking scheme of rhymes in which $1 \equiv 3$ and $3n - 1 \equiv 3n + 1 \equiv 3n + 3$ for $n = 1, 2, \ldots$.

35. Every incomplete n-line rhyme scheme Π corresponds to a singleton-free partition of $\{1, \ldots, n+1\}$ in which $(n+1)$ is grouped with all of Π's singletons. [H. W. Becker gave an algebraic proof in *AMM* **48** (1941), 702. Notice that $\varpi'_n = \sum_k \binom{n}{k}(-1)^{n-k}\varpi_k$, by the principle of inclusion and exclusion, and $\varpi_n = \sum_k \binom{n}{k}\varpi'_k$; we can in fact write $\varpi' = \varpi - 1$ in the umbral notation of exercise 23. J. O. Shallit has suggested extending Peirce's triangle by setting $\varpi_{n(n+1)} = \varpi'_n$; see exercises 38(e) and 33. In fact, ϖ_{nk} is the number of partitions of $\{1, \ldots, n\}$ with the property that $1, \ldots, k-1$ are not singletons; see H. W. Becker, *Bull. Amer. Math. Soc.* **58** (1952), 63.]

36. $\exp(e^z - 1 - z)$. (In general, if ϑ_n is the number of partitions of $\{1, \ldots, n\}$ into subsets of allowable sizes $s_1 < s_2 < \cdots$, the exponential generating function $\sum_n \vartheta_n z^n/n!$ is $\exp(z^{s_1}/s_1! + z^{s_2}/s_2! + \cdots)$, because $(z^{s_1}/s_1! + z^{s_2}/s_2! + \cdots)^k$ is the exponential generating function for partitions into exactly k parts.)

37. There are $\sum_k \binom{n}{k}\varpi'_k\varpi'_{n-k}$ possibilities of length n, hence 784,071,966 when $n = 14$. (But Pushkin's scheme is hard to beat.)

38. (a) Imagine starting with $x_1 x_2 \ldots x_n = 01 \ldots (n-1)$, then successively removing some element b_j and placing it at the left, for $j = 1, 2, \ldots, n$. Then x_k will be the kth most recently moved element, for $1 \le k \le |\{b_1, \ldots, b_n\}|$; see exercise 5.2.3–36. Consequently the array $x_1 \ldots x_n$ will return to its original state if and only if $b_n \ldots b_1$ is a restricted growth string. [Robbins and Bolker, *Æquat. Math.* **22** (1981), 281–282.]

In other words, let $a_1 \ldots a_n$ be a restricted growth string. Set $b_{-j} \leftarrow j$ and $b_{j+1} \leftarrow a_{n-j}$ for $0 \le j < n$. Then for $1 \le j \le n$, define k_j by the rule that b_j is the k_jth distinct element of the sequence $b_{j-1}, b_{j-2}, \ldots$. For example, the string $a_1 \ldots a_{16} = $ 0123032303456745 corresponds in this way to the σ-cycle 6688448628232384.

(b) Such paths correspond to restricted growth strings with $\max(a_1, \ldots, a_n) \le m$, so the answer is $\{\begin{smallmatrix} n \\ 0 \end{smallmatrix}\} + \{\begin{smallmatrix} n \\ 1 \end{smallmatrix}\} + \cdots + \{\begin{smallmatrix} n \\ m \end{smallmatrix}\}$.

(c) We may assume that $i = 1$, because the sequence $k_2 \ldots k_n k_1$ is a σ-cycle whenever $k_1 k_2 \ldots k_n$ is. Thus the answer is the number of restricted growth strings with $a_n = j - 1$, namely $\{\begin{smallmatrix} n-1 \\ j-1 \end{smallmatrix}\} + \{\begin{smallmatrix} n-1 \\ j \end{smallmatrix}\} + \{\begin{smallmatrix} n-1 \\ j+1 \end{smallmatrix}\} + \cdots$.

(d) If the answer is f_n we must have $\sum_k \binom{n}{k} f_k = \varpi_n$, since σ_1 is the identity permutation. Therefore $f_n = \varpi'_n$, the number of set partitions without singletons (exercise 35).

(e) Again ϖ'_n, by (a) and (d). [Consequently $\varpi'_p \bmod p = 1$ when p is prime.]

39. Set $u = t^{p+1}$ to obtain $\frac{1}{p+1}\int_0^\infty e^{-u} u^{(q-p)/(p+1)}\, du = \frac{1}{p+1}\Gamma(\frac{q+1}{p+1})$.

40. We have $g(z) = cz - n \ln z$, so the saddle point occurs at n/c. The rectangular path now has corners at $\pm n/c \pm mi/c$; and $\exp g(n/c + it) = (e^n c^n/n^n)\exp(-t^2 c^2/(2n) + it^3 c^3/(3n^2) + \cdots)$. The final result is $e^n(c/n)^{n-1}/\sqrt{2\pi n}$ times $1 + n/12 + O(n^{-2})$.

(Of course we could have obtained this result more quickly by letting $w = cz$ in the integral. But the answer given here applies the saddle point method mechanically, without attempting to be clever.)

41. Again the net result is just to multiply (21) by c^{n-1}; but in this case the *left* edge of the rectangular path is significant instead of the right edge. (Incidentally, when $c = -1$ we cannot derive an analog of (22) using Hankel's contour when x is real and positive, because the integral on that path diverges. But with the usual definition of z^x, a suitable path of integration does yield the formula $-(\cos \pi x)/\Gamma(x)$ when $n = x > 0$.)

42. We have $\oint e^{z^2} dz/z^n = 0$ when n is even. Otherwise both left and right edges of the rectangle with corners $\pm\sqrt{n/2} \pm in$ contribute approximately

$$\frac{e^{n/2}}{2\pi(n/2)^{n/2}} \int_{-\infty}^{\infty} \exp\left(-2t^2 - \frac{(-it)^3}{3}\frac{2^{3/2}}{n^{1/2}} + \frac{(it)^4}{n} - \cdots\right) dt,$$

when n is large. We can restrict $|t| \le n^\epsilon$ to show that this integral is $I_0 + (I_4 - \frac{4}{9}I_6)/n$ with relative error $O(n^{9\epsilon-3/2})$, where $I_k = \int_{-\infty}^{\infty} e^{-2t^2} t^k \, dt$. As before, the relative error is actually $O(n^{-2})$; we deduce the answer

$$\frac{1}{((n-1)/2)!} = \frac{e^{n/2}}{\sqrt{2\pi}(n/2)^{n/2}}\left(1 + \frac{1}{12n} + O\left(\frac{1}{n^2}\right)\right), \qquad n \text{ odd}.$$

(The analog of (22) is $(\sin \frac{\pi x}{2})^2/\Gamma((x-1)/2)$ when $n = x > 0$.)

43. Let $f(z) = e^{e^z}/z^n$. When $z = -n + it$ we have $|f(z)| < e n^{-n}$; when $z = t + 2\pi in + i\pi/2$ we have $|f(z)| = |z|^{-n} < (2\pi n)^{-n}$. So the integral is negligible except on a path $z = \xi + it$; and on that path $|f|$ decreases as $|t|$ increases from 0 to π. Already when $t = n^{\epsilon-1/2}$ we have $|f(z)|/f(\xi) = O(\exp(-n^{2\epsilon}/(\log n)^2))$. And when $|t| \ge \pi$ we have $|f(z)|/f(\xi) < 1/|1 + i\pi/\xi|^n = \exp(-\frac{n}{2}\ln(1 + \pi^2/\xi^2))$.

44. Set $u = na_2 t^2$ in (25) to obtain $\Re \int_0^\infty e^{-u} \exp(n^{-1/2}c_3(-u)^{3/2} + n^{-1}c_4(-u)^2 + n^{-3/2}c_5(-u)^{5/2} + \cdots) \, du/\sqrt{na_2 u}$ where $c_k = (2/(\xi+1))^{k/2}(\xi^{k-1} + (-1)^k(k-1)!)/k! = a_k/a_2^{k/2}$. This expression leads to

$$b_l = \sum_{\substack{k_1+2k_2+3k_3+\cdots=2l \\ k_1+k_2+k_3+\cdots=m \\ k_1,k_2,k_3,\ldots\ge 0}} \left(-\frac{1}{2}\right)^{l+m} \frac{c_3^{k_1}}{k_1!}\frac{c_4^{k_2}}{k_2!}\frac{c_5^{k_3}}{k_3!}\cdots,$$

a sum over partitions of $2l$. For example, $b_1 = \frac{3}{4}c_4 - \frac{15}{16}c_3^2$.

45. To get $\varpi_n/n!$ we replace $g(z)$ by $e^z - (n+1)\ln z$ in the derivation of (26). This change multiplies the integrand in the previous answer by $1/(1 + it/\xi)$, which is $1/(1 - n^{-1/2}a(-u)^{1/2})$ where $a = -\sqrt{2/(\xi+1)}$. Thus we get

$$b_l' = \sum_{\substack{k+k_1+2k_2+3k_3+\cdots=2l \\ k_1+k_2+k_3+\cdots=m \\ k,k_1,k_2,k_3,\ldots\ge 0}} \left(-\frac{1}{2}\right)^{l+m} a^k \frac{c_3^{k_1}}{k_1!}\frac{c_4^{k_2}}{k_2!}\frac{c_5^{k_3}}{k_3!}\cdots,$$

a sum of $p(2l) + p(2l-1) + \cdots + p(0)$ terms; $b_1' = \frac{3}{4}c_4 - \frac{15}{16}c_3^2 + \frac{3}{4}ac_3 - \frac{1}{2}a^2$. [The coefficient b_1' was obtained in a different way by L. Moser and M. Wyman, *Trans. Royal Soc. Canada* (3) **49**, Section 3 (1955), 49–54, who were the first to deduce an asymptotic series for ϖ_n. Their approximation is slightly less accurate than the result of (26) with n changed to $n+1$, because it doesn't pass exactly through the saddle point. Formula (26) is due to I. J. Good, *Iranian J. Science and Tech.* **4** (1975), 77–83.]

46. Equations (13) and (31) show that $\varpi_{nk} = (1 - \xi/n)^k \varpi_n (1 + O(n^{-1}))$ for fixed k as $n \to \infty$. And this approximation also holds when $k = n$, but with relative error $O((\log n)^2/n)$.

47. Steps (H1, H2, ..., H6) are performed respectively $(1, \varpi_n, \varpi_n - \varpi_{n-1}, \varpi_{n-1}, \varpi_{n-1}, \varpi_{n-1} - 1)$ times. The loop in H4 sets $j \leftarrow j - 1$ a total of $\varpi_{n-2} + \varpi_{n-3} + \cdots + \varpi_1$ times; the loop in H6 sets $b_j \leftarrow m$ a total of $(\varpi_{n-2} - 1) + \cdots + (\varpi_1 - 1)$ times. The ratio ϖ_{n-1}/ϖ_n is approximately $(\ln n)/n$, and $(\varpi_{n-2} + \cdots + \varpi_1)/\varpi_n \approx (\ln n)^2/n^2$.

48. We can easily verify the interchange of summation and integration in

$$\frac{e\varpi_x}{\Gamma(x+1)} = \frac{1}{2\pi i} \oint \frac{e^{e^z}}{z^{x+1}} \, dz = \frac{1}{2\pi i} \oint \sum_{k=0}^{\infty} \frac{e^{kx}}{k! \, z^{x+1}} \, dz$$

$$= \sum_{k=0}^{\infty} \frac{1}{k!} \frac{1}{2\pi i} \oint \frac{e^{kz}}{z^{x+1}} \, dz = \sum_{k=0}^{\infty} \frac{1}{k!} \frac{k^x}{\Gamma(x+1)}.$$

49. If $\xi = \ln n - \ln \ln n + x$, we have $\beta = 1 - e^{-x} - \alpha x$. Therefore by Lagrange's inversion formula (exercise 4.7–8),

$$x = \sum_{k=1}^{\infty} \frac{\beta^k}{k} \, [t^{k-1}] \left(\frac{f(t)}{1 - \alpha f(t)} \right)^k = \sum_{k=1}^{\infty} \sum_{j=0}^{\infty} \frac{\beta^k}{k} \alpha^j \binom{k+j-1}{j} [t^{k-1}] f(t)^{j+k},$$

where $f(t) = t/(1 - e^{-t})$. So the result follows from the handy identity

$$\left(\frac{z}{1 - e^{-z}} \right)^m = \sum_{n=0}^{\infty} \left[\begin{matrix} m \\ m-n \end{matrix} \right] \frac{z^n}{(m-1)(m-2)\ldots(m-n)}.$$

(This identity should be interpreted carefully when $n \geq m$; the coefficient of z^n is a polynomial in m of degree n, as explained in *CMath* equation (7.59).)

    The formula in this exercise is due to L. Comtet, *Comptes Rendus Acad. Sci.* (A) **270** (Paris, 1970), 1085–1088, who identified the coefficients previously computed by N. G. de Bruijn, *Asymptotic Methods in Analysis* (1958), 25–28. Convergence for $n \geq e$ was shown by Jeffrey, Corless, Hare, and Knuth, *Comptes Rendus Acad. Sci.* (I) **320** (1995), 1449–1452, who also derived a formula that converges somewhat faster.

    (The equation $\xi e^{\xi} = n$ has complex roots as well. We can obtain them all by using $\ln n + 2\pi i m$ in place of $\ln n$ in the formula of this exercise; the sum converges rapidly when $m \neq 0$. See Corless, Gonnet, Hare, Jeffrey, and Knuth, *Advances in Computational Math.* **5** (1996), 347–350.)

50. Let $\xi = \xi(n)$. Then $\xi'(n) = \xi/((\xi+1)n)$, and the Taylor series

$$\xi(n+k) = \xi + k\xi'(n) + \frac{k^2}{2}\xi''(n) + \cdots$$

can be shown to converge for $|k| < n + 1/e$.

    Indeed, much more is true, because the function $\xi(n) = -T(-n)$ is obtained from the tree function $T(z)$ by analytic continuation to the negative real axis. (The tree function has a quadratic singularity at $z = e^{-1}$; after going around this singularity we encounter a logarithmic singularity at $z = 0$, as part of an interesting multi-level Riemann surface on which the quadratic singularity appears only at level 0.) The derivatives of the tree function satisfy $z^k T^{(k)}(z) = R(z)^k p_k(R(z))$, where $R(z) = T(z)/(1 - T(z))$ and $p_k(x)$ is the polynomial of degree $k - 1$ defined by $p_{k+1}(x) = (1+x)^2 p_k'(x) + k(2+x)p_k(x)$. For example,

$$p_1(x) = 1, \quad p_2(x) = 2 + x, \quad p_3(x) = 9 + 10x + 3x^2, \quad p_4(x) = 64 + 113x + 70x^2 + 15x^3.$$

(The coefficients of $p_k(x)$, incidentally, enumerate certain phylogenetic trees called Greg trees: $[x^j]\,p_k(x)$ is the number of oriented trees with j unlabeled nodes and k labeled nodes, where leaves must be labeled and unlabeled nodes must have at least two children. See J. Felsenstein, *Systematic Zoology* **27** (1978), 27–33; L. R. Foulds and R. W. Robinson, *Lecture Notes in Math.* **829** (1980), 110–126; C. Flight, *Manuscripta* **34** (1990), 122–128.) If $q_k(x) = p_k(-x)$, we can prove by induction that $(-1)^m q_k^{(m)}(x) \geq 0$ for $0 \leq x \leq 1$. Therefore $q_k(x)$ decreases monotonically from k^{k-1} to $(k-1)!$ as x goes from 0 to 1, for all $k, m \geq 1$. It follows that

$$\xi(n+k) = \xi + \frac{kx}{n} - \left(\frac{kx}{n}\right)^2 \frac{q_2(x)}{2!} + \left(\frac{kx}{n}\right)^3 \frac{q_3(x)}{3!} - \cdots, \qquad x = \frac{\xi}{\xi+1},$$

where the partial sums alternately overshoot and undershoot the correct value if $k > 0$.

51. There are two saddle points, $\sigma = \sqrt{n+5/4} - 1/2$ and $\sigma' = -1 - \sigma$. Integration on a rectangular path with corners at $\sigma \pm im$ and $\sigma' \pm im$ shows that only σ is relevant as $n \to \infty$ (although σ' contributes a relative error of roughly $e^{-\sqrt{n}}$, which can be significant when n is small). Arguing almost as in (25), but with $g(z) = z + z^2/2 - (n+1)\ln z$, we find that t_n is well approximated by

$$\frac{n!}{2\pi} \int_{-n^\epsilon}^{n^\epsilon} e^{g(\sigma) - a_2 t^2 + a_3 it^3 + \cdots + a_l(-it)^l + O(n^{(l+1)\epsilon - (l-1)/2})}\,dt, \qquad a_k = \frac{\sigma+1}{k\sigma^{k-1}} + \frac{[k=2]}{2}.$$

The integral expands as in exercise 44 to

$$\frac{n!\,e^{(n+\sigma)/2}}{2\sigma^{n+1}\sqrt{\pi a_2}}(1 + b_1 + b_2 + \cdots + b_m + O(n^{-m-1})).$$

This time $c_k = (\sigma+1)\sigma^{1-k}(1 + 1/(2\sigma))^{-k/2}/k$ for $k \geq 3$, hence $(2\sigma+1)^{3k}\sigma^k b_k$ is a polynomial in σ of degree $2k$; for example,

$$b_1 = \frac{3}{4}c_4 - \frac{15}{16}c_3^2 = \frac{8\sigma^2 + 7\sigma - 1}{12\sigma(2\sigma+1)^3}.$$

In particular, Stirling's approximation and the b_1 term yield

$$t_n = \frac{1}{\sqrt{2}}n^{n/2}e^{-n/2+\sqrt{n}-1/4}\left(1 + \frac{7}{24}n^{-1/2} - \frac{119}{1152}n^{-1} - \frac{7933}{414720}n^{-3/2} + O(n^{-2})\right)$$

after we plug in the formula for σ — a result substantially more accurate than equation 5.1.4–(53), and obtained with considerably less labor.

52. Let $G(z) = \sum_k \Pr(X = k)z^k$, so that the jth cumulant κ_j is $j!\,[t^j]\ln G(e^t)$. In case (a) we have $G(z) = e^{e^{\xi z} - e^{\xi}}$; hence

$$\ln G(e^t) = e^{\xi e^t} - e^\xi = e^\xi(e^{\xi(e^t-1)} - 1) = e^\xi \sum_{k=1}^\infty (e^t - 1)^k \frac{\xi^k}{k!}, \qquad \kappa_j = e^\xi \sum_k \left\{{k \atop j}\right\}\xi^k\,[j \neq 0].$$

Case (b) is sort of a dual situation: Here $\kappa = j = \varpi_j\,[j \neq 0]$ because

$$G(z) = e^{e^{-1}-1} \sum_{j,k} \left\{{k \atop j}\right\}e^{-j}\frac{z^k}{k!} = e^{e^{-1}-1} \sum_j \frac{(e^{z-1} - e^{-1})^j}{j!} = e^{e^{z-1}-1}.$$

[If $\xi e^\xi = 1$ in case (a) we have $\kappa_j = e\varpi\,[j \neq 0]$. But if $\xi e^\xi = n$ in that case, the mean is $\kappa_1 = n$ and the variance σ^2 is $(\xi+1)n$. Thus, the formula in exercise 45 states that the mean value n occurs with approximate probability $1/\sqrt{2\pi\sigma}$ and relative error $O(1/n)$. This observation leads to another way to prove that formula.]

53. We can write $\ln G(e^t) = \mu t + \sigma^2 t^2/2 + \kappa_3 t^3/3! + \cdots$ as in Eq. 1.2.10–(23), and there is a positive constant δ such that $\sum_{j=3}^{\infty} |\kappa_j| t^j/j! < \sigma^2 t^2/6$ when $|t| \leq \delta$. Hence, if $0 < \epsilon < 1/2$, we can prove that

$$[z^{\mu n+r}] G(z)^n = \frac{1}{2\pi} \int_{-\pi}^{\pi} \frac{G(e^{it})^n \, dt}{e^{it(\mu n+r)}}$$

$$= \frac{1}{2\pi} \int_{-n^{\epsilon-1/2}}^{n^{\epsilon-1/2}} \exp\left(-irt - \frac{\sigma^2 t^2 n}{2} + O(n^{3\epsilon-1/2})\right) dt + O(e^{-cn^{2\epsilon}})$$

as $n \to \infty$, for some constant $c > 0$: The integrand for $n^{\epsilon-1/2} \leq |t| \leq \delta$ is bounded in absolute value by $\exp(-\sigma^2 n^{2\epsilon}/3)$; and when $\delta \leq |t| \leq \pi$ its magnitude is at most α^n, where $\alpha = \max |G(e^{it})|$ is less than 1 because the individual terms $p_k e^{kit}$ don't all lie on a straight line by our assumption. Thus

$$[z^{\mu n+r}] G(z)^n = \frac{1}{2\pi} \int_{-\infty}^{\infty} \exp\left(-irt - \frac{\sigma^2 t^2 n}{2} + O(n^{3\epsilon-1/2})\right) dt + O(e^{-cn^{2\epsilon}})$$

$$= \frac{1}{2\pi} \int_{-\infty}^{\infty} \exp\left(-\frac{\sigma^2 n}{2}\left(t + \frac{ir}{\sigma^2 n}\right)^2 - \frac{r^2}{2\sigma^2 n} + O(n^{3\epsilon-1/2})\right) dt + O(e^{-cn^{2\epsilon}})$$

$$= \frac{e^{-r^2/(2\sigma^2 n)}}{\sigma\sqrt{2\pi n}} + O(n^{3\epsilon-1}).$$

By taking account of κ_3, κ_4, ... in a similar way we can refine the estimate to $O(n^{-m})$ for arbitrarily large m; thus the result is valid also for $\epsilon = 0$. [In fact, such refinements lead to the "Edgeworth expansion," according to which $[z^{\mu n+r}] G(z)^n$ is asymptotic to

$$\frac{e^{-r^2/(2\sigma^2 n)}}{\sigma\sqrt{2\pi n}} \sum_{\substack{k_1+2k_2+3k_3+\cdots=m \\ k_1+k_2+k_3+\cdots=l \\ k_1,k_2,k_3,\ldots \geq 0 \\ 0 \leq s \leq l+m/2}} \frac{(-1)^s (2l+m)^{\underline{2s}}}{\sigma^{4l+2m-2s} 2^s s!} \frac{r^{2l+m-2s}}{n^{l+m-s}} \frac{1}{k_1! \, k_2! \, \ldots} \left(\frac{\kappa_3}{3!}\right)^{k_1} \left(\frac{\kappa_4}{4!}\right)^{k_2} \cdots \, ;$$

the absolute error is $O(n^{-p/2})$, where the constant hidden in the O depends only on p and G but not on r or n, if we restrict the sum to cases with $m < p - 1$. For example, when $p = 3$ we get

$$[z^{\mu n+r}] G(z)^n = \frac{e^{-r^2/(2\sigma^2 n)}}{\sigma\sqrt{2\pi n}} \left(1 - \frac{\kappa_3}{2\sigma^4}\left(\frac{r}{n}\right) + \frac{\kappa_3}{6\sigma^6}\left(\frac{r^3}{n^2}\right)\right) + O\left(\frac{1}{n^{3/2}}\right),$$

and there are seven more terms when $p = 4$. See P. L. Chebyshev, *Zapiski Imp. Akad. Nauk* **55** (1887), No. 6, 1–16; *Acta Math.* **14** (1890), 305–315; F. Y. Edgeworth, *Trans. Cambridge Phil. Soc.* **20** (1905), 36–65, 113–141; H. Cramér, *Skandinavisk Aktuarietidsskrift* **11** (1928), 13–74, 141–180.]

54. Formula (40) is equivalent to $\alpha = s \coth s + s$, $\beta = s \coth s - s$.

55. Let $c = \alpha e^{-\alpha}$. The Newtonian iteration $\beta_0 = c$, $\beta_{k+1} = (1 - \beta_k) c e^{\beta_k}/(1 - c e^{-\beta_k})$ rises rapidly to the correct value, unless α is extremely close to 1. For example, β_7 differs from $\ln 2$ by less than 10^{-75} when $\alpha = \ln 4$.

56. (a) By induction on n, $g^{(n+1)}(z) = (-1)^n \left(\dfrac{\sum_{k=0}^{n} \binom{n}{k} e^{(n-k)z}}{\alpha(e^z - 1)^{n+1}} - \dfrac{n!}{z^{n+1}}\right).$

(b) $\sum_{k=0}^{n} \binom{n}{k} e^{k\sigma}/n! = \int_0^1 \dots \int_0^1 \exp(\lfloor u_1 + \dots + u_n \rfloor \sigma)\, du_1 \dots du_n$
$$< \int_0^1 \dots \int_0^1 \exp((u_1 + \dots + u_n)\sigma)\, du_1 \dots du_n = (e^\sigma - 1)^n/\sigma^n.$$
The lower bound is similar, since $\lfloor u_1 + \dots + u_n \rfloor > u_1 + \dots + u_n - 1$.

(c) Thus $n!\,(1 - \beta/\alpha) < (-\sigma)^n g^{(n+1)}(\sigma) < 0$, and we need only verify that $1 - \beta/\alpha < 2(1 - \beta)$, namely that $2\alpha\beta < \alpha + \beta$. But $\alpha\beta < 1$ and $\alpha + \beta > 2$, by exercise 54.

57. (a) $n + 1 - m = (n+1)(1 - 1/\alpha) < (n+1)(1 - \beta/\alpha) = (n+1)\sigma/\alpha \le 2N$ as in answer 56(c). (b) The quantity $\alpha + \alpha\beta$ increases as α increases, because its derivative with respect to α is $1 + \beta + \beta(1 - \alpha)/(1 - \beta) = (1 - \alpha\beta)/(1 - \beta) + \beta > 0$. Therefore $1 - \beta < 2(1 - 1/\alpha)$.

58. (a) The derivative of $|e^{\sigma+it} - 1|^2/|\sigma + it|^2 = (e^{\sigma+it} - 1)(e^{\sigma-it} - 1)/(\sigma^2 + t^2)$ with respect to t is $(\sigma^2 + t^2) \sin t - t(2 \sin \frac{t}{2})^2 - (2 \sinh \frac{\sigma}{2})^2 t$ times a positive function. This derivative is always negative for $0 < t \le 2\pi$, because it is less than $t^2 \sin t - t(2 \sin \frac{t}{2})^2 = 8u \sin u \cos u (u - \tan u)$ where $t = 2u$.

Let $s = 2 \sinh \frac{\sigma}{2}$. When $\sigma \ge \pi$ and $2\pi \le t \le 4\pi$, the derivative is still negative, because we have $t \le 4\pi \le s^2 - \sigma^2/(2\pi) \le s^2 - \sigma^2/t$. Similarly, when $\sigma \ge 2\pi$ the derivative remains negative for $4\pi \le t \le 168\pi$; the proof gets easier and easier.

(b) Let $t = u\sigma/\sqrt{N}$. Then (41) and (42) prove that

$$\int_{-\tau}^{\tau} e^{(n+1)g(\sigma+it)}\, dt =$$

$$\frac{(e^\sigma - 1)^m}{\sigma^n \sqrt{N}} \int_{-N^\epsilon}^{N^\epsilon} \exp\left(-\frac{u^2}{2} + \frac{(-iu)^3 a_3}{N^{1/2}} + \dots + \frac{(-iu)^l a_l}{N^{l/2-1}} + O(N^{(l+1)\epsilon - (l-1)/2})\right) du,$$

where $(1 - \beta)a_k$ is a polynomial of degree $k - 1$ in α and β, with $0 \le a_k \le 2/k$. (For example, $6a_3 = (2 - \beta(\alpha + \beta))/(1 - \beta)$ and $24a_4 = (6 - \beta(\alpha^2 + 4\alpha\beta + \beta^2))/(1 - \beta)$.) The monotonicity of the integrand shows that the integral over the rest of the range is negligible. Now trade tails, extend the integral over $-\infty < u < \infty$, and use the formula of answer 44 with $c_k = 2^{k/2} a_k$ to define $b_1, b_2, \dots$.

(c) We will prove that $|e^z - 1|^m \sigma^{n+1}/((e^\sigma - 1)^m |z|^{n+1})$ is exponentially small on those three paths. If $\sigma \le 1$, this quantity is less than $1/(2\pi)^{n+1}$ (because, for example, $e^\sigma - 1 > \sigma$). If $\sigma > 1$, we have $\sigma < 2|z|$ and $|e^z - 1| \le e^\sigma - 1$.

59. In this extreme case, $\alpha = 1 + n^{-1}$ and $\beta = 1 - n^{-1} + \frac{2}{3}n^{-2} + O(n^{-3})$; hence $N = 1 + \frac{1}{3}n^{-1} + O(n^{-2})$. The leading term $\beta^{-n}/\sqrt{2\pi N}$ is $e/\sqrt{2\pi}$ times $1 - \frac{1}{3}n^{-1} + O(n^{-2})$. (Notice that $e/\sqrt{2\pi} \approx 1.0844$.) The quantity a_k in answer 58(b) turns out to be $1/k + O(n^{-1})$. So the correction terms, to first order, are

$$\frac{b_j}{N^j} = [z^j] \exp\left(-\sum_{k=1}^{\infty} \frac{B_{2k} z^{2k-1}}{2k(2k-1)}\right) + O\left(\frac{1}{n}\right),$$

namely the terms in the (divergent) series corresponding to Stirling's approximation

$$\frac{1}{1!} \sim \frac{e}{\sqrt{2\pi}}\left(1 - \frac{1}{12} + \frac{1}{288} + \frac{139}{51840} - \frac{571}{2488320} - \dots\right).$$

60. (a) The number of m-ary strings of length n in which all m digits appear is $m!\,\genfrac{\{}{\}}{0pt}{}{n}{m}$, and the inclusion-exclusion principle expresses this quantity as $\binom{m}{0}m^n - \binom{m}{1}(m-1)^n + \dots$. Now see exercise 7.2.1.4–37.

(b) We have $(m-1)^n/(m-1)! = (m^n/m!)m\exp(n\ln(1-1/m))$, and $\ln(1-1/m)$ is less than $-n^{\epsilon-1}$.

(c) In this case $\alpha > n^{\epsilon}$ and $\beta = \alpha e^{-\alpha}e^{\beta} < \alpha e^{1-\alpha}$. Therefore $1 < (1-\beta/\alpha)^{m-n} < \exp(nO(e^{-\alpha}))$; and $1 > e^{-\beta m} = e^{-(n+1)\beta/\alpha} > \exp(-nO(e^{-\alpha}))$. So (45) becomes $(m^n/m!)(1+O(n^{-1})+O(ne^{-n^{\epsilon}}))$.

61. Now $\alpha = 1 + \frac{r}{n} + O(n^{2\epsilon-2})$ and $\beta = 1 - \frac{r}{n} + O(n^{2\epsilon-2})$. Thus $N = r+O(n^{2\epsilon-1})$, and the case $l = 0$ of Eq. (43) reduces to

$$n^r \left(\frac{n}{2}\right)^r \frac{e^r}{r^r\sqrt{2\pi r}}\left(1+O(n^{2\epsilon-1})+O\left(\frac{1}{r}\right)\right).$$

(This approximation meshes well with identities such as $\left\{{n\atop n-1}\right\} = \binom{n}{2}$ and $\left\{{n\atop n-2}\right\} = 2\binom{n}{4} + \binom{n+1}{4}$; indeed, we have

$$\left\{{n\atop n-r}\right\} = \frac{n^{2r}}{2^r r!}\left(1+O\left(\frac{1}{n}\right)\right) \qquad \text{as } n\to\infty$$

when r is constant, according to formulas (6.42) and (6.43) of *CMath*.)

62. The assertion is true for $1 \le n \le 10000$ (with $m = \lfloor e^{\xi}-1\rfloor$ in 5648 of those cases). E. R. Canfield and C. Pomerance, in a paper that nicely surveys previous work on related problems, have shown that the statement holds for all sufficiently large n, and that the maximum occurs in *both* cases only if $e^{\xi} \bmod 1$ is extremely close to $\frac{1}{2}$. [*Integers* **2** (2002), A1:1–A1:13; **5** (2005), A9:1.]

63. (a) The result holds when $p_1 = \cdots = p_n = p$, because $a_{k-1}/a_k = (k/(n+1-k)) \times ((n-\mu)/\mu) \le (n-\mu)/(n+1-\mu) < 1$. It is also true by induction when $p_n = 0$ or 1. For the general case, consider the minimum of $a_k - a_{k-1}$ over all choices of $(p_1,\ldots,p_n)$ with $p_1 + \cdots + p_n = \mu$: If $0 < p_1 < p_2 < 1$, let $p_1' = p_1 - \delta$ and $p_2' = p_2 + \delta$, and notice that $a_k' - a_{k-1}' = a_k - a_{k-1} + \delta(p_1 - p_2 - \delta)\alpha$ for some α depending only on $p_3,\ldots,p_n$. At a minimum point we must have $\alpha = 0$; thus we can choose δ so that either $p_1' = 0$ or $p_2'=1$. The minimum can therefore be achieved when all p_j have one of three values $\{0,1,p\}$. But we have proved that $a_k - a_{k-1} > 0$ in such cases.

(b) Changing each p_j to $1 - p_j$ changes μ to $n - \mu$ and a_k to a_{n-k}.

(c) No roots of $f(x)$ are positive. Hence $f(z)/f(1)$ has the form in (a) and (b).

(d) Let $C(f)$ be the number of sign changes in the sequence of coefficients of f; we want to show that $C((1-x)^2 f) = 2$. In fact, $C((1-x)^m f) = m$ for all $m \ge 0$. For $C((1-x)^m) = m$, and $C((a+bx)f) \le C(f)$ when a and b are positive; hence $C((1-x)^m f) \le m$. And if $f(x)$ is any nonzero polynomial whatsoever, $C((1-x)f) > C(f)$; hence $C((1-x)^m f) \ge m$.

(e) Since $\sum_k \left[{n\atop k}\right]x^k = x(x+1)\ldots(x+n-1)$, part (c) applies directly with $\mu = H_n$. And for the polynomials $f_n(x) = \sum_k \left\{{n\atop k}\right\}x^k$, we can use part (c) with $\mu = \varpi_{n+1}/\varpi_n - 1$, if $f_n(x)$ has n real roots. The latter statement follows by induction because $f_{n+1}(x) = x(f_n(x) + f_n'(x))$: If $a > 0$ and if $f(x)$ has n real roots, so does the function $g(x) = e^{ax}f(x)$. And $g(x) \to 0$ as $x \to -\infty$; hence $g'(x) = e^{ax}(af(x) + f'(x))$ also has n real roots (namely, one at the far left, and $n-1$ between the roots of $g(x)$).

[See E. Laguerre, *J. de Math.* (3) **9** (1883), 99–146; W. Hoeffding, *Annals Math. Stat.* **27** (1956), 713–721; J. N. Darroch, *Annals Math. Stat.* **35** (1964), 1317–1321; J. Pitman, *J. Combinatorial Theory* **A77** (1997), 279–303.]

64. We need only use computer algebra to subtract $\ln \varpi_n$ from $\ln \varpi_{n-k}$.

65. It is ϖ_n^{-1} times the number of occurrences of k-blocks plus the number of occurrences of ordered pairs of k-blocks in the list of all set partitions, namely $\left(\binom{n}{k}\varpi_{n-k} + \binom{n}{k}\binom{n-k}{k}\varpi_{n-2k}\right)/\varpi_n$, minus the square of (49). Asymptotically, $(\xi^k/k!)(1+O(n^{4\xi-1}))$.

66. (The maximum of (48) when $n = 100$ is achieved only for the three partitions $7^1 6^2 5^4 4^6 3^7 2^6 1^4$, $7^1 6^2 5^4 4^6 3^8 2^5 1^3$, $7^1 6^2 5^4 4^7 3^6 2^6 1^3$.)

67. The expected value of M^k is ϖ_{n+k}/ϖ_n. By (50), the mean is therefore $\varpi_{n+1}/\varpi_n = n/\xi + \xi/(2(\xi+1)^2) + O(n^{-1})$, and the variance is

$$\frac{\varpi_{n+2}}{\varpi_n} - \frac{\varpi_{n+1}^2}{\varpi_n^2} = \left(\frac{n}{\xi}\right)^2 \left(1 + \frac{\xi(2\xi+1)}{(\xi+1)^2 n} - 1 - \frac{\xi^2}{(\xi+1)^2 n} + O\left(\frac{1}{n^2}\right)\right) = \frac{n}{\xi(\xi+1)} + O(1).$$

68. The maximum number of nonzero components in all parts of a partition is $n = n_1 + \cdots + n_m$; it occurs if and only if all component parts are 0 or 1. Then the values of $l + 1 = n$ and $b = mn_1 + (m-1)n_2 + \cdots + n_m$ reach their maximum. [Thus it's best to choose names of the multiset elements so that $n_1 \le n_2 \le \cdots \le n_m$.]

69. At the beginning of step M3, if $k > b$ and $l = r - 1$, go to M5. In step M5, if $j = a$ and $(v_j - 1)(r - l) < u_j$, go to M6 instead of decreasing v_j.

70. (a) $\left|{n-1 \atop r-1}\right| + \left|{n-2 \atop r-1}\right| + \cdots + \left|{r-1 \atop r-1}\right|$, since $\left|{n-k \atop r-1}\right|$ contain the block $\{0, \ldots, 0, 1\}$ with k 0s. The total, also known as $p(n-1, 1)$, is $p(n-1) + \cdots + p(1) + p(0)$.

(b) Exactly $N = \left\{{n-1 \atop r}\right\} + \left\{{n-2 \atop r-2}\right\}$ of the r-block partitions of $\{1, \ldots, n-1, n\}$ are the same if we interchange $n-1 \leftrightarrow n$. So the answer is $N + \frac{1}{2}(\{{n \atop r}\} - N) = \frac{1}{2}(\{{n \atop r}\} + N)$, which is also the number of restricted growth strings $a_1 \ldots a_n$ with $\max(a_1, \ldots, a_n) = r - 1$ and $a_{n-1} \le a_n$. And the total is $\frac{1}{2}(\varpi_n + \varpi_{n-1} + \varpi_{n-2})$.

71. $\lfloor \frac{1}{2}(n_1+1) \ldots (n_m+1) - \frac{1}{2} \rfloor$, because there are $(n_1+1) \ldots (n_m+1) - 2$ compositions into two parts, and half of those compositions fail to be in lexicographic order unless all n_j are even. (See exercise 7.2.1.4–31. Formulas for up to 5 parts have been worked out by E. M. Wright, *Proc. London Math. Soc.* (3) **11** (1961), 499–510.)

72. Yes. The following algorithm computes $a_{jk} = p(j, k)$ for $0 \le j, k \le n$ in $\Theta(n^4)$ steps: Start with $a_{jk} \leftarrow 1$ for all j and k. Then for $l = 0, 1, \ldots, n$ and $m = 0, 1, \ldots, n$ (in any order), if $l + m > 1$ set $a_{jk} \leftarrow a_{jk} + a_{(j-l)(k-m)}$ for $j = l, \ldots, n$ and $k = m, \ldots, n$ (in increasing order).

(See Table A–1. A similar method computes $p(n_1, \ldots, n_m)$ in $O(n_1 \ldots n_m)^2$ steps. Cheema and Motzkin, in the cited paper, have derived the recurrence relation

$$n_1 p(n_1, \ldots, n_m) = \sum_{l=1}^{\infty} \sum_{k_1, \ldots, k_m \ge 0} k_1 p(n_1 - k_1 l, \ldots, n_m - k_m l),$$

but this interesting formula is helpful for computation only in certain cases.)

Table A–1
MULTIPARTITION NUMBERS

n	0	1	2	3	4	5	6	n	0	1	2	3	4	5
$p(0,n)$	1	1	2	3	5	7	11	$P(0,n)$	1	2	9	66	712	10457
$p(1,n)$	1	2	4	7	12	19	30	$P(1,n)$	1	4	26	249	3274	56135
$p(2,n)$	2	4	9	16	29	47	77	$P(2,n)$	2	11	92	1075	16601	325269
$p(3,n)$	3	7	16	31	57	97	162	$P(3,n)$	5	36	371	5133	91226	2014321
$p(4,n)$	5	12	29	57	109	189	323	$P(4,n)$	15	135	1663	26683	537813	13241402
$p(5,n)$	7	19	47	97	189	339	589	$P(5,n)$	52	566	8155	149410	3376696	91914202

73. Yes. Let $P(m,n) = p(1,\ldots,1,2,\ldots,2)$ when there are m 1s and n 2s; then $P(m,0) = \varpi_m$, and we can use the recurrence

$$2P(m,n+1) = P(m+2,n) + P(m+1,n) + \sum_k \binom{n}{k} P(m,k).$$

This recurrence can be proved by considering what happens when we replace a pair of x's in the multiset for $P(m,n+1)$ by two distinct elements x and x'. We get $2P(m,n+1)$ partitions, representing $P(m+2,n)$, except in the $P(m+1,n)$ cases where x and x' belong to the same block, or in $\binom{n}{k}P(m,n-k)$ cases where the blocks containing x and x' are identical and have k additional elements.

Notes: See Table A–1. Another recurrence, less useful for computation, is

$$P(m+1,n) = \sum_{j,k} \binom{n}{k}\binom{n-k+m}{j} P(j,k).$$

The sequence $P(0,n)$ was first investigated by E. K. Lloyd, *Proc. Cambridge Philos. Soc.* **103** (1988), 277–284, and by G. Labelle, *Discrete Math.* **217** (2000), 237–248, who computed it by completely different methods. Exercise 70(b) showed that $P(m,1) = (\varpi_m + \varpi_{m+1} + \varpi_{m+2})/2$; in general $P(m,n)$ can be written in the umbral notation $\varpi^m q_n(\varpi)$, where $q_n(x)$ is a polynomial of degree $2n$ defined by the generating function $\sum_{n=0}^\infty q_n(x) z^n/n! = \exp((e^z + (x+x^2)z - 1)/2)$. Thus, by exercise 31,

$$\sum_{n=0}^\infty P(m,n)\frac{z^n}{n!} = e^{(e^z-1)/2} \sum_{k=0}^\infty \frac{\varpi_{(2k+m+1)(k+m+1)}}{2^k} \frac{z^k}{k!}.$$

Labelle proved, as a special case of much more general results, that the number of partitions of $\{1,1,\ldots,n,n\}$ into exactly r blocks is

$$n!\,[x^r z^n]\,e^{-x+x^2(e^z-1)/2} \sum_{k=0}^\infty e^{zk(k+1)/2}\frac{x^k}{k!}.$$

75. The saddle point method yields $Ce^{An^{2/3}+Bn^{1/3}}/n^{55/36}$, where $A = 3\zeta(3)^{1/3}$, $B = \pi^2\zeta(3)^{-1/3}/2$, and $C = \zeta(3)^{19/36}(2\pi)^{-5/6}3^{-1/2}\exp(1/3 + B^2/4 + \zeta'(2)/(2\pi^2) - \gamma/12)$. [F. C. Auluck, *Proc. Cambridge Philos. Soc.* **49** (1953), 72–83; E. M. Wright, *American J. Math.* **80** (1958), 643–658.]

76. Using the fact that $p(n_1,n_2,n_3,\ldots) \geq p(n_1+n_2,n_3,\ldots)$, hence $P(m+2,n) \geq P(m,n+1)$, one can prove by induction that $P(m,n+1) \geq (m+n+1)P(m,n)$. Thus

$$2P(m,n) \leq P(m+2,n-1) + P(m+1,n-1) + eP(m,n-1).$$

Iterating this inequality shows that $2^n P(0,n) = (\varpi^2 + \varpi)^n + O(n(\varpi^2+\varpi)^{n-1}) = (n\varpi_{2n-1}+\varpi_{2n})(1+O((\log n)^3/n))$. (A more precise asymptotic formula can be obtained from the generating function in the answer to exercise 73.)

78. 3 3 3 3 2 1 0 0 0
1 0 0 0 2 2 3 2 0   (because the encoded partitions
2 2 1 0 0 2 1 0 2   must all be (000000000))
2 1 0 2 2 0 0 1 3

79. There are 432 such cycles. But they yield only 304 different cycles of set partitions, since different cycles might describe the same sequence of partitions. For example, (000012022332321) and (000012022112123) are partitionwise equivalent.

80. [See F. Chung, P. Diaconis, and R. Graham, *Discrete Mathematics* **110** (1992), 52–55.] Construct a digraph with ϖ_{n-1} vertices and ϖ_n arcs; each restricted growth string $a_1 \ldots a_n$ defines an arc from vertex $a_1 \ldots a_{n-1}$ to vertex $\rho(a_2 \ldots a_n)$, where ρ is the function of exercise 4. (For example, arc 01001213 runs from 0100121 to 0110203.) Every universal cycle defines an Eulerian trail in this digraph; conversely, every Eulerian trail can be used to define one or more universal sequences of restricted growth on the elements $\{0, 1, \ldots, n-1\}$.

An Eulerian trail exists by the method of Section 2.3.4.2, if we let the last exit from every nonzero vertex $a_1 \ldots a_{n-1}$ be through arc $a_1 \ldots a_{n-1}a_{n-1}$. The sequence might not be cyclic, however. For example, no universal cycle exists when $n < 4$; and when $n = 4$ the universal sequence 000012030110100222 defines a cycle of set partitions that does not correspond to any universal cycle.

The existence of a cycle can be proved for $n \geq 6$ if we start with an Eulerian trail that begins $0^n xyx^{n-3}u(uv)^{\lfloor (n-2)/2 \rfloor}u^{[n \text{ odd}]}$ for some distinct elements $\{u, v, x, y\}$. This pattern is possible if we alter the last exit of $0^k 121^{n-3-k}$ from $0^{k-1}121^{n-2-k}$ to $0^{k-1}121^{n-3-k}2$ for $2 \leq k \leq n-4$, and let the last exits of 0121^{n-4} and $01^{n-3}2$ be respectively $010^{n-4}1$ and $0^{n-3}10$. Now if we choose numbers of the cycle *backwards*, thereby determining u and v, we can let x and y be the smallest elements distinct from $\{0, u, v\}$.

We can conclude in fact that the number of universal cycles having this extremely special type is huge — at least

$$\left(\prod_{k=2}^{n-1} (k!\, (n-k))^{\{ {n-1 \atop k} \}} \right) \Big/ \left((n-1)!\, (n-2)^3 3^{2n-5} 2^2 \right), \qquad \text{when } n \geq 6.$$

Yet none of them are known to be readily decodable. See below for the case $n = 5$.

81. Noting that $\varpi_5 = 52$, we use a universal cycle for $\{1, 2, 3, 4, 5\}$ in which the elements are 13 clubs, 13 diamonds, 13 hearts, 12 spades, and a joker. One such cycle, found by trial and error using Eulerian trails as in the previous answer, is

$$(\spadesuit\spadesuit\spadesuit\spadesuit\spadesuit\spadesuit\diamondsuit\diamondsuit\heartsuit\text{J}\spadesuit\diamondsuit\heartsuit\diamondsuit\heartsuit\spadesuit\clubsuit\spadesuit\diamondsuit\clubsuit\spadesuit\diamondsuit\diamondsuit\clubsuit\heartsuit\spadesuit\heartsuit\diamondsuit\spadesuit\clubsuit\spadesuit\clubsuit\diamondsuit\spadesuit\diamondsuit\diamondsuit\clubsuit\diamondsuit\spadesuit\spadesuit\heartsuit\diamondsuit\heartsuit\heartsuit\heartsuit\spadesuit\diamondsuit\heartsuit\heartsuit\spadesuit\spadesuit\diamondsuit\diamondsuit).$$

(In fact, there are essentially 114,056 such cycles if we branch to $a_k = a_{k-1}$ as a last resort and if we introduce the joker as soon as possible.) The trick still works with probability $\frac{47}{52}$ if we call the joker a spade.

82. There are 13644 solutions, although this number reduces to 1981 if we regard

$$\boxed{} \equiv \boxed{} \equiv \boxed{}, \quad \boxed{} \equiv \boxed{}, \quad \boxed{} \equiv \boxed{}.$$

The smallest common sum is $5/2$, and the largest is $25/2$; the remarkable solution

$$\boxed{} + \boxed{} + \boxed{} + \boxed{} + \boxed{} = \boxed{} + \boxed{} + \boxed{} + \boxed{} + \boxed{} = \boxed{} + \boxed{} + \boxed{} + \boxed{} + \boxed{}$$

is one of only two essentially distinct ways to get the common sum 118/15. [The special cases with common sums $5/2$ and 10 had been noticed earlier by H. E. Dudeney in *Strand* **68** (1924), 422, 530.]

SECTION 7.2.1.6

1. It could "see" a left parenthesis at the left of every internal node and a right parenthesis at the bottom of every internal node. Alternatively, it could associate right parentheses with the *external* nodes that it encounters—except for the very last □; see exercise 20.

2. Z1. [Initialize.] Set $z_k \leftarrow 2k - 1$ for $0 \le k \le n$. (Assume that $n \ge 2$.)

   Z2. [Visit.] Visit the tree-combination $z_1 z_2 \ldots z_n$.

   Z3. [Easy case?] If $z_{n-1} < z_n - 1$, set $z_n \leftarrow z_n - 1$ and return to Z2.

   Z4. [Find j.] Set $j \leftarrow n-1$ and $z_n \leftarrow 2n-1$. While $z_{j-1} = z_j - 1$, set $z_j \leftarrow 2j - 1$ and $j \leftarrow j - 1$.

   Z5. [Decrease z_j.] Terminate the algorithm if $j = 1$. Otherwise set $z_j \leftarrow z_j - 1$ and go back to Z2. ▮

3. Label the nodes of the forest in preorder. The first $z_k - 1$ elements of $a_1 \ldots a_{2n}$ contain $k - 1$ left parentheses and $z_k - k$ right parentheses. So there is an excess of $2k-1-z_k$ left parentheses over right parentheses when the "worm" first reaches node k; and $2k - 1 - z_k$ is the level (or depth) of that node.

Let $q_1 \ldots q_n$ be the inverse of $p_1 \ldots p_n$, so that node k is the q_kth node in postorder. Since k occurs to the left of j in $p_1 \ldots p_n$ if and only if $q_k < q_j$, we see that c_k is the number of nodes j that precede k in preorder but follow it in postorder, namely the number of proper ancestors of k; again, this is the level of k.

Alternative proof: We can also show that both sequences $z_1 \ldots z_n$ and $c_1 \ldots c_n$ have essentially the same recursive structure as (5): $Z_{pq} = (Z_{p(q-1)} + 1^p)$, $1(Z_{(p-1)q} + 1^{p-1})$ when $0 \le p \le q$; and $C_{pq} = C_{p(q-1)}$, $(q-p)C_{(p-1)q}$. (Consider the mate of the last, next-to-last, etc., left parenthesis.)

Incidentally, the formula '$c_{k+1} + d_k = c_k + 1$' is equivalent to (11).

4. Almost true; but $d_1 \ldots d_n$ and $z_1 \ldots z_n$ occur in *decreasing* order, while $p_1 \ldots p_n$ and $c_1 \ldots c_n$ are increasing. (This lexicographic property for a sequence of permutations $p_1 \ldots p_n$ is not automatically inherited from lexicographic order of the corresponding inversion tables $c_1 \ldots c_n$; but the result does hold for this particular class of $p_1 \ldots p_n$.)

5. $d_1 \ldots d_{15} = 0\,2\,0\,0\,2\,0\,0\,1\,0\,3\,2\,0\,1\,0\,4$; $z_1 \ldots z_{15} = 1\,2\,5\,6\,7\,10\,11\,12\,14\,15\,19\,22\,23\,25\,26$; $p_1 \ldots p_{15} = 2\,1\,5\,4\,8\,10\,9\,7\,11\,6\,13\,15\,14\,12\,3$; $c_1 \ldots c_{15} = 0\,1\,0\,1\,2\,1\,2\,3\,3\,4\,2\,1\,2\,2\,3$.

6. Match up the parentheses as usual; then simply curl the string up and around until a_{2n} becomes adjacent to a_1, and notice that the distinction between left and right parentheses can be reconstructed from the context. Letting a_1 correspond to the bottom of the circle, as in Table 1, yields the diagram shown. [A. Errera, *Mémoires de la Classe Sci. 8°*, *Acad. Royale de Belgique* (2) **11**, 6 (1931), 26 pp.]

7. (a) It equals $))()\ldots()$; setting $a_1 \leftarrow$ '(' will restore the initial string. (b) The initial binary tree (from step B1) will have been restored, except that $l_n = n + 1$.

8. $l_1 \ldots l_{15} = 2\,0\,4\,5\,0\,7\,8\,0\,10\,0\,0\,13\,0\,15\,0$; $r_1 \ldots r_{15} = 3\,0\,0\,6\,0\,12\,11\,9\,0\,0\,0\,0\,14\,0\,0$; $e_1 \ldots e_{15} = 1\,0\,3\,1\,0\,2\,2\,0\,1\,0\,0\,2\,0\,1\,0$; $s_1 \ldots s_{15} = 1\,0\,1\,2\,1\,0\,5\,3\,0\,1\,0\,0\,3\,0\,1\,0$.

9. Node j is a (proper) ancestor of node k if and only if $j < k$ and $s_j + j \ge k$. (As a consequence, we have $c_1 + \cdots + c_n = s_1 + \cdots + s_n$.)

10. If j is the index z_k of the kth left parenthesis, we have $w_j = c_k + 1$ and $w_{j'} = c_k$, where j' is the index of the matching right parenthesis.

11. Swap left and right parentheses in $a_{2n} \ldots a_1$ to get the mirror image of $a_1 \ldots a_{2n}$.

12. The mirror reflection of (4) corresponds to the forest

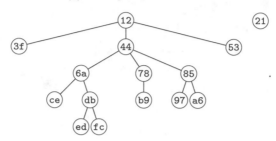

But the significance of transposition is clearer, forest-wise, if we draw right-sibling and left-child links horizontally and vertically, then do a matrix-like transposition:

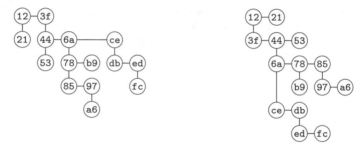

13. (a) By induction on the number of nodes, we have $\mathrm{preorder}(F^R) = \mathrm{postorder}(F)^R$ and $\mathrm{postorder}(F^R) = \mathrm{preorder}(F)^R$.

(b) Let F correspond to the binary tree B; then $\mathrm{preorder}(F) = \mathrm{preorder}(B)$ and $\mathrm{postorder}(F) = \mathrm{inorder}(B)$, as noted after 2.3.2–(6). Therefore $\mathrm{preorder}(F^T) = \mathrm{preorder}(B^R) = \mathrm{postorder}(B)^R$ has no simple relationship to either $\mathrm{preorder}(F)$ or $\mathrm{postorder}(F)$. But $\mathrm{postorder}(F^T) = \mathrm{inorder}(B^R) = \mathrm{inorder}(B)^R = \mathrm{postorder}(F)^R$.

14. According to answer 13, $\mathrm{postorder}(F^{RT}) = \mathrm{preorder}(F) = \mathrm{preorder}(B)$ when F corresponds naturally to B; and $\mathrm{postorder}(F^{TR}) = \mathrm{preorder}(F^T)^R = \mathrm{postorder}(B)$. Therefore the equation $F^{RT} = F^{TR}$ holds if and only if F has at most one node.

15. If F^R corresponds naturally to the binary tree B', the root of B' is the root of F's rightmost tree. The left link of node x in B' is to the leftmost child of x in F^R, which is the rightmost child of x in F; similarly, the right link is to x's left sibling in F.

Note: Since B corresponds naturally to F^{RT}, answer 13 tells us that $\mathrm{inorder}(B) = \mathrm{postorder}(F^{RT}) = \mathrm{postorder}(F^R)^R = \mathrm{preorder}(F)$.

16. The forest $F \mid G$ is obtained by placing the trees of F below the first node of G in postorder. Associativity follows because $F \mid (G \mid H) = (H^T G^T F^T)^T = (F \mid G) \mid H$. Notice, incidentally, that $\mathrm{postorder}(F \mid G) = \mathrm{postorder}(F)\,\mathrm{postorder}(G)$, and that $F \mid (GH) = (F \mid G)H$ when G is nonnull.

17. Any nonnull forest can be written $F = (G \mid \cdot)H$, where $\cdot$ denotes the 1-node forest; then $F^R = H^R(G^R \mid \cdot)$ and $F^T = (H^T \mid \cdot)G^T$. In particular we cannot have $F^R = F^T$ unless H is the null forest Λ, since the first tree of H^R can't be $H^T \mid \cdot$; and G must then also be Λ. Furthermore $F = F^T$ if and only if $G = H^T$. In that case we cannot also have $F^R = F^{RT}$ unless $G = \Lambda$; the first tree of G^{TR} would otherwise have more nodes than G itself.

It appears to be true that we cannot have $F^{RT} = F^{TR}$ unless $F = F^R$. Under that assumption, $F^{RT} = F^{TR}$ if and only if F and F^T are both self-conjugate. David Callan has discovered two infinite families of such forests, with parameters $i, j, k \geq 0$:

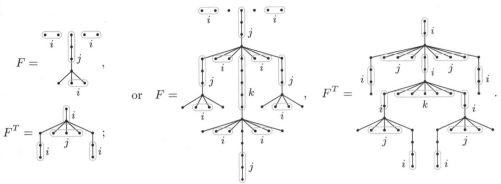

(In these examples, $i = 2$, $j = 3$, and $k = 5$.) Are there any other cases?

18. The $C_{15} = 9{,}694{,}845$ forests are partitioned into 20,982 classes. The largest is a cycle of length 58,968, one of whose elements is $((\,)(\,)((\,)))(\,)()((\,)((\,))()()())()$. The shortest are six two-element classes (corresponding to exercise 17), consisting of

$$()()()()()()()()()()()(), \qquad ()()()()(((\,))()()()()))()()(),$$
$$()()()(((((()()()())))))()()(), \qquad ()()(((((((()()()()))))))))()(),$$
$$()(((\,))(((((\,))())()))((\,()))(), \qquad ()((((((((((\,)))))))))))()(),$$

and their transposes. The somewhat strange strings $((((((\,()))))))()()()()()()()$, $()()()()()()((((((\,())))))))$, and $((((((\,()()()()()()()())))))))$ each have wedge-shaped binary trees and form a unique class of size 3. The path that runs from $()(((()(()()))(()((())())))()$ to $(((()())(()())(())(()())(()())()$ has 3120 elements, one of which is (2). According to the conjecture in answer 17, the shortest possible cycle has length 6; when $n = 15$ there are 66 such cycles. (The next-shortest cycle, which is unique, has length 10 and includes $()(()()()())()((((())()))((())).)$

19. The transformation from F_j to F_{j+1} by Algorithm P can be paraphrased as follows: "Find the last node in preorder, say x, that has a left sibling, say y. Remove x from its family and make it the new rightmost child of y. And if $x < n$, change all of x's descendants $x + 1$, ..., n into trivial one-node trees."

The transformation that takes F_j^R into F_{j+1}^R can therefore be stated as follows, if we recall that the kth node of F_j in preorder is the kth-from-last node of F_j^R in postorder: "Find the first node in postorder, say x, that has a right sibling, say y. Remove x from its family and make it the new leftmost child of y. And if $x > 1$, change all of x's descendants $x - 1$, ..., 1 into trivial one-node trees."

Similarly, we can paraphrase the transformation from G_j to G_{j+1} that is specified by Algorithm B: "Find j, the root of the leftmost nontrivial tree; then find k, its rightmost child. Remove k and its descendants from j's family, and insert them between j and j's right sibling. Finally, if $j > 1$, make j and its right siblings all children of $j - 1$, and $j - 1$ a child of $j - 2$, etc."

When this transformation changes the left-sibling/right-child representation from G_j^{RT} to G_{j+1}^{RT} (see exercise 15), it turns out to be identical to the transformation that takes F_j^R to F_{j+1}^R in the left-child/right-sibling representation. Therefore $G_j^{RT} = F_j^R$, because this identity clearly holds when $j = 1$.

(It follows that the sequence of tables $e_1 \ldots e_{n-1}$ for the binary trees generated by Algorithm B is exactly the sequence of tables $d_{n-1} \ldots d_1$ for the parenthesis strings generated by Algorithm P; this phenomenon is illustrated in Tables 1 and 2.)

Several symmetries between lists of forests have been explored by M. C. Er in *Comp. J.* **32** (1989), 76–85.

20. (a) This assertion, which generalizes Lemma 2.3.1P, is readily proved by induction.

(b) The following procedure is, in fact, almost identical to Algorithm P:

T1. [Initialize.] Set $b_{3k-2} \leftarrow 3$ and $b_{3k-1} \leftarrow b_{3k} \leftarrow 0$ for $1 \leq k \leq n$; also set $b_0 \leftarrow b_N \leftarrow 0$ and $m \leftarrow N - 3$, where $N = 3n + 1$.

T2. [Visit.] Visit $b_1 \ldots b_N$. (Now $b_m = 3$ and $b_{m+1} \ldots b_N = 0 \ldots 0$.)

T3. [Easy case?] Set $b_m \leftarrow 0$. If $b_{m-1} = 0$, set $b_{m-1} \leftarrow 3$, $m \leftarrow m - 1$, and go to T2.

T4. [Find j.] Set $j \leftarrow m - 1$ and $k \leftarrow N - 3$. While $b_j = 3$, set $b_j \leftarrow 0$, $b_k \leftarrow 3$, $j \leftarrow j - 1$, and $k \leftarrow k - 3$.

T5. [Increase b_j.] Terminate the algorithm if $j = 0$. Otherwise set $b_j \leftarrow 3$, $m \leftarrow N - 3$, and return to T2. ∎

[See S. Zaks, *Theoretical Comp. Sci.* **10** (1980), 63–82. In that article, Zaks pointed out that it is even easier to generate the sequence $z_1 \ldots z_n$ of indices j such that $b_j = 3$, using an algorithm virtually identical to the answer to exercise 2, because a valid ternary tree combination $z_1 \ldots z_n$ is characterized by the inequalities $z_{k-1} < z_k \leq 3k - 2$.]

21. For this problem we can essentially combine Algorithm P with Algorithm 7.2.1.2L. We shall assume for convenience that $n_t > 0$ and $n_1 + \cdots + n_t > 1$.

G1. [Initialize.] Set $l \leftarrow N$. Then for $j = t, \ldots, 2, 1$ (in this order), do the following operations n_j times: Set $b_{l-j} \leftarrow j$, $b_{l-j+1} \leftarrow \cdots \leftarrow b_{l-1} \leftarrow 0$, and $l \leftarrow l - j$. Finally set $b_0 \leftarrow b_N \leftarrow c_0 \leftarrow 0$ and $m \leftarrow N - t$.

G2. [Visit.] Visit $b_1 \ldots b_N$. (At this point $b_m > 0$ and $b_{m+1} = \cdots = b_N = 0$.)

G3. [Easy case?] If $b_{m-1} = 0$, set $b_{m-1} \leftarrow b_m$, $b_m \leftarrow 0$, $m \leftarrow m - 1$, and return to G2.

G4. [Find j.] Set $c_1 \leftarrow b_m$, $b_m \leftarrow 0$, $j \leftarrow m - 1$, and $k \leftarrow 1$. While $b_j \geq c_k$, set $k \leftarrow k + 1$, $c_k \leftarrow b_j$, $b_j \leftarrow 0$, and $j \leftarrow j - 1$.

G5. [Increase b_j.] If $b_j > 0$, find the smallest $l \geq 1$ such that $b_j < c_l$, and interchange $b_j \leftrightarrow c_l$. Otherwise, if $j > 0$, set $b_j \leftarrow c_1$ and $c_1 \leftarrow 0$. Otherwise terminate.

G6. [Reverse and spread out.] Set $j \leftarrow k$ and $l \leftarrow N$. While $c_j > 0$, set $b_{l-c_j} \leftarrow c_j$, $l \leftarrow l - c_j$, and $j \leftarrow j - 1$. Then set $m \leftarrow N - c_k$ and go back to G2. ∎

This algorithm assumes that $N > n_1 + 2n_2 + \cdots + tn_t$. [See *SICOMP* **8** (1979), 73–81.]

22. Note first that d_1 can be increased if and only if $r_1 = 0$ in the linked representation. Otherwise the successor of $d_1 \ldots d_{n-1}$ is obtained by finding the smallest j with $d_j > 0$ and setting $d_j \leftarrow 0$, $d_{j+1} \leftarrow d_{j+1} + 1$. We may assume that $n > 2$.

K1. [Initialize.] Set $l_k \leftarrow k + 1$ and $r_k \leftarrow 0$ for $1 \leq k < n$; also set $l_n \leftarrow r_n \leftarrow 0$.

K2. [Visit.] Visit the binary tree represented by $l_1 l_2 \ldots l_n$ and $r_1 r_2 \ldots r_n$.

K3. [Easy cases?] Set $y \leftarrow r_1$. If $y = 0$, set $r_1 \leftarrow 2$, $l_1 \leftarrow 0$, and return to K2. Otherwise if $l_1 = 0$, set $l_1 \leftarrow 2$, $r_1 \leftarrow r_2$, $r_2 \leftarrow l_2$, $l_2 \leftarrow 0$, and return to K2. Otherwise set $j \leftarrow 2$ and $k \leftarrow 1$.

K4. [Find j and k.] If $r_j > 0$, set $k \leftarrow j$ and $y \leftarrow r_j$. Then if $j \neq y - 1$, set $j \leftarrow j + 1$ and repeat this step.

K5. [Shuffle subtrees.] Set $l_j \leftarrow y$, $r_j \leftarrow r_y$, $r_y \leftarrow l_y$, and $l_y \leftarrow 0$. If $j = k$, go to K2.

K6. [Shift subtrees.] Terminate if $y = n$. Otherwise, while $k > 1$, set $k \leftarrow k - 1$, $j \leftarrow j - 1$, and $r_j \leftarrow r_k$. Then while $j > 1$, set $j \leftarrow j - 1$ and $r_j \leftarrow 0$. Return to K2. ∎

(See the analysis in exercise 45. Korsh [*Comp. J.* **48** (2005), 488–497; **49** (2006), 351–357; **54** (2011), 776–785] has shown that this algorithm, Algorithm P, and Algorithm B can all be extended to t-ary trees in interesting ways.)

23. (a) Since z_n begins at $2n - 1$ and goes back and forth C_{n-1} times, it ends at $2n - 1 - (C_{n-1} \bmod 2)$, when $n > 1$. Furthermore the final value of z_j is constant for all $n \geq j$. Thus the final string $z_1 z_2 \ldots$ is 1 2 5 6 9 11 13 14 17 19 $\ldots$, containing all odd numbers $< 2n$ except 3, 7, 15, 31, $\ldots$.

    (b) Similarly, the preorder permutation that characterizes the final tree is $2^k \, 2^{k-1}$ $\ldots$ 1 3 5 6 7 9 10 $\ldots$, where $k = \lfloor \lg n \rfloor$. Forestwise, node 2^j is the parent of 2^{j-1} nodes $\{2^{j-1}, 2^{j-1} + 1, \ldots, 2^j - 1\}$, for $1 < j \leq k$, and the trees $\{2^k + 1, \ldots, n\}$ are trivial.

    Note: If Algorithm N is restarted at step N2 after it has terminated, it will generate the same sequence, but backwards. Algorithm L has the same property.

24. $l_0 l_1 \ldots l_{15} = 2\,0\,1\,0\,3\,0\,0\,6\,5\,0\,8\,0\,0\,12\,11\,4$; $r_1 \ldots r_{15} = 0\,15\,0\,10\,7\,0\,0\,9\,0\,14\,13\,0\,0\,0\,0$; $k_1 \ldots k_{15} = 0\,0\,2\,2\,4\,5\,5\,4\,8\,4\,10\,11\,11\,10\,2$; $q_1 \ldots q_{15} = 2\,1\,15\,4\,3\,10\,8\,5\,7\,6\,9\,14\,11\,13\,12$; and $u_1 \ldots u_{15} = 1\,2\,3\,1\,0\,0\,5\,0\,3\,1\,0\,0\,1\,0\,10$. (If nodes of the forest F are numbered in postorder, k_j is the left sibling of j; or, if j is the leftmost child of p, $k_j = k_p$. Stated another way, k_j is the parent of j in the forest F^{TR}. And k_j is also $j - 1 - u_{n+1-j}$, the number of elements to the left of j in $q_1 \ldots q_n$ that are less than j.)

25. Taking a cue from Algorithms N and L, we want to extend each $(n-1)$-node tree to a list of two or more n-node trees. The idea in this case is to make n a child of $n - 1$ in the binary tree at the beginning and the end of every such list. The following algorithm uses additional link fields p_j and s_j, where p_j points to the parent of j in the forest, and s_j points to j's left sibling or to j's rightmost sibling if j is the leftmost in its family. (These pointers p_j and s_j are, of course, not the same as the permutations $p_1 \ldots p_n$ in Table 1 or the scope coordinates $s_1 \ldots s_n$ in Table 2. In fact $s_1 \ldots s_n$ is the permutation λ of exercise 33 below.)

M1. [Initialize.] Set $l_j \leftarrow j + 1$, $r_j \leftarrow 0$, $s_j \leftarrow j$, $p_j \leftarrow j - 1$, and $o_j \leftarrow -1$ for $1 \leq j \leq n$, except that $l_n \leftarrow 0$.

M2. [Visit.] Visit $l_1 \ldots l_n$ and $r_1 \ldots r_n$. Then set $j \leftarrow n$.

M3. [Find j.] If $o_j > 0$, set $k \leftarrow p_j$ and go to M5 if $k \neq j - 1$. If $o_j < 0$, set $k \leftarrow s_j$ and go to M4 if $k \neq j - 1$. If $k = j - 1$ in either case, set $o_j \leftarrow -o_j$, $j \leftarrow j - 1$, and repeat this step.

M4. [Transfer down.] (At this point k is j's left sibling, or the rightmost member of j's family.) If $k \geq j$, terminate if $j = 1$, otherwise set $x \leftarrow p_j$, $l_x \leftarrow 0$, $z \leftarrow k$, and $k \leftarrow 0$ (thereby detaching node j from its parent and heading for the top level). But if $k < j$, set $x \leftarrow p_j + 1$, $z \leftarrow s_x$, $r_k \leftarrow 0$, and $s_x \leftarrow k$ (thereby detaching node j from k and going down a level). Then set $x \leftarrow k + 1$, $y \leftarrow s_x$, $s_x \leftarrow z$, $s_j \leftarrow y$, $r_y \leftarrow j$, and $x \leftarrow j$. While $x \neq 0$, set $p_x \leftarrow k$ and $x \leftarrow r_x$. Return to M2.

M5. [Transfer up.] (At this point k is j's parent.) Set $x \leftarrow k + 1$, $y \leftarrow s_j$, $z \leftarrow s_x$, $s_x \leftarrow y$, and $r_y \leftarrow 0$. If $k \neq 0$, set $y \leftarrow p_k$, $r_k \leftarrow j$, $s_j \leftarrow k$, $s_{y+1} \leftarrow z$, and $x \leftarrow j$; otherwise set $y \leftarrow j - 1$, $l_y \leftarrow j$, $s_j \leftarrow z$, and $x \leftarrow j$. While $x \neq 0$, set $p_x \leftarrow y$ and $x \leftarrow r_x$. Return to M2. ∎

Running time notes: We can argue as in exercise 44 that step M3 costs $2C_n + 3(C_{n-1} + \cdots + C_1)$ mems, and that steps M4 and M5 together cost $8C_n - 2(C_{n-1} + \cdots + C_1)$, plus twice the number of times $x \leftarrow r_x$. The latter quantity is difficult to analyze precisely; for example, when $n = 15$ and $j = 6$, the algorithm sets $x \leftarrow r_x$ exactly $(1, 2, 3, 4, 5, 6)$ times in respectively $(45, 23, 7, 9, 2, 4)$ cases. But heuristically the average number of times $x \leftarrow r_x$ should be approximately $2 - 2^{j-n}$ when j is given, therefore about $(2C_n - (C_n - C_{n-1}) - (C_{n-1} - C_{n-2})/2 - (C_{n-2} - C_{n-3})/4 - \cdots)/C_n \approx 8/7$ overall. Empirical tests confirm this predicted behavior, showing that the total cost per tree approaches $265/21 \approx 12.6$ mems as $n \to \infty$.

26. (a) The condition is clearly necessary. And if it holds, we can uniquely construct F: Node 1 and its siblings are the roots of the forest, and their descendants are defined inductively by noncrossing partitions. (In fact, we can compute the depth coordinates $c_1 \ldots c_n$ directly from Π's restricted growth string $a_1 \ldots a_n$: Set $c_1 \leftarrow 0$ and $i_0 \leftarrow 0$. For $2 \leq j \leq n$, if $a_j > \max(a_1, \ldots, a_{j-1})$, set $c_j \leftarrow c_{j-1} + 1$ and $i_{a_j} \leftarrow c_j$, otherwise set $c_j \leftarrow i_{a_j}$.)

(b) If Π and Π' satisfy the noncrossing condition, so does their greatest common refinement $\Pi \vee \Pi'$, so we can proceed as in exercise 7.2.1.5–12(a).

(c) Let $x_1, \ldots, x_m$ be the children of some node in F, and let $1 \leq j < k \leq m$. Form F' by removing $x_{j+1}, \ldots, x_k$ from their family and reattaching them as children of $x_{j+1} - 1$, the rightmost descendant of x_j.

(d) Obvious, by (c). Thus the forests are ranked from bottom to top by the number of nonleaf nodes they contain (which is one less than the number of blocks in Π).

(e) Exactly $\sum_{k=0}^{n} e_k(e_k - 1)/2$, where $e_0 = n - e_1 - \cdots - e_n$ is the number of roots.

(f) Dualization is similar to the transposition operation in exercise 12, but we use left-sibling and right-child links instead of left-child and right-sibling, and we transpose about the *minor* diagonal:

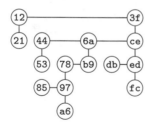 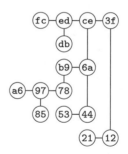

("Right" links now point downward. Notice that j is the rightmost child of k in F if and only if j is the left sibling of k in F^D. Preorder of F^D reverses the preorder of F, just as postorder of F^T reverses postorder of F.)

(g) From (f) we can see that F' covers F if and only if F^D covers F'^D. (Therefore F^D has $n + 1 - k$ leaves if F has k.)

(h) $F \bar{\wedge} F' = (F^D \bar{\vee} F'^D)^D$.

(i) No. If it did, equality would necessarily hold, by duality. But, for example, $0101 \bar{\wedge} 0121 = 0000$ and $0101 \bar{\vee} 0121 = 0123$, while $\text{leaves}(0101) + \text{leaves}(0121) \neq \text{leaves}(0000) + \text{leaves}(0123)$.

[Noncrossing partitions were first considered by H. W. Becker in *Math. Mag.* **22** (1948), 23–26. G. Kreweras proved in 1971 that they form a lattice; see the references in answer 2.3.4.6–3.]

27. (a) This assertion is equivalent to exercise 2.3.3–19.

(b) If we represent a forest by right-child and left-sibling links, preorder corresponds to inorder of the binary tree (see exercise 2.3.2–5), and s_j is the size of node j's right subtree. Rotation to the left at any nonleaf of this binary tree decreases exactly one of the scope coordinates, and the amount of decrease is as small as possible consistent with a valid table $s_1 \ldots s_n$. Therefore F' covers F if and only if F is obtained from F' by such a rotation. (Rotation in the left-child/right-sibling representation is similar, but with respect to postorder.)

(c) Dualization preserves the covering relation but exchanges left with right.

(d) $F \top F' = (F^D \perp F'^D)^D$. Equivalently, as noted in exercise 6.2.3–32, we can independently minimize the left-subtree sizes.

(e) The covering transformation in answer 26(c) obviously makes $s_j \le s'_j$ for all j.

(f) True, because $F \wedge F' \ltimes F \dashv F \perp F'$ and $F \wedge F' \ltimes F' \dashv F \perp F'$.

(g) False; for example, $0121 \vee 0122 = 0123$ and $0121 \top 0122 = 0122$. (But we do have $F \top F' \dashv F \vee F'$, by taking duals in (f).)

(h) The longest path, of length $\binom{n}{2}$, repeatedly decreases the rightmost nonzero s_j by 1. The shortest, of length $n-1$, repeatedly sets the leftmost nonzero s_j to 0.

Answer 6.2.3–32 gives many references to the literature of Tamari lattices.

28. (a) Just compute $\min(c_1, c'_1) \ldots \min(c_n, c'_n)$ and $\max(c_1, c'_1) \ldots \max(c_n, c'_n)$, because $c_1 \ldots c_n$ is a valid sequence if and only if $c_1 = 0$ and $c_j \le c_{j-1} + 1$ for $1 < j \le n$.

(b) Obvious because of (a). *Note:* The elements of any distributive lattice can be represented as the order ideals of some partial ordering. In the case of Fig. 62, that partial ordering is shown at the right, and a similar triangular grid with sides of length $n-2$ yields Stanley's lattice of order n.

(c) Take a node k of F that has a left sibling, j. Remove k from its family and place it as a new right child of j, followed by its former children as new children of j; the former children of k retain their own descendants. (This operation corresponds to changing)(to () in a nested parenthesis string. Thus a "perfect" Gray code for parentheses corresponds to a Hamiltonian path in the cover graph of Stanley's lattice. Exactly 38 such paths exist when $n = 4$, namely $(8, 6, 6, 8, 4, 6)$ from 0123 to $(0001, 0010, 0012, 0100, 0111, 0120)$ respectively.)

(d) True, because the cover relation in (c) is left-right symmetric. (We have $F \subseteq F'$ if and only if $w_j \le w'_j$ for $0 \le j \le 2n$, where the worm depths w_j are defined in exercise 10. If $w_0 \ldots w_{2n}$ is the worm walk of F, its reverse $w_{2n} \ldots w_0$ is the worm walk of F^R. Notice that the cover relation changes just one coordinate w_j. One can compute $F \cap F'$ and $F \cup F'$ by taking min and max of the w's instead of the c's.)

(e) See exercise 9. (Thus $F \perp F' \subseteq F \cap F'$, etc., as in exercise 27(f).)

Notes: Stanley introduced this lattice in *Fibonacci Quarterly* **13** (1975), 222–223. Since three important lattices are defined on the same elements, we need three notations for the different orderings; the symbols $\ltimes$, $\dashv$, and $\subseteq$ adopted here are intended to be reminiscent of the names of Kreweras, Tamari, and Stanley (who is Стэнли in Russia).

29. If we paste six regular pentagons together, we get 14 vertices whose coordinates after suitable rotation and scaling are respectively

$$p_{1010} = p_{\bar{0}000}^- = p_{3000}^* = p_{2\bar{1}00}^{*-} = (-1, \sqrt{3}, 2/\phi);$$

$$p_{0010} = p_{3100}^* = (\phi^{-2}, \sqrt{3}\,\phi, 0); \quad p_{3010} = p_{0\bar{1}00}^- = (0, 0, 2); \quad p_{3210} = p_{0\bar{2}00}^- = (2, 0, 2/\phi);$$

$$p_{0210} = p_{3200}^* = (\sqrt{5}, \sqrt{3}, 0); \quad p_{1000} = p_{2000}^* = (-\phi^2, \sqrt{3}/\phi, 0);$$

here $(x, y, z)^*$ means $(x, -y, z)$ and $(x, y, z)^-$ means $(x, y, -z)$. But then the three 4-edged "faces" are not squares; in fact, they don't even lie in a plane.

(One can however get a similar-looking solid, with true squares but irregular pentagons, by gluing together two suitable tetrahedra and lopping off the three glued-together corners. Alternative sets of coordinates for the associahedron, of substantial mathematical interest but less appealing to the eye, are discussed by Günter Ziegler in his *Lectures on Polytopes* (New York: Springer, 1995), example 9.11.)

30. (a) $\bar{f}_{n-1} \ldots \bar{f}_1$, because internal node j in symmetric order has a nonempty right subtree if and only if internal node $j + 1$ in symmetric order has an empty left subtree.

(b) By answer 26(f), the general canopy $1^{p_1} 0^{q_1+1} 1^{p_2+1} 0^{q_2+1} \ldots 1^{p_k+1} 0^{q_k}$ arises from binary trees whose nodes in symmetric order have the specification $R^{p_1} N L^{q_1} B R^{p_2} N L^{q_2} B \ldots R^{p_k} N L^{q_k}$, where B means "both subtrees are nonempty," R means "the right subtree is nonempty but not the left," L means "the left subtree is nonempty but not the right," and N means "neither subtree is nonempty."

The number $f(p_1, q_1; \ldots; p_k, q_k)$ of such trees is $\binom{p_1+q_1}{p_1}$ when $k = 1$; otherwise it's

$$[p_1 > 0] f(p_1 - 1, q_1; \ldots; p_k, q_k) + \sum_{j=1}^{k-1} f(p_1, q_1; \ldots; p_j, q_j) f(p_{j+1}, q_{j+1}; \ldots; p_k, q_k)$$
$$+ [q_k > 0] f(p_1, q_1; \ldots; p_k, q_k - 1).$$

And in particular, $f(1, 0; 0, 0; 1, 0; 5, 3; 0, 0; 0, 0; 0, 2; 0, 0; 1, 2) = 114044694$.

(c) $d_j = 0$ if and only if $c_{j+1} > c_j$, by exercise 3.

(d) In general, the canopy of $F \perp F'$ is $f_1 \ldots f_{n-1} \wedge f'_1 \ldots f'_{n-1}$, by exercise 27(a); the canopy of $F \top F'$ is $f_1 \ldots f_{n-1} \vee f'_1 \ldots f'_{n-1}$, by (a) and exercise 27(d).

[The fact that complements always exist in the Tamari lattice is due to H. Lakser; see G. Grätzer, *General Lattice Theory* (1978), exercise I.6.30. X. G. Viennot coined the nice term "canopy"; see arXiv:0905.3081 [math.CO] (2009), 12 pages.]

31. (a) 2^{n-1}; see exercise 6.2.2–5.

(b) $c_1 \leq \cdots \leq c_n$; $d_1, \ldots, d_{n-1} \leq 1$; $e_j > 0$ implies $e_j + \cdots + e_n = n - j$; $k_{j+1} \leq k_j + 1$; $p_1 \leq \cdots \leq p_j \geq \cdots \geq p_n$ for some j; $s_j > 0$ implies $s_j = n - j$; $u_1 \geq \cdots \geq u_n$; $z_{j+1} \leq z_j + 2$. (Other constraints, which apply in general, whittle down the number of possibilities to 2^{n-1} in each case. For example, $u_1 \ldots u_n$ must be a valid sequence of scope coordinates.)

(c) True in only n cases out of 2^{n-1}. (But F^T *is* degenerate.)

(d) The degenerate forest with canopy $f_1 \ldots f_{n-1}$ has $c_{j+1} = c_j + f_j$. Elements $j < k$ are siblings if and only if $f_j = f_{j+1} = \cdots = f_{k-1} = 0$. Thus if F'' is the degenerate forest with canopy $f_1 \ldots f_{n-1} \wedge f'_1 \ldots f'_{n-1}$, then $F'' \preccurlyeq F$ and $F'' \preccurlyeq F'$; hence $F'' \preccurlyeq F \wedge F' \dashv F \perp F'$. And we also have $F \perp F' \dashv F''$ by (b). A similar argument proves that $F \vee F' = F \top F'$ is the degenerate forest with canopy $f_1 \ldots f_{n-1} \vee f'_1 \ldots f'_{n-1}$.

Thus, when the Kreweras and Tamari lattices are restricted to degenerate forests, they become identical to the Boolean lattice of subsets of $\{1, \ldots, n-1\}$. [This result, in the case of Tamari lattices, is due to George Markowsky, *Order* **9** (1992), 265–290, whose paper also shows that Tamari lattices enjoy many further properties.]

32. Suppose F and F' have scope coordinates $s_1 \ldots s_n$ and $s'_1 \ldots s'_n$. Call index j *frozen* if $s_j < s'_j$ or $j = 0$. We want to specify the values of the frozen coordinates and maximize the others. Let $s_0 = n$, and for $0 \leq k \leq n$ let

$$s''_k = s_j - k + j, \quad \text{where } j = \max\{i \mid 0 \leq i \leq k, i \text{ is frozen, and } i + s_i \geq k\}.$$

Since $s_k \leq s_j - (k - j)$ for $0 \leq k - j \leq s_j$, we have $s''_k \geq s_k$, with equality when k is frozen.

The scopes $s_0'' s_1'' \ldots s_n''$ correspond to a valid forest according to the condition of exercise 27(a). For if $k \geq 0$ and $0 \leq l \leq s_k'' = s_j - k + j$ and $s_{k+l}'' = s_{j'} - k - l + j'$, we have $s_{k+l}'' + l \leq s_k''$ if $0 \leq j' - j \leq s_j$, because $s_{j'} + j' - j \leq s_j$ in that case. And we can't have $j > j'$ or $j' > j + s_j$, because $j + s_j \geq k + l \geq j'$.

Let F''' be a forest with scopes satisfying $s_k \leq s_k''' \leq s_k''$. Then $\min(s_k', s_k''') = s_k$, because $s_k = s_k''$ when k is frozen, otherwise $s_k = s_k'$.

Conversely, if F''' is a forest with $F' \perp F''' = F$, we must have $s_k \leq s_k''' \leq s_k''$. For $s_k''' < s_k$ would imply $s_k''' < s_k'$. And if k is minimal with $s_k''' > s_k''$, we have $s_k'' = s_j - k + j$ for some frozen j with $0 \leq j \leq k$ and $j + s_j \geq k$. Then $s_j''' \geq s_j$ implies $k - j \leq s_j'''$, hence $s_k''' + k - j \leq s_j'''$. If $j < k$ we have $s_j''' \leq s_j'' = s_j$, a contradiction. But $j = k$ implies $\min(s_k''', s_k') > s_k$.

To get the first semidistributive law, apply this principle with F replaced by $F \perp G$ and F' replaced by F; then the hypotheses $F \dashv G \dashv F''$ and $F \dashv H \dashv F''$ imply that $F \dashv G \top H \dashv F''$. The second semidistributive law follows by taking duals in the first.

(Ralph Freese suggests calling F'' the *pseudo-complement* of F' over F.)

33. (a) Let $k\lambda = \texttt{LLINK}[k]$ if $\texttt{LLINK}[k] \neq 0$, otherwise $\texttt{RLINK}[k-1]$ if $k \neq 1$, otherwise the root of the binary tree. This rule defines a permutation because $k\lambda = j$ if and only if $k = \text{parent}(j) + [j \text{ is a right child}]$, or $k = 1$ and j is the root. Also $k\lambda \geq k$ when $\texttt{LLINK}[k] = 0$ and $k\sigma\lambda \leq k$ when $\texttt{RLINK}[k] = 0$. [For a generalization to t-ary trees, see P. H. Edelman, *Discrete Math.* **40** (1982), 171–179.]

(b) Using the representation of (2) in answer 26(f), we see that $\lambda(F)$ is $(3\,1)(2)$ $(12\,6\,4)(5)(11\,7)(14\,13)(9\,8)(15)(10)$ in that case. In general the cycles are the families of the forest, in decreasing order within each cycle; nodes are numbered in preorder. [See Dershowitz and Zaks, *Discrete Math.* **62** (1986), 215–218.]

(c) $\lambda(F^D) = \rho\sigma\lambda(F)\rho$, where ρ is the "flip" permutation $(1\,n)(2\,n-1)\ldots$, because the dual forest interchanges $\texttt{LLINK} \leftrightarrow \texttt{RLINK}$ and flips the preorder numbering.

(d) The cycle breakup $(x_j\,x_k)(x_1 \ldots x_m) = (x_1 \ldots x_j x_{k+1} \ldots x_m)(x_{j+1} \ldots x_k)$ corresponds to answer 26(c).

(e) By (d), each covering path corresponds to a factorization of $(n \ldots 2\,1)$. Let q_n denote the number of such factorizations. Then we have the recurrence $q_1 = 1$ and $q_n = \sum_{l=1}^{n-1}(n-l)\binom{n-2}{l-1}q_l q_{n-l}$, because there are $n-l$ choices with $k - j = l$ by which the first transposition breaks the cycle into parts of sizes l and $n-l$, then $\binom{n-2}{l-1}$ ways to interleave the subsequent factors. The solution is $q_n = n^{n-2}$, because

$$\sum_{l=1}^{n-1}\binom{n-1}{l}l^{l-1}(y-l)^{n-1-l} = \lim_{x \to 0}\sum_{l=1}^{n-1}\binom{n-1}{l}(x+l)^{l-1}(y-l)^{n-1-l}$$

$$= \lim_{x \to 0}\frac{(x+y)^{n-1} - y^{n-1}}{x} = (n-1)y^{n-1}.$$

[See J. Dénes, *Magyar Tudományos Akadémia Matematikai Kutató Intézetének Közleményei* **4** (1959), 63–70. It is natural to seek a correspondence between factorizations and labeled free trees, since there also happen to be n^{n-2} of the latter. Perhaps the simplest is the following, given $(1\,2 \ldots n) = (x_1\,y_1) \ldots (x_{n-1}\,y_{n-1})$ where $x_j < y_j$: Suppose the cycle containing x_j and y_j in $(x_j\,y_j) \ldots (x_{n-1}\,y_{n-1})$ is $(z_1 \ldots z_m)$, where $z_1 < \cdots < z_m$. If $y_j = z_m$, let $a_j = z_1$, otherwise let $a_j = \min\{z_i \mid z_i > x_j\}$. Then one can show that $a_1 \ldots a_{n-1}$ is a "wake-up sequence" for parking $n - 1$ cars, and exercise 6.4–31 connects it to free trees.]

34. Each covering path from bottom to top is equivalent to a Young tableau of shape $(n - 1, n - 2, \ldots, 1)$, so we can use Theorem 5.1.4H. (See exercise 5.3.4–38.)

[The enumeration of such paths in Tamari lattices remains mysterious; the relevant sequence is 1, 1, 2, 9, 98, 2981, 340549, ...]

35. Multiply by $n + 1$, then see *AMM* **97** (1990), 626–630.

36. We might as well generalize to t-ary trees for arbitrary $t \geq 1$, by making obvious amendments to steps T1–T5. Let $C_n^{(t)}$ be the number of t-ary trees with n internal nodes; thus $C_n = C_n^{(2)}$ and $C_n^{(t)} = ((t - 1)n + 1)^{-1}\binom{tn}{n}$. If h of the degrees b_j are changed between visits, we have $h \geq x$ in $C_{n-x}^{(t)}$ cases. So the easy case occurs with probability $1 - C_{n-1}^{(t)}/C_n^{(t)} \approx 1 - (t-1)^{t-1}/t^t$, and the average number of times $b_j \leftarrow 0$ in step T4 is $(C_{n-1}^{(t)} + \cdots + C_1^{(t)})/C_n^{(t)} \approx (t-1)^{t-1}/(t^t - (t-1)^{t-1})$, or 4/23 when $t = 3$.

Indeed, we can also study the t-ary recursive structure $A_{pq}^{(t)} = 0\,A_{p(q-1)}^{(t)},\ t\,A_{(p-1)q}^{(t)}$ when $0 \leq (t-1)p \leq q \neq 0$, generalizing (5). The number of such degree sequences, $C_{pq}^{(t)}$, satisfies the recurrence (21) except that $C_{pq}^{(t)} = 0$ when $p < 0$ or $(t-1)p > q$. The general solution is

$$C_{pq}^{(t)} = \frac{q - (t-1)p + 1}{q + 1}\binom{p+q}{p} = \binom{p+q}{p} - (t-1)\binom{p+q}{p-1},$$

and we have $C_n^{(t)} = C_{n((t-1)n)}^{(t)}$. The triangle for $t = 3$ begins as shown at the right.

[The "Fuss–Catalan numbers" $C_n^{(t)}$ were first studied by N. Fuss, *Nova acta acad. scient. imp. Pet.* **9** (1791), 243–251.]

1				
1				
1	1			
1	2			
1	3	3		
1	4	7		
1	5	12	12	
1	6	18	30	
1	7	25	55	55
1	8	33	88	143

37. The basic lexicographic recursion for all such forests is

$$A(n_0, n_1, \ldots, n_t) = 0\,A(n_0 - 1, n_1, \ldots, n_t),$$
$$1\,A(n_0, n_1 - 1, \ldots, n_t),\ \ldots,\ t\,A(n_0, n_1, \ldots, n_t - 1)$$

when $n_0 > n_2 + 2n_3 + \cdots + (t-1)n_t$ and $n_1, \ldots, n_t \geq 0$; otherwise $A(n_0, n_1, \ldots, n_t)$ is empty, except that $A(0, \ldots, 0) = \epsilon$ is the sequence consisting of the empty string alone. Step G1 computes the first entry of $A(n_0, \ldots, n_t)$. We want to analyze five quantities:

  C, the number of times G2 is executed (the total number of forests);
  E, the number of times G3 goes to G2 (the number of easy cases);
  K, the number of times G4 moves some b_i into list c;
  L, the number of times G5 compares b_j with some c_i;
  Z, the number of times G5 sets $c_1 \leftarrow 0$.

Then the loop in step G6 sets $b_{l-c_j} \leftarrow c_j$ a total of $K - Z - n_1 - \cdots - n_t$ times.

Let n be the vector $(n_0, n_1, \ldots, n_t)$, and let e_j be the unit vector with 1 in coordinate position j. Let $|n| = n_0 + n_1 + \cdots + n_t$ and $\|n\| = n_1 + 2n_2 + \cdots + tn_t$. Using this notation we can rewrite the basic recurrence above in the convenient form

$$A(n) = 0\,A(n - e_0),\ 1\,A(n - e_1),\ \ldots,\ t\,A(n - e_t) \qquad \text{when } |n| > \|n\|.$$

Consider the general recurrence relation

$$F(n) = f(n) + \left(\sum_{j=0}^{t} F(n - e_j)\right)[|n| > \|n\|],$$

with $F(n) = 0$ whenever the vector n has a negative component. If $f(n) = [|n| = 0]$, then $F(n) = C(n)$ is the total number of forests. Answer 2.3.4.4–32 tells us that

$$C(n) = \frac{(|n| - 1)!\,(|n| - \|n\|)}{n_0!\,n_1!\ldots n_t!} = \sum_{j=0}^{t} (1 - j) \binom{|n| - 1}{n_0, \ldots, n_{j-1}, n_j - 1, n_{j+1}, \ldots, n_t},$$

generalizing the formula for $C_{pq}^{(t)}$ in answer 36 (which is the case $n_0 = (t-1)q + 1$ and $n_t = p$). Similarly, we obtain recurrences for the other quantities $E(n)$, $K(n)$, $L(n)$, and $Z(n)$ needed in our analysis by choosing other kernel functions $f(n)$:

$f(n) = [|n| = n_0 + 1 \text{ and } n_0 > \|n\|]$ yields $F(n) = E(n)$;
$f(n) = [|n| > n_0]$ yields $F(n) = E(n) + K(n)$;
$f(n) = [|n| = \|n\| + 1]$ yields $F(n) = C(n) + K(n) - Z(n)$;
$f(n) = \sum_{1 \le j < k \le t} n_j [n_k > 0]$ yields $F(n) = L(n)$.

The symbolic methods of exercise 2.3.4.4–32 do not seem to yield quick solutions to these more general recurrences, but we can readily establish the value of $C - E$ by noting that $b_m + m < N$ in step G2 if and only if the previous step was G3. Therefore

$$C(n) - E(n) = \sum_{j=1}^{t} C(n - f_j), \qquad \text{where } f_j = e_j - (j-1)e_0;$$

this sum counts the subforests in which $n_1 + \cdots + n_t$, the number of internal (nonleaf) nodes, has decreased by 1. Similarly we can let

$$C^{(x)}(n) = \sum \{C(n - i_1 f_1 - \cdots - i_t f_t) \mid i_1 + \cdots + i_t = x\}$$

be the number of subforests having $n_1 + \cdots + n_t - x$ internal nodes. Then we have

$$K(n) - Z(n) = \sum_{x-1}^{|n|} C^{(x)}(n),$$

a formula analogous to (20), because $k - [b_j = 0] \ge x \ge 1$ in step G5 if and only if $b_{m-x} > 0$ and $b_{m-x+1} \ge \cdots \ge b_m$. Such preorder degree strings are in one-to-one correspondence with the forests of $C^{(x)}(n)$ if we remove $b_{m-x+1} \ldots b_m$ and an appropriate number of trailing 0s from the string $b_1 \ldots b_N$.

From these formulas we can conclude that the Zaks–Richards algorithm needs only $O(1)$ operations per forest visited, whenever $n_1 = n_2 + \cdots + n_t + O(1)$, because $C(n - f_j)/C(n) = n_j n_0^{j-1}/(|n| - 1)^{\underline{j}} \le 1/4 + O(|n|^{-1})$ when $j > 1$. Indeed, the value of K is quite small in nearly all cases of practical interest. However, the algorithm can be slow when n_1 is large. For example, if $t = 1$, $n_0 = m + r + 1$, and $n_1 = m$, the algorithm essentially computes all r-combinations of $m + r$ things; then $C(n) = \binom{m+r}{r}$ and $K(n) - Z(n) = \binom{m+r}{r+1} = \Omega(mC(n))$ when r is fixed. [To ensure efficiency in all cases, we can keep track of trailing 1s; see Ruskey and Rœlants van Baronaigien, *Congressus Numerantium* **41** (1984), 53–62.]

Exact formulas for K, Z, and (especially) L do not seem to be simple, but we can compute those quantities as follows. Say that the "active block" of a forest is the rightmost substring of nonzero degrees; for example, the active block of 302102021230000000 is 2123. All permutations of the active block occur equally often. Indeed, let $D(n)$ denote the sum of "trailing zeros(β) $- 1$" over all preorder degree strings β for forests of specification n. Then a block with n'_j occurrences of j for $1 \le j \le t$ is active in exactly $D(n - n'_1 f_1 - \cdots - n'_t f_t) + [n'_1 + \cdots + n'_t = n_1 + \cdots + n_t]$ cases. For example, given the string 3021020000, we can insert 21230000 in three places to obtain a forest with active block 2123. The contributions to K and L when the active block is flush left (not preceded by any 0s) can be computed as in exercise 7.2.1.2–6, namely

$$k(n) = w(e_{n_1}(z) \ldots e_{n_t}(z)), \qquad l(n) = w\left(e_{n_1}(z) \ldots e_{n_t}(z) \sum_{1 \le i < j \le t} (n_i - zr_i(z))r_j(z)\right)$$

in the notation of that answer. Analogous contributions occur in general; therefore

$$K(n) = k(n) + \sum D(n-n')k(n'), \quad L(n) = l(n) + \sum D(n-n')l(n'), \quad Z(n) = \sum D(n-n'),$$

summed over all vectors n' such that $n'_j \le n_j$ for $1 \le j \le t$ and $|n'| - \|n'\| = |n| - \|n\|$ and $n'_1 + \cdots + n'_t \le n_1 + \cdots + n_t - 2$.

It remains to determine $D(n)$. Let $C(n; j)$ be the number of forests of specification $n = (n_0, \ldots, n_t)$ in which the last internal node in preorder has degree j. Then we have

$$C(n) = \sum_{j=1}^{t} C(n; j) \text{ and } C(n + e_1; 1) = C(n + e_2; 2) = \cdots = C(n + e_t; t) = C(n) + D(n).$$

From this infinite system of linear equations we can deduce that $C(n) + D(n)$ is

$$\sum_{i_2=0}^{n_2} \cdots \sum_{i_t=0}^{n_t} (-1)^{i_2 + \cdots + i_t} \binom{i_2 + \cdots + i_t}{i_2, \ldots, i_t} C(n + (1 + i_2 + \cdots + i_t)e_1 - i_2 f_2 - \cdots - i_t f_t).$$

Simpler expressions would of course be desirable, if they exist.

38. Step L1 obviously uses $4n + 2$ mems. Step L3 exits to L4 or L5 exactly $C_j - C_{j-1}$ times with a particular value of j; therefore it costs $2C_n + 3\sum_{j=0}^{n}(n - j)(C_j - C_{j-1}) = 2C_n + 3(C_{n-1} + \cdots + C_1 + C_0)$ mems. Steps L4 and L5 jointly cost a total of $6C_n - 6$. Therefore the entire process involves $9 + O(n^{-1/2})$ mems per visit.

39. A Young tableau of shape (q, p) and entries y_{ij} corresponds to an element of A_{pq} that has left parens in positions $p + q + 1 - y_{21}, \ldots, p + q + 1 - y_{2p}$ and right parens in positions $p + q + 1 - y_{11}, \ldots, p + q + 1 - y_{1q}$. The hook lengths are $\{q + 1, q, \ldots, 1, p, p - 1, \ldots, 1\} \setminus \{q - p + 1\}$; so $C_{pq} = (p + q)!(q - p + 1)/(p!(q + 1)!)$ by Theorem 5.1.4H.

40. (a) $C_{pq} = \binom{p+q}{p} - \binom{p+q}{p-1} \equiv \binom{p+q}{p} + \binom{p+q}{p-1} = \binom{p+q+1}{p}$ (modulo 2); now use exercise 1.2.6–11. (b) By Eq. 7.1.3–(36) we know that $\nu(n \And (n + 1)) = \nu(n + 1) - 1$.

41. It equals $C(wz)/(1 - zC(wz)) = 1/(1 - z - wzC(wz)) = (1 - wC(wz))/(1 - w - z)$, where $C(z)$ is the Catalan generating function (18). The first of these formulas, $C(wz) + zC(wz)^2 + z^2C(wz)^3 + \cdots$, is easily seen to be equivalent to (24). [See P. A. MacMahon, *Combinatory Analysis* 1 (Cambridge Univ. Press, 1915), 128–130.]

42. (a) Elements $a_1 \ldots a_n$ determine an entire self-conjugate nested string $a_1 \ldots a_{2n}$, and there are $C_{q(n-q)}$ possibilities for $a_1 \ldots a_n$ having exactly q right parentheses. So the answer is

$$\sum_{q=0}^{\lfloor n/2 \rfloor} C_{q(n-q)} = \sum_{q=0}^{\lfloor n/2 \rfloor} \left(\binom{n}{q} - \binom{n}{q-1}\right) = \binom{n}{\lfloor n/2 \rfloor}.$$

(b) Exactly $C_{(n-1)/2}$ [n odd], because a self-transpose binary tree is determined by its left subtree. And (c) has the same answer, because F is self-dual if and only if F^R is self-transpose.

43. $C_{pq} = C_q - \binom{q-p-1}{1}C_{q-1} + \cdots = \sum_{r=0}^{q-p}(-1)^r\binom{q-p-r}{r}C_{q-r}$, by induction on $q - p$.

44. The number of mems between visits is $3j - 2$ in step B3, $h + 1$ in step B4, and 4 in step B5, where h is the number of times $y \leftarrow r_y$. The number of binary trees with $h \geq x$, given j and x, is $[z^{n-j-x-1}]C(z)^{x+3}$ when $j < n$, because we get such trees by attaching $x+3$ subtrees below $j+x+1$ internal nodes. Setting $x = 0$ tells us that a given value of j occurs $C_{(n-j-1)(n-j+1)} = C_{n+1-j} - C_{n-j}$ times, using (24) and exercise 43. Thus $\sum j$ over all binary trees is $n + \sum_{j=1}^{n}(C_{n+1-j} - C_{n-j})j = C_n + C_{n-1} + \cdots + C_1$. Similarly, $\sum(h + 1)$ is $\sum_{j=1}^{n-1}\sum_{x=0}^{n-j-1}C_{(n-j-x-1)(n-j+1)} = \sum_{j=1}^{n-1}C_{(n-j-1)(n-j+2)} = \sum_{j=1}^{n}(C_{n-j+2} - 2C_{n-j+1}) = C_{n+1} - (C_n + C_{n-1} + \cdots + C_0)$. So overall, the algorithm costs $C_{n+1} + 4C_n + 2(C_{n-1} + \cdots + C_1) + O(n) = (26/3 - 10/(3n) + O(n^{-2}))C_n$ mems.

45. Each of the easy cases in step K3 occurs C_{n-1} times, so the total cost of that step is $3C_{n-1} + 8C_{n-1} + 2(C_n - 2C_{n-1})$ mems. Step K4 fetches r_i a total of $[z^{n-i-1}]C(z)^{i+2} = C_{(n-i-1)n}$ times; summing for $i \geq 2$ gives $C_{(n-3)(n+1)} = C_{n+1} - 3C_n + C_{n-1}$ mems altogether in that loop. Step K5 costs $6C_n - 12C_{n-1}$. Step K6 is a bit more complicated, but one can show that the operation $r_j \leftarrow r_k$ is performed $C_n - 3C_{n-1} + 1$ times when $n > 2$, while the operation $r_j \leftarrow 0$ is performed $C_{n-1} - n + 1$ times. The total number of mems therefore comes to $C_{n+1} + 7C_n - 9C_{n-1} + n + 3 = (8.75 - 9.375/n + O(n^{-2}))C_n$.

Although this total is asymptotically worse than that of Algorithm B in answer 44, the large negative coefficient of n^{-1} means that Algorithm B actually wins only when $n \geq 58$; and n won't ever be that big.

Skarbek has, however, improved Algorithm B to the following Algorithm B*, which generates the trees in reverse order and uses an auxiliary table $c_1 \ldots c_n$:

B1*. [Initialize.] Set $l_k \leftarrow c_k \leftarrow 0$ and $r_k \leftarrow k+1$ for $1 \leq k < n$; also set $l_n \leftarrow r_n \leftarrow 0$, and set $r_{n+1} \leftarrow 1$ (for convenience in step B3*).

B2*. [Visit.] Visit the binary tree represented by $l_1 l_2 \ldots l_n$ and $r_1 r_2 \ldots r_n$.

B3*. [Find j.] Set $j \leftarrow 1$. While $r_j = 0$, set $l_j \leftarrow c_j \leftarrow 0$, $r_j \leftarrow j+1$, and $j \leftarrow j+1$. Then terminate the algorithm if $j > n$.

B4*. [Demote r_j.] Set $x \leftarrow r_j$, $r_j \leftarrow r_x$, $r_x \leftarrow 0$, $z \leftarrow c_j$, $c_j \leftarrow x$. If $z > 0$, set $r_z \leftarrow x$; otherwise set $l_j \leftarrow x$. Return to B2*. ∎

If the values of r_1 and c_1 are maintained in registers, this algorithm needs only $4C_n + C_{n-1} + 4(C_{n-1} + C_{n-2} + \cdots + C_0) + 3n - 6 = (67/12 + 73/(24n) + O(n^{-2}))C_n$ mems to generate all C_n trees. [See W. Skarbek, *Fundamenta Informaticæ* **75** (2007), 505–536.]

46. (a) Going to the left from $\widehat{pq}$ increases the area by $q - p$.

(b) The leftward steps on a path from $\widehat{nn}$ to $\widehat{00}$ correspond to the left parentheses in $a_1 \ldots a_{2n}$, and we have $q - p = c_k$ at the kth such step.

(c) Equivalently, $C_{n+1}(x) = \sum_{k=0}^{n} x^k C_k(x) C_{n-k}(x)$. This recurrence holds because an $(n + 1)$-node forest F consists of the root of the leftmost tree together with a k-node forest F_l (the descendants of that root) and an $(n - k)$-node forest F_r (the remaining trees), and because we have

$$\text{internal path length}(F) = k + \text{internal path length}(F_l) + \text{internal path length}(F_r).$$

(d) The strings of $A_{p(p+r)}$ have the form $\alpha_0)\alpha_1) \ldots \alpha_{r-1})\alpha_r$ where each α_j is properly nested. The area of such a string is the sum over j of the area of α_j plus $r - j$ times the number of left parens in α_j.

Notes: The polynomials $C_{pq}(x)$ were introduced by L. Carlitz and J. Riordan in *Duke Math. J.* **31** (1964), 371–388; the identity in part (d) is equivalent to their formula

(10.12). They also proved that

$$C_{pq}(x) = \sum_r (-1)^r x^{r(r-1)-\binom{q-p}{2}} \binom{q-p-r}{r}_x C_{q-r}(x),$$

generalizing the result of exercise 43. From part (c) we have the infinite continued fraction $C(x, z) = 1/(1 - z/(1 - xz/(1 - x^2z/(1 - \cdots))))$, which G. N. Watson proved is equal to $F(x, z)/F(x, z/x)$, where

$$F(x, z) = \sum_{n=0}^{\infty} \frac{(-1)^n x^{n^2} z^n}{(1 - x)(1 - x^2) \dots (1 - x^n)};$$

see *J. London Math. Soc.* (2) **4** (1929), 39–48. We have already encountered the same generating function, slightly disguised, in exercise 5.2.1–15.

The internal path length of a forest is the "left path length" of the corresponding binary tree, namely the sum over all internal nodes of the number of left branches on the path from the root. The more general polynomial

$$C_n(x, y) = \sum x^{\text{left path length}(T)} y^{\text{right path length}(T)},$$

summed over all n-node binary trees T, seems to obey no simple additive recurrence like the one for $C_{nn}(x) = C_n(x, 1)$ studied in this exercise; but we do have $C_{n+1}(x, y) = \sum_k x^k C_k(x, y) y^{n-k} C_{n-k}(x, y)$. Therefore the super generating function $C(x, y, z) = \sum_n C_n(x, y) z^n$ satisfies the functional equation $C(x, y, z) = 1 + zC(x, y, xz)C(x, y, yz)$. (The case $x = y$ was considered in exercise 2.3.4.5–5.)

47. $C_n(x) = \sum_q x^{\binom{q-p}{2}} C_{pq}(x) C_{(n-q)(n-1-p)}(x)$ for $0 \leq p < n$.

48. Let $\bar{C}(z) = C(-1, z)$ in the notation of exercise 46, and let $\bar{C}(z)\bar{C}(-z) = F(z^2)$. Then $\bar{C}(z) = 1 + zF(z^2)$ and $\bar{C}(-z) = 1 - zF(z^2)$; so $F(z) = 1 - zF(z)^2$, and $F(z) = C(-z)$. It follows that $C_{pq}(-1) = [z^p] C(-z^2)^{\lceil (q-p)/2 \rceil}(1 + zC(-z^2))^{[q-p \text{ even}]}$, which is $(-1)^{(p/2)} C_{(p/2)(q/2-1)}[p \text{ even}]$ when q is even, $(-1)^{\lfloor p/2 \rfloor} C_{\lfloor p/2 \rfloor \lfloor q/2 \rfloor}$ when q is odd. A perfect Gray code through the strings of A_{pq} can exist only if $|C_{pq}(-1)| \leq 1$, because the associated graph is bipartite (see Fig. 62); $|C_{pq}(-1)|$ is the difference between the sizes of the parts, because each perfect transposition changes $c_1 + \cdots + c_n$ by ± 1.

49. By Algorithm U with $n=15$ and $N=10^6$, it is ()(()())((((()())))(((((())()))).

50. Make the following changes to Algorithm U: In step U1, also set $r \leftarrow 0$. In step U3, test if $a_m = $ ')' instead of testing if $N \leq c'$. In step U4, set $r \leftarrow r + c'$ instead of $N \leftarrow N - c'$. And omit the assignments to a_m in steps U3 and U4.

The string in (1) turns out to have rank 3141592. (Who knew?)

51. By Theorem 7.2.1.3L, $N = \binom{\bar{z}_1}{n} + \binom{\bar{z}_2}{n-1} + \cdots + \binom{\bar{z}_n}{1}$; hence $\kappa_n N = \binom{\bar{z}_1}{n-1} + \binom{\bar{z}_2}{n-2} + \cdots + \binom{\bar{z}_n}{0}$, since $\bar{z}_n \geq 1$. Now note that $N - \kappa_n N$ is the rank of $z_1 z_2 \dots z_n$, because of (23) and exercise 50. (For example, let $z_1 \dots z_4 = 1256$, which has rank 6 in Table 1. Then $\bar{z}_1 \dots \bar{z}_4 = 7632$, $N = 60$, and $\kappa_4 60 = 54$. Notice that N is fairly large, because $\bar{z}_1 = 2n - 1$; Fig. 47 shows that $\kappa_n N$ usually *exceeds* N when N is smaller.)

52. The number of trailing right parentheses has the same distribution as the number of leading left parentheses, and the sequence of nested strings that begin with '$(^k)$' is

$(^k)A_{(n-k)(n-1)}$. Therefore the probability that $d_n = k$ is $C_{(n-k)(n-1)}/C_n$. We find

$$\sum_{k=0}^{n} \binom{k}{t} C_{(n-k)(n-1)} = \sum_{k=0}^{n}\left(\binom{2n-1-k}{n-1} - \binom{2n-1-k}{n}\right)\binom{k}{t}$$

$$= \binom{2n}{n+t} - \binom{2n}{n+t+1} = C_{(n-t)(n+t)}$$

using Eq. 1.2.6–(25), and it follows that the mean and variance are respectively equal to $3n/(n+2) = 3 - 6/(n+2)$ and $2n(2n^2 - n - 1)/((n+2)^2(n+3)) = 4 + O(n^{-1})$. [The moments of this distribution were first calculated by R. Kemp in *Acta Informatica* **35** (1998), 17–89, Theorem 9. Notice that $c_n = d_n - 1$ has essentially the same behavior.]

53. (a) $3n/(n+2)$, by exercise 52. (b) H_n, by exercise 6.2.2–7. (c) $2-2^{-n}$, by induction.

(d) Any particular (but fixed) sequence of left or right branches has the same distribution of steps before a leaf is encountered. (In other words, the probability that a node with Dewey binary notation 01101 occurs is the same as the probability that 00000 occurs.) Thus if $X = k$ with probability p_k, each of the 2^k potential nodes on level k is external with probability p_k. The expected value $\sum_k 2^k p_k$ is therefore the expected number of external nodes, namely $n+1$ in all three cases. (One can of course also verify this result directly, with $p_k = C_{(n-k)(n-1)}/C_n$ in case (a), $p_k = \begin{bmatrix} n \\ k \end{bmatrix}/n!$ in case (b), and $p_k = 2^{-k+[k=n]}$ in case (c).)

Notes: The average level of a leaf turns out to be $\Theta(\sqrt{n})$, $\Theta(\log n)$, and $\Theta(n)$ in these three cases; thus it is longer when the expected time to hit the leftmost leaf is shorter! The reason is that ubiquitous "holes" near the root force other paths to be long. Case (a) has an interesting generalization to t-ary trees, when $p_k = C^{(t)}_{(n-k)((t-1)n-1)}/C^{(t)}_n$ in the notation of answer 36. Then the mean distance to the leftmost leaf is $(t+1)n/((t-1)n+2)$, and it is instructive to prove via telescoping series that

$$\sum_k t^k C^{(t)}_{(n-k)((t-1)n-1)} = \binom{tn}{n}.$$

54. Differentiating with respect to x we have

$$C'(x, z) = zC'(x, z)C(x, xz) + zC(x, z)(C'(x, xz) + zC_{/}(x, xz)),$$

where $C_{/}(x, z)$ denotes the derivative of $C(x, z)$ with respect to z. Thus $C'(1, z) = 2zC'(1, z)C(z) + z^2 C(z)C'(z)$; and since $C'(z) = C(z)^2 + 2zC(z)C'(z)$ we can solve for $C'(1, z)$, obtaining $z^2 C(z)^3/(1-2zC(z))^2$. Therefore $\sum(c_1 + \cdots + c_n) = [z^n]C'(1, z) = 2^{2n-1} - \frac{1}{2}(3n+1)C_n$, in agreement with exercise 2.3.4.5–5. Similarly we find

$$\sum(c_1 + \cdots + c_n)^2 = [z^n]C''(1, z) = \left(\frac{5n^2 + 19n + 6}{6}\right)\binom{2n}{n} - \left(1 + \frac{3n}{2}\right)4^n.$$

Thus the mean and variance are $\frac{1}{2}\sqrt{\pi}n^{3/2} + O(n)$ and $(\frac{5}{6} - \frac{\pi}{4})n^{3/2} + O(n)$, respectively.

55. Differentiating as in answer 54, and using the formulas of exercises 46(d) and 5.2.1–14 together with $[z^n]C(z)^r/(1-4z) = 2^{2n+r} - \sum_{j=1}^{r} 2^{r-j}\binom{2n+j}{n}$, yields

$$C'_{p(p+r)}(1) = [z^p]\left((r+1)\frac{z^2 C(z)^{r+3}}{1-4z} + \binom{r+1}{2}\frac{zC(z)^{r+2}}{\sqrt{1-4z}}\right)$$

$$= [z^p]\left((r+1)\frac{C(z)^{r+1} - 2C(z)^r + C(z)^{r-1}}{1-4z} + \binom{r+1}{2}\frac{C(z)^{r+1} - C(z)^r}{\sqrt{1-4z}}\right)$$

$$= (r+1)\left(2^{2p+r-1} - \binom{2p+r+1}{p} - \sum_{j=1}^{r-1} 2^{r-1-j}\binom{2p+j}{p}\right) + \binom{r+1}{2}\binom{2p+r}{p-1}.$$

56. Use 1.2.6–53(b). [See *BIT* **30** (1990), 67–68.]

57. $2S_0(a,b) = \binom{2a}{a}\binom{2b}{b} + \binom{2a+2b}{a+b}$ by 1.2.6–(21). Exercise 1.2.6–53 tells us that

$$\sum_{k=a-m}^{a} \binom{2a}{a-k}\binom{2b}{b-k} k = (m+1)(a+b-m)\binom{2a}{m+1}\binom{2b}{a+b-m};$$

therefore $2S_1(a,b) = \binom{2a}{a}\binom{2b}{b}\frac{ab}{a+b}$. And since $b^2 S_p(a,b) - S_{p+2}(a,b) = S_p(a,b-1)$, we find $2S_2(a,b) = \binom{2a+2b}{a+b}\frac{ab}{2a+2b-1}$; $2S_3(a,b) = \binom{2a}{a}\binom{2b}{b}a^2 b^2/(a+b)^2$. Formula (30) follows by setting $a = m$, $b = n - m$, and $C_{(x-k)(x+k)} = \binom{2x}{x-k} - \binom{2x}{x-k-1}$.

Similarly, the average of w_{2m-1} is $\sum_{k\geq0}(2k-1)C_{(m-k)(m+k-1)}C_{(n-m-k+1)(n-m+k)}$ divided by C_n, namely

$$\frac{2S_3(m,n+1-m) - S_2(m,n+1-m)}{m(n+1-m)C_n} = \frac{m(n+1-m)}{n}\binom{2m}{m}\binom{2n+2-2m}{n+1-m}/\binom{2n}{n} - 1.$$

[R. Kemp, *BIT* **20** (1980), 157–163; H. Prodinger, *Soochow J. Math.* **9** (1983), 193–196.]

58. Summing over cases in which the left subtree has k internal nodes, we have

$$t_{lmn} = [l=m=n=0] + \sum_{k=0}^{m-1} C_k t_{(l-1)(m-k-1)(n-k-1)} + \sum_{k=m}^{n-1} C_{n-1-k} t_{(l-1)mk}.$$

Thus the triple generating function $t(v,w,z) = \sum_{l,m,n} t_{lmn} v^l w^m z^n$ satisfies

$$t(v,w,z) = 1 + vwzC(wz)t(v,w,z) + vzC(z)t(v,w,z);$$

and the analogous linear relation for $t(w,z) = \partial t(v,w,z)/\partial v \,|_{v=1}$ follows, because $t(1,w,z) = \sum_{n=0}^{\infty}\sum_{m=0}^{n} C_n w^m z^n = (C(z) - wC(wz))/(1-w)$ and $zC(z)^2 = C(z) - 1$. Algebraic manipulation now yields

$$t(w,z) = \frac{C(z) + wC(wz) - (1+w)}{(1-w)^2 z} - \frac{2wC(z)C(wz)}{(1-w)^2} - \frac{C(z) - wC(wz)}{1-w},$$

and we obtain the formula $t_{mn} = (m+1)C_{n+1} - 2\sum_{k=0}^{m}(m-k)C_k C_{n-k} - C_n$. Now

$$\sum_{k=0}^{m-1}(k+1)C_k C_{n-1-k} = \frac{m}{2n}\binom{2m}{m}\binom{2n-2m}{n-m}$$

can be proved as in exercise 56, and it follows that

$$t_{mn} = 2\binom{2m}{m}\binom{2n-2m}{n-m}\frac{(2m+1)(2n-2m+1)}{(n+1)(n+2)} - C_n, \qquad \text{for } 0 \leq m \leq n.$$

[P. Kirschenhofer, *J. Combinatorics, Information and System Sciences* **8** (1983), 44–60. For higher moments and generalizations, see W. J. Gutjahr, *Random Structures & Algorithms* **3** (1992), 361–374; A. Panholzer and H. Prodinger, *J. Statistical Planning and Inference* **101** (2002), 267–279. Note that the generating function $t(v,w,z)$ yields

$$t_{lmn} = \sum_{k}\binom{l}{k}C_{(m-k)(m-1)}C_{(n-m-l+k)(n-m-1)}.$$

Using the fact that $\sum_k \binom{k}{r}C_{(n-k)(m-1)} = C_{(n-r)(m+r)}$ when $m \geq 1$, we obtain the formula $t_{mn} + C_n = \sum_k (k+1)C_{(m-k)(m-1)}C_{(n-m)(n-m+k+1)}$, a sum that can therefore (surprisingly) be expressed in closed form.]

59. $T(w,z) = \dfrac{w\big(C(z)-C(wz)\big)}{(1-w)} - wzC(z)C(wz)+zC(z)T(w,z)+wzC(wz)T(wz)$

$$= \frac{w\big((C(z)+C(wz)-2)/z - (1+w)C(z)C(wz) - (1-w)(C(z)-C(wz))\big)}{(1-w)^2}.$$

Hence $T_{mn} = t_{mn} - \sum_{k=m}^{n} C_k C_{n-k}$. [Is there a combinatorial proof?] And

$$T_{mn} = \binom{2m}{m}\binom{2n+2-2m}{n+1-m}\frac{4m(n+1-m)+n+1}{2(n+1)(n+2)} - \frac{1}{2}C_{n+1} - C_n, \quad \text{for } 1 \le m \le n.$$

60. (a) It is the number of right parentheses in co-atoms. (Therefore it is also the number of k for which $w_{2k-1} < 0$ in the associated "worm walk.")

(b) For convenience let $d(\text{'('}) = +1$ and $d(\text{')'}) = -1$.

A1. [Initialize.] Set $i \leftarrow j \leftarrow 1$ and $k \leftarrow 2n$.

A2. [Done?] Terminate the algorithm if $j > k$. Otherwise set $a_j \leftarrow \text{'('}$, $j \leftarrow j+1$.

A3. [Atom?] If $b_i = \text{')'}$, set $s \leftarrow -1$, $i \leftarrow i+1$, and go to A4. Otherwise set $s \leftarrow 1$, $i \leftarrow i+1$, and while $s > 0$ set $a_j \leftarrow b_i$, $j \leftarrow j+1$, $s \leftarrow s+d(b_i)$, $i \leftarrow i+1$. Return to A2.

A4. [Co-atom.] Set $s \leftarrow s+d(b_i)$. Then if $s < 0$, set $a_k \leftarrow b_i$, $k \leftarrow k-1$, $i \leftarrow i+1$, and repeat step A4. Otherwise set $a_k \leftarrow \text{')'}$, $k \leftarrow k-1$, $i \leftarrow i+1$, and return to A2. ∎

(c) The defect-11 inverse of (1) is $(())((()))))(()(()))(()))(((.$ In general we find it by locating the subscript m just before the lth-from-last right parenthesis, and the indices $(u_0, v_0), \ldots, (u_{s-1}, v_{s-1})$ of matching parentheses such that $u_j \le m < v_j$.

I1. [Initialize.] Set $c \leftarrow j \leftarrow s \leftarrow 0$, $k \leftarrow m \leftarrow 2n$, and $u_0 \leftarrow 2n+1$.

I2. [Scan right to left.] If $k = 0$, go to I5; if $a_k = \text{')'}$, go to I3; if $a_k = \text{'('}$, go to I4.

I3. [Process a ')'.] Set $r_j \leftarrow k$, $j \leftarrow j+1$, $c \leftarrow c+1$. If $c = l$, set $m \leftarrow k-1$, $s \leftarrow j$, and $u_s \leftarrow k$. Then decrease k by 1 and return to I2.

I4. [Process a '('.] (At this point the left parenthesis a_k matches the right parenthesis $a_{r_{j-1}}$.) Set $j \leftarrow j-1$. If $r_j > m$, set $u_j \leftarrow k$ and $v_j \leftarrow r_j$. Then decrease k by 1 and return to I2.

I5. [Prepare to permute.] Set $i \leftarrow j \leftarrow 1$, $k \leftarrow 2n$, and $c \leftarrow 0$.

I6. [Permute.] While $j \ne u_c$, set $b_i \leftarrow a_j$, $i \leftarrow i+1$, $j \leftarrow j+1$. Then terminate if $c = s$; otherwise set $b_i \leftarrow \text{')'}$, $i \leftarrow i+1$, $j \leftarrow j+1$. While $k \ne v_c$, set $b_i \leftarrow a_k$, $i \leftarrow i+1$, $k \leftarrow k-1$. Then set $b_i \leftarrow \text{'('}$, $i \leftarrow i+1$, $k \leftarrow k-1$, $c \leftarrow c+1$, and repeat step I6. ∎

Notes: The fact that exactly C_n balanced strings of length $2n$ have defect l, for $0 \le l \le n$, was discovered by P. A. MacMahon [*Philosophical Transactions* **209** (1909), 153–175, §20], then rediscovered by K. L. Chung and W. Feller [*Proc. Nat. Acad. Sci.* **35** (1949), 605–608], using generating functions. A simple combinatorial explanation was found subsequently by J. L. Hodges, Jr. [*Biometrika* **42** (1955), 261–262], who observed that if $\beta_1 \ldots \beta_r$ has defect $l > 0$ and if $\beta_k = \alpha_k^R$ is its rightmost co-atom, the balanced string $\beta_1 \ldots \beta_{k-1} (\beta_{k+1} \ldots \beta_r) \alpha_k'^R$ has defect $l-1$ (and this transformation is reversible). The efficient mapping in the present exercise is similar to a construction of M. D. Atkinson and J.-R. Sack [*Information Processing Letters* **41** (1992), 21–23].

61. (a) Let $c_j = 1 - b_j$; thus $c_j \le 1$, $c_1 + \cdots + c_N = f$, and we must prove that

$$c_1 + c_2 + \cdots + c_k < f \qquad \text{if and only if} \qquad k < N$$

holds for exactly f cyclic shifts. We can define c_j for all integers j by letting $c_{j\pm N} = c_j$. Let us also define Σ_j for all j by letting $\Sigma_0 = 0$ and $\Sigma_j = \Sigma_{j-1} + c_j$; then $\Sigma_{j+Nt} = \Sigma_j + ft$, and $\Sigma_{j+1} \le \Sigma_j + 1$. It follows that for each integer x there is a smallest integer $j = j(x)$ such that $\Sigma_j = x$. Moreover, $j(x) < j(x+1)$; and $j(x+f) = j(x) + N$. Thus the desired condition holds if and only if we shift by $j(x) \bmod N$ for $x = 1, 2, \ldots$, or f. (The history of this important lemma is discussed in answer 2.3.4.4–32.)

(b) Start with $l \leftarrow m \leftarrow s \leftarrow 0$. Then for $k = 1, 2, \ldots, N$ (in this order) do the following: Set $s \leftarrow s + 1 - b_k$; and if $s > m$, set $m \leftarrow s$, $j_l \leftarrow k$, and $l \leftarrow (l+1) \bmod f$. The answers are $j_0, \ldots, j_{f-1}$, by the proof in part (a).

(c) Start with any string $b_1 b_2 \ldots b_N$ containing n_j occurrences of j for $0 \le j \le t$. Apply a random permutation to this string, then apply the algorithm of part (b). Choose randomly between $(j_0, \ldots, j_{f-1})$ and use the resulting cyclic shift as a preorder sequence to define the forest.

[See L. Alonso, J. L. Rémy, and R. Schott, *Algorithmica* **17** (1997), 162–182, for an even more general algorithm.]

62. Bit strings $(l_1 \ldots l_n, r_1 \ldots r_n)$ are valid if and only if $b_1 \ldots b_n$ is valid in exercise 20, where $b_j = l_j + r_j$. Therefore we can use exercise 61. [See J. F. Korsh, *Information Processing Letters* **45** (1993), 291–294.]

63.

64. $X = 2k + b$ where $(k, b) = (0, 1), (2, 1), (0, 0), (5, 1), (6, 0), (1, 1)$; eventually $L_0 L_1 \ldots L_{12} = 5\ 11\ 3\ 4\ 0\ 7\ 9\ 8\ 1\ 6\ 10\ 12\ 2$.

65. See A. Panholzer and H. Prodinger, *Discrete Mathematics* **250** (2002), 181–195; M. Luczak and P. Winkler, *Random Structures & Algorithms* **24** (2004), 420–443.

66. (a) "Shrink" the white edges, merging the nodes that they connect. For example,

are the ordinary trees that correspond to the eleven Schröder trees depicted for $n = 3$. Under this correspondence a left link means, "Here is a child"; a white right link means, "Look here for more children"; a black right link means, "Here's the last child."

(b) Mimic Algorithm L, but between rotations use an ordinary Gray binary code to run through all color patterns of whatever right links are present. (The case $n = 3$ has, in fact, been illustrated in the example.)

Note that Schröder trees also correspond to series-parallel graphs, as in (53). They do, however, impose an order on the edges and/or superedges that are joined in parallel; so they correspond more precisely to series-parallel graphs *as embedded in the plane* (and with edges and vertices unlabeled, except for s and t).

67. $S(z) = 1 + zS(z)\big(1 + 2(S(z) - 1)\big)$, because $1 + 2(S(z) - 1)$ enumerates the right subtrees; therefore $S(z) = (1 + z - \sqrt{1 - 6z + z^2})/(4z)$.

Notes: We've seen Schröder numbers in exercise 2.3.4.4–31, where $G(z) = zS(z)$; and in exercise 2.2.1–11, where $b_n = 2S_{n-1}$ for $n \ge 2$ and where we found the recurrence $(n-1)S_n = (6n - 3)S_{n-1} - (n-2)S_{n-2}$. They grow asymptotically as explored in exercise 2.2.1–12. A triangle of numbers S_{pq}, analogous to (22), can be used to generate random Schröder trees. These numbers satisfy

$$S_{pq} = S_{p(q-1)} + S_{(p-1)q} + S_{(p-2)q} + \cdots + S_{0q} = S_{p(q-1)} + 2S_{(p-1)q} - S_{(p-1)(q-1)}$$

$$= \frac{q-p+1}{q+1} \sum_{k=0}^{p} \binom{q+1}{p-k}\binom{p-1}{k} 2^k = \sum_{k=0}^{p} \left(\binom{q}{p-k}\binom{p-1}{k} - \binom{q}{p-k-1}\binom{p-1}{k-1} \right) 2^k$$

$$= [w^p z^q]\, S(wz)/(1 - zS(wz));$$

the double generating function on the last line is due to Emeric Deutsch. Many other properties of Schröder trees are discussed in Richard Stanley's *Enumerative Combinatorics* **2** (1999), exercise 6.39.

68. A single row that contains only the empty string ϵ. (The general rule (36) for going from $n-1$ to n converts this row into '0 1', the pattern of order 1.)

69. The first $\binom{6}{3} = 20$ rows are the Christmas tree pattern of order 6, if we ignore the '10' at the beginning of each string. The pattern of order 7 is a bit more difficult to see; but there are $\binom{7}{3} = 35$ rows in which the leftmost entry begins with 0. Disregard the rightmost string in all such rows, and ignore the 0 at the beginning of each remaining string. (Other answers are also possible.)

70. If σ appears in column k of the Christmas tree pattern, let σ' be the string in column $n-k$ of the same row. (If we think of parentheses instead of bits, this rule takes the mirror reflection of the free parentheses in the sense of answer 11, by (39).)

71. $M_{t,n}$ is the sum of the t largest binomial coefficients $\binom{n}{k}$, because each row of the Christmas tree pattern can contain at most t elements of S, and because we do get such a set S by choosing all strings σ with $(n-t)/2 \le \nu(\sigma) \le (n+t-1)/2$. (The formula

$$M_{t,n} = \sum_{n-t \le 2k \le n+t-1} \binom{n}{k}$$

is about as simple as possible; however, special formulas like $M_{2,n} = M_{n+1}$ hold for small t, and we also have $M_{t,n} = 2^n$ for $t > n$.)

72. You get $M_{s,n}$, the same number as in the previous exercise. In fact, one can prove by induction that there are exactly $\binom{n}{n-k} - \binom{n}{k-s}$ rows of length $s + n - 2k \ge 0$.

73. 01100100100000000100101001100, 111001011011111111101101011100; see (38).

74. By the lexicographic property, we want to count the number of rows whose rightmost elements have the respective forms $0*^{29}$, $10*^{28}$, $110*^{27}$, $111000*^{24}$, $11100100*^{22}$, $111001010*^{21}$, $11100101100*^{19}$, $111001011010*^{18}$, $1110010110110*^{17}$, ..., namely all 30-bit strings that precede $\tau = 111001011011111111101101011100$.

If θ has p more 1s than 0s, the number of Christmas tree rows ending with $\theta*^n$ is the same as the number of rows ending with 1^p*^n; and this is $M_{p+1,n}$, by exercise 71, because all such rows are the n-step descendants of the starting row '$0^p\,0^{p-1}1\,\ldots\,1^p$'.

Consequently the answer is $M_{0,29} + M_{1,28} + M_{2,27} + M_{1,24} + \cdots + M_{12,3} + M_{13,2} = \sum_{k=1}^{21} M_{2k-1-z_k,\,n-z_k} = 0 + \binom{28}{14} + \binom{27}{14} + \binom{27}{13} + \binom{24}{12} + \cdots + 8 + 4 = 84867708$, where $(z_1, \ldots, z_{21}) = (1, 2, 3, 6, \ldots, 27, 28)$ is the sequence of places where 1s occur in τ.

75. We have $r_1^{(n)} = M_{n-2}$, because row $r_1^{(n)}$ is the bottom descendant of the first row in (33). We also have $r_{j+1}^{(n)} - r_j^{(n)} = M_{j,n-1-j} - M_{j-1,n-2-j} = M_{j+1,n-2-j}$ by the formula in answer 74, because the relevant sequence $z_1 \ldots z_{n-1}$ for row $r_j^{(n)}$ is $1^j 01^{n-1-j}$. Therefore, since $M_{j,n}/M_n \to j$ for fixed j as $n \to \infty$, we have

$$\lim_{n \to \infty} \frac{r_j^{(n)}}{M_n} = \sum_{k=1}^{j} \frac{k}{2^{k+1}} = 1 - \frac{j+2}{2^{j+1}}.$$

And we've also implicitly proved that $\sum_{k=0}^{n} M_{k,n-k} = M_{n+1} - 1$.

76. The first $\binom{2n}{n}$ elements of the infinite sequence

$$Q = 1313351313351335355713133513133513353557131335133535571335355735575779\ldots$$

are the row sizes in the pattern of order $2n$; this sequence $Q = q_1 q_2 q_3 \ldots$ is the unique fixed point of the transformation that maps $1 \mapsto 13$ and $n \mapsto (n-2) \, n \, n \, (n+2)$ for odd $n > 1$, representing two steps of (36).

Let $f(x) = \limsup_{n \to \infty} s(\lceil x M_n \rceil)/n$ for $0 < x \le 1$. This function apparently vanishes almost everywhere; but it equals 1 when x has the form $(q_1 + \cdots + q_j)/2^n$, because of answer 72. On the other hand if we define $g(x) = \lim_{n \to \infty} s(\lceil x M_n \rceil)/\sqrt{n}$, the function $g(x)$ appears to be measurable, with $\int_0^1 g(x)\,dx = \sqrt{\pi}$, although $g(x)$ is infinite when $f(x) > 0$. (Rigorous proofs or disproofs of these conjectures are solicited.)

77. The hint follows from (39), by considering worm walks; so we can proceed thus:

X1. [Initialize.] Set $a_j \leftarrow 0$ for $0 \le j \le n$; also set $x \leftarrow 1$. (In the following steps we will have $x = 1 + 2(a_1 + \cdots + a_n)$.)

X2. [Correct the tail.] While $x \le n$, set $a_x \leftarrow 1$ and $x \leftarrow x + 2$.

X3. [Visit.] Visit the bit string $a_1 \ldots a_n$.

X4. [Easy case?] If $a_n = 0$, set $a_n \leftarrow 1$, $x \leftarrow x + 2$, and return to X3.

X5. [Find and advance a_j.] Set $a_n \leftarrow 0$ and $j \leftarrow n - 1$. Then while $a_j = 1$, set $a_j \leftarrow 0$, $x \leftarrow x - 2$, and $j \leftarrow j - 1$. Stop if $j = 0$; otherwise set $a_j \leftarrow 1$ and go back to X2. ∎

78. True, by (39) and exercise 11.

79. (a) List the indices of the 0s, then the indices of the 1s; for instance, the bit string in exercise 73 corresponds to the permutation 1 4 5 7 8 10 11 12 13 20 23 25 29 30 2 3 6 9 14 15 16 17 18 19 21 22 24 26 27 28.

(b) Using the conventions of (39), the P tableau has the indices of left parentheses and free parentheses in its top row, other indices in the second row. Thus, from (38),

$$P = \begin{array}{|c|c|c|c|c|c|c|c|c|c|c|c|c|c|c|c|c|c|c|c|c|c|c|}
\hline
1 & 2 & 3 & 6 & 8 & 9 & 11 & 12 & 13 & 14 & 15 & 16 & 17 & 18 & 19 & 21 & 22 & 24 & 26 & 27 & 28 \\
\hline
4 & 5 & 7 & 10 & 20 & 23 & 25 & 29 & 30 \\
\cline{1-9}
\end{array}$$

[See K.-P. Vo, *SIAM J. Algebraic and Discrete Methods* **2** (1981), 324–332, for a generalization to chains of submultisets.]

80. This curious fact is a consequence of exercise 79 together with Theorem 6 in the author's paper on tableaux; see *Pacific J. Math.* **34** (1970), 709–727.

81. Suppose σ and σ' belong respectively to chains of length s and s' in the Christmas tree patterns of order n and n'. At most $\min(s, s')$ of the ss' pairs of strings in those chains can be in the biclutter. Furthermore, because of (39), those ss' pairs of strings actually constitute exactly $\min(s, s')$ chains in the Christmas tree pattern of order $n + n'$, when they are concatenated. Therefore the sum of $\min(s, s')$ over all pairs of chains is $M_{n+n'}$, and the result follows. We have incidentally proved the nonobvious identity

$$\sum_{j,\,k} \min(m+1-2j, n+1-2k)\, C_{j(m-j)}\, C_{k(n-k)} = M_{m+n}.$$

Notes: This extension of Sperner's theorem was proved independently by G. Katona [*Studia Sci. Math. Hungar.* **1** (1966), 59–63] and D. J. Kleitman [*Math. Zeitschrift* **90** (1965), 251–259]. See Greene and Kleitman, *J. Combinatorial Theory* **A20** (1976), 80–88, for the proof given here and for further results.

82. (a) There is at least one evaluation in each row m; there are two if and only if $s(m) > 1$ and the first evaluation yields 0. Thus if f is identically 1, we get the minimum, M_n; if f is identically 0, we get the maximum, $M_n + \sum_m [s(m) > 1] = M_{n+1}$.

(b) Let $f(\chi(m, n/2)) = 0$ in the $C_{n/2}$ cases where $s(m) = 1$; otherwise let $f(\chi(m, a)) = 1$, where a is defined by the algorithm. When n is odd, this rule implies that $f(\sigma)$ is always 1; but when n is even, $f(\sigma) = 0$ if and only if σ is first in its row. (To see why, use the fact that the row containing σ'_j in (41) always has size $s - 2$.) This function f is indeed monotonic; for if $\sigma \le \tau$ and if σ has a free left parenthesis, so does τ. For example, in the case $n = 8$ we have

$$f(x_1, \ldots, x_8) = x_8 \vee x_6 x_7 \vee x_4 x_5 (x_6 \vee x_7) \vee x_2 x_3 (x_4 (x_5 \vee x_6 \vee x_7) \vee x_5 (x_6 \vee x_7)).$$

(c) In these circumstances (45) is the solution for all n.

83. At most 3 outcomes are possible in step H4 — in fact, at most 2 when $s(m) = 1$. [See exercise 5.3.4–31 for sharper bounds; in the notation of that exercise, there are exactly $\delta_n + 2$ monotone Boolean functions of n Boolean variables.]

84. For this problem we partition the 2^n bit strings into M_n blocks instead of chains, where the strings $\{\sigma_1, \ldots, \sigma_s\}$ of each block satisfy $\|A\sigma_i^T - A\sigma_j^T\| \ge 1$ for $i \ne j$; then at most one bit string per block can satisfy $\|A\sigma^T - b\| < \frac{1}{2}$.

Let A' denote the first $n-1$ columns of A, and let v be the nth column. Suppose $\{\sigma_1, \ldots, \sigma_s\}$ is a block for A', and number the subscripts so that $v^T A' \sigma_1^T$ is the minimum of $v^T A' \sigma_j^T$. Then rule (36) defines appropriate blocks for A, because we have $\|A(\sigma_i 0)^T - A(\sigma_j 0)^T\| = \|A(\sigma_i 1)^T - A(\sigma_j 1)^T\| = \|A'\sigma_i^T - A'\sigma_j^T\|$ and

$$\|A(\sigma_j 1)^T - A(\sigma_1 0)^T\|^2 = \|A'\sigma_j^T + v - A'\sigma_1^T\|^2$$
$$= \|A'(\sigma_j - \sigma_1)^T\|^2 + \|v\|^2 + 2v^T A'(\sigma_j - \sigma_1)^T \ge \|v\|^2 \ge 1.$$

[And more is true; see *Advances in Math.* **5** (1970), 155–157. This result extends a theorem of J. E. Littlewood and A. C. Offord, *Mat. Sbornik* **54** (1943), 277–285, who considered the case $m = 2$.]

85. (Solution by Günter Rote.) The vector space V can be represented as

$$\{x \mid Ax = 0\}$$

for some $m \times n$ matrix A. Let v_j be the jth column of A, and notice that v_j cannot be zero because V contains no unit vectors. We can therefore assume that $\min(\|v_1\|, \ldots, \|v_n\|) = 1$, after multiplying A by an appropriate constant. Exercise 84 now applies.

Conversely, the basis with $m = 1$ and $x_{j1} = (-1)^{j-1}$ yields M_n solutions. [This result has application to electronic voting; see Golle's Ph.D. thesis (Stanford, 2004).]

86. First reorder the 4-node subtrees so that their level codes are 0121 (plus a constant); then sort larger and larger subtrees until everything is canonical. The resulting level codes are 0 1 2 3 4 3 2 1 2 3 2 1 2 0 1, and the parent pointers are 0 1 2 3 4 3 2 1 8 9 8 1 12 0 14.

87. (a) The condition holds if and only if $c_1 < \cdots < c_k \geq c_{k+1} \geq \cdots \geq c_n$ for some k, so the total number of cases is $\sum_k \binom{n-1}{n-k} = 2^{n-1}$.

(b) Note that $c_1 \ldots c_k = c'_1 \ldots c'_k$ if and only if $p_1 \ldots p_k = p'_1 \ldots p'_k$; and in such cases, $c_{k+1} < c'_{k+1}$ if and only if $p_{k+1} < p'_{k+1}$.

88. Exactly A_{n+1} forests are visited, and A_k of them have $p_k = \cdots = p_n = 0$. Therefore O4 is performed A_n times; and p_k is changed $A_{k+1} - 1$ times in step O5, for $1 \leq k < n$. Step O5 also changes p_n a total of $A_n - 1$ times. The average number of mems per visit is therefore only $2 + 3/(\alpha-1) + O(1/n) \approx 3.534$, if we keep p_n in a register. [See E. Kubicka, *Combinatorics, Probability and Computing* **5** (1996), 403–417.]

89. If step O5 sets $p_n \leftarrow p_j$ exactly Q_n times, it sets $p_k \leftarrow p_j$ exactly $Q_k + A_{k+1} - A_k$ times, for $1 < k < n$, because every prefix of a canonical $p_1 \ldots p_n$ is canonical. We have $(Q_1, Q_2, \ldots) = (0, 0, 1, 2, 5, 9, 22, 48, 118, 288, \ldots)$; and one can show that $Q_n = \sum_{d \geq 1} \sum_{1 \leq c < n/d - 1} a_{(n-cd)(n-cd-d)}$, where a_{nk} is the number of canonical parent sequences $p_1 \ldots p_n$ with $p_n = k$. But these numbers a_{nk} remain mysterious.

90. (a) This property is equivalent to 2.3.4.4–(7); vertex 0 is the centroid.

(b) Let $m = \lfloor n/2 \rfloor$. At the end of step O1, set $p_{m+1} \leftarrow 0$, and also $p_{2m+1} \leftarrow 0$ if n is odd. At the end of step O4, set $i \leftarrow j$ and while $p_i \neq 0$ set $i \leftarrow p_i$. (Then i is the root of the tree containing j and k.) At the beginning of step O5, if $k = i + m$ and $i < j$, set $j \leftarrow i$ and $d \leftarrow m$.

(c) If n is even, there are no bicentroidal trees with $n + 1$ vertices. Otherwise find all pairs $(p'_1 \ldots p'_m, p''_1 \ldots p''_m)$ of canonical forests on $m = \lfloor n/2 \rfloor$ nodes, with $p'_1 \ldots p'_m \geq p''_1 \ldots p''_m$; let $p_1 = 0$, $p_{j+1} = p'_j + 1$, and $p_{m+j+1} = (p''_j + m + 1)[p''_j > 0]$ for $1 \leq j \leq m$. If $p''_j = 0$, $p_{j+m+1} = 0'$ is the second centroid. (Two incarnations of Algorithm O will generate all such sequences. This algorithm for free trees is due to F. Ruskey and G. Li; see *SODA* **10** (1999), S939–S940.)

91. Use the following recursive procedure $W(n)$: If $n \leq 2$, return the unique n-node oriented tree. Otherwise choose positive integers j and d so that a given pair (j, d) is obtained with probability $d A_d A_{n-jd}/((n-1)A_n)$. Compute random oriented trees $T' \leftarrow W(n-jd)$ and $T'' \leftarrow W(d)$. Return the tree T obtained by linking j clones of T'' to the root of T'. [*Combinatorial Algorithms* (Academic Press, 1975), Chapter 25. For random free trees, see H. S. Wilf, *Journal of Algorithms* **2** (1981), 204–207.]

92. Not always. [R. L. Cummins, in *IEEE Trans.* **CT-13** (1966), 82–90, proved that the graph of $S(G)$ always contains a cycle; see also C. A. Holzmann and F. Harary, *SIAM J. Applied Math.* **22** (1972), 187–193. But their constructions are unsuitable for efficient computation, because they require foreknowledge of the parity of the sizes of intermediate results.]

93. Yes. Step S7 undoes step S3; step S9 undoes the deletions of step S8.

94. For example, we can use depth-first search, with an auxiliary table $b_1 \ldots b_n$:

i) Set $b_1 \ldots b_n \leftarrow 0 \ldots 0$, then $v \leftarrow 1$, $w \leftarrow 1$, $b_1 \leftarrow 1$, and $k \leftarrow n - 1$.

ii) Set $e \leftarrow n_{v-1}$. While $t_e \neq 0$, do the following substeps:

    a) Set $u \leftarrow t_e$. If $b_u \neq 0$, go to substep (c).

    b) Set $b_u \leftarrow w$, $w \leftarrow u$, $a_k \leftarrow e$, $k \leftarrow k - 1$. Terminate if $k = 0$.

    c) Set $e \leftarrow n_e$.

iii) If $w \neq 1$, set $v \leftarrow w$, $w \leftarrow b_w$, and return to (ii). Otherwise report an error: The given graph was not connected.

We could actually terminate as soon as substep (b) reduces k to 1, since Algorithm S never looks at the initial value of a_1. But we might as well test for connectivity.

95. The following steps perform a breadth-first search from u, to see if v is reachable without using edge e. An auxiliary array $b_1 \ldots b_n$ of arc pointers is used, which should be initialized to $0 \ldots 0$ at the end of step S1; we will reset it to $0 \ldots 0$ again.

i) Set $w \leftarrow u$ and $b_w \leftarrow v$.

ii) Set $f \leftarrow n_{u-1}$. While $t_f \neq 0$, do the following substeps:
 a) Set $v' \leftarrow t_f$. If $b_{v'} \neq 0$, go to substep (d).
 b) If $v' \neq v$, set $b_{v'} \leftarrow v$, $b_w \leftarrow v'$, $w \leftarrow v'$, and go to substep (d).
 c) If $f \neq e \oplus 1$, go to step (v).
 d) Set $f \leftarrow n_f$.

iii) Set $u \leftarrow b_u$. If $u \neq v$, return to step (ii).

iv) Set $u \leftarrow t_e$. While $u \neq v$, set $w \leftarrow b_u$, $b_u \leftarrow 0$, $u \leftarrow w$. Go to S9 (e is a bridge).

v) Set $u \leftarrow t_e$. While $u \neq v$, set $w \leftarrow b_u$, $b_u \leftarrow 0$, $u \leftarrow w$. Then set $u \leftarrow t_e$ again and continue step S8 (e is not a bridge).

Two quick heuristics can be used before starting this calculation: If $d_u = 1$, then e is obviously a bridge; and if $l_{l_e} \neq 0$, then e is obviously a nonbridge (because there's another edge between u and v). Such special cases are detected readily by the breadth-first search, yet experiments by the author indicate that both heuristics are definitely worthwhile. For example, the test on l_{l_e} typically saves 3% or so of the total running time.

96. (a) Let e_k be the arc $k - 1 \to k$. The steps in answer 94 set $a_k \leftarrow e_{n+1-k}$ for $n > k \geq 1$. Then at level k we shrink e_{n-k}, for $1 \leq k < n - 1$. After visiting the (unique) spanning tree $e_{n-1} \ldots e_2 e_n$, we unshrink e_{n-k} and discover quickly that it is a bridge, for $n - 1 > k \geq 1$. Thus the running time is linear in n; in the author's implementation it turns out to be exactly $102n - 226$ mems for $n \geq 3$.

However, this result depends critically on the order of the edges in the initial spanning tree. If step S1 had produced "organ-pipe order" such as

$$e_{n/2+1} \, e_{n/2} \, e_{n/2+2} \, e_{n/2-1} \, \cdots \, e_{n-1} \, e_2$$

in positions $a_2 \ldots a_{n-1}$ when n is even, the running time would have been $\Omega(n^2)$, because $\Omega(n)$ of the bridge tests would each have taken $\Omega(n)$ steps.

(b) Now a_k is initially e_{n-k} for $n > k \geq 1$, where e_1 is the arc $n \to 1$. The spanning trees visited, when $n \geq 4$, are respectively $e_{n-2} \ldots e_1 e_n$, $e_{n-2} \ldots e_1 e_{n-1}$, $e_{n-2} \ldots e_2 e_{n-1} e_n$, $e_{n-2} \ldots e_3 e_{n-1} e_n e_1$, $\ldots$, $e_{n-1} e_n e_1 \ldots e_{n-3}$. Following the tree $e_{n-2} \ldots e_{k+2} e_{n-1} e_n e_1 \ldots e_k$ the computations move down to level $n - k - 3$ and up again, for $0 \leq k \leq n - 4$; the bridge tests are all efficient. Thus the total running time is quadratic (in the author's version, exactly $35.5n^2 + 7.5n - 145$ mems, for $n \geq 5$).

Incidentally, P_n is $board(n, 0, 0, 0, 1, 0, 0)$ in the notation of the Stanford Graph-Base, and C_n is $board(n, 0, 0, 0, 1, 1, 0)$; the SGB vertices are named 0 through $n - 1$.

97. Yes, when $\{s, t\}$ is $\{1, 2\}$, $\{1, 3\}$, $\{2, 3\}$, $\{2, 4\}$, or $\{3, 4\}$, but not $\{1, 4\}$.

98. $A' = $; this is the "dual planar graph" of the planar graph A.

(The near trees of A' are complements of the spanning trees of A, and vice versa.)

99. The stated method works, by induction on the size of the tree, for essentially the same reasons that it worked for n-tuples in Section 7.2.1.1 — but with the additional proviso that we must successively designate each child of an uneasy node.

Leaf nodes are always passive, and they are neither easy nor uneasy; so we will assume that the branch nodes are numbered 1 to m in preorder. Let $f_p = p$ for all branch nodes, except when p is a passive uneasy node for which the nearest uneasy node to its right is active; in the latter case, f_p should point to the nearest active uneasy node to its left. (For purposes of this definition, we imagine that artificial nodes 0 and $m + 1$ are present at the left and right, both of which are uneasy and active.)

F1. [Initialize.] Set $f_p \leftarrow p$ for $0 \leq p \leq m$; also set $t_0 \leftarrow 1$, $v_0 \leftarrow 0$, and set each z_p so that $r_{z_p} = d_p$.

F2. [Select node p.] Set $q \leftarrow m$; then while $t_q = v_q$ set $q \leftarrow q - 1$. Set $p \leftarrow f_q$ and $f_q \leftarrow q$; terminate the algorithm if $p = 0$.

F3. [Change d_p.] Set $s \leftarrow d_p$, $s' \leftarrow r_s$, $k \leftarrow v_p$, and $d_p \leftarrow s'$. (Now $k = v_s \neq v_{s'}$.)

F4. [Update the values.] Set $q \leftarrow s$ and $v_q \leftarrow k \oplus 1$. While $d_q \neq 0$, set $q \leftarrow d_q$ and $v_q \leftarrow k \oplus 1$. (Now q is a leaf that has entered the config if $k = 0$, left it if $k = 1$.) Similarly, set $q \leftarrow s'$ and $v_q \leftarrow k$. While $d_q \neq 0$, set $q \leftarrow d_q$ and $v_q \leftarrow k$. (Now q is a leaf that has left the config if $k = 0$, entered it if $k = 1$.)

F5. [Visit.] Visit the current config, represented by all the leaf values.

F6. [Passivate p?] (All uneasy nodes to p's right are now active.) If $d_p \neq z_p$, return to step F2. Otherwise set $z_p \leftarrow s$, $q \leftarrow p - 1$; while $t_q = v_q$, set $q \leftarrow q - 1$. (Now q is the first uneasy node to the left of p; we will make p passive.) Set $f_p \leftarrow f_q$, $f_q \leftarrow q$, and return to F2. ▮

Although step F4 may change uneasy nodes to easy nodes and vice versa, the focus pointers need not be updated, because they're still set correctly.

100. A complete program, called GRAYSPSPAN, appears on the author's website. Its asymptotic efficiency can be proved by using the result of exercise 110 below.

102. If so, ordinary spanning trees can be listed in a *strong revolving-door order*, where the edges that enter and leave at each step are adjacent.

Interesting algorithms to generate all the oriented spanning trees with a given root have been developed by Harold N. Gabow and Eugene W. Myers, *SICOMP* **7** (1978), 280–287; S. Kapoor and H. Ramesh, *Algorithmica* **27** (2000), 120–130.

103. (a) Toppling increases $(x_0, x_1, \ldots, x_n)$ lexicographically, but does not change $x_0 + \cdots + x_n$. If we can topple at both V_i and V_j, either order gives the same result.

(b) Adding a grain of sand changes the 16 stable states as follows:

Given 0000 0001 0010 0011 0100 0101 0110 0111 1000 1001 1010 1011 1100 1101 1110 1111

+ 0001 0001 0010 0011 0001 0101 0110 0111 0101 1001 1010 1011 1001 1101 1110 1111 1101

+ 0010 0010 0011 0001 0010 0110 0111 0101 0110 1010 1011 1001 1010 1110 1111 1101 1110

+ 0100 0100 0101 0110 0111 1000 1001 1010 1011 1100 1101 1110 1111 0100 0101 0110 0111

+ 1000 1000 1001 1010 1011 1100 1101 1110 1111 0100 0101 0110 0111 1000 1001 1010 1011

The recurrent states are the nine cases with $x_1 + x_2 > 0$ and $x_3 + x_4 > 0$. Notice that repeated addition of 0001 leads to the infinite cycle 0000 → 0001 → 0010 → 0011 → 0001 → 0010 → $\cdots$; but the states 0001, 0010, and 0011 are *not* recurrent.

(c) If $x = \sigma(x + t)$ then also $x = \sigma(x + kt)$ for all $k \geq 0$. All components of t are positive; thus $x = \sigma(x + \max(d_1, \ldots, d_n)t)$ is recurrent. Conversely, suppose

$x = \sigma(d + y)$, where all $y_i \geq 0$; then $d + y + t$ topples to $x + t$ and it also topples to $\sigma(d) + y + t = d + y$. Therefore $\sigma(x + t) = \sigma(d + y) = x$.

(d) There are $N = \det(a_{ij})$ classes, because elementary row operations (exercise 4.6.1–19) triangularize the matrix while preserving congruence.

(e) There are nonnegative integers $m_1, \ldots, m_n, m'_1, \ldots, m'_n$ such that

$$x + m_1 a_1 + \cdots + m_n a_n = x' + m'_1 a_1 + \cdots + m'_n a_n = y, \text{ say.}$$

For sufficiently large k, the vector $y + kt$ topples in $m_1 + \cdots + m_n$ steps to $x + kt$, and in $m'_1 + \cdots + m'_n$ steps to $x' + kt$. Therefore $x = \sigma(x + kt) = \sigma(x' + kt) = x'$.

(f) The triangularization in (d) shows that $x \equiv x + Ny$ for arbitrary vectors y. And toppling preserves congruence; hence every class contains a recurrent state.

(g) Since $a = a_1 + \cdots + a_n$ in a balanced digraph, we have $x \equiv x + a$. If x is recurrent, we see in fact that every vertex topples exactly once when $x + a$ reduces to x, because the vectors $\{a_1, \ldots, a_n\}$ are linearly independent.

Conversely, if $\sigma(x + a) = x$ we must prove that x is recurrent. Let $z_m = \sigma(ma)$; there must be some positive k and m with $z_{m+k} = z_m$. Then every vertex topples k times when $z_m + ka$ reduces to z_m; hence there are vectors $y_j = (y_{j1}, \ldots, y_{jn})$ with $y_{jj} \geq d_j$ such that $(m + k)a$ topples to y_j. It follows that $x + n(m + k)a$ topples to $x + y_1 + \cdots + y_n$, and $\sigma(x + y_1 + \cdots + y_n) = \sigma(x + n(m + k)a) = x$.

(h) Treating subscripts cyclically, the spanning trees with arcs $V_j \to V_0$ for $j = i_1$, $\ldots, i_k$ have $n - k$ other arcs: $V_j \to V_{j-1}$ for $i_l < j \leq i_l + q_l$ and $V_j \to V_{j+1}$ for $i_l + q_l < j < i_{l+1}$. The recurrent states, similarly, have $x_j = 2$ for $j = i_1, \ldots, i_k$, and $x_j = 1$ for $i_l < j < i_{l+1}$, except that $x_j = 0$ when $j = i_l + q_l$ and $q_l > 0$.

(i) In this case state $x = (x_1, \ldots, x_n)$ is recurrent if and only if $(n - x_1, \ldots, n - x_n)$ solves the parking problem in the hint, because $t = (1, \ldots, 1)$, and a sequence that doesn't get parked leaves a "hole" that stops $x + t$ from toppling to x.

Notes: This sandpile model, introduced by Deepak Dhar [*Phys. Review Letters* **64** (1990), 1613–1616], has led to many papers in the physics literature. Dhar noted that, if M grains of sand are introduced at random, each recurrent state is equally probable as $M \to \infty$. The present exercise was inspired by the work of R. Cori and D. Rossin, *European J. Combinatorics* **21** (2000), 447–459.

Sandpile theory proves that every digraph D yields an abelian group whose elements correspond somehow to the oriented spanning trees of D with root V_0. In particular, the same is true when D is an ordinary graph, with arcs $u \to v$ and $v \to u$ whenever u and v are adjacent. Thus, for example, we can "add" two spanning trees; and some spanning tree can be regarded as "zero." An elegant correspondence between spanning trees and recurrent states, in the special case when D is an ordinary graph, has been found by R. Cori and Y. Le Borgne, *Advances in Applied Math.* **30** (2003), 44–52. But no simple correspondence is known for general digraphs D. For example, suppose $n = 2$ and $(e_{10}, e_{12}, e_{20}, e_{21}) = (p, q, r, s)$; then there are $pr + ps + qr$ oriented trees, and the recurrent states correspond to generalized two-dimensional toruses as in exercise 7–137. Yet even in the "balanced" case, when $p + q \geq s$ and $r + s \geq q$, no easy mapping between spanning trees and recurrent states is apparent.

104. (a) If $\det(\alpha I - C) = 0$, there is a vector $x = (x_1, \ldots, x_n)^T$ such that $Cx = \alpha x$ and $\max(x_1, \ldots, x_n) = x_m = 1$ for some m. Then $\alpha = \alpha x_m = c_{mm} - \sum_{j \neq m} e_{mj} x_j \geq c_{mm} - \sum_{j \neq m} e_{mj} = 0$. (Incidentally, a real symmetric matrix whose eigenvalues are nonnegative is called *positive semidefinite*. Our proof establishes the well-known fact that any real symmetric matrix with $c_{mm} \geq |\sum_{j \neq m} c_{mj}|$ for $1 \leq m \leq n$ has this property.) Thus $\alpha_0 \geq 0$; and $\alpha_0 = 0$ because $C(1, \ldots, 1)^T = (0, \ldots, 0)^T$.

(b) $\det(xI - C(G)) = x(x - \alpha_1) \ldots (x - \alpha_{n-1})$; and the coefficient of x is $(-1)^{n-1}n$ times the number of spanning trees, by the matrix tree theorem.

(c) $\det(\alpha I - C(K_n)) = \det((\alpha - n)I + J) = (\alpha - n)^{n-1}\alpha$ by exercise 1.2.3–36; here J is the matrix of all 1s. The aspects are therefore $0, n, \ldots, n$.

105. (a) If $e_{ij} = a + be'_{ij}$ we have $C(G) = naI - aJ + bC(G')$. And if C is any matrix whose row sums are zero, the identity

$$\det(xI + yJ - zC) = \frac{x + ny}{x} z^n \det((x/z)I - C)$$

can be proved by adding columns 2 through n to column 1, factoring out $(x + ny)/x$, subtracting y/x times column 1 from columns 2 through n, then subtracting columns 2 through n from column 1. Therefore, by setting $x = \alpha - na$, $y = a$, $z = b$, $a = 1$, and $b = -1$, we find that G has the aspects $0, n - \alpha_{n-1}, \ldots, n - \alpha_1$. (In particular, this result agrees with exercise 104(c) when G' is the empty graph $\overline{K_n}$.)

(b) Sort $\{\alpha'_0, \ldots, \alpha'_{n'-1}, \alpha''_0, \ldots, \alpha''_{n''-1}\}$ into order. (An easy case, for variety.)

(c) Here $\overline{G} = \overline{G'} \oplus \overline{G''}$, so G's aspects are $\{0, n' + n'', n'' + \alpha'_1, \ldots, n'' + \alpha'_{n'-1}, n' + \alpha''_1, \ldots, n' + \alpha''_{n''-1}\}$ by (a) and (b). (In particular, G is $K_{m,n}$ when $G' = \overline{K_m}$ and $G'' = \overline{K_n}$, hence the aspects of $K_{m,n}$ are $\{0, (n-1) \cdot m, (m-1) \cdot n, m+n\}$.)

(d) $C(G) = I_{n'} \otimes C(G'') + C(G') \otimes I_{n''}$, where I_n denotes the $n \times n$ identity matrix and $\otimes$ denotes the direct product of matrices. The aspects of $C(G)$ are $\{\alpha'_j + \alpha''_k \mid 0 \leq j < n', 0 \leq k < n''\}$; for if A and B are arbitrary matrices whose eigenvalues are $\{\lambda_1, \ldots, \lambda_m\}$ and $\{\mu_1, \ldots, \mu_n\}$, respectively, the eigenvalues of $A \otimes I_n + I_m \otimes B$ are the mn sums $\lambda_j + \mu_k$. *Proof:* Choose S and T so that $S^- A S$ and $T^- B T$ are triangular. Then use the matrix identity $(A \otimes B)(C \otimes D) = AC \otimes BD$ to show that $(S \otimes T)^-(A \otimes I_n + I_m \otimes B)(S \otimes T) = (S^- A S) \otimes I_n + I_m \otimes (T^- B T)$. (In particular, repeated use of this formula shows that the aspects of the n-cube are $\{\binom{n}{0} \cdot 0, \binom{n}{1} \cdot 2, \ldots, \binom{n}{n} \cdot 2n\}$, and Eq. (57) follows from exercise 104(b).)

(e) When G is a regular graph of degree d, its aspects are $\alpha_j = d - \lambda_{j+1}$, where $\lambda_1 \geq \cdots \geq \lambda_n$ are the eigenvalues of the adjacency matrix $A = (a_{ij})$. The adjacency matrix of G' is $A' = B^T B - d' I_{n'}$, where $B = (b_{ij})$ is the $n \times n'$ incidence matrix with entries $b_{ij} = [\text{edge } i \text{ touches vertex } j]$, and where $n = n'd'/2$ is the number of edges. The adjacency matrix of G is $A = BB^T - 2I_n$. Now we have

$$x^n \det(xI_{n'} - B^T B) = x^{n'} \det(xI_n - BB^T);$$

this identity follows from the fact that the coefficients of $\det(xI - A)$ can be expressed in terms of trace(A^k) for $k = 1, 2, \ldots$, via Newton's identities (exercise 1.2.9–10). So the aspects of G are the same as those of G', plus $n - n'$ aspects equal to $2d'$. [This result is due to E. B. Vakhovsky, *Sibirskiĭ Mat. Zhurnal* **6** (1965), 44–49; see also H. Sachs, *Wissenschaftliche Zeitschrift der Technischen Hochschule Ilmenau* **13** (1967), 405–412.]

(f) $A = A' \otimes A''$, so the aspects are $\{d''\alpha'_j + d'\alpha''_k - \alpha'_j\alpha''_k \mid 0 \leq j < n', 0 \leq k < n''\}$.

(g) $A(G) = I_{n'} \otimes A'' + A' \otimes I_{n''} + A' \otimes A'' = (I_{n'} + A') \otimes (I_{n''} + A'') - I_n$ yields the aspects $\{(d''+1)\alpha'_j + (d'+1)\alpha''_k - \alpha'_j\alpha''_k \mid 0 \leq j < n', 0 \leq k < n''\}$.

(h) When G' is regular, we can make $S^- A' S$ a diagonal matrix with entries $d' - \alpha'_j$, while simultaneously $S^- J_{n'} S$ is a diagonal matrix with entries $(n', 0, \ldots, 0)$, because $(1, \ldots, 1)^T$ is an eigenvector of both A' and $J_{n'}$. Thus, by the formula of answer 7–96(c), the aspects turn out to be $\{d + (d' - \alpha'_j n'[j=0])(d'' - \alpha''_k) + (d' - \alpha'_j)(d'' - \alpha''_k - n''[k=0]) \mid 0 \leq j < n', 0 \leq k < n''\}$, where $d = d'(n'' - d'') + (n' - d')d''$.

(i) A similar argument yields the scaled aspects $\{n''\alpha'_j \mid 0 \le j < n'\}$ of G', together with n' copies of shifted aspects $\{d'n'' + \alpha''_k \mid 1 \le k < n''\}$ of G''.

106. (a) If α is an aspect of the path P_n, there's a nonzero solution $(x_0, x_1, \ldots, x_{n+1})$ to the equations $\alpha x_k = 2x_k - x_{k-1} - x_{k+1}$ for $1 \le k \le n$, with $x_0 = x_1$ and $x_n = x_{n+1}$. If we set $x_k = \cos(2k-1)\theta$, we find $x_0 = x_1$ and $2x_k - x_{k-1} - x_{k+1} = 2x_k - (2\cos 2\theta)x_k$; hence $2 - 2\cos 2\theta = 4\sin^2\theta$ will be an aspect if we choose θ so that $x_n = x_{n+1}$ and so that the x's are not all zero. Thus the aspects of P_n turn out to be $\sigma_{0n}, \ldots, \sigma_{(n-1)n}$.

We must have $\alpha_1 \ldots \alpha_{n-1} = n$, by exercise 104(b), since $c(P_n) = 1$; therefore

$$c(P_m \square P_n) = \prod_{j=1}^{m-1} \prod_{k=1}^{n-1} (\sigma_{jm} + \sigma_{kn}).$$

(b, c) Similarly, if α is an aspect of the cycle C_n, there's a nonzero solution to the stated equations with $x_n = x_0$. For this case we try $x_k = \cos 2k\theta$ and find solutions when $\theta = j\pi/n$ for $0 \le j < \lceil n/2 \rceil$. And $x_k = \sin k\theta$ gives further, linearly independent solutions for $\lceil n/2 \rceil \le j < n$. The aspects of C_n are therefore $\sigma_{0n}, \sigma_{2n}, \ldots, \sigma_{(2n-2)n}$; and we have

$$c(P_m \square C_n) = n \prod_{j=1}^{m-1} \prod_{k=1}^{n-1} (\sigma_{jm} + \sigma_{(2k)n}), \quad c(C_m \square C_n) = mn \prod_{j=1}^{m-1} \prod_{k=1}^{n-1} (\sigma_{(2j)m} + \sigma_{(2k)n}).$$

Let $f_n(x) = (x + \sigma_{1n}) \ldots (x + \sigma_{(n-1)n})$ and $g_n(x) = (x + \sigma_{2n}) \ldots (x + \sigma_{(2n-2)n})$. These polynomials have integer coefficients; indeed, $f_n(x) = U_{n-1}(x/2+1)$ and $g_n(x) = 2(T_n(x/2 + 1) - 1)/x$, where $T_n(x)$ and $U_n(x)$ are the Chebyshev polynomials defined by $T_n(\cos\theta) = \cos n\theta$ and $U_n(\cos\theta) = (\sin(n+1)\theta)/\sin\theta$. The calculation of $c(P_m \square P_n)$ can be reduced to the evaluation of an $m \times m$ determinant, because it is the resultant of $f_m(x)$ with $f_n(-x)$; see exercise 4.6.1–12. Similarly, $\frac{1}{n}c(P_m \square C_n)$ and $\frac{1}{mn}c(C_m \square C_n)$ are the respective resultants of $f_m(x)$ with $g_n(-x)$ and of $g_m(x)$ with $g_n(-x)$.

Let $\alpha_n(x) = \prod_{d\backslash n} f_d(x)^{\mu(n/d)}$; thus $\alpha_1(x) = 1$, $\alpha_2(x) = x + 2$, $\alpha_3(x) = (x + 3) \times (x + 1)$, $\alpha_4(x) = x^2 + 4x + 2$, $\alpha_5(x) = (x^2 + 5x + 5)(x^2 + 3x + 1)$, $\alpha_6(x) = x^2 + 4x + 1$, etc. By considering so-called field polynomials one can show that $\alpha_n(x)$ is irreducible over the integers when n is even, otherwise it is the product of two irreducible factors of the same degree. Similarly, if $\beta_n(x) = \prod_{d\backslash n} g_d(x)^{\mu(n/d)}$, it turns out that $\beta_n(x)$ is the square of an irreducible polynomial when $n \ge 3$. These facts account for the presence of fairly small prime factors in the results. For example, the largest prime factor in $c(P_m \square P_n)$ for $m \le n \le 10$ is 1009; it occurs only in the resultant of $\alpha_6(x)$ with $\alpha_9(-x)$, which is $662913 = 3^2 \cdot 73 \cdot 1009$.

107. There are $(1, 1, 2, 6, 21)$ nonisomorphic graphs for $n = (1, \ldots, 5)$; but we need consider only cases with $\le \frac{1}{2}\binom{n}{2}$ edges, because of exercise 105(a). The surviving cases when $n = 4$ are free trees: The star is the complement of $K_1 \oplus K_3$, with aspects 0, 1, 1, 4; and P_4 has aspects $0, 2 - \sqrt{2}, 2, 2 + \sqrt{2}$ by exercise 106. There are three free trees when $n = 5$: The star has aspects 0, 1, 1, 1, 5; P_5's aspects are $0, 2 - \phi, 3 - \phi, 1 + \phi, 2 + \phi$; and the aspects of ⟝ are $0, r_1, 1, r_2, r_3$, where $(r_1, r_2, r_3) \approx (0.52, 2.31, 4.17)$ are the roots of $x^3 - 7x^2 + 13x - 5 = 0$.

Finally, there are five cases with a single cycle: ⟝ is $K_1 \longrightarrow (K_2 \oplus \overline{K_2})$, so its aspects are 0, 1, 1, 3, 5; C_5 has aspects $0, 3 - \phi, 3 - \phi, 2 + \phi, 2 + \phi$; ⟝ has aspects $0, r_1, r_2, 3, r_3$; its complement ⟝ has aspects $0, 5 - r_3, 2, 5 - r_2, 5 - r_1$; and the aspects of ⟝ turn out to be $0, (5 - \sqrt{13})/2, 3 - \phi, 2 + \phi, (5 + \sqrt{13})/2$.

108. Given a digraph D on vertices $\{V_1, \ldots, V_n\}$, let e_{ij} be the number of arcs from V_i to V_j. Define $C(D)$ and its aspects as before. Since $C(D)$ is not necessarily symmetric, the aspects are no longer guaranteed to be real. But if α is an aspect, so is its complex conjugate $\bar{\alpha}$; and if we order the aspects by their real parts, again we find $\alpha_0 = 0$. The formula $c(D) = \alpha_1 \ldots \alpha_{n-1}/n$ remains valid if we now interpret $c(D)$ as the *average* number of *oriented* spanning trees, taken over all n possible roots V_j. The aspects of the transitive tournament $\vec{K_n}$, whose arcs are $V_i \to V_j$ for $1 \leq i < j \leq n$, are obviously $0, 1, \ldots, n-1$; and those of its subgraphs are equally obvious.

The derivations in parts (a)–(d) of answer 105 carry over without change. For example, consider $K_1 \!\!-\!\! \vec{K_3}$, which has aspects $0, 2, 3, 4$; this digraph D has $(2, 4, 6, 12)$ oriented spanning trees with the four possible roots, and $c(D)$ is indeed equal to $2 \cdot 3 \cdot 4/4$. Notice also that the digraph ⟶⟶ is its own complement, and that it has the same aspects as $\vec{K_3}$.

Directed graphs also admit another family of interesting operations: If D' and D'' are digraphs on disjoint sets of vertices V' and V'', consider adding a arcs $v' \to v''$ and b arcs $v'' \to v'$ whenever $v' \in V'$ and $v'' \in V''$. By manipulating determinants as in answer 105(a), we can show that the resulting digraph has aspects $\{0, an'' + bn', an'' + \alpha_1', \ldots, an'' + \alpha_{n'-1}', bn' + \alpha_1'', \ldots, bn' + \alpha_{n''-1}''\}$. In the special case $a = 1$ and $b = 0$, we can conveniently denote the new digraph by $D' \to D''$; thus, for example, $\vec{K_n} = K_1 \to \vec{K_{n-1}}$. The digraph $K_{n_1} \to K_{n_2} \to \cdots \to K_{n_m}$ on $n_1 + n_2 + \cdots + n_m$ vertices has aspects $\{0, n_m \cdot s_m, \ldots, n_2 \cdot s_2, (n_1-1) \cdot s_1\}$, where $s_k = n_k + \cdots + n_m$.

The aspects of the oriented path $\vec{P_n}$ from V_1 to V_n are obviously $0, 1, \ldots, 1$. The oriented cycle $\vec{C_n}$ has aspects $\{0, 1 - \omega, \ldots, 1 - \omega^{n-1}\}$, where $\omega = e^{2\pi i/n}$.

There is also a nice result for arc digraphs: The aspects of D^* are obtained from those of D by simply adding $\tau_k - 1$ copies of the number σ_k, for $1 \leq k \leq n$, where τ_k is the in-degree of V_k and σ_k is its out-degree. (If $\tau_k = 0$, we *remove* one aspect equal to σ_k.) The proof is similar to, but simpler than, the derivation in answer 2.3.4.2–21.

Historical remarks: The results in exercises 104(b) and 105(a) are due to A. K. Kelmans, *Avtomatika i Telemekhanika* **26** (1965), 2194–2204; **27**, 2 (February 1966), 56–65; English translation in *Automation and Remote Control* **26** (1965), 2118–2129; **27** (1966), 233–241. Miroslav Fiedler [*Czech. Math. J.* **23** (1973), 298–305] introduced exercise 105(d), and proved interesting results about the aspect α_1, which he called the "algebraic connectivity" of G. Germain Kreweras, in *J. Combinatorial Theory* **B24** (1978), 202–212, enumerated spanning trees on grids, cylinders, and toruses, as well as oriented spanning trees on directed toruses such as $\vec{C_m} \,\square\, \vec{C_n}$. An excellent survey of graph aspects was published by Bojan Mohar in *Graph Theory, Combinatorics and Applications* (Wiley, 1991), 871–898; *Discrete Math.* **109** (1992), 171–183. For a thorough discussion of important families of graph eigenvalues and their properties, including a comprehensive bibliography, see *Spectra of Graphs* by D. M. Cvetković, M. Doob, and H. Sachs, third edition (1995).

109. Perhaps there is also a sandpile-related reason; see exercise 103.

110. By induction: Suppose there are $k \geq 1$ parallel edges between u and v. Then $c(G) = kc(G_1) + c(G_2)$, where G_1 is G with u and v identified, and G_2 is G with those k edges removed. Let $d_u = k + a$ and $d_v = k + b$.

Case 1: G_2 is connected. Then $ab > 0$, so we can write $a = x + 1$ and $b = y + 1$. We have $c(G_1) > \alpha\sqrt{x + y + 1}$ and $c(G_2) > \alpha\sqrt{xy}$, where α is a product over the other $n - 2$ vertices; and it is easy to verify that

$$k\sqrt{x + y + 1} + \sqrt{xy} \geq \sqrt{(x + k)(y + k)}.$$

Case 2: There are no such u and v for which G_2 is connected. Then every multi-edge of G is a bridge; in other words, G is a free tree except for parallel edges. In this case the result is trivial if there's a vertex of degree 1. Otherwise suppose u is an endpoint, with $d_u = k$ edges $u - v$. If $d_v > k + 1$, we have $c(G) = kc(G_1) > \alpha k \sqrt{x}$ where $d_v = k + 1 + x$, and it is easy to check that $k\sqrt{x} > \sqrt{(k-1)(k+x)}$ when $x > 0$. If $d_v = k$ we have $c(G) = k > \sqrt{(k-1)^2}$. Finally if $d_v = k + 1$, let $v_0 = u$, $v_1 = v$, and consider the unique path $v_1 - v_2 - \cdots - v_r$ where $r > 1$ and v_r has degree greater than 2; only one edge joins v_j to v_{j+1} for $1 \leq j < r$. Again the induction goes through.

[Other lower bounds on the number of spanning trees have been derived by A. V. Kostochka, *Random Structures & Algorithms* **6** (1995), 269–274.]

111. 2 1 5 4 11 7 9 8 6 10 15 12 14 13 3.

112. Either p appears on an even level and is an ancestor of q, or q appears on an odd level and is an ancestor of p.

113. prepostorder(F^R)=postpreorder(F)^R and postpreorder(F^R)=prepostorder(F)^R.

114. The most elegant approach, considering that the forest might be empty, is to set things up so that CHILD(Λ) points to the root of the leftmost tree, if any. Then initiate the first visit by setting Q $\leftarrow$ Λ, L $\leftarrow$ -1, and going to step Q6.

115. Suppose there are n_e nodes on even levels and n_o nodes on odd levels, and that n'_e of the even-level nodes are nonleaves. Then steps (Q1, ..., Q7) are performed respectively $(n_e + n_o, n_o, n'_e, n_e, n'_e, n_o + 1, n_e)$ times, including one execution of Q6 because of answer 114.

116. (a) This result follows from Algorithm Q.

(b) In fact, non-ordinary nodes strictly alternate between lucky and unlucky, beginning and ending with a lucky one. *Proof:* Consider the forest F' obtained by deleting the leftmost leaf of F, and use induction on n.

117. Such forests are precisely those whose left-child/right-sibling representation is a degenerate binary tree (exercise 31). So the answer is 2^{n-1}.

118. (a) t^{k-2}, for $k > 1$; luckiness occurs only near extreme leaves.

(b) An interesting recurrence leads to the solution $(F_k + 1 - (k+1) \bmod 3)/2$.

119. Label each node x with the value $v(x) = \sum \{ 2^k \mid k$ is an arc label on the path from the root to $x\}$. Then the node values in preorder are exactly the Gray binary code Γ_n, because exercise 113 shows that they satisfy recurrence 7.2.1.1–(5).

(If we apply the same value labeling to the ordinary binomial tree T_n and traverse it in preorder, we simply get the integers 0, 1, ..., $2^n - 1$.)

120. False: Only four of the "hollow" vertices in the illustration can appear next to the two "square" vertices, in a Hamiltonian cycle; one hollow pair is therefore out of luck. [See H. Fleischner and H. V. Kronk, *Monatshefte für Mathematik* **76** (1972), 112–117.]

121. Furthermore, there is a Hamiltonian path from u to v in T^2 if and only if similar conditions hold; but we retain u and/or v in $T^{(\prime)}$ if they have degree 1, and we require that the path in (i) be inside the path from u to v (excluding u and v themselves). Condition (ii) is also strengthened by changing 'vertices of degree 4' to 'dangerous vertices', where a vertex of $T^{(\prime)}$ is called dangerous if it either has degree 4 or has degree 2 and equals u or v. The smallest impossible case is $T = P_4$, with u and v chosen to be the non-endpoints. [*Časopis pro Pěstování Matematiky* **89** (1964), 323–338.]

Consequently T^2 contains a Hamiltonian cycle if and only if T is a *caterpillar*, namely a free tree whose derivative is a path. [See Frank Harary and A. J. Schwenk, *Mathematika* **18** (1971), 138–140.]

122. (a) We can represent an expression by a binary tree, with operators at the internal nodes and digits at the external nodes. If binary trees are implemented as in Algorithm B, the essential constraint imposed by the given grammar is that, if $r_j = k > 0$, then the operator at node j is $+$ or $-$ if and only if the operator at node k is $\times$ or $/$. Therefore the total number of possibilities for a tree with n leaves is $2^n S_{n-1}$, where S_n is a Schröder number; namely 10,646,016 when $n = 9$. (See exercise 66, but interchange left with right.) We can rather quickly generate them all, encountering exactly 1641 solutions. Only one expression, namely $1 + 2/((3-4)/(5+6) - (7-8)/9)$, does the job with no multiplications; twenty of them, such as $(((1-2)/((3/4) \times 5 - 6)) \times 7 + 8) \times 9$, require five pairs of parentheses; only 15 require no parentheses whatever.

(b) Now there are $1 + \sum_{k=1}^{8} \binom{8}{k} 2^{k+1} S_k = 23{,}463{,}169$ cases, and 3366 solutions. The shortest, of length 12, was found by Dudeney [*The Weekly Dispatch* (18 June 1899)], namely $123 - 45 - 67 + 89$; but he wasn't sure at the time that it was best. The longest solutions have length 27; there are twenty of them, as mentioned above.

(c) The number of cases rises dramatically to $2 + \sum_{k=1}^{8} \binom{8}{k} 4^{k+1} S_k = 8{,}157{,}017{,}474$, and there now are 97,221 solutions. The longest, which is unique, has length 40: $(((((.1/(.2 + .3))/.4)/.5)/(.6 - .7))/(.8 - .9)$. There are five amusing examples such as $.1 + (2 + 3 + 4 + 5) \times 6 + 7 + 8 + .9$, with seven $+$'s; furthermore, there are ten like $(1 - .2 - .3 - 4 - .5 - 6) \times (7 - 8 - 9)$, with seven $-$'s.

> *There is in fact very little principle in the thing,*
> *and there is no certain way of demonstrating*
> *that we have got the best possible solution.*
> — HENRY E. DUDENEY (1899)

Notes: Marie Leske's *Illustriertes Spielbuch für Mädchen*, first published in 1864, contained the earliest known appearance of such a problem; in the eleventh edition (1889), the fact that $100 = 1 + 2 + 3 + 4 + 5 + 6 + 7 + 8 \times 9$ was the solution to puzzle 16 in section 553. See also the references in exercise 7.2.1.1–111.

Richard Bellman explained in *AMM* **69** (1962), 640–643, how to handle the special case of part (a) in which the operators are restricted to be either $+$ and $\times$, without parentheses. His technique of dynamic programming can be used also in this more general problem to reduce the number of cases being considered. The idea is to determine the rational numbers obtainable from every subinterval of the digits $\{1, \ldots, n\}$, having a given operator at the root of the tree. We can also save a good deal of computation by discarding cases for the subintervals $\{1, \ldots, 8\}$ and $\{2, \ldots, 9\}$ that cannot lead to integer solutions. In this way the number of essentially different trees to consider is reduced to (a) 2,735,136 cases; (b) 6,813,760; (c) 739,361,319.

Floating point arithmetic is unreliable in this application. But the exact rational arithmetic routines of Section 4.5.1 do the job nicely, never needing to work with an integer greater than 10^9 in absolute value.

123. (a) 2284; but $2284 = (1 + 2 \times 3) \times (4 + 5 \times 67) - 89$. (b) 6964; but $6964 = (1/.2) \times 34 + 5 + 6789$. (c) 14786; but $14786 = -1 + 2 \times (.3 + 4 + 5) \times (6 + 789)$. [If we allow also a minus sign at the left of the expression, as Dudeney did, we actually obtain 1362, 2759, and 85597 additional solutions to problems 122(a), (b), and (c), including nineteen longer expressions in case (a) such as $-(1-2) \times ((3+4) \times (5 - (6-7) \times 8) + 9)$.

With such an extension, the smallest unreachable numbers in the present problem become (a) 3802, (b) 8312, and (c) 17722.] The total number of representable integers (positive, negative, or zero) turns out to be (a) 27,666; (b) 136,607; (c) 200,765.

124. Horton–Strahler numbers originated in studies of river flows: R. E. Horton, *Bull. Geol. Soc. Amer.* **56** (1945), 275–370; A. N. Strahler, *Bull. Geol. Soc. Amer.* **63** (1952), 1117–1142. Many tree-drawing ideas are explored and illustrated in a classic paper by Viennot, Eyrolles, Janey, and Arquès, *Computer Graphics* **23**, 3 (July 1989), 31–40.

SECTION 7.2.1.7

1. Perhaps under hexagram 21, "crunching" (▤); however, the ancient commentators related this hexagram more to law enforcement than to the interaction of electrons.

2. (a) For the first nucleotide in the codon, let (T, C, A, G) be respectively represented by (⚏,⚏,⚏,⚏); represent the second nucleotide, similarly, by (⚎,⚎,⚎,⚎); represent the third by (⚍,⚍,⚍,⚍); and superimpose those three representations. Thus, for example, hexagram number 34 is ䷡ = ⚏ + ⚎ + ⚍; it represents the codon TTC, which maps to the amino acid F. Under this correspondence, hexagrams 34 through 54 inclusive map into the respective values (F, G, L, Q, W, D, S, −, P, Y, K, A, I, T, N, H, M, R, V, E, C). Moreover, the three hexagrams that map to '−' are numbers 1, 9, and 41, namely ䷀, ䷤, and ䷨, which mean "creation," "taming," and "removal of excess" in the *I Ching*—all quite appropriate for the notion of completing a protein.

(b) Consider the $\binom{64}{6,6,6,4,4,4,4,4,3,3,2,2,2,2,2,2,2,2,2,1,1} \approx 2.3 \times 10^{69}$ ways to permute the elements of the $4 \times 4 \times 4$ genetic code array. Exactly

$$240288040217578979000399368196455132845166871875018555392000000 \approx 2.4 \times 10^{63}$$

of them contain at least one run of 21 distinct consecutive elements. [Using the principle of inclusion and exclusion one can show that any multiset $\{(n_1+1) \cdot x_1, \ldots, (n_r+1) \cdot x_r\}$ with r distinct elements and $n_r = 0$ has exactly

$$(n+1)\binom{n}{n_1, \ldots, n_r}r! - \sum_{k=1}^{r}(n+1-k)k!(r-k)!\, a_k \sum_{\substack{0 \le d_1, \ldots, d_r \le 1 \\ d_1 + \cdots + d_r = k}} \binom{n-k}{n_1-d_1, \ldots, n_r-d_r}$$

such permutations, where $n = n_1 + \cdots + n_r$ and a_k is the number of indecomposable permutations with k elements (exercise 7.2.1.2–100).] Thus only about one out of every million permutations has the stated property.

But there are $4!^3\binom{6}{2,2,2} = 1244160$ ways to represent codons as in part (a), and most of them correspond to different permutations of the amino acids (except for interchanging the representations of T and C in third position).

Empirically, in fact, about 31% of all permutations of the 64 hexagrams turn out to have suitable codon mappings. Thus the construction in part (a) gives no reason to believe that the authors of the *I Ching* anticipated the genetic code in any way.

3. Since $F_{31} - 10^6 = F_{28} + F_{22} + F_{20} + F_{18} + F_{16} + F_{14} + F_9$, the millionth is

⌣⌣⌣⌣⌣⌣−⌣⌣⌣−−−−−⌣⌣⌣−⌣⌣.

Going the other way is easier: $F_{31} - (F_5 + F_8 + F_{10} + F_{16} + F_{18} + F_{27} + F_{30}) = 314159$.

4. One of the two appearances of במדיר on line 4 should be במדיך; similarly, one ירדמב on line 8 should be ירמדב. And the six cases with rightmost letters ךנ appear twice, in lines 3 and 4, while the cases with rightmost בנ are missing. These glitches are probably typographical and/or scribal errors, not made by Donnolo himself.

5. The last one should have been ⟨𝄞⟩, not ⟨𝄞⟩.

6. The nth value m_n in Mersenne's list agrees with $n!$ only for $1 \le n \le 13$ and $15 \le n \le 38$. Mersenne knew that $14! = 87178291200 \ne m_{14} = 8778291200$, because he inserted the missing '1' in his personal copy of the book (now owned by the Bibliothèque Nationale; a facsimile was published in 1963). But the other errors in his table were not merely typographical, because they propagated into subsequent entries, except in the case of m_{50}: $m_{39} = 39! + 10^{26} - 10^{10}$; $m_{40} = 40m_{39}$; $m_{41} = 41m_{40} - 4 \cdot 10^{25} - 14 \cdot 10^{11}$; $m_n = nm_{n-1}$ for $n = 42, 43, 44, 46, 47, 48, 49, 55, 60$, and 62; $m_{50} = 50m_{49} + 10^{66}$; $m_{51} = 51 \cdot 50 \cdot m_{49}$. When he computed $m_{45} = 9 \cdot 45 \cdot m_{44} - 10^{40} + 10^{29}$, he apparently decided to take a shortcut, because it's easy to multiply by 5 or by 9; but he multiplied *twice* by 9. Most of his errors indicate an unreliable multiplication technique, which may have depended on an abacus: $m_{52} = 52m_{51} + 5 \cdot 10^{56} - 2 \cdot 10^{47} + 10^{34}$; $m_{53} = 53m_{52} - 4 \cdot 10^{29}$; $m_{54} = 54m_{53} + 10^{16}$; $m_{57} = 57m_{56} + 10^{33} + 10^{24}$; $m_{58} = 58m_{57} + 10^{67} - 10^{35} + 10^{32} + 11 \cdot 10^{26}$; $m_{59} = 59m_{58} + 10^{66} + 10^{49} - 10^{28}$; $m_{61} = 61m_{60} - 5 \cdot 10^{81}$; $m_{63} = 63m_{62} + 10^{82} - 10^{74}$; $m_{64} = 64m_{63} + 3 \cdot 10^{81} + 10^{67} + 2 \cdot 10^{38} - 2 \cdot 10^{33} - 10^{23}$.

The remaining case, $m_{56} \approx 10.912m_{55}$ is baffling; it is $\equiv 56m_{55}$ (modulo 10^{17}), but its other digits seem to satisfy neither rhyme nor reason. Can they be easily explained?

Notes: Athanasius Kircher must have copied from Mersenne when he tabulated $n!$ for $1 \le n \le 50$ on page 157 of his *Ars Magna Sciendi* (1669), because he repeated all of Mersenne's mistakes. Kircher did, however, list the values $10m_{14}$, $m_{45}/10$, and $10m_{49}$ instead of m_{14}, m_{45}, and m_{49}; perhaps he was trying to make the sequence grow more steadily. It is not clear who first calculated the correct value of $39!$; exercise 1.2.5–4 tells the story of $1000!$.

7. The basic permutations are 12345, 13254, 14523, 15432, 12453, 14235, 15324, 13542, 12534, 15243, 13425, 14352. But then we find that all 60 of the even permutations are both alive and dead, because (9) differs by an even permutation from (8). (Moreover, if we somehow repair the case $n = 5$, half of the live permutations for $n = 6$ will turn out to be odd.)

8. For example, we can replace (9) by

$$a_na_3 \ldots a_{n-1}a_2a_1, \ a_1a_4 \ldots a_na_3a_2, \ \ldots, \ a_{n-1}a_2 \ldots a_{n-2}a_1a_n,$$

thus flipping the ends and cyclically shifting the other elements in the permutations of (8). This modification works because all permutations have the correct parity, and because the live and dead ones both have a_1 in every possible position. (We essentially have a dual Sims table for the alternating group, as in Eq. 7.2.1.2–(32); but our elements are named $(n, n-1, \ldots, 1)$ instead of $(0, 1, \ldots, n-1)$.)

A simpler way to generate permutations with the proper signs was published by É. Bézout [*Mémoires Acad. Royale des Sciences* (Paris, 1764), 292]: Each permutation $\pm a_1 \ldots a_{n-1}$ of $\{1, \ldots, n-1\}$ yields n others, $\pm a_1 \ldots a_{n-1}a_n \mp a_1 \ldots a_{n-2}a_na_{n-1} \pm \cdots$. G. W. Leibniz had in fact discovered this rule in an unpublished manuscript dated 12 January 1684; see E. Knobloch, *Archive for Hist. Exact Sciences* **12** (1974), 142–173.

9. $(٠, ١, ٢, ٣, ٤, ٥, ٦, ٧, ٨, ٩)$; or perhaps we should say $(٩, ٨, ٧, ٦, ٥, ٤, ٣, ٢, ١, ٠)$. *Notes:* A different system was used for the index numbers of the equations; for example, '‌ل' stood for 200. Moreover, it should be noted that (11) is actually a transcription of al-Samaw'al's work into *modern* Arabic; Ahmad and Rashed based their work on a 14th-century copy that used similar but older forms of the digits: $(٥, ١, ٢, ٣, ۴, ٨, ٦, ٧, ٨, ٩)$. Al-Samaw'al himself may well have used numerals of an even earlier vintage.

10. If the 56 cases were equally likely, the answer would be $56H_{56} \approx 258.2$, as in the coupon collector's problem (exercise 3.3.2–8). But $(6, 30, 20)$ cases occur with the respective probabilities $(1/216, 1/72, 1/36)$; so the correct answer turns out to be

$$\int_0^\infty \left(1 - (1 - e^{-t/216})^6 (1 - e^{-t/72})^{30} (1 - e^{-t/36})^{20}\right) dt \approx 546.6,$$

about 42% of the upper bound $216H_{216}$. [See P. Flajolet, D. Gardy, and L. Thimonier, *Discrete Applied Math.* **39** (1992), 207–229.]

11. It tabulates the $\binom{6}{3} = 20$ combinations of (b, c, d, B, C, D) taken three at a time; furthermore, they appear in lexicographic order if we regard $b < c < d < B < C < D$. The letter t (𝕥) means "shift from lowercase to uppercase." [See A. Bonner, *Selected Works of Ramon Llull* (Princeton: 1985), 596–597.] There are two typos: 'd' should be 'b' at the beginning of line 6; 'c' should be 'd' at the end of line 18. Line 1 would have been more consistent with the others if Llull had presented it as

$$\boxed{\,\mathfrak{b}\,}\;\boxed{\,c\,}\;\boxed{\,\eth\,}\;\boxed{\,\mathfrak{t}\,} \;;$$

but in that line, of course, no case shift was needed.

12. Multiply Poinsot's cycle by 5 and add 2 (mod 7).

13. It's best to have just n lines when there are n different letters:

$$\begin{array}{c} a.\ aa.\ aaa \\ \hline b.\ ab.\ aab.\ aaab.\ bb.\ abb.\ aabb.\ aaabb \end{array}$$

Then, assigning the weights $(a, b) = (1, 4)$ gives the numbers 1 through 11 as in (18). (The first line of (16) should also be omitted.) Similarly, for $\{a, a, a, b, b, c\}$ we would implicitly give c the weight 12 and add the additional line

$$c.\ ac.\ aac.\ aaac.\ bc.\ abc.\ aabc.\ aaabc.\ bbc.\ abbc.\ aabbc.\ aaabbc.$$

[J. Bernoulli *almost* did it right in *Ars Conjectandi*, Part 2, Chapter 6.]

14. ABC ABD ABE ACD ACE ACB ADE ADB ADC AEB AEC AED BCD BCE BCA BDE BDA BDC BEA BEC BED BAC BAD BAE CDE CDA CDB CEA CEB CED CAB CAD CAE CBD CBE CBA DEA DEB DEC DAB DAC DAE DBC DBE DBA DCE DCA DCB EAB EAC EAD EBC EBD EBA ECD ECA ECB EDA EDB EDC. It's a genlex ordering (see Algorithm 7.2.1.3R), proceeding cyclically through the letters not yet used.

[A similar ordering had been used to form all 120 permutations of five letters in a kabbalistic work entitled *Sha'ari Tzedeq*, ascribed to the 13th-century author Natan ben Sa'adyah Har'ar of Messina, Sicily; see *Le Porte della Giustizia* (Milan: Adelphi, 2001).]

15. After j we place the $(n-1)$-combinations of $\{j, \ldots, m\}$ with repetition, so the answer is $\binom{(m+1-j)+(n-1)-1}{n-1} = \binom{m+n-j-1}{n-1}$. [Jean Borrel, also known as Buteonis, pointed this out on pages 305–309 of his early book *Logistica* (Lyon: 1560). He tabulated all throws of n dice for $1 \leq n \leq 4$, then used a sum over j to deduce that there are $126 + 70 + 35 + 15 + 5 + 1 = 252$ distinct throws for $n = 5$, and 462 for $n = 6$.]

16. N1. [Initialize.] Set $r \leftarrow n$, $t \leftarrow 0$, and $a_0 \leftarrow 0$.

　N2. [Advance.] While $r \geq q$, set $t \leftarrow t + 1$, $a_t \leftarrow q$, and $r \leftarrow r - q$. Then if $r > 0$, set $t \leftarrow t + 1$ and $a_t \leftarrow r$.

　N3. [Visit.] Visit the composition $a_1 \ldots a_t$.

　N4. [Find j.] Set $j \leftarrow t$, $t - 1$, $\ldots$, until $a_j \neq 1$. Terminate the algorithm if $j = 0$.

　N5. [Decrease a_j.] Set $a_j \leftarrow a_j - 1$, $r \leftarrow t - j + 1$, $t \leftarrow j$; return to N2. ∎

For example, the compositions for $n = 7$ and $q = 3$ are 331, 322, 3211, 313, 3121, 3112, 31111, 232, 2311, 223, 2221, 2212, 22111, 2131, 2122, 21211, 2113, 21121, 21112, 211111, 133, 1321, 1312, 13111, 1231, 1222, 12211, 1213, 12121, 12112, 121111, 1132, 11311, 1123, 11221, 11212, 112111, 11131, 11122, 111211, 11113, 111121, 111112, 1111111.

Nārāyaṇa's sutras 79 and 80 gave essentially this procedure, but with the strings reversed (133, 223, 1123, ...), because he preferred decreasing colex order. [Śārṅgadeva, in *Saṅgītaratnākara* §5.316–375, had previously developed an elaborate theory for the set of all compositions (rhythms) that can be formed from the basic parts $\{1, 2, 4, 6\}$.]

17. The number V_n of visits is $F^{(q)}_{n+q-1} = \Theta(\alpha_q^n)$; see exercise 5.4.2–7. The number X_n of times step N4 tests $a_j = 1$ satisfies $X_n = X_{n-1} + \cdots + X_{n-q} + 1$, and we find $X_n = V_0 + \cdots + V_n = (qV_n + (q-1)V_{n-1} + \cdots + V_{n-q+1} - 1)/(q-1) = \Theta(V_n)$. The number Y_n of times step N2 sets $a_t \leftarrow q$ satisfies the same recurrence, and we find $Y_n = X_{n-q}$. And the number of times step N2 finds $r = 0$ turns out to be V_{n-q}.

18. It was MDCLXVI in Roman numerals, where M > D > C > L > X > V > I.

19. Lines 329 and 1022. (Puteanus included 139 such verses among his list of 1022.)

20. With 'tria' preceding 'lumina', there are $5! \times 2! \times (11, 12, 12, 16)$ ways having a dactyl in the (1st, 2nd, 3rd, 4th) foot, respectively; with 'lumina' preceding 'tria' there are $5! \times 2! \times (16, 12, 12, 11)$. So the total is 24480. [Leibniz considered this problem near the end of his *Dissertatio de Arte Combinatoria*, and came up with the answer 45870; but his argument was riddled with errors.]

21. (a) The generating function $1/((1 - zu - yu^2)(1 - zv - yv^2)(1 - zw - yw^2))$ is clearly equal to $\sum_{p,q,r,s,t\geq 0} f(p, q, r; s, t) u^p v^q w^r z^s y^t$.

(b) If 'tibi' is $\smile\smile$ and 'Virgo' is $--$, the number is $3! \, 3!$ times $\sum_{k=0}^{3}(f(2k+1, 6 - 2k, 2; 3, 3) + f(2k, 6 - 2k, 2; 2, 3))$, namely $36((7+7) + (9+5) + (10+5) + (14+7)) = 2304$. Otherwise 'tibi' is $\smile-$, 'Virgo' is $-\smile$, and the number is $2! \, 3!$ times $\sum_{k=0}^{3}(f(2k, 5 - 2k, 2; 3, 2) + f(2k, 6 - 2k, 1; 3, 2))$, namely $12((7+6) + (5+4) + (4+4) + (0+6)) = 432$.

(c) The fifth foot begins with the second syllable of 'cælo', 'dotes', or 'Virgo'. Hence the additional number is $3! \, 3! \sum_{k=0}^{2} f(2k, 5 - 2k, 2; 3, 2) = 36(7 + 5 + 4) = 576$, and the grand total is $2304 + 432 + 576 = 3312$.

22. Let $\alpha \in \{\text{quot}, \text{sunt}, \text{tot}\}$, $\beta \in \{\text{cælo}, \text{dotes}, \text{Virgo}\}$, $\sigma = \text{sidera}$, and $\tau = \text{tibi}$. Prestet's analysis was essentially equivalent to that of Bernoulli, but he forgot to include the 36 cases $\alpha\alpha\tau\beta\beta\sigma\beta$. (In his favor one can say that those cases are poetically sterile; Puteanus found no use for them.) The 1675 edition of Prestet's book had also omitted all permutations that end with $\tau\beta$.

Wallis divided the possibilities into 23 types, $T_1 \cup T_2 \cup \cdots \cup T_{23}$. He claimed that his types 6 and 7 each yielded 324 verses; but actually $|T_6| = |T_7| = 252$, because his variable i should be 7, not 9. He also counted many solutions twice: $|T_3 \cap T_5| = 72$, $|T_2 \cap T_7| = |T_5 \cap T_7| = |T_3 \cap T_6| = |T_6 \cap T_{10}| = 36$, and $|T_{11} \cap T_{12}| = |T_{12} \cap T_{13}| = |T_{14} \cap T_{15}| = 12$. He missed the 36 possibilities $\alpha\beta\beta\alpha\sigma\alpha\tau\beta$ (19 of which were used by Puteanus). And he also missed all the permutations of exercise 21(c); Puteanus had used 250 of those 576. The Latin edition of Wallis's book, published in 1693, corrected several typographic errors in this section, but none of the mathematical mistakes.

Whitworth and Hartley omitted all cases with 'tibi' $= \smile-$ (see exercise 19), possibly because people's knowledge of classical hexameter was beginning to fade.

[Speaking of errors, Puteanus actually published only 1020 distinct permutations, not 1022, because lines 592 and 593 in his list were identical to lines 601 and 602. But he would have had no trouble finding two more cases — for example, by changing 'tot sunt' to 'sunt tot' in lines 252, 345, 511, 548, 659, 663, 678, 693, or 797.]

23. Reading each diagram left-to-right, so that $12|345 \leftrightarrow$ ▥, we get

24. His rule was: For $k = 0, 1, \ldots, n-1$, and for each combination $0 < j_1 < \cdots < j_k < n$ of $n-1$ things taken k at a time, visit all partitions of $\{1, \ldots, n-1\} \backslash \{j_1, \ldots, j_k\}$ together with the block $\{j_1, \ldots, j_k, n\}$. His order for $n = 5$ was:

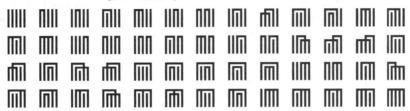

But strictly speaking, the answer to this exercise is "No" — because Honda's rule is not complete until the order of the combinations is specified. He generated combinations in *colex* order (lexicographic on $j_t \ldots j_1$). Lexicographic order on $j_1 \ldots j_t$ would also be consistent with the list given for $n = 4$, but it would put ▥ ▥ before ▥ ▥. *Reference:* T. Hayashi, *Tôhoku Math. J.* **33** (1931), 332–337.

25. No; (28) misses $14|235$ (the top-bottom reflection of its second pattern).

26. Let a_n be the number of indecomposable partitions of $\{1, \ldots, n\}$, and let a'_n be the number that are both indecomposable and complete. These sequences begin $\langle a_1, a_2, \ldots \rangle = \langle 1, 1, 2, 6, 22, 92, 426, \ldots \rangle$, $\langle a'_1, a'_2, \ldots \rangle = \langle 0, 1, 1, 3, 9, 33, 135, \ldots \rangle$; and the answer to this exercise is $a'_n - 1$ for $n \geq 2$. It turns out that a_n is also the number of symmetric polynomials of degree n in noncommuting variables. [See M. C. Wolf, *Duke Math. J.* **2** (1936), 626–637, who also tabulated indecomposable partitions into k parts.]

   If $A(z) = \sum_n a_n z^n$, and if $B(z) = \sum_n \varpi_n z^n$ is the non-exponential generating function for Bell numbers, we have $A(z)B(z) = B(z) - 1$, hence $A(z) = 1 - 1/B(z)$. And the result of exercise 7.2.1.5–35 implies that $\sum_n a'_n z^n = zA(z)/(1 + z - A(z)) = z(B(z) - 1)/(1 + zB(z))$. Unfortunately $B(z)$ has no especially nice closed form, although it does satisfy the interesting functional relation $1 + zB(z) = B(z/(1 + z))$. Notice that indecomposable set partitions with $n > 1$ correspond to vacillating tableau loops with no three consecutive λs equal to zero (see exercise 7.2.1.5–27).

27. The problem is ambiguous because genji-ko diagrams are not well defined. Let's require all vertical lines of a block to have the same height; then, for example, $145|236$ has no single-crossing diagram because ▥ is not allowed.

   The number of partitions with no crossing is C_n (see exercise 7.2.1.6–26). For one crossing, the elements of the two blocks that cross must appear within the restricted growth string as either $x^i yx^j y^k$ or $x^i y^{j+1} xy^k$ or $x^i y^j xy^k x^l$, where $i, j, k, l > 0$.

   Suppose the pattern is $x^i yx^j y^k$. There are $t = i + j + k + 2$ "slots" between the $i + 1 + j + k$ elements of this pattern, and the number of ways to fill these slots with noncrossing partitions is $\sum_{i_1+\cdots+i_t=n-i-j-k-1} C_{i_1}\ldots C_{i_t}$. We can express this number as

$$[z^{n-i-j-k-1}]\,C(z)^{i+j+k+2} = C_{(n-i-j-k-1)n}$$

by Eq. 7.2.1.6–(24). Summing on k gives $C_{(n-i-j-2)(n+1)}$; then summing on j and i gives $C_{(n-4)(n+3)}$.

Similarly, the other two patterns contribute $C_{(n-5)(n+3)}$ and $C_{(n-5)(n+4)}$. The total number of single-crossing partitions is therefore $C_{(n-5)(n+3)} + C_{(n-4)(n+4)}$.

28. Order the divisors of $cbbaaa$ by their number of prime factors and then colexicographically: $1 \prec a \prec b \prec c \prec aa \prec ba \prec ca \prec bb \prec cb \prec aaa \prec baa \prec caa \prec bba \prec cba \prec cbb \prec baaa \prec caaa \prec bbaa \prec cbaa \prec cbba \prec bbaaa \prec cbaaa \prec cbbaa \prec cbbaaa$. For every such divisor d, in decreasing order, let d be the first factor; recursively append all factorizations of $cbbaaa/d$ whose first factor is $\preceq d$.

If the divisors had been ordered lexicographically (namely $1 < a < aa < aaa < b < ba < \cdots < cbbaa < cbbaaa$), Wallis's algorithm would have been equivalent to Algorithm 7.2.1.5M with $(n_1, n_2, n_3) = (1, 2, 3)$. He probably chose his more complicated ordering of the divisors because it tends to agree more closely with ordinary numerical order when $a \approx b \approx c$; for example, his ordering is precisely numerical when $(a, b, c) = (7, 11, 13)$. By generating the divisors according to his somewhat complex scheme, Wallis was essentially generating multiset combinations, which we noted in Section 7.2.1.3 are equivalent to bounded compositions. [*Reference: A Discourse of Combinations* (1685), 126–128, with two typographic errors corrected.]

29. The factorizations $edcba$, $edcb \cdot a$, $edca \cdot b$, ..., $e \cdot d \cdot c \cdot b \cdot a$ correspond respectively to

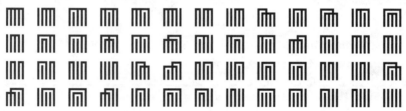

30. The coefficient is zero unless $i_1 + 2i_2 + \cdots = n$; in that case it is $\binom{m}{k} a_0^{m-k} \binom{k}{i_1, i_2, \ldots}$ where $k = i_1 + i_2 + \cdots$. (Consider $(a_0 z)^m$ times $(1 + (a_1/a_0)z + (a_2/a_0)z^2 + \cdots)^m$.)

31. The order produced by that algorithm is decreasing lexicographic, the reverse of (31), if we assume that partitions $a_1 \ldots a_k$ have $a_1 \geq \cdots \geq a_k$; de Moivre's was increasing *colexicographic*.

32. $20 \cdot 1 = 1 \cdot 7 + 13 \cdot 1 = 2 \cdot 7 + 6 \cdot 1 = 1 \cdot 10 + 10 \cdot 1 = 1 \cdot 10 + 1 \cdot 7 + 3 \cdot 1 = 2 \cdot 10$. In general, Boscovich suggested starting with $n \cdot 1$ and computing the successor of $a \cdot 10 + b \cdot 7 + c \cdot 1$ as follows: If $c \geq 7$, the successor is $a \cdot 10 + (b+1) \cdot 7 + (c-7) \cdot 1$; otherwise if $c + 7b \geq 10$, the successor is $(a + 1) \cdot 10 + (c + 7b - 10) \cdot 1$; otherwise stop.

> *"I may,"* said Poirot in a completely unconvinced tone, *"be wrong."*
> — AGATHA CHRISTIE, *After the Funeral* (1953)

— HARPO MARX, *The Cocoanuts* (1925)
— MARCEL MARCEAU, *Baptiste* (1946)

APPENDIX A

TABLES OF NUMERICAL QUANTITIES

Table 1

QUANTITIES THAT ARE FREQUENTLY USED IN STANDARD SUBROUTINES
AND IN ANALYSIS OF COMPUTER PROGRAMS (40 DECIMAL PLACES)

$$\sqrt{2} = 1.41421\ 35623\ 73095\ 04880\ 16887\ 24209\ 69807\ 85697-$$
$$\sqrt{3} = 1.73205\ 08075\ 68877\ 29352\ 74463\ 41505\ 87236\ 69428+$$
$$\sqrt{5} = 2.23606\ 79774\ 99789\ 69640\ 91736\ 68731\ 27623\ 54406+$$
$$\sqrt{10} = 3.16227\ 76601\ 68379\ 33199\ 88935\ 44432\ 71853\ 37196-$$
$$\sqrt[3]{2} = 1.25992\ 10498\ 94873\ 16476\ 72106\ 07278\ 22835\ 05703-$$
$$\sqrt[3]{3} = 1.44224\ 95703\ 07408\ 38232\ 16383\ 10780\ 10958\ 83919-$$
$$\sqrt[4]{2} = 1.18920\ 71150\ 02721\ 06671\ 74999\ 70560\ 47591\ 52930-$$
$$\ln 2 = 0.69314\ 71805\ 59945\ 30941\ 72321\ 21458\ 17656\ 80755+$$
$$\ln 3 = 1.09861\ 22886\ 68109\ 69139\ 52452\ 36922\ 52570\ 46475-$$
$$\ln 10 = 2.30258\ 50929\ 94045\ 68401\ 79914\ 54684\ 36420\ 76011+$$
$$1/\ln 2 = 1.44269\ 50408\ 88963\ 40735\ 99246\ 81001\ 89213\ 74266+$$
$$1/\ln 10 = 0.43429\ 44819\ 03251\ 82765\ 11289\ 18916\ 60508\ 22944-$$
$$\pi = 3.14159\ 26535\ 89793\ 23846\ 26433\ 83279\ 50288\ 41972-$$
$$1° = \pi/180 = 0.01745\ 32925\ 19943\ 29576\ 92369\ 07684\ 88612\ 71344+$$
$$1/\pi = 0.31830\ 98861\ 83790\ 67153\ 77675\ 26745\ 02872\ 40689+$$
$$\pi^2 = 9.86960\ 44010\ 89358\ 61883\ 44909\ 99876\ 15113\ 53137-$$
$$\sqrt{\pi} = \Gamma(1/2) = 1.77245\ 38509\ 05516\ 02729\ 81674\ 83341\ 14518\ 27975+$$
$$\Gamma(1/3) = 2.67893\ 85347\ 07747\ 63365\ 56929\ 40974\ 67764\ 41287-$$
$$\Gamma(2/3) = 1.35411\ 79394\ 26400\ 41694\ 52880\ 28154\ 51378\ 55193+$$
$$e = 2.71828\ 18284\ 59045\ 23536\ 02874\ 71352\ 66249\ 77572+$$
$$1/e = 0.36787\ 94411\ 71442\ 32159\ 55237\ 70161\ 46086\ 74458+$$
$$e^2 = 7.38905\ 60989\ 30650\ 22723\ 04274\ 60575\ 00781\ 31803+$$
$$\gamma = 0.57721\ 56649\ 01532\ 86060\ 65120\ 90082\ 40243\ 10422-$$
$$\ln \pi = 1.14472\ 98858\ 49400\ 17414\ 34273\ 51353\ 05871\ 16473-$$
$$\phi = 1.61803\ 39887\ 49894\ 84820\ 45868\ 34365\ 63811\ 77203+$$
$$e^\gamma = 1.78107\ 24179\ 90197\ 98523\ 65041\ 03107\ 17954\ 91696+$$
$$e^{\pi/4} = 2.19328\ 00507\ 38015\ 45655\ 97696\ 59278\ 73822\ 34616+$$
$$\sin 1 = 0.84147\ 09848\ 07896\ 50665\ 25023\ 21630\ 29899\ 96226-$$
$$\cos 1 = 0.54030\ 23058\ 68139\ 71740\ 09366\ 07442\ 97660\ 37323+$$
$$-\zeta'(2) = 0.93754\ 82543\ 15843\ 75370\ 25740\ 94567\ 86497\ 78979-$$
$$\zeta(3) = 1.20205\ 69031\ 59594\ 28539\ 97381\ 61511\ 44999\ 07650-$$
$$\ln \phi = 0.48121\ 18250\ 59603\ 44749\ 77589\ 13424\ 36842\ 31352-$$
$$1/\ln \phi = 2.07808\ 69212\ 35027\ 53760\ 13226\ 06117\ 79576\ 77422-$$
$$-\ln \ln 2 = 0.36651\ 29205\ 81664\ 32701\ 24391\ 58232\ 66946\ 94543-$$

Table 2

QUANTITIES THAT ARE FREQUENTLY USED IN STANDARD SUBROUTINES
AND IN ANALYSIS OF COMPUTER PROGRAMS (40 HEXADECIMAL PLACES)

The names at the left of the "=" signs are given in decimal notation.

$0.1 = 0.1999\ 9999\ 9999\ 9999\ 9999\ 9999\ 9999\ 9999\ 9999\ 999A-$

$0.01 = 0.028F\ 5C28\ F5C2\ 8F5C\ 28F5\ C28F\ 5C28\ F5C2\ 8F5C\ 28F6-$

$0.001 = 0.0041\ 8937\ 4BC6\ A7EF\ 9DB2\ 2D0E\ 5604\ 1893\ 74BC\ 6A7F-$

$0.0001 = 0.0006\ 8DB8\ BAC7\ 10CB\ 295E\ 9E1B\ 089A\ 0275\ 2546\ 0AA6+$

$0.00001 = 0.0000\ A7C5\ AC47\ 1B47\ 8423\ 0FCF\ 80DC\ 3372\ 1D53\ CDDD+$

$0.000001 = 0.0000\ 10C6\ F7A0\ B5ED\ 8D36\ B4C7\ F349\ 3858\ 3621\ FAFD-$

$0.0000001 = 0.0000\ 01AD\ 7F29\ ABCA\ F485\ 787A\ 6520\ EC08\ D236\ 9919+$

$0.00000001 = 0.0000\ 002A\ F31D\ C461\ 1873\ BF3F\ 7083\ 4ACD\ AE9F\ 0F4F+$

$0.000000001 = 0.0000\ 0004\ 4B82\ FA09\ B5A5\ 2CB9\ 8B40\ 5447\ C4A9\ 8188-$

$0.0000000001 = 0.0000\ 0000\ 6DF3\ 7F67\ 5EF6\ EADF\ 5AB9\ A207\ 2D44\ 268E-$

$\sqrt{2} = 1.6A09\ E667\ F3BC\ C908\ B2FB\ 1366\ EA95\ 7D3E\ 3ADE\ C175+$

$\sqrt{3} = 1.BB67\ AE85\ 84CA\ A73B\ 2574\ 2D70\ 78B8\ 3B89\ 25D8\ 34CC+$

$\sqrt{5} = 2.3C6E\ F372\ FE94\ F82B\ E739\ 80C0\ B9DB\ 9068\ 2104\ 4ED8-$

$\sqrt{10} = 3.298B\ 075B\ 4B6A\ 5240\ 9457\ 9061\ 9B37\ FD4A\ B4E0\ ABB0-$

$\sqrt[3]{2} = 1.428A\ 2F98\ D728\ AE22\ 3DDA\ B715\ BE25\ 0D0C\ 288F\ 1029+$

$\sqrt[3]{3} = 1.7137\ 4491\ 23EF\ 65CD\ DE7F\ 16C5\ 6E32\ 67C0\ A189\ 4C2B-$

$\sqrt[4]{2} = 1.306F\ E0A3\ 1B71\ 52DE\ 8D5A\ 4630\ 5C85\ EDEC\ BC27\ 3436+$

$\ln 2 = 0.B172\ 17F7\ D1CF\ 79AB\ C9E3\ B398\ 03F2\ F6AF\ 40F3\ 4326+$

$\ln 3 = 1.193E\ A7AA\ D030\ A976\ A419\ 8D55\ 053B\ 7CB5\ BE14\ 42DA-$

$\ln 10 = 2.4D76\ 3776\ AAA2\ B05B\ A95B\ 58AE\ 0B4C\ 28A3\ 8A3F\ B3E7+$

$1/\ln 2 = 1.7154\ 7652\ B82F\ E177\ 7D0F\ FDA0\ D23A\ 7D11\ D6AE\ F552-$

$1/\ln 10 = 0.6F2D\ EC54\ 9B94\ 38CA\ 9AAD\ D557\ D699\ EE19\ 1F71\ A301+$

$\pi = 3.243F\ 6A88\ 85A3\ 08D3\ 1319\ 8A2E\ 0370\ 7344\ A409\ 3822+$

$1° = \pi/180 = 0.0477\ D1A8\ 94A7\ 4E45\ 7076\ 2FB3\ 74A4\ 2E26\ C805\ BD78-$

$1/\pi = 0.517C\ C1B7\ 2722\ 0A94\ FE13\ ABE8\ FA9A\ 6EE0\ 6DB1\ 4ACD-$

$\pi^2 = 9.DE9E\ 64DF\ 22EF\ 2D25\ 6E26\ CD98\ 08C1\ AC70\ 85GG\ A3FE+$

$\sqrt{\pi} = \Gamma(1/2) = 1.C5BF\ 891B\ 4EF6\ AA79\ C3B0\ 520D\ 5DB9\ 383F\ E392\ 1547-$

$\Gamma(1/3) = 2.ADCE\ EA72\ 905E\ 2CEE\ C8D3\ E92C\ D580\ 46D8\ 4B46\ A6B3-$

$\Gamma(2/3) = 1.5AA7\ 7928\ C367\ 8CAB\ 2F4F\ EB70\ 2B26\ 990A\ 54F7\ EDBC+$

$e = 2.B7E1\ 5162\ 8AED\ 2A6A\ BF71\ 5880\ 9CF4\ F3C7\ 62E7\ 160F+$

$1/e = 0.5E2D\ 58D8\ B3BC\ DF1A\ BADE\ C782\ 9054\ F90D\ DA98\ 05AB-$

$e^2 = 7.6399\ 2E35\ 376B\ 730C\ E8EE\ 881A\ DA2A\ EEA1\ 1EB9\ EBD9+$

$\gamma = 0.93C4\ 67E3\ 7DB0\ C7A4\ D1BE\ 3F81\ 0152\ CB56\ A1CE\ CC3B-$

$\ln \pi = 1.250D\ 048E\ 7A1B\ D0BD\ 5F95\ 6C6A\ 843F\ 4998\ 5E6D\ DBF4-$

$\phi = 1.9E37\ 79B9\ 7F4A\ 7C15\ F39C\ C060\ 5CED\ C834\ 1082\ 276C-$

$e^\gamma = 1.C7F4\ 5CAB\ 1356\ BF14\ A7EF\ 5AEB\ 6B9F\ 6C45\ 60A9\ 1932+$

$e^{\pi/4} = 2.317A\ CD28\ E395\ 4F87\ 6B04\ B8AB\ AAC8\ C708\ F1C0\ 3C4A+$

$\sin 1 = 0.D76A\ A478\ 4867\ 7020\ C6E9\ E909\ C50F\ 3C32\ 89E5\ 1113+$

$\cos 1 = 0.8A51\ 407D\ A834\ 5C91\ C246\ 6D97\ 6871\ BD29\ A237\ 3A89+$

$-\zeta'(2) = 0.F003\ 2992\ B55C\ 4F28\ 88E9\ BA28\ 1E4C\ 405F\ 8CBE\ 9FEE+$

$\zeta(3) = 1.33BA\ 004F\ 0062\ 1383\ 7171\ 5C59\ E690\ 7F1B\ 180B\ 7DB1+$

$\ln \phi = 0.7B30\ B2BB\ 1458\ 2652\ F810\ 812A\ 5A31\ C083\ 4C9E\ B233+$

$1/\ln \phi = 2.13FD\ 8124\ F324\ 34A2\ 63C7\ 5F40\ 76C7\ 9883\ 5224\ 4685-$

$-\ln \ln 2 = 0.5DD3\ CA6F\ 75AE\ 7A83\ E037\ 67D6\ 6E33\ 2DBC\ 09DF\ AA82-$

Several interesting constants with less common names have arisen in connection with the analyses in the present book. Those constants have been evaluated to 40 decimal places in Eqs. 7.1.4–(90) and 7.2.1.5–(34), and in the answer to exercise 7.1.4–191.

Table 3

VALUES OF HARMONIC NUMBERS, BERNOULLI NUMBERS, AND FIBONACCI NUMBERS, FOR SMALL VALUES OF n

n	H_n	B_n	F_n	n
0	0	1	0	0
1	1	1/2	1	1
2	3/2	1/6	1	2
3	11/6	0	2	3
4	25/12	−1/30	3	4
5	137/60	0	5	5
6	49/20	1/42	8	6
7	363/140	0	13	7
8	761/280	−1/30	21	8
9	7129/2520	0	34	9
10	7381/2520	5/66	55	10
11	83711/27720	0	89	11
12	86021/27720	−691/2730	144	12
13	1145993/360360	0	233	13
14	1171733/360360	7/6	377	14
15	1195757/360360	0	610	15
16	2436559/720720	−3617/510	987	16
17	42142223/12252240	0	1597	17
18	14274301/4084080	43867/798	2584	18
19	275295799/77597520	0	4181	19
20	55835135/15519504	−174611/330	6765	20
21	18858053/5173168	0	10946	21
22	19093197/5173168	854513/138	17711	22
23	444316699/118982864	0	28657	23
24	1347822955/356948592	−236364091/2730	46368	24
25	34052522467/8923714800	0	75025	25
26	34395742267/8923714800	8553103/6	121393	26
27	312536252003/80313433200	0	196418	27
28	315404588903/80313433200	−23749461029/870	317811	28
29	9227046511387/2329089562800	0	514229	29
30	9304682830147/2329089562800	8615841276005/14322	832040	30

For any x, let $H_x = \sum_{n \geq 1} \left(\dfrac{1}{n} - \dfrac{1}{n+x} \right)$. Then

$$H_{1/2} = 2 - 2\ln 2,$$

$$H_{1/3} = 3 - \tfrac{1}{2}\pi/\sqrt{3} - \tfrac{3}{2}\ln 3,$$

$$H_{2/3} = \tfrac{3}{2} + \tfrac{1}{2}\pi/\sqrt{3} - \tfrac{3}{2}\ln 3,$$

$$H_{1/4} = 4 - \tfrac{1}{2}\pi - 3\ln 2,$$

$$H_{3/4} = \tfrac{4}{3} + \tfrac{1}{2}\pi - 3\ln 2,$$

$$H_{1/5} = 5 - \tfrac{1}{2}\pi\phi^{3/2}5^{-1/4} - \tfrac{5}{4}\ln 5 - \tfrac{1}{2}\sqrt{5}\ln\phi,$$

$$H_{2/5} = \tfrac{5}{2} - \tfrac{1}{2}\pi\phi^{-3/2}5^{-1/4} - \tfrac{5}{4}\ln 5 + \tfrac{1}{2}\sqrt{5}\ln\phi,$$

$$H_{3/5} = \tfrac{5}{3} + \tfrac{1}{2}\pi\phi^{-3/2}5^{-1/4} - \tfrac{5}{4}\ln 5 + \tfrac{1}{2}\sqrt{5}\ln\phi,$$

$$H_{4/5} = \tfrac{5}{4} + \tfrac{1}{2}\pi\phi^{3/2}5^{-1/4} - \tfrac{5}{4}\ln 5 - \tfrac{1}{2}\sqrt{5}\ln\phi,$$

$$H_{1/6} = 6 - \tfrac{1}{2}\pi\sqrt{3} - 2\ln 2 - \tfrac{3}{2}\ln 3,$$

$$H_{5/6} = \tfrac{6}{5} + \tfrac{1}{2}\pi\sqrt{3} - 2\ln 2 - \tfrac{3}{2}\ln 3,$$

and, in general, when $0 < p < q$ (see exercise 1.2.9–19),

$$H_{p/q} = \frac{q}{p} - \frac{\pi}{2}\cot\frac{p}{q}\pi - \ln 2q + 2 \sum_{1 \leq n < q/2} \cos\frac{2pn}{q}\pi \cdot \ln\sin\frac{n}{q}\pi.$$

*Reader, if you ever have to start a computing laboratory,
be warned by me and do not take as a computer an accountant,
no matter how honest and efficient. Your computer must work
to so and so many significant figures, whether the significance
of the digits begins six places before or six places after the
decimal point. Your accountant works to cents, and he will work to cents
until hell freezes over. Whatever numbers our accountant computed
he kept at all stages to exactly two places after the decimal point ...*

*This was his conscience, that he should be accurate to the last cent;
and he simply could not understand that physical quantities are not
measured in cents but on a sliding scale of values in which
the cents of one problem might be the dollars of another.*

— NORBERT WIENER, I am a Mathematician (1956)

INDEX TO NOTATIONS

In the following formulas, letters that are not further qualified have the following significance:

j, k	integer-valued arithmetic expression
m, n	nonnegative integer-valued arithmetic expression
p, q	binary-valued arithmetic expression (0 or 1)
x, y	real-valued arithmetic expression
z	complex-valued arithmetic expression
f	integer-valued, real-valued, or complex-valued function
G, H	graph
S, T	set or multiset
$\mathcal{F}, \mathcal{G}$	family of sets
u, v	vertex of a graph
α, β	string of symbols

The place of definition is either a page number in the present volume or a section number in another volume. Many other notations, such as K_n for the complete graph on n vertices, appear in the main index at the close of this book.

Formal symbolism	Meaning	Where defined
$V \leftarrow E$	give variable V the value of expression E	§1.1
$U \leftrightarrow V$	interchange the values of variables U and V	§1.1
A_n or $A[n]$	the nth element of linear array A	§1.1
A_{mn} or $A[m, n]$	the element in row m and column n of rectangular array A	§1.1
$(R?\ a{:}\ b)$	conditional expression: denotes a if relation R is true, b if R is false	96
$[R]$	characteristic function of relation R: $(R?\ 1{:}\ 0)$	§1.2.3
δ_{jk}	Kronecker delta: $[j = k]$	§1.2.3
$[z^n]\, f(z)$	coefficient of z^n in power series $f(z)$	§1.2.9
$z_1 + z_2 + \cdots + z_n$	sum of n numbers (even when n is 0 or 1)	§1.2.3
$a_1 a_2 \ldots a_n$	product or string or vector of n elements	
$(x_1, \ldots, x_n)$	vector of n elements	
$\langle x_1 x_2 \ldots x_{2k-1} \rangle$	median value (middle value after sorting)	75

Formal symbolism	Meaning	Where defined
$\sum_{R(k)} f(k)$	sum of all $f(k)$ such that relation $R(k)$ is true	§1.2.3
$\prod_{R(k)} f(k)$	product of all $f(k)$ such that relation $R(k)$ is true	§1.2.3
$\min_{R(k)} f(k)$	minimum of all $f(k)$ such that relation $R(k)$ is true	§1.2.3
$\max_{R(k)} f(k)$	maximum of all $f(k)$ such that relation $R(k)$ is true	§1.2.3
$\bigcup_{R(k)} S(k)$	union of all $S(k)$ such that relation $R(k)$ is true	
$\sum_{k=a}^{b} f(k)$	shorthand for $\sum_{a \le k \le b} f(k)$	§1.2.3
$\{a \mid R(a)\}$	set of all a such that relation $R(a)$ is true	
$\sum\{f(k) \mid R(k)\}$	another way to write $\sum_{R(k)} f(k)$	
$\{a_1, a_2, \ldots, a_n\}$	the set or multiset $\{a_k \mid 1 \le k \le n\}$	
$[x \mathrel{..} y]$	closed interval: $\{a \mid x \le a \le y\}$	§1.2.2
$(x \mathrel{..} y)$	open interval: $\{a \mid x < a < y\}$	§1.2.2
$[x \mathrel{..} y)$	half-open interval: $\{a \mid x \le a < y\}$	§1.2.2
$(x \mathrel{..} y]$	half-closed interval: $\{a \mid x < a \le y\}$	§1.2.2
$\lvert S \rvert$	cardinality: the number of elements in S	
$\lvert f \rvert$	number of solutions (when f is Boolean): $\sum_x f(x)$	207
$\lvert x \rvert$	absolute value of x: $(x \ge 0?\ x: -x)$	
$\lvert z \rvert$	absolute value of z: $\sqrt{z\bar{z}}$	§1.2.2
$\lvert \alpha \rvert$	length of α: m if $\alpha = a_1 a_2 \ldots a_m$	
$\lfloor x \rfloor$	floor of x, greatest integer function: $\max_{k \le x} k$	§1.2.4
$\lceil x \rceil$	ceiling of x, least integer function: $\min_{k \ge x} k$	§1.2.4
$x \bmod y$	mod function: $\bigl(y = 0?\ x: x - y\lfloor x/y \rfloor\bigr)$	§1.2.4
$\{x\}$	fractional part (used in contexts where a real value, not a set, is implied): $x \bmod 1$	§1.2.11.2
$x \equiv x' \pmod{y}$	relation of congruence: $x \bmod y = x' \bmod y$	§1.2.4
$j \backslash k$	j divides k: $k \bmod j = 0$ and $j > 0$	§1.2.4
$S \setminus T$	set difference: $\{s \mid s \text{ in } S \text{ and } s \text{ not in } T\}$	
$S \setminus t$	shorthand for $S \setminus \{t\}$	
$G \setminus U$	G with vertices of the set U removed	13
$G \setminus v$	G with vertex v removed	13
$G \setminus e$	G with edge e removed	13
G / e	G with edge e shrunk to a point	463
$S \cup t$	shorthand for $S \cup \{t\}$	
$S \uplus T$	multiset sum; e.g., $\{a, b\} \uplus \{a, c\} = \{a, a, b, c\}$	§4.6.3
$\gcd(j, k)$	greatest common divisor: $(j = k = 0?\ 0: \max_{d \backslash j, d \backslash k} d)$	§1.1
$j \perp k$	j is relatively prime to k: $\gcd(j, k) = 1$	§1.2.4

Formal symbolism	Meaning	Where defined
A^T	transpose of rectangular array A: $A^T[j,k] = A[k,j]$	
α^R	left-right reversal of string α	
α^T	conjugate of partition α	394
x^y	x to the y power (when $x > 0$): $e^{y \ln x}$	§1.2.2
x^k	x to the k power: $\left(k \geq 0?\ \prod_{j=0}^{k-1} x: 1/x^{-k}\right)$	§1.2.2
x^-	inverse (or reciprocal) of x: x^{-1}	§1.3.3
$x^{\bar{k}}$	x to the k rising: $\Gamma(x+k)/\Gamma(k) =$ $\left(k \geq 0?\ \prod_{j=0}^{k-1}(x+j): 1/(x+k)^{\overline{-k}}\right)$	§1.2.5
$x^{\underline{k}}$	x to the k falling: $x!/(x-k)! =$ $\left(k \geq 0?\ \prod_{j=0}^{k-1}(x-j): 1/(x-k)^{\underline{-k}}\right)$	§1.2.5
$n!$	n factorial: $\Gamma(n+1) = n^{\underline{n}}$	§1.2.5
$\binom{x}{k}$	binomial coefficient: $(k < 0?\ 0: x^{\underline{k}}/k!)$	§1.2.6
$\binom{n}{n_1,\ldots,n_m}$	multinomial coefficient (when $n = n_1 + \cdots + n_m$)	§1.2.6
$\left[\begin{smallmatrix} n \\ m \end{smallmatrix}\right]$	Stirling cycle number: $\sum_{0 < k_1 < \cdots < k_{n-m} < n} k_1 \ldots k_{n-m}$	§1.2.6
$\left\{\begin{smallmatrix} n \\ m \end{smallmatrix}\right\}$	Stirling subset number: $\sum_{1 \leq k_1 \leq \cdots \leq k_{n-m} \leq m} k_1 \ldots k_{n-m}$	§1.2.6
$\left\langle\begin{smallmatrix} n \\ m \end{smallmatrix}\right\rangle$	Eulerian number: $\sum_{k=0}^{m}(-1)^k \binom{n+1}{k}(m+1-k)^n$	§5.1.3
$\left|\begin{smallmatrix} n \\ m \end{smallmatrix}\right|$	m-part partitions of n: $\sum_{1 \leq k_1 \leq \cdots \leq k_m}[k_1 + \cdots + k_m = n]$	399
$(\ldots a_1 a_0 . a_{-1} \ldots)_b$	radix-b positional notation: $\sum_k a_k b^k$	§4.1
$\Re z$	real part of z	§1.2.2
$\Im z$	imaginary part of z	§1.2.2
$\bar{z}$	complex conjugate: $\Re z - i\,\Im z$	§1.2.2
$\neg p$ or $\sim p$ or $\overline{p}$	complement: $1 - p$	49
$\sim x$ or $\overline{x}$	bitwise complement	135
$p \wedge q$	Boolean conjunction (and): pq	49
$x \wedge y$	minimum: $\min\{x, y\}$	63
$x \,\&\, y$	bitwise AND	134
$p \vee q$	Boolean disjunction (or): $\overline{\overline{p}\overline{q}}$	49
$x \vee y$	maximum: $\max\{x, y\}$	63
$x \mid y$	bitwise OR	134
$p \oplus q$	Boolean exclusive disjunction (xor): $(p + q) \bmod 2$	50
$x \oplus y$	bitwise XOR	134
$x \mathbin{\dot-} y$	saturating subtraction, x monus y: $\max\{0, x - y\}$	§1.3.1′
$x \ll k$	bitwise left shift: $\lfloor 2^k x \rfloor$	135
$x \gg k$	bitwise right shift: $x \ll (-k)$	135
$x \ddagger y$	"zipper function" for interleaving bits, x zip y	147

Formal symbolism	Meaning	Where defined
$\log_b x$	logarithm, base b, of x (defined when $x > 0$, $b > 0$, and $b \neq 1$): the y such that $x = b^y$	§1.2.2
$\ln x$	natural logarithm: $\log_e x$	§1.2.2
$\lg x$	binary logarithm: $\log_2 x$	§1.2.2
λn	binary logsize (when $n > 0$): $\lfloor \lg n \rfloor$	142
$\exp x$	exponential of x: $e^x = \sum_{k=0}^{\infty} x^k / k!$	§1.2.9
ρn	ruler function (when $n > 0$): $\max_{2^m \backslash n} m$	140
νn	sideways sum (when $n \geq 0$): $\sum_{k \geq 0} ((n \gg k) \,\&\, 1)$	143
$\langle X_n \rangle$	the infinite sequence $X_0, X_1, X_2, \ldots$ (here the letter n is part of the symbolism)	§1.2.9
$f'(x)$	derivative of f at x	§1.2.9
$f''(x)$	second derivative of f at x	§1.2.10
$H_n^{(x)}$	harmonic number of order x: $\sum_{k=1}^{n} 1/k^x$	§1.2.7
H_n	harmonic number: $H_n^{(1)}$	§1.2.7
F_n	Fibonacci number: $(n \leq 1?\ n\!: F_{n-1} + F_{n-2})$	§1.2.8
B_n	Bernoulli number: $n!\, [z^n]\, z/(1 - e^{-z})$	§1.2.11.2
$\det(A)$	determinant of square matrix A	§1.2.3
$\text{sign}(x)$	sign of x: $[x > 0] - [x < 0]$	
$\zeta(x)$	zeta function: $\lim_{n \to \infty} H_n^{(x)}$ (when $x > 1$)	§1.2.7
$\Gamma(x)$	gamma function: $(x - 1)! = \gamma(x, \infty)$	§1.2.5
$\gamma(x, y)$	incomplete gamma function: $\int_0^y e^{-t} t^{x-1}\, dt$	§1.2.11.3
γ	Euler's constant: $-\Gamma'(1) = \lim_{n \to \infty} (H_n - \ln n)$	§1.2.7
e	base of natural logarithms: $\sum_{n \geq 0} 1/n!$	§1.2.2
π	circle ratio: $4 \sum_{n \geq 0} (-1)^n / (2n + 1)$	§1.2.2
∞	infinity: larger than any number	
Λ	null link (pointer to no address)	§2.1
$\emptyset$	empty set (set with no elements)	
ϵ	empty string (string of length zero)	
ϵ	unit family: $\{\emptyset\}$	273
ϕ	golden ratio: $(1 + \sqrt{5})/2$	§1.2.8
$\varphi(n)$	Euler's totient function: $\sum_{k=0}^{n-1} [k \perp n]$	§1.2.4
$x \approx y$	x is approximately equal to y	§1.2.5
$G \cong H$	G is isomorphic to H	14
$O(f(n))$	big-oh of $f(n)$, as the variable $n \to \infty$	§1.2.11.1
$O(f(z))$	big-oh of $f(z)$, as the variable $z \to 0$	§1.2.11.1
$\Omega(f(n))$	big-omega of $f(n)$, as the variable $n \to \infty$	§1.2.11.1
$\Theta(f(n))$	big-theta of $f(n)$, as the variable $n \to \infty$	§1.2.11.1

Formal symbolism	Meaning	Where defined
$\overline{G}$	complement of graph (or uniform hypergraph) G	26
G^T	converse of digraph G (change '$\longrightarrow$' to '$\longleftarrow$')	§7.2.2.3
$G \mid U$	G restricted to the vertices of set U	13
$u - v$	u is adjacent to v	13
$u \nmid v$	u is not adjacent to v	13
$u \longrightarrow v$	there is an arc from u to v	18
$u \longrightarrow^* v$	transitive closure: v is reachable from u	159
$d(u, v)$	distance from u to v	16
$G \cup H$	union of G and H	26
$G \oplus H$	direct sum (juxtaposition) of G and H	26
$G - H$	join of G and H	26
$G \longrightarrow H$	directed join of G and H	26
$G \square H$	Cartesian product of G and H	27
$G \otimes H$	direct product (conjunction) of G and H	28
$G \boxtimes H$	strong product of G and H	28
$G \triangle H$	odd product of G and H	28
$G \circ H$	lexicographic product (composition) of G and H	28
e_j	elementary family: $\{\{j\}\}$	273
$\wp$	universal family: all subsets of a given universe	275
$\mathcal{F} \cup \mathcal{G}$	union of families: $\{S \mid S \in \mathcal{F}$ or $S \in \mathcal{G}\}$	273
$\mathcal{F} \cap \mathcal{G}$	intersection of families: $\{S \mid S \in \mathcal{F}$ and $S \in \mathcal{G}\}$	273
$\mathcal{F} \setminus \mathcal{G}$	difference of families: $\{S \mid S \in \mathcal{F}$ and $S \notin \mathcal{G}\}$	273
$\mathcal{F} \oplus \mathcal{G}$	symmetric difference of families: $(\mathcal{F} \setminus \mathcal{G}) \cup (\mathcal{G} \setminus \mathcal{F})$	273
$\mathcal{F} \sqcup \mathcal{G}$	join of families: $\{S \cup T \mid S \in \mathcal{F}, T \in \mathcal{G}\}$	273
$\mathcal{F} \sqcap \mathcal{G}$	meet of families: $\{S \cap T \mid S \in \mathcal{F}, T \in \mathcal{G}\}$	273
$\mathcal{F} \boxplus \mathcal{G}$	delta of families: $\{S \oplus T \mid S \in \mathcal{F}, T \in \mathcal{G}\}$	273
$\mathcal{F}/\mathcal{G}$	quotient (cofactor) of families	273
$\mathcal{F} \bmod \mathcal{G}$	remainder of families: $\mathcal{F} \setminus (\mathcal{G} \sqcup (\mathcal{F}/\mathcal{G}))$	273
$\mathcal{F} \, \S \, k$	symmetrized family, if $\mathcal{F} = e_{j_1} \cup e_{j_2} \cup \cdots \cup e_{j_n}$	274
$\mathcal{F}^\uparrow$	maximal elements of $\mathcal{F}$: $\{S \in \mathcal{F} \mid T \in \mathcal{F}$ and $S \subseteq T$ implies $S = T\}$	276
$\mathcal{F}^\downarrow$	minimal elements of $\mathcal{F}$: $\{S \in \mathcal{F} \mid T \in \mathcal{F}$ and $S \supseteq T$ implies $S = T\}$	276
$\mathcal{F} \nearrow \mathcal{G}$	nonsubsets: $\{S \in \mathcal{F} \mid T \in \mathcal{G}$ implies $S \not\subseteq T\}$	276
$\mathcal{F} \searrow \mathcal{G}$	nonsupersets: $\{S \in \mathcal{F} \mid T \in \mathcal{G}$ implies $S \not\supseteq T\}$	276
$\mathcal{F} \swarrow \mathcal{G}$	subsets: $\{S \in \mathcal{F} \mid T \in \mathcal{G}$ implies $S \subseteq T\} = \mathcal{F} \setminus (\mathcal{F} \nearrow \mathcal{G})$	669
$\mathcal{F} \nwarrow \mathcal{G}$	supersets: $\{S \in \mathcal{F} \mid T \in \mathcal{G}$ implies $S \supseteq T\} = \mathcal{F} \setminus (\mathcal{F} \searrow \mathcal{G})$	669

Formal symbolism	Meaning	Where defined
$X \cdot Y$	dot product of vectors: $x_1y_1 + x_2y_2 + \cdots + x_ny_n$, if $X = x_1x_2\ldots x_n$ and $Y = y_1y_2\ldots y_n$	12
$X \subseteq Y$	containment of vectors: $x_k \leq y_k$ for $1 \leq k \leq n$, if $X = x_1x_2\ldots x_n$ and $Y = y_1y_2\ldots y_n$	135
$\alpha \diamond \beta$	melding of truth tables	218
$\alpha(G)$	independence number of G	35
$\gamma(G)$	domination number of G	673
$\kappa(G)$	vertex connectivity of G	§7.4.1.3
$\lambda(G)$	edge connectivity of G	§7.4.1.3
$\nu(G)$	matching number of G	§7.5.5
$\chi(G)$	chromatic number of G	35
$\omega(G)$	clique number of G	35
$c(G)$	number of spanning trees of G	482
▌	end of algorithm, program, or proof	§1.1

And to auoide the tediouse repetition of these woordes : is equalle to :
I will sette as I doe often in woorke use, a paire of paralleles,
or Gemowe lines of one lengthe, thus: =====,
bicause noe .2. thynges, can be moare equalle.
— ROBERT RECORDE, *The Whetstone of Witte* (1557)

Prof. Le Gendre, in the treatise that we shall often have occasion to cite,
used the same sign for both equality and congruence.
To avoid ambiguity we have made a distinction.
— C. F. GAUSS, *Disquisitiones Arithmeticæ* (1801)

Someone told me that each equation I included in the book
would halve the sales.
— STEPHEN HAWKING, *A Brief History of Time* (1987)

A reader who has temporarily forgotten the definition of, say, "z"
in an argument can at least guess that it should be a complex number.
— TERENCE TAO, *Google Buzz feed* (20 March 2010)

APPENDIX C

INDEX TO ALGORITHMS AND THEOREMS

*[An inverted list] provides duplicate, redundant information
in order to speed up secondary key retrieval.*
— DONALD E. KNUTH, *Sorting and Searching* (1973)

APPENDIX D

INDEX TO COMBINATORIAL PROBLEMS

The purpose of this appendix is to present concise descriptions of the major problems treated in the present book, and to associate each problem description with the name under which it can be found in the main index. Some of these problems can be solved efficiently, while others appear to be very difficult in general although special cases might be easy. No indication of problem complexity is given here.

Combinatorial problems have a chameleon-like tendency to assume many forms. For example, certain properties of graphs and hypergraphs are equivalent to other properties of 0–1 matrices; and an $m \times n$ matrix of 0s and 1s can itself be regarded as a Boolean function of its index variables (i, j), with 0 representing FALSE and 1 representing TRUE. Each problem also has many flavors: We sometimes ask only whether a solution to certain constraints exists at all; but usually we ask to see at least one explicit solution, or we try to count the number of solutions, or to visit them all. Often we require a solution that is optimum in some sense.

In the following list — which is intended to be helpful but by no means complete — each problem is presented in more-or-less formal terms as the task of "finding" some desired objective. This characterization is then followed by an informal paraphrase (in parentheses and quotation marks), and perhaps also by further comments.

Any problem that is stated in terms of directed graphs is automatically applicable also to undirected graphs, unless the digraph must be acyclic, because an undirected edge $u \text{---} v$ is equivalent to the two directed arcs $u \longrightarrow v$ and $v \longrightarrow u$.

• <u>Satisfiability</u>: Given a Boolean function f of n Boolean variables, find Boolean values $x_1, \ldots, x_n$ such that $f(x_1, \ldots, x_n) = 1$. ("If possible, show that f can be true.")

• <u>kSAT</u>: The satisfiability problem when f is the conjunction of clauses, where each clause is a disjunction of at most k literals x_j or $\bar{x}_j$. ("Can all the clauses be true?") The cases 2SAT and 3SAT are most important. Another significant special case arises when f is a conjunction of *Horn clauses*, each having at most one nonnegated literal x_j.

• <u>Boolean chain</u>: Given one or more Boolean functions of n Boolean values $x_1, \ldots, x_n$, find $x_{n+1}, \ldots, x_N$ such that each x_k for $n < k \leq N$ is a Boolean function of x_i and x_j for some $i < k$ and $j < k$, and such that each of the given functions is either constant or equal to x_l for some $l \leq N$. ("Construct a straight-line program to evaluate a given set of functions, sharing intermediate values.") ("Build a circuit to compute a given collection of outputs from the inputs 0, 1, $x_1, \ldots, x_n$, using 2-input Boolean gates with unlimited fanout.") The goal is usually to minimize N.

• <u>Broadword chain</u>: Like a Boolean chain, but using bitwise and/or arithmetic operations on integers modulo 2^d instead of Boolean operations on Boolean values; the given value of d can be arbitrarily large. ("Work on several related problems at once.")

• <u>Boolean programming</u>: Given a Boolean function f of n Boolean variables, together with given weights $w_1, \ldots, w_n$, find Boolean values $x_1, \ldots, x_n$ such that $f(x_1, \ldots, x_n) = 1$ and $w_1 x_1 + \cdots + w_n x_n$ is as large as possible. ("How can f be satisfied with maximum payoff?")

• Matching: Given a graph G, find a set of disjoint edges. ("Pair up the vertices so that each vertex has at most one partner.") The goal is usually to find as many edges as possible; a "perfect matching" includes all the vertices. In a bipartite graph with m vertices in one part and n vertices in the other, matching is equivalent to selecting a set of 1s in an $m \times n$ matrix of 0s and 1s, with at most one selected in each row and at most one selected in each column.

• Assignment problem: A generalization of bipartite matching, with weights associated with each edge; the total weight of the matching should be maximized. ("What assignment of people to jobs is best?") Equivalently, we wish to select elements of an $m \times n$ matrix, at most one per row and at most one per column, so that the sum of selected elements is as large as possible.

• Covering: Given a matrix A_{jk} of 0s and 1s, find a set of rows R such that we have $\sum_{j \in R} A_{jk} > 0$ for all k. ("Mark a 1 in each column and select all rows that have been marked.") Equivalently, find an implicant of a monotone Boolean function, given its clauses. The goal is usually to minimize $|R|$.

• Exact cover: Given a matrix A_{jk} of 0s and 1s, find a set of rows R such that $\sum_{j \in R} A_{jk} = 1$ for all k. ("Cover with mutually orthogonal rows.") The perfect matching problem is equivalent to finding an exact cover of the transposed incidence matrix.

• Independent set: Given a graph or hypergraph G, find a set of vertices U such that the induced graph $G \mid U$ has no edges. ("Choose unrelated vertices.") The goal is usually to maximize $|U|$. Classical special cases include the 8 queens problem, when G is the graph of queen moves on a chessboard, and the no-three-on-a-line problem.

• Clique: Given a graph G, find a set of vertices U such that the induced graph $G \mid U$ is complete. ("Choose mutually adjacent vertices.") Equivalently, find an independent set in $\overline{G}$. The goal is usually to maximize $|U|$.

• Vertex cover: Given a graph or hypergraph, find a set of vertices U such that every edge includes at least one vertex of U. ("Mark some vertices so that no edge remains unmarked.") Equivalently, find a covering of the transposed incidence matrix. Equivalently, find U such that $V \setminus U$ is independent, where V is the set of all vertices. The goal is usually to minimize $|U|$.

• Dominating set: Given a graph, find a set of vertices U such that every vertex not in U is adjacent to some vertex of U. ("What vertices are within one step of them all?") The classic 5-queens problem is the special case when G is the graph of queen moves on a chessboard.

• Kernel: Given a directed graph, find an independent set of vertices U such that every vertex not in U is the predecessor of some vertex of U. ("In what independent positions of a 2-player game can your opponent force you to remain?") If the graph is undirected, a kernel is equivalent to a maximal independent set, and to a dominating set that is both minimal and independent.

• Coloring: Given a graph, find a way to partition its vertices into k independent sets. ("Color the vertices with k colors, never giving the same color to adjacent points.") The goal is usually to minimize k.

• Shortest path: Given vertices u and v of a directed graph in which weights are associated with every arc, find the smallest total weight of an oriented path from u to v. ("Determine the best route.")

• <u>Longest path</u>: Given vertices u and v of a directed graph in which weights are associated with every arc, find the largest total weight of a simple oriented path from u to v. ("What route meanders the most?")

• <u>Reachability</u>: Given a set of vertices U in a directed graph G, find all vertices v such that $u \longrightarrow^* v$ for some $u \in U$. ("What vertices occur on paths that start in U?")

• <u>Spanning tree</u>: Given a graph G, find a free tree F on the same vertices, such that every edge of F is an edge of G. ("Choose just enough edges to connect up all the vertices.") If weights are associated with each edge, a *minimum spanning tree* is a spanning tree of smallest total weight.

• <u>Hamiltonian path</u>: Given a graph G, find a path P on the same vertices, such that every edge of P is an edge of G. ("Discover a path that encounters every vertex exactly once.") This is the classic knight's tour problem when G is the graph of knight moves on a chessboard. When the vertices of G are combinatorial objects — for example, tuples, permutations, combinations, partitions, or trees — that are adjacent when they are "close" to each other, a Hamiltonian path is often called a Gray code.

• <u>Hamiltonian cycle</u>: Given a graph G, find a cycle C on the same vertices, such that every edge of C is an edge of G. ("Discover a path that encounters every vertex exactly once and returns to the starting point.")

• <u>Traveling Salesrep Problem</u>: Find a Hamiltonian cycle of smallest total weight, when weights are associated with each edge of the given graph. ("What's the cheapest way to visit everything?") If the graph has no Hamiltonian cycle, we extend it to a complete graph by assigning a very large weight W to every nonexistent edge.

• <u>Topological sorting</u>: Given a directed graph, find a way to label each vertex x with a distinct number $l(x)$ in such a way that $x \longrightarrow y$ implies $l(x) < l(y)$. ("Place the vertices in a row, with each vertex to the left of all its successors.") Such a labeling is possible if and only if the given digraph is acyclic.

• <u>Optimum linear arrangement</u>: Given a graph, find a way to label each vertex x with a distinct integer $l(x)$, such that $\sum_{u - v} |l(u) - l(v)|$ is as small as possible. ("Place the vertices in a row, minimizing the sum of the resulting edge lengths.")

• <u>Knapsack problem</u>: Given a sequence of weights $w_1, \ldots, w_n$, a threshold W, and a sequence of values $v_1, \ldots, v_n$, find $K \subseteq \{1, \ldots, n\}$ such that $\sum_{k \in K} w_k \leq W$ and $\sum_{k \in K} v_k$ is maximum. ("How much value can be carried?")

• <u>Orthogonal array</u>: Given positive integers m and n, find an $m \times n^2$ array with entries $A_{jk} \in \{0, 1, \ldots, n-1\}$ and with the property that $j \neq j'$ and $k \neq k'$ implies $(A_{jk}, A_{j'k}) \neq (A_{jk'}, A_{j'k'})$. ("Construct m different $n \times n$ matrices of n-ary digits in such a way that all n^2 possible digit pairs occur when any two of the matrices are superimposed.") The case $m = 3$ corresponds to a latin square, and the case $m > 3$ corresponds to $m - 2$ mutually orthogonal latin squares.

• <u>Nearest common ancestor</u>: Given nodes u and v of a forest, find w such that every inclusive ancestor of u and of v is also an inclusive ancestor of w. ("Where does the shortest path from u to v change direction?")

• <u>Range minimum query</u>: Given a sequence of numbers $a_1, \ldots, a_n$, find the minimum elements of each subinterval $a_i, \ldots, a_j$ for $1 \leq i < j \leq n$. ("Solve all possible queries concerning the minimum value in any given range.") Exercises 150 and 151 of Section 7.1.3 show that this problem is equivalent to finding nearest common ancestors.

• <u>Universal cycle</u>: Given b, k, and N, find a cyclic sequence of elements x_0, x_1, $\ldots$, x_{N-1}, x_0, $\ldots$ of b-ary digits $\{0, 1, \ldots, b-1\}$ with the property that all combinatorial arrangements of a particular kind are given by the consecutive k-tuples $x_0 x_1 \ldots x_{k-1}$, $x_1 x_2 \ldots x_k$, $\ldots$, $x_{N-1} x_0 \ldots x_{k-2}$. ("Exhibit all possibilities in a circular fashion.") The result is called a de Bruijn cycle if $N = b^k$ and all possible k-tuples appear; it's a universal cycle of combinations if $N = \binom{b}{k}$ and if all k-combinations of b things appear; and it's a universal cycle of permutations if $N = b!$, $k = b-1$, and if all $(b-1)$-variations appear as k-tuples.

In most cases we have been able to give a set-theoretic definition that describes the problem completely, although the need for conciseness has often led to some obscuring of the intuition behind the problem.

— M. R. GAREY and D. S. JOHNSON, *A List of NP-Complete Problems* (1979)

INDEX AND GLOSSARY

Indexes need not necessarily be dry.

— HENRY B. WHEATLEY, *How to Make an Index* (1902)

When an index entry refers to a page containing a relevant exercise, see also the *answer* to that exercise for further information. An answer page is not indexed here unless it refers to a topic not included in the statement of the exercise.

THIS BOOK was composed on an HP Compaq 2510p with Computer Modern typefaces, using the TEX and METAFONT software as described in the author's books *Computers & Typesetting* (Reading, Mass.: Addison–Wesley, 1986), Volumes A–E. The illustrations were produced with John Hobby's METAPOST system. Some names in the index were typeset with additional fonts developed by Yannis Haralambous (Greek, Hebrew, Arabic), Olga G. Lapko (Cyrillic), Frans J. Velthuis (Devanagari), Masatoshi Watanabe (Japanese), and Linbo Zhang (Chinese).

ASCII CHARACTERS

	#0	#1	#2	#3	#4	#5	#6	#7	#8	#9	#a	#b	#c	#d	#e	#f	
#2x		!	"	#	$	%	&	'	(	)	*	+	,	−	.	/	#2x
#3x	0	1	2	3	4	5	6	7	8	9	:	;	<	=	>	?	#3x
#4x	@	A	B	C	D	E	F	G	H	I	J	K	L	M	N	O	#4x
#5x	P	Q	R	S	T	U	V	W	X	Y	Z	[	\	]	^	_	#5x
#6x	`	a	b	c	d	e	f	g	h	i	j	k	l	m	n	o	#6x
#7x	p	q	r	s	t	u	v	w	x	y	z	{	|	}	~	▪	#7x
	#0	#1	#2	#3	#4	#5	#6	#7	#8	#9	#a	#b	#c	#d	#e	#f	

MMIX OPERATION CODES

	#0	#1	#2	#3	#4	#5	#6	#7	
#0x	TRAP $5v$	FCMP v	FUN v	FEQL v	FADD $4v$	FIX $4v$	FSUB $4v$	FIXU $4v$	#0x
	FLOT[I] $4v$		FLOTU[I] $4v$		SFLOT[I] $4v$		SFLOTU[I] $4v$		
#1x	FMUL $4v$	FCMPE $4v$	FUNE v	FEQLE $4v$	FDIV $40v$	FSQRT $40v$	FREM $4v$	FINT $4v$	#1x
	MUL[I] $10v$		MULU[I] $10v$		DIV[I] $60v$		DIVU[I] $60v$		
#2x	ADD[I] v		ADDU[I] v		SUB[I] v		SUBU[I] v		#2x
	2ADDU[I] v		4ADDU[I] v		8ADDU[I] v		16ADDU[I] v		
#3x	CMP[I] v		CMPU[I] v		NEG[I] v		NEGU[I] v		#3x
	SL[I] v		SLU[I] v		SR[I] v		SRU[I] v		
#4x	BN[B] $v+\pi$		BZ[B] $v+\pi$		BP[B] $v+\pi$		BOD[B] $v+\pi$		#4x
	BNN[B] $v+\pi$		BNZ[B] $v+\pi$		BNP[B] $v+\pi$		BEV[B] $v+\pi$		
#5x	PBN[B] $3v-\pi$		PBZ[B] $3v-\pi$		PBP[B] $3v-\pi$		PBOD[B] $3v-\pi$		#5x
	PBNN[B] $3v-\pi$		PBNZ[B] $3v-\pi$		PBNP[B] $3v-\pi$		PBEV[B] $3v-\pi$		
#6x	CSN[I] v		CSZ[I] v		CSP[I] v		CSOD[I] v		#6x
	CSNN[I] v		CSNZ[I] v		CSNP[I] v		CSEV[I] v		
#7x	ZSN[I] v		ZSZ[I] v		ZSP[I] v		ZSOD[I] v		#7x
	ZSNN[I] v		ZSNZ[I] v		ZSNP[I] v		ZSEV[I] v		
#8x	LDB[I] $\mu+v$		LDBU[I] $\mu+v$		LDW[I] $\mu+v$		LDWU[I] $\mu+v$		#8x
	LDT[I] $\mu+v$		LDTU[I] $\mu+v$		LDO[I] $\mu+v$		LDOU[I] $\mu+v$		
#9x	LDSF[I] $\mu+v$		LDHT[I] $\mu+v$		CSWAP[I] $2\mu+2v$		LDUNC[I] $\mu+v$		#9x
	LDVTS[I] v		PRELD[I] v		PREGO[I] v		GO[I] $3v$		
#Ax	STB[I] $\mu+v$		STBU[I] $\mu+v$		STW[I] $\mu+v$		STWU[I] $\mu+v$		#Ax
	STT[I] $\mu+v$		STTU[I] $\mu+v$		STO[I] $\mu+v$		STOU[I] $\mu+v$		
#Bx	STSF[I] $\mu+v$		STHT[I] $\mu+v$		STCO[I] $\mu+v$		STUNC[I] $\mu+v$		#Bx
	SYNCD[I] v		PREST[I] v		SYNCID[I] v		PUSHGO[I] $3v$		
#Cx	OR[I] v		ORN[I] v		NOR[I] v		XOR[I] v		#Cx
	AND[I] v		ANDN[I] v		NAND[I] v		NXOR[I] v		
#Dx	BDIF[I] v		WDIF[I] v		TDIF[I] v		ODIF[I] v		#Dx
	MUX[I] v		SADD[I] v		MOR[I] v		MXOR[I] v		
#Ex	SETH v	SETMH v	SETML v	SETL v	INCH v	INCMH v	INCML v	INCL v	#Ex
	ORH v	ORMH v	ORML v	ORL v	ANDNH v	ANDNMH v	ANDNML v	ANDNL v	
#Fx	JMP[B] v		PUSHJ[B] v		GETA[B] v		PUT[I] v		#Fx
	POP $3v$	RESUME $5v$	[UN]SAVE $20\mu+v$		SYNC v	SWYM v	GET v	TRIP $5v$	
	#8	#9	#A	#B	#C	#D	#E	#F	

$\pi = 2v$ if the branch is taken, $\pi = 0$ if the branch is not taken